St John's College, Cambridge

Register of Twentieth-Century Johnians

Volume I, 1900–1949

First published in Great Britain by St John's College, Cambridge, 2004

Designed and printed by Cambridge Printing, the printing business of Cambridge University Press
www.cambridgeprinting.org

Copies may be obtained from the Biographical Assistant, St John's College, Cambridge, CB2 1QA

A catalogue record for this book is available from the British Library

ISBN 0-9501085-7-X

Editor's Note

The Biographical Archive of St John's College contains information on every member of the College – over 30,000 in total – since comprehensive admissions records began in 1629, with some notes on members before that. It combines information on birth, parents, schooling and academic career, drawn from College and University sources, with notes on later lives and careers and an *ad hoc* collection of press cuttings, letters, and miscellaneous documents.

In 1997 work commenced on the *Register of Twentieth-Century Johnians*, drawing on the information the College holds and creating a work of reference covering all members of the College who were admitted between 1900 and 1999. This volume includes those whose names appear in the College Admissions Registers in the first half of the century. The entries include the basic details recorded for every person entered in the Admissions Registers, together with brief information on College and University career, supplemented wherever possible by information on later occupations, achievements, marriages and children. This information has been put together from the details held in the Biographical Archive, which have been entered onto a Biographical Database. Members have had an opportunity to update the information the College holds on them via printouts of their records from the Database, which have been sent out with invitations to Johnian Dinners. During the last two years the individual entries in the *Register* have also been checked, where possible, by either the individual concerned or by a member of their family. In addition, further research has been undertaken where necessary.

The entries appear alphabetically by surname at admission, and take the following form:

Surname at admission; title at the time of writing, or at the time of their death; forenames at admission; name changes; year admitted; date and place of birth; father's name and occupation; mother's maiden name and occupation*; details of marriage and children; subject(s) studied at St John's; degrees awarded whilst resident at St John's; other university degrees; professional qualifications; fellowships of learned societies and fellowships or memberships of professional institutions or associations; tutor(s) at St John's; Johnian relatives; educational background; career; appointments; awards; honours; publications; and, where applicable, date of death.

Where names appear in brackets this denotes a change of name after they were admitted to the College, or an indication of the name they are known by (owing to an official name change, the preference of a middle name, or the use of a shortened name or nickname).

At the back of the book there is a list of members arranged by the year their names were entered in the College Admissions Registers. In some cases this may be different from the year the person matriculated or came into residence. A list of abbreviations used in the book precedes the main text.

---

* Details of parents are as recorded at the time the Admissions Register was completed. Mother's occupation was not generally recorded at the time, but in some cases may subsequently have been provided to the College.

During the war years there were many who came up to Cambridge for short courses slanted towards aeronautical, military or naval matters. Even though they spent only a short time at St John's they were officially listed as members of the College. Every person who was admitted to membership of the College between 1900 and 1949, for whatever reason and however long they stayed in residence, is included in this publication. There are a number of people, particularly from the period of the First World War, who were admitted to membership of the College but never had the opportunity to come up to study because they went to serve in the war, and were killed in action. The war years altered the course of people's lives, and this is reflected in the history of the College and its members, and therefore in the entries included here.

It has not been possible, and indeed it is not the aim of this publication, to undertake a detailed analysis of the family backgrounds of Johnians. The compilation of the information alone has been a huge task, and analysing the data would take some time, but as a result of seeing the draft version I am aware that some members of College have already expressed an interest in researching this further, and this interest is welcomed. It can briefly be stated that the professions of the fathers of students who came up to the College are varied and interesting, and show that in the early twentieth century St John's was welcoming the sons of labourers, lawyers, medics, farmers, tradesmen, civil servants, teachers and academics, military men, clergymen, as well as gentlemen of independent means, to name but a few of the positions listed. This, as well as an examination of the educational background of twentieth-century Johnians, makes it apparent that the College drew its members from a wide range of backgrounds. At a time when debate continues about widening access to higher education, and particularly to universities such as Oxford and Cambridge, it is worth noting the diversity evident in this record.

Work on this project has led to the College renewing contact with many members whom we had previously lost touch with, and also making contact with the relatives of many Johnians who are no longer alive. The project has therefore enabled the College to foster new relationships, as well as updating our biographical records.

As a result of seeing the draft *Register*, many Johnians have been in touch to say how much they have enjoyed looking up the entries for their friends and contemporaries and seeing what they went on to do. Some have enquired if it is possible to make contact with them, and it is very satisfying when we are able to help with this. Address information is not included in the book; many members of the College do not want this sort of detail to be published, and it would have been necessary to gain the permission of all those involved. Address information changes frequently, with the College receiving many address changes on a daily basis, and the *Register* is intended to be a record which can be consulted in years to come. Although there will inevitably be some information which could be added in the future, the aim has been to produce a work which is accurate at the time of writing, and does not contain information which will go out of date.

A biographical record such as this can never be said to be complete, as more details will come to light regarding the lives and careers of those listed within its pages. Those who have experience of compiling biographical information themselves, through genealogical research for example, will realise that it is sometimes difficult to establish facts regarding people's lives. Even when details are written down, certain printed sources are not always reliable, and sometimes even the information contained in official documents, such as birth certificates, is rejected by family members as being incorrect. When trying to respect the wishes of relatives of an individual it is sometimes difficult to reach a conclusion, particularly if conflicting information is received. Similarly, in some instances there appear to be discrepancies in the information contained in the entries for members of the same family. This can sometimes be explained by the fact that people came up to the College at different times; for example, the entries for two brothers might show different occupations for their father because his job changed after his first son arrived at St John's. There are several examples where brothers coming up to the College have spelt their parents' names differently, or where a father and son who are both Johnians have provided conflicting information. Where possible I have endeavoured to resolve these problems, but often when the Admissions Register has been checked the discrepancy appears there as well, and it has not been possible to establish which information is correct.

I have presented the facts that I have, whilst abiding by the wishes of the person concerned or their family. This has meant that although I have attempted to retain a certain style and format for the entries, the information is more detailed in some cases than in others. Where there is very little information it may be because the College does not have any further details, and it has not been possible to find any more information through further research, but in some cases it is because I have received a specific request only to publish certain facts. The College will continue to gather information on the lives of those mentioned in this volume.

I would like to thank all members of College who have commented on their entries, and the friends and relatives of Johnians, for their support and interest in the project. I would also like to thank those who volunteered to provide additional help through proofreading etc, or who have shown their support in other ways during the process of compiling the book, including many Johnians who were admitted to the College after 1950 who do not appear in this volume, and members of staff, past and present.

Fiona Colbert
Biographical Assistant

July 2004

Abbreviations

AA	Architectural Association	AICTA	Associate, Imperial College of Tropical Agriculture
AAC	Army Air Corps	AIDS	Acquired Immune Deficiency Syndrome
AAF	Auxiliary Air Force	AIIC	Association Internationale des Interpretes de Conference (International Association of Conference Interpreters)
AAG	Assistant Adjutant-General		
AAR	Associated Australian Resources		
AAS	American Astronomical Society	AIF	Australian Imperial Force
AB	Bachelor of Arts	AIL Fr	Associate, Institute of Linguists (in French)
ABC	Australian Broadcasting Commission	AIP	American Institute of Physics
ABRO	Army in Burma Reserve of Officers	AIRC	Associazione Italiana per la Ricerca sul Cancro (Italian Association for Cancer Research)
AC	Companion, Order of Australia		
ACA	Associate, Institute of Chartered Accountants	ALA	Associate, Library Association
ACAS	Advisory, Conciliation and Arbitration Service	ALFSEA	Allied Land Forces South East Asia
ACE	Association of Consulting Engineers	AM	Member, Order of Australia
ACGI	Associate, City and Guilds of London Institute	AMAP	Arctic Monitoring and Assessment Programme
ACIArb	Associate, Chartered Institute of Arbitrators	AMC	Association of Municipal Corporations
ACII	Associate, Chartered Insurance Institute	AMICE	Associate Member, Institution of Civil Engineers
ACIS	Associate, Institute of Chartered Secretaries and Administrators	AMIEE	Associate Member, Institution of Electrical Engineers (now MIEE)
ACMA	Associate, Chartered Institute of Management Accountants	AMIMechE	Associate Member, Institution of Mechanical Engineers
		AMInstCE	Associate Member, Institution of Civil Engineers
ACP	African, Caribbean and Pacific Group of States	AMN	Ahli Mangku Negara (Member Of The Most Distinguished Order Of The Defender Of The Realm, Federation of Malaysia)
ACT	Australian Capital Territory		
AD	Anno Domini (in the year of the Lord)		
ADC	Aide-de-Camp	AMP	Advanced Management Programme
Adj	Adjutant	AMRTPI	Associate Member, Royal Town Planning Institute
ADRDE	Air Defence Research and Development Establishment	AMTPI	Associate Member, Town Planning Institute (later AMRTPI)
AEA	Atomic Energy Authority	ANRPC	Association of Natural Rubber Producing Countries
AECMA	Association Européene des Constructeurs de Matériel Aérospatial	ANU	Australian National University
		ANZAAS	The Australian and New Zealand Association for the Advancement of Science
AEI	Associated Electrical Industries		
AEPS	Arctic Environmental Protection Strategy	AO	Officer, Order of Australia
AERE	Atomic Energy Research Establishment	APS	American Physical Society
AFB	Air Force Base	APTC	Army Physical Training Corps
AFC	Air Force Cross	AQMG	Assistant Quartermaster General
AFHQ	Allied Force Headquarters	ARAM	Associate, Royal Academy of Music
AFRAeS	Associate Fellow, Royal Aeronautical Society	ARANZ	Archives and Records Association of New Zealand
AFRC	Agricultural and Food Research Council	ARAS	Associate, Royal Astronomical Society
AG	Aktiengesellschaft (company suffix, Germany, Austria)	ARBS	Associate, Royal Society of British Sculptors
AGARD	Advisory Group for Aerospace Research and Development	ARC	Agricultural Research Council
		ARCM	Associate, Royal College of Music
AHA(T)	Area Health Authority (Teaching)	ARCO	Associate, Royal College of Organists
AIC	Associate, Institute of Chemistry	ARCS	Associate, Royal College of Science

ARIAS	Associate, Royal Incorporation of Architects in Scotland	BLA	British Liberation Army
ARIBA	Associate, Royal Institute of British Architects	BLEU	Blind Landing Experimental Unit
ARIC	Associate, Royal Institute of Chemistry	BLitt	Bachelor of Literature
ARICS	Professional Associate, Royal Institution of Chartered Surveyors	BM	Bachelor of Medicine
		BMA	British Medical Association
ARP	Air Raid Precautions/Protection	BMH	British Military Hospital
ARPS	Associate, Royal Photographic Society	BOA	British Optical Association
ARSCM	Associate, Royal School of Church Music	BOAC	British Overseas Airways Corporation
ASM	American Society of Metals	BOTB	British Overseas Trade Board
ASME	Association for the Study of Medical Education; American Society of Mechanical Engineers	BP	British Petroleum
		BPharm	Bachelor of Pharmacy
ASRY	Arab Shipbuilding and Repair Yard	BPsS	British Psychological Society
ASWE	Admiralty Surface Weapons Establishment	BR	British
ATC	Air Training Corps	BS	Bachelor of Surgery; Bachelor of Science
ATII	Associate Member, Chartered Institute of Taxation	BSA	Annual of the British School at Athens
ATL	Association of Teachers and Lecturers	BSc	Bachelor of Science
AUT	Association of University Teachers	BSI	British Standards Institution
AUWE	Admiralty Underwater Weapons Establishment	Bt	Baronet
AVS	Army Veterinary Service	BTH	British Thomson-Houston
AWRE	Atomic Weapons Research Establishment	BVetMed	Bachelor of Veterinary Medicine
AWS	American Welding Society	BVI	British Virgin Islands
b	born	CA	Chartered Accountant (Scotland and Canada)
BA	Bachelor of Arts	CACTM	Central Advisory Committee on Training for the Ministry
BAAS	British Association for the Advancement of Science		
BAFTA	British Academy of Film and Television Arts	CB	Companion, Order of the Bath
BAO	Bachelor of Art of Obstetrics	CBC	Canadian Broadcasting Corporation
BAOR	British Army of the Rhine	CBE	Commander, Order of the British Empire
BAT	British American Tobacco	CBI	Confederation of British Industry
BAUS	British Association of Urological Surgeons	CBIM	Companion, British Institute of Management
BBC	British Broadcasting Corporation	CBiol	Chartered Biologist
BC	Before Christ; British Columbia	CC	Companion, Order of Canada; City Council; County Council
BCG	Bacille Calmette Guérin (immunisation against tuberculosis)		
		CCF	Combined Cadet Force
BCh/BChir	Bachelor of Surgery	CCFP	Certificate in Family Medicine, College of Family Physicians of Canada
BCom	Bachelor of Commerce		
BCS	British Computer Society	CChem	Chartered Chemist
BCURA	British Coal Utilization Research Association	CCIM	Certified Commercial Investment Member
BD	Bachelor of Divinity	CCIR	Consultative Committee on International Radio
BDS	Bachelor of Dental Surgery	CDipAF	Certified Diploma in Accounting and Finance
BEA	British European Airways	CEd/CertEd	Certificate in Education
BEAMA	British Electrical and Allied Manufacturers' Association	CEDR	Centre for Effective Dispute Resolution
		CEGB	Central Electricity Generating Board
BICERI	British Internal Combustion Engine Research Institute	CEng	Chartered Engineer
		CENTO	Central Treaty Organisation
BEd	Bachelor of Education	CEO	Chief Executive Officer
BEF	British Expeditionary Force	CERN	Organisation (formerly Centre) Européenne pour la Recherche Nucléaire (European Organisation for Nuclear Research)
BEng	Bachelor of Engineering		
BICC	British Insulated Callender's Cables		
BIM	British Institute of Management	CEYMS	The Church of England Young Men's Society
		CF	Chaplain to the Forces

CH	Companion of Honour		CUNY	City University of New York
ChB	Bachelor of Surgery		CUOTC	Cambridge University Officers' Training Corps
CIArb	Chartered Institute of Arbitrators		CUP	Cambridge University Press
CID	Criminal Investigation Department		CUSIA	Cambridge University Society for International Affairs
CIE	Companion of the Eminent Order of the Indian Empire		CVCP	Committee of Vice-Chancellors and Principals of the Universities of the United Kingdom
CIMgt	Companion, Institute of Management		CVO	Commander, Royal Victorian Order
CIPA	Chartered Institute of Patent Agents		d	died
CIPM	Companion, Institute of Personnel Management		DA	Diploma in Anaesthesia
CIWEM	Chartered Institution of Water and Environmental Management		DAAG	Deputy Assistant Adjutant-General
			DADGT	Deputy Assistant Director-General of Transportation
CM	Master of Surgery		DADMS	Deputy Assistant Director of Medical Services
CMath	Chartered Mathematician		DADRT	Deputy Assistant Director of Railway Traffic
CMG	Commander, Order of St Michael and St George		DAgr	Doctor of Agriculture
CMHC	Canada Mortgage and Housing Corporation		DAQMG	Deputy Assistant Quartermaster General
CMS	Church Mission Society		DArch	Doctor of Architecture
CNAA	Council for National Academic Awards		DAV	Dayanand Anglo-Vedic (Non-governmental educational body, India)
CND	Campaign for Nuclear Disarmament			
CNISF	Conseil National des Ingénieurs et des Scientifiques de France (National Council of Engineers and Scientists of France)		DAvMed	Diploma in Aviation Medicine
			DC	District of Columbia
			DCH	Diploma in Child Health
CNRS	Centre National de la Recherche Scientifique (National Centre for Scientific Research)		DCL	Doctor of Civil Law
			DCRE	Deputy Commander Royal Engineers
Co	Company		DD	Doctor of Divinity
C of E	Church of England		DE	Doctor of Engineering
contrib	contributor; contributions to		DEA	Department of Economic Affairs
CPA	Chartered Patent Agent		DEconSc	Doctor of Economic Science
CPhys	Chartered Physicist		DEng	Doctor of Engineering
CPRE	Campaign to Protect Rural England (formerly Council for the Preservation of Rural England/Council for the Protection of Rural England)		DES	Department of Education and Science
			DFC	Distinguished Flying Cross
			DGMS	Director-General, Medical Services
CRA	Commander, Royal Artillery		DHA	District Health Authority
CRCP(C)	Certificant, Royal College of Physicians of Canada		DHL	Doctor of Humane Letters; Doctor of Hebrew Letters
CRE	Commander, Royal Engineers		DHMSA	Diploma in the History of Medicine (Society of Apothecaries)
CRO	Commonwealth Relations Office			
CSE	Certificate of Secondary Education		DHSS	Department of Health and Social Services
CSI	Companion, Order of the Star of India		DIC	Diploma of Imperial College
CSIR	Council for Scientific and Industrial Research (now CSIRO)		DIH	Diploma in Industrial Health
			DipAA	Diploma in Archive Administration
CSIRO	Commonwealth Scientific and Industrial Research Organisation (previously CSIR)		DipAgr	Diploma in Agriculture
			DipAgSci	Diploma in Agricultural Science
CSM	Company Sergeant-Major		DipAnth	Diploma in Anthropology
CSS	Catholic Secondary School		DipArch	Diploma in Architecture
CStJ	Commander, Most Venerable Order of the Hospital of St John of Jerusalem		DipChemEng	Diploma in Chemical Engineering
			DipEd	Diploma in Education
CTO	Chief Transport Officer		DipEdPsy	Diploma in Educational Psychology
CU	Cambridge University		DipGeog	Diploma in Geography
CUAC	Cambridge University Athletics Club		DipLib	Diploma in Librarianship
CUAS	Cambridge University Air Squadron		DipMathStats	Diploma in Mathematical Statistics
CUBC	Cambridge University Boat Club		DipTheol	Diploma in Theology
CUMS	Cambridge University Musical Society			

DipTropAgr	Diploma in Tropical Agriculture		EC	European Community; European Commission
dis	dissolved		ECAFE	Economic Commission for Asia and the Far East
div	divorced		ECTEL	European Telecommunications and Professional Electronics Industry (The Trade Association for the Electronic Capital Goods Industry in the European Economic Area)
DJAG	Deputy Judge Advocate-General			
DL	Deputy Lieutenant			
DLit/DLitt	Doctor of Literature; Doctor of Letters			
DLO	Diploma in Laryngology and Otology		ED	Efficiency Decoration
DLS	Doctor of Library Science		ed	edited
DM	Doctor of Medicine		EEA	Electronic Engineering Association (The Trade Association of the Electronic Capital Goods Industry)
DMilSci	Diploma in Military Science			
DMJ	Diploma in Medical Jurisprudence		EEC	European Economic Community
DMR	Diploma in Medical Radiology		EEF	Engineering Employers' Federation
DMRD	Diploma in Medical Radiological Diagnostics		EEG	Electroencephalography
DMRE	Diploma in Medical Radiology and Electrology		EMI	Electric and Musical Industries Ltd
DMRT	Diploma in Medical Radio-Therapy		EMS	Emergency Medical Service
DMus	Doctor of Music		Eng	England
DNA	DeoxyriboNucleic Acid		ENT	Ear, Nose and Throat
DNMR	Deputy National Military Representative		EPA	European Patent Attorney
DO	Diploma in Ophthalmology		EPI	European Patent Institute
DoE	Department of the Environment		ERD	Emergency Reserve Decoration (Army)
DoI	Department of Industry		ESF	European Science Foundation
DObstRCOG	Diploma of Royal College of Obstetricians and Gynaecologists		ESRC	Economic and Social Research Council
			ETH	Eidgenössiche Technische Hochschule (Swiss Federal Institute of Technology)
DOMS	Diploma in Ophthalmic Medicine and Surgery			
DOrthRCS	Diploma in Orthodontics, Royal College of Surgeons		Eumetsat	European Organisation for the Exploitation of Meteorological Satellites
DPA	Diploma in Public Administration; Doctor of Public Administration			
			EurIng	European Engineer (conferred by FEANI)
			EuroCASE	European Council of Applied Science and Engineering
DPH	Diploma in Public Health		FAA	Fellow, Australian Academy of Science
DPh/DPhil	Doctor of Philosophy		FAAAS	Fellow, American Association for the Advancement of Sciences
DPM	Diploma in Psychological Medicine			
DPsych	Doctor of Psychology		FACC	Fellow, American College of Cardiology
DQMG	Deputy Quartermaster-General		FACCA	Fellow, Association of Certified and Corporate Accountants
DRCOG	Diploma of Royal College of Obstetricians and Gynaecologists			
			FACR	Fellow, American College of Radiology
Dr Eng	Doctor of Engineering		FACS	Fellow, American College of Surgeons
Dr rer nat	Doctor of Natural Science		FACVT	Fellow, American College of Veterinary Toxicologists
DSB	Defence Signals Bureau		FAIM	Fellow, Australian Institute of Management
DSC	Distinguished Service Cross		FAO	Food and Agriculture Organisation
DSc	Doctor of Science		FAPA	Fellow, American Psychology Association
DSIR	Department of Scientific & Industrial Research		FAPS	Fellow, American Physical Society
DSO	Distinguished Service Order		FAPsS	Fellow, Australian Psychological Society
DSR	Department of Scientific Research		FARCS	Faculty of Anaesthetists, Royal College of Surgeons of England
DST	Director of Supplies and Transport			
DTA	Diploma in Tropical Agriculture		FASCE	Fellow, American Society of Civil Engineers
DTD	Directorate of Technical Development		FBA	Fellow, British Academy
DTech	Doctor of Technology		FBCS	Fellow, British Computer Society
DTI	Department of Trade and Industry		FBICSc	Fellow, British Institute of Cleaning Science
DTM&H	Diploma in Tropical Medicine and Hygiene		FBIM	Fellow, British Institute of Management
DUniv/DU	Doctor of the University		FBMA	Fellow, British Medical Association
DVetMed	Doctor of Veterinary Medicine		FBOA	Fellow, British Optical Association

FBPsS	Fellow, British Psychological Society
FC	Football Club
FCA	Fellow, Institute of Chartered Accountants
FCAM	Fellow, Communications, Advertising and Marketing Foundation
FCASI	Fellow, Canadian Aeronautics and Space Institute
FCCP	Fellow, American College of Chest Physicians
FCFP	Fellow, College of Family Physicians of Canada
FCI	Fellow, Institute of Commerce
FCIArb	Fellow, Chartered Institute of Arbitrators
FCIB	Fellow, Corporation of Insurance Brokers
FCII	Fellow, Chartered Insurance Institute
FCIM	Fellow, Chartered Institute of Marketing
FCIOB	Fellow, Chartered Institute of Building (formerly Institute of Building, see also FIOB)
FCIPA	Fellow, Chartered Institute of Patent Agents
FCIS	Fellow, Institute of Chartered Secretaries and Administrators
FCIT	Fellow, Chartered Institute of Transport
FCIWEM	Fellow, Chartered Institution of Water and Environmental Management
FCMI	Fellow Chartered Management Institute
FCO	Foreign and Commonwealth Office
FConsE	Fellow, Association of Consulting Engineers
FCOphth	Fellow, College of Ophthalmologists
FCP	Fellow, College of Preceptors
FCPath	Fellow, College of Pathologists
FCS/FChemSoc	Fellow, Chemical Society (now absorbed into Royal Society of Chemistry)
FCSD	Fellow, Chartered Society of Designers
FEAF	Far East Air Force
FEANI	Fédération Européene d'Associations Nationales d'Ingénieurs (European Federation of National Engineering Associations)
FEng	Fellow of Engineering (later FREng)
FFA	Fellow, Faculty of Actuaries (in Scotland); Fellow, Institute of Financial Accountants
FFARCS	Fellow, Faculty of Anaesthetists, Royal College of Surgeons of England
FFCM	Fellow, Faculty of Community Medicine
FFOM	Fellow, Faculty of Occupational Medicine, Royal College of Physicians
FFOMI	Fellow, Faculty of Occupational Medicine, Royal College of Physicians of Ireland
FFPHM	Fellow, Faculty of Public Health Medicine
FFR	Fellow, Faculty of Radiologists (now see FRCR)
FGS	Fellow, Geological Society
FGSM	Fellow, Guildhall School of Music and Drama
FHA	Fellow, Institute of Health Service Administrators
FHKCP	Fellow, Hong Kong College of Physicians
FIA	Fellow, Institute of Actuaries
FIAgrE	Fellow, Institution of Agricultural Engineers
FIArb	Fellow, Institute of Arbitrators
FIB	Fellow, Institute of Bankers
FIBA	Fellow, Institute of Business Administration, Australia
FIBiol	Fellow, Institute of Biology
FIBP	Fellow, Institute of British Photographers
FICE	Fellow, Institution of Civil Engineers
FICeram	Fellow, Institute of Ceramics
FIChemE	Fellow, Institution of Chemical Engineers
FICS	Fellow, Institute of Chartered Secretaries
FIDE	Fédération Internationale des Échecs (International/World Chess Federation)
FIEAust	Fellow, Institution of Engineers, Australia
FIEE	Fellow, Institution of Electrical Engineers
FIEEE	Fellow, Institute of Electrical and Electronics Engineers (NY)
FIEI	Fellow, Institution of Engineers of Ireland
FIES	Fellow, Illuminating Engineering Society; Fellow, Institution of Engineers and Shipbuilders in Scotland
FIFST	Fellow, Institute of Food Science and Technology
FIGO	International Federation of Gynaecology and Obstetricians
FIIM	Fellow, Institution of Industrial Managers
FIM	Fellow, Institute of Materials (now FIMMM)
FIMA	Fellow, Institute of Mathematics and its Applications
FIMarE	Fellow, Institute of Marine Engineers
FIMC	Fellow, Institute of Management Consultants
FIMechE	Fellow, Institution of Mechanical Engineers
FIMgt	Fellow, Institute of Management
FIMinE	Fellow, Institution of Mining Engineers
FIMM	Fellow, Institution of Mining and Metallurgy
FIMMM	Fellow, Institute of Materials, Minerals and Mining (formerly FIM)
FIMS	Fellow, Institute of Mathematical Statistics
FInstD	Fellow, Institute of Directors
FInstE	Fellow, Institute of Energy
FInstM	Fellow, Institute of Marketing (now see FCIM)
FInstP	Fellow, Institute of Physics
FInstPet	Fellow, Institute of Petroleum
FIOB	Fellow, Institute of Building (now Chartered Institute of Building, see also FCIOB)
FIOCES	Fédération Internationale des Organisations de Correspondances et d'Echanges Scolaires (International Federation for School Correspondence and Exchange Organisations)
FIoD	Fellow, Institute of Directors
FIOP	Fellow, Institute of Printing
FIPA	Fellow, Institute of Practitioners in Advertising
FIPENZ	Fellow, Institution of Professional Engineers, New Zealand
FIPlantE	Fellow, Institute of Plant Engineers
FIProdE	Fellow, Institution of Production Engineers

FIRC	Fondazione Italiana per la Ricerca sul Cancro (Italian Foundation for Cancer Research)
FIREE	Fellow, Institution of Radio and Electrical Engineers
FIRI	Fellow, Institution of the Rubber Industry
FIS	Fellow, Institute of Statisticians
FIStructE	Fellow, Institution of Structural Engineers
FIWES	Fellow, Institution of Water Engineers and Scientists
FJP	Federation of Jewish Philanthropies
FKC	Fellow, King's College, London
FLA	Fellow, Library Association
FLS	Fellow, Linnean Society
FMedSci	Fellow, Academy of Medical Sciences
FNA	Fellow, Indian National Science Academy
FOR	Fellowship of Operational Research
FOREST	Freedom Organisation for the Right to Smoke Tobacco
FPhysS	Fellow, Physical Society
FRACGP	Fellow, Royal Australian College of General Practitioners
FRACP	Fellow, Royal Australasian College of Physicians
FRACS	Fellow, Royal Australasian College of Surgeons
FRAeS	Fellow, Royal Aeronautical Society
FRAgS	Fellow, Royal Agricultural Societies (of England, Scotland and Wales)
FRAI	Fellow, Royal Anthropological Institute
FRAM	Fellow, Royal Academy of Music
FRAS	Fellow, Royal Astronomical Society
FRCA	Fellow, Royal College of Anaesthetists
FRCGP	Fellow, Royal College of General Practitioners
FRCM	Fellow, Royal College of Music
FRCO	Fellow, Royal College of Organists
FRCO(CHM)	Fellow, Royal College of Organists with Diploma in Choir Training
FRCOG	Fellow, Royal College of Obstetricians and Gynaecologists
FRCOphth	Fellow, Royal College of Ophthalmologists
FRCP	Fellow, Royal College of Physicians, London
FRCPath	Fellow, Royal College of Pathologists
FRCPC	Fellow, Royal College of Physicians and Surgeons of Canada
FRCPCH	Fellow, Royal College of Paediatrics and Child Health
FRCPE/FRCPEd	Fellow, Royal College of Physicians of Edinburgh
FRCPI	Fellow, Royal College of Physicians of Ireland
FRCPsych	Fellow, Royal College of Psychiatrists
FRCR	Fellow, Royal College of Radiologists
FRCS	Fellow, Royal College of Surgeons of England
FRCSC	Fellow, Royal College of Surgeons of Canada
FRCSE/FRCSEd	Fellow, Royal College of Surgeons of Edinburgh
FRCVS	Fellow, Royal College of Veterinary Surgeons
FREconS	Fellow, Royal Economic Society
FREng	Fellow, Royal Academy of Engineering
FRES	Fellow, Royal Entomological Society of London
FRGS	Fellow, Royal Geographical Society
FRHistS	Fellow, Royal Historical Society
FRHS	Fellow, Royal History Society
FRIBA	Fellow, Royal Institute of British Architects
FRIC	Fellow, Royal Institute of Chemistry
FRICS	Fellow, Royal Institution of Chartered Surveyors
FRINA	Fellow, Royal Institution of Naval Architects
FRIPHH	Fellow, Royal Institute of Public Health and Hygiene
FRMetS	Fellow, Royal Meteorological Society
FRMS	Fellow, Royal Microscopical Society
FRNCM	Fellow, Royal Northern College of Music
FRPS	Fellow, Royal Photographic Society
FRS	Fellow, Royal Society
FRSA	Fellow, Royal Society of Arts
FRSAI	Fellow, Royal Society of Antiquaries in Ireland
FRSAMD	Fellow, Royal Scottish Academy of Music and Drama
FRSanI	Fellow, Royal Sanitary Institute
FRSC	Fellow, Royal Society of Canada; Fellow, Royal Society of Chemistry
FRSCM	Fellow, Royal School of Church Music
FRSE	Fellow, Royal Society of Edinburgh
FRSH	Fellow, Royal Society for Promotion of Health
FRSL	Fellow, Royal Society of Literature
FRSM	Fellow, Royal Society of Medicine
FRSNZ	Fellow, Royal Society of New Zealand
FRSocMed	Fellow, Royal Society of Medicine
FRSSAf	Fellow, Royal Society of South Africa
FRSTM&H	Fellow, Royal Society of Tropical Medicine and Hygiene
FRTS	Fellow, Royal Television Society
FRVA	Fellow, Rating and Valuation Association
FSA	Fellow, Society of Antiquaries
FSE	Fellow, Society of Engineers
FSLTC	Fellow, Society of British Leather Technologists and Chemists
FSRHE	Fellow, Society for Research into Higher Education
FSS	Fellow, Royal Statistical Society
FTCD	Fellow, Trinity College Dublin
FTCL	Fellow, Trinity College of Music, London
FTI	Fellow, Textile Institute
FTII	Fellow, Chartered Institute of Taxation
FTS	Fellow, Australian Academy of Technological Sciences and Engineering
GB	Great Britain
GBE	Knight or Dame Grand Cross, Order of the British Empire
GCB	Knight/Dame Grand Cross of the Order of the Bath
GCCS	Government Code and Cipher School
GCE	General Certificate of Education
GCHQ	Government Communications Headquarters

GCMG	Knight Grand Cross, Order of St Michael and St George		IBRD	International Bank of Reconstruction and Development
GCSE	General Certificate of Secondary Education		ICA	Institute of Chartered Accountants
GEC	General Electric Company		ICAEW	Institute of Chartered Accountants in England and Wales
GHQ	General Headquarters		ICAS	Institute of Chartered Accountants of Scotland
GHQME	General Headquarters, Middle East		ICE	Institution of Civil Engineers
GLAA	Greater London Arts Association		ICFC	Industrial and Commercial Finance Corporation
GLC	Greater London Council		ICI	Imperial Chemical Industries
GM	George Medal		ICIPE	The International Centre of Insect Physiology and Ecology
GMC	General Medical Council		ICL	International Computers Ltd
GOC	General Officer Commanding		ICO	International Coffee Organisation
GP	General Practitioner		ICSSR	Indian Council of Social Science Research
GPO	General Post Office		ICTA	Imperial College of Tropical Agriculture
GS	General Staff		IDC	Imperial Defence College, London
GSO	General Staff Officer		IEE	Institution of Electrical Engineers
HAA	Heavy Ak Ak		IEEE	Institute of Electrical and Electronics Engineers
HAC	Honourable Artillery Company		IEI	Institution of Engineers of Ireland
HBM	His/Her Britannic Majesty/Majesty's		IEME	Inspectorate of Electrical and Mechanical Engineering
HCF	Honorary Chaplain to the Forces		IFAD	International Fund for Agricultural Development
HEFCE	Higher Education Funding Council for England		IFIP	International Federation for Information Processing
HF	High Frequency		IGS	International Glaciological Society
HGCA	Home-Grown Cereals Authority		IHBC	Institute of Historic Building Conservation
HH	His/Her Highness		IILS	International Institute for Labour Studies
HHD	Doctor of Humanities (US)		ILA	International Law Association
HM	His/Her Majesty/Majesty's		ILEA	Inner London Education Authority
HMC	Headmasters' and Headmistresses' Conference; Historical Manuscripts Commission		IMA	Institute for Mathematics and its Applications
HMG	His/Her Majesty's Government		IMechE	Institution of Mechanical Engineers
HMOCS	His/Her Majesty's Overseas Civil Service		IMO	International Maritime Organisation
HMS	His/Her Majesty's Ship		IMS	Indian Medical Service
HMSO	Her Majesty's Stationery Office		INSA	Indian National Science Academy
HMT	His/Her Majesty's Tug		INSEAD	Institut Européen d'Administration des Affairs (European Institute of Business Administration)
HMUDE	HM Underwater Detection Establishment		IPC	International Publishing Corporation
Hon	Honorary/Honourable		IPFA	Institute of Public Finance and Accountancy
HQ	Headquarters		IPPS	Institute of Physics and the Physical Society
HQRA	Headquarters Royal Artillery		IRA	International Reading Association
HRH	His/Her Royal Highness		IREE	Institution of Radio and Electrical Engineers
HSH	Her Serene Highness		IRQPC	International Rubber Quality and Packing Conference
HV	High Voltage		IRSG	International Rubber Study Group
IAAM	The Incorporated Association of Assistant Masters		IRV	Indian Reserve Volunteers
IACO	Inter-African Coffee Organisation		ISCA	Indian Science Congress Association
IAEA	International Atomic Energy Agency		ISM	Incorporated Society of Musicians
IAMANEH	Member, British Representative to International Association for Maternal and Neonatal Health		ISO	Imperial Service Order
IAMC	Indian Army Medical Corps		IT	Information Technology
IAPS	Incorporated Association of Preparatory Schools		ITV	Independent Television
IARO	Indian Army Reserve of Officers		IUC	International Undergraduate Committee
IASC	International Arctic Science Committee		IUCAA	Inter-University Centre for Astronomy and Astrophysics
IBA	Independent Broadcasting Authority			
IBM	International Business Machines Corporation			

IUCN	World Conservation Union (formerly International Union for the Conservation of Nature and Natural Resources)
IUPAC	International Union of Pure and Applied Chemistry
IUPAP	International Union of Pure and Applied Physics
IUPC	Inter-University and Polytechnic Council for Higher Education Overseas
JAG	Judge Advocate General
JCR	Junior Common Room
JP	Justice of the Peace
Jr	Junior
JRAMC	Journal of the Royal Army Medical Corps
JTC	Junior Training Corps
KBE	Knight Commander, Order of the British Empire
KC	King's Counsel
KCB	Knight Commander, Order of the Bath
KCHS	Knight Commander, Order of the Holy Sepulchre
KCIE	Knight Commander, Order of the Indian Empire
KCL	King's College London
KCMG	Knight Commander, Order of St Michael and St George
KCSG	Knight Commander, Order of St Gregory the Great
KCSI	Knight Commander, Star of India
KCVO	Knight Commander, Royal Victorian Order
KHS	Knight, Order of the Holy Sepulchre
KLJ	Knight, Order of St Lazarus of Jerusalem
KOYLI	King's Own Yorkshire Light Infantry
KRRC	King's Royal Rifle Corps
KSA	Kingdom of Saudi Arabia
KSJ	Knight, Sovereign Order of St John of Jerusalem (Knights Hospitaller)
KSLI	The King's (Shropshire Light Infantry)
KStJ	Knight, Most Venerable Order of the Hospital of St John of Jerusalem
Kt	Knight Bachelor
(L)	Electrical
LAA	Light Anti-Aircraft
LAAA	Liverpool Annals of Archaeology and Anthropology
LAC	Leading Aircraftman
LAg	Licentiate in Agriculture
LAMTPI	Legal Associate Member, Town Planning Institute
LCC	London County Council
LDS	Licentiate in Dental Surgery
LDSRCS	Licenciate in Dental Surgery, Royal College of Surgeons of England
LHD	Literarum Humaniorum Doctor (Doctor of Literature)
LittD	Doctor of Literature; Doctor of Letters
LLB	Bachelor of Laws
LLD	Doctor of Laws
LLM	Master of Laws
LMBC	Lady Margaret Boat Club
LMCC	Licentiate, Medical Council of Canada
LMS	London Mathematical Society
LMSSA	Licentiate in Medicine and Surgery, Society of Apothecaries
LNER	London and North Eastern Railway
LRAM	Licentiate, Royal Academy of Music
LRCP	Licentiate, Royal College of Physicians, London
LRCS	Licentiate, Royal College of Surgeons of England
LRFPS	Licentiate, Royal Faculty of Physicians and Surgeons
LSE	London School of Economics and Political Science
LSHTM	London School of Hygiene and Tropical Medicine
Lt	Lieutenant
Lt Cdr	Lieutenant Commander
LTCL	Licentiate, Trinity College of Music, London
Lt Col	Lieutenant Colonel
Ltd	Limited
LTh	Licentiate in Theology
LVO	Lieutenant, Royal Victorian Order
m	married
MA	Master of Arts
MACE	Member of the Association of Consulting Engineers
MACostE	Member, Association of Cost Engineers
MAFF	Ministry of Agriculture, Fisheries and Food
MAIChE	Member, American Institute of Chemical Engineers
MArch	Master of Architecture
MASCE	Member, American Society of Civil Engineers
MASME	Member, American Society of Mechanical Engineers
MATM	Master in Air Transport Management
MB	Bachelor of Medicine
MBA	Master of Business Administration
MBCS	Member, British Computer Society
MBE	Member, Order of the British Empire
MBIM	Member, British Institute of Management
MC	Military Cross
MCC	Marylebone Cricket Club
MCH	Malayan Certificate of Honour
MChir	Master of Surgery
MCIArb	Member, Chartered Institute of Arbitrators
MCIM	Member, Canadian Institute of Mining
MCIT	Member, Chartered Institute of Transport
MCIWEM	Member, Chartered Institution of Water and Environmental Management
MCMI	Member, Chartered Management Institute
MCom/MComm	Master of Commerce
MConsE	Member, Association of Consulting Engineers
MCSCE	Member, Canadian Society for Civil Engineering
MD	Doctor of Medicine
MDCM	Doctor of Medicine and Master of Surgery

ME	Middle East	MM	Military Medal
MEd	Master of Education	MNAS	Member, National Academy of Sciences (US)
MEF	Middle East Force	MNZIE	Member, New Zealand Institute of Engineers
MEng	Master of Engineering	MO	Medical Officer
MFCM	Member, Faculty of Community Medicine	MOD	Ministry of Defence
MFOM	Member, Faculty of Occupational Medicine	MOH	Medical Officer of Health
MGB	Motor Gun Boat	MORS	Military Operations Research Society
MGC	Machine Gun Corps	MP	Member of Parliament
MHA	Methodist Homes for the Aged	MPBW	Ministry of Public Buildings and Works
MHCIMA	Member, Hotel Catering and Institutional Management Association	MPH	Master of Public Health
MI	Myocardial Infarction	MPhil	Master of Philosophy
MIBiol	Member, Institute of Biology	MPMI	Member, Project Management Institute
MICE	Member, Institution of Civil Engineers	MRAeS	Member, Royal Aeronautical Society
MIChemE	Member, Institution of Chemical Engineers	MRC	Medical Research Council
MIE	Member, Institution of Engineers	MRCGP	Member, Royal College of General Practitioners
MIEE	Member, Institution of Electrical Engineers	MRCOG	Member, Royal College of Obstetricians and Gynaecologists
MIEI	Member, Institution of Engineers of Ireland	MRCP	Member, Royal College of Physicians
MIEM	Master of Industrial Engineering and Management	MRCPath	Member, Royal College of Pathologists
MIERE	Member, Institution of Electronic and Radio Engineers (later MIEE)	MRCPE	Member, Royal College of Physicians, Edinburgh
MIGasE	Member, Institution of Gas Engineers	MRCPsych	Member, Royal College of Psychiatrists
MIL	Member, Institute of Linguists	MRCS	Member, Royal College of Surgeons of England
MIM	Member, Institute of Metals	MRCVS	Member, Royal College of Veterinary Surgeons
MIMA	Member, Institute of Mathematics and its Applications	MRIA	Member, Royal Irish Academy
MIMarE	Member, Institute of Marine Engineers	MRIC	Member, Royal Institute of Chemistry
MIMarEST	Member, Institute of Marine Engineering, Science and Technology	MRIN	Member, Royal Institute of Navigation
		MRPharmS	Member, Royal Pharmaceutical Society
MIMechE	Member, Institution of Mechanical Engineers	MRSL	Member, Royal Society of Literature
MIMgt	Member, Institute of Management	MRTPI	Member, Royal Town Planning Institute
MIMinE	Member, Institute of Mining Engineers	MS/MSc	Master of Science
MInstCE	Member, Institution of Civil Engineers	MSAICE	Member, South African Institution of Civil Engineers
MInstE	Member, Institute of Energy	MSC	Manpower Services Commission
MInstMgt	Member, Institute of Management	MSCI	Member, Society of Chemical Industry
MInstP	Member, Institute of Physics	MScTech	Master of Science and Technology
MInstT	Member, Institute of Transport	MS(EE)	Master of Science (Electrical Engineering)
MInstW	Member, Institute of Welding	MTh	Master of Theology
MIOP	Member, Institute of Printing	MusB	Bachelor of Music
MIPD	Member, Institute of Personnel and Development	MusD	Doctor of Music
MIPM	Member, Institute of Personnel Management (now MIPD)	MVO	Member, Royal Victorian Order
		N	North/Northern
MIStructE	Member, Institution of Structural Engineers	NAAS	National Agricultural Advisory Service
MIT	Massachusetts Institute of Technology	NADFAS	National Association of Decorative and Fine Arts Societies
MITI	Member, Institute of Translation and Interpreting		
MITMA	Member, Institute of Trade Mark Agents	NALGO	National and Local Government Officers' Association
MIWEM	Member, Institution of Water and Environmental Management	NASA	National Aeronautics and Space Administration
		NATO	North Atlantic Treaty Organization
MIWES	Member, Institution of Water Engineers and Scientists	NCCL	National Council for Civil Liberties
MLitt	Master of Letters	NCO	Non-Commissioned Officer
		NDIC	National Defence Industries Council
MLS	Master of Library Studies	NE	North East

NEA	Nuclear Energy Agency	PGCE	Post Graduate Certificate of Education
NECZAM	National Education Company of Zambia	PhB	Bachelor of Philosophy
NEDO	National Economic Development Office	PhD	Doctor of Philosophy
NER	North Eastern Railway	PLA	Port of London Authority
NERC	Natural Environment Research Council	plc	Public Limited Company
NFU	National Farmers' Union	PMO	Principal Medical Officer
NHS	National Health Service	PNEU	Parents' National Educational Union
NI	Northern Ireland	POW	Prisoner of War
NIESR	National Institute of Economic and Social Research	PPS	Proceedings of the Prehistoric Society
NL	No Liability (company suffix, Australia)	PR	Public Relations
NSERC	Natural Sciences and Engineering Research Council, Canada	PSA	Property Services Agency
NSM	Non-Stipendiary Minister	PSMO	Principal School Medical Officer
NSPCC	National Society for the Prevention of Cruelty to Children	PTO	Principal Technical Officer
		Pty	Proprietary (company suffix, Australia, Southern Africa)
NSW	New South Wales	QALAS	Qualified Associate, Chartered Land Agents' Society
NT	New Testament	QC	Queen's Council
NTS	New Testament Studies	QHP	Queen's Honorary Physician
NUI	National University of Ireland	QMG	Quarter Master General
NV	Naamlose Vennootschap (Limited Company, Netherlands)	QS	Quarter Sessions
		QUB	Queen's University, Belfast
NW	North West/North Western	QVO	Queen Victoria's Own
NWFP	North-West Frontier Province	QVR	Queen Victoria's Rifles
NY	New York	RA	Royal Artillery; Royal Academician
NYC	New York City	RAC	Royal Armoured Corps; Regiment d'Artillerie Coloniale (Colonial Artillery Regiment)
NZ	New Zealand		
OBE	Officer, Order of the British Empire	RACD	Royal Army Chaplains' Department
OC	Officer Commanding	RADA	Royal Academy of Dramatic Art
OCAMAC	Oxford Centre for Advanced Materials and Composites	RAE	Royal Aircraft Establishment; Royal Aerospace Establishment; Royal Aeronautical Establishment
OCS	Officer Candidates School	RAEC	Royal Army Educational Corps
OCTU	Officer Cadet Training Unit	RAF	Royal Air Force
ODM	Ministry of Overseas Development	RAFVR	Royal Air Force Volunteer Reserves
OECD	Organisation for Economic Co-operation and Development	RAFVR(T)	Royal Air Force Volunteer Reserves (Training Branch)
		RAM	(Member of) Royal Academy of Music
OEEC	Organization for European Economic Co-operation	RAMC	Royal Army Medical Corps
OJHF	Old Johnian Henley Fund	RAOC	Royal Army Ordnance Corps
OM	Order of Merit	RAPC	Royal Army Pay Corps
Op	Opus	RARDE	Royal Armament Research and Development Establishment
OR	Operational Research		
OStJ	Officer, Most Venerable Order of the Hospital of St John of Jerusalem	RASC	Royal Army Service Corps
		RAVC	Royal Army Veterinary Corps
OTC	Officers' Training Corps	RC	Roman Catholic
OTU	Operational Training Unit	RCA	Royal College of Art
OUP	Oxford University Press	RCAF	Royal Canadian Air Force
PA	Personal Assistant	RCDS	Royal College of Defence Studies
PC	Privy Counsellor	RCGP	Royal College of General Practitioners
PCE	Postgraduate Certificate of Education	RCM	Royal College of Music
PE	Physical Education	RCNVR	Royal Canadian Naval Volunteer Reserves
PED	Doctor of Physical Education	RCOG	Royal College of Obstetricians and Gynaecologists
PEng	Registered Professional Engineer (Canada)	RCP	Royal College of Physicians

RCPath	Royal College of Pathologists		RSCM	Royal School of Church Music
RCPCH	Royal College of Paediatrics and Child Health		RSE	Royal Society of Edinburgh
RCPI	Royal College of Physicians of Ireland		RSGS	Royal Scottish Geographical Society
RCPSG	Royal College of Physicians and Surgeons of Glasgow		RSM	Royal Society of Medicine
RCR	Royal College of Radiology		RSME	Royal School of Military Engineering
RCS	Royal College of Surgeons in England; Royal College of Science		RSO	Resident Surgical Officer
			RSPCA	Royal Society for the Prevention of Cruelty to Animals
RCSI	Royal College of Surgeons in Ireland			
RCT	Royal Corps of Transport		RSRE	Royal Signals and Radar Establishment
RD	Royal Naval and Royal Marine Forces Reserve Decoration		RTO	Railway Transport Officer; Railway Traffic Officer
			RTS	Royal Television Society
RDI	Royal Designer for Industry		RUSI	Royal United Services Institute for Defence Studies (formerly Royal United Service Institution)
RE	Royal Engineers			
REMAP	Rehabilitation Engineering Movement Advisory Panels		RWA	Royal West of England Academy
			SA	South Africa
REME	Royal Electrical and Mechanical Engineers		SACS	South African Communication Service
RFA	Royal Field Artillery		SAS	Special Air Service
RFC	Royal Flying Corps; Rugby Football Club		SBAC	Society of British Aerospace Companies
RFU	Rugby Football Union		SBL	Society of Biblical Literature
RGA	Royal Garrison Artillery		SBStJ	Serving Brother, Most Venerable Order of the Hospital of St John of Jerusalem
RGS	Royal Geographical Society; Royal Grammar School			
RHA	Regional Health Authority; Royal Horse Artillery		ScD	Doctor of Science
			SCM	Student Christian Movement
RHQ	Regimental Headquarters		SDO	Senior Dental Officer
RHS	Royal Historical Society		SDP	Social Democratic Party
RIA	Royal Irish Academy		SE	South East/South Eastern
RIBA	(Member of) Royal Institute of British Architects		SEAC	South-East Asia Command
RICS	Royal Institute of Chartered Surveyors		SERC	Science and Engineering Research Council
RIIA	Royal Institute of International Affairs		SHAEF	Supreme Headquarters Allied Expeditionary Force
RINR	Royal Indian Naval Reserves		SHAPE	Supreme Headquarters Allied Powers Europe
RINVR	Royal Indian Naval Volunteer Reserves		SHO	Senior House Officer
RMA	Royal Military Academy		SJC	St John's College, Cambridge
RMC	Royal Military College		SJD	Doctor of Juridical Science
RMCS	Royal Military College of Science		SM	Master of Science
RMO	Resident Medical Officer; Regimental Medical Officer		SMN	Seri Maharaja Mangku Negara (Malaysia)
RMS	Royal Medical Society		SNTS	Studiorum Novi Testamenti Societas (Society for New Testament Studies)
RN	Royal Navy/Royal Naval			
RNAF	Royal Naval Air Force		SOAS	School of Oriental and African Studies
RNAS	Royal Naval Air Service		SOE	Special Operations Executive
RNB	Royal Naval Barracks		SORE	Staff Officer, Royal Engineers
RNC	Royal Naval College		SOTS	Society for Old Testament Study
RNH	Royal Naval Hospital		SPCK	Society for the Promotion of Christian Knowledge
RNLI	Royal National Lifeboat Institution		SPG	Society for the Propagation of the Gospel in Foreign Parts
RNR	Royal Naval Reserve			
RNVR	Royal Naval Volunteer Reserve		SRC	Science Research Council
RNVSR	Royal Naval Volunteer Supplementary Reserve		SS	Saints; Steamship
RoSPA	Royal Society for the Prevention of Accidents		SSRC	Social Sciences Research Council
RRS	Royal Research Ship		SSS	Special Signals Service
RSA	Royal Society of Arts		STC	Senior Training Corps
RSAMD	Royal Scottish Academy of Music and Drama		STD	*Sacrae Theologiae Doctor* (Doctor of Sacred Theology)
RSC	Royal Society of Canada		SWPA	South Western Pacific Area

TA	Territorial Army
TAF	Tactical Air Force
TAVRA	Territorial Auxiliary and Volunteer Reserve Association
TCD	Trinity College, Dublin
TD	Territorial Efficiency Decoration
TEC	Training and Enterprise Council
TES	Times Educational Supplement
TF	Territorial Force
ThM	Master of Theology
TI	Texas Instruments
TPR	Town Planning Review
trans	translated
TRE	Telecommunications Research Establishment
TSB	Trustee Savings Bank
TSO	Technical Staff Officer
TV	Television
UAE	United Arab Emirates
UC	University of California
UCCA	Universities Central Council on Admissions
UCH	University College Hospital (London)
UCL	University College, London
UCLA	University of California at Los Angeles
UCLES	University of Cambridge Local Examinations Syndicate
UCW	University College of Wales
UEA	University of East Anglia
UFAW	Universities Foundation for Animal Welfare
UFO	Unidentified Flying Object
UGC	University Grants Committee
UJA	United Jewish Appeal
UK	United Kingdom
UKAEA	United Kingdom Atomic Energy Authority
UKNMR	United Kingdom National Military Representative
UMIST	University of Manchester Institute of Science and Technology
UN	United Nations
UNCITRAL	United Nations Commission on International Trade Law
UNCTAD	United Nations Conference on Trade and Development
UNDP	United Nations Development Programme
UNEDO	United Nations Economic Development Organisation
UNESCO	United Nations Educational, Scientific and Cultural Organisation
UNICEF	United Nations Children's Fund
UNIDO	United Nations Industrial Development Organisation
UNO	United Nations Organization
UNRRA	United Nations Relief and Rehabilitation Administration
UR Church	United Reformed Church
US	United States
USA	United States of America
USAF	United States Air Force
USN	United States Navy
USNR	United States Naval Reserve
USPG	United Society for the Propagation of the Gospel
USSR	Union of Soviet Socialist Republics
UWA	University of Western Australia
VD	Volunteer Officers' Decoration; Royal Naval Volunteer Reserve Officers' Decoration (later VRD); Victorian Decoration
VetMB	Bachelor of Veterinary Medicine
VR	Volunteer Reserves
VRD	Royal Naval Volunteer Reserve Officers' Decoration
WEA	Workers' Educational Association
WHO	World Health Organization
WO	War Office; Warrant Officer
WS	Writer(s) to the Signet
WWI	World War I
WWII	World War II
YMCA	Young Men's Christian Association

A

AALDERS, Willem Jan Goossen (1923) Born 21 January 1907, son of Elisa Justinus Aalders, Shipbroker, and Bartha Johanna Cruyff. **Subject(s):** Economics; BA 1926. **Tutor(s):** E A Benians. **Educ:** Hoogere Burgerschool, Rotterdam, Holland.

AARONS, Frank Lewis Frankel (1918) Born 23 May 1900, The Gunyah, Carew Road, Wallington, Surrey; son of Frank Henry Aarons, Solicitor, and Daisy Frankel. **Tutor(s):** E E Sikes. **Educ:** St Winifred's, Kenley; Uppingham.

ABBOTT, Dr John Cave (1938) Born 27 December 1919, Old Somersby, Grantham; son of John Cave Abbott, Farmer, and Jeannie Stothard. **Subject(s):** Geography; BA 1946; MA 1949. **Tutor(s):** J S Boys Smith. **Educ:** Elementary School, Old Somersby; King's School, Grantham. **Career:** Chief, Marketing Service, Food and Agriculture Organisation of the UN. **Awards:** Newcome Exhibition, SJC 1938. **Publications:** *Politics & Poverty: a critique of the Food and Agriculture Organisation of the UN*, Routledge, London. Died 19 January 1994.

ABEL, John Percival (1943) Born 5 December 1925, 5 Royal Crescent, Harrogate, Yorkshire; son of Percival George Abel, Bank Cashier, and Hilda Jones. **Tutor(s):** C W Guillebaud. **Educ:** Lawrence House School, St Anne's; Shrewsbury School.

ABEYEWARDENA, Charles Christopher Patrick Perera (1919) Born 17 March 1900, Closenberg, Mayalle, Galle District, Ceylon; son of Francis Perera Abeyewardena, Merchant and Landed Proprietor, and Crawford Margarita Macdonald Perera de Soysa. **Tutor(s):** E A Benians. **Educ:** Prince of Wales College, Moratuwa; Government Training College, Colombo; Trinity College, Colombo; Royal College, Colombo.

ABHAYARATNA, Walter Patrick Leopold (1928) Born 21 September 1906, Colombo, Ceylon; son of Arthur Edwin Abhayaratna, and Lilian Adelaide Gunawardene. **Tutor(s):** J M Wordie. **Educ:** Government Training College, Colombo; Royal College, Colombo; Ceylon University College; Survey Department, Ceylon Training School.

ABSALOM, Harold John (1932) Born 18 September 1914, 40 Belmont Road, Ellacombe, Torquay; son of John Knight Absalom, Director of Goodbody's Cafés, Plymouth, and Frances Mary Spurgeon. **Subject(s):** Engineering; BA 1935. **Tutor(s):** J S Boys Smith. **Educ:** Plymouth College; Bootham School, York. Died 24 March 1989.

ABSOLON, Canon Peter Chambers (1948) Born 13 July 1927, Colkirk, Norfolk; son of Alfred George Absolon, Captain, RASC, Inspector, Gloucester Aircraft Company, and May Pearson; m Joan James, 1951 (d August 2001); 4 sons (Paul, James, Timothy and Philip), 1 daughter (Rachel). **Subject(s):** Theology; BA 1950; MA 1955. **Tutor(s):** C W Guillebaud. **Johnian Relatives:** brother of Michael John Absolon (1951). **Educ:** Primary and secondary schools, Southampton; Cheltenham Grammar School; Lincoln Theological College. **Career:** Lieutenant, Sherwood Foresters (National Service) 1946–1948; Ordained Deacon, Gloucester 1953, Priest 1954; Curate, Yate, Gloucestershire 1953–1956; Priest in Charge, St Andrew, Bosthall Heath, Kent 1956–1960; Vicar, St John's, Erith, Kent 1961–1967; Team Vicar, Strood, Kent (Adviser in Social Action) 1967–1981; Field Work Teacher for Social Work Courses, Kent University and mid-Kent College; Vicar, Holy Trinity, Gillingham, Kent 1981–1991. **Appointments:** Industrial Chaplain, Erith, Kent 1960–1967; Founder, Hands Volunteer Scheme 1969; Co-founder and Chairman, Medway Action Committee for the Homeless 1972; Honorary Canon, Rochester Cathedral 1979–1991; Member, Kent University School of Continuing Education Social Work Committee. **Publications:** 'The Exodus Affair: Hamburg 1947', *The Journal of Holocaust Education* Vol 6, No 3, 1997. Died 26 June 2001.

ACKERY, Professor Duncan Melville (1949) Born 11 August 1930, 129 Tulse Hill, Norwood, London; son of William Melville Ackery, Chartered Accountant, and Ruth Frances Carlisle. **Subject(s):** Natural Sciences; BA 1952; MA 1971; MB 1956; BChir 1956; MSc (Birmingham). **Tutor(s):** G C L Bertram. **Educ:** Dulwich College Preparatory School; Newport Grammar School; Dauntsey's School, West Lavington. **Career:** Surgeon Commander, RN; Consultant in Nuclear Medicine, Southampton University Hospital 1974–1992. **Appointments:** Honorary Clinical Professor of Nuclear Medicine, Southampton University 1989.

ACOSTA, George Alfred (1924) Born 3 April 1905, City of Mexico; son of Alfonso Acosta, First Secretary, Mexican Embassy, Brazil, and Catherine Oreglia. **Tutor(s):** E E Sikes. **Educ:** Sevenoaks School, Kent.

ACTESON, Henry William Alec (1943) Born 2 May 1925, The Firs, Dewlish, Dorset; son of William Henry Acteson, Cashier, Midland Bank, and Elizabeth Goldstone; m Marilyn Margaret Kramer, 10 November 1958, Regina, Saskatchewan, Canada. BA 1946; MA 1950. **Tutor(s):** S J Bailey. **Educ:** Christchurch School, Ilford; County High School, Ilford; Ulverston Grammar School.

ACTON, Henry (1909) Born 2 February 1890, New Hampton Road, Wolverhampton, Staffordshire; son of George Herbert Acton, Sub-Inspector of Schools, and Harriet Slater. **Subject(s):** Mathematics; BA 1912. **Tutor(s):** L H K Bushe-Fox. **Educ:** Tettenhall National School, Wolverhampton; Wolverhampton Higher Grade School; Wolverhampton Grammar School.

ACWORTH, Donald George William (1920) Born 9 June 1902, 9 Kingswood Villas, Gillingham, Kent; son of George Pelham Aufrère Acworth, Clerk in Holy Orders, and Maud Elizabeth Booth; m (1) Margaret Larken, 9 May 1931, Bushey Parish Church (d 1947), (2) Katharine Parker, 18 March 1949, London; 3 daughters (Angela, Carol and Susan). BA 1923; MA 1933. **Tutor(s):** E E Sikes. **Educ:** Westerleigh School, St Leonards on Sea; Radley College, Abingdon. **Career:** Joined company 1923, Member, Household Appliances Department 1926, Manager, Domestic Cooker Department 1933, Manager, Export Department 1948, Director, ten overseas subsidiary companies 1954, Director, all overseas companies and export sales 1957, GEC. **Appointments:** Chairman, BEAMA cooker section 1946–1947; Founder member, IEE Utilisation Section Committee; Member, several BSI Committees connected with heating and cooking.

ADAM, Kenneth (1926) Born 1 March 1908, 61 Caledon Road, Nottingham; son of Edward Percy Adam, Schoolmaster, and Ethel Jean Saunders; m Ruth King, 24 May 1932, East Bridgford, Nottinghamshire (d 1977); 3 sons (Clive, Piers and Nicholas), 1 daughter (Corinna). **Subject(s):** History; BA 1929. **Tutor(s):** E A Benians. **Educ:** Stanley Road Preparatory School, Nottingham; High School, Nottingham. **Career:** Reporter, *Manchester Guardian* 1930; Home News Editor, BBC 1934–1936; Special Correspondent, *The Star* 1936–1940; Press Officer, BOAC 1940–1941; Head of Publicity 1941–1950, Controller, *Light Programme* 1950–1955, BBC; Manager, Hulton Press 1955–1957; Controller, Television Programmes, BBC 1957–1968; Head, BBC Television 1961. **Appointments:** President, Cambridge Union Society, Lent Term 1930; Visiting Professor of Communications, Temple University, Philadelphia 1968; Chairman, *Free Speech*, ITV. Died 18 October 1978.

ADAMS, Alexander Francis Lucas (1935) Born 17 April 1916, 17 Elm Park Mansions, Chelsea, London; son of Alexander Hector Adams, Hotel Proprietor, and Hilare Caroline Matheson Lucas. **Subject(s):** History; BA 1938; MA 1942. **Tutor(s):** J S Boys Smith. **Educ:** St Augustine's Abbey School, Ramsgate; Ampleforth College.

ADAMS, Christopher Douglas (1949) Born 23 April 1927, 12 Lynedoch Crescent, Glasgow; son of Douglas Kinchin Adams, Physician, and Winifred Audrey Hirst; m Janet Dora Sydney Donovan, 1951; 1 son (Douglas Noël b 11 March 1952, d 11 May 2001). BA 1951; MA 1961.

Tutor(s): C W Guillebaud. **Johnian Relatives:** father of Douglas Noël Adams (1971). **Educ:** Kelvinside Academy; Ardureck Preparatory School; Trinity College, Glenalmond. **Career:** Ordained Priest; RN 1944–1946.

ADAMS, Frank (1904) Born 7 August 1885, Hull, Yorkshire; son of George Adams, Engineer, and Rebecca Mayo; m; 1 son, 2 daughters. **Subject(s):** Natural Sciences; BA 1907; MA 1911. **Tutor(s):** D MacAlister. **Educ:** Hymers College; Beverley Road School. **Career:** Master, County School, Caernarvonshire 1908–1910; Master, William Hulme's Grammar School, Manchester 1910–1950. Died 9 June 1975.

ADAMS, John Bernard Pye (1909) Born 15 November 1890, St John's, Cedars Road, Beckenham, Kent; son of Harold John Adams, Civil Servant, and Georgina Pye. **Subject(s):** Classics/Economics; BA 1912. **Tutor(s):** E E Sikes. **Educ:** Clare House School, Beckenham; Malvern College. **Career:** Warden and Assistant Educational Adviser, Hostel for Indian Students, South Kensington; Royal Welsh Fusiliers 1914; Temporary Captain 1915–1917. **Awards:** Latin Ode and Greek Epigram 1911; Browne Medal for Greek Epigram, University of Cambridge 1912. **Publications:** Various articles in *The Eagle*. Died 27 February 1917 (killed in action).

ADAMS, Norman Stuart (1947) Born 13 October 1925, Greenbank Nursing Home, Plymouth; son of William Stuart Adams, Electrical Draughtsman, and Janie Amelia Miller; m Sheila; 2 sons (John and Christopher Douglas). **Subject(s):** History; BA 1949; MA 1979. **Tutor(s):** F Thistlethwaite. **Educ:** Montpelier School, Plymouth; Devonport High School. **Career:** Dye Stuffs, Special Chemicals and Organics Divisions 1950–1975, Products Marketing Manager (Chemicals) 1975–1980, ICI; Industrial Marketing Consultancy Company 1980. **Awards:** Universities Prize Essay Competition, Royal Asiatic Society 1949. Died 14 March 1993.

ADAMSON, Dr Cuthbert (1915) Born 1 May 1896, The Vicarage, South Westoe, Westoe, Durham; son of Cuthbert Edward Adamson, Clerk in Holy Orders, and Clara Isabel Haggie. **Subject(s):** History/Medicine; BA 1919; MA 1937; BChir 1937; MB 1937; MRCS; LRCP. **Tutor(s):** R P Gregory. **Johnian Relatives:** son of Cuthbert Edward Adamson (1867); brother of Edward Blythman Adamson (1908) and of Francis Douglas Adamson (1910). **Educ:** Durham School. **Career:** Lieutenant, King's Own Yorkshire Light Infantry, Salonika 1914–1918; Honorary Consultant Physician, Durham Hospital Group; House Appointments, Royal Victoria Infirmary, Newcastle, and the Princess Mary Maternity Hospital, Newcastle; GP, Durham; TA, France, Kumasi (Gold Coast) and the Invasion of Europe, WWII; Senior Hospital Medical Officer, Dryburn Hospital; Medical Officer, Sherburn Hospital; Medical Officer, St Hild's Training College. Died 7 February 1970.

ADAMSON, The Revd Edward Blythman (1908) Born 20 May 1889, Westoe, South Shields, Durham; son of Cuthbert Edward Adamson, Clerk in Holy Orders, and Clara Isabel Haggie. BA 1911; MA 1915. **Tutor(s):** J R Tanner. **Johnian Relatives:** son of Cuthbert Edward Adamson (1867); brother of Francis Douglas Adamson (1910) and of Cuthbert Adamson (1915). **Educ:** The High School, South Shields; Wells Theological College. **Career:** Ordained Deacon 1912; Curate, Ryhope 1912–1916; Priest 1914; Curate, Houghton le Spring 1916–1918; Perpetual Curate, Grangetown 1918–1944; Vicar, Greatham 1944; Master, Greatham Hospital 1944; Rural Dean, Hartlepool 1945. **Appointments:** Honorary Canon, Durham Cathedral.

ADAMSON, Francis Douglas (1910) Born 8 October 1891, The Vicarage, Westoe, South Shields, Durham; son of Cuthbert Edward Adamson, Clerk in Holy Orders, and Clara Isabel Haggie. BA 1913. **Tutor(s):** J R Tanner. **Johnian Relatives:** son of Cuthbert Edward Adamson (1867); brother of Edward Blythman Adamson (1908) and of Cuthbert Adamson (1915). **Educ:** Durham School. **Career:** Enlisted in the Public Schools and Universities Battalion of the Royal Fusiliers; commissioned into the Army; Second Lieutenant, Border Regiment 1915. Died 17 November 1915 (killed in action).

ADAMSON, James Henry (1918) Born 2 December 1896, Crosby Road, North Waterloo, Liverpool; son of Joseph Adamson, Merchant and Director, Chemical Company, and Mary Fishwick. BA 1920; MA 1925; CChem; FRIC. **Tutor(s):** E E Sikes. **Educ:** Bishop's Court School, Freshfield; St Cuthbert's College, Ushaw. Died 19 May 1981.

ADCOCK, Cecil Milton (1926) Born 27 March 1909, Castellana 39, Madrid, Spain; son of Cecil Philip Adcock, Company Director, and Violet Marianne Bartholomew. **Subject(s):** Natural Sciences; BA 1930; MA 1935. **Tutor(s):** M P Charlesworth. **Johnian Relatives:** brother of Reginald Adcock (1930). **Educ:** Sunnydown School, Guildford; Malvern College.

ADCOCK, Reginald (1930) Born 7 June 1911, Castellana 43, Madrid, Spain; son of Cecil Philip Adcock, Merchant, and Violet Marianne Bartholomew. **Subject(s):** Modern and Medieval Languages. **Tutor(s):** C W Guillebaud. **Johnian Relatives:** brother of Cecil Milton Adcock (1926). **Educ:** Sunnydown School, Guildford; Malvern College.

ADDEY, John Michael (1939) Born 15 June 1920, 41 Weston Street, Barnsley; son of Francis Addey, General Manager, Cooperative Society, and Jane Eliza Coldwell. **Subject(s):** Economics; BA 1942; MA 1946. **Tutor(s):** C W Guillebaud. **Educ:** St Mary's School, Barnsley; Ackworth School. Died March 1982.

ADDISON, Cecil James Sim (1933) Born 21 August 1908, Omachie Hill, Parish of Monifield, Forfarshire; son of William Addison, Post Office Sorting Clerk and Telegraphist, and Helen Sim. **Subject(s):** Classics; BA 1935. **Tutor(s):** R L Howland. **Educ:** University of Edinburgh; Edinburgh Provincial Training College. **Career:** Linguist, Intelligence Service; Assistant Lecturer in Latin, University of Liverpool 1937–1941; Administrative Principal, Ministry of Works and Buildings 1941; Assistant Lecturer in Classics, University College, Dundee 1947. **Awards:** Scholarship, SJC; College Prize, SJC.

ADENEY, Eric Leonard (1905) Born 21 August 1888, 3 Mount Zion, Tunbridge Wells, Kent; son of Edwin Leonard Adeney, Physician, and Florence Mary Hobbs. BA 1910; MA 1932. **Tutor(s):** D MacAlister. **Educ:** Private Tuition. Died 4 November 1953.

ADENEY, Noel Frederick (1919) Born 26 November 1897, Helouan, Cairo, Egypt; son of Frederick Field Adeney, Clerk in Holy Orders, Church Missionary, and Selina Rosalie Savage; m Betty Holborn Gray Wardle, 23 July 1925, St Botolph, Aspley Guise; 1 son, 2 daughters. **Subject(s):** Medical Sciences; BA 1921; MA 1925; BChir 1925; MB 1925; MRCS; LRCP 1923; FRCS 1928. **Tutor(s):** E E Sikes. **Johnian Relatives:** son of Frederick Field Adeney (1884). **Educ:** Bushey House, Monkton Combe; Monkton Combe School, Bath. **Career:** Commissioned into the Royal Field Artillery, fought on the Somme and Passchendaele (Mentioned in Despatches); Director, Thoracic Unit, Southampton Hospital; House Surgeon, Royal Victoria and West Hampshire Hospital, Bournemouth; Honorary Surgeon, Cornelia and East Dorset Hospital, Poole; Consulting Thoracic Surgeon, Royal Hampshire County Hospital, Winchester, Isle of Wight, Dorset and Bournemouth CC, Royal National Sanatorium, Ventnor and Bournemouth; House Surgeon, St Mary's Hospital; Clinical Assistant, St Peter's Hospital; Surgical Clinical Assistant, Brompton Chest Hospital; Consulting Surgeon, Blandford Hospital; Resident Medical Officer, Three Counties Mental Hospital, Arlesey; House Surgeon, Bolingbroke Hospital. **Awards:** Scholarship, SJC 1915. **Honours:** Legion d'Honneur 1999. **Publications:** 'Scope of Thoracic Surgery', *Medical Press Circular*. Died 9 July 1999.

ADKINS, Edward William Orton (1931) Born 28 February 1913, Courtauld Road, Bocking, Braintree, Essex; son of Edward William Adkins, Physics Master, Elland Secondary School, and Edith Hird; m Margaret; 1 son, 1 daughter. **Subject(s):** Natural Sciences; BA 1934; MA 1939; BChir 1939; MB 1939; FRCS 1941; LRCP 1937; Fellow, British Orthopaedic Association; MRCS. **Tutor(s):** J M Wordie. **Educ:** Hollyside

House School, Braintree; County High School, Braintree; Huddersfield Grammar School. **Career:** Consultant Orthopaedic Surgeon, Derbyshire Royal Infirmary; Senior Registrar (Orthopaedic), Norfolk and Norwich and Addenbrooke's Hospitals; University Demonstrator in Anatomy 1938–1946; Surgeon Specialist, RAMC 1940; Consultant Orthopaedic Surgeon, Derbyshire City Hospital 1948. **Appointments:** Executive Committee, British Orthopaedic Association 1969–1970. **Awards:** Scholarship, SJC. Died 29 May 1998.

ADYE, Alan Michael (1944) Born 21 August 1927, 1 Kelvin Road, Clydach, Glamorganshire; son of John William Adye, Works Manager, and Dorothy Mabel Christian. **Subject(s):** Mechanical Sciences; BA 1947; MA 1951; MICE; MASME; MASCE. **Tutor(s):** S J Bailey. **Educ:** Swansea Grammar School; Wycliffe College. **Career:** Director of Marine Technology, SRC. **Honours:** OBE. Died 21 October 1987.

AGARWAL, Prem Prakash (1938) Born 30 November 1917, Kalka, Punjab, India; son of Rai Sahib Madho Ram Agarwal, Personal Assistant, and Kala Vati. **Subject(s):** Mathematics; BA 1940. **Tutor(s):** J M Wordie. **Educ:** DAV High School, Lucknow, India; Government Jubilee Inter-College, Lucknow, India; Lucknow University, India. **Career:** Secretary to Government Finance Department, Bihar 1949.

AHMED, Mohamed Mursi (1931) Born 1 December 1908, Mazata Sharq, Balyana District, Girga Province, Egypt; son of Mursi Ahmed, Police Detective, and Zainab Abu Bahr. **Tutor(s):** J M Wordie. **Educ:** Assuit Secondary School, Egypt; The Egyptian University, Cairo; University of Edinburgh.

AINLEY, Kendrick Edward Denison (1913) Born 1 January 1894, 57 Grange Road West, Birkenhead, Cheshire; son of Edward Theodore Ainley, Chemist, and Mary Hemingway. **Subject(s):** Mathematics. **Tutor(s):** L H K Bushe-Fox. **Educ:** King Edward VI Grammar School, Bury St Edmunds. **Career:** Second Lieutenant, 1st East Lancashire Field Company, RE, Egypt and Dardanelles 1914–1915. **Awards:** Scholarship, SJC. Died 11 May 1915 (killed in action at Gallipoli).

AINSCOW, Nigel Richard (1946) Born 14 April 1928; son of Harold Mason Ainscow, Clerk in Holy Orders, and Doris Birch (by adoption). **Subject(s):** Modern and Medieval Languages; BA 1949; MA 1953. **Tutor(s):** C W Guillebaud. **Educ:** Brockhurst, Church Stretton; Shrewsbury School. **Career:** Schoolmaster, Magdalene College School, Brackley 1950–1954; Schoolmaster, Lausanne, Switzerland 1954–1955; Schoolmaster, Ellesmere College, Shropshire 1955–1986.

AIREY, George William Edwin (1928) Born 3 January 1910, Cleveland House, Springwood Road, Roundhay, Leeds, Yorkshire; son of Edwin Airey, Builder and Contractor, and Edith Annie Greaves; 2 sons, 2 daughters. BA 1931; MA 1935. **Tutor(s):** J M Wordie. **Johnian Relatives:** nephew of John Robinson Airey (1903). **Educ:** Morlands School, Headingley; Roundhay High School, Leeds; The Leys School, Cambridge. **Career:** Major, RA, WWII. **Awards:** TD.

AIREY, Dr John Robinson (1903) Born 25 April 1868, 18 Chambers Street, Hunslet, Leeds, Yorkshire; son of John Robinson Airey, Builder, and Elizabeth Robinson; m; 1 daughter. **Subject(s):** Natural Sciences; BA 1906; MA 1910; ScD 1926; ScD (London). **Tutor(s):** D MacAlister. **Johnian Relatives:** uncle of George William Edwin Airey (1928). **Educ:** Yorkshire College, Leeds; Blenheim Council School, Leeds; Central High School, Leeds; Borough Road Training College, London. **Career:** Master, Porth County School, Glamorgan 1896–1903; Morley Secondary School 1906–1912; Principal, West Ham Technical Institute 1912–1918; Principal, City of Leeds Training College 1918–1933. **Appointments:** Member and Secretary, British Association Mathematical Tables Committee; Joint Editor, *The Philosophical Magazine*; Fellow, Royal Astronomical Society; Fellow, Edinburgh Mathematical Society. **Awards:** Foundation Scholarship, SJC; Wright's Prize, SJC 1904, 1905; Hocking Prize, SJC 1905; Hughes Prize, SJC 1906. Died 16 September 1937.

AITCHISON, Dr Alastair Gordon (1945) Born 7 August 1920, 31 South Terrace, Littlehampton, Sussex; son of John Gordon Aitchison, Commander, RN, and Eveline Betty Sutherland; m Marguerite Lucy Sloper, 16 February 1955. **Subject(s):** Natural Sciences; BA 1948. **Tutor(s):** G C L Bertram. **Johnian Relatives:** brother of Timothy John Aitchison (1947). **Educ:** Furnie Close Preparatory School, New Milton; Cranleigh School. **Career:** Lieutenant, Royal Marines 1940–1944; London Timber Firm 1944–1945. Died 13 February 1981.

AITCHISON, David Ridsdale (1941) Born 15 April 1923, Shanghai, China; son of George Lilburn Aitchison, Headmaster, Nieh Chih Kuei School, and Winifred Holmes. **Subject(s):** Mathematics; BA 1947. **Tutor(s):** J M Wordie. **Educ:** Cathedral School, Shanghai; St Albans School. Died 15 August 1988.

AITCHISON, Timothy John (1947) Born 19 July 1928, Wray House Nursing Home, South Leigh Road, Warblington, Hampshire; son of John Gordon Aitchison, Commander, RN, and Eveline Betty Sutherland (late Forbes); m June Rosemary Whitfield, 1955; 1 daughter (Susan Jane b 1960). BA 1950; MA 1954; FRICS; FRVA. **Tutor(s):** G C L Bertram. **Johnian Relatives:** brother of Alastair Gordon Aitchison (1945). **Educ:** Emsworth House, Emsworth; Westbury House, West Meon; Charterhouse. **Career:** Chartered Surveyor, W B Mason, Manor Farm, Bedhampton 1946–1947; Antique Dealer. Died 14 February 2001.

AITKEN, The Revd William McCrae (1941) Born 2 May 1923, 116 Park Street, London; son of David McCrae Aitken, Orthopaedic Surgeon, and Alice Garret-Smith; m Faith Marion Morton, 7 December 1957, Calabar, Nigeria. **Subject(s):** Mechanical Sciences; BA 1944; MA 1948; BD (Glasgow) 1949. **Tutor(s):** S J Bailey. **Educ:** Arnold House Preparatory School, St John's Wood; Sedbergh School. **Career:** Headmaster, St Andrews High School, Ndola; Master, Fettes College, Edinburgh 1950. **Awards:** Townsend Scholarship, SJC; Lupton and Hebblethwaite Exhibition, SJC 1940. Died 11 August 1994.

AKEROYD, Frederick Bromley (1931) Born 2 May 1913, Surrey Mount, Batley, Yorkshire; son of William Talbot Akeroyd, Soap Manufacturer, and Carrie Bromley; m Olive Hopper; 1 son (Frederick Michael b 10 November 1941). **Subject(s):** Natural Sciences; BA 1934; MA 1945. **Tutor(s):** M P Charlesworth. **Johnian Relatives:** father of Frederick Michael Akeroyd (1960); grandfather of Frederick Anthony Akeroyd (1986). **Educ:** Batley Girls' Grammar School (Kindergarten); Batley Grammar School. **Career:** RAMC 1939–1945; Principal, Group General Medical Practice, North Yorkshire 1945–1978. **Appointments:** Mayor, Whitby 1979. Died 27 November 1995.

AKIWUMI, The Rt Hon Lord Justice Akilano Molade (1947) Born 22 February 1927, 23 Lutterodt Street, Accra, Ghana; son of Augustus Molade Akiwumi, Barrister-at-Law, and Helen Kabuki Ocansey. **Subject(s):** Economics/Law; BA 1950; MA 1978. **Tutor(s):** F Thistlethwaite. **Educ:** Government Boys' School, Accra; Achimota College. **Career:** Called to the Bar, Lincoln's Inn 1951; Crown Counsel, Ghana 1951–1960; Circuit Judge, Ghana 1960–1962; High Court Judge, Ghana 1962–1964; Legal Secretary, East African Common Services Organization, Kenya 1964–1969; Regional Legal Adviser, United Nations Economic Commission for Africa 1969–1987; High Court Judge, Kenya 1987–1994; Judge of Court of Appeal, Kenya 1994–2001; Lord Justice of the Court of Justice of the Common Market for Eastern and Southern Africa 1995–2001; Lord President of the Court of Justice of the Common Market for Eastern and Southern Africa 2001. **Appointments:** Member, Honourable Society of Lincoln's Inn. **Publications:** Articles on legal aspects of economic co-operation in East Africa including 'Judicial Aspects of Economic Integration Treaties in Africa', *The Hague Academy of International Law, Colloquium*, 1972; 'The East African Community', *Journal of World Trade Law*, 1972; 'The Development of the Legislative Process in East African Integration', *Afrika Spectrum*, Deutsches Institut für Afrika-Forschung, Hamburg; 'The Role of the Public Servant in the East African Community',

The International Political Science IXth World Congress; 'A Plea for the Harmonization of African Investment Laws', School of Oriental and African Studies, University of London.

AKROYD, Peter Swainson (1920) Born 20 December 1900, Wavendon House, Wavendon, Woburn Sands, Bedfordshire; son of Swainson Howden Akroyd, Member of London Stock Exchange, and Evelyn Fanny King; m Elinor, 16 October 1946, Nicosia, Cyprus. **Tutor(s):** E E Sikes. **Educ:** The Knoll, Woburn Sands; Eton College. Died 23 February 1951.

ALCOCK, Alfred Samuel Mackenzie (1932) Born 27 December 1912, 91 Oxford Road, Linthorpe, Middlesbrough; son of Alfred Edwin Alcock, Mechanical Engineer, and Jessie Donald Mackintosh. BA 1935; MA 1939. **Tutor(s):** J S Boys Smith. **Educ:** Preparatory School, Sedbergh; Sedbergh School.

ALCOCK, Dr Robert Saxelby (1927) Born 14 November 1907, 29 Briar Road, Ecclesall, Sheffield, Yorkshire; son of Robert Alcock, Schoolmaster, and Caroline Saxelby; m Ludovika Jordan, 1934 (d 1999); 1 son (Robert Nicholas b 24 August 1938), 1 daughter (Isabel b 14 October 1945). **Subject(s):** Natural Sciences; BA 1930; MA 1934; PhD 1934. **Tutor(s):** C W Guillebaud. **Johnian Relatives:** father of Robert Nicholas Alcock (1956). **Educ:** Woodseats Council School, Sheffield; Central Secondary School, Sheffield. **Career:** Biochemist, Food Testing Laboratory, Barry, Glamorgan 1939–1946; Ministry of Supply; Ministry of Aviation; Board of Trade. **Awards:** Exhibition, SJC 1926; Scholarship 1930; Hughes Prize, SJC 1930. **Honours:** ISO 1967. Died 27 January 2000.

ALDCROFT, James Stuart (1919) Born 24 September 1899, 52 King Street, Stretford, Lancashire; son of William Hancock Aldcroft, General Manager and Actuary, Refuge Insurance Company, and Elizabeth Miller Gadd. **Tutor(s):** E E Sikes. **Educ:** Private School, Stretford; Manchester Grammar School. Died 1966.

ALDERSON, Denis Fordred (1929) Born 25 June 1911, 41 Queen's Walk, Nottingham; son of Reginald Alderson, Doctor of Medicine, and Mabel Elizabeth Inga Imeson. BA 1932. **Tutor(s):** M P Charlesworth. **Educ:** St Peter's School, Seaford; Marlborough College.

ALESSANDRINI, Goffredo (1922) Born 19 November 1904, Cairo, Egypt; son of Ermele Alessandrini, Engineer and Public Works Contractor, and Laura Pizzagalli. **Tutor(s):** E Cunningham. **Educ:** Gymnasium, Milan, Italy; Elementary Italian Schools, Alexandria; Royal Italian Lyceum, Alexandria.

ALEXANDER, Aaron (1908) Born 12 October 1888, Pretoria, Transvaal, South Africa; son of Abraham Alexander, General Merchant, and Flora Lewin; m Victoria; 2 sons (Lionel and Dicky), 1 daughter (Eileen). **Subject(s):** Law; BA 1912; MA 1919; LLB 1912; LLM 1919. **Tutor(s):** L H K Bushe-Fox. **Johnian Relatives:** brother of Morris Alexander (1897); father of Arthur Louis Lionel Alexander (1947) and of Anthony Victor Alexander (1949). **Educ:** Normal College; South African College; Cape of Good Hope University. **Career:** Lecturer, Cairo University; Called to the Bar, Inner Temple 1913; International Lawyer, Cairo, Egypt 1913. **Awards:** George Long Prize, University of Cambridge 1912. **Honours:** Order of the Nile. Died 12 September 1945.

ALEXANDER, Anthony Victor (1949) Born 17 September 1928, 4 Montagu Place, London; son of Aaron Alexander, Barrister-at-Law, and Victoria Mosseri; m Hélène Esther Adda; 1 daughter (Susannah). **Subject(s):** Modern Languages/Law; BA 1952; MA 1991; LLB 1953. **Tutor(s):** C W Guillebaud. **Johnian Relatives:** nephew of Morris Alexander (1897); son of Aaron Alexander (1908); brother of Arthur Louis Lionel Alexander (1947). **Educ:** The Dragon School, Oxford; Harrow School; The English School, Cairo, Egypt. **Career:** Royal Signals Corps 1947–1949; Sedgwick Collins & Co 1954–1968 (Director 1964–1968); Managing Director, Non Marine Division, Sedgwick Collins Holdings Ltd 1968–1973; Chairman, Sedgwick Forbes UK and

Director, Sedgwick Forbes Holdings 1973–1977; Deputy Chairman, Sedgwick Forbes Ltd 1977–1978; Chairman, Underwriting Services and Special Services, Sedgwick Group 1978–1984; Director, Sedgwick Group 1978–1989; ARV Aviation 1985–1988. **Appointments:** Director, Securicor Group and Securicor Services 1976–1996; Member, Overseas Projects Board 1978–1979; Deputy Chairman 1981–1982, Chairman 1982–1987, British Insurance Brokers Association; Member, British Invisible Exports Council 1983–1990; Member, Marketing of Investments Board 1985–1986; Director, Securities and Investments Board 1986–1989; Chairman of Trustees, Victor Adda Foundation and Fan Museum Trust. **Honours:** CBE 1987. Died 17 August 1999.

ALEXANDER, Archibald Corbet Fleming (1923) Born 27 March 1903, Bagan Luar, Province Wellesley, Federated Malay States; son of Edward Mathew Alexander, Merchant, Federated Malay States, and Isobel Tarbet Fleming Struthers. **Tutor(s):** B F Armitage. **Educ:** The Wells House, Malvern Wells; Shrewsbury School; Private Tuition.

ALEXANDER, Arthur Louis Lionel (1947) Born 15 July 1925, 4K Bickenhall Mansions, London; son of Aaron Alexander, Barrister-at-Law, and Victoria Mosseri; m Barbara Ramsay Green, 29 May 1952; 3 daughters (Susan b 1955, Margaret b 1957 and Janet b 1963). **Subject(s):** Law; BA 1949; MA 1962; LLB 1950. **Johnian Relatives:** son of Aaron Alexander (1908); brother of Anthony Victor Alexander (1949). **Educ:** English School, Cairo, Egypt; Dragon School, Oxford; Harrow School. **Career:** Called to the Bar, Inner Temple 1951; Legal Assistant, Office of the Solicitor of Inland Revenue 1957; Criminal Work 1958–1963, General Tax Work 1963–1968, Inland Revenue; Secretary, Law Commission's Working Party on Codification of the Criminal Law 1968–1970; General Tax Work 1970; Assistant Solicitor until 1986, Inland Revenue. **Appointments:** Supervisor in Law, SJC 1951; Chair, Social Security Appeals Tribunal 1986–1998. **Awards:** MacMahon Law Studentship 1951–1955; Brunt Trophy for Gliding 1951; Scholarship, SJC. **Publications:** (jointly) *The Law of Clubs*. Died 11 August 1999.

ALEXANDER, Sir Charles Gundry (1941) Born 5 May 1923, Oaklands, Crofton, Orpington, Kent; son of Sir Frank Alexander, 1st Bt, Shipbroker, JP, and Elsa Mary Collett; m (1) Mary Neale, 1944, (2) Eileen Ann Stewart, 1979; (1) 1 son (Richard b 1947), 1 daughter (Jennifer b 1949). BA 1944; MA 1948. **Tutor(s):** S J Bailey. **Educ:** Bishop's Stortford College. **Career:** Lieutenant, RN Cadet, SJC, North Atlantic and Far East 1943–1946; Chairman, Alexander Shipping Company Ltd 1959–1987. **Appointments:** Chairman, Governor's Care Ltd 1975–1986; Master, Merchant Taylors' Company 1981–1982; Deputy Chairman, Houlder Brothers & Co 1980–1988; Prime Warden, Shipwrights' Company 1983–1984.

ALEXANDER, Donald William (1932) Born 26 October 1913, 35 Beresford Road, Chingford; son of John Budge Alexander, Physician and Surgeon, and Hilda Willson Bailey. **Subject(s):** Classics/Modern and Medieval Languages; BA 1935; MA 1970. **Tutor(s):** R L Howland. **Educ:** Mistley Place, Manningtree; Shrewsbury School. **Career:** Director of Audio-Visual Aids, University of Dundee; Founder, Documentary Technicians' Alliance (DATA) 1944–1951; Ran National Coal Board Film Unit 1951–1963. **Awards:** Scholarship, SJC. Died 20 July 1993.

ALEXANDER, George Baker (1926) Born 25 September 1907, 96 Sackville Street, Barnsley, Yorkshire; son of George Glover Alexander, Barrister-at-Law, and Mary-Ann Goldthorpe Baker. **Subject(s):** Natural Sciences; BA 1930. **Tutor(s):** J M Wordie. **Educ:** Holgate Grammar School for Barnsley and District; The Grammar School, Leeds. **Publications:** *The Geology of Gibraltar*.

ALEXANDER, Dr John Amyas (1945) Born 27 January 1922, Steyning, Sussex; son of Charles Amyas Alexander, Electrical Engineer, and Lily Blackman. ScD 1990; BA (Pembroke) 1948; MA (Pembroke) 1953; PhD (Pembroke) 1960; Honorary Doctorate of Arts (Khartoum, Sudan) 2000. **Educ:** Haywards Heath Elementary School; Varndean School,

Brighton; Pembroke College, Cambridge. **Career:** Title B Fellow 1976–1986, Lecturer in Archaeology 1978–1986, Title E Fellow 1986–, SJC; Lecturer in Archaeology 1977–1986, University of Cambridge. **Appointments:** Supervisor in Archaeology, SJC 1976–1978; President, European Forum for African Archaeology, Rome; Vice-President, Council for British Archaeology 1991; Vice-Chairman, Society for Archaeological Research in the Sudan 1994. **Awards:** Centenary Medal of the University of Khartoum 1999. **Publications:** 'Roman Cambridge, Excavations on Castle Hill, 1956–1982', Cambridgeshire Antiquarian Society, March 2000; 'Archaeology and History of the Ottoman Turks in the Sudan', *Adumantu I*, Riadh, Saudi Arabia; 'The Ottoman Turkish Frontier in the Middle Nile Valley', *Adumantu I*, Riadh, Saudi Arabia.

ALEXANDER, The Revd Philip George (1905) Born 11 May 1883, Princetown, Lydford, Devon; son of George Edward Alexander, Civil Servant, and Charlotte Rowe. BA 1908. **Tutor(s):** E E Sikes. **Johnian Relatives:** brother of Ralph Cleave Alexander (1905). **Educ:** Wellington State School, New Zealand; State School, Palmerston North, New Zealand. **Career:** Ordained Deacon 1908; Curate, Christ Church, Barton Hill, Bristol 1908–1910; Ordained Priest 1909; Curate, Downend 1910–1912; Chaplain, RN 1912–1916 (HMS *Blenheim* 1912; HMS *Falmouth* 1912–1913; HMS *Hampshire* 1914–1916). Died 5 June 1916 (lost at sea with HMS *Hampshire*).

ALEXANDER, The Revd Ralph Cleave (1905) Born 11 May 1881, Princetown, Lydford, Devon; son of George Edward Alexander, Civil Servant, and Charlotte Rowe. BA 1908. **Tutor(s):** E E Sikes. **Johnian Relatives:** brother of Philip George Alexander (1905). **Educ:** Lower School, Weymouth College; State School, Palmerston North, New Zealand. **Career:** Ordained Deacon 1909; Curate, St Matthias, Plymouth 1909–1913; Ordained Priest 1910; Chaplain, RN 1913–1917 (HMS *Southampton* 1913; HMS *Hermione* 1913; HMS *Russell* 1914; HMS *Indus* 1915; HMS *Campania* 1916; HMS *Dublin* 1916–1917); Vicar, Luppett 1918–1923; Vicar, Shaugh Prior, Plymouth 1939–1943. Died 1943.

ALLAN, Derek Scott (1936) Born 15 March 1917, The Darland, 7 Brunswick Drive, Harrogate; son of Douglas Allan, Surgeon, and Mildred Hermine Gunn; m Rosemary Taylor, 1940; 1 son, 2 daughters. BA 1939; MA 1943. **Tutor(s):** C W Guillebaud. **Johnian Relatives:** nephew of Walter Beattie Allan (1892); son of Douglas Allan (1901). **Educ:** Sunderland Girls' High School; Bow School, Durham; Haileybury College. **Career:** RA 1939–1946; Captain Instructor-in-Gunnery, BLA and BAOR, Northern Europe 1944–1946; Science Master and Head of Department, various State Schools 1947–1966; Director, Health Food Company 1966–1972; Research, Oxford 1972. **Appointments:** Member, Footlights. **Publications:** (with J B Delair) *When the Earth Nearly Died*, Gateway, 1995 (later republished as *Cataclysm: Compelling Evidence of a Cosmic Catastrophe in 9500 BC*, Bear & Co, 1997).

ALLAN, Dr Douglas (1901) Born 10 September 1882, Sunderland; son of William Allan, Engineer and MP for Gateshead, and Jane Beattie; m Mildred Hermine Gunn; 1 son (Derek Scott b 15 March 1917). BA 1904; MRCS 1909. **Tutor(s):** D MacAlister. **Johnian Relatives:** brother of Walter Beattie Allan (1892); father of Derek Scott Allan (1936). **Educ:** Durham School. **Career:** Clinical Assistant, Guy's Hospital; Senior Medical Officer, Furness Officers' Hospital, Harrogate; Chief Medical Officer for Sunderland 1934.

ALLAN, Gilbert Francis (1938) Born 22 February 1918, Academy House, Kilsyth, Stirlingshire; son of James Allan, Schoolmaster, and Bertha Tulloch. **Subject(s):** Mathematics; BA 1946. **Tutor(s):** J M Wordie. **Educ:** Kilsyth Academy; University of Glasgow.

ALLAN, Peter Gerald (1944) Born 3 October 1926, 278 Willis Street, Wellington, New Zealand; son of George Allan, Textile Engineer, and Marie Emilie Rettéré; 5 children. **Subject(s):** Mechanical Sciences; BA 1947; MA 1951. **Tutor(s):** S J Bailey. **Educ:** English School, Cairo, Egypt; King's School, Ely. **Career:** REME 1947–1950; Rank Precision Industries

1950–1958; Senior Consultant, PA Management Consultants 1958–1966; Marketing Manager, Ideal Standard, 1966–1970; Allan & Co 1970–1995. **Appointments:** Director, British Hospital, Paris Levallois; President, British Chamber of Commerce and Industry 1994. **Honours:** OBE 1996; Chevalier de la Legion d'Honneur 2002.

ALLDRED, Reginald Alan (1915) Born 17 January 1897, Holbeach Hurn, Lincolnshire; son of Frederick Alldred, Schoolmaster, and Emma Fletcher Harris; m Marjorie. **Subject(s):** Mathematics; BA 1921; MA 1945. **Tutor(s):** L H K Bushe-Fox. **Johnian Relatives:** brother of Stanley Douglas Alldred (1919). **Educ:** Holbeach St Luke's Council School; Moulton Grammar School, Lincolnshire; Pocklington School. **Career:** Lieutenant, Royal North Lancashire Regiment 1915–1918; Railway Traffic Officer. **Awards:** Open Exhibition, SJC 1915; Dowman Exhibition, SJC 1915; Scholarship, SJC 1920; College Prize, SJC 1920. Died 3 May 1964.

ALLDRED, Stanley Douglas (1919) Born 24 March 1899, Holbeach Hurn, Lincolnshire; son of Frederick Alldred, Schoolmaster, and Emma Fletcher Harris; m Victoria Tonge-Smith, 1921, Brighton Parish Church. **Subject(s):** Mathematics. **Tutor(s):** E A Benians. **Johnian Relatives:** brother of Reginald Alan Alldred (1915). **Educ:** Moulton Grammar School, Lincolnshire; Pocklington School. **Career:** Artist's Rifles Training Corps 1917; Second Lieutenant, RFA, served in Ireland 1918. **Awards:** Dowman Exhibition, SJC; Scholarship, SJC 1920; College Prize, SJC 1920. Died 9 December 1923.

ALLEBONE, Dr Philip (1939) Born 1 July 1921, Rushden, Northamptonshire; son of Arthur Allebone, Boot Manufacturer, and Ada Mary Roberts; m 15 October 1949; 4 children. BA 1942; MA 1948; BChir 1948; MB 1948; DObstRCOG; MRCGP. **Tutor(s):** R L Howland. **Johnian Relatives:** father of Sam Philip Harcourt Allebone (1974); grandfather of Sophie Mary Allebone-Webb (1998). **Educ:** Kimbolton School.

ALLEN, Albert William (1901) (admitted as a Non-Collegiate Student 1900) Born 5 October 1880, Rockland, All Saints, Attleborough, Norfolk; son of Luther Allen, Leather Cutter, and Mary Ann Bloy. BA 1903; MA 1907. **Tutor(s):** D MacAlister. **Educ:** Pupil Teacher's Centre, Norwich Technical School. **Career:** Director of Education, Hornsey 1911–1938. **Appointments:** Member, NALGO Standing Joint Committee.

ALLEN, The Revd Alexander Drake (1905) Born 30 May 1878, The Vicarage, Moss, Campsall, Yorkshire; son of Francis Hordern Allen, Clerk in Holy Orders, and Elizabeth Horne Wright. BA 1908; MA 1913. **Tutor(s):** J R Tanner. **Educ:** King's School, Ely; The Grammar School, Clitheroe. **Career:** Ordained Deacon 1908; Curate, Worksop 1908–1909; Curate, All Saints, Nottingham 1909–1913; Ordained Priest 1910; Curate, St Michael and All Angels, Sutton in Ashfield 1913–1923; Vicar, Kneesall 1923–1938; Vicar, Maplebeck 1932–1938; Honorary Canon of Halloughton, Southwell Cathedral 1933; Rural Dean, Southwell 1936–1937; Rural Dean, Norwell 1937–1938; Rector, Holme Pierrepont with Adbolton, Nottinghamshire 1938–1948. Died 6 December 1972.

ALLEN, His Honour Anthony Kenway (1937) Born 31 October 1917, 45 Ryfold Road, Wimbledon Park; son of Charles Valentine Allen, Solicitor, and Edith Kenway; m Maureen Murtough, 1975. **Subject(s):** Law; BA 1940. **Tutor(s):** C W Guillebaud. **Educ:** Freiburg University, Germany; St George's College, Weybridge; Grenoble University, France. **Career:** Wing Commander, RAF Special Intelligence 1939–1945; Mentioned in Despatches June 1945; Called to the Bar, Inner Temple 1947; Circuit Judge 1978–1990. **Honours:** OBE (Military) 1946. Died 5 January 2003.

ALLEN, Charles Richards (1906) Born 3 May 1885, 10 Horbury Crescent, Notting Hill Gate, Middlesex; son of James Allen, MP, New Zealand, and Mary Jane Hill Richards. **Tutor(s):** L H K Bushe-Fox. **Johnian Relatives:** son of James Allen (1874). **Educ:** Wanganui Collegiate School, New Zealand; University of Otago, New Zealand. **Career:** Author and Playwright. **Publications:** six novels, four plays.

ALLEN, Douglas Geoffrey Glenn (1925) Born 27 December 1906, Elphin Lodge, 55 BC Lines, Umballa, India; son of Sydney Glenn Allen, Colonel, RAMC, and Elsie Annette Watkin. **Subject(s):** Natural Sciences; BA 1929; MA 1933. **Tutor(s):** J M Wordie. **Educ:** Lindsmere School, Eastbourne; Epsom College. **Career:** London Scottish Assurance Company 1923–1924; Clerical and Analytical Laboratories, London 1924–1925.

ALLEN, Dr Francis (1912) Born 5 July 1894, 80 Devonshire Road, Forest Hill, Surrey; son of Francis William Allen, Outfitter, and Mary Winder; m Ann Codrington. BA 1915; MA 1923. **Tutor(s):** R P Gregory. **Educ:** Haberdashers' Aske's Hatcham Boys' School; Guy's Hospital. **Career:** Clinical Assistant, Great Ormond Street Hospital; Medical Officer, St Pancras School Clinic, and Whittington College, Highgate; Honorary Medical Officer, Santa Claus Home for Invalid Children, Highgate; House Physician and House Surgeon, Skin Department, St Bartholomew's Hospital; Resident Medical Officer, Brighton Sanitorium. **Publications:** 'Cancer from the Point of View of a General Practitioner', *Public Health*, 1926. Died 2 November 1955.

ALLEN, Francis Donald (1943) Born 13 February 1925, 43 Midland Road, Wellingborough, Northamptonshire; son of Ralph Allen, Wholesale Fruit and Potato Merchant, and Rose Ellen Wild; m Delma Lavinia Cherry, 2 June 1949, Wellingborough; 1 son (David Russell b 6 April 1953). **Subject(s):** Mathematics/Mechanical Sciences; BA 1946; MA 1950. **Tutor(s):** S J Bailey. **Educ:** All Saints' School, Wellingborough; Wellingborough School. **Career:** Aero gas turbine engine component research and development: Joseph Lucas, Burnley 1945–1949; de Havilland, Bristol Siddeley, Rolls-Royce 1949–1988.

ALLEN, The Revd Francis Williams (1900) Born 3 November 1878, Tupsley, Herefordshire; son of Thomas Williams Allen, Bank Manager, and Maria Louise Barker; m Mary Fleming St John, 25 April 1911, Dinmore Chapel; 2 sons. BA 1903; MA 1929. **Tutor(s):** C E Graves. **Johnian Relatives:** grandson of Joseph Henry Barker (1828); father of John Francis Allen (1930). **Educ:** Hereford Cathedral School. **Career:** Ordained Deacon 1904; Curate and Chaplain, Stoke Newington, Lugano (Switzerland), Bodenham, then West Malvern 1904–1911; Ordained Priest 1905; Vicar, Claverdon 1911–1916; Rector, Harborough Magna 1916–1920; Rector, Charwelton with Fawsley 1920–1937; Rector and Vicar, Culworth, Northamptonshire 1937–1941. Died 17 November 1970.

ALLEN, Frank (1947) Born 5 June 1925, 223 Burnsall Road, Bradford, Yorkshire; son of Ernest George Allen, Weaving Overlooker, and Laura Constance Lilian Blakeborough; m Dorothy May Mason-Jones; 2 sons (Robert and David). **Subject(s):** Mathematics; BA 1949; MA 1993; FACCA. **Tutor(s):** J M Wordie. **Educ:** Hanson Junior School, Bradford; Belle Vue High School, Bradford. **Career:** Captain, 8th Gurkha Rifles, Indian Army 1943–1947; Accountant, A Guinness, Son and Co 1951–1983. Died 1 October 2002.

ALLEN, Frank Stanley (1938) Born 16 April 1919, 5 Presburg Road, New Malden, Kingston, Surrey; son of Herbert Stanley Allen, Professor of Natural Philosophy, and Jessie Euphemia Macturk; m Mary Patricia Pomona Mackenzie, 30 April 1951, Kilmadock East Church, Doune, Perthshire; 2 daughters (Marian Patricia b 13 May 1952 and Alice Margaret b 1 April 1959). **Subject(s):** History; BA 1941; MA 1945; Agriculture Diploma, North of Scotland College of Agriculture 1946. **Tutor(s):** S J Bailey; J S Boys Smith. **Johnian Relatives:** cousin of Roland Stanley Maxwell (1920), Ian Stanley Maxwell (1936) and of Malcolm Stanley Maxwell (1939). **Educ:** St Katherine's Kindergarten, St Andrews; St Salvator's School, St Andrews; Manor House School, Clapham. **Career:** Fife and Forfar Yeomanry and Warwickshire Yeomanry; Battle of El Alamein 1942; Farmer 1946. **Appointments:** JP, Aberdeen; Vice-Chairman, Valuation Appeal Committee, Grampian Region.

ALLEN, Geoffrey Austin (1905) Born 3 June 1887, Greenstead Hall, Halstead, Essex; son of Robert Allen, Gentleman, and Tryphena Luke.

Subject(s): Natural Sciences; BA 1908. **Tutor(s):** D MacAlister. **Educ:** Aldenham School. **Career:** Master, Grammar School, Wotton-under-Edge; Private, London Regiment 1914; Second Lieutenant, Essex Regiment 1915–1916. Died 1 July 1916 (killed in action on the Somme).

ALLEN, Geoffrey Reginald Cowley (1944) Born 27 August 1926, 28 Kinfauns Road, Ilford, Essex; son of Arthur Reginald Allen, House Builder and Decorator, and Blanche Annie Pratt. **Subject(s):** Mathematics; BA 1950; MA 1952. **Tutor(s):** J M Wordie. **Educ:** Bedford Modern School; Goodmayes Council School; Brentwood School.

ALLEN, James Edmund Percival (1901) Born 14 September 1881, Clyde Street, Dunedin, New Zealand; son of James Allen, Landowner, Member, House of Representatives, and Mary Jane Hill Richards. **Subject(s):** Law; BA 1904; LLB 1905. **Tutor(s):** L H K Bushe-Fox; D MacAlister. **Johnian Relatives:** son of James Allen (1874). **Educ:** Wanganui Collegiate School, New Zealand. **Career:** Admitted to Inner Temple 1906.

ALLEN, John Francis (1930) Born 20 August 1912, Leyland Cottage, Claverdon, Stratford-on-Avon; son of Francis Williams Allen, Clerk in Holy Orders, and Mary Fleming St John. **Subject(s):** Theology; BA 1933; MA 1961. **Tutor(s):** M P Charlesworth. **Johnian Relatives:** great grandson of Joseph Henry Barker (1828); son of Francis Williams Allen (1900). **Educ:** St Michael's College, Tenbury; St Edward's School, Oxford. **Career:** Assistant Master, St Paul's Cathedral Choir School 1933; Master, West Downs Preparatory School, Winchester 1938; Headmaster, Nottingham High School 1947–1975. Died 3 September 1988.

ALLEN, Professor John Frank (1938) Born 6 May 1908, 117 Harvard Avenue, Winnipeg; son of Frank Allen, Professor of Physics, University of Manitoba, and Sarah Estelle Harper; m Elfriede Hiebert, 1933 (div 1947); 1 adopted son (Hugh John). **Subject(s):** Physics; MA 1938; BA (Manitoba) 1928; MA (Toronto) 1930; PhD (Toronto) 1933; Honorary DSc (Manitoba) 1979; Honorary DSc (Heriot-Watt University) 1984; FPhysS 1945; FAPS 1948; FRSE 1948; FRS 1949. **Educ:** Secondary High School, Winnipeg; University of Manitoba, Canada; University of Toronto, Canada; California Institute of Technology, Pasadena, USA. **Career:** Research Assistant, Royal Society Mond Laboratory, University of Cambridge 1938–1944; Ministry of Supply 1938–1945; Title B Fellow and College Lecturer in Physics 1944–1947, SJC; Lecturer in Physics, University of Cambridge 1944–1947; Professor of Natural Philosophy 1947–1978 (Emeritus 1978), University of St Andrews. **Appointments:** Supervisor in Physics, SJC 1941–1945; Lecturer at over twenty conferences world-wide; Chairman, Very-low Temperature Commission, International Union of Pure and Applied Physics; Member, British National Committee for Physics. **Publications:** Four papers on Physiological Optics and Acoustics; numerous papers on low temperatures. Died 22 April 2001.

ALLEN, John Piers (1930) Born 30 March 1912, 34 Ashburnham Mansions, Chelsea, London; son of Percy Allen, Author, Journalist and Lecturer, and Marjorie Isabel Agnes Nash; m (1) Modwena Sedgwick, 1937, (2) Anne Preston, 1945, (3) Margaret Wootton, 1982; (1) 2 sons, (2) 2 sons, 2 daughters. **Tutor(s):** E A Benians. **Educ:** Willington School, Putney; Northcliffe House, Bognor Regis; Aldenham School. **Career:** Stage Actor and Theatre Director 1931–1939; Engineering Lieutenant, RNVR 1939–1945; Director, Producer and Administrator, Glyndebourne Children's Theatre 1945–1951; Writer and Producer, Programming for Schools, BBC 1951–1961; HM Inspector of Schools 1961–1972; Principal, Central School of Speech and Drama 1972–1978; Visiting Lecturer, City University 1979–1983; Visiting Professor, Westfield College, University of London 1979–1983; Visiting Lecturer, University College, Scarborough. **Appointments:** Chairman, UNESCO Children's Theatre Committee; Founder, National Association of Drama Training (Chairman, Accreditation Board 1979–1983); Chairman, Council for Dance Education and Training 1982–1995; Chairman, Old Meeting House Arts Centre, Helmsley; Founder President, 1812 Theatre Company, Helmsley. **Honours:** OBE 1979.

Publications: *Going to the Theatre*, 1949; *Three Medieval Plays*, 1956; *Masters of British Drama*, 1957; *Masters of European Drama*, 1962; Trends in *Education: Drama* (government report), 1968; *Drama in Schools*, 1978; *A History of the Theatre in Europe*, 1983. Died 4 January 2002.

ALLEN, Lucien Arthur (1907) Born 28 December 1888, 13 Beauclerc Road, Hammersmith, Middlesex; son of Arthur William Allen, Artist, and Emily Last; m Elizabeth Maude Crawford, 14 October 1916, St Mark's, Seremban, Federated Malay States (d 23 November 1962); 1 son (Lucien), 1 daughter (Margaret). **Subject(s):** Mathematics; BA 1910. **Tutor(s):** L H K Bushe-Fox. **Educ:** Brondesbury Preparatory School; Merchant Taylors' School. **Career:** Cadet, Federated Malay States 1912–1915; Acting Secretary to Resident, Negeri Sembilan 1915–1918; Assistant District Officer, Kuantan 1918–1919; Assistant District Officer, Lower Perak 1920; British Resident, Brunei 1921–1923; Assistant District Officer, Ipoh 1924; Deputy Public Prosecutor, Negeri Sembilan and Pahang 1924; British Adviser, Perelis 1928–1930; Officer, Class II 1929; Acting District Officer, Klang 1931; Acting General Adviser, Johor 1937–1938; Acting Deputy Commissioner of Lands, Federated Malay States 1938; Japanese POW; Controller of Rubber, Federated Malay States and Straits Settlements 1939–1945. **Honours:** OBE 1931. Died 17 September 1971.

ALLEN, The Revd Richard de Courcy (1936) Born 18 October 1915, 128 Harley Street, London; son of Richard William Allen, Physician, and Beatrice Mary Harston. **Subject(s):** History; BA 1939; MA 1946. **Educ:** Hill Top Court School, Seaford; The Chalet, Peasenhall; Epsom College; Bible Churchman's Missionary and Theological College, Bristol; Wycliffe Hall, Oxford. **Career:** Tutor, Oak Hill College, Southgate; Private, Suffolk Regiment; Commissioned, Royal West Kent Regiment; Major, General Montgomery's Staff, El Alamein, WWII; Ordained Deacon 1954; Ordained Priest 1955.

ALLEN, Robert Willoughby John (1933) Born 30 December 1914, Junin, Province of Buenos Aires, Argentina; son of Robert Willoughby Long Allen, Mechanical Engineer, and Constance Mary Josephine Butler; m Joan Leslie Drysdale, 6 April 1948, San Martin de Tours, Buenos Aires; 3 sons (Nicholas, David and James). **Subject(s):** Economics/Geography; BA 1936. **Tutor(s):** J M Wordie; C W Guillebaud. **Educ:** Woodlands Preparatory School, Deganwy; Repton School, Derby. **Career:** Clerk, A Sherriff & Co 1936–1949; Second Lieutenant, rising to Lieutenant, Queen Victoria's Rifles – POW 1940–1945; Member, London Stock Exchange 1945–1976; Browning Todd 1949–1951; Partner, Vivian Grey 1955–1957; Partner, Akroyd & Smithers 1957–1976; Farmer 1976–1994.

ALLEN, Ronald Charles Tucker (1927) Born 17 February 1909, Ansford, Castle Cary, Somerset; son of George Claude Allen, Farmer, and Elizabeth Lilian Bond; m Margaret; 3 sons (Mark, James and Roger), 1 daughter (Lucy). BA 1930; MA 1934; AMICE. **Tutor(s):** J M Wordie. **Johnian Relatives:** cousin of James Allen (1874). **Educ:** Sherborne Preparatory School; Sherborne School. **Career:** Nigerian Civil Service; Concrete Manufacturer; Assistant Civil Engineer, Air Ministry 1935. Died 9 July 1989.

ALLEN, William Francis Atwell (1946) Born 20 May 1924, Alexandria, Egypt; son of Atwell Hayes Allen, Lieutenant Colonel, RAOC, and Grace Stanley May Adams. **Subject(s):** Mechanical Sciences; BA 1949; MA 1953; MEng (British Columbia) 1975. **Tutor(s):** R L Howland. **Johnian Relatives:** great grandson of John Couch Adams (1839). **Educ:** Boundary Oak, Portsmouth; St John's School, Leatherhead. Died 20 August 1997.

ALLEN, William Ruskin (1919) Born 6 December 1895, Broadmoor Road, Crowthorne, Berkshire; son of John William Allen, Publisher, Longmans, and Annie Laura Butcher; m Joan Woodhouse, 22 October 1931, Gold Coast. BA 1921. **Tutor(s):** E A Benians. **Educ:** Ranelagh School, Bracknell; Private Tuition, Rouen, France. **Career:** Inspector of Schools, Gold Coast. Died 26 June 1954.

ALLISON, Harold (1948) Born 15 July 1927, Wyngarth, Pocklington, Yorkshire; son of Harold Allison, Building Contractor, and Irene Arnold; 2 sons (David Nicholas b 1955 and Ian Martin b 1957). BA 1950; MA 1978. **Tutor(s):** C W Guillebaud. **Johnian Relatives:** father of Ian Martin Allison (1976). **Educ:** Pocklington Grammar School. **Career:** Chartered Accountant.

ALLITT, Peter James (1943) Born 26 June 1925, Manor House, Newton, Wisbech, Cambridgeshire; son of Herbert John Allitt, Farmer, and Margaret Alice Rose. BA 1946; MA 1950. **Tutor(s):** C W Guillebaud. **Educ:** Wisbech High School; Wisbech Grammar School; Kimbolton School.

ALLNATT, John Edward (1938) Born 18 March 1919, The Haven, Cheap Street, Newbury; son of Alfred Ernest Allnatt, Managing Director, Building Contractors, and Edith Elliott; m Mary. **Subject(s):** Modern and Medieval Languages; BA 1945; MA 1948. **Tutor(s):** C W Guillebaud. **Educ:** St Wilfrid's, Seaford; The College, Vavey; Charterhouse; Leighton Park. Died 12 April 1977.

ALLON, John Philip Hilton (1941) Born 20 August 1922, Middlesbrough, Yorkshire; son of John Brock Allon, Solicitor and Town Clerk, and Henrietta Elizabeth Hilton. BA 1946; MA 1949. **Tutor(s):** C W Guillebaud. **Educ:** High School, Dudley; Ashton House, Wolverhampton; Mill Mead, Shrewsbury; Shrewsbury School. **Awards:** Exhibition, SJC.

ALLOTT, Cecil Bertram Scott (1905) Born 28 April 1886, Victoria Street, Heckmondwike, Yorkshire; son of Smith Allott, Schoolmaster, and Mary Hannah Scott; m; 2 daughters. **Subject(s):** Natural Sciences; BA 1908; MA 1913; BSc (London) 1908. **Tutor(s):** D MacAlister. **Educ:** Wheelwright Grammar School, Dewsbury. **Career:** Master, King's School, Canterbury 1911–1916; Research, Woolwich Arsenal 1916–1919; Lecturer, Woolwich Polytechnic 1917–1919; Master, Clifton College, Bristol 1920–1922; Senior Science Master, Hymers College, Hull 1922–1949. **Appointments:** Chairman, Newland High School Parents' Association. **Awards:** Exhibition, SJC. Died 23 June 1949.

ALLPRESS, Kenneth Peter (1937) See PRESS.

ALLSOP, Raymond (1935) Born 10 January 1917, 59 Circular Road, New Moston, Manchester; son of Frank Allsop, Corporal, MGC, and Beatrice Lines. **Subject(s):** Classics; BA 1938; MA 1942. **Tutor(s):** R L Howland. **Educ:** St James's Infant School; St Owen's Bluecoat School; Hereford Cathedral School. **Career:** Second Lieutenant, RA, WWII. **Awards:** Somerset Exhibition, SJC. Died 26 March 1942 (killed on active service).

ALLSOPP, Herbert Leslie (1917) Born 11 October 1899, 21 Springfield Road, Coventry; son of Benjamin Allsopp, Commercial Traveller, and Alice Emily Cave; m Joyce Agnes Hawkes, 28 December 1935, St Mary's Moseley, Birmingham; 3 daughters (Elizabeth, Anne and Lesley). **Subject(s):** Mathematics/Natural Sciences; BA 1920; MA 1924. **Tutor(s):** E E Sikes. **Johnian Relatives:** son-in-law of William John Hawkes (1900). **Educ:** Wheatley Street Council School; Earlsdon County School; Bablake Secondary School. **Career:** Physics Master, Wellingborough School 1933; Director, Carlisle and Gregson, University Services and Titirs 1957. **Awards:** Hoare Exhibition, SJC. **Honours:** OBE (Military) 1944; TD. Died 20 January 1959.

ALMOND, Harry Hudson (1948) Born 10 April 1928, 5 Willows Avenue, Lytham, Lancashire; son of William Almond, Stockbroker, and Norah Kathleen Duckett; m Daphne Joy Borrett, 11 April 1953, St Martin in the Fields; 2 sons (Jeremy b 17 June 1956 and Paul b 20 November 1961), 1 daughter (Fiona b 7 May 1959). **Subject(s):** Modern and Medieval Languages. **Tutor(s):** C W Guillebaud. **Educ:** Charney Hall, Grange-over-Sands; Shrewsbury School. **Career:** Lance Corporal, The Loyal Regiment 1946–1948; Worked for a large London brewery. **Appointments:** Captain, LMBC 1950–1951; Rowed Bow, winning Cambridge Crew, University Boat Race 1950 and 1951; Secretary, CUBC 1951; Rowed Bow,

Great Britain Olympic Coxless Four, Olympic Regatta, Helsinki 1952. **Awards:** Ladies Plate, Henley Royal Regatta 1949; Grand Challenge Cup (with LMBC), Henley Royal Regatta 1951; Gold Medal (with Great Britain Eight), European Championships, Macon 1951.

AMES, George Ernest (1938) Born 12 June 1920, Bewers Field, Birch, Colchester; son of George Ames, Inspector of Schools, and Vera Una Grady; m Evelyn Claire Smith, 21 September 1946; 2 daughters (Katherine Vivien b 6 February 1960 and Charlotte Ellen b 1 October 1963). **Subject(s):** Economics; BA 1941; MA 1945. **Tutor(s):** C W Guillebaud. **Educ:** Hurst House Preparatory School, Chesterfield; Ernest Bailey School; Brentwood School. **Career:** RA, 51st (Highland) Division, Eighth Army, served in Middle East, France and Germany Campaigns and finally as Staff Officer, War Crimes Administration, South East Asia Command, demobilised with rank of Major (Mentioned in Despatches) 1940–1946; Served Articles 1947–1950; Admitted Solicitor 1950; Assistant Solicitor 1950–1956; Local Secretary, High Wycombe, Oxford, Reading and Windsor, Number 3 (Southern) Legal Aid Area 1956–1960; Partner, Hartley Russell & Co 1960–1968; Company Secretary 1968–1978; Own property companies and Licensee 1978–1994; Charitable work 1994–. **Appointments:** Member, Falcons; Honorary Secretary, Reading and District Solicitors Association 1957–1968; Honorary Secretary, Romilly Association 1963–1968; Honorary Treasurer, Reading Cricket and Hockey Club 1962–1964; Lecturer, Company Law, Basingstoke and Reading Technical Colleges; Undertook classes, HM Borstal, Reading; Chairman, Charity Tendring Dial 1995–1998; President, Tendring Dial Credit Union.

AMIN, Mahmoud Loutfy (1929) Born 15 July 1909, Beni Shebl, Zagazig District, Sharqiya Province, Egypt; son of Aly Mansour Amin, Director, Daira Princes Mohammed Aly Ibrahim and Seif El Din. BA 1932. **Tutor(s):** C W Guillebaud. **Educ:** Said El Awal School, Alexandria; Abassia Secondary School, Alexandria, Egypt; Foad El Awal Secondary School, Cairo, Egypt.

AMSDEN, Richard Sidney (1939) Born 18 July 1920, 44 Milton Park, Highgate, London; son of Clifford Sendall Amsden, Head of Tithe Division, Queen Anne's Bounty Office, and Margaret Forbes Ferguson; m; 3 children. BA 1947; MA 1949; CEng; FIEE. **Tutor(s):** J S Boys Smith. **Educ:** Norfolk House School, London; Highgate Junior School, London; Highgate School, London. **Career:** Graduate trainee, then Director, Messrs Binnie, Deacon & Gowley 1942–1949; Civil Engineering Contractor, Contract Manager, then Director 1949–1980; Founder and Chairman, Chiltern Open Air Museum, Chalfont St Giles 1975–1994. Died 7 September 1997.

ANABTAWI, Wasfi Sadeq (1927) Born 1902, Nablus, Palestine; son of Shaikh Sadeq al Anabtawi, Merchant, and Ferida Anabtawi; 1 son (Maher Anabtawi). **Subject(s):** History/Geography; BA 1930; MA 1934. **Tutor(s):** E A Benians. **Educ:** Turkish Government School, Nablus; Palestine Government School, Nablus; English College, Jerusalem; American University, Beirut. **Career:** Finance Minister for King Hussein of Jordan.

ANAND, Dr Nitya (1948) Born 1 January 1925, Lyallpur, India; son of Bhai Balmukand, Professor, Agricultural College, Lyallpur, and Katar Devi; m Swarn Wadhawan, 27 November 1954, New Delhi, India; 2 sons (Neeraj b 25 May 1956 and Naveen b 25 September 1960), 1 daughter (Soniya b 9 September 1962). PhD 1951; BSc (Punjab) 1943; MSc (Delhi) 1945; PhD (Bombay) 1948. **Tutor(s):** J M Wordie. **Educ:** DAS High School, Lyallpur; Government College, Lahore; St Stephen's College, Delhi; Department of Chemical Technology, University of Bombay. **Career:** Rockfeller Foundation Fellow and Research Associate, Department of Bacteriology and Immunology, Harvard Medical School, Boston, USA; Scientist 1951–1974, Director 1974–1984, Scientist Emeritus 1985, Central Drug Research Institute, Lucknow. **Appointments:** Consultant to WHO, UNCTAD and UNIDO; Chairman, Indian Pharmacopoeia Committee 1981–2002; Member,

Scientific Advisory Committee to the Cabinet, Government of India 1981–1983; Member, Scientific and Technical Advisory Committee for Human Reproduction, WHO 1981–1984; Chairman, WHO Steering Committee for Chemotherapy of Malaria 1983–1987; Member, American Chemical Society, Indian Chemical Society and American Association for Cultivation of Science; Fellow, Indian National Science Academy, New Delhi; Fellow, Indian Academy of Sciences, Bangalore; Fellow, The National Academy of Sciences, Allahabad. **Awards:** Amrut Mody Research Award 1973; Acharya P C Ray and J C Ghosh Medals of Indian Chemical Society; Vishwakarma Medal, Indian National Science Academy; J B Chatterjee Gold Medal, Tropical School, Calcutta; K G Naik Gold Medal, Baroda University; Madhya Pradesh Government National Nehru Award for contribution to Science 1992; Raj Kristo Dutt Memorial Award, Indian Science Congress Association 1997; Uttar Pradesh Government, Vigyan Gaurav Award 2000. **Publications:** (jointly) *Art in Organic Synthesis*, 1969, Holden Day Inc, California; (ed) *Chemotherapy of Parasitic Sciences*; (ed jointly) *Chemotherapy and Immunology in the Control of Malaria, Filarians and Leishmaniasis*, 1984, Tata McGraw Hill, New Delhi; (ed) *Approaches to Design and Synthesis of Antiparasitic Drugs*, Elsevier, Amsterdam, 1999; 30 book chapters; 400 research papers; 120 national/international patents.

ANDERSON, Alexander Bruce (1919) Born 25 September 1899, Gortlie, Dickoya, Ceylon; son of John Anderson, Tea Planter, and Florence Brooke. BA 1923; MA 1927. **Tutor(s):** E E Sikes. **Educ:** Charters Towers; Lancing College.

ANDERSON, Godfrey Alard (1926) Born 5 September 1907, Yew Tree House, Winchelsey, Sussex; son of John Coussmaker Anderson, Barrister-at-Law, and Minnie Storr. **Subject(s):** Mechanical Sciences; BA 1929. **Tutor(s):** J M Wordie. **Educ:** Charters Towers, East Grinstead; Rugby School. **Career:** British Aluminium Company, Kinlochleven.

ANDERSON, John Dacre (1948) Born 12 February 1928, Beechwood, Cross Lane, Bebington, Cheshire; son of Laurence Robert Dacre Anderson, Director, Lever's Cattle Foods Ltd, and Margaret Alice Wynn-Evans; m Valerie Grant Howard, 1955; 3 sons (Mark Dacre b 1959, Jonathan St Clair b 1961 and Nicholas James b 1965), 1 daughter (Catherine Sheelah b 1957). BA 1951; MA 1977. **Tutor(s):** G C L Bertram. **Johnian Relatives:** grandson of William Paley Anderson (1843); son of Laurence Robert Dacre Anderson (1905); brother of Anthony Laurence Anderson (1953); brother of David Paley Anderson (1957). **Educ:** Hillstone School, Malvern; Rugby School.

ANDERSON, Laurence Robert Dacre (1905) Born 10 August 1886, Winsford, Somerset; son of William Paley Anderson, Vicar of Winsford, and Catherine Hubbersty; m Margaret Alice Wynne-Evans, 8 February 1927, St Mary's, Chester; 3 sons (John Dacre b 12 February 1928, Anthony Laurence b 23 December 1932 and David Paley b 19 October 1936). **Subject(s):** Classics/History; BA 1908; MA 1919. **Tutor(s):** E E Sikes. **Johnian Relatives:** son of William Paley Anderson (1843); father of John Dacre Anderson (1948), Anthony Laurence Anderson (1953) and of David Paley Anderson (1957). **Educ:** St George's School, Ascot; Rugby School. **Career:** 11th Brigade, RFA; Captain; Lever Brothers, Soap Manufacturers; Sunderland Scholar, Faculty of Commerce, Birmingham University 1909. **Honours:** MC 1918. Died 20 May 1971.

ANDERSON, Thomas Bruce (1949) Born 27 May 1928, 8c Minimi Yamati, Nagasaki, Japan; son of George Anderson, Surveyor, Lloyd's Register of Shipping, and Hilda Muriel Bruce; m Sheila; 2 sons (Jeremy and Nicholas). **Subject(s):** Classics/Law; BA 1952; MA 1956. **Tutor(s):** R L Howland. **Educ:** Hamilton Academy, Lanarkshire; King Edward's School, Birmingham. Died 17 July 1988.

ANDERSON, Professor William Blair (1936) (admitted to Trinity College 1899) Born 28 July 1877, Aberdeen; son of William Blair Anderson, Photographic Artist and Inventor, and Isabella Jane Drennan Irvine Barr. BA 1903 (Trinity); MA 1908 (Trinity). **Educ:** University of

Aberdeen; Gordon College, Aberdeen; Trinity College, Cambridge. **Johnian Relatives:** uncle of Hugh Craigmyle Middleton (1940). **Career:** Assistant Lecturer in Classics, The Victoria University of Manchester 1903–1906; Professor of Latin, Queen's University, Kingston, Canada 1903–1913; Professor of Imperial Latin 1913–1929, Hulme Professor of Latin 1929–1936, University of Manchester; Kennedy Professor of Latin, University of Cambridge 1936–1942; Title C Fellow 1936–1942, Title E Fellow 1942–1959, SJC. **Awards:** Scholarship; Browne Medal for Greek Epigram 1902. **Publications:** (ed) *Livy: Book IX*, Pitt Press, 1909 (3rd edition, 1928); (trans) *Sidonius Apollinaris: Poems and Letters*, Harvard University Press, 1936. Died 9 December 1959.

ANDERSON, William Douglas Laing (1944) Born 14 May 1925, Blantyre, Nyasaland Protectorate; son of Robert John Anderson, Tobacco Leaf Merchant, and Mary Hill Wilson; m (1) Patricia Doreen Lewis, 2 March 1956, Seria, Brunei (d 12 September 1964), (2) Gillian Mary Cunnew (née Trimming), 16 January 1993, Westcott, Surrey; (1) 2 sons (David and Clive), 1 daughter (Jean). **Subject(s):** Mechanical Sciences; BA 1949; MA 1954; MIEE. **Tutor(s):** S J Bailey. **Educ:** Perth Academy; St Mary's School, Melrose; Purley County School; University College, Exeter.

ANDERSON, William Thomas (1929) Born 6 December 1910, 6 Rosebery Avenue, South Shields, County Durham; son of Matthew Brack Anderson, Builder and Contractor, and Nora Marguerite Baker. **Subject(s):** Mechanical Sciences; BA 1932; MA 1936. **Tutor(s):** J M Wordie. **Educ:** St Nicholas School, South Shields; Tonstall School, Sunderland; Durham School. **Appointments:** Secretary, University Rugby Fives Society.

ANDREWARTHA, Kenneth (1949) Born 19 March 1929, 8 North Road, Egremont, Cumberland; son of James Henry Andrewartha, Corporation Labourer, and Sarah Elizabeth Frears; m 1976. **Subject(s):** Modern and Medieval Languages; BA 1952; MA 1956; PGCE (London) 1954. **Tutor(s):** C W Guillebaud. **Educ:** Infant School, Egremont; Woolwich Road Schools, Bexleyheath; National School, Whitehaven; Erith County Grammar School. **Career:** Translations Department, then Area Secretary for Europe, Scripture Gift Mission. Died 8 April 1995.

ANDREWS, Bernard Keith (1943) Born 19 March 1925, 37 Essex Road, Watford; son of Bernard John Andrews, Chartered Accountant, and Dorothy Phillips. **Educ:** Stanborough Park Preparatory School; Watford Grammar School.

ANDREWS, David Mark (1949) Born 9 May 1931, Lezayre, Grove Lane, Timperley, Cheshire; son of Ernest Andrews, Mechanical Engineer, and May Whiteley. **Subject(s):** Modern and Medieval Languages; BA 1952. **Tutor(s):** C W Guillebaud. **Johnian Relatives:** brother of John Malcolm Andrews (1955). **Educ:** Oswald Road School, Manchester; Gwydyr House School, St Annes on Sea; King Edward's School, St Annes on Sea; King William's College, Isle of Man; Manchester Grammar School; The British School, Montevideo; Cuddesdon Theological College, Oxford. **Career:** Joint Services Russian Course, Bodmin, RN, then Cambridge Russian Course, Intelligence Corps 1952–1954; Assistant Master (later Head), Modern Languages Department, St Benedict's School, Ealing 1956–1986.

ANDREWS, James Collingwood (1909) Born 8 February 1890, Avondale, Finchley New Road, Hampstead; son of Edward Collingwood Andrews, Surgeon, and Elizabeth Jane Tucker; m Annie Campell Inglis, 22 October 1915, Dailly Parish Church. **Subject(s):** Natural Sciences; BA 1912; MA 1919; MRCS; LRCP 1919. **Tutor(s):** J R Tanner. **Johnian Relatives:** son of Edward Collingwood Andrews (1880). **Educ:** Oundle School. **Career:** House Surgeon and Clinical Assistant for Medical Out-patients, London Hospital; Clinical Assistant, St John's Hospital for Diseases of the Skin; Anaesthetist, Queen Mary's Maternity Home, Hampstead; Captain and Adjutant, attached to the London Regiment, RAMC, WWI. **Appointments:** Member, Hampstead Medical Society. **Honours:** MC. Died 21 September 1976.

ANDREWS, John Henry (1941) Born 31 December 1922, Churston, St Johns Road, Driffield, Yorkshire; son of Thomas Andrews, Technical Chemist, and Edith Maud Covell. **Subject(s):** Natural Sciences; BA 1949; MA 1951. **Tutor(s):** C W Guillebaud. **Educ:** Driffield Church of England School; Bridlington School. Died 23 July 1995.

ANDREWS, Dr Peter Searell (1942) Born 15 April 1925, Amherst, Ashburton, Devon; son of Reginald Stanley Andrews, Managing Director, Edwin Tuckers & Sons Ltd, Maltsters, and Violet Searell; m; 4 sons, 1 daughter. **Subject(s):** Natural Sciences; BA 1945; MA 1957; MB 1948; BChir 1948; MD 1957; FRCPath; DMJ 1970. **Tutor(s):** S J Bailey. **Educ:** Hillside School, Ashburton; The Wilderness, Ashburton; Ashburton Grammar School; Wycliffe College, Stonehouse. **Career:** Middlesex Hospital Medical School 1944–1948; Trainee Junior Doctor, Surgical and Pathology posts, Middlesex Hospital 1948–1950; Captain, RAMC 1950–1952; Junior Lecturer in Pathology, Middlesex Hospital (Pathology Department) 1953–1958; Member, External Scientific Staff, MRC 1955–1958; Consultant Pathologist, Kettering General Hospital 1958–1990; Home Office Pathologist for East Midlands 1970–1990. **Publications:** *Rodent Ulcers Induced by X-rays Irradiation*, MD thesis, 1957; contributions to medical journals on Radiosensitivity of Tumours, Chondromalacia Patellae, Q Fever Endocarditis, Sudden Infant Death Syndrome and Hospital Autopsy Rates.

ANDREWS, Philip Kenneth Aylmer (1935) Born 2 February 1916, The Corran, Lochgilphead, South Knapdale, Argyll; son of James Alford Andrews, Physician, and Ala Lilian Emma Walker; m Joancita Hampton, 1940; 3 sons (Roderick Philip Alford b 18 September 1941, Norman Howard b 28 September 1943, and Grant Franklin b 6 May 1945), 2 daughters (Claire Frances b 15 June 1947, d 9 December 1975 and Cherry Elaine b 17 February 1949). **Subject(s):** Medicine; MB; BS 1944; MRCS; LRCP 1946; Graduate Diploma, Health Administration 1970. **Tutor(s):** R L Howland. **Johnian Relatives:** son of James Alford Andrews (1894); brother of Ronald Alford Andrews (1928); uncle of Peter Alford Andrews (1955) and of Michael Laurence Alford Andrews (1957). **Educ:** Stowe School. **Career:** GP, Tunbridge Wells 1946–1965; GP, Tasmania 1965–1969; Deputy Director, Department of Veterans' Affairs, Tasmania 1969–1984. Died 9 February 1983.

ANDREWS, Dr Ronald Alford (1928) Born 30 May 1909, Ratcliffe Hall, Syston, Barrow, Leicestershire; son of James Alford Andrews, Surgeon, and Ala Lilian Emma Walker; m (1) Rosemary Hansen Bay, 1934, (2) Jill Bannerman, 1983; (1) 2 sons (Peter Alford b 31 October 1936 and Michael Laurence Alford b 14 June 1939), (2) 1 stepson (Matthew). BA 1931; MA 1937; MB 1937; BChir 1937; MRCS Eng 1934; DM 1945; LRCP 1934. **Tutor(s):** M P Charlesworth. **Johnian Relatives:** son of James Alford Andrews (1894); brother of Philip Kenneth Aylmer Andrews (1935); father of Peter Alford Andrews (1955) and of Michael Laurence Alford Andrews (1957). **Educ:** Park House School, Paignton; Stowe School. **Career:** Surgeon Lieutenant Commander, RNVR, WWII; GP, Bexhill-on-Sea 1934–1967; Deep-water sailing yachtsman (many voyages, including a circumnavigation 1969–1972); Locum GP, New South Wales, Tasmania 1980–1990. **Appointments:** Cambridge Cruising Club (as undergraduate); Founder Member (later President), Bexhill-on-Sea Sailing Club 1947; Member, Royal Cruising Club 1952 (Commodore 1977–1979). **Publications:** About 30 articles on various aspects of cruising, deep-water sailing and navigation published in yachting journals including *The Royal Cruising Club Journal* and *Yachting Monthly*. Died 6 December 1997.

ANGEL, Dr Joseph Harold (1941) Born 2 April 1923, 85 Harehills Avenue, Leeds; son of Isidore Angel, Clothier, and Cecilia Schapiro; m Helen Webster, June 1962; 1 son (Jonathan Mark), 1 daughter (Jessica Clare Isabel). **Subject(s):** Natural Sciences; BA 1944; BChir 1948; MB 1948; MD 1959; MRCP 1954; FRCP 1973. **Tutor(s):** S J Bailey. **Educ:** Beechfield Junior Boys' School; Doncaster Grammar School. **Career:** Assistant Professor of Medicine, State University of New York 1957–1958; Staff Member, MRC's Tuberculosis Research Unit

1959–1962; Consultant Physician, Watford General Hospital 1964–1989; Consultant Physician, Harefield Hospital 1966–1989. **Awards:** Raymond Horton-Smith Prize for MD, University of Cambridge 1959. **Publications:** Papers on tuberculosis and on endocrine disorders.

ANGELBECK, Edward Norman James (1941) Born 26 November 1923, 1 Queens Road, Sudbury, Suffolk; son of Edward James Angelbeck, Schoolmaster, and Violet Elsie Maltby; m Nancie Phyllis Marion Houghton; 1 son (Nigel b 3 January 1950), 1 daughter (Kate b 16 November 1952). **Subject(s):** Natural Sciences; BA 1945; MA 1948; Diploma in Agriculture (Cantab) 1948. **Tutor(s):** C W Guillebaud. **Educ:** The Lymes Preparatory School, Sudbury; Sudbury Grammar School. **Career:** University of Cambridge Soil Science Department 1943–1946; National Agricultural Advisory Service (changed to Agricultural Development and Advisory Service) 1948–1983; District Advisory Officer, Blofield and Flegg District, Norfolk 1948; District Advisory Officer, Sudbury District, Suffolk 1955; Senior Advisory Officer, Worcestershire 1961; Deputy Regional Director, West Midlands 1983; Freelance Agricultural Journalist 1983. **Appointments:** Churchwarden, Stoulton with Drakes Broughton 1984–2001; President, Sudbury Grammar School Old Boys' Association 1991–; Lay Chairman, Pershore Deanery 1992–1996; Chairman, British Guild of Agricultural Journalists 2001.

ANSTEY, Professor Roger Thomas (1945) Born 1 February 1927, 5 Castle Hill, Maidenhead, Berkshire; son of John Frank Anstey, District Goods Manager, Great Western Railway, and Ethel Mary Thomas; m Avril Mary Louise; 1 son (Charles), 2 daughters (Rosalind and Louise). **Subject(s):** History; BA 1950; MA 1952; PhD (London) 1957. **Tutor(s):** J M Wordie. **Educ:** Alwyn Road Council School, Maidenhead; Penlee House, Plymouth; Plymouth College; Shrewsbury School. **Career:** Lecturer in Modern History, University College, Ibadan 1952–1957; Lecturer in History 1958–1966, Lecturer in Modern History 1966–1968, University of Durham; Professor of Modern History, University of Kent 1968–1979. **Appointments:** Visiting Professor, University of British Columbia 1966–1967. **Publications:** *Britain and the Congo in the 19th Century*, 1962; *King Leopold's Legacy: The Congo under Belgian Rule 1908–1960*, 1966; *The Atlantic Slave Trade and British Abolition*, 1975. Died 26 January 1979.

ANTHONY, Dr Arthur Lawrence (1908) Born 27 February 1890, Grove Road, Hawthorn, Bourke, Victoria, Australia; son of Arthur Frederick Anthony, Mariner, and Helen Dick; m Eveleen. MRCS; LRCP 1914. **Tutor(s):** J R Tanner. **Educ:** Bishop's Stortford College. **Career:** Chief Medical Officer, Ashanti Goldfields Corporation; Lieutenant, then Captain, RAMC 1914; Assistant Physician, Duff House Sanitorium. Died 25 February 1938.

ANTIA, Merwanji Jamshedji (1909) Born 15 June 1888, Bombay, India; son of Jamshedji Merwanji Antia, Secretary. **Subject(s):** Economics/History/Law; BA 1912; MA 1916. **Tutor(s):** J R Tanner. **Educ:** Elphinstone College, Bombay, India. **Career:** Called to the Bar, Gray's Inn 1914; Lecturer, College of Commerce 1915–1921 (Professor from 1919); Indian Educational Service 1921–1932 (Officiating Principal from 1928); Secretary, Accountancy Diploma Board 1932; Professor, Sydenham College (Principal 1940).

ANTROBUS, Harvey (1910) Born 10 June 1891, Berkeswell, Meridan, Warwickshire; son of Alfred Antrobus, Farmer, and Hannah Mary Worsley; m (1) Dora Elsie Upton (dis 1934), (2) Edna Lucy Chard, 1934; (1) 2 sons (Guy and Michael), (2) 2 daughters (Celia and Yvonne). **Subject(s):** Mathematics; BA 1913; MA 1919. **Tutor(s):** L H K Bushe-Fox. **Educ:** Maxstoke Parish School; Coleshill Grammar School; Birmingham University. **Career:** Lieutenant, RE, WWI. Died 9 April 1959.

APPLEBY, His Honour Judge Brian John (1948) Born 25 February 1930, Ernesto, Cavendish Road, Broughton, Manchester; son of Ernest Joel Appleby, Dental Supplies Agent, and Gertrude Nepolsky; m Rosa

Helena Flitterman, 1958; 1 son, 1 daughter. **Subject(s):** Law; BA 1951; QC 1971. **Tutor(s):** F Thistlethwaite. **Educ:** Bramcote Hall School, Nottinghamshire; Singleton Hill School, Manchester; Uppingham School. **Career:** Called to the Bar, Middle Temple 1953; Conservative Councillor 1955–1960; Deputy Chairman, Nottinghamshire QS 1970–1971; Recorder, Crown Court 1972–1988; Bencher, Middle Temple 1980; Circuit Judge, Midland and Oxford Circuit 1988. **Awards:** Johnson Exhibition, SJC 1948.

APPLEBY, Mark (1929) Born 5 August 1910, Embleton, Alnwick, Northumberland; son of Mark Appleby, Quarry Owner, and Wilhelmina Armstrong; m Lettice Emily, 1937; 2 daughters. **Subject(s):** Mathematics/Mechanical Sciences; BA 1932; MA 1936. **Tutor(s):** J M Wordie. **Educ:** The Duke's School, Alnwick; Clifton College. **Career:** Intelligence Service, WWII; Lecturer, Downing College, Cambridge; Professor of Mathematics, University of Valletta, Malta 1936. **Appointments:** Governor, Clifton College. **Awards:** George Cross replica from the Maltese Government in recognition of War work. Died 23 January 1994.

APPLETON, Anthony (1943) Born 3 October 1925, 17 Laira Street, Warrington, Lancashire; son of Robert Appleton, Newsagent and Tobacconist, and Ethel Hampson. **Tutor(s):** C W Guillebaud. **Educ:** Bolton Council School, Warrington; Warrington Secondary School; Boteler Grammar School, Warrington.

APPLETON, Sir Edward Victor (1911) Born 6 September 1892, 41 Maperton Street, Bradford, Yorkshire; son of Peter Appleton, Yarn Warehouseman, and Mary Wilcock; m (1) Jessie Longson, 1915, (2) Helen Allison, 24 March 1965, Canongate Kirk, Edinburgh; (1) 2 daughters. **Subject(s):** Natural Sciences; BA 1914; MA 1918; Honorary degrees from Oxford, Cambridge, Aberdeen, Birmingham, Leeds, Brussels, Cincinnati, Dalhousie, Laval and Montreal; FRS 1935; Hon MICE; Hon FRCSE 1955. **Tutor(s):** J R Tanner. **Educ:** Hanson Secondary School, Bradford. **Career:** Private, West Yorkshire Regiment, RE, WWI; Foundress Fellow, SJC 1919–1925; Assistant Demonstrator in Experimental Physics, University of Cambridge 1920–1925; Sublector, Trinity College, Cambridge 1922; Wheatstone Professor of Physics, KCL 1924–1936; Jacksonian Professor of Natural Philosophy, University of Cambridge 1936–1939; Title C Fellow, SJC 1936–1939; Secretary, Department of Scientific and Industrial Research 1939–1949; Principal and Vice-Chancellor, University of Edinburgh 1949. **Appointments:** Honorary Fellow, SJC 1946; President, International Scientific Radio Union; Chairman, BBC Scientific Advisory Committee; Member, Pontifical Academy of Sciences; President, British Association; Deputy Lieutenant, County of the City of Edinburgh; President, Radio Industry Council 1955–1957. **Awards:** Scholarship, SJC; Wiltshire Prize, University of Cambridge 1913; Hughes Medal, Royal Society 1933; Charles Chree Medal and Prize, Physical Society 1947; Nobel Prize for Physics 1947; US Medal of Merit 1947; James Alfred Ewing Medal, Institution of Civil Engineers 1948; Royal Medal, Royal Society 1950; Albert Medal, RSA 1950; Gunning Victoria Jubilee Prize, Royal Society of Edinburgh 1956–1960; Medal of Honour, American Institute of Radio Engineers 1962; Hutchinson Research Studentship; Valdemar Poulsen Gold Medal, Danish Academy of Technical Sciences; Kelvin Medal, Joint Engineering Institutions 1963; Keith Medal, Royal Scottish Society of Arts; Faraday Medal, Institute of Electrical Engineers. **Honours:** KCB 1941; GBE 1946; Cross of Freedom of Norway 1947; Officer of the Legion of Honour 1947. Died 21 April 1965.

APPLEWHAITE, Charles Trueman (1909) Born 8 January 1891, South Pickenham, Swaffham, Norfolk; son of Charles Mundy Applewhaite, Estateowner and Colonel, 4th Battalion, Norfolk Militia, and Mary Florence Mills. **Tutor(s):** L H K Bushe-Fox. **Educ:** Suffield Park, Cromer; Harrow School.

ARCHBOLD, John William (1926) Born 25 April 1908, 22 Fenkle Street, Alnwick, Northumberland; son of John Archbold, Master Draper, and Alice Markham; m Hilda Irene Benham, 2 July 1942; 1 son (Robert b

7 July 1947), 1 daughter (Alison b 22 February 1945). **Subject(s):** Mathematics; BA 1929; MA 1933. **Tutor(s):** J M Wordie. **Johnian Relatives:** father of Robert John Archbold (1965). **Educ:** The Duke's School, Alnwick; Manchester Grammar School. **Career:** Meteorological Office, WWII; Senior Lecturer in Mathematics, UCL 1970. **Awards:** Scholarship, SJC. Died 11 December 1989.

ARCHER, Geoffrey Clifford (1924) Born 2 May 1906, Croft House, Swan Lane, Lockwood, Huddersfield, Yorkshire; son of George Archer, Baptist Minister, and Ada Emeline Higgs. **Subject(s):** Mathematics; BA 1927; MA 1931. **Tutor(s):** J M Wordie. **Educ:** King James' Grammar School, Almondbury.

ARCHER-HIND, Laurence (1914) Born 18 March 1895, Little Newnham, Cambridge; son of Richard Dacre Archer-Hind, Fellow, Trinity College, and Laura Pocock; m Mary Honor Yarborough, 29 December 1920. **Tutor(s):** E E Sikes. **Educ:** King's College Choir School; Fonthill Preparatory School; Haileybury College. **Career:** Second Lieutenant, Lincolnshire Regiment 1914–1915; Teacher, Pellatt's Preparatory School, Dorset 1916. Died 20 March 1923.

ARD, Horace Herbert William (1904) Born 10 December 1885, Castle House, Naas, County Kildare; son of William Ard, Excise Officer, and Mary Maud Alexandra Harpur. **Tutor(s):** J R Tanner; C E Graves. **Educ:** Sherborne School; Perse School, Cambridge.

ARGYLE, The Revd Douglas Causer (1936) Born 25 January 1917, The Vicarage, Rawtenstall, Lancashire; son of Frank Wilkinson Argyle, Clerk in Holy Orders, and Margaret Sara Causer; m (1) Marjorie Joan Naish, 2 August 1951, St Francis Church, Salisbury, (2) Margaret Joan Oliver, 1989, Bibury Church; (1) 1 son (Andrew Nicholas). **Subject(s):** Classics/Geography; BA 1939; MA 1943. **Tutor(s):** J M Wordie; R L Howland. **Johnian Relatives:** son of Frank Wilkinson Argyle (1900); brother of Robert Murray Argyle (1937) and of Geoffrey Vaughan Argyle (1947); father of Andrew Nicholas Argyle (1971); uncle of Alastair Vaughan Argyle (1971) and of Duncan Murray Argyle (1973); grandfather of Victoria Clare Argyle (2001). **Educ:** Old Hall School, Wellington; Marlborough College. **Career:** Ordained 1941; Curate, Somercotes (Derbyshire); Army Chaplain; Assistant Master and Chaplain, Repton School 1947–1959; Chaplain and Assistant Master, Gresham's School, Holt, Norfolk 1959–1974; Rector, Eastleach and Southrop, Gloucestershire 1974–1982. **Awards:** Sizarship, SJC.

ARGYLE, The Revd Frank Wilkinson (1900) Born 24 September 1880, 1 Nelson Terrace, Great Yarmouth, Norfolk; son of John William Argyle, Merchant, and Mary Catherine Bower; m Margaret Sara Causer, 26 October 1910, Aston; 3 sons (Douglas Causer b 25 January 1917, Robert Murray b 14 October 1918 and Geoffrey Vaughan b 27 September 1925). BA 1903; MA 1907. **Tutor(s):** D MacAlister. **Johnian Relatives:** father of Douglas Causer Argyle (1936), Robert Murray Argyle (1937) and of Geoffrey Vaughan Argyle (1947); grandfather of Alastair Vaughan Argyle (1971), Andrew Nicholas Argyle (1971) and of Duncan Murray Argyle (1973); great grandfather of Victoria Clare Argyle (2001). **Educ:** Great Yarmouth Grammar School; Epsom College; Ridley Hall, Cambridge. **Career:** Curate, St Paul's, Onslow Square 1905–1910; Vicar, Christ Church, Wellington 1910–1913; Vicar, Rawtenstall 1913–1923; Surrogate 1915; Rural Dean, Rossendale 1920–1923; Vicar, Christ Church, Blackpool 1923–1932; Rector, March 1932–1934; Vicar, Leyland 1934–1938; Rural Dean, Leyland 1935–1936 Rector, Sevenoaks 1938; Rural Dean, Sevenoaks 1942–1945; Vicar, Cold Harbour, Surrey 1954. Died 20 November 1969.

ARGYLE, Geoffrey Vaughan (1947) Born 27 September 1925, Christ Church Vicarage, Queen Street, Blackpool, Lancashire; son of Frank Wilkinson Argyle, Clerk in Holy Orders, and Margaret Sara Causer; m Elisabeth Dorothy Vellacott, 29 December 1951; 3 sons (Alastair Vaughan b 1 December 1952, Duncan Murray b 1 August 1955 and Patrick Graham), 1 daughter (Rachel Alice). **Subject(s):** Geography; BA 1949; MA 1954. **Tutor(s):** J M Wordie. **Johnian Relatives:** son of Frank Wilkinson Argyle (1900); nephew of Frederick Donald Coggan (1928); brother of Douglas Causer Argyle (1936) and of Robert Murray Argyle (1937); father of Alastair Vaughan Argyle (1971); uncle of Andrew Nicholas Argyle (1971); father of Duncan Murray Argyle (1973); great uncle of Victoria Clare Argyle (2001). **Educ:** The Old Hall, Wellington; Marlborough College; Guy's Hospital Medical School. **Career:** Coldstream Guards 1944–1947; Schoolmaster 1951–1985.

ARGYLE, Robert Murray (1937) Born 14 October 1918, The Vicarage, Rawtenstall; son of Frank Wilkinson Argyle, Clerk in Holy Orders, and Margaret Sara Causer. **Subject(s):** Geography; BA 1947; MA 1949. **Tutor(s):** R L Howland. **Johnian Relatives:** son of Frank Wilkinson Argyle (1900); brother of Douglas Causer Argyle (1936) and Geoffrey Vaughan Argyle (1947); uncle of Alastair Vaughan Argyle (1971), Andrew Nicholas Argyle (1971) and of Duncan Murray Argyle (1973); great uncle of Victoria Clare Argyle (2001). **Educ:** The Old Hall, Wellington; Marlborough College. **Career:** RNVR, HMS *Hood*, WWII; Biology Teacher and Housemaster, Bradfield College, Berkshire 1947–1984. **Appointments:** President, The Hawks Club 1946. Died 5 February 2000.

ARIAS, Dr Harmodio (1907) Born 13 July 1885, Penonome, Republic of Panama; son of Antonio Arias, Landowner and Merchant, and Carmen Madrid; m Rosario Guardia; 2 sons (Harmodio and Roberto). **Subject(s):** Law; BA 1909; LLB 1909; LLD (London). **Tutor(s):** L H K Bushe-Fox. **Johnian Relatives:** father of Harmodio Arias (1935) and of Roberto Emilio Arias (1935). **Educ:** Escuela de Penonome, Panama; Colegio del Istruo, Panama; Catholic Collegiate School, Lytham; University School, Southport; LSE. **Career:** Under-Secretary of Foreign Affairs, Panama 1912–1915; Member, Commission on Codification of Laws in Panama 1915–1916; Professor of Roman and Comparative Law, Panama Law School 1916–1917; Representative of Panama, League of Nations 1920; Deputy to National Assembly of Panama 1924–1928; Representative of Uruguay to Bolivarian Congress 1926; Minister Plenipotentiary of Panama to the USA 1931; President, Republic of Panama 1932–1936. **Publications:** *The Doctrine of Continuous Voyages*, 1909; *The Panama*, 1911; publisher of the daily paper, *The Panama American*. Died 23 December 1962.

ARIAS, Harmodio (1935) Born 6 September 1917, Ancon Hospital, Panama; son of Harmodio Arias, President, Republic of Panama, and Rosario Guardia. **Subject(s):** Economics; BA 1938. **Tutor(s):** J M Wordie. **Johnian Relatives:** son of Harmodio Arias (1907); brother of Roberto Emilio Arias (1935). **Educ:** Balboa School; Raenford Military Academy, Puente, California; The Peddie School, Hightstown, New Jersey; Columbia University.

ARIAS, Dr Roberto Emilio (Tito) (1935) Born 26 October 1918, Panama City, Panama; son of Harmodio Arias, President, Republic of Panama, and Rosario Guardia; m (1) Querube, (2) Margot Fonteyn, 1955, Panamanian Consulate, Paris (d 1991); (1) 1 son (Roberto), twin daughters (Querube and Roseta). **Subject(s):** Economics and Law; BA 1938; Doctorat d'Etat (Sorbonne); Columbia University. **Tutor(s):** C W Guillebaud. **Johnian Relatives:** son of Harmodio Arias (1907); brother of Harmodio Arias (1935). **Educ:** Balboa School; Raenford Military Academy, Puente, California; The Peddie School, Hightstown, New Jersey. **Career:** Called to the Bar, Panama 1939; Fifth Circuit, Court of Appeals, USA 1941; Editor, *El Panama-Americana* 1942–1946; Counsellor to Panama Embassy, Chile 1947; Publisher, *La Hora* 1948–1968; Delegate to the UN Assembly, New York 1953–1955; Panamanian Ambassador to the Court of St James's 1955–1958 and 1960–1962; Elected Deputy to the National Assembly of Panama 1962–1968. Died 22 November 1989.

ARIS, Douglas Heath (1915) Born 16 July 1896, Crowhurst, Wickham Road, Sutton, Surrey; son of Charles Joseph Aris, Assistant to Manager, Discount Company, and Emily Augusta Pollock. **Tutor(s):** E E Sikes.

Educ: Merton Court School, Sidcup; City of London School. **Awards:** Scholarship, SJC 1914. **Publications:** 'The Passing of Boyhood', *The Eagle*, 37, 1916.

ARMITAGE, Bernard William Francis (1909) Born 6 July 1890, 271 Mansfield Road, Basford, Nottinghamshire; son of William Armitage, Corn Merchant, and Annie Clara Harris. BA 1913; MA 1918; MRCS; LRCP 1918. **Tutor(s):** J R Tanner. **Educ:** Nottingham High School; Gresham's School, Holt; University College, Bangor. **Career:** Ashton Fellow, SJC 1919–1925; House Surgeon, St Bartholomew's Hospital; Medical Advisor, Olympic Games, Antwerp 1920; Assistant Medical Officer, Croydon Mental Hospital 1934. **Appointments:** Tutor, SJC 1919–1925. Died 25 August 1976.

ARMITAGE, Brian (1948) Born 14 February 1928, Wood Lynn, Newton Park, Brighouse, Yorkshire; son of Herbert Armitage, Silk-waste Spinner, and Ada Pratt; m Ruth; 4 daughters. **Subject(s):** Natural Sciences/Law; BA 1950; MA 1957. **Tutor(s):** G C L Bertram. **Educ:** St Chad's Elementary School, Brighouse; Hipperholme Grammar School; Oundle School. Died 28 March 2002.

ARMITAGE, Edward John (1937) Born 4 May 1920, 207 Gray's Inn Road, London; son of Joseph Armitage, Architectural Sculptor, and Muriel Vice; m Marthe Cleyndert, 20 January 1951, St Anne's, Kew. BA 1940; MA 1944; Dip Arch (Edinburgh) 1948; Dip (London) 1950; FRIBA. **Tutor(s):** J S Boys Smith. **Educ:** Magdalen House School, Wandsworth; King's College Junior School, Wimbledon; St Paul's School, West Kensington. Died 20 November 1992.

ARMSTRONG, Alfred Elliott (1923) Born 8 October 1895, Colman, Clones, County Monaghan, Ireland; son of William Armstrong, Farmer, and Elizabeth West. **Tutor(s):** E E Sikes. **Educ:** Clones High School; Private Tuition; RMA, Woolwich.

ARMSTRONG, Bernard (1921) Born 19 April 1903, 277 Burley Road, Burley, Kirkstall, Leeds; son of Alfred Armstrong, Clerk in Holy Orders, and Linda Kate Reid. BA 1926; MA 1937. **Tutor(s):** B F Armitage. **Educ:** Preparatory School and Bristol Cathedral School.

ARMSTRONG, David John (1948) Born 20 November 1927, 55 Lancaster Gate, Paddington, London; son of Godfrey George Armstrong, Ports Adviser to the Government of India, and Margaret Eleanor Gardiner; m Jane Merrick Soper, 23 June 1956, St Bartholomew's, Leigh, Surrey; 4 sons (Robert David b 21 September 1958, James Edward b 14 April 1960, Charles Roland b 15 June 1961 and Richard Michael b 17 August 1962), 2 daughters (Elizabeth Jane b 21 May 1957 and Emily Margaret b 21 July 1969). **Subject(s):** Mechanical Sciences; BA 1950; MA 1955. **Tutor(s):** R L Howland. **Educ:** Fonthill Preparatory School, East Grinstead; Breeks Memorial School, Ootacamund, India; Bradfield College. **Career:** Manager, Structures and Foundations Design, HV Transmission Department, British Columbia Hydro, until 1993. **Appointments:** Vice-Chairman 1988–1990, Chairman 1990–1991, Canadian Electrical Association; Treasurer, National Academy of Older Canadians.

ARMSTRONG, Edmund Clarence Charles (1932) Born 17 February 1914, 73 Park Avenue, Donnybrook, Dublin; son of Edmund Clarence Richard Armstrong, Keeper of Irish Antiquities, and Bluemantle Pursuivant, College of Arms, and Mary Frances Cruise; m Dorice Austin, Trincomalee, 1951 (d 1983); triplet sons (Sean, Mark and Patrick b 1954). **Subject(s):** French/Spanish; BA 1935. **Tutor(s):** J S Boys Smith. **Educ:** Borlase School, Marlow; St Edmund's College, Ware. **Career:** RN, WWII; Civil Servant, Admiralty. Died 3 September 2001.

ARMSTRONG, George Trevor (1947) Born 13 September 1928, 12 Forster Road, Beckenham, Kent; son of John Leonard Armstrong, Chartered Accountant, and Maud Evelyn Mildred Atkinson; m 1965 (div). BA 1949; BVetMed (London) 1960. **Tutor(s):** G C L Bertram. **Educ:** Abbey School, East Grinstead; Haileybury College.

ARMSTRONG, Gerard Bruce (1941) Born 19 March 1923, 19 Warwick Square, Carlisle; son of William Herbert Fletcher Armstrong, Director of Public Instruction, Punjab, and Dorothy Lottie Hornell. **Tutor(s):** C W Guillebaud. **Educ:** The Hill School, Westerham; Pilgrims, Westerham; The Hall School, Hampstead; King's School, Canterbury. **Career:** Second Lieutenant, RAC, King's Dragoon Guards 1941–1944. Died 24 January 1944 (killed in action in Italy).

ARMSTRONG, John Barton (BARTON-ARMSTRONG) (1941) Born 8 April 1923, Cowpen Bewley, Stockton, County Durham; son of John Leonard Armstrong, Chartered Accountant, and Maud Evelyn Mildred Atkinson. BA 1944; MA 1948. **Tutor(s):** S J Bailey. **Educ:** The Abbey School, Beckenham; Haileybury College.

ARMSTRONG, John Dickson (1943) Born 27 June 1924, Ainthorpe, Eldon Grove, West Hartlepool; son of Herbert Armstrong, Corn Merchant, and Elizabeth Dickson. **Tutor(s):** C W Guillebaud. **Educ:** Rosebank Preparatory School, West Hartlepool; King's School, Canterbury. **Career:** Sub-Lieutenant, RNVR, WWII. Died 29 April 1945 (killed in action in HMS *Goodall*).

ARNELL, Oliver Roach (1906) (migrated to Gonville & Caius College) Born 26 August 1888, Whitecliff, Sandown, Ryde, Isle of Wight; son of William Thomas Arnell, Merchant Miller and JP, and Henrietta Gibbings. **Subject(s):** Mathematics; BA (Gonville & Caius) 1910. **Tutor(s):** L H K Bushe-Fox. **Educ:** Berkhamsted School; Dudley House, Sandown.

ARNISON, Thomas Mitchell (1929) Born 10 September 1910, Dorset House, Penrith, Cumberland; son of Charles Arnison, Solicitor, and Jean Currie Mitchell; m Dora Elizabeth Reynolds, May 1938, High Wycombe; 1 son (Nicholas b 1 November 1948), 2 daughters (Lisette b 20 February 1940, d 2 December 2000 and Gillian b 9 February 1947). **Subject(s):** Law; BA 1932; MA 1980. **Tutor(s):** M P Charlesworth. **Johnian Relatives:** great uncle of Robert John Allcock (1986). **Educ:** Penrith Grammar School; Charney Hall, Grange-over-Sands; Sedbergh School. **Career:** Officer, Border Regiment, WWII; Commandant of POW Camps in North Africa, then Italy 1942–1945; Solicitor, Arnison and Co (family firm), Penrith, Cumbria. **Appointments:** Governor, later Solicitor to the Governors, Sedbergh School; Trustee, Old Sedberghian Trust Fund. **Awards:** Lupton and Hebblethwaite Exhibition, SJC 1929. Died 28 June 1989.

ARNOLD, Erik Stennett (1919) Born 23 August 1897, 44 Inglis Road, Ealing, Middlesex; son of George Arnold, Jeweller, Silversmith, and Sophia Emily Jones. **Subject(s):** Classics. **Tutor(s):** E E Sikes. **Educ:** Darton House School, Ealing; Bowden House School, Seaford; Tonbridge School. **Career:** Probationary Flight Sublieutenant, RNAF, coastal defence work, Isle of Thanet 1916–1917; Eastern Mediterranean Squadron, RNAS 1917 (wounded); RAF 1918 (wounded); Captain in charge of stores, No 5 Stores Depot, RAF, Earls Court, London 1918–1919; N M Rothschild and Sons, Merchants and Bankers. **Awards:** Scholarship, SJC 1915. Died 17 April 1951.

ARNOLD, John Corry (1900) Born 8 April 1881, The Manse, Dunmurry, Drumbeg, County Antrim; son of Robert James Arnold, Presbyterian Clergyman, and Eliza Wilson; m Alice Emily; 4 sons (Patrick, Michael, Hugh and Christopher). **Subject(s):** Classics; BA 1903. **Tutor(s):** C E Graves. **Educ:** Royal Belfast Academical Institution. **Career:** Called to the Irish Bar 1906; Called to the Bar, Inner Temple 1911; Captain, Northumberland Fusiliers, WWI; Ministry of Pensions, WWI. **Appointments:** Secretary, Vice-President and President, Cambridge Union Society 1903. Died 24 September 1962.

ARNOLD, John Henry (1905) Born 31 July 1887, Maxstoke, Coleshill, Warwickshire; son of John Arnold, Farmer, and Harriett Betteridge. BA 1908; MA 1912. **Tutor(s):** C E Graves; J R Tanner. **Educ:** The Grammar School, Coleshill. **Career:** Master, St Faith's School, Cambridge 1909–1913; Master, Northampton School 1913–1920; Master, Brighton

College 1920–1923; Joint Headmaster, Brighton College Preparatory School 1923–1932.

ARNOLD, William Aubrey (1925) Born 18 March 1908, 2 Lutterworth Road, Northampton; son of William Arnold, Shoe Manufacturer, and Annie Hawes; m Winifred Catherine Bent; 1 son (William Robin Graham b 4 December 1935). **Subject(s):** Modern and Medieval Languages/Law; BA 1928. **Tutor(s):** E A Benians. **Johnian Relatives:** father of William Robin Graham Arnold (1955). **Educ:** Northampton Grammar School; Mill Hill School. **Career:** Shoe Manufacturer.

ARNOTT, Edward Whinstone (1902) Born 7 May 1883, 15 Commercial Street, Aberdare, Glamorganshire; son of Edward Arnott, Gentleman, and Janet Williams; m Julia. BA 1905; MA 1912. **Tutor(s):** D MacAlister. **Educ:** Wycliffe College, Stonehouse. **Career:** Called to the Bar, Inner Temple 1913; Major, RFA (TF) (Mentioned in Despatches), WWI. **Honours:** OBE. Died 31 December 1950.

ARNOTT, Hugh Whitehorn (1935) Born 20 August 1916, 8 Albion Road, South Hampstead, London; son of Robert James Arnott, Journalist, and Nora Whitehorn; m Christine Margaret Lowthian, July 1947; 3 sons (Peter John b 1948, Michael Hugh b 1950, and Richard James b 1954). **Subject(s):** Mathematics; BA 1938; MA 1942; DipEd (Oxford). **Tutor(s):** J M Wordie **Educ:** Sheringham House School, Hampstead; St Paul's School. **Career:** Mathematics Teacher, Head of Mathematics Department, King Edward VII School, Lytham St Annes 1947–1975. **Awards:** Scholarship, SJC. Died 26 November 1994.

ARNOTT, Ronald Whiston John (1919) Born 2 August 1900, Rockliffe, Radyr, Glamorganshire; son of William Thomas Arnott, Gentleman, and Mary Lewis. **Tutor(s):** E A Benians. **Johnian Relatives:** brother of Trevor Arnott (1920). **Educ:** Monmouth Grammar School; Christ's College, Brecon; Wycliffe College, Stonehouse. **Career:** 2nd Battalion, Artist's Rifles Officers Training Corps 1918–1919.

ARNOTT, Trevor (1920) Born 23 February 1902, Rockliffe, Radyr, Glamorganshire; son of William Thomas Arnott, Accountant, and Mary Lewis. **Tutor(s):** E E Sikes. **Johnian Relatives:** brother of Ronald Whiston John Arnott (1919). **Educ:** Wycliffe College, Stonehouse; The Grammar School, Monmouth.

ARROW, John William Frederick (1926) Born 27 May 1907, 80 Grenville Street, Toronto, Canada; son of Frederick Arrow, Accountant, and Lilian Frances Jones-Henry; m (1) Ebba Roll, 1934, (2) Marjorie Joyce Pilkington; 3 daughters (Susan, Frances and Prudence). **Subject(s):** English/History; BA 1929; FRSA. **Tutor(s):** E A Benians. **Educ:** Brentwood School. **Career:** Director, Overseas General Division, Ministry of Information 1942–1946. **Publications:** *Young Man's Testament*, 1932. Died 31 October 1958.

ARTHUR, Dr Allan Charles (1940) Born 18 May 1922, Mandala, Kilmacolm, Renfrewshire; son of Allan Arthur, Electrical Engineer, and Margaret Evelyn Anderson; m Joan Mary Parry, 14 April 1950, Northampton. **Subject(s):** Natural Sciences; BA 1943; MA 1947; BChir 1946; MB 1946; MB (Glasgow); BChir (Glasgow); MRCP (Edinburgh). **Tutor(s):** R L Howland. **Educ:** St Columba School, Kilmacolm; Glasgow Academy; Loretto School. **Career:** Assistant Physician, Falkirk and District Royal Infirmary; Honorary Physician, Armida Hospital, New South Wales, Australia; Lieutenant, RAMC 1946–1948.

ARTHUR, William Todd (1947) Born 26 August 1920, Pretoria, South Africa. **Subject(s):** Mechanical Sciences; BA 1949; MA 1978; BSc (Witwatersrand) 1941. **Tutor(s):** J M Wordie. **Educ:** University of the Witwatersrand, Johannesburg, South Africa. **Career:** South African Engineering Corps 1941–1945. **Honours:** MC.

ARULANANDOM, Dr Victor Ross (1933) Born 30 March 1914, Seremban, Federated Malay States; son of Sinnappan Ponnusamy Arulanandom, Railway Clerk, and Amirtham Ammal. **Subject(s):** Natural Sciences; BA 1936; MA 1960; BChir 1942; MB 1942. **Tutor(s):** R L Howland. **Educ:** The Methodist Girls' School, Federated Malay States; The Victoria Institution, Federated Malay States.

ARUNDEL, Dennis Drew (ARUNDELL) (1919) Born 22 July 1898, Ormefield, Long Lane, Finchley; son of Arundel Drew Arundel, Army Gymnastic Staff and Box Manufacturer, and Rosa Lucy Campbell. **Subject(s):** Classics; BA 1921; MA 1925; MusB 1923; FRCM. **Tutor(s):** E E Sikes. **Educ:** Stoke Newington Collegiate School; Beechmont Preparatory School, Sevenoaks; Tonbridge School. **Career:** Lieutenant, RGA 1914–1919; Fellow and Deputy Organist, SJC 1923–1929; Lecturer in Music and English Drama; Actor, Composer, Producer, Writer for theatre, radio, films and television; Member, Old Vic Company 1926–1950; First Lord Peter Wimsey in Dorothy L Sayers's *Busman's Honeymoon* 1937; Chief Producer, RCM Opera School 1959–1973; Resident Opera Producer and Coach, Royal Northern College of Music, Manchester 1974; Producer and translator of operas, arranger and composer of original works, chiefly with Sadler's Wells and the BBC 1959–1989. **Awards:** Sizarship; Browne Medal for Latin Epigram, University of Cambridge 1920; Winchester Reading Prize, University of Cambridge 1921. **Honours:** OBE 1978. **Publications:** *The Story of Sadler's Wells 1683–1964*, 1965. Died 10 December 1988.

ASCHAFFENBURG, Herr Wilhelm Arthur (1908) Born 20 November 1889, Essen, Ruhr, Prussia; son of Eugen Aschaffenburg, Journalist, and Paula Heinemann. **Tutor(s):** J R Tanner. **Educ:** Gymnasium, Hannover.

ASEM, Alfred Kofi (1943) Born 20 June 1918, Tsito, Gold Coast, British West Africa; son of Joseph Komla Kodzo Asem, Farmer, and Afua Gbo Addae. BA 1946; MA 1965. **Educ:** Presbyterian School, Kumasi, Tsito; Presbyterian Senior Boarding School, Blengo; Mfantsi Pim (Methodist Secondary School), Cape Coast; Agricultural Training Centre, Kumasi.

ASH, Dr Arthur Edward Michael (1935) See WIGGINS.

ASHBEE, John Michael Neville (1942) Born 5 February 1924, 41 Western Road, Brentwood; son of John Harold Neville Ashbee, Schoolmaster, and Katherine McCulloch Thomson. BA 1948; MA 1984. **Tutor(s):** C W Guillebaud. **Educ:** Brentwood School.

ASHBROOKE, Philip Biden Derwent (1942) Born 23 August 1925, 5 Roland Gardens, South Kensington; son of Philip Ashbrooke, Concert Director, and Gladys Derwent Moger; m Veronica Phillipa Stourton, 1954; 1 son (Auberon Francis Biden b 1956); 1 daughter (Sophy b 1959). **Subject(s):** Law; BA 1949; MA 1951. **Tutor(s):** S J Bailey. **Johnian Relatives:** father of Auberon Francis Biden Ashbrooke (1975). **Educ:** Orme School, Holland Park; Westminster School. **Career:** Captain, 8th King's Royal Irish Hussars 1944–1947; ADC to Governor of Kenya 1946–1947; Called to the Bar, Gray's Inn 1950; Legal Advisor, Shell International 1956–1982. Died 1 January 1993.

ASHBY, Francis Cyril (1922) Born 15 August 1903, 93 Aston Lane, Handsworth, West Bromwich, Staffordshire; son of Frank Ashby, Manufacturer, and Clementina Pickering. BA 1925. **Tutor(s):** E Cunningham. **Educ:** King Edward's Grammar School; Malvern College. **Career:** Managing Director, Frank Ashby & Sons Ltd. Died December 1952.

ASHBY, Hugh King (1929) Born 11 May 1911, The Poplars, Bishopthorpe, Yorkshire; son of Edgar Ashby, Dental Surgeon, and Mary Thompson; m Birthe; 3 sons (Peter, Michael and James). **Subject(s):** Natural Sciences; BA 1932; MA 1965. **Tutor(s):** C W Guillebaud. **Johnian Relatives:** brother of Richard Thompson Ashby (1927). **Educ:** Gresham's School, Holt. **Career:** Agricultural Officer, Senior Agricultural Officer, Federation of Malaya 1950. Died 19 December 1987.

ASHBY, Major Richard Thompson (1927) Born 15 January 1909, The Poplars, Bishopthorpe, Yorkshire; son of Edgar Ashby, Dental Surgeon, and Mary Thompson; m Elizabeth Stuttard Sagar, 2 November 1945, Canterbury. **Subject(s):** Natural Sciences; BA 1930; MA 1956. **Tutor(s):** C W Guillebaud. **Johnian Relatives:** brother of Hugh King Ashby (1929). **Educ:** Gresham's School, Holt. **Career:** Mountain Battery, RA, Abbottabad, North West Frontier Province, India, WWII. Died September 1983.

ASHBY, Michael Louis (1945) Born 24 May 1927, 20 Glazbury Road, North End, London; son of Cyril Francis Ashby, Medical Practitioner, and Kathleen Paula Rees; m Victoria Smeeton, 1969; 1 son (David b 1973), 1 daughter (Melanie b 1970). **Subject(s):** Natural Sciences/Physics; BA 1948; MA 1964. **Tutor(s):** C W Guillebaud. **Johnian Relatives:** brother of Peter James Ashby (1947). **Educ:** PNEU School, Rustington; Dorset House Preparatory School, Littlehampton; Epsom College. **Career:** Technical post, Development of Cyclotron, Austin Wing, Cavendish Laboratory 1948–1952; Electronic Engineer, Marconi Defence Systems, Stanmore, Middlesex 1953–1992. **Awards:** Major Scholarship, SJC 1945.

ASHBY, The Revd Norman (1902) Born 21 November 1881, Argyll Villa, Grosvenor Road, Scarborough; son of Richard Ashby, Dentist, and Rosina King; m Nora Mary Harington. BA 1907; MA 1910. **Tutor(s):** C E Graves; J R Tanner. **Johnian Relatives:** uncle of John Berkeley Harington (1940). **Educ:** Oliver's Mount School; Carisbrooke House, Scarborough. **Career:** Ordained Deacon 1908; Ordained Priest 1910; Lance Corporal, RAMC, WWI; Diocese of St Albans 1929–1935; Rector, Thorley, Bishop's Stortford 1938. Died 1 February 1946.

ASHBY, Peter James (1947) Born 15 September 1925, Batu Gajah Hospital, Perak, Federated Malay States; son of Cyril Francis Ashby, Medical Practitioner, and Kathleen Paula Rees. **Subject(s):** Natural Sciences; BA 1949. **Tutor(s):** G C L Bertram. **Johnian Relatives:** brother of Michael Louis Ashby (1945). **Educ:** PNEU School, Rustington; All Hallows School, Rousdon.

ASHE, The Revd Francis Patrick Bellesme (1934) Born 15 January 1915, All Saints Parsonage, Boudjah, Smyrna, Turkey; son of Robert Pickering Ashe, Clerk in Holy Orders, and Edith Blackler; m Marion Islay Bamber (née Johnston), 1950; 4 sons (Robert b 1953, Francis b 1953, Andrew b 1958 and David b 1963), 3 daughters (Lois b 1951, Islay b 1958 and Ruth b 1959). **Subject(s):** Modern and Medieval Languages/Theology; BA 1937; MA 1941. **Tutor(s):** J S Boys Smith. **Johnian Relatives:** nephew of Henry Ashe (1864); son of Robert Pickering Ashe (1876); cousin of George Hamilton Ashe (1899). **Educ:** Whitgift School, Croydon; Westcott House, Cambridge 1937. **Career:** Ordained Deacon 1940; Curate, St Mary's, Woolwich 1940–1944; Ordained Priest 1941; Relief Work, Greece 1944–1946; Bishop of Southwark's Chaplain to Youth 1946–1950; Vicar, St John the Evangelist, Blindley Heath 1950–1956; Vicar, Otley, Yorkshire 1956–1964; Vicar, St Mary's, Leamington Spa 1964–1971; Rector, Church Stretton with All Stretton and Little Stretton, Hereford 1971–1974. **Appointments:** Founder and Director, Project Vietnam Orphans 1968; Founder and Director, Christian Outreach, 1980. **Publications:** *Teddy Brown Stories*, Kingsway.

ASHE, Percy (1921) Naval Applicant.

ASHENDEN, Michael Roy Edward (1946) Born 12 December 1921, 69 Westover Road, Wandsworth, London; son of Frederick Roy Ashenden, Bank Clerk, and Rose Kate Dora Michael; m (1) Carol Simpson, 1951 (dis), (2) Sylvia June Woodward, 1975; 1 son (Gavin Roy Pelham), 4 daughters (Claire Louise Ann, Katharine Jane, Juliet and Helen Rachael). **Subject(s):** Law; BA 1948; MA 1968. **Tutor(s):** F Thistlethwaite. **Educ:** Maidstone Grammar School; Bethany School, Goudhurst. **Career:** Lieutenant, RNVR 1946; Called to the Bar, Middle Temple 1948; Pupil with Marvyn Everett 1949; Chambers with Alan King-Hamilton 1950; Shell International Chemicals Ltd 1951–1974; Shell International Petroleum Company Ltd, Legal Division 1974–1981.

ASHFORTH, John Vincent (1949) Born 13 November 1930, 15 Wilson Street, Darlington; son of John Ashforth, Foreman, Roll Turner, and Evelyn May Stokes; m Margaret Vera Leiper, 1956, King's College Chapel, University of Aberdeen; 2 sons (David b 1959 and Stephen b 1961), 1 daughter (Jill b 1964). **Subject(s):** Natural Sciences/ Mathematics; BA 1952; MA 1956. **Tutor(s):** J M Wordie. **Educ:** Thompson Street School; Alderman Leach School; Gladstone Street School; Queen Elizabeth Grammar School. **Career:** Ferranti (Edinburgh) 1952–1989.

ASHTON, Cyril Lea (1938) Born 29 July 1920, 92 Burlington Avenue, Oldham; son of Fred Ashton, Corporate Accountant, and Annie Lea. **Subject(s):** Modern and Medieval Languages; BA 1941; MA 1945. **Tutor(s):** C W Guillebaud. **Educ:** Werneth Council School, Oldham; Hulme Grammar School, Oldham. **Career:** Army Service 1940–1946; Languages Master 1946–1954, Head of Modern Languages 1954–1967, Vice-Master 1967–1980, The Hulme Grammar School, Oldham. **Appointments:** Member, Hawks Club; Member, Eagles.

ASHTON-CROSS, Desmond Ian Cyril (1937) Born 5 August 1896, 29 Ennismore Gardens, Knightsbridge; son of John Ashton Cross, Barrister-at-Law, and Clarice Gordon de Vohl. MA 1936. **Educ:** St Paul's Preparatory School, London; St Paul's School, London; University of Edinburgh. **Career:** Lecturer in Law, University of Cambridge. Died 11 January 1975.

ASHWORTH, Dr Nigel Whittaker (1946) Born 13 January 1928, Blue Bell Cottage, Welshpool, Montgomeryshire; son of Edward Whittaker Ashworth, Medical Practitioner, Colonel, RAMC, and Hilda Frances Jefferson; m (1) Rachel Evelyn Allesbrook, 28 April 1954, Church of St Mary Magdalen, Lillington, Leamington Spa, (2) Norma Margaret Couper (née Bailey), 31 January 1970. **Subject(s):** Natural Sciences; BA 1949; MA 1953; BChir 1952; MB 1952. **Tutor(s):** G C L Bertram. **Career:** Chief Medical Adviser, Shell International Petroleum Company Ltd 1978–1985; Principal Medical Officer, Department of Health, Wellington, New Zealand 1985–1986; Senior Medical Officer, Civil Aviation Authority, New Zealand 1989–1996.

ASHWORTH, Thomas Holmes Evelyn Battersby (1941) Born 15 July 1922, 2 Kymberley Road, Harrow-on-the-Hill; son of Bernard Joseph Bartley Ashworth, Civil Servant, and Evelyn Isabel Battersby. **Subject(s):** Law; BA 1947; MA 1968; FIB. **Tutor(s):** S J Bailey. **Educ:** Sacred Heart Convent, Wealdstone; Salvatorian College, Harrow Weald; Ampleforth College, York. **Career:** RAF 1941–1946; Called to the Bar, Lincoln's Inn 1954. **Honours:** CBE; DFC. Died 28 February 1988.

ASKEY, Dr Stephen Grange (1907) Born 3 January 1888, Beech Villa, Bishop's Road, Highgate, Hornsey, Middlesex; son of Frederick Day Askey, Solicitor, and Grace Leigh Grange; m Jeanette Billing; 1 son (John). **Subject(s):** Natural Sciences; BA 1910; MA 1914; MB BCh 1914; MD 1919; MRCS; LRCP (St Thomas' Hospital) 1913. **Tutor(s):** J R Tanner. **Educ:** Tollington Schools, Muswell Hill, London; Birkbeck College, London. **Career:** Captain, RAMC (TF); House Physician, St Thomas' Hospital; Senior Obstetric House Physician; Clinical Assistant, Children's Surgical Out-Patients' Department, Casualty Officer, and Resident Anaesthetist. **Appointments:** Vice-President, Society of Ornamental Turners 1949. **Publications:** 'A Case of Mikulicz' Disease', *Lancet*, 1920; 'Methods of Quinine Administration in Malaria', *Medical Times*, 1921; 'A Case of Streptococcal Meningitis – Recovery', *Lancet*, 1923. Died 24 June 1978.

ASPIN, The Revd Albert (1900) Born 6 December 1878, 67 Guide, Lower Darwen, Lancashire; son of James Aspin, Coal Miner, and Elizabeth Holden; m; 1 son (Noel), 1 daughter (Kathleen). BA 1903; MA 1907. **Tutor(s):** C E Graves. **Johnian Relatives:** nephew of William Holden (1880). **Educ:** Manchester Central School; Manchester Pupil Teachers' Centre. **Career:** Ordained Deacon 1903; Curate, Middleton 1903–1909; Ordained Priest 1905; Vicar, Birch in Hopwood 1906–1916; Vicar,

Todmorden 1916–1928; Vicar, St Anne's on Sea 1928–1950. **Appointments:** Canon Emeritus, Blackburn Cathedral 1955; Provincial Rank, Lancashire Western Freemasons. Died May 1961.

ASPINALL, William Briant Philip Pryce (1930) Born 5 May 1912, Jesmond Dene, Crowthorne, Berkshire; son of William Pryce Aspinall, Organist and Music Master, and Ethel Eleanor Ravenscroft; m (1) Aileen FitzGerald, (2) Phyllis Hill; (1) 1 son (Bill). **Subject(s):** Modern and Medieval Languages; BA 1933; MA 1938. **Tutor(s):** C W Guillebaud. **Educ:** St Hilary's, Crowthorne, Berkshire; Malvern House, Reading; Crowthorne Towers, Crowthorne; Royal Masonic School, Bushey. **Career:** Lieutenant Colonel, Intelligence Corps 1940–1945; Headmaster, Sutton Valence School 1950–1953; Headmaster, Windsor School, British Army of the Rhine 1953–1958; Headmaster, King Richard School, Cyprus 1959–1960; Headmaster, Queen's School, Rheindahlen 1960–1972. **Honours:** OBE 1945. Died 31 December 1989.

ASTBURY, Dr Norman Frederick (1926) Born 1 December 1908, 14 Uttoxeter Road, Longton, Staffordshire; son of William Edwin Astbury, Potter's Turner, and Clara Dean; m Nora Enid Wilkinson, 31 August 1933, Normacot Parish Church; 3 sons (Norman Eric b 6 September 1934, Julian b 28 May 1940 and Nigel b 13 December 1946), 1 daughter (Charmian b 8 March 1939). **Subject(s):** Natural Sciences (Physics); BA 1929; MA 1933; ScD 1954; CEng; FIEE; CPhys; FInstP; FRSA; Honorary FICeram. **Tutor(s):** J M Wordie. **Johnian Relatives:** father of Julian Astbury (1958). **Educ:** Normacot C of E School; Longton High School, Stoke-on-Trent. **Career:** Staff, National Physical Laboratory 1929–1939; Staff, HM Anti-Submarine Experimentation Establishment 1939–1945; Director of Research, J Sankey & Sons Ltd and Guest Keen & Nettlefold Ltd 1945–1949; Professor of Applied Physics, NSW University of Technology 1949–1951; Professor of Physics, University of Khartoum 1951–1956; RAE 1956–1957; Deputy Director of Research, British Ceramic Research Association 1957–1960; Director, British Ceramic Research Association 1960–1973. **Appointments:** Member, National Council for Technological Awards 1958–1964; President, British Ceramic Society 1960; Member, Inter-Services Metallurgical Research Council 1962–1964; Council Member, IPPS 1963–1966; Member, National Council for Academic Awards 1964–1966; Chairman, Committee, Directors of Research Associations 1964–1966; Member, Joint Services Non-Metallic Materials Research Board 1964–1969; Vice-President, Parliamentary and Scientific Committee 1965–1968; Member, Construction Research Advisory Council, DoE 1968–1971. **Awards:** Scholarship, SJC. **Honours:** CBE 1968. **Publications:** *Industrial Magnetic Testing*, 1952; *Electrical Applied Physics*, 1956. Died 28 October 1987.

ASTLE, Edward William Browne (1928) Born 17 November 1910, 57 Manchester Road, Northwich, Chester; son of Oswald Astle, Manager of Chemical Works, and Rachel Josephine Allison. **Subject(s):** Modern and Medieval Languages; BA 1931; MA 1936. **Tutor(s):** M P Charlesworth. **Educ:** Seymour Road Council School; Manchester Grammar School. **Awards:** Scholarship, SJC 1927. Died 26 December 1996.

ASTORGA, Don Eduardo Antonio (1942) Born 5 August 1912, Santiago, Chile; son of Maximo R Astorga, Farmer and Florinda Barriga; m Nena. **Tutor(s):** C W Guillebaud. **Educ:** Universidad de Chile, Chile; Instituto Nacional, Santiago, Chile.

ATHANASSOFF, Vladimir (1930) Born 11 December 1909, Sofia, Bulgaria; son of George Athanassoff, Engineer, Director of Granitoid Ltd, and Danka Slavova. **Tutor(s):** C W Guillebaud. **Educ:** Preparatory School, Sofia; States Gymnasium, Sofia; Robert College, Constantinople.

ATKINS, The Revd Hugh Leslie (1900) Born 22 July 1882, The Litten, Newbury, Berkshire; son of John Atkins, Clerk in Holy Orders and Headmaster, and Annie Sophie Dalby. BA 1903; MA 1913. **Tutor(s):** E E Sikes. **Educ:** The Grammar School, Newbury. **Career:** Ordained Deacon 1906; Curate, Freemantle, Hertfordshire 1906–1915; Ordained Priest

1908; Curate, Scholing 1915–1921; Rector and Vicar, Abbotstone, Hampshire 1925.

ATKINSON, Gerald (1911) Born 5 October 1892, 137 Stoneferry Road, Sutton, Hull, Yorkshire; son of George William Atkinson, Engine Fitter, and Mary Ann Rundle; 2 sons. **Subject(s):** Natural Sciences; BA 1914. **Tutor(s):** L H K Bushe-Fox. **Educ:** Stoneferry Council School; Chapman Street Council School; Hymers College, Hull. **Career:** Pioneer, RE (Special Brigade), Mentioned in Despatches, WWI; Science Master, Bablake School, Coventry (Deputy Head from 1930) 1914–1958. Died 4 November 1966.

ATKINSON, Henry Noel (1908) Born 25 December 1888, The Vicarage, Audlem, Cheshire; son of Arthur Atkinson, Clerk in Holy Orders, and Ursula Mary Hillyard. **Tutor(s):** E E Sikes. **Educ:** Charterhouse. **Career:** Second Lieutenant, 3rd Battalion, Cheshire Regiment 1913–1914. **Honours:** DSO 1915. Died 22 October 1914 (missing, presumed killed in action).

ATKINSON, James Arthur Lionel (1930) Born 5 October 1911, Bendigo, Victoria, Australia; son of Evelyn John Rupert Atkinson, of private means, and Marguerite Carre. BA 1933; MA 1937. **Educ:** Ivanhoe Grammar School, Melbourne; Courtenay Lodge, Abingdon. **Career:** Surgeon, Brisbane. Died 27 April 1977.

ATKINSON, James Robert (1935) Born 17 February 1916, Park View, Stanley Park Road, Wallington, Surrey; son of James William Atkinson, Deputy Superintending Engineer, Post Office, and Florence Smerdon; m Mona Rolt Wheeler, 7 September 1939. **Subject(s):** Mathematics/Natural Sciences/Physics; BA 1938; MA 1945; FRMetS 1946; FInstP 1947; FRSE 1969. **Tutor(s):** C W Guillebaud. **Educ:** Barrow Hedges School, Carshalton; Dulwich College Preparatory School; Leeds Grammar School. **Career:** Research Scientist, Radar Telecommunications Research Establishment 1938–1945; Nuclear Physics Research Department 1945, Senior Lecturer, Natural Philosophy 1954, University of Glasgow; Project Manager, Dounreay Materials Testing Reactor 1955; Assistant Director of Research, British Ship Research Association 1963; Assistant Director 1976, Deputy Director 1976–1983, Institute of Offshore Engineering, Heriot-Watt University. **Appointments:** Lectured on aspects of nuclear physics in Rumania, Greece, Turkey, Italy and USA from 1945. **Awards:** Mathematics Prize 1935; Scholarship, SJC 1936–1937.

ATKINSON, The Revd Myles (1904) (admitted as a Non-Collegiate Student 1903) Born 29 August 1883, 9 Market Place, Dalton-in-Furness, Lancashire; son of Benjamin Atkinson, Butcher, and Sarah Birkett. BA 1906; MA 1910. **Tutor(s):** D MacAlister. **Educ:** Dalton Free School; Dalton Pupil Teacher's Centre. **Career:** Assistant Master, West Hartlepool Upper Grade School 1906; Ordained Deacon 1908; Curate, St Ambrose, Pendleton 1908–1911; Ordained Priest 1909; Curate, Christ Church, Salford 1911–1919; Vicar, Woodborough 1912–1930; Vicar, Pilling, Lancashire 1930.

ATKINSON, Myles Birkett (1930) Born 15 June 1912, 22 Bentley Lane, Meanwood, Leeds; son of James Birkett Atkinson, Clerk in Holy Orders, and Annie Garstang. **Subject(s):** Mathematics/Mechanical Sciences; BA 1933; MIMechE. **Tutor(s):** J M Wordie. **Educ:** Ermysted's Grammar School, Skipton. **Career:** Chartered Engineer.

ATKINSON, Peter Doughton (1941) Born 31 October 1923, 17 Mere Road, Blackpool, Lancashire; son of George Frederick Atkinson, Civil Engineer, and Dorothy Norah Allen; m Margaret Newbury, 1946; 2 sons (David and Richard), 1 daughter (Janet). **Subject(s):** Mechanical Sciences; BA 1944; MA 1948; FBCS; FIEE. **Tutor(s):** S J Bailey. **Educ:** The School in the Sun, Lytham; Pembroke School, Lytham; Arnold School, Blackpool. **Career:** Temporary Experimental Officer, Admiralty Signals Establishment 1943–1946; Development Engineer, Research Laboratories of Elliott Brothers (London) Ltd 1946–1952; Group

Leader, British Tabulating Machine Company Ltd 1952–1954; Joint Head, Measurement Division, Tube Investments Ltd Technology Centre 1954–1959; Manager, Engineering Programmes, IBM United Kingdom Laboratories 1959–1973; Manager, IBM United Kingdom Scientific Centre, Peterlee 1973–1982; Staff Assistant to Laboratory Director, IBM United Kingdom Laboratories 1982–1984; Manager, Information Technology Centre, Portsmouth City Council 1984–1986; Administrator of Management Challenge (Schools' Business Game Competition), British Institute of Management (part time) 1986–1992. **Awards:** Heaviside Premium (jointly). **Publications:** (with H M Gale) 'A Theoretical and Experimental Study of the Series Connected Magnetic Amplifier', *Proceedings of the Institution of Electrical Engineers*, 1949; (with E H Frost Smith) Chapters 5, 6 and 7, ed M G Say, *Magnetic Amplifiers and Saturable Reactors*, George Newnes, 1954; (with R W Hynes) 'Analysis and Design of a Linear Differential Transformer', *The Elliott Journal*, August 1954; (with A V Hemingway) 'An Even-Harmonic Magnetic Amplifier and Applications to Measurement and Control', *Electronic Engineering*, November, 1954; 'Note on the Optimum Input Winding Resistance of a Magnetic Amplifier employing Voltage Feedback', *The Elliott Journal*.

ATKINSON, Terence Wickham (1937) Born 13 March 1918, 13 Princes Gate, Knightsbridge; son of Christopher Atkinson, Physician, and Winifred Ann Wickham; m Mary. **Subject(s):** Modern and Medieval Languages; BA 1940; MA 1944. **Tutor(s):** C W Guillebaud. **Educ:** St Neot's School, Eversley, Basingstoke; Marlborough College. **Career:** Assistant Master, Worksop College. Died July 1959.

ATKINSON, William (1934) Born 30 August 1915, 7 Hawthorne Place, Clitheroe; son of George Atkinson, Schoolmaster, and Lucy Makin; m Marian Ellen Wallace; 2 daughters (Elizabeth and Christine). **Subject(s):** Modern and Medieval Languages; BA 1937; MA 1956. **Tutor(s):** C W Guillebaud. **Educ:** Council School, Clitheroe; Clitheroe Royal Grammar School; Carnegie PE College, Leeds. **Career:** Head of PE, Blackpool Grammar School 1938–1940; Staff Sergeant, APTC 1940–1943; Commission Intelligence Corps 1943–1946; Service in Italy (Captain Field Security) 1944–1945; Head of PE, Blackpool Grammar School 1946–1960; Head of Languages, Fleetwood Grammar School 1960–1974.

ATTLEE, Wilfred Ormiston (1936) Born 17 June 1917, 2 Rose Hill, Dorking; son of Edmund Waller Attlee, Corn Merchant, and Hilda Mary Ormiston. **Subject(s):** Natural Sciences; BA 1939; MA 1943; MRCS; LRCP. **Tutor(s):** R L Howland. **Johnian Relatives:** cousin of Guthrie Philip Easten (1928). **Educ:** Nevill House School, Eastbourne; Marlborough College. **Career:** Honorary Major RAMC; GP.

ATTRILL, James Bernard (1942) Born 8 January 1924, 5 Nevada Terrace, Gillingham; son of Albert Henry Attrill, Civil Engineer, and Dora Olive Musselwhite; m Patricia, 2 sons (Peter and William). **Subject(s):** Natural Sciences; BA 1949; FRIC 1954. **Tutor(s):** C W Guillebaud. **Educ:** Dockyard School, Bermuda; Marian Vian Junior Mixed School, Beckenham; Beckenham and Penge County School; City of Bath Boys' School. **Career:** Editor, *The Analyst* 1954–1973. Died 10 May 1976.

ATTWOOD, Cyril (1941) Born 25 November 1922, 7 Stour Hill, Quarry Bank, Brierley Hill, Staffordshire; m Phyl, 1944; 1 daughter (Kay b 1953). **Subject(s):** Natural Sciences; BA 1944; MA 1948; PGCE. **Tutor(s):** C W Guillebaud. **Educ:** Netherend Infants' School, Cradley; Orchard Lane Boys' School, Lye; King Edward VI School, Stourbridge. **Career:** Army 1943; RE, GHQ India, Saigon Control Commission, Alfsea, War Office 1944–1947; Chemistry Teacher, Bancrofts School, Essex 1949–1951; Head of Science and House Master, King William College, Isle of Man 1951–1983.

ATTWOOLL, Victor William (1943) Born 9 December 1925, 322 Lonsdale Avenue, East Ham, Essex; son of Victor John Glen Attwooll, Port of London Authority Writer, and Beatrice Catherine Ellen

Holdway. **Subject(s):** Natural Sciences; BA 1946. **Tutor(s):** C W Guillebaud. **Educ:** Upminster Council School; Palmer's Endowed School, Grays.

AUBRY, Carl Paul (1908) Born 1 April 1889, Sedbergh, Yorkshire; son of Paul Aubry, Assistant Master, Sedbergh School, and Jeanette Frederika Curti; m Ethel Hey Montford, 24 May 1917, Itteringham, Norfolk. **Subject(s):** Classics; BA 1911; MA 1921. **Tutor(s):** J R Tanner, E E Sikes. **Educ:** Sedbergh School. **Career:** Master, West House Preparatory School, Edgbaston 1911; Lieutenant, RGA, WWI; Equipment Officer, Royal Horse Artillery 1918; Education Staff 1918–1919; Joint Headmaster, West House School. Died 12 December 1956.

AULER, Herr Kurt Max Friedrich Robert (1908) Born 21 September 1890, Alsterstrasse, Hamburg, Germany; son of Karl Lorenz Auler, Colonel of Engineers, and Marie Fanny Charlotte Wieladn. **Tutor(s):** L H K Bushe-Fox. **Educ:** Grossherzogliches Gymnasium, Freiburg im Breisgau, Germany.

AUSTIN, Dr Kingsley David (1949) Born 19 November 1928, Silver Birch, Witherley Road, Atherstone, Warwickshire; son of Harold Denham Austin, Hat Manufacturer, and Constance Jessie Broadbridge. **Subject(s):** Natural Sciences; BA 1952; BChir 1956; MB 1957. **Educ:** Atherstone North Council School; Atherstone Grammar School; Repton School.

AUSTIN, William Norman (1929) Born 26 November 1910, 18 Byfield Gardens, Barnes, Surrey; son of William John Austin, Building Surveyor, and Alice Mary Richmond Read. **Tutor(s):** M P Charlesworth. **Educ:** Colet Court Preparatory School; St Paul's School, London; St Bartholomew's Hospital.

AVERILL, Charles Edward (1905) Born 21 June 1886, Holly Grove, Cheadle, Staffordshire; son of Charles Averill, Gentleman, and Amelia Newbon. BA 1913. **Tutor(s):** D MacAlister. **Johnian Relatives:** brother of Thomas Henry Averill (1909). **Educ:** Penfillan House, Folkestone; Denstone College.

AVERILL, Thomas Henry (1909) Born 26 October 1889, Hazlewall, Cheadle, Staffordshire; son of Charles Averill, Gentleman Farmer, and Amelia Newbon. BA 1912; MA 1918. **Tutor(s):** L H K Bushe-Fox. **Johnian Relatives:** brother of Charles Edward Averill (1905). **Educ:** Denstone College. **Career:** Lieutenant, North Staffordshire Regiment, WWI.

AVERY, Eric Nugent (1926) Born 8 May 1907, Alford, Lincolnshire; son of Leonard Roy Avery, Bank Manager, and Florence Seaton Loweth; m Freda Connolly, 19 October 1944, Melbourne. **Subject(s):** Law; BA 1930; MA 1944. **Tutor(s):** E A Benians. **Educ:** Hill Stone School, Great Malvern; Sedbergh School; College of Chinese Studies, Peking; Princeton University. **Career:** Asiatic Petroleum Company (Royal-Dutch/Shell joint operating company), China 1930–1939; various managerial posts 1939–1947, General Manager 1947, later Managing Director then Chairman 1951–1955, The Shell Company of Australia. **Appointments:** Chairman, Claremont Petroleum NL; Director, Associated Australian Resources Ltd; Life member, Australian Petroleum Exploration Association. **Awards:** Exhibition, SJC 1925; Lupton and Hebblethwaite Exhibition, SJC 1926; Henry P Davison Scholarship (Economics), Princeton 1928. **Honours:** OBE 1970. Died January 1986.

AVERY, Ernest Victor (1919) Born 2 April 1899, 18 Claribel Road, Brixton, London; son of Arthur Ernest Avery, Secretary to a Building Contractor, and Daisy Trott. **Subject(s):** Mathematics; BA 1922; MA 1926. **Tutor(s):** E A Benians. **Educ:** Private Schools; Dulwich Hamlet London County Council School; Wilson's Grammar School, Camberwell. **Career:** Officer Cadet School, Exeter 1917–1918; Second Lieutenant, RFA, Reserve Brigade, Luton 1918; Second Lieutenant, 44th Brigade RFA, France. **Awards:** Sizarship, SJC 1917.

AVERY, Richard Francis (1929) Born 26 January 1911, 30 Handen Road, Lee, Kent; son of Frank Arthur Avery, Clerk, Lloyds of London, and Mabel Minnie Parsons; m Dorothea Cecilia Wharton, 2 September 1939; 1 son (Charles Henry Francis b 26 December 1940). **Subject(s):** History/Modern and Medieval Languages; BA 1932; MA 1936; FRES 1945. **Tutor(s):** E A Benians. **Johnian Relatives:** father of Charles Henry Francis Avery (1959); grandfather of Victoria Jane Avery (1988). **Educ:** St Dunstan's College, Catsford, London; Boys' High School, Southend-on-Sea. **Career:** Air Raid Warden, ARP, later in Anti-Aircraft Unit, WWII; Teacher, Finland 1932–1934; English Teacher, Berlitz School, Berne, Switzerland 1934–1936; Assistant Editor, Commonwealth Institute of Entomology 1936. **Awards:** Exhibition, SJC 1928. **Honours:** Defence Medal. Died 19 September 1993.

AVIS, Anthony Charles (1946) Born 22 May 1927, The Ship Inn, Gaywood, Norfolk; son of Charles Avis, Farmer, Publican, Property Dealer and Carter, and Alice Mary Langley; m Helen-Lela Kyriacopoulou, 1958; 1 son (Charles b 1959), 1 daughter (Alice b 1962). **Subject(s):** Classics/Law; BA 1949; MA 1953; LLB 1950; LLM 1985. **Tutor(s):** F Thistlethwaite. **Educ:** Gaywood Council School; King Edward VII Grammar School, King's Lynn. **Career:** Assorted labouring jobs, USA and Canada 1950–1952; articled to Basil Cozens-Hardy, Solicitors, Norwich 1952–1954; Solicitor, Private Practice, Norfolk 1954–1956; Brewing Industry 1956–1987; Director, Hammonds United Breweries Ltd, Bradford, West Yorkshire 1956; succession of brewery company directorships including Chairman, Castletown Brewery Ltd, Isle of Man 1979–1986. **Appointments:** Council Member, Brewers Society 1960–1987; Director, Lawgate Properties Ltd 1987, Crescent Estates Ltd; The Box Tree Restaurant, Ilkley Ltd 1966. **Publications:** *A Reminiscence of King Edward VII Grammar School, King's Lynn, Norfolk*, 1991; *Supplement to A reminiscence of King Edward VII Grammar School, King's Lynn, Norfolk*, 1993; *Gaywood – A Norfolk Village Childhood*, 1994; *Gaywood Remembered – A Pictorial Recollection*, 1995; *The Brewer's tale – an Account of a Yorkshire Brewery; The Brewing Industry 1950–1990*, 1997; *Timothy Bentley – Master Brewer of Yorkshire*, 1998; *The Journey – an autobiography*, 1999; *Gaywood Past – Some Historical Notes*, 1999; *Miscellanea*, 2001. Died 30 March 2004.

AXFORD, Ernest Coleman (1921) Born 10 March 1904, Trenarlett, St Tudy, Bodmin, Cornwall; son of Thomas Axford, Farmer, and Jane Coleman. **Subject(s):** English/Law; BA 1925; MA 1931; Teachers Diploma (London University). **Tutor(s):** E A Benians. **Johnian Relatives:** father of Martin Thomas James Axford (1952) and of Roger Francis Ernest Axford (1953). **Educ:** Braughton School, Lewes; Manor House School, Clapham. **Career:** Teacher, Manor House School; Teacher, Wath-upon-Dearne Grammar School; Teacher, Wallasey Grammar School; Teacher, King Edward School, Nuneaton; Teacher, Darlington Grammar School; Headmaster, Callington County School, Cornwall; Headmaster, Ossett Grammar School 1944. **Publications:** *The Vital Year*, 1960.

AYLETT, Arthur Denis (1927) Born 21 May 1908, 19 Hungerford Road, Islington, London; son of Arthur John Aylett, Master Builder, and Hannah Josephine Henman; 1 son (Nigel). **Subject(s):** Modern and Medieval Languages/Law; BA 1930; MA 1934. **Tutor(s):** M P Charlesworth. **Educ:** Bedford School; Highgate School. **Awards:** Exhibition, SJC. Died 28 February 1990.

AYLMER, Michael Leycester (1943) Born 28 October 1925, 174 Sutherland Avenue, Paddington, London; son of Guy Aylmer, Deputy Conservator of Forests, Sudan Civil Service, and Christabel Henrietta Rushbrooke. BA 1946. **Tutor(s):** C W Guillebaud. **Educ:** Horton, Biggleswade; Copthorne, Sussex; Winchester College.

AYTON, George Edward (1934) Born 29 November 1915, 2 Glebe Road, Darlington, Durham; son of Charles Edward Ayton, Schoolmaster, and Mildred Agnes Bartle; m Gwendoline Hawker, 9 August 1947, Wolborough, Devon; 4 sons (Philip, Nicholas, Michael and Richard), 1 daughter (Elizabeth). **Subject(s):** Modern and Medieval Languages/Geography; BA 1937; MA 1947. **Tutor(s):** C W Guillebaud. **Johnian Relatives:** father of Philip Kenneth Ayton (1967) and of Michael Frank Ayton (1976). **Educ:** Queen Elizabeth Grammar School, Darlington. **Career:** Teacher, Draks and Wellington, Somerset; Colonial Service, Education Officer, Head of Education, Kenya Police Force, and Head Teacher, Machakos, Kisii, Kapsabet and Kabianga, Kenya 1949–1963; Colonial Service, Education Officer and Head of Geography, King's College, Budo, Uganda 1967–1973. Died 5 July 2000.

B

BABB, Burland Arthur (1925) Born 1 January 1907, 114 Trowbridge Road, Bradford-on-Avon, Wiltshire; son of Thomas Henry Babb, Schoolmaster, and Daisy Agnes Herbert. BA 1928. **Tutor(s):** E E Sikes. **Educ:** Alfriston Council School; Bedford Modern School.

BABBAGE, Iver Reginald (1942) Born 13 May 1910, 7 Lyme Gardens, Lower Weston, Bath; son of William Henry Thomas Babbage, Engineer's Draughtsman, and Kate Copping. BSc (Bristol) 1930. **Educ:** Bathforum School, Bath; City School, Bath; Bristol University. **Career:** Flight Lieutenant, RAF; Instructor at Initial Training Wing.

BACHERT, The Revd Louis Richard Arthur (1900) Born 1 June 1877, Hamburg, Germany; son of Simon Theodore Bachert, Clergyman, and Elizabeth Anne Griffiths. BA 1903. **Tutor(s):** D MacAlister. **Educ:** Private Tuition. **Career:** Ordained Deacon 1904; Ordained Priest 1905.

BADCOCK, Arthur Lawrence (1913) Born 25 June 1894, The Rectory, Walgrave, Northamptonshire; son of Thomas Badcock, Clerk in Holy Orders, and Theodosia Downes. **Tutor(s):** R P Gregory. **Educ:** Stoke House Preparatory School; Radley College. **Career:** Second Lieutenant, 15th Battalion, Northamptonshire Regiment; transferred to 6th Battalion, King's Own Yorkshire Light Infantry; Machine Gun Officer. Died 13 October 1915 (killed in action in Flanders).

BADR-EL-DIN, Abd El Latif Mohammed (1936) Born 13 July 1909, Cairo, Egypt; son of Mohammed Badr-El-Din, Secretary of Parquet Mixed Courts, Egypt, and Zubra Suka. **Tutor(s):** C W Guillebaud. **Educ:** Mansoura Primary School; Moharram Bey Primary School; Abbasieh Secondary School; Higher School of Agriculture, Goza; University of Edinburgh.

BAGCHI, Satis Chandra (1901) Born 1 May 1882, Chota Naypore, Bengal, India; son of Roger Bagchi, Contractor, and Narayani Dhole. **Subject(s):** Mathematics; BA 1904; LLB 1906. **Tutor(s):** D MacAlister. **Educ:** General Assembly Institution, Calcutta; Bihar National College, Patna. **Career:** Called to the Bar, Gray's Inn 1907.

BAGLEY, James Harold (1939) Born 17 May 1921, 135 Dentons Green Lane, St Helens; son of Harold Bagley, Confidential Clerk, and Alice Trotter. **Subject(s):** Mathematics; BA 1942; MA 1947. **Tutor(s):** S J Bailey. **Educ:** Haydock Richard Evans Infants and Mixed Schools; Grammar School, Ashton-in-Makerfield.

BAGSHAWE, John Leslie (1924) Born 5 December 1905, son of Frederick William Bagshawe, Colonel, Indian Army, and Catherine Sinclair Grove. **Subject(s):** Modern and Medieval Languages; BA 1927; MA 1935. **Tutor(s):** E E Sikes. **Educ:** Ellerslie, Bickington, Devon; Marlborough College. **Awards:** Exhibition, SJC 1923.

BAILEY, Professor David Earle (1942) Born 20 June 1924, 10 St Kilda's Road, Stoke Newington; son of Arthur Edwin Bailey, Pharmaceutical Chemist, and Helena Eliza Earle, Teacher; m Florence Betty Bailey, 1948; 3 sons (Alan, Peter and Michael). **Subject(s):** Mathematics; BA 1945; MA 1949; PhD (Edinburgh) 1953; FIMA; CMath. **Tutor(s):** S J Bailey. **Educ:** Quainton Hall School, Harrow; Merchant Taylors' School. **Career:** Admiralty Gunnery Establishment, Teddington 1944–1946;

Assistant Master, Fettes College, Edinburgh 1946–1952; Head of Mathematics Department, Highgate School 1952–1955; Head of Assessment Group, Weapons Research Division, A V Roe & Co 1955–1960; Head of Mathematics Department, Bristol College of Science and Technology 1960–1964; Professor of Numerical Analysis and Computing, University of Bath 1964–1981.

BAILEY, George Herbert (1928) Born 22 May 1909, Boston Road, Holbeach, Lincolnshire; son of Fred Bailey, Smallholder, and Annie Hollingsworth; m Evelyn. **Subject(s):** English/Geography; BA 1931; MA 1943. **Tutor(s):** M P Charlesworth. **Johnian Relatives:** brother of Joseph Eric Bailey (1937); uncle of Christopher Martin Bailey (1966). **Educ:** Holbeach Council School; Sutton Bridge School; Spalding Grammar School. **Career:** Headmaster, Dunstable Grammar School 1949; Headmaster, Woolverstone Hall, Ipswich 1960. Died 1982.

BAILEY, Joseph Eric (1937) Born 8 June 1918, Middle Farm, Wingland, Lincolnshire; son of Fred Bailey, Farmer, and Annie Hollingsworth. **Subject(s):** English; BA 1940; MA 1944. **Tutor(s):** J S Boys Smith. **Johnian Relatives:** brother of George Herbert Bailey (1928); father of Christopher Martin Bailey (1966). **Educ:** Sutton Bridge School; Spalding Grammar School.

BAILEY, Ronald Headley (1947) Born 16 April 1926, 13 Buckingham Road, Leicester; son of Ernest Headley Bailey, Shoe Pressman, and Ethel Millicent Ainge. **Subject(s):** English; BA 1949; MA 1954. **Tutor(s):** F Thistlethwaite. **Educ:** Raunds Elementary School; Wellingborough Grammar School.

BAILEY, Professor Stanley John (1919) Born 19 June 1901, Great Gobions Farm, Stapleford, Hertfordshire; son of John Bailey, Farmer, and Evelyn Mary Campkin; m (1) Kathleen Aimée Hamilton, 1926 (d 1949), (2) Wilhemina Leeksma, 1952; 1 son (John Christopher Leeksma b 7 January 1956). **Subject(s):** Natural Sciences/Law; BA 1922; LLB 1923; MA 1926; LLM 1930; LLD 1959. **Tutor(s):** E A Benians. **Johnian Relatives:** father of John Christopher Leeksma Bailey (1975). **Educ:** Caldicott School, Hitchin; Manor House School, Clapham; Grammar School, Reigate; Queen's College, Taunton; Guy's Hospital Medical School. **Career:** Called to the Bar, Inner Temple 1922; On staff of Messrs Gibson & Weldon, Law Tutors 1922–1926; Lecturer, University College of Wales, Aberystwyth, then Reader in English Law, University of Birmingham 1926–1931; Title B Fellow and Lecturer in Law 1931–1950, Title C Fellow 1950–1968, Title D Fellow 1968–1980, SJC; Lecturer in Law 1934–1946, Reader in Law 1946–1950, Rouse Ball Professor of English Law 1950–1968, University of Cambridge. **Appointments:** Director of Studies 1934–1950, Tutor 1939–1946, SJC; Senior Proctor, University of Cambridge 1936–1937. **Publications:** (ed) *Cambridge Legal History* Series and *Cambridge Law Journal; Law of Wills*, 1935. Died 16 August 1980.

BAILEY, Trevor Edward (1946) Born 3 December 1923, Westcliff-on-Sea; son of Bertrand Fothergill Bailey, Civil Servant, and Muriel Elsie Reed; m Greta Maureen Hay, 1948; 2 sons, 1 daughter. **Subject(s):** History/English; BA 1948; MA 1991. **Tutor(s):** F Thistlethwaite. **Johnian Relatives:** grandfather of Laura Kate Hurley (2003). **Educ:** Alleyn Court Preparatory School, Westcliff-on-Sea; Dulwich College. **Career:** Royal Marines 1942–1945; School Teacher 1945–1946; Essex Cricket Team 1946–1967; England Test Cricketer 1949–1959; Journalist 1950–2000; Cricket and Football Correspondent, *Financial Times* 1966–1981; Commentator, *Test Match Special*, BBC Radio 4 1967–1999; PR Director 1970–2000. **Appointments:** Assistant Secretary, Essex County Cricket Club 1949, later Secretary until 1967; Founding Director, Essex Radio; Manager, Cricket Supporters Tours 1971–1999; Freeman, Borough of Southend 2000. **Honours:** CBE. **Awards:** Football Association Amateur Cup Medal (with Walthamstow Avenue) 1952. **Publications:** *Playing to Win*, Hutchinson's Library of Sports and Pastimes, 1954; (with D R Willcox) *Cricketers in the Making*, Hutchinson's Library of Sports and Pastimes, 1955; *Trevor Bailey's*

Cricket Book, Frederick Muller, 1959; *The Greatest Of My Time*, 1968; *Sir Gary, A Biography*, Harper Collins, 1976; *A History of Cricket*, Allen & Unwin, 1978; (with Fred Trueman) *From Larwood to Lillee*, Collins Queen Anne Press, 1983; *Wickets, Catches and the Odd Run*, Collins, 1986; (with Fred Truman) *The Spinner's Web*, Willow, 1988; *The Greatest Since My Time*, Hodder & Stoughton, 1989.

BAILLIE, John Gilroy (1924) Born 3 September 1896, 3 Belhaven Terrace, Edinburgh, Scotland; son of James Brand Baillie, Compositor, and Elizabeth Dickson Gilroy; m Helen Ruth Maclean, 25 June 1927, Athens; 1 son (Ian Maclean Gilroy b 26 May 1932), 1 daughter (Noreen Elizabeth Gilroy b 20 January 1930). **Tutor(s):** E A Benians. **Johnian Relatives:** father of Ian Maclean Gilroy Baillie (1952). **Educ:** Hugh Middleton Evening Institute, London; Battersea Polytechnic, London; Morley College, London. **Career:** Assistant Clerk, HM Office of Works 1914; Civil Service Rifles, serving in France, Greece and Mesopotamia (POW) 1914–1919; Transfer to Foreign Office 1919–1924; Probationer Vice-Consul, Levant; Served in Constaninople, Athens, Piraeus, Smyrna, Bushire, Ahwaz, Tabriz, Buenos Aires 1924–1937; Acting Consul-General, Buenos Aires 1937; Consul, Tabriz 1938–1942; Consul, Ahwaz 1942–1943; Consul, Baghdad 1943–1947; Consul, Vienna 1947–1949; Minister to Republic of Liberia 1949–1951; Consul-General, Gothenburg 1951–1955. Died 7 March 1960.

BAIN, Graham Ward (1910) Born 6 June 1891, Villa Stone, 3 Viale de' Colli, Florence, Italy; son of Edward Joseph Bain, Captain, RN, and Ella Gilmer Stone; m Joan Isobel Cumming; 1 daughter (Pamela). **Subject(s):** Modern and Medieval Languages; BA 1914; MA 1926. **Tutor(s):** E E Sikes. **Johnian Relatives:** second cousin of John Neville Ritchie (1899), William Traill Ritchie (1901) and of Charles Henry Ritchie (1907); second cousin, once removed, of James McLaren Ritchie (1927), Ian MacFarlane Ritchie (1932), Brian William Thomas Ritchie (1935), Kenneth John Stewart Ritchie (1938), and of Alexander James Otway Ritchie (1948); cousin of Joseph Bain (1949). **Educ:** Victoria College, Jersey; Marlborough College. **Career:** Indian Civil Service 1914–1926, including various magistrate posts, and military duty 1917–1919; Assistant Master, Marlborough College 1927–1931; Assistant Master and Head of Modern Languages, Repton College 1931; Intelligence Department, War Office, WWII. **Publications:** *The Wicked Flea: A Comedy*. Died 26 February 1955.

BAIN, Joseph (1949) Born 26 April 1928, Mount Pleasant, St David's, Pembrokeshire; son of John Bain, Assistant Master, Marlborough College, and Frances Preece; m Priscilla Blunt, 25 July 1972, Chapel of Hartlebury Castle, Worcester. **Subject(s):** Modern and Medieval Languages/English; BA 1952; MA 1956. **Tutor(s):** C W Guillebaud. **Johnian Relatives:** second cousin of John Neville Ritchie (1899), William Traill Ritchie (1901) and of Charles Henry Ritchie (1907); cousin of Graham Ward Bain (1910); second cousin, once removed, of James McLaren Ritchie (1927), Ian MacFarlane Ritchie (1932), Brian William Thomas Ritchie (1935), Kenneth John Stewart (1938) and of Alexander James Otway Ritchie (1948). **Educ:** St David's Voluntary School; Haverfordwest Grammar School; Marlborough College. **Career:** Assistant Master 1954–1962, Housemaster 1962–1973, Stowe School; Assistant Master, Winchester College 1974–1988. **Awards:** Exhibition, SJC 1946. **Publications:** Various articles for literary reference books.

BAINES, Guy Harrison (1930) Born 16 September 1911, The Vicarage, Rainford Road, St Helens; son of Albert Baines, Clerk in Holy Orders, and Mabel Harrison; m Jane Ward; 2 sons, 2 daughters. **Subject(s):** Natural Sciences; BA 1933; MA 1938; BChir 1938; MB 1938; FRCS 1939. **Tutor(s):** M P Charlesworth. **Johnian Relatives:** son of Albert Baines (1890); brother of Roger Holford Baines (1925); uncle of Stephen Christopher Baines (1964). **Educ:** Mostyn House Park School; Charterhouse. **Career:** Mobile Surgical Unit, Burma; Lieutenant Colonel, Surgical Division, 25th General Hospital; Various surgical posts, St Thomas' Hospital 1936–1938; Surgical Registrar, Resident Surgical Officer, Queen Elizabeth Hospital, Birmingham 1938; RAMC,

Parachutist with the First Airborne Division, North Africa, Italy and Sicily 1943; Assistant Surgeon, United Birmingham Hospitals 1946; Lecturer in Surgery, University of Birmingham 1952. Consultant Urologist, United Birmingham Hospitals. **Awards:** Hector Mackenzie Exhibition, St Thomas' Hospital 1933. Died 13 December 1984.

BAINES, Canon Roger Holford (1925) Born 1 April 1907, St George's Vicarage, Sidmouth Road, Newcastle-under-Lyme; son of Albert Baines, Clerk in Holy Orders, and Mabel Harrison; m Geraldine Mary Gordon Fisher, 3 April 1940; 3 sons. **Subject(s):** History/Theology; BA 1929; MA 1932. **Tutor(s):** E A Benians. **Johnian Relatives:** son of Albert Baines (1890); brother of Guy Harrison Baines (1930); father of Stephen Christopher Baines (1964). **Educ:** Mostyn House School, Parkgate, Cheshire; Charterhouse, Godalming, Surrey; Westcott House, Cambridge. **Career:** Ordained Deacon 1930; Curate, Chilvers Coton, Nuneaton 1930; Priest, Coventry Cathedral 1931; CMS, Uganda 1935–1939; Curate-in-charge, Gipton, Leeds 1939; Vicar, Beeston, Leeds 1943; Vicar, St Peter's, Harrogate 1947–1966; Rural Dean, Knaresborough 1954; Honorary Canon, Ripon Cathedral 1956; Licensed to officiate, Hereford 1966–1982; Ceased to officiate 1997. Died 18 June 1999.

BAIRSTOW, John Holroyd (1927) Born 23 December 1908, The Croft, Halifax, Yorkshire; son of John Bairstow, Member, Stock Exchange, and Georgina Beatrice Holroyd. **Subject(s):** Law; BA 1930; LLB 1931. **Tutor(s):** M P Charlesworth. **Educ:** Southcliffe School, Filey; Sedbergh School. **Career:** Admitted Solicitor 1933. **Awards:** Exhibition, SJC. Died 4 August 1968.

BAKAR, Abu (BIN TAMIN) (1939) Born 1 September 1920, Kampong Kedah, Parit Buntar, Federated Malay States; son of Tamin bin Haji Abdullah, Headteacher, and Yah binti Ahmad. **Subject(s):** Law; BA 1942. **Tutor(s):** C W Guillebaud. **Educ:** Malay School, Parit Tok Ngah; King Edward VII School, Taiping. **Awards:** Colonial Scholarship. Died 11 December 1942.

BAKAR, Dr Abu (PAWANCHEE) (1948) Born 25 January 1917, 28 Jones Road, Penang, Malaya; son of Pawanchee bin Hamad Noordin, Government Servant, and Khatijah binti Man; m Wan Noor Binte; 5 children. **Subject(s):** Archaeology and Anthropology; BA 1950; MA 1965; Diploma (Raffles College, Singapore) 1940. **Tutor(s):** C W Guillebaud. **Educ:** Hillview English School, Penang; Government English School, Penang; Hutchings School, Penang; The Free School, Penang; Raffles College, Singapore. **Career:** Biographical Assistant, Raffles Museum, Singapore 1940–1941; Officer and Musketry Instructor 1942–1945; Biographical Assistant, Raffles Museum, Singapore 1945–1948; Colonial Administrative Service 1948–1950; Assistant Secretary in Various Ministries 1950–1956; Acting Deputy Secretary, Ministry of Commerce and Industry 1956; Principal Assistant Secretary, Ministry of Education 1956–1957; Permanent Secretary, Ministry of Commerce and Industry 1957–1958; Senior Trade and Cultural Representative of Singapore to Indonesia 1961–1963; Permanent Secretary (Economic Development), Ministry of Finance 1963–1965; Permanent Secretary, Ministry of Foreign Affairs 1965; Permanent Secretary for Foreign Affairs, Singapore 1965; Ambassador Extraordinary and Plenipotentiary, and Permanent Representative of Singapore to the United Nations in New York 1965–1966; Permanent Secretary, Ministry of Foreign Affairs 1966–1967; Deputy Chairman, Malaysian Rubber Exchange, Kuala Lumpur 1967–1977; Chairman, Malaysian Rubber Exchange, Kuala Lumpur 1977–1979; Chairman/ Managing Director, Intercommerce Sdn Berhad 1980; Consultant to Rubber Industry, Shipping and International Trade. **Appointments:** President, Football Association of Singapore; Secretary to Muslim Advisory Board; Member, Chinese Advisory Board; Member, Hindu Advisory Board; Member, Port Authority of Singapore 1956–1967 (also Chairman, Highest Tender Board); Chairman, Roads Committee; Chairman, Development Planning Sub-Committee; Chairman, Tariff Committee; Chairman, Drafting Committee; Leader of Delegations overseas including ECAFE and the Colombo Plan; Committee Member for Planning, Jurong Industrial Estate; Member, Malaysian Delegation, IRSG 1968; Member, Malaysian Delegation, IRQPC; Member, Malaysian Delegation, ANRPC 1970; Member, Malaysian Delegation, IRA; Chairman, Freight Committee, Rubber Industry of Malaysia and Singapore 1970; Director and Chairman, Executive Council, Malaysian National Reinsurance Berhad 1973–1985; Member and Leader, Freight Committee of Rubber Industry of Malaysia; Director and Shareholder, various Transport Companies including Shipping Lines. **Awards:** British Council Scholarship 1948. **Honours:** 1930–45 Star; Pacific Star; War Medal 1939–1945, Oak Leaf. **Publications:** Book on the Malay Kris.

BAKER, Berkeley Edward (1946) Born 27 November 1921, New Asylum Inn, Fulbourn, Cambridgeshire; son of Edward Baker, Sub-Postmaster, and Nora Wilce; 1 son, 1 daughter. **Subject(s):** Economics; BA 1948; MA 1953. **Tutor(s):** C W Guillebaud. **Educ:** Fulbourn Council School; Cambridge and County High School. **Career:** Assistant, Cambridge University Library 1938–1941; Flight Lieutenant, RAF 1942–1946; Cadbury 1948–1950; Allen & Hanbury Ltd (pharmaceuticals) 1950–1968; Director, various Glaxo companies 1968–1981; Director, DEE Corporation Ltd 1981–1984.

BAKER, David King (1944) Born 11 July 1926, 87 Fordwych Road, Hampstead, London; son of Paul William Baker, Engineer, and Judith Dart Francis. **Subject(s):** Mechanical Sciences; BA 1949; MA 1951; MIMechE. **Tutor(s):** J M Wordie. **Johnian Relatives:** nephew of Henry Lyn Harris (1911); cousin of Henry Stephen Lyn Harris (1938); cousin of Nicholas King Harris (1940); cousin of Simon Joscelyn Fulke Harris (1950). **Educ:** King's School, Peterborough; St Christopher School, Letchworth. **Career:** RE 1945–1948; Engineering Design, Baker Perkins Ltd 1951–1970. **Appointments:** RE Cadet, SJC 1944–1945.

BAKER, Derek Collingwood (1919) Born 21 October 1901, 45 Elgin Mansions, London; son of Henry Edwin Baker, Engineer, and Mary Fawcett; m. **Subject(s):** Law; BA 1924; MA 1927; LLB 1924. **Tutor(s):** E E Sikes. **Educ:** Ovingham School, Rollingdene; Rugby School. **Career:** Called to the Bar, Middle Temple 1925; Barrister, Oxford Circuit; Director, Mariot Mouldings 1968. Died 9 March 1973.

BAKER, Frank Bernard (1918) Born 19 August 1900, 4 Belvoir Terrace, Cambridge; son of Henry Frederick Baker, Fellow, SJC, and Lily Isabella Homfield Klopp. **Subject(s):** Mathematics; BA 1921; MA 1925. **Tutor(s):** E E Sikes. **Johnian Relatives:** son of Henry Frederick Baker (1883); brother of Ralph Homfield Baker (1914). **Educ:** St Faith's, Cambridge; Bedale's School; Norwich Grammar School. **Career:** Chief Assistant, Aerodynamics Department, Handley Page Ltd; Aerodynamics Specialist, Flight Development Department, Fairey Aviation Company Ltd, Heston; Master, Oundle School 1922–1926; Master, Malvern School 1926; Senior Technical Instructor, BOAC and BEA Central Training School, Aldermaston 1947. **Awards:** Dowman Sizarship, SJC 1918. Died January 1953.

BAKER, James Alison (1929) Born 22 February 1908, 93 Eaton Place, Chelsea, Middlesex; son of Louis Samuel Baker, Lieutenant Colonel, Indian Army, and Florence Jane Alison. **Tutor(s):** C W Guillebaud. **Educ:** Winton House, Winchester; Oundle School; Royal College of Science, London. **Career:** Colonial Agricultural Officer, Kedah, Armoured Unit, Kedah Volunteer Defence Force. Died WWII (killed in action in Malaya).

BAKER, Dr Martyn Wilfred (1902) Born 20 March 1883, 7 Dorset Place, Newport, Monmouthshire; son of William Alfred Baker, Iron and Steel Manufacturer, and Alice Fennell; m Alice Mary. BA 1905; MA 1912; BChir 1909; MB 1912; LRCP; MRCS 1908. **Tutor(s):** D MacAlister. **Educ:** Coombe Down School, Bath; Wycliffe College. **Career:** Junior Obstetric Physician, St Thomas' Hospital 1910; Consulting Surgeon, East Surrey Hospital; Captain, RAMC, WWI. Died 20 March 1960.

BAKER, Ralph Homfield (1914) Born 19 November 1895, 4 Belvoir Terrace, Cambridge; son of Henry Frederick Baker, Fellow, SJC, and Lily Isabella Homfield Klopp. **Subject(s):** Economics/History. **Tutor(s):** R P Gregory. **Johnian Relatives:** son of Henry Frederick Baker (1883); brother of Frank Bernard Baker (1918). **Educ:** Perse School, Cambridge; Bedale's School. Died 1 July 1965.

BAKER, Richard Geoffrey (1949) Born 3 May 1929, Penwortham, Lancashire; son of Richard Baker, Electrical Engineer, and Elizabeth Ellen Caunce; m Dorothy Margaret Jolly, 24 July 1954, Preston; 2 sons (Richard b 6 January 1958 and Matthew b 16 December 1958), 1 daughter (Julia b 24 April 1955). **Subject(s):** Mechanical Sciences; BA 1952; MA 1956; FICE; CDipAF. **Tutor(s):** R L Howland. **Educ:** St Andrew's Elementary School, Preston; Preston Grammar School. **Career:** Commissioned Service, RE 1948–1949; Engineer, John Laing & Son 1952–1957; Port of Bristol Authority Engineer's Authority (final post, Chief Engineer) 1957–1980; Deputy Port Director, Port of Bristol Authority 1980–1985. **Appointments:** Member, CNISF.

BALCOMB, The Revd Herbert Francis George (1902) Born 25 November 1882, 29 Richmond Road, Hammersmith, London; son of George Albert Balcomb, Inland Revenue Supervisor, and Annie Frances Patterson. **Subject(s):** Mathematics; BA 1905. **Tutor(s):** D MacAlister. **Educ:** St Paul's School. **Career:** Ordained Deacon 1910; Ordained Priest 1911; Rector, Hindlip with Martin Hussingtree 1929; Rural Dean, Wich 1934–1948. **Awards:** Exhibition, SJC 1901. Died 1972.

BALDRY, Robert Ashley (1914) Born 11 July 1895, Methwold, Norfolk; son of William Ashley Baldry, Master Builder, and Dorothea Jane Greenacre; m Kathleen Smith, 1927; 1 son (John), 3 daughters (Jane, Mary and Shirley). **Subject(s):** Natural Sciences/Geology; BA 1920; MA 1925; FRGS; FGS. **Tutor(s):** R P Gregory. **Educ:** Methwold Elementary School; Thetford Grammar School. **Career:** Corporal, Special Brigade, RE, WWI; Geologist, eventually Chief Geologist, Lobitos Oilfields, Peru 1921–1947. **Honours:** Croix de Guerre. Died 29 July 1952.

BALDWIN, Professor Ernest Hubert Francis (1928) Born 29 March 1909, 167 Tredworth Road, Gloucester; son of Hubert Charles Baldwin, Orchestral Pianist, and Nellie Victoria Hailes; 1 son (Nigel), 1 daughter (Nicola). **Subject(s):** Natural Sciences; BA 1931; PhD 1934; ScD 1967. **Tutor(s):** J M Wordie. **Educ:** Calton Road Council School, Gloucester; The Crypt School, Gloucester. **Career:** Title A Fellow, SJC 1936–1941; Lecturer in Biochemistry, University of Cambridge 1936–1950; Professor of Biochemistry, UCL 1950. **Appointments:** Supervisor in Biochemistry, SJC 1936–1941; Fellow, New York Academy of Sciences. **Awards:** Exhibition, SJC; Hutchinson Research Studentship; Henry Humphries Prize for Research; European Cortina-Ulisse Prize 1952. **Publications:** *An Introduction to Comparative Biochemistry*, 1937; *Dynamic Aspects of Biochemistry*, 1947; *The Nature of Biochemistry*. Died 6 December 1969.

BALDWIN, John Anthony Ingthorpe (1933) Born 23 August 1914, The Vicarage, Long Load, Somerset; son of John Montgomery Baldwin, Clerk in Holy Orders, and Margaret Adelaide Mackenzie Mullen; m Edna Phyllis Newman, 6 September 1939 (d 1992); 1 son (John Melville b 27 October 1940), 1 daughter (Lynne Rosemary b 11 March 1943). **Subject(s):** Classics/Theology; BA 1936. **Tutor(s):** R L Howland. **Johnian Relatives:** father-in-law of Clive William Gordon Armstrong (1962). **Educ:** The Mall School, Strawberry Hill; St John's School, Leatherhead. **Career:** Private Tutor 1936–1937; Regular Officer, RASC 1937; BEF, served at Dunkirk, in India, Egypt, Palestine, Greece, Vienna, WWII, later Jamaica, Hong Kong, Suez; retired as Lieutenant Colonel 1958; Health and Safety Executive Officer 1958–1980; Called to the Bar, Gray's Inn 1974; Seconded by MOD to Bahrain to write Factory Act 1976–1978; Seconded by MOD to The Seychelles to write Factory Act 1979–1980. **Awards:** Various active service medals. Died 23 April 2002.

BALDWIN, Nelson Mills (1941) Born 17 March 1923, 16 Hartington Road, Chorlton-cum-Hardy, Manchester; son of Nelson Baldwin,

General Manager, Insurance Company, and Alice Mills. **Subject(s):** Law. **Tutor(s):** S J Bailey. **Educ:** Fairdene School, Coulsdon; Tonbridge Preparatory School, Yardley Court; Tonbridge School. **Career:** Solicitor of the Supreme Court 1948. **Appointments:** Chairman, Speedway Control Board 1964; Chief Executive, Royal Automobile Club 1971. **Honours:** OBE 1977. Died 18 April 1987.

BALDWIN, Group Captain Philip Harold (1936) Born 24 September 1917, 35 Kingswood Road, Wimbledon, Surrey; son of Harold Arthur Baldwin, Bank Official, and Elizabeth Alice Sharpe, Schoolmistress; m (Constance) Pamela Springfield, 31 October 1959, St Columba's, Pont Street, London; 1 son (Alan Charles), 1 daughter (Anne Elizabeth). **Subject(s):** Modern and Medieval Languages/Archaeology and Anthropology; BA 1939; MA 1943; DipEd 1967. **Tutor(s):** C W Guillebaud. **Johnian Relatives:** father of Alan Charles Baldwin (1981); father-in-law of Alice Rachel Caroline Tregear (Baldwin) (1982). **Educ:** Merton Elementary School and Church of England Central School; Rutlish School, Merton. **Career:** RAF 1939–1967; First Commanding Officer, 177 Squadron, WWII; 231 Group Headquarters 1944; Commanding Officer, Ranchi, Bihar; appointments to Ambala, Quetta and Air Headquarters India, until 1947; Commanding Officer, RAF Aberporth, West Wales; Group Captain 1960–1962; Defence Attaché, British Embassy, Rio de Janeiro, Brazil 1960–1962; Air Attaché, Madrid and Lisbon 1963–1965; D/UKNMR, SHAPE 1965–1967; French and Spanish Master, Chipping Campden School 1967–1974. **Appointments:** University Air Squadron 1937–1939; Wing Commander, University Air Squadron 1950–1953. **Awards:** County Scholarship to SJC. **Honours:** OBE 1954. Died 3 August 2003.

BALIGH, Amrullah Nafez (1938) Born 12 September 1918, Cairo, Egypt; son of Mohamed Hilmy Eff Baligh, Landowner, and Amiena Sayed Ahmed. **Tutor(s):** J S Boys Smith. **Educ:** Egyptian Preparatory and Primary Schools; Victoria College, Alexandria; Battersea Polytechnic.

BALL, Charles Olin (1918) American Student.

BALL, Dr David Hamilton (1949) Born 17 July 1931; m Karen Rutter; 4 children. **Subject(s):** Natural Sciences; BA 1952; BChir 1955; MB 1956; DObstRCOG (London) 1960; DIH (Society of Apothecaries) 1960. **Tutor(s):** G C L Bertram. **Educ:** Repton School. **Career:** House Physician and House Surgeon, London Hospital 1955–1956; Surgeon Lieutenant, RN 1956–1959; GP, New Milton, Hampshire 1960; Senior Partner, New Milton Health Centre 1971–1991. **Appointments:** Member, Royal College of Practitioners 1964–; Trustee, Oakhaven Hospice, Lymington, Hampshire 1991–1997; Medical Audit Facilitator, Hampshire 1992–1996; Medical Member, Tribunal Service, Lord Chancellor's Office 1996–2001; Chairman, The Grange Church Society, Christchurch, Hampshire 1997–2001.

BALL, Edward Fernley Gawen (1919) Naval Officer.

BALL, Ernest Frederick (1923) Born 16 November 1905, Lynsted, Queen's Avenue, Maidstone, Kent; son of Frederick Leonard Ball, Civil Engineer, and Alice Packman; m Dorothy Forbes MacLeod, 1945; 2 sons (William Frederick and John Macleod), 1 daughter (Alice Elizabeth). **Subject(s):** Mathematics/Mechanical Sciences; BA 1928; MA 1932; AMICE 1931. **Tutor(s):** B F Armitage. **Johnian Relatives:** father of William Frederick Ball (1963) and of John Macleod Ball (1966). **Educ:** Briary Preparatory School, Westgate; Maidstone Grammar School; Mill Hill School. **Career:** Articled to Dr Herbert Lapworth, Consulting Engineer 1928–1931; Civil Engineer and Manager, then Managing Director, A H Ball & Co, Civil Engineering Contractors, Farnham, Surrey 1931–1970; Officers Emergency Reserve, in succession with No 87 Bomb Disposal Section, No 10 Bomb Disposal Company, and Army Bomb Disposal School, Ripo, (latterly a Captain) 1940–1945. **Appointments:** Non-executive Director, The Lead Wool Co Ltd, Snodland, Kent; Non-executive Director, The Mid-Kent Water Company. Died 12 May 1975.

BALLANCE, Dr Michael Heudebourck (1945) Born 27 March 1928, Westmead, The Avenue, Potters Bar, Middlesex; son of Heudebourck Ballance, Stockjobber, and Rachel Mary Page; m Selina Maltby, 17 March 1959, Chelsea Old Church, London; 1 son (James b 1961), 2 daughters (Elizabeth b 1961 and Alexia Susan b 1964). **Subject(s):** Classics; BA 1948; MA 1954; PhD (Edinburgh) 1962; FSA 1990. **Tutor(s):** J M Wordie; R L Howland. **Johnian Relatives:** father of Alexia Susan Ballance (1982). **Educ:** The Grange, Stevenage; Oundle School; University of Edinburgh. **Career:** Rome Scholar in Classical Studies, British School at Rome 1948–1950; Sub-Lieutenant (National Service) 1951–1952; Field Archaeology, Turkey 1953–1957; Assistant Director and Librarian, British School of Rome 1957–1962; Classics Teacher and Curator of Myers Museum, Eton 1962–1986; Research Associate, Institute of Archaeology, Oxford 1990–2000. **Awards:** Major Scholarship, SJC 1945; John Stewart of Rannoch Scholarship in Greek and Latin, University of Cambridge 1947; Leverhulme Research Grant 1961. **Publications:** material from journeys in Turkey 1953–1962, 1992, 1994, 1996.

BALLANTYNE, John Andrew (1934) Born 3 May 1912, 96 York Drive, Glasgow; son of John George Ballantyne, Schoolmaster, and Marguerite Marie Mathilde Eugénie Stephanie Vander Meersch; m Joyce; 1 son (Graham), 1 daughter (Clare). **Subject(s):** Classics; BA 1936; MA 1948. **Tutor(s):** R L Howland. **Educ:** Ayr Academy; University of Edinburgh. **Career:** Lieutenant, RAC 1939–1943; POW, Tunisia 1943–1944; Liaison Officer to Italian Partisan Brigade 1944–1945; Assistant Director of Education for Norfolk, then Cheshire 1945–1948; Headmaster, Newbury Grammar School, Berkshire 1948–1960; Headmaster, Cranbrook School, Kent 1960. **Appointments:** Vice-President, Berkshire Rugby Football Union; Chairman, Berkshire County Combined Cadet Force Committee; Member, Berkshire County Cricket Club Committee. **Awards:** Graves Prize, SJC; Exhibition, SJC. **Honours:** MBE. Died 7 November 1960.

BALLINGER, Maurice (1936) Born 28 February 1917, Swallowbeek, North Hykeham, Branston, Lincolnshire; son of Harold Ballinger, Mechanical Engineer, and Annie Burns. **Subject(s):** Natural Sciences; BA 1938; MA 1942; FIMC. **Tutor(s):** J M Wordie. **Educ:** Southolme Private School; Hulme Grammar School. **Awards:** Scholarship, SJC 1937.

BALLS, Jack Lawrence (1932) Born 1 October 1913, The Priory Nursing Home, Newmarket Road, Cambridge; son of William Lawrence Balls, Chief Botanist, Ministry of Agriculture, Egypt, and Florence Edith Tyrrell. **Tutor(s):** J M Wordie. **Johnian Relatives:** son of William Lawrence Balls (1900). **Educ:** Entry House School, Diss; Junior School, Holt; Gresham's School, Holt.

BALLS, Dr William Lawrence (1900) Born 3 September 1882, Garboldisham, Norfolk; son of William Balls, Schoolmaster, and Emma Mary Lawrence; m Edith Tyrrell, 18 August 1909, St Mary's, Diss; 1 son (Jack Lawrence b 1 October 1913). **Subjects:** Natural Sciences; BA 1903; MA 1907; ScD 1916; FRS 1923. **Tutor(s):** D MacAlister. **Johnian Relatives:** father of Jack Lawrence Balls (1932). **Educ:** King Edward VI Middle School, Norwich. **Career:** Designer, Cotton Research Board, Egypt; Designer, Spinning Test Mill, Giza, Egypt; Botanist, Khedival Agriculture Society, Egypt 1904–1910; Foundress Fellow, SJC 1909–1913; Botanist, Department of Agriculture, Egpytian Government 1911–1913 and 1927–1933; Head, Experimental Department, Fine Cotton Spinners' Association, Bollington, Cheshire 1915–1926; Director, Botanical Section, Egyptian Ministry of Agriculture 1933–1937. **Appointments:** Honorary Fellow, SJC 1955–1960. Council, British Empire Cotton Corporation; Chief of the Experimental Department of the Fine Cotton Spinners' Association; Honorary Fellow, Textile Institute. **Awards:** Scholarship, SJC 1901; Walsingham Medal 1906. **Honours:** Order of the Medjidieh, Third Class 1914; CBE 1924; First Class, Order of Agriculture, Egypt 1947. **Publications:** *The Cotton Plant in Egypt* (1912); *The Development and Properties of Raw Cotton* (1915); *Handbook of Spinning Tests for Cotton Growers* (1920); *Studies of Quality in Cotton* (1928); *The Yield of a Crop* (1953). Died 18 July 1960.

BALMAIN, Graham Coumbe (1943) Born 4 April 1926, 22 Oakington Avenue, Wembley, London; son of William Andrew Balmain, Research Chemist, and Nancy Ada Coumbe. **Tutor(s):** C W Guillebaud. **Educ:** University College School, Hampstead; Felsted School.

BAMBAH, Professor Ram Prakash (1948) Born 30 September 1925, Jammu, India; son of Shri Bhagat Ram Bambah, Indian Railways, and Lajwati; m Saudamini Parija; 2 daughters (Bindu and Sucharu). **Subject(s):** Mathematics; PhD 1950; ScD 1970; BA (Punjab) 1943; MA (Punjab) 1945. **Tutor(s):** J M Wordie. **Educ:** MB High School, Wazirabad; KC Arya High School, Sialkot; Government College, Lahore (Panjab University). **Career:** Lecturer, Delhi University 1947–1948; 1851 Exhibition Scholarship, UCL 1950–1951; Title A Fellow, SJC 1952–1955; Reader 1952–1958, Professor 1958–1985, Vice Chancellor 1985–1991, Professor Emeritus 1993, Panjab University, Chandigarh; Professor, Ohio State University 1964–1970. **Appointments:** Member, Institute for Advanced Study, Princeton 1952–1954; Visiting Associate Professor/Professor, Notre Dame University 1957–1958; President, Indian Mathematical Society 1969; Visiting Professor, Ohio State University frequently 1970–1983 and 1991–1992; Member, UGC 1976–1979; Fellow and Vice-President, INSA 1979–1980; General President, ISCA 1983–1984; Fellow, Indian Academy of Sciences; Fellow, National Academy of Sciences of India; Fellow, Third World Academy of Sciences 1993; Member, Board of Trustees, *The Tribune* group of newspapers, Chandigarh; Chairman, Governing Body, IUCAA, Pune 1997–. **Awards:** 1851 Exhibition Scholarship 1948–1950; Srinivasa Ramanujan Medal, INSA 1979; Distinguished Service Award, Mathematics Association of India 1984; Meghnad Saha Award for Theoretical Sciences, UGC-Hari Om Trust 1986; Padma Bushan Award 1988; Ramanujan Memorial Lecture Award, Indian Mathematical Society 1993; Ramanujan Birth Centenary Award, Indian Science Congress 1994 (Gold Medal); Jawaharlal Nehru Birth Centenary Lecture Award, ISCA 1997; Aryabhata Medal, INSA 1998. **Publications:** (ed, with V C Dumir and R J Hans Gill) *Number Theory*, INSA and Hindustan Book Agency, New Delhi, 2000; more than 70 papers in research journals.

BAMBAWALE, Bhargao Amrit (1923) Born 3 November 1903, Narsinghpur, Central Provinces, India; son of Rao Bahadur Amrit Ramchandra Bambawale, District Superintendent of Police, and Bhima Tarte. **Subject(s):** Natural Sciences; BA 1925; MA 1931. **Tutor(s):** E Cunningham. **Educ:** Craddock High School, Wardha, India; Government High School, Yeotmal; Patwardham High School, Nagpur; Morris College with Victoria College of Science, Nagpur. Died 30 May 1975.

BAMBER, John (1949) Born 17 November 1928, The Vicarage, Crowle, Worcestershire; son of John Reginald Bamber, Clerk in Holy Orders, and Mary Monks; m Daphne Margaret Smyth, 29 January 1955, St Mark's Church, Nairobi; 3 sons (Jeremy John b 2 March 1956, Nigel Peter b 10 March 1962, and Julian Mark b 1 January 1968), 2 daughters (Deborah Jane b 12 June 1957 and Jennifer Clare b 25 November 1959). **Subject(s):** Mathematics. **Tutor(s):** J M Wordie. **Johnian Relatives:** grandson of John Bamber (1886); son of John Reginald Bamber (1919); father of Jeremy John Bamber (1975); grandfather of Simon John Bamber (2002). **Educ:** Wollaston Preparatory School; Wollaston Church of England School; King Edward VI School, Stourbridge. **Career:** Royal Signals 1948–1949; British American Tobacco, Kenya 1953, Tanganyika 1962, Uganda 1965, Nigeria 1969, London 1974. **Appointments:** Treasurer, Tobacco Trade Benevolent Association 1989.

BAMBER, Canon John Reginald (1919) Born 8 January 1900, The Vicarage, Crowle, Worcestershire; son of John Bamber, Clerk in Holy Orders, and Florence May Holland; m Mary Monks, 27 April 1927, Radcliffe Parish Church, Lancashire; 1 son (John b 17 November 1928), 1 daughter (Rosemary Margaret b 8 November 1930). **Subject(s):** History; BA 1922; MA 1927. **Tutor(s):** E E Sikes. **Johnian Relatives:** son of John Bamber (1886); father of John Bamber (1949); grandfather of

Jeremy John Bamber (1975); great grandfather of Simon John Bamber (2002). **Educ:** Norman House School, West Didsbury; Manchester Grammar School; Victoria University, Manchester; Ridley Hall, Cambridge 1922. **Career:** Ordained Deacon 1923; Curate, Christ Church, Salford 1923–1926; Ordained Priest, Manchester 1924; Curate, Stretford 1926–1927; Vicar, Crowle 1927–1933; Vicar, Wollaston, Worcestershire 1933–1939; Chaplain to the army, served in France, taken prisoner at Dunkirk, became Chaplain to large prison camp in Germany 1939–1945; Vicar, Holy Trinity, Malvern 1948. **Appointments:** Patron, St John the Baptist, Crowle 1942–1979; Member, CACTM 1950s; Honorary Canon, Worcester Cathedral 1956; Member of Convocation 1961–1969; Visitor on Preaching, Worcester Ordination College 1960s. **Honours:** MBE 1946. Died 8 February 1979.

BAMBROUGH, John Renford (1945) Born 29 April 1926, 4 Edward Street, Tunstall, Durham; son of John Renford Bambrough, Electrician, and Mary Kearton; m Moira Mahoney, 30 July 1952, St Nicholas's Church, Bishopwearmouth, Sunderland; 4 children. **Subject(s):** Classics; BA 1948; MA 1952. **Tutor(s):** R L Howland. **Educ:** New Silksworth Council School; Ryhope Secondary School; Bede Collegiate School, Sunderland. **Career:** 'Bevin Boy', Wearmouth Colliery (National Service); Title A Fellow 1950–1952, Title B Fellow 1952–1986, Lecturer in Moral Sciences 1962–1991, Title D Fellow 1986–1999, SJC; Assistant Lecturer in Classics 1957–1962, Lecturer in Classics 1962–1966, Lecturer in Moral Sciences (Philosophy) 1966–1991, University of Cambridge. **Appointments:** Tutor 1952–1964, Supervisor in Classics and Moral Sciences 1955–1962, Director of Studies in Moral Sciences/Philosophy 1959–1991, Dean of College 1964–1979, President 1979–1983, SJC; Stanton Lecturer in Philosophy of Religion, University of Cambridge 1962; Member, Council for the Accreditation of Teacher Education 1984–1987; President, Aristotelian Society 1989–1990; O R and Eva Mitchell Visiting Distinguished Professor of Philosophy, Trinity University, San Antonio, Texas 1993. **Awards:** Scholarship, SJC; John Stewart of Rannoch Scholarship in Classics, University of Cambridge 1947; Henry Carrington and Bentham Dumont Koe Studentship, University of Cambridge 1948. **Publications:** (ed) *The Cambridge Review*, 1951 onwards; 'Universals and Family Resemblances', *Proceedings of the Aristotelian Society* 61, 1961; *Reason, Truth and God*, 1969; *Moral Scepticism and Moral Knowledge*, 1979; (ed) *Philosophy*, 1973–1994. Died 17 January 1999.

BANCROFT, George Charles (1926) Born 21 June 1908, 11 Via Mazzini, Legnano, Italy; son of George Kerslake Bancroft, Mechanic, and Edith Thewlis. BA 1929. **Tutor(s):** E A Benians. **Educ:** Wild's Preparatory School, Oldham; Oldham Grammar School; New College, Harrogate.

BANE-SINHJI, Kumar Shri (1928) Born 19 August 1908, Wadhwan City, Kathiawar, India; son of Thakore Sahib Shri Jaswant Sinhji, Ruler of Wadhwan State, India, and Shreemati Sundarba. BA 1931; MA 1936. **Tutor(s):** C W Guillebaud. **Educ:** Rajkumar College, Rajkot; The Boys High School, Panchgani, Bombay, India.

BANISTER, Harry (1922) Born 12 April 1882, Orchard Street, St Annes-on-Sea, Lancashire; son of John Ratcliffe Banister, Schoolmaster, and Mary Grady; m Idwen Thomas, 6 December 1916, Llandegai Village Church. MSc 1924; PhD 1926; BSc (London) 1904. **Tutor(s):** E A Benians. **Educ:** Grammar School, St Annes-on-Sea; University College of North Wales. **Career:** Headmaster, Queen's Collegiate School, Benares, Indian Educational Service 1908–1924; Inspector of Schools, Indian Educational Service 1910; Military Service 1914–1919; Lecturer in Experimental Psychology, University of Cambridge 1926–1947. **Appointments:** Director of Studies in Moral Sciences and Supervisor in Psychology, SJC 1934–1947; Honorary Consultant Psychologist to the Papworth Village Settlement. **Publications:** *Introduction to Statistics*; *Emotions and Sentiments*. Died 19 January 1963.

BANISTER, Thomas Roger (1909) Born 8 February 1890, 7 Lombard Terrace, Preston, Lancashire; son of William Banister, Clerk in Holy Orders, and Mary Alice Grime. **Subject(s):** History/Economics; BA 1912. **Tutor(s):** J R Tanner. **Johnian Relatives:** uncle of David Banister Lockhart Smith (1946). **Educ:** Trent College. **Career:** Chinese Maritime Customs. Died 20 November 1955.

BANKS, Dr Arthur Ashton (1945) Born 4 February 1925, 68 Estcourt Street, Hull; son of Frederick Banks, Fireman, and Carrie Louise Ashton; m Beryl; 1 son (Nigel). PhD 1948; BSc (London) 1945; ARIC; CChem. **Tutor(s):** J M Wordie. **Educ:** Estcourt Street Elementary School, Hull; Hull Grammar School; Royal College of Science, South Kensington. **Career:** OR Analyst, ICI. Died 28 December 1994.

BANKS, James Dallaway (1935) Born 3 January 1917, Derrymore, Barton Wood Road, Lymington; son of Cyril Banks, Captain, RAMC, and Edith Ellen Dallaway; m (1) Winifred, (2) Janette; 2 sons (Christopher and John), 1 daughter (Susan). **Subject(s):** Mathematics; BA 1938; MA 1942. **Tutor(s):** C W Guillebaud. **Educ:** Salterhebble Council School, Halifax; Heath Grammar School, Halifax; Nottingham High School. **Career:** Indian Civil Service 1939–1947; Hospital Administrator 1947–1973; Assistant Secretary, Department of Health 1973–1975. **Awards:** Scholarship, SJC. Died 17 October 1985.

BANKS, Kenneth Charles (1927) Born 7 March 1909, 43 Rugby Road, Leamington, Warwickshire; son of Archibald James Banks, Civil Servant, and Edith Kate Collins; m Nona. **Subject(s):** History; BA 1930; MA 1943. **Tutor(s):** E A Benians. **Educ:** St Joseph's High School, Reading; Reading Collegiate School; Reading School. **Appointments:** Director, Engineering Employers London Association; Local Councillor. **Awards:** Scholarship, SJC. Died 4 January 1986.

BANSALL, Harry Allan (1946) Born 1 December 1921, 3 Prospect Terrace, Norton, Stockton-on-Tees; son of John Wilson Bansall, Chartered Civil Engineer, and Katherine Malcolm Aitken; m Irmgard Karoline Martha Meyer, 8 September 1962. BA 1948; MA 1953; CEng. **Tutor(s):** R L Howland. **Educ:** Orleton Preparatory School, Scarborough; Durham School. **Career:** Works Engineer, ICI. **Appointments:** JP. Died 1995.

BANSALL, Ian Aitken (1939) Born 10 February 1920, Links Parade, Carnoustie, Angus; son of John Wilson Bansall, Chartered Civil Engineer, and Katherine Malcolm Aitken. **Tutor(s):** R L Howland. **Educ:** Orleton School, Scarborough; Durham School. **Career:** Lieutenant, Durham Light Infantry, WWII. Died June 1944 (killed in action).

BARBASH, Hezekiah (Hedley) (1914) Born 27 February 1895, 53 Martin Street, Nether Hallam, Sheffield; son of Mendel Barbash, Export Merchant, and Olga Katz. **Subject(s):** Natural Sciences; BA 1917; BChir 1921; MB 1921; MRCS; LRCP 1919; FRCS 1926. **Tutor(s):** R P Gregory. **Johnian Relatives:** uncle of Anthony Seymour Valentine (1948). **Educ:** Netherthorpe Council School, Sheffield; Central Secondary School, Sheffield; City of London School. **Career:** Doctor, St Bartholomew's Hospital 1921; Registrar, Northampton General Hospital 1920s; Northampton General Hospital and Mapperly Hospital, Nottingham 1930–1931; GP, Beeston, Nottingham 1932–1961. **Awards:** Foundation Scholarship, SJC 1916. Died 25 August 1970.

BARBER, Bernard Anson (1939) Born 27 May 1920, Elmwood Anson Road, Manchester; son of George Carlisle Barber, Medical Practitioner, and Louisa Parker; m Diana Lee-Barber, 17 August 1946. **Tutor(s):** R L Howland. **Johnian Relatives:** brother of Wilfred Carlisle Barber (1926); uncle of Neil Carlisle Barber (1953). **Educ:** Moor Allerton School, Manchester; Repton School.

BARBER, Cyril Arthur (1903) Born 30 May 1885, 3 High View, Harrogate, Yorkshire; son of Francis Barber, Solicitor, and Alice Mary Womersley. BA 1909. **Tutor(s):** D MacAlister. **Educ:** Oakshade, Reigate; Reading School; Royal Naval School.

BARBER, Denis Ian (1944) Born 8 March 1926, 24 Torrington Park, North Finchley, Middlesex; son of Ernest Albert Barber, Insurance Clerk, and Celia Maud Wallis. **Tutor(s):** J M Wordie. **Educ:** Highgate Junior School; Highgate School.

BARBER, James Bertram (1926) Born 16 November 1907, McArthy House, Kandy, Ceylon; son of Charles Cyril Barber, Planter, and Edith van Langenberg; m Lily (Lee) Marie Northway, 1936, Brompton Oratory; 1 son (David Michael b 31 August 1939), 1 daughter (June Mary b 16 June 1941). BA 1929. **Tutor(s):** E A Benians. **Johnian Relatives:** father-in-law of William Brian Stallard (1958). **Educ:** St Joseph's College, Colombo; St Edmund's College, Ware. **Career:** Colonial Service, Uganda. Died 29 December 1940.

BARBER, John Stuart (1940) Born 1 June 1922, 26a Lunham Road, Norwood; son of Philip Stanley Barber, Produce Broker and Underwriter, Lloyd's, and Iris Ada Stuart Baker. **Tutor(s):** S J Bailey. **Educ:** Junior King's School, Canterbury; Shrewsbury School. **Career:** Flying Officer, RAF 1940–1943. Died 1943.

BARBER, Wilfred Carlisle (1926) Born 2 June 1907, 51 Princess Road, Moss Side, Manchester; son of George Carlisle Barber, Medical Practitioner, and Louisa Parker; 1 son, 1 daughter. **Subject(s):** Natural Sciences; BA 1929; MA 1933; MB 1933; BChir 1933; MRCS 1932; LRCP 1932; FRCS 1935; FACS 1965. **Tutor(s):** M P Charlesworth. **Johnian Relatives:** brother of Bernard Anson Barber (1939); father of Neil Carlisle Barber (1953). **Educ:** The Grammar School, Hulme; Sutton Valence School. **Career:** Surgeon, RAMC, Kenya 1939–1945; Professor of Surgery, University of Baghdad 1946–1949; Consultant Surgeon, The Nairobi Hospital, Kenya, and to the British Forces, HH The Aga Khan Hospital, and the Kenyatta National Hospital 1949–1975. Died 1 August 1975.

BARBOR, Dr Ronald Charles Blair (1928) Born 1 May 1910, 67 Lower Leeson Street, Dublin, Ireland; son of Charles James Barbor, Banker, and Helen Jane Hamilton Blair; m Yvonne; 4 children. MB 1937; BChir 1937; MRCS Eng 1934; FRSM; LRCP 1934. **Tutor(s):** M P Charlesworth. **Educ:** The Hawthorns, Merstham; Earlywood, Ascot; Rugby School. **Career:** Manipulative Physician, Charterhouse Clinic; Assistant, Department of Physical Medicine; House Officer, Physical, Gynaecology & Obstetrics Department, St Thomas' Hospital; Captain, RAMC; Consulting Orthopaedic Physician, Wimpole Street; GP. **Appointments:** Council, International Federation of Manual Medicine; Chairman, British Association of Manipulative Medicine. **Publications:** *Treatment for Chronic Low Back Pain*; *Pain Arising from Ligaments of Lower Back*. Died 13 September 1989.

BARBOSA DA SILVA, Edmundo Penna (1939) Born 11 February 1917, Curvelo, Minas Gerais, Brazil; son of Alexandre Barbosa da Silva, Estate Owner and Breeder, and Izabel Augusta de Oliveira Penna. **Tutor(s):** C W Guillebaud. **Educ:** Externato e Seni Internato; Faculdade de Direito da Universidade do Brasil.

BARBOUR, Dr Gavin Butler (1929) Born 19 March 1912, 255a Old Kent Road, Southwark; son of Thomas Barbour, Medical Practitioner, and Dorothy Elizabeth Fidgin; m J A Bouquet, 22 September 1945, New Delhi. BA 1932; BChir 1937; MD 1937. **Tutor(s):** M P Charlesworth. **Johnian Relatives:** brother of Thomas Lawson Barbour (1927). **Educ:** Brightlands Preparatory School; Mill Hill School. **Career:** Private, HAC; Second Lieutenant, RFA, WWII.

BARBOUR, Dr George Brown (1912) Born 22 August 1890, 24 Melville Street, Edinburgh; son of Alexander Hugh Freeland Barbour, Physician and Lecturer in Gynaecology, and Margaret Nelson Brown. BA 1917; MA 1921; MA (Edinburgh) 1911; PhD (Columbia) 1929; FRSE. **Tutor(s):** R P Gregory. **Johnian Relatives:** brother of Robert Freeland Barbour (1921). **Educ:** Merchiston Castle; University of Edinburgh. **Career:** British Army Overseas 1914–1919; Professor of Geology, Peking University 1920–1922; Professor of Applied Geology, Peiyang University, Tientsin 1922–1923; Professor of Geology, Yenching University, Peking 1923–1932; Lecturer, Columbia University 1928–1929; Acting Professor, Stanford University 1935; Associate Professor of Geology 1937, Professor, and Dean of College of Liberal Arts 1938, University of Cincinnati. **Appointments:** Visiting Lecturer, University of Cincinnati 1923–1933; Visiting Physiographer, Rockefeller Foundation, Peiping 1934; Honorary Lecturer, University of London 1934–1937; Fellow or Honorary Member of Scientific Societies in France, Belgium, China, Finland and SA. **Awards:** Mons Star. Died 12 July 1977.

BARBOUR, Dr Robert Freeland (1921) Born 27 March 1904, West Colinton House, Colinton, Edinburgh; son of Alexander Hugh Freeland Barbour, Physician, and Margaret Nelson Brown; m Constance Speer, 25 October 1930, Lakeville, Connecticut. **Subject(s):** Moral Sciences; BA 1925; MA 1935; MB (Edinburgh) 1929; ChB (Edinburgh) 1929; FRCPE; FRCPsych; FRCP (London). **Tutor(s):** E A Benians. **Johnian Relatives:** brother of George Brown Barbour (1912). **Educ:** The Academy, Edinburgh; Gresham's School, Holt. **Career:** Lecturer in Psychology, Bristol University 1947. Died 3 December 1989.

BARBOUR, Dr Thomas Lawson (1927) Born 29 June 1909, 255a Old Kent Road, Southwark, London; son of Thomas Barbour, Physician, and Dorothy Elizabeth Fidgin. **Subject(s):** Natural Sciences; BA 1930; MB 1938; BChir 1938. **Tutor(s):** M P Charlesworth. **Johnian Relatives:** brother of Gavin Butler Barbour (1929). **Educ:** Darvel, Scotland; City of London School; Mill Hill School.

BARCLAY, Cuthbert (1919) Born 27 February 1898, Wapella, 61 Silverdale, Sydenham, Kent; son of Henry James Barclay and Mary Allen Stoneham; m Marguerite Suzanne Carmen Senne; 2 daughters (Jaqueline and Micheline). **Subject(s):** Natural Sciences; BA 1921; MA 1927. **Tutor(s):** E E Sikes. **Educ:** West Hill School, Sydenham; Dulwich College. **Career:** Second Lieutenant, Royal Field Artillery 1917–1919; Lieutenant Royal Field Artillery 1919; Geneticist to United States Rubber Plantations Inc, Kisaran, Sumatra 1923. **Awards:** Research Studentship, Empire Cotton Growing Corporation 1922. Died 8 May 1969.

BARCLAY, Norman Veitch Lothian (1943) Born 5 October 1925, 3 Claremont Terrace, Glasgow; son of James Barclay, Whisky Exporter, and Florence Winifred Lothian; m (1) Joan Margaret Helen Ann Ogg, February 1955, St Moritz, Switzerland (div 1967), (2) Therese de las Casas, October 1969; (1) 3 sons (James b 29 August 1955, Rupert George Maxwell Lothian b 2 February 1957 and Jeremy b 15 February 1958), (2) 2 sons (Maxwell b 20 October 1970 and Alexander b 29 September 1974). BA 1949; MA 1978; CA. **Tutor(s):** S J Bailey. **Johnian Relatives:** father of Rupert George Maxwell Lothian Barclay (1975). **Educ:** Troon School; Glasgow Academy; Dreghorn Castle, Edinburgh; Harecroft Hall, Seascale; Trinity College, Glenalmond. **Career:** Captain, RE, Malaya and Japan 1944–1946; Articled to Thomson McClintock, Glasgow; business career in cork manufacturing, bottle closures and plastic moulding; Owner, Daniel Montgomery and Sons from 1950s; Owner, Aberdeen Comb Works 1966–1973; Director, Macfarlane Group 1974–1995. **Appointments:** Captain, and driver of four man bob, British Olympic Bobsleigh Team, Winter Olympics 1964; President, British Bobsleigh Association, 1990s. Died 28 March 1997.

BARDSLEY, The Revd Edwin Roy (1946) Born 13 March 1924, 106 Gardner Road, Prestwich, Lancashire; son of James Bardsley, Schoolmaster, and Annie Barlow; m 1953; 4 children. BA 1947; MA 1952. **Tutor(s):** C W Guillebaud. **Educ:** Bury Grammar School, Lancashire. **Career:** Royal Marines 1942–1945; Curate, St Mary's, Oldham 1949–1953; Priest, St George's, Harold Hill, Essex 1953–1958; Vicar, St John, Moulsham, Chelmsford 1958–1974; Chaplain, Chelmsford and Essex Hospital 1958–1974; Rector, Marwood with Bittadon, Barnstaple, Devon 1974–1977; Priest, Weare Gifford with

Landcross, Littleham and Monkleigh, Diocese of Exeter 1977–1980; Rural Dean, Hartland 1979–1980; Vicar, St Andrew's, Tiverton, Exeter 1980–1986; Chaplain, East Devon Further Education College 1980–1989. Died 19 June 1997.

BARDSLEY, Richard Geoffrey (1948) Born 9 July 1928, Rozel, Broadoak Road, Stockport, Cheshire; son of Herbert Bardsley, Sanitary and Electrical Engineer, and Gladys Irene Solly; m Elda Shantz, 1957; 3 children (Kathryn, Alex and Alyson). **Subject(s):** Modern and Medieval Languages/History; BA 1950; MA 1955. **Educ:** Barn Lea High School; Stockport Grammar School. **Career:** National Service 1946–1948; Overseas Department, Bank of England 1952–1956; Hanover Bank, New York 1957; President and CEO, Industrial Indemnity Finance Corporation, San Francisco 1985–1993; Executive Recruiter and Volunteer, International Executive Service Corps 1993–2000. Died 14 August 2000.

BARGH, The Revd George Edward Norman (1943) Born 9 March 1925, Elton Nursing Home, Harrogate, Yorkshire; son of Miles Taylor Bargh, Insurance Broker, and Gertrude Waterhouse; m Margaret Thomas; 2 sons, 2 daughters. **Subject(s):** Mathematics/Law; BA 1948; MA 1950; LLB (Leeds) 1950; Law Society Final 1951. **Educ:** High Harrogate College; Ripon Grammar School; The Leys School, Cambridge. **Career:** Home Guard 1942–1944; Petty Officer, RN 1944–1947; Solicitor, Temple and Bargh 1951–1974; Bursar, Wesley House 1974–1980; Priest (NSM), Ulverston, Cumbria 1982–1986; Priest, Egton-cum-Newland and Lowick, Diocese of Carlisle 1986–1990.

BARGRAVE-WEAVER, Dr Derek (1941) See WEAVER.

BARKBY, Joseph Ewart (1927) Born 22 March 1909, 21 Lathom Road, Southport, Lancashire; son of Joseph Thomas Barkby, Primitive Methodist Minister, and Maggie Ann Hartley. BA 1930. **Tutor(s):** C W Guillebaud. **Educ:** Durston House, Ealing; Mill Hill School. **Career:** Lieutenant, RNVR, WWII. Died 10 July 1945.

BARKER, John Townsend (1921) Born 5 September 1903, 55 Bunyan Road, Hitchin, Hertfordshire; son of John Henry Barker, Joinery Manufacturer and Timber Merchant, and Annie Maria Townsend. **Subject(s):** Economics; BA 1924; MA 1928. **Tutor(s):** E A Benians. **Johnian Relatives:** brother of Philip Townsend (1917). **Educ:** The Friends' School, Saffron Walden; Bootham School, York. **Appointments:** JP. Died 11 September 1996.

BARKER, Paul Stuart (1942) Born 22 January 1925, Annie Walthew Nursing Home, Didsbury Road, Heaton Norris; son of Roy Barker, Structural Engineer, and Bessie Green. **Subject(s):** Economics; BA 1948; MA 1950. **Tutor(s):** C W Guillebaud. **Educ:** Bowdon College, Cheshire; PNEU School, Hornchurch; Brentwood School.

BARKER, Philip Townsend (1917) Born 4 March 1899, 55 Bunyan Road, Hitchin, Hertfordshire; son of John Henry Barker, Timber Merchant and Joinery Manufacturer, and Annie Maria Townsend. BA 1923. **Tutor(s):** E E Sikes. **Johnian Relatives:** brother of John Townsend Barker (1921). **Educ:** Friends' School, Saffron Walden; Regent Street Polytechnic. **Career:** Second Lieutenant, RFA, WWI. Died 1 January 1981.

BARKER, Roland Richard Sinclair (1936) Born 5 March 1917, 144 St John's Road, Deptford, London; son of John Barker, Bricklayer, and Wilhelmina Sinclair; m Mary Joy Mardles, 13 June 1944, Farnborough. **Subject(s):** Modern and Medieval Languages; BA 1939; MA 1943; Diploma in Mathematics (Mathematical Association); Teacher's Diploma (University of London) 1947. **Tutor(s):** C W Guillebaud. **Educ:** Ravensbourne LCC Elementary School; Colfe's Grammar School, Lewisham. **Career:** Housemaster, Alleyn's School 1947–1977. **Appointments:** County Councillor, Somerset County Council 1985–1993.

BARKER, Stuart John (1949) Born 18 August 1928, Forest Hydro, Forest Road, Walthamstow, Essex; son of Sidney George Barker, Commercial Clerk, and Lilian Maud Rayner; m Daphne M Banks, 10 August 1956, New Malden, Surrey; 2 sons (Christopher Stuart b 12 August 1960 and Andrew John b 7 February 1962), 2 daughters (Anne Elizabeth b 9 January 1959 and Judith Alison b 8 January 1965). **Subject(s):** Natural Sciences; BA 1952; MA 1956. **Tutor(s):** E Miller; W A Deer; G C L Bertram. **Educ:** Selwyn Avenue Elementary School, Walthamstow; Sir George Monoux Grammar School, Walthamstow. **Career:** Technical Management, ICI Plastics Division. **Awards:** Minor Scholarship, SJC 1946. **Publications:** *Polyacetal Resins*, Iliffe, for the Plastics Institute, 1970.

BARKER, William Thomas (1949) Born 15 December 1928, 104 Glenthorne Avenue, Croydon, Surrey; son of William Barker, Secretary, Agricultural Implements Manufacturer, and Hyla Bronwen Thomas. **Subject(s):** Classics/Law; BA 1952. **Tutor(s):** R L Howland. **Educ:** Urmston Council School; Victoria Park Council School, Stretford; Manchester Grammar School. **Career:** Civil Servant, MAFF; Administrative Branch, Home Civil Service 1952. **Awards:** Patchett Scholarship, SJC.

BARLOW, Charles Gerald (1922) Born 3 May 1903, 12 High Lane, Chorlton-cum-Hardy, Withington, Lancashire; son of George Simpson Barlow, Accountant, and Fanny Jane Clegg. **Subject(s):** Natural Sciences; BA 1925; MA 1929; CChem; MRIC. **Tutor(s):** E A Benians. **Johnian Relatives:** brother of Harold Ernest Barlow (1920). **Educ:** High School, Chorlton-cum-Hardy; South Manchester School; Rhos-on-Sea Preparatory School; King William's College, Isle of Man. **Career:** Research Chemist, J Lyons & Co Ltd. Died 4 January 1989.

BARLOW, Christopher Matthew (1920) Born 21 September 1898, 102 Castle Street, Cambridge; son of Henry Theodore Edward Barlow, Clerk in Holy Orders, and Margaret Brown. BA 1923; MA 1928. **Tutor(s):** B F Armitage. **Johnian Relatives:** son of Henry Theodore Edward Barlow (1882). **Educ:** RMA, Woolwich; King's College Choir School, Cambridge; Felsted School. **Career:** Royal Field Artillery, France 1916–1918; Farmer, Kenya 1920–1922; Administrative Officer, Nigerian Political Service 1926–1930. **Honours:** MC 1918. Died 9 February 1930.

BARLOW, Harold Ernest (1920) Born 25 November 1900, 12 High Lane, Chorlton-cum-Hardy, Withington, Lancashire; son of George Simpson Barlow, Accountant, and Fanny Jane Clegg; m Gladys; 1 son (Michael). **Subject(s):** Economics/History; BA 1923; MA 1929. **Tutor(s):** E A Benians. **Johnian Relatives:** brother of Charles Gerald Barlow (1922). **Educ:** High School, Chorlton-cum-Hardy; South Manchester Preparatory School; Manchester Grammar School; HMS *Conway* School Ship; King William's College, Isle of Man. **Career:** J Lyons & Co Ltd, Cadby Hall, Hammersmith 1923; Assistant Secretary, J Lyons & Co Ltd, Cadby Hall, Hammersmith 1926; Secretary, J Lyons & Co Ltd, Cadby Hall, Hammersmith 1954–1963. **Appointments:** Member, National Federation of Property Owners. **Awards:** Choral Studentship, SJC. Died 4 October 1965.

BARLOW, Percival Smith (1902) Born 8 April 1878, Pocklington, Yorkshire; son of George Edward Barlow, Chemist, and Sarah Elliot Patterson; m; 2 sons. BA 1905; MA 1909; BSc (Victoria) 1897. **Tutor(s):** D MacAlister. **Educ:** Pocklington School; Yorkshire College, Leeds (part of The Victoria University). **Career:** Master, Normanton Grammar School 1898–1901; Government Training and Secondary School, Cairo 1905–1910; Oundle School 1910–1913; Headmaster, Hastings Grammar School 1913–1935; Captain, 5th Royal Sussex Regiment (TF), Palestine 1917–1919; Captain and Adjutant, RE, WWI. **Appointments:** Supervisor in Physics, SJC 1904–1905. Died 29 October 1935.

BARLOW, Peter Gordon Rigby (1941) Born 2 April 1923, Edenside, High Street, Golborne, Lancashire; son of Samuel Gordon Barlow, Cotton Yarn Merchant, and Eunice Hodson Rigby; m Joan Mary Collins,

25 March 1950; 1 son (Richard Peter Gordon), 1 daughter (Caroline Mary). **Subject(s):** Mechanical Sciences; BA 1947; MA 1949; FICE; MIE (Malaysia). **Tutor(s):** S J Bailey. **Johnian Relatives:** father of Richard Peter Gordon Barlow (1971). **Educ:** Newton-in-Makerfield Grammar School; Mostyn House School, Parkgate; Shrewsbury School. **Career:** Partner, Coode and Partners, Consulting Engineers 1967–1985.

BARNARD, Professor George Alfred (1933) Born 23 September 1915, 44 Winns Terrace, Walthamstow, Essex; son of Frederick Charles Barnard, Cabinet Maker and Joinery Worker, and Ethel Clarissa Lawrence; m (1) Helen J Davis, (2) Mary M L Jones; (1) 2 sons (Paul b 1943, Tom b 1945 and Henry b 1948), (2) 1 son (Neil b 1956). **Subject(s):** Mathematics; BA 1936; MA 1940; DSc (London) 1963; Honorary Doctor of Mathematics (Waterloo) 1983; DUniv (Open) 1986, (Essex) 1994; Honorary DSc (City) 1991. **Tutor(s):** J M Wordie. **Educ:** Winns Avenue Elementary School, Walthamstow; Sir George Monoux Grammar School, Walthamstow; Princeton University, USA. **Career:** Research Physicist, Plessey Company, Ilford 1940–1942; Department of the Controller of Physical Research and Signals Development, Ministry of Supply 1942–1945; Lecturer in Mathematics 1945–1947, Reader in Statistics 1948–1954, Professor of Statistics 1954–1966, Imperial College, London; Professor of Mathematics, University of Essex 1966–1975 (Emeritus 1975); Professor of Statistics, University of Waterloo, Canada 1975–1981. **Appointments:** Member, International Statistical Institute 1952 (Honorary Member 1996); Statistical Advisor, British Standards Institution 1954; Chairman, Institute of Statisticians 1960–1962; President, Operational Research Society 1962–1964; Member, UCG 1967–1972; President, Institute of Mathematics and its Applications 1970; Member, Computer Board 1970–1972; Member, SSRC 1971–1974; Council Member and President 1952, 1962, President 1971–1972, Honorary Fellow 1993, Royal Statistical Society; Fellow, American Statistical Association; Fellow, Institute of Mathematical Statistics; Fellow, American Association for the Advancement of Science; Member, Reconstituted Advisory Committee for Management Efficiency in the National Health Service; Member, Scientific Advisory Council on the scientific aspects of research for the Police Service. **Awards:** Baylis Studentship, SJC 1937; Guy Medal in Silver, Royal Statistical Society 1958; Guy Medal in Gold, Royal Statistical Society 1975; Gold Medal, Institute of Mathematics and its Applications 1986; Deming Medal, American Society for Quality Control 1991. **Publications:** (ed) *The Foundations of Statistical Inference*, 1962; papers in *Journal of the Royal Statistical Society*, *Technometrics* and *Biometrika*. Died 30 July 2002.

BARNARD, Henry Benjamin (1919) Born 12 January 1900, 217 Elgin Avenue, Paddington, London; son of John Henry Barnard, Copper Merchant, and Beatrice Barnett; m Berneice MacLeod Phillips, 24 March 1950. **Tutor(s):** E E Sikes. **Educ:** Ascot House, Brighton; Colet Court, Hammersmith; Clifton College. **Career:** Second Lieutenant, RASC 1914–1918. Died 2 February 1962.

BARNARD, John Marles Sedgwick (1919) Born 22 July 1900, 147 Westbourn Avenue, Sculcoates, Hull, Yorkshire; son of Adam Sedgwick Barnard, Electrical Engineer, and Muriel Marles-Thomas; m Cecilia Maud Cooke; 2 sons (Mark Cary Sedgwick b 23 March 1932 and John Marles Herbert b 16 February 1934). **Subject(s):** Mathematics; BA 1922; MA 1926. **Tutor(s):** E A Benians. **Johnian Relatives:** father of Mark Cary Sedgwick Barnard (1950) and of John Marles Herbert Barnard (1952); uncle of Anthony Nevin Barnard (1957). **Educ:** Queen Mary's Grammar School, Walsall; Willaston School, Nantwich. **Awards:** Sizarship 1919.

BARNES, Frederick George (1948) Born 23 December 1917, 6 St Edmund's Church Street, Salisbury; son of Francis George Barnes, Building Contractor, and Edith Carpenter; m Mary Gray, 11 April 1942, Dulwich; 2 sons (Alastair b 22 April 1948 and Nigel b 7 November 1949). BA 1950; MA 1967. **Tutor(s):** R L Howland. **Educ:** Dulwich Hamlet School; Alleyn's School, Dulwich. **Career:** British Army Royal Signals.

BARNES, Geoffrey George (1905) Born 1 September 1886, Pennycomequick, Plymouth, Devon; son of Reuben Barnes, Sub-inspector of Schools, and Annie Lloyd. **Subject(s):** Mathematics/Natural Sciences; BA 1908. **Tutor(s):** D MacAlister. **Educ:** Devonport High School; Owen's School, Islington. **Career:** Major, London Regiment (Post Office Rifles), wounded twice, Mentioned in Despatches, WWI. **Awards:** Scholarship, SJC.

BARNES, George Victor (1936) Born 4 June 1917, The Rectory, Clipsham; son of Joseph Sedgwick Barnes, Rector, Clipsham, and Francess Esther Woodhouse; m Barbara Ruth Shead, 1940; 1 son (Anthony Sedgwick b 1946), 1 daughter (Felicity Ann b 1949). **Johnian Relatives:** son of Joseph Sedgwick Barnes (1883). **Subject(s):** Mathematics; BA 1939; MA 1944. **Tutor(s):** J M Wordie. **Educ:** Clipsham C of E School; Stamford School. **Career:** Mathematics Master 1939–1982 (Head of Department 1961–1982) Churchers College, Petersfield; Royal Signals 1940–1946. **Awards:** Marquess of Exeter Exhibition, SJC 1936.

BARNES, Hugh Michael Francis (BARNES-YALLOWLEY) (1948) Born 10 September 1928, London; son of Francis Harold Barnes, Insurance, and Phyllis Louise; m Anne, 11 October 1958; 2 sons, 2 daughters. **Subject(s):** Political Economy/Economics; BA 1950; MA 1955. **Tutor(s):** C W Guillebaud. **Educ:** Kimbolton School, Huntingdonshire. **Career:** Director, Alexander Howden Group Ltd 1964–1977; Chairman, J Arpel & Company Ltd 1970–1978; Managing Director, Community Reinsurance Corporation Ltd 1973–1983; Chairman, Solar Group Ltd 1974–1978; Chairman, Sterling Offices (London) Ltd 1974–1978; Director, Alexander Howden Group Ltd 1978; Director, Lyon Group Ltd 1984–1986; Director, Bennett Barnes (Underwriting Agencies Ltd) 1987–1991. **Appointments:** Liveryman, Worshipful Company of Carpenters 1950; Member 1956–1968, President 1964, London Junior Chamber of Commerce; Governor 1973, Chairman 1983–1990, Dockland Settlements; Liveryman, Company of Insurers 1980–1999; Common Councilman for the Ward of Coleman Street 1986–2000; Governor, City of London School 1987–1995; Governor, Christ's Hospital 1988–1993; Chairman, Coleman Street Ward Club 1989; Master, Worshipful Company of Carpenters 1991–1992; Governor, Bridewell Royal Hospital (King Edward's School) 1991–2000; Committee Member, Langbourn Ward Club; Life Member, City Livery Club; Churchwarden, St Peter's Church, West Firle 1992; Chairman of Governors, Building Crafts College 1993; Member, Lewes and Seaford Deanery Synod 1997; Member, Chichester Diocesan Synod 2000. **Honours:** Officer, Order of St John.

BARNES, James Albert (1922) Born 6 August 1904, 5 Cock Pit, Longfield Road, Todmorden, Yorkshire; son of Richard Barnes, Cotton Twister and Drawer, and Rachel Wade. **Subject(s):** History; BA 1925; MA 1929. **Tutor(s):** E A Benians. **Educ:** Robinwood Council School, Todmorden; Cornholme Council School, Todmorden; Todmorden Secondary School. **Career:** Senior History Master, Clitheroe Royal Grammar School 1927–1964. Died 29 December 1994.

BARNES, James Haydn (1914) Born 26 March 1894, 42 Ryland Road, Edgbaston, Worcestershire; son of Jabez Barnes, Brass Manufacturer, and Maud Sarah Wright. **Subject(s):** Modern and Medieval Languages; BA 1920. **Tutor(s):** E E Sikes. **Educ:** King Edward's School, Birmingham; High School, Harrow; University College School, London. **Career:** House Master, Kingswood School, Bath 1921–1923; Modern Languages Master, Kingswood School, Bath 1921–1957; Teacher, Nigeria 1957.

BARNES, Professor John Arundel (1936) Born 9 September 1918, 27 Coley Hill, Reading; son of Thomas Daniel Barnes, Company Director, and Mabel Grace Nash; m Helen Frances Bastable; 3 sons, 1 daughter. **Subject(s):** Mathematics/Archaeology and Anthropology; BA 1939; MA 1943; MA (Oxon) 1947; DPhil (Oxon) 1951; FBA 1981. **Tutor(s):** J M Wordie. **Johnian Relatives:** father of Ian Murray Barnes (1970). **Educ:** Cloonavon House School; Reading School; Christ's Hospital; University of Cape Town; Balliol College, Oxford. **Career:** RN (Mentioned in Despatches) 1940–1946; Research Officer, Rhodes-Livingstone Institute 1946–1949; Lecturer 1949–1951, Honorary Research Assistant 1951–1953, Department of Anthropology, UCL; Title A Fellow, SJC 1950–1953; Simon Research Fellow, Manchester University 1951–1953; Reader in Anthropology, LSE 1954–1956; Professor of Anthropology, Sydney University 1956–1958; Professor of Anthropology, Research School of Pacific Studies, ANU, Canberra 1958–1969; Overseas Fellow, Churchill College, Cambridge 1965–1966; Fellow, Churchill College 1969–; Professor of Sociology 1969–1982 (Emeritus 1982–), University of Cambridge. **Appointments:** Member, Academy of the Social Sciences in Australia; Visitor, Institute for Social and Economic Change, Bangalore 1975; Visiting Professor, Delhi School of Economics, University of Delhi; Visiting Fellow, Research School of Social Sciences, ANU 1979–1980 and 1985–1992; Visiting Professor, Department of Sociology, University of New England; Visiting Scholar, Deakin University 1985; Visiting Professor, School of Social Sciences, Flinders University of South Australia 1990; Program Visitor, Sociology, Research School of Social Sciences, ANU 1993–1998. **Awards:** Scholarship, SJC 1936–1937; Wellcome Medal, Royal Anthropological Institute 1950; Rivers Medal, Royal Anthropological Institute 1959. **Honours:** DSC 1944. **Publications:** *Marriage in a Changing Society*, 1951; *Politics in a Changing Society*, 1954; *Inquest on the Murngin*, 1967; *Sociology in Cambridge*, 1970; *Three Styles in the Study of Kinship*, 1971; *Social Networks*, 1972; *The Ethics of Inquiry in Social Science*, 1977; *Who Should Know What?*, 1979; *Models and Interpretations*, 1990; *A Pack of Lies*, 1994.

BARNES, John Down (1941) Born 23 September 1922, 18 Chestnut Grove, New Earswick, Huntington, Yorkshire; son of Thomas Searle Barnes, Schoolmaster, and Dorothy Mary Radcliffe Drew. **Subject(s):** Economics; BA 1949; MA 1951. **Tutor(s):** C W Guillebaud. **Johnian Relatives:** brother of Robert Searle Barnes (1937). **Educ:** New Earswick School; Archbishop Holgate's Grammar School, York; Bootham School, York.

BARNES, Robert Searle (1937) Born 3 July 1919, 86 Chestnut Grove, New Earswick; son of Thomas Searle Barnes, Schoolmaster, and Dorothy Mary Radcliffe Drew. **Subject(s):** Law; BA 1941; MA 1944. **Tutor(s):** C W Guillebaud. **Johnian Relatives:** brother of John Down Barnes (1941). **Educ:** New Earswick School, York; Archbishop Holgate's School, York; Bootham School, York. **Career:** Admitted Solicitor 1950. Died 4 June 1968.

BARNETT, Alec (1920) Born 30 September 1901, 4 Dogo Street, St John, Cardiff, Glamorgan; son of David Percival Barnett, Shipowner, and Theodora Fothergill. **Tutor(s):** E A Benians. **Educ:** Repton Preparatory and Senior School.

BARNETT, Dr Anthony Michael (1933) Born 28 September 1914, 1 Heightley Villas, Kings Road, Cheltenham; son of Charles Sherborne Barnett, Fish, Game and Poultry Dealer, and Muriel Elizabeth Holborow; m Margaret. **Subject(s):** Natural Sciences; BA 1936; MA 1945; MRCS 1940; LRCP 1940. **Tutor(s):** R L Howland. **Educ:** Brandon House School, Cheltenham; Wycliffe College, Stonehouse. **Career:** Surgeon Lieutenant Colonel, RNVR; Senior House Surgeon, St Thomas' Hospital Orthopaedic Unit; Medical Officer, Colonial Service, Tanganyika 1946. Died 21 October 1994.

BARNETT, Richard David (1948) Born 24 July 1922, Trewen, Pentyrch, Glamorganshire; son of Andrew Philip Barnett, Stock Broker, and Dilys Delia Evans. **Subject(s):** Geography; BA 1950; MA 1955. **Tutor(s):** J M Wordie. **Educ:** Elm Tree House School, Llandaff; Llandaff Cathedral School; Dulwich College. **Career:** Captain, RA 1942–1947; Assistant Master, St Faith's School, Cambridge 1947–1948.

BARNETT, Dr Stephen Frank (1938) Born 10 August 1915, 16 Natal Road, Edmonton, Middlesex; son of Herbert Barnett, Clerk, and Lily May Kent. MA 1964; BSc Vet (London) 1938; PhD (London); MRCVS.

Tutor(s): R L Howland. **Educ:** Trinity County School, London; Royal Veterinary College, London. **Career:** Lecturer in Veterinary Parasitology, University of Cambridge 1964; Reserved Fellowship, Title B, Wolfson College, Cambridge 1978. **Awards:** Colonial Veterinary Scholarship. Died 18 August 1981.

BARRACLOUGH, Professor Geoffrey (1936) Born 10 May 1908, Bradford, Yorkshire; son of Walter Barraclough, Merchant, and Edith Mary Brayshaw. **Subject(s):** History; MA 1936; BA 1932 (Oxon); MA 1933 (Oxon). **Educ:** Oriel College, Oxford; Bootham School. **Career:** Title B Fellow and Lecturer in History, SJC 1936–1945 (on war service 1940–1945); Lecturer in History, University of Cambridge 1937–1945; Professor of Mediaeval History, University of Liverpool 1946–1956; Stevenson Professor of International History, London University 1956–1963; Title B Fellow and Lecturer in History 1962–1967, SJC; Assistant Director of Research in History, University of Cambridge 1966–1967; Chichele Professor of History, University of Oxford 1970; Fellow, Merton College, Oxford. **Appointments:** Director of Studies in History, SJC 1939–1945; series of chairs and lectureships, at California and Brandies among others 1963–1970. **Awards:** Harmsworth Senior Scholarship; Bryce Research Studentship 1931. **Publications:** *Mediaeval Germany*; *The Origins of Modern Germany*; *Factors in German History*, 1947; *History in a Changing World*, 1955; *The Mediaeval Papacy*, 1968; *Times Atlas of World History*. Died 26 December 1984.

BARRACLOUGH, The Revd Peter (1942) Born 21 March 1925, 29 Morlais Street, Roath Park, Cardiff; son of Charles Edwin Barraclough, Minister of Religion, and Grace Helen Borthwick Clarke; m Jean Rhodda Williams; 2 daughters. **Subject(s):** Natural Sciences; BA 1945; MA 1949. **Tutor(s):** C W Guillebaud. **Educ:** Roath Park Elementary School; Cardiff High School. **Career:** Minister, Van Road English Congregational Church, Caerphilly 1949–1953; Pastor, Tacket Street Congregational Church, Ipswich 1953; Minister, Hampstead Garden Suburb Free Church 1961. **Appointments:** Associate Professional Member, Society of Analytical Psychology (London). Died 20 December 1992.

BARRADELL-SMITH, Walter (1900) Born 21 February 1881, Training College, St Giles', Gillesgate, Durham; son of Samson Barradell-Smith, Clerk in Holy Orders, and Ann Whitfield Collins; 1 son (Richard). **Subject(s):** Classics; BA 1903. **Tutor(s):** D MacAlister. **Johnian Relatives:** brother of Sydney Barradell-Smith (1898). **Educ:** Durham School. **Career:** Assistant Master, Mulgrave Castle School 1903–1904; Assistant Master, Glasgow Academy 1907–1914; Lieutenant, Scottish Rifles, France 1917–1919. **Publications:** (under the name of Richard or Lilian Bird) Numerous plays and novels. Died 5 November 1965.

BARRAN, Arthur Haworth (1930) Born 14 April 1911, The Elms, Chapel-Allerton, Leeds, Yorkshire; son of Philip Austyn Barran, Engineer, and Dorothy Currer Briggs; m Rosa Greenwood, 27 March 1945, St Oswald's Church, Guiseley. **Subject(s):** Economics/Natural Sciences; BA 1933. **Tutor(s):** J M Wordie. **Educ:** Stancliffe Hall, Matlock; Repton School. **Career:** Anglo-Iranian Oil Company, Baghdad 1939; West Yorkshire Regiment 1941; Branch Manager, Rafidain Oil Company, Basra, Iran 1948; Manager, Khanaquin 1951; Senior Assistant, Lubricants Branch of the Distribution Department, London Office 1952; Branch Manager 1955; Manager, Regional Division, Marketing Department 1961; Regional Co-ordinator, Australasia and Far East 1963; Managing Director, BP New Zealand 1966.

BARRETT, The Revd Hugh Scott (1906) Born 3 March 1887, Blundell Sands, Great Crosby, Lancashire; son of Sir William Scott Barrett, Colliery Owner, and Julia Louisa Colville; m Dorothy Gertrude Farrar, 27 September 1916, Trinity Church, West Hampstead; 3 sons, 1 daughter. **Subject(s):** Classics/Law; BA 1909; MA 1952. **Tutor(s):** E E Sikes. **Educ:** Aldenham School. **Career:** Called to the Bar, Inner Temple 1911; Major, 6th The King's (Liverpool) Regiment (TF) (twice Mentioned in Despatches) 1914–1918; Deputy Judge Advocate-General, Army of the Rhine 1919–1923; In China 1927; In Egypt 1935; In

Palestine 1936; Deputy Judge Advocate-General, Middle East 1941–1943; Ordained Deacon and Priest 1952. **Honours:** OBE; CBE 1939. Died 30 July 1958.

BARRETT, Hugh Tremearne (1919) Born 15 November 1901, 4 Coolhurst Road, Crouch End, Hornsey; son of Walter Tremearne Barrett, Merchant Manager of Limited Companies, and Emily Wright. **Tutor(s):** E A Benians. **Educ:** King's School, Bruton; Highgate School; Army College, Heath End, Farnham.

BARRETT, John Henry (1931) Born 21 July 1913, 12 Portland Street, King's Lynn; son of John Ambrose Barrett, Brewer and Soldier, and Evelyn Marion Back; m Ruth Mary; 3 sons (Michael b 1942, Richard b 1947 and Robert b 1951), 1 daughter (Jane b 1941). **Subject(s):** Geography; BA 1935; MA 1952; Honorary MSc (Wales); FIBiol. **Tutor(s):** C W Guillebaud. **Educ:** Eversley School, Southwold; Repton School. **Career:** Warden, Dale Fort Field Centre, Pembrokeshire 1947–1968; Director, Countryside Unit, Broad Haven, Pembrokeshire 1970–1974. **Appointments:** Museum of Wales Council 1965–1990; National Trust Council Executive Conservation Panel 1980–1987; Linnaean Society 1996; Council for the Preservation of Rural Wales 1998. **Awards:** National Park Award 1989; H H Bloomer Award of the Linnean Society (contribution to field biology) 1996; Rural Wales Award by the Council of the Preservation of Rural Wales. **Honours:** MBE. **Publications:** *Some of My Days*; (jointly) *Pocket Guide to Seashore*, Collins, 1958; *Life on the Sea Shore*, Collins, 1974; *Handguide to the Sea Coast*, Collins 1981; *Identifying Flowers Common along the Coast Path*, Pembrokeshire Coast National Park, Barret & Nimmo, 1988; *The Pembrokeshire Coast Path*, Countryside Commission, 1974. Died 8 February 1999.

BARRETT, Laurence Ambrose (1934) Born 28 October 1915, 12 Portland Street, King's Lynn; son of John Ambrose Barrett, Brewer, and Evelyn Marion Back; m Evelyn Mary Maingay; 1 son (Timothy). **Subject(s):** Law; BA 1937. **Tutor(s):** C W Guillebaud. **Educ:** Eversley School, Southwold; Repton School. **Career:** Royal Norfolk Regiment, later POW in Singapore 1939–1945; Solicitor, Francis & Back (later Daynes, Chittock & Back) 1947–1976. **Appointments:** Trustee, Norwich CEYMS; Captain, Norfolk Cricket Club 1951–1954. Died 16 December 1976.

BARRETT, Dr Leonard Middleton (1944) Born 11 June 1927, 9 Humbledon View, Sunderland, County Durham; son of Leonard Wilson Barrett, Licentiate of Dental Surgery, and Margery Ann Middleton; m Lisl Margaret Sussman, 1952; 3 children. **Subject(s):** Natural Sciences/Clinical Medicine; BA 1947; MA 1955; BChir 1955; MB 1955; MRCS (Eng); LRCP (London). **Tutor(s):** S J Bailey; G C L Bertram. **Educ:** Tonstall Preparatory School, Sunderland; Strathallan School, Perthshire. **Career:** Medical Officer, RAMC 1951–1953; GP, Nidderdale, North Yorkshire 1953–1987.

BARRETT, Peter Thomas (1943) Born 27 October 1925, 59 Costa Street, South Bank, Middlesbrough; son of John Thomas Barrett, Police Constable, and Frances May Barratt. **Subject(s):** Natural Sciences; BA 1949; MA 1951. **Tutor(s):** C W Guillebaud. **Educ:** Saltburn Council School; Coatham School, Redcar.

BARRETT, Sidney Thomas (1912) Born 15 December 1892, Crossvale, Alltwalis, Llanfihangel-ar-arth, Cardiganshire; son of Thomas Barrett, Farmer, and Catherine Jones. BA 1915. **Tutor(s):** R P Gregory. **Educ:** Pencader; Taunton Grammar School.

BARRETT, Dr Wilfred Phillips (1924) Born 11 June 1906, Victoria Street, Chatteris, Cambridge; son of John Thomas Barrett, Tailor, and Clara Phillips. **Subject(s):** Modern and Medieval Languages/English; BA 1927; MA 1931; PhD 1932. **Tutor(s):** E A Benians. **Educ:** St Luke's Church of England School, Cambridge; Cambridge and County Boys' School, Cambridge. **Awards:** Wood and Hare Exhibition 1925; Scholarship, SJC 1926; College Prize, SJC 1926; Strathcona Studentship,

SJC 1927. **Publications:** (ed and trans, into English from original Latin and French documents) *The trial of Jeanne d'Arc*, Routledge, 1931; *Chart of Plays, 1584 to 1623*, CUP, 1934. Died January 1978.

BARRETT-GREENE, Alan Henry (1913) Born 10 October 1895, 53 Manor House Road, Newcastle upon Tyne, Northumberland; son of Henry Barrett-Greene, Journalist, and Alice Jane Patterson; m Brenda Bowers, 6 July 1927, Wolstanton Parish Church. BA 1918; MA 1923. **Tutor(s):** E E Sikes. **Educ:** Denstone College Preparatory School; Repton School. **Career:** Behara Land Company, Alexandria, Egypt; 5th Battalion, North Staffordshire Regiment (TF) (final rank of Lieutenant) and Training Reserve Battalion 1915–1918; Assistant County Arm Officer 1941; County Welfare Officer (rank of Lieutenant Colonel) 1942. **Appointments:** County Secretary, Soldiers', Sailors' and Airmen's Families Association 1947. **Honours:** OBE 1969. Died 14 January 1991.

BARRITT, William Vernon (1903) Born 20 March 1884, Brown Street, Colne, Lancashire; son of Isaac Barritt, Schoolmaster, and Alice Wood; m; 1 daughter. **Subject(s):** Natural Sciences; BA 1906; MA 1910. **Tutor(s):** D MacAlister. **Educ:** Nelson Municipal High School. **Career:** Captain, RAMC (TF), WWI; Head Teacher, St Austell County School 1922–1944. Died 1970s.

BARRON, Professor Donald Henry (1937) Born 9 April 1905, Flandreau, South Dakota, USA; son of George E Barron, Farmer, and Mae Luella Reed; m Marie Annette La Courciere, 22 October 1932; 2 daughters (Marie Annette and Donna Marie). MA 1935; ScD 1974; BA (Carleton College) 1928; MS (Iowa) 1929; PhD (Yale) 1932; FRCOG. **Educ:** Carleton College, Minnesota; Yale University; Iowa State College. **Career:** Assistant, Plant Physiology, Iowa State College 1928–1929; Assistant, Biology, Yale University; Instructor, Anatomy, Albany Medical College 1932–1933; National Research Council Fellow 1933–1934, Demonstrator in Anatomy 1935–1937, Lecturer in Anatomy 1937–1940, University of Cambridge; Title B Fellow, SJC 1937–1940; Assistant Professor, Zoology 1940–1942, Associate Professor, Zoology 1942–1943, University of Missouri; Associate Professor, Physiology 1943–1947, Assistant Dean 1945–1948, Professor of Physiology 1947–1969, Yale School of Medicine; Professor of Obstetrics and Gynaecology, University of Florida 1971–1993. **Appointments:** Supervisor in Anatomy and Physiology, SJC 1937–1940; Linacre Lecturer 1966. Died 23 August 1993.

BARRON, John (1944) Born 3 December 1926, 26 Chantrey Road, West Bridgford, Nottingham; son of James Arthur Holder, Printer's Compositor, and Winifred Alliss Lumb; m (1) Hazel Mary Taverner, 1951, (2) Ann; (1) 2 children. **Subject(s):** Natural Sciences/Physics; BA 1947; MA 1951. **Tutor(s):** C W Guillebaud. **Educ:** Henry Mellish Secondary School, Bulwell; Loughborough College School. **Career:** Lecturer, Department of Engineering, University of Cambridge. **Awards:** Scholarship, SJC. Died 2 September 1998.

BARRON, John Reginald Bernard (1938) Born 27 March 1918, 13 Prince's Gate, Knightsbridge, London; son of John Bernard Barron, Company Director and Manager, and Elinor Anne Popham Blyth; m Marjorie. **Tutor(s):** J S Boys Smith. **Educ:** St Aubyn's, Rottingdean; Harrow School; RMA, Woolwich. **Career:** Captain, RE 1939–1943. Died May 1943 (killed in action, Bon Peninsula).

BARR-SIM, Albert Derek (1947) Born 20 January 1922, Llanberis, Westgate Bay Avenue, Westgate-on-Sea; son of Albert Edward Barr-Sim, Group Captain, RAF, and Helen Grant MacMahon. **Tutor(s):** C W Guillebaud. **Educ:** St George's School, Folkestone; Cheltenham College; Old Rectory College, Hawarden. **Career:** POW, Singapore, WWII.

BARRY, William Henry (1929) Born 30 May 1911, Boston, Massachusetts, USA; son of William Henry Barry, Company Director, and Gertrude Martin. **Tutor(s):** J M Wordie. **Educ:** Lycée Janson de Sailly, Paris; Private Tuition, Courtenay Lodge, Sutton Courtenay.

BARTHOLOMEW, Alick Nairne (1949) Born 5 January 1930, Nairne Lodge, Duddingston, Edinburgh; son of John Bartholomew, Cartographic Publisher, and Marie Antoinette Sarolea; m (1) Ann, 1955, (2) Mari, 1994; (1) 1 son (James), 2 daughters (Sara and Kate). **Subject(s):** Geography/Geology; BA 1952; MA 1956. **Tutor(s):** J M Wordie. **Educ:** The Edinburgh Academy; University of Chicago, School of Business Administration. **Career:** National Service Commission, Gordon Highlanders 1948–1949; Senior Editor, US Publishers McGraw Hill, Alfred Knopf, Houghton Mifflin, Macmillan 1953–1971; Director, Viktor Gollancz 1967–1969; Publisher, Turnstone Press 1971–1982; Practising Transpersonal Psychotherapist 1979–1992; Publisher, Gateway Books 1982–1999; Consultant Editor, Literary Agent and Author 2000–. **Appointments:** Member, Scientific and Medical Network. **Publications:** (ed) *Crop Circles: Harbingers of World Change*, 1991; *Kombucha Tea for Your Health and Healing*, 1998; *Hidden Nature*, 2003.

BARTHOLOMEW, Walter (1936) Born 24 March 1918, 15 Russell Street, Batley, Yorkshire; son of William Bartholomew, Lance Corporal, 3rd Battalion, KOYLI, and Elsie Edna Stead. **Subject(s):** History; BA 1939; MA 1947; Postgraduate Diploma of Education, Leeds 1946. **Tutor(s):** J S Boys Smith. **Educ:** Batley Parish Church School; Batley Grammar School. **Career:** Headmaster, Northcliffe School, Shipley 1952–1974; Headmaster, Wrose Brow Middle School 1974.

BARTLETT, Dr Denis James (1944) Born 31 August 1925, 9 Storey's Way, Cambridge; son of Frederic Charles Bartlett, Professor of Experimental Psychology, and Emily Mary Smith, Director of Studies/Research Fellow, Newnham College; m Brigid Catherine Clare Davison, 31 October 1970, SJC Chapel; 1 son (Robin Kerry Charles b 1975), 1 daughter (Wendy Hazel Margaret b 1972). **Subject(s):** Natural Sciences/Clinical Medicine; BA 1947; MA 1953; BChir 1956; MB 1956; PhD 1961. **Tutor(s):** G C L Bertram; S J Bailey. **Johnian Relatives:** son of Frederic Charles Bartlett (1912); brother of Hugh Frederic Bartlett (1941). **Educ:** St Faith's School, Cambridge; Gresham's School, Holt; St Bartholomew's Hospital, London. **Career:** Research Fellow, Institute of Animal Physiology, Babraham 1962–1963; Head, MRC Population Genetics Research Unit, Oxford 1963–1968; Principal Cytogeneticist, Addenbrooke's Hospital, Cambridge 1975–1989. **Appointments:** Council Member, Association of Clinical Cytogeneticists 1982–1984; Editor, *Journal of Reproduction and Fertility* 1968–1975. **Publications:** Various papers, reports and chapters.

BARTLETT, Sir Frederic Charles (1912) Born 20 October 1886, Stow-on-the-Wold, Gloucester; son of William Bartlett, Master Boot Maker, and Temperance Matilda Howman; m Emily Mary Smith, 31 August 1920, All Saints' Church, Cambridge; 2 sons (Hugh and Denis). **Subject(s):** Moral Sciences; BA 1915; MA 1919; BA (London) 1910; MA (London) 1912; Honorary DPhil (Athens) 1937; Honorary DSc (Princeton) 1947; Honorary DPsych (Louvain) 1949; Honorary DSc (London) 1949; Honorary LLD (Edinburgh) 1961; Honorary DSc (Oxford) 1962; Honorary Doctorate (Padua) 1965; FRS 1932. **Tutor(s):** E E Sikes. **Johnian Relatives:** father of Hugh Frederic Bartlett (1941) and of Denis James Bartlett (1944). **Educ:** London University. **Career:** Lupton Fellow 1917–1926, Title B Fellow 1926–1931, Title C Fellow 1931–1952, Title E Fellow 1952–1957, Title D Fellow 1957–1969, SJC; Assistant Demonstrator of Experimental Psychology 1914, Reader in Experimental Psychology and Director of Psychological Laboratory 1922–1931, Professor of Experimental Psychology 1931–1952, University of Cambridge; Honorary Director, MRC Applied Psychology Unit 1966. **Appointments:** Director of Moral Science Studies, SJC 1919–1931; Chairman, Industrial Health Research Board 1948. **Awards:** Baly Medal and Huxley Medal 1943; Longacre Award of American Aero-Medical Association for work on psychology of aviation 1952; Royal Medal of the Royal Society 1952; Gold Medal of International Academy of Aviation Medicine 1964. **Honours:** Kt 1948. **Publications:** *Psychology and Primitive Culture*, 1923; *Pyschology and the Soldier*, 1927; *Remembering: A Study in Experimental and Social Psychology*, 1932; *The Problem of Noise*, 1934; *Political Propaganda*, 1941; *The Mind at Work*

and Play, 1951; *Thinking: An Experimental and Social Study*, 1958; Editor, *British Journal of Psychology*, 1924–1948; more than 200 published papers and many lectures to international societies. Died 30 September 1969.

BARTLETT, Hugh Frederic (1941) Born 25 February 1923, 9 Storey's Way, Cambridge; son of Frederic Charles Bartlett, Professor of Experimental Psychology, Cambridge, and Emily Mary Smith; m Rebecca Dickinson, 5 July 1953, Parish Church, Billericay; 1 step-daughter (Jane). **Subject(s):** Natural Sciences/Mechanical Sciences; BA 1944; MA 1947; Master of Engineering (University of Sydney) 1989; FIREE; MIEE; FIEAust. **Tutor(s):** J M Wordie. **Johnian Relatives:** son of Frederic Charles Bartlett (1912); brother of Denis James Bartlett (1944). **Educ:** Bromsgrove School, Llanwrtyd Wells; St Faith's Preparatory School, Cambridge; Gresham's School, Holt; Gresham's School, Newquay. **Career:** Admiralty Signals Establishment, Haslemere, design of '600' series of ship-borne transmitters for RN 1941–1945; Marconi's Wireless Telegraph Company, Chelmsford 1947–1964; Manager, Transmitter Design Group, and later Manager of Advance Techniques Group, Amalgamated Wireless (Australasia), Sydney, Australia 1964–1976; Assistant Head, Electrical Engineering Department, Papua New Guinea University 1977–1978; Lecturer and Senior Lecturer 1978–1988, Temporary part-time Senior Lecturer 1988–1990, Part-time work for laboratory courses 1990–1996, Electrical Engineering Department, University of Sydney. **Appointments:** President, IREE, Australia 1979–1980; Member, CCIR, Australian National Study Group 4, 10/11; Deputy President 1988, President, IREE, and member of a number of Boards and Committees of the IREE and The IREE Society; Co-editor, *Journal of Electrical and Electronics Engineering*, Australia 1980–1989; Member, a number of government/industry committees including several Australian Preparatory Groups for World Administrative Radio Conferences. **Awards:** Scholarship, SJC.

BARTLETT, John Shirley (1918) Born 13 December 1900, 25 Melford Road, East Dulwich, Surrey; son of Frederick Robert Bartlett, Commercial Clerk, and Maud Elinor Rose. **Subject(s):** Mathematics/Mechanical Sciences; BA 1921. **Tutor(s):** E E Sikes. **Educ:** Goodrich Higher Grade; City of London School. **Career:** Ludlow Corporation, a manufacturer of jute, hemp and flax products 1926–1966. **Awards:** Exhibition, SJC 1918. Died 6 June 1997.

BARTON, Brian Austin (1943) Born 17 January 1925, 46 Peel Street, Hale, Altrincham, Cheshire; son of Arthur Barton, Engineer Grinder, and Ethel Royle. **Subject(s):** Mechanical Sciences; BA 1946; MA 1950. **Tutor(s):** S J Bailey. **Educ:** Parochial Boys' School, Lymm; Lymm Grammar School. **Awards:** Hudson's Bay Scholarship 1948–1949.

BARTON, Frederick Sherbrooke (1914) Born 13 May 1895, 53 Waldeck Road, Carrington, Basford, Nottinghamshire; son of Edwin Henry Barton, Professor of Physics, and Mary Ann Stafford; m Violet Hedges, 20 June 1927, St Laurence's Church, Reading. **Subject(s):** Mathematics/Natural Sciences; BA 1919; MA 1922; MIEE; FInstP. **Tutor(s):** R P Gregory. **Johnian Relatives:** father of John Stafford Barton (1952). **Educ:** Nottingham High School. **Career:** Lieutenant (Technical Officer), RFC then RAF 1914–1918; Adviser on Defence Supplies to the UK High Commissioner in Canada 1941–1946; Principal Director of Electronic Research and Development, Ministry of Supply 1955. **Honours:** CBE 1953. Died 6 June 1969.

BARTON, Dr George Paterson (1948) Born 13 May 1925, 10 Cameron Street, Ponsonby, Auckland, New Zealand; son of Frazer Burnett Barton, Presbyterian Minister, and Jeanie Cordiner Reid; m Margaret Ailsa Begg, Dunedin, 2 January 1948; 3 sons (David Steven b 18 June 1951, John Campbell b 9 December 1952 and Paul Howard b 22 January 1956). **Subject(s):** International Law; PhD 1953; BA (New Zealand) 1948; LLB (New Zealand) 1948; LLM (New Zealand) 1950; Honorary LLD (Victoria) 1987; QC. **Tutor(s):** F Thistlethwaite; G C L Bertram. **Educ:** Ponsonby Primary School, Auckland, New Zealand; Gore Public School,

New Zealand; Gore High School, New Zealand; Otago Boys' High School, New Zealand; Otago University, Dunedin, New Zealand; Victoria University College, Wellington, New Zealand. **Career:** Law Clerk, Crown Law Office 1945; Law Clerk, Webb, Richmond, Swan & Bryan 1945–1947; Law Clerk, J J & Denis McGrath 1947–1948; Barrister: Supreme (now High) Court of New Zealand 1948, Western Samoa 1981, Cook Islands 1984, Sabah 1988, Sarawak 1992; Associate Officer, Human Rights Division, Secretariat, United Nations, New York 1950–1952; Senior Lecturer in English and New Zealand Law, Victoria University College, Wellington, New Zealand 1953–1955; Law Partnership, Morison Spratt Taylor & Co 1955–1959; Senior Lecturer in English and New Zealand Law 1959–1966, Reader in Law 1967–1968, Professor of Jurisprudence and Constitutional 1968–1976, Dean, Faculty of Law 1971–1973, Victoria University of Wellington, New Zealand; Queen's Counsel 1990. **Appointments:** Member, New Zealand Council of Law Reporting 1977–1983; Member, Disciplinary Committee of the New Zealand Law Society 1979–1983; Member, New Zealand Law Practitioners Disciplinary Tribunal 1983–1989; Representative of Commonwealth Lawyers' Association on Advisory Group of Commonwealth Human Rights Initiative 1989–1993; President, Bible Society in New Zealand 1996–1997; one of 8 World Vice-Presidents of the United Bible Societies 1996; Knox College Fellowship 1999. **Awards:** Junior University Scholarship, University of New Zealand 1941; Senior Scholarship in Law, University of New Zealand 1948; Humanitarian Trust Fund Studentship, University of Cambridge 1948–1950; Nuffield Fellowship 1963–1964.

BARTON, James Edward (1918) Born 21 May 1901, Cleveland, Oakley Street, Shrewsbury, Shropshire; son of James Herbert Cooper Barton, Solicitor and Schoolmaster, and Mary Louisa Harries. **Tutor(s):** E E Sikes. **Johnian Relatives:** son of James Herbert Cooper Barton (1887). **Educ:** St Ninian's School, Moffat; Blundell's School.

BARTON, Major John Holland (1933) Born 27 June 1915, Sutton St Edmund, Wisbech, Cambridgeshire; son of Samuel Barton, Schoolmaster, and Marjorie Holland; 4 children. **Subject(s):** Modern and Medieval Languages/Economics; BA 1937; MA 1942. **Tutor(s):** C W Guillebaud. **Educ:** Elementary School, Sutton St Edmund; The Grammar School, Spalding. **Career:** DAQMG, RASC, Singapore 1945–1950; Manager, country estate in Norfolk 1950–1960; Fund-raiser for Warwick University 1960–1964; Administrator, University of Hull 1964–1982.

BARTON, John Percival (1930) Born 18 January 1912, The Vicarage, Fernhurst, Sussex; son of Douglas Reginald Barton, Clerk in Holy Orders, and Eleanor Mabel Lucey. **Subject(s):** English. **Tutor(s):** E A Benians. **Educ:** St Edmund's Preparatory School, Grayshott; Shrewsbury House School, Long Ditton; King's College School, Wimbledon.

BARTRUM, Peter Clement (1930) Born 4 December 1907, 12 Heath Mansions, Hampstead; son of Clement Osborn Bartrum, Worsted Coating Manufacturer, and Kate Isabel Shattock. **Tutor(s):** J M Wordie. **Educ:** St John's House Preparatory School, Hampstead; South Kensington Preparatory School; Clifton College; The Queen's College, Oxford.

BARVE, Sadashiv Govind (1934) Born 27 April 1914, Jasqaon, Satara District, Bombay, India; son of Rao Bahadur Govind Raghunath Barve, Assistant Commissioner, Provincial Civil Service, and Annapurna Bai. **Subject(s):** Economics; BA 1936. **Tutor(s):** C W Guillebaud. **Educ:** Vernacular-Municipal School, Poona; New English School, Poona; Fergusson College, Poona.

BASS, Roger Arthur (1904) Born 24 April 1884, 7 Eastbourne Terrace, Paddington, London; son of Roger Bass, Gentleman, and Thomasina Sarah Sophia Green. **Tutor(s):** D MacAlister. **Educ:** Lindisfarne, Blackheath; St Alban's School. Died 18 May 1939.

BASSETT, Eric George (1933) Born 27 December 1914, 12 Wendron Street, Helston, Cornwall; son of Ervin Bassett, Wholesale Butcher, and Louise Williams. **Subject(s):** Geography/English; BA 1936; MA 1940; Bachelor of Divinity (London) 1957. **Tutor(s):** C W Guillebaud. **Johnian Relatives:** father of Ervin John Bassett (1970). **Educ:** Helston County School; Truro School. **Career:** Senior Lecturer, Faculty of Educational Studies, Portsmouth Polytechnic; RAF (ground staff), twice Mentioned in Despatches 1940–1945.

BASSETT, Stephen James (1919) Born 12 September 1899, Salem Street, Nashville, Tennessee, USA; son of Colin Sharp Bassett, Clerk in Holy Orders, and Mary Caroline Stephen Kane; m Marian Shaw, 17 October 1946, Irstead, Norfolk. **Tutor(s):** E A Benians. **Educ:** Trematon School, Eastbourne; Felsted School. **Career:** RAF 1917–1919.

BATCHELOR, Major Richard Ernest (1943) Born 22 March 1925, 32 Grove Street, New Fletton, Peterborough; son of Walter Richard Batchelor, Master Baker, and Constance Louise Todd Mead; m Dorothy Joan Beckett, 9 April 1951, St Mark's, Peterborough; 1 son (Simon Richard b 6 January 1953). **Subject(s):** Engineering/History/Geography; BA 1948; MA 1950; PGCE 1951. **Tutor(s):** C W Guillebaud; F Thistlethwaite; J M Wordie. **Educ:** All Souls' Elementary School, Peterborough; The King's School, Peterborough. **Career:** RE 1943–1947 (Cadet 1943, Second Lieutenant, Bengal Sappers and Miners 1945, reached rank of Captain); Regular Officer, RAEC 1951–1966; Secondary School Teacher, Harrogate Granby Park School (later Harrogate Granby High School) 1966–1986. **Awards:** Munsteven Exhibition, SJC 1943. **Publications:** *History of Yorkshire*, 1973. Died 31 March 2003.

BATCHELOR, Dr Robert (1942) Born 8 December 1924, 3 Church Hill, Brierley Hill, Staffordshire; son of Samuel Batchelor, Intaglio Engraver, and Florence Ada Jones; m Marion Joyce Stacey, Lambourn, Berkshire; 1 son (David), 2 daughters (Rebecca and Susan). **Subject(s):** Natural Sciences/Physics; BA 1945; MA 1949; PhD Neutron Physics 1967; CPhys; FInstP 1969. **Tutor(s):** C W Guillebaud. **Johnian Relatives:** father of David Anthony Batchelor (1974). **Educ:** Church of England School, Brierley Hill; Mill Street Junior School, Brierley Hill; King Edward VI School, Stourbridge. **Career:** Government Scientist; Scientific Officer, Admiralty Research Laboratory, Teddington 1944–1947; AERE, Harwell 1947–1956 (Senior Scientific Officer 1952–1956); Principal Scientific Officer, AWRE, Aldermaston 1956–1960; Banded Officer, Atomic Energy of Canada, Chalk River, Canada 1958–1959 (sabbatical); Divison Head, European Commission 1973; Commission of the European Communities, Establishment of Geel, Belgium 1973–1976; Superintendent, Ministry of Defence Headquarters, London 1976–1979; Director, Establishment of Geel, Belgium, Commission of the European Communities 1979–1984. **Appointments:** UK Member, European and American Nuclear Data Committee (2 years as Executive Secretary) 1961–1970. **Awards:** Minor Scholarship, SJC 1941; State Scholarship 1942. **Publications:** 23 original publications in scientific journals; 4 contributions to scientific books. Died 20 February 2003.

BATE, William Kendal (1928) Born 2 September 1908, Berg Street, Potchefstroom, Transvaal, South Africa; son of Charles Veale Bate, Newspaper Proprietor and Journalist, and Elizabeth Jane Turpin. **Tutor(s):** C W Guillebaud. **Educ:** Potchefstroom Boys College; Park Town School, Johannesburg; St Andrews College, Grahamstown.

BATES, Eric William (1944) Born 13 September 1926, Westgate Street, Southery, Norfolk; son of Frederick William John Bates, Constructional Engineer, and Marjorie May Osler; m Margaret Dorothy Geraldine Sargent, December 1951; 1 son (Richard John Sargent), 3 daughters (Margaret Anne Sarah, Mary Jane Geraldine and Elizabeth Susan Clare). **Subject(s):** Mechanical Sciences; BA 1947; MA 1951; CEng; FICE. **Tutor(s):** S J Bailey. **Johnian Relatives:** father of Richard John Sargent Bates (1972). **Educ:** Southery Elementary School; King Edward VII School, King's Lynn. **Career:** RE 1947–1949; Sir William Halcrow, Consultants 1949–1953; A E Farr, rising via acquisitions to Executive Director, Bovis Civil Engineering 1953–1980. Died 1 July 1980.

BATES, Captain Kingsley Darwin (1919) Born 24 January 1901, The Willows, Huyton, Lancashire; son of Darwin Bates, Electrical Engineer, and Alice Wilson; m Mary. BA 1922. **Tutor(s):** E E Sikes. **Educ:** Liverpool College for Girls Kindergarten; Colet House School, Rhyl, North Wales; Sedbergh School. **Awards:** Lupton and Hebblethwaite Exhibition, SJC 1919. Died 16 June 1942.

BATES, Martin Vernon (1938) Born 21 September 1919, 43 Azalea Road, Blackburn; son of Percy Vernon Bates, Schoolmaster, and Doris Helen Taylor; m Patricia Birkhead, 28 April 1945, Holmfirth, Yorkshire. BA 1946. **Tutor(s):** J M Wordie. **Educ:** Beach Hill School, Luton; Milton House Preparatory School, Waterloo, Liverpool; Luton Modern School, Luton; Royds Hall School, Huddersfield. **Career:** Lieutenant, RNVR.

BATESON, Professor Gregory (1922) Born 9 May 1904, Merton House, Grantchester, Cambridgeshire; son of William Bateson, Biologist, and Caroline Beatrice Durham; m (1) Margaret Mead, 1936 (div 1950), (2) Elizabeth Summer, 1951 (div 1958), (3) Lois Cammack, 1961; (1) 1 daughter (Mary Catherine b 1939), (2) 2 children, (3) 1 daughter. **Subject(s):** Anthropology/Natural Sciences; BA 1926; MA 1930. **Tutor(s):** B F Armitage. **Johnian Relatives:** grandson of William Henry Bateson (1829); son of William Bateson (1879); brother of Martin Bateson (1918); distant cousin of Stuart Latham Bateson (1920) and of David Stuart Bateson (1974). **Educ:** Charterhouse; Geneva University; University of California Medical School. **Career:** Anthropological fieldwork, New Britain 1927–1928; Lecturer in Linguistics, University of Sydney, Australia 1928; Fieldwork, New Guinea 1929–1930, 1932, 1939; Title A Fellow, SJC 1931–1936; Lecturer, University of Chicago 1934; Fieldwork, Bali 1936–1938; Anthropological Film Analyst, Museum of Modern Art, New York (analysing German propaganda films) 1942–1943; Lecturer, Columbia University 1943–1944; United States Office of Strategic Services, Southeast Asia 1944–1947; Lecturer, China, Burma, Sri Lanka, India 1946–1947; Lecturer, University of California, San Francisco 1948–1949; Research Associate, Psychiatry and Communications, Langley-Porter Clinic, San Francisco 1949–1951; Researcher, University of California Medical School 1949–1950; Ethnologist and Researcher on Alcoholism, Veterans Administration Hospital, Palo Alto, California 1949–1962; Associate Research Director in Ethnology, Communications Research Institute, Virgin Islands 1963–1964; Chief, Biological Relations Division, Oceanic Institute, Waimanalo, Hawaii 1964–1972; Professor of Anthropology and Ethnology, University of California, Santa Cruz 1972–1978; Scholar-in-Residence, Esalen Institute in California 1978–1980. **Appointments:** Guggenheim Fellow 1946–1947; Visiting Professor of Anthropology, New School for Social Research, New York 1946–1947; Visiting Professor, Harvard University 1947–1948; Visiting Professor of Anthropology, Stanford University 1951–1962; Member, Board of Regents, University of California, USA 1976–1978; Fellow, American Association for the Advancement of Science. **Awards:** Scholarship, SJC 1921; Anthony Wilkin Studentship, University of Cambridge 1927; Frieda Fromm-Reichmann Award for Research in Schizophrenia 1962; Career Development Award, National Institute of Mental Health 1964. **Publications:** *Naven*, CUP, 1936; *An Old Temple and a New Myth*, 1937; (with Margaret Mead) *Balinese Character: A Photographic Analysis*, New York Academy of Sciences, 1942; (with Jurgen Ruesch) *Communication: The Social Matrix of Psychiatry*, Norton, 1951; (ed) *Perceval's Narrative*, 1961; *Steps to an Ecology of Mind*, 1972; *Mind and nature: a necessary unity*, 1979; (with Mary Catherine Bateson) *Angels Fear*, Rider, 1988. Died 4 July 1980.

BATESON, Martin (1918) Born 1 September 1899, Norwich House, Panton Street, Cambridge; son of William Bateson, Director, John Innes Horticultural Institute, and Caroline Beatrice Durham. **Subject(s):** Natural Sciences; BA 1921. **Tutor(s):** E E Sikes. **Johnian Relatives:** grandson of William Henry Bateson (1829); son of William Bateson (1879); brother of Gregory Bateson (1922); distant cousin of Stuart Latham Bateson (1920) and of David Stuart Bateson (1974). **Educ:** St Faith's School, Cambridge; Rugby School. **Career:** Cadet, RFC/RAF 1917–1918. **Awards:** Scholarship, SJC 1917. Died 22 April 1922.

BATESON, Stuart Latham (1920) Born 7 July 1898, 30 Rosary Gardens, South Kensington, London; son of Alexander Dingwall Bateson, Barrister, KC, High Court Judge, and Isabel Mary Latham; m Marie Elphinstone Fleming Cullen, 9 June 1923, Alexandria, Dumbartonshire, 1 son (Alec John b 23 January 1925), 1 daughter (Isobel Joan b 8 January 1929). AMICE; AMIEE. **Johnian Relatives:** distant cousin of William Henry Bateson (1829), William Bateson (1879), Martin Bateson (1918) and of Gregory Bateson (1922); grandfather of David Stuart Bateson (1974). **Educ:** RN College, Keyham; Lockers Park, Hemel Hempstead; Rugby School. **Career:** Naval Officer; Commander 1934; Captain 1940–1949 (HMS *Latona* 1941, HMS *Ajax* 1941–1942, HMS *London* 1944–1946); Rear Admiral (L) 1949–1951. **Appointments:** Founder and Director, Royal Navy's Electrical Branch 1946–1951; Rutland County Commissioner for Boy Scouts 1953–1966 (Silver Acorn for specially distinguished services in scouting); Sheriff of Rutland 1953; Deputy Lieutenant for Rutland 1956; Vice Lieutenant for Rutland 1957. **Honours:** CBE 1948; CB 1950. Died 17 April 1980.

BATHE, Denys (1920) Born 11 February 1899, Claughton, Edgar Road, Margate, Kent; son of Henry Keassey Bathe, Surgeon, and Ada Louise Kittoe. **Tutor(s):** E A Benians. **Educ:** RMA, Woolwich; Eastfield House, Ditchling; Cheam School, Sutton; Wellington College. **Career:** Lieutenant, later Lieutenant Colonel, RE 1917. Died 1 February 1954.

BATTCOCK, Whalley Vowe (1930) Born 16 November 1913, 12 Kimbolton Avenue, St Peter, Bedford; son of Grenville Arthur Battcock, Solicitor, and Margaret Hester Vowe Peake. **Subject(s):** Mechanical Sciences; BA 1934. **Tutor(s):** J M Wordie. **Educ:** Rushmon, Bedford; Lambrook, Bracknell; Radley College.

BATTERBURY, George Anthony (1929) Born 22 June 1911, Rokeby, The Downs, Wimbledon, Surrey; son of Geoffrey Richard Batterbury, Schoolmaster, and Margaret Elizabeth Olive. **Subject(s):** Geography; BA 1933; MA 1936. **Tutor(s):** E A Benians. **Educ:** Rokeby, Wimbledon; The King's School, Canterbury. **Awards:** Exhibition, SJC 1928.

BATTING, Frank Merlin (1943) Born 29 July 1925, 58 Highmoor Road, Caversham, Reading; son of Walter John Batting, Bank Cashier, and Kathleen Atkinson; 2 sons (Richard and Nigel), 1 daughter (Carol). **Subject(s):** Mechanical Sciences; BA 1949; MA 1951; MIEE. **Tutor(s):** C W Guillebaud. **Educ:** Marlborough House, Reading; Grenham House, Birchington; St Lawrence College, Courteenhall. **Career:** CU Engineers' Association Register; Standard Telephone and Cables Ltd 1951–1961; Lecturer in Agricultural Engineering, University of Reading 1961–1963; Electronic Design Engineer, various firms, until 1990. **Appointments:** Driver, Meals on Wheels 1990–; Secretary, South Hertfordshire Branch, REMAP Charity 1990–.

BAUMANN, Francis Edgar (1933) Born 12 September 1914, Abberley, Chenies Lane, Ruislip; son of Karl Baumann, Mechanical Engineer, and May Marion Comfort. **Subject(s):** Mathematics/Mechanical Sciences; BA 1936; MA 1946. **Tutor(s):** J M Wordie. **Educ:** Caius House School, Urmston, Manchester; Paxton House, St Neots; Oundle School. **Awards:** Scholarship, SJC.

BAXTER, Arthur Douglas (1927) Born 20 January 1910, 3 Oxford Terrace, Edinburgh, Scotland; son of Arthur Wellesley Baxter, Merchant, and Margaret Rankin MacWhirter; m Elizabeth Annand, 4 October 1968, London. **Tutor(s):** M P Charlesworth. **Educ:** Kingsmead, Seaford; Loretto School, Musselburgh.

BAXTER, Arthur Harold Young (1900) Born 8 January 1879, No 167 Clifton Road, Aston Manor, Birmingham; son of George Baxter, Butcher, and Fanny Elizabeth Smith; m Doris. **Subject(s):** Classics; BA 1903; MA 1907. **Tutor(s):** E E Sikes. **Educ:** Mason University College; King Edward's Grammar School. **Career:** Ordained Deacon 1904. Died 1966.

BAXTER, Jeremy Richard (1949) Born 20 January 1929, 19 Kokine, Rangoon, Burma; son of Andrew Patterson Baxter, East India Merchant, and Anne Winifred Dixon; m Faith Elizabeth Graham, 1965; 2 sons, 1 daughter. **Subject(s):** Classics; BA 1952. **Tutor(s):** R L Howland. **Educ:** Clifton Hall Preparatory School, Midlothian; Sedbergh School. **Career:** Administrative Branch, Home Civil Service; Assistant Principal, Post Office 1952; Assistant Private Secretary to Postmaster-General 1956; Private Secretary to Assistant Postmaster-General 1957; Principal, Post Office 1958; Principal, Treasury 1964; Assistant Secretary, Post Office 1967; Director, Postal Personnel 1971; Director of Personnel, European Commission 1973–1981; Secretary, Post Office 1982–1984.

BAYLEY, Arthur Desmond Charles (1929) Born 13 October 1912, Nowshera, NW Frontier Province, India; son of Arthur Frederick Bayley, Captain, 89th Battery, RFA, and Constance Vera Hall; m (1) Audrey Goldsmith, 1936 (d 1940), (2) Eileen Price, 1944 (d 1990); (2) 3 daughters (Gillian, Joanna Mary d 1954 and Joanna Francis). **Subject(s):** Natural Sciences; BA 1934. **Tutor(s):** J M Wordie. **Johnian Relatives:** cousin of Anthony Hugo Wood (1952). **Educ:** St Alban's School, Lyme Regis; Rugby School. **Career:** Mond Nickel Company Ltd, Clydach, South Wales 1934–1945; Non-ferrous Branch, Allied Control Commission, Germany 1945–1947; Superintendent of Development, Metallurgical Division, The Consolidated Mining and Smelting Company of Canada Ltd, Trail, British Columbia 1947–1954; Assistant Consulting Metallurgist, Anglo-American Corporation of South Africa Ltd, Kitwe, Northern Rhodesia 1954–1958; monitoring world-wide business interests, KC Irvine (Canada), St John New Brunswick; building smelters in Rajistan, Turkey and Chile, UN Industrial Development Organisation. Died 1982.

BAYLEY, Cornelius Felix (1920) Born 16 October 1901, Uppingham Rutland; son of Cornelius Bayley, Chemist, and Isabel Cotterel. **Subject(s):** Natural Sciences; BA 1923; MA 1927. **Tutor(s):** B F Armitage. **Educ:** Uppingham Elementary School; Oakham School. **Awards:** Exhibition, SJC.

BAYLY, Denis Gibson (1944) Born 4 March 1926, 83 Aden Grove, Stoke Newington, London; son of Edwin Arthur Bayly, Cabinet Maker, and Helen Gibson. **Subject(s):** Mathematics; BA 1948. **Tutor(s):** J M Wordie. **Educ:** Oldfield Road Infant School; Church Street Junior School; Owen's School, Islington.

BAZELEY, Henry Paulle (1923) Born 5 May 1905, 11 Morrab Road, Penzance, Cornwall; son of Walter Bazeley, Ship Owner and Merchant, and Catherine Ethel Bennetts. **Subject(s):** Economics; BA 1926. **Tutor(s):** E A Benians. **Educ:** West Cornwall College, Penzance; Wycliffe College, Stonehouse.

BEACALL, Thomas (1900) Born 15 May 1881, Walton on the Hill, Liverpool; son of Thomas Beacall, Schoolmaster, and Eleanor Rebecca Holtaway; m Margaret. **Subject(s):** Natural Sciences; BA 1904. **Tutor(s):** J E Sandys. **Educ:** Crypt Grammar School; Merchant Venturers' Technical College, Bristol. **Career:** Clerk, Patent Office 1904; Superintending Examiner, Patent Office 1939. Died 1952.

BEALE, Cyril (ELMES BEALE) (1907) Born 8 May 1888, Ivanhoe, Westbourne, Holdenhurst, Bournemouth; son of John Elmes Beale, Fancy Goods Dealer, Alderman, Mayor of Bournemouth, and Sarah Hussey Brickell; m Aileen Laura Lee Packer, 1917; 2 sons (John and Ron), 1 daughter (Pam). **Subject(s):** History; BA 1910; MA 1915. **Tutor(s):** J R Tanner. **Johnian Relatives:** father of John Elmes Beale (1939). **Educ:** Weymouth College. **Career:** Beale's 1913; Captain, Royal Berkshire Regiment, Public Schools Battalion; attached Devon Regiment (wounded) (mentioned in Secretary of State's list, for valuable services in connection with the war), WWI; Joint Managing Director, J E Beale Ltd 1919. **Appointments:** Honorary Secretary, Bournemouth Rotary Club; President, Bournemouth Chamber of Trade 1931; President, Bournemouth Rotary Club 1935; Co-opted Member for Westbourne Ward 1942; Member and Vice-Chairman, Bournemouth Education Committee; Chairman, Higher Education Sub-committee; Governor, Bournemouth School for Girls; Governor, Talbot Heath School; Governor, University College, Southampton; Council Member, Southern College of Art. Died 30 January 1945.

BEALE, John Elmes (1939) Born 11 June 1919, Purley, Stirling Road, Bournemouth; son of Cyril Elmes Beale, Director of Private Company, and Aileen Laura Lee Packer. **Tutor(s):** J S Boys Smith. **Johnian Relatives:** son of Cyril Elmes Beale (1907). **Educ:** Wychwood Preparatory School, Bournemouth; Bishop's Stortford College.

BEALE, John Montagu (1924) Born 20 February 1907, Farndale, Alum Chine Road, Bournemouth; son of John Bennett Cole Beale, Fancy Goods Dealer, and Alice Ethel Holmes. **Subject(s):** Economics; BA 1928; MA 1932. **Tutor(s):** E A Benians. **Educ:** Bournemouth Boys' School; Mill Hill School. **Appointments:** Chairman, Bournemouth Bench of Magistrates 1968–1971. Died 9 October 1993.

BEALE, Norman Bewsey (1933) Born 20 October 1914, Bowness, Stirling Road, Bournemouth; son of Harold Hubert Beale, Company Director, and Dorothy Margaret Dyke; m Elaine; 1 son (Nigel), 1 daughter (Vanessa). **Subject(s):** Economics/History; BA 1936; MA 1940. **Tutor(s):** C W Guillebaud. **Educ:** Wychwood School, Bournemouth; Bishop's Stortford College. **Career:** Chairman, J E Beale Ltd, Carlton Hotels Ltd. Died 1 March 1990.

BEARCROFT, John Fortescue (1928) Born 30 March 1908, Victoria Nursing Home, Cairo, Egypt; son of William Fortescue Bearcroft, Engineer, and Rose Constance Tindall. **Subject(s):** Mechanical Sciences; BA 1930. **Tutor(s):** J M Wordie. **Educ:** English School, Cairo; Victoria College, Alexandria; Marlborough House, Reading; Wellington College, Berkshire; RMA, Woolwich. Died 4 September 1932.

BEARD, Arthur John (1912) Born 10 November 1892, Beccles, Suffolk; son of Arthur Willis Beard, Gentleman, and Annie Bella Sims; m Florence Lomax, 11 July 1917, Holy Trinity, Kensington Gore. **Subject(s):** Classics; BA 1918. **Tutor(s):** E E Sikes. **Johnian Relatives:** son of Arthur Willis Beard (1878). **Educ:** Felsted School. **Career:** Captain, Border Regiment (Essex) (wounded twice), WWI; Officer Cadet Battalion, WWI; Wing Commander, RAF 1939–1945; General Manager and Secretary, Liverpool Philharmonic Society 1945. **Honours:** MC 1918.

BEARD, Edwin Cyril (1909) Born 20 May 1891, 2 John Street, St Mary at the Walls, Colchester; son of Reginald Benjamin Beard, Master Ironmonger, and Eleanor Griffin. **Subject(s):** History; BA 1912. **Tutor(s):** J R Tanner. **Educ:** Royal Grammar School, Colchester. **Career:** Articled to the Town Clerk of Colchester; Lieutenant, University Battalion, Essex Regiment (TF) 1914–1917. Died 26 March 1917 (killed in action at Battle of Gaza).

BEARD, Dr Trevor Cory (1938) Born 11 May 1920, 17 Sandhurst Road, Gloucester; son of George Francis Beard, Bookseller, and Katharine Elizabeth Spear; m Joan Emilie Frankau, 2 November 1946, St Marylebone Parish Church; 2 sons, 2 daughters. **Subject(s):** Natural Sciences; BA 1941; MA 1945; BChir 1945; MB 1945; LRCP (London) 1944; MRCS (London) 1944; DObstRCOG 1946; MPH, Berkeley, California 1967; Honorary FRACGP (Australia) 1995. **Tutor(s):** R L Howland. **Educ:** Preparatory School, Gloucester; Crypt Grammar School, Gloucester; Berkeley, California. **Career:** St Bartholomew's Hospital, London 1941–1944; House Physician, St Bartholomew's Hospital, London 1944–1945; Rotating RMO in Medicine, Surgery and Casualty, Hertford County Hospital 1945; RMO (Obstetrics) City Of London Maternity Hospital 1945–1946; Captain, RAMC, Italy and UK 1947–1948; Group General Practice, Broxbourne, Hertfordshire 1949–1950; Solo Private General Practice, Campbell Town, Tasmania 1951–1972; Senior Medical Officer, Community Health Branch, Commonwealth Department of Health, Australia 1972–1985; Consultant to Better Health Commission, Canberra 1985–1986; Research Associate,

Department of Community Health, University of Tasmania 1987–1988; Senior Research Fellow, Menzies Centre for Population Health Research, University of Tasmania 1988–. **Appointments:** Member, British and Australian Medical Association 1944–; Member, Royal Society of Tasmania 1955–1972 and 1987–; Founder, Secretary and Life Member, Tasmanian Hydatids Eradication Council 1962–1996; Elected to California Chapter of Delta Omega 1967; Elected to Convocation, ANU 1977; Honorary Life Member, Australian Veterinary Association 1980; Member High Blood Pressure Research Council of Australia 1982; Founder and Member, Salt Skip Incorporated 1983–1998; Honorary Life Member, International Association of Hydatidosis 1988; Honorary Fellow, Royal Australian College of General Practitioners 1995; Honorary Life Member, Australian Nutrition Foundation 1997; Inaugural Jo Rogers Oration, Australian Nutrition Foundation 1997; Oration, 8th Annual General Meeting, Royal Australian College of General Practitioners. **Awards:** Free Place Scholarship, Crypt Grammar School, Gloucester 1930; Shuter Scholarship to St Bartholomew's Hospital, London 1941; FH Faulding Memorial Prize for research in general practice 1965; Winston Churchill Memorial Fellowship 1966; RM Johnson Memorial Medal, Royal Society of Tasmania 1987. **Honours:** OBE 1966. **Publications:** Numerous articles in learned journals.

BEATON, Sir Cecil Walter Hardy (1922) Born 14 January 1904, 21 Langland Gardens, Finchley Road, Hampstead, Middlesex; son of Ernest Walter Hardy Beaton, Timber Agent, and Merchant, and Esther Sisson. **Tutor(s):** B F Armitage. **Educ:** Heath Mount, Hampstead; St Cyprian's, Eastbourne; Harrow School. **Career:** Photographer, Stage and Costume Designer. **Awards:** Nieman Marcus 'Oscar', 1965, for costume design for *My Fair Lady*. **Honours:** CBE 1957; Kt 1972. **Publications:** *The Gainsborough Girls* (A Play); *Photobiography*, 1951; *Persona Grata*, 1953; *The Glass of Fashion*, 1954; *It Gives me Great Pleasure*, 1955; *Various Diaries*; *My Bolivian Aunt*, 1971. Died 18 January 1980.

BEATTIE, Hugh Ronald Montgomerie (1939) Born 21 May 1916, 59 Morningside Road, Edinburgh; son of Hugh Montgomerie Beattie, Master Mariner, and Elizabeth Dishart. **Tutor(s):** C W Guillebaud. **Educ:** James Gillespie's High School, Edinburgh; University of Edinburgh; Institute of Historical Research and UCL. **Awards:** Colonial Service Probationer. Died 6 February 1961.

BEATTY, Dr Anthony Carlyle (1942) Born 13 August 1923, 1 Northcote Mansions, Hampstead; son of Cyril Carlyle Beatty, Physician, and Constance Hermine Despard. **Subject(s):** Natural Sciences; BA 1948; MA 1966; MB 1952; BChir 1952. Died 1 December 1992.

BEATTY, Dr Richard Alan (1934) Born 26 April 1915, 13 Chilworth Buildings, Stranmillis Road, Belfast; son of Richard Thomas Beatty, Lecturer at Queen's University, Civil Servant, and Evelyn Berrett; m (1) Barbara Gomme, 1941, (2) Margaret Ore, 1953; (1) 1 son, 1 daughter, (2) 1 son, 1 daughter. **Subject(s):** Natural Sciences; BA 1937; MA 1941; PhD 1950; FRSE 1963. **Tutor(s):** C W Guillebaud. **Johnian Relatives:** father of Angus James Beatty (1960) and of Richard Calderwood Beatty (1973). **Educ:** The Mall School, Strawberry Hill, London; St Paul's School, London. **Career:** War service 1940–1946; Senior Principal Scientific Officer, Agricultural Research Council, Honorary Senior Lecturer, University of Edinburgh 1958; Research Fellow, Senior Lalor Fellow, Marine Biology Laboratory, Woods Hole, Massachusetts 1964. **Appointments:** Council of Management and Editorial Board, *Journal of Reproduction and Fertility*, 1959; Editorial staff, *Cytogenetics* 1961; Corrispondente estero della Societa Italiana per il Progresso della Zootecnica 1963. **Awards:** Scholarship, SJC 1936–1937; Keith Prize, Royal Society of Edinburgh 1962. **Publications:** over 100 scientific publications in genetics and reproduction; 2 books.

BEAUCHAMP, Guy Evelyn Louis Beachim (1923) Born 28 April 1904, Norton Hall, Midsomer Norton, Somerset; son of Louis Beachim Beauchamp, Colliery Proprietor, and Janet Trotman. **Tutor(s):** E E Sikes. **Educ:** Malvern College; Private Tuition, Plyhouse, Tisbury.

BEAUMONT, Henry Francis (1947) Born 23 July 1925, 36 New Cross Road, Stamford, Lincolnshire; son of Percy James Beaumont, Clerk in Holy Orders, and Elizabeth Rowbotham; m Anne Bagott Lindfield, 27 July 1953, Gloucester Cathedral. **Subject(s):** Classics; BA 1949; MA 1957. **Tutor(s):** R L Howland. **Educ:** Stamford High School; Stamford School. **Career:** Member of Staff, King's School, Gloucester 1951–1992 (Head of Classics 1951–1985, Housemaster of Dulverton House 1957–1978, Head of Middle School 1975–1985). **Appointments:** Coach, King's School Gloucester Rowing Club 1951–1985; Umpire, Amateur Rowing Association 1963–1995.

BEAUMONT, John Robert (1949) Born 30 March 1929, 336 Upper Richmond Road, Mortlake, Surrey; son of Norman Charles Beaumont, Textile Merchant, and Amy Alexandra Tyler; m Gloria York, 10 December 1955; twin daughters (Nicola and Fiona). **Subject(s):** Agriculture; BA 1952; MA 1961. **Tutor(s):** R L Howland. **Educ:** St Martin's Preparatory School; Shepperton School; Charterhouse. **Career:** Second Lieutenant, The Royal Regiment of Artillery, Assistant Adjutant, 57th Bhurtpore Mountain Mule Battery 1947–1949; PA to Sir George Stapledon, Dunns Farm Seeds 1952–1954; Sales and Marketing Manager, Plastics Division, Distillers Co Ltd 1954–1966; Sales and Marketing Manager, Plastics Division, Dow Chemical 1966–1969; Sales and Marketing Manager, British American Tobacco 1969–1973; Sales and Marketing Director, Shires Ltd, Chloride Group 1973–1976; Sales and Marketing Director, Pressalit UK 1977–1980; Agent, Building Products 1980–2001; Author 2001. **Publications:** Books on Bosham and spritsail barges.

BEAUMONT, Kenneth (1930) Born 17 August 1913, 31 Upper Green Lane, Brighouse, Yorkshire; son of Joe Beaumont, Builders Material Merchant, and Edith Annie Oates. **Subject(s):** Law; BA 1934; MA 1944; LLB 1935. **Tutor(s):** C W Guillebaud. **Educ:** Miss Bottomley's Private School, Brighouse; St Andrew's School, Brighouse; Ashville College, Harrogate. Died 1 December 1996.

BEAUMONT, William Hugh (1944) Born 10 August 1926, 27 Welbeck Street, London; son of William Beaumont, Physician, and Winifred Beaton; m Elizabeth Cutts, 28 April 1962, St Helen's Church, Clifford Chambers, Warwick; 2 sons (Richard Mark and Timothy John), 1 daughter (Amanda Claire). **Subject(s):** Natural Sciences; BA 1947; MA 1951; DipAgr 1948. **Tutor(s):** C W Guillebaud. **Educ:** University College School; Cranbrook School; Northern Polytechnic, London. **Career:** Research Assistant, Unilever 1948–1953; Technical Adviser, Cooper Technical Bureau 1953–1960; Head, Nutrition Research Unit, Wellcome Trust 1960–1972; Pig Farmer 1972–1990. **Appointments:** Consultant Secretary to British Association of Feed Supplement and Additive Manufacturers Ltd until 2002. **Publications:** 'Vitamin A Status of Beef Cattle', *Veterinary Record*, 1963; 'The Use of the Anabolic Agent Zeranol as a Growth Promoter for Cattle', *Veterinary Record*, 1974.

BEAVAN, Dr John Allan (1926) Born 29 January 1908, 9a Albany Road, Cardiff, Glamorgan; son of Thomas Albert Beavan, Architect, and Emilia Hargrave Johnson. **Subject(s):** Mathematics/Mechanical Sciences; BA 1930; MA 1942. **Tutor(s):** J M Wordie. **Educ:** Llansamor Court School, Cardiff; Monkton House School, Cardiff; The High School, Cardiff. **Awards:** Exhibition, SJC 1926.

BECKETT, John Norton (1901) Born 17 June 1882, 3 Piper's Row, Wolverhampton, Staffordshire; son of John Fellows Beckett, Leather Merchant, and Clara Norton. **Subject(s):** Mathematics/Natural Sciences; BA 1904; MA 1919. **Tutor(s):** D MacAlister. **Educ:** Monmouth Grammar School. **Career:** Civil Service 1905. Died 6 July 1956.

BECKETT, Peter Henry Robert Osborne (1937) Born 18 May 1917, Grosvenor House Nursing Home, Southampton; son of Osborne Beckett, Malayan Civil Service, and Frances Pennefather Rowe. **Subject(s):** Mechanical Sciences; BA 1939. **Tutor(s):** J S Boys Smith. **Educ:** St Cuthbert's, Malvern; Wellington College; RMA, Woolwich. Died 1 January 1987.

BECKLEY, Verey Alfred (1914) Born 3 September 1893, Bloemfontein, South Africa; son of William Henry Beckley, Assistant Market Master, and Georgina Horne Antill. **Subject(s):** Natural Sciences; BA 1916; MA 1920. **Tutor(s):** R P Gregory. **Johnian Relatives:** father of Verey Robert Sidley Beckley (1949). **Educ:** Boys High School, Pretoria; Boshof Government School; Grey College School, Bloemfontein, South Africa; Grey University College, Bloemfontein, South Africa. **Career:** Lieutenant, RGA 1914. **Awards:** Exhibition, SJC 1916. **Honours:** MC.

BECKLEY, Verey Robert Sidley (1949) Born 23 May 1924, Grootfontein, Middleburg, Cape Province, South Africa; son of Verey Alfred Beckley, Agricultural Chemist, and Doris Witherington Sidley. **Tutor(s):** G C L Bertram. **Johnian Relatives:** son of Verey Alfred Beckley (1914). **Educ:** Parklands School, Nairobi; King's School, Worcester; Prince of Wales School, Nairobi. **Career:** Colonial Service Course; Agricultural Officer, Kenya 1950. Died 22 September 1953.

BEER, Professor John Bernard (1948) Born 31 March 1926, 69 Longspring, Watford, Hertfordshire; son of John Bateman Beer, Civil Servant, Ministry of Labour, and Eva Chilton; m Professor Dame Gillian Patricia Kempster (née Thomas), 7 July 1962, St Benet's Church, Cambridge; 3 sons (Daniel b 13 December 1965, Rufus b 22 February 1968 and Zachary b 3 August 1971). **Subject(s):** English/Natural Sciences; BA 1950; MA 1955; PhD 1957; LittD 1995; FBA 1994. **Tutor(s):** F Thistlethwaite; A G Lee. **Educ:** Norvic Preparatory School; Callowland Junior School; Watford Grammar School. **Career:** Title A Fellow, SJC 1955–1958; Lecturer, University of Manchester 1958–1964; Fellow 1964–1993 (Emeritus 1993), Peterhouse, Cambridge; Lecturer 1964–1978, Reader in English Literature 1978–1987, Professor of English Literature 1987–1993 (Emeritus 1993), University of Cambridge. **Appointments:** British Academy Chatterton Lecturer 1964; Visiting Professor, University of Virginia 1975; Leverhulme Emeritus Fellow 1995–1996, University of Cambridge. **Publications:** *Coleridge the Visionary*, 1959; *The Achievement of E M Forster*, 1962; (ed) *Coleridge's Poems*, Everyman, 1962; *Blake's Humanism*, Manchester University Press, 1968; *Blake's Visionary Universe*, Manchester University Press, 1969; (ed) *Coleridge's Variety: Bicentenary Studies*, Macmillan, 1974; *Coleridge's Poetic Intelligence*, Macmillan, 1977; *Wordsworth and the Human Heart*, Macmillan, 1978; *Wordsworth in Time*, Faber, 1979; (ed) *E M Forster: A Human Exploration*, Macmillan, 1979; (ed) *Aids to Reflection* (Collected Coleridge), Princeton University Press, 1993; *Romantic Influences: Contemporary – Victorian – Modern*, Macmillan, 1994; (ed) *Questioning Romanticism*, John Hopkins University Press, 1995; *Providence and Love: Studies in Wordsworth, Channing, F W H Myers, George Eliot and Ruskin*, OUP, 1998; (ed) *Coleridge's Writings on Religion and Psychology*, Palgrave, 2002.

BEERS, Robert Stewart Ross (1948) Born 20 February 1928, 25 Roxborough Avenue, Harrow, Middlesex; son of Herbert Stewart Beers, Attaché, American Embassy, Washington, and Winsome Mary Ross; m Margaret Eve Perry, 4 February 1956, Tillington Church, West Sussex; 2 sons (Melville Robert Ross b 10 August 1958 and Clive David George b 30 June 1961). **Subject(s):** Archaeology and Anthropology/English Literature; BA 1950; MA 1978. **Tutor(s):** C W Guillebaud. **Educ:** St John's School, Pinner; Christ's Hospital. **Career:** RAF; District Commissioner, HM Overseas Civil Service, Sierra Leone 1952–1961; Deputy Registrar, General Medical Council 1962–1988; Administrative Adviser, Medical Protection Society 1988–1993.

BEEVERS, Thomas (1938) Born 20 November 1919, 8 Birch Grove, Acton; son of Thomas Beevers, Bank Manager, and Alice Maude Sadler. **Subject(s):** Modern and Medieval Languages; BA 1947; MA 1949. **Tutor(s):** C W Guillebaud. **Educ:** Tonbridge School; Newcastle Preparatory School. **Career:** Lieutenant, 1st Airborne Division, WWII; Assistant Master, Loretto School 1949.

BEGGS, Dr Robert David Irving (1929) Born 30 July 1911, Carling Avenue, Ottawa, Ontario, Canada; son of William Beggs, Physician and Surgeon, and Katharine Irving. BA 1932; BChir 1938; MB 1938; FRCS

1946. **Tutor(s):** M P Charlesworth. **Educ:** Ashbury College, Ottawa; Seafield Park, Farnham; The Wells House, Malvern; Loretto School, Musselburgh.

BEHARRELL, George David (1940) Born 9 May 1922, Enfield Nursing Home, Durban, Natal, South Africa; son of George Edward Beharrell, Sales Director, and Barbara Waddington. **Subject(s):** Mechanical Sciences; BA 1944. **Tutor(s):** S J Bailey. **Educ:** Packwood, Hockley Heath; Uppingham School. **Career:** Overseas Engineering Department, Dunlop 1946–1949; Engineer (later General Manager), Dunlop Rim and Wheel Company 1949–1966; General Works Manager, Dunlop UK Tyre Group Factory 1966.

BEHREND, Stanley William Emile (1927) Born 15 November 1908, Calcutta, India; son of Ernest Stanley Behrend, Mercantile Assistant, Graham's Trading Company, and Fanny Eliza Ward. **Tutor(s):** C W Guillebaud. **Educ:** St Paul's School, Darjeeling, India; Felsted School.

BEITH, Gilbert (1901) Born 12 May 1882, Belfield Lodge, Fallowfield, Rusholme, Lancashire; son of John Alexander Beith, Merchant, and Janet Fleming. BA 1904; Passed Final Exam, Law Society 1908. **Tutor(s):** D MacAlister. **Johnian Relatives:** brother of John Hay Beith (1895). **Educ:** Fettes College, Edinburgh. Died 21 July 1960.

BELGRAVE, Arthur Cyril (1903) Born 15 December 1884, Waterloo Street, South Cummingsburg, Georgetown, Demerara; son of Henry de Castro Belgrave, Municipal Accountant, and Emelia Lockheath McCreath; m Guitza; 3 sons (Derek, Cedric and Raymond), 1 daughter (Nadine). **Subject(s):** Mathematics/Natural Sciences; BA 1906. **Tutor(s):** J R Tanner; C E Graves. **Educ:** Queen's College, Demerara. **Career:** Civil Servant, Post Office 1908. Died 13 October 1955.

BELGRAVE, Herbert Alan (1913) Born 9 October 1893, Bridgetown, Barbados; son of George Gordon Belgrave, Merchant, and Mary Anne Hinds. **Subject(s):** Natural Sciences. **Tutor(s):** R P Gregory. **Educ:** Harrison College, Barbados; Queen's Royal College, Trinidad.

BELGRAVE, William Norman Cummins (1909) Born 17 April 1891, Fontabelle, Barbados, West Indies; son of Joshua Cummins Forde Belgrave, Merchant's Clerk, and Rhoda Evelyn. **Subject(s):** Natural Sciences; BA 1913; Diploma in Agriculture 1912. **Tutor(s):** L H K Bushe-Fox. **Educ:** Harrison College, Barbados. **Career:** Assistant Mycologist to Government of Federated Malay States 1915; Head, Division of Soil and Plant Physiology, Federated Malay States 1927; Assistant to Director, Agricultural Department, Federated Malay States 1930; Division of Agricultural Chemistry 1930; Chief Research Officer 1931. **Appointments:** Delegate to Second Imperial Mycological Conference 1929. Died 13 October 1955.

BELL, George Alexander (1925) Born 17 September 1906, Oak Cottage, Dean Row, Wilmslow, Cheshire; son of Joseph Bell, Chartered Accountant, and Ethel Harker; m Joyce Millicent Jennison Byrom; 1 son (Christopher John b 24 January 1939). **Subject(s):** Classics/Law; BA 1929; MA 1934. **Tutor(s):** E E Sikes. **Johnian Relatives:** brother of Joseph Howard Bell (1922); father of Christopher John Bell (1957). **Educ:** Beechfield School, Wilmslow; The Ryleys School, Alderley Edge; Sedbergh School; Princeton University. **Awards:** Honorary Exhibition, SJC 1924; Open Exhibition 1925; Henry P Davison Scholarship, Princeton University 1927. **Career:** Bletchley Park, WWII. Died 2 October 1986.

BELL, Sir (George) Raymond (1934) Born 13 March 1916; son of William Bell, Head of Commerce and Banking, Bradford Technical College, and Christabel Appleton; m Joan Elizabeth Coltham, 30 October 1944; 2 sons, 2 daughters. **Subject(s):** History/Law; BA 1937; MA 1960. **Tutor(s):** J S Boys Smith. **Johnian Relatives:** brother of William Rupert Graham Bell (1939). **Educ:** Bradford Grammar School. **Career:** Assistant Principal, Civil Service 1938; Ministry of Health 1938–1939;

Transferred to Treasury 1939; Lieutenant, RNVR 1941–1944; Treasury Representative on the staff of the British High Commissioner, Ottawa 1945–1948; Assistant Secretary 1951; Counsellor, UK Permanent Delegation, Brussels Conference 1961–1962 and 1970–1972; Deputy Secretary, HM Treasury 1966–1972; Vice-President, European Investment Bank 1973–1978. **Appointments:** Secretary (Finance), Office of HM High Commissioner for the UK in Canada 1945–48; Honorary Vice-President, European Investment Bank 1978. **Awards:** Scholarship, SJC 1936–1937. **Honours:** CB 1967; KCMG 1973. Died 18 February 2002.

BELL, George Trafford (1930) Born 9 March 1913, 205B Bluff, Yokohama, Japan; son of George Herbert Bell, Merchant, and Veronica Jessie Bell. **Subject(s):** Natural Sciences; BA 1934. **Tutor(s):** C W Guillebaud. **Educ:** The Ryleys School, Alderley Edge; Sedbergh School. Died 5 May 1984.

BELL, Gordon John (1942) Born 27 November 1923, Hardy Cottages, Coventry Road, Hinckley; son of John Bell, Company Director, and Ada Mary Jenkins; m Kaia Ringness, 1953; 2 sons, 1 daughter. **Subject(s):** Natural Sciences; BA 1948; MA 1971. **Tutor(s):** C W Guillebaud. **Educ:** St Cecilia's Private School, Hinckley; Coventry Preparatory School; Hinckley Grammar School. **Career:** Director, Royal Observatory, Hong Kong; Commanding Officer, Hong Kong AAF 1951–1965; Scientific Adviser, Hong Kong Government 1981. **Appointments:** JP; Honorary Commodore 1977; Honorary Fellow, Hong Kong Institute of Engineers. **Honours:** OBE. Died 6 May 1981.

BELL, Henry Esmond (1931) Born 10 January 1913, 40 Haslingden Drive, Manningham, Bradford; son of Harry Bryen Bell, Bank Manager, and Agnes Cockburn Dobie; m Edith Margaret McDowell, 1937; 1 son, 1 daughter. **Subject(s):** History; BA 1934; MA 1938. **Tutor(s):** E A Benians. **Educ:** Bradford Girls' Grammar School Kindergarten; Bradford Grammar School. **Career:** Temporary Assistant Keeper, Public Record Office 1935–1937; Lecturer in History, Newcastle Division, University of Durham 1937–1940; 10th Hussars, Army Education Corps; Staff Officer, Civil Affairs 1940–1946 (attached to Monuments, Fine Arts and Archives sub-commission for Italy 1944–1946); Fellow 1946–1964, Tutor and Librarian 1958, New College, Oxford; Visiting Professor, University of South Carolina 1959. **Awards:** Scholarship, SJC. **Publications:** *Italian Archives During the War and at its Close,* 1947; *Introduction to the History of the Court of Wards and its Liveries,* 1953. Died 27 August 1964.

BELL, Hubert Graham (1947) Born 18 December 1919, Nursing Home, Bodenham Road, Hereford; son of Harry Graham Bell, Automobile Engineer, and Grace Effingham Laughton. **Subject(s):** Mechanical Sciences; BA 1949; MA 1954. **Tutor(s):** R L Howland. **Educ:** Westminster Cathedral Choir School; Bristol Grammar School; RMA, Woolwich. **Awards:** Special Prize from New York Society of Model Engineers 1948 (for Radio Controlled working model of 'J' Class destroyer).

BELL, Ivan Crosland (1919) Born 1 April 1899, Huntly, Herschel Road, Cambridge; son of Walter George Bell, Fellow and Assistant Tutor, Trinity Hall, Cambridge, and Constance Mary Westlake; m Mitsuko Ishiwara, Tokyo, Japan, 1945; 1 son (John Bertrand Walter b 1945), 2 daughters (Constance Mabel Hilda b 1946 and Betty Margaret b 1951). **Subject(s):** Mathematics/Moral Sciences; BA 1922. **Tutor(s):** E E Sikes. **Educ:** Preparatory School, Colwall; Leighton Park School, Reading; King's College Choir School, Cambridge. **Career:** Farmer (for War effort) 1918–1919; Master, Batley Grammar School 1923–1929; Teacher of English in various schools and Universities in Japan (first position was at the First High School, Tokyo) 1929–1976. **Honours:** Order of the Rising Sun, Japan 1976. Died 25 July 1983.

BELL, Joseph Howard (1922) Born 27 February 1905, Oak Cottage, Dean Row, Wilmslow, Cheshire; son of Joseph Bell, Chartered Accountant, and Ethel Harker. BA 1926. **Tutor(s):** E Cunningham. **Johnian Relatives:** brother of George Alexander Bell (1925); uncle of

Christopher John Bell (1957). **Educ:** The Ryleys School, Alderley Edge; Sedbergh School. **Career:** Chartered Accountant; Apprentice to Mather and Platt 1927.

BELL, Canon Richard Eardley Thomas (1902) Born 3 December 1882, 48 Port Street, Bengeworth, Worcestershire; son of James Leonard Bell, Merchant, and Isabella Frances Bateman. **Subject(s):** Classics; BA 1905; MA 1909. **Tutor(s):** D MacAlister. **Educ:** St Paul's School, London. **Career:** Ordained Deacon 1906; Curate, West Ham 1906–1917; Ordained Priest 1907; Vicar, St Mary, Birkenhead 1920–1927; Vicar, St John with St Stephen, Reading 1927–1947; Vicar, Nettlebed 1947; Rural Dean, Henley 1950. Died 18 October 1975.

BELL, Thomas Edward (1946) Born 5 September 1921, Silkstone Common, Barnsley, Yorkshire; son of William Bell, Police Constable, and Florence Annie Shaw. **Subject(s):** Modern and Medieval Languages; BA 1947; MA 1958. **Tutor(s):** C W Guillebaud. **Educ:** Rawcliffe Bridge Council School; Goole Grammar School; Keighley Grammar School. **Career:** Sub-Lieutenant, RNVR.

BELL, Thomas Osmond (1905) Born 6 February 1888, Hay House, Earls Colne, Essex; son of Thomas Sampson Bell, Farmer, and Agnes Barnard. **Subject(s):** Natural Sciences; BA 1908. **Tutor(s):** D MacAlister. **Educ:** The Grammar School, Earls Colne. **Career:** Lecturer in Botany, School of Agriculture, Potchefstroom, Transvaal 1909; Captain, Essex Regiment, WWI; Farmer, Earls Colne, Essex until 1965. **Appointments:** Chairman, Earls Colne Parish Council; Chairman of Governors, Earls Colne Grammar School. Died 22 December 1965.

BELL, William Rupert Graham (1939) Born 29 May 1920, 22 Sydenham Road, Stockton-on-Tees, Durham; son of William Bell, Head of Banking and Commerce, Bradford Technical College, and Christabel Appleton; m Molly Bolton, 1950; 2 daughters. **Subject(s):** Economics; BA 1947; MA 1985. **Tutor(s):** C W Guillebaud. **Johnian Relatives:** brother of George Raymond Bell (1934). **Educ:** Bradford Grammar School. **Career:** RA (Mentioned in Despatches) 1940–1945; Assistant Principal 1948–1949, Principal 1949–1959, Assistant Secretary 1959–1966, Ministry of Fuel and Power; Under-Secretary, Ministry of Power 1966–1970; DTI 1970–1972; Deputy Principal, Civil Service College 1972–1975; Under-Secretary, Department of Industry 1975–1980. **Honours:** CB 1978. Died 6 October 1996.

BELLIS, Bertram Thomas (1948) Born 4 May 1927, St John's Manse, Seaton Road, Arbroath, Forfarshire; son of Thomas John Bellis, Methodist Minister, and Mary Ann Hine; m Joan Healey, 1952; 2 sons (Robert John b 1954 and Peter Timothy b 1957). **Subject(s):** Mathematics; BA 1951; MA 1955; FIMA 1964; FRSE 1972. **Tutor(s):** J M Wordie. **Johnian Relatives:** father of Peter Timothy Bellis (1975). **Educ:** Central Elementary School, Kendal; Westwood Preparatory School, Bath; Kingswood School, Bath. **Career:** Naval Rating 1946–1948; Mathematics Master, Rossall School 1951–1955; Head, Mathematics Department and Housemaster, Highgate School 1955–1965; Headmaster, Daniel Stewart's College, Edinburgh 1965–1972; Principal, Daniel Stewart's and Melville College 1972–1975; Headmaster, The Leys School, Cambridge 1975–1986. **Appointments:** Schoolmaster Fellow, Balliol College, Oxford 1963; Founding Director, Mathematics in Education and Industry Schools Project 1963–1965; Chairman, Scottish Education Department Committee on Computers and the Schools (reports: 1969 and 1972); President, Mathematical Association 1971–1972; Council Member, Institute of Mathematics and its Applications 1975–1979; Member, Educational Research Board, SSRC 1975–1980; Governor, Queenswood School 1980–1992; Governor, St John's College School 1981–1986. **Awards:** Exhibition, SJC 1945.

BELLMAN, The Revd Alexander Frederick (1909) Born 27 October 1890, The Vicarage, Staplefield, Cuckfield, Sussex; son of Arthur Frederick Bellman, Clerk in Holy Orders, and Ada Fanny Barnes. BA 1912; MA 1919. **Tutor(s):** E E Sikes. **Educ:** Haileybury College; Cambridge Clergy

Training School. **Career:** Deacon 1913; Curate, Dewsbury Moory 1913–1919; Priest 1914; Temporary CF 1916–1919; Curate, Thornhill Lees, in charge of Savile Town 1919–1923; Honorary Chaplain 1923; Vicar, Birkenshaw with Hunsworth 1923–1936; Vicar, Almondsbury 1936–1940; Honorary Canon, St Cuthbert, Wakefield Cathedral 1949. Died 8 May 1972.

BELSHAM, Ian Rollo Bernard (1944) Born 20 October 1926, St Mary's Road, Liss, Petersfield; son of Sydney James Belsham, Insurance Official, and Margaret Helen Read. **Tutor(s):** J M Wordie. **Educ:** St Norbert's Preparatory School; The King's School, Canterbury. **Appointments:** RAF Cadet, SJC.

BELSHAW, Dr Stanley Ainscow (1919) Born 30 March 1897, 52 Grey Mare Lane, Bradford, North Manchester; son of Thomas Belshaw, Clerk in Holy Orders, and Clarinda Ainscow; m Gladys. BA 1921; MRCS 1925; LRCP 1925. **Tutor(s):** E A Benians. **Johnian Relatives:** son of Thomas Belshaw (1887). **Educ:** Hoylake College; Dean Close School, Cheltenham. **Career:** Physician and Honorary Anaesthetist, Hertford County Hospital. Died 24 December 1989.

BENCE, Ronald Ivor (1926) Born 12 February 1908, 19 Rosevine Road, Wimbledon, Surrey; son of Edgar Henry Bence, Mechanical Engineer, and Alice Eva Frances Tansley. **Tutor(s):** M P Charlesworth. **Educ:** King Edward's School, Birmingham.

BENDER, Eugene Jacob (1945) Born 8 October 1923, St Louis, Missouri, USA; son of Ben Bender, Policeman, and Eva Levin; m Rowena Bloomberg (d 1971); twin daughters (Karen and Kathy). BA (Illinois) 1944; MA (Illinois) 1948. **Tutor(s):** C W Guillebaud. **Educ:** East St Louis High School, Illinois, USA; University of Illinois, Urbana, USA. **Career:** US Army, European Theater 1944–1946; Development Work, Social Service Organisations 1948–1986. **Publications:** *Military Holsters of World War II*, Taylor Publishing Company, 1984; *Luger Holsters and Accessories of the 20th Century*, Taylor Publishing Company, Dallas, 1992.

BENIANS, Hubert Michael (1943) Born 2 September 1925, London; son of Hubert Joseph Benians, Architect, and Eileen Theodora Dodd; m Rachael Clarke, 1950, Petersfinger, Salisbury; 3 sons (Timothy Michael b 1953, Mark Richard b 1956 and Peter Warren b 1959). **Subject(s):** RE Short Course; BSc Eng (London); CEng; MIMechE. **Tutor(s):** C W Guillebaud. **Johnian Relatives:** nephew of Ernest Alfred Benians (1899); cousin of Richard Gore Benians (1934), Martin Ackland Benians (1938) and of Peter Roy Benians (1942); brother of Robin Christopher Benians (1947). **Educ:** Marlborough House School, Hawkhurst; Eastbourne College; Regent Street Polytechnic, London. **Career:** Graduate Apprentice 1953, Technical Export Sales 1955, D Napier & Son Ltd, Acton; Autoklean & Beldam Ltd, Hounslow 1966; Guest Industrials Ltd, London 1966; Founder, Ben Implex (GB) Ltd, Denmead, Hampshire 1980.

BENIANS, The Revd Martin Ackland (1938) Born 16 September 1919, 26 Mount Park Road, Ealing; son of Ernest Alfred Benians, Master, SJC, and Sylvia Mary Dodd; m Elisabeth Grant Matthews, 1949; 1 son (Andrew Hamilton), 1 daughter (Catherine Lindsay). **Subject(s):** History; BA 1941; MA 1945; Theology, AM Course, Wesley House; Ridley Hall, Short Course 1959. **Tutor(s):** J S Boys Smith; S J Bailey. **Johnian Relatives:** son of Ernest Alfred Benians (1899); cousin of Richard Gore Benians (1934), Peter Roy Benians (1942), Hubert Michael Benians (1943) and of Robin Christopher Benians (1947). **Educ:** King's College Choir School, Cambridge; The Leys School, Cambridge. **Career:** Methodist Ministry 1944–1959; Second Minister, Frome, Somerset 1944–1947; Chaplain, Culford School, Bury St Edmunds and East Anglian Girls' School 1947–1949; Minister Ebenezer Circuit, Newcastle, Staffordshire 1949–1955; Ridley Hall, Cambridge 1958; Ordained Deacon 1959; Curate, St George's Headstone, Harrow 1959–1962; Ordained Priest 1960; Rector, Salhouse and Rackheath

Parishes, Norwich Diocese 1962–1989; Officiated, All Saints Church, Upper Sheringham 1992–2000; Voluntary Chaplain, Norwich Cathedral. **Appointments:** Member, Norfolk Railway Society and Gauge 'O' Guild; Norwich Branch, Prayer Book Society.

BENIANS, Peter Roy (1942) Born 5 March 1924, 43 Brixton Hill, London; son of Percy Stephen Benians, Schoolmaster, and Dorothy May Victoria Johnson; m Edna Gladys Clark. **Subject(s):** Natural Sciences; BA 1945; MA 1949; CertEd (Cantab) 1947. **Tutor(s):** C W Guillebaud. **Johnian Relatives:** nephew of Ernest Alfred Benians (1899); cousin of Martin Ackland Benians (1938), Richard Gore Benians (1934), Hubert Michael Benians (1943) and of Robin Christopher Benians (1947). **Educ:** Bethany House School, Goudhurst; St George's School, Tunbridge Wells. **Career:** Schoolmaster; Assistant Master 1948–1951, Headmaster, Senior Department 1951–1957, Principal 1957–1965, St George's School, Tunbridge Wells, Kent; Assistant Master, Stowmarket Grammar School 1965–1968; Assistant Master 1968–1976, Deputy Head 1976–1982, Head 1983, Trueloves School, Ingatestone, Essex (Shaftesbury Society School for Physically Handicapped); Brentwood School, Essex 1983–1986.

BENIANS, Dr Richard Gore (1934) Born 4 June 1916, The Mount, Goudhurst, Kent; son of Thomas Herbert Cecil Benians, Physician, and Amy Frances Rogers; m Edith Florence; 3 children. **Subject(s):** Natural Sciences; BA 1937; MA 1941; MB 1940; BChir 1940; MD 1951; MRCP 1947; FRCP (London) 1971. **Tutor(s):** R L Howland. **Johnian Relatives:** nephew of Ernest Alfred Benians (1899); cousin of Martin Ackland Benians (1938), Peter Roy Benians (1942), Hubert Michael Benians (1943) and of Robin Christopher Benians (1947). **Educ:** Hilden Oaks, Tonbridge; Yardley Court Preparatory School, Tonbridge; Tonbridge School. **Career:** Captain, RAMC, Africa and Italy 1941–1946; Assistant Chief Physician, Bradford Chest Clinic 1954–1959; Assistant Geriatrician, Bradford Hospital Group 1954–1959; Consultant Geriatrician and Physician, Southend-on-Sea 1959–1981. **Awards:** Prize in Psychological Medicine 1938–1939. Died 27 December 2003.

BENIANS, Dr Robin Christopher (1947) Born 18 June 1929, 6 Anglesea Terrace, Hastings, Sussex; son of Hubert Joseph Benians, Architect, and Eileen Theodora Dodd. **Subject(s):** Natural Sciences; BA 1950; BChir 1953; MB 1954; MA 1954; MD 1974. **Tutor(s):** R H Winfield; G C L Bertram. **Johnian Relatives:** nephew of Ernest Alfred Benians (1899); cousin of Richard Gore Benians (1934), Martin Ackland Benians (1938) and of Peter Roy Benians (1942); brother of Hubert Michael Benians (1943). **Educ:** The Grove, Goudhurst; Marlborough House, Hawkhurst; Canford School. **Career:** Consultant in child, adolescent and family psychiatry, Luton Child Guidance Clinic 1964–1971, then Ealing Child and Family Consultation Service 1971–1989; part-time Consultant to Barnardo's 1964–1996; part-time locum consultant in NHS, mainly medico-legal 1989–. **Appointments:** Honorary Secretary, Wandsworth Association for Mental Health 1971–1986. **Awards:** Van Heyden de Lancey Medico-Legal Prize 1985. **Publications:** 'Psychological aspects of burns in children' (MD Dissertation), 1974; 'Medico Legal Aspects of Contact between Children and families of Origin and others who have been important in their lives', *Medicine, Science and the Law*, 1987.

BENNETT, Albert Joseph (1931) Born 9 April 1913, 52 Stourbridge Road, Lye, Worcestershire; son of Albert James Bennett, Journeyman Baker, and Alice Whitlock. **Subject(s):** Economics/Mathematics; BA 1934; MA 1938; FHA; MIPM. **Tutor(s):** J M Wordie. **Educ:** Stambermill Church of England School, Lye; King Edward VI School, Stourbridge. **Career:** Secretary, National Health Service Staff Commission 1972–1975; Vice-Chairman, Paddington and North Kensington Health Authority 1982–1985. **Awards:** Baylis Scholarship, SJC. **Honours:** CBE.

BENNETT, Donald Edward (1949) Born 2 December 1929, 27 Southill Road, Chatham, Kent; son of Franklin Edward Bennett, Joiner, HM Dockyard, and Elsie May Harban; m Joyce Rosemarie Yale, 18 June 1955

(d 2001); 1 son (Mark b 1959). **Subject(s):** Archaeology and Anthropology; BA 1952; MA 1957. **Tutor(s):** A G Lee. **Educ:** Glencoe Road School, Chatham; Sir Joseph Williamson's Mathematical School, Rochester. **Career:** Administration, University of Ghana 1957–1962; Administration, University of Newcastle upon Tyne 1962–1967. **Appointments:** Committee of Vice-Chancellors and Principals of Universities of UK 1967–1986; Secretary, Overseas Research Students Awards Scheme 1986–2003.

BENNETT, The Revd George Anselm (1900) Born 23 December 1880, 25 Westgate Terrace, Brompton, Middlesex; son of John Bennett, Clerk in Holy Orders, and Ella Ann Heath Allin. **Subject(s):** Theology; BA 1903; MA 1907. **Tutor(s):** D MacAlister. **Educ:** Dean Close School, Cheltenham. **Career:** Ordained Deacon 1904; Curate, Reddenhall 1904–1909; Ordained Priest 1905; Vicar, St Mary's, Devonport 1918–1951.

BENNETT, Professor George Macdonald (1913) Born 25 October 1892, Upper Lindum Road, Lincoln; son of John Ebeneezer Bennett, Baptist Minister, and Hannah Martha Grange; m Doris. **Subject(s):** Natural Sciences; BA 1915; MA 1919; FRS 1947. **Tutor(s):** R P Gregory. **Educ:** East London College. **Career:** Researcher, British Dyes Ltd, and Ministry of Munitions 1915–1918; Beresford Fellow, SJC 1917–1923; Research Chemist and Head of Laboratories, Messrs Strange and Graham Ltd 1918–1921; Demonstrator in Chemistry, Guy's Hospital Medical School 1921–1924; Lecturer in Organic Chemistry, Sheffield University 1924–1928; Senior Lecturer, Sheffield University 1928–1931; Frith Professor, Sheffield University 1931–1938; Professor of Chemistry, KCL 1938–1945; Government Chemist 1945. **Awards:** Hutchinson Research Studentship, SJC 1916. **Honours:** CB. Died 9 February 1959.

BENNETT, Hilary Romaine (1920) Born 14 January 1901, 50 Alexandra Road, Wimbledon, Surrey; son of Cyril Frederick Bennett, Grain Broker, and Bertha Mary Govett. **Tutor(s):** E A Benians. **Educ:** Highfield School, Liphook; Lancing College; Private Tuition.

BENNETT, John Antony (1942) Born 28 July 1924, Fraser Memorial Home, Colombo, Ceylon; son of John Emil Bennett, Captain, Corps of Military Police, and Alice Marie Robinson. **Tutor(s):** C W Guillebaud. **Educ:** Colet Court Preparatory School; Glengorse Preparatory School; Eastbourne College. **Career:** RA, WWII; Administrative Officer, Nigeria 1947.

BENNETT, John Seabrook (1946) Born 15 April 1924, Balrampur Hospital, Lucknow, United Provinces, India; son of John Reginald William Bennett, Judge, Allahabad High Court, India, and Margaret Winifred Seabrook. **Tutor(s):** G C L Bertram. **Educ:** Edinburgh Academy; Clifton College; La Martiniere College, Lucknow.

BENNETT, Dr Michael Haynes (1946) Born 22 February 1928, 12 Alexandra Road, Stockton Heath, Cheshire; son of William George Bennett, Assistant Manager, Westminster Bank Ltd, Wigan, and Alice Taberner. **Subject(s):** Natural Sciences; BA 1949; MA 1953; MB 1952; BChir 1952; MRCPath 1964; FRCPath 1976. **Tutor(s):** G C L Bertram. **Educ:** Stockton Heath Council School; Westleigh Preparatory School, Lower Walton, Warrington; Wigan Grammar School. **Career:** Consultant Histopathologist, Mount Vernon Hospital until 1989. **Appointments:** Associate Research Fellow, Mount Vernon Hospital, UCL 1989. Died 9 May 1992.

BENNETT, Peter Luddington (1936) Born 9 November 1917, Twickenham, Middlesex; son of Edward Protheroe Bennett, Assistant Education Officer, London County Council, and Sarah Thirlwall Luddington. **Subject(s):** Mechanical Sciences; BA 1940. **Tutor(s):** J S Boys Smith. **Johnian Relatives:** brother of Philip Roger Luddington Bennett (1940). **Educ:** Caterham School; Whitgift School. **Career:** Engineer Lieutenant, RNVR, 1941. Died 12 December 1941 (lost at sea with HMS *Repulse*).

BENNETT, Philip Roger Luddington (1940) Born 3 September 1922, 55 Glencairn Road, Streatham, London; son of Edward Protheroe Bennett, Assistant Education Officer, London County Council, and Sarah Thirlwall Luddington; 2 sons (Philip and Joshua), 3 daughters (Chrystine, Elizabeth and Rachel). **Subject(s):** Mechanical Sciences; BA 1943; MA 1953; MBA (Harvard) 1951. **Tutor(s):** S J Bailey. **Johnian Relatives:** brother of Peter Luddington Bennett (1936). **Educ:** Fairdene Kindergarten School; Caterham School; Whitgift School, Croydon. **Career:** Engineer, Crompton Parkinson Ltd, manufacturing electrical engineers; Consultant for Medical Schools and Hospitals. **Appointments:** Consultant on Planning Expansion of Medical Schools at Stanford University, Washington, Oklahoma, Colorado, George Washington University, Brown University, University of New York and Chicago Medical School.

BENOY, James Francis (1913) Born 10 July 1894, Seabrook, Hythe, Kent; son of James Benoy, Army Chaplain, and Florence Frances Ann Percival. **Tutor(s):** E E Sikes. **Johnian Relatives:** son of James Benoy (1882). **Educ:** Brentwood Grammar School; Ovingdean High School, Brighton; Woodbridge School, Suffolk. **Career:** Lieutenant, South Staffordshire Regiment (wounded twice, Mentioned in Despatches), then Captain, Special List (Brigade Bombing Officer), WWI. **Awards:** Sizarship, SJC.

BENSON, George Enoch (1913) Born 31 October 1894, 14 Webster Road, Bermondsey, Surrey; son of Joseph Benson, Leather Dresser, and Jane Banks. **Subject(s):** Mathematics. **Tutor(s):** R P Gregory. **Educ:** Keeton's Road LCC School; St Olave's Grammar School. **Career:** Enlisted in Rifle Brigade 1914. **Awards:** Exhibition, SJC. Died 9 May 1915 (killed in action in the fight for the Aulers Ridge, near Fromelles).

BENSON, Henry Frederick Hamlyn (1929) Born 9 July 1911, 17 Ederline Avenue, Norbury, Croydon; son of Walter Hamlyn Benson, Wholesale Mantle Maker and Costumier, and Daisy Garnett. BA 1932. **Tutor(s):** M P Charlesworth. **Educ:** St Edmund's School, Hindhead; The Leys School, Cambridge.

BENSON, The Revd Theodore Ernest (1921) Born 10 June 1902, 5 Brighton Street, Barrow-in-Furness, Lancashire; son of Ernest Moore Benson, Clerk in Holy Orders, and Blanche Beatrice Matthews. **Subject(s):** Classics; BA 1924; MA 1940. **Tutor(s):** E E Sikes. **Johnian Relatives:** son of Ernest Moore Benson (1894). **Educ:** Liverpool College; St Lawrence College, Ramsgate; Ridley Hall, Cambridge. **Career:** Ordained Deacon 1925; Curate, Greyfriars, Reading 1925–1928; Ordained Priest 1926; Curate, All Saints, Preston, Lancashire 1928–1930; China Inland Mission, Tahsien, Diocese of East Szech 1931–1935; Kaifeng, Diocese of Honan 1935–1936 and Wahhsien, Diocese of East Szech 1936–1939; Diocesan Registrar; Principal, Bible Training Institute, Langchung; Dean, Chungking Theological Seminary 1931–1949; Tutor, Clifton Theological College, Bristol 1949–1958; Curate, Christ Church, Surbiton Hill 1958–1959. **Awards:** Scholarship, SJC. Died 1979.

BENSTEAD, Alfred Sydney (1914) Born 14 August 1888, 194 Victoria Street, Grimsby, Lincolnshire; son of Alfred Benstead, Coal Merchant, and Louisa Roberts Blow; m Edith Mildred Armstrong. **Subject(s):** Modern and Medieval Languages; BA 1918; MA 1921; BA (London) 1912; University College, Aberystwyth. **Tutor(s):** E E Sikes. **Johnian Relatives:** father of John Gordon Benstead (1939); grandfather of Richard John Rand Benstead (1971). **Educ:** Collegiate School, Grimsby; Municipal College, Grimsby; University College of Wales, Aberystwyth. **Career:** Form Master, Brigg Grammar School 1911; Assistant, École de Garçons, Montélimar, France 1912; French Master, Secondary School, Chippenham 1913; Lieutenant, Lincolnshire Regiment, then Major, General List (Commandant, Reception Camp), WWI; Senior French Master and House Master, Exeter School 1919–1923; Headmaster, Batley Grammar School 1923. **Appointments:** JP; Member, Executive Committee of the Yorkshire ATC; Member, Civil Committee, Batley (185) Squadron; Member, Batley Youth Committee; Member, Advisory

Committee, Batley and District Boy Scouts' Association; Chairman, Boy Scouts' Local Association. **Awards:** Wood Exhibition 1914. Died 6 November 1971.

BENSTEAD, Dr John Gordon (1939) Born 17 May 1921, 8 Raleigh Road, Exeter; son of Alfred Sydney Benstead, Headmaster, and Edith Mildred Armstrong; m Nancy Carver, 9 January 1946; 1 son (Richard), 1 daughter (Ursula). BA 1942; MA 1946; MB 1946; BChir 1946; MD 1950; FRCPath. **Tutor(s):** R L Howland. **Johnian Relatives:** son of Alfred Sydney Benstead (1914); father of Richard John Rand Benstead (1971). **Educ:** Preparatory Department, Girls' Grammar School, Batley; Batley Grammar School. **Career:** Home Office Pathologist; Demonstrator in Bacteriology, University of Leeds 1946; Consultant Pathologist, Southport Group of Hospitals 1951. Died 13 January 1987.

BENTALL, Reginald George (1924) Born 16 October 1905, The Firs, Richmond Road, Kingston, Surrey; son of George Anthony Bentall, of independent means, and Bessie Jacobs. BA 1927. **Tutor(s):** B F Armitage. **Educ:** King's College School, Wimbledon Common.

BENTALL, William Douglas (1915) Born 20 August 1896, Southend-on-Sea, Essex; son of William Bentall, Farmer, and Emily Mary Jolly. **Tutor(s):** L H K Bushe-Fox. **Educ:** Lindisfarne College, Westcliff-on-Sea; Mill Hill School. **Career:** Second Lieutenant, King's Own Yorkshire Light Infantry 1915. Died 16 September 1916 (killed in action in the Battle of the Somme).

BENTLEY, Arthur James (1907) Born 21 September 1888, Lake View, Ambleside, Westmorland; son of James Bentley, Schoolmaster, and Mary Morrell. BA 1910; MA 1937. **Tutor(s):** E E Sikes. **Educ:** Ambleside Kelsick Endowed School; St Bees Grammar School. **Career:** Master, St Ninian's School, Moffat 1910–1913; Cargilfield, Midlothian 1913–1914; Captain, Border Regiment; King Edward VII School 1919–1922; King's School, Worcester 1922. **Honours:** Military Cross and Bar 1918.

BENTLEY, John Brian (1932) Born 28 April 1914, Haworth, London Road, Mitcham, Surrey; son of Harold Bentley, Medical Practitioner, and Hannorah Marie Louise Constable; 1 son (Nick), 1 daughter (Susan). **Subject(s):** Modern and Medieval Languages; BA 1935; MA 1939. **Tutor(s):** E A Benians. **Johnian Relatives:** son of Harold Bentley (1893). **Educ:** Wimbledon High School; King's College Junior School, Wimbledon; Shrewsbury School. **Career:** Schoolmaster of Language, Lambrook School, Berkshire 1937–1981; Gunner Officer 1939–1945. Died 3 December 1981.

BENTLEY, John Hardy (1927) Born 1 August 1908, 72 Fitzjohns Avenue, Hampstead, London; son of Alfred Hardy Bentley, Solicitor, and Ethel Johnston. **Tutor(s):** E A Benians. **Educ:** The Hall, Hampstead; Amesbury School, Hindhead; Marlborough College.

BENTLEY, The Revd John Henry (1903) Born 20 March 1884, 12 Mowbray Street, Durham; son of John Bentley, Clerk in Holy Orders, and Margaret Ann Gray Niddry; m (1) Gertrude Angela Gotley, 7 August 1913 (d 1924), (2) Marjorie Wainwright, 4 May 1927 (d 1967). **Subject(s):** Oriental Languages/Theology; BA 1906; MA 1910. **Tutor(s):** J R Tanner; C E Graves. **Johnian Relatives:** brother of Reginald Arthur Bentley (1907). **Educ:** Pocklington School. **Career:** Ordained Deacon 1907; Curate, St Mark, Broomhall, Sheffield 1907–1910; Ordained Priest 1908; Lecturer and Librarian, Lichfield Theological College and Chaplain, St John, Lichfield 1910–1912; Tutor, Lichfield Theological College 1912–1916; Vicar, Milnsbridge 1916–1918; RAF Chaplain 1918–1919; Rector, Souldern 1918–1929; Rector, Layham, Suffolk 1929. **Appointments:** Secretary, Churchman's Union 1923–1927. **Awards:** John Stewart of Rannoch Scholarship in Hebrew, University of Cambridge 1903; Second Jeremie Septuagint Prize 1906; Steel Studentship (Graduate Candidate for Holy Orders), University of Cambridge 1906; Tyrwhitt Hebrew Scholarship, University of Cambridge 1907; Mason Prize for Biblical Hebrew, University of Cambridge 1908. **Publications:** *The Intelligent Use of the Psalms*; *A Scheme of Bible and Prayer Book Study*, 1915. Died April 1968.

BENTLEY, The Revd Reginald Arthur (1907) Born 19 January 1888, Woodside Cottage, Witton Gilbert, Durham; son of John Bentley, Clerk in Holy Orders, and Margaret Anne Gray Niddry; m Edith Frances Peto, 16 October 1917, Sykehouse, Yorkshire. BA 1911; MA 1915. **Tutor(s):** J R Tanner. **Johnian Relatives:** brother of John Henry Bentley (1903). **Educ:** Thorne Grammar School. **Career:** Ordained Deacon 1911; Curate, St Mark, Broomhall, Sheffield 1911–1915; Ordained Priest 1912; Curate, Halifax 1915–1918; Curate, Chipping Campden 1918–1922; Rector, Oddington, Gloucestershire 1922–1948; Rector, Todenham with Lemington 1948–1956. Died 23 May 1956.

BENTLEY-LLEWELLYN, Nathaniel James (1943) See LLEWELLYN.

BERESFORD, Gilbert Adrian (1907) Born 12 May 1886, 21 Hereford Square, Brompton, London; son of Edward Aden Beresford, Clerk in Holy Orders, and Annie Mary Moore. BA 1910. **Tutor(s):** J R Tanner. **Johnian Relatives:** son of Edward Aden Beresford (1875); nephew of John Jervis Beresford (1875); brother of Hans Aden Beresford (1903). **Educ:** Repton School. **Career:** Lieutenant, RFA, WWI.

BERESFORD, Hans Aden (1903) Born 18 January 1884, 21 Hereford Square, Brompton, London; son of Edward Aden Beresford, Clerk in Holy Orders, and Annie Mary Moore. BA 1907; MA 1911. **Tutor(s):** J R Tanner; C E Graves. **Johnian Relatives:** son of Edward Aden Beresford (1875); nephew of John Jervis Beresford (1875); brother of Gilbert Adrian Beresford (1907). **Educ:** Marlborough College. **Career:** Ordained Deacon 1909; Curate, Heath Town, Wolverhampton 1909–1912; Ordained Priest 1911; Rector, Maulden 1913–1922; CF 1916–1917; Rector, Hoby with Rotherby 1922; Rural Dean, Goscote 1940. Died 25 March 1949.

BERKOWITZ, Dr Sidney Maschelle (1937) Born 23 September 1911, 222 South 4th, Terre Haute, Indiana; son of Harrison Berkowitz, Retail Luggage Merchant, and Rosa Loeser. PhD 1939; BA (Cincinnati) 1933; Degree of Rabbi (Hebrew Union College, Cincinnati) 1936. **Educ:** Hebrew Union College, Cincinnati; University of Cincinnati, Ohio. **Career:** Rabbi, Hebrew Union College 1928–1936; Chaplain, US Air Corps 1942–1946. **Appointments:** Executive Board of Central Board of American Rabbis; President, Child Guidance Center, Youngstown, Ohio; President, Mohoning County Advisory Board of Aid for the Aged; Member, Major's Committee on Human Relations; Member, Ohio Citizen's Council for Health and Welfare. Died 1983.

BERLESCU-BEZA, Constantin (BEZA-DAPONTE) (1941) Born 27 September 1920, Bucharest, Roumania; son of Constantin Berlescu and Athena Daponte; BA 1944; MA 1951. **Tutor(s):** S J Bailey. **Educ:** Licée Gh Lazar, Bucharest; University of Bucharest.

BERNARD, George Henry Brian (1900) Born 21 April 1883, Durban, Natal, South Africa; son of William Crowdy Bernard, Gentleman, and Margaret Amy Wersing. **Subject(s):** Mechanical Sciences; BA 1903. **Tutor(s):** E E Sikes. **Educ:** High School, Durban, South Africa.

BERNARD, Henry Claude (1912) Born 21 October 1893, 2 Spencer Terrace, Fishponds, Bristol, Gloucestershire; son of Claude Bernard, Surgeon, and Margaret Newton. **Subject(s):** Mathematics. **Tutor(s):** L H K Bushe-Fox. **Educ:** Redlands School, Bristol; Grammar School, Thame. **Career:** Second Lieutenant, 7th Battalion, Gloucestershire Regiment 1915; attached Worcestershire Regiment. Died 3 September 1916 (killed in action).

BERRIDGE, Evan Denys (1921) Born 13 September 1902, 13 Elsenham Street, Wandsworth, London; son of Jesse Berridge, Clerk in Holy Orders, and Edna Adeline Dell. **Subject(s):** Classics; BA 1924; MA 1928. **Tutor(s):** E E Sikes. **Educ:** Whitehall College, Witham; Forest School, Walthamstow; St John's School, Leatherhead. **Career:** Assistant Master,

Wolverhampton Grammar School 1925; Perse School 1925; Epsom College 1932. **Awards:** Nunn Exhibition, SJC; Abbott Scholarship, University of Cambridge 1922. Died 11 October 1979.

BERRY, Donald (1948) Born 27 August 1928, 36 Newtown Avenue, Royston, Yorkshire; son of William Berry, Miner, and Grace Lilian Walker; m Margaret Frances Emere; 3 sons (John, Peter and Simon). **Subject(s):** History; BA 1950; MA 1955. **Tutor(s):** F Thistlethwaite. **Educ:** Royston Junior School; Barnsley Grammar School. **Career:** Works Manager, S Maw, Son & Sons 1951–1967; Management Consultant, W D Scott & Sons 1967–1969; Principal Officer, Management Services 1969–1972, Manager, London Factories 1972–1978, Assistant Controller, in charge of Engineering Supplies and Transport 1978–1989, British Telecom.

BERRY, Dr Gerard John (1948) Born 7 November 1926, Morecambe, Lancashire; son of John Robinson Berry, Grocer's Manager, and Lucy Agnes Hindley; m Sylvia Wells, 1955; 4 sons, 1 daughter. **Subject(s):** Economics; BA 1950; MA 1955; MA (Surrey) 1983; PhD (Surrey) 1991. **Tutor(s):** C W Guillebaud. **Educ:** St Mary's Roman Catholic School, Morecambe; Preston Catholic College; Morecambe Grammar School. **Career:** RAF 1945–1948; Insolvency Practitioner, Morgan & Co 1951–1952; Marks & Spencer 1952–1957; Area Manager/Deputy Managing Director, Etam Ltd 1952–1971; Retail Director, Tricoville Ltd 1972–1984; Bursar, Farnborough Hill Trust 1984–1995; Part-time Tutor, Adult Education Centre, University of Surrey 1993–2000; Part-time Tutor, WEA Lincoln 1996. **Appointments:** Governor, Farnborough Hill Trust 1995–2001.

BERRY, Canon Oscar Keith de la Tour (DE BERRY) (1926) Born 12 October 1907, The Mount, Monken Hadley, East Barnet, Hertfordshire; son of Oscar Cohu de Berry, Accountant, and Ellen Maria Maddox; m Betty; 2 sons, 2 daughters. **Subject(s):** History/English; BA 1929; MA 1933. **Tutor(s):** E A Benians. **Educ:** St Andrew's School, East Grinstead; Marlborough College; Ridley Hall, Cambridge. **Career:** Vicar, St Aldate's, Oxford; Ordained Deacon 1930; Curate, St Mary, Islington 1930–1935; Ordained Priest 1931; Vicar, St George, Battersea, with St James, Nine Elms 1935–1939; Vicar, Immanuel, Streatham 1939–1951; Chaplain, Sutton Emergency Hospital 1940; Honorary Canon, Christ Church Cathedral, Oxford; Honorary Curate, St Paul's, Portman Square; Honorary Curate, All Souls, Langham Place. **Publications:** *The Making of a Christian.* Died 16 May 1993.

BERTIN, Reginald James Edmund (1939) Born 25 July 1920, 2 Avebury Road, Leytonstone, Essex; son of Reginald Brackstone Bertin, Clerk in Holy Orders, and Ethel Chadwick; m Mollie Stewart Bromhead, August 1948; 2 daughters (Janet Hilary Christine and Katherine Rosemary). **Subject(s):** Economics; BA 1942; MA 1946; MusB (London) 1957; DipEd (London); FRCO(CHM). **Tutor(s):** J S Boys Smith. **Educ:** West Ham High School; Forest School; Royal College of Music. **Career:** War Service, 33 Field Regiment, RA (Technical Assistant, D-Day, 6 June 1944, later service in Europe, Egypt, Palestine) 1942–1947; Chairman, Trinity College of Music, Eastbourne Centre; Director of Music, Archbishop Tenison's Grammar School 1948–1957; Eastbourne Parish Church Organist and Choirmaster 1957–1962; Director of Music, Eastbourne Grammar School 1957–1983; Chairman and Conductor, Southbourne Choir of Eastbourne 1958–1985; Organist and Choirmaster, St Saviour and St Peter's Church, Eastbourne 1967–1984; Director/Founder, Renaissance Singers of Eastbourne 1977–2000.

BERTRAM, Dr George Colin Lawder (1929) Born 27 April 1911, Riversfield, Stephenson Terrace, Worcester; son of Francis George Lawder Bertram, Deputy Director of Civil Aviation, Air Ministry, and Mabel Catherine Smith; m (Cicely) Kate Ricardo, 28 September 1939, Upper Beeding, Sussex (d July 1999); 4 sons (Mark b 1942, Brian b 1944, Roger b 1946 and William b 1950). **Subject(s):** Natural Sciences; BA 1932; MA 1937; PhD 1939. **Tutor(s):** C W Guillebaud. **Johnian Relatives:** father of Mark Harry Ricardo Bertram (1961) and of Brian

Colin Ricardo Bertram (1962); uncle of Robert Campbell Bosanquet (1962) and of Nicholas Delisle Burns (1963); father of Roger Charles Ricardo Bertram (1964) and of William Halsey Ricardo Bertram (1968); grandfather of Hal Alexander Bertram (1989) and of Jessica Catharine Bertram (1994). **Educ:** Berkhamsted School. **Career:** Biologist, British Graham Land Expedition, Antarctic 1934–1937; Chief Fisheries Officer, Colonial Office, Palestine 1940–1943; Fisheries Consultant, Anglo-American Middle East Supply Centre, Cairo 1943–1945; Title B Fellow, SJC 1945–1972; Director, Scott Polar Research Institute, Cambridge 1949–1957; General Secretary, Galton Institute 1957–1964; Title E Fellow 1972–1978, Title D Fellow 1978–2001, SJC. **Appointments:** Tutor 1945–1965, Senior Tutor 1965–1972, SJC; Governor, Berkhamsted School 1953–1985; Visiting Professor, University of Otago, New Zealand 1957; President, Arctic Club 1963; Honorary General Secretary, Royal Geographical Society 1965–1971; President, Antarctic Club 1966 and 1994; College Representative, University Appointments Board 1969; Governor, Sedbergh School 1973–1982. **Awards:** Exhibition, SJC 1929; Slater Studentship 1933; Polar Medal 1937; Murchison Grant, Royal Geographical Society 1957; Carter Medal, Galton Institute. **Publications:** *Army Handbook on Cold Weather Equipment*; *Arctic & Antarctic: A Prospect of the Polar Regions*, 1939, 1958; *Adam's Brood: Hopes and Fears of a Biologist*, 1959; *In Search of Mermaids: The Manatees of Guyana*, 1963; *Antarctica, Cambridge, Conservation and Population: A Biologist's Story*, 1987; *Memories and Musings of an Octogenarian Biologist*, 1994; *Antarctica 60 Years Ago*, 1996; numerous papers on arctic, zoological and population topics. Died 11 January 2001.

BERTSCHINGER, Dr Max (1948) Born 20 March 1913, Effretikon, Illnau, Canton of Zürich, Switzerland; son of Alfred Bertschinger, Stationmaster, and Katarina Müller. **Tutor(s):** J M Wordie. **Educ:** Primary Schools, Effretikon and Thalwil; Secondary School, Sargans; Zürich Cantonal School; Zürich University. **Career:** Teacher of English and German, Aargauische Kantonsschule, Aarau 1940–1941; Appenzell am Rhein Kantonsschule, Trogen 1941–1945; Kantonsschule Realgymnasium, Zürich 1945–1948.

BERWIN, Stanley Jack (1944) Born 18 March 1926, 9 Leopold Street, Leeds; son of Louis Berwin, Wholesale Clothier, and Celia Moran; m Rosalie Myers; 1 son (Nicholas), 1 daughter (Dorothy). **Tutor(s):** J M Wordie. **Educ:** Cowper Street School; Moortown Council School; Roundhay High School. **Career:** Articled under Lord Donald Wade, Booth & Co; Founding Partner, Berwin, Leighton & Co; Founder, S J Berwin & Co, Solicitors 1966–; Director, N M Rothschild's, Merchant Bank 1970. **Appointments:** RN Cadet.

BEST, The Revd Isaac James (1902) Born 20 June 1883, Silverwell House, Great Bolton, Lancashire; son of William Best, Architect, and Jane Alcock; m Queenie; 1 son, 2 daughters. BA 1906. **Tutor(s):** C E Graves; J R Tanner. **Educ:** The Church Institute, Bolton. **Career:** Ordained Deacon 1911; Curate, Portsmouth 1911–1914; Curate, St Denys, Southampton 1914–1922; Rector, Highclere 1922–1927; Assistant Master, Highfield School, Liphook, Hampshire 1931. Died 31 January 1960.

BETHELL, Alexander Duke (1911) Born 23 January 1893, 38 Hill Street, Stourbridge, Worcestershire; son of Thomas Duke Bethell, Cashier of County Court, and Elizabeth Lyall Barrie; m Mildred Lucie; 2 daughters. **Subject(s):** Classics; BA 1914. **Tutor(s):** E E Sikes. **Johnian Relatives:** uncle of Douglas Brian Parkes (1951). **Educ:** King Edward's School, Stourbridge. **Career:** Manager, De Clermont and Donner Ltd, Leeds Branch; District Officer, Administrative Service, British Somaliland and Kenya Protectorates 1914; Chief Commercial Advisor to the Ethiopian Government 1942. **Awards:** Exhibition, SJC.

BEVAN, Eric James (1914) Born 27 November 1894, 2 Greencroft Gardens, South Hampstead, Middlesex; son of James Alfred Bevan, Clerk in Holy Orders, and Annie Susan Woodall; m Margaret;

1 daughter (Nancy). **Subject(s):** Classics/History; BA 1921; MA 1939. **Tutor(s):** E E Sikes. **Educ:** Great Yarmouth Grammar School. **Career:** Second Lieutenant, King's Own Yorkshire Light Infantry, WWI; Master, Wycliffe College, Stonehouse 1921. **Awards:** Sizarship, SJC. Died 13 April 1984.

BEVAN, Guy Theodore Molesworth (1909) Born 17 March 1890, St Andrew's Vicarage, Stoke Newington, London; son of Henry Edward James Bevan, Clerk in Holy Orders, and The Hon Charlotte Josephine Elizabeth Molesworth; m Jean Munro Martin, 11 August 1920. BA 1912; MA 1927. **Tutor(s):** J R Tanner. **Johnian Relatives:** son of Henry Edward James Bevan (1873); brother of Rupert Charles Molesworth Bevan (1919). **Educ:** Malvern College. **Career:** Major, RE (Mentioned in Despatches), WWI. Died June 1974.

BEVAN, Llewelyn Vaughan (1923) Born 6 January 1905, Garden Walk, Chesterton, Cambridge; son of Penry Vaughan Bevan, University Demonstrator and Fellow, Trinity College, and Hilda Cornelia Few; m Molly. **Subject(s):** Classics; BA 1927; MA 1945. **Tutor(s):** E E Sikes. **Johnian Relatives:** brother of Owen Vaughan Bevan (1928). **Educ:** Englefield Green School; Bedford School. **Awards:** Exhibition, SJC. Died 29 June 1987.

BEVAN, Owen Vaughan (1928) Born 9 February 1909, Hillside, Egham, Surrey; son of Penry Vaughan Bevan, Fellow, Trinity College, Cambridge, and Hilda Cornelia Few; 2 sons, 2 daughters. **Subject(s):** History; BA 1931; MA 1935. **Tutor(s):** E A Benians. **Johnian Relatives:** brother of Llewelyn Vaughan Bevan (1923). **Educ:** Bedford School. **Career:** Assistant Master, Denstone College 1932–1934; Assistant Master 1934–1973, Vice-Master 1969–1973, Bedford School. **Awards:** Exhibition, SJC 1927; College History Prize 1929. Died 19 April 2004.

BEVAN, Rupert Charles Molesworth (1919) Born 31 January 1899, Upper Chelsea Rectory, 141 Sloane Street, London; son of Henry Edward James Bevan, Clerk in Holy Orders, and Charlotte Josephine Elizabeth Molesworth. **Tutor(s):** E E Sikes. **Johnian Relatives:** son of Henry Edward James Bevan (1873); brother of Guy Theodore Molesworth Bevan (1909). **Educ:** St Augustine's, Eastbourne; Old Malt House, Matravers; Repton School. **Career:** Rubber Planter, Sua Betong Estate, Port Dickson, Negri Sembilan, Federated Malay States; Grenadier Guards 1917; Lieutenant, Grenadier Guards 1919. Died 2 February 1963.

BEVERIDGE, Dr William John Morton (1928) Born 5 July 1911, 18 Dundonald Street, Edinburgh; son of Alexander William Morton Beveridge, Manager, Bank of Scotland, and Esther Pitt. **Subject(s):** Natural Sciences; BA 1932; MA 1942; BChir 1942; MB 1942; MRCS (Edinburgh) 1935; LRFPS (Glasgow) 1935; LRCP (Edinburgh) 1935. **Tutor(s):** M P Charlesworth. **Educ:** Glasgow Academy; Glasgow University. **Career:** House Surgeon, Royal Infirmary, Stirling; House Physician, Connaught Hospital, London; Assistant Bacteriologist, Royal Infirmary, Edinburgh; Emergency Bacteriology Service, Department of Health, Scotland. Died 13 June 1949.

BEWICK, William Alfred Malcolm (1949) Born 28 December 1930, 2 Kingston Road, Romford, Essex; son of William Leslie Bewick, Bank Clerk, and Edna Edith Bray. **Tutor(s):** A G Lee. **Educ:** Upminster Primary School; Caterham School.

BEWLEY, Edward Clibborn (1920) Born 2 December 1902, Ardenvohn, Cowper Road, Rathmines, Dublin; son of Thomas Watson Bewley, Biscuit Manufacturer, and Elisabeth Bevington Clibborn. **Subject(s):** Mathematics; BA 1924; MA 1928; FSA. **Tutor(s):** E E Sikes. **Educ:** St Stephen's Green School, Dublin; The Downs School, Colwall, Malvern; Bootham School, York. Died 29 November 1979.

BEZA-DAPONTE, Constantin (1941) See BERLESCU-BEZA.

BHANDARI, Dharm Pal (1930) Born 28 September 1908, Lahore, India; son of Rai Gobind Ram Bhandari, Punjab Civil Service, and Shrimati Malan Devi. **Subject(s):** Natural Sciences; BA 1932; MA 1937. **Tutor(s):** C W Guillebaud. **Educ:** Sanatan High School, Lahore; DAV High School, Lahore; Forman Christian College, Lahore.

BHANSALI, Mansen Damoder (1916) Born 7 November 1898, Bombay, India; son of Damoder Dharmadas Bhansali, and Hurkorebai Vithaldas Gaujawalla; 1 daughter. **Subject(s):** Mathematics/Law; BA 1919; MA 1923; LLB 1920. **Tutor(s):** E E Sikes. **Educ:** New High School, Bombay, India; Scottish High School, Bombay; Dulwich College. **Career:** Assistant Collector and Magistrate, Indian Civil Service, Bombay (Officiating Deputy Secretary to Government, Finance Department 1931) 1923–1936; Officiating Registrar of Co-operative Societies, Bombay 1936; Commissioner of Excise 1936; Registrar 1938; Ex-officio Joint Secretary to Government of Bombay, Revenue Department 1939. **Awards:** Exhibition, SJC 1916; Foundation Scholarship, SJC. Died 17 May 1961.

BHIDE, Mahadeva Vishnu (1904) Born 13 February 1883, Poona, India; son of Vishnu Sakharam Bhide, Banker. **Subject(s):** Mathematics; BA 1907; BA (Bombay). **Tutor(s):** J R Tanner; C E Graves. **Educ:** Fergusson College, Poona, India; University of Bombay, India. **Career:** Assistant Commissioner, Amritsar 1908; Assistant Censor, Bombay 1915–1919; Postal Censor, Lahore 1919; Officiating Legal Remembrancer, Secretary to Government Legislative Department 1925; Judge, Lahore High Court 1927–1936; Chief Justice, High Court, Patiala 1943–1945; Chief Justice, High Court, Indore 1945.

BIBBY, Howard Morton (1936) Born 20 July 1918, 32 Ashburton Road, Claughton; son of John Pye Bibby, Director of Bibby and Sons Ltd, Seed Crushers, and Doris Dent Harker; m Constance Wooldridge, 13 February 1948, Christchurch, Willaston. **Subject(s):** Natural Sciences; BA 1939; MA 1943. **Tutor(s):** J M Wordie. **Johnian Relatives:** father of Colin Joseph Bibby (1967). **Educ:** The Leas, Hoylake; Oundle School. Died 6 April 1997.

BICKERTON, Dr Derek (1943) Born 25 March 1926, Maternity Home, Bebington, Cheshire; son of Thomas Bickerton, Estate Clerk, and Hilda Ashall. **Subject(s):** English/History; BA 1949; MA 1968; PhD 1976. **Tutor(s):** C W Guillebaud. **Educ:** Westbourne Preparatory School, Prenton; Calday Grange Grammar School. **Career:** Schoolmaster, Barbados 1959. **Awards:** Minor Scholarship, SJC 1942. **Publications:** *Payroll*, Eyre and Spottiswoode, 1959.

BICKFORD, Colonel Nicholas (1925) Born 2 August 1907, Cromwell House, 298 Hayden's Road, Wimbledon, Surrey; son of Nicholas Seymour Bickford, Physician and Surgeon, and Christine Ann Macdonald. **Tutor(s):** M P Charlesworth. **Educ:** Rokeby, The Downs, Wimbledon; Eastbourne College; Middlesex Hospital. **Career:** Civilian Medical Officer to the Junior Leaders' Training Regiment (RA); RAMC, served in India, Burma, Korea, twice Mentioned in Despatches. **Appointments:** Member, Executive Committee, Nuneaton Division, BMA. Died 1 March 1973.

BIGGS, Charles Edward James (1923) Born 5 February 1902, 49 Beauval Road, Lordship Lane, Dulwich, Surrey; son of James Douglas Biggs, Civil Servant, and Mary Elizabeth Cockerill. **Tutor(s):** B F Armitage. **Educ:** Christ's College, Finchley; Erith County School; South Eastern Agricultural College, Wye; Imperial College of Science, South Kensington. **Career:** Agricultural Officer, Uganda 1924; Senior Agricultural Officer, Uganda 1931; Deputy Director of Agriculture, Tanganyika 1942; Director of Agriculture, Tanganyika 1949. **Publications:** *Planning a Native Holding, Experiments on the Maintenance of Soil Fertility*.

BIGNALL, Dr John Reginald (1932) Born 14 October 1913, 35 Russell Road, Nottingham; son of Walter Bignall, Hosiery Manufacturer, and Nellie Cockayne; m Ruth Thirtle, 1939, 1 son, 3 daughters. **Subject(s):**

Natural Sciences; BA 1935; MA 1939; BChir 1939; MB 1939; MD 1947; FRCP 1961. **Tutor(s):** R L Howland. **Educ:** Elementary School; The High School, Nottingham. **Career:** Dean, Institute of Diseases of the Chest; Major, RAMC, Middle East and Mediterranean 1941–1946; Consultant Physician, Brompton Hospital 1957–1979. Died 2000.

BILLINGER, Hector Fussell (1911) Born 18 October 1893, 8 Rope Walk, Neath, Glamorganshire; son of James Fussell Billinger, Bookseller, and Margaret Jane Thomas. **Subject(s):** History; BA 1914. **Tutor(s):** L H K Bushe-Fox. **Educ:** County School, Cambridge. **Career:** Master, Royal Masonic School, Bushey; Second Lieutenant, East Lancashire Regiment 1914; Acting Adjutant 1916. Died 23 November 1916 (killed in action).

BILSBY, Herbert (1927) Born 4 November 1907, Regent Road, Spalding, Lincolnshire; son of Charles Burton Bilsby, Master Carpenter and Builder, and Lizzie Maria Loughton. **Subject(s):** English/Geography; BA 1930; MA 1934. **Tutor(s):** M P Charlesworth. **Educ:** Spalding Central Council School; Spalding Grammar School.

BILSLAND, The Rt Hon Lord Alexander Steven (Lord Bilsland of Kinrara) (1910) Born 13 September 1892, 28 Park Circus, Glasgow, Scotland; son of William Bilsland, Bread and Biscuit Manufacturer, and Agnes Ann Steven; m Amy Colville, 1922. Honorary LLD (Glasgow) 1948, (Aberdeen) 1956. **Tutor(s):** L H K Bushe-Fox. **Johnian Relatives:** cousin of James Alexander Bilsland (1906); brother of William Blair Bilsland (1908). **Educ:** Glasgow Academy; Park School, Glasgow. **Career:** Captain, 8th Cameronians (Scottish Rifles, TF), France and Palestine, later Staff Captain, WWI; Chairman, Bilsland Brothers Ltd; Director, Hillington Industrial Estates; Director, Colvilles Ltd; Director, later President, Scottish Amicable Life Assurance Society; Director, John Brown & Co Ltd; Director and Chairman, Glasgow Stockholders Trusts Ltd; Chairman, Scottish National Trust Ltd; Director, Union Bank 1924; Chairman, Union Bank 1935; Director, Burmah Oil Co Ltd 1947–1966; Chairman, Scottish Industries Exhibition 1949; Chairman, Scottish Industrial Estates Ltd 1955; Governor, Bank of Scotland 1957–1966. **Appointments:** President, Glasgow Chamber of Commerce 1933–1935; Commissioner for Western District of Scotland, Civil Defence Regional Organisation 1940–1944; Vice-Chairman, Council for Art and Industry; Chairman, Executive Council of the Scottish Council (Development and Industry) until 1955; Freeman, City of Aberdeen 1956; Honorary Associate, Royal Institute of British Architects; Chairman, Scottish Council 1955; Chairman, Scottish Economic Committee; President, Boys Brigade Battalion; Member, Royal Company of Archers (Queen's Body Guard for Scotland); Honorary Fellow, SJC 1955–1970; DL; JP. **Awards:** St Mungo Prize 1949. **Honours:** MC; Baron of Kinrara 1950; Kt 1955. Died 10 December 1970.

BILSLAND, James Alexander (1906) Born 27 October 1887, 5 Kelvingrove Terrace, Glasgow; son of Alexander Bilsland, Bread and Biscuit Manufacturer, and Jane Colville. **Subject(s):** Mechanical Sciences; BA 1909. **Tutor(s):** L H K Bushe-Fox. **Johnian Relatives:** cousin of William Blair Bilsland (1908) and of Alexander Steven Bilsland (1910). **Educ:** Park School, Glasgow; Glasgow Academy; Glasgow University.

BILSLAND, William Blair (1908) Born 18 July 1888, 3 Lynedoch Place, Glasgow, Scotland; son of William Bilsland, Bread and Biscuit Manufacturer, and Agnes Ann Steven. **Tutor(s):** L H K Bushe-Fox. **Johnian Relatives:** cousin of James Alexander Bilsland (1906); brother of Alexander Steven Bilsland (1910). **Educ:** Glasgow Academy; University of Glasgow.

BINGEMANN, Alfred Mervyn (1921) Naval Officer.

BINGHAM, Francis Denis (1919) Naval Officer.

BINGLEY, The Revd Gerald Arthur (1911) Born 5 December 1892, 281 Trinity Road, Wandsworth, Surrey; son of Frederick Thomas Bingley, Slate Merchant, and Fanny Headland; m Mildred Helen Gardiner, 5 June 1926, St Nicholas, Southfleet, Kent. BA 1914; MA 1919. **Tutor(s):** J R Tanner. **Educ:** Hurstleigh, Tunbridge Wells; Ridley Hall, Cambridge. **Career:** Deacon 1920; Curate, Newchapel 1920–1923; Priest 1922; Curate, Southfleet 1923–1936; Curate, Bramford with Burstall 1926–1928; Vicar, Capel, Surrey 1928–1945; Vicar, Chevithorne, Devon 1945–1949; Rector, Burstow, Surrey 1949.

BINNIAN, James Anthony (1949) Born 13 February 1929, Oldnall Road, Kidderminster, Worcestershire; son of James Binnian, Steel Manufacturer, and Alice Muriel Richards; m Celia. **Subject(s):** History/Law; BA 1952; MA 1956. **Tutor(s):** A G Lee. **Educ:** The Downs School, Colwall; Lea House School, Kidderminster; Uppingham School. Died 3 March 1999.

BINNIE, Dr Mark (1939) Born 14 February 1921, 20 Edward Gardens, Cardonald, Paisley; son of Mark Binnie, Engineer, and Mary Reid Drummond; 1 son, 1 daughter. **Subject(s):** Natural Sciences; BA 1942; MB 1950; BChir 1950. **Tutor(s):** R L Howland. **Educ:** Giffnock School; Strathallan School. **Career:** GP, Chippenham, Slough 1972. Died 21 May 1972.

BINNING, Dr Rex Austin (1926) Born 26 August 1908, 22 French Street, Southampton; son of Frederick George Binning, Pawnbroker and Jeweller, and Sarah Ellen Waters; (2) Nancy Louise Repard, 27 May 1948, Hove, (3) Geraldine Mary Matthews, 25 September 1959, Brighton; 4 children. BA 1931; MA 1944; MRCS 1934; LRCP 1934; FFARCS 1953. **Tutor(s):** M P Charlesworth. **Educ:** Western District School, Fremantle, Southampton; King Edward VI Grammar School, Southampton; Wycliffe College, Stonehouse. **Career:** Private Practice, Hove 1936; Honorary Anaesthetist, Royal Alexandra Hospital for Sick Children; Clinical Assistant Anaesthetist, Royal Sussex County Hospital 1937; Major, RAMC 1939–1945. **Appointments:** Chairman, South Eastern Society, and Southern Society of Anaesthetists; Chairman, Brighton and Mid-Sussex BMA; President, Brighton and Sussex Medico-Chirurgical Society; Councillor, Borough of Hove; Chairman, Brighton and Hove Regency Society. **Publications:** *Use of Rechargeable Batteries for Laryngoscopes; Flowmeters, Can they be Improved?; Anaesthetics, almost 50 years in retrospect.* Died 19 November 1988.

BINNS, Sir Arthur Lennon (1911) Born 31 March 1891, 19 Cavendish Street, Grimsby, Lincolnshire; son of John Binns, Post Office Clerk, and Sarah Ann Bowder. **Subject(s):** Natural Sciences; BA 1914; MA 1922; BSc (London). **Tutor(s):** E E Sikes. **Educ:** Diocesan High School, Grimsby; Welholme School, Grimsby; Municipal College, Grimsby. **Career:** Captain, Lincolnshire Regiment (wounded), later with RE, WWI; Science Master, King Edward's School, Birmingham; Education Officer, Barking, Essex 1921–1925; Education Officer, Ealing, Middlesex 1925–1936; Education Officer, West Riding 1936–1945; Chief Education Officer, Lancashire 1945. **Appointments:** President, Association of Directors of Education; Fleming Committee on Public Schools; Ministry of Education Committee on Standard Construction for Schools. **Honours:** MC; CBE 1945; Kt 1954. Died 23 September 1971.

BINNS, George (1942) Born 27 October 1924, 19 Woodlands, Golders Green, London; son of Arthur George Binns, Clothier, and Evelyn Watson. **Tutor(s):** C W Guillebaud. **Educ:** Laneside School, Golders Green; Tenterden Tower, Hendon; Eastbourne College.

BINNS, Professor Howard Reed (REES) (1928) Born 3 August 1909, Rumeli-Hissar, Constantinople, Turkey; son of Cuthbert Evelyn Binns, Merchant, and Edith Mildred Edwards; m Katharine Vroom Lawson, 1935; 1 son, 1 daughter. **Subject(s):** Natural Sciences; BA 1931; MA 1935; BSc (Edinburgh); MRCVS 1934. **Tutor(s):** J M Wordie. **Johnian Relatives:** father of Richard Mark Binns (1957). **Educ:** Community School, Constantinople; Bootham School, York. **Career:** Veterinary Officer, Nyasaland, Malawi until 1940; Veterinary Officer, Palestine 1940; Deputy Director, Veterinary Research, Palestine 1947; Director,

East African Veterinary Research Organisation, Kenya 1947–1967; Professor of Veterinary Micro-Biology 1969–1974; Director, Centre for International Programmes, University of Guelph, Canada 1969–1974. **Honours:** OBE 1948; CMG 1958. Died 29 April 1987.

BINNS, Michael Ferrars Elliott (1941) See ELLIOTT-BINNS.

BIN TAMIN, Abu (1939) See BAKAR.

BIRBECK, Harold Leslie (1920) Born 25 October 1901, Regent Place, London Road, Stoke-on-Trent; son of Charles James Birbeck, Art Director, and Alice Mary Salmon. **Subject(s):** Mathematics; BA 1923; MA 1929. **Tutor(s):** E A Benians. **Educ:** Boothen, Church School, Stoke; St Peter's Church School; Orme Boys' School, Newcastle-under-Lyme.

BIRD, Charles Kellam (1919) Born 21 July 1897, Corby, Lincolnshire; son of George Bird, Master Wheelwright, and Sarah Anne Hannam; m Constance Roberts, 1927, York; 2 sons (Geoffrey Kellam b 20 January 1931, d 25 September 1969 and Stephen Christopher Kellam b 11 May 1934), 1 daughter (Mary b 1929, d 1929). **Subject(s):** Mathematics; BA 1921; MA 1926. **Tutor(s):** E A Benians. **Johnian Relatives:** father of Geoffrey Kellam Bird (1951) and Stephen Christopher Kellam Bird (1954). **Educ:** Corby Council School; King's School, Grantham. **Career:** Honourable Artillery Company, France 1916–1919; LNER (formerly NER) 1922–1957, various positions including: Chief Staff Clerk to the District Superintendent, Leeds 1926; North Eastern Area Representative, Clearing House and Classification Committee, then Assistant to Chief General Manager for Rates and Statistics, Rates Office, York 1928–1934; Assistant Goods Manager, Southern Area 1934–1943; Acting Goods Manager 1943–1947; Acting Divisional General Manager 1947; Chief Regional Officer, Eastern Region 1947–1957; General Manager, Eastern Region 1955. **Awards:** Newcome Exhibition, SJC 1915; Scholarship, SJC 1915. **Honours:** CBE 1957. Died 28 February 1958.

BIRD, Douglas Joseph (1912) Born 14 April 1894, 7 Willis Road, St Andrew the Less, Cambridge; son of Herbert Flack Bird, Vinegar Maker, and Emma Jessie Martin; m Marjorie; 1 son (John). **Tutor(s):** R P Gregory. **Educ:** Gresham's School, Holt.

BIRD, Francis George (1925) Born 11 October 1905, Elan House, Gladstone Road, Gloucester; son of William Henry Bird, Schoolmaster, and Ada May Matthews; m Grace Freda Mary Preen, 5 August 1931, Gloucester; 1 son (David), 1 daughter (Margaret). **Subject(s):** Mathematics; BA 1928; MA 1933. **Tutor(s):** J M Wordie. **Johnian Relatives:** father of David Richard John Bird (1957); grandfather of Richard David James Bird (1988). **Educ:** St Luke's Elementary School, Gloucester; The Crypt School, Gloucester. **Career:** Assistant Master, St Paul's School, London 1928 (Club President 1935, Boarding Housemaster 1939). **Awards:** Exhibition, SJC. Died 15 July 1943.

BIRKETT, Alan Abbott (1944) Born 2 March 1926, 1 Shelley Terrace, Lewes, Sussex; son of Alan Birkett, Accountant, and Eva Abbott. **Tutor(s):** J M Wordie. **Educ:** Woodstock Road House School; Latham's Preparatory School; Magdalen College School, Oxford. **Career:** Sub-Lieutenant, RNVR. Died 23 September 1946.

BIRTLES, George Duncan (1943) Born 5 April 1926, La Casita, Lees Road, Bramhall, Cheshire; son of Duncan Whitridge Birtles, Export Manager, and Bertha Padfield; m Brenda Baughen; 2 daughters. **Subject(s):** History; BA 1946; MA 1951; CEd; FRSA. **Tutor(s):** C W Guillebaud. **Johnian Relatives:** brother of Gordon Padfield Birtles (1949). **Educ:** Stockport Grammar School. **Career:** Assistant Master, Solihull School 1947–1956; Chief Assistant Education Officer, Solihull 1956–1958; Deputy Borough Education Officer, Edmonton 1959–1964; Deputy Director, Educational Services, London Borough of Redbridge 1964–1988; Reader, Church of England 1989. **Awards:** Choral Scholarship, SJC.

BIRTLES, Gordon Padfield (1949) Born 20 January 1930, The Homestead, Patch Lane, Stockport, Cheshire; son of Duncan Whitridge Birtles, Director, Messrs William Cannan Ltd, Manchester, and Bertha Padfield; m Ellinor Mary Fairbairn, 18 April 1953, The Cathedral Church of St Mary, Edinburgh; 1 daughter (Caroline). **Subject(s):** History; BA 1952; MA 1978; MIPM. **Tutor(s):** A G Lee. **Johnian Relatives:** brother of George Duncan Birtles (1943). **Educ:** Syddall Park Preparatory School; Stockport Grammar School. **Career:** Market Research and Economic Forecasting Executive, Metal Box Co Ltd 1952–1956; Marketing Executive, Christian Salvesen & Co Ltd 1956–1959; Head of Personnel, Coates, Lorilleax, Total, GW Sun Chemical Inc 1959–1970; Founder and Managing Director, SITA Technology Ltd 1970. **Awards:** Major Scholarship, SJC 1948. **Publications:** (ed) Training programmes for numerous industries around the world; (ed) 28 textbooks on Polymeric Materials; (ed) series of books on various subjects.

BISDEE, James Sutherland Mitchell (1913) Born 9 January 1895, Oatlands, Tasmania; son of Thomas Gamaliel Bisdee, Gentleman, and Edith Sutherland Mitchell. **Tutor(s):** R P Gregory. **Educ:** Fairleigh Grammar School, Weston; Bedford Grammar School. **Career:** Trooper, King Edward's Horse; Lieutenant, Royal Field Artillery, WWI. Died 22 November 1959.

BISHOP, Dr Laurence Jack (1946) Born 29 October 1915, 1 Apsley Terrace, Horn Lane, Acton, Middlesex; son of Laurence Frank Bishop, Motor Engineer, and Laura Secrett Hunniball. **Subject(s):** Natural Sciences; BA 1948; MA 1959; MB 1959; BChir 1959; LMSSA 1952. **Tutor(s):** G C L Bertram. **Educ:** Fairburn Preparatory School, Bristol; All Saints' School, Bristol; University of Bristol. **Career:** Resident Medical Officer, York Clinic, Guy's Hospital; District Medical Officer, Monserrat, British West Indies 1963.

BISHOP, Terence Alan Martyn (1947) Born 10 November 1907, Homelea, Sandon, Essex; son of Cosby Martyn Bishop, Civil Servant, and Constance Augusta Mercer. MA 1947; FBA 1971. **Educ:** Rutlish School, Merton; Christ's Hospital; Keble College, Oxford. **Career:** Master, Glenalmond College 1930–1931; RA 1940–1945; Lecturer in Medieval History, Balliol College, Oxford 1945–1946; Reader in Palaeography and Diplomatic, University of Cambridge 1947–1975. **Publications:** (ed) *Facsimiles of English Royal Writs to AD 1100*, 1957; *Scriptores Regis*, 1961; *English Caroline Minuscule*, 1971. Died 29 March 1994.

BISHOP, William Douglas (1927) Born 25 October 1907, 47 Moscow Court, Paddington, London; son of William Battlescombe Bishop, Mining Engineer, and Julie McKechnie. **Tutor(s):** C W Guillebaud. **Educ:** Colet Court, London; Beechmont, Sevenoaks; Cheltenham College.

BLACK, Peter Robert (1945) Born 1 May 1919, 141 Stoke Road, Averstoke, Hampshire; son of Francis George Hamilton Rollo Black, Surgeon-captain, RN, and Violet Isabel Mackie; m Betty; 1 son (Duncan), 1 daughter (Julia). **Subject(s):** Economics/History; BA 1947. **Tutor(s):** J M Wordie. **Educ:** Little Appley School, Ryde; Bloxham School, Oxfordshire; McTinniswoods, Camberley. **Career:** Teacher, Bassingham Village College; Lieutenant, RN, HMS *Melbreak* and HMS *Reading* 1940–1945. **Publications:** *Mirabel, Once Upon a Time*, 1980. Died 20 July 1984.

BLACK, Robert Andrew Stransham (1920) Born 17 January 1902, 40 Queens Gate Terrace, Kensington, London; son of Robert James Black, Landed Proprietor, and Ellen Cecilia La Touche. **Tutor(s):** E E Sikes. **Educ:** St Andrew's School, Eastbourne; Eton College.

BLACK, Stuart Gordon (1910) Born 22 September 1890, Swiss Villa, Cockington, Torquay, Devon; son of George Black, Bachelor of Medicine, University of Edinburgh, and Marion Reid; m Laurie. **Subject(s):** Physics/Mechanics; BA 1920; ARPS; FIBP; FRPS 1935.

Tutor(s): J R Tanner. **Educ:** Private Tuition. **Career:** Air Mechanic, RNAS, WWI; Photographer. **Appointments:** Member, London Salon of Photography 1949. Died 20 December 1961.

BLACKBURN, Professor Julian Murray (1930) Born 5 December 1903, 79 The Drive, Hove, Sussex; son of Ernest Murray Blackburn, of independent means, and Fanny Julia Reid. PhD 1933; BSc (LSE). **Tutor(s):** E A Benians. **Educ:** Copthorne School, Crawley; Kingsgate School, Winchester; LSE.

BLACKMAN, Professor Geoffrey Emett (1921) Born 17 April 1903, 58 Scarsdale Villas, Kensington, London; son of Vernon Herbert Blackman, Professor of Plant Physiology and Pathology, and Edith Delta Emett; m Audrey Babette Seligman, 8 October 1931, All Saints' Church, Fulham. **Subject(s):** Natural Sciences; BA 1925; BA (Oxon) 1945; MA (Oxon) 1945; FRS 1959. **Tutor(s):** B F Armitage. **Johnian Relatives:** nephew of Frederick Frost Blackman (1887) and of Sidney Spencer Farwell Blackman (1891); son of Vernon Herbert Blackman (1892); brother of John Vernon Blackman (1925); cousin of Peter Francis Blackman (1938). **Educ:** Leass High School; Rokeby Preparatory School, Wimbledon; King's College School, Wimbledon. **Career:** Agricultural Research Council, WWII; Consultant, Rubber Research Institute of Malaya; Head, Botany Section, Jealotts Hill Agricultural Research Station 1927–1935; Lecturer, Plant Ecology, Imperial College, London 1935–1945; Fellow, St John's College, Oxford 1945; Sibthorpian Professor of Rural Economy, University of Oxford 1945–1970 (Emeritus 1970); Director, Agricultural Research Council Unit of Experimental Agronomy 1950. **Appointments:** Secretary, Biology War Committee; US National Academy of Sciences Committee on the Effects of Herbicides in Vietnam. Died 8 January 1980.

BLACKMAN, John Vernon (1925) Born 28 October 1906, 58 Scarsdale Villas, Kensington, London; son of Vernon Herbert Blackman, Professor of Plant Physiology and Pathology, ICL, and Edith Delta Emett. **Subject(s):** Natural Sciences. **Tutor(s):** J M Wordie. **Johnian Relatives:** nephew of Frederick Frost Blackman (1887) and of Sidney Spencer Farwell Blackman (1891); son of Vernon Herbert Blackman (1892); brother of Geoffrey Emett Blackman (1921); cousin of Peter Francis Blackman (1938). **Educ:** Rokeby Preparatory School, Wimbledon; King's College School, Wimbledon.

BLACKMAN, Dr Peter Francis (1938) Born 16 November 1918, 26 Trinity Street, Cambridge; son of Frederick Frost Blackman, Reader in Botany, Cambridge, and Elsie Chick. **Subject(s):** Mechanical Sciences; BA 1941; MA 1945; PhD (UCL). **Tutor(s):** J S Boys Smith. **Johnian Relatives:** son of Frederick Frost Blackman (1887); nephew of Sidney Spencer Farwell Blackman (1891) and of Vernon Herbert Blackman (1892); cousin of Geoffrey Emett Blackman (1921) and of John Vernon Blackman (1925). **Educ:** Hildersham House, Ramsgate; Rugby School; UCL. **Career:** BTH Works, Rugby 1937–1938; RAF 1940; Lecturer, Electrical Engineering Department, Imperial College, London; Co-Founder and Technical Director, Feedback. Died 4 February 2001.

BLACKWELL, Sir Basil Davenport (1939) Born 8 February 1922, 72 Hollyshaw Lane, Whitkirk, Leeds, Yorkshire; son of Alfred Blackwell, Engineer Manager, and Hilda Kathleen Sophia Bretherick (later Mrs Lloyd); m Betty Meggs, 4 September 1948, Holy Trinity Church, Exmouth; 1 daughter (Susan). **Subject(s):** Mathematics; BA 1942; MA 1946; BSc (London) 1948; FIMechE 1959; FRAeS 1964; CIMgt 1972; FREng 1978; Honorary DSc (Bath) 1984. **Tutor(s):** J M Wordie; S J Bailey. **Educ:** Cowper Street School, Leeds; Moortown School, Leeds; Leeds Grammar School, Leeds. **Career:** Experimental Officer, Department of Scientific Research, Admiralty 1942–1945; Technical Assistant, Rolls-Royce Ltd gas turbine division 1945–1949; Design and Development Engineer (finally Deputy Chief Engineer), Engine Division, Bristol Aeroplane Company Ltd 1949–1960; Business Manager 1960–1963, Technical Sales Director 1963–1965, Bristol-Siddeley Engines Ltd; Managing Director, Small Engine Division, Rolls-Royce Ltd (formerly Bristol-Siddeley) 1965–1970; Commercial Director, Westland Aircraft Ltd 1970–1972; Managing Director, Westland Helicopters Ltd 1972–1974; Vice-Chairman and Chief Executive, Westland plc (formerly Westland Aircraft Ltd), and of Westland Helicopters Ltd, British Hovercraft Corporation, Normalair-Garrett Ltd 1974–1985; Chairman and Chief Executive, Westland plc 1985. **Appointments:** President, Adams Society, SJC 1941–1942; Council Member, BIM, CBI, NDIC, EEF, SBAC; Vice-President 1978, President 1979 and 1980, Deputy President 1980, SBAC; Liveryman, Worshipful Company of Coachmakers 1980–; Vice-President, EEF 1983–1985; President, AECMA 1984–1985 (President d'honneur 1985–); President, Johnian Society 1985; Chairman, Astrid Trust 1986–1993; Council Member 1986–1995, Honorary Fellow 2001, Bath University. **Awards:** Exhibition, SJC 1940; Scholarship, SJC 1941; Hughes Prize, SJC 1942; British Gold Medal, Royal Aeronautical Society 1982; Chancellor Medal, Bath University 1997. **Honours:** Kt 1983. **Publications:** (jointly) *The Global Challenge of Innovation*, 1991; contributor to professional journals.

BLACKWELL, Michael James (1947) Born 28 June 1925, 17 Lawn Road, Hampstead; son of Herbert James Blackwell, Schoolmaster, and Elizabeth Timperley. **Subject(s):** Natural Sciences; BA 1949; MA 1954. **Tutor(s):** G C L Bertram. **Educ:** Harrow Weald Junior School; University College School; St Albans School. **Career:** Senior Meteorological Officer, Meteorological Office Research Unit, attached to the School of Agriculture, Cambridge. **Awards:** Polar Medal 1964.

BLACKWOOD, John Barry (1945) Born 19 April 1927, Lis-na-cool, Castlehill Road, Belfast; son of Terence Alexander Blackwood, Mill Manager, and Jessie Wellwood. **Tutor(s):** C W Guillebaud. **Educ:** Campbell College Preparatory School; Campbell College, Belfast.

BLADWELL, Ernest Wilfrid (1913) Born 15 June 1895, Bath, Somerset; son of Joseph Ambrose Bladwell, Builder's Merchant, and Alice Mary Jane Palmer. **Tutor(s):** R P Gregory. **Educ:** Wycliffe College, Stonehouse. **Career:** Corporal, RE, WWI.

BLAIKLEY, David James (1932) Born 2 April 1914, Talsarnau, Nether Street, Finchley, Middlesex; son of Alexander John Blaikley, Bank Manager, and Adelaide Miller; m Margaret Nancy Bergius, 19 October 1939, St Barnabas Church, North Finchley; 2 daughters (Fiona b 25 August 1941 and Shuna 24 February 1944). **Subject(s):** Mechanical Sciences; BA 1935; MA 1942. **Tutor(s):** J S Boys Smith. **Johnian Relatives:** brother of Robert Marcel Blaikley (1935); cousin of Arthur James Thomson (1937); uncle of John Brotherton Conybeare (1958). **Educ:** Holmwood Preparatory School; Christ's College, Finchley. **Career:** Consulting Civil Engineer. Died 1 October 1974.

BLAIKLEY, Robert Marcel (1935) Born 1 October 1916, Talsarnau, Nether Street, Finchley, Middlesex; son of Alexander John Blaikley, Bank Manager, and Adelaide Miller; m Alice Mary (Molly) Duncan, 1942; 1 son (Derrick Robert b 1944), 1 daughter (Marion b 1948). **Subject(s):** Mathematics/Economics; BA 1938; MA 1942. **Tutor(s):** J M Wordie. **Johnian Relatives:** brother of David James Blaikley (1932); cousin of Arthur James Thomson (1937); uncle of John Brotherton Conybeare (1958). **Educ:** Holmwood, Finchley; Christ's College, Finchley. **Career:** 112 Field Regiment RA 43rd Division, wounded in battle for Hill 112, later posted to India 1940–1946; Inland Revenue 1946–1948; General Register Office, Somerset House 1948–1965; transferred to Diplomatic Service as Counsellor 1965; on loan to Colonial Office as Head of Defence Department 1965–1966; Head of Aviation and Telecommunications Department, Commonwealth Office 1966–1968; Deputy High Commissioner, Kingston, Jamaica 1968–1971; Deputy High Commissioner, Accra, Ghana 1971–1973. Died 11 July 2003.

BLAIR, Dr Alexander Tritton (1923) Born 24 May 1905, Helmsley, Yorkshire; son of Alexander Campbell Blair, Physician and Surgeon, and Beatrice Mary Tritton. BA 1927; MB 1935; BChir 1935. **Tutor(s):** B F Armitage. **Educ:** Clifton House, Harrogate; St Peter's School, York. Died 28 October 1977.

BLAIR-MCGUFFIE, James Carruthers (1921) See MCGUFFIE.

BLAKE, Anthony Roger Morley (1942) Born 30 April 1924, Rosemead, Marine Parade, Leigh-on-Sea; son of Arthur Blake, Metal Merchant's Traveller, and Winifred Mabel Morley. **Tutor(s):** C W Guillebaud. **Educ:** Beverley College; Westcliff High School; Hertford Grammar School.

BLAKE, David Eustace (1943) Born 27 April 1925, Wade Cottage, Havant, Hampshire; son of Philip Blake, Dental Surgeon, and Marjorie Flora Down; m Sally Ruth Nicholson, 21 July 1954, St Peter's, Titchfield. **Tutor(s):** C W Guillebaud. **Johnian Relatives:** brother of John Philip Blake (1936). **Educ:** Emsworth House; Aldenham School. **Career:** RE Cadet.

BLAKE, Dr Ernest Oscar (1943) See BRIEGER.

BLAKE, John Philip (1936) Born 17 November 1917, 132½ High Street, Portsmouth; son of Philip Blake, Dental Surgeon, and Marjorie Flora Down. **Subject(s):** Mathematics; BA 1939. **Tutor(s):** J M Wordie. **Johnian Relatives:** brother of David Eustace Blake (1943). **Educ:** Emsworth House Preparatory School; Aldenham School. **Career:** Captain, Royal Marine Commando 1939–1944. **Honours:** MC. Died 3 June 1944 (killed in action in Italy).

BLAKE, John Raymond (1920) Born 21 May 1899, Leyton House, Harpenden, Hertfordshire; son of William Henry Blake, Medical Practitioner, and Elizabeth Alice Twynam. **Tutor(s):** E A Benians. **Educ:** Hardinwick School, Harpenden; St George's School, Harpenden; Aldenham School.

BLAKELEY, Frank Roland (1914) Born 22 June 1896, Alpine Villas, Normanton, Yorkshire; son of Frank Blakeley, Draper, and Ada Eliza Bikerdike. **Tutor(s):** E E Sikes. **Educ:** Normanton Grammar School. **Career:** POW, escaped to Denmark; Second Lieutenant, Somerset Light Infantry; Indian Infantry. Died 18 February 1917 (killed in action).

BLAKSTAD, Gabriel Clifford Clark (1930) Born 1 September 1911, Sunnyside, 155 Stockton Road, West Hartlepool; son of Björn Blakstad, Timber Agent, and Eliza Clark; m Alice Monica Margaret McGrath, 1 September 1936. **Subject(s):** Economics/Mathematics; BA 1933; MA 1948. **Tutor(s):** J M Wordie. **Educ:** High School, West Hartlepool; Durham School. **Career:** Customs and Excise Department, Federated Malay States, Taiping; Senior Customs Officer, Colonial Customs Service; Probationer, Government Monopolies Department, Straits Settlements 1933; Stationed in Butterworth, Province Wellesley 1938–1940; Transferred to Singapore 1940; Food Supply work 1941–1942; POW, Changi Gaol, Singapore 1943. **Awards:** Baker Exhibition, SJC 1930. Died 1 January 1990.

BLANCH, Joseph William (1927) Born 21 February 1905, Viña del Mar, Valparaiso, Chile, South America; son of Joseph Little Blanch, Merchant, and Ada Rosa Smyth. **Tutor(s):** C W Guillebaud. **Educ:** Stanmore Park; Harrow School.

BLANCHARD, Paul Harwood (1942) Born 24 December 1923, St Ann's Hospital, Cleveland, Ohio, USA; son of Walter Joseph Blanchard, Consulting Engineer, and Marguerite Duce. **Subject(s):** Natural Sciences; BA 1948; MA 1950. **Tutor(s):** C W Guillebaud. **Educ:** St Dunstan's School, Golders Green; Arnold House School, St John's Wood; Charterhouse.

BLANCHE, Eugene Hornby (1918) American Student.

BLAND, Ernest John (1922) Born 20 April 1903, 32 Lyndewode Road, Cambridge; son of John Graves Bland, Accountant, and Elizabeth Maud Diver. **Subject(s):** Mathematics; BA 1925; MA 1933. **Tutor(s):** E Cunningham. **Educ:** The Perse School, Cambridge. Died 6 September 1977.

BLANFORD, Edward Oliver Trenchard (1931) Born 4 September 1913, Thandiani, Hazara, North-West Frontier Province, India; son of Charles Edward Blanford, Captain, RA, and Vida May Trenchard; m Lucie Shiach, 30 April 1954, St Sylvester's Catholic Church, Elgin. **Subject(s):** Natural Sciences (Psychology); BA 1935. **Tutor(s):** J M Wordie. **Educ:** St Edmund's School, Grayshott; Sherborne School. **Career:** Management Apprentice with J Lyons; Industrial Engineer; National Union of Manufacturers; General Commercial Manager of Coal Machinery Division of Joy-Sullivan; Acting General Manager; Managing Director 1963.

BLANSHARD, Dr Gerald Phoenix (1943) Born 6 February 1926, Princess Street, Adwick-le-Street, Yorkshire; son of William Blanshard, Retailing, and Eva Jones Phoenix, Retailing; m May Simpson Bisset, 3 April 1956, Aberdeen; 4 sons (Keith Simpson b 28 March 1957, Nigel Gove b 21 May 1958, Jonathan David b 12 January 1961 and Gavin William b 21 August 1963). **Subject(s):** Natural Sciences; BA 1946; MA 1955; MB 1949; BChir 1949; MD 1955; MRCP 1955; FRCP 1975; Licentiate, Medical Council, Canada 1958. **Tutor(s):** S J Bailey. **Educ:** Adwick-le-Street Council School; Bridlington School. **Career:** Research Fellow in Medicine, Harvard 1958; Consultant Physician, Hillingdon Hospital, Uxbridge 1964; Consultant Physician, St John and St Elizabeth Hospital, London 1966; Retired 1993. **Publications:** Various medical papers.

BLANSHARD, Herbert Lewis (1911) Born 17 November 1877, 22 Norwood Street, Scarborough, Yorkshire; son of William Noble Blanshard, Banker's Clerk, and Eliza Dodds. **Subject(s):** Economics. **Tutor(s):** J R Tanner. **Educ:** St Martin's School, Scarborough; Belgrave School, Scarborough. Died 3 June 1913.

BLAXTER, Augustus Pearce Llewellyn (1910) Born 9 September 1891, 59 Oakley Road, Islington, London; son of Augustus Pearce Blaxter, Mechanical Engineer, and Eliza Emily Davies; m Enid Elvet Lewis, 26 July 1916, Welsh Tabernacle, King's Cross; 2 sons (Cyril and Peter). **Subject(s):** Natural Sciences; BA 1913; MA 1934. **Tutor(s):** J R Tanner. **Johnian Relatives:** brother of Cyril Glyndwr Blaxter (1921) and of Royston Blaxter (1924); father of Peter Llewellyn Blaxter (1937). **Educ:** University College School, London. **Career:** Commissioned, 11th Battalion, Middlesex Regiment 1914; Lieutenant and Adjutant, 1st Garrison Battalion, Northamptonshire Regiment, serving in Gallipoli and Palestine, WWI; Instructor, Small Arms School, Shaincliffe (final rank of Captain), WWI; Engineer, Managing Director, later Chairman, Barnett & Foster Ltd (soft drinks bottling company). Died 14 December 1972.

BLAXTER, Cyril Glyndwr (1921) Born 29 June 1904, 5 Canonbury Park South, Islington, London; son of Augustus Pearce Blaxter, Engineer, and Eliza Emily Davies. BA 1926; MA 1935. **Tutor(s):** B F Armitage. **Johnian Relatives:** brother of Augustus Pearce Llewellyn Blaxter (1910) and of Royston Blaxter (1924); uncle of Peter Llewellyn Blaxter (1937). **Educ:** Miss Wane's Preparatory School, Potters Bar; Elstree School; Harrow School. **Appointments:** Librarian, University Pitt Club 1925–1926.

BLAXTER, Peter Llewellyn (1937) Born 17 February 1918, 37 Highbury New Park, London; son of Augustus Pearce Llewellyn Blaxter, Engineer, and Enid Elvet Lewis; m Joan Patricia Barr, 7 July 1943, London. BA 1940; MA 1944; BChir 1944; MB 1944; MRCS; LRCP London 1943; DOMS 1949; FRCS 1951; FRCOphth 1989. **Tutor(s):** R L Howland. **Johnian Relatives:** son of Augustus Pearce Llewellyn Blaxter (1910); nephew of Cyril Glyndwr Blaxter (1921) and of Royston Blaxter (1924). **Educ:** Elstree School; Tonbridge School. **Career:** Senior Registrar, Eye Department, Guy's Hospital; Ophthalmic Surgeon, Manchester Victoria Jewish Hospital; Consultant Surgeon, Manchester Royal Eye Hospital 1954–1983. **Appointments:** Council Member and Vice-President, RSM (Department of Ophthalmology); Member, Ophthalmic Society UK; Court of Examiners, Royal College of Surgeons 1971–1997; President, Ophthalmological Society North of England; Master, Worshipful Company of Founders 1973; Master, Oxford Ophthalmological Congress 1974–1975. Died 3 May 1997.

BLAXTER, Royston (1924) Born 3 September 1907, 5 Canonbury Park South, Islington, London; son of Augustus Pearce Blaxter, Engineer, and Eliza Emily Davies. **Tutor(s):** B F Armitage. **Johnian Relatives:** brother of Augustus Pearce Llewellyn Blaxter (1910) and of Cyril Glyndwr Blaxter (1921); uncle of Peter Llewellyn Blaxter (1937). **Educ:** Verulum, Potters Bar; Elstree; Harrow School.

BLENCH, Dr John Wheatley (1947) Born 17 July 1926, 4 Bridge Street, Berwick-upon-Tweed; son of John Blench, Grocer, and Frances Fisackerly, Primary School Teacher. **Subject(s):** English; BA 1949; MA 1954; PhD 1956. **Tutor(s):** F Thistlethwaite. **Educ:** Bell Tower School, Berwick; St Mary's Church of England School, Berwick; The Grammar School, Berwick. **Career:** Assistant, Department of English Literature, University of Edinburgh; Lecturer in English, University of Aberdeen. **Publications:** Articles in *Cambridge Journal* and *Review of English Studies*. **Awards:** Major Scholarship, SJC.

BLENKINSOP, John Rowell (1926) Born 7 January 1907, 19 Cromwell Terrace, Gateshead, County Durham; son of John Mathewson Blenkinsop, Clerk in Coal-exporting firm, and Annie Douglas Rowell; m Erica Sheila Mary Ranalow, 10 September 1938, Chelsea Old Church. **Subject(s):** Modern and Medieval Languages/English; BA 1929; MA 1938. **Tutor(s):** M P Charlesworth. **Educ:** Royal Grammar School, Newcastle Upon Tyne. **Awards:** Scholarship, SJC. Died March 1970.

BLICK, Harry Moffat (1920) Born 18 October 1902, Claremont, Grange Road, Ashton-upon-Mersey, Cheshire; son of George Henry Watts Blick, India-Rubber Manufacturer, and Agnes Moffat. **Tutor(s):** B F Armitage. **Educ:** Sale High School; Denstone College.

BLICK, John David (1949) Born 17 June 1931, 1 South Constitution Street, Aberdeen; son of John Blick, Mechanical Engineer, and Mary Adams. **Subject(s):** Mathematics; BA 1952; MA 1956. **Tutor(s):** W A Deer. **Educ:** Hill School, Dovercourt; Church of England School, Bilton; Harwich County High School, Dovercourt.

BLISS, Alfred Howard (1919) Born 26 February 1899, 51 Moor Road, Rushden, Northamptonshire; son of Alfred Thomas Bliss, Elementary Schoolmaster, and Harriett Elizabeth Gadd; m (1) Sylvia Vera Henry, 1928 (d 1947), (2) Eugenie, 22 September 1949, St Mark's Church, Cambridge; (1) 1 son (Michael), 1 daughter (Oonagh Jane). **Subject(s):** Classics; BA 1921. **Tutor(s):** E E Sikes. **Educ:** Kingsthorpe National School; Kingsthorpe Grove School; Northampton School. **Career:** Broadcast Song Recitals under the name of Peter Howard; Civil Servant, Ministry of National Insurance 1921–1959; Schoolmaster, Sexey's School, Blackford, Somerset 1959–1961. Died 6 May 1961.

BLOCH, Arnold (1945) Born 8 August 1928, 1 Synagogue House, Queen Street, Portsea; son of Mendel Bloch, Jewish Minister of Religion, and Golda Swift; m Elaine. **Subject(s):** Oriental Languages/Law; BA 1948; MA 1952; LLB 1949; LLB (Melbourne). **Tutor(s):** C W Guillebaud. **Educ:** Heygate Street Elementary School; Peter Symond's School, Winchester. **Career:** Barrister and Solicitor, Supreme Court, Victoria 1952–1981; Industry and Commerce 1981–1985. **Appointments:** Chairman, Victoria Jewish Board of Deputies; President, Mount Scopus Memorial College. **Awards:** Rogerson Exhibition 1945. **Honours:** Member, General Division of the Order of Australia. Died 15 February 1985.

BLOOD, Terence Fitzgerald (1934) Born 15 July 1915, 18 Pembroke Road, Dublin; son of Horace Fitzgerald Blood, Medical Practitioner, and Gladys Mary Mason. **Subject(s):** Agriculture; BA 1937; MA 1941. **Tutor(s):** R L Howland. **Educ:** Shardlow Hall; Repton School. **Career:** Colonial Service, Nigeria and Gambia 1939–1947; Agricultural Adviser in the West Country & London, MAFF 1948–1980.

BLOOMER, Leonard (1918) Born 19 October 1888, Blackwell, Bromsgrove; son of George Frost Bloomer, Professor of Music, and Eliza Jane Yeats. **Tutor(s):** R P Gregory. **Educ:** King Edward VI School, Stratford-upon-Avon. **Career:** Lieutenant, Royal Warwickshire Regiment.

BLOW, Dr Roland John (1946) Born 22 March 1922, 47 Ladysmith Road, St Albans, Hertfordshire; son of Charles Edward Blow, Ladies' and Children's Outfitters, and Laura Florence Neale; m Nan Lewis, 16 February 1952, Church of St Bartholomew the Less, St Bartholomew's Hospital, London; 1 son. **Subject(s):** Natural Sciences; BA 1949; MA 1954; BChir 1953; MB 1954; MRCS (London); LRCP (London) 1953; DIH (Society of Apothecaries, London) 1969; MFOM (RCP London) 1978. **Educ:** Garden Fields School, St Albans; St Albans School; University of Birmingham. **Career:** RE (reached rank of Captain) 1940–1945; Medical Student, then Doctor, St Bartholomew's Hospital 1950–1957; GP 1957–1966; Industry (final post Senior Medical Officer, ITT (UK)) 1972–1985. **Awards:** Croix de Guerre, with Silver Star August 1944.

BLUMHARDT, Edward Henry Fenwick (MILLS) (1910) Born 31 May 1891, The Rectory, Brimington, Chesterfield, Derbyshire; son of Edward Keane Blumhardt, Clerk in Holy Orders, and Frances Margaret Mills; m Phyllis Walker, 25 September 1915, Ashtead Parish Church (d 26 April 1968); 1 daughter (Anne). **Subject(s):** History/Modern and Medieval Languages; BA 1913; MA 1919. **Tutor(s):** J R Tanner. **Educ:** Malvern College. **Career:** Lieutenant, Northumberland Fusiliers (TF), WWI; Secretary, University Library, Cambridge; Foundress Fellow, SJC 1919–1922; Librarian, University of Birmingham 1921. **Awards:** Scholarship, SJC. **Publications:** 'Sainte Anne D'Auray', *The Eagle*, 34. Died 8 May 1978.

BLUNT, William Gwyn (1927) Born 28 May 1909, 3 Church Place, Nanty-glo, Monmouthshire; son of William Blunt, Schoolmaster, and Mary Elizabeth Williams. **Subject(s):** Mathematics; BA 1930; MA 1946. **Tutor(s):** J M Wordie. **Educ:** The County School, Abertillery; Hereford Cathedral School. **Career:** Assistant Master, Royal Academical Institution, Belfast 1931; Headmaster, Mathematical Department, Royal Academical Institution, Belfast 1954. **Appointments:** Member, Mathematical Association of Great Britain. **Awards:** Somerset Exhibition, SJC 1927. Died February 1992.

BOAG, John Wilson (1933) Born 20 June 1911, 18 Culbord Street, Elgin; son of John Boag, Master Mariner, and Margaret Anne Byers. **Tutor(s):** J S Boys Smith. **Educ:** Langside School, Glasgow; Queen's Park School, Glasgow; Glasgow University.

BOATMAN, John Herbert (1926) Born 31 March 1908, Golf House, Sheringham, Norfolk; son of Charles Henry Boatman, Assistant Superintendent, Prudential Assurance Company, and Charlotte Abdy; m (1) Gwenneth Pamela Scales, 24 September 1934, Bromley, Kent (div 1953), (2) Margaret Hearn, 3 October 1953, Bromley, Kent; (1) 2 sons (John Leslie b 23 September 1935 and Michael George Christopher b 17 August 1939), (2) Twin daughters (Rosemary Jane b 29 December 1955 and Margaret Ann b 30 December 1955, d 1 November 2002). **Subject(s):** Modern and Medieval Languages/English; BA 1929. **Tutor(s):** M P Charlesworth. **Johnian Relatives:** father of Michael George Christopher Boatman (1959). **Educ:** Church of England School, Spalding; The Grammar School, Spalding. **Career:** Inland Revenue (final position of Senior Inspector of Taxes) 1929–1973; Dis-established Civil Servant, St Albans 1973–1978. **Awards:** Exhibition, SJC. Died 14 March 1996.

BOCKS, Shirley John (1938) Born 15 May 1917, 31 St Joseph's Street, Grandpass, Colombo, Ceylon; son of Eugine Richard Bocks, Locomotive Driver, and Euline Victoria Perera. **Subject(s):** Mathematics; BA 1940; MA 1948. **Tutor(s):** J M Wordie. **Educ:** St Anthony's School, Dannatogoda; St Benedict's College, Colombo, Ceylon; Ceylon University College, Ceylon. **Career:** Irrigation Department 1940–1961; Assistant Director of Hydrology, Department of Inland Waterways, Ministry of Transport and Aviation, Nigeria 1961. **Awards:** Ceylon Government Scholarship.

BODDINGTON, Vincent Coke (1905) Born 16 April 1886, The Cottage, Titley, Kington, Herefordshire; son of Arthur Cavendish Onslow Boddington, Gentleman, and Lucy Theodora Coke; m Florence Garrett Bastard, 6 November 1915, St Mary Abchurch, London. BA 1908. **Tutor(s):** E E Sikes. **Educ:** Hereford Cathedral School; Shrewsbury School. **Career:** Ordained Deacon 1910; Ordained Priest 1911; Temporary CF, 4th Class, RACD (TF) 1914–1917. **Awards:** Choral Studentship, SJC. Died 13 March 1917 (died of tuberculosis contracted on active service).

BODE, Karl Ernst Franz (1935) Born 24 November 1912, Bönnien, Hanover, Germany; son of Franz Bode, Bankontrolleur, and Martha Lagershausen. **Tutor(s):** C W Guillebaud. **Educ:** Andreas-oberreae Schule, Hildesheim; Universities of Bonn and Cologne; University of Vienna; University of Berne. **Awards:** Strathcona Research Exhibition, SJC.

BODINGTON, George Christopher (1945) Born 11 April 1927, Lima House, Bath Road, Reading, Berkshire; son of George Lewis Redner Bodington, Barrister-at-Law, and Elsie Winifred Wheatley; m Joyce Morris, 21 April 1951. **Tutor(s):** J M Wordie. **Educ:** Denny School, Boulogne sur Siene; Rose Hill School, Tunbridge Wells; St Peter's School, York.

BOLDERSTON, William Northcott (1904) Born 7 February 1884, Newquay, Cornwall; son of George Bolderston, Wesleyan Minister, and Sarah Mary Northcott. **Subject(s):** Modern and Medieval Languages; BA 1907; MA 1911; Docteur des Lettres, Rennes University 1913. **Tutor(s):** D MacAlister. **Educ:** Grammar School, Newbury; Trowbridge High School; Harleigh House School, Bodmin; Wesleyan Day School, Coad's Green. **Career:** Master, Belfast Royal Academical Institution 1912. **Publications:** *La Vie de Saint Remi, poeme du 13 e Sicele, Par Richier*, Oxford.

BOLSTER, Richard Vary Campbell (1931) Born 10 May 1912, Woodlands, Meopham, Strood, Kent; son of Richard Bolster, Major, RA, and Vary Cargill Finley. **Tutor(s):** J M Wordie. **Educ:** New Beacon School, Sevenoaks; Tonbridge School.

BOLT, The Revd David Dingley (1948) Born 22 November 1918, Alexandra Maternity Nursing Home, Plymouth; son of Reginald Dingley Bolt, Civil Engineer's Clerk, and Dorothy Cissie Norris; m Joan Mary Johnston, 2 April 1946, St Andrew's Church, Plymouth; 4 children. **Subject(s):** Law; LLB 1958; LLM 1985. **Tutor(s):** J M Wordie. **Educ:** Princetown School; Tavistock Grammar School; Plymouth Technical College; Westcott House, Cambridge. **Career:** Barclays Bank 1935–1939; Officer, Devon Regiment 1940–1946; Kings African Rifles 1942–1945; Captain, Army 1944–1946; District Officer, Resident Magistrate and High Court Judge, HM Colonial Service, Nyasaland 1946–1970; Called to the Bar, Grays Inn 1953; Barrister-at-Law 1953; Ordained Deacon 1968; Ordained Priest (Non-Stipendiary Minister) 1969; Non-Stipendiary Priest, Malawi 1969–1970; Curate, Good Shepherd, Cambridge 1970–1971; Priest, St Nicholas, Great Wilbraham and St John, Little Wilbraham with St George, Six Mile Bottom 1971–1974; Vicar, St Nicholas, Great Wilbaham; Rector, St John, Little Wilbraham with St George, Six Mile Bottom 1974–1986; Rural Dean of Quy 1975–1981; Permission to Officiate, Parish of The Ascension, Cambridge 1986. **Appointments:** Associate, Institute of Bankers 1939.

BOLTON SHAW, Brian Worsley (1944) See SHAW.

BOMPAS, Major William Michael Gwynnett (1939) Born 16 November 1920, Seaton, Devon; son of Cecil Henry Bompas, Indian Civil Service, and Nita Frances Goode; m (1) Denise Mustard, 1947 (div 1977), (2) Ghislaine de Cicco 1980 (div 1992), (3) Anne Summer 1994 (div 1996), (4) Ellen-Ann Simpson, 1997. **Subject(s):** Natural Sciences/Mechanical Sciences; BA 1954; MA 1960; CEng 1965; MIMechE 1965. **Tutor(s):** R L Howland; J M Wordie. **Johnian Relatives:** grandson of Henry Mason Bompas (1854). **Educ:** Bishop's Stortford College Preparatory School; Tormore Preparatory School, Upper Deal; Merchant Taylors', Northwood. **Career:** RA Field Branch 1940–1960 (War service with 1st Army, Tunisia; final appointment, on Military Directing Staff, RMCS, with rank of Local Lieutenant Colonel 1956–1960); Assistant Director of Research (Lubricants), Esso Petroleum Company Research Department 1960–1968; Secretary, CU Engineering Department 1968–1976; Secretary, Queen Elizabeth College, University of London (now part of KCL) 1976–1985.

BOND, Brian Willoughby (1913) Born 15 January 1894, Ballygarive, Longford, Ireland; son of Willoughby James Bond, JP, and Mary Rosa Kerr Bond; m Cicely Ingeborg Arendrup Grenside, 15 June 1926; 1 son (Julian Patrick Willoughby b 17 March 1928, d 26 October 1992). **Tutor(s):** L H K Bushe-Fox. **Johnian Relatives:** great great nephew of Alexander Perry Bond (1800); grandson of James Willoughby Bond (1856); great uncle of Stephen Francis Bond (1991). **Educ:** Gresford School, Wrexham; Malvern College. **Career:** Captain, Connaught Rangers 1914–1915; Assistant District Commissioner, Kenya 1920. **Awards:** Scholarship, SJC. **Honours:** MC 1919. Died 19 August 1963.

BOND, Derek Arthur (1948) Born 25 January 1928, 24 Beaconsfield Road, Great Yarmouth; son of Percival Arthur Bond, Area Retail Manager, and Jessie Mabel Constance Van Houten. **Subject(s):** History; BA 1950; MA 1955. **Tutor(s):** F Thistlethwaite. **Educ:** Priory School, Great Yarmouth; Great Yarmouth Grammar School; Sir John Leman School, Beccles. Died 16 October 1997.

BOND, Ralph Norman (1919) Born 31 August 1900, 2 Priory Villas, Morecambe, Lancashire; son of Ralph Bond, Jeweller and Qualified Optician, and Elizabeth England. **Subject(s):** Classics; BA 1922; MA 1929. **Tutor(s):** E E Sikes. **Educ:** Morecambe National School (Elementary); Royal Grammar School, Lancaster. **Career:** Permanent Secretary, Ministry of Posts and Information, Ceylon; Cadet, Ceylon Civil Service 1923; Ceylon Civil Service, Puttalam Kachahri 1924; Ceylon Civil Service, Hambantota 1924; Office Assistant, Badulla Kachahri 1926; Political Magistrate, Gampola 1930; Assistant Government Agent, Mullaittivu 1931. **Awards:** Scholarship, SJC 1918. **Honours:** OBE 1950; CMG 1953. Died 6 August 1984.

BONE, Lieutenant Commander Cyril Cornelius (1922) Born 5 September 1904, 24 Devonshire Place, Marylebone, London; son of Henry Peters Bone, Member, London Stock Exchange, and Lilian Maude Watney; m Sheila. **Tutor(s):** E Cunningham. **Educ:** Holland House, Hove; Malvern College. **Career:** Lieutenant Commander, RNVR. Died 8 February 1941.

BONNER, Colin Abbott (1938) Born 27 July 1919, Streatham Manor, Leigham Avenue, Streatham; son of Stanley Abbott Bonner, General Manager of Bank, and Marie Maxwell Denning. **Tutor(s):** C W Guillebaud. **Educ:** Downside Preparatory School, Purley; Lancing College. **Career:** Navy, HMS *Hood* 1939–1941. Died May 1941 (missing, believed killed, in HMS *Hood*).

BONSALL, Geoffrey Weatherill (1947) Born 2 December 1924, Wuchang, Hubei, China; son of Bramwell Seaton Bonsall, Methodist Minister, and Hannah Ada Mary Dale. **Subject(s):** Oriental Studies (Chinese); BA 1949; MA 1954; MLS (University of Hawaii) 1969. **Tutor(s):** C W Guillebaud. **Johnian Relatives:** brother of Leonard Dale Bonsall (1938); uncle of Christopher John Bonsall (1970) and David Charles Bonsall (1974). **Educ:** City of Norwich Secondary School; The Leys School, Cambridge. **Career:** Friends' Ambulance Unit 1943–1947 (China 1945–1947); Japanese Library, SOAS, London University 1955; Deputy Librarian, University of Hong Kong 1955–1969; Director, Hong Kong University Press 1970–1979. **Awards:** Studentship, Scarborough.

BONSALL, Leonard Dale (1938) Born 23 September 1919, Kuling, KinKiang, China; son of Bramwell Seaton Bonsall, Methodist Minister, and Hannah Ada Mary Dale; m Nellie Wee; 2 sons (Christopher and David). **Subject(s):** Economics/Law; BA 1943; MA 1946. **Tutor(s):** C W Guillebaud. **Johnian Relatives:** brother-in-law of Chong Jin Wee (1935); brother of Geoffrey Weatherill Bonsall (1947); father of Christopher John Bonsall (1970) and of David Charles Bonsall (1974). **Educ:** Kimbolton School. **Career:** Friends' Ambulance Unit, China 1944–1946; Senior Partner, Messrs Jaques and Lewis 1950–1984. **Appointments:** Member, Law Society's Working Party on Conveyancing 1963–1966. Died 23 April 1984.

BONSER, Geoffrey Alwyn Gershom (1907) Born 3 February 1888, Westfield House, Sutton in Ashfield, Nottinghamshire; son of George Gershom Bonser, gentleman of independent means, and Dorothy Ann Sims; m Lilian Prime, 3 July 1918. **Subject(s):** Natural Sciences; BA 1910; LRCP 1914. **Tutor(s):** J R Tanner. **Educ:** King's School, Worcester. **Career:** Attached to the First Eastern Hospital, Cambridge; Acting House Surgeon, Addenbrooke's Hospital 1915; Captain, RAMC, attached to the 12th Norfolks, Egypt and Palestine Campaign. Died 29 September 1918 (killed in action near Armentières).

BONSEY, The Revd William (1930) Born 17 February 1912, The Rectory, Morecambe; son of William Henry Bonsey, Clerk in Holy Orders, and Ernestine Colville Learmonth Gilchrist; BA 1933. **Tutor(s):** E A Benians. **Johnian Relatives:** son of William Henry Bonsey (1892). **Educ:** Belmont School, Clayton; Lancing College, Shoreham; Ely Theological College. **Career:** Ordained Deacon 1935; Curate of Weeke 1935–1937; Ordained Priest 1936; Curate of Moordown 1937; Chaplain, RNVR 1939–1941. Died 22 May 1941 (missing, presumed killed, on active service in HMS *Gloucester*).

BOOKER, The Revd Edward (1900) Born 9 April 1881, 206 Rommany Road, Norwood, Surrey; son of Edward Charles Booker, Carpenter, and Matilda Parker. **Subject(s):** Classics; BA 1903; MA 1912. **Tutor(s):** C E Graves. **Educ:** City of London School. **Career:** Ordained Deacon 1907; Curate, Great Yarmouth 1907–1919; Ordained Priest 1908. Died 4 February 1919.

BOOTH, Ernest (1913) Born 7 September 1894, 22 Wandsworth Bridge, Fulham, Middlesex; son of George William Booth, Director of Company, and Martha Kershaw; m Dora Clarkson Lawe, 22 December 1922, St John's Church, Bedfordshire; 1 son (Stephen Dion), 1 daughter (Shirley). **Subject(s):** History/Law; BA 1920; MA 1932; LLB 1932. **Tutor(s):** L H K Bushe-Fox. **Johnian Relatives:** brother-in-law of Francis Walsham Lawe (1913); father of Stephen Dion Booth (1942). **Educ:** Froebel Educational Institute, London; Latymer Upper School. **Career:** Lieutenant, Middlesex Regiment, and MGC 1914–1918; Senior Partner, Samuel Tonkin, Booth and Co, Solicitors 1929. **Awards:** Scholarship, SJC. Died 16 October 1983.

BOOTH, Dr Guy Herman (1941) Born 27 August 1923, 52 High Street, Bridlington, Yorkshire; son of Albert Edwin Booth, Army Officer, and May Hermon. **Subject(s):** Natural Sciences; BA 1945; MA 1948; PhD 1952. **Tutor(s):** C W Guillebaud. **Educ:** Bridlington High School; Bridlington School. Died 23 September 1989.

BOOTH, John Charles Hedley (1923) Born 11 February 1905, 8 Ravensworth Crescent, Low Fell, Gateshead, Durham; son of Lancelot Hedley Booth, Solicitor, and Gertrude Hulton; m (1) Winfred Eva Nimmo, 5 April 1934, Castle Eden, County Durham (d 21 November 1965), (2) Constance Mary Dove (d 1995); (1) 2 sons (Roger John Nimmo b 20 January 1935 and Jonathan Charles Norleigh b 18 March 1943), 1 daughter (Ethne Freda b 3 September 1938). **Subject(s):** Law; BA 1925; MA 1931. **Tutor(s):** E A Benians. **Johnian Relatives:** brother of Norleigh Booth (1926); father of Roger John Nimmo Booth (1955); uncle of Neil Lancelot Booth (1958). **Educ:** Newcastle Preparatory School; Durham School. **Career:** Paterson, Simons and Co Ltd,

Merchants, Singapore 1927–1930; J Brown and Sons Ltd, Brass Founders, Middlesbrough 1931 (Managing Director 1939); Board Member 1936, Deputy Chairman 1950, Joint Managing Director 1953, J Nimmo & Sons, Brewers. **Appointments:** Chairman, Sedgefield Conservative Association 1949–1950; High Sherriff of County Durham 1963–1964; Chairman, Stockton Race Course; Member, Race Course Association; Member, Race Course Betting Control Board; President, Teesside and South-West Durham Chamber of Commerce; President, Teesside Industrial Development Board. Died September 1974.

BOOTH, Nathaniel Barton (1942) Born 22 June 1924, Delamere, Lancaster Avenue, Farnham, Surrey; son of Lionel Barton Booth, Principal Scientific Officer, Ministry of Aircraft Production, and Phyllis Petley Duncan. **Subject(s):** Classics; BA 1947; MA 1949. **Tutor(s):** C W Guillebaud. **Educ:** Edgeborough School, Guildford; Betteshanger School, Eastry; Sedbergh School. **Awards:** Scholarship, SJC.

BOOTH, Norleigh (1926) Born 7 August 1908, Carr Hill House, Gateshead, County Durham; son of Lancelot Hedley Booth, Solicitor, and Gertrude Evelyn Hulton; Dorothy Barham, 1933; 2 sons (Piers Norleigh and Neil Lancelot), 1 daugher (Charlotte). **Subject(s):** Law; BA 1929; MA 1933; LLB 1930; Hon DCL (Newcastle) 1970. **Tutor(s):** E A Benians. **Johnian Relatives:** brother of John Charles Hedley Booth (1923); uncle of Roger John Nimmo Booth (1955); father of Neil Lancelot Booth (1958). **Educ:** Durham School. **Career:** Partner, Watson, Burton, Booth and Robinson, Solicitors, Newcastle upon Tyne 1930–1974; RNVR 1941–1945. **Appointments:** Council Member, King's College, Newcastle 1949–1974 (Vice Chairman 1966–1974). Died July 1988.

BOOTH, Paul Rupert (1947) Born 15 July 1928, Delamere, Lancaster Avenue, Farnham, Surrey; son of Lionel Barton Booth, Principal Scientific Officer, RAE, and Phyllis Petley Duncan. **Subject(s):** Natural Sciences; BA 1950. **Tutor(s):** G C L Bertram. **Educ:** Barfield Preparatory School; Yorebridge Grammar School; Richmond Grammar School; Sedbergh School.

BOOTH, Stephen Dion (1942) Born 20 October 1923, 2 Sutton Court, Chiswick, Middlesex; son of Ernest Booth, Solicitor, and Dora Clarkson Lawe. **Tutor(s):** S J Bailey. **Johnian Relatives:** son of Ernest Booth (1913); nephew of Francis Walsham Lawe (1913). **Educ:** Froebel Educational Institute, London; St Paul's School; Bedford School. **Career:** Flying Officer, RAFVR 1942–1944. Died 3 December 1944 (killed in collision during air operations off South Burma coast).

BOOTHEWAY, George Hartley (1919) Born 9 June 1900, Catlow Hall Street, Oswaldtwistle, Lancashire; son of George Bootheway, Director, firm of Cotton Machinists, and Sarah Helen Hartley; m Grace Hewitt, 23 December 1929, St George's Cathedral, Cape Town. **Subject(s):** Mechanical Sciences; BA 1922; MA 1926; BSc (Manchester). **Tutor(s):** E A Benians. **Johnian Relatives:** brother of Kenneth Charles Hartley Bootheway (1931). **Educ:** Secondary School, Accrington; Manchester University. Died October 1973.

BOOTHEWAY, Kenneth Charles Hartley (1931) Born 15 February 1914, Norwood, Park Lane, Oswaldtwistle, Yorkshire; son of George Bootheway, Director, firm of Cotton Machinists, and Sara Helen Hartley; m Christiane Michel, 15 February 1944, Military Chapel, Beirut. **Subject(s):** Mechanical Sciences; BA 1935; MA 1940. **Tutor(s):** J M Wordie. **Johnian Relatives:** brother of George Hartley Bootheway (1919). **Educ:** Preparatory School, Grange-over-Sands; Rugby School.

BOOTH-JONES, Charles Ellison (1947) Born 12 December 1919, 40 Upper Fitzwilliam Street, Dublin; son of Arthur Edward Booth Jones, RAMC, and Agnes Hawks; m Anthea Phyllis Baker, 17 October 1942; 1 son (Christopher Charles b 1943), 1 daughter (Anthea Jane Christina b 1947). **Subject(s):** Mechanical Sciences; BA 1949; MA 1960. **Tutor(s):** R L Howland. **Educ:** Southsea Preparatory School; Dover College; RMA, Woolwich. **Career:** 1st Royal Signals 1939, retired as Lieutenant Colonel

1961; Second Head, Mathematics Department, Brighton College Junior School 1962–1971; Senior Master, Edinburgh House School 1971–1984. **Publications:** *The Beaver Book of Brain Ticklers*, Hamlyn, 1977; *More Brain Ticklers*, 1978; *Even More Brain Ticklers*, 1980; *Casse-Tête Énigmes et Devinettes*, Chanteeler, 1981; *Puzzelen en Spelen met Getallen*, Zuidnederlandse, 1981.

BOOTY, Bernard Kenneth (1936) Born 9 June 1917, Llanberis, Manor Close, Ruislip; son of Hubert Ernest Booty, Incorporated Accountant, and Kathleen Mary Heath. **Subject(s):** Classics; BA 1939. **Tutor(s):** R L Howland. **Educ:** Parkfield, Haywards Heath; Malvern College. **Awards:** Scholarship, SJC 1936–1937. Died May 1978.

BORCHARDT, Roger John (1937) Born 4 August 1918, Allerton House, Bath Road, Cheltenham; son of Walter Gustav Borchardt, Schoolmaster, and Sarah Broughall Williams; m Joan Andrews, November 1939. **Subject(s):** Mathematics; BA 1940. **Tutor(s):** J M Wordie. **Educ:** Cheltenham College Junior School; Cheltenham College. **Career:** RN 1939–1940. Died 12 October 1940 (killed in action on HMS *Ajax*).

BOSWORTH, Thomas Owen (1903) Born 28 March 1882, Spratton, Northamptonshire; son of Thomas Jones Bosworth, Gentleman, and Annie Worthington. **Subject(s):** Natural Sciences; BA 1906; MA 1914. **Tutor(s):** E E Sikes. **Educ:** St Cuthbert's School, Worksop; Market Bosworth Grammar School. **Career:** Geologist; Master, Northampton and County Technical School 1908. **Awards:** Exhibition, SJC 1903–1905; Hutchinson Scholarship 1907–1909; Harkness Scholarship, University of Cambridge 1908. Died 18 January 1929.

BOTT, John David (CONSTANCE) (1946) Born 1 March 1923, Cologne, Germany; son of John Ernest Bott, Engineer, and Elsie Constance. **Subject(s):** Natural Sciences; BA 1948; MA 1953. **Tutor(s):** J M Wordie. **Educ:** Abbassia School, Cairo; Elementary School, Feltham; Ashford County School. **Career:** Laboratory Manager; Lieutenant, RNVR, Fleet Air Arm 1942–1946.

BOTTERO, Victor William Kenneth (1943) Born 6 April 1925, Clifton Hotel, Promenade, Southport; son of Umberto Bottero, Hotel Manager, and Ellen Olive Archer. **Tutor(s):** C W Guillebaud. **Educ:** Summerville Kindergarten; Terra Nova Preparatory School; Sedbergh School.

BOUMPHREY, John Michael Howorth (1948) Born 27 April 1927, The Bungalow, Eastham, Wirral, Cheshire; son of Frank Victor Boumphrey, Dentist, and Alice Margaret Howorth; m Mary Jill Stones (née Harris), 1969; 1 son (Michael Edward b 1970). **Subject(s):** History; BA 1951; MA 1955; PGCE 1955. **Tutor(s):** A G Lee; F Thistlethwaite. **Educ:** Mostyn House School, Parkgate, Wirral; Sedbergh School. **Career:** History and English Teacher, public and comprehensive schools.

BOURNE, Charles Beresford (1945) Born 19 February 1921, Barbados, British West Indies; son of Beresford Bourne, Clerk in Holy Orders, and Lilian May Ward; m Barbara Farmer, 20 August 1949; 1 son (Peter), 2 daughters (Frances and Angela). **Subject(s):** Law; LLB 1947; LLM 1985; BA (Toronto) 1945; SJD (Harvard Law School) 1970; Honorary LLD (British Columbia) 1993; FRSC. **Educ:** The Lodge School, Barbados; University of Toronto. **Career:** Assistant Professor of Law, University of Saskatchewan 1947–1950; Associate Professor 1950–1957, Professor of Law 1957–1986 (Emeritus 1986), Legal Counsel and Adviser to the President on Faculty-University Relations 1975–1986, University of British Columbia, Vancouver, Canada. **Appointments:** Member, English Bar (Middle Temple) 1947; Member, Bar of Barbados 1949; Member, Bar of British Columbia 1957; Member, Committee of the International Law Association on International Rivers 1958–1966; Editor-in-Chief, *Canadian Yearbook of International Law* 1962–1993; Academic-in-Residence, Legal Bureau, Department of External Affairs, Ottawa 1971–1972; Honorary Solicitor and Member, Board of Governors, Vancouver School of Theology 1971–1980; Member, Permanent Court of Arbitration, The Hague 1978–1984; Chairman, International Law Association's Committee on International Water Resources 1990–2000; President, Canadian Branch, ILA; President, Canadian Council on International Law. **Publications:** *International Water Law*; (ed Patricia Wouters) *Selected Writings of Professor Charles B Bourne*, 1997.

BOWDEN, Harold Treacher (1919) Born 20 November 1897, Rochford House, Ramsgate, Kent; son of Reginald Treacher Bowden, Physician and Surgeon, and Ada Blanche Campbell. **Subject(s):** Natural Sciences (Chemistry); BA 1921; AIC. **Tutor(s):** E A Benians. **Educ:** St Lawrence College, Ramsgate; Salisbury School. **Career:** Pioneer, Special Brigade, RE 1915–1919; Science Master, Oratory School, Caversham 1924.

BOWEN, Evan Roderic (1933) Born 6 August 1913, The Elms, Priory Street, Cardigan; son of Evan Bowen, Grocer, and Margaret Ellen Twiss. **Subject(s):** Law; BA 1935; MA 1940; Honorary LLD (Wales) 1972; QC 1952. **Tutor(s):** C W Guillebaud. **Educ:** Cardigan Council School; University College of Wales, Aberystwyth. **Career:** Practised at the Bar with chambers in Cardiff 1940; HM Forces 1940–1945; on staff of Judge Advocate-General MP, County of Cardigan 1945–1966; Recorder, Carmarthen 1950; Recorder, Merthyr Tydfil 1953–1960; Recorder, Swansea 1960–1964; Recorder, Cardiff 1964–1967. **Appointments:** Chairman, Welsh Parliamentary Party 1955; Chairman, Montgomeryshire QS 1959–1971; Deputy Chairman, Ways and Means, House of Commons 1965–1966; Social Security (formerly National Insurance) Commander 1967–1986; President, St David's University College, Lampeter 1977–1992; Honorary Fellow, Trinity College, Carmarthen 1992; Master Emeritus, Middle Temple 1998; Member, Court of the National Museums and of the University of Wales. Died 18 July 2001.

BOWEN, John Leslie (1935) See GEBHARD.

BOWEN, Leslie Harold (1907) Born 3 November 1888, Rochford, Strensham Road, Moseley, Kings Norton, Worcestershire; son of John Bowen, Master Builder, Alderman, High Sherriff, and Catherine (Kate) Julia Townsend. BA 1910. **Tutor(s):** J R Tanner. **Johnian Relatives:** brother of William Henry Bowen (1930); uncle of Leslie Harold Bowen (1935); uncle of John Leslie Gebhard (1935) and of Thomas Jim Bowen (1936). **Educ:** Queen's College, Taunton. **Career:** Ryland, Martineau and Carslake, of Birmingham, Solicitors; Corporal, London Regiment (Queen Victoria's Rifles) 1914; 1st Lincolnshire Regiment, France; Second Lieutenant, 3rd Lincolnshire Regiment 1915. Died 22 December 1915 (killed in action).

BOWEN, Leslie Harold (1935) Born 22 March 1917, 24 Lensfield Road, Cambridge; son of William Henry Bowen, Consulting Surgeon, and Kathleen Edith Clark. **Subject(s):** Classics/Law; BA 1938. **Tutor(s):** R L Howland. **Johnian Relatives:** nephew of Leslie Harold Bowen (1907); son of William Henry Bowen (1930); cousin of John Leslie Gebhard (1935) and of Thomas Jim Bowen (1936). **Educ:** Miss Borrer's School; St Faith's, Cambridge; Marlborough. **Career:** Member of Home Guard and farmer, WWII. Died 23 October 1942.

BOWEN, Colonel Thomas Jim (1936) Born 21 July 1917, Ingleside, Strensham Hill, Moseley, Birmingham; son of Thomas Oliver Bowen, Builder, and May Baragwanath; m Anne Bowen, 1950; 2 sons, 1 daughter. BA 1939; MA 1943. **Tutor(s):** C W Guillebaud. **Johnian Relatives:** nephew of Leslie Harold Bowen (1907) and of William Henry Bowen (1930); cousin of John Leslie Gebhard (1935) and of Leslie Harold Bowen (1935). **Educ:** West House School, Edgbaston; The Leys School, Cambridge. **Career:** Army Officer, Worcestershire Regiment, 1st Battalion 1939–1968; Colonel, The Worcestershire Regiment 1967–1970; Steward to the Dean and Chapter and Administrator of Worcester Cathedral 1970–1982; Colonel, The Worcestershire and Sherwood Foresters Regiment 1972–1977. **Appointments:** High Sheriff of Hereford and Worcester 1980. **Honours:** MC; Commander, Order of South Arabia 1967. Died 14 May 2001.

BOWEN, William Henry (1930) Born 20 July 1878, 16 Edwardes Street, Balsall Heath, King's Norton, Worcestershire; son of John Bowen, Builder and Contractor, and Catherine (Kate) Julia Townsend; m Kathleen Edith Clark, 1914; 2 sons, 1 daughter. MA 1928; MB (London) 1901; BS 1902; MS 1904; MRCS 1901; LRCP 1901; FRCS 1903; FRSM. **Johnian Relatives:** brother of Leslie Harold Bowen (1907); father of Leslie Harold Bowen (1935); uncle of John Leslie Gebhard (1935) and of Thomas Jim Bowen (1936). **Educ:** The High School, Birmingham; Guy's Hospital, London. **Career:** University Teacher; Surgeon, Addenbrooke's Hospital, Cambridge; Honorary Consulting Surgeon, Royston Hospital; Honorary Surgeon, Research Hospital, Cambridge; Surgeon, East London Hospital for Children, Shadwell; Surgeon, Royal Ear Hospital, London. **Awards:** Gold Medal in Surgery 1902. **Publications:** 'Traumatic subdural haemorrhage', *Guy's Hospital Reports*, Volume 59; 'Experimental analysis of the growth of cancer', *Procedures of the Royal Society*, 78, 1906; 'Five cases of perforation of the large bowel', *Guy's Hospital Reports*, 1922; 'The Mayo and Crile Clinics: with special reference to thyroid surgery', *British Journal of Surgery*, 1923; *Appendicitus: a critical study*, 1937; *Charles Dickens and his Family: a sympathetic study*, 1956. Died 31 December 1963.

BOWER, Alan John (1938) Born 23 January 1920, Hillside, College Lane, Woking; son of Arthur Robert Bower, Master Printer, and Eleanor May Oldaker; m Florence Mary Brydon, 12 January 1943, Aberfeldy; 1 son (Ian Bruce b 15 October 1943), 1 daughter (Rona Mary b 7 May 1947). **Subject(s):** Natural Sciences; BA 1941; MA 1945. **Tutor(s):** R L Howland. **Johnian Relatives:** father of Ian Bruce Bower (1962). **Educ:** Wallops School, Weybridge; Ewell Castle School; Tonbridge School. **Career:** Publisher; Master Printer. **Honours:** MC. Died 7 December 1978.

BOWER, Anthony Hugh Brian (1947) Born 4 June 1929, 3 Whitehall Gardens, Victoria Avenue, Kingston upon Hull; son of Anthony Bower, Schoolmaster, and Helen Pearson McIntosh; m Margareta Anne Payne, 1964 (dis 1981); 1 son (Anthony b 1969, d 1998), 1 daughter (Stephanie b 1967). **Subject(s):** Natural Sciences/Mechanical Sciences; BA 1950; MA 1954; CEng; MIEE. **Tutor(s):** G C L Bertram; W A Deer. **Johnian Relatives:** great grandson of Anthony Bower (1842). **Educ:** Froebel House Preparatory School, Hull; Hymers College, Hull. **Career:** National Service 1950–1952; British Telecommunications Research 1953–1955; Engineering Division, BBC 1955–1988. **Awards:** Major Scholarship, SJC 1946.

BOWER, Thomas Henry (1933) Born 24 April 1911, 87 Burcot Road, Ecclesall, Sheffield; son of William Henry Bower, Schoolmaster, and Mary Elizabeth Bailey. **Subject(s):** Natural Sciences; BA 1935; MA 1967; BSc; MSc; Diploma in Education (Sheffield). **Tutor(s):** J M Wordie. **Educ:** Meersbrook Bank School, Sheffield; Firth Park Secondary School, Sheffield; Sheffield University. **Career:** Petroleum Geologist 1937–1970; Consulting Geologist/Lecturer in Geology in University of West Indies, St Augustine, Trinidad, and self-employed Agriculturalist 1970. Died 2 November 1988.

BOWES, John Foster Lyon (1940) Born 3 February 1921, Nursing House, Eldon Grove, West Hartlepool; son of Geoffrey Foster Bowes, Bank Manager, Barclays Bank Ltd, and Susan Bevan; m Phyllis Margaret Findlay-Smith, 10 April 1948; 1 son (Simon), 1 daughter (Susan). **Subject(s):** History; BA 1943; MA 1947. **Tutor(s):** C W Guillebaud. **Educ:** The Downs School, Malvern; Bryanston School. **Career:** RAF 1941–1945; British Military Administration Civil Affairs Officer 1945–1947; Assistant Master, Lathallan School, Fife 1948–1949; Housemaster, Second Master, Cheltenham College 1949–1981. **Appointments:** Honorary Secretary, Cheltonian Society 1981–1991; Chairman of Governors, The Downs School, Malvern 1983–1986; Member, Cheltenham College Council 1986–1991. **Awards:** King's Commendation for Valuable Service in the Air.

BOWLE, Brian Edward (1925) Born 29 November 1906, 1 Cleeve Villas, Butter Row, Rodborough, Gloucestershire; son of James Edward Pori

Bowle, Master Tailor, and Mabel Ellen Bruton. **Subject(s):** Natural Sciences; BA 1928; MA 1935. **Tutor(s):** J M Wordie. **Educ:** Amberley Parochial School; Marling School, Stroud. **Awards:** Exhibition, SJC 1925.

BOWLEY, John Lindsay William (1929) Born 26 July 1910, The Trellis, Bickley, Bromley, Kent; son of Alfred William Bowley, Member, London Stock Exchange, and Mary Lindsay Bristow. **Tutor(s):** J M Wordie. **Educ:** Bickley Park School; Amesbury School, Hindhead; Marlborough College.

BOWMAN, James Eric (1920) Born 6 March 1901, 6 Barn Hill, Stamford, Lincolnshire; son of Edward Stuart Bowman, Master Builder, and Florence Mabel Simken. **Subject(s):** Mathematics; BA 1923; MA 1927. **Tutor(s):** B F Armitage. **Educ:** Stamford School. **Career:** Assistant Master, later Bursar, Eastbourne College. **Awards:** Exhibition, SJC. Died 13 February 1965.

BOWN, John Henry Edgar (1933) Born 1 June 1914, Woburn Lodge, Oak Hill, Surbiton; son of Joseph Edgar Bown, Acting Deputy Inspector General, Indian Police, and Beryl Iolanthi Sedgley. **Tutor(s):** E A Benians. **Educ:** Glyngarth School, Cheltenham; Cheltenham College; Wycliffe College, Stonehouse.

BOX, Dr Antony William (1931) Born 6 February 1913, Bridge House, Stratford-on-Avon; son of William Frederick Box, Surgeon, and Constance Marion Roberts. BA 1934; MB 1938; BChir 1938. **Tutor(s):** M P Charlesworth. **Educ:** The King's School, Canterbury; Wrekin College, Wellington.

BOXALL, Randolph Leonard (1940) Born 11 August 1922, Clerkspool, Wiveliscombe, Somerset; son of Leonard Edwin Boxall, Gum exporter from the Sudan, and Beatrice Helena Jewell. **Tutor(s):** J M Wordie. **Educ:** Taunton School; Ashburton College. **Career:** Called to the Bar, Inner Temple 1951.

BOYCE, Peter McConnell (1936) Born 13 August 1918, Darjeeling; son of William Henry Boyce, Indian Civil Service, and Nora Isabella Gardiner. **Subject(s):** Mathematics/Economics; BA 1939. **Tutor(s):** J M Wordie. **Educ:** Flint House, Seaford; Miss Holland's School, Wimbledon; King's College Junior School, Wimbledon; King's College School, Wimbledon. **Career:** Indian Civil Service 1940–1948; Colonial Civil Service, Nigeria 1948–1958; Solicitor in private practice 1958–1979. **Awards:** Scholarship, SJC 1936–1937.

BOYD, Leslie Stanthorne (1930) Born 14 February 1913, The Hollies, Melrose, Roxburgh, Scotland; son of Robert Edwin Boyd, Yarn Merchant, and Margaret Sophia Davidson. **Subject(s):** Modern and Medieval Languages; BA 1935; MA 1938. **Tutor(s):** C W Guillebaud. **Educ:** The Abbey School, Melrose; St Mary's School, Melrose; Merchiston Castle School, Edinburgh. Died 10 July 1975.

BOYDELL, James Stephen (1948) Born 28 February 1927, 28 Winter Street, Horwich, Lancashire; son of James Boydell, Coal Hewer, and Lucy Wildish. **Subject(s):** History; BA 1950; MA 1970. **Tutor(s):** F Thistlethwaite. **Educ:** Lord Street Council School, Horwich; St Catherine's Church of England School; Rivington and Blackrod Grammar School.

BOYES, Albert Edgar (1940) Born 20 February 1921, 15 Ramsey Street, Scarborough; son of Albert Boyes, Organist and Plasterer, and Mary Ann Barker; m (1) Joyce Bell, 5 June 1948, Crumpsall Park Methodist Church (d), (2) Mary Davies Padfield, 16 April 1966; (1) 1 son (Martin b 1955), 1 daughter (Miriam b 1953). **Subject(s):** Natural Sciences; BA 1943; MA 1947. **Tutor(s):** J M Wordie. **Educ:** Gladstone Road Council School; High School for Boys, Scarborough. **Career:** Imperial Chemical Industries Ltd 1942–1978 (Research Manager, Plastics Division 1972–1978). **Awards:** Scholarship, SJC; Wright's Prize, SJC 1941.

BOYES, William Edward (1930) Born 1 March 1913, Lismore, Granville Road, Barnet, Hertfordshire; son of William Archibald Boyes, Solicitor and Clerk to the Magistrates, and Ethel Gilling; m Margaret Ilott, 1 July 1944, All Saints' Church, Hertford; 2 sons (William Osborn b 27 October 1949 and Richard Mark Edward b 25 September 1950), 1 daughter (Margaret Jane b 23 September 1945). **Subject(s):** Modern and Medieval Languages/Law; BA 1934; MA 1957. **Tutor(s):** C W Guillebaud. **Johnian Relatives:** grandson of William Osborn Boyes (1863); father of William Osborn Boyes (1967). **Educ:** Preparatory School, Granville Road, Barnet; Preparatory School, Norman Court, Little Heath, Potters Bar; Aldenham School. **Career:** Admitted Solicitor 1937; Practice, Barnet, Hertfordshire; Clerk to the Barnet Magistrates 1960–1967. **Appointments:** President, Hertfordshire Law Society. Died 16 August 1967.

BOYLE, The Revd David Harrop (1902) (admitted as a Non-Collegiate Student 1901) Born 3 May 1875, 32 Tutbury Street, Manchester, Lancashire; son of John Boyle, Mechanic (Engineer), and Mary Elizabeth Harrop. **Subject(s):** Natural Sciences/History; BA 1904; MA 1908; BSc (Manchester) 1896. **Tutor(s):** D MacAlister. **Educ:** Roby Pupil Teachers' Centre, Manchester; Owens College, Manchester. **Career:** Teacher, Birley Street Board School, Manchester 1896–1898; Curate, St Thomas, Hyde 1904–1906; Priest, Chester 1905; Tutor, Chester Diocesan Training College 1906–1911; Licensed Preacher, Diocese of Chester 1906–1918; Assistant Chaplain, Chester Diocesan Training College 1906–1922; Vice-Principal 1911–1922; Assistant Diocesan Inspector of Schools, Chester 1916–1919; Vicar, St James, Congleton 1918–1919; Vicar, St Matthew, Stockport 1922–1929; Assistant Diocesan Inspector of Schools, Chester 1923–1929; Vicar, Moulton 1929–1930; Rector, St Peter, Chester 1930–1932; Vicar, Toft 1932–1935; Chaplain, Felixstowe College 1935–1938; Rector, St John the Evangelist, Moffat 1938–1944; Permission to Officiate, Diocese of Cheshire 1945.

BOYNS, The Revd Martin Laurence Harley (1947) (admitted to Emmanuel College 1945) Born 6 July 1926, 85 Woodcote Road, Wallington, Surrey; son of Kenneth Harley Boyns, Wesleyan Methodist Minister, and Violet Irene Watson; m Susan Carter, 4 June 1955, St Peter's Church, Woodmansterne; 2 sons (Timothy b 1958 and Nicolas b 1963), 1 daughter (Sarah Jane b 1960). **Subject(s):** History; BA 1949; MA 1951; Cambridge Ordination Course 1952. **Tutor(s):** R L Howland. **Johnian Relatives:** brother of Richard Wallis Harley Boyns (1941); father of Nicolas John Harley Boyns (1981). **Educ:** Laneside Preparatory School, Golders Green; Leas House Preparatory School, Golders Green; Downside Preparatory School, Purley; Kingswood School, Bath; Emmanuel College, Cambridge; Ridley Hall, Cambridge. **Career:** RN 1945–1947; Ordained Deacon 1952; Curate, Woodmansterne, Surrey 1952–1955; Priest 1953; Curate, Holy Trinity with Christ Church, Folkestone, Kent 1955–1958; Vicar, Duffield, Derbyshire 1958–1971; Vicar, Rawdon, West Yorkshire 1971–1976; Chaplain, Woodlands Hospital, Rawdon (Bradford Royal Infirmary) 1971–1976; Rector, Melton, Suffolk 1976–1985; Rector, St Gerrans with St Anthony in Roseland, Cornwall 1985–1992. **Appointments:** Honorary Chaplain, Missions to Seamen 1987; Relief Chaplain, Port of Rotterdam, Netherlands 1993.

BOYNS, Richard Wallis Harley (1941) Born 10 June 1922, Rickmansworth, Hertfordshire; son of Kenneth Harley Boyns, Methodist Minister, and Violet Irene Watson; m Joan Timperley, 3 April 1959, Caxton Hall; 1 daughter (Elizabeth b 25 November 1960). **Subject(s):** History; BA 1947; MA 1950. **Tutor(s):** C W Guillebaud. **Johnian Relatives:** brother of Martin Laurence Harley Boyns (1947); uncle of Nicolas John Harley Boyns (1981). **Educ:** Tenterden Hall Preparatory School; Kingswood School. **Career:** Fleet Air Arm 1942–1946; House Master and Senior Master, King William's College, Isle of Man 1948–1983. Died 2 June 1986.

BOYS SMITH, The Revd Dr John Sandwith (1919) Born 8 January 1901, The Vicarage, Hordle, Hampshire; son of Edward Percy Boys Smith, Clerk in Holy Orders, and Charlotte Cecilia Sandwith; m Gwendolen Sara Wynn, 1942 (d 1994); 2 sons (John Wynn b 14 February 1943 and Stephen Wynn b 4 May 1946). **Subject(s):** Economics/Theology; BA 1922; MA 1926; Hon LLD (Cantab) 1970. **Tutor(s):** E A Benians. **Johnian Relatives:** son of Edward Percy Boys Smith (1881); father of John Wynn Boys Smith (1961) and of Stephen Wynn Boys Smith (1964); grandfather of Sarah Jane Boys Smith (1995). **Educ:** Furzie Close School, New Barton; Sherborne School. **Career:** Title A Fellow 1927–1933, Chaplain 1927–1934, Title B Fellow 1933–1940 and 1944–1959, Title C Fellow 1940–1944, Master 1959–1969, Title D Fellow 1969–1991, SJC; Lecturer in Theology 1931–1940, Ely Professor of Divinity 1940–1943, Vice-Chancellor 1963–1965, University of Cambridge. **Appointments:** Director of Studies and Supervisor in Theology 1927–1952, Praelector 1929–1931, Assistant Tutor 1931–1934, Tutor 1934–1939, Junior Bursar 1939–1944, Senior Bursar 1944–1959, Director of Studies in Moral Sciences 1947–1959, SJC; Stanton Lecturer in the Philosophy of Religion, University of Cambridge 1934–1937; Canon Emeritus, Ely Cathedral 1948; Honorary Fellow, Darwin College 1969–1991. **Awards:** Naden Studentship, SJC 1922; Burney Scholarship, University of Cambridge 1924. **Publications:** (with J M Creed) *Religious Thought in the Eighteenth Century*, 1934; *Memories of St John's College Cambridge 1919–1969*, 1983. Died 3 November 1991.

BRACKETT, Arthur William Keith (1913) Born 24 June 1894, 69 Queen's Road, Tunbridge Wells, Kent; son of Arthur William Brackett, Chartered Surveyor, and Emily Gertrude Lindsey; m Phyllis Mansell, 25 July 1931, Holy Trinity Church, Hastings; 1 son (Barry). **Subject(s):** Law; BA 1920; MA 1924; LLB 1920. **Tutor(s):** E E Sikes. **Educ:** Stanley Road Preparatory School; Tonbridge School. **Career:** Lieutenant, Queen's Own, Royal West Kent Regiment (wounded) 1914–1918; Solicitor, Menneer, Idle, Brackett and Williams, Hastings. **Appointments:** Prime Warden, Worshipful Company of Blacksmiths. Died 5 November 1964.

BRADBEER, John Wyatt (1945) Born 9 August 1927, 32 Linden Road, Redland, Bristol; son of Ernest Gustave Bradbeer, Physician, and Edyth Hetty Chaplin; m Sheila Attfield; 1 son (Robin Wyatt), 1 daughter (Sharon). **Subject(s):** Natural Sciences; BA 1948; MA 1952; MB 1951; BChir 1951; FRCS. **Tutor(s):** S J Bailey. **Educ:** XIV Preparatory School, Bristol; Ryeford Hall, Stonehouse; Wycliffe College, Stonehouse. **Career:** Consultant Surgeon, Mayday Hospital, Thornton Heath, Surrey 1966–1989. **Appointments:** Member, Court of Examiners, Royal College of Surgeons of England 1982–1988.

BRADDELL, Lionel Henry (1936) Born 11 March 1912, Highgrove, Ashburton, Devonshire; son of Lionel Braddell, Gentleman Farmer, and Mabel Elizabeth Bridge. **Tutor(s):** J M Wordie. **Educ:** Aymestrey Court, Worcester; Aldenham School; TCD. **Awards:** Colonial Probationer.

BRADDOCK, Joseph Edward (1920) Born 29 May 1902, 25 Drakefield Road, Upper Tooting, Surrey; son of Thomas Alfred Braddock, Gas Meter Manufacturer and Director, and Lucy Mary Bailey; m Murial Hilda Stuart Legg, 29 December 1925, St Leonard's, Streatham; 1 daughter. BA 1923; MA 1940. **Tutor(s):** B F Armitage. **Educ:** The New Beacon, Sevenoaks; Uppingham School. **Career:** Author, Lecturer, and BBC script writer; Tutor, Yardley Court School, Tonbridge 1934. **Publications:** *The Wise Shepherd and other poems*; *The Pilgrim Shadow*; *Bright Ghost*; *Swanhild*; *Footpaths of the Kent-Sussex Border*; *The Greek Phoenix*.

BRADFORD, John Eric (1929) Born 9 December 1910, 3 Park Terrace, Cambridge; son of Marcus Dennis Bradford, Director of Companies, and Kate Newens; 2 daughters. BA 1932; MA 1936. **Tutor(s):** C W Guillebaud. **Educ:** The Perse Preparatory School, Cambridge; The Perse School, Cambridge. **Career:** Cambridgeshire Regiment, POW, WWII; Owner, University Arms Hotel, Cambridge; Director, Cambridge Electric Supply Company, Cambridge Waterworks Company, and Grawbridge Water Work Company. Died 11 March 1998.

BRADING, George Thomas Robert (1944) Born 3 November 1926, 92 Boundaries Road, Balham; son of Thomas Brading, Technical Manager, Vickers, Armstrong Ltd, and Gladys Mary Saunders. **Subject(s):** Modern and Medieval Languages; BA 1949; MA 1951. **Tutor(s):** J M Wordie. **Educ:** West Jesmond Council School; Newcastle upon Tyne Royal Grammar School.

BRADLEY, David John (1938) Born 22 February 1913, Chicago, Illinois, USA; son of Harold Cornelius Bradley, Professor of Biochemistry, Wisconsin, and Mary Josephine Crane; m Elizabeth Bancroft McLane, 26 April 1941, USA. **Tutor(s):** J S Boys Smith. **Educ:** Wisconsin High School, Madison; Le Rosey, Switzerland; Dartmouth College, Hanover.

BRADLEY, Dr Rupert Stevenson (1924) Born 5 August 1907, 65 Moor View, Devonport, Devonshire; son of Robert Bradley, Chief Gunnery Instructor, RN, and Ellen Mary Berry. **Subject(s):** Natural Sciences (Chemistry); BA 1927; MA 1931; ScD 1954; FRIC. **Tutor(s):** J M Wordie. **Educ:** Elmham Council School; The Priory School, Great Yarmouth; The Grammar School, Great Yarmouth. **Career:** Senior Lecturer in Chemistry, University of Leeds 1950; Reader in Inorganic Chemistry 1959. Died 19 August 1993.

BRADLOW, Emanuel Percy (1927) Born 15 March 1906, Railway Road, New Doornfontein, Johannesburg, South Africa; son of David Adolph Bradlow, Merchant and Jeweller, and Annie Rebecca Greenberg. **Subject(s):** Law; BA 1929; MA 1952; BA (Witwatersrand) 1926; Honorary Doctor of Commerce (Witwatersrand). **Tutor(s):** C W Guillebaud. **Educ:** King Edward VII School, Johannesburg; University of Witwatersrand, Johannesburg. **Career:** Barrister-at-Law, Inner Temple, London; Chairman, Bradlow's Stores Ltd. **Appointments:** President, Johannesburg Chamber of Commerce; President, Associated Chambers of Commerce of South Africa. Died 17 December 1988.

BRADSHAW, Peter Malcolm Clark (1948) Born 14 September 1928, 26 Lockwood Street, Driffield, Yorkshire; son of Peter Sheperdson Bradshaw, Master Miller and Master Baker, and Margaret Annie Clark; m Annie Burns Gair, 8 August 1959, Ashington, Northumberland; 3 sons (Quintin Paul b 16 November 1962, Adrian Peter b 10 July 1964 and Jeremy Simon b 5 March 1967). **Subject(s):** Natural Sciences/ Geography; BA 1951; MA 1955. **Tutor(s):** G C L Bertram; W A Deer; E Miller. **Educ:** Driffield Council School; Pocklington School. **Career:** Intelligence Corps 1946–1948; Martins Bank, London 1952–1955; Schoolmaster in Science 1955–1989; Examiner in Sciences, University of Cambridge Local Examinations Syndicate 1962; Head, Chemistry Department, Wells Cathedral School 1967–1989.

BRADY, Frank (1903) Born 1 July 1885, The Square, Barnstaple, Devon; son of John Brady, Railway Contractor, and Elizabeth Holloway. **Tutor(s):** J R Tanner; C E Graves. **Educ:** Prior Park School, Bath.

BRAILOWSKY, Vadime (1924) Born 23 December 1905, Odessa, Russia; son of David Brailowsky, Banker and Landed Proprietor, and Nathalie Konelsky. **Tutor(s):** J M Wordie. **Educ:** La Lycée Carnot, Paris.

BRAIN, Kenneth Roy (1924) Born 22 June 1898, Watling Street, Wilncote, Warwickshire; son of Robert Brain, Grocer and Draper, and Mary Elizabeth Kimberlin; m Ethel Joyce Seward, 1926. **Subject(s):** Mathematics; BA 1926; MA 1930; BSc (London) 1921; MSc (Battersea Polytechnic) 1923. **Tutor(s):** J M Wordie. **Educ:** Queen Elizabeth's Grammar School, Tamworth; UCL. **Career:** Headmaster, Holmfirth Secondary School, Yorkshire; Master, Blandford Secondary School, Dorset 1922; Master, St John's College, Battersea 1922–1924; Master, Batley Grammar School 1926–1931.

BRAIN, Michael Benjamin (1929) Born 13 April 1910, Cwrt-yr-Ala, Michaelstone-le-Pit, Cardiff; son of William Henry Brain, Master Brewer, and Ethel Mary Hall. BA 1932; MA 1936. **Tutor(s):** C W Guillebaud. **Educ:** Harris Hill, Newbury; Repton School. Died 24 April 1971.

BRAITHWAITE, Bernard Sedgwick (1930) Born 8 June 1913, St James', The School House, Baldersby, Yorkshire; son of Thomas John Braithwaite, Schoolmaster, and Mary Moore Sedgwick, Housewife; m (1) Biddie Mary (d 1959), (2) Yvonne Madge Erna, 1971; (1) 2 sons (John Dawson and David Dawson), (2) 2 stepsons (Nicholas b 30 November 1951 and Christopher Charles b 18 November 1955), 1 stepdaughter (Susan Ann b 11 September 1953). **Subject(s):** Natural Sciences; BA 1935; MA 1939; DipEd 1937. **Tutor(s):** J M Wordie. **Johnian Relatives:** stepfather of Nicholas Leng-Smith (1970) and of Christopher Charles Leng Smith (1974). **Educ:** Church of England School, Baldersby; Kirkby Malham School; Sedbergh School. **Career:** Lecturer, Extra-Mural Department, London University 1937–1938; Master, Christ's Hospital, Horsham 1938–1939; Flying Officer, RAF 1939–1940; Administrative Assistant to Director of Education, Derbyshire 1939–1943; Deputy Director of Education, East Sussex 1943–1950; Chief Education Officer, East Sussex 1950–1966; Director of Education, Bahamas 1967–1968; General Education Specialist, World Bank, Washington DC 1968–1971; Educational Planning Consultant to: World Bank; UNESCO; British Council; and independently in Guyana, Gambia, Israel, Australia, Malaysia, South Korea, Nigeria, Tanzania, Bangladesh, Peru, Somalia, the Philippines and Indonesia 1971–1989. **Appointments:** Council Member, London Institute of Education; Member, Advisory Committee on Social Welfare for the Colonies; Member, Executive of the Association of Education Committees of the UK 1952–1966; Member, School Broadcasting Council of the BBC 1958–1966; Ford Foundation Fellowship in USA 1960; Council Member, University of Sussex 1960–1967; Chairman, Council, South East Regional Exams Board, CSE 1963–1966; Chairman, Schools Television Committee, Independent Television Authority 1963–1967; Visiting Professor of Education, State University of New York 1963; University of Manitoba 1967; Lecturer on Georgian furniture and porcelain for Cambridge University Extra-Mural Studies Board and the WEA. **Awards:** Scholarship, SJC 1935–1936. **Publications:** Contribution to *Open Learning*, UNESCO. Died 21 September 2001.

BRAITHWAITE, John Geden North (1945) Born 5 October 1920, Ashville, Etherley Lane, Bishop Auckland, County Durham; son of Frank Braithwaite, Stationer and Bookseller, and Edith Muriel North; m Dorothy Gargate, August 1947, Elvet Church, Durham. **Subject(s):** Natural Sciences; BA 1947; MA 1952. **Tutor(s):** C W Guillebaud. **Educ:** High School, Bishop Auckland; Cockton Hill Council School, Bishop Auckland; King James I Grammar School, Bishop Auckland. **Career:** Flight Lieutenant, RAF 1939–1945; Physicist, The Environmental Research Institute of Michigan, until 1982.

BRAITHWAITE, John Vernon (1931) Born 26 December 1912, Strafford House, West Street, Boston, Lincolnshire; son of John Braithwaite, Physician and Surgeon, and Clara Beatrice Webster; m Nancy Phyllis Scatchard (d 1995); 2 sons (Norman John and William Thomas). **Tutor(s):** M P Charlesworth. **Johnian Relatives:** father of Norman John Braithwaite (1964). **Educ:** Horton Preparatory School, Biggleswade; Shrewsbury School; Medical Training (London). **Career:** Squadron Leader and Acting Wing Commander (final ranks), RAF, WWII. Died 1975.

BRAMWELL, Eric Arundell (1924) Born 9 April 1906, Sample Oak Cottage, Shalford, Surrey; son of Ernest Bramwell, Clerk in Holy Orders, and Louisa Anne Arundell. **Tutor(s):** J M Wordie. **Educ:** St Neots Eversley Private School; Charterhouse.

BRAMWELL, Hartley (1941) Born 3 April 1924, 12 Prince Edward Road, South Shields; son of Hartley Bramwell, Managing Secretary, Co-operative Society, and Florence Littlewood; m Leigh Cooper, 1951; 2 daughters (Victoria b 1952 and Andrea b 1955). **Subject(s):** Law; BA 1947; MA 1949; Qualified Solicitor; LAMTPI. **Tutor(s):** S J Bailey. **Educ:** Mortimer Road School, South Shields; High School for Boys, South Shields. **Career:** Pilot, Fleet Air Arm with the Home, East Indies and British Pacific Fleets 1942–1946; Solicitor, Hampshire County Council 1950–1954; Senior

Assistant Solicitor, Devon County Council, Exeter 1954–1964; County Solicitor and Secretary, Royal County of Berkshire 1974–1977; Senior Lecturer in Law, Associate Professor, University of Hong Kong 1977–1983; Legal Consultant, Mortgage Corporation 1988–1989. **Publications:** *Conveyancing in Hong Kong*, Butterworths, 1981.

BRANCH, Newton Kemal (1931) Born 7 September 1912, Walford House, Mersea Road, Colchester, Essex; son of Alfred Ernest Branch, Director General, Royal Animal Breeding Station, and Ada Loomas Hill. **Subject(s):** Law; BA 1934. **Tutor(s):** M P Charlesworth. **Educ:** Colchester Kindergarten; Heathfield, Keston; Marlborough College.

BRAND, Dr Boris Peter (1943) See BRANDHENDLER.

BRANDENBURGER, Peter Hugh (1938) Born 16 October 1919, 199 Melrose Avenue, Kilburn, London; son of Fritz Moritz Brandenburger, Bank Manager, and Hilda Bregman. **Tutor(s):** C W Guillebaud. **Educ:** University College School, Hampstead.

BRANDER, Michael William (1941) Born 8 May 1924, Edinburgh; son of Francis Robert Brander and Anne Anderson Johnston; m Lady Evelyn Jean Blanche Balfour, 11 December 1948; 1 son (Andrew Michael), 2 daughters (Kathleen and Ann). **Subject(s):** History/Economics/Law; BA 1946; MA 1949. **Tutor(s):** C W Guillebaud. **Johnian Relatives:** cousin of Ian Calthrop Brander (1952); father of Andrew Michael Brander (1967). **Educ:** South Kensington Preparatory School; Haileybury College. **Career:** Volunteered for Royal Armoured Corps 1942; Commissioned 10th Royal Hussars 1943; Wounded in action with 8th Army in Italy in 1944 and invalided out; PA, Directors of Anglo-American Corporation of South Africa 1947–1949; Managed own stud farm 1950–1955; Full time author 1955; Managing Director, The Gleneil Press 1995. **Appointments:** Captain, Home Guard 1950–1954. **Publications:** *The Language of the Field*, 1997; *Brander's Original Guide to Scotch Whisky*, 2000; numerous works including biography, history, travel, and Scottish and Country Life.

BRANDHENDLER, Dr Boris Peter Conradin Frederick Anatole (BRAND, Boris Peter) (1943) Born 30 May 1925, Queen Charlotte's Hospital, Paddington; son of Boris Mark Brandhendler, West African Merchant, and Louise Renan; m Kathleen Mary Knight, 1960; 1 daughter (Elizabeth Mary b 1961). **Subject(s):** Natural Sciences; BA 1946; MA 1950; PhD 1953; BSc (London) 1948; FRPS 1971. **Tutor(s):** C W Guillebaud. **Educ:** Essendine Elementary School; North Paddington Central School; Polytechnic Secondary School, London. **Career:** Research Chemist, Philips Lamps Ltd, Mitcham, Surrey 1945–1948 (developed first settling process for phosphors in television tubes in Europe); Senior Research Chemist, Organics Division, ICI/Zeneca 1952–1983 (worked on copper phthalocyanine pigments, biocides, fungicides and colour photography, invented Monastral Fast Blue RF used to produce blue paint for houses, cars and nitrocellulose lacquers, the bacterialcide Proxel GXL and the fungicide Densil S, discovered delta polymorphic crystalline form of copper phthalocyanine, and worked on Monastral Fast Blue B, used to produce motorway signs in the UK and other countries in Europe); Part-time Lecturer in Chemistry, Salford College of Advanced Technology 1954–1967; Part-time Lecturer in Chemistry, John Dalton College, Manchester 1964–1967. **Publications:** numerous articles in *Transactions of the Faraday Society* and *Journal of Photographic Science*, and many patents.

BRANFORD, Robert Richard (1939) Born 11 July 1920, Evelyn Hall, Mussoorie, Punjab, India; son of Richard Branford, Farmer, and Joyce Evelyn Cobbold. **Subject(s):** History; BA 1947. **Tutor(s):** J S Boys Smith. **Educ:** King's College Choir School, Cambridge; Marlborough College. **Career:** Nigerian Colonial Service. Died 29 August 1949.

BRANFORD, Professor William Richard Grenville (1945) Born 19 January 1927, 17 Winn Road, Southampton; son of Francis William Branford, Lieutenant, RN, and Catherine Miller; m Jean Gordon-

Brown, 1952; 1 son, 1 daughter. **Subject(s):** English; BA 1948; MA 1952; BEd (Cape Town) 1950; PhD (Natal) 1961. **Tutor(s):** S J Bailey. **Johnian Relatives:** great grandson of Abraham Hill (1835); great grand nephew of Isaac Hill (1843); great nephew of Edwin Hill (1862); grandson of Frank Hill (1880). **Educ:** Hilton College, Natal, South Africa; St Mark's Diocesan School, George, South Africa; St Andrew's College, South Africa. **Career:** Stellenbosch University 1951; Lecturer in English, University of Natal 1952–1959; Senior Lecturer, Rhodes University and Examiner, English Higher, Joint Matriculation Board 1964–1965; Director, Institute for Study of English in Africa 1964–1971; English Language 1966–1971; Professor of Linguistics 1972–1976; Professor and Head of Department of Linguistics and English Language 1977–1990, Professor Emeritus 1990, Rhodes University. **Appointments:** General Editor, Rhodes University Project for *Dictionary of South African English on Historical Principles*; South African Member, Editorial Advisory Board, *Oxford English Dictionary* 1985; Honorary Research Associate in Linguistics, University of Cape Town. **Publications:** *Judgement of the Lion*; *The Elements of English*, 1967; *Structure, Style & Communication*, 1980; (with Jean Branford) *Dictionary of South African English*, 1993.

BRASH, Edward John Yelverton (1907) Born 21 May 1888, 2 Northernhay Place, Exeter, Devon; son of Edward Alexander Brash, Surgeon, and Blanche Gregory; m Gwendoline Bartlett, 7 July 1916, St Margaret's, Lee. **Subject(s):** Natural Sciences; BA 1910; MB; BChir 1916; LRCP (St Bartholomew's) 1913; MRCS 1913. **Tutor(s):** J R Tanner. **Educ:** Exeter School. **Career:** House Surgeon and House Physician, Addenbrooke's Hospital, Cambridge; Acting Major, RAMC (TF); Surgeon Specialist, 41st General Hospital, Salonica. **Honours:** Order of St Sava, 4th Class (Serbia).

BRASHER, Christopher William (1947) Born 21 August 1928, 121 Parade Street, Kingston, Georgetown, British Guiana; son of William Kenneth Brasher, Electrical Engineer, and Katie Howe; m Shirley Bloomer; 1 son (Hugh), 2 daughters (Kate and Amanda). **Subject(s):** Natural Sciences; BA 1951; MA 1978; DUniv (Stirling) 1989; Honorary DSc (Kingston) 1996. **Tutor(s):** G C L Bertram. **Johnian Relatives:** son of William Kenneth Brasher (1919). **Educ:** Oakley Hall, Cirencester; Rugby School. **Career:** Junior Executive, Mobil Oil Company 1951–1957; Sports Editor 1957–1961, Columnist 1961–1991, *The Observer*; BBC TV Reporter, *Tonight* 1961–1965; Editor, *Time Out* and *Man Alive* 1964–1965; Head, General Features, BBC TV 1969–1972; Chairman, Brasher Leisure Ltd 1977–2003; Managing Director, Fleetfoot Ltd 1979–1995; Chairman, Berghaus Ltd 1993–1998; Chairman, The Brasher Boot Company Ltd 1993–2001. **Appointments:** Captain, Cambridge University Hare and Hounds; President, CUAC; Secretary, then President, Cambridge University Mountaineering Club; Co-founder 1979, Trustee 1983–1992 and 1996, The John Muir Trust; Trustee, London Marathon Charitable Trust 1981; Founder 1981, Race Director 1981–1995, Chairman 1981–1995, President 1995–2003, The London Marathon; Vice-President 1984–2003, British Orienteering Federation; Trustee, The Knoydart Foundation; Chairman, The Chris Brasher Trust 1988; Chairman, The Petersham Trust 1999. **Awards:** Olympic Gold Medal (3,000m Steeplechase) 1956; Sports Writer of the Year (British Press Awards) 1968 and 1976. **Honours:** National Medal of Honour, Finland 1975; OStJ 1995; CBE 1996. **Publications:** (with Sir John Hunt) *The Red Snows*, 1960; *Sportsmen of Our Time*, 1962; *Diaries of the Olympics – Tokyo*, 1964; *Mexico*, 1968; *Munich*, 1972. Died 28 February 2003.

BRASHER, William Kenneth (1919) Born 31 March 1897, 128 Cotham Brow, Bristol, Gloucestershire; son of Charles William James Brasher, Doctor of Medicine, and Mabel Marion Westlake; m Katie Howe, 1922; 2 sons (Peter Howe b 23 March 1924 and Christopher William b 21 August 1928), 2 daughters (Elizabeth Furneaux b 21 August 1925 and Francis Margaret b 24 January 1931). BA 1921. **Tutor(s):** E A Benians. **Johnian Relatives:** father of Christopher William Brasher (1947). **Educ:** Preparatory School, Clifton; Clifton College. **Career:** South Midland Division, Signal Company, RE, including service in France 1915–1919 (Lieutenant 1916); Design and Development Department, Marconi's Wireless Telegraph Co 1919–1922; Assistant Engineer, Chief Engineer, then Government Electrical Inspector, Post Office, British Guyana 1922–1939; Served in British Guinea on secondment to the Government of Iraq 1928, and in Palestine 1933; Secretary, Institution of Electrical Engineers 1939–1962. **Honours:** CBE 1951; Commander of the Order of King Leopold II, Belgium 1963. Died 24 May 1972.

BRATHERTON, Dr David Georges (1938) Born 4 July 1919, Saint Leu La Forêt, Seine et Oise, Pontoise, France; son of Harry Bratherton, Gown Manufacturer, and Marguerite Moffat; m Mary Ineson (d 1985); 1 son (John David b 1959), 1 daughter (Wendy Joan b 1948). **Subject(s):** Natural Sciences; BA 1941; MA 1955; MB, BChir (Manchester) 1944; FRCR. **Tutor(s):** C W Guillebaud. **Johnian Relatives:** father of John David Bratherton (1980). **Educ:** Halton Bank Council School, Salford; Eccles Grammar School; Manchester Grammar School. **Career:** Assistant Medical Officer, Radium Institute, Bradford; Consultant Radiotherapist, Holt Radium Institute, Manchester; Director, Department of Radiotherapy and Oncology; Chairman, Consultant Staff, Addenbrooke's Hospital; Consultant Radiotherapist and Assistant Director, Radiotherapeutic Centre, East Anglian Regional Hospital Board 1955; Associate Lecturer in Clinical Medicine, University of Cambridge 1976–1981 and 1981–1986; Director, Arthur Rank Hospice 1981–1984. **Appointments:** Fellow, Faculty of Radiologists (now, Royal College of Radiologists). **Awards:** Exhibition, SJC 1937. Died 15 November 1991.

BRATT, John Bernard (1933) Born 26 July 1902, 195 Berners Street, Aston Manor, Birmingham; son of John Thomas Daniel Bratt, Jeweller, and Florence Lily Jennings Haynes. **Subject(s):** Natural Sciences; BA 1935; BSc (London) 1933. **Tutor(s):** J M Wordie. **Educ:** Birmingham Midland Institute; Birmingham Central Technical College.

BRAUNHOLTZ, Hermann Justus (1908) Born 12 October 1888, Sydney House, Chesterton Road, Cambridge; son of Eugen Gustav Wilhelm Braunholtz, Reader in Romance, University of Cambridge, and Elisabeth Charlotte Dorothea Breul; m Joan Margaret Raymont, 25 June 1932, Hampstead; 1 son, 1 daughter. **Subject(s):** Classics/Modern and Medieval Languages; BA 1911; MA 1919. **Tutor(s):** E E Sikes. **Educ:** Oundle School; Mr T R Goodchild's Preparatory School, Cambridge. **Career:** Lance Corporal, RAMC, WWI; Assistant Keeper 1913, Keeper, Department of Oriental Antiquities and Ethnography until 1938, Keeper, Department of Ethnography 1938–1953, British Museum. **Appointments:** Honorary Editor 1926–1935, President 1937–1939 and 1941–1943, Royal Anthropological Institute; Member and President, International African Institute. **Honours:** CBE 1951. **Publications:** 'History of Ethnography on the Museum after 1793', *British Museum Quarterly*, 18, 1953. Died 4 June 1963.

BRAY, Dr Basil Richard (1932) Born 27 June 1914, 14 Burngreave Road, Sheffield; son of Frederick Richard Bray, Medical Practitioner, and Joan Jewell Willing; m Anthea Wolstenholme. **Subject(s):** Natural Sciences; BA 1935; MA 1939; MB 1939; BChir 1939; MRCS; LRCP. **Tutor(s):** R L Howland. **Educ:** Birkdale Preparatory School, Sheffield; The Leys School, Cambridge. **Career:** Surgeon Lieutenant, RNVR 1939–1941. Died 22 May 1941 (killed in action in HMS *Greyhound*, off Crete).

BRAY, George James (1943) Born 12 May 1925, 20 East Road, Shoreditch; son of George John Bray, Compositor, and Rose Fuller. **Tutor(s):** C W Guillebaud. **Educ:** Popham Road School, London; Highbury County School, London.

BRAY, John Clive Russell (1945) Born 5 April 1920, Lane Cove Road, Ryde, New South Wales; son of Reginald Norman Russell Bray, Marine Engineer, and Julia Catherine Carstens. **Subject(s):** English; BA 1948; MA 1952. **Tutor(s):** C W Guillebaud. **Educ:** Eastwood, New South Wales; Stanmore, New South Wales; HMS *Conway*. **Career:** Cadet, Peninsular and Oriental Steamship Company 1938–1939; Flight Sergeant, RAF, then POW 1939–1945; Lecturer in English, Fouad I University, Cairo, Egypt 1948–1952; Schoolmaster, English School, Nicosia 1956. Died 16 February 1958.

BRAYBROOK, Clifford Herbert (1936) Born 26 October 1917, 2 Sheringham Avenue, Romford, Essex; son of Herbert Braybrook, Civil Servant, and Annie Edith Beach; m Sylvia Ridley, 1951; 2 daughters (Diana and Monica). **Subject(s):** Mathematics; BA 1939; MA 2002. **Tutor(s):** J M Wordie. **Educ:** London Road Council School, Romford; St Edward's C of E School, Romford; Royal Liberty County School, Romford; Purley County School. **Career:** Radar Officer, Ordinance Corps Workshop, and Staff Officer, 21 Army Group, RAOC and REME (discharged as Major) 1940–1946; Section Leader, Group Leader, and Manager, Systems Division, Mullard Research Laboratories (later Philips) 1946–1980.

BRAYSHAW, John Derwent (1941) Born 1 September 1922, Mottram Cottage, Dean Row, Wilmslow; son of Edmund Russel Brayshaw, Managing Director of Machine Tool Company, and Winifred Maude Barber. **Subject(s):** Natural Sciences; BA 1945; MA 1948. **Tutor(s):** C W Guillebaud. **Educ:** Sidcot Friends' School, Somerset; Manchester Grammar School. Died August 1973.

BRAYSHAY, Sidney (1903) Born 18 April 1885, Stockton-on-Tees, County Durham; son of William Brayshay, Solicitor, and Mary Louisa Davison; m Olga Margaret Exner, 24 January 1928, Singapore. **Subject(s):** Mechanical Sciences; BA 1906. **Tutor(s):** D MacAlister. **Educ:** Ripon Grammar School. **Career:** Technical Instructor, Public Works Department, Kuala Lumpur 1911; Assistant Engineer 1914; Lieutenant, RE 1918; Executive Engineer in charge of the Technical School, Kuala Lumpur 1920–1928; Acting Senior Engineer, Hydraulics, Selangor 1930. Died 12 June 1946.

BRAZIER, Leslie Frederick (1943) Born 28 July 1925, Upper Heath, Hampstead, London; son of Charles Herbert Brazier, Civil Servant, Post Office, and Emily Muriel Howard. **Subject(s):** Modern and Medieval Languages/Economics; BA 1948; MA 1952. **Tutor(s):** C W Guillebaud. **Educ:** Alperton Council School; University College School. **Career:** RAF Cadet. **Awards:** Exhibition, SJC 1943.

BREARLEY, Joseph (1928) Born 13 July 1909, 46 Blakeridge Lane, Batley, Yorkshire; son of Herbert Brearley, Master Draper, and Sarah Caroline Elstub. **Subject(s):** English; BA 1931; MA 1938. **Tutor(s):** M P Charlesworth. **Educ:** Carlinghow Council School, Batley; Batley Grammar School.

BREDDY, Denis Charles George (1949) Born 18 December 1929, Bury Hill Farm, Mangotsfield, Gloucestershire; son of Lawford Breddy, Farmer, and Gertrude Maud Church. **Subject(s):** Mechanical Sciences; BA 1952. **Tutor(s):** G C L Bertram. **Educ:** Downend Elementary School, Bristol; Clifton College Preparatory School; Clifton College.

BREFFIT, Reginald Ernest (1919) Born 30 September 1900, The Upper Close, St Mary in the Marsh, Norwich; son of Walter Breffit, Clerk in Holy Orders, and Ethel Maud Long; 1 son. BA 1922; MA 1926. **Tutor(s):** E E Sikes. **Educ:** The King's School, Canterbury; Norfolk House School, Beaconsfield. **Career:** Inspector, Educational Officer, Wiltshire Police Force; Constable, Wiltshire Police Force 1926; Superintendent, Devizes 1935; Chief Constable, East Sussex 1936. Died 24 June 1976.

BRENNAND, Arthur Fynes (1923) Born 25 March 1904, Mayfield, Blandford, Dorset; son of William Arthur Bedford Brennand, Solicitor, and Ida Norah Katharine Fynes-Clinton. **Subject(s):** Mechanical Sciences; BA 1926. **Tutor(s):** E Cunningham. **Educ:** Dane Court Preparatory School, Parkstone; The King's School, Canterbury. Died 1 October 1987.

BRERETON, John Jerningham (1927) Born 18 April 1908, 7 Cannon Place, Hampstead, London; son of Cloudesley Shovel Henry Brereton, Divisional Inspector, London County Council, and Maud Adeline Ford; m Audrey Jean Masshall Woode, 31 July 1937; 3 daughters (Margaret, Elizabeth and Jennifer). **Subject(s):** Natural Sciences; BA 1930; MA

1959; DipAgr 1932. **Tutor(s):** J M Wordie. **Johnian Relatives:** son of Cloudesley Shovel Henry Brereton (1883). **Educ:** Pinewood, Farnborough; Oundle School; The Rothamstead Agricultural Institute. **Career:** 6th Norfolk Home Guard 1939–1945. Died 4 January 1984.

BRETHERTON, Leonard Francis (1927) Born 17 May 1909, Winscombe, Park End Road, Gloucester; son of Francis Hawkins Bretherton, Solicitor; and Laura Jane Aldridge. **Subject(s):** Mechanical Sciences; BA 1930. **Tutor(s):** J M Wordie. **Educ:** Preparatory School, Gloucester; Wycliffe College, Stonehouse.

BREWER, Cyril Griffith (1920) Born 12 February 1900, Bentley Villa, Meanwood, Leeds, Yorkshire; son of Griffith Brewer, Chartered Patent Agent, and Beatrice Hilda Swanston. BA 1923; MA 1927. **Tutor(s):** B F Armitage. **Educ:** Wellesley House School, Broadstairs; Felsted School. **Career:** Pilot Officer, RAFVR, Balloon Command 1940; Air Ministry 1941; Squadron Leader and Liaison Officer to Public and Secondary Schools; Housemaster, Cotswold (Approved) School, Ashton Keynes, Swindon. **Appointments:** Member, Selection Boards for Short Course Cadets. Died 10 March 1982.

BREWER, Godfrey Noel (1921) Naval Officer.

BREWSTER, Alan Roulston (1937) Born 18 March 1919, Braeside, Beechwood Avenue, Londonderry; son of Frederick Charles Brewster, Director of Public Company, and Jane Macfarlane Roulston; m Angela Mary Wyncoll, 21 December 1943. **Tutor(s):** J M Wordie. **Educ:** Doyle College, Londonderry; Portora Royal School, Enniskillen. **Career:** RASC, WWII.

BREWSTER, Flying Officer John (1935) Born 16 March 1916, Winsley Hurst, Ripley, Harrogate; son of Thomas Fox Brewster, of independent means, and Katherine May Harrison. BA 1938. **Tutor(s):** C W Guillebaud. **Educ:** Heddon Court, Barnet; Repton School. **Career:** Flying Officer, RAF, WWII. Died April 1941 (killed on active service).

BREWSTER, The Revd Leslie George (1921) Born 11 September 1903, 16 Marjorie Grove, Clapham Common, Surrey; son of Henry George Brewster, Commercial Clerk, and Alice Mary Hignett. **Subject(s):** English/Theology; BA 1926; MA 1930; MRCS 1952; LRCP 1952. **Tutor(s):** E A Benians. **Johnian Relatives:** father of David John Brewster (1957); grandfather of Elizabeth Jean McDonnell (1982) and of Sarah Elizabeth Snyder (1984). **Educ:** Manor House School, Clapham; Ridley Hall, Cambridge; St Mary's Hospital School, Paddington. **Career:** Ordained Deacon 1927; Curate, Holy Trinity, Eastbourne 1927–1931; Ordained Priest 1928; Lecturer and Curate, Watford 1932–1934; Vicar, St Paul, Walcot, Bath 1934–1938; Vicar, Christ Church, Southport 1938–1943; GP until retirement. Died September 1974.

BRIAN, Frederick Reginald Hugh (1912) Born 15 April 1893, Abbassia, Cairo, Egypt; son of Hyla Edwin Brian, Senior Master, Military School, Cairo, and Annie Elliott. **Subject(s):** Mathematics; BA 1915; MA 1926. **Tutor(s):** L H K Bushe-Fox. **Educ:** Berkhampstead School. **Career:** Lieutenant, RGA, WWI.

BRICE-SMITH, Dr Harold Francis (1908) Born 3 September 1889, 3 Whitton Terrace, Rothbury, Northumberland; son of Brice Smith, Clerk in Holy Orders, and Kate Emily Middleton; m Norah May Shrimpton, 28 March 1932, All Saints, Hameringham; BA 1911; MA 1921; BChir 1915; MRCS; LRCP 1921. **Tutor(s):** J R Tanner. **Johnian Relatives:** brother of Rollo Brice-Smith (1905) and of John Kenneth Brice-Smith (1915). **Educ:** The Grammar School, Bury St Edmunds. **Career:** Captain, RAMC (wounded twice, Mentioned in Despatches), WWI; Middlesex Hospital 1934. **Honours:** MC 1918. Died 4 November 1972.

BRICE-SMITH, John Kenneth (1915) Born 11 February 1894, The Rectory, Hameringham, Lincolnshire; son of Brice Smith, Clerk in Holy

Orders, and Kate Emily Middleton. **Tutor(s):** E E Sikes. **Johnian Relatives:** brother of Rollo Brice-Smith (1905); brother of Harold Francis Brice-Smith (1908). **Educ:** Cranleigh School; Quy Vicarage, Cambridge. **Career:** Second Lieutenant, 7th Battalion, Lincolnshire Regiment 1914–1915. Died 11 September 1915 (of wounds received in action in the Ypres Salient 6 September 1915).

BRICE-SMITH, Rollo (1905) Born 21 August 1886, 3 Whitton Terrace, Rothbury, Northumberland; son of Brice Smith, Clerk in Holy Orders, and Kate Emily Middleton. **Subject(s):** Classics; BA 1908; MA 1912. **Tutor(s):** J R Tanner; C E Graves. **Johnian Relatives:** brother of Harold Francis Brice-Smith (1908) and of John Kenneth Brice-Smith (1915). **Educ:** Pocklington School. **Career:** Headmaster, Llandaff Cathedral School 1911; Joint Headmaster, Brightlands, Newnham on Severn 1932. Died 7 November 1964.

BRICKSTOCK, Dr Alan (1948) Born 11 June 1930, Sandfield House, 12 Stream Road, Wordsley, Kingswinford, Stourbridge; son of Ernest Llewellyn Brickstock, Garage Proprietor, and Ethel Ward; m (1) Josephine Berry Moxley, 1956, (2) Ivy Rolls, 1968; (1) 1 son (Richard John), 1 daughter (Elizabeth). **Subject(s):** Mathematics; BA 1951; MA 1955; PhD 1955. **Tutor(s):** J M Wordie. **Educ:** Orchard Lane School, Lye; King Edward VI Grammar School, Stourbridge. **Career:** Procurement Executive, Ministry of Defence 1954–1990. **Awards:** Minor Scholarship, SJC 1947. Died 7 May 2002.

BRIDGE, James Haslam Newham (1946) Born 8 February 1925, 671 Oldham Road, Newton Heath, Manchester; son of James Bridge, Cotton Salesman, and Gertrude Whittle. **Subject(s):** Economics; BA 1947. **Tutor(s):** C W Guillebaud. **Educ:** Barneslea Private School; Manchester Grammar School. **Career:** Sub-Lieutenant, Fleet Air Arm.

BRIDGEFORD, George Macrae (1924) Born 25 July 1906, 32 Olive Road, Cricklewood, Hendon, Middlesex; son of John Macrae Bridgeford, Seed Merchant, and Phoebe Georgina Gunn; m Alison Bond, 8 February 1958, St John the Baptist, West Byfleet, Surrey. **Subject(s):** Natural Sciences; BA 1927; MA 1945. **Tutor(s):** B F Armitage. **Educ:** Haberdashers' Aske's School, Hampstead. **Career:** Warner, Barnes & Co Ltd, Manila 1927; Manila Manager 1938; Interned by the Japanese, WWII. **Appointments:** Technical Advisory Committee, Philippine Sugar Control Board. **Awards:** Exhibition, SJC.

BRIEF, Morris (1927) Born 22 January 1908, 5 Sheba Street, Spitalfields, London; son of Joseph Brief, Cabinet Maker (Journeyman), and Dinah Boimel. **Subject(s):** Mathematics; BA 1930. **Tutor(s):** J M Wordie. **Educ:** Underwood Street London County Council School; Central Foundation School; East London College. **Awards:** Scholarship, SJC 1926.

BRIEGER, Dr Ernest Oskar (BLAKE, Ernest Oscar) (1943) Born 6 June 1923, Herrnprotsch, Breslau, Germany; son of Ernest Brieger, Physician, and Kate Friedenthal; m Mavis Renwick, 7 June 1952, Caldecote Parish Church; 2 sons, 1 daughter. **Subject(s):** History; BA 1949; MA 1951; PhD 1953. **Tutor(s):** C W Guillebaud. **Educ:** Dragon School, Oxford; The Leys School, Cambridge. **Career:** Temporary Captain, The Queen's Royal Regiment, WWII; Lecturer in History, University of Nottingham 1952; Lecturer, then Reader in History, University of Southampton 1959. **Publications:** (ed) *Liber Eliensis*, RHS Camden Third Series, 1953; *The Cartulary of the Priory of St Denys near Southampton*, ed, Southampton Record Series, 1981. Died 7 June 2000.

BRIERLEY, Alan Corns (1941) Born 2 May 1923, 100 Burlington Avenue, Oldham; son of John Corns Brierley, Lecturer in Mechanical Engineering, University of Manchester, and Ethel Mills; m Valerie Margaret Norris, 1949; 2 sons (Paul Norris b 10 April 1951 and Mark Richard b 9 October 1953), 1 daughter (Sarah Elizabeth b 15 March 1957). **Subject(s):** Modern and Medieval Languages/History; BA 1947. **Tutor(s):** C W Guillebaud. **Johnian Relatives:** father of Paul Norris

Brierley (1969). **Educ:** Werneth Council School, Oldham; Hulme Grammar School, Oldham. **Career:** Lieutenant, RA 1942–1945; United Steel Companies (subsequently BSC) 1948–1982.

BRIGGS, Dr Arthur John (1938) Born 8 April 1920, Cedar Lawn, North End Road, Hampstead; son of William Arthur Briggs, Clerk in Holy Orders, and Emily Hoole. **Subject(s):** Natural Sciences; BA 1941; BChir 1944; MB 1944; MRCS; LRCP. **Tutor(s):** R L Howland. **Educ:** Loughborough Grammar School; Cheltenham College. **Career:** RAMC 1944–1946; GP, Beeston, Nottinghamshire 1946; Medical Officer, Treasury Medical Service 1966.

BRIGGS, Geoffrey Hugh (1943) Born 14 April 1926, Denison Hall, Leeds; son of Harry Briggs, Colliery Surface Electrician, and Charlotte Irene Black; m Judith de la Mare, 1950; 2 sons (Nicholas b 1957 and Peter b 1963). **Subject(s):** Classics; BA 1947; MA 1950; DipLib (London) 1949; DipAA (London) 1950; ALA 1951. **Tutor(s):** C W Guillebaud. **Educ:** Rochester Cathedral Choir School; King's School, Rochester; Ashby de la Zouche Grammar School. **Career:** Assistant Librarian, University of London Library 1949–1954; Deputy Librarian, Victoria University of Wellington, New Zealand 1954–1967; Deputy Librarian, University of Calgary, Alberta, Canada 1967–1969; University Librarian, Carleton University, Ottawa, Canada 1969–1991. **Awards:** Choral Studentship, SJC.

BRIGGS, Professor George Edward (1912) Born 25 June 1893, 24 Agscough Street, Grimsby, Lincolnshire; son of Walter Thomas Briggs, Coal Carter, and Susan Townend; m Nora Burman, 1 May 1920, Cleethorpes; 1 son (Peter George Briggs b 16 October 1923), 1 daughter (Janet Mary b 13 November 1927. **Subject(s):** Natural Sciences; BA 1915; MA 1920; FRS 1935. **Tutor(s):** R P Gregory. **Johnian Relatives:** father of Peter George Briggs (1941). **Educ:** Welholme County School; Grimsby Municipal College. **Career:** Sergeant-Instructor, RE (Signals) 1916–1919; Demonstrator in Plant Physiology 1919–1926, Lecturer in Botany 1926–1937, Reader in Plant Physiology 1937–1946, Professor of Plant Physiology 1946–1948, Professor of Botany 1948–1960, University of Cambridge; Gregson Fellow 1920–1926, Title B Fellow 1926–1937, Title C Fellow 1937–1960, Title D Fellow 1960, SJC. **Appointments:** Supervisor in Botany 1920–1926, Steward 1935–1946, Acting Senior Bursar 1943, President 1952–1963, SJC; Member, Council of the Senate 1941–1946, Chairman, Botanic Garden Syndicate, University of Cambridge. **Awards:** Frank Smart Prize for Botany, University of Cambridge 1914; Frank Smart Studentship, University of Cambridge 1915; Gedge Prize, University of Cambridge 1920; Allen Scholarship, University of Cambridge 1920; Slater Research Studentship. Died 8 February 1985.

BRIGGS, James Hillsdon (1932) Born 8 April 1914, 39 Lee Crescent, Edgbaston, Birmingham; son of Cecil Francis Briggs, Civil Servant, and Elizabeth Kitty Thompson. **Subject(s):** Mathematics/Natural Sciences; BA 1935; MA 1939; FIEE. **Tutor(s):** J M Wordie. **Educ:** Acocks Green Council School; Camp Hill Grammar School, Birmingham; King Edward VI School, Birmingham. **Career:** Carrier Communications Development Laboratory, General Electric Company 1935–1937; RAE; Air Ministry Research Department; TRE, Malvern; Chairman, Inter-services Radio Measurement Committee 1937–1955; Superintendent, Ground Radar Department, Radar Research Establishment 1955–1961; Director of Electronics, Research and Development, Ministry of Aviation 1961. **Awards:** Scholarship, SJC. Died 2 November 1987.

BRIGGS, Peter George (1941) Born 16 October 1923, 9 Brunswick Walk, Cambridge; son of George Edward Briggs, Fellow and Professor of Botany, and Nora Burman; m Mary Coome Kidd (d 1995); 2 sons, 1 daughter. **Subject(s):** Mechanical Sciences; BA 1946; MA 1949; MIEE. **Tutor(s):** C W Guillebaud. **Johnian Relatives:** son of George Edward Briggs (1912). **Educ:** Chesterton Preparatory School, Cambridge; King's School, Cambridge; The Leys School, Cambridge. **Career:** Electrical

Engineer; Ministry of Supply 1942–1945; Development Engineer, Elliott Brothers 1948–1952; International Computers Ltd 1952–1970 (Chief Engineer 1967–1973); Partner, Rainback Engineering & Brig-Ayd Controls 1974. **Appointments:** Member, Tewin Village Hall Committee. Died 16 August 2003.

BRIGGS, The Revd William Arthur (1900) Born 2 January 1878, Kirkby Folly, Nottinghamshire; son of George Briggs, Draper, and Betsy Anne Hardstaff. **Subject(s):** Natural Sciences; BA 1903; MA 1909. **Tutor(s):** D MacAlister. **Educ:** University College, Nottingham. **Career:** Science Lecturer, Diocesan Training College, York 1903; Ordained Deacon 1904; Ordained Priest 1905; RN Chaplain, various parishes and ships 1905–1928; Rector, Long Whatton 1928–1933; Rector, Stanford on Soar 1933.

BRIGGS CONSTABLE, William (1942) See CONSTABLE.

BRIGHT, Gerald Emery (1944) Born 17 May 1926, Lutton, Cornwood, Devon; son of James Bright, Police Sergeant, Devon Constabulary, Dartmouth, and Edith Dobbs; 2 children. **Subject(s):** History; BA 1948; MA 1950; PGCE 1952. **Tutor(s):** J M Wordie. **Educ:** Totnes Grammar School; Launceston College; Dartmouth Grammar School. **Career:** RN Cadet/Sub-Lieutenant 1943–1947; Dean Close, Cheltenham 1949; Assistant Master, Exmouth School, Headmaster, Hook Norton, Oxfordshire 1956–1960; Headmaster, Broadclyst, Devon 1960–1970; Headmaster/Principal, Ivybridge Community College, Devon 1970–1987; Course Director/Consultant, Community Education Development Centre and University of Exeter 1987–1993.

BRIGHT, Dr Peter Hayne (1941) Born 24 September 1922, 1 Norfolk Road, Bury St Edmunds, Suffolk; son of Wilfred James Bright, Headmaster, and Gertrude Elizabeth Jones; m Elizabeth. **Subject(s):** Natural Sciences; BA 1944; MA 1948; BChir 1948; MB 1948. **Tutor(s):** S J Bailey. **Johnian Relatives:** brother of Michael Valentine Bright (1956). **Educ:** The Grammar School, Chipping Campden; Wycliffe College. Died 12 June 2004.

BRIGHTMAN, Geoffrey (1925) Born 18 May 1908, Cintra, Sandpit Lane, Sandridge, St Albans, Hertfordshire; son of William Henry Brightman, Solicitor, and Minnie Boston Way; m Doris Thatcher. **Subject(s):** Classics/Law; LLB 1930. **Tutor(s):** E E Sikes. **Johnian Relatives:** brother of John Anson Brightman (1927); uncle of Christopher Anthony John Brightman (1966). **Educ:** Doon House, Westgate-on-Sea; Marlborough College. **Career:** Partner, London law firm; RNVR; own solicitor's practice, Lewes, WWII. Died 10 September 1977.

BRIGHTMAN, The Rt Hon Lord John Anson (1927) Born 20 June 1911, Cintra, Sandpit Lane, Sandridge, St Albans, Hertfordshire; son of William Henry Brightman, Solicitor, and Minnie Boston Way; m Roxane Ambatielo, 1945, Chapel of the British Embassy, Istanbul; 1 son. **Subject(s):** Law; BA 1932; MA 1972. **Tutor(s):** M P Charlesworth. **Johnian Relatives:** brother of Geoffrey Brightman (1925); father of Christopher Anthony John Brightman (1966). **Educ:** Doon House, Westgate-on-Sea; Marlborough College. **Career:** Assistant Master of Mathematics, Magdalen Preparatory School, Broadstairs 1928–1929; Called to the Bar, Lincoln's Inn 1932; Barrister, Lincoln's Inn 1932–1970; Sub-Lieutenant, RNVR, HMS *Martinetta* 1939–1941; Staff, Anti-submarine Warfare Training Base, Tobermory 1941–1943; Lieutenant, HMS *Barle*, 48th Escort Group, Atlantic and Mediterranean 1943–1944; Staff Course, Royal Naval Staff College, Greenwich 1944; Assistant Naval Attaché, Ankara, Turkey; Lieutenant Commander 1944–1945; Staff of Lord Louis Mountbatten, SEAC 1945–1946; QC 1961–1970; Bencher, Lincoln's Inn 1966; Attorney General, Duchy of Lancaster 1969–1970; Judge, High Court of Justice, Chancery Division 1970–1979; Judge, National Industrial Relations Court 1971–1974; Lord Justice of Court of Appeal 1979–1982; Lord of Appeal in Ordinary 1982–1986. **Appointments:** Secretary, then President, SJC Law Society; Master, University Law Society Moots 1930–1932; Member, General Council of the Bar 1956–1960 and 1966–1970; Honorary Fellow, SJC 1982; Chairman, Tancred's Foundation 1982–1996; Chairman of numerous House of Lords Committees 1983–1995; Fellow, Royal Geographical Society 1993; Member, Advisory Committee, Institute of Advanced Legal Studies 2000; Honorary Fellow, Royal Geographical Society 2001. **Honours:** Kt 1970; PC 1979; Baron and Life Peer 1982. **Publications:** 'Historical Sites in Franz Josef Land', *Circumpolar Journal*, 1997; 'Drafting Quagmires', *Statute Law Review*, 2002.

BRIND, Arthur Henry (1944) Born 4 July 1927, 10 Lewis Street, Barry, Glamorganshire; son of Thomas Henry Brind and Nellie Winifred Blanche Lawrence; m Barbara Harrison, 31 August 1954, Biddenham Church, Bedfordshire; 1 son, 1 daughter. **Subject(s):** History; BA 1947; MA 1951. **Tutor(s):** C W Guillebaud; F Thistlethwaite. **Johnian Relatives:** father of Oliver Henry Brind (1980). **Educ:** Romilly Boys' School; County School for Boys, Barry. **Career:** HM Forces 1947–1949; Colonial Administrative Service, Gold Coast/Ghana 1950–1960; Regional Secretary, Transvolta/Togoland 1959–1960; HM Diplomatic Service 1960–1987; Acting High Commissioner, Uganda 1972–1973; High Commissioner, Mauritius 1974–1977; Ambassador, Somali Democratic Republic 1977–1980; High Commissioner, Malawi 1983–1987. **Appointments:** Visiting Research Fellow, RIIA 1981–1982. **Honours:** CMG 1973; Grand Commander, Order of Lion of Malawi 1985. **Publications:** *Soviet Policy in the Horn of Africa*, 1983; *Lying Abroad, Diplomatic Memoirs*, 1999.

BRISCOE, Dr Arnold Daly (1918) Born 2 July 1900, London Street, Whitefield, Lancashire; son of Arnold Daly Briscoe, Brewer, and Ellen Lord; m Doris Winifred Nicholson, 15 September 1925, St Cyprian's Church, Brockley (d 14 April 1985); 1 son (John Hubert Daly b 19 March 1933), 3 daughters (Dorothy Anne Daly b 5 June 1928, Susan Marjorie Daly b 15 September 1930 and Elizabeth Jane Daly b 21 May 1936). **Subject(s):** Natural Sciences; BA 1921; MA 1933; BChir 1933; MB 1933; MRCS 1924; LRCP 1924. **Tutor(s):** E E Sikes. **Johnian Relatives:** father of John Hubert Daly Briscoe (1951). **Educ:** Clyde House School, Hereford; Hereford Cathedral School. **Career:** Assistant House Surgeon, North Ormsby Hospital, Middlesbrough 1924; Clinical Assistant, Children's Department, St Thomas' Hospital 1924; GP, Downderry, Cornwall 1925–1931; TA (Mentioned in Despatches 1940) 1928–1945; GP, Woodbridge, Suffolk 1932–1965. **Appointments:** Chairman, Woodbridge Urban District Council 1973; Chairman, Libraries, Museums, Records and Amenities Committee, Suffolk County Council 1974–1978; Chairman, Suffolk Coastal District Council 1977–1978; First Honorary Freeman, Woodbridge 2001. **Awards:** Somerset Exhibition, SJC 1918; Red Cross Voluntary Service Medal and Bar. **Honours:** TD with two bars; Coronation Medal 1953; Silver Jubilee Medal 1977. **Publications:** *A Stuart Benefactress, Sarah, Duchess of Somerset*, 1973; *A Tudor Worthy, Thomas Seckford of Woodbridge*, 1979; *A Marian Lord Mayor, Sir Thomas White*, 1982. Died 25 January 2002.

BRISTOW, George (1942) Born 21 May 1924, 6 Corporation Road, Carlisle; son of George Bristow, Clerk, and Hilda Mary Andrews; m Kathleen. **Subject(s):** Geography; BA 1948; MA 1965. **Tutor(s):** C W Guillebaud. **Educ:** Kendal Street School, Carlisle; National School, Clitheroe; St James' School, Clitheroe; Clitheroe Royal Grammar School. **Career:** Colonial Officer, New Hebrides and Christmas Island. **Honours:** MBE. Died 20 September 1999.

BRITTAIN, Percival Bernard (1921) Born 5 December 1901, 31 Grove Road, Wanstead, Essex; son of Percival Frederic Brittain, Electrical Engineer, and Ethel Harriet Catterson. **Tutor(s):** B F Armitage. **Educ:** Wychwood, Bournemouth; Eastbourne College.

BRITTON, Roland Henfrey Glanville (1925) Born 30 September 1906, Strathmena, Little Stanmore, Middlesex; son of Frank Leonard Britton, of independent means, and Thirza Annie Chapman; m Norah Jocelyn (d 16 January 1951). **Tutor(s):** E E Sikes. **Educ:** Glengorse, Meads, Eastbourne; Bedford School.

BROAD, Percival Gordon (1901) Born 31 December 1882, The Plantation, Warlingham, Godstone, Surrey; son of Harrington Evans Broad, Accountant and Auditor, and Zillah Broad; m Joyce Winifred (d 1968), 2 sons (Tim and Kit), 1 daughter (Dawn). BA 1904; MA 1910. **Tutor(s):** J R Tanner; C E Graves. **Educ:** Uppingham School. **Career:** Forest Department, Bombay Burma Trading Company 1904; Chartered Accountant 1932.

BROAD, Philip (1921) Born 18 January 1903, 223 Barnsley Road, Sheffield, Yorkshire; son of Thomas Tucker Broad, Congregational Minister, MP, and Margaret Cooper. **Subject(s):** Modern and Medieval Languages; BA 1924. **Tutor(s):** E E Sikes. **Johnian Relatives:** brother of Stephen Broad (1927). **Educ:** Private Tuition; Mill Hill School, London; Clifton College. **Career:** Master, Glasgow Academy 1925; Third Secretary, Tokyo 1926, Second Secretary 1931, Foreign Office; Counsellor, Foreign Service Branch A, Grade VI 1950. **Awards:** Scholarship, SJC 1920.

BROAD, Stephen (1927) Born 16 June 1908, 223 Barnsley Road, Sheffield, Yorkshire; son of Thomas Tucker Broad, Congregational Minister, and Margaret Cooper. **Subject(s):** Modern and Medieval Languages/History; BA 1930. **Tutor(s):** M P Charlesworth. **Johnian Relatives:** brother of Philip Broad (1921). **Educ:** Bootham School, York.

BROADBENT, Dr Bernard (1918) Born 15 May 1899, The School House, Benwick, Cambridge; son of Benjamin Broadbent, Schoolmaster, and Maud Litchfield. **Subject(s):** Natural Sciences; BA 1920; MA 1925; BChir 1925; MB 1925; MRCS; LRCP; DPH. **Tutor(s):** E E Sikes. **Educ:** Benwick Council School; March Grammar School. Died 4 December 1982.

BROADBENT, Sir Ewen (1942) Born 9 August 1924, 23 Vesta Road, Brockley, London; son of Wilfred Broadbent, Baptist Minister, and Mary Ewen; m Barbara David, 1951; 1 son. **Subject(s):** Modern and Medieval Languages; BA 1948; MA 1950. **Tutor(s):** C W Guillebaud. **Educ:** Queens Road Council School, Nuneaton; King Edward VI Grammar School, Nuneaton. **Career:** Captain, Gordon Highlanders 1943–1947; Air Ministry 1949; Private Secretary to Secretary of State for Air 1955–1959; Ministry of Defence 1965–1984; Private Secretary to Secretary of State for Defence 1967–1968; Assistant Under-Secretary of State 1969–1972; Department Under-Secretary of State (Air) 1972–1975; Department Under-Secretary of State (Civilian Management) 1975–1982; Second Permanent Under-Secretary of State, Ministry of Defence 1982–1984; Chairman, International Military Services Ltd 1991–1993. **Appointments:** Trustee, RAF Museum 1985. Chairman, Look Ahead Housing Association 1988; Chairman, Council for Voluntary Welfare Work 1989; Vice-Chairman, RUSI Council 1990; Trustee, Maxwell Pensioner Trust, 1992. **Honours:** CMG 1965; CB 1973; KCB 1984. **Publications:** *The Military and Government from Macmillan to Heseltine*, 1988. Died 27 February 1993.

BROADBENT, Professor Thomas Arthur Alan (1921) Born 31 May 1903, 7 Front Street, Consett, County Durham; son of George Thomas Broadbent, Grocer, and Harriett Carey; m Nita; 1 son (Richard), 1 daughter (Frances). **Subject(s):** Mathematics; BA 1924; MA 1928. **Tutor(s):** E A Benians. **Educ:** Consett Council School; Consett Secondary School. **Career:** Mathematics Lecturer, Reading University 1926–1935; Editor, *The Mathematical Gazette* 1929–1955; Assistant Professor of Mathematics, Royal Naval College, Greenwich 1935–1956; Professor of Mathematics, Royal Naval College, Greenwich 1956–1967. **Appointments:** Council Member, LMS 1947–1951; President, Mathematical Association 1953; Gresham Professor of Mathematics, City of London 1956–1968. **Awards:** Scholarship, SJC. Died 27 January 1973.

BROADHEAD, Denis Lumb (1935) Born 17 November 1916, 120 Rochdale Road, Plumstead, London; son of James Arthur Broadhead, Schoolmaster, and Nellie Lumb. **Tutor(s):** R L Howland. **Educ:** Private School; Leiston Secondary School, Suffolk; The Leys School, Cambridge.

BROCK, Byron Britton (1928) Born 1 July 1904, Kingston, Ontario, Canada; son of Reginald Walter Brock, Head of Geology Department, University of British Columbia, and Mildred Gertrude Britton. **Tutor(s):** J M Wordie. **Educ:** Kitsilano School, Vancouver; King Edward School, Vancouver; Royal Naval College of Canada, Esquimalt; University of British Columbia, Vancouver.

BROCK, Eric George (1911) Born 19 March 1893, 26 Marine Crescent, Waterloo, Lancashire; son of George Albert Brock, Congregational Minister, and Minnie Constance Winzar. **Subject(s):** Mathematics; BA 1914. **Tutor(s):** L H K Bushe-Fox. **Educ:** Merchant Taylors' School, Crosby. **Career:** Second Lieutenant, later Captain, King's (Liverpool Regiment, TF), WWI. **Honours:** MC 1916. Died 31 July 1917 (killed in action).

BROCK, Werner Gottfried (1939) Born 28 March 1901, Charlottenburg, Berlin; son of Gustav Brock, Medical Practitioner, and Hermine Salomons. **Educ:** University of Freiburg; University of Gottingen; University of Vienna; University of Berlin; University of Munich; University of Jena; University of Heidelberg; Kaiser Friedrich Schule, Berlin. Died 21 June 1974.

BROCKBANK, Birkett (1903) Born 18 February 1883, 3 North Road, Clayton, Audenshaw, Lancashire; son of John Birkett Brockbank, Warehouseman, and Elizabeth Hyde. **Subject(s):** Natural Sciences; BA 1906; MA 1910. **Tutor(s):** D MacAlister. **Educ:** Birley Street Higher Grade School, Manchester; Pupil Teachers' Centre, Manchester; Queen Street Board School, Manchester.

BROCKBANK, James Tyrrell (1939) Born 14 December 1920, St Mary's Lodge, York; son of James Lindow Brockbank, HM Inspector of Schools, and Harriet Elizabeth Tyrrell; m Pamela Margaret Oxley Parker, 11 November 1950, Faulkbourne, Essex; 4 sons (Richard b 15 January 1952, Nicholas b 2 March 1954, James b 10 June 1957 and Christopher b 10 June 1959). **Subject(s):** Natural Sciences; BA 1942; MA 1946. **Tutor(s):** J M Wordie. **Johnian Relatives:** father of Richard John Brockbank (1970). **Educ:** St Peter's Preparatory School, York; St Peter's School, York. **Career:** Sherwood Foresters, then Inns of Court 'Devil's Own' Regiment, WWII; Articled to Town Clerk of York 1946–1947; Assistant Solicitor, Wolverhampton 1948–1951; Assistant Clerk, Hertfordshire 1951–1954; Deputy Clerk, Nottinghamshire 1954–1961; Clerk of the Peace, Durham 1961–1971; Clerk, Durham County Council 1961–1974; Clerk to the Lieutenancy 1964–1988; DL, Durham 1970; Member, Local Government Boundary Commission for England 1976–1985; High Sheriff, Durham 1989; Solicitor; Vice Lord Lieutenant of Durham 1990–1995. Died 24 December 1995.

BROCKLEHURST, Frederick (1935) Born 26 August 1917, 22 Union Street, Broughton, Salford; son of Arthur Brocklehurst, Sergeant, RGA, Clerk, and Janet Horton. **Subject(s):** Modern and Medieval Languages; BA 1938. **Tutor(s):** C W Guillebaud. **Educ:** Grecian Street Council School, Salford; Manchester Grammar School. **Awards:** Scholarship 1934.

BRODIE, Douglas Spencer (1924) Born 3 April 1906, Fairholme, Garforth, Yorkshire; son of James Brodie, Vinegar Brewer, and Jessie Spencer. BA 1927. **Tutor(s):** J M Wordie. **Educ:** Ghyll Royd, Ilkley; Fettes College, Edinburgh.

BRODIE, Ian Eustace (1919) Naval Officer.

BROMFIELD, Joseph Dicken (1911) Born 22 September 1893, Upper Bar, Newport, Shropshire; son of William Bromfield, Master Plumber, and Margaret Dicken. **Subject(s):** History. **Tutor(s):** J R Tanner. **Educ:** Newport Grammar School. **Awards:** Careswell Scholarship, Newport School. Died 14 February 1912.

BROMHEAD, Michael Bernard (1942) Born 30 May 1924, 5 Gresham Gardens, Golder's Green, London; son of Bernard Henry Bromhead, Film Studio Manager, and Dorothy Violet Webster. **Tutor(s):** C W Guillebaud. **Educ:** St Dunstan's School; Arnold House School; Charterhouse.

BROMWICH, John I'Anson (1934) Born 8 December 1915, 1 Selwyn Gardens, Cambridge; son of Thomas John I'Anson Bromwich, University Lecturer in Mathematics, and Agnes Bertha Bellis. **Subject(s):** Archaeology and Anthropology/History; BA 1937; MA 1941. **Tutor(s):** J S Boys Smith. **Johnian Relatives:** son of Thomas John I'Anson Bromwich (1892). **Educ:** King's College School, Cambridge; Bromsgrove School. **Career:** Title A Fellow, SJC 1949–1954; Assistant Lecturer in English 1949–1954, Lecturer in English 1956, University of Cambridge; Fellow, University College (Wolfson College), Cambridge 1965. **Appointments:** Supervisor in Anglo-Saxon 1952–1978, Director of Studies in Anglo-Saxon 1974–1978, SJC. **Awards:** Scholarship, SJC 1937. **Honours:** TD 1950. Died 25 December 1990.

BROOK, Dr Alexis (1937) Born 24 January 1920, Devon Nook, Barrowgate Road, Brentford; son of Solomon Brook, Electrical Engineer, Company Director, and Ida Judelson; m (1) Maureen Senior 1950 (d 1981), (2) Ruth Klauber, 1984; (1) 1 son (Timothy John b 1955), 1 daughter (Rebecca Jane b 1952). **Subject(s):** Natural Sciences; BA 1941; MA 1944; MB 1949; BChir 1949; FRCPsych. **Tutor(s):** R L Howland. **Educ:** Gunnersbury Preparatory School, London; St Paul's School, London. **Career:** Registrar, Maudsley Hospital 1951–1953; Senior Registrar, Napsbury Hospital 1953–1956; Senior Hospital Medical Officer 1956–1960, Consultant 1960–1971, Cassel Hospital; Consultant, St Bartholomew's 1971–1977; Consultant 1971–1985, Chairman 1979–1985, Tavistock Clinic. **Publications:** Miscellaneous papers on the role of a psychotherapist in general practice; psychological aspects of disorders of the gut; psychological aspects of disorders of the eye.

BROOKE, Donald Guest (1930) Born 10 March 1906, 30 Winsor Terrace, Beckton, South East Ham, Essex; son of William Holford Brooke, Clerk in Holy Orders, and Mildred Flory. **Tutor(s):** E A Benians. **Educ:** Worksop College.

BROOKE, Edward Newton (1922) Born 13 October 1902, Fernside, Lightcliffe, Hipperholme, Yorkshire; son of Newton Brooke, Manufacturer and Company Director, and Edith Sutcliffe. BA 1925. **Tutor(s):** B F Armitage. **Johnian Relatives:** brother of William Aspinall Newton Brooke (1923). **Educ:** Bradford Grammar School; West Hill Preparatory School, Repton; Repton School.

BROOKE, John Claude (1928) Born 20 August 1910, 1 Romola Road, Herne Hill, Surrey; son of William Brooke, Master Mariner, and Ethel Alice Marion Davies; m Peggy; 2 sons (David and Andrew), 1 daughter (Felicity). **Subject(s):** Modern and Medieval Languages (French, Spanish); BA 1931; MA 1935. **Tutor(s):** M P Charlesworth. **Educ:** Northfield Preparatory School, Herne Hill; Alleyn's School, Dulwich. **Career:** Teacher, Royal Liberty School, Romford 1932–1935; Education Officer, Newcastle upon Tyne 1935–1940; Director of Education, Hyde 1940–1945; Deputy Education Officer 1945–1957, Chief Education Officer 1957–1974, Worcestershire. **Appointments:** Honorary Secretary, National Association of Education Officers 1964–1970; President, Society of Education Officers. **Awards:** Minor Scholarship 1927; Esme Howard Graduate Research Scholarship (held *in absentia* at the Residencia des Estudiantes, University of Madrid) 1931–1932. Died 2 February 1983.

BROOKE, Sidney (1916) Born 4 September 1897, 203 Cheetham Villas, Cheetham North, Manchester, Lancashire; son of Louis Victor Brooke, Photographer, and Esther Goldinger. **Subject(s):** Law; BA 1919; LLB 1921. **Tutor(s):** E E Sikes. **Educ:** St Luke's School, Manchester; Southall Street School, Manchester; North Manchester Preparatory School; Manchester Grammar School. **Awards:** Somerset Exhibition, SJC 1916.

BROOKE, William Aspinall Newton (1923) Born 15 December 1904, Fernside, Lightcliffe, Hipperholme, Yorkshire; son of Newton Brooke,

Company Director, and Edith Sutcliffe. BA 1926; MA 1931. **Tutor(s):** B F Armitage. **Johnian Relatives:** brother of Edward Newton Brooke (1922). **Educ:** Bradford Grammar School; Repton School. Died 8 January 1982.

BROOKE, Professor Zachary Nugent (1902) Born 1 February 1883, Fernhead, Thicket Road, Sutton, Surrey; son of George Brooke, Barrister, and Alice Elizabeth Nicholas; m Rosa Grace Stanton, 1 July 1919, St Mary's, Hambleden; 3 sons (Michael, Nicholas and Christopher). **Subject(s):** Classics/History; BA 1905; MA (Gonville & Caius) 1909; LittD (Gonville & Caius) 1932; FBA 1940. **Tutor(s):** E E Sikes. **Educ:** Arlington House Preparatory School, Brighton; Bradfield College. **Career:** Fellow, Gonville & Caius College 1908; Captain, East Surrey Regiment and General List (Intelligence), WWI; Lecturer in History 1926–1944, Professor of Medieval History 1944, University of Cambridge. **Appointments:** Praelector, Gonville & Caius College 1914–1928; Librarian, Gonville & Caius College 1928–1944; Ford Lecturer, Trinity College 1930. **Awards:** Gladstone Prize, University of Cambridge 1906; Winchester Reading Prize, University of Cambridge 1906; Lightfoot Scholarship, University of Cambridge 1907. **Publications:** (Joint ed) *Cambridge Medieval History*, 1921; *The English Church and the Papacy, 1066–1200*, 1931; *A History of Europe, 911 to 1198*, 1938. Died 7 October 1946.

BROOKES, Alexis Michael Panther (1931) Born 14 June 1913, 6 Churchfield Road, Ealing, Middlesex; son of Claud James Brookes, Medical Practitioner, and Frances Magan; m Laura Thomas, 7 September 1946, East Molesey; 1 son (David Michael b 22 January 1951), 2 daughters (Hilary b 26 September 1948 and Sue b 4 May 1955). **Subject(s):** Mechanical Sciences/Natural Sciences; BA 1934; MA 1938. **Tutor(s):** J M Wordie. **Johnian Relatives:** father of David Michael Brookes (1969). **Educ:** Norland Place School, Holland Park Avenue, London; Mr Wilkinson's Preparatory School, 10 Orme Square, London; Westminster School. **Career:** English Electric Company 1937; Metrology Department, National Physical Laboratory 1939–1946; Demonstrator in Engineering 1946–1949, Lecturer in Engineering 1949–1980, Special Pro-Proctor for Motor Vehicles 1951–1954, University of Cambridge; Title B Fellow 1948–1980, Lecturer 1954–1980, Title D Fellow 1980–2002, SJC. **Appointments:** Supervisor in Mechanical Sciences 1946–1952, Junior Bursar 1952–1963, Director of Studies in Engineering 1969–1971, SJC; Senior Treasurer, LMBC. Died 19 April 2002.

BROOKES, Ralph Caldecott (1913) Born 30 August 1891, Congleton, Cheshire; son of George Oakden Brookes, of independent means, and Annie Heywood. **Subject(s):** Mechanical Sciences; BA 1916. **Tutor(s):** L H K Bushe-Fox. **Educ:** King's Choir School, Cambridge; Colchester Royal Grammar School; Cranleigh School; Dulwich College. **Career:** Royal Naval Division, WWI; Lecturer, Department of Electrical Engineering, University of Liverpool 1931.

BROOKS, Dr Edwin (1949) Born 1 December 1929, 6 Romilly Avenue, Barry, Glamorganshire; son of Edwin Brooks, Foreman Blacksmith, Great Western Railway, and Agnes Elizabeth Campbell; m Winifred Hazel Soundie, 1956; 4 sons, 2 daughters. **Subject(s):** Geography; BA 1952; MA 1956; PhD 1958; FAIM 1983; FIBA 1984; ACIS 1995. **Tutor(s):** J M Wordie. **Educ:** Romilly School, Barry; Barry Grammar School. **Career:** National Service, Singapore 1948–1949; Assistant Lecturer in Geography, University of Liverpool 1954–1966; Councillor, Birkenhead 1958–1967; MP (Lab), Bebington 1966–1970; Lecturer in Geography 1970–1972, Senior Lecturer 1972–1977, University of Liverpool; Dean, School of Business and Liberal Studies 1977–1982, Director, Albury-Wodonga Campus 1981–1982, Dean, School of Commerce 1982–1988, Riverina College of Advanced Education, New South Wales; Deputy Principal, Charles Sturt University, Riverina 1988–1989; Director and Deputy Chairman, Riverina Health Service 1994–1996. **Publications:** *This Crowded Kingdom*, 1973; (ed) *Tribes of the Amazon Basin in Brazil*, 1973.

BROOKS, The Revd John Cowell (1928) Born 20 June 1909, Oldfield Cottage, Liskeard Gardens, Blackheath, London; son of William Charles Brooks, Chartered Accountant, and Mabel Eveline Cowell; m Waveney Cremer, 16 January 1971, St Paul's, Canterbury; 2 daughters (Amy Isabelle Bradford b 21 December 1971 and Rosalind Fiona Bradford b 13 June 1975). **Subject(s):** Classics/English; BA 1931; MA 1935. **Tutor(s):** M P Charlesworth. **Johnian Relatives:** brother-in-law of Edward Earle Raven (1909); brother of Maxwell Peter Brooks (1933); uncle of John Martin Brooks Earle Raven (1956). **Educ:** Stratheden House School, Blackheath; St Wilfrid's School, Bexhill; Tonbridge School. **Career:** Assistant Master, Wycliffe College, Stonehouse, Gloucestershire 1931–1936; Assistant Master, Sedbergh School, Yorkshire 1936–1941; Lieutenant, RNVR 1941–1945; Mirfield Theological College 1946–1947; Ordained Deacon 1947–1948; Curate, St Barnabas, Wood End, Northolt 1947–1954; Ordained Priest 1948; Vice-Principal and Lecturer in Church History, Cuddesdon College, Oxford 1954–1961; Rector, Church of the Holy Nativity, Ndola, Zambia 1961–1971; Chaplain, Dover College 1971–1974; Rector, Tilmanstone and Northbourne with Betteshanger and Ham 1974–1986. **Awards:** College Reading Prize 1930. Died 30 October 2001.

BROOKS, Maxwell Peter (1933) Born 4 December 1914, Oldfield Cottage, Liskeard Gardens, Blackheath, London; son of William Charles Brooks, Chartered Accountant, and Mabel Eveline Cowell; m Anna Pamela Whitworth, 10 June 1939; 2 sons (Anthony William b 19 January 1944 and Peter Martin b 21 February 1946). BA 1936. **Tutor(s):** R L Howland. **Johnian Relatives:** brother-in-law of Edward Earle Raven (1909); brother of John Cowell Brooks (1928); uncle of John Martin Brookes Earle Raven (1956). **Educ:** St Wilfrid's, Little Common and Hawkhurst; Tonbridge School. **Career:** Captain, RA, WWII; Rugby player, Harlequins and Kent; Chartered Accountant 1948; Marketing. Died 6 June 1971.

BROOM, Dr Trevor (1943) Born 20 March 1926, Wolverhampton; son of Henry Cliff Broom, Production Engineer, and Ruby Mary Jane Webster; m Jean Margaret, 1957; 1 son (Andrew), 3 daughters (Alison, Susan and Katherine). **Subject(s):** Natural Sciences/Metallurgy; BA 1946; MA 1950; PhD (Birmingham); FIM; FREng 1985. **Educ:** Woodfield Avenue Elementary School, Wolverhampton; St George Secondary School, Bristol. **Career:** Director of Operations 1971–1981, Director-General of Research Division 1981–1986, CEGB. **Awards:** Major Scholarship, SJC 1943. **Honours:** OBE 1975. **Publications:** Papers in Materials Science (Metallurgy); *A History of Solva*, 2nd edition, Trevor Broom, 2002; *Notes for a History of Solva: Part I, The 19th Century*, Trevor Broom, 1995 (revised); *Notes for a History of Solva: Part II, The Churches and Chapels of Whitchurch*, Broom, 2000.

BROOME, Frank Milnes (1919) Born 14 April 1898, 70 Old Road, Stockport, Lancaster; son of Frank Broome, Manager, Cotton Mill, and Mary Jane Milnes. **Tutor(s):** E A Benians. **Educ:** Derby Road School, Stockport; Wellington School, Stockport; Manchester Grammar School.

BROOME, Kenneth Reginald (1943) Born 19 May 1925, 41 Rushey Green, Catford; son of Reginald Alexander Broome, Accountant, and Violet Frances Paull; m Heather Claire Platt, 27 January 1946; 1 son, 5 daughters. **Subject(s):** Mechanical Sciences; BA 1947; MA 1960. **Tutor(s):** S J Bailey. **Educ:** LCC School, Kilmorie Road; Perry Rise Preparatory School; St Dunstan's College, Catford. **Career:** Consulting Engineer, K R Broome & Associates, Woodside, California.

BROOME, Philip Gordon (1925) Born 23 April 1905, Platt Rectory, Rusholme, South Manchester; son of Harold Holkan Broome, Lieutenant Colonel, Indian Medical Service, and Clara Alice Finney. **Tutor(s):** J M Wordie. **Educ:** Rugby School; RMA, Woolwich.

BROOME, Richard Neville (1927) Born 25 May 1909, The Rectory, Birkin, Yorkshire; son of Harold Holkar Broome, Lieutenant Colonel, Indian Medical Service, and Clara Alice Finney; m Tamsin; 2 sons

(Nicholas and John), 1 daughter (Juliet). **Subject(s):** Classics/Law; BA 1930. **Tutor(s):** M P Charlesworth. **Educ:** St Cuthbert's Preparatory School; Rugby School. **Career:** Malayan Civil Service; Japanese Occupied Malaya 1944, WWII. **Honours:** OBE; MC (WWII). Died 13 January 1986.

BROOMHEAD, Ivor William (1942) Born 7 December 1924, 6 Mansfield Crescent, Armthorpe, Doncaster; son of Frederick William Broomhead, Mechanical Engineer, and Florence Elizabeth Percival; m Dorothea Primrose Wagstaff, 1950; 1 son (Anthony David William b 9 October 1954), 2 daughters (Amanda Rosemary b 25 September 1951 and Susan Carolyn b 14 September 1963). **Subject(s):** Natural Sciences; BA 1945; MA 1949; BChir 1948; MB 1948; MChir 1958; FRCS 1954. **Tutor(s):** S J Bailey. **Johnian Relatives:** son-in-law of John Edward Pretty Wagstaff (1911); father-in-law of Jonathan Phillips (1970); father of Anthony David William Broomhead (1973). **Educ:** Armthorpe Council School; Doncaster Grammar School; University College Hospital Medical School, London. **Career:** Demonstrator in Anatomy, University of Cambridge 1950–1952; Resident Assistant Surgeon, UCH 1955–1957; Senior Registrar in Plastic Surgery, St Thomas' Hospital and The Hospital for Sick Children, Great Ormond Street 1957–1963; Consultant Plastic Surgeon, The Hospital for Sick Children, Great Ormond Street 1963–1987; Guy's Hospital 1968–1987, Royal Masonic Hospital 1974–1986. **Appointments:** Consultant Advisor in Plastic Surgery to the Chief Medical Officer of the DHSS 1976–1985; Representative, British Association of Plastic Surgeons on the Council of the Royal College of Surgeons of England 1980–1989; President, Plastic Surgery Section, Royal Society of Medicine 1981; President, British Association of Plastic Surgeons 1985. **Awards:** State Scholarship 1942; Marmaduke Shield Scholarship in Human Anatomy 1944; Major Scholarship, SJC 1945; Entrance Scholarship, University College Hospital Medical School 1945; Goldsmid Prize in Obstetrics and Gynaecology 1948. **Publications:** Chapter on Injuries of the Face and Jaws, *Clinical Surgery*, Robb & Smith, 1965; Chapter on Cleft Lip and Palate, *Operative Surgery*, Robb & Smith, 1976; Chapter on Protruding Ears, *Operative Surgery*, Robb & Smith, 1976; Chapter on Congenital Defects of the Scalp, *Plastic Surgery in Infancy and Childhood*, Mustarde & Jackson, 1988; Papers on Cleft Lip and Palate, Nerve Supply of Soft Palate, Reconstruction of the Ear, Epidermolysis Bullosa Congenita, Haemangiomata.

BROSTOFF, Daniel Victor (1948) Born 1 February 1928, Park House, 1 Neasden Lane, Willesden, London; son of Harry Brostoff, Medical Practitioner, and Judith Dorothie Umanski; m Erica Rees, 1 April 1966, Hampstead, London; 1 son (Alexander Max Rhys (Sacha) b 21 September 1972). BA 1951; MA 1955; PhD (London) 1955; DIC. **Tutor(s):** G C L Bertram. **Johnian Relatives:** nephew of Louis Rosenhead (1928); cousin of Martin David Rosenhead (1953) and of Jonathan Vivian Rosenhead (1956). **Educ:** Perse School, Cambridge; Roundhay School, Leeds; Willesden County School; Imperial College, London. **Career:** Senior Editor, Hutchinson Publishing Group 1964–1976; Marketing Manager, Flowtron Aire Ltd 1976; Director, Therafield Ltd 1985; Antique Restorer 1990–1998. Died 21 January 2004.

BROTHERTON, Clifford (1919) Born 21 July 1901, 125 Whitley Street, Dewsbury, Yorkshire; son of James Edward Brotherton, Decorator and Dealer in Antiques, and Edith Annie Lucas; m Minnie Crowther, St Martin's, Brighouse, Yorkshire, c1930; 1 son (John Michael b 7 December 1935), 1 daughter (Margaret Jean b 4 April 1942). **Subjects:** Mechanical Sciences/Mathematics; BA 1922. **Tutor(s):** E A Benians. **Johnian Relatives:** father of John Michael Brotherton (1956). **Educ:** Boothroyd Lane Council School, Dewsbury; Wheelwright Grammar School, Bewsbury. **Career:** Hydraulic Engineer. **Awards:** Sizarship, SJC 1919. Died 31 August 1960.

BROUGH, Dr James Nuttall (1948) Born 18 April 1928, 4 Birch Polygon, Rusholme, Manchester; son of Frederick Albert Brough, Professional Violinist, and Lilian Oliver Popplewell, Singer and Pianist; m Patricia

Elizabeth Glover, 23 June 1951, Christ Church, Woodford; 3 sons (Lester James b 5 January 1956, d 4 July 1976, Harvey Frederick Glover b 24 October 1957 and Rex Edward b 31 October 1960), 1 daughter (Teresa Susan b 11 July 1952). **Subject(s):** Natural Sciences; BA 1950; PhD 1955. **Tutor:** G C L Bertram. **Educ:** Heaton Moor Council School; Stockport Grammar School. **Career:** Work on synthetic fibres, then Technical and Production Management, Courtaulds. **Appointments:** Examiner in Chemistry for 30 years; Chamber of Commerce and Industry Representative, City of Coventry Education Committee and Further Education and Schools Sub-Committees; Governor, primary schools, Coventry Technical College and Coundon Court Secondary School. **Awards:** Scholarship, SJC 1950; Wright's Prize, SJC. Died 19 September 1990.

BROUGH, Professor John (1939) Born 31 August 1917, 22 Peel Street, Lochee, Dundee; son of Charles Brough, Teacher, and Elizabeth Small McKenzie; m Marjorie Allan Robertson, 1939; 1 daughter. **Subject(s):** Classics/Oriental Languages; BA 1941; MA 1945; Classics (Edinburgh) 1939; DLitt (Edinburgh) 1945; FBA. **Tutor(s):** R L Howland. **Educ:** Morgan Academy, Dundee; High School, Dundee; University of Edinburgh. **Career:** Agriculture 1940–1943; Assistant in Agricultural Research 1943–1944; Assistant Keeper, Department of Oriental Books and Manuscripts, British Museum 1944–1946; Title A Fellow, SJC 1945–1948; Lecturer in Sanskrit 1946–1948, Professor of Sanskrit, Head of Department of India, Pakistan and Ceylon, SOAS 1948–1967, Head, SOAS, University of London; Title C Fellow 1967–1984, SJC; Professor of Sanskrit, University of Cambridge 1967–1984. **Appointments:** President, Philological Society 1960–1963. **Awards:** Brotherton Sanskrit Prize, University of Cambridge 1942; Bendall Sanskrit Exhibition 1941 and 1942. **Publications:** *Selections from Classical Sanskrit Literature*, 1951; *The Early Brahmanical System of Gotra and Pravara*, 1953; *The Gandharr Dharmapada*, 1962; *Poems From the Sanskrit*, Penguin, 1968; Articles in *Chamber's Encyclopædia*, *Encyclopædia Britannica*, and in specialist journals. Died 9 January 1984.

BROWN, Alastair Houghton (1934) Born 14 December 1915, 1 Parkside Gardens, Wimbledon; son of Percy Houghton Brown, Barrister-at-Law, and Elizabeth Annie Malcolm. **Subject(s):** Economics/Law; BA 1937. **Tutor(s):** C W Guillebaud. **Educ:** Rose Hill School, Benstead; Uppingham. **Career:** Called to the Bar 1938–1939; Lieutenant, 10th Royal Hussars 1939–1941. Died 25 January 1942 (killed in action in Libya).

BROWN, Alec John Charles (1917) Born 15 February 1900, 29 Princess May Road, Stoke Newington, Middlesex; son of John Edward Brown, Schoolmaster, and Alice Elizabeth Goodwin; m Milena Voultchevitch. **Subject(s):** Modern and Medieval Languages; BA 1920. **Tutor(s):** E E Sikes. **Educ:** Somerleyton Elementary School; Fressingfield Elementary School; Eye Grammar School; Leiston County Secondary School. **Career:** Lecturer, Belgrade University; Correspondent, *The Times*; Adviser to the Yugoslav Directory of Information; Writer and Translator: published poems, novels and translations, notably of Pasternak's *Safe Conduct*, and Remizov's *The Fifth Pestilence*. **Publications:** *The Honest Bounder*; *The Hollow Mountain*; *Angelo's Moon*; *Yugoslav Life and Landscape*. Died September 1962.

BROWN, Dr Alexander Carnegie (1919) Born 9 March 1899, 4 Ferndale Road, Brixton, Surrey; son of Johnston Carnegie Brown, Clerk in Holy Orders, and Jessie Tindall; m Ella Mary Wright, 15 September 1925, St Paul's, Cambridge; 1 son (Ian b 6 February 1934), 2 daughters (Jean and Nancy). BA 1921; MRCS; LRCP 1924. **Tutor(s):** E E Sikes. **Johnian Relatives:** son of Johnston Carnegie Brown (1882); brother of George Carnegie Brown (1925); father of Ian Graham Carnegie Brown (1952). **Educ:** German School, Jerusalem; Trent College, Derbyshire. **Career:** Honorary Surgeon, Ripon Cottage Hospital 1927; Certified Factory Surgeon; Medical Officer, Analby Road Infirmary, Hull; House Surgeon, Addenbrooke's, Cambridge until 1964. Died 14 April 1985.

BROWN, Andrew Torrance (1947) Born 15 January 1929, Manor House, Ferryhill, Durham; son of Frederick Andrew Brown, Medical Practitioner, and Marjorie Ann Ruff. **Subject(s):** Natural Sciences; BA 1950. **Tutor(s):** G C L Bertram. **Educ:** Bow Preparatory School, Durham; Durham School.

BROWN, Arthur Edward (1903) Born 5 April 1884, 34 Castle Street, Cambridge; son of Edward Blomfield Brown, Watchmaker, and Dove Crisp. **Subject(s):** History/Law; BA 1906; MA 1912; LLB 1907. **Tutor(s):** J R Tanner; C E Graves. **Educ:** Higher Grade School, King Street. **Career:** Called to the Bar, Inner Temple 1912; Professor of Politics, Cotton College, Assam 1914; Professor of Public and Private International Law, Calcutta University 1919–1923; Special Duty, Legislative Department, Indian Government 1920–1923; Earle Law College, Gauhati 1923–1935. **Awards:** Scholarship, SJC 1905; Whewell Scholarship in International Law, University of Cambridge 1908; Commended for Yorke Prize, University of Cambridge 1910. Died 6 January 1939.

BROWN, Bernard Henry Kingsmill (1933) Born 26 April 1914, The Rectory, Rickinghall, Diss; son of Henry Kingsmill Brown, Clerk in Holy Orders, and Margaret Cecilia Wilson; m Elizabeth Barbara Wells, 10 June 1950, St Andrew's Church, Boxford; 3 sons. BA 1936; FGSM; FRAM. **Tutor(s):** J S Boys Smith. **Educ:** St George's Chapel Choir School; Tonbridge School. **Career:** Professor of Trumpet, Guildhall School of Music. Died 11 March 1983.

BROWN, Christopher Wilkinson (1911) Born 15 November 1892, The Vicarage, Embsay, Yorkshire; son of Charles Vernon Brown, Clerk in Holy Orders, and Alice Hannah Wilkinson. **Subject(s):** History; BA 1914. **Tutor(s):** E E Sikes. **Educ:** Pocklington School. **Career:** Second Lieutenant 1914, Lieutenant 1915, later Captain, 3rd Royal Scots Fusiliers (wounded twice), WWI. **Awards:** Dowman Exhibition, SJC. Died 30 April 1916 (killed in action).

BROWN, Cyril Maitland Ash (1933) Born 21 December 1906, Fullarton Road, Frewville, Adelaide, Australia; son of William Jethro Brown, Professor of Law, University of Adelaide, and Aimee Marie Loth; BA 1935; MA 1954; BA (Adelaide) 1932. **Tutor(s):** E A Benians. **Johnian Relatives:** son of William Jethro Brown (1887). **Educ:** St Peter's Collegiate School, Adelaide; St Mark's College, University of Adelaide; St Stephen's House, Oxford. Died 1 January 1977.

BROWN, David Eric (1939) Born 13 October 1920, The Nursing Home, 29 Henley Road, Ipswich, Suffolk; son of Cecil Jermyn Brown, Schoolmaster, and Gladys Muriel Smith. **Subject(s):** Geography; BA 1944. **Tutor(s):** R L Howland. **Educ:** St Mary's Preparatory School, Melrose; Sedbergh School.

BROWN, Edward Richardson (1914) Born 31 August 1895, 22 Taftonville, Ecclesall, Bierlow, Sheffield, Yorkshire; son of William Edward Brown, Schoolmaster, and Edith Madeline Collinson; m (1) Norah Casson Simpson, (2) Peggy Arline Loughman, 1932 (div 1942); (1) 1 son (Donald b May 1921), (2) 2 sons (Aldric Loughman b 20 February 1934 and Robert Louis b 16 October 1938). **Subject(s):** Mathematics; BA 1917; BA (London); Qualified Cost Accountant. **Tutor(s):** L H K Bushe-Fox. **Johnian Relatives:** father of Aldric Loughman Brown (1952). **Educ:** Penketh School; Ackworth School; Manchester Grammar School. **Career:** Master, Hastings Grammar School 1920–1925; Master, Blackburn Grammar School 1925–1926; Master, King Edward VI School, Sheffield 1929; Master, Kingswood Grammar School, Bristol; Cost Accountant, Douglas Motors; Publican, Three Horseshoes, Burbage, Wiltshire. Died December 1967.

BROWN, Edward Walter William (1930) Born 13 September 1899, St Mary's Lodge, 1 Hornsey Park Road, Middlesex; son of Edward William Brown, Surveyor, and Ada Mary Ann Stevens. **Tutor(s):** J M Wordie. **Educ:** Verulam School, Potters Bar; County School, Dover. **Career:** Army 1916–1919.

BROWN, Eric Metcalfe (1912) Born 22 February 1892, Barkley West, Cape Colony, South Africa; son of William Thomas Tilbrook Brown, Merchant, and Amy Rayner. **Subject(s):** Law. **Tutor(s):** L H K Bushe-Fox. **Educ:** Kingswood College; Rhodes College, Grahamstown. **Career:** London Rifle Brigade; Bedfordshire Regiment; Lieutenant, Tank Corps, WWI. Died 30 September 1917 (killed in action).

BROWN, Frederick Bamford (1949) Born 28 June 1919, Brinkworth, Wiltshire; son of Frederick Charles Brown, Grocer, and Lucy Frances Winfield. BSc (Bristol) 1949. **Tutor(s):** G C L Bertram. **Educ:** Cheltenham Grammar School; Bristol University.

BROWN, Frederick (Freddie) Richard (1929) Born 16 December 1910, Lima, Peru, South America; son of Roger Grounds Brown, Businessman, and Inez Anita Milne; m Marjorie Elizabeth Palmer, 9 June 1945, St James-the-Less, Stubbings, Maidenhead. **Tutor(s):** C W Guillebaud. **Educ:** St Peter's School, Chile; St Perans School, Maidenhead; The Leys School, Cambridge. **Career:** Cricketer, Surrey 1931–1948, Northamptonshire 1949–1953; England Test Cricketer 1931–1953 (22 matches) (Captain 1949, 1950, 1951); Lieutenant, RASC (POW Italy), WWII. **Appointments:** England Test Selector 1951–1953 (Chairman 1953); President, MCC 1971–1972; Chairman, Cricket Council 1974–1979; Chairman, National Cricket Association 1977; President, English Schools Cricket Association. **Honours:** MBE; CBE 1980. Died 24 July 1991.

BROWN, Dr George Carnegie (CARNEGIE BROWN) (1925) Born 28 January 1906, Jerusalem, Palestine; son of Johnston Carnegie Brown, Clerk in Holy Orders, and Jessie Tindall. BA 1928; MA 1949; MRCS 1933; LRCP 1933; LMSSA 1931. **Tutor(s):** M P Charlesworth. **Johnian Relatives:** son of Johnston Carnegie Brown (1882); brother of Alexander Carnegie Brown (1919); uncle of Ian Graham Brown (1952). **Educ:** German School, Jerusalem; Hurst Court, Ore, Hastings; The Leys School, Cambridge. **Career:** Clinical Assistant, ENT Department, House Surgeon, Surgical Unit, Resident Anaesthetist, St Mary's Hospital. Died 26 March 1964.

BROWN, George Colin Woods (1919) Born 14 January 1900, Acacia, Harcourt Road, Wallington, Surrey; son of George Andrew Brown, City Manager, Insurance Firm, and Annie Louise Tindall. **Subject(s):** Natural Sciences; BA 1922. **Tutor(s):** E E Sikes. **Educ:** Dower House School, Wallington; Whitgift Grammar School, Croydon. Died November 1969.

BROWN, Dr Herbert Harris (1925) Born 23 November 1908, 52 Griffiths Road, Wimbledon, Surrey; son of John Norman Brown, Examiner of Patents, and Jane Cheesman; m Hildegard. **Subject(s):** Natural Sciences; BA 1930; MA 1934; PhD (Glasgow) 1938. **Tutor(s):** J M Wordie. **Educ:** George Watson College, Edinburgh; King's College School, Wimbledon; Kingsbridge Grammar School; Brentwood School. **Career:** Assistant Lecturer in Zoology, Glasgow University 1931–1936; Colonial Services 1936–1948; Colonial (now Commonwealth) Development Corporation 1948–1951; FAO, UN (Department of Fisheries, Rome) 1951–1969. **Awards:** Scholarship, SJC. **Honours:** OBE 1946. Died 1995.

BROWN, Ian Michael (1944) Born 8 August 1926, Victoria Nursing Home, Cleveleys, Thornton, Lancashire; son of Vance Auberon Brown, Electrical Engineer, and Eleanor Purcer Smith, Doctor. **Subject(s):** Natural Sciences; BA 1947; BChir 1953; MB 1953. **Tutor(s):** S J Bailey. **Educ:** Elementary School, Cheadle; South Manchester School; Manchester Grammar School. **Career:** Consultant Anaesthetist, Stockport and Buxton Hospital Group 1963. Died 15 February 1989.

BROWN, James Clifford (1941) Born 18 August 1923, Ipswich, Suffolk; son of Henry John Brown, Musician, and Lois Smith, Teacher. **Subject(s):** Music/English; BA 1946; MA 1949; MusB 1946; FRCO 1948. **Tutor(s):** C W Guillebaud. **Educ:** Nacton Road Elementary School, Ipswich; Northgate Grammar School, Ipswich. **Career:** Lecturer,

Department of Music 1948–1971, University Organist 1948–1983, Senior Lecturer, Department of Music 1972–1983, University of Leeds. **Appointments:** Chorus pianist, Leeds Philharmonic Society 1949–1951; President, Ipswich Choral Society 1989–1999; Honorary Life Member, Leeds Organists' Society. **Awards:** Choral Studentship 1941–1942, 1946; John Stewart of Rannoch Music Scholarship, University of Cambridge 1942; Organ Studentship 1947; William Barclay Squire Prize 1947; Read Prize for FRCO Result. **Publications:** Various choral works including *The Baptism of Christ*; orchestral works; piano, organ and vocal pieces; chamber works.

BROWN, John Gordon Leonard (1930) Born 25 June 1912, 1 Dell Road, Grays, Essex; son of Leonard Brown, Master Builder and Contractor, and Jessie Eliza Mumford; m Joan Frances Hargreaves, 30 September 1939; 1 son (Christopher John Gordon), 2 daughters (Susan Margaret and Angela Mary). **Subject(s):** Law; BA 1934; MA 1938. **Tutor(s):** J M Wordie; S J Bailey. **Johnian Relatives:** father of Christopher John Gordon Brown (1963). **Educ:** Bridge Road School, Grays; Palmers School, Grays. **Career:** Brachers, Solicitors of Maidstone 1937–1992 (Senior Partner 1968–1977); Solicitor of the Supreme Court 1937–1992; Commissioned 17/21 Lancers 1941. **Awards:** McMahon Studentship, SJC 1937. Died 18 February 2001.

BROWN, Kenneth Douglas (1945) Born 25 September 1924, 26 Hexham Road, West Norwood, London; son of Harold George Brown, Wholesale Provision Merchant, and Irene Elsie Attrill. **Subject(s):** Classics; BA 1948; MA 1952. **Tutor(s):** C W Guillebaud. **Educ:** Dulwich College Preparatory School; Dulwich College.

BROWN, Kenneth Long (LONG-BROWN) (1922) Born 14 February 1903, 7 Queen's Avenue, Muswell Hill, Hornsey, Middlesex; son of Alfred Long Brown, Member of the London Stock Exchange, and Kate Grant Weston; m Marjorie Phillips, 1930; 2 daughters (Rosemary and Patricia). **Subject(s):** Mathematics; BA 1925; MA 1929. **Tutor(s):** E Cunningham. **Johnian Relatives:** brother of Norman Long Brown (1920). **Educ:** Tollington School, Muswell Hill; Ovingdean School, Brighton; Malvern College. **Career:** Chartered Accountant; Assistant Secretary, Secretary, Managing Director, Phillips Rubber Soles and Heels. Died 10 November 1963.

BROWN, Michael Evelyn (1948) Born 29 September 1928, 62 Westerfield Road, Ipswich; son of Keith William Brown, Timber Merchant, and Nora Evelyn Taylor; m Joan Goadby, 11 August 1956, Compton, Surrey; 1 son (Jonathan William b 20 July 1961), 1 daughter (Charlotte Miranda b 10 April 1959). **Subject(s):** Geography; BA 1950; MA 1979. **Tutor(s):** F Thistlethwaite. **Educ:** St Mary's School, Melrose; Blundell's School, Tiverton. **Career:** Suffolk Regiment 1947; William Brown & Co, Ipswich 1950 (Director 1964, Managing Director 1978). **Appointments:** Chairman, National Sawmilling Association 1973–1975; President, Timber Trade Federation 1982–1984.

BROWN, Michael John Hilton (1949) Born 15 December 1926, Forest Dene, Kimberley Road, Chingford, Essex; son of Charles Hilton Leonard Brown, Actuary, and Louisa Nock. **Subject(s):** Mechanical Sciences; BA 1952. **Tutor(s):** R L Howland. **Educ:** Dulwich College Preparatory School; Dulwich College. **Career:** Shell UK.

BROWN, Norman Long (LONG-BROWN) (1920) Born 25 July 1901, 7 Queen's Avenue, Muswell Hill, Hornsey, Middlesex; son of Alfred Long Brown, Member, London Stock Exchange, and Kate Grant Weston; m Honoria Mabelle Blain, 31 July 1931, South Nutfield. **Subject(s):** Law; BA 1924; MA 1927; LLB 1925; LLM 1985. **Tutor(s):** E A Benians. **Johnian Relatives:** brother of Kenneth Long Brown (1922). **Educ:** Swiss Government School, Neuchatel; Tollington School, Muswell Hill; Ovingdean Hall, Brighton; Charterhouse. **Career:** Called to Bar, Inner Temple 1930; Barrister, Probate and Divorce Court, Western Circuit; Historian of Cheam School. **Appointments:** Registrar of Charterhouse. Died 23 September 1995.

BROWN, Sidney Kemp (1919) Born 28 July 1900, 8 Woodsley Terrace, Leeds, Yorkshire; son of Francis Henry Brown, Clerk to 'Flounders' Educational Trust, and Mary Sophia Longmaid; m Edith Mary Hargreaves; 1 son (Richard Kemp b 20 August 1933). **Subject(s):** History; BA 1922; MA 1927. **Tutor(s):** E A Benians. **Johnian Relatives:** father of Richard Kemp Brown (1953). **Educ:** Lyddon Villa School, Leeds; Letchworth School; Bootham School, York. **Career:** Teacher, Boys' Grammar School.

BROWN, Vivian Fox (1940) Born 24 August 1922, Murree, Punjab, India; son of Henry Noel Brown, Lieutenant Colonel, Royal Corps of Signals, and Constance Mary Fox Andrews. **Tutor(s):** C W Guillebaud. **Educ:** Bishop's Stortford College.

BROWNE, Alan Chapman Lloyd (1930) Born 14 February 1907, 33 The Common, Woolwich, Kent; son of William Lloyd Browne, Lieutenant Colonel, and Alice Fancourt Orde Browne; m Sheila Rosemary Lloyd, 7 February 1950, St Saviour's, London. **Tutor(s):** J M Wordie. **Educ:** RMA, Woolwich; St Hugh's School, Bickley; Shirley House School, Charlton; Cheltenham College. **Career:** Apprentice, Armstrong Siddeley Motors Ltd, Coventry 1925–1928.

BROWNE, Barrington (1910) Born 19 February 1892, 60 Sankey Street, Warrington, Lancashire; son of Birch Browne, Master Hair Dresser, and Henrietta Priestnall. **Subject(s):** Classics; BA 1913; MA 1923. **Tutor(s):** E E Sikes. **Educ:** Warrington British School; Boteler Grammar School, Warrington. **Career:** Second Lieutenant, RASC, WWI; Master, 2nd Master and House Master, Dewsbury Wheelwright Boys' Grammar School. Died 18 August 1955.

BROWNLEE, Kenneth Alexander (1937) Born 4 August 1918, 254 Linthorpe Road, Middlesbrough; son of James Brownlee, Physician and Surgeon, and Gertrude Mary Wilks. **Subject(s):** Natural Sciences/Mathematics; BA 1940; MA 1944. **Tutor(s):** J M Wordie. **Educ:** Middlesbrough High School; Durham School. **Career:** Royal Ordnance Factories, WWII; Professor of Statistics, University of Chicago. **Publications:** *Industrial Experimentation*, 1946.

BROWNSON, George Stephen (1913) Born 13 May 1894, 24 Wood Lane, Hyde, Cheshire; son of Thomas Brownson, Solicitor, and Frances Harrison. **Subject(s):** Law; BA 1917; MA 1921; LLB 1920. **Tutor(s):** L H K Bushe-Fox. **Educ:** Hyde Grammar School; Manchester Grammar School. **Career:** Solicitor, T & G S Brownson, Hyde, Cheshire. Died 21 October 1942.

BROWNSON, Dr Roger Dawson Dawson-Duffield (1902) Born 21 March 1884, St John's Lodge, Sharlston, Wakefield, Yorkshire; son of Frank Brownson, Clerk in Holy Orders, and Margaret Dawson de Coverdale Dawson-Duffield; m Gwenllian Clare Rice, 26 September 1911. **Subject(s):** Natural Sciences; BA 1905; BChir 1911; MB 1911; MRCS; LRCP 1908. **Tutor(s):** D MacAlister. **Johnian Relatives:** son of Frank Brownson (1881). **Educ:** Warwick School. **Career:** Captain, RAMC Special Reserve 1914–1918. Died 21 October 1918.

BROWNSON, Thomas Kerfoot (1908) Born 25 April 1885, Thorncliffe, Hyde, Cheshire; son of George Brownson, Clothier, and Alice Jane Kerfoot. BA 1912. **Tutor(s):** L H K Bushe-Fox. **Educ:** Hyde Grammar School; Tettenhall College, Staffordshire.

BRUCE, George (1927) Born 11 June 1908, Station Road, Hetton-le-Hole, County Durham; son of George Bruce, Proprietor of a Drapery Establishment, and Lily Atkinson; m Joan Crosby. **Subject(s):** English/History; BA 1930; MA 1934. **Tutor(s):** E A Benians. **Educ:** Houghton le Spring Elementary School; Technical School, Durham; Ashville College, Harrogate. **Career:** English and History Master, Ashville College 1930; Educational Corps, TA, WWII; Secretary, University Entrance and School Examinations Council, University of London 1959; Died 16 November 1968.

BRUCE, Harold Trefusis (1949) Born 1 June 1929, Greenbank Cottage, Kingsmead Avenue, Cuddington; son of Albert Bruce, Chartered Accountant, and Lylie Helen Williams; m Ann. **Subject(s):** Mechanical Sciences; BA 1952; MA 1956. **Tutor(s):** R L Howland. **Educ:** Coombrook School, Hemel Hempstead; Heath Brow Preparatory School, Hemel Hempstead; Truro School. **Appointments:** Honorary Secretary, Basildon Constituency Labour Party; Member, OJHF. Died 1 January 1995.

BRUCE, Oswald (1901) Born 3 December 1883, Chilton House, Northfleet, Kent; son of George Barclay Bruce, Civil Engineer, and Virginia Emma Walker. **Tutor(s):** D MacAlister. **Educ:** Upper Canada College, Toronto, Canada; Chatham House School, Ramsgate.

BRUCE, Victor Walter (1945) Born 11 November 1918, 176 Waterloo Road, Middlesbrough; son of Walter Bruce, Shipping Superintendent, and Esther Leckonby Embleton; m Thérèse Willième; 3 sons (Christopher b 5 September 1961, Alan b 4 May 1972 and Derek b 20 January 1974). BA 1948; MA 1952; MS (UCLA) 1949. **Tutor(s):** C W Guillebaud. **Career:** RAFVR 1939–1945; Chief, Human Resources Division, Organisation of Agricultural Services, Food and Agriculture Organisation, UN.

BRUCE-JOHNSTON, Roy Grego (1923) Born 20 August 1905, 19 Manchester Street, Marylebone, London; son of George Bruce-Johnston, of independent means, and Louie Susannah Grego; m Margaret Evelyn Helmore Palmer, 20 August 1929, Upton Parish Church, Norfolk. **Subject(s):** History; BA 1927; MA 1931. **Tutor(s):** E A Benians. **Educ:** The Chiltons, Halton, Tring; Malvern College. **Career:** History Master 1932, Housemaster 1949, Dover College. Died June 1976.

BRUCE JONES, Thomas Dunlop (1938) Born 2 May 1920, Castlehill, Larbert, Stirling, Scotland; son of John Cumming Bruce Jones, Timber Merchant, and Dorothy Euphemia Mitchell Dunlop; m Patricia Leslie Denny, 1 November 1952, Dumbarton; 4 daughters (Veronica b 1953, Victoria b 1956, Claire b 1958 and Juliet b 1966). **Subject(s):** Economics; BA 1941; MA 1945; FICS. **Tutor(s):** C W Guillebaud. **Johnian Relatives:** cousin of Thomas Dunlop (1930) and of William Beckett Dunlop (1933). **Educ:** Ardvreck School, Crieff; Rugby School. **Career:** Qualified Chartered Secretary; RA 1940–1946; Jones & Campbell Ltd 1948; Director, James Jones and Sons Ltd 1950; Jones Buckie Shipyard Ltd 1953–1995; Finance Director, Hume Timber Merchants 1957–1967; Founding Managing Director, Jones Campbell Ltd 1967–1982. **Honours:** MC.

BRUCE LOCKHART, Logie (1940) Born 12 October 1921, 2 Vicarage Road, Rugby, Warwickshire; son of John Harold Bruce Lockhart, Headmaster, Sedbergh School, and Alwina Mona Ivy Brougham; m Josephine (Jo) Agnew, 1944; 2 sons (Rhuraidh and Duncan), 3 daughters (Jennifer, Fiona and Kirsty). **Subject(s):** Modern and Medieval Languages; BA 1946; MA 1955. **Tutor(s):** C W Guillebaud. **Johnian Relatives:** uncle of James Robert Bruce Lockhart (1960) and of Alastair Kim Bruce Lockhart (1965). **Educ:** Cargilfield, Edinburgh; Sedbergh School. **Career:** RMC, Sandhurst 1941–1942; 9th Sherwood Foresters 1942–1944; 2nd Household Cavalry (Lifeguards) 1944–1945; Assistant Master, Tonbridge School 1947–1955; Headmaster, Gresham's School, Holt, Norfolk 1955–1982. **Appointments:** Sponsor, National Council for Educational Standards. **Awards:** Exhibition, SJC 1939; Wright's Prize, SJC; Lupton and Hebblethwaite Exhibition, SJC 1940; Larmor Award, SJC 1947; Scholarship, SJC. **Publications:** *Pleasures of Fishing*, 1980; *Stuff and Nonsense, Observations of a Norfolk Scot*, The Larks Press, 1996; Sundry articles in *Country Life*, *Field*, *TES*, *Scotsman*, *The Times*, *Telegraph*.

BRUCKLAND, Norman Ernest (1947) Born 11 February 1929, 4 Cheddington Road, Edmonton, London; son of John Ernest Bruckland, Trolleybus Conductor, and Lily Hull, Quality Controller; m Kathleen Crosby, 1953; 1 son (Andrew John b 1955), 1 daughter (Christina Mary b 1958). **Subject(s):** History; BA 1950; MA 1991. **Tutor(s):** F Thistlethwaite. **Educ:** Silver Street School, Edmonton; Latymer School, Edmonton. **Career:** HM Inspector of Taxes 1950–1955; Secretariat, Institute of Chartered Accountants in England and Wales 1955–1970; National Partnership Secretary, Grant Thornton 1971–1989; Occasional freelance magazine journalist and consultant to business and institutions 1989–1997. **Publications:** (jointly) *The Management & Development of an Accountant's Practice*, Longman Professional.

BRUCKNER, Edgar Thomas (1947) Born 22 November 1929, Prague; son of Egon Bruckner, Businessman, and Edith Maria Schonfeld. **Subject(s):** Modern and Medieval Languages/Economics; BA 1950; MA 1954. **Tutor(s):** C W Guillebaud. **Educ:** Little Abbey Preparatory School; Aldenham School.

BRUFORD, Professor Walter Horace (1912) Born 14 July 1894, 4 Alexandra Street, Salford, Lancashire; son of Francis James Bruford, Drainage Inspector, and Annie Fox; m Gerda Hendrick, 1952 (d 1976); 1 son, 2 daughters. **Subject(s):** Modern and Medieval Languages; BA 1915; MA 1920; Honorary LLD (Aberdeen) 1958; Honorary DLitt (Newcastle) 1969; Honorary DLitt (Edinburgh) 1974; FBA 1963. **Tutor(s):** E E Sikes. **Johnian Relatives:** father of Alan James Bruford (1957). **Educ:** Manchester Grammar School. **Career:** Assistant Master, Manchester Grammar School 1915; Intelligence Division, Admiralty, with rank of Lieutenant, RNVR, WWI; Research, University of Zurich; Bishop of Peterborough's Fellow, SJC 1920–1923; Lecturer in German 1920–1929, Reader 1923, University of Aberdeen; Professor of German, University of Edinburgh 1929–1951; Seconded to Foreign Office 1939–1943; Schroeder Professor of German, University of Cambridge 1951–1961; Title C Fellow 1951–1961, Title E Fellow 1961–1966, SJC. **Appointments:** Honorary Fellow, Institute of Germanic Studies, London University; Corresponding Member, Deutsche Akademie fur Sprache und Dichtung 1957; President, Modern Language Association 1959; Saechsische der Wissenschaften, Leipzig 1965; Modern Humanities Research Association 1965; English Goethe Society 1965–1975. **Awards:** Bendall Sanskrit Exhibition 1914; Tiarks German Scholarship, University of Cambridge 1919; Goethe-Medal in Gold, Goethe-Institut, Munich 1958. **Publications:** (with J J Findlay) *Sound and Symbol*, 1917; *Germany in the 18th Century*, 1935; *Die Gesellschaftlichen Grundlagen der Goethezeit*; *Chekhov and his Russia*, 1948; two chapters in (ed W Rose) *Essays on Goethe*; *Theatre, Drama and Audience in Goethe's Germany*; *Literary Interpretation in Germany*, 1952; *Goethe's Faust* (introd, revised and annotated, in Everyman's Library); *Chekhov, Studies in Modern European Literature and Thought*, 1957; *The Organisation and Rise of Prussia and German Consitutional and Social Development, 1795–1830*, Cambridge Modern History, New Series, Volumes 7 and 9; *Culture and Society in Classical Weimar*, 1959; *Deutsche Kultur der Goethezeit*; *The German Tradition of Self-Cultivation: Bildung from Humboldt to Thomas Mann*, 1975; Various articles and reviews in Modern Language Periodicals. Died 28 June 1988.

BRYAN, John Lindsay (1919) Born 26 May 1896, 32 St George's Road, Beckenham, Kent; son of Lindsay Edward George Bryan, Solicitor, Lieutenant Colonel (Manchester Regiment, TF), and Emily Beatrice Johnson; m Irene Innes Pocock, 1927 (d 1982); 1 son (Patrick John b 25 June 1929). BA 1921; MA 1925. **Tutor(s):** E E Sikes. **Johnian Relatives:** father of Patrick John Bryan (1948). **Educ:** Abbey School, Beckenham; St Andrew's School, Eastbourne; Rugby School. **Career:** Private, HAC, France (took part in first battle of Ypres, wounded) 1914; Second Lieutenant 1915, Lieutenant 1916, 5th Battalion, Manchester Regiment, served in Gallipoli 1915, and Belgium (Mentioned in Despatches); Seconded to 127th Machine Gun Company, Egypt and France 1916–1918; 42nd Machine Gun Battalion 1918–1919; Acting Captain March 1918; acting Major November 1918; Cricketer, Kent 1919–1932; Schoolmaster, St Andrew's Preparatory School, Eastbourne 1922–1982; Served throughout WWII, including Dunkirk (Mentioned in Despatches), rose to rank of Lieutenant Colonel, Royal Armoured Corps. **Honours:** MC 1918. Died 23 April 1985.

BRYAN, Patrick John (1948) Born 25 June 1929, 25 Meads Street, Eastbourne; son of John Lindsay Bryan, Schoolmaster, and Irene Innes Pocock; m Georgina Shirley Burt, 1955; 3 sons (Richard Lindsay b 1957, Peter Nigel b 1960 and Nicholas George b 1964). **Subject(s):** Archaeology and Anthropology; BA 1951; MA 1955; PGCE (London) 1951. **Tutor(s):** R L Howland. **Johnian Relatives:** son of John Lindsay Bryan (1919). **Educ:** St Andrew's School, Eastbourne; Rugby School; London University. **Career:** Education Officer, Colonial Service; Work in Northern Rhodesia 1952–1961; Teacher, Suffolk and Cheltenham 1961–1989. **Awards:** Major Scholarship, SJC 1947.

BRYCE, The Hon Robert Broughton (1932) Born 27 February 1910, Toronto, Canada; son of Robert Alexander Bryce, Mining Engineer, and Edna Gertrude Baxter. **Subject(s):** Economics; BA 1935; MA 1939. **Tutor(s):** C W Guillebaud. **Educ:** Fern Avenue Public School, Toronto; University of Toronto Schools; Faculty of Engineering, University of Toronto; Harvard. **Career:** Public Service of Canada 1937–1974. **Appointments:** Member, Queen's Privy Council for Canada 1984. **Honours:** Companion of the Order of Canada 1967. Died 30 July 1997.

BRYDEN, John Whitfield (1942) Born 27 February 1924, 13 Frodsham Street, Tranmere, Birkenhead; son of John Whitfield Bryden, Electric Tram Driver, and Annie Harris. **Subject(s):** Natural Sciences. **Tutor(s):** C W Guillebaud. **Educ:** Mersey Park School; Birkenhead Institute.

BRYERS, Richard Hugh Castellain (1930) Born 13 September 1911, St John's Rectory, Launceston, Tasmania; son of John Shaw Bryers, Clerk in Holy Orders and Private Tutor, and Charlotte Susan Newman; m Phyllis Hankin, 7 July 1938. **Subject(s):** History; BA 1933. **Tutor(s):** C W Guillebaud. **Johnian Relatives:** son of John Shaw Bryers (1894). **Educ:** Temple Grove School, Eastbourne; Harrow School. **Career:** King's Own Royal Regiment 1933–1963; Captain and Adjutant 1940; Served in Iraq, India and Burma 1941–1944; General Staff Officer and Temporary Lieutenant Colonel 1944; British Joint Staff Mission, Washington 1950–1952; Served in Korea 1953–1956; Commander, 5 Battalion Malay Regiment 1954–1956; Commander, Land Forces in the Persian Gulf 1960–1963; Commander, Land Forces in the Persian Gulf 1977–1989. **Appointments:** Deputy President, Red Cross, Suffolk Branch 1977–1989. **Honours:** CBE.

BRYSON, Robert (1925) Born 12 June 1902, 245 Westbourne Avenue, Gateshead, County Durham; son of Robert Bryson, Railroad Engineer, and Sarah Jane Davidson. **Tutor(s):** J M Wordie. **Educ:** North Heaton School; Heaton Technical School; Skerry's College; Rutherford Technical College.

BUCHANAN, Alexander Maclaurin (1932) Born 6 March 1913, Robinsfield, Baldernock, Stirling; son of Hugh Reid Buchanan, Solicitor, and Jean Hill Maclaurin; BA 1937. **Tutor(s):** R L Howland. **Educ:** The High School, Glasgow. **Career:** Colonel, RAMC.

BUCHANAN, Angus Batts (1934) Born 26 August 1915, Silverhurst, Wynberg, Cape Colony, South Africa; son of James Buchanan, Manufacturing Confectioner, and Hilda West Batts. **Subject(s):** Natural Sciences; BA 1937; MA 1941. **Tutor(s):** C W Guillebaud. **Johnian Relatives:** brother of Donald Batts Buchanan (1925) and of Ian Batts Buchanan (1938). **Educ:** Western Province Preparatory School, Claremont; Highbury Hill Crest, Natal; Michaelhouse Balgowan, Natal.

BUCHANAN, Donald Batts (1925) Born 5 September 1906, Newlands Road, Claremont, Wynberg, Cape Colony, South Africa; son of James Buchanan, Manufacturing Confectioner, and Hilda West Batts; m; 1 stepson. **Subject(s):** Economics; BA 1928; MA 1932. **Tutor(s):** E A Benians. **Johnian Relatives:** brother of Angus Batts Buchanan (1934) and of Ian Batts Buchanan (1938). **Educ:** Hazelmere, Cape Town, South Africa; Western Provinces Preparatory School, Cape Town, South Africa; Hilton College, Natal, South Africa. Died October 1993.

BUCHANAN, Ian Batts (1938) Born 3 January 1920, Silverhurst, Wynberg, Cape Colony, South Africa; son of James Buchanan, Manufacturing Confectioner, and Hilda West Batts. **Subject(s):** Economics. **Tutor(s):** C W Guillebaud. **Johnian Relatives:** brother of Donald Batts Buchanan (1925) and of Angus Batts Buchanan (1934). **Educ:** Western Province Preparatory; Diocesan College, Rondebosch.

BUCHANAN, John MacAlister (1931) Born 17 January 1912, Robinsfield, Parish of Baldernock, Stirlingshire, Scotland; son of Hugh Reid Buchanan, Solicitor, and Jean Hill Maclaurin. **Subject(s):** History; BA 1934. **Tutor(s):** E A Benians. **Educ:** The High School, Glasgow. Died 23 December 1984.

BUCHANAN, Robert Donald (1917) Born 29 October 1899, 1 Sydney Terrace, Bradpole, Dorset; son of Edgar Simmons Buchanan, Clerk in Holy Orders, and Margaret Lyne. **Subject(s):** History; BA 1921; MA 1934. **Tutor(s):** E E Sikes. **Educ:** Downs School, Colwall; Leighton Park School. Died 6 April 1978.

BUCKATZSCH, Erich John Metius (1949) Born 6 November 1917, Asquith, Saskatchewan, Canada; son of Hugo Metius Buckatzsch, Mechanical Engineer, and Mabel Chappell. **m** Wilma. BA (Oxon) 1939; MA (Oxon) 1943. **Educ:** High Storrs Grammar School, Sheffield; Balliol College, Oxford. **Career:** Nuffield Research Fellow, Department of Applied Economics. Died 8 August 1954.

BUCKINGHAM, John (1914) Born 23 December 1894, North Aller, South Molton, Devon; son of John Mortimer Buckingham, Yeoman, and Mary Downing. **Subject(s):** Mathematics; BA 1921; MA 1924. **Tutor(s):** R P Gregory. **Johnian Relatives:** brother of Raymond Buckingham (1916). **Educ:** Sunnyhill School, Ilfracombe; Berkhamsted School. **Career:** Director of Programmes and Planning, RN Scientific Service, Admiralty 1959. **Appointments:** Chief Scientific Officer, RN Scientific Service 1946. **Awards:** Exhibition, SJC. **Honours:** CB 1953. Died 23 November 1982.

BUCKINGHAM, Raymond (1916) Born 26 January 1897, North Aller, South Molton, Devon; son of John Mortimer Buckingham, Yeoman, and Mary Downing. **Subject(s):** Mathematics; BA 1921; MA 1926. **Tutor(s):** R P Gregory. **Johnian Relatives:** brother of John Buckingham (1914). **Educ:** Sunnyhill School, Illfracombe; Berkhamsted School. **Awards:** Scholarship, SJC 1915. Died 1974.

BUCKINGHAM, Professor Richard Arthur (1929) Born 17 July 1911, 17 Cecil Road, Norwich; son of George Herbert Buckingham, Managing Director, and Alice Mary Watson King; m Christina O'Brien; 1 son, 2 daughters. **Subject(s):** Mathematics; BA 1932; PhD 1937; FBCS; FPhysS. **Tutor(s):** J M Wordie. **Johnian Relatives:** father of Richard Hugh Buckingham (1961). **Educ:** Bracondale School, Norwich; Gresham's School, Holt. **Career:** Lecturer in Mathematics, UCL 1948; Reader in Physics 1951; Director, University of London Computer Unit 1957; Scientific Translation Editor, Pergamon Press 1962; Professor of Computing Science 1963, Director, Institute of Computer Science 1964–1974, University of London; Professor of Computer Education 1974–1978 (Emeritus 1978–1994), Birkbeck College, London. **Awards:** Scholarship, SJC 1928. **Publications:** *Numerical Methods*, 1959. Died 13 August 1994.

BUCKLAND, Mervyn William Lancelot (1946) Born 18 July 1920, Victoria Street, Staple Hill, Mangotsfield; son of Lancelot Percy Buckland, Motor Engineer, and Nellie Frances Tyler; m Constance. BA 1969; MA 1972. **Tutor(s):** F Thistlethwaite. **Educ:** Kingswood School. Died 13 March 1992.

BUCKLEY, John (1919) Born 11 June 1898, Kenyon House, Wellington Street, Gorton; son of John Buckley, Company Director, Master Brewer, and Emma French. **Tutor(s):** E E Sikes. **Educ:** Croxton, Southport; St John's School, Leatherhead. **Career:** Lieutenant (Pilot in Aeroplanes and Air Ships), RFC and RAF, England and France 1917–1919. Died 16 December 1937.

BUCKLEY, William (1920) Born 7 October 1903, 71 Ripponden Road, Oldham, Lancashire; son of Llewellyn Buckley, Cotton Merchant, and Sarah Henthorne; m; 1 son. BA 1924; MA 1946; MRCS 1928; LRCP 1928; FRCS. **Tutor(s):** B F Armitage. **Educ:** Hulme Grammar School, Oldham; King Edward VII School, Lytham. **Career:** Assistant Thoracic Surgeon, Nottinghamshire County Council and Nottingham City Council; Plastic Surgery Unit for war casualties; GP, Worksop. Died 14 November 1956.

BUCKLEY, William Howell (1914) Born 7 February 1896, Penyfai, Llanelly, Carmarthen; son of William Joseph Buckley, Brewer, and Muriel Howell. **Tutor(s):** L H K Bushe-Fox. **Educ:** St Andrew's School, Tenby; Cothiel House, Abingdon; Radley College. **Career:** Second Lieutenant, 6th (Inniskilling) Dragoons (wounded), WWI.

BUCKNELL, Douglas Wentworth (1926) Born 18 December 1905, Argreah, Redmyre Road, Strathfield, New South Wales, Australia; son of William Wentworth Bucknell, Civil Servant and Landowner, and Fanny Fox; m Mary. BA 1929; MA 1933. **Tutor(s):** J M Wordie. **Educ:** The King's School, Paramatta. Died 16 May 1968.

BUDD, Bernard Wilfred (1931) Born 18 December 1912, 12 Kingsland Road, Millom, Cumberland; son of William Robert Arscott Budd, United Methodist Minister, and Florence Daisy Hewson; m Margaret Alison Burgin, 29 April 1944, Harpenden Methodist Church. **Tutor(s):** J M Wordie. **Educ:** Cardiff High School; West Leeds High School.

BUDDEN, Dr Kenneth George (1933) Born 23 June 1915, 76 Shadwell Road, North End, Portsmouth; son of George Easthope Budden, Engineer and Civil Servant, Admiralty, and Hannah Gertrude Homer Rea; m Nicolette Ann Lydia de Longesdon Longsdon, 1947, St James' Church, Wield, Hampshire. **Subject(s):** Natural Sciences; BA 1936; MA 1940; PhD 1940; BSc with External General Honours (London) 1935; Honorary Doctorate (University of Düsseldorf) 1985; MIEE 1946; FInstP 1946; FPhysS 1946, FRS 1966. **Tutor(s):** J M Wordie. **Educ:** North End High School, Portsmouth; St Paul's Church of England School, Barrow-in-Furness; Victoria Road School, Barrow-in-Furness; Secondary School, Portsmouth; The Grammar School, Portsmouth. **Career:** Research, University of Cambridge 1936–1939; Telecommunications Research Establishment 1939–1941; British Air Commission, Washington, DC 1941–1944; Air Command, South-East Asia 1945; Delanium Limited 1945–1947; Demonstrator in Physics 1947–1953, Lecturer in Physics 1953–1965, Reader in Physics 1965–1982 (Emeritus 1982), University of Cambridge; Title B Fellow 1947–1982, Lecturer in Physics 1956–1982, Title D Fellow 1982–, SJC. **Appointments:** Supervisor in Physics 1947–1956, Director of Studies in Physics 1961–1977, SJC. **Awards:** Scholarship, SJC 1933; Wright's Prize, SJC 1934–1935; Hughes Prize, SJC 1936; Hockin Prize, SJC 1936; Henry Humphreys Prize, SJC 1938; Heinrich Hertz Medal, American Institute of Electrical and Electronics Engineers 1993; Gold Medal, The Royal Astronomical Society 1999. **Publications:** *Radio Waves in the Ionosphere*, 1961; *The Wave-Guide Mode Theory of Wave Propagation*, 1961; *Lectures in Magnetoionic Theory*, 1964; *The Propagation of Radio Waves*, 1985; numerous papers in scientific journals on the propagation of radio waves.

BULLARD, Jack Alfred Arthur (1942) Born 20 July 1924, 14 Sutton Road, Watford, Hertfordshire; son of Arthur John Bullard, Grocer, and Alice Violet Saltwell. **Tutor(s):** S J Bailey. **Educ:** Watford Fields Council School; Watford Grammar School.

BULLEN, Frederick John (1911) Born 23 February 1893, Cromer, Norfolk; son of Arthur Herbert Bullen, Music Seller, and Eleanor Lydia Grand Artis; m Joyce Capper; 1 son. **Subject(s):** Natural Sciences; BA 1914; MA 1931. **Tutor(s):** L H K Bushe-Fox. **Johnian Relatives:** father of John Jaques Bullen (1946). **Educ:** Cromer Council School; Paston

Grammar School, North Walsham. **Career:** Lieutenant, RGA, later with Ministry of Munitions, WWI; Science Master, Kendal Grammar School 1914; Appointment Department, Ministry of Labour 1919; Managing Director, Barronia Metals Company, Hereford 1946.

BULLEN, Dr John Jaques (1946) Born 29 June 1920, Ruislip, Middlesex; son of Frederick John Bullen, Managing Director, Metals Company, and Joyce Capper. PhD 1949; MRCVS 1942. **Tutor(s):** J M Wordie. **Johnian Relatives:** son of Frederick John Bullen (1911). **Educ:** Northwood Preparatory School; Dauntsey's School, West Lavington; Royal Veterinary College, London. **Career:** Captain, RAVC; Demonstrator in Bacteriology and Research Assistant, Research Institute in Animal Pathology, Berkshire 1942–1944.

BULLEN, Professor Keith Edward (1931) Born 29 June 1906, Ponsonby, Auckland, New Zealand; son of George Sherrar Bullen, Journalist, and Maud Hannah Burfoot; m Mary Pressley; 1 son, 1 daughter. PhD 1937; BSc (New Zealand) 1928; MA (New Zealand) 1928; FRS 1949. **Tutor(s):** J M Wordie. **Educ:** Bayfield District School, Auckland; Auckland Grammar School; Auckland University College. **Career:** Master, Auckland Grammar School 1926–1927; Lecturer in Mathematics, Auckland University College 1927–1931 and 1934–1940; Lecturer in Mathematics, University of Melbourne 1940–1945; Professor of Applied Mathematics, University of Sydney 1945. **Appointments:** Fellow, Royal Astronomical Society. **Awards:** Hector Medal for Outstanding Scientific Work, Royal Society of New Zealand 1952; William Bowie Medal for Unselfish Co-operation in Research, American Geophysical Union 1961. **Publications:** *An Introduction to the Theory of Seismology*; *The Earth's Density*, 1975. Died 23 September 1976.

BULLER, Christopher Anson (1944) Born 30 October 1926, 31 York Place, Chorlton-upon-Medlock, Manchester; son of John Frederick Buller, Coffee Planter, and Leila Margaret Samuels. **Tutor(s):** J M Wordie. **Educ:** St George's, Windsor Castle; Felsted School.

BULLERWELL, Dr Robert Alexander Finlay (1933) Born 25 September 1914, 7 Jubilee Terrace, Bedlington Station, Northumberland; son of Robert George Alexander Bullerwell, Elementary Schoolmaster, and Susan May Finlay; m Edith Thelma. **Subject(s):** Natural Sciences; BA 1936; MA 1940; DipEd (Sheffield) 1937; PhD (London) 1953. **Tutor(s):** J M Wordie. **Educ:** Bedlington Station Council School; The Grammar School, Morpeth. **Career:** Science Master, Prior Park College, Bath 1938; Flight Lieutenant, RAF Meteorological Service 1940; University Demonstrator in Chemistry, promoted to Lecturer, then Senior Lecturer, Royal Free Hospital School of Medicine 1946–1976; University Teacher 1976. **Publications:** Several papers in Journals of the Chemical and Polarographic Societies.

BULLOCK, Albert Holden (1938) Born 9 September 1920, 143 Higher Antley Street, Accrington, Lancashire; son of Harold Bullock, Master Plumber, and Anne Holden. BA 1941. **Tutor(s):** J M Wordie. **Educ:** St Peter's School, Accrington; Accrington Grammar School. **Career:** Air Commodore, RAF Technical Branch. **Honours:** OBE 1960.

BUNCE, John Victor (1941) Born 18 September 1922, 7 Keslake Road, Kensal Rise, London; son of John Percival Bunce, Engineer's Draughtsman, and Gwendoline Denning Bown. **Subject(s):** Modern and Medieval Languages; BA 1946. **Tutor(s):** C W Guillebaud. **Educ:** Royal Masonic Junior School, Bushey; Royal Masonic Senior School, Bushey.

BUNT, Arthur Percival (1909) Born 4 February 1891, West Holme, Camborne, Cornwall; son of Jabez Henry Harvey Bunt, Bank Manager, and Mary Frances Rule; m Ethel Tonking, 24 July 1918, Wesleyan Church, Penzance; 1 son (John), 2 daughters (Monica and Barbara). BA 1913; MA 1918. **Tutor(s):** L H K Bushe-Fox. **Johnian Relatives:** father of John Percival Bunt (1943). **Educ:** Private School, Penzance; Truro College. **Career:** Captain and Adjutant, Duke of Cornwall's Light Infantry, WWI; Barrister-at-Law; Company Director. Died 28 January 1947.

BUNT, John Percival (1943) Born 22 December 1925, 13 Mount Park Crescent, Ealing, London; son of Arthur Percival Bunt, Barrister-at-Law, Company Director, and Ethel Tonking, Concert Pianist. **Subject(s):** Natural Sciences; BA 1946; MA 1950. **Tutor(s):** C W Guillebaud. **Johnian Relatives:** son of Arthur Percival Bunt (1909). **Educ:** Notting Hill High School, Ealing; Harrow View House, Ealing; Oundle School. **Career:** Electronics Engineer, digital computer development; Technical Manager, Computing Division 1955–1960, Divisional Manager, Mobile Computing Division 1960–1965, Elliott Brothers Ltd, London; Joint General Manager, Elliott Space & Weapon Automation Ltd 1965–1969; Technical Director, Marconi-Elliott Computer Systems Ltd (later GEC Computers Ltd) 1969–1972. **Appointments:** Member, Editor of journal *The Upland Goose*, and President, Falkland Islands Philatelic Study Group. **Awards:** Minor Scholarship, SJC 1943. **Publications:** *War Stamp Overprints of the Falkland Islands 1918–1920*, 1981; *The De la Rue Definitives of the Falkland Islands, 1901–1929*, 1986. Died 2 July 2002.

BURCH, William Edward Victor (1925) Born 24 May 1907, 56 Westover Road, Wandsworth, Surrey; son of William Isaac Burch, Managing Director, Lanston Monotype Company Ltd, and Amy Frances Snarey; 1 son (Stephen), 1 daughter (Gillian). BA 1928; MA 1932. **Tutor(s):** J M Wordie. **Educ:** Highfield School, Wandsworth Common; Cranleigh School. Died 15 January 1982.

BURDEN, Donald Fletcher (1935) Born 20 January 1917, Grammar School House, Keldgate, Beverley; son of Charles Henry Burden, Schoolmaster, and Constance Fletcher; m Elizabeth; 1 son (Jeremy b 5 June 1952), 1 daughter (Rachel b 21 November 1957). **Subject(s):** History/Law; BA 1938; MA 1946; Solicitors final examination 1940. **Tutor(s):** J S Boys Smith. **Educ:** Beverley High School; Beverley Grammar School. **Career:** RN 1940–1945; Solicitor, family firm, Percy Hibbert and Burden, Hyde 1946–1989. **Appointments:** Treasurer, University Liberal Club; Actively associated with Liberal Party Council. **Awards:** Exhibition, SJC 1936–1937. **Publications:** Founder and first Editor, *The New Radical*. Died 26 August 2001.

BURDON-COOPER, Alick McLaurin Monteath (1925) Born 9 June 1907, 22 The Circus, Bath, Somerset; son of John Burdon-Cooper, Ophthalmic Surgeon, and Teresa McLaurin Monteath; m Christian Anna Lily Campbell-Colquhoun, 29 March 1937, Crieff, Perthshire; 1 son (John Archibald b 12 January 1938), 1 daughter (Kirsteen Anna b 22 February 1940). **Subject(s):** Mathematics/Economics; BA 1929; MA 1933; BSc (London). **Tutor(s):** J M Wordie. **Johnian Relatives:** father of John Archibald Burdon-Cooper (1958). **Educ:** Wellesley House, Bath; Hamilton House, Bath; Monkton Combe Junior School, Bath; Oundle School. **Career:** Accountant, Pilkington Bros, St Helens; Army, Middle East, WWII; Partner, Wenham Bros and Co, Chartered Accountants, Birmingham and London 1947–1961; Founding Director and Chairman, Westler Foods Ltd, Yorkshire. Died 14 December 1978.

BURGESS, The Revd Frederick William (1930) Born 6 May 1912, Myless, Worrin Road, Shenfield, Essex; son of Arthur Frederick Burgess, Schoolmaster, and Stephanie Pratt; m Joan Margaret Dyke, 1951; 1 son (Edmund b 1957), 1 daughter (Sarah b 1954). **Subject(s):** Theology/Mathematics; BA 1933; MA 1937; FRCO 1942. **Tutor(s):** J M Wordie. **Educ:** Brentwood School. **Career:** Vicar, Great Oakley, Diocese of Chelmsford; Ordained Deacon 1936; Curate, St Mary, Walthamstow 1936; Assistant Master, King's School, Ely 1938–1947; Ordained Priest 1939; Chaplain, Abingdon School 1947–1957; Rector, North and South Lopham, Norfolk 1957; Rector, Great Oakley with Wix (SJC Living) until 1982. **Awards:** Scholarship, SJC 1930. Died 11 January 1991.

BURGESS, Thomas Charles (1926) Born 9 February 1908, 38 Kent Street, Broughton, Salford, Lancashire; son of Charles William Burgess, Warehouseman, and Maria Cardwell; m Hilda Holder; 2 sons, 1 daughter. **Subject(s):** Classics; BA 1930; MA 1936. **Tutor(s):** M P Charlesworth. **Johnian Relatives:** father of John Cardwell Burgess (1965). **Educ:** Grecian Street Elementary School; Manchester Grammar

School. **Career:** Assistant Master, Reading and Birkenhead Schools; Squadron Leader, Intelligence, RAF, Belgium, Holland and Germany, WWII; Housemaster, King Edward's School, Birmingham 1935–1951; Headmaster, Five Ways Grammar School 1951. **Awards:** Graves Prize, SJC; Scholarship, SJC. Died September 1963.

BURGIN, David Harding (1949) Born 21 June 1928, 1 Prout Grove, Willesden, Middlesex; son of Alfred Burgin, Member, London Stock Exchange, and Doris Harding. **Subject(s):** History; BA 1952; MA 1973. **Tutor(s):** A G Lee. **Educ:** Kingswood School, Bath; University College School, London. **Career:** Black & Decker Ltd 1964; Managing Director, Schick Incorporated (UK) Ltd 1964.

BURKE, Anthony Edgerton (1944) Born 1 May 1926, 10 College Road, Harrow, Middlesex; son of Albert Edgar Burke, Bank Clerk, and Violet Burgess; m Janet Elizabeth Phillips, 1961; 1 son (Andrew James b 1964). **Subject(s):** Mechanical Sciences; BA 1947; MA 1963; FIMechE. **Tutor(s):** S J Bailey. **Johnian Relatives:** father of Andrew James Burke (1983). **Educ:** St Mildred's School, Pinner; St John's School, Pinner; Merchant Taylors' School. **Career:** Engineering Manager, Rank-Xerox Ltd 1986.

BURKETT, Richard Southern (1935) Born 21 April 1916, 12 Park Parade, Sunderland; son of Richard Southern Burkett, Chartered Accountant, and Mabel Emily Crabtree. **Subject(s):** History/Law; BA 1938; MA 1949. **Tutor(s):** J S Boys Smith. **Educ:** Roker Preparatory School; Tonstall School, Sunderland; Ashville College, Harrogate.

BURKITT, Harold Gale (1939) Born 16 October 1920, Woodside House, Witton Park, Bishop Auckland; son of Harold Burkitt, Land Agent, and Florence Blodwyn Maud Powell; 4 daughters. **Tutor(s):** C W Guillebaud. **Johnian Relatives:** brother of Henry Gale Stewart Burkitt (1932) and of William Gale Burkitt (1935). **Educ:** Bow School, Durham; Durham School. **Career:** Captain 1939–1945; Farmer 1945–1959. Died November 1959.

BURKITT, Lieutenant Colonel Henry Gale Stewart (1932) Born 25 May 1913, 12 Otterburn Terrace, Newcastle upon Tyne; son of Harold Burkitt, Land Agent and Valuer, and Florence Blodwyn Maud Powell; m Margaret Alison Campbell Black, 21 January 1956, Christ Church, Kensington. **Subject(s):** Classics/Archaeology and Anthropology; BA 1935; MA 1939. **Tutor(s):** R L Howland. **Johnian Relatives:** brother of Harold Gale Burkitt (1939) and of William Gale Burkitt (1935). **Educ:** Bow School, Durham; Durham School. **Career:** Lieutenant, Indian Army, 3/17th Dogra Regiment 1936. Died 13 December 1987.

BURKITT, William Gale (1935) Born 2 April 1916, Glenholme, Bishop Auckland, Durham; son of Harold Burkitt, Estate Agent, Chartered Surveyor, and Florence Blodwyn Maud Powell; m Gillian Patricia Guttrall Garland, 2 April 1947. **Subject(s):** Geography; BA 1938; MA 1942; Graduate, BIM. **Tutor(s):** J M Wordie. **Johnian Relatives:** brother of Henry Gale Stewart Burkitt (1932); brother of Harold Gale Burkitt (1939). **Educ:** Bow School, Durham; King James I School, Bishop Auckland. Died 9 December 1980.

BURLEY, Percival Leslie (1923) Born 15 June 1905, Glenthorne, 1 Charles Street, Petersfield, Southampton; son of Percy Clement Burley, Solicitor, and Augusta Edith Gammon; m Ruth; 1 son (Richard), 1 daughter (Jenny). **Subject(s):** Law; BA 1927; MA 1930; LLB 1928. **Tutor(s):** E A Benians. **Educ:** Churchers College, Petersfield; The Leys School, Cambridge. **Career:** Partner, Burley and Geach Solicitors; Squadron Leader, Pathfinder Squadron, WWII. **Appointments:** Vice-Chairman, Petersfield Town Council; President, Petersfield Chamber of Commerce. Died 26 August 1976.

BURLING, Edward James Poynter (1912) Born 22 January 1889, 39 Russell Square, Cambridge; son of Edward Mason Burling, Hotel Proprietor, and Christiana Pointer. **Tutor(s):** L H K Bushe-Fox. **Educ:**

Truro College; Haverfordwest Grammar School. **Career:** Captain (Aeroplane Officer), RFC/RAF (Mentioned in Despatches), WWI. **Awards:** Bronze Medal, Royal Humane Society 1922. **Honours:** DSC 1919; DFC; French Croix de Guerre.

BURLING, Philip Cecil George (1934) Born 13 September 1915, 1 Edinburgh Road, Carshalton, Surrey; son of George Alfred Burling, Civil Servant, and Mary Rice-Jones; m Patricia; 4 sons (Julian, Andrew, Mark and Francis), 1 daughter (Margaret). **Subject(s):** Natural Sciences; BA 1937; MA 1974. **Tutor(s):** J M Wordie. **Educ:** Sutton Preparatory School; Exeter School. Died 21 April 1987.

BURN, Ernest William (1916) Born 16 April 1897, 6 Ninth Avenue, Heaton, Newcastle upon Tyne, Northumberland; son of William Burn, Jeweller's Assistant, and Martha Anne Taylor. **Subject(s):** Mathematics; BA 1921; MA 1928. **Tutor(s):** E E Sikes. **Educ:** Private School, Newcastle; Royal Grammar School, Newcastle upon Tyne. **Career:** Master, Hulme Grammar School, Manchester 1922–1930; Master, Nelson School, Wigton, Cumberland 1930. **Awards:** Scholarship, SJC 1915.

BURN, Macdonald (1941) Born 3 December 1922, 81 Main Street, Spittal, Berwick-on-Tweed; son of Alexander Charles Burn, Agricultural Chemist, and Catherine Fraser Macdonald; m Sheila Mary Waterhouse, August 1948. **Subject(s):** English; BA 1946; MA 1948. **Tutor(s):** C W Guillebaud. **Educ:** Spittal Council School; Berwick Grammar School. **Career:** Assistant Master, Paston School, North Walsham.

BURNETT, Sir David Humphery (1935) Born 27 January 1918, Rockfield Cottage, Oxted, Godstone, Surrey; son of Leslie Trew Burnett, 2nd Baronet, Chartered Surveyor, and Joan Humphery; m Geraldine Elizabeth Mortimer Fisher, 21 July 1948; 3 sons (Charles David b 18 May 1951, John and Robert (d)). BA 1938; MA 1942; ARICS 1948; FIMgt; FBIM 1968; FRICS 1970; FLS 1979. **Tutor(s):** J M Wordie. **Educ:** Lee School, Oxted; Bowden House School, Seaford; Harrow School. **Career:** HM Lieutenant of the City of London; Second Lieutenant, then GSO, Major and Temporary Lieutenant Colonel GSO1, 60th Anti-aircraft Regiment, RA (France, North Africa, Sicily and Italy), Mentioned in Despatches, 1939–1945; Partner, David Burnett & Son, Chartered Surveyors 1947–1950; Director, Proprietors of Hay's Wharf Ltd 1950–1980 (Chairman 1965–1980); Director, Guardian Royal Exchange Assurance 1967–1988; Director, London and Thameshaven Oil Wharves, The Marine Insurance Company, Hymatic Dredges and Malterbury Investments. **Appointments:** Member, Port of London Authority 1962–1975; Master, Company of Watermen and Lightermen of the River Thames 1964; Chairman, London Association of Public Wharfingers 1964–1971; Master, Girdlers' Company 1970; Council Member, Brighton College 1971–1993; Chairman, South London Botanical Institute 1976–1981 (President 1985). **Honours:** MBE 1945; TD. Died 19 May 2002.

BURNETT, Donald Fenn (1931) Born 27 February 1912, 64 Blackman Lane, Leeds, Yorkshire; son of Ernest William Burnett, Builder, and Ellen Fenn; m Elizabeth. **Subject(s):** Mathematics/Natural Sciences; BA 1934; MA 1938. **Tutor(s):** J M Wordie. **Educ:** Cowper Street Council School; The Grammar School, Leeds. **Career:** Lecturer in Physics and Assistant in Physical Training, St Luke's Training College, Exeter 1939.

BURNETT, Donald Stuart (1948) Born 22 May 1927, Kotagiri, Nilgiri District, South India; son of Wilfrid Henry Burnett, Methodist Minister, and Jennie Stuart Cressy; m Joan Freeman; 1 son (Charles Stuart Freeman), 1 daughter (Susan Elisabeth). **Subject(s):** Geography; BA 1949; MA 1954; PGCE (London). **Tutor(s):** J M Wordie. **Johnian Relatives:** father of Charles Stuart Freeman Burnett (1969). **Educ:** Hebron School, Coonoor, Nilgiris; Ilfracombe Grammar School; Kingswood School, Bath. **Career:** RN 1946–1948; Teacher, Prior's Court 1951–1956; Teacher, Alliance High School for African Boys, Kenya 1956–1960; Head, Geography Department, Sale Grammar School for

Boys 1961–1975; Senior Master, Sale County Grammar School for Boys 1971–1984. **Publications:** *A Revision Notebook of East African Geography*, OUP, 1964.

BURNETT, Reginald Penrith (1921) Born 16 May 1900, 21 Eshton Terrace, Clitheroe, Lancashire; son of Penrith Burnett, Clerk in Holy Orders, and Ethel Maud Rush. **Tutor(s):** E A Benians. **Educ:** King Edward's School, Birmingham; Ordination Test School, Knutsford. **Career:** Army 1918–1919.

BURNEY, Christopher Arthur Geoffrey (1935) Born 16 June 1917, Beech Cottage, Fleet, Hampshire; son of Arthur Edward Cave Burney, Lieutenant Colonel, RA, and Dorothy Norton; m Julia Burrell, 2 February 1946. **Tutor(s):** C W Guillebaud. **Educ:** Heddon Court, Cockfosters; Bilton Grange, Rugby; Wellington College; Grenoble, France; Santander, Spain.

BURNS, Ian Forrest (1931) Born 26 November 1913, 3a Lothian Road, Poona, India; son of William Burns, Economic Botanist to Government of India, and Margaret Forrest Aitchison. **Subject(s):** Modern and Medieval Languages; BA 1934; LDS. **Tutor(s):** C W Guillebaud. **Educ:** Viewpark School, Edinburgh; Morrison's Academy, Crieff, Scotland. **Appointments:** RCS Edinburgh 1941.

BURNS, John Carlyle (1947) Born 12 February 1926, 3 Lloyd Avenue West, Mount Albert, Auckland, New Zealand; son of Walter Allan Burns, Plumber, and Mary Eleanor Clarke; m Eleanor Freda Myers, 1952; 1 son (Keith Howard b 1956), 1 daughter (Hilary Jane b 1958). **Subject(s):** Mathematics; BA 1949; MA 1982; BSc (New Zealand) 1944; MSc (New Zealand) 1945; PhD (Manchester) 1952. **Tutor(s):** J M Wordie. **Educ:** Gladstone School, Auckland, New Zealand; Mount Albert Grammar School, Auckland, New Zealand; Auckland University College, New Zealand. **Career:** Junior Lecturer in Mathematics, Auckland University College 1946–1947; Senior Lecturer/Associate Professor, Victoria University College 1952–1962; Senior Lecturer/Reader, Department of Mathematics, ANU 1963–1969; Professor of Mathematics, Royal Military College, Canberra, Faculty of Military Studies, University of New South Wales, Sydney 1969–1986; Emeritus Professor, University of New South Wales 1986. **Appointments:** Dean of Faculty, University of New South Wales 1973–1978. **Awards:** Scholarship, SJC; Adams Essay Prize; Bernhard H Neumann Award, Australian Mathematics Trust. **Publications:** *Seeking Solutions*, Australian Mathematics Trust, 2000; approximately 30 papers in mathematical journals.

BURNS, Robert James (1941) Born 26 November 1922, London; son of Robert Edward Burns, Colonial Civil Servant, Gold Coast Colony, and Jessie Dallachy Mackenzie; m Eleanor Teasdale, 4 October 1944, Toronto (d 1983); 2 sons, 2 daughters. **Subject(s):** Economics; BA 1948; MA 1953; MComm (Toronto) 1954. **Tutor(s):** S J Bailey; C W Guillebaud. **Educ:** St Giles' Preparatory School, St Leonards-on-Sea; Sutton Valence School. **Career:** RAF Navigator and Navigation Instructor, WWII; Ontario Hydro; BC Hydro; CMHC; self employment as an economic consultant.

BURR, Captain Frederick Godfrey (1908) Born 24 August 1890, Shirrenden, Horsmanden, Kent; son of Frederick William Burr, Lieutenant Colonel, Royal Scots Fusiliers, and Euphemia Campbell. BA 1911. **Tutor(s):** E E Sikes. **Educ:** St Andrew's School, Eastbourne; Harrow. **Career:** Captain, 7th Battalion, Royal Scots Fusiliers 1914–1915. Died 26 September 1915 (killed in action in the Battle of Loos).

BURRELL, John Hugh (1912) Born 17 August 1893, 25 The Avenue, Crossgate, Durham; son of John George Burrell, Architect and Surveyor, and Mary Caldcleugh; m Elise Vernon (d 3 June 1962); 1 daughter (Mary). BA 1915. **Tutor(s):** E E Sikes. **Educ:** Bailey School, Durham; Durham School. **Career:** 17th Division, Staff Sergeant-Major (Musketry), 1914–1915; Second Lieutenant, 8th Durham Light Infantry 1915;

Lieutenant 1917; Acting Captain and Adjutant 1917–1918; Served with BEF in France 1916–1918; Mentioned in Despatches 1918; POW 1918; Assistant Principal, Home Office 1920–1928; Principal 1928; various secretarial or similar positions in the Home Office. **Honours:** CBE 1948. Died 13 June 1965.

BURROW, Felix George Marton (1933) Born 1 February 1914, Brookfield House, West Kirby, Cheshire; son of George Albert Burrow, Leather Merchant, and Mary Sibylla Hull. **Subject(s):** History. **Tutor(s):** J S Boys Smith. **Educ:** Somerville School, New Brighton; King Edward VII School, Lytham. Died 25 July 1935.

BURROW, Geoffrey Robert France (1942) Born 30 August 1924, 287 Halifax Road, Brighouse, Yorkshire; son of Robert Burrow, Waterworks Engineer, and Marion Gertrude France. **Tutor(s):** C W Guillebaud. **Educ:** Chichester High School; Victoria College, Jersey; Bedford School.

BURSILL, Claude (1945) Born 26 July 1920, Oak Lawn, Christchurch Road, Mortlake, Surrey; son of Bernard Bursill, Merchant, and Thekla Weber; m Vera Morgan (d 2 April 1981); 1 son (Mark Eliot, d 23 August 1971), 1 daughter (Charmian b 19 February 1945). **Subject(s):** Natural Sciences; BA 1947; MA 1952. **Tutor(s):** J M Wordie. **Educ:** East Sheen County School; Birkbeck College; UCL. **Career:** Geological Assistant, Anglo-Iranian Oil Company, England and Scotland 1939–1940; RAFVR 1941–1942; Technical Assistant, Ignition Research Department 1942–1945, Head, Chemical Section, Engine Research Department 1945, D Napier and Son, Aero-engine Manufacturers; Chief Geologist, Anglo-American Corp of South Africa Ltd 1953–1960; Science Advisor, Board of Directors, Rank Organization 1960–1963; Executive Director, New Brunswick Research and Productivity Council 1963–1983; Scientific Adviser (Energy) EEC (part-time) 1984–1988. **Publications:** Associated with Anglo-American Corp and New Brunswick Research.

BURSTALL, Aubrey Frederic (1923) Born 15 January 1902, 102 Bristol Road, Edgbaston, Birmingham; son of Henry Frederic William Burstall, Professor of Mechanical Engineering, Birmingham, and Lilian Maud Adley; m Nora Elizabeth Boycott, 15 December 1923. PhD 1925; MSc (Birmingham); DSc (Melbourne); MIMechE. **Tutor(s):** E Cunningham. **Johnian Relatives:** son of Henry Frederic William Burstall (1886). **Educ:** Rathvilly Preparatory School, Northfield; King Edward's High School, Birmingham; University of Birmingham. **Career:** Synthetic Ammonia and Nitrates Ltd, Billingham (later ICI) 1925–1933; Technical Advisor, Aluminium Plant and Vessel Company of Wandsworth, London 1933–1936; Professor of Engineering, Melbourne University 1936; Professor of Mechanical and Marine Engineering, King's College, Newcastle 1945. Died June 1984.

BURT, Professor Sir Cyril Lodovic (1913) Born 3 March 1883, Westminster; son of Cyril Cecil Barrow Burt, Physician, and Martha Decima Evans; m Joyce Muriel Woods. MA (Oxon); Teachers' Diploma (Oxon) 1908; FBA 1950. **Educ:** Warwick Grammar School; Christ's Hospital; Jesus College, Oxford. **Career:** Assistant Lecturer in Physiology and Lecturer in Experimental Psychology, University of Liverpool 1908–1913; Assistant in Experimental Psychology, University of Cambridge 1913–1914; Psychologist to London County Council (Education Department) 1913–1932; Professor of Education, University of London 1924–1931; Charles Spearman Professor of Psychology, UCL 1931–1950. **Appointments:** Fellow Commoner, SJC 1913–1914; President, BPsS 1942; First President, Mensa; Founding Editor, *British Journal of Statistical Psychology* 1947–1963. **Awards:** John Locke Scholarship in Mental Philosophy, University of Oxford; Thorndike Prize, American Psychological Association 1971. **Honours:** Kt 1946. **Publications:** *Distribution and Relations of Educational Abilities*, 1917; *Mental and Scholastic Tests*, 1921; *The Young Delinquent*, 1925; *How the Mind Works*, 1933; *The Subnormal Mind*, 1935; *The Backward Child*, 1937; *The Factors of the Mind*, 1940; over 300 articles, lectures and book chapters. Died 10 October 1971.

BURTON, Arnold James (1935) Born 3 November 1917, 173 Chapeltown Road, Leeds; son of Montague Maurice Burton, Company Director, and Sophia Amelia Marks; m (1) E M Rennie, 1940, (2) B H Flatau, 1950, (3) Jean Marie Rosenthall, 25 August 1994; (1) 1 son (Alexander Simon James), (2) 3 sons (Jeremy John, Nicholas Anthony and Mark Timothy). **Subject(s):** Geography; BA 1939; MA 1943. **Tutor(s):** J M Wordie. **Johnian Relatives:** father of Nicholas Anthony Burton (1971) and of Mark Timothy Burton (1973). **Educ:** Grosvenor House School, Harrogate; Clifton College, Bristol; The Berkshire School, Sheffield, USA. **Career:** RAF 1939–1945; Director, Montague Burton Ltd 1945–1983. **Appointments:** Chairman, and later President, Council of Multiple Shops Federation 1945–1983; Member, Associate Committee of the Royal Automobile Club 1974–1989.

BURTON, Charles Alan (1931) Born 26 September 1912, 169 Waterloo Street, Georgetown, Demerara, British Guiana; son of Charles Montagu Burton, Government Medical Officer, and Irma Marguerite Ann Seedorff. **Subject(s):** Modern and Medieval Languages/Law; BA 1934. **Tutor(s):** C W Guillebaud. **Johnian Relatives:** brother of John Henry Montagu Burton (1928). **Educ:** Hillside School, Reigate; Repton School.

BURTON, Dennis Arthur Edward (1928) Born 21 November 1910, Fairfield House, Castleford, Yorkshire; son of Arthur Cornelius Burton, Dealer in Cattle Medicines, and Daisy Vernon Sharp. **Subject(s):** Modern and Medieval Languages (French and Spanish); BA 1931; MA 1937. **Tutor(s):** C W Guillebaud. **Johnian Relatives:** father of Anthony Levesley Burton (1965). **Educ:** Old Hall School, Hornsea; Pocklington School. **Awards:** Dowman Exhibition, SJC 1928. Died 1 November 1985.

BURTON, Canon Humphrey Phillips Walcot (1907) Born 12 May 1888, Woodfield House, Kidderminster, Worcestershire; son of John Richard Burton, Clerk in Holy Orders, and Mary Henrietta Anne Dashwood Walcot; m (1) Hilda Kathleen Marchand, 10 September 1913, Holy Trinity, Lyonsdown, New Barnet (d 1950), (2) Jane Loft (née Johnson), 9 October 1950, St James, Louth; (1) 3 daughters (Joan Mary Walcot b 2 August 1914 (d 1974), Barbara Kathleen Walcot b 4 October 1918 and Margaret (Peggy) Irene b 20 October 1921), (2) 2 stepsons (Edmund Martin Boswell Loft b 22 March 1925, John Patrick Boswell Loft b 16 August 1926), 1 stepdaughter (Katherine Frances Boswell Loft b 4 March 1923). **Subject(s):** History; BA 1910; MA 1914. **Tutor(s):** J R Tanner. **Johnian Relatives:** brother-in-law of Geoffrey Isidore Charles Marchand (1907); stepfather of Edmund Martin Boswell Loft (1946). **Educ:** Hereford Cathedral School. **Career:** Deacon, Chester, 1912; Curate, St Mary, Stockport 1912–1913; Ordained Priest, Lincoln 1913; Curate, Frodingham 1913–1921; Temporary CF, 4th Class, RACD, 1915–1919; Vicar, Crosby 1921–1928; Rector, Louth with Welton le Wold, and Chaplain, Louth Workhouse and Surrogate 1928; Proctor in Convocation for Lincoln and Rural Dean, Louthesk West 1929; Prebendary of Louth, Lincoln Cathedral 1934–1951; Rector, Withcall 1938. **Appointments:** President of the Union 1911; Organising Secretary, Stepney Council of Public Welfare 1911–1912; Select Preacher, University of Cambridge 1939; Canon Emeritus 1952. **Awards:** Naden Studentship, SJC; Open Exhibition, SJC; Somerset Exhibition, SJC. **Publications:** (autobiography) *Weavers of Webs*, Monckton Publications, 1955. Died 15 December 1957.

BURTON, John Henry Montagu (1928) Born 7 February 1911, 34 Main Street, Georgetown, Demerara; son of Charles Montagu Burton, Government Medical Officer, and Irma Marguerite Ann Seedorff. BA 1932. **Tutor(s):** C W Guillebaud. **Johnian Relatives:** brother of Charles Alan Burton (1931). **Educ:** Hillside School, Reigate; Repton School.

BURTON, Thomas Edmund (1943) Born 10 November 1926, 1a Blackburn Avenue, Bridlington, Yorkshire; son of James Burton, Postman, and Janie Hope. **Subject(s):** Moral Sciences/Law; BA 1949; MA 1961. **Tutor(s):** C W Guillebaud. **Educ:** Oxford Street Elementary School, Bridlington; Bridlington School.

BURTON, William Glynn (1939) Born 19 April 1916, Reeth, Richmond, Yorkshire; son of Wilfred Glynn Burton, Schoolmaster, and Florence Hannah Collitt; m Mariella, 1 daughter (Agneta). MA 1947; BSc (Leeds) 1938; DSc (Leeds) 1968. **Tutor(s):** C W Guillebaud. **Educ:** Topcliffe Church of England School; Thirsk Secondary School; University of Leeds. **Career:** Deputy Director and Head of the Plant Physiology and Biochemistry Division, ARC, Food Research Institute, Norwich 1976. **Awards:** Agricultural Research Scholarship. Died 9 July 1989.

BURY, Dr Henry Philip Roberts (1948) Born 24 November 1929, 5 Avenue Terrace, Southend-on-Sea, Essex; son of Henry Cyril Bury, Municipal Clerk, and Gladys Roberts; m Mary Catherine Hegarty, 29 February 1960; 4 sons (Henry John and James Michael b 28 January 1961, Richard Patrick b 13 February 1963 and David Philip b 6 January 1965), 1 daughter (Catherine Margaret b 1 August 1973). BA 1951; MSc 1957; BChir 1958; MB 1958. **Tutor(s):** G C L Bertram. **Johnian Relatives:** father of David Philip Bury (1984). **Educ:** Branwood House Private School; Eccles Grammar School; Manchester Grammar School. **Career:** Registrar in Clinical Pathology, Children's Hospital, Sheffield 1960–1962; Lecturer in Pathology, University of Sheffield 1962–1969; Consultant, Histopathology, Castle Hill Hospital, Cottington, 1969–1994. **Appointments:** Crewdson-Benington Studentship 1952. **Awards:** Somerset Exhibition, SJC 1947.

BURY, Patrick James (1937) Born 16 February 1919, 36 Sydney Street, Chelsea; son of Edward Basil Bury, Clerk in the Foreign Office, and Phyllis Edwalyn de Kay. **Subject(s):** Classics; BA 1948. **Tutor(s):** R L Howland. **Educ:** Spyway School, Langton Matravers; Westminster School. **Awards:** Major Scholarship, SJC 1936; Marquess of Salisbury Exhibition, SJC 1937.

BUSH, Richard Eldon (1909) Born 16 June 1891, St Ringer's, Keynsham, Somerset; son of Philip Wathen Bush, Solicitor, and Maria Louisa Bremridge. **Subject(s):** History. **Tutor(s):** J R Tanner. **Educ:** Ormonde House School, Dursley; Malvern College.

BUSHE-FOX, Patrick Loftus (1925) Born 4 May 1907, 15 Madingley Road, Cambridge; son of Loftus Henry Kendal Bushe-Fox, Fellow and Tutor, SJC, and Theodora Willoughby. **Subject(s):** History; BA 1928; MA 1932; LLB 1932; LLM 1935. **Tutor(s):** E A Benians. **Johnian Relatives:** son of Loftus Henry Kendal Bushe-Fox (1882). **Educ:** King's College Choir School, Cambridge; Charterhouse. **Career:** Called to the Bar, Inner Temple 1932; Ministry of Economic Warfare 1941–1945; Control Office for Germany and Austria 1945–1947; German Section 1947–1950, Assistant Legal Advisor 1950–1960, Legal Counsellor 1960–1967, Foreign Office. **Awards:** Whewell Scholarship, University of Cambridge 1928. **Honours:** CMG 1963. Died 2 June 1982.

BUSHELL, Herbert Donald (1912) Born 31 October 1892, 16 Finchley Road, Walworth, Southwark, Surrey; son of Herbert Henry Gams Bushell, Tobacconist, and Emma Amelia Neale. **Tutor(s):** E E Sikes. **Educ:** County Secondary School, Holloway. Died 7 March 1913.

BUSHELL, William (1919) Born 5 October 1898, 26 Cross Street, Rhodes, Manchester; son of James Bushell, Clerk, and Elizabeth Daniels. BA 1921. **Tutor(s):** E A Benians. **Educ:** North Manchester Preparatory School; Manchester Grammar School.

BUSVINE, Robert Lewis (1949) Born 8 February 1929, 34 Golders Manor Drive, Golders Green, London; son of John Lewis Busvine, Furrier, and Dorothy Lewis Hind; m Ann (d 16 January 1999); 2 sons (Nicholas John Lewis b 13 May 1960 and Douglas Carl), 1 daughter (Joanna Franklin). **Subject(s):** History/Economics; BA 1952; MA 1961; FIMC. **Tutor(s):** A G Lee. **Johnian Relatives:** father of Nicholas John Lewis Busvine (1979). **Educ:** La Sagesse Convent, Golders Green; Queen Elizabeth's Grammar School, Barnet. **Career:** Management Consultant/Director, Busvine Associates Ltd. **Awards:** Minor Scholarship, SJC 1946. Died 30 May 2004.

BUTCHER, George Laidman (1948) Born 22 November 1926, Loke Road, King's Lynn, Norfolk; son of George Frederick Butcher, Schoolmaster, and Rose Laidman; m Sheila Florence Porter, 1952, King's Lynn, Norfolk; 3 sons (Paul b 1955, Peter b 1957 and Timothy b 1958), 1 daughter (Elizabeth b 1961). BA 1950; MA 1974. **Tutor(s):** F Thistlethwaite. **Educ:** St James's School, King's Lynn; King Edward VII Grammar School, King's Lynn. **Career:** Instruction in Small Arms and Infantry Weapon Training, School of Infantry, Warminster and Small Arms School, Hythe, Royal Norfolk Regiment 1945–1948; Cambridge Institute of Education 1950–1952; English Department, Kingswood Grammar School, Bristol 1952–1958; English Department, Aylesbury Grammar School, Buckinghamshire 1958–1972; Extra-Mural Tutor, Aylesbury College of Further Education and Co-ordinator, BBC Adult Literacy Scheme 1972–1977; Head, Adult Education Centre 1977–1985; Consultant, British Telecom's Management Training College, Milton Keynes 1985–1990.

BUTCHER, Professor Harold John (1938) Born 6 September 1920, 49 Bond Road, Southampton; son of Thomas Harold Butcher, HM Senior Inspector of Taxes, and Lily Rose Hand. **Subject(s):** Classics; BA 1941; PhD (Manchester); Diploma in Education (Manchester). **Tutor(s):** R L Howland. **Educ:** St Anselm's Preparatory School; Whitgift School; University of Manchester. **Career:** Ministry of Education and LCC Education Department 1947–1952; Lecturer in Education, University of Manchester 1956–1963; Lecturer in Psychology, University of Edinburgh 1966; Professor of Higher Education, University of Manchester 1966; Department of Developmental Psychology, Sussex University. **Awards:** Exhibition, SJC 1937. **Publications:** *Sampling in Educational Research*, Statistical Guides in Educational Research No 3, Manchester University Press, 1966; (ed with H B Pont) *Educational research in Britain*, University of London Press, 1968; (with Raymond Bernard Cattell) *The prediction of achievement and creativity*, Bobbs-Merrill, 1968; (with James Freeman and Thomas Christie) *Creativity. A selective review of research*, Research into higher education monographs No 5, Society for Research into Higher Education, 1968; *Human intelligence: its nature and assessment*, Manuals of modern psychology, Methuen, 1970; (ed with D E Lomax) *Readings in human intelligence*, Manuals of modern psychology, Methuen, 1972; (with Ernest Rudd) *Contemporary problems in higher education. An account of research*, McGraw Hill, 1972; (ed with John Sants) *Developmental psychology. Selected readings*, Penguin modern psychology readings, Penguin, 1975.

BUTLER, Basil Richard Ryland (1949) Born 1 March 1930, Plover Hill House, Hexham, Northumberland; son of Hugh Montagu Butler, Headmaster, Queen Mary's School, Walsall, and Annie Isabel Wiltshire; m Lilian Joyce Haswell, 26 June 1954; 1 son (Richard b 1957), 2 daughters (Clare b 1960 and Helen b 1964). **Subject(s):** Natural Sciences; BA 1952; MA 1956; FREng; FIMM; FInstPet 1965; Honorary FIChemE 1991. **Tutor(s):** W A Deer; E Miller. **Educ:** Queen Mary's School, Walsall; Denstone College. **Career:** British Army; Petroleum Engineer, Trinidad Leaseholds Ltd, West Indies 1954–1957; Production Engineer, Reservoir Engineer, then (from 1964) Chief Petroleum Engineer, Kuwait Oil Company 1958–1968; Operations Manager, BP Colombia Inc, Bogota 1968–1970; Operations Manager and Vice President, BP Alaska Inc 1970–1972; General Manager of Operations, Kuwait Oil Company 1972–1975; Manager, Ninian Developments, BP Petroleum Development Company Ltd, London 1975–1976; Director, Sullom Voe Association and Manager, Sullom Voe Terminal, Shetland Island 1976–1978; General Manager, Exploration and Production, BP Petroleum Development Ltd, Aberdeen 1978–1980; Chief Executive, BP Petroleum Development Ltd, London 1980–1986; Director, BP International Ltd 1981; Managing Director and Chief Executive 1981–1986, Chairman 1986–1989, BP Exploration Company Ltd; Managing Director, British Petroleum Company plc 1986–1991; Chairman 1991–1995, Director 1991–1998, BP Solar International; Director, Murphy Oil Corporation, Arkansas 1991–2002; Director 1991–1998, Chairman 1993–1998, Brown and Root Ltd; Chairman, Devonport Management Ltd and Devonport Royal Dockyard

1992–1994; Chairman, KS Biomedix plc 1995–2001. **Appointments:** Fellow 1985–, Council Member 1994–, Honorary Secretary for International Affairs 1995–1998, Senior Vice-President 1996–1999, Chairman, Membership Committee 1999–2002, Royal Academy of Engineering; Member, Committee for Middle East Trade 1985–1993; Consultant, World Bank; Liveryman, Shipwrights' Company 1988; Member, CBI Council; Member, Offshore Industry Advisory Board; President, Institute of Petroleum 1990–1992; Member, European Science and Technology Assembly; Chairman, Environment Committee of the Business and Industry Advisory Committee to the OECD, Paris 1991; Chairman, EuroCASE 1992–1997; Honorary Member, Spanish Royal Academy of Engineering 1999; Fellow, Institute of Materials, Mining and Metallurgy; Fellow, Institute of Petroleum; Honorary Fellow, Institution of Chemical Engineers; Member, Advisory Board, Tyndall Centre, University of East Anglia. **Honours:** OBE 1976; CBE 1997.

BUTLER, The Venerable Cuthbert Hilary (1932) Born 8 March 1913, 16 Wantage Road, Reading, Berkshire; son of William Edward Butler, Wine Merchant, and Bertha Alice Bowman; m Josephine Mary Stubbs, 1942; 4 sons (Jeremy, Mark, Andrew and Sebastian), 2 daughters (Raphaelle and Veronica). **Subject(s):** History/Theology; BA 1935; MA 1939. **Tutor(s):** J S Boys Smith; E A Benians. **Johnian Relatives:** brother of Felix John Butler (1925); uncle of Julia Catherine Copley (1982). **Educ:** No IX Preparatory School, Reading; Reading School. **Career:** Ordained Deacon 1940–1941; Curate, Preston, Sussex 1940–1942; Ordained Priest 1941; Chaplain, RAFVR 1942–1946; Vicar, St Matthias, Preston 1947–1951; Rector, Crawley, Sussex 1951–1958; Rector, Oliver, British Columbia, Canada 1958–1961; Canon Lecturer, Christ Church Cathedral, Victoria, British Columbia 1961–1971; Director of Program, Diocese of British Columbia 1971–1978; Archdeacon of Columbia, British Columbia 1977–1978. **Awards:** Exhibition, SJC; College Reading Prize 1934; Burney Prize, University of Cambridge 1936; Naden Studentship, SJC 1937; Burney Studentship, University of Cambridge 1937–1938; Gladstone Memorial Studentship, University of Cambridge 1939–1940.

BUTLER, Felix John (1925) Born 27 December 1905, 16 Wantage Road, Reading, Berkshire; son of William Edward Butler, Wine Merchant, and Bertha Alice Bowman. **Subject(s):** History; BA 1928; MA 1937; BSc (London) 1939. **Tutor(s):** E A Benians. **Johnian Relatives:** brother of Cuthbert Hilary Butler (1932). **Educ:** Wilson Elementary School, Reading; Reading School. **Awards:** Scholarship, SJC 1924. Died 17 February 1997.

BUTLER, Francis Herbert Culverhouse (1919) (admitted to Selwyn College 1914) Born 10 July 1894, Morda Road, Oswestry, Shropshire; son of Herbert William Butler, Assistant County Surveyor, and Sophia Victoria Frey; m Eleanor Madeline Beck, 18 August 1925, Ropley Parish Church; 1 son (Richard), 1 daughter (Elizabeth). **Subject(s):** Natural Sciences; BA 1921; MA 1924. **Tutor(s):** E E Sikes. **Johnian Relatives:** father of Richard Francis Culverhouse Butler (1944). **Educ:** Peter Symond's School, Winchester. **Career:** Lieutenant, Temporary Captain, Royal Hampshire Regiment (served in Palestine and Mesopotamia) (Mentioned in Despatches 1917) 1914–1918; Chemistry Teacher, Dulwich College 1922–1930; Inspector of Schools 1930; Founder, Council for the Promotion of Field Studies 1943; Director and Secretary, Council for the Promotion of Field Studies 1947–1960. Died 14 November 1970.

BUTLER, Dr George (1942) Born 11 March 1924, Thorn Edge Farm, Trawden, Lancashire; son of Richard Butler, Farmer, and Rebecca Lofthouse. **Subject(s):** Natural Sciences; BA 1945; MA 1949. **Tutor(s):** C W Guillebaud. **Educ:** Rimington Council School; Queen Mary's Grammar School, Clitheroe.

BUTLER, Ian Edward (1949) Born 13 November 1929, Tezpur, Assam, India; son of Stanley Gordon Butler, Indian Service of Engineers, and Janet Muir Morrison; 1 son (Gordon Thomas b 1963). **Subject(s):**

Economics; BA 1952; MA 1956. **Tutor(s):** G C L Bertram. **Johnian Relatives:** father of Gordon Thomas Butler (1981); father-in-law of Henrietta Lucy Butler (1982). **Educ:** The Limes School, Croydon; Heath Mount, Woodhall Park; Caterham School.

BUTLER, John David (1940) Born 23 September 1921, 29 Friars Street, Sudbury, Suffolk; son of Gerald Snowden Butler, Director, Ordnance Factories, India, and Helen Veronica Shaw. **Tutor(s):** C W Guillebaud. **Educ:** Dorset House, Littlehampton; Oundle School. **Career:** Captain, Gurkha Rifles 1940–1944. **Award:** Munsteven Exhibition, SJC 1940. Died June 1944 (killed in action in Burma).

BUTLER, Richard Francis Culverhouse (1944) Born 31 July 1926, Belford House, Ropley, Hampshire; son of Francis Herbert Culverhouse Butler, Inspector of Schools, London County Council, and Eleanor Madeleine Beck; m Yvonne Mary Chamberlain, 1958, Portsmouth Cathedral; 2 daughters (Mary and Sarah). **Subject(s):** Natural Sciences; BA 1948; MA 1951; CEng; FIEE; MInstMgt. **Tutor(s):** C W Guillebaud. **Johnian Relatives:** son of Francis Herbert Culverhouse Butler (1919). **Educ:** Baston School, Hayes Common; Carn Brea Preparatory School, Bromley; Gresham's School, Holt. **Career:** Commissioned REME 1947–1970; Regular Army Commission 1949–1970; Research and Development, and Management, MOD and working with industry (rank of Lieutenant Colonel) 1966; Vickers plc, Medical Engineering 1970–1974 (Managing Director 1973–1974); Engineering Director, Vickers plc, Design and Projects, Eastleigh 1974–1985; Director, Hampshire Technology Centre 1981; Director, ITW Consultants 1986–1995.

BUTLER, Ronald Crossley (1946) Born 21 September 1927, 121 Manchester Road, Oldham, Lancashire; son of William Crossley Butler, Butcher, and Alice Barnes. **Subject(s):** English. BA 1949. **Tutor(s):** F Thistlethwaite. **Educ:** Thames Road Junior School, Blackpool; Blackpool Grammar School. **Awards:** Minor Scholarship, SJC 1945.

BUTLER, Rupert Donovan Weeden (1919) Born 13 December 1900, 23 Donkin Street, Port Elizabeth, Cape Colony, South Africa; son of Thomas Harrison Butler, Medical Practitioner, and Ellen Reed; m Molly; 1 son (Philip Roderick b 7 May 1933), 1 daughter. BA 1922; MRCS; DOMS; LRCP. **Tutor(s):** E A Benians. **Johnian Relatives:** father of Philip Roderick Butler (1951). **Educ:** Beech Lawn, Leamington; Stoneygate School, Leicester; King Edward's School, Birmingham; Oundle School. **Career:** Birmingham and Midland Eye Hospital: House Surgeon 1926, Consultant 1931; Major, RAMC: France 1939–1940, Royal United Hospital, Bath 1940–1942, Northern Ireland 1942–1945; Consultant Ophthalmic Surgeon, Birmingham and Midland Eye Hospital, the Women's Hospital and Stourbridge Hospital 1965. **Appointments:** Director, Birmingham School of Orthoptics; President, Midland Ophthalmological Society. Died 26 February 1978.

BUTSON, Dr Arthur Richard Cecil (1940) Born 24 October 1922, International Hospital, Hankow, China; son of Cecil Walter Butson, Consulting Engineer, and Doris Neave Stanton-Cook; m Eileen Callon, 30 June 1967; 1 son (Andrew Richard), 2 daughters (Sarah Louise and Caroline Frances). **Subject(s):** Natural Sciences; BA 1943; MA 1947; BChir 1945; MB 1945; MD 1951; FRCS; FRCSC; FACS. **Tutor(s):** R L Howland. **Educ:** Hankow Private School; English School, Château-d'Oex, Switzerland; The Downs School, Colwall; Leighton Park School, Reading. **Career:** Surgical Registrar, University College Hospital Medical School, London; Surgical Training, London and Montreal 1948–1952; Surgical Practice, Hamilton, Ontario 1953–2001. **Appointments:** President, SJC Medical Society 1941–1942; Private, Cambridge University Dispatch Riders Unit and Home Guard 1941–1942; Medical Officer, Falkland Islands Dependencies Survey mapping coastline Antarctic peninsula 1946–1948; Brigade Surgeon to St John Ambulance and former Provincial Surgeon 1973–1987; Clinical Professor of Surgery, McMaster University Medical School 1970–1994; Canadian Militia, ending as Lieutenant Colonel and Commanding

Officer, Hamilton Militia Medical Company, then Area Surgeon, Central Canada 1956–1982; Queen's Honorary Surgeon 1977–1979; Represented Canada on Interallied Confederation Officers Medical Reserves (NATO Reserve Officers Organisation) 1980–1984; Honorary Colonel 23 (Hamilton) Medical Company 1989–1997; Member, Victoria Cross and George Cross Association. **Awards:** Albert Medal, Scott Polar Research Institute, Cambridge; Twice won trophy for best medical company in Canada. **Honours:** Canadian Forces Decoration; Polar Medal; Officer of Order of Military Merit, Canada; CStJ; Canadian Forces Decoration; George Cross; Queen's Silver Jubilee Medal. **Publications:** 'Acclimatisation to Cold in the Antarctic', *Nature*, 1949; 'Utilization of High-Fat-Diet at Low Temperatures', *Lancet*, 1950; 'Regeneration of the cervical sympathetic', *British Journal of Surgery*, 1950; 'Use of Intra articular Hydrocortisone in Orthopedic Conditions', *Canadian Medical Association Journal*, 1954; (jointly) 'Clinical Trial of High Dosage Vitimin E in Human Muscular Dystrophy', *Canadian Medical Association Journal*, 1960; 'Effects and Prevention of Frostbite in Wound Healing', *Canadian Journal of Surgery*, 1975; 'An Evaluation of Intermittent Pneumatic Calf Compression in Prevention of Deep Venous Thrombosis in General Abdominal Surgery', *American Journal of Surgery*, 1981; 'Familial Multiple Polyposis Coli with Multiple Associated Tumours', *Diseases of the Colon and Rectum*, 1983; 'The Clinical Use of Antishock Trousers', *Canadian Medical Association Journal*, 1983; *Handbook on the Administration of Oxygen*, St John Ambulance Publication; *A History of the Military Medical Units of Hamilton, Ontario, in Peace and War 1900–90*, 1990; 'The Healthy Heart: Facts on Meat Consumption', *Cardiology*, 1998.

BUTT, Sam (1907) Born 30 May 1889, Grimsby, Lincolnshire; son of Walter William Butt, Hotelkeeper, and Eugenie Annie Sophia Kennedy. **Tutor(s):** J R Tanner. **Educ:** Collegiate School, Grimsby; The Grammar School, Old Clee, Grimsby.

BUTTERWORTH, The Revd Albert Wilson (1920) Born 11 October 1901, Sigra, Benares, India; son of Albert Butterworth, Clerk in Holy Orders, and Annie Eliza Banks; m Anne May Spicer (d 1947); 1 son (Hugh). **Subject(s):** Economics/History; BA 1923; MA 1927. **Tutor(s):** E A Benians. **Educ:** Hereford Cathedral Preparatory and Senior Schools; Dean Close School, Cheltenham; Ridley Hall, Cambridge. **Career:** Ordained Deacon 1924; Curate, Frodingham 1924–1930; Ordained Priest 1925; Priest in Charge, St Hugh, Old Brumby 1927–1930; Curate, St John the Baptist, Croydon and Priest in Charge, Waddon District Church 1930–1931; Rector, St Giles, Colchester 1931–1939; Chaplain, Public Assistance Institution, Colchester 1933; Vicar, St Paul, Chatham 1939–1942; Chaplain, HM Borstal Institution, Rochester 1940–1942; Vicar, St James, Croydon 1942–1951; Rector, Plaxtol 1951–1956; Rector, Much Birch with Little Birch, Herefordshire 1956–1964; Rector, Felton with Preston Wynne and Ullingswick, Herefordshire 1964–1967. Died 22 November 1979.

BUTTERWORTH, Sir George Neville (1929) Born 27 December 1911, Belmont House, Belmont, Hastings, Sussex; son of George Richard Butterworth, Incorporated Accountant, and Hannah Wright; m Barbara Mary Briggs, 1947; 2 sons. **Subject(s):** Economics/Mathematics; BA 1933; MA 1969. **Tutor(s):** J M Wordie. **Educ:** Laton House School, Hastings; The Grange Preparatory School, St Helens, Ore; Malvern College. **Career:** Commercial Director; English Sewing Cotton Company (Tootal) 1933; Managing Director 1966–1968, Chairman 1968–1974, Tootal Textile Group. **Appointments:** DL, Greater Manchester, 1974; High Sheriff, Greater Manchester 1975. **Honours:** Kt 1973. Died 25 May 1995.

BUTTERWORTH, John (1923) Born 21 September 1905, 27 Brooklands Road, Burnley, Lancashire; son of John Butterworth, Cotton Manufacturer, and Marie Eugénie Faivre. **Subject(s):** Mathematics/Natural Sciences; BA 1926. **Tutor(s):** B F Armitage. **Educ:** Mostyn House School, Parkgate; Radley College, Abingdon. **Awards:** Exhibition, SJC 1922.

BUTTLE, Professor Gladwin Albert Hurst (1919) Born 11 April 1899, Park View, Godstone, Surrey; son of William Buttle, Solicitor, and Mary Wilby Ward; m Eva Korella, 1936; 1 son (Richard). **Subject(s):** Natural Sciences; BA 1921; MA 1926; Honorary MD (Louvain) 1945; MB 1967; BChir 1967; MRCS (UCL) 1924; LRCP (UCL) 1924; FRCP (London) 1970; FRSocMed. **Tutor(s):** E E Sikes. **Educ:** Whitgift Grammar School, Croydon; RMA, Woolwich. **Career:** RMA Cadet Battalion 1916–1918; School of Military Engineering 1st Reserve Battalion, Chatham 1918; Haynes Park Signal Depot, Bedford 1918–1919; Bedford 'A' Signal Depot 1919; 459th Field Company, RE, Midland Division, BAOR 1919; Pharmacologist, Wellcome Physiological Research Laboratories, Beckenham 1924–1939; Lieutenant Colonel, RAMC, adviser in Blood Transfusion, MEF and BLA 1940–1945; Wellcome Professor of Pharmacology, School of Pharmacy, University of London 1946–1966; Professor 1948–1960 (Emeritus 1960), St Bartholomew's Hospital Medical School; Visiting Professor of Pharmacology in Mexico City, Addis Ababa, and Riyadh 1965–1977; Expert, FAO, Mexico City 1967–1969; Professor of Pharmacology, Addis Ababa 1972–1974; Professor of Pharmacology, Riyadh University 1974–1978. **Appointments:** Member, British Pharmacological Society 1932; Co-founder and Chairman, Buttle Trust for Children 1953–1974; British Pharmacopoeia Codex Action and Uses Committee; MRC Drug Safety Committee; Colonial Office Leprosy Committee; Ministry of Agriculture Food Additives Committee; Medical Consultant to MOD. **Honours:** OBE 1942 (Military). **Publications:** Contributions on chemotherapy and pharmacology to medical journals. Died 3 May 1983.

BUTTLE, William Roland (1937) Born 14 February 1918, Kirkleby, Malton, Yorkshire; son of William Roland Buttle, Farmer, and Grace Earl Parmley. **Subject(s):** Classics; BA 1940; MA 1944. **Tutor(s):** R L Howland. **Educ:** Southcliffe Preparatory School, Filey; Tunstall School, Sunderland; Durham School. **Awards:** Baker Exhibition, SJC 1937. Died 25 March 1974.

BUTTON, Arnold Elliot (1908) Born 29 June 1888, 34 Great Portland Street, Marylebone, Middlesex; son of Henry Elliot Button, Musician, and Nora Harvey Marshall. BA 1911. **Tutor(s):** J R Tanner. **Educ:** St Paul's School, London. **Career:** Air Mechanic, RAF, WWI. **Appointments:** Member, Fédération Aéronautique Internationale. Died 14 January 1964.

BUTTON, John Carr (1933) Born 1 August 1915, 125 Gainsborough Road, Monks, Coppenhall, Cheshire; son of Leonard Joseph Button, Electrical Engineer, and Dorothy Mary Holmes; m Joan. **Subject(s):** Natural Sciences; BA 1936; MA 1940. **Tutor(s):** C W Guillebaud. **Educ:** Edleston Road School, Crewe; County Secondary School, Crewe; The Leys School, Cambridge. Died 26 February 1973.

BUTZER, Heinrich Wilhelm Viktor (1930) Born 23 December 1911, Deininghausen, Dortmund, Germany; son of Heinrich Butzer, Engineer, and Martha Rave. **Tutor(s):** C W Guillebaud. **Educ:** Dortmund Vorschule; Dortmund Gymnasium.

BUXTON, Gurney Harry Lionel (1930) Born 30 October 1911, 128 Cambridge Street, Norwich; son of Henry James Buxton, Master House Furnisher, and Rosetta Elizabeth Locke. **Subject(s):** Mathematics; BA 1933. **Tutor(s):** J M Wordie. **Educ:** Crooks Place School, Norwich; City of Norwich School. **Awards:** Scholarship, SJC 1929.

BUXTON, Dr Peter Howroyd (1936) Born 17 December 1918, 40 Merton Hall Road, Wimbledon; son of Oliver James Buxton, Chartered Secretary, and Gladys Howroyd; m Aline M L Kennedy, 17 December 1949, Parish Church, Barnes. **Subject(s):** Natural Sciences; BA 1939; MA 1952; MB 1942; BChir 1942; MD 1952. **Tutor(s):** J M Wordie. **Educ:** St Andrew's School, Meads, Eastbourne; Bradfield College. **Career:** Consultant Pathologist, Regional Neurosurgical Unit, Walton Hospital, Liverpool 1960.

BYGATE, Noel (1940) Born 7 December 1921, 18 Sherwood Crescent, Rotherham, Yorkshire; son of Reginald Bygate, Attendant, Liverpool Public Museum, and Alice Wright, Teacher; 3 children. **Subject(s):** English/History; BA 1947; MA 1950. **Tutor(s):** C W Guillebaud. **Educ:** Hoylake Church of England School; Hoylake Parade School, Preparatory Department; Calday Grange Grammar School. **Career:** Intelligence Corps, The King's Regiment (India), and Lancashire Fusiliers (reaching rank of Captain) 1940–1946; Teacher, Beckenham and Penge Grammar School 1949–1958; Teacher, Hastings Grammar School (subsequently called William Parker School) 1958–1983 (Head of English Department 1958–1969, Deputy Head 1969). **Publications:** (co-author) *History of Hastings Grammar School.*

BYRNE, Douglas Norman (1942) Born 30 January 1924, Cowes, Isle of Wight; son of Leonard William Byrne, Engine Room Artificer, RN, and Clarice Evelyn Noak; m Noreen Thurlby Giles, 1949; 1 son (Richard William), 1 daughter (Rosemary Alison). **Subject(s):** Classics; BA 1949; MA 1952. **Tutor(s):** C W Guillebaud; R L Howland. **Johnian Relatives:** father of Richard William Byrne (1969). **Educ:** Lyndhurst Road School, Portsmouth; Portsmouth Grammar School. **Career:** Pilot, RAF 1943–1946; Assistant Principal 1949–1952, Principal 1952–1955, Ministry of Supply; Board of Trade 1955–1961; Cabinet Office 1961–1964; Assistant Secretary, Board of Trade 1964–1966; Monopolies and Mergers Commission 1966–1969; Department of Trade and Industry 1969–1974; Under-Secretary and Head of Mechanical Engineering, Fair Trading, Competition Policy and Marine Divisions in Departments of Trade, Industry, Prices and Consumer Protection, and Transport 1974–1984. **Appointments:** RAF Cadet, SJC 1942–1943; Captain, LMBC 1947–1948; Honorary Secretary, Johnian Society 1949–1984. **Awards:** Exhibition, SJC 1941; Scholarship, SJC 1947; Sir Joseph Larmor Award, SJC 1948; Wright's Prize, SJC 1948.

BYRNE, James John (1941) Born 12 August 1918, 1 Catherine Street, Waterford, Ireland; son of Michael Byrne, Sergeant, Royal Irish Constabulary, and Josephine Hamill. MSc 1948. **Tutor(s):** C W Guillebaud. **Educ:** St Kieran's College, Kilkenny; National University of Ireland.

BYRNE, Patrick Charles (1938) Born 4 November 1911, 251 Clonliffe Road, Dublin; son of Patrick Byrne, Police Sergeant, and Kate Weir. BA (Dublin) 1935. **Tutor(s):** C W Guillebaud. **Educ:** O'Connell School, Dublin; Emo Park, Portarlington; University College, Dublin.

BYRON-SCOTT, The Revd Wallace (1904) Born 1 June 1885, 40 Cecil Street, New Somerby, Lincolnshire; son of Alexander Byron-Scott, Commercial Clerk, and Charlotte Burrell. BA 1908; MA 1911. **Tutor(s):** C E Graves; J R Tanner. **Educ:** Gainsborough Grammar School. **Career:** Ordained Deacon 1912; Curate, Lanteglos with St Adwenna 1912–1914; Ordained Priest 1913; Chaplain, Giggleswick School 1915–1933; Chaplain and Divinity Lecturer, Ripon Training College 1933–1940; Vicar, Masham, Yorkshire 1940–1960. **Appointments:** Examining Chaplain to Bishop of Ripon 1945; Honorary Canon, Ripon Cathedral 1949. Died 1972.

BYTHELL, Denis William Prestwich (1929) Born 10 January 1911, Beech Hill, Singleton Road, Broughton, Lancashire; son of William James Storey Bythell, Doctor of Medicine, and Theodora Prestwich. BA 1932; MA 1942. **Tutor(s):** J M Wordie. **Johnian Relatives:** son of William James Storey Bythell (1890). **Educ:** Nevill Holt Preparatory School; Uppingham School.

BYWATERS, Bruce William Draper (1936) Born 28 May 1918, 17 Logan Road, Bristol; son of Hubert William Bywaters, Industrial Chemist, and Olive Robertson. **Subject(s):** Natural Sciences/Economics; BA 1939; MA 1943. **Tutor(s):** C W Guillebaud. **Educ:** Redland Collegiate School, Bristol; XIV School, Bristol; Wakefield Grammar School. **Awards:** Scholarship, SJC 1936–1937. Died 6 May 2004.

BYWATERS, Keith Robertson (1939) Born 4 March 1922, 30 Henleaze Avenue, Bristol; son of Hubert William Bywaters, Director and Works Manager, and Olive Robertson. **Subject(s):** Law. BA 1943; MA 1946. **Tutor(s):** S J Bailey. **Educ:** Wakefield Grammar School; King Arthur VII School, Sheffield.

C

CADBURY, Charles Lloyd (1944) Born 3 November 1926, 46 Edgbaston Park Road, Birmingham; son of Paul Strangman Cadbury, Managing Director, Cadbury Brothers Ltd, Cocoa and Chocolate Manufacturers, and Rachel Eveline Wilson; m Jillian Ransome, Stafford, 8 January 1958; 4 children. **Subject(s):** Natural Sciences/Economics; BA 1949; MA 1977. **Tutor(s):** C W Guillebaud. **Johnian Relatives:** son of Paul Strangman Cadbury (1914). **Educ:** West House School, Birmingham; Leighton Park School. **Career:** Friends' Ambulance Unit 1945–1948; Director, Cadbury Brothers Ltd 1950–1970; Owner, Wayfarers Foods Ltd, Redditch 1971–1975; Various Housing Associations 1976–1989; Director, South East Lancashire Housing Association 1980–1985; Clerk, Lench's Trust (Birmingham) 1985–1989. **Appointments:** JP. Died 16 January 2000.

CADBURY, Paul Strangman (1914) Born 3 November 1895, 4 Arthur Road, Edgbaston, Warwickshire; son of Barrow Cadbury, Cocoa Manufacturer, and Geraldine Southall; m Rachel Eveline Wilson, 24 June 1919, Friend's Meeting House, George Road, Birmingham. **Tutor(s):** E E Sikes. **Johnian Relatives:** father of Charles Lloyd Cadbury (1944). **Educ:** West House School, Birmingham; Leighton Park School. **Career:** Friends' Ambulance Unit 1914–1918; Cadbury Brothers (Vice-Chairman 1944, Chairman 1959) 1919–1965. **Appointments:** Chairman, Birmingham City Council's Reconstruction Committee; Honorary Secretary, West Midlands Group on Post-war Reconstruction and Planning; Chairman, Friends' Ambulance Unit 1939–1948; Member, Royal Commission on Local Government in the Greater London Area 1957–1960. **Honours:** CBE 1948. Died 24 October 1984.

CADDICK, Sydney David (1900) Born 14 November 1881, Church Street, Bilston, Staffordshire; son of Silas Caddick, Butcher, and Mary Ann Dickin. BA 1903; MA (Sidney Sussex) 1908. **Tutor(s):** J E Sandys. **Educ:** Denstone College, Staffordshire. **Career:** Master, Handel Lodge, Southampton 1903–1907; Master, Southampton Grammar School 1908–1931. Died 16 January 1931.

CADLE, Harry Sidney (1913) Born 3 June 1894, Windsor Lodge, Leigham Valley Road, Streatham, Surrey; son of Henry Sidney Cadle, Inspector of Taxes, and Kate Vaux; m Phyllis Mary Fowell Swan, 2 April 1921. **Tutor(s):** E E Sikes. **Johnian Relatives:** son of Henry Sidney Cadle (1882). **Educ:** Dulwich College Preparatory School; Dulwich College. **Career:** Second Lieutenant, 7th Battalion, Royal Welsh Fusiliers 1914; Lieutenant, East Surrey Regiment; Captain 1916; attached to Labour Corps until 1919; Assistant Inspector of Taxes 1920; Inspector 1923; Senior Inspector 1944. **Awards:** Scholarship, SJC.

CADMAN, Dr Donald Spencer (1935) Born 28 March 1917, Coniston, Alexandra Road, Wellington, Shropshire; son of Thomas Cadman, Printing Works Manager, and Betsy Adelaide Cadman; m Mary. **Subject(s):** Natural Sciences; BA 1938; BChir 1941; MB 1941; FRCP. **Tutor(s):** C W Guillebaud. **Johnian Relatives:** brother of Samuel Parkes Hubert Cadman (1925). **Educ:** Constitution Hill Council School, Wellington; Adams Grammar School, Newport. **Career:** Part-time Physician, Department of Cardiac Medicine, St Thomas' Hospital 1951. **Awards:** Scholarship, SJC 1936–1937.

CADMAN, Samuel Parkes Hubert (1925) Born 15 November 1906, Bennets Bank, Wellington, Shropshire; son of Thomas Cadman, Works Manager, and Betsy Adelaide Cadman. **Subject(s):** Natural Sciences/Economics; BA 1928. **Tutor(s):** J M Wordie. **Johnian Relatives:** brother of Donald Spencer Cadman (1935). **Educ:** Constitution Hill Council

School, Wellington; Newport Grammar School. **Awards:** Scholarship, SJC. Died 6 November 1973.

CAIRNS, Dr Richard (1924) Born 9 July 1906, 53 Lovaine Place, Newcastle upon Tyne, Northumberland; son of Ralph Cairns, Proprietor of a Motor Garage, and Grace Hardie. BA 1929; BChir 1933; MB 1942. **Tutor(s):** B F Armitage. **Educ:** New College, Harrogate.

CALDWELL, Dr John (1927) Born 8 May 1903, 19 Clive Place, Penarth, Glamorganshire; son of Peter Caldwell, Analytical Chemist, and Emily Phillips. PhD 1931; BSc (Glasgow) 1925; DSc (Glasgow); PhD (Glasgow). **Tutor(s):** J M Wordie. **Educ:** Kilmarnock Academy; Glasgow University. **Career:** Professor of Botany, University of Exeter 1947. **Awards:** Carnegie Research Fellow in Botany; Donaldson Research Scholarship in Biology, Glasgow 1925–27. Died 26 August 1974.

CALLANDER, Henry Ronald Burn (1947) Born 6 November 1921, Syrencot House, Figheldean, Amesbury, Wiltshire; son of William Henry Burn Callander, Major, Royal Scots Greys, and Mary Hermione Christian Garforth. **Tutor(s):** C W Guillebaud. **Educ:** St David's, Reigate; Eton.

CALLARD, Sir Eric John (1932) Born 15 March 1913, 162 Union Street, Torquay; son of Frank Callard, Master Baker and Confectioner, and Ada Mary Fawkes; m Pauline Mary Pengelly, 1938; 3 daughters. **Subject(s):** Mechanical Sciences; BA 1935; MA 1973; CEng; Honorary DSc (Cranfield Institute of Technology) 1974; FRSA 1970; CIMgt; Honorary FIMechE; FBIM 1966. **Tutor(s):** J S Boys Smith. **Educ:** Primary Department, Torquay Grammar School; Richmond Lodge; Montpelier School, Paignton; Queen's College, Taunton. **Career:** ICI Ltd 1935–1947; Ministry of Aircraft Production 1942; ICI Paints Division 1947–1964 (Joint Managing Director 1955–1959, Chairman 1959–1964); Non-executive Chairman, British Home Stores 1976–1982. **Appointments:** Chairman, Delegation Board, ICI (Hyde) Ltd 1959; Director, Pension Funds Securities Ltd 1963–1967; Director, Imperial Metal Industries Ltd 1964–1967; Council Member, BIM, 1964–1969; Council Member, Manchester University Business School 1964–1971; Chairman, ICI (Europa) Ltd 1965–1967; Council Member, Export Council for Europe, 1965–1971; Member, CBI Steering Committee on Europe, 1965–1971; Director, Imperial Chemicals Insurance Ltd 1966–1970; Member, Council of Industry for Management Education, 1967–1973; Member, Cambridge University Appointments Board 1968–1971; Member, CBI Overseas Committee 1969–1971; Member, Royal Institution of Great Britain 1971; Director 1964–1975, Deputy Chairman 1967–1971, Chairman 1971–1975, ICI Ltd; Chairman 1967–1971, President 1971–1976, Industrial Participation Association; Honorary Member 1966, President 1969–1971, Vice-President 1971, Manchester Business School Association; Director, Midland Bank Ltd 1971–1987; Member, Trustee, Civic Trust 1972–1975; Member, Governor, London Business School 1972–1975; Member, British Shippers' Council 1972–1975; Director, Ferguson Industrial Holdings 1975–1986; Director, Commercial Union Assurance Company 1976–1983; Member, Hansard Society Commission on Electoral Reform 1975–1976; Member, Committee of Inquiry into Industrial Democracy 1976–1977; Director, Equity Capital for Industry 1976–1984. Died 21 September 1998.

CALLAWAY, Dr Archibald Charles (1947) Born 22 December 1917, Timaru, New Zealand; son of Archibald Charles Callaway, Farmer, and Mabel Adams; m Helen Ann Lund, 4 November 1950; 3 sons, 1 daughter. **Subject(s):** Economics; BA 1949; BCom (Canterbury); MCom (Canterbury); PhD (Harvard) 1959. **Tutor(s):** C W Guillebaud. **Educ:** Lake Coleridge School; Christchurch West High School; Canterbury University College; Balliol College, Oxford. **Career:** 1st Canterbury Regiment 1940–1941; 6th Field Regiment 1941–1944; Assistant Lecturer in Economics, Massey Agricultural College, New Zealand 1947; Tutor in Economics, University of Oxford 1955; Member, Centre for International Studies, MIT 1959; Research Professor,

Nigerian Institute of Social and Economic Research 1967–1972; Research Associate, Queen Elizabeth House, Oxford 1972–1978; Senior Associate Member, St Anthony's College 1972–1978; Leader, UNESCO Educational Planning Team, Federal Ministry of Education, Lagos 1978. Died 16 July 1987.

CALLENDER, Reginald Henry (1912) (admitted as a Non-Collegiate Student 1911) Born 31 August 1892, Bishopton, County Durham; son of Henry Callender, Butcher and Cattle Dealer, and Jessie Gertrude Mills. **Subject(s):** History; BA 1914. **Tutor(s):** L H K Bushe-Fox. **Educ:** Grammar School, Stockton-on-Tees. **Career:** Master, Bromley School 1914; Second Lieutenant, 17th Battalion, Durham Light Infantry, then 9th Battalion, WWI. Died 5 October 1915.

CALLENDER, Thomas Ormiston (1915) Born 28 December 1896, Ormiston, Erith, Kent; son of Thomas Octavius Callender, Electrical Engineer, and Bessie Emmeline Pinnock; m Dorothy. **Tutor(s):** L H K Bushe-Fox. **Educ:** Shirley House School, Charlton; Little Hermitage, Rochester. **Career:** Royal Marines 1915–1918; Manager, Marine Department, Callender's Cable and Construction Company Ltd (later Director) 1928–1941. **Appointments:** Member, Kent County Council. Died 10 May 1941.

CALVERT, Edward (1906) Born 13 August 1887, Burgh by Sands, Cumberland; son of Robert Calvert, Master Mariner, and Fanny Maria Blaylock. **Subject(s):** Natural Sciences; BA 1909; MB 1913; MRCS; LRCP 1912. **Tutor(s):** J R Tanner. **Educ:** The Grammar School, St Bees. **Career:** Lieutenant, Indian Medical Service 1913–1915; Captain, Indian Medical Service 1915–1924; Major, Indian Medical Service 1924–1930.

CALVERT, James Michael (1933) Born 6 March 1913, Rohtak, Punjab, India; son of Hubert Calvert, Deputy Commissioner, Rohtak, and Oclanis O'Brien. **Subject(s):** Mechanical Sciences; BA 1935; MA 1963; CEng; FRHistS; MICE. **Tutor(s):** J S Boys Smith. **Johnian Relatives:** brother of Sidney Denis Calvert (1930). **Educ:** Lynchmere School, Eastbourne; Bradfield College; RMA, Woolwich. **Career:** Major, RE 1933; Brigadier; Hallsworth Research Fellow, University of Manchester 1971–1972. **Appointments:** Freedom of the City of London. **Honours:** DSO and bar; Legion d'Honneur (Officier); Croix de Guerre avec Palme; American Silver Star; Ordre de Leopold II (Commandant); Silver Star (USA); Cross of Liberty, Norway. **Publications:** *Prisoner of Hope*, 1952; *Fighting Mad*, 1964; *Dictionary of Battles*; *Lord Slim*. Died 26 November 1998.

CALVERT, John Harold Knowles (1937) Born 3 May 1916, London; son of Harold William Calvert and Edith Anne Johnston. **Subject(s):** Mechanical Sciences; BA 1939. **Tutor(s):** J S Boys Smith. **Educ:** Duncan Grammar School, Canada; University School, Canada; Royal Military College of Canada. **Career:** Second Lieutenant, RE, WWII.

CALVERT, Colonel Sidney Denis (1930) Born 14 May 1910, 71 King's Road, Rochdale, Lancashire; son of Hubert Calvert, Indian Civil Servant, and Oclanis O'Brien; m Mollie; 1 son (Michael), 1 daughter (Clare). **Subject(s):** Mechanical Sciences; BA 1932. **Tutor(s):** J M Wordie. **Johnian Relatives:** brother of James Michael Calvert (1933). **Educ:** Lynchmere School, Eastbourne; Clifton College; RMA, Woolwich. **Career:** Colonel, RE. **Honours:** OBE 1953; CBE 1960. Died 29 October 1989.

CALVIN, Archibald Augustus (1931) Born 2 December 1907, Hamilton, Wentworth, Ontario, Canada; son of Delano Dexter Calvin, Architect, and Eleanor Elizabeth Malloch. **Tutor(s):** E A Benians. **Educ:** A Dame's School, Toronto; University of Toronto Schools; Queen's University, Kingston, Canada.

CALVIOU, Peter Michael (1949) Born 30 May 1929, 114 Godstone Road, Purley, Surrey; son of Henri Jean Calviou, Cable Operator, and Dorothy Maud Kitching; m Audrey West, 9 October 1965; 1 son (Michael Colin b 1969), 1 daughter (Louise Jacqueline b 1966). **Subject(s):** Modern Languages/Philology; BA 1952; MA 1956. **Tutor(s):** J M Wordie. **Johnian Relatives:** father of Michael Colin Calviou (1987). **Educ:** Keinton Mandeville Council School; Hindhayes School, Street; Pinnerwood Park School, Pinner; St Julian's School, Carcavelos, Portugal; École Française de Lisbonne, Lisbon; Caterham School. **Career:** Intelligence Corps 1947–1949; Stubbs Ltd, London (Director from 1961) 1952–1968; Personnel Manager, Reporting Manager, Reporter Training Manager, Register Editor, Producer of Management Ratios, Dun & Bradstreet Ltd 1968–1984; Systems Analyst, Dun & Bradstreet European Business Information Centre 1984–1990. **Appointments:** Director, Woodside Bridge Club, Amersham.

CAMBRIDGE, Harold William George (1935) Born 13 October 1916, 61 Cecil Road, Gloucester; son of George Henry Walter Cambridge, Carpenter, and Ellen Maude Waspe; m March 1941; 6 children. **Subject(s):** Classics; BA 1938. **Tutor(s):** R L Howland. **Educ:** Linden Road School, Gloucester; Crypt School, Gloucester. **Career:** Major, Royal Tank Regiment, Control Commission Germany (Intelligence) 1939–1947; Senior Classics Master, Careers Advisor, Sir John Talbot School 1949–1980. **Appointments:** County Councillor (Shropshire) 1981–1993; Associate County Council Member 1988–1993. **Awards:** Scholarship, SJC. Died 13 July 2000.

CAMERON, Alexander Maurice (1921) Born 30 May 1898, 27 Brunswick Gardens, Kensington, London; son of Sir Maurice Alexander Cameron, Major, RE, and Ethel Georgiana Ancrum. **Tutor(s):** E E Sikes. **Educ:** Hill Side, Godalming; Wellington College; RMA, Woolwich.

CAMERON, Donald Ian (1928) Born 3 April 1910, son of John Cameron, Rector, Multon Grammar School, and Annie Cameron. **Subject(s):** Natural Sciences; BA 1931; MA 1958. **Tutor(s):** J M Wordie. **Educ:** The King's School, Paramatta, New South Wales.

CAMERON, John Alexander (1938) Born 26 September 1917, 198 Wanstead Park Road, Ilford; son of James Smith Cameron, Assistant Superintendent Engineer, Royal Mail, and Mary Ann MacDonald. **Tutor(s):** J S Boys Smith. **Educ:** The Park School, Ilford; Christ's Hospital, Horsham; Northampton Polytechnic Institute.

CAMERON, Noël Roy Scott (1919) Born 27 December 1891, St Helens, 2 Dennington Park Road, Hampstead, Middlesex; son of Donald Gordon Cameron, Managing Director of Public Company, and Helen Elizabeth Archer. BA 1922; MA 1926. **Tutor(s):** E A Benians. **Educ:** The Grammar School, Brighton. **Career:** Assistant Master, Preparatory Schools 1908–1913; Assistant Master, Wellesley House, Broadstairs 1913–1914; Private, 14th Battalion, The London Regiment, London Scottish, England and France 1916–1917; Second Lieutenant, 390 Siege Battery, RGA, Italy and England 1917–1919; Schoolmaster, St Bees School 1922–1928; Schoolmaster, Trinity College, Glenalmond 1928–1952; House Master, Trinity College, Glenalmond 1930–1949; Sub-warden, Trinity College, Glenalmond 1949–1952. Died 7 January 1963.

CAMPBELL, Adrian Hugh Ward (1941) Born 20 March 1923, 6 Selwyn Gardens, Cambridge; son of Archibald Young Campbell, Professor of Greek, University of Liverpool, and Agnes Olwen Ward; m Irene Chedd, Dorset; 4 daughters (Catherine, Sally, Rosemary and Alison). **Tutor(s):** C W Guillebaud. **Johnian Relatives:** son of Archibald Young Campbell (1904); cousin of Colin Campbell (1942) and of Alasdair Boyd Macneill Campbell (1958). **Educ:** Chinthurst School, Tadworth; Bryanston School, Dorset; Bath Academy of Art. **Career:** Actor; Art Teacher; Artist (painter).

CAMPBELL, Professor Alexander Elmslie (1949) Born 12 May 1929, New Haven, Connecticut, USA; son of John Young Campbell, Professor of New Testament, Westminster College, Cambridge, and Anna Emma Wickert; m (1) Sophia Anne Sonne, 1956 (d 1972), (2) Juliet Jeanne d'Auvergne Collings, 1983; 1 son, 1 daughter. **Subject(s):** History; BA 1952; MA 1956; PhD 1956; MA (Oxon) 1959; FRHS 1970. **Tutor(s):**

A G Lee. **Educ:** Paisley Grammar School; Perse School, Cambridge. **Career:** Fellow, King's College, Cambridge 1955–1959; Second Secretary, HM Foreign Service 1958–1960; Fellow and Tutor in Modern History 1960–1972, Emeritus Fellow 1981–2002, Keble College, Oxford; Director of American Studies 1972–1984, Professor of American History 1972–1987 (Emeritus 1987–2002), University of Birmingham. **Appointments:** Visiting Professor, Hobart and William Smith Colleges, New York 1970; Visiting Professor, Columbia University 1975; Member, Institute for Advanced Study, Princeton 1975; Visiting Professor, University of Kansas 1976; Visiting Professor, Stanford University 1977. **Awards:** Exhibition, SJC 1946; Hutton Prize, SJC 1950; Scholarship, SJC 1951; Earle Prize 1951; Smith-Mundt Studentship, Harvard University 1953–1954; Laski Studentship, SJC 1954. **Publications:** Various books, including *Great Britain and the United States, 1895–1903*; (ed) *Expansion and Imperialism,* 1970; *America Comes of Age: The Era of Theodore Roosevelt,* 1971; (ed) *The USA in World Affairs,* 1974; articles and reviews in collections and journals. Died 16 August 2002.

CAMPBELL, Professor Archibald Young (1904) Born 18 April 1885, Clydesdale Bank House, Blantyre, Lanarkshire; son of George Campbell, Bank Agent, and Rose Young Henderson; m Agnes Olwen Ward, 18 June 1912, Cambridge; 1 son (Adrian Hugh Ward b 20 March 1923), 2 daughters (Laura and Stella (Clare)). **Subject(s):** Classics; BA 1907; MA 1911. **Tutor(s):** D MacAlister. **Johnian Relatives:** father of Adrian Hugh Ward Campbell (1941); uncle of Colin Campbell (1942) and of Alasdair Boyd Macneill Campbell (1958). **Educ:** Hamilton Academy; Fettes College, Edinburgh. **Career:** Assistant Lecturer in Classics, University of Liverpool 1908–1909; Lecturer in Classics, University College, Reading 1909–1911; Foundress Fellow 1910–1922, Lecturer 1911–1922, SJC; Gladstone Professor of Greek, University of Liverpool 1922–1950; Part-time teacher, University of Bristol 1954. **Publications:** *Horace: A New Interpretation,* 1924; *Poems,* 1926; *Horati Carmina XX,* 1934; (ed) *Aeschylus' Agamemnon,* 1936; *Verse Translation,* 1940; Edition of *Horace's Odes and Epodes,* with Latin notes, 1945; *Euripides' Helena,* 1950; many contributions to classical periodicals. Died 19 February 1958.

CAMPBELL, Colin (1942) Born 31 May 1924, 27 Halpin Road, Rangoon, Burma; son of George Riddoch Campbell, Representative, Ministry of Shipping, India, Burma, Ceylon, and Cynthia May Berry. **Subject(s):** History. **Tutor(s):** C W Guillebaud. **Johnian Relatives:** nephew of Archibald Young Campbell (1904); cousin of Adrian Hugh Ward Campbell (1941) and of Alasdair Boyd Macneill Campbell (1958). **Educ:** Elstree School; Harrow School. **Career:** Lieutenant, 3rd Battalion, Scots Guards 1942–1945. Died 17 February 1945 (of wounds received in action in North-West Europe).

CAMPBELL, Dr Colin Guy Hirst (1905) Born 8 July 1887, High Street, Saddleworth, Yorkshire; son of Colin George Campbell, Surgeon, and Annie Ethel Hirst. **Subject(s):** Natural Sciences; BA 1908; MA 1934; MD 1934; MRCS; LRCP 1912; DPH 1932. **Tutor(s):** E E Sikes. **Educ:** Hodder School; Stonyhurst College. **Career:** Captain, RAMC, WWI; House Surgeon and House Physician, Westminster Hospital; Medical Officer, Iraq Health Service; Member, Ankylomiastosis Commission, Trinidad 1914; Senior Assistant, Department of Venereal Diseases, London Hospital 1950. **Awards:** Scholarship, Westminster Hospital 1909. Died 5 July 1973.

CAMPBELL, Donald (1938) Born 6 September 1919, 68 Idmiston Road, West Norwood, London; son of Donald Campbell, Dental Surgeon, and Victoria May Heard; m Brenda Fabian Mallett, 1947; 2 sons (Neil and Roy), 1 daughter (Jill). **Subject(s):** Classics; BA 1941; MA 1958; Honorary MSc (Hull) 1987. **Tutor(s):** R L Howland. **Educ:** Brightlands Preparatory School, West Dulwich; Dulwich College; University of Hull. **Career:** Buildings Officer, Assistant to Registrar 1947, Director of Works 1984, University of Hull. **Appointments:** Chairman, then Honorary Secretary, Hull Civic Society 1969–1994. **Awards:** Minor Scholarship, SJC 1937; Centenary Citizen Award, Hull City Council 1998. **Publications:** Various articles for *Campaign Freedom For Feet.*

CAMPBELL, Donald John (1925) Born 29 October 1903, Schoolhouse, Strathchur, Argyllshire, Scotland; son of Peter Campbell, Schoolmaster, and Catherine MacRae; m Una Jessie Philip. **Subject(s):** Classics; BA 1928; MA (Aberdeen) 1925; DLitt (Aberdeen). **Tutor(s):** M P Charlesworth. **Educ:** Culloden School; Royal Academy, Inverness; Aberdeen University. **Career:** Assistant to the Professor of Humanity at Aberdeen 1925–1931; Lecturer in Latin, University of Edinburgh 1931. **Publications:** (ed) 2nd book of Pliny's *Natural History*. Died 26 June 1939.

CAMPBELL, Frank William Argyll (1937) Born 10 November 1916, Government Hill, Singapore; son of James Argyll Campbell, Research Staff, National Institute for Medical Research, and Annie Beatrice Cowell. **Tutor(s):** R L Howland. **Educ:** University College School; Guy's Hospital. Died 13 March 1996.

CAMPBELL, Dr Hugh (1935) Born 24 October 1916, 102 City Road, Holborn, London; son of Hugh Campbell, Banker's Clerk, and Annie Clement Spence; m Sybil Marian Williams, 1946 (d 1988); 2 sons. **Subject(s):** Natural Sciences; BA 1938; MA 1942; PhD 1946. **Tutor(s):** J M Wordie. **Johnian Relatives:** brother-in-law of Daniel Douglas Eley (1938). **Educ:** University College School. **Career:** Research, Department of Colloid Science, University of Cambridge 1938–1945; Head of Physical Chemistry, Research Group, May and Baker Ltd 1945–1961; Lecturer, West Ham Technical College 1949–1954; Research Manager, Chloride Electrical Storage Company Ltd 1961–1965; Managing Director, Alkaline Batteries Ltd 1965–1967; Electric Power Storage Ltd 1968–1971; Director, Chloride Electrical Storage Company Ltd 1968–1971; Industrial Adviser, Department of Trade and Industry 1971–1974; Career Consultant in Paris and London 1974–1978. **Awards:** Scholarship, SJC 1937. **Publications:** Papers on various subjects in scientific journals. Died 10 October 1998.

CAMPBELL, James Duncan Donald (1926) Born 18 March 1908, 1029 Linden Avenue, Victoria, British Columbia; son of Duncan Edward Campbell, Druggist, and Beatrice McDonald. **Subject(s):** Law; BA 1929; MA 1950. **Tutor(s):** C W Guillebaud. **Educ:** St Helliers School, Victoria; Boys' Central School, Victoria; The High School, Victoria; Brentwood College, Victoria. Died 12 April 1980.

CAMPBELL, John Charles Kenneth (1941) Born 25 October 1923, Downham Market, Norfolk; son of Kenneth Charles Campbell, Engineer, and Edna Gaynor Parry. **Tutor(s):** S J Bailey. **Educ:** Cumnor House, Purley; Carn Brea Preparatory School, Bromley; Canford School.

CAMPBELL, John Hope (1942) Born 8 June 1923, 22 Hermitage Gardens, Edinburgh; son of John Hope Campbell, WS, and Margaret Jane Syme; m Ethel Margaret Joan Loudon. **Subject(s):** Law; BA 1948. **Tutor(s):** S J Bailey. **Educ:** Cargilfield, Barnton; Sedbergh School. **Career:** Articled to a Solicitor, Edinburgh.

CAMPBELL, John Macleod (1937) Born 4 May 1918, 7 Cornwall Mansions, Kensington Court; son of William Macleod Campbell, Colonel, 5th Suffolk Regiment, and Rachel Dorothy Charles; m (1) Penelope, 1942 (dis 1946), (2) Erita Elvira, 1950 (d 1982), (3) Edith Joan, 1985; 1 son (Peter). **Subject(s):** History; BA 1940; MHCIMA. **Tutor(s):** R L Howland. **Educ:** Highfield School, Liphook; Denstone College, Uttoxeter. **Career:** Army Officer 1939–1948; School of Catering, Zurich 1949–1950; Hotel management and industrial catering 1950–1982. Died 31 January 2003.

CAMPBELL, John Murray Martin (1947) Born 24 July 1928, Cherangani, Kenya Colony; son of Ronald John Martin Campbell, Accountant, and Olive Bernice Martin. **Subject(s):** Geography; BA 1951. **Tutor(s):** J M Wordie. **Educ:** Kitale Primary School; Prince of Wales School, Nairobi.

CAMPBELL, Merville O'Neale (1946) Born 30 June 1925, Culloden Road, St Michael, Barbados; son of Dudley Fitzgerald Campbell, Hotel Assistant, and Eva Viola Tull. **Subject(s):** Mathematics; BA 1949; MA 1953. **Tutor(s):** J M Wordie. **Educ:** St Matthias Boys' School, Barbados; Combermere School, Barbados; Harrison College, Barbados. **Career:** Assistant Lecturer in Mathematics 1951, Lecturer in Mathematics 1953, University College of the Gold Coast, Ghana; Lecturer in Mathematics, University College of Ghana 1961.

CAMPBELL, Robert (1931) Born 19 June 1905, 37 University Road, Belfast, Ireland; son of Sir John Campbell, Surgeon, and Emily Frances Fitzsimons (formerly Chestnut). **Tutor(s):** C W Guillebaud. **Educ:** Royal Belfast Academical Institution; University of Edinburgh.

CAMPION, Brigadier Donald (1923) Born 18 November 1898, 5 Cromer Terrace, Kingsthorpe, Northamptonshire; son of Bernard Campion, Barrister-at-Law, and Rose Lees; m Anne Joyce Martin, 18 December 1923, Great Houghton, Northamptonshire. **Tutor(s):** E E Sikes. **Educ:** Marlborough College; RMC, Woolwich. **Career:** Captain 1929; General Staff Officer, Aar Office 1932; Brevet Major 1936; RE, WWII. Died 17 January 1964.

CANHAM, Edwin Dillon Frank (1900) Born 12 March 1879, Barrowby, Grantham; son of Henry Robert Field Canham, Clerk in Holy Orders, and Emma Marie James; m Agnes Francis Armstrong, 5 September 1923, St Matthews, Lee, Devon. BA 1905. **Tutor(s):** J E Sandys. **Johnian Relatives:** son of Henry Robert Field Canham (1870). **Educ:** Bourne Grammar School; University College, Nottingham; St John's School, Leatherhead. **Career:** Mathematics Teacher, Upland House Preparatory School, Epsom 1903–1929; Mathematics Teacher, Westhill Park School, Titchfield, Hampshire 1929. **Awards:** Sizarship, SJC. Died 30 March 1955.

CANN, Colonel Charles Alfred (1922) Born 18 January 1904, 1 Lumley Street, Oxford Street, London; son of Charles Edwin Cann, Motor Carriage Builder, and Amelia Sarah Martin; m Grace Elizabeth Jennings; 2 sons (Charles Richard b 3 February 1937 and David John b 3 May 1944). BA 1925; MA 1929; CEng; FIMechE. **Tutor(s):** E Cunningham. **Johnian Relatives:** father of Charles Richard Cann (1957) and of David John Cann (1963). **Educ:** Christ's College, Finchley; Owens School, Islington. **Career:** Mechanical Engineer; Colonel. Died 28 December 1982.

CANN, Denis Moore (1920) Naval Officer.

CANNELL, Anthony John (1938) Born 3 November 1920, Boundary House, Langley, Loddon; son of Frederick John Cannell, Farmer and Seed Merchant, and Dorothy Frances Blyth. **Subject(s):** Natural Sciences; BA 1941. **Tutor(s):** C W Guillebaud. **Johnian Relatives:** brother of Michael Frederick Cannell (1947). **Educ:** Town Close House Preparatory School, Norwich; The Leys School, Cambridge. **Career:** Agricultural Seed Trade, Norfolk. Died 24 April 1988.

CANNELL, Michael Frederick (1947) Born 30 March 1925, Boundary House, Langley, Loddon; son of Frederick John Cannell, Seed Merchant, and Dorothy Frances Blyth; 1 daughter. **Subject(s):** Modern and Medieval Languages; BA 1949; MA 1954. **Tutor(s):** C W Guillebaud. **Johnian Relatives:** brother of Anthony John Cannell (1938). **Educ:** Town Close House Preparatory School, Norwich; The Leys School, Cambridge. **Career:** RAF, WWII; Headmaster, Alice Hoffmann School. Died 31 March 1999.

CANNON, Brian Norris (1949) Born 20 August 1928, Cooklands, Capel, Kent; son of Charles Louis Cannon, Police Constable, and Irene Amy Spencer; m Ann; 1 son (Mark), 1 daughter (Margaret). **Subject(s):** Classics; BA 1952; MA 1956. **Tutor(s):** R L Howland. **Johnian Relatives:** brother of Harold Charles Cannon (1950); father of Margaret Anna Buckham Cannon (1984). **Educ:** Slade School, Tonbridge; Methodist School, Canterbury; Sevenoaks Grammar School. Died November 1978.

CANNY, Professor Martin Joseph Patrick (1949) Born 14 May 1931, 147 Darling Point Road, Darling Point, Woollahra, New South Wales; son of Alan Joseph Canny, Medical Practitioner, and Isabella Broughton Ebsworth. **Subject(s):** Natural Sciences; BA 1952; MA 1956; PhD 1956. **Tutor(s):** W A Deer. **Educ:** Fairfield, Bellevue Hill, New South Wales; Malvern School, Hunter's Hill; The Scots College Preparatory School; The Scots College. **Career:** University Demonstrator in Botany 1955; Senior Research Chemist, Imperial Chemical Industries of Australia and New Zealand, Melbourne 1957–1960; Senior Assistant in Research in Botany 1959; Lecturer in Botany, University of Cambridge 1960–1964; Foundation Professor of Botany, Monash University, Australia 1964–1986. **Appointments:** Royal Society and Nuffield Fellowship, Makerere College, Uganda 1964; Visiting Professor, University College, London University 1969; Fulbright Fellowship, Visiting Colleague, University of Hawaii 1972; Visiting Professor, University of Bristol 1975; Visiting Professor, University of Edinburgh 1982; NSERC International Award, Carleton University, Ottawa 1982, 1983; Canadian Commonwealth Fellowship, Carleton University 1985; Honorary Research Professor, Carleton University 1986–1999; Tansley Lecturer, Universities of Edinburgh, Lancaster, Bangor, Cambridge, Oxford 1988; Diploma Asociación de Técnicos Azucareros de Cuba 1999; Profesor Invitado, Universidad de la Habana, Cuba 1999; Visiting Fellow, ANU 1999. **Awards:** Sir Joseph Larmor's Plate 1952. **Publications:** *Phloem Translocation*, CUP, 1973; over 100 scientific papers.

CANTOPHER, John Keily (1934) Born 7 November 1914, 207 Pitshanger Lane, Ealing; son of William Joseph Cantopher, Stockbroker, and Edith Mary Keily. **Subject(s):** Economics; BA 1937. **Tutor(s):** C W Guillebaud. **Educ:** Beaumont College, Old Windsor; Harewood, Bexhill on Sea.

CAPRON, Evelyn Charles (1921) Naval Officer.

CARADON, Lord Hugh Mackintosh (1925) See FOOT.

CARDENAS, Professor Martin (1945) Born 12 November 1899, Cochabamba, Bolivia, South America; son of Daniel Cardenas, Farmer, and Peregrina Hermosa. **Educ:** High School, Cochabamba; Natural History Institute, La Paz, Bolivia. **Career:** Professor of Natural Sciences, Normal Institute, La Paz 1922–1930; Professor of Plant Genetics and Phytopathology, University of Cochabamba, 1930–1937; Professor of Botany, Agricultural School, and Rector, Simon Bolivar University 1937–1944.

CARDNO, Professor James Alexander (1938) Born 5 January 1915, Parkhill, Longside, Aberdeenshire; son of James Cardno, Farmer, and Williamina Mary Daniel. **Subject(s):** Moral Sciences; BA 1940; MA 1946; MA (Aberdeen); FBPsS 1962; FAPsS 1966; FAPA 1972. **Tutor(s):** C W Guillebaud. **Educ:** Kinellar Public School; Private Tuition; Kintore Higher Grade Public School; Aberdeen Grammar School; University of Aberdeen. **Career:** Psychological Laboratory, University of Cambridge 1940–1941; Temporary Assistant Principal, Board of Trade 1941–1944; Assistant Specialist, Ministry of Information, Reference Division 1944; Specialist, Ministry of Information 1944–1946; Director of Social Studies, University of Sydney 1946–1950; Senior Lecturer in Psychology, University of Tasmania 1950–1953; Professor, University of Tasmania 1953; Clerk in Holy Orders, Diocese of Tasmania 1973. **Appointments:** Honorary Priest Assistant, St David's Cathedral, Hobart; Chairman, Psychological Registration Board, Tasmania 1977.

CARDWELL, Alfred George (1908) Born 11 February 1889, Broomfield House, Halifax Road, Dewsbury, Yorkshire; son of George Stephenson Cardwell, Colliery Proprietor, and Sarah Ann Hill. BA 1912. **Tutor(s):** E E Sikes. **Educ:** Leadhall House, Harrogate; Bromsgrove School.

CARE, Henry Clifford (1911) Born 2 February 1892, 99 Alma Road, Sheerness, Kent; son of William John Care, Draughtsman, and Alice Mary Allen. **Subject(s):** Mathematics/Natural Sciences; BA 1914.

Tutor(s): J R Tanner. **Educ:** University College School. **Career:** Civil Service 1914; Lieutenant (Technical Officer), RAF, WWI; Director of Finance, War Office 1948. **Awards:** Scholarship, SJC. **Honours:** CB 1948. Died 10 November 1979.

CARLISLE, Dr Raymond (1948) Born 5 August 1928, The Crossways, Birstall, Leicestershire; son of Cyril Dan Carlisle, Insurance Inspector, and Emily Halse; m Helen Claire Ullyet, 23 May 1989, Acton; 3 daughters (Lena Birgitta b 15 May 1961, Ulla Hildegard b 26 September 1962 and Kristina Maria b 31 December 1964). **Subject(s):** Natural Sciences; BA 1951; MA 1967; BChir 1956; MB 1957; MD 1967. **Tutor(s):** G C L Bertram. **Educ:** Birstall Council School; Loughborough College School. **Career:** Junior Pathologist, Dulwich Hospital 1957; Resident Pathologist SHO, Westminster Hospital and Medical School 1958–1959; Medical Registrar, General Medicine and Rheumatology, St Stephen's Hospital, London 1959–1962; Research Fellow, State University and Buffalo General Hospital, Buffalo, New York 1962–1965; Senior Registrar, Cardiology, Regional Cardiac Unit, Newcastle upon Tyne 1965–1967; Clinical Research Fellow, Sahlgren's Hospital, Göteborg, Sweden 1971; Research Fellow in Cardiology and Honorary Consultant, Queen Elizabeth Medical Centre, Birmingham 1973–1974; Senior Lecturer and Consultant 1967–1972, Reader and Consultant 1972–1975, Department of Medicine, University College Hospital and University of Ibadan, Nigeria 1972–1975; Honorary Consultant Cardiologist, Northwick Park Hospital, Harrow 1976–1979; Medical Officer, Health Headquarters, Department of Health and Social Security, London 1975–1980; Professor in Medicine and Consultant, University Teaching Hospital and University of Zambia, Lusaka 1980–1984; Consultant, Internal Medicine and Cardiology, King Fahad Armed Forces Hospital, Jeddah, KSA 1984–1985; Consultant, Internal Medicine and Cardiology, Tawam Hospital, Al Ain, Abu Dhabi, UAE 1986–1988; Senior Consultant Cardiologist, Quatif Central Hospital 1988–1989; Medical Director of Health Screening Services, The Haven Green Clinic, London 1990–1999; Locum Assistant GP, London 1990–2002.

CARLYLL, Dr Hildred Bertram (CARLILL) (1900) Born 21 January 1882, 1 Courthorpe Villas, Warple Road, Wimbledon, Surrey; son of Stephen Green Carlyll, Merchant, and Henrietta Frederica Anne Gale; m Mildred Constance Godfrey, 3 June 1922, St Margaret's, Westminster; 1 son (John), 2 daughters (Elizabeth and Susan). BA 1903; MA 1909; MB 1909; BChir 1909; MD 1913; LRCP 1907; MRCP 1911; MRCS 1911; FRCP 1939; . **Tutor(s):** D MacAlister. **Educ:** Harrow School. **Career:** Surgeon Lieutenant, RN (Mentioned in Despatches), WWI; Neurologist and Psychiatrist, Royal Naval Hospital; Hunterian Professor, Royal College of Surgeons 1918; Physician, Westminster Hospital 1919. **Appointments:** Honorary Secretary, Neurological Section, BMA 1922. **Publications:** Medical papers on syphilis, epilepsy, nerve palsies, hysteria. Died 16 April 1942.

CARMICHAEL, Donald Dewar (1937) Born 8 June 1918, Holmcroft, Claredon Place, Dunblane; son of Alastair McPherson Carmichael, Public Works Contractor, and Elizabeth Campbell Dewar. **Tutor(s):** J S Boys Smith. **Educ:** St Mary's School, Dunblane; Edinburgh Academy.

CARMICHAEL, Donald Macaulay (1936) Born 22 May 1908, Manse of Farr, Bettyhill, Sutherland, Scotland; son of Dugald Carmichael, Minister of the Church of Scotland, and Agnes Macmillan Macaulay; m Margaret Parkinson, 20 December 1949. **Tutor(s):** J S Boys Smith. **Johnian Relatives:** brother of Hugh Carmichael (1933). **Educ:** Reay Public School; Thurso Academy; University of Edinburgh.

CARMICHAEL, Dr Hugh (1933) Born 10 November 1906, Manse of Farr, Bettyhill, Sutherland, Scotland; son of Dugald Carmichael, Minister of the Church of Scotland, and Agnes Macmillan Macaulay; m Margaret Elizabeth May Maclennan, 23 October 1937; 2 sons (Dugald Macauley and Hugh Alexander Lorne), 2 daughters (Margaret Lind and Elizabeth Agnes). MA (by incorporation) 1939; PhD 1936; BSc (Edinburgh) 1929; FRSC. **Tutor(s):** J M Wordie. **Johnian Relatives:** brother of Donald

Macaulay Carmichael (1936). **Educ:** Reay Public School; Thurso Academy; University of Edinburgh. **Career:** Carnegie Research Fellow, The Physics Laboratory, University of Edinburgh 1929–1933; Clerk Maxwell Research Fellow 1933–1937, University Demonstrator in Physics 1937–1944, University of Cambridge; Title A Fellow, SJC 1936–1940 (on War service from 1939); Meteorological Office, Hankey Scheme 1940–1944; Senior Principal Scientific Officer, Ministry of Supply, Atomic Energy Mission to Canada 1944–1950; Principal Research Officer, Head of General Physics Branch, Atomic Energy of Canada Ltd 1950–1971. **Appointments:** Supervisor in Physics, SJC 1936–1940; Member, Inter-Union Commission on Solar-Terrestrial Physics; Member, Canadian Association of Physicists; Member, American Geophysical Union. **Awards:** Clerk Maxwell Studentship 1934. **Publications:** Scientific and technical reports and papers on cosmic radiation, space physics, solar flares, nuclear reactor control and instrumentation, fused silica micro-balance, nuclear physics, radioactive contamination control. Died 16 January 1995.

CARNEGIE, James (1935) Born 10 February 1913, Lancaster Cottage, Turriff, Aberdeenshire; son of James Carnegie, Farmer, and Annabella Margaret Troup; m Isobel Margaret McKinnon, 1953; 1 son (Robert John), 3 daughters (Margaret, Catherine and Alison). **Subject(s):** Classics; BA 1938; MA 1942; MA (Aberdeen) 1934. **Tutor(s):** R L Howland. **Johnian Relatives:** father of Robert John Alexander Carnegie (1984). **Educ:** Turriff Secondary School; University of Aberdeen. **Career:** Assistant Lecturer in Greek, University of Manchester 1939–1940; Field Security Intelligence Corps, North Africa and Italy 1940–1946; Lecturer, then Senior Lecturer of Greek, University of Glasgow 1946–1978. **Awards:** Ferguson Scholarship 1935; Craven Scholarship, University of Cambridge 1937; Hallam Prize, University of Cambridge 1937; Prendergast Greek Studentship, University of Cambridge 1938; Fullarton, Moir & Gray Scholarship 1938; Second Chancellor's Classical Medal, University of Cambridge 1938. Died 25 August 2002.

CARNEGIE BROWN, Dr George (1925) See BROWN.

CARNELL, Canon Geoffrey Gordon (1937) Born 5 July 1918, 100 Rupert Street, Norwich; m Mary Elizabeth Boucher Smith, 1945; 2 sons (Martin b 1946 and Andrew b 1948). **Subject(s):** History/Theology; BA 1940; MA 1944. **Tutor(s):** J S Boys Smith. **Educ:** Colman Road Elementary School, Norwich; City of Norwich School; Cuddesdon College, Oxford. **Career:** Ordained Deacon 1942; Ordained Priest 1943; Assistant Curate, Abington, Northampton 1942–1949; Chaplain and Lecturer in Divinity, St Gabriel's College, Camberwell 1949–1953; Rector, Isham with Great and Little Harrowden, Northamptonshire 1953–1971; Rector, Boughton, Northampton 1971–1985. **Appointments:** Examining Chaplain to Bishop of Peterborough 1962–1986; Director, Post-Ordination Training and Ordinands 1962–1986; Non-Residentiary Canon, Peterborough Cathedral 1965–1985 (Emeritus 1985–); Librarian, Peterborough Diocese 1968–1993; Chaplain to High Sheriff of Northamptonshire 1972–1973; Ecclesiastical History Society 1979–; Chaplain to The Queen 1981–1988; Vice-Chairman, Northants Record Society 1982–1989; Chaplain to the Mayor of Kettering 1988–1989; Church of England Record Society 1992–. **Awards:** Minor Scholarship, SJC 1936; Lightfoot Scholarship, University of Cambridge 1940; Naden Studentship 1940. **Publications:** *The Bishops of Peterborough: 1541–1991*, 1993.

CARNES, Gerald Lambton (1930) Born 23 September 1912, Marsden Hall, Whitburn, South Shields; son of Charles Spearman Carnes, Mining Engineer, and Eileen Hannah Darke. **Tutor(s):** C W Guillebaud. **Educ:** Rugby School; Orleton School, Scarborough.

CARO, John Everard (Jack) (1924) Born 23 February 1906, Earlstown Villa, Mottram in Longendale, Cheshire; son of William Caro, Accountant, and Eva Daynes; m (1) Cicely Marshall (d 1968), (2) Myrtle, 1970; (1) 2 sons (Terence Everard b 1 November 1930 and John Andrew b 2 April 1932). **Subject(s):** Classics/History; BA 1927. **Tutor(s):** E E Sikes. **Johnian Relatives:** father of John Andrew Caro

(1952). **Educ:** North Manchester Grammar School; Manchester Grammar School. **Career:** Inland Revenue until 1970 (retired with the grade of Senior Principal Inspector); Consultant, Country Landowners Association 1970–1986. **Awards:** Somerset Exhibition, SJC. Died November 1997.

CARPENTER, The Revd Bernard Linley (1945) Born 11 November 1927, Highfield, Park Place, Newbridge, Monmouthshire; son of Herbert James Carpenter, Lecturer in Engineering, and Sarah Davies. **Subject(s):** Theology; BA 1949; MA 1952. **Tutor(s):** C W Guillebaud. **Educ:** Tynewydd Primary School, Newbridge; Lewis' School, Pengam; Séminaire St Sulpice, Paris. **Career:** Ordained Priest 1956; Served in the following parishes of the Roman Catholic diocese of Clifton: Fishponds (Bristol), St Mary's (Bath), Our Lady, Lawrence Weston (Bristol), St Osmund's (Salisbury), St Joseph's (Bridgwater), St Mary's (Stow-on-the-Wold), St Patrick's (Corsham), St Catharine's (Frome) 1956–1997.

CARPENTER, The Revd Charles Gordon (1908) Born 6 December 1888, 4 Keith Grove, Shepherd's Bush, London; son of Charles Percy Carpenter, Leather Merchant, and Zillah Eliza Cook; m Evelyn May; 2 sons (Russell and Robert). **Subject(s):** Mathematics; BA 1911; MA 1919. **Tutor(s):** L H K Bushe-Fox. **Johnian Relatives:** father of Robert Gordon Carpenter (1951). **Educ:** Emanuel School, Wandsworth Common; City of London School. **Career:** Assistant Master, Highgate School 1914; Baptist Missionary Society, India, Serampore and Delhi 1915–1929; Master, Portsmouth Grammar School 1930–1945; Master, Roan School 1945. Died 2 March 1979.

CARR, Charles Raymond (1949) Born 18 June 1931, St Andrews, Fife; son of Charles Telford Carr, University Lecturer in German, and Marian Frances Hilton Roscoe, Schoolteacher; m Joan Emily Pedrick Allinson, 26 February 1955, Arusna, Tanzania; 2 sons (Neil Stephen b 3 December 1955 and Michael Nicholas b 4 April 1962). **Subject(s):** Modern and Medieval Languages; BA 1952; MA 1956. **Tutor(s):** C W Guillebaud. **Educ:** New Park School, St Andrews; Rugby School. **Career:** Various positions in Uganda, Kenya, Tanzania, Sudan, Malaysia, Netherlands, Antilles, Ghana, London and the Hague, Royal Dutch, Shell Group 1952–1984; Canada Life Assurance 1985–1993.

CARR, Harold (1946) Born 1 July 1917, 3 Leazes Crescent, Newcastle upon Tyne; son of Joseph Carr, Jeweller, and Ethel Wilson. MB (Durham); BSc (Durham) 1939. **Tutor(s):** G C L Bertram. **Educ:** Private School, Herne Bay; Modern School, Newcastle upon Tyne; University of Durham. **Career:** RAF, WWII.

CARR, John Wooltorton (1935) Born 30 May 1916, St Leonards, Church Square, City of St Kilda, Victoria, Australia; son of Claude Ambrose Carr, Stockbroker and Company Director, and Gladys Marie Korb. **Subject(s):** Mechanical Sciences; BA 1938. **Tutor(s):** J S Boys Smith. **Educ:** Miss Hammond's School, Bromley; PNEU School, Bournemouth; St Michael's, Uckfield; Wycliffe College. **Career:** Pilot Officer, RAFVR 1939–1941. Died August 1941 (killed on active service).

CARRIS, Bertram Dudley (1936) Born 23 October 1917, 102 Dudley Road, Withington, Manchester; son of Austin Francis Carris, Printer's Engineer and Director of Companies, and Maud White; m Mary Pinnell, June 1947. **Subject(s):** Economics. **Tutor(s):** C W Guillebaud. **Johnian Relatives:** brother of Harold Edward Carris (1927). **Educ:** Belmont Preparatory School, Mill Hill, London; Harrow School. **Career:** Lieutenant, Scots Guards (wounded and taken prisoner in Libya 1942), WWII; Jack Barclay Ltd, Rolls-Royce and Bentley Retailers 1945.

CARRIS, Harold Edward (1927) Born 7 July 1909, 45 Alderley Road, Flixton, Lancashire; son of Austin Francis Carris, Corresponding Clerk, and Maud White; m Marjorie. BA 1930. **Tutor(s):** C W Guillebaud. **Johnian Relatives:** brother of Bertram Dudley Carris (1936). **Educ:** Wrekin College, Wellington; Mill Hill School. **Career:** Squadron Leader, RAF; Managing Director, Beaden and Co, Printers. Died 29 July 1959.

CARROLL, Patrick Milne (1937) Born 3 December 1919, 123 Earls Court Road, Kensington; son of Charles Michael Carroll, Mining Engineer, and Louisa Margaret Milne. **Subject(s):** Law; BA 1940. **Tutor(s):** C W Guillebaud. **Educ:** St Augustine's Abbey School, Ramsgate; Ampleforth College. **Career:** Second Lieutenant, RAC (Yeomanry), WWII. Died 22 July 1942 (killed in action in Libya).

CARRUTHERS, Kenneth St Clare (1909) (admitted as a Non-Collegiate Student 1908) Born 6 January 1885, Tellicherry, Malabar, South India; son of Herbert St Clare Carruthers, Colonel, Indian Medical Service, and Minnie Alice Lowe Nedham. **Subject(s):** Natural Sciences; BA 1911; MA 1915. **Tutor(s):** L H K Bushe-Fox. **Educ:** Colet Court; St Paul's School; Manchester University.

CARSE, William (1923) Born 23 August 1899, 7 Johnstone Street, Paisley, Renfrewshire, Scotland; son of Robert Allison Carse, Butcher, and Agnes Simpson Mitchell; m Helen Knox Beaton, 1928; 1 son. **Tutor(s):** E A Benians. **Educ:** John Neilson School, Paisley; The Grammar School, Paisley; The High School, Glasgow. **Career:** Wellington Military College 1917–1918; Indian Army, Madras, South Persia 1918–1920; HM Consular Service, USA, Guatemala, Germany, Portuguese East Africa, Portugal and Portuguese West Africa 1923–1937; Consul General, Luanda, Angola 1937–1939; Consul, Tenerife 1939–1943; Consul-General, Reykjavik, Iceland 1943–1945; British Political Mission, Hungary 1945–1946; Consul–General, Tabriz, Persia 1946–1947; Consul General, Ahwaz, Persia 1948; Deputy High Commissioner for UK, Peshawar, Pakistan 1948–1951; Consul General, São Paulo, Brazil 1951–1956.

CARSLAW, Ronald McGregor (1919) Born 17 June 1900, 8 Park Avenue, Glasgow, Scotland; son of William Henderson Carslaw, Engineer, and Margaret (Maggie) Kay. BA 1922; MA 1926; PhD 1930. **Tutor(s):** E A Benians. **Educ:** Glasgow Academy; Mercheston Castle School, Edinburgh. **Career:** Cadet, Edinburgh University Officers Training Corps (Artillery Unit) 1918; Pupil, Farm, Perthshire 1919. Died 1973.

CARSON, Brian Hardy (1922) Born 19 June 1903, East Bank, Frodsham, Cheshire; son of Cyril Hardy Carson, Engineer in charge of a Railway, NSW, Australia, and Florence Celenia Royle. **Subject(s):** Mathematics/Law; BA 1925 (Corpus Christi). **Tutor(s):** E Cunningham. **Educ:** Colet House, Rhyl; The King's School, Junior and Senior, Canterbury. Died 4 February 1944.

CARSON, James Eric Rutherford (1937) Born 28 May 1915, Mexico City, Mexico; son of William English Carson, Journalist, and Margaret Davies. **Tutor(s):** C W Guillebaud. **Educ:** Rhydykeanau Elementary School; Aberystwyth County School; University College of Wales, Aberystwyth.

CARSWELL, Alexander (1935) Born 6 July 1917, The Grange, Falkirk; son of Allan Alexander Carswell, Gentlemen's Outfitter, and Mary Aitken Towers. **Subject(s):** Law; BA 1938; MA 1942. **Tutor(s):** C W Guillebaud. **Educ:** Selma House, Falkirk; Falkirk High School; Strathallan School, Forgandenny. **Career:** Argyll and Sutherland Highlanders, WWII. Died WWII.

CARTER, Charles Christopher (1902) Born 3 March 1882, 81 Walton Lane, Kirkdale, Lancashire; son of Christopher Anthony Carter, Clerk in Holy Orders, and Lavinia Elizabeth Mordecai; m Emily Wright, 2 April 1907, Spondon Parish Church. BA 1905. **Tutor(s):** D MacAlister. **Johnian Relatives:** son of Christopher Anthony Carter (1872); brother of William Herbert Carter (1908). **Educ:** Anfield Road Board School, Liverpool. **Career:** Assistant Master 1908–1926, Headmaster 1926–1946, St Saviour's Church of England Day School. **Appointments:** President, National Association of Schoolmasters. Died 18 January 1948.

CARTER, Sir Charles Frederick (1938) Born 15 August 1919, 277 Clifton Road, Rugby; son of Frederick William Carter, Engineer (FRS), and Edith Mildred Cramp; m Janet Shea, 1944 (d 2000); 1 son, 2 daughters.

Subject(s): Mathematics/Economics; BA 1944; MA 1946; Honorary DEconSc (National University of Ireland) 1968; Honorary DSc (New University of Ulster) 1979, (Lancaster) 1979, (QUB) 1980; Honorary LLD (TCD) 1980, (Liverpool) 1982; FBA 1970; Honorary MRIA. **Tutor(s):** J M Wordie; C W Guillebaud. **Johnian Relatives:** son of Frederick William Carter (1892); brother of Geoffrey William Carter (1928) and of James Roger Carter (1930); uncle of Michael Francis Carter (1963); great uncle of Andrew Nicholas Carter (2000). **Educ:** Lawrence Sheriff School, Rugby; Rugby School. **Career:** Friends' Relief Service 1941–1945; Lecturer in Statistics, University of Cambridge 1945–1951; Fellow, Emmanuel College, Cambridge 1947–1951; Professor of Applied Economics, The Queen's University, Belfast 1952–1959; Stanley Jevons Professor of Political Economy and Cobden Lecturer, University of Manchester, 1959–1963; Vice-Chancellor, University of Lancaster 1963–1979. **Appointments:** Member, UN Expert Committee on Commodity Trade 1953; Chairman, Science and Industry Committee, RSA, British Association and Nuffield Foundation 1954–1959; Joint Editor, *Journal of Industrial Economics* 1955–1961; Member, Capital Investment Advisory Committee, Republic of Ireland 1956; Member, British Association Committee on Metric System 1958; Member, Council for Scientific and Industrial Research 1959–1963; Member, Commission on Higher Education, Republic of Ireland 1960–1967; Joint Editor, *Economic Journal* 1961–1970; Member, Heyworth Committee on Social Studies 1963; Member, Advisory Council on Technology 1964–1966; Chairman, Joint Committee of the Universities and the Accountancy Profession 1964–1970; Chairman, Schools' Broadcasting Council 1964–1971; Honorary Fellow, Emmanuel College, Cambridge 1965; Chairman, North-West Economic Planning Council 1965–1968; Trustee, Joseph Rowntree Memorial Trust 1966–1994 (Vice-Chairman 1981–1994); President, Manchester Statistical Society 1967–1969; Trustee, Sir Halley Stewart Trust 1969 (Chairman 1986–1997); Member, North Western Postal Board 1970–1973; Chairman, Advisory Board of Accountancy Education 1970–1976; Secretary-General, Royal Economic Society 1971–1975; Chairman, Centre for Studies in Social Policy 1972–1978; Chairman, Post Office Review Committee 1976–1977; Chairman, Northern Ireland Economic Council 1977–1987; Editor, *Policy Studies* 1980–1988; President, BAAS 1981–1982; Chairman, Rosehill Theatre Trust 1984–1998; Chairman, Learning from Experience Trust 1986–1992 and 1994–1998; Chairman, Council, Goldsmiths' College, University of London 1988–1994; President, British Society 1989; President, Policy Studies Institute 1989–1997; Companion, Operational Research Society. **Awards:** Exhibition, SJC 1936; Baylis Scholarship, SJC 1937. **Honours:** Kt 1978. **Publications:** *The Science of Wealth*, 1960, 3rd edn 1973; (with W B Reddaway and J R N Stone) *The Measurement of Production Movements*, 1948; (with G L S Shackle and others) *Uncertainty and Business Decisions*, 1954; (with A D Roy) *British Economic Statistics*, 1954; (with B R Williams) *Industry and Technical Progress*, 1957; *Investment in Innovation*, 1958; *Science in Industry*, 1959; (with D P Barritt) *The Northern Ireland Problem*, 1962, 2nd edn 1972; *Wealth*, 1968; (with G Brosan and others) *Patterns and Policies in Higher Education*, 1971; *On Having a Sense of all Conditions*, 1971; (with J L Ford and others) *Uncertainty and Expectation in Economics*, 1972; *Higher Education for the Future*, 1980; (with J H M Pinder) *Policies for a Constrained Economy*, 1982; (with P John) *A New Accord*, 1992; *Members One of Another*, 1996; articles in *The Economic Journal*, etc. Died 27 June 2002.

CARTER, Sir Derrick Hunton (1924) Born 7 April 1906, 9 George Street, Wolverhampton, Staffordshire; son of Arthur Hunton Carter, Physician, and Winifred Ida Macmeikan; m (1) Phyllis Best, 1933, (2) Madeline O'Callaghan 1948 (d 1992); (1) 1 son, 1 daughter, (2) 1 daughter. **Subject(s):** Mechanical Sciences; BA 1927; MA 1955. **Tutor(s):** E A Benians. **Educ:** The Wells House, Malvern Wells; Haileybury College. **Career:** Civil Engineer, Dominion Bridge Company, Montreal 1927–1928; Research Engineer, Billingham Division, ICI 1928–1933; Assistant Sales Controller, ICI, London 1933–1938; Second Lieutenant, 27th (London Electrical Engineers) Battalion RE, TA 1936; Assistant Sales Manager, ICI 1938–1939; 1st War Advanced Class; Major, Tank

Design Department, RA; Commander (Lieutenant Colonel), Armament Wing, DTD, Lulworth 1942–1945; Assistant Sales Manager 1945–1947, Sales Control Manager, General Chemicals Division 1947, Managing Director, General Chemicals Division 1953, Chairman, General Chemicals Division 1961, Chairman, Mond Division 1964, ICI; Chairman, United Sulphuric Acid Corporation Ltd 1967–1971; BICERI Ltd 1967–1990; Director Avon Rubber Company Ltd 1970–1981; Director, Stothert & Pitt Ltd 1971–1979; Chairman, Torrance & Sons Ltd 1971–1979; Chairman, Remploy Ltd 1972–1976. **Appointments:** Member, Executive Committee, Gloucestershire Council for Small Industries in Rural Areas 1970–1986; Freeman, City of London 1973; Liveryman, Worshipful Company of Coachmakers and Coach Harness Makers 1973; Member, Council of Management, National Star Centre for Disabled Youth 1977–1982; Vice-President, Gloucestershire Association of Boys' Clubs. **Honours:** TD 1952; Kt 1975. Died 8 December 1997.

CARTER, Douglas (1929) Born 4 December 1911, 6 Neal Street, Horton, Bradford; son of Albert Carter, Optician, and Mabel Smith; m Alice Le Mesurier, 20 April 1935, Church of the Beheading of St John the Baptist, Westbourne, Emsworth, Hampshire (d 1986); 3 sons (Michael Norman b 12 July 1936, Charles Douglas b 17 May 1939, d 4 April 1994 and Stephen Kirby b 6 August 1944), 1 daughter (Harriet Mabel Frederica b 25 May 1942). **Subject(s):** History/Economics; BA 1933. **Tutor(s):** E A Benians. **Johnian Relatives:** father of Charles Douglas Carter (1957); father-in-law of Guy Roper Jillings (1957). **Educ:** Ashfield High School, Bradford; The Grammar School, Bradford. **Career:** Assistant Principal 1934–1939, Principal 1939–1943, Assistant Secretary 1943–1946, Controller, Import Licensing Department 1949–1954, Distribution of Industry Division 1954–1957, Industries and Manufactures Division 1957–1960, Commercial Relations and Exports Division 1960–1963, Under-Secretary 1963–1965, Tariff Division 1965, Under-Secretary 1970–1971 (Department of Trade and Industry), Board of Trade. **Appointments:** Secretary, Imperial Shipping Committee 1935–1938; Chairman, Committee of Experts in Enemy Property Custodianship, Inter-Allied Reparations Agency, Brussels 1946–1949. **Awards:** Scholarship, SJC 1928; Wrenbury Research Scholarship, 1933. **Honours:** CB 1969. **Publications:** Articles in bridge magazines. Died 20 January 1998.

CARTER, Edmund Brian (1948) Born 22 July 1927, 24 Water Street, Huddersfield; son of John Granville Carter, Builder's Merchant, and Winnifred Gill; m Maureen Cockhill, 26 June 1954, Farnley Tyas, Huddersfield; 1 son (Anthony Philip b 30 November 1958), 2 daughters (Hilary Ann b 4 June 1957 and Mary Elizabeth b 1 March 1963). BA 1951; MA 1956. **Tutor(s):** G C L Bertram. **Educ:** Oakes Council School, Huddersfield; Kirkheaton National School; Almondbury Grammar School. **Appointments:** President, Builders Merchants Federation 1984–1985; Master, Worshipful Company of Builders Merchants 1991–1992.

CARTER, Professor Geoffrey William (1928) Born 21 May 1909, 223 Clifton Road, Rugby, Warwickshire; son of Frederick William Carter, Engineer, and Edith Mildred Cramp; m Freda Lapwood, 1938; 1 son, 1 daughter. **Subject(s):** Mathematics/Mechanical Sciences; BA 1931; MA 1937; FIEE; FIEEE. **Tutor(s):** J M Wordie. **Johnian Relatives:** son of Frederick William Carter (1892); brother of James Roger Carter (1930) and of Charles Frederick Carter (1938); uncle of Michael Francis Carter (1963); great uncle of Andrew Nicholas Carter (2000). **Educ:** Laurence Sheriff Lower School, Rugby; Rugby School. **Career:** Researcher, British Thomson-Houston Company 1932–1945; Demonstrator, Oxford University 1945; Professor of Electrical Engineering and Head of Department, University of Leeds 1946–1974. **Appointments:** Chairman, University Christian Council. **Awards:** Scholarship, SJC 1927; Mayhew Prize, University of Cambridge 1931; Rex Moir Prize 1932. **Publications:** *The simple calculation of Electrical Transients*, 1944; *The electromagnetic field in its engineering aspects*, 1954; *Techniques of circuit analysis*, 1972. Died 18 February 1989.

CARTER, Henry Robison (1911) Born 7 October 1891, 2 Belgrave Square, Scarborough, Yorkshire; son of Henry Vandyke Carter, Deputy Surgeon General, Indian Medical Service, and Mary Ellen Robison; m Katherine Douglas, 1915. **Subject(s):** Classics; BA 1914. **Tutor(s):** E E Sikes. **Educ:** Haileybury College. **Career:** India Office 1916–1919; Farmer, Estate Manager 1919–1940. **Awards:** Charles Oldham Classical Scholarship, University of Cambridge 1915. **Publications:** 'Nonsense', *The Eagle*, 34; 'Homo Unius Libri', *The Eagle*, 35; '(A Parody of) Horace, Odes, I, xxix', *The Eagle*, 36; 'The Bombardment of Scarborough', *The Eagle*, 36.

CARTER, The Revd Henry Stewart (1923) Born 19 November 1904, 38 Springbourne Road, Toxteth Park, Liverpool; son of William Henry Carter, Bookkeeper, and Robina Gibson Stewart; m Norah Octavia Randall. **Subject(s):** History; BA 1926; MA 1930; Honorary DD (Meadville Theological College, Chicago); Honorary LittD (Emerson College, Boston). **Tutor(s):** E A Benians. **Educ:** St Michael's Council School; Morrison Council School; Liverpool Collegiate School. **Career:** Minister, Cambridge Unitarian Church. **Appointments:** Secretary, Hibbert Trust; Vice President, International Association for Religious Freedom; Member, Unitarian General Assembly Council. Died 10 August 1966.

CARTER, James Roger (1930) Born 11 October 1911, 227 Clifton Road, Rugby; son of Frederick William Carter, Electrical Engineer, and Edith Mildred Cramp; m Julia Marian Whitworth, 1940; 2 sons (John Nicholas and Michael Francis), 1 daughter (Anne Elizabeth). **Subject(s):** Natural Sciences/Economics; BA 1933; MA 1937. **Tutor(s):** J M Wordie. **Johnian Relatives:** son of Frederick William Carter (1892); brother of Geoffrey William Carter (1928) and of Charles Frederick Carter (1938); father of Michael Francis Carter (1963); grandfather of Andrew Nicholas Carter (2000). **Educ:** Tyntesfield, Rugby; Lower School of Lawrence Sheriff, Rugby; Rugby School. **Career:** Assistant, Mary Ward Settlement, London 1933–1935; Education Officer, Pontypool Educational Settlement 1935–1938; Representative of Friends Service Council (Society of Friends), Berlin 1938–1939; Warden of Pontypool Educational Settlement 1939–1944; Displaced Persons Division of United Nations Relief and Rehabilitation Administration 1944–1947; Entered Ministry of Education 1947; First Secretary, British Embassy, Washington 1949–1952; Principal, Kaimosi Teacher Training College, Kenya 1960–1962; Secretary, Kenya Education Commission 1962–1967; Educational Planning Adviser, Tanzania 1967–1971; University Planning Officer, University of Dar es Salaam 1971–1974. **Appointments:** Founder member, Britain-Tanzania Society 1975.

CARTER, Major William Herbert (1908) Born 2 August 1889, 25 Rockfield Road, Walton, Liverpool; son of Christopher Anthony Carter, Clerk in Holy Orders, and Lavinia Elizabeth Mordecai; m (2) Anita Rimmer, 2 August 1961, SJC Chapel. **Subject(s):** Mathematics/Natural Sciences; BA 1911. **Tutor(s):** L H K Bushe-Fox. **Johnian Relatives:** son of Christopher Anthony Carter (1872); brother of Charles Christopher Carter (1902). **Educ:** Anfield Road Board School, Liverpool; Liverpool College. **Career:** Indian Civil Service 1913–1927; Lieutenant, IARO, attached 6th Gurkha Rifles and 4th Assam Rifles, Captain, Special List (mentioned in Secretary of State's list, for valuable services in connection with the war) 1914–1918; Actuary, Duncan Fraser & Co 1927–1955. **Awards:** Scholarship, SJC; Bell Scholarship, University of Cambridge 1909. **Publications:** *Omar Khayyam* (translation). Died 31 March 1975.

CARTWRIGHT, Edgar David Beverley (1944) Born 21 October 1926, 38 Portland Road, Stoke Newington; son of Edgar Cartwright, Hotel Keeper, and Lucienne Tartanson. **Subject(s):** Natural Sciences; BA 1948. **Tutor(s):** C W Guillebaud. **Educ:** Downridge Kindergarten, Worthing; Xavierian College, Brighton; Worthing High School. **Career:** Assistant Director, Institute of Oceanographic Sciences, Bidston Observatory, Birkenhead.

CARTWRIGHT, Harry (1937) Born 16 September 1919, 48 Heald Place, Rusholme; son of Edwin Harry Cartwright, Clerk, and Agnes Alice Gillibrand; m Catharine Margaret Carson, Bradbury, 1950; 2 sons (Philip Hugh and Jonathan Harry). **Subject(s):** Mechanical Sciences; BA 1940; MA 1947; CEng; MIMechE; MIEE. **Tutor(s):** J S Boys Smith; S J Bailey. **Educ:** Beaver Road Municipal School, Manchester; William Hulme's Grammar School, Manchester. **Career:** RAF 1940–1946; Decca Navigator Company 1946–1947; English Electric Company 1947–1949; Design and Project Engineer 1949–1955, Chief Engineer 1955–1960, Department of Atomic Energy, Risley; Director in charge of UKAEA consultancy services on nuclear reactors 1960–1964; Director, Water Reactors 1964–1970; Director, Fast Reactor Systems 1970–1973; Director, Atomic Energy Establishment, Winfrith 1973–1983. **Appointments:** President, British Nuclear Energy Society 1979–1982; Vice-President 1980–1983, President 1983–1985, European Nuclear Society; Chairman of Governors, Purbeck School 1985–1988; Chairman of Trustees, Corfe Castle Charities 1991–1998. **Awards:** Exhibition, SJC 1938; Scholarship, SJC 1939; State Scholarship; Manchester City Scholarship. **Honours:** MBE (military) 1946; CBE (civil) 1979. **Publications:** Various technical papers.

CARUS, Alexander (1922) Born 13 October 1903, 27 Infirmary Road, Blackburn, Lancashire; son of Alexander Hubert Carus, Cotton Manufacturer, and Louisa Wilcock. BA 1925; MA 1929. **Tutor(s):** B F Armitage. **Educ:** Stonyhurst College.

CASE, Humphrey John (1937) Born 26 May 1918, Park Hill, Frome; son of George Reginald Case, Leather Manufacturer, and Margaret Helen Duckett; m (1) Margaret Adelia Eaton, 1942, (2) Jean Alison Orr, 1949, (3) Jocelyn Herickx; (2) 2 sons. **Subject(s):** English; BA 1940; MA 1945; FSA 1954. **Tutor(s):** J S Boys Smith. **Educ:** Winton House, Winchester; Charterhouse. **Career:** War Service 1939–1946; Assistant Keeper 1949–1957, Senior Assistant Keeper 1957–1969, Deputy Keeper, Department of Antiquities 1969–1973, Keeper, Department of Antiquities 1973–1982, Ashmolean Museum. **Appointments:** Vice-President, Prehistoric Society 1969–1973. **Publications:** Various papers.

CASH, Francis William (1926) Born 15 July 1906, Westerland, Alcester Road, Wallington, Surrey; son of Samuel Ernest Cash, Solicitor, and Edith Lilias Cash. BA 1929. **Tutor(s):** C W Guillebaud. **Educ:** The Dower House, Wallington; Beaumont House, Rickmansworth; Brighton College.

CASSELS, John Samuel de Oliveira (1907) Born 19 June 1888, Villa Nova de Gaya, Oporto, Portugal; son of Andrew Boys Cassels, Merchant, and Elizabeth Ann Kate Nixon. **Tutor(s):** J R Tanner. **Johnian Relatives:** nephew of William Wharton Cassels (1877); cousin of Wilfrid Gardiner Cassels (1913). **Educ:** Private Tuition.

CASSELS, Captain Wilfrid Gardiner (1913) Born 30 July 1893, Oporto, Portugal; son of Herbert Wynne Cassels, Merchant, and Edith de Saumarez de Haviland. **Subject(s):** Theology. **Tutor(s):** E E Sikes. **Johnian Relatives:** nephew of William Wharton Cassels (1877); cousin of John Samuel de Oliveira Cassels (1907). **Educ:** Trent College. **Career:** Second Lieutenant, Border Regiment 1914; Captain, Border Regiment 1916; Mentioned in Despatches 1914. Died 13 July 1916 (killed in action near Bouzencourt).

CASSON, Geoffrey Norman (1935) Born 9 June 1916, 41 Carsick Hill Road, Sheffield; son of Lionel Francis Casson, Steel Manufacturer's Buyer, and Jane Frances Norman. BA 1938; MA 1946; Cambridge Certificate of Education 1946. **Tutor(s):** C W Guillebaud. **Educ:** Birkdale Preparatory School, Sheffield; King's School, Ely. **Career:** Headmaster, St Petroc's School, Bude, Cornwall 1966. **Awards:** Reading Prize, SJC 1937. Died January 1986.

CASSON, Sir Hugh Maxwell (1928) Born 23 May 1910, 4 Crossfield Road, Hampstead; son of Randal Casson, Indian Civil Service, and Mary Caroline Man; m Margaret Macdonald Troup, 1938; 3 daughters. BA 1932; MA 1943; Honorary Doctorate (RCA) 1975; Honorary Doctorate (Southampton) 1977; Honorary LLD (Birmingham) 1977; Honorary DLitt (Sheffield) 1986; RIBA; FCSD; RDI 1951; RA 1970. **Tutor(s):** M P Charlesworth. **Johnian Relatives:** son of Randal Casson (1897). **Educ:** Wootton Court, Canterbury; Eastbourne College. **Career:** Architect, Private Practice 1937; Camouflage Officer, Air Ministry 1940–1944; Technical Officer, Ministry of Town and Country Planning 1944–1946; Private Practice, Senior Partner, Casson Conder & Partner 1946–1976; Director of Architecture, Festival of Britain 1948–1951; Professor of Environmental Design, Royal College of Art 1953–1975; Master of Faculty, RDI 1969–1971; Provost, Royal College of Art 1980–1986. **Appointments:** Honorary Fellow, SJC 1976; Member, Royal Danish Academy 1954; Member, Royal Fine Art Commission, 1960–1983; Honorary Associate, American Institute of Architects 1968; Member, Royal Mint Advisory Committee 1972–1999; Trustee, National Portrait Gallery 1976–1984; President, Royal Academy 1976–1984; Trustee, British Museum (National History) 1976–1986; Member of the Board, British Council 1977–1981; Honorary Member, Royal Canadian Academy of Arts 1980; Honorary Fellow, UCL 1983. **Awards:** Craven Scholarship, British School at Athens; Albert Medal, RSA 1984. **Honours:** Kt 1952; KCVO 1978; Italian Order of Merit 1980; CH 1985 . **Publications:** *New Sights of London*, London Transport, 1937; *Bombed Churches*, 1946; *Homes by the Million*, Penguin, 1947; (with Anthony Chitty) *Houses–Permanent and Prefabrication*, 1947; *Victorian Architecture*, 1948; *Inscape: the design of interiors*, 1968; (with Joyce Grenfell) *Nanny Says*, 1972; *Diary*, 1981; *Hugh Casson's London*, 1983; *Hugh Casson's Oxford*, 1988; *Japan Observed*, 1991; *Hugh Casson's Cambridge*, 1992; *The Tower of London: an artist's portrait*, 1993; Regular contributor as author and illustrator to technical and lay press. Died 16 August 1999.

CASTLE, Cecil Wells (1914) Born 5 June 1894, Calcutta, India; son of Roland Constantine Castle, Deputy Inspector General, Indian Police, and Amelia Doran. **Tutor(s):** E E Sikes. **Educ:** Durston House, Ealing; Orkney House, Bedford; Bradfield College; Cottington Brow School, Bexhill on Sea; Sandhurst College. **Career:** South Staffordshire Regiment 1915–1917. Died 3 August 1917 (killed in action).

CASTLE, The Revd Graham Hunt (1903) Born 18 April 1885, Avondale, 98 Redland Road, Westbury, Gloucestershire; son of Adam Cottam Castle, Solicitor, and Emma Catherine May Hunt. BA 1906; MA 1910. **Tutor(s):** C E Graves; J R Tanner. **Educ:** Clifton College. **Career:** Ordained Deacon 1908; Curate, St Mary, Portsea 1908–1911; Ordained Priest 1909; Curate, St James, Pokesdown 1911–1915; Curate, St Barnabas, Pimlico 1916–1919; Curate, Godshill 1921–1924; Vicar, St Agnes, Kennington Park 1924–1925. Died 8 May 1945.

CASWELL, Francis Emil George (1927) Born 2 September 1905, The Deanery, George Town, Demerara; son of Emil George Henry Caswell, Clerk in Holy Orders, and Ethel Morgan. **Tutor(s):** J M Wordie. **Educ:** St Edmund's School, Canterbury; Keble College, Oxford.

CATER, Ian Barwys Reid (1926) Born 13 March 1907, Zenda Cottage, Ashtead, Surrey; son of Herbert Elliott Cater, Company Director, and Ernestine Isabel Bourne; m Amy Forrest. **Subject(s):** Mathematics/Law; BA 1929; MA 1961. **Tutor(s):** J M Wordie. **Johnian Relatives:** nephew of Charles William Bourne (1864) and of Alfred Allinson Bourne (1867). **Educ:** Rokeby School, Wimbledon; King's College School, Wimbledon. **Career:** Lieutenant Colonel. Died 30 October 1985.

CATFORD, Sir John Robin (1944) Born 11 January 1923, 90 Langham Road, Teddington, Middlesex; son of Adrian Leslie Catford, Aero-Engine Designer, and Ethel Augusta Rolfe; m Daphne Georgina Darby; 21 August 1948; 3 sons (John Charles b 1949, Simon Leslie b 1956 and Francis James Robin b 1959); 1 daughter (Lucy Georgina b 1952). DipAgSci 1946; BSc (St Andrews) 1944. **Tutor(s):** C W Guillebaud. **Johnian Relatives:** father of John Charles Catford (1968). **Educ:** Denmead School, Hampton; Hampton Grammar School; University of St Andrews. **Career:** Department of Agriculture and Forest, Sudan Civil

Service 1946–1955; Secondment to White Nile Schemes Board 1952–1955; Various commercial posts (mainly in the UK) 1955–1966; MAFF 1966–1982 (Principal 1966, Assistant Secretary 1972, Under-Secretary 1979); Secretary for Appointments to the Prime Minister and Ecclesiastical Secretary to the Lord Chancellor 1982–1993. **Appointments:** Member, Chichester Diocesan Synod 1979–1984; Crafts Adviser, Radcliffe Trust 1993; Member, Chichester Cathedral Council 2001. **Honours:** CBE 1990; KCVO 1993.

CATHERWOOD, Robert Ernest Frederick (1947) Born 9 August 1928, Creagh, Bellaghy, Magherafelt, County Londonderry; son of Henry Ernest Catherwood, Merchant, and May Isabelle Sharp. BA 1950; MA 1962. **Tutor(s):** R L Howland. **Educ:** Campbell College Preparatory School; St Hilda's School, Belfast; Campbell College, Belfast.

CATTRELL, Victor Gordon (1943) Born 13 April 1924, 9 Milburn Street, Workington, Cumberland; son of Albert Victor Cattrell, Steelworks Maintenance Electrician, and Eleanor May Veevers; m Rosemary Wyatt Bagshawe, 19 May 1956. BA 1946; MA 1949. **Tutor(s):** C W Guillebaud. **Educ:** St Michael's Elementary School, Workington; County Secondary School, Workington.

CAUGHLEY, James Gilfillan (1939) Born 2 February 1905, Takapau, Hawkes Bay, New Zealand; son of James Caughley, Schoolmaster, and Annie Charlotte Shaw. **Tutor(s):** C W Guillebaud. **Educ:** Takapau Public School; Darmevirlze High School; Victoria University College; Canterbury University College.

CAUNCE, Fred (1932) Born 16 February 1911, 12 Bank Street, Golborne, Lancashire; son of Walter Caunce, Machinist in Engineering Works, and Edith Burrows. **Subject(s):** Mechanical Sciences; BA 1934; MA 1941; BSc (London). **Tutor(s):** J S Boys Smith. **Educ:** Ashton in Makerfield Grammar School; Wigan Mining and Technical College. **Awards:** Whitworth Senior Scholarship, London University.

CAVALIER, Francis Bernard (1909) Born 10 July 1889, 20 Clarence Square, Cheltenham; son of Anthony Ramsden Cavalier, Clerk in Holy Orders, and Mary Grey. **Tutor(s):** E E Sikes. **Educ:** Colet Court; St Paul's School. **Awards:** Sizarship, SJC.

CAVE, George Charles Montague Major (1939) Born 14 August 1920, Santos, Brazil; son of Charles Victor Cave, Superintendent, Western Telegraph Company, and Evelyn Florence Major. **Tutor(s):** C W Guillebaud. **Educ:** Norwood School, Exeter; Shrewsbury School. **Career:** Lieutenant, Devonshire Regiment and Commandos 1939–1943. Died 14 July 1943 (killed in action in Sicily).

CAVE, Richard (1924) Born 21 December 1905, 171 Wargrave Road, Newton in Makerfield, Lancashire; son of Thomas Ashton Cave, Commercial Traveller, and Elizabeth Aspinall; m Edith Marjorie Leech, 22 December 1928, St James's Church, West Derby, Liverpool; 1 son (Richard b 18 October 1929). **Subject(s):** Mathematics; BA 1927; MA 1931. **Tutor(s):** J M Wordie. **Johnian Relatives:** grandfather of Jennifer Ann Cave (Taylerson) (1987). **Educ:** Earlestown District C of E School; Leigh Grammar School. **Career:** Chief Examiner, Joint Matriculation Board of the Northern Universities; Assistant Mathematics Master, Liverpool Collegiate School 1927–1949; Lecturer in Mathematics and Statistics, City of Liverpool College of Commerce (Later Principal Lecturer) 1949–1966. **Awards:** Exhibition, SJC. Died 12 August 1976.

CAWTHORNE, Donald Ernest (1943) Born 11 September 1925, 11 West Clowes Street, Salford, Lancashire; son of Ernest Henry Cawthorne, Managing Director, Credit Clothing Company, and Elsie Mary Broad; m Jill Merrick, 5 October 1953. **Tutor(s):** C W Guillebaud. **Educ:** Gorse Hill Council School; Stretford Grammar School.

CELLAN-JONES, Alan James Gwynne (1949) Born 13 July 1931, 93 Walter Road, Swansea; son of Cecil John Cellan-Jones, Surgeon, and Lavinia Dailey; m Margaret Shirley Eavis, 2 April 1957; 3 sons (Rory b 1958, Simon b 1962 and Deiniol b 1965), 1 daughter (Lavinia b 1967). **Subject(s):** Natural Sciences; BA 1952; MA 1978; FRSA 1992. **Tutor(s):** G C L Bertram. **Educ:** Dragon School, Oxford; Charterhouse. **Career:** Director of Television, Theatre and Film; Head of Plays, BBC Television 1976–1979. **Appointments:** Chairman, BAFTA 1984–1995; Chairman, Directors Guild of Great Britain 1993–1995. **Awards:** Directors Guild of America Award 1976; American 'ACE' Award for *Oxbridge Blues* 1986. **Publications:** *The Novel on the Screen* (text of lecture at Swansea), University of Wales Press; various songs.

CHADWICK, Brian Lloyd (1910) Born 4 November 1890, Ashfield House, Dewsbury, Yorkshire; son of Thomas Lang Chadwick, Solicitor and Registrar of Dewsbury County Court, and Charlotte Mary Lloyd Davies; m Kathleen Muriel Fowler, 10 April 1953, St Edmundsbury Cathedral. **Subject(s):** Classics; BA 1913; MA 1952. **Tutor(s):** E E Sikes. **Educ:** Preparatory School, Oatlands, Harrogate; Shrewsbury School. **Career:** Second Lieutenant, RGA, WWI; Ministry of Labour, WWI.

CHADWICK, Morley (1908) Born 29 January 1891, St Margaret's Place, King's Lynn; son of George Richard Chadwick, Surgeon, and Marian Morley. **Subject(s):** Natural Sciences; BA 1911. **Tutor(s):** E E Sikes. **Johnian Relatives:** father of George Richard Chadwick (1958). **Educ:** Edward VII Grammar School, King's Lynn; Grammar School, Donington, Spalding. **Career:** Captain, RAMC, WWI.

CHADWICK, Dr Norman Ellis (1915) Born 21 July 1896, Willesden, Middlesex; son of Ellis Henry Chadwick, Sub-Inspector of Schools, and Esther Alice Miller. BA 1921; MA 1930; MB 1930. **Tutor(s):** E E Sikes. **Educ:** St Olave's Grammar School; City of London School. **Career:** MOH, Hove. **Awards:** Scholarship, SJC 1914.

CHADWICK, The Revd William Owen (1935) Born 20 May 1916, 15 Oaklands Road, Bromley, Kent; son of John Chadwick, Barrister-at-Law, and Edith Mary Horrocks; m Ruth Romaine Hallward, 1949; 2 sons, 2 daughters. **Subject(s):** Classics/History/Theology; BA 1939; MA 1942; DD 1955; Honorary FRSE, Honorary DD (St Andrews, Oxon, Wales); Honorary DLitt (Kent, Bristol, London, Leeds); Honorary LittD (UEA, Cambridge); Honorary Doctor of Letters (Columbia); Honorary LLD (Aberdeen); FBA 1962. **Tutor(s):** R L Howland. **Educ:** St Hugh's School, Bromley; Tonbridge School. **Career:** Ordained 1940; Curate, St John's, Huddersfield 1940–1942; Chaplain, Wellington College 1942–1946; Fellow, Trinity Hall, Cambridge 1947–1956; Master 1956–1983, Fellow 1983–, Selwyn College, Cambridge; Dixie Professor of Ecclesiastical History 1958–1968, Regius Professor of Modern History 1968–1983, Vice-Chancellor 1969–1971, University of Cambridge; Chancellor, University of East Anglia 1985–1994. **Appointments:** Honorary Fellow, SJC 1964; Chairman, Archbishops' Commission on Church and State 1966–1970; Honorary Member, American Academy of Arts and Sciences 1977; Trustee 1978–1994, Chairman 1988–1994, National Portrait Gallery; President, British Academy 1981–1985; Member, Royal Commission on Historical Manuscripts 1984–1991; Honorary Fellow, Trinity Hall, Cambridge; Honorary Fellow, Wolfson College, Cambridge. **Awards:** Naden Studentship, SJC; Scholarship, SJC 1938. **Honours:** KBE 1982; OM 1983. **Publications:** *John Cassian*, 1950; *From Bossuet to Newman*, 1957; *Victorian Miniature*, 1960; *The Reformation*, 1964; *The Victorian Church*, 1966, 1971; *The Secularization of the European Mind in the 19th Century*, 1976; *The Popes and European Revolution*, 1981; *Britain and the Vatican during the Second World War*, 1986; *Michael Ramsey*, 1990; *The Spirit of the Oxford Movement*, 1990; *The Christian Church in the Cold War*, 1992; *A History of Christianity*, 1995; *A History of the Popes 1830–1914*, 1998; *Lord Acton and History*, 1999; *The Early Reformation on the Continent*, 2001.

CHALKE, Dr Herbert Davis (1919) Born 15 June 1897, 12 The Parade, Porth, Ystradyfodwg, Glamorganshire; son of Richard David Chalke, Headmaster, Pupil Teacher Centre, Porth, and Naomi Davis; m Kathleen; 1 son. BA 1921; MA 1926; MRCS; LRCP 1924. **Tutor(s):** E E Sikes.

Educ: Rhondda County Intermediate School; University College, Cardiff. **Career:** RFC 1916–1918; Assistant Tuberculosis Physician, King Edward VII National Memorial Association; Assistant to Medical Officer of Health, Metropolitan Borough of Poplar; House Physician, Devonshire Hospital, Buxton; Assistant Medical Officer, Southern Hospital and River Hospitals, Metropolitan Asylums Board 1925–1979; Colonel, RAMC 1939–1945. **Appointments:** Fellow, BMA 1966; President, Society of Medical Officers of Health. **Awards:** USA Typhus Commission Medal; Mitchener Medal, RCS. **Honours:** OBE. **Publications:** Various, on hygiene and public health, tuberculosis, military medicine, medical history, alcoholism; Founder and Editor, *British Journal on Alcohol and Alcoholism.* Died 8 October 1979.

CHALLIS, The Revd James Dobb (1935) Born 11 October 1916, 30 Kimberly Street, Toxteth Park, Liverpool; son of John Frederick Challis, Clerk in Holy Orders, and Nellie Dobb. **Subject(s):** History/Theology; BA 1938; MA 1942. **Tutor(s):** J S Boys Smith. **Educ:** Hill House Preparatory School, Doncaster; Nottingham High School; Trent College; Ridley Hall, Cambridge. **Career:** Ordained Deacon 1940; Curate, Lenten 1940–1947; Ordained Priest, Southwell 1941; Perpetual Curate, St Chad, Derby 1947–1955; Rector, Holy Trinity, Chesterfield 1955; Vicar, St Phillip's Penn Fields 1967; Prebendary, Lincoln Cathedral 1980–1981. **Awards:** Barrow Exhibition. Died 29 December 1996.

CHAMBERLAIN, James Russell (1925) Born 1 January 1907, 399 Wellingborough Road, Northampton; son of James Thomas Chamberlain, Solicitor, and Elizabeth Dyson; m Kitty Louise Edwards, 1934; 1 son (Michael), 2 daughters (Anne and Rosemary). **Subject(s):** Law; BA 1928; MA 1958; LLB 1929. **Tutor(s):** E A Benians. **Educ:** Northampton Town and County School. **Career:** Solicitor, Supreme Court 1931–1932; Founder, P R E Smith, Chamberlain & Co, Wellingborough 1932 (spent over 60 years in practice); Acting Group Captain in charge of bomb disposal of all RAF Airfields in England and Wales, WWII. **Appointments:** President, Northamptonshire Law Society; President, Wellingborough Rotary Club; President, Wellingborough Rugby Club. **Awards:** Prize Exhibition (Law) 1926. Died 7 May 2000.

CHAMBERLAIN, Ralph (1927) Born 21 March 1909, Pinchbeck, Spalding, Lincolnshire; son of Robert Chamberlain, Agricultural Worker, and Fanny Pearce; m; 1 son, 1 daughter. **Subject(s):** Natural Sciences; BA 1930; MA 1959; DipAgr 1931. **Tutor(s):** C W Guillebaud. **Educ:** Central Council School, Spalding; The Grammar School, Spalding. **Career:** Head of Agricultural Zoology Department, Queen's University; Reader, Queen's University 1952; Assistant in Agricultural Zoology, Queen's University, Belfast, and the Ministry of Agriculture 1931–1944; Head of the Agricultural Entomology Division, NI Ministry of Agriculture 1944; Senior Principal Scientific Officer, NI Ministry of Agriculture 1957. **Awards:** Ministry of Agriculture and Fisheries Scholarship. Died March 1966.

CHAMBERS, John Frank (1936) Born 10 July 1917, 29 Jubilee Drive, Liverpool; son of John Chambers, Quarter Master Sergeant, Cotton Warehouseman, and Gertrude Hughes. **Subject(s):** History; BA 1939; MA 1960. **Tutor(s):** J S Boys Smith. **Educ:** St Margaret's School, Liverpool; Merchant Taylors' Girls' Preparatory School; Merchant Taylors' Boys' School, Great Crosby. **Awards:** Exhibition, SJC 1936–1937.

CHAMBERS, Oliver Ronald (1929) Born 2 April 1912, 29 Woodlands Park Road, King's Norton, Birmingham; son of Oliver John Chambers, Stock and Share Broker, Birmingham Stock Exchange and Caroline Elizabeth James. **Tutor(s):** J M Wordie. **Educ:** The Downs School, Colwall, near Malvern; Leighton Park School, Reading.

CHAMPION, Professor Frank Clive (1926) Born 2 November 1907, Cardinal Villa, Wolsey Road, Esher, Surrey; son of Frank Charles Champion, Superintendent of Assurance Agents, and Alice Killick; m Joan Mingay, 1936, (div 1951). **Subject(s):** Natural Sciences; BA 1929; MA 1933; PhD 1932. **Tutor(s):** J M Wordie. **Educ:** Elmside Preparatory

School, Redhill; Royal Grammar School, Guildford. **Career:** Assistant Lecturer in Physics, Nottingham University 1932–1934; Lecturer 1934, Reader 1948, Professor 1959, KCL. **Appointments:** Honorary Secretary, Atomic Scientists Association 1945–1948; Royal Society Visiting Professor, Malaysia 1967; Fellow, KCL 1970. **Publications:** *The Properties of Matter; University Physics.* Died 24 February 1976.

CHAMPNESS, John Alec (1928) Born 11 November 1910, Hill Cottage, Bencombe Road, Purley, Surrey; son of Clement Maurice Champness, Chartered Accountant, and Constance Harriet Duder. BA 1932. **Tutor(s):** C W Guillebaud. **Educ:** The Limes Preparatory School, Croydon; The Leys School, Cambridge. **Career:** Flying Officer, RAF, WWII. Died November 1940 (killed in action).

CHAN, Shu-Fung (1938) Born 25 August 1914, Canton, China; son of Chan Chai-Gnock, Chinese Army, and Young Zee. **Tutor(s):** C W Guillebaud. **Educ:** Preparatory School, Tong Hing; Hiong Ping Public School, Pei Hai; The Font Public School, Canton; Wah Yan English College, Hong Kong; Military College, Canton.

CHANG, Dr Tse-Chun (1943) Born 5 April 1918, Shanghai, China; son of Chang Chin, Government Official, and Kiang Yin-Tze. PhD 1948; BA (Tsinghua) 1940; FREconS. **Tutor(s):** C W Guillebaud. **Educ:** Tsinghua University. **Career:** Assistant in Statistics, Tsinghua University 1940–1943; International Monetary Fund, Washington DC 1947; Economic Affairs Officer 1948–1956, Chief, Section II, Economic Survey Branch 1956, United Nations. **Publications:** *Cyclical Movements in the Balance of Payment,* CUP, 1951.

CHANT, William Morton (1941) Born 12 March 1923, 274 Warwick Road, Carlisle; son of Arthur Guy Chant, Shropshire County Architect, and Jessie Elizabeth Brown. **Tutor(s):** S J Bailey. **Educ:** Prestfelde Preparatory School, Shrewsbury; Shrewsbury School; Shrewsbury Technical College.

CHAPMAN, Alfred Reginald Bewes (1913) Born 13 July 1895, Roseneath, Courtenay Park, Newton Abbot, Devon; son of Thomas Alfred Chapman, Bishop of Colchester, and Catherine Mary Bewes. **Tutor(s):** L H K Bushe-Fox. **Johnian Relatives:** brother of Cecil Anstis Bewes Chapman (1917) and of Edward Nowel Bewes Chapman (1919). **Educ:** Alton Preparatory School; Plymouth College; Rossall School. **Career:** Second Lieutenant, Loyal North Lancashire Regiment 1914–1916. Died 6 June 1916 (killed in action).

CHAPMAN, Arthur Salisbury (1920) Born 4 November 1903, 3 Redland Court, Redland, Bristol, Gloucestershire; son of Arthur Edward Chapman, Vicar and Rural Dean of Luton, and Ethelreda Mary Woodward. **Tutor(s):** E A Benians. **Johnian Relatives:** son of Arthur Edward Chapman (1887). **Educ:** Luton Preparatory School; Haileybury College.

CHAPMAN, Cecil Anstis Bewes (1917) Born 30 July 1900, Bristol, Somerset; son of Thomas Alfred Chapman, Bishop of Colchester, and Catherine Mary Bewes. **Tutor(s):** E E Sikes. **Johnian Relatives:** brother of Alfred Reginald Bewes Chapman (1913) and of Edward Nowel Bewes Chapman (1919). **Educ:** Bolton School. **Career:** RAF, WWI. Died 26 June 1918.

CHAPMAN, The Revd Canon Edward Nowel Bewes (1919) Born 27 December 1901, The Vicarage, Trinity Road, Bristol, Gloucestershire; son of Thomas Alfred Chapman, Bishop of Colchester, and Catherine Mary Bewes; m Mildred Mallord Turner, 1 June 1926, St Matthew's, Bayswater; 1 daughter (Catherine). **Subject(s):** History/Theology; BA 1923; MA 1926. **Tutor(s):** E E Sikes. **Johnian Relatives:** brother of Alfred Reginald Bewes Chapman (1913) and of Cecil Anstis Bewes Chapman (1917). **Educ:** Church Institute, Bolton; Bolton School. **Career:** Curate, St Matthew's, Bayswater 1925–1927; Curate, St Saviour, Westcliff on Sea 1930–1936; Minister, St Andrew, Westcliff on Sea 1930–1936; Rector, Harpurhey, Manchester 1936–1939; Rector,

Stretford, Manchester 1939–1946; Perpetual Curate, Emmanuel, Compton Gifford, Plymouth 1946–1952; Rector, St John, Pembroke, Bermuda 1952. Died 11 April 1966.

CHAPMAN, Lieutenant Colonel Frederick Spencer (1925) Born 10 May 1907, 33 Oakwood Court, Kensington, Middlesex; son of Frank Chapman, Solicitor, and Winifred Ormonde; m Faith Mary Townson, 31 January 1946, Church of the Redemption, New Delhi; 3 sons (Nicholas, Stephen and Christopher). **Subject(s):** English/History; BA 1929; MA 1934. **Tutor(s):** J M Wordie. **Johnian Relatives:** father of Nicholas Frank Spencer Chapman (1966) and of Stephen Ormond Spencer Chapman (1968); grandfather of Kathleen Rowan Spencer Chapman (1996). **Educ:** Clevedon House School, Ben Rhydding; Sedbergh School. **Career:** Ski Expert and Naturalist, British Arctic Route Expedition 1930–1931; Master, Aysgarth School, Bedale 1934–1936; Member, British Diplomatic Mission to Tibet 1936–1937; Housemaster, Gordonstoun 1937–1940; 5th Battalion, Scots Guards, Singapore 1940–1941; POW 1941; 1st Organising Secretary, Outward Bound Trust 1946; Headmaster, King Alfred School, Plön, Germany 1947; Headmaster, St Andrew's College, Grahamstown, South Africa 1956–1962; Warden, Pestalozzi Village Settlement, Battle, Sussex 1962–1966; Warden, and Lecturer, Department of Education, Wantage Hall 1966–1971. **Awards:** Polar Medal, Arctic Clasp 1931; Gill Memorial Award and Gold Medal, RGS 1941; Monro Park Medal, RSGS; The Sunday Times Special Award and Gold Medal 1949; Lawrence of Arabia Memorial Award, Central Asian Society. **Honours:** DSO and Bar; TD. **Publications:** *The Northern Lights*, 1934; *Watkins' Last Expedition*, 1934; *Lhasa: The Holy City*, 1938; *Helvellyn to Himalaya*, 1940; *Lightest Africa*, 1955; *The Jungle is Neutral*. Died 8 August 1971.

CHAPMAN, Commander George Critchett (1947) Born 21 August 1926, Flint; son of Frederick Critchett Chapman, Accountant, and Ruby Louise Potter; m Avril Veronica Clarke, 14 December 1957; 1 son (Edward John Critchett b 1961), 1 daughter (Mary Anne b 1959). **Subject(s):** Mechanical Sciences; BA 1949; MA 1955; CEng; MIEE. **Tutor(s):** R L Howland. **Johnian Relatives:** father of Edward John Critchett Chapman (1980). **Educ:** St Christopher's and St Dunstan's Schools, Burnham-on-Sea; Royal Naval Colleges Dartmouth and Manadon, Plymouth. **Career:** Midshipman (1944) to Commander (Weapons Engineer) RN 1940–1979; HM Ships *Ajax, MGB 658, Milne, Mameluke, Implacable, Loch Ruthven, Loch Veyatie, Victorious, Kent* and ashore posts including Devonport Dockyard, Britannia RNC Dartmouth, *Dolphin* (First Submarine Squadron), AUWE (Ikara project), MOD (Polaris/Chevaline project), *Defiance* (Acting Captain 1975). **Appointments:** Honorary Secretary, National Association of Water Power Users (UK) 1987–1996; Founder (and Life) Member, Association of (Independent) Electricity Producers 1987. **Honours:** OBE 1977. **Publications:** numerous contributions to publications of the Amateur Yacht Research Society etc, mostly on sailing hydrofoils.

CHAPMAN, Henry Bryan Parry (1944) Born 23 July 1925, 4 Springfield Road, Leicester; son of Alfred Chapman, Silk Manufacturer, and Mary Evangeline Parry Jones; m Genevieve Hennessy Chapman; 3 sons (Colin, Geoffrey and Owen); 1 daughter (Moira). **Subject(s):** Engineering; BA 1948; MA 1958; MS (Lehigh University, Pennsylvania, USA); MICE. **Tutor(s):** S J Bailey. **Educ:** Stoneygate School, Leicester; The Downs School, Colwall; Leighton Park School, Reading. **Career:** Civil and Structural Engineering; City and University Planning. **Appointments:** Member, American Planning Association.

CHAPMAN, Dr John Brian (1945) Born 8 February 1927, St Chad's Hospital, Edgbaston, Birmingham; son of Albert Ernest Chapman, Lecturer in Education, Birmingham University, and Gertrude Wilde; m Barbara Elsie Champion (d 2000); 3 sons (Jeremy, Michael Brian and Nicholas). **Subject(s):** Natural Sciences; BA 1948; BChir 1952; MB 1952; MA 1970; FRCGP; DObstRCOG. **Tutor(s):** G C L Bertram. **Johnian Relatives:** father of Michael Brian Chapman (1973). **Educ:** West House Preparatory School, Edgbaston; King Edward VI School, Birmingham.

Career: House Physician, House Surgeon, Casualty Surgical Officer, Middlesex Hospital, London; HQ, Malaya Command, RAMC 1953–1955; Obstetric House Officer, Mothers Hospital, London 1956; GP, Wrotham, Ightham, Kent 1957–1992; Trainer of Trainee GPs; Hospital Psychotherapy Practitioner, Maidstone, Tunbridge Wells 1964–1995. **Appointments:** Member, Kent Area Health Authority, later Tonbridge Wells Health Authority; Vice-Chairman, Kent Non Accidental Injury to Children Committee; Council Member and Provost, South Thames Faculty, RCGP; Medical Audit Facilitator, Kent; Member, Local Research Ethics Committee, Maidstone; Member, South Thames Multiple Centre Research Ethics Committee; Trustee, Joseph Weld Hospice, Dorchester; Chairman, Clinical Governance Committee, Joseph Weld Hospice; Primary School Governor. **Publications:** *Mother and Baby Groups in General Practice*; (jointly) *Ethics and Citizenship: some reflections from the Kent branch*, 1996.

CHAPMAN, Maurice Boswell (1927) Born 25 May 1907, Seonee, Chappala, Central Provinces, India; son of Robert Alexander Boswell Chapman, Indian Civil Service, and Constance Martha Crawford. **Subject(s):** Mechanical Sciences; BA 1930. **Tutor(s):** J M Wordie. **Johnian Relatives:** brother of Robert Geoffrey Chapman (1927). **Educ:** St Peter's Preparatory School, Weston-Super-Mare; Sherborne School; RMA, Woolwich; SMF, Chatham. **Career:** Second Lieutenant, RE 1927.

CHAPMAN, Robert Geoffrey (1927) Born 30 June 1909, 9 Pembridge Gardens, Kensington, London; son of Robert Alexander Boswell Chapman, Indian Civil Service, and Constance Martha Crawford. **Subject(s):** Classics/Economics; BA 1930. **Tutor(s):** M P Charlesworth. **Johnian Relatives:** brother of Maurice Boswell Chapman (1927). **Educ:** St Peter's School, Weston-Super-Mare; Sherborne School.

CHAPMAN, Rodney Harold Benbow (1945) Born 3 December 1926, 5 Woodland Avenue, Northampton; son of Bertram Charles Chapman, Commercial Traveller, and Laura Mabel Benbow; m Annette. **Subject(s):** Modern and Medieval Languages; BA 1948; MA 1952; PGCE (London) 1953. **Tutor(s):** C W Guillebaud. **Educ:** Waynflete House School, Northampton; Felsted School. **Career:** Schoolteacher, Ghana (Army Education Service) 1954–1962; Second Master, Kingham Hill School, Oxford; Head of Modern Languages 1962–1991. **Appointments:** Lieutenant Colonel, Officer in Charge of the Combined Cadet Force; Secretary, Old Boys Association, Kingham Hill School. Died 22 May 1991.

CHAPMAN-ANDREWS, Sir Edwin Arthur (1926) Born 9 September 1903, 11 Weirfield Road, Exeter, Devon; son of Arthur John Chapman-Andrews, Municipal Official, Exeter Education Authority, and Ada Allen; m Sadie Barbara Nixon, 1931; 2 sons, 2 daughters. **Subject(s):** Arabic/Persian/Russian. **Tutor(s):** C W Guillebaud. **Johnian Relatives:** father of John Andrew Chapman-Andrews (1962). **Educ:** St John's Hospital, Exeter; Hele's School, Exeter; UCL; University of Paris, Sorbonne. **Career:** Probationary Vice-Consul, Levant Consular Service 1926, Egypt 1928–1929, Abyssinia 1930, London 1931–1932, Kirkuk, Iraq and Rowanduz 1933–1935; Consul, Harrar, Abyssinia 1935–1937; Cairo, Egypt 1937–1940; Honorary Commission, Royal Sussex Regiment 1940; Liaison Officer on staff of Commander-in-Chief, Middle East, with Emperor Haile Selassie 1942; Head, Personnel Department, Foreign Office 1945; Inspector of Overseas Establishments 1946; British Minister (No 2) in the Embassy, Cairo 1947–1951; Head of Mission, Beirut 1951–1956; Ambassador to Karthum 1956–1961; Adviser, Massey-Ferguson (Holdings) Ltd 1962–1977; Director, Export Branch, Massey-Ferguson 1964–1977; Director, Mitchell Cotts (Export) 1965–1973; Director, John Carrington & Co Ltd 1972–1977. **Appointments:** Council Member, Royal Central Asian Society 1962–1969; Member, Committee for Middle East Trade (COMET) 1963–1968 (Chairman 1965–1968); Member, British National Export Council 1965–1968; Council Member, Lord Kitchener National Memorial Fund; Council Member, Anglo-Arab Association; Council Member, Royal Albert Hall. **Honours:** OBE 1936; CMG 1948; KCMG 1953; KStJ; KCSG (Papal). Died 10 February 1980.

CHAPPELL, Peter Stanley (1920) Born 3 December 1901, Quarwood, Lower Snell, Stow-on-the-Wold, Gloucestershire; son of Thomas Stanley Chappell, of independent means, and Christine Liebert. **Tutor(s):** B F Armitage. **Educ:** West Downs, Winchester; Eton College.

CHAPPLE, Dr Harold (1901) Born 13 February 1881, Kent Town, Adelaide, Australia; son of Frederic Chapple, Schoolmaster, and Elizabeth Sarah Hunter; m Irene Briscoe Arbuthnot Lane, 12 October 1911, St George's, Hanover Square; 2 sons. **Subject(s):** Natural Sciences; BA 1904; MA 1909; BChir 1910; MB 1911; MChir 1912; BSc (Adelaide) 1901; MRCS; LRCP 1908; FRCS 1910; FRSocMed; FRCOG. **Tutor(s):** D MacAlister. **Educ:** Prince Alfred College, Adelaide, Australia. **Career:** Captain, RAMC, WWI; Obstetric Surgeon, Guy's Hospital 1913; Consulting Gynaecologist, London Jewish Hospital. **Publications:** 'Treatment of Pelvic Inflammation by Auto-Inoculation', *Lancet*, 1913; 'Some Effects of Intestinal Stasis on the Female Generative Organs', *British Medical Journal*, 1914; *Midwifery*, 1917; *Diseases of Women*, 1918. Died 8 March 1945.

CHAPPLE, Dr Peter Arbuthnot Lane (1938) Born 19 June 1920, 18 Devonshire Street, London; son of Harold Chapple, Surgeon, and Irene Briscoe Arbuthnot Lane; m Dorothy Marguerite Sugden, 3 October 1942. **Tutor(s):** J S Boys Smith. **Educ:** Beachborough Park School; Rugby School.

CHARLESWORTH, Professor Geoffrey Brown (1939) Born 29 September 1920, Carr Head, Deepcar, Sheffield; son of Frank Charlesworth, Coal Mine Deputy, and Mary Hannah Brown. BA 1942; MA 1946. **Tutor(s):** J M Wordie. **Educ:** Deepcar National School; Penistone Grammar School. **Career:** Bletchley Park 1941–1945; Teacher of Mathematics and Science, The British Boys' School, Alexandria, Egypt 1945–1947; Associate Dean of Liberal Arts and Sciences 1967–1974, Professor of Mathematics 1974–1981, Hofstra University, Hempstead, New York, USA. **Awards:** Scholarship, SJC. **Publications:** *A Gardener Obsessed*, David Godine, 1994; *The Opinionated Gardener*, David Godins, 1988.

CHARLESWORTH, The Revd Martin Percival (1923) (admitted to Jesus College 1914) Born 18 January 1895, Eastham, Cheshire; son of Ambrose Charlesworth, Rector, Thurstaston, and Alice Maud Emily Whish. BA (Jesus) 1920; MA (Jesus) 1923; Honorary Degree (Wales) 1947; Honorary Degree (Bordeaux) 1948; FSA 1938; FBA 1940. **Educ:** Braeside School, West Kirby; Birkenhead School; Jesus College, Cambridge; The Graduate College, Princeton, USA. **Career:** Second Lieutenant, Labour Corps, WWI; Title B Fellow 1923–1950, Lecturer in Classics (*ad hoc*) 1921–1923, Lecturer in Classics 1923–1950, SJC; Lecturer in Classics 1926–1931, Laurence Reader in Classics (Ancient History) 1931–1950, University of Cambridge; Recruiting Officer, Bletchley Park, WWII; Ordained Deacon and Priest 1940. **Appointments:** Jane Eliza Proctor Visiting Fellow, Princeton 1921–1922; Tutor 1925–1931, Director of Studies in Classics 1925–1948, President 1937–1950, SJC; Martin Lecturer, Oberlin College, Ohio 1935. **Awards:** Bell Scholarship, University of Cambridge 1915; John Stewart of Rannoch Scholarship in Greek and Latin, University of Cambridge 1916; Craven Scholarship, University of Cambridge 1920; Chancellor's Classical Medal, University of Cambridge 1921; Hare Prize, University of Cambridge 1922. **Publications:** (ed) *Cambridge Ancient History*; *Trade Routes and Commerce of the Roman Empire*, 1924; *Five Men*, 1936; *The Lost Province*, 1949; *The Roman Empire*, OUP, 1951. Died 26 October 1955.

CHARLTON, Professor John Maxwell Town (1946) Born 29 July 1917, Keithock, Cote Green, Ludworth, Glossop; son of Henry Buckley Charlton, Professor of English Literature, Manchester, and Edith Foster Town; m Joyce. **Subject(s):** Classics; BA 1947; BA (Manchester) 1939. **Tutor(s):** R L Howland. **Educ:** Manchester Grammar School; Manchester University. **Career:** Captain, RE; Reader in Classics, University of North Staffordshire 1952; Professor of Classics, University of North Staffordshire 1959–1982. **Awards:** Exhibition, SJC 1938. Died 9 May 1983.

CHARLTON, William Hartley Denys (1924) Born 11 May 1905, Weathercote, Foxley Lane, Beddington, Surrey; son of Frederick William Charlton, Civil Servant, and Marion Butterworth. BA 1927; MA 1992. **Tutor(s):** E E Sikes. **Educ:** Falconbury School, Purley; Marlborough College; Courtenay Lodge, Sutton Courtenay.

CHARNOCK, William Henry (1920) Born 7 April 1902, 43 Pendleston Road, Walthamstow, Essex; son of Sydney Charnock, Schoolmaster, and Minnie Elizabeth Beeton; m Nancy; 1 son (Tony). **Subject(s):** Mechanical Sciences; BA 1923; MA 1927. **Tutor(s):** E E Sikes. **Educ:** Southey Hall Preparatory School, Worthing; Lancing College. **Career:** Junior Assistant to the District Engineer, LNER, Cambridge. Died 14 November 1959.

CHARTERS, Dr Alan Dumergue (1921) Born 26 March 1903, 24 St James Road, Edgbaston, Birmingham; son of Alfred Robert Charters, Headmaster, Preparatory School, and Evelyn Mary Williamson; m Susan Maude Dennison; 2 sons (John Dumergue b 9 May 1930, d 15 June 2000 and David Dennison b 16 December 1931). **Subject(s):** Natural Sciences; BA 1924; MA 1958; MB 1929; BChir 1929; MD 1933; MRCS 1927; LRCP 1927; MRCP 1946; FRCP 1958; DTM&H; Diploma in Medicine and Hygiene 1929; FRACP. **Tutor(s):** B F Armitage. **Johnian Relatives:** grandson of Robert Henry Charters (1847); son of Alfred Robert Charters (1884); father of John Dumergue Charters (1949) and of David Dennison Charters (1950). **Educ:** Westerleigh, St Leonards on Sea; Sedbergh School. **Career:** GP and Consultant Physician 1927–1996. **Appointments:** Emeritus Consultant Physician and Freeman, Sir Charles Gairdner Hospital, Perth, Australia. **Honours:** AM 1989. **Publications:** *Human Parasitology*; numerous articles in *British Medical Journal*, *Lancet* and others. Died 9 September 1996.

CHARTERS, Dr John Dumergue (1949) Born 9 May 1930, Mengo Hospital, Namirembe, Uganda; son of Alan Dumergue Charters, Consultant Physician, and Susan Maude Dennison, Registered Nurse. **Subject(s):** Natural Sciences; BA 1952; MA 1995; BChir 1955; MB 1956. **Tutor(s):** G C L Bertram. **Johnian Relatives:** great grandson of Robert Henry Charters (1847); grandson of Alfred Robert Charters (1884); son of Alan Dumergue Charters (1921); brother of David Dennison Charters (1950). **Educ:** St Andrew's School, Turi, Kenya; Kenton College, Nairobi; St Andrew's College, Grahamstown. **Career:** GP. **Publications:** (with Alan Dumergue Charters) article on heart disease. Died 15 June 2000.

CHASTENEY, Howard Everson (1907) Born 9 August 1888, 366 Alfreton Road, Hyson Green, Nottingham; son of Frederick Chasteney, Inspector of Schools, and Annie Hunter; m Ellen (d 1964); 2 daughters. **Subject(s):** Mathematics/Natural Sciences; BA 1910; MA 1914. **Tutor(s):** L H K Bushe-Fox. **Educ:** Masters Road Higher Elementary School; Nottingham High School. **Career:** HM Inspector of Factories, Sheffield 1913–1914; RE 1914–1918 (wounded); HM Inspector of Factories, Sheffield, Liverpool, then London 1918–1937; HM Deputy Superintending Inspector of Factories, Manchester 1937–1938; HM Deputy Chief Inspector of Factories, London 1938–1946; HM Chief Inspector of Factories, Ministry of Labour and National Service 1946–1947. Died 18 February 1947.

CHATTERJI, Amulya Kumar (1909) Born 11 May 1889, 73 Manicktolla Street, Calcutta, India; son of Aditya Kumaar Chatterji, Senior Professor of Philosophy, Bithune College, and Golap Kumari Bannerji. **Subject(s):** Mathematics; BA 1913. **Tutor(s):** L H K Bushe-Fox. **Educ:** The Hindi School of Calcutta, India; The General Assembly's Institution, Calcutta, India.

CHAUDHRY, Girdhari Lal (1910) Born 4 September 1892, Ludhiana, Punjab, India; son of Lala Anant Ram, Merchant and Honorary Magistrate. **Subject(s):** Mathematics/Law; BA 1913. **Tutor(s):** J R Tanner. **Educ:** Government High School, Lyallpur, India; Government College, Lahore.

CHAUDHURI, Shiva Kumar (1920) Born 23 October 1900, Calcutta, India; son of Sir Asutosh Chaudhuri, High Court Judge, and Prativa Tagore. **Tutor(s):** E A Benians. **Johnian Relatives:** son of Sir Asutosh Chaudhuri (1881). **Educ:** Hindu School, Calcutta; JB Institution, Calcutta; Mittra Institution, Calcutta; Presidency College, India; KCL.

CHAUMETON, John Bryan (1948) Born 25 August 1928, 24 Grosvenor Road, Church End, Finchley, Middlesex; son of John Charles Chaumeton, Chartered Accountant, and Hilda Greaves; m (1) Audrey Nella Chamberlain, 1955, (2) Janice Horlor, 1975 (d); (1) 2 sons (Paul Adrian b 1958 and Nigel Richard b 1960). **Subject(s):** Natural Sciences; BA 1951; MA 1955; FRICS. **Tutor(s):** G C L Bertram. **Educ:** Holmewood Preparatory School, Woodside Park; Bishop's Stortford College. **Career:** Chartered Surveyor.

CHECKLAND, Montmorency Beaumont (1902) Born 16 November 1883, 25 Ventnor Villas, Hove, Sussex; son of William Checkland, Colliery Proprietor, and Amy Beaumont. **Subject(s):** Law; BA 1907. **Tutor(s):** C E Graves; J R Tanner. **Educ:** Newton College; Uppingham School. **Career:** Called to the Bar, Inner Temple 1912; Lieutenant, West Somerset Yeomanry, attached Somerset Light Infantry 1914–1917. Died 17 August 1917 (killed in action at Langemarck).

CHEERS, Brian (1949) Born 2 April 1929, Radcliffe, Lancashire; son of Frank Cheers and Sarah Alice Mills; m Florence Margaret Bignell, 2 July 1955, Quebec City (d 27 July 1998); 1 daughter (Pamela Ruth b 14 December 1957). **Subject(s):** Mechanical Sciences; BA 1952; MA 1956. **Tutor(s):** R L Howland. **Johnian Relatives:** brother of Francis Cheers (1937); uncle of Christopher Francis Cheers (1981). **Educ:** Water Lane Council School, Radcliffe; Whitefield Junior Council School; Bury Grammar School. **Awards:** Exhibition, SJC. **Career:** Defence Scientist, Department of National Defence, Canada 1952–1989; Scientific Liaison Officer, Canadian Defence Research Staff, Washington 1968–1972.

CHEERS, Francis (1937) Born 9 March 1919, Radcliffe, Lancashire; son of Frank Cheers and Sarah Alice Mills; m (1) Margaret Rome Pleming, 26 June 1943, Oxford (d 26 September 1979), (2) Barbara Moore, 2 April 1983, Abingdon, Oxon; (1) 2 sons (John Christopher b 11 September 1945 and Christopher Francis b 21 April 1962), 4 daughters (Alison Margaret b 13 November 1946, Hilary Frances b 30 November 1949, Elizabeth Ina b 10 February 1951 and Penelope Ann b 12 January 1955). **Subject(s):** Mathematics/Mechanical Sciences; BA 1940; MA 1956. **Tutor(s):** J S Boys Smith. **Johnian Relatives:** brother of Brian Cheers (1949); father of Christopher Francis Cheers (1981). **Educ:** Radcliffe Central Council School; Bury Grammar School. **Career:** Scientific Officer, National Physical Laboratory, Teddington 1941–1947; Research Officer, Aerodynamics Laboratory and Gas Dynamics Laboratory, National Research Council, Canada 1947–1957; Lecturer in Engineering (Mechanical) 1958–1965, Senior Lecturer in Engineering 1965–1982, University of Manchester. **Awards:** Exhibition, SJC 1936; Scholarship, SJC 1939; College Prize, SJC 1939; Wright's Prize, SJC 1939. **Publications:** *Elements of Compressible Flow*, John Wiley and Sons, 1963. Died 8 June 1995.

CHEESE, The Revd William Gerard (1902) Born 9 June 1893, The Vicarage, New Bilton, Rugby, Warwickshire; son of James Albert Cheese, Clerk in Holy Orders, and Emily Powell. **Subject(s):** Classics; BA 1905. **Tutor(s):** E E Sikes. **Johnian Relatives:** son of James Albert Cheese (1847); brother of John Ethelstan Cheese (1896). **Educ:** Overslade School, Rugby; Temple Grove School, East Sheen; Clifton College. **Career:** Ordained Deacon 1906; Ordained Priest 1907; Temporary CF, 4th Class, RACD, WWI. Died 7 November 1918 (died of pneumonia contracted on active service).

CHEETHAM, Ernest Mark (1912) Born 1 June 1892, 69 Harrowgate Road, South Hackney, London; son of Joseph Ernest Cheetham, Printer's Manager, and Phoebe Ann Brandon. **Subject(s):** Mathematics/ Natural Sciences/Law; BA 1915. **Tutor(s):** R P Gregory. **Educ:** South

Norwood High School; Croydon Borough Secondary School; Tottenham County School; East London College. **Career:** Corporal, RE, WWI. **Honours:** MBE. Died 1971.

CHEETHAM, The Revd Canon Frederic Philip (1909) Born 16 July 1890, 77 Clova Road, West Ham, Essex; son of Walter Cheetham, Accountant, and Ann James; m Helen Elizabeth MacIntosh, 19 July 1930, Chingford Parish Church; 1 son (Philip Martin b 3 July 1938). **Subject(s):** Classics/Theology; BA 1912; MA 1916. **Tutor(s):** E E Sikes. **Johnian Relatives:** father of Philip Martin Cheetham (1959). **Educ:** City of London School; Ridley Hall, Cambridge. **Career:** Deacon 1914; Curate, St Barnabas, Mitcham 1914–1916; Priest 1915; Tutor, St Aidan's College 1916–1920; Temporary CF 1918–1919; Sub-Warden of the Theological Hostel and Lecturer, KCL 1920–1924; Principal, Egerton Hall, Manchester 1924–1939; Vicar, Hartford, Cheshire 1939–1958; Rural Dean, Middlewich 1951. **Appointments:** Examining Chaplain to the Bishop of Manchester 1924; Honorary Canon, Manchester Cathedral 1935–1939 (Emeritus 1939); Examining Chaplain to the Bishop of Chester 1945. **Awards:** Browne Medal for Greek Ode, University of Cambridge 1912; Bachelors' Carus Greek Testament Prize, University of Cambridge 1913; Second Jeremie Septuagint Prize, University of Cambridge 1914. Died 29 December 1970.

CHELL, Harold (1908) Born 10 May 1889, The Vicarage, Kneesall, Nottinghamshire; son of George Russell Chell, Clerk in Holy Orders, and Alice Pope Haines. BA 1913. **Tutor(s):** E E Sikes. **Johnian Relatives:** grandson of John Chell (1822); son of George Russell Chell (1856); brother of John Whyley Chell (1898). **Educ:** St Michael's College, Tenbury Wells; Shrewsbury School. **Career:** Student, St Mary's Hospital; Second Lieutenant, 8th Battalion, Royal Fusiliers (London Regiment) 1914–1915. Died 10 August 1915.

CHENG, Chao-tsung (1949) Born 10 July 1912, Foochow, Fukien, China; son of I-Chü Cheng, Lecturer in Chinese, Imperial College, Peking, and Mei-fang Chen. **Tutor(s):** C W Guillebaud. **Educ:** Trinity College, Foochow; Anglo-Chinese College, Foochow; Tsinghua University, Peiping. **Career:** Lecturer in English, National University of Amoy 1938–1939; Lecturer in English and Chinese, the Lester School, Shanghai 1939–1942; Assistant Professor of English and Chinese, Amoy 1943–1949.

CHESHIRE, Albert White (1939) Born 15 January 1920, Nagpur, Central Provinces, India; son of Francis Moreton Cheshire, Teacher, and Fanny Margaret Alexander White. **Subject(s):** Classics. **Johnian Relatives:** son of Francis Moreton Cheshire (1906); brother-in-law of Thomas Blythe Hutton (1932). **Educ:** St George's School, Harpenden. **Career:** Captain, RA, WWII. Died 29 November 1944 (died in India).

CHESHIRE, Francis Moreton (1906) Born 14 August 1877, 4 Calthorpe Road, Neithrop, Banbury, Oxfordshire; son of Stephen Cheshire, Baptist Minister, and Emily Rachel Horner; 2 sons, 2 daughters. **Subject(s):** History/Theology; BA 1909; MA 1926. **Tutor(s):** J R Tanner. **Johnian Relatives:** father-in-law of Thomas Blythe Hutton (1932); father of Albert White Cheshire (1939). **Educ:** Bishop's Stortford College. **Career:** Assistant Educational Advisor to Indian Students, India Office 1911; Lieutenant, 2nd Nagpur Rifles, Indian Defence Force, WWI; Principal, Morris College, Nagpur, Central Provinces 1914–1931; Master, St George's College, Harpenden 1931. Died 6 August 1971.

CHESTON, John Anthony (1943) Born 8 May 1925, 13 Pembroke Road, Clifton; son of Henry Leslie Cheston, Local Government Officer, and Effie May Bond. **Tutor(s):** S J Bailey. **Educ:** Portishead Kindergarten School; Portishead Council School; Colston's School, Bristol.

CHEW, Frederick Robert Gansel (1926) Born 4 May 1907, 2 Osterley Mansions, Spring Grove, Heston, Middlesex; son of Robert George Chew, Bank Manager, and Ethel Marion Symes; m Mrs Eva Maria Mohr; 1 son, 1 stepson. BA 1932; MA 1954. **Tutor(s):** J M Wordie. **Educ:**

Hamilton House, Ealing; Streete Court, Westgate-on-Sea; Sedbergh School. **Career:** Master, Salem School, Baden, Germany 1929–1933; Master, Gordonstoun School 1934–1959; Lieutenant Colonel, Seaforth Highlanders, WWII; Headmaster, Gordonstoun School 1959–1967. **Awards:** Freedom Cross of Norway, 1945. **Honours:** CVO 1968. Died 11 September 1970.

CHIDSON, Captain Lawrence Drury (1914) Born 5 November 1894, Chidson's Ranch, Tigardville, Portland, Oregon, USA; son of Charles Richard Chidson, Artist, and Norah O'Melia. **Subject(s):** Classics. **Tutor(s):** E E Sikes. **Educ:** Streatham Grammar School; Westminster Abbey Choir School; Dulwich College. **Career:** Enlisted, 5th East Surrey (Territorial) Regiment 1914; Second Lieutenant (1914), Lieutenant (1915), then Captain, King's Royal Rifle Corps 1914–1917 (Mentioned in Despatches). **Awards:** Entrance Scholarship, SJC 1913. **Honours:** MC 1916. Died 23 April 1917 (killed in action in France).

CHILDS, Patrick (1926) Born 7 March 1907, 6 Christchurch Gardens, Reading, Berkshire; son of William Macbride Childs, Vice-Chancellor of the University of Reading, and Emma Catherine Pollard. **Subject(s):** Mathematics/Mechanical Sciences; BA 1929; MA 1933. **Tutor(s):** J M Wordie. **Johnian Relatives:** father of Christopher Montgomery Childs (1959). **Educ:** Darlston Court, Swanage; Oakham School. **Career:** Assistant Master, Shrewsbury School 1929–1967; Housemaster 1946–1960. Died 20 March 1994.

CHILTON, Dr Cecil William (1933) Born 16 October 1914, Verona, Park Street, Kingswinford; son of Robert Chilton, Motor Omnibus Inspector, and Amy Elizabeth Lovejoy; m Althea. **Subject(s):** Classics/History; BA 1936; MA 1946; PhD (Hull) 1963. **Tutor(s):** R L Howland. **Educ:** Hill Street Church of England School, Brierley Hill; King Edward VI School, Stourbridge. **Career:** Schoolmaster 1937–1939; Captain, Worcestershire Regiment 1939–1945; Lecturer, Classics, Hull University 1948–1971; Faculty of Arts admissions officer, Hull University 1969–1973; Reader, Classics, Hull University 1971–1982. **Appointments:** Treasurer and President, Hull Branch, Classical Association. **Publications:** *Diogenes of Oenoanda: The Fragments*; *Early Hull Printers and Booksellers*. Died 25 May 1984.

CHIRGWIN, Eric Graham (1945) Born 2 March 1919, 210 Claughton Road, Birkenhead, Cheshire; son of William Alfred Chirgwin, Engine Fitter, and Alice Maxton; m Frances Mary Johnston, 27 December 1947. **Subject(s):** Theology; BA 1947; MA 1951; BA (Liverpool) 1939. **Tutor(s):** C W Guillebaud. **Educ:** Park High School, Birkenhead; Liverpool University. Died 19 July 1967.

CHIVERS, John (1945) Born 15 February 1927, Woodhouse, Impington, Cambridgeshire; son of John Stanley Chivers, Director of Chivers & Sons, Jam Manufacturers, and Mary Gambling Bird; m Judith; 1 son (Benjamin), 1 daughter (Annabel). **Subject(s):** Mechanical Sciences; BA 1948; MA 1952; DIC. **Tutor(s):** S J Bailey; R L Howland. **Educ:** St Faith's School, Cambridge; The Leys School, Cambridge. **Appointments:** Member, Impington Parish Council. Died 14 July 1985.

CHIVERS, William Douglas (1942) Born 6 November 1922, The Bungalow, Caswell Way, Swansea; son of William James Chivers, Wholesale Provision Merchant, and Theresa Ethel Davey. **Tutor(s):** C W Guillebaud. **Educ:** PNEU Junior School, Langland; Wycliffe College, Stonehouse. Died 1947.

CHONG, Professor Frederick (1937) Born 5 March 1915, Portman Street, Waterloo, Redfern, New South Wales, Australia; son of Percival Chong, Merchant, and Fan Ali Kow. **Subject(s):** Mathematics; BA 1939; MA 1943; MSc (Sydney) 1937; PhD (Iowa State) 1952; Hon DSc (Macquarie University, Australia) 1992; Hon DSc (Sydney) June 1999 (posthumously); FIMA; CMath 1976. **Tutor(s):** J M Wordie. **Educ:** Redfern Public School; Cleveland Street International High School; Fort Street High School; University of Sydney. **Career:** Lecturer in

Mathematics and Physics, New England University College 1940–1947; Senior Lecturer in Mathematics, University of Sydney 1948–1955; Professor of Mathematics, University of Auckland 1956–1965; Foundation Professor of Mathematics, Macquarie University 1965–1980. Died 14 May 1999.

CHOTZNER, John Raymond (COLCHESTER) (1927) Born 15 August 1907, Darjeeling, India; son of Alfred James Chotzner, High Court Judge, Calcutta, and Ethel Kathleen Lan Davis. **Subject(s):** Law; BA 1930. **Tutor(s):** C W Guillebaud. **Johnian Relatives:** son of Alfred James Chotzner (1892). **Educ:** St Cyprian's, Eastbourne; Harrow School; Imperial College of Science.

CHRISTIE, Alexander Kenneth (1939) Born 4 May 1920, 12 Friars Street, Shoeburyness, Essex; son of Alexander Christie, Locomotive Engine Driver, and Charlotte Sarah Smith; m Sheila Jean Sanders, 1961; 2 daughters (Alison Sarah b 1962 and Helen Margaret b 1964). **Subject(s):** Mathematics; BA 1947; MA 1949. **Tutor(s):** S J Bailey; G L C Bertram; J M Wordie. **Educ:** Hinguar Street Elementary School, Shoeburyness; High School for Boys, Southend-on-Sea. **Career:** Master, Sedbergh School 1947–1948; Master, Framlingham College 1948–1949; Master, Brighton College 1949–1952; Assistant Master, Dulwich College 1952–1980. **Awards:** Exhibition, SJC. Died 20 January 2001.

CHRISTIE, Dan Edwin (1937) Born 11 October 1915, Dover-Foxcroft, Maine, USA; son of Dan Foss Christie, Skilled Labourer, and Blanche Ellen Hamlin. **Tutor(s):** J M Wordie. **Educ:** Milo High School; Bowdoin College, Brunswick, USA. **Career:** Lecturer in Topology, Department of Mathematics, Bowdoin College, USA. Died 18 July 1975.

CHRISTIE, John Belford Wilson (1932) Born 4 May 1914, Allanton House, Newmains, Lanarkshire; son of John Aitkin Christie, Advocate, and Mary Belford; m Christine Isobel Syme Arnott; 4 daughters. **Subject(s):** Economics; BA 1935; LLB 1939 (Edinburgh); Honorary LLD (Dundee) 1977; KHS 1988; KCHS 1994. **Tutor(s):** C W Guillebaud. **Educ:** St Oran's School, Drummond Place, Edinburgh; Merchiston Castle School, Colinton. **Career:** RNVR 1936–1948; Admitted to Faculty of Advocates 1939; Sheriff–Substitute, Western Division of Dumfries and Galloway 1948–1955; Sheriff, Tayside, Central and Fife (formerly Perth and Angus), Dundee 1955–1983. **Appointments:** Member, Queen's College Council, University of St Andrews 1960–1967; Member, Parole Board for Scotland 1967–1973; Member, University Court 1967–1975 and Honorary Lecturer, Department of Private Law, University of Dundee. **Honours:** CBE 1981. Died 20 July 2002.

CHUA, Seng Chew (1932) Born 1 June 1912, 251 Telok Ayer Street, Singapore; son of Chua Gee Kheng, Merchant, and Goh Tim Hewnh. **Subject(s):** Mathematics; BA 1935; MA 1950. **Tutor(s):** J M Wordie. **Educ:** Chinese High School, Singapore; The Raffles Institution, Singapore.

CHURCHWARD, The Revd Arthur Cyril (1905) (initially Non-Collegiate) Born 10 July 1885, 2 St Lawrence Road, Notting Hill, London; son of Marcus Wellesley Churchward, Clerk in Holy Orders, and Mary Ella Woodall. BA 1907; MA 1912. **Tutor(s):** D MacAlister. **Johnian Relatives:** son of Marcus Wellesley Churchward (1879). **Educ:** Collegiate School, Malta. **Career:** Deacon 1908; Curate, St Paul, Newington 1908–1913; Priest 1909; Private, RASC, WWI; Missionary Priest, Universities Mission to Central Africa, Diocese of Nyasaland 1914–1921. Died 15 November 1921.

CLACK, Nicholas Barry Menzies (1949) Born 17 August 1930, Standlake, Oxfordshire; son of Leslie Alan Clack, Farmer, and Janet Mary Lardner Menzies; m Ann Martindell, 17 August 1957, Gaunt House, Standlake; 1 son (Toby b 8 April 1967), 1 daughter (Bryony b 1 February 1969). **Subject(s):** Mechanical Sciences; BA 1952; MA 1960; MSc (LSE) 1971–1972; CEng; MIEE; FIMgt. **Tutor(s):** R L Howland. **Educ:** Wycliffe College, Stonehouse; Royal Naval College, Dartmouth. **Career:** Captain,

RN (from Cadet) mainly in submarines, and staff appointments in Ministry of Defence and HM Naval Bases 1948–1984 (last appointment, Commodore, HMS *Drake*, RNB Devonport 1982–1984); General Administrator, Trinity College of Music 1984–1989; General Secretary, Distressed Gentlefolks' Aid Association 1989–1992. **Appointments:** Secretary, LMBC 1951–1952; Council of Governors, Wycliffe College 1979; Chairman, Education Committee; Administrator 1984–1989, Trustee 1989, Music Students' Hostel Trust Ltd; Chairman, Membership and Objets D'Art Committees, Army and Navy Club 1995–2001. **Publications:** 'Education and Training of Engineers in the Nuclear Industry', Institution of Mechanical Engineers, London, 5 December 1968.

CLANDILLON, Edmund John (1944) Born 25 October 1926, Montreal, Canada; son of John Clandillon, Canadian Pacific Railway, and Hilda Alice Martin. **Tutor(s):** J M Wordie. **Educ:** Waterloo with Seaforth Grammar School, Liverpool; Douglas High School, Isle of Man; Liverpool Collegiate School; Queen Elizabeth Grammar School, Hexham. **Appointments:** RAF Cadet, SJC.

CLAPIN, Basil Philip Waterlow (1938) Born 30 January 1918, Colville House, Tonbridge, Kent; son of Alfred Clifton Clapin, Schoolmaster, and Emily Lutwytch Waterlow. BA 1947; MA 1959. **Tutor(s):** J S Boys Smith. **Educ:** Hilden Gates, Tonbridge; Langley Place, St Leonards-on-Sea; Cheltenham College; RMA Woolwich. **Career:** Second Lieutenant, RE.

CLARIDGE, Marcus William (1922) Born 26 June 1904, Oaklands, Ampthill, Bedfordshire; son of William Claridge, Master Grocer, and Annie Barrett Brightman; m Stella Caroline Renwick. **Subject(s):** Mathematics; BA 1925; MA 1929. **Tutor(s):** E Cunningham. **Educ:** Bedford Modern School. **Career:** Auditor, Bombay, Baroda and Central India Railway, Church Gate, Bombay, India. Died 2 September 1936.

CLARK, Albert Edward (1920) Born 30 September 1901, 291 Hoxton Street, Hoxton Old Town, London; son of Charles Benjamin Clark, Master Butcher, and Maud Annie Worts; m Ann. **Subject(s):** History; BA 1923; MA 1927; FRHS. **Tutor(s):** E A Benians. **Educ:** London County Council School; Owens School, Islington. **Career:** Master, Taunton School 1924–1925; Merchant Taylors' School and St George's School, Harpenden 1925–1926; Queen Mary's Grammar School, Walsall 1926. Died 19 December 1991.

CLARK, Donald (1946) Born 14 October 1924, 60 Buckingham Street, Scunthorpe, Lincolnshire; son of John William Clark, Grocery Manager, and Caroline Annie Beard; m Patricia, 3 November 1951; 1 son (Michael John b 7 September 1952), 1 daughter (Susan Jacqueline b 3 July 1955). **Subject(s):** Mathematics; BA 1949; MA 1953; Diploma in Anthropology 1950; MBIM. **Tutor(s):** J M Wordie. **Johnian Relatives:** father of Michael John Clark (1970). **Educ:** Henderson Avenue Junior School, Scunthorpe; Scunthorpe Grammar School. **Career:** Markham Main Colliery, Armthorpe, Doncaster 1943–1946; Various positions in Industry 1950–1982; Director, Management Services 1974–1982; Professional Clarinettist 1982–2000. Died 29 August 2003.

CLARK, George Edward (1931) Born 6 August 1912, Baltrasna, St John's Road, Sandown, Isle of Wight; son of Cecil Clark, Journeyman Plumber, and Rosetta Wilson; m Margaret (Peggy), 26 July 1939; 2 sons (Alan b 16 May 1943 and Robert b 21 February 1949), 1 daughter (Rosemary b 22 May 1940). **Subject(s):** Mathematics; BA 1934; MA 1954. **Tutor(s):** J M Wordie. **Educ:** St John's Infant School, Sandown; Sandown Church of England School; Sandown County Secondary School. **Career:** Indian Civil Service 1936–1948; School Teacher, Lindisfarne College, Hastings, New Zealand 1954–1961; St Andrew's College, Christchurch, New Zealand 1961–1972. Died 1 September 2002.

CLARK, Harold Edward (1949) Born 25 October 1923, 1207 Lake Avenue, Elyria, Ohio, USA; son of Harold Melvin Clark, Salesman, and Gladys Alverda Dienst; m Leah Rose Caliri (d 1994). BA (Miami) 1949; Diploma (Sorbonne) 1951; PhD (Indiana) 1955. **Subject(s):** English.

Tutor(s): A G Lee. **Educ:** Elyria High School, Ohio, USA; Miami University, Oxford, Ohio, USA; Biarritz American University, France; Sorbonne, University of Paris, France; University of Heidelberg, Germany; Indiana University, USA. **Career:** 78th Infantry Division, US Army, Ardennes and Rhineland Campaigns 1943–1946; Assistant Professor of English, St Lawrence University, Canton, New York 1955–1961; Fulbright Lecturer in American Literature, Kiel University, Germany 1958–1959; Professor of English 1961–1985 (Emeritus 1985) Suffolk University, Boston, Massachusetts; Founder and Director, Collection of African American Literature, Suffolk University 1971–1985. **Awards:** Rotary Foundation Fellowship for Advanced Study 1949–1950. **Publications:** *Black Writers in New England*, National Park Service, Boston, Massachussetts, USA, 1985; *Dictionary Catalog of the Collection of African American Literature in the Mildred F Sawyer Library of Suffolk University*, Boston, Massachusetts, Suffolk University, 1996.

CLARK, Henry Robert Ernest (1910) Born 18 October 1891, Lorna Doone, Muswell Hill, Clerkenwell, Middlesex; son of William Henry Dennis Clark, Civil Servant, and Isabella Godwin Terry. **Subject(s):** History; BA 1913; LLB 1913. **Tutor(s):** E E Sikes. **Educ:** Barnet Grammar School; City of London School. **Career:** Second Lieutenant, 15th Battalion, London Regiment (Civil Servant Rifles) 1914; Machine-gun Officer, France 1915. Died 3 June 1915 (killed in action).

CLARK, Peter Kenneth (1947) Born 23 January 1926, 69 Radipole Road, Fulham, London; son of Percy Thomas Clarence Clark, Mechanical Engineer, and Elsie Gandee. **Subject(s):** Geography; BA 1949; MA 1974. **Tutor(s):** J M Wordie. **Educ:** Munster Road School, Fulham; Latymer Upper School, Hammersmith; Harvey Grammar School, Folkestone. **Career:** Meteorological work, RN.

CLARK, Dr Robert Edward David (1925) Born 25 December 1906, Lahore, India; son of Hamlet Edward Clark, Clerk in Holy Orders, Church Missionary Society, and Edith Sarah Panton; m Ethel Margaret Perry, 21 February 1947, Emmanuel Congregational Church. **Subject(s):** Natural Sciences; BA 1928; MA 1932; PhD 1932. **Tutor(s):** J M Wordie. **Educ:** Surrey House, Margate; St Andrew's, Southborough; St Lawrence College, Ramsgate. **Awards:** Exhibition, SJC. **Publications:** *The New International Dictionary of the Christian Church*. Died 18 November 1984.

CLARKE, Brian Aylmer (1923) Born 23 May 1905, 29 Tregunter Road, Kensington, London; son of Arthur Gerald Aylmer Clarke, of independent means, and Gladys Eva Bond. **Tutor(s):** E E Sikes. **Educ:** St Hugh's Preparatory School, Bickley; Private Tuition (I Wright Platt).

CLARKE, Brian Lawson (1944) Born 21 April 1926, 19 Shaftesbury Road, Coventry, Warwickshire; son of Lawson Clarke, Motor Works Manager, and May Lilian Lander. **Tutor(s):** J M Wordie. **Educ:** Rookery Road Council School, Handsworth; Handsworth Grammar School.

CLARKE, Charles Richard (1949) Born 15 April 1929, Woodhey, Bromborough, Cheshire; son of Charles Hugh Clarke, Technical Director, Lever Brothers, and Mavis Mary Gregory Short. **Tutor(s):** G C L Bertram. **Johnian Relatives:** brother of Donald Hugh Clarke (1944). **Educ:** The Dene School, Caterham; Oundle School.

CLARKE, Christopher Garrard (1919) Naval Officer.

CLARKE, Denis Horace Hilary (1933) Born 28 January 1915, 42 George Road, Erdington, Birmingham; son of Sir Horace William Clarke, Metallurgical Engineer, and Nellie Teresa Maud Flynn; m Louise Marie Schlinker, 5 April 1946, Edgbaston Old Church, Birmingham; 1 son (George Timothy Horace b 20 April 1949), 1 daughter (Maroussia Nancy b 29 March 1947). **Subject(s):** Mathematics/Mechanical Sciences; BA 1936; MA 1940; CEng, MIMechE, MIM. **Tutor(s):** J S Boys Smith. **Johnian Relatives:** father of George Timothy Horace Clarke (1968). **Educ:** Oundle School. **Career:** Director, James Booth and Delta Metal. Died September 1998.

CLARKE, Denis Lowther Lovell (1935) Born 14 September 1916, All Saints Vicarage, All Saints Street, Nottingham; son of Herbert Lovell Clarke, Clerk in Holy Orders, and Phyllis Mary Fulford; m Diana Godfrey, 1942; 1 son (Jeremy Francis b 1944). **Subject(s):** Classics; BA 1938; MA 1941; DipEd (London) 1939, MA (Oxon). **Tutor(s):** R L Howland. **Johnian Relatives:** great grandson of William Clarke (1822); great nephew of John Clarke (1866); grandson of Henry Lowther Clarke (1870); son of Herbert Lovell Clarke (1901); father of Jeremy Francis Clarke (1963). **Educ:** Forest Fields Preparatory School, Nottingham; West Leeds High School; Magdalen College School, Oxford. **Career:** Classics Teacher, Steyning Grammar School; Pioneer Corps and later Intelligence Corps, WWII; Head of Classics and Usher (second master), Magdalen College School, Oxford 1958–1978. **Appointments:** Member, Leander Club 1972–1976; Member, Foundation of Magdalen College, Oxford 1972–1978. Died 9 April 1992.

CLARKE, Desmond Frederick Aubrey (1919) Born 3 June 1896, 39 Maidstone Road, Rochester, Kent; son of Frederick William Alfred Clarke, Civil Servant, and Josephine Fitzgerald Moylan. **Subject(s):** History; BA 1920. **Tutor(s):** E A Benians. **Educ:** Shirley House School, Old Charlton; Dulwich College. **Publications:** *Reminiscences of Jerusalem and the Holy Land*, 1919. Died March 1984.

CLARKE, Donald (1913) Born 4 May 1895, 90 Easton Square, High Wycombe, Buckinghamshire; son of Arthur Joseph Clarke, Solicitor and Town Clerk, and Minnie Gibbs Peace. **Tutor(s):** L H K Bushe-Fox. **Educ:** Mill Hill. **Career:** Enlisted, Private, HAC 1914; Second Lieutenant (Observer Officer), RFC 1916. Died 26 August 1916 (killed in action).

CLARKE, Donald Hugh (1944) Born 15 May 1926, Rathmines, Bromborough, Cheshire; son of Charles Hugh Clarke, Technical Director, Lever Bros and Unilever Ltd, and Mavis Mary Gregory Short; m (2) Moyna (Paddy) Smith, 17 March 1967, London; (1) 2 daughters (Susan and Mary Louise), (2) 1 daughter (Samantha). BA 1948; MA 1951. **Tutor(s):** C W Guillebaud. **Johnian Relatives:** brother of Charles Richard Clarke (1949). **Educ:** Dene School, Caterham; Oundle School. **Career:** Assistant General Works Manager, Bromborough 1957–1959; Managing Director, Lever Bros (Nigeria) Ltd 1959–1963; Director, Van den Burghs and Jurgens Ltd, and General Works Manager, Bromborough 1963; Managing Director, Craigmillar; Owner and Manager, Littleglade Fresh Foods 1985–1987.

CLARKE, Harold John (1943) Born 31 May 1925, White Bungalow, Eastwood Road, Rayleigh; son of Herbert George Clarke, Bank Clerk, and Amy Ivy Collins. **Tutor(s):** S J Bailey. **Educ:** Essex House Kindergarten, Woodford; St Aubyn's Preparatory School, Woodford; Chigwell Grammar School.

CLARKE, The Revd Herbert Lovell (1901) Born 15 August 1881, Hedon, Yorkshire; son of Henry Lowther Clarke, Clerk in Holy Orders, and Alice Lovell Kemp; m Phyllis Mary Fulford; 1 son (Denis Lowther Lovell b 14 September 1916). **Subject(s):** Classics; BA 1904; MA 1908. **Tutor(s):** J R Tanner; C E Graves. **Johnian Relatives:** grandson of William Clarke (1822); nephew of John Clarke (1866); son of Henry Lowther Clarke (1870); father of Denis Lowther Lovell Clarke (1935); grandfather of Jeremy Francis Clarke (1963). **Educ:** Magdalen College School, Oxford; Batley Grammar School. **Career:** Deacon 1905; Curate, Lady Margaret Church (St John's College Mission), Walworth 1905–1907; Priest, Southwark 1906; Curate, Wimbledon 1907–1912; Vicar, All Saints, Nottingham 1912–1923; Army 1918–1919; Honorary CF 1919; Chaplain, HM Prison, Leeds 1923–1924; Vicar, St Bartholomew 1923–1933; Rector, Barwick-in-Elmet, Leeds 1933–1938; Rural Dean, Whitkirk 1938–1944; Archdeacon, Leeds 1940–1950; Vicar, Horsforth, Leeds 1944. Died 4 April 1962.

CLARKE, John Harrison (1912) Born 13 May 1893, 2 Gainsboro House, Lithos Road, Hampstead, Middlesex; son of John Folliott Mostyn Clarke, Civil Engineer, and Mary Foster Barham. BA 1919; MA 1923.

Tutor(s): L H K Bushe-Fox. **Educ:** West Heath School, Hampstead; University College School, Frognal; University Correspondence College, Cambridge. **Career:** Captain, Duke of Cornwall's Light Infantry, WWI (wounded); Schoolmaster, Solihull School; Headmaster, own Preparatory School, Somerset; St Christopher's School, Letchworth until 1958. Died 23 February 1976.

CLARKE, Philip Holmes (1947) Born 5 October 1929, 327 Hasland Road, Chesterfield, Derbyshire; son of Bernard Duchar Clarke, Sales Manager, and Ada Holmes, Tailoress; m Enid Young, 1953; 2 sons, 1 daughter. **Subject(s):** Natural Sciences/Chemical Engineering; BA 1952; MA 1956. **Tutor(s):** G C L Bertram. **Educ:** Hasland Junior School, Chesterfield; Chesterfield Grammar School. **Career:** Boots Pure Drug Company 1953–1954; ICI Ltd 1954–1986.

CLARKE, Captain Robert Shuttleworth (1909) Born 22 April 1890, Marstow, Herefordshire; son of William Shuttleworth Clarke, Clerk in Holy Orders, and Maria Brandram Jones. BA 1912. **Tutor(s):** J R Tanner. **Johnian Relatives:** son of William Shuttleworth Clarke (1870). **Educ:** Malvern College. **Career:** Assistant Master, Golden Parsonage Preparatory School, Hemel Hempstead; Lieutenant, 5th Battalion, King's Shropshire Light Infantry 1914; Captain 1915. Died 25 September 1915 (killed in action).

CLARKE, Roderick Ernest (1900) Born 26 September 1882, 28 Edward Street, Port of Spain, Trinidad; son of Ernest de Radcliffe Clarke, Deputy Registrar, Trinidad Supreme Court, and Louise Lamy. **Tutor(s):** D MacAlister. **Educ:** St Mary's College, Port of Spain, Trinidad.

CLARKE, Roy Rainbird (1932) Born 24 January 1914, 12 St Philip's Road, Norwich; son of William George Clarke, Journalist, and Edith Holden; m Sibyl Hastings Pye, 28 September 1939, Somerset. **Subject(s):** History/Archaeology and Anthropology; BA 1936; MA 1939. **Tutor(s):** E A Benians. **Educ:** King Edward VI School, Norwich. **Career:** Deputy Curator, Norwich Castle Museum; Lecturer and Author on Archaeology; Director of Museums, Norwich. **Awards:** Sizarship, SJC. Died 7 May 1963.

CLARKE, William Edward (1946) Born 13 January 1928, Newcroft, Hillside Crescent, Swansea; son of Daniel Leslie Clarke, Shipping Agent, and Enid Eveline Annie Beynon. **Tutor(s):** J M Wordie. **Educ:** Brynmill Elementary School, Swansea; Terrace Road Elementary School, Swansea; Swansea Grammar School.

CLAXTON, Patrick Fisher (1933) Born 13 March 1915, St Anns, Houndiscombe Villas, Plymouth; son of Ernest William Claxton, Engineer Captain, RN, and Kathleen O'Callaghan Fisher; m Jóna Gudrún Gunnarsdóttir; 2 daughters. **Subject(s):** Modern and Medieval Languages; BA 1936; FCIT. **Tutor(s):** C W Guillebaud. **Educ:** Seafield Park Preparatory School; Sutton Valence School. **Career:** RASC, Junior Officers' Course and RASC Driving School, Feltham 1936–1940; Adjutant 49 Division Column RASC and DAQMG Iceland Forces, attended Staff College, then War Office 1940–1942; GHQ, India 1943–1945; Singapore 1945–1946; WO 1946–1948; British Element Trieste Force 1949–1951; HQ, BAOR 1952–1954; RASC Officers' School 1955–1956; Amphibious Warfare HQ and Persian Gulf 1957–1958; Colonel, WO 1959–1960; Brigadier, WO 1961–1962; DST, BAOR 1963–1965; CTO, BAOR 1965–1966; Commandant, School of Transport, and ADC to the Queen 1966–1968; Transport Officer-in-Chief (Commandant); General Manager, Regular Forces Employment Association 1971–1981; Colonel Commandant, RCT 1972–1980. **Appointments:** General Manager, Regular Forces Employment Association 1971–1981; Governor and Member, Administrative Board, Corps of Commissionaires 1977–1990. **Honours:** OBE 1946; CB 1972. **Publications:** *The Regular Forces Employment Association 1885–1985*, 1985. Died 8 September 2000.

CLAY, Michael Nelson (1942) Born 4 January 1924, Acomb Nursing Home, Harrogate; son of James Harold Clay, Mine Owner, and Ruth Hetta

Nelson. **Tutor(s):** C W Guillebaud. **Johnian Relatives:** half brother of Ralston Nelson Hope Clay (Nelson) (1929). **Educ:** Girls' High School, Skipton; Oatlands Preparatory School, Harrogate; Shrewsbury School.

CLAY, Ralston Nelson Hope (1929) Born 30 May 1911, Cheswall, Nelson, Burnley; son of Alfred John Hope, Cotton Manufacturer, and Ruth Hetta Nelson. BA 1932; MA 1939. **Tutor(s):** J M Wordie. **Johnian Relatives:** half brother of Michael Nelson Clay (1942). **Educ:** Ghyll Royd, Ilkley; The Preparatory School, Sedbergh; The Leys School, Cambridge. Died 24 February 1986.

CLAY, Reginald Eustace (1922) Born 18 December 1898, 35 Quernmore Road, Stroud Green, Hornsey, Middlesex; son of Reginald Stanley Clay, Principal of the Northern Polytechnic, and Theodora Tilly. **Tutor(s):** E Cunningham. **Educ:** Tollington School; Highgate Grammar School; Imperial College of Science.

CLEARY, Denis Mackrow (1927) Born 20 December 1907, 143 Herbert Road, Plumstead, Woolwich, Kent; son of Frank Esmonde Cleary, Clerical Accountant, and Emmeline Marie Mackrow; m Barbara (d 9 February 1960). **Subject(s):** Mathematics; BA 1930; MA 1934. **Tutor(s):** J M Wordie. **Educ:** St Patrick's School, Plumstead; St Ignatius College, London; St Olave's Grammar School. **Career:** Assistant Principal 1931 and 1937, Resident Clerk 1934, India Office; Private Secretary to Permanent Under-Secretary of State 1936–1937; Ministry of Home Security 1940–1944; Assistant Secretary, Foreign Office (German section) 1946–1949; Office of the United Kingdom High Commissioner, India 1949–1951; Head, Western and United Nations Department, Commonwealth Relations Office 1953; British Deputy High Commissioner, Cyprus 1962. **Awards:** Scholarship, SJC 1926. **Honours:** CMG 1967. Died 1997.

CLEAVE, William Paul Oke (1930) Born 2 August 1911, 4 Gordon Road, Clifton, Bristol; son of Paul Rogers Cleave, Clerk in Holy Orders, and Constance Denby Allen. **Subject(s):** Modern and Medieval Languages/Geography; BA 1933; MA 1945. **Tutor(s):** C W Guillebaud. **Johnian Relatives:** son of Paul Rogers Cleave (1884); father of John William Oke Cleave (1957). **Educ:** Gresham's School, Holt. **Career:** Headmaster, St George's School, Windsor. Died 31 October 1977.

CLEGG, Harry James Rowland (1923) Born 15 August 1900, Handforth House, Handforth, Cheshire; son of Alfred Rowland Clegg, Cotton Spinner, and Henrietta Madge Donnell. BA 1924; MA 1928. **Tutor(s):** B F Armitage. **Educ:** Bilton Grange, Rugby; RNC Osborne; RNC Dartmouth. **Career:** Lieutenant Commander, RN. Died 26 January 1947.

CLELAND, Captain John Robert (1907) Born 4 November 1889, No 2, The University, Glasgow; son of Professor John Cleland, Regius Professor of Anatomy, Glasgow, and Ada Marion Spottiswood Balfour. BA 1911; MA 1920. **Tutor(s):** L H K Bushe-Fox. **Educ:** Kelvinside Academy, Glasgow. **Career:** Captain, RFA; Ordained Priest, Liberal Catholic Church 1923; Member, Tutorial Staff, Technological Institute of Great Britain 1948. Died 28 December 1952.

CLEMENT, Thomas Roy (1945) Born 28 February 1928, Howwell, Kirkcudbright; son of Thomas Graeme Clement, Farmer, and Margaret Gray. **Tutor(s):** C W Guillebaud. **Educ:** Kirkcudbright Academy; Belmont House School; Merchiston Castle School.

CLEMENTI, Dennis Montagu (1929) Born 13 January 1909, Malvern Lodge, Malvern Road, Cheltenham; son of John Clementi, Colonel, Indian Army and Augusta Warren Mildred Graham. BA 1931; MA 1946. **Tutor(s):** J M Wordie. **Johnian Relatives:** brother of Kenneth John Clementi (1933). **Educ:** Sherborne School; RMA, Woolwich.

CLEMENTI, Dr Kenneth John (1933) Born 20 February 1915, Malvern Lodge, Malvern Road, Cheltenham; son of John Clementi, Colonel, Indian Army, and Augusta Warren Mildred Graham; m Margaret

Victoria Frederick, 3 July 1970, Calgary, Alberta, Canada. **Subject(s):** Natural Sciences; BA 1936; MA 1969; BChir 1939; DPH (Toronto) 1969; MRCS (Eng); LRCP (London) 1940; MFCM 1970. **Tutor(s):** R L Howland. **Johnian Relatives:** brother of Dennis Montague Clementi (1929). **Educ:** Temple Grove, Eastbourne; Sherborne School. **Career:** Research Scientific Officer, Department of National Defence, Suffield Research Establishment, Alberta, Canada 1951–1956; Family Physician, own Medical Clinic, Milk River, Alberta 1956–1966; Medical Officer of Health, Medicine Hat, Alberta 1966–1984. **Appointments:** Secretary, Westmorland Branch of BMA 1947–1951; Director of Nutrition, Canada Survey for 3 prairie provinces 1970–1972. **Publications:** Various scientific papers. Died 12 October 2003.

CLEMENTS, Clement Lisle (1926) Born 4 November 1907, 9 York Terrace, Preston, Tynemouth, Northumberland; son of William Thomas Clements, Clerk in Holy Orders, and Hild Lisle Bentham. BA 1933; MA 1936. **Tutor(s):** M P Charlesworth. **Johnian Relatives:** son of William Thomas Clements (1894). **Educ:** Lickey Hills School, Rednal, Birmingham; Junior King's School, Canterbury; King's School, Canterbury.

CLEMENTS, Sir John Selby (1929) Born 25 April 1910, 1 Carlton Terrace, Childs Hill, Hendon, Middlesex; son of Herbert William Clements, Barrister-at-Law, and Mary Elizabeth Stevens; m (1) Inga Marca Willemer Ahlgren (div 1946), (2) Kay Hammond (d 1980). **Tutor(s):** E A Benians. **Educ:** St Paul's School, London. **Career:** Actor, first appeared on stage at the Lyric, Hammersmith 1930–1935; Founder, The Intimate Theatre, Palmers Green; West End Roles 1935; Director of plays and founder of a revue company for Entertainments National Service Association 1939–1945; Director, Chichester Festival Theatre 1966–1973; Acting roles in theatre, film and radio including *They Came to a City, Private Lives, Marriage a la Mode, The Beaux Stratagem, Man and Superman, The Rivals, Pygmalion, The Rape of the Belt, The Marriage-go-Round, We Beg to Differ, South Ridings, The Four Weathers, Things to Come, Oh, What a Lovely War,* and *Gandhi.* **Honours:** CBE 1956; Kt 1968. Died 6 April 1988.

CLEMENTSON, Peter George Alfred (1931) Born 21 June 1912, St Peter's Vicarage, Ravenscourt Park, Hammersmith; son of John Schofield Clementson, Clerk in Holy Orders, and Hilda Mary Godfrey. BA 1934; MA 1938. **Tutor(s):** E A Benians. **Johnian Relatives:** son of John Schofield Clementson (1878). **Educ:** Colet Court; Fraebel Institute, London; Belvedere, Hove; Tonbridge School. **Career:** Assistant Master 1935, Headmaster 1938, Terrington Hall, York.

CLEMOW, John (1930) Born 9 November 1911, 8 The Pines, Sheerness East, Sheppey, Minster; son of Joseph Thomas Clemow, Inspector of Shipwrights, and Grace Maud Varney, Nurse; m Ellen Frances Dorothy Hutchins, 1935; 1 daughter (Mary Patricia b 1940). **Subject(s):** Mathematics; BA 1933; MA 1937; CEng; FIEE; CMath; FIMA. **Tutor(s):** J M Wordie. **Educ:** Hyndland Higher Grade School, Glasgow; King's Road School, Rosyth; Senior Boys' School, Sheerness; Borden Grammar School, Sittingbourne; Military College of Science; US Army Fort Bliss, 2nd Guided Missile Course. **Career:** Head, Nuclear Physics Division, SRC; Teacher 1934–1939; Army Service 1939–1957; Colonel, with the honorary rank of Brigadier; RAE 1948–1951; Chief Engineer, Vickers Aircraft (weapons) 1957–1961; Director (Engineering) GEC (Electronics) 1961–1966. **Awards:** Scholarship, SJC 1929; Lefroy Gold Medal, Royal Artillery Institution 1955.

CLEVELAND, James Brian (1943) Born 29 January 1925, 75 Thornton Road, Rusholme, Manchester; son of Sydney Dyson Cleveland, Director, Manchester City Art Galleries, and Helen Plant; m Doreen Bristow, March 1947, Penn Parish Church, Wolverhampton; 1 son (Michael Andrew b 10 March 1956), 1 daughter (Janet Susan b 26 November 1952). **Subject(s):** Economics; BA 1948. **Tutor(s):** C W Guillebaud. **Educ:** Old Moat Lane Elementary School, Manchester; Manchester Grammar School; Stockport Grammar School. **Career:** RAF Navigator

Acting Flight Lieutenant, Empire Air Navigation School 1944–1947; Director, Worsted Division, Tootal Ltd; Managing Director, Bernard Wardle Fabrics Ltd; Managing Director, Merton Printers Co Ltd. **Appointments:** Director, Board, Bernard Wardle & Co Ltd; Director, Board, Vita-tex Co Ltd.

CLEWS, Professor Charles John Birkett (1946) Born 10 June 1912, 118 Brampton Road, East Ham, Essex; son of William Joseph Clews, Commercial Clerk, and Charlotte Birkett. BSc (London) 1932; PhD 1935. **Tutor(s):** J M Wordie. **Educ:** East Ham Technical College; Queen Mary College, University of London. **Career:** Royal Institution 1935–1936; Travelling Student, University of Vienna 1936–1937; Lecturer in Physics, Queen Mary College 1937–1940; Cavendish Laboratory 1940; Research, Ministry of Supply 1940–1941; Experimental Officer, ADRDE 1941–1942; Experimental Officer, Army Operational Research Group 1942–1945; Major, Scientific Intelligence Section, Field Force, in France, Belgium, Holland and Germany 1944–1945; Professor of Physics and Deputy Vice-Chancellor, University of Western Australia 1952.

CLIFF, Arnold Pearse (1910) Born 3 August 1891, 10 Springfield Terrace, Upton, Torquay; son of Albert Stephens Cliff, Tailor's Cutter, and Emma Pearse; m Femina Louise Rosenstein, 21 March 1956, London. **Subject(s):** Natural Sciences/Agriculture; BA 1913; LLB 1913. **Tutor(s):** L H K Bushe-Fox. **Educ:** Wollaston Road School, Stourbridge; King Edward VI Grammar School, Stourbridge. **Career:** Deputy Director of Agriculture, Bihar, India 1920; Secretary, Indian Central Jute Committee 1936. Died 27 January 1983.

CLIFFORD, Dudley Ronald (1947) Born 12 October 1926, 25 Park Place East, Sunderland; son of Charles Richard Clifford, Clerk, London and North Eastern Railway, and Bessie Brooks. **Subject(s):** Oriental Languages; BA 1949; MA 1959. **Educ:** Arthur Pease School, Darlington; Darlington Grammar School; Durham Choristers' School; Durham School. **Career:** Lieutenant, Intelligence Corps, HQ Malaya Command 1944–1947; Chinese Affairs, Malayan Civil Service 1951–1958; Education and Training Officer, John Bull Rubber Co, Leicester 1958–1960; Nyasaland Government Service 1961–1963; Northern Ireland Youth Employment Service Board 1964–1966. Appointments and Careers Advisory Officer, Queen's University, Belfast 1966–1986. **Awards:** Baker Exhibition, SJC 1944.

CLIFTON, Henry Tilden (1946) Born 24 September 1924, Grovebury Crossing, Grovebury Road, Leighton Buzzard, Bedfordshire; son of Henry Tilden Clifton and Annie Emma Crouch; m Pamela Mary Damment, 30 December 1947; 3 sons (David, Andrew and Nigel), 2 daughters (Susan and Judith). **Subject(s):** History; BA 1948; MA 1966. **Tutor(s):** F Thistlethwaite. **Educ:** Beaudesert Infants School, Leighton Buzzard; Pulford Junior School, Leighton Buzzard; Beaudesert Senior School; The Cedars School, Leighton Buzzard. **Career:** RN 1942–1946 (Commissioned 1943); postings in Portugal, Mexico, Chile, Canada, and India, J & P Coats Ltd; London Business School 1971; Manufacturing Manager, J & P Coats Ltd, Glasgow 1971–1979; Deputy Managing Director, Madura Coats, India 1980–1983.

CLISSOLD, The Revd William (1903) Born 7 September 1882, Rockness, Horsley, Stroud, Gloucestershire; son of Joseph Clissold, Brewer and Maltster, and Matilda Jane King. **Subject(s):** History; BA 1906. **Tutor(s):** D MacAlister. **Educ:** Wycliffe College. **Career:** Ordained Deacon 1907; Curate, St Nicholas, Birmingham 1907–1909; Ordained Priest 1908; Curate, St Barnabas, Balsall Heath 1909–1911; Curate, Lapworth 1911–1912; Curate, Verwod 1912–1915; Curate, St Faith's Mission, Rusape, South Rhodesia 1916–1922; Director, St Paul's Mission, Molepolole, Kimberley 1922–1928; Priest in Charge, Korogwe, Tanganyika 1930–1932; Archdeacon 1931–1932; Rector, St Margaret's River, Western Australia 1933–1939; SPG Deputation 1936–1938; Curate, St Filan, Kilmacolm, with St Mary, Bridge of Weir, Renfrewshire 1940–1941; Curate, St Mary's Cathedral, Glasgow 1941–1942; Vicar,

St Luke's, Holbeach Hurn, Lincolnshire 1945–1947; St Peter's Grange, St Leonards on Sea 1947–1949. Died 23 January 1949.

CLOSE, Professor Hubert Michael (1933) Born 22 December 1914, 18 Sneath Avenue, Golders Green; son of Hubert John Close, Chartered Surveyor, Inland Revenue, and Louise Drysdale Ellis; 1 son (Sahar Gul, adopted). **Subject(s):** History/English; BA 1936; MA 1945. **Tutor(s):** E A Benians. **Educ:** University College School, Hampstead. **Career:** Teacher, St Stephen's College, Delhi 1937–1940; Commissioned, Indian Army 1940–1946; English Teacher, Islamia College, Peshawar 1947–1977; Reader in English, University of Peshawar, Pakistan 1963; Teacher, Edwardes College, Peshawar 1977–1996. **Awards:** Third Year Essay Prize, SJC 1936; Sitara-I Imtiaz (Star of Pakistan), 1980. **Honours:** MC 1945; OBE 1983. **Publications:** *A Pathan Company*, National Book Foundation, Pakistan, 1994; *Attlee, Wavell, Mountbatten and the Transfer of Power*, National Book Foundation Pakistan, 1997; 'An Essay on Wavell'. Died 18 October 1999.

CLOTHIER, Peter Thompson (1928) Born 28 March 1910, Leigh Holt Street, Somerset; son of Samuel Thompson Clothier, Architect, and Esther Bright Clark. **Tutor(s):** E A Benians. **Educ:** Elmhurst County School, Street; Leighton Park School, Reading.

CLOUGH, Thomas (1906) Born 16 October 1887, 14 Brookville Road, Fulham, Middlesex; son of Thomas Clough, Artist and Designer, and Elizabeth Williams. **Subject(s):** Mathematics/Natural Sciences; BA 1909. **Tutor(s):** L H K Bushe-Fox. **Educ:** Latymer Upper School. **Career:** Indian Civil Service, Eastern Bengal and Assam 1911; Captain, IARO, attached 21st Cavalry, WWI. **Awards:** Bhaonagar Medal, University of Cambridge 1911.

CLOUTS, Philip (1911) Born 28 June 1890, 13 Hamilton Street, Inverness, Scotland; son of Louis Clouts, Merchant, and Dora Pickleman. **Subject(s):** Law; BA 1914; LLB 1914. **Tutor(s):** L H K Bushe-Fox. **Educ:** South African College School; South African College, Cape Town. **Career:** Called to the Bar, Inner Temple 1915.

CLOW, Sir Andrew Gourlay (1909) Born 29 April 1890, 8 Alford Place, Aberdeen; son of William McCallum Clow, Minister, Free Church of Scotland, and Annie Morton Loudon; m Ariadne Mavis Dunderdale, 3 June 1925, St John's Church, Newbury; 1 daughter. **Subject(s):** Mathematics; BA 1912; MA 1924. **Tutor(s):** L H K Bushe-Fox. **Educ:** Merchiston Castle School, Edinburgh. **Career:** Indian Civil Service 1913; Assistant Magistrate and Collector, United Provinces 1914; Assistant Record Officer and Assistant Settlement Officer 1917; Deputy Commissioner (Provincial) and Settlement Officer 1918–1919; Controller, Labour Bureau, Government of India, Delhi 1920; Under-Secretary 1923, Deputy Secretary 1924, Secretary 1928, Department of Industries, Government of India; Joint Secretary 1931, Secretary 1935–1938, Department of Industry and Labour; Last British Governor of Assam 1942–1947; Governor of Bombay 1946. **Appointments:** Member, Hunter Commission, investigating disturbances in the Punjab 1919; Adviser and Substitute Delegate, International Labour Conference, Geneva 1919; Member, Royal Commission on Labour in India 1929–1931; Member for Communications, Viceroy's Executive Council 1938–1942; UK Representative on UN Commission for Asia and the Far East 1947–1948; Chairman, Scottish Gas Board 1949–1956. **Awards:** Scholarship, SJC. **Honours:** CIE 1928; CSI 1935; Kt 1939; KCSI 1941. Died 31 December 1957.

COAD, Claude Norman (1902) Born 13 April 1884, Ebury Road, Batley, Yorkshire; son of George Chapman Coad, Wesleyan Minister, and Mary Ann Baines; m Florence. **Subject(s):** Natural Sciences; BA 1905; MA 1911; BChir 1910; MB 1910; MRCS; LRCP 1908. **Tutor(s):** D MacAlister. **Educ:** Tettenhall College; University College, Nottingham. **Career:** Deputy Commissioner of Medical Services, Ministry of Pensions; Captain, RAMC 1917. **Honours:** MC with Bar 1919. Died 19 August 1938.

COATES, David Wilson (1904) Born 11 April 1886, 35 Sibella Road, Clapham, Surrey; son of Fletcher Coates, Warehouseman, and Sarah Ann Wilson Boyes; m Mabel Rose Goodley, 1913; 3 sons (Peter, Alan and Michael), 2 daughters (Diana and Pamela). **Subject(s):** Law; BA 1907; MA 1911; LLB 1907. **Tutor(s):** C E Graves; J R Tanner. **Johnian Relatives:** father of Peter John Hurst Coates (1932) and of Michael Antony Wilson Coates (1940). **Educ:** Wycliffe College, Stonehouse. **Career:** Partner in Firm, Elles, Salaman, Coates and Co, Chartered Accountants; Chief Accountant, Coal Mines Department, Board of Trade 1917; Chief Accountant, Central Electricity Board 1927–1951; Finance Director, Coal Division, Ministry of Fuel and Power 1942–1943. **Appointments:** Member, Land Fertility Committee 1939–1941. **Honours:** CBE 1918. Died 5 August 1968.

COATES, Michael Antony Wilson (1940) Born 4 August 1922, Stirt Lodge, Bishop's Stortford, Hertfordshire; son of David Wilson Coates, Chartered Accountant, and Mabel Rose Goodley. **Subject(s):** Economics; BA 1943. **Tutor(s):** C W Guillebaud. **Johnian Relatives:** son of David Wilson Coates (1904); brother of Peter John Hurst Coates (1932). **Educ:** Dane Hall Preparatory School, Bishop's Stortford; Bishop's Stortford College Preparatory School; Lendrick School, Teignmouth; Radley College.

COATES, Peter John Hurst (1932) Born 2 February 1914, 6 Grosvenor Avenue, Carshalton; son of David Wilson Coates, Chartered Accountant, and Mabel Rose Goodley. **Tutor(s):** E A Benians. **Johnian Relatives:** son of David Wilson Coates (1904); brother of Michael Antony Wilson Coates (1940). **Educ:** Chantry Mount, Bishop's Stortford; Bishop's Stortford College; Wycliffe College, Stonehouse.

COBB, The Revd Peter Graham (1945) Born 17 June 1927, 25 Grove Road, Wimborne, Dorset; son of George Frank Cobb, Mineral Water Maker, and Leonora Evans; m Sian Mansel Thomas, 1963; 1 son (Matthew b 1970), 2 daughters (Joanna b 1964 and Sarah b 1965). **Subject(s):** Geography; BA 1948; MA 1952; Cambridge Certificate of Theology 1967. **Tutor(s):** J M Wordie. **Educ:** Winton and Moordown Council School; Bournemouth Secondary School. **Career:** Housemaster, Cowbridge Grammar School 1949–1966; Ordained Deacon 1968; Assistant Curate, Barry 1968–1971; Ordained Priest 1969; Inspector of Church Schools, Llandaff Diocese 1969–1981; Vicar, Penmark, with Porthkerry 1972–1981; Vicar, Magor & Redwick with Undy, Diocese of Monmouth 1982–1995. **Appointments:** Member, Ridley Hall, Cambridge. **Awards:** Exhibition, SJC 1945; Wright's Prize, SJC 1946. **Publications:** *At Cowbridge Grammar School 1949–1966*, Brown, Cowbridge; Music for String Groups, Piano Quintet, Voice and Piano, Voice and String Quartet, Monmouth Publishing.

COBBOLD, Robert Henry Wanklyn (1912) Born 3 December 1892, Earls Barton, Northamptonshire; son of Robert Russell Cobbold, Clerk in Holy Orders, and Mary Elizabeth Wanklyn. **Subject(s):** Classics. **Tutor(s):** E E Sikes. **Educ:** King's Choir School, Cambridge; Marlborough College. **Career:** Second Lieutenant, then Lieutenant, 6th Battalion, attached 2nd Battalion, Rifle Brigade 1914–1915. **Awards:** Foundation and Junior Scholarships, Marlborough College; Entrance Scholarship, SJC 1911. Died 9 September 1915 (killed in action at Fleurbaix, Flanders).

COBURN, Donald (1942) Born 16 June 1923, 1 Queens Road, Sudbury, Suffolk; son of Sidney Thomas Coburn, Engineer's Merchant, and Ellen Rosina Freeman; m Marjorie Northcott, 5 September 1947, Sydney Cathedral. BA 1945; MA 1948. **Tutor(s):** S J Bailey. **Educ:** East Finchley Grammar School; Pinner Park School; University College School.

COCHRAN, Professor William Gemmell (1931) Born 15 July 1909, 19 Belmont Drive, Rutherglen, Scotland; son of Thomas Cochran, Mineral Agent, London, Midland & Scottish Railway, and Jean Willock Gemmell. **Subject(s):** Mathematics; BA 1934; MA 1938; MA (Glasgow) 1931; Honorary Doctor of Laws (Johns Hopkins University) 1975. **Tutor(s):**

J M Wordie. **Educ:** Central Higher Grade School, Gourock; The High School, Glasgow; The University, Glasgow. **Career:** Statistician, Rothamsted Experimental Station 1934–1939; Professor of Mathematical Statistics, Iowa State College 1939–1946; Associate Director, Institute of Statistics, University of North Carolina 1946–1948; Professor of Biostatistics, School of Hygiene, Johns Hopkins University 1948–1957; Professor of Statistics, Harvard University 1957. **Appointments:** Member, American Academy of Arts and Sciences; Member, National Academy of Science. Died 29 March 1980.

COCHRANE, Robert Hope (1945) Born 7 April 1918, Funes, Rosario de Santa Fe, Argentina; son of James Cochrane, Engineer, and Georgina Taylor. BA 1948; MA 1952. **Educ:** Private Tutor, Argentina; City and Guilds College, South Kensington. **Career:** Apprentice, Central Argentine Railway 1934–1938; Sergeant Pilot, RAFVR 1940–1945. Died 1 February 1993.

COCKAYNE, Alan Harry (1943) Born 3 July 1925, 17 Chestnut Street, Gorton, Manchester; son of Harry Cockayne, Railway Clerk, LNER, and Annie Greensmith. **Subject(s):** Mathematics/Natural Sciences; BA 1946; MA 1950. **Tutor(s):** S J Bailey. **Educ:** Varna Street Elementary School; Manchester Grammar School. **Career:** Computer Manager. **Awards:** Townsend Scholarship, SJC 1942.

COCKBURN, Ian George Colin (1939) Born 28 April 1920, 22 North Grange Road, Leeds; son of Edward Colin Cockburn, Engineer, and Ivy Alice Fraser. **Subject(s):** Law; BA 1947; MA 1950. **Tutor(s):** J S Boys Smith. **Educ:** Moorlands School, Leeds; Oundle School. **Career:** Lieutenant, KOYLI 1939–1945; Served articles with Morrish and Company, Leeds; Solicitor, Simpson, Curtis & Company 1950–1952. Died 10 January 1952.

COCKBURN, William Derrick (1948) Born 17 January 1928, 27 Brighton Grove, Newcastle upon Tyne; son of William Huntley Cockburn, Insurance Agent, and Florence May Heron; m Gillian Pardoe, 11 June 1955, Southgate, London; 1 son (Richard b 27 April 1957, d 4 February 1992). **Subject(s):** History; BA 1950; MA 1955. **Tutor(s):** F Thistlethwaite. **Educ:** Westgate Hill Council School; Royal Grammar School, Newcastle upon Tyne.

COCKCROFT, Professor Sir John Douglas (1922) Born 27 May 1897, 154 Halifax Road, Langfield, Todmorden, Lancashire; son of John Arthur Cockcroft, Cotton and Linen Manufacturer, and Annie Maude Fielden; m Eunice Elizabeth Crabtree, 1925; 2 sons (John Haslam b 19 January 1927, d 11 October 1929 and Christopher b 14 January 1942); 4 daughters (Joan Dorothea b 5 October 1932, Jocelyn b 1 September 1934, Elisabeth Fielden b 23 March 1936 and Catherine Helena b 17 October 1941). **Subject(s):** Mathematics; BA 1924; MA 1928; PhD 1928; BSc (Manchester College of Technology); over 20 Honorary Degrees, including Honorary LLD (St Andrews) 1955; Honorary Degree (Coimbra University, Portugal); FRS 1936. **Tutor(s):** E Cunningham. **Johnian Relatives:** uncle of John Hoyle Cockcroft (1955), John Anthony Eric Cockcroft (1956) and of Robert Cockcroft (1958); father of Christopher Hugh John Cockcroft (1961); uncle of Frank Laurence Cockcroft (1962). **Educ:** Todmorden Elementary Schools; Todmorden Grammar School; Manchester University; Manchester College of Technology (now UMIST). **Career:** Royal Field Artillery, WWI; College Apprentice, Metropolitan-Vickers 1920–1922; Demonstrator in Physics 1929–1935, Lecturer in Physics 1935–1939, University of Cambridge; Title B Fellow, SJC 1933–1939; Chief Superintendent, Ministry of Supply Air Defence Research and Development Establishment 1939; Title C Fellow, SJC 1939–1946; Jacksonian Professor of Natural Philosophy, University of Cambridge 1939–1946; Assistant Director of Research, Ministry of Supply 1941–1944; Director, Atomic Energy Division, National Research Council of Canada, Montreal and Canadian Research Plant, Chalk River 1944–1946; Director, AERE, Harwell 1946–1958; Chairman, Defence Research Policy Committee 1952; First Master, Churchill College

1959–1967; President, Manchester College of Science and Technology (now UMIST) 1961; Chancellor, ANU, Canberra 1961–1965. **Appointments:** Supervisor in Mechanical Sciences 1929–1938, Supervisor in Physics 1931–1940, Junior Bursar 1933–1939, Honorary Fellow 1946–1967, SJC; Secretary, Department of Scientific and Industrial Research; President, Physical Society 1961–1962; President, British Association for the Advancement of Science 1961–1963; President, Institute of Physics; President, European Atomic Energy Society; President, Pugwash Conference. **Awards:** Sizarship, SJC; Hoare Exhibition 1922; Clerk Maxwell Scholarship 1926; Hopkins Prize, Cambridge Philosophical Society 1946; Nobel Prize 1951; Royal Medal of the Royal Society 1954; Kelvin Gold Medal 1956; Hughes Medal, Royal Society; Faraday Medal, Institution of Electrical Engineers; James Alfred Ewing Medal, Institution of Civil Engineers; Austrian Wilhelm Exner Medal 1961; Atoms-for-Peace Award 1961; US Medal of Freedom. **Honours:** CBE 1944; Kt 1948; Chevalier of the Legion of Honour 1950; KCB 1953; OM 1957. Died 18 September 1967.

COCKER, Thomas Bernard (1916) Born 12 May 1898, 29 King Street, Royton, Lancashire; son of Alphonso Cocker, Grocer, and Cicely Annie Mellor. **Subject(s):** Law/Classics; BA 1920; MA 1926; LLB 1921. **Tutor(s):** E E Sikes. **Educ:** Wesleyan Day School, Royton; Byron Street Council School, Royton; Hulme Grammar School. **Career:** Eastern Cadetship 1921; Police Magistrate and Deputy Registrar, Supreme Court, Singapore.

COCKERTON, John Penn (1931) Born 15 July 1912, The Butts, Bakewell, Derbyshire; son of Vernon Reilly Cockerton, Solicitor, and Edith Augusta Taylor. **Tutor(s):** J M Wordie. **Johnian Relatives:** grandson of John Cockerton (1826). **Educ:** The Preparatory School, Oakfield; Rugby School. Died 12 May 1944.

COFFEY, Dr Michael (1947) Born 30 May 1926, Ilkeston, Derbyshire; son of James Coffey, Schoolmaster, and Rose Lydia Swain; m Brigitte Stadelmann, 28 July 1962; 2 daughters (Margaret b 1964 and Monica b 1966). **Subject(s):** Classics; BA 1949; MA 1953; PhD 1954; BA (Manchester) 1947. **Tutor(s):** R L Howland. **Educ:** St Mary's Roman Catholic School, Horwich; Catholic College, Preston; Manchester University. **Career:** Assistant Lecturer, Department of Latin 1951–1954, Lecturer 1954–1967, Senior Lecturer 1967–1976, Acting Head of Department 1977–1978, Reader in Greek and Latin 1977–1991, Honorary Research Fellow in Latin and Greek 1991–, UCL. **Publications:** *Roman Satire*, 1989; (with Roland Mayer) *Seneca Phaedra*, Cambridge, 1990.

COGGAN, Rt Revd the Rt Hon Lord (Frederick) Donald (1928) Born 9 October 1909, 32 Croftdown Road, St Pancras, London; son of Cornish Arthur Coggan, Company Director and Company Secretary, and Fannie Sarah Chubb; m Jean Braithwaite Strain, 1935; 2 daughters (Ann b 1938 and Ruth b 1940). **Subject(s):** Oriental Languages; BA 1931; MA 1935; BD (Wycliffe College, Toronto) 1941; Honorary DD (Wycliffe College, Toronto) 1944; DD (Lambeth) 1957; Honorary DD (Leeds) 1958; Honorary DD (Cantab) 1962; Honorary DD (Aberdeen, Tokyo, Saskatoon, Huron, Hull) 1963; HHD (Princeton) 1966; Honorary DLitt (Lancaster) 1967; Honorary STD (General Theology Seminary, NY) 1967; Honorary DD (Manchester) 1972; Honorary LLD (Liverpool) 1972; Honorary DCL (Kent) 1975; DUniv (York) 1975; Honorary DD (Moravian Theology Seminary) 1976; Honorary DD (Virginia Theology Seminary) 1979. **Tutor(s):** M P Charlesworth; E A Benians. **Johnian Relatives:** uncle of Geoffrey Vaughan Argyle (1947). **Educ:** Merchant Taylors' School, London; Wycliffe Hall, Oxford. **Career:** Assistant Lecturer in Semitic Languages and Literature, University of Manchester 1931–1934; Ordained Deacon 1934; Curate, St Mary Islington 1934–1937; Ordained Priest 1935; Professor of New Testament, Wycliffe College, Toronto 1937–1944; Principal, London College of Divinity 1944–1956; Bishop of Bradford 1956–1961; Archbishop of York 1961–1974; Archbishop of Canterbury 1974–1980. **Appointments:** Chairman, Liturgical Commission 1960–1964; Honorary Fellow, SJC 1961–2000; Pro-Chancellor, York University

1962–1974; President, Society for Old Testament Study 1967–1968; Prelate, Order of St John of Jerusalem 1967–1990; Pro-Chancellor, Hull University 1968–1974; FKC 1975; Honorary Freeman, City of Canterbury 1976; First Life President, Church Army 1981. **Awards:** Exhibition, SJC 1927; John Stewart of Rannoch Scholarship in Hebrew, University of Cambridge 1928; Jeremie Septuagint Prize 1931; Naden Studentship 1931; First Tyrwhitt Hebrew Scholarship, University of Cambridge 1932; Mason Prize, University of Cambridge 1932. **Honours:** PC 1961; Royal Victorian Chain 1980; Baron (Life Peer) 1980. **Publications:** *A People's Heritage*, 1944; *The Ministry of the Word*, 1945; *The Glory of God*, 1950; *Stewards of Grace*, 1958; *Five Makers of the New Testament*, 1962; *Christian Priorities*, 1963; *The Prayers of the New Testament*, 1967; *Sinews of Faith*, 1969; *Word and World*, 1971; *Convictions*, 1975; *On Preaching*, 1978; *The Heart of the Christian Faith*, 1978; *The Name above All Names*, 1981; *Sure Foundation*, 1981; *Mission to the World*, 1982; *Paul: Portrait of a Revolutionary*, 1984; *The Sacrament of the Word*, 1987; *Cuthbert Bardsley: Bishop, Evangelist, Pastor*, 1989; *God of Hope*, 1991; *Voice From the Cross*, 1993; *The Servant-son*, 1995; *Meet Paul*, 1998; contributions to *Theology*, etc. Died 17 May 2000.

COGGIN, Maurice Edward Henry (1910) Born 11 October 1892, The Vicarage, Lemsford, Hatfield, Hertfordshire; son of Frederick Ernest Coggin, Clerk in Holy Orders, and Clara Lloyd. BA 1914; MA 1920. **Tutor(s):** E E Sikes. **Educ:** Woodlands Preparatory School, Folkestone; Winchester College; Eastbourne College.

COHEN, Jacob (1928) Born 8 February 1908, 23 Fieldgate Street, Whitechapel, London; son of Aaron Cohen, Master Cabinet Maker, and Betsy Eigenstein. **Subject(s):** Mathematics; BA 1930. **Tutor(s):** J M Wordie. **Educ:** Myrdle Street County Schools; Central Foundation School; East London College. **Awards:** Exhibition, SJC 1927. Died 15 March 1996.

COHEN, Leon Gaston (1919) Born 8 February 1901, Alexandria, Egypt; son of Samuel Judah Cohen, Cotton Shipper to Egypt, and Esther Schouschana. **Tutor(s):** E E Sikes. **Educ:** South Manchester School; Clifton College.

COLBY, John Bothway (1927) Born 17 December 1907, 331 London Road, Lowestoft, Suffolk; son of Joseph John Colby, Owner of Fishing Fleet, and Alice Mary Bothway. **Subject(s):** History; BA 1930. **Tutor(s):** E A Benians. **Educ:** Preparatory School, Shipmeadow; St Paul's School, London.

COLCHESTER, John Raymond Chotzner (1927) See CHOTZNER.

COLDWELL, Alan (1940) Born 15 December 1922, Kylemore, 34 Bradshaw Road, Honley, Huddersfield; son of John Coldwell, Master motor body builder, and Nelsie Gill. **Subject(s):** History; BA 1943. **Tutor(s):** C W Guillebaud. **Educ:** Honley National School; Holme Valley Grammar School.

COLE, Dr Brian Wilson (1946) Born 25 July 1928, 24 3rd Avenue, Melville, Johannesburg, South Africa; son of Henry John Cole, Gold Miner, and Dora Mary Wilson; m Margaret (d 1994); 2 sons, 1 daughter. **Subject(s):** Natural Sciences; BA 1949; MA 1953; MRCS; LRCP. **Tutor(s):** G C L Bertram. **Educ:** Church of England School, Driffield; Bridlington School. **Career:** GP, Bradford.

COLE, Geoffrey Alfred (1920) Born 19 July 1902, Westlecott Road, Swindon, Wiltshire; son of Samuel Barrett Cole, Outfitter, and Annie Gammon; m Edith Monica; 1 son (Brian), 1 daughter (Susan), 1 stepson (James), 1 stepdaughter (Anne). BA 1923; MA 1930. **Tutor(s):** B F Armitage. **Educ:** Wychwood, Bournemouth; Leighton Park School, Reading. Died 15 February 1973.

COLE, Geoffrey Bruce (1919) Born 12 October 1900, Claremont, Westbury on Trym, Bristol; son of Caleb Bruce Cole, Chocolate Manufacturer, and Edith Emily Shove. **Tutor(s):** E E Sikes. **Educ:** Harrow School; Private Tuition, Darnford, Swanage. Died 3 July 1963.

COLE, James Humphrey (1909) Born 22 January 1891, Brundall, Norwich; son of Herbert Henchman Cole, Solicitor, and Amy Gertrude Green. **Subject(s):** Mathematics; BA 1912. **Tutor(s):** L H K Bushe-Fox. **Educ:** King Edward VI Middle School, Norwich; Gresham's School, Holt. **Career:** Director, Geodetic Survey, Egypt 1943.

COLE, Kenneth Edward (1947) Born 12 April 1927, 24 Connaught Gardens, Muswell Hill, London; son of Edward Joseph Cole, Schoolmaster, and Florence Ellen Jenkins. **Tutor(s):** G C L Bertram. **Educ:** Highgate Junior School; Highgate School.

COLE, Ralph Turney (1903) Born 24 November 1884, Willow Bank, Paignton, Devon; son of Ralph Henry Cole, Gentleman, and Margaret Thomson. BA 1906. **Tutor(s):** D MacAlister. **Educ:** Plymouth and Mannamead College.

COLE, Reginald Alexander Lister (1919) Born 15 April 1898, Wing, Leighton Buzzard, Buckinghamshire; son of Alexander Barnett Farquharson Cole, Clerk in Holy Orders, and Edith Mary Lister; m Olive Elizabeth Russ, 29 March 1929, Middlesex; 1 son (John Alexander b 12 May 1931), 1 daughter (Daphne Olive b 15 April 1933). **Subject(s):** Mathematics/Natural Sciences; BA 1922. **Tutor(s):** E E Sikes. **Johnian Relatives:** son of Alexander Barnett Farquharson Cole (1888); grandfather of Andrew Timothy Cole (1976). **Educ:** St Michael's College, Tenbury; Bedford School. **Career:** Second Lieutenant, Signals Detachment, RE, France 1917–1919; Standard Telephones and Cables Ltd 1922–1963, including secondments to Chicago (with Parent Company IT&T), and Austria early 1920s; development of thermionic valves, North Woolwich 1930s, Ilminster 1940–1945; Head, Development Laboratory, Ilminster, post war; Managerial posts, Paignton, late 1950s–1963. **Awards:** Scholarship, SJC 1916. **Publications:** (with D P Dalzell) 'The hydrogen filled iron wire ballast lamp', *Electrical Communication*, October 1939; 'General principles of valve-crate design', *Electrical Communication*, September 1946. Died 13 August 1985.

COLE, Robert Templeman (1937) Born 14 December 1918, 20 Walpole Street, London; son of Percival Pasley Cole, Surgeon, and Amy Gladys Templeman; m Elspeth Alison Lydford Lawson 18 October 1947. BA 1940; MA 1944. **Tutor(s):** J S Boys Smith. **Educ:** Northwood Preparatory School; Harrow School. **Career:** Chairman, Conder Group plc.

COLE, William Arthur Stewart (1925) Born 21 May 1906, Banham, Attleborough, Norfolk; son of Frederick George Cole, Headmaster, Thetford Grammar School, and Elsie Margaret Wheeler. **Subject(s):** Geography/History; BA 1928. **Tutor(s):** E A Benians. **Johnian Relatives:** son of Frederick George Cole (1884). **Educ:** Thetford Grammar School. Died 16 November 1981.

COLE, Dr William Frederick (1946) Born 26 July 1917, Narrogin, Western Australia; son of Henry Francis Herbert Cole, Schoolmaster, and Muriel Anne Duffin. PhD 1949; BSc (UWA) 1938; MSc (UWA) 1940; DSc (UWA) 1969. **Tutor(s):** J M Wordie. **Educ:** Narrogin State School; Albany High School; University of Western Australia. **Career:** Radium Officer, Radon Laboratory, University of Western Australia 1941; Physicist, Munitions Supply Laboratories, Maribyrnong 1942–1946; Research Physicist, CSIRO Division Building Research 1949–1982; Research Fellow 1982–1984. **Awards:** Hackett Research Studentship 1946. **Publications:** (with J Shearer) 'Analysis of soil colloids by x-ray diffraction methods', *Royal Society of Western Australia Journal*, 1939–1940; (with J Shearer) 'X-ray analysis of some Tasmanian soil colloids', *Royal Society of Western Australia Journal*, 1939–1940; (with C S Gloe) 'The geology and physiography of the Malkup area', *Royal Society of Western Australia Journal*, 1939–1940; 'Results of a microscopic study of some soil colloids', *Royal Society of Western Australia Journal*, 1940–1941; 'X-ray analysis (by the powder method) and microscopic examination of the products of weathering of the Gingin Upper Greensandied', *Royal Society of Western Australia Journal*,

1940–1941; (with R T Prider) 'The alteration products of olivine and leucite in the leucite-lamproites from the West Kimberley area, Western Australia', *American Mineralogist*, 1942.

COLEGRAVE, Edward Henry Manby (1921) Naval Officer.

COLEMAN, Dr Francis Hayling (1927) Born 3 June 1908, Slade Hill, Wolverhampton, Staffordshire; son of Edward Hayling Coleman, Medical Practitioner, and Norah Winifred Clark Peel; 2 sons, 1 daughter. **Subject(s):** Natural Sciences; BA 1930; MA 1935; MB 1935; BChir 1935; MD 1944; MRCS 1933; MRCP 1936; LRCP 1933. **Tutor(s):** M P Charlesworth. **Johnian Relatives:** son of Edward Hayling Coleman (1891). **Educ:** Tettenhall College, Staffordshire; Oakfield, Rugby; Rugby School. **Career:** Wing Commander, RAFVR, WWII; GP. Died 23 February 1965.

COLEMAN, Canon Noel Dolben (1910) Born 11 December 1891, Bingham, Nottinghamshire; son of William Frederick Coleman, Clerk, and Phoebe Coleman; m Dorothy Margaret Charlotte Bobart, 31 May 1918; 2 daughters. **Subject(s):** Theology; BA 1913; MA 1917; MA (Durham) 1920. **Tutor(s):** L H K Bushe-Fox. **Educ:** Bingham National School; Brunt's Technical School, Mansfield; Minster Grammar School, Southwell; Wells Theological College. **Career:** Deacon 1915; Curate, Alfreton 1915–1916; Priest 1916; Curate, St Werburgh, Derby 1916–1918; Temporary CF, Palestine 1918–1919; Curate, Matlock 1919–1920; Honorary CF 1920; Lecturer in Theology and Hellenistic Greek, University of Durham 1920–1944; Chaplain, University College, Durham 1924–1944; Dean of Theology, Durham 1933–1934. **Appointments:** Examining Chaplain to the Bishop of Bradford 1931; Chairman, General Board of Faculties, Durham 1934–1935; Honorary Canon of St Sitha, Bradford Cathedral 1936; Member of Senate, Durham University 1938–1944; Editorial and Translation Superintendent, British and Foreign Bible Society 1944. **Awards:** Foundation Scholarship, SJC. **Publications:** (Contributor) *New Commentary on Holy Scripture*, Gore, 1928. Died 13 May 1948.

COLES, John Patrick (1947) Born 15 March 1926, The Parsonage, Sandycroft, Chester; son of Douglas Frederick Coles, Clerk in Holy Orders, and Margaret Pidgeon. **Subject(s):** Mathematics/Economics; BA 1948; MA 1953. **Tutor(s):** J M Wordie. **Educ:** Dane Court Preparatory School, Pyrford; St John's School, Leatherhead. **Career:** Headmaster, Royal Liberty School, Romford 1963–1989.

COLES, The Revd Victor John Hulbert (1909) Born 1 January 1891, Upton Lovell, Heytesbury, Wiltshire; son of Robert John Hulbert Coles, Gentleman, and Eleanor Mabel Read; m Cicely Gwladys Glover, 21 April 1914. **Subject(s):** Classics; BA 1912; MA 1916. **Tutor(s):** E E Sikes. **Educ:** Lord Weymouth's Grammar School, Warminster; Bedford Grammar School; Bishop's Hostel, Liverpool. **Career:** Deacon 1914; Curate, St Bridget, Wavertree 1914–1916; Priest 1915; Curate, Lancaster 1916–1920; Vicar, Dolphinholme 1920–1923; Curate in Charge, St Luke's Coventional District, Slyne with Hest 1933–1935; Vicar, St Luke's Coventional District, Slyne with Hest 1935–1943; Vicar, Podington with Farndish, Northamptonshire 1943. **Publications:** 'Greek verse', *The Eagle*, 33.

COLL Y SERNA, Charles Arthur (1926) Born 16 March 1907, Mendoza, Argentine Republic, South America; son of Arthur Coll y Serna, Engineer, and Sofia Benigas. **Subject(s):** Economics; BA 1929. **Tutor(s):** C W Guillebaud. **Educ:** Collegio de la Salle, Buenos Aires; Institut Vogt, St Gallen, Switzerland; Lyceum Alpinum, Zuorz, Switzerland.

COLLEY, David Bayley (1921) Naval Officer.

COLLIER, Frank Kenneth Gerald (1928) Born 24 March 1910, 58 Upper Richmond Road, Mortlake, Surrey; son of Frank Jackson Collier, Civil Engineer, and Mary Gladys Humphreys; m Gwendoline Halford, 1938; 2 sons. **Subject(s):** Natural Sciences (Geology); BA 1931; MA 1935;

DipEd (Oxon) 1945; FSRHE 1993. **Tutor(s):** C W Guillebaud. **Educ:** St Albans School, Lyme Regis; Aldenham School, Elstree. **Career:** Technical Translator, Stockholm 1931–1932; Schoolmaster 1933–1941; Royal Ordnance Factories 1941–1944; Physics Master, Lancing College 1944–1949; Lecturer, St Luke's College, Exeter 1949–1959; Principal, Bede College, University of Durham 1959–1975. **Appointments:** Editor, Education for Teaching 1953–1958; Fulbright Tour of Universities in USA 1963; Chairman, Association of Teachers in Colleges and Departments of Education 1964–1965; Visiting Professor of Education, Temple University, Philadelphia 1965, 1968; Consultant to Council for Educational Technology 1971–1980; British Council Tours (India, Brazil and Portugal) 1976–1979; Honorary Research Fellow, UEA 1978–1981; Lecture tours, USA, 1979, 1990; Study Tour, Kenya 1988. **Awards:** Exhibition, SJC 1928; Bonney Prize (Geology), SJC 1931. **Publications:** *The Science of Humanity*, 1950; *The Social Purposes of Education*, 1959; *New Dimensions in Higher Education*, 1968; (Editor) *Innovation in Higher Education*, 1974; (Editor) *Values and Moral Development in Higher Education*, 1974; (Editor) *Evaluating the New BEd*, 1978; (Editor) *The Management of Peer-Group Learning*, 1983; *A New Teaching, A New Learning: a Guide to Theological Education*, 1989; articles in educational and other journals. Died 10 August 1998.

COLLINGE, Professor Neville Edgar (1945) Born 18 December 1921, 35 Westbury Road, Crumpsall, Manchester; son of Edgar Thomas Collinge, Bank Cashier, and Constance Mabel Vallintine; m Mildred Elizabeth Owen, 1949; 1 son, 1 daughter. **Subject(s):** Classics; BA 1947; MA 1952; PhD 1967; BA (Manchester) 1942. **Tutor(s):** R L Howland. **Educ:** Crumpsall Lane Municipal Elementary School, Manchester; Manchester Grammar School; Manchester University; RMA Sandhurst. **Career:** Captain 44th Recce Regiment, Italy 1944–1945; Lecturer in Classics, University of Durham 1947–1969; Professor of Classics 1969–1974; Director of Linguistics 1971–1974, University of Toronto; Professor of Linguistics, University of Birmingham 1974–1979; Professor of Comparative Philology 1980–1987 (Emeritus 1987), University of Manchester. **Appointments:** Tutor, St Chad's College, Durham 1959–1967; Visiting Professor, University of Pennsylvania 1962; Visiting Lecturer, Yale University 1966. **Awards:** Patchett Scholarship, SJC 1941. **Honours:** MC. **Publications:** *The Structure of Horace's Odes*, OUP, 1961; *Collectanea Linguistica*, Mouton, 1970; *The Laws of Indo-European*, Benjamins, 1985; (ed) *An Encyclopaedia of Language*, Routledge, 1990; many articles.

COLLINGS, Hubert Dennis (1928) Born 3 March 1905, Sycamore Cottage, Chobham Road, Horsell, Surrey; son of Dudley Willis Collings, Medical Practitioner, and Mary Theresa Bond. **Subject(s):** Geography/Archaeology and Anthropology; BA 1931. **Tutor(s):** E A Benians. **Educ:** Lamsook School, Bracknell; Eversley School, Southwold; Dover College.

COLLINS, Derek Wilfred (1947) Born 5 June 1925, 18 King Street, King's Lynn, Norfolk; son of Wilfred John Collins, Draper's Warehouseman, and Lucy Louisa Bobbins. **Subject(s):** Economics/History; BA 1949. **Tutor(s):** F Thistlethwaite. **Educ:** St James's Elementary School, King's Lynn; King Edward VII Grammar School, King's Lynn.

COLLINS, Edward Lawrence (1904) Born 5 January 1880, 26 Freeland Street, Kirkdale, Lancashire; son of Edward Collins, Master Mariner, and Jane Plomer. **Tutor(s):** C E Graves; J R Tanner. **Educ:** Liverpool College.

COLLINS, Dr Ernest Jacob (1913) Born 9 September 1896, 11 Lime Tree Avenue, Penge, Surrey; son of Joseph Collins, Gardener, and Elizabeth Gibb. **Subject(s):** Agriculture; BA 1914; MA 1919; BSc (London); DSc (London) 1926. **Tutor(s):** R P Gregory. **Educ:** University College, Bangor; UCL. **Career:** John Innes Horticultural Institution (Council 1927–1931) 1915–1934. **Appointments:** Fellow, Linnean Society. Died 6 February 1939.

COLLINS, Francis Geoffrey (1931) Born 20 June 1914, 67, Pentubane Street, Cardiff; son of Frank Collins, United Methodist Minister, and

Alice Miriam Boatfield. **Subject(s):** Natural Sciences/Moral Sciences; BA 1935; MA 1939. **Tutor(s):** J M Wordie. **Educ:** Egerton House School, Exeter; Yalton School; The County School, Weston-Super-Mare; Sidcot School, Winscombe.

COLLINS, Henry Stanley (1917) Born 8 July 1900, The Elms, Merton Hall Road, Wimbledon, Surrey; son of Henry Noble Collins, Gentleman, and Eveline Mary Blunden; m Noelle. BA 1920; MA 1925. **Tutor(s):** E E Sikes. **Educ:** Hadfield House School; Ivy Bank School; University School, Hastings. **Career:** Methodist Minister, Plymouth. Died 10 April 1971.

COLLINS, The Revd James Frederick (1931) Born 3 October 1910, Durley Cottage, Manor Road, Sutton Coldfield; son of George Dawson Collins, Gold Stud Manufacturer, and Emily Marian Brown; m (1) Jean Wood, 1942, (2) Gwynnedd Nicholl, 1982; (1) 1 son (Christopher), 1 daughter (Jane). **Subject(s):** History/Theology; BA 1934; MA 1938. **Tutor(s):** E A Benians. **Educ:** Lindley Lodge, Nuneaton; Westcott House, Cambridge. **Career:** Cadet Officer, Pangbourne Nautical College 1924–1927; Cadet, White Star Line Company, Liverpool 1927–1930; Ordained Deacon 1935; Curate, Benwell 1935–1938; Ordained Priest, Newcastle 1936; Chaplain, RNVR 1936–1946; Chaplain, Missions to Seamen, Port Sudan 1938–1941; Curate, All Saints, Milford 1946–1947; Vicar, Rothwell with Orton 1947–1951; Surrogate 1948–1951; Rector, Bromham, Wiltshire 1951–1962; Vicar, Chisledon with Drayoot Foliat, Swindon 1962–1968; Director of Ordination Candidates, Diocese of Salisbury 1968–1974; Assistant Priest, St John's, Devizes 1968–1975; Permitted to Officiate, St Albans 1981–1995.

COLLINS, John Stratford (1901) Born 24 April 1882, 120 Alexandra Road, Hampstead, Middlesex; son of John Stratford Collins, Army General, Peshwar, India, and Margaret Arabella Jackson. BA 1904. **Tutor(s):** J R Tanner; C E Graves. **Educ:** Victoria College, Jersey. **Career:** Teacher, Downside College 1909. Died 2 February 1912.

COLLINS, Dr Leslie Arthur (1928) Born 18 June 1909, Fairlawn, The Green, St Leonards-on-Sea, Sussex; son of Henry Noble Collins, of independent means, and Eveline Mary Blunden. **Subject(s):** Natural Sciences; BA 1931; MA 1937; BChir 1937; MB 1937. **Tutor(s):** M P Charlesworth. **Johnian Relatives:** father of John Leslie Collins (1960); grandfather of Michael John Collins (1989). **Educ:** University School, Hastings; Sutton Valence School.

COLLINS, Martyn (1940) Born 28 March 1922, Hulse Road Nursing Home, Southampton; son of Ralph Sextus Collins, Builder and Estate Agent, and Evie Kezia Farmer; m (1) Anne Pocock, (2) Binnie Barns; (1) 2 sons (Benjamin and Oliver), 1 daughter (Antonia), (2) 1 son (Matthew), 1 daughter (Louise). **Subject(s):** Architecture; BA 1947; MA 1949. **Tutor(s):** C W Guillebaud. **Johnian Relatives:** nephew of Ebenezer Cunningham (1899); cousin of Morris Anskar Cunningham (1935). **Educ:** PNEU School; Oakmount Preparatory School, Southampton; Bembridge School. **Career:** Architect.

COLLINS, Neville Clarence (1947) Born 21 October 1925, 195 Hertford Road, Freezywater, Waltham Cross, Middlesex; son of Clarence William Collins, Clerk of Works, and Nellie Florence Bullerwell; m Geneviève Pauline Fontier. **Subject(s):** Modern and Medieval Languages; BA 1949; MA 1954; DipEd (Oxon) 1957; BA (Hons) Russian (Westminster) 1994. **Tutor(s):** C W Guillebaud. **Educ:** Corpus Christi School, Portsmouth; Wolmer's School, Kingston, Jamaica; Cheshunt Grammar School; School of Education, University of Oxford; University of Westminster. **Career:** War Service, RE 1943–1947; Teacher, UK and Nigeria 1951–1962; Education Officer, BBC 1963–1968; Producer, audio-visual materials, ILEA TV Centre 1968–1989.

COLLINSON, Michael (1944) Born 18 May 1926, Halifax, Yorkshire; m Sue Mayon Henshaw, 4 March 1989, Halifax; 1 son (Adam Grant b 20 January 1965), 1 daughter (Charlotte Elizabeth b 8 June 1970).

Subject(s): Law; BA 1949; MA 1951. **Tutor(s):** J M Wordie. **Educ:** Woodlands Preparatory School, Deganwy; Oundle School. **Career:** Solicitor. **Appointments:** RAF Cadet, SJC.

COLLINSON, Dr Roy Gladwin (1945) Born 24 April 1927, 8 Gladwin Street, Batley, Yorkshire; son of Norman Collinson, Wool Buyer, and Gertrude Mary Gladwin; m Joyce, 2 daughters (Frances and Deborah). **Subject(s):** Natural Sciences; BA 1948; MA 1951; PhD 1952. **Tutor(s):** C W Guillebaud. **Educ:** Purlwell Council School, Batley; Batley Grammar School. **Awards:** Major Scholarship, SJC. Died 5 June 1959.

COLLIS, Henry John Gurney (1932) Born 27 June 1913, 17 Osbourne Road, Newcastle upon Tyne; son of Arthur John Collis, Doctor of Medicine, and Dorothy Mary Wren Gurney; 1 son. **Subject(s):** Modern and Medieval Languages; BA 1935; MA 1939. **Tutor(s):** C W Guillebaud. **Educ:** Stoneygate Preparatory School, Leicester; Shrewsbury School. **Career:** Assistant Master, Clifton College Preparatory School 1935–1940; Northern Command then War Office 1940–1945; Founder Headmaster, The Eastbourne College Preparatory School, Ascham, Eastbourne 1945; Headmaster, Colet Court Preparatory School, St Paul's School, London 1957–1973. **Appointments:** Chairman, Incorporated Association of Preparatory Schools 1959; Director 1973, Chairman 1979–1981, National Association for Gifted Children; Commissioner for Education, Boy Scouts' Association; Chairman, National Cycling Committee on Road Safety; Council Member, Bible Reading Fellowship; Governor, St Edmund's School, Canterbury. **Awards:** USA-Page Scholarship under auspices of English Speaking Union 1952. Died 17 May 1994.

COLLISON, Lewis Herbert (1927) Born 30 July 1908, 338 High Road, Tottenham, London; son of William Herbert Collison, Grocer, and Florence Blanche Havill; m Edna Mollie Ivens, 1934; 2 daughters (June b 1937 and Jane b 1940). **Subject(s):** Classics/English; BA 1930; MA 1946. **Tutor(s):** M P Charlesworth. **Johnian Relatives:** brother of Victor Edward Collison (1936); father-in-law of David Nigel de Lorentz Young (1970). **Educ:** Mill Hill Junior School, London; Mill Hill School. **Career:** Assistant Master, Sedbergh School 1931–1940; Major, King's Own Royal Regiment 1940–1945; Housemaster, Sedbergh School 1946–1952; Headmaster, Liverpool College 1952–1970. **Appointments:** JP, Liverpool 1958–1970; Council Member, University of Liverpool 1963–1969. Died 21 November 1988.

COLLISON, Victor Edward (1936) Born 27 May 1917, 338 High Road, Tottenham, London; son of William Herbert Collison, Grocer, and Florence Blanche Havill; m Jane Elizabeth Riddell, 30 April 1957. BA 1939; MA 1978. **Tutor(s):** C W Guillebaud. **Johnian Relatives:** brother of Lewis Herbert Collison (1927). **Educ:** Belmont, Mill Hill Junior School; Mill Hill School. **Career:** Lieutenant Colonel, Royal West African Frontier Force 1940–1946; Her Majesty's Overseas Civil Service, Nigeria Provincial Commissioner 1940–1960; Bursar, Sedbergh School 1962–1977. **Appointments:** Clerk to the Governors, Sedbergh School, Cumbria. Died 4 February 1991.

COLMAN, Edwin Woodruff (1926) Born 19 March 1905, 934 N Church Street, Rockford, Illinois; son of Howard Darling Colman, Mechanical Engineer, and Bertha Emeline Maguire. **Tutor(s):** E A Benians. **Educ:** Grammar School; High School; Phillip Exeter Academy; Princeton University.

COLSON, The Revd Alexander Francis Lionel (1940) Born 6 September 1921, Simla, India; son of Lionel Hewitt Colson, Indian Police, and Isabel Amelia Denham; m Alice Ruth Mackay Sim, 1951; 1 son (Richard b 1955), 2 daughters (Mary b 1953 and Alice b 1958). **Subject(s):** Mechanical Sciences; BA 1943; MA 1961; Passed Staff College 1952. **Tutor(s):** S J Bailey. **Johnian Relatives:** great grandson of Charles Colson (1835); great nephew of Francis Henry Colson (1875); cousin of Charles Gordon Tulloch Colson (1910). **Educ:** Junior School, Cheltenham College; Oundle School. **Career:** Student Apprentice,

Messrs J I Thornycroft, Woolston, Southampton 1940; Regular Officer, RE (retired as Major) 1942–1960; Mentioned in Despatches 1945; Tyndale Hall Theological College 1960–1962; Ordained Deacon 1962; Curate, St Paul's, Slough 1962–1965; Ordained Priest 1963; Rector, Elmswell 1965–1973; Vicar, St Luke's, West Kilburn, with St Simon and St Jude 1973–1982; Rector, Thrandeston, Stuston, Brome and Oakley 1982–1986. **Awards:** Tyndale Hall Bible Diploma 1st Prize 1962. **Honours:** MBE (Military) 1945.

COLSON, Canon Charles Gordon Tulloch (1910) Born 10 October 1891, School House, Plymouth College, Compton Gifford, Devon; son of Francis Henry Colson, Fellow, SJC, and Maud Jane Anne Tulloch; m Elsie Florence Anderson, 24 April 1923, Christ Church, Lancaster Gate; 2 daughters (Mary Winifred b 1924 and Margaret Elsie b 1926). **Subject(s):** Theology; BA 1913; MA 1917. **Tutor(s):** J R Tanner. **Johnian Relatives:** grandson of Charles Colson (1835); son of Francis Henry Colson (1875); cousin of Alexander Francis Lionel Colson (1940). **Educ:** Plymouth College; Ely Theological College. **Career:** Ordained Deacon and Priest 1915; Curate, St Clement, Notting Hill 1915–1916; Curate, St John the Baptist, Holland Road, Kensington 1916–1919; Temporary CF 1918; Curate, Christ Church, Lancaster Gate 1920–1923; Curate in Charge of Northfleet 1923–1927; Vicar, Northfleet 1927–1931; Vicar, St Michael and All Angels with All Saints, Paddington 1931–1938; Rector, Winterslow 1938–1943; Vicar, Warminster 1943–1956; Rural Dean, Heytesbury 1946–1954; Rector, Upton Scudamore 1947–1956; Canon and Prebendary of Ruscombe Southbury, Salisbury Cathedral 1950–1956; Rector, Comrie, Diocese of Dunkeld 1956. **Appointments:** Secretary to Lord Mayor's Armenian Fund 1917–1920. Died 8 July 1968.

COLVIN, Gilbert Russell (1922) Born 1 October 1903, 37 Shakespeare Crescent, Manor Park, East Ham, Essex; son of Gilbert Colvin, Chartered Secretary, and Alice Sarah Engledow; m Doreen; 1 daughter (Angela), 2 sons (Charles and Andrew). **Subject(s):** Mathematics/ Economics; BA 1925; MA 1954. **Tutor(s):** E Cunningham. **Educ:** Brentwood School. **Career:** Director, Federation of Boot Manufacturers; Fatstock Marketing Corporation; Manfield & Sons; Traffic Apprentice, LNER. **Honours:** MBE 1941. Died 9 February 1990.

COLWILL, Dr Charles Kingsley (1918) Born 17 July 1899, 111 Wallwood Road, Leytonstone, Essex; son of Charles Colwill, Managing Director, and Kate Norman Button; m (1) Muriel Workingham, 11 July 1925, St Mary Abbot's, Kensington, (2) Dorothy. **Subject(s):** Natural Sciences; BA 1921; MA 1926; MB 1926; BChir 1926; MRCS; LRCP 1924. **Tutor(s):** E E Sikes. **Educ:** Oxford House School, Croydon; Whitgift Grammar School; Guy's Hospital Medical School, London. Died 9 March 1987.

COMBRIDGE, Anthony Theodore (1949) Born 16 January 1929, 58 Fengates Road, Redhill, Surrey; son of John Theodore Combridge, Registrar, KCL, and Norah Elizabeth Charlwood. **Subject(s):** Classics; BA 1952; MA 1956. **Tutor(s):** R L Howland. **Johnian Relatives:** son of John Theodore Combridge (1919). **Educ:** Hillside Preparatory School, Reigate; St Paul's School. **Career:** Assistant Master, Classics, Pocklington School, Yorkshire 1954–1958; Assistant Master, Cranleigh School, Surrey 1958–1967; Assistant Master, Sherborne School, Dorset 1968–1988. **Awards:** Montagu Butler Prize, University of Cambridge 1952.

COMBRIDGE, John Theodore (1919) Born 28 August 1897, Brighton, Sussex; son of Daniel Thomas Combridge, Butcher, and Rhoda Rebecca Gardner; m (1) Norah Elizabeth Charlwood, 30 December 1926, Galeed Chapel, Brighton, (2) Winifred Adelaide Cooke, 1972; (1) 1 son (Anthony), 2 daughters (Rosemary and Nancy). **Subject(s):** Mathematics; BA 1921; MA 1925; MSc (London) 1924. **Tutor(s):** E E Sikes. **Johnian Relatives:** father of Anthony Theodore Combridge (1949). **Educ:** Strathallan, Brighton; Taunton House School, Brighton; Brighton College. **Career:** Royal Army Cadet School 1916; Second Lieutenant, Royal Field Artillery 1917, served in France 1917–1919;

Demonstrator in Mathematics, City & Guilds Engineering College, Imperial College of Science 1923–1926; Assistant Lecturer then Lecturer in Mathematics 1926–1937, Assistant to the Secretary 1937–1947, Honorary Lecturer in Mathematics 1937–1962, Registrar 1947–1962, Fellow 1955, KCL. **Appointments:** President, Mathematical Association 1961–1962. **Awards:** Exhibition, SJC 1916. Died 10 December 1986.

COMBS, Sir Willis Ide (1938) Born 6 May 1916, Prahan, Melbourne, Australia; son of Willis Ide Combs and Ada Mary Quigley; m Grace Willis, 1942; 2 daughters. **Subject(s):** Modern and Medieval Languages; BA 1940. **Tutor(s):** C W Guillebaud. **Educ:** North School, Dannevirke; High School, Dannevirke; Victoria University College, Wellington New Zealand. **Career:** HM Forces 1940–1946; Member, Foreign Service 1947; First Secretary, Foreign Service 1948–1951; First Secretary and Consul, Rio 1951–1953; First Secretary and Consul (Chargé d'Affaires, 1954), Peking 1953–1956; Foreign Office 1956–1959; Counsellor (Commercial), Baghdad 1959–1963; Diplomatic Service Inspector 1963–1965; Counsellor, British Embassy, Rangoon 1965–1968; Under-Secretary of State, FCO 1968–1970; Ambassador to Indonesia 1970–1975. **Honours:** CMG 1962; KCVO 1974. Died 13 January 1994.

COMMON, Donald Keith (1945) Born 13 September 1927, 7 Dean Crescent, Stirling, Scotland; son of Ralph Lawson Keith Common, Dental Surgeon, and Beatrice Mary Heron; m Pat; 2 sons (Alistair and Peter) 1 daughter (Catherine). **Subject(s):** Mechanical Sciences; BA 1948; MA 1954; FIMechE. **Tutor(s):** S J Bailey; R L Howland. **Educ:** Stirling High School; Strathallan School, Forgandenny. **Career:** Apprentice, Harland Engineering, Alloa 1948–1951; Merz and McLellan, Consulting Engineers 1951–1959; Reactor Pressure Vessel Engineer 1959–1976, Quality Assurance Manager, Nuclear Plant Design 1976–1980, CEGB; Independent Consulting Engineer 1980. **Appointments:** Pressure Vessel Consultant, British Standards Institution. Died 11 June 1999.

COMMON, Francis Graeme (1930) Born 15 August 1912, 1 Beresford Park North, Sunderland; son of Charles Raymond Common, Iron Merchant and Graeme Blumer; m Margaret Enid Evans, 29 January 1944, St Michael's, Bishop's Stortford. **Tutor(s):** E A Benians. **Educ:** Sunderland High School; Corcester, Corbridge on Tyne; Felsted School.

COMRIE, Dr Leslie John (1919) Born 15 August 1893, Pukekohe, New Zealand; son of John Alexander Comrie, Merchant, and Lois Helen Smith; m Phyllis Betty Kitto, 1933; 1 son (Julian Kitto b 14 May 1935). PhD 1924; MA (New Zealand) 1915; FRS 1950. **Tutor(s):** E A Benians. **Johnian Relatives:** brother-in-law of Humphrey Davy Findley Kitto (1916) and of William Michael Herbert Greaves (1916); father of Julian Kitto Comrie (1956); uncle of George Richard Herbert Greaves (1961). **Educ:** Pukehoe High School; Auckland Grammar School; Auckland University College; University of New Zealand. **Career:** New Zealand Expeditionary Force 1916–1918; Sergeant, New Zealand Rifle Brigade, France 1918 (wounded); Lecturer in Astronomy and Computing, Swarthmore College and North Western University 1924–1925; Nautical Almanac Office 1925–1936: Deputy Superintendent 1926–1930, Superintendent 1930–1936; Founder and Managing Director, Scientific Computing Service Ltd 1937–1950. **Awards:** Isaac Newton Studentship, University of Cambridge 1921. **Publications:** *Chambers Six-Figure Mathematical Tables*, 1948. Died 11 December 1950.

CONCANNON, Edmond James Blake (1924) Born 27 March 1906, 69 Gloucester Terrace, Paddington, London; son of Edmond George Concannon, Stock Exchange, Lieutenant Colonel, HM Army, and Bertha Beckford Syvret Gosselin. **Tutor(s):** B F Armitage. **Educ:** Wootton Court, Canterbury; Eastbourne College.

CONDER, James Edward Bevill (1940) Born 23 June 1922, Kasauli, Punjab, India; son of Hugh Conder, Lieutenant Colonel, Indian Army, and Violet Mirelle Rowbotham. **Tutor(s):** C W Guillebaud. **Educ:** Ladies' College, Cheltenham; Junior School, Cheltenham College;

Cheltenham College. **Career:** Commissioned, Essex Regiment; served in North Africa (with 5th Hampshires) and Italy 1941–1945. **Honours:** MC 1943.

CONDER, John Marmaduke (1908) Born 10 May 1889, Chapdale, Clapham, Bentham, Yorkshire; son of John Denny Conder, Farmer, and Margaret Swindlehurst. **Subject(s):** Natural Sciences/Mathematics; BA 1911. **Tutor(s):** J R Tanner. **Educ:** Windermere Grammar School. **Career:** Assistant Commissioner, Burma 1914; Military Service 1918–1920; Officiating Sessions Judge 1922–1931.

CONNELL, Canon Ernest Oldham (1922) Born 4 August 1903, Redcourt, City of Prahran, Bourke County, Victoria, Australia; son of Ernest Henry Connell, Chairman, Shipping Company, and Mary Lilian Oldham; m Phyllis; 1 son (John), 3 daughters (Elizabeth, Anne and Margaret). **Subject(s):** Mathematics/Natural Sciences; BA 1925; MA 1929. **Tutor(s):** E E Sikes. **Johnian Relatives:** brother of Frank James Connell (1927) and of Reginald Morton Connell (1930); father of John Barr Stevenson Connell (1969). **Educ:** Merchiston Preparatory School, Edinburgh; Merchiston Castle School, Edinburgh. **Career:** Master, Shrewsbury School 1927; Master, Merchiston School 1927–1958. **Appointments:** Honorary Canon, St Mary's Cathedral, Edinburgh 1970. Died 16 March 1986.

CONNELL, Frank James (1927) Born 23 May 1910, Cobrilla, Dandenong Road, Caulfield, Bourke County, Victoria, Australia; son of Ernest Henry Connell, Lecturer in Medical Psychology, and Mary Lilian Oldham. **Subject(s):** Mechanical Sciences; BA 1931; MA 1935; ARIBA; ARIAS; AMTPI; AMRTPI. **Tutor(s):** J M Wordie. **Johnian Relatives:** brother of Ernest Oldham Connell (1922) and of Reginald Morton Connell (1930); uncle of John Barr Stevenson Connell (1969). **Educ:** Merchiston Castle Preparatory School, Edinburgh; Merchiston Castle Upper School, Edinburgh. **Career:** Superintendent, Town Planning Office, Scottish Development Department, Scottish Office, Edinburgh. Died 1 January 1992.

CONNELL, James Archibald (1936) Born 17 November 1917, 36a Beccaid Street, Braamfontein, Johannesburg, South Africa; son of John Connell, Professor of Music, Transvaal University, and Marion Baillie. **Tutor(s):** J M Wordie. **Educ:** Benges School, Hertford; Malvern College.

CONNELL, Reginald Morton (1930) Born 22 July 1911, Windara, Williams Road, Toorak, Melbourne, Victoria, Australia; son of Ernest Henry Connell, Medical Practitioner, and Mary Lilian Oldham. **Subject(s):** Modern and Medieval Languages/Economics. **Tutor(s):** C W Guillebaud. **Johnian Relatives:** brother of Ernest Oldham Connell (1922) and of Frank James Connell (1927); uncle of John Barr Stevenson Connell (1969). **Educ:** Merchiston Preparatory School, Edinburgh; Merchiston Castle School, Edinburgh. Died 23 December 1982.

CONNELL, William John Ramsay (1925) Born 24 February 1907, 19 Winton Drive, Glasgow; son of Allan MacGregor Connell, Shipbuilder, and Margaret Drake Ramsay; m (1) Eleanor Carve (div 1939), (2) Aurore Severi, 1950. **Tutor(s):** E A Benians. **Educ:** Sandroyd, Cobham; Harrow. Died 27 December 1960.

CONNELLY, George Fredrick (1940) Born 12 February 1921, 9 Drewry Road, Keighley, Yorkshire; son of Albert Connelly, Engineer, and Emma Lottey; m Mary Pennington, December 1943; 3 daughters (Lesley b 1949, Pamela b 1951 and Alison b 1953). **Subject(s):** Modern and Medieval Languages; BA 1947; MA 1949. **Tutor(s):** C W Guillebaud. **Educ:** Utley Council School, Keighley; Highfield Council School, Keighley; Keighley Boys' Grammar School. **Career:** Commissioned RA, transferred KOYLI, promoted to Captain, seconded as Liaison Officer to Dutch Army 1942–1946; Proctor and Gamble (progressing to Senior Management) 1947. **Appointments:** Various management board appointments in paper print and packaging industries 1964–1980.

CONSTABLE, Professor Frederick Hurn (1920) Born 26 November 1901, 97 Brook Street, Southwark, Surrey; son of Frederick William Constable, Cashier, and Minnie Hurn; m Sance Helena Robson; 2 sons (John Hurn b 19 August 1934, d 18 November 1999 and David Noel b 20 December 1939). **Subject(s):** Mathematics/Natural Sciences; BA 1923; MA 1927; PhD 1926; ScD 1926; PhD (London) 1925. **Tutor(s):** B F Armitage. **Johnian Relatives:** father of David Noel Constable (1959); grandfather of Catherine Anna Elizabeth Constable (1986). **Educ:** Kettering Road Council School, Northampton; Northampton School. **Career:** Foundress Fellow, SJC 1925–1930; Research Department, Radiovisor Ltd, Letchworth 1931–1935; Professor of Physical Chemistry, University of Giza 1936–1939; Professor of Physical Chemistry, Istanbul University 1943–1975. **Awards:** Scholarship, SJC; Strathcona Research Studentship, SJC; Gordon Wigan Prize, University of Cambridge 1925. Died 5 November 1975.

CONSTABLE, William Briggs (BRIGGS CONSTABLE) (1942) Born 8 July 1924, 10 Coates Crescent, Edinburgh; son of William Briggs Constable, Major, RA, and Edith Selkirk Allan Oswald; m Barbara Flury; 4 sons (William, Adam, Peter and Bryce). **Subject(s):** Agriculture; BA 1948; MA 1950. **Tutor(s):** C W Guillebaud. **Educ:** Edinburgh Academy; Craigflower, Lorryburn, Fife; Sedbergh School. **Career:** Officer, RA, Burma and India WWII; Water conservation work, Bulawayo and Figtree 1951; Manager, pig farm, Lincolnshire; Manager, water engineering firm, Scotland. Died 6 March 2003.

CONSTABLE, Professor William George (1906) Born 27 October 1887, Derby; son of William George Samuel Constable, Schoolmaster, and Remeliah Isabella Webb; m Olivia Roberts, 29 May 1926; 2 sons (John b 21 June 1927 and Giles b 1 June 1929). **Subject(s):** History/Economics; BA 1909; MA 1919; Honorary DLitt (Nottingham); Honorary DLitt (New Brunswick, Canada). **Tutor(s):** L H K Bushe-Fox. **Johnian Relatives:** father of Giles Constable (1952). **Educ:** Derby School. **Career:** Called to the Bar, Inner Temple 1914; Major, Sherwood Foresters (Nottinghamshire and Derby Regiment) and Lancashire Fusiliers 1914–1918 (Mentioned in Despatches); Studies, Slade School of Fine Art 1919–1923; Lecturer, Wallace Collection 1923–1924; Assistant Director, National Gallery 1924–1931; Director, Courtauld Institute, University of London 1931–1936; Title E Fellow, SJC 1935–1937; Slade Professor of Fine Art, University of Cambridge 1935–1938; Curator of Paintings, Boston Museum of Fine Arts 1938–1957. **Appointments:** Honorary Fellow, SJC 1955; Member, Company of Goldsmiths 1937; Art Critic, *New Statesman*, *Saturday Review*, and *Burlington Magazine*; Special Advisor to American Commission for the Protection of Artistic and Historic Monuments in Europe, WWII; Honorary Member, Belgian Royal Academy of Arts. **Awards:** Exhibition, SJC; Whewell Scholarship for International Law, University of Cambridge 1909. **Honours:** Chevalier of the Legion d'Honneur; Commendatore of the Crown of Italy; Officer, Ordre des Arts et Lettres (France). **Publications:** *John Flaxman*, 1927; *Catalogue of the Marlay Bequest, Fitzwilliam Museum*, 1927; *Richard Wilson*, 1953; *The Painter's Workshop*, 1954; *Canaletto*, 1962. Died 3 February 1976.

CONSTANCE, John David (1945) See BOTT.

CONSTANT, Michael Brancovan (1934) Born 15 May 1916, Tetney, Lincolnshire; son of Marin Brancovan Constant, Manager, Petroleum Company, and Minnie Brocklebank; m Audrey Curtis, 1951; 1 son (Richard b 1954), 1 daughter (Anne b 1953). BA 1937; MA 1944. **Tutor(s):** C W Guillebaud. **Johnian Relatives:** father of Richard Michael Constant (1972). **Educ:** Sompting Abbotts, Worthing; Seafield Park, near Fareham; Sherborne School.

CONWAY, Professor John Seymour (1949) Born 31 December 1929, 3 Alberon Gardens, Golders Green, London; son of Geoffrey Seymour Conway, Civil Servant, Ministry of Education, and Elsie Phillips; m Ann Patricia Jefferies, 10 August 1957, St Peter's Church, Roydon, Essex; 1 son (David b 1958), 2 daughters (Jane b 1960 and Alison b 1965).

Subject(s): English/History; BA 1952; MA 1956; PhD 1956. **Tutor(s):** A G Lee. **Educ:** Bishop's Court, Formby; Arnold Lodge, Leamington; Larchfield School, Helensburgh; Sedbergh School. **Career:** International Relations, University of Manitoba 1955–1957; Modern European History and International Relations, Department of History, University of British Columbia, Vancouver 1957–1995; Smallman Visiting Professor, Department of History, University of Western Ontario, London, Ontario 1998. **Appointments:** Founding Member, Scholars' Conference on the German Church and the Holocaust 1970; Director, Association of Contemporary Church Historians 1995; Member, Editorial Boards of the journals *Kirchliche Zeitgeschichte* and the *Journal of Holocaust and Genocide Studies*; Chairman, Vancouver Branch of the Canadian Institute of International Affairs; Chairman, United Nations Association; Executive Vice-Chairman, Tibetan Refugee Aid Society of Canada; Member, Anglican Diocese of New Westminster's Refugee Liaison Committee. **Awards:** Lupton and Hebblethwaite Exhibition, SJC 1948. **Honours:** Queen's Silver Jubilee Medal 1977. **Publications:** *The Nazi Persecution of the Churches 1933–1945*, 1968 (translated into German, French and Spanish, and reissued in 1997); large number of articles dealing with the role of the European churches and the Vatican during the Holocaust, as well as on the topic of Christian-Jewish relations during the twentieth century.

COOK, Charles William (1945) Born 11 March 1927, 7 Craven Road, Reading, Berkshire; son of Henry Denman Cook, Mechanical Engineer, and Agneta Mary Cook. **Subject(s):** Mechanical Sciences; BA 1948; MA 1952. **Tutor(s):** S J Bailey; R L Howland. **Johnian Relatives:** grandson of Charles Henry Herbert Cook (1868). **Educ:** Reading School; Marlborough House, Reading; Leighton Park School, Reading. **Career:** Mechanical Engineer.

COOK, Raymond Baker (1933) Born 1 January 1915, Daisy Cottage, Holme Church Lane, Beverley; son of John William Cook, Manager, Wire Rope Works, and Laura Annie Baker. **Subject(s):** English; BA 1936. **Tutor(s):** J S Boys Smith. **Educ:** St Nicholas Infants School; Minster Boys' School; King Edward VII School, Lytham. Died 31 October 1969.

COOKE, Anthony Eskrigg (1925) Born 26 June 1907, Shirley, Bedford Road, Luton, Bedfordshire; son of Richard Edward Cooke, Solicitor, and Margaret Lindsay Heward; m Jeanie Pauline Durler. BA 1928. **Tutor(s):** M P Charlesworth. **Johnian Relatives:** father of David Anthony Durler Cooke (1961). **Educ:** Berkhamsted School. **Career:** Mechanical Engineer.

COOKE, Arthur Hunt (HUNT COOKE) (1924) Born 9 February 1906, Jhansi, United Provinces, India; son of Ebenezer Hunt Cooke, Medical Practitioner, and Katie Williams Jones. **Subject(s):** Modern and Medieval Languages; BA 1927; MA 1945. **Tutor(s):** E E Sikes. **Johnian Relatives:** son of Ebenezer Hunt Cooke (1881). **Educ:** Preparatory Branch, University College School; University College School, Hampstead. **Career:** Superintendent of Education, Abeokuta, Southern Nigeria (Colonial Service); HM Overseas Education (Nigeria and Mauritius). **Honours:** OBE. Died 17 December 1993.

COOKE, George Edward (1927) Born 24 December 1908, 7 Hampden Street, Beeston, Nottinghamshire; son of Enoch Samuel Cooke, Merchant, and Emma Hooton. **Subject(s):** Mechanical Sciences; BA 1930; MA 1934. **Tutor(s):** J M Wordie. **Educ:** West End House, Beeston; South Council School, West Bridgford; Mundella School, Nottingham. **Awards:** Scholarship, SJC 1929; Archibald Denny Prize, University of Cambridge 1930. Died July 1973.

COOKE, John Caister (1938) Born 26 January 1908, 31 Pinchbeck Road, Spalding, Lincolnshire; son of Earsham Turner Cooke, Coal Agent, and Evelyn Caister. BA 1938. **Tutor(s):** J M Wordie. **Educ:** Boston Grammar School; Ripon School; The Queen's College, Oxford. **Career:** Ferry Pilot, Air Transport Auxiliary 1939–1945.

COOKSLEY, The Revd George Antony Hawkes (1940) Born 1 June 1921, 1 Richmond Park Road, Clifton, Bristol; son of Frank Robert Cooksley, Clerk in Holy Orders, and Anna Evelyn Hawkes; m Barbara; 2 children. **Subject(s):** Classics/Theology; BA 1943. **Tutor(s):** R L Howland. **Educ:** Westbury House, West Meon; Cranleigh School. **Career:** Curate, St Peter, Harborne, Birmingham 1944–1950; Rector, North with South Lopham, Norfolk 1950–1952. Died 14 August 1952.

COOMBS, Arthur George (1903) Born 4 July 1884, Magdala Villa, Bridgwater, Somerset; son of John Coombs, Land Agent, and Mary Catherine Sercombe; m Dora Arnell, 4 January 1921, St Mary's, Brading, Isle of Wight. **Subject(s):** Natural Sciences; BA 1906; MA 1910; BSc (London) 1910. **Tutor(s):** D MacAlister. **Educ:** Queen's College, Taunton; Imperial College, London. **Career:** Major, RGA; Science Master, Wolverhampton Grammar School 1906–1909; Master, Berkhamsted School 1911–1924; Headmaster, Barnard Castle School 1924. **Honours:** DSO; Belgian Croix de Guerre. Died 31 July 1974.

COOP, Wilfrid (1902) Born 29 October 1882, 158 Albemarle Street, Ashton under Lyne, Lancashire; son of John Hague Coop, Cattle Dealer, and Sarah Ogden. **Subject(s):** Classics; BA 1905; MA 1909. **Tutor(s):** D MacAlister. **Educ:** Manchester Grammar School. **Career:** Master, Birkenhead School 1906; Private, then Lieutenant, 10th (Scottish) Battalion, King's Liverpool Regiment (TF) 1915. Died 24 June 1915 (of wounds received in action in the Ypres Salient 16 June 1915).

COOPER, Cyril George (1923) Born 4 August 1904, Ferndale, St Margaret's Road, Longfleet, Poole, Dorset; son of Walter Percy Cooper, Timber Merchant's Manager, and Annie Eliza Mabey; m Elsie Lacey, 1929; 1 daughter (Shirley Ann). **Subject(s):** Natural Sciences; BA 1926; MA 1933. **Tutor(s):** J M Wordie. **Educ:** Portsmouth Grammar School. **Career:** Anglo-Saxon Petroleum Company 1927. Died 16 October 1988.

COOPER, Harold (1908) Born 25 February 1890, Compstall, Werneth, Cheshire; son of William Cooper, Life Assurance Agent, and Emma Bowden; m Dorothy Joyce Richardson, 18 April 1925; 1 son (Michael John Richardson b 15 October 1930). **Subject(s):** Modern and Medieval Languages; BA 1911; MA 1919. **Tutor(s):** E E Sikes. **Johnian Relatives:** father of Michael John Richardson Cooper (1949). **Educ:** Manchester Grammar School. **Career:** Captain, Unattached List TF (OTC), and Intelligence Corps, WWI; Bishop's Stortford College; St Lawrence College, Ramsgate; Manchester Grammar School 1919–1924; Assistant Master, Harrow School 1924. **Awards:** Tiarks German Scholarship, University of Cambridge 1911.

COOPER, John Napier (1939) Born 12 September 1921, Kephissia, Greece; son of Gordon Cooper, Major; Civil Engineer, and Olive Thorp; 1 son. **Subject(s):** Mechanical Sciences; BA 1942; MA 1946; MICE. **Tutor(s):** J S Boys Smith. **Educ:** Andover Preparatory School; Kimbolton School. **Career:** Civil Servant; Air Ministry 1948–1958; Central Electricity Generating Board 1960–1982. **Awards:** Lucy Ingram Exhibition. Died 27 March 1987.

COOPER, John Sydney (1945) Born 4 May 1927, 52 Hastings Road, Maidstone, Kent; son of Sydney Cooper, Incorporated Accountant, and Gladys Minnie Hollis; m Ann Silvers, 1955; 4 daughters. **Tutor(s):** J M Wordie. **Johnian Relatives:** brother of Michael Leonard Cooper (1950). **Educ:** Marist Convent, Hythe; Ash Eton School, Folkestone; Cranbrook School; Staff College, Camberley; RMCS, Shrivenham. **Career:** Joined Army 1945; Commissioned, RA 1947; Served Middle East, North Africa, Far East, Gibraltar, Germany, and Ministry of Defence, London; finally Director, Proof and Experimental Establishment; retired as Brigadier 1980; Diocesan Secretary (C of E), Gloucester 1980–1985; Diocesan Secretary, Chichester 1985–1992.

COOPER, Dr Michael George (1945) Born 13 August 1927, 25 Park Place East, Sunderland; son of George Marsden Cooper, Schoolmaster, and Kathleen Clayburn, Schoolmistress; m Elizabeth Helen Kent, 18 July 1970, SJC Chapel; 2 daughters (Katherine Marie b 1973 and Anne Hazel b 1976). **Subject(s):** Mathematics; BA 1948; MA 1952; PhD 1970; ScD 1986; MA (Oxon); DPhil (Oxon); MICE; FIMechE. **Tutor(s):** J M Wordie. **Educ:** St Olave's Preparatory School; Erith County School; City of London School. **Career:** Rolls-Royce 1949–1950; New Zealand Ministry of Works and Hydro Electric Design 1951–1954; Atomic Energy Authority 1955–1957; Lecturer in Engineering, University of Cambridge 1957–1978; Title B Fellow 1962–1978, Lecturer in Mechanical Sciences 1962–1974, Lecturer in Engineering 1974–1978, SJC; Senior Research Officer, Oxford 1978–1987; Fellow, Wolfson College, Oxford 1979–1987. **Awards:** Strathcona Scholarship, SJC 1945. **Publications:** *Risk, Man-made Hazards to Man*, OUP, 1985; various contributions to journals.

COOPER, Michael John Richardson (1949) Born 15 October 1930, Arden, South Hill Avenue, Harrow, Middlesex; son of Harold Cooper, Assistant Master, Harrow School, and Dorothy Joyce Richardson, Housewife; m Sheila; 2 sons (Jonathan and Anthony). **Subject(s):** Natural Sciences; BA 1952; MA 1959. **Tutor(s):** G C L Bertram. **Johnian Relatives:** son of Harold Cooper (1908). **Educ:** Orley Farm School, Harrow; Harrow School. **Career:** Schoolmaster, later Head of Chemistry Department, Dean Close School, Cheltenham 1959–1985. **Appointments:** Founder, RN section, and later Contingent Commander, CCF, Dean Close School, Cheltenham. **Publications:** *A Practical Chemistry for Schools*, OUP; contributions to the Royal Chemistry Society's magazine *Chemistry in Britain*. Died 10 November 2002.

COOPER, Peter Brian (1945) Born 21 September 1927, Charing Cross Hospital, King William Street, Strand; son of Frank Lakin Cooper, Schoolmaster, and Lily Evelyn Bryan. **Subject(s):** Modern and Medieval Languages; BA 1948; MA 1952. **Tutor(s):** C W Guillebaud. **Educ:** Sharnbrook Council School; Bedford Modern School. **Career:** Head of Music, Mable Fletcher Technical College, Liverpool 1968.

COOPER, Thomas (1904) Born 17 September 1887, Ford Bank, London Road, Buxton, Derbyshire; son of Thomas Cooper, Provision Merchant, and Caroline Simpson. BA 1907; MA 1928. **Tutor(s):** E E Sikes. **Educ:** Buxton College. **Career:** Master, Blatchington School 1907–1910; Felsted School 1910–1949. Died 11 February 1949.

COOPER, Thomas Bruce (1926) Born 6 March 1908, The Hurst, Quorndon, Leicestershire; son of John Bruce Cooper, Engineer, and Violet Mary Gordon. BA 1929. **Tutor(s):** J M Wordie. **Educ:** St Bede's, Eastbourne; South Kensington Preparatory School; Repton School. **Career:** Wing Commander and Group Captain, RAF, WWII. **Honours:** OBE; DFC 1942. Died 5 March 1949.

COPLEY, Dr Arthur Charles (1919) Born 27 October 1902, Durban, Natal, South Africa; son of Stanley Copley, Medical Practitioner, and Kate Gwendoline Fowler. **Subject(s):** Natural Sciences; BA 1923; MA 1926; BChir 1926; MB 1927; MRCS (Guy's Hospital) 1925; LRCP (Guy's Hospital) 1925; FRCS 1930. **Tutor(s):** E A Benians. **Educ:** The High School, Durban; Hilton College, Natal. **Career:** Lieutenant Colonel, South African Medical Corps; Senior Visiting Surgeon, Addington Hospital; Visiting Surgeon, Renishaw Hospital; Consulting Surgeon, Sir J L Hulett and Sons 1925–1939; Surgeon, South African Forces 1939–1945. **Appointments:** President, Natal Coastal Branch of Medical Association. Died November 1961.

CORBETT, Andrew James Gerald (1930) Born 14 December 1912, Agra, India; son of Basil Andrew Corbett, Lieutenant Colonel, Indian Army, and Veronique Eleanor. **Subject(s):** Natural Sciences; BA 1934; MA 1944. **Tutor(s):** J M Wordie. **Educ:** Naish House Preparatory School, Burnham on Sea; Oundle School.

CORBETT, Arthur Edward (1900) Born 16 February 1881, Castle Street, Nenagh, County Tipperary, Ireland; son of Martin Corbett, Merchant, and Susan Mary Burke. BA 1903. **Tutor(s):** E E Sikes. **Educ:** Clongowes Wood College; University College, Dublin.

CORBETT, George Ernest (1942) Born 14 May 1924, 51 Bankfield Street, Bolton; son of George Henry Corbett, Admiralty Accountant, and Lynda Holden. **Subject(s):** Law; BA 1947. **Tutor(s):** S J Bailey. **Educ:** County School, Harrow; Bolton Municipal Secondary School.

CORBY, Sir Frederick Brian (1949) Born 10 May 1929, 17 Coleman Street, Raunds, Northamptonshire; son of Charles Walter Corby, Clerk in Shoe Factory, and Millicent Pentelow; m Elizabeth Mairi McInnes, 1 August 1952; 1 son (Nicholas b 1960), 2 daughters (Fiona b 1955 and Jane b 1957). **Subject(s):** Mathematics; BA 1952; MA 1956; Honorary DSc (City) 1989; Honorary DLitt (National Council for Academic Affairs) 1991; Honorary DSc (Hertfordshire) 1996; FIA 1955. **Tutor(s):** J M Wordie. **Johnian Relatives:** brother-in-law of Archibald Alastair McInnes (1942); grandfather of Alistair James Baker (2002). **Educ:** Raunds Church of England School; Kimbolton School. **Career:** Prudential Assurance Company Ltd/Prudential Corporation plc 1952–1995 (Deputy General Manager 1974–1976, General Manager 1976–1979, Group General Manager 1979–1982 Prudential Assurance Company Ltd; General Manager 1982–1985, Chief Executive 1982–1990, Director 1982–1990, Prudential Corporation Ltd; Chairman, Prudential Assurance Company Ltd 1985–1989; Chairman, Prudential Corporation plc 1990–1995). **Appointments:** Member, SJC Appeal Finance Committee; Vice President, Institute of Actuaries 1979–1983; Chairman, Association of British Insurers 1985–1987; Director, Bank of England 1985–1993; Visitor, Hatfield Polytechnic 1991–1992; President, Confederation of British Industry (CBI) 1990–1992; President, Geneva Association 1990–1994; Chairman, South Bank Board 1990–1998; First Chancellor, University of Hertfordshire 1992–1996; President, National Institute of Economic and Social Research 1994–; Governor, National Association of Security Dealers Inc 2001–. **Honours:** Kt 1989. **Publications:** Contributions to *Journal of Institute of Actuaries* and *Journal of the Geneva Association*.

CORBY, Harold Douglas Lane (1936) Born 19 May 1913, Melrose, Headington, Oxford; son of Edward William Corby, Tobacconist, and Gertrude Emily Walker. **Educ:** Church Street School, Oxford; Headington C of E School, Oxford; City of Oxford School; Ontario Agricultural College, Canada.

CORCUERA, Carlos Loizaga (1926) Born 12 June 1906, 17 Calle de Buenavista, City of Mexico; son of Carlos Loizaga Corcuera y Palomar, Architect, and Ana Riba y Cervantes; 1 son (Santiago Corcuera Cabezut). **Subject(s):** Mathematics; BA 1929. **Tutor(s):** J M Wordie. **Educ:** High School, Guadalajara, Mexico; Institute Guadalajara, Mexico; California Institute of Technology, Pasadena, California. **Career:** Oil Industry Engineer, Mexico.

CORDER, Philip (1912) Born 5 March 1891, 10 Kensington Terrace, Sunderland, County Durham; son of Herbert Corder, Insurance Broker, and Mary Grace Dymond; m Johanna Adrianna van der Mersch, 1915. **Subject(s):** Modern and Medieval Languages; BA 1915; MA 1919; DLitt 1951; Certificate of Mechanical Engineering (Bristol) 1912. **Tutor(s):** E E Sikes. **Educ:** Sunderland High School; Friends' School, Acworth; Friends' School, Bootham; University of Bristol. **Career:** Senior English Master, Northampton County School, 1915; English Master, later Housemaster, Bootham School 1918. **Appointments:** Honorary Curator, Malton Museum; Assistant Secretary, Society of Antiquities of London; President, Royal Archeological Institute 1954–1957. **Publications:** Editor, *Antiquaries' Journal, Archaeologica* and *Research Reports*. Died 28 May 1961.

CORLETT, Dr David Ernest (1945) Born 27 February 1927, 30 Highbury, Monkseaton, Northumberland; son of Ernest William Corlett, Marine Engineer, and Elsie Blanche Barnett; m (1) Sheila Nancy Topham, 19 December 1953, St Andrew's Church, Keighley, Yorkshire (d 1979), (2) Susan Williamson, 19 February 1983; (1) 1 son (Simon), 1 daughter (Jane), (2) 1 son (James). **Subject(s):** Natural Sciences; BA 1948; MA 1952; MB 1954; BChir 1954; DCH; DObstRCOG; MRCGP. **Tutor(s):**

G C L Bertram. **Educ:** Bygate Road Elementary School, Monkseaton; Royal Grammar School, Newcastle upon Tyne. **Career:** Medical Practitioner, Hospital House Appointments for 2 years, then GP; Part-time Medical Referee, DHSS/Benefits Agency 1981–1997. Died April 2002.

CORMACK, Professor Allan MacLeod (1947) Born 23 February 1924, 103 Becker Street, Bellevue, Johannesburg, Transvaal, South Africa; son of George Cormack, Electrical Engineer, and Amelia MacLeod; m Barbara Jeanne Seavey, 1950; 1 son (Robert); 2 daughters (Margaret and Jean). BSc (Cape Town) 1944; MSc (Cape Town) 1945; Honorary DSc (Tufts University) 1980; FAAAS 1980. **Tutor(s):** J M Wordie. **Educ:** Observatory Junior School, Johannesburg; Rondebosch Preparatory School; Grey Junior School, Port Elizabeth; Rondebosch High School, Cape Town; University of Cape Town. **Career:** Lecturer, University of Cape Town 1950–1956; Research Fellow, Harvard University 1956–1957; Assistant Professor 1957–1960, Associate Professor 1960–1964, Professor of Physics 1964–1980, Chairman, Physics Department 1968–1976, University Professor 1980, Tufts University. **Appointments:** Fellow, American Physical Society 1964; Honorary Member, Swedish Neuroradiological Society 1979; Member, National Academy of Sciences 1983; Foreign Fellow, Royal Society of South Africa 1983; Nelson Medical Lecturer, University of California, Davis 1985; South African Institute of Physics 1985; Watkins Visiting Professor, Wichita State University 1986; American Association of Physicists in Medicine 1988; Honorary Fellow, SJC 1993. **Awards:** Ballou Medallist, Tufts University 1978; (Jointly) Nobel Prize for Medicine 1979; Medal of Merit, University of Cape Town 1980; Mike Hogg Medallist, University of Texas 1981; US National Medal of Science 1990. **Publications:** Articles on nuclear and particle physics, computed tomography, and related mathematics. Died 7 May 1998.

CORNEY, John Victor (1941) Born 8 January 1923, Stockton Heath, Cheshire; son of Leonard George Corney, Colonial Civil Servant, Malaysia, and Hilda Fletcher; m Jean Margaret Cox, 30 April 1949, RMA Chapel, Sandhurst; 2 sons (J H Bruce b 24 April 1952 and R G Toby b 29 December 1958), 2 daughters (Susan C J b 26 July 1950 and C Lucy b 13 July 1964). **Subject(s):** Mechanical Sciences; BA 1944; MA 1948; FICE; FIMechE. **Tutor(s):** S J Bailey. **Johnian Relatives:** son of Leonard George Corney (1905). **Educ:** Charterhouse. **Career:** Engineer Officer, RN 1943–1946; Chartered Civil Engineer 1951–1988; Resident Engineer, Kariba Dam, Southern Rhodesia and Roseires Dam, Sudan; Partner responsible for Bombay Naval Dockyard Breakwater; Mina Zayed Harbour, Abu Dhabi; ASRY Dry Dock, Bahrain and Ruwais Naval Base, Oman. **Appointments:** Member, Panel of Reservoirs (Safety Provisions) Act 1930; Consultant to UNESCO on Philae Temples, Egypt and Lybian National Museum; Engineering Advisory Panel, Second Severn Crossing.

CORNEY, Leonard George (1905) Born 27 March 1886, 29 Lovely Lane, Warrington, Lancashire; son of Alfred Corney, Schoolmaster, and Elizabeth Steele Miller; m Hilda Fletcher, 1921; 1 son (John Victor b 8 January 1923), 1 daughter (Judith Anne b 9 April 1928). **Subject(s):** Classics; BA 1908. **Tutor(s):** E E Sikes. **Johnian Relatives:** father of John Victor Corney (1941). **Educ:** Wycliffe School, Warrington; Boteler Grammar School, Warrington. **Career:** Examiner, Colonial Audit Branch, Exchequer and Audit Department, Gold Coast 1910–1916; Acting Assistant Colonial Secretary 1916–1917; Gold Coast Regiment 1917–1918; Senior Assistant Auditor, then Acting Auditor 1919; Deputy Auditor 1920–1930; Assistant Director, Central Office 1930–1931; Deputy Auditor, Straits Settlements and Federated Malay Straits 1931–1940; Acting Financial Secretary 1940–1947; POW 1942–1945. **Appointments:** Salaries Commissioner, Aden and Somaliland. **Honours:** CMG 1946. Died 13 August 1955.

CORNWALL, Dr Ian Wolfran (1928) Born 28 November 1909, Westcliffe, Coonoor, Nilgeri Hills, South India; son of John Wolfran Cornwall, Lieutenant Colonel, Indian Medical Service, and Effie Esme Sinclair;

m (1) Anna Margareta (née Callear), 1937 (d 1967), (2) Mary L Reynolds (née Miller), 1974; 2 sons. **Subject(s):** Modern and Medieval Languages; BA 1931; Diploma (London) 1947; PhD (London) 1952. **Tutor(s):** M P Charlesworth. **Educ:** Horris Hill School, Newton, Newbury; Wellington College, Berkshire; Institute of Archaeology, University of London. **Career:** Teacher, Stafford School, Bushey Heath; Vacuum Cleaner Salesman 1931; Clerk, then manufacturer of pharmaceuticals 1931–1939; Postal and Telegraph Censor, Press Censor 1939–1945; Secretary 1948–1951, Researcher and Lecturer in Environmental Archaeology 1951–1965, Reader in Human Environment 1965–1974, Institute of Archaeology, University of London. **Appointments:** Life Member, Geologists' Association. **Awards:** Carnegie Medal, Library Association 1960; Henry Stopes Memorial Medal, Geologists' Association 1970. **Publications:** *Bones for the Archaeologist*, 1956 (revised edition 1975); *Soils for the Archaeologist*, 1958; *The Making of Man*, 1960; *The World of Ancient Man*, 1964; *Hunter's Half Moon* (fiction), 1967; *Prehistoric Animals and their Hunters*, 1968; *Ice Ages*, 1970; contributions to specialist journals. Died 18 November 1994.

CORNWELL, Derek John (1937) Born 28 April 1919, The Vicarage, Little Heath; son of Frank Barnard Cornwell, Merchant, and Maud Christian Williams; m Vivian Katherine Kitson, 7 December 1946. **Subject(s):** Economics; BA 1940; MA 1944. **Tutor(s):** C W Guillebaud. **Educ:** Brentwood School. Died 1 September 1990.

CORSELLIS, Henry Alexander (1928) Born 17 November 1909, 11 Preston Park Avenue, Preston, Brighton; son of Arthur Henry Nicholas Corsellis, Officer in 4th Dragoon Guards, and Elizabeth Annie Stewart. BA 1931. **Tutor(s):** C W Guillebaud. **Johnian Relatives:** brother of John Arthur Nicholas Corsellis (1933). **Educ:** Preparatory School, Haywards Heath; Haileybury College. **Career:** Admitted Solicitor 1935. Died 26 February 1982.

CORSELLIS, Professor John Arthur Nicholas (1933) Born 30 January 1915, Holt End, Kingsclere, Southampton; son of Arthur Henry Nicholas Corsellis, Major, 4th Cavalry Reserve Regiment, and Elizabeth Annie Stewart; m 1947; 1 son, 1 daughter. **Subject(s):** Modern Languages. **Tutor(s):** C W Guillebaud. **Johnian Relatives:** brother of Henry Alexander Corsellis (1928). **Educ:** Hillcrest Preparatory School, Haywards Heath; Haileybury College. **Career:** Consultant in Neuropathology, Runwell Hospital, Essex 1954–1976; Senior Lecturer, Department of Neuropathology, Institute of Psychiatry 1960–1963; Professor of Neuropathology 1976–1979; Honorary Consultant in Neuropathology, Runwell Hospital 1979–1985. **Publications:** *Mental Illness and the Ageing Brain*, 1962; *The Aftermath of Boxing*, 1973. Died 27 October 1994.

CORT, John Leonard Patchett (1903) Born 2 March 1883, 22 Northenden Road, Sale, Cheshire; son of John Patchett Cort, Clerk in Holy Orders, and Beatrice Catherine Russell; m Alice Margaret Masse, 4 April 1959. BA 1907; MA 1921. **Tutor(s):** C E Graves; J R Tanner. **Johnian Relatives:** grandson of Jonathon Johnson Cort (1846) and of James Russell (1849); son of John Patchett Cort (1876). **Educ:** Shrewsbury School. **Career:** Assistant Master, Brigg Grammar School 1907; Lieutenant, RASC, WWI; Honorary Lieutenant (Administrative Officer), RAF, WWI; Headmaster, Ashley House School, Worksop 1938; Mostyn House Preparatory School, Parkgate 1944. Died 14 September 1960.

COSGROVE, Dr Edward Cecil (1920) Born 27 April 1902, St Coca's, Kilcock, County Kildare, Ireland; son of Edward Cosgrove, Medical Practitioner, Coroner, and Agusta Cuffe; m Jessie; 2 sons (Duncan and Michael), 1 daughter (Sheila). BA 1923; MA 1958; MRCS (St Bartholomew's) 1928, LRCP (St Bartholomew's) 1928. **Tutor(s):** B F Armitage. **Educ:** Hodder Place School; Stonyhurst College. **Career:** House Physician, Warneford Hospital, Leamington, and Sussex County and Children's Hospital, Brighton; Physician, Royal Hospital, Nuxton. Died 22 May 1962.

COSH, Dr Frederick Sydney (1929) Born 1 July 1911, 69 Ashley Hill, Bristol; son of Godwin Fred Cosh, Company Director, and Joyce Amie Milsom. **Subject(s):** Natural Sciences; BA 1932; MB 1937; BChir 1937. **Tutor(s):** M P Charlesworth. **Johnian Relatives:** cousin of John Arthur Cosh (1933). **Educ:** Fellesford House Boys' School, Bristol; Cotham Secondary School; London Hospital. **Career:** GP, Chard, Somerset. **Awards:** Macaulay Scholarship 1928. Died 1974.

COSH, Dr John Arthur (1933) Born 17 June 1915, 39 Chesterfield Road, Bristol; son of Arthur Strode Cosh, Chemist and Druggist, and Ellen Jänisch; m Kate Jackson; 2 sons (Nicholas and Ian), 1 daughter (Claire). **Subject(s):** Natural Sciences; BA 1936; MA 1950; MB 1940; BChir 1940; MD 1951; MRCP 1947; FRCP (London) 1964. **Tutor(s):** R L Howland. **Johnian Relatives:** cousin of Frederick Sydney Cosh (1929); brother-in-law of Frederic Sinclair Jackson (1933). **Educ:** Littleton House, Knowle; The Grammar School, Bristol. **Career:** Junior Hospital posts, Lambeth and Winchester Hospitals; Surgeon Lieutenant, RNVR (Mentioned in Despatches) 1942–1946; Lecturer in Medicine, University of Bristol 1953–1957; Assistant Physician, United Bristol Hospitals 1953–1957; Consultant Physician, Bath Hospitals 1957–1979. **Appointments:** Member of Committee of Directors, Bristol Cancer Help Centre 1980–1990. **Awards:** Open Exhibition, SJC 1933; Scholarship, SJC 1934; University Scholarship, St Thomas' Hospital 1936–1939; Heberden Medal 1979. **Publications:** (with J V Lever) *Rheumatic Diseases and the Heart*, Springer, 1988; various papers on rheumatic diseases in medical journals.

COSSERAT, Eric Cyril (1925) Born 21 June 1906, son of Wilford Arthur Peloquin Cosserat, District Engineer, and Constance Adeline Mary Cockburn. BA 1929. **Tutor(s):** J M Wordie. **Educ:** St Paul's School, Darjeeling, India; Warwick School.

COSTAIN, Dr Cecil Clifford (1947) Born 16 June 1922, Ponoka, Alberta, Canada; son of Henry Hudson Costain, General Manager, Saskatchewan Breeders' Association, and Mary Elida Eakin. PhD 1952; BA (Saskatchewan) 1946; MA (Saskatchewan) 1947. **Tutor(s):** J M Wordie. **Educ:** Haultain Public School, Saskatoon; Nutana Collegiate Institute, Saskatoon; University of Saskatchewan. **Career:** Lieutenant Commander, Royal Canadian Navy 1941–1945. **Honours:** DSC. Died 18 December 1991.

COSTELLO, The Revd Kevin (1944) Born 3 November 1923, 18 St Andrew's Avenue, Droylesden, Lancashire; son of Henry Costello, Insurance Superintendent, and Susannah Rylance. **Subject(s):** Mathematics/History; BA 1947; MA 1951. **Tutor(s):** J M Wordie. **Educ:** De La Salle College, Pendleton; St John's College, Kintbury. **Career:** Headmaster, De La Salle College, Sheffield, 1954–1960; Auxiliary Provincial of the English Province of the De La Salle Brothers 1961.

COSTER, Hendrik Paulus (1946) Born 22 November 1919, The Hague, Holland; son of Dirk Coster, Professor of Physics, University of Groningen, and Lina Maria Wijsman. PhD (Utrecht) 1945. **Tutor(s):** J M Wordie. **Educ:** University of Groningen; University of Leyden; University of Utrecht. **Career:** Shell Studentship for work in Geophysics.

COTTON, The Revd John Horace Brazel (1948) Born 30 April 1928, Charnwood, 59 Thrale Road, Streatham, Surrey; son of John Horace Cotton, Taxation Officer, ICI, and Nora Kathleen Trevor; m Margaret Elizabeth Hutchinson, 2 October 1954; 3 sons (John Howard Lewis and Jeremy David b 31 May 1956 and Robert Lloyd b 2 January 1958). **Subject(s):** Mechanical Sciences; BA 1950; MA 1976; MIMechE; MACostE; CEng. **Tutor(s):** R L Howland. **Educ:** The Abbey School, Beckenham; Winchester House School, Brackley; Malvern College. **Career:** Vacuum Oil Company Ltd, Coryton Refinery 1951–1955; ICI Ltd Plastics Division, Division Cost Engineer 1955–1982; Ordained, St Albans Abbey 1981; Curate, Hertford Hundred Group of Parishes 1981–1987; Rector 1987–1996. **Appointments:** Chaplain 1983, Master 1986–1987 and 1999, Worshipful Company of Joiners and Ceilers; Member, Court of City University, London 2000–.

COTTON, The Revd Robert Hugh Alban (1908) Born 2 November 1888, 40 Spencer Square, Ramsgate, Kent; son of Charles Cotton, Surgeon, and Adelaide Leigh. BA 1911. **Tutor(s):** J R Tanner. **Educ:** Wellesley House, St Peter's Thanet; Malvern House, Keraney; Sutton Valence School; Scholae Cancellarii, Lincoln. **Career:** Deacon 1912; Curate, Calstock 1912–1915; Priest 1913; Curate, St Peter, Ealing 1915–1916; Curate, Holy Innocents, Hammersmith 1917; Second Lieutenant, RASC, WWI. **Awards:** Robins Exhibition; Philpott Exhibition, Scholae Cancellarii, Lincoln 1911. Died 12 October 1918 (died at Taranto of pneumonia).

COULSON, Bernard William Harrison (1930) Born 24 May 1911, 11 Cecil Road, Rochester, Kent; son of Lewis John Coulson, Farmer and Agricultural Merchant, and Florence Susannah Campbell; m Muriel Gertrude Pryor, 1941 (d 1996); 3 sons (Edmund John Harrison b 1945, Robert Anthony Harrison b 1947 and Edward William Harrison b 1955). **Subject(s):** Natural Sciences; BA 1933; MA 1937; BSc (London); DipEd (London). **Tutor(s):** J M Wordie. **Johnian Relatives:** uncle of Charles Lewis Harrison Coulson (1960) and of Francis Owen Harrison Coulson (1966); father of Edward William Harrison Coulson (1973). **Educ:** University School, Rochester; Mathematical School, Rochester; The King's School, Rochester; Institute of Education, Birkbeck College, London. **Career:** Dauntsey's School, Devizes 1934–1947; Head of Biology Department, Oundle School 1948–1971. **Appointments:** Schoolmaster Fellow Commoner 1968. Died 16 March 2003.

COULSON, Douglas Joseph (1936) Born 12 September 1917, 14 Market Place, Pocklington; son of Fred Coulson, Florist and Fruiterer, and Grace Allison; m Betty; 1 son (John), 1 daughter (Jane). **Subject(s):** English/Geography; BA 1939; MA 1946; DipEd (Cambridge). **Tutor(s):** J S Boys Smith. **Educ:** Pocklington C of E School; Pocklington School. **Career:** Lieutenant Colonel, RA; served in India and Burma 1939–1946; Assistant Master, Merchant Taylors' School, Moor Park 1946–1952; Headmaster, Adams Grammar School, Shropshire 1952–1962; Headmaster, Collyer's School, Horsham 1962–1965; Headmaster, Queen Elizabeth's Grammar School, Blackburn 1965–1977. **Appointments:** JP. Died 31 July 1977.

COULTON, Dr George Gordon (1919) (admitted to St Catharine's College 1877) Born 15 October 1858, King's Lynn, Norfolk; son of John James Coulton, Solicitor, and Sarah Radley; m. Rose Dorothy Ilbert, 1903 (d 1959); 2 daughters (Mary and Bridget). LittD 1928; BA 1881 (St Catharine's); MA 1890 (St Catharine's); Hon DLitt (Durham) 1920; Hon LLD (Edinburgh) 1931, (Queen's University, Kingston, Ontario) 1942; FBA 1929. **Educ:** Lycée Imperial, St Omer; Felsted School; St Catharine's College, Cambridge; Heidelberg University. **Career:** Preparatory Schoolmaster, Malvern Wells; Deacon 1883; Priest 1884; Curate, Offley 1883, Rickmansworth 1884; Assistant Master, Llandovery College 1885–1887; Assistant Master, Sherborne School 1889–1892; Assistant Master, Sedbergh School 1892–1893; Assistant Master, Dulwich College 1893–1896; Assistant Master, South Lynn, Eastbourne 1897–1910; Lecturer in English, University of Cambridge 1919–1934; Foundress Fellow 1919–1926, Title B Fellow 1926–1947, SJC. **Appointments:** Birkbeck Lecturer in Ecclesiastical History, Trinity College, Cambridge 1910; Honorary Fellow, St Catharine's College, Cambridge 1922–1947; Lowell Lecturer, Boston, Massachusetts 1923; Davies Lecturer, Aberystwyth 1923; Ford's Lecturer, Oxford 1930–1931; Rhind Lecturer, Edinburgh 1931; Guest Professor of History, Toronto University 1940–1944. **Awards:** Scholarship, St Catharine's College 1877. **Publications:** *A Strong Army in a Free State*, 1900; *Public Schools and Public Needs*, 1901; *Friars Lantern*, 1906; *From St Francis to Dante*, 1906; *Chaucer and His England*, 1908; *The main illusions of pacifism*, 1916; *The Case for Compulsory Military Service*, 1917; *Christ, St Francis and to-day*, 1919; *Five Centuries of Religion*, 1923; *Life in the Middle Ages*, 1928; *Art and the Reformation*, 1928; *Crusades, commerce and adventure*, 1930; *Romanism and truth*, 1930; *The medieval scene*, 1930; *Papal infallibility*, 1932; *Scottish abbeys & social life*, 1933; *Medieval Panorama*,

1938; *Inquisition and liberty*, 1938; *Europe's apprenticeship: a survey of medieval Latin with examples*, 1940; *Fourscore Years*, 1943; General Editor, *Cambridge Studies in Medieval Life and Thought*; occasional writer, *The Guardian*. Died 4 March 1947.

COULTOUS, Frederick David (1944) Born 18 May 1926, 48 King Street, Eccleshill, Bradford, Yorkshire; son of Herbert Coultous, House Decorator, and Elsie Margaret Rowlands. **Subject(s):** Theology; BA 1949; MA 1952. **Tutor(s):** J M Wordie. **Johnian Relatives:** brother-in-law of Ernest Roland Walmsley (1948). **Educ:** Eccleshill Parish Church School; Belle Vue High School, Bradford. **Appointments:** RN Cadet, SJC. Died 29 November 1989.

COURT, Kenneth Frank (1944) Born 14 March 1926, New Church College, Devonshire Street, Islington; son of Arthur Frank Court, District Manager, Navy Army and Air Force Institute, and Alice Maud Carter; m Sybil; 2 sons (Andrew and David), 1 daughter (Jenny). **Subject(s):** English; BA 1949. **Tutor(s):** J M Wordie. **Educ:** Westleigh School, Southend-on-Sea; Woodside Junior School, Croydon; Walton on Thames Central School; Prescot Grammar School, Lancashire. **Career:** Managing Director, specialist textile firm. **Appointments:** RAF Cadet, SJC. Died 8 October 2000.

COUSEN, Cecil (1931) Born 14 April 1913, 13 Cornwall Terrace, Manningham, Bradford; son of Herbert Cousen, Stuff Merchants Traveller, and Mary Stead. **Subject(s):** Mathematics. **Tutor(s):** C W Guillebaud. **Educ:** The Grammar School, Bradford; Woodhouse Grove School.

COUTIE, George Angus (1949) Born 15 August 1929, Prestwich, Lancashire; son of Richard Porteous Coutie and Catherine Dall; m Heather Wood, 24 April 1954; 2 daughters (Jane b 1957 and Margaret b 1960). **Subject(s):** Mathematics; Diploma in Mathematical Statistics; BA 1952; MA 1956. **Tutor(s):** J M Wordie; J R Bambrough. **Educ:** Prestwich Park View Council School; Manchester Grammar School. **Career:** Royal Army Ordnance Corps 1947–1949; Statistician, later Management Services Manager, Organics Division, ICI 1953–1986. **Awards:** Scholarship, SJC.

COUTINHO, Fritz Herbert (1929) Born 19 December 1910, Hamburg, Germany; son of Felix Coutinho, Steel and Metal Export Merchant, and Hedwig Reinhardt. **Tutor(s):** C W Guillebaud. **Educ:** Vorschule Bertram, Hamburg; Gelehrten Schule des Johanneums, Hamburg.

COUTTS, Sir Walter Fleming (1935) Born 30 November 1912, 1 Fonthill Road, Aberdeen; son of John William Coutts, Minister, United Free Church, and Rose Fleming; m Janet Elizabeth Jamieson, 1942; 1 son, 1 daughter. MA (St Andrews) 1934. **Tutor(s):** J S Boys Smith. **Educ:** Glasgow Academy; University of Andrews. **Career:** District Officer, Kenya 1936; Secretariat, Kenya 1946; District Commissioner, Kenya 1947; Administrator, St Vincent, West Indies 1949–1955; Minister for Education, Labour and Lands, Kenya 1956–1958; Chief Secretary, Education, Labour and Lands, Kenya 1958–1961; Governor, Uganda 1961–1962; Governor-General and Commander-in-Chief, Uganda 1962–1963; Chairman, Metal Industries 1965–1969; Assistant Vice-Chancellor (Administration), Warwick University 1969–1971; Chairman, Pergamon Press 1972–1974; Chairman, Grindlays (Commercial) Holdings 1974–1978. **Appointments:** Special Commissioner for African Elections February 1955; Director, Assam Investments 1964–1978; Secretary to Dulverton Trust 1966–1969; Director, Inchcape (East Africa) Ltd 1970–1978; Director, The Farmington Trust 1971–1978. **Honours:** MBE 1949; CMG 1953; Kt 1961; KCMG 1961; GCMG 1962. Died 4 November 1988.

COVERLEY, Leonard James (1933) Born 6 November 1914, 52 Holly Road, Northampton; son of James Coverley, Foreman Joiner, and Agnes Dean Perrett. **Subject(s):** Classics; BA 1936; MA 1947. **Tutor(s):** R L Howland. **Educ:** Stimpson Avenue School, Northampton; Stamford

School. **Career:** Senior Classical Master, Chelmsford Hall, Eastbourne 1936–1940; RAMC 1940–1943; Lecturer in Classics, University of Cairo, Giza, Egypt 1943–1946; Research Student, London University 1946; Acting Headmaster, Chelmsford Hall, Eastbourne. 1947. **Awards:** Marquess of Exeter Exhibition, SJC. Died 2 January 1997.

COWAN, John (1935) Born 28 September 1916, Bayfield, Stawford Road, Bowden, Altrincham; son of Andrew Wallace Cowan, Constructional Engineer, and Charlotte Mervyna Pillman. **Subject(s):** Economics/Moral Sciences; BA 1938. **Tutor(s):** C W Guillebaud. **Educ:** St Monica's School, Edinburgh; Cargilfield, Edinburgh; Fettes College, Edinburgh.

COWBURN, Richard Edridge (1928) Born 25 July 1908, 24 Chapel Street, Belgrave Square, London; son of Frank Cowburn, Tea Planter, and Emily Varley; m Catharine Elizabeth Biscoe, 17 November 1944. **Tutor(s):** M P Charlesworth. **Educ:** St Ronan's, West Worthing; Lancing College, Sussex.

COWEN, Harold Wolfe (1924) Born 7 April 1906, 100 Commercial Road, St George in the East, London; son of Marcus Woolf Cowen, Medical Practitioner, and Ray Brenda Myers; m Raymonde. BA 1928; MA 1931; MRCS (University College Hospital) 1931; LRCP (University College Hospital) 1931. **Tutor(s):** B F Armitage. **Educ:** Ascot House, Brighton; The Perse School, Cambridge. Died 3 April 1968.

COWEN, Lieutenant Painton Sydney (1936) Born 28 April 1918, Johannesburg; son of Walter Painton Cowen, Mining Engineer, and Amy Margaret Marshall; m Doris Pamela. **Tutor(s):** J S Boys Smith. **Johnian Relatives:** brother of Roderick Cowen (1946). **Educ:** Diocesan College, Cape Town; Heathfield Preparatory School, Kent; Oundle School. **Career:** Lieutenant, Royal Marines 1939–1942. Died December 1942 (killed on active service).

COWEN, Roderick (1946) Born 29 March 1927, Fyzabad, Trinidad, West Indies; son of Walter Painton Cowen, Mining Engineer, and Amy Margaret Marshall. **Tutor(s):** G C L Bertram. **Johnian Relatives:** brother of Painton Sydney Cowen (1936). **Educ:** Western Province Preparatory School; Tyenhanger Lodge, Seaford; Diocesan College, Cape Town.

COWLEY, Ralph Alexander (1936) Born 6 February 1917, 21 Beaumont Terrace, Spennymore, Durham; son of John Embleton Cowley, Marine Engineer, and Phyllis Mary Brown. **Subject(s):** History/Moral Sciences; BA 1939. **Tutor(s):** J S Boys Smith. **Educ:** King's Street Council School, Spennymoor; Royal Grammar School, Newcastle upon Tyne. **Career:** Temporary Sub-Lieutenant, RN 1939–1940. **Awards:** Sizarship, SJC. Died 1 June 1940 (killed in action off Dunkirk in HM Minesweeper *Skipjack*).

COWPER, Alfred William Noel (1923) Born 26 December 1905, 3 Beaconsfield Terrace, Hythe, Kent; son of Alfred Edward Cowper, Company Director, and Lucy Alice Barson. **Subject(s):** Economics; BA 1931. **Tutor(s):** E E Sikes. **Johnian Relatives:** brother of Michael Roy Cowper (1934). **Educ:** Dunstun House School, Ealing; The Pilgrims Preparatory School, Westerham; Sedbergh School. **Career:** Solicitor. Died 1981.

COWPER, Joseph Herbert (1919) Born 7 April 1900, 1 Plotina Terrace, South Shields, Durham; son of Joseph Cowper, General Merchant, and Margaret Elizabeth Scott Beck Dove. **Tutor(s):** E E Sikes. **Educ:** Mr Wilkinson's, Eslington Tower, Jesmond; Aldenham School. **Career:** Cadet, RFA 1918–1919.

COWPER, Michael Roy (1934) Born 22 October 1916, 22 Mount Avenue, Ealing; son of Alfred Edward Cowper, Company Director, and Lucy Alice Barson; m Margaret. **Subject(s):** Law; BA 1937; MA 1942; LLB 1938; LLM 1985. **Tutor(s):** C W Guillebaud. **Johnian Relatives:** brother of Alfred William Noel Cowper (1923). **Educ:** Manor House, Horsham; Rugby School. **Career:** Solicitor. Died 31 July 1993.

COX, David (1932) Born 13 September 1913, 20 Sheep Street, Wellingborough; son of George James Cox, Boot and Shoe Manufacturer, and Florence Mary Stevens. **Subject(s):** Natural Sciences; BA 1935; MA 1953. **Tutor(s):** J M Wordie. **Educ:** Wellingborough School.

COX, Professor Sir David Roxbee (1942) Born 15 July 1924, Hall Road Nursing Home, Handsworth; son of Sam Roxbee Cox, Die-Sinker, and Lilian Esther Braines; m Joyce Drummond, 21 August 1948, St Mary's, Keighley; 3 sons, 1 daughter. **Subject(s):** Mathematics; BA 1946; MA 1950; PhD (Leeds) 1947; various Hon DSc; FRS 1973; Hon FBA 1997. **Tutor(s):** S J Bailey. **Educ:** St Michael's School, Birmingham; Handsworth Grammar School. **Career:** RAE 1944–1946; Wool Industries Research Association 1946–1950; Assistant Lecturer in Mathematics (Statistics), Statistical Laboratory, University of Cambridge 1950–1955; Visiting Professor, University of North Carolina 1955–1956; Reader in Statistics 1956–1960, Professor of Statistics 1961–1966, Birkbeck College, London; Editor, *Biometrika* 1966; Professor of Statistics 1966–1988, Head of Department of Mathematics 1970–1974, SERC Senior Research Fellow 1983–1988, Imperial College, London; Warden, Nuffield College, Oxford 1988–1994. **Appointments:** President, Bernoulli Society 1979–1981; Royal Statistical Society 1980–1982; Foreign Member, Royal Danish Academy of Sciences and Letters 1983; Foreign Honorary Member, American Academy of Arts and Sciences 1974; Foreign Associate, US National Academy of Science 1988; Honorary Fellow, SJC 1989; Foreign Member, Indian National Academy of Science 1992; Council Member, Royal Society 1994–1996; President, International Statistical Institute 1995–1997. **Awards:** Major Scholarship 1941. **Honours:** Kt 1985. **Publications:** (jointly) *Statistical Methods in the Textile Industry*, 1949; *Planning of Experiments*, 1958; (jointly) *Queues*, 1961; *Renewal Theory*, 1962; (jointly) *Theory of Stochastic Processes*, 1965; (jointly) *Statistical Analysis of Series of Events*, 1966; *Analysis of Binary Data*, 1970; (jointly) *Theoretical Statistics*, 1974; (jointly) *Problems and Solutions in Theoretical Statistics*, 1978; (jointly) *Point Processes*, 1980; (jointly) *Applied Statistics*, 1981; (jointly) *Analysis of Survival Data*, 1984; papers in *Journal of The Royal Statistical Society, Biometrika*, etc.

COX, Henry Talbot (1921) Born 14 September 1902, Georgetown, Demerara, British Guiana; son of Henry Soper Cox, Barrister-at-Law, and Georgina Alice Maud Etheridge; m Jean; 1 son (Peter). **Subject(s):** Natural Sciences; BA 1924; MA 1934; BChir 1934; MB 1934; MD 1940; MRCS 1926; LRCP 1926; FRCSEd 1933; FRCS. **Tutor(s):** B F Armitage. **Johnian Relatives:** son of Henry Soper Cox (1889). **Educ:** Preparatory School, St Albans; St Albans School. **Career:** House Surgeon, St Thomas' Hospital, London; Junior resident posts, Bradford and Liverpool; Assistant Medical Officer, Booth Hall, Manchester; Resident Surgical Officer, Withington Hospital, later Consultant Surgeon 1932–1967; Consultant Surgeon, Wythenshawe Hospital 1950–1969. **Appointments:** President, Manchester Medical Society 1958–1959. **Publications:** Several articles. Died 5 January 1984.

COX, Horace Beresford (1901) Born 7 August 1882, Roslyn Villa, Millbrook Road, Freemantle, Southampton; son of Charles Cox, Printer and Publisher, and Rosa Bartlett. **Tutor(s):** D MacAlister. **Educ:** Dean Close School, Cheltenham. **Career:** Lieutenant Colonel, RGA (TF), WWI. **Honours:** OBE.

COX, Robert Mundy (1921) Naval Officer.

CRADOCK, Leonard (1920) Born 1 March 1902, Mayfield, Ruswarp, Whitby, Yorkshire; son of Leonard Cradock, of independent means, and Mary Braithwaite. **Tutor(s):** E E Sikes. **Educ:** Orleton, Scarborough; Uppingham School.

CRADOCK, Rt Hon Sir Percy (1946) Born 26 October 1923, Greenfield Farm, Byers Green, County Durham; son of Alfred James Cradock, Colliery Cashier, and Caroline Elizabeth Robinson; m Birthe Marie Dyrland, 1953. **Subject(s):** English/Law; BA 1948; MA 1952; LLB 1951;

LLM 1985. **Tutor(s):** F Thistlethwaite. **Educ:** Byers Green Council School; Alderman Wraith School, Spennymoor. **Career:** RAF 1946; Superviser in Law, University of Cambridge 1951–1954; Called to the Bar, Middle Temple 1953; HM Diplomatic Service 1954; Foreign Office 1954–1957; Kuala Lumpur 1957–1961; Hong Kong 1961; First Secretary, Peking 1962; Foreign Office 1963–1966; Councillor and Head of Chancery, Peking 1966–1968; Chargé d'Affaires, Peking 1968–1969; Head of Planning Staff, FCO 1969–1971; Under-Secretary, Cabinet Office 1971–1975; Ambassador, East Germany 1976–1978; Leader, UK Delegation, Test Ban Discussions 1977–1978; Ambassador, Republic of China 1978–1983; Continuing responsiblity for negotiations over future of Hong Kong 1983–1984; Prime Minister's Foreign Affairs Adviser 1984–1992; Chairman, Joint Intelligence Committee 1985–1992. **Appointments:** President, Cambridge Union 1950; Honorary Fellow, SJC 1982. **Awards:** Exhibition, SJC 1941. **Honours:** CMG 1968; KCMG 1980; GCMG 1983; PC 1993. **Publications:** *Recollections of the Cambridge Union*; *Experiences of China*, 1994; *In Pursuit of British Interests*, 1997; *Know Your Enemy*, 2002.

CRAFER, Charles Thomas (1919) Born 19 January 1899, Langham, Norfolk; son of Charles Crafer, Farmer, and Margaret Cooke. **Tutor(s):** E A Benians. **Educ:** Miss Cook's School, Lynfield, Hunstanton; Wellingborough School. **Career:** RFA Cadet School, Exeter 1917; Second Lieutenant, RFA, served in France 1918–1919.

CRAGG, Francis Talbot (1936) Born 7 August 1918, 49 West View, Elland, Yorkshire; son of William Talbot Cragg, Owner, Providence Mills, Elland, and Ethel Horsman. **Subject(s):** Economics/Law; BA 1939. **Tutor(s):** C W Guillebaud. **Educ:** Bowden House School, Seaford; Uppingham School.

CRAGG, John Norman (1944) Born 28 February 1926, Crossbar, Morland, Westmorland; son of Benjamin Cragg, Gardener, and Elsie Lightfoot. **Tutor(s):** J M Wordie. **Educ:** Arnside National School; Heversham Grammar School.

CRAGGS, Ernest Wade Foxton (HALL-CRAGGS) (1919) Born 1 May 1896, The Poplars, Woodlands Road, Middlesbrough; son of Ernest Hall Craggs, Naval Architect and Engineer, and Emma Ida Bertholde Trechmann; m (1) Agnes Sidney Wilkins, 25 June 1925, (2) Joan Johnstone; (1) 1 son (Ernest Christopher Bernard b 20 November 1926), 1 daughter (Priscilla). **Subject(s):** Mechanical Sciences; BA 1922; MA 1958. **Tutor(s):** E E Sikes. **Johnian Relatives:** son of Ernest Hall Craggs (1881); nephew of George Craggs Craggs (1902); brother of Richard Berthold Trechmann Craggs (1922); father of Ernest Christopher Bernard Hall-Craggs (1944); uncle of John Francis Hall-Craggs (1953). **Educ:** Beechmont, Sevenoaks; Charterhouse. **Career:** Managing Director, Coronium Metal Company Ltd, Reading. Died 1 September 1959.

CRAGGS, George Craggs (1902) Born 11 July 1874, Woodlands, Middlesbrough, Yorkshire; son of Henry Foxton Craggs, Shipbuilder, and Isabella Hall. BA 1905. **Tutor(s):** C E Graves; J R Tanner. **Johnian Relatives:** uncle of Ernest Wade Foxton Craggs (1919) and of Richard Berthold Trechmann Craggs (1922); great uncle of Ernest Christopher Bernard Hall-Craggs (1944) and of John Francis Hall-Craggs (1953). **Educ:** Leys School, Cambridge; Woodhouse Grove School; High School, Middlesbrough. **Career:** Soldering Fluids Factory Manager. Died 29 April 1941.

CRAGGS, Professor James Wilkinson (1949) Born 3 February 1920, 2 Glenthorne Road, Sunderland; son of Thomas Gibson Craggs, Schoolmaster, and Margaret Wilkinson. PhD 1955; BSc (Manchester) 1941; PhD (Manchester) 1947. **Tutor(s):** J M Wordie. **Educ:** Barnes' School, Sunderland; Sunderland Bede Collegiate School; University of Manchester. **Career:** Lecturer in Mathematics, St Andrews University; Lecturer in Mathematics, King's College, Newcastle upon Tyne 1954; Professor of Mathematics, University of Leeds 1961; Professor of Engineering Mathematics, University of Melbourne 1967; Professor of

Mathematics, Southampton University until 1989. **Awards:** Senior 1851 Exhibition.

CRAGGS, Richard Berthold Trechmann (HALL-CRAGGS) (1922) Born 2 March 1903, Woodlands Road, Middlesbrough, Yorkshire; son of Ernest Hall Craggs, Naval Architect and Engineer, and Emma Ida Bertholde Trechmann; m Gwendolen Oliver, July 1930; 1 son (John Francis b 20 September 1931), 2 daughters (Anne Emma and Marion Gwendolen). **Subject(s):** Mathematics/Mechanical Sciences; BA 1925; MA 1929; MIMechE. **Tutor(s):** E Cunningham. **Johnian Relatives:** son of Ernest Hall Craggs (1881); nephew of George Craggs Craggs (1902); brother of Ernest Wade Foxton Craggs (1919); uncle of Ernest Christopher Bernard Hall-Craggs (1944); father of John Francis Hall-Craggs (1953). **Educ:** Beechmont, Sevenoaks; Shrewsbury School. **Career:** Thomas Hedley and Co Ltd, Trafford Park, Manchester 1937; T Hedley and Co, Collingwood Street, Newcastle upon Tyne 1951. **Appointments:** Engineers' Association, University of Cambridge. Died 16 August 1962.

CRAIG, Dr Douglas Stuart (1941) Born 23 November 1923, Benmore, Mill Road, Bebington, Cheshire; son of Robert Craig, Chemical Engineer, and Hilda Elizabeth Wood. **Subject(s):** Natural Sciences; BA 1944; MA 1948; BChir 1948; MB 1948. **Tutor(s):** C W Guillebaud. **Educ:** Mostyn House School, Parkgate; Radley College.

CRAIG, James Alan (1926) Born 8 September 1904, Waterhead of Dryfe, Hutton, Dumfriesshire, Scotland; son of Edward James Craig, Farmer, and Janet Greenshields Hamilton. **Tutor(s):** E A Benians. **Educ:** Wallace Hall Academy; Edinburgh Academy; West of Scotland Agricultural College; Institute of Research in Agricultural Economics, Oxford.

CRAIG, Norman Vincent (1924) Born 12 September 1906, Eldon Green, Ballyrobert, County Down, Ireland; son of Vincent Craig, Architect, and Millicent Bowring Wimble. BA (Magdalene) 1928; MA (Magdalene) 1938. **Tutor(s):** B F Armitage. **Johnian Relatives:** brother of Terence Vincent Craig (1921). **Educ:** Amesbury School, Hindhead; Gresham's School, Holt. **Career:** Called to the Bar, Inner Temple 1930; Northern Circuit.

CRAIG, Terence Vincent (1921) Born 23 December 1902, Eldon Green, Ballyrobert, County Down, Ireland; son of Vincent Craig, Architect, and Millicent Bowring Wimble; m (1) Diana Skimming, 1933, (2) Pam; 2 sons (Tom and Dick), 1 daughter (Amanda). BA 1925; MA 1928. **Tutor(s):** B F Armitage. **Johnian Relatives:** brother of Norman Vincent Craig (1924). **Educ:** Mount Alington, Hindhead; Wellington College; Home Place, Holt. Died 17 December 1963.

CRAIG, Thomas Bird (1922) Born 18 July 1903, Kasauli, Punjab, India; son of Charles William Craig, Railway Advisor to the Rajpura, and Julia Merceron Burton; m 1937 (d 1954); 2 daughters. **Subject(s):** Agriculture; BA 1925. **Tutor(s):** E A Benians. **Educ:** Hill House Preparatory School, St Leonards on Sea; Haileybury College. **Career:** Chief Land Inspector, Lands Department, Rhodesia 1963. Died 27 April 1972.

CRAIK, Dr Kenneth James William (1936) Born 29 March 1914, 10 Trinity Street, Leith; son of James Bowstead Craik, Writer to the Signet, and Marie Sylvia Robson. PhD 1940. **Tutor(s):** J S Boys Smith. **Educ:** Edinburgh Academy; University of Edinburgh. **Career:** Title A Fellow, SJC 1941–1945 (leave of absence on war service 1941–1945); Director, Unit for Research in Applied Psychology, Cambridge 1944. **Appointments:** Shaw Fellowship 1936; Chairman, Target Tracking Panel, Ministry of Supply. **Publications:** *The Nature of Explanation*, CUP, 1943; *Mechanisms of the Mind*, CUP, 1966. Died 7 May 1945.

CRANE, Charles David (1938) Born 2 July 1919, Kingsdene, Sutton on Hull, Yorkshire; son of Charles James Crane, Insurance Broker, and Jessie Richardson. **Subject(s):** History. **Tutor(s):** J S Boys Smith. **Johnian Relatives:** brother of James Alfred Crane (1932). **Educ:** The High School, Hull; Hymers College, Hull. **Awards:** Exhibition, SJC 1937.

CRANE, James Alfred (1932) Born 31 May 1914, Charleston, Anlaby Road, Kingston-upon-Hull; son of Charles James Crane, Insurance Broker and Member of Lloyds, and Jessie Richardson. **Subject(s):** Economics/Law. **Tutor(s):** C W Guillebaud. **Johnian Relatives:** brother of Charles David Crane (1938). **Educ:** The High School, Hull; Hymers College, Hull.

CRANLEY, John Desmond (1921) Born 3 July 1903, 81 Orchard Road, Southsea, Hampshire; son of James David William Henry Fry Cranley, Engineer Commander, RN, and Florence Louise Sanderson. **Tutor(s):** E A Benians. **Educ:** Portsmouth Grammar School; Royal Naval College, Osborne; Royal Naval College, Dartmouth.

CRAUFORD, Clive Lane (1938) Born 9 February 1919, 40 Leeside Avenue, Muswell Hill, London; son of William Harold Lane Crauford, Architect, and Phyllis Maud Prince. **Subject(s):** Economics. **Tutor(s):** C W Guillebaud. **Educ:** Norfolk House School; Highgate School. **Career:** Major 1939–1945; Stockbroker 1946. **Honours:** MC.

CRAUFORD, Leonard George (1904) Born 1 February 1886, Brittania Theatre, Hoxton, Middlesex; son of Alfred Lane Crauford, Theatrical Manager, and Georgina Pigott. **Subject(s):** Law; BA 1907; MA 1912; LLB 1907. **Tutor(s):** D MacAlister. **Educ:** University College School, London. **Career:** Sapper, RE (London Electrical Engineers, TF), WWI.

CRAVEN, Arthur (1937) Born 26 October 1916, Calside, Paisley; son of David Edwin Craven, Electrical Engineer, and Elizabeth Ayston; 1 son. **Subject(s):** Modern and Medieval Languages; BA 1939; MA 1943. **Tutor(s):** C W Guillebaud. **Educ:** South School, Paisley; Pallion School, Sunderland; Bendanell Council School, Leeds; City of Leeds School; University of Leeds. **Career:** Senior Modern Languages Master and Housemaster, St Peter's School, York 1946–1967. Died 10 September 1967.

CRAVEN, William Anthony Hubert (1922) Born 25 January 1904, 77 Elizabeth Street, Belgravia, London; son of The Hon Charles Eric Craven, Lieutenant, Scots Guards, and Amalia Kolowratek. **Tutor(s):** B F Armitage. **Educ:** Beaumont College, Windsor; Horne Place, Holt.

CRAWFORD, Arthur Dennis Benjamin (1932) Born 4 December 1913, High Street, Wolstanton, Staffordshire; son of Hubert Benjamin Crawford, Hyde and Skin Broker, and Norah Wilkinson Shorter. **Tutor(s):** J M Wordie. **Educ:** The Grammar School, Wolverhampton; The Leys School, Cambridge. **Career:** Director, Mullins Ltd, Dudley; Major, 10th Gurka Rifles, Far East 1939–1945. Died March 1966.

CRAWFORD, John Aikman (1925) Born 24 November 1906, 98 Polwarth Terrace, Edinburgh, Scotland; son of Harry George Crawford, Wine Merchant, and Annie Marguerita Ferguson; 2 daughters (Rosemary and Brigit), 1 stepdaughter (Gill). **Subject(s):** Mathematics; BA 1928. **Tutor(s):** J M Wordie. **Educ:** Edinburgh Academy; Malvern College. Died 4 December 1988.

CRAWFORD, Dr Maurice Paterson (1924) Born 8 July 1906, Darjeeling, India; son of William Monod Crawford, Indian Civil Service, and Annie Paterson. **Subject(s):** Natural Sciences; BA 1927; MB; BAO; BCh. **Tutor(s):** B F Armitage. **Johnian Relatives:** son of William Monod Crawford (1894); brother of William Glasgow Crawford (1919). **Educ:** Ashleigh House School; Clanrye Preparatory School; Royal Academical Institution, Belfast. **Career:** Various House Posts, lastly at General Lying-In Hospital, York Road, London; Private Practice, Bexley, Kent; GP, Minchinhampton, Gloucestershire. **Appointments:** Honorary Member, British Red Cross Society; Honorary Secretary, Dartford Division, BMA. Died 12 December 1977.

CRAWFORD, Dr Robert (1932) Born 17 August 1913, The Shieling, Maybole, Ayrshire, Scotland; son of John Crawford, Boot and Shoe Manufacturer, and Agnes Alexander, Piano Teacher; m Paula, 21 July 1951, 3 children. **Subject(s):** Natural Sciences; BA 1935; MA 1940; MB 1940; BChir 1940; MD 1954; MRCOG 1950, FRCOG 1965. **Tutor(s):** R L Howland. **Educ:** Cambusdown Preparatory School, Alloway, Scotland; Loretto School, Musselburgh, Scotland. **Career:** Squadron Leader, RAF Medical Branch 1940–1945; Consultant Obstetrician and Gynaecologist, South Essex Group of Hospitals 1955–1979. Died 5 July 2000.

CRAWFORD, William Glasgow (1919) Born 28 April 1902, Lanauli, Bombay Presidency, India; son of William Monod Crawford, Indian Civil Service, and Annie Paterson; 1 son, 2 daughters. **Subject(s):** Natural Sciences; BA 1923. **Tutor(s):** E A Benians. **Johnian Relatives:** son of William Monod Crawford (1894); brother of Maurice Paterson Crawford (1924). **Educ:** Clanrye School, Belfast; Royal Academical Institution, Belfast. **Career:** Assistant Conservator in Indian Forest Service, Burma, Indian Civil Service 1925; Deputy Conservator, Indian Forest Service, Burma, Indian Civil Service 1931; RAF, then Lieutenant Colonel, Army, Burma, WWII; Ministry of Agriculture, England; Fruit-Farmer, New Zealand. Died July 1968.

CRAWLEY-BOEVEY, Richard Martin (1927) Born 31 July 1908, Simla, India; son of Edward Martin Crawley-Boevey, Captain, 1st Royal Sussex Regiment, and Rosalie Winifred Margaret Sartorius. **Tutor(s):** E A Benians. **Educ:** St Cyprian's, Eastbourne; Summersdale, Chichester; Chillon College, Villeneue, Vaud, Switzerland.

CRAWLEY-BOEVEY, Thomas (Tim) Michael Blake (1949) Born 29 September 1928, St Albans, Hertfordshire; son of Sir Launcelot Valentine Hyde Crawley-Boevey, Baronet, and Elizabeth Goodeth Innes; m Laura Coelingh, 1957 (d 1979); 2 sons (Thomas Hyde b 1958 and William Walstan b 1960). **Subject(s):** English; BA 1952; MA 1956. **Tutor(s):** A G Lee. **Johnian Relatives:** father of William Walstan Crawley-Boevey (1978). **Educ:** St Peter's Court, Broadstairs; Wellington College. **Career:** Second Lieutenant, Durham Light Infantry 1948; Shipping Agent 1952–1961; Consumers' Association 1961–1982; Editor, *Money Which?* 1968–1976; Editor, *Which?* 1976–1982; Editor-in-chief, *Which?* 1980–1982; Council Insurance Ombudsman Bureau 1985. **Appointments:** Master, Girdlers' Company 1992–1993.

CRAWSHAW, Derek Anthony John (1948) Born 6 November 1927, Staines, Middlesex; son of Charles Herbert Crawshaw, Colonel, Army Educational Corps, and Margaret Elizabeth Howie; m Bridget Mary. BA 1950; MA 1956. **Tutor(s):** J M Wordie. **Educ:** Seabrook Lodge, Hythe; Dover College Junior School; Peter Symonds School, Winchester; Dover College. **Career:** Second Lieutenant, RA 1946–1948. Died 6 May 1996.

CREED, John Leslie (1946) Born 6 April 1928, The Hostelry, The College, Ely; son of John Martin Creed, Clerk in Holy Orders, and May Geraldine Lilley; m Jean, 4 children. **Subject(s):** Classics; BA 1950; MA 1953. **Tutor(s):** R L Howland. **Johnian Relatives:** son of John Martin Creed (1919). **Educ:** Ely High School Preparatory Department; Hillbrow, Rugby; Marlborough College. **Career:** Lecturer in Classics, University of Reading 1950–1965; Lecturer in Classics 1965–1967, Senior Lecturer in Classics 1967, University of Lancaster. **Appointments:** Provost of Colleges, University of Lancaster. **Awards:** John Stewart of Rannoch Scholarship in Greek and Latin, University of Cambridge 1949. Died 5 May 1990.

CREED, Canon John Martin (1919) (admitted to Gonville & Caius College 1908) Born 14 October 1889, Leicester; son of Colin John Creed, Clerk in Holy Orders, and Etheldreda Wright Spackman; m May Geraldine Lilley, 22 June 1927, Hereford Cathedral. BA (Caius) 1911; MA (Caius) 1915. **Johnian Relatives:** father of John Leslie Creed (1946). **Educ:** Wyggeston School, Leicester; Gonville & Caius College, Cambridge. **Career:** Lecturer in Divinity, University of Cambridge; Curate, St Paul's, Manningham, Bradford 1913–1919; Drosier Fellow, Gonville & Caius College, Cambridge 1914–1919; CF 1917–1919; Foundress Fellow 1919–1926, Dean 1919–1926, Lecturer in Theology

1922–1926, Title B Fellow 1926, Title C Fellow 1926–1940 SJC; Ely Professor of Divinity, University of Cambridge 1926–1940. **Appointments:** Examining Chaplain to Bishop of Wakefield 1919–1923; Examining Chaplain to the Bishop of Edmundsbury and Ipswich 1923; Examining Chaplain to the Bishop of Truro 1935. **Awards:** Ramage Research Studentship 1912–1914. **Publications:** *Commentary on St Luke's Gospel*, 1930 (with J Boys-Smith); *The Divinity of Jesus Christ*, 1938. Died 17 February 1940.

CREEK, Ernest George (1928) Born 11 May 1910, 68 Ingare Road, Beccles, Suffolk; son of Ernest George Creek, Horticultural Instructor, and Maud Mary Leverett; m Dorothy Margaret Headland, 1941; 2 sons (Peter and John), 3 daughters (Anne, Elizabeth and Rosemary). **Subject(s):** Modern and Medieval Languages/Economics; BA 1931; FCA. **Tutor(s):** C W Guillebaud. **Educ:** Feoffment Boys' School, Bury St Edmunds; East Anglian School, Bury St Edmunds. **Career:** Indian Civil Service, rising from District Officer to District Magistrate in Bengal (now Bangladesh) 1933–1947; Chartered Accountant 1952–1971. **Awards:** Newman Scholarship; West Suffolk University Scholarship; Open Exhibition, SJC. Died 13 January 2003.

CREES, James Harold Edward (1901) Born 21 July 1882, 12 Richmond Terrace, Clapham Road, Kennington, Surrey; son of James Stephens Crees, Schoolmaster, and Annie Sophia Davis; m Amy Mary Martin, 8 August 1925, Hereford Cathedral. **Subject(s):** Classics/History; BA 1904; MA 1908; BA (London) 1902. **Tutor(s):** C E Graves; J R Tanner. **Educ:** Westminster School; University of London. **Career:** Assistant Master, Wyggeston School 1907; Headmaster, Crypt Grammar School 1911–1919; Headmaster, Hereford Cathedral School 1919–1940. **Appointments:** Examiner in Ancient History, University of London 1911–1915. **Awards:** Thirlwall Prize, University of Cambridge 1906. **Publications:** Books on Ancient History and Literature. Died 29 December 1941.

CRELLIN, Colonel Douglas (1908) Born 4 March 1890, 47 Victoria Street, Douglas, Isle of Man; son of John Crellin, Merchant, and Elizabeth Jane Kneen; m Bertha. **Subject(s):** Natural Sciences; BA 1911; MRCS; LRCP 1916. **Tutor(s):** J R Tanner. **Educ:** Tollington School, London. **Career:** Major, RAMC. **Honours:** MC for Gallantry, Passchendaele 1918. Died 15 May 1952.

CRIBB, Robert James Preston (1944) Born 1 April 1927, 28 Clifton Road, Wood Green, London; son of George Preston Cribb, Clerk, HM Office of Works, and Dilys Tudor Rhys. **Subject(s):** Natural Sciences; BA 1947; MA 1955. **Tutor(s):** C W Guillebaud. **Educ:** Cheadle Hulme Council School; Bramhall Council School; Skep Preparatory School, Stoke-on-Trent; King's School, Chester. Died 25 January 1986.

CRICHTON, John Wallis (1947) Born 3 May 1923, Stanborough, Hatfield, Hertfordshire; son of Samuel George Crichton, Policeman, and Rosina Elizabeth Wallis; m Janet. BA 1949; MA 1959. **Tutor(s):** G C L Bertram. **Educ:** Handride Senior School, Welwyn Garden City; Alleyne's Grammar School, Stevenage. Died 13 February 1982.

CRICK, Dr Anthony Frederick (1941) Born 4 August 1923, Chilcombe, Park Road, Hale, Cheshire; son of Louis Graham Minden Crick, Chemical Manufacturer, and Winifred Moxon Walker. **Subject(s):** Natural Sciences; BA 1944; BChir 1947; MB 1947. **Tutor(s):** S J Bailey. **Johnian Relatives:** son of Louis Graham Minden Crick (1910); brother of John Louis Mingaye Crick (1947). **Educ:** St Ronan's Preparatory School, Sussex; Marlborough College. **Career:** GP.

CRICK, John Louis Mingaye (1947) Born 11 October 1924, Chilcombe, Tabley Road, Knutsford, Cheshire; son of Louis Graham Minden Crick, Manufacturing Chemist, and Winifred Moxon Walker; m Anne. **Subject(s):** Economics; BA 1949; MA 1958. **Johnian Relatives:** son of Louis Graham Minden Crick (1910); brother of Anthony Frederick Crick (1941). **Educ:** St Ronan's Preparatory School, Sussex;

Marlborough College. **Career:** Articled to Chartered Accountant 1941–1943; Scots Guards 1943–1947; Accountant. Died 17 February 1995.

CRICK, Louis Graham Minden (1910) Born 21 March 1891, St George's, Roundhay, Leeds; son of Frederick William Crick, Clerk in Holy Orders, and Margaret Graham Wilson; m Winifred Moxon Walker, 20 February 1915, St Luke's, Chesterton; 2 sons (Anthony Frederick b 4 August 1923 and John Louis Mingaye b 11 October 1924). BA 1913. **Tutor(s):** J R Tanner. **Johnian Relatives:** father of Anthony Frederick Crick (1941) and of John Louis Mingaye Crick (1947). **Educ:** Pocklington School. **Career:** Lieutenant, Cheshire Regiment (TF), WWI; Manufacturing Chemist. Died 27 November 1972.

CRIDDLE, Sidney James (1941) Born 1 July 1923, Elmfield Villas, Carcroft, Adwick le Street; son of Sidney Leedham Criddle, Colliery Manager, and Annie Mary Ashford. **Tutor(s):** C W Guillebaud. **Educ:** Adwick le Street School; Drax Grammar School.

CRIPPS, Sir (Cyril) Humphrey (1934) Born 2 October 1915, 4 Northlands Street, Camberwell, London; son of Sir Cyril Thomas Cripps, Chairman, Pianoforte Supplies Ltd, and Lady Amy Elizabeth Humphrey; m Dorothea Casson Cook, 1942; 3 sons (Robert, John d 1989 and Edward), 1 daughter (Eleanor d 1994). **Subject(s):** Natural Sciences; BA 1937; MA 1948; Honorary ScD (Nottingham) 1975; Honorary LLD (Cantab) 1976; FRS; FCS 1935; CChem; FRIC 1977; FRSC 1979. **Tutor(s):** J M Wordie. **Johnian Relatives:** father of Edward James Spencer Cripps (1971). **Educ:** Northampton Town and County Grammar School. **Career:** Managing Director 1960–1979, Chairman 1979–2000, Pianoforte Supplies Ltd, Roade, Northampton; Director 1966–1997, Chairman 1973–1996, Velcro Industries NV; Chairman, Air BVI 1971–1986; Co Founder and Chairman, Cripps Foundation 1979–2000. **Appointments:** Life Member, Court, University of Nottingham 1953; Freeman, City of London 1957; Liveryman, Worshipful Company of Wheelwrights 1957 (Court Member 1970, Master 1982); Foundation Governor, Bilton Grange Preparatory School 1957–1980; Honorary Fellow, Cripps Hall, Nottingham University 1959; Member, Northamptonshire County Council 1963–1981 (Leader of Independents until 1974); Governor, Northampton Grammar School 1963–1974; Governor, Northampton High School for Girls 1966–1992; Honorary Fellow, SJC 1966–2000; President, Johnian Society 1966; Board Member, Northampton Development Corporation 1968–1985; Trustee, Cripps Postgraduate Medical Centre, Northampton General Hospital 1969–1974; Honorary Fellow, Selwyn College, Cambridge 1971; Honorary Fellow, Magdalene College, Cambridge 1971; Member of Trust, Peterborough Cathedral 1975–1995; Member of Trust, All Saints Church, Northampton 1975–1985; Governor, Northampton School for Boys 1977–1981; Honorary Fellow, Queens' College, Cambridge 1979; Liveryman, Worshipful Company of Tallow Chandlers 1983; High Sheriff, Northamptonshire 1985–1986; DL, Northamptonshire 1986–1996; Chairman, Northampton Old Grammar School Foundation 1988–1996; Trustee, University of Nottingham Development Trust 1990–1993. **Honours:** Kt 1989. Died 14 April 2000.

CRIPPS, The Revd Richard Seymour (1904) Born 21 May 1886, Cricklewood, Hendon, Middlesex; son of Richard Augustus Cripps, Analytical Chemist, and Madeline Eliza Emma Edwards; m Annie Eveline Skinner, 21 June 1916; 2 sons (Keith Richard John b 24 June 1921 and Michael Frank Douglas b 21 May 1928), 2 daughters (Audrey Madeline b 18 March 1919 and Rosemary Helen b 11 September 1929). **Subject(s):** Theology; BA 1907; MA 1912; BD 1929. **Tutor(s):** D MacAlister. **Johnian Relatives:** grandfather of Peter Richard Cripps (1981). **Educ:** York Place School, Brighton. **Career:** Ordained Deacon 1912; Curate, St Philip, Cambridge 1912–1915; Ordained Priest 1913; Curate, St Michael, Southfields 1916–1918; Vicar, Horningsea 1918–1929; Vicar, Holy Trinity, Anerley 1929–1939; Vicar, Priors Marston and Priors Hardwick 1939–1944; Vicar, Burwell, Cambridge 1944–1954. **Appointments:** Hulsean Preacher 1935; Examiner in

Theology, St David's College, Lampeter, Cambridge and London University; Lecturer to Society for Old Testament Study. **Awards:** John Stewart of Rannoch Scholarship in Hebrew, University of Cambridge 1906; Hebrew Prize, University of Cambridge 1907; Steel Studentship, University of Cambridge 1907; Mason and Wright's Prizes; Naden Studentship. **Publications:** *A Critical and Exegetical Commentary on the Book of Amos*, 1929; Contributions to *Encyclopaedia Britannica*, *Chambers Encyclopaedia* and *Story of the Bible*. Died 23 September 1954.

CRISP, Edmund Theodore (1939) Born 10 July 1921, 5 Wellgarth Road, Knowle, Bristol; son of Edmund Robert Crisp, Commercial Artist, and Theodora Fraser Millar; m Dorothy Ramsay 1948; 1 son (Edmund Nigel Ramsay b 1952), 2 daughters (Lalage b 1949 and Pamela b 1955). **Subject(s):** Natural Sciences; BA 1942; MA 1946. **Tutor(s):** J M Wordie. **Johnian Relatives:** father of Edmund Nigel Ramsay Crisp (1970); uncle of Alexander Malcolm Ramsay (1975), grandfather of Charlotte Madeleine Duffryn Crisp (2001). **Educ:** Wells Road Elementary School, Bristol; Cotham Secondary School, Bristol. **Career:** Industrial Chemist; Senior Executive, ICI 1947–1981; General Manager, Corpus Christie Petrochemical Company, Houston, USA 1978–1981.

CRITTALL, Richard Guy Berrington (1930) Born 27 July 1912, 49 Wickham Way, Beckenham, Kent; son of Richard Godfrey Crittall, Central Heating Engineer, and Ethel May Guy; m Marjorie Judson, 15 February 1945, Naples. **Subject(s):** Engineering; BA 1933; MA 1937. **Tutor(s):** J M Wordie. **Educ:** Wellesley House, Broadstairs; Repton School.

CROFT, Eric David (1925) Born 15 January 1907, 3 Lyndhurst Road, Withycombe, Raleigh, Exmouth, Devon; son of William Morley Croft, Shop Proprietor, and Emma Catherine Cram; m Catherine Margaret Croft, 23 July 1952, St Stephen's Comely Bank Church, Edinburgh. **Subject(s):** Natural Sciences; BA 1928; MA 1932; BSc (London) 1927. **Tutor(s):** J M Wordie. **Educ:** National School, Exmouth; Hele's School, Exeter; Exeter School. **Career:** Secretary, Public Transport Association 1930–1931; Editorial Staff 1931–1934, Technical Editor 1934–1938, *Manchester Guardian Commercial*; Secretary and President, British Hotels and Restaurants Association 1947–1972. **Appointments:** Joint Secretary (Employers' side), National Council for the Omnibus Industry; Member, Roads Improvement Association; Member, Industrial Tribunals; Member, Value Added Tax Tribunals. **Awards:** Vidal Exhibition, SJC. **Honours:** MBE. Died 24 February 1999.

CROFT, Kenneth Stuart Bayne (1941) Born 19 September 1922, 159 Monks Road, Lincoln; son of William Croft, Builder, and Florence Kate Draper; m Madeline M Lyon, 3 April 1948. **Subject(s):** Modern and Medieval Languages; BA 1946; MA 1948. **Tutor(s):** C W Guillebaud. **Educ:** Lincoln School. **Career:** Assistant Spanish Master, King Edward VI School, Southampton 1949. **Appointments:** Schoolmaster Fellow, Trinity Hall, Cambridge, Easter Term 1966; Master, Winchester and Portsmouth Diocesan Guild of Church Bellringers 1977. Died 12 May 1984.

CROFT, The Revd Canon Peter Gardom (1943) Born 21 October 1925, 38 Witton Street, Northwich, Cheshire; son of Gerald William Croft, Boot and Shoe Retailer, and Frances Elizabeth Martin; m Beryl Brazier, 1947; 1 son (Simon b 1960), 1 daughter (Sarah b 1964). **Subject(s):** English; BA 1948; MA 1950. **Tutor(s):** C W Guillebaud. **Johnian Relatives:** father-in-law of David Lawrence McMullen (1959). **Educ:** Davenham Church of England School; Sir John Deane's Grammar School, Northwich; Wells Theological College. **Career:** Deacon 1952–1953; Curate, Rugby St Andrew 1952–1958; Ordained Priest 1953; Vicar, Stockingford 1958–1965; Vicar, St Stephen, Little Harwood, Blackburn, Lancashire 1965; Canon-Theologian, Blackburn Cathedral 1965; Rector, Washington in the Washington Group of Parishes, Tyne & Wear 1965–1978; Communications Officer, Diocese of Sheffield 1978–1983; Canon Residentiary and Sub-Dean, Guildford Cathedral 1983–1994; General Secretary, Modern Churchman's Union 1985–1989.

Appointments: Secretary, Parish and People 1974–1999. **Publications:** Various booklets including: *Rural Deaneries*, Prism Pamphlet, 1962; *A Primer for Teams*, British Council of Churches, 1979; *The Parish Magazine Inset*, Parish and People, 1993; *Folk Religion*, Modern Churchman's Union, 1981; *The Rise of the Deanery*, Parish and People, 1996; *A Victorian Church Newspaper*, 2000. Died 6 April 2001.

CROFTS, John James (1942) Born 29 April 1920, 15 Vyvyan Terrace, Clifton; son of John Ernest Victor Crofts, on Staff of John Lewis, formerly Professor of English, and Sibyl Ann Hony. **Subject(s):** Modern and Medieval Languages; BA 1948; MA 1958. **Tutor(s):** C W Guillebaud. **Educ:** Wycliffe College; Bristol University; University of Edinburgh.

CROFTS, John Raymond (1925) Born 23 July 1906, 3 Church Road, Highgate, Middlesex; son of Thomas Robert Norman Crofts, Headmaster, and Emily May Thomas-Moore. **Subject(s):** Mathematics; BA 1928. **Tutor(s):** J M Wordie. **Educ:** Strathedin House, Blackheath; Royal Masonic School, Bushey; Bengeo School, Hertford; Rugby School. **Career:** Assistant Master, Royal Masonic School, Bushey; Assistant Master, Uppingham School 1929–1966. **Awards:** Sizarship, SJC. Died 21 May 1988.

CROLE-REES, The Revd Herbert Stanley (1903) Born 3 August 1881, 59 Loftus Road, Shepherd's Bush, London; son of Charles Crole-Rees, Wine Merchant, and Charlotte Elizabeth Rhind. BA 1906; MA 1912. **Tutor(s):** J R Tanner; C E Graves. **Educ:** Lindenthorpe, Broadstairs; Mercer's School, Holborn. **Career:** Ordained Deacon 1906; Curate, Lady Margaret, Walworth 1906–1908; Ordained Priest 1907; Chaplain, RN 1908–1929 (HMS *Ocean* 1908–1909; HMS *Kent* 1909–1912; HMS *Vivid* 1912; Chaplain, Youth Training Establishment 1913–1914; HMS *Victoria* 1914–1915; HMS *Australia* 1915; HMS Hospital Ship, China 1915; HMS *Hercules* 1915–1916; HMS *Impregnable* 1917–1919; Chaplain, HM Dockyard, Hong Kong 1919–1923; HMS *Bermuda* 1923–1924; HMS *Thunderer* 1925; Royal Naval Barracks, Chatham 1925–1929); Diocesan Chaplain for Church Extension, Rochester 1929–1932; Vicar, Herne Hill 1934–1937; Diocese of Cape Town 1944.

CROMPTON, John William Richardson (1926) Born 14 May 1908, Rivington Hall, Rivington, Lancashire; son of Andrews Crompton, Landed Proprietor and JP, and Teresa Richardson Moss. **Tutor(s):** J M Wordie. **Educ:** Cressbrook, Kirkby Lonsdale, Westmorland; Sedbergh School.

CRONE, Gerald Roe (1919) Born 16 September 1899, Kensal Lodge, Kensal Rise, Willesden, Middlesex; son of John Smythe Crone, Physician and Surgeon, and Nina Gertrude Roe; m Helen May Ward, 9 February 1932, All Saints Church, Granby, Nottinghamshire; 2 sons (Robin Fitzgerald b 21 May 1934 and Hugh Donal b 31 March 1936). **Subject(s):** History; BA 1922; MA 1929; FRGS. **Tutor(s):** E A Benians. **Johnian Relatives:** father of Robin Fitzgerald Crone (1952) and of Hugh Donal Crone (1954). **Educ:** Kilburn Grammar School. **Career:** Librarian, then also Map Curator, Royal Geographical Society. **Appointments:** Council Member, Hakluyt Society; Member, Institute of British Geographers; Treasurer, Irish Literary Society of London. **Awards:** Research Medal, Royal Scottish Geographical Society; Victoria Medal, Royal Geographical Society, 1966; Treasurer, Irish Literary Society of London. Died 6 October 1982.

CROOK, John (1947) Born 22 March 1929, Hooton Cottage, Wigan Road, Standish, Lancashire; son of Robert Burton Crook, Clothing Manufacturer's Manager, and Gladys Morton Latham; m; 2 sons (David and Robert); 1 daughter (Barbara). **Subject(s):** Natural Sciences; BA 1950; MA 1955; BChir 1953; MB 1954; FRCA. **Tutor(s):** G C L Bertram. **Educ:** Mariebonne Council School; Woodfield Preparatory School; Wigan Grammar School. **Career:** Consultant Anaesthetist, Wigan and Leigh Hospital Group 1965–1990; Consultant Anaesthetist, Wrightington Hospital 1965–1994.

CROOK, Professor John Anthony (1939) Born 5 November 1921, 77 Oakmead Road, Balham, London; son of Herbert Crook, Musician (clarinet, ex Army), and Hilda Naomi Flower. **Subject(s):** Classics; BA 1947; MA 1949; Honorary Doctorate (University of Freiburg im Breisgau) 1995; FBA 1970–1980. **Tutor(s):** R L Howland. **Educ:** St Mary's, Balham; Dulwich College. **Career:** Private and Corporal, 9th Royal Fusiliers 1941–1943; POW, Stalag VIIIB 1943–1945; Sergeant, RAEC 1945; Research Student, Balliol College, Oxford 1947–1948; Assistant Lecturer in Classics 1948–1949, Lecturer 1949–1951, Reading University; Title A Fellow 1951–1953, Title B Fellow 1953–1979, Lecturer in Classics 1953–1979, Title C Fellow 1979–1984, Title D Fellow 1984–, SJC; Assistant Lecturer in Classics 1953–1955, Lecturer in Classics 1955–1971, Reader in Roman History and Law 1971–1979, Brereton Reader 1974–1979, Professor of Ancient History 1979–1984 (Emeritus 1984), University of Cambridge. **Appointments:** Tutor 1956–1964, Director of Studies 1966–1977, Secretary, College Council 1969–1971, Praelector 1966–1971 and 1976–1977, President 1971–1975, SJC. **Awards:** John Stewart of Rannoch Scholarship in Greek and Latin, University of Cambridge 1941; Craven Studentship, University of Cambridge 1947. **Publications:** *Consilium Principis*, 1955; *Law and Life of Rome*, 1967; *Legal Advocacy in the Roman World*, 1995; (contributor) *The Cambridge Ancient History*, 2nd edition, Vol IX, 1994, Vol X, 1996.

CROOKSHANK, Alexander Oldfield (1940) Born 23 February 1921, 41 Kidbrooke Park Road, Blackheath; son of Arthur Chichester Crookshank, Clerk in Holy Orders, and Harriet Dorothea Mary Oldfield. **Tutor(s):** J M Wordie. **Educ:** Placelands, East Grinstead; Glengorse, Battle; Eastbourne College. **Career:** Second Lieutenant, Maritime Regiment, RA 1940–1942. Died August 1942 (killed at sea).

CROOME, John Capel (1919) Naval Officer.

CROSBY, John (1923) Born 8 August 1905, 1 Osborne Villas, Newcastle upon Tyne, Northumberland; son of John Crosby, Wholesale Baker and Confectioner, and Jessie Evelyn Carr Angus. **Tutor(s):** B F Armitage. **Educ:** Newcastle Modern School; New College, Harrogate.

CROSS, Professor Sir Barry Albert (1947) Born 17 March 1925, West Combe, Windermere Road, Coulsdon, Surrey; son of Hubert Charles Cross, Cashier, Life Assurance Office, and Elsie May Richards; m Audrey Lilian Crow, 1949; 1 son (Nigel), 2 daughters (Penelope and Jennifer). **Subject(s):** Natural Sciences; BA 1949; MA 1953; PhD 1953; ScD (Corpus Christi) 1964; MRCVS; FRS 1975. **Tutor(s):** G C L Bertram. **Johnian Relatives:** brother of John Arthur Cross (1945). **Educ:** Clifton House Preparatory School, Coulsdon; Reigate Grammar School; Royal Veterinary College. **Career:** Demonstrator in Applied Anatomy 1951, Lecturer in Veterinary Anatomy 1955, University of Cambridge; Fellow, Corpus Christi College, Cambridge 1962–1967 and 1974–1994; Professor of Anatomy, University of Bristol, 1967–1974; Director, Agricultural Institute of Animal Physiology, Babraham, Cambridge 1974–1986; Director, Animal Physiology and Genetic Research, Agricultural and Food Research Council 1986. **Appointments:** Supervisor in Physiology, SJC 1958–1967; Member, Government Farm Animal Welfare Advisory Committee 1975; Honorary Fellow, Royal Agriculture Society for England; Secretary, Zoological Society of London 1992. **Awards:** Gedge Prize, University of Cambridge 1952; Bledisloe Veterinary Award 1982. **Honours:** Chevalier Order of Dannenbrog 1968; Commander d'Honneur de l'Ordre du Bontemps de Médoc et des Graves 1973; CBE 1981; KBE 1989. Died 27 April 1994.

CROSS, David Anderson (1944) Born 19 July 1926, Ixworth, Suffolk; son of Stanley William Cross, Farmer, and Doris Laura Ware; m Madeline Sally Dennis, 19 October 1957, All Saints Church, Stansfield; 1 son (Richard David Henry b 10 July 1961), 1 daughter (Sarah Jane b 7 July 1959). **Subject(s):** Agriculture; BA 1947; MA 1951. **Tutor(s):** C W Guillebaud. **Johnian Relatives:** brother of John Stanley Cross (1947). **Educ:** Eversley School, Southwold; Uppingham School.

CROSS, Professor John Arthur (1945) Born 10 May 1927, 84 Windermere Road, Coulsdon, Surrey; son of Hubert Charles Cross, Assurance Clerk, and Elsie May Richards; m Maureen; 3 daughters (Helen, Ann and Julia). **Subject(s):** History; BA 1948; MA 1952; BSc (London) 1956; PhD (London) 1965; DipEd (Liverpool). **Tutor(s):** F Thistlethwaite. **Johnian Relatives:** brother of Barry Albert Cross (1947). **Educ:** Clifton House Preparatory School, Coulsdon; St Anne's Preparatory School, Coulsdon; Reigate Grammar School. **Career:** Central Office of Information; Lecturer in Politics, Welsh College of Advanced Technology; Lecturer in Politics 1964–1975, Professor of Politics, and Head of Department 1975–1988, University College, Cardiff. **Publications:** *Whitehall and the Commonwealth*, Routledge & Kegan Paul, 1967; *Sir Samuel Hoare: A Political Biography*, Cape, 1977; *Lord Swinton*, 1982. Died 2 August 1988.

CROSS, John Stanley (1947) Born 30 May 1925, Ixworth, Suffolk; son of Stanley William Cross, Farmer, and Doris Laura Ware; m Janet Patricia Devilt, 1961; 2 sons (Nicholas b 1962 and Anthony b 1968), 1 daughter (Philippa b 1964). **Subject(s):** Agriculture; BA 1950; MA 1970. **Tutor(s):** G C L Bertram. **Johnian Relatives:** brother of David Anderson Cross (1944). **Educ:** Eversley School, Southwold; Uppingham School. **Career:** Farmer. **Appointments:** Marketing Advisor to Minister of Agriculture 1980–1982; Chairman, Eastern Counties Farmers Ltd; Chairman, HGCA Cereals Research; Chairman, Morley Research Centre; Trustee, John Innes Research Institute. **Honours:** CBE 1978.

CROSSLEY, Alan Francis (1924) Born 25 March 1905, 103 Highbury Hill, Islington, London; son of Walter Haigh Crossley, Clerk in the Patent Office, and Emily Jane Charlotte Spencer; m Joan R. **Subject(s):** Mathematics; BA 1927; MA 1931. **Tutor(s):** J M Wordie. **Educ:** Drayton Park London County Council School; Owen's School, Islington. **Career:** Principal Scientific Officer, Meteorological Office; Technical Officer, Meteorological Office, Air Ministry 1939–1945. **Awards:** Exhibition, SJC. **Honours:** ISO 1966. Died June 1983.

CROSSLEY, Frank Leggo (1926) Born 9 January 1909, Brinnington Road, Stockport, Cheshire; son of Joseph Crossley, Minister of the United Methodist Church, and Carrie Louise Leggo. **Subject(s):** Law; BA 1929. **Tutor(s):** E A Benians. **Educ:** South Bank Elementary School, York; Gladstone Road School, Scarborough; Scarborough High School.

CROSSMAN, Professor Edward Robert Francis Ward (1944) Born 16 September 1925, Whiteshill, Hambrook, Winterbourne; son of Francis Ward Crossman, Medical Practitioner, and Alice Reid; m Patricia; 3 sons (Francis Hedley Danvers, Robert Edward and Martin John), 1 daughter (Lucia Edna Alice). **Subject(s):** Natural Sciences/Moral Sciences; BA 1950; MA 1952; PhD (Birmingham) 1956. **Tutor(s):** C W Guillebaud. **Educ:** Ravenswood Preparatory School, Tiverton; Shrewsbury School. **Career:** RAF, WWII; Lecturer in General Psychology, Exeter College, Oxford; Lecturer in Psychology, University of Reading 1959; Faculty member 1964, Chairman, Department of Industrial Engineering and Operations Research 1969–1970, Professor of Industrial Engineering and Operations Research until 1987 (Emeritus 1987), University of California, Berkeley. **Awards:** Minor Scholarship, SJC 1944; Passingham Prize 1951; Kenneth Craik Endowment, SJC 1961. Died 5 February 2001.

CROSTHWAIT, Michael Leland (1936) Born 20 August 1916, Banu, Mussoorie, India; son of Leland George Crosthwait, Lieutenant Colonel, Indian Army, and Katherine Rosa Mau. **Subject(s):** Mechanical Sciences; BA 1938; MA 1961; MICE. **Tutor(s):** J S Boys Smith. **Educ:** St Peter's School, Eastbourne; Wellington College; RMA Woolwich. **Career:** Fellow and Bursar, Darwin College 1970. **Honours:** MBE. Died 1 November 1996.

CROSTHWAITE, Charles Noel (1932) Born 8 June 1914, Nathiagali, North-West Frontier Province, India; son of Charles Gilbert Crosthwaite, Lieutenant Colonel, Indian Army, and Joan Becher. **Subject(s):** Modern and Medieval Languages; BA 1935. **Tutor(s):** C W Guillebaud. **Educ:** Mr Batley, Wichwood, Bournemouth; Dunchurch Hall, Rugby; Shrewsbury School.

CROSTHWAITE, Hugh (1942) Born 2 February 1923, The Rectory, Welton le Marsh, Lincolnshire; son of Joseph Nixon Crosthwaite, Clerk in Holy Orders, and Mabel Eveline Camm. **Subject(s):** Classics; BA 1945; MA 1966. **Tutor(s):** C W Guillebaud. **Educ:** St Michael's College, Tenbury; Stamford School.

CROSTON, Arthur Kenneth (1938) Born 28 February 1916, 17 Cornett Road, Liverpool; son of Thomas Arthur Croston, Director, Legal and Commercial Stationers, and Elizabeth Danson. **Subject(s):** English; BA 1940; MA 1944; BA (Liverpool) 1938. **Tutor(s):** J S Boys Smith. **Educ:** Longmore Road Elementary School, Aintree; Manor Road Elementary School, Wallasey; Wallasey Grammar School; University of Liverpool. **Career:** Lieutenant, RA 1940–1945; Assistant Lecturer in English Literature, University of Sheffield 1945–1950; Professor of English, University College of the West Indies 1950–1960; Senior Assistant Registrary, Office of the General Board 1960–1970; Fellow, St Edmund's House 1970. **Awards:** Strathcona Studentship, SJC 1940. **Publications:** Several, mainly on the Elizabethan and Stuart periods. Died 14 November 1991.

CROTHERS, John Clemens (1927) Born 15 October 1909, 6 Grosvenor Road, Batley, Yorkshire; son of Hamilton Crothers, Private Secretary and Town Councillor for Batley, and Dora Clemens. **Subject(s):** Law; BA 1930; MA 1934. **Tutor(s):** C W Guillebaud. **Educ:** Batley Girls Preparatory Grammar School, Batley; The Grammar School, Batley.

CROUCH, Bernard Cyril (1926) Born 26 February 1908, 6 Oakwood Gardens, Seven Kings, Ilford, Essex; son of Henry Charles Crouch, Journalist, and Lillian Eleanor Joel. **Subject(s):** English/Law; BA 1929. **Tutor(s):** M P Charlesworth. **Educ:** Gidea Park College; Brentwood School.

CROWDER, The Venerable Norman Harry (1945) Born 20 October 1926, Nottingham, England; son of Laurence Smethurst Crowder, Chartered Accountant, and Frances Annie Hicks; m Pauleen Florence Alison Styles, 16 December 1971; 1 son (Richard Laurence Robert b 1973). **Subject(s):** Classics/Theology; BA 1948; MA 1952. **Tutor(s):** R L Howland. **Educ:** Nottingham High School; Theological Training, Westcott House, Cambridge. **Career:** Curate, Radcliffe-on-Trent, Nottingham 1952–1955; Residential Chaplain to Bishop of Portsmouth 1955–1958; Assistant Chaplain, then Chaplain, Canford School, Wimborne, Dorset 1959–1972; Vicar, St John's, Ryde, Isle of Wight 1972–1975; Director of Education, Portsmouth Diocese and Canon Residentiary, Portsmouth Cathedral 1975–1985; Archdeacon of Portsmouth 1985–1993; Chaplain, Salisbury Cathedral School 1993–1999.

CROWLEY, John Yarborough (1931) Born 5 November 1912, 15 South Park Hill, Croydon, Surrey; son of Charles Edmund Lucas Crowley, Brewer, and Beatrice Cicely Hooke; m Anne Young, 1 June 1946, St Andrew's, Burnham-on-Sea. **Subject(s):** Modern and Medieval Languages; BA 1934. **Tutor(s):** C W Guillebaud. **Educ:** St Anselm's College, Croydon; Eversley, Tunbridge Wells; Bradfield College. Died January 1984.

CROWLEY-MILLING, Michael Crowley (1935) Born 7 May 1917, Wilton House, East Parade, Rhyl, North Wales; son of Thomas William Crowley-Milling, Solicitor and Notary, and Lillian May Chinnery; m Gee Dickson, 1957. **Subject(s):** Mechanical Sciences; BA 1938; MA 1942. **Tutor(s):** J M Wordie. **Educ:** Kingsland Grange, Shrewsbury; Radley College, Abingdon. **Career:** Electrical Engineer, Metropolitan-Vickers Electrical Company Ltd 1938–1963; Director, Daresbury Nuclear Physics Laboratory 1963–1971; CERN, Geneva 1971–1983 (responsible for control system for Super Proton Synchrotron (SPS) 1971–1976, SPS division leader 1977–1978, Director, Acceleration Program 1979–1980); Consultant 1981–1985; Director, Crowley Consultants 1984; Consultant, Los Alamos National Laboratory, USA 1985–1989; Consultant, Elettra Laboratory, Trieste, Italy 1988–1992; Stanford Linear Accelerator Centre, Stanford University 1991–1994; Consultant, Superconducting Super Collider Laboratory, Dallas, USA 1998. **Appointments:** Secretary, LMBC 1937; Captain, LMBC 1938. **Awards:** IEE Crompton Premium 1959; Institute of Physics, Glazebrook Medal 1981. **Honours:** CMG 1982 (for services to science). **Publications:** *Accelerator Control Systems*, 1986; *Accelerator & Large Experimental Physics Control Systems*, 1990; *John Bertram Adams – Engineer Extraordinary*, Gordon & Breach, 1993; many articles in scientific journals and considerable number of patents.

CROWTHER, Denys James (1935) Born 17 April 1917, 57 De Frevile Avenue, Chesterton, Cambridge; son of James Arnold Crowther, Professor of Physics, University of Reading, and Florence Maud Billinger. **Subject(s):** Geography; BA 1938; MA 1942. **Tutor(s):** C W Guillebaud. **Johnian Relatives:** son of James Arnold Crowther (1902). **Educ:** Marlborough House, Reading; Leighton Park School, Reading. **Career:** Special Trainee, Metropolitan Vickers Electrical Company Ltd, and later Technical Assistant, Education Department 1939; Flying Officer, RAFVR 1942–1945; Section Leader, Education Department 1951; Personnel Manager, Metropolitan Vickers Electrical Company Ltd. Died 16 December 1992.

CROWTHER, Edward Ramsden (1929) Born 8 December 1910, Rob Royd, Golcar, Huddersfield; son of Ramsden Heppenstall Crowther, Woollen Manufacturer, and Marion Shaw; 3 children. BA 1932. **Tutor(s):** J M Wordie. **Educ:** Moslyn House School; Shrewsbury School.

CROWTHER, Dr Herbert Arnold (1915) Born 10 November 1895, 32 Greenmount Street, Hunslet, Leeds; son of William Scarlett Crowther, Schoolmaster, and Ellen Maria Jewitt; 1 daughter. **Subject(s):** Natural Sciences; BA 1918; MA 1930; MRCS; LRCP. **Tutor(s):** R P Gregory. **Educ:** Armley Park School; Cockburn High School, Leeds; Bradford Grammar School. **Career:** Chest Physician, South Yorkshire; Medical Superintendent, Devon and Cornwall Sanatorium, Didsworthy, South Brent 1921; Consultant Tuberculosis Officer, West Riding 1930. **Awards:** Scholarship, SJC 1914. Died 24 April 1976.

CROWTHER, Professor James Arnold (1902) Born 28 August 1883, Corporation Street, Baths, Brightside, Sheffield; son of James William Crowther, Pawnbroker and Clothier, and Martha Annie Nadin; m Florence Maud Billinger, 1912, Cambridge; 2 sons (Alan and Denys). **Subject(s):** Natural Sciences; BA 1905; MA 1909; ScD 1915; FInstP. **Tutor(s):** D MacAlister. **Johnian Relatives:** father of Denys James Crowther (1935). **Educ:** Royal Grammar School, Sheffield. **Career:** Fellow, SJC 1908–1914; Assistant Demonstrator in Experimental Physics 1912–1924, Lecturer in Physics Applied to Medical Radiology 1921–1924, University of Cambridge; Professor of Physics 1924–1946 (Emeritus 1946–1950), University of Reading. **Appointments:** Supervisor in Physics, SJC 1914–1917; Vice-President, Institute of Physics. **Publications:** *Handbook of Industrial Radiology*, 1944; a number of textbooks. Died 25 March 1950.

CROWTHER, Dr Joseph Stanley (1927) Born 2 December 1907, 44 Thryberg Street, Bradford, Yorkshire; son of Thomas Edward Crowther, Wholesale Fruit Merchant, and Mary Hannah Baines. **Subject(s):** Natural Sciences; BA 1930; MRCP 1949; MD 1950; FRCP 1971. **Tutor(s):** J M Wordie. **Educ:** Hanson Secondary School, Bradford; University College Hospital. **Career:** Buyer, Harrods 1930–1938; RAMC; Posts at Central Middlesex, Chase Farm, and Clare Hall Hospitals; Consultant Chest Physician, Nottingham Chest Clinic and Ransom Hospital, Mansfield 1961. Died 22 August 1981.

CRUICKSHANK, Donald Edward (1906) Born 2 November 1887, 6 Lorton Terrace, London; son of George Edwin Cruickshank, Barrister, and Sarah Maria Tylor. **Subject(s):** Mathematics; BA 1909. **Tutor(s):** J R Tanner. **Johnian Relatives:** son of George Edwin Cruickshank (1866); brother of George Malcolm Cruickshank (1905). **Educ:** Linton House School; Queen Elizabeth's School, Barnet; Aldenham School. **Career:** Assistant with Nicholson and Corlette, Lincoln's Inn; School of the Architectural Association 1909; Private, Public Schools Battalion, Royal

Fusiliers 1914; Second Lieutenant, Border Regiment; attached Wiltshire Regiment. **Awards:** Banister Fletcher Bursary 1912. Died 9 April 1916 (killed in action in Mesopotamia).

CRUICKSHANK, Professor Durward William John (1947) Born 7 March 1924, 329 Norwood Road, Herne Hill, London; son of William Durward Cruickshank, Medical Practitioner, and Margaret Ombler Meek, Medical Practitioner; m Marjorie Alice Travis, 1953 (d 1983); 1 son (John Durward b 1959), 1 daughter (Helen Margaret b 1957). **Subject(s):** Mathematics; BA 1949; MA 1954; ScD 1961; BSc (London) 1944; Diploma (Loughborough College) 1944; PhD (Leeds) 1952; FRS 1979; FRSC; CChem. **Tutor(s):** J M Wordie. **Johnian Relatives:** second cousin of Charles Parrington Prest (1918); father of John Durward Cruickshank (1978). **Educ:** Brightlands Preparatory School, Dulwich; Ovingdean Preparatory School, Brighton; St Lawrence College, Ramsgate; St Lawrence College, Courteenhall. **Career:** Engineering Assistant, Inter-Services Research Bureau, SOE and Admiralty 1944–1946; Research Assistant, Chemistry Department 1946–1947, Lecturer in Mathematical Chemistry 1950–1957, Reader in Mathematical Chemistry 1957–1962, University of Leeds; Title A Fellow, SJC 1953–1956; Joseph Black Professor of Chemistry, University of Glasgow 1962–1967; Professor of Chemistry, UMIST 1967–1983 (Emeritus 1983–). **Appointments:** Treasurer 1966–1972, General Secretary 1970–1972, International Union of Crystallography. **Awards:** Chemical Society Award for Structural Chemistry 1978; 1st Dorothy Hodgkin Prize, British Crystallographic Association 1991; Companion of UMIST 1992. **Publications:** numerous papers on crystallography.

CRUICKSHANK, George Malcolm (1905) Born 18 November 1885, 6 Lorton Terrace, London; son of George Edwin Cruickshank, Barrister, and Sarah Maria Tylor; m Alice Mary Beck, 9 June 1921, Old Jordans, Buckinghamshire; 1 daughter (Rowena). **Subject(s):** Mechanical Sciences; BA 1908; MA 1912; AMICE. **Tutor(s):** J R Tanner; C E Graves. **Johnian Relatives:** son of George Edwin Cruickshank (1866); brother of Donald Edward Cruickshank (1906). **Educ:** Aldenham School. **Career:** Patent Agent and Engineer; Proprietor, Cruickshank and Co, Dublin; Manager, Marks and Clerk, Patent Agents, Glasgow. Died 8 May 1980.

CUBBON, Dr Henry Thomas (1912) Born 29 March 1893, 1 Dashwood Terrace, Neithrop, Banbury, Oxfordshire; son of Henry Cubbon, Congregational Minister, and Hannah Spencer Walker. BA 1915; BChir 1921; MB 1921; Diploma in Medical Radiology and Electrology 1921; MRCS; LRCP 1918. **Tutor(s):** R P Gregory. **Johnian Relatives:** son of Henry Cubbon (1884). **Educ:** Westminster School; Hitchin Grammar School. **Career:** Dresser, RAMC, WWI; Honorary 2nd Electro-Therapist, Royal Sussex County Hospital, Brighton; Honorary Radiologist, Haywards Heath Hospital, and other Brighton hospitals. Died 5 June 1961.

CULE, Eric William (1926) Born 23 September 1907, Broncleri, The Parade, Ton Pentre, Ystrady-fo dwg, Glamorgan; son of Edgar Cule, Solicitor, and Lizzie Chichton Johnson. **Tutor(s):** E A Benians. **Educ:** Rhondda Council School; Rhondda Secondary School; Belmont, Mill Hill; Mill Hill School.

CULLEN, Alfred Edgar (1902) Born 18 April 1883, 5 Arthur Street, Nottingham; son of Alfred Cullen, Hosiery Manufacturer, and Elizabeth Briggs. **Subject(s):** Natural Sciences; BA 1905; BChir 1910; MB 1910; LRCP; MRCS 1908. **Tutor(s):** D MacAlister. **Educ:** The High School, Nottingham. **Career:** Doctor, Western Australia 1934. **Awards:** Scholarship, SJC 1901.

CULLEN, The Revd Augustus Pountney (1908) Born 16 September 1889, 39 Wellington Street, Barton St Mary, Gloucestershire; son of Augustus Henry Cullen, Congregational Minister, and Edith Jane Pountney; m Jean Naomi Batchan, 9 October 1919, Tientsin Anglo-Chinese College; 1 son (Patrick Arthur Augustus b 8 April 1927), 3 daughters (D Enid b 11 January 1921, E Rowena b 2 January 1923 and E Joanna b 5 September

1930). **Subject(s):** Classics; BA 1911; MA 1954; BA (Oxford) 1913. **Tutor(s):** E E Sikes. **Johnian Relatives:** father of Patrick Arthur Augustus Cullen (1948). **Educ:** South Manchester Grammar School; Bishop's Stortford College; Mansfield College, Oxford. **Career:** Assistant Master, Oundle School 1911; Assistant Master, Eltham College, London 1912–1913; YMCA in Le Havre and Rouen 1914–1915; Ordained in the Congregational Ministry, 1916; Educational Missionary of the London Missionary Society at the Tientsin Anglo-Chinese College, China 1916 and 1947–1950; On deputation, Furlough 1939–1940; Interned by the Japanese at Weihsien, Northern China 1942–1945. **Publications:** *Making China's Men*; *Memoir of Lavington Hart*. Died 4 September 1960.

CULLEN, Patrick Arthur Augustus (1948) Born 8 April 1927, Tientsin, North China; son of Augustus Pountney Cullen, Educational Missionary in China, and Jean Naomi Batchan; m Margaret Lois Inglis, 6 January 1962, Congregational Church, Sanderstead, Surrey; 1 son (Nicholas), 1 daughter (Anna). **Subject(s):** Languages; BA 1950; MA 1961; DipEd (Cambridge) 1952. **Tutor(s):** C W Guillebaud. **Johnian Relatives:** son of Augustus Pountney Cullen (1908). **Educ:** Tientsin Grammar School, China; Bishop's Stortford College. **Career:** Sergeant Instructor, RAEC 1946–1948; Assistant, Oberschule am Leibnizplatz, Bremen 1952–1953; In charge, English for Schools Broadcasts, Radio Bremen 1953–1954; Christ's Hospital, Horsham 1954–1987 (Housemaster, Christ's Hospital, Horsham 1960–1971, Head, German Department, Christ's Hospital, Horsham 1972–1987); External Oral Examiner, German GCSE Advanced Level, UCLES 1989–2000 and Oxford Delegacy 1990–1997. **Publications:** *Learn German Quickly*, McGibbon & Kee, 1964.

CULLIS, Leonard (1902) Born 25 January 1884, Budbrook, Warwickshire; son of Edwin Cullis, Headmaster, and Eliza Ann Harrison. **Subject(s):** Mathematics; BA 1905; MA 1911; FRAeS. **Tutor(s):** D MacAlister. **Educ:** Warwick School. **Career:** Lieutenant, IARO; attached 23rd Sikh Pioneers, WWI. Died 15 August 1957.

CULPIN, Claude (1928) Born 26 September 1910, Sutton Road, Newton, Leverington, Cambridgeshire; son of John Edward F Culpin, Farm Foreman, and Hannah Gathergood. **Subject(s):** Natural Sciences; BA 1931; MA 1935; FIAgrE. **Tutor(s):** C W Guillebaud. **Johnian Relatives:** brother of Stanley Culpin (1936). **Educ:** Thorney Boys' School; Wisbech Grammar School. **Honours:** OBE. Died 11 November 1995.

CULPIN, Stanley (1936) Born 21 April 1914, Thorney, Peterborough; son of John Edward Culpin, Farm Foreman, and Hannah Gathergood. **Tutor(s):** C W Guillebaud. **Johnian Relatives:** brother of Claude Culpin (1928). **Educ:** Wisbech Grammar School; East Anglian Institute of Agriculture, Chelmsford.

CULSHAW, Dr Frank Hubert (1928) Born 22 March 1910, 1 Derby Road, Wesham, Kirkham, Lancashire; son of Frank Culshaw, Master, Poor Law Institution, and Eleanor Rogers. **Subject(s):** Natural Sciences; BA 1931. **Tutor(s):** M P Charlesworth. **Educ:** Saner Street, Hull; Hymers College, Hull. **Career:** Resident Anaesthetist and House Surgeon, Addenbrooke's Hospital 1934. Died 10 November 1934.

CULTON, John Greenwood (1944) Born 12 June 1926, 37 Parkfield Road, Toxteth Park, Liverpool; son of James Culton, Cashier, Shipping Merchants, and Charlotte Emily Greenwood. **Tutor(s):** J M Wordie. **Educ:** Sudley Road School, Liverpool; Pinner Park School; Oakington Manor School; Wembley County School; Ewart High School, Newton Stewart; Dorking County School.

CUMMINS, Cresswell Arthur (1902) Born 5 April 1883, 80 Whitecross Street, London; son of Walter Henry Cummins, Draper, and Mary Ellen Gale. **Subject(s):** Natural Sciences; BA 1905; MA 1909. **Tutor(s):** D MacAlister. **Educ:** Charterhouse; Christ's Hospital. **Career:** Education Department, Southern Nigeria 1905; Inspector of Schools, Southern Nigeria 1907–1923.

CUMMINS, Francis John (1914) Born 24 February 1895, St James' College, Bargate, Grimsby, Lincolnshire; son of Richard Henry Cummins, Clerk in Holy Orders, and Evangeline Hester Maria Hall. **Subject(s):** Mathematics; BA 1920; MA 1927. **Tutor(s):** L H K Bushe-Fox. **Educ:** Clee Grammar School; Stamford School. **Career:** Captain, Dorset Regiment 1914–1918; Master, Stamford School 1920–1926; Bedford School 1926–1958. **Awards:** Exeter Exhibition, SJC. Died 24 November 1960.

CUNLIFFE, Herbert (1933) Born 11 October 1903, 174 Main Street, Billinge; son of John Cunliffe, Collier, and Mary Arkwright. **Tutor(s):** J M Wordie. **Educ:** Sutton Manor Elementary School; St Helens Municipal Technical School; Manchester University.

CUNNINGHAM, Cyril (1943) Born 21 March 1925, King George V Merchant Seamen's Memorial Hospital, Floriana, Malta; son of George Cunningham, Messenger, National Provincial Bank, and Ethel Waters. **Tutor(s):** S J Bailey. **Educ:** Hollydale Road School, London; Brockley Central School; Greenwich Commercial Evening Institute.

CUNNINGHAM, Professor John Arthur (1900) Born 13 August 1877, Millfield House, Buncrana, County Donegal; son of John Cunningham, Irish Land Commissioner, and Nora O'Donel Long. **Subject(s):** Physics and Chemistry; BA 1902; MA 1908; BA (Ireland). **Tutor(s):** D MacAlister. **Educ:** High School, Dublin; Academical Institution, Derry; Royal College of Science, Ireland. **Career:** Member, Indian Educational Service 1903–1911; Professor of Physics, University of Calcutta 1903–1911. **Awards:** Studentship, SJC 1900. Died 3 July 1911.

CUNNINGHAM, Morris Anskar (1935) Born 11 March 1916, Wayside, Huntingdon Road, Cambridge; son of Ebenezer Cunningham, Fellow and Lecturer, and Ada Collins; 1 son (Stephen Walter), 2 daughters (Ann and Jane). **Subject(s):** Moral Sciences; BA 1938; MA 1942; MA (London) 1948; DipEdPsy (London) 1949. **Tutor(s):** J S Boys Smith. **Johnian Relatives:** son of Ebenezer Cunningham (1899); cousin of Martyn Collins (1940); father of Stephen Walter Cunningham (1964). **Educ:** St Faiths, Cambridge; St George's School, Harpenden; UCL. **Career:** Principal Clinical Child Psychologist, The Crichton Royal Hospital, Dumfries 1958. **Awards:** Wright's Prize, SJC 1936; Scholarship, SJC 1937; Newcome Prize, SJC 1937; Strathcona Studentship, SJC 1938.

CUNNINGHAM, Thomas Sheriff (1923) Born 25 September 1905, Cragston, Stewarton, Ayrshire, Scotland; son of Alexander Cunningham, Cotton Business, and Sarah Marie Ann Sheriff. **Tutor(s):** B F Armitage. **Educ:** Sandroys, Cobham; Bradfield College.

CURNOW, John Michael (1941) Born 15 August 1923, 46 Sherbourne Road, Blackpool, Lancashire; son of William Iggulden Curnow, Schoolmaster, and Edith Eveline Hall. **Tutor(s):** C W Guillebaud. **Educ:** Cleveley's College; Blackpool Grammar School. Died 6 October 1950.

CURRAN, Sir Samuel Crowe (1937) Born 23 May 1912, Casement Street, Ballymena, Antrim; son of John Curran, Blast Furnace Foreman, and Sarah Owens Crowe; m Joan Elizabeth Strothers, 7 November 1940 (d 10 February 1999); 3 sons (John Strothers b 17 July 1947, Charles Samuel b 17 October 1948, James Crowe b 1 November 1951), 1 daughter (Sheena Margaret b 16 March 1945). PhD 1941; MA (Glasgow) 1933; BSc (Glasgow) 1934; PhD (Glasgow) 1937; DSc (Glasgow) 1950; FRSE; FEng; FInstP; Hon FIEE 1989; FRS. **Tutor(s):** J M Wordie. **Johnian Relatives:** uncle of Alan Hamilton Curran (1969); grandfather of David Charles Curran (1996). **Educ:** Netherton Public School, Wishaw; Berryhill Public School, Wishaw; Wishaw High Secondary School; University of Glasgow. **Career:** Cavendish Laboratory, University of Cambridge 1937–1939; RAE 1939–1940; Ministry of Aircraft Production and Ministry of Supply 1940–1944; Manhattan Project (Ministry of Supply), University of California 1944–1945; Natural Philosophy, Glasgow University 1945–1955;

UKAEA 1955–1958; Chief Scientist, Atomic Weapons Research Establishment 1958–1959; Principal, Royal College of Science and Technology, Glasgow 1959–1964; Principal and Vice-Chancellor, University of Strathclyde 1964–1980. **Appointments:** President, Scottish Society for the Mentally Handicapped 1954–1998; Member, Council for Scientific and Industrial Research 1962–1965; Chairman, Advisory Committee on Medical Research 1962–1975; Director, Scottish Television 1964–1982; Member, SRC 1965–1968; Member, Advisory Council on Technology 1965–1970; Director, Cetec Systems Ltd 1965–1977; Chairman, Advisory Board on Relations with Universities 1966–1970; Chief Scientific Adviser to the Secretary of State for Scotland 1967–1977; Director, Hall Thermotank Ltd 1969–1976; Director, General Steels Division, British Steel Company 1970–1973; Director, International Research and Development Company Ltd 1970–1978; Honorary Fellow, SJC 1971–1998; Honorary President, Scottish Polish Cultural Association 1972–1998; Member, Oil Development Council for Scotland 1973–1978; Chairman, Deputy Chairman, Electricity Council 1977–1979; Member, Advisory Committee on Safety of Nuclear Installations 1977–1980; Chairman, Electricity Supply Research Council 1978–1980; Member, Radioactive Waste Management Advisory Committee 1978–1981; Member, Advisory Council of A Power for Good 1978–1998; Member, UK National Commission for UNESCO, and Education Advisory Committee 1978–1998; Deputy Chairman, Electricity Supply Research Council 1980–1982; Visiting Professor in Energy Studies, University of Glasgow 1980–1988; Director, Nuclear Structures (Protection) Ltd 1981–1998; President, St Andrews' Society, Glasgow 1982–1988; Member, Standing Commission on Scottish Economy 1987–1998; Fellow, University of Strathclyde 1990–1998; President, Institute of Environmental Safety 1992; Freeman, Motherwell and Wishaw 1966; Freeman, City of Glasgow 1980. **Awards:** St Mungo Prize, City of Glasgow. **Honours:** Commander of the Royal Order of St Olav, Norway 1966; Commander, Order of Polish People's Republic 1976; Kt. **Publications:** (with J D Craggs) *Counting Tubes*, 1949; *Luminescence and the Scintillation Counter*, 1953; *Alpha, Beta and Gamma Ray Spectroscopy*, 1964; (jointly) *Energy Resources and the Environment*, 1976; (with J S Curran) *Energy and Human Needs*, 1979; *Issues in Science and Education*, 1988. Died 25 February 1998.

CURRANT, Dr Eric James (1925) Born 20 July 1906, 11 Brook Street, Luton; son of Percy William Currant, Manufacturer of Straw Hats, and Annie Tearle; m Lena Lints-Smith; 3 daughters. BA 1928; MA 1936; BChir 1936; MB 1936; MRCS; LRCP. **Tutor(s):** B F Armitage. **Educ:** Bedford School; The Leys School, Cambridge. **Career:** Clinical Medical Officer, Community Health Service, South East Hampshire Area; London Hospital; Superintendent, Victoria Leprosy Hospital, Dichpalli, India 1949–1954; Medical Officer, Dr Barnardo's Homes 1954–1958; Director, Leprologist to Government of Northern Rhodesia 1958–1961; Deputy Medical Director, Lingfield Hospital School for children suffering from Epilepsy 1963–1971. Died 24 May 1993.

CURRIE, James Donald Maxwell (1920) Born 30 July 1901, Larkfield, Wardie Road, Leith, Edinburgh; son of James Currie, Shipowner, and Gertrude Barclay Peterkin. BA 1923; MA 1927. **Tutor(s):** B F Armitage. **Educ:** Edinburgh Academy; Cargilfield, Cramond Bridge; Rugby School. **Career:** Chairman, Currie Line Ltd. Died 27 November 1943.

CURRY, Basil John Elmitt (1920) Born 6 August 1898, Perth Cottage, Queen Victoria Street, Cape Town, Cape of Good Hope; son of John Henry Curry, Architect, and Rosalie Perrin. BA 1923; MA 1927. **Tutor(s):** E E Sikes. **Educ:** Limes School, Croydon; Aldro School, Eastbourne; Oundle School.

CURTIS, Allan Raymond (1941) Born 20 December 1922, 73 Pix Road, Letchworth, Hertfordshire; son of Raymond Arthur Curtis, Civil Servant, and Emma Elizabeth Johnson; m Margaret Fisher, 8 May 1958, near Billericay, Essex; 1 son (David b 18 December 1959), 2 daughters (Hilary b 10 April 1961 and Ruth b 13 January 1964). **Subject(s):**

Mathematics; BA 1947; MA 1949; Special RE Course; FIMA; CMath. **Tutor(s):** J M Wordie. **Johnian Relatives:** father of David Curtis (1978). **Educ:** St Mary's School, Hendon; Westbury School, Letchworth; Chase Side School, Enfield; Enfield Grammar School. **Career:** Second Lieutenant, RE 1942–1943; Lieutenant 1943; Field Company Platoon Commander, Normandy 1944; Field Company Platoon Commander, Germany 1945; Tutorial teaching of undergraduate mathematics for various Cambridge Colleges 1948–1951; Title A Fellow, SJC 1950–1953; Lecturer in Applied Mathematics, University of Sheffield 1952–1956; Principal Scientific Officer, Theoretical Physics Division, UKAEA, The Harwell Laboratory 1957–1963; Leader, Computing Group, Theoretical Physics Division 1961–1963; Scientist in Planetary Sciences Section, Jet Propulsion Laboratory, California Institute of Technology, Pasadena, California, USA 1962; Head of Mathematics Branch, UKAEA Banded staff, Theoretical Physics Division, later appointed to Senior Staff 1963–1974; Leader, Applied Mathematics Group 1974–1987, Senior Research Scientist 1986–1987, Computer Sciences and Systems Division, AERE; Managing Director and Senior Consultant, ARC Scientific Limited 1987. **Appointments:** Sub-warden, Stephenson Hall, University of Sheffield 1954–1956; Visitor, Centre for Mathematical Analysis and School of Mathematical Sciences, ANU, Canberra March–May 1990. **Awards:** Exhibition, SJC; Adams Prize, University of Cambridge; Rayleigh Prize, University of Cambridge. **Publications:** (with R M Goody) 'Spectral line shape and its effect on atmospheric transmissions', *Quarterly Journal of the Royal Meteorological Society*, 1954; (with R M Goody) 'Thermal radiation in the upper atmosphere', *Proceedings of the Royal Society*, 1966; (with M J D Powell) 'On the convergence of exchange algorithms for calculating minimax approximations', *Computer Journal*, 1966; (with M R Osborne) 'The construction of minimax rational approximations to functions', *Computer Journal*, 1966; (with E M Chance, G M Clore and E P Shephard) 'Numerical Solution of the Hodgkin-Huxley Equations in a Moving Coordinate System: Simulation of Nerve Impulse Transmission over Long Distances', *Journal of Computer Physics*, 1981; 'Analysis of covariance after non-linear least-square fitting', *IMA Journal of Numerical Analysis*, 1987; numerous other research papers, reports, conference contributions and chapters in books.

CURTIS, Dr Geoffrey Carew (1938) Born 8 June 1919, 89 Wightman Road, Hornsey; son of William Edward Curtis, Professor of Physics, and Adeline Mary Grace Mitchell; m Margaret Shirley Snelling, 24 September 1954; 3 children. **Subject(s):** Natural Sciences; BA 1941; MA 1945; PhD (London) 1951; MInstP. **Tutor(s):** J M Wordie. **Educ:** Comrie House School, North Finchley; Royal Grammar School, Newcastle upon Tyne. **Career:** Principal Scientific Officer, UKAEA. **Awards:** Major Scholarship, SJC 1937. Died 5 October 1983.

CURTIS, Ronald Edgar (1940) Born 5 March 1922, 2 Industry Cottages, Barnwood, Gloucestershire; son of Samuel Curtis, Blacksmith, and Lucy Hale. BA 1948; MA 1958. **Tutor(s):** J M Wordie. **Johnian Relatives:** father of Timothy John Morant Curtis (1981). **Educ:** Holmer Church of England School; Hereford Cathedral School. **Career:** Squadron Leader (pathfinder), RAF 1940–1945; Trainee Line Manager, then Management Consultant, manufacturing industry; own business as Agent for several continental metal component companies. **Honours:** DSO; DFC and Bar.

CURTLER, Ernest Alfred (1919) Born 19 November 1895, 295 High Street, West Bromwich, Staffordshire; son of Alfred Thomas Curtler, Bank Clerk, and Sarah Alma Cole. **Subject(s):** Economics/Agriculture; BA 1921; MA 1926. **Tutor(s):** E A Benians. **Educ:** Bristol Grammar School. **Career:** 6th Somerset Light Infantry 1914; Second Lieutenant, 1st Somerset Light Infantry 1915; Demobilised with the rank of Lieutenant 1919; Assistant Agriculturalist, Malay (transferred to Central Experimental Station, Serdang 1922) 1921–1930; Assistant Agriculturalist; later Agricultural Officer, Cameron Highlands 1930. **Appointments:** Lieutenant, Malay States Volunteer Regiment. Died 20 July 1937.

CURZON-SIGGERS, Canon William Arthur (1913) Born 8 April 1891, Hamilton, Victoria, Australia; son of William Curzon-Siggers, Clerk in Holy Orders, and Annie Brook. **Subject(s):** Law; BA 1915; LLB 1915; LLM 1921; BA (New Zealand) 1912; MA (New Zealand) 1913. **Tutor(s):** L H K Bushe-Fox. **Educ:** Dunedin Collegiate School; Selwyn Collegiate School; Otago Boys High School; Otago University College, University of New Zealand. **Career:** Air Mechanic, RFC, WWI; Called to the Bar, Inner Temple 1916; Tutor, Selwyn College, Dunedin, New Zealand 1928; Deacon and Priest, Dunedin; Sub-Warden, Selwyn College, Dunedin, and Curate in Charge, Holy Innocents, Leith Valley 1928–1933; Lecturer in International Law, University College, University of New Zealand 1928–1960; Chaplain and Superintendent, Anglican Orphanage, Dunedin 1933–1934; Vicar, North-East Valley and Examining Chaplain to the Bishop of Dunedin 1934–1945; Canon, St Paul's Cathedral, Dunedin 1945. **Appointments:** Member, Standing Commission of the Church of the Province of New Zealand 1940–1958 (Chairman 1954–1958). **Awards:** MacMahon Law Studentship, SJC 1916. Died 20 February 1969.

CUSHING, William Ewart Whitrick (1909) Born 19 October 1891, Pople Street, Wymondham, Norfolk; son of James William Cushing, Master Coach Painter, and Edith Emily Croxen; 2 sons. **Subject(s):** Modern and Medieval Languages; BA 1912; MA 1920. **Tutor(s):** J R Tanner. **Educ:** The Grammar School, Swaffham. **Career:** Schoolmaster, Northumberland; Second Lieutenant, 9th Norfolks; initially with 13 Squadron, then Recording Officer, 85 Squadron, RFC 1916.

CUSSINS, Dr Wilfred Denys (1944) Born 20 June 1927, 34 Walmgate, York; son of Reginald Cussins, Radio and Electrical Engineer, and Edith Anderson. **Subject(s):** Mechanical Sciences; BA 1947; MA 1951; PhD 1953. **Tutor(s):** S J Bailey. **Educ:** St Lawrence's School, York; Nunthorpe Secondary School, York. **Awards:** Charles Lamb Prize 1947.

CUSTANCE, Richard Martin (1946) Born 13 August 1926, The Rectory, Little Bealings, Suffolk; son of Martin Custance, Clerk in Holy Orders, and Kathleen Paulley; m Frances Joy Gloag, 17 September 1947. **Subject(s):** Mechanical Sciences; BA 1948; MA 1953. **Tutor(s):** R L Howland. **Educ:** Kilvinton Hall, Enfield Chase; Bromsgrove School. **Career:** Testing Laboratories, Summerfield House, Bennet Lane, Elstree 1951; Costain Concrete Company Ltd 1959. Died 4 April 1989.

CUTTING, Ernest Melville (1901) Born 22 August 1882, Constitution, Barbados, West Indies; son of Ernest Augustine Cutting, Clerk in Holy Orders, and Emmeline Pendrall Barrow; m Dora. **Subject(s):** Natural Sciences; BA 1904; MA 1908. **Tutor(s):** D MacAlister. **Educ:** Harrison College, Barbados. **Career:** Senior Lecturer in Botany, UCL. Died 2 October 1957.

CUTTS, Anson Bailey (1929) Born 4 January 1905, 140 Laurel Avenue, Minneapolis, Minnesota; son of Anson Bailey Cutts, Businessman, and Edna Browning Stokes. PhB (Yale) 1928. **Tutor(s):** M P Charlesworth. **Educ:** Blake School for Boys, Minneapolis; West School, Minneapolis; Yale University. **Career:** Lifetime Fellow, Winston Churchill Memorial and Library, Westminster College, Fulton, Missouri.

D

DA CUNHA, His Honour John Wilfrid (1940) Born 6 September 1922, Lauriston, Wash Lane, Timperley, Cheshire; son of Frank da Cunha, Physician and Surgeon, Consul for Portugal, and Lucy Finnerty; m Janet Savatard, 1953; 1 son, 4 daughters. **Subject(s):** Law; BA 1943; MA 1955; Barrister-at-Law 1948. **Tutor(s):** S J Bailey. **Educ:** Bishop's Court, Freshfield; Stonyhurst College; Manchester University, Faculty of Law. **Career:** 23rd Hussars, RAC 1942–1947, wounded Normandy 1944; Judge Advocate's Department (War Crimes) 1946–1947; Honorary Major; Called to the Bar, Middle Temple 1948; Circuit Judge (formerly Judge of County Courts) 1970–1992. **Appointments:** Governor, Mount Carmel School, Alderley Edge 1962–1978; Chairman, Local Appeal Tribunal, Ministry of Social Security (Wigan) 1964–1968; Assistant

Recorder, Oldham County Borough Quarter Sessions 1966–1970; Chairman, Industrial Tribunals 1966–1970; JP, Lancashire 1968; Deputy Chairman, Lancashire County Quarter Sessions 1968–1971; Commissioner, Northern Ireland (Emergency Provisions) Act 1973; Member, Appeals Tribunal, Northern Ireland; Parole Board 1976–1978; President, Bristol Medico-Legal Society 1989–1991; Criminal Injuries Compensation Board 1992–1997.

D'AGUIAR, John Edward (1923) Born 13 April 1903, Lisbon, Portugal; son of John George d'Aguiar, Medical Practitioner, and Philomena Maria de Freitas. **Tutor(s):** E A Benians. **Educ:** Bishop's Court, Freshfield, Liverpool; Stonyhurst College.

DAIN, John (1940) Born 30 June 1921, 68 St Agnes Road, Moseley, Birmingham; son of Frederick William Dain, Inspector of Taxes, and Edith Dorothy Jackson. **Subject(s):** Mathematics; BA 1943; MA 1947. **Tutor(s):** J M Wordie. **Educ:** Moortown Preparatory School, Leeds; Ingledew College, Leeds; Northwood Preparatory School; Merchant Taylors' School. **Career:** TRE 1942–1946; AERE 1946–1954; English Electric Valve Company 1954. **Awards:** Baylis Scholarship, SJC 1939.

DAKIN, Robert Humphrey (1948) Born 18 April 1927, 27 Springhill Road, Sheffield; son of Herbert Dakin, Chartered Accountant, and Lilian Constance Cooper; m Denny G G Jones, 26 March 1969. **Subject(s):** English; BA 1950; MA 1955. **Tutor(s):** F Thistlethwaite. **Educ:** Ecclesall Church School; King Edward VII School, Sheffield; Worksop College. **Career:** Headmaster, Mowden Hall School, Stocksfield, Northumberland 1959. Died 13 November 1998.

DALÁL, Sir Ardeshir Rustomji (1905) Born 24 April 1884, Bombay, India; son of Rustomji Jehangir Dalál, Exchange Broker, and Aimai Dorabji Baman Behram; m Manekbai Wadia, 1912; 1 son, 2 daughters. **Subject(s):** Natural Sciences; BA 1907; MA 1919. **Tutor(s):** D MacAlister. **Educ:** Elphinstone College, Bombay; Fort High School. **Career:** Assistant Collector, Superintendent of Land Records, Indian Civil Service 1908–1921; Deputy Secretary, Government Finance Department 1925–1926; Member, Indian Legislative Assembly 1927; Collector and Municipal Commissioner for Bombay 1928–1931; President, Indian Chamber of Commerce, Calcutta 1938–1939; President, Indian Science Congress Association 1941; Director, Planning and Development Department, India, and Member, Executive Council 1944–1946. **Appointments:** Director, Tata Sons Ltd; Director, Tata Iron and Steel Company 1931–1942; President, Calcutta Rotary Club 1937–1938; Director, Andhra Valley Power Supply Company. **Honours:** Kt 1939; KCIE 1946. Died 8 October 1949.

DALBY, Robert (1921) Naval Officer.

DALE, Frank (1907) Born 17 April 1888, Saxmundham, Suffolk; son of Sam Dale, Monumental Stonemason, and Milly Harriet Smith. **Subject(s):** Classics/History; BA 1910; MA 1925. **Tutor(s):** E E Sikes. **Educ:** Wyndham House School; Woodbridge School. **Career:** Assistant Master, Woodbridge School 1911; Assistant Master, Berkhamstead School 1915; Private, HAC, then Second Lieutenant, King's Own Scottish Borderers, WWI. Died 21 December 1965.

DALVI, Ganpat Vishvanath (1935) Born 11 June 1913, Baroda, India; son of Vishvanath Ganpat Dalvi, Barrister-at-Law, and Sulabha Vasindevrao Bhandarkar. **Subject(s):** Natural Sciences; BA 1937. **Tutor(s):** C W Guillebaud. **Johnian Relatives:** son of Vishvanath Ganpat Dalvi (1906). **Educ:** Elphinstone College, Bombay, India; Royal Institute of Science, Bombay; Government Law College, Bombay. **Career:** Called to the Bar, Lincoln's Inn 1939; Principal, Siddharth College of Law, University of Bombay 1960.

DALVI, Vishvanath Ganpat (1906) Born 27 August 1886, Baroda, India; son of Ganpat Jagannath Dalvi, Book-keeper and Accountant, and Rewabai; m Sulabna Vasindevrao Bhandarkar; 1 son (Ganpat b 11 June

1913). **Subject(s):** Mathematics; BA 1909; LLB 1911. **Tutor(s):** L H K Bushe-Fox. **Johnian Relatives:** father of Ganpat Vishvanath Dalvi (1935). **Educ:** Elphinstone High School; Elphinstone College.

DALZELL, Donald Percy (1916) Born 30 August 1898, 273 Lamaha Street, North Cummingsburg, Georgetown, Demerara; son of John Dalzell, Shipping Company's Manager, and Ethel Blanche Forster. **Subject(s):** Mathematics/Mechanical Sciences; BA 1921; MA 1926; CEng; MIEE. **Tutor(s):** E E Sikes. **Educ:** Belvedere College; Anerley College; Royal Masonic School, Bushey. **Awards:** Exhibition, SJC 1916. Died 25 March 1988.

DANCKWERTS, Professor Peter Victor (1948) Born 14 October 1916, Southsea; son of Victor Hilary Danckwerts, Vice-Admiral, RN, and Joyce Middleton; m Lavinia Macfarlane, 1960. MA 1948; BA (Oxon) 1938; SM (MIT) 1948; CEng; FIChemE; FRS 1969. **Educ:** Stubbington House, Fareham; Winchester College; Balliol College, Oxford; MIT. **Career:** Sub-Lieutenant, RNVR 1940–1945; Demonstrator in Chemical Engineering, University of Cambridge 1948; Deputy Director of Research and Development, Industrial Group, Atomic Energy Authority 1954–1956; Professor of Chemical Engineering Science, Imperial College of Science and Technology, London 1956; Shell Professor of Chemical Engineering, University of Cambridge 1959–1977; Fellow, Pembroke College, Cambridge 1959–1977 (Emeritus 1977). **Appointments:** Honorary Member, American Academy of Arts and Sciences 1964; President, Institution of Chemical Engineers 1965–1966. **Honours:** MBE 1943; George Cross 1940. **Publications:** *Gas-Liquid Reactions*, 1970. Died 25 October 1984.

DANIEL, Professor Glyn Edmund (1932) Born 23 April 1914, Lampeter View, Lampeter Wefrey, Narberth, Pembrokeshire; son of John Daniel, Headmaster, and Mary Jane Edmunds; m Ruth Langhorne, 12 September 1946. **Subject(s):** Archaeology and Anthropology; BA 1935; MA 1939; PhD 1938; LittD 1962; FBA. **Tutor(s):** J M Wordie. **Johnian Relatives:** uncle of Richard Tristan Bailey Langhorne (1959); husband of Ruth Daniel (1998). **Educ:** Llantwit Major Public Elementary School; Boys' County School, Barry. **Career:** Wing Commander, Photo-reconnaissance, RAF, India (Mentioned in Despatches); Title A Fellow 1938–1947, Title B Fellow 1947–1974, Lecturer in Archaeology and Anthropology 1954–1974, Title C Fellow 1974–1976, Title D Fellow 1976–1986, SJC; Assistant Lecturer, Faculty of Archaeology and Anthropology 1945–1948, Lecturer in Archaeology 1948–1974, Disney Professor of Archaeology 1974–1981, University of Cambridge. **Appointments:** Assistant Supervisor in Archaeology and Anthropology 1938–1940, Supervisor in Archaeology and Anthropology 1946–1954, Steward 1946–1955, Director of Studies in Archaeology and Anthropology 1947–1974, SJC; Member, Arts Theatre Trust 1954; Department of Environment Committee on Archaeological Rescue Projects in Cambridgeshire, Essex and Hertfordshire; President, Royal Anthropological Institute; Emeritus Fellow, Leverhulme Trust 1985; Director, Anglia Television; Director, Cambridge Arts Theatre. **Awards:** Wallenberg Prize 1938; Allen Scholarship 1937. **Publications:** *The Three Ages*, 1942; *A Hundred Years of Archaeology*, 1950; *The Prehistoric Chamber Tombs of England and Wales*, 1950; (with S Piggott) *A Picture Book of Ancient British Art*, 1951; *Lascaux and Carnac*, 1955; (ed) *Myth or Legend*, 1955; (with T G E Powell) *Barclodiad y Gawres*, 1956; *The Megalith Builders of Western Europe*, 1958; *The Prehistoric Chamber Tombs of France*, 1960; (with Colin Renfrew) *The Idea of Prehistory*, 1961, revised edition 1986; *The Hungry Archaeologist in France*, 1963; (with S P O'Riordain) *New Grange and the Bend of the Boyne*, 1964; (ed with I L Foster) *Prehistoric and Early Wales*, 1964; *Man Discovers his Past*, 1966; *The Origins and Growth of Archaeology*, 1967; *The First Civilisations*, 1968; *Archaeology and the History of Art*, 1970; *Megaliths in History*, 1973; (ed, jointly) *France before the Romans*, 1974; *A Hundred and Fifty Years of Archaeology*, 1975; *Cambridge and the Back-Looking Curiosity: an inaugural lecture*, 1976; *A Short History of Archaeology*, 1981; (ed) *Towards a History of Archaeology*, 1981; *Some Small Harvest* (memoirs), 1986; articles in archaeological journals; (ed John D Evans,

Barry Cunliffe and Colin Renfrew) *Festschrift: Antiquity and Man*, 1981. Died 13 December 1986.

DANIEL, Professor Peter Maxwell (1930) Born 14 November 1910, 1A Upper Wimpole Street, Marylebone, London; son of Peter Lewis Daniel, Consultant Surgeon, and Beatrice Laetitia Herskind; m (1) Sarah Shelford, (2) F Dawn Bosanquet; (1) 2 sons, 3 daughters, (2) 1 son, 1 daughter. BA 1938; MA 1940; BChir 1942; MB 1942; BSc (London) 1961; MA (Oxon); DM (Oxon); DSc (London); MRCP 1954; FRCP; FRCS; FRCPath; FRCPsych; FLS; FIBiol. **Tutor(s):** M P Charlesworth. **Educ:** St Cross School, Walton on the Heath; Westminster School. **Career:** Honorary Consultant Pathologist, Radcliffe Infirmary, Oxford 1948–1956; Senior Research Officer, University of Oxford 1949–1956; Honorary Consultant in Neuropathology to the Army at Home 1952–1977; Honorary Consultant Neuropathologist, Bethlem Royal and Maudsley Hospitals 1956–1976; Professor of Neuropathology (later Emeritus), University of London, Institute of Psychiatry, Maudsley Hospital 1957–1976; Senior Research Fellow, Department of Applied Physiology and Surgical Science, Hunterian Institute, RCS 1976–1998; Emeritus Physician, Bethlem Royal and Maudsley Hospitals 1977–1998; Visiting Senior Research Fellow, St Thomas' Hospital Medical School 1981–1998. **Appointments:** Liveryman, Society of Apothecaries 1952–1999; Editorial Board, *Journal of Neurology, Neurosurgery and Psychiatry* 1953–1964; Editorial Board, *Journal of Physiology* 1958–1965; Council Member, Neonatal Society 1959–1961; President, British Neuropathological Society 1963–1964; Erasmus Wilson Lecturer, RCS, 1964; Council Member 1966–1969, Honorary Member 1985, Association of British Neurologists; Member, Board of Governors, Bethlem Royal and Maudsley Hospitals 1966–1975; President 1966, Trustee 1971–1998, Honorary Member 1985, Harveian Society London; Chairman, Academic Board, Institute of Psychiatry 1966–1970; Editorial Board, *Journal of Neuroendocrinology* 1966–1977; Council Member, Royal Microscopical Society 1968–1972; President, Neurological Section, RSM 1970–1971; Council Member, Charing Cross Hospital Medical School 1972–1985; Editorial Board, *Brain* 1974–1976; Vice-Chairman, Central Academic Council, British Postgraduate Medical Federation 1975–1976; Emeritus Fellow, Leverhulme Trust 1978–1980; President, Osler Club 1979–1982; President, Section of History of Medicine, RSM 1979–1982; Editorial Board, *Quarterly Journal of Experimental Physiology* 1980–1984; Honorary Member, Physiological Society 1981; Member, Board of Studies in Physiology, University of London 1981; Honorary Librarian, Royal College of Pathologists 1981–1998; Council Member 1981–1998, Honorary Librarian 1984–1990, President 1987–1988, Medical Society of London; Member, Library Committee, Linnean Society 1987–1998; Life Member, Anatomical Society of Great Britain. **Awards:** John Hunter Medal and Triennial Prize 1946–1948. **Publications:** *Studies of the Renal Circulation*, 1947; *The Hypothalamus and Pituitary Gland*, 1975; papers in various medical and scientific journals. Died 19 November 1998.

DANIELLI, Professor James Frederic (1941) Born 13 November 1911, 36 Swinderby Road, Wembley, Middlesex; son of James Frederic Danielli, Civil Servant, and Helena Hollins; m Mary; 2 children. PhD 1942; BSc (London) 1931; PhD (London) 1933; DSc (London) 1938; FRS 1957. **Educ:** The County School, Wembley; UCL; Princeton University. **Career:** Title A Fellow, SJC 1942–1945; University Reader in Cell Physiology, Royal Cancer Hospital, London 1946–1947; Physiologist, Marine Biological Laboratory, Plymouth 1947–1949; Professor of Zoology, KCL 1949–1960; Fellow, UCL 1960; Director, Centre for Theoretical Biology, State University of New York 1962–1980; Head, Life Sciences Department, Worcester Polytechnic Institute, USA 1974. **Publications:** (with Hugh Davson) *The Permeability of Natural Membranes*, 1943. Died 22 April 1984.

DANIELS, Cyril Ernest (1929) Born 4 June 1912, 6 Avenue Mansions, Park Avenue, Willesden, Middlesex; son of John Alfred Daniels, Dry Goods Merchant, and Dorothy Edith Ernst. **Subject(s):** Economics/Moral Sciences; BA 1934. **Tutor(s):** J M Wordie. **Educ:** Sunbury House; St Bede's, Eastbourne; Berrystead, Oundle; Oundle School.

DANIELS, John Michael Ewan (1938) Born 4 June 1919, Grasmere, Queen Anne's Place, Bush Hill Park; son of Percy Leigh Daniels, Farmer, and Mary Agnes Hobbs. **Subject(s):** Modern and Medieval Languages; BA 1941. **Tutor(s):** C W Guillebaud. **Educ:** The Abbey, Beckenham; Repton School. **Career:** Pilot Officer, RAFVR 1939–1941. **Awards:** Exhibition, SJC 1937. Died August 1941 (killed in action).

DANNATT, Peter Conrad (1947) Born 3 October 1928, 31 Marlborough Road, Stretford, Manchester; son of Cecil Dannatt, Electrical Engineer, and Winifred Ethel Flear; m Elizabeth Unsworth; 2 sons (Timothy Mark b 1 March 1958 and Andrew Howard Guy b 5 June 1962), 1 daughter (Lorna Kate b 30 January 1959). **Subject(s):** Mechanical Sciences; BA 1950; MA 1991; MIEE. **Educ:** Altrincham Grammar School. **Career:** Electrical Engineer, Electrical and Nuclear Industries to 1960. **Awards:** Major Scholarship, SJC 1946.

D'ANTAL, Andrew Louis (1930) Born 24 January 1912, 1 Alma Utea, Budapest; son of Ladislas d'Antal, Financier, and Elizabeth Gartner; m Fleur; 1 son (Stephen), 1 daughter (Linda). **Subject(s):** Economics. **Tutor(s):** C W Guillebaud. **Educ:** Preparatory School, Budapest; Berthold's Gymnasium, Freiburg in Breisgain; Norton House, Rottingdean; Cranbrook School, Kent. Died 27 June 1988.

D'ARCY, John Robert (1949) Born 5 March 1929, Bunmichael, Brittany Road, Hove, Sussex; son of Thomas Norman D'Arcy, Surgeon Rear Admiral, RN, and Eleanor Lennox Broadbent; m Pamela Boulding, 4 June 1955, St Simon Zelotes Church, Chelsea (d 1995); 2 sons (William b 25 February 1957, and James b 7 August 1959). **Subject(s):** Law; BA 1952. **Tutor(s):** A G Lee. **Educ:** The School, Malvern Link; St Edward's School, Oxford. **Career:** Called to the Bar, Inner Temple 1953; Captain, British Overseas Airways Corporation (later British Airways); Instructor on DC10 simulators; General Manager, Flight Crew, BOAC; Chief Pilot, Flight Crew, British Airways; Flight Manager, Concorde/707 until 1984; Operations Manager, Cyprus Airways 1984–1986. **Appointments:** Freeman, City of London. **Awards:** Choral Studentship, SJC.

DARK, Geoffrey Fairfax (1931) Born 2 September 1913, 127 Sidwell Street, Exeter, Devon; son of Alexander Pedler Dark, Master Wood Carver, and Mabel Maud Pope. **Subject(s):** History. **Tutor(s):** E A Benians. **Educ:** Egerton School, Exeter; Exeter School.

DARLING, Ralph McIntire (1918) American Student.

DARLING, Thomas Young (1940) Born 5 February 1922, Queen Victoria Hospital, Johannesberg, South Africa; son of Thomas Darling, Farmer and Company Director, and Christian Margaret Shepherd; m Anna Margaret Maclean, 28 June 1952, Edinburgh; 1 son, 3 daughters. **Subject(s):** Mechanical Sciences; BA 1947; MA 1964; MICE 1952; FICE 1964; ACII 1970. **Tutor(s):** S J Bailey. **Johnian Relatives:** brother of William Hunter Darling (1948). **Educ:** Oakleigh Park Preparatory School, Whetstone; Loretto School. **Career:** Served, RE, India and Burma 1940–1946; seconded to Queen Victoria's Own Madras Sappers and Miners 1942; demobbed with rank of Major; Sir Alexander Gibb & Partners, Consulting Civil Engineers 1949–1954; Contract Civil Engineer, Geo Wimpey, then J L Kier 1954–1969; Director, Capital & Metropolitan, Insurance Brokers, Edinburgh 1970–1972; Part-time lecturer, Civil Engineering Department, Edinburgh University 1970–1991; Partner, Darling, Young and Partners, Advisers in Personal Finance 1973–1991; Director, Albyn Associates 1991. **Appointments:** Elder, Braid Church 1967; Congregational Stewardship Promoter for 20 years; Elder, Edinburgh Presbytery for 12 years; Member, Church of Scotland Trust (Chairman 1986–1991); Chairman, Church of Scotland Insurance Company; Member, Edinburgh Merchant Company 1968; Representative on Melville Trust for the Care and Cure of Cancer for 20 years, latterly as Chairman; Member 1976, President 1992–1993, Edinburgh Rotary Club; Honorary Fellow, Edinburgh University 1991; Chairman, Edinburgh Parkinson Society 1994; Member, New Club; Member, Edinburgh Angus Club. Died 24 June 1995.

DARLING, William Hunter (1948) Born 2 October 1927, Los Kop, Northumberland Road, New Barnet, Hertfordshire; son of Thomas Darling, Farmer and Company Director, and Christian Margaret Shepherd; m Susan Chloe Dixon, 22 April 1970. **Subject(s):** Agriculture; BA 1950; MA 1955. **Tutor(s):** G C L Bertram. **Johnian Relatives:** brother of Thomas Young Darling (1940). **Educ:** Beaufort Lodge Preparatory School, Barnet; St Christopher's School, Letchworth; Loretto School. **Career:** Second Lieutenant, Royal Tank Regiment, India 1947; Farmer, Greys, Royston, Hertfordshire 1952–1985. **Appointments:** Honorary Secretary, Royal Forestry Society, Gloucestershire; JP, Royston 1965–1984; Chairman, Hertfordshire NFU 1961–1962; Founder Member, later Chairman, and President, Hertfordshire/Middlesex Trust for Nature Conservation 1965–1984; Member, Forestry Commission Regional Advisory Committee 1974–1985. **Awards:** Nuffield Farming Scholarship, New Zealand/Australia 1956.

DARLINGTON, Dr Alfred Frankland Dean (1919) Born 3 February 1897, 55 Bond Street, Leigh, Lancaster; son of William Henry Robertson Darlington, Private Secretary and Schoolmaster, and Ellen Frankland; m Gwendoline Pearl. BA 1921; MA 1927; MB 1925; BChir 1925. **Tutor(s):** E E Sikes. **Educ:** Warrington Grammar School; City of London School. **Career:** Physician, Children's Department, Cheltenham General Eye and Children's Hospital; Senior Obstetric House Physician, St Thomas' Hospital; House Surgeon, Coventry and Warwick Hospital. **Honours:** MC. Died 15 April 1979.

DARLINGTON, William Aubrey Cecil (1909) Born 20 February 1890, Queen's College, Trull, Taunton; son of Thomas Darlington, Fellow, SJC and HM Inspector of Schools, and Annie Edith Bainbridge; m Marjorie Sheppard, 3 November 1918, St James', Piccadilly; 1 daughter. **Subject(s):** Classics/Modern and Medieval Languages; BA 1912; MA 1926. **Tutor(s):** E E Sikes. **Johnian Relatives:** son of Thomas Darlington (1882). **Educ:** The Grammar School, Aberystwyth; Shrewsbury School. **Career:** Master, St Michael's School, Westgate-on-Sea 1913; Captain and Adjutant, Northumberland Fusiliers (TF) (wounded), then War Office, WWI; Dramatic Critic, *Daily Telegraph* 1920–1968. **Publications:** *I do what I like, an Autobiography*, 1947; Various contributions to *The Eagle*, and to *Punch*; *Alf's Button* (short stories). Died 24 May 1979.

DARMON, Dr Stanley Edward (1942) Born 25 January 1924, New Town, Spilsby; son of Walter Norriss Darmon, Joiner, and Ruby Constance Sadie Codd; m Jean Agnes Southerst; 1 son (James), 1 daughter (Anne). **Subject(s):** Natural Sciences; BA 1945; PhD Spectroscopy 1948. **Tutor(s):** C W Guillebaud. **Educ:** King Edward VI Grammar School, Spilsby. **Career:** Research Fellow, Leeds University 1946–1951; Brewer 1951–1977, Director 1977–1982, Guinness plc.

DARWALL, Michael Theodore Dyott (1935) Born 1 October 1916, Dogpole, Barclay Oval, Woodford Wells, Essex; son of Dyott Whateley Darwall, Clerk in Holy Orders, and Lucy Willacy; m Joan Chennell Diggle, 1940 (d 1996); 2 sons (Edward Chennell Dyott b 1944 and George Howard Dyott b 1946). **Subject(s):** Engineering; BA 1938; MIMechE 1946. **Tutor(s):** J S Boys Smith. **Johnian Relatives:** grandson of Henry George Willacy (1869); father of George Howard Dyott Darwall (1965). **Educ:** The Knoll, Woburn Sands; Shrewsbury. **Career:** Junior Technical Assistant, London Passenger Transport Board (Railways) 1938; Officer Cadet, RE 1940; Second Lieutenant, RAOC 1941; Lieutenant, REME on formation 1942; Captain, REME 1944; Reckitt and Colman, Hull, Yorkshire 1946; Westinghouse Brake and Signal Company, Chippenham, Wiltshire 1950; Motor Industry Research Association, Nuneaton, Warwickshire 1969–1981.

DARWIN, John Henry (1904) Born 27 October 1884, St Briabel, Queen's Grove, Southsea, Hampshire; son of Samuel Brothers Darwin, Secretary and Superintendent, Gas Company, and Evelyn Gesina Grobbee. **Subject(s):** Classics; BA 1907. **Tutor(s):** E E Sikes. **Educ:** Charterhouse.

Career: Assistant Magistrate and Collector, United Provinces, India 1909–1917; Military Service 1918–1919; Deputy Director of Civil Supplies, United Provinces 1919–1921; Magistrate and Collector 1921–1927; Deputy Secretary, Government General Branch 1927–1936; Reforms Commissioner 1936–1937. **Awards:** Scholarship, SJC 1904. **Honours:** CIE 1932.

DAS GUPTA, Professor Charu Chandra (1944) Born 6 September 1908, Dinajpur, Bengal, India; son of Hem Chandra Das Gupta, Professor of Geology, Presidency College, Calcutta, and Mrinaliné Roy. **Subject(s):** History; PhD 1946; BA (Calcutta) 1929; MA (Calcutta) 1931; PhD (Calcutta) 1944. **Tutor(s):** J M Wordie. **Educ:** South Suburban School, Calcutta; Presidency College, Calcutta; Calcutta University. **Career:** Professor of History, Carmichael College, Rangpur; Principal, Government College, Darjeeling.

D'ASSIS-FONSECA, Honorio Bingham (FONSECA) (1948) Born 19 February 1926, Toledo, Ohio, USA; son of Honorio José Muschamp d'Assis Fonseca, Mechanical Engineer, and Helen Vera Bingham Bingham-Hall. **Tutor(s):** C W Guillebaud. **Educ:** Bowdon College, Cheshire; Ascham House School, Gosforth; Durham School. **Career:** Captain, RA, India. Died 17 November 1967.

DAVENPORT, Arthur (1915) Born 19 April 1897, 17 Southmoor Road, St Giles, Oxford; son of William Arthur Davenport, Bank Cashier, and Jane Prestidge. **Tutor(s):** L H K Bushe-Fox. **Educ:** Abingdon School. **Career:** Lieutenant, Rifle Brigade, attached to Tank Corps 1915–1918. **Awards:** Scholarship, SJC 1914. Died 23 August 1918 (killed in action near Boyelles).

DAVEY, John (1930) Born 19 March 1911, 13 Beckbury Street, Farsley, North Bierley; son of Percy Davey, Grocery Inspector, and Edith Waters. **Subject(s):** History; BA 1933; MA 1937. **Tutor(s):** E A Benians. **Educ:** Pudsey Secondary School; Fulneck Secondary School; Ashville College, Harrogate. **Awards:** Exhibition, SJC 1929.

DAVID, Illtyd (1917) Born 6 March 1894, The Post Office, Nantymoel, Llandyfodwg, Glamorganshire; son of Edward David, Postmaster, and Jane Evans; m Eira Cole Morgan, 28 April 1943, St James' Church, Swansea; 1 son (Edward Illtyd). **Subject(s):** Law; BA 1920; MA 1924; LLB 1920; BA (Wales) 1916; LLD (Dublin) 1923; MA (Wales) 1930. **Tutor(s):** E E Sikes. **Johnian Relatives:** father of Edward Illtyd David (1965). **Educ:** Intermediate School, Barry; University College, Aberystwyth. **Career:** Called to the Bar, Inner Temple 1924; Organiser of Adult Education and Lecturer, Tutorial Classes Committee, University Colleges of Swansea and Aberystwyth 1924; Head of Extramural Studies, University College of Swansea 1941–1960; Senior Staff Tutor, University Extension, University College of Swansea 1951.

DAVID, John (1948) Born 6 August 1927, The Corner House, Llanharry, Glamorganshire; son of Thomas Edward David, Farmer, and Viva Taylor; m 8 July 1967; 1 son (Jonathan), 2 daughters (Joanna and Helen). **Subject(s):** Chemical Engineering; BA 1951; MA 1955; MEng 1992. **Tutor(s):** G C L Bertram. **Educ:** Llanharry Council School; Cowbridge Grammar School, Glamorgan.

DAVID, John Ernest Awelrydd (1928) Born 31 October 1910, 91 High Street, Walthamstow, Essex; son of Joseph Andrew David, Journalist, and Annie Wynne Hird. **Tutor(s):** M P Charlesworth. **Educ:** Herneville Preparatory School; Dulwich College; St Bartholomew's Hospital Medical School.

DAVIDGE, Professor Henry Thomas (1902) Born 9 November 1871, Teddington, Middlesex; son of Henry Thomas Davidge, of independent means, and Eliza West; m Louisa Annie Dexter, 29 July 1898, St Leonard's, Streatham. BSc (London) 1898; ARCS; MIEE. **Tutor(s):** D MacAlister. **Educ:** Tiffin's School, Kingston upon Thames. **Career:** Professor of Electricity, Royal Ordnance College, London 1903–1918;

Professor, UCL 1918–1936; Head of Engineering, Seafield Technical College, Crofton; Lecturer, Department of Engineering, University of Cambridge. **Publications:** *Optical Instruments*; *Wireless Telegraphy*; *Meteorological Instruments*; *Electricity and National Welfare*. Died 15 July 1957.

DAVIDSON, Alan Salisbury (1919) Born 5 September 1900, 76 Hill Street, North Adelaide, South Australia; son of Allan Arthur Davidson, Mining Engineer, and Charlotte Beeston; m Vi, 1925. BA 1922; MA 1930. **Tutor(s):** E E Sikes. **Educ:** Tollington School, Fetherdown. **Career:** Keffi Consolidated Tin Mines, Jos, Northern Nigeria 1922. **Appointments:** Freeman, City of London; Member, Glazier's Company; Fellow, Royal Philatelic Society; Member, British Society of Australian Philatelists. Died 17 June 1989.

DAVIDSON, Alexander Craig Lennox (1935) Born 5 February 1914, Shell Cove Road, North Sydney, New South Wales, Australia; son of Alexander Davidson, Merchant, and Annie Brown Craig. **Tutor(s):** C W Guillebaud. **Educ:** Headfort School, Killara; King's School, Parramatta; University of Sydney.

DAVIDSON, Angus Garth (1938) Born 20 December 1919, 18 Roker Park Terrace, Sunderland, Durham; son of Oswald Rae Davidson, Company Director, and Ethel Robinson Swan; m (1) Alison Yora Priestly, 29 August 1952, Cheltenham Parish Church (div 1968), (2) Wendy Susan Orford, 23 December 1968; (1) 1 son (Simon b 1956), 1 daughter (Teresa b 1953), (2) 1 son (Angus Alexander b 1974). BA 1942; MA 1945; Diploma of Architecture (Birmingham); RIBA. **Tutor(s):** J S Boys Smith. **Johnian Relatives:** brother of Stephen Moriarty Davidson (1927); uncle of Roderick Macdonald Davidson (1958). **Educ:** Claremont House, Sunderland; Oswestry Grammar School, Oswestry; Warwick School; Birmingham University. **Career:** Architect, Berkshire County Architects Office; Architect, Coventry City Architects; Architect, Private Practice; Principal Architect (Territorial), Department of Education and Science 1965–1981. Died 30 May 2001.

DAVIDSON, Dr Donald Georges (1939) Born 14 February 1921, 74 Bromyard Road, Worcester; son of George Davidson, Physician and Surgeon, and Violette Wykes. **Subject(s):** Natural Sciences; BA 1942; MB 1946; BChir 1946. **Tutor(s):** R L Howland. **Educ:** Packwood Haugh; Shrewsbury School. **Career:** GP.

DAVIDSON, Francis Stanley (1948) Born 6 May 1928, Deneholme, Denewell Avenue, Low Fell, Gateshead; son of Francis Thomas Bowie Davidson, Mechanical Engineer, and Ruth Greer McHugh; m (1) Ann Veronica Gilbert, St Luke's, Torquay, 15 August 1951 (div), (2) Jean Ann Reid, 6 November 1961; 2 sons (Roderick and Andrew), 2 daughters (Kate and Veronica). **Subject(s):** Natural Sciences; BA 1950; MA 1957; MBIM. **Tutor(s):** G C L Bertram. **Educ:** Musgrave Private School, Low Fell, Gateshead; Newcastle Royal Grammar School. **Career:** Procter and Gamble 1951–1954; Mars 1954–1955; PA Consultants 1955–1961; Managing Director, small engineering firm 1961–1964; Chief Industrial Consultant, ICFC 1964–1971; Self-employed 1971–1979; Economic Development Office, Breckland Council 1979–1993. **Appointments:** General Manager, European Study Conferences Ltd. Died 23 June 2000.

DAVIDSON, James Johnston (1924) Born 13 October 1902, 120 Mid Stocket Road, Aberdeen, Scotland; son of James Davidson, Bank Accountant, and Elizabeth Elphinston Johnston. **Subject(s):** Classics; BA 1927; MA (Aberdeen). **Tutor(s):** E E Sikes. **Educ:** Fettercairn Public School; Robert Gordon's College; Aberdeen University.

DAVIDSON, Dr James Wightman (1938) Born 1 October 1915, 46 Upland Road, Kelburn, Wellington, New Zealand; son of George Wightman Davidson, Representative, British Manufacturers, and Edith Mabel Brown. PhD 1942. **Tutor(s):** J S Boys Smith. **Educ:** Croydon Diocesan School, Wellington, New Zealand; Hereworth School,

Havelock North; Waitaki Boys' High School, Oamoru; Victoria University College, Wellington, New Zealand. **Career:** Professor of Pacific History, ANU, Canberra; Political Assistant to the Governor of Samoa; Consultant to the Constitution Planning Committee of Papua New Guinea; Title A Fellow, SJC 1944–1951; Lecturer in History, University of Cambridge 1947. **Appointments:** Australian and New Zealand Association for the Advancement of Science 1957. **Awards:** Open Strathcona Studentship, SJC. Died 8 April 1973.

DAVIDSON, John Peter Archibald (1935) Born 8 November 1916, 77 The Peak, Hong Kong; son of Edgar Davidson, Solicitor, and Eva Geraldine Crew. **Subject(s):** Law. **Tutor(s):** J M Wordie. **Educ:** Peak School, Hong Kong; St Christopher's School, Eastbourne; Charterhouse. **Career:** Flight Lieutenant, RAFVR 1939–1941. **Awards:** Harmsworth Law Scholarship; MacMahon Law Studentship. Died January 1941 (killed on active service).

DAVIDSON, Malcolm Norman (1940) Born 31 January 1922, Anglo-American Hospital, Cairo, Egypt; son of Sydney Herbert Davidson, Inspector, Ministry of Interior, Egypt, and Sarah Yuill Cunningham; m Helen Audrey Lynas, 14 September 1949; 1 son (John), 2 daughters (Sarah and Susannah). **Subject(s):** Law; BA 1947. **Tutor(s):** R L Howland. **Educ:** Monrae Grange, Kilkeel; Tonbridge School. **Career:** Captain, RAOC 1942–1943; Clerk to East Africa Central Legislative Assembly, Nairobi, HM Colonial Administrative Service. Died 25 June 1958.

DAVIDSON, Percy Maurice (1921) Born 5 March 1902, 98 Ramsden Road, Balham, London; son of Percy Davidson, of independent means, and Helen Mary Gray. **Subject(s):** Natural Sciences (Physics); BA 1924; PhD (London). **Tutor(s):** B F Armitage. **Educ:** Balham Grammar School; King's College School, Wimbledon. **Career:** Lecturer in Physics, University College of Swansea 1929–1964; Professor of Theoretical Physics, University College of Swansea 1964. **Awards:** Scholarship, SJC 1920.

DAVIDSON, Dr Stephen Moriarty (1927) Born 22 October 1910, 2 Azalea Terrace South, Sunderland, County Durham; son of Oswald Rae Davidson, Managing Director, Outfitters, and Ethel Robinson Swan; m Kathleen Flora Macdonald, 10 October 1936, Cambridge; 1 son (Roderick Macdonald b 2 January 1938), 1 daughter (Patricia Mary b 20 September 1939). BA 1931; MA 1936; MB 1936; BChir 1936; MRCS 1934; LRCP 1934. **Tutor(s):** M P Charlesworth. **Johnian Relatives:** brother of Angus Garth Davidson (1938); father of Roderick Macdonald Davidson (1958). **Educ:** Argyle House School, Sunderland; Ashville College, Harrogate. **Career:** Private Medical Practice, Plymouth 1936–1969; Surgeon Lieutenant Commander, RNVR 1939–1944. **Appointments:** JP, Plymouth 1960. Died 26 April 1998.

DAVIE, Geoffrey Bowcher (1929) Born 24 May 1911, Mentmore House, Uxbridge Road, Kingston, Surrey; son of Mervyn Bowcher Davie, Underwriter (Member of Lloyd's), and Evelyn Constance Warren. **Subject(s):** Modern and Medieval Languages. **Tutor(s):** C W Guillebaud. **Educ:** St Wilfred's School, Bexhill on Sea; Repton School. **Career:** Lieutenant (Aeroplane Officer), RNVR, Fleet Air Arm, HMS *Formidable*, WWII. Died 8 May 1941 (killed in action in the Middle East).

DAVIES, Arthur Lloyd (1919) Born 13 April 1898, The Rectory, Denbigh; son of Daniel Davies, Vicar and Rural Dean, and Frances Hester Mary Ellis; m Barbara Walker, 28 July 1925, St James's Church, Nantglyn. **Subject(s):** Mechanical Sciences; BA 1922; MA 1944. **Tutor(s):** E A Benians. **Johnian Relatives:** son of Daniel Davies (1883); brother of Noel Gordon Davies (1929). **Educ:** Praetoria House, Folkstone; Shrewsbury School; RMC, Woolwich. **Career:** Second Lieutenant, RFA 1916, served in France, Captain of his Battery, WWI; Engineer and Assistant Manager, Brunner Mond's Middlewich Works 1925. **Honours:** MC 1917, with Bar 1918. Died 20 July 1989.

DAVIES, Arthur Thomas (1912) Born 25 February 1893, 86 Manchester Road, Nelson, Lancashire; son of Thomas Davies, Bookseller, and Elizabeth Parker. **Subject(s):** Natural Sciences (Physics); BA 1915; MA 1921. **Tutor(s):** R P Gregory. **Educ:** Carr Road Elementary School, Ely; Secondary School, Nelson.

DAVIES, Ben (1945) Born 26 August 1926, Barberry Hill, Eirias, Colwyn Bay, Denbighshire; son of Benjamin Davies, Director of a Limited Company, and Euphemia Cameron Macpherson; m Isobel Matilda Alexander, 10 May 1952. **Tutor(s):** J M Wordie. **Educ:** St Wilfrid's School, Seaford; Upper Canada College, Toronto; Shrewsbury School.

DAVIES, Bernard Sydney (1920) Naval Officer.

DAVIES, David Edgar (1944) Born 28 August 1925, 1 Chatsworth Avenue, Walton, Liverpool; son of Daniel Davies, Tannery Company's Commercial Traveller, and Elizabeth Morgan. **Subject(s):** Modern and Medieval Languages; BA 1948; MA 1950. **Tutor(s):** C W Guillebaud. **Educ:** Warbreck Council School, Liverpool; Alsop High School, Liverpool.

DAVIES, David Idwal (1930) Born 22 July 1911, 4 Carr Mount, Rawtenstall, Lancashire; son of David Rhoslwyn Davies, Unitarian Minister, and Jane Grey Jones; m Josephine. **Subject(s):** Classics/Philosophy; BA 1933; MA 1948; Teaching Diploma (Manchester). **Tutor(s):** M P Charlesworth. **Educ:** Blackley Municipal School; The Grammar School, Manchester; University of Manchester. **Career:** Head of Department of English and General Studies, Hull College of Technology; Assistant Lecturer in Classics, Egyptian University, Cairo; Master, Drogheda Grammar School 1935; Assistant Master, Egyptian Government Secondary Schools 1935–1938; Master, Zickel's Hohere Privatschule, Berlin 1938; Wittingehame College, Brighton 1939–1940; Dauntsey's School, Wiltshire 1940; Intelligence Officer, RAF, Middle East 1941–1945; Classical Master, Audenshaw Grammar School, Manchester 1946. **Awards:** Scholarship, SJC. Died 2 August 1979.

DAVIES, The Revd David Richard (1900) Born 17 June 1881, Pandy, Ystradyfodwg, Glamorganshire; son of Richard Davies, Draper, and Martha Jenkins; m Anita Mary. BA 1903; MA 1907. **Tutor(s):** C E Graves; J R Tanner. **Educ:** St John's School, Ystrad Meurig. **Career:** Dean, St Michael's College, Aberdare 1904; Vicar, Oakwood, Surrey; Curate, St James, Latchford 1904–1906; Priest 1905; Curate, Lymm 1906–1907; Curate, Kendal 1907–1909; Curate, Heysham with St John, Sandylands 1909–1913; Vicar, Finsthwaite 1913–1923; Vicar, Broughton in Amounderness, Lancashire 1923. Died 17 March 1947.

DAVIES, Professor David Richard Seaborne (1925) Born 26 June 1904, Talafor, South Beach, Pwllheli, Carnarvonshire; son of David Seaborne Davies, Master Mariner, and Gladys Davison. **Subject(s):** Law; BA 1927; MA 1931. **Tutor(s):** E A Benians. **Educ:** Pwllheli Elementary School; Pwllheli Council School; University College, Aberystwyth. **Career:** Lecturer, later Reader in Law, LSE 1929–1945; Nationality Division, Home Office, WWII; MP for Caernarvon Boroughs 1945; Professor of Common Law, Faculty of Law, Warden of Derby Hall, Dean of Law Faculty 1945, Public Orator 1950–1955, Pro-Vice-Chancellor 1956–1960, University of Liverpool. **Appointments:** President, Society of Public Teachers of Law 1960–1961; Cooley Lectureship, University of Michigan 1962; High Sheriff of Caernarvonshire 1967–1968; Member, Criminal Law Revision Committee; Magistrate. **Awards:** Yorke Prize, University of Cambridge 1928. Died 21 October 1984.

DAVIES, Professor David Vaughan (1944) (admitted to Trinity Hall 1937) Born 28 October 1911, Dolfonddu, Cemmaes, Machynlleth; son of Joshua Davies, Farmer, and Mary Emma Ryder; m Ruby Bertha Ernest, 1940; 2 sons (Michael and Christopher), 1 daughter (Elizabeth). MA (Trinity Hall) 1937; MB, BS (London) 1935; DSc (London) 1961; MRCS, LRCP (1935); FRCS (1963). **Educ:** Cemmaes Council School; Towyn County School; UCL; University College Hospital. **Career:** Demonstrator in Anatomy 1937–1939, Lecturer 1939–1948, University of Cambridge; Title B Fellow 1944–1948, Supervisor in Anatomy 1941–1947, Lecturer in Anatomy 1946–1948, SJC; Arris and Gale Lecturer, Royal College of Surgeons, London 1945; Professor of Anatomy 1948–1969, Sub-Dean 1958–1966, St Thomas' Hospital Medical School, University of London; Fellow, UCL 1956. **Appointments:** High Sheriff of Montgomeryshire 1961–1962; President, Anatomical Society 1965–1967; President, Montgomeryshire Society, London; Member, London Welsh Association; Vice-President, Clwb y Cymry. **Awards:** Gold Medal in Physiology 1932; Ferrier Scholarship 1933 and 1934. **Publications:** (ed) *Gray's Anatomy*; *Synovial Joints*, 1961. Died 16 July 1969.

DAVIES, Denis Laidlaw (1928) Born 20 December 1909, Wellington Street, Woollahra, Sydney, New South Wales, Australia; son of Reginald Laidlaw Davies, Medical Practitioner, and Phyllis Parbury. **Subject(s):** History; BA 1931. **Tutor(s):** C W Guillebaud. **Educ:** The King's School, Parramatta, Sydney, Australia.

DAVIES, Denys Martin Owen (1943) Born 15 November 1925, St Paul's Vicarage, Llanelly, Wales; son of John Thomas Davies, Clerk in Holy Orders, and Gwenonwy Owen; m April Rosamond Addison, 23 March 1957; 2 sons (Geraint Thomas Owen b 1959 and Martin Peter Owen b 1961), 2 daughters (Rosamond Mary b 1957 and Alys Helen b 1962). **Subject(s):** Mechanical Sciences; BA 1950; MA 1973; MICE. **Tutor(s):** S J Bailey. **Johnian Relatives:** nephew of Franklin Kidd (1909). **Educ:** King's College Choir School, Cambridge; Llandovery College; Birmingham Central Technical College. **Career:** Lieutenant, RE, India, Burma and Malaya 1945–1948; Assistant Design Engineer, Cobb and Whakamaru Hydro-Electric Schemes 1952–1953, Assistant Engineer, Atiamuri Hydro-Electric Scheme 1954–1955, Ministry of Works, New Zealand; Section Engineer 1955–1956, Assistant Design Engineer, Loch Shin Hydro-Electric Scheme, Scotland 1956–1957, Section Engineer, Bridges, Gt Ouse Flood Protection Scheme 1957–1960, Murdoch MacDonald and Partners, London; Deputy Resident Engineer, Ford Motor Company Press Shop and Assembly Plant, Liverpool 1960–1963, Consultant's Site Representative, Ford Motor Company Transmission Plant, Liverpool 1963–1964, Resident Engineer, Boulton and Paul Ltd, Factory Extension, Lowestoft 1965–1966, Posford Pavry and Partners, London; Deputy Manager, Docks and Estate, Hutchinson Estate and Dock Company (Widnes) Ltd 1966–1967; Construction Engineer and Acting Water Engineer, Public Works Department Western District, Government of Fiji 1968–1970; Assistant to Project Manager, Guyana Sea Defences, Sir William Halcrow and Partners, London 1971–1973; Project Civil Engineer, Guyana Electricity Corporation Re-development Scheme 1973–1974, Senior Engineer, Specifications, Conditions of Contract, Contract Documents and Project Procedures 1974–1975, The Shawinigan Engineering Company, Montreal; Resident Engineer for Civil Works of the Nuclear Island, Cordoba Nuclear Power Station, Argentina, Atomic Energy of Canada Ltd, Toronto, seconded by Canatom Inc of Montreal 1975–1978; Senior Engineer, Construction Co-ordination, Korean Nuclear Power Station 1978–1979, Senior Engineer, Administration and Procurement, Montreal, Rumanian Nuclear Power Station 1979–1980, Canatom Inc, Montreal; Chief Resident Engineer, Bani Walid Wool Textile Complex, Libya, Haiste International, Leeds 1980–1982; Chief Buildings and Civil Engineer, Al Jubail Industrial City Sea Water Cooling Operation and Maintenance Contract, Resource Sciences Arabia Ltd 1983–1984; Manager, 'El Almendral' Estate, San Roque, Cadiz, Spain from 1985; Resident Engineer, Lyonaise des Eaux, Gibraltar Sea Water Pumping Station, Northumbria Consultants 1991.

DAVIES, Eric (1908) Born 30 September 1889, Ingleton, Grassendale Road, Grassendale, Liverpool; son of Alfred Thomas Davies, JP, Civil Servant, and Margaret Esther Nicholas. **Subject(s):** Law; BA 1911; LLB 1911. **Tutor(s):** L H K Bushe-Fox. **Educ:** Waterloo High School, Blundellsands; Bishop's Stortford College. **Career:** Bristows Law Firm 1911–1961 (Partner 1922); Admitted Solicitor 1914; Commissioned Second Lieutenant, Nottinghamshire Yeomanry 1914; sailed with Regiment to Alexandria 1915; fought at Gallipoli 1915; fought at Gaza and Jerusalem 1917. **Appointments:** Member, Law Society 1920; Member, Goschen Committee on Trade Marks 1933; Council Member, Law Society 1936–1958; Member 1940, Commissioned Second Lieutenant 1943, Home Guard; Chairman, Legal Aid Sub-Committee, Citizens Advice Bureaux, National Council of Social Services 1941–1947; Member, Denning Committee on Procedure in Matrimonial Causes 1946; Member, Solicitors' Disciplinary Committee 1951–1959. Died 1 November 1978.

DAVIES, Frank (1925) Born 29 May 1907, 19 Russell Road, Hendon, Middlesex; son of Bertram Davies, Solicitor's Articled Clerk, and Elizabeth Annie Peacock. **Subject(s):** Natural Sciences (Physics); BA 1928; MA 1939; BSc (London) 1928. **Tutor(s):** J M Wordie. **Educ:** Algernon Road Elementary School; Hendon County School. **Johnian Relatives:** uncle of Barry Lyn Davies (1957). Died 28 June 1986.

DAVIES, Hugh Sykes (SYKES DAVIES) (1928) Born 17 August 1909, Wesley Manse, West Street, Prescott, Lancashire; son of Thomas Seaton Davies, Wesleyan Minister, and Kate Sykes; m Fay; 2 daughters (Kate and Judith). **Subject(s):** Classics/English; BA 1931; MA 1935. **Tutor(s):** M P Charlesworth. **Educ:** Highgate Grammar Preparatory School; Kingswood School, Bath. **Career:** Ministry of Food, WWII; Lecturer in English, University of Cambridge 1936; Title A Fellow 1933–1936, Title B Fellow 1936–1976 (leave of absence for war service 1940–1945), Lecturer in English 1946–1976, Title D Fellow 1976–1984, SJC. **Appointments:** Assistant Supervisor in English 1933–1934, Supervisor in English 1934–1947, Director of Studies in English 1937–1970, SJC. **Awards:** Scholarship, SJC; Jebb Studentship 1931; Le Bas Prize, University of Cambridge 1933. **Publications:** *Realism in the Drama*, 1933; *Surrealism*, 1936; *Macaulay's Marginalia to Lucretius*, 1937; *No Man Pursues*, 1950; *Grammar without Tears*, 1951; *Full Fathom Five*, 1956; *The Papers of Andrew Melmoth*, 1960. Died 6 June 1984.

DAVIES, Ian Leonard (1942) Born 2 June 1924, 26 Porthkerry Road, Barry, Glamorganshire; son of Harry Leonard Davies, Schoolmaster, and Janet Doris Hellings; m Hilary Dawson, 22 September 1951, Leckhampton, Cheltenham; 2 sons, 2 daughters. **Subject(s):** Mechanical Sciences/Mathematics; BA 1945; MA 1949; FIEE. **Tutor(s):** S J Bailey; J M Wordie. **Johnian Relatives:** godfather of Adrian Hearle (1977). **Educ:** Romilly Road Elementary School, Barry; Barry County School for Boys; University College, Cardiff. **Career:** Scientific Civil Servant; Chartered Electrical Engineer; various posts at TRE, Malvern 1944–1945, BLEU, Martlesham 1945–1947, TRE (later the Royal Radar Establishment) 1949–1969 (Head of Quantum and Microwave Electronics 1960–1963, Head of Airborne Radar Department 1963–1969); Imperial Defence College 1970; Assistant Chief Scientific Adviser (Projects), Ministry of Defence 1971–1972; Deputy Controller, Electronics 1973, and Deputy Controller, Air Systems D 1973–1975, Procurement Executive, Ministry of Defence; Director, Admiralty Underwater Weapons Establishment, Portland, Dorset 1975–1984; After retirement: part-time Consultant to Ministry of Defence 1985–1989; part-time Technical Adviser to Monopolies and Mergers Commission 1986; Various voluntary part time jobs with local organisations. **Appointments:** Chairman, Electronics Division, IEE 1975–1976. **Awards:** State Scholarship 1941; Scholarship, SJC 1944; Wright's Prize, SJC 1944; IEE Heaviside Premium 1952. **Honours:** CB 1983. **Publications:** Various papers on Information Theory, Radar and Lasers.

DAVIES, Idris John (1940) Born 13 August 1922, 10 Sunnyside Road, Bridgend, Glamorganshire; son of Idris Evan Davies, Quarry Owner and Contractor, and Alice Maud Power; m Beryl Baylis, 25 April 1946. BA 1947; MA 1950. **Tutor(s):** R L Howland. **Educ:** Oldcastle Boys' School, Bridgend; The Grammar School, Cowbridge. Died 7 December 1949.

DAVIES, Ivor Glyndwr (1912) Born 15 September 1891, Bryngarw House, Porth, Ystradyfodwg, Glamorganshire; son of Ivor Henry Davies, Physician, and Sarah Ann Thomas. BA 1915; MA 1919. **Tutor(s):** L H K Bushe-Fox. **Educ:** Private Tuition. Died 9 July 1977.

DAVIES, Professor Jack (1948) Born 24 August 1919, 72 Markham Avenue, Carcroft, Adwick le Street, Yorkshire; son of William Davies, Colliery Clerk, and Mary Boyce. MA 1947; BSc (Leeds) 1941; MD (Iowa) 1943; ChB (Leeds) 1944, MD (Leeds) 1950. **Educ:** Doncaster Grammar School; University of Leeds; University of Iowa. **Career:** Associate Professor of Anatomy, Washington University, St Louis; Demonstrator in Anatomy 1947–1949, Lecturer in Anatomy 1949–1951, University of Cambridge; Title B Fellow 1949–1951, Supervisor in Anatomy 1948–1951, SJC; Assistant Professor of Anatomy, University of Iowa 1951–. **Appointments:** Secretary, Washington University Medical Society; Society for Experimental Biology and Medicine; American Association of Anatomists.

DAVIES, Jack Gale Wilmot (1930) Born 10 September 1911, Heathfield, Broadclyst, Devonshire; son of Langford George Davies, Medical Practitioner, and Lily Barnes Green; m Georgette O'Dell (née Vanson); 1 son. **Subject(s):** Classics; BA 1933; MA 1937; Honorary DLitt (City). **Educ:** Stratheden House School, Blackheath; Langley Place, St Leonards on Sea; Tonbridge School. **Career:** Middlesex Regiment: Captain, Major, Lieutenant Colonel 1941, Colonel 1943, Central Mediterranean Force 1944, South-East Asia Command 1945; Title E Fellow, SJC 1959–1968; Chief Psychologist, Directorate of the Selection of Personnel, War Office; Non-executive Director, Portals Holdings. **Appointments:** Amateur Cricketer, Kent (99 matches) 1934–1951; Secretary, Appointments Board (now the Careers Service) 1952, Deputy Pro-Chancellor 1984–1989, University of Cambridge. Executive Director, Bank of England 1969–1970; Treasurer 1976, President 1986 (subsequently life Vice-President), MCC. **Awards:** Scholarship, SJC 1929. **Honours:** OBE 1946. Died 5 November 1992.

DAVIES, The Revd Canon John Howard (1947) Born 19 February 1929, 3 Belsize Avenue, Ealing, Middlesex; son of Jabez Howard Davies, Clerk, Petroleum Company, and Sarah Violet Gardiner; m Ina Mary, 1956 (d 4 October 1985); 4 sons (John Clement Stanley b 23 November 1957 d 23 August 1999, Michael James Bernard b 19 August 1959, Peter Thomas Justin b 13 April 1962 and Christopher Francis Paul George b 1 June 1968 d 12 February 1974). **Subject(s):** Music/Theology; BA 1950; MA 1954; BD (Nottingham); Cambridge Ordination Course 1955. **Tutor(s):** C W Guillebaud. **Johnian Relatives:** father of John Clement Stanley Davies (1976) and of Michael James Bernard Davies (1978). **Educ:** Beaconsfield Road Elementary School, Southall; Southall Grammar School; Westcott House, Cambridge. **Career:** Ordained Deacon 1955; Succentor, Derby Cathedral 1955–1958; Ordained Priest 1956; Chaplain, Westcott House, Cambridge 1958–1963; Lecturer in Theology 1963–1974, Senior Lecturer 1974–1981, Director of Studies in Theology 1981–1994, Southampton University; Canon Theologian, Winchester Cathedral 1981–1991. **Appointments:** Public Preacher, Diocese of Winchester 1964; Member, Archbishop's Commission on Church Music 1988–1992. **Awards:** Choral Studentship, SJC 1947; John Stewart of Rannoch Scholarship, University of Cambridge 1949–1951; Naden Studentship 1951–1952. **Publications:** *A Letter to Hebrews*, 1967; (contributor) 'In Tune with Heaven' (report of Archbishop's Commission on Church Music).

DAVIES, Laurence Hector (1936) Born 28 May 1911, 51 Molyneux Road, Waterloo, Liverpool; son of Henry James Yates Davies, Local Government Official, and Florence Elizabeth Hector; m Helen Garden, 18 December 1948. **Subject(s):** English; BA 1939; MA 1943. **Tutor(s):** J S Boys Smith. **Educ:** Liverpool College. **Awards:** Choral Scholarship, SJC. Died 13 May 1983.

DAVIES, Noel Gordon (1929) Born 31 August 1910, The Vicarage, Wrexham; son of Daniel Davies, Lord Bishop of Bangor, and Frances Hester Mary Ellis; m Joan Douthet. **Tutor(s):** J M Wordie. **Johnian Relatives:** son of Daniel Davies (1883); brother of Arthur Lloyd Davies (1919). **Educ:** Colet House, Rhyl; Shrewsbury School. **Career:** Second Engineer Officer, SS *Stone Street* (Panama). Died 13 September 1942 (killed at sea).

DAVIES, Norman Frederick (1942) Born 29 August 1924, 11 Carlisle Street, Birkenhead; son of Joseph Herbert Samuel Davies, Foreman Baker, and Jane Davies. **Tutor(s):** C W Guillebaud. **Educ:** Claughton Higher Grade School; Birkenhead School.

DAVIES, Patrick Taylor (1948) Born 10 August 1927, Tilbhoom, India; son of Andrew Taylor Davies, Tea-planter, and Olive Kathleen Mary Hobson; m Marjorie Eileen Wilkinson, 9 May 1959, Wickersley, Yorkshire; 2 daughters (Jennifer b 10 December 1960 and Susan b 10 October 1962). **Subject(s):** Mathematics; BA 1950; MA 1991. **Johnian Relatives:** grandson of John Bayley Davies (1859). **Educ:** Shrewsbury School; Trinity College, Oxford. **Career:** Lieutenant, RA, Nigeria; Lieutenant, RA (TA), Shropshire Battery 1945–1952; HM Colonial Administration Service, Nigeria 1952–1979; Permanent Secretary, Kano State 1970–1979; Chief Inspector, Area Courts, Kano State 1972–1979. **Honours:** OBE 1967; CMG 1978.

DAVIES, Richard Morgan (1911) Born 24 May 1892, The Post Office, Llandyssil, Cardiganshire; son of Richard Morgan Davies, Postmaster, and Adelaide Reid. BA 1914. **Tutor(s):** E E Sikes. **Educ:** College School, Lampeter. **Career:** Master, Langton Maltravers Preparatory School 1914; Lieutenant, RFA (wounded twice), WWI.

DAVIS, Colin Geoffrey (1942) Born 16 February 1925, St George's Avenue, Northampton; son of Sidney James Davis, Shoe Manufacturer, and Alice Dewhurst. **Subject(s):** Natural Sciences; BA 1949; MA 1951. **Tutor(s):** C W Guillebaud. **Educ:** Wainfleet School, Northampton; Oundle School.

DAVIS, Edward Derek (1944) Born 16 September 1926, 532 Rochdale Road, Royton, Lancashire; son of Joseph Davis, Cotton Yarn Salesman, and Mabel Haslam; m Joyce Chapman, 1953; 3 children. **Subject(s):** History; BA 1948; MA 1951; University of Cambridge Teaching Certificate 1951. **Tutor(s):** J M Wordie. **Educ:** Werneth Council School, Oldham; Hulme Grammar School, Oldham. **Career:** Teacher, Buxton, Derbyshire 1951–1953; Assistant Director of Education, Chester 1953–1955; Head of Department, Bailey School, Fleetwood 1955–1961; Senior Lecturer, Newcastle upon Tyne Teacher Training College 1961–1964; Principal Lecturer, Craigie College of Education, Ayr, Scotland 1964–1979. **Appointments:** RN Cadet, SJC.

DAVIS, Harold (1914) Born 8 September 1895, 2 Wood Hill, Northampton; son of Charles William Davis, India Rubber Merchant, and Florence Stoker; m Aileen; 5 children. **Subject(s):** Mathematics. **Tutor(s):** L H K Bushe-Fox. **Educ:** Wellingborough School. **Career:** Lieutenant, Somerset Light Infantry (TF), WWI; attached 3rd Gurkha Rifles, Indian Army, WWI. **Awards:** Scholarship, SJC. Died 18 July 1937.

DAVIS, Harold James (1908) Born 19 April 1889, Waverton, Cheshire; son of Richard Henry Davis, Schoolmaster, and Ellen Louisa Davis. **Subject(s):** Mathematics; BA 1911; MA 1923. **Tutor(s):** L H K Bushe-Fox. **Educ:** Waverton Church of England School; The King's School, Chester. **Career:** Master, Oswestry School 1912–1913; Master, Altrincham County High School 1913–1914; Sergeant, Royal Welsh Fusiliers, WWI; Lecturer in Mathematics, University College, Southampton 1914–1921; Lecturer in Mathematics, Bradford Technical College 1921–1924; Haberdashers' Aske's School, Hatcham (Vice-Master 1928) 1924–1954. **Appointments:** Examiner, Welsh Board. **Awards:** Open Scholarship, SJC. Died 18 January 1954.

DAVIS, Sir Herbert (1909) Born 12 March 1891, 31 Sandbrook Road, Stoke Newington, London; son of James Davis, Ivory Turner, and Ann Studdeard; m Eva Fitzgerald Radford; 2 daughters. **Subject(s):** Natural Sciences/History; BA 1912. **Tutor(s):** J R Tanner. **Educ:** The Grocers' School; Hackney Downs Secondary School, London; Birkbeck College, London. **Career:** Assistant Buyer, Jurgens 1918–1927; Secretary, Margarine Union 1927–1929; Board, Unilever 1937. **Honours:** CBE 1941; Kt 1943. Died 20 February 1972.

DAVIS, Michael Gerard (1942) Born 15 September 1924, Maternity Hospital, Singapore; son of John Michael Davis, Naval Stores Officer, and Helen Burke. **Tutor(s):** C W Guillebaud. **Educ:** Wimbledon College.

DAVIS, Dr Paul John Reginald (1932) Born 18 December 1913, 38 Brompton Square, Kensington, London; son of Leopold Clement John Davis, Antique Dealer, and Jessica (Jessie) Thomas; 1 daughter (Elizabeth). **Subject(s):** Classics; BA 1936; MA 1939; MB, BChir 1940. **Tutor(s):** R L Howland. **Educ:** Rosehill School, Banstead; Tonbridge School. **Career:** Captain, RAMC. **Honours:** MBE 1945. Died 4 August 1992.

DAVIS, Peter Brian (1944) Born 22 October 1926, 21a Alton Road, Oxton, Birkenhead; son of Victor Samuel England Davis, Headmaster, Latymer's School, and Lois Ellen Ponting. **Subject(s):** Mechanical Sciences; BA 1947; MA 1951; MICE 1954; FICE 1970; MBIM 1973; FBIM 1980. **Johnian Relatives:** son of Victor Samuel England Davis (1914); father of Edward John Davis (1971). **Educ:** Kilvinton Hall Preparatory School; Latymer's School, Edmonton. **Career:** Stressman, Sir Frederick Handley Page 1948; National Service, RE, Malaya 1948–1950; Indentured Graduate Assistant to Chief Civil Engineer, British Rail Eastern Region, King's Cross 1950–1955; work on Bridges, Permanent Way and then Electrification, Stratford (East London) District 1955–1958; Assistant District Engineer, Sheffield 1958–1966; Divisional Civil Engineer, Stratford 1966–1972; Assistant Chief Civil Engineer 1972–1974, Chief Civil Engineer 1974–1989, Assistant General Manager 1989–1991, York.

DAVIS, Dr Peter Sidney (1940) Born 1 December 1922, St George's Avenue, Northampton; son of Sidney James Davis, Managing Director, Shoe Manufacturers, and Alice Dewhurst (née Marsden); m Valerie Elizabeth Martin, February 1948; 2 sons. **Subject(s):** Natural Sciences; BA 1943; MA 1947; MB 1946; BChir 1946; MRCP. **Tutor(s):** R L Howland. **Educ:** Wainfleet House School, Northampton; Oundle School. **Career:** Major, RAMC, WWII; Medical Registrar, Neurological Unit, St George's Hospital; Senior Registrar, Departments of General Medicine, Rheumatology, and Physical Medicine, West London Hospital 1952. **Awards:** Bulkeley Medal and Prize. Died April 1961.

DAVIS, Dr Richard James Lance (1946) Born 25 April 1921, Bank Wood, Duffield, Derbyshire; son of Lancelot Samuel Davis, Hosiery Manufacturer, and Phyllis Emily Meakin; m Evelyn Athol Vaughan, 16 August 1949, St Wystan's Church, Repton. **Subject(s):** Natural Sciences; BA 1949; MA 1967; BChir 1952; MB 1952; MRCGP 1976. **Tutor(s):** G C L Bertram. **Johnian Relatives:** grandfather of Johanna Katherine Warnke (1996). **Educ:** Winchester Home School, Brackley; Repton School.

DAVIS, Victor Samuel England (1914) Born 6 December 1896, 32 Park Street, Melford within Salisbury, Wiltshire; son of Albert Sidney Davis, Clerk, and Annie Louise England; m Lois Ellen Ponting; 1 son (Peter Brian b 22 October 1926). **Subject(s):** Modern and Medieval Languages; BA 1917; MA 1923; Diploma (Lille) 1922. **Tutor(s):** E E Sikes. **Johnian Relatives:** father of Peter Brian Davis (1944); grandfather of Edward John Davis (1971). **Educ:** Private Tuition; St Thomas' Clergy School, Salisbury; Bishop Wordsworth's School, Salisbury. **Career:** Master, Whitney Grammar School 1918–1920; Master, Dauntsey's School, Wiltshire 1920–1925; Master, Birkenhead School 1925–1929; Headmaster, Latymer School, Edmonton 1929. Died 1 June 1971.

DAVISON, Bruce Munro (1925) Born 23 April 1908, Thornbury, Caterham, Surrey; son of John Usher Davison, Gentleman, and Meliscent Gunn; 2 sons (Andrew and Mark). **Subject(s):** Mathematics/Law; BA 1929; MA 1938; FCA 1933. **Tutor(s):** M P Charlesworth. **Johnian Relatives:** brother of Jack Gunn Davison (1922). **Educ:** St Winifred's, Kenley; The Dene, Caterham; Malvern College. **Career:** Chartered Accountant. **Appointments:** School Governor; local politics; British Legion. Died 23 September 2000.

DAVISON, Deryck Porter (1943) Born 9 April 1925, 37 Rothbury Street, Scarborough, Yorkshire; son of Joseph William Davison, Printer, and Doris Porter; m Joyce Mary Bailey, 22 August 1951, Alfreton (d 1985); 1 son (Stephen Patrick b 6 January 1954), 1 daughter (Barbara b 25 February 1956). **Subject(s):** Mathematics; BA 1946; MA 1950. **Tutor(s):** S J Bailey. **Educ:** Gladstone Road Council School, Scarborough; Scarborough High School. **Career:** Mathematics Teacher, Head of Mathematics 1963–1975, Director of Studies 1975–1981, Bridlington School.

DAVISON, Professor Edward Lewis (1919) Born 28 July 1898, 22 Harcourt Drive, Glasgow, Scotland; son of Edwin Tetlaw Shields, Ship Stores and Oil Merchant, and Evelyn Mary Davison; m Natalie Eva Weiner, 27 April 1926, New York. **Subject(s):** English; BA 1921; MA 1925; Honorary DLitt (Colorado) 1934. **Tutor(s):** E A Benians. **Johnian Relatives:** father of Peter Hubert Davison (1949). **Educ:** Stanhope School, South Shields. **Career:** RN, rose to Lieutenant 1914–1918; Editor, *The Challenge* (London literary and political review) 1922–1926; General Manager, *Guardian* 1924; frequent contributor to *The London Mercury*; Assistant Professor, Wassar College 1926–1927; McBride Lecturer, Western Reserve; Barrow Lecturer, Georgia; Moddy Lecturer, Chicago; John Simon Guggenheim Memorial Fellow Poetry, Europe 1930; Visiting Professor of English Literature, University of Miami; Director, Writers' Conference, Boulder 1935–1942; Professor of English Literature, University of Colorado 1935–1946; Lieutenant Colonel, administering project for the re-education of 370,000 German prisoners of war in the US 1939–1945; George M Laughlin Professor of English Literature, Washington and Jefferson College 1946; Dean, Washington and Jefferson College 1947–1949; Professor of English, Hunter College 1950; Director, School of General Studies, Hunter College 1953. **Appointments:** President, Poetry Society of America 1955–1956. **Honours:** Legion of Merit. **Publications:** Author of eight volumes of verse, including *Harvest of Youth*, *The Heart's Unreason* and *The Ninth Witch*; *Collected Poems*, Harper's, 1940. Died 8 February 1970.

DAVISON, Jack Gunn (1922) Born 1 July 1906, Thornbury, Caterham, Surrey; son of John Usher Davison, Gentleman, and Meliscent Gunn. **Tutor(s):** B F Armitage. **Johnian Relatives:** brother of Bruce Munro Davison (1925). **Educ:** St Winifred's, Kenley; The Dene, Caterham; Malvern College.

DAVISON, Peter Hubert (1949) Born 27 June 1928, 107 East 76th Street, New York, USA; son of Edward Lewis Davison, Author, and Natalie Eva Wiener; m Jane Auchincloss Truslow, 7 March 1959. **Tutor(s):** A G Lee. **Johnian Relatives:** son of Edward Lewis Davison (1919). **Educ:** University Hill School, Boulder; Fountain Valley School, Colorado Springs; Harvard University, Cambridge, USA. **Career:** Assistant to the Director, Harvard University Press; Editor, Harcourt, Brace & Co 1950; Associate Editor, Atlantic Monthly Press, Boston 1957. **Awards:** Fulbright Scholarship.

DAVISON, Robert (1931) Born 17 November 1912, 3 Ash Villas, Dunstan on Tyne, Durham; son of Thomas Atkinson Davison, Engineers' Clerk, and Grace Davison, Primary School Teacher; m M Eileen Power, 10 August 1940; 2 sons (John and Peter). **Subject(s):** Modern and Medieval Languages; BA 1934; MA 1938. **Tutor(s):** C W Guillebaud. **Educ:** The Council School, North Heaton; Royal Grammar School, Newcastle upon Tyne. **Career:** Modern Languages Teacher/Housemaster, Northampton and Worcester Royal Grammar Schools 1934–1940; Commissioned, RNVR 1940–1947; Senior Lecturer, Modern Languages, RMA, Sandhurst 1947–1975. Died 30 May 2000.

DAVY, Arthur (1947) Born 26 December 1929, 60 Sharrow Street, Broomhall, Sheffield; son of Ernest Harry Davy, Table Blade Maker, and Winifred Harmon. **Subject(s):** Natural Sciences; BA 1953. **Tutor(s):** G C L Bertram. **Educ:** St Barnabas Council School, Cecil Road; Thorpe Salvin Council School; Woodhouse Grammar School.

DAVY, Clifton Lionel (1914) Born 7 April 1895, School Street, Darfield, Yorkshire; son of Frederick Younge Davy, of independent means, and Lilian Crossley. **Tutor(s):** E E Sikes. **Educ:** Wesley College; Sligo Grammar School. **Career:** Second Lieutenant, West Yorkshire Regiment 1914; Captain, MGC 1914. **Honours:** MC 1916.

DAWES, Alan (1944) Born 11 January 1926, 138 Highfields, North Wingfield, Derbyshire; son of Alfred Dawes, Schoolmaster, and Madge Watson; m Joan Pindar, 9 August 1951; St Stephen's Church, Steeton. **Subject(s):** Law; BA 1947; MA 1951; LLB 1948; LLM 1985. **Tutor(s):** S J Bailey. **Educ:** Old Leake School; Crowland Senior School, Peterborough; Spalding Grammar School; King's School, Peterborough. **Career:** Consultant, Legal Practice, Buckle Mellow; Director, Norwich & Peterborough Building Society. **Awards:** Munsteven Exhibition, SJC. Died 14 November 1995.

DAWES, Herbert Edwin Tonge (1900) Born 11 February 1881, Long Sutton, Lincolnshire; son of Edwin Dawes, Brewer, and Kate Tonge. BA 1903; MB 1910; BChir 1910; LRCP; MRCS. **Tutor(s):** D MacAlister. **Educ:** Dover College Junior School; Dover College. **Career:** Senior Obstetric Officer and Resident House Surgeon, St Thomas' Hospital 1907. Died 4 November 1930.

DAWS, Hubert Gordon (1944) Born 12 December 1925, 71 Noel Street, Nottingham; son of Hubert Hope Daws, Clerk in Holy Orders, and Maud Mabel Lucy Tomlinson. **Tutor(s):** J M Wordie. **Educ:** St Michael's School, Surrey; Weymouth College; Wellingborough School.

DAWSON, Ambrose Middleton (1905) Born 14 May 1886, Clarendon Park Road, Knighton, Leicestershire; son of Ambrose Pudsey Dawson, Clerk in Holy Orders and Schoolmaster, and Mary Middleton. **Subject(s):** Mathematics; BA 1908. **Tutor(s):** D MacAlister. **Educ:** Kibworth Grammar School; Sedbergh School. **Career:** Assistant Master, Reigate Grammar School 1908–1912; Victoria College, Jersey 1913; Captain, Hampshire Regiment (TF) 1914–1917. **Honours:** MC 1917. Died 21 April 1968.

DAWSON, Ernest John (1936) Born 21 October 1917, 820 Manchester Road, Castleton, Lancashire; son of Ernest Jaques Dawson, Boot and Shoe Maker, and Emily Ashworth. **Subject(s):** Natural Sciences; BA 1939; MA 1966. **Tutor(s):** J S Boys Smith. **Educ:** St David's Preparatory School; College School, Colwyn Bay; Rydal School, Colwyn Bay.

DAWSON, John Kenneth Nettleton (1947) Born 3 October 1925, 5 The Crescent, Belper, Derbyshire; son of Edward Nettleton Dawson, Schoolmaster, and Mabel Hurt, Bank Clerk; m Nancy Lonsdale, 23 June 1956, Uxbridge; 1 son (Michael b 1963), 2 daughters (Susan b 1961 and Janet b 1965). **Subject(s):** English/Law; BA 1949; MA 1954; LLB 1951; Solicitor 1953. **Tutor(s):** F Thistlethwaite. **Educ:** Long Row Elementary School, Belper; Herbert Strutt Secondary School, Belper. **Career:** Royal Signals 1944–1947, commissioned 1945, Palestine and Egypt; Legal and Administrative posts, Cambridge City Council 1953; Somerset County Council 1954–1955; Bedfordshire County Council 1955–1983 (Deputy County Secretary 1973–1983). **Appointments:** Chairman, Bedfordshire County Beekeepers Association 1996. **Awards:** Exhibition, SJC 1942; Foundation Scholarship 1950; MacMahon Law Studentship 1950.

DAWSON, The Revd Ralph Sigismund (1919) Born 9 October 1899, 70 Franklin Road, Harrogate, Yorkshire; son of Sigismund Theodore Dawson, Clerk in Holy Orders, and Harriet Maud Wallace; m Freda. BA 1923; MA 1927. **Tutor(s):** E A Benians. **Educ:** Balliol House Preparatory School, Harrogate; St Peter's School, York; Ridley Hall, Cambridge. **Career:** Ordained Deacon 1925; Curate, Emmanuel Church, Southport 1925–1929; Ordained Priest, Liverpool 1926; Private Chaplain to Bishop of Liverpool 1929–1935; Vicar, Filey 1935–1937; Chaplain, St Edward, King and Martyr, Cambridge 1939–1957. Died 4 September 1968.

DAWSON, Reginald Thomas (1904) Born 17 January 1885, 2 Somerset Place, Russel Road, Great Yarmouth, Norfolk; son of William Frederick Charles Dawson, Merchant, and Margaret Rachel Welch. **Subject(s):** Natural Sciences; BA 1907; MA 1911. **Tutor(s):** D MacAlister. **Educ:** The Grammar School, Great Yarmouth. **Career:** Lieutenant, Edinburgh Academy OTC, WWI. **Awards:** Exhibition, SJC 1903.

DAWSON, Sidney Cooper (1930) Born 9 May 1909, 15 St Leonard's Road, Sculcoates, Kingston upon Hull; son of Thomas Cooper Dawson, Chief Inspector of Weights and Measures, and Margaret Matthew. **Subject(s):** Mechanical Sciences; BA 1933. **Tutor(s):** J M Wordie. **Educ:** Bede Collegiate School, Sunderland; Technical College, Sunderland. **Career:** Apprentice Engineer, Messrs Doxford & Son Ltd, Engineer Works, Sunderland.

DAY, Cyril Rupert (1915) Born 23 March 1896, Buckland Hill, Maidstone, Kent; son of Herbert John Day, Artist, and Myra Cooper. **Tutor(s):** E E Sikes. **Educ:** Maidstone Grammar School; Leighton Park School.

DAY, Dennis Ivor (1911) Born 10 February 1892, Rheola, Cemetery Road, St Ives, Huntingdonshire; son of George Dennis Day, Solicitor, and Margaret Jane Davis. **Subject(s):** Mathematics. **Tutor(s):** J R Tanner. **Johnian Relatives:** son of George Dennis Day (1879); brother of George Lewis Day (1910); brother-in-law of Laurance Edgar Tanner (1910); brother of Miles Jeffrey Game Day (1915). **Educ:** Repton School. **Career:** Royal Naval Division 1914; Second Lieutenant, attached to the 24th Division, Royal Field Artillery 1914. Died 7 October 1915 (of wounds received in action at Vermelles 25 September 1915).

DAY, George Lewis (1910) Born 2 December 1890, Rheola, Cemetery Road, St Ives, Huntingdonshire; son of George Dennis Day, Solicitor, and Margaret Jane Davis; m Dorothy Gwendoline (d 22 November 1959); 1 daughter (Sheila). **Subject(s):** History; BA 1913; MA 1913. **Tutor(s):** J R Tanner. **Johnian Relatives:** son of George Dennis Day (1879); brother-in-law of Laurance Edgar Tanner (1910); brother of Dennis Ivor Day (1911) and of Miles Jeffrey Game Day (1915). **Educ:** Repton School. **Career:** Major, Huntingdonshire Cyclist Battalion, WWI; attached Gloucestershire Regiment (Mentioned in Despatches), WWI; Solicitor, Day & Son, St Ives 1919; Town Clerk, St Ives 1940–1960. **Appointments:** Honorary Freeman, St Ives 1965. Died 28 March 1972.

DAY, Miles Jeffrey Game (1915) Born 1 December 1896, Rheola, Cemetery Road, St Ives, Huntingdonshire; son of George Dennis Day, Solicitor, and Margaret Jane Davis. **Tutor(s):** L H K Bushe-Fox. **Johnian Relatives:** son of George Dennis Day (1879); brother of George Lewis Day (1910); brother-in-law of Laurance Edgar Tanner (1910); brother of Dennis Ivor Day (1911). **Educ:** Slepe Hall, St Ives; Sandroyd, Cobham; Repton School. **Career:** Flight Lieutenant, RNAS 1917; Acting Flight Commander 1918. **Honours:** DSC. **Publications:** Poems in *The Spectator* and *Cornhill*, 1917. Died 27 February 1918 (killed in action).

DAY, Neville John (1948) Born 4 June 1925, 61 Carlyle Road, Cambridge; son of Edward John Day, Grocer, and Elsie May Favell; m Joan Arnold, July 1961, Girton, Cambridge; 1 daughter (Alison b June 1962). **Subject(s):** Classics; BA 1950; MA 1955; CEng; MIMechE. **Tutor(s):** R L Howland; A G Lee. **Educ:** St Luke's School, Cambridge; Perse School for Boys, Cambridge; Enfield Technical College. **Career:** Commissioned, REME 1945–1948; UKAEA 1960–1966; Legal and Patents Advisor, Atomic Power Construction Company 1966–1970; Legal Advisor, Nuclear Power Company Ltd 1970–1975; Called to the Bar, Lincoln's Inn 1975; Legal Advisor, National Nuclear Corporation 1975–1983. **Awards:** Cambridgeshire Minor Scholarship 1936; Samuel Nunn Travel Exhibition 1950.

DÉ, Birendra Nath (1903) Born 27 March 1882, Habibpur, District of Midnapore, India; son of Rajendra Lal Dé, Landowner, and Jogendra Burdhan; m Shanta Shila Mallik; 1 son (Debi Kumar b 7 February 1913). **Subject(s):** Mathematics; BA 1906. **Tutor(s):** D MacAlister.

Johnian Relatives: father of Debi Kumar Dé (1930). **Educ:** Presidency College, Calcutta, India. **Career:** Assistant Commissioner and Settlement Officer, United Provinces 1906–1919; Excise Commissioner 1919; Deputy Commissioner 1919–1925; Excise Commissioner and Superintendent of Stamps 1925–1926; Deputy Commissioner and Revenue Secretary to the Government, Central Provinces 1926–1927; Financial Secretary 1927–1928; Officiating Commissioner 1928.

DE, Debesh Chandra (1944) Born 1 June 1919, Hazaribagh, Chota Nagpur, Bihar, India; son of Bankim Chandra De, Advocate, High Court, Patna, and Niharbále Mitra. **Subject(s):** Mathematics; BA 1946; MA 1950; BSc (Patna) 1938; MSc (Patna) 1940. **Tutor(s):** J M Wordie. **Educ:** Miller School, Patna; Bihar National College, Bankipur; Science College, Patna; Patna University.

DÉ, Debi Kumar (1930) Born 7 February 1913, Jubbulpore, Central Provinces, India; son of Birendra Nath Dé, Commissioner, Indian Civil Service, and Shanta Shilla Mallik. **Subject(s):** Mathematics; BA 1935. **Tutor(s):** J M Wordie. **Johnian Relatives:** son of Birendra Nath Dé (1903). **Educ:** St Paul's School, Darjeeling, India.

DEANE, The Revd James Killen (1905) Born 19 September 1886, 201 Grays Inn Road, London; son of John Henry Deane, Surgeon, and Margaret Ann Killen. BA 1910; MA 1913. **Tutor(s):** J R Tanner; C E Graves. **Educ:** Dean Close School, Cheltenham. **Career:** Ordained Deacon 1910; Curate, St Matthew, Islington 1910–1913; Ordained Priest 1911; Curate, All Saints, Harlesden 1913–1917; Organising Secretary, Colonial and Continental Church Society, Eastern District 1917–1923; Rector, Clophill 1923–1925; Vicar, Malmesbury Abbey and St Mary, Westport, Wiltshire 1925–1944; Vicar, St Paul's, East Molesey 1944–1949. Died 1948.

DEAR, John Colin (1935) Born 21 June 1913, Rotorua, New Zealand; son of William John Finn Dear, Public Accountant, and Mary Elizabeth Anne Slatyer. **Subject(s):** Mathematics; BA 1937; MA 1942. **Tutor(s):** J M Wordie. **Educ:** Primary School, Helensville; King's School, Auckland; Mount Albert Grammar School, Auckland; Auckland College, University of New Zealand.

DEARDEN, Dr John Robert Biffin (1919) Born 25 May 1897, 62 Alexandra Crescent, Dewsbury, Yorkshire; son of Henry Dearden, Borough and Water Engineer, and Constance Ruth Dora Biffin. BA 1921; BChir 1924. **Tutor(s):** E A Benians. **Educ:** Willaston School, Nantwich; Wheelwright School.

DEARDEN, John Royds (1921) Born 8 July 1903, Locliff, Ashburton, Canterbury, New Zealand; son of Peregrine Robert Dearden, Sheep Farmer, and Annie Abbott Grigg. BA 1924. **Tutor(s):** B F Armitage. **Educ:** Brandon House, Cheltenham; Cheltenham College Junior School; Sherborne School. **Career:** Planter, Colonial Agricultural Service, Nigeria; British-American Tobacco Company, Madras 1925.

DE BOER, George (1939) Born 28 July 1920, 1 Park Avenue, Perry Street, Hull; son of Hessel de Boer, Fitter (foreman), and Ethel Sergeant, Telephonist; m Margaret Nield, 12 April 1952 (d 26 September 2000); 1 son (John b 1957), 1 daughter (Bridget Mary b 1954). **Subject(s):** Geography; BA 1942; MA 1946. **Tutor(s):** J M Wordie. **Johnian Relatives:** father of John de Boer (1976). **Educ:** St George's Road Council School, Hull; Hymers College, Hull. **Career:** Lecturer in Geography 1948–1964, Senior Lecturer in Geography 1964–1967, Reader in Geography 1967–1982 (Emeritus 1982), University of Hull. **Awards:** College Scholarship 1941. **Publications:** Papers in journals and contributions to books.

DE DIRSZTAY, Gedeon (1908) Born 4 August 1890, 29 Nagy János utea, Budapest, Hungary; son of Bela de Dirsztay, Landowner, and Irene Brull. **Tutor(s):** L H K Bushe-Fox. **Educ:** Gymnasium, Budapest.

DEE, Robert John (1949) Born 6 June 1929, Queen Mary Nursing Home, Derby; son of Thomas Pride Dee, Chemical Engineer, and Winifred Mary Latham; m Maureen Joan Smith, 18 June 1955, Southend-on-Sea; 2 sons (Clifford b 1959 and Stephen b 1964), 2 daughters (Alison b 1957 and Caroline b 1961). **Subject(s):** Mechanical Sciences; BA 1952; MA 1956; CEng; FIMechE; PEng (Ontario, Canada). **Tutor(s):** R L Howland. **Educ:** Darley Abbey Church of England School, Derby; Chislehurst and Sidcup County School for Boys; Brigg Grammar School; Ipswich School. **Career:** Royal Signals 1947–1949; Junior Engineer, Vacuum Oil Company 1952–1954; Graduate Apprentice 1954, Design Engineer 1955–1958, Plant Engineer 1958–1959, ICI Ltd; Engineer II 1959–1967, Reactor Shift Manager 1963–1964, Assistant Manager, DIDO Reactor 1964–1967, UKAEA; Senior Design Engineer, Shawinigan Engineering Company, Montreal, Canada 1967–1969; Mechanical Design Engineer 1969–1972, Supervising Mechanical Design Engineer 1972–1974, Ontario Hydro, Toronto, Canada; Senior Design Engineer (Nuclear) 1974–1992, Senior Consultant and Acting Manager 1992–1993, Pickering NGS Engineering Department. **Appointments:** Chairman, Central Canada Branch 1980–1982 and 1992–1994, Chairman, Western Branch 1996–1998, IMechE. **Awards:** Scholarship, SJC 1952; IMechE 150th Anniversary Gold Medal 1997.

DEER, Professor William Alexander (1934) Born 26 October 1910, 82 St Ives Road, Rusholme, Manchester; son of William Deer, Grey Cloth Maker-up, and Davina Cunningham; m (1) Margaret Kidd, 1939, (2) Rita Tagg, 1973; 2 sons, 1 daughter. PhD 1937; MSc (Manchester); Honorary DSc (Aberdeen) 1983; FRS 1962; FGS. **Tutor(s):** J M Wordie. **Educ:** Ducie Avenue Central School, Manchester; Manchester Central High School; Victoria University of Manchester. **Career:** Title A Fellow, SJC 1939–1947 (suspended for war service 1941–1946); RE 1940–1946; Title B Fellow, SJC 1947–1950; Professor of Geology, Manchester University 1950–1961; Title C Fellow, SJC 1961–1966; Demonstrator in Mineralogy and Petrology 1946–1949, Lecturer in Mineralogy and Petrology 1949–1950, Professor of Mineralogy and Petrology 1961–1978 (Emeritus 1978), Vice-Chancellor 1971–1973, University of Cambridge; Master, Trinity Hall, Cambridge 1966–1975. **Appointments:** Petrologist, British East Greenland Expedition 1935–1936; Tutorial Bursar 1946–1949, Supervisor in Mineralogy, Petrology and Geology 1946–1950, Junior Bursar 1947–1949, Tutor 1949–1950, Honorary Fellow 1969, SJC; Leader, NE Baffin Land Expedition 1948; Percival Lecturer, University of Manchester 1953; Joint Leader, East Greenland Geological Expedition 1953; Leader, British East Greenland Expedition 1966; Trustee, British Museum (Natural History) 1967–1975; President, Mineralogical Society 1967–1970; Member, NERC 1968–1971; President, Geological Society 1970–1972; Member, Marshall Aid Commemoration Commission 1973–1979; Honorary Fellow, Trinity Hall, Cambridge 1978. **Awards:** Strathcona Studentship, SJC 1934; 1850 Exhibition Senior Studentship 1938; Murchison Fund, Geological Society 1945; Bruce Medal, Royal Society of Edinburgh 1948; Murchison Medal, Geological Society 1974. **Publications:** *Rock-forming Minerals*, 5 vols, (jointly) 1962–1963, 6 vols 2nd edition 1978–2002; *Introduction to Rock-forming Minerals*, 1966, 2nd edition, 1992; papers in *Mineralogy and Petrology*.

DE GARIS, Leslie (1944) Born 16 November 1926, Guernsey, Channel Islands; son of William Arthur de Garis, Tomato Industry, and Lilian Maude Le Couteur. **Tutor(s):** J M Wordie. **Educ:** Sarel Preparatory School; Intermediate School; Elizabeth College, Guernsey. **Appointments:** RAF Cadet, SJC.

DEHN, Harold Bruce (1935) Born 1 September 1916, 22 Cranes Park Avenue, Surbiton; son of Frank Bernard Dehn, Chartered Patent Agent, and Irma Becker. **Subject(s):** Law; BA 1938; MA 1966; Passed the Final Examination of the Law Society, November 1947. **Tutor(s):** J S Boys Smith. **Johnian Relatives:** brother of Stanley Gustav Dehn (1930). **Educ:** Shrewsbury House School, Surbiton; Rossall School. Died 16 June 1996.

DEHN, Michael Harold (1949) Born 27 November 1930, Malvern Cottage, 8 Malvern Grove, Withington, Manchester; son of Harold Gustav Dehn, Cotton Shipping Merchant, and Phyllis Mary Arning; m Jill. **Subject(s):** Economics/Law; BA 1952; MA 1965. **Tutor(s):** C W Guillebaud. **Educ:** Beech Hall School, Macclesfield; Glaston Tor School, Glastonbury; Aldenham School. **Career:** Branch Manager, National Employers' General Insurance Association Ltd. Died 3 June 1971.

DEHN, Stanley Gustav (1930) Born 22 February 1913, Oakleigh, Balgores Lane, Romford, Essex; son of Frank Bernhard Dehn, Chartered Patent Agent, and Irma Becker; m Avril Symes-Thompson, 14 October 1950, St George's, Hanover Square (d 1988); 2 sons (Edmund b 1952 and Stephen b 1958). **Subject(s):** Mechanical Sciences; BA 1934; MA 1938; FCIPA 1939. **Tutor(s):** J M Wordie. **Johnian Relatives:** brother of Harold Bruce Dehn (1935). **Educ:** Shrewsbury House School, Surbiton; Malvern College. **Career:** German Patent firm 1936; Major, XIX London Regiment, WWII; Senior Partner, Frank B Dehn & Co 1964; Patent Attorney 1982. **Honours:** TD. Died 5 August 1999.

DE LA MOTTE, Edward Septimus George (1920) Born 23 January 1901, 8 Trumpington Street, Cambridge; son of Vital de la Motte and Susanna Agnes Miller; m Mabel; 1 son (John). **Subject(s):** Mathematics/ Mechanical Sciences; BA 1923. **Tutor(s):** E A Benians. **Educ:** Bedford Kindergarten; Holm Leigh Preparatory School, Buxton; Corchester Preparatory School, Corbridge on Tyne; St Bees School, Cumberland. **Career:** Civil Engineer and Railway Surveyor; Marines, RNVR (special duties in the underground movement in South Africa) WWII. Died 27 January 1958.

DE LANDA, Francis Joseph (1922) Born 13 April 1903, Mexico City, South America; son of Guillermo de Landa y Escaardon, Gentleman, and Sofia Osio. **Tutor(s):** B F Armitage. **Educ:** Preparatory School, Biarritz, France; Stoneyhurst College; Private Tuition, London. Died 2 December 1944.

DE LA TORRE, Fernando (1949) Born 18 February 1927, Calle Covarrubias 5, Madrid, Spain; son of Silverio de la Torre, Civil Engineer, and Caridad Fé Alba; m Gillian Duncan; 3 daughters (Joanne, Elena and Alicia). **Subject(s):** Economics/Geography/Modern Languages; BA 1953; MA 1956. **Tutor(s):** C W Guillebaud. **Educ:** Girton Village School; Impington Village College; Perse School, Cambridge.

D'ELBOUX, Raymond Herbert (1919) Born 6 January 1894, 37 Haldon Road, Wandsworth, Surrey; son of Herbert Clare D'Elboux, Gentleman, and Lydia Alice Kent; m Eleanor de Trafford, 2 October 1922, Westminster Cathedral (d 1955); 2 daughters (Ursula and Susan). **Subject(s):** History; BA 1921; MA 1945. **Tutor(s):** E A Benians. **Johnian Relatives:** brother-in-law of Cuthbert Henry de Trafford (1919). **Educ:** County School for Boys, Beckenham, Kent; Strand School, KCL; KCL. **Career:** Inns of Court Officers Training Corps 1915; 4th Reserve Battalion, The Buffs 1915–1916; Lieutenant, 1st Loyal North Lancashire Regiment 1916–1919; Assistant Master, County School, Bexhill. **Appointments:** FSA. **Honours:** MC, WWI; Bronze Medal, Royal Humane Society, WWI. Died 5 January 1961.

DELGADO, Gregorio Alexander (1926) Born 13 May 1907, 98 Morningside Avenue, New York, USA; son of Jose Manuel Delgado, Physician, and Mary Alexandra Mitchell; m Frances, 20 August 1959. **Subject(s):** History; BA 1929. **Tutor(s):** E A Benians. **Educ:** St Peter's School, York.

DEL MAR, Ronald Henry (1933) Born 23 April 1915, Hampstead, London; son of Max Del Mar, Brush Manufacturer, and Vera Del Mar; m Pauline Elizabeth Arthur, 1946; 1 son (Christopher), 1 daughter (Antonia). **Subject(s):** Natural Sciences/Chemistry; BA 1936; MA 1941; CChem; FRSC. **Tutor(s):** C W Guillebaud. **Johnian Relatives:** father of Christopher Bernard Del Mar (1971). **Educ:** The Hall, Hampstead; Marlborough College; Philosophy Department, LSE. **Career:**

Management Trainee, Unilever 1937–1939; Senior Technical Assistant to the Director of Ordnance Factories 1939–1945; various executive positions, Unilever, UK and South Africa 1945–1968; Director and Chemicals Coordinator, Unilever Ltd and Unilever NV 1968–1976. **Awards:** Scholarship, SJC; Hutchinson Studentship, SJC 1936–1937.

DE MEL, Louis Hilton Vere (1930) Born 2 April 1912, The Whist Bungalow, Katahena Ward, Colombo, Ceylon; son of Frederic Joseph de Mel, Barrister-at-Law, and Cecilia Louisa Engeltina Pieris. **Tutor(s):** C W Guillebaud. **Johnian Relatives:** son of Frederic Joseph de Mel (1897). **Educ:** St Thomas' College, Colombo, Ceylon; Private Tuition, London.

DENHAM, The Revd Joseph Percival (1908) Born 14 May 1889, 14 Holland Grove, North Brixton, London; son of William Denham, Secretary, Homes for Working Boys, Kennington, and Susannah Hitching. BA 1911; MA 1920. **Tutor(s):** J R Tanner. **Educ:** Merchant Taylors' School, London. **Career:** Ordained Deacon 1912; Curate, Whitburn 1912–1914; Priest 1913; CF, 4th Class, RACD (Mentioned in Despatches), WWI; Aldershot 1923–1926; Catterick 1927–1929; Egypt 1929–1934; Plymouth 1934–1936; Vicar, Broadhembury, Honiton 1936–1940; Vicar, Ipplepen, Exeter 1940–1945; Hursley, Hampshire 1945–1949; Rector, Dunsfold, Surrey 1949. Died 16 August 1975. **Awards:** Hebrew Prize, University of Cambridge 1910; Reading Prize, University of Cambridge 1910.

DENHOLM, Group Captain George Lovell (1928) Born 20 December 1908, Tidings Hill, Bo'ness, West Lothian, Scotland; son of William Andrew Denholm, Ship Broker and Timber Merchant, and Minnie Scott Lovell. BA 1931. **Tutor(s):** J M Wordie. **Educ:** Cargilfield School, Cramond Bridge; Fettes College, Edinburgh. **Career:** RAF. **Honours:** DFC. Died 16 June 1997.

DENISON, Professor Norman (1943) Born 3 May 1925, 64 Wakefield Road, Ossett, Yorkshire; son of Ernest Denison, Merchant, and Elizabeth Richards; 1 son, 1 daughter. **Subject(s):** Modern and Medieval Languages; BA 1949; MA 1951; PhD 1955. **Tutor(s):** C W Guillebaud. **Educ:** Welholme School, Grimsby; Wintringham Secondary School. **Career:** Intelligence Corps, RE 1943–1947; Assistant-Lector in English, Helsinki University 1951–1952; Studied Finnish 1952–1954; Assistant Lecturer in German, University College of Wales, Aberystwyth 1956–1959; Lecturer in General Linguistics, Glasgow University 1959; Director of Language Studies, LSE 1964–1972; Chairman, Linguistics Department, Vorstand des Instituts fur Sprachwissenschaft 1972–1992, Professor of General and Applied Linguistics 1972–1993 (Emeritus 1993), Karl-Franzens University of Graz, Austria. **Appointments:** Overseas Visiting Scholar, SJC Lent 1976; Member, Academic Steering Committee, Centre for Research on Plurilingualism, University of Udine, Italy 1994–.

DENMAN, Eric Edward (1948) Born 19 August 1927, 18 Honister Avenue, Newcastle upon Tyne; son of Albert Edward Denman and Gertrude Ann Harrison. **Subject(s):** Natural Sciences; BA 1951; MA 1960; BChir 1954; MB 1954. **Tutor(s):** G C L Bertram. **Johnian Relatives:** brother of George Roy Denman (1942). **Educ:** Harrow County School. **Career:** Consultant Orthopaedic Surgeon, Swindon and Cirencester area 1965.

DENMAN, Sir (George) Roy (1942) Born 12 June 1924, 10 Lisburn Road, Liverpool; son of Albert Edward Denman and Gertrude Ann Harrison; m Moya Frances Gabrielle Lade, 2 April 1966, St Peter's, Ightham, Kent; 1 son, 1 daughter. **Subject(s):** Modern and Medieval Languages; BA 1947; MA 1953. **Tutor(s):** C W Guillebaud. **Johnian Relatives:** brother of Eric Edward Denman (1948). **Educ:** Harrow County School. **Career:** Royal Signals (final rank of Major) 1943–1946; Board of Trade 1948; Private Secretary to Minister, Board of Trade 1950–1952; Served in HM Embassy Bonn and UK delegation to Geneva 1957–1960 and 1965–1967; Under-Secretary, Board of Trade 1967–1970; Member, negotiating delegation, EEC 1970–1972; Deputy Secretary, DTI

1970–1974; British Overseas Trade Board 1972–1975; Department of Trade 1974–1975; Second Permanent Secretary, Cabinet Office 1975–1977; Director-General of External Affairs, EEC Commission 1977–1982; EC Ambassador to US 1982–1989. **Appointments:** Business Fellow, Kennedy School, Harvard 1989–1990. **Awards:** Minor Scholarship, SJC 1941. **Honours:** CMG 1968; CB 1972; KCB 1977.

DENNEY, The Revd Anthony Howe (1948) Born 30 January 1918, Newton Cottage, Sturminster Newton, Dorset; son of Owen Lindsey Denney, Automobile Engineer, and Grace Isabelle Dumbrell; 3 children. **Subject(s):** Theology; BA 1950. **Tutor(s):** C W Guillebaud. **Educ:** South Lodge Preparatory School, Lowestoft; King's School, Ely; KCL. **Career:** Ordained Deacon to St Andrew's, Chesterton 1949; Curate, St Andrew's, Chesterton, Cambridge 1949–1952; Ordained Priest 1950; Curate, St Mary Stoke, Ipswich 1952–1953; Curate, Trimley St Martin 1953–1956; Rector, Trimley St Martin 1956–1962; Research Officer, Children's Council, Church of England Board of Education 1962–1970; Deputy Director 1970, Director 1971, Religious Education, Diocese of Coventry; Curate-in-Charge, Lower Shuckburgh with Wolfhampcote, Flecknoe and Upper Shuckburgh, Diocese of Coventry 1970–1973; Curate-in-Charge, Marton (with Birdingbury 1971–1973), Diocese of Coventry 1973. **Appointments:** Associate, KCL 1948; Honorary Canon, Coventry Cathedral 1974. **Awards:** George Williams Prize, University of Cambridge 1949. **Publications:** (ed) *Sibton Abbey Estates: Select Documents, 1325–1509,* Suffolk Records Society, 1960; *Children in Need,* SCM Press, 1966; (ed) *Seeing in the Dark,* Church Information, 1969; *Working with Children* (Library of Pastoral Care), Society for Promoting Christian Knowledge, 1971; *Militaria: Collecting Print and Manuscript,* Photo Precision, 1973; *When Father is Away,* Priory Press, 1973; *Truancy and School Phobias,* Priory Press, 1974.

DENNING, Brigadier Gordon Masey (1924) Born 23 June 1906, 26 Ravenswood Road, Redland, Bristol, Gloucestershire; son of Harry Denning, Provision Merchant, and Sarah Madeline Gordon; m Joyce, 1933; 1 son (Michael), 1 daughter (Gillian). BA 1927; MA 1955; MRCS (St Mary's) 1934; LRCP (St Mary's) 1934. **Tutor(s):** B F Armitage. **Johnian Relatives:** father of Michael Gordon Denning (1955). **Educ:** Albert Villas School, Clifton; Clifton College; The Abbey, Portishead. **Career:** Deputy Director and Brigadier, Medical Services, RAMC, WWII; Senior Medical Officer, Sandhurst; Medical Liaison Officer, British Army Staff, Washington, USA; Staff Medical Officer, Allied Forces, Norway, and for SHAPE; Posts at the Tower of London and Millbank 1963–1972. Died 26 July 1986.

DENNIS, Stratford Hercules (1919) Naval Officer.

DENNY, George Andrew Willert (1923) Born 19 August 1904, Woodfoot, Belton Road, Foots Cray, Kent; son of George Willert Denny, Railway Agent, and Mary Ann Lowe; 1 son (George). **Subject(s):** Classics; BA 1926; MA 1930. **Tutor(s):** E E Sikes; M P Charlesworth. **Johnian Relatives:** father of George Denny (1956). **Educ:** Sidcup High School; Merton Court Preparatory School; Shrewsbury School; Penpellan House, Folkestone. **Career:** Master, Bradfield College 1926–1927; Master, King Edward VI School, Chelmsford 1927; Lecturer in Classics, Queen Mary College, London 1947. **Awards:** Exhibition, SJC; Browne Medal for Greek Epigram, University of Cambridge 1925. Died 22 June 1971.

DE NOBRIGA, Alexander Percy (1946) Born 24 August 1924, Port of Spain, Trinidad, British West Indies; son of George de Nobriga, Managing Director, and Hazel May Moody; m Anne Birbeck, October 1952. BA 1948; MA 1953. **Tutor(s):** G C L Bertram. **Educ:** Yardley Court Preparatory School, Tonbridge; Tonbridge School. **Career:** Business Appointment, West Indies 1952. **Appointments:** Secretary, Hereford Herd Book Society. Died 1998.

DENSHAM, Dr Arnold Thomas (1900) Born 7 February 1882, Strode House, Tyndall's Park Road, Westbury, Bristol; son of Henry Densham, Tanner, and Jane Sharland Gibbings. **Subject(s):** Natural Sciences; BA

1903; MA 1907; BChir 1907; LRCP 1907; MRCS 1907; LDSRCS 1915. **Tutor(s):** C E Graves. **Educ:** Clifton College. **Career:** Lieutenant, Indian Medical Service 1907–1909; Chief Assistant, Dental Department, St Bartholomew's Hospital; Clinical Assistant and Assistant House Surgeon, Guy's Hospital; Lieutenant, RAMC 1917–1919. Died 13 October 1948.

DENSON, John Boyd (1948) Born 13 August 1926, 50 Carley Road, Southwick, Sunderland; son of George Denson, Conservative Agent for Cambridge, and Alice Boyd; m Joyce Symondson, 1957. **Subject(s):** English/Oriental Languages; BA 1949; MA 1955. **Tutor(s):** F Thistlethwaite. **Educ:** Paston House, Cambridge; Cambridge and County High School; St George's College, Weybridge; Perse School, Cambridge. **Career:** Diplomatic Service: Hong Kong, Peking, Tokyo, Helsinki, Washington 1951–1969; Head, Far Eastern Department, Foreign Office and Acting Chargé d'Affaires 1969–1971; Diplomatic Service, Laos 1971–1972; Consul General, Athens 1973–1977; HM Ambassador, Katmandu, Nepal 1977–1983. **Honours:** CMG; OBE. Died 24 April 1992.

DENT, John Chisholm (1942) Born 3 February 1924, Redcote, Plough Lane, Coulsdon; son of Alfred Carey Dent, Lubricating Oil Manufacturer, and Janie de Carle Chisholm; m Hazel. **Subject(s):** Modern and Medieval Langauges; BA 1948; MA 1951; Certificate in Education (Huddersfield) 1952. **Tutor(s):** C W Guillebaud. **Educ:** Downside Lodge, Purley; Downside, Purley; Whitgift Grammar School, Croydon; Epsom College, Epsom, Surrey; Huddersfield Teacher Training College. **Career:** Queen's Royal Regiment, Intelligence Corp 1943–1947; Industrial experience (J Clark) 1948–1951; Lecturer, Dockyard Technical College, Chatham 1952–1959; Further Education (Adult and Community Education), Cumberland Community College 1959–1974; Principal, Cumbria Community College 1974–1982. Died 24 June 1998.

DENTON, Sir Eric James (1941) Born 30 September 1923, 53 Denby Street, Bentley, Doncaster, Yorkshire; son of George Denton, Fitter at Colliery, and Mary Anne Ogden; m Nancy Emily Wright, 1946; 2 sons, 1 daughter. **Subject(s):** Natural Sciences; BA 1944; MA 1964; ScD 1964; BSc (London); PhD (London); Hon DSc (Exeter) 1976; Hon DSc (Göteborg) 1978; FRS 1964. **Tutor(s):** C W Guillebaud. **Educ:** Cooke Street School, Bentley; Doncaster Grammar School; UCL. **Career:** Lecturer in Physiology 1948–1956, Lecturer in Biophysics 1953, University of Aberdeen; Physiologist 1956–1974, Director 1974–1987, Marine Biological Association Laboratory, Plymouth; Royal Society Research Professor, University of Bristol 1964–1974 (Honorary Professor 1975); Fellow, University College, London 1965. **Appointments:** Member, Royal Commission on Environmental Pollution 1973–1976; Honorary Secretary, Physiological Society 1963–1969. **Awards:** Royal Medal, Royal Society 1987; Frink Medal, Zoological Society of London 1987; International Prize for Biology, Japan Society for the Promotion of Science 1989. **Honours:** CBE 1974; Kt 1987. **Publications:** 'Buoyancy mechanisms of sea creatures', *Endeavour*, January 1963; scientific papers in *Journal of Marine Biological Association*, etc.

DENYER, Charles Leonard (1915) Born 15 May 1887, Portfield, Oving, Sussex; son of Henry Denyer, Draper's Assistant, and Anne Ryan; m Ida Nellie. **Subject(s):** History; BA 1918; MA 1923. **Tutor(s):** L H K Bushe-Fox. **Educ:** Lancastrian Boys' School, Chichester; Portsmouth Grammar School; St Paul's College, Cheltenham. **Career:** Assistant Master, Rossall School 1918–1926; Headmaster, Robert May's Grammar School, Odiham 1926–1929; Headmaster, Andover Grammar School, Hampshire 1929.

DE POTIER, Adrian (1942) Born 5 July 1921, Oeleghem, Antwerp, Belgium; son of Gwijde Constantinus de Potier, of independent means, and Camélia Diamaldis; m Barbara Janet Gwendolen Welch, 27 July 1950. **Tutor(s):** C W Guillebaud. **Educ:** Raynes Park County School; Bournemouth Municipal College.

DE QUINCEY, William Bertram (1932) Born 23 September 1913, Avonhurst, Chislehurst, Kent; son of Bertram De Quincy Quincey,

Solicitor, and Martha Kate Woodall. BA 1936; MA 1939; CEng; MIGasE. **Tutor(s):** J S Boys Smith. **Educ:** Sunnydown, Guildford; St Wilfred's, Seaford; Shrewsbury School. **Career:** Gas and Water Engineer. **Appointments:** Member, American Institute of Gas Engineers. **Honours:** MBE 1989. Died 20 November 1991.

DE ROMERO Y DORREGO, Manuel (1924) Born 4 May 1905, San Sebastian, Spain; son of Don Jose Romero y Sein, Senator and Barrister, and Ana Maria Dorrego vida Guren. Died 13 June 1924.

DE SILVA, Dr Harry Reginald (1926) Born 8 June 1898, Pensacola, Florida, USA; son of Harry Grant De Silva, Life Insurance Agent, and Mary Stearns Comings. PhD 1928; Masters Degree (Harvard). **Tutor(s):** C W Guillebaud. **Educ:** Pensacola High School; University of Florida; Harvard University. **Career:** Lecturer in Psychology, McGill University, Montreal, Canada 1922–1924.

DE SILVA, Hettihewagé Benedict (1937) Born 20 April 1915, Aranwab, Ceylon; son of Mahenderam Hettihewagé Alexander de Silva, Inspector of Post Offices, and Punchinona Gunawardena. **Tutor(s):** J M Wordie. **Educ:** St Thomas' College, Ceylon; St Joseph College, Colombo; University College, Columbo.

DE SILVA, The Rt Hon Lucien Macull Dominic (1911) Born 25 April 1893, Moratuwella, Ceylon; son of Lindamullagé Gabriel de Silva, Merchant, and Kanapathilijanaralalage Maria Theodora de Silva; m Anne C Edwards, 1930. **Subject(s):** Mathematics; BA 1914; MA 1939. **Tutor(s):** L H K Bushe-Fox. **Educ:** Royal College, Colombo, Ceylon; Trinity College, Kandy. **Career:** President, Carius Commissions, Ceylon, WWII; Called to the Bar, Gray's Inn 1916; KC Ceylon Bar 1931; Solicitor General, Ceylon 1931–1934; Acting Attorney General, Ceylon 1932–1934; Puisne Justice, Supreme Court, Ceylon 1933–1934; KC 1938. **Appointments:** Delegate of Ceylon, Commonwealth Conference on Citizenship 1947; Delegate of Ceylon, Commonwealth Relations Conference 1949; Privy Councillor 1953; Bencher, Gray's Inn 1953; Honorary Fellow, SJC 1956. Died 28 November 1962.

DE SILVA, Neil Marcus (1929) Born 31 July 1911, The Leete, Rosmead Place, Colpetty, Colombo, Ceylon; son of Lindamulage Benedict Felix de Silva, Barrister-at-Law, and Lindamulage Bridget Mildred Millicent de Silva. **Subject(s):** Law; BA 1932. **Tutor(s):** C W Guillebaud. **Educ:** Royal College, Colombo.

DE SOUZA, Aniceto Emmanuel (1901) Born 10 August 1883, Rangoon, Burma; son of Eduardo Maçial de Souza, Physician and Surgeon, and Theda Thereza Lefevre. **Tutor(s):** D MacAlister. **Johnian Relatives:** brother of Eduardo Valentine de Souza (1900). **Educ:** Rangoon College; St Paul's School, London.

DE SOUZA, Eduardo Valentine (1900) Born 14 February 1882, Rangoon, Burma; son of Eduardo Maçial de Souza, Physician and Surgeon, and Theda Thereza Lefevre. BA (Downing) 1905. **Tutor(s):** D MacAlister. **Johnian Relatives:** brother of Aniceto Emmanuel de Souza (1901). **Educ:** St Paul's School, London; Downing College, Cambridge.

DE SOUZA SANTOS, Marcello Damy (1938) Born 14 June 1914, Campinas, Estado de São Paulo, Brazil; son of Haraldo Egydio de Souza Santos and Maria de Souza Damy. **Educ:** Gymnasio do Estado em Campinas; Gymnasio do Estado em São Paulo; University of São Paulo. **Awards:** British Council Scholarship.

DE STYRCEA, Jonel (1929) Born 16 May 1909, Czernowitz, Bucovina, Romania; son of Le Baron Jean V de Styrcea, Master of Ceremonies, Royal Court of Roumanie, and Bertha (Comtesse) de Vismes et de Ponthieu. **Subject(s):** Modern and Medieval Languages; BA 1932. **Tutor(s):** C W Guillebaud. **Educ:** Le Rosey (Institut Carnal), Canton de Vaud, Switzerland; Geneva College, Switzerland. **Career:** Official to King of Romania. Died 1988.

DE TRAFFORD, Cuthbert Henry (1919) Born 11 June 1897, Littlebourne, Canterbury, Kent; son of Humphrey Edward de Trafford, Master Brewer, and Magdalene Ann Mary Arnold. **Tutor(s):** E A Benians. **Johnian Relatives:** brother-in-law of Raymond Herbert D'Elboux (1919). **Educ:** Downside School, Bath. **Career:** Rifleman, 16th Battalion, The London Regiment 1915–1918 (home service 1915–1916, France 1916–1917, hospitalised in England with trench feet 1918). Died 9 November 1956.

DE VOS, Pieter Jacobus Gerhard (1946) Born 15 March 1916, Zastron, Orange Free State, South Africa; son of Phillippus Albertus Myburgh de Vos, Minister, Dutch Reformed Church, and Marguerite Jeanette de Villiers. BSc (Stellenbosch) 1936; MSc (Stellenbosch) 1937; DSc (Stellenbosch) 1942. **Tutor(s):** J M Wordie. **Educ:** Zastron Middlebare Skool; Stellenbosch High School; Stellenbosch University. **Career:** Lecturer in Physics 1940–1946.

DEW, Canon William Harold (1921) Born 3 June 1902, 51 Beaconsfield Terrace, Northampton; son of William Dew, Furnishing Buyer, Draper's Assistant, and Ada Jane Pettett. **Subject(s):** Natural Sciences; BA 1924; MA 1928; BSc (London). **Tutor(s):** B F Armitage. **Educ:** Northampton School; Westcott House, Cambridge. **Career:** Lecturer, Northampton College of Technology; Ordained Deacon 1926; Curate, St Mary's, Nottingham 1926–1929; Ordained Priest 1927; Curate, Holy Trinity, Formby 1929–1930; Curate, Christ Church, Hoxton, and Warden, Maurice Hostel 1930–1934; Assistant Chaplain, Bede College, Durham, and Chaplain, St Hilda's College 1934–1936; Vicar, St Hilda's, Millfield 1936–1941; Vicar, Barrow on Soar, Leicestershire 1941–1964; Rural Dean, Akely East 1956; Honorary Canon, Leicester Cathedral 1960. **Awards:** Scholarship, SJC. Died 5 September 1990.

DEWAR, Thomas Wright (1938) Born 17 September 1919, Alderley, Hillpark, Glasgow; son of James Chalmers Dewar, Distiller, and Jean Campbell Burnet; m Ann Primrose Aitken, 1956. **Subject(s):** History; BA 1947; MA 1949. **Tutor(s):** J S Boys Smith; F Thistlethwaite. **Educ:** Craigflower, Torryburn, Scotland; Loretto School, Musselburgh, Scotland. **Career:** Subaltern, Royal Scots Fusiliers 1940–1942; POW 1942–1945; Captain, Royal Scots Fusiliers 1945–1946; Schoolmaster, Woodbridge School 1948–1951; Schoolmaster, Larchfield School, Helensburgh 1951–1962; Headmaster, The Abbey School, Woodbridge, Suffolk 1962–1986. **Publications:** *Norfolk Front Line*, Woodthorpe Publishing, 1998.

DE WATTEVILLE, Kenneth William (1924) Born 4 April 1899, Kingussie, Invernessshire, Scotland; son of Walter Frederick de Watteville, Medical Practitioner, and Mary Flora MacKenzie; m Enid Purchas, 9 December 1924, All Saint's, Cambridge. **Tutor(s):** E E Sikes. **Educ:** Fettes College, Edinburgh.

DEWES, John Gordon (1945) Born 11 October 1926, Heathfield, Cross Lane, Latchford Without, Cheshire; son of Herbert John Salisbury Dewes, Commercial Traveller, and Kathleen Ida Matthews; m Ann Shirley Henderson, 10 April 1954; 2 sons (Timothy John b 6 January 1956 and Anthony Roy b 2 June 1957), 3 daughters (Deborah Mary b 16 July 1959, Carolyn Sarah b 15 October 1964 and Philippa Margaret b 30 August 1966). **Subject(s):** Law/Geography; BA 1950; MA 1952; DipTheol 1990. **Tutor(s):** J M Wordie. **Johnian Relatives:** descendant of Symonds d'Ewes (1618); father of Timothy John Dewes (1975) and of Anthony Roy Dewes (1976). **Educ:** Stockton Lodge School, Stockton Heath, Warrington; Hydneye House, Hastings; Aldenham School, Elstree. **Career:** England Test Cricketer 1948–1951; Schoolmaster, Tonbridge School 1951–1953; Schoolmaster and House Tutor, Rugby School 1953–1958; Headmaster, Barker College, Hornsby, NSW, Australia 1958–1963; Schoolmaster and Careers Master, Dulwich College 1963–1986; Lecturer, Open University 1971–1996. **Awards:** Larmor Award, SJC 1950.

DE WET, Professor Jacobus Stephanus (1937) Born 1 July 1913, Rousville, Buitenkant Straat, Orange Free State; son of Jacobus Rees de

Wet, Attorney at Law, and Ellen Johanna de Roux; m Madge; 2 sons, 1 stepson. BA 1937 (by incorporation); BSc (Cape Town) 1935; BA (Oxford) 1937; PhD (Princeton) 1940. **Tutor(s):** J M Wordie. **Educ:** Smithfield Secondary School; University of Cape Town; Balliol College, Oxford. **Career:** Lecturer in Applied Mathematics, University of Cape Town 1940–1942; Professor of Mathematics, University of Pretoria 1942–1946; ICI and College Research Fellow 1946–1971, Fellow 1947–1971 (Emeritus 1971), Tutor in Mathematics 1947–1971, Vice Master 1971, Balliol College, Oxford; Dean, Faculty of Science, University of Cape Town 1971–1982. **Appointments:** Technical Adviser to the Royal South African Navy 1940–1946; Council Member 1975, Assistant Principal 1975, University of Cape Town; Adviser to Council for Scientific and Industrial Research, South Africa 1982–1985; Curator, Bodleian Library, Pro-Proctor 1958–1960, University of Oxford. **Awards:** Rhodes Scholarship 1935–1937. Died 7 January 1995.

DEWEY, Leonard (1943) Born 16 May 1925, 8 Oxford Street, Saltburn by the Sea, Yorkshire; son of William Parkin Dewey, Accountant, and Edith Liddell; 2 children. **Subject(s):** Mechanical Sciences; BA 1946. **Tutor(s):** S J Bailey. **Johnian Relatives:** father of Adrian Christopher Dewey (1979). **Educ:** Linthorpe Elementary School, Middlesbrough; Acklam Hall Secondary School, Middlesbrough; Worksop College. **Career:** Project Manager, Petrochemicals Division, ICI Ltd.

DEWHURST, Arthur (1948) Born 9 October 1926, 453 Whalley New Road, Blackburn, Lancashire; son of William Dewhurst, Mill Manager, and Ethel Sharples; m Joan Riley, 1 August 1953, St Gabriel's Church, Blackburn, 1 August 1953; 1 son (Mark b 4 May 1962, d 14 December 1974), 1 daughter (Alison b 23 January 1965). **Subject(s):** History; BA 1950; MA 1955. **Tutor(s):** F Thistlethwaite. **Educ:** St Gabriel's Junior School, Blackburn; Clitheroe Royal Grammar School. **Career:** Organist and Choirmaster, St John's Church, Blackburn 1952–1961; St Peter's Secondary School, Blackburn 1952–1961; Headmaster, Sandford School, Wareham 1961–1966; Organist and Choirmaster, Lady St Mary, Wareham 1963–1966; Headmaster, Whittle-le-Woods School, Preston 1966–1968; Headmaster, Milford-on-Sea School 1968–1971; Headmaster, Kendal Central Primary School 1971–1974; Headmaster, Rottingdean Junior and Middle School 1974–1976; Headmaster, Salesbury, Blackburn 1976–1984.

DEWICK, The Revd Edward Chisholm (1903) Born 13 November 1884, 2 Southwick Place, Paddington, Middlesex; son of Edward Samuel Dewick, Clerk in Holy Orders, and Emily Chisholm; m Hilda Clara Schaeffer, 20 December 1920, Bengal. BA 1906; MA 1910; BD 1938; DD 1950. **Tutor(s):** C E Graves; J R Tanner. **Johnian Relatives:** son of Edward Samuel Dewick (1862). **Educ:** Merchant Taylors' School. **Career:** Ordained Deacon 1908; Curate, St Peter, Norbiton 1908–1911; Priest 1909; Tutor and Dean 1911–1919, Vice-Principal 1915–1916, Principal 1917, St Aidan's College, Birkenhead; Lecturer in Ecclesiastical History, Liverpool University 1911–1919; Examining Chaplain to Bishop of Peterborough 1916–1919; Acting Principal, St Paul's Missionary College 1919–1924; Fellow, Calcutta University 1920–1923; Principal, St Andrew's College and Chaplain, Christ Church, Gorakhpur 1934–1938; Lecturer, Hislop College and Warden, YMCA Hostel, Nagpur 1938–1945; Lecturer, St Andrew's House, Pampisford 1946. **Appointments:** Secretary, Student Christian Association of India 1923–1925; Literature Secretary, YMCA, India, Burma and Ceylon 1925–1934; Hulsean Lecturer 1946–1948. **Awards:** First Jeremie Septuagint Prize 1907; Hulsean Prize, University of Cambridge 1908. **Publications:** *Primitive Christian Eschatology*, 1912; *Christ's Message in Times of Crisis*, 1917; *The Indwelling God*, 1938. Died 14 June 1958.

DE WINTON, Charles Francis Seton (1929) Born 7 May 1910, Lynford, Richmond Road, New Barnet, Hertfordshire; son of Charles Lucien Wragg de Winton, Agent to a Furnishing Manufacturer, and Florence Alice Bruer. **Subject(s):** Modern and Medieval Languages/English; BA 1932; MA 1936. **Tutor(s):** C W Guillebaud. **Educ:** Norman Court, New Barnet; Branksome, Godalming; Kilcott, Godalming; Charterhouse, Godalming. **Awards:** Team Exhibition 1928.

DEXTER, John Alfred (1949) Born 2 May 1929, 64 Scotgate, Stamford; son of Alfred Dexter, Garage Proprietor, and Dorothy May Towns; m Hazel Mary Kirkup, 20 August 1953, St Paul's Church, Cambridge; 1 son (Mark Nicholas). **Subject(s):** Classics; BA 1952; MA 1956. **Tutor(s):** R L Howland. **Educ:** St John's School, Stamford; Bluecoat School, Stamford; Stamford School. **Career:** Head of Classics, King's School, Peterborough 1962–1994. **Awards:** Exhibition, SJC.

DE YARBURGH-BATESON, The Rt Hon Lord Richard Arthur (Lord DERAMORE) (1929) Born 9 April 1911, 103 Ebury Street, Belgrave District, London; son of George Nicholas de Yarburgh-Bateson, 4th Baron Deramore, and Muriel Katharine Duncombe; m Janet Mary Ware, 28 August 1948; 1 daughter (Ann Katherine Peel b 1950). **Subject(s):** Architecture; BA 1932; MA 1936; RIBA 1936; AA Diploma 1936; ARIBA 1937. **Tutor(s):** E A Benians. **Johnian Relatives:** brother of Stephen Nicholas de Yarburgh-Bateson (Lord Deramore) (1922). **Educ:** Evelyn's, Hillingdon; Harrow School; Craighurst, Southwold; Architectual Association School. **Career:** Salaried Partner, Arthur W M Kenyon 1938–1939; RAFVR, 14 Squadron 1942; Pilot Officer 1943; Navigation Instructor, 13 OTU 1944; 14 Squadron 1944–1945; Christopher Nicholson FRIBA 1946–1947; Associate of Eli Mayorcas FRIBA and P H Laurence ARIBA 1946–1948; Assistant County Architect, Hertfordshire County Council 1948–1952; Partner, HG Cherry FRIBA 1952–1965; Cherry & Deramore 1965–1970; Practised in Buckinghamshire and North Yorkshire 1970–1982. **Appointments:** Architectural Association 1932–1939; Auxiliary Fire Service, London 1939; Council Member, Architectural Association 1951–1954; Governor 1964–1988, Manager 1965–1970, Heslington Primary School; Governor, Tudor Hall School, Banbury 1966–1975; Council Member, Queen Mary's School, Helmsley 1977–1985; Fellow, Woodard Schools (Northern Division) 1978–1984; President, Vale of Pickering Art Club 1979–97; Management Committee, Pury Cust Nursing Home, York 1976–1984 (Chairman 1983–1984); Prayer Book Society. **Awards:** winner, *Telegraph Magazine* Mystery Story Competition 1975. **Publications:** (jointly) *Winged Promises: A History of 14 Squadron, RAF, 1915–1945*, 1996; *Still Waters*, 1997; articles in architectural and motoring journals; stories in *London Mystery Magazine*.

DE YARBURGH-BATESON, Lord Stephen Nicholas (Lord DERAMORE) (1922) Born 18 May 1903, 5 South Eaton Place, Eaton Square, London; son of George Nicholas de Yarburgh-Bateson, 4th Baron Deramore, and Muriel Katherine Duncombe; m Nina Marion Macpherson-Grant, 1929; 1 daughter (Jane). **Tutor(s):** B F Armitage. **Johnian Relatives:** brother of Richard Arthur de Yarburgh-Bateson (Deramore) (1929). **Educ:** Wixenford School; Harrow School. **Career:** Partner, Cazenove and Ackroyd, London; Squadron Leader, RAFVR and Senior Controller, 4 Group, Bomber Command (Mentioned in Despatches), WWII. **Appointments:** Member, Derwent Rural Council; Parish Councillor; Life Member, Red Cross Society. Died 23 December 1964.

DHAVLE, Shankar Balaji (1901) Born 3 October 1882, Bergal, Belgaum District, Bombay, India; son of Balaji Shripad Dhavle, Government Servant; m Kashibal. **Subject(s):** Mathematics; BA 1904. **Tutor(s):** J R Tanner; C E Graves. **Educ:** Rajaran College, Kolhapur; Elphinstone College, Bombay. **Career:** Indian Civil Service 1906–1942; Adviser to His Highness the Rajasheb of Sangli, Bombay 1942.

DHENIN, Air Marshal Sir Geoffrey Howard (1936) Born 2 April 1918, 24 Treharne Road, Caerau Maesteg, Bridgend, Glamorganshire; son of Lewis Richard Dhenin, Master Baker, Corporal, Glamorgan Yeomanry, and Lucy Ellen Dagg, Teacher; m (1) Claude Andrée Evelyn Rabut, Paris, 1946 (d 1996), (2) Syvia Howard, Maidenhead, May 2002; 2 sons (1 deceased), 2 daughters. **Subject(s):** Natural Sciences; BA 1939; MA 1957; MB 1942; BChir 1942; MD 1957; DPH (London); FFCM 1975; FRAeS 1971; MRCS; LRCP. **Tutor(s):** R L Howland. **Educ:** Plasnewydd Elementary School, Maesteg, Wales; Hereford Cathedral School; Guy's Hospital. **Career:** RAF, Bomber Command, 2nd TAF, Mentioned in Despatches 1943–1945; Pilot Training 1945–1946; Various Medical

Officer Pilot appointments 1946–1958; Staff College, Bracknell 1958–1959; Command, Princess Mary's RAF Hospital, Akrotiri, Cyprus 1960–1963; Command, RAF Hospital, Ely 1963–1966; PMO Air Support Command 1966–1968; Director of Health and Research, RAF 1968–1970; Deputy DGMS, RAF 1970–1971; PMO Strike Command 1971–1973; DGMS, RAF 1974–1978. **Appointments:** Fellow, International Academy of Aerospace Medicine 1972; QHP 1970–1978; Adviser to Saudi Arabian National Guard 1978–1979. **Awards:** Open Scholarship in Classics, SJC 1936–1937; CStJ 1974. **Honours:** GM 1943; AFC 1953; Bar 1957; KBE 1975. **Publications:** (ed) *Textbook of Aviation Medicine*, 1978.

DIAMOND, Professor Jack (1935) Born 22 June 1912, 1 Bangalore Villas, Borstal, Rochester; son of Alfred John Diamond, Mechanic, and Jessie Mary Kitchingham. DSc (Heriot Watt); MSc 1938; FIMechE. **Tutor(s):** J S Boys Smith. **Educ:** Dunikier School, Kircaldy; King's Road School, Kircaldy; Junior Technical School, Chatham; HM Dockyard School, Chatham; Chatham Technical Institute; Medway Technical College, Gillingham; City and Guilds Engineering College, London. **Career:** Demonstrator in Engineering, University of Cambridge 1937–1945; Engineer Officer, RN 1939–1944; AERE, Harwell 1946–1952; Professor of Mechanical Engineering, University of Manchester 1952–1960; Beyer Professor of Mechanical Engineering, University of Manchester 1960–1977. Died 27 June 1990.

DIAMOND, John Gilbert (1932) Born 10 October 1914, 49 Lindsay Road, Dublin; son of Henry Diamond, Civil Servant, Ministry of Home Affairs, Belfast, and Nellie Irvine; BA 1936; MA 1940. **Tutor(s):** J M Wordie. **Educ:** Dr Hilda's Preparatory School, Belfast; Campbell College, Belfast.

DIANDERAS, Roberto (1941) Born 9 May 1911, Chincha Alta, Peru, South America; son of Domingo Dianderas, Industrial Manager, and Carolina Chumbiauca. **Tutor(s):** C W Guillebaud. **Educ:** Colegio Nacional Pardo, Chincha Alta, Peru; Escuda Militar de Chonillos. **Awards:** British Council Scholarship.

DIAS, Ponnahannedigey Christopher Edward Arnold (1925) Born 27 March 1906, Pattia South, Panadura Town, Kalulara District, Ceylon; son of Ponnahannedigey Charles Edward Arnold Dias, Merchant and Proprietary Planter, and Vidanalagey Beatrice Frances Catherine De Mel. **Tutor(s):** E A Benians. **Educ:** The Royal College, Colombo.

DICHMONT, Ian Alexander (1938) Born 4 April 1920, Jambo Grove Road, Green Point, Cape of Good Hope; son of Archibald Alexander William Dichmont, Solicitor and Notary Public, and Daisy Esther Harris. **Subject(s):** Law; BA 1946; MA 1949. **Tutor(s):** C W Guillebaud. **Educ:** Green and Sea Point High School, South Africa; Diocesan College, Rondebosch, South Africa. **Career:** War service, POW Italy, WWII.

DICK, Gordon Ian Brand (1924) Born 7 March 1906, Bourneville, Highfield, Headington, Oxon; son of John Reid Dick, Electrical Engineer, and Annetta Brand; m Rosemary Elizabeth Wilson, 15 September 1934, St Chad's Church, Pattingham; 3 sons (Robert Ian b 17 July 1939, John Brand b 23 April 1946, d 11 December 1987 and Charles Richard b 13 May 1950). **Subject(s):** Mechanical Sciences; BA 1927; MA 1947. **Tutor(s):** B F Armitage. **Johnian Relatives:** brother-in-law of Richard William Russell Wilson (1921); father of Robert Ian Dick (1958), John Brand Dick (1964) and of Charles Richard Dick (1969). **Educ:** Marlborough House, Reading; Leighton Park School, Reading. **Career:** Managing Director, later Chairman, W Lucy & Co Ltd, Manufacturing Electrical Engineers and Ironfounders, Oxford. Died 3 September 1990.

DICKENS, John Raymond (1931) Born 16 September 1914, 19 Birchfield Road, Northampton; son of John Dickens, Director of John Dickens and Company, Printers, and Constance Maud Stiff; m 1941; 1 son

(Timothy), 2 daughters (Jane and Sue). **Subject(s):** Natural Sciences; BA 1936. **Tutor(s):** J M Wordie. **Educ:** Waynflete House School, Northampton; Town and County School; Oakham School. **Career:** Director, John Dickens and Company, Printers. **Appointments:** Secretary, Northampton Association of Master Printers; Council Member, Northamptonshire Chamber of Commerce; Member, Northampton Rotary Club.

DICKINSON, Alan (1944) Born 14 December 1925, 76 Ravenswood Road, Newcastle upon Tyne; son of John Dickinson, Accountant, and Eveline Annie Purves; m Joyce Heir, 15 July 1949, Jesmond Parish Church, Newcastle upon Tyne; 1 son (Christopher b 20 July 1956), 2 daughters (Caroline b 10 February 1954 and Jacqueline b 20 November 1958). **Subject(s):** History; BA 1948; MA 1950. **Tutor(s):** J M Wordie. **Johnian Relatives:** father of Christopher John Dickinson (1974). **Educ:** Royal Grammar School, Newcastle upon Tyne. **Career:** RN Cadet; RNVR Sub-Lieutenant, Colonial Service, Ministry of Finance, Nyasaland; Proprietor, Kirkstone Foot Hotel, Ambleside; Assistant Registrar, University of East Anglia. **Awards:** Exhibition, SJC 1944. **Honours:** MBE 1960. Died 5 February 1999.

DICKINSON, Allan William (1944) Born 29 January 1926, Cark Bridge, Cark-in-Cartmel, Lancashire; son of William Dickinson, Relieving Officer and Registrar of Births and Deaths, and Mabel Hutton; m Margaret G Bell, 1951; 1 son (Jonathan Martin b 1954). **Subject(s):** Mechanical Sciences; BA 1947; MA 1951; CEng; FIMechE 1959. **Tutor(s):** S J Bailey. **Educ:** Flookburgh and Holker Church of England Schools; Lightburn Council School, Ulverston; Ulverston Grammar School. **Career:** Army Service 1947; Commissioned REME 1948; 2nd OC, 3 Medium Workshop, BAOR, Hanover 1948; OC, 31 REME Workshop, 7th Armoured Division 1949; Technician, Admiralty Development Establishment, Barrow-in-Furness 1949; Development Engineer Fire Hose, Bentham Factory 1953–1958, Chief Engineer, New Hose and Belting Factory, Newcastle upon Tyne 1958–1963, George Angus Co Ltd; Chief Engineer and Project Manager, New Tyre and Footwear Factory, Burton-on-Trent 1963–1967, General Manager, Carlisle 1967–1983, Pirelli Ltd; Director, Local Enterprise Agency 1983. **Appointments:** Member, Northern Economic Planning Council; Chairman, Communications Panel 1971–1979; DTI Enterprise Counsellor 1988–1995.

DICKINSON, James Stanley (1948) Born 12 February 1926, 11 West Lawn, Sunderland, County Durham; son of Stanley Dickinson, Marine Engine Builder, and Bertha Cramlington Ranken; m Fay Nelson, 5 April 1956, Humshaugh, Northumberland; 1 son (John Robert b 1958), 1 daughter (Marjorie Louise b 1960). BA 1950; MA 1955. **Tutor(s):** R L Howland. **Educ:** Aysgarth School; Sedbergh School; University of Edinburgh. **Career:** Commissioned, RA, Indian Army; Managing Director, S Tyzack & Co Ltd, Sunderland 1955–1968; Farmer 1969–. **Appointments:** Member, winning Inter Service Team (TA) 1951; Director, Charles W Taylor & Sons Ltd 1966–1998.

DICKINSON, Michael George Heneage (1949) Born 21 February 1929, 15 Camden Crescent, Bath; son of George Heneage Dickinson, Goldsmith, and Ethel Marjorie Millard. **Subject(s):** Mechanical Sciences; BA 1952; MA 1956. **Tutor(s):** R L Howland. **Educ:** St Christopher's School, Bath; Marlborough College. Died 1 January 2003.

DICKINSON, Patrick John (1938) Born 28 August 1919, Upper Barian, Murree Hills, Punjab, India; son of John Dickinson, Major, Indian Army, and Ethel Mary Elise Sharpe. **Tutor(s):** J S Boys Smith. **Educ:** King's College School, Wimbledon. Died 28 May 1984.

DICK-READ, Dr Grantly (1908) See READ.

DICKS, Dr Henry Victor (1920) Born 27 April 1900, Pernau, Estonia, Russia; son of Julius Dicks, Shipbroker and Merchant, Vice-Consul, Pernau, and Gabriele Wilhelmina Magda Plath; m (Pretoria) Maud

Jeffrey, 19 November 1927, St Andrew's Holborn; 2 sons, 2 daughters. **Subject(s):** Natural Sciences; BA 1923; MA 1927; MB 1927; MD 1930; MRCS (St Bartholomew's) 1926; LRCP (St Bartholomew's) 1926; FRCP (St Bartholomew's) 1947; FRCPsych 1971. **Tutor(s):** B F Armitage. **Educ:** Preparatory School, Pernau, Estonia; Gymnasium, Riga Latvia; St Katherine's School, Classical Division, Petrograd, Russia. **Career:** Artists Rifles, 2nd Battalion, BEF, then Interpreter, Military Intelligence 1918–1920; House Physician, Medical Professorial Unit 1926–1927, Junior Demonstrator in Pathology and Baly Research Scholarship 1928–1930, St Bartholomew's; House Physician, Bethlem Royal Hospital 1927–1928; Clinical Assistant 1927–1928, Physician 1928–1946, Assistant Medical Director 1934–1946, The Tavistock Clinic; Psychiatric Specialist, Stanborough, Hertfordshire 1939–1941; Command Psychiatrist, London District, rank of Major, RAMC 1941–1946; Adviser and Researcher on German Morale, Military Intelligence 1942–1944; Adviser on Morale Intelligence, Psychological Warfare Division, SHAEF 1944–1945; Adviser on German Personnel, Intelligence Branch, Control Commission for Germany 1945–1946; First Nuffield Professor of Psychiatry, University of Leeds 1946; Consultant Psychiatrist, General Infirmary, Leeds and West Riding Mental Hospitals' Board 1946–1948; Consultant Psychiatrist, Adult Department 1948–1965, Educational Secretary and Head, Marital Unit 1948–1965, The Tavistock Clinic; Senior Research Officer (Professorial level), Centre for Research in Collective Psychopathology, Columbus Centre, University of Sussex 1966–1970. **Appointments:** Council, Royal Medico-Psychological Association 1947–1950; Council, National Association of Mental Health 1948–1952; Honorary Secretary Medical Section, BPsS; various BMA Posts; Foundation Fellow, Royal College of Psychiatrists. **Awards:** Scholarship, SJC 1923; Brackenbury Scholarship in Medicine 1925; Kirkes Prize and Gold Medal, St Bartholomew's 1925. **Publications:** numerous chapters and articles in various publications including *Lancet*, *Modern Trends in Psychological Medicine*, and *British Journal of Medical Psychology*. Died 22 July 1977.

DICKSON, Edward Chambre (1937) Born 29 July 1918, Woodville, Lytham; son of Alfred Eric Dickson, Chartered Land Agent and Surveyor, and Kathleen Yates; m Joyce Mary Houghton, 21 April 1951; 1 son (Peter), 1 daughter (Daphne). **Subject(s):** Economics. **Tutor(s):** C W Guillebaud. **Educ:** Bigshott School, Wokingham; Marlborough College. **Career:** Captain, 88th Field Regiment, RA 1939–1945.

DIGGLE, James (1934) Born 20 August 1915, Oakhurst, Rochdale Road East, Heywood; son of James Stanley Diggle, Civil Engineer, and Dorothy Mary Mellalieu; m Margaret Hood, 1938, 2 sons (Richard and Peter), 2 daughters (Julia and Lorna). **Subject(s):** Law; BA 1937; MA 1943. **Tutor(s):** C W Guillebaud. **Johnian Relatives:** brother of William Mellalieu Diggle (1929). **Educ:** Wadham House, Hale; Terra Nova, Birkdale; Seafield School, Lytham; Canford School. **Career:** Stockbroker, Manchester; Major, RASC WWII. **Appointments:** Member, Royal British Legion; Member, St George's Masonic Lodge; Sidesman, Warden and Treasurer, St Peter's Church, Prestbury. **Honours:** TD. Died 10 August 1999.

DIGGLE, Dr William Mellalieu (1929) Born 9 October 1909, Oakhurst Heywood, Bury; son of James Stanley Diggle, Consulting Civil Engineer, and Dorothy Mary Mellalieu; m Alice Mitchell; 2 sons (Anthony and John). BA 1932; MA 1956; MRCS; LRCP. **Tutor(s):** M P Charlesworth. **Johnian Relatives:** brother of James Diggle (1934). **Educ:** Mr Thompson's School, St Annes-on-Sea; Arnold House School, Llandulas; Canford School, Wimborne. **Career:** Member, Social Security Medical Board; GP, Cheshire 1939–1968; RNVR 1940–1946; Police Surgeon, Chester 1947–1968. Died 29 November 1995.

DIMOCK, Eric John (1926) Born 21 May 1908, Home Farm, Stretham, Isle of Ely, Cambridgeshire; son of John Dimock, Farmer, and Rosetta Adelaide Shrive; m (1) Constance Ethel Jacobs, 1936, Singapore (d 1966), (2) Joan Stevens, 1970, Ely; 2 daughters (Joan Elizabeth b 19 January 1937 and Jill b 26 July 1940, d 21 February 1993). BA 1929; MA

1949. **Tutor(s):** E A Benians. **Johnian Relatives:** father-in-law of Peter Arthur Jackson (1957). **Educ:** Glebe House, Hunstanton; The King's School, Ely. **Career:** Rubber Planter, Malaya 1929–1942; Volunteer Force, Singapore; Japanese POW, Changi Prison, Singapore, then work on railway 1942–1945; Ministry of Agriculture and Fisheries 1946–1970. Died 14 July 1991.

DINGLE, John Rodney (1949) Born 20 September 1929, 2 Queen's Avenue, Hornsey, London; son of William Warren Dingle, Accountant and Secretary, and Evelyn Bertha Guillebaud; m June Ley, 1975; 2 stepdaughters (Alison b 1964 and Kathryn b 1967). **Subject(s):** Modern and Medieval Languages; BA 1952; MA 1956; CertEd (Cambridge) 1953. **Tutor(s):** C W Guillebaud. **Johnian Relatives:** second cousin, once removed, of Claude William Guillebaud (1909) and of Walter Henry Guillebaud (1909). **Educ:** Brooklands, Tonbridge; The Abbey School, Beckenham; Christ's Hospital. **Career:** Sergeant, Wiltshire Regiment 1948–1949; Master, Bryanston School, Dorset 1953–1970; Master, Exmouth Community College 1971–1989; Head of Modern Languages, Exmouth Community College 1987–1989. **Awards:** GB Gold Medal VIII European Championships, Macon 1951. **Publications:** *Distilled Enthusiasms*, Arthur Ransome Society, 1992; *Renewed Enthusiasms*, Arthur Ransome Society, 1999.

DINGLE, Professor Robert Balson (1943) Born 26 March 1926, 163 Hyde Road, Gorton, Manchester; son of Edward Douglas Dingle, Physician, and Nora Gertrude Balson; m Helen Glenronnie Munro, 7 January 1958. **Subject(s):** Natural Sciences; BA 1946; PhD 1951; FRSE 1961. **Tutor(s):** C W Guillebaud. **Educ:** St George's School, Boscombe; West Preston Manor School, Rustington; Gorse Cliff Preparatory School, Boscombe; Bournemouth Secondary School. **Career:** Title A Fellow, SJC 1948–1952; Senior Student, Exhibition of 1851 1952; Chief Assistant to Professor R Kronig, Technical University of Delft, Holland 1953; Reader in Theoretical Physics, University of Western Australia, Perth 1954–1960; First Professor of Theoretical Physics, St Andrews University 1960. **Appointments:** Visiting Professor, University of Alberta, University of California, and University of Western Australia 1968–1969. **Awards:** Major Scholarship, SJC 1943. **Publications:** *Asymptotic Expansions: their derivation and interpretation*, 1973; contributions to learned journals.

DINSMORE, John Francis (1919) Born 17 August 1898, Crebilly House, Ballymena, Antrim; son of John Dinsmore, Mill Owner, Woollen Manufacturer, and Ethel Constance Hossack. **Tutor(s):** E E Sikes. **Educ:** Mourne House; Uppingham School. **Career:** Army 1916–1919.

DIRAC, Professor Gabriel Andrew (1942) Born 13 March 1925, Budapest, Hungary; son of Richard Balazs, Book Publisher, and Margit Wigner; m Rosemarie Elisabeth; 1 son, 3 daughters. **Subject(s):** Mathematics; BA 1946; MA 1949. **Tutor(s):** S J Bailey. **Johnian Relatives:** stepson of Paul Adrien Maurice Dirac (1921). **Educ:** The Leys School, Cambridge; Horty Miklos Street Elementary School, Budapest; Protestant Gymnasium, Budapest; Perse School, Cambridge. **Career:** Lecturer in Mathematics, University of Toronto; Lecturer in Mathematics, KCL 1953; Erasmus Smith's Professor of Mathematics, TCD 1965; Professor of Pure Mathematics, University College, Swansea 1966–1971; Professor of Mathematics, University of Aarhus, Denmark 1971. **Awards:** Rayleigh Prize, University of Cambridge 1950. Died 20 July 1984.

DIRAC, Professor Paul Adrien Maurice (1921) Born 8 August 1902, Monk Road, Bristol; son of Charles Adrien Ladislas Dirac, School Teacher, and Florence Hannah Holten; m Margit Wigner; 2 stepchildren, 2 daughters. PhD 1926; BSc (Bristol); FRS 1930; Honorary Doctor, Moscow University 1966. **Tutor(s):** M P Charlesworth. **Johnian Relatives:** stepfather of Gabriel Andrew Dirac (1942). **Educ:** Bishop Road School, Bristol; Merchant Venturers' Secondary School, Bristol; Bristol University. **Career:** Title A Fellow 1927–1932, Title C Fellow 1932–1969, Title D Fellow 1969–1984, SJC; Lecturer in Mathematics

1929–1932, Praelector in Mathematical Physics 1929–1932, Lucasian Professor of Mathematics 1932–1969 (Emeritus 1969–1984), University of Cambridge; Professor of Physics, Florida State University 1971–1984. **Appointments:** Praelector in Mathematical Physics 1929–1932, SJC; Member, Pontifical Academy of Sciences 1961; Honorary Fellow, Bar-Ilan University, Israel. **Awards:** Exhibition, SJC; Hopkins Prize, Cambridge Philosophical Society 1927–1930; Nobel Prize for Physics (with Schroedinger) 1933; Royal Medal, Royal Society 1939; Copley Medal 1952; Rabindranath Tagore Birth Centenary Plaque, Asiatic Society of Bengal; Max Planck Medal, German Physics Institute; J Robert Oppenheimer Memorial Prize, Miami Center for Theoretical Studies. **Honours:** OM 1973. **Publications:** *Principles of Quantum Mechanics*, 1930, new edition 1982; *Development of Quantum Theory*, 1971; *General Theory of Relativity*, 1975; *Directions in Physics*, 1978; papers on quantum theory. Died 20 October 1984.

DITCHAM, Anthony Greville Fox (1946) Born 25 July 1922, 52 Kelvin Avenue, Palmers Green, London; son of Vivian Ashley Ditcham, Civil Servant, and Irene May Robinson. **Tutor(s):** F Thistlethwaite. **Educ:** Broomfield Park College, Southgate; Highfield College, Leigh-on-Sea; HMS *Worcester* Nautical Training College. **Career:** Colonial Service.

DIVER, John (1930) Born 22 December 1911, 35 Chandos Road, Willesden Green, Middlesex; son of Oswald Francis Diver, Actuary, and Ada Noverre. **Subject(s):** Natural Sciences; BA 1933; BChir 1936; MB 1937. **Tutor(s):** M P Charlesworth. **Johnian Relatives:** son of Oswald Francis Diver (1894). **Educ:** Froebel Educational Institute, Hammersmith; Gresham's School, Holt. **Career:** Obstetric Officer, St Mary's Hospital; House Physician, Woolwich Memorial Hospital; House Surgeon, St Mary's Hospital and Paddington Green Children's Hospital; Captain, RAMC 1939–1945. Died 29 May 1945 (died of beriberi, Changi POW Hospital, Singapore).

DIXON, Brian Fenton (1946) Born 30 November 1923, Fairholm, Rawdon, Horsforth, Yorkshire; son of Joseph Frederick Dixon, Bank Cashier, and Gertrude Jefferies; m Grace. BA 1948; MA 1953; FRICS; FRGS; FIArb. **Tutor(s):** J M Wordie. **Johnian Relatives:** brother of James Neville Dixon (1941). **Educ:** Rawdon Church School; Aireborough Grammar School. **Career:** Chartered Surveyor and Planning Consultant. Died 29 August 1989.

DIXON, Cuthbert (1906) Born 23 January 1887, Pelau Leazes, St Giles, Durham; son of James Dixon, Clerk in Holy Orders, and Emma Mickley. BA 1914. **Tutor(s):** J R Tanner. **Educ:** St Paul's School. **Career:** Captain, Royal Scottish (wounded), then employed with Officer Cadet Battalion, WWI; Assistant Master, Merchiston Castle School, Edinburgh; Master, Clifton Hall School, Edinburgh; First Headmaster of Newpark School, St Andrews 1933–1949. Died 7 May 1949.

DIXON, Douglas Gilbert (1908) Born 30 March 1890, 96 Queen's Road, Peckham, London; son of Joseph Briggs Dixon, Board Schoolmaster, and Mary Elizabeth Brown. **Tutor(s):** E E Sikes. **Educ:** Battersea Grammar School; Birkbeck College. **Career:** Fruit farming, Canada 1909.

DIXON, Foster Hickman (1929) Born 14 July 1912, 9 Coronation Road, Bristol; son of Thomas Benjamin Dixon, Medical Practitioner, and Bessie Norah Lane. **Tutor(s):** M P Charlesworth. **Educ:** Avondale Preparatory School, Clifton; Clifton College.

DIXON, James Neville (1941) Born 20 February 1922, Fairholm, Rawdon, Leeds; son of Joseph Frederick Dixon, Bank Cashier, and Gertrude Jefferies. **Subject(s):** Economics; BA 1944; MA 1947; FCA. **Tutor(s):** J M Wordie. **Johnian Relatives:** brother of Brian Fenton Dixon (1946). **Educ:** Aireborough Grammar School, Guiseley. **Career:** Senior Partner, Messrs Armitage & Norton, Chartered Accountants. **Appointments:** JP. Died 31 July 1978.

DIXON, John Lindley (1949) Born 12 March 1930, 158 Woodsley Road, Leeds; son of Sidney Frank Dixon, Schoolmaster, and Marie Durham Schaerer. **Subject(s):** Mathematics; BA 1952; MA 1956. **Tutor(s):** R L Howland. **Educ:** Leeds Grammar School; Mill Hill School. **Career:** Colonial Survey Service, Entebbe, Uganda 1952–1962; Organist, St John's Church, Entebbe 1952–1963; Servicer of keyboard instruments (helped instal pipe organ, St John's Cathedral, Fort Portal, Uganda 1957, overhauled 1991); Administrative Assistant, later Estates Officer, Anglican Church of Uganda 1963–1970; Assistant Organist, Namirembe Cathedral until 1970; Bursar, Lubiri Secondary School, Kampala 1973–1980; Full Time Piano Tuner and Organ Servicer 1981–; Organist, All Saints Cathedral, Nairobi 1982–. **Appointments:** President, Uganda Society 1968–1969; Honorary Treasurer, Nairobi Music Society 1987; Founder Member, Chairman and Treasurer, Uganda Student Christian Hostels Association. **Awards:** Minor Scholarship, SJC 1946. **Publications:** one article in *Empire Survey Review*, October 1959, and several on organs.

DIXON, William Maxwell (1944) Born 22 October 1925, Hawklemass, Whittingham, Northumberland; son of Henry Dixon, Grocer, and Elizabeth Green. BA 1949; MA 1954; FICE. **Tutor(s):** S J Bailey. **Educ:** Whittingham Elementary School; Rock Lodge Preparatory School, Roker; Durham School; Christ Church, Oxford. **Career:** Area Manager, Sir Robert McAlpine and Sons Ltd. Died 11 March 1993.

DOBBIE, Dr Joseph Hume Leslie (1921) Born 30 April 1902, 21 Murrayfield Avenue, Edinburgh, Scotland; son of Sir Joseph Dobbie, Solicitor, Supreme Court, and Alice Elizabeth Sharp. BA 1924; Diploma in Medical Radiology and Electrology 1935. **Tutor(s):** B F Armitage. **Educ:** Russell House, Trinity, Edinburgh; Edinburgh Academy; Oundle School. **Career:** House Surgeon, Radcliffe Infirmary, Oxford; Resident Anaesthetist, Addenbrooke's Hospital, Cambridge; Resident, in charge of Children's Wing, Leith Hospital, Edinburgh; Assistant Lecturer in Radiotherapy, University of Manchester 1952. **Appointments:** Deputy Director, Holt Radium Institute, Manchester; Fellow, Royal College of Radiologists. **Publications:** *The Treatment of Malignant Disease by Radiotherapy*, 1963. Died 17 September 1984.

DOBBS, Leonard George (1920) Born 8 June 1901, 13 Cheyne Gardens, Chelsea, Middlesex; son of George Cumberland Dobbs, Company Director and Publisher, and Rosalind Heyworth Potter. **Subject(s):** Mathematics/Natural Sciences; BA 1923. **Tutor(s):** E E Sikes. **Johnian Relatives:** brother of Sealey Patrick Dobbs (1919). **Educ:** Preparatory School, Oxford; The Grange, Folkestone; Bedales School, Petersfield. **Career:** Assistant Master, Lady Manners School, Bakewell 1925. Died 2 March 1945.

DOBBS, Sealey Patrick (1919) Born 28 February 1900, 13 Cheyne Gardens, Chelsea, London; son of George Cumberland Dobbs, Publisher, and Rosalind Heyworth Potter. **Subject(s):** Mathematics/Economics; BA 1922. **Tutor(s):** E E Sikes. **Johnian Relatives:** brother of Leonard George Dobbs (1920). **Educ:** Oxford Preparatory School; Winchester College; Marlborough College; KCL; RMA, Woolwich. **Awards:** Research Studentship, Ratan Tata Foundation tenable at LSE 1925.

DOBSON, Robert Arthur (1920) Born 15 May 1900, 115 Bath Street, Ilkeston, Derbyshire; son of Arthur Dobson, Surgeon, and Charlotte Lucas. BA 1923; MA 1927. **Tutor(s):** E A Benians. **Educ:** Winchester House School; Shrewsbury School; Highcliffe School, Nottingham.

DOCKRAY, Dr John Vernon (1919) (Admitted Trinity College 1917) Born 8 May 1899, Windhill Place, Bishop's Stortford, Hertfordshire; son of John Smalley Dockray, Doctor of Medicine, and Florence Marie Humphreys; m (1) Evelyn Mary Gayton, 23 June 1926, St Michael's Church, Bishop's Stortford, (2) Mary Frances Wrinch, 13 December 1945. **Subject(s):** Natural Sciences; BA 1922; MA 1925; MRCS 1925; LRCP 1925. **Tutor(s):** E A Benians. **Educ:** The School, Bishop's

Stortford; Trinity College, Cambridge; RMC, Sandhurst. **Career:** Second Lieutenant, East Kent Regiment 1918–1919; Royal Mail Lines Ltd; Honorary Medical Officer, Bishop's Stortford Hospital; House Physician, County Hospital, Hertford; RNVR. **Appointments:** CUOTC, WWI. **Honours:** OBE. Died 29 December 1948.

DODD, The Revd Canon Rowland Pocock (1905) Born 14 April 1886, Broadhurst Gardens, Hampstead, Middlesex; son of Francis William Dodd, Clerk in Holy Orders, and Mary Selina Fuller; m (1) Frances Mary Wooldridge (d 1919), (2) Leila Kathleen Rawlinson, 14 September 1926, All Saints Church, Banstead; 2 sons (Charles Nathanael b 1 March 1930 and Peter Curwen b 9 June 1933). **Subject(s):** Classics/Theology; BA 1908; MA 1919. **Tutor(s):** D MacAlister. **Johnian Relatives:** father of Peter Curwen Dodd (1954). **Educ:** Dean Close Memorial School, Cheltenham. **Career:** Ordained Deacon 1911; Curate, Christ Church, Patricroft 1911–1913; Ordained Priest 1912; Sub-Warden, St Anselm's Hostel, Manchester 1913–1914; Curate, St Chrysostom, Victoria Park, Manchester 1913–1914; Temporary CF, 3rd Class, RACD (wounded, Mentioned in Despatches) 1914–1918; Curate, St Mary, Prestwich 1914–1919; Chaplain, SJC 1919–1920; SPG Missionary, Cawnpore 1920–1928; Examining Chaplain to Bishop of Lucknow 1926–1928; Vice-Principal, Knutsford Test School, Hawarden 1928–1930; Licence to Officiate, Diocese of Bath and Wells 1930–1931; Rector, Tarporley, Cheshire 1931–1945; Rector, Freshwater, Isle of Wight 1945–1956; Rural Dean, West Wight 1951–1956. **Appointments:** Honorary Canon, Portsmouth Cathedral 1954. **Awards:** Scholarship, SJC. **Honours:** MC 1917. Died 2 April 1975.

DODD, Walter Prichard (1908) Born 18 November 1888, Penbryn, Llangollen, Denbighshire; son of Walter Gummow Dodd, Insurance Clerk, and Margaret Eleanor Dodd; 2 sons (Mervyn and Dennis). **Subject(s):** Classics; BA 1911; MA 1920. **Tutor(s):** E E Sikes. **Educ:** Llangollen County School; Wrexham County School; University College of Wales. **Career:** Lieutenant, Royal Welsh Fusiliers; Master, George Watson's College, Edinburgh; Headmaster, Colwyn Bay Secondary School; Master, Woodhouse Grove School 1911–1913; Master, Newbury Grammar School 1913–1915. **Awards:** Open Scholarship, SJC. **Honours:** MC. Died 8 March 1963.

DODERET, William (1913) Born 30 September 1862, Madras, India; son of Frederick Doderet, Public Works Department, Madras, and Emily Elizabeth Newland. **Educ:** Melsungen, Germany; University College School, London; Wren and Gurney's; Balliol College, Oxford. **Career:** University Teacher, Marathi.

DOGGART, William Edward (1907) Born 6 April 1888, 19 Fred Street, Broughton, Salford, Lancashire; son of Hugh Doggart, House Painter, and Elizabeth McAnergeny. **Subject(s):** Moral Sciences; BA 1910. **Tutor(s):** L H K Bushe-Fox. **Educ:** Marlborough Road Board School, Salford; Salford Central Higher Grade School; Salford Technical School.

DOHERTY, Dr Michael Verran (1938) Born 12 July 1919, Streatham Manor, Leigham Avenue, Streatham, London; son of John William Doherty, Dental Surgeon, and Helen Grace Verran. BA 1941. **Tutor(s):** R L Howland. **Educ:** Mill Hill Preparatory School; Gresham's School, Holt.

DOHOO, Roy McGregor (1938) Born 3 September 1919, Tullynessle, Devonshire Road, Hornchurch, Essex; son of Arthur Godfrey Dohoo, Principal Assistant, Education Office, London County Council, and Helen McGregor; m Alice Rosemary Makin, 12 March 1949; 1 son (Ian Robert b 1952), 1 daughter (Sheila Mary b 1950). **Subject(s):** Mathematics; BA 1941; MA 1945; FIEE; CEng; PEng. **Tutor(s):** J M Wordie. **Educ:** City of London School. **Career:** British Army RAOC 1941–1943; REME 1943–1947 (Demobilised as Major); Experimental Officer, Air Ministry 1947–1948; Scientific and Senior Scientific Officer, Ministry of Supply Armament Design 1948–1952; Defence Scientific Service Officer, Defence Research Board, Canada 1952–1969; Seconded to RAND Corporation, Santa Monica, California 1957–1959; Canadian

National Defence College 1968–1969; Department of Communications, Canada 1969–1977 (retired as Director General, Space Program); Consultant, Satellite Communications; President, Roy M Dohoo Ltd 1977–1992. **Awards:** Beaufoy Scholarship 1938–1941.

DOLBY, Arthur (1939) Born 6 February 1920, 92 Cark Road, Keighley, Yorkshire; son of John Thomas Dolby, Railway Clerk, and Harriet Taylor. **Subject(s):** Modern and Medieval Languages; BA 1946. **Tutor(s):** C W Guillebaud. **Educ:** Eastwood Council School, Keighley; Boys' Grammar School, Keighley. Died 20 January 2004.

DOLEY, John Oliver (1935) Born 25 April 1918, 144 Waterloo Road, Wolverhampton; son of Walter Oliver Doley, Engineer's Wood Patternmaker, and Mabel Florence Priest. **Subject(s):** Mathematics; BA 1938; MA 1942. **Tutor(s):** J M Wordie. **Educ:** St Peter's Collegiate School, Wolverhampton; Wolverhampton Grammar School. **Awards:** Scholarship, SJC 1936–1937. Died 16 December 1989.

DOLLMAN, Hereward Chune (1907) Born 10 March 1888, Hove House, Newton Grove, Bedford Park, Middlesex; son of John Charles Dollman, Artist, and Mary Jane Fletcher. **Tutor(s):** L H K Bushe-Fox. **Johnian Relatives:** brother of John Guy Dollman (1905). **Educ:** Colet Court, Hammersmith; St Paul's, London.

DOLLMAN, Captain John Guy (1905) Born 4 September 1886, Bedford Park, Acton, Middlesex; son of John Charles Dollman, Artist, and Mary Jane Fletcher; m Violet Holloway, 1916. **Subject(s):** Natural Sciences; BA 1908. **Tutor(s):** D MacAlister. **Johnian Relatives:** brother of Hereward Chune Dollman (1907). **Educ:** St Paul's School. **Career:** Assistant, Department of Zoology, British Museum 1907–1915; Inns of Court OTC Regiment 1915–1919; Work on large mammals and big game animals, Natural History Museum 1919. **Appointments:** Member, panel of advisers to British delegation to International Conference for the Preservation of the Flora and Fauna of Africa 1933; Exhibition Secretary, Civil Service Exhibitions of Arts; broadcast as Uncle Guy on *Children's Hour*. **Awards:** Exhibition, SJC. **Publications:** *Catalogue of the Selous Collection of Big Game in the British Museum (Natural History)*; (ed) R Lydekker, *The Game Animals of Africa*; (ed) R Lydekker, *The Great and Small Game of India, Malaya, Burma and Tibet*; (with R Lydekker) *Game Animals of Indian Sub-Continents*; (ed, with J B Burlace) R Ward, *Records of Big Game*; articles in journals including *Proceedings of the Linnean Society*. Died 21 March 1942.

DOMVILLE, Alan Ratcliffe (1947) Born 25 August 1924, Glendale, Pine Grove, Prestwich, Manchester; son of Sydney Thomas Domville, HM Inspector of Taxes, and Margaret Mary Trafford; m Alice Diana; 2 daughters (Ann and Jean). **Subject(s):** Natural Sciences; BA 1949; MA 1954; MIEE; CEng. **Tutor(s):** G C L Bertram. **Johnian Relatives:** brother-in-law of Kenneth James Le Couteur (1938). **Educ:** Bickerton House School, Birkdale; Bolton School, Lancashire; Dunnow Hall, Newton by Bowland; Kingsmoor School, Glossop.

DONALD, James Mackie (1936) Born 23 December 1917, 131 Boness Road, Grangemouth; son of David Angus Donald, Civil Engineer, and Isabella Brimer Mackintosh Mackie; m Jean Valentine Moir Scott. **Subject(s):** Law/Economics; BA 1939; MA 1967. **Tutor(s):** C W Guillebaud. **Educ:** Hurst Grange, Stirling; Sedbergh School. **Career:** Argyll and Southern Highlanders, TA 1939; Commissioned Leicestershire Yeomanry, 8th Army (Western Desert and Italy) 1940; Captain and Adjutant, 154 Leicester Yeomanry Field Regiment, RA (Mentioned in Despatches) until 1946; Sales and Marketing, Sale, Tilney and Co 1947–1959; Northern Division Sales Manager, AEI Hotpoint Ltd 1959–1961; Managing Director, AEI Gala Appliances Pty Ltd, Australia 1961–1963; Sales Director, AEI Hotpoint Ltd 1963–1965; Marketing Director, TI Creda Ltd 1965–1970; Managing Director, Royal Albert, Allied English Potteries 1970–1973; Management and Marketing Consultant, Europe 1973–1983. **Appointments:** Captain, Berkshire Golf Club 1977; President, Berkshire Golf Club 1991–1994.

DONALDSON, Professor William Anderson (1948) Born 20 January 1927, 23 Woodend Avenue, Cathcart, Glasgow; son of John William Anderson Donaldson, Merchant, and Jean Marguerite Smith; m Constance Wilson, 15 July 1965, Bearsden; 1 son (Alan John b 11 January 1967), 1 daughter (Laura Caroline b 12 January 1972). **Subject(s):** Mathematics; BA 1950; MA 1983; MA (Glasgow) 1946; DipMathStats 1951. **Tutor(s):** J M Wordie. **Educ:** Queen's Park Secondary School, Glasgow; Glasgow University. **Career:** Assistant Lecturer in Mathematics 1946–1948, Lecturer in Mathematics 1951–1955, University of Glasgow; Chief Mathematician, then Data Processing Manager, Scottish Factories, Rolls-Royce Ltd 1955–1962; Senior Lecturer, Reader, then (from 1971) Professor and Head of the Department of Operational Research, University of Strathclyde 1962–1987; Visiting Professor, University of Toronto 1988–1989. **Appointments:** National Computing Centre Education Committee 1966–1967; Scottish Education Department, Computer Studies in School Curriculum Committee 1967–1971; BCS, Systems Analysis and Professional Qualification Exam Boards 1967–1971; Engineering Industry Training Board, Computer Training Policy Committee 1968–1971; Member, then Chairman, Scottish Advisory Committee on Computers in the Health Service 1970–1983; Advisory Panel on Information Processing 1974–1981; Member then Chairman, Information and Computer Services Advisory Group 1975–1984; Vice-President, Operational Research Society 1978–1980; Chairman, Scottish Health Information Review Committee 1982–1984. **Honours:** OBE 1983. **Publications:** *Operational Research Techniques*, Volume I, 1969 and Volume II, 1974, Business Books, London; various papers, journals, and reports.

DONNE, The Revd Reginald Felix (1907) Born 17 September 1887, The Vicarage, Welland, Malvern Wells, Worcestershire; son of John Matthew Donne, Clerk in Holy Orders, and Letitia Gray-Jones. BA 1911; MA 1926. **Tutor(s):** J R Tanner. **Educ:** Hereford Cathedral School; Wells Theological College. **Career:** Ordained Deacon 1913; Curate, St Paul's, Crewe 1913–1914; Curate, Corsham 1914–1917; Ordained Priest 1915; Curate, Cockfield 1924–1928; Rector, Wootton Rivers, Marlborough 1928. Died 2 July 1936.

DONOGHUE, The Revd Matthew James (1940) Born 25 March 1917, 1 Hill Road, Bathgate, West Lothian, Scotland; son of Michael Donoghue, Insurance Agent, and Margaret O'Donnell. **Subject(s):** English/History; BA 1943; MA 1947. **Tutor(s):** C W Guillebaud. **Educ:** St Mary's School, Bathgate; St Joseph's College, Dumfries; Oscott College, Birmingham; Grand Seminaire, Constances; St Edmund's House, Cambridge.

DONOVAN, Edmund Lawrence (1907) Born 2 October 1887, Riston, Skirlaugh, Yorkshire; son of Jeremiah Alexander Donovan, Clerk in Holy Orders, and Esther Bell O'Callaghan. BA 1910; MA 1914. **Tutor(s):** J R Tanner. **Educ:** Pocklington School. **Career:** Second Lieutenant, East Yorkshire Regiment (Cyclist Battalion, TF), then Lieutenant, King's African Rifles, WWI.

DONOVAN, Philip Anthony (1944) Born 2 June 1919, 94 Regents Park Road, London; son of Henry Rupert Donovan, Farmer, and Winifred Alice Bacon; m Hilda Margaret (June) Bell, 12 June 1946. BSc (St Andrews) 1943. **Tutor(s):** C W Guillebaud. **Educ:** Waderer Beach School, Natal; Milton School, Bulawayo; University of St Andrews. **Career:** Department of Agriculture, Cape St Mary, Gambia, British West Africa; Inspector, AC Cossor Ltd 1943–1944.

DORMAN, Richard Bostock (1948) Born 8 August 1925, 77 Eastgate Street, Stafford; son of John Ehrenfried Dorman, Engineer, and Madeleine Louise Bostock, Dentist; m Anna Illingworth, 1950; 1 son (Paul b 1963), 2 daughters (Julia b 1953 and Deborah b 1959). **Subject(s):** Russian and Modern Greek; BA 1951. **Tutor(s):** C W Guillebaud. **Educ:** Sedbergh School. **Career:** H M Forces 1944–1948; Assistant Principal 1951–1955, Principal 1955–1958, War Office; Commonwealth Relations Office 1958–1960; First Secretary, British

High Commission, Nicosia (Diplomatic Service) 1960–1964; Deputy High Commissioner, Freetown 1964–1966; South East Asia Department, Foreign Office 1967–1968; NATO Defence College, Rome 1968–1969; Counsellor, Addis Ababa 1969–1973; Commercial Counsellor, Bucharest 1974–1977; Counsellor, Pretoria, South Africa 1977–1982; High Commissioner, Vanuatu 1982–1985; Founder and Chairman (from 1990), British Friends of Vanuatu 1986–1999. **Awards:** Minor Scholarship, SJC 1943. **Honours:** CBE 1984; Medal of National Merit, Vanuatu 1999.

DORWARD, Adam Paterson (1941) Born 11 June 1922, Ardenleigh, Galashiels, Selkirkshire; son of Adam Paterson Dorward, Wholesale Clothier, and Isabella Fairgrieve. **Tutor(s):** C W Guillebaud. **Johnian Relatives:** brother of Arthur Fairgrieve Dorward (1943); uncle of Richard Munro Dorward (1962) and of James Fairgrieve Dorward (1964). **Educ:** Galashiels Academy; St Mary's, Melrose; Sedbergh School.

DORWARD, Arthur Fairgrieve (1943) Born 3 March 1925, Ardenleigh, Galashiels; son of Adam Paterson Dorward, Wholesale Clothier, and Isabella Fairgrieve. **Subject(s):** Modern and Medieval Languages; BA 1948; MA 1991. **Tutor(s):** C W Guillebaud. **Johnian Relatives:** brother of Adam Paterson Dorward (1941); uncle of Richard Munro Dorward (1962) and of James Fairgrieve Dorward (1964). **Educ:** St Mary's Preparatory School, Melrose; Sedbergh School. **Career:** RAF Cadet.

DOUBLEDAY, John Gordon (1947) Born 27 November 1920, 163 West Road, Southend-on-Sea, Essex; son of Douglas Collins Doubleday, Managing Director, Potato Merchants, and Edith Howgego. **Tutor(s):** J M Wordie. **Educ:** Alleyne Court Preparatory School, Westcliff on Sea; Bedford School. **Career:** Colonial Service Course; Ministry of Health 1939–1941; Flight Lieutenant, RAF 1941–1947.

DOUGLAS, Brian Kirkbride (1935) Born 18 August 1914, Milverton Lodge, Victoria Park, Manchester; son of William Robert Douglas, Surgeon Lieutenant, RAMC, and Margaret Kirkbride. **Subject(s):** Music; MusB 1938. **Tutor(s):** C W Guillebaud. **Educ:** The Leas (Dealtry's), Hoylake; Uppingham School; Grimes Tutorial College, Manchester.

DOUGLAS, David Hamilton (1949) Born 11 June 1929, Victoria Hospital, Hong Kong; son of William Ewart Douglas, Chartered Civil Engineer, and Amelia Hamilton; m Hazel Mary Edgar, 3 July 1958, St Andrew's Cathedral, Singapore; 2 daughters (Louise b 3 July 1961 and Joanna b 24 March 1964). **Subject(s):** Modern and Medieval Languages; BA 1952; MA 1959. **Tutor(s):** C W Guillebaud. **Johnian Relatives:** son of William Ewart Douglas (1909); brother of Ian Kenneth Hamilton Douglas (1942). **Educ:** Durston House Preparatory School, Ealing; Derby Academy, Hingham, USA; Monkton Coombe School. **Career:** Intelligence Corps 1947–1949; Far-East Representative for Henry Hopes, Singapore 1954–1961; Opened and started Window Factory for Henry Hopes in Calcutta, India 1962–1963; Management Consultant, Associated Industrial Consultants 1963–1969. Died 25 March 2001.

DOUGLAS, Ian Kenneth Hamilton (1942) Born 21 December 1923, French Hospital, Hong Kong; son of William Ewart Douglas, Civil Engineer, and Amelia Hamilton. BA 1945; MA 1966; CEng; MIMechE. **Tutor(s):** S J Bailey. **Johnian Relatives:** son of William Ewart Douglas (1909); brother of David Hamilton Douglas (1949). **Educ:** Durston House Preparatory School, Ealing; St Paul's School; Bath Technical College. Died 11 April 1997.

DOUGLAS, John (1913) Born 9 May 1894, North Terrace, Birstall, Leeds, Yorkshire; son of Charles Douglas, Engineer, and Helen Hogg Ellison. **Subject(s):** Mathematics/Mechanical Sciences; BA 1920. **Tutor(s):** L H K Bushe-Fox. **Educ:** Bradford Grammar School. **Career:** Second Lieutenant, RE 1915; Somme Campaign, France 1916; Artillery Observer, RFC; Lieutenant (Aeroplane Officer), RAF (wounded); trained as pilot, RAF 1918; Apprentice, Metropolitan-Vickers Electric Company Ltd, Manchester 1920–1922.

DOUGLAS, William Ewart (1909) Born 27 October 1889, 30 Market Street, Wellingborough, Northamptonshire; son of George Douglas, Master Printer, and Adah Loakes. **Subject(s):** Mechanical Sciences; BA 1913; MA 1945. **Tutor(s):** L H K Bushe-Fox. **Johnian Relatives:** father of Ian Kenneth Hamilton Douglas (1942) and of David Hamilton Douglas (1949). **Educ:** Victoria Board School, Wellingborough; Wellingborough Grammar School.

DOW, James Crown (1942) Born 1 June 1924, 14 The Barons, St Margaret's, Twickenham; son of Robert Dow, Medical Practitioner, and Estelle Norah Howard Murphy. **Subject(s):** English; BA 1948; MA 1950. **Tutor(s):** C W Guillebaud; F Thistlethwaite. **Johnian Relatives:** grandson of Henry Howard Murphy (1868). **Educ:** The Mount School, Kersal; St Ronan's Preparatory School, Prenton; Calday Grange Grammar School, West Kirby. **Career:** RAF 1943–1947; Insurance and International Reinsurance 1949–1987. **Appointments:** Royal Insurance Group; Secretary, British Insurance (Atomic Energy) Committee; JP 1963; Lay-Magistrate, Inner London Juvenile Courts 1963–1989; Custodian Trustee, Rainer Foundation (voluntary) 1979–1995. **Awards:** Chartered Insurance Institute's Travelling Scholarship 1951. **Publications:** *Nuclear Energy and Insurance*, Witherby, London 1989.

DOW, James Findlay (1929) Born 13 May 1911, Glenlean, Montgomery Road, Newlands, Cathcart, Renfrewshire; son of John Archibald Dow, Wholesale Wine and Spirit Merchant, and Jessie Archibald Harkness; m (2) Jean Millbank, 28 November 1952, Shoeburyness; 2 sons (Ian and Hamish), 3 daughters (Alison, Emma and Lindsey). **Subject(s):** Natural Sciences; BA 1932; BChir 1935; MB 1936; FRCP. **Tutor(s):** M P Charlesworth. **Johnian Relatives:** brother of John Alexander Dow (1936). **Educ:** High School, Glasgow; Strathallan School, Forgandenny; Middlesex Hospital. **Career:** House posititions, Middlesex and Brompton Hospitals 1936–1939; Resident Assistant Physician 1939; Honorary Assistant Physician 1946, St George's Hospital Consultant; Consultant, London Life. **Appointments:** Chairman, Medical Committee, King Edward VII Hospital for Officers. Died 24 September 1983.

DOW, John Alexander (1936) Born 18 June 1918, 19 Montgomery Road, Glasgow, Scotland; son of John Archibald Dow, Wine and Spirits Merchant, and Jessie Archibald Harkness; 1 son, 2 daughters. **Subject(s):** Economics/Law; BA 1939; MA 1978. **Tutor(s):** C W Guillebaud. **Johnian Relatives:** brother of James Findlay Dow (1929). **Educ:** Glasgow Academy; Strathallan School, Forgandenny. **Career:** Lieutenant, RNVR 1939–1945; Scottish Sales Manager, Hiram Walker and Sons Ltd 1972; Past Visitor of the Incorporation of Maltmen; Regional Director UK, Hiram Walker International Company. **Appointments:** Treasurer, Scottish Wine and Spirit Merchants Benevolent Institution 1952–1965; Director, Scottish Wine and Spirit Merchants Benevolent Institution, 1962; Vice-president, Scottish Wholesale Wine Distributors Association 1967–1970; President, Scottish Wine and Spirit Merchants Benevolent Institution 1969–1970. Died 2 February 1995.

DOWELL, Keith Walton (1935) Born 13 June 1917, 6 Ravensdale Avenue, North Finchley, London; son of Albert Walton Dowell, Company Director, and Marjorie Frances Wilson; m Sheila. BA 1939; MA 1943. **Tutor(s):** J M Wordie. **Johnian Relatives:** brother of Peter Derrick Dowell (1939). **Educ:** St Dunstan's School, London; Kent House School, Eastbourne; Oundle School. Died 14 February 1974.

DOWELL, Peter Derrick (1939) Born 23 August 1921, 362 Finchley Road, Hampstead, London; son of Albert Walton Dowell, Glass Manufacturer, and Marjorie Frances Wilson. **Subject(s):** Economics. **Tutor(s):** C W Guillebaud. **Johnian Relatives:** brother of Keith Walton Dowell (1935). **Educ:** Kent House School, Eastbourne; St Bede's School, Eastbourne; Oundle School.

DOWER, John Gordon (1919) Born 2 September 1900, 1 Ashburn Place, Ilkley, Yorkshire; son of Robert Shillito Dower, Iron Merchant, and Mary

Amelia Cobb Hearnshaw; m Pauline Trevelyan, 3 September 1929, Cambo Church, Northumberland; 2 sons (Michael Shillito Trevelyan b 15 November 1933 and Robert Charles Philips b 27 October 1938), 1 daughter (Susan Florence b 5 January 1931). **Subject(s):** History; BA 1923; MA 1930; ARIBA 1930. **Tutor(s):** E A Benians. **Johnian Relatives:** son of Robert Shillito Dower (1892); father of Michael Shillito Trevelyan Dower (1954), and of Robert Charles Philips Dower (1958); grandfather of Thomas Calverley Dower (1990). **Educ:** Ghyll Royd School, Ilkley; The Leys School, Cambridge. **Career:** Architect and Planner; Civil Servant. **Appointments:** Drafting Secretary of Standing Committee on National Parks of CPRE 1934. **Awards:** Exhibition, SJC 1918. **Publications:** 'The Dower Report' (white paper on National Parks in England and Wales), 1945. Died 3 October 1947.

DOWLING, Dr Edmund John (1939) Born 20 March 1921, Benoni, Transvaal, South Africa; son of Edward Dowling, Doctor of Medicine, and Dorothy Wilson; m Elizabeth Howorth, 6 February 1951; 3 sons (Edward, Jonathan and Peter). BA 1942; MA 1946; MB 1948; BChir 1948. **Tutor(s):** R L Howland. **Educ:** St Dunstan's, Benoni, Transvaal; Fulwood Grammar School, Preston; Colet Court, London; St Paul's School, London. **Career:** St Thomas' Hospital, London 1942–1945; RAMC 1945–1947; Clinical Assistant, St Thomas' Hospital, London 1948; GP 1949–1967; Medical Staff, Government Service 1967–1983. Died 17 February 2003.

DOWNER, Edward George (1943) Born 6 September 1925, 4 Davigdor Road, Hove, Sussex; son of Harold George Downer, Surgeon, and Claudia Phyllis Clowes; m Yvonne Catherine Claudet, 29 March 1947. **Tutor(s):** C W Guillebaud. **Educ:** Westwood School; Claremont Preparatory School; Windlesham House School; Marlborough College.

DOWNS, James (1917) Born 30 March 1899, 70 South Parade, Pudsey, Yorkshire; son of John W Downs, Worsted Manufacturer, and Mary Dorman; m Kathleen Maud Whitley, 9 June 1925, Arthington; 3 sons, 1 daughter. **Subject(s):** Natural Sciences; BA 1921; MA 1925. **Tutor(s):** E E Sikes. **Johnian Relatives:** uncle of John Patrick Downs (1944) and of Peter William Musgrave (1947). **Educ:** New College, Harrogate. **Career:** Family firm, Downs, Coulter & Co Ltd (textile manufacturers) 1922, became Joint Managing Director. Died 31 December 1975.

DOWNS, John Patrick (1944) Born 26 July 1926, Sowden House, Thornton, Bradford, Yorkshire; son of William Downs, Worsted Manufacturer of Downs, Coulter & Co Ltd, and Janet Lindsay Dick; 3 sons. **Subject(s):** Natural Sciences; BA 1950; MA 1952. **Tutor(s):** C W Guillebaud. **Johnian Relatives:** nephew of James Downs (1917); cousin of Peter William Musgrave (1947). **Educ:** Grosvenor House School, Harrogate; Ashville College, Harrogate; The Leys School, Cambridge. **Career:** Director, Downs, Coulter & Co Ltd, Textile Manufacturers, Bradford, West Yorkshire 1950–1989. Died 27 January 2001.

DOWNSBROUGH, Dr Frank Keith (1943) Born 4 September 1925, 4 Oakdene Terrace, Moston, Manchester; son of Ernest Downsbrough, Engineer's Draughtsman, and Agnes Emma Holroyd, Chiropodist; m Elizabeth Marshall, 29 November 1958; 1 son (Miles b 13 September 1965), 1 daughter (Julie Rose b 21 July 1961). **Subject(s):** Natural Sciences; BA 1946; MA 1950; MB ChB (Leeds) 1953; DMRD (London) 1958; FRCP (Canada) 1972. **Tutor(s):** C W Guillebaud. **Educ:** Queensbury Council School; Bradford Grammar School; Leeds University Medical School. **Career:** Research Chemist in Flue Gas Washing, Battersea Power Station 1945–1947; Diagnostic Radiologist 1958; Consultant Radiologist, Leeds Regional Hospital Board 1961–1967; Diagnostic Radiology Specialist, Ontario 1967–1970; Diagnostic Radiology Specialist, Alberta 1970–1972; Consultant Radiologist, Oxford Regional Health Authority 1972–1975; Diagnostic Radiology Specialist, Alberta 1975–2002. **Awards:** Exhibition, SJC; West Riding County Major Scholarship 1943; Silver Cup, London Power Company Athletic Games 1947. **Publications:** 'A case of Double Arterio-venous Fistula', *British Medical Journal*, 1962.

DOYLE, Harold John (1934) Born 7 July 1916, 25 Willow Grove, Beverley; son of Harry Doyle, Assistant Superintendent, Hull Post Office, and Ann Maria Hall; m; 3 children. **Subject(s):** English/History; BA 1937; MA 1941. **Tutor(s):** J S Boys Smith. **Educ:** Holland House; St Mary's Church of England School; Beverley Grammar School. **Career:** Elwell County Secondary School 1939; RN 1939–1945; Assistant Master, Glyn County School, Elwell 1947–1950; Headmaster, St Mary's Church of England Boys' School, Merton 1951–1963; Headmaster, Rivermead Secondary Boys' School, Kingston, Surrey 1963.

DRAKE, Dr Brian John (1944) Born 13 July 1926, 7 Belvoir Road, Cambridge; son of Frederick William Drake, Scientific Instrument Maker, and Grace Emily Ayers, School Teacher; m Vibeke Engelbrekt-Pedersen, 30 May 1960, Nærum, Denmark; 2 sons (Laurence b 3 January 1963 and Marcus b 18 July 1966). **Subject(s):** Natural Sciences; BA 1948; MA 1951; MA (Oxon) 1951; BM (Oxon) 1953; BCh (Oxon) 1953; DObstRCOG 1957; LRAM 1966; ARCM 1966. **Tutor(s):** C W Guillebaud; G C L Bertram. **Johnian Relatives:** cousin of Michael John Drake (1962); father of Laurence Karsten Drake (1982) and of Marcus John Drake (1985). **Educ:** Milton Road School, Cambridge; Perse School, Cambridge. **Career:** Military Service 1946–1948 (Royal Signals 1946–1947, Officer, RAEC and Head of Science, Duke of York's Royal Military School, Dover 1947–1948); Medical Student, United Oxford Hospitals Clinical School and Balliol College, Oxford 1950–1953; House Physician, Radcliffe Infirmary, Oxford 1953–1954; House Surgeon, Addenbrooke's Hospital 1954; Obstetrical House Surgeon, Reading 1954–1955; SHO, Accident Service, Radcliffe Infirmary 1956–1957; GP, Histon 1957–1989; Clinical Assistant, Department of Venereology, Addenbrooke's Hospital 1959–1973; Consultant in Genito-Urinary Medicine, Bedford Hospital 1966–1991. **Appointments:** President, Cambridge Medical Society 1984–1985.

DRANE, Arthur Benjamin (1935) Born 7 June 1917, 11 Quarry Road, Wandsworth, London; son of Benjamin Edgar Drane, Clerk, and Maud Edla Paterson; 3 children. **Subject(s):** History/English; BA 1938; MA 1942. **Tutor(s):** J S Boys Smith. **Educ:** Preparatory School, Gidea Park; City of Norwich School. **Career:** Teacher, Oxford and Staffordshire 1938–1939; Commissioned Officer, Royal Tank Regiment 1939–1945; Head of English Department, Nunthorpe School, York 1949–1961. Died 5 April 1961.

DRAPER, John Robert (1900) Born 28 December 1877, Bradley Hall, Eccleston, Chorley, Lancashire; son of Thomas Draper, Farmer, and Mary Schofield; m Nellie Dixon, 7 July 1906, St Matthew's, Upper Clapton. **Subject(s):** Natural Sciences; BA 1903; BChir 1906; MB 1906. **Tutor(s):** J E Sandys. **Educ:** Harris Institute, Preston; St John's College, Battersea. **Career:** Surgeon, Barry Accident and Surgery Hospital 1934–1941; Medical Officer, London Terminal Aerodrome, Croydon 1936. **Publications:** *Yellow Fever and Aircraft*. Died 3 March 1951.

DRAPER, Philip Johnson (1940) Born 16 August 1921, School House, Martin, Lincolnshire; son of Sydney Harold Draper, Schoolmaster, and Elsie Johnson. **Educ:** Stamford School. **Career:** Captain, RE 1940–1944. **Awards:** Marquess of Exeter Exhibition, SJC. Died 6 June 1944 (killed in action in Normandy).

DRAYSON, Harold Percy (1925) Born 19 March 1905, 74 Marlborough Mansions, Hampstead, Middlesex; son of Alfred Percy Drayson, Diamond Merchant, and Dorothy Frances Johns; m Renee Lecoq, 7 June 1945, Paris. **Tutor(s):** J M Wordie. **Educ:** Wellington College; RMA, Woolwich.

DRAYTON, William John (1928) Born 3 September 1910, 51 Old Tiverton Road, Exeter, Devon; son of Henry Godwin Drayton, Master Bookseller, and Emma Rose Hetty Brealy. BA 1931. **Tutor(s):** C W Guillebaud. **Educ:** Norwood School, Pennsylvania, Exeter; Exeter School. **Awards:** Vidal Exhibition, SJC 1928.

DRESSLER, Patrick Edward (1945) Born 30 May 1924, Huntington, Indiana, USA; son of Edward Earl Dressler, Auditor, and Ann Frances Yochem. **Tutor(s):** C W Guillebaud. **Educ:** Harvard University. **Career:** Sergeant, US Army.

DREVER, Professor Harald Irving (1934) Born 17 March 1912, Edinburgh; son of James Drever, Professor of Psychology, and Annie May Watson. **Subject(s):** Geology; PhD 1938. **Tutor(s):** J M Wordie. **Johnian Relatives:** brother of James Drever (1932); uncle of James Irving Drever (1961). **Educ:** Gullane School; Royal High School, Edinburgh; University of Edinburgh. **Career:** Senior Lecturer in Geology, Professor of Geology, University of St Andrews. Died 4 October 1975.

DREVER, Professor James (1932) Born 29 January 1910, Edinburgh; son of James Drever, Professor of Psychology, and Annie May Watson; m Joan Isobel Mackay Budge; 1 son (James Irving), 1 daughter (Alison Irving). **Subject(s):** Moral Sciences; BA 1934; MA 1958; MA (Edinburgh) 1932. **Tutor(s):** J S Boys Smith. **Johnian Relatives:** brother of Harald Irving Drever (1934); father of James Irving Drever (1961). **Educ:** Royal High School, Edinburgh; University of Edinburgh. **Career:** Assistant in Philosophy, University of Edinburgh; Lecturer, Newcastle University; RN; Professor of Psychology, University of Edinburgh 1944; Principal and Vice Chancellor, Dundee University 1964–1978. **Appointments:** Editor, *British Journal of Psychology* until 1961; President, BPsS 1960–1961; Member, Committee on Higher Education (the Robbins Committee). Died 5 November 1991.

DREWE, Brian Sydney (1932) Born 21 August 1914, 14 Merivale Road, Harrow; son of William Sydney Drewe, Manager to a Music Publisher, and Florence Jane Lake. **Subject(s):** English; BA 1935; MA 1939; LLB (London); FTCL; ARCM; LRAM. **Tutor(s):** J S Boys Smith. **Educ:** London County Council School, North Kensington; Christ's Hospital, Horsham. **Career:** Fellow, Trinity College of Music, London; Secretary, Charing Cross Hospital Medical School. **Appointments:** JP. **Awards:** Choral Scholarship, SJC. **Honours:** ERD; TD. Died 24 July 1990.

DRINKWATER, Allen Paul (1928) Born 8 February 1909, Rothay, 31 Derby Road, Tolworth, Surbiton, Surrey; son of Paul Drinkwater, Member, London Stock Exchange, and Margaret Anna Allen; m Peggy Blewett. **Subject(s):** Natural Sciences; BA 1931. **Tutor(s):** C W Guillebaud. **Educ:** Clayesmore School, Winchester. **Career:** Lieutenant, Educational Adviser, RNVR. Died 18 February 1945 (killed on active service at Lagos while attempting to save life).

DRUCE, Cyril Lemuel (1904) Born 27 April 1883, Church Green, Witney, Oxfordshire; son of Lemuel Druce, Provisions Merchant, and Annie Eva Rowles; m (1) Irene Gladys Ashleigh Smith, 11 April 1921, St Martin in the Fields, (2) Doris. **Subject(s):** Modern and Medieval Languages; BA 1907; MA 1920. **Tutor(s):** D MacAlister. **Educ:** Witney Grammar School; All Saints' School, Bloxham. **Career:** Master, Cambridge County School 1907; Assistant Master, University College School, Hampstead 1920. Died 23 July 1960.

DRUMMOND, John Berney (1914) Born 28 June 1895, 10 Arlington Villas, Kemp Town, Brighton, Sussex; son of Charles Maltby Drummond, of independent means, and Clara Bell. **Subject(s):** Mathematics; BA 1917; MA 1922. **Tutor(s):** L H K Bushe-Fox. **Educ:** Brighton College. **Career:** Sapper, RE 1917–1919; Tutor, General Engineering College, London 1919; Vice-Principal, Windlesham High School, Southern Cross, Brighton. Died 2 September 1937.

DRUMMOND, Octavio Almeida (1946) Born 21 June 1912, Rio de Janeiro, Brazil; son of Henrique Fox Drummond, Engineer, and Maria Moretzhon Almeida. **Tutor(s):** G C L Bertram. **Educ:** Colegio Baptista, Rio de Janeiro; Gymnasio do Estado, São Paulo; Escola Superior de Agricultura, Minas Geraes.

DRYSDALE, The Revd George Frederick (1902) Born 28 June 1879, Milsey Bank, Crouch Hill, Middlesex; son of George Drysdale, Presbyterian Minister, and Jane Jobbins. BA 1905; MA 1930. **Tutor(s):** D MacAlister. **Educ:** Kurnella School, Bournemouth. **Career:** Ordained Deacon 1911; Ordained Priest 1913; Vicar 1918–1937, Curate 1949–1955, Whitminster. Died 3 March 1962.

DUCE, Dr Alan Godfrey (1944) Born 21 February 1927, 128 Cambridge Street, Leicester; son of Owen Alfred Duce, Inland Revenue Clerk, and Edith Gertrude Heath. **Subject(s):** Natural Sciences; BA 1947; MA 1951; PhD 1951. **Tutor(s):** C W Guillebaud. **Educ:** Derby School; Bemrose School, Derby.

DUCHESNE, Charles Samuel Collier (1919) Born 7 March 1900, Merdon, Surrey Road, Bournemouth; son of Ernest Collier Duchesne, Superintendent, Working Men's College, and Fanny Elizabeth Colman. **Subject(s):** Classics/History; BA 1922; MA 1926. **Tutor(s):** E E Sikes. **Educ:** Highgate Junior School; Letchworth School; Bishop's Stortford College. **Career:** Schoolmaster, Taunton School 1922–1924; Schoolmaster, Chigwell School 1924–1925; Schoolmaster, Bembridge School 1925–1926; Schoolmaster, Eltham College 1926. **Awards:** Exhibition, SJC 1918. Died 15 July 1987.

DUCKWORTH, The Revd Canon John Noel (1946) (admitted to Jesus College 1932) Born 25 December 1912, Swinefleet, Goole, Yorkshire; son of Peter Duckworth, Clerk in Holy Orders, and Mary Gertrude Sumner. **Subject(s):** History; BA 1935 (Jesus); MA 1939 (Jesus). **Johnian Relatives:** godfather of Paul Bratley (1958). **Educ:** Lincoln School; Jesus College, Cambridge; Ridley Hall, Cambridge. **Career:** Ordained Deacon 1936; Curate, Church of the Transfiguration, Newington, Yorkshire 1936–1939; Ordained Priest 1937; Chaplain, Cambridgeshire Regiment, taken prisoner by the Japanese after the fall of Singapore, twice Mentioned in Despatches 1939–1945; Chaplain, SJC 1946–1948; Chaplain and Lecturer in Divinity, Achimota Training College 1948–1951; Senior Warden, Senior Tutor and Dean, University College of the Gold Coast 1948–1951; Canon of Accra 1955–1958; Chaplain, Pocklington School, Yorkshire 1961; Chaplain, Churchill College, Cambridge 1961–1973. Died 24 November 1980.

DUDLEY, Professor Donald Reynolds (1928) Born 3 March 1910, 9 North Street, Smethwick, Staffordshire; son of John Joseph Dudley, Schoolmaster, and Emma Jane Reynolds; m Eryl; adopted daughters (Susan and Mary). **Subject(s):** Classics; BA 1931; MA 1935. **Tutor(s):** M P Charlesworth. **Educ:** King Edward's High School, Birmingham. **Career:** Schoolmaster, Eton College; Title A Fellow, SJC 1935–1937; Lecturer in Classics, Reading University 1937–1944; Director of Extra-Mural Studies 1944, Professor of Latin 1955, Dean of Arts Faculty 1958–1961, University of Birmingham. **Appointments:** Visiting Lecturer, Tulane University, USA 1953; Fellow, Society of Antiquaries of London; Worcester Frereday Fellow, St John's College, Oxford; Bailiff, King Edward's School. **Awards:** Scholarship, SJC; Hare Prize, University of Cambridge 1936. Died 31 August 1972.

DUDLEY, John George (1939) Born 9 October 1920, 40 Upper Fitzwilliam Street, Dublin; son of Harold Benson Dudley, Rubber Planter, and Florence Villiers Kingsley Dobbyn. **Subject(s):** Geography; BA 1942; MA 1946. **Tutor(s):** R L Howland. **Educ:** Rockport, Craigavad, Ireland; Worksop College, Nottingham. **Awards:** Sizarship, SJC.

DUELL, Charles Halliwell (1927) Born 20 July 1905, New Rochelle, New York, USA; son of Holland Sackett Duell, Lawyer, and Mabel Halliwell. **Subject(s):** English. **Tutor(s):** M P Charlesworth. **Educ:** Riversdale County School, New York; The Hotchkiss School, Lakeville; Yale University.

DUFF, William Leslie Gordon (1934) Born 13 July 1916, Chelston, Kilmacolm, Renfrewshire, Scotland; son of Thomas Lawrie Duff, Shipowner, and Margaret Harvey McLachlan; m Helen Fullarton, 10

June 1955; 2 sons (Malcolm b 1957 and Alasdair b 1959). **Subject(s):** Economics; BA 1937; CA 1947. **Tutor(s):** C W Guillebaud. **Educ:** Dardenne Preparatory School, Kilmacolm; Merchiston Castle School, Edinburgh. **Career:** 52nd (Lowland) Infantry Division (Cameronians), served in North-West Europe, Mentioned in Despatches 1941–1946; Accountant, Finance Director, Collins Publishers, Glasgow 1948–1976. **Appointments:** Member of Council, Institute of Chartered Accountants of Scotland 1966–1968.

DUFFIELD, Henry William (1914) Born 22 September 1895, Baghdad, Turkish Arabia; son of Charles Edward Duffield, General Manager, Egyptian Markets, Cairo, and Mary Elizabeth Johnston. **Tutor(s):** E E Sikes. **Educ:** Grenham House, Birchington on Sea; Felsted School. **Career:** Second Lieutenant, Duke of Cornwall's Light Infantry; Captain, MGC, WWI.

DUKES, Dr Maurice Nelson Graham (1948) Born 2 November 1930, 23 Dodworth Road, Barnsley, Yorkshire; son of Joseph Harmer Dukes, Principal, Brierley Hill Technical School, and Iris Davidson; m (1) Matthina Anna Greup, 1956, The Netherlands, (2) Elisabet Helsing, 1988, Norway; (1) 1 son (Michael Gerald Harmer b 1958), 1 daughter (Matthea Johanna Meijnouda b 1962). **Subject(s):** Natural Sciences/Law; BA 1951; MA 1955; LLB 1957; LLM 1985; MRCS LRCP (London) 1955; MD (Leiden) 1963. **Tutor(s):** G C L Bertram. **Educ:** Hill Street School, Stourbridge; King Edward's Grammar School, Stourbridge; University of Leiden. **Career:** Medical Director and Research Director in the Pharmaceutical Industry 1957–1972; Medical Director, Netherlands Board for the Evaluation of Medicines 1972–1982; Regional Officer for Pharmaceuticals, World Health Organisation, Copenhagen 1982–1992; Professor of Drug Policy Science, University of Groningen 1986–1995; Professor of Drug Policy Studies, University of Oslo 1995–. **Honours:** Knight in the Order of Oranje-Nassau (The Netherlands) 2000. **Publications:** Editor in Chief, *Meyler's Side Effects of Drugs*, 1975–; *Side Effects of Drugs Annuals*, 1977–1993; *Responsibility for Drug-Induced Injury*, 1988, 1998; *The Law and Ethics of the Pharmaceutical Industry*, 2004; 300 scientific and legal papers on medicines and drug safety.

DUMAS, Arthur Blair (1913) Born 20 March 1895, Charlton, Kent; son of Robert Dumas, Marine Engineer, and Edith Marriott. **Tutor(s):** R P Gregory. **Educ:** Stafford Grammar School; Sutton Coldfield Grammar School; Daniel Stewart's School, Edinburgh; Berkhamsted School. **Career:** Captain, Royal Warwickshire Regiment.

DUNANT, The Revd Charles Edward (1931) Born 16 August 1911, 71 South Norwood Hill, Croydon, Surrey; son of Edouard Dunant, Stock Exchange Worker, and Dora Elizabeth Mosley. **Subject(s):** Modern and Medieval Languages; BA 1934. **Tutor(s):** J S Boys Smith. **Educ:** Château d'Oex, Switzerland; Vevey College; Dover College Junior School; Dover College; KCL. **Career:** Chaplain, Community of Vienna with Prague and Budapest; Ordained Deacon 1940; Curate, St Saviour, Poplar 1940–1947; Priest, London 1941; Chaplain, RN, HMS *Phoebe* 1947–1950, HMS *Raleigh* 1950–1952; 3rd Commando Brigade, Royal Marines 1952; HMS *Hornet* 1954; Vicar, Holy Trinity Church, North Shields 1962.

DUNCAN, Angus Henry (1949) Born 29 September 1928, 46 Weoley Hill, Selly Oak, Birmingham; son of William Ogilvy Duncan, Chartered Patent Agent and Consulting Engineer, and Agnes Stirling Henry; m Pauline Mary Harding, 1955; 2 daughters (Rachel b 1963 and Celia b 1966). **Subject(s):** Natural/Mechanical Sciences; BA 1952; MA 1956; MIMechE 1956; AMIEE. **Tutor(s):** G C L Bertram. **Educ:** West House School, Edgbaston; Oundle School. **Career:** Trained with Gill, Jennings & Every, Chartered Patent Agents, Chancery Lane, London 1952–1954; Barker, Brettell & Duncan, Chartered Patent Agents, Birmingham 1954–1991 (Chartered Mechanical Engineer 1957–1991, Partner 1957–1988, Senior Partner 1988–1991). **Appointments:** Council Member, Chartered Institute of Patent Agents 1976–1986 (President

1985–1986); Council Member, European Patent Institute 1979–1989 (Vice-President 1985–1989); Member, Smallpeice Trust. **Awards:** Munsteven Exhibition, SJC 1947; Gill Prize 1956. Died 19 December 2001.

DUNCAN, Sir Arthur Bryce (1927) Born 27 August 1909, Newlands, Parish of Kirkmahor, Dumfriesshire, Scotland; son of John Bryce Duncan, Farmer, and Adeline Agnes McKerrow; m Isabel Mary Kennedy-Moffat, 1936. BA 1930. **Tutor(s):** C W Guillebaud. **Educ:** Old College, Windermere; Rugby School. **Career:** Convenor, Dumfriesshire County Council 1961–1968. **Appointments:** Chairman, Nature Conservancy 1953–1961; Deputy Lord Lieutenant 1967–1969; Lord Lieutenant 1969–1970; Chairman, Gallaway Cattle Society of Great Britain and Ireland; President, Royal Smithfield Club. **Honours:** Kt 1961. Died 2 November 1984.

DUNCAN, Cyril John (1935) Born 27 June 1916, 287 Ongar Road, Brentwood, Essex; son of Frank Reuben Duncan, Quartermaster Sergeant, RE, and Bessie Holmes; m 1940; 1 son, 1 daughter. **Subject(s):** Mathematics/Natural Sciences; BA 1938; MA 1950; FRPS 1945; FIOP 1964; FRMS 1948. **Tutor(s):** J M Wordie. **Johnian Relatives:** brother of Frank Alan Duncan (1932). **Educ:** Springleigh House School, Exeter; St John's Hospital, Exeter; Huntingdon Road School, Grantham; St John's, Spitalgate, Grantham; King's School, Grantham. **Career:** Kodak Ltd 1938–1940; RAE, Farnborough 1940–1946; Director, Department of Photography, King's College, Newcastle upon Tyne 1947–1979; Director, Computer Typesetting Project 1965–1970. **Appointments:** National Council for Educational Technology; Council for National Academic Awards. Died 17 February 1979.

DUNCAN, Frank Alan (1932) Born 17 January 1913, 165 Warley Road, Great Warley, Essex; son of Frank Reuben Duncan, Contractor's Agent, and Bessie Holmes; 1 son, 1 daughter. **Subject(s):** Mechanical Sciences; BA 1935; MA 1951; FIMechE; MBIM. **Tutor(s):** J S Boys Smith. **Johnian Relatives:** brother of Cyril John Duncan (1935). **Educ:** The King's School, Grantham. **Career:** British United Shoe Machinery Company, Leicester 1935–1954; Director and General Manager, Mellor Bromleys Ltd 1954; Resident Director, T Grieve & Co Ltd (offshoot of Bentley Engineering Group); Director, Economic Stampings Ltd, Leicester 1958. **Appointments:** President, Leicester Association of Engineers; Vice-Chairman, Engineering Advisory Committee, Leicester College of Technology. **Awards:** Newcome Exhibition, SJC. Died 2 December 1968.

DUNCOMBE, Dr Eliot (1934) Born 30 May 1916, Nassau; son of Frederick Arthur Cyril Duncombe, Civil Servant, and Helen Daphne Rhiannon Eliot; m Joyce H Tucker, 1944; 3 sons. **Subject(s):** Mechanical Sciences; BA 1937; MA 1943; PhD (Pittsburgh) 1965. **Tutor(s):** J S Boys Smith. **Educ:** Convent Preparatory School, Abingdon; King Edward VI School, Stratford-on-Avon; University of Pittsburgh, USA. **Awards:** Scholarship, SJC 1937. Died 16 September 2002.

DUNK, Harry Wormald (1933) Born 3 September 1915, Victoria Crescent, Barnsley; son of Albert Dunk, Master Builder and Public Works Contractor, and Wilhelmina Greenwood Wormald. **Subject(s):** Modern and Medieval Languages; Law; BA 1936; MA 1946. **Tutor(s):** E A Benians. **Educ:** St Mary's, Barnsley; Rossall Preparatory School; Rossall School. **Career:** Articled Solicitor, Rotherham 1936–1939; Second Lieutenant, KOYLI 1939–1945 (Lieutenant 1941, Captain 1944); Admitted Solicitor; Partner, Messers Gichard & Co 1945–1979. Died 2 September 1979.

DUNKERLEY, The Revd Cecil Lawrence (1911) Born 18 January 1892, Welford House, Bakewell, Derbyshire; son of William Herbert Cecil Dunkerley, Clerk in Holy Orders, Archdeacon, and Mary Beatrice Taylor; m Kathleen Olive Pott, 4 January 1922, St Mary's, Great Milton, Oxon; 1 son (David), 1 daughter (Margaret). BA 1914; MA 1921. **Tutor(s):** E E Sikes. **Johnian Relatives:** brother of Lionel Ernest Brooke Dunkerley (1919). **Educ:** Hereford School; Wells Theological College.

Career: Captain, Queen's Own, Royal West Kent Regiment, served in Gallipoli, Egypt and Palestine; attached to the Staff, 3rd Division, 1918; Deputy Assistant Provost Marshal, Egyptian Expeditionary Force 1919; Deacon 1921; Curate, St Mary, Bryanston Square 1921–1924; Priest 1922; Curate, Binfield 1924–1927; Vicar, Laleham 1927–1931; Rector, Iver Heath 1931–1936; Rector, Paulerspury, Northamptonshire 1938–1954; Rector, Collingtree with Courteenhall, Northamptonshire 1954. **Awards:** Somerset Exhibition, SJC. **Honours:** MC at the Battle of Gaza 1917. Died 1 September 1978.

DUNKERLEY, Gerald (1943) Born 19 February 1921, 23 Sycamore Terrace, York; son of Leonard Dunkerley, Engineer's Buyer, and Ethel King; m Pamela. **Subject(s):** Economics; BA 1945; MA 1950. **Tutor(s):** C W Guillebaud. **Educ:** Eboracum Preparatory School, York; Archbishop Holgate's Grammar School, York; Bootham School. **Career:** Head of Engineering Staff Administration, BBC Broadcasting House; Sub-Lieutenant, RNVR, serving on coastal vessels 1939–1943. Died 3 January 1993.

DUNKERLEY, Lionel Ernest Brooke (1919) Born 10 August 1899, Penang, Straits Settlements, Malaysia; son of William Herbert Cecil Dunkerley, Clerk in Holy Orders, and Mary Beatrice Taylor; m Dorothy Elizabeth Louise King, 2 May 1931, St George's, Paris. BA 1922; MA 1928. **Tutor(s):** E E Sikes. **Johnian Relatives:** brother of Cecil Lawrence Dunkerley (1911). **Educ:** The Cathedral School, Hereford. **Career:** No 11 Officer Cadet Battalion, Pirbright 1918–1919; Second Lieutenant, 1919; Assistant District Commissioner, Sierra Leone 1929; District Commissioner, Sierra Leone 1936. **Awards:** Somerset Exhibition, SJC 1918. Died 1 September 1965.

DUNKLEY, Sir Herbert Francis (1905) Born 2 July 1886, Earls Barton, Northamptonshire; son of Charles Dunkley, Boot and Shoe Manufacturer, and Eliza Robinson; m Gwendoline Scott Willows Wilson, 1912 (d 1956). **Subject(s):** Mathematics/Natural Sciences; BA 1908; MA 1920. **Tutor(s):** E E Sikes. **Educ:** The Grammar School, Wellingborough. **Career:** Indian Civil Service; Assistant Commissioner, Burma 1910; Registrar, Chief Court, Lower Burma 1919–1921; District and Sessions Judge 1922; Called to the Bar, Lincoln's Inn 1922; Officiating Registrar, High Court, Rangoon 1926; Acting Judge, High Court, Rangoon 1933.

DUNKLEY, Kenneth Lawrance (1926) Born 21 January 1907, 50 Jalland Street, Hull, Yorkshire; son of John Weightman Dunkley and Sarah Susan Lawrance; m Marjorie; 1 son (Peter). **Subject(s):** Mathematics; BA 1929. **Tutor(s):** J M Wordie. **Educ:** Humber Street School, Hull; Spalding National School; Boulevard Secondary School, Hull; Hymers College, Hull. **Awards:** Scholarship, SJC; Mayhew Prize, University of Cambridge 1929. Died 14 September 1951.

DUNLOP, Andrew Fergus (1919) Born 10 November 1901, 14 Chichele Road, Willesden, Middlesex; son of Andrew Dunlop, East India Merchant, and Isabella Agnes Kinninmont; m Gwendolen Elizabeth Coit, 17 March 1926, Ethical Church, London; 2 sons (Malcolm b 17 February 1927 and Robert b 22 June 1929). BA 1923. **Tutor(s):** B F Armitage. **Johnian Relatives:** brother of John Kinninmont Dunlop (1910); father of Robert Fergus Dunlop (1949). **Educ:** Lady Margaret's School, Willesden Lane, London; Mill Hill School. **Career:** Opera Singer 1934–1939; Major, KRRC, Political Warfare Executive 1942–1945; Director, Visitors' Department, British Council. **Appointments:** Chairman 1962–1976, President 1977–1981, Slough Philharmonic Orchestra. **Honours:** OBE 1957; TD. Died 27 November 1980.

DUNLOP, Sir John Kinninmont (1910) Born 6 April 1892, 14 Chichele Road, Willesden, Middlesex; son of Andrew Dunlop, East India Merchant, and Isabella Agnes Kinninmont; m Agnes Maitland Walker, 19 April 1922, St Oswald's Church, Backford, Cheshire (died 1948); 1 son (John). **Subject(s):** History/Law; BA 1913; MA 1926; PhD (Queen Mary College, London); LLB 1913. **Tutor(s):** J R Tanner. **Johnian**

Relatives: brother of Andrew Fergus Dunlop (1919); uncle of Robert Fergus Dunlop (1949). **Educ:** Mill Hill School. **Career:** Major, Rangers (12th London) MGC, served in France and USA (mentioned three times in dispatches); Commanding Officer, the Rangers 1935–1937; AAG TA, War Office 1937; Regional Commissioner, Italy 1943, Deputy Regional Commissioner, Hamburg 1947–1949, Land Commissioner, Hamburg 1949–1952, HM Consul-General, Hamburg 1952–1956. **Appointments:** Chairman, Anglo-German Association; President, Kent Archeological Society. **Honours:** MC; Order of St Anne of Russia, 4th Class; CMG 1952; KBE 1956. **Publications:** Various on the British Army; *The Pleasant Town of Sevenoaks*, 1964. Died 26 April 1974.

DUNLOP, John Ralph Renton (1937) Born 18 September 1917, 3 Mulberry Walk, Chelsea; son of George Gerald Derne Dunlop, Clerk in Holy Orders, and Ruth Mary Haslam; m Mary Jean Davie, 24 June 1947, Ilminster Parish Church, Somerset; 1 daughter (Jane Virginia). **Subject(s):** Mechanical Sciences; BA 1940; MA 1944. **Tutor(s):** J S Boys Smith. **Educ:** St Ronan's School, Worthing; Forres, Swanage; Bryanston School, Blandford; Ottershaw College, Chertsey. **Career:** Pilot Officer, RAFVR, POW Japan, later Flying Officer, RAF (Technical Engineering Branch) 1940–1945; Service in Singapore 1941–1942; POW, Java and Japan 1942–1945; Engineering Company, Essex 1946–1957; Unigate Transport and Engineering Division (sometime Sectional Chief Transport Engineer) 1958–1982.

DUNLOP, Robert Fergus (1949) Born 22 June 1929, 1 Tor Gardens, Kensington, London; son of Andrew Fergus Dunlop, and Gwendolen Elizabeth Coit; m Jane Clare McManus, 23 September 1966, St James' Church, Horton, Gloucestershire; 1 son (Simon b 18 September 1967), 2 daughters (Kate b 2 August 1969 and Jessica b 28 March 1972). BA 1952; MA 1956; Sloan Fellow, MBA (MIT) 1960; MRAeS; CEng. **Tutor(s):** R L Howland. **Johnian Relatives:** nephew of John Kinninmont Dunlop (1910); son of Andrew Fergus Dunlop (1919). **Educ:** Pinewood School, Farnborough; Marlborough College. **Career:** Second Lieutenant, RA 1947–1949; Flight Lieutenant, 501 Squadron, Royal Auxiliary Air Force 1952–1957; Bristol Aeroplane Company, British Aircraft Corporation, and British Hovercraft Corporation 1952–1970; Lonrho Plc 1970–1994 (Deputy Chairman 1991–1994); Acting Chairman, The Observer Ltd. **Honours:** Air Efficiency Award.

DUNLOP, Sir Thomas (1930) Born 11 April 1912, 20 Queen's Gate, Dowanhill, Partick, Lanarkshire, Scotland; son of Thomas Dunlop, Shipowner, and Mary Elizabeth Beckett; m Adda Mary Alison Smith, 1947; 1 son, 2 daughters. BA 1933; CA. **Tutor(s):** C W Guillebaud. **Johnian Relatives:** brother of William Beckett Dunlop (1933); cousin of Thomas Dunlop Bruce Jones (1938). **Educ:** Kelvinside Academy; Craigflower, Torryburn; Shrewsbury School. **Career:** Chartered Accountant, McClelland Ker & Co 1937–1938; Partner, Thomas Dunlop and Sons, Ship Owners and Insurance Brokers, Glasgow 1938–1986; Major, Royal Signals 1939–1945. **Appointments:** Director, Glasgow & Clyde Shipowners' Association 1950s; Deacon of the Incorporation of Bakers of Glasgow 1955; Governor, Hutchesons' School 1957–1980; Chairman, Trustee Savings Bank of Glasgow 1960s; Executive Committee, Erskine Hospital; Vice President, Royal Alfred Seafarers' Society; Honorary Agent of the Shipwrecked Mariners' Society; Chairman, Underwriters' Association of Glasgow; Director, Merchant's House (and their Representative on the Hutchesons' Educational Trust); Member, Board of Management, Royal Hospital for Sick Children; Chairman, Renfrew Rates Valuation Appeals Commission; Member, Committee of Princess Louise Scottish Hospital, Erskine; Life Member, Royal Clyde Yacht Club; District Commissioner of the Lanark and Renfrew Branch of the Pony Club. **Honours:** Order of St John 1965. Died 18 August 1999.

DUNLOP, William Beckett (1933) Born 6 March 1915, 20 Queens Gate, Dowanhill, Partick, Glasgow; son of Thomas Dunlop, Ship Owner, and Mary Elizabeth Beckett; m Charmian Katherine Chauncy, 22 March 1947. **Subject(s):** Law; BA 1936. **Tutor(s):** C W Guillebaud. **Johnian Relatives:** brother of Thomas Dunlop (1930); cousin of Thomas

Dunlop Bruce Jones (1938). **Educ:** Kelvinside Academy, Glasgow; Craigflower, Torryburn, Scotland; Rugby School. **Career:** Captain, Royal Horse Artillery, WWII. Died 1 January 1960.

DUNN, John Stanley (1919) Born 25 April 1898, 63 Gloucester Street, Pimlico, London; son of John Moulton Dunn, Master Butcher, and Ada Elizabeth Kauffman; m Constance Edith Wade, 10 July 1928, Wesley Church, Cambridge. **Subject(s):** Natural Sciences; BA 1921; MA 1925. **Tutor(s):** E E Sikes. **Educ:** Sir Walter St John's School, Battersea. **Awards:** Dowman Scholarship, SJC 1916. Died 22 April 1967.

DUNN, Professor Peter MacNaughton (1947) Born 23 June 1929, Metchley Abbey, Harborne, Birmingham; son of Naughton Dunn, Orthopaedic Surgeon, and Ethel Violet Jackson, Nurse; m Judy Lunt, 22 July 1961; 2 sons (Robert and John), 1 daughter (Sara). **Subject(s):** Natural Sciences; BA 1950; MA 1955; BChir 1953; MB 1954; MD 1969; DObstRCOG 1958; DCH 1963; MRCP 1974; FRCP 1979; FRCOG 1983; FRCPCH 1996. **Tutor(s):** G C L Bertram. **Johnian Relatives:** uncle of James MacNaughton Stuart (1968). **Educ:** Edgbaston High School; West House School; Marlborough College. **Career:** National Service, RMO Gurkha Rifles, Malaya 1955–1957; Senior Research Fellow, Cardiovascular Research Institute, San Francisco 1966–1967; Director, Academic Neonatal Service 1968–1988, Professor of Perinatal Medicine and Child Health 1987 (Emeritus 1991), University of Bristol. **Appointments:** Consultant, WHO (Health Statistics and Family Health) 1970–1993; Consultant, Task Force on Appropriate Technology for Maternal and Child Health 1982–1995; British Paediatric Representative, European Association of Perinatal Medicine 1972–1984; Member, Scientific Committee 1972–1974, 1978–1982, 1986–1988, 1990–1992, 1994–1996; Chairman, European Association of Perinatal Medicine Working Party on Perinatal Audit 1990–1996; Founder, British Association of Perinatal Medicine 1976; Inaugural President, British Association of Perinatal Medicine 1980–1984; Co-ordinator and Member, International Paediatric Association's Expert Advisory Panel on Perinatology and Neonatology 1977–1983; Chairman, FIGO Committee on Perinatal Epidemiology and Health Statistics 1979–1988 and Member of other FIGO committees including FIGO Ethics in Human Reproduction Committee 1985–2000; Member, Ethics Committee, World Federation of Perinatal Medicine 1999–2002; British Representative, IAMANEH 1986–1994; Founder and Inaugural President, British Society for the History of Paediatrics and Child Health 2002; President, South West Paediatric Club 1988–1990; President, Bristol Medico-Chirurgical Society 1993–1994; President, Bristol Medico-Historical Society 1999–2003. **Awards:** De Snoo-van't Hoogerhuis Medal and Prize, The Netherlands 1983; British Orthopaedic Association Gold Medal 1986; James Spence Medalist 2001 (RCPCH). **Publications:** More than 400 publications on perinatal medicine; co-editor of 12 books; contributor to 123 medical reports.

DUNNICLIFF, Harry (1923) Born 11 November 1903, 76 Wellington Street, Long Eaton, Derbyshire; son of Charles Edwin Dunnicliff, Lace Manufacturer, and Jessie Emma Fullalove. **Subject(s):** Natural Sciences; BA 1926; MA 1930. **Tutor(s):** B F Armitage. **Educ:** Derby Road School, Long Eaton; The High School, Nottingham. **Awards:** Exhibition, SJC 1923.

DUNSTON, Professor Arthur John (1947) Born 17 January 1922, Dellwood, Liebenrood Road, Reading, Berkshire; son of Frederick Arthur Dunston, Hardware Salesman, and Lilian Grace Avery; m (1) Margaret Barr Watson, 1 March 1944, (2) Lynette Meryl McAuley, 1 December 1961; 1 son (Colin b 28 August 1948), 1 daughter (Cynthia b 1 April 1951). **Subject(s):** Classics; BA 1949; MA 1953; BA (Reading) 1947. **Tutor(s):** R L Howland. **Educ:** Reading School; Reading University. **Career:** Lieutenant, Queen's Royal Regiment, WWII; Assistant Lecturer, UCL 1949–1951; Lecturer in Classics, Reading University 1951–1953; Professor of Latin 1953–1986 (Emeritus 1986–2000), Deputy Vice-Chancellor 1982–1986, University of Sydney. **Awards:** Cavaliere nell'Ordine al merito della Repubblica Italiana. Died 5 February 2000.

DUPONT, Jack Norman (1938) Born 10 December 1919, Fairmount, Marine Parade, Saltburn; son of Alfred Norman Dupont, Company Director, and Rachel Evelyn Puckrin. **Subject(s):** History; BA 1941; MA 1945. **Tutor(s):** J S Boys Smith. **Educ:** St Aubyn's, Woodford Green; Claremont School, Hove; Bishop's Stortford College. Died March 1979.

DURANT, William Maitland (1908) Born 14 August 1889, Hadleigh, Suffolk; son of William Friend Durant, Congregational Minister, and Mary Handyside Young; m Olive. **Subject(s):** History; BA 1911; MA 1925; LLB 1913. **Tutor(s):** J R Tanner. **Educ:** Mill Hill School. **Career:** MGC, First East Gloucestershire Regiment, France; Admitted Solicitor 1919. Died 25 July 1948.

DURBIN, Professor James (1942) Born 30 June 1923, 9 Lacey Street, Widnes, Lancashire; son of George William Durbin and Lucy Winefrid Coffey; m Anne Dearnley Outhwaite, 1958; 2 sons, 1 daughter. **Subject(s):** Mathematics; BA 1947; MA 1949; Diploma in Mathematical Statistics 1948; Doctor *Honoris Causa* (National University of Tucuman, Argentina) 2001; FIMS 1958; FBA 2001. **Tutor(s):** S J Bailey; J M Wordie. **Johnian Relatives:** father of Richard Michael Durbin (1979). **Educ:** Wade Deacon Grammar School, Widnes. **Career:** Army Operational Research Group 1943–1945; Boot and Shoe Trade Research Association 1945–1947; Department of Applied Economics, University of Cambridge 1948–1949; Assistant Lecturer, then Lecturer in Statistics 1950–1953, Reader in Statistics 1953–1961, Professor of Statistics 1961–1988 (Emeritus 1988), LSE. **Appointments:** Visiting Professor, University of North Carolina 1959–1960, Stanford University 1960, University of Wisconsin 1965, Johns Hopkins University 1965–1966, University of Washington 1966, ANU 1970–1971, University of California, Berkeley 1971, University of Cape Town 1978, UCLA 1984, University of California, Santa Barbara 1989, National University of Singapore 1989–1990, University of Trento, Italy 1991, Ohio State University 1993; Member, International Statistical Institute 1955 (President 1983–1985, Honorary Member 1999); Fellow, American Statistical Association 1960 (Board of Directors 1980–1982); Research Fellow, US Bureau of the Census 1992; Statistics Canada 1994; Moscow Academy of Sciences 1995; Statistics NZ 1997; Member, ESRC 1983–1986 (Chairman, Research Resources and Methods Committee 1982–1985); Fellow, Econometric Society 1967; Vice President 1969–1970 and 1972–1973, President 1986–1987, Royal Statistical Society. **Awards:** Guy Medal in Bronze 1966, in Silver 1976. **Publications:** *Distribution Theory for Tests based on the Sample Distribution Function*, 1973; (with S J Koopman) *Time Series Analysis by State Space Methods*, 2001; articles in statistical journals, including *Biometrika*, and the *Journal of the Royal Statistical Society*.

DURHAM, Peter Walter (1935) Born 30 January 1917, Yew Trees, Bolsterstone, Sheffield; son of John Durham, Municipal Accountant, and Jennie Holt. **Subject(s):** Economics/Law; BA 1938. **Tutor(s):** C W Guillebaud. **Educ:** Preparatory Schools; Repton School. **Career:** Captain, Royal Tank Regiment 1939–1942. Died 24 October 1942 (killed in action at El Alamein).

DURLEY, Thomas Clifford (1923) Born 8 May 1904, 36 Peel Street, Sculcoates, Hull, Yorkshire; son of Clifford Hall Durley, Engineer, and Hannah Elizabeth Hornsby; m Mollie; 1 son (Richard), 2 daughters (Julia and Angela). **Subject(s):** Mathematics/Mechanical Sciences; BA 1926. **Tutor(s):** J M Wordie. **Educ:** Newland Avenue School, Hull; Eton House Preparatory School, Hull; Hymers College, Hull. **Career:** Trussed Concrete Steel Company 1937; Reinforced Concrete Steel Company 1952; Durley, Hill and Partners 1959. **Awards:** Exhibition, SJC. Died 27 February 1964.

DUTTA, Indu Bhushan (1901) Born 11 May 1882, Comilla, Tipperah District, Bengal, India; son of Kailas Chandra Dutta, Vakeel of High Court, Bengal. **Tutor(s):** C E Graves; J R Tanner. **Educ:** Presidency College, Calcutta University.

DUTTON, Harold (1907) Born 1 June 1888, Fearnhead, Warrington, Lancashire; son of Henry Hewitt Dutton, Estate Agent and Insurance Inspector, and Beatrice Thornton; m Marjorie Youatt; 1 son (James Edward b 2 February 1934). **Subject(s):** Classics/History; BA 1910; LLB 1911. **Tutor(s):** E E Sikes. **Johnian Relatives:** father of James Edward Dutton (1952). **Educ:** The Grammar School, Warrington. **Career:** Lieutenant, North Staffordshire Regiment and MGC, WWI; Farmer. Died 24 May 1977.

DYER, The Revd Charles Henry (1903) Born 25 October 1876, Tokyo, Japan; son of Henry Dyer, Engineer, and Mary Euphemie Aquart Ferguson; m (1) Beatrix Ada Warwick, 7 October 1908 (d 1928), (2) Margaret Amelia Paisley (née Brownlee) 24 June 1921 (d 1941). BA 1905; MA 1910; MA (Glasgow) 1899. **Tutor(s):** D MacAlister. **Educ:** Glasgow University; Edinburgh Theological College. **Career:** Ordained Deacon 1901; Curate, St Andrew's, Glasgow 1901–1903; Ordained Priest 1902; Curate, All Saints, Cambridge 1903–1904; Curate, St Andrew's, Chesterton 1908–1912; Curate, St Ninian's, Glasgow 1908–1912; Curate, Leyland 1913–1917; Vicar, Whittle-le-Woods, Lancashire 1917–1923; Vicar, Great Wilbraham 1923–1929; Permission to Officiate, Diocese of Ely 1929. Died 16 September 1950.

DYKE MARSH, Henry St George (1914) Born 30 November 1894, 8 Castle Yard, Windsor Castle; son of Henry Dyke Marsh, Major, Military Knight of Windsor, and Edith Macan. **Tutor(s):** L H K Bushe-Fox. **Educ:** Scaitcliffe School; Wellington College. **Career:** Sapper, RE (Meteorological Section), WWI. **Awards:** Exhibition, SJC.

DYMOND, Edmund Gilbert (1918) Born 30 July 1900, Maisydderwen, Hirwain, Aberdare; son of Edmund Robert Dymond, Civil Engineer, and Dorothy Emma Harris; m Alice More, 17 December 1927, Princeton, USA. **Subject(s):** Natural Sciences; BA 1921; MA 1926. **Tutor(s):** E E Sikes. **Educ:** Packwood Haugh, Hockley Heath. **Career:** Title A Fellow, SJC 1925–1931; Demonstrator in Physics, University of Cambridge 1927–1931; Lecturer in Physics 1932–1948, Reader in Physics 1948–1952, Department of Natural Philosophy, University of Edinburgh; Kew Observatory, developing and perfecting the British Radiosonde 1939–1945. **Appointments:** International Education Board Fellowship to Göttingen and Princeton 1924–1925; Supervisor, SJC 1926–1931. Died 26 October 1952.

DYNES, Max Russell (1919) Born 31 December 1892, Moorefield, Ontario, Canada; son of Edward Dynes, Conveyancer and Municipal Clerk, and Lizzie Boothe. **Subject(s):** Economics; BA 1922. **Tutor(s):** E A Benians. **Educ:** Public School, Moorefield, Ontario, Canada; High School, Drayton, Ontario, Canada; Moose Jaw Normal School, Saskatchewan, Canada. **Career:** Private, 229th Ontario Battalion, Canadian Forces, promoted to Physical Training Staff 1917; RFC 1917–1918; Second Lieutenant, RAF 1918; 29th Wing, RAF, 58th Training Defence Squadron, Cranwell, Lincolnshire 1919.

DYSON, Dr Alan (1938) Born 29 May 1920, 124 York Drive, Glasgow; son of Fred Dyson, Lecturer, Imperial College, and Winifred Gertrude Greenwood; m Wendy; 1 son (Peter), 1 daughter (Pauline). **Subject(s):** Mathematics; BA 1941; MA 1945; ScD 1978. **Tutor(s):** J M Wordie. **Educ:** Blakesley House School; Rutlish School, Merton. **Awards:** College Prize, SJC 1939. Died 11 January 1989.

E

EAGLES, Frank Mortimer (1921) Born 27 September 1902, 122 Kyrle Road, Battersea, London; son of Edwin Mortimer Eagles, Headmaster, and Cecilia Eliza Borchardt; m Lily Constance Clarke, 1 January 1927, St Stephen's Bush Hill Park, Enfield; 2 sons (Peter Mortimer b 23 April 1931 and David Mortimer b 27 May 1935), 2 daughters (Sheila Margaret b 17 May 1928 and Anne Constance b 25 May 1944). **Subject(s):** Natural Sciences; BA 1924; MA 1928; KCL 1925. **Tutor(s):** B F Armitage. **Johnian Relatives:** son of Edwin Mortimer Eagles (1881); brother of

Jack Mortimer Eagles (1919); father of Peter Mortimer Eagles (1950), and of David Mortimer Eagles (1953); grandfather of Michael Eagles (1977). **Educ:** The Grammar School, Enfield. **Career:** Ordained Deacon 1926; Curate, Christ Church, Hoxton 1926–1930; Ordained Priest 1927; Head, Maurice Hostel (the College Mission) 1927–1930; Curate, St Paul, Winchmore Hill 1930–1932; Minister, South Whitchurch, Edgware 1932–1936; Vicar, St Michael and All Angels, Enfield 1936–1944; Rector, Murston, Kent 1944–1954; Vicar, Pulloxhill with Flitton, Bedfordshire 1954. Died 9 August 1960.

EAGLES, Jack Mortimer (1919) Born 16 July 1898, 34 Sotheby Road, Islington, London; son of Edwin Mortimer Eagles, Schoolmaster, and Cecilia Eliza Borchardt; m Margery Moxon, 14 August 1923. **Subjects:** Mathematics/Natural Sciences. **Tutor(s):** E A Benians. **Johnian Relatives:** son of Edwin Mortimer Eagles (1891); brother of Frank Mortimer Eagles (1921); uncle of Peter Mortimer Eagles (1950), and of David Mortimer Eagles (1953); great uncle of Michael Eagles (1977). **Educ:** Battersea Grammar School; Enfield Grammar School; Northampton Institute, University of London. **Career:** No 13 Officers Cadet Battalion, Newmarket 1917; Second Lieutenant, 3rd Battalion, attached to 11th Battalion, The Queen's Regiment, served in Italy and France 1917–1918; Assistant Master, Sedbergh School 1922–1944; Headmaster, Marling School, Stroud. Died 2 April 1953.

EARL, Lionel Richard Franklyn (1926) Born 17 May 1907, 48 Hillside Road, Streatham, Surrey; son of Edward Franklyn Earl, Civil Servant, and Winifred Jane. **Subject(s):** Classics; BA 1929. **Tutor(s):** M P Charlesworth. **Educ:** Limes Preparatory School, Croydon; Oakham School. **Awards:** Scholarship, SJC. Died 23 September 1986.

EARLE, Francis John Wansford (1935) Born 17 October 1916, The Vicarage, Wansford, East Yorkshire; son of Albert Earle, Clerk in Holy Orders, and Grace Emily Middleton. **Subject(s):** Theology/Law; BA 1938; MA 1946. **Tutor(s):** J S Boys Smith. **Educ:** Orleton Preparatory School, Scarborough; Repton School. **Career:** War service, POW Italy, WWII.

EARLE, Sir George Foster (1908) Born 8 February 1890, Newgate House, Cottingham, Hull; son of John Hudson Earle, Cement Manufacturer, and Alice Edith Bainbridge; m (1) George Daphne Fitzgeorge, St Peter's, Eaton Square, 9 December 1915, (2) Margery Schroder, 1931. **Tutor(s):** L H K Bushe-Fox. **Johnian Relatives:** second cousin of Maxwell Jackson (1882); cousin of Ronald Emerson Maxwell Jackson (1920) and of Myles Allen Maxwell Jackson (1926). **Educ:** Thornhaugh Preparatory School, Swanage; Harrow School, Middlesex. **Career:** Secretary and Director, G & T Earle Ltd, Hull 1914; Lieutenant, RASC, France, WWI; 13th Hussars, Mesopotamia, WWI; Director, British Portland Cement Manufacturers Ltd 1922 (Managing Director 1937); Chairman, Managing Director, Associated Portland Cement Manufacturers and British Portland Cement Manufacturers 1956. **Appointments:** Vice President, Institute of Directors 1954; President, Aims of Industry 1954. **Honours:** CBE 1951; Kt 1954. Died 11 December 1965.

EARLE, Thomas Jeffrey (1938) Born 2 October 1919, Mersham Bitterne; son of Francis William Earle, Lieutenant Colonel, and Marie Blanche Lyne Stivens. **Tutor(s):** J M Wordie. **Educ:** The Hall, Hampstead; Winchester College. **Career:** Sub-Lieutenant, RNVR 1939–1940. Died 8 June 1940 (killed in action in HMS *Glorious*).

EARNSHAW, Dr David Anthony (1949) Born 28 December 1930, Niddamoor, Old Lees Road, Hebden Bridge, Yorkshire; son of Harry Earnshaw, Accountant and Secretary, and Amy Bramley; m Gillian Jane Cook. **Subject(s):** Natural Sciences; BA 1952; MA 1958; MB 1955; BChir 1955; FRCGP. **Tutor(s):** G C L Bertram. **Educ:** New School, Halifax; Heath Grammar School, Halifax. **Career:** General Medical Practitioner, Earl Shilton, Leicester 1960–1989. **Appointments:** Fellow, BMA; Council Member, BMA 1987–1989.

EARP, Dr John Rosslyn (1910) Born 5 September 1891, Riber, Matlock, Derbyshire; son of John Oswald Earp, Forage Merchant, and Catherine Lavinia Hands; m Kathleen M Goodliffe; 4 children. BA 1913; MA 1920; MRCS; LRCP 1917. **Tutor(s):** E E Sikes. **Johnian Relatives:** brother of Freeling Oswald Millns Earp (1912). **Educ:** Riber Castle, Matlock; Kingsmead School, Hoylake; Bridlington Grammar School. **Career:** Director of Health, New Mexico State, USA; Assistant Resident Medical Officer, City of London Chest Hospital, Victoria Park; Anglo-Belgian Ambulance, WWI; Medical Journalist, London and Geneva; Director, Division of Public Health, New York 1937. **Awards:** Silver Medal, Hygiene and Public Health; Mons Medal. **Publications:** 'The Student who Smokes'; 'Tobacco, Health and Efficiency', *Lancet*, 1925; 'Letters from France', *The Eagle*, 39. Died 19 May 1941.

EARP, Freeling Oswald Millns (1912) Born 30 December 1892, Riber, Matlock, Derbyshire; son of John Oswald Earp, Wool Stapler, and Catherine Lavinia Hands. **Subject(s):** Natural Sciences; BA 1915. **Tutor(s):** E E Sikes. **Johnian Relatives:** brother of John Rosslyn Earp (1910). **Educ:** Riber Castle School; Kingsmead School, Hoylake; Bridlington Grammar School. **Career:** Science Master, Westminster School 1919–1949. Died 4 January 1964.

EASON, Thomas William (1935) Born 16 March 1916, 153 Wingrove Avenue, Newcastle upon Tyne; son of James Eason, Building Contractor, and Georgina Mark Forster Farbridge; m 1947; 1 daughter. **Subject(s):** Modern and Medieval Languages (French/German); BA 1938; MA 1945; DipEd (London); CertEd (London). **Tutor(s):** C W Guillebaud. **Educ:** Wingrove Council School, Newcastle; Royal Grammar School, Newcastle. **Career:** Hanseatic Scholar, Universities of Hamburg and Göttingen 1938–1940; Teacher, Midhurst Grammar School 1940; Army Service, France and England 1940–1941; 8th Army 1942–1945; Intelligence Officer, BAOR 1945–1947; Head of Modern Languages, College of St Mark and St John, Chelsea 1947–1954; Headmaster, Primary School, Friskney, Lincolnshire 1954–1959; in charge of Secondary Teacher-training Course, Edge Hill College, Ormskirk, Lancashire 1959–1965; Research for Ministry of Education, Institute of Education, University of London 1965–1971; Research, Edge Hill College 1971–1981. **Appointments:** Member, Lincoln Diocesan Education Committee; Chairman, Friends of the Arvon Foundation; Chairman, Arvon Centres Ltd. **Awards:** Exhibition, SJC 1935–1938; Strathcona Travel Exhibition, SJC 1937; Goldsmiths' Travelling Award 1937, for the study of baroque architecture. **Publications:** poems in *The Eagle*, *Poetry Chicago* and elsewhere; journal articles/research reports on educational philosophy and teacher training.

EASTEN, Guthrie Philip (1928) Born 4 August 1909, Arcola, Saskatchewan, Canada; son of Jon Atkins Easten, Clerk in Holy Orders, and Nora Ethel Attlee; m Margaret L Peat, 30 August 1938 (d 1996). **Subject(s):** Mechanical Sciences; BA 1931; MA 1935; MIEE; CEng. **Tutor(s):** J M Wordie. **Johnian Relatives:** nephew of John Attlee (1886), Bartram Waller Attlee (1887) and of Wilfrid Henry Waller Attlee (1894); cousin of Wilfrid Ormiston Attlee (1936). **Educ:** Radnor School, Redhill; Nevill House School, Eastbourne; St Peter's School, York. **Career:** Engineer and Physicist, Ferranti Ltd, Manchester 1931–1935; Admiralty, later Ministry of Defence, London 1935–1939; Royal Naval Scientific Service 1935–1969; Ministry of Defence, Bath 1939–1944, Teddington 1944–1953, Portsmouth 1953–1969. **Appointments:** Master, University of Cambridge Guild of Change Ringers 1929–1930; Honorary Secretary, LMBC 1930–1931. **Awards:** Sizarship, SJC 1928. Died 27 March 2001.

EASTICK, Bernard Charles Douglas (1935) Born 1 December 1916, Malford Lodge, Malford Road, Snaresbrook, Essex; son of Frederick Charles Eastick, Sugar Refiner, and Clarisse Elvira Smith; m Myra Hall, December 1941 (d January 2000); 1 son, 2 daughters. **Tutor(s):** J M Wordie. **Johnian Relatives:** son of Frederick Charles Eastick (1908); nephew of Douglas Martineau Eastick (1924). **Educ:** Yardley Court School, Tonbridge; Tonbridge School. **Career:** Sugar Refiner;

Commissioned 4th Battalion, Royal Berkshire Regiment 1936; 8th Army, France, North Africa and Italy 1939–1946 (Mentioned in Despatches 1945). **Appointments:** Member, Leander Club; Member, Hawks Club; Royal Channel Islands Yacht Club; Liveryman, Grocers' Company; Société Jersiaise; National Trust for Jersey; International Camellia Society; Freeman, City of London, June 1939. **Awards:** Winner of Wyfold Challenge Cup, Henley Royal Regatta 1939. **Honours:** MBE 1946; TD 1950.

EASTICK, Douglas Martineau (1924) Born 11 September 1905, 63 Preston Road, Leytonstone, Essex; son of Charles Esau Eastick, Analytical Chemist, and Elvina Rosa Duling. **Tutor(s):** B F Armitage. **Johnian Relatives:** brother of Frederick Charles Eastick (1908); uncle of Bernard Charles Douglas Eastick (1935). **Educ:** Holyrood School, Bognor; Uppingham School. Died 25 November 1957.

EASTICK, Frederick Charles (1908) Born 23 September 1889, Farimount, High Road, Leyton, Essex; son of Charles Esau Eastick, Analytical Chemist, and Elvina Rosa Duling; m Clarissa Elvira; 1 son (Bernard Charles Douglas b 1 December 1916). **Subject(s):** Natural Sciences; BA 1911; MA 1915. **Tutor(s):** J R Tanner. **Johnian Relatives:** brother of Douglas Martineau Eastick (1924); father of Bernard Charles Douglas Eastick (1935). **Educ:** Chigwell School. **Career:** Sugar Refiner. Died 15 August 1970.

EASTMAN, Hugh Leonard (1946) Born 11 March 1926, 34 Chip Hill Road, Bolton, Lancashire; son of Alec Charles Eastman, Congregational Minister, and Muriel Clara Cook. **Subject(s):** Natural Sciences; BA 1948; MA 1954. **Tutor(s):** G C L Bertram. **Educ:** Thundersley Council School, Essex; Caterham School, Surrey. **Career:** Chartered Patent Agent.

EASTON, The Revd Frank Reginald James (1902) Born 20 March 1883, 31 Noel Street, Hyson Green, Basford, Nottinghamshire; son of James George Easton, Clerk in Holy Orders, and Mary Ann Merrick; m Winifred Hastings Baylis, 2 July 1914, West Wickham. BA 1905; MA 1909. **Tutor(s):** C E Graves; J R Tanner. **Johnian Relatives:** son of James George Easton (1872); brother of James William Easton (1906). **Educ:** Queen Elizabeth's Grammar School, Faversham. **Career:** Ordained Deacon 1907; Ordained Priest 1909; Vicar, St Luke, Cleckheaton 1919–1928; Rector, Stoke Prior, and Vicar, Docklow 1928–1936; Vicar, Long Grove, Herefordshire 1936–1942. Died 1942.

EASTON, James William (1906) Born 30 December 1886, Great Yarmouth, Norfolk; son of James George Easton, Clerk in Holy Orders, and Mary Ann Merrick; 1 daughter. BA 1909; MA 1913. **Tutor(s):** J R Tanner. **Johnian Relatives:** son of James George Easton (1872); brother of Frank Reginald James Easton (1902). **Educ:** Faversham Grammar School. **Career:** Schoolmaster, Connaught House Preparatory School 1910–1915; Lieutenant, RGA, WWI; Hendon County School 1920–1947. Died 25 August 1966.

EBERHART, Professor Richard Ghormley (1927) Born 5 April 1904, Austin, Mower County, Minnesota, USA; son of Alpha La Rue Eberhart, Secretary to a Packing House, and Lena Lowenstein; m Helen Elizabeth Butcher, 29 August 1941; 1 son (Richard Butcher), 1 daughter (Margaret). **Subject(s):** English; BA 1929; MA 1933; BA (Dartmouth) 1926; Honorary LittD (Dartmouth) 1954; Honorary LittD (Skidmore) 1966; Honorary LittD (Wooster) 1969; Honorary LittD (Colgate) 1974; Honorary DHL (Franklin Pierce) 1978; Honorary LittD (St Lawrence) 1985. **Tutor(s):** M P Charlesworth. **Educ:** Austin High School, Minnesota, USA; Dartmouth College, Hanover, USA; University of Minnesota, Minneapolis, USA. **Career:** Tutor to son of King Prajadhipok of Siam; Assistant Manager (later Vice-President and Member, Board of Directors), Butcher Polish Company, Boston, Massachusetts; English Teacher, St Mark's School, Southborough, Massachusetts 1933–1941; Teacher, Cambridge School, Kendall Green, Massachusetts 1941–1944; Lieutenant Commander, USN Reserve 1942–1946; Poet in Residence and Visiting Professor, University of

Washington 1952–1953; Professor, University of Connecticut 1953–1954; Poet in Residence and Visiting Professor of English, Wheaton College 1954–1955; Resident Fellow (Professor), Creative Writing and Christian Gauss Lecturer, Princeton 1955–1956; Professor of English and Poet in Residence at Dartmouth College 1956. **Appointments:** Founder, Poets' Theatre Inc, Cambridge, Massachusetts 1950; Advisory Committee on the Arts, National Cultural Center (later John F Kennedy Memorial Center), Washington 1959; Member, American Academy and Institute of Arts and Letters 1960; Elliston Lecturer on Poetry, University of Cincinnati 1961; Honorary Consultant in American Letters, The Library of Congress 1963–1969; Member, National Academy of Arts and Sciences 1967; Fellow, Academy of American Poets 1969; Honorary Member, Alpha Chapter, Massachusetts 1967; Visiting Professor, University of Washington 1967 and 1972; Honorary President, Poetry Society of America 1972; Participant, Poetry International, London 1973; Distinguished Visiting Professor, Florida University 1974; Visiting Professor Columbia University 1975; Regents Professor, University of California, Davis 1975; First Wallace Stevens Fellow, Timothy Dwight College, Yale 1976; Poet Laureate, New Hampshire 1979–1984; World Academy of Arts and Culture, Republic of China 1981; Member, American Academy of Arts and Letters 1982; Exhibition, Dartmouth College Library 1984; Honorary Fellow, SJC 1986; International Poets Academy, Madras, India 1987. **Awards:** President's Medallion, Florida University 1977; Shelley Memorial Prize; Robert Frost Medal, Poetry Society of America 1986; Sarah Josepha Hale Award, Richards Library, Newport, New Hampshire 1982; Pulitzer Prize 1966; New York Quarterly Poetry Day Award 1980; National Book Award 1977; Bollingen Prize 1962. **Publications:** *A Bravery of Earth*, 1930; *Reading the Spirit*, 1936; *Selected Poems*, 1951; *Undercliff: Poems, 1946–1953*, Chatto and Windus, 1953; *Great Praises*, 1957; *Collected Poems, 1930–1960*; *Collected Verse Plays*, 1962; *The Quarry*, 1964; *Selected Poems, 1930–1965, New Directions*, 1965; *Thirty One Sonnets*, 1967; *Shifts of Being*, 1968; *Fields of Grace*, 1972 (National Book Award nominee 1973); *Poems to Poets*, 1975; *Collected Poems 1930–1976*, 1976; *Collected Poems 1930–86*, 1988; *To Eberhart from Ginsberg: a letter about 'Howl'*, 1956, 1976; *Of Poetry and Poets* (criticism), 1979; *Ways of Light*, 1980; *Survivors*, 1980; *Four Poems*, 1980; *New Hampshire/Nine Poems*, 1980; *Chocorua*, 1981; *Florida Poems*, 1981; *The Long Reach*, 1984; *Maine Poems*, 1989; *New and Collected Poems*, 1990; *Recorded Readings of his Poetry*, 1961, 1968.

EBERLIE, Dr (Wilhelm, later William) Felix (1910) Born 3 March 1892, 7 Beresford Terrace, Islington, Middlesex; son of Johann Jakob Eberli, Insurance Agent, and Harriette Ada Lucy Perryman; m Winifred Maud Spinks, 19 July 1917, St Mary's Church, Harrogate (d 4 April 1968); 2 sons ((William) John Dymoke b 26 November 1920 and Richard Frere b 28 May 1932), 2 daughters (Elizabeth Mary Frances b 30 January 1922 and Margaret Felicia b 6 March 1929). BA 1913; MB 1922; BChir 1922; MRCS 1916; LRCP 1916. **Tutor(s):** J R Tanner. **Johnian Relatives:** father of (William) John Dymoke Eberlie (1939) and of Richard Frere Eberlie (1953). **Educ:** Sutton Valence School. **Career:** Honorary Medical Officer, Bute Hospital and Children's Hospital, Luton; Surgeon Sub-Lieutenant, RN Volunteer Reserve 1914–1918; St Bartholomew's Hospital 1916; GP, Luton 1922–1959. **Appointments:** President, Bedfordshire Branch, BMA 1939; Member, Bedfordshire Executive Council; Chairman, Local Medical Committee; Luton Borough Council 1946; Chairman, Medical Subcommittee, Luton and Dunstable Hospital 1948–1959. Died 16 February 1986.

EBERLIE, Dr (William) John Dymoke (1939) Born 26 November 1920, 55 Granada Road, Southsea; son of (William) Felix Eberlie, Medical Practitioner, and Winifred Maud Spinks; m Doreen Mary Jewell, 3 September 1949, Totnes, Devon; 2 sons (Peter Dymoke b 1950 and William Michael b 1954), 1 daughter (Susan b 1951). **Subject(s):** Natural Sciences/Medicine; BA 1942; MA 1948; MB 1948; BChir 1948; MRCP 1950; MRCS 1944; LRCP 1944; FRSTM&H 1955. **Tutor(s):** R L Howland. **Johnian Relatives:** son of (Wilhelm, later William) Felix Eberlie (1910); brother of Richard Frere Eberlie (1953). **Educ:** The New

Beacon, Sevenoaks; Sherborne School. **Career:** House Surgeon, St Bartholomew's Hospital and Wellhouse Hospital, Barnet 1942–1944; Surgeon Lieutenant, RNVR, Devonport 1945–1946; Medical Officer, Nyasaland, Nigeria 1952–1960; GP, Norwich 1960–1966; GP, Colborne, Ontario 1966–1986. Died 26 March 1999.

EDDOWES, Dr Alfred Bowman (1919) Born 3 August 1901, 7 Eardley Crescent, Brompton, London; son of Alfred Eddowes, Medical Practitioner, and Ellen Atkin; m Penelope Cynthia Clarke, 29 April 1930, St Mark's, North Audley Street; 2 sons (David b 24 August 1933 and Hugh b 26 February 1936). **Subject(s):** Natural Sciences; BA 1922; MA 1933; MB 1933; BChir 1933. **Tutor(s):** E E Sikes. **Johnian Relatives:** father of Hugh Eddowes (1954). **Career:** St George's Hospital, London; GP, Woodford Green, Essex 1934. **Awards:** Scholarship, SJC 1918. Died 28 January 1993.

EDDY, Lambert Wellington (1934) Born 1 June 1913, 12 Mitchell Hill Terrace, Truro; son of William Lambert Eddy, Schoolmaster, and Marion Pascoe Wellington. **Subject(s):** Mathematics; BA 1937; MA 1941. **Tutor(s):** J M Wordie. **Educ:** Daniell Road Chapel School, Truro; Truro School; University College, Exeter. **Awards:** Exhibition, SJC; Scholarship, SJC 1937. Died 1 January 1950.

EDDY, Spencer (1926) Born 26 May 1907; son of Spencer Eddy, Secretary to the American Embassy in Berlin, and Lurline Elizabeth Spreckels. BA 1929; MA 1933. **Tutor(s):** E A Benians. **Educ:** Private Tuition, Paris; Harrow School; Private Tuition, Pitsen, Essex. **Career:** Investment Business, New York 1943–1945; Military Intelligence 1943–1945.

EDEN, Dr Alfred (1930) Born 24 May 1912, Brook Street, Soham, Cambridge; son of George Eden, Agricultural Workman, and Lillie Pitches; m Eva; 2 sons (Robert and Anthony), 1 daughter (Judy). **Subject(s):** Natural Sciences; BA 1933; MA 1937; PhD 1939; DipAgr 1934; CChem; FRIC; FRSC. **Tutor(s):** C W Guillebaud. **Educ:** Boys' Council School, Soham; The Grammar School, Soham. **Career:** Biochemist, MAFF. **Honours:** ISO. Died 14 April 1986.

EDEN, John Forbes (1947) Born 9 March 1929, Nuwara Eliya, Ceylon; son of Thomas Eden, Scientific Officer, Tea Research Institute, and Eleanor Dundas Harford. **Subject(s):** Law; BA 1950; MA 1967. **Tutor(s):** F Thistlethwaite. **Educ:** Collegiate School of St Peter, Adelaide; Forres School, Swanage. **Career:** Consultant Solicitor.

EDGAR, John David (1935) Born 31 December 1915, Kirkee, Poona, India; son of David Keethoek Edgar, Lieutenant Colonel, RE, and Eva Constance Macnab Miles; m Suzanne Constance Pictor, 15 October 1946; 1 son (Martin), 2 daughters (Virginia and Louise). **Subject(s):** Mechanical Sciences; BA 1937. **Tutor(s):** J S Boys Smith. **Educ:** Tormore School, Deal; Cheltenham College; RMA, Woolwich. **Career:** Captain, RE, then POW, Singapore 1939–1945. **Awards:** Scholarship, SJC 1936–1937; Wright's Prize, SJC 1937. Died 21 June 1964.

EDGAR, Samuel Gairdner Gibson (1919) Born 22 June 1899, The Manse, Milngavie, Dumbartonshire; son of John Edgar, Minister, Church of Scotland, and Eleanor Grant Harper. **Subject(s):** Law; BA 1923; MA 1926. **Tutor(s):** E A Benians. **Educ:** Glasgow Academy; Rossall School, Lancashire. **Career:** The Argyle and Sutherland Highlanders and RAF 1917–1919; Deputy Director and Assistant Editor, Statutory Publications Office, Westminster. **Honours:** CBE 1964. Died 12 November 1991.

EDINGER, John Philip (1921) Born 15 June 1903, The Elms, Station Road, Epping, Essex; son of William Henry Edinger, Civil Engineer, and Hannah Ruth Violet Allen. **Tutor(s):** E Cunningham. **Educ:** Eastbourne College.

EDMONDS, Harold (1902) Born 23 April 1883, 4 The Terrace, Richmond, Surrey; son of Robert Edmonds, Solicitor, and Emma Iredell. BA 1905; MA 1909. **Tutor(s):** C E Graves; J R Tanner. **Educ:**

Stamford School. **Career:** Ordained Deacon 1906; Curate, Aston 1906–1910; Ordained Priest 1907; Curate, Edgbaston 1910–1916. Died 26 July 1916.

EDMONDS, Sydney Arthur (1903) Born 7 January 1881, 55 Albert Road, Morice Town, Devonport, Devon; son of Tobias George Edmonds, RN, and Harriet Melinda Martin. **Tutor(s):** D MacAlister. **Educ:** Stoke Public School, Devonport; Royal College of Science, Dublin.

EDMUNDS, Paul Roberts (1923) Born 18 November 1903, Columbus, Ohio, USA; son of George Edgar Edmunds, in business, and Margaret Roberts. **Tutor(s):** E A Benians. **Educ:** Hill School, Pottsdam, Pennsylvania, USA; Detroit Preparatory School; Princetown Tutoring School, USA.

EDRIDGE-GREEN, Dr Frederick William (1904) Born 14 December 1863, 29 Stock Orchard Crescent, Holloway, Middlesex; son of Thomas Allen Green, China Manufacturer, and Maria Smith; m Minnie Jane Hicks, 1893. MB (Durham) 1887; BS (Durham) 1887; MD (Durham) 1889; MRCS; LRCP 1887; FRCP 1892. **Tutor(s):** D MacAlister. **Educ:** Totteridge Park; Private Tuition; St Bartholomew's Hospital; Durham University. **Career:** Hunterian Professor 1911, Arris and Gale Lecturer 1921–1922, Royal College of Surgeons; Special Adviser on Colour Vision and Eyesight, Board of Trade; Ophthalmic Surgeon to Pensions Board. **Appointments:** Beit Memorial Research Fellow. **Awards:** Thomas Gray Memorial Prize 1936. **Honours:** CBE. **Publications:** *Physiology of Vision*, 1920; *Card Test for Colour Blindness*, 1920; *Cause, Prevention and Cure of Myopia*, 1925; *Science and Pseudo-Science*, 1933. Died 17 April 1953.

EDSALL, John Tileston (1924) Born 3 November 1902, 346 S 16th Street, Philadelphia, Pennsylvania, USA; son of David Linn Edsall, Physician, Dean of Harvard Medical School, and Margaret Harding Tileston. BA (Harvard) 1923; MD (Harvard) 1928. **Tutor(s):** B F Armitage. **Educ:** Milton Academy; Browne and Nichols School, Cambridge, USA; Harvard College; Harvard Medical School. **Career:** Tutor in Biochemistry 1928, Assistant Professor 1932–1938, Associate Professor 1938–1951, Professor 1951, Harvard University; Editor-in-Chief, *Journal of Biological Chemistry* 1958. **Appointments:** J S Guggenheim Memorial Foundation Fellow, California Institute of Technology 1940–1941; Fulbright Lecturer, University of Cambridge 1952; J S Guggenheim Memorial Foundation Fellow, Harvard 1954–1956; Visiting Professor, College de France, Paris 1955; Member, American Chemical Society, American Society of Biological Chemists; Member, American Academy of Arts and Sciences.

EDWARDES, Eric Grant (1918) Born 28 January 1896, Sawston, Cambridge; son of Henry Grant Edwardes, of independent means, and Mary Ellen Lucy Pursell. **Tutor(s):** R P Gregory. **Educ:** St Edmund's College, Ware; Ealing Priory School; Private Tuition, Auckland, New Zealand; University Tutorial College, Red Lion Square, London.

EDWARDS, Anderson Colin Talbot (1927) Born 24 August 1908, The Vicarage, Culgaith, Cumberland; son of John Talbot Edwards, Clerk in Holy Orders, and Ethel Gertrude Smith; m Juliet; 1 son (Vernon), 2 daughters (Joanna and Claire). **Subject(s):** History/Law; BA 1930; MA 1963. **Tutor(s):** E A Benians. **Johnian Relatives:** son of John Talbot Edwards (1886). **Educ:** Lime House, Wetheral, Carlisle; Rossall School. **Career:** Colonial Service, Nigeria and Malawi. Died 7 November 1971.

EDWARDS, Arthur Bertie Duncan (1922) Born 29 April 1898, 151 Commercial Road, Landport, Portsmouth, Hampshire; son of Joseph Arthur Edwards, Manager, Engineering Firm, and Rosa May Duncan. **Tutor(s):** E E Sikes. **Educ:** Portsmouth Secondary School; St George's College, London.

EDWARDS, Dr Arthur Tudor (1908) Born 7 March 1890, 94 Oxford Street, Swansea, Glamorganshire; son of William Edwards, Draper, and Mary Thomas; m Evelyn Imelda Chichester. **Subject(s):** Natural Sciences; BA 1911; MA 1915; MChir (Middlesex) 1913; MRCS; LRCP; FRCS 1915. **Tutor(s):** J R Tanner. **Johnian Relatives:** brother of William Griffith Edwards (1911). **Educ:** Mill Hill School. **Career:** Surgical Registrar, Middlesex Hospital until 1914; Major, RAMC, France 1915–1919; Assistant Surgeon, Westminster Hospital, and Brompton Hospital for Diseases of the Chest; Consultant, King Edward VII's Sanitorium at Midhurst; Consultant, Queen Alexandra's Hospital, Millbank; Civilian Consultant, RAF, and Advisor for Thoracic Casualties for the Ministry of Health. **Appointments:** Honorary Fellow, American Society of Thoracic Surgeons; President, Society of Thoracic Surgeons; Council, Royal College of Surgeons 1943. **Awards:** University Entrance Scholarship; Senior Broderip Scholarship to Middlesex. **Publications:** 'Intrathoric New Growths', *British Journal of Science*, 1927; 'After Results of Surgical Procedure in Cases of Pulmonary Tuberculosis', *British Journal of Science*, 1928; 'Technique of Pulmonary Abcess', *British Journal of Science*, 1929; Articles on chest surgery in Hutchinson and Stevens' *Index of Treatment, and in Medical Annual*. Died 25 August 1946.

EDWARDS, David St John (1937) Born 16 April 1917, Ravenswood Nursing Home, Ilfracombe; son of Herbert Lawrence Edwards, Captain RN, and Eleanore Barnewall O'Hea; m Kathleen Mary Miller, 24 November 1947; 1 son (Simon St John), 2 daughters (Lucinda and Angela). **Subject(s):** Mechanical Sciences; BA 1939; MA 1956. **Tutor(s):** J S Boys Smith. **Educ:** Fernden Preparatory School, Haslemere; Wellington College; RMA Woolwich. **Career:** Second Lieutenant, RE 1937; retired as Lieutenant Colonel 1959; Director, Lep Transport Ltd and subsidiaries 1960–1982.

EDWARDS, Edward John Paul (1941) Born 21 June 1922, Kellacott, Padstow, Cornwall; son of Thomas Smale Edwards, Commander, RN, and Edith Shaw. **Subject(s):** English; BA 1947. **Tutor(s):** C W Guillebaud. **Educ:** Speedwell Preparatory School, New Milton; King Edward VII School, King's Lynn. **Career:** Assistant Master, King's Lynn Grammar School.

EDWARDS, Geoffrey Richard (1910) Born 13 July 1891, 71 Lowth Road, Camberwell, Surrey; son of Richard Edwards, Civil Servant (Savings Bank), and Lucy Rebecca Baskerville; m Margaret Elizabeth Simon, 1924; 2 sons, 1 daughter. **Subject(s):** Mathematics/Natural Sciences; BA 1913; MA 1926. **Tutor(s):** L H K Bushe-Fox. **Johnian Relatives:** father of John Martin Baskerville Edwards (1945). **Educ:** Alleyn's School, Dulwich; St Paul's School, London. **Career:** Imperial Forest Service, India 1913–1916; Pilot, RFC, then Lieutenant (Aeroplane Officer), RAF (wounded, POW) 1916–1920; Pilot, International Aeronautical Commission, Germany 1918–1920; Assistant to the Secretary, National Physical Laboratory, Teddington 1921–1925. **Appointments:** General Secretary, RSM 1925–1951; Honorary Fellow, RSM; Editor, *Catholic Medical Guardian* 1938–1942; Director, Institute of Travel Agents; Governor, St John's School, Apethorpe, Northamptonshire. **Honours:** OBE 1949; Military Cross First Class of Czechoslovakia; Officer of the Order of the Orange Nassau; Commander of the Order of the Crown, Belgium. Died 10 December 1961.

EDWARDS, George Hewlett Dawes (1931) Born 26 May 1909, The Vicarage, Crossens, Southport; son of George Zachary Edwards, Clerk in Holy Orders, and Helen Amelia Dawes. **Tutor(s):** M P Charlesworth. **Educ:** Holmwood School, Formby; Merchant Taylors' School, Liverpool.

EDWARDS, James (Jimmy) Keith O'Neill (1938) Born 23 March 1920, 17 Woodlands Road, Barnes, London; son of Reginald Walter Kenrick Edwards, Lecturer in Mathematics, and Phyllis Keith Cowan; m Valerie Seymour, 5 November 1958 (div 1969). BA 1941; MA 1945. **Tutor(s):** J S Boys Smith; R L Howland. **Educ:** Ranelagh House School; St Paul's Cathedral Choir School; King's College School, Wimbledon. **Career:** RAF 1940–1946; Music Hall: Windmill Theatre 1946; Adelphi Theatre 1950–1951, 1952–1954, 1954–1955, 1960–1961; Radio and Television: *Take it From Here*, BBC 1948–1959; *Does The Team Think?*, BBC 1957–1977; *Whack-O!*, BBC TV 1957–1961, 1971–1972; *Seven Faces of*

Jim 1961–1962; *Six More Faces of Jim* 1962–1963; *Bold as Brass* 1964; *John Jorrocks Esq*, BBC2 1966; *Fosset Saga* 1969; *The Glums*, LWT 1979; Films: *Three Men in a Boat* 1957; *Bottoms Up* 1960; *Nearly a Nasty Accident* 1961; *The Plank* 1979; *Rhubarb* 1980; *It's Your Move* 1982; Stage: *Big Bad Mouse*, Shaftesbury 1966–1968; *Halfway up the Tree*, Queen's 1968; *Maid of the Mountains*, Palace 1972; *Hulla Balloo*, Criterion 1972; *Doctor in the House* 1978; *Oh! Sir James!* 1979; *Oliver!*, Toronto 1983. **Appointments:** Lord Rector of Aberdeen University 1951–1954; Founder, Handle Bar Club for men with large moustaches. **Awards:** Choral Scholarship, SJC. **Honours:** DFC. **Publications:** *Take It From Me*, 1952; *Six of the Best*, 1984. Died 8 July 1988.

EDWARDS, Dr John Llewelyn Jones (1944) Born 16 May 1918, Great Darkgate Street, Aberystwyth, Wales; son of David Edwards, Superintendent of Police, and Sarah Jones; m Monica; 2 sons (Mark and Stephen), 1 daughter (Alexandra). **Subject(s):** Law; BA 1947; MA 1952; LLD 1964; PhD (London) 1954; LLB (Wales); Honorary LLD (Ontario) 1982, (Nova Scotia) 1984. **Educ:** Council School, Aberystwyth; Central School, Lampeter; Tregaron Secondary School; University College of Wales, Aberystwyth. **Career:** Assistant Lecturer in Law, UCL 1947; Called to the Bar, Middle Temple 1948; Reader in Law, Queen's University, Belfast 1954; Dunn Professor of Law, Dalhousie University, Nova Scotia 1958; Professor of Law 1963, Director, Criminology Centre, Law Faculty 1963–1976, University of Toronto; Called to the Bar, Ontario, Canada 1971; Harry T Klein Distinguished Professor of Law, Northern Kentucky University 1987. **Publications:** *Law Officers of the Crown*, 1964. Died September 1994.

EDWARDS, John Martin Baskerville (1945) Born 6 November 1926, 44 Catherine Street, Westminster; son of Geoffrey Richard Edwards, Secretary, Royal Society of Medicine, and Margaret Elizabeth Simon. **Tutor(s):** J M Wordie. **Johnian Relatives:** son of Geoffrey Richard Edwards (1910). **Educ:** Avisford, Arundel; Ampleforth College, York. **Appointments:** RAF Cadet, SJC.

EDWARDS, Norman Henry (1948) Born 18 May 1927, British Hospital, Samuel Street, Woolwich; son of Henry William Edwards, Taxi-driver, then Master Grocer, and Mary Margaret Cheesley; m (1) Valerie Anne Howie, (2) Armelle Therese de Cugnac Dampierre; (1) 1 daughter (Nicola Jane), (2) 3 sons (Paul Norman, Mark Henry and Christopher Arnaud), 1 daughter (Pascalle Mary). **Subject(s):** Modern and Medieval Languages/Economics; BA 1950; MA 1955. **Tutor(s):** C W Guillebaud. **Educ:** St Peter's School, Westminster; St Michael's School, Westminster; Emanuel School, Wandsworth. **Career:** Corporal, Army Intelligence Corps; Staff Interpreter, NATO 1953–1961; Freelance Interpreter 1961. **Appointments:** Member, AIIC.

EDWARDS, Robert Cleveland (1927) Born 4 July 1908, Buen Iden 1644, Buenos Aires, Argentina; son of Jason Holroyd Edwards, Senior Accountant, Buenos Aires Western Railway, Argentina, and Ellen Anne Clark. **Subject(s):** Modern and Medieval Languages/Economics; BA 1930. **Tutor(s):** M P Charlesworth. **Educ:** St George's College, Quilemas, Buenos Aires, Argentina; Berkhampsted School.

EDWARDS, William Griffith (1911) Born 14 June 1891, The Elms, Swansea, Glamorganshire; son of William Edwards, Draper, and Mary Thomas. BA 1914; AMICE. **Tutor(s):** J R Tanner. **Johnian Relatives:** brother of Arthur Tudor Edwards (1908). **Educ:** Mill Hill School. **Career:** Flight Lieutenant, RAF; Wolseley Motors (Vickers Ltd), Birmingham 1926; Hordern Mason and Edwards Ltd 1935. Died April 1938.

EDWARDS-TAYLOR, Sherwood (1920) Born 11 May 1901, 17 Southwood Avenue, Highgate, Hornsey, Middlesex; son of Thomas Edwards Taylor, Steel Manufacturer, and Emily Hesford. **Tutor(s):** B F Armitage. **Educ:** Ebor School, Bexhill; Highgate School.

EGNER, William Edward (1931) Born 20 February 1911, 22 Monkton Road, Jarrow, Durham; son of George August Egner, Pork Butcher, and

Catherine Stolz; 1 son (Geoffrey William b 28 November 1941). **Subject(s):** Mathematics; BA 1933; MA 1938; BSc; FIMA; CMath. **Tutor(s):** J M Wordie. **Johnian Relatives:** father of Geoffrey William Egner (1960). **Educ:** Jarrow Secondary School; Armstrong College, Newcastle upon Tyne. **Career:** Chartered Mathematician. **Appointments:** JP. **Honours:** CBE. Died 13 February 1997.

EL-BAKRI, Essayid (El-sayid) Ahmed Morad (1920) Born 16 March 1897, Cairo, Egypt; son of Essayid Abdulhamid el-Bakri, Manager, el-Bakri Lords Estates, and Essayida Zakia el-Moweilhia. BA 1923. **Tutor(s):** B F Armitage. **Educ:** Khediveh School, Cairo, Egypt; Nasrich School, Cairo, Egypt. **Career:** Co-operative Section, Ministry of Agriculture. **Publications:** *Agricultural Production in Egypt*.

ELEY, Dr Alan John (1923) Born 23 September 1904, 28 Carlisle Road, Romford, Essex; son of George Clement Eley, Assistant to the Director of Education for Essex, and Alice Bushby. **Subject(s):** Mathematics; BA 1926; MA 1930; DMR; MB (St Bartholomew's) 1944; BS (St Bartholomew's) 1944. **Tutor(s):** E Cunningham. **Educ:** Albert Road Council School, Romford; Brentwood School. **Career:** Schoolmaster, City of London School for Boys until 1938; Surgeon Lieutenant, RNVR until 1947; Director, Ministry of Health Mass Radiography Unit; Senior, then Principal Medical Officer, Ministry of Health. **Appointments:** Chairman, Chelmsford Community Health Council. Died 3 July 1985.

ELEY, Professor Daniel Douglas (1938) Born 1 October 1914, 16 Lumley Road, Wallasey, Cheshire; son of Daniel Eley, Advertising Agent, and Fanny Allen Ross; m Brenda May Williams, 1942; 1 son (Roderick b 1944). **Subject(s):** Natural Sciences; PhD 1940; ScD 1954; BSc (Manchester) 1934; MSc (Manchester) 1935; PhD (Manchester) 1937; FRS 1964; FRSC; CChem. **Tutor(s):** J M Wordie. **Johnian Relatives:** brother-in-law of Hugh Campbell (1935). **Educ:** West Bridgford Elementary School, Nottingham; West Bridgford County Secondary School; Christ's College, Finchley; University of Manchester. **Career:** Department of Colloid Science, Cambridge University Research for Ministry of Supply 1940–1945; Lecturer in Colloid Chemistry 1945, Reader in Biophysical Chemistry 1951, Bristol University; Professor of Physical Chemistry 1954–1980 (Emeritus 1980), Emeritus Dean, Faculty of Pure Science 1959–1962, University of Nottingham. **Appointments:** Darbishire Fellow 1936; Reilly Lecturer, University of Notre Dame (USA) 1950; Council Member, Faraday Society 1951–1954, 1960–1963; Sir Jesse Boot Foundation Lecturer, Nottingham University 1955 and 1981; Meetings Secretary 1961–1963, Honorary Secretary 1963–1965, Vice-President 1963–1966, British Biophysical Society; Lecturer, Royal Australian Chemical Institute 1967; Scientific Assessor to Sub-Committee on Coastal Pollutions, House of Commons Select Committee on Science and Technology 1967–1968; Corresponding Member, Bavarian Academy of Sciences 1971; Sir Eric Rideal Lecturer, Society of Chemical Industry 1975; Leverhulme Emeritus Fellow 1981; Honorary Member, British Biophysical Society 1983. **Awards:** Woodiwiss Scholarship, Manchester University 1933; Department of Scientific and Industrial Research Senior Award 1937; Medal, University of Liège 1950; Mercer Scholarship, Manchester University 1934. **Honours:** OBE 1961. **Publications:** (ed) *Adhesion*, 1961; various papers in *Transactions of the Faraday Society*, *Proceedings of the Royal Society*, *Journal of the Chemical Society*, *Journal of Biochemistry*, *Nature* etc.

ELGOOD, John Lawson Alsager (1941) Born 25 April 1923, 6 Northwick Park Road, Harrow, Middlesex; son of Vivian Arthur Alsager Elgood, Solicitor, and Doris Gabrielle Lawson Lewis; m Eleanor Maud Garland Wylde, 1 April 1944. **Tutor(s):** S J Bailey. **Educ:** Orley Farm School, Harrow; St Andrew's, Eastbourne; Harrow School. **Career:** Solicitor, Willcock's & Co, Strand. Died 23 March 1960.

ELGOOD, Ronald Lloyd (1943) Born 28 August 1925, 20 Colebrooke Road, Bexhill, Sussex; son of Cyril Lloyd Elgood, Medical Practitioner, and Ethel Helen Hunt. **Subject(s):** Law; BA 1948; MA 1961. **Tutor(s):**

C W Guillebaud. **Educ:** Durlston Court, Swanage; Bradfield College. **Career:** RAF Cadet; Consultant Solicitor.

ELIAS, Charles Frederick (1944) Born 18 June 1926, Holt House, North Road, Grassendale Park, Liverpool; son of Charles Frederick Elias, Chartered Surveyor, and Alice Symonds McKnight. **Subject(s):** Mechanical Sciences; BA 1947; MA 1953. **Tutor(s):** S J Bailey; R L Howland. **Johnian Relatives:** great nephew of Lewis Williams (1857); brother-in-law of Frank Samuel Jennings Hollick (1929). **Educ:** Braeside Preparatory School, West Kirby; University of Toronto Schools; Calday Grange Grammar School, West Kirby. **Career:** OC RHQ Squadron 32 Assault Engineer Regiment, RE 1948; Chartered Civil Engineer, MICE 1952, working with various consulting civil engineers, local authorities and the Welsh Water Authority 1978–1983. **Appointments:** Proprietor of the Athenaeum, Liverpool.

ELIZAGA Y ROMERO RUBIO, Lorenzo Manuel Porfirio (1923) Born 11 April 1903, 5/6 Calle de San Andres, Mexico City; son of Lorenzo Elizaga, Lawyer, and Sofia Romero Rubio. **Tutor(s):** B F Armitage. **Educ:** École Spéciale d'Architecture, Paris, France; Colegio de los Padres Maristas, Mexico.

ELLIOT, Anthony Russel Pontifex (1948) Born 6 June 1929, St Bartholomew's Hospital, London; son of Russell Augustus Pontifex Elliot, Departmental Manager, Leather Merchants and Tanners, and Doris Alexandra Tomlinson; m Daphne C Wilkinson, 2 September 1953, Winchmore Hill Congregational Church, London; 2 children. **Subject(s):** History/Arabic and Persian; BA 1952; MA 1955; FCII; FInstM. **Tutor(s):** A G Lee, F Thistlethwaite. **Educ:** Highfield Road Elementary School, Winchmore Hill; Enfield Grammar School. **Career:** Manager, International Department, Sun Alliance & London Insurance Group 1975–1980; Managing Director, Willis Faber (Underwriting Management) Ltd 1980–1983; Private Consultant 1983. **Appointments:** Freeman, City of London 1982. **Awards:** Minor Scholarship, SJC 1947.

ELLIOT SMITH, Grafton Latimer (1922) Born 24 September 1903, Ismailia Quarter, Cairo, Egypt; son of Grafton Elliot Smith, Professor of Anatomy, University of London, and Kate Emily Macredie. BA 1925. **Tutor(s):** E A Benians. **Johnian Relatives:** son of Grafton Elliot Smith (1896); brother of Stephen Elliot Smith (1930). **Educ:** St Peter's School, York; Ladyham House School, Manchester; St Olave's Preparatory School, York. **Career:** Sudan Political Service. Died 29 March 1964.

ELLIOT SMITH, Stephen (1930) Born 12 December 1910, 4 Willow Bank, Rusholme, Manchester; son of Grafton Elliot Smith, Professor of Anatomy, and Kate Emily Macredie. **Subject(s):** Natural Sciences; BA 1932. **Tutor(s):** J M Wordie. **Johnian Relatives:** son of Grafton Elliot Smith (1896); brother of Grafton Latimer Elliot Smith (1922). **Educ:** Moor Allerton School, Manchester; Stanmore Park School, Middlesex; Oundle School. Died 27 December 1935.

ELLIOTT, John Dickerson (1922) Born 16 February 1903, 37 West 71st Street, New York, USA; son of John George Elliott, Merchant Importer, and Aline Dickerson. **Tutor(s):** E E Sikes. **Educ:** Private Schools, Hove, Holt and Hayes.

ELLIOTT, John Sinclair (1949) Born 12 April 1931, 31 Victoria Avenue, Sunderland; son of Edward Elliott, Deputy Treasurer, Easington Rural District Council, and Georgina Sinclair; m Sheila Mary Robinson, 1 October 1966, Chapel Royal of St Peter ad Vincula, Tower of London; 2 daughters (Julia b 1967 and Vanessa b 1974). **Subject(s):** French/ Music/Archaeology and Anthropology; BA 1952; MA 1956; MCIT; MATM. **Tutor(s):** C W Guillebaud. **Educ:** A J Dawson Grammar School, Wellfield; Durham School. **Career:** British Airways 1966–1988. **Awards:** Baker Exhibition, SJC; Choral Studentship, SJC.

ELLIOTT, Dr William Alexander (1928) Born 30 September 1910, 33 Oak Road, Crumpsall, North Manchester; son of William Elliott,

Inspector of Schools, and Jane Read Chester; m Dorothy. **Subject(s):** Natural Sciences; BA 1931; MA 1935; BChir 1934; MB 1934; MD 1938. **Tutor(s):** M P Charlesworth. **Educ:** King Edward's Grammar School, Birmingham; King Edward's High School, Birmingham. Died 4 March 1977.

ELLIOTT-BINNS, Dr Christopher Plunkett Elliott (1943) Born 25 December 1924, The Rectory, North Cadbury, Somerset; son of Leonard Elliott Elliott-Binns, Clerk in Holy Orders, and Anna Scott Kilner. **Subject(s):** Natural Sciences/Moral Sciences; BA 1946; MA 1974; MB 1948; BChir 1948; MD 1974. **Tutor(s):** S J Bailey. **Johnian Relatives:** brother of Michael Ferrars Elliott Elliott-Binns (1941); uncle of John Richard Elliott-Binns (1969). **Educ:** Windlesham House; Harrow School.

ELLIOTT-BINNS, Michael Ferrars Elliott (BINNS) (1941) Born 17 August 1923, The Rectory, North Cadbury, Somerset; son of Leonard Elliott Elliott-Binns, Clerk in Holy Orders, and Anna Scott Kilner; m Marjorie Alison Carey, 9 November 1948, St Pancras Church, London; 1 son (John), 2 daughters (Barbara and Penelope). **Subject(s):** Law; BA 1947; MA 1969. **Tutor(s):** C W Guillebaud. **Johnian Relatives:** brother of Christopher Plunkett Elliott Elliott-Binns (1943); father of John Richard Elliott-Binns (1969). **Educ:** Windlesham House; Winchester College. **Career:** Commissioned Field Artillery 1942–1945; Called to the Bar, Middle Temple 1948–1949; Assistant Secretary, Church Assembly 1949–1963; Legal Secretary 1963–1970; Assistant Secretary, General Synod 1970–1976; Coordinator, Chiswick Family Rescue 1978–1980; Funding Worker, Brixton Circle Projects 1981–1983. **Awards:** Minor Scholarship, SJC 1940; McMahon Studentship, SJC. **Publications:** *The Layman in Church Government*, 1956, 1964; *A Guide to the Pastoral Measure*, 1969; *The Layman and his Church*, 1970, 1974; *North Downs Church*, 1983; *Realisation* (includes poems written during time at SJC), 1993; *Finding Through War*, 1995 (published for Royal Star and Garter Home, poems from it are published in *The Eagle* 1996); 2 plays professionally performed. Died 14 February 2003.

ELLIOTT-SMITH, John (1922) Born 3 April 1901, The Rowans, Ashley Road, Epsom, Surrey; son of Alfred Elliott Sidney Smith, Solicitor, and Amy Robinson. **Tutor(s):** E E Sikes. **Educ:** Private School, Weybridge; Repton School.

ELLIS, Arthur Isaac (1903) Born 10 April 1883, 26 Grafton Street, Marylebone, Middlesex; son of John Nott Pyke Ellis, Landed Proprietor, and Lucy Shakson. **Subject(s):** Classics/History; BA 1906; MA 1910. **Tutor(s):** C E Graves; J R Tanner. **Educ:** University College School, London. **Career:** Captain, Royal Fusiliers, WWI; Superintendent of Reading Room, Department of Printed Books 1909, Keeper of Printed Books 1948, British Museum. **Honours:** CBE 1949. Died 1 February 1963.

ELLIS, David Edmund (1943) Born 16 August 1926, 30 Pretoria Road, Streatham; son of Algernon Reginald Ellis, Civil Servant, Lord Chancellor's Department, and Grace Goodwin; m Elizabeth. BA 1947; MA 1950; ARIBA; AA Diploma (London). **Tutor(s):** C W Guillebaud. **Educ:** Ravensbury Preparatory School, Mitcham; Rutlish School, Wimbledon; Perse School, Cambridge.

ELLIS, George Rayner (1919) Born 5 October 1897, 384 Edgware Road, Paddington, Middlesex; son of Leonard Wale Ealand (later Ellis), Journalist, and Florence Caroline Rayner; m Gwendoline Hilda MacRobert, 1935; 1 son (George Francis Rayner b 11 August 1939), 1 daughter (Caroline Rayner b 29 September 1937). **Subject(s):** Modern and Medieval Languages; BA 1922; MA 1931. **Tutor(s):** E A Benians. **Johnian Relatives:** father of George Francis Rayner Ellis (1961). **Educ:** Lindisfarne College, Westcliffe; Latymer Upper School, Hammersmith. **Career:** Army 1916–1919; Editorial Writer 1926–1941, Editor 1941–1951, Editor-in-Chief 1951–1953, *Rand Daily Mail*, South Africa. Died 6 November 1953.

ELLIS, Dr John Matthew (1931) Born 26 February 1913, 148 Meadow Head, Ecclesall Bierlow, Yorkshire; son of Edward Matthew Ellis, Bank Manager, and Dora Ethel Wharmby; m Evelyn Mary Head (née Ford), 17 December 1947. **Subject(s):** Natural Sciences; BA 1934; MA 1938. **Tutor(s):** J M Wordie. **Educ:** King Edward VII School, Sheffield; Giggleswick School. **Career:** Skin Consultant, Gloucester Infirmary; Medical Officer, 43rd Reconnaissance Unit; Special Commendation from Field Marshal Montgomery, WWII. Died 1 November 1956.

ELLIS, Keith Stanley (1948) Born 9 September 1927, 12 Merlin Way, Sheffield; son of Ernest Ellis, Sheet Steel Parer, and Ruth Miriam Thraves. **Subject(s):** History; BA 1950. **Tutor(s):** F Thistlethwaite. **Educ:** King Edward VII School, Sheffield.

ELLIS, Oliver Bernard (1916) Born 20 June 1898, Kirby Road, Leicester; son of Bernard Ellis, Merchant, and Isabel Clare Evans. **Tutor(s):** E E Sikes. **Educ:** Wyggeston School, Leicester; Sidcot School; Bootham School, York. **Career:** Royal Naval Air Service 1916; Active Service 1917. Died 20 May 1917 (shot down behind enemy lines).

ELLIS, Rowland (1922) Born 14 March 1904, The Windmill, 49 St Peter's Street, St Albans; son of William George Ellis, of independent means, and Ada Louise Freezer. **Subject(s):** History. **Tutor(s):** E A Benians. **Educ:** Westville Road School, Shepherd's Bush; Latymer Upper School, Hammersmith. **Awards:** Scholarship, SJC.

ELLISON, Michael John (1935) Born 17 December 1916, 116 Sutherland Avenue, Paddington, London; son of John Ellison, Surgeon, and Dorothy Lambert; m Elizabeth Oliver (née Hempson), 15 April 1950, Rottingdean. **Subject(s):** Economics/Law; BA 1938. **Tutor(s):** R L Howland. **Educ:** Bigshotte School, Wokingham; Magdalene Court, Broadstairs; Stowe School. **Career:** Messrs Bristows Cooke & Carpmael, London. Died 25 March 1982.

ELLISON, Roger John (1941) Born 6 August 1922, 2B Oxford and Cambridge Mansions, London; son of John Ellison, Surgeon, and Dorothy Lambert; m Dorothy Stella Simmonds, 29 December 1951. **Subject(s):** History; BA 1945; MA 1947. **Tutor(s):** C W Guillebaud. **Educ:** Egerton House, London; Wellesley House, Broadstairs; Stowe School. **Awards:** Scholarship, SJC.

ELMES BEALE, Cyril (1907) See BEALE.

ELMS, Charles Francis (1942) Born 5 October 1923, 37 Carville Terrace, Willington, Durham; son of Charles William Elms, Motor Bus Proprietor, and Martha Fox; m Dorothy. **Subject(s):** Natural Sciences; BA 1945; MA 1949. **Tutor(s):** C W Guillebaud. **Educ:** Willington Council School; Cockton Hill Council School; Bishop Auckland Grammar School. **Career:** Midshipman, RNVR, HMS *Victory*, HMS *Mercury* 1944–1945; Sub-Lieutenant, HMS *Calliope* 1945; Assistant Principal, Post Office 1948; Private Secretary to Assistant Postmaster General 1949; Managing Director, Reliance Systems Ltd. Died 25 December 1998.

EL-RICABY, Mohammed Akram (1919) Born 15 June 1899, Damascus, Syria; son of Ali Riza Pasha El-Ricaby, General and Chief Administrator. **Tutor(s):** E A Benians. **Educ:** College de Freres, Jerusalem; Schools at Acca and Damascus; School of Hadicaii, Meswerat; Royal School, Medina; Royal Schools of Baghdad and Basrah; Mission Laïque Française, Bayruth; Royal School, Aleppo; Special Courses in Arabic, Damascus; Turkish Agricultural School. **Career:** Traction and Statistics Office, Hedjaz Railway (military service) 1916–1917.

ELSLEY, Jack Leslie (1947) Born 24 July 1923, 35 Ringwood Road, Eastbourne, Sussex; son of Harry Oswald Elsley, Ironmonger's Manager, and Grace Adeline Lukes. **Subject(s):** Physics. **Tutor(s):** G C L Bertram. **Educ:** St Philip's Church of England School, Eastbourne; All Souls Elementary School; Eastbourne Grammar School. **Career:** Laboratory

Assistant, Cavendish Laboratory, Cambridge 1941; Marketing and Sales, Electronics Industry 1950. Died 12 February 1993.

ELSWORTH, Walter Leslie (1927) Born 25 December 1908, 5 Alma Place, Thornbury, East Bradford, Yorkshire; son of Thomas Elsworth, Secretary and Building Society Manager, and Sarah Alice Downes; m Phyllis Grace Macklin, 29 August 1935, Ilford; 1 son (John David b 17 January 1939), 1 daughter (Doreen Anne b 5 December 1936). **Subject(s):** Classics; BA 1930; MA 1937. **Tutor(s):** M P Charlesworth. **Johnian Relatives:** father of John David Elsworth (1958). **Educ:** Hanson Junior Council School, Bradford; Bradford Grammar School. **Career:** Assistant Master, Holyhead County School 1930–1944; Senior Classics Master, Wolstanton County Grammar School, Newcastle 1944–1954; Headmaster, King Edward VI Grammar School, Morpeth, Northumberland 1954. **Awards:** Exhibition, SJC 1927; Scholarship, SJC 1929; Browne Medal for Greek Epigram, University of Cambridge 1930. Died 18 February 1993.

ELY, Trevor Howorth Anthony (1920) Born 20 June 1901, Grafton House, Hereford; son of William Anthony Silvester Ely, of independent means, and Louisa Frances Haselden Wood; m Madeleine Denny, 1927, Cambridge (d 1964); 1 son (Richard), 4 daughters (June, Rosamund, Alicia and Annette). **Subject(s):** Agriculture/Botany; BA 1923. **Tutor(s):** B F Armitage. **Educ:** The Cathedral School, Hereford; Hill Side, West Malvern; Malvern College; Private Tuition. **Career:** Schoolmaster, Ross Grammar School; Schoolmaster, Hereford Cathedral School. Died February 1985.

EMBLETON, Professor Clifford (1949) Born 11 May 1931, Highfield, 11 Fairacres Road, Bebington; son of Arthur Thomas Embleton, Shipping Clerk, and Constance Fitzgerald; m (1) Davina Caroline Cherry, 19 May 1956, (2) Dr Christine Hamann, February 1991; 3 sons. **Subject(s):** Geography; BA 1952; MA 1956; PhD 1956; FRCO 1949. **Tutor(s):** J M Wordie. **Educ:** Stanton Road Council School, Bebington; Birkenhead School. **Career:** Assistant Lecturer in Geography, Bedford College, London 1956; Professor of Geography, until 1988 (Emeritus 1988–1990), King's College, University of London; Leverhulme Fellow 1992–1994. **Awards:** Grant from Philip Lake Fund 1953. **Publications:** (with Professor Cuchlaine King) *Glacial and Periglacial Geomorphology*, 1968; (with Alan Mountjoy) *Africa: A Geographical Study*, 1965. Died 4 July 1994.

EMELÉUS, Professor Karl George (1919) Born 4 August 1901, 18 Gough Street, Poplar, Middlesex; son of Karl Henry Emeléus, Pharmacist, and Ellen Biggs; m Florence Mary Chambers, 1929; 3 sons, 1 daughter. **Subject(s):** Natural Sciences; BA 1922; MA 1926; PhD 1926; Honorary ScD (Dublin) 1958; Honorary ScD (Ulster) 1986; FInstP; MRIA. **Tutor(s):** E A Benians. **Educ:** Collegiate School, St Leonards; The Grammar School, Hastings. **Career:** Lecturer in Experimental Physics 1927–1933, Professor, Dean and Head of Department, Faculty of Applied Science and Technology 1933–1966, University of Belfast. **Appointments:** Governor, Armagh Observatory. **Awards:** Open Exhibition, SJC 1919. **Honours:** CBE. **Publications:** More than 250. Died 18 June 1989.

EMERY, John Nicholas (1933) Born 12 August 1913, Wormley Lodge, Hertfordshire; son of George Frederick Emery, Barrister-at-Law, and Mary Ethel Taylor; m Helen Margaret Pratt (née Lyons), 31 December 1943; 1 son (Peter), 1 daughter (Catherine-Anne). **Subject(s):** Natural Sciences; BA 1936; MA 1950. **Tutor(s):** J M Wordie. **Educ:** King's College Choir School, Cambridge; Oldfield, Swanage; St Peter's School, York. **Career:** Flight Lieutenant 1939–1945; Head, Science Department, Trinity College, Glenalmond 1974. Died 25 August 1982.

EMERY, Richard Seabrook (1948) Born 2 March 1930, 38 Sydney Road, Richmond, Surrey; son of Frank William Seabrook, Chartered Accountant, and Marjorie Frances Baker; m Jill Neary, 12 February 1955, West Dean, Chichester; 2 daughters (Tessa Jane and Clare

Frances). **Tutor(s):** G C L Bertram. **Educ:** The Manor House, Horsham; Radley College. **Career:** Publisher; Manager, R J Acford & Woodman-Marshall 1953–1967; Director, then Managing Director, William Heinemann Medical Books 1967–1982.

EMMS, Geoffrey Donald (1925) Born 15 May 1906, 91 Baxter Avenue, Southend, Essex; son of Harry Donald Hastings Emms, Secretary of John Williams Ltd, and Kate Mary Dann. **Subject(s):** Natural Sciences; BA 1928; MA 1933. **Tutor(s):** J M Wordie. **Educ:** Private School, Southend; City of Norwich School; Imperial College of Science and Technology. **Career:** Regular Commission, RAF 1930; Mentioned in Despatches 1932; Administrative Duties, Electrical and Wireless School 1933; Flight Lieutenant 1934; Air Ministry 1936–1938; Squadron Leader, RAF 1938–1940. **Awards:** Exhibition, SJC. Died 1940 (killed in action).

ENDERBY, Dr George Edward Hale (1934) Born 9 June 1915, Birklea, Spilsby Road, Skirbeck, Boston;. son of George Alfred Enderby, Consulting Optician, and Gertrude Hale; m Dorothy Frances Grocock, 1940; 1 son (David), 2 daughters (Diana and Jane). **Subject(s):** Natural Sciences; BA 1937; MA 1941; MB 1941; BChir 1941; DA 1943; FFARCS 1953; FRCA. **Tutor(s):** R L Howland. **Johnian Relatives:** father of David Hale Enderby (1960). **Educ:** Kingswood School, Bath; Boston Grammar School; Medical School, Guys Hospital; Northwestern University, USA; Duke University, USA. **Career:** Emergency Medical Service, WWII; Guy's Hospital; Pembury Hospital, Kent; Plastic and Reconstructive Surgery Unit, Rooksdown House, Basingstoke; Royal National Orthopaedic Hospital, Stanmore; Metropolitan Ear, Nose and Throat Hospital; Consultant Anaesthetist, Queen Victoria Hospital, East Grinstead 1951; Private Practice, until 1984. **Appointments:** Lecturer in Anaesthetics, America, Australia, South Africa, Canada, Europe 1950s/1960s; Captain 1965, President 1972–1973, Medical Golfing Society; Examiner for final fellowship examination 1976–1981, Council Member 1977–1983, FARCS; President, Anaesthetic Section, RSM; Expert witness, Medical Defence Union 1984. **Awards:** Scholarship, SJC; Guy's Hospital Entrance Scholarship; Leonard Lubbock Prize; United Hospital Entrance Scholarship; Gold Medal, FARCS; Gold Medal, RCM. **Publications:** Chapter in Gray, Nunn and Utting, *Textbook of Anaesthesia*; *Hypotensive Anaesthesia*, 1984; numerous papers on anaesthesia in medical journals. Died 30 December 2003.

ENGELBRECHT, Petrus Albertus (1923) Born 5 August 1905, Rotterdam, Holland; son of Willem Anton Engelbrecht, Shipbroker and Steamship Agent, and Elisabeth Margaretha Lycklama a Nijeholt. BA 1926; MA 1939. **Tutor(s):** E A Benians. **Educ:** Hogere Burgerschool, Rotterdam. Died 23 October 1977.

ENGLAND, Arthur Francis John (1925) Born 21 May 1907, 312 Beverley Road, East Sculcoates, Hull, Yorkshire; son of Arthur Creyke England, Vicar of Hessle, Canon of York Minster, and Jessie Rawlings Brangwin. **Tutor(s):** E E Sikes. **Educ:** Kindergarten, Hull; Worksop College. **Career:** Captain, South Lancashire Regiment, WWII; Acting Major, Malay Regiment.

ENGLEDOW, Professor Sir Frank Leonard (1910) Born 20 August 1890, 8 Etta Street, Deptford, Kent; son of Henry Engledow, Police Sergeant, and Elizabeth Prentice; m Mildred Remmeline Roper, 1921 (d 1956); 4 daughters. **Subject(s):** Natural Sciences; BA 1913; MA 1919; BSc (UCL) 1910; FRS 1946. **Tutor(s):** L H K Bushe-Fox. **Educ:** Upland Council School, Bexley Heath; Dartford Grammar School; UCL. **Career:** Lieutenant Colonel (retiring rank), Queen's Own, Royal West Kent Regiment, then Adjutant Mesopotamian Expeditionary Force (Mentioned in Despatches) 1914–1918; Director of Agriculture, Mesopotamia 1918–1919; Plant Breeding Institute, Cambridge 1919; Foundress Fellow 1919–1926, Title B Fellow 1926–1930, Title C Fellow 1930–1957, Title D Fellow 1957–1985, SJC; Lecturer in Agriculture 1926–1930, Drapers Professor of Agriculture 1930–1957, University of Cambridge; Liaison Officer, Ministry of Agriculture 1940.

Appointments: Director of Studies in Agricultural Science 1920–1930, Senior Bursar's Assistant 1922–1924, SJC; Colonial Office work, Nigeria, the West Indies, Malaya, Kenya, Tanganyika and Uganda; work for the Indian Tea Association, Assam; report on the Agricultural Development of Southern Rhodesia for the Government; Member, West India Royal Commission 1938; Managing Trustee, Nuffield Foundation 1943; UK Delegate, United Nations Conference on Food and Agriculture, Hot Springs 1944; President, British Federation of Manufacturing Industries Research Association; Chairman, Food Investigation Board, Department of Scientific and Industrial Research. **Honours:** Croix de Guerre 1918; CMG 1935; Kt 1944. **Publications:** (ed) *Britain's Future in Farming*, 1980. Died 3 June 1985.

ENGLEFIELD, Frederick Ronald Hastings (1910) Born 5 February 1891, 33 Southbrook Road, Lee, Kent; son of Frederick William Englefield, Solicitor, and Frances Maud Hastings Robinson. **Subject(s):** Modern and Medieval Languages; BA 1913. **Tutor(s):** J R Tanner. **Educ:** Mill Hill School. **Career:** Lieutenant, Hampshire Regiment, WWI.

ENGLISH, Frederick Hubert (1911) Born 19 August 1890, Holt, Norfolk; son of Arthur William English, Builder, and Alice Fox. **Subject(s):** Modern and Medieval Languages; BA 1914; MA 1925. **Tutor(s):** E E Sikes. **Educ:** Norwich Municipal Secondary School. **Career:** Second Lieutenant, Aldenham School OTC, WWI; Assistant Master, Aldenham School 1915–1949.

ENGLISH, Michael (1942) Born 7 November 1924, Tydd St Mary, Lincolnshire; son of Stanley Arthur English, Schoolmaster, and Ethel Sly; m Marjorie Lockwood; 1 son (Julian Michael), 1 daughter. **Subject(s):** English; BA 1947; MA 1957; FIPA; FCAM. **Tutor(s):** C W Guillebaud; F Thistlethwaite. **Johnian Relatives:** father of Julian Michael English (1969). **Educ:** Tydd St Mary School; Spalding Grammar School. **Career:** Indian Army 1943–1946; Business career in advertising agencies as Copywriter, Executive, and Managing Director 1948; Chairman and Chief Executive, Ted Bates Ltd 1971–1983. **Appointments:** President, Institute of Practitioners in Advertising 1979–1981. **Awards:** Minor Foundation Scholarship, SJC.

ENNALS, John Arthur Ford (1936) Born 21 July 1918, Mellish Road, Walsall; son of Arthur Ford Ennals, Master Draper, and Jessie Edith Taylor; m Judith Garde Wilson, 7 July 1952; 1 son, 1 daughter. **Subject(s):** History/Moral Sciences; BA 1939; MA 1956. **Tutor(s):** J S Boys Smith. **Educ:** Lowercroft School, Walsall; Queen Mary's Grammar School, Walsall. **Career:** War Correspondent; Joined mission to Yugoslavia to link up with Tito's partisans 1939–1945; General Secretary, World Federation of United Nations Associations 1946–1956; General Secretary and Tutor in International Relations, Ruskin College, Oxford 1956–1966; Director General, United Nations Association of the United Kingdom 1966–1970; Director, United Kingdom Immigrants Service 1970–1983. **Appointments:** Chairman, Anti-Apartheid Movement. **Awards:** Scholarship, SJC 1936–1937. Died 14 September 1989.

ENNOS, Frederick Raine (1909) Born 9 July 1890, 29 Brooke Road, West Hackney, Stoke Newington; son of Frederick William Ennos, Solicitor's Clerk, and Emma Raine; m Ethel May Saunders, 14 June 1919; 2 sons (John Frederick b 27 February 1921 and Anthony Edward b 12 June 1924). **Subject(s):** Natural Sciences; BA 1912; BSc (London) 1912. **Tutor(s):** L H K Bushe-Fox. **Johnian Relatives:** grandfather of Richard Aiton Ennos (1973). **Educ:** Birkbeck School, Kingsland; Parmiter's School, Victoria Park; St Olave's Grammar School. **Awards:** Wright's Prize, SJC 1910; Wiltshire Prize, University of Cambridge 1911.

ENTWISTLE, Roy (1920) Born 1 July 1901, 22 Cooperation Street, Bacup, Lancashire; son of Fred Entwistle, Schoolmaster, and Alice Jane Soffe. **Subject(s):** Classics/English; BA 1923; MA 1945. **Tutor(s):** E E Sikes. **Educ:** Morton St Paul's Church of England School; Manchester Grammar School. **Awards:** Open and Somerset Exhibitions, SJC 1920.

EPPS, The Revd Stanley Moorcroft (1919) Born 26 December 1900, 107 Helix Road, Brixton Hill, Brixton, Surrey; son of Walter Maxted Epps, Architect, and Florence Mary Moorcroft; 1 daughter (Mary). **Subject(s):** Mathematics/Natural Sciences; BA 1922; MA 1926. **Tutor(s):** E A Benians. **Educ:** Upton College, Bexley Heath; Mercer's School, Hilborn; KCL; Dorchester Missionary College. **Career:** Deacon 1923; Curate, St Mark, New Brompton 1923–1926; Priest 1924; Curate, Gravesend 1926–1930; Chaplain, Training Ship Arethusa 1935–1936; Chaplain, RN 1936; HMS *Victory*, for RN Barracks, Portsmouth 1936–1937; HMS *Malaya* 1937–1939; HMS *Nelson* 1939–1941; RN Artificers Training Establishment 1941–1943; HM Signal School 1943–1946; HMS *Dryad* 1946–1951; Vicar, St Oswald, Coney Hill, Gloucester 1951–1956; Vicar, Wimborne Minster, Dorset 1956. Died 13 March 1993.

ERICKSON, Professor John (1949) Born 17 April 1929, 250 Taylor Street, South Shields; son of Henry Erickson, Shipwright, and Jessie Heyes; m Ljubica Petrovic, 18 July 1957; 1 son ((Ian) Mark b 16 April 1964), 1 daughter (Amanda Jane b 20 August 1962). **Subject(s):** History; BA 1952; MA 1958; FRSE 1982; FBA 1985; FRSA 1991. **Tutor(s):** A G Lee. **Educ:** Gilbert Street School, South Shields; Mortimer Road School, South Shields; South Shields High School; St John's College, Oxford University. **Career:** Research Fellow, St Anthony's College, Oxford 1956–1958; Lecturer in Modern History, University of St Andrews 1958–1962; Lecturer, Senior Lecturer and Reader, Department of Government, University of Manchester 1962–1967; Reader and Lecturer in Higher Defence Studies 1967, Professor of Politics 1969–1988, University Endowment Fellow and Director, Centre for Defence Studies 1988–1996, University of Edinburgh. **Appointments:** Visiting Professor, Russian Research Center, University of Indiana 1967; Visiting Professor, Texas A&M University 1981; Visiting Professor, Department of History, Yale University; President, Association of Civil Defence and Emergency Planning Officers 1981; Honorary Fellow, Aerospace Academy, Ukraine 1995; Honorary Fellow, Defence Studies, and Professor Emeritus, University of Edinburgh 1996–2002. **Awards:** Minor Scholarship, SJC 1946. **Publications:** *The Soviet High Command 1918–1941*, 1962; *Storia dello Stato Maggiore Sovietico*, 1963; (ed) *The Military-Technical Revolution*, 1966; (ed) *The Armed Services and Society*, 1970; *Soviet Military Power*, 1971; *Stalin's War with Germany: The Road to Stalingrad*, 1975; (ed) *Soviet Military Power and Performance*, 1979; *Stalin's War with Germany: The Road to Berlin*, 1983; (ed) *Barbarossa: The Axis and the Allies*, 1994; (jointly) *The Soviet Armed Forces 1918–1992: A Research Guide to Soviet Sources*, 1997; (jointly) *The Russian Front 1941–1945*, 1999; (introduction) *Invasion 1940*, 2000; (with Ljubica Erickson) *The Eastern Front in Photographs 1941–1945*, 2001. Died 10 February 2002.

ESCANDON Y SALAMANCA, Manuel (1922) Born 4 June 1897, Paris, France; son of Manuel Escandon y Barron, Marques de Villa Vieja, and Petronilla Salamanca y Hurtado de Zaldivar. **Tutor(s):** B F Armitage. **Educ:** Beaumont College; Private Tuition, Bournemouth.

ESCHELBACHER, Hermann Friedrich (ASHBROOK) (1935) Born 2 April 1912, Freiburg, Germany; son of Max Eschelbacher, Rabbi, and Bertha Kahn. **Tutor(s):** J S Boys Smith. **Educ:** Staatliches Hohenzellerugymnasium, Düsseldorf. **Career:** Antiquarian bookseller.

ESCRITT, Colonel George Stanley (1929) Born 29 December 1909, 18 Victoria Street, Hull; son of Charles Henry Escritt, Grocer, and Edith Charlotte Richardson; 1 son, 1 daughter. **Subject(s):** Mathematics/Mechanical Sciences; BA 1932; MA 1942. **Tutor(s):** J M Wordie. **Educ:** Newland Avenue Council School, Hull; Hymers College, Hull. **Career:** Army, France and Burma (Colonel 1945) WWII, then War Office; Researched Guided Missiles 1932–1955; Physics Teacher, Hymers College, Hull 1961–1970. **Awards:** Scholarship, SJC. Died 6 January 1970.

ESPLEY, Frank Alan (1938) Born 8 November 1919, 64 Higher Antley Street, Accrington, Lancashire; son of Arthur James Espley, Director of Limited Companies, and Eliza Edith Thornber; m Gladys; 2 sons, 2 daughters. BA 1941; MA 1994. **Tutor(s):** C W Guillebaud. **Johnian Relatives:** brother of Gilbert Thornber Espley (1931), Herbert Noel Espley (1933) and of William Arthur Espley (1943). **Educ:** Woodnook Council School, Accrington; Accrington Grammar School; Price's School, Fareham. **Career:** Lieutenant Colonel, Air-Despatch, RASC. **Appointments:** Secretary, Ulster Farmers' Union 1964–1985.

ESPLEY, Gilbert Thornber (1931) Born 16 May 1913, 62 Higher Antley Street, Accrington, Lancashire; son of Arthur James Espley, Director of Limited Companies, and Eliza Edith Thornber; m Gertrude Anne McNeillie, 1943, Prestwick, Ayrshire; 1 son (David), 2 daughters (Elizabeth and Pamela). **Subject(s):** Natural Sciences; BA 1934; Pharmacy Degree (Leeds). **Tutor(s):** J M Wordie. **Johnian Relatives:** brother of Herbert Noel Espley (1933), Frank Alan Espley (1938) and of William Arthur Espley (1943). **Educ:** Woodnook Council School; Accrington Grammar School; Leeds University. **Career:** Joint Managing Director, Thornbers (Chemists) Ltd 1946–1978; Managing Director, Nash Drug Company Ltd 1978–1984. **Publications:** section on stock control and buying, *Retail Pharmacists' Handbook*. Died 11 February 1994.

ESPLEY, Herbert Noel (1933) Born 18 January 1915, 62 Higher Antley Street, Accrington, Lancashire; son of Arthur James Espley, Company Director, and Eliza Edith Thornber; m Mary (Mollie) Heys, 1938, Accrington; 2 sons (Ian Noel b 1940 and Peter David b 1945), 1 daughter (Patricia Mary b 1942). **Subject(s):** Natural Sciences; BA 1936. **Tutor(s):** J M Wordie. **Johnian Relatives:** brother of Gilbert Thornber Espley (1931), Frank Alan Espley (1938) and of William Arthur Espley (1943). **Educ:** Woodnook Council School, Accrington; Accrington Grammar School; Harris Institute, Preston. **Career:** Pharmacist; Joint Managing Director, Thornbers (Chemists) Ltd 1946–1978; Chairman, H N Espley & Sons (Chemists) Ltd 1978–1993. Died October 1993.

ESPLEY, William Arthur (1943) Born 30 March 1923, Holly Mount, Hollins Lane, Accrington, Lancashire; son of Arthur James Espley, Company Director, and Eliza Edith Thornber. **Subject(s):** Law; BA 1946; MA 1965. **Tutor(s):** S J Bailey. **Johnian Relatives:** brother of Gilbert Thornber Espley (1931), Herbert Noel Espley (1933) and of Frank Alan Espley (1938). **Educ:** Accrington Grammar School; Price's School, Fareham. **Career:** Articled to Barlow, Norris and Jenkin, Solicitors 1940; practised in Eastbourne for many years. Died 21 July 1990.

EUGENIDES, Eustathuis (1934) Born 1 September 1914, Stavrodromion Parish, Constantinople; son of Stephen E Eugenides, Banker, and Helen Leonidas Zarifis. **Subject(s):** Economics. **Tutor(s):** C W Guillebaud. **Educ:** First Public School, Athens; National University of Athens; École des Hautes Études Commerciales de la Chambre de Commerce, Paris.

EVANS, Albert Dan (1920) Born 25 May 1902, 10 Springbourn Road, Toxteth Park, Liverpool, Lancashire; son of Albert Edward Evans, Schoolmaster, and Katherine Eleanor Jones; m Henriette Milloud, 21 August 1926. **Subject(s):** History; BA 1923; MA 1961. **Tutor(s):** E A Benians. **Educ:** Dovedale Road School, Liverpool; Liverpool Collegiate School. **Career:** Secretariat, United Nations, New York. **Awards:** Scholarship, SJC 1919; Whewell Scholarship, University of Cambridge 1923, 1925.

EVANS, Albert Ernest (1903) Born 28 December 1882, Sydenham House, Ebbw Vale, Monmouthshire; son of William Evans, Provisions Merchant, and Jane James. **Tutor(s):** D MacAlister. **Johnian Relatives:** brother of Edgar David Evans (1901). **Educ:** Wycliffe College, Stonehouse.

EVANS, David Dunston Silian (1941) Born 31 May 1923, The Vicarage, Rhosymedre, Cefn, Denbighshire; son of David Thomas Silian Evans, Clerk in Holy Orders, and Katherine Dunston; 3 children. **Subject(s):** Economics; BA 1947; MA 1949. **Tutor(s):** C W Guillebaud. **Educ:** Preparatory School, Sherborne; St John's School, Leatherhead; St Peter's

School, York. **Career:** Advertising Agency business; Supplier of crested products to universities and schools until 1992.

EVANS, David Hubert Raymond (1927) Born 5 April 1909, 1 Berkeley Villas, St James Crescent, Swansea, Glamorgan; son of Thomas Evans, Managing Director of Flour Millers, and Sara Letitia Evans; m Iris May Boswell, 10 April 1931, Cardiff; 2 sons (Russell b 27 April 1936 and Nigel b 18 July 1938), 1 daughter (Gaenor b 29 July 1937). **Subject(s):** Law; BA 1931; MA 1936; LLB 1932. **Tutor(s):** J M Wordie. **Johnian Relatives:** father of Russell Thomas Forrester Evans (1956) and of Nigel James Forrester Evans (1957); grandfather of Polly Patricia Evans (1989) and of Sophie Caroline Evans (1992). **Educ:** Craig-y-Nos Preparatory School, Swansea; Cheltenham College; Aberystwyth University. **Career:** Solicitor, Evesham, London and Newmarket; Substantive Major and Temporary Lieutenant Colonel (final ranks), Worcestershire Regiment 1940–1946; Motor car manufacturing, Oxford. Died 17 April 1968.

EVANS, Edgar David (1901) Born 15 December 1879, Sydenham House, Ebbw Vale, Monmouthshire; son of William Evans, Grocer and Draper, and Jane James. BA 1904. **Tutor(s):** D MacAlister. **Johnian Relatives:** brother of Albert Ernest Evans (1903). **Educ:** Wycliffe College, Stonehouse; University College, Aberystwyth. **Career:** Lieutenant, Middlesex Regiment, Labour Corps, and RGA, WWI; Civil Engineer.

EVANS, Geoffrey David (1944) Born 20 April 1926, Orchard Lea, Nether Street, Finchley, Middlesex; son of Rhys David Evans, Director, Provisions Manufacturer, and Margaret Dorothea Lidstone; m Rachel Tower, 1 February 1957. **Tutor(s):** J M Wordie. **Educ:** Oakleigh Park Preparatory School; Tonbridge School.

EVANS, Dr George Clifford (1930) Born 22 June 1913, The Manse, Brook Lane, Golcar, Yorkshire; son of George Evans, Baptist Minister, and Hannah Holderness; m J Margaret Heufield, 1940 (d 26 December 2001); 1 son (Peter), 2 daughters (Elisabeth and Ruth). **Subject(s):** Natural Sciences; BA 1934; MA 1938; PhD 1938; ScD 1974. **Tutor(s):** J M Wordie. **Johnian Relatives:** father of Peter John Holderness Evans (1968); grandfather of Perran John Horrell (1990). **Educ:** Preparatory School, Huddersfield; Derby School; Wyggeston School, Leicester; Hulme Grammar School, Manchester. **Career:** Title A Fellow 1938–1948 (suspended 1939–1946 while on war service), Title B Fellow 1948–1979, Lecturer in Botany 1949–1979, Title D Fellow 1979–, SJC; University Demonstrator in Plant Physiology 1937–1946, Lecturer in Plant Physiology 1945–1977, Reader in Experimental Ecology, Department of Botany 1977–1979 (Emeritus 1979–), University of Cambridge; Sub-Lieutenant 1939, Lieutenant 1940, Lieutenant Commander 1943–1945, RNVR. **Appointments:** Supervisor in Botany 1946–1949, Bursar in Charge of College Buildings 1952–1966, SJC; Member, Cambridge Philosophical Society; Member, British Ecological Society (President 1975–1976); Member, British Photobiological Society (Chairman 1979–1981); Member, Society for Experimental Biology. **Awards:** Scholarship, SJC 1933; Frank Smart Prize, University of Cambridge 1934; Frank Smart Studentship, University of Cambridge 1936; Henry Humphreys Prize, SJC 1937. **Publications:** *The Quantitative Analysis of Plant Growth*, 1972, Blackwell Scientific Publications; (ed) *Light as an Ecological Factor*, 1965; *Light as an Ecological Factor II*, 1976; articles in scientific publications such as *The Journal of Ecology* and *The New Phytologist*.

EVANS, Herbert Clyde (1909) (admitted as a Non-Collegiate Student 1908) Born 26 April 1883, North Town Belt, Oamaru, New Zealand; son of John Thomas Evans, Ship Merchant, and Emma Edy Shacklock; m Constance Irene Johnson, 25 March 1913. **Subject(s):** Moral Sciences/Law; BA 1911. **Tutor(s):** L H K Bushe-Fox. **Educ:** Gisborne Public School; Gisborne High School. **Career:** Mercantile Service; Russian Navy, Russo-Japanese War; Called to the Bar, Inner Temple 1914; Lecturer to Officers, Admiralty; Lieutenant Commander, RNVR, Nelson Battalion, Royal Naval Division (Mentioned in Despatches), WWI. Died 5 June 1915 (killed in action in Gallipoli).

EVANS, Horace Wynne (1935) Born 7 December 1914, Blodwen Villas, Holywell; son of David Edward Evans, Grocer Master, Second Lieutenant, and Louvera Victoria Hannah Hughes. **Tutor(s):** C W Guillebaud. **Educ:** Holywell Council School; Holywell County School; University College, Aberystwyth.

EVANS, Howell Thomas (1902) Born 6 November 1877, Cwmbwrla, nr Swansea, Wales; son of John Evans, Tin Refiner, and Mary Jane Thomas; 4 sons (Myrddin, David Meurig, Lyn and Rhys). **Subject(s):** History/Moral Sciences; BA 1904; MA 1908. **Tutor(s):** J R Tanner; C E Graves. **Johnian Relatives:** grandfather of Anthony Howell Meurig Evans (1954); great grandfather of James Frederick Meurig Evans (1987). **Educ:** University College of Wales, Aberystwyth. **Career:** Master, Swansea Secondary School 1900–1902; Master, Wellington College, Shropshire 1902–1904; Carmarthen Grammar School 1904–1905; Master, Cardiff High School for Boys 1905–1917; Headmaster, Aberayron County School 1917–1944. **Publications:** numerous books including *History of England and Wales*, 1910; *Making of Modern Wales*, 1912; *Wales and the Wars of the Roses*, Cambridge, 1915; Schools series: *Once Upon a Time*, 1929; *At Such and Such a Time*, 1931; *Long Long Ago*, 1932; *The Time of Expansion*, 1933. Died 1950.

EVANS, Hugh Everard (1940) Born 30 August 1922, Cougham Hall, King's Lynn, Norfolk; son of Norman Paget Evans, Major, RA, and Marion Julia Patterson. **Subject(s):** Mechanical Sciences; BA 1944; MA 1947. **Tutor(s):** S J Bailey. **Educ:** Westbourne House, Folkestone; King's Mead, Seaford; Marlborough College. Died March 1987.

EVANS, Ifor Leslie (1920) Born 17 January 1897, 16 Clifton Street, Aberdare, Glamorganshire; son of William John Evans, Merchant Taylor, and Mary Elizabeth Milligan; m Ruth Jolles; 1 son, 1 daughter. **Subject(s):** Economics/History; BA 1922; MA 1925; Honorary DLitt (University of Malta) 1948. **Tutor(s):** E A Benians. **Educ:** KP Oberrealschule, Suhl i Thür, Germany; Wycliffe College, Stonehouse; Private Tuition; Lyceé de Beauvais, France; Untersuchungsgefängnis zu, Nürnberg, Germany (POW); Kriegsgefangenenlager, Ruhleben, Germany (POW). **Career:** Foundress Fellow 1923–1929, Title B Fellow 1929–1934, Supervisor in History 1929–1934, SJC; Visiting Lecturer, Graduate School of Economics, Washington, and Visiting Professor, Post-Graduate Institute of International Studies, Geneva 1924–1929; Lecturer, Economic History, University of Cambridge 1926–1934; Principal, University College of Wales, Aberystwyth (later Vice-Chancellor) 1934. **Appointments:** Acting Senior Bursar, SJC 1930–1931; Member, Faculty Board of Economics, University of Cambridge 1931–1934. **Awards:** Strathcona Studentship, SJC; Whewell Scholarship, University of Cambridge 1921, 1923; Leverhulme Research Fellowship 1948. **Publications:** Prepared an edition of *Welsh Folk Songs*. Died 31 May 1952.

EVANS, The Revd Jenkin (1900) (Admitted as Non-Collegiate Student 1899) Born 6 October 1864, Kilybebyll, Pontardawe, Swansea, Glamorganshire; son of William Evans, Farm Bailiff, and Catherine Jones. BA 1902; MA 1923. **Tutor(s):** E E Sikes. **Educ:** Carmarthen Training College; Kilybebyll Board School. **Career:** Ordained deacon 1902; Curate and vicar in various Welsh parishes 1902–1935; Ordained priest 1904.

EVANS, Michael David Thompson (1947) Born 13 June 1924, Leamington House, Dover College, Dover; son of Thomas Henry Thompson Evans, Schoolmaster, Clerk in Holy Orders, and Mary Priscilla Pearson, Domestic Manager of Boarding Schools; m Anne Hollingsworth, 17 September 1960, Northiam, Sussex; 4 daughters (Caroline Thompson b 21 July 1961, Susan Thompson b 20 August 1962, Jane Thompson b 12 December 1966 and Gillian Thompson b 6 August 1969). **Subject(s):** Law; BA 1949; MA 1955; War Office course in Turkish, 1942–1943; MA (London) 1993. **Tutor(s):** F Thistlethwaite. **Johnian Relatives:** brother of Roland Thompson Evans (1931). **Educ:** Seabrook Lodge, Hythe; The Depperhaugh, Hoxne; Shrewsbury School;

SOAS, London. **Career:** Foreign Office Official, Turkey 1944–1946; Called to the Bar, Lincoln's Inn 1950–1952; Solicitor and Partner, Cameron Markby 1956–1987. **Appointments:** Council Member and Spokesman on problems caused by rent acts, British Property Federation; Director, Property Holding and Investment Trust Plc.

EVANS, Percy Edwin (1907) Born 15 September 1888, Church Aston, Newport, Shropshire; son of Edwin Evans, Schoolmaster, and Maria Haywood. **Subject(s):** Natural Sciences; BA 1910; MA 1918. **Tutor(s):** J R Tanner. **Educ:** The Grammar School, Newport. **Career:** Assistant Master, Royal College, Colombo 1914. **Awards:** Sizarship, SJC.

EVANS, Rhys David (1912) Born 12 June 1893, 96 Park Road, Hampstead, Middlesex; son of David Evans, Tradesman, and Rachel Evans; m Margaret; 1 son (Geoffrey). BA 1915; MA 1919. **Tutor(s):** E E Sikes. **Educ:** William Ellis School, Gospel Oak. **Career:** Second Lieutenant, King's Royal Rifle Corps, POW, WWI. Died 4 March 1957.

EVANS, Roland Thompson (1931) Born 12 September 1913, 10 Myrtle Hill Terrace, Cork, Ireland; son of Thomas Henry Thompson Evans, Housemaster, and Mary Priscilla Pearson. **Subject(s):** Natural Sciences; BA 1934; FCIS. **Tutor(s):** J M Wordie. **Johnian Relatives:** brother of Michael David Thompson Evans (1947). **Educ:** Dover College Junior School; Mill Hill School. **Career:** Commissioned, RA (reached rank of captain) 1939; GSO3 to CRA, Eighth Armoured Division, Egypt; Secretary, Mutual Finance Ltd 1948. Died March 1970.

EVANS, Dr Theophilus Islwyn (1917) Born 14 May 1898, The School House, Aberbeeg, Monmouthshire; son of Theophilus Evans, Schoolmaster, and Mary Gwendoline Watkins; m Clarissa. **Subject(s):** Medicine; BA 1920; MA 1931; BChir 1931; MB 1931; MRCS; LRCP. **Tutor(s):** E E Sikes. **Educ:** Intermediate School, Abertillery; University College, Abertillery; University College of Wales, Aberystwyth. **Career:** Clinical Assistant, Electro-Cardiographical Department, St Thomas' Hospital; GP, Gellicrug, Abertillery. Died 18 November 1966.

EVANS, William Emrys (1911) Born 7 December 1878, 15 New Pits, Mountain Ash, Glamorganshire; son of James Evans, Engine Driver, and Elizabeth Bevan. **Subject(s):** Natural Sciences (Geology). **Tutor(s):** L H K Bushe-Fox. **Educ:** Cardiff and Aberystwyth University Colleges; Pontypridd Pupil Teachers' Centre. **Career:** Lieutenant, RGA, WWI; Lecturer in Geography and Physics, Caerleon Training College 1914.

EVANS, Commander Vincent (1942) Born 31 May 1924, Crosby House, Great Crosby, Lancashire; son of Frederick Augustus Evans, Physician and Surgeon, Major RAMC, and Olwen Violet Davies. BA 1945; MA 1949; FIMarE. **Tutor(s):** S J Bailey. **Educ:** Crosby Preparatory School; Merchant Taylors' School, Crosby. **Career:** Chief Engineer HM Ships Hotham, Whitesand Bay, Vidal and Triumph; RN to Commander 1944–1977; Officers' Association, Employment Consultant 1977–1990. **Appointments:** Chairman, London Philharmonic Choir 1987–1991.

EVANS-ATKINSON, Norman (1919) Born 25 January 1893, Ashfield, Bewerley, Yorkshire; son of Charles Evans-Atkinson, Solicitor, Notary, County Court Registrar, and Agnes Fanny Clayton. **Tutor(s):** E E Sikes. **Educ:** Ellesmere Preparatory School, Harrogate; The College, Harrogate; Sedbergh School; Leeds University.

EVATT, George Raleigh Kerr (1900) Born 30 September 1883, Woolwich, Kent; son of George Joseph Hamilton Evatt, Surgeon General, RAMC, and Sophia Mary Frances Kerr. **Tutor(s):** D MacAlister. **Educ:** Cheltenham College; privately educated. **Career:** Second Lieutenant 1904, Lieutenant 1906, Middlesex Regiment; Lieutenant, Northern Nigeria, West African Frontier Force 1909–1913; Captain, 1st Middlesex Regiment 1914. Died 13 November 1914 (killed in action near Armentières).

EVE, Stephen Theodore (1929) Born 22 November 1911, 4 Fairfield Road, Croydon, Surrey; son of William Harold Eve, Chartered Land

Surveyor, and Ada Gertrude Price; m Betty V Rank, 8 March 1948, St Michael's Church, London. BA 1933. **Tutor(s):** C W Guillebaud. **Educ:** Hillside, Reigate; Tonbridge School. **Career:** Lieutenant Colonel, 4th Queen's Own Hussars. **Honours:** MBE; MC. Died 5 April 1987.

EVELYN-JONES, Lorence (1925) Born 3 December 1907, Whyteleafe Grange, Warlingham, Godstone, Surrey; son of Frank Evelyn-Jones, Solicitor, and Lavinia Walthew; 1 son (Colin), 1 daughter (Inga). BA 1928. **Tutor(s):** J M Wordie. **Educ:** Clare House, Beckenham; St Cyprian's, Eastbourne; Rugby School. Died 20 October 1993.

EVERATT, Reginald William (1907) Born 23 June 1885, Rhyl, Flintshire, Wales; son of William Robert Everatt, Schoolmaster, and Clara Elisabeth King. **Tutor(s):** J R Tanner. **Educ:** University College, Bangor, Wales.

EVERETT, John Frederick (1931) Born 19 May 1912, 4 Gordon Road, Boscombe, Bournemouth, Hampshire; son of John Lawrence Everett, Mechanical Engineer, and Florence Louise Cowie; m Ellen Vivienne Koster, 12 August 1939; 2 sons (David John b 1942 and Anthony Robert b 1950), 1 daughter (Rosemary Julia b 1943). **Subject(s):** Natural Sciences; BA 1934; MA 1938. **Tutor(s):** J M Wordie. **Educ:** Preparatory House, Cranleigh; Cranleigh School. **Career:** Demonstrator in Medical Biology, University of Durham College of Medicine 1935–1936; Assistant Master, Felsted School 1936–1939; Served in Army 1939–1946; Assistant Master, Queen Elizabeth School, Wimborne 1946; Administrative Assistant, Newcastle upon Tyne Education Department 1946–1948; Assistant Director of Education, Wiltshire 1949–1955; Deputy Chief Education Officer, Wiltshire 1955–1969; Chief Education Officer, Wiltshire 1969–1977; Consultant, British Council 1978–1980. **Appointments:** TA 1947–1967; Chairman, West Wiltshire Group, CPRE 1959–1990; President, Bath and District Branch, Royal Signals Association. **Awards:** Exhibition, SJC 1930. **Honours:** MBE; TD. Died 2 September 2002.

EVERETT, Group Captain Leslie Scott (1926) Born 13 April 1907, Holveton, Bodmin, Cornwall; son of John Hugo Everett, Post Office Overseer, and Hilda Fanny Scott. **Subject(s):** Natural Sciences; BA 1929; MRCS (King's College Hospital) 1931; LRCP (King's College Hospital) 1931. **Tutor(s):** J M Wordie. **Educ:** Bodmin Church of England School; Bodmin County School; Plymouth College. **Career:** Squadron Leader, RAF; Wing Commander 1946; Group Captain 1955. **Awards:** Exhibition, SJC. Died 14 January 1986.

EVERY, Austin Rimmington (1912) Born 14 December 1892, Lewes, Sussex; son of John Henry Every, Engineer, and Jessie Maria Mond; m Amy Louise Jackson, 9 September 1950, Lewes. BA 1915; MA 1942. **Tutor(s):** L H K Bushe-Fox. **Johnian Relatives:** brother of John Morris Every (1904). **Educ:** Tonbridge School; Brighton Municipal Technical School. Died 1 April 1968.

EVERY, John Morris (1904) Born 10 March 1886, 25 St John's Terrace, St John's, Lewes, Sussex; son of John Henry Every, Iron Founder, and Jessie Maria Mond. BA 1909; MA 1914. **Tutor(s):** D MacAlister. **Johnian Relatives:** brother of Austin Rimmington Every (1912). **Educ:** Tonbridge School. **Career:** Mechanical and Constructional Engineer of Phoenix Iron Works, Lewes. Died 1964.

EVES, The Revd Ralph Shakespeare (1913) (admitted to Trinity Hall 1906) Born 7 August 1887, London; son of Arthur Edward Eves, Solicitor, and Susie Smith. BA (Trinity Hall) 1909; LLB 1909 (Trinity Hall); MA (Trinity Hall) 1913. **Educ:** Merchant Taylors' School. **Career:** Curate, St Michael and All Angels, Beckenham 1911–1913; Chaplain, SJC 1913–1915; Head, Wellington College Mission, Walworth 1915–1916; Vicar, St Michael and All Angels, Beckenham 1916–1920; Librarian, Pusey House, Oxford 1920–1922; Vicar, All Souls, Clapton Park 1922–1928; Vicar, St Barnabas, Pimlico 1928–1931; Vicar, St Alban, Holborn 1931–1947. **Appointments:** Proctor in Convocation for London 1930–1931; Commissary for the Bishop of Riverina, New South Wales from 1930. Died 2 January 1947.

EWBANK, The Revd Alan Maurice (1919) Born 21 April 1901, 8 Webster Gardens, Ealing, Middlesex; son of Alan Ewbank, Clerk in Holy Orders, and Grace Catherine Davies. **Subject(s):** Classics; BA 1923; MA 1927. **Tutor(s):** E E Sikes. **Johnian Relatives:** grandson of Alfred Lloyd Vandyke Ewbank (1860); son of Alan Ewbank (1889). **Educ:** Owens School, Islington; St Paul's School, London; Colet Court, London; London College of Divinity. **Career:** Curate, St Saviour, Tollington Park, London 1927–1930; Ordained Priest 1928. Died 6 March 1930.

F

FAGNANI, Henry Hutchinson (1921) Born 25 September 1896, 11 Aldridge Road Villas, St Mary, Paddington, London; son of Henry Bulwer Fagnani, Steel Merchant, and Catherine Ann Hutchinson. **Tutor(s):** E E Sikes. **Educ:** Linton House School, London; Merchant Taylors' School, London.

FAHEY, Edmund Joseph Francis (1945) Born 15 July 1921, Chicago, Illinois, USA; son of John Fahey, Motorman, Chicago Surface Lines Inc, and Beatrice. **Tutor(s):** C W Guillebaud. **Educ:** Loyola Academy, Chicago; Loyola University, Chicago; University of Connecticut. **Career:** Private, First Class, US Army.

FAIRBAIRN, Professor Walter McArthur (1949) Born 5 April 1928, 113 Kenilworth Avenue, Glasgow; son of John William Fairbairn, Schoolmaster, and Catherine Livingstone McFarlane; m Barbara M Thomson, 11 September 1953, Glasgow; 2 sons (David b 1954 and Gordon b 1956), 1 daughter (Margaret b 1958). **Subject(s):** Mathematics; BA 1951; MA 1980; MA (Glasgow) 1948; PhD (Birmingham) 1953; FInstP; CPhys. **Tutor(s):** J M Wordie. **Educ:** Shawlands Academy; Glasgow High School; Glasgow University. **Career:** Assistant Lecturer in Mathematics 1948–1949, Lecturer in Mathematics 1953–1958, University of Glasgow; Title A Fellow, SJC 1956–1959; Lecturer in Mathematics, Manchester College of Sciences and Technology, Manchester University 1958–1964; Visiting Lecturer in Physics, Johns Hopkins University, Baltimore, USA 1962–1963 and 1979; Senior Lecturer, then Professor in Theoretical Physics 1964–1993, Deputy Vice-Chancellor 1984–1993, University of Lancaster; Visiting Professor, University of Waterloo, Ontario 1969–1970; Visiting Professor, University of New South Wales, Canberra 1980. **Awards:** Mayhews Prize; Adams Memorial Prize 1950.

FAIRBANK, James (1914) Born 21 September 1895, Appleton-le-Street, York; son of James Arthur Fairbank, Landowner and Farmer, and Elizabeth Watson. BA 1922. **Tutor(s):** R P Gregory. **Educ:** Mount Academy, Malton; Grammar School, Malton. **Career:** Private, RASC (Mechanical Transport), WWI.

FAIRHEAD, Dr Russell Wale (1944) Born 9 February 1927, Lynton, Winmarleigh Road, Preston, Lancashire; son of John William Fairhead, Civil Servant, General Post Office, and Evelyn Winifred Wale; m Heather Fuzzey, 1955; 1 son (Anthony Russell b 8 October 1957), 2 daughters (Joanne Fraser b 4 September 1959 and Harriet 14 April 1966). **Subject(s):** Natural Sciences; BA 1947; MA 1982; MB 1949; BChir 1949. **Tutor(s):** S J Bailey. **Johnian Relatives:** father of Anthony Russell Fairhead (1976). **Educ:** Redland View Preparatory School, Bristol; Bristol Grammar School; Lower School of John Lyon, Harrow; Exeter School. **Career:** House Appointments and Senior Resident Medical Officer, Westminster Hospital; Surgeon Lieutenant, RNVR; GP, Exeter; Physician, Royal Western Counties Hospital Group; Police Surgeon, Devon and Cornwall Constabulary; Senior Medical Officer, KwaZulu Health Service. **Appointments:** President, Devon and Exeter Medical Society. **Awards:** Sizarship, SJC; Vidal Exhibition, SJC.

FAIRHURST, Harry (1947) Born 15 August 1923, Newton-in-Makerfield, Lancashire; son of Benjamin Adzhead Fairhurst, Schoolmaster, and Ivy Seddon; 3 children. **Subject(s):** History; BA 1949; MA 1954. **Tutor(s):**

F Thistlethwaite. **Johnian Relatives:** brother of Jack Fairhurst (1940). **Educ:** St John the Baptist School, Oldham; Hulme Grammar School. **Career:** Captain, Airborne Signals, NW Europe and Palestine (Mentioned in Despatches), WWII; Manchester Public Libraries 1949–1951; Assistant Librarian, Brotherton Library, University of Leeds 1951–1956; Deputy Librarian, University College of Rhodesia and Nysasland 1956–1962; Librarian, University of York 1962. Died 27 April 1986.

FAIRHURST, Jack (1940) Born 20 April 1922, Newton-le-Willows, Lancashire; son of Benjamin Adzhead Fairhurst, Schoolmaster, and Ivy Seddon; 3 sons, 1 daughter. **Subject(s):** History; BA 1947; MA 1961. **Tutor(s):** C W Guillebaud. **Johnian Relatives:** brother of Harry Fairhurst (1947). **Educ:** Hey St John's Church of England School, Oldham; Hulme Grammar School, Oldham. **Career:** 1/8 Gurkha Rifles, Indian Army, Burma, Java 1941–1946; Colonial Service, Northern Rhodesia 1949–1966; Deputy Director (Administration), Estate Management and Building Service 1970–1989, Administrative Duties, McDonald Institute for Archeological Research 1990–1999, University of Cambridge. **Awards:** Sizarship, SJC. **Honours:** MBE for public service in Northern Rhodesia 1961; OBE for public service in Northern Rhodesia and Zambia 1965; Order of Distinguished Service, Zambia 1966.

FAIRLESS, Thomas Arnold Ashbridge (1936) Born 10 July 1902, 11 St Rollox Street, Hebburn on Tyne, Durham; son of Thomas Fairless, Grocer, and Sarah Ann Ashbridge; m Joan Marchant Chetwynd. **Subject(s):** Moral Sciences; BA 1939; MA 1943. **Tutor(s):** J S Boys Smith. **Educ:** Wesleyan Council School, Hebburn on Tyne; Dodmire Council School, Darlington; Higher Grade School, Darlington; Junior Technical School, Darlington. **Career:** Engineering Draftsman, Darlington 1917; Warden, the People's College, Blackburn, Lancashire 1947. Died 1974.

FAIRWEATHER, David Armstead (1930) Born 5 June 1913, Netergate, Pencisely Road, Llandaff, Glamorganshire; son of Paul Fairweather, Ship-owner/Lloyds Underwriter, and Mary Alice Sherratt. **Subject(s):** Modern and Medieval Languages; BA 1934. **Tutor(s):** C W Guillebaud. **Educ:** College Preparatory School, Cardiff; Pensionnat St Pierre, Calais; Winchmore Hill School, London; Canton Secondary School, Cardiff; Perse School, Cambridge.

FALCON, Michael (1922) Born 14 December 1903, Villa Friedia, Dwars Street, Sunnyside, Pretoria, South Africa; son of William Falcon, Headmaster, Hilton College, Natal; and Nora Amelia Rust; 2 children. **Subject(s):** Natural Sciences; BA 1925; MA 1929; Associate of the Royal School of Mines. **Tutor(s):** B F Armitage. **Johnian Relatives:** son of William Falcon (1892). **Educ:** Highbury Preparatory School, Hillcrest, South Africa; Hilton College; Natal University College, Pietermaritzburg. **Career:** Surveyor, Shift Boss, and Mine Overseer, Van Ryn Deep, Benoni 1927–1938; Major, Mines Engineering Brigade, South African Corps, WWII; Assistant Technical Advisor, Transvaal Chamber of Mines 1938–1951; Technical Advisor, Transvaal Chamber of Mines 1951. **Appointments:** President, Chemical, Metallurgical and Mining Society (South Africa) 1946–1947; Chairman, South African Executive Committee of the 7th Commonwealth Congress. **Publications:** *Aspects of Organization in the Witwatersrand Gold Mining Industry, with Special References to Labour*. Died 25 March 1961.

FAREWELL, John Freke (1924) Born 13 May 1899, Wormwood Scrubbs; son of John Raymond Farewell, Prison Commissioner, Home Office, and Florence Isabel Morey. **Tutor(s):** E E Sikes. **Educ:** Connaught House, Weymouth; Cheltenham. Died 19 April 1969.

FARLEY, John Robert (1938) Born 3 February 1920, 32 Lynford Gardens, Ilford, Essex; son of Fred Arthur Farley, Methodist Minister, and Frances Clara Deans. **Tutor(s):** C W Guillebaud. **Educ:** Rochester University School; Cowling Council School; Ermysted's Grammar School, Skipton; Blackpool Grammar School.

FARMER, Dr Bertram Hughes (1934) Born 18 March 1916, The Cliff, Malmesbury, Wiltshire; son of Seymour Farmer, Baptist Minister, and Mary Martha Hughes; m Anne Stewart, 1947 (d 1995). **Subject(s):** Geography; BA 1937; MA 1941; Honorary DLitt (Peradeniya, Sri Lanka) 1981. **Tutor(s):** J M Wordie. **Educ:** Stainsbridge College, Malmesbury; Malmesbury Secondary School Preparatory Department; Malmesbury Secondary School. **Career:** Major, RE (Mentioned in Despatches) 1939–1945; Lecturer in Geography, University College, Swansea 1946–1948; Teaching Officer 1948, Demonstrator in Geography 1948–1952, Lecturer in Geography 1952–1967, Director, Centre of South Asian Studies 1964–1983, Reader in South Asian Geography 1967–1983 (Emeritus 1983), University of Cambridge; Title B Fellow 1948–1977, Lecturer 1956–1983, Title D Fellow 1977–1996, SJC. **Appointments:** Supervisor 1948–1977, Director of Studies in Geography 1952–1977, Tutor 1958–1961, President 1967–1971, SJC; Governor, School of Oriental and African Studies, University of London; Member, Land Commission, Ceylon 1955–1958; Chairman, Gal Oya Project Evaluation Committee, Ceylon 1966–1967; President, Institute of British Geographers 1972. **Awards:** Scholarship, SJC 1936–1937; Wright's Prize, SJC 1937; Gill Award 1954; Leverhulme Research Grant 1963; Victoria Medal, Council of the Royal Geographical Society. Died 6 February 1996.

FARMER, Frank Reginald (1933) Born 18 December 1914, 92 Stanley Road, Gloucester; son of Frank Henry Farmer, Foreman Platelayer on Railway, and Minnie Godson; m Betty Smart, 1939; 1 son, 2 daughters. **Subject(s):** Mathematics; BA 1936; FInstP 1965; Honorary FSE 1974; FRS 1981. **Tutor(s):** J M Wordie. **Educ:** Carlton Road Council School, Gloucester; Crypt School, Gloucester. **Career:** Kestner Evaporator and Engineering Company 1936–1946; Director, Safety Reliability Directorate, Atomic Energy Authority (formerly Department of Atomic Energy) 1947–1979; Editor, *Reliability Engineering* 1980. **Appointments:** Foreign Associate, National Academy of Engineers USA 1980. **Awards:** Churchill Gold Medal 1974. **Honours:** OBE 1967. **Publications:** *Nuclear Reactor Safety*, 1977. Died 10 June 2001.

FARR, Peter James (1939) Born 20 May 1921, Darnall's Hall, Weston, Hitchin, Hertfordshire; son of Charles Edgar Farr, Farmer, and Elsie Maud Edmondson; BA 1943; MA 1946. **Tutor(s):** J S Boys Smith. **Educ:** Wychwood School, Bournemouth; Uppingham School.

FARR, Peter John (1943) Born 25 April 1926, 6 Holcombe Avenue, King's Lynn, Norfolk; son of Bert Richard Farr, Company Director, and Norah Mary Spreckley. **Subject(s):** Mechanical Sciences; BA 1946; MA 1967. **Tutor(s):** S J Bailey. **Educ:** St Faith's School, Cambridge; Aldenham School.

FARRAR, The Revd John Evelyn (1929) Born 7 April 1912, 49 Dudley Road, Moss Side South, Manchester; son of Fred Farrar, Schoolmaster, and Grace Winder; m Betty Gwillim Howard Tripp; 2 daughters. **Subject(s):** English/Moral Sciences; BA 1934; MA 1937; BA (Oxon) 1934. **Tutor(s):** M P Charlesworth. **Educ:** Crimsworth School, Manchester; Arnold House School, Blackpool. **Career:** Assistant Minister, Emmanuel Congregational Church, Cambridge 1937–1943; Director, London Missionary Society 1940; Minister, Macclesfield Congregational Church 1943–1965; Minister, Bollington Congregational Church 1948–1965; Minister, Leek United Reformed Church 1965–1977. **Publications:** *A Note on the History of Congregationalism in Macclesfield*; *History of Bollington Congregational Church.* Died 6 February 1987.

FARRAR, Reginald Hodson (1942) Born 27 February 1924, 1 St Margaret's Road, Horsforth, Yorkshire; son of George Fielding Farrar, Municipal Clerk, and Hilda Mary Hodson. **Subject(s):** Mathematics; BA 1948; MA 1950. **Tutor(s):** S J Bailey. **Educ:** Horsforth National School; Leeds Modern School. **Career:** Captain, Royal Signals 1943–1947; Senior Mathematics Master, Malvern College 1960–1984.

FAULKNER, Dr Donald (1934) Born 11 September 1915, 14 Westcroft Terrace, Bideford, Devon; son of Herbert Faulkner, United Methodist Minister, and Marion Sarvent; 1 daughter (Margaret). **Subject(s):** Natural Sciences; BA 1937; MA 1941; PhD 1940. **Tutor(s):** J M Wordie. **Educ:** Hornby Street Elementary School, Heywood; Central Higher School, Heywood; Heywood Grammar School; Cotham Secondary School, Bristol. **Career:** Title A Fellow, SJC 1940–1946 (on War Service 1940–1945); Research and Development Department, Distillers Company, Epsom; Work concerned with plastics and polymers. **Awards:** Scholarship, SJC 1936–1937; Hughes Prize, SJC 1937. Died 13 December 1994.

FAULKNER, John Herbert (1931) Born 30 August 1913, El Oro, Mexico; son of Herbert William Faulkner, Mining Engineer, and Marianna Amy May Booth; m Sheila; 2 daughters. BA 1934; MA 1973. **Tutor(s):** E A Benians. **Educ:** Brightlands, Dulwich; Shrewsbury School. **Career:** Served with the army in India, Normandy, Palestine, Singapore, Austria, and Germany; wounded during the Normandy Landings; Retired as Lieutenant Colonel 1958; Teacher, Hardye's School, Dorchester, Dorset 1958–1972. Died 1 September 1994.

FAULKS, John Michael (1949) Born 8 January 1928, Commonfield Cottage, Newent, Gloucestershire; son of Henry Faulks, Farm Labourer, and Edith Mary Holford. **Subject(s):** Mechanical Sciences; BA 1952; MA 1956. **Tutor(s):** R L Howland. **Johnian Relatives:** brother of Philip James Faulks (1933). **Educ:** Picklenash Elementary School, Newent; Rendcomb College, Cirencester. **Awards:** John Bernard Seeley Prize in Aeronautics 1952.

FAULKS, Philip James (1933) Born 12 August 1914, Brass Hills, Newent, Gloucestershire; son of Henry Faulks, Stockman, and Edith Mary Holford. **Subject(s):** Natural Sciences; BA 1936; MA 1940. **Tutor(s):** C W Guillebaud. **Johnian Relatives:** brother of John Michael Faulks (1949). **Educ:** Gloucestershire County Council School, Newent; Grammar School, Newent. **Career:** Lecturer in Botany, University of Aberdeen 1947.

FAWKES, Dr Marmaduke Ayscough (1933) Born 6 December 1915, Westholm, Biggar Bank, Walney, Barrow-in-Furness; son of Marmaduke Fawkes, Physician and Surgeon, and Linda Esperanza Funnell. **Subject(s):** Natural Sciences; BA 1937; MA 1940; BChir 1941; MB 1941; DPH 1951 (London); DTM&H (Conjoint board); MFCM 1972, Faculty of Community Medicine. **Tutor(s):** R L Howland. **Educ:** Highfield School, Liphook; Epsom College. **Career:** Principal Health Officer, Federal Government of Nigeria; Major, Indian Medical Service; Venereal Diseases Specialist, Trinidad 1951; Medical Officer of Health, Federation of Nigeria 1955. **Appointments:** Specialist in Community Medicine, South-West Thames Regional Health Authority. **Awards:** SBStJ 1960. Died 12 February 1993.

FAYERMAN, Alec George Percy (1904) Born 9 January 1885, 20 Adelaide Road, Leamington, Warwickshire; son of George Metcalfe Fayerman, Estate Agent, Surveyor and Auctioneer, and Ellen Elizabeth Ball. **Tutor(s):** E E Sikes. **Educ:** Bowood House Preparatory School, Leamington Spa; Leamington College, Leamington Spa; Hereford Cathedral School. **Career:** Major, Royal Warwickshire Regiment (TF), WWI.

FAYLE, Dr Brian William Knott (1949) Born 4 May 1930, St Brenda's Nursing Home, Clifton Park, Clifton, Bristol; son of Benjamin William Day Fayle, Medical Practitioner, and Isabelle Bryson Spiers Flett. BA 1952; MA 1956; BChir 1956; MB 1957. **Tutor(s):** G C L Bertram. **Educ:** Aymestrey School, Rushwick; Sherborne School.

FEARNSIDE, Kenneth (1937) Born 28 May 1919, 47 Station Road Ossett; son of David Fearnside, Café Proprietor, and Florence Haigh; m Marjorie Butcher, 1945; 2 daughters (Rosemary Agnes and Sarah Margaret Jane). **Subject(s):** Natural Sciences; BA 1940; MA 1944; AFRAeS 1962;

FIEE. **Tutor(s):** C W Guillebaud. **Johnian Relatives:** father-in-law of John Henry Parker (1967). **Educ:** South Ossett Church of England School; St Mary's Church of England School, Scarborough; Scarborough High School. **Career:** Signals/Radar Officer, RAF 1940–1946; AERE 1947–1950; Technical Director, Isotope Developments Ltd 1950–1953; Smiths Aviation Division: Systems Studies, Guided Weapons Department 1953–1957, Research Manager 1957–1959, Director of Research 1959–1961; Director, Plessey Company 1961–1968. **Appointments:** Captain, Bredon Cricket Club. **Awards:** Major Scholarship, SJC 1936; Hocken Prize in Physics. Died 17 August 1983.

FEATHER, Clive Edward (1934) Born 27 November 1915, 45 Church Road, Hove; son of Morris Feather, Company Director, Government Clothing Contractor, and Sabina Zelinski. **Subject(s):** Modern and Medieval Languages; BA 1937; MA 1941. **Tutor(s):** C W Guillebaud. **Educ:** The Hall, London; Eton College. **Awards:** Exhibition, SJC.

FEATHER, Peter Kelk (1922) Born 7 May 1904, Fairlea, Halifax, Yorkshire; son of Jackson Herbert Feather, Worsted Spinner, and Ruth Illingworth. **Tutor(s):** E A Benians. **Educ:** Hill Head School, Shrewsbury; Malvern College.

FELL, Arnold (1923) Born 12 June 1905, 8 Salisbury Street, Skipton, Yorkshire; son of John Charles Fell, Lead Manufacturer, and Susanna Hodgson. **Tutor(s):** B F Armitage. **Educ:** Preparatory School, Sedbergh; Hellesdown School, Norwich.

FELL, Eric Whineray (1931) Born 22 September 1901, Mayfield, Ulverston, Lancashire; son of Alfred Fell, Accountant, and Mary Elizabeth Winder; m Margaret E Taylor, 7 December 1943, Friends' Meeting House, Malton. BSc (Birmingham); MSc (Birmingham) 1926. **Tutor(s):** J M Wordie. **Educ:** St Aubyn's Preparatory School, Barrow-in-Furness; Haileybury College; University of Birmingham; Technische Hochschule, Aachen, Germany. **Career:** Apprentice, Vickers Naval Construction Works 1919–1923; Wiggin Metallurgical Scholar, University of Birmingham 1923–1925; Research Metallurgist, United Steel Companies 1929–1931. **Appointments:** Andrew Carnegie Scholar, Iron and Steel Institute 1925; Robert Blair Fellow, London County Council 1926.

FELTON, Percy William (1909) Born 27 January 1891, Underhill Cottage, Oswestry, Shropshire; son of William Felton, Contractor, and Jane Hill; m Sarah Joan Bartlett, 7 June 1917, Brighton; 1 son (William Fowler b 2 August 1913). **Subject(s):** Natural Sciences; BA 1912; MA 1939; BSc (London) 1912. **Tutor(s):** J R Tanner. **Johnian Relatives:** uncle of Peter Bartlett Collier Watson (1926); father of William Fowler Felton (1936). **Educ:** Oswestry School. **Career:** Director, Ronuk Works, Brighton 1923; Director, Hilton Rider and Co Ltd 1946. Died 20 November 1969.

FELTON, Dr William Fowler (1936) Born 2 August 1918, 5 College Terrace, Brighton; son of Percy William Felton, Director of Ronuk Ltd, and Sarah Joan Bartlett; m Felicity Anne Hamilton, 17 March 1945, St Michael's Church, Great Billington, Bedfordshire; 2 sons (Michael and Timothy), 3 daughters (Sarah, Jane and Joanna). **Subject(s):** Natural Sciences; BA 1939; MA 1943; BChir 1942; MB 1942; DPH (London); DIH (Society of Apothecaries). **Tutor(s):** R L Howland. **Johnian Relatives:** son of Percy William Felton (1909); cousin of Peter Bartlett Collier Watson (1926). **Educ:** Mowden School, Brighton; Charterhouse. **Career:** House Surgeon, Middlesex Hospital 1942; PMO, Ministry of Supply 1952; Hallmark Cards Ltd UK (eventually Managing Director and Chairman of Hallmark Europe) 1952–1968; Consultant in Genito-urinary medicine 1976–1983. **Appointments:** Honorary Consultant, St Thomas' Hospital 1986. **Honours:** Knight of the Royal Order of George I of the Hellines (with swords).

FENN, Charles Henry (1935) Born 19 June 1907, 155 Grove Lane, Camberwell, London; son of Robert William Fenn, Commercial Traveller, and Jennie Elizabeth Boxley. **Tutor(s):** J S Boys Smith. **Educ:** Beckenham Council School, Kent; Beckenham County School; Sutton County School, Surrey.

FENTON, Richard Coote (1939) Born 21 May 1921, 1 Lancaster Road, Hampstead; son of John Edward Fenton, Sales Manager, and Ida Elizabeth Mullins; m Mary Jo; 2 daughters (Helen Elizabeth and Ruth Catharine), 4 stepchildren. BA 1942; MA 1946. **Tutor(s):** C W Guillebaud. **Educ:** Highwood School, Mill Hill; St George's School, Windsor; Cranleigh School. **Career:** Ministry of Economic Warfare and Foreign Office 1941–1947; British Schering Company 1947–1951; British Manager, Pfizer Ltd 1951–1952; Vice-President, Pfizer Corporation 1952–1962; Chairman and Managing Director of British Subsidiary, Pfizer Corporation, Director of all other associated companies in Europe and America 1952–1967; Chairman, Pfizer Ltd 1956–1961; President, International Pfizer Corporation 1962–1967; Independent Entrepreneur 1968. Died 2 November 2002.

FENWICK-SMITH, Peter (1941) See SMITH.

FERGUSON, Professor John (1939) Born 2 March 1921, Windlehurst, Anson Road, Rusholme, Manchester; son of Allan Hitchen Ferguson, Assistant Professor of Physics, and Nesta Thomas; m Elnora Dixon, 1950. **Subject(s):** Classics; BA 1942; MA 1947; BD (London). **Tutor(s):** R L Howland. **Educ:** Bishop's Stortford College Preparatory School; Bishop's Stortford College. **Career:** Professor of Classics, University College of Ibadan, Nigeria; University of Minnesota 1956–1969; Professor and Dean of Faculty of Arts, Open University 1969–1979; President, Selly Oak Colleges, Birmingham 1979–1986. **Appointments:** Chairman, United Nations Association of Great Britain 1980. **Awards:** Scholarship, SJC. **Publications:** More than fifty books on classics and education. Died 22 May 1989.

FERGUSON, Thomas Barker (1945) Born 24 July 1927, 2 Green Avenue, Blackpool, Lancashire; son of Duncan Ferguson, Marine Engineer, and Mabel Lizzie Barker; m Angela Mary Saddington, 30 October 1952, St Michael's Church, Crich, Derbyshire; 1 son (Duncan b 1954), 2 daughters (Anne b 1955 and Fiona b 1961). **Subject(s):** Mechanical Sciences; BA 1948; MA 1952. **Tutor(s):** S J Bailey; R L Howland. **Educ:** Roseacre Council School, Blackpool; Arnold School, Blackpool. **Career:** Technical Assistant, Rolls-Royce Ltd, Derby 1948–1953; Assistant Technical Manager, Bryan Donkin Co Ltd, Chesterfield 1953–1959; Lecturer in Mechanical Engineering 1959–1964, Senior Lecturer in Mechanical Engineering 1964–1984, Honorary Senior Lecturer in Mechanical Engineering 1984–, University of Sheffield. **Publications:** *The Centrifugal Compressor Stage*, Butterworth, 1963; papers on turbo machinery.

FERGUSSON, Dr John Douglas (1928) Born 5 December 1909, The Hydropathic Establishment, Great Malvern, Worcestershire; son of John Newbery Fraser Fergusson, Physician and Surgeon, and Mildred Gladys Mercer; m (1) Alice Maartensz, (2) Myrtle Mason (née Body), 23 April 1969, London; (1) 2 sons. **Subject(s):** Natural Sciences; BA 1931; MA 1945; MB 1934; BChir 1934; MD 1946; MRCS 1934; LRCP 1934; FRCS 1936. **Tutor(s):** M P Charlesworth. **Johnian Relatives:** son of John Newbery Fraser Fergusson (1899); nephew of Argyll Fergusson (1899) and of Louis Roy Fergusson (1902). **Educ:** Mount House School, Plymouth; Malvernhurst School, Malvern; St Peter's School, York. **Career:** Central Middlesex Hospital 1934. **Appointments:** Hunterian Professor, RCS 1945–1946; Founder and Secretary, British Association of Urological Surgeons 1957–1960; President, British Association of Urological Surgeons 1970–1972. **Awards:** Sutton-Sams Prize, St Thomas' Hospital; St Peter's Medal, British Association of Urological Surgeons; Cheselden Medal, St Thomas' Hospital. **Publications:** (ed) *British Journal of Urology*. Died 20 April 1979.

FERGUSSON, Louis Roy (1902) Born 11 January 1885, Sutherland Villa, Wick, Caithness, Scotland; son of John Campbell Fergusson, Physician, Malvern Hydropathic Establishment, and Christina Mackie. BA 1906. **Tutor(s):** D MacAlister. **Johnian Relatives:** brother of John Newbury Fraser Fergusson (1899) and of Argyll Fergusson (1899); uncle of John Douglas Fergusson (1928). **Educ:** Cherbourg Boys' School; Malvern College. **Career:** Headmaster's Secretary 1912, Bursar 1913, Rossall School; Lieutenant, RFA, then Captain, Special List, WWI; Captain, 8th Worcestershire Regiment 1920.

FERGUSSON, Sydney George (1939) Born 3 April 1920, 15 Barefoot Street, Ripon; son of Leonard Pratt Fergusson, Grocer, and Ellen May Routledge. **Tutor(s):** J M Wordie. **Educ:** West Riding County Council School, Ripon; Ripon Grammar School.

FERNANDO, Charles Herbert Zuleski (1910) Born 28 June 1892, Colombo, Ceylon; son of Charles Matthew Fernando, Barrister-at-Law, and Jane Maria de Soysa. **Subject(s):** Law; BA 1913. **Tutor(s):** L H K Bushe-Fox. **Johnian Relatives:** son of Charles Matthew Fernando (1885). **Educ:** St Joseph's College, Colombo. **Career:** Called to the Bar, Lincoln's Inn 1913.

FERRIDAY, Thomas Bennett (1921) Born 24 July 1894, School House, Kinglsey, Stoke-on-Trent, Staffordshire; son of Moses Ferriday, Schoolmaster, and Elizabeth Bennett. BA 1923; MA 1947. **Tutor(s):** E E Sikes. **Educ:** Kingsley Edward School; RMA, Woolwich; High School, Leek. **Career:** Lieutenant, Royal Corps of Signals; Brevet Major, Signal Unit, Huddersfield; Intelligence Officer, Civil Defence Control Room, Southern Region, Ministry of Home Security; Instructor, Army Signal Training Centre 1923–1925; Captain, Wireless Interception Unit, Palestine 1926; Company Commander, India 1927–1930; Retired 1931; Recalled to Signal Unit, Catterick Camp 1939; Instructor, Signal Section, Cambridge University STC 1940–1941; Assistant Master, Nottingham Bluecoat School 1946.

FERRIS, Samuel Bernard Clutton (1908) Born 1 December 1890, 59 St Andrews, Hillingdon, Middlesex; son of John Spencer Ferris, Physician and Surgeon, and Mary Clutton. BA 1911. **Tutor(s):** J R Tanner. **Educ:** Cheltenham College; Eastbourne College. **Career:** Second Lieutenant, 11th Cavalry Reserve, 10th Hussars 1914–1915. Died 6 April 1915 (accidentally killed).

FERRIS, William Edward (1907) Born 14 April 1889, 1 West View Cottages, West Road, Bury St Edmunds; son of George Francis Ferris, Drum Major, and Esther Cooper. **Subject(s):** Natural Sciences; BA 1910. **Tutor(s):** J R Tanner. **Educ:** Municipal Secondary School, Norwich.

FETTES, Peter (1934) Born 28 December 1913, 184 Burmah Road, Penang, Straights Settlements; son of James Dollery Fettes, Engineer, and Margaret Hood Moffat Johnstone; m; 1 daughter. **Subject(s):** Modern Languages Tripos; BA 1937. **Tutor(s):** C W Guillebaud. **Educ:** St Peter's School, Weston-Super-Mare; Royal College of Music, London; Bradfield College. **Career:** Radio Announcer and Newsreader; Announcer, Midland Regional BBC 1937; RAF 1939–1945; Announcer, *The Light Programme*, BBC 1945.

FEWINGS, John Albert (1906) Born 19 March 1887, The Grammar School, Bugle Street, Southampton; son of James Fewings, Headmaster, and Lydia Mary Blackmur; m Cordelia. **Subject(s):** Mathematics/ Natural Sciences; BA 1909; MA 1913. **Tutor(s):** J R Tanner. **Johnian Relatives:** brother of Percy James Fewings (1901). **Educ:** Bedford Grammar School. **Career:** Second Lieutenant, RGA, WWI; Headmaster, St Andrew's School, Meads, Eastbourne. Died 24 February 1946.

FEWINGS, John Atkinson (1936) Born 12 February 1918, Holly House, Staple Street, Hern Hill, Kent; son of Arthur Blackmur Fewings, Superintending Inspector, Ministry of Agriculture and Fisheries, and Lucy Mabel Atkinson. **Tutor(s):** R L Howland. **Educ:** Glen Garth Preparatory School, Cheltenham; St Andrew's, Eastbourne; Rugby.

FEWINGS, Percy James (1901) Born 24 May 1882, The Grammar School, Southampton; son of James Fewings, Headmaster, Southampton Grammar School, and Lydia Mary Blackmur. **Subject(s):** Natural Sciences; BA 1904. **Tutor(s):** D MacAlister. **Johnian Relatives:** brother of John Albert Fewings (1906). **Educ:** King Edward VI Grammar School, Southampton. **Career:** Science Master, Mansfield Grammar School 1904–1909; City of Norwich School 1911.

FFRENCH MULLEN, Christopher Richard (1943) Born 26 November 1925, 36 Upper Mount Street, Dublin; son of Ernest Ffrench Mullen, Planter, and Winifred Margaret Pope. **Tutor(s):** C W Guillebaud. **Educ:** St Bede's Preparatory School, Rugeley; The Oratory School, Reading; Dominican College, Newbridge; Foyle College, Londonderry.

FIDLER, Dr John Carter (1933) Born 21 September 1907, Main Street, Haltwhistle, Northumberland; son of William Corn Fidler, Solicitor's Clerk, and Jessie Carter; PhD 1937; BSc (Durham) 1929; PhD (Durham) 1932. **Tutor(s):** C W Guillebaud. **Educ:** Hexham Grammar School; Carlisle Technical School; Armstrong College, Newcastle upon Tyne. **Career:** Research Student, Armstrong College 1929–1930; Earl Grey Fellow, Armstrong College; Covent Garden Laboratory of the Food Investigation Organisation 1936. **Awards:** Ottesen Medal 1959. **Honours:** OBE 1957.

FIELD, Arthur Michael Cary (1929) Born 24 March 1910, 32 St James' Road, Edgbaston; son of Arthur Perrott Cary Field, Schoolmaster, and Ethelwyn Mary Bullock; m Mary. **Subject(s):** History; BA 1932. **Tutor(s):** E A Benians. **Johnian Relatives:** son of Arthur Perrott Cary Field (1886). **Educ:** West House School, Edgbaston; Tonbridge School. **Career:** Library Assistant, Institute of Historical Research, University of London 1948. **Awards:** Exhibition, SJC. Died 3 November 1982.

FIELD, Derek Harold (1941) Born 26 March 1923, 79 St Pancras, Chichester, Sussex; son of Harold Field, Farmer and Horse Dealer, and Edith Muriel Harrison; m Catherine Rosemary Jones, 1948; 4 sons (Christopher b 1951, Godfrey b 1953, Stephen b 1956 and Mark b 1960). **Subject(s):** Mechanical Sciences; BA 1944; MA 1948; CEng; MICE. **Tutor(s):** S J Bailey. **Educ:** Marlborough College; Westbury House, West Meon. **Career:** REME, Mentioned in Despatches, Palestine 1943–1947; Design Engineer, Bridge Department, Dorman Long 1947–1953; Engineer, Bridge over River Tagus, Portugal 1949–1951; Works Manager, Director and General Manager, Shelton Iron and Steel 1953–1978; Director, North Staffordshire Chamber of Commerce and Industry 1980–1984; TSB England and Wales 1983–1988. **Appointments:** High Sheriff of Staffordshire 1989–1990; DL, Staffordshire 1991; Mayor, Ancient Corporation of Hanley 1992; President, Chamber of Commerce and Industry; President, Stone Lawn Tennis and Squash Club; President, Stone Conservative Association. Died 30 July 1999.

FIELD, George Arthur Charles (1921) Born 17 July 1903, 18 Chambers Road, Southport, Lancashire; son of Francis George Elwes Field, Clerk in Holy Orders, and Alice Jane de Ville Owen; m Elsie Muriel Murray, 1 January 1933, Johore Bahru, Malaya; 1 son (Jonathan), 2 daughters (Wendy and Susan). **Subject(s):** History; BA 1925. **Tutor(s):** B F Armitage. **Johnian Relatives:** grandson of Thomas Field (1840); nephew of Dudley Thomas Bousquet Field (1884) and of Arthur Perrott Cary Field (1886); son of Francis George Elwes Field (1887); brother of Thomas Richard Owen Field (1922); father of Jonathan Mostyn Murray Field (1956). **Educ:** Gresham's School, Holt. **Career:** Chinese Government Salt Administration 1925; Assistant Superintendent of Customs, Sarawak 1930; Superintendent 1931; Civilian Internee 1941–1945; Commissioner of Trade and Customs, Sarawak 1946. Died 12 February 1972.

FIELD, Hubert Astley (1919) Born 10 September 1898, 99 Blackburn Road, Darwen, Lancashire; son of Edgar Alfred Field, Medical Practitioner, and Henrietta Beeson. **Subject(s):** Natural Sciences; BA 1921. **Tutor(s):** E A Benians. **Educ:** Woodham Grove School, Bradford;

Manchester Grammar School. **Career:** Master, Blackburn Grammar School 1921–1923; Manchester Grammar School 1923–1963. **Awards:** Somerset Exhibition, SJC 1916.

FIELD, Thomas Richard Owen (1922) Born 9 December 1899, Newham House, Truro, Cornwall; son of Francis George Elwes Field, Clerk in Holy Orders, and Alice Jane de Ville Owen; m Constance Joyce Wood, 27 November 1959, St Stephen's, Rochester Row, Westminster. **Subject(s):** Modern and Medieval Languages/English; BA 1925. **Tutor(s):** E E Sikes. **Johnian Relatives:** grandson of Thomas Field (1840); nephew of Dudley Thomas Bousquet Field (1884); nephew of Arthur Perrott Cary Field (1886); son of Francis George Elwes Field (1887); brother of George Arthur Charles Field (1921); uncle of Jonathan Mostyn Murray Field (1956). **Educ:** West House School, Edgbaston; Oundle School. **Career:** Indian Army 1918–1922; Assistant Master, Imperial Service College, Windsor 1925–1929; Harrow School 1929–1939; Ministry of Aircraft Production, WWII; Principal, Finance Division, Ministry of Supply 1951. **Publications:** 'The Lists of Love', *The Eagle*, 43; 'What are the Wild Waves Saying', *The Eagle*, 43; 'Despair', *The Eagle*, 44. Died 12 March 1989.

FIELD, William Patrick McDonnell (1947) Born 20 July 1926, Oxford House Nursing Home, Clarendon Road, Watford, Hertfordshire; son of Gordon Field, Civil Engineer, Electricity Board, Watford, and Mercy Rudd Vince; m Madeleine Hay, 14 September 1968, Cheltenham; 1 son (Roger Philip b 1971), 1 daughter (Caroline Sarah b 1972). **Subject(s):** Modern and Medieval Languages; BA 1950; MA 1954. **Tutor(s):** R L Howland. **Educ:** Watford Grammar School; Christ's Hospital. **Career:** Intelligence Corps (cryptanalyst and translator), Bletchley Park and Austria 1944–1947; GCHQ, Eastcote 1950–1953; French teacher, New Zealand 1953–1954; DSB, Melbourne, Australia 1954–1958; English teacher, Germany 1958–1959; English Teacher (TEFL), Bournemouth; Linguist Specialist, GCHQ, Cheltenham 1959–1967; GCHQ, Cyprus 1967–1968; GCHQ, Cheltenham 1968–1973; Departments of Environment (Housing) and Transport (Road Safety and Carriage of Dangerous Goods), London 1973–1988; Dangerous Goods Branch, Economic Commission for Europe (UNO), Geneva 1990–1991. **Awards:** Major Scholarship, SJC 1944; Henry Arthur Thomas Travel Award, University of Cambridge 1948–1949. **Publications:** *Conquest of the Underwater World*, 1974, David & Charles (translation of Hans Hass, *Welt unter Wasser*).

FIELDING, Raymond (1947) Born 29 November 1925, 53 Thompson Street, Shipley, Yorkshire; son of Henry Fielding, Woollen Warehouseman, and Sarah Lee; m Dorothy Christine Sharp, 1959; 2 sons (Andrew John and Stephen Charles). **Subject(s):** English/History; BA 1949; MA 1954. **Tutor(s):** F Thistlethwaite. **Educ:** Albert Road Junior School, Shipley; The Salt High School, Shipley. **Career:** Head of English Department, Baines School, Poulton-le-Fylde. **Publications:** (edited with E L Black), *Practice Papers in English Language*, 1967, John Murray.

FIGUEIREDO, José Borges (1901) Born 28 May 1883, São Paolo, Brazil; son of José Borges Figueiredo and Maria Augusta Paião. **Tutor(s):** C E Graves; J R Tanner. **Educ:** Oakfield School, Crouch End; Escola Americana, Brazil.

FILMER, Walter George Harry (1913) Born 30 September 1894, 6 Castlenau Gardens, Barnes, Surrey; son of Walter George Filmer, Commercial Traveller, and Phoebe Lobjoit. **Subject(s):** Mathematics; BA 1920. **Tutor(s):** L H K Bushe-Fox. **Educ:** Springfield College, Acton; Latymer Upper School. **Career:** Captain and Adjutant, The Buffs, East Kent Regiment (Mentioned in Despatches), WWI. **Honours:** MBE.

FILMER, William Edmund (1925) Born 10 February 1906, 4 Devonshire Road, Toxteth Park, Liverpool, Lancashire; son of Reginald Harold Filmer, Fancy Box Manufacturer, and Caroline Hall. **Subject(s):** Mathematics/Natural Sciences; BA 1928. **Tutor(s):** J M Wordie. **Educ:** Rosehill School, Banstead; Lancing College.

FILTNESS, Donald Dunstan (1937) Born 10 September 1918, Clovelly Nursing Home, Ditton Court Road, Southend-on-Sea; son of William Edward Filtness, Assistant Clerk to the Armourers and Braziers Company, and Mabel Constance Mackay. **Subject(s):** Mathematics; BA 1940. **Tutor(s):** J M Wordie. **Educ:** Chalkwell Hall Council School, Leigh-on-Sea; High School for Boys, Southend-on-Sea. **Awards:** Baylis Scholarship, SJC 1936.

FINCH, Captain Frank Richard (1942) Born 7 February 1924, 387 Wigan Road, Ashton-in-Makerfield; son of Frank Finch, Accounts Clerk, Lancashire Associated Collieries, and Elizabeth Ellen Gaskell; m Glady Annie Metcalfe, 13 August 1948 (d December 1999); 1 son (Peter b 1952), 2 daughters (Alexandra b 1950 and Susan b 1954, d 1991). **Subject(s):** Natural Sciences; BA 1945; MA 1949; MBIM. **Tutor(s):** C W Guillebaud. **Educ:** St Peter's Church of England Elementary School, Bryn; The Grammar School, Ashton-in-Makerfield. **Career:** RN (retired as Captain) 1946–1971; Academic Registrar, South Bank Polytechnic 1971–1978; Academic Registrar, Chelsea College, London University 1978–1984.

FINCH, Henry Kingsley (1902) Born 31 May 1883, 7 Priory Terrace, Wellesley Road, St Mary at the Walls, Colchester, Essex; son of Henry Finch, Doctor, and Helen Georgina Gazeley. **Subject(s):** Classics; BA 1905; MA 1910. **Tutor(s):** D MacAlister. **Educ:** Bedford Grammar School. **Career:** Ordained Deacon 1908; Curate, Alfreton 1908–1912; Priest 1909; Curate, St Mary, Nottingham 1912–1914; CF 1915–1917. Died 11 November 1917.

FINCH, Peter Charles (1925) Born 27 August 1905, Cortessy House, Norfolk; son of Charles Hugh Finch, Brewer, and Mildred Bertha Long. **Tutor(s):** B F Armitage. **Educ:** South Lodge, Enfield; Winton House, Winchester; Harrow School; Home Place, Holt.

FINK, Dr Frederick William (1935) Born 27 March 1912, Newark, New Jersey, USA; son of Colin Garfield Fink, Professor, Columbia University, New York, and Lottie Catherine Muller. MSc 1938. **Tutor(s):** J M Wordie. **Educ:** Lincoln School of Teachers College; Cornell University. Died 11 April 1998.

FINKELSTEIN, Maurice Moores Behr (1926) Born 27 May 1908, 40 Nelson Road South, Great Yarmouth, Norfolk; son of Samuel Meyer Finkelstein, Herring Agent or Fish Merchant, and Rachel Lewis. **Subject(s):** Natural Sciences; BA 1929. **Tutor(s):** C W Guillebaud. **Educ:** High School, Great Yarmouth; Duncan House School, Great Yarmouth; The Grammar School, Great Yarmouth. **Awards:** Exhibition, SJC.

FINLAY, Dr David Thornton (1948) Born 14 December 1929, The Gables, Honiton, Devon; son of James Ernest Finlay, Medical Practitioner, and Florence Lucy Flamank. **Subject(s):** Natural Sciences; BA 1951; MA 1955; BChir 1954; MB 1955. **Tutor(s):** G C L Bertram. **Educ:** Ravenswood Preparatory School, Tiverton; Epsom College.

FINLAY, James Stimpson (1919) Born 3 April 1901, 219 Cavehill Road, Belfast, Ireland; son of Robert Hugh Forsythe Finlay, Managing Director, Messrs A Finlay Ltd, and Margaret Finlay Stimpson. BA 1922; MA 1931. **Tutor(s):** E A Benians. **Educ:** Rockport Preparatory School, Craigard; Dover College, Junior School (Preparatory School); Heversham School; Monkton Combe School; Presbyterian College, Belfast. **Career:** Ordained Minister, John White Memorial Congregational Church, Belfast 1935; in business, South America; Professor of Languages, University of Montevideo; Editor, *World Crusade*, the organ of the World's Evangelisation Crusade.

FINLAYSON, Dr John Richard Terrell (1947) Born 25 January 1929, Ambleside, 26 Downs Court Road, Purley; son of Thomas Campbell Finlayson, Technical Director, and Doris Mabel Ashby Terrell; m; 2 daughters, 3 stepchildren. BA 1950; MA 1954; BChir 1953; MB 1954.

Tutor(s): G C L Bertram. **Educ:** Glengorse Preparatory School, Battle; Tonbridge School. **Career:** GP, Coventry. **Appointments:** National Medical Adviser to the Samaritans. Died 22 November 1987.

FINNEGAN, Dr Thomas (1922) Born 30 May 1901, Kelvin House, Botanic Avenue, Belfast, Ireland; son of John Maxwell Finnegan, Secretary to Queen's University, Belfast, and Susan Wilson Dobbin; m; 3 sons, 2 daughters. **Subject(s):** Classics/Theology; BA 1924; MA 1928; Honorary LLD (TCD). **Tutor(s):** E E Sikes. **Educ:** Methodist College, Belfast; Queen's University, Belfast. **Career:** Lecturer in Classics, Magee University College, Londonderry; Principal, Cumberland Lodge, Windsor; President, Selly Oak Colleges, Birmingham, USA; Professor of Latin and Greek, Magee College 1930; President, Magee College 1946. Died 11 November 1964.

FINNIE, John (1947) Born 24 July 1924, Strath, Tulloch, Meldrum, Aberdeenshire; son of William Pratt Milne Finnie, Farm Bailiff, and Joan McGarrol. **Tutor(s):** C W Guillebaud. **Educ:** Greenfield Council School; St Mary's Church of England School, Greenfield; The Hulme Grammar School, Oldham. **Career:** Lieutenant, RNVR.

FINUCAN, Henry Maurice (1940) Born 6 July 1917, Warry Street, Valley, Brisbane; son of Michael Thomas Finucan, Wholesale Merchant, and Margaret Mary O'Brien. BA (Oxon) 1939. **Tutor(s):** J M Wordie. **Educ:** Gregory Terrace College, Brisbane; University of Queensland, Brisbane; Balliol College, Oxford.

FISHER, Charley (1902) Born 4 October 1883, Bulk, Lancashire; son of John Fisher, Farmer, and Susannah McNeal. BA 1907. **Tutor(s):** J R Tanner; C E Graves. **Career:** Ordained Deacon 1910; Ordained Priest 1911.

FISHER, Frederic Browell (1907) Born 17 August 1888, The Vicarage, Fulham, Middlesex; son of Frederic Horatio Fisher, Clerk in Holy Orders, and Agnes Jeune Jackson; m Joan Ethel Pike, 13 November 1920, St Martin in the Fields. **Subject(s):** Classics; BA 1910. **Tutor(s):** E E Sikes. **Educ:** Bengeo School; Marlborough College. **Career:** Bank of Bengal 1911; Lieutenant, IARO, attached to 5th Gurkha Rifles. **Awards:** Foundation Scholarship, Marlborough 1902. Died 10 December 1936.

FISHER, George Walter Peter (1936) Born 19 August 1917, St Paul's Road, Clifton, Bristol; son of Alfred George Timbrell Fisher, Consulting Surgeon, and Grace Ellen Bond. **Subject(s):** English; BA 1939; MA 1962. **Tutor(s):** R L Howland. **Educ:** Private Tuition, London; Westminster School; St Thomas' Hospital. **Career:** Commander, 'M' Battery, Royal Horse Artillery 1954–1956.

FISHER, Graham Russel (RUSSEL-FISHER) (1924) Born 21 September 1905, 6 Alexandra Road, South Withington, Manchester; son of Wilfred Harold Fisher, Solicitor, and Alcide Eleanore Fernande Leroy. **Subject(s):** English/Law; BA 1927; MA 1931. **Tutor(s):** E E Sikes. **Educ:** Private School, Penrith; Penrith Grammar School; Durham School. Died 30 January 1987.

FISHER, John Derbyshire (1934) Born 16 February 1916, Poplar House, Sutton on Trent, Newark; son of Hedley Fisher, Director, J D Marsden Ltd, and Jessie Marsden; 2 sons. **Tutor(s):** R L Howland. **Educ:** Broadgate School, Nottingham; The Leys School, Cambridge. **Career:** RAMC, 6th Airborne Division 1939–1945; Nottingham General Hospital; Medical Officer, Nottingham University 1946–1974. **Appointments:** Master, Royal Sussex Masonic Lodge; Founder Member, Nottingham University Lodge; Member, Grand Provincial Lodge; Vice-President, Climbing Club; Member, Trent Sailing Club. **Honours:** MC. Died 30 January 1974.

FISHER, Kenneth John (1945) Born 26 June 1927, Glenside House, Ulverston, Cumbria; son of Stanley Joseph Fisher, Solicitor, and

Gertrude Isabel Ridding, Teacher; m Mary Florence Towers, 8 May 1954; 1 son (Stephen John b 6 October 1957), 1 daughter (Anne Rosemary b 24 April 1956). **Subject(s):** Law; BA 1950; MA 1978; LLB 1951; LLM 1985. **Tutor(s):** S J Bailey. **Educ:** Durham House School, Barrow-in-Furness; The Craig, Windermere; Uppingham. **Career:** Sub-Lieutenant, RNVR 1945–1948; Admitted Solicitor 1953; Senior Partner, Kendall & Fisher 1972–1997. **Appointments:** Clerk to the General Commissioners of Taxes, Lonsdale North; Chairman, Agricultural Land Tribunal (Northern Area); Chairman, Supplementary Benefits Appeal Tribunal; Member, Cumbria Family Health Services Authority; Chairman, Cumbria Medical Services Committee; Member, South Cumberland Health Council; Chairman, Social Security Appeal Tribunal; Chairman, Dalton and District Recreational Charity Trust; Chairman, Furness Probation Support Group; Member, Furness Hospital NHS Trust 1994–1995; Chairman, Area Committee, The Legal Aid Board; Clerk to Billincoat Charities and Dalton Free School Trustees; President, Dalton Town Band; President, North Lonsdale Law Association; Life Governor, Imperial Cancer Research Fund; Honorary Solicitor to St Mary's Hospice; Chairman of Governors, Chetwynde School. **Awards:** Sir Joseph Larmor Award, SJC.

FISHER, Dr Michael George Penton (1949) Born 21 November 1930, 67 Brunswick Place, Hove, Sussex; son of William Alexander Penton Fisher, Principal Scientific Officer, Farnborough, and Anna Elizabeth Romere; m Nuala, 1957; 1 son (Robert), 1 daughter (Caroline). **Subject(s):** Natural Sciences (Medicine); BA 1952; MA 1978; MB 1956; BChir 1955; DObstRCOG; DCH; DAvMed; MFOM 1980. **Tutor(s):** G C L Bertram. **Johnian Relatives:** son of William Alexander Penton Fisher (1920); brother of Edward Anthony La Salle Fisher (1959). **Educ:** North Farnborough Elementary School; Clifton House, Harrogate; Farnborough Grammar School; Wrekin College; Middlesex Hospital Medical School. **Career:** House Officer, NHS; Medical Branch, RAF, including tours in Hong Kong, the Maldives, Germany and USA (served at the British Embassy on the Air Attaché's staff, subsequently on exchange with the USAF at Andrews AFB) 1956–1985; Commanding Officer, Princess Mary's RAF Hospital, Halton 1983–1985; Medical Division, Civil Aviation Authority, Head of Clinics and Occupational Health Service 1985–1995; Aviation Medical Adviser to Aircrew Underwriting Agencies Ltd 1997. **Appointments:** Member, BMA; RAF Club and Association of Authorised Aviation Medical Examiners; Society of Occupational Medicine. **Awards:** Strathcona Scholarship, SJC 1952; Fox Linton Award for Flight Safety. **Publications:** Various papers on Aviation Medicine.

FISHER, William Alexander Penton (1920) Born 8 March 1901, Woodside, Alum Chine Road, Bournemouth; son of George Penton Fisher, Art Master, and Kate Isabel Penton; m Anna Elizabeth Romère; 2 sons (Michael George Penton b 21 November 1930 and Edward Antony La Salle b 5 December 1938). **Subject(s):** Mathematics/Mechanical Sciences; BA 1923. **Tutor(s):** B F Armitage. **Johnian Relatives:** father of Michael George Penton Fisher (1949) and of Edward Anthony La Salle Fisher (1959). **Educ:** Brighton Grammar School; Bournemouth School. **Career:** Gravity surveyor, Anglo-Saxon Petroleum Company; Member, Cambridge University Engineers' Association Register 1937; Principal Scientific Officer, RAE, Farnborough 1948. **Awards:** Scholarship, SJC 1919. Died 6 October 1969.

FISON, Alexander Key (1910) Born 2 August 1891, 14 Dean Road, Willesden, Middlesex; son of Alfred Henry Fison, Lecturer in Physics, Guy's Hospital, London, and Alice Maud Williamson; m Mabel Rose Gates, 25 April 1925, St Gabriel, Cricklewood; 1 son (John). **Subject(s):** Mathematics; BA 1913. **Tutor(s):** L H K Bushe-Fox. **Johnian Relatives:** brother-in-law of Bernard William Gilbert (1910); uncle of Roger Key Gilbert (1948). **Educ:** Norfolk House, Beaconsfield; Aldenham School. **Career:** Captain, Essex Regiment, WWI; Chartered Accountant, Partner in Knox, Cropper and Caomlany. **Honours:** Chevalier, Legion of Honour; MC 18 July 1917; Croix de Guerre 1919. Died 17 September 1965.

FITZHERBERT, Lord Basil Francis Nicholas (STAFFORD) (1949) Born 7 April 1926, Hamlash, Shortfield Common, Frensham, Surrey; son of Thomas Charles Fitzherbert, Gentleman, and Helen Beryl Frances Waters; m Morag Nada Campbell, 16 June 1952; 3 sons, 3 daughters. **Tutor(s):** R L Howland. **Educ:** Avisford, Arundel; Ampleforth College. **Career:** Lieutenant, Scots Guards 1945–1947; Director, Barclays Bank 1982. **Appointments:** President, Staffordshire Country Landowners' Association; Show Director, Staffordshire Agricultural Society. Died 8 January 1986.

FITZHERBERT, Henry (1926) Born 30 August 1908, Park Hall, Manchester, Jamaica; son of Godfrey White Fitzherbert, Planter, and Anna Rachel Pile; m Elizabeth; 2 sons (Nicholas and Simon). **Tutor(s):** M P Charlesworth. **Educ:** École Nouvelle de la Suisse, Romand Chailly, Lausanne, Switzerland; Private Tuition. Died 28 June 1960.

FLACK, Alan William (1932) Born 1 November 1913, 36 Manor Road, Stoke Newington, London; son of William Thomas Flack, Local Government Officer, and Helen Tossell; m Joan. **Subject(s):** Mathematics/Natural Sciences; BA 1935; MA 1966; BSc (London) 1935. **Tutor(s):** J M Wordie. **Educ:** The Grammar School, Stoke Newington; City of London School. **Career:** Lecturer in Physics and Astronomy, University of Canterbury, New Zealand; Indian Civil Service 1935–1947. **Awards:** Exhibition, SJC. Died 20 December 1980.

FLECK, Fritz (1913) Born 18 July 1895, 24 Dom Strasse, Cologne, Germany; son of Hugo Fleck, Amtsgerichsrat, and Rosa Strakosch. **Tutor(s):** L H K Bushe-Fox. **Educ:** Konigliche Friedrich Wilhelms Gymnasium, Cologne.

FLEET, The Revd Charles Stanley (1906) Born 26 July 1888, 70 Upland Road, Lordship Lane, Camberwell, Surrey; son of Oswald Charles Fleet, Banker's Clerk, and Jane Elizabeth Turner; m Dorothy Alice Sharp, 19 September 1913, Gillingham Parish Church. BA 1909; MA 1913. **Tutor(s):** J R Tanner. **Johnian Relatives:** brother of William Walter Strong Fleet (1903). **Educ:** Dulwich College. **Career:** Ordained Deacon 1911; Ordained Priest 1912; Curate, Gillingham 1913; Curate, Bovey Tracey 1914; Curate, High Week 1915; CF, 4th Class, RACD (Mentioned in Despatches) 1916–1918; Vicar, Charlestown 1919–1922; Vicar, St German's 1922; Vicar, Abingdon 1925–1926; Vicar, Newquay 1926–1934; Vicar, St Sithney, Helston, Cornwall 1934–1938. **Honours:** MC 1918. Died 9 April 1959.

FLEET, George (1942) Born 4 July 1907, Stone Croft Cottages, Piltdown, Fletching, Uckfield; son of George Fleet, Joiner, and Ellen Camfield; m Elsie Uren; 2 sons (Stephen George b 28 September 1936 and Robin John b 8 September 1939). **Subject(s):** Geography; BA 1944; MA 1948; BA (London) 1928. **Tutor(s):** C W Guillebaud. **Johnian Relatives:** father of Stephen George Fleet (1955) and of Robin John Fleet (1959). **Educ:** Uckfield Grammar School; Westminster College, London. **Career:** Instructor, Initial Training Wing; Flight Lieutenant, RAFVR; Headmaster, Ongar Secondary School, Essex; Inspector of Schools, East Sussex Education Committee. Died 4 April 1976.

FLEET, The Revd William Walter Strong (1903) Born 31 March 1881, 1 Albert Villas, Upland Road, Camberwell, Surrey; son of Oswald Charles Fleet, Banker's Clerk, and Jane Elizabeth Turner; m Beatrice Mary Whelpdale, 10 September 1912, Woking Parish Church. BA 1906; MA 1910. **Tutor(s):** J R Tanner; C E Graves. **Johnian Relatives:** brother of Charles Stanley Fleet (1906). **Educ:** Alleyn's School, Dulwich. **Career:** Ordained Deacon 1907; Curate, Woking 1907–1920; Ordained Priest 1908; Vicar, Marchwood, Hampshire 1921–1928; Diocesan Inspector of Schools, Winchester 1928. Died 23 January 1944.

FLEMING, David Johnstone (1920) Born 23 February 1902, 137 Bede Burn Road, Jarrow-on-Tyne, County Durham; son of James Fleming, Marine Engineering Draughtsman, and Catherine Johnstone; m Hester Leonie Cliff, 26 March 1934, Singapore Cathedral. **Subject(s):** Natural Sciences; BA 1923; MA 1966. **Tutor(s):** B F Armitage. **Johnian Relatives:** brother of John Fleming (1921). **Educ:** County Secondary School, Jarrow. **Career:** POW, Siam; Eastern Smelting Company, Penang, Malaysia 1924–1941; Buyer, then Area Sales Manager, Durham Chemicals Group, Birtley, County Durham 1947–1968. Died 14 June 1984.

FLEMING, Sir John (1921) Born 2 May 1904, Melville Drive, Motherwell, Dalziel, Lanarkshire, Scotland; son of James Fleming, Chief Marine Engineering Draughtsman, and Catherine Johnstone; m Jean Law Gillitt, 1930. **Subject(s):** Mechanical Sciences/Mathematics; BA 1925; MA 1957. **Tutor(s):** E Cunningham. **Johnian Relatives:** brother of David Johnstone Fleming (1920). **Educ:** County Secondary School, Jarrow. **Career:** Instructor Lieutenant, RN 1925; Instructor Lieutenant Commander, RN 1931; Instructor Commander, Seconded to the Naval Weather Service 1939; Fleet Meteorological Officer to Allied Naval Commander, Expeditionary Force 1944; Assistant, then Deputy Director, Naval Weather Service 1945–1952; Instructor Captain, RN 1950; Fleet Instructor Officer and Fleet Meteorological Officer, Home Fleet 1950; Command Instructor Officer, The Nore 1951; Education Department, Admiralty 1952; Instructor Rear Admiral and Director, Naval Education Service 1956–1960. **Honours:** DSC 1944; KBE 1960. Died 3 November 1994.

FLEMMING, Arthur Adrian Greig (1920) Born 29 January 1902, 4 Kingston Road, Bradford-on-Avon, Wiltshire; son of Charles Edward Stewart Flemming, Medical Practitioner, and Anna Maria Catharine Hayward. **Tutor(s):** B F Armitage. **Educ:** The King's School, Bruton.

FLETCHER, Frank Cecil (1922) Born 27 September 1903, 31 Queen's Crescent, Lincoln; son of John Francis Fletcher, Civil Servant, and Kate Dawson. **Subject(s):** Modern and Medieval Languages; BA 1925. **Tutor(s):** E E Sikes. **Educ:** Infants' School, Urmston; Caius House, Urmston; Manchester Grammar School. **Awards:** Scholarship, SJC 1921.

FLETCHER, John Norman (1906) Born 19 March 1889, 5 Conduit Road, St Paul, Bedford; son of William Charles Fletcher, HM Inspector of Schools, and Kate Edith Penny. **Tutor(s):** L H K Bushe-Fox. **Johnian Relatives:** brother of Philip Fletcher (1922). **Educ:** The Leas, Holylake; Berkhamsted; Greenbank, Sifton Park, Liverpool.

FLETCHER, Philip (1922) Born 3 March 1903, 37 Cable Road, Hoylake cum West Kirby, Cheshire; son of William Charles Fletcher, HM Inspector of Secondary Schools, and Kate Edith Penny. **Subject(s):** Mathematics; BA 1925; MA 1931; MA (Princeton). **Tutor(s):** E Cunningham. **Johnian Relatives:** son of William Charles Fletcher (1883); brother of John Norman Fletcher (1906). **Educ:** Homefield Preparatory School, Sutton; Highgate School. **Career:** Master, Marlborough College 1926–1930; Assistant Master, Geelong Grammar School, Corio, Victoria, Australia 1931–1933; 2nd Master, Cheltenham College 1934–1945; Headmaster, Prince of Wales's School for Europeans, Kabete, Nairobi, Kenya 1945; Worthing Boys' School, Sussex 1961. **Appointments:** Jane Eliza Procter Visiting Fellowship, Princeton 1925. **Awards:** Scholarship, SJC; College Prize, SJC 1925. **Honours:** OBE 1960. Died 15 February 1976.

FLETCHER, Thomas Charles (1911) Born 28 June 1892, Scarrington, Nottinghamshire; son of George Arthur Fletcher, Gentleman, and Kate Annie Tabeser. **Tutor(s):** J R Tanner. **Educ:** Nottingham High School; Gresham's School, Holt.

FLETCHER, William Bruce (1943) Born 9 October 1925, Bankfield, Singleton, Lancashire; son of Alfred Fletcher, Public Works Contractor, and Evelyn Gladys Robinson; m; 5 children, 3 stepchildren. BA 1946; MA 1950. **Tutor(s):** S J Bailey. **Educ:** The School in the Sun, Lytham; Lawrence House School, St Anne's; Shrewsbury School. **Career:** Housebuilder.

FLINT, John Edgar (1948) Born 17 May 1930, Montreal, Canada; son of Alfred Edgar Flint, French Polisher, and Sarah Pickup. **Subject(s):** History; BA 1952; MA 1955. **Tutor(s):** F Thistlethwaite. **Educ:** Barnoldswick Modern School; Moat Road Intermediate School, Leicester; Alderman Newton's School, Leicester. **Career:** Lecturer in History, KCL 1959.

FODEN, Raymond Davidson (1941) Born 3 June 1923, 30 Leyland Road, Lee, London; son of William Bertram Foden, Civil Servant, and Zélie Lemmy; m Muriel, 2 September 1950; 3 daughters (Gillian, Alison and Jean). BA 1944. **Tutor(s):** C W Guillebaud. **Johnian Relatives:** son of William Bertram Foden (1911). **Educ:** Carn Brea Preparatory School, Bromley; Dulwich College. **Career:** Captain, REME, Middle East Branch 101, Lines of Communication Area, India Command 1945; Engineer, Halls, London; Chief Engineer, Westons Biscuits, Slough; Chief Engineer, Telomex, Horsham and Okehampton; co-founder, Morgan and Foden, engineering consultancy partnership. **Appointments:** Member, Parochial Church Council, and member, Church Choir, Crediton, Devon. Died 23 September 2003.

FODEN, William Bertram (1911) Born 19 September 1892, 1 High Street, Newcastle, Staffordshire; son of William Genders Foden, Hatter and Outfitter, and Rosa Annie Davidson Fox; m Zélie Lemmy; 1 son (Raymond Davidson b 3 June 1923), 1 daughter (Vivienne b 2 June 1927). **Subjects:** Mathematics/Natural Sciences; BA 1914. **Tutor(s):** J R Tanner. **Johnian Relatives:** father of Raymond Davidson Foden (1941). **Educ:** Newcastle High School. **Career:** Gunner, RGA, WWI; Civil Service 1915; Assistant Under-Secretary of State, Air Ministry 1945. **Awards:** Scholarship, SJC. **Honours:** CB 1945. Died 6 September 1981.

FOGG, Professor Gordon Elliott (Tony) (1940) Born 26 April 1919, Langar, Bingham, Nottinghamshire; son of Revd Leslie Charles Fogg, Methodist Minister, and Doris Mary Elliott; m Elizabeth Beryl Llechid Jones, 7 July 1945 (d 1997); 1 son (Timothy Dolben b 1951), 1 daughter (Elizabeth Helen b 1947). PhD Plant Physiology 1943; ScD 1966; BSc (London) 1939; Hon LLD (Dundee) 1974; FIBiol 1963; FRS 1965. **Tutor(s):** C W Guillebaud; J M Wordie. **Educ:** Dulwich College; Queen Mary College, University of London. **Career:** Assistant, Seaweed Survey of British Isles, Marine Biological Association 1942–1943; Plant Physiologist, Fison's Pest Control Ltd 1943–1945; Assistant Lecturer, Lecturer, then Reader in Botany, UCL 1945–1960; Professor of Botany, Westfield College, London 1960–1971; Professor and Head of Department of Marine Biology, University College of North Wales, Bangor 1971–1985; Professor Emeritus, University of Wales 1985. **Appointments:** Rockefeller Fellow 1954; Botanical Secretary, Society of Experimental Biology 1957–1960; President, British Phycological Society 1961–1962; Chairman, Scientific Advisory Committee, British Antarctic Survey 1971–1984; President, Section K, British Association 1973; Chairman, Council of Freshwater Biological Association 1974–1985; Fellow, Queen Mary & Westfield College 1976; President, Institute of Biology 1976–1977; Trustee, British Museum (Natural History) 1976–1985; Member, Royal Commission on Environmental Pollution 1979–1985; NERC 1981–1982; Trustee, Royal Botanic Gardens 1983–1989; Leverhulme Emeritus Fellow 1986. **Awards:** Strathcona Research Exhibition 1940. **Honours:** CBE 1983. **Publications:** *The Metabolism of Algae*, 1953; *The Growth of Plants*, 1963; *Photosynthesis*, 1968; (with W D P Stewart, P Fay and A E Walsby) *The Bluegreen Algae*, 1973; (with B Thake) *Algal Cultures and Phytoplankton Ecology*, 1987; (with D Smith) *The Explorations of Antarctica*, 1990; *A History of Antarctic Science*, CUP, 1992; *The Biology of Polar Habitats*, 1998; (ed) *Penguin's New Biology*; approximately 150 papers in scientific journals.

FOGGON, James Joseph (1941) Born 13 August 1923, Netherton, Harbottle, Rothbury, Northumberland; son of James Mackay Foggon, Farm Horseman, and Isabella White; m H Lewer, 18 January 1958. **Tutor(s):** C W Guillebaud. **Educ:** Thomlinson's Church of England School, Rothbury; King Edward VI Grammar School, Morpeth. **Career:** Lieutenant, RN 1946; Chief of Electrical Engineering, HM Naval Dockyard, Hong Kong 1951; Lieutenant Commander; Torpedo Experimental Establishment, Greenock 1958. **Honours:** MBE 1967.

FONSECA, Honorio Bingham (1948) See D'ASSIS-FONSECA.

FOOT, Hugh Mackintosh (Lord CARADON) (1925) Born 8 October 1907, 1 Lipson Terrace, Plymouth; son of Isaac Foot, Solicitor and MP for Bodmin, and Eva Mackintosh; m Florence Sylvia Tod; 3 sons, 1 daughter. **Subject(s):** History/Law; BA 1929. **Tutor(s):** E A Benians. **Educ:** Kindergarten, Plymouth; Ferns School, Swanage; Leighton Park School, Reading. **Career:** Administrative Officer, Palestine Government 1929–1937; Attached to the Colonial Office 1938–1939; Assistant British Resident, Trans-Jordan 1939–1942; British Military Administration, Cyrenaica 1943; Colonial Secretary, Cyprus 1943–1945; Colonial Secretary, Jamaica 1945–1947; Chief Secretary, Nigeria 1947–1951; Captain-General and Governor-in-Chief, Jamaica 1951–1957; Governor and Commander-in-Chief, Cyprus 1957–1960; Ambassador and Adviser, UK Mission to the UN and UK representative on Trusteeship Council 1961–1962; Consultant, Special Fund of the United Nations 1963–1964; Minister of State for Foreign and Commonwealth Affairs, and Permanent UK Representative at the UN 1964–1970; Consultant, UN Development Programme 1971–1975. **Appointments:** President, Cambridge Union Society, Easter Term 1929; Honorary Fellow, SJC 1960; Member, UN Expert Group on South Africa 1964; Visiting Fellow, Princeton, Harvard and Georgetown Universities. **Honours:** OBE 1939; CMG 1946; KCMG 1951; KStJ 1952; KCVO 1953; GCMG 1957; Baron (Life Peer) 1964; PC 1968. **Publications:** *A Start in Freedom*, 1964. Died 5 September 1990.

FOOTTIT, Edward Hall (1928) Born 10 May 1909, Westborough, Lincolnshire; son of Edward Hall Foottit, Rector of Westborough, and Eleanor Guy Huchinson; m Zoe Ruth Welch 1939 (d 1995); 2 sons (Robert Edward b 13 May 1942 and George Thomas Welch b 29 May 1948), 3 daughters. **Subject(s):** Law/History; BA 1931; MA 1944. **Tutor(s):** E A Benians. **Johnian Relatives:** father of Robert Edward Foottit (1960) and of George Thomas Welch Foottit (1967). **Educ:** Lincoln School. **Career:** Qualified as Solicitor 1935; Solicitor, Browetts of Coventry.

FOOTTIT, Raymond Langdon Carter (1923) Born 12 February 1904, 31 Mount Vale, York; son of Cecil Carter Foottit, Bank Manager, and Edith Mary Langdon; m Rose Marie Hodgson, 1 April 1946. **Subject(s):** Mathematics/Economics; BA 1926. **Tutor(s):** E Cunningham. **Educ:** Archbishop Holgate's School, York; St Peter's School, York; Abingdon School, Berkshire. Died 21 August 1971.

FORBES, Alastair (1927) Born 21 March 1910, Springbank, Whitworth, Rochdale, Lancashire; son of Thomas John Lawson Forbes, Surgeon, and Mary Scholfield Welsh. BA 1931; MA 1935. **Tutor(s):** J M Wordie. **Educ:** University School, Southport; The Leys School, Cambridge. **Career:** Second-hand Bookseller. Died March 1964.

FORBES, Peter Ronald Anthony (1946) Born 16 September 1915, Belper, Derbyshire; son of William Stronach Foster Forbes, RN, and Helen Margaret Strutt. **Tutor(s):** G C L Bertram. **Educ:** Northaw Place, Potters Bar; Stowe School; RMC, Sandhurst.

FORBES, Richard Lumsden (1936) Born 29 February 1916, Seaforth, Seabank Road, Nairn, Scotland; son of Richard Robert Forbes, Colonel, and Jessie Wilson Paton. **Subject(s):** Mechanical Sciences; BA 1938; MA 1963. **Tutor(s):** J S Boys Smith. **Educ:** Pinewood, Farnborough; Haileybury College; Army College; RMA. **Career:** Second Lieutenant, RE.

FORD, Dennis Howard (1949) Born 16 April 1928, 129 Tulse Hill, London; son of Frederick George Ernest Ford, Chartered Civil Engineer, and Nellie Charlotte Hill; m (1) Elizabeth Mary Wallis, 18 August 1960, St Margaret's Church, Topsham (d 6 October 1988), (2) Elisabeth

Herring, 4 April 1992; 1 son (Christopher James), 1 daughter (Jennifer Mary). **Subject(s):** Classics; BA 1952; MA 1956; DipEd 1953. **Tutor(s):** R L Howland. **Educ:** Dulwich College Preparatory School, London; Dulwich College. **Career:** Teacher, Housemaster and Librarian, Oundle School 1953–1992. **Appointments:** Treasurer, St Peter's Church, Oundle 1980–2003. **Awards:** Minor Scholarship, SJC 1946.

FORD, John Henry Ford (1932) Born 7 January 1913, Normanhurst, Langley Park, Mill Hill, Middlesex; son of Albert Steeds Ford Ford, News Agent Proprietor/Journalist, and Daisy Letitia Smith. **Subject(s):** Economics/Law; BA 1935; MA 1939. **Tutor(s):** C W Guillebaud. **Johnian Relatives:** cousin of John Ford Northcott (1892); nephew of Albert Francis Smith (1914). **Educ:** St Dunstan's Preparatory School, Worthing; Dover College. **Career:** Company Secretary, Marshall of Cambridge; RAF 1940–1958 (Wing Commander 1947); Commander, Cambridge University Air Force Squadron 1956. **Awards:** 3rd Gordon Shephard Memorial Prize, RAF 1958. **Honours:** DFC; AFC.

FORD, Richard Brutton (1919) Born 27 October 1899, Exeter, Devon; son of Mortimer Ford, Solicitor, and Amy Platt; m Vera Gleason; 1 son (Peter Evan Brutton b 25 August 1932). **Johnian Relatives:** father of Peter Evan Brutton Ford (1951). **Educ:** Cheltenham College Junior School; Royal Naval College, Dartmouth. **Career:** Commander, RN 1914–1923; Messrs Bousteads, Malaya 1923–1932; RN 1934–1946. Died 1988.

FORESTIER-WALKER, Edmond Annesley (1940) Born 27 May 1922, Rainridge Farm, Reston Grafton, Hampshire; son of Edmond Alec Forestier-Walker, Colonel, and Eileen de Renzy Channer. **Tutor(s):** C W Guillebaud. **Educ:** New Beacon, Sevenoaks; Felsted School.

FORGAN, Thomas Adrian (1928) Born 31 March 1909, Moorside, Pipers Lane, Heswall, Cheshire; son of Thomas Henry Forgan, Cotton Merchant, and Dora Stretch Warrington; m E Ann. **Subject(s):** Natural Sciences; BA 1931; MA 1968. **Tutor(s):** C W Guillebaud. **Educ:** St Fileans, Heswall; Berkhamsted School. Died 19 December 1992.

FORGE, Geoffrey Baynton (1942) Born 12 June 1909, Swan Street, West Malling, Kent; son of George Baynton Forge, Medical Practitioner, and Eleanor Annie Tyer. **Subject(s):** Geography; BA 1945; BA (London) 1931. **Tutor(s):** C W Guillebaud. **Educ:** Rottingdean Preparatory School; Cranbrook School. **Career:** Assistant Master, Kingston Grammar School; Flight Lieutenant, RAF; Instructor, Initial Training Wing.

FORRESTER, Basil Holden (1932) Born 16 September 1913, Townfield House, Sandy Lane, Leyland, Preston; son of William James Holden Forrester, Cotton Manufacturer, and Constance Law. **Subject(s):** Economics. **Tutor(s):** C W Guillebaud. **Johnian Relatives:** brother of Robert Michael Forrester (1937). **Educ:** The Ryleys School, Alderley Edge; Clifton College. Died 1978.

FORRESTER, Dr Robert Michael (1937) Born 15 May 1919, Townfield House, Sandy Lane, Leyland; son of William James Holden Forrester, Cotton Manufacturer, and Constance Law; m Marion; 4 children. **Subject(s):** Natural Sciences; BA 1940; MA 1944; BChir 1943; MB 1943; MD 1955; FRCP. **Tutor(s):** R L Howland. **Johnian Relatives:** brother of Basil Holden Forrester (1932). **Educ:** Victoria College, Manchester University; The Ryleys School, Alderley Edge; Clifton College. **Career:** Royal Enniskillen Dragoon Guards, Captain, RAMC, and Staff Captain, War Office, WWII; Consultant Paediatrician, Wigan and Leigh Hospitals, and to the Royal National Institute for the Blind mid–1950s–1980. **Appointments:** Chairman, Warnock Committee on Education for the Handicapped. Died 21 June 2003.

FORRESTER, William Herbert (1939) Born 14 February 1921, 27 Oxford Street, Barrow-in-Furness; son of William Forrester, Director, and Mary Louisa Last; m Dorothy Margaret Edmondson, 24 February 1945,

Madras, India. BA 1942. **Tutor(s):** J S Boys Smith. **Educ:** St Paul's Church School, Barrow-in-Furness; Oxford Street Elementary School, Barrow-in-Furness; Barrow-in-Furness Grammar School.

FORSE, John (1940) Born 2 August 1922, 51 Streathbourne Road, Balham, London; son of William Thomas Forse, Mechanical Engineer, and Lilian Pagdin; m Kathleen Betty Edwards, 24 September 1946, Barnham, Sussex; 2 sons (Bill and Tim). BA 1943; MA 1947. **Tutor(s):** S J Bailey. **Johnian Relatives:** half-brother of William Arthur Forse (1932); father of William Cambray Forse (1970). **Educ:** Beulah House High School; King's College Junior and Senior Schools. Died 15 August 1989.

FORSE, William Arthur (1932) Born 27 November 1913, 41 Longley Road, Tooting, Surrey; son of William Thomas Forse, Engineer, and Mabel Rose Mattock. **Subject(s):** Engineering; BA 1935. **Tutor(s):** J S Boys Smith. **Johnian Relatives:** half-brother of John Forse (1940); uncle of William Cambray Forse (1970). **Educ:** Highfield School, Wandsworth; Framlingham College. Died 10 December 1936.

FORSTER, Charles Arthur (1942) Born 23 September 1924, 7 Vere Street, Salford; son of Ernest Henry Forster, Railway Superintending Inspector, and Mary Elizabeth Biden; m Barbara Temple, 1948; 2 sons (b 1949 and 1952), 1 daughter (b 1955). **Subject(s):** Mechanical Sciences; BA 1945; MA 1949; BSc (London) 1947; MSc (London) 1949; FBCS. **Tutor(s):** S J Bailey. **Educ:** Seedley Council School; Manchester Grammar School. **Career:** Aeronautics, De Havillands (aircraft) 1944–1950; English Electric (GEC) (guided weapons) 1950–1961; Computer Software, Ferranti (ICL) 1961–1963; Elliotts (GEC) 1963–1966; ITT 1966–1967; Senior Consultant, Sema Group 1968–1982. **Awards:** Baylis Scholarship, SJC 1941; John Bernard Seely Prize, University of Cambridge 1944.

FORSTER, The Revd Dr Kenneth (1944) Born 3 January 1927, 55 Westbourne Grove, Hessle, East Yorkshire; son of Charles Edward Forster, Shipwright, and Gertrude May Millington; m June Margaret Bouskill, 25 July 1953 (d 2 July 2003); 1 daughter (Frances Irene b 1964). **Subject(s):** Mathematics/Physics; BA 1950; MA 1952; PGCE 1951; MSc (Salford) 1977; PhD (Salford) 1980; MInstP 1967; CPhys. **Tutor(s):** J M Wordie. **Educ:** Hessle Church of England School; Hessle Council Senior School; Beverley Grammar School; North East Ordination Course. **Career:** Sergeant/Instructor, Royal Signals 1945–1948; Assistant Master for Physics, Kingston High School, Hull 1951–1959; Lecturer in Physics 1959–1966, Senior Lecturer in Physics 1966–1976, Hull College of Technology; Senior Lecturer in Physics, Humberside College of Higher Education, Hull 1976–1987; Ordained Deacon, York Minster 1986; Assistant Curate (NSM), All Saints' Church, Hessle, East Yorkshire 1986–1992; Ordained Priest, All Saints' Church, Hessle, East Yorkshire 1987; Chaplain (part-time), Humberside Polytechnic, Hull 1987–1991; Chaplain, University of Humberside 1991–1992; Assistant Curate (NSM), St Mary's Church, Sculcoates, Hull 1992–1994.

FORSTER, Oliver Matthew (1928) Born 24 March 1910, Sedgefield House, Sedgefield, County Durham; son of Matthew Forster, Brewer and Maltster, and Hannah Theodosia Bagley; m Helen; 2 daughters (Ann and Sheila). **Subject(s):** Classics; BA 1931; MA 1935. **Tutor(s):** M P Charlesworth. **Educ:** Old Hall School, Wellington; Sedbergh School. **Awards:** Scholarship, SJC. Died 4 October 1988.

FORWARD, Nigel Stewart (1945) Born 19 May 1923, Northwood Cottage, Farnham Common, Buckinghamshire; son of Ernest Lionel Forward, Medical Inspector, Ministry of Pensions, and Aileen Frances Middlemiss; m Stella Mary Castor, 1945; 2 daughters (Miranda Jane b 22 January 1952 and Tamsin Mary 20 August 1960). **Subject(s):** Mathematics; BA 1947; MA 1968. **Tutor(s):** J M Wordie. **Educ:** Gayhurst Preparatory School, Gerrard's Cross; Marlborough College. **Career:** Foreign Office at Bletchley 1941–1945; Ministry of Defence (with periods of secondment to HM Treasury and Atomic Energy

Authority) 1947–1957; UK Delegation to NATO, Paris, Foreign Office 1957–1960; Assistant Secretary, Ministry of Defence 1960–1963 and 1965–1967; Private Secretary to Mr Ian Macleod, Sir Selwyn Lloyd and Mr Herbert Bowden 1963–1965; Civil Service Department, Machinery of Government Division 1969–1972; Under-Secretary, Department of Employment 1972–1977; Secretary, Royal Commission on the Distribution of Income and Wealth 1977–1980. **Appointments:** Co-founder and Secretary 1982–1997, Friends of Ridgeway; Part-time British Executive Service Overseas 1987–1991. **Awards:** Baylis Scholarship, SJC 1940. **Publications:** *The Field of Nations*, Macmillan, 1970; *An A to Z of Income and Wealth*, HMSO, 1980.

FOSBROOKE, Henry Albert (1927) Born 10 October 1908, Ordsall Hall, Salford; son of Henry Leonard Fosbrooke, Clerk in Holy Orders, and Elizabeth Gardiner Malcolm; 2 children. **Subject(s):** Economics/Archaeology and Anthropology; BA 1930; MA 1934. **Tutor(s):** E A Benians. **Educ:** Pocklington School. **Career:** Cadet, Tanganyika Territory 1931; Assistant District Officer 1933; Military service 1938–1941; District Officer 1943; Director of the Rhodes-Livingstone Institute, Northern Rhodesia 1955; Consultant Socio-Ecologist, Maasai Pastoral Rehabilitation, Ngorongoro Conservation Area, Tanzania 1994–1995; Consultant Socio-Ecologist, Mkomazi eviction of Maasai, Legal and Human Rights Centre, University of Dar es Salaam 1994–1995. **Awards:** Dowman Exhibition, SJC.

FOSTER, Andrew Brisbin (1926) Born 3 January 1903, 6306 Overbrook Avenue, Philadelphia, Pennsylvania, USA; son of Frank Brisbin Foster, President of Congoleum-Nairn Company, and Edith Lanigan. **Subject(s):** History; BA 1929; MA 1933; BSc (Dartmouth) 1926. **Tutor(s):** E A Benians. **Educ:** Protestant Episcopal Academy, Philadelphia; Dartmouth College, New Hampshire. **Career:** Head, Commonwealth Branch, US State Department, Washington 1952. Died 8 October 1963.

FOSTER, Brian Stanley (1945) Born 20 November 1927, 128 Harlaxton Road, Grantham, Lincolnshire; son of Stanley Foster, Haircutter and Tobacconist, and Rachel Mary Blower; m Judith Patricia Lowe (d 2002); 1 son, 2 daughters. **Subject(s):** Law; BA 1949; MA 1952. **Tutor(s):** S J Bailey. **Educ:** Huntingtower Road Council School, Grantham; King's School, Grantham. **Career:** Solicitor. **Appointments:** Deputy Lieutenant, Lincolnshire 1973. **Awards:** TD.

FOSTER, The Revd Edward James Graham (1931) Born 21 January 1912, The Vicarage, Acton Turville, Gloucestershire; son of James Richard Foster, Clerk in Holy Orders, and Alice Norton Lees; m Constance Lily Doncaster, 3 July 1948, Mexborough Parish Church; 1 son, 2 daughters. BA 1934; MA 1938; MusB 1935. **Tutor(s):** J M Wordie. **Johnian Relatives:** son of James Richard Foster (1894). **Educ:** Crescent House, Brighton; Merton Court, Sidcup; St John's School, Leatherhead; Wells Theological College 1935. **Career:** Assistant Organist, Emmanuel College, Cambridge 1934–1935; Ordained Deacon 1937; Curate, Kidderminster 1937; Ordained Priest, Worcester 1938; Priest, Astwood Bank with Cookhill 1943–1945; Chaplain and Lecturer in Music, Chester College 1945–1950; Vicar, St John's, Balby, Doncaster 1951–1967; Vicar, Ashford-in-the-Water with Sheldon, Derby 1967–1978.

FOSTER, Eric (1941) Born 15 January 1923, 148 Bolton Street, Oldham, Lancashire; son of Edward Foster, House Painter and Decorator, and Annie Hurst. **Subject(s):** Natural Sciences/Physics; BA 1944; MA 1948; MIEE. **Tutor(s):** C W Guillebaud. **Educ:** Alexandra Road Council School, Oldham; Oldham Municipal High School. **Career:** A C Cossor Ltd 1943–1947; British Insulated Callenders, Cables Ltd 1948–1952; Ferranti Ltd 1952–1987.

FOSTER, Herbert Frederick Brudenell (1927) Born 8 May 1908, Littlemoor, Queensbury, Halifax, Yorkshire; son of Herbert Anderton Foster, Alpaca and Mohair Spinner and Manufacturer, and Frances Edith Agnes Brudenell Bruce; m Christine Lucas-Tooth, 28 November

1945, St Paul's, Knightsbridge. **Tutor(s):** C W Guillebaud. **Educ:** Wiscenford, Wokingham; Radley College.

FOSTER, Kenneth John (1935) Born 23 July 1917, 33 Cam Road, Cambridge; son of William Henry Foster, Private Tutor, and Rose Hall. **Subject(s):** Law; BA 1938; MA 1942. **Tutor(s):** R L Howland. **Educ:** Milton Road Council School; The Perse School, Cambridge.

FOSTER, Laurence Edward Anderton (1925) Born 21 April 1906, Northowram Hall, Halifax, Yorkshire; son of Edward Hornby Foster, Worsted Manufacturer, and Florence Ruth Anderton. BA 1928; MA 1932. **Tutor(s):** J M Wordie. **Educ:** St George's, Broadstairs; Bradfield College, Holt; Private Tuition, Holt.

FOSTER, Reginald John (1946) Born 16 June 1921, Henwood Manor, Tettenhall, Staffordshire; son of Wilfrid Lionel Foster, Major, RA, and Evelyn Mary Cammell; m Iona Patricia Fairs; 1 son, 4 daughters. **Subject(s):** Mechanical Sciences; BA 1948; MA 1957. **Tutor(s):** R L Howland. **Educ:** Kent House, Eastbourne; Winchester College. **Career:** Night fighter pilot, Squadron Leader, Test Pilot, RAE 1941–1946; Various managerial appointments, British Oxygen Company (now The BOC Group) 1950–1968; Marketing Director, then Managing Director, Henry Sykes 1968–1975; Regional Manager, Tanzania, Kenya, Zambia, Nigeria and Pakistan, The BOC Group 1975–1984. **Honours:** DFC and Bar; AFC.

FOSTER, Robert Douglas (1910) Born 2 May 1890, 1 Westbourne Road, Selby, Yorkshire; son of Robert John Foster, Flax Spinner, and Ellen Gertrude Govrill. BA 1913. **Tutor(s):** J R Tanner. **Educ:** St Peter's School, York. **Career:** Second Lieutenant, 6th Lincolnshire Regiment 1914. **Awards:** Choral Studentship, SJC. Died 6 August 1915 (missing, presumed killed in action, at Sulva Bay, Gallipoli).

FOSTER, Thomas Hartley (1920) Born 23 November 1902, 2 Duke Street, Tavistock, Devon; son of Joseph Henry Foster, Glass and China Merchant, and Mabel Lucy Carter; 1 daughter (Daphne E). **Subject(s):** Mathematics; BA 1923; MA 1929. **Tutor(s):** E E Sikes. **Educ:** Spring Hill Preparatory School; Tavistock Grammar School. **Career:** Master, St Edmund's College, Ware 1923–1924; Master, St Peter's School, York 1925; Master, King Edward VI Grammar School, Louth 1925. Died 2 February 1995.

FOSTER, William Henry (1902) (admitted as Non-Collegiate Student 1901) Born 20 October 1866, 54 Springback Gardens, Bolton, Lancashire; son of James Foster, Spindle Maker, and Mary Ellen Mounsey. **Subject(s):** Natural Sciences; BA 1903; MA 1907; BA (London) 1890; BSc (London) 1903. **Tutor(s):** D MacAlister. **Educ:** Manchester Grammar School; University of London. Died 29 November 1948.

FOSTER, The Revd William Roy (1918) Born 5 June 1899, 302 Crystal Palace Road, East Dulwich, Camberwell, Surrey; son of William Alfred Foster, Commercial Clerk, and Florence Victoria Cottee. **Subject(s):** Moral Sciences/Theology; BA 1921; MA 1925. **Tutor(s):** E E Sikes. **Educ:** Alleyn's School, Dulwich. **Career:** Bishop's College, Cheshunt 1922; Deacon 1923; Curate, All Saint's, Wimbledon 1923–1927; Priest 1924; Priest Vicar, Southwark Cathedral 1927–1928; Succentor 1928–1935; Curate, All Saints, Margaret Street, and Master of the Choir School 1935–1950; Vicar, St Augustine, Queen's Gate, Kensington 1950–1965. **Awards:** Choral Studentship, SJC. Died 14 June 1976.

FOUNTAIN, Christopher Osborn (1927) Born 29 December 1907, The Shoehorn, Orpington, Kent; son of Henry Fountain, Principal Assistant Secretary, Board of Trade, and Agnes Maud Laughton Leishman; m Joan Margaret Brewers Goodhart, 5 March 1953, St Andrew's Church, Calcutta. **Subject(s):** Economics/Classics; BA 1930. **Tutor(s):** M P Charlesworth. **Educ:** Gadebridge Park, Boxmoor; Oundle School. **Awards:** Exhibition, SJC 1926.

FOURNIER D'ALBE, Eugene Robert (1947) Born 9 March 1925, Westgate House, Palace Road, Kingston, Surrey; son of Edmund Edward Fournier d'Albe, Physicist, and Yolande Hanman. **Subject(s):** Oriental Languages (Sanskrit and Tibetan); BA 1949; MA 1954. **Tutor(s):** F Thistlethwaite. **Educ:** Catherine Street School, St Albans; St Albans School.

FOWLER, John Anthony (1938) Born 15 June 1919, Wotton Lodge Nursing Home, Gloucester; son of Eric Francis Tiernay Fowler, Solicitor, and Edith Mary Thompson; m Carol Withers, 15 June 1950, Cheadle Hulme, Cheshire; 1 son (Christopher John b 1954), 1 daughter (April Jane b 1951). **Subject(s):** Natural Sciences; BA 1941; MA 1945; FRSC. **Tutor(s):** J M Wordie. **Johnian Relatives:** father of Christopher John Fowler (1972). **Educ:** King's School, Gloucester; Crown East Court, Aymestry; Malvern College. **Career:** Shift Chemist, ICI Explosives Division, Kilmarnock, Ayrshire 1941–1945; Technical Service Dept, ICI Dyestuffs Division (later ICI Organics Division), Blackley, Manchester 1945–1969; Manager, Special Chemicals Business Area, ICI Organics Division, Blackley, Manchester 1969–1976; General Commissioner of Taxes, Manchester Salford 1977–1994. **Publications:** Numerous publications in technical press.

FOX, Basil Norman (1947) Born 22 July 1927, Long Eaton, Derbyshire; son of George Norman Fox, Managing Director, and Emily Kathleen Wootton; m Brenda Mary Greville Cooke, 1955; 1 son (Adam), 2 daughters (Catherine and Julia). **Subject(s):** Agriculture; BA 1950; MA 1955. **Tutor(s):** G C L Bertram. **Educ:** Ockbrook Moravian School; Loughborough Grammar School; Wellingborough School. **Career:** Farming 1950–1959; Agricultural Representative, Shell Chemical Company 1959–1960; Shell International Company, London 1960–1987, International Agricultural Public Affairs Co-ordinator 1980–1987; Director General, International Agricultural Training Programme 1987–1997.

FOX, Donald Douglas (1946) Born 19 September 1921, 3 Parkhouse, Holly Park, London; son of Douglas Percival Fox, Shipping Clerk, and Edith Beatrice James; m Joan Mary Weedon, 3 March 1961, St James's Church, Piccadilly. **Subject(s):** Economics; BA 1948; MA 1991. **Tutor(s):** C W Guillebaud. **Educ:** Enfield Convent School; Chase Side School; Enfield Grammar School. **Career:** Sub-Lieutenant, RNVR 1940–1946; Executive, Mobil Oil Company 1950–1985. Died 29 May 2002.

FOXALL, Dennis Arthur (1939) Born 11 July 1921, 10 Park Street, Halesowen, Worcester; son of Arthur Thomas Foxall, Press Toolsetter, and Miriam Smith; 1 son (Simon). **Subject(s):** History; BA 1942; MA 1947. **Tutor(s):** J S Boys Smith. **Educ:** Corbett Street Council School, Smethwick; Holly Lodge High School, Smethwick. **Career:** Assistant Master, Dean Close School, Cheltenham 1949–1959; Headmaster, Adam's Grammar School, Wem Salop 1959–1960; Headmaster of Forest School, Snaresbrook 1960. Died 28 June 2000.

FOXWORTHY, Alfred William (1925) Born 7 October 1906, 16 Francis Road, Leyton, Essex; son of Alfred William Foxworthy, Master Mariner, Merchant Service, and Margaret Ann Harrison. **Subject(s):** Mathematics; BA 1928. **Tutor(s):** J M Wordie. **Johnian Relatives:** grandfather of Duncan William Gordon Blackburn (1980). **Educ:** Elwick Road Upper Grade Elementary School; Merchant Taylors' School, Crosby. **Awards:** Exhibition, SJC.

FRANCE, Kenneth Robertson (1935) Born 16 February 1917, 9 Marchmont Terrace, Glasgow; son of William Galbraith France, Chartered Accountant, and Ellinor Alice Robertson Smith. **Subject(s):** Law; BA 1938. **Educ:** Kelvinside Academy, Glasgow; Bilton Grange, Rugby; Uppingham School. **Career:** Partner, Moncrieff Warren Patterson & Co, Solicitors, Glasgow; Second Lieutenant, 64th Anti-Tank Regiment, RA; Captain, 2nd Defence Regiment, RA; Staff Captain, ADC to Major General Green, Chief of Staff to Lord Gort 1939–1945. **Awards:** Wright's Prize, SJC 1936; Scholarship, SJC 1937. Died 5 October 1976.

FRANCE, Norman Hoole (1923) Born 2 March 1904, 5 Lycemoon Villas, Kowloon, Hong Kong, China; son of John Hoole France, Clerk in Holy Orders, and Elizabeth Elliott. **Subject(s):** History; BA 1926; MA 1930. **Tutor(s):** E A Benians. **Johnian Relatives:** uncle of Simon John France (1951). **Educ:** Oakmount, Portswood, Southampton; The King's School, Ely; Felsted School. **Career:** Professor of History, Hong Kong University; Hong Kong Volunteer Defence Force, WWII. **Appointments:** Jane Eliza Procter Visiting Fellow, Princeton University 1926. **Awards:** Scholarship, SJC. Died December 1941 (killed in Hong Kong during the Japanese attacks).

FRANCIS, Dr Clement Alexander (1919) Born 3 March 1898, Sherwood, Queensland, Australia; son of Henry Alexander Francis, Ear, Nose and Throat Surgeon, and Lilian Agate; m Patricia Marion Margaret Stewart, 1 February 1930, Holy Trinity Church, Guildford; 1 son (Stewart), 2 daughters (Janet and Sheila). BA 1921; MA 1929; MB 1929; BChir 1929; MRCS; LRCP 1925. **Tutor(s):** E E Sikes. **Johnian Relatives:** son of Henry Alexander Francis (1883); father of Stewart Alexander Clement Francis (1958). **Educ:** Mostyn House School, Parkgate; St Edward's School, Oxford; St Bartholomew's Hospital, London. **Career:** Lieutenant, Royal Field Artillery 1917–1919; Senior Surgeon, Ear, Nose and Throat Department, Children's Hospital, Plaistow; Surgeon in charge, Allergy Clinic, Metropolitan Ear, Nose and Throat Hospital, London; international authority on allergic diseases; continued the work which his father pioneered, of treating asthma by lightly cauterising the nasal septum. **Appointments:** Captain, LMBC 1921; Treasurer and Council Member, British Association of Allergists; Member, MCC, Marylebone Rotary Club, Junior Carlton Club; Senior Honorary Secretary, Hunterian Society. **Publications:** 'Prognosis of Operations for the Removal of Nasal Polypi in Asthma', *Practitioner*, 1929, and numerous other papers to medical journals, on asthma and hay-fever; *Asthma*, W M Heineman, Medical Books, 1950. Died 27 November 1951.

FRANCIS, Hugh Elvet (1929) Born 28 March 1907, Glanafon, Cemmaes, Montgomeryshire; son of Maurice Evan Francis, JP, Farmer, and County Councillor, and Ellen Jones; m Frances Bowen, 28 September 1932; 3 sons (Hugh, Timothy and Richard), 1 daughter (Elizabeth). **Subject(s):** Law; LLB 1931; LLM 1985; LLB (Wales) 1929; QC 1960. **Tutor(s):** C W Guillebaud. **Johnian Relatives:** father of Hugh Bowen Francis (1953). **Educ:** Cemmaes Council School; Machynlleth County School; University College of Wales, Aberystwyth. **Career:** Equity Draughtsman and Conveyancer, Lincoln's Inn; Called to the Bar, Gray's Inn 1932; Practised at Chancery Bar 1932–1939 and 1945–1979; Lieutenant Colonel, JAG Branch 1939–1945; Bencher, Gray's Inn 1956; Chairman, Performing Rights Tribunal 1969; Treasurer, Gray's Inn 1974. **Appointments:** Chancellor, County Palatine of Durham 1969. **Publications:** (ed) *Lindley on Partnership*. Died 7 June 1986.

FRANCIS, Dr John Harvey (1919) Born 24 October 1899, Moira House, Arnold, Nottinghamshire; son of Harvey Francis, Medical Practitioner, and Jessie Abell Usher; m H Marion Francis. BA 1921; MA 1926. **Tutor(s):** E E Sikes. **Johnian Relatives:** brother of Reginald Harvey Francis (1923). **Educ:** Langley Place, St Leonards on Sea; Rugby School. **Career:** Army. **Awards:** Exhibition, SJC 1916. Died 17 April 1991.

FRANCIS, Reginald Harvey (1923) Born 1 November 1905, Front Street, Arnold, Nottinghamshire; son of Harvey Francis, Medical Practitioner, and Jessie Abell Usher; m Aylmer. BA 1926. **Tutor(s):** B F Armitage. **Johnian Relatives:** brother of John Harvey Francis (1919). **Educ:** Langley Place, St Leonards on Sea; Rugby School. Died 21 January 1990.

FRANKLAND, Edward Raven Percy (1937) Born 14 June 1918, Needle House, Ravenstonedale, Westmorland; son of Edward Percy Frankland, Novelist, Artist, and Landowner, and Maud Metcalfe-Gibson; m Juliet Camilla Brown, 3 June 1959, Effingham. **Tutor(s):** J S Boys Smith. **Educ:** Park House School, Paignton; Sedbergh School. **Awards:** Lupton and Hebblethwaite Exhibition, SJC 1937.

FRANKLIN, Eric Stanley (1925) Born 22 July 1907, The Savoy Hotel, Mussoorie, India; son of Edward Stanley Franklin, Electrical Engineer, and Isabel Edith Cushing. **Tutor(s):** J M Wordie. **Educ:** Hamilton House, Bath; Kent House, Eastbourne; Oundle School.

FRANKLIN, Harold Walter (1915) Born 13 March 1898, Rectory Road, Rickmansworth, Hertfordshire; son of Hector George Franklin, Clerk, and Alice Amelia Stephens. **Subject(s):** Mathematics/Mechanical Sciences; BA 1920; MA 1945. **Tutor(s):** L H K Bushe-Fox. **Educ:** Colne Valley High School, Rickmansworth; Watford Grammar School. **Career:** Air Mechanic, RNAS, WWI; Various aircraft firms 1922–1932; Lecturer in Mechanical and Aeronautical Engineering, Northampton Polytechnic 1932; Reader, Northampton College of Advanced Technology until 1962. **Awards:** Scholarship, SJC 1914. Died 21 October 1962.

FRANKLIN, Dr Mervin Clarence (1931) Born 2 May 1905, Te Aroha, New Zealand; son of John Franklin, Farmer, and Matilda Wharfe. PhD 1933; BSc (University of New Zealand) 1927, MSc (University of New Zealand) 1928. **Tutor(s):** J M Wordie. **Educ:** Pukekohe District High School, New Zealand; Auckland Grammar School; Auckland University College. **Career:** Analyst, Dominion Laboratory 1927; Staff Member, Canterbury Agricultural College 1930–1931.

FRANKLIN, Roland Arthur Ellis (1944) Born 5 May 1926, 5 Pembridge Place, London; son of Ellis Arthur Franklin, Banker, and Muriel Frances Waley; m Nina Stoutzker, 23 June 1949. **Tutor(s):** J M Wordie. **Educ:** Devon House; Oundle School.

FRANKLIN, Thomas Bedford (1901) Born 7 September 1882, The Grove, Shutlanger, Towcester, Northamptonshire; son of Charles Henry Blunt Franklin, Gentleman Farmer, and Annie Watson; m Horatia Horne. BA 1904; MA 1939. **Tutor(s):** E E Sikes. **Educ:** Wellingborough Grammar School; Magdalen College, Brackley. **Career:** Master, Fettes College, Edinburgh 1907–1921; Founder and Officer, Fettes College OTC (twice mentioned in Secretary of State's list, for valuable services in connection with the war), WWI; 2nd South Staffordshire Regiment 1916; Headmaster, Stancliffe High School, Matlock 1921–1933. Died 11 August 1960.

FRASER, Donald (1931) Born 30 September 1913, Stourton Grange, Stourton, Rothwell, Yorkshire; son of Kenneth Fraser, Managing Director, Yorkshire Copper Works, and Alice Gertrude Woodall; m Ruth; 3 sons (Andrew, James and David). BA 1935; MA 1938. **Tutor(s):** M P Charlesworth. **Johnian Relatives:** brother of Kenneth Fraser (1926) and of Gordon Fraser (1928). **Educ:** St Poran's, Maidenhead; Oundle School. Died 31 May 1977.

FRASER, Donald Stuart (1906) Born 13 September 1887, 2 Hampton Villas, King Edward Road, Rochester, Kent; son of Roderick Fraser, Master Tailor, and Mary Ellen Hammond; m Kathleen Brown, 23 May 1919, Bywell St Peter's, Northumberland. **Subject(s):** History; BA 1909. **Tutor(s):** J R Tanner. **Educ:** Dulwich College Preparatory School; Dulwich College. **Career:** Collector and Assistant Magistrate, Indian Civil Service, Bengal and Peshawar 1910–1925; Second Lieutenant, 22nd Cavalry Guides, IARO, WWI; Tobacco Planter, Glen Somerset, Macheke, Southern Rhodesia.

FRASER, Gordon (1928) Born 26 February 1911, Ben Wyvis, North Park Grove, Roundhay, Leeds; son of Kenneth Fraser, Managing Director, Yorkshire Copper Works, and Alice Gertrude Woodall. BA 1931; MA 1935. **Tutor(s):** C W Guillebaud. **Johnian Relatives:** brother of Kenneth Fraser (1926) and of Donald Fraser (1931). **Educ:** Oundle School. **Career:** Director, UNESCO, Paris; Bookseller and Publisher 1935; Founder and Head, Gordon Fraser, greeting card firm 1938; Intelligence Officer, Palestine, Western Desert, and British Military Mission, Yugoslavia 1939–1945. Died 27 June 1981.

FRASER, Ian Richardson (1937) Born 12 December 1918, 42 Clarence Road, St Pancras; son of James Fraser, Minister, and Madge Silvers Richardson; m; 1 son (Martin), 2 daughters (Bridgette and Sarah). **Subject(s):** Modern and Medieval Languages; BA 1940; MA 1958. **Johnian Relatives:** nephew of Patrick Playfair Laidlaw (1900); son of James Fraser (1901); nephew of Hugh Alexander Lyon Laidlaw (1904), Charles Glass Playfair Laidlaw (1907) and of Walter Sibbald Laidlaw (1909); cousin of Christophor Charles Fraser Laidlaw (1940). **Educ:** LCC Elementary School, Haverstock Hill, London; University College School, Hampstead. **Career:** Assistant Master, Bristol Grammar Junior School 1945–1961; Headmaster, Brentwood Junior School, Essex. Died 10 August 1993.

FRASER, The Revd James (1901) Born 9 April 1883, 36 Leinster Square, London; son of James Fraser, Member, Lloyd's, and Sarah Georgina McBride; m Madge Silvers Richardson, 1911; 2 sons (Ian b 12 December 1918 and Hamish). BA 1906; MA 1909. **Tutor(s):** D MacAlister. **Johnian Relatives:** brother-in-law of Patrick Playfair Laidlaw (1900), Hugh Alexander Lyon Laidlaw (1904), Charles Glass Playfair Laidlaw (1907) and of Walter Sibbald Laidlaw (1909); father of Ian Richardson Fraser (1937); uncle of Christophor Charles Fraser Laidlaw (1940). **Educ:** Linton House School. **Career:** Vicar, Kentish Town, London 1914; Moderator of Presbyterian Church in England 1938. Died 1 September 1966.

FRASER, Keith (1922) Born 5 December 1903, 5 Butler Road, Harrow, Middlesex; son of Leslie McGregor Fraser, Mechanical Engineer, and Edith Maud Marsh; m Grace. **Subject(s):** Law; BA 1925; MA 1929. **Tutor(s):** E Cunningham. **Educ:** The Knoll, Woburn Sands; Oundle School. Died 31 October 1967.

FRASER, Kenneth (1926) Born 16 July 1908, 58 Shaftesbury Avenue, Street Lane, Leeds, Yorkshire; son of Kenneth Fraser, Managing Director, Leeds & Yorkshire Copper Works, and Alice Gertrude Woodall. **Subject(s):** Law; BA 1929; MA 1933; LLB 1930; LLM 1985. **Tutor(s):** C W Guillebaud. **Johnian Relatives:** brother of Gordon Fraser (1928) and of Donald Fraser (1931). **Educ:** Blackpool High School; Moorlands School, Leeds; Orleton School, Scarborough; Oundle School. **Career:** Admitted Solicitor 1932. Died 4 July 1990.

FRASER, Simon Barron (1945) Born 14 October 1926, 38 Primrose Mansions, Battersea, London; son of Robert Fraser, Mechanical Engineer, and Agnes Esmé Ashton Iredale; m Prunella Hodgson, 23 May 1959. BA 1948; MA 1952. **Tutor(s):** C W Guillebaud. **Educ:** South Kensington Preparatory School; Hythe House, Bexhill; Seafield Park, Fareham; Bryanston School.

FRAZER, Andrew Keith (1945) Born 27 August 1927, Moorlands Hall Maternity Home, Dewsbury; son of William Mowll Frazer, Barrister-at-Law and Professor of Hygiene, Liverpool University, and Gladys Mary Gubbins; m (2) Anne; (1) 2 sons (Scot and Kit), (2) 1 son (Andrew), 1 daughter (Alison). **Subject(s):** Natural Sciences; BA 1948; MA 1952. **Tutor(s):** G C L Bertram. **Educ:** Braeside Preparatory School, West Kirby; Buckenhurst Preparatory School, Liverpool; Liverpool College; Shrewsbury School. **Career:** Honorary Assistant Neurosurgeon, Royal Perth Hospital 1959–1965; Consultant Neurosurgeon, University Hospital of Wales, Cardiff 1973–1987. **Appointments:** Lieutenant Commander, Royal Australian Navy; Welsh Representative, General Medical Council 1981–1985. Died 15 September 1987.

FREAN, Dr Henry George (1900) Born 11 January 1883, 137 Macquarie Street North, Sydney, New South Wales, Australia; son of George Moore Frean, Gentleman, and Emily Sophia Kemp. **Subject(s):** Natural Sciences; BA 1904; MA 1908; MB 1908; BChir 1908; LRCP; MRCS 1908; FRCS 1910; Diploma in Ophalmology (Oxford) 1913. **Tutor(s):** D MacAlister. **Educ:** Dean Close School, Cheltenham. **Career:** Clinical Assistant, Pathologist, and Demonstrator in Anatomy, London and Oxford; Captain, RAMC, Egypt and the Caucasus; Eye Specialist. Died 18 June 1922.

FREDERICK, Captain Thomas (1912) Born 7 March 1893, Moulton, Acle, Norfolk; son of Henry Penrice Frederick, Solicitor, and Margaret Beevor. **Tutor(s):** E E Sikes. **Educ:** Rosslyn House Preparatory School, Walton, Felixtowe; Edgeborough Preparatory School, Guildford; Aldenham School. **Career:** Second Lieutenant, then Captain, Norfolk Regiment 1915–1917. **Awards:** Platt Scholarship, Aldenham. **Honours:** MC. Died 14 December 1917.

FREDJOHN, Dennis (1943) Born 22 February 1925, 36 Poynders Road, Clapham, Surrey; son of Maurice Harry Fredjohn, General Merchant, and Dorothy Maud Battey; m Pamela Jill Samms, December 1947; 1 son, 2 daughters. **Subject(s):** History; BA 1947; MA 1952. **Tutor(s):** C W Guillebaud. **Educ:** Dulwich Hamlet School; Archbishop Sumner's School; Westminster City School, London. **Career:** Aluminium Industry in England and Canada, including work with Texas Instruments; Founded Indalex in conjunction with the Pillar Group; Managing Director, Pillar Holdings (subsequently RTZ); UK Managing Director, Alusuisse; Chairman, Capital Ventures. **Appointments:** RAF Cadet, SJC; Member, SJC Appeal Finance Committee; Founder, Cambridge Colleges Fund; Member, Doctors and Dentists Review Body; Member, Gloucester Cathedral Appeal Committee; Member, University of Gloucester Development Committee; Chairman, Redmarley Village Hall; Council Member, Lloyd's of London. Died 23 December 2001.

FREEMAN, Alan Douglas (1942) Born 16 August 1923, 43 George Street, Basingstoke, Hampshire; son of Leonard James Freeman, Engineering Clerk, and May Mills; m Diana Maxine Tracey Johnson, 12 September 1950, The Church of St Mary the Virgin, Silchester; 1 daughter (Andrea Leonora Tracey). **Subject(s):** Mathematics; BA 1948; MA 1977; ACA; FCA 1962. **Tutor(s):** S J Bailey; J M Wordie. **Educ:** Brook Street Council School; Queen Mary's School, Basingstoke. **Career:** Lieutenant, then Captain, 8th Army Troops RE, Sicily, Italy and Austria 1942–1945; Military Operational Research Unit 1946; Articled to Turquand Youngs, Chartered Accountants 1948; Vickers Ltd 1953; management and financial control assignments in the UK, Middle East, and Far East, Production-Engineering Ltd (later P-E) 1954–1972; International Aeradio Ltd (subsidiary of BOAC) 1972–1978; Financial Director, BOAC 1978; Financial Planning Manager, British Airways 1979; in retirement, various directorships and independent consulting assignments 1980. **Publications:** 'Pressure Distribution over a Double-Wedge Aerofoil in Supersonic Flight', *Technical Note Aero 1870*, HMG, RAE, Farnborough, 1947. **Awards:** Minor Scholarship, SJC 1940.

FREEMAN, Eric John (1939) Born 27 September 1921, The Dingle, Wake Green Road, Moseley, Birmingham; son of Frederick Allwood Freeman, Commercial Clerk, and Lilian Amy Jarvis. **Subject(s):** Classics; BA 1942; MA 1946. **Tutor(s):** R L Howland. **Educ:** College Road Council School, Moseley; King's Edward's High School, Birmingham. **Career:** Deputy Director responsible for Administration and Planning, later Director of History of Medicine and Librarian, Wellcome Institute for the History of Medicine. **Appointments:** Bishop and LeFanu Memorial Lecturer 1996. **Awards:** Scholarship, SJC.

FREEMAN, Jack Greenfield (1924) Born 15 August 1906, 14 Wimborne Gardens, Ealing, Middlesex; son of Edmund Freeman, Mantle Manufacturer, and Fanny Cloudelsey. BA 1927. **Tutor(s):** E A Benians. **Educ:** Amesbury, Hindhead; Tonbridge School.

FREEMAN, Ronald Walter (1946) Born 28 November 1924, 102 City Road, London; son of Albert Walter Freeman, Commercial Clerk, and Hilda Mary Chipperfield; m Margaret Edith Gay, 1952; 3 daughters. **Subject(s):** Natural Sciences; BA 1948; MA 1953. **Tutor(s):** G C L Bertram. **Educ:** Garfield Road School; Minchenden Secondary School; Birkbeck College. **Awards:** Exhibition, Plastics Industry.

FREKE, Cecil George (1906) Born 8 October 1887, 378 Coldharbour Lane, Brixton, Surrey; son of Cecil Henry Freke, Chemist, and Alice Reding; m Judith Mary Marston; 1 son (John), 1 daughter (Biddy).

Subject(s): Mathematics; BA 1909; BSc (London) 1911. **Tutor(s):** L H K Bushe-Fox. **Johnian Relatives:** father of John Henry Freke (1943). **Educ:** Merchant Taylors' School. **Career:** Assistant Magistrate and Controller, Indian Civil Service 1911–1919; Assistant to Director-General of Commercial Intelligence, then Director-General, Indian Government 1919–1924; Deputy Secretary, then Secretary, Finance Department, Indian Government 1924–1932; Director, British National Committee, International Chamber of Commerce 1946–1954; Secretary, Iraq Currency Board 1949. Died 3 June 1974.

FREKE, John Henry (1943) Born 2 May 1925, Calcutta, India; son of Cecil George Freke, Indian Civil Service, and Judith Mary Marston. **Subject(s):** Economics; BA 1948; MA 1950. **Tutor(s):** C W Guillebaud. **Johnian Relatives:** son of Cecil George Freke (1906). **Educ:** King's Mead, Seaford; Westminster School; Rugby School. **Career:** RE Cadet.

FREME, Herbert Michael More (1919) Born 10 August 1902, Kingston Hill, Surrey; son of Pericles Freme, Member, London Stock Exchange, and Blanche Flora Isabella Freme. **Tutor(s):** E E Sikes. **Educ:** Vernon House School, London; St Edmund's College, Ware; University College School, Hampstead.

FRENCH, Dr Edward Brodie (1930) Born 9 May 1912, Ranmore, Burgh Heath Banstead, Surrey; son of Ronald Edgar French, Medical Practitioner, and Dorothy Brodie Ford; m Yvonne; 4 sons (Michael, John, Robert and Andrew). **Subject(s):** Natural Sciences; BA 1934; MB 1937; BChir 1937; FRCPEd 1957; FRCP 1960. **Tutor(s):** M P Charlesworth. **Johnian Relatives:** father of Michael Edward French (1960). **Educ:** Chinthurst School, Tadworth; St Anselm's School, Croydon; Tonbridge School. **Career:** Guy's Hospital 1934–1943; RAMC, France & Far East, finishing as Commanding Officer of BMH Singapore and Adviser in Medicine to SEAC 1941–1946; St Mary's Hospital 1947–1948; Lecturer in Medicine, University of Edinburgh 1948–1950; Physician, Northern Group of Hospitals, Edinburgh 1948–1977; Physician, Western, Northern and Eastern General Hospitals 1948–1977; Senior Lecturer in Medicine 1950–1952, Reader in Medicine 1968–1977, University of Edinburgh. **Awards:** Scholarship, SJC 1933. **Publications:** (contributor) *Davidson's Textbook Principles*; (contributor) *Practice of Medicine and Macleod's Clinical Examination*. Died 22 June 2000.

FRENCH, Reginald Thomas George (1900) Born 30 January 1881, 62 Harvard Road, Hilton Green, Lewisham, Kent; son of Thomas French, Civil Servant, and Annie Eliza Simmons; m Hilda Parke, 1907 (d 16 March 1957); 2 sons (Arthur and Thomas). **Subject(s):** Natural Sciences; BA 1903; MA 1940. **Tutor(s):** J E Sandys. **Johnian Relatives:** father of Thomas Worden French (1937). **Educ:** Plassey Road Board School; Central Foundation School, City Road, London. **Career:** Examining Staff, Patent Office 1903–1914; Ministry of Munitions 1915–1918; Secretary, Nitrogen Products Committee 1917–1919; Secretary, Water Power Resources Committee, Board of Trade 1919–1920; Governor, Central Foundation School 1951. **Honours:** OBE 1918; CBE 1941. Died 7 November 1965.

FRENCH, Thomas Worden (1937) Born 19 September 1917, 70 Mackenzie Road, Beckenham; son of Reginald Thomas George French, Secretary to the Electricity Commissioners, and Hilda Parke; m Muriel Elizabeth Jane Evans, 1952; 2 daughters (Hilary and Charlotte). **Subject(s):** Classics/Archaeology and Anthropology; BA 1940; MA 1944; Honorary Doctorate (York) 1997; FSA 1960. **Tutor(s):** R L Howland. **Johnian Relatives:** son of Reginald Thomas George French (1900). **Educ:** The Hall, Sydenham; Dulwich College. **Career:** Major, RA 1940–1946; Seconded to Monuments, Fine Arts and Archives Sub-Commission of the War Office, working in Greece and the Dodecanese 1944–1946; Assistant Keeper, Greek and Roman Department, British Museum 1946–1947; Senior Architectural Investigator, Royal Commission on Historical Monuments (England) 1947–1980. **Appointments:** Founder Member and first Secretary, Vernacular

Architecture Group 1953; Council Member, Yorkshire Archaeological Society 1964–1995; Member, Local Advisory Committee for the Dean and Chapter of York Minster 1980–1990; Trustee, York Glaziers Trust 1982; Honorary Member, Vernacular Architecture Group 1986; Member, York Diocesan Advisory Committee for the Care of Churches 1986–1998; Member, York Minster Fabric Advisory Committee 1991; Member, UK Committee of the Corpus Vitrearum Medii Aevi 1993. **Awards:** Africa Star with Eighth Army Clasp; Victory Medal; Queen's Silver Jubilee Medal 1977; Italy Star. **Publications:** Articles in various journals including 'Archaeology in the Dodecanese 1939–46', *Journal of Hellenic Studies*; 'Losses and survivals in the Dodecanese', *Annual of the British School at Athens*; 'The Herbert House, York', *Yorkshire Archaeological Journal*; 'Observations on some Medieval Glass in York Minster', *Antiquaries Journal*; 'Houses to 1650, City of York III', *Royal Commission on Historical Monuments (England)*. Died 18 February 2001.

FRENCH, William Arthur Liveing (1918) Born 25 January 1896, 135 Walmersley Road, Bury, Lancashire; son of William French, Chemist, and Amelia Annie Whybrow. **Subject(s):** History; BA 1920. **Tutor(s):** E E Sikes. **Educ:** Lancaster Grammar School; Mostyn House School, Parkgate, Chester; St Bees School; Harris Institute, Preston. Died 6 June 1938.

FREUNDLICH, Dr Herbert Frederick (1948) Born 19 June 1909, Leipzig, Germany; son of Herbert Max Finlay Freundlich, Professor of Chemistry, and Marie Mann. MA 1947; PhD 1971; Diplom-Ingenieur (Zürich) 1934. **Educ:** Real Gymnasium, Berlin-Lichterfelde; Technische Hochschule, Berlin; Eidgenossische Technische Hochschule, Zürich. **Career:** Atomic Energy Project, Canada 1940; Physicist, Department of Radiotherapeutics 1947; Principal Physicist, United Bristol Hospitals 1951.

FROWDE, Russell (1935) Born 15 March 1917, 14 Somerset Avenue, Blackpool; son of John Cameron Frowde, Company Secretary, and Lily Rushworth. **Tutor(s):** R L Howland. **Educ:** Higham Hall, Nuneaton; Harecroft Hall, Gosforth; St Wilfrid's, Seaford; Shrewsbury School.

FRY, Percival John Margrie (1942) Born 23 March 1924, 48 Dorothy Road, Battersea, London; son of Adrian Claud Fry, Civil Servant, and Doris Irene Tresidder. **Subject(s):** Modern and Medieval Languages; BA 1946; MA 1949. **Tutor(s):** C W Guillebaud. **Educ:** Hotham Road LCC School, Putney; Christ's Hospital. **Awards:** Exhibition, SJC 1941. **Honours:** OBE 1969.

FRYER, Sydney Ernest (1900) Born 17 July 1881, Portobello Barracks, Rathmines, Dublin, Ireland; son of William Fryer, Army Schoolmaster, and Emma Ann Kenna. **Subject(s):** Classics; BA 1903. **Tutor(s):** C E Graves; J R Tanner. **Educ:** St Olave's School, Southwark. **Career:** Assistant Master, Bishop's College School, Quebec 1903; Department of Public Instruction, Egypt 1906; Assistant Master, Ealing County School 1918. **Awards:** Sizarship, SJC.

FRYERS, John Lawrence (1908) Born 13 August 1889, 72 Brondesbury Road, Willesden, Middlesex; son of John Fryers, Railway Officer, and Harriet Aikman. **Subject(s):** Modern and Medieval Languages; BA 1911; MA 1929. **Tutor(s):** E E Sikes. **Educ:** Merchant Taylors' School. **Career:** Master, Queen's College, Taunton 1912–1913; Master, Merchant Taylors' School 1913–1950; Captain, Intelligence Corps, France and Italy, WWI. **Honours:** MC. Died 4 January 1959.

FUAD, The Hon Mr Justice Kutlu Tekin (1949) Born 23 April 1926, Nicosia, Cyprus; son of Mustapha Fuad Bey, Supreme Court Judge, Cyprus, and Belkis Hilmi; m Indji Izzet, 16 November 1952; 2 sons, 1 daughter. **Subject(s):** Law; BA 1951; MA 1956. **Tutor(s):** G C L Bertram; A G Lee. **Educ:** Temple Grove Preparatory School, Uckfield; Marlborough College. **Career:** Lieutenant, KRRC, UK, North Africa and Palestine 1944–1948; Called to the Bar, Inner Temple 1952 (Honorary Bencher 1993); Magistrate, Cyprus 1953–1956; Colonial Legal Service 1953–1962; Resident Magistrate, Senior Crown Counsel, Legal Draftsman, and Director of Public Prosecutions, Uganda 1956–1963; Judge of the High Court, Uganda 1963–1972; Director, Legal Division, Commonwealth Secretariat 1972–1980; Judge of the High Court, Hong Kong 1980–1982; Justice of Appeal, Hong Kong 1982–1988; Vice-President, Court of Appeal, Hong Kong 1988–1993; President, Court of Appeal, Brunei, Negara Brunei Darussalam 1993–2000; Non-Permanent Judge, Hong Kong Court of Final Appeal 1997–; *Ad hoc* Judge, European Court of Human Rights 2000. **Appointments:** Chairman, Law Reform Committee; Chairman, Visitation Committee, Makerere University College; Chairman, Disciplinary Committee, Law Council; President, Industrial Court; Member, Faculty Board, Faculty of Law, Makerere University; Member, Law Reform Commission, Hong Kong 1983–1989; President, Hong Kong Family Law Association 1986–1993. **Honours:** CBE 1993; Member of the Most Honourable Order of the Crown of Brunei, First Class.

FUCHS, Sir Vivian Ernest (1924) Born 11 February 1908, Recluse Lodge, Freshwater, Isle of Wight; son of Ernest Fuchs, of independent means, and Violet Anne Watson; m (1) Joyce Connell, 1933 (d 1990), (2) Eleanor Honnywill, 1991; (1) 1 son (Peter Ernest Kay b 2 June 1940), 2 daughters (Hilary Anne b 17 February 1936, d 2002 and Rosalind b 17 February 1938, d 1946). **Subject(s):** Natural Sciences; BA 1929; MA 1933; PhD 1937; ScD 1959; Honorary LLD (Edinburgh) 1958; Honorary DSc (Durham) 1958, (Cantab) 1959, (Leicester) 1972; Honorary ScD (Swansea) 1971; Honorary LLD (Birmingham) 1974; FRS 1974. **Tutor(s):** J M Wordie. **Johnian Relatives:** father of Peter Ernest Kay Fuchs (1959). **Educ:** Asheton Preparatory School, Tenterden; Brighton College. **Career:** Geologist, Cambridge East Greenland Expedition 1929; Geologist, Cambridge Expedition to East African Lakes 1930–1931; Geologist, East African Archaeological Expedition 1931–1932; Leader, Lake Rudolf Rift Valley Expedition 1933–1934; Leader, Lake Rukwa Expedition 1937–1938; Second Lieutenant, Cambridgeshire Regiment, TA 1939; Served in West Africa 1942–1943; Staff College, Camberley 1943; Served in North-West Europe (despatches), demobilized as Major 1944–1946; Leader, Falkland Islands Dependencies Survey (Antarctica) 1947–1950; Director, Falkland Islands Dependencies Scientific Bureau 1950–1955; Leader, Commonwealth Trans-Antarctic Expedition 1955–1958; Director, British Antarctic Survey 1958–1973. **Appointments:** Council Member 1958–1961, Vice-President 1961–1964, President 1982–1984, Honorary Vice-President 1985–1999, RGS; President, IGS 1963–1966; Honorary Fellow, Wolfson College, Cambridge 1970; President, BAAS 1972; Honorary Fellow, SJC 1983; Freedom of the City of London 1983. **Awards:** Cuthbert Peek Grant, RGS 1936; Founder's Gold Medal, RGS 1951; Silver Medal RSA 1952; Polar Medal 1953, Clasp 1958; Special Gold Medal, RGS 1958; Richthofen Medal (Berlin) 1958; Kirchenpauer Medal (Hamburg) 1958; The Royal Scottish Geographical Society Gold Medal 1958; Société de Géographie (Paris) Gold Medal 1958; Sociedad Chilena de Historia y Geografia Medal 1958; Brussels Exposition Universelle and International Algemene Werelotentoonstelling 1958; Plancius Medal (Amsterdam) 1959; Egede Medal (Copenhagen) 1959; Hubbard Medal, National Geographic Society (Washington) 1959; Explorers Club Medal (New York) 1959; Geographical Society (Chicago) Gold Medal 1959; Prestwich Medal, Geological Society of London 1960. **Honours:** Kt 1958. **Publications:** (with E Hillary) *The Crossing of Antarctica*, 1958; *Antarctic Adventure*, 1959; (ed) *Forces of Nature*, 1977; *Of Ice and Men*, 1982; (ed) *Oxford Illustrated Encyclopedia: The Physical World*, 1985; *A Time to Speak* (autobiography), 1990; geographical and geological reports and papers in scientific journals. Died 11 November 1999.

FUCHS, Dr Wolfgang Heinrich Johannes (1933) Born 19 May 1915, Munich, Germany; son of Martin Erick Fuchs, Formerly Councillor (Stadtrat) of Breslau, and Alice Margaret Manasse; m Dorothee Rausch von Traubenberg. **Subject(s):** Mathematics; BA 1936; PhD 1941. **Tutor(s):** J M Wordie. **Educ:** Johannes Gymnasium, Paradies Strasse, Breslau; Grunewald Gymnasium, Herberts Strasse, Berlin; University of Zurich. **Career:** Fellow, University of Aberdeen 1938; Assistant Lecturer in Mathematics, University of Wales, Swansea 1944–1947; Senior Lecturer in Pure Mathematics, University of Liverpool 1947–1948; Professor of Mathematics, Cornell University 1950–1985 (Emeritus 1985). **Awards:** Guggenheim Fellowship 1955; Fulbright-Hays Fellowship 1973; Humboldt Fellowship 1978. **Publications:** More than 65 papers in complex function theory and related areas; editor of several mathematical journals, notably the *Proceedings of the American Mathematical Society*. Died 24 February 1997.

FUDGE, Harry Vincent (1936) Born 20 July 1918, 123 North Road, Kirkmanshulme, Manchester; son of Harry Fudge, Coal Merchant, and Martha Walmsley. **Tutor(s):** J M Wordie. **Educ:** Meliden Church of England School; Rhyl County School.

FULLJAMES, The Revd Owen Ralph (1920) Born 22 August 1901, 42 Cottage Grove, Southsea, Hampshire; son of Gilbert Fulljames, Pawnbroker and Jeweller, and Edith Marion Totterdell; m (1) Julia Marray, 25 June 1927, St Jude, Southsea, (2) Joan. **Subject(s):** History; BA 1923; MA 1927. **Tutor(s):** E A Benians. **Educ:** Kindergarten, Portsmouth High School; Private School, Southsea; St Paul's Cathedral School; Sutton Valence School; Ridley Hall, Cambridge. **Career:** Rector, St Mary's, Hornsey; Assistant Master, St Paul's Cathedral Choir School 1924–1925; Ordained Deacon 1926; Curate, St John the Evangelist, Redhill 1926–1929; Ordained Priest 1927; Chaplain, RN, serving in Sandhurst, *Victory*, Portsmouth, *Drake* and *Rodney* 1930–1936; Assistant Master, Rugby School 1935–1954; Chaplain, RNVR 1937–1940; Chaplain, Rugby School 1946; Priest in Charge, Holy Trinity, Kingsway 1959; Honorary Chaplain, Bishop of London 1959. **Honours:** VRD. Died 11 January 1990.

FURNESS, John Bernard (1939) Born 24 October 1921, 70 Countess Street, Accrington, Lancashire; son of Richard Dickinson Furness, Book-keeper, and Jane Slater. **Subject(s):** Mathematics; BA 1942; MA 1946; FIA. **Educ:** Hyndburn Park Council School, Accrington; Accrington Grammar School. **Career:** Group Business Secretary, Equity and Law Assurance Society Ltd.

FYNES-CLINTON, Hugh Arthur (1932) Born 8 January 1913, St. James' Vicarage, Layland, Lancashire; son of Charles Edward Fynes-Clinton, Clerk in Holy Orders, and Quenilda Mary Shaw. **Subject(s):** Classics/Theology; BA 1935; MA 1939. **Tutor(s):** R L Howland. **Johnian Relatives:** son of Charles Edward Fynes-Clinton (1888). **Educ:** Hulme Grammar School, Oldham; Worksop College. **Career:** Inspector of Native Schools, Southern Rhodesia. Died 20 July 1990.

FYSON, Harold (1924) Born 15 January 1906, High Street, Isleham, Cambridgeshire; son of Ernest Fyson, Farmer and Coal Merchant, and Mary Elizabeth Flatt; m Ruby Deborah; 2 daughters (Gillian Elizabeth and Esther M Paige). **Subject(s):** Mathematics; BA 1927; MA 1931; FRGS. **Tutor(s):** J M Wordie. **Educ:** Isleham National School; Cambridge and County School. **Career:** Assistant Master, Elstree School; Surveyor, Nigeria 1933; Assistant Master, Mercers' School 1949; Schoolmaster, Collyer's School, Horsham 1962. **Awards:** Scholarship, SJC 1923. Died 1 May 1996.

FYZEE, Professor Asif (Asaf) Ali Ashgar (1922) Born 10 April 1899, Matheran, Bombay, India; son of Ali Ashgar Hasanli Fyzee, Landowner. **Subject(s):** Oriental Languages; BA 1925; MA 1929. **Tutor(s):** E A Benians. **Educ:** St Xavier's High School, Bombay, India; St Xavier's College, Bombay; Government Law School, Bombay. **Career:** Called to the Bar, Middle Temple 1924; Legal Practice, Bombay High Court 1926–1938; Professor of Law, Bombay 1929–1932; Principal, Bombay Law College 1938–1947; Perry Professor of Jurisprudence 1938–1947; Member, Bombay Public Service Commission 1947–1949; Indian Ambassador to Egypt 1949–1951; Member, Union Public Service Commission, New Delhi 1952; Visiting Professor, Institute of Islamic Studies, McGill University, Montreal 1958–1959. **Appointments:** President, Bombay Rotary Club 1947–1948; Commonwealth Visiting

Fellow, SJC 1962–1963; Honorary Secretary, Islamic Research Association; Fellow, University of Bombay; Honorary Member, Deutsche Morgenlandische Gesellschaft, Marburg. **Publications:** *Introduction to Muhammadan Law*, OUP, 1931; *Ismaili Law of Wills*, OUP, 1933; *Islamic Culture*, 1944. Died 23 October 1981.

G

GABRIEL, Philip Llewelyn (1938) Born 9 January 1920, Fern Villa, Lodge Road, Caerleon, Newport; son of Jacob Rees Gabriel, History Tutor, and Annie Morgan; m Ina. **Subject(s):** Mathematics; BA 1941; MA 1959. **Tutor(s):** J M Wordie. **Educ:** Caerleon Endowed School; Hereford Cathedral School. **Career:** Senior Assistant Actuary, Legal-General Assurance Society. Died 21 January 1992.

GACCON, William Edward (1921) Born 8 November 1902, 37 Caeran Road, Newport, Monmouthshire; son of John Augustus Gaccon, Organist and Music Teacher, and Alice Emily Gait. **Subject(s):** Classics; BA 1924; MA 1932. **Tutor(s):** E E Sikes. **Educ:** Llandaff Cathedral School; Hereford Cathedral School. **Career:** Master, Worcester College for the Blind 1925; Master, St Mark's School, Southborough, Massachusetts, USA 1931; RNVR 1940–1945. **Awards:** Exhibition, SJC. Died 27 March 1978.

GAJENDRA SINGH, Bhanwar (1934) Born 26 August 1912, Kunadi, Kotah State, Rajputana, India; son of Kanwar Chandra Sen, Private Secretary to HH Maharaj Sahib of Kotah. **Subject(s):** Law; BA 1936; MA 1949; LLB 1937. **Tutor(s):** C W Guillebaud. **Educ:** Mayo College, Ajmere, India. **Career:** District and Sessions Judge, United States of Rajasthan; Collector and District Magistrate, Commissioner, Indian Administrative Service, Union Government of India. **Appointments:** Member, Board of Revenue; Member, Board of Governors, Mayo College, Ajmere.

GALBRAITH, Alexander Henderson (1923) Born 29 December 1904, 3 Colebrook Terrace, Hillhead, Glasgow, Scotland; son of William Brodie Galbraith, Chartered Accountant, and Annie Jack Dunlop. **Subject(s):** History/Law; BA 1926. **Tutor(s):** E A Benians. **Educ:** Harrow School.

GALBRAITH, Ian Robertson (1937) Born 23 April 1919, 5 Broomknowe Terrace, Kilmacolm; son of John Galbraith, Lawyer, and Mabel Tarbet Robertson. **Subject(s):** Economics/Law; BA 1940; MA 1944. **Tutor(s):** C W Guillebaud. **Educ:** Strathallan School.

GALBRAITH, Walter Anderson (1941) Born 19 August 1922, 7 Woodside Terrace, Glasgow; son of Walter Weir Galbraith, Consulting Surgeon, and Lucy Evelyn Anderson. BA 1947; MA 1950. **Tutor(s):** S J Bailey. **Educ:** Ayton House Preparatory School, Glasgow; Glasgow Academy; Hurst Grange Preparatory School, Stirling; Harrow School.

GALE, Alexander John (1928) Born 31 January 1909, 6 Grosvenor Terrace, Newington, London; son of Alexander Alfred Gale, Fish Merchant, and Cecilia Porter; m Muriel. **Subject(s):** Mathematics; BA 1931; MA 1935. **Tutor(s):** J M Wordie. **Educ:** Merton Church of England School; King's College School, Wimbledon. Died 24 April 1989.

GALE, Conrad Arthur Lewis (1915) Born 18 May 1895, Belleville, Barbados, British West Indies; son of Valence Gale, Journalist, and Clara Alsop Chenery. **Tutor(s):** R P Gregory. **Educ:** Harrison College, Barbados; Chatham House, Ramsgate.

GALE, The Revd Cuthbert Courtenay (1908) Born 11 December 1883, High Street, Tenterden, Kent; son of James Randolph Courtenay Gale, Clerk in Holy Orders, and Mary Simpson Jago. BA 1911. **Tutor(s):** E E Sikes. **Johnian Relatives:** son of James Randolph Courtenay Gale (1876). **Educ:** Sutton Park School; Eltham College. **Career:** Ordained Deacon 1912; Curate, Yeovil with Priston 1912–1914; Priest 1913; Curate, St John the Evangelist, Redhill 1914–1915; Captain, RASC 1915–1918. Died 20 February 1926.

GALE, Professor Ernest Frederick (1933) Born 15 July 1914, 27 Avondale Road, Luton; son of Ernest Francis Edward Gale, Solicitor's Accountant, and Nellie Annie Tomlin; m Eiry Mair Jones, 28 August 1937; 1 son (David Anthony b 1944). **Subject(s):** Natural Sciences; BA 1936; PhD 1939; ScD 1947; BSc (London); FRS 1953. **Tutor(s):** J M Wordie. **Johnian Relatives:** father of David Anthony Gale (1962). **Educ:** Central Council School, Weston-Super-Mare; County School, Weston-Super-Mare. **Career:** Research in Biochemistry, University of Cambridge 1936–1938; Beit Memorial Fellow 1941; Scientific Staff, MRC 1943; Reader in Chemical Microbiology, University of Cambridge 1949–1960; Director, MRC Unit for Chemical Microbiology 1948–1962; Title A Fellow 1941–1944, Title E Fellow 1949–1953, Title C Fellow 1953–1988, SJC; Professor of Chemical Microbiology 1960–1981 (Emeritus 1981), University of Cambridge. **Appointments:** Herter Lecturer, Johns Hopkins Hospital, Baltimore, USA 1948; Commonwealth Travelling Fellow, Hanna Lecturer, Western Reserve University 1951; Member, Food Investigation Board 1954–1958; Meetings Secretary 1954–1958, International Representative 1963–1967, President 1967–1969, Honorary Member 1978, Society for General Microbiology; Harvey Lecturer, New York 1955; Leeuwenhoek Lecturer, Royal Society, London 1956; Member, International Union of Biochemistry Commission on Enzymes 1957–1961; Visiting Fellow, ANU 1964–1965; Malcolm Lecturer, Syracuse University 1967; M Stephenson Memorial Lecturer 1971; Linacre Lecturer, SJC 1973; Squibb Lecturer, Nottingham University 1986. **Awards:** Scholarship, SJC 1935; Senior Studentship, Royal Commission for Exhibition of 1851 1939. **Publications:** *Chemical Activities of Bacteria*, 1947; *The Molecular Basis of Antibiotic Action*, 1972, 2nd edition 1981; scientific papers in *Biochemical Journal, Journal of General Microbiology, Biochimica et Biophysica Acta*, etc.

GALE, Ian Walter Valence (1945) Born 9 July 1927, Abingdon, Dalkeith Road, St Michael, Barbados; son of Conrad Arthur Louis Gale, Editor, Barbados Advocate, and Ena May Duley. **Subject(s):** History/Law; BA 1948; MA 1967. **Tutor(s):** C W Guillebaud. **Educ:** The Lodge School, St John, Barbados. **Career:** Called to the Bar, Inner Temple 1949.

GALLIMORE, Alfred Smithson (1919) Born 31 March 1897, The Bank, Market Place, Long Eaton, Derbyshire; son of James Orpe Gallimore, Bank Manager, and Harriet Maude Smithson. **Subject(s):** Classics; BA 1921. **Tutor(s):** E E Sikes. **Educ:** Riber Castle, Mattock; Aldenham School. **Appointments:** Exhibition, SJC 1915.

GALLOWAY, Antony Lennox (1948) Born 24 September 1917, 9 Inverna Court, Kensington; son of Lennox Galloway, Lieutenant Colonel, RA, and Eileen Rosetta Reed; m Ursula Lund, 9 June 1956. **Subject(s):** Engineering/Mechanical Sciences; BA 1950; MA 1955; CEng; MIEE. **Tutor(s):** R L Howland. **Educ:** Sandroyd School, Cobham; Repton School; RMA, Woolwich. **Career:** Lieutenant Colonel. Died 19 February 1997.

GALT, Robert Brownlie (1913) Born 31 May 1894, North Delting, Riversdale Road, Poulton-cum-Seacombe, Chester; son of Charles Galt, Wine Merchant, and Ada Maria Davies. **Tutor(s):** E E Sikes. **Educ:** Elleray Park School, Wallasey; Malvern College. **Career:** Second Lieutenant, King's (Liverpool Regiment) (wounded), WWI. **Awards:** Scholarship, SJC.

GAMBLE, John Christopher (1929) Born 25 December 1910, Windlehurst, St Helens; son of Sir David Gamble, Farmer, and Eveline Frances Josephine Cole. **Subject(s):** Modern and Medieval Languages. **Tutor(s):** C W Guillebaud. **Johnian Relatives:** brother of William Gamble (1932). **Educ:** Packwood Haugh, Hockley Heath; Shrewsbury School.

GAMBLE, William (1932) Born 21 April 1913, Windlehurst, St Helens; son of Sir David Gamble and Eveline Frances Josephine Cole; m Christine Mary Permain, 27 November 1948, St Michael's Church, Camberley. **Subject(s):** History; BA 1935; MA 1947. **Tutor(s):** E A Benians. **Johnian Relatives:** brother of John Christopher Gamble

(1929). **Educ:** Etonhurst, Weston-super-Mare; Shrewsbury School. Died 4 December 1993.

GAMBLEN, Professor Frank (1936) Born 22 May 1913, Fire Station, South Perth, Australia; son of Horace Gamblen, Storekeeper, and Louisa Sampson. **Subject(s):** Mathematics; BA 1938; MA 1942; MSc (Western Australia); DipEd. **Tutor(s):** J M Wordie. **Educ:** State School, South Perth, Australia; Perth Modern School, Perth, Australia; University of Western Australia, Australia. **Career:** Mathematics Staff, University of Western Australia 1938–1978. **Appointments:** Visiting Professor, University of Kansas 1957; Honorary Fellow, St George's College, University of Western Australia; Carnegie Travelling Fellow. Died 1 November 1996.

GAMGEE, Joseph Leonard (1922) Born 12 August 1903, 28 Rotton Park Road, Edgbaston, Birmingham; son of Leonard Parker Gamgee, Surgeon and Professor, Birmingham University, and Margaret Williams; m Audrey; 1 son (Oliver), 2 daughters (Margaret and Jill). BA 1926; MA 1929. **Tutor(s):** B F Armitage. **Educ:** Edgbaston Church of England School; Edgbaston Preparatory School; King Edward's School, Birmingham. **Career:** Barrister-at-Law; Chairman, English Copper Mines in Spain. **Appointments:** President, Mental Health Appeals Tribunal. Died 16 March 1984.

GAMINARA, Albert William (1932) Born 1 December 1913, Tumaco, Republic of Colombia, South America; son of Albert Sydney Gaminara, Merchant, and Catherine Helen Copeman; m Monica Watson, 24 February 1947, Harlow Parish Church; 1 son, 3 daughters. **Subject(s):** Mathematics/Law; BA 1935; MA 1939. **Tutor(s):** J M Wordie. **Educ:** Cranbrook College, Ilford; City of London School; Oriel College, Oxford University. **Career:** Administrative Cadet, Sierra Leone, HM Overseas Civil Service 1936; Principal, Colonial Office 1947–1950; Administrative Officer, Northern Rhodesia 1950; Administrative Secretary, Government of Northern Rhodesia 1961–1963; Secretary to the Cabinet 1964; Adviser, Cabinet Office, Zambia 1965. **Appointments:** Member, Legislative Council, Northern Rhodesia 1963. **Honours:** CMG 1963. Died 22 December 1993.

GANDY, Henry (1904) Born 6 October 1884, 6 The Mount, Ecclesall, Bierlow, Yorkshire; son of Charles Gandy, Minister of Catholic Apostolic Church, and Emily Senneck. **Subject(s):** Classics; BA 1907; MA 1911. **Tutor(s):** C E Graves; J R Tanner. **Educ:** Royal Grammar School, Newcastle upon Tyne. **Career:** Solicitor, Wilkinson and Marshall, Newcastle upon Tyne 1910–1939.

GANN, Henry Charles (1921) Naval Officer.

GARABEDIAN, Dikran Garabed (1908) Born 15 September 1887, Diarbekir, Armenia; son of Stephan Garabedian, Anglican Churchman, and Oghida Zorian. **Subject(s):** Modern and Medieval Languages; BA 1911; MA 1915. **Tutor(s):** E E Sikes. **Educ:** Armenian School, Diarbekir; University of Toulouse; Syrian Protestant College, Beyrouth; University of Paris. **Career:** Taylorian Lecturer in French, Taylor Institution, Oxford 1914–1920; Tutor and Lecturer in French, St Catherine's Society, Oxford 1953. **Publications:** *The Sonnets of Shakespeare*, French Translation, Clarendon Press. Died 18 June 1963.

GARBETT, Peter (1948) Born 3 February 1928, 71 Newborough, Scarborough; son of Leopold Claude Garbett, Hotel Proprietor, and Mary Victoria Coopland; m Ann Barbara Forrest, 1963; 2 sons. BA 1950; MA 1955; FICE. **Tutor(s):** R L Howland. **Educ:** Eccles Grammar School; Scarborough College; Worksop College Preparatory School; Lisvane School, Scarborough; St Peter's School, York. **Career:** Mott MacDonald 1951–1990.

GARCIA, Leopold Basil Ronald (1900) Born 15 September 1882, Cromwell Road, Fitzhugh, Milbrook, Southampton; son of Charles Garcia, Mineral Water Maker, and Ellen Soffe. **Tutor(s):** C E Graves; J R

Tanner. **Johnian Relatives:** brother of George Henry Russell Garcia (1889). **Educ:** Southampton Grammar School.

GARDINER, Dennis Malcolm (1943) Born 8 June 1925, 61 Chadwick Road, Westcliff-on-Sea, Essex; son of Benjamin Isaac Gardiner, Dried Fruit Broker, and Florence Hilda Fowler. BA 1948. **Tutor(s):** C W Guillebaud. **Educ:** Tollington Boys' School, London; Saffron Walden Grammar School; King Edward VI School, Bury St Edmunds. **Career:** Lotus and Delta Shoe Company; RN Cadet. **Awards:** Exhibition, SJC.

GARDINER, Gilbert Claydon (1924) Born 30 April 1905, Victoria House, Anson Road, Islington, Middlesex; son of Alfred George Gardiner, Author and Journalist, and Ada Claydon. **Subject(s):** English; BA 1927. **Tutor(s):** B F Armitage. **Educ:** University College School Hampstead; The Leys School, Cambridge; LSE. Died 20 September 1981.

GARDINER, Henry Rolf (1921) Born 5 November 1902, 56 Fitz George Avenue, Fulham, London; son of Alan Henderson Gardiner, Egyptologist, and Hedwig Rosen; m Mariabella (Marabel) Honor Hodgkin, Autumn 1932; 2 sons, 1 daughter. **Subject(s):** Modern and Medieval Languages; BA 1924. **Tutor(s):** E A Benians. **Educ:** West Downs, Winchester; Rugby School; Bedales School, Petersfield. **Career:** Farmer of the 1500 acre Springhead Estate. **Appointments:** Member, Dorset County Council 1937–1946; President, Dorset Federation of Young Farmers' Clubs 1944–1946; Joint Chairman, Dorset and Somerset Rural Industries Committee 1951–1969; Member, National Executive, Soil Association; Chairman, Dorset Branch, Council for the Protection of Rural England 1957–1967 (President 1970–1971); Chairman, Dorset Branch, County Landowners' Association 1961–1963; High Sheriff of Dorset 1967–1968; Honorary Member, Institute of Landscape Architects 1971. **Awards:** Lenne Gold Medal for Landscape Husbandry, Goethe Foundation 1971. **Publications:** *The Second Coming and other Poems*, 1921; *World Without End*, 1932; *England herself – ventures in rural restoration*, 1943; *Love and Memory, A Garland of Poems*, 1960; *Water Springing from the Ground*, 1972; contributions to periodicals etc. Died 26 November 1971.

GARDINER, The Revd James Aitken (1949) Born 14 March 1925, St James's Manse, Orchard Street, Falkirk; son of William Gardiner, Minister, United Free Church of Scotland, and Jessie Thomson Hutson; m Mary Murray, 12 July 1952, King's College Chapel, Old Aberdeen. **Subject(s):** Theology and Religious Studies; BA 1951; MA 1956; MA (Aberdeen), 1949. **Tutor(s):** C W Guillebaud. **Educ:** Rothesay Academy; Bellahouston Academy; Hamilton Academy; Gordon Schools, Huntley; Aberdeen University. **Career:** RAF 1944–1947; Licensed to Preach the Gospel by the Presbytery of Strathbogie, and as a probationer for the Holy Ministry 1953; Minister, Parish of Dyke and Moy, Elginshire; Lecturer in New Testament Studies, University College, Ibadan, Nigeria; Temporary Lecturer in Religious Education, Moray House College of Education, Edinburgh.

GARDINER, John David (1926) Born 11 March 1909, son of Alfred Charles Gardiner, Commercial Business, and Lucy Margaret Holyman. BA 1931. **Tutor(s):** J M Wordie. **Educ:** Falconbury Preparatory School; Courtenay Lodge, Sutton Courtenay.

GARDINER, Kenneth John Rattray (1909) Born 19 July 1889, 3 Albion Villas, Alperton, Middlesex; son of William Rattray Gardiner, Merchant, and Edith Ann Bull. **Subject(s):** Engineering. **Tutor(s):** L H K Bushe-Fox. **Educ:** School of the Reformed Churches, St Petersburg; Eastbourne College; Crystal Palace Engineering School. **Career:** Engineer, Norton Griffiths and Co, Baku, South Russia; Town Surveyor, Bloemfontein, South Africa; Public Works Division, Nairobi, Kenya; Lieutenant, RE (Tunnelling Company), then Captain, King's African Rifles 1915–1917. Died 1 February 1917 (died of dysentery on HM Hospital Ship).

GARDINER, Brigadier Richard Aylmer (1931) Born 21 June 1911, Dalhousie, Punjab; son of Richard Gardiner, Brigadier, Indian Army, and Amelia Mary Tyler; m Marguerite (Peggy) Rochfort, 1938; 2 sons

(Noel and Piers). **Subject(s):** Mechanical Sciences; BA 1933; MA 1938; FSA; MIOP; FRICS; FRGS 1937. **Tutor(s):** J S Boys Smith. **Educ:** St Christopher's School, Eastbourne; Stowe School, Buckingham; RMA, Woolwich. **Career:** Commissioned, RE 1931–1963; Chief of Geographic Section, Allied Force Headquarters, Fontainbleau 1961–1963; Director of Map Production and Publications, Ordnance Survey 1963–1966; Keeper of the Map Room, Royal Geographical Society 1966–1978. **Appointments:** President, British Cartographic Society 1968–1970; Chairman, Royal Society's Cartography Sub-committee 1971–1977. **Honours:** MBE. Died 22 November 1978.

GARDNER, Dr Eric Kay (1931) Born 24 March 1913, 15 Park Crescent, Church End, Finchley; son of Edward Shillito Gardner, Woollen Agent, and Mary Sophia Kay; m Catherine Winifred Baker; 1 son (Andrew), 2 daughters (Angela and Priscilla). **Subject(s):** Natural Sciences; BA 1934; MA 1973; BChir (St Bartholomew's Hospital) 1939; MB 1939; FRCS 1948; FFARCS 1952. **Tutor(s):** M P Charlesworth. **Educ:** St Lawrence College Junior, Ramsgate; St Lawrence College. **Career:** House Officer 1938–1941; Resident Anaesthetist 1941–1942, Resident Surgical Officer 1942–1948, St Margaret's Hospital, Epping; Consultant Anaesthetist, Whipps Cross Hospital 1948–1957; Consultant Anaesthetist, Barnet General Hospital 1957–1976; Medical Adviser, National Advice Centre, Council for Postgraduate Medical Education 1976–1983; Medical Adviser, London Ambulance Service 1978–1988.

GARDNER, Major Jack Montfort Stanley (1913) Born 27 April 1894, St Thomas' Vicarage, Hyde, Cheshire; son of Walter Richard Gardner, Clerk in Holy Orders, and Ella Stanley Scott; m Violet Marion Jackson; 2 sons (Brian and Richard), 2 daughters (June and Valerie). **Tutor(s):** L H K Bushe-Fox. **Educ:** Southey Hall, Worthing; King Edward's School, Stratford-on-Avon; Durham School. **Career:** Hunts Cyclist Battalion 1914; rose to rank of Captain; 124th Baluchistan Regiment, Indian Army 1915; served on North West Frontier and in Persia until 1934. **Awards:** Baker Exhibition, SJC. **Honours:** MBE. Died 27 May 1935.

GARDNER, John Bardsley (1927) Born 26 October 1908, 30 Elm Park Road, Winchmore Hill, Southgate, Middlesex; son of James Chaloner Gardner, Chartered Accountant, and Clara Elizabeth Brodersen. **Subject(s):** English; BA 1930; MA 1934. **Tutor(s):** M P Charlesworth. **Educ:** Oldfield School, Swanage; The Leys School, Cambridge. Died 18 January 1979.

GARDNER, John Edmund (1948) Born 20 November 1926, St Stephen's House, Seaton Delaval, Northumberland; son of Cyril John Gardner, Clerk in Holy Orders, School Chaplain, and Lena Henderson; m Margaret Mercer, 1952, St Paul's, Oxford (d 1997); 1 son (Simon), 2 daughters (Alexis and Miranda). **Subject(s):** Theology; BA 1951; MA 1955. **Tutor(s):** C W Guillebaud. **Educ:** St Stephen's House, Oxford; Mr Cottam's Preparatory School, Newcastle upon Tyne; King Alfred's School, Wantage. **Career:** Professional Magician 1943–1944; Lieutenant, Royal Marines (transferred from Fleet Air Arm) 1944; Ordained Deacon 1953; Assistant Curate, Christ Church, Frome 1953–1955; Ordained Priest 1954; Chaplain, RAF 1955–1957; Assistant Priest (curate), Evesham 1957–1958; Released from Holy Orders 1958; Theatre Critic/Theatrical Journalist 1959–1963; Author of thrillers and continuation of the James Bond novels; Toured USA, lecturing on Shakespeare. **Publications:** The Bond Novels: *Licence Renewed; For Special Services; Icebreaker; Role of Honour; Nobody Lives for Ever; No Deals, Mr Bond; Scorpius; Win, Lose, or Die; Brokenclaw; The Man from Barbarossa; Death is For Ever; Never Send Flowers; SeaFire; Cold; Licence to Kill* (from the Screenplay); *Goldeneye* (from the Screenplay). The Boysie Oakes Books: *The Liquidator; Understrike; Amber Nine; Madrigal; Founder Member; Traitor's Exit; Air Apparent; A Killer for a Song.* The Derek Torry Novels: *A Complete State of Death; The Corner Men.* The Moriarty Journals: *The Return of Moriarty; The Revenge of Moriarty.* The Herbie Kruger Novels: *The Nostradamus Traitor; The Garden of Weapons; The Quiet Dogs; Maestro; Confessor.* Other Novels: *Golgotha; Flamingo; The Dancing Dodo; The Werewolf Trace; To Run a Little Faster;*

Every Night's a Bullfight; The Censor; Day of Absolution; Blood of the Fathers (as Edmund McCoy); *Bottled Spider.* The Generations Trilogy: *The Secret Generations; The Secret Houses; The Secret Families.* Autobiography: *Spin The Bottle.* Collected short stories: *The Assassination File; Hideaway.*

GARLE-BROWNE, John Babington (1900) Born 24 January 1881, Bufton Lodge, Ratby, Leicestershire; son of John Garle-Browne, House Proprietor, and Sarah Louise Davies. **Subject(s):** History; BA 1903. **Tutor(s):** C E Graves. **Educ:** Pocklington School.

GARNER, Sir Henry (Harry) Mason (1911) Born 3 December 1891, The Breach, Donnington-le-Heath, Leicestershire; son of William Garner, Grocer, and Annie Gadsby; m Hilda Annie Green, 1921; 1 son (Henry Clifford), 1 daughter. **Subject(s):** Mathematics; BA 1914; MA 1919. **Tutor(s):** L H K Bushe-Fox. **Johnian Relatives:** father of Henry Clifford Garner (1940). **Educ:** Grammar School, Market Bosworth. **Career:** Sub-Lieutenant, RNVR, WWI; Deputy Director of Scientific Research, Ministry of Aircraft Production 1942–1945; Principal Director of Scientific Research, Ministry of Supply 1946–1949; Researched Chinese Lacquer and Cloisonné in retirement. **Appointments:** Honorary Secretary of Oriental Ceramic Society 1951–1967; President, Oriental Ceramic Society 1968–1971. **Awards:** Marmaduke Levitt Scholarship, University of Cambridge 1911; Isaac Newton Studentship, University of Cambridge 1915; Smith's Prize, University of Cambridge 1916. **Honours:** CB 1942; KBE 1951. **Publications:** *Oriental Blue and White*, 1964; *Chinese and Japanese Cloisonné Enamels*, 1967; (with Margaret Medley and photographs by William B Gruber and Rupert P Leach) *Chinese Art in Three-dimensional Colour*, 1969; *Ryukyu Lacquer*, 1972; *Chinese and Associated Lacquer from the Garner Collection*, 1973; *Chinese Export Art in Schloss Ambras*, 1975; *Chinese Lacquer*, 1979. Died 8 August 1977.

GARNER, Henry Clifford (1940) Born 14 July 1922, Mount Pleasant, College Town, Sandhurst, Berkshire; son of Henry Mason Garner, Civil Servant, and Hilda Annie Green. **Subject(s):** Mathematics; BA 1944; MA 1956. **Tutor(s):** J M Wordie. **Johnian Relatives:** son of Henry (Harry) Mason Garner (1911). **Educ:** St Felix School, Felixstowe; Westminster School. **Awards:** Major Scholarship, SJC 1939; Marquess of Salisbury Exhibition, SJC 1940.

GARNETT, The Revd Philip Robert Mauleverer (1923) Born 23 January 1906, 16 Bold Street, Warrington, Lancashire; son of Philip Carlisle Garnett, Master Cabinet Maker, and Emilie Ayre Watson. **Subject(s):** Economics; BA 1927; MA 1931. **Tutor(s):** J M Wordie. **Educ:** Eagle House, Sandhurst; Cheltenham College; Ridley Hall, Cambridge. **Career:** Assistant Master, Oakley Hall, Cirencester 1928; Ordained Deacon 1952; Curate, St Mary, Sholing, Hampshire 1953; Ordained Priest 1953; Curate, Kirby Moorside, Yorkshire; Vicar, Ledsham with Fairburn, Yorkshire 1957.

GARRETT, Edward John (1934) Born 11 February 1915, Hill View, Barnetts Road, Knock, Belfast; son of Edward John Garrett, Estate Agent and Accountant, and Margaret Hamilton Hislop. **Subject(s):** Mathematics; BA 1937; MA 1941. **Tutor(s):** J M Wordie. **Johnian Relatives:** brother of Henry Hamilton Garrett (1935); great uncle of Owen John Garrett (1990) and of Charlotte Anne Garrett (1994). **Educ:** Freshford, Knock, Belfast; Campbell College, Belfast. **Career:** Assistant Master, Methodist College, Belfast 1937–1948; Second Lieutenant (later Major), RA, 8th (Belfast) Heavy Anti-Aircraft Regiment 1939–1946; Schoolmaster, Campbell College 1948. Died April 1986.

GARRETT, Henry Hamilton (1935) Born 20 September 1917, Hill View, Barnetts Road, Belfast; son of Edward John Garrett, Estate Agent and Accountant, and Margaret Hamilton Hislop. **Subject(s):** Natural Sciences; BA 1939; MA 1943; LLB (London) 1952. **Tutor(s):** J M Wordie. **Johnian Relatives:** brother of Edward John Garrett (1934); great uncle of Charlotte Anne Garrett (1994) and of Owen John Garrett (1990).

Educ: Freshford, Knock, Belfast; Campbell College, Belfast. **Career:** Principal Officer, Department of Education.

GARROOD, John Francis (1944) Born 20 June 1926, Langdale, 625 London Road South, Lowestoft, Suffolk; son of Charles Henry Garrood, Marine and Mechanical Engineer, and Ruby Eveline Schwank. **Subject(s):** History/Law; BA 1949; MA 1953. **Tutor(s):** J M Wordie; F Thistlethwaite. **Educ:** South Lodge School, Lowestoft (later Old Buckenham Hall School); Oundle School. **Career:** Sub-Lieutenant, RNVR 1945–1947; Lieutenant, then Lieutenant Commander, RNVSR; Admitted Solicitor 1956; Partner, Lyus, Burne & Lyus, Diss, Norfolk 1960–1966; Assisted Legal Practices in Southwold and Lowestoft 1966–1972; Self-employed in Local Government (legal) 1972–1979. **Appointments:** RN Cadet, SJC; Cambridge University Naval Division 1944–1945; Honorary Secretary, Southwold Sailing Club 1970–1974; Lieutenant Commander, RNR 1973; Vice-Commodore 1976, Commodore 1977, Southwold Sailing Club.

GARROULD, Ivor George Bayes (1920) Born 19 May 1901, 12 Brondesbury Park, Willesden, Middlesex; son of Arthur Henry Garrould, Government and Hospital Contractor, and Jessie Emma Marline Davies; 3 sons. **Tutor(s):** E E Sikes. **Johnian Relatives:** brother-in-law of Eric William Winch (1919); uncle of Thomas Beverley Charles Winch (1950). **Educ:** Lindisfarne College, Westcliff-on-Sea; Bishop's Stortford College. **Career:** Director, E & R Garrould, London; Intelligence Corps 1939–1945.

GARTON, Arthur Ernest James (1928) Born 14 March 1909, 1 Gordon Street, St Pancras, London; son of John Arthur Garton, Clerk in Holy Orders, and Hilda Jane Collins. BA 1931. **Tutor(s):** M P Charlesworth. **Educ:** Stoke House, Seaford; The Cathedral School, Hereford. **Awards:** Exhibition, SJC 1928.

GASKELL, Peter Monks (1940) Born 6 March 1921, 112 Park Road, Hindley, Lancashire; son of Peter Gaskell, Colliery Agent, and Edith Alice Monks. **Tutor(s):** J M Wordie. **Educ:** Terra Nova, Birkdale; Rydal School, Conway.

GASKELL, William Harriman Craig (1931) Born 11 June 1914, Melrose, Naini Tal, United Provinces, India; son of William Gaskell, Indian Civil Services, Opium Agent, and Euphemia Craig. **Subject(s):** Modern and Medieval Languages/Economics; BA 1936. **Tutor(s):** C W Guillebaud. **Johnian Relatives:** son of William Gaskell (1891); cousin, once removed, of John Macmaster Pitkethly (1974). **Educ:** Shrewsbury House, Ditton Hill; Rugby School. **Career:** Director, WH Everett and Son Ltd; Director, Country Book Club Ltd; Captain, RASC.

GASPER, Philip Arnold (1914) Born 2 August 1893, Calcutta, India; son of Donald Malcolm Gasper, Printer, and Leah Mary Teil. **Subject(s):** Modern and Medieval Languages/History; BA 1917; MA 1921; Diploma in Education (Oxford) 1928. **Tutor(s):** E E Sikes. **Educ:** Doveton College, Calcutta, India; St Xavier's College, Calcutta, India; Scottish Churches College, Calcutta India; Presidency College, Calcutta, India. **Career:** Master, Churcher's College, Petersfield 1918; Cheltenham Grammar School 1919–1921; Varndean School, Brighton 1921. **Awards:** Exhibition, SJC 1916. **Publications:** 'Icelandic Studies', *The Eagle*, 1916; 'Cervantes', *The Eagle*, 1917.

GATHORNE, The Revd Christopher (1902) Born 30 December 1882, Wenhaston, Suffolk; son of Richard Gathorne, Clerk in Holy Orders, and Jessie Taylor. BA 1905; MA 1909. **Tutor(s):** J R Tanner; C E Graves. **Johnian Relatives:** brother of John Naylor Gathorne (1898). **Educ:** Pocklington School. **Career:** Ordained Deacon 1907; Ordained Priest 1910; Curate, Nuthurst 1910–1914; Curate, Kirby Lonsdale 1914–1916; Curate, St John, Workington 1916–1921; Curate, Holy Trinity, Carlisle 1922–1924; Vicar, Lupton with Hutton Roof 1924–1937. Died 10 August 1950.

GATTY, Hugh Percival Wharton (1925) Born 4 February 1907, The Vicarage, Offley, Hitchin, Hertfordshire; son of Percival Edmund Gatty, Clerk in Holy Orders, and Alice Mabel Wellwood Ker. **Subject(s):** History; BA 1928; MA 1932. **Tutor(s):** E A Benians. **Johnian Relatives:** nephew of Frederick Alfred Gatty (1874) and of Albert Augustus Gatty (1876); son of Percival Edmund Gatty (1886); cousin of Philip Vincent Gatty (1921). **Educ:** Northaw Place, Potters Bar; Harrow School. **Career:** Foreign Office, WWII; Title A Fellow 1931–1936, Title B Fellow and Lecturer in History 1936–1945 (leave of absence on war service 1940–1945), Title E Fellow 1945–1948, SJC. **Appointments:** Supervisor in History 1932–1936, Librarian 1937–1948, SJC; Secretary, Cambridge and County Folk Museum; Secretary, Walpole Society. **Awards:** Exhibition, SJC; Taylor Studentship 1929; Strathcona Studentship, SJC 1930. Died 18 March 1948.

GATTY, Oliver (1935) Born 5 November 1907, 45 Onslow Gardens, London; son of Stephen Herbert Gatty, Chief Justice of Gibraltar, and Katharine Morrison; m Penelope Noel Tower. **Johnian Relatives:** great grandson of Alexander John Scott (1786). **Educ:** St Peter's Court, Broadstairs; Winchester; Balliol College, Oxford. **Career:** Tutorial Fellow, Balliol College, Oxford 1930–1933. Died 5 June 1940.

GATTY, Philip Vincent (1921) Born 18 August 1901, Frognal End, Frognal Gardens, Hampstead; son of Frederick Alfred Gatty, Calico Printer and Dyer, and Frances Minna Woolfield Irwin; m Helen. BA 1924; MA 1928. **Tutor(s):** E A Benians. **Johnian Relatives:** son of Frederick Alfred Gatty (1874); nephew of Albert Augustus Gatty (1876) and of Percival Edmund Gatty (1886); cousin of Hugh Percival Wharton Gatty (1925). **Educ:** Radley College. Died 6 January 1972.

GAUDIE, Martyn (1943) Born 17 January 1925, Wohelo, Gypsy Lane, Nunthorpe, Ormesby, Yorkshire; son of Norman Gaudie, Director and Secretary, Sugar Manufacturers, and Eva Mary Briggs; m Marjorie Hall, 14 May 1964, St Andrew's Methodist, Hardwick, Stockton-on-Tees; 3 sons (Angus b 18 February 1965, Robert b 17 May 1969 and Hugh b 12 June 1974), 1 daughter (Elspeth b 3 September 1966). **Subject(s):** Economics/Geography/Agriculture. BA 1949; MA 1955. **Tutor(s):** C W Guillebaud; G C L Bertram. **Educ:** Collingwood Preparatory School; Friends' School, Great Ayton; Bootham School, York. **Career:** Land Work as Conscientious Objector 1943–1947; Lecturer, Warden and Sports Officer, Askham Bryan Agricultural College, York 1950–1958; Farm Manager, Agricultural Research Station, Nungua, University of Ghana 1958–1962; Farmer, Stamfrey Farm, West Rounton, Northallerton, North Yorkshire 1963–1993. **Appointments:** Member, Ghana Test Match Team v Sierra Leone, Freetown 1961; Captain, Dons University of Ghana Cricket Team 1960–1962; Chairman, Northallerton National Farmers' Union; Chairman, Brompton Discussion Society; Prison Visitor, Young Offenders' Institution Northallerton 1996–.

GAUSSEN, John MacCulloch (1912) Born 25 July 1893, The Parsonage, Orphan Drive, West Derby, Lancaster; son of Charles Edward Gaussen, Clerk in Holy Orders, and Mary Newbold. BA 1918; MA 1924. **Tutor(s):** E E Sikes. **Johnian Relatives:** son of Charles Edward Gaussen (1874). **Educ:** Berkhampstead School. **Career:** Major, Royal Warwickshire Regiment (TF), France (wounded, Mentioned in Despatches), then Instructor, Officer Cadet School, Cambridge, WWI; Master, Brighton College; Master, Preparatory School, Godalming; Master, then Headmaster, Brighton Preparatory School. Died 26 January 1970.

GAVINS, Raymond Cedric (1949) Born 8 January 1930, Stone Place Farm, Skellingthorpe, Lincolnshire; son of John Hansard Gavins, Garthman on farm, and Myra Helen Sarah Measures; m Jean Mary Booth, 1955, Sheffield; 1 son (Michael Richard b 1964), 2 daughters (Jillian Anne b 1958 and Carol Jane b 1961). **Subject(s):** Modern and Medieval Languages; BA 1952; MA 1956. **Tutor(s):** C W Guillebaud. **Educ:** Church of England School, Stapleford; Fulletby Church of England School; Ewerby Church of England School; Carres Grammar School, Sleaford; King's School, Grantham. **Career:** Sergeant, RE

1948–1949; Assistant Master, Modern Languages 1954–1956, Head of Modern Languages 1957–1962, Carres Grammar School, Sleaford; Head of Modern Languages, Batley Grammar School 1962–1966; Senior Lecturer, Head of Modern Languages, Derby College of Art and Technology 1966–1981; Head of Division of Modern Languages, Derbyshire College of Higher Education 1981–1990; Head of Division of Modern Languages 1990–1991, Part-time Lecturer 1991–1995, University of Derby. **Awards:** Newcome Exhibition, SJC 1948.

GAY, Michael Algar Parrish (1944) Born 17 November 1926, Highlands, Hare Street, Romford, Essex; son of Alfred William Gay, Solicitor, and Doris Eva Parrish; m Zena Mavis Sloman, 12 July 1952. **Tutor(s):** J M Wordie. **Educ:** Falconbury, Little Common; Felsted School. **Career:** Wilkinson, Chater & Co. **Appointments:** RAF Cadet, SJC.

GAZE, Edwin Howard (1900) Born 2 May 1882, 14 Balfour Road, Highbury New Park, Islington, London; son of Edwin Robert Gaze, Cotton Goods Warehouseman, and Helen Knight. BA 1903. **Tutor(s):** J E Sandys. **Educ:** Paston Grammar School, North Walsham. **Career:** Master, Kidderminster Grammar School 1904.

GAZE, Geoffrey Atkinson (1900) Born 19 July 1881, Carrow Hill, Norwich, Norfolk; son of William Geoffrey Gaze, Solicitor, and Margaret Kate Atkinson. **Tutor(s):** E E Sikes. **Educ:** King Edward VI Middle School, Norwich; Oundle School. **Career:** Clerk, Queen Anne's Bounty Office 1902; Captain, London Regiment (Civil Service Rifles) 1914–1916. **Awards:** Munsteven Exhibition, SJC. Died 15 September 1916 (killed in action).

GEAKE, The Revd Anthony (1904) Born 14 May 1884, Eglington Villa, Compton Gifford, Devon; son of Edward Geake, Gentleman, and Henrietta Nancy Raby; m Emily Paget Martin, 14 February 1912, St Martin's, Gospel Oak, London. **Subject(s):** History; BA 1907; MA 1911. **Tutor(s):** J R Tanner; C E Graves. **Educ:** Sutton Valence School. **Career:** Ordained Deacon 1908; Curate, St Paul, Onslow Square 1908–1910; Ordained Priest 1909; Curate, St Paul, Bournemouth 1910–1911; Rector, Little Yeldham 1912–1913; Rector, Hackford and Vicar, Whitwell 1913–1932; Rector, Dengie with Asheldam 1932–1942; Rector, Burston with Shimpling, Norfolk 1942–1948.

GEARY, Professor Alfred (1912) Born 15 December 1893, Barwell, Hinckley, Leicestershire; son of William Geary, Shoe-Clicker, and Catherine Pickering; m Gladys Swithenbank. **Subject(s):** Mathematics; BA 1915; MA 1919; MSc (UCL) 1928. **Tutor(s):** L H K Bushe-Fox. **Johnian Relatives:** uncle of Richard Arthur Radford (1938) and Roger Nicholas Radford (1944). **Educ:** Barwell Church of England School; Barwell Wesleyan School; Market Bosworth Grammar School; UCL. **Career:** Teacher, Bishop Stolgate's School, York; Teacher, Eltham College; Lecturer in Mathematics, Northampton Polytechnic, London 1926–1956 (Head, Mathematics Department 1928). **Appointments:** Examiner for various boards; Founder Member, Institute of Mathematics and its Applications. **Publications:** *Mathematics for Technical Students*; *Advanced Mathematics for Technical Students*. Died 15 May 1978.

GEBHARD, John Leslie (BOWEN) (1935) Born 12 July 1915, Durban, South Africa; son of Norman Leslie Gebhard, Technical Manager, and Florence May Bowen; m Elaine Winbolt Lewis, 31 May 1941; 3 sons. **Subject(s):** Economics/Law; BA 1938; MA 1942. **Tutor(s):** C W Guillebaud. **Johnian Relatives:** nephew of Leslie Harold Bowen (1907) and of William Henry Bowen (1930); cousin of Leslie Harold Bowen (1935) and of Thomas Jim Bowen (1936). **Educ:** Southlea, Malvern; Bromsgrove School. **Career:** Articled to a Solicitor 1938; Embodied with HAC, commissioned in Royal Warwickshire Regiment 1939; served in France 1940; Seconded to Indian Army 1942–1945; served in Burma; twice Mentioned in Despatches 1942–1945; passed the Final examination of the Law Society 1947; admitted as Solicitor 1947; Solicitor's Office, Customs and Excise 1950–1970; Legal Adviser, British Joint Services Liaison Organisation, Bonn, West Germany 1970–1978.

Appointments: Winfield Society. **Honours:** MC 1945 (Karen resistance); OBE 1966. **Publications:** *Undercover in the Jungle*, William Kimber, 1978. Died 16 February 2002.

GEDDES, Archibald (1949) Born 31 March 1927, 10 Janefield Place, Beith, Ayrshire, Scotland; son of Archibald Geddes, Wood Machinist, and Elizabeth Kennedy Fulton. **Subject(s):** Mathematics; BA 1951; MA 1955. **Tutor(s):** J M Wordie. **Educ:** Beith Academy; Speir's School, Beith; Glasgow University. **Career:** Lecturer in Mathematics, University of Glasgow 1953; Title A Fellow, SJC 1955–1958. **Awards:** Scholarship, SJC 1951; Rayleigh Prize, University of Cambridge 1953. Died 5 April 1985.

GENDERS, Antony Clive (1936) Born 1 June 1917, 43 Fossdale Road, Sheffield; son of William Henry Genders, Managing Director, and May Peat, Timber Merchant; m Celia Meakin. **Subject(s):** Economics; BA 1939; MA 1943. **Tutor(s):** C W Guillebaud. **Educ:** Birkdale Preparatory School, Sheffield; King's School, Ely. **Career:** Established Berowne School, Stratford-upon-Avon. Died 21 September 1999.

GENDERS, William Roy (1932) Born 21 January 1913, 43 Fossdale Road, Sheffield; son of William Henry Genders, Timber Merchant, and May Peat. **Tutor(s):** C W Guillebaud. **Educ:** Birkdale School, Sheffield; The King's School, Ely. **Awards:** Heritage Award for restoring Northborough Manor. **Publications:** *League Cricket in England*; *Worcestershire County Cricket*; 50 gardening books. Died 28 September 1985.

GENGE, Dr Donald Sealy Gilbert (1925) Born 16 December 1905, 89 Lansdowne Road, Croydon, Surrey; son of George Gilbert Genge, Doctor of Medicine, and Catherine Wheeldon. BA 1929; MA 1932; MB 1943; BChir 1943. **Tutor(s):** M P Charlesworth. **Educ:** The College, Eastbourne; The University Tutorial College, London. Died 1993.

GENGE, James Robert (1930) Born 7 July 1912, Victoria, British Columbia, Canada; son of Lawrence Arthur Genge, Merchant, and Gertrude Alice Rithet; 1 son (Brian), 3 daughters (Alice, Pamela and Jennifer). **Subject(s):** Mathematics/Economics; BA 1934; MA 1937. **Tutor(s):** J M Wordie. **Educ:** Cranleigh House School, Oak Bay, Victoria, British Columbia; Brentwood College, Victoria, British Columbia. **Career:** RCNVR, WWII; Rithet Consolidation, Vice-President 1939–1945; President and Owner, Rithet Consolidated. Died 23 October 1997.

GENT, Derek Frederick (1947) Born 10 February 1929, 26 Southernhay, West Exeter; son of Fred Gent, Farmer, and Margery Mary Coombe; m Miriam Senior, 1955; 3 children. BA 1950. **Tutor(s):** G C L Bertram. **Educ:** St Peter's School, Exmouth; Blundell's School, Tiverton. **Career:** Farmer. **Appointments:** Liberal Democrat District Councillor, East Devon District.

GENT, Grande Ufficiale Harold Arthur (1924) Born 31 July 1905, 8 Grove Street, Wellingborough, Northamptonshire; son of Jabez Gent, Table Water Manufacturer, and Louisa Agnes Hewitt; m Maria Teresa Marzi, 5 December 1956, Verona; 1 son (John Anthony b 19 August 1957), 1 daughter (Diana Elizabeth b 21 January 1959). BA 1927. **Tutor(s):** E E Sikes. **Johnian Relatives:** father of John Antony Gent (1975). **Educ:** The Board School, Bedford; Bedford Modern School. **Career:** Managing Director, Laboratori Glaxo, Verona, Italy 1932–1970; Army, served in Africa, Middle East and Italy, WWII. **Awards:** Grande Ufficiale of the Italian Republic 1968. **Honours:** CBE 1968. Died 13 August 1987.

GEORGE, Bryan Henry (1941) Born 7 April 1923, 273 Nithsdale Road, Glasgow; son of Reginald Harry George, Divisional Secretary, Scottish National Council, and Catherine Gladys Ackland. BA 1944; MA 1948; CEng; MIMechE; FInstD; MIMgt; FBICSc. **Tutor(s):** S J Bailey. **Educ:** Kilmarnock Academy; Strathallan School.

GEORGE, John Key Durancé (1945) Born 16 April 1924, Burnt House, Stubbington, Fareham, Hampshire; son of Arthur Swynfen Durancé George, Commander, RN, and Hilda Ker Finlay. **Tutor(s):**

F Thistlethwaite. **Educ:** Fernden School, Haslemere; Wellington College. **Career:** Lieutenant, 27th Lancers, Middle East 1943–1945. Died 11 April 1946.

GEORGE, John Trevor (1914) Born 17 March 1895, Bronhadren, Stow Park, Newport, Monmouthshire; son of Jonathan George, Clerk in Holy Orders, and Lavinia Lamb; m Olive. **Tutor(s):** E E Sikes. **Educ:** Oakfield House School, Newport; Clifton College. **Career:** Ministry of Pensions; Captain, Monmouthshire Regiment 1914–1917. **Honours:** MC. Died 22 September 1965.

GEORGE, Professor Thomas Neville (1926) Born 13 May 1904, 30 Pentrepoth, Morriston, Swansea, Glamorganshire; son of Thomas Rupert George, Schoolmaster, and Lizzie Evans; m Sarah Davies, 1932. PhD 1928; DSc (Wales); Honorary D és Sc (Rennes); Honorary LLD (Wales); FRS 1963. **Tutor(s):** J M Wordie. **Educ:** Swansea Municipal Secondary School; Swansea Grammar School; University College of Swansea. **Career:** Fellow, University of Wales until 1926; Geological Survey 1930–1933; Professor of Geology, University College, Swansea 1933–1946; Professor of Geology, University of Glasgow 1947. **Appointments:** President, Association of University Teachers of GB and NI 1959; President, Paleontological Association 1962–1964; President, Geological Society of London 1968–1970; President, Association of Teachers of Geology 1970–1971; Board, Geological Survey of GB; Chairman, Mineral Resources Panel of the Scottish Council; Vice President, Royal Society of Edinburgh; President, Glasgow Geological Society; Council Member, BAAS; Woodward Visiting Lecturer, Yale; Visiting Scholar of Columbia, Ohio and Missouri Universities. **Awards:** Lyell Medal, Geological Society of London 1963; Kelvin Prize, Royal Philosophical Society 1975. **Publications:** *Evolution in Outline*, 1951; *Regional Geology Handbook of North Wales*, 1961; *Regional Geology Handbook of South Wales*, 1969. Died 18 June 1980.

GEORGE, William Ewart (1921) Naval Officer.

GERRARD, Dr John Anthony Fraser (1945) Born 5 March 1924, Northern Hospital Liverpool; son of Cecil Balfour Gerrard, Controller of Transportation (Shipping), Ministry of Supply, and Julia Nellie Fraser. PhD 1950; BSc (London) 1944. **Tutor(s):** J M Wordie. **Educ:** Elm Hall Drive Private School; Quarry Bank High School, Liverpool; Ewell Castle School; City of London Freemen's School, Ashstead Park; Imperial College of Science and Technology. **Career:** Geophysicist, Colonial Service, Uganda 1948.

GERRARD, Raymond Ormesher (1935) Born 24 September 1916, Exford, Temple Drive, Swinton, Manchester; son of Clement Thomas Gerrard, Master Builder, and Alice Ormesher; m (1) Jane Chamberlain, 1939, (2) Jean Lyle, 1965; (1) 2 daughters (Gail Patricia b 1941 and Prudence Jane b 1946). **Subject(s):** Economics/Law; BA 1938; MA 1942; FIOB 1959. **Tutor(s):** C W Guillebaud. **Educ:** The Downs, Colwall, Malvern; Bryanston School, Blandford. **Career:** Second Lieutenant, RE, 110th East Lancaster Army Troops 1939–1942; Captain, RE, Field Engineer Airfield Construction 1942–1944; Major Staff Officer, RE, New Delhi HQ, India (airfield construction) 1944–1945; Major, RE, attached to the RAF in India 1945–1946; Director J Gerrard & sons, Manchester 1956–1968; Director, British Engine Insurance, Manchester 1966–1976; Director, Fram Group, London 1968–1972; Director, Fairclough Group, Northwich 1972–1979; Director, Trafford Park Estates, Manchester 1979–1998; Management Consultant to Architects Halliday Meechan 1979–1998; Director, Central Manchester Development Corporation 1988–1997. **Appointments:** Leader, Home Builders Mission from Britain to Canada, organised by Department of Trade and Commerce, Ottawa, Canada 1964; Chairman, Team Services, London 1988–1996; Chairman, Manchester Phoenix Institute 1987–1994; Chairman, Manchester Initiative 1992–2000; Salford Governing Body, Royal College of Advanced Technology; Member, Salford University Council; Chairman, Manchester Guardian Society for the Protection of Trade; Chairman, Manchester Guardian Society Charitable Trust; Trustee,

Northwest Civic Trust; Trustee and Chairman, Worsley Civic Trust; Trustee, Salford and Trafford Groundwork Trust. **Honours:** OBE 1992.

GERSON, Guillaume Hubert Auguste (1916) Born 12 August 1895, Antwerp, Belgium; son of Alphonse Francois Jean Gerson, Commissionaire en Marchandises, and Hortense Marie Josèphe Pieraerts. **Subject(s):** History/Modern and Medieval Languages/Geography; BA 1919; MA 1930. **Tutor(s):** E E Sikes. **Educ:** St John Berchmann's College, Antwerp; Abbey of Mooredsons.

GETTY, Professor Robert John (1928) Born 5 February 1908, Mettican, Errigal, Coleraine, County Londonderry, Ireland; son of William Getty, Farmer, and Martha May Crowe; m Margaret Wood. **Subject(s):** Classics; BA 1930; MA 1934; BA (Belfast) 1928; FRSC 1956. **Tutor(s):** M P Charlesworth. **Educ:** Coleraine Academical Institution; Queen's University, Belfast. **Career:** Assistant in Latin, University of Aberdeen 1930–1934; Lecturer in Latin, University of Liverpool 1934–1937; Title B Fellow and Lecturer in Classics, SJC 1937–1947 (leave of absence on war service 1940–1945); Faculty Assistant Lecturer in Classics 1939–1947; Lecturer in Classics 1947, University of Cambridge; Air Ministry, Foreign Office 1940–1945; Professor of Latin 1947–1951, Professor of Classics and Head of Department 1951–1958, University College, University of Toronto; First Paddison Professor of Classics, University of North Carolina 1958. **Appointments:** Visiting Professor, University of Chicago, Summer 1949; Executive Committee, Classical Association of the Middle West and South; Member, Societies of the Promotion of Hellenic and Roman Studies; Member, Classical Association; Member, Association Guillame Bude; Société des Études Latines; President, American Philological Society; Director, Vice-President, American Philological Association. **Publications:** *The Lost St Gall MS of Valerius Flaccus*, 1934; *M Annaei Lucani de Bello Civili Liber I*, CUP, 1940, reprinted 1955 with corrigenda. Died 24 October 1963.

GHEY, Geoffrey William Essington (1923) Born 9 February 1905, Berwyn Lodge, Broadstone, Canford, Dorset; son of William Essington Ghey, Commercial Traveller, and Jane Glasgow; m Eileen Mackinnon, 1936; 1 son (Peter Lachlan b 13 February 1939). **Subject(s):** Mechanical Sciences; BA 1926; MA 1930; MIEE. **Tutor(s):** B F Armitage. **Johnian Relatives:** cousin once removed, of Philip Henry Ratcliffe Ghey (1927); father of Peter Lachlan Ghey (1958). **Educ:** Wychwood School, Bournemouth; Sedbergh School. **Career:** Lecturer, Royal Naval College, Dartmouth 1926–1967 (Director of Studies 1957). **Awards:** Lupton and Hebblethwaite Exhibition, SJC. **Honours:** MBE. **Publications:** (with J Goodier) *Electromagnetism*, 1952. Died November 1984.

GHEY, Dr Philip Henry Ratcliffe (1927) Born 2 July 1909, North Friary Nursing Home, Plymouth, Devon; son of Samuel Henry Ratcliffe Ghey, Insurance Company District Manager, and Alice Porter; m E M Ruth McKee, 1941; 1 son (Peter b 1947). **Subject(s):** Natural Sciences; BA 1930; MA 1934; BChir 1934; MB 1934; MChir 1938; MRCS 1933; LRCP 1933; FRCS 1935. **Tutor(s):** M P Charlesworth. **Johnian Relatives:** Cousin once removed, of Geoffrey William Essington Ghey (1923); cousin of Peter Lachlan Ghey (1958). **Educ:** Mount House School, Plymouth; Kelly College, Tavistock; Plymouth Technical College. **Career:** Resident Surgical Officer, Prince of Wales Hospital, Plymouth; Consulting Surgeon, United Cambridge Hospitals, and other neighbouring hospitals; RAMC 1938; Associate Lecturer in Surgery, University of Cambridge 1949; Surgeon Specialist, Sarwak 1964. Died 14 March 1992.

GHOSH, Mahim Chandra (1900) Born 20 January 1880, Nikla, Mymensingh, Bengal; son of Nabin Chandra Ghosh, Zemindar, and Digambari Rai. **Subject(s):** Mathematics; BA 1903; MA 1911; BA (Calcutta). **Tutor(s):** D MacAlister. **Johnian Relatives:** brother of Bimal Chandra Ghosh (1896). **Educ:** Presidency College, Calcutta. **Career:** Magistrate and Judge, India 1904–1932; Called to the Bar, Inner Temple 1911.

GIBBINS, Thomas William Horn (1903) Born 18 July 1884, Bondgate, Alnwick, Northumberland; son of Thomas William Horn Gibbins, Collector, and Margaret Gallon. BA 1906. **Tutor(s):** D MacAlister. **Educ:** Morpeth Grammar School.

GIBBONS, Thomas James (1930) Born 14 July 1911, Perth, Western Australia; son of John Martin Gibbons, Gold Miner, and Florence Caroline James; m Joan McNeil, 9 October 1954; 1 son (Julian). **Subject(s):** English; BA 1933; MA 1941. **Tutor(s):** M P Charlesworth. **Educ:** Ladysmith Road School, Exeter; Exeter School. **Career:** Naval Interpreter in French and Modern Greek (Advanced Level); Civil Service, Immigration Officer; Teacher, Technical Colleges and Adult Education; Police Interpreter; Examiner, Royal Society of Arts in French, German and Italian; English Master, Andros Grammar School, Greece; Temporary Acting Sub-Lieutenant, RNVR, retired as Lieutenant Commander RN 1952. **Appointments:** UK Battle of Crete Veteran 1990; President, Dover Anglo-French Association 1991.

GIBBS, Alan Edward Russell (1941) Born 2 November 1921, Hellesdon Links Estate, Norwich, Norfolk; son of Arthur Gibbs, Architect and General Sales Manager, and Dorothy Agnes Rowe. **Tutor(s):** S J Bailey. **Johnian Relatives:** father of Fiona Russell Gibbs (Boult) (1983). **Educ:** The Grammar School, Norwich; Queen Elizabeth's School, Barnet; Norwich High School; King Edward VI School, Birmingham. **Career:** Articled with Slater and Downing, Cambridge 1940.

GIBBS, John Morel (1930) Born 17 August 1912, Eastcliffe, Park Road, Penarth, Glamorganshire; son of John Angel Gibbs, Major, Shipowner, and Susan Gladys Morel; m Sheila Margaret Newton, 1937, Penarth; 5 sons. **Subject(s):** Law; BA 1934; MA 1938; Social Sciences Course (UCL); Clinical Psychology Training (Guy's Hospital); MA (London University) 1940; Doctorate of Humane Letters (Union College, Kentucky, USA) 1964. **Tutor(s):** C W Guillebaud. **Johnian Relatives:** father of John Newton Gibbs (1960), William Malcolm Gibbs (1963), Andrew Goldsworthy Gibbs (1965) and of Simon Edward Gibbs (1967); grandfather of Jessica Faith Gibbs (1995). **Educ:** King Alfred's School, Penarth, South Wales; Caldicott School, Hitchin; The Leys School, Cambridge. **Career:** Called to the Bar 1935; Senior Psychologist, Hertfordshire Psychiatric and Child Guidance Service 1941–1945; Lecturer in Psychology, University College, Cardiff 1945–1977. **Appointments:** Methodist Local Preacher, Sunday School Superintendent and Class Leader in local Church; Vice-President, Methodist Conference 1958; Chairman, Board of Management for Methodist Residential Schools; Treasurer, Methodist Division of Education and Youth; Chairman, Central Council in Education and Training for Social Work in Wales; President, Contemporary Art Society for Wales 1995. **Honours:** OBE 1967. **Publications:** (with Sheila Gibbs) *Militant and Triumphant, a pageant of the Church*, Methodist Youth Department, London, 1948; *Patterns of Residential Care for Children*, National Children's Home, 1968; *Morels of Cardiff: the History of a Family Shipping Firm*, National Museum of Wales, 1982; *James Pyke Thompson: The Turner House Penarth 1888–1988*, National Museum of Wales, 1990; (with Sheila Gibbs) *Trinity Methodist Church, Penarth: a Portrait*, Methodist Publishing House, Peterborough, 1994. Died 16 June 1996.

GIBBY, David (1922) Born 27 January 1890, Clyn Llewelyn, Llancefn, Pembrokeshire; son of William Gibby, Farmer, and Martha Morris. MSc 1924. **Tutor(s):** B F Armitage. **Educ:** Narberth County School; University College of Wales.

GIBSON, Dr Alan Calvert (1944) Born 2 August 1926, 58 Selborne Road, Dudley, Worcestershire; son of Eric Calvert Gibson, Bank Manager, and Kathleen West; m Joyce, 1951; 3 daughters (Janet, Jane and Sally). **Subject(s):** Natural Sciences; BA 1947; MA 1951; BChir 1950; MB 1950; MRCP (Ed) 1956; DPM (Dunelm) 1956; FRCP (Ed) 1971; FRCPsych 1977. **Tutor(s):** S J Bailey. **Educ:** Durston House, Ealing; St Paul's School; St Mary's Hospital Medical School. **Career:** Casualty Physician,

St Mary's Hospital 1951; Senior Hospital Medical Officer, Runwell Hospital, Essex 1958; Consultant Psychiatrist, Herrison Hospital Group, Dorchester 1963; Consultant Psychiatrist, Bournemouth and East Dorset Hospitals 1966; Honorary Lecturer, Southampton University 1976–1981; Medical Director, Bowden House Clinic, Harrow-on-the-Hill 1981–1984. **Appointments:** Member, Mental Health Review Tribunal 1986–1999; Member, Parole Board 1989–1992. **Publications:** Various papers on Old Age Psychosis, Stress Disorders and Hypertension; numerous papers on Tardive Dyskinesia, 1974–1988; chapter on Tardive Dyskinesia, research and treatment, SP Medical and Scientific Books, New York, 1990.

GIBSON, Charles Edward Dehany (1935) Born 19 April 1917, 13 Cornwall Terrace, Regent's Park, London; son of Ralf Sumner Gibson, Admiralty Recruiting Staff Officer, and Anne Christina Bernard; m Susan Veronica Whitelegge, 4 April 1964, All Saints Church, Martin, Hampshire. BA 1939; MA 1943. **Tutor(s):** C W Guillebaud. **Educ:** Mr Barnard, Alpine Cottage, Arveyes sur Bex, Switzerland; Mr Andrews, Picket Post, Ringwood; Marlborough College; Mrs Croome Smith, Bristol.

GIBSON, George (1938) Born 10 December 1919, 12 Stamford Grove, Handsworth, Birmingham; son of Albert Ernest Gibson, Toolmaker Journeyman, and Sarah Ann Young. **Subject(s):** Economics; BA 1942; MA 1945. **Tutor(s):** J M Wordie. **Educ:** Westminster Road Council School, Birmingham; Handsworth Grammar School. **Career:** Pilot Officer, RAF 1939; POW Germany 1942. Died 1966.

GIBSON, Humphrey Graeme (1925) Born 9 November 1906, son of Edward Marriott Gibson, Engineer, and Margaret Favre McCallum; m Rosemary Rachel Earle, 10 June 1939. **Subject(s):** Mechanical Sciences/Mathematics; BA 1928. **Tutor(s):** J M Wordie. **Educ:** Hazelwood, Limpsfield; Oundle School. **Career:** Assistant to the Maintenance Engineer, Metropolitan Cammel Carriage Wagon and Finance Company Ltd, Birmingham 1928–1930; Candy Filter Company Ltd 1930–1940; Second Lieutenant, RE 1940; Staff Captain (Mechanic), GHQ, Cairo 1941–1943; Deputy Assistant Director of Works (Electrician and Mechanic), GHQ, Paiforce, Baghdad 1943–1944; Service Engineer's Department, Anglo-Iranian Oil Company Ltd, Abadan, Persia 1944–1945; Inspector, Royal Engineer Machinery, to Commander, RE, Larkhill, Salisbury Plain 1945–1946; Deputy Manager, Cairo, Associated British Manufacturers (Egypt) Limited, Cairo 1946.

GIBSON, John Milne (1944) Born 16 August 1926, 14 Whitehall Road, Harrow, Middlesex; son of John Gibson Gibson, Civil Servant, Air Ministry, and Edith Auld. **Subject(s):** Geography; BA 1949; MA 1951. **Tutor(s):** J M Wordie. **Educ:** Northwood Preparatory School; Marlborough College. **Appointments:** RN Cadet, SJC.

GIBSON, Dr John Nevill (1945) Born 1 May 1927, 22 Rosemont Road, Acton, Middlesex; son of John Torbet Smith Gibson, Medical Practitioner, and Vera Constance Squire; m Diana Mary Bateman, 27 July 1951. **Subject(s):** Natural Sciences; BA 1948; MB 1951; BChir 1951; MChir 1966. **Tutor(s):** S J Bailey. **Johnian Relatives:** brother of William Russell Gibson (1950). **Educ:** Hillbrow, Eastbourne; Charterhouse. **Career:** Consultant General Surgeon, Tunbridge Wells Hospital Group 1966. Died 25 November 1996.

GIBSON, Sir Ronald George (1930) Born 28 November 1909, 359 Portsmouth Road, Southampton; son of George Edward Gibson, Master Chemist, and Gladys Muriel Prince; m Dorothy Elizabeth Alberta Rainey, 1934; 2 daughters. BA 1932; MA 1952; Honorary LLD (Wales) 1965; Honorary DM (Southampton) 1980; MRCS; FRCS 1968; FRCGP 1967; LRCP; FRSA 1983. **Tutor(s):** M P Charlesworth. **Educ:** Banister Court School; Osborne House School; Mill Hill School. **Career:** Lieutenant Colonel, RAMC (Emergency Reserve); Principal Medical Officer, Italian Somaliland 1944–1945; Medical Officer, Winchester College and St Swithun's School, Winchester 1950–1977; GP, until 1977. **Appointments:** Council Member, BMA 1950–1972 (Chairman, Representative Committee 1963–1966, Chairman, Council 1966–1971); First Provost, South-East England Faculty, RCGP 1954; RCS 1962–1967; Standing Medical Advisory Committee 1966–1976 (Chairman 1972–1976); Health Services Council 1966–1976 (Vice-Chairman 1972–1976); James Mackenzie Lecturer, RCGP 1967; Master, Court of Assistants, Worshipful Society of Apothecaries of London 1971 (Liveryman 1964, Master 1980); Tribunal on Alleged Atrocities, Northern Ireland 1971; Personal Social Services Council, DHSS 1973–1976; Member, GMC 1974–79; Governor, Eastleigh College of Further Education 1977–1985; Chairman, Medical Insurance Agency 1977–1982; Chairman, Medical Information Revision Panel, British Library 1978–1982; Member, Court, University of Southampton 1979–1986; DL, Hampshire 1983; Director and President, Brendoncare Foundation 1983–1989; High Steward, Winchester Cathedral 1985–1989; Advisory Council on Misuse of Drugs; Chairman, Steering Committee on Barbiturates; Chairman, Advisory Committee, Drug Surveillance Research Unit, Southampton University. **Awards:** Butterworth Gold Medal, BMA 1956; Gold Medal, BMA 1970. **Honours:** OBE 1961; CBE 1970; Kt 1975. **Publications:** *Care of the Elderly in General Practice*, 1956; *The Satchel and the Shining Morning Face*, 1971; *The One with the Elephant*, 1976; *Adolescence*, 1978; *The Family Doctor, His Life and History*, 1981. Died 27 June 1989.

GIESECKE, Herr Ernest Franz Rudolph Hans (1910) Born 2 June 1892, Klein Wanz Leben Bezirk Magdeburg Preassen, Germany; son of Ernest Giesecke, Oekonomierat, and Maria Oesterreich. **Tutor(s):** J R Tanner. **Educ:** Real Gymnasium, Rostock.

GIFFORD, David Ross (1942) Born 4 October 1924, Marienburg, Cologne; son of Jack Ross Gifford, Lieutenant Colonel, RA, and Joyce Maud Stevens. **Tutor(s):** C W Guillebaud. **Educ:** Glengorse, Battle, Sussex; Imperial Service College; King's School, Bruton.

GILANI, Abdulla (1935) Born 28 May 1916, Calcutta, India; son of Shaikh Abu Nash Gilani, Freight Broker, and Kamarunnesa. **Subject(s):** Natural Sciences; BA 1938; MA 1947. **Tutor(s):** R L Howland. **Educ:** St Xavier's College, Calcutta.

GILBERT, Sir Bernard William (1910) Born 28 September 1891, 58 Bunbury Street, Nottingham; son of Harry Gilbert, Hosiery Warehouseman, and Mary Ellen Atkin; m Janet Maude Fison, 12 December 1925, St Mary's, Amersham; 1 son (Roger Key b 27 June 1930), 3 daughters (Phoebe, Rosemary and Margaret). **Subject(s):** Mathematics; BA 1913; MA 1952. **Tutor(s):** L H K Bushe-Fox. **Johnian Relatives:** brother-in-law of Alexander Key Fison (1910); father of Roger Key Gilbert (1948). **Educ:** West Bridgford Higher Grade School; Nottingham High School. **Career:** Royal Horse Artillery, RGA, WWI; Second Secretary, responsible for home finance and supply; HM Treasury 1914–1957: Principal Assistant Secretary 1934, Under-Secretary 1939, Joint Second-Secretary responsible for supply services 1944, Member, Economic Planning Board 1947–1957 (Chairman 1953). **Appointments:** Honorary Fellow, SJC 1952. **Honours:** KCB 1946; GCB 1950. Died 7 November 1957.

GILBERT, David Hew (1949) Born 13 October 1928, 6 Cleveland Road, Hillingdon, Uxbridge, Middlesex; son of Herbert Gilbert, Civil Servant, Post Office, and Margaret Haining Hyslop Wales. **Subject(s):** English; BA 1952. **Tutor(s):** C W Guillebaud. **Educ:** Oak Farm Elementary School; Bishopshalt School.

GILBERT, David Martyn (1949) Born 18 April 1928, 91 Hertford Road, Enfield, Middlesex; son of Arthur Gilbert, Chartered Surveyor, and Ethel Florence Martyn. **Subject(s):** Modern and Medieval Languages; BA 1952. **Tutor(s):** C W Guillebaud. **Educ:** Inglemere School, Enfield; Junior House, Felsted; Felsted School. **Career:** Royal Marines 1947–1949.

GILBERT, Keith Reginald (1933) Born 19 December 1914, 40 York Road, Edgbaston, Birmingham; son of Harry Reginald Gilbert, Coal and Coke Factor, and Elsie Winifred Forrester; m (1) Lucy Auerbach, (2) Electra Michelaidou. **Subject(s):** Mathematics; BA 1936; MA 1940. **Tutor(s):** J M Wordie. **Educ:** West House School, Edgbaston; King Edward's High School, Birmingham. **Career:** Research Assistant, Royal School of Mines, Imperial College 1936–1938; RAFVR 1939–1945; Assistant Chief Research Engineer, CAV Ltd 1945–1973; Assistant Keeper 1955, Deputy Keeper 1955, Keeper of Mechanical and Civil Engineering 1962, Science Museum. **Appointments:** President, Newcomen Society. Died 11 June 1973.

GILBERT, Robert Greenway (1946) Born 9 January 1925, Hollybush Lane, Tittensor, Stoke-on-Trent; son of George Alfred Gilbert, Clerk in Holy Orders, and Muriel Kate Greenway. **Subject(s):** Law; BA 1948; MA 1953. **Tutor(s):** F Thistlethwaite. **Educ:** South Manchester Grammar School; Wells Cathedral School; Rugby School.

GILBERT, Dr Roger Key (1948) Born 27 June 1930, Hethermead, Westanley Road, Amersham, Buckinghamshire; son of Bernard William Gilbert, Second Secretary, HM Treasury, and Janet Maud Fison; m Carol Cynthia Coon, 31 March 1956, Watertown, Connecticut, USA. BA 1951; MA 1955; MB 1954; BChir 1954. **Tutor(s):** G C L Bertram. **Johnian Relatives:** son of Bernard William Gilbert (1910); nephew of Alexander Key Fison (1910). **Educ:** Springfield Grange Farm School, The Lee, Great Missenden; Beacon School, Chesham Bois; Merchant Taylors' School. **Career:** Member, Board of Governors, College of American Pathologists.

GILBERT, Thomas (1926) Born 28 November 1908, The Rectory, Marston Sicca, Warwickshire; son of Joseph Guest Gilbert, Clerk in Holy Orders, and Alice Louise Greene. **Tutor(s):** J M Wordie. **Educ:** Private Tuition, Bowers Gifford; Mostyn House, Parkgate; Harrow School.

GILBERT, William Hamish (1936) Born 28 December 1917, Belmont Terrace, Port Elizabeth, South Africa; son of William Gilbert, Surgeon, and Eleanor Elizabeth Scurlock. **Tutor(s):** R L Howland. **Educ:** Hazelbrae Preparatory School, Port Elizabeth; Cambersdown Preparatory School, Ayr; St Andrews Preparatory School, Grahamstown; St Andrews College, Grahamstown; Rhodes University College, South Africa.

GILCHRIST, John Stirling (STIRLING-GILCHRIST) (1918) Born 1 January 1899, Hamilton, Scotland; son of James Gilchrist, Varied business interests, and Margaret Stirling; m Odilia de Ortuzar, 27 March 1926, All Souls, Langham Place. **Subject(s):** Law; BA 1920; MA 1948; LLB 1920. **Tutor(s):** R P Gregory. **Educ:** The Grammar School, Hamilton; Glasgow University. **Career:** Member of the Inner Temple; Casualty Medical Officer and Clinical Assistant, Middlesex Hospital; Assistant Medical Officer, LCC Mental Hospital, Bexley; Senior Medical Officer Neurological and Psycho-therapeutic Clinic, Sunderland, and Clinic for Nervous Disorders, Derby.

GILCHRIST, Reginald Thomas (1927) Born 22 May 1909, 345 Derby Street, Bolton, Lancashire; son of Robert Munn Gilchrist, Medical Practitioner, and Selina Leach. **Subject(s):** Law; BA 1930; MA 1935. **Tutor(s):** M P Charlesworth. **Johnian Relatives:** brother of Robert Munn Gilchrist (1920) and of Ronald Renshaw Gilchrist (1922); father of James Michael Gilchrist (1957). **Educ:** Dreghorn Castle School, Colenton; Uppingham School. **Career:** Solicitor with Renshaw, Gilchrist & Co, Fleetwood. Died 19 March 1985.

GILCHRIST, Dr Robert Munn (1920) Born 15 October 1902, 345 Derby Street, Bolton; son of Robert Munn Gilchrist, Physician and Surgeon, and Selina Leach. BA 1923; MA 1928; MB 1928; BChir 1928; MRCS (St Bartholomew's) 1926; LRCP (St Bartholomew's) 1926. **Tutor(s):** B F Armitage. **Johnian Relatives:** brother of Ronald Renshaw Gilchrist (1922) and of Reginald Thomas Gilchrist (1927);

uncle of James Michael Gilchrist (1957). **Educ:** Sunninghill Council School, Bolton; Bolton Grammar School; Manchester Grammar School. **Career:** Honorary Colonel, Indian Medical Service; Clinical Assistant, Brompton Hospital for Diseases of the Chest; Honorary Physician, Bromley and District Hospital; Honorary Physician, St Bartholomew's Hospital. **Appointments:** Member, BMA. Died 1973.

GILCHRIST, Ronald Reid (1942) Born 1 September 1924, 7 Kirklee Road, Glasgow; son of Hector Gordon Gilchrist, Lieutenant Colonel, Engineer, and Erica Lestock Reid. BA 1945; MA 1949. **Tutor(s):** S J Bailey. **Educ:** Glasgow Academy; Harrow View House, Ealing; Loretto School. **Career:** Engine Research Department, Bristol Aeroplane Company; AEC Ltd, Southall; Works Director, Tubes Ltd 1958; Managing Director, Tube Products Ltd 1966; Chairman, Helliwells Ltd 1966; Chief Executive, Australian Institute of Management 1975–1988.

GILCHRIST, Ronald Renshaw (1922) Born 19 July 1904, 345 Derby Street, Bolton; son of Robert Munn Gilchrist, Physician and Surgeon, and Selina Leach. **Subject(s):** Law; BA 1926; MA 1930. **Tutor(s):** B F Armitage. **Johnian Relatives:** brother of Robert Munn Gilchrist (1920) and of Reginald Thomas Gilchrist (1927); uncle of James Michael Gilchrist (1957). **Educ:** Sunning Hill School; Bolton Grammar School; Mill Hill School. Died 30 June 1971.

GILES, Sidney Herbert (1942) Born 4 March 1924, 127 Knatchbull Road, Camberwell, London; son of Percy Albert Giles, Accountant, and Blanche Lizzie Carpenter; m Sheila Binns, 3 August 1954; 1 son (David Nicholas b 1962), 1 daughter (Caroline Elizabeth b 1958). **Subject(s):** Modern and Medieval Languages; BA 1948; MA 1980; MCIT. **Tutor(s):** C W Guillebaud. **Educ:** Dulwich Hamlet School; Alleyn's School, Dulwich. **Career:** Captain, Royal Signals 1943–1947; Management Trainee, British Rail, North East Region; Freight Depot Management, Dewsbury and Darlington 1948–1956; Transport Manager, Dorman Long (Steel) Ltd and British Steel 1956–1982; Director and Chief Executive, Teesside and District Chamber of Commerce and Industry 1984–1990.

GILL, Alan (1942) Born 1 September 1923, 2 Beechwood Crescent, Leeds; son of Edwin Lister Gill, Overseer, GPO Telegraphs, and Jane Parker; m Rose Heath, 1948; 3 sons. **Subject(s):** Mathematics; BA 1945; MA 1995. **Tutor(s):** S J Bailey. **Educ:** Brudenell Road Council School, Leeds; Leeds Modern School. **Career:** Experimental Officer, Royal Naval Scientific Service 1943–1946; HM Inspector of Taxes, retired with rank of Senior Principal Inspector of Taxes (Assistant Director, Inland Revenue) 1946–1983.

GILL, Cecil Gervase Hope (1914) Born 14 December 1894, Jabalpore, Central India; son of Charles Hope Gill, Bishop of Travancore, and Mary Madge Thopp; m Colina, 1937. BA 1921; MA 1944. **Tutor(s):** E E Sikes. **Educ:** Wychwood School, Bournemouth; Windlesham House, Brighton; King William's College, Isle of Man; Brighton College. **Career:** Captain, Royal Monmouthshire RE, Flanders, Egypt and Palestine 1914–1919; Probationer Vice Consul, Levant Consular Service, Morocco, Tangier, Casablanca, Saffi, and Tetuan 1920–1923; Diplomat, Middle East 1939–1945. Died 20 January 1984.

GILL, George Austin (1914) Born 17 January 1893, Bloemfontein, South Africa; son of Henry Frederick Gill, General Manager of Dairy, and Winifred Ethel Austin. **Subject(s):** Natural Sciences; BA 1916; MA 1920. **Tutor(s):** R P Gregory. **Educ:** Bedford Grammar School; Grey College School, Bloemfontein, South Africa; Grey University College, Bloemfontein, South Africa. **Career:** Lieutenant, RGA. **Honours:** MC 1917; MC with Bar 1918.

GILL, Colonel Gordon Harry (1900) Born 2 April 1882, 17 St Margaret Bank, Rochester, Kent; son of John Edwin Gill, Ship builder and Ship owner, and Ellen Stewart Hayman. **Educ:** Rochester Grammar School;

Paris and Anglo-Saxon, Auteuil. **Career:** Second Lieutenant, Royal Munster Fusiliers; served in South African War 1901–1902; Lieutenant, RASC 1906; Captain 1912; Deputy Assistant Quartermaster-General 1914–1919; Major 1916; Brevet-Colonel 1918; Chief Instructor, RASC Training College 1925–1929; Officer Commanding, RASC, Colchester; Lieutenant Colonel 1930; Colonel 1932; Assistant Quartermaster-General, Scottish Command 1932–1934; Assistant Director of Supplies and Transport, Eastern Command 1934–1938; Aide-de-Camp to the King 1936–1938; Retired 1938; Re-employed 1939 (Mentioned in Despatches 1940). **Honours:** DSO 1917; Order of Aviz, Portugal 1918; Chevalier Legion d'Honneur; CMG 1919.

GILL, Reginald George (1903) Born 8 October 1885, Wavertree, Loats Road, Clapham, Surrey; son of George Reginald Gill, Publisher, Director of Public Company, Mary Jane Oakes. BA 1908. **Tutor(s):** D MacAlister. **Educ:** City of London School. **Career:** Called to the Bar, Lincoln's Inn 1909.

GILL, Professor Stanley (1943) Born 26 March 1926, Teralta Nursing Home, Church Walk, Worthing; son of Walter Campbell Gill, Schoolmaster, and Rhoda Harriet Mitchell. **Subject(s):** Mathematics/Natural Sciences; BA 1947; MA 1950; PhD 1953. **Tutor(s):** C W Guillebaud. **Educ:** Broadwater Junior School, Worthing; Worthing High School. **Career:** National Physical Laboratory 1947–1950; Title A Fellow, SJC 1952–1955; Assistant in Research, University of Cambridge 1952–1955; Ferranti Ltd 1955–1964; Professor of Automated Data Processing, Manchester College of Science and Technology 1963–1964; Professor of Computing Science, Imperial College 1964–1970; Chairman, Software Sciences Holdings Ltd 1970. **Appointments:** Visiting Assistant Professor, University of Illinois 1953–1954; Council Member and President, BCS. Died 5 April 1975.

GILLESPIE, Charles Bainbridge (1921) Born 8 February 1905, Greystoke, Morpeth, Northumberland; son of James John Gillespie, Chartered Accountant, and Annie Bainbridge; m Molly Wilson, 6 June 1929, St John the Baptist, Alnmouth; 2 sons, 1 daughter. **Subject(s):** History; BA 1926; MA 1930. **Tutor(s):** E A Benians. **Johnian Relatives:** son of James John Gillespie (1889); father of Brian John Gillespie (1951). **Educ:** Aysgarth School, Newton-le-Willows, York; Uppingham School. **Career:** Chartered Accountant, Gillespie Brothers and Co, Newcastle, London and Morpeth. Died 14 May 1937.

GILLESPIE, John Kenneth (1945) (admitted to Selwyn College 1943) Born 28 June 1925, Egerton, Ashford, Kent; son of Douglas Gillespie, Civil Engineer, and Hilda Pullman, Housewife; 1 daughter. **Subject(s):** Mechanical Sciences; BA 1949; MA 1951. **Tutor(s):** S J Bailey. **Educ:** Rocklands School, Hastings; Cranbrook School. **Career:** Oil Company Executive; various Directorships, Chevron Corporation, Belgium and UK 1973–1984.

GILLESPIE, John Ronald (1942) Born 27 June 1924, Shanghai, Hong Kong; son of Ronald Dare Gillespie, Director, Imperial Chemical Industries, and Kathleen Little. **Tutor(s):** S J Bailey. **Educ:** West Downs, Winchester; Loretto School. **Career:** Pilot Officer, RAF. Died 7 October 1944 (killed in action).

GILLESPIE, Dr Robert Pollock (1925) Born 22 November 1903, 33 Thomson Avenue, Johnstone, Renfrewshire, Scotland; son of Thomas Gillespie, Master Butcher, and Jane Pollock; m Mary Isabel Bowman, 29 June 1937, Glasgow; 1 son (Alastair b 1945), 3 daughters (Lorna b 1940, Marjorie b 1943 and Janet b 1946). PhD 1932; BSc (Glasgow) 1924; MA (Glasgow) 1924; FRSE 1932. **Tutor(s):** J M Wordie. **Johnian Relatives:** father of Thomas Alastair Gillespie (1962). **Educ:** Paisley Grammar School; Glasgow University. **Career:** Assistant Lecturer, University of Glasgow 1928; Meteorological Branch, RAF, WWII; Senior Lecturer in Mathematics, University of Glasgow 1962–1969. **Appointments:** Member, University Court, University of Glasgow (by election) 1966–1969. Died 1 January 1977.

GILLETT, Anthony Walter (1932) Born 16 July 1912, 102 Banbury Road, St Giles, Oxford; son of Arthur Bevington Gillett, Banker, and Margaret Clark; m Jean. **Subject(s):** Mechanical Sciences; BA 1936; MA 1945. **Tutor(s):** J S Boys Smith. **Educ:** Lynham's School, Oxford; Leighton Park School, Reading. Died 3 December 1992.

GILLETT, Kenneth Arthur (1941) Born 21 September 1922, Bridge Road, Long Sutton, Holbeach, Lincolnshire; son of George Archer Gillett, Agricultural Worker, and Florence Nobbs. **Subject(s):** Modern and Medieval Languages; BA 1947; MA 1950. **Tutor(s):** C W Guillebaud. **Educ:** Long Sutton Council School; Spalding Grammar School.

GILLSON, Professor Albert Henry Steward (1908) Born 4 December 1889, 37 Grafton Street, Cambridge; son of Henry Dennis Gillson, Carpenter, and Eleanor Mary Pinner. **Subject(s):** Mathematics; BA 1911. **Tutor(s):** L H K Bushe-Fox. **Educ:** Brunswick County School, Cambridge; Cambridge and County School; Slade School of Art. **Career:** Instructor Lieutenant, RN, WWI; Royal Canadian Air Force; President, University of Manitoba; Dawson College, St John's, Quebec; Professor of Mathematics and Dean of Arts and Sciences, McGill University, Montreal 1920–1948. **Awards:** Tyson Gold Medal for Astronomy, University of Cambridge 1911; Isaac Newton Studentship for Research, University of Cambridge 1913. Died 10 September 1954.

GILMAN, Edgar Ivan (1942) Born 28 June 1923, 36 Bingham Road, Nottingham; son of George Edgar Gilman, Bank Manager, and Mildred Kate Griffiths. **Subject(s):** History; BA 1947; MA 1949. **Tutor(s):** C W Guillebaud. **Educ:** Mapperley Plains School, Nottingham; Nottingham High School. **Career:** Assistant Master, Pavement School, Nottingham. Died 23 January 1994.

GILMORE, Paul Carl (1949) Born 5 December 1925, Lethbridge, Alberta, Canada; son of John Alexander Gilmore, Baker, and Emma Alberdina Mueller; m Maryke G Worp, 12 June 1954; 1 son (Ian Alexander), 1 daughter (Karen Maryke). **Subject(s):** Maths; BA 1951; MA 1955; BA (British Columbia) 1949; Dr of Mathematics (Amsterdam) 1953. **Tutor(s):** J M Wordie. **Educ:** North Vancouver High School; University of British Columbia, Vancouver. **Career:** Military Service, RCAF 1943–1946; NSERC Post-Doctoral Fellow, Department of Mathematics, University of Toronto, Canada 1951–1953; Assistant Professor of Mathematics, Pennsylvania State University, State College, Pennsylvania, USA 1955–1958; Research Mathematician and Manager, Thomas J Watson Research Centre, IBM, Yorktown Heights, New York, USA 1958–1977; Professor and Head 1977–1984, Professor 1984–1990 (Emeritus 1990), Department of Computer Science, University of British Columbia, Vancouver. **Awards:** University of British Columbia Exchange Scholarship, SJC 1949; Lanchester Prize, Operational Research Society of America 1963, with Ralph Gomory; Testimonial on Parchment by the Royal Humane Society for rescuing a man from the Cam, 24 April 1951. **Publications:** *Logicism Renewed: Logical Foundations for Mathematics and Computer Science* (research monograph), 2003, Association for Symbolic Logic; a number of papers on mathematics and its applications in various journals.

GIRLING, Frank Aldous (1919) Born 10 July 1898, Noverons, Brightlingsea, Essex; son of Frank Disney Girling, Farmer, and Ellen Violet Aldous; m Susan. **Tutor(s):** E E Sikes. **Johnian Relatives:** brother of John Robert Girling (1918). **Educ:** Woodbridge School, Suffolk. **Career:** Farmer. Died 1 January 1966.

GIRLING, John Robert (1918) Born 11 February 1900, Brightlingsea, Essex; son of Frank Disney Girling, Farmer, and Ellen Violet Aldous. **Tutor(s):** E E Sikes. **Johnian Relatives:** brother of Frank Aldous Girling (1919). **Educ:** Woodbridge School.

GIRLING, Michael Stuart (1949) Born 14 June 1929, 81 Kenton Road, Wembley, Middlesex; son of Arthur Stuart Girling, Bank Clerk, and Mildred Georgina Edmondson; m Audrey Helen Bosker, 7 August 1954,

St Luke's Church, Chelsea; 1 son (Christopher b 20 December 1958), 2 daughters (Sarah Jane b 22 September 1955 and Kate Alison b 7 September 1960). **Subject(s):** Mathematics; BA 1952; MA 1956. **Tutor(s):** J M Wordie. **Educ:** The Abbey, East Grinstead; Harrow School. **Career:** Master, Wellington School 1953–1959; Master, Woolverstone Hall, Ipswich 1959–1964; Head of Mathematics, Tulse Hill School, London 1964–1968; HM Inspector of Schools 1968–1988. **Awards:** Minor Scholarship, SJC 1947.

GITTINS, Dr Peter Robert (1944) Born 27 November 1925, Mure Hospital, Nagpur, Central Provinces, India; son of Robert John Gittins, Medical Practitioner, and Eileen Mary Little, Medical Practitioner; 3 children. **Subject(s):** Natural Sciences; BA 1947; MA 1950; BChir 1950; MB 1950; DObstRCOG. **Tutor(s):** S J Bailey. **Educ:** Westhill School, Selly Oak; Stanley House School, Birmingham; The Downs School, Colwall; Leighton Park School, Reading. **Career:** Medical Practitioner; Founder and Medical Director, The Robert Nursing Home, Birmingham.

GLASGOW, Dr Eric Lawrence Harper (1942) Born 10 June 1924, 101 Harehills Avenue, Leeds; son of William Ewart Glasgow, HM Inspector of Taxes, and Sybil Maud Thompson Harper. **Subject(s):** History; BA 1945; MA 1949; PhD (Manchester) 1951. **Tutor(s):** C W Guillebaud. **Educ:** Priory School, Leeds; Bickerton House School, Birkdale; University Correspondence College, Cambridge. **Career:** Lundie Reader, St Deiniol's Library, Hawarden 1970–1986; Historian and Literacy Researcher; Tutor, North West Region, The Open University 1974–1978; Tutor in English Literature, University of London 1984–2002. **Publications:** Various, including many articles on local and regional history; two articles published by the Austrian Byron Society, and contributions to *Biblio, Modern Greek, The Haileyburian, Salzburg Studies in Literature, Victorians Institute Journal, Library Review, Contemporary Review, Library History, Reference Reviews, History* and *The Eagle*.

GLASSOW, Professor Francis Solomon (1935) Born 12 February 1917, 12 Oakland Road, West Jesmond, Newcastle Upon Tyne; son of Solomon Glassow, Book Traveller, and Hannah Clark Firman; m Winifred Rewcastle; 1 son (Nicholas b 1949), 2 daughters (Anna b 1944 and Karen b 1948). **Subject(s):** Natural Sciences; BA 1938; MA 1942; MB 1942; BChir 1942; MRCS 1942; LRCP 1942; FRCS 1952; FRCS (Canada) 1953; LMCC (Canada) 1953. **Tutor(s):** R L Howland. **Educ:** West Jesmond Council School; Newcastle Royal Grammar School. **Career:** Captain, RAMC, 15th Scottish Infantry Division 1942–1946 (Normandy Landings June 1944); Senior Surgical Registrar, Newcastle Royal Victoria Infirmary and Newcastle General Hospital 1946–1952; Surgeon, Shouldice Hospital, Toronto 1953–1986. **Appointments:** Speciality Hernia Surgeon; Hunterian Professor, Royal College of Surgeons of England 1983; Honorary Life Member, Ontario Medical Association; Honorary member, Minneapolis Surgical Society 1985. **Awards:** Kitchener Scholarship, 1935–1938; Sizarship, SJC 1935–1938. **Publications:** Twenty-five surgical publications in various surgical journals in Canada, USA, Britain and Mexico, on topics related to Hernia Surgery.

GLEADOW, Edward Purdy (1928) Born 18 March 1911, Ferriby, Yorkshire; son of Robert Ward Gleadow, Brewer, and Marian Huffam; m Mary Gates, 1955; 1 son (Edward Peter). **Subject(s):** History; BA 1933; MA 1937. **Tutor(s):** E A Benians. **Johnian Relatives:** uncle of Jonathan Gleadow Clarke (1957). **Educ:** Meadowcroft School, Windermere; Orleton School, Scarborough; Trinity College, Glenalmond. **Career:** Schoolmaster 1933–1939; Green Howards 1939–1948; RAEC 1948–1966; Retired Officer 1966–1977; Education Adviser, Regular Commissions Board 1960–1977. **Honours:** MBE 1947.

GLEAVE, George Eric (1916) Born 21 September 189626 Brynn Street, St Helens, Lancashire; son of John Gleave, Surveyor, and Margaret Jane Robinson. **Tutor(s):** E E Sikes. **Johnian Relatives:** brother of John

Wallace Gleave (1909) and of Thomas Reginald Gleave (1913). **Educ:** Southport College; Prescot Grammar School; Bishop Wilson's College. **Career:** Second Lieutenant, Royal Lancashire Regiment. **Honours:** MC for conspicuous gallantry 1918.

GLEAVE, The Revd Canon John Wallace (1909) Born 21 October 1890, Haresfinch, Windle St Helens, Lancashire; son of John Gleave, Builder and Land Agent, and Margaret Jane Robinson. **Subject(s):** Theology; BA 1912; MA 1922. **Tutor(s):** J R Tanner. **Johnian Relatives:** brother of Thomas Reginald Gleave (1913) and of George Eric Gleave (1916). **Educ:** Merchant Taylors' School, Crosby. **Career:** Deacon 1913; Diocesan Chaplain and Vice-Principal, Bishop Wilson Theological College, Isle of Man 1913–1915; Priest 1914; Domestic Chaplain to the Bishop 1915–1916; Principal, Bishop Wilson Theological College, Isle of Man 1915–1917; Temporary CF 1916–1920; Curate, St Mark, Sheffield 1921–1924; Succentor, Coventry Cathedral 1924–1927; Vicar, St Paul, Walsall 1927–1931; Vicar, St Mark, Sheffield 1931; Honorary Canon, Sheffield Cathedral 1939. **Awards:** Wright's Prize, SJC 1910; Carus University Prize; Naden Studentship 1912.

GLEAVE, Thomas Reginald (1913) Born 17 July 1894, 26 Brynn Street, St Helens, Lancashire; son of John Gleave, Estate Agent, and Margaret Jane Robinson. **Tutor(s):** R P Gregory. **Johnian Relatives:** brother of John Wallace Gleave (1909) and of George Eric Gleave (1916). **Educ:** Southport College; Prescot Grammar School. **Career:** Second Lieutenant, later Captain (1916) 5th (Territorial) Battalion, Prince of Wales' Volunteers, South Lancashire Regiment, WWI. Died 10 October 1916 (killed in action).

GLEDSTONE, The Revd Frederick Farrar (1904) Born 30 June 1885, Consett, County Durham; son of Thomas Liddle Gledstone, Bank Manager, and Annie Elizabeth Farrar. **Subject(s):** Classics/Theology; BA 1907; MA 1911. **Tutor(s):** E E Sikes. **Educ:** Durham School. **Career:** Ordained Deacon 1910; Curate, Rotherhithe 1910–1919; Ordained Priest 1911; Chaplain and Vice-Principal, St Paul's Missionary College, Burgh 1920–1924; SPG Missionary, Dornakal 1924–1947; Registrar 1938–1947, Honorary Canon 1940–1947, Diocese of Dornakal; Archdeacon, Deccan 1947; Curate, Tynemouth 1949–1955. **Awards:** Scholarship, SJC 1904; Carus Greek Testament Prize, University of Cambridge 1909. Died 7 December 1963.

GLEN, John Douglas (1941) Born 30 April 1924, 23 Carmichael Place, Glasgow; son of Archibald Glen, Managing Director, and Margaret Stevenson Cameron Hardie. **Subject(s):** Economics. **Tutor(s):** C W Guillebaud. **Educ:** Moray Place School, Glasgow; Glasgow Academy; Warriston School, Moffat; Craigend Park School, Edinburgh; Strathallan School, Perthshire.

GLEN, Robert Muir (1926) Born 17 March 1909, 16 Park Circus, Glasgow, Scotland; son of Robert Muir Glen, Master Calico Printer, and Marguerite Milne Crichton; m Sylvia Clarissa Forman, 16 September 1950, St Peter's, Vere Street, London. **Subject(s):** Natural Sciences; BA 1930. **Tutor(s):** J M Wordie. **Educ:** Kelvinside Academy, Glasgow; Warriston, Moffat; Loretto School, Musselburgh.

GLEN, William Burns Cowan (1920) Born 5 June 1901, 17 Mansion House Road, Langside, Cathcart, Renfrewshire; son of Richard Bartlett Glen, Merchant and Shipowner, and Louisa McArthur Cowan; m Esme. **Tutor(s):** E E Sikes. **Educ:** Glasgow Academy; Fettes College, Edinburgh. Died 22 February 1958.

GLIDDEN, Herbert Harrison (1918) American Student.

GLOVER, Colin Merriam (1929) Born 26 March 1912, 25 Highbury Place, Islington, London; son of James Alison Glover, Medical Officer, Ministry of Health, and Katharine Merriam. BA 1933; MA 1936. **Tutor(s):** J M Wordie. **Johnian Relatives:** son of James Alison Glover (1894); cousin of Terrot Reaveley Glover (1888); brother of Eric Charles

Glover (1935) and of Michael Alison Glover (1940); father of Christopher Whelpdale Merriam Glover (1959). **Educ:** Heathmount, Hampstead; Tyttenhanger Lodge, Seaford; Oundle School. **Career:** British Xylonite Company Ltd 1933; Works Manager, BA Plastics Ltd 1948–1961 (Works Director 1950, Managing Director 1957); Managing Director, British Xylonite Company Ltd 1961; Managing Director, Bakelite Xylonite Ltd 1963; Executive Director, Lloyd's Register of Shipping.

GLOVER, Eric Charles (1935) Born 5 October 1917, 23 Rosslyn Hill, Hampstead, London; son of James Alison Glover, Physician, Captain, RAMC, and Katharine Merriam; m Jean Mary Lochore, 10 August 1943 (d 1994); 2 sons, 1 daughter. **Subject(s):** Natural Sciences; BA 1938; MA 1942; MB; BChir 1946; FRCS 1950; Diploma of Ophthalmic Medicine and Surgery. **Tutor(s):** R L Howland. **Johnian Relatives:** cousin of Terrot Reaveley Glover (1888); son of James Alison Glover (1894); brother of Colin Merriam Glover (1929) and of Michael Alison Glover (1940); uncle of Christopher Whelpdale Merriam Glover (1959). **Educ:** Tyttenhanger Lodge, Seaford; Oundle School. **Career:** Surgeon Captain, RNR; Consultant Ophthalmic Surgeon, King Edward VII Hospital, Windsor; House Surgeon, Mount Vernon Hospital 1941; Surgeon Lieutenant, RNVR 1942–1946; House Surgeon, Middlesex Hospital 1946; Served, RNR 1946–1968; House Surgeon and RSO Moorfields Eye Hospital 1947–1949; Chief Clinical Assistant, Moorfields 1949–1976; Consultant Ophthalmic Surgeon, King Edward VII Hospital, Windsor 1951–1982; Surgeon Captain PMO, London Division 1962–1965; Honorary Surgeon to HM The Queen 1968; Honorary Adviser in Ophthalmology, RNLI 1974–1987. **Appointments:** Committee Member, CUMS; SJC Medical Society; President, Windsor Medical Society 1967–1968. **Honours:** VRD. Died 26 February 1998.

GLOVER, Michael Alison (1940) Born 20 May 1922, Hampstead; son of James Alison Glover, Medical Officer, and Katharine Merriam; m Daphne Bowring, 1 September 1945, Holy Trinity, Brompton; 1 daughter (Stephanie). **Subject(s):** History; BA 1947; MA 1949. **Tutor(s):** C W Guillebaud. **Johnian Relatives:** cousin of Terrot Reaveley Glover (1888); son of James Alison Glover (1894); brother of Colin Merriam Glover (1929) and of Eric Charles Glover (1935); uncle of Christopher Whelpdale Merriam Glover (1959). **Educ:** Tyttenhanger Lodge School, Seaford; The Hall School, Hampstead; Oundle School. **Career:** Captain, The Sherwood Foresters, POW Germany, WWII; Military Historian. **Publications:** *Wellington's Peninsular Victories*, 1963; *Britannia Sickens*, 1971; *That Astonishing Infantry, The Peninsular War 1807–1814*, 1974; *Wellington's Army in the Peninsula*, 1977; *The Napoleonic Wars: An Illustrated History*, 1979; and many others. Died 25 September 1990.

GLOVER, Roderick Lewis (1924) Born 17 June 1907, 17 Belsize Park, Hampstead, London; son of Lewis Gladstone Glover, Medical Practitioner, and Mary Mildred Glover; m Joan Weight, 16 September 1947. BA 1928. **Tutor(s):** E E Sikes. **Johnian Relatives:** son of Lewis Gladstone Glover (1886). **Educ:** St John's House, Shepherd's Walk, London; Tyttenhanger School, Seaford; Rugby School.

GLYN, Charles Reginald (1913) Born 4 March 1895, Broom Hills, Dartford Heath, Dartford, Kent; son of Lewis Edward Glyn, Member of His Majesty's Council, and Mary Eliza Dugdale. **Tutor(s):** L H K Bushe-Fox. **Johnian Relatives:** brother of John Westray Wilson Glyn (1915). **Educ:** Streete Court Preparatory School, Westgate-on-Sea; Haileybury College. **Career:** Royal Military Hospital 1914; Second Lieutenant, Hodson's Horse (110th Mahrattas), Indian Army 1914–1917. Died 9 January 1917 (killed in action in Mesopotamia).

GLYN, John Westray Wilson (1915) Born 6 September 1897, Dartford, Kent; son of Lewis Edmund Glyn, King's Counsel, and Mary Eliza Dugdale; m Mary Faith Butts, 4 June 1924, Stilton Parish Church. **Tutor(s):** L H K Bushe-Fox. **Johnian Relatives:** brother of Charles Reginald Glyn (1913). **Educ:** Shrewsbury School.

GNAU, Howarth Widman (1923) Born 10 August 1900, 309 Hancock East, Detroit, Michigan, USA; son of George Joseph Gnau, Insurance Underwriter, and Adele Rosalie Widman. **Tutor(s):** E A Benians. **Educ:** Harvard University Graduate Course; Detroit University School, University of Michigan.

GOBBITT, The Revd Reginald Henry Sutton (1914) (Readmitted 1919) Born 6 September 1891, Beccles, Suffolk; son of Henry Sutton Gobbitt, Master Grocer and Draper, and Clementia Elizabeth Goff. **Subject(s):** History; BA 1920; MA 1925. **Tutor(s):** E A Benians; L H K Bushe-Fox. **Educ:** Ipswich Middle School; Ipswich School. **Career:** Associate, Institute of Chartered Accountants 1913; Paymaster Lieutenant, RNR 1914–1918; Deacon then Priest, Southwark; Curate, St Luke, Eltham 1921–1925; Organising Director, Industrial Christian Fellowship, South-west Area, and Public Preacher, Diocese of Bristol 1925–1930; Vicar, St Martin, Knowle 1930–1943; Rector, Wallingford, Berkshire 1943–1951. **Honours:** MBE 1918. Died 16 March 1951.

GODDARD, Professor Laurence Stanley (1939) Born 25 April 1917, Paddington, Sydney, New South Wales; son of Horace Cleveland Goddard, Boat Builder, and Clara Kitt; m Joan Ward, 1955; 3 sons, 1 daughter. PhD 1947; BSc (Sydney) 1939. **Tutor(s):** J M Wordie. **Educ:** Fort Street Boys' High School, Sydney; Sydney University. **Career:** Telecommunications Research Establishment, Swanage, Dorset 1941–1942; Research Mathematician, EMI Laboratories, Hayes, Middlesex 1942–1945; Lecturer, then Senior Lecturer in Mathematics, University of St Andrews 1947–1949; Senior Lecturer in Mathematics, University of Aberdeen 1949–1956; Operational Research Officer, ICI Ltd, Millbank then Metals Division, Birmingham 1956–1959; Professor of Mathematics, University of Tasmania 1959–1967; Professor of Mathematics, University of Salford 1967–1982. Died March 1996.

GODJEVATZ, Dragutin (1917) Born 2 January 1896, Belgrade, Serbia; son of Vladimir Godjevatz, Hardware Merchant, and Vukosawa Mihanovitch. **Tutor(s):** E E Sikes. **Educ:** Primary School, Belgrade; Secondary School, Belgrade; University of Grenoble.

GODWIN, William Henry (1942) Born 29 November 1923, 50 Elsham Road, Kensington, London; son of George Stanley Godwin, Barrister-at-Law, and Dorothy Alicia Purdon. **Subject(s):** English; BA 1945; MA 1948. **Tutor(s):** C W Guillebaud. **Educ:** St Paul's Preparatory School; Lycée Français de Londres. **Awards:** Minor Scholarship, SJC 1941.

GOFFE, Reginald (1928) Born 13 December 1908, 69a King's Road, Chelsea, Middlesex; son of Ernest Edward Goffe, Warehouseman, and Gertrude Ruth Ward. **Subject(s):** History; BA 1931. **Tutor(s):** E A Benians. **Educ:** Sloane School, Chelsea; St Luke's School, Chelsea. **Awards:** Sizarship 1928.

GOLD, Ernest (1900) Born 24 July 1881, Berkswell, Warwickshire; son of John Gold, Farmer, and Ellen Peckett; m Catherine Lockerbie Harlow, 4 July 1907, Edinburgh (d 1973); 1 daughter (Mary). **Subjects:** Mathematics/Natural Sciences; BA 1903; MA 1907; FRS 1918. **Tutor(s):** D MacAlister. **Educ:** Mason University College, Birmingham; Coleshill Grammar School. **Career:** Mathematics Lecturer, City of London Technical College 1904; Fellow, SJC 1906–1912; Schuster Reader in Dynamical Meteorology, University of Cambridge 1907–1910; Superintendent of Statistics, Meteorological Office 1910; Captain 1915, Lieutenant Colonel 1918, RE (Meteorological Section) WWI; Deputy Director, Meteorological Office, Air Ministry 1940. **Appointments:** President, International Commission for Synoptic Weather Information 1919–1947; President, Meteorological Sub-Commission of International Commission for Aerial Navigation 1922–1939; President, Royal Meteorological Society 1934–1936. **Awards:** International Meteorological Organisation Prize 1958; Symons Gold Medal, Royal Meteorological Society 1926; American Medal of Freedom with Silver Palms 1946. **Honours:** DSO 1916; OBE; CB 1942. **Publications:** Physical and Meteorological Papers and Reports in the *Proceedings of the Royal Society, Reports of British Association*, etc. Died 30 January 1976.

GOLDEN, Lieutenant Colonel Harold Arthur (1919) Born 14 January 1896, College Avenue, Heigham, Norwich; son of Arthur Robert Golden, Assistant Headmaster, City of Norwich School, and Margaret Mary Pybus; m Freda Mary Lightfoot, 3 May 1929, St Cuthbert's Church, Carlisle; 1 daughter (Susannah). **Subject(s):** Mechanical Sciences; BA 1921. **Tutor(s):** E A Benians. **Educ:** City of Norwich School. **Career:** RE, served in India, Egypt and Palestine; seconded to Egyptian Army; rose to Captain; Instructor, RMA, Woolwich 1914–1935; Chief Constable of Shropshire 1935–1946; Chief Constable of Wiltshire 1946–1963. **Honours:** OBE; CBE 1960. Died 18 April 1976.

GOLDIE, Professor Alfred William (1939) Born 10 December 1920, 106 Broad Street, Coseley, Staffordshire; son of Albert Goldie, Fitter (machine tools), and Olive Alice Caddick; m Mary Kenyon, 1944; 1 son (John), 2 daughters (Isobel and Helen). **Subject(s):** Mathematics; BA 1942; MA 1946. **Educ:** Christ Church School, Coseley; Wolverhampton Grammar School. **Career:** Mathematics Lecturer, Nottingham University 1946; Research Associate, Yale 1948–1960; Algebra Reader, Newcastle University 1960–1961; Professor of Mathematics, Leeds University 1961–1987 (Emeritus 1987). **Appointments:** Visiting Professor, University of Paris 1968–1969.

GOLDIE, Dr Archibald Hayman Robertson (1910) Born 7 July 1888, Bathvill College, Armadale, Bathgate, Linlithgowshire, Scotland; son of Andrew Goldie, Minister, United Free Church of Scotland, and Isabella Gillies Robertson; m (1) Marion Nairne Wilson (d 3 February 1948), (2) Nellie Carruthers, 5 April 1952. **Subject(s):** Mathematics; BA 1913; MA (St Andrews); DSc (St Andrews) 1936. **Tutor(s):** L H K Bushe-Fox. **Educ:** Glenisla Public School; Gantsherrie Church School, Coatbridge; Harris Academy, Dundee; St Andrews University. **Career:** Falmouth Observatory, Meteorological Office 1913; Senior Professional Assistant, Observatory, Eskdalemuir, Scotland 1915; Major, Meteorological Section, RE (Mentioned in Despatches) WWI; Superintendent, Aviation Services Division, Meteorological Office; Head, Meteorological Office, Edinburgh 1924; Deputy Director, Meteorological Office, Air Ministry 1938–1953. **Appointments:** Vice-President, Royal Society of Edinburgh; Secretary, International Association for Geodesy and Geophysics. **Awards:** Dux Medal. **Honours:** CBE 1951. **Publications:** Revised the *Abercromby Book on Weather*. Died 24 January 1964.

GOLDIE-SCOT, Captain William Norton Longman (1939) Born 10 February 1920, Planetree, Gatehouse-of-Fleet, Kirkcudbrightshire; son of Thomas Goldie Goldie-Scot, Physician, and Alice Phillips. **Educ:** St Ninian's Preparatory School, Moffat; Fettes College, Edinburgh. **Career:** Captain, Artillery Officer, Italy and India 1939–1945; Administrative Officer to the Gold Coast, Colonial Service 1947.

GOLDSMITH, Colin Cecil (1949) Born 25 July 1931, Esher, Surrey; son of Ernest Cecil Goldschmidt, Metal Merchant, and Sybil Hescott; m Patricia Mary Christine Kerley, 23 April 1955; 1 son, 4 daughters. **Subject(s):** Mathematics; BA 1952; MA 1956; FIMA; CMath. **Tutor(s):** J M Wordie; J R Bambrough. **Johnian Relatives:** father of Paul William Goldsmith (1974). **Educ:** St Christopher's, Hove; Saltus Grammar School, Bermuda; Charterhouse. **Career:** Instructor Officer, RN 1952–1955; Mathematics Teacher, Marlborough College, Wiltshire 1955–1991; British Council Mathematics Consultant to Czech and Slovak Bi-lingual Schools 1993–1998. **Appointments:** Member 1961, Trustee 1980, Deputy Chairman 1991, School Mathematics Project. **Awards:** Baylis Scholarship, SJC 1948. **Publications:** Co-author and/or editor of many school textbooks.

GOLDSTEIN, Dr David John (1948) Born 9 March 1928, Brunswick Nursing Home, 9 Brunswick Walk, Cambridge; son of Sydney Goldstein, Professor of Applied Mathematics, University of Cambridge, and Rosa Rachel Sass. **Subject(s):** Natural Sciences; BA 1951; MA 1955. **Tutor(s):** G C L Bertram. **Johnian Relatives:** son of Sydney Goldstein (1922). **Educ:** King's College School, Cambridge; Dartington Hall, Totnes; Manumit School, Pawling, New York, USA; The Cambridge School; Leighton Park School. **Career:** Part-time Lecturer, Chemical Engineering, MIT.

GOLDSTEIN, Professor Sydney (1922) Born 3 December 1903, 57 Morpeth Street, West Sculcoates, Hull, Yorkshire; son of Abraham Joseph Goldstein, Furniture Dealer, and Hilda Jacobs; m Rosa R Sass, 1926, Johannesburg; 1 son, 1 daughter. **Subject(s):** Mathematics; BA 1925; MA 1929; PhD 1928; Honorary DEng (Purdue) 1967; Honorary DSc (Case Institute of Technology) 1967; Honorary DSc (The Technion, Israel) 1969; Honorary DSc (Leeds) 1973; FRS 1937. **Tutor(s):** E Cunningham. **Johnian Relatives:** father of David John Goldstein (1948). **Educ:** Eton House School, Hull; Argyle House School, Sunderland; Bede Collegiate School, Sunderland; University of Leeds. **Career:** Rockefeller Fellow, University of Göttingen 1928–1929; Lecturer in Applied Mathematics, Manchester University 1929–1931; Title A Fellow 1929–1932, Deputy Lecturer in Mathematics 1931–1932, Assistant Lecturer in Mathematics 1932–1933, Title B Fellow and Lecturer in Mathematics 1933–1945 (leave of absence on war service 1939–1944), SJC; Lecturer in Mathematics 1931–1939, Stokes Lecturer in Mathematics 1939–1945, University of Cambridge; Leverhulme Research Fellow, California Institute of Technology 1938–1939; Aerodynamics Division, National Physics Laboratory 1939–1945; Beyer Professor of Applied Mathematics, Manchester University 1945–1950; Professor of Applied Mathematics, Technion Israel Institute of Technology, Haifa 1950–1955; Gordon McKay Professor of Applied Mathematics 1955–1970 (Emeritus 1970), Harvard. **Appointments:** Council Member, Royal Society 1945–1947; Chairman, Aeronautical Research Council 1946–1949; Visiting Professor, Brown University 1947; Wright Brothers Lecturer, Institute of Aeronautical Sciences 1947; Visiting Professor, University of Michigan 1947–1950; Visiting Professor, University of Maryland 1950; Vice President, Technion Israel Institute of Technology, Haifa 1951–1955; Visiting Lecturer of Applied Science, Harvard University 1952; Visiting Professor, University of Virginia 1952; Gordon McKay Visiting Lecturer in Applied Science, Harvard University 1954; Honorary Fellow, SJC 1965; Honorary Fellow, Royal Aeronautical Society 1971; Honorary Fellow, Weizmann Institute of Science 1971; Honorary FIMA 1972; Honorary Member, ASME 1981; Foreign Member, Finnish Scientific Society; Foreign Member, Royal Netherlands Academy of Sciences and Letters. **Awards:** Scholarship, SJC; Hughes Prize, SJC 1925; Baylis Studentship, SJC 1925; Mayhew Prize, University of Cambridge 1925; Adams Memorial Prize, University of Cambridge 1925; Smith's Prize, University of Cambridge 1927; Isaac Newton Studentship, University of Cambridge 1927; Timoshenko Medal, American Society of Mechanical Engineers. **Publications:** Editor, *Modern Developments in Fluid Dynamics*, 1938; *Lectures on Fluid Mechanics*, 1960. Died 22 January 1989.

GOLDWATER, Dr Harry Gerald (1914) Born 19 September 1892, Dublin, Ireland; son of William Goldwater, Hotel Proprietor, and Dora Harmel. **Subject(s):** Medicine; MB BChir 1937; BA (Rhodes) 1913; MRCS 1923; LRCP 1923. **Tutor(s):** R P Gregory. **Educ:** Uitenhage High School; Rhodes University College, Grahamstown. **Career:** Second Lieutenant, RGA, WWI; Middlesex Hospital.

GONEHALLI, Venkanna Hosnabaik (1906) Born 23 October 1881, Hanehalli, Kanara, India; son of Hosnabaik Honnappanaik Gonehalli, Landholder. **Subject(s):** Natural Sciences; BA 1908; MA 1912. **Tutor(s):** J R Tanner. **Educ:** Elphinstone College, Bombay. **Career:** Divisional Inspector of Agriculture, Bombay Government 1910.

GONZALEZ, Alphonso (1929) Born 10 April 1911, 14 Calle de Lima, Chorillos, Lima, Peru; son of Vicente Gonzalez Obregoso, Landowner, and Rosa Pardo. **Tutor(s):** C W Guillebaud. **Educ:** St John's Beaumont Preparatory School, Windsor; Beaumont College, Windsor.

GOODALL, Dr John Francis (1928) Born 10 February 1911, 47 Savile Park Road, Halifax; son of Herbert Goodall, Worsted Coating Manufacturer, and Agnes Elizabeth Rees; m Joyce Rhodes, 1938 (d 1962); 2 sons (Robert and Jeremy), 2 daughters (Frances and Alison). BA 1932; MB 1937; BChir 1937; MD 1940. **Tutor(s):** C W Guillebaud. **Educ:** Halifax Grammar School; Ashville College, Harrogate. **Career:** GP, Skipton 1938–1942 and 1945–1983 (Practice Manager, in retirement); Major, Army Medical Corps (served in The King's Own Regiment, India) 1942–1945. **Appointments:** Senior Partner, Fisher Medical Centre, Skipton, North Yorkshire 1972–1983. Died 5 February 2003.

GOODALL, Peter Bentley (1942) Born 9 October 1923, Ashingtons, Lady's Close, Watford; son of Ralph Alexander Goodall, Produce Merchant, and Mary Bentley Clements; m Tessa Humphreys, 10 March 1962. **Tutor(s):** S J Bailey. **Educ:** Streete Court, Westgate; Westbury Manor, Brackley; Radley College.

GOODCHILD, Arthur James Poulton (1945) Born 6 March 1925, Queen Mary Nursing Home, Derby; son of Arthur James Poulton Goodchild, First Officer, Merchant Service, and Violet Elizabeth Gibson. BSc (London) 1945. **Educ:** Rydal School, Weymouth; Weymouth Grammar School; Derby School; Derby Technical College; University College, Nottingham. **Career:** Colonial Agricultural Service.

GOODE, James Edward (1949) Born 27 April 1929, Okonite Villas, Pennygate, Spalding, Lincolnshire; son of James Goode, Schoolmaster, and Gladys Nora Rebecca Skinner; m Alice. **Subject(s):** English/Law; BA 1952; MA 1956. **Tutor(s):** A G Lee. **Johnian Relatives:** brother of John Goode (1942). **Educ:** Spalding Grammar School. **Career:** Solicitor; Partner in Andrews, Stanton and Ringrose, Lincolnshire 1960. Died 19 April 1996.

GOODE, John (1942) Born 10 January 1925, Okonite Villas, Pennygate, Spalding; son of James Goode, Schoolmaster, and Gladys Nora Rebecca Skinner. **Subject(s):** Modern and Medieval Languages; BA 1945; MA 1949. **Tutor(s):** C W Guillebaud. **Johnian Relatives:** brother of James Edward Goode (1949). **Educ:** Spalding Grammar School; Worksop College. **Career:** Master, Rossall School 1960.

GOODE, John Basil (1925) Born 28 April 1906, 6 Stanmore Road, Edgbaston, Birmingham, Warwickshire; son of John Howard Goode, Bank Manager, and Grace Isabel Warner. **Subject(s):** Natural Sciences (Physics); BA 1928. **Tutor(s):** J M Wordie. **Educ:** Chigwell House School, Edgbaston; King Edward's School, Birmingham. **Career:** Senior Principal Scientific Officer, Royal Armament Research and Development Establishment, Ministry of Defence. **Honours:** OBE 1967.

GOODE, The Revd Reginald Henry (1908) Born 14 December 1888, 3 Tenison Road, St Andrew the Less, Cambridge; son of George Goode, Assistant Librarian, University Library, and Emily Grace Warland; m Mary Calley Drysdale, 1916. **Subject(s):** Natural Sciences; BA 1911; MA 1919. **Tutor(s):** L H K Bushe-Fox. **Educ:** Preparatory School and De Freville Grammar School, Cambridge; Warkworth House School, Cambridge. **Career:** Lieutenant, MGC, then Ministry of Labour 1914–1918; Ordained Deacon 1919; Curate, Wombell 1919–1922; Priest 1920; Priest in Charge, Waterhole Mission, Athabasca 1922–1925; Rector, Morton, Essex (with Little Laver 1933) 1925; Chaplain, LCC Residential School, Ongar 1933; Rector, Houghton Conquest with Houghton Gildaple, Bedfordshire 1946–1951; Rector, Marston Mortayne, Bedfordshire 1951–1955; Vicar, Great with Little Hormead, and Rector, Wyddial 1955. **Publications:** *Fossil Flora of the Pembrokeshire Coalfield*, 1913. Died 27 April 1969.

GOODE, Robert Charles Jeffrey (1928) Born 12 December 1909, 5 Carisbrook Road, Hastings, Sussex; son of Richard Almond Jeffrey Goode, Civil Servant, and Agnes Codrington. **Subject(s):** Natural Sciences; BA 1931. **Tutor(s):** J M Wordie. **Educ:** Livingstone, Rhodesia; The Grammar School, Caistor; Oakham School; McGill University, Canada. **Career:** Geduld Proprietary Mines Ltd, Dersley, Transvaal. **Awards:** Johnson Exhibition, SJC 1928.

GOODERSON, Richard Norman (1934) Born 3 March 1915, 22 Booth Street, Handsworth, Birmingham; son of Arthur Herbert Gooderson, Bank Manager, and Clarice Mary Judge; m Marjorie Nash, 1939; 2 sons, 1 daughter. **Subject(s):** Law; BA 1937; LLD (St Catharine's) 1977. **Tutor(s):** C W Guillebaud. **Educ:** Northampton Town and County School; St Catharine's College, Cambridge. **Career:** Assistant Commissioner in the Punjab 1938–1945; Called to the Bar, Inner Temple 1946–1948; Fellow of Law 1948–1982, St Catharine's College, Cambridge. **Appointments:** Tutor and President 1948–1982, Senior Tutor 1965–1967, St Catharine's College, Cambridge. **Awards:** George Long Prize for Roman Law, University of Cambridge 1936; Scholarship, SJC 1936–1937; Hughes Prize, SJC 1937; George Long Prize for Jurisprudence, University of Cambridge 1937; Bhaonagar Medal, University of Cambridge 1938. **Publications:** *Alibi*, 1977. Died 25 January 1982.

GOODHAND, Ian Frank (1948) Born 22 June 1928, Karachi, India; son of Frank William Goodhand, Bank Manager, Eastern Bank, Colombo, and Kathleen Smith; m Estella, 1951; 1 son (Christopher b 1952), 1 daughter (Christine b 1954). **Subject(s):** Geography; BA 1950; MA 1955. **Tutor(s):** J M Wordie; B H Farmer. **Educ:** Truro School. **Career:** RAF 1946–1948; Management Trainee, Works/Production Manager, Training Course Director, J Lyon & Co Ltd 1951–1964; Company Director, Building Supplies and Services, Guest Keen & Nettlefolds Ltd and Sub-Group Director, GKN Engineering & Contracting Ltd 1964–1976; Turriff Corporation, Main Board Director 1976–1980; Self-Employed Consultancy 1980–1983; Willis Faber & Dumas Ltd Human Resources, Contracts, and Internal Projects 1983–1993.

GOODLET, Dr Brian Laidlaw (1930) Born 13 March 1903, Petrograd, Russia; son of Charles William Goodlet, ex-Civil Servant, Russian Imperial Government, and Agnes Mary Laidlaw; m Norah McCormick, 1932; 2 sons, 2 daughters. **Subject(s):** Mechanical Sciences; BA 1932; MA 1937; ScD 1958. **Tutor(s):** J M Wordie. **Educ:** The Imperial School, Petrograd, Russia; University of Sheffield. **Career:** Professor of Electrical Engineering, Cape Town; Fitter's Apprentice, Vickers Ltd, Sheffield 1919–1922; Special Trainee, Metropolitan Vickers Ltd, Manchester 1922–1924; Associateship of Engineering, University of Sheffield 1923; Technical Assistant, Research Department 1923–1927, Section Leader, Vickers Ltd 1927–1930; Chief Engineer and Director, Brush Electrical Engineering Company Ltd 1937–1950; Commander, South African Naval Force on African and East Indies Stations 1941–1946; Head of Engineering Research and Development Department, Harwell 1950–1956. **Appointments:** FRSSAf 1945; Chairman, Admiralty's Naval Educational Advisory Committee 1952. **Awards:** Thomas Hawkesby Gold Medal, Institute of Mechanical Engineers. **Honours:** OBE 1944. Died 27 October 1961.

GOODMAN, William Wolf (1923) Born 26 June 1900, Poplar Street, Memphis, Tennessee, USA; son of Abe Goodman, Banker, and Bobye Wolf. **Tutor(s):** E A Benians. **Educ:** Memphis Public School; Memphis University School; Culver Military Academy, Indiana; University of Pennsylvania; Law School, Harvard University.

GOODRAM, Alan James Sloman (1942) Born 8 November 1923, 62 Vale Road, Ramsgate; son of William Valentine Goodram, Schoolmaster, and Nancy Maud Sloman. **Tutor(s):** C W Guillebaud. **Educ:** Chatham House School, Ramsgate.

GOODRICH, The Revd Harold Spencer (1912) Born 9 October 1892, 152 Vincent Road, Ecclesall Bierlow, Sheffield, Yorkshire; son of Ernest Lincoln Goodrich, Commercial Clerk, and Alice Spencer; m Gertrude Alice Hornby; 1 son (Philip), 2 daughters (Margaret and Joan). **Subject(s):** History; BA 1915; MA 1919. **Tutor(s):** E E Sikes. **Johnian Relatives:** father-in-law of Henry Arthur Wickstead (1932); father of Philip Harold Ernest Goodrich (1949); grandfather of Arthur Timothy John Wickstead (1973). **Educ:** Ecclesall National School; Central Secondary School, Sheffield; Westcott House, Cambridge. **Career:** Rural Dean, Beltisloe;

Deacon 1916; Curate, Ardsley, Barnsley 1916–1919; Priest 1917; Curate, St Andrew, Derby 1919–1922; Vicar, Pleasley Hill 1923–1934; Rector, Irnham and Vicar, Corby, Grantham 1934; Vicar, Canwick, Lincolnshire 1963. **Appointments:** Director of Studies, Diocesan Clerical Study Group and Area Inspector of Church Schools 1944; appointed to a Prebendal Stall, Lincoln Cathedral 1946. **Publications:** *Thomas Field, DD: A Memoir*, 1937. Died 8 September 1964.

GOODRICH, The Right Reverend Philip Harold Ernest (1949) Born 2 November 1929, The Vicarage, Pleasley Hill, Mansfield, Nottinghamshire; son of Harold Spencer Goodrich, Clerk in Holy Orders, and Gertrude Alice Hornby; m Margaret Bennett, 10 September 1960; 4 daughters (Joanna, Philippa, Rosalind and Olivia). **Subject(s):** History; BA 1952; MA 1956. **Tutor(s):** A G Lee. **Johnian Relatives:** son of Harold Spencer Goodrich (1912); brother-in-law of Henry Arthur Wickstead (1932); uncle of Arthur Timothy John Wickstead (1973). **Educ:** King's School, Grantham; Stamford School; Cuddesdon Theological College, Oxford. **Career:** Ordained 1954; Curate, Rugby Parish Church 1954–1957; Chaplain, SJC 1957–1961; Rector, South Ormsby Group of Parishes, Lincolnshire 1961–1968; Vicar, Bromley Parish Church, Kent 1968–1973; Bishop Suffragan of Tonbridge 1974–1982; Diocesan Director of Ordinands, Rochester 1974–1982; Bishop of Worcester 1982–1996. **Appointments:** Chairman, The Children's Society 1990–1997; Member, House of Lords 1986–1996; Bishop Protector, world wide Anglican Franciscan Order 1990–1996; Produced eight lectures for St Giles-in-the-Fields entitled 'The Great Moments of Life' Autumn 1997. **Awards:** Larmor Award, SJC. Died 22 January 2001.

GOODWIN, Eric Anthony (1942) Born 17 April 1924, 6 Tudor Terrace, Aberdare; son of Frederick Charles Goodwin, Mining Engineer, and Dora Horner; m Jane Lonsdale, Uxbridge; 2 sons (Thomas and Richard). **Subject(s):** Law; BA 1951; MA 1954. **Tutor(s):** S J Bailey. **Johnian Relatives:** father of Richard Michael Goodwin (1976). **Educ:** Town Council School, Aberdare; Hereford Cathedral School. **Career:** Midlothian Border Horse and Airborne Division, Germany, India and Palestine; Local Government and Water Authority Solicitor. Died 6 December 1976.

GOODWIN, John Charles Hill (1946) Born 14 October 1927, Langhill, Manchester Road, Sheffield; son of Stuart Coldwell Goodwin, Steel Manufacturer, and Florence Nellie Hill. BA 1949. **Tutor(s):** F Thistlethwaite. **Educ:** St Anselm's Preparatory School, Bakewell; Oundle School.

GOODY, Professor John Rankine (1938) Born 27 July 1919, 59 Bridge Avenue, Hammersmith, London; son of Harold Ernest Goody, Electrical Engineer, and Lilian Rankine; m Juliet Mitchell; 1 son, 4 daughters. **Subject(s):** English; BA 1946; MA 1949; PhD 1954; ScD 1969; Diploma in Anthropology (Cantab) 1947; BLitt (Oxon) 1952; FBA 1976. **Tutor(s):** J S Boys Smith. **Johnian Relatives:** brother of Richard Mead Goody (1939); stepfather of Polly Miranda Rossdale (1997). **Educ:** Handside School, Welwyn Garden City; St Albans School; Balliol College, Oxford; RMA, Sandhurst. **Career:** HM Forces 1939–1946; Lieutenant, 1st Battalion, Sherwood Foresters, POW, Middle East, Italy and Germany 1942–1945; Educational Administration, Hertfordshire Education Authority 1947–1949; Assistant Lecturer 1954–1959, Lecturer in Archaeology and Anthropology 1959–1971, Director, African Studies Centre 1966–1973, Smuts Reader in Commonwealth Studies 1971–1978, William Wyse Professor of Social Anthropology 1973–1984 (Emeritus 1984–), University of Cambridge; Title B Fellow 1961–1973, Lecturer in Archaeology and Anthropology 1963–1973, Title C Fellow 1973–1984, Title E Fellow 1984–, SJC. **Appointments:** Supervisor in Archaeology and Anthropology 1958–1963, Director of Studies in Social and Political Studies 1969–1972, SJC; Foreign Honorary Member, American Academy of Arts and Sciences 1980; Member, Academia Europaea 1991; Member, Ordre des Palmes Academiques 1993; Officier dans l'Ordre des Arts et Lettres 2001;

Citoyen d'Honneur de Bouzigues, Herault 2002. **Awards:** Anthony Wilkin Studentship, University of Cambridge 1951; Allen Scholarship, University of Cambridge 1952; The International Prize of the Fyssen Foundation for Anthropology and Cognition 1990; Gold Medal of the Swedish Society for Anthropology and Geography 1991. **Publications:** *The Social Organisation of the LoWiili*, 1956; (ed) *The Developmental Cycle in Domestic Groups*, 1958; *Death, Property and the Ancestors*, 1962; (ed) *Succession to High Office*, 1966; (with J A Braimah) *Salaga: the struggle for power*, 1967; (ed) *Literacy in Traditional Societies*, 1968; *Comparative Studies in Kinship*, 1969; *Technology, Tradition and the State in Africa*, 1971; *The Myth of the Bagre*, 1972; (with S J Tambiah) *Bridewealth and Dowry*, 1973; (ed) *The Character of Kinship*, 1973; (ed) *Changing Social Structure in Ghana*, 1975; *Production and Reproduction*, 1977; *The Domestication of the Savage Mind*, 1977; (with S W D K Gandah) *Une Recitation du Bagré*, 1981; *Cooking, Cuisine and Class*, 1982; *The Development of the Family and Marriage in Europe*, 1983; *The Logic of Writing and the Organization of Society*, 1986; *The Interface between the Oral and the Written*, 1987; *The Oriental, the Ancient and the Primitive*, 1990; *The Culture of Flowers*, 1993; *The Expansive Moment*, 1995; *The East in the West*, 1996; *Jack Goody: l'homme, l'écriture et la mort*, 1996; *Representations and Contradictions*, Oxford, 1997; *The Power of the Written Word*, Smithsonian University Press, 2000; *The European Family: an historico-anthropological essay*, Blackwells, 2000; *A Myth Revisited: the Third Bagre*, 2003; *Islam in Europe*, 2003; *Capitalism and Modernity: the Great Debate*, 2004; contributions to learned journals.

GOODY, Professor Richard Mead (1939) Born 19 June 1921, 19 Brockswood Lane, Welwyn Garden City, Hertfordshire; son of Harold Ernest Goody, Electrical Engineer, and Lilian Rankine; m Elfriede Koch, 11 September 1946; 1 daughter (Brigid Rankine). **Subject(s):** Natural Sciences; BA 1942; MA 1946; PhD 1950; Honorary MA (Harvard) 1958; FAAAS 1959. **Tutor(s):** J M Wordie. **Johnian Relatives:** brother of John Rankine Goody (1938). **Educ:** Handside School, Welwyn Garden City; St Albans School. **Career:** Scientific Officer, Ministry of Aircraft Production, Boscombe Down 1942–1946; Title A Fellow, SJC 1950–1953; Reader in Meteorology, Imperial College 1953–1958; Director, Blue Hill Observatory, and Abbott Lawrence Rotch Professor of Dynamical Meteorology 1958–1970, Director, Center for Earth and Planetary Physics 1970–1972, Mallinckrodt Professor of Planetary Physics 1970–1991, Gordon McKay Professor of Applied Physics 1980–1991 (Emeritus 1991–), Harvard University. **Appointments:** Member, The Royal Meteorological Society; Member, US National Academy of Sciences 1970; Fellow, American Meteorological Society 1970; Fellow, American Geophysical Union 1975; Distinguished Visiting Scientist, Jet Propulsion Laboratory 1977–; John C Lindsay Memorial Lecturer, Goddard Space Flight Center 1978; Visiting Fellow, St Cross College, Oxford 1984 and 1988; Visiting Professor, Wolfson College, Oxford, Trinity Term 1986; Halley Lecturer, University of Oxford 1987; Honorary Member, International Radiation Commission 1988; Member, American Philosophical Society 1997; Priestley Lecturer, CSIRO, Melbourne, Australia 1999; Honorary Member, American Meteorological Society 1999; National Associate of the National Academies 2001. **Awards:** Buchan Prize, Royal Meteorological Society 1958; 50th Anniversary Medal, American Meteorological Society 1970; Cleveland Abbe Award, American Meteorological Society 1977; Public Service Medal, NASA 1980; William Bowie Medal, American Geophysical Union 1998. **Publications:** *The Physics of the Stratosphere*, CUP, 1954; *Atmospheric Radiation*, Clarendon Press, Oxford, 1964 (2nd edition 1989); (with J C G Walker) *Atmospheres*, Prentice-Hall, New Jersey, 1972; *Principles of Atmospheric Physics and Chemistry*, OUP, 1995.

GOOLDEN, Hugh Joseph (1912) Born 11 January 1893, 48 Barkston Gardens, Brompton, Middlesex; son of Charles Joseph Goolden, of independent means, and Isabel Asmit; m Kathleen Mary; 1 son (Godfrey). **Subject(s):** Classics; BA 1916; MA 1919. **Tutor(s):** E E Sikes. **Educ:** Down House, Westgate-on-Sea; Shrewsbury School. **Career:** Rifleman, King's Royal Rifle Corps (wounded), WWI; Barrister-at-Law; Called to the Bar, Inner Temple 1925. Died 4 October 1965.

GORDIN, Peter (1938) Born 5 November 1919, Grosmont, Anlaby Park, Hull; son of George William Gordin, Inspector of Taxes, and Alma Lucy Kettle; m (1) Elisabeth Collins, 5 May 1942, St Mary at the Walls, Colchester (d 1962), (2) Joan Forbes Borrie, 12 August 1963, St Margaret's, Rochester; 3 children. **Subject(s):** History; BA 1946; MA 1949. **Tutor(s):** J S Boys Smith; F Thistlethwaite. **Educ:** St Hilda's School, Carshalton; Limes School, South Croydon; Oakham School. **Career:** Duke of Cornwall's Light Infantry 1939–1945; Teacher and Second Master, King's School, Rochester, Kent 1947–1983. **Awards:** Minor Scholarship, SJC 1937; Johnson Exhibition, SJC 1937.

GORDON, Dr Edward Francis Strathearn (1912) Born 23 December 1893, 2 Lennox Street, Edinburgh; son of The Hon Arthur Gordon, Minister, Church of Scotland, and Emily Olga Marian Constant; m (1) Florence Phyllis Milholland, 18 February 1927, Holy Trinity, Brompton, (2) Margaret Joan Sargent, 22 April 1963. BA 1915; MA 1920; MRCS; LRCP 1917; FRSM. **Tutor(s):** R P Gregory. **Educ:** Merchiston Castle Preparatory School; Merchiston Castle School. **Career:** House Physician, Clinical Assistant, Children's Department, and House Surgeon, Skin and Venereal Departments, St Bartholomew's; Temporary Surgeon Lieutenant, RN; Medical Officer, Navy, Army and Air Force Institutes 1934.

GORDON, Ernest Harold (1926) Born 14 September 1907, 37 Charter Street, Gillingham, Kent; son of George Gordon, Engine Fitter, HM Dockyard, and Matilda Louisa Adelaide Pett; m (1) Jean Alexander, 1933 (d 1986), (2) Gwendoline Law, 1990. **Subject(s):** Mathematics; BA 1929; MA 1978. **Tutor(s):** J M Wordie. **Educ:** Richmond Road Council School, Gillingham; Sir J Williamson's Mathematical School, Rochester. **Career:** Called to the Bar, Middle Temple 1947; Principal Inspector of Taxes, Somerset House, until 1957; Messrs Slaughter and May 1957–1978. **Awards:** Exhibition, SJC 1926. Died 29 October 2003.

GORDON, Ian Robert (1942) Born 5 September 1924, Waterloo House, Blyth, Northumberland; son of William Ingram Gordon, Medical Practitioner, and Frances Eva Swan; m Joyce. BA 1947; MA 1949. **Tutor(s):** C W Guillebaud. **Educ:** Kindergarten School, Blyth; Tynemouth Boys' School; Corchester Preparatory School; Sedbergh School. **Career:** Bomb and Mine Disposal Squad, RNVR 1942; Farmer, Devon 1952–1964; Overseas Development Agency, went to Zambia, Botswana and the Sudan, Island of Nevis, West Indies, as a member of the corps of specialists 1965. **Publications:** *Animal Husbandry in Central Africa*, NECZAM, 3 vols. Died 28 May 1996.

GORDON, William Roger (1942) Born 14 June 1924, 122 King Street, Dukinfield, Cheshire; son of Charles Napier Gordon, Medical Practitioner, and Mary Lockhart; m Yolanda Osborn, 27 June 1959, Havana, Cuba. BA 1948; MA 1950. **Tutor(s):** S J Bailey. **Educ:** Dragon School, Oxford; Rugby School.

GORMAN, Patrick (1941) Born 16 April 1923, 89 High Street, Croydon, Surrey; son of Thomas Gorman, Metropolitan Police Officer, CID, and Dorothy Sarah Gasse-Gordon. **Tutor(s):** S J Bailey. **Educ:** Selhurst Grammar School.

GORRINGE, Allan Lindsay (1903) Born 20 January 1884, Seaford, Eastbourne, Sussex; son of Edward Joseph Gorringe, Farmer, and Eunice Brown; m Edith Alice Leeds Saunders; 1 son (John Allan Lindsay b 28 November 1918). BA 1907. **Tutor(s):** D MacAlister. **Johnian Relatives:** father of John Allan Lindsay Gorringe (1937). **Educ:** Manor House School, Clapham. **Career:** Assistant Master, Repton House School 1915–1918. Died 22 November 1918.

GORRINGE, John Allan Lindsay (1937) Born 28 November 1918, The Pastures, Repton; son of Allan Lindsay Gorringe, Schoolmaster, and Edith Alice Leeds Saunders. **Subject(s):** Economics; BA 1940; MA 1944; MB, ChB (Edinburgh) 1951; MRCP (Edinburgh) 1954. **Tutor(s):** C W

Guillebaud. **Johnian Relatives:** son of Allan Lindsay Gorringe (1903). **Educ:** Meadows School, Amersham; Port Regis School, Broadstairs; Radley College. **Career:** RA 1939–1946; Director, Clinical Investigation Department, Parke, Davis, and Company; SHO, later Registrar, Pneumoconiosis Research Unit, MRC.

GOTTSTEIN, Herr Kurd Felix Waldemar (1911) Born 14 February 1894, Cosel, Germany; son of Leo Gottstein, General Direktor, Königliche Kommercienrat, and Hedwig Behrend. **Tutor(s):** L H K Bushe-Fox. **Educ:** Gymnasium, Breslau, Germany.

GOUDY, Alexander Porter (1944) Born 17 May 1926, Great Shelford, Cambridgeshire; son of Alexander Porter Goudy, Lecturer in Russian, Clare College, Cambridge, and Clara Eisenstein; m Maude Ferguson, 1958, Colombo; 2 daughters (Gillian b 1960 and Jacqueline b 1964). **Subject(s):** Mechanical Sciences; BA 1947; MA 1951; FICE; CEng; PEng (Malaysia); MIE (Malaysia); FCIWEM. **Tutor(s):** S J Bailey. **Educ:** King's College School, Cambridge; The Leys School, Cambridge; Perse School, Cambridge. **Career:** RE 1947–1949; Civil/Water Engineer, Binnie & Partners, Consulting Engineers (including service in Hong Kong, Malaysia, India, Nepal, Singapore and Pakistan) 1949–1991; Independent Consultant 1991–2001.

GOUGH, Gordon (1946) Born 27 May 1928, 12 Pelham Terrace, Pelham Road, Gravesend, Kent; son of William George Gough, Night Officer, Thames Nautical Training College, and Edith Mabel Asker. **Subject(s):** Natural Sciences; BA 1949; MA 1953. **Tutor(s):** G C L Bertram. **Educ:** Cecil Road School, Gravesend; County School, Gravesend. **Awards:** Minor Scholarship, SJC 1945.

GOUGH, Henry Joseph (1902) Born 25 February 1883, Hill View, Woodbridge, Suffolk; son of George Gough, Gentleman, and Margaret Fitzpatrick. **Tutor(s):** D MacAlister. **Educ:** Woodbridge School. **Awards:** Scholarship 1901. Died 7 January 1903.

GOUGH, Dr John Richard (1944) Born 4 April 1926, 39 Clarence Road, Teddington, Middlesex; son of Herbert John Gough, Director General, Ministry of Supply, and Sybil Holmes. **Subject(s):** Natural Sciences; BA 1947; MA 1951; MB 1950; BChir 1950. **Tutor(s):** S J Bailey. **Educ:** Mall School, Strawberry Hill; Stubbington School, Fareham; Felsted School.

GOULD, Douglas Harold Mellor (1917) Born 15 March 1900, 14 Fitzwilliam Street West, Huddersfield, Yorkshire; son of Charles Thomas Gould, Grocer, and Mary Elizabeth Mellor. **Tutor(s):** E E Sikes. **Educ:** Huddersfield College of Music; Huddersfield Collegiate School; New College, Harrogate. **Career:** Organist: Halifax Parish Church, Leeds Parish Church, St James's Church, Brighouse; Organist and Director of Music, Elland Parish Church 1935.

GOULD, Lionel John (1942) Born 6 November 1907, 37 Bletchley Road, Fenny Stratford, Buckinghamshire; son of William John Gould, Stationer, and Alice Lillian Verney. **Subject(s):** Geography; BA 1944; MA 1948; BSc (London) 1933. **Tutor(s):** C W Guillebaud. **Educ:** Bletchley Council School; County School, Wolverton; Technical College; University of Reading; KCL; LSE. **Career:** Instructor, Initial Training Wing; Flight Lieutenant, RAF 1941; Schoolmaster, Technical College.

GOUPILLE, Joseph Philippe (1926) Born 16 October 1906, Beau Bassin, Plaines Wilhems, Mauritius; son of Pierre Henri Goupille, Director of Rogers & Co, and Lydie Rousset. **Tutor(s):** E A Benians. **Educ:** Royal College, Mauritius.

GOVIER, Leonard John (1943) Born 4 July 1925, 387 Monks Road, Heavitree, Exeter; son of Francis Leonard Govier, Assistant Clerk, County of Devon Insurance Committee, and Emilie Ellen Hopkins, Ladies' Tailoress; m Marguerite Kathleen Frampton, 4 July 1953, Richmond Parish Church, Surrey; 2 daughters (Christine Beatrice Ellen and Jacqueline Marguerite Ann). **Subject(s):** Natural Sciences; BA 1946; MA 1950; FOR; MORS; FSS. **Tutor(s):** C W Guillebaud. **Educ:** Ladysmith Road School, Exeter; Exeter School. **Career:** Scientist, Research Department, Climax Rock Drill and Engineering Works Ltd, Carn Brea 1945–1947 (under Dr E J B Willey (1925), Research Manager); Physicist, Metallurgy Laboratory, Armstrong Siddeley Motors Ltd, Coventry 1947–1949; Technical Sales Representative, Technical Sales Department 1951–1952; Manufacturing Assistant, Co-ordination and Economics Department 1952–1956, Head, Corporate Analysis Division, Co-ordination and Economics Department 1956–1960, Head, Mathematical Developments Division and Central OR Group, Corporate Planning Department 1960–1967, Company Management Scientist 1967–1970, ESSO Petroleum Company Ltd, London; Lecturer, Department of Computational and Statistical Science, University of Liverpool 1970–1975; Principal Assistant Planner, Borough Planning Group, Department of Planning and Communications, London Borough of Camden 1975–1976; Lecturer and Postgraduate Officer, Department of Computation, UMIST 1976–1982. **Publications:** numerous articles and conference reports in various journals.

GOWARD, Frank Kenneth (1938) Born 30 August 1919, 1 Daw Green Avenue, Crigglestone, Wakefield; son of Frank Goward, Colliery under-manager, and Mary Elsie Kaye; 2 children. **Subject(s):** Natural Sciences; BA 1941; MA 1947. **Tutor(s):** C W Guillebaud. **Educ:** Crigglestone Council School; Wakefield Grammar School. **Career:** Telecommunications Research Department, Malvern 1940–1945; AERE 1945–1954. **Awards:** Major Scholarship, SJC 1937. Died 10 March 1954.

GOWER, Dudley George (1922) Born 28 April 1903, 54 Thistlewaite Road, Lower Clapton, London; son of George Herbert Gower, Fish Merchant, and Ethel Elizabeth Barton. BA 1925; MA 1934. **Tutor(s):** E E Sikes. **Educ:** High School, Walthamstow; Monoux School, Walthamstow; St John's College, Hurstpierpont; Milton Abbas School, Blandford.

GRAAFF, Dr Johannes de Villiers (1947) Born 19 February 1928, Muizenberg, Cape Province, South Africa; son of David Pieter de Villiers Graaff, Baronet, Company Director, and Magdalena Susannah van Heerden; m Clare Thomson, 7 July 1951, St Bene't's Church, Cambridge. PhD 1950; BA (Cape Town) 1946. **Tutor(s):** J M Wordie. **Educ:** Western Province Preparatory School; Diocesan College, Rondebosch; University of Cape Town. **Career:** Economics Teacher, University of the Witwatersrand; Title A Fellow, SJC 1951–1954; Assistant Lecturer in Economics, University of Cambridge 1951–1952; Overseas Fellow, Churchill College, Cambridge 1964–1965.

GRABHAM, George Wallington (1913) Born 29 November 1895, Witham, Essex; son of George Wallington Grabham and Constance Ethel Josephine Crane; m Edith Norah, 20 November 1916. **Tutor(s):** R P Gregory. **Educ:** The Cedars, Stanway; Repton School. **Career:** Lieutenant, RASC (Mechanical Transport), WWI.

GRACIE, Captain Henry Stewart (1920) Born 6 August 1901, Marsh Villa, Leonard Stanley, Gloucestershire; son of George Stewart Gracie, Master Mariner, and Edith Helen Witchell; m Dorothy Constance (d 18 July 1960). **Subject(s):** Mathematics; BA 1923; MA 1952; FSA. **Tutor(s):** E E Sikes. **Educ:** Marling School, Stroud; St Anne's, Redhill; Pocklington School. **Career:** Instructor Captain, RN; Director of Studies and Dean, Royal Naval College, Greenwich 1952–1956. **Awards:** Exhibition, SJC. **Honours:** CB 1956. Died 7 February 1979.

GRAETZ, Dr Gerhard Hermann Arnold (1922) Born 16 June 1904, Vicarage House, East Lane, Wembley, Middlesex; son of Max Paul Robert Graetz, Manager of Banking House, and Clara Arnold; m Annie Sutherland; 1 son (Paul). BA 1926; MA 1933; BChir 1932; MB 1933; MRCS (St Barts) 1929; LRCP (St Barts) 1929. **Tutor(s):** B F Armitage. **Educ:** Colet Court, London; St Paul's School, London. **Career:** House

Physician, Devon and Exeter Hospital; House Surgeon and Resident Medical Officer, Connaught Hospital, Walthamstow; Anaesthetist, Huddersfield Royal Infirmary. Died 16 August 1960.

GRAHAM, Graeme Scott (SCOTT GRAHAM) (1921) Born 19 September 1902, Hyndford Villa, Hyndford Street, Dundee, Scotland; son of James Alexander Graham, Solicitor and Notary Public, and Grace Jane Scott; m Olive Irene Ridd; 1 son (Peter James b 24 October 1936). BA 1924; MA 1954. **Tutor(s):** E A Benians. **Johnian Relatives:** father of Peter James Scott Graham (1956). **Educ:** Seafield House Preparatory School, Broughty Ferry; Uppingham School, Newport; Emberton House, Newport Pagnal.

GRAHAM-MARTIN, Captain Hugh Noël (1940) Born 23 December 1921, 150 Princes Road, Toxteth Park, Liverpool; son of John Graham Martin, Medical Practitioner, and Gertrude Jane Montgomery; m (1) Cynthia Brooke McVeagh, 11 June 1945, (2) Mercedes; 2 sons (Charles and John), 1 daughter (Annabel). BA 1943. **Tutor(s):** S J Bailey. **Educ:** Mr Dobie's, Heswell, Cheshire; Marlborough College. Died 7 April 1988.

GRAIL, Captain Clifford George (1909) (admitted as a Non-Collegiate Student 1908) Born 27 September 1890, Sowdley, East Dean, Gloucestershire; son of George Henry Grail, Assistant Superintendent to the Prudential Assurance Company, and Mary Ann Lewis. **Subject(s):** Modern and Medieval Languages; BA 1911; Cambridge Teachers' Diploma 1910. **Tutor(s):** E E Sikes. **Educ:** Sowdley Elementary School; Newnham Elementary School; Newport Grammar School. **Career:** Modern Languages Master, Bromley School, Kent and French Lecturer, Bromley School of Science and Art 1911–1914; Second Lieutenant, 7th Battalion, Prince of Wales' (North Staffordshire) Regiment 1914; Lieutenant 1915; Captain 1915. Died 23 July 1915 (killed in action at Gallipoli).

GRANGE, George William Keith (1916) Born 6 February 1897, New England, St Ann, Jamaica, British West Indies; son of George Spence Grange, Clerk in Holy Orders, and Lillian Augusta Susan Smythe. **Subject(s):** Mathematics; BA 1919. **Tutor(s):** E E Sikes. **Educ:** Potsdam School, Jamaica. **Career:** Assistant Master, Durham School 1919–1922.

GRANGER-TAYLOR, Jerry (1937) See TAYLOR.

GRANT, Cecil Charles l'Estrange (1921) Naval Officer.

GRANT, Francis Henry Symons (1902) Born 18 September 1883, 103 Wickersley Road, Battersea, Surrey; son of George Grant, Contractor, and Mary Elizabeth Symons; m Alice Maude May Broadhurst, 1910 (d 1950). **Subject(s):** Natural Sciences/History; BA 1905; MA 1929. **Tutor(s):** D MacAlister. **Educ:** Basnett Grove School, Battersea; Westminster City School, London. **Career:** Secretary's Office 1906, Regional Director, Home Counties 1939, GPO; Controller-General, Posts and Telecommunications Branch, Control Commission for Germany 1945–1946. **Honours:** CBE 1942. Died 5 December 1963.

GRANT, Geoffrey John Cardross (1942) Born 2 October 1924, Balgreen, Townhead Street, Hamilton, Lanarkshire; son of Donald Cardross Grant, Major, The Cameronians, and Beatrice Irene Despard; m Barbara Elizabeth Ann Phipps, 13 January 1945. **Tutor(s):** C W Guillebaud. **Educ:** Oakley Hall, Cirencester; Haileybury College. **Career:** Flight Sergeant, RAFVR, WWII. Died March 1945 (killed in action).

GRANT, Malcolm Leith (1948) Born 8 November 1927, 29 The Close, Norwich, Norfolk; son of Alastair Forbes Grant, Manager, King's Lynn Beet Sugar Factory, and Margaret Mountfield Sims; m Ursula Burnet, 1975, Edinburgh; 1 son (Neil b 30 May 1978). **Subject(s):** English/History; BA 1950. **Tutor(s):** F Thistlethwaite. **Johnian Relatives:** brother of Neil David Mountfield Grant (1958). **Educ:** Thorpe House School, Norwich; King Edward VI School, Norwich. Died 29 October 1992.

GRANT, Robert Sturge (1929) Born 27 January 1909, Lanas Terrace, Newton le Willows, Yorkshire; son of Archibald Sturge Grant, Headmaster, Hillside School, Reigate, and Dorothy Clarke. **Subject(s):** Mechanical Sciences; BA 1931; MA 1962. **Tutor(s):** J M Wordie. **Educ:** Willington School, Putney; Tormore School, Upper Deal; The King's School, Canterbury; RMA, Woolwich. **Career:** Second Lieutenant, RE 1929; Brigadier, until 1969. Died 1973.

GRAVESON, George Stanley (1933) Born 10 May 1915, 14 Rawson Avenue, Farnworth, Lancaster; son of George Adam Graveson, Ironmonger, and Charlotte Ann Davison; m (2) Jeanne, 1973; (1) 3 sons. **Subject(s):** Natural Sciences; BA 1936; MA 1947; MD; FRCP. **Tutor(s):** R L Howland. **Educ:** Kearsley St John's Elementary School; The Grammar School, Farnworth. **Career:** Chief Assistant in Neurology, Manchester Royal Infirmary 1939; Wing Commander and Neuropsychiatrist, RAF 1939–1945; Lecturer in Neurology, Manchester University 1945–1950; Consultant Neurologist, Wessex; Founder, Wessex Neurological Centre 1950–1976. Died 16 April 1976.

GRAY, Frank Truan (1945) Born 22 October 1920, Prince Frederick, Maryland, USA; son of John Basil Gray, Judge, Circuit Court, and Aimée Atlee Truan. **Tutor(s):** C W Guillebaud. **Educ:** Calvert County High School; Princeton University. **Career:** Lieutenant, 9th Air Force, US Forces.

GRAY, Dr Oliver (1919) Born 23 January 1899, 16 Berkeley Terrace, Glasgow, Scotland; son of Albert Alexander Gray, Physician, and Mabel Henderson; m Marjorie Carr; 1 daughter. BA 1921; MA 1953; MD. **Tutor(s):** E E Sikes. **Educ:** Glasgow Academy; Bootham School, York. **Career:** Ambulance driver, French Unit, Italian Alps, then RN 1914–1918; House-appointments, Glasgow; GP, Campbeltown 1924–1928; GP, Haselmere 1928–1958; Served, hospital ships 1939–1945. **Appointments:** JP, Surrey. **Awards:** BMA Scholarship 1950. **Honours:** MBE (for bravery in rescuing the wounded at the Normandy Landings). Died 28 January 1964.

GRAY, Richard Anthony Pereira (1920) Born 27 February 1902, 3 Northernhay Place, Exeter, Devon; son of Joseph Anthony Wenceslaus Pereira Gray, GP, and Grace Blanche Francis; m Mavis Shrimpton; 1 son, 1 daughter. **Subject(s):** Natural Sciences; BA 1923; MA 1928; BChir 1929; MB 1929. **Tutor(s):** B F Armitage. **Johnian Relatives:** brother of Sydney Joseph Pereira Gray (1917); uncle of Denis John Pereira Gray (1954) and of Robert Jonathan Pereira Gray (1958); great uncle of Timothy John Pereira Gray (1990). **Educ:** Norwood School, Pennsylvania; Exeter School. **Career:** GP 1931. **Appointments:** Chairman, Exeter Division, BMA; President, Devon and Exeter Medical Society; Founder Member, Royal College of General Practitioners. **Awards:** Knight of St John 1974. Died 18 April 1980.

GRAY, Dr Sydney Joseph Pereira (1917) Born 14 June 1899, 29 Belmont Road, Exeter, Devon; son of Joseph Anthony Wenceslaus Gray, GP, and Grace Blanche Francis; m Alice Evelyn Cole; 2 sons (Denis John Pereira b 2 October 1935 and Robert Jonathan Pereira b 6 May 1939). **Subject(s):** Natural Sciences; BA 1921; MA 1925; MRCS; LRCP (St Bartholomew's) 1925; FRCSEd 1929. **Tutor(s):** E E Sikes. **Johnian Relatives:** brother of Richard Anthony Pereira Gray (1920); father of Denis John Pereira Gray (1954) and of Robert Jonathan Pereira Gray (1958); grandfather of Timothy John Pereira Gray (1990). **Educ:** Norwood School, Exeter; Exeter School. **Career:** House positions at St Bartholomew's and Royal Northern Hospital; Honorary Medical Officer to the Exeter Dispensary; GP, Exeter 1932. **Awards:** Vidal Exhibition, SJC 1918. Died 17 March 1975.

GRAYSON, John Richard (1915) Born 14 August 1894, 7 Stanhope Road, Westoe, South Shields, Durham; son of John Grayson, Schoolmaster, and Isabella Hunter. **Tutor(s):** L H K Bushe-Fox. **Educ:** Westoe Senior School; St Cuthbert's, Worksop; Westoe Secondary School.

GREAR, Ernest John Lantsbery (1910) Born 26 April 1891, 252 Dalston Lane, Hackney, London; son of Thomas Grear, Congregational Minister, and Mary Alice Lantsbery. **Subject(s):** History; BA 1913; MA 1928. **Tutor(s):** J R Tanner. **Educ:** Bishop's Stortford College; Mill Hill School. **Career:** Lecturer, University of Dijon 1914; Lieutenant, Middlesex Regiment (The Prince of Wales' Own), and MGC (wounded twice), WWI; Royal Army Ordnance Corps, WWII; Master, Wath Grammar School 1956. Died 15 October 1973.

GREATOREX, Thomas William (1933) Born 21 June 1914, 3 Manor Drive, Halifax, Yorkshire; son of Robert Wilkinson Greatorex, Surgeon, and Mildred Helena Nash. BA 1936. **Educ:** Woodlands School, Deganwy, North Wales; Sedbergh School. **Career:** Lieutenant, RAMC 1939–1941. Died May 1941 (of wounds received on active service in the Middle East).

GREAVES, Professor William Michael Herbert (1916) Born 10 September 1897, Industry, St Joseph, Barbados, British West Indies; son of Eustace Charles Greaves, Physician and Surgeon, and Maggie Bleuitt Campbell Parker; m Caroline Grace Kitto, 1926; 1 son (George Richard Herbert b 3 June 1941). **Subject(s):** Mathematics; BA 1919; MA 1923; FRS 1943. **Tutor(s):** E E Sikes. **Johnian Relatives:** brother-in-law of Humphrey Davy Findley Kitto (1916); uncle of Julian Kitto Comrie (1956); father of George Richard Herbert Greaves (1961). **Educ:** The Lodge School, Barbados; Codrington College, Barbados. **Career:** Foundress Fellow, SJC 1922–1925; Chief Assistant, Greenwich Royal Observatory 1924–1938; Astronomer Royal for Scotland; Professor of Astronomy, Edinburgh; Director, Royal Observatory, Blackford Hill 1938–1955. **Appointments:** Secretary, Section A, BAAS 1924–1931; President, Royal Astronomical Society 1947–1949. **Awards:** Wright's Prize, SJC; Tyson Medal for Astronomy, University of Cambridge 1919; Second Smith's Prize, University of Cambridge 1921; Isaac Newton Studentship, University of Cambridge 1921–1923. Died 24 December 1955.

GREEN, Arthur Norman (1939) Born 20 May 1921, 90 New Road, Croxley Green, Rickmansworth, Hertfordshire; son of Arthur Green, Managing Director, and Emma Mildred Dove Smith. BA 1942. **Tutor(s):** J M Wordie. **Educ:** Oak House Preparatory School, Croxley Green; Watford Grammar School.

GREEN, Charles John Sanders (1938) Born 9 June 1919, Sunnymead, Beaconsfield Road, Clacton-on-Sea; son of Algernon Sanders Green, Medical Practitioner, and Elizabeth Hall Pargiter. BA 1941. **Tutor(s):** R L Howland. **Educ:** Beaudesert Park, Minchinhampton; Marlborough College. **Career:** Surgeon Lieutenant, RNVR, WWII. Died October 1944 (missing, presumed killed, on active service).

GREEN, Charles Norman (1932) Born 10 January 1913, 80 Dale Street, Lancaster; son of James William Green, Schoolmaster, and Lucy Bottomley. **Subject(s):** Mathematics; BA 1935; MA 1939. **Tutor(s):** J M Wordie. **Educ:** Boys' National School, Lancaster; Royal Grammar School, Lancaster.

GREEN, Dr Charles Roger Heyden (1939) Born 6 January 1922, Knuston Hall, Irchester, Wellingborough; son of Charles William Sidney Green, Shoe Manufacturer, and Josephine Sara Frederique Van der Heyden; m Joan Muriel Oliver, 1 December 1945, Emmanuel Church, Northwood, Middlesex; 3 daughters. BA 1943; MA 1949; DObstRCOG 1948; MB 1944; BChir 1944. **Tutor(s):** R L Howland. **Johnian Relatives:** nephew of Reginald Kersey Green (1919) and of Donald Cecil Green (1924). **Educ:** Lydgate House School, Hunstanton; Oundle School. **Career:** Postgraduate Clinical Appointments, Middlesex Hospital; Clinical Assistant, Obstetric Department, West Suffolk Hospital; Captain, RAMC, Egypt and Palestine 1945–1948; GP, Bury St Edmunds, Suffolk 1948–1986 (Senior Partner 1965–1986).

GREEN, Daniel Ezra (1934) Born 12 May 1917, 37 Highbury Place, London; son of Joshua Green, General Merchant, and Louisa Deborah Horn. **Subject(s):** Law; BA 1937; MA 1946. **Tutor(s):** C W Guillebaud.

Register of Twentieth-Century Johnians, 1900–1949

Educ: English School, Na'adi; English School, Cairo. **Career:** Farmer; Writer. **Awards:** Scottish Arts Council Bursary. **Publications:** *The Politics of Food*, 1975.

GREEN, Donald Cecil (1924) Born 8 December 1902, Rushden, Northamptonshire; son of Charles Arthur Kersey Green, Boot and Shoe Manufacturer, and Mary Catherine Sanders. **Tutor(s):** B F Armitage. **Johnian Relatives:** brother of Reginald Kersey Green (1919); uncle of Charles Roger Heyden Green (1939). **Educ:** Farm House School; Mill Hill School.

GREEN, The Revd Ernest William (1902) Born 6 September 1881, 59 Bloomfield Road, Maida Vale, London; son of William Herbert Green, Clergyman, and Ann Andre; m Miranda Mary Wilkinson, 8 March 1915, The Citadel, Cairo; 1 son, 1 daughter. BA 1906; MA 1910. **Tutor(s):** E E Sikes. **Career:** Ordained Deacon 1907; Curate, Holy Trinity Eastbourne 1907–1910; Priest 1909; CF 1910–1930; Senior Chaplain, Aldershot 1919–1923; Vicar, Dunston, Stafford 1930–1934; Vicar, Chipping Campden, Gloucestershire 1934–1936. **Appointments:** Chaplain, local Freemasons Lodge; Member, Diocesan Association for Moral Welfare. **Honours:** OBE 1919. Died 22 February 1936.

GREEN, Frederick Arthur (1928) Born 26 August 1909, 80 Dale Street, Lancaster; son of James William Green, Schoolmaster, and Lucy Bottomley. **Subject(s):** Mathematics; BA 1931. **Tutor(s):** J M Wordie. **Educ:** Boys' National School, Lancaster; Royal Grammar School, Lancaster. **Awards:** Exhibition, SJC 1928.

GREEN, Gilbert Wilson (1942) Born 12 September 1924, Bridgethorpe, Clock House Lane, Bedfont, Middlesex; son of Robert Charles Green, Builder, and Mary Frances Coffee, Teacher; m Julian Elizabeth Quick, 5 September 1950, St James' Church, Longborough, Gloucestershire; 4 sons. **Subject(s):** Natural Sciences; BA 1945; MA 1949; FGS. **Tutor(s):** C W Guillebaud. **Educ:** Pembroke House, Hampton; St Paul's School. **Career:** Geologist, HM Geological Survey 1945; Senior Geologist in charge of Field Mapping and Training, Jamaica Geological Survey Department, Kingston 1969–1971; District Geologist, Central and South Midlands Field Unit, British Geological Survey, Keyworth, Nottingham 1974–1982. **Appointments:** Government Assessor, Jamaica; Blue Mountains Water Supply Scheme (Kingston); Project Manager, Fieldwork, South East Essex (Third London Airport) Project 1971–74. **Publications:** Various maps in different scales; *North Exmoor Floods*, 1955; *British Regional Geological Handbook – Bristol & Gloucester Region*, 3rd edition, 1992; various other publications.

GREEN, Gordon Leonard (1949) Born 15 July 1929, Kentdale Nursing Home, Kendal, Westmorland; son of Thomas Farrimond Green, Headmaster, Bootham School, and Jessie Doris Leonard; m Sally. **Subject(s):** English/Modern and Medieval Languages; BA 1952. **Tutor(s):** A G Lee. **Educ:** Leominster Grammar School; Bootham School. Died 6 February 1976.

GREEN, Professor Harry Norman (1934) Born 21 September 1902, 605 London Road, Sheffield; son of Harry Green, Master Baker, and Beatrice Holmshaw. MA 1934; MB 1924 (Sheffield); BChir (Sheffield) 1924; BSc (Sheffield) 1925; MSc (Sheffield) 1926; MD 1927 (Sheffield). **Educ:** Central School, Sheffield; University of Sheffield. **Career:** Clinical Assistant, Royal Infirmary, Sheffield 1926–1933; University Demonstrator in Pathology 1934–1935; Professor of Pathology, University of Sheffield 1935–1954; Lieutenant Colonel, RAMC 1944–1945; Professor of Experimental Pathology and Cancer Research, University of Leeds; Consultant, Cancer Research & Human Pathology, Leeds General Infirmary 1954–1965. **Publications:** *Immunological Aspects of Cancer*. Died 16 May 1967.

GREEN, Henry Edward Beck (1915) Born 18 October 1886, Clenchwarton, Norfolk; son of Edward Green, Farmer, and Lucy Becks. **Subject(s):** Moral Sciences; BA 1920; MA 1930. **Tutor(s):** E E Sikes.

Educ: Sutton Bridge Boys' School; Moulton Grammar School; Kings Lynn Pupil Teachers' Centre; St John's College, York.

GREEN, Horace Norman (1926) Born 7 September 1908, 3 Broomfield Grove, Rotherham, Yorkshire; son of Charles Horace Green, Master Builder, and Sarah Ann Martin. **Subject(s):** Law; BA 1929; MA 1933. **Tutor(s):** E A Benians. **Educ:** New College, Harrogate.

GREEN, Professor James Alexander (1947) Born 26 February 1926, Rochester, New York, USA; son of Frederick Charles Green, Drapers Professor of French, University of Cambridge, and Mary Balairdie Gilchrist; m Margaret Lord, 2 August 1950, St Andrew's, Girton; 1 son (Alastair James); 2 daughters (Jane Margaret and Sally Ann). PhD 1951; BSc (St Andrews) 1944; FRSE 1968; FRS 1987. **Tutor(s):** J M Wordie. **Educ:** Bedford Park School, Toronto; Perse School, Cambridge; St Andrews University. **Career:** Scientific Officer, Foreign Office, Bletchley Park 1944–1945; Assistant, Aerodynamics Department, RAE, Farnborough 1945–1946; Temporary Master, Oswestry High School 1946; Demonstrator, St Andrews University 1946–1947; Lecturer in Mathematics 1950–1959, Senior Lecturer in Mathematics 1959–1963, Manchester University; Reader in Mathematics, University of Sussex 1964–1965; Professor of Mathematics 1965–1991 (Emeritus 1991), University of Warwick. **Appointments:** Member, Editorial Board, *Journal of Algebra* 1965–1975. **Awards:** Major Scholarship, SJC 1944.

GREEN, Martin Burgess (1945) Born 21 September 1927, 61 Balfour Road, Ealing, Middlesex; son of Joseph William Elias Green, Confectioner and Tobacconist, and Hilda Brewster. **Subject(s):** English; BA 1948; MA 1952; PhD (Michigan). **Tutor(s):** F Thistlethwaite. **Educ:** Northfields School, West Ealing; Weston Lullingfield School; Priory School, Shrewsbury. **Career:** Lecturer in English, University of Birmingham 1965. **Publications:** *A Mirror for Anglo-Saxons*, Longman, 1961.

GREEN, Norman (1906) Born 11 October 1887, 47 Cranmer Road, Cumberland, Kennington, Surrey; son of George Edwin Green, Bootmaker, and Louisa Ellen Ekens. **Subject(s):** Natural Sciences; BA 1909; MA 1913. **Tutor(s):** J R Tanner. **Educ:** St Olave's Grammar School. **Career:** Master, Crewkern Grammar School 1911–1914; Master, Huish's School, Taunton 1914–1916; Lieutenant, Sherwood Foresters (Nottinghamshire and Derby Regiment) (wounded), WWI; Captain, General List, WWI; Chemist, HM Factory, Queensferry 1916–1918; Assistant Master, Acton County School 1919–1944. Died 30 December 1944.

GREEN, Dr Reginald Arthur (1947) Born 22 April 1917, 27 Horsham Avenue, Friern, Barnet, Middlesex; son of Arthur Green, Bank Cashier, and Emma Race; m Margaret Rangdale Scott, August 1946, Gosforth, Newcastle upon Tyne (d November 2000); 1 son (Timothy David b November 1947), 1 daughter (Clare Frances Rangdale b March 1950). PhD 1950; MRCVS (London) 1938; BSc (London) 1946. **Tutor(s):** G C L Bertram. **Educ:** Tenterden Hall Preparatory School, Hendon; Highgate School; Royal Veterinary College, London; Birkbeck College. **Career:** Veterinary Surgeon 1938–1945; Research Student in Zoology 1947–1950, University Demonstrator in Zoology 1949–1952, University Lecturer in Veterinary Anatomy and Anatomy 1952–1982, University of Cambridge; Title B Fellow and Lecturer in Veterinary Anatomy and Anatomy 1971–1982, Title E Fellow 1982, SJC. **Appointments:** Acting Tutor for Engineers 1972–1973, Tutor for Natural Scientists 1973–1982, SJC.

GREEN, Reginald Kersey (1919) Born 12 February 1896, Rushden, Northamptonshire; son of Charles Arthur Kersey Green, Boot Manufacturer and Leather Merchant, and Mary Catherine Sanders; m Phyllis Natalie Mary, 14 April 1932, Parish Church of St Michael, Sittingbourne. BA 1921; MA 1926. **Tutor(s):** E E Sikes. **Johnian Relatives:** brother of Donald Cecil Green (1924); uncle of Charles Roger Heyden Green (1939). **Educ:** New College, Harrogate. Died 27 May 1960.

GREEN, Stewart (1941) Born 13 August 1923, 76 Clarkehouse Road, Sheffield; son of Douglas Green, Physician and Surgeon, and Ethel Siddell. **Tutor(s):** S J Bailey. **Educ:** Birkdale Preparatory School, Sheffield; St Bees School; Uppingham School.

GREEN, Major Stuart Montague (1907) Born 6 June 1888, 122 Broomspring Lane, Ecclesall, Bierlow, Sheffield; son of Aaron Asher Green, Rabbi, Hampstead Synagogue, and Ada Jacob; m Constance Juliet Bacharach, 9 December 1919, Hampstead Synagogue. **Subject(s):** Classics; BA 1910. **Tutor(s):** E E Sikes. **Educ:** University College Preparatory School, London; St Paul's School, London. **Career:** Called to the Bar, Inner Temple 1912; Captain, London Regiment (Kensington Battalion) (wounded, Mentioned in Despatches), WWI. Died 14 May 1949.

GREEN, William Otis (1929) Born 18 October 1909, Cranbrook, British Columbia, Canada; son of Frank William Green, Doctor of Medicine, and Lillian Barbara Staples. BA 1933. **Tutor(s):** M P Charlesworth. **Educ:** Kingsley House Preparatory School; Brentwood College, Victoria, Canada.

GREENE, Edward Reginald (1923) Born 26 November 1904, São Paulo, Brazil; son of Edward Greene, Managing Director, Brazilian Warrant Company, and Eva Stutzer. BA 1926. **Tutor(s):** E A Benians. **Educ:** Berkhamsted School; Bedale's School, Petersfield.

GREENER, Paul (1944) Born 24 April 1926, Maternity Home, Museum Road, Oxford; son of William Greener, Clerk in Holy Orders, and Luna Wilkinson; m (1) Angela Jane Gray, 31 January 1959, St Peter's, Ruddington, Nottinghamshire; (2) Daphne Aspinall, 24 December 1991, Okehampton; (1) 2 sons (Andrew William Henry b 26 June 1962 and Alastair Paul b 3 October 1963), 1 daughter (Prudence Jane Elizabeth b 28 December 1959). **Subject(s):** Engineering/Agriculture; BA 1950; MA 1952. **Tutor(s):** J M Wordie. **Educ:** Exeter School. **Career:** RE, India and Palestine 1945–1948; Working Farmer 1951–1982; Diocesan Cartographer, Statistician/Records, Exeter Diocesan Board of Finance 1983–1997. **Appointments:** RE Cadet, SJC 1944–1945. **Publications:** *Drewsteignton Millennium Picture Book*; *A Study of Seventeenth Century Drewsteignton*.

GREENHALGH, Arthur Ward (1928) Born 3 August 1910, 58 Seymour Road, Bolton, Lancashire; son of William Arthur Greenhalgh, Master Cotton Spinner, and Rhoda Ward. **Subject(s):** Law; BA 1931; MA 1935. **Tutor(s):** E A Benians. **Educ:** Bolton School; The Leys School, Cambridge. **Career:** Solicitor, Bolton; Admitted Solicitor 1934. Died 25 February 1957.

GREENSTREET, Anthony John (1949) Born 12 August 1928, St Barnabas Nursing Home, Saltash, Cornwall; son of Norman Bernard de Medina Greenstreet, Surgeon-Commander, RN, and Kathleen Mary Pryn; m Anne Millin Selby, 15 April 1961, Camberley; 1 son (James John Pryn b 8 July 1965), 2 daughters (Rosanna Clare b 23 November 1963 and Miranda Frances Jane b 28 June 1969). **Subject(s):** English/History; BA 1952; MA 1956. **Tutor(s):** A G Lee. **Johnian Relatives:** grandson of William John Greenstreet (1879); son of Norman Bernard de Medina Greenstreet (1912). **Educ:** Mount House Preparatory School, Plymouth and Tavistock; Sherborne School. **Career:** Administrative Assistant, Bengal Chamber of Commerce and Industry, Calcutta 1952–1955; Export Sales Executive, Aero Research Ltd, Duxford 1956–1957; Eastern Federation of Building Trades Employers, Cambridge 1958; Assistant Secretary, Joint Iron Council, London 1958–1962; Deputy Director, Engineering Employers Federation, London 1962–1991.

GREENSTREET, Dr Norman Bernard de Medina (1912) Born 29 January 1894, Downfield, Stroud, Gloucestershire; son of William John Greenstreet, Headmaster, then Journalist and Editor, and Ethel de Medina Spender; m Kathleen Mary Pryn, August 1921, Buckland Monachorum, Devon; 1 son (Anthony John b 12 August 1928), 1 daughter (June de Medina b 30 January 1927). BA 1915; MA 1919;

MRCS; LRCP 1918. **Tutor(s):** R P Gregory. **Johnian Relatives:** son of William John Greenstreet (1879); father of Anthony John Greenstreet (1949). **Educ:** Marling School, Stroud; University College, Reading. **Career:** Second Lieutenant, Norfolk Regiment (TF), WWI; RN 1915–1948 (Surgeon Commander 1934). Died 10 November 1980.

GREENUP, The Revd Basil William (1927) Born 13 July 1908, St John's Hall, Avenell Road, Highbury, Middlesex; son of Albert William Greenup, Clerk in Holy Orders, and Evelyn Helen Heron. BA 1930; MA 1937. **Tutor(s):** M P Charlesworth. **Johnian Relatives:** son of Albert William Greenup (1885). **Educ:** St Peter's School, Eastbourne; Merchant Taylors' School, London. **Career:** Steward, Services Hospital, Greenwich; Assistant Appeal Secretary and Secretary, Appeal Committee, St Thomas' Hospital; Teacher, Dulwich College Preparatory School 1935. **Awards:** Exhibition, SJC 1926; John Stewart of Rannoch Scholarship in Hebrew, University of Cambridge 1927.

GREENWOOD, Alan Frederic (1923) Born 4 March 1905, 6 Park Avenue, Barrowford, Lancashire; son of Fred Greenwood, Headmaster, and Mary Stansfield. **Subject(s):** Law; BA 1926; MA 1930; LLB 1927. **Tutor(s):** E A Benians. **Educ:** Whitefield Council School, Nelson; Woodhouse Grove School, Bradford. **Career:** Admitted Solicitor 1930; Assistant Solicitor, Leeds Corporation 1930–1935; Deputy Town Clerk, Gloucester 1935–1939; Town Clerk, Leamington Spa 1939–1946; Assistant Secretary, Local Government Boundary Commission 1946–1949; Assistant Secretary, Development Commission and Agricultural Research Council 1949–1951; Colonial Office Adviser on Local Government to the Gold Coast 1951–1953; Permanent Secretary, Ministry of Local Government and Justice, Gold Coast/Ghana 1953–1960; Special Commission, Ghana 1960–1963; UN Adviser on Local Government, Uganda 1964–1966; UN Adviser on Local Government, Zambia 1966–1970. **Honours:** OBE 1946. Died 23 February 1983.

GREENWOOD, Guy Kenneth (1947) Born 9 July 1925, The Vicarage, Howick, Natal, South Africa; son of Frank Braithwaite Greenwood, Clerk in Holy Orders, and Margaret Moser. **Subject(s):** History; BA 1949; BEd. **Tutor(s):** F Thistlethwaite. **Educ:** Lime House School, Wetheral; Uppingham School. **Career:** Administrative Assistant, East Sussex and Northumberland, 1961; Assistant Education Officer, Dorset 1961–1967; Director of Education, Westmorland 1967.

GREENWOOD, Roger Paul (1942) Born 14 October 1923, Port Kembla, Illawarra, New South Wales; son of Harold Paul Greenwood, Engineer, and Katherine Phebe Stansfield. **Tutor(s):** C W Guillebaud. **Educ:** Grosvenor House School, Harrogate; Winchester House School, Brackley; Uppingham School.

GREENWOOD, William Henry (1935) Born 14 March 1917, 58 Heath Crescent, Halifax, Yorkshire; son of Edwin Greenwood, Managing Director, W H Greenwood Ltd, and Florence Dale; m Audrey, Tempest Blackburn, 10 December 1943; 2 sons, 2 daughters. **Subject(s):** Natural Sciences; BA 1938; MA 1945; MRCS, LRCP (London) 1942. **Tutor(s):** R L Howland. **Educ:** Heath Grammar School, Halifax; Rydal School, Colwyn Bay; Caldecott School, Hitchin; Leeds University Medical School. **Career:** Meanwood Park EMS Hospital 1941–1942; Major, RAMC, Palestine and Greece 1942–1944; Assistant GP, Shifnal, Shropshire 1944–1945; GP, Bedale, North Yorkshire 1945–1975; Medical Practitioner, Mowbray Grange OAP Hospital 1960–1975; Medical Practitioner, Vom Bacon Factory, Leeming Bar 1960–1975.

GREEVES, John Anthony de Maine (1946) Born 20 December 1927, Coolnashee, Crawfordsburn, County Down, Northern Ireland; son of John Ronald Howard Greeves, Company Director, Lieutenant Colonel, RE, and Lisbeth Snowden Demaine; m Georgina Dorothy Simpson, 20 July 1957; 1 son (John Peter Arthur), 2 daughters (Elaine Nicola and Elizabeth Caroline). **Subject(s):** Mechanical Sciences; BA 1949; MA 1976; European Engineer; CEng; FICE; FCIWEM; FCIArb; MConsE; FIEI. **Tutor(s):** R L Howland. **Educ:** Rockport Preparatory School,

Craigavad; Campbell College, Belfast. **Career:** Assistant Engineer, Sir William Halcrow & Partners; Engineer/Agent, John Graham (Dromore); Partner and subsequently Senior Partner, Ferguson and McIlveen, Consulting Civil Engineers; Professional Arbitrator and Conciliator; Major, RE (TA). **Appointments:** Honorary Colonel 74 (Antrim Artillery) Engineer Regiment (V); Chairman, (Northern Ireland) National Employers' Liaison Committee TAVRA; President and Chairman of Trustees, Church of Ireland Young Men's Society; Director, Herdmans Holdings plc; Director, Enterprise Ulster; Trustee, Homes for the Blind (Northern Ireland); Chairman, many professional bodies. **Publications:** Various professional papers.

GREGOROWSKI, William Reinhold (1939) Born 10 June 1921, Rosehill, Herschel Walk, Kenilworth, Cape Province, South Africa; son of Lennox Fyfe Gregorowski, Advocate, and Mary Craig Russell. **Subject(s):** Economics; BA 1947; MA 1950. **Tutor(s):** C W Guillebaud. **Educ:** Waterkloof House Preparatory School, Pretoria, South Africa; Diocesan College, Rondebosch, South Africa.

GREGORY, Alan Thomas (1946) Born 13 October 1925, 1 Oriental Street, Poplar, London; son of Lloyd Thomas Gregory, Ship's Butcher, and Florence Eugenie Abbott; m (1) Pamela Douglas Scott, 1952 (d 1986), (2) Marion Newth (née Nash), 1988; (1) 1 son, 2 daughters. **Subject(s):** Classics; BA 1948; MA 1978. **Tutor(s):** R L Howland. **Educ:** Thomas Street Junior School; Dulwich College. **Career:** Directed on to coal mining on conscription 1944–1946; Ministry of Power 1948–1970; British Petroleum 1971; General Manager, BP Italiana 1972–1973; Director, Government and Public Affairs 1975–1985; Director, BP UK and Ireland 1980–1985 (Chairman, BP Oil Ltd 1981–1985; Director, BP Chemical International Ltd 1984–1985); National Home Loans Corporation 1985–1991; Director, Willis Corroon (formerly Willis Faber) plc 1987–1997. **Appointments:** Member, Industrial and Economic Affairs Committee, General Synod 1980–1985; Churchwarden, St Mary's, Stoke D'Abernon, Surrey 1988–1990; Chairman, NATO Petroleum Planning Committee 1967–1970; Governor, Queen Mary College, London University 1981–1987; President, Institution of Petroleum 1982–1984; University Commissioner 1988–1995; Chairman, Willis Faber Pension Trustees Board 1992–1997; National Home Loans Corporation 1985–1991. **Awards:** Hawkesbury Burberry Prize 1948; Exhibition, SJC 1943. **Honours:** CBE 1984.

GREGORY, Arthur Reginald (1909) Born 12 May 1890, 9 Grove Place, Weston-Super-Mare, Somerset; son of Arthur William Gregory, Commercial Traveller, and Angel Beatrice Weeks. **Subject(s):** Natural Sciences; BA 1912. **Tutor(s):** J R Tanner. **Educ:** St Olave's School, Southwark. **Career:** Captain, Border Regiment (TF) (wounded), WWI. Died 19 October 1967.

GREGORY, Donald Leonard (1930) Born 12 June 1911, Coogee, Ragstone Road, Slough; son of Leonard Gregory, Head Postmaster, and Beryl Darvill. **Subject(s):** History/Classics; BA 1933; MA 1937. **Tutor(s):** M P Charlesworth. **Educ:** Intermediate School, Llandrindod Wells; The Cathedral School, Hereford. **Career:** Lecturer, School of Education, University of Manchester 1959. **Awards:** Somerset Exhibition, SJC 1929.

GREGORY, Dr Eric (1945) Born 5 January 1928, 99 Harvey Lane, Golborne, Lancashire; son of Henry Percy Gregory, Steelworks Salesman, and Ellen Waterworth. **Subject(s):** Natural Sciences; BA 1948; MA 1952; PhD 1954. **Tutor(s):** C W Guillebaud. **Johnian Relatives:** brother of Frank Gregory (1939). **Educ:** Arnold School, Blackpool. **Awards:** Economic Co-operation Administration Technical Assistance Programme Scholarship to Michigan University, 1951.

GREGORY, Frank (1939) Born 12 December 1920, 14 Charles Street, Golborne, Warrington, Lancashire; son of Henry Percy Gregory, Iron and Steel Salesman, and Ellen Waterworth; m (1) Mary McNaught, 11 March 1944 (div 1963), (2) Gillian Weston Perkins, 30 January 1965; 1 son (Nigel Peter b 1967), 1 daughter (Clare Elizabeth b 1969).

Subject(s): Mathematics; BA 1942; MA 1946. **Tutor(s):** J M Wordie. **Johnian Relatives:** brother of Eric Gregory (1945). **Educ:** Arnold Preparatory School, Blackpool; Arnold Senior School, Blackpool. **Career:** Army, RE (final rank of Captain) 1940–1946; Commercial Department, Rio Tinto Plc, London 1948–1974; Managing Director and Chief Executive, Sogemin Ltd, London 1974–1985.

GREGORY, Professor Geoffrey (1949) Born 14 March 1929, 4 Osborne Grove, Stockport Etchells, Cheshire; son of Gilbert Gregory, Municipal Clerk, and Minnie Louisa Haag; m Brenda Syers; 3 daughters (Janet Ruth, Sarah Helen and Katherine Anne). **Subject(s):** Maths; BA 1952; MA 1956; PhD (Stanford). **Tutor(s):** J M Wordie. **Educ:** Orchard Preparatory School, Gatley; Shadow Moss Elementary School, Moss Nook, Manchester; Manchester Grammar School. **Career:** Staff Tutor, Institute for Engineering Production, University of Birmingham 1957–1959; Senior Lecturer in Statistics, University of Melbourne 1959–1968; Senior Research Fellow in Operational Research, University of Lancaster 1968–1972; Professor of Management Science, Loughborough University of Technology 1973–1990. **Appointments:** British Aerospace Visiting Professor in Management Science, Universiti Utara, Malaysia 1992; Commonwealth Secretariat Visiting Professor in Management Science, Universiti Brunei, Darussalam 1996. **Awards:** Baylis Scholarship, SJC 1946. **Publications:** *Mathematical Methods in Management*, John Wiley & Sons, 1983; *Decision Analysis*, Pitman, 1988; numerous articles in professional journals.

GREGORY, John Henry (1921) Born 17 March 1904, 23 High Street, Highgate, St Pancras, Middlesex; son of Henry Lonsdale Gregory, Physician and Surgeon, and Mary Elizabeth Munsey. **Tutor(s):** B F Armitage. **Johnian Relatives:** son of Henry Lonsdale Gregory (1891). **Educ:** Cholmeley School, Highgate. Died 30 September 1923.

GREGORY, William Charles Edward (1947) Born 15 April 1903, 32 Mansel Street, Briton Ferry, Glamorganshire; son of Charles Edward Gregory, Barber, and Gwladys Hall; 3 daughters. **Subject(s):** Economics; BA 1949; MA 1954. **Educ:** Neath Road Elementary School, Briton Ferry. **Career:** Itinerant Barber, Wales and USA 1917–1940; Ambulance Driver, Civil Defence 1940–1942; Lecturer to HM Forces 1942–1946; Editor, *Man and Metal*, 1946–1947; Organising Tutor, Extra-Mural Studies, University College, Cardiff 1959.

GREGORY-SMITH, The Revd Thomas Gregory (1927) See SMITH.

GREGSON, Howard Davenport (1946) Born 8 September 1923, 6 Highfield Avenue, Golders Green, Middlesex; son of William Gregson, Mechanical and Marine Engineer, and Isabelle Mary Davenport; m Susan Lunn, 1956; 1 son (Peter), 2 daughters (Nicola and Philippa). **Subject(s):** Mechanical Sciences; BA 1948; MA 1958; MICE; CEng. **Tutor(s):** R L Howland. **Educ:** The Hall, Hampstead; Colet Court, Hammersmith; St Paul's School. **Career:** Commissioned, RE 1943; served NW Europe 1944–1945; Adjutant, 61st Division, RE 1946; Instructor, Mons Officer Cadet School 1948–1951; Second in command, 32 Fortress Squadron, Gibraltar 1951–1953; Instructor, Royal School of Military Engineering 1953–1955; OC 50 Field Squadron 1956; Long Civil Engineering Course, RSME 1956–1958; DCRE, Dharan, Nepal 1958–1959; Staff of Command Works Officer, Singapore 1959–1961; OC 65 Corps Field Park Squadron 1961–1963; BAOR, TSO II, RARDE 1963–1964; Assistant Master 1964–1968, Housemaster 1968–1978, Careers Master 1978–1984, Cranleigh School; Assistant Master, Rosemead School, Littlehampton 1984–1988.

GREIG, Murray Thomson (1936) Born 23 April 1908, Kirin, Manchukuo, China; son of James Alexander Greig, Medical Practitioner, and Isabella Thomson Wallace. BSc (New Zealand); MB (New Zealand); ChB (New Zealand); FRCS England; FRACS. **Educ:** Wellington College, New Zealand; Victoria University College, New Zealand; Otago University College, New Zealand. **Career:** University Demonstrator in Anatomy; Surgeon, Waikato Hospital, Hamilton, New Zealand 1948–1973. Died 19 March 2000.

GRIBBIN, Brigadier Kenneth David (1938) Born 8 April 1919, Oxford; son of Thomas Mangnall Gribbin, Clerk in Holy Orders, and Edith Fanny Hoare; m Marian Senior, July 1945, Jerusalem; 1 son (b 1949), 1 daughter (b 1946). **Subject(s):** Mathematics/Mechanical Sciences; BA 1949; MA 1966; CEng; MIEE. **Tutor(s):** J M Wordie. **Educ:** Ladybarn House Preparatory School, Manchester; Gadebridge Park, Hemel Hempstead; Marlborough College. **Career:** Commissioned Second Lieutenant, Royal Signals, Middle East and Italy 1939–1946; Army Staff College, Haifa 1945; Joint Services Staff College Latimer 1956; Various staff appointments in Germany, Singapore and UK; Retired from Army as Brigadier 1969. **Appointments:** Secretary General, Cancer Research Campaign 1969–1984. **Awards:** Sizarship, SJC. **Honours:** MBE (Military) 1954; OBE (Civil) 1981.

GRICE, Dennis Neve (1930) Born 3 March 1912, 49 Webster Gardens, Ealing, Middlesex; son of Neve Joseph Grice, Leather Merchant, and Agnes Ethel Webster; m Margaret Peal. BA 1933. **Tutor(s):** M P Charlesworth. **Educ:** Stratton Park School; Uppingham School. **Career:** RAF 1931–1940 (commissioned Pilot Officer in Reserve of Air Force Officers 1931, promoted to Flying Officer, RAFVR 1932). Died 8 August 1940 (died as a result of air operations).

GRICE, Norman (1912) Born 14 April 1893, 1 Elmwood Place, Eccleshill, Bradford, Yorkshire; son of Septimus Jonathan Grice, Clerk, and Harriett Gale Tansley. **Tutor(s):** R P Gregory. **Educ:** Bradford Grammar School. **Career:** Captain, North Yorkshire Regiment (TF) (wounded three times), WWI.

GRIFFIN, Dr Ewart Maxse (1927) Born 21 August 1907, 53 Logan Road, Bristol; son of Richard Clarke Griffin, Baptist Minister, and Elizabeth Emily Batt; m Doreen Mary Shea, 16 July 1936, Uppingham. **Subject(s):** Natural Sciences; BA 1930; MA 1935; MB 1935; BChir 1935; MD 1947; MRCS 1933; LRCP 1933. **Tutor(s):** M P Charlesworth. **Educ:** Bishop Road Council School, Bristol; North Bristol Central School; Taunton School. **Career:** Factory Doctor, Uppingham District, Rutland 1952.

GRIFFITH, George Hugh Clarence (1948) Born 21 August 1929, Bridgetown, Barbados, British West Indies; son of Herman Clarence Griffith, Local Government Officer, Barbados, and Edith Glencora Griffith; m (1) Eileen Emrey, 1952, (2) Gerlinde Zimnick, 1972, Bahamas; (1) 2 daughters (Lesley b 1953 and Kim b 1967). **Subject(s):** Law; BA 1951; MA 1955; LLB 1958; LLM 1985. **Tutor(s):** J M Wordie. **Educ:** Wesley Hall School; Harrison College, Barbados. **Career:** Called to the Bar, Gray's Inn 1959; Parliamentary Counsel, Jamaica 1959–1968; Legal Draftsman, Bahamas 1968–1974; Parliamentary Counsel 1974–1983, Chief Parliamentary Counsel 1983–1997, Bermuda; Legal Consultant, Attorney-General's Chambers, Barbados 1997–. **Awards:** Barbados Scholarship 1947.

GRIFFITH, The Revd William Graham Allix (1919) Born 20 August 1898, The Rectory, Treswell, Nottinghamshire; son of William Haig Griffith, Clerk in Holy Orders, and Ethel Agnes Graham. **Subject(s):** Classics; BA 1921; MA 1926. **Tutor(s):** E A Benians. **Career:** Cadet 1917; North and Derby Regiment 1917, served in France 1918; BAOR, England and France 1918–1919; Lieutenant, 17th Battalion, Worcester Regiment, Rouelles 1919; Bishops' College, Cheshunt 1926; Deacon 1926; Curate, Beverley Minster 1926–1929; Priest 1927; Curate, Scarborough 1929–1934; Vicar, St John the Evangelist, Drypool 1934–1942; Vicar, Rudby, Cleveland with Middleton 1942–1947; Vicar, St Columba, Scarborough 1950–1962; Vicar, St Olave, York 1962. **Awards:** Lupton and Hebblethwaite Exhibition, SJC 1917.

GRIFFITHS, David Thomas (1920) Born 10 October 1896, Orchard Street, Brecknock, Wales; son of David Thomas Griffiths, Manual Instructor, Brecon Schools, and Alice Davis. BA 1922. **Tutor(s):** E A Benians. **Educ:** Mount Street School, Brecon; Brecon County School. **Career:** Probationer, Indian Forest Service (while at SJC); Deputy Conservator, Burma; Assistant Conservator, Indian Forest Service 1923; Officiating Deputy Conservator 1924.

GRIFFITHS, The Revd George Arthur Mence (1908) Born 18 March 1891, 4 Bournevale Road, Streatham, Surrey; son of Harry Griffiths, Wholesale Tea Dealer, and Florence Annie Parker; m Una Kathleen. **Subject(s):** History; BA 1911; MA 1915. **Tutor(s):** E E Sikes. **Educ:** Laleham School, Margate; University College, Aberystwyth; Ripon Clergy College; Clergy Training School, Cambridge. **Career:** Ordained Deacon 1914; CF, 4th Class, RACD, WWI; Curate, St Matthew, Hammersmith 1914–1917; Priest 1915; Curate, Tring 1918–1920; Curate, St John the Divine, Chatham 1920–1921; Curate, St John the Baptist, Margate 1921–1928; Vicar, Bearsted, Kent 1928–1940; Vicar, St Giles in the Wood, Devon 1940–1946; Vicar, Lynton 1946–1949; Curate, Wrington, Somerset 1949–1956. Died 28 October 1965.

GRIFFITHS, Gordon Craven (1924) Born 16 June 1905, 38 Melville Road, Edgbaston, Birmingham; son of Alfred Cornforth Griffiths, Stockbroker, and Beatrice Emily Craven. **Tutor(s):** E E Sikes. **Educ:** Church of England College, Edgbaston; West House School, Edgbaston; St Andrews, Eastbourne; Malvern College.

GRIFFITHS, The Revd Hugh Peregrine (1909) Born 9 August 1890, Prospect House, Bishop's Castle, Shropshire; son of William Henry Griffiths, Clerk in Holy Orders, and Mary Newill. **Subject(s):** Theology; BA 1912; MA 1918. **Tutor(s):** J R Tanner. **Educ:** Merchant Taylors' School; Ridley Hall, Cambridge. **Career:** Deacon 1913; Curate, Braintree 1913–1918; Priest 1914; Curate, St Peter, Clerkenwell 1918–1921; Curate, Holy Trinity, Richmond 1921–1923; Chaplain and Director, Allen Gardner Memorial Institute, South American Missionary Society, Los Cocos 1923–1929; Curate, St Paul, St Albans 1929–1930; Vicar, St Minver with St Michael and St Enodoc, Wadebridge 1930–1946; Vicar, Axmouth, Devon 1946.

GRIFFITHS, John David (1944) Born 28 October 1926, St Aubin, West Avenue, Stockton Heath, Cheshire; son of John Calvert Griffiths, Wholesale Drapery Sales Manager, and Nellie Foers Bennett. **Tutor(s):** C W Guillebaud. **Educ:** Stockton Lodge Preparatory School; Wade Deacon Grammar School, Widnes.

GRIFFITHS, Dr Peter (1946) Born 22 February 1928, 1 High Street, Clydach Vale, Rhondda, Glamorgan; son of William Griffiths, Grocer, and Elsie Florence Love; m Gwyneth Margaret Roberts, 11 July 1953, Holy Trinity Church, Cambridge; 1 son (Hugh b 1957), 2 daughters (Jane b 1954 and Ruth b 1955). **Subject(s):** Natural Sciences; BA 1949; MA 1953; MB 1952; BChir 1952; DObstRCOG 1957. **Tutor(s):** G C L Bertram. **Educ:** Cwmclydach Elementary School, Clydach Vale; Porth County School; Pontypridd Grammar School. **Career:** House Surgeon, All Saints Urological Centre, Southwark 1952–1953; Short Service Commission as Station MO, 11 Group, Fighter Command, RAF 1953–1956; House Surgeon, Luton Maternity Hospital 1956–1957; Trainee GP, Wood Green, London 1957–1958; Assistant GP, Bletchley, Buckinghamshire 1958–1959; GP, Principal, Wickford, Essex 1959–1992.

GRIFFITHS, Rt Hon the Lord William Hugh (1942) Born 26 September 1923, 90 Harley Street, London; son of Sir Hugh Ernest Griffiths, Consulting Surgeon, and Doris Eirene Griffiths; m (1) Evelyn Krefting, 1949 (d 1998), (2) Heather, Baroness Brigstocke, January 2000; (1) 1 son, 3 daughters. **Subject(s):** Law; BA 1948; MA 1965; Honorary LLD (Wales) 1987; Honorary LLD (De Montfort) 1993; QC 1964. **Tutor(s):** S J Bailey. **Educ:** Arnold House, St John's Wood; Charterhouse. **Career:** Welsh Guards 1942–1946; Called to the Bar, Inner Temple 1949; Recorder of Margate 1962–1964; Recorder of Cambridge 1964–1970; Member, Advisory Council on Penal Reform 1967–1970; Treasurer of the Bar Council 1968–1969; Bencher 1971; Judge of the High Court of Justice, Queen's Bench Division 1971–1980; Judge, National Industrial Relations Court 1973–1974; Vice-Chairman, Parole Board 1976–1977;

Member, Chancellor's Law Reform Committee 1976–1993; Lord Justice of Appeal 1980–1985; Chairman, Security Commission 1985–1992; Lord of Appeal in Ordinary 1985–1993. **Appointments:** Honorary Fellow, SJC 1985; Chairman, Tribunal of Inquiry on Ronan Point 1968; Honorary Member, Canadian Bar Association 1981; President, Senate of the Inns of Court and the Bar 1982–1984; Honorary Fellow, American Institute of Judicial Administration 1985; American College of Trial Lawyers 1988; President, MCC 1991–1992; Captain, Royal and Ancient Golf Club 1993–1994; Chairman, Lord Chancellor's Advisory Committee on Legal Education and Conduct 1991–1993. **Honours:** MC 1944; Kt 1971; Privy Counsellor 1980; Baron (Life Peer) 1985.

GRIGG, Sir Percy James (1909) Born 16 December 1890, 4 Danby Terrace, Withycombe Raleigh, Exmouth, Devon; son of Frank Alfred Grigg, Builder, and Jane Elizabeth Crocker; m Gertrude Charlotte Hough, 1919. **Subject(s):** Mathematics; BA 1912; MA 1943; Honorary LLD (Bristol) 1946. **Tutor(s):** L H K Bushe-Fox. **Educ:** British Elementary School, Boscombe; Bournemouth. **Career:** British Executive Director, International Bank for Reconstruction and Development; RGA; Treasury 1913; Principal Private Secretary to the Chancellors of the Exchequer 1921–1930; Chairman, Board of Customs and Excise 1930; Chairman, Board of Inland Revenue 1930–1934; Finance Member, Government of India 1934–1939; Permanent Under-Secretary of State for War 1939–1942; Secretary of State for War 1942–1945; MP (National Party), East Cardiff 1942–1945; Director, Imperial Tobacco Company 1947; Director, Prudential Assurance Company 1948; Director, National Provincial Bank 1949 (Deputy Chairman 1957); Director, Distillers Company 1950; Chairman, Bass, Mitchells and Butlers 1961. **Appointments:** Honorary Fellow 1943; Honorary Master of the Bench, Middle Temple 1953. **Honours:** KCB 1932; KCSI 1936. **Publications:** *Prejudice and Judgement.* Died 5 May 1964.

GRIGSON, Pawlet St John Baseley (1901) Born 12 June 1882, Rickinhall Inferior, Suffolk; son of Baseley Hales Grigson, Clerk in Holy Orders, and Annette Hammond Wigg; m Kathleen Monica Bagnall, 16 September 1919, All Saints', Great Fransham. BA 1904. **Tutor(s):** D MacAlister. **Educ:** Bury St Edmunds Grammar School. **Career:** Bombay and Burma Trading Corporation 1908; Captain, IARO, attached 70th Burma Rifles, WWI. Died 12 April 1952.

GRIMES, The Revd Gerald Hubert (1902) Born 4 June 1883, The Vicarage, Stanton upon Hine Heath, Shropshire; son of Patrick Grimes, Clerk in Holy Orders, and Sarah Tabberer Bloor. BA 1905; MA 1932. **Tutor(s):** E E Sikes. **Johnian Relatives:** brother of Henry Sydney King Grimes (1902). **Educ:** King's School, Chester; Hereford Cathedral School. **Career:** Ordained Deacon 1908; Curate, Much Wenlock 1908–1913; Priest 1909; Vicar, Lee Brockhurst 1917–1947; Chaplain to the Wem Union 1921–1935; Vicar, Battlefield with Albrighton, Shropshire 1943.

GRIMES, Henry Sydney King (1902) (admitted to Jesus College 1901) Born 22 August 1881, The Vicarage, Stanton upon Hine Heath, Shropshire; son of Patrick Grimes, Clerk in Holy Orders, and Sarah Tabberer Bloor. BA (Jesus) 1910. **Tutor(s):** E E Sikes. **Johnian Relatives:** brother of Gerald Hubert Grimes (1902). **Educ:** King's School, Chester; Hereford Cathedral School.

GRIMSDELL, Eric Hedley McKenzie (1926) Born 8 May 1909, 21a Sedgemere Villas, East End Road, East Finchley, Middlesex; son of Ernest Hedley Grimsdell, Wholesale Manufacturing Optician, and Ada McKenzie. BA 1930. **Tutor(s):** C W Guillebaud. **Johnian Relatives:** brother of Richard Lucian Grimsdell (1930). **Educ:** Fern Bank, Finchley; Tenlerden Hall, Henden; Mill Hill School.

GRIMSDELL, Richard Lucian (1930) Born 16 September 1913, Grasmere, Windermere Avenue, Finchley, Middlesex; son of Ernest Hedley Grimsdell, Wholesale Manufacturing Optician, and Ada McKenzie. BA 1934. **Tutor(s):** M P Charlesworth. **Johnian Relatives:**

brother of Eric Hedley McKenzie Grimsdell (1926). **Educ:** Fern Bank, Church End, Finchley; Tenterden Hall, Hendon; Mill Hill School.

GRINT, Leslie Alfred (1940) Born 26 December 1921, The Corner, Lound, Lowestoft, Suffolk; son of Arthur Grint, Engine Driver, and Alice Louisa James; m Margaret Evans, 29 July 1950. **Subject(s):** Classics/Moral Sciences; BA 1947. **Tutor(s):** R L Howland. **Educ:** Lound Voluntary School; Lowestoft Secondary School. **Career:** Appointments Officer, University of York. **Awards:** Burney Prize, University of Cambridge 1950. Died 31 May 1971.

GROSE, Richard John Hicks (1938) Born 1 August 1919, Wimblish Hall, Saffron Walden, Essex; son of Henry Hicks Grose, Farmer and Forage Merchant, and Kathleen Margaret Hayes. **Subject(s):** Law; BA 1941; MA 1945. **Tutor(s):** R L Howland. **Educ:** Newport Grammar School; Walden Grammar School; Wycliffe College, Stonehouse. **Career:** Called to the Bar, Middle Temple 1948.

GROSS, Dauve (1947) Born 12 August 1925, 69 Finch Road, Handsworth, Birmingham; son of Gershon Gross, Manufacturer's Agent, and Bertha Gluckin; m Jane. **Subject(s):** Law; BA 1949; LLB 1950. **Educ:** Westminster Road Council School; Birmingham Hebrew School; King Edward's High School, Birmingham. **Career:** Solicitor. Died 11 July 1991.

GROVE, Leslie Stevenson (1938) Born 15 August 1919, Cartref, Market Street, Kingswinford; son of Harold Victor Grove, Steel Works Representative, and Ethel Mary Bowdler. **Subject(s):** History; BA 1941; MA 1946. **Tutor(s):** J S Boys Smith. **Educ:** Church of England Elementary School, Kingswinford; King Edward's School, Stourbridge. **Career:** Director of Personnel, Industrial Electrical Division, Tube Investments. Died 20 October 1980.

GRUBB, John Burlingham (1925) Born 28 September 1906, The Croft, Burnt Green, Alvechurch, Worcestershire; son of David Burlingham Grubb, Company Director, and Marian Poynting. **Subject(s):** English/Modern and Medieval Languages; BA 1929. **Tutor(s):** E E Sikes. **Educ:** Downs School, Colwall; Brunnaker School, King's Norton; Bootham School, York. **Awards:** Scholarship, SJC 1924.

GUEST, Dr George Howell (1947) Born 9 February 1924, 18 Friars Avenue, Bangor, North Wales; son of Ernest Joseph Guest, Commercial Traveller, and Gwendolen Brown; m Nancy (Nan) Talbot, 1959; 1 son (David Stephen Benedict b 8 June 1963), 1 daughter (Elizabeth Mary Helen b 11 October 1965). **Subject(s):** Music; BA 1949; MA 1954; MusB 1950; MusD (Lambeth) 1977; Honorary DMus (Wales) 1989; FRCO 1942. **Tutor(s):** C W Guillebaud. **Johnian Relatives:** father of David Stephen Benedict Guest (1982); father-in-law of Catherine Jane Boulton (1983). **Educ:** Friars School, Bangor; Chester Cathedral Choir School; King's School, Chester. **Career:** RAF 1942–1946; Sub-Organist, Chester Cathedral 1944–1947; Organist and Choirmaster 1951–1991, Title B Fellow, Lecturer in Music 1956–1988, Title D Fellow 1988–2002, SJC; Assistant Lecturer in Music 1953–1956, Lecturer in Music 1956–1982, University of Cambridge. **Appointments:** Supervisor and Director of Studies in Music, SJC 1956–1988; Examiner, Associated Board of Royal Schools of Music 1959–1992; Council Member, Royal College of Organists 1964; Director, Berkshire Boys Choir, USA 1967 and 1970; Honorary FRSCM 1973; University Organist 1974–1991; Aelod er Anrhydedd, Gorsedd y Beirdd Eisteddfod Genedlaethol Cymru 1977; Director, Arts Theatre, Cambridge 1977–1990; President, Royal College of Organists 1978–1980; President, Cathedral Organists' Association 1980–1982; Council Member, RSCM 1983–1999; President, Friends of Cathedral Music 1983; Director, Côr Cenedlaethol Ieuenctid Cymru 1984; Artistic Director, Llandaf Festival 1985; President, Incorporated Association of Organists 1987–1989; Honorary Fellow, University of Wales, Bangor; Honorary Fellow, Royal Canadian College of Organists 1991; Honorary Fellow, Welsh College of Music and Drama 1992; Honorary Fellow, University of Wales, Aberystwyth; Honorary Member,

RAM; conducted concerts and seminars in the USA, Canada, Japan, Australia, Brazil, South Africa, Patagonia (Argentina), the Philippines, the USSR and most European countries. **Awards:** John Stewart of Rannoch Scholarship in Sacred Music, University of Cambridge 1948; John Edwards Memorial Award, Guild for Promotion of Welsh Music 1989. **Honours:** CBE 1987. Died 20 November 2002.

GUEST-WILLIAMS, The Revd Alyn Arthur (1907) Born 22 January 1888, King's School, South Street, Durham; son of Samuel Blackwell Guest-Williams, Clerk in Holy Orders, and Catherine Gray; m Harriett Beeching (d 1949), 19 June 1917, Norwich Cathedral. BA 1910; MA 1914. **Tutor(s):** E E Sikes. **Johnian Relatives:** brother of Warren Kirkham Guest-Williams (1906). **Educ:** Durham School. **Career:** Ordained Deacon 1911; Curate, Binfield 1911–1914; Ordained Priest 1912; Minor Canon and Precentor, Norwich Cathedral 1914–1919; Officiating Minister, Norwich War Hospital 1917–1918; Rector, Trowell 1919–1926; Rector, Christleton, Cheshire 1926–1949. **Awards:** Choral Studentship, SJC. Died 26 June 1974.

GUEST-WILLIAMS, Warren Kirkham (1906) Born 11 November 1886, The Schools, South Street, Durham; son of Samuel Blackwell Guest-Williams, Clerk in Holy Orders, and Catherine Gray. **Subject(s):** Classics; BA 1909. **Tutor(s):** E E Sikes. **Johnian Relatives:** brother of Alyn Arthur Guest-Williams (1907). **Educ:** Durham School. **Career:** Assistant Superintendent, Public Works Department, India, then Assistant Traffic Superintendent, Indian State Railways 1911; Captain, RTO, and DADRT, East Bengal IRV Rifles until 1920. Died 10 December 1920.

GUGENHEIM, Peter Gerhard Arthur Fritz (1941) Born 6 August 1921, Berlin, Germany; son of Hans Gugenheim, in Commerce, and Klara Lucie Gerson. **Subject(s):** Natural Sciences. **Tutor(s):** J M Wordie. **Educ:** Private Preparatory School, Berlin; Collége Royal Français, Berlin; Cheltenham College. Died September 1970.

GUILLEBAUD, Claude William (1909) Born 2 July 1890, The Rectory, Yatesbury, Calne, Wiltshire; son of Erneste Delabere Guillebaud, Clerk in Holy Orders, and Mabel Louisa Marshall; m Marie Therese Prunner; 2 daughters (Philomena b 22 July 1926 and Claudia b 5 October 1929). **Subject(s):** Economics; BA 1912; MA 1916. **Tutor(s):** J R Tanner. **Johnian Relatives:** nephew of Alfred Marshall (1861); twin brother of Walter Henry Guillebaud (1909); uncle of Peter Delabere Guillebaud (1932); second cousin, once removed, of John Rodney Dingle (1949); great uncle of John Guillebaud (1958). **Educ:** Repton School; Hulme Hall, University of Manchester. **Career:** Title A Fellow 1915, Title B Fellow 1926–1957, Lecturer in Economics 1946–1957, Title D Fellow 1957–1971, SJC; Lecturer in Economics and Politics 1926–1945, Lecturer in Economics 1945–1955, Reader in Economics and Politics 1956–1957, University of Cambridge. **Appointments:** Supervisor in Economics 1921–1947, Assistant Tutor 1926–1929, Praelector 1926–1929, Tutor 1929–1956, Director of Studies in Economics 1935–1957, Senior Tutor 1953–1956, SJC; Supreme Economic Council, Paris 1919–1920; Secretary, Committee on Prices under Profiteering Acts 1920–1922; Senior Proctor 1932–1933, University of Cambridge; Chairman, numerous Wages Boards/Councils 1940–1955; Chairman, Court of Inquiry into Railway Wages 1951; Member, Industrial Disputes Tribunal 1952; Member, Royal Commission on Scottish Affairs 1954; Independent Member, Agricultural Wages Boards for England, Wales, and Scotland 1956; Chairman, Committee of Inquiry into the Cost of the National Health Service 1956; Chairman, Railway Pay Committee of Inquiry 1960. **Awards:** Adam Smith Prize, University of Cambridge 1915. **Honours:** CBE 1948. **Publications:** Th*e Works Council: A German Experiment in Industrial Democracy*, 1928; *The Economic Recovery of Germany 1933–1938*, 1939; (ed) *Cambridge Economic Handbook, 1946–1958*; (ed) *Alfred Marshall, Principles of Economics*, Variorum Edition, 1961; *The Wages Council System in Great Britain*, 2nd edition, 1962; *Economic Survey of the Sisal Industry of Tanganyika*, 2nd edition, 1967; *The Role of the Arbitrator in Industrial Wage Disputes*, 1970. Died 23 August 1971.

GUILLEBAUD, Peter Delabere (1932) Born 19 April 1914, Combe Royal, Bath; son of Harold Ernest Guillebaud, Archdeacon of Ruanda-Urundi, Missionary and Bible Translator, and Margaret Lindesay Gamul Edwards. **Subject(s):** Mathematics; BA 1935; MA 1939. **Tutor(s):** J M Wordie. **Johnian Relatives:** nephew of Claude William Guillebaud (1909) and of Walter Henry Guillebaud (1909); father of John Guillebaud (1958). **Educ:** Monkton Combe Junior School; Monkton Combe School. **Career:** Bible Translator and Missionary with Church Mission Society 1940–1980; Founder of first Protestant Secondary School in Rwanda (then Ruanda-Urundi). Died 7 November 1996.

GUILLEBAUD, Walter Henry (1909) Born 2 July 1890, The Rectory, Yatesbury, Calne, Wiltshire; son of Erneste Delabere Guillebaud, Clerk in Holy Orders, and Mabel Louisa Marshall; m (1) Alice Betty Stocks, 1916 (d 1919), (2) Dorothy Joyce Young, 1921; 2 daughters (Jean Margaret b 1923 and Alison Ruth b 1925). **Subject(s):** Natural Sciences; BA 1912; Diploma in Agriculture; Diploma in Forestry. **Tutor(s):** J R Tanner. **Johnian Relatives:** nephew of Alfred Marshall (1861); twin brother of Claude William Guillebaud (1909); uncle of Peter Delabere Guillebaud (1932); second cousin, once removed, of John Rodney Dingle (1949); great uncle of John Guillebaud (1958). **Educ:** Repton School; Hulme Hall, University of Manchester. **Career:** Assistant Inspector, Board of Agriculture and Fisheries 1914–1919; Forestry Commission: Research Officer 1919 (later Chief Research Officer), Deputy Surveyor in charge of the Forest of Dean 1939–1943, Director of Research and Education 1943, Deputy Director-General 1948. **Appointments:** Secretary, Congregational Church, Gerrards Cross 1944; Secretary, Retired Men's Club, Gerrards Cross 1949. **Honours:** CBE 1951. Died November 1973.

GUINNESS, The Revd Canon Gordon Meyer (1920) Born 1 April 1902, 51 Bow Road, Bow, London; son of Henry Grattan Guinness, Doctor of Medicine, and Annie Reed; m Grace Bewes, 12 September 1935, St John's Church, Tunbridge Wells; 3 sons (Robin b 7 March 1938, Garry b 27 September 1940 and Christopher b 5 February 1943), 2 daughters (Ann b 20 August 1936 and Dawn b 18 January 1946). **Subjects:** History/Theology; BA 1924; MA 1928. **Tutor(s):** E A Benians. **Johnian Relatives:** father of Robin Gordon Guinness (1957). **Educ:** Dulwich College; The Leys School, Cambridge; Ridley Hall, Cambridge. **Career:** Missionary to India and Nepal; Ordained Deacon 1925; Curate, St Saviour, Stoke next Guilford 1925–1927; Ordained Priest 1926; Secretary, Regions Beyond Missionary Union 1927–1928; Curate, St John, Tunbridge Wells 1929–1933; Curate in Charge, Bishop Hannington Memorial District, Hove 1934–1939; Minister 1939–1943; Vicar, St John, Tunbridge Wells 1943–1951; Vicar, St John the Evangelist, Boscombe 1951–1966; Vicar, Christ Church, Winchester 1965–1971. **Appointments:** Honorary Canon, Winchester Cathedral 1964–1971 (Emeritus 1971). **Publications:** *Israel, Egypt, Russia and God* (pamphlet); *The Quest for the Nepal Border*, Marshall & Co, 1928. Died February 1980.

GUISE, Charles Alexander Leonard (1932) Born 31 July 1907, Burleigh, Minchin Hampton, Gloucestershire; son of John Dougal Guise, East India Merchant, and Laura Lilian Buckland; MA (inc) 1932. **Tutor(s):** R L Howland. **Educ:** Winton House, Winchester; Winchester College; Trinity College, Oxford.

GUNN, Sir John Currie (1937) Born 13 September 1916, 19 Kelvinside Gardens, East Glasgow; son of Richard Robertson Gunn, Merchant Taylor, and Jane Blair Currie; m Betty Russum 1944 (d January 2002); 1 son (John Michael Ferguson b 8 June 1954). **Subject(s):** Mathematics; BA 1939; MA 1946; MA (Glasgow) 1937; Honorary DSc (Loughborough); DUniv (Open University) 1989; FRSE 1959. **Tutor(s):** J M Wordie. **Johnian Relatives:** father of John Michael Ferguson Gunn (1975). **Educ:** Glasgow Academy; Glasgow University. **Career:** Title A Fellow, SJC 1943–1948 (suspended for War Service 1943–1945; supernumerary 1945–1948); Admiralty, WWII; Lecturer in Mathematics,

University of Manchester 1945–1946; Department of Applied Mathematics, UCL 1946–1949; Cargill Professor of Natural Philosophy 1949–1982, Head of Department 1973–1982, Dean of Faculties 1989–1991, University of Glasgow. **Appointments:** Member, Glasgow University Court 1966–1971; UK Delegate to CERN Council 1966–1968; Member, SRC 1968–1972; Member, Open University, Academic Advisory Committee 1970; Member Computer Board 1971–1978. **Awards:** Mayhew Prize, University of Cambridge; Glazebrook Medal, Institute of Physics 1984. **Honours:** CBE 1976; Kt 1982. **Publications:** Papers on mathematical physics in various scientific journals. Died 26 July 2002.

GUNN, Sidney George (1932) Born 30 March 1913, Crosses Road, Long Sutton, Lincolnshire; son of Walter Gunn, Fruit Grower, and Clara Louisa Milnes; m Leah, 1940; 3 sons (Michael, Stuart and Andrew). **Subject(s):** Modern and Medieval Languages; BA 1935. **Tutor(s):** J S Boys Smith. **Educ:** Long Sutton Council School; The Grammar School, Spalding. **Career:** Head of Modern Languages, Lancaster Royal Grammar School 1938–1978; War service, RN, Telegraphist in North Atlantic, then Lieutenant, France and India. **Appointments:** Member, Lincoln Wellington Athletic Club (represented England in 1 mile run 1938). Died 27 January 2003.

GUNSON, Gerald (1946) Born 25 July 1926, 7 Diamond Terrace, Agbrigg Road, Wakefield, Yorkshire; son of George Herbert Gunson, Surveyor to the County Council, and Alice May Pepper. **Subject(s):** Natural Sciences; BA 1948; MA 1953. **Tutor(s):** R L Howland. **Educ:** Starbeck School; Snapethorpe School; Silcoates School; Royal Naval Courses, University of Edinburgh; Loughborough College; Engineering College, Keyham. Died March 1984.

GUNSTON, David (1921) Born 16 June 1901, Warkworth Lodge, Warkworth Terrace, Cambridge; son of William Hewison Gunston, Mathematics Lecturer and Private Tutor, and Letitia Dougan; m Ethel Ross Miller, 8 April 1925, Great St Mary's, Cambridge. **Subject(s):** Mathematics/Mechanical Sciences; BA 1924; MA 1928. **Tutor(s):** E Cunningham. **Johnian Relatives:** son of William Hewison Gunston (1875); nephew of Thomas Wilson Dougan (1875). **Educ:** St Faith's School, Cambridge; Felsted School. **Career:** Baker, Perkins & Co Ltd, Westwood Works, Peterborough 1937. Died 3 July 1976.

GUPPY, Ronald James (1935) Born 7 July 1916, 84 Halkett Place, St Helier, Jersey; son of James George Guppy, Compositor, and Hilda May Journeaux; m Elsie Fuller, 1943; 1 son, 1 daughter. **Subject(s):** Mathematics; BA 1938. **Tutor(s):** J M Wordie. **Johnian Relatives:** father of Paul Michael Guppy (1967). **Educ:** St Luke's Elementary School, Jersey; Victoria College, Jersey. **Career:** Captain, RE, RA 1939–1945; Home Office; Private Secretary to two Home Secretaries 1946; Assistant Under-Secretary of State 1961; Assistant Under-Secretary of State for the Department of Education 1967–1969; Secretary to Royal Commission on the Constitution 1969–1973; Receiver for the Metropolitan Police District 1974–1976. **Awards:** Scholarship, SJC 1936–1937. **Honours:** CB 1967. Died 27 January 1977.

GURNEY, Maurice Patrick (1919) (Readmitted 1922) Born 12 June 1893, 15 Pond Terrace, Chelsea, London; son of Jason Gurney, Wine Merchant, and Marion Wilhelmina Adie. **Subject(s):** Modern and Medieval Languages; BA 1923. **Tutor(s):** E E Sikes. **Educ:** Belmont, Hove; Stonyhurst College; Mauresea, Roehampton; St Mary's Hall, Stonyhurst.

GURUSWAMI, Krishnaswami Reddiar (1912) Born 20 June 1894, Kannivadi, Dindigul Taluk, Madura, Madras Presidency, India; son of Krishnaswami Reddi, Landowner. **Subject(s):** Moral Sciences; BA 1916; MA 1928. **Tutor(s):** L H K Bushe-Fox. **Educ:** S R School, Kannivadi; Municipal High School, Dindigul, India; Pachaiyappa's College, Madras. **Publications:** 'Good God!', *The Eagle*, 36; 'The Sole Difference', *The Eagle*, 37; 'Rangan', *The Eagle*, 37; 'Kanthi', *The Eagle*, 38. Died March 1975.

GUTHRIE, Dr Colin Bain (1949) Born 2 March 1931, Samne, Peru; son of John Guthrie, Sugar Technologist, and Evelyne Francis Howard; m Kathleen Ann Pike, 23 October 1957. **Subject(s):** Mechanical Sciences/Engineering; BA 1952; PhD (Michigan). **Tutor(s):** R L Howland. **Educ:** Barrhead High School; Private School, Jamaica; Private School, Trinidad; The Lodge School, Barbados; Strathallan School; Michigan State University. Died 12 October 1998.

GUTHRIE-JONES, David (1935) Born 8 April 1917, Kooinda, Dolgelley, Merioneth, North Wales; son of Rowland Guthrie-Jones, Solicitor, and Mari Elizabeth Griffith; m Joyce Noble, 1946 (d 1967); 1 son, 2 daughters. **Subject(s):** Law; BA 1938; MA 1942. **Tutor(s):** C W Guillebaud. **Johnian Relatives:** brother of Edward Guthrie-Jones (1930) and of Griffith Winston Guthrie-Jones (1935); uncle of Edward Patrick Guthrie-Jones (1958). **Educ:** Dolgelley Grammar School; Bootham School, York. **Career:** Solicitor, London 1946–1987.

GUTHRIE-JONES, Edward (1930) Born 2 June 1912, Llysmynach, Dolgelley, Merioneth; son of Rowland Guthrie-Jones, Solicitor, and Mari Elizabeth Griffith; m Joan Lloyd Evans, July 1937, Horeb Chapel, Dyffryn Ardudwy, Merioneth; 2 sons (Edward Patrick b 19 June 1938 and David Ifan b 6 September 1943). BA 1934; MA 1938. **Tutor(s):** J M Wordie. **Johnian Relatives:** brother of David Guthrie-Jones (1935) and of Griffith Winston Guthrie-Jones (1935); father of Edward Patrick Guthrie-Jones (1958). **Educ:** Meithrinfa School, Aberystwyth; Dolgelly Grammar School; Bootham School, York. **Career:** Apprentice, Metropolitan Vickers Company Ltd, Manchester 1934–1936; Thornycroft Ltd until 1961; Midland Motor Cylinder Company until 1977. Died 6 December 1994.

GUTHRIE-JONES, Griffith Winston (1935) Born 24 September 1914, Kooinda, Dolgelley, Merioneth, North Wales; son of Rowland Guthrie-Jones, Solicitor, and Mari Elizabeth Griffith. **Subject(s):** History; BA 1937; MA 1941; MA (by incorporation); LLB (Wales); QC 1963. **Tutor(s):** C W Guillebaud. **Johnian Relatives:** brother of Edward Guthrie-Jones (1930) and of David Guthrie-Jones (1935); uncle of Edward Patrick Guthrie-Jones (1958). **Educ:** Dolgelley Grammar School; Bootham School, York; University College, Aberystwyth. **Career:** Called to the Bar, Gray's Inn 1939; War Service, North Africa and Italy, then Yugoslavia as the artillery observation end of combined operations 1939–1945; Major, staff of the Judge Advocate General, Germany 1945; Judge Advocate, Italy 1946; Deputy Chairman, Court of Quarter Sessions, Cumberland 1963. **Appointments:** Supporting Speaker, Election 1950–1951; Conservative and National Liberal Candidate, Wrexham Division, By-Election 1955. Died 4 August 1996.

GUTSELL, Leslie Charles (1930) Born 9 November 1911, 111 Marsala Road, Lewisham, Kent; son of Charles Alexander Gutsell, Draughtsman to Electrical Engineer, and Rose Evelyn Brush; BA 1933; MA 1937. **Tutor(s):** M P Charlesworth. **Educ:** London County Council School, East Dulwich; Alleyn's School, Dulwich. **Awards:** Choral Scholarship, SJC. Died 2 January 1983.

GUTTRIDGE, Professor George Herbert (1917) Born 6 August 1898, 18 Cavendish Square, Margaret Street, Hull, Yorkshire; son of Frederick William Hamilton Guttridge, United Methodist Minister, and Eleanor Cowley Peace; m Eleanor Mann. **Subject(s):** History; BA 1920; MA 1925. **Tutor(s):** E E Sikes. **Educ:** Wilmslow College; Nottingham High School. **Career:** Second Lieutenant, RGA 1917–1918; Lecturer in British Empire History, Board of Military Studies 1921–1922; Lecturer, Economics Tripos 1923–24; Choate Memorial Fellow, Harvard University 1922–1923; Assistant Professor of Modern History, University of California 1925–1931; Associate Professor, University of California 1931–1942; Professor of English History, University of California 1942–1958; Sather Professor of History, University of California 1958–1965. **Awards:** Prince Consort Prize,

University of Cambridge 1922. **Publications:** *Colonial Policy of William III*, 1922; *David Hartley, MP*, 1926; *American Correspondence of a Bristol Merchant*, 1934; *English Whiggism and the American Revolution*, 1942; *Early Career of Lord Rockingham*, 1952; *Correspondence of Edmund Burke, Vol III*, 1961. Died 7 February 1969.

GWILT, George David (1946) Born 11 November 1927, 39 Polwarth Gardens, Edinburgh, Scotland; son of Richard Lloyd Gwilt, Actuary, and Ethel Marjory Beveridge Mair; m Ann Dalton Sylvester, 1956; 3 sons (Richard, Philip and Christopher). **Subject(s):** Mathematics; BA 1949; MA 1953; FFA 1952; FBCS. **Tutor(s):** G C L Bertram. **Johnian Relatives:** brother of David William Gwilt (1951). **Educ:** Norland Place, London; Gillsland Park, Edinburgh; Edinburgh Academy; Dollar Academy; Dragon School, Oxford; St Mary's Preparatory School, Melrose; Sedbergh School. **Career:** Clerk 1949–1956, Assistant Official 1956–1957, Assistant Actuary 1957–1962, Statistician 1962–1964, Mechanisation Manager 1964–1969, Systems Manager 1969–1972, Deputy Pensions Manager 1972–1973, Pensions Actuary 1973–1977, Assistant General Manager and Pensions Manager 1977–1978, Assistant General Manager (finance) 1978–1979, General Manager 1979–1984, Chief Executive 1979–1988, Managing Director and Actuary 1984–1988, Standard Life Assurance Company; Deputy Chairman, Associated Scottish Life Offices 1986–1988; Special Advisor in Scotland, Citicorp 1989–1991. **Appointments:** Trustee, TSB, South of Scotland 1966–1983; Non-Executive Director, Hammerson Property Investment and Development Corporation 1979–1994; Non-Executive Director, European Assets Trust NV 1979–2000; President, Faculty of Actuaries 1981–1983; Member, Monopolies & Mergers Commission 1983–1987; Non-Executive Director, Scottish Mortgage and Trust 1983–1998; Convenor, Scottish Poetry Library Association 1988–2001; Non-Executive Director, Hodgson Martin 1989–2000. **Awards:** Major Scholarship, SJC 1945.

GWYN, John David (1939) Born 11 June 1922, Hillside, Cowbridge, Glamorganshire; son of Arthur William Gwyn, Solicitor, and Elsie Isabel David. **Subject(s):** Law; BA 1942. **Tutor(s):** S J Bailey. **Educ:** Pontfaen Primary School; Cowbridge Grammar School. **Career:** Lieutenant, Welch Regiment 1942–1943. **Awards:** MacMahon Law Studentship. Died 2 December 1943 (killed on active service in Italy).

GWYNN, Brian Purnell (1938) Born 25 February 1919, Dormansland, Lingfield, Surrey; son of William Purnell Gwynn, Colonel, RAMC, and Harriet Margaret Hutchinson; m Jennifer Mary Lorimer King, 1970. **Subject(s):** History; BA 1941; MA 1945. **Tutor(s):** J S Boys Smith. **Educ:** St Andrew's School, Tenby; Bedford School. **Career:** Company Secretary, Iranian Oil Participants 1978. **Awards:** Exhibition, SJC 1937. Died 4 January 1999.

GWYNNE, Hubert Llewelyn (1911) Born 2 May 1892, Westwood Road, Leek, Staffordshire; son of Clement Thomas Gwynne, Solicitor, and Mary Adeline Jones. **Subject(s):** History; BA 1914. **Tutor(s):** E E Sikes. **Educ:** Newcastle High School. **Career:** Articled to Arthur Shaw; Second Lieutenant, North Staffordshire Regiment 1915–1916. **Awards:** Subsizarship, SJC; McMahon Law Studentship 1916. Died 18 November 1916 (killed in action at Grandcourt).

GWYNNE-TIMOTHY, Kenneth Gordon Rupert (1949) Born 21 May 1925, Halifax, Nova Scotia; son of Gordon Ronald Gwynne-Timothy, Schoolmaster, and Dorothy Mabel Wilhelmena Zwicker; 1 son (John); 2 daughters (Heather and Janet). **Subject(s):** Law; BA 1951; MA 1955; LLB 1952; LLM 1985; BA (Toronto); QC 1966. **Tutor(s):** G C L Bertram. **Johnian Relatives:** uncle of Kenneth Gordon Gwynne-Timothy (1988). **Educ:** Crescent Preparatory School; University of Toronto Schools; Trinity College, University of Toronto. **Career:** Partner, Holden, Murdoch & Finlay; Called to the Bar, Gray's Inn 1953; Osgoode Hall (Ontario Bar) 1954; Adjunct Professor, Faculty of Management Studies, University of Toronto.

HABAKKUK, Sir Hrothgar John (1933) Born 13 May 1915, 42 Park Road, Barry; son of Evan Guest Habakkuk, Education Secretary, and Annie Bowen; m Mary Richards, 12 August 1948, Gloucester (d 16 August 2002); 1 son, 3 daughters. **Subject(s):** History; BA 1936; MA 1940; Honorary LittD 1973; Honorary DLitt (Wales) 1971, Honorary DLitt (Pennsylvania) 1975, Honorary DLitt (Kent) 1978, Honorary DLitt (Ulster) 1988; FBA 1965; FRHistS. **Tutor(s):** E A Benians. **Johnian Relatives:** father of David John Habakkuk (1968). **Educ:** The County School, Barry. **Career:** Fellow, Pembroke College, Cambridge 1938–1950; Temporary Civil Servant, Foreign Office 1940–1942; Board of Trade 1942–1946; University Lecturer, Faculty of Economics, University of Cambridge 1946–1950; Chichele Professor of Economic History, Oxford; Fellow, All Souls College 1950–1967; Principal, Jesus College, Oxford 1967–1984; Vice-Chancellor, Oxford University 1973–1977; President, UC Swansea 1975–1984; Pro Vice-Chancellor, Oxford University 1977–1983; Fellow, All Souls, Oxford 1988–2001. **Appointments:** Director of Studies in History and Librarian, Pembroke College, Cambridge 1946–1950; Member, Grigg Committee on Departmental Records 1952–1954; Visiting Lecturer, Harvard University 1954–1955; Member, Advisory Council on Public Records 1958–1970; Ford Research Professor, University of California, Berkeley 1962–1963; Member, SSRC 1967–1971; Member, National Libraries Committee 1968–1969; Honorary Fellow, SJC 1971; Honorary Fellow, Pembroke College 1973; Member, Administration Board, International Association of Universities 1975–1985; Chairman, Committee of Vice Chancellors and Principals of Universities of UK 1976–1977; President, Royal Historical Society 1976–1980; Chairman, Advisory Group on London Health Services 1980–1981; Chairman, Oxfordshire District Health Authority 1981–1984; Ford Lecturer 1984–1985; Honorary Fellow, University College Swansea 1991; Foreign Member, American Philosophical Society; Foreign Member, American Academy of Arts and Sciences; Honorary Fellow, All Souls, Oxford 2002. **Awards:** Strathcona Studentship, SJC 1937; Amy Mary Preston Read Scholarship 1938. **Honours:** Kt 1976. **Publications:** *American and British Technology in the Nineteenth Century*, 1962; *Population Growth and Economic Development since 1750*, 1971; *Landowners: marriage, debt and the estates system 1650–1950*, 1994; articles and reviews. Died 3 November 2002.

HABICH, Leopold Sylvester Morrice (1904) Born 12 October 1887, 5 Rogers Street, Cape Town, South Africa; son of Martin Carl Albert Habich, Agent, and Florence Cecilia Morrice. **Subject(s):** Natural Sciences; BA 1907. **Tutor(s):** D MacAlister. **Educ:** South African College School.

HACKETT, George Reginald (1940) Born 1 September 1914, 4 Somer's Road, Halesowen, Worcester; son of George Hackett, Steel Bar Inspector of steel works, and Ethel May Brittain. **Subject(s):** Geography; BA 1942; MA 1946; BSc (Birmingham) 1935. **Tutor(s):** C W Guillebaud. **Educ:** Tenter Street Elementary School, Halesowen; Halesowen Grammar School; University of Birmingham. **Career:** Education Officer, RAF; Master, Shaftesbury Grammar School 1945.

HACKING, Dr Peter Michael (1947) Born 1 May 1929, Innisfree, Hillview Gardens, Hendon, Middlesex; son of James Thompson Hacking, Manager, Garage and Motor Engineers, and Ethel May Haddock; m Helen, 1953; 2 sons (Nigel b 1956 and Jeremy b 1960), 1 daughter (Julie b 1954). **Subject(s):** Natural Sciences; BA 1950; MA 1959; MB 1953; BChir 1953; MD 1962; FRCR 1960. **Tutor(s):** G C L Bertram. **Educ:** Ravensfield College, Hendon; Norwood School, Exeter; Exeter School. **Career:** Consultant Diagnostic Radiologist; Head of Radiology Departments, Royal Victoria Infirmary and University of Newcastle upon Tyne 1977–1988. **Awards:** Vidal Exhibition, SJC 1947; Scholarship, SJC 1949.

HADINGHAM, Frank Edward (1929) Born 25 April 1912, Earsham, Norfolk; son of Herbert William Hadingham, Farmer, and Flora Marie Newham; m Nora Katheen Brown; 2 sons (Michael Frank and Jeremy

John), 2 daughters (Penelope Ann and Bridget Jane). **Subject(s):** English; BA 1932; MA 1936. **Tutor(s):** M P Charlesworth. **Educ:** Earsham Elementary School; St Cross, Suffolk Elementary School; Bungay Grammar School. **Career:** Senior English Master, Bungay Grammar School. **Awards:** Open Exhibition, SJC 1929; Foundation Scholarship, SJC 1931.

HADLAND, John Kynaston Phipps (1926) Born 5 December 1907, Riversdale, Gaywood Road, King's Lynn, Norfolk; son of Richard Phipps Hadland, Clerk in Holy Orders, and Helen Margaret Metcalfe. **Subject(s):** History; BA 1929. **Tutor(s):** M P Charlesworth. **Johnian Relatives:** son of Richard Phipps Hadland (1892). **Educ:** Brunswick, Haywards Heath; Cheltenham College.

HAGGARD, Michael Verner (1941) Born 1 February 1924, 1 Hillside, Charmouth, Dorset; son of Daniel Amyand Haggard, Coffee Estate Manager, and Phoebe Haggard; m Nancie Lyle, 23 July 1949, St Luke's Church, Sydney Street, London; 2 sons (Andrew Doveton b 1951 and Ian Beattie b 1952). **Subject(s):** Economics; BA 1944; MA 1948. **Tutor(s):** C W Guillebaud. **Educ:** Aldeburgh Lodge School; Private Tuition; Gresham House School, Kilmarnock. **Career:** Assistant Advertising Manager, Moss Bros, Covent Garden 1944–1945; Assistant to the Director of Information at the Empire Industries Association and British Empire League, Whitehall 1945; Organising Secretary, Empire Industries Association 1956; Shell & BP Marketing Services, Africa 1956. Died 8 April 2000.

HAGGER, The Revd Canon Norman Watson (1912) Born 2 November 1893, Tolleshunt Major, Essex; son of Watson Hagger, Clerk in Holy Orders, and Mary Ann Elizabeth Fenner; m Charlotte Maria James, 12 June 1918, Church Crookham, Hampshire; 1 son (John). **Subject(s):** Theology; BA 1915; MA 1920. **Tutor(s):** E E Sikes. **Educ:** Highfield, Leigh-on-Sea; Forest School; Bishop's College, Cheshunt. **Career:** Captain, Royal Sussex Regiment, then with Officer Cadet Battalion, WWI; Deacon 1920; Curate, St James, Forest Gate 1920–1923; Priest 1921; Curate, Witham 1923–1928; Licence to Officiate, Diocese of Lincoln 1928–1937; Priest Vicar, Lincoln Cathedral (Honorary from 1937) 1928–1937; Chaplain, HM Prison, Lincoln 1929–1937; Lecturer, Bishop's Hostel, Lincoln 1931–1942; Rector, Coningsby, Lincolnshire 1937–1959; Perpetual Curate, Tattershall with Thorpe 1954–1959; Rural Dean, Gartree, Lincoln 1938–1959; Canon and Prebendary of Buckden in Lincoln Cathedral 1950; Vicar, Witham-on-the-Hill 1959–1964. Died 10 January 1972.

HAGGIS, Bernard Murray (1943) Born 12 October 1924, 51 Woodland Way, Mill Hill, Middlesex; son of Bernard Haggis, Solicitor, and Grace Johnston Davidson; m Sheila Mary Hellewell, 28 July 1981. **Subject(s):** Modern and Medieval Languages; BA 1948; MA 1954. **Tutor(s):** C W Guillebaud. **Educ:** University College School.

HAGON, David Olaf (1949) Born 30 May 1929, 12 Folds Drive, Sheffield; son of Thomas Hagon, Representative of Firth-Vickers Stainless Steels Ltd, and Rachel Romanie Fourneau; m Judith Sarah Louise Humphreys; 1 son (Charles William Benedict b 14 April 1967), 1 daughter (Tamsin Christian Rebecca b 11 December 1970). **Subject(s):** Natural Sciences/Chemical Engineering; BA 1952; MA 1961; MEng 1992; MIChemE; RoSPA Licentiate. **Tutor(s):** G C L Bertram. **Johnian Relatives:** father of Charles William Benedict Hagon (1985). **Educ:** Dore and Totley High School, Sheffield; King Edward VII School, Sheffield; University School, Southport; Wycliffe College, Stonehouse. **Career:** Works Manager; ICI 1953–1984. **Publications:** 'FN Curves-Risk', *Transactions of the Institutions of Chemical Engineering Research Design*, Volume 62, 1984.

HAGUE, Michael Taylor (1947) Born 20 April 1929, Atalaye, Grange Avenue, Oldham, Lancashire; son of William Taylor Hague, Cotton Spinner, and Kathleen Hood. **Subject(s):** Law; BA 1950. **Tutor(s):** F Thistlethwaite. **Johnian Relatives:** brother of David William Taylor

Hague (1953). **Educ:** Bilton Grange Preparatory School; Rugby School. **Career:** Solicitor.

HAIGH, Frederick Thomas Stretton (1926) Born 11 December 1907, 20 Alexandra Road, Leicester; son of Thomas Frederick Haigh, Auctioneer, and Alice Stretton. **Subject(s):** Economics; BA 1929. **Tutor(s):** E A Benians. **Educ:** Stoneygate Preparatory School; Wyggeston Grammar School, Leicester.

HAIGH, Dr Harry (1931) Born 24 May 1913, 10 Myrtle Villas, Sowerby Bridge, Yorkshire; son of Willie Haigh, Woollen Manufacturer, and Alice Sharp; 2 sons, 2 daughters. **Subject(s):** Natural Sciences; BA 1934; MA 1941; BChir 1937; MB 1937; DTM&H; DObstRCOG. **Tutor(s):** M P Charlesworth. **Johnian Relatives:** father of Willie Haigh (1957). **Educ:** Crossley and Porter School, Halifax; Rydal School, Colwyn Bay. **Career:** Missionary Doctor, Methodist Hospital, Ituk Mbang, Eastern Nigeria 1940–1969. **Honours:** MBE 1956. Died 13 May 1969.

HAIG-THOMAS, David (1928) Born 1 December 1908, 41 Princes Gardens, Knightsbridge, London; son of Peter Haig-Thomas, of independent means, and Maud Frances Nelson; m Nancy Bury; 2 sons (Tony and Geoffrey). **Tutor(s):** E A Benians. **Johnian Relatives:** uncle of Hugo Alistair Christian Haig-Thomas (1971). **Educ:** St David's School, Reigate; Eton College. **Career:** Rowed for England, Los Angeles Olympics 1932; Explorer, including expeditions to Abyssinia (with Wilfred Thesiger), and the Arctic (joining Ernest Shackleton's expedition, as photographer and ornithologist, later undertaking his own expedition, during which he discovered a new island off the Canadian coast, now named after him); Eskimo Linguist, Iceland; Commando, Parachute Regiment, No 4 Commando and 6th Airborne Division. **Publications:** *I Leap Before I Look*, Putnam, 1936; *Tracks in the Snow*, Hodder & Stoughton, 1939. Died 6 June 1944 (killed in action in Normandy).

HAIR, Professor Paul Edward Hedley (1943) Born 27 January 1926, 28 Edwin Street, Amble, Northumberland; son of Thomas Edward Couchman Hair, Probation Officer, and Florence Hedley; m Margaret Robinson, 5 December 1959; 1 son (Christopher b 1963), 1 daughter (Ruth b 1966). **Subject(s):** History; BA 1948; MA 1950; BA (by incorporation) (Oxon) 1955; DPhil (Oxon) 1955; FRHistS. **Tutor(s):** C W Guillebaud. **Educ:** Tweedmouth East Council School; Berwick-upon-Tweed Grammar School; Balliol College and Nuffield College, Oxford. **Career:** Mine Worker, Ashington Colliery 1944–1947; Student Bursar, Nuffield and Balliol Colleges, Oxford 1949–1953; Research Fellow, University of Ibadan, Nigeria 1952–1955; Lecturer, Teacher Training, Fourah Bay College, Sierra Leone 1955–1959; Teacher, Bottisham Village College 1959–1961; Lecturer, University of Sierra Leone 1961–1963; Senior Lecturer in African History, University of Khartoum 1963–1965; Lecturer, Senior Lecturer, Reader 1965–1979, Ramsay Muir Professor of Modern History 1979–1990 (Emeritus 1990–2001), Department of History, University of Liverpool. **Appointments:** Chairman, Liverpool Medical History Society 1984–1994; Chairman, Local Population Studies Society 1985–1992; Chairman, Liverpool Society for the History of Science and Technology 1985–1989; Member, Fontes Historiae Africanae Committee, British Academy 1985; General Editor, Liverpool Historical Studies, Liverpool Historical Essays 1987–1994, 1997; President, Hakluyt Society 1992–1997; Chairman, Historical Society of Lancashire and Cheshire 1993–1996; Chairman, Liverpool NHS Trusts Archives Committee 1995. **Awards:** Ada Carr Steven Bursary of the Edinburgh Borderers' Association 1936; Major Scholarship, SJC 1942; Bell and Abbott Exhibition 1943. **Publications:** *The Early Study of Nigerian Languages*, 1967; *Before the Bawdy Court*, 1972; (ed, with Roger Anstey) *Liverpool, The African Slave Trade and Abolition*, 1976 and 1989; *The Westward Enterprise*, 1978; *East of Mina*, 1988; (ed) *Coals on Rails*, 1988; *To Defend Your Empire*, 1990; (ed) *Barbot on Guinea*, 1992; *English Seamen and Traders in Guinea 1553–1565*, 1992; *The Founding of the Castelo de São Jorge da Mina*, 1994; (ed, with Roy Bridges) *Compassing the Vaste Globe* *of the Earth*; *Africa Observed*, 1997; *Africa Encountered: European contacts and evidence 1450–1700*, Variorum, Aldershot, 1997; (ed, with D P Gamble) *The Discovery of River Gambra by Richard Jobson, 1623*, 1999; (ed) *Hawkins in Guinea 1567–1568*, 2000. Died 13 August 2001.

HAKIM, Meherban Hormasjee (1904) Born 3 December 1885, Bombay, India; son of Hormasjee Mervanjee Hakim, Lieutenant Colonel, Indian Medical Sevice, and Shireenbai Rustomjee Kama. **Tutor(s):** D MacAlister. **Educ:** St Joseph's College, Coonoor, India; Forest School, Walthamstow.

HAKKI, Dr Ahmed (1949) Born 11 January 1932, Paris, France; son of Abdal Rahman Hakki, Egyptian Minister to Italy, and Aicha Aly Hussein Pasha. **Subject(s):** Natural Sciences; BA 1952; MA 1956; BChir 1958; MB 1959; DPM (Eng); MRCPsych. **Tutor(s):** G C L Bertram. **Johnian Relatives:** brother of Aref Hakki (1953). **Educ:** Victoria College, Cairo, Egypt. **Career:** Psychiatrist, Chief Intensive Care Unit, Bronx Psychiatric Center, New York; Clinical Assistant Professor of Psychiatry, Albert Einstein College of Medicine, Bronx, New York.

HALE, The Revd James Leonard Ramsay (1921) Born 29 May 1901, 21 Coningsby Road, Walton, Liverpool; son of William Ramsay Hale, Secretary for Higher Education, Cheshire County Council, and Clara Helen Price; m Jessie Griffith, 25 June 1932, St Michael with St Olave, Chester. **Subject(s):** English/Moral Sciences; BA 1925; MA 1947. **Tutor(s):** B F Armitage. **Educ:** College School, Chester; King's School, Chester; University of Liverpool. **Career:** Assistant Master, County High School for Boys, Altrincham 1932; Ordained Deacon 1950; Curate, Altrincham 1950–1953; Ordained Priest 1951; Curate, Bowden, Cheshire 1957–1964; Rector, St Leonard, Colchester 1964. **Publications:** 'The Voyager', *The Eagle* 43, 1924. Died 7 May 1972.

HALES, Professor Anton Linder (1931) Born 1 March 1911, Mossel Bay, Cape Province; son of James Hales, Manufacturer's Representative, and Sarah Elizabeth Rudd; m (1) Marjorie Jacoba de Villiers Carter, 1936 (d 1957), (2) Denise Lynne Adcock; (1) 4 sons (James, Andrew, Peter and John), (2) 2 sons (Marc Anton and Colin Adcock). **Subject(s):** Mathematics; BA 1933; MA 1952; BSc (Cape Town); MSc (Cape Town); PhD (Cape Town) 1936. **Tutor(s):** J M Wordie. **Educ:** Hazelbrae Preparatory School; Grey Institute High School; Pretoria Boys High School; Green and Sea Point High School; University of Cape Town. **Career:** Department of Applied Mathematics, Johannesburg 1930–1931; Junior, then Senior Lecturer, Department of Mathematics, University of the Witwatersrand 1930–1940; Lieutenant, 42 Geological Section, South African Engineer Corps 1941–1942; Instrument Section, War Supplies, South Africa 1942–1945; Senior Research Officer, Bernard Price Institute of Geophysical Research, University of the Witwatersrand 1946–1949; Professor of Applied Mathematics, Head of Department of Mathematics, University of Cape Town 1949–1954; Director, Bernard Price Institute of Geophysical Research, University of the Witwatersrand 1954–1962; Professor of Geophysics 1962–1969, 1969–1973 and 1978–1982, Interim Vice-President for Academic Affairs, University of Texas, Dallas; Director, Research School of Earth Sciences, ANU, Canberra 1973–1978.

HALFORD, Richard Frederick (1919) Born 6 November 1897, 69 Clifton Hill, Marylebone, London; son of Bernhard Frederick Halford, Insurance Broker, and Hilda Rebecca Behrend. **Tutor(s):** E E Sikes. **Educ:** West Heath School, Hampstead; Belsize School, Hampstead; Clifton College. **Career:** Army, WWI. Died 1978.

HALKET, Peter Buchanan (1948) Born 8 March 1928, Stone Field, Kidbrooke Grove, Charlton, London; son of James Pitcairn Halket, Naval Architect, and Elvire Corthals. BA 1950; MA 1958. **Tutor(s):** R L Howland. **Educ:** Rodney House School, Alverstoke; Ryde School; Falmouth Grammar School. **Career:** Partner, Explorer Films 1961–1992; Proprietor, Venture Film Services 1974–1982; Headmaster, Lanesborough School, Guildford 1976–1978; Deputy Headmaster, St John's College Preparatory School 1978–1988.

HALL, The Revd Alfred Francis (1906) Born 20 February 1887, 17 Mowbray Road, Willesden, Middlesex; son of Frederick Hall, Banker's Clerk, and Ethel Jane Mary Francis; m Katharine Gertrude Dobbie, 10 May 1921, New Zealand. **Subject(s):** Natural Sciences; BA 1909; MA 1913. **Tutor(s):** J R Tanner. **Educ:** Dulwich College. **Career:** Ordained Deacon 1910; Curate, St Peter, Upton Cross, West Ham 1910–1913; Ordained Priest 1911; Curate, Havelock, New Zealand 1915–1919; Curate, Woodville, New Zealand 1919–1920; Vicar, Opotiki, New Zealand 1921–1925; Vicar, Tauranga, New Zealand 1925–1932; Canon, St Chad, Diocese of Waiapu, New Zealand 1932; Vicar, Gisborne, New Zealand 1932–1938; Archdeacon, Waiapu, New Zealand 1949. **Awards:** Choral Studentship, SJC; Winchester Reading Prize, University of Cambridge 1910.

HALL, Bruce (1937) Born 29 December 1918, 4 Harris View, Penrhiwceiber; son of George Henry Hall, MP for Aberdare, Merthyr Tydfil, and Margaret Jones. BA 1941. **Tutor(s):** C W Guillebaud. **Educ:** Penrhiwceiber Elementary School; Cowbridge Grammar School; University of Cardiff.

HALL, Denys James Nicholas (1938) Born 11 October 1919, The Vicarage, Frizington, Cumberland; son of John Hall, Clergyman, and Alice Laura Fisher; m Margaret Thompson, 1957; 1 son (John b 1962), 1 daughter (Elizabeth b 1960). **Subject(s):** History/Geography; BA 1945; MA 1947. **Tutor(s):** J S Boys Smith. **Educ:** Durham Cathedral Choir School; Durham School. **Career:** Military service, demobilised as Captain 1940–1946; Took part in Normandy Landing 1944; Assistant Master, St John's College, Johannesburg 1947–1950; Assistant Master and Housemaster, Ottershaw School, Chertsey, Surrey. **Appointments:** Member, CUMS.

HALL, The Revd Edgar Bernard (1942) Born 11 May 1924, Grove House, Garstang Road, Preston; son of John Wesley Hall, Methodist Minister, and Evelyn Blake. BA 1945; MA 1949. **Tutor(s):** C W Guillebaud. **Educ:** Redby Council School, Sunderland; Devonshire Road Council School, Blackpool; Boys' Grammar School, Blackpool; Royal Grammar School, Newcastle upon Tyne.

HALL, Professor George Garfield (1947) Born 5 March 1925, 24 Cyprus Park, Belfast; son of Richard Hall, Presbyterian Minister, and Margaret Hall Sayers; m Doreen Hastings, 28 June 1951, Belfast; 1 son (Richard b 1962), 2 daughters (Honor b 1956 and Hazel b 1958). MA 1950; PhD 1951; ScD 1990; BSc (Belfast) 1946; Honorary DEng (Kyoto) 1989; DSc *honoris causa* (NUI, Maynooth) 2004; CMath; FIMA. **Tutor(s):** J M Wordie. **Educ:** Girton Lodge School, Belfast; Mountpottinger Public Elementary School, Belfast; Regent House School, Newtownards; Methodist College, Belfast; Queen's University, Belfast. **Career:** Assistant in Research in Theoretical Chemistry 1950–1955, Title A Fellow 1953–1956, SJC; Lecturer in Mathematics, Imperial College, London 1955–1962; Research, University of Uppsala 1957–1958; Professor of Applied Mathematics 1962–1982 (Emeritus 1982), Dean of Pure Science 1972–1975, Nottingham University; Professor of Quantum Molecular Science, Kyoto University, Japan 1983–1988. **Appointments:** Council, IMA 1968–1971; Visiting Professor, University of Kansas 1969–1979; Spiers Lecturer, Chemical Society 1972; Computer Consultative Committee, Department of Education and Science 1972–1976; International Academy of Quantum Molecular Science 1974; Executive Committee, International Society for Quantum Biology 1977–1980; Chair, Joint Mathematical Council, 1979–1981; Mathematics Committee, CNAA 1980–1983; Lennard-Jones Lecturer, Royal Society of Chemistry 1988. **Publications:** *Matrices and Tensors*, (a volume of the *International Encyclopedia of Physical Chemistry and Chemical Physics*), Pergamon, 1963; *Applied Group Theory*, Longman, 1965; *Molecular Solid-State Physics*, Springer, 1991; 200 papers in various journals; special issue of *International Journal of Quantum Chemistry*, Volume 74, 1999.

HALL, The Revd George Noel Lankester (1910) Born 25 December 1891, White Horse Street, Baldock, Hertfordshire; son of George Hall, Corn Merchant, and Kate Lankester. **Subject(s):** Classics/Theology; BA 1913;

MA 1918. **Tutor(s):** E E Sikes. **Educ:** Bedford Kindergarten; Bedford Grammar School; Bishop's College, Cheshunt. **Career:** Deacon 1917; Curate, Christ Church, Luton 1917–1919; Priest 1918; Vice Principal, Ely Theological College 1919–1925; SPG Missionary, Ranchi 1925–1926 and 1930; SPG Missionary, Itki 1926–1928; Examining Chaplain to the Bishop of Chota Nagpur 1926–1936; Furlough 1931; SPG Missionary, Itki 1932–1936; Lord Bishop, Chota Nagpur 1936–1957; Fellow, St Augustine's College, Canterbury 1957–1960. **Awards:** Lightfoot Studentship, University of Cambridge 1916. **Publications:** *The Seven Root Sins*, 1936; 'Ode on the Immediate Prospect of the Easter Vacation', *The Eagle*, 32. Died 12 May 1962.

HALL, Hedley Walter (1934) Born 3 October 1907, West View, Farsley, Leeds; son of Walter Hall, Free Methodist Minister, and Julia Florence Copestake. **Tutor(s):** R L Howland. **Educ:** Council School, Leeds and Goole; Secondary School, Goole; Shebbear College, Beaworthy; KCL; UCH.

HALL, James Griffith (1912) Born 15 September 1893, Newton Oystermouth, Glamorganshire; son of Griffith Jenkin Hall, Gentleman, and Mary Elizabeth Jones. **Subject(s):** Law; BA 1915; MA 1921; LLB 1915. **Tutor(s):** L H K Bushe-Fox. **Educ:** Brynmill Board School; Cheltenham House Private School; Swansea Grammar School; Queen's College, Taunton. **Career:** Assistant Secretary, Consolidated Signal Co Ltd 1919; Secretary, Westinghouse Garrard Ticket Machines Ltd, H Hewins Ltd, and the Railway Brakes and Signals Industrial and Export Group; Secretary of merged company, Westinghouse Brake Company Ltd 1930.

HALL, John (1944) Born 2 August 1927, 11 Braidfauld Gardens, Glasgow; son of John Hall, Shipbroker, and Dorothy Cunningham Tullis Brodie; m Mary Elizabeth Butters, 26 January 1954. **Subject(s):** Law; BA 1949; MA 1951. **Tutor(s):** S J Bailey. **Educ:** Glasgow Academy; Strathallan School. Died 8 April 1989.

HALL, John Challice (1945) Born 23 January 1928, 27 Wonford Road, Exeter; son of Haddon Alfred Hall, Commercial Traveller, and Ida Jane Challice. **Subject(s):** Law; BA 1948; MA 1952; LLB 1951. **Tutor(s):** S J Bailey. **Educ:** The Garden School, Exeter; Exeter School. **Career:** Title B Fellow 1955–1988, Lecturer 1955–1992, Title D Fellow 1988–1992, SJC; Lecturer in Family Law, University of Cambridge 1960–1988. **Appointments:** Tutor 1961–1983, Director of Studies in Law 1970–1989, Senior Tutor 1972–1983, Director of Studies in Law (Admissions) 1990–1991, SJC; Secretary, Johnian Society 1983–1992; Recorder 1990; JP. Died 2 May 1992.

HALL, John Frank Austin (1944) Born 7 April 1926, 124 Greengate Street, Oldham, Lancashire; son of Frank Hall, Cotton Waste Dealer, and Jessie Coyne; m Sheila Broadbent, 16 August 1969. **Subject(s):** Modern and Medieval Languages; BA 1948; MA 1951. **Tutor(s):** J M Wordie. **Educ:** Lydgate National School; Hulme Grammar School, Oldham.

HALL, John Kenneth (1942) Born 12 January 1925, 12 Lime Grove, Bury, Lancashire; son of Norman Hall, Research Chemist, ICI, and Norah Hall; m Betty Kathleen Wykes, 21 June 1952; 2 daughters. **Subject(s):** Natural Sciences; BA 1945; MA 1949. **Tutor(s):** C W Guillebaud. **Johnian Relatives:** brother of David Malcolm Hall (1950). **Educ:** Claremont Preparatory School, Huddersfield; Kirkheaton National School; Almondbury Grammar School, Huddersfield. **Career:** Chemical Engineer, ICI, Trafford Park, Grangemouth and Huddersfield, then, ICI India, Calcutta 1960–1967. Died 1967.

HALL, Major General Kenneth (1936) Born 29 July 1916, 41 School Road, Sale, Chester; son of Frank Hall, Chemist, and Hannah Clayton; m Celia; 2 sons. **Subject(s):** Economics/History; BA 1939. **Tutor(s):** J S Boys Smith. **Educ:** Worksop College. **Career:** Commissioned, Royal Tank Regiment 1940–1949; Royal Army Education Corps 1949–1972; Commandant, Army School of Education 1955–1956; Commandant,

RAEC Centre 1971–1972; Director of Education, Ministry of Defence 1972–1982; Colonel Commandant, RAEC 1978. **Awards:** Sizarship, SJC. **Honours:** CB 1976; OBE. Died 12 December 1987.

HALL, Leonard Graham (1935) Born 25 February 1917, 33 Victoria Street, Grimsby; son of William Edwin Hall, Jeweller, and Nellie Alice Smith; m Betty Minns; 2 sons (William and John), 1 daughter (Rosalind). **Subject(s):** Mathematics; BA 1938; MA 1945; FIA. **Tutor(s):** J M Wordie. **Educ:** Humberstone Foundation School, Cleethorpes. **Career:** Clerical Medical and General Life Assurance Society 1938–1939; Meteorologist, RAF (then POW) 1939–1945; Clerical Medical and General Life Assurance Society 1945–1990 (Deputy General Manager 1961–1975; General Manager 1975–1982 Non-Executive Director 1982–1990). **Appointments:** Chairman, Society of Investment Analysts 1969–1971; Vice-President, Institute of Actuaries 1970–1973; Chairman, Life Offices Association 1979–1981; Master, Worshipful Company of Actuaries 1984–1985; various directorships, mainly in the fields of investment, pension funds and life assurance. **Publications:** *The Role and Responsibilities of the Institutional Investor*, International Congress of Actuaries, Sydney, 1984.

HALL, Michael Lindsay Bracebridge (1936) Born 5 January 1918, The Rectory, Weddington, Nuneaton; son of Bracebridge Lindsay Hall, Clerk in Holy Orders, and Harriet Emily Timmis; m Brenda Mary Hallam, 2 July 1943, Coulsdon Parish Church. **Subject(s):** History; BA 1939; MA 1943. **Tutor(s):** J S Boys Smith. **Johnian Relatives:** son of Bracebridge Lindsay Hall (1894); uncle of Richard Antony Bracebridge Hall (1958); great uncle of Jonathan Patrick Bracebridge Hall (1987). **Educ:** Norfolk House Preparatory School, Beaconsfield; St Edward's School, Oxford. **Career:** Captain, Royal Warwickshire Regiment; Assistant Master, Ascham, Eastbourne College Preparatory School 1946–1950; Headmaster, Junior School, Ardingly College, Haywards Heath 1950–1955; Headmaster, Homefield Preparatory School, Sutton, Surrey 1955–1963; Children's Secretary and Editor, Children's Publications 1963–1973, Distribution Manager 1973–1981, USPG; Governing Council, Church School 1981–1984; Finance and General Purposes Committee, Church Schools Company Ltd 1984–1991.

HALL, Reginald John Ratcliff (1936) Born 1 July 1917, 181 Moseley Road, St Martin's, Birmingham; son of George Victor Hall, Assistant Dairy Manager, and Constance Irene Ratcliffe. **Subject(s):** Modern and Medieval Languages; BA 1939; MA 1968. **Tutor(s):** C W Guillebaud. **Educ:** Moseley Road Council School, Birmingham; Golden Hillock Road Council School, Birmingham; King Edward's Grammar School, Birmingham; King Edward VI High School, Birmingham. **Career:** War service, POW, WWII. **Awards:** Scholarship, SJC 1936–1937. Died 1979.

HALL, Richard de Zouche (1927) Born 10 August 1908, 30 Reservoir Road, Prenton, Birkenhead, Cheshire; son of Arthur William Hall, Manager to Cotton Merchants, and Beatrice Margaret de Zouche; m Penelope Janet Young, 1941, Calne; 2 daughters (Penelope Mary and Janet). **Subject(s):** Classics/Law; BA 1930; MA 1934; LLB 1932. **Tutor(s):** M P Charlesworth. **Educ:** Mr Kingdon's Preparatory School, Prenton; Birkenhead School; Liverpool University. **Career:** Solicitor and Town Clerk, Halifax 1948–1974. **Appointments:** Honorary Freeman, Halifax 1973. **Publications:** *Star Queen*, 1994.

HALLACK, William Collin (1904) Born 31 March 1886, Krausen Street, Cape Town, South Africa; son of William Hallack, Bank Auditor, and Amy Collin. BA 1907. **Tutor(s):** C E Graves; J R Tanner. **Educ:** The High School, Sea Point.

HALL-CRAGGS, Dr Ernest Christopher Bernard (1944) Born 20 November 1926, Lima House, Bath Road, Reading, Berkshire; son of Ernest Wade Foxton Hall-Craggs, Mechanical Engineer, and Agnes Sidney Wilkins; m Mary; 5 children. **Subject(s):** Natural Sciences; BA 1948; MB 1949; BChir 1949; MA 1959; PhD (London) 1965. **Tutor(s):** S J Bailey. **Johnian Relatives:** grandson of Ernest Hall Craggs

(Hall-Craggs) (1881); grand nephew of George Craggs Craggs (1902); son of Ernest Wade Foxton Hall-Craggs (1919); nephew of Richard Berthold Trechmann Hall-Craggs (1922); cousin of John Francis Hall-Craggs (1953). **Educ:** Abbey School, Reading; High School, Wimbledon; Chafyn Grove, Salisbury; Charterhouse. **Career:** Junior Surgical Specialist, RAMC, Malaya 1952–1954; Medical Officer, Colonial Service, Uganda 1955; Lecturer in Anatomy, Makerere University College of East Africa 1959–1963; Lecturer in Anatomy 1963–1965, Senior Lecturer in Anatomy 1965–1971, University Reader in Anatomy 1971–1975, UCL; Visiting Lecturer in Physiology, London Foot Hospital 1969–1975; Professor and Head, Division of Gross Anatomy, University of Maryland School of Medicine 1975–1986; Tutor in Anatomy, St Edmund Hall and Worcester Colleges, University of Oxford. **Appointments:** Wellcome Research Fellow 1971; Faculty Member, Alpha Omega Alpha Honor Medical Society 1982. **Awards:** Wellcome Research Travel Grant 1974. Died 2 June 2000.

HALL-CRAGGS, Richard Berthold Trechmann (1922) See CRAGGS.

HALLIDAY, Ernest (Hal) (1934) Born 2 January 1916, 4 Naburn Street, Kingston upon Hull; son of Frederick William Halliday, Engineer, and Carrie Spalding; m Margaret Cograve 1941, 2 sons. **Subject(s):** History; BA 1937; MA 1969. **Tutor(s):** J S Boys Smith. **Johnian Relatives:** father of John Frederick Halliday (1961). **Educ:** Selby Elementary School, Hull; Hymers College, Hull. **Career:** HM Inspector of Taxes, Yorkshire; Captain (final rank), Royal Corps of Signals, WWII; Civil Service: retired as Assistant Secretary, in charge of Personnel, Department of Health. **Appointments:** Member, West Wickham Residents' Association. Died 15 July 1993.

HALLIDAY, Philip James (1938) Born 21 July 1920, Claremont, Albert Road, Wilmslow, Cheshire; son of Donald Dunn Halliday, Chartered Accountant, and Elizabeth Wright. **Subject(s):** Economics; BA 1941. **Tutor(s):** C W Guillebaud. **Educ:** Earnseat School, Arnside; Bootham School, York. **Career:** Pilot Officer, RAFVR WWII. Died 25 December 1941.

HALLIWELL, Wilfred Newbold (1909) Born 15 September 1889, 17 Belle Vue Terrace, Bury, Lancashire; son of Robert Halliwell, Colliery Agent, and Ada Newbold; m Verna Ada Esme Twentyman, 30 September 1915, St Laurence, Kirby Misperton. **Tutor(s):** J R Tanner. **Johnian Relatives:** nephew of William Taylor Newbold (1869). **Educ:** St Bees School. **Career:** Second Lieutenant, Yorkshire Regiment 1915–1916. Died 21 September 1916 (killed in action).

HALL-SMITH, Dr George Waldo (1925) Born 19 April 1906, Northwold, Stanley Road, Sutton, Surrey; son of Percy Hall-Smith, Medical Practitioner, and Christine Helga Sharr. BA 1928; MB 1933; BChir 1933; MRCS (Guy's) 1931; LRCP (Guy's) 1931. **Tutor(s):** B F Armitage. **Educ:** Arnold House School; Abbotsholme School; The Leys School, Cambridge. Died 1 March 1990.

HALSEY, Edward James (1920) Born 20 August 1901, Exeter Villa, St Mary's, Newmarket, Suffolk; son of William James Halsey, Trainer of Racehorses, and Ellen Lee; m Anna. **Subject(s):** Natural Sciences; BA 1923. **Tutor(s):** B F Armitage. **Educ:** Private Tuition, Cambridge; Perse School, Cambridge. **Awards:** Scholarship, SJC. Died 8 April 1989.

HALSEY, Reginald Tom (1907) Born 19 February 1888, Romsdal House, Brunswick, Gloucester; son of Sydney Halsey, Corn Merchant, and Florence Annie Grist; m Violet Harris, 17 August 1920, All Souls' Church, Langham Place, London. **Subject(s):** Classics/Modern and Medieval Languages; BA 1910; MA 1920. **Tutor(s):** E E Sikes. **Educ:** Greenhill School, Moseley; Oundle School. **Career:** Assistant in English, Lycée la Tour d'Auvergne, Quimper 1911–1912; Chalet-Biensis, Montreux 1913; English School, Freiburg im Breisgau 1914; Lieutenant, 8th Cheshire Regiment, Gallipoli; Master, Sedbergh School 1918–1919; Bishop's Stortford 1919; Hurstpierpoint College 1919–1920; Manchester

Grammar School 1920; Guildford Grammar School 1921; Bishop Vesey's Grammar School, Sutton Coldfield 1921–1928; Co-Principal, Chester College, Harrow 1931.

HALSON, Geoffrey Robert (1949) Born 8 May 1929, Somerton, Ashton Road, Newton-in-Makerfield; son of Robert Halson, Electrician, and Lilian Shallcross. **Tutor(s):** A G Lee. **Educ:** Earlstown District Junior School; Newton-le-Willows Grammar School.

HAMBLIN, Henry Joel (1932) Born 25 December 1913, 18 Coronation Avenue, Stapleton, Bristol; son of Walter George Hamblin, Mechanical Engineer (Manager), and Kathleen Young, Housewife; m Gwendoline Offer, 24 December 1931, Oxford; 1 daughter (Jane b 1 September 1946). **Subject(s):** Mechanical Sciences; BA 1935; MA 1968; FIAgrE. **Tutor(s):** C W Guillebaud. **Johnian Relatives:** uncle of Richard Charles Offer (1966). **Educ:** Wendover School, Fishponds; Bristol Grammar School, Bristol. **Career:** Petters Ltd, Yeovil 1935–1938; Institute for Research in Agricultural Engineering, Oxford 1938–1942; Machinery Tester, National Institute of Agricultural Engineering 1942–1945; Designed and developed agricultural machinery as Head of the Mechanical Engineering Department, Head of the Engineering Division, then Deputy Director, National Institute of Agricultural Engineering, Silsoe, Bedfordshire 1945–1973. **Appointments:** Honorary Fellow, Royal Agricultural Society of England. **Awards:** Hughes Prize, SJC; Townsend Scholarship, SJC 1931. **Honours:** OBE 1960. Died 10 November 2001.

HAMBLING, Andrew (1948) Born 13 January 1930, Calcutta; son of Victor Frederick Hambling, Clerk in Holy Orders, and Hilda May Storey; m Helen Whitelaw Hamilton Purvis, 21 April 1962, St Nicholas Church, Ringwould, Kent; 1 son (Roderick b 16 November 1963), 1 daughter (Rebecca b 12 August 1965). **Subject(s):** History; BA 1951; MA 1955. **Tutor(s):** A G Lee. **Educ:** Worcester Cathedral Choir School; Worcester Cathedral King's School. **Career:** Schoolmaster, Haileybury School 1956–1991 (Housemaster 1967–1982, Head of History 1978–1988, Second Master 1985–1991); Archivist, Haileybury School 1998.

HAMBRIDGE, Dr Rhodes (1933) Born 29 October 1913, Colinville, Newcastle Street, Rose Bay, Woollahra, New South Wales, Australia; son of Frank Hambridge, Metallurgical Accountant, Adelaide Steam Ship Company, and Alice May Cavill; m Patricia (Patsy) Marion Baker, 27 June 1940, West London Register Office, Paddington; 1 son (Allan Mark b 30 May 1942), 2 daughters (Catherine Anne b 30 May 1944 and Rachel Marion b 9 November 1949). BA 1940; MA 1943; MRCS 1942; LRCP 1942. **Tutor(s):** R L Howland. **Educ:** North Sydney Church of England Grammar; North Sydney Boys' High School; The King's School, Parramatta; Sydney University; St George's Hospital, London; Brompton Chest Hospital. **Career:** B1 Grade, Sector 6, Non-tuberculosis Thoracic Surgical Unit, Harefield Hospital (Sanatorium) 1944; Temporary Probationary Surgeon Lieutenant, RNVR, Medical Officer in charge of Chest Wards, RNH Herne Bay, New South Wales, 1944–1946; Assistant Chest Physician, Surrey County Council 1946–1947; Tuberculosis Specialist, Australian Red Cross, New South Wales Division 1948–1951; Consultant Chest Physician, Newcastle Regional Hospital Board, covering West Cumberland, working initially from Workington Infirmary then West Cumberland Hospital, Whitehaven (involved with the introduction of the Chest Service, including BCG and Mass X-ray) 1952–1978. **Appointments:** Captain, LMBC 1935, Member, London Rowing Club 1937 (selected for the England VIII). **Awards:** Gold Medal, Empire Games, Sydney 1938. Died 29 September 1993.

HAMILTON, Arthur James Stanley (1901) Born 27 December 1882, Glenthorn, Carlton Road, Southampton; son of James Thomas Hamilton, Stockbroker, and Rosa Ellen Train; m Winifred Louisa Chisholm Dalton (d 1966); 1 son (Richard Neville Dalton b 1913, d 2000). **Subject(s):** Law; BA 1905; MA 1912; LLB 1905. **Tutor(s):** D MacAlister. **Educ:** Southampton Grammar School; Bedford Grammar School. **Career:** Called to the Bar, Lincoln's Inn 1911.

HAMILTON, John Dennys (1934) Born 18 January 1916, Nagpur, Central Provinces, India; son of Kismet Leland Brewer Hamilton, Indian Civil Service, and Ruth Madeleine Dennys; m Esme Pettit, 1947 (d 19 April 1992); 3 sons (David Anthony b 23 December 1950, Roger John b 25 March 1952 and Adrian Dennys b 13 August 1957), 2 daughters (Rosemary Lynne b 26 January 1949 and Briony Claire b 29 January 1954 d 24 September 1956). **Subject(s):** Modern and Medieval Languages/Economics; BA 1937. **Tutor(s):** J S Boys Smith. **Johnian Relatives:** son of Kismet Leland Brewer Hamilton (1902); brother of Michael Brewer Hamilton (1946); father of Roger John Hamilton (1970). **Educ:** Eagle House, Sandhurst; Wellington College. **Career:** Colonial Service Nigeria and Gambia 1938–1959; Captain, Nigeria Regiment 1939–1943; Teaching in UK 1960–1966. Died 21 May 2000.

HAMILTON, Kismet Leland Brewer (1902) Born 13 August 1883, Ahmednagar, India; son of William Robarts Hamilton, Barrister, Bombay and London, and Lilian Fanny Louisa Brewer; m Ruth Madeleine Dennys (d 23 June 1985); 2 sons (John Dennys b 18 January 1916 and Michael Brewer b 25 August 1922). **Subject(s):** Classics/History; BA 1905; MA 1909. **Tutor(s):** E E Sikes. **Johnian Relatives:** father of John Dennys Hamilton (1934) and of Michael Brewer Hamilton (1946); grandfather of Roger John Hamilton (1970). **Educ:** Tonbridge School. **Career:** Indian Civil Service; Commissioner, Political Agent 1907–1936. **Awards:** Exhibition, SJC. **Honours:** CIE 1934. Died 16 April 1966.

HAMILTON, Lester Dewie Goodchild (1944) Born 27 January 1926, Sedgeford, King's Lynn; son of Edward McDonald Hamilton, Engineer, and Ethel Louise Carter. **Subject(s):** Natural Sciences; BA 1947. **Tutor(s):** C W Guillebaud. **Educ:** Sedgeford School; King Edward VII Grammar School, King's Lynn.

HAMILTON, Michael Brewer (1946) Born 25 August 1922, Simla, India; son of Kismet Leland Brewer Hamilton, Indian Civil Service, and Madeleine Ruth Dennys; m June Ormrod, 22 July 1947; 2 sons (William Dennys Ormrod b 27 January 1957 and Charles Mortimer b 26 February 1964). **Subject(s):** Economics/Modern Languages; BA 1948; MA 1953. **Tutor(s):** C W Guillebaud. **Johnian Relatives:** son of Kismet Leland Brewer Hamilton (1902); brother of John Dennys Hamilton (1934); uncle of Roger John Hamilton (1970). **Educ:** Hordle House, Milford on Sea; Sherborne School. **Career:** Indian Army; Captain, Scinde Horse (Indian Armoured Corps) 1941–1946; Colonial Service, HMOCS, Solomon Islands 1950–1967; Registrar of Co-operative Societies.

HAMMOND, John Edwin (1949) Born 9 January 1929, Worcester; son of Godfrey Edwin Hammond, China Warehouseman, and Clara Elizabeth Smith; m Kathleen Mary Crompton, 15 August 1953; 3 daughters (Rosalind Guinevere b 1956, Rachel Amaryllis b 1960 and Rhiannon Rowena b 1964). **Subject(s):** Classics; BA 1952; MA 1956; BA (London) 1968. **Educ:** St John's School, Worcester; St Martin's School, Hereford; Lord Scudamore's School, Hereford; Hereford Cathedral School. **Career:** Senior Classics Master, Buxton College 1953–1956; Classics Master, Grove Park School, Wrexham 1957–1966; Head of Classics, King Edward VI Grammar School, Morpeth 1967–1972; Senior Classics Master, Loughborough High School 1972–1990.

HAMPTON, Sidney (1920) Born 26 April 1897, 5 Copper Hill Terrace, Hamble, Southampton; son of William Hampton, Carpenter and House Surveyor, and Ellen Kean Lenfant; m Nina Marion, 1 December 1928, Holy Trinity Church, Brompton. BA 1923; MA 1928. **Tutor(s):** E A Benians. **Educ:** University College, Southampton; Hamble National School. **Career:** Lieutenant, RNVR; Called to the Bar, Inner Temple 1925.

HANCOCK, Charles Magin Coulter (1925) Born 26 May 1907, Penkerris, St Agnes, Cornwall; son of George Coulter Hancock, Solicitor, and Ada Branwell; m Alison; 2 sons (George and Richard), 1 stepdaughter (Rosemary). **Subject(s):** Law; BA 1928; MA 1964. **Tutor(s):** E A Benians. **Educ:** St Peter's Manor House, Horsham; Malvern College. Died 6 December 1986.

HAND, Henry Sheerman (1912) Born 8 July 1893, Aston Clinton, Tring, Buckinghamshire; son of John Henry Hand, Butler, and Charlotte Sheerman. **Subject(s):** Modern and Medieval Languages; BA 1915. **Tutor(s):** E E Sikes. **Educ:** Berkhampstead School. **Career:** Master, Berkhampstead School 1915. **Awards:** Choral Studentship, SJC; John Stewart of Rannoch Scholarship in Music, University of Cambridge 1915; Second Winchester Reading Prize, University of Cambridge 1915.

HANMER, Stephen Henry (1925) Born 22 September 1906, The Rectory, Grendon, Warwickshire; son of Hugh Hanmer, Clerk in Holy Orders, and Margaret Maude Ethelston. BA 1928. **Tutor(s):** E A Benians. **Johnian Relatives:** son of Hugh Hanmer (1882). **Educ:** Ashampstead School; Shrewsbury School. **Career:** Admitted Solicitor 1932; Partner, Longueville & Co, Solicitors, Oswestry, Shropshire. Died 14 September 1980.

HANNAH, Gerald Rainsford (1924) Born 18 October 1905, Lota, Torwood Gardens, Torquay, Devon; son of Walter Rainsford Hannah, of independent means, and Ada Valentine Clayton Cockburn. **Tutor(s):** E A Benians. **Educ:** Chillon College, Villeneuve, Switzerland; Wychwood Preparatory School, Bournemouth; Sherborne School.

HANSEN, Erwin Gunther (1936) Born 2 April 1913, 9 Southgrove Terrace, Ventnor, Isle of Wight; son of Albert Bernhard Hansen, Banker, and Marie Claire Blais de la Montague Selwyn. **Subject(s):** Mechanical Sciences; BA 1939; MA 1952. **Tutor(s):** J S Boys Smith. **Educ:** Maxigymnasium, Munich, Germany; Stella Matutina, Feldkirch; Humanistiches Gymnasium, Kreuzgasse.

HANSFORD, John Talbot (1940) Born 16 January 1922, 21 Montagu Gardens, Wallington, Surrey; son of Richard Vernon Hansford, Post Office Engineer, and Elsie May Talbot; m Dorothy Owen, 1947; 1 son, 4 daughters. **Subject(s):** Mathematics; BA 1943; MA 1947; BSc (London) 1949; PGCE. **Tutor(s):** J M Wordie. **Johnian Relatives:** brother of Richard Norman Hansford (1936). **Educ:** The Elms Kindergarten School, Wallington; Homefield Sutton Preparatory School; Christ's Hospital. **Career:** War Service, RAF and Industry 1942–1946; Schoolmaster, University College School 1947–1955; Schoolmaster, Salford Grammar School 1955–1960; Headmaster, Bury Grammar School, Lancashire 1960–1969; Headmaster, King Edward's School, Witley, Surrey 1969–1980; Headmaster, Christ's Hospital 1985–1986. **Awards:** Scholarship, SJC.

HANSFORD, Richard Norman (1936) Born 31 October 1917, 9 Rangemore Road, Inverness, Scotland; son of Richard Vernon Hansford, Post Office Engineer, and Elsie May Talbot. **Subject(s):** Mathematics/Mechanical Sciences; BA 1939; MA 1943; FIEE. **Tutor(s):** J S Boys Smith. **Johnian Relatives:** brother of John Talbot Hansford (1940). **Educ:** The Elms, Beddington; Homefield, Sutton; Shrewsbury School. **Career:** RN Scientific Service, HM Underwater Detection Establishment, Portland, Dorset; Electrical Engineer for GPO, Admiralty and Atomic Energy; Constructor, Christian Missionary Radio Station, Seychelles; Part-time Assistant, King Edward's School, Witley. **Appointments:** Civil Service UKAEA. **Awards:** Scholarship, SJC 1936–1937. Died 14 August 1979.

HANSON, James (1909) Born 4 August 1889, 4 North Porter Street, Ancoats, Lancashire; son of James Hanson, Gas Engineer, and Sarah Jones. **Subject(s):** Modern and Medieval Languages; BA 1912. **Tutor(s):** E E Sikes. **Johnian Relatives:** brother of Richard Harold Hanson (1911). **Educ:** St George's School, Manchester; Municipal Secondary School, Manchester; Manchester Pupil Teachers' College. **Career:** Master, Merchant Taylors' School 1912; Lieutenant, Coldstream Guards and General Staff, WWI; Modern Languages Master, Mill Hill School 1914–1920.

HANSON, Richard Harold (1911) Born 2 September 1891, 4 North Porter Street, Ancoats, Lancashire; son of James Hanson, Gas Engineer, and Sarah Jones. **Tutor(s):** E E Sikes. **Johnian Relatives:** brother of James Hanson (1909). **Educ:** Manchester Pupil Teachers' College.

HARBINSON, George Chamberlain (1927) Born 28 July 1909, Tower Road, Larne, County Antrim, Ireland; son of William John Reid Harbinson, Steamship Owner, and Margaret Caroline Stevenson Chamberlain. **Subject(s):** Mechanical Sciences; BA 1931. **Tutor(s):** J M Wordie. **Johnian Relatives:** brother of William Kenneth Harbinson (1925) and of Gerald Edward Harbinson (1931). **Educ:** Edgeborough Preparatory School, Guildford; Marlborough College. **Career:** Engineer, Metrovicks then Permutit 1948; Farmer, Kerrera, 1959; Managing Director, Macallan Distillery, Speyside 1959–1975. Died 26 September 1996.

HARBINSON, Gerald Edward (1931) Born 26 October 1912, Ivy Bank, Larne Harbour, Antrim, Ireland; son of William John Reid Harbinson, Company Director, and Margaret Caroline Stevenson Chamberlain; m Pamela Mary Webster, 5 August 1944, St Patrick's Church, Antrim. **Tutor(s):** J M Wordie. **Johnian Relatives:** brother of William Kenneth Harbinson (1925) and of George Chamberlain Harbinson (1927). **Educ:** Kindergarten, Sutton May; Edgeborough Preparatory School, Guildford; Marlborough College.

HARBINSON, William Kenneth (1925) Born 11 July 1906, Lisvarna, Larne, County Antrim, Ireland; son of William John Reid Harbinson, Director, Larne Harbour Ltd, and Margaret Caroline Stevenson Chamberlain; m (1) Muriel Higson (d), (2) Muriel Wilson; 3 sons (John, Denys and Christopher), 2 daughters (Judith and Joanna). **Subject(s):** Modern and Medieval Languages; BA 1929. **Tutor(s):** E E Sikes. **Johnian Relatives:** brother of George Chamberlain Harbinson (1927) and of Gerald Edward Harbinson (1931). **Educ:** Edgeborough, Guildford; Marlborough College. **Career:** Company Director. Died 14 November 2000.

HARBOUR, Harold Ernest (1929) Born 5 December 1910, 411 Edgware Road, Paddington; son of John Harbour, Tobacconist, and Julia Jane Wood; m Mary McManus, 21 October 1936, Dar es Salaam, Tanganyika; 4 sons (Peter b 17 June 1939, Christopher b 8 December 1940, d 1986, Anthony b 26 June 1943 and Michael b 4 July 1945), 2 daughters (Margaret b 22 December 1937 and Mary b 17 February 1947). **Subject(s):** Natural Sciences; BA 1932; MA 1959. **Tutor(s):** C W Guillebaud. **Johnian Relatives:** father of Peter John Harbour (1957); grandfather of Claire Maria Jane Harbour (Lyell) (1983). **Educ:** London County Council School, Campbell Street; Haberdashers' Aske's Hampstead School. **Career:** Colonial Scholarship, Royal Dick Veterinary College, Edinburgh; Colonial Veterinary Service, Singida, Tanganyika 1936–1939; Veterinary Investigation Officer, Bangor then East of Scotland 1939–1946; Veterinary Advisory Service, Research Department, Cooper, McDougal and Robertson (later Wellcome), Berkhamsted (where he developed vaccine against foot and mouth disease), then Director of Veterinary Research, Wellcome 1946–1975. **Appointments:** Editor, *Research in Veterinary Science*; Founder Member, Veterinary Research Club. **Awards:** Scholarship, Haberdashers' Aske's Hampstead School; Exhibition, SJC 1929. Died 19 February 2000.

HARCOURT, Robert Albert Foyson (1939) Born 16 January 1920, 16 Queen's Road, Norwich; son of Sidney Robert Harcourt, Wine and Spirit Merchant, and Ellen Kate Foyson. **Tutor(s):** J S Boys Smith. **Educ:** Gothic House School; City of Norwich School.

HARDEN, Charles George Stuart (1923) Born 31 October 1906, Levona, Myrtlefield Park, Belfast, County Antrim, Ireland; son of Charles Stuart Harden, Solicitor, and Mary McKinney. **Subject(s):** Economics/Mathematics; BA 1928; MA 1932. **Tutor(s):** E E Sikes. **Educ:** Mostyn House School, Parkgate; St Bees School. **Career:** Second Master and Senior Housemaster, Worksop College, Nottinghamshire; Master, Mourne Grange, Kilkeel, County Down 1928–1929; Headmaster, St Bees School 1946. Died 16 March 1991.

HARDERN, Leslie Harry (1921) Born 4 November 1903, 3 Brighton Street, Barrow-in-Furness, Lancashire; son of David Harry Hardern, Commercial Clerk, and Violet Keen; m Lilian. **Subject(s):** Modern and Medieval Languages/Economics; BA 1924. **Tutor(s):** E A Benians. **Educ:** St Paul's School, Barrow-in-Furness; Municipal Secondary School, Barrow-in-Furness. **Career:** Linen Thread Company, Glasgow, and in Italy; Founder, Dress-manufacturing Company, Manchester; Public Relations, Gas Light & Coke Company; Farmer. **Appointments:** Founder Member and 18th President, Institute of Public Relations. Died November 1974.

HARDING, Douglas Arthur (1930) Born 6 December 1911, 32 Gaynesford Road, Forest Hill, Sydenham, Kent; son of Arthur George Harding, Clerk to London County Council, and Mabella Meta Sly; m Dorothy May Mallender; 1 son, 2 daughters. **Subject(s):** Natural Sciences; BA 1933; MA 1959. **Tutor(s):** C W Guillebaud. **Johnian Relatives:** father of Robert Douglas Harding (1963). **Educ:** Whitgift Grammar School, Croydon. **Career:** Research Engineer, National Physical Laboratory, British Hydromechanics Research Association. **Awards:** Scholarship, SJC. Died 14 August 1973.

HARDING, Sir George William (1945) Born 18 January 1927, Highgate, London; son of Lieutenant Colonel George Richardson Harding, and Grace Henley Darby; m Sheila Margaret Ormond Riddel, 1955, Chelsea, London; 4 sons (Rupert b 1956, Simon and Martin b 1957 and James b 1962). **Subject(s):** Classics; BA 1950; MA 1955. **Tutor(s):** J M Wordie; R L Howland. **Educ:** Byron House, Highgate; Peterborough Lodge, Hampstead; Tyttenhanger Lodge, Seaford, Sussex; Aldenham School, Hertfordshire. **Career:** Royal Marines 1945–1948; HM Foreign Service, Singapore 1951–1952, Burma 1952–1955, Paris 1956–1959, Santo Domingo 1960–1963, Mexico City 1967–1970, Paris 1970–1974; Ambassador, Peru 1977–1979; Assistant Under-Secretary of State, Foreign and Commonwealth Office 1979–1981; Ambassador to Brazil 1981–1984; Deputy Under-Secretary of State, Foreign and Commonwealth Office 1984–1986; Chairman, First Spanish Investment Trust 1987–1996; Thai-Euro Fund 1988–1997; Non-executive Director, Lloyds Bank plc 1988–1993. **Appointments:** Visiting Fellow, Harvard Centre for International Affairs 1986; Chairman, British-Thai Business Group 1995–1997; Chairman, Margaret Mee Amazon Trust 1988–1994; Chairman, Anglo-Peruvian Society 1987–1989; Chairman, Brazilian Chamber of Commerce 1988–1991; Member, Trilateral Commission 1988–1993; Vice-President, Royal Geographical Society 1990; Council Member, Royal Institute of International Affairs 1990. **Awards:** Sir Joseph Larmor Award, SJC 1950. **Honours:** CVO 1972; CMG 1977; KCMG 1983.

HARDING, Harold Frederick (1932) Born 23 September 1908, 18 Clerk Street, North East Valley, Dunedin, New Zealand; son of George William Henry Harding, Clerk in Holy Orders, and Ida Maud Williams. **Subject(s):** Moral Sciences; BA 1934; MA 1940; BA 1932, MA 1933 (New Zealand). **Tutor(s):** J S Boys Smith. **Johnian Relatives:** son of George William Henry Harding (1895). **Educ:** Dunedin Preparatory School, Christchurch; Christ's College; Canterbury College, Christchurch. **Career:** Ordained Deacon 1934; Curate, St John the Evangelist with St Saviour, Fitzroy Square, London 1934–1938; Ordained Priest 1935; Vicar, St Chad, Linwood 1938–1941; CF, New Zealand; served with 23rd Battalion in Italy; twice decorated 1941–1945; Chaplain, St Catharine's College, Cambridge 1946; Vicar, Philipstown, Christchurch 1948; Vicar, Anderson's Bay, New Zealand 1972. **Honours:** DSO; MBE. Died 23 September 1972.

HARDING, James William (1924) Born 12 June 1906, 52 Alderson Road, Wavertree, Liverpool; son of James Harding, Clerk, and Elizabeth Taliasen Prosser. **Subject(s):** Mathematics; BA 1927; MA 1943. **Tutor(s):** J M Wordie. **Educ:** Crosby Council School; Christ Church School, Waterloo; Merchant Taylors' School, Crosby. **Career:** Assistant Master, Denbigh County School 1927. **Awards:** Exhibition, SJC. Died 6 October 1966.

HARDING, The Revd Walter Harry (1906) Born 11 December 1886, Wivenhoe, Nightingale Road, Wood Green, Middlesex; son of Hugo Lee Harding, Clerk in Holy Orders, and Minnie Emily Ellis. **Subject(s):** Classics; BA 1909; MA 1913. **Tutor(s):** E E Sikes. **Educ:** City of London School. **Career:** Ordained Deacon 1910; Curate, St James', Norlands, Kensington 1910–1914; Ordained Priest 1911; Curate, St John's, Hendon 1914–1916; Temporary CF, 4th Class, RACD 1916–1922; Curate, Frimley 1923–1928; Chaplain, Holloway Sanatorium, Virginia Water 1928–1948; Vicar, Northleigh, Oxfordshire 1948–1962. Died 2 August 1962.

HARDING, William Iliff (1900) Born 9 March 1882, Eden House, Maybank Road, Woodford, Essex; son of Charles Frederick Harding, Ironmonger, and Catharine Hyatt; m Marion Elizabeth Allen, 30 September 1909, St Mark's, Surbiton. **Subject(s):** History; BA 1903; MA 1907. **Tutor(s):** C E Graves. **Educ:** Woodford House School. Died 29 May 1948.

HARDINGHAM, The Revd John (1900) Born 27 April 1880, North Lodge, North End, Crayford, Kent; son of Edward Hardingham, Bank Accountant, and Sarah Vincent. BA 1903. **Tutor(s):** J R Tanner; C E Graves. **Educ:** St Olave's Grammar School, London. **Career:** Ordained Deacon 1904; Curate and Priest, St Paul, Finsbury, St Mary, Whittlesey, St John, Buckhurst Hill, and St Edmund, Southwold 1904–1916; Ordained Priest 1905; Temporary CF 1916–1921; Vicar, Wenhaston, Suffolk 1926–1932; Vicar, Thorington 1932; Rural Dean, North Dunwich 1947.

HARDISTY, Charles William (1911) Born 18 January 1893, 16 Great Cheetham, Street West, Broughton, Salford; son of Charles Henry Hardisty, Schoolmaster, and Sarah Maria Hancock; m Dorothy Mayhew Girling. **Subject(s):** Modern and Medieval Languages; BA 1914. **Tutor(s):** E E Sikes. **Educ:** Manchester Grammar School. **Career:** Assistant Master, King William's College, Isle of Man 1914–1915; Army, then Naval Intelligence Service 1916–1919; HM Customs and Excise 1919–1954 (Commissioner from 1946). **Honours:** CB 1950. Died 1974.

HARDMAN, John Alan (1943) Born 23 February 1925, Kelowna, Llanerch Road, Llandillo-yn-Rhos; son of George Edward Hardman, Schoolmaster, and Edith Richardson. **Subject(s):** History; BA 1949; MA 1954. **Tutor(s):** S J Bailey. **Educ:** Froebelian School, Rhos-on-Sea; Rydal Junior School; Rydal School.

HARDMAN, Wilfrid Henry (1913) Born 27 July 1894, 12 Denton Road, Hornsey, Middlesex; son of Henry Hardman, Shipping Clerk, and Minnie Jane Shubrook; m Mary Ellen Webb; 1 son (Richard Henry b 6 August 1934), 1 daughter (Ann Elizabeth b 29 September 1928). **Tutor(s):** R P Gregory. **Johnian Relatives:** father of Richard Henry Hardman (1955). **Educ:** Christ's Hospital. **Career:** Major, RE; Mentioned in Despatches 1914–1918; Ministry of Transport 1920–1923; Treasury 1923; Ministry of Labour 1923–1957; Assistant Secretary, Employment Policy Department and Labour Supply Department, Ministry of Labour 1923–1957. **Honours:** CBE; MC. Died 15 November 1968.

HARDY, Dr Douglas (1942) Born 22 June 1923, 256 Furlong Road, Goldthorpe, Rotherham; son of Wilfred Hardy, Foreman Bricklayer, and Mabel Hadley. **Subject(s):** Natural Sciences; BA 1945; MA 1948. **Tutor(s):** C W Guillebaud. **Educ:** Greengates Council School; Bradford Grammar School. **Awards:** Major Scholarship, SJC 1941. Died 1991.

HARDY, Gordon Sidey (1902) Born 19 February 1884, 6 Waveney Terrace, Great Yarmouth, Norfolk; son of Charles Millice Hardy, Baptist Minister, and Ellen Jotchman; m Veronica Rimington, 1915; 1 son, 1 daughter. **Subject(s):** Mathematics/Natural Sciences; BA 1905. **Tutor(s):** C E Graves; J R Tanner. **Educ:** Mill Hill School. **Career:** Collector and Customs Service, Central Board of Revenue, Indian Civil Service 1907–1933. **Appointments:** Governor, Mill Hill School. **Honours:** CIE 1931. Died 9 September 1936.

HARESIGN, Arthur Sneath (1938) Born 14 November 1919, Money Bridge, West Pinchbeck, Spalding; son of Isaac Haresign, Farmer, and Alice Maud Sneath. **Subject(s):** Modern and Medieval Languages; BA 1941; MA 1945. **Tutor(s):** C W Guillebaud. **Educ:** Pinchbeck East Church of England School; Spalding Grammar School. **Career:** Sixth Form Modern Languages Master, The King's School, Macclesfield 1941–1977. **Awards:** College Prize, SJC 1939; Wright's Prize, SJC 1941; Foundation Scholarship, SJC 1941.

HARINGTON, John Berkeley (1940) Born 13 September 1921, Station Family Hospital, Cliffden, Muree, India; son of Frederick John Harington, Major, and Olive Isabel Deane. BA 1948; MA 1950. **Tutor(s):** J M Wordie. **Johnian Relatives:** nephew of Norman Ashby (1902). **Educ:** Lanbrook Preparatory School; Maiden Erlegh School, Reading.

HARKER, Dr Maurice John (1919) Born 3 June 1898, Shirley, Cedars Road, Teddington; son of Albert John Harker, Bank Manager, and Augusta Annie Winzar; m Margaret Denise Franklin, 5 June 1928, St Paul's, Withington. BA 1923; MA 1928; MB 1928; BChir 1928; MRCS; LRCP 1925. **Tutor(s):** E E Sikes. **Educ:** Berkhamsted; The Towers, Dovercourt; St Paul's School, London. **Career:** Army 1917–1919; Resident Anaesthetist, St Bartholomew's Hospital; Addenbrooke's Hospital, Cambridge; Anaesthetist, Shropshire Orthopaedic Hospital, Oswestry. Died 13 May 1967.

HARKER, Dr Robert Ian (1947) Born 2 August 1926, 6 Claremont Terrace, Glasgow, Scotland; son of George Percival Harker, Grain Merchant's Manager, and Hilda McAldowie; m Marina Adele Pundt, 5 June 1955; 3 daughters (Elizabeth, Jennifer and Alexandra). **Subject(s):** Natural Sciences; BA 1949; MA 1954; PhD 1954. **Tutor(s):** G C L Bertram. **Johnian Relatives:** brother of Norrison Alexander Harker (1951). **Educ:** Carn Brea Preparatory School, Bromley; Repton School. **Career:** Geologist; Professor, University of Pennsylvania; Sub-Lieutenant, HMS *Kestrel*, RNVR 1946–1947; Assistant Professor of Geology, Pennsylvania State University 1953–1956; Senior Scientist, Johns Manville Corporation 1956–1962; President, Tem-Pres Research, State College, Pennsylvania 1962–1970; Professor of Geology, University of Pennsylvania 1970–1996. **Awards:** Distinguished Teaching Award, College of General Studies; Lindback Teaching Award, School of Arts and Sciences. **Publications:** Approximately 50 papers in professional journals.

HARKNESS, Kenneth Lanyon (1921) Naval Officer.

HARLEY, James Macgregor Bruce (1949) Born 21 April 1928, 27 Daresbury Road, Chorlton-cum-Hardy, Manchester; son of Robert Bruce Harley, Research Chemist, and Helen Laurie Macgregor; m Barbara Corinna Ellis, 7 November 1953. BSc (St Andrews) 1949. **Tutor(s):** G C L Bertram. **Educ:** Reddiford School, Pinner; Stafford's School, Harrow Weald; St Faith's School, Cambridge; St John's School, Pinner; Merchant Taylors' School; St Andrews University. **Career:** Colonial Service Course; Research Officer (Entomologist), East Africa High Commission 1950.

HARMAN, Dr John Bishop (1926) Born 10 August 1907, 108 Harley Street, London; son of Nathaniel Bishop Harman, Medical Practitioner, and Katherine Chamberlain; m Anna Spicer, 1946; 4 daughters. **Subject(s):** Natural Sciences (Pathology); BA 1929; MA 1933; BChir 1932; MD 1937. **Tutor(s):** M P Charlesworth. **Johnian Relatives:** son of Nathaniel Bishop Harman (1895); brother of Roger Chamberlain Harman (1929) and of Michael Boys Harman (1933). **Educ:** Oundle School; University of Strasbourg. **Career:** Resident Assistant Physician, St Thomas' Hospital; Consultant Staff (by election) 1938; Royal Marsden Hospital 1947. **Appointments:** President, Medical Defence Union 1976–1981; 2nd Vice-President, Royal College of Physicians 1981–1982. **Awards:** Frank Smart Prize for Zoology, University of Cambridge 1928. **Publications:** (ed) *National Formulary*. Died 13 November 1994.

HARMAN, Michael Boys (1933) Born 29 September 1914, 108 Harley Street, London; son of Nathaniel Bishop Harman, Surgeon, and Katherine Chamberlain; m Sheila Margaret Wilmot, 11 September 1948, St Margaret's Church, Bagendon. **Subject(s):** History; BA 1936; MA 1940. **Tutor(s):** E A Benians. **Johnian Relatives:** son of Nathaniel Bishop Harman (1895); brother of John Bishop Harman (1926) and of Roger Chamberlain Harman (1929). **Educ:** Fretherne House School, London; Norman Court, London; Oundle School. Died 27 June 1993.

HARMAN, Roger Chamberlain (1929) Born 12 August 1911, 108 Harley Street, London; son of Nathaniel Bishop Harman, Opthalmic Surgeon, and Katherine Chamberlain. **Subject(s):** History/Economics; BA 1933. **Tutor(s):** E A Benians. **Johnian Relatives:** son of Nathaniel Bishop Harman (1895); brother of John Bishop Harman (1926) and of Michael Boys Harman (1933). **Educ:** Fretherne House School, London; Oundle School. Died 2 October 1941.

HARMER, John William (1921) Born 8 January 1903, 7 Wontner Road, Balham, Surrey; son of John Thomas Harmer, Technical Book Keeper and Accountant, and Bertha Baker; 1 son (Carey Francis John). **Subject(s):** Mathematics; BA 1924; MA 1928; FRAS. **Tutor(s):** E A Benians. **Johnian Relatives:** father of Carey Francis John Harmer (1957); grandfather of Quentin John Harmer (1989). **Educ:** London County Council School, Hearneville Road; City of London School. **Career:** Headmaster, Torquay Grammar School 1936–1966. **Awards:** Scholarship, SJC 1920. Died 9 May 1995.

HARPER, David Neale (1934) Born 21 March 1916, 7 St Barnabas Road, Cambridge; son of Harold Hori Harper, Joint Governing Director, King & Harper, and Mabel Alice Bell. **Subject(s):** Economics. **Tutor(s):** C W Guillebaud. **Educ:** St Faith's School, Cambridge; The Leys School, Cambridge. **Career:** Pilot Officer, RAF 1939–1941. Died February 1941.

HARPER, Wallace Russell (1923) Born 27 May 1905, Gainsborough, Lincolnshire; son of Joseph Thomas Harper, Manager to a Timber Merchant, and Gladys Mary Smithson; m Gladys Mackenzie. **Subject(s):** Natural Sciences; BA 1926. **Tutor(s):** B F Armitage. **Johnian Relatives:** father of Colin Mackenzie Harper (1958). **Educ:** The Grammar School, Gainsborough; Gresham School, Holt. **Career:** Physics Department, Bristol University 1931–1932; Admiralty; Imperial College, London, WWII. **Awards:** Scholarship, SJC. Died 15 June 1970.

HARPUR, Richard Latimer (1944) Born 5 August 1926, Home Farm House, Burton Latimer, Kettering, Northamptonshire; son of John Latimer Harpur, Land Agent, and Lilian Doris Constance Hack; m Janet Dorothy Phillipps; 3 sons (Philip, James and George). **Subject(s):** Agriculture; BA 1947; MA 1950. **Tutor(s):** C W Guillebaud. **Educ:** Wellingborough School. **Career:** Agriculturist/Farmer; Development Manager and New Products Manager, Fisons Pest Control Ltd, Harston. **Appointments:** JP.

HARRAP, Michael Leslie (1944) Born 22 July 1926, 2a Broad Walk, Buxton, Derbyshire; son of Frank Leslie Harrap, Company Director, and Elsie Clayton; m Ann Morton, 5 September 1957. BA 1947; MA 1951. **Tutor(s):** S J Bailey. **Educ:** Holmleigh Preparatory School, Buxton; Shrewsbury School.

HARRIES, David John (1947) Born 22 December 1928, 68 Connaught Road, Cardiff; son of David John Harries, Surgeon, and Estelle Maud Lilian Band; m (1) Tanis Sara Smith, 1966, Bristol (div 1980), (2) Pamela Green, 1988, Cardiff; (1) 1 son (Stephen b 1960), 1 daughter (Siân b 1963). **Subject(s):** Natural Sciences; BA 1950; MA 1954; BDS (Bristol) 1956; LDSRCS (Eng) 1956; DOrthRCS (Eng) 1973. **Tutor(s):** G C L Bertram. **Educ:** Richmond Collegiate School, Cardiff; Brightlands, Newnham; Bromsgrove School; Bristol University. **Career:** Pilot Officer, RAF 1951–1952; Principal in General Practice, Cardiff 1956–1966; Dental Adviser, Dental Practice Board, Eastbourne 1966–1970; Eastman Dental Hospital and Royal Dental Hospital 1970–1972; Orthodontic Adviser, Dental Practice Board, Eastbourne 1972–1978; Principal, Orthodontic Practice, North Wales 1978–1981; SDO in Orthodontics, Cheshire Area Health Authority 1981–1984; Principal, Orthodontic Practice, South Wales 1984–1993. **Appointments:** in retirement: Lay Assessor of Retirement and Children's Homes, South Glamorgan; Advocate, Age Concern.

HARRIS, Alfred Stanley (1943) Born 18 September 1925, Maternity Home, Bradford Road, Batley, Yorkshire; son of Mark Harris, Civil Servant, and Ada Link. **Subject(s):** Natural Sciences; BA 1946; MA 1950; CChem; MRIC. **Tutor(s):** C W Guillebaud. **Educ:** Park Road Council School, Batley; Batley Grammar School. **Career:** Chief Chemist, British Chrome & Chemicals. Died 16 August 1984.

HARRIS, Brian Kempster (1925) Born 7 January 1906, Bryn Ogwen, Garth Bangor, Caernarvonshire; son of David Robert Harris, Principal, Normal Training College, Bangor, and Evelyn Elizabeth Kempster; m Primrose Marshall Eaton, 11 August 1938; 1 son, 2 daughters. **Subject(s):** Natural Sciences/Physics; BA 1928; MA 1932. **Tutor(s):** J M Wordie. **Johnian Relatives:** son of David Robert Harris (1896); father of Nigel Brian Westbeech Harris (1967); grandfather of Charles Scott Armstrong (1990). **Educ:** Friars School, Bangor, Wales; Oundle School. **Career:** Assistant Master, Haileybury College 1929–1932; Assistant Master, Head of Physics Department and Housemaster, Oundle School 1932–1971. **Publications:** *Foundations of Physics* (O level text book), 1989. Died 22 November 2003.

HARRIS, Colin Spurge (1924) Born 11 November 1905, Victoria Road, Buckhurst Hill, Essex; son of Booth Harris, Chemical Manufacturer, and Florence Emily Spurge. BA 1927. **Tutor(s):** B F Armitage. **Educ:** The Grammar School, Chigwell; Mill Hill School. Died 4 March 1993.

HARRIS, David Burnsall (1939) Born 11 June 1921, 58 Woodstock Road, Golders Green, London; son of Frank Pollard Harris, Wesleyan Minister, and Dora Lloyd Snape. **Subject(s):** Economics; BA 1942; MA 1946; ACA 1948. **Tutor(s):** C W Guillebaud. **Educ:** Reddiford Preparatory School, Pinner; Terry's Preparatory. **Career:** Accountant. Died 23 June 1957.

HARRIS, David Russell (1949) Born 23 March 1928, City Road Hospital, London; son of Henry Albert Harris, Fellow, SJC, Professor of Anatomy, and Margaret Susan Webb; m Janet M Wood, 27 August 1955, Felixstowe Parish Church; 2 sons, 1 daughter. BA 1953; MA 1956; Qualified Schoolmaster, UK Ministry of Education 1963. **Tutor(s):** G C L Bertram. **Johnian Relatives:** son of Henry Albert Harris (1937). **Educ:** King's Choir School, Cambridge; Perse School, Cambridge. **Career:** Fleet Air Arm, RNAS (last ship HMS *Illustrious*); Overseas Consultant, Hunting Technical Services, Africa, Middle East and Pakistan 1954–1962; Technical Officer (Soils) Food and Agricultural Organisation of the UN, Africa and Middle East 1964–1972; Senior Land Husbandry Officer, Northern Region, Government of Malawi 1973–1979; Senior Consultant, ULG Consultants Ltd 1980–1991; Self Employed Associate Consultant, ULG 1991. **Appointments:** Member, Norfolk Broads Authority Consultative Committee; Member, Management Committee, Littlehall Museum, Lavenham; Active Life Member, Suffolk Preservation Society, county branch of CPRE; land use, waste and water advisor.

HARRIS, Desmond John (1948) Born 13 August 1927, 47 Nelson Road, Durban, Natal, South Africa; son of Augustus John Harris, Senior Clerk, South African Railways and Harbours Administration, and Mabel Jenkinson; m Elsie Stella MacSymon, 4 July 1953, St Bene't's, Cambridge. **Subject(s):** Mathematics; BA 1950; MA 1954; BSc (Cape Town) 1947. **Tutor(s):** J M Wordie. **Educ:** Durban Preparatory High School; Durban High School; University of Cape Town. **Career:** Lecturer in Mathematics, University of Natal, Durban, South Africa 1954–1957; Lecturer in Mathematics, University of Durham 1957–1959; Lecturer in Mathematics, University College of Wales, Cardiff 1959–1994. **Publications:** Various papers in mathematical journals.

HARRIS, Edward Brian (1934) Born 2 February 1916, 25/1 Rowland Road, Calcutta; son of Albert Edward Harris, Artist, and Ethel Annie Issard; m Elizabeth Tyndall, 8 September 1939; 2 sons (Nicholas Tyndall b 1946 and Simon Mannering b 1951). **Subject(s):** Modern and Medieval Languages; BA 1938; MA 1947. **Tutor(s):** C W Guillebaud. **Johnian Relatives:** father of Simon Mannering Harris (1969). **Educ:** Little Meads, Wootton Bassett; Royal Masonic School, Bushey. **Career:** Master, Brighton Grammar School 1947–1981. **Awards:** Scholarship, SJC 1936–1937. Died 2 October 1984.

HARRIS, Edward Sewell (1914) Born 29 October 1895, South View House, Yeadon, Yorkshire; son of Henry Harris, Actuary, and Margaret Prideaux Naish; 1 daughter. **Subject(s):** Mathematics; BA 1917; MA 1921; BSc (London) 1923. **Tutor(s):** L H K Bushe-Fox. **Johnian Relatives:** brother of Henry Lyn Harris (1911); uncle of Henry Stephen Lyn Harris (1938), Nicholas King Harris (1940) and of Simon Joscelyn Fulke Harris (1950); great uncle of Adrian King Harris (1968). **Educ:** West Leith School, Hampstead; Leighton Park School. **Career:** On Staff, Beechcroft Settlement, Birkenhead 1921; First Warden, Percival Guildhouse, Rugby (Community Centre of Adult Education) 1926; First Secretary, Watling Community Association 1942. **Appointments:** JP. **Awards:** Scholarship, SJC. Died October 1983.

HARRIS, George Henry Gordon (1946) Born 3 November 1922, 12 Fishpond Lane, Holbeach, Lincolnshire; son of George Henry Harris, Grocer and General Dealer, and Lily Ethel Hawes; m Christine Mary Wilcox; 2 daughters (Penelope Jane and Rosamund Georgia). BA 1948. **Tutor(s):** C W Guillebaud. **Educ:** Holbeach School; Moulton Grammar School; Spalding Grammar School; University of Edinburgh. **Career:** RAF Pilot, Bomber Command, Flight Commander, 101 Squadron, Flight Lieutenant 1941–1946; Assistant Appointments Secretary, Liverpool University. Appointments Secretary, Glasgow University; Graduate Recruitment and Training Manager, Mobil Oil Co; Supervising Consultant, Management Recruitment, Development and Appraisal, PA Management Consultants Ltd; Managing Director, Canny Bowen (UK headhunters); Chairman, Amrop International (worldwide headhunters); Retired 1986. **Honours:** DFC 1944.

HARRIS, Professor Henry Albert (1937) Born 13 September 1886, Rhymney; son of Henry Harris, Bessemer Steel Works Manager, and Sarah Thomas; m Margaret Llewelyn Webb, 1912; 2 sons (Celfyn and David), 3 daughters (Eluned (d October 2001), Dalbren, and Anne). MA 1934; BSc (Cardiff) 1907; MB, BS (London) 1921; DSc (London) 1929; MD (London) 1933; Board of Education Certificate in the Theory and Practice of Teaching; MRCS 1920; MRCP 1920. **Johnian Relatives:** father of David Russell Harris (1949). **Educ:** Abermorlais Elementary School, Merthyr Tydfil; Merthyr Intermediate School; University College, Cardiff. **Career:** Part time Demonstrator, UCL; Ernest Hart Memorial Scholar for Research, British Medical Association 1921–1923; Rockefeller Medical Foundation Fellow for Research 1925–1926; Assistant Professor, UCL 1927; Clinical Assistant to Child Welfare clinic and Assistant to Director of the Medical Unit, UCH; Hunterian Professor, Royal College of Surgeons 1931; Professor of Clinical Anatomy, University College Hospital 1931; Professor of Anatomy, University of Cambridge 1934–1951 (Emeritus 1951); Title C Fellow 1937–1951, Title E Fellow 1951–1968, SJC; Professor of Anatomy, Cairo; Professor of Anatomy, Khartoum until 1956. **Appointments:** Aris and Gale Lecturer, Royal College of Surgeons 1929; William Julius Mickle Fellow and Alvarenga Prize 1930. **Awards:** Entrance Scholarship, University of Cardiff; Bucknill Scholarship, UCL 1916; Junior Gold Medals in anatomy and physiology, UCL; Senior Gold Medals in Anatomy and Physiology, UCL; Cluff Memorial Prize 1918; Senior Fellowes Gold Medal in Clinical Medicine 1920; Alvarenga Prize, RCP 1930; Symington Prize, Anatomical Association 1930. Died 10 September 1968.

HARRIS, Henry Lyn (1911) Born 16 September 1892, 13 Northdale Road, Frizinghall Heaton, Bradford, Yorkshire; son of Henry Harris, Insurance Clerk, and Margaret Prideaux Naish; m Eleanor Anna Baker,

15 May 1916, Friends Meeting House, Acton, London; 3 sons (Henry Stephen Lyn, Nicholas King and Simon Joscelyn Fulke). **Subject(s):** History; BA 1914; LLB 1915. **Tutor(s):** J R Tanner. **Johnian Relatives:** brother of Edward Sewell Harris (1914); father of Henry Stephen Lyn Harris (1938) and of Nicholas King Harris (1940); uncle of David King Baker (1944); father of Simon Joscelyn Fulke Harris (1950); grandfather of Adrian King Harris (1968). **Educ:** Leighton Park School, Reading. **Career:** Headmaster, St Christopher School, Letchworth 1925–1954.

HARRIS, Professor Henry Stephen Lyn (1938) Born 22 January 1920, 14 Randall Road, Clifton, Bristol; son of Henry Lyn Harris, Headmaster, and Eleanor Anna Baker, Headmistress; m Margaret Hingeley, 6 January 1945, the Friends Meeting House, Golders Green; 2 sons (Anthony b 1948 and Kester b 1956), 2 daughters (Jenny b 1949 and Jill b 1951). **Subject(s):** Mechanical Sciences; BA 1941; MA 1945; MICE 1946. **Tutor(s):** J S Boys Smith. **Johnian Relatives:** son of Henry Lyn Harris (1911); nephew of Edward Sewell Harris (1914); brother of Nicholas King Harris (1940); cousin of David King Baker (1944); brother of Simon Joscelyn Fulke Harris (1950); uncle of Adrian King Harris (1968). **Educ:** St Christopher School, Letchworth. **Career:** Metropolitan Water Board 1941–1946; District Engineer, Southern Railway of Peru 1946–1950; Research, Engineering Department 1950–1952, Demonstrator in Engineering 1952–1954, Lecturer in Engineering 1954–1972, University of Cambridge; Title B Fellow and Lecturer in Mechanical Sciences, SJC 1962–1972; Professor of Engineering, University of Lancaster 1972–1985 (Emeritus 1985). **Appointments:** Sabbatical, Sydney Opera House 1964–1965; Tutor, SJC 1965–1972; Sabbatical, Ministry of Works and Development, New Zealand 1983. **Awards:** Scholarship, SJC 1940. Died 27 March 2002.

HARRIS, Henry Wilson (1902) Born 21 September 1883, 3 Eton Place, Plymouth, Devon; son of Henry Vigurs Harris, House Decorator, and Fanny Wilson; m Florence (d 1962); 1 daughter (Anne). **Subject(s):** Classics; BA 1905; MA 1909. **Tutor(s):** D MacAlister. **Educ:** Plymouth College. **Career:** Master, Leighton Park School 1906; Editor, *London Daily News* 1909–1932; Editor, *The Spectator* 1932. **Appointments:** President, Union Society 1905; MP for Cambridge 1945. **Awards:** Scholarship, SJC 1901. Died 11 January 1955.

HARRIS, John Corbett (1922) Born 29 July 1904, The Vicarage, Llanfachreth, Merionethshire; son of John Harris, Clerk in Holy Orders, and Blanche Corbett. BA 1926; MA 1930. **Tutor(s):** E A Benians. **Educ:** Llandaff Cathedral School; Clive House, Prestatyn; Shrewsbury School; Private Tuition, Holt. **Career:** Licensee, Green Man Inn, Trumpington; Gunner, RA, WWII. Died 1942 (killed in action in the Middle East).

HARRIS, John Frederick (1910) Born 17 February 1891, 16 Brunswick Terrace, Castle Church, Staffordshire; son of Frederick Harris, Art Master, and Adelaide Lucy Horton Knight. **Subject(s):** History; BA 1914. **Tutor(s):** J R Tanner. **Educ:** Chatham House School, Ramsgate; Denstone College. **Career:** Teacher, North Devon School, Barnstaple; Tutor to the sons of Sir Henry Babington Smith 1913–1914; Master, Sherborne Preparatory School 1915. **Awards:** Exhibition, SJC 1909. **Publications:** numerous contributions to *The Eagle*; *Samuel Butler, Author of Erewhon: the Man and his Work*. Died 15 January 1919.

HARRIS, Nicholas King (1940) Born 5 August 1922, Northcote, Westbury on Trym, Bristol; son of Henry Lyn Harris, Schoolmaster, and Eleanor Anna Baker; m Cathleen Adrienne Joll; 1 son (Adrian b 21 May 1949). **Subject(s):** Economics/History; BA 1943; MA 1947; MA (Oxon) 1949; DipEd (Oxford). **Tutor(s):** C W Guillebaud. **Johnian Relatives:** son of Henry Lyn Harris (1911); nephew of Edward Sewell Harris (1914); brother of Henry Stephen Lyn Harris (1938); cousin of David King Baker (1944); brother of Simon Joscelyn Fulke Harris (1950); father of Adrian King Harris (1968). **Educ:** St Christopher's School, Letchworth. **Career:** Headmaster, St Christopher's School, Letchworth 1954–1980. Died 1980.

HARRIS, Noël Hedley Vicars (1921) Born 22 November 1901, The Gate House, Rugby, Warwickshire; son of Charles Frederick Harris, Solicitor, and Evelyn Clara Vicars. BA 1924. **Tutor(s):** B F Armitage. **Educ:** Charterhouse; Courtenay Lodge. **Career:** Sudan Plantations Syndicate 1924; District Reclamation Officer, Game Department, Tanganyika 1927; Secretary-librarian, Tsetse Reserve 1929; Assistant Director 1932; Secretary, Lands and Mines 1937; Captain, Military Service 1939–1943; Assistant Chief Secretary 1945; Director of Establishments 1949.

HARRIS, Peter Medley John (1945) Born 15 January 1922, Woodside Nursing Home, Plymouth; son of Leonard Harris, Picture Dealer, and Evelyn Medley Wood. **Subject(s):** English; BA 1947; MA 1952. **Tutor(s):** F Thistlethwaite. **Educ:** Hoe Grammar School, Plymouth; Sidcot School; Leighton Park School. **Career:** Audit Office, London Passenger Transport Board 1939–1940; Novice, Anglican Benedictine Community, Nashdom, Buckinghamshire 1940–1941; Navigator, RAF 1941–1944; Educational work, Borneo. **Honours:** DFC 1944.

HARRIS, William Anderton (1919) Born 1 September 1896, 3 William Street, Newark on Trent, Nottinghamshire; son of Herbert Samuel Harris, Grocer, and Ann Jackson. **Subject(s):** History/Economics; BA 1922. **Tutor(s):** E A Benians. **Educ:** Boultham Council School; St Peter at Gowts National School; Lincoln School. **Career:** Middlesex Regiment and MGC; Journalist; Founder, *Youth*, Proprietor and Editor, *The Old Cambridge* (undergraduate journal). Died 2 September 1923.

HARRIS-JONES, Frank (1945) Born 9 July 1928, 8 Elm Street, Troedyrhiew, Merthyr Tydfil; son of Gladstone Penn Jones, Timekeeper, and Una Harris. BA 1950; MA 1963. **Tutor(s):** J M Wordie. **Educ:** Abermorlais School, Merthyr Tydfil; Cyfartha Castle School, Merthyr Tydfil. **Career:** Merchant Banker, South America 1950–1960; Secretary, Appointments Board, University of Hull 1961–1971; Registrar and Secretary, Institute of Science and Technology 1971, Dean of Students (part-time) 1994, Public Orator 1994–1998, University of Wales, Cardiff. Died 22 January 2000.

HARRISON, Beverley Thelwall (1927) Born 3 August 1909, The Little House, Burnham, Buckinghamshire; son of Robert George Harrison, Solicitor, and Mabel Gertrude Thelwall. **Subject(s):** Law; BA 1930; MA 1936. **Tutor(s):** C W Guillebaud. **Educ:** Mrs Hayman, Brackley; Gresham's School, Holt.

HARRISON, Eric (1940) Born 19 April 1921, 44 Lister Avenue, Doncaster; son of John William Harrison, Railway Locomotive Driver, LNER, and Clarice Ducker; m Gwynneth Roberts, 1944; 1 son (John Harrison), 2 daughters (Enid Walton and Mary Erricker). **Subject(s):** Mathematics; BA 1943; MA 1947. **Tutor(s):** J M Wordie. **Educ:** Hyde Park Boys' School, Doncaster; Stirling Street Junior Boys' School, Doncaster; The Grammar School, Doncaster. **Career:** Senior Mathematical Master, Boteler Grammar School, Warrington 1955–1979. **Awards:** Scholarship, SJC.

HARRISON, Francis Burton (1939) Born 7 February 1921, Malacanan Palace, Manila, Philippine Islands; son of Francis Burton Harrison, Governor General, Phillipine Islands, and Salena Elizabeth Wrentmore. **Subject(s):** Mathematics. **Tutor(s):** J M Wordie. **Educ:** Elstree School; Château de Changins, Switzerland.

HARRISON, Gilbert Henry (1935) Born 26 February 1915, 1 Holmer Terrace, Holmer, Hertfordshire; son of Henry Harrison, Bandsman, 9th Lancers, and Hilda Cross West. **Subject(s):** Classics/History; BA 1938; MA 1942. **Tutor(s):** R L Howland. **Educ:** St Owen's Council School; Hereford Cathedral School.

HARRISON, John Dashwood St Clair (1940) Born 1 October 1921, 39 Palmerston Place, Edinburgh, Scotland; son of Theodore St Clair Harrison, Colonial Civil Servant, Lagos, Nigeria, and Janet Mary Love Strettell; m Morag Cameron; 2 sons, 2 daughters. **Subject(s):**

Economics; BA 1947; MA 1949. **Tutor(s):** C W Guillebaud. **Educ:** Lathallan School, Colinsburgh; Marlborough College. **Career:** GCHQ 1941–1945; Apprentice, Qualified Assistant, Manager, Thomson McLintock & Co, Chartered Accountants, London 1947–1967; Partner 1967–1986.

HARRISON, Michael Beverley Leeds (1928) Born 30 June 1910, 104 Marine Parade, Worthing, Sussex; son of Henry Leeds Harrison, Medical Practitioner, and Geraldine Margaret Sanderson; m Myrtle Irene Knowlman, 21 August 1944, St Barnabas, Finchley. **Subject(s):** Natural Sciences (Biochemistry); BA 1931; MA 1959. **Tutor(s):** J M Wordie. **Johnian Relatives:** son of Henry Leeds Harrison (1880). **Educ:** Elstree School; Tonbridge School.

HARRISON, Milton (1923) Born 26 June 1891, Chapel Terrace, Lumb, Newchurch, Lancashire; son of James Harrison, Cotton Loom Jobber, and Mary Alice Wilson. **Tutor(s):** E A Benians. **Educ:** Elementary School, Newchurch, Pendle; Nelson Technical School; Nelson Tutorial Classes. **Career:** Psychologist. **Awards:** Exhibition, SJC.

HARRISON, Wilfred Hugh Lane (1922) Naval Officer.

HARRISON, William (1925) Born 8 June 1905, 35 King's Bench Street, Hull, Yorkshire; son of William Aaron Harrison, Motor Agent, and Betsy Ann Blashill. **Subject(s):** Mathematics; BA 1928. **Tutor(s):** J M Wordie. **Educ:** Chillern Street Council School, Hull; Hymers College, Hull.

HARRISS, Kendal Bushe (1927) Born 10 January 1909, Kelonna, British Columbia; son of Reginald Edmund Harriss, Army Officer, and Alice Maude Mary Gorson; m Joan Alcestis Meynell, 11 September 1939, London. **Tutor(s):** E A Benians. **Educ:** Brunswick School, Haywards Heath; Imperial Service College, Windsor; Courtenay Lodge, Sutton Courtenay.

HARROCKS, Dr Donald Raymond (1942) Born 16 December 1923, 55 Mount Road, Wallasey, Cheshire; son of David Henry Harrocks, Building Contractor, and Violet Hill. **Subject(s):** Natural Sciences; BA 1945; MA 1949; MB 1949; BChir 1949. **Tutor(s):** S J Bailey. **Educ:** St Christopher's School, Bournemouth; Wychwood School, Bournemouth; Clifton College, Bristol; Stirling House, Bournemouth; Middlesex Hospital. **Career:** Medical Practitioner.

HARRY, John (1947) Born 6 August 1924, 10 Colebrooke Avenue, Ealing, Middlesex; son of William Arthur Harry, Chief of Securities Section, Lloyds Bank Ltd, and Winifred Hannah Jenkins; m Audrey Eileen Meyrick, 25 June 1960, All Saints, Banstead Parish Church, Surrey; 1 son (Martyn b 19 February 1964), 1 daughter (Jennifer b 10 February 1966). **Subject(s):** Natural Sciences; BA 1949; MA 1955; CPA. **Tutor(s):** G C L Bertram. **Educ:** Durston House, Ealing; St Paul's School. **Career:** Research Biochemist, Patent Department, Distillers Company Ltd Research Centre, Great Burgh, Epsom (qualifying as a Patent Agent 1956) 1950–1958; Patents Manager, BP Chemicals Ltd 1958–1985; Senior Debt Counsellor, Horsham Citizens Advice Bureau 1985–1997. **Appointments:** Manager, Horsham Symphony Orchestra 1980; Secretary, Highland Fieldcraft Training Centre Association 2000.

HART, Dr Edward Watson (1930) Born 19 September 1910, 33 Camphill Avenue, Parish of Cathcart, Glasgow; son of Maxwell Mure Hart, Contractor, Coal Shipper, and Elizabeth Alexander Watson; m Peggy; 2 daughters (Hazel and Mandie). **Subject(s):** Natural Sciences; BA 1933; MA 1937; MB 1937; BChir 1937; MD 1937; FRCP. **Tutor(s):** M P Charlesworth. **Educ:** Glasgow Academy; St Andrew's School; Strathallan School, Forgandenny; Glasgow University. **Career:** Middlesex and Brompton Hospitals, and Great Ormond Street 1937–1939; Lieutenant Colonel Army Transfusion Service, France, Northern Ireland, India 1939–1945; Part-time Lecturer, Middlesex Hospital Medical School 1945–1973; Physician, Children's Department Middlesex Hospital and Hampstead General Hospital 1945–1973; Lecturer, Paediatrics, Royal

Free Hospital School of Medicine 1961. **Appointments:** Secretary, British Paediatric Association 1959–1965. **Honours:** MBE 1948. Died 23 May 1986.

HART, Eric Leslie (1937) Born 5 July 1918, 34 Kingscourt Road, Streatham; son of Jabez Leslie Nathaniel Hart, Engineer, and Nellie Dora Fisk. **Subject(s):** History; BA 1940; MA 1944. **Tutor(s):** J S Boys Smith. **Educ:** Streatham Grammar School; Alleyns School, Dulwich. **Awards:** Choral Studentship, SJC. Died 8 May 1994.

HART, The Revd Henry St John (1931) Born 15 April 1912, Station Road, Holt, Norfolk; son of John Henry Arthur Hart, Clerk in Holy Orders, Fellow and Lecturer, SJC, and Katharine Mary Gwatkin; m Shirley Gillian Barnes, 21 August 1969, Round Church, Cambridge. **Subject(s):** Theology and Religious Studies; BA 1934; MA 1938; BD 1954. **Tutor(s):** J S Boys Smith. **Johnian Relatives:** great grandson of Richard Gwatkin (1810); grandson of Thomas Gwatkin (1858); great nephew of Charles Edward Graves (1858) and of Henry Melvill Gwatkin (1863); son of John Henry Arthur Hart (1895); nephew of Francis Ley Gwatkin (1895) and of Edward Arthur Gwatkin (1897); brother of Richard William Kennett Hart (1930). **Educ:** Lady Manners School, Bakewell; The Grammar School, Leeds. **Career:** Fellow 1936, Chaplain 1936–1950, Dean 1940–1950 and 1955–1972, Vice-President 1978–1979, Queens' College, Cambridge; Reader in Hebrew and Intertestamental Studies, University of Cambridge 1972–1979; Licenced to Officiate, Norwich 1980–1986; Permission to Officiate 1986. **Awards:** Scholarship, SJC; Hughes Exhibition, SJC 1932; Naden Studentship 1934; Crosse Studentship 1935.

HART, Kenneth Forster (1939) Born 29 March 1921, 45 Wigan Road, Golborne, Warrington, Lancashire; son of William Hart, Coal Miner, and Mabel Cartwright; m Nancie; 2 children. **Subject(s):** Mathematics; BA 1942; MA 1946; Teacher's Certificate (Westminster) 1946. **Tutor(s):** J M Wordie. **Educ:** Golborne Parochial School; Newton-in-Makerfield Grammar School; Westminster College. **Career:** RAF, North Africa and Italy 1941–1946; Deputy Head, King's School, Chester 1950–1966; Head of Maths, Padgate Teacher Training College 1966–1976. Died 16 November 2003.

HART, Richard William Kennett (1930) Born 28 January 1911, Cintra Lodge, Little Shelford, Cambridgeshire; son of John Henry Arthur Hart, Clerk in Holy Orders, Fellow and Lecturer, SJC, and Katharine Mary Gwatkin. **Subject(s):** English; BA 1933. **Tutor(s):** E A Benians. **Johnian Relatives:** great grandson of Richard Gwatkin (1810); grandson of Thomas Gwatkin (1858); great nephew of Charles Edward Graves (1858) and of Henry Mellvill Gwatkin (1863); son of John Henry Arthur Hart (1895); nephew of Francis Ley Gwatkin (1895) and of Edward Arthur Gwatkin (1897); brother of Henry St John Hart (1931). **Educ:** Lady Manners School, Bakewell; The Grammar School, Leeds. Died 4 August 1933.

HARTLEY, Anthony Vivian (1947) Born 23 August 1926, The Nursing Home, East Hoathley, Sussex; son of Edward Holland Hartley, Tobacco Grower, and Marjorie Godwin Birchenough. **Tutor(s):** J M Wordie. **Educ:** King's School, Macclesfield; Birkenhead School. **Career:** Captain, Rajput Regiment, Indian Army; Colonial Service Course, Nigeria.

HARTREE, Colin William (1919) Born 27 September 1898, Trumpington, Cambridgeshire; son of William Hartree, Officer of Munitions Inventions Department, and Eva Rayner. **Subject(s):** Mathematics. **Tutor(s):** E E Sikes. **Johnian Relatives:** brother of Douglas Rayner Hartree (1915). **Educ:** St Faith's School, Cambridge; Bedales School, Petersfield. Died 9 February 1920.

HARTREE, Professor Douglas Rayner (1915) Born 27 March 1897, 33 Chesterton Road, Chesterton, Cambridge; son of William Hartree, Private Tutor, and Eva Rayner; m Elaine Charleton, 1923; 2 sons, 1 daughter. **Subject(s):** Mathematics/Natural Sciences; BA 1921; MA 1926; PhD 1926; FRS 1932. **Tutor(s):** R P Gregory. **Johnian Relatives:** brother of Colin William Hartree (1919). **Educ:** St Faith's School, Cambridge; Bedales School, Petersfield. **Career:** Lieutenant, RNVR, Anti-aircraft Experimental Section, Munitions Inventions Department 1916–1918; Bayley Fellow, SJC 1924–1927; Fellow, Christ's College, Cambridge 1928; Demonstrator in Physics, University of Cambridge 1928–1929; Beyer Professor of Applied Mathematics, Manchester University 1929–1937; Professor of Theoretical Physics, Manchester University 1937–1945; Seconded to Ministry of Supply, ran a computing service making use of the Manchester Differential Analyser 1939–1945; Professor of Engineering Physics, Manchester University 1945–1946; Plummer Professor of Mathematical Physics, University of Cambridge 1946–1958. **Appointments:** Assistant Supervisor in Physics 1924–1925, Supervisor in Physics 1925–1928, SJC; Kelvin Lecturer in the Institution of Electrical Engineers 1943; Acting Chief, Institute of Numerical Analysis 1948. **Awards:** Scholarship, SJC 1914. **Publications:** *Numerical Analysis*; *Calculating Instruments and Machines*; *Calculation of Atomic Structures*; Papers in *Proceedings of the Cambridge Philosophical Society*, and *Proceedings of the Royal Society*. Died 12 February 1958.

HARTREE, Dr Edward Francis (1939) Born 13 October 1910, London; son of Francis Rawlinson Hartree, Insurance Clerk, and Emma Florence Fay. MA 1939; BSc (London) 1932; PhD (London) 1933. **Educ:** Hendon County School; Imperial College of Science and Technology. **Career:** Assistant in Research in Parasitology, Molteno Institute 1938–1948, Assistant Director of Research in Cellular Biology 1948–1952, University of Cambridge; Visiting Professor, University of Auckland 1976. **Awards:** Ciba Medal, Biochemical Society 1976.

HARTRIDGE, Dr Gerald (1938) Born 24 August 1920, 3 Millington Road, Cambridge; son of Hamilton Hartridge, Professor of Physiology, St Bartholomew's Medical College, and Kathleen Adéle Wilson. BA 1941; MA 1945; MB 1945; BChir 1945. **Tutor(s):** R L Howland. **Educ:** King's Choir School, Cambridge; Orme Square School, London; Harrow School.

HARTWELL, Sir Charles Herbert (1922) Born 25 April 1904, 25 Hartford Road, East Finchley, Middlesex; son of Alfred Hartwell, Civil Servant, Post Office, and Alice Annie Harvey. **Subject(s):** Mathematics/Law; BA 1925. **Tutor(s):** E Cunningham. **Educ:** East Finchley Grammar School; Squires Lane Council School; Finchley County School. **Career:** Various posts, Ceylon Civil Service 1926–1940; Administrative Secretary, Palestine Administrative Service 1940–1942; Controller of Imports, Exports and Exchange, Ceylon Civil Service 1942–1947; Director of Establishment, Kenya 1947; later Deputy Chief Secretary, Minister of Education, Labour and Lands 1947–1955; Chief Secretary, Uganda 1955–1960; Chairman, Civil Service Commission, Northern Rhodesia 1960. **Honours:** CMG 1954; Kt 1960. Died 13 August 1982.

HARVEY, Donald George Robert (1937) Born 6 March 1919, 4 Orchard Drive, Lewisham; son of George Alfred Sydney Harvey, Engineer, and Dora Annie Speyer. **Subject(s):** Mechanical Sciences. **Johnian Relatives:** brother of Gordon Columba Harvey (1940). **Educ:** St Wilfrid's Preparatory School, Hawkhurst; Rugby School. **Career:** Lieutenant, WWII. Died August 1944 (killed in action).

HARVEY, Gordon Columba (1940) Born 23 July 1921, 4 Orchard Drive, Lewisham; son of George Alfred Sydney Harvey, Engineer, and Dora Annie Speyer; m Beryl Davies, 28 June 1947. **Tutor(s):** S J Bailey. **Johnian Relatives:** brother of Donald George Robert Harvey (1937). **Educ:** St Wilfrid's Preparatory School, Hawkhurst; Rugby School.

HARVEY, Henry Norman Martin (1949) Born 8 January 1920, 7 Penrith Road, Basingstoke, Hampshire; son of Willian Norman Harvey, Poultry Farmer, and Gertrude Margaret Watson. **Tutor(s):** J M Wordie. **Educ:** West Ayton Elementary School, Scarborough; Scarborough High School. **Career:** Major, Gurkha Rifles; Colonial Service Course; Police Officer, Tanganyika 1947.

HARVEY, John Allen (1922) Born 20 August 1900, Roslyn, Dunedin, New Zealand; son of Charles William Norman Harvey, Stockbroker and Sharebroker, and Charlotte Bloomfield McGill; m Audrey Helen Sois Sanguinetti, 11 November 1929, Kuala Lumpur; 2 sons (Michael John b 19 November 1930 and William Robin b 13 June 1932), 2 daughters (Gillian Frances b 14 November 1939 and Alison Victoria Featherstone b 1 May 1945). **Subject(s):** History; BA 1929; MA (New Zealand) 1922. **Tutor(s):** E A Benians. **Johnian Relatives:** father of Michael John Harvey (1950). **Educ:** Christ's College Grammar School, Christchurch, New Zealand; Otago University College, Dunedin, New Zealand. **Career:** Cadet, Federated Malay States; Open Civil Service Examination 1924; Member, Malayan Civil Service 1925–1955; Head, Lands and Mines Department, Kaduna, Northern Provinces, Nigeria 1942–1944; Military Administrator, Cocos Islands (Indian Ocean) and subsequently Senior Civil Affairs Officer, British Military Administration, Malaya 1945–1946; First Chief Social Welfare Officer on return of Civil Government 1946–1947; Commissioner of Lands, Malaya 1947; British Advisor, Pahang 1948; Commissioner of Lands, Chairman, Rural Board for Singapore Island and Member, Legislative Council, Singapore 1949–1953; British Adviser, Pahang 1953–1954; Controller of the Household of HM the Yang di Pertuan Agong of the Federation of Malaya 1957–1961. Died 20 March 1991.

HARWOOD, Herbert Clifton Fairfax (1926) Born 18 July 1907, Botanic Gardens Street, Curepipe, Plaines Wilhelms, Mauritius; son of Samuel Davenport Fairfax Harwood, Lecturer at Wye Agricultural College, and Agnes Marguerite Peromat. BA 1930. **Tutor(s):** M P Charlesworth. **Johnian Relatives:** son of Samuel Davenport Fairfax Harwood (1897). **Educ:** St Hugh's School, Bickley; Radley College. Died 31 January 1961.

HASELER, The Revd Digby Bertram (1919) Born 30 July 1897, King's Norton, Worcestershire; son of Rowland Haseler, Clerk in Holy Orders, and Catherine Round. **Subject(s):** History; BA 1922; MA 1929. **Tutor(s):** E E Sikes. **Educ:** Shrewsbury Priory Secondary Council School; Hereford Cathedral School; Westcott House, Cambridge. **Career:** King's Shropshire Light Infantry 1916–1918; Ordained Deacon 1929; Curate, St John's, Hackney 1929–1935; Ordained Priest 1930; Rector, Stapleton, Shropshire 1935–1946; Rector, Brandesburton 1945–1952; Vicar, Holme on Spalding Moor, Yorkshire 1953. **Awards:** Somerset Exhibition, SJC 1916. **Publications:** 'At a British Cemetery in Flanders', *The Eagle*, 1920; 'A Chanty', *The Eagle*, 1920. Died 25 October 1978.

HASKETT, Ronald Walter (1944) Born 16 February 1927, Kutelamara, High Street, West End, Southampton; son of Garnett Haskett, Machinist, and Ethel Louisa Bailey. **Subject(s):** Natural Sciences; BA 1948; MA 1971. **Tutor(s):** C W Guillebaud. **Educ:** West End Elementary School, Southampton; Shirley School, Southampton; Taunton's School, Southampton.

HASLAM, The Revd Reginald Kingdon (1909) Born 25 December 1885, Ashling Villas, Knighton, Leicestershire; son of Herbert Kingdon Haslam, Clerk in Holy Orders, and Florence Helen Hempel. **Subject(s):** History; BA 1912; MA 1918. **Johnian Relatives:** brother of Victor Kingdon Haslam (1906); uncle of Richard Alleyn Kingdon Haslam (1949). **Educ:** Sutton Park School; Stamford School. **Career:** Ordained Deacon 1913; Missioner, Pembroke College Mission, Newington 1913–1920; Ordained Priest 1914; Temporary CF 1916–1919; Vicar of the Lady Margaret, Walworth 1921–1927; Curate in charge, St Olave's Mission Church, Mitcham 1927–1929; Minister 1929–1931; Vicar 1931–1938; Licence to officiate, Diocese of Grahamstown, South Africa 1938–1940; Curate, Basingstoke 1940–1943; Curate in charge 1943–1946, Vicar 1946–1954, St Mark, Surbiton; Rector, Aller with Pitney-Lortie, Somerset 1954. Died 26 January 1971.

HASLAM, Richard Alleyn Kingdon (1949) Born 19 December 1929, Dulwich, London; son of Victor Kingdon Haslam, Schoolmaster, and Helena Mary Cottrell-Dormer; m (Winifred) Judith Manning, 9 April

1964, St Peter's Church, St Albans; 1 son, 2 daughters. **Subject(s):** Natural Sciences; BA 1952; MA 1956; CertEd (Cambridge) 1953. **Tutor(s):** G C L Bertram. **Johnian Relatives:** son of Victor Kingdon Haslam (1906); nephew of Reginald Kingdon Haslam (1909). **Educ:** New College School, Oxford; St Petroc's School, Bude; Sedbergh School. **Career:** Master, Ashville College, Harrogate 1953–1955; Master, Bournmouth School for Boys 1955–1959; Master, Dennis Memorial Grammar School, Onitsha, East Nigeria 1959–1963; Master, Leighton Park School, Reading 1963–1964; Master, South-East Essex County Technical High School 1964–1967; Head of Chemistry, Oswestry School 1967–1991.

HASLAM, Victor Kingdon (1906) Born 20 September 1887, Cross Road, Knighton, Wigston, Leicestershire; son of Herbert Kingdon Haslam, Clerk in Holy Orders, and Florence Helen Hempel; m Helena Mary Cottrell-Dormer; 2 sons (Nigel Christopher Kingdon b 16 January 1920, d 23 January 1996 and Richard Alleyn Kingdon b 19 December 1929), 1 daughter (Helen Rosemary Kingdon b 25 August 1921). **Subject(s):** Theology; BA 1909; MA 1955. **Tutor(s):** E E Sikes. **Johnian Relatives:** brother of Reginald Kingdon Haslam (1909); father of Richard Alleyn Kingdon Haslam (1949). **Educ:** Stamford School. **Career:** Master, Springfield Preparatory School 1909–1914; Lieutenant, RGA, WWI; Master, Barnard Castle School 1921–1926; Master, Rushmoor, Bedford 1926–1928; Master, Alleyn's School, Dulwich 1928–1954. Died 1 January 1966.

HASSAN, Salvador (1946) Born 26 August 1921, Tangier, Morocco; son of Samuel Hassan, Banker, and Victoria Nahon. **Subject(s):** Law; LLB 1949. **Tutor(s):** F Thistlethwaite. **Educ:** Lycée Regnault, Tangier; Repton School.

HASSAN, Tengku Abdullah (1931) Born 16 October 1912, Kota Bahru, Kelantan, Malaya; son of Tengku Hassan Bin Ungku Mohamed, Government Pensioner, Magistrate, and Tengku Embong Binti Sultan Muhammad. **Subject(s):** Law; BA 1934; MA 1937. **Tutor(s):** C W Guillebaud. **Educ:** Majlis Ugama English School; Victoria Bridge School, Singapore; Raffles Institution, Singapore.

HASSÉ, Dr Henry Ronald (1903) Born 27 July 1884, Ballykennedy, Ahoghill, County Antrim, Ireland; son of Leonard Gadow Hassé, Moravian Clergyman, and Annie Ball; m Kathleen Norah Kershaw, 1912. **Subject(s):** Mathematics; BA 1906; MA 1910; BSc (Manchester) 1903; MSc (Manchester) 1906. **Tutor(s):** J R Tanner; C E Graves. **Educ:** Fulneck Moravian School, Leeds; Ownes College, Manchester. **Career:** Assistant Lecturer in Mathematics, University of Liverpool 1908–1910; Ashton Fellow, SJC 1910–1916; Lecturer in Mathematics, Manchester University 1910–1919; Professor of Mathematics 1919–1949, Dean, Faculty of Science 1926–1930, Bristol University. **Awards:** Isaac Newton Studentship, University of Cambridge 1907; Honourable Mention for Smith's Prize, University of Cambridge 1908. Died 16 June 1955.

HASTIE, John Williams (1933) Born 12 March 1912, Columbia Hospital, Washington DC; son of Donald Hastie, Salesman, and Helen Moss Williams. **Tutor(s):** J S Boys Smith. **Educ:** The Grammar School, Cheshire; The High School, New Haven; Yale University, New Haven.

HASWELL, Anthony James Darley (1941) Born 4 August 1922, Srinagar, Kashmir, India; son of Chetwynd Henry Haswell, Brigadier, RE, and Dorothy Edith Berry; m Angela Mary Murphy, 1957; 3 sons, 1 daughter. **Subject(s):** Law; BA 1944; MA 1947. **Tutor(s):** S J Bailey. **Educ:** Little Appley School, Ryde; Cheltenham College Junior School; Winchester College. **Career:** Solicitor of the Supreme Court; Admitted Solicitor 1949; RAC Legal Department 1949; Army Legal Corps 1949–1981; Private Practice, London and Cornwall 1950–1951; Commissioned, Army Legal Services Staff List (Captain) 1952; Temporary Major 1956; Lieutenant Colonel 1967. **Appointments:** Insurance Ombudsman 1981–1989; Liveryman, Worshipful Company of Insurers 1987; Freeman, City of London 1987; Chairman, Appeals Tribunals, Financial Intermediaries, Managers and Brokers Regulatory Association 1989;

Deputy Chairman, Money Management Council 1994–1999. **Honours:** OBE 1985. **Publications:** Insurance Ombudsman Bureau annual reports for years 1981–1988; miscellaneous articles in industry journals.

HATTEN, Arthur William (1900) Born 12 March 1880, Hurstmonceux, Sussex; son of Charles William Hatten, Clerk in Holy Orders, and Rozalie Jane Palmer de Verinne. **Subject(s):** Classics; BA 1903. **Tutor(s):** E E Sikes. **Educ:** Grantham School. Died 5 February 1916.

HATTERSLEY, William Hanchett (1908) Born 26 October 1887, 6 Bateman Street, Cambridge; son of William Oliver Hattersley, Grocer, and Elizabeth Mary Palmer. **Tutor(s):** L H K Bushe-Fox. **Educ:** Perse Grammar School, Cambridge; Framlingham College. **Career:** Actor (under stage name Mr Eric Howard); roles include Alaric Chichester in *Peg o' my Heart.*

HATTON-ELLIS, Alfred Willmott Balfour (1920) Born 4 November 1898, West View, Lymm, Cheshire; son of Joseph Alfred Hatton-Ellis, Lieutenant, Army Motor Reserve of Officers, and Florence Martha Mawson; m Bridget Faith Mary Henry, 7 November 1942, St Mary's, Torquay. BA 1923; MA 1928. **Tutor(s):** E A Benians. **Johnian Relatives:** father of Gerald Willmott Hatton-Ellis (1964). **Educ:** Private Tuition, Crowborough and Eastbourne. **Career:** Carlton Publicity, Kingsway 1924; Lord Thomas Ltd 1926; British Celanese Ltd, Hanover Square 1928; Agricultural Economist, Seale Hayne Agricultural College, Newton Abbot 1945–1949. Died 7 March 1954.

HAUGHTON, Michael Frederick (1944) Born 10 May 1926, Braemar, Linney Road, Bramhall, Cheshire; son of Herbert Haughton, Textile Designer, and Alice Vivian Whitehead. **Subject(s):** English; BA 1948; MA 1951. **Tutor(s):** J M Wordie. **Johnian Relatives:** father of Dominic Stephen St John Haughton (1978). **Educ:** Westwood Preparatory School; Kingswood School; Philadelphia Textile Institute. **Career:** Brooklyn Museum; Museum of Modern Art, New York; Fairchild Publications. **Appointments:** RN Cadet, SJC. **Awards:** Goodwin Travelling Fellowship 1950.

HAUPT, Alden Morgan (1934) Born 18 January 1916, 161 East 79 Street, New York; son of Walter Clerk Haupt, Physician, and Mary Alden Morgan. **Tutor(s):** C W Guillebaud. **Educ:** Parker School, Chicago; Latin School, Chicago; Middlesex School, Concord, Massachusetts; Harvard University.

HAVILAND, Denis William Garstin Latimer (1929) Born 15 August 1910, 14 Lanark Mansions, North Paddington, London; son of William Alexander Haviland, Artist, and Edyth Louise Latimer, Artist. **Subject(s):** Modern and Medieval Languages/History; BA 1933; MA 1940; CIMgt; FRSA; FIIM. **Tutor(s):** E A Benians. **Johnian Relatives:** stepbrother of Hugo William Arbouin Repard (1929). **Educ:** Seafield School, Collington; Rugby School. **Career:** London Midland and Scottish Railway 1934–1939; Colonel, RE 1940–1946; Principal, Control Office for Germany and Austria; Head, German General Economic Department, Foreign Office 1945–1950; Under-Secretary (Air), Ministry of Supply; Deputy Secretary, Ministry of Aviation 1950–1959; Joint Managing Director and Deputy Chairman, Chairman and Managing Director, Staveley Industries Ltd 1965–1969; Director, Organised Office Designs Ltd 1972–2000. **Appointments:** Chairman, Preparatory Commission European Launcher Development Organisation 1962–1964; Director, Short Bros Ltd 1964–1981; Council Member, BIM 1967–1983; Committee Member, Cranfield Institute of Technology 1970–1983; Member, Management Studies Board 1974–1979, Member, Business and Management Committee and Academic Committee, 1979–1993, CNAA; Chairman, Professional Standards Committee 1975–1982; Founding Chairman, Confederation of Healing Organisations 1981–1990; Founding Chairman, Holistic Cancer Council 1984–1986; Council and Executive Committee Member, British Complementary Medicine Association 1990–1992. **Awards:** Verulam Gold Medal, BIM 1984. **Honours:** CB 1957. Died 30 May 2000.

HAWCRIDGE, Robert Stuart (1905) Born 8 June 1887, 37 Windsor Street, Barrow-in-Furness, Lancashire; son of Thomas Arthur Hawcridge, School Board Superintendent, and Emma Ratcliffe. BA 1909; MA 1913. **Tutor(s):** C E Graves; J R Tanner. **Educ:** Manchester Grammar School; University of Manchester. **Career:** Classics and Art Master, and House Master, North Manchester School; Master, Batley Grammar School, Yorkshire 1912; Corporal, 2nd Sportsman's Battalion, 24th Royal Fusiliers 1915–1916. **Appointments:** Lecturer in Industrial History, Workers' Educational Association. **Awards:** Shakespeare Society's Prize, Manchester Grammar School 1904; Procter Reading Prize, Manchester Grammar School 1905; Exhibition, SJC. Died 28 July 1916 (killed in action near Delville Wood).

HAWKES, William John (1900) Born 4 February 1882, Fairlight, Queen's Road, Clevedon, Somerset; son of Edward Clifford Hawkes, Clerk in Holy Orders, and Agnes Henrietta Jefferies; m Jessie Louisa Allen, 19 December 1908, Carshalton; 1 daughter (Joyce Agnes). **Subject(s):** Classics; BA 1903; MA 1907. **Tutor(s):** E E Sikes. **Johnian Relatives:** father-in-law of Herbert Leslie Allsopp (1917). **Educ:** Exeter School. **Career:** Headmaster, Woodroughs School, Moseley, Birmingham 1901. **Publications:** *Preparatory Latin Grammar Papers.* Died 12 December 1943.

HAWKINS, Michael Oliver Slade (1948) Born 11 May 1928, 27 Cumberland Park, Acton, Middlesex; son of Lewis Brackstone Hawkins, Bank Clerk, Bank of England, and Vera Margaret Kate Havinden; m Sheila Rosemary Skoyles, 3 November 1956, Christ Church, Little Heath, Hertfordshire; 2 sons (Simon b 21 May 1960 and Jeremy b 27 February 1962), 1 daughter (Charlotte b 29 December 1965). **Subject(s):** Economics; BA 1950; MA 1988. **Tutor(s):** C W Guillebaud, F Thistlethwaite. **Educ:** Wycliffe Junior School, Stonehouse; Wycliffe College, Stonehouse. **Career:** Colonial Administrative Officer, Kenya and Botswana 1951–1972; Local Government Officer, Hampshire County Council 1972–1983. **Appointments:** Permanent Secretary, Ministry of Works and Communications, Botswana 1966–1972; Assistant County Secretary, Hampshire County Council 1973–1983.

HAWORTH, Christopher Matthew (Kit) (1931) Born 31 December 1911, Disley, Stockport, Chester; son of Harold Wilfred Haworth, Clerk in Holy Orders, and Mary Katherine Matthew. **Subject(s):** Classics; BA 1934; MA 1938. **Tutor(s):** M P Charlesworth. **Educ:** Arnold House School, Llandulas; Pocklington School. **Career:** Master, Exeter School 1935–1936; Master, High Wycombe Royal Grammar School 1936–1975 (Senior Classics Master 1946–1975); Captain, Royal Northumberland Fusiliers 1940–1946. **Awards:** Foundation Scholarship, SJC. **Publications:** (with Leslie J Ashford) *The History of the Royal Grammar School High Wycombe 1562–1962*, Governors of the Royal Grammar School, High Wycombe, 1962. Died 17 August 1975.

HAWORTH, Dr Fred (1946) Born 26 April 1923, 167 Livesey Branch Road, Blackburn, Lancashire; son of Lawrence Haworth, Smallholder, and Mary Ellen Moore, Weaver; m Margaret Fisher, 11 November 1944; 2 sons (Ian b 1 January 1946 and Roger b 20 September 1949). **Subject(s):** Agricultural Science; DipAgSci 1947; BSc (Liverpool) 1943; DPhil (Liverpool) 1947. **Tutor(s):** G C L Bertram. **Johnian Relatives:** father of Ian Haworth (1964). **Educ:** Gregson Lane Elementary School, Preston; Balshaws Grammar School, Leyland; Liverpool University. **Career:** Imperial College of Tropical Agriculture, Trinidad, Colonial Research Service 1947–1950; Research Chemist, Tea Research Institute, Ceylon 1950–1953; Soil Chemist, National Vegetable Research Station, Wellesbourne 1953–1965; Project Manager, FAO/UNDP Agricultural Research Institute, Ethiopia 1965–1967; Director, Research, Caroni Ltd, Trinidad 1967–1971; Senior Research Officer, FAO/UNDP, Thailand 1973–1976; Technical Consultant, IBRD 1976–1979; Senior Research Officer, International Service for National Agricultural Research, Hague, Netherlands 1980–1985; Technical Consultant, Hague, Netherlands 1985–1987. **Awards:** Scholarship, SJC; Colonial Agricultural Scholarship, Cambridge; T H Middleton Prize 1947.

HAWS, Edward Thomas (1944) Born 19 January 1927, 31 Cheltenham Road, Southend-on-Sea, Essex; son of Edward Haws, Ironmonger's Manager, and Phyllis Annie Thomas; m Moira Jane Forbes, 26 August 1950; 2 sons (Gordon Forbes b 12 July 1951 and Tony David b 29 January 1958, d 1995), 1 daughter (Linda Jane b 22 March 1954). **Subject(s):** Mechanical Sciences; BA 1947; MA 1951; FREng; FICE; FIPENZ; CEng; FConsE. **Tutor(s):** S J Bailey. **Educ:** Thorpe Elementary School, Southend-on-Sea; Southend-on-Sea High School. **Career:** Sir Alexander Gibb & Partners 1947–1963; Resident Engineer, Meig Dam; Resident Engineer, Atiamuri Power Project; Engineer in charge, Tongariro River Power Development 1963–1978; Director, Soil Mechanics Ltd; Managing Director, Engineering and Resources Consultants; Stabilising Val de la Mare Dam, Jersey; Hari Rud Irrigation, Afghanistan; Chowilla Dam, South Australia; Director and Consultant, Rendel Palmer & Tritton, Consulting Engineers 1978–1992; Project Engineer, Mersey Tidal Power Barrage; Manager, Thames Barrier Project; Manager, Arakundo/Jambu Aye Irrigation Project. **Appointments:** Member, All Reservoirs Panel under Reservoirs Act 1971–; Chairman, International Commission on Large Dams Committee on the Environment 1979–1993; Chairman, British Dam Society and British Hydromechanics Research Association; Consultant, All Reservoirs Panel 1992–; Vice-President, International Commission on Large Dams 1993–1996. **Awards:** Exhibition, SJC 1944; Scholarship, SJC 1945. **Publications:** 'Diaphragm Walls', *Civil Engineering for Underground Rail Transport*, 1990; 44 technical papers; Parsons Memorial Lecture, Royal Society and RSE, 1996.

HAWTON, Sir John Malcolm Kenneth (1923) Born 18 September 1904, 46 Battersea Rise, South West Battersea, Surrey; son of John Francis Hawton, Accountant General's Department, GPO, and Marie Sarah Cocks; m Hilda Cawley; 1 daughter. **Subject(s):** Classics; BA 1926; MA 1930. **Tutor(s):** E E Sikes. **Educ:** Emanuel School, Wandsworth Common. **Career:** Master, University College School 1926–1927; Ministry of Health 1927; Called to the Bar 1931; Permanent Secretary, Ministry of Health 1951–1960; Chairman, British Waterways Board 1963–1968. **Honours:** CB 1947; KCB 1952. Died 7 January 1982.

HAY, Alexander Charles de Prudrik (1929) Born 11 March 1910, 17 North Gardner Street, Partick, Lanarkshire, Scotland; son of Alexander James Hay, Clerk in Holy Orders, and Carolina Isabella Esther Bastianini. **Subject(s):** History; BA 1932; MA 1936. **Tutor(s):** E A Benians. **Educ:** The High School, Hawick; Westcott House, Cambridge. **Career:** Ordained Deacon 1934; Curate, St Paul, Cullercoats 1934–1936; Ordained Priest 1935; Curate, St Nicholas Cathedral Church, Newcastle upon Tyne 1937–1939; Chaplain and Master, Dame Allan's School, Newcastle 1939; Vicar, Heddon on the Wall, Northumberland 1963; Honorary Canon of Newcastle Cathedral 1970. Died 14 February 1989.

HAY, Andrew Mackenzie (1948) Born 9 April 1928, 16 Cowley Street, Westminster, London; son of Ewen James Mackenzie Hay, East India Merchant, and Bertine Louise Vavasseur Buxton; m (1) Jennifer Mary Dimoline, 27 June 1950, (2) Louise Warner, 30 January 1957, (3) Sharman Douglas, 1968, (4) Catherine Newman, 30 July 1977. **Subject(s):** Economics; BA 1950; MA 1955. **Tutor(s):** C W Guillebaud. **Educ:** Byron House, Highgate, London; Betteshanger School, Eastry; Blundell's School, Tiverton. **Career:** Second Lieutenant, Army Education Corps; Commodities Trader, London and Ceylon 1950–1953; Merchant Banking Executive 1954–1980; President, British-American Chamber of Commerce 1966–1968; President, Calvert Vavasseur & Co 1968–1980; International Trade Consultant 1980–2001. **Appointments:** Vice-Principal, Calvert Vavasseur & Co Inc, NYC 1954–1961; President, Calvert-Peat Inc NYC 1978; HM Honorary British Consul 1987; Dean of Oregon Consular Corps 1991; President, American Importers Association 1977–1979; President, Philippine American Chamber of Commerce; President, British American Chamber of Commerce. **Awards:** World Affairs Council Willard de Weese Award 1992. **Honours:** CBE. **Publications:** *A Century of Coconuts; Confessions of an Honorary Consul*, 1999. Died 2 May 2001.

HAY, Captain David (1926) Born 18 January 1909, Midhurst, Sussex; son of Thomas Hay, Headmaster, and Amy Charlotte Tabram. **Subject(s):** English/History; BA 1930; MA 1934. **Tutor(s):** M P Charlesworth. **Johnian Relatives:** son of Thomas Hay (1892). **Educ:** King Edward VI School, Chelmsford. **Career:** Group Captain. Died 9 June 1989.

HAY, James Foulis (1929) Born 27 March 1912, 62 Great George Street, Glasgow; son of David Allan Hay, Chartered Accountant, and Frances Margaret Walker; 1 daughter (Susan). BA 1932; MA 1936. **Tutor(s):** C W Guillebaud. **Educ:** Glasgow Academy. Died 26 April 1972.

HAY, Michael (1929) Born 19 June 1911, King Edward VI School, Chelmsford; son of Thomas Hay, Headmaster, and Amy Charlotte Tabram. **Subject(s):** Modern and Medieval Languages/Geography; BA 1932; MA 1936. **Tutor(s):** J M Wordie. **Johnian Relatives:** son of Thomas Hay (1892). **Educ:** King Edward VI School, Chelmsford.

HAY, Robert Malcolm (1941) Born 28 February 1923, Grange Fell, Leigh Woods, Bristol; son of Robert Bruce Hay, Mechanical Engineer, and Henrietta Margaret Mylne; m Colette Lucille Cantrill, 8 August 1949, Portsmouth. BA 1944; MA 1947. **Tutor(s):** S J Bailey. **Educ:** Gayhurst School, Gerrard's Cross; Oundle School. **Career:** Laboratory, British Electrical and Allied Industries Research Association 1940.

HAY, William (1948) Born 25 August 1926, 13 Southfield, St Andrews, Fife; son of William Hay, Joiner, and Margaret McDonald Taylor; 1 son, 1 daughter. **Subject(s):** Classics; BA 1950; MA 1957. **Tutor(s):** R L Howland. **Educ:** Madras College, St Andrews; Fettes College, Edinburgh. **Career:** Colonial Administrative Service, Tanganyika 1952–1962; Ford Motor Company 1963–1967; Laporte Industries 1967–1989. **Awards:** Major Scholarship, SJC 1945.

HAY, The Revd William King (1904) Born 22 June 1884, 44 Fern Avenue, Byker, Newcastle upon Tyne; son of Thomas Hay, Clerk, and Isabella Catherine Ewing. **Subject(s):** History; BA 1907; MA 1912. **Tutor(s):** J R Tanner; C E Graves. **Johnian Relatives:** brother of Thomas Hay (1892). **Educ:** The Royal Grammar School, Newcastle upon Tyne. **Career:** Ordained Deacon 1907; Curate, Christ Church, Patricroft 1907–1909; Ordained Priest 1908; Curate, Hurworth 1909–1911; Assistant Master, Newcastle Grammar School 1911–1913; Curate, St Aubin, Jersey 1916–1917. Died 21 January 1917.

HAYBURN, Edward Francis (1925) Born 29 October 1907, Walmer House, Walmer Villas, Manningham, Bradford, Yorkshire; son of Edward George Hayburn, Company Director, and Mary Wilkinson. BA 1929. **Tutor(s):** J M Wordie. **Johnian Relatives:** cousin of Geoffrey Rex Liebert (1924). **Educ:** Woodlands School, Deganwy, North Wales; Rugby School.

HAYGARTH, Harold John (1936) Born 4 July 1917, 39 Westhouse Grove, West Kirby, Wirral; son of Harold Haygarth, Schoolmaster, and Lizzie Walker. **Subject(s):** Mathematics/Mechanical Sciences; BA 1939; MA 1943. **Tutor(s):** J M Wordie. **Educ:** Kingsmead School, Meols Hoylake; Calday Grange Grammar School, West Kirby. **Career:** Lieutenant, RNVR; 1939–1943. **Awards:** Scholarship, SJC. Died 12 December 1943 (killed on active service).

HAYMAN, Christopher Hartley (1937) Born 17 February 1919, Dudley Nursing Home, Leeds; son of Perceval Mills Cobham Hayman, Barrister-at-law, and Susan Moon Hartley. **Subject(s):** Economics. **Tutor(s):** J S Boys Smith. **Johnian Relatives:** brother of Perceval Ecroyd Cobham Hayman (1934). **Educ:** Winchester House, Brackley; Bradfield College; Heidelberg University. **Career:** Captain, 9th The Queen's Royal Lancers, RAC 1941–1943. Died 26 April 1943 (killed in action).

HAYMAN, Professor Henry John Godfrey (1936) Born 22 September 1917, 28 Somali Road, Hampstead, London; son of Philip Godfrey Hayman, Merchant, and Kate Abrahams; m Berta Perlmutter, 1953.

Subject(s): Natural Sciences; BA 1939; MA 1943; PhD (Jerusalem) 1947. **Tutor(s):** C W Guillebaud. **Educ:** Brondesbury and Kilburn High School Kindergarten, London; Wykeham House School, London; University College School, London. **Career:** Lecturer, Hebrew University 1963–1967; Book-Statistical Thermodynamics, Elsevier 1967–1968; Associate Professor 1968–1988, Professor Emeritus 1988, Hebrew University. **Awards:** Exhibition, SJC 1936–1937; Junior Scholarship, SJC 1938.

HAYMAN, His Honour John David Woodburn (1937) Born 24 August 1918, Johannesburg, Transvaal, South Africa; son of Israel Hayman, Solicitor, and Ethel Loewenstark; m Jane Davison; 2 sons, 4 daughters. **Subject(s):** Law; BA 1940; MA 1944; LLB 1943; LLM 1985. **Tutor(s):** C W Guillebaud. **Johnian Relatives:** father of Christopher David Hayman (1978). **Educ:** King Edward VII School, Johannesburg, South Africa. **Career:** Service with South African Forces 1940–1942; Called to the Bar, Middle Temple 1945; Lecturer in Law, University College of Wales, Aberystwyth; Lecturer in Law, Leeds University; Lecturer in Law, University of Cambridge; Circuit Judge 1976–1992.

HAYMAN, The Revd Canon Perceval Ecroyd Cobham (1934) Born 22 March 1915, Rusholme, Manchester; son of Perceval Mills Cobham Hayman, Barrister-at-law, and Susan Moon Hartley; m Sylvia Mary Gamble, October 1939; 1 daughter (Susan Caroline). **Subject(s):** History/English; BA 1937; MA 1941. **Tutor(s):** J S Boys Smith. **Johnian Relatives:** brother of Christopher Hartley Hayman (1937). **Educ:** Winchester House School, Brackley; Stowe School; Lincoln Theological College. **Career:** Ordained Deacon 1950–1951; Ordained Priest 1951; Chaplain, Marlborough College 1954–1963; Rector, Rogate with Terwick, Chichester, Sussex 1963–1981; Rural Dean, Midhurst, Sussex 1972–1981; Canon and Prebendary, Chichester Cathedral. 1977–1981. Died 12 May 1996.

HAYMANN, Professor Walter Kurt (HAYMAN) (1943) Born 6 January 1926, Cologne, Germany; son of Franz Samuel Haymann, Emeritus Professor of Law, University of Cologne, and Ruth Mathilde Hensel; m (1) Margaret Riley Crann, September 1947 (d 1994); (2) Waficka Katifi, May 1995 (d 2001); (1) 3 daughters. **Subject(s):** Mathematics; BA 1946; MA 1951; ScD 1956; Honorary DSc (Exeter) 1981; Honorary DSc (Birmingham) 1985; Honorary Dr rer nat (Giessen) 1992; Honorary DPhil (Uppsala) 1992; Honorary DSc (National University of Ireland) 1997; FRS 1956. **Tutor(s):** J M Wordie. **Johnian Relatives:** father-in-law of Alexander Simon Wassermann (1967). **Educ:** Humanistic Gymnasium, Cologne, Germany; Gordonstoun School. **Career:** Lecturer, King's College, Newcastle upon Tyne 1947; Title A Fellow, SJC 1947–1950; Lecturer 1947–1953, Reader 1953–1956, University College, Exeter; Professor of Pure Mathematics 1956–1985 (Emeritus 1985), Dean, Royal College of Science 1978–1981, Imperial College, London; Professor (Part-time) 1985–1993 (Emeritus 1993), University of York; Senior Research Fellow, Imperial College 1995–. **Appointments:** Visiting Lecturer, Brown University, USA 1949–1950; Visiting Lecturer, Stanford University, USA 1950 and 1955; Visiting Lecturer, American Mathematical Society 1961; Co-founder, with Mrs Hayman, British Mathematical Olympiad; Vice-President, London Mathematical Society 1982–1984; Foreign Member, Finnish Academy of Science and Letters; Foreign Member, Accademia Nazionale dei Lincei, Rome; Corresponding Member, Bavarian Academy of Science. **Awards:** Major Scholarship, SJC 1942; Wright's Prize, SJC 1944; Earle Prize 1945; Baylis Studentship 1946; Twisden Studentship, Trinity College, Cambridge 1946; First Smith's Prize, University of Cambridge 1948; Adams Prize, University of Cambridge 1949; Junior Berwick Prize 1955; Senior Berwick Prize 1964; de Morgan Medal, London Mathematical Society 1995. **Publications:** *Multivalent Functions*, Cambridge, 1958 (2nd expanded edition, 1994); *Meromorphic Functions*, Oxford, 1964; *Research and Problems in Function Theory*, London, 1967; *Subharmonic Functions*, II Volumes, Academic Press, 1976 and 1989; about 190 papers in various mathematical journals.

HAYNES, Philip Francis (1923) Born 21 May 1905, 8 St Michael's Road, Maidstone, Kent; son of Bernard William Haynes, Iron Merchant, and Ethel Mary Hills; m Norah Vivienne Willshire; 1 son (Patrick d 1937), 1 daughter (Sarah). **Tutor(s):** E A Benians. **Educ:** St Peter's School, Seaford; Haileybury College. **Career:** Captain, 4th Battalion, Queens Royal West Kent Regiment, (later POW), WWII; Chairman, Haynes Brothers Ltd, Maidstone. Died 5 August 1987.

HAYTER, William Duncan Cary (1923) Born 26 March 1906, Compton Pauncefote, Somerset; son of William Percy Hayter, Farmer, and Mary Newbury Coles. **Tutor(s):** B F Armitage. **Educ:** The King's School, Bruton. Died 4 June 1971.

HAYWARD, John Ralph Goodwin (1919) Born 7 June 1901, Weatherall House, Well Walk, Hampstead, Middlesex; son of Frederick George Hayward, gentleman of independent means, and Augusta Beatrice Rooth. **Tutor(s):** E E Sikes. **Educ:** Heath Mount School, Hampstead; Malvern College; Private Tuition, Reading.

HAYWARD, Maurice John (Jack) (1925) Born 2 February 1906, Poona, India, son of Maurice Henry Weston Hayward, Indian Civil Service, and Alice Christine Barber; m Lady Patricia Mary Stopford; 1 son (Richard), 3 daughters (Bridget, Caroline and Sarah). **Subject(s):** Economics/History; BA 1928. **Tutor(s):** E A Benians. **Johnian Relatives:** grandson of Robert Baldwin Hayward (1846); son of Maurice Henry Weston Hayward (1886); uncle of Frank Antony Peet (1941). **Educ:** Copthorne School, Sussex; Marlborough College. **Career:** Colonial Service 1929–1957; Eastern Cadet, Malayan Civil Service 1929; Assistant District Commissioner, Tanjong Malim, Perak; Assistant Adviser, Besut, Trengganu; Assistant District Officer, Bukit Mertajam, Province Wellesley 1934; Magistrate, Seremban, Negri Sembilan 1936; Secretary to the Resident, Kuala Lipis, Pahang 1938; District Officer, Kuala Lipis, Pahang 1941; POW Malaya and Thailand 1942–1945; Principal Secretary, Federal Treasury, Malaya; Principal Secretary, Federal Secretariat, Malaya; British Adviser, Perlis 1950; British Adviser, Trengganu; British Adviser, Pahang; Resident Commissioner, Malacca; Assistant Secretary, Magistrates Association 1957; Committee Clerk, Archivist, Dunstable Town Council. **Appointments:** Church Warden, St Mary the Virgin, Haddenham, Bucks. **Awards:** Scholarship, SJC 1924. Died 3 September 2001.

HAYWARD, Roger Kendrick (1945) Born 15 December 1927, 19 Shenbourne Road, Acocks Green, Birmingham; son of William Herbert Hayward, Deputy Director of Education for Bolton, and May Higgs; m Rachel Christian Erskine, 2 July 1956. BA 1950; MA 1952; FICE; MRIN; MIE (Aust). **Tutor(s):** S J Bailey; R L Howland. **Educ:** Hartfield Crescent School, Birmingham; Bolton School. **Career:** Partner, Halcrow International Partnership (Consulting Engineers). Died 21 July 1985.

HEAD, James Lawrence (1918) American Student.

HEAD, Kenneth Harold (1945) Born 10 May 1927, Cradley Heath, Staffordshire; son of Harold Robert Head, Cashier, Mechanical Engineering Works, and Hilda Errington; m Beryl Totney, June 1949; 1 son (Christopher Paul Errington); 1 daughter (Rosalind Margaret). **Subject(s):** Mechanical Sciences; BA 1948; MA 1952; CEng; FICE 1968; FGS. **Tutor(s):** S J Bailey; R L Howland. **Educ:** Old Hill Junior Mixed Council School; King Edward VI School, Stourbridge. **Career:** Robert M Douglas (Contractors) Ltd, Birmingham 1949–1960; Engineer-in-Charge, Soil Mechanics Laboratory, Mangla Dam Project (Pakistan), Binnie and Partners 1960–1966; Laboratory Manager, Soil Mechanics Ltd, Chelsea, then Bracknell 1966–1978; Senior Engineer, ELE Technical Services Ltd 1978–1984; Independent Consultant in Geotechnical Testing and Training 1984; Drafting Consultant for BS 1377:1990, Methods of test for soils for civil engineering purposes. **Awards:** State Scholarship 1944; Exhibition, SJC 1945. **Publications:** *Manual of Soil Laboratory Testing*, 3 vols, 1980–1986, 2nd edition 1992–1998; *Soil Technicians Handbook*, 1989.

HEALD, William Margetson (1913) Born 21 August 1894, The Rectory, Chale, Isle of Wight, Hampshire; son of Charles William Heald, Clerk in Orders, and Charlotte Jolliffe. BA 1916; MRCS; LRCP. **Tutor(s):** R P Gregory. **Educ:** Allen House, Guildford; Marlborough College. **Career:** Lieutenant, RAMC 1918; 91st Field Ambulance; Medical Officer, 16th Battalion, Lancashire Fusiliers. **Awards:** Exhibition, SJC. Died 8 September 1918 (of wounds received in action on the Somme 22 August 1918).

HEALEY, Robert Geoffrey (1933) Born 10 August 1914, Moorcroft, Manchester Road, Heywood; son of John William Healey, Cotton Spinner, Rope and Twine Manufacturer, and Eleanor Mason; m Barbara. **Subject(s):** Economics; BA 1936; MA 1940. **Tutor(s):** C W Guillebaud. **Educ:** Wycliffe College, Stonehouse. **Career:** Rope and Twine Manufacturer; Artillery, served in Italy 1939–1945. Died 10 August 1962.

HEAP, Alan (1941) Born 20 September 1922, 111 Swan Lane, Lockwood, Huddersfield, Yorkshire; son of Joshua Heap, Grocer, and Celia Maria Rawlinson. **Subject(s):** Mechanical Sciences; BA 1944; MA 1948. **Tutor(s):** S J Bailey. **Educ:** Mount Pleasant Elementary School, Huddersfield; Huddersfield College. Died 6 February 1993.

HEARLE, Professor John William Stanley (1943) Born 5 June 1925, The Cottage, Elmbridge Road, Wotton Without Gloucester; son of William Henry Trounce Hearle, Manager, Agricultural Cooperative Society, and Esther Christine Stanley; m (1) Marjorie Joyce Pebody, 1955 (d 1982), (2) Ann Maureen Ashworth, 1985; 3 sons (David J, Adrian D and R Marcus), 1 stepson (Stephen J Ashworth), 1 stepdaughter (Catherine E Sheehan). **Subject(s):** Natural Sciences/Physics; BA 1947; MA 1950; ScD 1973; PhD (Manchester) 1952; FInstP 1961; FTI. **Johnian Relatives:** father of Adrian Donald Hearle (1977); uncle of Geoffrey Hugh Griffiths (1977). **Educ:** Wotton School, Gloucester; Crypt Grammar School, Gloucester. **Career:** RAE 1945–1946; British Cotton Industry Research Association (Shirley Institute) 1946–1948; Department of Textiles, UMIST 1949–1985; Professor of Textile Technology and Chairman of Department 1974–1985 (Emeritus 1985), Professorial Fellow 1985, UMIST; Dean, Faculty of Technology, University of Manchester 1979–1980; Chairman, Tension Technology International Ltd 1986–1995, later Senior Consultant. **Appointments:** Post-doctoral Fellow, Clemson University, South Carolina 1953; Fellow 1960, Honorary Fellow 1984, Vice-President 1978–1990, Chairman of Council 1993–1995, Vice-Chairman 1991–1993 and 1995–1996, Honorary Life Member 1998, Editor-in-Chief, *Textile Insitute Journal* 1987–2000, Textile Institute; Visiting Associate Professor of Mechanical Engineering, MIT 1963–1964; Consultant, DuPont 1970–2000; Honorary Member, Fiber Society (USA) and British Society of Rheology; Director, NATO Advanced Study Institute on Mechanics of Flexible Fibre Assemblies, Greece 1979; Chairman, Mellor Archaeological Trust; Distinguished Visiting Professor of Mechanical Engineering 1986–1988, Visiting Professor in Materials Science Program 1989–1990, University of Delaware; Visiting Scientist, Research Division of Fibers Department, DuPont 1989–1990. **Awards:** Warner Medal, Textile Institute 1967. **Publications:** (with W E Morton) *Physical Properties of Textile Fibres*, 1962, 1975, 1993; (with P Grosberg and S Backer) *Structural Mechanics of Fibers, Yarns and Fabrics*, 1969; *Polymers and their Properties*, 1982; (with B Lomas and W Cooke) *Atlas of Fibre Fracture and Damage to Textiles*, 1989, 2000; (with L Hollick and D K Wilson) *Yarn Texturing Technology*, 2001; editor and contributor to other books; 250 research papers and many general articles.

HEARN, Harry Robert (1949) Born 23 March 1927, 1 The Avenue, Beckenham, Kent; son of Harry Hearn, Butcher, and Edith Marion Cooper. BA 1952; MA 1956. **Tutor(s):** G C L Bertram. **Educ:** Clare House School, Beckenham; Sutton Valence School. **Awards:** Robins Exhibition 1949. **Honours:** OBE 1972.

HEARN, Captain Robert Cecil (1911) Born 30 October 1892, 3 St James', Hatcham, Surrey; son of Charles Henry Hearn, Commercial Traveller, and Florence Maria Perry. **Subject(s):** Classics; BA 1914. **Tutor(s):** E E

Sikes. **Educ:** St Olave's Grammar School. **Career:** Lieutenant 1916, Acting Captain 1917, then Captain, London Regiment (Blackheath and Woolwich Battalion). **Honours:** MC 1917. Died 30 April 1918 (killed in action near Jerusalem).

HEATH, Ernest Alfred John (1919) Born 8 April 1899, 77 Hillfield Road, West Hampstead, London; son of Alfred Heath, Schoolmaster, and Florence Kate Whiddington; m (2) Gladys Hale, 19 June 1943; Holy Trinity, Bayswater; twin sons (b 1944). **Subject(s):** Mathematics; BA 1921; MA 1929; FIA. **Tutor(s):** E E Sikes. **Educ:** Lower School of John Lyon, Harrow; Harrow County Secondary School; Merchant Taylors' School. **Career:** Manager and Actuary, Medical Sickness Annuity and Life Assurance Society 1944. **Awards:** Scholarship, SJC 1917. Died 8 April 1984.

HEATH, Karl Edwin (1935) Born 18 September 1916, 11 Howard Street, Lincoln; son of George Thomas Heath, Ladies' Costumier, and Ethel Chatterton; m Grace Pepper. **Subject(s):** History/Law; BA 1938; MA 1942. **Tutor(s):** J S Boys Smith. **Johnian Relatives:** brother-in-law of Allan Hulme (1936); uncle of Edward Christopher Hulme (1965). **Educ:** Rosemary Lane School; Westgate School; North District School; Lincoln School. **Career:** RE, served with BEF in France, WWII; History and Economics teacher, Preston Grammar School 1944–1946; Lecturer, University of West Indies 1946–1952; Director, Shell Oilfield Schools, Venezuela 1952–1955; Lecturer in Philosophy, Lancaster Polytechnic (later University of Coventry) 1955–1981. **Appointments:** Founder and General Secretary, United Nations Association of Jamaica 1949; Founder and Chairman, Jamaica Council for Civil Rights 1950. **Awards:** Exhibition, SJC 1934; UN World Essay Prize while at UN Headquarters, New York 1950. **Publications:** *Ask the Parson*, GW Foote & Co – National Secular Society.

HEATLEY, Dr Norman George (1928) Born 10 January 1911, Selwyn House, Marton Place, Woodbridge, Suffolk; son of Thomas George Heatley, Veterinary Surgeon, and Grace Alice Symonds; m Mercy I Bing, 18 December 1944; 3 sons (Christopher, Piers and Jonathan), 2 daughters (Rose and Tamsin). **Subject(s):** Natural Sciences; BA 1932; MA 1936; PhD 1937; MA (Oxon) 1947; Honorary DM (Oxon) 1990. **Tutor(s):** C W Guillebaud. **Educ:** St Felix, Felixstowe; Westbourne House, Folkestone; The Grange, Folkestone; Tonbridge School, Kent. **Career:** Biochemical research (Senior Research Officer, later University Lecturer), Sir William Dunn School of Pathology, University of Oxford 1939–1978; Nuffield (Penicillin) Research Fellow 1948–1978, Supernumerary Fellow 1978–1982, Honorary Fellow 1982–2004, Lincoln College, Oxford. **Appointments:** Honorary Fellow, SJC 1992–2004. **Awards:** Benn Wolfe Levy Studentship in Biochemistry, University of Cambridge 1935; Rockefeller Fellowship 1939; Philip Walker Studentship in Pathology, Oxford 1942. **Honours:** OBE 1978. **Publications:** author/co-author of 65 scientific papers. Died 5 January 2004.

HEATON, The Revd Frederick Alphonse Arthur Will (1906) Born 22 September 1887, 7 Rochester Terrace, Kentish Town, Middlesex; son of William Cartledge Heaton, Clerk in Holy Orders, and Harriet Mary Milton; m Winifred Mary (d 1929). **Subject(s):** Theology; BA 1909. **Tutor(s):** E E Sikes. **Educ:** King's School, Canterbury; Worth Matravers Vicarage. **Career:** Ordained Deacon 1910; Curate, St Michael, Edmonton 1910–1911; Ordained Priest 1911; Curate, St Sepulchre, Holborn 1911–1912; Curate, St Michael, Golders Green 1914–1920; Vicar, Tong 1920–1926; Vicar, St Michael, Tenterden 1926. Died 23 November 1953.

HEBDITCH, Gerald Edward William (1949) Born 24 April 1929, Aldonvale, Hendford Hill, Yeovil, Somerset; son of Harold Oliver Hebditch, Garage Proprietor, and Lily Ethel Bartle; m Janice Aitken, 1962; 1 daughter (Tamsin Rowena b 1974). **Subject(s):** Natural Sciences; BA 1952; MA 1957. **Tutor(s):** G C L Bertram. **Educ:** Yeovil Preparatory and Collegiate School; Yeovil School. **Career:** Radar Fitter,

RAF 1947–1949; Exploration Seismologist, Shell International Petroleum Company 1952–1956; Assistant Physics Master, Peter Symonds School, Winchester 1957; Assistant Physics Master, Dulwich College, London 1957–1961; Head of Physics, City of Leeds Training College 1962–1964; Head of Science, City of Leeds and Carnegie College 1965–1974; Education Advisor in charge of teachers' college, as part of UNESCO project, Irian Barat (West Irian – now Irian Jaya), Indonesia (sabbatical) 1969–1970; Senior Advisor, Leeds Education Authority 1974–1977; County Advisor, Education Department of Humberside County Council 1978; Director, Dorset Education-Industry Partnership 1989–1994. **Appointments:** Non-executive Director, Headteacher Into Industry Ltd 1991; Associate Director, Southern Science and Technology Forum (Bournemouth University) 1995; Work on various committees, mostly education/industry liaison. Died 14 December 1999.

HEDGECOCK, Arthur Thomas (1909) Born 24 February 1890, 19 South Road, Faversham, Kent; son of Arthur Thomas Hedgecock, Farmer, and Evelyn Maria Hartley. **Subject(s):** Mathematics/Natural Sciences; BA 1912; MA 1920. **Tutor(s):** L H K Bushe-Fox. **Educ:** Sheldwich National Schools, Faversham; Wreight's School, Faversham. **Career:** Master, Radley College 1913–1946; Lieutenant, Irish Guards, WWI. Died 23 April 1970.

HEDLEY, Charles Stephens (1925) Born 24 August 1906, Hillside, Loudwater, Chipping Wycombe, Buckinghamshire; son of George Henry Hedley, Paper Manufacturer, and Elizabeth Stephens; m (1) Jane Margaret Hobbs, 27 June 1936, St Mary Magdalene, Stoke Bishop, Bristol (dis 1945), (2) Joan Vivian More (née Hatton Smith), 8 July 1949, London; (1) 2 daughters (Priscilla Jane b 10 July 1937 and Sarah Mary-Anne b 4 July 1940, d 8 January 1994), (2) 1 son (Giles Henry b 18 April 1950, d 12 April 1981), 3 stepsons (Thomas b 17 September 1941, Roger V b 13 August 1943 and Charles b 25 October 1946). **Subject(s):** Economics; BA 1928; MA 1932. **Tutor(s):** J M Wordie. **Johnian Relatives:** son-in-law of Victor William John Hobbs (1905); stepfather of Roger Vivian More (1962). **Educ:** Braidlee, Stoke Bishop; Marlborough College. **Career:** RE (Sappers), serving at Dunkirk, North Africa, and finally at Aldershot 1939–1945; Paper Manufacturer, St Anne's Mill, Bristol, then Hedge Mill, Loudwater, High Wycombe. **Appointments:** Member, Dunkirk Veterans' Association; Member, Leander Club; Steward, Henley Royal Regatta; Member, Buckinghamshire County Council; Magistrate for Wycombe (sometime Chair, Wycombe Bench); President, Flackwell Heath Golf Club. **Honours:** MC. Died 21 August 1976.

HEDLEY, The Revd Percy Little (1917) Born 27 March 1900, Darlington, County Durham; son of John Hedley, Railway Agent, and Annie Bella Rutherford. **Subject(s):** Classics; BA 1920; MA 1925. **Tutor(s):** E E Sikes. **Educ:** Elementary School, Darlington; Elementary School, Mirfield; Grammar School, Mirfield; Huddersfield College. **Awards:** Jeremie Septuagint Prize 1922.

HEESOM, Dudley Stone (1920) Born 14 May 1903, 142 Station Road, Redhill, Surrey; son of Edwin Ernest Darley Heesom, Dental Surgeon, and Maude Agnes Miller. **Subject(s):** History; BA 1926; MA 1935. **Tutor(s):** E A Benians. **Educ:** Radnor School, Redhill; The Junior King's School, Canterbury; The King's School, Canterbury. **Career:** History Master, Oundle School 1927–1968; Housemaster, Oundle School 1939–1956. **Awards:** HP Davison Scholarship from University of Cambridge to Princeton University 1925–1926. Died 1986.

HEFFERNAN, Dr Herbert Nesbitt (1931) Born 21 October 1913, St Thomas' Mount, Madras, India; son of Herbert William Heffernan, Lieutenant Colonel, Indian Army, and Grace Elizabeth Macdonald; m Ilse Mathilde Kizitaff, 5 June 1959 (d 1997); 1 son (Ranald Robin b 1966), 1 daughter (Anthea Moly b 1966). BA 1936; MA 1938; MRCS; LRCP 1942; MRCPsych 1972. **Tutor(s):** M P Charlesworth. **Educ:** Mr S A Phillips' Preparatory School, The Old Ride; Wellington College, Crowthorne; St Bartholomew's Hospital. **Career:** Honorary Lieutenant Colonel, RAMC 1949; Consultant Psychiatrist, Thames Regional Health Authority 1964. **Honours:** MBE 1970.

HEIMANN, Herman Paul (1910) Born 6 August 1888, Bloemfontein, Orange River Colony, South Africa; son of Julius Heimann, and Sarah Norden. **Subject(s):** Law; BA 1913; MA 1917; LLB 1913. **Tutor(s):** L H K Bushe-Fox. **Educ:** Marist Brothers, Gildburg and Port Elizabeth, South Africa; South African School and College, Cape Town, South Africa. **Career:** Private, Essex Regiment, WWI; Called to the Bar, Inner Temple 1914. Died 17 January 1981.

HELLINGS, Geoffrey Stuart (1907) Born 21 June 1888, Rockholme, Leckhampton, Gloucestershire; son of Robert Carnal Hellings, Hatter and Hosier, and Eliza Fisher Wright. **Subject(s):** Classics; BA 1910. **Tutor(s):** E E Sikes. **Educ:** Cheltenham Grammar School; Christ's Hospital, Horsham. **Career:** Cadet, Federated Malay States 1911; Studied Chinese in Canton 1912–1914; Lieutenant, Duke of Cornwall's Light Infantry 1915–1919; Acting Assistant District Officer, Kinta 1919; Magistrate, Batu Gajah 1919; Protector of Chinese, Perak 1920; Protector of Chinese, Selangor 1921–1923; Controller of Labour and Protector of Chinese, Johor 1923; Officer, Class III 1923; Class II, Protector of Chinese, Selangor and Pahang 1928; Collector of Estate Duty, Federated Malay States; also Acting District Officer, Ulu Langat 1929; Acting Official Assignee and Registrar of Companies 1930; Magistrate, Ipoh 1932. **Awards:** Christ's Hospital Exhibition, University of Cambridge 1907; John Stewart of Rannoch Scholarship in Greek and Latin, University of Cambridge 1909.

HELLIWELL, Leslie (1949) Born 12 November 1928, Bridge House, Haworth, Keighley, Yorkshire; son of Herbert Helliwell, Worsted Roller Coverer, and Mary Craven; m Irene Raistrick, 1954; 1 son (Christopher), 2 daughters (Catherine and Jessica). **Subject(s):** English; BA 1952; MA 1956. **Tutor(s):** A G Lee. **Educ:** Howarth Council School; Keighley Grammar School. **Career:** Teacher, The City School, Lincoln 1953–1957; Head of Department and Librarian, The King's School, Pontefract 1957–1968; Head of English Department, Withernsea High School 1968–1985. **Appointments:** Chairman, Committee promoting Professional Arts Events 1976–1984; Chairman of Governors, South Holderness School 1991–1994; Member, Branch Officer, Council Member, IAAM (later ATL); SDP and later Liberal Democrat Activist (Branch Officer, Constituency Secretary, Election Agent); Parish Councillor and Chairman, Holderness District Commitee of the Local Councils Assocation.

HEMMINGS, Henry (1919) Born 1 May 1899, 109 Upper Thrift Street, Northampton; son of George Hemmings, Chief Clerk, Northamptonshire County Council, and Jennie Cottam Carruthers; 1 daughter. **Subject(s):** Natural Sciences; BA 1921; MA 1938. **Tutor(s):** E E Sikes. **Educ:** Stimpson Avenue Council School, Northampton; The Grammar School, Northampton. **Career:** Second Lieutenant, Army; Inns of Court Officers Training Corps 1917; No 16 Officer Cadet Battalion 1917–1918; 3rd Battalion, Oxford and Bucks Light Infantry 1918; 11th Sherwood Foresters 1918; 71st POW Company 1918. **Awards:** Exhibition, SJC 1917; Harkness Scholarship, University of Cambridge 1922. Died 16 September 1997.

HEMMINGS, John (1941) Born 10 July 1923, 35 Avonmore Avenue, Mossley Hill, Liverpool; son of Fred Hemmings, Officer of Customs and Excise, and Annie Amelia Hambrook, Schoolmistress; m Sheila Margaret Urquhart, 19 May 1945, Lancaster; 3 sons (Richard Francis b 18 November 1948, David b 1 May 1951 and Andrew b 21 August 1953), 1 daughter (Sarah Margaret b 17 May 1956). **Subject(s):** Modern and Medieval Languages; BA 1946; MA 1948; DipEd (Edinburgh) 1948; MEd (Manchester) 1977. **Tutor(s):** C W Guillebaud. **Johnian Relatives:** brother of Robert Frederick Hemmings (1943); father of Richard Francis Hemmings (1966). **Educ:** Dovedale Road Council School, Mossley Hill; Beaver Road Council School, Didsbury; Manchester Grammar School. **Career:** Captain, Manchester Regiment,

Holland and Germany (Mentioned in Despatches) 1942–1945; Assistant Master, Rawtenstall and Bacup Grammar School 1948–1951; Senior German Master, Bolton County Grammar School 1952–1957; Deputy Headmaster, Halesowen Grammar School 1957–1967; Headmaster, Hathershaw School, Oldham 1967–1976. **Awards:** Scholarship, SJC. Died 22 August 1982.

HEMMINGS, Robert Frederick (1943) Born 20 August 1925, 35 Avonmore Avenue, Mossley Hill, Liverpool; son of Fred Hemmings, Officer of Customs and Excise, and Annie Amelia Hambrook; m Margaret Joyce Woods, 1960; 2 children. **Subject(s):** Natural Sciences; BA 1946; MA 1950; MIEE. **Tutor(s):** C W Guillebaud. **Johnian Relatives:** brother of John Hemmings (1941); uncle of Richard Francis Hemmings (1966). **Educ:** Dovedale Road Council School, Liverpool; Beaver Road Council School, Didsbury, Manchester; Manchester Grammar School. **Career:** Instructor and Captain, Royal Signals, RMA Sandhurst 1946–1948; College Apprentice, Metropolitan Vickers 1948–1950; Research Assistant, Department of Physics, Imperial College, London 1950–1951; Fusion Research, Sub Section Leader, Reports and Publications, AEI Research Laboratory, Aldermaston 1951–1963; Chief Engineer, AEI Transformer Division 1963–1971; Principal Engineer, Reports and Publications, Ferranti Ltd 1971–1975; Senior Design Engineer, Kennedy and Donkin 1975–1981; Senior Engineer, GEC Turbine Generators 1981–1990. **Awards:** Minor Scholarship, SJC.

HEMMINGS, William Oliver Chambers (1934) Born 11 June 1915, 116 Westbourne Road, Sheffield; son of Isaac Hemmings, Director of Limited Company, and Mary Elizabeth Hunter Chambers. **Subject(s):** Classics/Law; BA 1937. **Tutor(s):** R L Howland. **Educ:** Westbourne Preparatory School, Sheffield; Oakham School. **Career:** Flying Officer, RAF 1937–1939. **Awards:** Exhibition, SJC. Died 26 June 1939.

HENCKEN, Dr Hugh O'Neill (1924) Born 8 January 1902, 30 West 87th Street, New York, USA; son of Albert Charles Hencken, Insurance Broker, and Mary Creighton O'Neill. **Subject(s):** English; BA 1926; MA 1931; PhD 1930; ScD 1972. **Tutor(s):** E E Sikes. **Educ:** Brunswick School, Treenwich; The Hill School, Pottstown; Princeton University. **Career:** Curator, European Archaeology, Peabody Museum, Harvard; Director, American School of Prehistoric Research 1945–1972. **Appointments:** Honorary Fellow, SJC 1969. **Publications:** *The Archaeology of Cornwall*, 1932. Died 31 August 1981.

HENDERSON, Ian Montrose (1947) Born 7 September 1927, Farvic Mine, Gwanda, Southern Rhodesia; son of Herbert Stephen Henderson, Cattle Rancher, and Helen Joan Davison. BA 1950; MA 1954. **Tutor(s):** G C L Bertram. **Educ:** Rhodes Estate Preparatory School, Bulawayo; Plumtree School, Southern Rhodesia.

HENDERSON, Brigadier James Lomas (1923) Born 27 November 1897, 8 Homefield Road, Chiswick, Middlesex; son of William Henderson, Master Jeweller, and Ada Anne Cain. **Subject(s):** Economics; BA 1925; MA 1941. **Tutor(s):** J M Wordie. **Career:** Brigadier, Royal Signals. **Awards:** Legion of Merit (America). **Honours:** OBE. Died 25 February 1988.

HENDERSON, Dr John Anthony (1934) Born 15 February 1915, 51 Lexham Gardens, Kensington, London; son of Arthur Francis Henderson, Major, 27th Light Cavalry, Indian Army, and Muriel Hanbury; m (1) Barbara Joan Hart, 1944, St Martin-in-the-Fields, (2) Miriam Karlin, 1974; (1) 1 son, 2 daughters. **Subject(s):** Medicine; BA 1937; MA 1960; MB; MRCOG 1949; FRCOG 1985; MRCS 1941; LRCP 1941; FRSocMed; FRSC. **Tutor(s):** R L Howland. **Johnian Relatives:** grandson of Edward Erskine Henderson (1888). **Educ:** King's Mead, Seaford; Pinewood, Farnborough; Bryanston, Blandford. **Career:** Physician; Personal Physician to Prime Ministers Alec Douglas-Home and Margaret Thatcher; Surgeon Lieutenant, RNVR. **Honours:** CBE 1991. Died 14 May 1992.

HENDERSON, Mervyn (1901) Born 13 March 1883, Surbiton Hill, Surrey; son of John Young Henderson, Merchant, and Isabel McQueen Drynan. BA 1906; MA 1910. **Tutor(s):** D MacAlister. **Educ:** Montrose College, Brixton Hill; Heidelberg College. **Career:** Third Principal, Emmanuel College, University of Queensland 1923–1954.

HENDERSON, Percival (1901) Born 17 September 1884, Derwent House, Honley, Huddersfield; son of John Henderson, Bookkeeper, and Emily Haigh. **Subject(s):** Natural Sciences; BA 1904; MA 1908. **Tutor(s):** D MacAlister. **Educ:** College Higher Grade School, Huddersfield. **Career:** Called to the Bar, Gray's Inn 1914; Captain, RE, WWI.

HENDRY, James Frank Williamson (1934) Born 13 July 1915, 4 Clifton Place, Glasgow; son of James Hendry, Professor of Midwifery, University of Glasgow, and Harriet Elizabeth Williamson; BA 1937. **Tutor(s):** C W Guillebaud. **Johnian Relatives:** brother of Joseph McInnes Hendry (1937) and of John Robin Napier Hendry (1939). **Educ:** Kelvinside Academy; Loretto School. **Career:** Architect, Glasgow, then Devon. Died 21 August 1993.

HENDRY, John Robin Napier (1939) Born 25 November 1920, 12 Claremont Terrace, Glasgow; son of James Hendry, Professor of Obstetrics and Gynaecology, University of Glasgow, and Harriet Elizabeth Williamson. BA 1943; MA 1971. **Tutor(s):** J M Wordie. **Johnian Relatives:** brother of James Frank Williamson Hendry (1934) and of Joseph McInnes Hendry (1937). **Educ:** Kelvinside Academy, Glasgow; Loretto Preparatory School; Loretto Upper School. Died 1 August 1992.

HENDRY, Dr Joseph McInnes (1937) Born 14 November 1918, Acomb Court, Great Ouseburn; son of James Hendry, Professor of Obstetrics and Gynaecology, University of Glasgow, and Harriet Elizabeth Williamson. BA 1940; MA 1977. **Tutor(s):** R L Howland. **Johnian Relatives:** brother of James Frank Williamson Hendry (1934) and of John Robin Napier Hendry (1939). **Educ:** Loretto School. **Career:** Orthopaedic Consultant Surgeon.

HENRY, David (1946) Born 19 April 1925, Caedre, Caedre Street, Bridgend, Glamorganshire; son of Thomas Glanffrwd Henry, Chief Sanitary Inspector, Midhurst District Council, and Hylda Frances Williams; 1 son, 1 daughter. **Subject(s):** History; BA 1948; MA 1953. **Tutor(s):** F Thistlethwaite. **Educ:** Sir Joseph Williamson's Mathematical School, Rochester; Midhurst Grammar School. **Career:** Prince of Wales Own Ghurka Rifles 1943–1946; Assistant Postal Controller, Class II, Home Counties 1950–1955; Assistant Postal Controller, Class I, Home Counties 1955; Assistant Postal Controller, Class I, Belfast until 1961; Head Postmaster, Norwich 1961–1966; Postal Controller, Midland Region 1966.

HENRY, Howard Francis (1924) Born 1 May 1904, Oakleigh, Chorleywood, Rickmansworth, Hertfordshire; son of John Howard Henry, Mining Engineer, and Caroline Theresa James. **Subject(s):** Mathematics/Modern and Medieval Languages; BA 1927; MA 1931; BSc (London) 1924; ACGI. **Tutor(s):** J M Wordie. **Johnian Relatives:** grandson of George Henry (1866). **Educ:** Dean Close School, Cheltenham; Imperial College of Science, City and Guilds Engineering Department. **Career:** Assistant Master, King William's College, Isle of Man 1927–1933. Died 30 June 1933.

HENRY, Dr Norman Fordyce McKerron (1934) Born 23 December 1909, Maddison Place, Grangemouth, Stirlingshire; son of William Miller Henry, Teacher, and Christina May Anderson. PhD 1938. **Educ:** Aberdeen Grammar School; Aberdeen University. **Career:** University Demonstrator in Mineralogy and Petrology 1938–1946, University Lecturer 1946–1977, University of Cambridge; Title B Fellow 1960–1972, College Lecturer in Mineralogy and Petrology 1962–1972, Title E Fellow 1972–1983, SJC. **Appointments:** Founding Member, SJC Food and Wine Society (now the Norman Henry Society), Supervisor in

Mineralogy and Petrology 1938–1962, Steward 1961–1969, Praelector 1961 and 1971–1975, SJC. **Awards:** Bonney Award, SJC 1937. **Publications:** *Microscopic Study of Opaque Minerals,* 1972; *International Tables for X-Ray Crystallography;* (joint ed) *Use and Occupancy of Rooms in St John's College 1936–1976,* 1985. Died 10 July 1983.

HENRY, William David Murray (1909) Born 22 February 1892, 5 Duke Street, Bloomsbury, London; son of David Murray Henry, Solicitor, and Agnes Sarah Sloman. BA 1912. **Tutor(s):** L H K Bushe-Fox. **Educ:** The Grammar School, Wellingborough. **Career:** Captain, RASC, WWI. Died 4 February 1959.

HENSLOW, Cyril John Wall (1905) Born 28 February 1886, Zeals St Martin, Mere, Wiltshire; son of Leonard Ramsay Henslow, Rector, Zeals St Martin, and Susan Wall. BA 1910; MA 1913. **Tutor(s):** E E Sikes. **Johnian Relatives:** grandson of John Stevens Henslow (1813); son of Leonard Ramsay Henslow (1850); brother of Raymond Benedict Wall Henslow (1899). **Educ:** Royal Naval Academy; Lancing College; Collegia Beda, Rome. **Career:** Ordained Priest 1912; Society of Divine Compassion 1914; Benedictine Community, Pershore, Worcester 1920. Died 1976.

HENSMAN, John Cyril (1919) Born 18 April 1898, 7 Red Lion Square, Stamford, Lincolnshire; son of John William Hensman, Master Baker and Confectioner, and Louisa Laxton; m Edna Irene Pendered, 29 May 1928, Wesleyan Church, Raunds. **Subject(s):** Natural Sciences; BA 1921; MA 1925. **Tutor(s):** E E Sikes. **Educ:** St Nicholas Elementary School; Stamford School. **Career:** RGA and RE 1917–1919; Assistant Master, Rotherham Grammar School 1923–1924; Science Master, Aldenham School 1924–1928; Assistant House Master 1926–1928; Headmaster, Scottish Collegiate School, Calcutta 1928.

HENSTOCK, Professor Ralph (1941) Born 2 June 1923, 21 The Colliery, Newstead, Nottinghamshire; son of William Henstock, Colliery Stoker, and Mary Ellen Bancroft; m Marjorie Jardine, 1949; 1 son (John Patrick b 1952). **Subject(s):** Mathematics; BA 1944; MA 1948; PhD (London) 1948; FSS. **Tutor(s):** S J Bailey. **Educ:** Newstead Council School; Henry Mellish County Secondary School, Bulwell. **Career:** Experimental Officer, Ministry of Supply 1943–1946; Assistant, Department of Mathematics, Bedford College, London 1947–1948; Lecturer in Mathematics, Birkbeck College, London 1948–1951; Lecturer in Mathematics, Queen's University, Belfast 1951–1956; Lecturer in Mathematics, University of Bristol 1956–1960; Senior Lecturer in Pure Mathematics, Queen's University, Belfast 1960–1964; Senior Lecturer in Mathematics, University of Lancaster 1964–1970; Professor of Pure Mathematics 1970–1988 (Emeritus 1988), University of Ulster. **Appointments:** Member, London Mathematical Society and American Mathematical Society; Member, International Advisory Board, Mathematica Japonica 1992. **Awards:** State Scholarship 1941–1943 and 1947; Scholarship, SJC 1943. **Publications:** *Lectures on the Theory of Integration,* World Scientific, 1988; *The General Theory of Integration,* Clarendon, OUP, 1991; 47 papers on Pure Mathematics; reviews of many papers in mathematical reviews.

HENTON, Guy Robin Plenderleith (1948) Born 10 December 1927, Thornton Heath, Croydon, Surrey; son of Arthur Herbert Henton, Company Secretary, and Dorothy Fanny Charlotte Plenderleith. **Subject(s):** Modern and Medieval Languages/History. **Tutor(s):** C W Guillebaud. **Educ:** Woodside Elementary School, Croydon; Christ's Hospital. **Career:** Sergeant, RASC.

HENTON, Richard (1933) Born 3 August 1914, 28 Granville Road, Frizinghall, Bradford; son of Meanwell Henton, Schoolmaster, and Mary Elizabeth Bland. **Subject(s):** History/Law. **Tutor(s):** E A Benians. **Educ:** Frizinghall School; The Grammar School, Bradford.

HEPBURN, Dr Fred (1945) Born 9 April 1927, Tanfield View, Stanley, County Durham; son of Thomas Hepburn, Grocery Proprietor, and Emily Isabel Seed. **Subject(s):** Natural Sciences; BA 1948; MA 1952;

MSc 1953; PhD (Nottingham) 1959. **Tutor(s):** G C L Bertram. **Educ:** Stanley Front Street Junior School; Alderman Wood Secondary School, Stanley. **Career:** Research Assistant in Meteorological Physics 1948–1951; Demonstrator, Physics Department 1951–1952, Assistant Lecturer in Physics 1952–1955, Lecturer in Physics 1955–1960, University of Nottingham; Lecturer in Medical Physics, Medical Faculty, Leeds University 1960–1985. **Awards:** Minor Scholarship 1945. **Publications:** 9 papers on low and high frequency features of 'atmospherics' 1953–1960; 20 papers on electro physiological monitoring and therapeutic equipment and techniques in cardiology, including the organisation and functioning of an early and effective Cardiac Pacing Implementation and Monitoring Centre (1965–1971).

HEPTONSTALL, Cyril Philip (1943) Born 7 July 1924, 27 Marshfield Road, Goole, Yorkshire; son of Robert Allatt Heptonstall, Solicitor, and Mary Aline Dixon; m Cora Arline Mary Smith, 24 April 1954, St Mary's Cathedral, Edinburgh; 1 son (Hugh b 1 October 1956, d 1995), 2 daughters (Julia and Anna). **Subject(s):** Law; BA 1947; MA 1950; LLB 1949; LLM 1985. **Tutor(s):** C W Guillebaud. **Johnian Relatives:** father of Hugh Heptonstall (1975). **Educ:** Drax Grammar School; King's School, Grantham; Tonbridge School. **Career:** Called to the Bar, Inner Temple 1951; Solicitor 1956–1994. Died 19 October 2000.

HEPWORTH, Arthur Jackson (1930) Born 1 August 1911, Croft House, Rotherham, York; son of Frank Arthur Hepworth, Surgeon, and Hilda Constance Jackson. **Tutor(s):** M P Charlesworth. **Johnian Relatives:** son of Frank Arthur Hepworth (1897). **Educ:** The Knoll, Woburn Sands; Eastbourne College.

HERBAGE, Deryk Livingston (1920) Born 14 June 1901, The Bank House, Woking, Surrey; son of Walter Herbage, Bank Manager, and Ruth Anne Livingston; m Anna Maria Josepha. **Subject(s):** Natural Sciences; BA 1923. **Tutor(s):** E E Sikes. **Johnian Relatives:** brother of Julian Livingston Herbage (1922). **Educ:** Fretherne House School, Hampstead; Rossall School, Fleetwood. Died 5 April 1964.

HERBAGE, Julian Livingston (1922) Born 10 September 1904, Bank House, Woking, Surrey; son of Walter Herbage, Bank Manager, and Ruth Anne Livingston; m Anna Instone, 14 December 1944. **Tutor(s):** B F Armitage. **Johnian Relatives:** brother of Deryk Livingston Herbage (1920). **Educ:** South Kensington Preparatory School; Royal Naval College, Osborne; Royal Naval College, Dartmouth. **Career:** Assistant, London Station, BBC (later BBC's Musicologist) 1927–1946; Assistant Director of Music, BBC 1940. Died 17 January 1976.

HERD, Thomas Brodie (1936) Born 23 September 1917, 2 Dalgliesh Road, Dundee; son of Thomas Herd, Chairman, Distillers Company Ltd, and Elizabeth Smith Simon. **Tutor(s):** C W Guillebaud. **Educ:** Arnhall College, Dundee; Merchiston Castle School.

HEREWARD, Dr Hugh Gordon (1939) Born 10 November 1920, 102 City Road, London; son of Alexander Francis Hereward, Master Mariner, and Gladys Elizabeth Potter Garnett; m Frances Penley, 1942 (d 1997); 2 sons (Christopher b 1944 and William b 1946), 1 daughter (Frances b 1948). **Subject(s):** Natural Sciences; BA 1942; MA 1947; PhD 1950. **Tutor(s):** J M Wordie. **Educ:** Claremont House School, London; Chigwell School, Birmingham; King Edward's High School, Birmingham. **Career:** Scientific Officer, DSIR, Montreal 1942–1946; CERN, Geneva 1954–1976. **Awards:** Scholarship, SJC.

HERON, Michael (1936) Born 27 September 1919, 1 South View, Billingham, Stockton, Durham; son of John McMichael Heron, Textile Manufacturer, and Nora Cheseldine; m (1) Camilla Fraser, 1951 (div 1985), (2) Bernadette Anthony Hone, 1986. **Subject(s):** Economics; BA (TCD) 1949. **Tutor(s):** R L Howland. **Educ:** Froebelian School, Ilkley; Wells Preparatory School; Durham School; Munich University; Uppsala University; TCD. **Career:** Sub-Lieutenant RNVR 1946–1949; International Labour Office, Geneva 1951–1954; Freelance Translator,

Majorca 1954–1957; Civic Trust, London 1957–1960; Freelance Translator 1960–1965; English Teacher, British Institute, Valencia 1965–1970; Consular Officer, British Vice-Consulate, Alicante 1970–1974; British Vice-Consul, British Consulate, Alicante 1978.

HERRICK, Herbert John Charles (1923) Born 12 May 1904, 42 Edmund Street, Seedley, Salford, Manchester; son of James Herrick, Accountant, and Esther Andrew. **Subject(s):** Classics/English; BA 1926. **Tutor(s):** E E Sikes. **Educ:** Halton Bank School; Manchester Grammar School. **Awards:** Exhibition, SJC 1923.

HERRIDGE, Geoffrey Howard (1923) Born 22 February 1904, Overton Farm, Maisemore, Gloucestershire; son of Edward Herridge, Farmer, and Mary Elizabeth Welford. **Subject(s):** Mathematics; BA 1926; MA 1930. **Tutor(s):** E Cunningham. **Educ:** Crypt Grammar School, Gloucester. **Career:** Joined Turkish (Iraq) Petroleum Company Ltd 1926; General Manager, Middle East 1947; Director, Iraq Petroleum Company Ltd and Associated Companies 1953; Managing Director 1957; Deputy Chairman 1963; President, Institute of Petroleum 1964. **Awards:** Scholarship, SJC 1922. **Honours:** CMG 1962. Died 1 March 1997.

HERRMANN, Paul Millington (1911) Born 11 November 1891, 21 Jraumaumweg, Hohenfelde, Hamburg, Germany; son of Paul Millington Herrmann, Bank Manager, and Lydia Eliza Millington. **Tutor(s):** J R Tanner. **Educ:** Gymnasium, Wurzen Germany; University of Leipzig.

HERVEY, Maurice William Bethell (1919) Naval Officer.

HERZL, Hans (1910) Born 10 June 1891, Vienna, Austria; son of Theodor Herzl, Publicist, Litterateur, Doctor of Law, and Julie Naschauer. **Subject(s):** Classics; BA 1914. **Tutor(s):** E E Sikes. **Johnian Relatives:** uncle of Stephan Theodore Neumann (1936). **Educ:** Ascott House School; Clifton College. **Career:** Private, Middlesex Regiment, WWI. Died October 1930.

HERZOG, Albert Ludwig Ewald (1911) Born 12 July 1893, Barmen, Germany; son of Ewald Herzog, Doctor of Chemistry, and Bertha Vogeler. **Tutor(s):** E E Sikes. **Educ:** Primary School, Barmen; Gymnasium, Barmen.

HESSE, Ernest Paul (1926) Born 18 September 1905, Pohlandstrusse 24ii, Dresden, Germany; son of Paul Friedrich Wilhelm Hesse, Merchant, and Anna Elsbeth Kögler. **Tutor(s):** M P Charlesworth. **Educ:** Dreikoenigschule, Dresden; University of Innsbruck; University of Gottingen.

HESSELGREAVES, John Wainwright (1921) (Migrated to Christ's College 1921) Born 25 June 1904, 40 Stansfield Road, Todmorden, Yorkshire; son of George Edward Hesselgreaves, Schoolmaster, and Jessie Greenwood. **Subject(s):** Mathematics/Natural Sciences; BA (Christ's) 1925; MA (Christ's) 1932. **Tutor(s):** E Cunningham. **Educ:** Todmorden National School; Todmorden Secondary School; Christ's College, Cambridge. **Awards:** Scholarship, Christ's College 1921.

HETHERINGTON, Robert Newett (1931) Born 8 April 1913, Dallas, Malone, Belfast, Ireland; son of Robert Hetherington, Linen Manufacturer, and Mary Emmeline Newett. **Subject(s):** Medicine; BA 1934; MA 1938. **Tutor(s):** M P Charlesworth. **Educ:** Shrewsbury School; Mourne Grange, Kilkeel, Ireland. **Career:** Doctor.

HEUGHAN, Donald Malcolm (1949) Born 15 May 1926, Hatherleigh, Moorlands Avenue, Dewsbury, Yorkshire; son of George Heughan, Pharmacist, and Annie Idle, School Teacher; m (1) Margaret Crook, 1951 (dis 1982), (2) Jer Bilimoria, 1982; (1) 1 son (Malcolm b 1952), 1 daughter (Anne b 1956), (2) 2 stepdaughters. **Subject(s):** MSc 1952; BSc (Dunelm) 1947; CEng; MIMechE; MRAeS; FCMI; FREng. **Tutor(s):** J M

Wordie. **Educ:** Wheelwright Grammar School, Dewsbury; King's College, Durham University, Newcastle upon Tyne. **Career:** First Research Engineer, British (now Malayan) Rubber Producers' Research Association, Welwyn Garden City 1951–1954; Aerodynamicist, Functional Test Engineer, Manager, Technical Services Department, Acting Manager, Design Division, de Havilland Aircraft Company, Hatfield 1954–1961; Management Consultant, Senior Consultant, Manager, Associated Industrial Consultants Ltd 1961–1970; Director and Chief Executive, Furniture Development Council and Furniture Industry Research Association, Stevenage 1970–1991. **Appointments:** Honorary Liveryman, Worshipful Company of Furniture Makers 1971; Trustee, MacRobert Trust of Tarland, Aberdeenshire 1964; Freeman, City of London. **Publications:** 'Non Destructive Testing of Flat Bonded Rubber Mountings', *Transactions of the Institute of the Rubber Industry*, 1953; 'An Experimental Study of a Symmetrical Aerofoil with a Rear Suction Slot and a Retractable Flap', *Journal of the Royal Aeronautical Society*, 1953; 'Furniture Production', George Bray Memorial Lecture, Institute of Production Engineers 1972; (contributor) *The MacRobert Trusts 1943–1993*.

HEUSTON, Professor Robert Francis Vere (1946) Born 17 November 1923, 87 Lower Baggot Street, Dublin; son of Vere Douglas Heuston, Manager of the Registry Department, Guinness' Brewery, and Dorothy Helen Coulter; m Bridget Nancy Ward-Perkins (née Boland), 1962; 4 stepdaughters. LLB (TCD) 1945; DCL (Oxon) 1970; MRIA. **Educ:** Earlsfort House School, Dublin; St Columba's College, Rathfarnham; TCD. **Career:** Tutor for Admissions and Lecturer in Jurisprudence, Pembroke College, Cambridge; Called to the Bar, King's Inns 1947 (Honorary Bencher 1983), Gray's Inn 1951 (Honorary Bencher 1988); Fellow and Tutor in Law, Pembroke College, Oxford 1947–1965; Professor of Law, Southampton University 1965–1970; Regius Professor of Law, TCD 1970–1983; Arthur Goodhart Professor of Legal Science, University of Cambridge 1986–1987. **Appointments:** Visiting Fellow, All Souls College, Oxford; Member, Law Reform Committee for England and Wales 1968–1970; Member, Law Reform Committee of Ireland 1975–1981. **Publications:** (ed) 11th–20th editions of *Salmond and Heuston on Torts*; *Lives of the Lord Chancellors*, Vols I and II, 1964–1987; *Essays on Constitutional Law*, 1961. Died 21 December 1995.

HEWARD, Arthur Brian Augustus (1917) Born 15 July 1900, Brockville, Ontario, Canada; son of Arthur Richard Graves Heward, Assistant Secretary, CPRR Coy, and Sarah Efa Jones. BA 1921; MA 1964. **Tutor(s):** E E Sikes. **Educ:** Lower Canada College; Courtenay Lodge School. Died 4 March 1982.

HEWITT, Charles Geoffrey (1944) Born 24 February 1926, 62 Erwood Road, Levenshulme, Manchester; son of Charles Hewitt, Textile Export Merchant's Shipping Clerk, and Norah Milwain Emery. **Subject(s):** Natural Sciences; BA 1950; MA 1952. **Tutor(s):** C W Guillebaud. **Educ:** Alma Road Elementary School; Manchester Grammar School.

HEWLETT, Alfred Lionel (1919) Born 18 May 1902, Haigh Cottage, Haigh, Lancashire; son of Alfred Hewlett, Iron Merchant, and Amy Burrows. **Tutor(s):** E A Benians. **Educ:** Rydal Mount School, Colwyn Bay.

HEWLETT, Donald Marland (1939) Born 30 August 1920, Northenden, Cheshire; son of Thomas Henry Hewlett, MP, JP, City of Manchester, and Bertha Alice Marland; m (1) Christine Pollon, (2) Diana Greenwood, (3) Thérèse McMurray; (2) 2 sons (Jonathan and Mark), 1 daughter (Sophie), (3) 1 son (Patrick), 1 daughter (Siobhan). **Subject(s):** Geography. **Tutor(s):** J M Wordie. **Educ:** Mostyn House School, Parkgate; Clifton College, Bristol. **Career:** Ordinary Seaman 1940–1941; Sub-Lieutenant, RNVR 1941–1943; Fleet Air Arm 1943–1944; Lieutenant, Meteorological Officer, RNVR 1944–1946; Actor, RADA 1947–1948; Oxford Playhouse Repertory Company 1950–1952; Appeared in many plays on Tour and West End, including: *Look Who's Here* (Fortune Theatre); *And Another Thing* (Fortune

Theatre); *Grab Me a Gondola* (Lyric Theatre); *Wind in the Willows* (Sadler's Wells); *Two Into One* (Shaftesbury Theatre); Films and TV, including: Colonel Reynolds in *It Ain't Half Hot Mum*; Lord Meldrum in *You Rang M'Lord*; *Saving Grace*; *Callan*; *Touch of Class*; *Carry on Behind*; *Great Train Robbery*; *Lovejoy*; *Coronation Street*; *Protectors*; *Avengers*. **Appointments:** Prominent member, The Footlights; entertained troops; Founder, The Kirkwall Arts Club. **Awards:** Athene Seyler Prize for comedy.

HEY, William Rennie (1922) Born 29 March 1904, 16 Princess Street, Nelson, Lancashire; son of William Rennie Hey, Cotton Manufacturer and Town Councillor, and Barbara Elizabeth Matthews. **Subject(s):** History; BA 1925; MA 1933. **Tutor(s):** E A Benians. **Educ:** Bradshaw Street Council School; Nelson Secondary School; Rydal Mount School, Colwyn Bay.

HEYWOOD, Henry Thomas (1932) Born 21 September 1913, Allithwaite, Cartmel, Lancashire; son of Edmund Heywood, Auxiliary Postman and Woodman, and Nellie Walker. **Subject(s):** Natural Sciences/Economics; BA 1935. **Tutor(s):** J M Wordie. **Educ:** Allithwaite C of E School; Victoria Grammar School, Ulverston. **Career:** Senior Inspector of Taxes, Newcastle 2nd District. **Awards:** Scholarship, SJC. Died 28 September 1957.

HEYWOOD-WADDINGTON, Dr Michael Broke (1947) Born 24 April 1929, 7 St Catherine Road, Littlehampton, Sussex; son of William Broke Heywood-Waddington, Medical Practitioner, and Edna Madeleine Goddard. **Subject(s):** Natural Sciences; BA 1950; MA 1978; BChir 1953; MB 1953; FRCS 1960. **Tutor(s):** G C L Bertram. **Educ:** Dorset House, Littlehampton; Epsom House. **Career:** Consultant Orthopaedic and Traumatic Surgeon, Chelmsford and St Helena Hospital Group 1967–1992. **Appointments:** President, Orthopaedic Section, Royal Society of Medicine; Regional Orthopaedic Adviser, Royal College of Surgeons. **Awards:** Major Scholarship, SJC 1946.

HIBBERD, Andrew Stuart (1912) Born 5 September 1893, Canford Magna, Dorset; son of William Henry Hibberd, Farmer, and Mary Catherine Edney; m Alice Mary Chichester, 31 July 1923 (d 1977). BA 1917; MA 1937; FRSA. **Tutor(s):** R P Gregory. **Educ:** Wimborne Grammar School; Weymouth College. **Career:** Lieutenant, Dorset Regiment, later Captain and Adjutant, 25th Punjabis, Indian Army, Gallipoli, Mesopotamia, Waziristan 1914–1922; Announcer, BBC 1924–1951. **Awards:** Choral Scholarship, SJC. **Honours:** MBE 1935. **Publications:** *This – is London* (Autobiography). Died 1 November 1983.

HIBBERT, Francis Dennis (1925) Born 18 August 1906, The College, Denstone, Staffordshire; son of Francis Aidan Hibbert, Clerk in Holy Orders, and Hilda Kate Wykes. **Subject(s):** History/Geography; BA 1928; MA 1969. **Tutor(s):** E A Benians. **Johnian Relatives:** son of Francis Aidan Hibbert (1886). **Educ:** Denstone College; Bloxham School. **Career:** Colonial Service 1929; Education Officer, Nigeria 1958. **Appointments:** Chairman, Public Service Commission, Kaduna, Northern Nigeria. **Awards:** Sizarship, SJC. **Honours:** CMG 1958. Died November 1975.

HIBBERT, John Desmond (1934) Born 16 December 1914, Nazirabad, India; son of Oswald Yates Hibbert, Colonel, Queen's Own Royal West Kent Regiment, and Violet Marion Watson Pike. **Subject(s):** Mechanical Sciences; BA 1936; MA 1941; MICE. **Tutor(s):** J S Boys Smith. **Johnian Relatives:** brother of Richard Oswald Hibbert (1933). **Educ:** Highfield School, Liphook; Shrewsbury School; RMA, Woolwich. **Career:** Lieutenant Colonel, RE 1960. Died 22 April 2001.

HIBBERT, Richard Oswald (1933) Born 16 December 1914, Nasirabad, India; son of Oswald Yates Hibbert, Lieutenant Colonel, HM Army, and Violet Marion Watson Pike; 1 son (John), 1 daughter. **Subject(s):** Classics; BA 1936. **Tutor(s):** R L Howland. **Johnian Relatives:** brother

of John Desmond Hibbert (1934). **Educ:** Highfield School, Liphook; Shrewsbury School. **Career:** Indian Civil Service 1937–1948. **Appointments:** President, College Classical Society. Died 1979.

HICKS, Dr Anthony Rayner Harvey (1937) Born 5 April 1919, Milton Lodge, Great Baddow, Chelmsford; son of Joseph Harvey Hicks, Company Director, and Evely Elizabeth Rayner. **Subject(s):** Medicine; BA 1940; MA 1966; MB BChir 1949. **Tutor(s):** R L Howland. **Educ:** Alleyn Court School, Westcliff-on-Sea; Felsted School. **Career:** General Medical Practitioner. **Appointments:** Commissioner, St John's Ambulance, County of Surrey. **Honours:** Commander of the Order of St John of Jerusalem. Died 11 July 1992.

HICKS, Colonel Arthur Lionel (1931) Born 6 September 1910, 21 West Avenue, Gosforth, Northumberland; son of William Herbert Percy Hicks, Ship Broker, and Kathleen Louise Newbury; m Margaret; 1 son (Nigel), 2 daughters (Carol and Ann). **Subject(s):** Mechanical Sciences; BA 1933; MA 1959; MIMechE; MICE; MIEE. **Educ:** Newcastle Preparatory School; Ascham House School, Newcastle; St Peter's School, York; RMA, Woolwich. **Career:** Gazetted Second Lieutenant, RE, rising to Colonel, Consulting Engineer 1931. **Honours:** OBE. Died 23 April 1986.

HICKS, Ernest Philip (1936) Born 20 December 1917, 84 Station Road, Bill Quay, Felbrig, Gateshead; son of John Henry Hicks, Newsagent, and Edith May Gunton; m Joyce Elsie Loveridge, 1977, Mapledurham. **Subject(s):** Mathematics; BA 1939; MA 1943; FIMA 1964; CMath 1992. **Tutor(s):** J M Wordie. **Educ:** Bill Quay Council School; Jarrow County Secondary School. **Career:** Member, Richard Beeching's (later Lord Beeching) Rocket Research Group, Aberporth; Member, AWRE 1946; Meteorological Planner, involved in Woomera H-bomb tests; Scientific Attaché, Washington; Specialist in nuclear explosion safety studies; Head, Theoretical Group, Dounreay Experimental Reactor Establishment; Safety specialist in development of fast reactor fuels; Head, Theoretical Analysis Group, Springfields Nuclear Power Development Laboratories, UKAEA, Preston. **Awards:** Scholarship, SJC 1936–1937. **Honours:** American Medal of Freedom. Died 24 March 1995.

HICKS, The Revd Francis William (1905) Born 18 May 1886, 16 Hawthorn Road, Gosforth, Northumberland; son of William Searle Hicks, Architect, and Annie Alice Adamson. **Subject(s):** Classics; BA 1908. **Tutor(s):** D MacAlister. **Educ:** Durham School. **Career:** Ordained Deacon 1909; Curate, St Aidan, Leeds 1909–1912; Ordained Priest 1910; Incumbent of Arcola, Saskatchewan, Canada 1912–1913; Incumbent of Manor, Saskatchewan, Canada 1913–1915; Temporary Chaplain, RN 1915–1919 (HMS *Princess Margaret*, HMS *Dreadnought*, then HMS *Woolwich*); Curate, Helmsley 1921–1925; Vicar, Bramham, Yorkshire 1925–1929; Vicar, Eglingham 1940–1944; Canon and Chancellor, St Paul's Anglican Cathedral, Malta 1944. **Awards:** Exhibition, SJC. Died 24 January 1960.

HIGGINS, Dr Frank Edmund (1908) Born 20 July 1885, Cudnell, Charlton Kings, Gloucestershire; son of Francis Edmund Higgins, Leather Goods Manufacturer, and Emma Amelia Bate; m Violet Lucy Bailey, 28 April 1917. **Subject(s):** Natural Sciences; BA 1912; BChir 1923; MB 1923; MRCS; LRCP 1915. **Tutor(s):** L H K Bushe-Fox. **Johnian Relatives:** brother of Frederick Alfred Raymond Higgins (1903). **Educ:** Cheltenham Grammar School. **Career:** Lieutenant, RAMC, WWI; Surgeon, St Leonard's Hospital, Sudbury; Resident Obstetric House Physician, Block VIII St Thomas' Hospital.

HIGGINS, Frederick Alfred Raymond (1903) Born 5 December 1883, Cudwell, Charlton Kings, Gloucestershire; son of Francis Edmund Higgins, Trunk Maker, and Emma Amelia Bate. **Subject(s):** Mathematics; BA 1906. **Tutor(s):** D MacAlister. **Johnian Relatives:** brother of Frank Edmund Higgins (1908). **Educ:** Cheltenham Grammar School. **Career:** Temporary Science Master, Eton College 1907; Master, Clifton College 1908–1909. Died 19 March 1909.

HIGGINS, Larratt Tinsley (1949) Born 4 February 1924, Sewell, Rancagua, Santiago, Chile; son of Larratt Tinsley Higgins, Mining Engineer, Braden Copper Company, and Edna Earle Ambrose; m May Patricia Hourigan, 24 July 1951, Belfast. **Subject(s):** Economics; BA 1951; MA 1956; BA (Toronto) 1949. **Educ:** The American Schools, Sewell and Rancagua; Public School, Baltimore; St Peter's School, Villa Alemana, Chile; Trinity College School, Port Hope; Trinity College, Toronto.

HIGGINSON, Graham Kenrick (1944) Born 12 February 1925, 2 The Beeches, Acton Park, Wrexham; son of Samuel Sidney Higginson, Deputy Clerk, Rural District Council, and Eleanor Kenrick. **Tutor(s):** S J Bailey. **Educ:** Acton Park Council School, Wrexham; Grove Park County School, Wrexham. **Career:** 6th Battalion, Royal Welch Fusiliers, WWII. Died 1 October 1944 (killed in action in North-West Europe).

HIGGINSON, Herbert Walmsley (1929) Born 23 November 1910, 25 Chester Street, Wrexham; son of Henry Higginson, Motor Garage Proprietor, and Emily Mary Smith; m Margaret Elizabeth Freeman, 1937; 1 son, 2 daughters. **Subject(s):** Law; BA 1932; MA 1977; LLB 1933; LLM 1985. **Tutor(s):** C W Guillebaud. **Educ:** Colet House, Rhyl; Haileybury College. **Career:** Solicitor 1935; Second Lieutenant, then Captain, 24 Lancers (Mentioned in Despatches) 1941–1944; Major, GSO2 11 Armoured Division 1945–1946; Partner 1947–1977; Senior Partner, Herbert Smith & Co 1971–1977. **Appointments:** Master, City of London Solicitors' Company 1969–1970. **Honours:** MC 1945; CBE 1981. **Publications:** Contributor to *Buckley on the Companies Act*, 2000.

HIGGINTON, John Martin (1912) Born 8 October 1893, 85 Lennard Road, Beckenham, Kent; son of Arthur John Higginton, Insurance Surveyor, and Edith Martha Bennett. BA 1915; MA 1921. **Tutor(s):** R P Gregory. **Educ:** Whitgift Grammar School.

HIGGS, Geoffrey William Hawley (HAWLEY-HIGGS) (1944) Born 27 April 1926, 60 Cold Overton Road, Oakham, Rutland; son of Percy Edward Higgs, Headmaster, and Maud Cooper. **Subject(s):** Natural Sciences; BA 1947. **Tutor(s):** C W Guillebaud. **Educ:** Oakham School. Died 1 September 1998.

HIGGS, Sydney Limbrey (1912) Born 12 September 1892, 29 Griffel Avenue, Streatham, Surrey; son of John Limbrey Higgs, Solicitor, and Florence Alice Martin; m Betty Chune Howard, 24 December 1927, St James's, Norland Square (d 21 February 1954); 1 daughter (Jennifer), 2 step-daughters (Pamela and Yolande). BA 1915; MA 1919; LRCP; MRCS 1917; FRCS. **Tutor(s):** L H K Bushe-Fox. **Educ:** Whitgift School, Croydon. **Career:** Surgeon, RN 1917–1920; Assistant Surgeon, Orthopaedic Department, St Bartholomew's, later Head of Department 1920–1937; Military Orthopaedic Hospital, Shepherd's Bush; Surgeon, Royal National Orthopaedic Hospital; Surgeon in charge of Hertfordshire Orthopaedic Clinics; Consulting Surgeon, Bishop's Stortford Hospital, and British Red Cross Clinic for Rheumatism, Regent's Park; Heritage Hospitals and Schools, Chailey; Hertfordshire County Sanitorium, Ware Park; Watford Peace Memorial Hospital; Letchworth Hospital; Yateley Hospital; Demonstrator in Anatomy, St Bartholomew's Medical School; Surgeon, Queen Mary's, Roehampton. **Appointments:** President, Orthopaedics Section, Royal Society of Medicine 1940–1941; President, Heberden Society 1947 and 1948; President, British Orthopaedic Association 1950. **Publications:** 'Treatment of Stiff Joints', *Journal of the Chartered Society of Massage and Medical Gymnastics*, 1924; 'Treatment and Results of Fractures of the Upper End of the Femur', *Procedures of the Royal Society of Medicine*, 1927; 'Hammer Toe', *Post-Graduate Medical Journal*, 1931; 'Fractures of the Femur', *Practioner*, 1931. Died 21 November 1977.

HIGHET, Hugh Campbell (1931) Born 3 April 1913, Bangkok, Siam; son of Hugh Campbell Highet, Oculist, and Emma Robinow; m Nancie Mary (d 1996); 2 daughters (Jill Penelope b 2 November 1939 and Hilary Barbara b 2 October 1943). **Subject(s):** Natural Sciences; BA 1935. **Tutor(s):** J M Wordie. **Educ:** Hazelhurst, Frant; Shrewsbury School. **Career:** Research Chemist (concerned notably with the development of styrene and PVC in Britain) 1935–1953; Training Officer, Distillers 1953–1967; Training Officer, BP Chemicals 1967–1973. Died 18 September 2001.

HIGHFIELD-JONES, Philip (1912) Born 29 July 1893, Penn Fields, Upper Penn, Staffordshire; son of Benjamin Highfield-Jones, Manufacturer, and Eliza Storey; m Muriel Read, 10 March 1931. BA 1916; MA 1919. **Tutor(s):** R P Gregory. **Educ:** Berkhamsted School. **Career:** Lieutenant, South Staffordshire Regiment; Major, South Staffordshire, TA, WWI. **Honours:** MC 1917. Died 26 June 1951.

HIGNETT, Reginald Arthur (1923) Born 5 April 1904, Derwent House, Derwent Road, West Derby, Liverpool; son of Arthur Walton Hignett, Tobacco Manufacturer, and Annie Gertrude Smith. **Tutor(s):** E E Sikes. **Educ:** Holmwood School, Formby; Harrow School.

HIGSON, Leslie Arthur (1912) Born 15 May 1893, Bistre, Buckley, County Flint; son of Alfred Higson, Schoolmaster, and Emily Millin. **Subject(s):** Mathematics; BA 1920. **Tutor(s):** L H K Bushe-Fox. **Educ:** Duncombe Road Higher Grade School; Christ's Hospital. **Career:** Captain, Middlesex Regiment (wounded twice), WWI. **Awards:** Scholarship, SJC.

HILARY, Robert Jephson (1912) Born 28 May 1893, Oak Villas, Dry Hill Park, Tonbridge, Kent; son of Henry Hilary, Mathematics Master, Tonbridge School, and Alice Cecilia Jephson; m Nita Margaret MacMahon, 2 August 1923, St John's, East Dulwich. **Subject(s):** Classics; BA 1915. **Tutor(s):** E E Sikes. **Johnian Relatives:** son of Henry Hilary (1866). **Educ:** Yardley Court Preparatory School; Tonbridge School. **Career:** Lieutenant, The Buffs (East Kent Regiment) (wounded), WWI; Assistant Master of Classics, Westminster (Housemaster from 1925) 1923–1937. Died 15 March 1937.

HILL, Arthur David Frank (1945) Born 24 February 1927, 43 Winterhey Lane, Horwich, Lancashire; son of Arthur Edward Hill, Dentist, and Edith Gartside. **Subject(s):** Mechanical Sciences; BA 1948; MA 1952. **Tutor(s):** S J Bailey; R L Howland. **Educ:** St Monica's School, Camberley; Bolton School; Clifton House School, Harrogate.

HILL, Charles Kenneth (1946) Born 3 October 1920, Bloemfontein, Orange Free State, South Africa; son of Charles Harmon Hill, Attorney, and Kathleen Ellen Deale, Secretary; m Jean Farre Ballantine, 5 July 1950, Claremont, Cape Town, South Africa. **Subject(s):** Maths; BA 1948; MA 1952; BSc (Rhodes) 1941; MSc (Rhodes) 1942. **Tutor(s):** J M Wordie. **Educ:** St Andrew's School, Bloemfontein, South Africa; Rhodes University College, Grahamstown, South Africa. **Career:** South African Forces (Temporary Sergeant, Sergeant, SSS, SACS) 1942–1945; Lecturer in Mathematics, University of Natal, Durban, South Africa 1942–1961. **Appointments:** Founder Member, Liberal Party, South Africa. Died 15 June 2002.

HILL, Eric Desmond Hume Darley (1923) Born 6 October 1904, 12 Hume Street, Dublin, Ireland; son of Edwin Darley Hill, Managing Director, Northern Banking Company, and Deborah Overend. BA 1926; MA 1930. **Tutor(s):** E Cunningham. **Educ:** Rockport, Craigavad; Shrewsbury School.

HILL, Eric Grenville (1949) Born 1 March 1929, Meadway, Hillside Walk, Brook Street, South Weald, Essex; son of Hubert Grenville Hill, Insurance Broker, and Lily Victoria Roberts; m Wanda Moore, 1976. **Subject(s):** Law/Natural Sciences; BA 1952; MA 1957; LLB 1953; Bar Finals 1954; Solicitors Finals 1976; LLM 1985. **Tutor(s):** E Miller; W A Deer. **Educ:** Brentwood School; St George's School, Harpenden; Urwick Orr Management College; Columbia University, New York. **Career:** National Service 1947–1949; Called to the Bar 1954; Admitted Solicitor

1976; Manager, Group Patent Department, International Licensing and Joint Ventures, Group Planning, Mergers and Acquisitions, Director, Finnish Peroxides, Laporte Industries 1956–1976; Formed Grenville Hill, Solicitors 1976–1994. **Appointments:** Harpenden Urban District Councillor; Hertfordshire County Councillor; Kensington and Chelsea Borough Councillor; Parliamentary Candidate, General Election, October 1974; various school governorships and further education appointments; Member, The Bow Group; Special Mentor, The Prince's Trust; Member, Royal Lymington Yacht Club; Co-founder and past Commodore, Port Solent Yacht Club; Co-founder and proprietor, Alderney Stud. Died 22 July 2002.

HILL, Ernest Gordon (1935) Born 3 January 1917, 65 Wednesbury Road, Walsall; son of Matthew Ernest Hill, Clerk, and Edith Emily Beech; 1 daughter. **Subject(s):** History; BA 1938; MA 1947. **Tutor(s):** J S Boys Smith. **Educ:** Willow House; Queen Mary's Grammar School, Walsall. **Career:** Saffron Waldon Grammar School; March Grammar School; Royal Leicestershire Regiment, seconded to the King's African Rifles, WWII; Senior History Master and Deputy Headmaster, Joseph Leckie Comprehensive School, Walsall 1954; Headmaster, Waverley Grammar School, Birmingham 1954–1959; Headmaster, Harrogate Grammar School. 1959. **Awards:** Goldsmith Exhibition, SJC 1936; College Prize, SJC.

HILL, The Revd Henry Gordon (1948) Born 14 December 1921, Kingston, Ontario, Canada; son of Henry Knox Hill, Lieutenant Commander, Royal Canadian Navy, and Kathleen Elizabeth Cunningham. **Subject(s):** Theology; BA 1950; MA 1954; BA (Queen's) 1945; LTh (Trinity College, Toronto) 1948. **Tutor(s):** C W Guillebaud. **Educ:** Queen's University, Kingston, Canada; Trinity College, University of Toronto, Canada; Appleby College, Oakville Canada. **Career:** Primate of Canada, Episcopal Liaison with Non-Chalcedonian Church; Deacon 1948; Priest, Ely for Ontario 1950; Curate, Belleville 1950–1951; Rector, Adolphustown, Sandhurst, Ontario 1951–1952; Chaplain, SJC 1952–1955; Senior Curate, St Peter's Church, Wisbech 1955; Bishop of Ontario 1975–1981; Co-Chairman, Anglican-Orthodox Joint Doctrinal Commission 1980. **Appointments:** Associate Professor of History, Canterbury College, Kingston, Ontario 1961; Bishop of Ontario 1975–1981; Co-Chairman, Anglican-Orthodox Joint Doctrinal Commission 1980. **Awards:** KLJ 1980.

HILL, Ivan Conrad (1925) Born 22 January 1906, 84 Gwendolen Road, Leicester; son of Wilfrid Lawson Hill, Boot and Shoe Manufacturer, and Annie Jane England; m (1) Alexandrina Ewart, 1931 (div 1962), (2) Sheila Houghton, 1963; (1) 4 daughters. **Subject(s):** History/Law; BA 1928. **Tutor(s):** M P Charlesworth. **Educ:** Wyggeston School, Leicester; Oakham School. **Career:** Joint Managing Director, Kelsall & Kemp Ltd 1933; Samuel Courtauld & Co Ltd 1962–1966; Illingworth Morris & Co Ltd 1976–1980; Convoy Woollen Company Ltd 1984–1990. **Appointments:** Liveryman, Worshipful Company of Weavers 1938; Chairman, Wool Industries Research Association 1950–1953; Member, Monopolies and Restrictive Practices Commission, and Monopolies Commission 1951–1963; Chairman, British Rayon Research Association 1956–1961; Chairman, Industrial Coal Consumers Council until 1965. **Awards:** Johnson Exhibition, SJC.

HILL, Sir John McGregor (1945) Born 21 February 1921, Westminster Nursing Home, 50 Liverpool Road, Chester; son of John Campbell Hill, Inspector of Schools, and Margaret Elizabeth Park; m Nora Eileen Hellet, 1947; 2 sons, 1 daughter. PhD 1949; Honorary DSc (Bradford) 1981; Honorary FICE 1977; FInstP; FRS 1981; Honorary FIEE 1981; FEng 1982; FREng; FInstE. **Tutor(s):** J M Wordie. **Educ:** Broomfield House School, Kew Gardens; Richmond County School; KCL. **Career:** Flight Lieutenant, RAF 1941; Cavendish Laboratory, Cambridge 1946; Member for Production 1946–1967; Lecturer, London University 1948; UKAEA 1950; Member for Production 1964; Chairman 1967–1981; Chairman, British Nuclear Fuels 1971–1983; Member, Nuclear Power Advisory Board 1973–1981; Institute of Energy 1974; Amersham

International 1975–1988; Foreign Associate, US National Academy of Engineering 1976; Sylvanus Thompson Medal, Institute of Radiology 1978; Aurora Holdings 1984–1988; President, British Nuclear Forum 1984–1989; Rea Brothers Group 1987–1995. **Appointments:** Member, Advisory Council on Technology 1968–1970; Energy Commission 1977–1979; Foreign Associate, US Academy of Engineering 1982. **Awards:** Melchett Medal, Institute of Energy 1974; Sylvanus Thompson Medal, Institute of Radiology 1978. **Honours:** Kt 1969; Legion d'Honneur 1985.

HILL, John Robertshaw (1902) Born 18 September 1883, 28 White's View, Manningham, Bradford; son of Thomas Rawson Hill, Stuff Manufacturer, and Sarah Jane Robertshaw. **Subject(s):** Natural Sciences; BA 1906. **Tutor(s):** C E Graves; J R Tanner. **Educ:** Bradford Grammar School. **Career:** Government Chemist, Federated Malay States 1910; Davy-Faraday Laboratory, Royal Institution 1913–1914; Private, West Yorkshire Regiment, then Second Lieutenant, RE (Special Brigade), WWI. Died 6 May 1917 (killed in action).

HILL, Philip Eustace Lionel (1929) Born 5 March 1910, Burroway Street, Neutral Bay, North Sydney, Australia; son of Leslie Noel Hill, Stock Breeder/Grazier, and Elsie Marian Manchee. BA 1932. **Tutor(s):** C W Guillebaud. **Educ:** The King's School, Parramatta, Sydney. Died 1970.

HILL, Richard Baird (1944) Born 8 October 1926, Military Hospital, New Road, Woolwich; son of Richard Hill, Major, Royal Fusiliers, and Rebecca Martha Harris. **Tutor(s):** J M Wordie. **Educ:** Hounslow Heath Junior School; Isleworth County School.

HILL, Robert William McLeavy (1946) Born 2 May 1928, 157 University Road, Belfast; son of James Herbert Hill, Civil Engineer, and Margaret Sisson; m Susan Mary Kottler; 1 son (Charles), 2 daughters (Mary and Katie). BA 1949; MA 1974. **Tutor(s):** G C L Bertram. **Educ:** Elm Park, Killylea; Campbell College, Portrush. **Career:** Founder and Consultant, Cotswold Seeds Ltd, Moreton in Marsh, Gloucestershire.

HILL, Roger Frank (1943) Born 19 December 1925, Blairgowrie, Coonoor, South India; son of Cecil Robert Hill, Manager, Imperial Bank of India, and Mabel Ellen Butcher. **Tutor(s):** C W Guillebaud. **Educ:** Great Yarmouth Grammar School; Bishop's Stortford College.

HILL, Rowland (1926) Born 15 July 1907, Highmead House, Blakeney, Gloucestershire; son of Rowland Hill, Medical Practitioner, and Maude Amanda Minns. BA 1930; MRCS 1933; LRCP 1933. **Tutor(s):** M P Charlesworth. **Educ:** Dean Close School, Cheltenham. **Career:** Practice in Barnes; Flying Officer, RAF, then Flight Lieutenant, RAFVR, WWII.

HILL, Stanley (1931) Born 21 August 1912, 112 Smedley Road, Cheetham; son of Joseph Evan Hill, Retail Draper's Manager, and Maria Beardsall; m Ellen Rose; 1 son (John), 1 daughter (Margaret). **Subject(s):** Natural Sciences; BA 1934; MA 1938. **Tutor(s):** J M Wordie. **Educ:** Cheetham Collegiate School; Manchester Grammar School. **Career:** Radar work, WWII; Deputy Director of Research, Tate & Lyle; Mathematics Teacher, Caterham Grammar School. **Awards:** Scholarship, SJC. **Publications:** Various scientific papers. Died 16 February 2002.

HILL, William Edward (1906) Born 28 July 1886, Bridgend, Haverthwaite, Colton, Lancashire; son of Edward Joseph Hill, Schoolmaster, and Mary Agnes Croasdale; m Nora Gray; 1 son. **Subject(s):** Natural Sciences; BA 1909; BSc; FRCS. **Tutor(s):** E E Sikes. **Educ:** Browidge Endowed School; The High School, Ulverston; The Higher Grade School, Barrow-in-Furness; The Grammar School, Kendal. **Career:** Master, Merchiston Castle School, Edinburgh 1911–1913; Director, Lansil Ltd, Lancaster 1927–1947. **Awards:** Sizarship, SJC. Died 23 October 1947.

HILLER, Alan Menzies (1913) Born 30 March 1895, Shanghai, China; son of Henry King Hiller, Civil Engineer, and Charlotte Ellen Menzies. **Tutor(s):** L H K Bushe-Fox. **Educ:** German School, Shanghai; The Leas, Hoylake; Berkhamsted School. **Career:** Second Lieutenant, 3rd Queen's Royal West Surrey Regiment, WWI. Died 16 May 1915 (killed in action).

HILLIER, Dr Thomas Lucas (1913) Born 20 January 1895, 3 Elmdale Road, St Michael, Bristol, Somerset; son of Thomas Hillier, Gentleman, and Julia Lucas; m Dorothy McCabe; 3 sons. **Subject(s):** Medicine; BA 1918; BChir 1922; MB 1922; MRCS; LRCP (London). **Tutor(s):** R P Gregory. **Educ:** St Goar Preparatory School, Clifton; Wycliffe College, Stonehouse. **Career:** Surgeon Lieutenant, RN 1918; Medical Officer, Mission Hospital, Paoning (China Inland Mission); GP, Cornwall. Died 2 November 1990.

HILLS, Kenneth Arthur (1945) Born 23 December 1926, 6 Wille Cottages, South Street, Lewes, Sussex; son of Arthur William Hills, Journeyman Stonemason, and Eva Mary Godden; m Ruth Evans, 7 June 1963, Richmond, Surrey. **Subject(s):** Geography/History; BA 1948; MA 1952; Cambridge Certificate of Education 1951. **Tutor(s):** F Thistlethwaite. **Educ:** South Malling Junior School, Lewes; Central School, Lewes; Lewes County Grammar School for Boys. **Career:** Teacher, Lewes County Grammar School for Boys 1951–1955; Employee, Director, Managing Director, Ginn and Company, Schoolbook Publishers 1955–1972; Managing Director, Hart Davis Educational 1973–1983; Director, Granada Publishing 1975–1983; Editorial Director, Collins Educational 1983–1985. **Appointments:** Chairman, Educational Publishers Council 1985. **Publications:** 24 History and Geography books for children.

HILLS, Walter Hyde (1935) Born 28 September 1917, Drylaw, Hitchen Hatch Lane, Sevenoaks, Kent; son of James Stuart Hills, Wholesale Druggist, and Bessie Sinclair Thompson; m Renata Barshall, 6 October 1943, Hampstead Parish Church (d 2002); 1 son (Nicholas b 1947), 1 daughter (Andrea b 1950). **Subjects:** Natural Sciences/Biochemistry; BA 1938; MA 1952; CChem; FRSC; FRIC. **Tutor(s):** J M Wordie. **Educ:** Knole School, Sevenoaks; Sutton Valence School; Staff College, Camberley. **Career:** Employee, Director, Managing Director, John Bell Hills and Lucas Ltd 1938–1966; RA 1939–1946; Schoolmaster, Worth 1966–1975; Head of Science, Kent College 1975–1984; Assistant Master and Librarian, West Heath 1984–1997. **Honours:** TD 1942; MBE (Military) 1945. Died 30 January 2003.

HILLYER, Reginald Arthur Nicholas (1920) Born 18 December 1897, 30 Buxton Road, Croydon, Surrey; son of Nicholas Hillyer, Schoolmaster, and Sophia Ann Sunnuck. **Tutor(s):** E E Sikes. **Educ:** The High School, Southend-on-Sea.

HILTON, Herbert Geoffrey (1936) Born 1 May 1917, Cotswold, Stafford Road, Oakengates, Wombridge, Shropshire; son of Herbert Hilton, Iron and Steel Works Engineer, and Winifred Westwood. **Subject(s):** Mechanical Sciences; BA 1939; MA 1943. **Tutor(s):** J S Boys Smith. **Educ:** Haughton Hall Preparatory School, Shifnal; Wellington Grammar School; Adams Grammar School, Newport. **Career:** Lieutenant, RN 1946; Engineer, John Summers and Sons Steelworks 1946. **Honours:** DSC 1946.

HILTON, Joseph Raymond (1945) Born 1 September 1927, 38 Winmarleigh Gardens, Leigh, Lancashire; son of Wilfred Hilton, Director, James Hilton & Son Ltd, and Mary Ann Baxendale; m Joan Margaret Young; 2 daughters (Susan and Julia). **Subject(s):** Mechanical Sciences; BA 1948; MA 1970; CEng; MIMechE. **Tutor(s):** S J Bailey; R L Howland. **Educ:** King Street Elementary School, Leigh; Leigh Grammar School. **Career:** Chartered Engineer; Engineering Director, Siebe Gorman & Co Ltd 1969–1978; Technical Director, Racal Safety Ltd 1978–1992. **Appointments:** Director, Founder and First Chairman, UK Branch, Internatioinal Society for Respiratory Protection. **Publications:** *Albert and the Elephant* and other Albert monologues.

HILTON, Philip Trevor (1928) Born 23 March 1911, 137 Loughborough Road, Leicester; son of Stephen Hilton, Boot Factor, and Edith Kate Crawford. **Subject(s):** Economics; BA 1932. **Tutor(s):** C W Guillebaud. **Educ:** Wyggeston Grammar School.

HIMELY, Luis Sigismund (1928) Born 28 November 1906, Occitania, Macagua, Cuba; son of William Charles Himely, Surgeon, and Violet Emily Brune. **Tutor(s):** J M Wordie. **Educ:** Richmond Lodge School, Torquay; Newton College, Newton Abbot; University of Bristol, Faculty of Engineering. **Career:** Captain, Federated Malay States Volunteer Force, POW Malaya, WWII.

HINDE, Professor Robert Aubrey (1942) Born 26 October 1923, Gurney Court, Magdalen Street, Norwich, Norfolk; son of Ernest Bertram Hinde, Medical Practitioner, and Isabella Taylor; m (1) Hester Cecily Coutts, 1948, Register Office, Bromley (dis 1971), (2) Joan Gladys Stevenson, 1971, Cambridge; (1) 2 sons (Francis Ronald John b 1950 and Jonathan Robert b 1958), 2 daughters (Katherine Gwendolen Isabel b 1952 and Miranda Elizabeth b 1954), (2) 2 daughters (Larissa Jane b 1972 and Camilla Anne b 1974). **Subject(s):** Natural Sciences/Zoology; BA 1947; MA 1952; ScD 1961; BSc (London); DPhil (Oxon); Honorary ScD (Université Libre, Brussels) 1974, (University of Paris, Nanterre) 1978, (Stirling) 1991, (Göteborg) 1991, (Edinburgh) 1992, (Western Ontario) 1996, (Oxon) 1998; FRS 1974; Honorary FBPsS 1981; Honorary FRCPsych 1988; Honorary FTCD 1990; Honorary FBA 2002. **Tutor(s):** J M Wordie. **Johnian Relatives:** father of Francis Ronald John Hinde (1968). **Educ:** Unthank College, Norwich; Oundle School. **Career:** Flight Lieutenant, Coastal Command, RAF 1941–1945; Research Assistant, Edward Grey Institute, University of Oxford 1948–1950; Curator, Ornithological Field Station (now Sub-Department of Animal Behaviour), Madingley, Cambridge 1950–1964; Title A Fellow 1951–1954, Title B Fellow 1958–1963, Lecturer in Zoology 1962–1963, Title E Fellow 1963–1989, Master 1989–1994, Title D Fellow 1994–, SJC; Royal Society Research Professor, University of Cambridge 1963–1989; Honorary Director, MRC Unit on Development and Integration of Behaviour 1970–1989. **Appointments:** Supervisor in Zoology 1955–1962, Steward 1956–1958, Tutor 1958–1963, SJC; Foreign Honorary Member, American Academy of Arts and Sciences 1974; Honorary Fellow, American Ornithologists' Union 1976; Honorary Foreign Associate, National Academy of Sciences, USA 1978; Hitchcock Professor, University of California 1979; Green Visiting Scholar, University of Texas 1983; Council Member, Royal Society 1985–1987; Honorary Fellow, Balliol College, Oxford 1986; Honorary Member, Association for the Study of Animal Behaviour 1987; Deutsche Ornithologische Gesellschaft 1988; Croonian Lecturer, Royal Society 1990; Member, Academia Europaea 1990. **Awards:** Munsteven Exhibition, SJC 1942; Scholarship, SJC 1947; Scientific Medal, Zoological Society 1961; Leonard Cammer Medal in Psychiatry, Columbia College, New York 1980; Osman Hill Medal, Primate Society of Great Britain 1980; Albert Einstein Award for Psychiatry, Albert Einstein College of Medicine, New York 1987; Huxley Medal, Royal Anthropological Institute 1990; Distinguished Scientific Contribution Award, Society for Research in Child Development 1991; Distinguished Career Award, International Society for the Study of Personal Relationships 1992; Frink Medal, Zoological Society of London 1992; G Stanley Hall Medal of the American Psychological Association 1993; Royal Medal, Royal Society 1996; Society's Medal, Association for the Study of Animal Behaviour 1997; Bowlby/Ainsworth Award in Child Development 2003. **Honours:** CBE 1988. **Publications:** *Animal Behaviour: a Synthesis of Ethology and Comparative Psychology*, 1966; (ed) *Bird Vocalizations: their relations to current problems in biology and psychology*, 1969; (joint ed) *Short Term Changes in Neural Activity and Behaviour*, 1970; (ed) *Non–Verbal Communication*, 1972; (joint ed) *Constraints on Learning*, 1973; *Biological Bases of Human Social Behaviour*, 1974; (joint ed) *Growing Points in Ethology*, 1976; *Towards Understanding Relationships*, 1979; *Ethology: its nature and relations with other sciences*, 1982; (jointly) *Defended to Death*, 1982; (ed and contributor) *Primate Social Relationships: an integrated approach*, 1983; (joint ed) *Social Relationships and Cognitive Development*, 1985; *Individuals, Relationships* *and Culture, 1987;* (joint ed) *Relationships within Families,* 1988; (joint ed) *Aggression and War,* 1989; (joint ed) *Education for Peace,* 1989; (ed and contributor) *The Institution of War,* 1991; (joint ed) *Co–operation and Prosocial Behaviour,* 1991; (joint ed) *War: a necessary evil?,* 1994; *Relationships: a dialectical perspective,* 1997; *Why gods persist: a scientific approach to religion,* Routledge, London and New York, 1999; (ed, with J Rotblat) *Eliminating the Causes of War,* Pugwash Occasional Papers, 2001; *Why Good is Good: the sources of morality,* Routledge, London and New York, 2002; (joint author) *War No More,* Pluto Press, 2003; sundry papers in biological, psychological and anthropological journals.

HINE, Francis Jopson (1942) Born 25 September 1921, Brathay, Scotforth Road, Lancaster; son of William Jopson Hine, Optician, and Mabel Ewan. **Tutor(s):** S J Bailey. **Johnian Relatives:** brother of Peter Ewan Hine (1942). **Educ:** Preparatory School, Lancaster; Friends' School, Lancaster; Oakmount School, Arnside; Lancaster Royal Grammar School; University of Manchester.

HINE, Peter Ewan (1942) Born 29 May 1924, Brathay, Scotforth Road, Lancaster; son of William Jopson Hine, Optician, and Mabel Ewan. **Tutor(s):** C W Guillebaud. **Johnian Relatives:** brother of Francis Jopson Hine (1942). **Educ:** Preparatory School, Lancaster; Lancaster Royal Grammar School.

HINES, James Wilfred (1939) Born 31 March 1921, Aldham Hall, Colchester; son of Herbert James Hines, Farmer, and Elizabeth Helen Robinson; m Pauline Estelle Gunary, 12 November 1955, Edwardstone, Suffolk (d 4 December 1991); 1 son (Ricard Adam). **Subject(s):** Agriculture; BA 1947; MA 1949. **Tutor(s):** C W Guillebaud. **Educ:** Mistley Place, Manningtree; Rugby School. **Career:** Farmer 1948–1989.

HINSLEY, Professor Sir Francis Harry (1937) Born 26 November 1918, 28 Rowland Street, Walsall; son of Thomas Henry Hinsley, Walsall Cooperative Society, and Emma Adey; m Hilary Brett; 2 sons (Hugo and Charles), 1 daughter (Clarissa). **Subject(s):** History; BA 1944; MA 1946; Honorary DLitt (University of Witwatersrand) 1985; Honorary DMilSci (Royal Roads Military College, Canada) 1987; FBA 1981. **Tutor(s):** J S Boys Smith. **Johnian Relatives:** uncle of Richard Nicholas Hinsley Pugh (1965); father of Hugh Edward Hinsley (1968). **Educ:** Wolverhampton Road Elementary School, Walsall; Queen Mary's Grammar School, Walsall. **Career:** Foreign Office, including intelligence work at Bletchley Park 1939–1946; Title A Fellow 1944–1949 (suspended on war service 1944–1946), Title B Fellow 1949–1969, Lecturer in History 1950–1969, SJC; Lecturer in History 1949–1965, Reader in the History of International Relations 1965–1969, Professor of the History of International Relations 1969–1983 (Emeritus 1983), Vice-Chancellor 1981–1983, University of Cambridge; Title C Fellow 1969–1979, Master 1979–1989, Title D Fellow 1989–1998, SJC. **Appointments:** Supervisor in History 1948–1950, Director of Studies in History 1954–1969, Steward 1955–1956, Tutor 1956–1963, SJC; Lees-Knowles Lecturer on Military Science, Trinity College, Cambridge 1970–1971; Editor, *The Historical Journal* 1960–1971; UK Representative, Provisional Academic Committee for European University Institute 1973–1975; President, SJC 1975–1979; Trustee, British Museum 1984–1989; Honorary Fellow, Darwin College, Cambridge 1987. **Awards:** Exhibition, SJC 1936; Scholarship, SJC. **Honours:** OBE 1946; Kt 1985. **Publications:** *Command of the Sea,* 1950; *Hitler's Strategy,* 1951; (ed) *New Cambridge Modern History,* Volume XI, 1962; *Power and the Pursuit of Peace,* 1963; *Sovereignty,* 1966; *Nationalism and the International System,* 1973; (ed) *British Foreign Policy under Sir Edward Grey,* 1977; (jointly) *British Intelligence in the Second World War,* Volume 1, 1979, Volume 2, 1981, Volume 3 (Part 1), 1984, (Part 2), 1988, Volume 4, 1990, abridged edition 1993; (ed) *Codebreakers: the inside story of Bletchley Park,* 1993. Died 16 February 1998.

HINTON, Arthur Russell (1921) Born 15 February 1904, 26 Park Road, Middlesbrough, Yorkshire; son of Amos Humphrey Hinton, Grocer and Provision Merchant, and Irene Christine Russell; m Muriel Fletcher, 23

April 1930, Park Wesleyan Church, Middlesbrough; 3 sons, 2 daughters. BA 1925. **Tutor(s):** E Cunningham. **Johnian Relatives:** brother of John Hinton (1937). **Educ:** Caldicott School, Hitchin; Mill Hill School. Died 2 April 1974.

HINTON, John (1937) Born 22 January 1919, Southcote, Cambridge Road, Middlesbrough; son of Amos Humphrey Hinton, Grocer and Provision Merchant, and Irene Christine Russell; m Dulcis Hammond, 19 October 1946. BA 1940; MA 1944. **Tutor(s):** J M Wordie. **Johnian Relatives:** brother of Arthur Russell Hinton (1921). **Educ:** Caldicott School, Hitchin; Mill Hill School; Miss Collingwood's Private Preparatory School. **Career:** Royal Corps of Signals 1939–1945; Amos Hinton & Sons Ltd 1945–1969 (Director 1948–1969). Died 9 August 1969.

HINTON, William Kirtland (1919) Born 1 May 1901, Grove Hill, Middlesbrough, North Yorkshire; son of William Henry Hinton, Managing Director, Amos Hinton & Sons, Grocer, and Mary Charlotte Mascall; m Alida Mary; 3 sons (William Patrick Crane b 28 May 1931, David Anthony b 27 May 1934 and Jolyon Kirtland b 13 September 1943), 1 daughter (Jane b 2 April 1929). **Subject(s):** Mathematics/Economics; BA 1922. **Tutor(s):** E A Benians. **Johnian Relatives:** father of William Patrick Crane Hinton (1951) and of David Anthony Hinton (1954). **Educ:** Private School, Southbrooke; Preparatory School, Sedbergh; Mill Hill School, London. Died 2 August 1983.

HIPPS, Nathaniel (1925) Born 14 July 1908, 152 Harehills Avenue, Leeds, Yorkshire; son of Paul Hipps, Master Tailor, and Fanny Rubinstein. **Tutor(s):** M P Charlesworth. **Educ:** Leeds Grammar School; Cranford College; Clifton College.

HIRJEE, Rustom (1908) Born 13 May 1889, Mandalay, Burma; son of Hirjee Nowrojee Hirjee, Advocate. **Tutor(s):** L H K Bushe-Fox. **Educ:** St Peter's School, Mandalay, Burma; Denstone College.

HIRON, The Rev John Bennett (1901) (admitted as Non-Collegiate Student 1900) Born 21 December 1860, Deddington, Oxfordshire; son of John Samuel Hiron, Stationer, and Mary Bennett. BA 1903; MA 1907; BA (London) 1888. **Tutor(s):** D MacAlister. **Educ:** Derby School; Hereford School. **Career:** Ordained Deacon 1896; Ordained Priest 1898; Preacher, Ely Diocese 1902–1928. Died 24 April 1939.

HIRST, Geoffrey Audus Nicholson (1922) Born 14 December 1904, Redhill, Shireoaks Road, Headingley, Leeds; son of Edward Audus Hirst, Colonel, and Eleanor Maud Nicholson. **Tutor(s):** E E Sikes. **Educ:** Bramcote, Scarborough; Charterhouse. **Career:** Managing Director, Hirst, Brooke and Hirst Ltd, (Manufacturing Chemists) 1930; Conservative MP (Independent in 1966) for Shipley 1950–1970; Chairman, Conservative Party Parliamentary Trade and Industry Committee; Chairman, Film Industry Committee. **Appointments:** President, Leeds Chamber of Commerce 1952–1954; Honorary Member, Bradford Chamber of Commerce Council; Honorary Vice President, National Chamber of Trade. Died 17 June 1984.

HIRST, William Henry (1949) Born 20 February 1928, 351 Hainton Avenue, Grimsby, Lincolnshire; son of Algernon Henry Hirst, Milliner, and Charlotte Kitching. **Subject(s):** Natural Sciences/Chemical Engineering; BA 1952. **Tutor(s):** G C L Bertram. **Educ:** St Martin's Preparatory School, Grimsby; Humberstone Foundation School, Clee. Died 1993.

HITCHING, Wilfrid Wallace (1915) Born 10 September 1895, 33 Alice Street, Sale, Cheshire; son of Wilfrid Wallace Hitching, Commercial Traveller, and Florence Emily Thomas; m Hilda Doris May. **Subject(s):** Law; BA 1921; LLB 1921. **Tutor(s):** L H K Bushe-Fox. **Johnian Relatives:** father of James Wallace Hitching (1962). **Educ:** Sale High School; Orphan Schools, Cheadle; Hulme Hall. **Career:** Second

Lieutenant, 152nd Siege Battery, RGA, France 1916. **Awards:** Scholarship, SJC; Squire Law Studentship 1915; Wright's Prize, SJC 1920; Whewell Scholarship, University of Cambridge 1921, 1923.

HO, Maung Kway Foung (1936) Born 20 March 1913, Rangoon; son of Ho Kim Kyone, Merchant, and Kyiang Sin. **Tutor(s):** C W Guillebaud. **Educ:** St John's Convent, Rangoon; St Paul's School, Rangoon; Bramcote Hall Preparatory School, Nottinghamshire; Trent College, Derbyshire; University College, Rangoon University. **Awards:** International Colonial Service Probationer.

HO, Shai Chuen (1911) Born 12 May 1891, 3 Old Bailey Street, Hong Kong; son of Fuk Ho, Manager, Merchant's Office, and Lau-Ying Lo. **Subject(s):** Medicine. BA 1914; LMSSA 1918. **Tutor(s):** L H K Bushe-Fox. **Johnian Relatives:** brother of Shai Leung Ho (1907). **Educ:** King's College School. **Career:** Physician. Died 29 April 1938.

HO, Shai Leung (1907) Born 7 November 1888, 21 Hollywood Road, Hong Kong; son of Fuk Ho, Manager, Merchant's Office, and Lau-Ying Lo. **Subject(s):** Architecture/Civil Engineering. **Tutor(s):** L H K Bushe-Fox. **Johnian Relatives:** brother of Shai Chuen Ho (1911). **Educ:** Tulse Hill School; King's College School, London. Died 21 December 1933.

HOARE, Henry George Wishart (1931) Born 11 June 1912, Ravenscraig, 12 Gayton Road, Harrow; son of Henry Gilbert Hoare, Baptist Minister, and Maude Inglis Wishart; m Georgina R Tod (d 1995); 3 daughters. **Subject(s):** Natural Sciences; BA 1934; MA 1941; MB 1938; BChir 1938; FRCS; FRCS (Edinburgh) 1939; FCOphth 1989; FRCOphth 1993. **Tutor(s):** M P Charlesworth. **Educ:** Roborough School, Eastbourne; Colet Court School, London; The Leys School, Cambridge. **Career:** Consulting Ophthalmic Surgeon, Gwent Area Health Authority. Died 29 July 1999.

HOBBS, Alan Victor (1913) Born 8 December 1894, 130 Old Christchurch Road, Bournemouth, Hampshire; son of Alfred Ernest Hobbs, Pharmaceutical Chemist, and Mary Octavia Warwick. **Subject(s):** Mathematics. **Tutor(s):** L H K Bushe-Fox. **Educ:** King Charles's School, Tunbridge Wells; Skinner's School; Tonbridge School. **Career:** Enlisted in Royal West Kent Regiment; gazetted Second Lieutenant, 10th (Service) Battalion, the Royal Sussex Regiment 1914; RFC 1915. Died 15 December 1915 (shot down over Valencienne by the German Pilot Immelmann).

HOBBS, Leonard Paul (1943) Born 9 November 1924, Sherwood, Streetsbrook Road, Shirley, Birmingham; son of Leonard Hobbs, Clerk and Telegraphist, and Sybil Agnes Slade. BA 1947; MA 1949. **Tutor(s):** S J Bailey. **Educ:** Hall Green Council School; Moseley Secondary School; Solihull School. **Awards:** Minor Scholarship, SJC 1942.

HOBBS, Victor William John (1905) Born 23 January 1887, 78 St Michael's Hill, Bristol; son of Edwin Ernest Hobbs, Insurance Surveyor, and Jane Elizabeth Deborah Barns; m Frances Gwendoline Croom-Johnson, 3 September 1912; 1 daughter (Jane Margaret Hobbs b 20 May 1914). **Subject(s):** Law; BA 1908; MA 1913; LLB 1909. **Tutor(s):** D MacAlister. **Johnian Relatives:** father-in-law of Charles Stephens Hedley (1925). **Educ:** Clifton College, Bristol. **Career:** Assistant Master, Llandaff Cathedral School 1909; Called to the Bar, Inner Temple 1909; Assistant Master (Modern Languages), Highgate School 1912–1915; Lieutenant, 6th The Buffs (East Kent Regiment, TF), WWI. Died 9 August 1918 (killed in action at Morlancourt).

HOBDEN, David Henry William (1940) Born 13 July 1921, 19 Route des Soeurs, Shanghai, China; son of Frank Hobden, Accountant, Cable and Wireless Ltd, and Marguerite Clara Dowdall; m Vera (d 1998); 4 children. **Subject(s):** Modern and Medieval Languages; BA 1946; MA 1949. **Tutor(s):** C W Guillebaud. **Johnian Relatives:** brother-in-law of Raymond Arthur Lyttleton (1937). **Educ:** Cathedral School, Shangai;

Dane Court, Parkstone; Canford School, Wimborne; Hotel School, Lucerne. **Career:** Pilot Officer, RCAF, WWII; Civil Servant, International Labour Organization, Geneva; Editor, English language edition, *International Labour Review*. **Awards:** Sizarship, SJC. Died 30 September 1999.

HOBSON, Antony John (1937) Born 2 April 1919, Wingate, Kirby Muxloe; son of Charles Thornton Hobson, Cost Accountant, and Gladys May Marson. BA 1940; MA 1946. **Tutor(s):** J S Boys Smith. **Johnian Relatives:** father of Christopher John Hobson (1967). **Educ:** Woodlands School, Deganwy; Shrewsbury School. **Career:** War service, POW Java, WWII.

HOBSON, Patrick James (1947) Born 14 April 1925, 23 Private Road, Nottingham; son of Sidney Hobson, Timber Merchant, and Hilda Mary Scanlan; m Jeanne Barbara Culpin, 1 July 1950. **Subject(s):** English; BA 1949; MA 1954. **Tutor(s):** F Thistlethwaite. **Educ:** Waverley School, Nottingham; Leighton Park School. **Career:** Sub-Lieutenant, RN, WWII; Second Master, Oratory School 1953–1962. Died 27 August 1982.

HOBSON, Stanley Wakefield (1929) Born 13 May 1910, 50 Malcolm Street, Newcastle upon Tyne; son of John Thomas Hobson, Plumber, and Mary Ellen Wakefield. **Subject(s):** Modern and Medieval Languages/Economics; BA 1932; MA 1937. **Tutor(s):** C W Guillebaud. **Educ:** Heaton Park Road Council School, Newcastle; Royal Grammar School, Newcastle. **Career:** Director of Education, Kingston-upon-Hull 1952–1974. **Appointments:** Senior Member, Hull University Council. Died September 1982.

HOCKEY, The Revd Harold Hibbet Hubert (1900) Born 26 January 1879, Beccles, Suffolk; son of Alfred Knibbs Hockey, Schoolmaster, and Emma Bridgman; m Edith Grace Murrell; 1 daughter (Elizabeth). BA 1903; MA 1910. **Tutor(s):** D MacAlister. **Educ:** The College, Beccles. **Career:** Ordained Deacon 1905; Curate, All Saints, Eastbourne 1905–1908; Ordained Priest 1909. Died 15 January 1936.

HOCKIN, John Russell Ayscoghe (1925) Born 11 March 1902, The Park Farm, Mathon, Herefordshire; son of Arthur Ayscoghe Hockin, Farmer, and Kathleen Maud Paine. BA 1928. **Tutor(s):** E A Benians. **Educ:** Bedford School; Leighton Park School, Reading. Died 20 August 1942.

HODGE, James (1938) Born 5 July 1920, 11 Fore Street, St Austell, Cornwall; son of Harry Faull Hodge, Ironmonger, and Edith Coath, School Teacher; m Betty Hood, 24 October 1945, Reigate; 2 daughters (Alison b 1948 and Margaret b 1950). **Subject(s):** Mechanical Sciences; BA 1941; MA 1945; CEng; FIMechE; MRAeS; MASME; FRSA. **Tutor(s):** J S Boys Smith; S J Bailey. **Educ:** West Hill Council School, St Austell; County School, St Austell. **Career:** Project Engineer, Power Jets Ltd 1941–1945; Design Engineer, Gas Turbine Department, English Electric Company, Rugby 1945–1946; Scientific Officer, AERE, Harwell 1946–1948; Senior Consultant, later Chief Engineer, Power Jets (Research and Development) Ltd 1948–1958; Visiting Professor of Mechanical Engineering, Columbia University, New York 1953 and 1954; Group Chief Engineer, later Engineering Director and Research Director, Holman Group, Camborne 1958–1974; Reader in Engineering, Cornwall Technical College 1971–1974. **Appointments:** Honorary Secretary, University Engineering Society; Chairman 1961–1976, then President until 1981, Cornish Engine Preservation Society (later The Trevithick Society); Honorary Treasurer 1962–1989, President 1989–, RNLI Penlee; Bard of the Cornish Gorsedd (Bardic name 'Ynjnor Ayr' meaning 'Engineer of air') 1979; Trustee, Penlee Lifeboat Disaster Fund 1981; Founder Chairman, REMAP Cornwall; Kemp Memorial Lecturer, Exeter University 1988. **Awards:** Scholarship, SJC 1940; College Prizes 1939, 1940. **Publications:** *Gas Turbine Cycles & Performance Estimation*, Butterworth, 1955; *Richard Trevithick*, Shire Books, 1973; numerous papers in the technical press.

HODGE, Professor Sir William Vallance Douglas (1923) Born 17 June 1903, 1 Church Hill Place, Edinburgh, Scotland; son of Archibald James Hodge, Searcher of Public Records, and Jenny Vallance; m Kathleen Anne Cameron, 1929; 1 son, 1 daughter. **Subject(s):** Mathematics; BA 1925; MA 1930; ScD 1950 (Pembroke); Honorary DSc (Bristol 1957; Leicester 1959; Sheffield 1960; Liverpool 1961; Exeter 1961; Wales 1961); Honorary LLD (Edinburgh) 1958; FRS 1938; FRSE. **Tutor(s):** E Cunningham. **Educ:** George Watson's College, Edinburgh; University of Edinburgh. **Career:** Lecturer, Bristol University 1926–1931; Title A Fellow, SJC 1930–1933; Lecturer in Mathematics 1933–1936, Lowndean Professor of Astronomy and Geometry 1936–1970 (Emeritus 1970–1975), University of Cambridge; Fellow 1935–1970, Master 1958–1970, Pembroke College, Cambridge. **Appointments:** President, London Mathematical Society 1947–1949; President, Cambridge Philosophical Society 1947–1949; Visiting Lecturer, Harvard University 1950; Vice-President, International Mathematical Union 1954–1958; President, Mathematical Association 1955; Physical Secretary, Royal Society 1957–1965; President, International Congress of Mathematicians, Edinburgh 1958; Foreign Honorary Member, American Academy of Arts and Sciences 1958; Foreign Associate, US National Academy of Sciences 1959; Vice-President, Royal Society 1959–1965; Honorary Fellow, SJC 1964–1975; Foreign Member, Royal Danish Academy 1966; Honorary Fellow, Pembroke College, Cambridge 1970; Foreign Member, American Philosophical Society. **Awards:** Ferguson Scholarship 1924; Smith's Prize, University of Cambridge 1927; Senior Studentship 1931; 1851 Exhibition, SJC; Adams Prize, University of Cambridge 1936; Berwick Prize, London Mathematical Society 1952; Royal Medal, Royal Society 1957; De Morgan Medal, London Mathematical Society 1959; Gunning Victoria Jubilee Prize, Royal Society of Edinburgh 1968; Copley Medal, Royal Society 1974. **Honours:** Kt 1959. **Publications:** *Theory and Applications of Harmonic Integrals*, 1941 (2nd edition, 1952); (with D Pedoe) *Methods of Algebraic Geometry*, Volume 1 1947, Volume 2 1952, Volume 3 1954; numerous papers in British and foreign mathematical journals. Died 7 July 1975.

HODGES, The Revd Charles Frederic (1903) Born 20 April 1885, The Vicarage, Stoke by Nayland, Suffolk; son of George Hodges, Archdeacon of Sudbury, and Agnes Helena Sanders; 3 sons (David, Anthony and John), 2 daughters (Fay and Petronella). BA 1907; MA 1919. **Tutor(s):** J R Tanner; C E Graves. **Johnian Relatives:** son of George Hodges (1871). **Educ:** Bury St Edmunds School. **Career:** Ordained Deacon 1909; Curate, St Augustine, South Hackney 1909–1910; Curate, Nayland 1910–1911 and 1913–1915; Ordained Priest 1911; Curate, Willesden 1911–1913; Curate, St Matthew, Ipswich 1915–1916; Curate, St Mary Magdalene, St Leonards, Sussex 1916–1921; Vicar, Ospringe 1921–1944; Rector, Ickham, Kent 1944–1956. **Appointments:** Editor, *Ickham Review* (Parish Magazine). Died 28 June 1964.

HODGES, Professor Henry Woolmington Mackenzie (1938) Born 19 July 1920, The Blocks, Deddington, Oxfordshire; son of George Montague Williams Hodges, Physician and Surgeon, and Barbara Kathleen Webber; Diploma in Archaeology (London University). **Tutor(s):** R L Howland. **Educ:** Eversley School, Tunbridge Wells; Kimbolton School. **Career:** Royal Naval Air Branch; Assistant Lecturer, The Queen's University of Belfast 1953–1957; Lecturer, Archaeological Technology Institute, London 1957–1974; Professor of Artefacts Conservation, Queen's University, Kingston, Ontario 1974–1988; Secretary-General, International Institute for Conservation 1988–1994. **Appointments:** Fellow, International Institute of Conservation 1960. **Publications:** *Artefacts*, 1964; *Technology in the Ancient World*, 1970. Died 19 May 1997.

HODGESS, Frederick Henry (1942) Born 23 September 1904, 1 Grosvenor Place, Plymouth; son of Cecil Stanley Hodgess, Pawnbroker, and Mabel May Hodge. BA 1944; MA 1948; BSc (London) 1924. **Tutor(s):** C W Guillebaud. **Educ:** St Paul's Church of England School, Plymouth; High Street Council School, Plymouth; Devonport High School; Borough Road Training College, Isleworth; Battersea Technical Institute. **Career:** Instructor, Initial Flight Wing; Master, Purley County Secondary School, Old Coulsdon 1948–1954. Died 11 March 1954.

HODGETTS, Robert Bartley (1937) Born 10 November 1918, Ladbroke Nursing Home, Southend-on-Sea; son of Bartley Hodgetts, Master Mariner, and Florence Harriet Stagg; m (1) A K Jeffreys, 1945, (2) Frances Grace Pepper, 1949; (1) 1 daughter, (2) 2 daughters. **Subject(s):** History; BA 1941; MA 1985. **Tutor(s):** J S Boys Smith. **Johnian Relatives:** father of Gabrielle Julia Frances Hodgetts (1982); uncle of Charlotte Amanda York Brown (1987). **Educ:** Crosby Road Council School, Great Crosby; Merchant Taylors' School, Great Crosby. **Career:** RNVR, Fleet Air Arm 1940–1945; Assistant Principal 1947–1951, Principal 1951–1964, Assistant Secretary 1964–1973, Ministry of National Insurance; Under-Secretary, DHSS, 1973–1978. **Appointments:** Clerk to Worshipful Company of Glaziers 1979–85. **Awards:** Exhibition, SJC 1936; Scholarship, SJC.

HODGKISS, Derek Saunders (1948) Born 16 August 1926, 6 Grange Road, Pendleton, Salford, Lancashire; son of William James Hodgkiss, Registrar, Salford Royal Technical College, and Mabel Annie Saunders; m Marjorie Pauline Smith, 2 April 1955, Irlams-o'th'-Height, Salford; 2 sons (Richard William b 6 January 1956 and John Patrick b 15 May 1958). **Subject(s):** History; BA 1950; MA 1955. **Tutor(s):** F Thistlethwaite. **Educ:** Broomhouse Lane School, Salford; Manchester Grammar School. **Career:** Bury Grammar School, Lancashire 1953–1988 (Head, History Department 1962–1975, Second Master 1975–1988). **Awards:** Somerset Exhibition, SJC.

HODGSON, James (1948) Born 14 October 1925, Glenmore Maternity Home, Sea Point, Cape Town, South Africa; son of Frederick Warmingham Hodgson, Civil Servant, and Lucy Elizabeth Challenor; m (1) Patricia Reed, St Mary's, Prestbury, Cheltenham, 26 March 1951, (2) Dawn Giles, 21 July 1979. BA 1950; MA 1974. **Tutor(s):** F Thistlethwaite. **Educ:** St Hilda's School, Bahia Blanca, Argentina; Backford School; John Stocker School, Exeter; Exeter School. **Career:** RA, India and Germany; The Post Office 1950; Director, External Telecommunications Executive, the Post Office 1969; Vice-Chairman, British Telecom, until 1985. **Appointments:** Director, Cable and Wireless Ltd 1970. **Awards:** Scholarship, SJC. **Honours:** CBE 1983. Died 25 May 1999.

HODGSON, John Richard Patrick (1947) Born 29 December 1925, The Long Cottage, Barnet Lane, Totteridge, Hertfordshire; son of Richard William Hodgson, Post Office Clerk, and Mary Ann O'Brien.

HODGSON, Dr Oliver Ernest Fenner (1942) Born 16 March 1924, 22 High Street, Andover, Hampshire; son of Ronald George Keith Hodgson, Medical Practitioner, and Dorothy Margaret Greig, Medical Practitioner. **Subject(s):** Natural Sciences; BA 1945; MA 1965; MB 1948; BChir 1948; FRCPsych. **Tutor(s):** S J Bailey. **Educ:** Harcourt School; Epsom College. **Career:** Consultant Psychiatrist, Fulbourn and Addenbrooke's Hospitals, Cambridge 1960; Associate Lecturer, Faculty of Clinical Medicine 1981–1986; Emeritus Consultant Psychiatrist, Addenbrooke's Hospital, Cambridge 1986.

HODGSON, Thomas Riley (1938) Born 20 November 1915, Towngate, Clifton in Hartshead, Brighouse, Yorkshire; son of Raymond Hodgson, Grocer's Clerk, and Sarah Ellen English. **Tutor(s):** J S Boys Smith. **Educ:** St Andrew's Church School, Brighouse; Cowper Street Council School; Leeds Grammar School; University of Leeds. **Career:** Observer, Coastal Command (Pilot Officer), RAF 1939–1941. **Awards:** Open Strathcona Exhibition, SJC. Died 17 May 1941 (killed in a flying accident).

HOFFMAN, Wallace Benjamin (1945) Born 14 August 1915, Denver, Colorado, USA; son of Wallace Hoffman, Editor, and Louella Fern Evans. BA (Denver) 1941. **Tutor(s):** C W Guillebaud. **Educ:** University of Denver. **Career:** Sergeant, US Army.

HOFMANN, Johannes Alfred Franz Georg (1913) Born 13 May 1891, Griez, Germany; son of Franz Heinrich Hofmann, Furstlicher Landgerichtsprasident, and Charlotte Pauline Malwina Weber. **Tutor(s):** R P Gregory. **Educ:** Griez Gymnasium; Munich University.

HOGAN, Claude Douglas Devereux (1905) Born 26 July 1886, Anson Road, Penang, Straits Settlements; son of Reginald Arthur Philip Hogan, Barrister-at-Law, and Annie Amelia Somerville Shropshire. BA 1908; LLB 1909. **Tutor(s):** E E Sikes. **Johnian Relatives:** brother of Reginald Victor John Somervill Hogan (1904). **Educ:** Private Tuition, Germany; Reading School.

HOGAN, Reginald Victor John Somervill (1904) Born 26 August 1885, Penang, Straits Settlements; son of Reginald Arthur Philip Hogan, Barrister-at-Law, and Annie Amelia Somerville Shropshire. BA 1907. **Tutor(s):** E E Sikes. **Johnian Relatives:** brother of Claude Douglas Devereux Hogan (1905). **Educ:** Konigliches Gymnasium, Dusseldorf; Reading School. **Career:** Admitted to Middle Temple 1906; Called to the Bar 1909; Lieutenant, East Lancashire Regiment, later Captain, RAF (wounded twice), then Staff Officer, 3rd Grade, Air Ministry, WWI.

HOGG, Denis Broadbery (1944) Born 28 July 1926, 17 Middleton Park Square, Hunslet, Leeds; son of Herbert William Hogg, Electrician, and Mabel Ethel Broadbery. **Tutor(s):** J M Wordie. **Educ:** Talbot Road School, Roundhay; Roundhay School. **Appointments:** RE Cadet, SJC.

HOGGAN, Ralph Walter (1918) Born 5 June 1900, Comely Bank, College Road, Dulwich, Surrey; son of Walter Hoggan and Mary Bonnar Elder; m Lilian Alice Thurston, 3 September 1927, St Stephen's, Dulwich. **Subject(s):** Mathematics; BA 1922. **Tutor(s):** E E Sikes. **Educ:** Dulwich Preparatory School; Dulwich College.

HOLBARD, Cyril Arthur (1927) Born 10 March 1908, 9 Rowston Street, Cleethorpes, Lincolnshire; son of Arthur Ernest Holbard, ex soldier, and Annie Elizabeth Grant. **Subject(s):** Natural Sciences; BA 1930; MA 1934. **Tutor(s):** J M Wordie. **Educ:** Elementary School, Stamford; Stamford School. **Awards:** Marquess of Exeter Exhibition, SJC.

HOLDEN, Arthur Alfred (1924) Born 26 January 1906, St Augustine's Rectory, Junction Street, Newton, Manchester; son of William Holden, Clerk in Holy Orders, and Kate Dibb. **Tutor(s):** E E Sikes. **Johnian Relatives:** son of William Holden (1880); nephew of Richard Holden (1880); brother of Norman Victor Holden (1909), John Railton Holden (1911) and of William Richard Holden (1921). **Educ:** Moston Lane Municipal School, Manchester; Manchester Grammar School.

HOLDEN, Brian Astbury (1942) Born 27 January 1924, Princess Mary Maternity Hospital, Newcastle upon Tyne; son of Charles William Holden, Printer's Reader, and Annie Astbury. **Subject(s):** Natural Sciences; BA 1945; MA 1949. **Tutor(s):** C W Guillebaud. **Educ:** Arthur's Hill Elementary School, Newcastle upon Tyne; Royal Grammar School, Newcastle upon Tyne. **Career:** RN 1944–1946; Development Engineer, Ferrograph Company 1947–1955; Chief Engineer, Burgess Micro Switch Company 1955–1984.

HOLDEN, Frank (1911) Born 24 November 1893, 24 East Hill Street, Barnoldswick, Yorkshire; son of Blackburn Holden, Cotton Manufacturer, and Mary Ellen Dickinson. **Subject(s):** Natural Sciences; BA 1914; MA 1925. **Tutor(s):** L H K Bushe-Fox. **Educ:** High School, Barnoldswick; Modern School, Southport; Nelson Secondary School.

HOLDEN, Henry Francis (1914) Born 5 February 1896, Melview, Orchard Road, Erdington, Warwickshire; son of Sydney Holmwood Holden, Electrical Engineer, and Sophia Henrietta Gregg. **Subject(s):** Natural Sciences; BA 1920; MA 1923. **Tutor(s):** R P Gregory. **Educ:** Handsworth Grammar School; King Edward VI School. **Career:** Lieutenant, South Staffordshire Regiment 1914. **Awards:** Scholarship,

SJC; Hughes Prize, SJC 1920; Hutchinson Studentship, SJC 1920; Benn W Levy Studentship 1921.

HOLDEN, John Railton (1911) Born 28 August 1891, 754 Rochdale Road, St George's, Manchester; son of William Holden, Clerk in Holy Orders, and Kate Dibb. **Tutor(s):** J R Tanner. **Johnian Relatives:** son of William Holden (1880); nephew of Richard Holden (1880); brother of Norman Victor Holden (1909), William Richard Holden (1921) and of Arthur Alfred Holden (1924). **Educ:** Manchester Grammar School; College of Agriculture and Horticulture, Holmes Chapel. **Career:** Royal Fusiliers (Public Schools Battalion), Second Lieutenant, RE (TF), later Lieutenant (Aeroplane Officer), RAF, WWI.

HOLDEN, Norman Victor (1909) Born 30 March 1890, 754 Rochdale Road, Manchester, Lancashire; son of William Holden, Clerk in Holy Orders, and Kate Dibb. **Subject(s):** History; BA 1912. **Tutor(s):** J R Tanner. **Johnian Relatives:** son of William Holden (1880); nephew of Richard Holden (1880); brother of John Railton Holden (1911), William Richard Holden (1921) and of Arthur Alfred Holden (1924). **Educ:** Manchester Grammar School. **Career:** Master, Central High School for Boys, Manchester; History Master, Manchester Grammar School; Form Master, Junior Preparatory School, Manchester; Lieutenant, 6th Lancashire Fusiliers 1914 (declined a Captaincy). **Appointments:** Organising Secretary, Manchester and District Scouts' Association. **Awards:** Somerset Exhibition, SJC. Died 5 June 1915 (of wounds received in action in Gallipoli on 4 June).

HOLDEN, William Richard (1921) Born 27 October 1903, St Augustine's Rectory, Junction Street, Newton, Manchester; son of William Holden, Clerk in Holy Orders, and Kate Dibb. **Subject(s):** Modern and Medieval Languages/History; BA 1925; MA 1929. **Tutor(s):** E E Sikes. **Johnian Relatives:** son of William Holden (1880); nephew of Richard Holden (1880); brother of Norman Victor Holden (1909), John Railton Holden (1911) and of Arthur Alfred Holden (1924). **Educ:** Public Elementary School, Manchester; The Grammar School, Manchester. Died 5 October 1975.

HOLDICH, Cyril Leslie (1932) Born 16 February 1914, 65 Huntingdon Road, Coventry; son of Henry Holdich, Machine Tool Maker, and Alice Ellen Mills. **Subject(s):** Natural Sciences; BA 1935; MA 1974. **Tutor(s):** J M Wordie. **Educ:** Earlson Elementary School, Coventry; Bablake School, Coventry.

HOLDING, Daniel John (1945) Born 16 March 1928, 33 Ashburn Road, Stockport, Cheshire; son of Daniel Holding, Cotton Cloth Merchant's Cashier, and Nelly Hyde; m Aileen Elisabeth Weber, 28 July 1953; 2 sons (Stephen James b 1957 and John Benjamin b 1960), 2 daughters (Rachel Joy b 1954 and Sarah Marjorie b 1956). **Subject(s):** Mechanical Sciences; BA 1948; MA 1955; CMath FIMA; PGCE (Manchester) 1952; Cert Theol (Manchester) 1953. **Tutor(s):** S J Bailey; R L Howland. **Educ:** Heaton Moor Council School; Manchester Grammar School. **Career:** Research Technician, A V Roe 1948–1951; Assistant Master, Hookergate Grammar School 1953–1955; Assistant Master, Cheadle Hulme School 1955–1958; Head, Mathematics Department, Exeter School 1959–1967; Principal Lecturer and Head of Department of Mathematical Studies, University College of St Martin, Lancaster 1968–1985. **Appointments:** Visiting Lecturer, International School, Geneva August 1964; Visiting Lecturer, University of Botswana, Bechuanaland and Swaziland July 1966; Secretary, North Lancashire Group, Lancashire Wildlife Trust 1988–; Chairman, Heysham Heritage Association 1995–. **Awards:** Baylis Scholarship, SJC 1945. **Publications:** (co-author) School Mathematics Project, CUP, 1964–1975; The Investigations Book, CUP, 1992; educational computer software, CUP, 1985–1986.

HOLDSWORTH, The Revd John Alexander Philip (1941) Born 1 September 1922, The Vicarage, South Benfleet, Essex; son of William Henry Holdsworth, Clerk in Holy Orders, and Ethel Mary Harris. **Subject(s):** English; BA 1947; MA 1949. **Tutor(s):** C W Guillebaud.

Educ: Rochdale Grammar School; Durham School. **Career:** Deacon, Priest, Curate, All Saints', Wigan 1953. **Awards:** Exhibition, SJC. Died April 1983.

HOLGATE, James William (1933) Born 20 January 1915, 14 Richmond Road, St Annes on Sea, Lancaster; son of Arthur Holgate, Merchant and Manufacturer, Agriculturist, and Emma Boardman; BA 1936; MA 1940. **Tutor(s):** C W Guillebaud. **Educ:** Ormskirk Grammar School; English Grammar School, Château d'Oex, Switzerland; Royal Grammar School, Clitheroe.

HOLLAND, Graham Lambert (1948) Born 20 December 1924, Auckland, New Zealand; son of Daniel Daley Holland, Literary Editor, *New Zealand Herald*, and Rachel Colquhoun Elliffe. BA 1950; BSc (New Zealand) 1945; MSc 1947. **Tutor(s):** J M Wordie. **Educ:** Owairaka Primary School; Mt Albert Grammar School; Auckland University College. **Career:** Lubricants Supply and Economics, Shell International. Died October 1994.

HOLLEY, Geoffrey Evelyn Windham (1938) Born 12 August 1917, Pietermaritzburg, Natal, South Africa; son of James Hunt Holley, Wattle Planter, and Emily Frances Georgina Norman; 1 daughter. **Subject(s):** Economics; BA 1940. **Tutor(s):** C W Guillebaud. **Educ:** Cordwallis Preparatory School, Pietermaritzburg; Michaelhouse, Balgowan; Rhodes University College, Grahamstown South Africa. Died 1 August 1988.

HOLLICK, Dr Frank Samuel Jennings (1929) Born 17 November 1910, 197 Stamford Street, Stretford, Manchester; son of Samuel Mee Hollick, Minister, Catholic Apostolic Church, and Agnes Mary Jennings; m Alison Cunningham Dew Elias, 12 January 1946, West Kirby Presbyterian Church; 3 sons, 1 daughter, 1 foster daughter. **Subject(s):** Natural Sciences; BA 1932; MA 1936; PhD 1936. **Tutor(s):** J M Wordie. **Johnian Relatives:** brother-in-law of Charles Frederick Elias (1944). **Educ:** Armsworth Kindergarten; Moor Allerton Preparatory School, West Didsbury; Manchester Grammar School. **Career:** Title A Fellow 1935–1941, Supervisor in Zoology 1935–1949, Title B Fellow 1941–1972, Lecturer in Zoology 1949–1972, Title D Fellow 1972–2001, SJC; Demonstrator in Zoology 1937–1945, Lecturer in Zoology 1945–1972, University of Cambridge. **Awards:** Somerset Exhibition, SJC 1929; Strathcona Studentship, SJC 1934. Died 28 May 2001.

HOLLINGS, Christopher Ingham (1949) Born 12 October 1928, 10 Orchard Drive, Blackheath, London; son of Harold Hollings, Controller of Research, and Alice Carter; m Elizabeth Marie Bap, 23 May 1953. BA 1952. **Tutor(s):** C W Guillebaud. **Johnian Relatives:** brother of John Carter Hollings (1947). **Educ:** Belmont House, Blackheath; Yardley Court, Tonbridge; Tonbridge School.

HOLLINGS, John Carter (1947) Born 19 December 1923, 40 Tyrwhitt Road, Deptford; son of Harold Hollings, Research Chemist, Gas Company, and Alice Carter. BA 1949; MA 1954. **Tutor(s):** G C L Bertram. **Johnian Relatives:** brother of Christopher Ingham Hollings (1949). **Educ:** Belmont House; Tonbridge School.

HOLLINGS, John Shaw (1941) Born 29 April 1923, 7 Rawlinson Road, Southport, Lancashire; son of Henry Shaw Hollings, Mantle Manufacturer, and Kate Ellen Brown. **Subject(s):** Mechanical Sciences; BA 1944; MA 1948; CEng; FIMechE. **Tutor(s):** S J Bailey. **Johnian Relatives:** brother of Peter Shaw Hollings (1934). **Educ:** Terra Nova School, Birkdale; Stowe School. **Career:** Chief Designer, Rolls-Royce and Associates Ltd 1959; Engineering Director, Rolls-Royce Motors' Car Division, Crewe 1960. Died 23 July 1997.

HOLLINGS, Peter Shaw (1934) Born 24 November 1915, Oakdene, Windsor Road, Chorley, Lancashire; son of Henry Shaw Hollings, Mantle Manufacturer, and Kate Ellen Brown; 2 daughters. **Subject(s):** Natural Sciences; BA 1937; MA 1941; LMSSA 1943 (Middlesex); FRCSE

1947. **Tutor(s):** R L Howland. **Johnian Relatives:** brother of John Shaw Hollings (1941). **Educ:** Terra Nova School, Birkdale; The Leys School, Cambridge. **Career:** Guest Hospital, Dudley; Royal Hampshire County Hospital, Winchester; Royal Hospital, Wolverhampton. 1943–1951; Senior Surgeon, Ear, Nose and Throat Department, Durham and North West Durham Hospital 1951–1956. Died 18 June 1956.

HOLLINGWORTH, Henry Neville (1923) Born 29 January 1905, St Barnabas Vicarage, Lovely Lane, Warrington, Lancashire; son of John Henry Garside Hollingworth, Clerk in Holy Orders, and Charlotte Boulton Pickering. **Subject(s):** Classics/Theology; BA 1926; MA 1930. **Tutor(s):** E E Sikes. **Educ:** Manchester Grammar School; Westcott House, Cambridge. **Career:** Ordained Deacon 1928; Curate, Mirfield 1928–1931; Ordained Priest 1929; Curate, St John, Bulawayo 1931–1937; Vicar, St Thomas, Batley 1937–1943; Vicar, Holy Trinity, Halifax 1943–1955; Vicar, St Peter, Handsworth, Birmingham 1955. **Appointments:** Warden, St Deniol's Library, Hawarden; Chief Inspector of Religious Education, Diocese of Wakefield. **Awards:** Patchett Scholarship, SJC. Died 1971.

HOLMBERG, Eric Robert Reginald (1936) Born 24 August 1917, 30 North Street, Ventnor, Isle of Wight; son of Karl Robert Holmberg, Assistant in Hardware Store and served in Canadian Army, and Edith Jane May Williams; m Wanda Erna Reich, 1940; 1 son, 1 daughter. **Subject(s):** Mathematics; BA 1939; MA 1944; PhD (Imperial College, London) 1951. **Tutor(s):** J M Wordie. **Johnian Relatives:** father of Stephen Roger Mark Holmberg (1975). **Educ:** Sandown Grammar School. **Career:** Mine Design Department, Admiralty 1940–1945; Admiralty Gunnery Establishment 1945–1950; Operational Research Department, Admiralty 1950–1958; Chief Superintendent, Army Operational Research Group 1956–1961; Director, Army Operational Science and Research, subsequently Assistant Chief Scientist (Army), Ministry of Defence 1961–1972; Deputy Chief Scientist (Army), Ministry of Defence 1972–1977. **Publications:** *The Trouble with Relativity*, 1986; papers in *Procedures of the Royal Astronomical Society*.

HOLMES, Cecil Ewart (1935) Born 29 May 1916, 23 Vernon Terrace, Brighton; son of Henry Raymond Joy Holmes, Captain, Royal Sussex Regiment and Poultry Farmer, and Eveline Mackintosh. **Subject(s):** Classics/English; BA 1938. **Tutor(s):** R L Howland. **Educ:** Dragon School, Oxford; Sedbergh School. **Career:** Newsreader, BBC 1945.

HOLMES, Eusebius (1944) Born 23 December 1926, Rotherholme, Wensleydale Road, Hampton, Middlesex; son of Eusebius Holmes, Research Chemist, National Physical Laboratory, and Mary Elizabeth Sammons; m Shirley Erica Parkinson, 16 May 1953; 2 sons (Simon Eusebius b 12 April 1957 and Robert Patrick b 9 August 1962), 2 daughters (Sarah Caroline b 4 October 1959 and Elizabeth Rachel b 7 May 1964). **Subject(s):** Natural Sciences; BA 1950. **Tutor(s):** C W Guillebaud. **Johnian Relatives:** father of Simon Eusebius Holmes (1976) and of Robert Patrick Holmes (1981). **Educ:** Kingston Grammar School. **Awards:** Sir Joseph Larmor Award, SJC 1950.

HOLMES, Professor George Arthur (1945) Born 22 April 1927, 2 Portland Street, Aberystwyth; son of John Holmes, Watchmaker, and Margaret Thomas; m (Evelyn) Anne Klein, 19 December 1953; 2 sons (Peter d 1968 and Nicholas), twin daughters (Susan and Catherine). **Subject(s):** History; BA 1948; MA 1952; PhD 1953; MA (Oxon) 1954; FBA 1985. **Tutor(s):** F Thistlethwaite. **Johnian Relatives:** father of Nicholas Jonathan Holmes (1982). **Educ:** Aberystwyth Council School; Ardwyn County School; University College of Wales, Aberystwyth. **Career:** Title A Fellow, SJC 1951–1954; Tutor, Modern History 1954–1962, and Librarian, St Catherine's Society, Oxford; Fellow and Tutor 1962–1989, Vice-Master 1969–1971, Emeritus Fellow 1990, St Catherine's College, Oxford; Chichele Professor of Medieval History, University of Oxford 1989. **Appointments:** Member, Institute for Advanced Study, Princeton 1967–1968; Visiting Professor, Harvard University Centre for Italian Renaissance Studies, Florence 1995;

Chairman, Board of the Warburg Institute, London University 1993–1995; Chairman, Victoria County History Committee, Institute of Historical Research 1979–1989; Joint Editor, *English Historical Review* 1974–1981; Delegate, OUP 1982–1991. **Awards:** Minor Scholarship, SJC 1945; Ellen MacArthur Prize for Economic History, University of Cambridge 1957; Serena Medal for Italian Studies, British Academy 1993. **Publications:** *The Estates of the Higher Nobility in Fourteenth-Century England*, 1957; *The Later Middle Ages*, 1962; *The Florentine Enlightenment 1400–1450*, 1969; *Europe: hierarchy and revolt 1320–1450*, 1975; *The Good Parliament*, 1975; *Dante*, 1980; *Florence, Rome and the Origins of the Renaissance*, 1986; (ed) *The Oxford Illustrated History of Medieval Europe*, 1988; *The First Age of the Western City 1300–1500*, 1990; (ed) *Art and Politics in Renaissance Italy*, 1993; *Renaissance*, 1996; (ed) *The Oxford Illustrated History of Italy*, 1997; articles in learned journals.

HOLMES, Dr John (1918) Born 14 December 1896, High Bank House, Gorton, Lancaster; son of John Holmes, Wholesale Grocer, and Elizabeth Grace Hall; 2 sons, 1 daughter. MRCP 1926. **Tutor(s):** E E Sikes. **Educ:** Manchester Grammar School. **Career:** Army, rose to Sergeant-Major (discharged on medical grounds) 1914–1917; House appointments, East London Hospital and City of London Hospital for Diseases of the Heart and Lungs 1924–1927; GP and Physician, Southport General Infirmary 1927–1962. **Appointments:** President, Southport Medical Society 1952; Chairman, Medical Board, Southport General Infirmary 1947–1949. Died 24 January 1976.

HOLMES, John Maxwell Wilson (1949) Born 31 March 1930, 9 Dapdune Crescent, Guildford, Surrey; son of Hugh Holmes, Pharmacist, and Phoebe Gwenllien Bond, Pharmacist; m Valerie Gould, 4 August 1954, Upton Church, Torquay; 2 daughters (Helen Mary Wilson and Katherine Amanda). BA 1952; MA 1956; CEng; FIEE. **Tutor(s):** R L Howland. **Educ:** Cockington School, Torquay; Torquay Grammar School; Taunton School. **Career:** Commander, RN 1948–1980; Chief Project Manager, British Aerospace 1980–1990; Consultant/Company Director.

HOLMES, Lockhart Eastwood (1919) Born 7 August 1900, 49 Radnor Drive, Liscard, Cheshire; son of Livingstone Holmes, Director, Public Company, and Helen Eastwood Tilston. **Tutor(s):** E A Benians. **Educ:** Manor House Private School; Wallasey Grammar School; Sedbergh School. **Career:** Partner, Charlton and Bagshaw, Liverpool; Agricultural Advisor to Estonian Government 1921; Served on Board, Liverpool Corn Trade Association Ltd 1945–1948; Represented National Federation of the Corn Trade Association in Washington 1949; President of Board, Liverpool Corn Trade Association Ltd 1952.

HOLT, James Garfield (1920) Born 25 October 1901, Axholme, Egerton Park, Tranmere, Cheshire; son of Louis Holt, West African Merchant's Clerk, and Florence Mary Holt. BA 1923. **Tutor(s):** E E Sikes. **Educ:** Mostyn House School, Park Gate, Shrewsbury; Shrewsbury School.

HOLT, Peter Fox (1939) Born 24 January 1921, 10 College Road, Harrow; son of Guy Marriner Whittell Holt, Solicitor, and Margery Burton Bailey; m Margaret Harvey, 3 January 1959. **Subject(s):** Natural Sciences; BA 1943. **Tutor(s):** C W Guillebaud. **Educ:** Orley Farm School, Harrow; Rugby School. Died 4 January 1991.

HOLTHOUSE, The Revd Cuthbert Lempriere (1906) Born 10 April 1887, 85 Gower Street, St Pancras, London; son of Edwin Hermus Holthouse, and Harriet Emily Hesketh; m (1) Phyllis Margaret Marchant, 6 May 1919 (d 1942), (2) Frances Theodora Daniell, 7 February 1944. **Subject(s):** Mathematics; BA 1909; MA 1914. **Tutor(s):** E E Sikes. **Educ:** Highgate School; Haileybury College. **Career:** Ordained Deacon 1910; Assistant Missioner, Lady Margaret Church, Walworth 1910–1914; Ordained Priest 1911; Curate, Lewisham 1914–1918; Temporary CF, 4th Class, RACD 1918–1919; Vicar, St Augustine, Saskatchewan 1919–1921; Rector, Broadview 1921–1925;

Examining Chaplain to Bishop of Qu'Appelle 1921–1935; Rector, Balcarres 1925–1932; Rector, Estevan 1932–1935; Vicar, North Holmwood, Surrey 1935–1942; Vicar, Chertsey 1942–1949; Rural Dean, Chertsey 1946–1949; Vicar, Hursley, Hampshire 1949–1957. **Awards:** Sizarship, SJC. Died 8 February 1967.

HOLTTUM, Dr Richard Eric (1914) Born 20 July 1895, Linton, Cambridgeshire; son of Richard Holttum, Draper and JP, and Florence Bradley; m Ursula Massey, June 1927, Saffron Walden; 2 daughters. **Subject(s):** Natural Sciences; BA 1920; MA 1927; ScD 1951; Honorary DSc (University of Singapore) 1954. **Tutor(s):** R P Gregory. **Educ:** Linton Elementary School; Friends' School, Saffron Walden; Bootham School, York. **Career:** Honorary Research Associate, Royal Botanic Gardens, Kew, and Rijksherbarium, Leiden, Holland; Assistant Director 1922, Acting Director 1923 and 1925, Director 1925–1949, Botanic Gardens, Singapore; Professor of Botany, University of Malaya 1949–1954. **Appointments:** District Governor, Singapore 1941–1942 and 1948–1949. **Awards:** Wright's Prize, SJC 1916; Frank Stuart Prize for Botany 1920; Victoria Medal of Honour, Royal Horticultural Society; Gold Medals from Linnaean Society, Orchid Society of America, Orchid Society of South East Asia; Robert Allerton Award from Pacific Tropical Botanical Garden, Hawaii 1975. **Publications:** *Orchids of Malaya*, 1953; *Gardening in the Lowlands of Malaya*, 1953, *Plant Life in Malaya*, 1954; *Ferns of Malaya*; *Gardening in the Tropics*; *The Zingiberaceae of the Malay Peninsula*, and various books and papers on orchids, ferns, bamboos, gingers. Died 18 September 1990.

HOLTZAPFFEL, John George Holtzapffel (BUDD) (1907) Born 6 August 1888, 4 Chapel Place, Long Acre, London; son of George William Holtzapffel, Civil Engineer, and Florence Annie Weedon. **Subject(s):** Natural Sciences; BA 1910; MA 1914. **Tutor(s):** L H K Bushe-Fox. **Educ:** Kindergarten School; Melville Hall, Hampstead; Merchant Taylors' School. **Career:** Captain, London Regiment (Royal Fusiliers), WWI. Died 2 April 1968.

HOMAN, Dr George Maxwell (1938) Born 8 January 1920, Riversdale, Telegraph Road, Heswall, Cheshire; son of St George Marriott Leslie Homan, GP, and Agnes Maxwell Burns; BA 1941; MA 1945; MRCS; LRCP London; Diploma in Laryngology and Otology. **Tutor(s):** R L Howland. **Educ:** St Filian's, Heswall; Moorland House, Heswall; Malvern College. **Career:** Major, RAMC; GP, NHS. Died 1996.

HONE, Arthur Robert (1934) Born 18 February 1915, 338 Kingston Road, Merton, Surrey; son of Arthur Malcolm Hone, Bricklayer, and Ellen Louise Chastney. **Subject(s):** Modern and Medieval Languages; BA 1937; MA 1945. **Tutor(s):** C W Guillebaud. **Educ:** Cottenham Park Church School; Raynes Park Council School; Rutlish Secondary School, Merton. **Awards:** Scholarship, SJC 1936–1937.

HONEYBALL, Frederick Ralph (1910) (migrated to Selwyn College) Born 31 December 1890, 4 St George's Place, Deal, Kent; son of Frederick Thomas Honeyball, Estate Agent, and Kate Chennell. **Tutor(s):** L H K Bushe-Fox. **Educ:** Glen Coil School, Deal; St Bees School.

HONEYBOURNE, Harry Cecil (1903) Born 17 December 1883, 2 Hooper Street, Cambridge; son of John William Charles Honeybourne, Schoolmaster, and Virginia Marsh; m Daisy Sandiland, 16 August 1911, St Paul's Church, De Beauvoir Town. **Subject(s):** Natural Sciences; BA 1906; MA 1910. **Tutor(s):** D MacAlister. **Johnian Relatives:** brother of Victor Cyril Honeybourne (1899). **Educ:** KCL; Royal Grammar School, Guildford. **Career:** Captain and Adjutant, London Regiment (Blackheath and Woolwich Battalion), WWI.

HOOD, Alastair Moar (1941) Born 14 August 1923, Newton Bank, Douglas Street, Largs, Ayrshire; son of Alexander Hood, Company Director, and Jessie Moar Metcalfe. **Tutor(s):** S J Bailey. **Educ:** The Dene, Caterham; Glasgow High School; Bishop's Stortford College.

HOOD, Edwin John (1948) Born 24 November 1926, 284 Stratford Road, Birmingham; son of Edwin John Hood, Motor Engineer's Salesman, and Isabelle Kate Mary Davies. **Subject(s):** Classics. BA 1950. **Tutor(s):** R L Howland. **Educ:** Stechford Elementary School, Birmingham; King Edward's School, Birmingham. **Career:** Accountant. **Awards:** Exhibition, SJC 1944. Died 28 June 2003.

HOOK, Charles Wilfrid Theodore (1911) Born 5 April 1892, 147 London Road, Lowestoft, Suffolk; son of Frederic Joseph Hook, Advertising Manager, and Jessie Cushing Crosskill. **Subject(s):** Mathematics; BA 1914. **Tutor(s):** L H K Bushe-Fox. **Educ:** Lowestoft College for Boys; Higher Grade School, Cambridge; Cambridge and County School. **Career:** Lieutenant, The Buffs (East Kent Regiment, TF), later Captain, Special List (Trench Mortar Battery), WWI.

HOPKIN, Professor Sir (William Aylsham) Bryan (1933) Born 7 December 1914, The Cot, St Brides-super-Ely, Glamorganshire; son of William Hopkin, Cashier, Land Agent's Office, and Lilian Blanche Cottele; m Renée Ricour, The 'Mairie' (Town Hall), Marcq-en-Baroeul, Nord, France, 6 September 1938; 2 sons (John Edward b 28 December 1940 and Richard Douglas b 6 September 1944). **Subject(s):** Economics; BA 1936; MA 1952. **Tutor(s):** E A Benians; C W Guillebaud. **Educ:** Christchurch Elementary School, Weston-super-Mare; Elementary School, St George-super-Ely; Barry County School. **Career:** Postgraduate Research, Economic Research Department, Manchester University 1936–1937; Ministry of Health 1938–1941; Prime Minister's Statistical Branch 1941–1945; Royal Commission on Population 1945–1948; Economic Section, Cabinet Office 1948–1950; Central Statistical Office 1950–1952; Director, National Institute of Economic and Social Research 1952–1957; Secretary, Council on Prices, Productivity, and Incomes 1957–1958; Deputy Director, Economic Section, HM Treasury 1958–1965; Economic Planning Unit, Mauritius 1965; Ministry of Overseas Development 1966–1967; Director-General of Economic Planning, ODM 1967–1969; Director General, DEA 1969; Deputy Chief Economic Adviser, HM Treasury 1970–1972; Professor of Economics, University College Cardiff 1972–1974 and 1977–1982; Head of Government Economic Service and Chief Economic Advisor, HM Treasury 1974–1977. **Appointments:** Honorary Fellow, SJC 1982; Member, Commonwealth Development Corporation 1972–1974; Chairman, Manpower Services Committee for Wales 1978–1979; Honorary Professorial Fellow, University College, Swansea 1988. **Awards:** Wrenbury Scholarship 1936. **Honours:** CBE 1961; Kt 1971.

HOPPER, Michael Thompson (1948) Born 1 June 1929, Freiston, Boston, Lincolnshire; son of Stanley Thompson Hopper, Watchmaker, Jeweller and Silversmith, and Gwendolen Mary Creasey; m Janet. **Subject(s):** Engineering; BA 1951; MA 1960; CEng; MIEE. **Tutor(s):** R L Howland. **Educ:** Trinity Private School, Boston; Boston Grammar School; Stamford School. **Career:** Weapons Engineer Officer 1947–1979, Commander 1968–1979, RN; Directorate, Surface Weapons Projects (Naval), ASWE, Portsdown, Cosham, Hampshire 1975–1978.

HORBERRY, Winston Robert (1933) Born 6 March 1915, 1 Dunrobin Terrace, Sea Point, Cape of Good Hope, South Africa; son of William Horberry, Drapers Manager and Silk Buyer, and Elizabeth Bruce Anderson. **Subject(s):** Natural Sciences; BA 1936. **Tutor(s):** C W Guillebaud. **Educ:** Boys' High School, Rondebosch, South Africa; The Grammar School, Thorne; Woodham Grove School, Apperly Bridge.

HORE, Henry (Harry) Sinclair (1935) Born 28 April 1917, Borehead, Old Braid Road, Colinton, Midlothian; son of Henry James Hore, WS, and Aimée Hay Sinclair. **Subject(s):** Modern and Medieval Languages. **Tutor(s):** C W Guillebaud. **Educ:** The Hill School, Colinton Road; Cargilfield School, Midlothian; Uppingham.

HORI, Timothy Keishi (1901) Born 23 September 1878, Oita, Japan; son of Joan Hori, Doctor, and Tai Yukimatsu. BA (Non-Collegiate) 1906.

Tutor(s): J R Tanner; C E Graves. **Educ:** Osaka Higher English School; Holy Trinity Divinity School.

HORLINGTON, Brigadier Frank (1913) Born 23 December 1893, 7 East Parade, Sedgefield, Durham; son of John Soulsby Horlington, Relieving Officer, and Elizabeth Blythman. BA 1917; MA 1950. **Tutor(s):** E E Sikes. **Educ:** Darlington Grammar School; Stockton Secondary School. **Career:** Lieutenant, RFA (TF), later Staff Lieutenant, WWI. **Honours:** OBE; TD. Died 19 October 1958.

HORLOCK, Professor Sir John Harold (1946) Born 19 April 1928, 16 The Broadway, Edmonton, Middlesex; son of Harold Edgar Horlock, Undertaker, and Olive Margaret Kissner; m Sheila Joy Stutely, 8 June 1953; 1 son (Timothy John b 4 January 1958); 2 daughters (Alison and Jane). **Subject(s):** Mechanical Sciences; BA 1949; MA 1953; ScD 1975; PhD 1955; Honorary DSc (Heriot-Watt) 1980, (Salford) 1981, (University of East Asia) 1987, (CNAA) 1991, (De Montfort University) 1995; Honorary DUniv (Open University) 1991; Honorary DEng (Liverpool) 1987; Honorary DE (Cranfield) 1997; FEng 1977; FRS 1976. **Tutor(s):** R L Howland. **Johnian Relatives:** father of Timothy John Horlock (1977). **Educ:** High Field Road School, Winchmore Hill; Raglan School, Edmonton; Latymer's School, Edmonton. **Career:** Rolls-Royce 1949–1951; Demonstrator in Engineering 1954–1956, Lecturer in Engineering 1956–1958, University of Cambridge; Title A Fellow, SJC 1954–1957; Harrison Professor of Mechanical Engineering, University of Liverpool 1958–1967; Professor of Engineering 1967–1974, Director, Whittle Laboratory 1971–1974, University of Cambridge; Title C Fellow, SJC 1967–1974; Vice-Chancellor, Salford University 1974–1980; Vice-Chancellor 1981–1990, Fellow 1990–2001, Open University; Pro-Chancellor, UMIST 1995–2001. **Appointments:** Member, SJC Appeal Finance Committee; College Supervisor in Mechanical Sciences 1955–1958, Honorary Fellow 1988, SJC; Vice-President, Royal Society 1982–1985 and 1992–1997; Honorary Fellow, UMIST 1991; Treasurer, Royal Society 1992–1997; Fellow, ASME (USA); Honorary Foreign Associate, National Academy of Engineers, USA. **Awards:** Rex Moir Prize; James Clayton Prize, IMechE 1962; Thomas Hawksey Gold Medal, IMechE, 1969; Arthur Main Prize, IMechE, 1997; R Tom Sawyer Award, ASME 1997; James Ewing Medal, ICE 2001. **Honours:** Kt 1996.

HORNAK, Hermann Bernhardt (1931) Born 31 March 1912, Naples, Italy; son of Bernhardt Hornak, Army Officer, and Lucy Steinheimer. **Tutor(s):** C W Guillebaud. **Educ:** Ginnasio Bosetti-Boselli, Milan; Canford School, Wimborne.

HORNE, John William (1900) Born 11 July 1877, 22 Cradley Road, Netherton, Dudley, Worcestershire; son of Dennis Horne, Anchor Smith, and Elizabeth Faulkner. **Tutor(s):** D MacAlister. **Educ:** Dudley School. **Career:** Master, St John's College, Grimsargh, Preston.

HORNE, Professor Michael Rex (1939) Born 29 December 1921, 11 Prebend Street, Leicester; son of Ernest Horne, Congregational Minister, and Katie Smeeton, School Teacher; m Dorcas Mary Hewett, 14 August 1947; 2 sons (John Gregory b 4 October 1952 and Barnabas Robert), 1 daughter (Sara Josephine), 1 adopted daughter (Shanti Margaret b 1966). **Subject(s):** Mechanical Sciences; BA 1942; MA 1946; PhD 1950; ScD 1956; MSc (Manchester); Honorary DSc (Salford) 1981; FEng; FIStructE; FICE; FRS 1981; FREng. **Tutor(s):** S J Bailey. **Johnian Relatives:** father of John Gregory Horne (1970). **Educ:** Wolverton Council School; Park Council School, Boston, Lincolnshire; Boston Grammar School, Lincolnshire; Leeds Grammar School. **Career:** Assistant Engineer, River Great Ouse Catchment Board 1941–1945; Scientific Officer, British Welding Research Association 1945–1951; Assistant Director of Research in Engineering 1951–1956, Lecturer in Engineering 1957–1960, University of Cambridge; Title B Fellow 1957–1960, SJC; Professor of Civil Engineering 1960–1983 (Emeritus 1983–2000), University of Manchester. **Appointments:** Supervisor in Mechanical Sciences 1953–1950 and 1957–1960, SJC; Institution of Civil Engineers, Telford Premiums 1956, 1966, 1978; Chairman, North

West Branch, Institution of Structural Engineers 1969–1970; Member, Merrison Committee on Box Girders 1970–1973; Beyer Professor, University of Manchester 1978–1983; President, Institution of Structural Engineers 1980–1981; President, Section G, BAAS 1981–1982; Chairman, Government Review of Public Utility Streetworks Act 1984; Royal Society Visiting Professor, University of Hong Kong 1986. **Awards:** Archibald Denny Prize, University of Cambridge; John Winbolt Prize, University of Cambridge 1944; Henry Adams Award 1970; Diploma 1971, Bronze Medal 1973, Gold Medal 1986, Institution of Structural Engineers; Oscar Faber Bronze Medal 1972; Baker Gold Medal, ICE 1977. **Honours:** OBE 1981. **Publications:** (with J F Baker and J Heyman) *The Steel Skeleton*, 1956; (with W F Merchant) *The Stability of Frames*, 1965; *The Plastic Theory of Structures*, 1971; (with L J Morris) *Plastic Design of Low Rise Frames*, 1981; papers on structures, strength of materials and particulate theory of soils to learned journals. Died 6 January 2000.

HORNE, Roderick Rees Kimball (1929) Born 2 August 1911, Warburton, Granville Road, North Finchley; son of Roderick William Horne, Director, Limited Company, and Daisy Kate Vidler; 1 son (Michael). **Tutor(s):** C W Guillebaud. **Educ:** Harewood Preparatory School, Bexhill on Sea; Haileybury College. **Career:** Smyth-Horne Ltd, Bookbinders' Machinery Dealers. Died 19 August 1958.

HOROWITZ, Solomon (1900) Born 6 September 1881, Brzezany, Austria; son of Jacob Horowitz, Merchant, and Sarah Eiger. **Subject(s):** Classics/Moral Sciences/Law; BA 1903; MA 1932. **Tutor(s):** J E Sandys. **Educ:** Manchester Grammar School. **Career:** Called to the Bar, Inner Temple 1907; Head, S Horowitz & Co, Advocates, Jerusalem; Died 15 February 1956.

HORRELL, John Ernest Bryant (1943) Born 28 May 1925, Ivyhurst, Raunds, Northamptonshire; son of Arthur Leslie Horrell, Squadron Leader, RAF and Shoe Manufacturer, and Dorothy Irene Kathleen Bremmer. BA 1946; MA 1950. **Tutor(s):** S J Bailey. **Educ:** Wellingborough School.

HORRIDGE, Professor George Adrian (1946) Born 12 December 1927, 238 Tullibardine Road, Sheffield; son of George William Horridge, Motor Cycle Agent, and Olive Stray; m Audrey Lightburne; 1 son (Jonathan Mark), 3 daughters (Alison, Naomi and Rebecca). **Subject(s):** Natural Sciences; BA 1949; MA 1953; PhD 1954; ScD 1968; FRS 1969. **Tutor(s):** G C L Bertram. **Johnian Relatives:** father of Jonathan Mark Horridge (1975). **Educ:** Ecclesall Church Elementary School, Sheffield; King Edward VII School, Sheffield. **Career:** Scientific Officer, then Senior Scientific Officer, RAE, Farnborough 1953–1954; Title A Fellow, SJC 1953–1956; Lecturer, then Reader in Zoology 1956–1969, Director, Gatty Marine Laboratory 1960–1969, St Andrews University; Professor of Biology 1969–1993 (Emeritus 1993), Executive Director, Centre for Visual Sciences 1987–1990, University Fellow 1994–1997, ANU, Canberra. **Appointments:** Visiting Associate Professor, University of California, Los Angeles; Fellow, Center for Advanced Study in the Behavioral Sciences, Stanford University, California 1959–1960; Visiting Full Professor, Yale University 1965; Examiner in Biology, Universiti Sains, Penang and University of Malaya, Kuala Lumpur, Malaysia, 1972–1984; Visiting Fellow, Balliol College, Oxford 1973–1974; Chief Scientist, US Research Ship Alpha Helix, Moluccas 1975; Visiting Fellow, Churchill College, Cambridge 1976–1977 and 1993–1994; Fellow, Marine Biology Laboratory, Woods Hole, Massachusetts; Royal Society Visiting Professor, University of St Andrews 1992; Member, Cambridge Philosophical Society; Member, Physiological Society; Member, Society for Experimental Biology; Member, Society for Nautical Research; Fellow, Australian Academy of Science 1972. **Awards:** Major Scholarship, SJC; 1851 Exhibition, SJC 1954; Scientific Medal, Zoological Society 1968. **Honours:** Centenary Medal (Australia) 2003. **Publications:** (with T H Bullock) *The Structure and Function of the Nervous Systems of Invertebrates*, 2 Volumes, Freeman, San Francisco, 1965; *Interneurons*, Freeman, San Francisco, 1968; (ed) *The Compound*

Eye of Insects, Oxford, 1975; *The Prahu, Traditional Sailing Boat of Indonesia*, Oxford in Asia, Kuala Lumpur, 1981, 1986; *Sailing Craft of Indonesia*, Oxford in Asia, 1986; *Outrigger Canoes of Bali and Madura, Indonesia*, Bishop Museum Press, Honolulu, 1987; (ed, jointly) *Natural and Low-level Seeing Systems*, OUP, 1993; over 250 papers on sciences, the Indonesian Prahu, and other topics.

HORSFALL, Thomas Mendelssohn (1919) Naval Officer.

HORSFIELD, John (1943) Born 4 August 1925, Sunnyside Nursing Home, Hinderton Road, Neston, Cheshire; son of Edgar Charles Horsfield, Bank Cashier, and Constance Muriel Watson; m Olive Gwyneth Ballinger, 1952; 2 sons (David b 1954 and Ian b 1959), 1 daughter (Jill b 1957). **Subject(s):** Mechanical Sciences; BA 1946; MA 1950; MICE. **Educ:** Silverdene Preparatory School, Bebington; Calday Grange Grammar School, West Kirby. **Career:** Apprenticed to Wilson Lovatt and Sons Ltd, Contractors 1948–1965; George Wimpey 1965–1966; Wilson Lovatt 1966–1971; Tarmac Construction 1971–1989.

HORSFIELD, William Donald (1944) Born 19 April 1926, 29 Dean Terrace, Ryton, Durham; son of Reginald Horsfield, Schoolmaster, and Lilian Snowball; m; 2 daughters. **Subject(s):** Mechanical Sciences; BA 1947; MA 1963; CEng; MRAeS. **Tutor(s):** J S Bailey. **Educ:** Catchgate Boys' School, Annfield Plain; Alderman Wood School, Stanley. **Career:** Blackburn Aircraft, Brough 1947–1951; Aerodynamics Team 1951, Flight Test Department 1954, Chief Aerodynamicist 1961, Special Director, Aerodynamics 1977, English Electric, Warton and its successor companies; Executive Director Engineering, Warton Division, British Aerospace 1979–1986. **Awards:** Major Scholarship, SJC 1944. Died 26 December 1990.

HORSFORD, Eric John (1941) Born 31 July 1923, Crossways Farm, Roxham, Downham, Norfolk; son of John Tom Horsford, Insurance Agent, and Helen Mary Richardson. **Subject(s):** Mechanical Sciences; BA 1944. **Tutor(s):** S J Bailey. **Educ:** Denver Council School; Wormegay Council School; King Edward VII School, King's Lynn.

HORTON, Professor Frank (1901) Born 20 August 1878, Handsworth, Birmingham; son of Albert Horton, Schoolmaster, and Kate Louisa Carley; m (1) Vera Fulton, 18 July 1911, St Paul's Pro-Cathedral, Wellington, New Zealand, (2) Ann Catherine Davies, 1939; (1) 1 daughter (Ngaire). BA 1903; MA 1908; ScD 1914; BSc (London) 1899; DSc (London) 1903; MSc (Birmingham) 1923. **Tutor(s):** D MacAlister. **Educ:** King Edward's School. **Career:** Lecturer in Physics, Cavendish Laboratory, Cambridge 1905–1914; Ashton Fellow, SJC 1905–1914; Professor of Physics 1916–1946, Vice-Chancellor 1939–1945, London University. **Appointments:** Supervisor in Natural Sciences (Physics) 1906–1914. **Awards:** Clerk Maxwell Scholarship 1906; 1851 Research Scholarship; Mackinnon Research Studentship, Royal Society; Allen Scholarship, University of Cambridge 1904. Died 31 October 1957.

HORTON-SMITH-HARTLEY, Percival Hubert Graham (1915) Born 27 September 1896, 8 Upper Westbourne Terrace, Hyde Park, London; son of Percival Horton-Smith-Hartley, Physician and Fellow, SJC, and Lucy Josephine Hartley; m Mary Grizel Buchanan, 2 August 1923. **Subject(s):** Modern and Medieval Languages; BA 1922; MA 1926. **Tutor(s):** L H K Bushe-Fox; E E Sikes. **Johnian Relatives:** son of Percival Horton-Smith-Hartley (1886). **Educ:** Summerfield, Oxford; Eton College. **Career:** Captain, Coldstream Guards 1915–1918; Master, Eton College 1922–1956; Served with Military Government in Italy 1939–1945. **Appointments:** Master, Worshipful Company of Ironmongers 1953–1954. **Awards:** Scholarship, SJC 1914. **Honours:** OBE 1945. Died 3 January 1977.

HOSIE, James Findlay (1934) Born 22 August 1913, East Church Street, Buckie, Banffshire; son of James Hosie, Classical Master, and Ann

Reid; m Barbara Mary Mansell, 1951. **Subject(s):** Mathematics; BA 1936; MA (Glasgow). **Tutor(s):** J M Wordie. **Educ:** Dunabastair Public School; Arns Public School; Cumbernauld Public School; Kilsyth Academy; Glasgow University. **Career:** Indian Civil Service 1938–1947; Principal, Ministry of Defence 1947–1956; Assistant Secretary, Ministry of Defence, London 1956–1958; Assistant Secretary QMG to the Forces, War Office 1958–1961; Office of Minister for Science, later Department of Education and Science 1961–1965; Director, SRC 1965–1974. **Honours:** MBE 1946; OBE 1955; CBE 1972. Died 31 October 1993.

HOSIER, Dr John (1947) Born 18 November 1928, 85 Sunnymead Road, Kingsbury, London; son of Harry John William Hosier, Founded Hosier & Dickenson, and Constance Irene Richmond, Violinist; m Biddy Baxter. **Subject(s):** English/Music; BA 1950; MA 1954; Honorary MusD (City University) 1986; FRCM 1981; FRNCM 1985; FGSM 1978; FRSA 1976; Honorary RAM 1980; Honorary FTCL 1986. **Tutor(s):** F Thistlethwaite. **Educ:** The Fayent Junior School; Preston Manor County School, Wembley. **Career:** Teacher, British Council, Ankara, Turkey 1951–1953; Music Producer, BBC Radio for schools 1953–1959; Adviser on Educational Music Programmes, ABC, Sydney, Australia 1959–1960; Senior and Executive Music Producer, BBC Educational Television 1960–1973; Senior Inspector for Music, ILEA and Director of Centre for Young Musicians 1973–1976; Principal, Guildhall School of Music and Drama 1978–1989; Director and Member of Council, Hong Kong Academy for Performing Arts (Fellow 1993) 1989–1993. **Appointments:** Music Director, Footlights Club 1950; Founder Member and Vice-Chairman, UK Council for Music Education and Training 1975–1981; Member, Gulbenkian Enquiry into training musicians 1978; Member, Council of Management, Royal Philharmonic Society 1982–1989; Governing Body, Chetham's School 1983–1988; Member, Music Panel, GLAA 1984–1986; Member, Music Panel, British Council 1984–1988; Vice-Chairman, Kent Opera 1985–1987; Committee Member, Hong Kong Philharmonic Orchestra 1990–1993; Member, Conservatoires Advisory Group, HEFCE 1993–1997; Board Member, Trinity College of Music 1993–1997; Member, Court, Musicians' Company 1993–2000; Trustee, Kathleen Ferrier Memorial Scholarship Fund 1994–2000; Chairman, Music Panel, Caird Scholarship Trust 1995–2000; Trustee, Southeast Music Schemes 1997–2000; President, ISM 1998; Director, Early Music Centre 1994–2000; Director, the Barbican; Chairman, Performing Arts Panel, HEFCE; President, Incorporated Society of Musicians 1997–1998; President, ISM 1998–1999; President, Incorporated Society of Musicians 1998–1999. **Honours:** CBE 1994. **Publications:** Numerous books including (with Yehudi Menuhin) *The Instruments of the Orchestra*; articles on music in educational journals; wrote and arranged music for many radio and television programmes and produced several documentaries for BBC2. Died 27 March 2000.

HOSKING, Dr Anthony John (1949) Born 25 July 1930, Glenside, Carlisle Avenue, St Albans; son of Arthur Robert Hosking, Printer's Reader, and Ivy Olive Rose Daniells; m (Marjorie) Anne Briggs, 22 July 1955, St Saviours, St Albans; 1 son (David John b 11 April 1959), 1 daughter (b 25 May 1957). **Subject(s):** Natural Sciences; BA 1952; MA 1969; LRCP (London) MRCS (Eng) 1956; MB, BChir 1957. **Tutor(s):** G C L Bertram. **Educ:** Bernard's Heath School, St Albans; St Albans School. **Career:** GP, West Cambridgeshire 1959–1995.

HOSKYN, Dr Charles Henry (1932) Born 10 October 1912, 69 Clifton Road, Rugby; son of Charles Reginald Hoskyn, Medical Practitioner, and Helen Parker; m Heather Stott; 1 son (Peter), 1 daughter (Hazel). BA 1935; MA 1946; BChir 1946; MB 1946; MD 1949; MRCS (St Bartholomew's); LRCP (St Bartholomew's). **Tutor(s):** R L Howland. **Educ:** Oakfield School, Rugby; Hildenham School, Broadstairs; Bedford School. **Career:** Lieutenant Colonel, RAMC 1939–1945; Medical Officer, National Dock Labour Board; Assistant Medical Officer, Austin Motor Company; Medical Superintendant, Royal Mail Lines 1949. **Honours:** OBE. Died 17 December 1960.

HOSMER, Henry Barnes (1925) Born 13 April 1907, Boston, Massachusetts, USA; son of Sidney Hosmer, Electrical Engineer, and Clara Marie Barnes. **Tutor(s):** E A Benians. **Educ:** Woodwards School, Boston; Messrs Noble & Greenhough; Pomfret School; Yale College, New Haven.

HOTCHIN, Philip Lowther (1948) Born 16 March 1927, 39 Chapeltown, Pudsey, Yorkshire; son of Arthur Hotchin, Registrar of Births, Marriages and Deaths, and Elizabeth Clark. BSc (Leeds). **Tutor(s):** R L Howland. **Educ:** Pudsey Greenside School; Pudsey Grammar School; University of Leeds.

HOVIL, Guy Oscar (1920) Born 8 March 1901, 9 Court Road, West Norwood, London; son of Frank Hovil, Civil Engineer, Egyptian State Railways, and Helen Lilian Benekendorff; m Marjorie Elsie Barton, 14 April 1928, St Mary's, Kuala Lumpur, Malaysia. BA 1923; MA 1961. **Tutor(s):** E E Sikes. **Educ:** Westerleigh, Hollington Park Road, St Leonards-on-Sea; Sedbergh School. **Career:** Flying Officer, Malayan Volunteer Air Force (later POW in Java), WWII; Hoblyn & King, London; Assistant, Guthrie & Co, Kuala Lumpar, Malaysia 1924–1927; Charles Bradbourne & Co, Stock Brokers, Malaysia 1927–1940. **Awards:** Lupton and Hebblethwaite Exhibition, SJC. Died 11 May 1963.

HOW, Canon John Charles Halland (1900) Born 16 September 1881, 6 Prospect Villas, London Road, Forest Hill, Kent; son of Charles How, Draper, and Elizabeth Halland; m (1) Naomi Junie Katherine, 1925 (d 1938), (2) Barbara Colcutt, 1939; (1) 1 son (Martin), 1 daughter (Ruth). **Subject(s):** Oriental Languages/Theology; BA 1903; MA 1907; Honorary DD (Glasgow) 1943. **Tutor(s):** C E Graves. **Educ:** Christ Church Choir School, Oxford; Pocklington School. **Career:** Lecturer in Hebrew, SJC 1906–1920 (Lectureship suspended while on military service 1917–1919); Lecturer in Hebrew 1907–1913, Precentor 1907–1920, Trinity College, Cambridge; Chaplain, Palestine and Egypt (military service) 1917–1919; Lecturer (open lectures), Cambridge 1922–1926; Rector, Liverpool 1926–1935; Vicar and Rural Dean, Brighton 1935–1938; Bishop, Glasgow and Galloway 1938; Primus of Episcopal Church of Scotland 1946–1951. **Appointments:** Director of Studies in Hebrew and Oriental Languages, SJC 1920–1922. **Awards:** John Stewart of Rannoch Hebrew Scholarship, University of Cambridge 1901; Tyrwhitt Scholarship, University of Cambridge 1904; Mason Prize for Biblical Hebrew, University of Cambridge 1904. **Publications:** *The Sung Eucharist*; *Christian and Churchman*; *Personal Discipleship and the Way of Prayer*. Died 22 May 1961.

HOWARD, Sir Henry Fraser (1923) (admitted to Trinity Hall 1893) Born 20 July 1874, Shide, Whippingham, Isle of Wight; son of Henry Howard, Gentleman, and Margaret Fraser; m Mabel Rosa Roney-Dougal, 19 June 1913, All Saints', Margaret Street, London (d 9 March 1923); 2 sons, 3 daughters. **Subjects:** Classics; MA 1924; BA (Trinity Hall) 1897. **Educ:** Aldenham School; Trinity Hall, Cambridge. **Career:** Various posts, Indian Civil Service 1897–1925 (including Assistant Magistrate and Collector, Bengal 1897; Superintendent, Revision of Imperial Gazetteer for Bengal 1904; Under-Secretary to the Government of India, Finance Department 1905; Collector of Customs, Calcutta 1909–1913; Controller of Currency, India 1914–1916; Secretary to the Government of India, Finance Department 1917–1920; Controller of Finance, India Office 1920–1923; Title B Fellow and Senior Bursar, SJC 1923–1943. **Appointments:** Coach, LMBC; Treasurer, CUBC; President, Cambridgeshire Rowing Association 1924–1943; Member, Assessment Committee, Borough of Cambridge 1925; Member 1925–1942, Chairman 1932–1942, River Cam Conservancy; Member, Town Council (served on various committees including Finance and Public Works) 1930; Member, Financial Board, University of Cambridge 1933; Trustee, Cambridge municipal charities. **Awards:** Exhibition, Trinity Hall 1893; Scholarship, Trinity Hall 1894. **Honours:** CIE 1913; CSI 1919; KCIE 1923. **Publications:** *Handbook of Criminal Procedure*; *India and the Gold Standard*; *An Account of the Finances of the College of St John the Evangelist in the University of Cambridge, 1511–1926*, 1935; Articles in *Imperial Gazetteer*. Died 19 October 1943.

HOWARD, Horace Reginald (1912) (admitted to Selwyn College 1911) Born 3 July 1892, Willenhall, Staffordshire; son of George Howard, Lockmaker, and Mary Hulse. **Tutor(s):** L H K Bushe-Fox. **Educ:** Tettenhall College; Queen Mary's School, Walsall.

HOWARD, Jack Wesley (1918) American Student.

HOWARD, John (1930) Born 2 October 1911, 11 Leighton Street, Moston, North Manchester; son of Frederick Howard, Pressure Gauge Dial Writer, and Edith Smith. **Subject(s):** Modern and Medieval Languages; BA 1933; MA 1937. **Tutor(s):** C W Guillebaud. **Educ:** Manchester Grammar School; Sale High School. **Awards:** Exhibition, SJC 1929.

HOWARD, Richard Samuel (1922) Born 4 July 1904, Gonvena, Wadebridge, Cornwall; son of Richard Howard, of independent means, and Marion Augusta Holman. BA 1925; MA 1950. **Tutor(s):** E Cunningham. **Educ:** Braidlea, Clifton; Marlborough College. **Career:** Radio Engineer, Standard Telephones and Cables, Hendon 1926; Radio Engineer, Marconi Osram Valve Company 1929; Radio Engineer, Lissen Ltd 1932. Died November 1986.

HOWARTH, Professor John Lee (1942) Born 8 June 1924, Westhoughton, Lancashire; son of John Howarth and Elsie Lee; m (1) Phyllis Mary Harrison, 26 December 1946, (2) Enid Bogner, 4 December 1961, (3) Dr Faith Gabelnick, 3 June 1993; 3 sons (John Norman b 1951, David Lee b 1953 and Samuel Carl b 1963), 1 daughter (Rachel b 1965). **Subject(s):** Mathematics/Natural Sciences; BA 1945; MA 1949; BSc (London) 1948; MSc (London) 1950; PhD (London) 1963; Honorary DSc (State University of New York) 1994; FInstP. **Tutor(s):** C W Guillebaud. **Educ:** Rivington and Blackrod Grammar School; University of London. **Career:** Junior Scientific Officer, RAE, Farnborough, Hampshire 1945–1946; Research Physicist, BSA Group Research Centre, Sheffield 1946–1947; Assistant Physicist and Senior Physicist, Sheffield National Centre for Radiotherapy 1947–1953; Head, Radiation Physics Department, Lovelace Foundation for Medical Research and Education, Albuquerque 1953–1964; Professor of Physics and Director, General Honours Program 1964–1978, Associate Professor of Radiology (Physics), School of Medicine 1968–1978, University of New Mexico, Albuquerque; Professor of Physics and Director, General Honours Program, University of Maryland College Park 1978–1989; Distinguished Visiting Professor, State University of New York College, Plattsburgh 1992–1993. **Publications:** numerous articles in various journals including *Journal of Scientific Instruments*, *British Journal of Radiology*, *Indian Journal of Radiology*, *American Journal of Roentgenology*, *Annals of the New York Academy of Sciences*, *Radiation Research*, and *Archives of Pathology*.

HOWARTH, Professor Leslie (1945) (admitted to Gonville & Caius College 1930) Born 23 May 1911, 14 Crooked Shore, Bacup, Lancashire; son of Fred Howarth, Civil Engineer, Borough Council, and Elizabeth Ellen Matthews; m Eva Priestley, 1934; 2 sons (Peter David b 17 February 1944 and Michael John b 8 January 1948). **Subject(s):** Mathematics; BA (Gonville & Caius) 1933; PhD (King's) 1936; MA (King's) 1937; BSc (Manchester) 1931; FRS 1950. **Johnian Relatives:** brother of Ronald Matthews Howarth (1938). **Educ:** Accrington Grammar School; Manchester University; Gonville & Caius College, Cambridge. **Career:** Berry-Ramsey Research Fellow, King's College, Cambridge 1936–1945; Lecturer in Mathematics, University of Cambridge 1936–1949; Work on turbulence, California Institute of Technology 1937–1938; External Ballistics Department Ordnance Board 1939–1942; Armament Research Department 1942–1945; Title B Fellow and College Lecturer, SJC 1945–1949; Profesor of Applied Mathematics 1949–1964, Dean, Faculty of Science 1957–1960, Henry Overton Wills Professor of Mathematics and Head, Department of Mathematics 1964–1976, University of Bristol. **Appointments:** Stokes Lecturer 1949. **Awards:** Adams Prize, University of Cambridge; Smith's Prize, University of Cambridge 1935. **Honours:** OBE 1955. **Publications:** (contributor) *Modern Developments in Fluid Dynamics*, 1938; (ed)

Modern Developments in Fluid Dynamics: high speed flow, 1953; 'Laminar Boundary Layers', *Handbuch der Physik*, Volume VIII, 1959. Died 22 September 2001.

HOWARTH, Ronald Matthews (1938) Born 14 May 1920, 71 Elmfield Street, Church, Accrington, Lancashire; son of Fred Howarth, Civil Engineer, and Elizabeth Ellen Matthews; m Dorothy Mary Clark, 1941 (d 1994); 1 son (Roger Mervyn), 1 daughter (Denise Mary). **Subject(s):** Mathematics; BA 1941; MA 1946; FRAeS. **Tutor(s):** J M Wordie. **Johnian Relatives:** brother of Leslie Howarth (1945). **Educ:** Hyndburn Park Council School, Accrington; Accrington Grammar School. **Career:** Managing Director, then Chairman, Bristol Aerojet Ltd, Banwell, Avon 1971–1985.

HOWE, Bruce (1938) Born 20 November 1912, 1833 M Street NW, Washington DC, USA; son of Walter Bruce Howe, Lawyer, and Mary Wortham Carlisle. **Tutor(s):** J M Wordie. **Educ:** St Alban's School, Washington DC; St Paul's School, Concord; Yale University; Harvard University.

HOWE, The Revd Canon David Randall (1948) Born 4 September 1924, Thurne Cottage, Ember Lane, Thames Ditton, Surrey; son of Randall Lionel Bentham Howe, Clerk in Holy Orders, and Emily Marjorie Barton. BA 1951; MA 1955. **Tutor(s):** C W Guillebaud. **Johnian Relatives:** grandson of Percy Frederic Barton (1887); brother of Jeremy Frederic Howe (1950) and of Richard Gerard Elliott Howe (1953); uncle of Michael Jeremy Howe (1985). **Educ:** Wells Theological College; King's College Choir School, Cambridge; Shrewsbury School. **Career:** Ordained Deacon 1953; Curate, Basingstoke 1953–1959; Ordained Priest 1954; Rector, Rotherwick, Hook and Greywell 1959–1970; Rector, Broughton cum Bossington 1970–1981; Rector, Broughton with Bossington and Mottisfont 1981–1986; Rector, Broughton, Bossington, Houghton and Mottisfont 1986–1989; Honorary Canon, Winchester Cathedral 1987–1989.

HOWE, George Arthur (1911) Born 7 June 1891, 27 Market Street, Buxton, Derbyshire; son of George Howe, Veterinary Surgeon and Sarah Agnes Smith; m Eveline Pinshon, 21 July 1921, Hooley Hill Methodist Church, Audenshaw; 1 son (James Turner b 8 July 1926), 1 daughter (Margaret b 1 May 1929). **Subject(s):** History/Law; BA 1914; MA 1918; LLB 1914. **Tutor(s):** J R Tanner. **Johnian Relatives:** father of James Turner Howe (1944). **Educ:** Denstone College. **Career:** Captain, Lancashire Fusiliers, WWI; Assistant Accountant, then General Secretary, White Star Line 1922; Accountant, Manchester Ship Canal 1934. Died 6 January 1979.

HOWE, James Turner (1944) Born 8 July 1926, 21 Montclair Drive, Wavertree, Liverpool; son of George Arthur Howe, Chief Accountant, Manchester Ship Canal, and Eveline Pinshon; m Ida Smith, 1953; 2 daughters (Christine b 18 April 1956 and Carolyn b 15 October 1959). **Subject(s):** Mechanical Sciences; BA 1947; FIEE. **Tutor(s):** S J Bailey. **Johnian Relatives:** son of George Arthur Howe (1911). **Educ:** Giggleswick School. **Career:** Captain, REME Army Apprentices School, Taunton 1947–1949; Area Manager, North Western Electricity Board, Manchester.

HOWE, Peter William Herbert (1946) Born 13 August 1928, 41 Rawcliffe Street, Blackpool; son of Benjamin Leslie Howe, Watchmaker, and Kathleen Eliza Haigh; m Ann Roberson, 1968; 1 son (Bruce), 2 daughters (Jennifer Sarah and Audrey Fiona). **Subject(s):** Maths; BA 1949; MA 1965; CEng; MRAeS; MIMA. **Tutor(s):** J M Wordie. **Educ:** Roseacre Elementary School, Blackpool; Arnold School, Blackpool. **Career:** Principal Scientific Officer, National Gas Turbine Establishment 1951–1980; Mathematics Teacher, Farnham College 1981. **Awards:** Exhibition, SJC 1946.

HOWELL, Illtyd Mark (1919) Born 8 May 1901, 23 Risca Road, Newport; son of Illtyd Howell, Iron and Oil Merchant, and Louisa Annett Mordey.

BA 1922; MA 1965. **Tutor(s):** E A Benians. **Educ:** Cheltenham House School; Newport; Newport Intermediate School; Wycliffe College, Stonehouse. **Career:** Chairman, Thos H Howell, stockholding company. Died 10 June 1989.

HOWELL, Malcolm Bardsley Warbeck (1938) Born 29 October 1919, 41 Lonsdale Road, Wolverhampton; son of Frederick Edwin Warbeck Howell, Solicitor and Town Clerk, and Marion Martha Bardsley. **Subject(s):** Economics. **Educ:** Old Hill, Wellington; Marlborough College.

HOWELL, Maurice Ives Berthon (1914) Born 28 October 1895, 37 West Hill, Wandsworth, Surrey; son of Thomas Arthur Ives Howell, Medical Practitioner, and Frances Elizabeth Margaret Berthon. **Tutor(s):** L H K Bushe-Fox. **Educ:** Leinster House, Putney Hill; Radley College. **Career:** Second Lieutenant, 1st Battalion, The Queen's Royal West Surrey Regiment 1914–1915. Died 25 September 1915 (killed in action at Givenchy).

HOWELL, Trevor Henry (1926) Born 6 October 1908, 13 Victoria Road, Barnsley, Yorkshire; son of Trevor Howell, GP, and Florence Davis; m Margaret; 2 sons, 2 daughters. MRCPE 1937. **Tutor(s):** M P Charlesworth. **Educ:** Orleton, Scarborough; Bradfield College, Berkshire. **Career:** GP, Hammersmith, later in Worthing until 1939; Deputy Surgeon, Royal Hospital, Chelsea, RAMC (Later posted to India and Burma), WWII; Consultant Physician, St John's Hospital, Battersea and Queen's Hospital, Croydon; Lecturer, St Bartholomew's, Guy's, Westminster, Charing Cross, and St George's Hospitals. **Appointments:** Founder, Care for the Elderly (later British Geriatrics Society); Fellow, American Geriatrics Society. **Awards:** Nuffield Foundation Research Fellowship 1945; Willard Owen Thompson Gold Medal, American Geriatrics Society; Founder's Medal, British Geriatrics Society; FE Williams Prize, RCP. **Publications:** *De Sedibus Morborum in Senecute*. Died May 1988.

HOWELLS, Professor Herbert Norman (1946) Born 17 October 1892, Lydney, Gloucestershire; son of Oliver Howells, Master Decorator, and Elizabeth Burgham; m Dorothy Goozee, 1920 (d 1975), 1 son (Michael Kendrick d 1935), 1 daughter (Ursula). MusD (Oxon) 1937; Honorary MusD (Cambridge) 1961; Hon DMus (RCM) 1982; Hon RAM 1947; Hon FRSCM 1963; FRCM; FRCO. **Educ:** St Mary's School, Lydney; Lydney Grammar School; Gloucester Cathedral; Royal College of Music. **Career:** Sub-organist, Salisbury Cathedral 1917; Assistant to Sir Richard Terry, editor of manuscripts of Tudor church music, and composer 1917–1920; Lecturer (later Professor of Composition), Royal College of Music 1920–1970; Director of Music, St Paul's Girls' School, Brook Green 1936–1962; Deputy Organist, SJC 1941–1945; King Edward Professor of Music, University of London 1950 (Emeritus 1962). **Appointments:** President, Incorporated Society of Musicians 1952; Honorary Fellow, Trinity College of Music 1956; President, Plainsong and Mediaeval Music Society; President, Royal College of Organists 1958–1959; Editor, *RCM Magazine*; Master, Worshipful Company of Musicians 1959 (first John Collard Fellow; elected to John Collard Life Fellowship 1959); Honorary Fellow, SJC 1962; Honorary Fellow, The Queen's College, Oxford 1977. **Awards:** Open Scholarship in Composition, Royal College of Music 1912; Grove Scholarship, Royal College of Music 1915; Bruce Scholarship, Royal College of Music 1916. **Honours:** CBE 1953; CH 1972. **Publications:** Selected compositions: *Sir Patrick Spens*; *Sine Nomine Procession*; *Puck's Minuet*; *Piano Concerto*; *Elegy for Strings*; *Concerto for Strings*; *Lady Audrey's Suite*; *Phantasy Quartet*; *Piano Quartet*; *Rhapsodic Quintet*; *First and Third Sonatas for violin and pianoforte*; *Lambert's Clavichord*; *In Green Ways*, five songs for Soprano and Orchestra; *Peacock Pie song-cycle*; *Sonata for Organ*; *Hymnus Paradisi*; *Missa Sabrinensis*; *Pageantry*; *A Kent Yeoman's Wooing Song*; *Four Organ Rhapsodies*; *Six Psalm Preludes*; *Music for a Prince* (for HRH Prince Charles); *Introit* (composed for Coronation Service, 1953); *Inheritance* (commissioned by The Arts Council of Great Britain for *A Garland for the Queen*, 1953);

An English Mass, 1955; *Howell's Clavichord* (20 pieces); *Missa Aedis Christi*; *Missa, Collegium Regale*; *Three Figures*; *Sequence for St Michael*; *Coventry Antiphon*; *Stabat Mater*; *The Coventry Mass*. Died 23 February 1983.

HOWELLS, Dr James Bletsoe (1943) Born 15 May 1925, 108 Kew Road, Richmond; son of William Spencer Howells, Chemist and Druggist, and Emily Louise Bletsoe; m (2) Jennie; (1) 2 sons, 1 daughter. **Subject(s):** Natural Sciences. **Tutor(s):** S J Bailey. **Educ:** Richmond Hill School; Gunnersbury Preparatory School; Aldenham School. **Career:** Consultant Radiologist, St James's Hospital, Balham 1962–1985. **Appointments:** Member, British Institute of Radiology. Died 24 September 1987.

HOWL, Oliver Brian (1941) Born 8 October 1922, 231 Tettenhall Road, Wolverhampton; son of Clifford Howl, Engineer, and Doris Savill; m Elizabeth Mary Caroline Dyke, 1956, Wolverhampton; 1 son (Oliver Jonathan Dyke), 1 daughter (Julia Caroline). **Subject(s):** Mechanical Sciences; BA 1944; MA 1948; MIMechE; CEng. **Tutor(s):** S J Bailey. **Johnian Relatives:** father-in-law of John Michael Rowland (1974). **Educ:** Packwood Haugh; Shrewsbury School; Rugby Technical College. **Career:** Engineer Lieutenant, RN; Lecturer in Physics, RMA, Sandhurst 1948; Engineer 1949, Managing Director 1956, Chairman 1969–1981, Lee Howl & Co. **Appointments:** Vice-Chairman, British Pump Manufacturers Association; Master, Staffordshire Beagles; Trustee, Ironbridge Gorge Museum; President, Greenflies Cricket Club.

HOWLAND, Robert Leslie (1924) Born 25 March 1905, 56 Marlborough Road, Watford, Hertfordshire; son of Robert Howland, Bristle Merchant, and Mary Helen Turner; m Eileen Tait, 11 September 1930, St Giles's Church, Stoke Poges; 2 sons (Robert Ifor Leslie b 20 March 1935 and Peter Leslie b 5 February 1940), 1 daughter (Judith b 7 July 1931, d 28 February 1990). **Subject(s):** Classics; BA 1928; MA 1931. **Tutor(s):** E E Sikes. **Johnian Relatives:** father of Robert Ifor Leslie Howland (1956) and of Peter Leslie Howland (1959). **Educ:** Shirley House, Watford; The Noble School, White Plains, New York, USA; Seafield House, Broughty Ferry; Shrewsbury School. **Career:** Master, Eton College; Title A Fellow 1929–1935, Assistant Lecturer in Classics 1930–1931, Lecturer in Classics 1931–1972, Title B Fellow 1935–1972, Title D Fellow 1972–1986, SJC; Assistant Lecturer in Classics 1936–1938, Lecturer in Classics 1938–1972, University Proctor 1951, University of Cambridge; Radar Fighter Controller, UK, Mediterranean and South East Asia, RAF, WWII; Warden, Madingley Hall 1965–1975. **Appointments:** Member, British National Athletic Team 1927–1939 (Captain 1934–1935), representing Britain in Shot Put; Assistant Supervisor in Classics 1930, Assistant Tutor 1931–1934, Tutor 1934–1965, Director of Studies in Classics 1948–1966, Senior Tutor 1956–1965, President 1963–1967, SJC. **Awards:** Scholarship, SJC 1924; Strathcona Research Studentship, SJC 1928. Died 7 March 1986.

HOWLES, Dr Ralph (1933) Born 5 February 1915, 591 Gorton Road, Reddish, Stockport; son of Arthur Howles, Farm Bailiff, and Hannah Hibbert Toplis; m Doris May Abbott, 16 August 1952, Holy Trinity Church, Bedford; 2 sons, 1 daughter. **Subject(s):** Natural Sciences; BA 1936; MA 1978; PhD 1940. **Tutor(s):** J M Wordie. **Educ:** Brookdale Park School, Manchester; Manchester Grammar School. **Career:** RN 1943–1945; ICI Penicillin Department, Manchester 1946–1947; Research Officer, Virology, Cheshunt Experimental & Research Station, Glasshouse Crops Research Institute, Littlehampton 1947–1961; Department of Agriculture, South Australia, eventually Senior Research Officer, Virology 1962–1977. **Appointments:** Secretary, SJC Natural Sciences Society; Treasurer of Croquet Club. **Awards:** Frank Smart Studentship, University of Cambridge 1938; Endowed the Hollinshead-Howles Prize for Natural Scientists 1966; Diploma from the French Ambassador in Australia for service at D Day; France and Germany Star. **Publications:** Technical notes on inactivation of virus in seed by dry heat treatment.

HOWORTH, Roland Heslop (1939) Born 9 July 1921, Aysgarth, Water Street, Leyland, Lancashire; son of Frederick Howorth, Architect, and Jane Heslop; m (1) Jean Alice Pickering, 1958 (d 1989), (2) Clarice Garnett, 1991; (1) 1 son (Christopher Paul b 1965), 1 daughter (Jane Margaret b 1966). **Subject(s):** Classics; BA 1942; MA 1947; BSc (Open) 2001. **Tutor(s):** R L Howland. **Educ:** Leyland Methodist School; Manchester Grammar School; Open University. **Career:** Assistant Lecturer in Classics 1947–1949, Lecturer 1949–1951, University College, Hull; Reader in Classics, University College of the Gold Coast 1951–1960; Assistant Director of Examinations, Civil Service Commission 1960–1966; Senior Assistant Director of Examinations 1966–1973; Head of Written Examination Unit 1973–1981. **Awards:** Patchett Scholarship, SJC 1938. **Publications:** 'The Origin of the Use of AN and KE in Indefinite Clauses', *Classical Quarterly*, January–April 1955.

HOWSON, Thomas Leslie (1940) Born 3 February 1915, 83 Bertram Road, Enfield, Middlesex; son of Herbert Howson, Bricklayer's Labourer, and Elizabeth Pearce. **Subject(s):** Geography; BA 1942; MA 1946; BSc (London) 1935. **Tutor(s):** C W Guillebaud. **Educ:** Bush Hill Park Boys' School; Enfield Grammar School; Goldsmiths' College, University of London. **Career:** Pilot Officer, RAF.

HOYLAND, Geoffrey (1912) Born 15 December 1889, 105 Gough Road, Edgbaston; son of John William Hoyland and Rachel Anna Somervell; m Dorothea Cadbury, 30 July 1919, Friends' Meeting House, Bourneville; 1 son (Hugh James b 13 August 1931). **Subject(s):** History; BA 1915; MA 1919. **Tutor(s):** R P Gregory. **Johnian Relatives:** half brother of William Frazer Hoyland (1926); father of Hugh James Hoyland (1950). **Educ:** King Edward's School, Birmingham; Birmingham University. **Career:** Master, Uppingham Junior School; Headmaster, The Downs School, Colwall, Malvern 1919–1940. **Awards:** Second Winchester Reading Prize, University of Cambridge 1915. Died 17 June 1965.

HOYLAND, William Frazer (1926) Born 11 January 1908, Kingsmead, Bristol Road, Selly Oak, King's Norton, Worcester; son of John William Hoyland, Principal of a Quaker Training College, and Josephine Taylor; m Phyllis Dow, 1937, Lewes; 1 adopted son (Mark), 1 adopted daughter (Christine). **Subject(s):** Natural Sciences; BA 1930; MA 1936. **Tutor(s):** J M Wordie. **Johnian Relatives:** half brother of Geoffrey Hoyland (1912); uncle of Hugh James Hoyland (1950). **Educ:** The Downs School, Colwall, Malvern; Bootham School, York. **Career:** Farmer, New Zealand; Assistant Master, Bryanston School 1930; Headmaster, Downs School, Colwall 1940–1952; Assistant Headmaster, Scots College, Wellington, New Zealand 1960–1972. Died 1981.

HOYLE, Professor Sir Fred (1939) (admitted to Emmanuel College 1933) Born 24 June 1915, 34 Gilstead, Bingley, Yorkshire; son of Benjamin Hoyle, Cloth Merchant, and Mabel Pickard; m Barbara Clark, 1939; 1 son (Geoff), 1 daughter (Elizabeth). **Subject(s):** Mathematics; MA 1940; BA 1936 (Emmanuel); Honorary ScD (East Anglia) 1967; Honorary DSc (Leeds) 1969; Honorary DSc (Bradford) 1975; Honorary DSc (Newcastle) 1976; FRS 1957; Honorary MRIA (Section of Science) 1977. **Johnian Relatives:** father of Geoffrey Hoyle (1961); father-in-law of Richard Anthony Lowndes (1961). **Educ:** Eldwick Council School; Bingley Grammar School; Emmanuel College, Cambridge. **Career:** British Admiralty 1939–1945; Title A Fellow 1939–1946 (suspended for war service 1941–1945), Title B Fellow 1946–1957, Title E Fellow 1957–1958, Title C Fellow, 1958–1972, SJC; Lecturer in Mathematics 1945–1958, Plumian Professor of Astronomy and Experimental Philosophy 1958–1972, Director, Institute of Theoretical Astronomy 1967–1973, University of Cambridge. **Appointments:** Honorary Fellow, SJC 1973–2001; Visiting Professor of Astrophysics, California Institute of Technology 1953 and 1954; Visiting Professor of Astronomy, California Institute of Technology 1956; Staff Member, Mount Wilson and Palomar Observatories 1957–1962; Visiting Associate in Physics, California Institute of Technology 1963; Honorary Member, American Academy of Arts and Sciences 1964; Member, SRC 1967–1972; Foreign Associate, US National Academy of Sciences 1969; Professor of Astronomy, Royal Institution of Great Britain 1969–1972; Vice-President, Royal Society 1970–1971; President, Royal Astronomical Society 1971–1973; Andrew D White Professor-at-Large, Cornell University 1972–1978; Honorary Research Professor, Manchester University 1972; Honorary Research Professor, University College, Cardiff 1975; Honorary Member, Mark Twain Society 1978; Member, American Philosophical Society 1980; Honorary Fellow, Emmanuel College, Cambridge 1983; Institute of Astronomy, University of Cambridge 1996; Addison White Greenaway Visiting Professor of Astronomy. **Awards:** Mayhew Prize, University of Cambridge 1936; Smith's Prize, University of Cambridge 1938; Goldsmith Exhibition 1938; Senior Exhibition, Royal Commission of 1851 1938; Royal Astronomical Society Gold Medal 1968; UN Kalinga Prize 1968; Bruce Gold Medal 1970; Royal Medal, Royal Society 1974; Sherman Fairchild Scholarship 1974–1975; Klumphe-Roberts Award 1977; Dag Hammarskjöld Gold Medal, Académie Diplomatique de la Paix 1986; Karl Schwarzehild Medal, German Astronomical Society 1992; Balzan Prize, Fondation Internationale Balzan 1994; Annenberg Award, Astronomy Education, AAS 1996; Crafoord Prize, Royal Swedish Academy of Sciences. **Honours:** Kt 1972. **Publications:** General: *Some Recent Researches in Solar Physics*, 1949; *The Nature of the Universe*, 1951; *A Decade of Decision*, 1953; *Frontiers of Astronomy*, 1955; *Man and Materialism*, 1956; *Astronomy*, 1962; *Star Formation*, 1963; *Of Men and Galaxies*, 1964; *Encounter with the Future*, 1965; *Galaxies, Nuclei and Quasars*, 1965; *Man in the Universe*, 1966; *From Stonehenge to Modern Cosmology*, 1972; *Nicolaus Copernicus*, 1973; *The Relation of Physics and Cosmology*, 1973; (with J V Narlikar) *Action–at–a–Distance in Physics and Cosmology*, 1974; *Astronomy and Cosmology*, 1975; 'Highlights in Astronomy', in *England, Astronomy Today*, 1975; *Ten Faces of the Universe*, 1977; *On Stonehenge*, 1977; *Energy or Extinction*, 1977; (with N C Wickramasinghe) *Lifecloud*, 1978; *The Cosmogony of the Solar System*, 1978; (with N C Wickramasinghe) *Diseases From Space*, 1979; (with G Hoyle) *Commonsense and Nuclear Energy*, 1979; (with J V Narlikar) *The Physics–Astronomy Frontier*, 1980; (with N C Wickramasinghe) *Space Travellers: the Bringers of Life*, 1981; *Ice*, 1981; (with N C Wickramasinghe) *Evolution from Space*, 1981; *The Intelligent Universe*, 1983; (with N C Wickramasinghe) *Archaeopteryx, the Primordial Bird: a case of fossil forgery*, 1986; (with N C Wickramasinghe) *Cosmic Life Force*, 1988; (with N C Wickramasinghe) *The Theory of Cosmic Grains*, 1991; (with N C Wickramasinghe) *Our Place in the Cosmos*, 1993; Novels: *The Black Cloud*, 1957; *Ossian's Ride*, 1959; (with J Elliot) *A for Andromeda*, 1962; (with G Hoyle) *Fifth Planet*, 1963; (with J Elliot) *Andromeda Breakthrough*, 1964; *October the First is Too Late*, 1966; *Element 79*, 1967; (with G Hoyle) *Rockets in Ursa Major*, 1969; (with G Hoyle) *Seven Steps to the Sun*, 1970; (with G Hoyle) *The Molecule Men*, 1971; (with G Hoyle) *The Inferno*, 1973; (with G Hoyle) *Into Deepest Space*, 1974; (with G Hoyle) *The Incandescent Ones*, 1977; (with G Hoyle) *The Westminster Disaster*, 1978; Children's stories with G Hoyle: *The Energy Pirate*, 1982; *The Giants of Universal Park*, 1982; *The Frozen Planet of Azuron*, 1982; *The Planet of Death*, 1982; *Comet Halley*, 1985; (with N C Wickramasinghe) *Cosmic Life Force*, 1988; Autobiography: *The Small World of Fred Hoyle*, 1986; *Home is Where the Wind Blows*, 1994; Play: *Rockets in Ursa Major*, 1962; Libretto: *The Alchemy of Love*; space serials for television; scientific papers. Died 20 August 2001.

HPA, Sao Hseng (1942) Born 16 December 1923, Yawnghwe, Southern Shan States, Burma; son of Sao Shwe Thaike, The Sawbwa of Yawnghwe. **Tutor(s):** S J Bailey. **Educ:** Private English School, Kalaw; Shan Chiefs' School, Taunggyi; The King's School, Canterbury.

HUCK, Dr Richard James (1934) Born 11 May 1915, 48 Dumbarton Road, Brixton Hill, London; son of James Francis Scott Huck, Naval Designer, and Frances Thomas; m Elizabeth Brennen Morris, 3 January 1952; 1 son (Angus James b 1957). **Subject(s):** Natural Sciences; BA 1937; MA 1941; MSc (London) 1950; PhD (London) 1959. **Tutor(s):** C W Guillebaud. **Educ:** Franciscan Road School, Tooting, London; Bec School, Beechcroft Road, London. **Career:** Physics Master, Leamington

College for Boys, Leamington Spa 1937–1939; Lecturer in Physics, Mathematics, and Chemistry, Faraday House Electrical Engineering College, Southampton Row, London 1939–1940; Temporary Experimental Officer, DSR Admiralty 1940–1945; Lecturer in Physics and Chemistry, Faraday House Electrical Engineering College, Southampton Row, London 1946–1947; Senior Lecturer and Deputy Head of Department, Physics Department, Battersea Polytechnic, London (later University of Surrey) 1947–1980; Chief Examiner in GCE Physics at Advanced and Special levels, University of London School Examinations Board 1960–1972. **Awards:** Open Scholarship, SJC; State Scholarship; Senior County Scholarship, London County Council 1933; Junior County Scholarship from London County Council 1926. **Publications:** 'Variational Methods in Inelastic Collisions', PhD thesis, 1959; *History of the Physics Department, Battersea Polytechnic and University of Surrey, 1906–1986, Eighty Years On*, 1986; Various scientific papers: (with Benjamin and Jenkins) 'Oxide-Coated Cathodes. Particle Size and Emission', *Procedures of the Physics Society*, 1938; 'The Effectiveness of Variational Methods for Inelastic Scattering Problems', *Procedures of the Physics Society*, 1957; (with E Thornton) 'Sutherland-Wassilyeva Coefficients for the Viscosities of Binary Rare-Gas Mixtures', *Procedures of the Physics Society*, 1967; (with E Thornton) 'Sutherland-Wassiyeva Coefficients for the Thermal Conductivities of Binary Rare-Gas Mixtures', *Procedures of 4th Symposium on Thermophysical Properties*, University of Maryland, USA, 1968; (with E A Johnson) 'Predictions for Sound Propagation in Disparate-Mass Gas-Mixtures', *Archives of Mechanics*, 1980; (with E A Johnson) 'Physical Properties of Double Sound Modes in Disparate-Mass Gas-Mixtures', *Rarefied Gas Dynamics, Progress in Astronautics and Aeronautics*, 1981.

HUDSON, George (1939) Born 4 April 1916, Moorlea, Lower Wycombe Road, Neutral Bay, North Sydney, Australia; son of George William Hudson, Timber Merchant, and Lena Lipman. **Subject(s):** Mechanical Sciences; BA 1942; MA 1946. **Tutor(s):** S J Bailey. **Educ:** King's School, Australia; Blundell's School, Tiverton; Royal School of Science, London University. **Career:** Acting Pilot Officer, RAF 1936–1938.

HUDSON, George Alexander (1949) Born 15 August 1930, Kandy Nursing Home, Kandy, Ceylon; son of Alexander Hudson, Tea Planter, and Katie Irene Hardwick. **Subject(s):** Economics; BA 1952. **Tutor(s):** C W Guillebaud. **Educ:** The Hill School, Nuwara Eliya, Ceylon; Uppingham School. Died 28 January 1994.

HUDSON, Robert Lindsay (1935) Born 3 July 1917, Hanley Villas, Isle of Man; son of Arthur Lindsay Hudson, Schoolmaster, and Alice Edith Wilson. **Subject(s):** Natural Sciences/Mechanical Sciences; BA 1938; MA 1942. **Tutor(s):** J M Wordie. **Educ:** Glossop Grammar School. **Career:** Headmaster, Edmonton School, London. **Awards:** Scholarship, SJC 1937. Died 6 July 1974.

HUDSON, Wilfred Faraday (1921) Born 21 May 1905, Alpina, Long Lane, Church End, Finchley, Middlesex; son of Thomas Charlton Hudson, Astronomer, HM Nautical Almanac Office, and Sarah Beatrice Brown. **Tutor(s):** B F Armitage. **Educ:** Muncaster School, Ashford; Finchley County Secondary School; Leighton Park School, Reading.

HUDSPITH, Hubert Corot (1929) Born 4 February 1911, 11 Kenilworth Road, Monkseaton; son of William Hudspith, Company Secretary, and Sarah Beall. **Subject(s):** History; BA 1932. **Tutor(s):** E A Benians. **Educ:** Royal Grammar School, Newcastle upon Tyne; The High School, Nottingham. **Awards:** Scholarship, SJC 1928.

HUGHES, Arnold (1906) Born 11 October 1887, The Briars, Lingard Road, Lewisham, Kent; son of Alexander Hughes, Optician, and Lucy Grimwade. **Subject(s):** Classics/History; BA 1909; MA 1914. **Tutor(s):** J R Tanner. **Educ:** St Olave's Grammar School, Southwark. **Career:** Assistant Master, Dean Close School, Cheltenham 1911–1913; Headmaster, Ying Wa College, Hong Kong 1913–1922. Died 23 August 1922.

HUGHES, Arthur (1935) Born 5 February 1916, 99 Wantage Road, Reading; son of Arthur Price Hughes, Methodist Minister, and Mary Sowerbutts; m Daphne. **Subject(s):** Modern and Medieval Languages; BA 1938; MA 1942; Member, Institute of Directors. **Tutor(s):** C W Guillebaud. **Educ:** Ellis Avenue School, Leicester; Abbeydale School, Sheffield; Rutlish School, Merton, London; Kingswood School, Bath. **Career:** Wing Commander 1951–1961; Commander, University Air Squadron 1953–1956. **Appointments:** Air Ministry for duty in the Department of the Chief of the Air Force. **Honours:** DFC; Legion d'Honneur; Croix de Guerre avec Palme. Died 27 March 1993.

HUGHES, Basil Frederick Murray (1915) Born 23 July 1896, St Peters' Vicarage, St Leonards-on-Sea, Sussex; son of Frederick George Hughes, Clerk in Holy Orders, and Mary Eleanor Burwood. **Tutor(s):** L H K Bushe-Fox. **Educ:** Fonthill, East Grinstead; Wellington College. **Career:** Flight Sub-Lieutenant, Royal Naval Air Service, WWI. Died 1 December 1915.

HUGHES, Harold (1943) Born 13 March 1910, Chapel House, Charles Street, Tredegar, Monmouthshire; son of William Hughes, Coal Miner, and Jennie Wathan. **Subject(s):** Geography; BA 1945; MA 1949; BSc (Wales) 1932; DipEd 1933. **Tutor(s):** C W Guillebaud. **Educ:** Tredegar Secondary School; University College of Wales, Aberystwyth. **Career:** RAF Cadet, SJC; Flight Lieutenant, Instructor, Initial Training Wing, RAF.

HUGHES, The Revd John Evans (1905) Born 24 July 1875, Esgaer, Gorwydd, Cardiganshire; son of Sarah Hughes. **Subject(s):** Theology; BA 1908; MA 1917. **Tutor(s):** J R Tanner. **Educ:** St John's College School, Ystrad Meurig. **Career:** Curate, Newtown, Montgomeryshire 1908–1910; Ordained Priest 1909; Curate, Hawarden 1910–1913; Vicar, Dolfor 1918–1922; Vicar, Holt, Denbighshire 1922–1927; Vicar, Llanwddyn 1927–1938; Vicar, Forden 1938–1948. **Awards:** Sizarship, SJC.

HUGHES, John Lawrence (1910) Born 16 April 1892, 53 St George's Terrace, Swansea, Glamorganshire; son of William Rogers Hughes, Commercial Traveller, and Margaret Richards. **Tutor(s):** J R Tanner. **Educ:** The Grammar School, Swansea; Lewisham School, Weston-Super-Mare. **Career:** Private, Royal West Kent Regiment 1914; Second Lieutenant, Welsh Regiment 1915; RFC, France 1917. Died 1 October 1917 (killed in action).

HUGHES, John Morgan (1943) Born 9 December 1925, Woodville, 13 Burgh Heath Road, Epsom, Surrey; son of Alfred Morgan Hughes, Dentist, and Monica Muncaster Jowett. **Tutor(s):** C W Guillebaud. **Educ:** Sherwood School, Epsom; Parkside School, East Horsley; Oundle School.

HUGHES, Professor John Victor (1934) Born 6 March 1910, 23 Alexandra Road, Grangetown, Yorkshire; son of John Henry Hughes, Blacksmith Journeyman, and Hannah Eliza Watson. **Subject(s):** Physics. **Tutor(s):** J M Wordie. **Educ:** Hugh Bell Boys' School, Middlesbrough; Middlesbrough High School for Boys; Royal College of Science, South Kensington. **Career:** Demonstrator, Royal College of Science 1931–1934; Senior Physicist, Pilkington Bros, Lancashire 1937–1941; Admiralty Signal Establishment, Radar 1941–1946; Assistant Professor of Physics, Queen's University, Kingston, Ontario 1946.

HUGHES, Percival Tryfen Maurice (1937) Born 25 May 1918, Hafod Unos, Bangor; son of Maurice Arthur Hughes, Clerk in Holy Orders, and Evelyn Myfanwy Edwardes. **Subject(s):** Classics; BA 1940. **Tutor(s):** R L Howland. **Educ:** Old Hall School, Wellington; Shrewsbury School. **Awards:** Major Scholarship, SJC 1936; Shrewsbury School Exibition 1937; Scholarship, SJC 1939; College Prize, SJC 1939.

HUGHES, Philip (1946) Born 26 February 1922, 25 Loughborough Road, Leicester; son of Arthur Price Hughes, Methodist Minister, and Mary Sowerbutts. **Subject(s):** English; BA 1948; MA 1953; Social Science Certificate (LSE). **Tutor(s):** F Thistlethwaite. **Educ:** Wimbledon Council

School; Churchtown Council School, Southport; King George V School, Southport; Stockport Secondary School; Kingswood School, Bath. **Career:** Probation Officer, HM Prison Service, Manchester; Advanced Social Casework Course, Tavistock Clinic 1956; Assistant Director of Welfare Services, Cyprus 1957; Deputy Children's Officer, Kent 1959–1964; Children's Officer, Greenwich 1964.

HUGHES-JONES, Oswald (1907) Born 13 November 1888, 21 Bentley Road, Liverpool; son of Robert Hughes-Jones, Shipbroker, and Margaret Eleanor Williams. **Subject(s):** Law; BA 1910; LLB 1910. **Tutor(s):** L H K Bushe-Fox. **Educ:** Liverpool College Upper School; Liverpool University. **Career:** Solicitor, Butcher and Barlow, Bury 1914. Died 1 April 1964.

HULL, Professor Gordon Ferrie (1905) Born 7 October 1876, Haldimand County, Ontario, Canada; son of John Hull, Teacher, and Jane Moore. BA (Toronto) 1892; PhD (Chicago) 1897. **Tutor(s):** J R Tanner. **Educ:** University of Toronto, Canada; University of Chicago, USA. **Career:** Professor of Physics, Dartmouth College, New Hampshire, USA 1905. **Appointments:** Fellow Commoner, SJC 1905.

HULME, Dr Alfred Cresswell (1930) Born 12 June 1905, 313 Bearwood Road, Smithwick, Staffordshire; son of Alfred John Hulme, Manager of Steel Rolling Mills, and Annie Cresswell, Teacher; m (2) Irene Nichols, 31 August 1973; 1 son (adopted 1945). PhD 1935; BSc (Birmingham); MSc (Birmingham); DSc (Birmingham). **Tutor(s):** J M Wordie. **Educ:** George Dixon's Elementary School; King Edward's School, Birmingham; University of Birmingham. **Career:** Ditton Laboratory, Food Investigation Board; Senior Principal Scientific Officer, Agricultural Research Council. **Awards:** Strathcona Award, SJC. Died 10 July 2000.

HULME, Allan (1936) Born 26 June 1917, Station Lane Cottages, Seaton Carew, West Hartlepool, Durham; son of Alfred Hulme, Railway Clerk, and Minnie Clarke; m Christine Annie Pepper. **Subject(s):** Natural Sciences; BA 1939; BChir 1942; MB 1942; FRCS 1947. **Tutor(s):** C W Guillebaud. **Johnian Relatives:** brother-in-law of Karl Edwin Heath (1935); father of Edward Christopher Hulme (1965). **Educ:** Romiley Council School; South Manchester School; Manchester Grammar School. **Career:** Consultant Neurosurgeon, South Western Regional Hospital Board, Frenchay Hospital, Bristol. **Awards:** Somerset Exhibition, SJC 1936.

HULME, Sidney (1920) Born 3 July 1901, 122 New Lane, Winton, Manchester; son of Frank Alfred Hulme, Clothing Manufacturer, and Annie Elizabeth Buck. **Subject(s):** Law; BA 1923; MA 1928; LLB 1923. **Tutor(s):** E A Benians. **Educ:** The Grammar School, Eccles; The Grammar School, Manchester; Rydal Mount School, Colwyn Bay. **Career:** Qualified as a Solicitor. **Awards:** Scholarship, SJC 1923; Mackrell Prize. Died 27 May 1977.

HULME, Thomas Ernest (1902) Born 16 September 1883, Gratton, Horton, Staffordshire; son of Thomas Hulme, Merchant, and Mary Young. **Subject(s):** Mathematics. **Tutor(s):** D MacAlister. **Educ:** Newcastle-under-Lyme High School. **Career:** Essayist; translator of Henri Bergson and others; aesthetic philosopher; imagist poet; Teacher, Berlitz School, Brussels; Private, Infantry, Honourable Artillery Company, Flanders 1914–1915; Second Lieutenant, Royal Marine Artillery Company, Belgium 1915–1917. **Awards:** Exhibition, SJC 1901. **Publications:** *The Complete Poetical Works of T E Hulme*, 1912 (five of his six poems); (Compiled by Sir Herbert Edward Read) *Speculations*, 1924 (essays); (ed Sir Herbert Edward Read) *Notes on Language and Style*, 1929 (essays); (ed Sam Hynes) *Further Speculations*, 1955; (ed Karen Csengeri) *The Collected Writings of T E Hulme*, Clarendon Press, 1994. Died 28 September 1917 (killed in action in Nieuport, Belgium).

HUME, Percy John (1904) Born 25 February 1886, 4 Warwick Terrace, Bulls Lane, Finchley, Middlesex; son of Richard John Hume, Accountant, and Phoebe Birch. **Subject(s):** Natural Sciences/Moral

Sciences; BA 1907. **Tutor(s):** J R Tanner; C E Graves. **Educ:** William Ellis Endowed School, Gospel Oak. **Career:** Civil Service, India Office 1910.

HUME, Peter Joseph (1936) Born 12 February 1914, Siward Crescent, Hull Road, York; son of Joseph Hume, Schoolmaster, and Bertha Frances Cooper. BA 1939. **Tutor(s):** J M Wordie. **Educ:** Bootham School. **Career:** Personnel Officer, Friends' Ambulance Unit 1939–1942. Died December 1942 (missing, presumed lost at sea).

HUMFREY, John Charles Willis (1900) Born 25 June 1879, Chester, Cheshire; son of Charles Humfrey, Chemist, and Annie Florence Whitter. **Subject(s):** Physics and Chemistry; BA 1902; BSc (Victoria). **Tutor(s):** D MacAlister. **Educ:** Kings School, Chester; University College, Liverpool; Victoria University. **Career:** Metallurgist, Messrs Sandberg, Consulting Engineers; Metallurgist, Baldwins Ltd 1902–1909; Assistant Metallurgist, National Physical Laboratory 1909–1913; Chief Analyst, Admiralty Inspection Office 1913–1919; Superintendent of Technical Application of Metals, Ministry of Supply 1946. **Honours:** OBE 1920.

HUMPHREY, Professor George (1947) Born 17 July 1889, Boughton under Blean, Kent; son of Edmund Alfred Humphrey, Schoolmaster, and Emily Anne Maddex; m (1) Muriel Miller, (2) Berta Hochberger (née Wolpert); 1 daughter (Anne). MA (Oxon); PhD (Harvard). **Educ:** St Saviour's School, Westgate-on-Sea; Faversham Grammar School; All Souls College, Oxford; Leipzig; Harvard. **Career:** Tutor, Borough Road College 1915; Professor of Classics, University of St Francis Xavier, Antigonish, Nova Scotia 1916–1918; Assistant Professor of Psychology, Wesleyan University, Middletown, Connecticut 1920–1924; Charlton Professor of Philosophy, Queen's University, Kingston, Ontario 1924–1947; Dominion Fellow, SJC 1947; Professor of Psychology, University of Oxford 1947–1956. **Appointments:** Director, Institute of Experimental Psychology; Secretary and President, Canadian Psychological Association. **Awards:** Cassell Scholarship to study at Leipzig. **Publications:** *The Nature of Learning*, 1933; *Thinking: Its Experimental Psychology*, 1951; *Story of a Man's Mind*, 1923; *The Chemistry of Thinking*, 1963. Died 24 April 1966.

HUNNYBUN, Kenneth Gresham (1935) Born 30 May 1917, 85 Scalby Road, Scarborough; son of Kenneth Hunnybun, Solicitor, and Charlotte Emily Juliet Williams; m Nancy Mabyn Bradley. **Subject(s):** Law; BA 1938; MA 1948. **Tutor(s):** R L Howland. **Educ:** Sandgate School, Esher; St Edmund's School, Hindhead; Wellington College. **Career:** Solicitor, Hunnybun & Sykes, Huntingdon. Died 23 July 1977.

HUNT, The Revd Alfred Garrod Leedes (1902) Born 16 October 1882, Christ Church Vicarage, St George's in the East, Middlesex; son of Alfred Leedes Hunt, Clerk in Holy Orders, and Mary Jane Ayshford. BA 1905; MA 1909. **Tutor(s):** C E Graves; J R Tanner. **Johnian Relatives:** son of Alfred Leedes Hunt (1872). **Educ:** Ipswich School. **Career:** Curate, Leyton 1906–1912; Chaplain to Bishop of Newcastle 1912–1915; Curate, Benwell 1915–1918; Curate, Christ Church, Leyton 1918–1928; Vicar, St Philip, Cambridge 1928–1962. Died 12 January 1962.

HUNT, David Edward (1949) Born 2 February 1931, 171 Newport Road, Cardiff; son of Albert Edward Hunt, Builder, and Jean McKergo; m Lesley Mary Roberts, 1964 (div July 1998); 2 sons (John and Michael), 1 daughter (Elizabeth). **Subject(s):** Maths/Economics; BA 1952; MA 1956; FCA; ATII. **Educ:** Monkton House, Cardiff; Hereford Cathedral School; Blundell's School, Tiverton. **Career:** Qualified as Chartered Accountant 1956; Second Lieutenant, Welch Regiment 1957; Partner, R H March & Son & Co, Chartered Accountants, Cardiff 1960–1962; Partner, Mann Judd & Co (later Touche Ross & Co) 1962–1989; Chartered Accountant (own practice), Llantwit Major, South Glamorgan 1989. **Appointments:** President, South Wales Chartered Accountants Students Society 1964–1965; Member, Chartered Institute of Taxation 1968; Secretary, Technical Advisory Committee, South Wales Society of Chartered Accountants 1970–1981; Treasurer, Vale of Glamorgan Conservative Association 1992–1993; Vice Chairman,

Llandaff Diocesan Board of Finance 1994; Treasurer of Women Priests for Wales 1994–1998; Lay Member, Governing Body, Church in Wales 1995. Died 31 October 2002.

HUNT, George William (1919) Born 21 June 1899, 30 Alfred Street, City of Gloucester; son of Charles George Hunt, Clerk on Midland Railway, and Charlotte Ann Williams. **Subject(s):** Classics; BA 1921; MA 1926. **Tutor(s):** E E Sikes. **Educ:** Crypt Grammar School, Gloucester. **Career:** RGA 1918–1919; Assistant Master, Cathedral School, Hereford 1921–1953. **Awards:** Dowman Sizarship, SJC 1918. Died November 1960.

HUNT, John Christopher Noel (1948) (admitted to Selwyn College 1945) Born 14 April 1927, Marratons, Morwenstow, Cornwall; son of Frederick Noel Hunt, Major, and Elizabeth Mary Holmes. BA 1950. **Educ:** Bedford School; Selwyn College, Cambridge. **Career:** Lieutenant, Royal Marines 1946–1948.

HUNT, Dr Leonard Bryan (1943) Born 20 April 1926, 276 Birchfield Road, Handsworth, Birmingham; son of Leonard Robert Hunt, Rope and Twine Manufacturer, and Elsie Mary Phipps; 2 sons. **Subject(s):** Natural Sciences; BA 1946; MA 1958; MB 1949; BChir 1949; DPH; FFPHM; DHMSA. **Educ:** King Edward's High School, Birmingham. **Career:** Short Service Commission, RAF 1950–1956; Medical Adviser, Pharmaceutical Industry 1959–1972; Senior Medical Officer, Department of Health 1972–1990; Consultant in Public Health Medicine, Barnet Health Authority 1990–1995. **Appointments:** Vice-Chairman, Association for Stammerers. **Publications:** Articles on public health and health care planning, including 'Self-help for Stutterers'.

HUNT, Brigadier Richard Swinton (1929) Born 12 December 1910, 11 Lynedock Place, Glasgow; son of Spencer Hunt, Lieutenant Colonel, Indian Medical Service, and Margaret MacGregor. BA 1932; MA 1936; FRCS. **Tutor(s):** M P Charlesworth. **Educ:** Mr Powys' Preparatory School, Sherborne; Sherborne School. **Honours:** MBE. Died 1987.

HUNT, Sidney Robert (1928) Born 23 January 1909, Long Wittenham, Cholsey, Berkshire; son of Sidney James Hunt, Gardener, and Emma Shorter. **Subject(s):** Mathematics; BA 1931. **Tutor(s):** J M Wordie. **Educ:** Long Wittenham Church of England Elementary School; Abingdon School. **Awards:** Scholarship, SJC 1927.

HUNT COOKE, Arthur Hunt (1924) See COOKE.

HUNTER, Brian Vincent (1939) Born 3 January 1920, Inner Meath Road Bray; son of John Frederick Hunter, Civil Servant, and Mary Mercer Rogers. **Subject(s):** English; BA 1946. **Tutor(s):** C W Guillebaud. **Educ:** Parkmount Preparatory School; Belfast Royal Academy; Fane Street Public Elementary School; Royal Academical Institution, Belfast. **Career:** Schoolmaster. **Awards:** Exhibition, SJC.

HUNTER, Sir Ernest John (1931) Born 3 November 1912, 19 Haldane Terrace, Newcastle Upon Tyne; son of George Ernest Hunter, Shipbuilder, and Elsie Emma May Edwards. **Subject(s):** Mechanical Sciences; BSc (Durham) 1935. **Tutor(s):** J M Wordie. **Educ:** Newcastle Preparatory School; Corchester School; Oundle School. **Career:** Apprentice, Wallsend Shipyard 1930–1931; Messers Swan, Hunter and Wigham Richardson Ltd (Shipbuilders) 1935–1937; Assistant Manager, Barclay, Curle & Co 1937; Assistant General Manager, Swan, Hunter & Wigham Richardson, Dry Docks Department 1941–1945; Director, Swan Hunter (Shipbuilders) 1945. **Appointments:** President, British Employers' Federation; President, Shipbuilding Employers' Federation 1956; Chairman, Tyne Shipbuilders' Association; Vice-Chairman, North-East Coast Ship Repairers' Association; Vice-President, North-East Coast Institution of Engineers and Shipbuilders; Freeman, City of London; Liveryman, Company of Shipwrights; Director, Glasgow Iron & Steel Company Ltd; Director, Mercantile Dry Dock Company Ltd; Director, Tyne Tanker Cleaning Company Ltd; Director Consett Iron Company Ltd; Director, Brims & Co Ltd; Chairman, MW Swinburne &

Sons Ltd; Chairman, Barclay, Curle & Co Ltd; Chairman, Wallsend Slipway and Engineering Company Ltd. **Honours:** CBE 1960; Kt 1964.

HUNTER, Professor John (1947) Born 11 August 1922, Dykehead Farm, Airdrie, Lanarkshire; son of Stephen Young Hunter, Farmer, and Agnes Waugh; m Brenda Laval Chesterton (Girton), 1952; 1 son (Keith b 1956), 1 daughter (Lynn b 1957). **Subject(s):** Mathematics; BA 1949; PhD 1953; MA (Glasgow) 1944; FIMA. **Tutor(s):** J M Wordie. **Educ:** Chapelside Primary; Airdrie Academy. **Career:** Lecturer, Senior Lecturer, and Professor of Mathematics, Glasgow University 1951–1986. **Appointments:** Bryce Fellowship, Glasgow University; Visiting Professor, Swarthmore College, Pennsylvania, USA 1964–1965; Visiting Professor, University of St Thomas, St Paul, Minnesota, USA 1986–1988; External Examiner in Mathematics and Maths Education for many British Universities and Colleges; Chairman of various working parties for Scottish Education Department; President, Edinburgh Mathematical Society; President, Glasgow Mathematical Association; Founder Member, Scottish Mathematical Council (Secretary, later Chairman). **Awards:** Rayleigh Prize, University of Cambridge; Bryce Fellowship, Glasgow University; Fulbright Scholarship 1964–1965. **Publications:** Research papers on Number Theory; various mathematical texts (University and School level).

HUNTER, Sir John Adams (1910) Born 30 October 1890, 29 Falmouth Road, Newcastle upon Tyne, Northumberland; son of John Main Hunter, Wine Merchant, and Janet Adams; m Catherine Gladys Greener. **Subject(s):** History; BA 1912. **Tutor(s):** J R Tanner. **Educ:** Royal Grammar School, Newcastle upon Tyne. **Career:** Various posts, including Assistant Secretary to the Government of Federated Malay States, Malayan Civil Service 1914–1938; Lieutenant-Governor, Malta 1938–1940; Governor, Commander-in-Chief, British Honduras 1940–1947. **Honours:** CMG 1940; KCMG 1942. Died 17 November 1962.

HUNTER, John Bowman (1909) Born 16 September 1890, Fernleigh, Oliver Grove, South Norwood, Croydon; son of James Hunter, Ship and Insurance Broker, and Mary Fernie Hastings Hood; m Hilda Margaret Whitfield, 6 September 1922, Beaconsfield Parish Church. **Subject(s):** Natural Sciences; BA 1912; MA 1920; BChir 1921; MB 1921; MChir 1922. **Tutor(s):** J R Tanner. **Johnian Relatives:** nephew of William Hunter (1887). **Educ:** Bedford Grammar School. **Career:** RAMC 1914–1919; House Posts, Royal Northern Hospital and Royal Chest Hospital; Thoracic Surgeon, Papworth Sanitorium 1928; King's College Hospital 1928; Group Officer in charge of Sector VII, Emergency Medical Service, WWII. **Appointments:** Honorary Secretary, Surgery Section, BMA 1931–1932; Deputy Vice Chancellor, University of London. **Awards:** Gold Medal, Clinical Medicine, University College Hospital. **Honours:** CBE; MC. **Publications:** (part editor) Rose and Carless's *Manual of Surgery*; 'Mortality of Acute Appendicitis', *British Medical Journal*, 1927; 'Action of Saliva and Gastric Juice on the Clotting of Blood', *British Journal of Surgery*, 1928; 'Treatment of Malignant Disease of the Hypopharanx', *Procedures of the Royal Society of Medicine*, 1932; 'Diagnosis and Treatment of Abscess of the Lung', *Procedures of the Royal Society of Medicine*, 1932. Died 16 September 1951.

HUNTER, Dr Michael James (1943) Born 1 February 1925, 14 St Symon's Avenue, Putney; son of William James Harcourt Hunter, Chartered Accountant, and Marjory Kate Millis; m Lois Olive June Anderson, 22 May 1954, Holy Trinity Brompton. BA 1947; MA 1950; MB 1950; BChir 1950; DObstRCOG 1955. **Tutor(s):** S J Bailey. **Educ:** Sandroyd School, Cobham; Rugby School. Died 11 September 1998.

HUNTER, Oscar Geldert (1926) Born 23 December 1907, Victoria Road, Darlaston, Staffordshire; son of Thomas Geldert Hunter, Commercial Clerk, and Emma Child. **Subject(s):** Classics; BA 1929; MA 1933. **Tutor(s):** M P Charlesworth. **Educ:** Hillary Street Council School, Walsall; Queen Mary's Grammar School, Walsall. **Career:** Deloitte Haskins & Sells Chartered Accountants (Partner 1952) until 1980.

HUNTER, Robert Stuart (1932) Born 27 August 1914, 56 Bentinck Street, Glasgow; son of Thomas Macmillan Hunter, Civil Engineer, and Mary Isabella Moody-Stuart; m Mary Henderson Cameron, 8 October 1949, Colinton Parish Church, Edinburgh; 2 sons (Gavin Stuart Cameron b 1953 and David Dickson b 1956), 1 daughter (Alison Mary b 1950). **Subject(s):** Mathematics/Law; BA 1935. **Tutor(s):** J M Wordie. **Educ:** Glasgow Academy. **Career:** Senior Partner, Kerr, McLeod and McFarlane 1973–1974; Partner in Charge, Deloitte's, Glasgow, and Member, Central Policy Committee 1974–1980. **Appointments:** Member, Institute of Chartered Accountants of Scotland 1940 (member, Ethics Committee). **Awards:** Scholarship, SJC 1935. Died 30 April 2003.

HUNTER, William Clayton (1927) Born 3 October 1908, 14 Broad Walk, Buxton, Derby; son of Robert Forgie Hunter, Photographic Dealer, and Maud May Clayton. **Subject(s):** History/English; BA 1930. **Tutor(s):** E A Benians. **Educ:** Buxton Council School; Lady Manners School, Bakewell; Sutton Valence School.

HUNTLEY, John Guy Henderson (1927) Born 7 November 1908, The Vicarage, Lund, Beverley, Yorkshire; son of Arthur Henderson Huntley, Clerk in Holy Orders, and Edith Mary Young. **Subject(s):** Natural Sciences; BA 1930. **Tutor(s):** J M Wordie. **Johnian Relatives:** son of Arthur Henderson Huntley (1890). **Educ:** High School, Hull; Hymers College, Hull; Maisons Lafitte, French Cours; Harvey's Preparatory School, Paris; Forest School, Walthamstow. **Career:** Crosse & Blackwell Ltd; later C & E Morton Ltd; Metal Box Company. Died 13 March 1954.

HURDMAN, Cyril (1915) Born 1 June 1896, 76 Newbridge Street, Wolverhampton, Staffordshire; son of George Edward Hurdman, Builder, and Eleanor Thomas. **Tutor(s):** L H K Bushe-Fox. **Educ:** St Jude's Church of England School, Wolverhampton; Wolverhampton Grammar School. **Career:** Commission, South Staffordshire Regiment, later with Royal Warwickshire Regiment 1915–1916. **Awards:** Scholarship, SJC 1914. Died 20 July 1916 (killed in action).

HURLL, John Patrick (1922) Born 31 October 1902, 5 Pitt Street, Edinburgh, Scotland; son of Hugh Beckett Hurll, Bank Agent, and Isabel Hurll. **Subject(s):** History; BA 1925. **Tutor(s):** E A Benians. **Educ:** Clifton Bank School, St Andrews; Sedbergh School. **Awards:** Exhibition, SJC 1922.

HURRELL, Arthur (1942) Born 11 May 1924, The Gables, Elswick Road, Newcastle upon Tyne; son of Arthur George Hurrell, Motor Engineer, and Esther Alsop Harrison; m Phyllis June Buckley, 1949; 3 sons, 1 daughter. **Subject(s):** Mechanical Sciences; BA 1945; MA 1949. **Tutor(s):** S J Bailey. **Johnian Relatives:** father of Timothy John Hurrell (1973). **Educ:** Westhill Private School; Bourneville Council School; King Edward's Grammar School, Birmingham; King Edward's High School, Birmingham. **Career:** Assistant Research and Development Engineer, Boulton Aircraft Armament Ltd 1944–1947; Assistant Master, King Edward's School, Birmingham 1947–1953; Senior Mathematics Master, Wallasey Grammar School 1953–1957; Principal, Queen Victoria School, Matavatocu, Suva, Fiji 1958–1960; Assistant Master, Marlborough College 1961–1976; Senior Maths Master, Sixth Form College, Ghana 1977–1979; Senior Lecturer, Mathematics Education, University of Lesotho 1979–1985. **Appointments:** Group Scout Master, King Edward's School 1947–1953; Group Scout Master, Wallasey Grammar School 1953–1957. **Awards:** Sir Joseph Larmor 1944. **Publications:** *Kuksar Conquered* (a booklet about his late son's mountaineering exploits); contributions to School Mathematics Project Publications and Macmillan Boleswa School Mathematics text books.

HURRY, Arthur Gordon (1912) Born 12 September 1893, Abbotsbrook, 43 Castle Road, Reading, Berkshire; son of Jamieson Boyd Hurry, Doctor of Medicine, and Gertrude Louisa Hill; m Rosemary Ingham Pickering, 1 July 1931, Studland Church, Dorset. BA 1918; MA 1924.

Tutor(s): R P Gregory. **Educ:** Hildershalm House School, Broadstairs; Marlborough College. **Career:** Lieutenant, Gloucestershire Regiment, attached to Royal Irish Regiment, WWI; St Bartholomew's Hospital 1933. Died 27 December 1982.

HURST, Dennis George (1944) Born 22 August 1926, California, Winlaton, Blaydon; son of James Hurst, Motor Bus Proprietor, and Marion Nixon. **Tutor(s):** J M Wordie. **Educ:** Winlaton Council School; Scorton Grammar School; Heversham Grammar School.

HURST, Donald Geoffrey (1937) Born 19 March 1911, The Manse, Truro Road, St Austell; son of George Leopold Hurst, Minister of Religion, and Sarah Ellen Inns. **Tutor(s):** J M Wordie. **Educ:** Lower School, Callender, Canada; Lower School, Vernon, Canada; High School, Buckingham, Canada; McGill University, Montreal.

HURST, The Revd Ronald Francis (1906) (initially Non-Collegiate) Born 7 October 1882, 128 Union Road, Oswaldtwistle, Lancashire; son of William Hurst, Director, Insurance Company, and Grace Robinson; m Evelyn Hardy, 13 September 1917. **Subject(s):** Moral Sciences; BA 1908; MA 1913. **Tutor(s):** E E Sikes. **Educ:** St Paul's School, Oswaldtwistle; Ridley Hall, Cambridge. **Career:** Deacon 1909; Curate, St Matthew, Bolton 1909–1911; Priest 1910; Curate, St Andrew, Cleveleys 1911–1912; Curate, St Mary, Crumpsall 1912–1914; Vicar, St Andrew, Cleveleys 1914–1947 (Surrogate from 1935); Temporary CF 1917–1919; Canon of Prestona, Blackburn Cathedral 1946–1949. Died 17 October 1949.

HUSAIN, Akhter (1924) Born 1 March 1902, Burhanpur, Central Provinces, India; son of Mian Bhai Abdul Husain, Indian Civil Service, and Zeynab. **Tutor(s):** E A Benians. **Educ:** Ansumani Islamia School, Damoh; St Joseph's Convent School, Saugor; HCH School, Burhanpur; Mohammedan Anglo Oriental College, Aligarh; Allahabad University; Muslim University, Aligarh.

HUSBAND, Anthony Dearden (1931) Born 8 October 1913, Lahore, India; son of George Staunton Husband, Captain, Indian Medical Service, and Bertha Walker; m Wendy Higgs, 1953. BA 1936; MA 1938; FRCS 1965. **Tutor(s):** M P Charlesworth. **Educ:** Park House, Paignton; Pinewood, Farnborough; Wellington College. **Career:** Conscientious Objector, Friends' Ambulance Unit 1939–1945; Surgeon, El Obeid, Sudan 1945–1965. Died 23 November 1972.

HUSSEY-FREKE, Ambrose Frederick (1929) Born 5 January 1910, Tientsin, North China; son of Frederick Hussey-Freke, Chinese Government Salt Revenue, Shanghai, and Evelyn Margaret Morton; m Mary Georgiana Codrington, 21 October 1950, Wroughton Parish Church, Wiltshire. **Subject(s):** Modern and Medieval Languages/Economics; BA 1932. **Tutor(s):** C W Guillebaud. **Educ:** Preparatory School, Hill Side, Godalming. Died 19 October 1986.

HUSTON, Frank Edward (1918) American Student.

HUTCHINGS, Raymond Francis Dudley (1942) Born 18 November 1924, 19 Valkyrie Road, Westcliff-on-Sea; son of Dudley Albert Hutchings, Senior Assistant, Metropolitan Water Board, and Winifred Alice Bennett. **Subject(s):** Economics; BA 1947; MA 1953. **Tutor(s):** C W Guillebaud. **Educ:** St Mary's PNEU School, Westcliff-on-Sea; Westcliff High School; St Christopher School, Letchworth.

HUTCHINS, Dr Philip Frank (1945) Born 5 July 1927, 43 Talbot Road, Northampton; son of Frank Hutchins, Boot Upper Manufacturer, and Emily Kate Payne. **Subject(s):** Natural Sciences; BA 1948; MA 1952. **Tutor(s):** C W Guillebaud. **Educ:** Stimpson Avenue School, Northampton; Northampton Town and County School. **Career:** Researcher into Sedimentary Petrology, Sedgwick Museum, Cambridge 1949; Petrologist, Cambridge Spitsbergen Expedition 1949. **Awards:** Amy Mary Preston Read Scholarship 1950. Died 2 November 1955.

HUTCHINSON, Arthur Lockwood (1946) Born 28 July 1920, Dufferin Hospital, Calcutta, India; son of Arthur Stanley Hutchinson, Methodist Minister, and Margery Moyle Parkes. **Subject(s):** History; BA 1948. **Tutor(s):** F Thistlethwaite. **Educ:** Altrincham County High School; Woodhouse Grove School, Apperley Bridge; Kingswood School, Bath. **Career:** Articled Chartered Accountant 1938–1940; RN 1940–1946; Foreign Staff, *The Times* 1949–1957; Foreign Duty Editor, Television News 1957–1960; Deputy Editor, *Ten O'Clock News* 1960–1963; Deputy Editor, Current Affairs (Sound), *Panorama* 1963–1964; Head, BBC Secretariat 1964–1967; Foreign News Editor 1967–1969, Head of Talks and Current Affairs Group 1969, BBC; Chief Assistant to the Managing Director, BBC Radio 1973. Died 15 September 1974.

HUTCHINSON, Francis Downes (1904) Born 18 September 1880, Castleton, Newton Heath, Lancashire; son of Thomas William Hutchinson, Clerk in Holy Orders, and Frances Massie. **Tutor(s):** C E Graves; J R Tanner. **Johnian Relatives:** son of Thomas William Hutchinson (1869). **Educ:** St Faith's School, Cambridge.

HUTCHINSON, Professor George William (1939) Born 16 February 1921, Farnsfield, Newark, Nottinghamshire; son of George Hutchinson, Farmer, and Louisa Ethel Saul; m Christine Anne Rymer, 1943 (div 1970); 2 sons. **Subject(s):** Natural Sciences; BA 1942; MA 1946; PhD 1952; FRAS; FRSA. **Tutor(s):** C W Guillebaud. **Johnian Relatives:** father of Patrick Alan Hutchinson (1966). **Educ:** Towyn Council School; Abergele County School. **Career:** Research worker and factory manager, cotton textile industry 1942–1947; Manager, Corsland and Pickstone Ltd, dyers and finishers, Bury, Lancashire 1946–1947; Cavendish Laboratory, Cambridge 1947–1952; Clerk Maxwell Scholarship, University of Cambridge 1949–1952; Nuffield Fellow 1952–1953; Lecturer in Natural Philosophy, University of Glasgow 1953–1955; Research Association of Stanford University, California 1954; Lecturer in Physics 1955–1957, Senior Lecturer in Physics 1957, University of Birmingham; Professor of Physics 1960–1985 (Emeritus 1985), Southampton University. **Appointments:** Member, National Executive Committee, AUT 1978–1984; Member, National Council, Campaign for Nuclear Disarmament 1981–1984; International Secretary, Scientists Against Nuclear Arms 1985–1990; Executive Committee, British Peace Assembly 1988–1992 (Acting Chairman 1990–1992, Chairman 1992); Executive Committee, World Disarmament Campaign UK 1988; Executive Committee, Labour Action for Peace 1990 (Membership Secretary 1992–1997); Visited Chernobyl to see and report on effects of nuclear disaster 1991; Executive of World Disarmament Campaign UK. **Awards:** Duddell Medal, Physical Society 1959. **Publications:** Papers on nuclear and elementary particle physics, nuclear instrumentation and cosmic rays, and disarmament and peace.

HUTCHINSON, Dr Henry Procter (1921) Born 13 June 1903, Burton Latimer, Northamptonshire; son of Edmund Hutchinson, Farmer, and Lydia Mary Davy; m Dolores Mary Durnford, 22 September 1934; 2 sons (David Procter b 1935 and Geoffrey Guy b 1938), 1 daughter (Amanda Mary b 1941). **Subject(s):** Natural Sciences; BA 1926; MA 1931; MB 1931; BChir 1931; MRCS 1929; MRCP 1931; LRCP 1929. **Tutor(s):** B F Armitage. **Johnian Relatives:** brother of Joseph Burtt Hutchinson (1920); uncle of Dennis Procter Hutchinson (1962). **Educ:** Ackworth School, Pontefract; Bootham School, York. **Career:** St Bartholomew's Hospital, London; Private Practice, Haywards Heath. **Awards:** Frank Smart Prize for Zoology, University of Cambridge 1926. Died 19 May 1980.

HUTCHINSON, Professor Sir Joseph Burtt (1920) Born 21 March 1902, Burton Latimer, Northamptonshire; son of Edmund Hutchinson, Farmer, and Lydia Mary Davy; m Martha Leonora Johnson, 1930, Malton, Yorkshire; 1 son (Dennis Procter b 13 June 1943), 1 daughter (Helga Leonora b 21 July 1939). **Subject(s):** Natural Sciences; BA 1923; MA 1931; ScD 1948; Honorary DSc (Nottingham) 1966; Honorary DSc (East Anglia) 1971; FLS 1939; FRS 1951; Foreign FNA 1974. **Tutor(s):** B F Armitage. **Johnian Relatives:** brother of Henry Procter Hutchinson

(1921); father of Dennis Procter Hutchinson (1962). **Educ:** Ackworth School, Pontefract; Bootham School, York; Cambridge School of Agriculture; Imperial College of Tropical Agriculture, Trinidad. **Career:** Assistant Geneticist, Empire Cotton Growing Corporation 1926–1933; Institute of Plant Industry at Indore, Central India 1933–1937; Geneticist for the Empire Cotton Growing Corporation, Trinidad 1937–1944; Lecturer, Imperial College of Tropical Agriculture, Trinidad 1937–1944; Adviser on Cotton to the British Caribbean Governments 1937–1944; Chief Geneticist, Empire Cotton Growing Corporation, Sudan Government Cotton Research Station, Shambat, Khartoum 1944–1947; Director, Cotton Research Station, Namulonge, Uganda 1949–1957; Drapers' Professor of Agriculture, University of Cambridge 1957–1969 (Emeritus 1969); Title C Fellow 1957–1969, Title E Fellow 1969–1988, SJC; Visiting Professor, Indian Agricultural Research Institute 1969–1970. **Appointments:** Member, Governing Body, The Plant Breeding Institute, Cambridge, The John Innes Institute, Norwich, The Friends' School, Saffron Walden, Norfolk Agriculture Station; Chair, Governing Council 1953, and Honorary Fellow 1957, Makerere College, University of East Africa; Member, Nature Conservancy 1960; Trustee, Lucy Cavendish College, Cambridge 1963; President, BAAS 1965–1966. **Awards:** Exhibition, SJC 1920; Queen's Coronation Medal, Uganda 1953; Royal Medal of the Royal Society 1967. **Honours:** CMG 1944; Kt 1956. **Publications:** (with R A Silow and S A Stephens) *Evolution of Gossypium and the Differentiation of the Cultivated Cottons*, OUP, 1947; (ed) *Essays on Crop Plant Evolution*, CUP, 1965; (ed) *Population and Food Supply*, CUP, 1969; *Farming and Food Supply: the Interdependence of Countryside and Town*, CUP, 1972; (ed) *Evolutionary Studies in World Crops*, CUP, 1974; *The Challenge of the Third World* (The Eddington Memorial Lecture delivered at the University of Cambridge, November 1974), CUP, 1975; (with A C Owers) *Change and Innovation in Norfolk Farming*, Packard Publishing, 1980. Died 16 January 1988.

HUTCHINSON, Miles (1944) Born 6 July 1926, Westleigh, Holme-on-Spalding Moor, Yorkshire; son of Miles Hutchinson, Medical Practitioner, and Constance Emily Drury; m Margaret Montgomery, 1954; 1 son (John b 1960). **Subject(s):** Natural Sciences; BA 1947; MA 1951; Post-Graduate Chemical Engineering Diploma (Bradford) 1949–1950. **Tutor(s):** C W Guillebaud. **Educ:** Holme Hall, Holme-on-Spalding Moor; Holme Council School; Bridlington School; Bradford Technical College. **Career:** Sergeant/Instructor, RAEC 1947–1949; Production Management, British Aluminium Company, Smelters Lochaber & Kinlochleven 1950–1966; Chemical Engineer (Technical), British Aluminium Burnt Island Alumina Plant 1966–1988.

HUTCHINSON, Richard Wyatt (1914) Born 22 December 1894, Heswall, Cheshire; son of Arthur Michael Hutchinson, Gentleman, and Evelyn Florence Coffee. **Subject(s):** Classics; BA 1920; MA 1924, FSA; FRAI. **Tutor(s):** E E Sikes. **Educ:** Somerville School, New Brighton; Birkenhead School. **Career:** Second Lieutenant, Labour Corps, France and Belgium 1914–1918; Archaeologist in Mycenae, Knossos, Iraq, Colchester, Traprain Law, Turkey and Poland from 1921; Curator, Villa Ariadne, Knossos, Crete 1934–1947; GHQME, Cairo 1941–1945; Lecturer in Classical Archaeology, Liverpool 1948–1951; Lecturer in Classics, University of Cambridge 1951. **Awards:** Exhibition, SJC; Craven Studentship, University of Cambridge 1921. **Publications:** *Prehistoric Crete*, 1962, Penguin; articles in numerous journals, including 'Two Etruscan Vases', *Annals of Archaeology and Anthropology*, 1930; 'Three Vases in Cambridge: An Attribution to Cyprus', *LAAA* 21, 1934; 'Sipylos and S-P-L-L', *Annales du Service des Antiquites de l'Egypte*, 1942; 'Battle-axes in the Aegean', *PPS* 16, 1950; 'Prehistoric Town Planning in Crete', *TPR* 21, 1950; 'Review of Alexiou (Kretika Chronika 1952)', *Antiquity* 28, 1954; 'A Tholos Tomb on the Kephala', *BSA* 51, 1956; 'A Late Minoan Tomb at Knossos', *BSA* 51, 1956. Died 4 April 1970.

HUTCHISON, Denis Charles (1927) Born 25 April 1909, 9 Wendover Road, Bromley, Kent; son of Stanley Hutchison, Solicitor, and Alice Mabel Holditch. **Subject(s):** Classics/Law; BA 1930; MA 1978. **Tutor(s):** M P Charlesworth. **Educ:** Bickley Park School; Malvern House School;

St Hugh's School, Bickley; Malvern College. **Career:** Solicitor. **Awards:** Scholarship, SJC 1926. Died 1998.

HUTTON, Herman Gardner (1926) Born 12 January 1909, 145 Victoria Road, Headingley, Leeds, Yorkshire; son of Albert Edward Hutton, Physician and Surgeon, and Dorothy Heap. BA 1930. **Tutor(s):** M P Charlesworth. **Educ:** The Grammar School, Leeds; Giggleswick School. Died 1 March 1983.

HUTTON, Professor John Henry (1936) Born 27 June 1885, West Haslerton, Yorkshire; son of Joseph Henry Hutton, Clerk in Holy Orders, and Clarissa Marshall Barwick; m (1) Stella Eleanora Bishop, 1920 (d 1944), (2) Maureen Margaret O'Reilly, 27 June 1946. **Subject(s):** Anthropology; MA (Oxon) 1919; DSc 1924; MA (by incorporation). **Educ:** Leatherhead School; Chigwell Grammar School; Worcester College, Oxford. **Career:** Indian Civil Service 1909–1936; Lecturer in Archaeology and Anthropology 1936–1937, William Wyse Professor of Social Anthropology 1937–1949, University of Cambridge; Fellow, St Catharine's College, Cambridge 1936–1951. **Appointments:** President, Royal Anthropological Institute 1929; Honorary Fellow, St Catharine's College, Cambridge 1951–1968. **Awards:** Rivers Memorial Medal (for fieldwork in the Naga Hills, Assam), Royal Anthropological Institute 1929. **Honours:** CIE 1920. **Publications:** *The Angami Nagas*, Macmillan, 1921; *The Sema Nagas*, Macmilan, 1921; *Diaries of two tours in the unadministered area east of the Naga Hills*, The Asiatic Society of Bengal, 1929; *Report on the Census of India*, 1931; 'An Outline of Chang Grammar', *Journal of the Asiatic Society of Bengal*, Vol 25, 1932; *A Primitive Philosophy of Life* (The Frazer Lecture 1938), Clarendon Press, 1938; *Caste in India: its Nature, Function and Origins*, CUP, 1946. Died 23 May 1968.

HUTTON, Patrick Hamilton (1949) Born 29 March 1930, Woodview, Charlton Avenue, Hersham, Walton on Thames; son of Peter Coats Hutton, Lieutenant Commander, RN, and Mary Hamilton Finch; m Felicity Todhunter; 1 son, 1 daughter. **Subject(s):** English/History; BA 1952; MA 1956; MA (Open University) 1998. **Tutor(s):** A G Lee. **Educ:** The Old Malthouse Preparatory School, Swanage; Winchester College. **Career:** English and History Teacher, King Edward's School, Birmingham 1952–1956; Housemaster, Achimota School, Ghana 1956–1959; Head of English Department, Woolverstone Hall, Inner London Education Authority's Boarding Grammar School, Suffolk 1960–1965; Head of English Department and Librarian, St Paul's School 1965–1969; Headmaster, St Marylebone Grammar School 1970–1978; Headmaster, Wolverhampton Grammar School 1978–1990; Established Hutton Books, Antiquarian and Second Hand Book Dealer, Launceston, Cornwall 1990–2000. **Appointments:** Member, HMC; Committee Member, National Council for Educational Standards; Liveryman, Merchant Taylors' Company 1991.

HUTTON, Percy Granville (1915) Born 20 February 1897, 81 Clyde Road, Didsbury, Withington, Manchester, Lancashire; son of William Percy Hutton, Wesleyan Minister, and Annie Anderson Rowson; m Wilhemina Beatrice Helen Laar, 14 February 1949. **Subject(s):** Law; BA 1921; LLB 1921. **Tutor(s):** E E Sikes. **Educ:** Arnold House School, Blackpool; Kingswood School, Bath. **Awards:** Dowman Sizarship, SJC 1915. Died 1 March 1983.

HUTTON, The Revd Robert Jermyn (1908) Born 12 February 1889, Newlands, Ridgway, Eckington, Derbyshire; son of John Jermyn Hutton, Scythe and Sickle Manufacturer, and Anna Sophia Simmons. BA 1911; MA 1920. **Tutor(s):** J R Tanner. **Educ:** Pocklington School; Cambridge Clergy Training School. **Career:** 1911; Deacon 1912; Curate, Christ Church, Ashton under Lyne 1912–1919; Priest 1913; Curate, Repton with Foremark 1919–1924; Perpetual Curate, Totley, Sheffield 1924. Died May 1947.

HUTTON, Thomas Blythe (1932) Born 28 May 1914, 275 Burley Road, Leeds; son of Frank Walter Hutton, Estate Manager, and Annie Blythe;

m Dorothy Cheshire, 2 sons. **Subject(s):** Natural Sciences; BA 1935; MA 1941; MB 1941; BChir 1941; FRCS 1947; FRCSE 1947; DLO. **Tutor(s):** C W Guillebaud. **Johnian Relatives:** son-in-law of Francis Moreton Cheshire (1906); brother-in-law of Albert White Cheshire (1939). **Educ:** Headingly Hill School, Leeds; The Grammar School, Leeds. **Career:** Assistant, Ear, Throat and Nose Department, St Thomas' Hospital; House Surgeon, St Thomas' Hospital 1936; Major, RAMC 1941–1945; First ENT consultant Wakefield Group Hospitals 1950–1970; Consultant Surgeon. **Honours:** ED. Died 16 August 1995.

HUTTON, Thomas Edward (1939) Born 10 January 1921, King Straithe Square, Kings Lynn; son of Thomas Oswald Powell Hutton, Physician, and Doris Field. **Tutor(s):** R L Howland. **Educ:** Barber's Preparatory School, Hunstanton; Aldeburgh Lodge; Shrewsbury School. **Career:** RN, WWII; Shell Oil; Chief Executive, Total. **Appointments:** Non-executive Director of British Rail; numerous other directorships. Died 10 October 2000.

HUXLEY, Professor Herbert Henry (1935) Born 29 July 1916, 15 Hazel Avenue, Brooklands, Cheshire; son of Henry Huxley, Engineer, and Amy Bland; m (1) Joan Mary Peers, 30 August 1941, Wesley Church, Cambridge, (2) Margaret Elizabeth Cox, 23 August 1975, Beckley, Sussex. **Subject(s):** Classics; BA 1939; MA 1942; MA (TCD) 1961. **Tutor(s):** R L Howland. **Johnian Relatives:** father of Martin Neil Huxley (1962). **Educ:** Manchester Grammar School; St Mary Magdalene's School, Ashton on Mersey; Sale High School, Brooklands; TCD. **Career:** Royal Army Pay Corps; Classical Master, Elizabeth College, Guernsey (evacuated to Buxton); Classical Master Worksop College, Nottinghamshire; Assistant Lecturer in Latin, University of Leeds 1944; Senior Lecturer in Latin 1951, Reader in Latin 1963, University of Manchester; Professor of Classics, University of Victoria, Vancouver Island, British Columbia 1968; Senior Leave Fellowship by the Canada Council 1970–1971. **Appointments:** Life Fellow, Internationales Institut für Kunstwissenschaften (Geneva and Zurich) 1961; Visiting Professor, University College 1971; Fellow, Fondazlone "Latinitas" (Vatican) 1977; Visiting Fellow, St Cross College, Oxford 1978; Visiting Fellow, St Edmund's House, Lent and Easter Term 1980; President, Virgil Society 1992–1994; Fellow, International Institute of Arts and Letters (Geneva). **Awards:** Exhibition, SJC; Scholarship, SJC 1937. **Publications:** Contributed an Alcaic Ode in praise of Horace for Niall Rudd's *Two thousand years alive: Essays for Horace's Bimillennium*, Bristol Classical Press, 1993; (with F J Lelievre) *Across Bin Brook*, 1993.

HUXTABLE, The Revd Michael George (1947) Born 23 April 1929, Mornington, Dean Lane, Weeke, Winchester; son of Kenneth Huxtable, Dental Surgeon, and Audrey Sybil Hill; m Barbara Mary Barclay Lyon, 11 April 1958, St Mary Magdalene, Milton, Hampshire; 2 sons (Christopher b 1961 and Peter b 1968), 2 daughters (Janet b 1959 and Helen b 1964). **Subject(s):** Natural Sciences; BA 1950; MA 1954. **Tutor(s):** G C L Bertram. **Johnian Relatives:** brother-in-law of Ian Barclay Lyon (1947). **Educ:** Horris Hill, Newbury; Marlborough College. **Career:** Assistant Master, Sedbergh School 1950–1954; Assistant Master, Wellington College, Berkshire 1954–1977; Director of Music, Chafyn Grove School, Salisbury 1977–1981; Physics Teacher, South Wiltshire Grammar School for Girls 1981–1983; Head of Physics, Royal Naval School, Haslemere 1984–1989; Reader, Church of England, St Paul's Church, Salisbury 1984–1990; Ordained Deacon, Non-Stipendiary Minister, licensed to St Paul's 1990; Priest, St Paul's, Salisbury 1991–2001.

HYAMS, Alexander (1902) Born 11 January 1884, Warsaw, Russia; son of David Hyams, Veterinarian, and Rose Zenenoff; 2 sons (Maurice Arnold and Cecil Francis). **Subject(s):** Natural Sciences; BA 1905; MA 1911. **Tutor(s):** C E Graves; J R Tanner. **Educ:** City of London School; Gravel Lane School, Houndsditch. **Career:** Corporation Road Classical School, Newport 1905–1912; Municipal Secondary School, Newport 1912–1944.

HYATT, John Hampden (1949) Born 12 June 1928, Heatherwood, Heathdene Road, Wallington, Surrey; son of Kenneth Edwin Hyatt, Civil Engineer, and Olive Guthrie; m Cynthia Mary Stevenson, 19 May 1962, Flamstead, Hertfordshire; 1 son (Michael John Guthrie b 1963), 2 daughters (Juliet Mary b 1964 and Susan Joanna b 1967). **Subject(s):** Engineering; BA 1952; MICE 1957; MNZIE 1967–1974. **Tutor(s):** R L Howland. **Educ:** PNEU School, Wallington; Hollingbury Court Preparatory School, Brighton; Cressbrook Preparatory School, Kirkby Lonsdale; Sedbergh School. **Career:** Civil Engineering Contractors, Dorman Long and Taylor Woodrow, John Howard & Co Ltd 1952–1966; Consulting Engineers, Freeman, Fox and Partners and Mekong Secretariat (United Nations), Thailand 1966–1990; Resident Engineer in charge of construction supervision (major projects included the Forth Road Bridge, Scotland, Auckland Harbour Bridge, New Zealand, The M5 Motorway in Somerset, The Humber Bridge, First Stage Expressway in Bangkok, Thailand, and the Huai Mong Irrigation Project). **Appointments:** Chairman, Society of Professional Engineers, Thailand 1978–1980. **Publications:** 'The Construction of the Din Daeng to Port Section of the First Stage Expressway System in Bangkok', *The Institution of Civil Engineers Proceedings Part I*, May 1983.

HYDE, Edgar Stanley (1923) Born 6 February 1906, 59 Newmarket Road, Waterloo, Ashton under Lyne, Lancashire; son of Harry Hyde, Wholesale Druggist and Drysalter, and Mary Jane Clarke. **Subject(s):** Natural Sciences; BA 1926; MA 1930. **Tutor(s):** B F Armitage. **Educ:** Manchester Grammar School; Sedbergh School. **Career:** Indian Civil Service 1947; Secretary, ICI 1947–1964; Fine Arts Dealer; Director of Manning Galleries Ltd, London 1966. **Appointments:** Chairman, Upper Mersey Navigation Commission. Died 10 May 1981.

HYDE, Dr Ernest William (1934) Born 8 January 1916, 10 Massey Road, Gloucester; son of William George Hyde, Flour Mill Manager, and Elsie Maud Smith; m Vera. **Subject(s):** Natural Sciences; BA 1937; MA 1941; BChir 1941; MB 1941; LRCP; DMR; MRCS. **Tutor(s):** R L Howland. **Educ:** Crypt School, Gloucester. **Career:** Middlesex Hospital; Radiologist, Derby 1941–1946; Radiologist, Gloucestershire Royal Infirmary and Eye Institution; Consultant Radiologist, Gloucestershire Royal Hospital 1946–1976. Died 1 October 1988.

HYDE, Ronald Harry Picton (1931) Born 6 October 1912, 7 Taunton Road, Ashton-Under-Lyne; son of Sir Harry Hyde, Chairman of Lancashire County Council, and Mary Jane Clarke; m Joan. **Subject(s):** History; BA 1934. **Tutor(s):** E A Benians. **Educ:** Smallwood Manor School; Sedbergh School. **Career:** Reporter, *Daily Express*, Manchester 1934–1939; Assistant News Editor, *Evening Standard* 1939–1940; News Editor, *Evening Standard* 1940–1972. **Awards:** Lupton and Hebblethwaite Exhibition, SJC. **Honours:** OBE 1971. Died 11 July 1995.

HYDE, Ronald William (1907) Born 11 August 1888, 11 Tackley Place, Saint Giles', Oxford; son of Alfred Hyde, Bank Manager, Cambridge, and Alice Mary White. **Tutor(s):** E E Sikes. **Educ:** Private Tuition. **Career:** Captain, Lincolnshire Regiment, later attached General Staff, Indian Army, then ADC, WWI.

HYNES, Dr Martin (1929) Born 11 January 1911, 220 Victoria Avenue, Hull; son of Martin Hynes, Farmer, and Mary Priestly; m (1) May Charlton, 13 May 1948, Nottingham, (2) Jean Lawson, 1963, London; (2) 2 sons. **Subject(s):** Natural Sciences; BA 1932; MB 1935; BChir 1935; MD 1938; FRCP 1957; MRCS 1935; FCPath 1964; LRCP (London) 1935. **Tutor(s):** M P Charlesworth. **Educ:** George Dixon's School, Birmingham; Beverley Grammar School; Middlesex Hospital. **Career:** Clinical Pathologist, Royal Northern Hospital; Clinical Pathologist, King Edward VII Hospital for Officers; Clinical Pathologist, Manor House Hospital; Reader in Medicine, University of Cambridge 1946–1950. **Appointments:** Examiner, Pathology Conjoint Board; Member, Association of Physicians, Great Britain; Member, Association of Clinical Pathologists; Eunice Oaks Research Fellow. **Honours:** MVO 1979. **Publications:** *Medical Bacteriology*, 8th Edition, 1964; *Diseases of the Blood*, Chamberlain's *Textbook of Medicine*, 1952; various papers on haemotology and bacteriology. Died 13 November 2000.

HYSLOP, James (1921) Born 13 November 1894, 84 Loreburn Street, Dumfries, Scotland; son of James Hyslop, Solicitor, and Margaret McKenzie. PhD 1925; MA (Glasgow); FRSE 1927. **Tutor(s):** E A Benians. **Educ:** St Michael Street School, Dumfries; The Academy, Dumfries; Glasgow University. **Career:** Lecturer in Mathematics, Glasgow. Died 17 November 1942.

I

IBRAHIM, Ahmad bin Mohamed (1936) Born 15 May 1916, Singapore; son of Mohamed Ibrahim bin Shaick Ismail, Medical Practitioner, and Hamidah binte Shaick Baboo. **Subject(s):** Economics/Law; BA 1939; MA 1962; BA (London) in Singapore 1935. **Tutor(s):** C W Guillebaud. **Educ:** St Anthony's Boys' School, Singapore; Victoria Bridge School, Singapore; Raffles Institution, Singapore; Raffles College, Singapore. **Career:** Ambassador to Egypt; Deputy Rector, International Islamic University; Lecturer in Law, Raffles University College 1947; Advocate-General, Singapore 1948–1953; Attorney-General, Singapore 1963–1967; Dean, Law Faculty, University of Malaya 1972; Dean, Law Faculty and Co-founder, International Islamic University 1983. **Awards:** Exhibition, SJC 1937; Wright's Prize, SJC 1937; George Long Prize, University of Cambridge 1938; Certificate of Honour at the Middle Temple Bar Finals; Tokoh Ma'al Hijrah Award 1988. **Publications:** Over 30 titles on Family and Islamic law and administration including: *Islamic Law in Malaya*, 1965; *Family Law*, 1999. Died 17 April 1999.

ILES, Gordon Butler (1927) Born 18 August 1908, Durdham, Granville Road, Sidcup, Kent; son of John Henry Iles, Newspaper Proprietor, and Eleanor Marion Bird; m (d April 1983). BA 1933; MA 1936. **Tutor(s):** M P Charlesworth. **Johnian Relatives:** brother of John Bird Iles (1925). **Educ:** St Dunstan's Preparatory School, Burnham; St Bede's, Eastbourne; Marlborough College. **Career:** Special Effects, J Arthur Rank Organisation; Founder, Artona Music Roll Company, Ramsgate; Chief UK Theoretician and Designer, Aeolian Company 1930–1938; Instructor and Wing Commander, RAF 1938. Died 1 August 1983.

ILES, John Bird (1925) Born 4 March 1907, Durdham, Granville Road, Foots Cray, Kent; son of John Henry Iles, Newspaper Proprietor, and Eleanor Marion Bird. BA 1928; MA 1955; AA Diploma; ARIBA. **Tutor(s):** E E Sikes. **Johnian Relatives:** brother of Gordon Butler Iles (1927). **Educ:** St Dunstan's, Burnham; St Bede's School, Eastbourne; Marlborough College. **Career:** Architect. Died 3 January 1985.

ILIFFE, John Kenneth (1949) Born 18 September 1931; son of George Kenneth Iliffe, Supervisor, Cable and Wireless Ltd, and Doris Howard Thompson; m Dorothy Bannister, 1955. **Subject(s):** Mathematics; BA 1952; MA 1957. **Tutor(s):** J M Wordie; J R Bambrough. **Educ:** Church School, Crosthwaite, Kendal; Parmiter's School; Chingford County High School; City of London School. **Career:** Computer Engineering, Rice Institute 1958–1961; Commercial Research and Development, Ferranti and ICL 1961–1981; Professor of Information Systems, London University 1981–1986; Computer Design Consultant 1986–1996. **Appointments:** Visiting Professor, Stanford, Syracuse, London, UC Davis and Rice University (formerly the Rice Institute). **Awards:** Major Scholarship, SJC 1948; Harry Goode Memorial Medal 2000, IEEE Computer Society. **Publications:** *Basic Machine Principles*, Macdonald-Elsevier, 1972; *Advanced Computer Design*, Prentice-Hall, 1982.

ILITCH, Milorad (1946) Born 27 September 1922, Belgrade, Yugoslavia; son of Sima Ilitch, Professor, Skin Diseases, and Draginja Nikolitch. **Tutor(s):** G C L Bertram. **Educ:** Gymnasium in Belgrade.

IMAM, Syed Naqui (1923) Born 30 August 1902, Naura, Patna, India; son of Ali Omam, Prime Minister, Nizam's Government, Hyderabad; m Aziza. **Subject(s):** Law; BA 1926; MA 1948. **Tutor(s):** E A Benians.

Educ: Oxford Preparatory School; Leighton Park School, Reading; Private Tuition; University of Manchester. Died 5 February 1959.

INABA, Naomichi (1922) Born 22 March 1900, Tokyo, Japan; son of Viscount Masamichi Inaba, Imperial Court of Japan, and Viscountess C Sakai. **Tutor(s):** E A Benians. **Educ:** Seisoku Middle School, Tokyo, Japan.

INABA, Viscount Masayashi (1927) Born 14 January 1906, son of Viscount Masanao Inaba, Master of Ceremonies, Imperial Court of Japan, and Viscountess Kazuko Inaba. BA 1930. **Tutor(s):** C W Guillebaud. **Johnian Relatives:** son of Masanao Inaba (1887). **Educ:** Private Tuition, Beckhythe, Overstrand; Morning Star School, Kojimachi, Tokyo, Japan.

INCE, Cecil Raymond Sidney (1935) Born 20 August 1916, Llanberis, Hazelwood Lane, Southgate, Middlesex; son of Sidney John Ince, Brewer's Bookkeeper, Gunner, RGA, and Catherine Margaret Griffiths; m Elizabeth. **Subject(s):** Mathematics; BA 1938; MA 1942; CEng, MIEE. **Tutor(s):** J M Wordie. **Educ:** The Convent School, Grays; Palmers School, Grays. **Appointments:** Chairman, Great Baddow Parish Church Council 1973; Chelmsford District Councillor 1973. Died 2 May 1985.

INCE, Charles Augustus (1942) Born 7 May 1923, Maternity Home, 62 Caeran Road, Newport, Monmouthshire; son of Harold David Ince, Jeweller, and Helen Mary Gaccon. **Subject(s):** Economics; BA 1948; MA 1950. **Tutor(s):** C W Guillebaud. **Educ:** The Choristers' School, Exeter; Monmouth School.

INCE, Ralph Edward (1924) Born 12 May 1905, 46 Eastern Road, Romford, Essex; son of Herbert Arthur Ince, Clerk to the Corporation of the City of London, and Mary Effie Carter. **Subject(s):** Mathematics; BA 1927; MA 1931. **Tutor(s):** J M Wordie. **Educ:** Salisbury Road Council School; Brentwood School. **Career:** Colonial Education Service, Malaya/Federated Malay States 1927; Director of Education, Singapore, until 1957. Died 10 July 1996.

INGRAM, William Mark (1936) Born 12 July 1918, Grammar School House, Kimbolton, Huntingdonshire; son of William Ingram, Schoolmaster, and Lucy Annie Miller-Inglis. **Subject(s):** Economics; BA 1939; MA 1943. **Tutor(s):** C W Guillebaud. **Educ:** Kimbolton School.

INKSETTER, James Gibson (1934) Born 28 July 1912, Hamilton, Ontario, Canada; son of George Addison Inksetter, Coffee Planter, and Marion Gibson; m Margaret Jane McCracken, 22 June 1941; 1 son (Tom), 1 daughter (Janet). **Subject(s):** English; BA 1936. **Tutor(s):** J S Boys Smith. **Educ:** Bennett High School, Buffalo; Yale University. **Career:** Department of Highways, Ontario, Canada 1941–1963. Died 25 October 1963.

INNES, Alexander (1928) Born 6 April 1910, 21 Grange Road, Edinburgh, Scotland; son of Peter David Innes, Chief Education Officer, Birmingham, and Maybelle Annie Stewart Wright; m Mary Christopher; 4 children. **Subject(s):** Natural Sciences; BA 1931; MA 1935; BChir 1935; MB 1938; FRCS. **Tutor(s):** M P Charlesworth. **Johnian Relatives:** father of Christopher David Innes (1989). **Educ:** Streatham Hill High School; West House Preparatory School, Edgbaston; King Edward VI School, Birmingham. **Career:** House Posts, St Bartholomew's Hospital; Surgical Registrar, Birmingham; Surgeon, Emergency Medical Service Hospitals 1940–1945; RAMC, India and Japan 1945–1947; Assistant Surgeon, then Consultant, United Birmingham Hospital 1947–1975. **Appointments:** President, CU Medical Society; Honorary Secretary and President, Moynihan Surgical Club; President, Association of Surgeons of Great Britain and Ireland; Fellow, British Orthopaedic Association; Member, Court of Examiners, Royal College of Surgeons; Vice-President, Medical Defence Union. **Awards:** Wright's Prize, SJC; Walsham and Brackenbury Prizes, St Bartholomew's; Senior Science Scholarship, St Bartholomew's. **Honours:** MBE. Died 11 October 1986.

INNS, Frederic Cutts (1937) Born 13 December 1917, Beryl Cottage, Station Road, Brimington; son of Charles Harold Inns, Branch Manager, Coke Oven Company, and Constance Cutts; m Rita. **Subject(s):** Modern and Medieval Languages; BA 1940; MA 1944. **Tutor(s):** C W Guillebaud. **Educ:** Brimington Central School; Chesterfield Grammar School. Died 21 February 1992.

INSTANCE, Michael Courage (1945) Born 3 June 1927, Madras, India; son of Arthur Louis Instance, Lieutenant, RINR, and Edith Stella Ziphen Courage. **Tutor(s):** J M Wordie. **Educ:** Belmont School, Falmouth; Exeter School.

IRELAND, William Francis (1906) Born 17 May 1887, 36 Hardington Road, West Derby, Lancashire; son of Francis Ireland, Clerk in Holy Orders, and Jessie Lyon. **Subject(s):** Classics; BA 1909; MA 1913. **Tutor(s):** E E Sikes. **Educ:** Clive House, Southport; Uppingham School. **Career:** Master, Mourne Grange, Kilkeel, County Down 1910; Ordained Deacon 1911; Ordained Priest 1912.

IREMONGER, Edward Victor (1905) Born 21 June 1887, The Yews, Norwood, Hayes, Middlesex; son of Edward Iremonger, Private Tutor, and Fanny West. **Subject(s):** Classics; BA 1908. **Tutor(s):** J R Tanner. **Educ:** Christ's Hospital. **Career:** Assistant Master, Ilkley Grammar School 1908–1909; Assistant Master, Bishop's College Preparatory School, Lennoxville, Quebec 1909–1915; Private, Universities and Public Schools Battalion, 21st Royal Fusiliers 1915; 9th Royal Fusiliers 1916; POW 1918. **Awards:** Goldsmith's Exhibition; Exhibition, SJC. **Honours:** Vellum Certificate for gallantry in the field 1917. Died 12 or 13 September 1918 (died in German hands at Le Quesnoy).

IRESON, Norman Wilfred (1943) Born 22 May 1924, Yarwell, Northamptonshire; son of Wilfrid Ireson, Bricklayer and Stone Mason, and Maria Billard. **Subject(s):** Economics; BA 1949; MA 1954. **Tutor(s):** C W Guillebaud. **Educ:** Yarwell Elementary School; Laxton Grammar School. **Appointments:** RAF Cadet, SJC.

IRVIN, Charles Watkinson (1930) Born 5 June 1912, West Road, Peterhead, Aberdeenshire, Scotland; son of Thomas William Irvin, Fish Salesman, and Christiana Leech-Watkinson; 2 sons. **Subject(s):** Mechanical Sciences; BA 1933. **Tutor(s):** E A Benians. **Educ:** Tynemouth School; The Leys School, Cambridge. **Career:** Daimler-Benz Works, Germany; Assistant Designer (later Chief Technical Adviser), Wallsend Slipway and Engineering Company 1938–1964; Major, RE 1939–1945. **Appointments:** Member, Tynemouth Branch, United Nations Association; Freemason. Died 16 July 1964.

IRVING, John Christopher (1907) Born 24 June 1888, Crowthorne, Sandhurst, Berkshire; son of Alexander Irving, Clerk in Holy Orders, and Elizabeth Susanna Percy. BA 1910. **Tutor(s):** J R Tanner. **Johnian Relatives:** brother of Percy Alexander Irving (1906). **Educ:** Trent College, Derbyshire. **Career:** Second Lieutenant, RGA, WWI; Journalist, Lincoln 1940. Died 25 November 1941.

IRVING, Percy Alexander (1906) Born 22 January 1885, Wellington College, Sandhurst, Berkshire; son of Alexander Irving, Clerk in Holy Orders, and Elizabeth Susanna Percy; m Anne Seatle Huddleston, 17 November 1941. BA 1909; MA 1921. **Tutor(s):** J R Tanner. **Johnian Relatives:** brother of John Christopher Irving (1907). **Educ:** Felsted School; UCL; KCL. **Career:** Second Lieutenant, then Lieutenant, Bedfordshire Regiment, later Captain, RE (Special Brigade) (wounded), WWI. Died 21 April 1961.

IRWIN, Captain William Livingstone (1903) Born 19 July 1884, The Manse, Bray, County Wicklow, Ireland; son of Charles Huston Irwin, Presbyterian Minister, and Jane Anderson Adams; m Margaret Tyson, 2 November 1940, Brighton. **Tutor(s):** D MacAlister. **Educ:** Dulwich College. **Career:** Captain, the Manchester Regiment 1940.

ISPAHANI, Mirza Abol Hassan (1920) Born 1902, Madras, India; son of Mirza Mohamed Ispahani, Merchant, and Sakeena Sultan; m (1) Ameneh Sultan Shushtary, 1930, (2) Ghamar Azimi, 1954; (1) 2 sons (Mirza Mohamed b 9 February 1931 and Mirza Zia b 19 September 1938), 1 daughter (Iran b 16 August 1932). **Subject(s):** Economics/Law; BA 1923; MA 1927; LLB 1923. **Tutor(s):** E A Benians. **Johnian Relatives:** father of Mirza Mohamed Ispahani (1949); uncle of Mirza Mohamed Ali Ispahani (1949) and of Shahpur Shirazi (1953). **Educ:** Vepery Convent, India; St Mary's European High School, India. **Career:** Called to the Bar, Inner Temple 1924; Family Business, M M Ispahani Ltd, Calcutta 1924, later Director; First Ambassador of Pakistan to the UN and the USA 1947–1952; High Commissioner of Pakistan in London 1952–1954; Minister of Industry and Commerce, Government of Pakistan 1954–1955; First Ambassador of Pakistan to the USA; formed, with his brother, Pakistan International Airlines. **Appointments:** Member, Calcutta City Corporation 1933–1935 and 1940; Elected to the Bengal Legislature 1937–1947; Deputy Mayor, Calcutta 1941–1942; Member, Working Committee, All-India Muslim League; Member, Indian Constituent Assembly. **Honours:** MBE 1944. **Publications:** *Quaid-e-Azam as I knew him*; *Jinnah – Ispahani Correspondence*; *27 Days in China*; *Leningrad to Samarkand*. Died 18 November 1981.

ISPAHANI, Mirza Mohamed (1949) Born 9 February 1931, Bombay; son of Mirza Abul Hassan Ispahani, Ambassador of Pakistan to the US, and Ameneh Sultan Shushtary; m (1) 1958 (dis 1973), (2) Shobha, 1995; (1) 1 son (Mirza Iraj b 22 November 1960), 3 daughters (Mahnaz b 3 January 1959, Farahnaz b 16 July 1963 and Lalehnaz b 31 March 1966), (2) 1 stepdaughter (Alizeh b 25 May 1986). BA 1952; MA 1956. **Tutor(s):** C W Guillebaud. **Johnian Relatives:** son of Mirza Abol Hassan Ispahani (1920); cousin of Mirza Mohamed Ali Ispahani (1949) and of Shahpur Shirazi (1953). **Educ:** St Xavier's College, Calcutta; La Matiniere, Lucknow; St Xavier's College, Calcutta; St Paul's School, Darjeeling. **Career:** Chairman, M M Ispahani Ltd, Pakistan (Family business). **Appointments:** Member, Hawks Club; Member, Eagles.

ISPAHANI, Mirza Mohamed Ali (1949) Born 23 July 1931, Bangalore, India; son of Mirza Mohmood Ispahani, Merchant, and Fatimah Sultan Kazerooni; m Ameneh Khaleeli, 1958; 1 son (Emaad b 1977), 1 daughter (Mariam b 1969). **Tutor(s):** C W Guillebaud. **Johnian Relatives:** nephew of Mirza Abol Hassan Ispahani (1920); cousin of Mirza Mohamed Ispahani (1949). **Educ:** St Xavier's College, Calcutta; La Martiniere, Lucknow; St Xavier's College, Calcutta. **Career:** Director, Ispahani Group of Companies, Bangladesh and Pakistan.

IVES, Arthur Lionel (1921) Born 9 October 1904, The Grange, Roundhay, Leeds, Yorkshire; son of Alfred Edward Ives, Company Director, and Beatrice Caroline Hill; m (1) Daphne (d 3 April 1953). BA (Downing) 1925; MA (Downing) 1929. **Tutor(s):** E A Benians. **Educ:** St George's Preparatory School, Roundhay; Rossal Preparatory School; Rossal School; Downing College, Cambridge.

IVES, Edward Kenneth (1926) Born 8 October 1907, Laural Bank, Guisely, Yorkshire; son of John Harry Ives, Woollen Manufacturer, and Emily Braithwaite. **Tutor(s):** J M Wordie. **Johnian Relatives:** brother of John Bapty Ives (1921); cousin of James Ives (1922). **Educ:** Clifton School, Harrogate; St Peter's School, Harrogate. **Career:** Woollen Manufacturer. Died 1968.

IVES, Francis Wilson Ernest (1926) Born 18 July 1908, St Saviour's Vicarage, Arkwright Street, Nottingham; son of William Ernest Ives, Clerk in Holy Orders, and Adelaide Emily Wilson. BA 1929; MA 1945. **Tutor(s):** M P Charlesworth. **Educ:** Clifton College.

IVES, Captain James (1922) Born 18 February 1904, Nutley, Rawdon, Yorkshire; son of Charles Albert Ives, Woollen Manufacturer, and Frances Alice Beecroft; m Dorothy. **Tutor(s):** E A Benians. **Johnian Relatives:** cousin of John Bapty Ives (1921); cousin of Edward Kenneth Ives (1926). **Educ:** Bamcote, Scarborough; Shrewsbury School. **Career:** Director, Family Woollen Firm; Captain Heavy Anti-Aircraft Battery, RA, TA. Died 6 January 1944 (died on active service).

IVES, John Bapty (1921) Born 30 July 1902, Oxford Road, Guisley, Yorkshire; son of John Harry Ives, Woollen Manufacturer, and Emily Braithwaite. BA 1924; MA 1928. **Tutor(s):** E A Benians. **Johnian Relatives:** cousin of James Ives (1922); brother of Edward Kenneth Ives (1926). **Educ:** Friends' School, Rawdon; Clifton House School, Harrogate; Sedbergh School; Stramongate School, Kendal. Died 19 January 1985.

IVILL, John (1948) Born 7 May 1928, 393 Aimsworth Road, Radcliffe, Lancashire; son of John Ivill, Shopkeeper, and Margaret Boardman; m Audrey Marie Hart, March 1955; 1 son (Richard), 2 daughters (Jennifer and Penelope). **Subject(s):** Modern and Medieval Languages; BA 1950; MA 1955. **Tutor(s):** C W Guillebaud. **Educ:** Whitefield Council School; Stand Grammar School, Whitefield. **Career:** Founder and Managing Director, H & B Wire Fabrications Ltd.

IVORY, James Harvey Trevithick (1939) Born 9 February 1921, Singapore, Straits Settlements; son of George Harry Ivory, Chartered Civil Engineer, and Ethel Irene Trevithick; m Daphne Marion Amelia Winnett, 18 November 1954; 1 son (John Bruce b 1959, d 1979), 1 daughter (Georgina Ann b 1956). **Subject(s):** Mechanical Sciences; BA 1947; MA 1949; FICE. **Tutor(s):** S J Bailey; R L Howland. **Educ:** Finnart Preparatory School, Newquay, Cornwall; Plymouth College. **Career:** Sapper/Cadet/Subaltern, RE 1940–1946; Assistant 1948–1952, Partner 1952–1958, Sole Principal 1958–1968, GH Ivory & Partners, Civil Engineering Consultants; Head of Technical Contracts, Oil Consortium, Tehran, Iran 1970–1972; Civil Engineering Consultant 1972–1977.

IYENGAR, Omeo (1918) Born 17 June 1900, Bangalore, India; son of R Iyengar, Superintendent, Opthalmic Hospital, and Herone Sen. **Subject(s):** Mathematics. **Tutor(s):** E E Sikes. **Educ:** Bishop Cotton School, Bangalore; Mill Hill School. Died 27 February 1922.

J

JACKLIN, James Valentine (1911) Born 17 July 1891, Northfields, Bassingbourn, Cambridge; son of Arnold James Jacklin, Builder, and Ellen Sarah Jennings. **Tutor(s):** J R Tanner. **Educ:** Hitchin Grammar School. **Career:** Captain, Essex Regiment, WWI. Died 11 January 1953.

JACKSON, Arthur David (1942) Born 27 July 1923, Coniston, Whitefield Road, Solihull, Birmingham; son of Stanley George Jackson, Pin Manufacturer, and Hilda Cross; m Helen Viola Palmqust, 1944; 1 daughter (Lynne Milburn). **Subject(s):** Mathematics; BA 1947; MA 1949; ACIS. **Tutor(s):** S J Bailey. **Educ:** Solihull School. **Career:** Managing Director, Newey Group Limited 1988. **Awards:** Major Scholarship, SJC 1941. Died 5 May 2002.

JACKSON, Charles Albert (1903) Born 8 May 1884, Hall Street, Bilston, Staffordshire; son of Joseph Jackson, General Dealer, and Emily Wilks. **Subject(s):** Natural Sciences; BA 1906; MA 1910. **Tutor(s):** D MacAlister. **Educ:** Wolverhampton Grammar School. **Career:** GPO 1907.

JACKSON, Francis William David (1949) Born 19 August 1928, Alltdinnie, Aboyne, Aberdeenshire; son of Brigadier Cecil Vivian Staveley Jackson, and Margaret Jean Davidson; m Sheila Jean Clark, 12 July 1969, Norbury. **Subject(s):** Modern and Medieval Languages (Russian); BA 1952; MA 1956; Diploma in Medieval Mongol 1953; CA. **Tutor(s):** C W Guillebaud. **Educ:** Belhaven Hill School, Dunbar; Trinity College, Glenalmond. **Career:** Royal Corps of Signals (National Service) 1947–1949; Chartered Accountant (Scottish) 1958; Partner, Turquands Barton Mayhew, and successor firm Ernst & Whinney 1973–1987.

Awards: Minor Scholarship, SJC 1945. **Publications:** 'Isandhlwana 1879 – The Sources Re-examined', *Journal of the Society for Army Historical Research*, 1963; various articles and book reviews in military historical journals.

JACKSON, Frank Storer (1928) Born 4 June 1910, 160 Clarence Road, Derby; son of John Jackson, Mechanical Engineer, and Gertrude Louise Bollen; m Doris; 1 daughter (Barbara). **Subject(s):** Mathematics/ Mechanical Sciences; BA 1931; MA 1935. **Tutor(s):** J M Wordie. **Johnian Relatives:** brother of John Eric Jackson (1923); uncle of Anthony John Bollen Jackson (1956). **Educ:** Milford House Preparatory School, Abergavenny; King Henry VIII Grammar School, Abergavenny. **Career:** Civil Engineer. Died 26 July 1996.

JACKSON, Dr Frederic Sinclair (1933) Born 10 August 1914, Rosslyn, Park Avenue, Knaresborough, Yorkshire; son of Percy Jackson, Bank Manager, and Ellen Preston; m Joan Ann Temperley, 19 May 1951, London; 2 daughters (Helen and Anthea). **Subject(s):** Mathematics/ Economics; BA 1936; MA 1966; BChir 1941; MB 1941; MRCP 1948; FRCP 1962. **Tutor(s):** J M Wordie. **Johnian Relatives:** brother-in-law of John Arthur Cosh (1933). **Educ:** Bingley Grammar School. **Career:** Cardiologist; RAF, Medical Officer, 17 Squadron, India and Burma; Consultant Cardiologist, Head of Department, Newcastle General Hospital 1951; Clinical Teacher in Medicine, King's College, Newcastle upon Tyne 1959. **Appointments:** Member, Newcastle Regional Hospital Board; Honorary Consulting Cardiologist, Newcastle Hospitals Group; Member, British Cardiac Society; Member, Alpine Club. Died 23 September 1999.

JACKSON, Gilbert Edward (1908) Born 2 March 1890, Hedon, Hull, Yorkshire; son of John Lowthian Jackson, Surgeon, and Ida Beatrice Bird; m (1) Margorie Lilian, 5 July 1921, St Mary the Virgin, Toronto, (2) Elizabeth Ewringmann, 1932; 1 son (John), 2 daughters (Mary and Joan). **Subject(s):** History/Economics; BA 1911; MA 1958. **Tutor(s):** J R Tanner. **Educ:** Denstone College. **Career:** President, Sentinel Securities of Canada Ltd, and Sentinel Associates Ltd; Director of Chris Hansen's of Canada Ltd, and Corporate Investors Ltd; Lecturer in Political Economy, University of Toronto (Professor 1926) 1911–1935; Queen's Own (Royal West Kent) Regiment 1916; 2nd Battalion, Mesopotamia 1916–1917; Second Lieutenant, 6th Loyal North Lancashire Regiment 1918–1919; Economist, Bank of Nova Scotia 1927–1935; Advisor to the Governors of the Bank of England 1935–1939; Head, Gilbert Jackson and Associates 1939; Acting Director, School of Commerce, McGill University 1940. **Appointments:** Secretary, Ontario Commission on Unemployment 1915; Chairman, Provincial Unemployment Service Council of Ontario 1921–1926; Member, Industrial Disputes Enquiry Commission 1941; National War Labour Board 1942; National Selective Service Advisory Board 1943–1945. **Awards:** Foundation Scholarship, SJC. **Honours:** Order of King Christian X of Denmark; OBE 1946. **Publications:** *An Economist's Confession of Faith*, Macmillan, 1935; *If Thine Enemy Hunger*, 1941; *Facts in the Case*, 1944. Died 16 June 1959.

JACKSON, The Revd Graeme Clark (1949) Born 17 February 1929, Firs Nursing Home, Kandy, Ceylon; son of The Revd George Basil Jackson, Methodist Missionary, and Harriet Agnes Anderton; m (1) Doreen Elsie Penna, 7 September 1956, Methodist Church, Kolluptiya, Colombo (dis 1983); (2) Elizabeth Marion Hale, 27 September 1986, Lambeth Mission; (1) 1 son (Alastair b 1962), 1 daughter (Gayle b 1958). **Subject(s):** Natural Sciences/Geography; BA 1952; MA 1979; BA (Bristol) 1955. **Tutor(s):** G C L Bertram. **Educ:** Kingswood, Kandy, Sri Lanka; Bournville Elementary School, Birmingham; Hebron, Coonoor, India; Richmond College, Galle, Sri Lanka; Lawrence Park High School, Toronto, Canada; Kingswood School, Bath. **Career:** Methodist Church, Sri Lanka 1955–1965 (Ordained Minister 1957); Asia Secretary, Deputy Director and Acting Director, Commission on Inter-Church Aid, Refugee and World Service of the World Council of Churches, Geneva 1966–1974; Asia Secretary and Personnel Secretary, Methodist Overseas Division, London 1974–1983; Coordinator, Vietnamese Programme,

Refugee Council, London 1983–1988; Programme Manager, Asia International Division, Help the Aged 1988–1994.

JACKSON, Harley Douglas (1907) Born 16 June 1888, 61 West Hill, Wandsworth, Surrey; son of Edward Harley Molineux Jackson, Clerk in Holy Orders, and Ellen Rathbone Orford Howe. BA 1910; MA 1919. **Tutor(s):** J R Tanner. **Johnian Relatives:** brother of John Edward Norman Jackson (1905). **Educ:** Pocklington School. **Career:** Classics Master, Diocesan College, Rondebosch, Cape Colony 1912.

JACKSON, The Revd John Edward Norman (1905) Born 27 September 1885, 4 Tavistock Terrace, Haldon Road, Wandsworth, Surrey; son of Edward Harley Molineux Jackson, Clerk in Holy Orders, and Ellen Rathbone Orford Howe. **Subject(s):** History; BA 1908; MA 1912. **Tutor(s):** C E Graves; J R Tanner. **Johnian Relatives:** brother of Harley Douglas Jackson (1907). **Educ:** Pocklington School. **Career:** Ordained Deacon 1909; Ordained Priest 1910; Curate, St Anthony, Byker 1910–1912; Curate, St Andrew, Newcastle upon Tyne 1912–1919; Temporary CF, 4th Class, RACD 1918–1919; Curate, Grasmere 1919–1922; Curate, Shrivenham with Watchfield 1922–1923; Curate, Malvern Link 1923–1924; Vicar, Bransdale with Farndale 1924–1926; Vicar, Yeddingham and Knapton 1926–1927; Rector, Normanby 1927–1932; Vicar, Hovingham 1932–1935; Vicar, St Mary Bishophill Junior, York 1935–1947; Chaplain, Bootham Park Mental Hospital 1944–1947; Vicar, Gilsland with Over Denton, Cumberland 1947–1951; Rector, Wetheral with Warwick, Carlisle 1951–1956. Died July 1964.

JACKSON, John Eric (1923) Born 14 March 1905, 144 Walbrook Road, Derby; son of John Jackson, Engineer, and Gertrude Louise Bollen; m Mary; 1 son (Anthony), 2 daughters (Dilys and Dinah). **Subject(s):** Mathematics; BA 1926; MA 1937; FRAS; FRICS. **Tutor(s):** J M Wordie. **Johnian Relatives:** brother of Frank Storer Jackson (1928); father of Anthony John Bollen Jackson (1956). **Educ:** Private School, Derby; Derby Municipal Secondary School; Abergavenny Grammar School. **Career:** Colonial Surveys (Sri Lanka) 1928; University Lecturer in Geodesy 1948; Fellow, Fitzwilliam House 1966. Died 1 February 1985.

JACKSON, Joseph Frank (1934) Born 19 February 1904, 31 Burnbury Road, Clapham, London; son of Joseph Charles Jackson, Schoolmaster, and Kate Charlotte Bateman; m Mary Davies Thompson. **Tutor(s):** C W Guillebaud. **Johnian Relatives:** brother-in-law of Wilfrid Jansen Thompson (1923); father of Richard Andrew Jackson (1966). **Educ:** Pinner Elementary School; Harrow County School; London University; Northern Polytechnic Institute. Died 7 September 1986.

JACKSON, Kenneth Greer (1923) Born 4 January 1905, This Kiare, Thorn Road, Bearsden, West Kilpatrick, County Dumbarton, Scotland; son of Stewart Douglas Jackson, Publisher, and Mary Hadfield Greer. **Subject(s):** Law; BA 1926; LLB 1927. **Tutor(s):** E A Benians. **Educ:** Junior School, Brighton College; Bootham School, York.

JACKSON, Professor Kenneth Hurlstone (1928) Born 1 November 1909, Melville, Lavender Vale, Beddington, Surrey; son of Alan Stuart Jackson, Authorised Clerk, London Stock Exchange, and Lucy Jane Hurlstone; m Janet Dall Galloway, 1936; 1 son, 1 daughter. **Subject(s):** Classics/ Archaeology and Anthropology; BA 1931; MA 1935; Litt D 1954; FBA 1957. **Tutor(s):** M P Charlesworth. **Johnian Relatives:** father of Alastar Hurlstone Jackson (1961). **Educ:** Whitgift Grammar School, Croydon; The County School, Sutton. **Career:** Studies in Bangor and Dublin 1932–1934; Title A Fellow, SJC 1934–1940; Assistant Lecturer in Celtic Studies 1937–1939; Lecturer in Celtic Studies 1939–1940 University of Cambridge; Associate, then full Professor of Celtic, University of Harvard 1940; British Censorship Office, Bermuda, WWII; Professor of Celtic Languages, Literature, History and Antiquities, Edinburgh 1950; Rede Lecturer 1964. **Appointments:** Honorary Fellow, SJC 1979. **Awards:** Scholarship, SJC 1928; Browne Medals for Greek Ode and Latin Epigram, University of Cambridge 1930 and 1931; Allen Scholarship, University of Cambridge 1933; Derek Allen Prize, British

Academy. **Honours:** CBE 1985. **Publications:** *Early Welsh Gnomic Poems*, 1935; *The Battle of Magh Leana*, 1938; *Scealta on mBlascaod (Tales from the Blaskets)*, 1939; *The Goddodin of Aneirin*; *Once Again Arthur's Battles*; *A Celtic Miscellany*, 1951; *Language and History in Early Britain*, 1953; *A Historical Phonology of Breton*, 1967; *The Vision of MacConglinne*, 1990. Died 20 February 1991.

JACKSON, Myles Allen Maxwell (1926) Born 30 September 1906, Ferriby, Yorkshire; son of Maxwell Jackson, Solicitor, and Maude Muschamp Vickers. **Tutor(s):** E A Benians. **Johnian Relatives:** son of Maxwell Jackson (1882); cousin of George Foster Earle (1908); brother of Ronald Emerson Maxwell Jackson (1920). **Educ:** The Old College, Windermere; Rossall School.

JACKSON, Reginald (1940) Born 16 November 1921, High Street, Market Weighton, East Yorkshire; son of Reginald Jackson, Cycle and Motor Engineer, and Elizabeth Featonby Robson (née Grant). **Tutor(s):** R L Howland. **Educ:** Market Weighton Church of England Boys' School; Pocklington School. **Career:** Lieutenant, 6th Battalion, The Green Howards 1940–1943. Died 28 July 1943 (killed in action in Sicily).

JACKSON, Richard Hoyle (1927) Born 6 January 1910, Wellington Lodge, Wellington Road, Oldham, Lancashire; son of Richard Hoyle Jackson, Master Cotton Spinner, and Alice Prockter Scott. **Subject(s):** Law; BA 1930; MA 1946; LLB 1931. **Tutor(s):** C W Guillebaud. **Educ:** Lawrence House Preparatory School; Repton School. **Career:** Wrigley, Clayson & Armstrongs of Oldham. Died 1 July 1985.

JACKSON, Professor Richard Meredith (1921) Born 19 August 1903, The Drive, Phippsville, Northampton; son of James Jackson, Solicitor, and Jennie May Parnell; m Lenli. **Subject(s):** Law; BA 1924; MA 1928; LLB 1924; LLD 1934; FBA 1966. **Tutor(s):** B F Armitage. **Educ:** Waynflete House Preparatory School, Northampton; Sidcot School, Somerset; Leighton Park School, Reading. **Career:** Qualified as Solicitor 1928; Title B Fellow 1946–1966, Lecturer in Law 1947–1970, Title C Fellow 1966–1970, Title D Fellow 1970–1986, SJC; Lecturer in Law 1934–1950, Reader in Public Law and Administration 1950–1966, Downing Professor of the Laws of England 1966–1970 (Emeritus 1970), University of Cambridge. **Appointments:** Assistant Supervisor in Law 1929–1932, Supervisor in Law 1932–1947 (leave of absence on war service 1941–1946), Director of Studies in Law 1950–1961, SJC; JP; Secretary, Royal Commission on Justices of the Peace 1946–1948; Various other Government Committees; Member and Vice-President, Council of the Magistrates' Association. **Awards:** McMahon Studentship, SJC; York Prize 1931. **Publications:** *History of Quasi-Contract in English Law*, 1936; *Machinery of Justice in England*, 1940. Died 8 May 1986.

JACKSON, Robert Flinders (1939) Born 17 July 1921, Hampden Way, Bilton, Rugby; son of Forbes Jackson, Electrical Engineer, and Olive Maude Hitchcock; m 1949; 3 children. **Subject(s):** Mechanical Sciences; BA 1942; MA 1951; FREng 1982; FIMechE; MIEE. **Tutor(s):** S J Bailey. **Educ:** Abingdon School. **Career:** Lieutenant, RN 1941–1946; Mentioned in Despatches 1945; Chief Pile Operator, Head of Research Reactor Division, Chief Engineer and Assistant Director, AERE 1946–1965; Director of Industrial Development, Director of Engineering, Deputy Managing Director, Northern Division of Atomic Energy Authority 1965–1985. **Appointments:** Secretary, LMBC 1940–1941; Vice President, Institute of Mechanical Engineers 1981–1987. **Honours:** CBE 1984.

JACKSON, Ronald Emerson Maxwell (MAXWELL-JACKSON) (1920) Born 6 March 1903, Ferriby, Yorkshire; son of Maxwell Jackson, Solicitor, and Maude Muschamp Vickers. BA 1926; MA 1930. **Tutor(s):** E A Benians. **Johnian Relatives:** son of Maxwell Jackson (1882); cousin of George Foster Earle (1908); brother of Myles Allen Maxwell Jackson (1926). **Educ:** The Old College, Windermere; Charterhouse. **Career:** Solicitor 1930. Died 5 May 1966.

JACOB, Anstey Ross (1912) Born 4 October 1893, Calcutta, India; son of Stephen Jacob, Indian Civil Servant, and Clara L Forlong. **Tutor(s):** E E Sikes. **Johnian Relatives:** brother of Philip Gordon Jacob (1894). **Educ:** Dulwich Preparatory; Dulwich College. **Career:** Second Lieutenant, Durham Light Infantry 1916. **Awards:** Major Scholarship, SJC. **Publications:** 'Possibly Pan in the Wilderness', *The Eagle*, 35. Died 18 September 1916 (killed in action).

JACOB, Bernard Binyon (1925) Born 10 September 1905, 15 Percy Terrace, Waterford, Ireland; son of Edwin Binyon Jacob, Stock Broker, and Jessie Elizabeth Baker. **Subject(s):** English/Geography; BA 1928; MA 1932. **Tutor(s):** E A Benians. **Educ:** Newton School, Waterford; Bootham School, York; Sidcot School, Winscombe. **Career:** Master, Woodbrooke, Birmingham 1928–1929; Master, Sandbach Grammar School, Cheshire 1929–1932; Master, Ashbourne Grammar School, Derbyshire 1932–1935; Master, Friends' School, Saffron Walden, Essex 1935–1963. Died 17 June 1976.

JACOBS, William Ernest Walter (CARPENTER-JACOBS) (1933) Born 12 September 1914, Novaya, Ulitsa, Odessa; son of William James Jacobs, Insurance Agent, and Amy Blanche Carpenter. **Subject(s):** English; BA 1936; MA 1940. **Tutor(s):** C W Guillebaud. **Educ:** Aldro School, Meads; Cranbrook School, Kent.

JACOBSEN, Ronald Norman (1947) Born 13 October 1917, Gisburn Place, Blackburn, Lancashire; son of Louis Jacobson, Master Tailor, and Elise Perls-Pieres. **Tutor(s):** J M Wordie. **Educ:** Wensley Fold School, Blackburn; Queen Elizabeth's Grammar School, Blackburn. **Career:** Major, Royal Northumberland Fusiliers; Colonial Service, Nigeria; Calico Printers Association Trainee 1936–1938; Master, Hexham Preparatory School 1938–1939.

JACOBSOHN, Arthur (1914) Born 31 August 1881, Courland; son of Heinrich Jacobsohn, and Lena Field. **Subject(s):** Law. **Tutor(s):** L H K Bushe-Fox. **Educ:** Boys' High School, Oudtshoorn; South African College, Cape Town. **Career:** Second Lieutenant, RASC 1914–1918.

JACQUEST, Samuel Percy (1907) Born 18 January 1888, Rockingham Road, Kettering, Northamptonshire; son of Samuel Frederick Jacquest, Contractor, and Susan Groome. **Subject(s):** Modern and Medieval Languages; BA 1910. **Tutor(s):** L H K Bushe-Fox. **Johnian Relatives:** uncle of Richard Calvert Wood (1932). **Educ:** The Grammar School, Kettering. **Career:** Headmaster, Terrace School, British Columbia; Headmaster, Greenwood School, British Columbia; English Master, Bishop's College, Lennoxville, Canada 1912; Canadian Field Artillery 1915–1916. Died 18 October 1916 (killed in action while at work in an ammunition pit).

JAGGER, Professor John Greenwood (1929) Born 16 October 1906, 33 Timson Street, Failsworth; son of John Ernest Jagger, Electrical Engineer, and Elizabeth Hartle; 1 son (John Charles Greenwood). **Subject(s):** Mechanical Sciences; BA 1931; MA 1935; BSc (Manchester) 1929; MSc (Manchester) 1935; FIMechE; MIEE. **Tutor(s):** M P Charlesworth. **Educ:** St John's C of E School, Failsworth; Oldham Municipal School; College of Technology, Manchester; Victoria University, Manchester. **Career:** Professor of Mechanical Engineering, University of Bradford (formerly Bradford Institute of Technology) 1964 (later Emeritus Professor). **Awards:** Rex Moir Prize 1931; Ricardo Prize, University of Cambridge 1931. Died 15 April 1999.

JAGO, Jack Alexander (1918) Born 2 May 1899, The Willows, Hutton, Essex; son of Sydney James Alexander Jago, Stockjobber, and Edith Hawys Tribe; m (1) Irene Valerie Christofora, (2) Moya. **Subject(s):** Natural Sciences; BA 1921; MA 1926. **Tutor(s):** E E Sikes. **Educ:** White Hall College, Witham; Merchant Taylors' School, London. **Career:** Instructor Commander, RN. **Awards:** Scholarship, SJC 1917. Died 4 November 1968.

JAHN, Richard Edgar (1944) Born 15 March 1927, 72 West Wycombe Road, High Wycombe, Buckinghamshire; son of Hermann Edgar Jahn, Artificial Flower Merchant, and Florence Dora Davis. **Subject(s):** Natural Sciences; BA 1947; MA 1951. **Tutor(s):** C W Guillebaud. **Educ:** Stanhope Junior School, Ealing; New Malden East Junior School; Raynes Park County School. **Career:** Systems Accountant, BOC Group 1950–1992.

JAMES, David Elidyn Howell (1935) Born 12 August 1915, Cefn Glas, Radyr, Glamorganshire; son of Howell Ewart James, Inspector, Ministry of Health, and Elizabeth Vaughan Hoskins. **Subject(s):** Law; BA 1937; MA 1948; LLB (Wales) 1935; DPA (London) 1949. **Tutor(s):** C W Guillebaud. **Educ:** College School Cardiff; Llandaff Cathedral School; Cardiff High School for Boys; University College of Wales, Aberystwyth. **Career:** Solicitor. Died 1991.

JAMES, Francis Arthur (1905) Born 22 May 1886, Curfew House, Haigh, Lancashire; son of Charles Henry James, Clerk in Holy Orders, and Emily Maria Donner. **Subject(s):** Mathematics; BA 1908; MA 1914. **Tutor(s):** E E Sikes. **Johnian Relatives:** son of Charles Henry James (1868). **Educ:** Cranleigh School. **Career:** Vice-Principal, Colvin Taludar's School, Lucknow 1909–1914; Second Lieutenant, 5th Manchester Regiment, Egypt and Gallipoli 1914–1915. Died 18 September 1915 (killed in action).

JAMES, Geoffrey Sargood (1941) Born 7 June 1924, 22 Horsham Avenue, Friern Barnet, London; son of Ralph Jordan James, Bank Clerk, and Olive Snow. **Subject(s):** Mathematics; BA 1944; Diploma in Mathematical Statistics 1948; FSS. **Tutor(s):** S J Bailey. **Educ:** Friar's Hill School, Friern Barnet; Oakleigh Park Preparatory School, Friern Barnet; Friends' School, Saffron Walden; Grammar School, Newton Abbot. **Career:** Radar Research, Malvern 1943–1946; National Physical Laboratory, Teddington 1948–1949; Assistant Lecturer in Mathematical Statistics 1949–1952, Lecturer in Mathematical Statistics 1952–1980, University of Leeds. **Awards:** Exhibition, SJC 1942; Scholarship, SJC 1943. **Publications:** Various research papers, mainly in *Biometrika*.

JAMES, Dr Gwilym (1900) Born 7 December 1879, Powell Street, Aberystwyth, Cardigan; son of Enoch James, Master Mariner, and Margaret Hopkins Jones; m Annie; 1 daughter (Margot). BA 1905; MA 1919; MRCS; LRCP 1911. **Tutor(s):** E E Sikes. **Educ:** University College of Wales, Aberystwyth. **Career:** House Surgeon, Queen's Hospital for Children; Captain, RAMC 1914–1918; Practice, Llanelly, Wales 1919–1943. Died 24 June 1949.

JAMES, Horace Meredith (1941) Born 3 December 1923, 10 Sycamore Road, Smethwick, Staffordshire; son of Sidney James, Vanman, and Louie Matthews. **Tutor(s):** C W Guillebaud. **Educ:** Boulton Road Elementary School; King Edward's High School, Birmingham. **Awards:** Scholarship, SJC. Died 29 May 1945.

JAMES, Leslie Hollins Prideaux (1942) Born 20 May 1924, Titagarh, Calcutta; son of Vyvyan Hector Prideaux James, Merchant's Assistant, and Ruth Hitchenson; m Audrey Kraft; 2 sons (Paul and Matthew). **Subject(s):** History; BA 1947. **Tutor(s):** C W Guillebaud. **Educ:** Winnington Elementary School, Cheshire; Davenham Elementary School, Cheshire; Hartford Elementary School, Cheshire; Sir John Dean's Grammar School, Northwich; Lincoln Theological College. **Career:** Flying training, RAF 1942–1943; No 5 Mobile Field Photographic Section, Normandy, Belgium, Holland and Germany 1944–1946; LAC Photographer 1944–1948; Demobilised 1946; Lincoln Theological College 1948–1949; Master in Charge, The Junior School, Bolton School (Boys' Division) 1967–1984.

JAMES, Professor Reginald William (1909) Born 9 January 1891, 151 Praed Street, Paddington, London; son of William George Joseph James, Umbrella Manufacturer, and Isabel Sarah Ward; m Anne Watson, 1936; 2 sons, 1 daughter. **Subject(s):** Natural Sciences; BA 1912; MA 1919; FRS 1955. **Tutor(s):** J R Tanner. **Educ:** Polytechnic Day School, London; City of London School. **Career:** Reader in Experimental Physics, Manchester University; Physicist, Shackleton Antarctic Expedition 1914; Captain, Sound Ranging Section, RE (Mentioned in Despatches) 1916–1918; Professor of Physics 1936–1957 (Emeritus 1957), Fellow 1949, Acting Principal 1956–1957, Vice-Chancellor, University of Cape Town. **Publications:** *The Optical Principles of the diffraction of X-Rays*. Died 7 June 1964.

JAMES, Thomas Cecil Garside (1937) Born 8 January 1918, Ashton under Lyne; son of Joshua James, Director and Secretary, Wholesale Druggists, and Evelina Walters; m Elsie Williams, 1941; 1 son, 2 daughters. **Subject(s):** History; BA 1940; MA 1944. **Tutor(s):** J S Boys Smith. **Johnian Relatives:** godfather of Julian Michael Bedford Morrell (1980). **Educ:** Albion School, Ashton under Lyne; Mossley Road Council School, Ashton under Lyne; Manchester Grammar School. **Career:** Principal Private Secretary to Secretary of State for Air 1951–1955; Assistant Secretary, Air Ministry 1955–1968; Civil Secretary, FEAF 1963–1966; Chief of Public Relations 1966–1968, Assistant Under-Secretary of State 1968–1977, MOD. **Appointments:** Member, Falcons; Member, Eagles. **Awards:** Exhibition, SJC 1936; Scholarship 1939; Strathcona Exhibition, SJC 1940. **Honours:** CMG 1966; Officers' Cross of the Order of Merit of the Republic of Poland for services to the history of the Polish Air Force 1998. **Publications:** *Battle of Britain*, 2000; *Growth of Fighter Command 1936–1940*, 2003.

JAMES, Professor William Owen (1924) Born 21 May 1900, Ravenscroft, Mount Pleasant Road, Tottenham, Middlesex; son of William Benjamin James, Headmaster, and Agnes Ursula Collins; m Gladys Macphail Redfearn, 1928. PhD 1927; BSc (London); FRS 1952. **Tutor(s):** J M Wordie. **Educ:** The Grammar School, Tottenham; University College, Reading. **Career:** Staff, Institute for Plant Physiology, Rothamsted 1925–1927; Demonstrator 1927–1946, Reader 1946–1958, Department of Botany, Oxford; Head of Botany, Imperial College 1958–1967. **Appointments:** Member, Editorial Panel, *Endeavour*. **Publications:** *Introduction to Plant Physiology*, 1931; *Plant Respiration*, 1953; (joint ed) *New Phytologist*; *Introduction to Plant Biology*; *Background to Gardening*; *Cell Respiration*, 1971. Died 15 September 1978.

JANES, Geoffrey Gilbert (1944) Born 24 June 1926, City Maternity Home, Westcotes Drive, Leicester; son of Gilbert Janes, Chief Sanitary Inspector, Reigate Corporation, and Evelyn Florence Woodard. **Subject(s):** Mechanical Sciences; BA 1947. **Tutor(s):** S J Bailey. **Educ:** North Bank Preparatory School, Reigate; St John's Church of England School, Redhill; Reigate Grammar School. **Career:** Manager, Inspection Department, F Perkins Ltd.

JAQUET, Brian Sidney (1921) Born 2 July 1902, Carisbrooke Park Road, Sidcup, Chislehurst, Kent; son of Robert Glover Jaquet, Accountant General, India Office, and Emily Rose Woods. **Subject(s):** Economics/Law; BA 1924; MA 1963; LLB 1924. **Tutor(s):** E A Benians. **Educ:** Stratheden House, Blackheath; Merton Court, Sidcup; Repton School. **Career:** Admitted Solicitor 1927; Messrs Sharpe Pritchard & Co, Chancery Lane. Died 25 April 1978.

JARCHOW, Frederick Carl (1929) Born 18 February 1911, Thirle, Claremont Road, Red Hill, Surrey; son of Frederick Jarchow, Grain Merchant, and Gertrude Mary Board. **Tutor(s):** M P Charlesworth. **Johnian Relatives:** cousin of Christopher John Frederick Jarchow (1898). **Educ:** Observatory House, Westgate-on-Sea; Brighton College.

JARDIN, Dennis William (1945) Born 13 June 1927, The Village, Hebron, Morpeth, Northumberland; son of Thomas Jardin, Blacksmith, and Charlotte Rogerson. **Subject(s):** Mechanical Sciences; BA 1948; MA 1977. **Tutor(s):** S J Bailey; R L Howland. **Educ:** Tritlington Church of England School; Morpeth Grammar School. **Career:** ICI 1948–1955; Teacher, Sir Joseph Williamson's Mathematical School, Rochester 1955–1987; Head of Science, Sir Joseph Williamson's Mathematical

School, Rochester 1970–1987. **Awards:** Exhibition, SJC 1945; Scholarship, SJC 1946.

JARMAN, Maurice Vernon (1944) Born 18 May 1927, 3 First Avenue, Gorton, Manchester; son of Arthur Ernest Jarman, Schoolmaster, and Ellen Perry; m Wennie Chan, 23 June 1977, Poole; 1 daughter (Sonata Marisa b 30 July 1979). **Subject(s):** Mechanical Sciences; BA 1947; MA 1951; MICE; MIMechE. **Tutor(s):** S J Bailey. **Johnian Relatives:** brother of Ronald Arthur Jarman (1942). **Educ:** Alma Park Elementary School; Manchester Grammar School. **Career:** Managing Director, Sime Darby Engineering, Singapore 1973–1976; Head, Continuing Education Department, Singapore Polytechnic 1983–1987. **Publications:** 'Empty Sea Containers. Quantifying the Problem and Proposing a Solution', 1999.

JARMAN, Ronald Arthur (1942) Born 17 March 1924, 3 First Avenue, Gorton, Manchester; son of Arthur Ernest Jarman, Schoolmaster, and Ellen Perry; m Stella Ross Harvey, 1950; 1 son (Bernard), 2 daughters (Rosemary and Heather). **Subject(s):** Mechanical Sciences; BA 1945; MA 1949. **Tutor(s):** S J Bailey. **Johnian Relatives:** brother of Maurice Vernon Jarman (1944). **Educ:** Alma Park Elementary School, Manchester; Manchester Grammar School. **Career:** Aero-Engineer Design Draftsman, Rolls-Royce, Derby 1945–1948; School Teacher, Steiner (Waldorf) School 1948–1988; Chairman, Steiner Schools Fellowship and Director of Education, Emerson College 1960–1990; Education Lecturer, Plymouth University, Emerson College and USA, Australia, Slovenia 1980–2000. **Appointments:** Round Table Society; Chairman, Steiner Schools Fellowship, Great Britain and Ireland; International Education Councils 1955–1980; Inaugurator, International Waldorf School Council 1970, and European Council of Steiner Waldorf Schools 1990; Initiator, Through Heart to Peace, Bosnian relief and therapy organisation 1994. **Awards:** Strathcona Scholarship, SJC 1941. **Publications:** *Teaching Mathematics in Rudolf Steiner Schools*, Hawthorn Press, 1998.

JARRATT, The Revd George Lansdell (1900) Born 26 January 1882, The Rectory, Goodleigh, Devon; son of Frederick Jarratt, Clerk in Holy Orders, and Jane Lucas. BA 1903; MA 1914. **Tutor(s):** D MacAlister. **Educ:** Exeter School. **Career:** Ordained Deacon 1927; Chaplain, Berkhamsted School 1927–1930; Ordained Priest 1928; Rector, Thornbury, Devon 1930–1950; Rector, Wytham, Berkshire 1955. Died 11 September 1961.

JARRATT, The Revd Thomas (1925) Born 20 November 1905, Ivydene, Bulstrode Avenue, Hounslow, Middlesex; son of Wilfrid Thomas Jarratt, Accountant, and Elsie Parker; m Audrey Ethel Brett. **Subject(s):** Classics/Theology; BA 1929; MA 1932. **Tutor(s):** M P Charlesworth. **Educ:** South Lodge School, Hounslow; Emanuel School, Wandsworth Common. **Career:** Cheshunt College, Cambridge; Minister, London Road Congregational Church, Lowestoft 1930–1938; Minister, Sevenoaks Congregational Church 1938. Died 2 November 1967.

JARVIS, Charles Hooper (1904) (Admitted as non-collegiate student 1903) Born 25 October 1881, Lothian Street, Heigham, Norwich, Norfolk; son of Charles Whorton Jarvis, Grocer and Draper, and Mary Ann Charlotte Hooper; m Alice Julia Allen; 1 son (Philip Charles b 3 March 1922). **Subject(s):** History/Law; BA 1906; MA 1910; LLB 1906; LLD (Dublin). **Tutor(s):** D MacAlister. **Johnian Relatives:** father of Philip Charles Jarvis (1940); grandfather of Mark Jarvis (1970). **Educ:** Higher Grade School, Norwich. **Career:** Master, Henry Smith's School, Hartlepool 1906–1910; History Lecturer, Leeds Training College 1910–1916; Local Inspector of Schools, Leeds 1919–1921; Director of Education, Wood Green, London 1921–1945. Died 24 October 1960.

JARVIS, Philip Charles (1940) Born 3 March 1922, 13 Elgin Road, Wood Green, London; son of Charles Hooper Jarvis, Director of Education, Borough of Wood Green, and Alice Julia Allen; m (1) Margaret (d 17 January 1998), (2) Anna Catherina, 30 October 1999; 2 sons (Mark and

Andrew). **Subject(s):** Mechanical Sciences; BA 1943; MA 1947; CEng; MIEE. **Tutor(s):** S J Bailey. **Johnian Relatives:** son of Charles Hooper Jarvis (1904); father of Mark Jarvis (1970). **Educ:** Rhodes Avenue School, Alexandra Park; Norfolk House Preparatory School, London; Highgate School; Morley Grammar School. **Career:** Birmingham District Manager, Central Electricity Generating Board 1964–1981.

JÁUREGUI, Julio Ventura (1927) Born 11 February 1909, Oruro, Bolivia, South America; son of Ezequiel Jáuregui, Estate Owner, Company Director and Manufacturer, and Tomasa Cusicanqui Reyes Ortiz. BA 1930; MA 1934. **Tutor(s):** J M Wordie. **Educ:** Colegio, San Calixto; University School, Hastings.

JAYAWARDANA, Andrew Cyril Joseph Perera Wijeratna (1913) Born 4 February 1894, Morotuwa, Ceylon; son of Bodiabadugey Gregory Perera W Jayawardana, Landed Proprietor, and Mary Gertrude Fernando. **Tutor(s):** L H K Bushe-Fox. **Educ:** Dr Joseph's College, Columbo.

JEAVONS, Professor Peter Machin (1939) Born 29 May 1920, 48 Reddings Road, Moseley, Birmingham; son of Ernest Victor Jeavons, Hardware Merchant, and Mary Weston Machin. BA 1942; MA 1946; Honorary DSc (Aston University) 1984; MB 1945; BChir 1945; MRCP; FRCPsych; DPM. **Tutor(s):** R L Howland. **Educ:** Edgbaston High School for Girls Kindergarten; Hallfield Preparatory School, Edgbaston; Stowe School. **Career:** Consultant Psychiatrist and Deputy Medical Superintendent, Birmingham Hospital Group; Visiting Professor, Department of Vision Sciences, Aston University 1980. Died 17 March 1997.

JEEJEEBHOY, Phiroze Jamshedji (1939) Born 2 December 1915, Deolali, Nasik District, India; son of Jamshedji Pestonji Bomanji Jeejeebhoy, Landowner, and Jaijee Dhondy. BA 1941; MA 1945. **Tutor(s):** C W Guillebaud. **Educ:** Zoroastrian Boarding High School, Deolali; St Xavier's College, Bombay, India; Sydenham College, Bombay, India.

JEEVES, Professor Malcolm Alexander (1948) Born 16 November 1926, 30 Priory Road, Stamford, Lincolnshire; son of Alexander Frederick Thomas Jeeves, Cashier, and Helena May Hammond; m Ruth Elisabeth Hartridge, 1955; 2 daughters (Sarah Marguerite Elizabeth b 7 May 1958 and Joanna Mary Helena b 1 March 1961). **Subject(s):** Natural Sciences/Moral Sciences; BA 1951; MA 1955; PhD 1957; Honorary DSc (Edinburgh) 1993; Honorary DUniv (Stirling) 1999; Honorary DSc (St Andrews) 2000; FRSE; FAPS; FBPsS 1958; FMedSci. **Tutor(s):** G C L Bertram. **Educ:** St George's School, Stamford; Stamford Bluecoat School; Stamford School. **Career:** Commissioned, Royal Lincolnshire Regiment 1945–1948; Research, Nuffield Unit for Ageing, Cambridge and Harvard 1951–1956; Rotary Foundation Fellow, Harvard University 1953–1954; Lecturer in Psychology, Leeds University 1956–1959; Foundation Professor of Psychology 1959–1969 and Dean 1962–1964, University of Adelaide; Foundation Professor of Psychology 1969–1993, Vice-Principal 1981–1985, Director, MRC Cognitive Neuroscience Research Group 1984–1989, Honorary Research Professor and Emeritus Professor of Psychology 1993, University of St Andrews. **Appointments:** Fellow, Advanced Study, Harvard 1953; Fellow, Australian Psychological Society 1964; Psychology Committee, Social Science Research Council, 1972–1976; President, Psychology Section, BAAS; Chairman, International Neuropsychological Symposium; Member, Science and Engineering Research Council 1985–1989; Neuroscience and Mental Health Board, MRC 1985–1989; Honorary Sheriff, Fife 1986–; Vice-President 1990–1993, President 1996–1999, RSE; Editor in Chief, *Neuropsychologia* 1990–1993; Foundation Fellow, Academy of Medical Science 1998. **Awards:** Marquess of Exeter Exhibition, SJC 1945; Burney Studentship, University of Cambridge 1951; Research Exhibition, SJC 1952; Fellowship for Advanced Study, Harvard 1953; Gregg Bury Prize (Philosophy) 1954; Kenneth Craik Prize, SJC 1955; Abbie Medal (Anatomy), Australia 1981; Cairns Medal (Neurology and Neurosurgery), Australia 1986. **Honours:** CBE 1992. **Publications:** (with Z P Dienes)

Thinking in Structures, 1965; *The Scientific Enterprise and Christian Faith*, 1968; (with Z P Dienes) *The Effects of Structural Relations on Transfer*, 1970; *Experimental Psychology – An Introduction for Biologists*, 1974; *Psychology and Christianity – The View Both Ways*, 1974; (with B Greer) *Analysis of Structural Learning*, 1983; *Behavioural Science – A Christian Perspective*, 1984; (ed with G Baumgartner) *Methods in Neuropsychology*, 1986; (with David Myers) *Psychology Through the Eyes of Faith*, 1987, 2002; *Mind Fields*, 1993; (ed and contributor) *Callosal Agenesis – A Natural Split Brain?*, 1994; *Human Nature at the Millennium*, 1997; (with R J Berry) *Science, Life and Christian Belief*, 1998; (ed) *From Cells to Souls*, 2003; (ed) *Human Nature*, 2003; more than 100 papers in scientific journals.

JEFFERIES, Dr John Trevor (1947) Born 2 April 1925, Kellerberrin, Western Australia; son of John Jefferies, Bank Manager, and Vera Emily Healy, Home Duties; m Charmian Candy, 10 September 1949; 2 sons (Stephen R and Trevor R), 1 daughter (Helen C). **Subject(s):** Natural Sciences; BA 1949; MA 1953; BSc (Western Australia) 1946; DSc (Western Australia) 1960; FAAAS; FRAS. **Tutor(s):** J M Wordie. **Educ:** Government State School, Dumbleyung; Government State School, Williams; Guildford Grammar School, Western Australia; Perth Technical College; University of Western Australia. **Career:** Research Officer, CSIRO, Australia 1949–1956; Research Associate, Sacramento Peak Observatory, New Mexico, USA 1956–1959; Staff Scientist, Joint Institute for Laboratory Astrophysics, Boulder, Colorado 1960–1964; Professor, Physics and Astronomy 1964–1983, Director, Institute for Astronomy 1967–1983, University of Hawaii; Director 1983–1987, Astronomer 1987–1992, National Optical Astronomy Observatories, Tucson, Arizona. **Awards:** Guggenheim Foundation Fellowship 1970. **Publications:** *Spectral Line Formation*, 1967; (ed) *Infrared Solar Physics*, 1994; over 100 papers in professional journals on solar and astrophysics.

JEFFERIS, Robert Stephen (1936) Born 30 December 1918, 5 Claremont Road, West Kirby, Cheshire; son of Arthur Frederick Jefferis, Company Director to Estate Owner, and Clara Alice Sutton; m Josephine, 4 sons (Robin, Stephen, John and Michael), 1 daughter (Marcia). **Subject(s):** Law. **Tutor(s):** J S Boys Smith. **Educ:** Braeside Preparatory School, West Kirby; Aldenham School. **Career:** Solicitor, Watford. Died 30 December 1982.

JEFFERSON, John Launcelot (1919) Born 6 September 1898, The Rectory, Kirkbampton, Cumberland; son of William Jefferson, Clerk in Holy Orders, and Mary Elizabeth Whittaker. **Subject(s):** Mechanical Sciences; BA 1921. **Tutor(s):** E E Sikes. **Educ:** Nelson School, Wigton. **Career:** Army 1916–1918. Died 6 January 1975.

JEFFERY, David Schofield (1946) Born 2 April 1921, 365 Pinner Road, Harrow, Middlesex; son of George Jeffery, Mathematician, and Elizabeth Schofield, Teacher; m Marion McKenzie, 13 June 1952; 1 son (Robert Schofield b 1956), 2 daughters (Ruth b 1953 and Susan b 1957). **Subject(s):** Natural Sciences; BA 1948; MA 1953; MB 1952; BChir 1952; DObstRCOG; MRCGP. **Tutor(s):** S J Bailey; G C L Bertram. **Johnian Relatives:** father of Robert Schofield Jeffery (1974). **Educ:** Northwood Preparatory School; Leighton Park School, Reading. **Career:** House appointments, University College Hospital and Ashford Hospital, Middlesex 1952–1954; GP, Old Windsor and Englefield Green, 1954–1987. **Appointments:** Honorary Secretary, Postgraduate Education Centre's Trustees, Windsor 1964–1987; Governor, Leighton Park School; Charity Treasurerships.

JEFFREYS, Professor Sir Harold (1910) Born 22 April 1891, School House, Fatfield, Harraton, Durham; son of Robert Hall Jeffreys, Schoolmaster, and Elizabeth Mary Sharpe; m Dr Bertha Swirles, 1940. **Subject(s):** Mathematics; BA 1913; MA 1917; DSc (Durham) 1917; Honorary LLD (Liverpool) 1953; Honorary ScD (Dublin) 1956; Honorary DCL (Durham) 1960; Honorary DSc (Southern Methodist University, Dallas) 1967; Honorary DPhil (Uppsala) 1977; FRS 1925; Hon FRSE; Hon FRSNZ. **Tutor(s):** L H K Bushe-Fox. **Educ:** Rutherford

College, Newcastle upon Tyne; Armstrong College, Newcastle upon Tyne. **Career:** Meteorological Office, London 1917–1922; Foundress Fellow 1914–1926, Assistant Lecturer in Mathematics 1922–1924, Lecturer in Mathematics 1924–1932, Title B Fellow 1926–1932, Title E Fellow 1932–1946, Title C Fellow 1946–1958, Title D Fellow 1958–1989, SJC; Cavendish Laboratory 1915–1917, Lecturer in Mathematics 1926–1931, Reader in Geophysics 1931–1946, Plumian Professor of Astronomy and Experimental Philosophy 1946–1958, University of Cambridge. **Appointments:** President, Royal Astronomical Society 1955–1957; President, International Seismological Association 1957–1960; Foreign Associate, US National Academy of Sciences; Foreign Associate, Accademia dei Lincei, Rome; Foreign Associate, Academy of Sciences, Stockholm; Foreign Associate, New York Academy of Sciences; Foreign Associate, American Academy of Arts and Sciences; Foreign Associate, Academie Royal de Belgique; Corresponding Member, American Geophysical Union; Corresponding Member, Geological Society of America; Corresponding Member, RIA; Honorary Member, Institute of Mathematics, Seismological Society of America; Honorary Member, Royal Meteorological Society; Honorary Corresponding Astronomer, Royal Observatory of Belgium 1984. **Awards:** Isaac Newton Studentship, University of Cambridge; Smith's Prize, University of Cambridge 1915; Adams Prize, University of Cambridge 1927; Buchan Prize, Royal Meteorological Society 1929; Gold Medal, Royal Astronomical Society 1937; Murchison Medal, Geological Society 1939; Victoria Medal, RGS 1942; Royal Medal, Royal Society 1948; Charles Lagrange Prize, Academie Royale de Sciences de Belgique 1948; Bowie Medal, American Geophysical Union 1952; Copley Medal, Royal Society; Vetlesen Prize 1962; Guy Medal, Royal Statistical Society 1963; Wollaston Medal, Geological Society 1964; Medal of Seismological Society of America 1979; Bakerian Lecturer, Royal Society; Grove Karl Gibert Award, Carnegie Institution of Washington 1962. **Honours:** Kt 1953. **Publications:** *The Earth: Its Origin, History and Physical Constitution*, 1924; *Operational Methods in Mathematical Physics*, 1927; *The Future of the Earth*, 1929; *Scientific Inference*, 1931; *Cartesian Tensors*, 1931; *Earthquakes and Mountains*, 1935; *Theory of Probability*, 1939; (with B Jeffreys) *Methods of Mathematics Physics*, 1946; *Asymptotic Approximations*, 1962; Papers on Astronomy, Geophysics, Theory of Scientific Method, and Plant Ecology, republished in *Collected Papers of Sir Harold Jeffreys*, Volumes 1–6, 1971–1977. Died 18 March 1989.

JEFFREYS, Robert Sydney (1906) Born 9 January 1888, Green Point, Cape Town, South Africa; son of George Ernest Jeffreys, Merchant, and Maria Johanna Herbert; m Dorothy. **Subject(s):** Law; BA 1909; LLB 1909. **Tutor(s):** L H K Bushe-Fox. **Educ:** Green and Sea Point Public School, Cape Town; Boys High School, Wynberg; Bedford Grammar School. **Career:** Called to the Bar, Gray's Inn 1910; Assistant Commissioner and JP, Rhodesia 1910–1922; Assistant Magistrate 1926; Judge, Protectorate Court, Nigeria 1939. Died 27 December 1959.

JEHANGIR, Jehangir Cowasji (1930) Born 15 November 1911, Gibbs House, Malabar Hill, Bombay, India; son of Sir Cowasjee Jehangir, Landowner and Industrialist, and Hirabai Hilla Hormorji Wadia; m Lady Bomanji. BA 1934. **Tutor(s):** E A Benians. **Johnian Relatives:** son of Cowasjee Jehangir (1897). **Educ:** St Xavier's High School, Bombay; Private Tuition. **Career:** Lecturer on Indian Affairs. **Appointments:** Honorary Liaison Officer to High Commissioner for India. Died 23 October 1944.

JEHU, Brigadier Ivor Stewart (1928) Born 21 October 1908, Strathmartine, Hepburn Gardens, St Andrews, Scotland; son of Thomas John Jehu, Professor of Geology, University of Edinburgh, and Annie Meston Stewart; m Joan Mary Rose Wier, 1944; 1 son, 1 daughter. **Subject(s):** History; BA 1931. **Tutor(s):** E A Benians. **Johnian Relatives:** son of Thomas John Jehu (1895). **Educ:** Edinburgh Academy; University of Edinburgh. **Career:** Sub-Editor, Glasgow *Herald* 1931–1932; Junior Assistant Editor, *The Times of India*, Bombay; Correspondent for *The Times, Daily Telegraph, Daily Mail, The Christian*

Science Monitor; Director of Public Relations, Defence Department, Government of India 1940–1942; Lieutenant Colonel, Indian Army 1940–1942; Brigadier and Head of Inter-Services Public Relations Directorate, India Command 1942–1945; Editor, *The Times of India* and Director, Bennett Coleman and Co (India) 1945–1952; Editor, *The Sunday News of India*, and the *Evening News of India* 1948–1950; Chief Information Officer, Ministry of Supply, UK; Chief Information Officer, Ministry of Aviation. **Honours:** CIE 1944. Died 7 October 1960.

JELLEY, Dr John Valentine (1946) Born 3 July 1918, Hampton in Arden, Warwickshire; son of James Valentine Jelley, Artist, and Edith Mary Brock. **Subject(s):** Physics; PhD 1951; BSc (Birmingham) 1940; FRAS. **Tutor(s):** J M Wordie. **Educ:** Solihull School; Birmingham University. **Career:** Radar Research, Malvern 1940–1944; Nuclear Physics Research, Canada 1944–1946; Principal Scientific Officer, AERE, Harwell 1951. **Appointments:** Member, European Physical Union; British Member, International Astronomical Union; Member, Institute of Navigation 1990.

JENKINS, Albert Ernest (1901) Born 29 October 1880, Abermolais School House, Newfoundland, Merthyr Tydfil, Wales; son of Jenkin Jenkins, Schoolmaster, and Elizabeth Owen. **Subject(s):** Classics; BA 1904; BA (London) 1900; MA (London) 1903. **Tutor(s):** D MacAlister. **Educ:** Abermolais School, Merthyr Tydfil.

JENKINS, Cecil (1920) Born 27 October 1900, 4 Hunters Buildings, Borough Road, Southwark, Surrey; son of Edgar Jenkins, Insurance Superintendent, and Ethel Cradick; m Helen Maud (d 22 October 1952). **Subject(s):** Natural Sciences; BA 1923; MA 1928. **Tutor(s):** B F Armitage. **Educ:** John Ruskin London County Council Elementary School, Camberwell; Merton Road London County Council School, Wandsworth; Westminster City School. **Career:** Master, King Edward VI School, Southampton; Master, Worthing Secondary School 1925. **Awards:** Exhibition, SJC. Died 17 January 1979.

JENKINS, Dr David Philip (1944) Born 13 May 1927, 37 Ladysmith Road, Cardiff; son of David Alban Jenkins, Municipal Clerk, and Marie Romola Thomas; m Marion Nicholas Jasper, 2 June 1952; 1 son (Huw David b 1962), 2 daughters (Bridget Mary b 1957, d 1988 and Elspeth Jane b 1959). **Subject(s):** Natural Sciences; BA 1947; MA 1952; PhD 1952; FBCS. **Tutor(s):** C W Guillebaud. **Johnian Relatives:** father-in-law of David Robert Wilkinson (1975). **Educ:** Cardiff High School; Rhondda County School, Porth. **Career:** Mathematics Division, TRE (Retired as Superintendent, Computing and Software Research Division, RSRE, Malvern) 1950–1982. **Awards:** Major Scholarship, SJC 1944.

JENKINS, Frederick (1904) Born 29 April 1881, Munsley, Herefordshire; son of Owen Francis Samuel Jenkins, Clerk in Holy Orders, and Elizabeth Langworthy. **Subject(s):** Natural Sciences; BA 1907. **Tutor(s):** D MacAlister. **Educ:** St John's School, Leatherhead. **Career:** Assistant Master, Great Ealing School; Assistant Master, West Kirby School; Assistant Master, Harrogate School; Assistant Master, Wye Agricultural College; Sellindge Agricultural College, Kent 1912. Died 8 July 1962.

JENKINS, Gwilym John (1934) Born 23 September 1915, 161 Kings Road, Cardiff; son of John Russell Jenkins, Schoolmaster, and Susan Batt. **Subject(s):** Mechanical Sciences; BA 1937; MA 1941. **Tutor(s):** J S Boys Smith. **Educ:** Radnor Road Boys' School; Cardiff High School.

JENKINS, Hammond Beaconsfield (1900) Born 23 April 1881, 308 Upper Parliament Street, Liverpool; son of Thomas Mutlow Jenkins, RN, and Rosa Mary Addison; m Edith; 1 daughter (Winifred Mary d 10 September 2000). **Subject(s):** Mechanical Sciences; BA 1903; MA 1908. **Tutor(s):** L H K Bushe-Fox; D MacAlister. **Educ:** Hoscote House School, West Kirby; Liverpool Institute. **Career:** Examiner, Education Office 1908; Assistant Secretary, Board of Education 1939. Died 30 September 1965.

JENKINS, Henry John (1949) Born 24 June 1930, Military Families Hospital, Scotton, Richmond, Yorkshire; son of William Henry Edwin Jenkins, Bandmaster, 2nd East Surrey Regiment, and Catherine Neale. **Subject(s):** English; BA 1952; MA 1956. **Tutor(s):** A G Lee. **Educ:** Horbury Council School; Ossett Grammar School. **Career:** Solicitor and Notary, Senior Partner, Messrs Cunningtons, Solicitors, Braintree, Essex. **Awards:** Exhibition, SJC 1947; Research Scholarship, Minnesota University.

JENKINS, Herbert Riches (1913) Born 23 December 1880, Ystradfychan House, Ystradyfodwg, Glamorganshire; son of William Jenkins, Mining Engineer, and Kate Elizabeth Riches. **Subject(s):** History; BA 1919; MA 1923. **Tutor(s):** L H K Bushe-Fox. **Educ:** Clifton College.

JENKS, George Bernard (1920) Born 23 March 1902, 28 Penn Road, Wolverhampton, Staffordshire; son of Albert Ernest Jenks, Manufacturer, and Annie Wright; m Sheila Margaret Carnegie-Brown. **Tutor(s):** E A Benians. **Johnian Relatives:** father of Robin Eric Jenks (1948). **Educ:** The Priory, Malvern; Lickey Hills School; Uppingham School. **Career:** Chairman and Managing Director of A E Jenks & Catlell Ltd 1938. Died 28 April 1956.

JENKS, Robin Eric (1948) Born 8 October 1928, Queen Victoria Nursing Institution, Wolverhampton; son of George Bernard Jenks, Director, Pressed Steel Manufacturing Company, and Sheila Margaret Carnegie-Brown. **Subject(s):** English; BA 1950; MA 1955. **Tutor(s):** R L Howland. **Johnian Relatives:** son of George Bernard Jenks (1920). **Educ:** Licky Hills School; Old Hall School; Upper Canada College, Toronto; Shrewsbury School.

JENKS, Walter Henry (1923) Born 26 December 1903, Hanover Lodge, Regents Park, London; son of Walter Jenks, of independent means, and Maud Marion Baker. **Tutor(s):** B F Armitage. **Educ:** Fretherne House, London; Heddon Court, Cockfosters, Barnet; Malvern College; Stirling House, Bournemouth.

JENKS, William Corfield (1922) Naval Officer.

JENKYN, Thomas Richard (1928) Born 4 March 1909, 131 Felbrigge Road, Goodmayes, Ilford, Essex; son of Richard Thomas Jenkyn, Paper Maker's Export Manager, and Edith Emily Engledow. **Subject(s):** Mathematics/Natural Sciences; BA 1931; MA 1940. **Tutor(s):** J M Wordie. **Educ:** Ilford College; Brentwood School.

JENNINGS, Jan McIlwraith (1924) Born 1 November 1906, Campbellfield, St Michaels, St Albans; son of Thomas Noel Gwyn Jennings, General Manager, Standard Bank of South Africa, and Mabel Andrina Janet McIlwraith. **Tutor(s):** B F Armitage. **Educ:** Western Province Preparatory School, Cape Town, South Africa; Kelly College, Tavistock; Private Tuition, Watford.

JENNINGS, John Rannard (1922) Born 5 May 1904, Thoresway, Caistor, Lincolnshire; son of John Thomas Jennings, Farmer, and Winifred Constance Sparkes; m Joan Audrey Read, 1929; 2 sons. BA 1925; MA 1947. **Tutor(s):** B F Armitage. **Educ:** Clevedon House School, Leeds; Gresham's School, Holt. **Career:** National Institute of Industrial Psychology 1927–1938; Secretary, National Institute for the Deaf 1938–1941; National Institute of Industrial Psychology 1941; Department of the Senior Psychologist to the Admiralty, HMS *Royal Arthur*, Skegness 1941–1945; Industrial Psychology, Department of Labour and Employment, New Zealand 1947; Vocational Guidance Centre, Wellington, New Zealand 1958. **Appointments:** Psychologist, Disabled Re-habilitation League, Auckland; Associate, BPsS; Founder, New Zealand Institute of Personnel Management. **Publications:** Many articles in psychological journals and by invitation in the *American Buros Mental Measurement Yearbook*. Died December 1998.

JERROME, Ronald Henry (1931) Born 2 April 1913, 60 Ulleswater Road, Southgate; son of Henry Abraham Jerrome, Clerk, Port of London

Authority, and Katherine Louisa Byworth. **Subject(s):** Mathematics; BA 1934. **Tutor(s):** J M Wordie. **Educ:** Glencourse, Eastbourne; Brunswick, Haywards Heath; The Cathedral School, Hereford. **Career:** Company Director. **Awards:** Somerset Exhibition, SJC 1931.

JERUSALEM, Georg (1908) Born 12 March 1886, Vienna, Austria; son of Josef Jerusalem, Manufacturer, and Hermine Vondörfer. BA 1910. **Tutor(s):** E E Sikes. **Educ:** Technical High School, Vienna, Austria; Manchester University.

JESSOP, Dennis Samuel Alfred Edwards (1925) Born 31 December 1907, 190 Aston Lane, Handsworth, Staffordshire; son of Harry Edwards Jessop, Medical Practitioner, and Fanny Susannah Simmons; m Margaret L Hutchinson, 1 April 1929, Church of Our Lady and the English Martyrs, Cambridge. BA 1928; MA 1932. **Tutor(s):** E A Benians. **Johnian Relatives:** brother of Harry Victor Edwards Jessop (1923); brother-in-law of Allan Noel Skelton (1925). **Educ:** Edgbaston Preparatory School; Malvern College. **Career:** Assistant Master, Hollylea Preparatory School, Liverpool 1931; Local Director, Brush Electrical Engineering Company Ltd, Loughborough, Leicestershire 1947. Died 6 December 1987.

JESSOP, Harry Victor Edwards (1923) Born 15 September 1905, 1 Tintern Road, Handsworth, Staffordshire; son of Harry Edwards Jessop, Medical Practitioner, and Fanny Susannah Simmons; m Hilda Mary (Bobbie) Applin, 30 November 1928, St Peter's, Belsize Square; 1 daughter (Sally-Ann). **Tutor(s):** B F Armitage. **Johnian Relatives:** brother of Dennis Samuel Alfred Edward Jessop (1925). **Educ:** Edgbaston Preparatory School; Malvern College. Died 26 January 1969.

JESTY, John Bedford (1938) Born 23 March 1920, Doddings Bere Regis; son of Frederick Thomas Jesty, Farmer, and Emily Rebecca Bedford. BA 1941. **Tutor(s):** J S Boys Smith. **Educ:** Pembroke Lodge, Southbourne; Beau-soleil, Villars, Switzerland; Weymouth College. Died 19 February 2003.

JEWELL, Edward Basil (1920) Born 2 November 1899, 15 Victoria Grove, Southsea, Hampshire; son of Edward Charles Jewell, Brewer, and Beatrice Ada Gale. **Tutor(s):** E A Benians. **Educ:** Monkton Combe School, Bath; RMC, Sandhurst; St John's Hall, Highbury.

JEWELL, Professor Peter Arundel (1945) Born 16 June 1925, 197 Burntwood Lane, Wandsworth, London; son of Percy Arundel Jewell, Builder, and Ivy Dorothea Enness; m Juliet Clutton-Brock, 1958; 3 daughters. **Subject(s):** Natural Sciences (Physiology with Pharmacology); BA 1947; MA 1951; PhD 1951; BSc (Reading) 1945; CBiol; FIBiol. **Tutor(s):** G C L Bertram. **Educ:** West Hill Elementary School; Wandsworth School; Chelsea Polytechnic; University of Reading. **Career:** Assistant in Research, Pharmacology, University of Cambridge 1947; Lecturer, Department of Pharmacology 1950–1960, Lecturer, Animal Husbandry and Veterinary Hygiene 1959, Royal Veterinary College, London; Research Fellow, Zoological Society of London 1960–1966; Professor of Biological Sciences, University of Nigeria 1966–1967; Senior Lecturer and Director of Conservation Course, UCL 1967–1972; Professor of Zoology, Royal Holloway College 1972–1977; Mary Marshall and Arthur Walton Professor of the Physiology of Reproduction, University of Cambridge 1977–1992; Title C Fellow, SJC 1977–1992; Title E Fellow, SJC 1992–1998. **Appointments:** Vice-President, Zoological Society of London 1991–1992; President Mammal Society 1991–1993; Vice-President, Rare Breeds Survival Trust 1991–1998. **Awards:** Gedge Prize, University of Cambridge 1950. **Publications:** (ed) *The Experimental Earthwork on Overton Down, Wiltshire, 1960*, BAAS, 1963; (with C Milner and J Morton Boyd) *Island Survivors: the Ecology of the Soay Sheep of St Kilda*, Athlone Press, 1974; (ed, with S Holt and D Hard) *Problems in Management of Locally Abundant Wild Mammals*, Academic Press, New York, 1981; scientific papers in *Journal of Animal Ecology, Journal of Physiology, Journal of Zoology, Ark* etc. Died 23 May 1998.

JIMÉNEZ, Manuel (1939) (admitted to Fitzwilliam College 1938) Born 30 May 1918, Madrid; son of Alberto Jiménez, Lecturer in Spanish, University of Oxford, and Natalia Bartolomé. **Subject(s):** Modern and Medieval Languages. **Educ:** Instituto Escuela, Madrid; Institucion Libre de Enseñanza, Madrid; Madrid University.

JOCE, John Burden Dunn (1901) Born 24 September 1881, Strand, Bideford, Devon; son of William Dunn Joce, Druggist, and Charlotte Saunder. **Subject(s):** Modern and Medieval Languages; BA 1904. **Tutor(s):** C E Graves; J R Tanner. **Educ:** Exeter School. **Career:** Assistant Master, Haileybury School 1914–1956; Lieutenant, RNVR, WWI.

JOHN, Basil Joseph (1921) Born 8 February 1902, Satara, India; son of Henry Celestine John, East India Merchant, and Mabel Teresa Shield. **Tutor(s):** E A Benians. **Educ:** St Mary's Convent, England's Lane, Hampstead; Convent of the Cross, Boscombe; Stonyhurst College.

JOHNS, Ewart Morien (1942) Born 21 November 1923, 17 Old Village Road, Barry, Glamorganshire; son of Thomas Giraldus Johns, Schoolmaster, and Gertrude Watkin Edwards; m Barbara Mary Tetley, 1949; 3 sons (b 1951, 1953 and 1961), 1 daughter (b 1964). **Subject(s):** Geography; BA 1947; MA 1949; DipEd (London) 1948; Honorary Doctorate of Arts (Dartington College of Arts, University of Plymouth) 2001. **Tutor(s):** C W Guillebaud. **Educ:** Romilly Elementary School, Barry; Barry Boys County School. **Career:** Lecturer and Senior Lecturer in Geography, University of Exeter 1948–1972; Lecturer in Geography, Oklahoma State University 1969–1970; Founding Head of Department of Visual Arts, University of Lancaster 1972–1983; Exhibitions of Paintings/Drawings/Sculpture 1961–2002 including Grabowski Gallery, London, others in London and in Exeter, Lancaster, Hull, Harrogate, Kendal, Leeds, Folkstone, Plymouth, and Totnes, and Retrospective Exhibitions at King's Lynn Arts Centre and Dartington College of Arts 2001. **Publications:** *British Townscapes*, Arnold, 1965; *50 Years of Art*, Dartington College of Arts, 2001.

JOHNS, John Gordon Peter Owen (1942) Born 18 April 1924, Bangkok, Siam; son of John Francis Johns, Far Eastern Consular Service, and Nora Lettice Liddle; m Megan Christine Terrey, 8 July 1950. **Subject(s):** Law; BA (Magdalene) 1948. **Tutor(s):** C W Guillebaud. **Educ:** Melbreck Pre-Preparatory School, Tilford; St Edmund's Preparatory School, Hindhead; Charterhouse. **Career:** Solicitor.

JOHNSON, Anthony Alfred (1945) Born 11 March 1927, 128 Lapwing Lane, Didsbury, Manchester; son of Carlton Spence Johnson, Hydraulic Packer, and Emily Ryland. **Tutor(s):** J M Wordie. **Educ:** Broomfield House School, Didsbury; Moor Allerton School, Didsbury; Cheadle Hulme School, Cheshire.

JOHNSON, Arthur Hazel Lionel (1934) Born 8 September 1916, Bownhill, Coronation Road, Rodborough, Stroud; son of Arthur Hazeldine Johnson, Draper, and Elsie Maud Gobey; m Joyce. **Subject(s):** Mathematics; BA 1937. **Tutor(s):** J M Wordie. **Educ:** Uplands Council School, Stroud; Marling School, Stroud. **Career:** Ministry of Food: Assistant Director, Deputy Director, Director of Cocoa, Chocolate and Sugar Confectionery Division 1939–1945; Management Committee, Rowntree & Co, York 1945–1950. **Awards:** Scholarship, SJC 1937; Wright's Prize, SJC 1937. Died 4 October 1950.

JOHNSON, Brian Gordon (1944) Born 24 December 1926, 160 Milton Road, Cambridge; son of William Frederick Edward Johnson, Chief Clerk, Emmanuel College, and Winifred Violet Ivy Chapman; m Pamela Mary Shaw, 14 July 1951; 2 sons (David and Paul). **Subject(s):** Mathematics/Music; BA 1950. **Tutor(s):** J M Wordie. **Educ:** Milton Road School, Cambridge; Perse School, Cambridge. **Career:** National Service, RE; Manager, JE Lyons Co 1951–1961. Died 1 May 1961.

JOHNSON, Colin Aylmer (1941) Born 26 July 1923, Birkdale, Southport, Lancashire; son of John Johnson, Cap and Hat Manufacturer, and

Margaret Aylmer. **Subject(s):** Law; BA 1947; MA 1949; LLB 1948. **Tutor(s):** S J Bailey. **Johnian Relatives:** brother of John Aylmer Johnson (1939). **Educ:** Terra Nova, Birkdale; Charterhouse. **Career:** RNVR 1942–1946; Solicitor, Laces & Co, Liverpool 1951. Died 11 March 1967.

JOHNSON, Cyril Jossé (1919) Born 16 August 1897, 37a Finsbury Square, London; son of Harold Jossé Johnson, Physician, and Emily Jane Foxwell; m Joyce Irene Pinnock, 14 July 1928, St Nicholas' Parish Church, Chislehurst. **Subject(s):** Modern and Medieval Languages; BA 1922; MA 1926. **Tutor(s):** E E Sikes. **Johnian Relatives:** nephew of Herbert Somerton Foxwell (1868), Edward Ernest Foxwell (1871) and of William Arthur Foxwell (1874). **Educ:** Dean Court, Byfleet; Felsted School, Essex. **Career:** Second Lieutenant, RE, served in France 1917; Lieutenant, RE, seconded to Intelligence Corps, WWI; Farmer. **Appointments:** Master, Worshipful Company of Pewterers, and the Worshipful Company of Tallow Chandlers. **Awards:** Scholarship, SJC 1915. Died 19 August 1980.

JOHNSON, Derek (1948) Born 21 June 1930, 18 Burton Road, Monk Bretton, Barnsley, Yorkshire; son of Ernest Arthur Johnson, Colliery Deputy, and Doris Haigh; m Betty Robinson, 1952; 2 sons, 1 daughter. **Subject(s):** History; BA 1951. **Tutor(s):** F Thistlethwaite. **Educ:** Littleworth Junior School, Barnsley; Barnsley and District Holgate Grammar School. **Career:** District Officer, HM Overseas Civil Service, Uganda 1951–1964; Administrative Manager, then Credit Manager, Total Oil GB Ltd 1965–1974; Manager, Commercial and Industrial Division, then Deputy to the Managing Director, Botswana Development Corporation 1974–1981; General Manager, Swaziland Sugar Association 1981–1991. **Honours:** Uganda Independence Medal. **Publications:** (contributor) *Looking Back at the Uganda Protectorate*.

JOHNSON, Dr Desmond Sidney (1943) Born 18 November 1924, 101 Bromley Road, Ecclesfield, Sheffield; son of Sidney Johnson, Schoolmaster, and Doris Smith. **Subject(s):** Natural Sciences; BA 1947; MA 1950; PhD (London). **Tutor(s):** C W Guillebaud. **Educ:** Ryecroft Council School; Mexborough Secondary School. **Career:** Lecturer in Zoology 1959, Reader in Zoology and Head of Department 1961, University of Malaya. **Awards:** Exhibition, SJC 1942; Frank Smart Prize for Zoology, University of Cambridge 1948.

JOHNSON, Eric Finnis (1914) Born 29 January 1896, 34 Great Coram Street, Bloomsbury, Middlesex; son of Henry John Finnis Johnson, Departmental Manager, and Harriett Annie Thomson; m Muriel; 1 daughter (Lesley). **Subject(s):** Mechanical Sciences; BA 1921; MA 1924. **Tutor(s):** L H K Bushe-Fox. **Educ:** Central Foundation School. **Career:** Lieutenant, Berkshire Regiment, POW, WWI; Port Commissioner, Calcutta 1923–1935; Port Engineer, Vizagapatam 1935–1939; Manager, European Works, Borax Consolidated Ltd 1939. Died 20 July 1967.

JOHNSON, Ernest William (1901) Born 16 March 1882, South Cave, Yorkshire; son of James Johnson, Teacher, and Carolina Stenson; 2 sons. **Subject(s):** Mathematics; BA 1904; MA 1920. **Tutor(s):** E E Sikes. **Educ:** South Cave Boys Church of England School; Hymers College, Hull. **Career:** Teacher, Municipal Secondary School, Manchester 1904–1909; Mathematics Teacher, Huddersfield College 1909; Mathematics Master, Central High School, Manchester, until 1942. Died 4 May 1943.

JOHNSON, Howard William (1942) Born 27 August 1924, 1 Stanford Avenue, Hassocks, Sussex; son of William Johnson, Motor Fitter, and Nellie Louie Willis Fry; m (1) Barbara Joan Stride, 1949 (d 1996), (2) Ruth Wallas; (1) 2 sons. **Subject(s):** Natural Sciences; BA 1945; FIA 1953. **Tutor(s):** C W Guillebaud. **Educ:** St Andrew's Senior Boys' School, Worthing; Ferring Church School; Seal School, Kent; Cowfold Church School; Worthing High School. **Career:** Lieutenant, Fleet Air Arm 1944–1947; various actuarial and management appointments with Equitable Life Assurance Society 1947–1985; Various Senior Management appointments and directorships of subsidiary companies, including Managing Director of University Life 1973–1985.

JOHNSON, John Aylmer (1939) Born 2 January 1921, 5 Knowsley Road, Southport, Lancashire; son of John Johnson, Hat and Cap Manufacturer, and Margaret Aylmer; m Faith Rosemary Rice-Jones, 1980. **Subject(s):** Law; BA 1942; MA 1946. **Tutor(s):** C W Guillebaud; S J Bailey. **Johnian Relatives:** brother of Colin Aylmer Johnson (1941). **Educ:** Somerville, Birkdale; Terra Nova School, Birkdale; Charterhouse. **Career:** Lieutenant, RNVR 1941–1946; Solicitor (Honours) 1949; Partner, Dodds Ashcroft (Solicitors) Liverpool 1952–1986; Consultant, Davies Wallis Foyster, Liverpool 1986–1995. **Appointments:** Governor, Terra Nova School, Holmes Chapel, Cheshire 1962–1986 (Chairman, 1967–1980); Chairman, Watson Prickard Ltd, Liverpool, 1984–1991. **Awards:** Senior Scholarship (Classics), Charterhouse; Foundation Scholarship, SJC 1947; Wright's Prize, SJC 1947.

JOHNSON, Professor John Charles (SPERRIN-JOHNSON) (1913) Born 2 October 1885, 109 Douglas Street, Cork, Ireland; son of Andrew Johnson, Coach Builder, and Kate McCarthy. **Tutor(s):** R P Gregory. **Educ:** Christian Brothers' College, Cork, Ireland; University College, Cork. **Career:** Professor of Botany, University College, Cork; Professor of Botany, University College, Auckland, NZ 1914.

JOHNSON, Leslie (1911) Born 23 February 1892, 287 Camden Road, Holloway; son of Benjamin Charles Johnson, Surveyor, and Maud Louise Hebblethwaite. **Subject(s):** Mechanical Sciences; BA 1914; MA 1918. **Tutor(s):** L H K Bushe-Fox. **Educ:** Highgate School. Died 25 January 1969.

JOHNSON, Malcolm MacDonald (1949) Subject(s): History; BA 1952; MA 1956. **Tutor(s):** A G Lee. **Career:** Esquire Bedell, University of Cambridge 1987–1997.

JOHNSON, Dr Martin Christopher (1915) Born 11 October 1896, Church Gate, Cheshunt, Hertfordshire; son of Ernest Wright Johnson, Congregational Minister, and Bertha Bell; m Elsie Wilkinson, 7 November 1962, Carrs Lane Church, Birmingham. **Subject(s):** Natural Sciences; BA 1922; MA 1926; DSc (Birmingham). **Tutor(s):** E E Sikes. **Educ:** Private School, Cheshunt; Perse Grammar School, Cambridge. **Career:** Lecturer, then Reader in Astrophysics, University of Birmingham 1924–1962. **Awards:** Exhibition, SJC 1915; Arnold Gerstenberg Studentship 1922. Died 26 November 1983.

JOHNSON, Maurice Alexander (1928) Born 8 June 1909, Waveney, St Mary's Road, Long Ditton, Surrey; son of Alexander William Johnson, Solicitor, and Caroline Price-Jones. BA 1931; MA 1935. **Tutor(s):** C W Guillebaud. **Educ:** Shrewsbury House, Ditton Hill; Oundle School. Died 19 January 1987.

JOHNSON, Sir Ronald Ernest Charles (1931) Born 3 May 1913, 8 Garnier Street, Landport, Portsmouth; son of Ernest Bertram Johnson, Leading Cook's Mate, HMS *Irresistible*, and Amelia Grace Kneller; m Elizabeth Gladys Nuttall, 11 September 1938, Southend-on-Sea; 3 sons (David b 27 October 1942, Paul b 14 June 1949 and Matthew b 20 September 1946, d 8 February 1977). **Subject(s):** Classics; BA 1934; MA 1938; Civil Service Exam. **Tutor(s):** M P Charlesworth. **Johnian Relatives:** father of David Charles Johnson (1964). **Educ:** Drayton Road Elementary School, Portsmouth; Portsmouth Grammar School. **Career:** Civil Servant, Scottish Office 1935; Intelligence Staff of Commander-in-Chief, Eastern Fleet 1944–1945; Secretary, Scottish Home and Health Department 1963–1972; Secretary, Commissions for Scotland 1972–1978. **Appointments:** Organist and Choirmaster, St Columba's-by-the-Castle 1952; Member, Board, Fire College, Moreton-in-Marsh; Chairman, Civil Service Savings Committee for Scotland 1963–1978; Chairman, Scottish Hospital Centre 1964–1972; President, Edinburgh Bach Society 1973–1986; Member, Scottish Records Advisory Council 1975–1978; Chairman, Fire Service Research & Training Trust 1976–1989; Committee on Administration of Sherrifdoms 1981–1982; Edinburgh Society of Organists 1980–1982; JP. **Awards:** Scholarship, Portsmouth Grammar School. **Honours:** CB 1961; Kt 1970. **Publications:** Articles in religious and musical journals. Died 8 March 1996.

JOHNSON, The Revd Vernon Yate (1910) Born 12 September 1891, 4 Osborne Terrace, Edinburgh, Scotland; son of James Yate Vernon Johnson, Consulting Engineer, and Agnes Symington; m Helen Aspinall, 28 July 1920, St Mary's, Horsell, Worthing. BA 1913; MA 1917. **Tutor(s):** J R Tanner. **Educ:** The Academy, Edinburgh; Tonbridge School; Tutorial College, Edinburgh; Bishop's Hostel, Farnham. **Career:** Deacon 1915; Curate, Horsell, Woking 1915–1922; Priest 1916; Temporary CF, 4th Class, RACD 1917–1919; Vicar, Nidd, Harrogate 1922–1928; Vicar, St Martin, Potternewton, Leeds 1928–1939; Chaplain, Ministry of Pensions Hospital, Leeds 1937–1939; Rector, St Cuthbert, Colington and St Mungo, Balerno 1939–1953; Canon, St Mary's Cathedral, Edinburgh 1952–1953. **Appointments:** Secretary, Diocesan Church Music Committee; Secretary, Leeds Clergy and Ministers Fraternal; Secretary, Leeds Area Committee, Missionary Council; Assistant Grand Chaplain, Surrey 1920; President, Scottish Ecclesiological Society 1949–1950. Died 11 October 1954.

JOHNSON, William Arthur (1930) Born 24 May 1911, 9 Bolton Road, Pendlebury, Swinton, Lancaster; son of Harold William Johnson, Teacher, and Emma Ruth Gartell. **Subject(s):** Natural Sciences; BA 1933; MA 1937. **Tutor(s):** C W Guillebaud. **Educ:** Halton Bank Council School, Salford; Manchester Grammar School. **Awards:** Exhibition, SJC 1930.

JOHNSTON, The Revd Alec Bowman (1903) Born 1 January 1884, Heighington, County Durham; son of John Johnston, Schoolmaster, and Sarah Simpson. **Subject(s):** Classics/Theology; BA 1906; MA 1910. **Tutor(s):** C E Graves; J R Tanner. **Educ:** Wolverhampton Grammar School. **Career:** Ordained Deacon 1907; Curate, St Anne, Bermondsey 1907–1910; Ordained Priest 1908; Acting Principal, Church Missionary Society, Calcutta 1911–1919; Vice-Principal 1921–1924, Acting Principal 1924–1926, Principal 1926–1934, Noble College, Masulipatam; Chaplain, St Mary, Masulipatam 1924–1926; Vicar, St Matthew with St James, Cambridge 1935–1940; Rector, Welney, Wisbech 1940. **Appointments:** Fellow, Calcutta University 1919. Died 24 June 1966.

JOHNSTON, David Kenneth (1939) Born 15 December 1920, Agra, United Provinces, India; son of Thomas Kenneth Johnston, Indian Civil Service, and Margaret King. **Tutor(s):** R L Howland. **Educ:** Packwood Haugh; Shrewsbury School. **Career:** Lieutenant, Durham Light Infantry, attached Devon Regiment, 6th Airborne Division 1941–1945; Adjutant, North Africa and Italy 1943. Died 24 March 1945 (killed in action).

JOHNSTON, Donald Vaughan (1901) Born 4 November 1882, Maesybar, Llansamlet, Wales; son of John Wallace Johnston, Draper, and Miriam Merchant. **Subject(s):** Mathematics; BA 1904; MA 1910. **Tutor(s):** D MacAlister. **Educ:** Swansea Grammar School. **Career:** Assistant Master, Ystalyfera County School, Cardiff High School; Headmaster, Newtown Intermediate School, Montgomeryshire; Headmaster, Lewis School, Pengam 1919–1926; Chief Inspector, Welsh Board of Education 1926.

JOHNSTON, Frank (1903) Born 10 November 1885, West View, Green Hill Road, Hampstead, Middlesex; son of Charles Johnston, Wine Merchant, and Harriette Lauder King. **Subject(s):** Law; BA 1907. **Tutor(s):** D MacAlister. **Educ:** Charterhouse. **Career:** Major, King's (Shropshire Light Infantry) WWI. Died 31 May 1918 (of wounds received in action).

JOHNSTON, George Arthur Patrick (1933) Born 16 May 1915, Fallowfield, Lurgan, County Armagh, Northern Ireland; son of John Johnston, Linen Manufacturer, and Annie Macoun; m. **Subject(s):** Modern and Medieval Languages/History; BA 1936; MA 1940. **Tutor(s):** C W Guillebaud. **Johnian Relatives:** brother of James Entwisle Johnston (1921). **Educ:** The College, Lurgan; Campbell College, Belfast. Died 1 August 1998.

JOHNSTON, George Robert Arthur McGarel (1935) Born 2 September 1916, 32 Whites Road, Bloemfontein, South Africa; son of Charles McGarel Johnston and Margaret Thompson. **Subject(s):** Economics/Archaeology and Anthropology; BA 1938. **Tutor(s):** C W Guillebaud. **Educ:** St Andrew's Preparatory School, Grahamstown, South Africa; Cheltenham College.

JOHNSTON, James Entwisle (1921) Born 19 February 1903, Annadale, Lurgan, County Armagh, Ireland; son of John Johnston, Linen Manufacturer, and Annie Macoun; m Mary Watson, 27 April 1946, St Helen's Bay Presbyterian Church, County Down. BA 1924. **Tutor(s):** E E Sikes. **Johnian Relatives:** brother of George Arthur Patrick Johnston (1933). **Educ:** Rockport Preparatory School, County Down; Shrewsbury School.

JOHNSTON, John Worthington (1927) Born 13 August 1904, Redford Delgany, Rathdown, County Wicklow, Northern Ireland; son of John Curry Johnston, Presbyterian Minister, and Edith Smith Smith. **Subject(s):** Theology; BA 1929; MA 1957; BA (TCD). **Tutor(s):** E A Benians. **Educ:** Mountjoy School, Dublin; St Andrew's College, Dublin; TCD; Magee College, Londonderry; Westminster College, Cambridge.

JOHNSTON, Malcolm Charteris (1914) Born 17 September 1895, Mount Warren, Torquay, Devon; son of John Charteris Johnston, Congregational Minister, and Catherine Macdonald Dow. **Subject(s):** History; BA 1920; MA 1925. **Tutor(s):** L H K Bushe-Fox. **Educ:** Torquay College; Mill Hill School. **Career:** Captain, RASC, WWI; Superintendent of Staff, Selfridges, Oxford Street. Died 20 March 1964.

JOHNSTON, The Hon Lord Robert Smith (KINCRAIG) (1936) Born 10 October 1918, Fulbar, Langlands Road, Glasgow, Scotland; son of William Turner Johnston, Wholesale Ironmonger, and Annie Robertson Smith; m (1) Margaret Joan Graham, 21 August 1943, Trinity Church, Pollokshields, Glasgow (deceased), (2) Margaret Ogg, 23 July 2003; 1 son (Alexander Graham b 1944), 1 daughter (Barbara b 1947). **Subject(s):** Law; BA 1939; LLB (Glasgow) 1942; QC (Scotland) 1955. **Tutor(s):** C W Guillebaud. **Educ:** Giffnock School, Renfrewshire; Strathallan School, Forgandenny, Scotland. **Career:** Called to Bar (Faculty of Advocates) 1942–1988; Extra Advocate-Depute 1951–1953; Advocate-Depute, Crown Office 1953–1955; Home Advocate-Depute 1959–1962; Sheriff Principal of Roxburgh, Berwick and Selkirk 1964–1970; Elevated to Judges Bench 1972; Senator, College of Justice, Scotland. **Appointments:** President, College Law Society 1938–1939; Member, Faculty of Advocates 1942; Dean, Faculty of Advocates of Scotland 1970–1972; Chairman, Review of Parole and related matters in Scotland 1988.

JOHNSTON, Sydney (1900) Born 16 February 1882, Hampstead, Middlesex; son of Charles Johnston, Wine Merchant, and Harriet Lander King; m Violet. BA 1903. **Tutor(s):** D MacAlister. **Educ:** Horton House, Northampton; Charterhouse. **Career:** Tea Planter, Kincora Estate, Ceylon 1911. Died 4 September 1937.

JOHNSTON, Vivian Dale (1931) Born 2 March 1912, Villa Devoto, Buenos Aires; son of Matthew Thomson Trotter Johnston, Manager, Cattle Breeding Establishment, and Winifred Mary Gardom. **Tutor(s):** J M Wordie. **Educ:** Winton House, Winchester; Sherborne School. **Career:** Apprentice, Railway Construction Works, Argentina 1930–1931.

JOHNSTONE, Alastair Ian Campbell (1935) Born 29 July 1917, 34 Albert Road, Marylebone, London; son of Charles Campbell Gosling Johnstone, Army Officer (Major), and Laura Mary Hemans. **Tutor(s):** R L Howland. **Educ:** Orley Farm School, Harrow; Harrow School.

JOHNSTONE, James Arthur (1935) Born 29 July 1913, 1 Bellevue Crescent, Ayr; son of Arthur James Johnstone, Solicitor, and Euphemia Tennant Fullarton; m Dorothy Christian Liddle Hacket, 6 July 1946,

St Columba's Church House, London; 1 son (Peter Tennant 1948). **Subject(s):** Mathematics. **Tutor(s):** J M Wordie. **Johnian Relatives:** father of Peter Tennant Johnstone (1966). **Educ:** Ayr Academy; University of Glasgow. **Career:** Department of Inland Revenue 1936; Assistant Secretary, Inland Revenue 1946–1964; Commissioner, Inland Revenue 1964–1973. **Appointments:** Secretary, Radcliffe Commission on the Taxation of Profits and Income 1952–1955; Chairman, Third Inland Revenue Ordinance Review Committee, Hong Kong 1976. **Publications:** (Co-author) *Comparative conflict resolution procedures in taxation; An Analytic Comparative Study*, Michigan Legal Studies. Died 25 July 1989.

JOHNSTONE, The Revd John Robert Maxwell (1926) Born 6 July 1907, The Vicarage, Queen's Road, Southbourne, Bournemouth; son of Philip Marmaduke Cramer Johnstone, Clerk in Holy Orders, and Emily Alexandra Galpin; m Vera. BA 1929; MA 1933. **Tutor(s):** J M Wordie. **Educ:** Cheltenham College Junior School; Cheltenham College; Cuddesdon College. **Career:** Vicar, Ashton Keynes; Ordained Deacon 1930; Curate, Otley 1930–1933; Ordained Priest 1931; Secretary, Church Missionary Society, Young People's Department 1933–1936; Vicar, Frizinghall, Bradford 1936–1944; Perpetual Curate, St Barnabas, Knowle 1945–1953; Vicar, St John the Baptist, Greenhill, Middlesex 1958–1962; Vicar, Ashton Keynes with Leigh, Swindon, Wiltshire 1962; Honorary Canon, Bristol Cathedral 1965; Residentiary Canon, Bristol Cathedral 1966. **Awards:** Choral Studentship, SJC.

JOHNSTONE, Captain Ronald David (1937) Born 10 August 1918, Ahmedabad Camp, India; son of Thomas White Johnstone, Chief Inspector of Factories, and Anne Morgan; m Mona Cornelius, 9 October 1942. **Subject(s):** Modern and Medieval Languages; BA 1940. **Tutor(s):** C W Guillebaud. **Educ:** Goodwich School; Ryeford Hall; Wycliffe College, Stonehouse. **Career:** Captain, Lothian and Border Horse, Royal Tank Regiment. **Honours:** MC. Died June 1944 (killed in action in Italy).

JOLLANS, John Lewis (1943) Born 2 July 1925, Scotter, Gainsborough, Lincolnshire; son of William Jollans, Cotton Merchant, and Rachel Baron; m Margaret. BA 1946; MA 1950; AICTA 1947; MIBiol 1973. **Tutor(s):** C W Guillebaud. **Johnian Relatives:** brother of William Mallinson Jollans (1942); father of Adam Nicholas Jollans (1977). **Educ:** Council School, Great Harwood; Council School, Birmingham; King Edward's School, Birmingham. **Career:** Research into animal husbandry and breeding, and senior lecturer, Kumasi College, Ghana; Geneticist, Messrs C & T Harris Ltd 1961; Research Officer, Centre for Agricultural Strategy, University of Reading 1976. **Appointments:** Associate, Imperial College of Tropical Agriculture 1947. Died 3 October 1987.

JOLLANS, William Mallinson (1942) Born 24 April 1924, Scotter, Gainsborough, Lincolnshire; son of William Jollans, Cotton Merchant, and Rachel Baron; m Joan Osbourn, 14 July 1951; 4 sons (Anthony, Alastair, Kenneth and Philip). **Subject(s):** Mechanical Sciences; BA 1945; MA 1949; CEng; FICE; FCIWEM. **Tutor(s):** S J Bailey. **Johnian Relatives:** brother of John Lewis Jollans (1943); uncle of Adam Nicholas Jollans (1977). **Educ:** Scotter Church of England School; Trent Boulevard Elementary School, West Bridgford; Great Harwood Council School, Lancashire; Dennis Road Elementary School, Birmingham; King Edward's High School, Birmingham. **Career:** County Water Engineer, Caithness County Council; Water Engineer and Manager, Huddersfield Borough Council; Director of Operations, Yorkshire Water Authority; Engineering Adviser, Water Aid 1986–2000.

JOLLY, Evelyn Hugh Parker (1904) Born 18 April 1886, 67 London Road, Ipswich, Suffolk; son of Henry John Parker Jolly, Miller and Merchant, and Mary Emily Lee; m Ida Carrie Cole, 26 November 1919, St Saviour's, Warwick Avenue. **Subject(s):** Natural Sciences/History; BA 1907. **Tutor(s):** D MacAlister. **Johnian Relatives:** brother of Leonard John Parker Jolly (1901). **Educ:** Framlingham College. **Career:** Judge, Magistrate, Judicial Commissioner, Indian Civil Service 1908–1934. Died 6 December 1962.

JOLLY, Keith (1948) Born 4 August 1927, Oak Villa, Duke Road, Rondebosch, Cape Town, South Africa; son of William Tasker Adam Jolly, Professor of Physiology, and Aimée Murray. **Subject(s):** Archaeology and Anthropology; BA 1950; MA 1954; BA (Cape Town) 1947. **Tutor(s):** J M Wordie. **Educ:** Micklefield Preparatory School; Camps Bay Preparatory School; Rondebosch High School; Diocesan College, Rondebosch. Died 16 September 1970.

JOLLY, Leonard John Parker (1901) Born 30 October 1882, High Street, Halstead, Essex; son of Henry John Parker Jolly, Miller and Merchant, and Mary Emily Lee. **Subject(s):** Natural Sciences; BA 1904. **Tutor(s):** D MacAlister. **Johnian Relatives:** brother of Evelyn Hugh Parker Jolly (1904). **Educ:** Framlingham College. **Career:** Indian Civil Service. Died 1914.

JONAS, Harry Oliver John Carter (1946) Born 11 May 1923, The Grange, Stevenage, Hertfordshire; son of Harry Carter Jonas, CBE, Land Agent, and Phyllis Juliet Nicolls; m (1) Jean Phyllis Cadman, 1945 (d 1974), (2) Alex, Lady Nunburnholme, 1948; 1 son, 2 daughters, 1 stepson. BA 1948; MA 1953; FRICS. **Tutor(s):** G C L Bertram. **Educ:** King's College School, Cambridge; Charterhouse. **Career:** RA 1941–1946; Chartered Surveyor 1949–1979; Senior Partner, Carter Jonas, Chartered Surveyors 1966–1979. **Appointments:** Crown Estate Receiver 1953–1979; Land Steward, Society of Merchant Venturers of Bristol 1965–1979.

JONES, Anthony Humphrey Lewis (1943) Born 30 June 1925, 2 Kingston Road, Swansea; son of Lewis Jones, Secretary, South Wales Steel Association, and Alice Maude Willis. **Tutor(s):** C W Guillebaud. **Educ:** Stouts Hill Preparatory School, Uley; Clifton College.

JONES, Anthony Lewis (1947) Born 17 August 1925, 9 Rosebury Crescent, Newcastle upon Tyne; son of Percy Louis Jones, Engineer, and Ethel Margaret Gillis. **Subject(s):** Law; BA 1949; LLB 1950. **Tutor(s):** C W Guillebaud. **Educ:** Newcastle Preparatory School; Oundle School. **Career:** Lieutenant, RA; Lawyer.

JONES, Dr Arthur Emrys (1937) Born 30 August 1920, 4 Warden Street, Kirkdale; son of Ellis Jones, Orthopaedic Fitter, and Sarah Jane Jones; m Mary Lewis; 1 son (Emrys b 1948), 1 daughter (Gwyneth b 1944). **Subject(s):** Mathematics; BA 1940. **Tutor(s):** J M Wordie. **Johnian Relatives:** uncle of Gareth David Jones (1969). **Educ:** Anfield Road School; Alsop High School. **Career:** Ballistics Section, Armaments Research Department 1940–1945; Rothamsted Experimental Station; Lecturer in Mathematics, Imperial College, London 1945–1947. **Awards:** Major Scholarship, SJC 1936. Died 7 May 1948.

JONES, Professor Sir Brynmor (1929) Born 20 September 1903, 4 Roberts Lane, Rhos, Wrexham; son of William Edward Jones, Schoolmaster, and Hannah Jane Roberts; m Dora Jones, 1933 (d 1987). PhD 1933; ScD 1948; BSc (Wales) 1925; PhD (Wales) 1928; Honorary LLD (Wales) 1968; Honorary LLD (Leeds) 1974; Honorary DLitt (Hull) 1972; FRSC. **Tutor(s):** J M Wordie. **Educ:** Sorbonne, Paris; The Grammar School, Ruabon; University College of North Wales, Bangor. **Career:** Fellow, University of Wales 1928–1931; Assistant Demonstrator, University of Cambridge 1930–1931; Lecturer in Organic Chemistry, University of Sheffield 1931–1946; Extra-Mural Research Team, Ministry of Supply 1940–1945; G F Grant Professor of Chemistry 1946–1956, Dean, Faculty of Science, and Deputy Principal 1949–1952, Vice-Principal 1952–1954, Pro-Vice-Chancellor 1954–1956, Vice-Chancellor 1956–1972, University College, Hull; Director, Yorkshire Television 1970–1972. **Appointments:** Council Member, Chemical Society 1945–1948 and 1953–1956; Senior Reporter, Annual Reports of Chemical Society 1948; President, Hull Literary and Philosophical Society 1955–1957; Member, Court of Universities of Nottingham and Sheffield 1956–1972; Governor, Hymers College 1956–1984; Member, East Riding Education Committee 1956–1974; Member, General Nursing Council 1960–1966; Chairman, Universities Council for Adult Education 1961–1965; Member, British Committee of Selection for Frank Know Fellowships to Harvard

University 1962–1972; Member, DSIR Postgraduate Training Awards Committee 1963–1965; Member, Academic Advisory Committee, Welsh College of Advanced Technology 1964–1967; Member, Provisional Council, University of East Africa and of University of Dar es Salaam 1964–1968; Member, GMC 1964–1974; Member, Kennedy Memorial Trust 1964–1974; Chairman, Visiting Grants Committee to Universities of Basutoland, Bechuanaland Protectorate and Swaziland 1965; Member, Provisional Council, University of Mauritius 1965–1967; Chairman, UGC and Ministry of Education Sub-Committee on Audio-Visual Aids 1965; Roscoe Lecturer, University of Manchester 1967; Chairman, Programme Committee on Higher Education, BBC Further Education Advisory Council 1967–1970; Member, Advisory Committee, Planning Committee and Council of Open University 1967–1972; Chairman, National Council for Education Technology 1967–1973; Member, Royal Commission on Higher Education in Ceylon 1969–1970; President, Association for Programmed Learning and Educational Technology 1969–1972; Member, India Committee of IUC and British Council 1972; Sir Philip Magnus Memorial Lecturer 1973; Governor, East Riding College of Agriculture 1977–1982; Chairman, Foundation Committee for Engineering Technology 1978; Chairman, Humberside Branch, British Digestive Foundation 1978; Chairman, Beverley Minster Restoration Appeal 1982; Governor, Pocklington School; Honorary FCP; President, Hull Civic Society; President, Hull Bach Choir; President, East Riding Local History Society; Chairman, Academic Council, BMA; Member, Universities Science and Technology Board; Member, Inter-University Council (and Executive) for Higher Education, Overseas; Member, University Council, Nairobi; Member, Hull Chamber of Commerce and Shipping. **Awards:** Leverhulme Research Fellowship 1939. **Honours:** Kt 1968. **Publications:** *University of Sheffield Record of War Work 1939–1945*; numerous papers on Physical Organic, and Organic Chemistry in the *Journal of the Chemical Society* and other scientific periodicals; articles and published lectures on new learning resources and Education Technology. Died 16 July 1989.

JONES, Cecil Henry Douglas (1936) Born 17 September 1916, Bronmeurig, Ystrad Meurig, South Cardiganshire; son of David John Jones, Clerk in Holy Orders, and Mary Elizabeth Roberts. **Subject(s):** Moral Sciences; BA 1938; MA 1953. **Tutor(s):** J S Boys Smith. **Educ:** St John's College, Ystrad Meurig; University College, Aberystwyth.

JONES, Professor Clement Workman (1945) Born 30 August 1920, 42 Kenmare Road, Toxteth Park, Liverpool; son of William Alfred Jones, Bank Clerk, and Ethel May Robinson; m Shina Stevenson, 1951 (d 1991); 1 son, 1 daughter. PhD 1948; BSc (Liverpool) 1940; MSc (Liverpool) 1945; CMath; FIMA. **Tutor(s):** J M Wordie. **Educ:** Holt School, Liverpool; University of Liverpool. **Career:** Weapon Development, Ministry of Supply 1940–1945; Lecturer in Applied Mathematics, University of Liverpool 1947–1956; Reader in Applied Mathematics 1956–1962, Professor of Mathematics Applied to Engineering 1962–1981 (Emeritus 1981), Imperial College, London. **Appointments:** Fellow, Cambridge Philosophical Society; Editor, later Trustee, *Quarterly Journal of Mechanics and Applied Mathematics*.

JONES, Cyril Greenslade (1936) Born 28 October 1917, Castle House, Broad Street, Rhos, Wrexham; son of Walter Frank Jones, Clerk, and Winifred Mary Greenslade. **Subject(s):** Classics; BA 1939. **Tutor(s):** R L Howland. **Educ:** Acton Park Council School, Wrexham; Wrexham County School, Wrexham; RMA, Sandhurst. **Career:** Officer, served in Alexandria, WWII; Factory Manager. **Awards:** Scholarship, SJC 1936–1937.

JONES, David Pritchard (1944) Born 26 September 1926, Barnsley, Yorkshire; son of Daniel Pritchard Jones, Assistant Master, Barnsley Grammar School, and Amy Ethel Smith. BA 1947; MA 1951; MA (Leeds). **Tutor(s):** J M Wordie. **Educ:** Wilthorpe Council School; Barnsley and District Holgate Grammar School; Ackworth School. **Career:** Senior Lecturer, in charge of Linguistics and Phonetics Section, Department of Modern Languages, Leeds Polytechnic 1976–1979.

JONES, The Revd David Treborth (1901) Born 3 July 1871, Treborth, Bangor; son of John Jones, Calvinistic Methodist Minister, and Jane Winifred Jones. **Subject(s):** Moral Sciences; BA 1904. **Tutor(s):** D MacAlister. **Educ:** St John's School, Menai Bridge; University College of Wales, Aberystwyth; Bala Theological College, Wales. **Career:** Calvinistic Methodist Minister 1906.

JONES, Dewi Roland (1949) Born 22 April 1929, 25 Palmer Street, Wrexham; son of Trevor Woodfine Jones, Draper, and Eleanor May Evans. **Subject(s):** Natural Sciences; BA 1952. **Tutor(s):** C W Guillebaud. **Educ:** Alexandra Council School, Wrexham; Grove Park Grammar School, Wrexham.

JONES, Douglass Gordon (1933) Born 14 September 1914, Randolph Lodge, Biddenden, Kent; son of Herbert Gordon Jones, of independent means, and Alice Mary Douglass; m (1) Mary Elsie Hoadley, 17 February 1940, Kuala Lumpur (d 30 November 1966), (2) Phyllis Maude Sorrentino (née Taylor), 24 July 1968, Biddenden; 2 sons (Christopher Gordon b 13 April 1942 and Hamlyn Gordon b 7 December 1947). **Subject(s):** Natural Sciences; BA 1936; MA 1973; DipAgr (Cantab). **Tutor(s):** J M Wordie. **Johnian Relatives:** father of Christopher Gordon Jones (1960) and of Hamlyn Gordon Jones (1966); grandfather of Julia Patricia Gordon Jones (2001). **Educ:** St Lawrence College, Ramsgate. **Career:** Colonial Agricultural Service, Malaya and Tanganyika; HM Overseas Civil Service 1938–1961; Japanese POW, Changi Prison, Singapore, WWII; Vice-Chairman, British Sulphur Corporation Ltd, London 1961–1978. **Appointments:** Associate, Imperial College of Tropical Agriculture, Trinidad. Died 16 September 1978.

JONES, Ernest Gibson (1926) Born 10 May 1908, North Cliffe, Ashbourne, Derbyshire; son of William Albert Hunt Jones, Corn Merchant, and Jessie Gibson. **Subject(s):** Mechanical Sciences/Mathematics; BA 1929. **Tutor(s):** J M Wordie. **Educ:** Junior House, St Bees; Preparatory School, Sedbergh; Sedbergh School. **Career:** Assistant to the Chief Accountant, Compania Primitiva de Gas, Buenos Aires 1931. Died 4 July 1934.

JONES, Ernest Loveday (1926) Born 15 May 1906, Bethel Farm, District of Bethulie, Orange Free State, South Africa; son of Ernest William Jones, Farmer, and Elizabeth Ann Cox. **Subject(s):** Law; BA 1928. **Tutor(s):** E A Benians. **Educ:** The Grammar School, Kettering; Wycliffe College, Stonehouse. **Career:** Solicitor.

JONES, Evan John (1942) Born 10 August 1924, Terrace, Bronant, Aberystwyth; son of Evan Jones, Builder, and Jane Morgan. **Subject(s):** Natural Sciences; BA 1945. **Tutor(s):** C W Guillebaud. **Educ:** Llanrhystyd Church of England School, Aberystwyth; County School, Ardwyn.

JONES, Frank Butler (1911) Born 1 December 1891, 143 Murdock Road, Handsworth, Staffordshire; son of George Butler Jones, Commercial Clerk, and Mary Stammers. **Subject(s):** Natural Sciences; BA 1914. **Tutor(s):** J R Tanner. **Educ:** Tollington Park School; Northern Polytechnic Institute. **Awards:** Scholarship, SJC.

JONES, Frederick Charles Dudley (DUDLEY-JONES) (1939) Born 24 April 1920, Danycoed Villa, Richmond Road, Mountain Ash; son of Evan David Jones, Colliery Fireman, and Mary Agnes Griffiths. **Tutor(s):** R L Howland. **Educ:** Duffryn Boys' School, Mountain Ash; Hereford Cathedral School. **Awards:** Somerset Exhibition, SJC 1939. Died 21 August 1997.

JONES, Sir Harry Ernest (1930) Born 1 August 1911, Puddle Dock, Silverstone, Towcester; son of Harry Charles Ofield Jones, Police Sergeant, and Helen Martin; m Phyllis Eva Dixon, 1935 (d 1987); 1 son, 1 daughter. **Subject(s):** Classics; BA 1933. **Tutor(s):** M P Charlesworth. **Educ:** Burton Latimer School; King's Cliffe School; Stamford School.

Career: Private Secretary to Minister Sir Milne Barbour 1931–1939; Assistant Principal 1937, Deputy Principal 1939, Principal Officer 1940, Assistant Secretary 1942, Permanent Secretary 1955, Industrial Development Adviser 1969, Ministry of Commerce, Northern Ireland Civil Service; Agent in Great Britain for Northern Ireland 1970–1976. **Awards:** Marquess of Exeter Exhibition, SJC 1930. **Honours:** CBE 1955; Kt 1971. Died 4 February 1998.

JONES, Hywel Francis (1946) Born 28 December 1928, Arfon, Glantawe Street, Morriston, Swansea; son of Brynmor Jones, Tinworker, and Maggie Beatrice Francis; m Marian Rosser Craven, 1959; 1 daughter (Sharon Elizabeth b 28 May 1960). **Subject(s):** Maths/Economics; BA 1949; MA 1953; IPFA 1953. **Tutor(s):** J M Wordie. **Educ:** Pentrepoeth Infants' School; Martin Street Boys' School; Bishop Gore Grammar School, Swansea. **Career:** Borough Treasurer's Department, Swansea 1949–1956; National Service, RAPC 1953–1955; Deputy County Treasurer, Breconshire 1956–1959; Assistant County Treasurer, Carmarthenshire 1959–1966; Borough Treasurer, Port Talbot 1966–1975; Member, Public Works Loan Board 1971–1975; Financial Adviser, AMC 1972–1974; Secretary, Commission for Local Administration in Wales 1975–1985; Commissioner for Local Administration in Wales 1985–1991. **Appointments:** Treasurer, Royal National Eisteddfod of Wales 1975–1995; Druid Member, Gorsedd of Bards 1977 (Treasurer from 1992); Member, Lord Chancellor's Advisory Committee for West Glamorgan 1990–1997. **Awards:** Minor Scholarship, SJC 1945.

JONES, Isaac Ernest (1913) Born 5 December 1893, 18 Lucretia Road, Kennington, London; son of Isaac Jones, Sanitary Inspector, and Jane Elizabeth Applebee; m Florence (Topsy). **Subject(s):** Mathematics/Natural Sciences; BA 1919; MA 1923; BSc (London). **Tutor(s):** R P Gregory. **Educ:** St James the Less Church School, Bethnal Green; Parminter's School; St Olave's School. **Career:** Rifleman, 12th London Regiment, reached rank of Major, Royal Welsh Fusiliers, Middle East, Mesopotamia and India (wounded) 1914–1918; National Secretary, National Federation for Building Trades Employers; Employer's Secretary, National Joint Council for the Building Industry; Secretary, Eastern Counties Federation of Building Trades Employers 1921. **Appointments:** Honorary Secretary, Building Industry's National Council. **Awards:** Sizarship, SJC. Died 27 July 1962.

JONES, Ivon Lewis Lloyd (1940) Born 26 February 1921, Hafod Wen Nantybwch, Tredegar, Monmouthshire; son of Lewis Jones, Schoolmaster, and Helen Jones. **Subject(s):** Law; BA 1948; MA 1950. **Tutor(s):** S J Bailey. **Educ:** Dukestown Council School; Georgetown Central Boys' Council School; Tredegar County School; Hereford Cathedral School. **Career:** Army, working on Russian intelligence, attached to Devonshire Regiment 1941–1947; Articled to Llewellyn and Hann, Solicitors, Merthyr 1949–1951; Ellis and Fairbairn, Southampton Row, London 1951. Died 18 April 1977.

JONES, James Dennis (1947) Born 27 February 1927, Church Street, Charlbury, Oxfordshire; son of James Clifford Jones, Inspector of Taxes, and Mary Constance Allen; m 17 July 1948; 3 children. **Subject(s):** Mechanical Sciences; BA 1949; MA 1954. **Tutor(s):** R L Howland. **Educ:** Charlbury Infant School; Charlbury Council School; Chipping Norton County School; No 1 Radio School, RAF, Cranwell. **Career:** RAF, final rank of Air Commodore 1943–1978. **Honours:** MBE 1973.

JONES, Sir John Kenneth Trevor (1932) Born 11 July 1910, Blythe Cottage, Abergavenny, Monmouthshire; son of John Jones, Cattle Dealer and Farmer, and Agnes Morgan; m Menna, 1940; 2 sons (John Cyril b 2 November 1941, Gerald Kenneth b 16 June 1943). **Subject(s):** Law; BA 1934; LLB (Wales) 1931; QC 1976. **Tutor(s):** C W Guillebaud. **Johnian Relatives:** father of John Cyril Jones (1959) and of Gerald Kenneth Jones (1962). **Educ:** Headford Road School, Abergavenny; King Henry VIII Grammar School, Abergavenny; University College of Wales, Aberystwyth. **Career:** Called to the Bar, Lincoln's Inn 1937; Major, RA

1939–1945; Legal Assistant, Home Office 1945; Home Office Legal Adviser. **Appointments:** Member, British/Irish Commission on Law Enforcement. **Honours:** CBE 1956; Kt 1965. Died 25 October 1995.

JONES, John Sharpley (1919) Born 14 May 1895, Vine Cottage, Tudor Road, Kingston on Thames, Surrey; son of Edward Jones, Civil Servant, and Ellen Sharpley; m Ethel Margaret Taylor, 31 January 1927, Bangalore, South India. **Subject(s):** Mathematics; BA 1921; MA 1925. **Tutor(s):** E A Benians. **Educ:** Emanuel School, Wandsworth; Royal College of Science, London University. **Career:** Research into ventilation of gold mines in Mysore, India; Research into jet engines, WWII; Carrier Engineering Company until 1960.

JONES, Lawrence Charles Kennedy Vaughan (1927) Born 4 December 1909, Veldsyde Ridge Road, Parktown, Johannesburg, South Africa; son of Henry Hastings Jones, Landowner, and Alice Carrie Harvey. **Subject(s):** History; BA 1931. **Tutor(s):** C W Guillebaud. **Educ:** Castle Park, Dalkey; Tonbridge School.

JONES, Leslie Edwin (GODFREY-JONES) (1932) Born 4 February 1910, 31 Lady Somerset Road, St Pancras, London; son of James Henry Jones, Manufacturer's Agent, and Lilian Mabel Powe; 2 children. **Subject(s):** Mathematics; BSc (London) 1930; MSc (London) 1932. **Tutor(s):** J M Wordie. **Educ:** Harrow County School; UCL. **Career:** Assistant Master, Aldenham School, and Officer, OTC 1934–1944; Assistant Master, Head of Mathematics, Rugby School 1944–1959; Headmaster, Marling School, Stroud 1959. **Awards:** Strathcona Exhibition, SJC 1932. **Honours:** TD and Bar. Died 29 August 1998.

JONES, Merlin Hywel (1926) Born 19 July 1908, 13 Pembroke Street, Pembroke Dock, Pembrokeshire; son of Trevor Hywel Jones, Schoolmaster, and Anna Elizabeth Robson. BA 1930; MA 1934. **Tutor(s):** J M Wordie. **Educ:** St Andrew's Preparatory School, Tenby; Albert Villas Preparatory School, Bristol; Oakham School. Died 24 February 1985.

JONES, Sir Pendril Charles Varier (1902) Born 24 February 1883, Glantaff House, Troedyrhiw, Glamorganshire; son of Charles Morgan Jones, Surgeon, and Margaret Jenkins. **Subject(s):** Natural Sciences; BA 1905; MA 1909; LRCP; MRCS 1910; MRCP 1929. **Tutor(s):** D MacAlister. **Career:** Founder and Medical Director, Papworth Village Settlement for Rehabilitation of Tuberculosis Sufferers. **Honours:** Kt 1931. **Publications:** *Tuberculosis and the Working Man*, 1915; *Industrial Colonies and Village Settlements for the Consumptive*, 1920, *Papworth: Administrative and Economic Problems in Tuberculosis*, 1925; *Significance of Temperature Variations in Tuberculosis*, 1926. Died 30 January 1941.

JONES, The Revd Richard Granville (1944) Born 26 July 1926, Laventie, Woodmancote, Dursley, Gloucestershire; son of Henry William Jones, Hotel Proprietor, and Ida Grace Wintle; m Kathleen; 3 daughters. **Subject(s):** Mechanical Sciences; BA 1947; MA 1951; BD (Manchester) 1953; DD (Hull) 1988. **Tutor(s):** S J Bailey. **Educ:** St Margaret's Kindergarten School, Rock; North Cornwall High School, Trebetherick; Truro School. **Career:** Probationer, Methodist Ministry, Plymouth East 1949–1950; Ordained as a Minister 1954; Minister, Sheffield, then Birkenhead 1955–1969; Tutor, then Principal, Hartley Victoria College 1969–1982; Chairman, East Anglia District, Methodist Church 1983–1993. **Appointments:** Editor, *The Epworth Review*; President, Methodist Conference 1988–1989. **Publications:** *Worship for Today*, 1968; *How Goes Christian Marriage?*, 1978; *Towards a Radical Church*, 1975; *Groundwork of Worship and Preaching*, 1980; *Groundwork of Christian Ethics*, 1984; *What to do?*, 1999.

JONES, Richard McNair (1905) Born 6 September 1886, 16 Pendennis Road, Streatham, Surrey; son of Barton Wilson Jones, Bank Clerk, and Frances Jane Emery; m Lois Mary Gritten, 28 April 1923, St Thomas' Church, Wandsworth; 1 son (Philip Humphrey McNair b 19 March 1925), 2 daughters (Florence Marian McNair b 23 March 1927 and

Ursula Mary McNair b 28 May 1933). **Subject(s):** Mathematics; BA 1908. **Tutor(s):** J R Tanner; C E Graves. **Johnian Relatives:** uncle of Robin Philip Williams (1948); great uncle of Anthony Geraint Williams (1977). **Educ:** Latymer School, Hammersmith. **Career:** Lieutenant, Northumberland Fusiliers (wounded), WWI; Actuary. **Awards:** Scholarship, SJC. Died 24 January 1977.

JONES, Dr Robert Francis (1904) Born 16 August 1886, Mathyrafal, Llangymen, Meifod, Montgomeryshire; son of John Maurice Jones, Farmer, and Jane; m Margaret May Moss, 30 March 1915, St Paul's, Walsall. **Subject(s):** Natural Sciences; BA 1907; MA 1917; BChir 1917; MB 1917; MRCS; LRCP 1911. **Tutor(s):** D MacAlister. **Educ:** Denstone College, Staffordshire; University College, Aberystwyth. **Career:** University Scholar, St George's Hospital 1907; Captain, RAMC, WWI; Medical Examiner, Midland Collieries' Indemnity Company; Medical Officer to Post Office; Assistant House Surgeon and Assistant House Physician, St George's Hospital. **Awards:** Webb Prize for Bacteriology 1911. **Publications:** *Bacteriology of Tigris Water*. Died 3 November 1960.

JONES, Dr Robert Peter Neil (1939) Born 26 January 1921, 71 Bolton Street, Oldham; son of Eric Jones, University Lecturer in Engineering, and Edith Purdy. **Subject(s):** Mechanical Sciences; BA 1942; MA 1946; PhD 1948. **Tutor(s):** S J Bailey. **Educ:** Mount School, Kersal; North Manchester Grammar School; Manchester Grammar School. **Career:** Assistant Director of Research 1958–1964; Lecturer, Mechanical Engineering, University of Liverpool 1964–1980. Died 18 June 1992.

JONES, Roland Norman (1937) Born 16 May 1919, 64 Rawlinson Road, Southport; son of Norman Jones, Architect, and Esther Cooper; m (1) Anna Hopland Brown, (2) Gabrielle Marshal; 5 children. BA 1940; MA 1944; MB BChir 1943; MChir 1948; FRCS 1948. **Tutor(s):** R L Howland. **Educ:** Malsis Preparatory School, Cross Hills; Croxton Preparatory School, Southport; Oundle School; St Thomas' Hospital, London. **Career:** Surgeon Lieutenant, RNVR, WWII; Consultant Surgeon, Colchester 1951–1982. Died October 2001.

JONES, Ronald Montague (MONTAGUE-JONES) (1930) Born 10 December 1909, St Albans School, Hertfordshire; son of Edgar Montague Jones, Headmaster, and Emmeline Mary Yates; m Barbara Elizabeth Margaret Gibbon, 1 November 1945, Kandy, Ceylon. BA 1933; MA 1937. **Tutor(s):** J M Wordie. **Educ:** St Albans School; RMA. **Career:** Second Lieutenant, RE 1930; Dorset County Councillor 1964. **Honours:** CBE. Died 1 August 1996.

JONES, Dr Ronald Morgan (1928) Born 21 June 1909, 1 Station Terrace, Penrhiwceiber, Llanwarno Mountain Ash, Glamorgan; son of Alfred Morgan Jones, Chemist and Druggist, and Edith Mary Morgan. **Subject(s):** Natural Sciences; BA 1931; MA 1936; BChir 1935; MB 1936. **Tutor(s):** M P Charlesworth. **Educ:** Council School, Penrhiwceiber; Jones West Monmouth School, Pontypool; Leighton Park School, Reading.

JONES, Sydney (1924) Born 26 July 1907, Queen's Terrace, Guiseley, Yorkshire; son of Alfred Edward Jones, Wholesale Clothier, and Louise Shepherd. BA 1927. **Tutor(s):** E A Benians. **Educ:** New College, Harrogate. **Career:** Director, Joseph May and Sons (Leeds). Died 12 August 1998.

JONES, Thomas Lovel (1923) Born 26 June 1905, 187 Newport Road, Cardiff, Glamorgan; son of William Edwin Jones, Shipowner, and Elsie Louise Wadley; m Rosemary Rutherford, 1930. **Tutor(s):** B F Armitage. **Educ:** Penarth Lodge; Liphook; Haileybury College. **Career:** Officer, Shropshire Yeomanry. **Appointments:** Member, Royal Thames Yacht Club. Died 11 June 1938.

JONES, William Havercroft (1902) Born 28 July 1869, Dolfawr, Llangollen, Wales; son of William Jones, Miller and Farmer, and Sarah Miller. **Tutor(s):** D MacAlister. **Educ:** Lower Grammar School, Llangollen; Ruabon Grammar School.

JONES, The Hon Sir William Lloyd Mars (MARS-JONES) (1937) Born 4 September 1915, Post Office, Llansannan; son of Henry Mars Jones, General Merchant, and Jane Lloyd; m Sheila Mary Felicity Cobon, 1947; 3 sons. **Subject(s):** Law; BA 1939; MA 1943; LLB (UCW Aberystwyth) 1936; Honorary LLD (UCW Aberystwyth) 1973; QC 1957. **Tutor(s):** C W Guillebaud. **Educ:** Llansannan Elementary School; Denbigh Secondary School; UCW, Aberystwyth. **Career:** Called to the Bar, Gray's Inn 1939; RNVR 1939–1945 (Lieutenant Commander 1945); Barrister-at-Law; Wales and Chester Circuit Judge 1947; Recorder, Birkenhead 1959–1965, Swansea 1965–1968, Cardiff 1968–1969; Judge, High Court of Justice, Queen's Bench Division 1969–1990; Presiding Judge, Wales and Chester Circuit 1971–1975. **Appointments:** President, Central Students' Representative Council, UCW 1936–1937; Member, Bar Council 1962; Deputy Chairman, Denbighshire Quarter Sessions 1962–1968; Member, Home Office Inquiry into allegations against Metropolitan Police Officers 1964; Bencher 1964, Treasurer 1982, Gray's Inn; Member, Home Secretary's Advisory Council on the Penal System 1966–1968; President, North Wales Arts Association 1976; President, UCW, Bangor 1983–1995; President, UCW Old Students' Association 1987–1988; President, London Welsh Trust 1989–1995. **Awards:** MacMahon Studentship 1939; Holker Senior Exhibition, Gray's Inn 1946. **Honours:** MBE (Military) 1945; Kt 1969. **Publications:** Contributor to *Atkins Encyclopedia of Court Forms and Precedents*. Died 10 January 1999.

JONES, William Percival (1920) Born 15 October 1902, Calcutta, India; son of Eustace Percival Jones, Registrar, Department of Commerce and Industry, India, and Agnes Heffernan. **Tutor(s):** B F Armitage. **Educ:** Loretto Convent, Simla, India; Stonyhurst College.

JOPSON, Professor Norman Brooke (1909) Born 20 January 1890, 12 Caledonian Road, Leeds, Yorkshire; son of Samuel Rolison Jopson, Travelling Representative for Manufacturing Firm, and Mary Alice Brooke. **Subject(s):** Modern and Medieval Languages/Oriental Languages; BA 1912; MA 1930. **Tutor(s):** E E Sikes. **Educ:** Merchant Taylors' School, Crosby; Wesley College, Sheffield. **Career:** Russian Army, later, War Office 1914–1919; Admiralty 1919–1920; Foreign Office 1920–1923; Member, Inter-Allied Plebiscite Commission for Klagenfurt; Comparative Reader, School of Slavonic Studies, University of London 1923–1937 (Professor 1936); Head, Department of Uncommon Languages, Postal and Telegraphic Censorship 1939–1945; Professor of Comparative Philology 1937–1954 (Emeritus 1955–1969), University of Cambridge; Title C Fellow 1937–1954, Title E Fellow 1954–1969, SJC. **Appointments:** President, Philological Society 1952. **Awards:** Bendal Sanskrit Exhibition 1913; Tiarks Scholarship 1913. **Publications:** *Spoken Russian*, 1939. Died 13 January 1969.

JORDAN-MOSS, Norman (1938) See MOSS.

JOSEPH, Felix Alexander (1913) Born 29 April 1890, son of Saul Abdulla Joseph, Bill and Bullion Broker and Merchant, and Sophia Gubbay; m Gladys Enid Abelson, 10 January 1923, West London Synagogue, Upper Berkeley Street, London; 2 sons (Anthony Felix Alexander b 25 November 1923 and Geoffrey Seymour Saul b 16 September 1925), 1 daughter (Wendy Adele Marguerite b 19 June 1929). **Subject(s):** Mathematics; BA 1917; MA 1921. **Tutor(s):** R P Gregory. **Johnian Relatives:** father-in-law of Robin Philip Williams (1948); grandfather of Anthony Geraint Williams (1977). **Educ:** Victoria English School, Hong Kong; Shanghai Public School. **Career:** Russo-Chinese Bank and Russo-Asiatic Bank, Shanghai and Hong Kong 1907–1914; Driver, HAC, attached to RE, WWI; Engineer; Businessman. Died 30 September 1949.

JOSHI, Dr Atmaram Bhairav (1947) Born 17 November 1916, Jubbulpore, Central Provinces, India; son of Bhairav Balwant Joshi, Schoolmaster, and Shanta Joshi; m Vimala Gangadhar Kawley, 7 May 1937, Wardha, India; 1 son (Jayant b 22 July 1955). **Subject(s):** PhD 1950; BSc (Nagpur) 1937; MSc (Nagpur) 1944. **Tutor(s):** G C L Bertram. **Educ:** Government High School, Raipur; College of Science,

Nagpur; Imperial Agricultural Research Institute, New Delhi. **Career:** Deputy Director General (Crop Sciences), Indian Council of Agricultural Research, New Delhi; Assistant Botanist, Imperial Agricultural Research Institute, New Dehli 1940–1977; Dean, Postgraduate School 1958–1976, Director 1972–1977, Indian Agricultural Research Institute, New Delhi; Project leader, UNDP/FAO Project on Improvement of Field Crop Productivity in Egypt, Cairo 1971–1972; Vice-Chancellor, Agriculture University, Rahuri, State of Maharashtra 1977–1980. **Appointments:** Associated with the Agharkar Research Institute, India. **Awards:** Padma Shri, Republic Day 1976; Borlaug Award 1976. **Publications:** About 300 publications, including *Sesamum*, Indian Council of Agricultural Research, New Delhi, India; *Breeding and Genetics of American Cotton*, Indian Council of Agricultural Research, New Delhi, India.

JOSHI, Surendra Vinayak (1927) Born 13 September 1905, Bombay, India; son of Vinayak Nilkanth Joshi, Export and Import Merchant, and Krishnabai Mogre. **Subject(s):** History; BA 1929; MA 1966; BA (Bombay). **Tutor(s):** E A Benians. **Educ:** The Wilson High School, Bombay; The Aryan Education Society's High School, Bombay; Elphinstone College, Bombay; University of Bombay.

JOSLIN, Professor David Maelgwyn (1942) Born 29 April 1925, 25 Wyndham Street, Barry; son of James John Joslin, Schoolmaster, and Mary Jenkins; m Mary Kidston. **Subject(s):** History; BA 1947. **Tutor(s):** C W Guillebaud. **Educ:** Holton Road Elementary School, Barry; Barry Boys' County School. **Career:** Fellow, Pembroke College, Cambridge 1951–1970; Assistant Lecturer in History 1954–1957, Lecturer in History 1957–1965, Professor of Economic History 1965–1970, University of Cambridge. **Appointments:** Director of Studies and Senior Tutor, Pembroke College, Cambridge 1951–1970. **Awards:** Scholarship, SJC; College Prize 1948. **Publications:** *A Century Of Banking in Latin America*, 1963. Died 15 October 1970.

JOWETT, Dr Edward Pearse (1932) Born 24 December 1913, Hankow, China; son of Hardy Jowett, Political Representative, Asiatic Petroleum Company, and Katherine Alice Wheatly; m Sheila. MB; BChir. **Tutor(s):** R L Howland. **Educ:** Wycliffe College, Stonehouse. Died 5 February 1989.

JOY, David Victor (1941) Born 15 July 1923, Bolobo, Leopold Province, Belgian Congo; son of Henry Charles Victor Joy, Medical Practitioner, and Gertrude Rosetta Gibbs. **Tutor(s):** S J Bailey. **Educ:** Southayes School, Bridport; Queen's College, Taunton.

JUCYS, Adolfas (1939) Born 30 August 1904, Klausgalvu, Salantai, Lithuania; son of Pranciskus Jucys, Farmer, and Barbara Jonkute; m Sofija Nezabitauskaite, 6 September 1934. **Tutor(s):** J M Wordie. **Educ:** Primary School, Salantai; High School, Plunge; University of Lithuania.

JUDGE, Edward Thomas (1926) Born 20 November 1908, 82 Upperton Road, Leicester; son of Thomas Oliver Judge, Master Jeweller, and Florence Gravestock; m Alice Gertrude Matthews; 2 sons. **Subject(s):** Mechanical Sciences; BA 1930; MA 1934. **Tutor(s):** J M Wordie. **Educ:** Mill Hill School, Leicester; Worcester Royal Grammar School. **Career:** Dorman, Long and Co Ltd, Middlesbrough 1930–1967 (Chief Technical Engineer 1937, Director 1947, Chairman and General Managing Director 1961–1967). **Appointments:** Member, North-Eastern Electricity Board 1952–1962; Representative of Minister of Transport, Board of the Tees Conservancy Commission; Honorary Vice President, Iron and Steel Institute 1958; President, British Iron and Steel Federation 1965–1967; Chairman, Reyrolle Parsons Ltd 1969–1974; President, British Electrical and Allied Manufacturers' Association 1970–1971; Director, Dorman Long Vanderbijl Corp Ltd; Director, Cleveland Scientific Institution; Director, Pilkington Brothers Ltd; Director, ETJ Consultancy Services; Director, Fibreglass Ltd; Director, The Zenith Electric Co Ltd; Director, BPB Industries Ltd. **Awards:** Bessemer Gold Medal, Iron & Steel Institute 1967. Died 8 January 1992.

JUKES, John Andrew (1936) Born 19 May 1917, 99D Addison Road, Kensington, London; son of Andrew Monroe Jukes, Captain, Indian Medical Service, and Gertrude Elizabeth King; m Muriel Child, 19 June 1943, Beddington Church; 2 sons, 2 daughters. **Subject(s):** Natural Sciences; BA 1939; MA 1948; BSc (Economics) LSE 1948; Fellow, Institution of Highway Engineers. **Tutor(s):** J M Wordie. **Educ:** Norland Place School, Kensington, London; Seabrook Lodge, Hythe; Shrewsbury School. **Career:** Cavendish Laboratory, Cambridge 1939; Radar and Operational Research 1939–1946; Research Department, LMS Railway 1946–1948; Economic Advisor, Cabinet Office and Treasury 1948–1954; British Embassy, Washington (Economic Advisor) 1949–1951; Economic Advisor to UKAEA 1954–1964; Deputy Director General 1964, Deputy Under-Secretary of State 1967, DEA; Director General, Research and Economic Planning, Ministry of Transport 1969–1970; Director General, Economics and Resources 1970–1972, Deputy Secretary (Environmental Protection) 1972–1974, Director-General, Highways 1974–1976, DEA; Department of Transport 1976–1977. **Appointments:** Chairman, Steering Group on Water Authority Economic and Financial Objectives 1973–1974; Member, CEGB 1977–1980; Representative for Sutton SDP on Council for Social Democracy 1982–1986; Member, Merton and Sutton DHA 1986–1990; Alliance (SDP) Councillor, and Chairman, Finance Sub-Committee, London Borough of Sutton 1986–1990; President, Sutton Liberal Democrats 1990–1993. **Awards:** Exhibition, SJC 1936–1937. **Honours:** CB 1968. Died 12 December 1997.

JULIAN, Professor Desmond Gareth (1943) Born 24 April 1926, 43 Croxteth Road, Liverpool; son of Frederick Bennett Julian, Medical Practitioner, and Jane Frances Galbraith. **Subject(s):** Natural Sciences; BA 1946; MA 1953; BChir 1948; MB 1948; MD 1954; Hon MD (Gothenburg) 1987; Hon MD (Edinburgh) 1997; MRCP 1952; FRCPE 1967; FRCP 1970; FRACP 1970; FACC 1985. **Tutor(s):** S J Bailey. **Educ:** Parkfield School, Liverpool; Leighton Park School, Reading. **Career:** Surgeon Lieutenant, RNVR 1949–1951; Registrar, Liverpool Cardiac and Thoracic Surgical Centres 1952–1955; Medical Registrar, National Heart Hospital 1955–1956; Research Fellow, Harvard Medical School, USA 1957–1958; Research Fellow, Peter Bent Brigham Hospital, Boston, USA 1957–1958; Senior Registrar, Royal Infirmary, Edinburgh 1958–1961; Consultant Cardiologist, Sydney Hospital, Australia 1961–1964; Consultant Physician, Royal Infirmary, Edinburgh 1964–1974; Professor of Cardiology, University of Newcastle upon Tyne 1975–1986; Medical Director, British Heart Foundation 1986–1993. **Appointments:** Member, MRC Systems Board 1980–1984; Editor, *European Heart Journal* 1980–1988; President, British Cardiac Society 1985–1987. **Awards:** Gold Medal, European Society of Cardiology 1998. **Honours:** CBE 1993. **Publications:** *Acute Myocardial Infarction*, 1967; *Cardiology*, 1972, 7th edition 1998; (ed) *Angina Pectoris*, 1975, 2nd edition 1984; contributions to medical journals, particularly on coronary disease and arrhythmias.

JUNG, Dr Leopold (YOUNG) (1943) Born 18 August 1926, Vienna, Austria; son of Samuel Jung, Medical Practitioner, and Marie Kessler; m (1) Fay Lilian Merskey, 1953 (d 1981), (2) Ruth Breslow, 1983 (d 1996), (3) Jo-Ellen Dana Turner, 1999; 2 sons (Philip and Joseph), 1 daughter (Sarah). **Subject(s):** Mathematics/Natural Sciences/Physics; BA 1946; MA 1950; MS(EE) (Johns Hopkins) 1956; Dr Eng (Johns Hopkins) 1959; Honorary Doctor of Humane Letters (Johns Hopkins) 1989; FAAAS; FREng. **Tutor(s):** S J Bailey. **Educ:** Friern Barnet Grammar School; Loughborough Grammar School; Sheffield City Grammar School; St Peter's School, York; Johns Hopkins University, USA. **Career:** Westinghouse Electric Company, Baltimore, USA 1953–1960; Stanford Research Institute 1960–1973; Staff Consultant, Naval Research Laboratory 1973–1981; Director for Research, Office of Secretary of Defense, Pentagon 1981–1994; Board of Directors and Technology Activites Board, Filtronic plc (UK) 1994–. **Appointments:** Distinguished Lecturer, IEEE Summer School, Leeds University 1966 and 1969; President, Microwave Theory and Techniques Society 1969; Visiting Professor, Technion, Israel 1970–1971; NATO/AGARD

Lecturer, University of Bologna, Italy 1971; Board of Directors 1971–1974 and 1979–1982, Executive Vice-President 1979, President and Chairman of the Board 1980, and Fellow, IEEE; Board of Governors, American Association of Engineering Societies 1980; Member, National Academy of Engineering (US). **Awards:** Major Scholarship, SJC 1943; BG Lamme Scholarship, Westinghouse Electric Company 1958; Microwave Prize 1964; Microwave Career Award 1984; The Woodrow Wilson Award for Distinguished Government Service 2001.

K

KAESTLIN, John Paul (1932) Born 2 October 1913, St Margarethen, Canton St Gall, Switzerland; son of George Henry Kaestlin, Manager, London and Eastern Trade Bank, and Margaret Cecily Bock. **Subject(s):** History/English; BA 1936; MA 1939. **Tutor(s):** E A Benians. **Educ:** Orme School, London; Bilton Grange, Rugby; Clifton College. **Career:** Sub-editor, *The Times*; Assistant Editor, Baltic and Scandinavian paper 1936–1939; Major, RA 1939–1947; DAAG, Control and Disbandment, German Armed Forces 1945–1946; DAAG, War Crimes Trials 1946–1947; Called to the Bar, Middle Temple 1959. **Honours:** MBE 1947. Died August 1963.

KALE, Dhundiraj Govind (1939) (admitted to Fitzwilliam House 1938) Born 5 October 1916, Satara, India; son of Sardar Govind Krishna Kale, Judge, and Sonntai Bal. BA (Bombay); MSc (London). **Tutor(s):** J M Wordie. **Educ:** High School, Poona; Sir Parashurambau College, Poona; Fergusson College, Poona; UCL; Fitzwilliam House, Cambridge. **Career:** Called to the Bar, Middle Temple 1944.

KALÉ, Vithal Dhondo (1911) Born 23 April 1892, Kolhapur, Bombay Presidency, India; son of Dhondo Sadashir Kalé, Subjudge and Magistrate. BA 1915; MA 1918. **Tutor(s):** J R Tanner. **Educ:** Poonah New School; Perse School, Cambridge.

KAMATH, Hundi Srinivasa (1926) Born 21 January 1905, Mangalore, Madras Presidency, India; son of Hundi Rama Kamath, Teacher and Landlord, and Anandi Bai. **Tutor(s):** J M Wordie. **Educ:** Canara High School, Mangalore; Government College, Mangalore; Presidency College, Madras, India; UCL.

KANE, Professor Prabhakar Pandurang (1949) Born 24 October 1929, Bombay, India; son of Pandurang Vaman Kane, Advocate, High Court, Bombay, and Subhadra Gopal Bal; m Mary Thomas, 26 September 1957, USA; 3 daughters (Rohini Dwivedi, Madhuri Kirloskar and Nandini Kane). **Subject(s):** Natural Sciences/Physics; BA 1951; MA 1955; BSc (Bombay) 1949; PhD (Rochester, USA) 1957. **Tutor(s):** E Miller; G C L Bertram. **Johnian Relatives:** uncle of Vaman Shankar Patwardhan (1946) and of Madhukar Shankar Patwardhan (1947); great uncle of Ranjan Madhukar Patwardhan (1979). **Educ:** High School, Bombay; Elphinstone College, Bombay; Royal Institute of Science, Bombay. **Career:** Assistant Professor, Wesleyan University, Connecticut, USA 1957–1959; Assistant Professor of Physics 1959–1966, Associate Professor of Physics 1966–1968, Professor of Physics 1968–1989 (Emeritus 1989), Indian Institute of Technology, Bombay. **Awards:** Sir Mangaldas Nathubai Technical Scholarship of the University of Bombay tenable at Cambridge 1949–1953; Hutchinson Studentship, SJC 1952–1953. **Publications:** Regional Editor, *Radiation, Physics and Chemistry*; *Applications of Radiation Physics* (manuscript); papers in *Reviews of Modern Physics, Nuclear Physics, Pramana, Physics Reports; Physical Review, Atomic and Nuclear Physics.*

KANT, Frederick William (1918) American Student.

KAPUR, Shikandhi (1938) Born 18 July 1920, Lalaguda Secunderabad, Deccan, India; son of Nauridh Rai Kapur, District Engineer, and Basauti Kapur. **Subject(s):** Law; BA 1941; MA 1945; LLB 1942. **Tutor(s):** C W Guillebaud. **Educ:** Bishop Cotton Boys' School, Bangalore; Hyderabad.

KATER, Sir Gregory Blaxland (1930) Born 15 May 1912, Nyrang, Cheeseman's Creek, Boree Shire, New South Wales, Australia; son of Norman William Kater, Company Chairman, and Jean Gaerloch MacKenzie; m Catherine Mary Ferris-Scott, 1937; 2 sons, 1 daughter. **Subject(s):** Mechanical Sciences; BA 1933; MA 1937; CEng. **Tutor(s):** J M Wordie. **Johnian Relatives:** brother of Norman Herman Murchison Kater (1930). **Educ:** Tudor House School, New South Wales; The King's School, Parramatta, Sydney, Australia. **Career:** Chairman, Electrical Equipment of Australia Ltd 1939; AIF, Middle East and New Guinea (wounded in Syria), demobilised as Major; Director 1950, Chairman 1957, Oil Search Ltd; Director 1951, Chairman 1956, Permanent Trustee Company Ltd; Chairman, Mercantile & General Reinsurance Company of Australia Ltd and Mercantile & General Life Reassurance Company of Australia Ltd 1957; Director 1963, Chairman 1976, Metal Manufacturers Ltd; Director, CSR Ltd 1949; Director, H E Kater & Son Pty Ltd, Merino Stud 1948; Director, Vickers Australia Ltd 1965; Director, Vickers Cockatoo Docks Pty Ltd 1972; Director, W R Carpenter Holdings Ltd 1970; Chairman, The Commercial Banking Company of Sydney Ltd, Australia. **Appointments:** Vice-President, New South Wales Society for Crippled Children 1950; Liveryman, Worshipful Company of Broderers, London. **Honours:** Kt 1974. Died 9 July 1978.

KATER, Norman Herman Murchison (1930) Born 26 March 1904, Sutton Forest, New South Wales, Australia; son of Norman William Kater, Sheep Farmer, and Jean Gaerloch MacKenzie. **Tutor(s):** C W Guillebaud. **Johnian Relatives:** brother of Gregory Blaxland Kater (1930). **Educ:** Killcott, Godalming; Tudor House School, New South Wales; The Armidale School, New South Wales; Church of England Grammar School, Sydney; University of Sydney. **Career:** Medical Officer, Royal Australian Air Force, SWPA; Wing Commander. **Honours:** MC.

KAUNTZE, John Travis (1933) Born 23 March 1915, 159 Windsor Road, Oldham; son of Henry Booth Kauntze, Veterinary Surgeon, and Elizabeth Bagley. **Educ:** Wilmslow Preparatory School; The Ryleys, Alderley Edge; Blundell's School, Tiverton.

KAVANAGH, Lieutenant Colonel George Charles MacMorrough (1920) Born 29 May 1896, Minnow Brook, Terenure, Rathfarnham, County Durham; son of William George Kavanagh, Gun Manufacturer, and Mary Jane Redmond; m Sheila. **Tutor(s):** E A Benians. **Educ:** Belvedere College, Dublin; TCD; RMA, Woolwich. **Career:** Second Lieutenant, RE 1916; Lieutenant 1917; Served in France and Belgium 1917–1918 (wounded); Captain 1926; Attached to Sudan Defence Force 1928–1933; Major 1935. **Awards:** Exhibition, SJC. Died 25 July 1937.

KEAST, John Harris (1925) Born 26 May 1906, 15 Moore Street, Strood, Rochester, Kent; son of John James Keast, RSPCA Inspector, and Frieda Nelly Betty Althaber; m Rita. **Subject(s):** Mathematics; BA 1928; MA 1932. **Tutor(s):** J M Wordie. **Educ:** Stanley Road, Nottingham; High Pavement, Nottingham; King Edward's School, Birmingham. **Career:** Surveyor, Nigeria, Colonial Service 1928; Assistant Director of Surveys, Colonial Service 1951; Director of Surveys, Eastern Region, Nigeria, Colonial Service 1956. **Awards:** Scholarship, SJC. Died May 1972.

KEEBLE, Cyril Francis Allan (1903) Born 14 February 1885, The Hall, Tattingstone, Holbrook, Suffolk; son of William Frederick Keeble, Farmer, and Olivia Jane Welton; m Sarah Elizabeth Sowerbutts; 1 son (Thomas Whitfield b 10 February 1918). **Subject(s):** History; BA 1906; MA 1930. **Tutor(s):** C E Graves; J R Tanner. **Johnian Relatives:** father of Thomas Whitfield Keeble (1937); grandfather of Giles Richard Gordon Keeble (1968). **Educ:** The Leys School, Cambridge. **Career:** Master, Bilton Grange, Rugby 1906–1908; Abbey School, Beckenham 1908–1910; Second Master, Rydal School, Colwyn Bay 1910–1915; Sedbergh School 1915–1925; Captain, 12th Battalion, Cheshire Home Guard; Captain, 4th Border Regiment; Education Officer, 155th Infantry Brigade 1918–1919; House Master, Roundhay School, Leeds and Lecturer in Spanish, Leeds School of Commerce 1925–1926;

Headmaster, Barrow-on-Soar Grammar School 1926–1929; Headmaster, Sir John Deane's Grammar School, Northwich, Cheshire 1929. **Awards:** Sizarship, SJC. **Honours:** MBE 1945. Died 1 April 1970.

KEEBLE, Dr Thomas Whitfield (1937) Born 10 February 1918, Pendeen, Sedbergh; son of Cyril Francis Allan Keeble, Headmaster, Sir John Deane's Grammar School, and Sarah Elizabeth Sowerbutts; m Ursula Madeline Scott Morris, 7 July 1945, St Margaret's Church, Roath; 2 sons (Roger and Giles). **Subject(s):** Modern and Medieval Languages (French and Spanish); BA 1945; MA 1952; PhD (KCL) 1948. **Tutor(s):** C W Guillebaud. **Johnian Relatives:** son of Cyril Francis Allan Keeble (1903); father of Giles Richard Gordon Keeble (1968). **Educ:** Humphrey Perkins Grammar School, Barrow-on-Soar; Baswick House, Stafford; Sir John Deane's Grammar School, Northwich. **Career:** Assistant Adjutant, 2nd Indian Field Regiment, 1941–1945; Assistant Principal, Commonwealth Relations Office 1948–1949; Private Secretary to Parliamentary Under-Secretary of State for Commonwealth Affairs 1949; First Secretary, UK High Commission in Pakistan at Lahore, Peshawar and Karachi 1950–1955; First Secretary, UK delegation to the UN, New York 1955–1959; Head of Defence and Western Department, Commonwealth Relations Office 1959–1960; British Deputy High Commissioner, Ghana 1960–1963; Head, Economic General Department, CRO 1963–1966; Commercial Minister, British Embassy, Buenos Aires 1966–1967; Honorary Research Associate, Institute of Latin American Studies, University of London 1967–1968; Minister, British Embassy, Madrid 1969–1971; Head, UN (Economic and Social) Department, FCO 1971–1972; Head, UN Department 1972–1974; Senior Directing Staff (Civil), National Defence College, Latimer 1974–1976; Acting Senior Clerk, Committee Office, House of Commons 1976–1983. **Appointments:** Freeman, City of London 1980; Member, Visual Arts Panel of Eastern Arts Association 1986–1991; Member, Kettle's Yard Committee 1987–1989. **Awards:** Sizarship, SJC 1937. **Publications:** *British Overseas Territories and South America, 1806–1914*, 1970; articles in *Hispanic Reviews*. Died 20 December 1994.

KEELEY, Thomas Clews (1913) Born 16 February 1894, Melrose, Wood End Road, Erdington, Warwickshire; son of Thomas Clews Keeley, Commercial Traveller, and Eliza Clews. **Subject(s):** Mathematics/Natural Sciences; BA 1916; MA 1920; FInstP. **Tutor(s):** R P Gregory. **Educ:** King Edward's School, Aston; King Edward's School, Birmingham. **Career:** Royal Aircraft Establishment 1917–1919; Tutor in Physics, University Demonstrator in Physics, University of Oxford 1924–1961; Fellow and Sub-Warden, Wadham College, Oxford 1941–1961. **Awards:** Hockin Prize, SJC 1916; Wright's Prize, SJC 1916. **Honours:** CBE 1944. Died 25 December 1988.

KEEN, Alfred Stewart (1927) Born 26 March 1907, Bannu, North West Frontier Province, India; son of William John Keen, Lieutenant Colonel, Indian Army, and Marion Beatrice Mills. **Subject(s):** Mechanical Sciences; BA 1930. **Tutor(s):** J M Wordie. **Johnian Relatives:** brother of Maxwell Frederick Arthur Keen (1922). **Educ:** Oxford Preparatory School; Haileybury College; RMA, Woolwich.

KEEN, Maxwell Frederick Arthur (1922) Born 27 November 1903, Miramshah, Tochi Valley, North West Provinces, India; son of William John Keen, Lieutenant Colonel, Indian Political Department, and Marion Beatrice Mills; m Joan, 1 son (David). **Subject(s):** Mechanical Sciences; BA 1925. **Tutor(s):** E Cunningham. **Johnian Relatives:** brother of Alfred Stewart Keen (1927). **Educ:** Oxford Preparatory School; Haileybury College. **Career:** Sudan Political Service. Died 2 January 1971.

KEFFORD, Edward Kingsley (1924) Born 16 May 1903, The Vicarage, Dullingham, Cambridgeshire; son of William Kingsley Kefford, Clerk in Holy Orders, and Henrietta Mabel Trigg; 2 sons (Neville Frederick and Michael Edward). BA 1927; MA 1931. **Tutor(s):** J M Wordie. **Johnian Relatives:** nephew of Edward John Kefford (1890); son of William Kingsley Kefford (1894); brother of Harry Kingsley Kefford (1921) and

of Richard William Kingsley Kefford (1927); father of Michael Edward Kingsley Kefford (1958) and of Neville Frederick Kingsley Kefford (1958). **Educ:** Grammar School, Wellingborough. **Career:** Headmaster, Edinburgh House Preparatory School, Hampshire 1935–1969. Died 25 January 1971.

KEFFORD, Harry Kingsley (1921) Born 30 May 1900, Coulthorn Lodge, Ospringe Road, Faversham, Kent; son of William Kingsley Kefford, Clerk in Holy Orders, and Henrietta Mabel Trigg. BA 1924; MA 1936. **Tutor(s):** E E Sikes. **Johnian Relatives:** nephew of Edward John Kefford (1890); son of William Kingsley Kefford (1894); brother of Edward Kingsley Kefford (1924) and of Richard William Kingsley Kefford (1927); uncle of Michael Edward Kingsley Kefford (1958) and of Neville Frederick Kingsley Kefford (1958). **Educ:** Wellingborough School. **Career:** Master, Elstree Preparatory School 1925. Died December 1975.

KEFFORD, Richard William Kingsley (1927) Born 2 November 1908, The Vicarage, Dullingham, Cambridgeshire; son of William Kingsley Kefford, Clerk in Holy Orders, and Henrietta Mabel Trigg. BA 1930; MA 1935. **Tutor(s):** J M Wordie. **Johnian Relatives:** nephew of Edward John Kefford (1890); son of William Kingsley Kefford (1894); brother of Harry Kingsley Kefford (1921) and of Edward Kingsley Kefford (1924); uncle of Michael Edward Kingsley Kefford (1958) and of Neville Frederick Kingsley Kefford (1958). **Educ:** Wellingborough School. Died 15 August 1997.

KEIDAN, Joshua Marcus (1930) Born 27 June 1912, 269 Legrams Lane, Horton, Bradford; son of Nathan Keidan, Master General Draper, and Dora Bloom; 2 sons. **Subject(s):** Classics/Law; BA 1933; MA 1937; LLB 1934; LLM 1985; LLM (London). **Tutor(s):** M P Charlesworth. **Educ:** Carlton Street School, Bradford; Bradford Grammar School. **Career:** Called to the Bar, Gray's Inn 1936; Ministry of Health 1938; War Service 1942–1946; DHSS. **Awards:** Scholarship, SJC 1929. Died 1 February 1998.

KEILLER, Patrick Lewis Laurence (1934) Born 20 December 1915, Stirling House, Horton Place, Kollupitiya, Colombo, Ceylon; son of Patrick Anderson Keiller, Agricultural Chemist, and Helen Laurence; m Kay, 1947 (d April 2002); 2 sons (Nigel b 1948 and Angus b 1957). **Subject(s):** Natural Sciences; BA 1937; MA 1950; DipGeog 1939; MIBiol 1958. **Tutor(s):** J M Wordie. **Educ:** Seafield House Preparatory School, Broughty Ferry, Scotland; Trinity College, Glenalmond; Bristol University. **Career:** British Expeditionary Force, France 1939, later serving in Nigeria, India and Burma; Colombo Commercial Company, Ceylon; Assistant Master, Biology, Ipswich School 1951–1957; Housemaster and Head of Biology Department, Loretto School, Musselburgh, East Lothian 1961–1975. **Appointments:** Chairman, Greens Committee, Member, General Council, Life Member, Royal and Ancient Golf Club. Died 28 July 2002.

KELDERS, Theodor Carl (1914) Born 17 February 1896, Elberfeld, Germany; son of Carl Theodor Kelders, Doctor of Laws, and Julie Maussner. **Tutor(s):** L H K Bushe-Fox. **Educ:** Gymnasium, Elberfeld; Gymnasium, Düsseldorf.

KELLAR, James Noel (1945) Born 22 August 1917, 45 Woodstock Road, Bristol; son of James Ballantyne Kellar, Captain, RFA, and Enid Frances Evans; m Mabel Anne Stephens; 1 son (Paul Roderick Noel b 2 June 1948), 1 daughter (Janet Susan b 27 October 1945). **Subject(s):** Physics/Chemistry; BSc (London) 1938; BSc (Reading) 1939. **Johnian Relatives:** father of Paul Roderic Noel Kellar (1967). **Educ:** Dauntsey's School, Devizes; University of Reading. **Career:** Sub-Lieutenant (Lieutenant 1942), RNVR (Special Branch) 1940–1945. Died 20 July 1948.

KELLETT, Dr John Reginald (1946) Born 26 March 1925, 2 Parrott Street, Tong, Bradford; son of Reginald Kellett, Textile Factory Manager, and Nellie Horsfield; m Margaret Webster, 1952; 1 son, 1 daughter.

Subject(s): History; BA 1949; MA 1953; PhD (London). **Tutor(s):** F Thistlethwaite. **Educ:** Dudley Hill Primary School; Bradford Grammar School; St John's College, Oxford. **Career:** Fleet Air Arm; Institute of Historical Research 1949–1952; Extra-mural Lecturer 1954–1958, Lecturer and Reader in Economic History 1958–1984, University of Glasgow. **Publications:** *Glasgow: A Concise History*, 1967; *The Impact of Railways on Victorian Cities*, 1969. Died 15 May 1991.

KELLOCK, John Denis Gilbert (1925) Born 23 August 1906, 36 York Avenue, Great Crosby, Lancashire; son of John Harold Kellock, General Merchant, and Alice Mary Louisa Edmondson; m Jean; 2 daughters. **Subject(s):** Modern and Medieval Languages/Economics; BA 1928; MA 1933. **Tutor(s):** E E Sikes. **Educ:** Holmwood School, Freshfield, Liverpool; Shrewsbury School. **Career:** Director, Gerrard and Reid, Bankers; Owner, Flower-growing Estate; Squadron Leader, RAF (received a Dutch Decoration), WWII; Liberal Candidate, St Ives Division, and North Buckinghamshire. **Awards:** Scholarship, SJC. Died 1 January 1959.

KELLOCK, Joseph Grigg (1922) Born 23 March 1904, Christchurch, New Zealand; son of William Plumer Kellock, Farmer, and Martha Clarissa Grigg; m Annie Winifred Gillespie, 12 July 1928, St James', Morpeth. **Subject(s):** Law; BA 1925; MA 1972. **Tutor(s):** E A Benians. **Johnian Relatives:** son in law of James John Gillespie (1889). **Educ:** Sherborne Preparatory School; Sherborne School. Died 19 June 1982.

KELLS, John Henry McKnight (1934) Born 8 September 1910, 110 Castlereagh Road, Belfast, Northern Ireland; son of Robert Kells, Dentist, and Lilian Jane McKnight; m Mary Elizabeth Cossey; 2 sons (Daniel b 1953 and Gerald b 1959), 1 daughter (Nancy b 1955). **Subject(s):** Classics; BA 1936; MA 1951. **Tutor(s):** R L Howland. **Educ:** Methodist College, Belfast; Queen's University, Northern Ireland. **Career:** Lecturer in Latin and Greek, and Reader 1937–1977, Tutor to Greek and Latin Departments 1952–1965, UCL; Chairman, London University Final Honours Examination in Classics 1967–1969; Head of Latin Department 1972–1973, Honorary Research Fellow (Greek) 1977, UCL. **Appointments:** Associate Member, Barnet Guild of Artists 1996 (exhibited paintings at Guild's Annual Exhibition 1998). **Publications:** (ed) *Sophocles, Electra*, Cambridge Greek and Latin Classics, 1973, with subsequent reprints; numerous articles and reviews in professional journals.

KELYNACK, Hilary Clifton (1934) Born 31 May 1915, Ivy Bank, Devonshire Avenue, Beeston, Nottingham; son of William Sydney Kelynack, Wesleyan Minister, and Annie Lilian Hayman; m Grace Fisher; 1 son (John), 1 daughter (Ann). BA 1937; MA 1941; MusB 1940; FRCO; Honorary FTCL. **Tutor(s):** C W Guillebaud. **Johnian Relatives:** son of William Sydney Kelynack (1898). **Educ:** Stationers' Company School, Hornsey; University College School, Frognal; Guildhall School of Music. **Career:** Acting College Organist and Choirmaster 1936–1938; Organist and Choirmaster, Jesus College, Cambridge 1938–1939; Director of Music, Monkton Coombe School 1943–1948; Music Master, Oundle School 1948–1952; Director of Music, Stowe School 1952–1960; Conductor Hertford Orchestra and Choral Society 1960–1977; Head of Music Department, Balls Park College of Education, Hertford 1966–1977. **Appointments:** Member, Board of Examiners, Trinity College of Music 1966–1982.

KEMBALL-COOK, Richard Bertie (1934) Born 6 March 1915, 39 Dorset Road, Merton, Wimbledon, London; son of Sir Basil Alfred Kemball-Cook, Director of Transports, Admiralty Department, and Nancy Annie Pavitt; 1 child. **Subject(s):** Mechanical Sciences; BA 1937; MA 1945. **Tutor(s):** J S Boys Smith. **Educ:** Cothill House Preparatory School; Shrewsbury School. **Career:** Apprenticed with Mather and Platt; Technical Officer on Anti-submarine warfare, Admiralty 1939–1945; Management Consultant with P-E Consulting Group 1946–1972; Independent Management Consultant 1972. **Awards:** Exhibition, SJC. **Publications:** *The Organisation Gap*.

KEMP, James Herbert (1931) Born 31 March 1912, Long Street, Dursley; son of Alfred James Kemp, Gentlemen's Outfitter, and Helen Frederica Martin Savage; m Mary Fallon, 1941; 1 son (Edwin Martin b 1945), 2 daughters (Sheelagh Brigid b 1943 and Ellen Jane b 1955). **Subject(s):** Natural Sciences; BA 1934. **Tutor(s):** J M Wordie. **Johnian Relatives:** father of Edwin Martin Kemp (1963); grandfather of James Martin Kemp (1996). **Educ:** Uley National School; Crypt School, Gloucester. **Career:** Chemist, British Colloids, The Crookes Laboratories, Park Royal 1934–1938; Chemistry Master, Kings School, Rochester 1938–1940; Chemist, Ministry of Aircraft Production 1940–1947; Senior Chemistry Master, Royal Grammar School, High Wycombe 1947–1949; Senior Chemistry Master, Crypt School, Gloucester 1949–1955; Senior Science Master, Downside School, Bath 1955–1977. **Awards:** Scholarship, SJC.

KEMP, Percy Vickerman (1910) Born 16 July 1892, 1 Salem Hill South, Sunderland, County Durham; son of James Vickerman Kemp, Clerk in Holy Orders, and Mary Royston Nicholson. **Subject(s):** Classics; BA 1913. **Tutor(s):** L H K Bushe-Fox. **Educ:** St John's School, Leatherhead; Westcott House, Cambridge. **Career:** Private, 19th Battalion, Royal Fusiliers 1915; Second Lieutenant, 4th Battalion, Durham Light Infantry 1916; Acting Captain 1918. **Awards:** Choral Studentship, SJC. Died 31 May 1918 (died of gas poisoning on active service).

KEMP, Ralph (1932) Born 14 March 1913, 3 Beaconsfield Terrace, St Stephens, Canterbury, Kent; son of Lawrence Kemp, Solicitor's Clerk, and Lillian Elizabeth Wilson; m Ruth Elizabeth Fletcher, 21 February 1945, St John's Church, Caterham. **Subject(s):** Classics; BA 1935. **Educ:** Simon Langton School, Canterbury; Christ's Hospital, Horsham. **Career:** Classics Master, Maidstone Grammar 1935–1973; Captain, RN 1939–1945. Died October 1984.

KEMP-KING, Paul Robert (1936) Born 27 May 1918, Netherleigh, Lancaster; son of George Kemp-King, Civil Servant, War Office, and Mary Lilian Wenonah Helme. **Subject(s):** Geography; BA 1940. **Tutor(s):** J M Wordie. **Johnian Relatives:** son of George Kemp-King (1899). **Educ:** Cressbrook, Kirkby Lonsdale, Westmorland; Naish House School, Burnham-on-Sea; Westminster School, London. Died April 1994.

KEMPSON, Gerald Peter (1942) Born 9 March 1924, White Cross Nursing Home, Edgbaston, Birmingham; son of Alwyn Maitland Kempson, Production Manager, Imperial Chemical Industries, and Anita Mary Tapper; m Christina Anne Turner, 1960; 2 sons (Paul Robert b 1962 and David Anthony b 1964). **Subject(s):** Natural Sciences; BA 1948. **Tutor(s):** C W Guillebaud. **Educ:** St George's School, North Foreland; Marlborough College. **Career:** Sub-Lieutenant, RNVR 1943–1946; Technical Officer, Henry Wiggin & Co 1949–1953; Technical Officer, ICI Metals 1955–1968; Store Proprietor 1968–1972; Financial Advisor, Imperial Life 1972–1993; Semi-professional Jazz Pianist 1993. **Appointments:** 1952 Mond Nickel Fellow.

KEMSLEY, John Edward Timothy (1937) Born 11 May 1919, Crouchman's, Shoeburyness; son of Arthur Unwin Kemsley, Gentleman, and Olive Armitage Goodman; m Pamela FitzGerald 24 July 1948. BA 1940. **Tutor(s):** C W Guillebaud. **Educ:** Aldeburgh Lodge, Suffolk; Charterhouse; Alpine College, Switzerland. Died 30 March 1978.

KENCHINGTON, Francis Ernest (1924) Born 24 April 1904, Hamilton Lodge, Hythe, Kent; son of George Kenchington, Dairyman, and Edith Marshman. **Tutor(s):** B F Armitage. **Educ:** St Leonard's C of E School, Hythe; Harvey Grammar School, Folkestone; South Eastern Agricultural College, Wye.

KENCHINGTON, Dr Noel Scott (1932) Born 25 September 1913, 61 Woodberry Crescent, Muswell Hill, Middlesex; son of Charles William Kenchington, Actuary, and Mary Edith Scott; m Barbara M Swaffield, 11 June 1947, Bromsgrove; 2 sons, 1 daughter. **Subject(s):** Medicine; BA 1935; MA 1939; MRCS 1940; LRCP 1940. **Tutor(s):** R L Howland. **Educ:**

Grey Friars School, Leamington Spa; Wycliffe College, Stonehouse; Birmingham University Medical School. **Career:** House Surgeon, Birmingham General Hospital 1940–1941; House Physician, Birmingham Queen Elizabeth Hospital 1941; RAMC, India and Burma 1941–1946; GP, Bromsgrove 1946–1978; Part-time Anaesthetist, Bromsgrove General Hospital 1950–1978. **Appointments:** Divisional Surgeon, Bromsgrove St John's Ambulance Service 1950s and 1960s; Member, Cambridge Medical Society; Magistrate, later Chairman, Bromsgrove Bench 1953–1983; Member, BMA; Chairman, Worcestershire Division, BMA 1977–1978; Secretary, Bromsgrove Choral Society. **Honours:** Officer, Order of St John. Died 29 October 2003.

KENDALL, Dr Guy Melville (1911) Born 2 July 1892, Tallyhoe, Athenry, County Galway, Ireland; son of Edward Kendall, JP, and Elizabeth Mary Hazell. **Subject(s):** Natural Sciences; BA 1914; MB 1917; LRCP; MRCS 1916; MRCP 1922. **Tutor(s):** J R Tanner. **Educ:** Epsom College. **Career:** Captain, RAMC, Mesopotamia, WWI; Resident Medical Officer, Victoria Hospital for Children; House Physician, Children's Department, and Casualty Officer, St Thomas' Hospital; Physician, Epsom Cottage Hospital 1934. **Awards:** Subsizarship, SJC. **Publications:** 'A Case of Ototic Meningitis', *British Medical Journal*, 1924 (with others); 'Adenoma of the Small Intestine', *British Journal of Surgery*, 1924. Died 3 December 1952.

KENDALL, Sir Maurice George (1926) Born 6 September 1907, 120 Mill Road, Kettering, Northamptonshire; son of John Roughton Kendall, Mechanical Engineer, and Georgina Jessie Brewer; m (1) Sheila Frances Holland Lester, 1933, (2) Kathleen Ruth Audrey Whitfield; (1) 2 sons, 1 daughter, (2) 1 son. **Subject(s):** Mathematics; BA 1929; MA 1935; ScD 1949; DUniv (Essex) 1968; DUniv (Lancaster) 1975; FBA 1970. **Tutor(s):** J M Wordie. **Johnian Relatives:** father of John Paul Holland Kendall (1957) and of James Darrell Phillipson Kendall (1968). **Educ:** St Mary's School, Kettering; Church of England School, Kettering; Central School, Derby; St Dunstan's Council School, Derby; Osmaston Council School, Derby. **Career:** Board, Corporation of Economic and Industrial Research (CEIR UK Ltd); Head, Economic Intelligence Branch, Ministry of Agriculture and Fisheries 1930–1941; Statistician 1941–1949, Joint Assistant General Manager 1947–1949, Chamber of Shipping; Professor of Statistics, University of London 1949–1961; Chairman, Scientific Control Systems Ltd 1967–1971; Chairman, Scientific Control Systems (Holdings) 1971–1972; Director, World Fertility Survey 1972–1980. **Appointments:** Fellow, British Computer Society; President, Royal Statistical Society 1960; President, Operational Research Society; President, Institute of Statisticians 1964; Fellow, London Graduate School of Business Studies; Fellow, American Statistical Association; Fellow, Econometric Society; Honorary Member, Market Research Society; Honorary Fellow, LSE 1975; Honorary Member, International Statistical Institute 1979. **Awards:** Gold Medal, Royal Statistical Society 1968; UN Peace Medal 1980. **Honours:** Kt 1974. **Publications:** Many on probability and statistics, including, *The Advanced Theory of Statistics*, 1943–1946; *Dictionary of Statistical Terms*; *Bibliography of Statistical Literature*; (General Editor) *Griffin's Statistical Monographs and Courses*; *Introduction to the Theory of Statistics*. Died 29 March 1983.

KENDALL, William Clarke (1943) Born 15 July 1925, Holm Nook, Ulverston, Lancashire; son of William Clarke Kendall, Solicitor, and Gladys Mary Deason. **Tutor(s):** C W Guillebaud. **Educ:** Earnseat School, Arnside; Sedbergh School.

KENDON, Frank Samuel Herbert (1919) Born 12 September 1893, Bethany House, Goudhurst, Kent; son of Samuel Kendon, Schoolmaster, and Ellen Susan Todman; m Elizabeth Cecilia Phyllis Horne, 19 April 1930, Goudhurst, Kent; 3 sons (Adam b 4 April 1934, Andrew b 8 December 1940 and Thomas Adrian b 14 December 1943), 1 daughter (Alice b 28 November 1931). **Subject(s):** English. **Tutor(s):** E A Benians. **Johnian Relatives:** uncle of Richard Donald Kendon (1943); father-in-law of John Christopher Stephens (1948); father of Adam Kendon (1952). **Educ:** Bethany House School, Goudhurst. **Career:** Pupil Teacher

and Assistant Master, Bethany House School until 1915; Sapper, RE Signal Service, Egypt 1915–1919; Editorial staff, *John O'London's Weekly* c1928–1935; Assistant Secretary to the Syndics, CUP 1935–1954; Title E Fellow, SJC 1948–1958. **Appointments:** Fellow, Royal Society of Literature 1946; Member, Panel of Literary Advisers to *The New English Bible* 1948. **Awards:** Seatonian Prize, University of Cambridge 1942, 1945 and 1946. **Publications:** *Mural Paintings in English Churches*, 1923; *Poems and Sonnets*, 1924; *Arguments and Emblems*, 1925; *A Life and Death of Judas Iscariot*, 1926; *The Small Years*, 1930; *The Adventure of Poetry*, 1932; *Tristram*, 1934; *The Cherry Minder*, 1935; *The Time Piece*, 1945; *Martin Makesure*, 1950; (posthumous) *Thirty Six Psalms: An English Version*, 1963. Died 28 December 1959.

KENDON, Richard Donald (1943) Born 2 September 1926, Rays Nursing Home, Strand, Ryde, Isle of Wight; son of Donald Henry Kendon, Electrical Engineer, Electric Power Company, and Katherine Grace Honess; 4 children. **Subject(s):** Mechanical Sciences; BA 1946; MA 1950; MIEE. **Johnian Relatives:** nephew of Frank Samuel Herbert Kendon (1919); cousin of Adam Kendon (1952). **Educ:** Bethany House School, Goudhurst; Truro School; Bromsgrove School. **Career:** East Midlands Electricity Board, Nottingham 1949–1988.

KENNEDY, Edward Gilbert (1925) Born 10 September 1906, Tientsin, North China; son of Frederick Arthur Kennedy, Merchant, and Florence Edith Robinson; m Rosa Gwynne Jones, 27 April 1935, Bombay. **Subject(s):** Law/History; BA 1928. **Tutor(s):** E A Benians. **Educ:** Tientsin Grammar School; Warwick School.

KENNEDY, Hewat Munro (1944) Born 12 September 1927, 12 Bridge Street, Hawick, Roxburghshire; son of Hewat Kennedy, Hosiery Manufacturer, and Patricia McDonald Munro. **Subject(s):** Mechanical Sciences; BA 1947. **Tutor(s):** S J Bailey. **Educ:** Hawick High School.

KENNEDY, John Reid (1929) Born 1 November 1910, Fernhill, Charmouth, Dorset; son of John Kennedy, Clerk in Holy Orders, and Ethel Mary Reid; m Diana Margaret Pass, 6 November 1954, Wootton Fitzpaine Church, Dorset; 2 sons (Colin and Alan), 1 daughter (Katherine). **Subject(s):** Law; BA 1932; LLB 1933; LLM 1985. **Tutor(s):** E A Benians. **Johnian Relatives:** brother of William Hall Kennedy (1929). **Educ:** Durlston Court (Preparatory) School, Swanage; Aldenham School, Elstree. **Career:** Solicitor 1936–1961; Major, Army (England and India) 1939–1946; Colonial Legal Service 1946; Custodian State Domain, Palestine 1947–1950; Colonial Legal Service, Dar es Salaam 1950–1961; Administrator General, Legal Department, Tanganyika 1958–1961. Died 25 March 2001.

KENNEDY, William Hall (1929) Born 24 September 1912, Fernhill, Charmouth, Dorset; son of John Kennedy, Clerk in Holy Orders, and Ethel Mary Reid; m Pauline Elizabeth Nott-Bower, 15 June 1946, St Mary's Church, Wimbledon; 2 daughters (Anne and Elizabeth). **Subject(s):** Classics/History; BA 1934; MA 1939. **Tutor(s):** R L Howland. **Johnian Relatives:** brother of John Reid Kennedy (1929). **Educ:** Marlborough College. **Career:** Dorset Regiment and 12th Indian Frontier Force Regiment 1940–1946; House Tutor, Senior Master and Head of the History Department, Aldenham School, Hertfordshire, until 1959; Headmaster, Kirkham Grammar School 1959–1972. **Awards:** Scholarship, SJC.

KENNY, Ronald Edmond (1924) Born 19 March 1906, 32 Bouverie Road West, Folkestone, Kent; son of Henry Torrens Kenny, Colonel, 32nd (Bombay) Lancers, and Zoe Fellows. **Subject(s):** Modern and Medieval Languages/History; BA 1929; MA 1958. **Tutor(s):** B F Armitage. **Johnian Relatives:** son of Henry Torrens Kenny (1876). **Educ:** Wellington College; Lausanne University.

KENRICK, Cecil John (1932) Born 29 November 1913, 17 Ampton Road, Edgbaston; son of Clive Kenrick, Holloware Manufacturer, and Frances Flore Goodman; BA 1935. **Tutor(s):** J M Wordie. **Educ:** Dornford, Langton Matravers; Shrewsbury School.

KENT, Alan (1942) Born 13 April 1925, 20 Dorset Street, Kingston-upon-Hull; son of Percy Edward Albert Kent, Company Director, and Denise Fowler; m Barbara Joan Dalley, 1964; 1 son (Jasper), 1 daughter (Phoebe). **Subject(s):** Natural Sciences/Chemical Engineering; BA 1949; MA 1951; MEng 1992. **Tutor(s):** C W Guillebaud; G C L Bertram. **Educ:** Francis Askew School, Hull; C of E School, Hessle; Pocklington School. **Career:** Chemical Process Research, development and design. **Appointments:** Birmingham Local Secretary, Mensa 1963–1964; Founder, organizer and editor, one-name Trethewy Society 1983–. **Publications:** Articles in various genealogical journals.

KENYON, Dr Harold Frederick (1930) Born 7 May 1911, Lane Head, Shipley; son of Walter Harold Kenyon, Secretary to a Worsted Manufacturing Company, and Ada Rosa Bransgrove; m Ida E Wilkinson, 7 January 1943; 1 son (William), 2 daughters (Eileen Mary and Margaret Eleanor). **Subject(s):** Natural Sciences; BA 1933; MA 1938; PhD 1938. **Tutor(s):** J M Wordie. **Educ:** West Riding Council School, Shipley; Private School, Chepstow; West Riding Council School, Denby Dale; The Grammar School, Penistone; Arnold House School, Blackpool. **Career:** Shell Refining & Marketing Company 1938–1948; Associated Electrical Industries 1948–1971. Died 5 November 2000.

KEOGH, John Denis (1935) Born 1 February 1918, Chung King, Szechwan, China; son of Denis Thomas Keogh, Merchant, and Annie Innocent. **Subject(s):** Law; BA 1938; MA 1942. **Tutor(s):** C W Guillebaud. **Educ:** St Augustine's Abbey School, Ramsgate; Beaumont College.

KEONG, Siew Tong (1934) Born 26 October 1913, Penang; son of Keong Yeok Kee, Merchant, and Choo Neoh Goh. **Tutor(s):** R L Howland. **Educ:** St Xavier's Institution, Penang.

KER, Robert Dermot Paton (1927) Born 15 March 1908, Johnstown, Newtownbarry, Union of Enniscothy, County Wexford, Ireland; son of John Paton Ker, Planter and Mine Owner, Malaysia, and Florence Mary Templeton. **Tutor(s):** E A Benians. **Educ:** St Edward's School, Oxford.

KERKHAM, Robin Kingsford (1928) Born 9 February 1910, The Laurels, Terrington St Clement, Norfolk; son of Robert Hugh Kerkham, Farmer and Landowner, and Mildred Johnson; m Mary Sylvia Major, 1937, Warwick; 1 son (William b 14 October 1938), 2 daughters (Ann b 29 May 1941 and Patricia b 5 April 1944). **Subject(s):** Natural Sciences, Agriculture; BA 1931; MA 1958; DipAgr 1932; AICTA 1932. **Tutor(s):** C W Guillebaud. **Johnian Relatives:** father of William David Kerkham (1957); uncle of Richard Hugh Kerkham (1959). **Educ:** King Edward VII School, King's Lynn; Bootham School, York. **Career:** Colonial Agricultural Service, Uganda 1934–1955; Farmer, Norfolk 1955. **Appointments:** Chairman, Norfolk Branch, National Farmers' Union 1975. **Awards:** Jubilee Medal as Chairman, West Norfolk District Council. **Honours:** OBE 1956. Died 1 July 1980.

KERMODE, Terence Lucas (1943) Born 17 December 1925, Bowsden, Prescot Road, St Helens, Lancashire; son of George Douglas Kermode, Schoolmaster, and Ida Fearn Sparks; m Sylvia Hunter-Jones, 1967; 3 stepsons. **Subject(s):** Mathematics; BA 1946; MA 1952. **Tutor(s):** S J Bailey; J M Wordie. **Educ:** Cowley School, St Helens; Rydal School. **Career:** Head of Department, Housemaster, Captain in CCF, Lancing College 1948–1971; Schoolmaster Fellow Commoner, Magdalene College, Lent Term 1967; Joint Headmaster, Heath Mount School 1971–1975; Head of Department and Computing, Bennett Memorial School 1975–1983; Head of Department, Woodbridge School 1983–1990. **Honours:** TD 1961. **Publications:** Articles in journals; poem in the *TES*.

KERROD, Norman (1940) Born 18 February 1922, 42 Victoria Avenue, Elland, Yorkshire; son of Clement Kerrod, Labourer/Butcher, and May Hadfield. **Subject(s):** English; BA 1943; MA 1948. **Tutor(s):** C W Guillebaud. **Educ:** Elland National School; Bentley Road Council School, Doncaster; Milnsbridge National Grammar School, Huddersfield; King James's Grammar School, Almondbury. **Awards:** Scholarship, SJC.

KERRUISH, Norman (1945) Born 15 January 1928, 36 Gidlow Avenue, Wigan, Lancashire; son of William Joseph Kerruish, Secretary, Cooperative Society, and Mabel Paul; m Marion Leyland, February 1950 (d 1980); 1 son (David b 1953), 1 daughter (Alison b 1958). **Subject(s):** Mathematics; BA 1948; MA 1952. **Educ:** Hindley Green Church of England School; Abram Grammar School. **Career:** Head, Mathematics and Computer Department, BTH Company, Rugby 1959–1965; Reader in Engineering Mathematics, Aston University 1965–1985.

KERSHAW, The Revd Arthur (1900) Born 13 July 1878, 2 Simson Hill, Heywood, Lancashire; son of John Kershaw, Engineer, and Elizabeth Whittaker. BA 1903; MA 1907. **Tutor(s):** E E Sikes. **Johnian Relatives:** father of Geoffrey Kershaw (1930). **Educ:** Private Tuition. **Career:** Ordained Deacon 1903; Ordained Priest 1905; Rector, All Saints, Stand, Manchester 1910.

KERSHAW, Cecil Aubrey (1919) Born 19 November 1898, 35 Mayflower Road, Clapham Road, Kennington, London; son of Joseph Crabb Kershaw, Commercial Traveller, and Florence Edith Lowen. **Subject(s):** Mechanical Sciences; BA 1922; MA 1926. **Tutor(s):** E A Benians. **Educ:** Collett House School, Bournemouth; The County School, Yeovil; Bournemouth School; Bournemouth Municipal College. **Career:** Assistant Engineer, Merz and McLellan, Consulting Engineers 1925; Northampton Polytechnic Institute, London 1937; ICI Ltd 1952.

KERSHAW, The Revd Geoffrey (1930) Born 25 March 1910, Lonsdale Terrace, Whitefield, Lancashire; son of Arthur Kershaw, Clerk in Holy Orders, and Annie Preston; m Edith. **Subject(s):** History/Theology; BA 1933; MA 1937. **Tutor(s):** E A Benians. **Johnian Relatives:** son of Arthur Kershaw (1900). **Educ:** Kersal School; Rossall Preparatory School; Rossall School; Bishop's College, Cheshunt. **Career:** Ordained Deacon 1934; Curate, Rochdale 1934–1939; Ordained Priest 1935; Chaplain, HM Forces (twice Mentioned in Despatches) 1939–1945; Vicar, St James, Heywood, Lancashire 1946–1951; Mayor, Heywood 1950–1951; Vicar, Holy Trinity, Littleborough, Lancashire 1951–1971; Canon, Manchester Cathedral 1966; Rector, Bride, Isle of Man 1971–1975. Died 5 October 1980.

KETTLEWELL, Geoffrey Wade (1943) Born 25 July 1925, Wensley Dene, 5 Kent Drive, Harrogate, Yorkshire; son of Frederick Thomas Kettlewell, Director of Woollen Mill, and Gladys Mary Wade. **Tutor(s):** C W Guillebaud. **Educ:** Grosvenor House School, Harrogate; Rydal School.

KEW, The Revd Norman Henry (1946) Born 6 July 1923, 12 Victoria Place, Victoria Road, Bristol; son of Frederick Archibald Kew, Minister of Religion, and Eva Bruce Bryant; m Geraldine. **Subject(s):** History; BA 1948; MA 1956. **Tutor(s):** F Thistlethwaite. **Educ:** Bedminster Down Elementary School; Redcliffe Church School; Bristol Grammar School; Caterham School. **Career:** Sub-Lieutenant, RNVR 1942–1945; Congregational Pastor, Stourbridge 1951; Army Chaplain, Banners Gate Congregational Church, Sutton Coldfield 1957. Died 7 March 1994.

KEY, Samuel (1927) Born 22 August 1908, 33 Cecil Street, West Derby, Liverpool; son of Max Key, Tailor's Machinist, and Esther Goldberg. **Subject(s):** Modern and Medieval Languages; BA 1930; MA 1949. **Tutor(s):** M P Charlesworth. **Educ:** Oulton School, Liverpool. **Awards:** Scholarship, SJC 1926.

KEYSELL, Francis Paul (1933) Born 13 August 1914, Scotts Hill House, Ware; son of Francis Olney Keysell, Provision Merchant, and Edith Jean Paul; m (1) Evelyn McCowen, (2) Diana Forbes, 8 July 1950; (1) 1 son (Francis Kerry). **Subject(s):** Law; BA 1936. **Tutor(s):** E A Benians. **Johnian Relatives:** father of Francis Kerry Keysell (1959). **Educ:** Bengeo School, Hertford; Mill Mead, Shrewsbury; Shrewsbury School. **Career:**

Provision Merchant; Admitted to the Middle Temple 1934; Called to the Bar 1938; Second Lieutenant, then Captain, RA, WWII.

KEYTE, The Revd Douglas Joseph Henry (1937) Born 16 February 1918, 47 Hall Street, Hockley; son of Joseph Henry Keyte, Storesman, and Amy Parker. **Subject(s):** Classics/Law; BA 1940; MA 1946; BA (School of Theology, Oxford) 1948. **Educ:** St Paul's School, Birmingham; Icknield Street School, Birmingham; Albert Road School, Birmingham; King Edward VI Grammar School, Aston; King Edward VI High School, Birmingham. **Career:** Curate, St Paul, Kersal 1948–1951; Priest in Charge, St Francis of Assisi, Newall Green, Wythenshawe 1951–1954; Chaplain and Assistant Master, King William's College, Isle of Man 1954–1957; Master, Adisadel College, Cape Coast, Ghana 1957–1961; Head of Classics, Girls' Grammar School, Sale 1962–1982; Honorary Curate, St George with St Barnabas, Charlestown, Salford 1975. **Awards:** Major Scholarship, SJC 1936.

KEYWORTH, Frederick Munday (1901) Born 20 September 1883, Dalhousie, Punjab, India; son of Edwin Keyworth, Lay Agent, CMS, and Mary Ann Munday. **Subject(s):** Classics; BA 1904. **Tutor(s):** E E Sikes. **Educ:** King's Lynn School. **Career:** Master, Royal Masonic School, Bushey 1904; Master, Free School, Penang 1905. **Awards:** Sizarship, SJC.

KHAN, Fazl Muhammed (1902) Born 19 May 1882, Basijaur, Hoshiarpur, Punjab, India; son of Nathe Khan, Landholder, and Nur Begam Khanam. **Subject(s):** Mathematics; BA 1905. **Tutor(s):** D MacAlister. **Educ:** Ludhiana School; Lahore Government College.

KHAN, Mahomed Ismail (1901) Born Agra, India; son of Nawab Mahomed Ishak Khan, Indian Civil Service, and Musamat Amival Zamani Begaun. BA 1905. **Tutor(s):** E E Sikes. **Educ:** Tonbridge School.

KHAN, Mohamed Islam-ullah (1907) Born 1866, Delhi, India; son of Mohamed Ikram-ullah Khan, Honorary Magistrate. **Tutor(s):** J R Tanner. **Educ:** Arabic High School, Delhi, India.

KHAN, Sahibzada Rashid Ali (1929) Born 8 February 1904, Lahore, India; son of Nawab Sir Zulfigar Ali Khan, Landholder, and Member, Indian Legislative Assembly, and Mahmood Sultan Begam. BA (Punjab) 1925. **Tutor(s):** E A Benians. **Educ:** Punjab University; Government College, Lahore; Aitchison Indian Chiefs College, Lahore. **Career:** Political career, Lahore.

KHAN, Sirdar Abdussamad (1936) Born 21 October 1916, Hyderabad, Deccan, India; son of Maolvi Khan Fazal Mahomed Khan, Director of Public Instruction, Hyderabad. **Subject(s):** Mathematics/Law; BA 1939; MA 1943. **Tutor(s):** J M Wordie. **Educ:** City High School; Nizam's College, Hyderabad.

KHANNA, Amrit Kumar (1942) Born 21 May 1924, 14 Burdwan Road, Calcutta; son of Nanda Lal Khanna, Landholder, and Sudharani Mahtab, Maharaj Kumari of Burdwan. **Subject(s):** Mechanical Sciences; BA 1945; MA 1949; MICE. **Tutor(s):** S J Bailey. **Johnian Relatives:** son of Nanda Lal Khanna (1920). **Educ:** Fernden, Haslemere; Wellington College, Berkshire. **Career:** Lieutenant Colonel. Died 5 July 1991.

KHANNA, Nanda Lal (1920) Born 4 April 1899, Lahore, India; son of Lalla Lant Ram Khanna, Banker and Zernindar, and Sham Devi. **Tutor(s):** E A Benians. **Johnian Relatives:** father of Amrit Kumar Khanna (1942). **Educ:** DAV School, Lahore; Government College, Lahore; Punjab University.

KHONG, Kam Tak (1904) Born 30 December 1884, Penang, Straits Settlements; son of Thye Cheng Khong, Tin Miner, Malaysia, and Ah Sen Chan; m Swee Chun Lam; 3 sons (Kit Yew b 5 May 1921, Kit Soon b 22 May 1924 and Kit Thong b 4 March 1927), 3 daughters (Soh Gaik b 30 October 1913, Winnie Sau Meng b 30 May 1920 and Helen Sau Yü b 4 October 1922). **Subject(s):** Natural Sciences; BA 1907; MB 1910; BChir 1910; MA 1913; MRCS (London); LRCP (London). **Tutor(s):** D MacAlister. **Johnian Relatives:** father of Kit Soon Khong (1946). **Educ:** Penang Free School; Anglo-Chinese School, Ipoh, Malaya. **Career:** Private Medical Practitioner 1910–1960. **Appointments:** Medical Superintendent, Perak Chinese Maternity Hospital 1921–1957; JP 1924; Member, Kinta Sanitary Board 1917–1921 and 1936–1941; Perak State Councillor 1932–1941; Federal Legislative Councillor, Malaya 1936–1941; Advisor, Federal Advisory Council to the Governor, Straits Settlement and High Commissioner, Federated Malay States 1936–1941. **Honours:** MCH 1932; MBE 1936; CBE 1947; Dato Kurnia Negara 1955. Died 5 October 1973.

KHONG, Kit Soon (1946) Born 22 May 1924, Chung Thye Phin Road, Ipoh, Perak, Malaya; son of Kam Tak Khong, Medical Practitioner, and Swee Chun Lam; m Hong Keow Khoo, 1964; 1 son (Kok Wai b 30 October 1967), 1 daughter (Pek Lan b 24 October 1965). **Subject(s):** Mechanical Sciences; BA 1949; MA 1953; FIES; FICE; FIWES; MIEM. **Tutor(s):** R L Howland. **Johnian Relatives:** son of Kam Tak Khong (1904). **Educ:** Anglo-Chinese School, Ipoh, Perak, Malaya; Raffles College, Singapore. **Career:** Assistant Engineer, Sir William Halcrow & Partners, UK 1949–1952; Assistant Engineer 1953–1959, Senior Engineer 1959–1964, City Council, Singapore; Superintending Engineer/Chief Water Engineer 1964–1970, General Manager 1970–1975, Public Utilities Board, Singapore; Principal, Ngee Ann Technical College, Singapore 1975–1982; World Bank Management Adviser to National Water Supply & Drainage Board, Sri Lanka 1983; Senior Contract Administrator, later Manager, Technology Transfer, Mass Rapid Transit Corporation, Singapore 1984–1989; Project Manager (Infrastructure), Night Safari, Singapore Zoological Gardens 1990–1997. **Appointments:** Member, Board of Directors, Singapore Zoological Gardens 1971–1982; Interviewer, Professional Interview, Institution of Civil Engineers, UK 1972 and 1976–1977; Member, Board of Governors, Singapore Armed Forces Reservist Association 1972–1981; Advisory Committee Member, Institution of Civil Engineers, UK, Singapore Branch 1972–1982; Panel Chairman/Member of Professional Review, Institution of Engineers, Singapore 1973–1982; Member, Disciplinary Committee, Professional Engineers Board 1981; Member, Institute of Education Council, Singapore 1981–1982. **Honours:** PPA (Public Administration Medal of Singapore).

KHOSLA, Krishna Kumar (1929) Born 12 April 1910, Lahore, Punjab, India; son of Ram Prasad Khosla, Professor of History, and Bhagwanti. **Subject(s):** Economics; BA 1932; MA 1936; BA (Patna, India) 1929. **Tutor(s):** C W Guillebaud. **Educ:** Government Aided School, Muzaffarpur; Greer Bhumihar Brahman College, Muzaffarpur.

KIDD, Professor Douglas Alexander (1934) Born 9 May 1913, Rowandale, Cults, Aberdeenshire; son of John Kidd, Grocer, and Lucy Gunn; m Margaret Miller Barr, 1942; 2 daughters (Alison and Aileen). **Subject(s):** Classics; BA 1936; MA 1951; MA (Aberdeen) 1934. **Tutor(s):** R L Howland. **Educ:** Cults Public School, Aberdeen; Robert Gordon's College, Aberdeen; Aberdeen University; Universities of Munich and Lund. **Career:** Assistant Lecturer in Latin 1938–1941, Lecturer in Latin 1945–1950, University of Aberdeen; Lieutenant, RNVR 1941–1945; Professor of Classics, University College of the Gold Coast (later renamed the University of Ghana) 1950–1957; Professor of Classics, University of Canterbury, New Zealand 1957–1979. **Appointments:** Founder, Dante Alighieri Society. **Awards:** Scholarship, SJC; Gold Medal from the Italian Department of Cultural Affairs, for services to Italian culture in New Zealand 1964. **Publications:** *Collins Latin Gem Dictionary*, 1957; *A Commentary on the Phaenomena of Aratus*, CUP, 1997. Died 27 December 2001.

KIDD, Dr Franklin (1909) Born 12 October 1890, 4 Linton Villas, Weston-Super-Mare, Somerset; son of Benjamin Kidd, Civil Servant, and Maud Emma Isabel Perry; m Mary Nest Owen, 20 April 1920, St David's Cathedral. **Subject(s):** Natural Sciences; BA 1912; MA 1916; DSc (London) 1917; FRS 1944. **Tutor(s):** J R Tanner.

Johnian Relatives: uncle of Denys Martin Owen Davies (1943). **Educ:** Tonbridge School. **Career:** Fellow, SJC 1913–1919; Food Investigation Board, Botany Laboratory, Cambridge 1918; Low Temperature Research Station, Cambridge 1922; 1 year tour of South Africa, Australia, New Zealand, Canada and USA to advise on export of Fruit 1927; Superintendent, Low Temperature Research Station, Cambridge 1934; Director of Food Investigation, Department of Scientific and Industrial Research 1947–1957; Title E Fellow, SJC 1950–1958. **Appointments:** Chairman, Royal Commission (SA) 1936; Chairman, Food Group, Society of Chemical Industry. **Awards:** Slater Studentship 1912; Frank Smart Prize for Biology, University of Cambridge 1912; Frank Smart Studentship, University of Cambridge 1913; Walsingham Medal, University of Cambridge 1913; Allen Scholarship, University of Cambridge 1916; Gedge Prize, University of Cambridge 1916. **Honours:** CBE 1950. **Publications:** *Almond in Peterhouse and other poems*, 1950; *The Peopled Earth*, 1965; Various contributions to *The Eagle* and scientific journals. Died 7 May 1974.

KIDD, Dr Fred (1938) Born 23 July 1919, 84 Exley Head, Keighley; son of Harry Kidd, Motor Transport, and Ellen Ambler; m Joyce Binns, 22 August 1942; 2 sons (John Anthony b 1944 and David Michael b 1945). **Subject(s):** Natural Sciences; BA 1941; MA 1945; PhD (Leeds) 1964; FTI. **Tutor(s):** C W Guillebaud. **Educ:** Ingrow Council School, Keighley; Keighley Boys' Grammar School. **Career:** Experimental Officer, Chemical Inspection Department, Ministry of Supply, Royal Ordnance Factory, Risley, Warrington 1941–1945; Deputy Research Superintendent, Sutcliffe Speakman and Co, Leigh 1945–1947; Senior Research Chemist, Armoride Ltd, Earby 1947–1949; Senior Research Chemist, British Brush Manufacturers Research Association Ltd 1949–1957; Research Chemist, Textile Industries, University of Leeds 1953–1962; Director of Research, British Brush Manufacturers Research Association Ltd 1957–1962; Senior Lecturer in Chemistry, Scottish Woollen Technical College, Galashiels 1962; Vice Principal and Head of Technology Department, Scottish College of Textiles, Galashiels 1969–1979. **Appointments:** Honorary Fellow, Scottish College of Textiles 1988; Honorary University Lecturer, University of Leeds. **Awards:** Minor Scholarship, SJC 1937; Prizes in 1939 and 1941; Service Medal of the Textile Institute, Manchester 1991. **Publications:** *Brushmaking Materials*, 1957. Died 20 September 2000.

KIDDLE, Frederick Edward (1918) American Student.

KIER, Hans Harold (1947) Born 5 February 1929, Tean Hurst, Chedsley, Cheadle, Staffordshire; son of Olaf Kier, Civil Engineer, and Gudrun Anna Carstensen. **Tutor(s):** R L Howland. **Educ:** Wimbledon Common Preparatory School; Loretto Junior School; Loretto School. Died 17 December 1947.

KIKUCHI, Taiji (1919) Born 27 September 1893, Hongo, Tokyo, Japan; son of Dairoku Yasuyuki Kikuchi, Privy Councillor, President, Imperial Academy of Japan, and Tatsu Fukuda. BA (Imperial University of Japan). **Tutor(s):** E A Benians. **Johnian Relatives:** son of Dairoku Yasuyuki Kikuchi (1873). **Educ:** Middle School of Higher Normal School, Tokyo; First High School, Tokyo; Imperial University of Japan. **Career:** Electrotechnical Laboratory, Department of Communications, Tokyo; Institute of Physical and Chemical Research, Japan; Advanced Student, Cavendish Laboratory. Died 2 March 1921.

KILFORD, William Kenneth (1935) Born 31 August 1916, 4 Havelock Street, Ilkeston, Derbyshire; son of William George Kilford, Chartered Surveyor, and Margaret Elsie Sinclair; m Ivy Joan Sadler, 1947; 1 son (Jonathan Michael), 1 daughter (Jane Caroline). **Subject(s):** Economics/Geography; BA 1938; MA 1942; CEng; MICE. **Tutor(s):** C W Guillebaud. **Johnian Relatives:** father of Jonathan Michael Kilford (1966). **Educ:** Kimbolton School. **Career:** Assistant in Surveyor's Department 1939–1940; HM Forces, RE, served in France, Belgium, Germany, demobbed rank of Captain 1940–1945; Engineering Assistant, Middleton, Lancashire 1946–1949; Senior Planning Assistant

Research, Warwickshire County Council 1949–1952; Deputy Area Planning Officer, South East Staffordshire County Council 1952–1953; Lecturer/Senior Lecturer, South West Essex Technical College/ South East Essex Regional College of Technology (became North East London Polytechnic) 1953–1971; Lecturer in Civil and Structural Engineering, University of Sheffield 1971–1981. **Awards:** Lucy Ingram Exhibition. **Publications:** *Elementary Air Survey*, 1963, 4th edition 1979.

KILNER, Dr John Goff (1941) Born 24 February 1923, 15 Albert Crescent, Bury St Edmunds, Suffolk; son of Henry Goff Kilner, GP, and Mabel Olive Simpson; m (1) Pamela Doreen Peckett, 2 July 1946 (d 1969), (2) Anne Wilkinson, 1971; 3 sons, 3 stepchildren. **Subject(s):** Natural Sciences; BA 1944; MA 1948; MB 1947; BChir 1947. **Tutor(s):** S J Bailey. **Educ:** Portland House School, Bury St Edmunds; Holyrood School, Bognor Regis; Oundle School. **Career:** GP, Bury St Edmunds. **Appointments:** Chairman, Epsom and Ewell Housing Association for the Elderly. Died 7 June 1987.

KIMBER, John Cowley Britton (1928) Born 17 September 1909, Pevensey Sluice, Bexhill, Sussex; son of John Kimber, Domestic Gardener, and Frances Cowley Britton; m Elizabeth. **Subject(s):** History/Geography; BA 1931; MA 1935. **Tutor(s):** E A Benians. **Educ:** The Grammar School, Hastings. **Career:** Squadron Leader, RAF; Schoolmaster, King's School, Gloucester 1931. Died 25 April 1985.

KIN, Harry Myo (1922) Born 12 November 1903, Rangoon, Burma; son of Maung Kin, Barrister-at-Law, and Than May. **Subject(s):** Law; BA 1928; MA 1929. **Tutor(s):** E A Benians. **Educ:** Diocesan Boys' High School, Rangoon, Burma.

KING, Alan Brasher (1948) Born 3 November 1926, 31 Midway Avenue, Bridlington, Yorkshire; son of Ebenezer Frederick King, Bank Clerk, and Ethel Longbottom. **Subject(s):** Music; BA 1949; MA 1958. **Tutor(s):** C W Guillebaud. **Educ:** Bridlington School. **Career:** RN 1945–1947; Assistant Organist, Emmanuel Church, Bridlington.

KING, Arthur David Newton (1948) Born 14 August 1930, 61 Tudor Gardens, Acton, Middlesex; son of Fred King, Executive Officer, and Katharine Elsie Newton. **Subject(s):** Mechanical Sciences; BA 1951; MA 1958. **Tutor(s):** R L Howland. **Educ:** Langton House, Worthing; Lyndhurst Road School, Worthing; Buxton College, Derbyshire. **Career:** Engineer, Timken Roller Bearings. Died 3 March 1988.

KING, Dennis Hoare (1919) Born 2 September 1897, 8 Springfield Road, Swindon, Wiltshire; son of Fred King, Schoolmaster, and Elizabeth Sarah Lelean; m Alice Mabel Griffin; 1 son (Roy Favell b 14 August 1925). **Subject(s):** Natural Sciences; BA 1921; MA 1925. **Tutor(s):** E A Benians. **Johnian Relatives:** father of Roy Favell King (1943). **Educ:** Swindon Secondary School. **Career:** Master, Northampton School 1921–1962. Died 19 August 1962.

KING, John Ernest (1928) Born 15 June 1909, The Rectory, Holt, Norfolk; son of Herbert Alfred King, Clerk in Holy Orders, and Clara Lucy Matilda Young; m (1) Mary Lillias Robbie, 27 December 1947, Edinburgh, (2) Helen Cochrane, 29 October 1970, Edinburgh. **Subject(s):** Moral Sciences; BA 1932; MA 1935. **Tutor(s):** E A Benians. **Johnian Relatives:** son of Herbert Alfred King (1889). **Educ:** Crosby House School, Sheringham; Gresham's School, Holt. **Career:** Assistant Master, The Edinburgh Academy 1949–1979. **Publications:** (ed Desmond Lee) *Wittgenstein's Lectures 1930–32 from the notes of John King and Desmond Lee*; *Ludwig Wittgenstein – Personal Recollections*, Blackwells. Died 5 July 1997.

KING, John Norman (1932) Born 29 November 1913, 15 Warmsworth Road, Balby, Doncaster; son of John James King, Commercial Traveller, and Agnes Mary Norman. **Tutor(s):** J M Wordie. **Educ:** Private School, Farnsley; Clifton House School, Harrogate; Sedbergh School.

KING, Raymond (1925) Born 26 March 1907, Bel-Air, Alderley Edge, Chester; son of Harold King, Manufacturer, and Mabel Louise Bennett. BA 1928. **Tutor(s):** E A Benians. **Educ:** Semer House, Biggleswade; Holmwood, Freshfield; Shrewsbury School.

KING, Dr Roy Favell (1943) Born 14 August 1925, 49 Cottarville, Weston Favell, Northampton; son of Dennis Hoare King, Schoolmaster, and Alice Mabel Griffin; m Sheila Griffiths, 1954; 1 son (John Christopher b 20 May 1955), 1 daughter (Kirsten Mary b 10 September 1958). **Subject(s):** Natural Sciences; BA 1947; MA 1950; PhD 1953; BSc (London) 1948. **Tutor(s):** C W Guillebaud. **Johnian Relatives:** son of Dennis Hoare King (1919); uncle of Geoffrey Hugh Griffiths (1977). **Educ:** Barry Road Junior School, Northampton; Northampton Town and County School. **Career:** ICI Research Fellow, Department of Geology, University of Birmingham 1952–1954; Lecturer, Reader, then Honorary Reader in Geophysics, University of Birmingham 1954. **Awards:** Major Scholarship, SJC 1942. **Publications:** Various publications on geophysics, including (with D H Griffiths) *Applied Geophysics for Geologists and Engineers*, Pergamon Press, 2nd edition 1981.

KINGDOM, William Alexander (1911) Born 26 October 1892, 59 London Road, Southwark, Surrey; son of James Kingdom, Tailor, and Charlotte Salter. **Subject(s):** Classics; BA 1914. **Tutor(s):** E E Sikes. **Educ:** St Olave's Grammar School. **Career:** Lieutenant, South Staffordshire Regiment and MGC (wounded), WWI.

KINGDON, Sir Donald (1902) Born 24 November 1883, 11 Via del Presto, Florence, Italy; son of Walter Kingdon, Artist, and Mary Billing; m Kathleen Moody, 1914; 1 son, 2 daughters. **Subject(s):** Law; BA 1905; LLB 1905. **Tutor(s):** C E Graves; J R Tanner. **Johnian Relatives:** brother of Campbell Kingdon (1897); father of Richard Donald Kingdon (1936). **Educ:** Eastbourne College. **Career:** Called to the Bar, Inner Temple 1905; Legal Assistant and Inspector of Schools, Gambia 1907; Acting Colonial Secretary, Gambia 1912; Acting Chief Justice, Uganda 1917 and 1918; Attorney-General, Gold Coast 1918; Member, Executive and Legislative Councils; Acting Colonial Secretary, Gold Coast 1919; Attorney-General, Nigeria 1921–1929; KC, Nigeria 1925; Acting Chief Secretary to the Government, Nigeria 1928 and 1929; Chief Justice, Nigeria 1929–1946; President, West African Court of Appeal 1936–1946. **Appointments:** Commissioner for Revised Edition, *Laws of the Gold Coast* 1920, *Laws of Nigeria* 1923, *Laws of Tanganyika* 1947, *Laws of Kenya* 1948, *Laws of Uganda* 1951, *Laws of British Guiana* 1953, *Laws of Gambia* 1955, *Laws of Nyasaland* 1957, *Laws of the Federation of Nigeria* 1958; Chairman, Committee appointed by East African High Commission to enquire into causes of failure of KAG and other vaccines prepared at Kabete 1949; Sole Commissioner to enquire into riots in Uganda 1949; Chairman, Commission to enquire into explosion at Mulago 1951. **Honours:** Kt 1931. Died 17 December 1961.

KINGDON, Richard Donald (1936) Born 10 July 1917, Entebbe, Uganda; son of Sir Donald Kingdon, Chief Justice of Nigeria, and Kathleen Moody; m Leslie. BA 1945. **Tutor(s):** C W Guillebaud. **Johnian Relatives:** nephew of Campbell Kingdon (1897); son of Donald Kingdon (1902). **Educ:** St George's, Broadstairs; Eastbourne College. Died 14 June 1952.

KINGSTON, John Samuel (1923) Born 3 January 1904, 16 Grandison Road, Battersea, Surrey; son of Thomas Kingston, Managing Director, Mayfair Catering Company Ltd, and Lucy Charlotte Sprigge. **Tutor(s):** E A Benians. **Educ:** St Paul's School, London; Manor House School, Clapham Common.

KINNEY, Raymond Harold (1918) American Student.

KIPPING, Stanley Arnold Brian (1948) Born 5 April 1928, 45 Fulbrook Road, Cambridge; son of Frederic Barry Kipping, Lecturer in Chemistry, University of Cambridge, and Margaret Gertrude Wilkins; m Joyce Evelyn Tudor, 10 August 1951; 1 son (John Brian b 1957), 2 daughters (Jennifer Anne b 1952 and Sally Margaret b 1960). **Subject(s):** Natural Sciences; BA 1950; MA 1955. **Tutor(s):** G C L Bertram. **Johnian Relatives:** son of Frederic Barry Kipping (1954). **Educ:** The Leys School, Cambridge. **Career:** RAF 1946–1948; Boots Pure Drug Co (later The Boots Company plc) 1951–1988 (Director 1973–1988, Director of Production 1978–1988). **Appointments:** Member, Nottingham Health Authority (Vice-Chairman 1991–1994) 1987–1994; Chairman, Nottinghamshire Family Health Services Authority and Vice-Chairman, North Nottinghamshire Health Authority 1994–1996; Council Member 1985–1997, Pro Chancellor 1994–1997, University of Nottingham; Special Organics Economics Development Committee, NEDO.

KIRBY, Frank (1937) Born 25 October 1919, Holmside, Stoneyhurst Road, Gosforth; son of Frank Kirby, Solicitor, and Lizzie Pearse. **Subject(s):** Economics. **Tutor(s):** C W Guillebaud. **Johnian Relatives:** twin brother of Harold Kirby (1937). **Educ:** Ascham House, Gosforth; Bootham School, York. **Career:** Farm work as conscientious objector, WWII; Bookseller.

KIRBY, Frederick Neville (1941) Born 9 August 1923, Redesdale House, Barmoor, Morpeth, Northumberland; son of Frederick Kirby, Highway Surveyor, and Marion Welsh Fortune; m Valerie Ann Challen, 5 September 1959, The Parish Church, Blisworth, Northamptonshire; 2 daughters (Alison Jane b 3 March 1965 and Frances Ann b 20 April 1970). **Subject(s):** Mechanical Sciences; BA 1944; MA 1948; CEng; FICE; FIMechE. **Tutor(s):** S J Bailey. **Johnian Relatives:** second cousin of William John Fortune Rawling (1958). **Educ:** King Edward VI Grammar School, Morpeth. **Career:** Chartered Engineer: CA Parsons & Co Ltd 1943–1952; Brush Electrical Engineering Co Ltd 1953–1957, F Perkins Ltd 1957–1962; Vickers Ltd, Barrow-in-Furness 1962–1966; The English Electric Co Ltd (subsequently The General Electric Co Ltd), Preston and Manchester 1967–1988. **Appointments:** Clayton Fellowship, Institution of Mechanical Engineers 1948; Goodwin Fellowship, SJC 1951. **Awards:** Scholarship, SJC 1943; College Prize, SJC 1943; Miller Prize, Institution of Civil Engineers 1946; Hughes Prize, SJC 1949; Ricardo Prize in Thermodynamics, University of Cambridge 1949.

KIRBY, Harold (1937) Born 25 October 1919, Holmside, Stoneyhurst Road, Gosforth; son of Frank Kirby, Solicitor, and Lizzie Pearse; m Evelyn Winifred Dodds, 29 July 1954; 1 son (Richard b 10 May 1955). **Subject(s):** Economics/Law; BA 1940; MA 1944. **Tutor(s):** C W Guillebaud. **Johnian Relatives:** twin brother of Frank Kirby (1937). **Educ:** Ascham House, Gosforth; Bootham School, York. **Career:** RN, WWII; Solicitor. **Publications:** Various.

KIRK, John Haydn (1909) Born 22 March 1890, 140 Leadenhall Street, London; son of John George Kirk, Architect and Surveyor, and Annie Jones; m Betty. BA 1912. **Tutor(s):** J R Tanner. **Educ:** Weymouth College. **Career:** Served, WWI; Assistant District Officer, Nigeria 1916. Died 4 August 1948.

KIRK, Dr Peter John Daniels (1948) Born 13 March 1930, 36 Burgate, Barton-on-Humber, Lincolnshire; son of Thomas Hobson Kirk, Medical Practitioner, and Ethel Winifred Daniels; m Sheila Elliott, March 1956; 3 children. **Subject(s):** Natural Sciences; BA 1951; BChir 1954; MB 1955. **Tutor(s):** G C L Bertram. **Educ:** New Hall Private School; Barton-on-Humber Grammar School; Bootham School; Middlesex Hospital. **Career:** Hartlepool General Hospital; Middlesbrough General Hospital; GP, Barton-on-Humber; GP, Burra, South Australia 1964; GP, Blackwood Clinic, Adelaide, South Australia, until 1992.

KIRKNESS, James Michael Percy (1928) Born 11 October 1910, 110 London Road, North End, Portsmouth; son of William Ronald Kirkness, Medical Practitioner, and Edith Mary Ashwell; m (1) Elizabeth

Knocker (d 1 December 1962), (2) Susannah Youell, 18 October 1963; (1) 2 sons (James and Bill), 2 daughters (Janet and Mary). **Subject(s):** Natural Sciences; BA 1932; MA 1954. **Tutor(s):** C W Guillebaud. **Johnian Relatives:** nephew of Lewis Hawker Kirkness (1901). **Educ:** Malfield Grange, Paddock Wood; Epsom College. **Career:** Manager, Overseas and Veterinary Services, Association of British Pharmaceutical Industry 1950–1975; Commander, RNR 1966. **Honours:** MBE; TD. Died 29 October 1990.

KIRKNESS, Lieutenant Colonel Lewis Hawker (1901) Born 14 November 1881, Kenwyn, 3 Spencer Hill, Wimbledon, Surrey; son of William Kirkness, Gentleman, and Emily Simons Soltau; m Idonea Frances Armstrong, 10 February 1917, St Mary's, Paddington. **Subject(s):** History; BA 1904; MA 1908; MInstT. **Tutor(s):** E E Sikes. **Johnian Relatives:** uncle of James Michael Percy Kirkness (1928). **Educ:** King's College School. **Career:** Assistant Traffic Superintendent, Madras Railways, 1906; District Traffic Superintendent 1909; Secretary to Agent, Madras and Southern Mahratta Railway 1911; Indian Volunteer Force; Sergeant Motor Cyclist; Lieutenant Colonel, Special List, attached to RE, then Assistant Director of Railways, Salonika Force (Mentioned in Despatches four times) 1914–1918; Deputy Transportation Superintendent, Madras and Southern Mahratta Railway 1924; Principal, Railway Staff College, Dehra Dun 1929; Secretary, Railway Department, Indian Government 1933–1936; Captain, 2nd Battalion, Madras and Southern Mahratta Railway Rifles, Auxiliary Force, India; Deputy Assistant Director of Transportation, Movement Control, War Office 1939–1945. **Appointments:** Member, Permanent Commission, International Railway Congress; Joint Secretary, Wedgwood Committee on Indian Railway Finance 1936–1937. **Honours:** 1914–1915 Star; British War and Victory Medals; Defence and War Medals; Order of the White Eagle, Fifth Class, with swords (Serbia) 1917; DSO 1918; OBE (Military) 1919; Medal for Military Merit, Third Class (Greece) 1919; Order of the White Eagle, Fourth Class (Serbia) 1920; Indian Volunteer Force Decoration (George V); Jubilee Medal 1935; CIE 1936; Coronation Medal 1937; Order of the White Eagle, Fourth Class (Czechoslovakia). **Publications:** *Principles of Absolute Block System*, 1929; Report on Road and Rail Competition in India. Died 24 January 1950.

KIRKWOOD, Thomas Miller (1927) Born 30 December 1906, Chunking, Szechwan, China; son of Thomas Kirkwood, Medical Practitioner, and Essie Maud Miller. **Subject(s):** Mathematics; BA 1930; MA 1944. **Tutor(s):** J M Wordie. **Educ:** Wesley College, Dublin; Emanuel School, Wandsworth Common, London; Institute of Actuaries, Staple Inn, London. **Career:** Actuarial Assistant to WP Phelps 1925–1927; Assistant Master, Rugby School 1930; Secretary to the Director of Public Works, Colonial Service, Malaya; Secretary to the Communications Board, Rivers Advisory Board, Fraser's Hill Development Committee, Colonial Service, Malaya; Assistant Secretary in Colonial Secretariat, Singapore 1930–1935; Director, The College, South Leigh, Oxon 1935–1939; Lieutenant Colonel, Royal Irish Dragoon Guards, WWII. Died 21 July 1978.

KIRKWOOD, Tristram Guy Hammett (1934) Born 10 November 1914, Boldrewood, Burghfield Common, Reading; son of Richard Hammett Kirkwood, Lieutenant Colonel, Devon Regiment, and Agnes Elizabeth Mary Alleyne; m Elizabeth; 1 son (Andrew), 2 daughters (Juliet and Jennifer). **Subject(s):** Mechanical Sciences; BA 1936. **Tutor(s):** J S Boys Smith. **Educ:** Swanbourne House School, Winslow; Wellington College, Berkshire; RMA, Woolwich. **Career:** Major, RE 1939–1944. Died November 1944 (killed in action in Western Europe).

KIRLOSKAR, Vinayak Ganesh (1906) Born 20 October 1885, Bombay, India; son of Ganesh Ramchandra Kirloskar, High Court Pleader, and Saraswatibai Ganesh Bhagurat. **Subject(s):** Mathematics; BA 1909. **Tutor(s):** L H K Bushe-Fox. **Educ:** University of Bombay; Jamkhandi High School; Sholapur High School; Elphinstone College, Bombay; Deccan College, Poona.

KITCHIN, Finlay Tower (1925) Born 21 December 1906, Ulverstone, Egmont Road, Sutton, Surrey; son of Finlay Lorimer Kitchin, Palaeontologist to HM Geological Survey, and Anna Louise Chamberlain. **Subject(s):** Law; BA 1928; MA 1931; LLB 1929; LLM 1985. **Tutor(s):** E E Sikes. **Johnian Relatives:** son of Finlay Lorimer Kitchin (1890). **Educ:** Clan Ridarde House School, Sutton; Homefield School, Sutton; Felsted School. **Career:** Solicitor, Supreme Court of England and Wales. Died 1986.

KITTEL, Professor Jerome Charles (1936) Born 18 July 1916, 1223 Bushwick Avenue, Brooklyn, New York; son of George Paul Kittel, Engineer, and Helen Lemler; m Muriel Agnes Lister, 23 June 1938; 2 sons (Peter and Timothy), 1 daughter (Ruth). **Subject(s):** Natural Sciences; BA 1938; MA 1993; PhD (Wisconsin) 1941. **Tutor(s):** J M Wordie. **Educ:** Englewood High School, Englewood, USA; Horace Mann School for Boys, Riverdale, New York; University of Wisconsin; MIT. **Career:** Consultant, E I Du Pont & Co; Consultant, RCA; Consultant, Westinghouse Corporation; Consultant, Hughes Aircraft Company; Consultant, Chevron Corporation; Research Physicist, Bureau of Ordnance 1940–1942; Head, Submarine Operations Research Group, US Navy, Washington 1943–1945; Physics Department, MIT 1945–1947; Bell Telephone Laboratories, Murray Hill, New Jersey 1947–1951; Professor, Department of Physics, University of California, Berkeley 1951–1978 (Emeritus 1978). **Appointments:** Guggenheim Fellow 1947, 1957, 1964; Member, US National Academy of Science 1957; Member, American Academy of Arts and Sciences 1957; Miller Fellow, University of California, 1959, 1960; Fellow, American Physics Society; Member, American Association of Physics Teachers; Member, American Institute of Physics (Board of Governors 1954–1958). **Awards:** Oliver Buckley Prize for Solid State Physics 1957; Oersted Medal 1972; Distinguished Teachers Award, University of California, Berkeley 1972; Oersted Medal, American Association of Physics Teachers 1978. **Publications:** *Introduction to Solid State Physics*, 7th edition, 1996; (with H Kroemer) *Thermal Physics*, 2nd edition, 1980; *Quantum Theory of Solids*, 1987.

KITTERMASTER, Dr Arthur Richard (1947) Born 18 January 1928, Prior's House, 51 Lillington Road, Leamington, Warwickshire; son of Harold Baxter Kittermaster, Colonial Service, and Winifred Elsie Rotherham; m Liz. **Subject(s):** Natural Sciences; BA 1950; MA 1973; MB 1953; BChir 1953; FRCPath 1976. **Tutor(s):** G C L Bertram. **Educ:** Ruzawi School, Southern Rhodesia; Lambrook School, Bracknell; Ridley College, St Catherine's, Canada; Shrewsbury School. **Career:** Consultant Pathologist, Kent & Sussex Hospital, Tunbridge Wells; Lecturer in Clinical Pathology, St Thomas' Hospital, London. Died 10 July 1998.

KITTO, Professor Humphrey Davy Findley (1916) Born 2 June 1897, Chaxhill, Westbury on Severn, Gloucestershire; son of Humphrey Davy Kitto, Schoolmaster, and Caroline Findley; m Ann Kraft, 1928; 1 son (John), 1 daughter (Jane). **Subject(s):** Classics; BA 1919; FBA 1955; FRSL 1957. **Tutor(s):** E E Sikes. **Johnian Relatives:** brother-in-law of William Michael Herbert Greaves (1916) and of Leslie John Comrie (1919); uncle of Julian Kitto Comrie (1956) and of George Richard Herbert Greaves (1961). **Educ:** Walmore Hill Council School; Crypt Grammar School. **Career:** Assistant to Professor of Greek, then Lecturer, Glasgow University 1921–1944; Professor of Greek, Bristol University 1944–1962; Taught at University of California, and at Brandeis University 1960–1964. **Appointments:** Visiting Scholar, Cornell, Brandeis, and University of California, Santa Barbara. **Awards:** Scholarship, SJC 1915; Wright's Prize, SJC; Hawksley Burbury Prize, SJC. **Publications:** *In the Mountains of Greece*, 1933; *Greek Tragedy*, 1939; *The Greeks*, 1951; *Form and Meaning in Drama*, 1956; *Poiesis*, 1966. Died 21 January 1982.

KITTO, John Lemon (1901) Born 24 October 1882, Porthleven, Sithney, Cornwall; son of James John Kitto, Ship Builder, and Elizabeth Jacka; m Violet. **Subject(s):** Natural Sciences; BA 1904; MA 1967. **Tutor(s):** D MacAlister. **Educ:** Truro College. **Career:** Lecturer, St Mark's College,

Chelsea 1907–1908; Assistant Librarian, House of Commons; Assistant Master, Beverley Grammar School 1910–1913; Leighton Park School 1932. Died 13 August 1971.

KNAPE SMITH, Thomas (1923) See SMITH.

KNEEL, Jack Alexander Charles (1945) Born 5 May 1927, 26 Southernhay West, Exeter; son of William Alexander Kneel, Managing Director, and Geraldine Kate Clapp. BA 1948; MA 1952. **Tutor(s):** S J Bailey. **Educ:** Norwood School, Exeter; Blundell's School, Tiverton.

KNIGHT, Astley Chadborn (1930) Born 18 November 1911, Pinetown, Durban, Natal, South Africa; son of Wilfred Edwyn Knight, Medical Practitioner, and Evelyn Louisa Chadborn. **Tutor(s):** M P Charlesworth. **Educ:** Highbury School, Natal.

KNIGHT, Bartholomew Francis (1935) Born 14 September 1917, Dalton House, Kendal, Westmorland; son of Francis Howard Knight, Schoolmaster, and Dorothy Cheney Ashcroft; m Audrey Ruscombe, 12 August 1949, Church of St Peter and St Paul, Ewhurst, Surrey; 1 son (Sebastian), 3 daughters (Celia, Erica and Olivia). BA 1938; MA 1951; BA (London) 1952; PGCE (London) 1955; Diploma in Applied Linguistics (Edinburgh) 1965. **Tutor(s):** J M Wordie. **Educ:** Stramongate School, Kendal; Whitgift Grammar School, Croydon; Bootham School, York. **Career:** Education Officer, Tanganyika-Tanzania 1952–1963; English Language Officer, British Council 1964–1967; Lecturer, School of Education, University of Leicester 1968; Principal, Brummana High School, Lebanon 1968–1975; Lecturer in English, British Council, Jeddah, Saudi Arabia 1976–1978. **Appointments:** Visiting Professor, University of Alexandria 1978–1979. **Honours:** OBE 1973. **Publications:** *York Notes on 'Jane Eyre'*, Longman York Press.

KNIGHT, Charles (1902) Born 14 November 1881, Astley Bridge, Lancashire; son of Robert Knight, Commercial Traveller, and Alice Ruth Holden. **Subject(s):** Moral Sciences; BA 1905; MA 1908. **Tutor(s):** D MacAlister. **Educ:** St Paul's National School; Bolton Church of England Educational Institution; Bolton Pupil Teacher's Centre. **Career:** Assistant Master, King Edward VI Grammar School, Guildford 1908–1933.

KNIGHT, Revd Dr David Arthur (1939) Born 12 March 1921, Laceby Rectory, Grimsby; son of Henry Wynyard Knight, Rector of Laceby and Canon of Lincoln, and Kate Elizabeth Bishopp; m Mary; 1 son (Robert), 1 daughter (Katharine). **Subject(s):** Moral Sciences. BA 1942; MA 1946; MSc (Leeds); PhD (Exeter) 1964. **Tutor(s):** R L Howland. **Johnian Relatives:** son of Henry Wynyard Knight (1884). **Educ:** Pocklington School; Oak Hill Theological College; Wells Theological College. **Career:** Armed Forces, Europe 1942; Royal Corps of Signals, 2nd British Army, Normandy Landing 11 June 1944, injured, Creully, 2 July 1944; Army Education Branch 1945; Discharged 1946; Engineer, BBC, Bristol 1946; Rehabilitation Officer, Ministry of Labour, Leeds 1951–1952; Consultant Clinical Psychologist at four Yorkshire mental hospitals and associated outpatient clinics 1951–1957; Research Psychologist, McGill University 1957–1961; PhD Program, University of Exeter 1961–1964; Chief Psychologist/Director, Mental Health Center, Wilmington, North Carolina 1964–1968; Psychologist, Board of Education, Annapolis 1968–1986; State Licensed Private Clinical Psychologist 1974; Director, Centre for Treatment of Abused Women and Pathological Personality 1979–2002; Part time Lecturer in Psychology, County Junior College 1977–1978; Founding Member, St Charles The Martyr Anglican Church 1981; Corporate Secretary/Executive Secretary, Traditional Anglican Church, Eastern United States Province 1985–2002; Director, Drug and Alcohol Program, Woodlawn Church, Baltimore 1993; Ordained Deacon 2001; Ordained Priest 2002. **Appointments:** Invited Psychologist Speaker, Third World Congress of Psychiatry, Montreal 1961, 'Placebo Effects and New Tranquilising Drugs'. **Awards:** Four War medals including Defence Medal and France and Germany Star; King

George VI medal for disabled ex-servicemen. **Publications:** *New England Journal of Medicine*, 1962; various chapters, papers and journals. Died 25 August 2003.

KNIGHT, Hugh Frederick Parker (1903) Born 7 January 1882, 11 Wellington Square, Cheltenham, Gloucester; son of Thomas William Knight, Private Tutor, and Kate Parker. **Tutor(s):** D MacAlister. **Educ:** Dean Close Memorial School, Cheltenham.

KNIGHT, Leslie Cartwright (1919) Born 8 April 1898, Church Street, Wellingborough, Northamptonshire; son of Luke Cartwright Knight, Estate Agent, and Julia Ellen Colledge; m Violet Mary Gibbard; 1 son (John), 1 daughter (Jean). BA 1921; MA 1928. **Tutor(s):** E A Benians. **Educ:** Wellingborough School. **Career:** Royal Artillery Officer Cadet School 1917; 6(A) Reserve Brigade, RFA, Glasgow 1917; Lieutenant, 218th Brigade, RFA 1917–1919; Brewer; Manager, Taylor Walker and Co Ltd. Died 2 June 1964.

KNIGHT, Dr Robert Lanier (1927) Born 8 March 1907, 18 Fishpond Road, Hitchin, Hertfordshire; son of Henry Knight, Civil Servant, and Nelly Pierce. Diploma of Agriculture (Wye). **Tutor(s):** C W Guillebaud. **Educ:** Belmont College; Woking County School; South Eastern Agricultural College, Wye; Imperial College of Tropical Agriculture, Trinidad. **Career:** Empire Growing Corporation. Sudan 1929–1954; Chief Geneticist, Sudan Government 1954; Head of Fruit Breeding Section, East Malling Research Station 1954. **Appointments:** Chairman, Agricultural Publications Committee, Sudan Ministry of Agriculture. **Awards:** Jones-Bateman Cup, Royal Horticultural Society 1969. **Honours:** OBE 1952. Died 15 February 1972.

KNOPP, The Revd Alexander Edward Robert (1929) Born 31 December 1909, 17 Ripley Road, Seven Kings, Ilford; son of James Alexander Knopp, Civil Servant, Post Office, and Ethel Loughborough; m Kathleen Dennison, 1938; 2 sons (John and Simon), 4 daughters (Judith, Rachel, Shirley and Rosemary). **Subject(s):** History/Theology; BA 1933; MA 1937. **Tutor(s):** E A Benians. **Johnian Relatives:** father of John Alexander Dennison Knopp (1959). **Educ:** Albert Road School, Romford; Brentwood School; Ridley Hall, Cambridge. **Career:** Ordained Deacon 1934; Curate, St Mary's, Loughton 1934–1938; Ordained Priest (Chelmsford) 1935; Curate, St Mary's, Prittlewell 1938–1940; Rector, Nevendon 1940; Curate, North Benfleet 1940–1941; Rector, North Benfleet with Nevendon 1941–1948; Vicar, St John's, Walthamstow 1948–1950; Vicar, Pampisford 1950–1959; Vicar, Babraham and Pampisford, Cambridgeshire (in plurality) 1950–1959; Rector, Quendon with Rickling, Essex 1959–1968; Rector, Great Yeldham 1968–1973; Rector, Great with Little Snoring, Norfolk 1973–1976; Permitted to Office, Diocese of Ely 1977.

KNOWLES, Dr Alan Keith (1944) Born 9 April 1927, Kelowna Nursing Home, Llannerch Road, Llandrillo yn Rhos, Colwyn Bay, Wales; son of Joseph Albert Knowles, Financial Secretary, Methodist Education Committee, and Ada Chew. **Subject(s):** Natural Sciences; BA 1947; MA 1951; BChir 1950; MB 1950; MRCS England 1951; LRCP, London; DObstRCOG 1956. **Tutor(s):** S J Bailey. **Johnian Relatives:** son of Joseph Albert Knowles (1913); uncle of Peter Marshall Shepherd (1966). **Educ:** Rydal School, Colwyn Bay. **Career:** Squadron Leader, Medical Branch, RAF; Medical Practitioner. **Appointments:** Medical Officer to the UEA 1965–1980; Member, Pathfinder Association; Fellow, Society of Antiquaries of London 1990. **Honours:** MBE 1996.

KNOWLES, John Clapham (1918) Born 1 November 1900, Ashlea, Bentham, Yorkshire; son of Thomas Knowles, Grocer, and Margaret Ellen Clapham; m Marjorie Elizabeth Hurst, 1929. BA (Manchester) 1922; ACA 1927; FCA 1933. **Tutor(s):** E E Sikes. **Educ:** Bentham Grammar School; Ackworth School, Pontefract; Bootham School, York; Manchester University. **Career:** Partner in firm of Bell, Watts, McCombie and Knowles, Chartered Accountants; Secretary, Air Chute of Great Britain Limited, Parachute Makers. Died 4 August 1960.

KNOWLES, Joseph Albert (1913) Born 16 November 1891, 19 Iredale Street, Cheetham, Lancashire; son of Joseph Knowles, Manager, and Ellen Smith; m Ada Chew; 1 son (Alan Keith b 9 April 1927), 1 daughter (Barbara b 27 October 1923). BA 1919; MA 1937. **Tutor(s):** R P Gregory. **Johnian Relatives:** father of Alan Keith Knowles (1944). **Educ:** Municipal Secondary School, Salford; École Normale, La Drôme; St Paul's College, Cheltenham. **Career:** Captain, Cheshire Regiment, fought at Gallipoli and on the Somme (wounded twice), WWI; Schoolmaster, Bishop's Stortford College 1919–1920; Schoolmaster, Rydal School 1920. **Appointments:** Financial Secretary, Methodist Education Committee. **Honours:** MC; OBE. Died 31 May 1963.

KNOX, Professor Bernard McGregor Walker (1933) Born 24 November 1914, 94 Hollings Road, Manningham, Bradford; son of Bernard Knox, Professional Pianist, and Rowena Walker, Nurse; m Betty Baur, 12 April 1939; 1 son (Bernard MacGregor). **Subject(s):** Classics; BA 1936; PhD (Yale) 1948; LHD 1983; LittD (Princeton); LHD (George Washington) 1977. **Tutor(s):** R L Howland. **Educ:** Hackford Road Elementary School, London; Battersea Grammar School, London. **Career:** French Battalion, XIth International Brigade, Madrid, November–December 1936; US Army, France and Italy 1944–1945; Assistant and Full Professor, Yale 1949–1960; Hillhouse Professor of Greek 1959; Director, Center for Hellenic Studies, Harvard, Washington DC 1960–1985. **Appointments:** Gugenheim Fellow; Sather Lecturer; Nellie Wallace Lecturer (Oxford). **Awards:** Scholarship, SJC; Decorated by the American, British, and French Governments for war service; Sixteenth Cosmos Club award by the Cosmos Club, Washington DC, USA; George Jean Nathan Prize for Dramatic Criticism. **Publications:** *Oedipus at Thebes*; *Oedipus the King*; *The Heroic Temper*; *Word and Action*; *Essays Ancient and Modern*; *The Oldest Dead White European Males*; *Backing into the Future*; (Editor) *The Norton Book of Classical Literature*; (Assistant Editor and Contributor) *The Cambridge History of Classical Literature*, Vol I.

KNOX, Sir Robert Uchtred Eyre (1908) (Readmitted 1919) Born 14 January 1889, Norton Court, Norton Fitzwarren, Taunton; son of Alexander Knox, Civil Servant, and Ruth Cooper; m Dorothy Margaret Hill, 19 April 1924. **Subject(s):** Natural Sciences; BA 1911. **Tutor(s):** J R Tanner; E E Sikes. **Educ:** Dulwich College. **Career:** Ceremonial Officer, HM Treasury; Captain, Suffolk Regiment, then War Office, WWI; Private Secretary to Sir Warren Fisher 1928; Secretary, Commissions and Committees concerned with the 1937 and 1953 Coronations. **Honours:** DSO 1916; CVO 1933; KCVO 1937; KCB 1953. Died 15 October 1965.

KOCH, Otto Erich Alfred (1937) Born 31 August 1919, Frankfurt am Main, Germany; son of Otto Koch, Jeweller, and Ida Kahn. **Subject(s):** Economics; BA 1940. **Tutor(s):** J S Boys Smith. **Educ:** Varrentrap Schule, Frankfurt; Goethe Gymnasium, Frankfurt; Cranbrook School. **Career:** Broadcaster, International Service 1944–1953, Public Affairs Department 1953–1967, Area Head, Arts and Science 1967–1971, Regional Director, Montreal 1971–1977, Canadian Broadcasting Corporation. **Publications:** *The French Kiss*, 1969; *The Leisure Riots*, 1973; *The Last Thing You Want to Know*, 1976; *Good Night, Little Spy*, 1979; *Kassandrus*, 1988; *Liebe und Mord auf Xananta*, 1992; *Icon in Love*, 1998; *Inside Seven Days – The Show That Shook the Nation*, 1986; *Deemed Suspect*, 1980; *Hilmar and Odette*, 1995; *The Brothers Hambourg*, 1997; *The Man Who Knew Charlie Chaplin*, 2000; *The Earrings*, 2002.

KOETTLITZ, Maurice (1921) Born 20 June 1903, 20 London Road, Dover, Kent; son of Maurice Koettlitz, Medical Practitioner, and Mabel Hannah Hodgson. BA 1924; MA 1929; BChir 1942; MB 1942. **Tutor(s):** B F Armitage. **Educ:** Dover College.

KOH, Kheng Seng (1902) Born 15 September 1885, Penang, Straits Settlements; son of Cheng Hooi Koh, Gentleman, and Say Tim Tan. **Subject(s):** Natural Sciences; BA 1905. **Tutor(s):** D MacAlister. **Educ:** Penang Free School.

KOINANGE, Peter Mbiyu (1936) Born Kiambaa, Kiamlu, Kenya, East Africa; son of Koinange wa Mbiyu, Senior Chief of Kiambu District, and Wambui wa Gikango; m Louise; 1 son (John). **Tutor(s):** C W Guillebaud. **Educ:** Alliance High School, Kikuyu, Kenya; Hampton Institute, Virginia, USA; Ohio Wesleyan College, Delaware; Teachers College, Columbia, USA. **Career:** Founder and Principal, Kenya Teachers' College, Githunguri 1939–1948; London Co-operative Society (machine minder and shop steward at processing dairy) 1951–1959; Director, Bureau of African Affairs, Ghana 1959–1960; Secretary General, Pan African Freedom Movement for East, Central and South Africa, Dar-es-Salaam 1961–1962; Minister for Pan African Affairs 1963–1964; MP, Kiambu 1963–1979; Minister of Education 1964–1966; Minister of State, Office of the President 1966–1978; Minister for Water Development 1978–1979. **Appointments:** Founder, Kenya African Union 1944.

KOONTZ, Patrick Duffy (1918) American Student.

KOUSMICHOFF, Constantine (1923) Born 17 April 1905, Petrograd, Russia; son of Viacheslav Kousmichoff, Tea Merchant, and Vera Bourakovitch. **Tutor(s):** J M Wordie. **Educ:** École Secondaire Russe, Paris.

KRAEMER, Adolf Ernst (1901) Born 5 May 1883, Hallescheslefer 21, Berlin, Germany; son of Justus Wilhelm Kraemer, Professor of Philosophy, and Friedericke Anna Noeldechen. **Tutor(s):** D MacAlister. **Educ:** Friedrich Wilhelm's Gymnasium, Berlin.

KRAGH, Alan Mackenzie (1943) Born 13 February 1925, Beclands, Tooting Bec Gardens, Streatham; son of Frederick Arthur Mackenzie Kragh, Electrical Engineer, and Lille Lawton. **Tutor(s):** C W Guillebaud. **Educ:** Hitherfield School; Dulwich College.

KRAUS, Martin (1905) Born 25 January 1884, Bacau, Romania; son of Charles Kraus, Warehouse Manager, and Sophia Kupferstein. **Subject(s):** Classics; BA 1908; BA 1905, MA (Manchester) 1906. **Tutor(s):** E E Sikes. **Educ:** Manchester Grammar School; Owens College, Manchester. **Career:** Headmaster, Manchester Jews' School 1910; Latin Master, Municipal Secondary School, Bolton 1932. **Awards:** Victoria Scholarship, 1906.

KRAUSE, Eric Sutherland (1939) Born 28 December 1919, 18 Banbury Terrace, South Shields; son of William Tate Martin Krause, Engineer and Director, and Evelyn Bown. **Subject(s):** Law and Economics; BA 1946. **Tutor(s):** J S Boys Smith. **Educ:** Westoe High School; South Shields High School; Royal Grammar School, Newcastle upon Tyne. **Career:** School of Biology, University of Leeds; Acting Director, International Labour Office (London Branch). **Awards:** Scholarship, SJC; Emergency Reserve Decoration.

KRONHEIMER, Dr Erwin Heinz (1946) Born 11 February 1928, Mannheim, Germany; son of Wilhelm Kronheimer, Lawyer, and Else Mezger; m Janet Harris, 30 June 1960, Hampstead; 1 son (Peter Benedict b 1963), 1 daughter (Claudia Ann b 1961). **Subject(s):** Mathematics/ Natural Sciences; BA 1949; MA 1953; PhD (Southampton) 1956. **Tutor(s):** J M Wordie. **Educ:** City of Oxford High School. **Career:** Lecturer in Mathematics, then Senior Lecturer in Mathematics, Birkbeck College, University of London 1953–1993. **Awards:** Baylis Scholarship, SJC 1945. **Publications:** Papers in various mathematical journals.

KUESTER, Hanns Ulrich Oskar (CHESTER) (1929) Born 6 April 1908, Breslau, Germany; son of Hans Adolph Kuester, Merchant, and Else Lessing, Farm Manager; m Elizabeth Dale Spafford, 1941; 1 son (Frank Theodor b 1947), 1 daughter (Moira Jane b 1949). **Subject(s):** Modern and Medieval Languages; BA 1932; MA 1936. **Tutor(s):** M P Charlesworth. **Johnian Relatives:** brother-in-law of Douglas Harold Spafford (1942). **Educ:** Gymnasium, Breslau; University of Breslau;

University of Kiel; TCD; University of Munich. **Career:** Head of Modern Languages, Ottershaw College 1932–1937; Head of Modern Languages, St Marylebone Grammar School 1937–1938; Head of Modern Languages, Aldenham School 1938–1940; Commander, Animal Transport Column, India; Interpreter in Urdu, then Japanese; Senior Intelligence Officer, Japanese POW Camp; Head of Modern Languages, Whitgift School 1947–1973; Chief Examiner in German, London University Schools Examination Department 1953–1973; Assistant Master in English, Nicolas Cusanus Gymnasium, Bergisch-Gladbach 1973–1975; Language Tutor, Cambridge Tutors VI Form College, Croydon 1979–1990 and 1995–1996. **Appointments:** Chairman, Anglo-German Association. **Awards:** Exhibition, SJC 1931. Died 8 December 2002.

KUIPERS, Professor John Dennis (1935) Born 9 July 1918, The White House, Manchester Road, Timperley, Cheshire; son of Joannes Kuipers, Manufacturer, and Marion Sewell; m Johanna Adriana de Roon; 3 sons (Francis b 1941, Adrian 1944 and Richard b 1946). **Subject(s):** Economics; BA 1938; MA 1942; MSc (London); DSc; LLD (Strathclyde); Hon LLD (Strathclyde) 1974. **Tutor(s):** C W Guillebaud. **Educ:** Miss Lowe's Preparatory School, Sale; Mostyn House School, Parkgate; City of London College, Moorfields, London; Radley College. **Career:** Assistant Director, Joint Managing Director, Chairman and Managing Director, Royal "de Betuwe" Ltd of Tiel, Holland; British Pro-consul, Amsterdam 1939–1940; Civilian Assistant, General Staff War Office 1940–1941 (Rank of Major 1941); Captain, General Staff, Royal Netherlands Army 1944–1945; Left full-time business to concentrate on international affairs 1965; President, Economic and Social Committee of the European Communities 1970; Visiting Professor, Strathclyde Business School 1973. **Appointments:** Committee Member 1960–1974, Member, Executive Committee and Vice-President 1970–1974, President, Foreign Affairs Council 1970–1974, Netherlands Federation of Industry; Member, Economic and Social Committee of the European Communities 1962–1974 (Member, Executive Committee 1964–1972, President, 1970–1972); Member, Presidential Council, Union of Industrial Federations of the EEC; Member, Administrative Committee, Business and Industry Advisory Committee to OECD. **Honours:** Knight in The Order of the Netherlands Lion; Officer of the Order of Oranje Nassau (Netherlands); Commander in the Order of Leopold II (Belgium); Commander in the Order of Merit (Italy). Died 21 September 1999.

KYLE, Dr David (1927) Born 9 August 1908, 11 Barns Street, Ayr, Scotland; son of David Kyle, Medical Practitioner, and Doreen May Welsh; 2 sons. **Subject(s):** Natural Sciences; BA 1930; MA 1935; FRCGP 1969. **Tutor(s):** M P Charlesworth. **Educ:** Newcastle Preparatory School; Shrewsbury School. **Career:** Surgeon, Breconshire War Memorial Hospital; Various house appointments in opthalmology, surgery and medicine, St Mary's Hospital 1935; GP, Brecon 1935. **Appointments:** Foundation Member, College of General Practitioners. **Awards:** Scholarship, SJC. **Honours:** OBE 1972. **Publications:** Chapters on abdominal swellings and surgery, *Encyclopaedia of General Practice*; *Contribution of a general-practitioner hospital*; *Personal Views*. Died 9 December 1977.

L

LACEY, Egerton Jeffery (1943) Born 2 November 1926, 3 Victoria Road, Upper Norwood, London; son of Frank Herbert Lacey, Lieutenant Colonel, and Barbara Frances Mary Allen. **Subject(s):** Law; BA 1948. **Tutor(s):** C W Guillebaud. **Educ:** Roxbury Preparatory School, Surbiton; Bedford School; University of Toronto. **Career:** Graphic Designer. Died 2 February 1996.

LACEY, Horace Marsden (1919) Born 20 June 1899, 4 Coulson Street, Chelsea, London; son of Henry Baker Lacey, Lecturer in Natural Science, and Gertrude Chapman; m Ursula E Eva, 1 June 1925, Essex Church, London. **Subject(s):** Natural Sciences/Anthropology; BA 1922; MA 1927.

Tutor(s): E A Benians. **Educ:** Latymer Upper School, Hammersmith; South Western Polytechnic, Chelsea. **Career:** Inns of Court Officers Training Corps 1918; Private, No 2 Officer Cadet Battalion, Cambridge 1918–1919; Private, London Scottish Regiment 1919; Camerons and 2nd and 3rd Gordon Highlanders 1919; Schoolmaster, Richmond School, Yorkshire 1922–1923; Schoolmaster, Wyggeston School, Leicester 1923–1960. **Appointments:** President, Leicester Model Railway Group. **Awards:** Sizarship, SJC 1917. Died 27 December 1977.

LACEY, Thomas Lewis Guthrie (1943) Born 17 November 1926, St Clare, Burkes Road, Beaconsfield, Buckinghamshire; son of Charles Frederick Lacey, Railway Official, and Jessie Brown Guthrie. **Tutor(s):** S J Bailey. **Educ:** Strathallan School.

LACK, Dr Christofer Cheyne (1931) Born 18 June 1913, 16 Devonshire Place, Marylebone; son of Harry Lambert Lack, Consulting Surgeon, and Kathleen Frances Rind; BA 1934; MA 1948; MRCS 1938; MRCP; FRCPsych; LRCP 1938. **Tutor(s):** M P Charlesworth. **Educ:** Miss Dale's, Hampstead; Arnold House School; Gresham's School, Holt. **Career:** Supernumerary First Assistant, Department of Neurology and Psychiatry, London Hospital; Clinical Assistant, Department of Psychiatry, King Edward VII Hospital, Windsor; Major, RAMC; Psychiatrist, King Edward Memorial Hospital, Ealing 1950. **Appointments:** Honorary Consulting Child Psychiatrist, London Hospital. **Publications:** 'Management of Convalescent Neurotics', *Journal of the Royal Army Medical Corps*, 1946. Died 23 June 1996.

LACSON, Domingo W (1911) Born 15 May 1889, Molo, Iloilo, Phillipines; son of Domingo Lacson, Proprietario. **Tutor(s):** L H K Bushe-Fox. **Educ:** Ateneo de Manila; Universidad Real de Santa Tomas, Manila.

LAIDLAW, Charles Glass Playfair (1907) Born 13 December 1887, Matlock House, 126 Green Lanes, Stoke Newington, London; son of Robert Laidlaw, Governent Doctor and JP, Seychelles, and Elizabeth Playfair. **Subject(s):** Natural Sciences; BA 1910; MA 1914. **Tutor(s):** L H K Bushe-Fox. **Johnian Relatives:** brother of George Muir Laidlaw (1897) and of Patrick Playfair Laidlaw (1900); brother-in-law of James Fraser (1901); brother of Hugh Alexander Lyon Laidlaw (1904) and of Walter Sibbald Laidlaw (1909); uncle of Christophor Charles Fraser Laidlaw (1940). **Educ:** Perse School, Cambridge. **Career:** Research in Plant Physiology, Imperial College of Science and Technology 1912–1914; Private, London Scottish Regiment 1914–1915. **Awards:** Minor Scholarship, SJC 1906; Foundation Scholarship, SJC 1909; Hutchinson Studentship, SJC 1911; Research Scholarship, Board of Agriculture and Fisheries 1912. **Publications:** (with R C Knight) 'A description of a recording porometer and a note of stomatal behaviour during wilting', *Annals of Botany*, Vol XXX, No CXVII, 1916. Died 3 April 1915 (from wounds received in action at Richebourg l'Avoué on 2 April).

LAIDLAW, Sir Christophor Charles Fraser (1940) Born 9 August 1922, 7 Alipore Road, Calcutta, India; son of Hugh Alexander Lyon Laidlaw, Managing Director, BP, and Sarah Georgina Fraser; m Nina Mary Prichard, 20 December 1952, St Mary's Church, Frensham, Surrey; 1 son (William Samuel Hugh b 3 January 1955), 3 daughters (Emma Katherine b 27 November 1953, Helena Mary Tertia b 29 April 1959 and Joanne Alice b 29 April 1959). **Subject(s):** Modern and Medieval Languages; BA 1947; MA 1953; FRSA 1996. **Tutor(s):** C W Guillebaud. **Johnian Relatives:** nephew of George Muir Laidlaw (1897), Patrick Playfair Laidlaw (1900) and of James Fraser (1901); son of Hugh Alexander Lyon Laidlaw (1904); nephew of Charles Glass Playfair Laidlaw (1907) and of Walter Sibbald Laidlaw (1909). **Educ:** Rose Hill School, Banstead; Rugby School. **Career:** Major on General Staff, Europe and Far East 1939–1945; Intelligence Corps 1941–1946; British Petroleum 1948; BP representative in Hamburg 1959–1961; General Manager, Marketing Department, BP 1963–1967; Director, Société Française, BP 1964–1985; Director, BP Trading 1967; President, BP Belgium 1967–1971; Director (Operations), BP 1971–1972; President,

BP Italiana 1972–1973; Managing Director, BP 1972–1981; President, BP Deutsche 1972–1983; Chairman, BP Oil 1977–1981; Deputy Chairman, BP 1980–1981; Chairman, BP Oil International 1981; Chairman, Boving & Co Ltd 1984–1986; Mercedes-Benz (UK) Ltd 1986–1993; Director, Daimler-Benz (UK) Ltd 1994; Director, Daimler-Chrysler (UK) Holdings Ltd 1999. **Appointments:** Honorary Fellow, SJC 1996; Director, Commercial Union Assurance 1978–1983; Member, International Council, INSEAD 1980; Director, Barclays Bank International 1980–1987; Chairman, ICL plc 1981–1984; Director, Barclays Bank plc 1981–1988; President, ICL France 1983; Director, Equity Capital for Industry Ltd 1983–1986; President, German Chamber of Industry and Commerce 1983–1986; Director, Amerada Hess Corporation 1983–1994; Barclays Merchant Bank Ltd 1984–1986; Chairman, UK Advisory Board, INSEAD 1984–1991; Director, Dalgety 1984–1992; Director, Redland 1984–1992; Director, TWIL Ltd 1985–1989; Chairman, Bridon 1985–1990; Director, Mercedes-Benz (UK) Ltd 1986–1993; Director, INSEAD 1987–1994; Master, Tallow Chandlers' Co 1988–1989; Trustee, International Spinal Research Trust 1991; Vice-President, British-German Association 1996; Vice-President 1997–1998, President 1998–1999, Johnian Society. **Honours:** Kt 1982.

LAIDLAW, Hugh Alexander Lyon (1904) Born 1 September 1885, 46 Shields Road, Pollockshields, Glasgow; son of Robert Laidlaw, Doctor and JP, Seychelles, and Elizabeth Playfair; m Sarah Georgina Fraser, 31 October 1914, St Paul's, Westbourne Grove; 1 son (Christophor Charles Fraser b 9 August 1922). **Subject(s):** Classics; BA 1907. **Tutor(s):** D MacAlister. **Johnian Relatives:** brother of George Muir Laidlaw (1897) and of Patrick Playfair Laidlaw (1900); brother-in-law of James Fraser (1901); brother of Charles Glass Playfair Laidlaw (1907) and of Walter Sibbald Laidlaw (1909); father of Christophor Charles Fraser Laidlaw (1940). **Educ:** Perse School, Cambridge; Paradise House School, Stoke Newington. **Career:** Managing Director, BP. Died 21 January 1931.

LAIDLAW, Sir Patrick Playfair (1900) Born 26 September 1881, Glasgow; son of Robert Laidlaw, Doctor, and Elizabeth Playfair. **Subject(s):** Natural Sciences/Medicine; BA 1903; MA 1909; BChir 1907; LRCP; MRCS; FRS 1927. **Tutor(s):** D MacAlister. **Johnian Relatives:** brother of George Muir Laidlaw (1897); brother-in-law of James Fraser (1901); brother of Hugh Alexander Lyon Laidlaw (1904), Charles Glass Playfair Laidlaw (1907) and of Walter Sibbald Laidlaw (1909); uncle of Christophor Charles Fraser Laidlaw (1940). **Educ:** The Leys School, Cambridge. **Career:** William Dunn Lecturer in Pathology 1914–1922; Demonstrator in Physiology and Assistant House Surgeon, Guy's Hospital; Pathologist 1934, Head, Department of Pathology and Bacteriology 1936, MRC. **Appointments:** Honorary Fellow, SJC 1940. **Awards:** Scholarship 1902; Gedge Prize, University of Cambridge 1906; Gold Medal for Clinical Medicine, Guy's Hospital 1906; Royal Society Royal Medal. **Honours:** Kt 1935. Died 20 March 1940.

LAIDLAW, Walter Sibbald (1909) Born 24 February 1889, 126 Green Lanes, Stoke Newington, London; son of Robert Laidlaw, Medical Practitioner, and Elizabeth Playfair. **Subject(s):** Mechanical Sciences; BA 1912. **Tutor(s):** L H K Bushe-Fox. **Johnian Relatives:** brother of George Muir Laidlaw (1897) and of Patrick Playfair Laidlaw (1900); brother-in-law of James Fraser (1901); brother of Hugh Alexander Lyon Laidlaw (1904) and of Charles Glass Playfair Laidlaw (1907); uncle of Christophor Charles Fraser Laidlaw (1940). **Educ:** Perse School, Cambridge. **Career:** Westinghouse, Manchester 1912; Private, Non-commissioned Officer, later Second Lieutenant, 203rd Field Company, RE (wounded) 1916–1917. Died 23 November 1917 (killed in action near Ypres).

LAING, Charles William (1942) Born 17 November 1923, 1 Valebrook, Sunderland; son of William Frederick Laing, Solicitor, and Dorothy Mary Morrow. **Tutor(s):** S J Bailey. **Johnian Relatives:** brother of Peter Elston Laing (1944). **Educ:** Grange School, Sunderland; Tonstall Preparatory School, Sunderland; Durham School. **Career:** Second Lieutenant, East Riding Yeomanry. Died 26 October 1944 (of wounds received in action).

LAING, Kenneth Macrae (1928) Born 15 January 1907, The Schoolhouse, Glenlivet, County Banff, Scotland; son of Thomas Laing, Schoolmaster, and Mary Dickson Simpson. **Subject(s):** Classics; BA 1931; MA (Aberdeen). **Tutor(s):** M P Charlesworth. **Educ:** Glenlivet Parish School; Mortlach Secondary School; Keith Grammar School; University of Aberdeen. **Awards:** Nunn Exhibition, SJC 1928.

LAING, Peter Elston (1944) Born 7 December 1926, 1 Valebrooke, Sunderland; son of William Frederick Laing, Solicitor, and Dorothy Mary Morrow; m Helen Rosemary Marett Tims, 28 July 1951, St Mary and St Michael, Trumpington, Cambridge; 1 son (Charles Elston), 1 daughter (Sarah Elizabeth Kristensen). **Subject(s):** Mechanical Sciences; BA 1950; MA 1952; PGCE 1954. **Tutor(s):** J M Wordie; R L Howland. **Johnian Relatives:** brother of Charles William Laing (1942). **Educ:** Tonstall School, Sunderland; Grosvenor House School, Harrogate; Durham School. **Career:** Lieutenant, RE 1945–1948; Technical Designs Assistant, Twyfords Ltd 1951–1952; Research Assistant, Furniture Development Council 1952–1953; Assistant Master, The Skinners School, Tunbridge Wells 1954–1959; Assistant Master, The Royal Tunbridge Wells Technical High School for Boys 1959–1972; Model Soldiers Business 1972–1989. **Appointments:** RE Cadet, SJC 1944–1945.

LAING, Rodney Ninian Warrington (1920) Born 10 December 1901, 16 Kensington Square, Kensington, London; son of Frederick Robert Ninian Laing, Barrister-at-Law, and Jane Hewett. BA 1923. **Tutor(s):** E A Benians. **Educ:** Lady Cross School, Seaford; Downside School, Bath. Died 7 February 1952.

LAIRD, Andrew John (1910) Born 13 September 1872, 33 Cumberland Street West, Glasgow, Scotland; son of James Laird, Master Mariner, and Louisa Graham MacGregor. MB (Glasgow); CM (Glasgow); MD (Glasgow). **Tutor(s):** E E Sikes. **Educ:** Glasgow University.

LAIT, John (1929) Born 17 July 1911, 11 Coventry Road, Bedworth, Warwickshire; son of Walter James Lait, Baptist Minister, and Amy Blackwell; m Mavis Waterhouse, 9 March 1940, Soham; 1 son (Andrew John b 7 July 1941), 2 daughters (Christine Mary b 27 August 1943 and Rosemary Ann b 1 March 1947). **Subject(s):** Mathematics; BA 1932; MA 1936; MIEE; MIERE. **Tutor(s):** J M Wordie. **Johnian Relatives:** father of Andrew John Lait (1960). **Educ:** Earlsdon Council School; Central Council School, Sutton in Ashfield; Queen Elizabeth Grammar School, Mansfield; Marling School, Stroud. **Career:** Principal Lecturer in Electronics, RMCS, Shrivenham until 1977; Part-time Library Consultant to Pergamon Press, Oxford 1977. **Awards:** Scholarship 1928. **Honours:** OBE 1971. Died 21 January 1988.

LAKE, Malcolm George (1943) Born 4 August 1924, Foul Anchor, Tydd St Giles, Isle of Ely; son of George Lake, Station Master, Yarmouth Beach Railway Station, and Betsy Ellen Victoria Ludlow. **Subject(s):** Economics; BA 1947. **Tutor(s):** C W Guillebaud. **Educ:** St Michael's Infant School, King's Lynn; St James's Primary School, King's Lynn; King Edward VII Grammar School, King's Lynn.

LAKE, Neville Robert Norris (1944) Born 5 January 1926, 3 The Avenue, Seaton, Devon; son of Frederick Lake, Motor Engineer, and Lilian Gladys Newton. BA 1949. **Tutor(s):** J M Wordie. **Educ:** Colyton Grammar School.

LAKSHNAKARA, Mom Chao (1922) Born 9 April 1902, Bangkok, Siam; son of HRH Prince Phrom Varamirak and Ann. BA 1925. **Tutor(s):** E A Benians. **Educ:** Private Tuition.

LÁL, Sir Manohar (1900) Born 31 December 1879, Fazilka, Ferozepore District, Punjab, India; son of Sital Perhad, Government Official. **Subject(s):** Moral Sciences; BA 1902; MA (Punjab). **Tutor(s):** J R Tanner; C E Graves. **Educ:** Punjab University. **Career:** Called to the Bar, Lincoln's Inn 1904; Principal, Randhir College, Karpurthala 1906–1909;

Minto Professor of Economics, Calcutta University 1909–1912; Minister of Education, Punjab Government 1927–1930; Finance Minister, Punjab 1937. **Appointments:** President, All-India Economic Conference 1935. **Awards:** Whewell Scholarship, University of Cambridge 1903; Cobden Prize, University of Cambridge 1904. **Honours:** Kt 1941. Died May 1949.

LÁLL, Panna (1904) Born 23 November 1883, Bareilly, United Provinces, India; son of Hazari Láll, Accountant, and Jiya Dayal; m Lakshmi Bai. **Subject(s):** Natural Sciences/Law; BA 1906; MA 1937; LLB 1907. **Tutor(s):** D MacAlister. **Educ:** Agra College. **Career:** Called to the Bar, Gray's Inn 1907; Assistant Magistrate and Collector, United Province 1907; Joint Magistrate 1917; Under-Secretary to Government 1917–1918; Forest Settlement Officer, Dehre Dun 1918; Investigator of Customary Law, Kumaon 1919; Secretary, United Provinces Excise Committee 1921; Magistrate and Collector 1923; Member, Indian Historical Records Commission 1926; Deputy Secretary, Industries Department, Government 1927; Secretary to Industries and Educational Departments, Government 1927; Member, United Provinces Legislative Committee 1927–1928; Officiating Commissioner 1931; Political Agent to the Maharaja of Benares 1931–1937; Commissioner 1938; Chief Secretary to Government, United Provinces 1939. **Appointments:** President, Numismatic Society of India 1934–1940; President, Historical Society, United Provinces 1939–1944. **Honours:** CIE 1939. **Publications:** *The Dates of Skandagupta and his Successors*; *Hindu Customary Law*; *Rhasa's Svapnavasavdatta* (translation).

LAMB, George Liston (1924) Born 31 October 1905, Bombay, India; son of George Lamb, Major, Indian Medical Service, and Patricia Napier Liston. **Subject(s):** Classics/Modern and Medieval Languages; BA 1928; MA 1939. **Tutor(s):** E E Sikes. **Educ:** Edinburgh Academy; Fettes College, Edinburgh. **Career:** Housemaster, Assistant Master 1927, Marlborough College. **Awards:** Exhibition, SJC. Died 26 July 1957.

LAMB, George Manners (1943) Born 16 January 1926, Wiesbaden, Germany; son of George Manners Lamb, Night Telephonist, and Annie Sanderson. **Tutor(s):** C W Guillebaud. **Educ:** St John's School, Devonport; St George's School, Plymouth; Garrison School, Bulford; St Mary's School, Berwick; Berwick Grammar School. Died 28 March 1945 (killed in action at the Rhine Bridgehead).

LAMBAH, Dr Paul (1934) Born 19 August 1915, 38 Lauriston Place, Edinburgh; son of Vishwa Mitra Lambah, Medical Practitioner, and Mary Wilson Black; BA 1938; MA 1978; MRCS; LRCP; DO. **Tutor(s):** R L Howland. **Educ:** Aldenham Park School, Bridgnorth; Tettenhall College; Epsom College. **Career:** Ophthalmologist; House Surgeon, Westminster Hospital 1942; Registrar, Wolverhampton Eye Infirmary 1962–1963. **Publications:** 'Some common causes of Eye Injury in the young', *Lancet*, 1962.

LAMBALLE, Oliver Ward (1933) Born 23 August 1914, 308 Linthorpe Road, Middlesbrough; son of Frederic William Lamballe, Lieutenant Colonel, RAMC, and Charlotte Jane Ward. **Tutor(s):** R L Howland. **Educ:** Bootham School, York.

LAMING, Eric Laird (1919) Born 15 June 1899, Keith Terrace, Blackhall, Cramond; son of Walter Cecil Laming, Headmaster, Nevill House School, and Frances Mabel Laird. **Subject(s):** Classics; BA 1921; MA 1928. **Tutor(s):** E E Sikes. **Johnian Relatives:** son of Walter Cecil Laming (1888). **Educ:** Kelvinside Academy, Glasgow; Oundle School. **Career:** Headmaster, Nevill House School, Eastbourne 1933–1960. **Awards:** Scholarship, SJC 1917; Wright's Prize, SJC 1920; Wood and Hare Exhibition 1920. Died 1 July 1986.

LAMPLUGH, The Revd Alfred Amoz Fletcher (1901) Born 24 March 1878, Ash, Farningham, Dartford, Kent; son of David Lamplugh, Clerk in Holy Orders, and Mary Jane Flitcroft Fletcher. **Subject(s):** History; BA 1904; MA 1920. **Tutor(s):** C E Graves; J R Tanner. **Johnian**

Relatives: son of David Lamplugh (1871); brother of Lancelot John Lamplugh (1904). **Educ:** Maidstone Grammar School. **Career:** Deacon 1906; Curate, Burley in Wharfedale 1906–1908; Priest 1907; Curate, St John the Baptist, Newtown 1909–1910; Curate, St Bartholomew, Stamford Hill 1910–1921; Curate, St Andrew, Deal 1921–1926; Curate, Whitstable 1926–1928; Vicar, Bekesbourne, Kent 1928–1948. **Awards:** Scholarship, Ripon Theological College. Died 7 February 1961.

LAMPLUGH, The Revd Lancelot John (1904) Born 19 February 1883, Farningham, Kent; son of David Lamplugh, Clerk in Holy Orders, and Mary Jane Flitcroft Fletcher. BA 1907. **Tutor(s):** C E Graves; J R Tanner. **Johnian Relatives:** son of David Lamplugh (1871); brother of Alfred Amoz Fletcher Lamplugh (1901). **Educ:** North Eastern County School, Barnard Castle. **Career:** Ordained Deacon 1908; Curate, Leithkirk 1908–1910; Ordained Priest 1909; Curate, St Andrew 1910–1914; Curate, Coseley 1914–1923; Curate, Wednesbury 1923–1925; Vicar, St Peter, West Bromwich 1925–1961. Died 17 April 1961.

LANDA Y OSIO, José de (1922) Born 28 May 1899, City of Mexico, South America; son of Guillermo de Landa y Escandon and Sofia Osio y del Barrio. **Tutor(s):** B F Armitage. **Educ:** Stonyhurst College; Private Tuition.

LANDELLS, Professor John Wingrave (1930) Born 20 September 1911, 6 Sunny Bank Road, Rusholme; son of William Landells, Journalist, and Jane Cardno Rait. **Subject(s):** Natural Sciences; BA 1933; MA 1939; BChir 1936; MB 1939. **Tutor(s):** M P Charlesworth. **Educ:** Manchester Grammar Preparatory School; King Arthur School, Musselburgh; John Watson's Institution, Edinburgh; Fettes College, Edinburgh. **Career:** Senior Lecturer, then University Reader in Morbid Anatomy 1957–1976, London Hospital Medical College; Professor of Pathology, University of Addis Ababa, Ethiopia 1976–1994. **Awards:** Scholarship, SJC 1929. **Honours:** OBE 1981. Died 3 November 1998.

LANDIN, Dennis Mould (1940) Born 23 August 1921, Kimbolton, Huntingdonshire; son of Wilfrid Mould Landin, Grocer, and Lavinia Squelch. **Tutor(s):** J M Wordie. **Educ:** Kimbolton School. **Career:** War service, WWII.

LANE, Edward Arthur (1929) Born 15 December 1909, Glenvar, Julians Road, Wimborne, Dorset; son of Edward Andrew Lane, Clerk in Holy Orders, and Mary Elizabeth Luby; 1 daughter. **Subject(s):** Classics; BA 1932; MA 1936. **Tutor(s):** M P Charlesworth. **Johnian Relatives:** son of Edward Andrew Lane (1891). **Educ:** Dalmeny School, Torquay; St John's School, Leatherhead; British School at Athens 1932. **Career:** Assistant Keeper, Ceramics Department, Victoria and Albert Museum 1934; Squadron Leader, Intelligence work, Air Ministry, WWII; Keeper, Ceramics Department, Victoria and Albert Museum 1950. **Appointments:** Visiting Professor, Alexandria University. **Awards:** Scholarship, SJC 1928; Abbot Exhibition 1929. **Publications:** *Early Islamic Pottery*, 1947; *French Faience and Greek Pottery*, 1948; *Style in Pottery*, 1948; *Italian Porcelain*, 1954; *Later Islamic Pottery*, 1957; *English Porcelain Figures of the Eighteenth Century*, 1961; (ed) *Faber Monographs on Pottery and Porcelain*. Died 7 March 1963.

LANE, Henry Clarence Horsburgh (1906) Born 16 December 1886, Graythorne, Thicket Road, Penge, Surrey; son of John MacDonald Lane, Indian Navy, and Margaret Augusta Powell. **Subject(s):** Classics; BA 1909; MA 1916. **Tutor(s):** E E Sikes. **Educ:** Dean Close School, Cheltenham. **Career:** Master, Pocklington School 1909–1910; Master, The King's School, Pontefract 1910–1912; Government Education Department, Federated Malay States 1912–1916; Second Lieutenant, Border Regiment 1916–1917. **Awards:** Choral Studentship, SJC. Died 10 July 1917 (killed in action).

LANG, Professor David Marshall (1942) Born 6 May 1924, Golf View, Chislehurst, Kent; son of David Marshall Lang, Medical Practitioner, and May Rena Wilson; m Janet Sugden, 11 February 1956, St Chad's

Church, Far Headingley, Leeds; 2 sons, 2 daughters. **Subject(s):** Modern and Medieval Languages; BA 1945; MA 1948; PhD 1949; LittD 1964; DLit (London) 1958; Honorary Doctor of Philological Sciences (Tbilisi State University, Georgia). **Tutor(s):** C W Guillebaud. **Johnian Relatives:** father of Andrew Marshall Lang (1977). **Educ:** Petergate, Weston-Super-Mare; St Wilfred's, Hawkhurst; Bath High School; Kingswood, Bath; St Christopher's School, Bath; Monkton Combe School. **Career:** Acting Vice-Consul, Tabriz, then Third Secretary to the British Embassy in Tehran 1944–1946; Title A Fellow, SJC 1945–1952; Part-time Research Lecturer in Georgian 1949–1954, Reader in Georgian 1954–1964, Professor of Caucasian Studies 1964–1984, SOAS; Warden, Connaught Hall, University of London 1956–1984. **Appointments:** Senior Fellowship, Russian Institute of Columbia University, New York 1952–1953; Honorary Secretary, Royal Asiatic Society, London 1962–1964; Visiting Professor of Caucasian Languages, University of California, Los Angeles 1964–1965. **Awards:** Major Scholarship, SJC 1941. **Publications:** *Studies of Numismatic History of the Georgians in Transcaucasia*, 1955; *Lives and Legends of the Georgian Saints*, 1956; *The Wisdom of Balavar*, 1957; *The Last Years of the Georgian Monarchy*, 1957; *The First Russian Radical*, 1959; *A Modern History of Georgia*, 1962; *The Georgians*, 1966; *Armenia, Cradle of Civilization*, 1970; (with C Burney) *The People of the Hills*, 1971; (with C J Walker) *The Armenians*, 1976; *The Bulgarians*, 1976; *The Armenians, a People in Exile*, 1981. Died 30 March 1991.

LANG, Ian Newcomb (1945) Born 9 December 1924, Kingswood, Upper Wrotham Road, Gravesend, Kent; son of Norman Granville Lang, Secretary, and Mildred Newcomb; m Marjie; 4 sons (Joe, Chunky, Matt and Greg). **Subject(s):** English; BA 1947; MA 1957. **Tutor(s):** C W Guillebaud. **Educ:** Modern School, Streatham; Norbury College; Sevenoaks Preparatory School; Kingswood School, Bath. **Career:** Service Organiser, BBC European English Service; RN 1944–1945; Head of Service, BBC Far Eastern Station, Singapore 1962. **Appointments:** Representative of the BBC in South East Asia. **Awards:** Winchester Reading Prize, University of Cambridge 1948. Died 8 January 1988.

LANG-ANDERSON, Brigadier William Grant (1922) Born 13 February 1898, The Grand Hotel, Glasgow, Scotland; son of Robert Lang-Anderson, Civil Engineer, and Mary Grant. **Tutor(s):** E A Benians. **Educ:** Ardvreck, Crieff; Victoria College, Alexandria, Egypt; Harrow School. **Career:** RE, France, Italy 1917; Public Works Department, North West Frontier Province; 14th Army, Calcutta and Burma, WWII; Chief Engineer, Public Works Department, Peshawar 1948.

LANGDON, Augustus John (1931) Born 20 April 1913, 111 Round Hill Crescent, Brighton; son of Cecil Langdon, Clerk in Holy Orders, and Elizabeth Mercer Hutchinson; m (2) Doris Edna Clinkard, 1949; (1) 2 daughters, (2) 1 son. **Subject(s):** Natural Sciences; BA 1934; MA 1942; FRICS. **Tutor(s):** C W Guillebaud. **Educ:** The Knoll, Woburn Sands; King's College Choir School, Cambridge; Berkhampsted School. **Career:** Chief Surveyor, Ministry of Agriculture; Assistant to J Carter Jonas & Sons, Oxford 1936–1937; Superintendent Lands Officer, Admiralty 1937–1945; Partner, J Carter Jonas & Sons, Oxford 1945–1948; Regional Land Commissioner, Ministry of Agriculture 1948–1965; Chief Surveyor, Agricultural Development and Advisory Service, MAFF 1971–1974; Surveyor for National Trust 1974–1976. **Appointments:** Chairman, Statutory Committee on Agricultural Valuation; Member, General Council, RICS; Member, Land Agency and Agricultural Divisional Council 1971–1975. **Publications:** (Contributor) ed R C Walmesley, *Rural Estate Management*; Fream's *Elements of Agriculture*, and professional and agricultural journals. Died 3 December 1992.

LANGFORD, David (1944) Born 3 March 1926, 25 Mornington Road, St Pancras, London; son of George Harry Langford, Railway Clerk, and Florence Emily Webb. **Tutor(s):** J M Wordie. **Educ:** William Ellis School, London; Tewkesbury Grammar School; St Alban's County School.

LANGHORNE, George Wilmot (1920) Born 2 March 1900, Lucknow, United Provinces, India; son of Frederick James Langhorne, Divisional Forest Officer, and Minnie Alice Hilton. **Tutor(s):** B F Armitage. **Educ:** Diocesan Boys' School, Nairi Tal, India; Bishop Collins' School, Bangalore, India; St Paul's School, Darjeeling; Courtenay Lodge, Sutton Courtenay.

LANGSTADT, Dr Erich (1934) Born 15 April 1910, Neheim, Westphalia; son of Adolf Langstadt, Merchant, and Minna Herz; m Florence. PhD 1938. **Tutor(s):** J S Boys Smith. **Educ:** Realgymnasium Neheim; University of Cologne; University of Freiburg; University of Marburg. **Career:** Librarian, Brotherton Library, Leeds University 1946–1975. **Awards:** Strathcona Research Exhibition, SJC. Died 13 February 1989.

LANGTON, The Revd Ernest William (1942) Born 12 May 1905, Cemetery Lodge, Bridlington, Yorkshire; son of Robert Langton, Superintendent of Cemetery, and Annie Elizabeth Horner. **Subject(s):** History; BA 1944. **Educ:** Beverley Grammar School; St John's College, York. **Career:** Divinity Master, Handsworth Grammar School, Birmingham; Curate, Leamington Spa; Master, Beverley Grammar School; Master, Oxford Street School, Bridlington 1924–1935; Master, Burlington School, Bridlington 1935–1941; Master, Ashville College, Harrogate 1941; Rector, Brandesburton 1958–1973. Died 2 March 1986.

LANGTON, The Revd Frederick Edward Palmer (1919) Born 13 October 1897, Ponteland Vicarage, Newcastle upon Tyne; son of Frederick William Langton, Clerk in Holy Orders, and Tryphena Viola Moseley Palmer. **Subject(s):** History/Theology; BA 1922; MA 1933. **Tutor(s):** E E Sikes. **Educ:** Sea Bank, Alnmouth; Durham School. **Career:** Second Lieutenant, RFC, France 1917–1918; Lieutenant, RAF 1918–1919; Assistant Librarian, Trinity College, Cambridge 1922–1923; Ordained Deacon 1924; Curate, St Michael, Shoreditch 1924–1925; Ordained Priest 1925; Curate, St Cuthbert, Kensington 1925–1931; Vicar, Holy Redeemer, Clerkenwell 1931–1948; Vicar, St Philip, Clerkenwell 1936–1947; Vicar, St Mary the Virgin, Pimlico 1948. **Appointents:** Chaplain, RNVR 1942–1946. **Awards:** Baker Exhibition, SJC 1916. Died 5 June 1972.

LANGTON, Harold McKee (1912) Born 4 October 1884, 9 Malborough Terrace, South Boulevard, Kingston upon Hull, Yorkshire; son of James Christopher Langton, Schoolmaster, and Caroline Anne McKee; m Ethel; 1 daughter (Muriel). **Subject(s):** Natural Sciences; BA 1915; MA 1920. **Tutor(s):** R P Gregory. **Educ:** Bradford Technical College; Hackney Technical Institution; East Ham Technical College. Died 16 March 1978.

LANGTON MAY, Cecil Hugh (1927) Born 20 July 1909, Forest House, East Horsley, Surrey; son of Peter Langton May, Stockbroker, and Ida Maude Sturdy. **Tutor(s):** C W Guillebaud. **Johnian Relatives:** son of Peter Langton May (1893); nephew of Frederick Sturdy May (1895) and of Herbert Richard Dudfield May (1897); brother of Ivan Langton May (1922); cousin of Richard Sturdy May (1928) and of Peter Dudfield May (1931). **Educ:** Boxgrove School, Guildford; Harrow School.

LANGTON MAY, Ivan (1922) Born 19 August 1903, Paxhill, Lindfield, Sussex; son of Peter Langton May, Stock Exchange, and Ida Maude Sturdy; m Betty Myra Heaver 21 October 1937. **Subject(s):** Law; BA 1925. **Tutor(s):** E E Sikes. **Johnian Relatives:** son of Peter Langton May (1893); nephew of Frederick Sturdy May (1895) and of Herbert Richard Dudfield May (1897); brother of Cecil Hugh Langton May (1927); cousin of Richard Sturdy May (1928) and of Peter Dudfield May (1931). **Educ:** Boxgrove School, Guildford; Harrow School. **Career:** RA, WWII; Costello, Parsons & Co. Died 27 November 1997.

LANKESTER, John Ernest (1941) Born 28 June 1923, Ipswich, Suffolk; son of Ernest Walter Lankester, Superintendent and Deputy Chief Constable, and Mabel Emily Cooper; m Anna Mir Vilardebó, 1947,

Seville; 3 daughters. **Subject(s):** Modern and Medieval Languages; BA 1944; MA 1948; CertEd (Cambridge) 1945. **Tutor(s):** C W Guillebaud. **Educ:** Northgate School, Ipswich. **Career:** British Council Officer, Council Service in Spain, France, Syria, Argentina and Tunisia 1945–1980; Lecturer, British Institute, Barcelona 1945–1947; Lecturer, British Institute, Seville 1947–1949; Assistant Regional Director, Toulouse 1949–1951; Lecturer/Assistant Director, Damascus 1951–1956; Director, Asociación Argentina de Cultura Británica, Córdoba 1956–1960; Deputy Director, British Council, Cambridge 1960–1969; Regional Director, British Council, Toulouse 1969–1971; Deputy Director, British Council Institute, Barcelona 1971–1975; British Council Director/Cultural Attaché, Tunisia 1975–1980.

LAPWOOD, Dr Ernest Ralph (1928) Born 23 September 1909, 39 Minstead Road, Erdington, Warwickshire; son of Ernest Lapwood, Handicraft Instructor, and Rose Allen; m Nancy Harper Stuckey, 1940, Chengtu; 2 sons, 2 daughters. **Subject(s):** Mathematics/Geography; BA 1931; MA 1944; PhD 1950. **Tutor(s):** J M Wordie. **Johnian Relatives:** father of Peter Ralph Lapwood (1961). **Educ:** Osborne Road Council School, Erdington; King Edward's School, Birmingham. **Career:** Mathematics Master, Medhurst College (London Missionary Society), Shanghai 1932; Mathematics Faculty, Yenching University 1936–1953; Inspector for Chinese Industrial Co-operatives 1939–1942; Assistant Lecturer in Mathematics 1953–1956, Lecturer in Mathematics 1956–1972, Reader in Theoretical Seismology 1972–1976 (Emeritus 1976), University of Cambridge; Fellow 1955, Vice-Master 1972–1976, Life Fellow 1976–1984, Emmanuel College, Cambridge. **Appointments:** Director of Studies, Emmanuel College, Cambridge 1955; Pro-Proctor 1956–1957, Proctor 1957, University of Cambridge; Chairman, UK National Sub-Committee for Seismology and the Physics of the Earth's Interior; Chairman, Committee for a Reference Earth-Model; Deputy-Chairman, British Association Committee for Seismology. **Awards:** Scholarship, SJC 1927. **Publications:** (with Nancy Lapwood) *Through the Chinese Revolution*, Spalding & Levy, 1954; (with Tatsuo Usami) *Free oscillations of the earth*, CUP, 1981. Died 11 April 1984.

LAPWORTH, Harold John (1939) Born 30 December 1919, 153 Coventry Road, Birmingham; son of Francis John Birch Lapworth, Master Tailor, and Lilian May Baker; m Olive Hewish, 1948; 1 daughter (Susan). **Subject(s):** Modern Languages (Spanish/German); BA 1947; MA 1950. **Tutor(s):** C W Guillebaud. **Educ:** Henwick House School, Birmingham; Jenkin's Street Council School, Birmingham; King Edward's Grammar School; King Edward's High School, Birmingham. **Career:** Assistant Modern Languages Master, Bexhill Grammar School for Boys 1948–1957; Head of Spanish/German Department, Queen Mary's Grammar School for Boys, Walsall 1957–1963; Senior Lecturer in Languages, South Dorset Technical College, Weymouth 1963–1980. **Awards:** Major Open Scholarship in Modern Languages, SJC 1938.

LARDNER, Thomas Harry Afolabi (1949) Born 18 June 1927, Lagos, Nigeria; son of Henry William Jonathan Lardner, Chief Clerk, and Mary Adekemi Randle. **Tutor(s):** C W Guillebaud. **Educ:** Church Missionary Society Grammar School, Lagos; King's College, Lagos. **Career:** Technical Assistant, King's College, Lagos.

LARMOUR, James (1926) Born 22 May 1906, 49 Castlereagh Street, Belfast, County Down, Ireland; son of James Larmour, Businessman, and Mary Bennett; m Mary Jane Brown; 1 son (James Martin b 16 November 1943, d 11 April 1971), 2 daughters (Jane and Patricia). **Subject(s):** Mathematics; BA 1929; MA 1935; BSc (Belfast) 1927. **Tutor(s):** J M Wordie. **Johnian Relatives:** father of James Martin Larmour (1963); great uncle of David Gordon Thomson (1987). **Educ:** Mountpottinger Elementary School; Methodist College, Belfast; Queen's University, Belfast. **Career:** Assistant Master, Christ's Hospital, Horsham 1929–1935; Assistant Master, Sixth Form Master, House Master (Troy House), Rugby School 1936–1969. **Publications:** *School Trigonometry*, Parts 1 and 2. Died 2 April 1989.

LARMUTH, Reginald Stone Ashley (1923) Born 4 April 1902, Holme Leigh, Church Road, Cheadle Hulme, Cheshire; son of Reginald Ashley Larmuth, Auctioneer, Valuer and Estate Agent, and Helen Louisa Stone Willacy; m Lucy; 1 daughter (Joanna). BA 1927; MA 1931; FIMechE; FIMarE. **Tutor(s):** E Cunningham. **Educ:** Cheadle Hulme High School; Ryley's School, Alderley Edge; King William's College, Isle of Man; Newton Heath Branch, Manchester School of Technology. Died 21 June 1995.

LASCELLES, Mr Justice Daniel Richard (1926) Born 17 September 1908, Harewood House, Grange Road, Darlington, County Durham; son of Alfred Lascelles, Toy Merchant, and Eleanor Jane Buckle. **Subject(s):** Law; BA 1929. **Tutor(s):** E A Benians. **Educ:** Chasemont Preparatory School; Darlington Grammar School; Durham School. **Career:** Called to the Bar, Inner Temple 1930; Farming 1931–1932; Administrative Branch, Sarawak, Colonial Civil Service 1932; Member, Supreme Court of Sarawak, North Borneo and Brunei 1952. **Honours:** CBE. Died 1 March 1984.

LASH, John Noel de Warrenne (1946) Born 28 December 1917, Sydenham; son of Ivan Richard de Warrenne Lash, Major, and Elsie Ethel. **Tutor(s):** G C L Bertram. **Educ:** Privately Educated, Palestine; RMC, Sandhurst.

LASKEY, Raymond John (1944) Born 12 February 1926, Folkestone House, Brent Street, Hendon, Middlesex; son of Albert William Laskey, Purchase Manager, Motor Car Engines, and Mabel Elsie Roe. **Tutor(s):** J M Wordie. **Educ:** Ravensfield College, Hendon; St George's School, Harpenden; Belmont School, Mill Hill; Oundle School. **Appointments:** RAF Cadet, SJC.

LASKI, Norman (1919) Born 13 February 1900, Cheetham Hill Road, Cheetham, North Lancashire; son of Noah Laski, Cotton Goods Exporter, and Sarah Gotliffe; m Viola; 2 daughters (Ann and Simone). BA 1921; MA 1948. **Tutor(s):** E E Sikes. **Educ:** Manchester Grammar School; Clifton College. **Career:** Director, Marks and Spencer Ltd. Died 22 July 1968.

LASLETT, Thomas Peter Ruffell (1935) Born 18 December 1915, 14 Glebe Road, Bedford; son of George Henry Ruffell Laslett, Baptist Minister, and Eveline Elizabeth Alden; m Janet Crockett Clark, 1947; 2 sons. **Subject(s):** History; BA 1938; MA 1942; LittD (Trinity) 1980; DUniv (Open) 1980, (Keele) 1993, (Tulane, USA) 2000; FBA 1979. **Tutor(s):** J S Boys Smith. **Educ:** Gartlet School, Watford; Grammar School, Watford; Taunton School. **Career:** RN 1940–1945; Lieutenant RNVR, Japanese Naval Intelligence, Bletchley Park 1943–1945; Producer, BBC, *Third Programme* talks 1946–1960; Title A Fellow, SJC 1948–1951; Assistant Lecturer in History, University of Cambridge 1950–1953; Fellow, Trinity College, Cambridge 1952; Co-Founder and Director, Cambridge Group for the History of Population and Social Structure 1964; Reader in Politics and the History of Social Structure, University of Cambridge 1966–1983. **Appointments:** Institute for Advanced Study, Princeton 1959–1960; Chairman, Viewers and Listeners Association of Great Britain 1962; Member, Government Committee on Foundation of Open University 1965; Center for Advanced Study in the Behavioural Sciences, California 1967–1968; Visiting Professor, Johns Hopkins University 1972; Visiting Professor, College de France, Paris 1976; Visiting Professor, Yale University 1977; Member, government institution of first University of the Third Age 1981; Visiting Professor, Nihon University, Tokyo 1992. **Awards:** First Year Essay Prize, SJC 1936; Scholarship, SJC 1936–1937; Wright's Prize, SJC 1937. **Honours:** CBE 1997. **Publications:** Founder and Chief Editor, *Philosophy, Politics and Society*, 1957 (6th series 1992); *Sir Robert Filmer*, 1949; *Locke's Two Treatises of Government*, 1960, 3rd edition 1988; *The World We Have Lost*, 1965, 3rd edn 1983; (with R Wall) *Household and Family in Past Time*, 1972; *Family Life and Illicit Love in Earlier Generations*, 1977; (with R M Smith and others) *Bastardy and its Comparative History*, 1980; (jointly) *Family Forms in Historic Europe*, 1983; *A Fresh Map of Life*, 1989, 2nd edition 1996; (with J Fishkin)

Justice between Age Groups and Generations, 1992; (with D Kertzer) *Ageing in the Past*, 1995. Died 8 November 2001.

LATHROP, Julian Langson (1918) American Student.

LATIF, Sarhan Carnrudin (1912) Born 18 October 1893, Bombay, India; son of Carnrudin Amirudin Abdul Latif, Pleader at Consular Court, Zanzibar, and Vazair Sheikhali. BA 1915. **Tutor(s):** R P Gregory. **Johnian Relatives:** brother of Alma Latifi (1898); uncle of Komair Latifi (1930). **Educ:** United Services College; Heidelberg, Germany; St Paul's School.

LATIFI, Komair (1930) Born 20 July 1912, No 2 Civil Lines, Delhi, India; son of Alma Latifi, Indian Civil Service, Barrister-at-Law, and Nasima Tyabji. BA 1933; MA 1937. **Tutor(s):** E A Benians. **Johnian Relatives:** son of Alma Latifi (1898); nephew of Sarhan Carnrudin Latif (1912). **Educ:** St Xavier's High School, Bombay, India; Bembridge School, Isle of Wight.

LA TOUCHE, Hugh Norman Digues (1910) Born 27 September 1890, Karnâl, India; son of James Norman Digues La Touche, Senior Inspector of Railways, Indian Public Works, and Aileen Harriet Etheredge. **Tutor(s):** L H K Bushe-Fox. **Educ:** Inholmes, Cheltenham; Grammar School, Ludlow. **Career:** Lieutenant, 63rd Palamcottah Light Infantry, Indian Army, WWI.

LAUGHLIN, Philip Herbert (1914) Born 22 April 1896, 23 St Giles Street, Northampton; son of Joseph Herbert Laughlin, Master Fruiterer, and Amy Elliott. **Subject(s):** Mathematics. **Tutor(s):** R P Gregory. **Educ:** St Giles's Council Schools, Northampton; Kettering Road County School; Northampton and County School. **Career:** Second Lieutenant, Royal West Surrey Regiment, Egypt and Palestine until 1917. **Awards:** Scholarship, SJC. Died 21 December 1917 (of wounds received in action near Jerusalem).

LAUNDER, Geoffrey William (1938) Born 24 March 1919, Glenville, Staplehurst, Kent; son of William George Launder, Chief Inspector of Schools, and Daisy Emma Shoobridge. **Subject(s):** Mechanical Sciences; BA 1947; MA 1949; CEng; MIEE; MICE. **Tutor(s):** J S Boys Smith. **Educ:** Bush Hill Park School, Enfield, London; Raglan School, Enfield, London; Manchester Grammar School; Hymers College, Hull. **Career:** Training Officer, BICC Ltd; Assistant Engineer, Railway Department, Colonial Service, Nigeria 1948.

LAURISTON, Richard Basil (1935) Born 26 January 1917, 27 Radcliffe Road, Haydon Bridge, Northumberland; son of Alexander Lauriston, Solicitor, and Nelly Ainsworth; m Monica Deacon, 1944; 3 sons. **Subject(s):** Law; BA 1938; MA 1942; LLB 1939; LLM 1985. **Tutor(s):** C W Guillebaud. **Educ:** High School, Middlesbrough; Sir William Turner's School, Redcar. **Career:** Royal Corps of Signals 1939–1945; Fielder, Le Riche and Co, Lincoln's Inn 1945–1948; Solicitor, Partner in father's firm 1948–1962; Senior Partner, Alex Lauriston & Son, Solicitors, Middlesbrough 1962–1976; Recorder of the Crown Court 1974–1982. **Appointments:** Permanent Chairman of Industrial Tribunals 1976–1989.

LAVERACK, Frederick Cyril (1943) Born 10 September 1925, Durham House, 102 Crouch Hill, Middlesex; son of Frederick William Reid Laverack, Bank of England, and Winifred Mary Rushworth. **Tutor(s):** C W Guillebaud. **Educ:** Hertford Grammar School; Bishop's Stortford College.

LAVERS, Norman Henry Stewart (1944) Born 27 March 1927, 10 Sandfield Road, St Albans, Hertfordshire; son of Charles Stewart Touzeau Lavers, Timber Merchant, and Elsie Smith. **Subject(s):** Mathematics. **Tutor(s):** J M Wordie. **Educ:** St John's Preparatory School, St Albans; St Alban's School.

LAVERY, The Revd Hugh (1943) Born 1 March 1916, 15 Lime Street, Waldridge, Chester-le-Street; son of Mark Lavery, Coal Hewer, and

Mary McCormick. **Subject(s):** History; BA 1946; MA 1950. **Tutor(s):** C W Guillebaud. **Educ:** St Cuthbert's School, Chester-le-Street; Towneley Memorial Central School, Stanley; Ushaw College, Durham; Gregorian University, Rome; Stonyhurst.

LAW, Dr Frank William (1919) Born 14 August 1898, Heston Lodge, Isleworth, Middlesex; son of Thomas Law, Director, Textile Warehouse Company, and Emma Janet MacRea; m Brenda Thomas, 25 May 1929, All Saints' Church, Blackheath; 1 son (Barry), 1 daughter (Brynhilde). **Subject(s):** Natural Sciences; BA 1922; MA 1926; MB 1927; BChir 1927; MD 1932; FRCS 1929; LRCP 1926; MRCS 1926; FRSM. **Tutor(s):** E A Benians. **Johnian Relatives:** father of Barry Thomas MacRea Law (1952). **Educ:** Hounslow Commercial College; Isleworth County School; St Paul's School, London; Middlesex Hospital. **Career:** Officer, RA, France and Flanders 1917–1918; Assistant Surgeon, Central London Ophthalmic Hospital; Ophthalmic Surgeon, Paddington Green Children's Hospital, and West Middlesex Hospital; Consulting Surgeon, Willesden Borough Council; Ophthalmologist, South Eastern Metropolitan Sector, Emergency Medical Service, WWI; Pathologist, Curator, and Assistant Medical Officer, Physico-therapeutical Department, Royal London Ophthalmic Hospital; Senior Ophthalmic Surgeon, Guy's Hospital; House Surgeon 1927, Senior Resident Officer 1928, Pathologist, Curator, Medical Officer in charge of Department of Physical Therapy, Senior Surgeon until 1963, Moorfields Eye Hospital. **Appointments:** Member, Committee of Management (later Board of Governors), Finance Committee, House Committee, Moorfields Eye Hospital; Member 1933, Court Assistant 1946, Warden 1951, Master 1955–1957, Worshipful Company of Spectacle Makers; Honorary Secretary 1938–1946, Council Member, Treasurer, President 1960–1962, Ophthalmological Society of the UK; Freedom, City of London 1938; Honorary Secretary, Council of British Ophthalmologists 1942–1944; Honorary Secretary 1944, President, Council Member, Faculty of Ophthalmologists; Honorary Member, Société Belge d'Ophtalmologie 1946; Secretary General, XVI International Ophthalmological Congress, London 1950; Exchange Professor, Johns Hopkins University, Baltimore, USA 1953; Honorary Visiting Ophthalmologist, Johns Hopkins Hospital, Baltimore, USA 1953; Council Member, Oxford Ophthalmological Congress (Master 1953–1955); Lecturer, Institute of Ophthalmology, London; Vice-Presisent, Section of Ophthalmology, later Fellow, RSM; Chairman, Committee of the Johnian Society 1956–1986, President, Johnian Society 1964; Honorary FBOA (BOA Foundation Lecturer 1957); Consulting Ophthalmologist, Royal Hospital, Chelsea; Consulting Ophthalmologist, King Edward VII Hospital for Officers; Honorary Consultant, Queen Alexandra Military Hospital, Millbank, until 1961; Honorary Consultant in Ophthalmology to the Army 1961–1963; Chairman, Opthalmic Nursing Board; Member, General Optical Council; Member, Hospital Committee, Ophthalmic Hospital of St John, Jerusalem; Examiner, Fellowship in Ophthalmology, RCS, Orthoptic Board; Member, Council of the European Opthalmological Society; Vice-President, International Association for the Prevention of Blindness; Consultant Adviser in Ophthalmology to four Ministries; Member, Société Française d'Ophtalmologie; Honorary Member, Greek Ophthalmological Society; Honorary Member, Pan-American Medical Association, Section of Ophthalmology; Honorary Member, American Medical Association; Honorary Member, Canadian Ophthalmological Society; Honorary Fellow, American Academy of Ophthalmology and Otolaryngology. **Awards:** Van Duyse Medal, Société Belge d'Ophtalmologie 1946. **Honours:** KStJ. **Publications:** *Ultra-Violet Therapy in Eye Disease*, John Murray, 1934; (with E Treacher Collins) *The History & Traditions of the Moorfields Eye Hospital*, Volume II, H K Lewis, 1975; many papers in medical and ophthalmological journals including the *British Journal of Ophthalmology*, *Modern Practice in Ophthalmology*, and *Practitioner*. Died 26 May 1987.

LAW, Kenneth Kitson (1943) Born 28 April 1925, 1 Carden Terrace, Aberdeen; son of Arthur Edward Law, Art Master, and Jane Annie Kitson. **Tutor(s):** C W Guillebaud. **Educ:** Harris Academy, Dundee; Dundee High School.

LAW, Dr William Alexander (1929) Born 22 August 1910, 5 Mansfield Place, Edinburgh; son of James Law, Dental Surgeon, and Agnes Jarvis; m (3) Patricia; 1 son (Bruce), 1 daughter (Alison), 2 stepsons (Andrew and James). **Subject(s):** Natural Sciences; BA 1932; MA 1936; BChir 1935; MB 1936; MD 1942; MRCS 1935; LRCP 1935; FRCS 1937. **Tutor(s):** M P Charlesworth. **Educ:** Malse's Hall, Cross Hills, Keighley; Giggleswick School. **Career:** Lieutenant Colonel, RAMC; Commanded a Mobile Field Surgical Unit in North Africa, Sicily and Italy, WWII; Associate Surgeon, Robert Jones and Agnes Hunt Hospital, Oswestry; Consultant Orthopaedic Surgeon to the London Hospital 1945–1975; Consultant Orthopaedic Surgeon, Royal Masonic Hospital, London 1963–1975; Consultant Orthopaedic Surgeon to the Italian Hospital 1975. **Appointments:** Hunterian Professor of Surgery 1963, Watson Jones Lecturer 1978, RCS; Fellow, British Orthopaedic Association; Effective Member, International Society of Orthopaedic Surgery and Traumatology; President, Caledonian Society; Life Governor of the Royal Scottish Corporation. **Awards:** Rockefeller Travelling Scholarship in Medicine 1946; Gold Medal, British Orthopaedic Association. **Honours:** OBE 1943 (Military); TD. **Publications:** *Osteoarthritis of the Hip*, 1969; *Some Landmarks in the Surgery of Rheumatism*, 1979. Died 30 October 1989.

LAWE, Francis Walsham (1913) Born 16 February 1894, Belgrave Terrace, Pinderlands, Stanley, Wakefield, Yorkshire; son of Thomas Haigh Lawe, Chief Clerk, Education Department, and Emma Jane Eason; m Marjorie Edwards, 12 September 1923, Hamstead Parish Church; 1 son. **Subject(s):** Economics; BA 1920; MA 1925; CIPM. **Tutor(s):** E E Sikes. **Johnian Relatives:** brother-in-law of Ernest Booth (1913); uncle of Stephen Dion Booth (1942). **Educ:** Clarendon Street National School, Wakefield; St John's National School, Wakefield; Wakefield Grammar School. **Career:** Captain, East Yorkshire Regiment; Liaison Officer to Portuguese army, then POW, East Prussia 1914–1918; Institute of Industrial Psychology 1920; Worked for Lyons 1923–1929; Director and General Manager, Harrods 1929–1955. **Appointments:** Council Member, Retail Distributors Association 1948–1958; Governor, College of Distributive Trades 1945–1970; Chairman, Retail Trades Education Council. **Honours:** CBE. Died 28 March 1982.

LAWLESS, Michael (1931) Born 6 June 1909, Cork Road, Fermay; son of Patrick Lawless, Officer, Royal Irish Constabulary, and Mary Breen; BSc (Ireland) 1930; MSc (Ireland) 1931. **Tutor(s):** J M Wordie. **Educ:** Christian Brothers School, Fermay; St Joseph's Seminary, Galway; University College, Galway.

LAWN, Dr Lawrence (1916) Born 8 November 1898, Kimberley, Cape Colony; son of James Gunson Lawn, Mining Engineer, and Mary Searle; m Olive Elizabeth Day, 30 August 1924, St Andrew's Street Baptist Chapel; 1 daughter (Olivia Mary). **Subject(s):** Medicine; BA 1920; MA 1923; BChir 1924; MD 1933; MRCS; LRCP. **Tutor(s):** E E Sikes. **Educ:** Redruth Secondary School; Exeter Grammar School; Bishop's Stortford College. **Career:** Clinical Assistant, Children's Clinic and Ear, Nose and Throat Clinic, St Thomas' Hospital; House Surgeon, Addenbrooke's Hospital. **Publications:** 'Early Action of Insulin in the Diabetic', *Biochemical Journal*, 1925. Died 7 March 1974.

LAWRANCE, Norman Macleod (1936) Born 15 May 1917, 70 Cambridge Terrace, Paddington, London; son of Norman Macleod Lawrance, Director of Balmoral (Ceylon) Estates Co Ltd, and Dorris Emily Partridge Webb; m Irene Audrey Herring, 14 July 1962; 2 daughters (Elizabeth Joyce and Anne Margaret). **Subject(s):** Mechanical Sciences; BA 1939; MA 1943; CEng; MIMechE; FInstE 1982. **Tutor(s):** J S Boys Smith. **Educ:** Ovingdean Hall, Brighton; Charterhouse; Maiden Erlegh, Reading. **Career:** Second Lieutenant (demobilised as Major), RASC, UK, France, and East Africa 1939–1946; Shell Petroleum Company Ltd, London 1946–1962; Engineer, Fuel Oil Experimental Station, Assistant Engineer Fuel Oil Technology Department 1955–1962; Superintending Engineer, Estates Department, Legal & General Assurance Society 1962–1972; Controller, Property Services 1973–1980; Property Services Manager 1980–1982.

LAWRENCE, Captain Eustace Henry (1932) Born 24 April 1913, Albion House, High Street, Knaresborough, Yorkshire; son of Edmund William Lawrence, Master Chemist, and Elizabeth Richmond. **Subject(s):** History/Archaeology and Anthropology; BA 1935. **Tutor(s):** E A Benians. **Educ:** Pocklington School. **Career:** Burmah Oil Company 1935–1939; Captain, 1st Burma Rifles; ADC to General Bruce Scott; Commandant of Camp, Upper Burmah 1939–1942. Died 1 May 1942 (killed in action).

LAWRENSON, Alexander Cameron (1929) Born 4 May 1910, 6 Village Terrace, South Shields, County Durham; son of Thomas Alfred Lawrenson, Headmaster, Westoe Secondary School, and Elsie Cameron. **Subject(s):** English/Modern and Medieval Languages; BA 1932; MA 1936. **Tutor(s):** M P Charlesworth. **Johnian Relatives:** son of Thomas Alfred Lawrenson (1886). **Educ:** St Nicholas Private School, South Shields; The High School, South Shields.

LAWRIE, Niculae (1943) See LITTMAN.

LAWS, Dr Gilbert James (1932) Born 20 June 1913, 6 Charnwood Road, Loughborough; son of Samuel Charles Laws, Principal, Northampton Polytechnic, London, and Ellen Phillipson; m Mary, 1 son (Kipps), 1 daughter (Su). **Subject(s):** Natural Sciences; BA 1935; MB 1940; BChir 1940. **Tutor(s):** R L Howland. **Johnian Relatives:** son of Samuel Charles Laws (1901). **Educ:** Woodfield Preparatory School, Wigan; The Grammar School, Wigan; Berkhamsted School. **Career:** Consultant Pathologist, Hexham Group of Hospitals 1951. Died 17 October 1989.

LAWS, John Richard Harwood (1947) Born 3 June 1925, 16 Horncliffe Road, Blackpool, Lancashire; son of Frederick Robert Laws, Schoolmaster, and Annetta Isabel Kirby. **Subject(s):** Modern and Medieval Languages; BA 1949; MA 1954. **Tutor(s):** C W Guillebaud. **Educ:** Arnold School, Blackpool. **Career:** Lieutenant, RA.

LAWS, Samuel Charles (1901) Born 5 February 1879, East Dereham, Norfolk; son of James John Laws, Outfitter, and Emily Bloy; m (1) Ellen Phillipson (d 1936), (2) Lucy Yvonne Sadler; (1) 1 son, 1 daughter. **Subject(s):** Physics and Chemistry; BA 1904; MA 1908; BSc (London) 1900; MSc (London) 1919. **Tutor(s):** D MacAlister. **Johnian Relatives:** father of Gilbert James Laws (1932). **Educ:** Norfolk County School; University College, Nottingham. **Career:** Assistant Lecturer in Physics, KCL 1904–1905; Head, Physics and Engineering Department, Blackburn Technical College 1905–1909; Principal, Loughborough Technical College 1909–1915; Principal, Wigan and District Mining and Technical College 1915–1924; Principal, Northampton Polytechnic, St John Street, London 1924–1947. Died 22 March 1963.

LAWSON, Dr John David (1941) Born 4 April 1923, Nursing Home, Saint Nicholas Street, Coventry; son of Ronald Latimer Lawson, Welding Engineer, and Ruth Houseman; m Kathleen Wyllie, 1949; 2 sons, 1 daughter. **Subject(s):** Mechanical Science; BA 1944; ScD Physics 1969; FInstP 1970; FRS 1983. **Tutor(s):** C W Guillebaud. **Educ:** Langdale School, Birches Barn Road, Wolverhampton; St George's School, Harpenden; Wolverhampton Grammar School. **Career:** Aerials Group, Telecommunications Research Establishment, Malvern 1943–1947; Accelerator Group, AERE, Malvern Branch 1947–1951; General Physics Division, AERE, Harwell 1951–1962; Applied Physics Divison, and later Technology Division, Rutherford Laboratory (later Rutherford Appleton Laboratory), Chilton, Oxon 1962–1987; Honorary Scientist on Retirement 1987. **Appointments:** Microwave Laboratory, Stanford, USA 1959–1960; Visiting Professor, Department of Physics and Astronomy, University of Maryland, USA 1971; Culham Laboratory, Technology Division 1975–1976. **Awards:** Thomas Young Medal, Institute of Physics 1985. **Publications:** *The Physics of Charged Particle Beams*, Clarendon Press, Oxford 1977, 2nd edn 1988; papers on various topics in applied physics in several journals.

LAWSON, Thomas Campbell (1932) Born 6 November 1912, 48 Albert Drive, Glasgow; son of Thomas Browlie Lawson, Wholesale Merchant (Jeweller), and Robina Innes Forsyth. **Subject(s):** Economics; BA 1935. **Tutor(s):** C W Guillebaud. **Educ:** Kelvinside Academy, Glasgow; Private Tuition, Switzerland; Brighton College. **Career:** Chartered Accountant, firm which became part of Grant Thornton; Captain, North Staffordshire Regiment, POW Germany, WWII.

LAXTON, Harold Raymond Wentworth (1948) Born 18 March 1928, 191 Lincoln Road, Peterborough; son of Harold Wadsley Laxton, Electrical and Mechanical Engineer, and Muriel Wentworth Collier; m Barbara; 3 sons (Simon, Tim and Chris), 1 daughter (Helen). **Subject(s):** History/Law; BA 1950; MA 1955. **Tutor(s):** F Thistlethwaite. **Johnian Relatives:** father of Timothy Raymond Laxton (1977). **Educ:** St Marks Junior School, Peterborough; King's School, Peterborough. **Career:** Able Seaman, RN 1951; Articled to Charles Greenwood, Solicitor, Peterborough; Head of Litigation Department 1951. **Appointments:** Member, Peterborough City Council 1962; Chairman, Finance Committee 1967; Deputy Mayor 1968; Leader, Council 1969; Member, Peterborough Development Corporation Board 1968; Mayor 1973. **Awards:** Munsteven Exhibition, SJC. Died 7 June 1980.

LAYARD, Arthur Frank Capel (1919) Naval Officer.

LAYCOCK, Dr Handley Theodore (1927) Born 5 October 1910, Lanchowfu, Kansu, China; son of Albert Penard Laycock, Medical Practitioner, and Winifred Hingston; m Winifred Worth, 1 January 1949, Garrison Church, Hargeisa, British Somaliland. **Subject(s):** Natural Sciences; BA 1932; MA 1936; BChir 1935; MB 1935; LRCP; FRCS. **Tutor(s):** M P Charlesworth. **Johnian Relatives:** son of Albert Penard Laycock (1895); brother of John Dixon Laycock (1930). **Educ:** St Paul's Preparatory School, Colet Court; St Paul's School, London. **Career:** Surgical Specialist in England, Malta, India, Burma, Nationalist China and South Africa (Natal); 14th Army, Mentioned in Despatches, WWII; Medical Officer (surgical), British Somaliland 1948–1950; Medical Officer, Tanganyika 1950–1954; Surgeon Specialist, Nyasaland 1954–1964; Surgeon Superintendent, Bay of Islands Hospital, Kawakawa, New Zealand 1964–1974.

LAYCOCK, Dr John Dixon (1930) Born 13 September 1912, 32 Milton Road, Highgate, London; Son of Albert Penard Laycock, Medical Practitioner, and Winifred Hingston; m Lina Tubby (née Burges), 28 July 1950, Ruislip Baptist Church. MRCS 1937; BS 1938; MB 1938; LRCP 1937. **Tutor(s):** M P Charlesworth. **Johnian Relatives:** son of Albert Penard Laycock (1895); brother of Handley Theodore Laycock (1927). **Educ:** Colet Court Preparatory School, London; St Paul's School, London. **Career:** Chief Assistant, Department of Anaesthetics, Casualty Clinical Assistant and Resident Anaesthetist, St Thomas' Hospital; Resident Anaesthetist, Hillingdon County Hospital; House Physician, Bolingbroke Hospital.

LAYMAN, Felix Herbert (1918) Born 21 October 1879, Bexley Heath, Kent; son of Henry Layman, Surveyor, and Harriet Papineau. **Subject(s):** Law; BA 1920; LLB 1920. **Tutor(s):** R P Gregory. **Educ:** Mr Patmore's Private School, Wallington; Hurstpierpoint. **Career:** South African Constabulary 1902. **Honours:** MC. Died 18 April 1936.

LAYTON, Professor David (1943) Born 20 January 1925, Cleveland Nursing Home, Darlington; son of Arnold Layton, Railway Clerk, and Margaret Calvert, Teacher; m Eva Margaret Howarth, 1950; 2 sons (Mark and Matthew), 1 daughter (Alison). **Subject(s):** Natural Sciences; BA 1947; MA 1955; MSc (London) 1955; DLit (London) 1997. **Tutor(s):** C W Guillebaud. **Educ:** Coatham School, Redcar. **Career:** Research Officer, Industrial Scientific Research 1945–1947; Science Teacher, Bolton County Grammar School 1947–1949; Science Teacher, Royal Grammar School, Newcastle upon Tyne 1949–1960; Lecturer in Science Education 1960–1970, Inaugural Director, Centre for Studies in Science Education 1970–1982, Professor of Science Education 1973–1989

(Emeritus 1989–), University of Leeds. **Appointments:** Honorary Member, Association for Science Education; Visiting Professor, Monash University, Australia 1977; Visiting Professor, University of British Columbia 1982 and 1989; Visiting Professor, University of Linköping, Sweden 1984; Visiting Professor, Queen's University, Kingston, Canada 1993. **Honours:** OBE 1988. **Publications:** *Science for the People*, 1973; *Interpreters of Science*, 1984; (with E Jenkins, S Magill and A Davey) *Inarticulate Science? Perspectives on the Public Understanding of Science*; (with E Jenkins and G McCulloch) *Technological Revolution? The politics of school science and technology since 1945*; (ed) *Innovations in Science and Technology Education* (5 vols), UNESCO, 1986–1994.

LAYTON, Frank Michael (1927) Born 10 June 1909, 38 Ablewell Street, Walsall, Staffordshire; son of Frank George Layton, Physician, and Dorothea Yonge. BA 1931; MA 1934. **Tutor(s):** J M Wordie. **Johnian Relatives:** brother of Ronald Allinson Layton (1920) and of Paul Henry Layton (1922). **Educ:** The Manor House, Horsham; Epsom College. **Career:** Schoolmaster; Probation Officer 1931. Died 5 October 1988.

LAYTON, His Honour Paul Henry (1922) Born 11 July 1905, 38 Ablewell Street, Walsall, Staffordshire; son of Frank George Layton, Physician and Surgeon, and Dorothea Yonge; m Frances Evelyn Weekes, 12 August 1950, St George's Church, Goderich, Ontario; 2 sons (Alexander and Geoffrey). **Subject(s):** Law; BA 1927; MA 1947. **Tutor(s):** B F Armitage. **Johnian Relatives:** brother of Ronald Allinson Layton (1920) and of Frank Michael Layton (1927). **Educ:** St Peter's School, Seaford; Epsom College; St Mary's Grammar School, Walsall. **Career:** Called to the Bar, Inner Temple 1929; Oxford Circuit, with Chambers in Birmingham 1930–1939; Commissioned, RAFVR (demobilised with rank of Squadron Leader) 1939–1945; Resumed practice at the Bar 1945; Recorder, Smethwick 1952–1964; Deputy Chairman, Staffordshire QS 1955–1965; Chairman, Agricultural Land Tribunal, West Midlands 1955–1965; Member, Mental Health Review Tribunal, Birmingham Region 1960–1965; Recorder, Walsall 1964–1965. **Appointments:** President, Medico-Legal Society 1983–1985. **Awards:** Paul Methuen Prize, Inner Temple 1929. Died 11 July 1989.

LAYTON, Ronald Allinson (1920) Born 25 June 1901, 38 Ablewell Street, Walsall, Staffordshire; son of Frank George Layton, Medical Practitioner, and Dorothea Yonge. BA 1925; MA 1947. **Tutor(s):** B F Armitage. **Johnian Relatives:** brother of Paul Henry Layton (1922) and of Frank Michael Layton (1927). **Educ:** Queen Mary's Grammar School, Walsall; St Peter's and St David's School, Seaford; Epsom College. **Career:** Assistant Master, St Martin's Preparatory School, Northwood, Middlesex; Partner in Norwood Preparatory School, Exeter. Died 1984.

LAZENBY, Eric Walter (1920) Born 20 February 1898, Middleborough, Bell County, Kentucky, USA; son of Walter Hebdon Lazenby, Secretary to a Limited Company, and Louisa Mary Marshall. **Tutor(s):** E E Sikes. **Educ:** King Edward VII School, Sheffield; Courtenay Lodge School, Abingdon.

LAZIER, Morley John Campbell (1928) Born 25 July 1903, Gonzales, Monterey County, California, USA; son of Arthur Kilgour Lazier, Businessman, and Nellie Ada McClory. **Tutor(s):** J M Wordie. **Educ:** Winnipeg Public Schools, Canada; Kelvin Technical High School, Winnipeg, Canada; University of Manitoba, Canada; University of Toronto, Canada.

LEACH, Donald Anthony (1947) Born 19 May 1925, 8 Gertrude Street, Grimsby, Lincolnshire; son of James Leach, Accountant, and Josephine Butt; m Joan; 1 son, 1 daughter. BA 1950. **Tutor(s):** G C L Bertram. **Educ:** Grove Park High School, Chiswick; Colet Court Preparatory School; St Paul's School. Died July 1999.

LEADMAN, Wilfrid Morley (1901) Born 24 August 1881, Boroughbridge, Yorkshire; son of Alexander Dionysius Hobson Leadman, Physician and Surgeon, and Annie Fountain Morley.

Subject(s): Theology; BA 1904. **Tutor(s):** J R Tanner; C E Graves. **Educ:** Pocklington School. **Awards:** John Stewart of Rannoch Scholarship in Hebrew, University of Cambridge 1902.

LEAKEY, Douglas Gray Bazett (1927) Born 18 October 1907, Kabete, Nairobi, Kenya, Africa; son of Harry Leakey, Clerk in Holy Orders and Canon of Mombassa, and Mary Bazett. **Subject(s):** Geography; BA 1931; MA 1949. **Tutor(s):** J M Wordie. **Johnian Relatives:** brother of Louis Seymour Bazett Leakey (1922). **Educ:** Gorse Cliff School, Boscombe; Weymouth College. **Career:** Assistant Conservator of Forests 1932–1955; Conservator of Forests, then Deputy Chief Conservator 1955–1962. **Honours:** OBE 1954.

LEAKEY, The Revd Herbert Nettleton (1909) Born 20 February 1890, Blaby Rectory, Wigston, Leicestershire; son of Charles Montague Leakey, Medical Practitioner, and Agnes Edwards. **Subject(s):** Classics; BA 1912. **Tutor(s):** J R Tanner. **Johnian Relatives:** brother of Richard John Montague Leakey (1919). **Educ:** Stamford School; Ripon Clergy College. **Career:** Deacon 1913; Curate, St Paul, Devonport 1913–1914; Priest 1914; Curate, Charles, Plymouth 1914–1917; Temporary CF, 4th Class, RACD, until 1917. **Awards:** Marquess of Exeter Exhibition, SJC 1909. Died 23 June 1917 (at Dar-es-Salaam, of sunstroke).

LEAKEY, Dr Louis Seymour Bazett (1922) Born 7 August 1903, Church Missionary Station, Kikuyu, Nairobi, Kenya, Africa; son of Harry Leakey, Clerk in Holy Orders, and Mary Bazett; m (1) Henrietta Wilfreda Avern, 1928, (2) Mary Douglas Nicol, 1936; (1) 1 son, 1 daughter; (2) 3 sons. **Subject(s):** Modern and Medieval Languages/Anthropology; BA 1926; MA 1929; PhD 1930; Honorary DSc (Oxford); FBA 1958. **Tutor(s):** E A Benians. **Johnian Relatives:** brother of Douglas Gray Bazett Leakey (1927). **Educ:** Gorse Cliff School, Boscombe; Sangeen Preparatory School, Bournemouth; Weymouth College. **Career:** Various Expeditions to East Africa 1925–1935; Title A Fellow, SJC 1929–1934; Head, African Section, Special Branch, CID, Kenya, WWII; Curator and Honorary Director, Coryndon Institute, Nairobi 1945–1961; Official Translator during part of the Trial of Jomo Kenyatta. **Appointments:** Herbert Spencer Lecturer, Oxford 1960–1961; Honorary Fellow, SJC 1966–1972; Trustee, National Parks of Kenya; Trustee, Kenya Wild Life Society; Vice President, East African Kennel Club. **Awards:** Viking Medal, Wenner-Gren Foundation, Royal Anthropological Institute 1962; Vega Medal, Swedish Society of Anthropology and Geography 1963; Founder's Royal Medal, Royal Geographical Society 1964; 1851 Exhibition Research Studentship; Swedish Andre Medal; Pitt-Rivers Memorial Medal, Royal Anthropological Institute; Henry Stopes Medal, Geological Society of London; Cuthbert Peek Medal, Royal Geographical Society; Sizarship, SJC. **Publications:** *The Stone Age Cultures of Kenya Colony; The Stone Age Races of Kenya; Adam's Ancestors; Stone Age Africa; Mau Mau and the Kikuyu; Defeating Mau Mau; Olduvai Gorge; Olduvai Gorge 1951–1961; Memoirs: White African, By The Evidence; Excavations at the Njoro River Cave.* Died 1 October 1972.

LEAKEY, Richard John Montague (1919) Born 27 November 1894, Caistor, Lincolnshire; son of Charles Montague Leakey, Medical Practitioner, and Agnes Edwards; m Edith Mary Down, 19 July 1923, St Decuman's, Watchet; 1 daughter (Sarah). BA 1921. **Tutor(s):** E E Sikes. **Johnian Relatives:** brother of Herbert Nettleton Leakey (1909). **Educ:** Stamford School; Callington School. Died 4 August 1981.

LEAN, James Hugh John (1938) Born 14 October 1919, 1 Richmond Park Road, Clifton, Bristol; son of James Vincent Lean, Farmer/Captain, Reserve Cavalry, and Contance Mary Holley; BA 1947. **Tutor(s):** J S Boys Smith. **Educ:** Naish House, Burnham-on-Sea; Malvern College; Petter Engineering Works, Yeovil.

LEAN, Leslie John Lawrance (1919) Born 28 July 1899, 34 Paddenswick Road, Hammersmith, Middlesex; son of John Frederick Lean, Accountant, and Florence Mary Platt; m Phoebe Weismann, 9 July 1929, St Anne's Church, Kew; 2 sons (John Leonard b 30 May 1930 and

Christopher b 5 December 1931), 1 daughter (Lois Elizabeth b 2 November 1938). **Subject(s):** History/Anthropology; BA 1921; MA 1925; BSc Econ (London); MInstT. **Tutor(s):** E A Benians. **Johnian Relatives:** father of Christopher Lean (1951). **Educ:** Latymer Upper School, Hammersmith. **Career:** Great Western Railway (later British Rail): initially based at Paddington Station, secondment to study the methods of the German Railways 1928–1930, Assistant Docks Manager, Cardiff Docks 1931–1942, four months in China studying the organisation of the Chinese Railways 1935, Manager, Millbay Docks 1942–1959, secondment to manage the port of Takoradi, the Gold Coast (now Ghana) 1943. **Awards:** Scholarship, SJC 1917. Died 24 July 1972.

LEAPER, Professor Robert Anthony Bernard (1940) Born 7 June 1921, 60 Manville Road, Balham, London; son of William Bambrick Leaper, Teacher under the London County Council, and Gertrude Ann Elizabeth Harriet Taylor, Teacher; m Elizabeth Arno, 1950; 2 sons, 1 daughter. **Subject(s):** English; BA 1949; MA 1951; MA (Oxon) 1960; Diploma, Public and Social Administration (Oxon) 1960; Docteur *Honoris Causa*, Université de Rennes 1987; DUniv (Surrey) 1992. **Tutor(s):** C W Guillebaud. **Educ:** Wimbledon College; Ratcliffe College, Leicester. **Career:** Coal Miner 1942–1945; Warden, St John Bosco Youth Centre, Stepney 1945–1947; Cadet Officer, Civil Service 1949–1950; Education Officer, Co-operative College, Stanford Hall, Loughborough 1950–1956; Principal, Social Welfare Training Centre, Zambia 1956–1960; Lecturer, Senior Lecturer, then Acting Director, Social Administration, University College, Swansea 1960–1970; Professor of Social Policy and Administration, University of Exeter 1970–1986; Professor Emeritus of Social Administration, Postgraduate Medical School, University of Exeter 1997–2002; Consultant, National Care Standards Commission 2002–2004. **Appointments:** Chairman, National Association of Councils of Voluntary Service 1958–1967; Chairman, South West Manpower Services Commission 1963–1980; Executive, later Vice-Chairman, National Council of Social Service 1964–1980; President, European Region, International Council on Social Welfare 1971–1979; Chairman, Area Board, MSC 1975–1986; Governor, Centre for Policy on Ageing 1982–1988; Visiting Lecturer, Roehampton Institute, University of Surrey 1986–1994; Visiting Professor of Social Policy, University of Surrey, Roehampton 1986–1997; Chairman, Exeter Age Concern 1996; Chairman, Age Concern England Training Committee 1996; Lay Inspector of Nursing and Residential Care Homes, Devon Health Authority 1999; Trustee, Positive Lifestyle 2000–; Fellow, Centre for Social Policy, Dartington Hall. **Awards:** Médaille de l'École Nationale de Santé France 1975. **Honours:** CBE 1975. **Publications:** *Communities and Social Change*, 1966; (ed/contributor) *Community Work*, 1968, 2nd edition 1971; *Community Work*, 1969, 2nd edition 1972; (ed) *Social Policy & Administration*, Blackwells, 1973–1993; (with Ann Glynn-Jones) *Growing Older in a South Devon Town*, University of Exeter, 1975; *Health, Wealth and Housing*, 1980; (ed) *The European Communities*, Blackwells, 1980; *European Social Policy in Soldatos & Lasok; Change and Continuity*, Exeter, 1984; (with A Yoder) *Community Care – Myths and Realities*, Martinus Nijhoff, 1985; *At Home in Devon*, University of Exeter Press, 1986; *Age Speaks for Itself*, 1988; *Age Speaks for Itself in Europe*, 1993; *Research project on European older people's perceptions of five European Cities*, Blackwells, Oxford, December 1993; published final report on *Age Speaks for Itself in Europe* with support of European Commission, Brussels, August 1995; *Training & Qualifications for work with older people*, 1998; *Research report on Employment over 50: a study in Teignbridge*, 1999.

LEATHEM, George (1901) Born 21 December 1881, 2 Queen's Square, Belfast, Ireland; son of John Gaston Leathem, Bank Cashier, and Mary Rendle Stone; m Lesla (d 1960). **Subject(s):** Mathematics; BA 1904; MA 1920. **Tutor(s):** D MacAlister. **Johnian Relatives:** brother of John Gaston Leathem (1891); uncle of John Gaston Leathem (1925) and of Terence Robert Leathem (1930). **Educ:** Royal Academical Institution, Belfast; Queen's College, Belfast. **Career:** Collector and Judge, Indian Civil Service 1906–1922. **Publications:** *Songs of the Double Star*, 1911. Died 4 January 1953.

LEATHEM, John Gaston (1925) Born 14 May 1906, 5 Harvey Road, Cambridge; son of John Gaston Leathem, Fellow and Senior Bursar, SJC, and Annie Muir McMullan. **Subject(s):** Classics; BA 1929; MA 1935. **Tutor(s):** E E Sikes. **Johnian Relatives:** son of John Gaston Leathem (1891); nephew of George Leathem (1901); brother of Terence Robert Leathem (1930). **Educ:** St Faith's School, Cambridge; Marlborough College. **Career:** Assistant Master, St Lawrence College, Ramsgate 1933–1939; Headmaster, King Edward VII Grammar School, King's Lynn 1939–1945; Headmaster, Taunton School 1945–1966. **Appointments:** President, Cambridge Union Society Lent Term 1929; JP, Somerset 1953. Died 13 July 1984.

LEATHEM, Terence Robert (1930) Born 31 July 1911, 5 Harvey Road, Cambridge; son of John Gaston Leathem, Fellow and Senior Bursar, SJC, and Annie Muir McMullan; m Mary Parkin; 1 son, 1 daughter. **Subject(s):** History/Modern and Medieval Languages; BA 1933; MA 1937. **Tutor(s):** C W Guillebaud. **Johnian Relatives:** son of John Gaston Leathem (1891); nephew of George Leathem (1901); brother of John Gaston Leathem (1925). **Educ:** St Faith's School, Cambridge; Marlborough College. **Career:** Teacher, King's College School, Wimbledon and Christ's Hospital, Horsham; TA 1937; Military Intelligence, working on the Ultra operation, Bletchley Park, decoding and assessing German radio communications 1940–1945; Headmaster, Ludlow Grammar School 1945–1950; Headmaster, Caterham School, Surrey 1950–1973. **Appointments:** Secretary, Easter Term 1932, Vice-President, Michaelmas Term 1932, President, Lent Term 1933, Cambridge Union Society. **Awards:** Sizarship, SJC. Died 11 September 1991.

LEATON, Esmond Harold (1948) Born 12 July 1928, Grosvenor Nursing Home, 42 Forest Road, Nottingham; son of John Esmond Leaton, Bank Officer, and Kathleen Goode; m Joy Suzanne; 4 sons (Nicholas, David, Peter and Christopher). **Subject(s):** Mathematics; BA 1950; MA 1955. **Tutor(s):** J M Wordie. **Educ:** Radcliffe House School, Nottingham; West Bridgford County Secondary School; Solihull Grammar School. **Career:** Assistant Master, Brighton College 1952–1954; Assistant Master, St Marylebone Grammar School 1954–1959; Lecturer, Avery Hill College of Education 1959–1966; UNESCO 1966–1974; Her Majesty's Inspector of Education 1974–1988. **Awards:** Minor Scholarship, SJC 1945.

LE COUTEUR, Professor Kenneth James (1938) Born 16 September 1920, St Helier, Jersey; son of Philip Le Couteur, Builder and Plate Glass Merchant, and Eva Gartrell, Teacher; m Enid Domville; 3 daughters (Caroline, Penelope and Mary). **Subject(s):** Mathematics; BA 1941; MA 1945; PhD 1949; FAA 1960. **Tutor(s):** J M Wordie. **Johnian Relatives:** brother-in-law of Alan Ratcliffe Domville (1947). **Educ:** Victoria College, Jersey, Channel Islands. **Career:** Bletchley Park, WWII; Title A Fellow, SJC 1945–1948; Turner and Newall Fellowship, University of Manchester 1948–1951; Reader in Theoretical Physics, University of Liverpool 1951–1955; Professor of Theoretical Physics, ANU, Canberra 1955–1985 (Emeritus 1985). **Awards:** Scholarship, SJC; Wright's Prize, SJC; Major Scholarship, SJC 1937; Mayhew Prize, University of Cambridge 1941. **Publications:** Scientific papers.

LEDGARD, The Revd Canon Thomas Callinan (1935) Born 22 July 1916, Evelyn Hall, Mussoorie, United Provinces, India; son of Ralph Gilbert Ledgard, Clerk in Holy Orders, and Winifred Edmund Callinan; m Aline Jeannette Hardy, 29 September 1942. BA 1938; MA 1950. **Tutor(s):** R L Howland. **Johnian Relatives:** nephew of Walter Hubert Ledgard (1893). **Educ:** Tonstall Preparatory School, Sunderland; Durham School; Westcott House, Cambridge. **Career:** Ordained Deacon, Durham 1939; Curate, Bishopswearmouth 1939–1942; Ordained Priest, Durham 1940; Curate, Ryhope 1942–1944; Vicar, St Michael and All Angels, Norton, Durham 1944–1946; Vicar, Warcop and Rector, Musgrave, Westmorland 1946–1950; Rector, Fulbourn, Cambridgeshire, 1950–1956; Vicar, Kirkby Lonsdale with Mansergh 1956–1959; Vicar, Cartmel 1969; Honorary Canon, Carlisle 1970; Priest in charge, Warcop, Musgrave, Soulby and Crosby Garret, Carlisle 1979–1982. **Awards:** Reading Prize, SJC 1937. Died 30 March 1999.

LEE, Arthur Guy (1937) Born 5 November 1918, 13 Prince's Gate, Knightsbridge; son of Harry Lee, Eye Specialist, and Mabel Ellis Allday; m Helen Elizabeth Whitley, 13 January 1945, Halifax Parish Church; 2 adopted sons (Robert Antony b 19 September 1952 and Timothy Guy b 6 August 1953). **Subject(s):** Classics; BA 1940; MA 1945. **Tutor(s):** R L Howland. **Johnian Relatives:** son of Harry Lee (1901). **Educ:** Glebe House, Hunstanton; Loretto School. **Career:** Captain, Royal Corps of Signals; Title A Fellow 1945–1948 (suspended for war service 1945–1946), Title B Fellow 1948–1982, Lecturer in Classics 1948–1982, Librarian 1961–1984, Title D Fellow 1982–, SJC; Lecturer in Classics, University of Cambridge 1949–1982. **Appointments:** Tutor 1949–1956, Praelector 1956–1961, SJC. **Awards:** McAulay Scholarship, SJC 1936; John Stewart of Rannoch Scholarship, University of Cambridge 1939; Browne Medal for Latin Ode, University of Cambridge 1939; Earle Prize 1939; Top Prize in the Certamen Vaticanum for a Latin poem on 'An Ascent by Spacecraft to the Moon', Latinitas, 1954. **Publications:** (ed) Ovid, *Metamorphoses*, CUP, 1953; (introduction and notes) Cicero, *Paradoxa Stoicorum*, Macmillan, 1953; (trans) *Ovid's Amores*, Murray, 1968; (ed and trans) *Tibullus: Elegies*, Lee, 1975, 2nd edition Cairns, 1982, 3rd edition, Cairns, 1990 including Book 3; (trans and notes) *Virgil's Eclogues*, Cairns, 1980, Penguin, 1984; (trans) *The Satires of Persius*, Cairns, 1987; (ed) *The Poems of Catullus*, World's Classics, 1991; (trans and notes) Propertius, *The Poems*, World's Classics, 1991; 'Calpurnius Siculus Eclogues', Boyle & Sullivan *Roman Poets of the Early Empire*, Penguin, 1991; (ed) *Horace: Odes and Carmen Saeculare*, Cairns, 1998.

LEE, Eric Hanson (1914) Born 7 November 1895, Whitchurch, Shropshire; son of Leonard Lee, Chemist, and Annie Elizabeth Hanson. **Tutor(s):** R P Gregory. **Educ:** Whitchurch Grammar School. **Career:** Second Lieutenant, King's Shropshire Light Infantry, France 1914–1916. Died 19 September 1916 (killed in action).

LEE, Harry (1901) Born 8 December 1882, Soothill Nether, Yorkshire; son of Arthur Lee, Blanket Manufacturer, and Phebe Ridgway; m Mabel Ellis Allday; 2 sons (Arthur Guy b 5 November 1918 and Miles Allday b 6 May 1914). BA 1905; MB 1910; BChir 1910; LRCP 1909; FRCS 1911. **Tutor(s):** L H K Bushe-Fox; D MacAlister. **Johnian Relatives:** father of Arthur Guy Lee (1937). **Educ:** Tettenhall College. **Career:** Captain, RAMC (TF), WWI; Ophthalmic Surgeon to Leeds Public Dispensary 1914; Lecturer in Ophthalmology, University of Leeds; Honorary Ophthalmic Surgeon, Leeds General Infirmary. **Appointments:** England Rugby player (war years). Died 11 January 1933.

LEE, Tun Sir Hau Shik (1921) Born 19 November 1902, Canton, China; son of Kwai Lim Lee, Chinese Government, and Kwoo Chun; m (1) Dawn Kathleen Glen, 1922 (d 1926), (2) Kwan Choi Lin, 1929; (1) 2 sons (Douglas Kim Kiu and Vivian Leslie Heong Kong), (2) 4 sons (Robert Kut Lung, George Yau Lung b 3 June 1931, Cecil Siew Lung b 27 February 1934, Thomas Mun Lung b 8 January 1938, and Alexander Yu Lung b 25 May 1939 d 31 October 1999), 2 daughters (Violet Suet Lan b 26 November 1932 and Jasmine Suet Ngor b 13 April 1936). **Subject(s):** Economics; BA 1924; MA 1978. **Tutor(s):** E A Benians. **Johnian Relatives:** father of Thomas Mun Lung Lee (1956) and of Alexander Yu Lung Lee (1957). **Educ:** The Christian College, Canton; Queen's College, Hong Kong. **Career:** Chief, Passive Defence Forces, Kuala Lumpur 1941; Colonel, Allied Armed Forces 1942–1945; Co-founder, Alliance Party 1949; Minister of Transport 1953–1956; Minister of Finance 1956–1959. **Appointments:** Council Member, Federated Malay States Chamber of Mines 1929–1955; President, Selangor Chinese Chamber of Commerce 1936–1955; JP 1938; President, Selangor Miners Club 1938; President, Miners Association, Negeri Sembilan, Selangor & Pahang 1938–1955; Member, Federal Finance Committee 1946–1956; Member, War Damage Commission 1946–1956; Member, Tin Advisory Committee 1946–1955; Member, Chinese Tin Mines Rehabilitation Loans Board 1946–1959; Member, Council of State, Selangor 1946–1947; President, All Malaya Chinese Mining Association 1946–1955; Member, Malayan Tin Delegation to all International Tin Meetings 1946–1960; Member, Malayan Union Advisory Council 1946–1947; President, Kuen Cheng

Girls' School 1945–1952; Member, Kuala Lumpur Sanitary Board 1946–1958; President, Associated Chinese Chambers of Commerce, Malaya and Singapore 1947–1955; Member, Director of Operations Committee 1948–1955; Member, Federal Executive Council 1948–1957; President, All Malaya Kochow Association 1949; President, Selangor Malaysian Chinese Association 1949–1956; President, United Lees Association 1949–1959; Member, Alliance Executive Committee and Alliance National Council 1953–1959; Member, Merdeka Mission to London (negotiating independence from the British) 1956; Chairman, Federal Finance Committee 1956–1959; Member, Financial Mission to London 1957; Chairman, Political, Organisation, Election and Membership Standing Sub-Committee, Malaysian Chinese Association 1957–1959; President, Federation of Malaya Red Cross Society 1957–1962; President, Federation of Malaya Olympic Council 1957–1959; President, Senior Golfers Society of Malaya 1957–1958, 1960–1963; President, Oxford and Cambridge Society 1959–1964; President, Malaysian Golf Association 1960–1975; President, Federation of Kwang Tung Associations 1962; President, Selangor Kwang Tung Association 1962; Vice President, Malaysian Zoological Society 1965; President, Royal Commonwealth Society 1969–1973; Honorary President, Wine and Food Society, Kuala Lumpar 1970; Vice Patron, Royal Commonwealth Society 1973; Patron, Malaysian Golf Association, 1975; Vice Chairman, Institute Bank Malaysia 1977; Chairman, China Press Limited, Kuala Lumpur; Chartered Bank Trustee Berhad, Kuala Lumpur; Development & Commercial Bank (Ltd), Berhad, Kuala Lumpur; Golden Castle Finance Corporation (Malaysia) Berhad, Kuala Lumpur; On Tai Development Sdn Berhad, Kuala Lumpur; Chairman, Board of Governors, Lady Templer Hospital, Kuala Lumpur; Director and Vice-Chairman, Golden Castle Finance Corporation Ltd, Singapore. **Awards:** Isaac Newton Studentship, 1921–1923. **Honours:** CBE 1948; KBE 1957; SMN 1959. Died 22 June 1988.

LEEMING, John Coates (1945) Born 3 May 1927, 94 Higher Wood Street, Middleton, Lancashire; son of James Arthur Leeming, Assistant Works Manager, and Harriet Coates; m (1) Dorothy Carter, 1949 (dis 1972); (2) Cheryl Elise Kendall Gillan, 1985; (1) 2 sons (Barry b 1950 and Peter b 1959). **Subject(s):** Mathematics; BA 1948; MA 1960. **Tutor(s):** J M Wordie. **Educ:** Durnford Street Council School; Elm Street Council School; Mills Hill Council School; Chadderton Grammar School. **Career:** Teaching 1948–1950; Civil Service, HM Customs and Excise 1950–1956; HM Treasury 1956–1958; HM Customs and Excise 1958–1967; World Bank (IBRD) Washington DC 1967–1970; Civil Service Department 1970–1975; Commissioner of Customs and Excise 1975–1978; DTI 1978–1985; British National Space Centre, serving as Director General on retirement 1985–1988; Consultant to aerospace companies and space agencies 1988–1997. **Awards:** Exhibition, SJC 1945; Scholarship, SJC 1946.

LEES, George Milne (1949) Born 8 November 1928, Woodfield Maternity Home, Manchester Road, Oldham, Lancashire; son of Fred Lees, Company Secretary, Cotton Mill, and Hilda Mary Schofield; m Olive Whitelegg, March 1953; 2 daughters (Helen b 1954 and Catherine b 1957). **Subject(s):** Modern and Medieval Languages; BA 1952; MA 1956. **Tutor(s):** C W Guillebaud. **Educ:** Byron Street Council School, Royton; Hulme Grammar School, Oldham. **Career:** Graduate Trainee, then Production Control in Drop Stamping Division, Daniel Doncaster & Sons Ltd, Sheffield 1952–1956; Senior Methods Engineer, Greengate & Irwell Rubber Co Ltd, Salford 1956–1957; Organisation and Methods Officer, National Coal Board, North West Division, Manchester 1957–1963; Commercial Computer Services Northern Sales Manager, IC Ltd (Manchester) 1963–1966; Management Services Manager and Spares Department Manager, Seddon Atkinson Vehicle Group Ltd 1966–1972; Managing Director, MPI (North Lancashire) Ltd 1972–1978; Sub-Postmaster, Stanton St John 1978–1993.

LEES, George Thomas (1914) Born 4 November 1895, 313 Oldham Road, Royton, Lancashire; son of John George Lees, Sub-manager, Cotton Spinning, and Alice Ann Clegg. **Subject(s):** Mathematics/Law;

BA 1920; LLB 1920. **Tutor(s):** L H K Bushe-Fox. **Educ:** Stanley Road Council School; Hulme Grammar School. **Career:** Called to the Bar, Gray's Inn 1922; On Parliamentary Register 1947. **Awards:** Exhibition, SJC; Adams Memorial Prize, SJC 1916.

LEES, Dr John Francis (1945) Born 22 October 1927, Queen Victoria Nursing Institution, Wolverhampton; son of Francis Charles Lees, Medical Practitioner, and Elizabeth Gaylor. **Subject(s):** Natural Sciences; BA 1948; BChir 1950; MB 1950; FFARCS 1963. **Tutor(s):** G C L Bertram. **Educ:** St John's Preparatory School, Alton Castle; Ratcliffe College. **Career:** Consultant Anaesthetist, St Helier Hospital, Carshalton, Surrey 1965–1993.

LEES, Roland James (1936) Born 3 December 1917, 30 Tame Street, West Bromwich, Staffordshire; son of Roland John Lees, Railway Signalman, and Ada Bell Jeavons. **Subject(s):** Natural Sciences; BA 1939; MA 1943; BSc (London) 1939. **Tutor(s):** C W Guillebaud. **Educ:** Hill Street Council School, Stourbridge; Brooks Street Council School, Stourbridge; King Edward VI Grammar School, Stourbridge. **Career:** Air Ministry Research Establishment, Dundee; Principal Scientific Officer, Ministry of Supply 1939–1959; Head of Instrument and Photographic Department, RAE; Deputy Director (Equipment), RAE, Farnborough 1959–1966; Director, Royal Radar Establishment, Malvern 1972. **Awards:** Scholarship, SJC 1936–1937; Wright's Prize, SJC 1937. Died 8 November 1985.

LEES, Ronald Samuel Mann (1939) Born 24 March 1920, 51 Chesterton Road, Cambridge; son of Samuel Lees, Professor of Mechanical Engineering, and Elsie Elizabeth Mann; m Annette. **Subject(s):** Natural Sciences; BA 1942. **Tutor(s):** J M Wordie. **Johnian Relatives:** son of Samuel Lees (1906). **Educ:** Durston House Preparatory School; Tonbridge School. **Career:** Flying Officer, RAF 1939–1944. Died 6 August 1944.

LEES, Professor Samuel (1906) Born 26 August 1885, Salford, Manchester; son of Samuel Henry Lees, Oil Merchant, and Sarah Hannah Shearman; m Elsie Elizabeth Mann; 2 sons. **Subject(s):** Mathematics; BA 1909; MA 1913. **Tutor(s):** L H K Bushe-Fox. **Johnian Relatives:** father of Ronald Samuel Mann Lees (1939). **Educ:** St Clement's School, Broughton; Central Board School, Manchester; Municipal School of Technology, Manchester. **Career:** Foundress Fellow, SJC 1912–1929; Reader in Applied Thermodynamics, University of Manchester 1913–1915; Engineer, Navy 1915–1918; Hopkinson Lecturer in Thermodynamics, University of Cambridge 1919–1929; Consultant Engineer to Silica Gel Ltd, Baltimore, USA 1929–1931; Professor of Mechanical Engineering, University of Birmingham 1931–1940. **Appointments:** Director of Studies in Engineering, SJC 1925–1929. **Awards:** Scholarship, SJC 1907; Hutchinson Studentship, SJC 1911; Rayleigh Prize and John Winbolt Prize, University of Cambridge 1911. Died 27 January 1940.

LEESER, Herbert (1907) Born 4 September 1888, Hildesheim, Hanover, Germany; son of Max Leeser, Bank Director and Royal Prussian Councillor of Commerce, and Selma Hein. **Tutor(s):** J R Tanner. **Educ:** Konigliches Gymnasium, Andreanum.

LEESON, Patrick George (1933) Born 17 July 1915, Darjeeling, Bengal, India; son of George William Leeson, Engineer and Naval Architect, and Bertha Medland Rendell; m Anne Pamela Foster, 27 July 1946, Malvern Priory, Great Malvern, Worcestershire; 1 son (George Rendall b 9 November 1951), 2 daughters (Lindsay Medland b 8 April 1947 and Cynthia Annette b 6 February 1949). **Subject(s):** Mechanical Sciences; BA 1936. **Tutor(s):** J S Boys Smith. **Educ:** Link School, Malvern; Malvern College. **Career:** Commissioned, Auxiliary Air Force, 605 Squadron, Castle Bromwich 1936; Flying Officer, then Flight Lieutenant, WWII, POW various camps including Stalag Luft 111; various managerial positions, International Division, British United Shoe Machinery Company, until 1965; Managing Director, Vaughan Crane Company (subsidiary of the Herbert Morris Group) 1965–1976. Died 12 May 1997.

LEE WARNER, Roland Paul (1911) Born 4 January 1893, 4 Howard Square, Eastbourne, Sussex; son of Sir William Lee Warner, Member, Council of India, and Ellen Paullina Holland. **Tutor(s):** J R Tanner. **Johnian Relatives:** son of William Lee Warner (1865). **Educ:** Rugby School; Slade School of Art. **Career:** Private, The Queen's (Royal West Surrey) Regiment, WWI; POW 1918. Died 8 February 1960.

LEFÈVRE, Edward (1920) Born 1 October 1901, 27 Spinkfield Road, Birkby, Huddersfield; son of William Lefèvre, 2nd Master and Senior Science Master, Huddersfield College, and Laura Ellen Green. **Subject(s):** Mathematics/Natural Sciences; BA 1923. **Tutor(s):** B F Armitage. **Educ:** Preparatory School (Private); Huddersfield College. **Awards:** Sizarship, SJC.

LEFTWICH, Richard Alfred (1924) Born 29 April 1906, Pentland View, Colinton, Edinburgh; son of Charles Gerrans Leftwich, Indian Civil Service, and Evadne Fawcus. BA 1927. **Tutor(s):** E A Benians. **Johnian Relatives:** son of Charles Gerrans Leftwich (1891). **Educ:** Durleston Court, Swanage; Shrewsbury School; Victoria College, Jersey.

LEGG, Francis Benjamin Stuart (1928) Born 31 August 1910, 15 Mitcham Park, Mitcham, Surrey; son of Arthur Stuart Legg, Solicitor, and Ethel Green; m Margaret Bonté Sheldon Amos, 19 March 1932; 3 sons (Thomas Stuart, Robert Alexander and Charles Francis), 1 daughter (Ruth Margaret). BA 1931; MA 1950. **Tutor(s):** J M Wordie. **Johnian Relatives:** father of Thomas Stuart Legg (1955). **Educ:** Rose Hill, Banstead; Marlborough College. **Career:** Empire Marketing Board Film Unit: Editor, *Coalface* (documentary) 1935; Editor, *Night Mail* (documentary) 1936; Film Producer, The Film Centre for Shell (including *The Rival World*, *A Light in Nature*, *Powered Flight*, *Three Dawns to Sydney* and *The Heartland*); Founder, Film Centre 1938–1939; National Film Board, Ottawa, Canada, with John Grierson 1939–1948. Died 23 July 1988.

LEGH-JONES, Peter Edward Legh (1943) Born 18 November 1924, 17 Wellington Square, Hastings; son of Edward Raymond Legh-Jones, Squadron Leader, RAF, and Gwendoline Violet Rosamond Cope; m Patricia Ann. **Tutor(s):** C W Guillebaud. **Educ:** Sacred Heart College, Hastings; Hastings Grammar School; Mayfield College. **Career:** Shell Oil Company, USA.

LEIGH, Philip Mark (1948) Born 2 January 1930, 2 Queensdown Road, Hackney, London; son of Morris Leigh, Cabinet Maker, and Rose Silverstein; m Jacqueline Freeman, 2 sons (Howard and Trevor), 1 daughter (Juliet). **Subject(s):** Law; BA 1951; MA 1955; FCIB. **Tutor(s):** F Thistlethwaite. **Educ:** Salisbury Road Elementary School; Royal Grammar School, High Wycombe; Haberdashers' Aske's School, Hampstead. **Career:** Managing Director, Bolton Building Society; Called to the Bar, Middle Temple 1952. **Appointments:** Member, Jewish Welfare Board; Member, Farrand Commission on Conveyancing; Vice-President, National Association of Estate Agents. Died 9 October 1987.

LEIGH-SARNEY, Harvey Frederick (1920) Born 23 March 1903, Heath View, Southborough, Kent; son of Frederick Elwyn Leigh Sarney, Tutor, and Florence Mary Jetter. **Tutor(s):** E E Sikes. **Educ:** Westerleigh School, St Leonards-on-Sea; Clifton College.

LE MAITRE, Sir Alfred Sutherland (1918) Born 13 June 1896, Flint Cottage, Rottingdean, Sussex; son of Alfred George Le Maitre, Headmaster of Preparatory School, and Katherine Cadell Bell; m Evelyn Elsie Martelli, 29 July 1931, Lincoln's Inn Chapel; 2 sons. **Subject(s):** Classics; BA 1920; MA 1925. **Tutor(s):** E E Sikes. **Educ:** St Salvators, St Andrews; Fettes College, Edinburgh. **Career:** 7th Battalion, Black Watch 1914–1918; Administration, Fleet Air Arm, Admiralty 1920; Member, Mission to HM Dockyards, Far East 1930; Head, Civil Establishments Branch, Admiralty 1938; Under-Secretary to Admiralty Delegation to Washington 1944; Principal Assistant Secretary 1945;

Under-Secretary 1946; Under-Secretary to the Board of Trade 1947–1948; Controller of Ground Services 1948–1957. **Awards:** Scholarship, SJC 1914. **Honours:** MC; CB 1945; KBE 1951. Died 22 March 1959.

LENDON, Dr Nelson Courtney (1927) Born 21 August 1909, Carvabius, Lanteglos, Camelford, Cornwall; son of Samuel Courtney Lendon, Farmer, and Clara Maud Roose; m Ellen Johnson Cramb McNeill; 2 sons (John Courtney b 10 August 1941 and Clive Courtney b 21 August 1942). **Subject(s):** Natural Sciences; BA 1930; MA 1935; BChir 1935; MB 1947; MD 1951; LMSSA, London; DPH, London. **Tutor(s):** M P Charlesworth. **Johnian Relatives:** father of John Courtney Lendon (1960). **Educ:** Miss Watson's Preparatory School, Camelford; Warwick School; St Mary's Hospital, Paddington. **Career:** Major, RAMC, WWII; Japanese POW, Burma/Siam Railway 1942–1945; Medical Officer, Queen Alexandra Hospital, Cosham, Hampshire 1950; General Medical Practitioner, South London then Kent, 1953 until retirement. **Appointments:** Chairman, Canterbury & East Kent Branch, English Speaking Union. **Awards:** Exhibition, SJC 1927; Sizarship, SJC 1927. **Publications:** *Drugs Aid* (Booklet). Died 14 March 1998.

LENNON, Derek Carlton (1946) Born 10 February 1928, Bampton Nursing Home, Barrack Road, Christchurch, Bournemouth, Hampshire; son of Joseph Lennon and Bessie May Carlton; m Sonja Zavadlav, 20 June 1953, Southampton; 2 daughters (Andria Melisanda b 12 May 1956, and Fiona Patrizia b 29 January 1961). **Subject(s):** Natural Sciences/Chemical Engineering; BA 1949; MA 1959; MEng 1992; MSCI; MAIChE. **Tutor(s):** G C L Bertram. **Educ:** Southbourne High School; Westbourne Preparatory School; Bournemouth School. **Career:** Military Service, Captain, Intelligence Corps 1951–1953; Director, Humphreys & Glasgow Ltd; Managing Director, later Chairman, Capital Plant International Ltd; Chairman, Capital Plant Investment Inc; Chairman, Oxford Virology plc; Director, Société de Construction d'Appareils pour Gaz a l'Eau et Gaz Industrielle. **Awards:** Major Scholarship, SJC 1945; Sir Stewart Goodwin Fellowship 1953.

LEONARD, John Gifford (1914) Born 26 January 1896, 20 Princess Road, South Hornsey, Middlesex; son of Charles Hare Leonard, Chemical Manufacturer, and Charlotte Rachel Butler. **Tutor(s):** R P Gregory. **Educ:** St Peter's, Broadstairs; Rugby School.

LEONARD, Percy James (1905) Born 15 January 1886, 1 Alexandra Road, Newport, Monmouthshire; son of William Frederick Leonard, Grocer, and Laura Howells. **Subject(s):** Natural Sciences; BA 1908. **Tutor(s):** D MacAlister. **Educ:** Newport Intermediate School. **Career:** Cranleigh School, Taunton School, then Carnarvon School 1913; Newport High School 1913–1915; Corporal, RASC, then Lieutenant, RGA 1915–1919; Mathematics Master, Southport Grammar School 1919–1922. **Awards:** Scholarship, SJC; Central Welsh Board Gold Medal 1905. Died 12 December 1922.

LESLIE, William (1919) Born 8 May 1901, 67 Osborne Place, Aberdeen, Scotland; son of William Leslie, of independent means, and Mary Barrow Stewart; m Avis Yalden Thomson, 31 September 1948. **Subject(s):** Modern and Medieval Languages/Economics; BA 1923; MA 1926. **Tutor(s):** E E Sikes. **Educ:** Aberdeen Grammar School; Mr Oldfield's Preparatory School, Torquay; Bishop's Stortford College.

LETHBRIDGE, Christopher John (1943) Born 18 March 1925, The Lodge, Waterbeach, Cambridgeshire; son of Thomas Charles Lethbridge, Honorary Keeper, Anglo-Saxon Antiquities, and Sylvia Frances Robertson. **Subject(s):** Natural Sciences; BA 1946; MA 1994. **Tutor(s):** S J Bailey. **Educ:** Stubbington House, Fareham; Wellington College. Died 1 February 1996.

LETHBRIDGE, John Anthony (1942) Born 29 December 1924, Bombay, India; son of John Louis Lethbridge, Indian Civil Service, and Eleanor Francesca Almeida. **Tutor(s):** C W Guillebaud. **Educ:** St Boniface's College, Plymouth.

LEUCHARS, John Noel (1934) Born 26 December 1915, Elmhurst, Cobham, Surrey; son of William Wood Leuchars, Barrister-at-Law, and Gwendoline Evelyn Flemming; m Elsa Hazel Parkes, 3 September 1949, Christ Church, Esher. **Subject(s):** Economics/Law; BA 1937. **Tutor(s):** C W Guillebaud. **Educ:** St Peter's Court, Broadstairs; Rugby School.

LEVERSEDGE, Leslie Frank (1923) Born 29 May 1904, Melton Constable, Norfolk; son of Frank Ernest Leversedge, Engineer, and Enid Daphney Eke; m; 2 sons, 3 daughters. BA 1926; MA 1930. **Tutor(s):** E A Benians. **Educ:** St Paul's School, Salafagar, Darjeeling; St Peter's School, York. **Career:** Barrister, Inner Temple 1936; Colonial Service, Northern Rhodesia 1960; British Council 1963–1975. **Honours:** CMG 1955. Died 12 June 1996.

LEVY, Cecil Herbert (LINDSEY) (1933) Born 25 January 1916, 24 Underwood Street, Spitalfields, London; son of Lewis Levy, Schoolmaster, and Dora Leah Herring; m Désirée; children. **Subject(s):** Law; BA 1937; MA 1940. **Tutor(s):** E A Benians. **Educ:** Goodall Road School; Leyton County High School. **Career:** RAF, WWII; Ministry of Labour. Died 12 March 2001.

LEVY, Leslie Charles (1906) Born 7 September 1888, Cliff Hill, Lucea, Hanover, Jamaica; son of Jacob Levy, Merchant, and Anna Lee. **Subject(s):** Law; LLB 1909. **Tutor(s):** L H K Bushe-Fox. **Educ:** Jamaica College, Kingston. **Career:** Gray's Inn 1909. **Awards:** Bacon Scholarship for Constitutional Law, Gray's Inn 1909.

LEVY, Dr Stanley Isaac (1909) Born 24 December 1890, 31 Islip Road, Kentish Town, Middlesex; son of David Levy, Master Fruiterer, and Catherine Parks; m Mary Victoria Emanuel. **Subject(s):** Natural Sciences; BA 1912; MA 1922; BSc (London) 1911; PhD (London) 1923; ARIC 1914; FRIC 1918; QC 1957. **Tutor(s):** J R Tanner. **Educ:** University College School, London; City of London School. **Career:** Chemical Assistant to Director General of Explosive Supplies 1914–1918; Called to the Bar 1927; Assistant Director of Filling Factories, Ministry of Supply 1939–1944. **Appointments:** Master of the Bench of the Middle Temple 1963; Meldola Medal Committee, Royal Institute of Chemistry 1956. **Publications:** *The Rare Earths*, 1915; *Modern Explosives*, 1920; *Incandescent Lighting*, 1922; *Introduction to Industrial Chemistry*, 1926. Died 12 November 1968.

LEWIN, Richard (1935) Born 20 August 1915, Sunny Croft River, Temple Ewell, Dover; son of Francis Hutchinson Laprimandaye Lewin, Governor, Dr Barnado's Homes, and Eva Gwenllian Hall. **Subject(s):** History/Moral Sciences; BA 1938; MA 1946; Diploma in Careers Guidance. **Tutor(s):** J S Boys Smith. **Educ:** Dover College Junior School; Dane Court School, Parkstone; Bryanston School; Ottershaw College, Chertsey. **Career:** Principal Careers Officer, Norfolk County Council. Died 11 June 1998.

LEWIS, Cecil Jack (1923) Born 29 July 1904, 34 Rectory Road, Walthamstow, Essex; son of Cecil Wilfred Lewis, Ostrich Feather Merchant, and Lizzie Edith Andrews. BA 1926; MA 1932; LLB 1927. **Tutor(s):** E E Sikes. **Educ:** Forest School, Walthamstow; Oswestry School, Salop; Brentwood School, Essex. **Career:** Consultant to Butcher & Barlow, Bank Street, Bury, Lancashire. **Awards:** Scholarship, SJC. Died 9 August 1988.

LEWIS, Charles Cedric Carr (1923) Born 11 December 1904, Lanherne, Axminster, Devon; son of Henry Charles Lewis, Bank Manager, and Beatrice Caroline Carr. **Subject(s):** English/Modern and Medieval Languages; BA 1927; MA 1930. **Tutor(s):** E E Sikes. **Educ:** Kingsland Grange, Shrewsbury; Exeter School.

LEWIS, David (1942) Born 21 October 1924, 61 Holliday Road, Handsworth, Birmingham; son of Benjamin Leo Lewis, Precious Stone Dealer, and Deborah Zeiman. **Subject(s):** Mathematics; BA 1945. **Tutor(s):** S J Bailey. **Educ:** Mrs Kimberley's Preparatory School,

Handsworth; George Dixon's Elementary School, Birmingham; King Edward's High School, Birmingham. **Career:** Research Department, Ministry of Aircraft Production, Millbank 1944–1947. Died 11 March 1947.

LEWIS, David Henry (1931) Born 23 February 1914, Dover Street, Bilston, Staffordshire; son of David Lewis, Ironfounder, and Mildred Clarissa Babb. BA 1935; MA 1939. **Tutor(s):** J M Wordie. **Educ:** Bilston High School; Secondary School, Ilfracombe; King Edward's High School, Birmingham. **Career:** Lieutenant Colonel, RA, TA. **Appointments:** Deputy Lieutenant for Staffordshire 1958. **Honours:** OBE (Military) 1954; TD. Died 24 January 1992.

LEWIS, David Lincoln (LINCOLN-LEWIS) (1925) Born 27 December 1906, Maesyffynon, Ystalyfera, Llanguicke, Glamorganshire; son of William James Lewis, GP, Medical Health Officer, Glamorgan, and Constance Mary Adeney. **Subject(s):** Natural Sciences; BA 1928; MA 1935; BChir 1935; MChir 1939; FRCS. **Tutor(s):** M P Charlesworth. **Johnian Relatives:** brother of Roland Swaine Lewis (1926) and of Edward Axford Lewis (1931). **Educ:** Ystalyfera Intermediate School; Epsom College. **Career:** Gynaecologist, Royal South Infirmary, Shrewsbury, Salop; St George's Hospital, Hyde Park Corner, London 1938. **Honours:** MC. Died 23 February 1998.

LEWIS, Dennis Stanley (1942) Born 25 June 1924, 143 Bethune Road, Stoke Newington, London; son of Keith Lewis, Manufacturing Furrier, and Mary Feldman. **Tutor(s):** S J Bailey. **Educ:** Tenterden Towers School, Hendon; Belmont Preparatory School, Mill Hill; St Paul's School.

LEWIS, Dudley George (1930) Born 8 May 1911, Rose Deep Mine, Germiston, Transvaal, South Africa; son of Harvey George Lewis, Chief Time Keeper, Rose Deep Mine, and Mary Ann Mitchel Fairweather. **Subject(s):** Geography/Economics; BA 1933. **Tutor(s):** C W Guillebaud. **Educ:** Glen Carn School, South Africa; Wycliffe College, Stonehouse. **Career:** Group Captain, RAF, WWII. **Honours:** Legion of Merit; DFC 1941.

LEWIS, Professor Dyfed (1947) Born 20 March 1926, Penfai, Traianmawr, Breconshire; son of David Lewis, Farmer, and Mary Jane Evans. **Subject(s):** Natural Sciences; BA 1949; MA 1953; MSc (Wales); PhD (Sheffield). **Tutor(s):** G C L Bertram. **Educ:** Brecon Grammar School; Cray Elementary School; University College of Wales, Aberystwyth. **Career:** Department of Microbiology, University of Sheffield 1949–1952; Member of Staff, Agricultural Research Council Institute of Animal Physiology 1952–1958; Lecturer in Agricultural Chemistry 1958–1961, Reader in Agricultural Chemistry 1961–1964, University of Nottingham; Professor of Agricultural Chemistry, University of Leeds 1964.

LEWIS, Dr Edmund Oliver (1906) (initially Non-Collegiate) Born 19 June 1882, Ton Pentre, Gelly, Ystradyfodwg, Glamorganshire; son of Edward Lewis, Colliery Overman, and Jane Thomas; m Mary Maud. **Subject(s):** Moral Sciences; BA 1907; MA 1911; BSc (Wales) 1903; DSc (London) 1910; MRCS; FRCP 1921. **Tutor(s):** J R Tanner. **Educ:** University College, Aberystwyth. **Career:** University Demonstrator in Experimental Psychology 1909–1911; Inspector under 1914 Mental Deficiency Act; Lord Chancellor's Medical Visitor in Lunacy. **Appointments:** Honorary Member, Royal Medico-Psychological Association. **Honours:** CBE 1957. Died 8 August 1965.

LEWIS, Edward Axford (1931) Born 24 June 1913, Tyrwaun, Ystalyfera, Llanguicke, Glamorganshire; son of William James Lewis, Medical Health Officer, Portadawe Union, and Constance Mary Adeney; m Margery. **Subject(s):** Law; BA 1935; LLB 1936. **Tutor(s):** J S Boys Smith. **Johnian Relatives:** brother of David Lincoln Lewis (1925) and of Roland Swaine Lewis (1926). **Educ:** County School, Ystalyfera; Epsom College. **Career:** Solicitor, Robin Thompson & Partners, Cardiff. Died 1981.

LEWIS, The Revd Frank Stanley (1923) Born 22 April 1904, 20 Newick Road, Lower Clapton, Hackney, Middlesex; son of Frank Thomas Lewis, Clerk in Holy Orders, and Sarah Ann Crooks. **Subject(s):** Mathematics/Theology; BA 1926; MA 1930. **Tutor(s):** E Cunningham. **Johnian Relatives:** father of Paul Lothian Lewis (1959). **Educ:** Private Tuition, Kensington; Preparatory School, Wokingham; Marlborough College; Westcott House, Cambridge. **Career:** Ordained Deacon 1928; Curate, St Anne, South Lambeth 1928–1931; Ordained Priest 1929; Curate, St Paul with St Mark, Deptford 1931–1934; Missioner, Wellington College Mission, Walworth 1934–1937; Vicar, St Mark, Walworth 1934–1941; Vicar, St Margaret, Putney 1941–1955; Vicar, Christ Church, Sutton 1956; Honorary Canon, Southwark Diocese. **Awards:** Scholarship, SJC 1922; Hare and Wood Exhibition 1926. Died 18 April 1991.

LEWIS, Frederick Victor (1937) Born 15 November 1918, 11 Everest Road, Great Crosby; son of Frederick Richard Lewis, Managing Director, and Edith Winifred Kerr; m Betty. **Subject(s):** Natural Sciences; BA 1940; MA 1944. **Tutor(s):** C W Guillebaud. **Educ:** St Fillans, Heswall; Oriel House, St Asaph; Oundle School. Died May 1983.

LEWIS, George Matthews (1933) Born 1 November 1914, 202 Birchfield Road, Handsworth, Birmingham; son of Frederick Charles George Lewis, Master Grocer, and Mabel Mary Matthews; m Bridget Mary, 25 October 1945, British Embassy Church in Vienna; 2 daughters (Gillian Mary b 1948 and Hilary Bridget b 1951). **Subject(s):** Mathematics/Mechanical Sciences; BA 1936; MA 1950; FICE; MIWEM. **Tutor(s):** J S Boys Smith. **Educ:** Fairfield House School, Yardley, Birmingham; Solihull School. **Career:** Howard Humphreys and Sons of Westminster, consulting Civil Engineers 1937–1938; TA, RE 1939–1946; Partner, Willcox Raikes and Marshall, Birmingham (later Mander, Raikes and Marshall). **Appointments:** University Engineering Society; SJC Chess Club. **Awards:** Scholarship, 1934; College Prizes; Exhibition, SJC; TD. Died 8 March 2003.

LEWIS, Gerald Brassington (1939) Born 10 December 1920, Wychwood, Heswall Hills, Cheshire; son of Frederick Richard Lewis, Managing Director, Wholesale Butchers, and Edith Winifred Kerr. **Subject(s):** Modern and Medieval Languages; BA 1942; MA 1946. **Tutor(s):** C W Guillebaud. **Educ:** St Fillans, Heswall, Cheshire; Oriel House, St Asaph, Wales; Oundle School. Died 1988.

LEWIS, Henry Godfrey (1900) Born 7 February 1880, Cape Town; son of Leon Lewis, Merchant, and Rose Rabinowitz. **Subject(s):** Law; BA 1903; LLB 1903. **Tutor(s):** D MacAlister. **Educ:** South African College. **Career:** Called to the Bar, Inner Temple 1904. **Awards:** Inns of Court Studentship 1904.

LEWIS, Hugh Gething (1919) Born 15 April 1901, Cathedral Road, Cardiff; son of Samuel Gething Lewis, Iron and Steel Merchant, and Jane Llewellyn. **Tutor(s):** E A Benians. **Educ:** Llandaff Cathedral School; Haileybury College.

LEWIS, Ian Alexander Darroch (1939) Born 13 August 1920, 17 Brompton Avenue, Toxteth Park, Liverpool; son of William Cudmore McCullagh Lewis, Professor of Inorganic Chemistry, and Jean Waterston Darroch. BA 1942; MA 1951; MInstP; MIEE; CEng. **Tutor(s):** J M Wordie. **Educ:** Calday Grange Grammar School, West Kirby. **Career:** Ministry of Defence. Died 17 October 1996.

LEWIS, Isaiah Leonard (1926) Born 11 May 1909, 73 Mildenhall Road, Lower Clapton, Middlesex; son of Judah Barnett Lewis, Schoolmaster, and Annie Kingstone. **Subject(s):** Law/Mathematics; BA 1929; MA 1933; BSc (London) 1927; QC. **Tutor(s):** J M Wordie. **Educ:** Millfields London County Council School; Hackney Downs Secondary School. **Career:** Admitted at the Middle Temple 1928; Called to the Bar 1932; Partner, Jaques & Lewis; Labour Candidate for Reigate (Surrey) 1935; Labour Candidate for Brentford-Chiswick 1951. **Awards:**

Goldsmith's Exhibition; Scholarship, SJC 1925; Wright's Prize for Mathematics, SJC 1928; MacMahon Law Studentship 1930. Died 2 February 1994.

LEWIS, John Cecil Wyn (1933) Born 20 September 1914, Glynteg, Eden Avenue, Swansea; son of John Emlyn Lewis, Wholesale Milliner, and Ethel May Webb; 4 children. **Subject(s):** Classics/English; BA 1937; MA 1990. **Tutor(s):** R L Howland. **Educ:** Llanyre Hall, Llandrindod; Brightlands, Newnham; Marlborough College. **Career:** English Teacher, Italy 1937–1938; English Teacher, Bedales School, Hampshire 1938–1940; War Service, RA 1940–1946; RAF Education Service 1948–1965; Head of Classics, Valley Grammar School 1968–1969; Rent Officer Service, Glamorgan 1970–1979.

LEWIS, John Morgan (1914) Born 11 July 1882, Panteg, Ystalyfera, Glamorganshire; son of David Lewis, Blacksmith, and Gwenllian Morgan. **Subject(s):** Modern and Medieval Languages; BA 1916; MA 1921; BA (Wales). **Tutor(s):** E E Sikes. **Educ:** Ystalyfera Intermediate School; University College of Wales, Aberystwyth; University of Paris. **Career:** Master, Cowley School, St Helens 1905–1912; Lycée de Vendome, France 1912–1913; Lieutenant, RGA 1914–1918; Leeds Grammar School 1920–1923; Headmaster, Rastrick Grammar School, Brighouse, Yorkshire 1923. **Awards:** Foundation Scholarship, SJC 1916.

LEWIS, Dr John Scott (1946) Born 14 September 1928, 14 Llanwonno Road, Stanleytown, Rhondda, Glamorganshire; son of William Francis Lewis, Schoolmaster, and Emma Irene Scott; m Constance Olivia Rees, 12 December 1955, Llandyri, Carmarthenshire (d 19 January 2001); 2 sons (Gareth Huw b 3 March 1958 and Jeremy William b 16 June 1961). **Subject(s):** Natural Sciences; BA 1949; MA 1956; BChir 1952; MB 1952; DObstRCOG; MRCGP. **Tutor(s):** G C L Bertram. **Educ:** Tylorstown Junior School; Rhondda County School, Porth. **Career:** House Posts, King's College Hospital, London and Addenbrooke's Hospital, Cambridge; Research Assistant, Obstetrics and Gynaecology, King's College Hospital, London; Demonstrator, Department of Anatomy, University of Cambridge; GP Principal, Llanelli 1958–1988; Part-time Medical Adviser, Benefits Agency 1988–1998.

LEWIS, Owen Calder (1938) Born 2 March 1920, Armadale, Victoria; son of Athol Hugh Lewis, Banker, and Margaret Elsie Calder; BA 1942; MA 1945. **Tutor(s):** C W Guillebaud. **Educ:** Sydney Church of England Grammar School, New South Wales, Australia; St Paul's, Hammersmith.

LEWIS, Captain Percy James (1903) Born 16 August 1884, 10 St Owen Street, Hereford; son of William Lewis, Miller and Corn Merchant, and Sarah Hannah Rhodes; m Noelle Minnie Pinson Buntine, 10 November 1934, St Peter's, Maritzburg, Natal; 2 sons (Robert James Pinson b 21 September 1936 and David Murray Rhodes b 19 July 1940). **Subject(s):** Classics; BA 1906; MA 1910. **Tutor(s):** E E Sikes. **Johnian Relatives:** father of David Murray Rhodes Lewis (1960) and of Robert James Pinson Lewis (1968). **Educ:** Hereford Cathedral School. **Career:** Master, Malvern College 1907–1914; Captain, Herefordshire Regiment (wounded twice), then employed by Officer Cadet Battalion, WWI; Farmer, Matapa, Bremersdorp, Swaziland 1921–1946. **Appointments:** Member, Swaziland Advisory Council; President, Swaziland Farmers' Association. **Honours:** OBE 1946. Died 17 February 1962.

LEWIS, Raymond Wilfred Logan (1937) Born 1 June 1918, 38 Carrick Road, Ayr; son of Fred Lewis, Civil Servant, and Jane Park Logan; m Margaret; 1 stepson (Andrew Kessler). **Subject(s):** Law; BA 1941; MA 1944. **Tutor(s):** R L Howland. **Educ:** Ayton House, Glasgow; Shrewsbury House. **Career:** Journalist and Photographer. **Appointments:** President, Association Scottish Motoring Writers; co-founder, Ayr Bay Sailing Club; Motoring Correspondent, *Ayrshire Post*. **Publications:** Plays and pageants; broadcast on BBC children's programmes; contributions to *Glasgow Herald*, *Scottish Field*, *Top Gear*. Died 8 January 2001.

LEWIS, Dr Rees Daniel Sidney (RHYS-LEWIS) (1934) Born 3 October 1916, Craigydrysni, Forest Lane, Hendy, Llanelly; son of William Sidney Lewis, Works Manager, and Margaret Mary Davies; m Heather; 1 son (Jonathan), 1 daughter (Georgina). **Subject(s):** Natural Sciences; BA 1937; MA 1941; MB 1942; BChir 1942; MD 1948; MRCS 1940; LRCP 1940; DMR 1942; FRCR 1975. **Tutor(s):** R L Howland. **Educ:** St David's School, Llanelly; The Grammar School, Pencader; The Cathedral School, Hereford. **Career:** Director Regional Radiotherapy Centre and Consultant in Radiotherapy, North-East Thames RHA; Honorary Chief Clinical Assistant Radiotherapy Department, London Hospital; Assistant Radiotherapist, St Thomas' Hospital, London; House Physician, Radiology and House Surgeon, St George's Hospital, London; Major, RAMC. **Appointments:** President, Radiology Section, Royal Medical Society; Fellow, RSM. **Awards:** Somerset Exhibition, SJC 1934. **Publications:** 'Regional Radiotherapy Centre: Scope & Limitations', *Procedures of the Royal Society of Medicine*, 1970. Died 14 June 2000.

LEWIS, Dr Roland Swaine (1926) Born 23 November 1908, Tyrwaun, Ystalyfera, Llanguicke, Glamorganshire, Wales; son of William James Lewis, Physician and Surgeon, and Constance Mary Adeney; m Christianna Brand, 1936; 1 daughter (adopted). **Subject(s):** Natural Sciences; BA 1929; MA 1945; MB 1945; BChir 1945; MRCS 1932; LRCP 1932; FRCS 1934. **Tutor(s):** M P Charlesworth. **Johnian Relatives:** brother of David Lincoln Lewis (Lincoln-Lewis) (1925) and of Edward Axford Lewis (1931). **Educ:** Ystalyfera County School; Epsom College; St George's Hospital Medical School, London. **Career:** Assistant Surgeon, Ear, Nose and Throat Department, King's College Hospital; Consultant Otolaryngologist, King's College Hospital and Mount Vernon Hospitals 1948–1972; part-time Lecturer in Oto-Rhino-Laryngology, King's College Hospital Medical School 1959. **Publications:** Chapters in medical text books; articles on cancer of the nose and throat in various medical journals. Died 24 February 2000.

LEWIS, William Peter (1943) Born 26 October 1924, 1 John Street, Treharris, Glamorganshire; son of Griffith Lewis, Screenman at colliery, and Gladys Targett. **Tutor(s):** C W Guillebaud. **Educ:** Treharris Central School; Quakers' Yard Secondary School, Treharris. **Career:** Schoolmaster.

LEWIS, William Russell (1947) Born 4 September 1926, 18 Van Road, Caerphilly, Glamorganshire; son of William John Lewis, Income Tax Collector, and Mary Hannah Lewis; m Alys Isabel Rees, 1964; 3 sons (Oliver, Martin and Daniel). **Subject(s):** History/Economics; BA 1950; MA 1955. **Tutor(s):** F Thistlethwaite. **Educ:** Twyn Junior School, Caerphilly; Caerphilly Boys' Grammar School. **Career:** NCO, Intelligence Corps, serving in India, Malaya, and Indonesia, WWII; Commissioned, RA 1945–1948; Stockbroker 1951–1957; Market Research 1957–1958; British Iron and Steel Federation 1958–1960; Press Officer, then Director, European Community Press Office, London 1960–1965; Leader Writer, *Daily Telegraph* 1965–1968; Director, Conservative Political Centre 1966–1975; Leader Writer, *Daily Mail* 1977–1992; General Director, Institute for Economic Affairs 1992; Director, Maastricht Referendum Campaign 1992–1993; Director, European Foundation 1995–1997; Director, FOREST 1997–. **Appointments:** Chairman, Bow Group 1958; President, Selsdon Group 1975–1979. **Publications:** *Industry and the Property Owning Democracy*, 1954; *Rome or Brussels?*, Institute of Economic Affairs, 1972; *The New Service Society*, Longmans, 1973; *The Reactionary Joke Book*, Wolff, 1973; *Margaret Thatcher*, Routledge, 1975 and 1983; *The Survival of Capitalism*, Institute for Study of Conflict, 1977; *Tony Benn*, Associated Business Press, 1978; *The Official Shop Steward's Joke Book*, Futura, 1980; *Anti-Racism, A Mania Explored*, Quartet Books, 1988; *A Memoir of FC Scott*, Westmorland Gazette, 1989; *The Environmental Alphabet*, Adam Smith Institute, 1993; *The Deadweight State*, Economic Research Council, 1998; *Challenge from Europe – Britain, the Commonwealth and the Free Trade Area*; *Master Eurocrat – The Making of Jacques Delors*; *The Myth of Europe*.

LEWIS-BOWEN, Gerard Arthur (1924) Born 3 April 1906, Clynfiew, Manordwy, Pembrokeshire; son of Thomas Edward Lewis-Bowen, Annuitant, and Ruth Beardmore; m Phyllis Ethel Maude Bredee, 21 April 1928, St Mark's Church, Cambridge; 1 son, 1 daughter. **Subject(s):** Mechanical Sciences; BA 1927; MA 1985; FICE 1956; MICE 1932. **Tutor(s):** J M Wordie. **Johnian Relatives:** father of Edmund Harold Philip Lewis-Bowen (1951). **Educ:** Chilverton Elms Preparatory, Dover; Haileybury College. **Career:** Practical Training, London North Eastern Railway, York 1928; District Engineer, Nizam's State Railway, Hyderabad State, Deccan 1929–1947; District Engineer, Sudan Railways, Khartoum 1947–1954; Deputy Municipal Engineer, Mombasa, Kenya 1954–1960; Sir Owen Williams & Partners (consulting engineers), London and Rugby 1961–1976. **Appointments:** Cambridge University Engineers' Association. Died 30 July 1996.

LEYLAND, Eric (1938) Born 6 July 1920, 180 Cansfield Grove, Ashton in Makerfield, Lancashire; son of Herbert Leyland, Hairdresser, and Glenella Fairhurst; m Madge Parkinson, 9 April 1943; 1 son (Christopher Mark b 1949). **Subject(s):** Natural Sciences; BA 1941; MA 1945. **Tutor(s):** J M Wordie. **Johnian Relatives:** father of Christopher Mark Leyland (1968). **Educ:** Evans Council School, Ashton in Makerfield; Ashton in Makerfield Grammar School. **Career:** Schoolteacher, Buxton College (final position Deputy Head) 1946–1982. Died 26 October 1996.

LEYLAND, Robert Clive (1921) Born 10 April 1903, Claridge's Hotel, Brook Street, London; son of Christopher John Leyland, Director, Parsons Marine Steam Turbine Company, and Helen Dora Cayley. **Tutor(s):** E E Sikes. **Educ:** Evelyn's, Uxbridge; Royal Naval College, Osborne; Royal Naval College, Dartmouth; Apprentice, Parsons Marine Steam Turbine Company.

LICKERISH, Leslie Arthur (1937) Born 12 April 1918, Midland Road, Thrapston; son of Arthur Lickerish, Master Printer, and Doris Blackwell. **Subject(s):** Natural Sciences; BA 1940; MA 1946. **Tutor(s):** C W Guillebaud. **Educ:** Snibston Council School; Coalville Grammar School; Wyggeston Boys' School, Leicester. **Career:** Pest Control Ltd, Harston, Cambridgeshire 1948–1954; Senior Scientific Officer, East Malling Research Station. **Awards:** Minor Scholarship, SJC 1936.

LIEBERT, Geoffrey Rex (1924) Born 9 November 1905, 22 Marlborough Road, Manningham, Bradford; son of Martin Liebert, Chemical Manufacturer, and Elise Maud Heilborn. **Subject(s):** Classics/ Modern and Medieval Languages; BA 1928; MA 1935. **Tutor(s):** E E Sikes. **Johnian Relatives:** cousin of Edward Francis Hayburn (1925). **Educ:** Day School, Manchester; Woodlands School, Deganwy, North Wales; Uppingham School. **Awards:** Scholarship, SJC 1923. Died 1988.

LIEU, Nyam Nyi (1931) Born 14 September 1910, Shanghai, China; son of Ong Sung Lieu, Merchant and Mineowner, and Soo Tsung Yih. **Subject(s):** Economics; BA 1934. **Tutor(s):** C W Guillebaud. **Educ:** St John's YMCA School, Shanghai, China; St John's University Middle School, Shanghai, China; St John's University, Shanghai, China.

LIGHT, Lovell Hillier Benjamin (1923) Born 21 July 1904, The Limes, Tillingham, Southminster, Essex; son of Leonard William Light, Physician and Surgeon, and Winifred Elizabeth Sharp; m Colyenn Audrey Bell (née Norman), 14 September 1946, London. MRCS (St Thomas' Hospital) 1932; LRCP (St Thomas' Hospital) 1932. **Tutor(s):** B F Armitage. **Educ:** Felsted School. **Career:** Medical Practitioner, Burnham on Crouch 1935. Died 6 July 1975.

LIGHTFOOT, Arthur Wilfrid (1921) Born 29 September 1902, Fern Lea, Norton, Stockton, County Durham; son of Percy William Lightfoot, Glass and China Dealer, and Annie Borrow. **Subject(s):** Mechanical Sciences; BA 1924. **Tutor(s):** E Cunningham. **Educ:** North Eastern County School, Barnard Castle.

LILLEY, James (1926) Born 13 December 1906, Ballykeel, Moneyrea, Comber, County Down, Ireland; son of William John Lilley, Farmer, and Eleanor Irvine. **Tutor(s):** E A Benians. **Educ:** Campbell College, Belfast. **Career:** Farmer.

LILLEY, Dr Samuel (1936) Born 25 June 1914, 18 Ebington Gardens, Belfast; son of William Edward Campbell Lilley, Manager, Linen Trade, and Elizabeth Wilhelmina Shaw. **Subject(s):** Physics; PhD 1939; BSc (Belfast) 1935; MSc (Belfast) 1936. **Tutor(s):** J M Wordie. **Educ:** Mounthotlinger, Belfast; Royal Belfast Academical Institution; Queen's University, Belfast. **Career:** Mathematical research into external ballistics 1939–1945; Title A Fellow, SJC 1940–1948 (suspended while on war service 1940–1945); Resident Staff Tutor, Extra Mural Department, University of Birmingham 1950–1956; Senior Staff Tutor in Science, Department of Adult Education, University of Nottingham 1956–1979; Writer and broadcaster on scientific subjects. **Publications:** *Men, Machines and History*, Cobbett Press, 1948. Died 11 November 1987.

LILLIE, Denis Gascoigne (1906) Born 27 August 1884, 77 Queen's Gate, South Kensington; son of John Gascoigne Lillie, Gentleman, and Eliza Macan. **Subject(s):** Natural Sciences; BA 1909; MA 1914. **Tutor(s):** L H K Bushe-Fox. **Educ:** United Services College, Westward Ho!; University of Birmingham. **Career:** Marine Biologist, Captain Scott's Antarctic Expedition 1910. Died 13 May 1963.

LILLIS, Francis Barry (1935) Born 21 October 1916, 28 Adelaide Road, Dublin; son of Francis James Lillis, Stock Broker, and Claire Renee Wogan-Brown. **Subject(s):** History; BA 1938. **Tutor(s):** C W Guillebaud. **Educ:** The Oratory Preparatory School, Reading; Ampleforth College, York; Private Tuition, France.

LIM, Guan Cheng (1904) Born 24 May 1886, China Street, Penang, Straits Settlements; son of Tek Suan Lim, Merchant, and Gok Lo Yuh. **Subject(s):** Natural Sciences; BA 1907; BChir 1910; MB 1911. **Tutor(s):** D MacAlister. **Educ:** Penang Free School.

LIM, Kheng Kooi (1928) Born 27 February 1910, 18 Stewart Lane, Penang, Straits Settlements; son of Lim Ewe Chaing, Merchant, and Chan San Leng. **Subject(s):** Law; BA 1931; LLB 1934. **Tutor(s):** C W Guillebaud. **Educ:** The Free School, Penang. **Awards:** Wright's Prize, SJC 1929; Hughes Prize, SJC 1931; McMahon Law Studentship, SJC 1932.

LINCOLN, Louis John (1925) Born 30 June 1906, Curepipe Road, Plaines Wilhelms, Mauritius; son of Pierre Louis Eugene Lincoln, Civil Servant, and Marie Julia Blanche. **Subject(s):** Law; BA 1928; MA 1951. **Tutor(s):** E A Benians. **Johnian Relatives:** cousin of René Lincoln (1924). **Educ:** Royal College, Mauritius. **Career:** Barrister-at-Law, Middle Temple; Professional Assistant to the Attorney-General, Mauritius; District and Stipendiary Magistrate; President, Criminal Intermediate Court; Judge of the Supreme Court; TA, WWII. Died 15 April 1971.

LINCOLN, Norman (1904) Born 12 April 1885, 81 George Street, Croydon, Surrey; son of John George Lincoln, Solicitor, and Annie Susannah King. BA 1907. **Tutor(s):** C E Graves; J R Tanner. **Educ:** Pocklington School. **Career:** Assistant Secretary to the Agent of the Bombay-Baroda Railway 1909; Lieutenant, IARO, attached Mahrattas and Railway Battalion, Indian Defence Force, WWI.

LINCOLN, René (1924) (matriculated as Non-Collegiate Student 1923) Born 23 November 1898, son of Edgar Lincoln, Sworn Broker, and Edmée J De Cordemoy de Froham. BA 1926; MA 1930. **Tutor(s):** B F Armitage. **Johnian Relatives:** cousin of Louis John Lincoln (1925). **Educ:** Royal College, Mauritius; School of Agriculture, Mauritius.

LINCOLN-LEWIS, David (1925) See LEWIS.

LINDARS, The Revd Frederick Chevallier (Barnabas) (1942) Born 11 June 1923, Stanbridge Vicarage, Leighton Buzzard; son of Walter St John Lindars, Clerk in Holy Orders, and Rose Chevallier. **Subject(s):** Oriental Languages/Theology; BA 1945; MA 1948; BD 1961; DD 1973. **Tutor(s):** C W Guillebaud. **Educ:** Altrincham Grammar School; Westcott House, Cambridge. **Career:** War service 1943–1945; Ordained Deacon 1948; Ordained Priest 1949; Curate, St Luke's, Pallion, Sunderland 1948–1952; Member, Society of St Francis 1952–1991 (Guardian 1970–1985); Assistant Curate, St Bene't's, Cambridge; Assistant Lecturer in Divinity, University of Cambridge 1966–1978; Fellow and Dean, Jesus College, Cambridge 1976–1978. **Appointments:** Member, General Synod; Member, SNTS (Assistant Secretary 1962–1975); Member, SOTS (President 1986); T W Manson Memorial Lecturer, Manchester University 1974; Canon Theologian, Leicester Cathedral 1977; Rylands Professor of Biblical Criticism and Exegesis, Manchester University 1978; Ethel M Wood Lecturer, University of London 1983. **Awards:** Rogerson Scholarship, SJC 1941. **Publications:** 'Matthew, Levi, Lebbaeus and the Value of the Western Text', *NTS* 4, 1958; 'The Holy Spirit in Romans', *Church Quarterly Review* 161, 1960; *New Testament Apologetic: The Doctrinal Significance of the Old Testament Quotations*, SCM/Westminster Press, 1961; 'The Composition of John XX', *NTS* 7, 1961; *Behind the Fourth Gospel*, 1971; *The Gospel of John*, 1981; *The new look on the Son of Man*, 1981; *Christ and salvation*, 1982; *Jesus Son of Man*, 1983; *John*, 1990; *The theology of the Letter to the Hebrews*, 1991. Died 21 October 1991.

LINDBERGH, Frederick Michael St Leger (1945) Born 11 November 1920, Onder Kopjes, Oxford Road, Parktown, Johannesburg; son of Albert Victor Lindbergh, Publisher, and Gladys Mary York St Leger. **Tutor(s):** C W Guillebaud. **Johnian Relatives:** cousin of Wilfred Henry Frederick Robinson (1937); brother of John Victor Lindbergh (1938). **Educ:** Ridge Preparatory School, Johannesburg; Diocesan College, Cape Town. **Career:** Lieutenant, South African Armoured Corps, Middle East 1939–1945; Farmer, Transvaal, South Africa, with an interest in the preservation of game.

LINDBERGH, John Victor (1938) Born 17 April 1919, Crawford Lea, Muizenburg, South Africa; son of Albert Victor Lindbergh, Publisher, and Gladys Mary York St Leger. **Tutor(s):** J S Boys Smith. **Johnian Relatives:** cousin of Wilfred Henry Frederick Robinson (1937); brother of Frederick Michael St Leger Lindbergh (1945). **Educ:** Ridge Preparatory School, Johannesburg; Diocesan College, Cape Town. **Career:** Pilot, South African Air Force 1939–1943. Died March 1943 (killed in action).

LINDON, Denis Norman (1948) Born 11 July 1928, Maternity Hospital, Singapore Straits Settlements; son of Norman Lidstone Lindon, Deputy Commissioner of Police, Federated Malay States, and Dorothy Minnie Shave; m Mary Prudence Houghton Brown; 1 son, 2 daughters. **Subject(s):** Natural Sciences/Law; BA 1950; MA 1957. **Tutor(s):** G C L Bertram. **Johnian Relatives:** father of Paul Vere Lindon (1981). **Educ:** Exeter School. **Career:** Second Lieutenant, Royal Signals, BAOR; UK Marketing Director, Major International Pharmaceutical Company; Sometime General Commissioner of Income Tax in Surrey. **Awards:** Vidal Exhibition, SJC 1946.

LINDSAY, Robert James Forsythe (1918) American Student.

LINDSELL, Major John (1911) Born 13 November 1892, Bearton, Hitchin, Hertfordshire; son of Edward Barber Lindsell, Solicitor and Land Agent, and Maria Elizabeth Tuke; m Rosemary Croft (d 24 December 1947). **Subject(s):** Mathematics/Natural Sciences; BA 1914. **Tutor(s):** L H K Bushe-Fox. **Educ:** Uppingham School. **Career:** Captain, Loyal North Lancashire Regiment, France 1914–1918; Major, the Loyal Regiment. **Honours:** MC 1917. Died 14 October 1959.

LINDSEY, Cecil Herbert (1933) See LEVY.

LINDSEY, Peter Kenneth John (1947) Born 1 April 1923, Lindwood, Lympstone, Devon; son of Kenneth Charles Lindsey, Surgical Instrument Maker, and Kate Mary Woodroffe; m Jean Swindells, 6 June 1959. **Tutor(s):** C W Guillebaud. **Educ:** St Peter's Court, Burgess Hill; Sutton Valence School. **Career:** Colonial Administration Course.

LINE, Timothy Charles (1948) Born 26 February 1931, Brunswick Nursing Home, Cambridge; son of James Line, Fellow, Emmanuel College, Cambridge, and Dorothy Beatrice Gertrude Dimmock; m Birgitta Christina Wendela Wachtmeister, 1968; 2 sons, 2 daughters. **Subject(s):** Natural Sciences; BA 1951; MA 1955. **Tutor(s):** G C L Bertram. **Johnian Relatives:** father of Charles Edward Rütger Line (1988); father-in-law of Sophie Anne Jennifer Green (1989). **Educ:** St Nicholas School, Cambridge; St Faith's School, Cambridge; Peter Symond's School, Winchester; Perse School, Cambridge. **Career:** Lieutenant, later Commander, RN 1951–1970 (Weapons/Electrical); Sonar development, HMUDE Portland 1956–1966; IBM 1970–1990 (Product Manager, IBM Personal Computer 1983–1987); Independent Consultant 1991–2001. **Awards:** Major Scholarship, SJC 1947.

LINES, Alfred James (1944) Born 31 December 1926, Delhi, India; son of Alfred Lines, Director of Civil Engineering, Indian Railway Board, and Gwendoline Mary Aldridge. **Subject(s):** Mechanical Sciences; BA 1947. **Tutor(s):** S J Bailey. **Educ:** Tormore School, Deal; Cranleigh School.

LINFOOT, Dr Edward Hubert (1948) Born 8 June 1905, Sheffield; son of George Edward Linfoot, Musical Adviser, Sheffield Education Committee, and Laura Edith Clayton; m Joyce Dancer, 1935; 1 son (John Sebastian), 1 daughter (Margaret). ScD (by incorporation) 1948; BA (Oxon) 1926; DPhil (Oxon) 1928; DSc (Oxon) 1948. **Educ:** Hunter's Bar Council School, Sheffield; King Edward VII School, Sheffield; Balliol College, Oxford. **Career:** Göttingen University 1928–1929; Jane Eliza Procter Fellow 1929–1930; University of Princeton 1929–1931; Lecturer in Mathematics, University of Bristol 1932–1948; John Couch Adams Astronomer 1948, Assistant Director, Observatory 1948–1970, University of Cambridge; Fellow, University College, Cambridge (later Wolfson College) 1966. **Appointments:** Jane Eliza Procter Visiting Fellow University of Princeton 1929–1931. **Awards:** Junior Mathematical Scholarship 1924; Senior Mathematical Scholarship 1928. **Publications:** *Recent Advances in Optics* 1955; *Fourier Methods in Optical Image Evaluation*, 1964. Died 14 October 1982.

LINGFORD, Kenneth (1933) Born 28 July 1916, Burnholme, Cotherston, Startforth, Yorkshire; son of Herbert Muschamp Lingford, Baking Powder Manufacturer, and Dorothea Mary Saville. **Subject(s):** Economics, Law; BA 1937; MA 1941. **Tutor(s):** C W Guillebaud. **Educ:** Friends School, Stramongate, Kendal; Bootham School, York.

LINNELL, Charles Darby (1902) Born 1 March 1877, 78 Branstone Road, Burton on Trent, Stafford; son of John Edward Linnell, Clerk in Holy Orders, and Emmeline Elizabeth Darby. **Subject(s):** Modern and Medieval Languages; BA 1903; BA (London) 1895; MA (London) 1889. **Tutor(s):** D MacAlister. **Johnian Relatives:** brother of John Wycliffe Linnell (1899) and of Robert McCheyne Linnell (1900). **Educ:** Bedford Modern School. **Career:** Lektor in English, Handelhochschule, Cologne 1904; Master, St John's School, Leatherhead 1908–1917; Censor Staff, France 1917–1919; Modern Languages Master, Bedford Modern School 1920–1963. Died 25 September 1963.

LINNELL, Maurice Edward (1933) Born 15 August 1914, Peterborough Road, Crowland, Lincolnshire; son of Isaiah Linnell, Farm Labourer, and Lizzie Beeken. **Subject(s):** Modern and Medieval Languages, Economics; BA 1936; MA 1940. **Tutor(s):** C W Guillebaud. **Educ:** Crowland Council School; Spalding Grammar School.

LINNELL, Robert McCheyne (1900) Born 16 February 1881, Burton on Trent, Stafford; son of John Edward Linnell, Clerk in Holy Orders, and Emmeline Elizabeth Darby. BA 1904; MRCS; LRCP (London) 1907;

Diploma in Public Health 1909; Diploma in Tropical Medicine 1910. **Tutor(s):** D MacAlister. **Johnian Relatives:** brother of John Wycliffe Linnell (1899) and of Charles Darby Linnell (1902). **Educ:** Bedford Modern School. **Career:** Medical Officer, Rossall School 1910–1911; Lieutenant, RAMC Special Reserve 1911; RAMC 1914–1915. Died 16 March 1915 (died of meningitis contracted while working among soldiers with the disease).

LINNEY, Duncan Stuart (1947) Born 10 May 1920, Pietersburg, Transvaal, South Africa; son of Duncan Linney, Inspector of Schools, and Renette Johanna Margharita Biccard. BA (Witwatersrand) 1941. **Tutor(s):** C W Guillebaud. **Johnian Relatives:** son of Duncan Linney (1896). **Educ:** Rustenburg Primary School; Pietersburg High School; University of Witwatersrand.

LINNEY, George (1948) Born 10 September 1928, Ferham House, Kimberworth Road, Rotherham, Yorkshire; son of George William Linney, Steelworker, and Freda Elizabeth Whitehead, Master Baker; m Annette Marjorie Stacey, 2 July 1955, St Mary's Church, Greasbrough, Rotherham. **Subject(s):** Modern and Medieval Languages; BA 1950; MA 1956. **Educ:** Ferham Road Council School, Rotherham; Rotherham Grammar School. **Career:** RAEC 1946–1948; Sales Manager, Hot Rolled Strip, Narrow Strip Product Unit, British Steel Corporation 1976–1981; Field Sales Manager, Narrow Strip 1981–1982.

LIPKIND, Goodman (1901) Born 27 June 1875, 20 St Mark's Street, Whitechapel; son of John Lipkind, Property Dealer, and Rebecca Tuckmann. BA (London). **Tutor(s):** D MacAlister. **Educ:** Jews College, London.

LISTER, Dr John (1938) Born 8 August 1920, 3 Station Road, Cambus, Alloa, Clackmannanshire; son of Thomas Lister, Chartered Accountant, and Anna Rebecca Black; m (1) Eileen Doris Trafford, 3 July 1943, (2) Moyra Jacobson, 2000; (1) 3 sons (Thomas Andrew b 1944, Ian Whitson b 1948 and Robert William b 1953). **Subject(s):** Natural Sciences; BA 1941; MA 1952; BChir 1943; MB 1943; MD 1952; FRCP London. **Tutor(s):** R L Howland. **Johnian Relatives:** father of Thomas Andrew Lister (1963) and of Robert William Lister (1971). **Educ:** Hazelwood Lane School, Palmers Green; Norfolk House Preparatory School, Muswell Hill; The Hall, Hampstead; St Paul's School; St Bartholomew's Hospital, London. **Career:** RAMC 1943–1946; Senior Registrar, Royal Free Hospital 1948–1953; Consultant Physician, King Edward VII Hospital, Windsor and East Berkshire District 1953–1984; Postgraduate Medical Dean, North West Thames Region, University of London 1972–1984; Linacre Fellow, Royal College of Physicians of London 1985–1991. **Appointments:** Honorary Fellow, American College of Physicians; London Correspondent, *New England Journal of Medicine* 1952–1980. **Publications:** Various, on Diabetes Mellitus and postgraduate medical education.

LISTER, Tom (1906) Born 10 May 1887, Ouzlewell, Thornhill, Yorkshire; son of Ben Lister, Mould Fitter, Glass Works, and Annie Louisa Marsden; m Isabelle Mary. **Subject(s):** Natural Sciences/Mathematics/History; BA 1909. **Tutor(s):** J R Tanner. **Educ:** Wheelwright Grammar School, Dewsbury. **Career:** Assistant Commissioner and Secretary, Burma and Federated Malay States, Indian Civil Service 1911–1921; Officiating Deputy Commissioner, then Deputy Commissioner 1922–1929; Officiating Secretary to Government Revenue Department, Burma 1929–1930. **Appointments:** Delegate, Burma Round Table Conference 1931. **Honours:** CIE 1932. Died 26 March 1945.

LITHERLAND, The Revd Geoffrey (1929) Born 19 January 1911, Stanley Road, Knutsford, Cheshire; son of William Litherland, Costs Estimating Clerk, and Martha Elizabeth Duggins; m Averil, 1942 (d 1984); 2 sons (Peter and Martin), 1 daughter (Margaret). **Subject(s):** Natural Sciences; BA 1932; MA 1936; BD (London). **Tutor(s):** J M Wordie. **Educ:** Yorston Lodge, Knutsford; Altrincham Grammar School. **Career:** Methodist Minister; Warden, Wesley Deaconess Order; Headmaster,

Queen's College, Bahamas; Theology Teacher, Southlands College. **Awards:** Scholarship, SJC 1928. Died 1991.

LITLER-JONES, Robert Clouston Martland (1934) Born 12 December 1915, 48 Rodney Street, Liverpool; son of Thomas Caldwell Litler-Jones, Surgeon, and Isabel Clouston Thin. BA 1937; MA 1943. **Tutor(s):** C W Guillebaud. **Educ:** Abberley Hall Preparatory School, Worcester; Rugby School.

LITTLE, Bryce (1918) American Student.

LITTLEBOY, Gerald (1915) Born 18 September 1896, 8 North Square, Newport Pagnell, Buckinghamshire; son of Francis Littleboy, Bank Director, and Lucy Ann Brown; m Gwendolen Florence Richardson; 1 son (Michael Francis b 7 July 1931). **Subject(s):** Mathematics; BA 1921; MA 1925. **Tutor(s):** L H K Bushe-Fox. **Johnian Relatives:** father of Michael Francis Littleboy (1949); grandfather of William Regnar Littleboy (1979). **Educ:** Downe Preparatory School; Bootham School, York. **Career:** Senior Mathematical Master, Friends' School, Great Ayton 1921–1926; Lady Manners School, Bakewell 1926–1927; Sidcot School, Winscombe 1927–1934; Headmaster, Saffron Walden School 1934–1955. **Appointments:** Administrator, Friends' Educational Council. Died 1 June 1962.

LITTLEBOY, Michael Francis (1949) Born 7 July 1931, Hedgeway, Winscombe, Somerset; son of Gerald Littleboy, Headmaster, Friends' School, Saffron Walden, and Gwendolen Florence Richardson; m Judith Ann Isles, 2 sons (Patrick Ronald and William Regnar b 18 November 1961); 1 daughter (Anna Katharine). **Subject(s):** Mathematics/English; BA 1952; MA 1956. **Tutor(s):** J M Wordie. **Johnian Relatives:** son of Gerald Littleboy (1915); father of William Regnar Littleboy (1979). **Educ:** Friends' School, Saffron Walden; Bootham School, York. **Awards:** Exhibition, SJC 1948.

LITTLEWOOD, James (1940) Born 21 October 1922, 244 Shaw Road, Royton, Lancashire; son of Thomas Littlewood, Cotton Mill Secretary, and Sarah Jane Penhall; m Barbara Shaw, 9 August 1950; 2 sons (David b 1955 and Peter b 1957), 1 daughter (Pamela b 1953). **Subject(s):** Modern Languages/Economics; BA 1943; MA 1947. **Tutor(s):** C W Guillebaud. **Johnian Relatives:** father of David John Littlewood (1974). **Educ:** Byron Street Council School, Royton; Manchester Grammar School. **Career:** Army 1942–1947; HM Treasury 1947–1967; Seconded to the Cabinet Office 1955–1967; Department for National Savings 1967–1981 (Director of Savings 1972–1981). **Appointments:** Secretary, Committee on Administrative Tribunals and Enquiries 1955–1957; Colombo Plan Conference Secretariat 1955 and 1959. **Awards:** Scholarship, SJC. **Honours:** CB 1973. Died 14 January 1998.

LITTMAN, Niculae (LAWRIE) (1943) Born 22 February 1922, 46 Bd Carol, Bukarest, Roumania; son of Georges Littman, Lieutenant, Free French Forces, and Margot Benzal. **Tutor(s):** C W Guillebaud. **Educ:** Clementa School, Bukarest; Liceul St George, Bukarest; Maiden Erlegh, Reading.

LIVERSIDGE, Charles (1924) Born 9 June 1906, Belmont, Lepton, Huddersfield; son of Norman Liversidge, Worsted Cloth Manufacturer, and Margaret Alice Wade. **Tutor(s):** E E Sikes. **Educ:** Woodlands School, Deganwy; Malvern College.

LIVESEY, Professor Derek Leonard (1940) Born 21 July 1923, 71 Chorley New Road, Horwich, Lancashire; son of Leonard Livesey, Builder's Clerk, and Florence Nicholson Ellison; m Lois; 1 daughter. **Subject(s):** Natural Sciences; BA 1943; PhD 1947. **Tutor(s):** J M Wordie. **Educ:** Lord Street Council School, Horwich; St Catherine's Church of England School, Horwich; Rivington and Blackrod Grammar School. **Career:** Assistant Professor of Physics, University of British Columbia 1960. Died 20 March 1992.

LIVESEY, Harry Talboys (1943) Born 20 July 1924, 22 Preston Street, Bolton; son of Harry Livesey, Operative Cotton Spinner, and Harriet Mary Cox. **Tutor(s):** C W Guillebaud. **Educ:** Victoria Council School, Bolton; Bolton Municipal Secondary School.

LIVESLEY, Dr Robert Kenneth (1944) Born 30 May 1926, Kuling, Kiukiang, China; son of Ernest Henry Livesley, Methodist Minister, and Bertha Weaver; m Valerie Margaret Thomas, 1953; 1 son, 2 daughters. **Subject(s):** Mechanical Sciences; BA 1947; MA 1951; PhD (Manchester) 1954. **Tutor(s):** S J Bailey. **Educ:** Barnstaple Grammar School; Kingswood School. **Career:** Apprentice, Metropolitan-Vickers Electrical Company 1947–1949; Demonstrator in Engineering Mathematics 1949–1952, Research Assistant, Computing Laboratory 1952–1955, University of Manchester; Demonstrator in Engineering 1955–1956, Lecturer in Engineering 1956–1993, University of Cambridge; Fellow, Churchill College, Cambridge 1960. **Appointments:** Director of Studies and Post-graduate Tutor, Churchill College, Cambridge 1960; Member, BCS. **Awards:** Major Scholarship, SJC 1944; Charles Lamb Prize, Electrical Engineering 1946; Ricardo Prize, Heat and Heat Engines, University of Cambridge 1947. **Publications:** 5 books; numerous papers on structural analysis, computational methods and engineering mathematics.

LLEWELLYN, David William Alun (1921) Born 17 April 1903, Dunraven House, Montem Road, Forest Hill, London; son of David William Llewellyn, Headmaster, and Elizabeth Jane Lewis; m Lesley Diane. **Subject(s):** History/English/Law; BA 1924; MA 1928; FRSAI. **Tutor(s):** E A Benians. **Educ:** Stillness Road School, Forest Hill; Alleyn's School, Dulwich. **Career:** Author of Novels, Short Stories, Science Fiction, Plays, Politics, Travel; Called to the Bar, Lincoln's Inn 1927; Legal Translator, Geneva Secretariat, League of Nations 1937–1939; Secretary, Central Valuation Board, Coal Nationalisation 1947–1949. **Appointments:** Member, British Commonwealth Industries Association 1935–1969; Council, Poetry Society of Great Britain. **Awards:** Exhibition, SJC; Chancellor's English Medal, University of Cambridge 1923. **Publications:** *The Deacon*, 1934; *The Strange Invaders*, 1934, 1977; *Confound their Politics*, 1934; *History of the Union Society of London*; *The Soul of Cezar Azan*, 1938; *Jubilee John*, 1939; *The Tyrant from Below*, 1957; *Ways to Love*, 1957; *Shell Guide to Wales*, 1969, 1972, 1977; *Celtic Christianity*, 1978; *Man and Mind*, 1980; *Tim Twice*, 1981. Died 27 November 1988.

LLEWELLYN, Nathaniel James (BENTLEY-LLEWELLYN) (1943) Born 7 June 1917, 3 The Poplars, Gladstone Street, Abertillery; son of Nathaniel James Llewellyn, Secretary of Education, Abertillery, and Ann Thomas. **Subject(s):** Natural Sciences; BA 1945; MA 1950. **Tutor(s):** C W Guillebaud. **Educ:** Llanelli County Intermediate School; University College, Swansea; UCL. **Career:** Geologist; Officer, RE, WWII. Died 17 March 1998.

LLEWELLYN, William John Michael (1931) Born 16 January 1912, Wellington House, Hereford; son of Arthur Henry Llewellyn, District Valuer, Inland Revenue, and Martha Helen Scott. **Subject(s):** Classics/English; BA 1934. **Tutor(s):** M P Charlesworth. **Educ:** Durlaston Court, Swanage; Shrewsbury School. **Awards:** Exhibition, SJC.

LLOYD, Charles Brian Murray (1947) Born 11 March 1927, 10 Onslow Avenue Mansions, Richmond, Surrey; son of Murray Tenison Lloyd, Australian Representative, Anglo-Iranian Oil Company, and Elizabeth Mary Rowe; m (1) Felice Rosemary Benjamin, 4 August 1951 (d 31 March 1954), (2) Waltraud; (1) 1 son, (2) 2 sons. **Subject(s):** Modern and Medieval Languages. **Tutor(s):** F Thistlethwaite. **Johnian Relatives:** son of Murray Tenison Lloyd (1908). **Educ:** Shore School, Australia; Adwalton, Melbourne; St Bede's, Eastbourne; Sydney Church of England Grammar School. **Career:** Shipping Director, Modders Ltd; Shipping Director, Wheelock Maritime Ltd, Hong Kong; Co-Founder, Lloyd International Airways. **Appointments:** President, LMBC. Died 19 July 1995.

LLOYD, David Demarest (1931) Born 6 June 1911, 527 West Street, New York; son of David Lloyd, Literary Agent, and Eliza Shore Mathews; m Charlotte Westwood, 1940; 2 children. **Subject(s):** Economics; BA (Harvard) 1931. **Tutor(s):** E A Benians. **Educ:** Somerville High School, New Jersey; Plainfield High School, New Jersey; Harvard College, Cambridge, Massachusetts; Harvard Law School. **Career:** Author; US Government, the White House 1948. **Awards:** Charles and Julia Henry Fund Studentship. **Publications:** *Son and Stranger*, Bodley Head, London, 1950.

LLOYD, Dr Ernest Llewelyn (1912) Born 8 August 1893, Bryn Celyn, St Asaph, Denbighshire, Wales; son of Llewelyn Lloyd, Cathedral Organist, and Emily Jones; 2 sons. **Subject(s):** Classics; BA 1919; MA 1922; MB Edinburgh 1932; ChB Edinburgh 1932; Diploma in Tropical Medicine and Health 1937. **Tutor(s):** E E Sikes. **Johnian Relatives:** cousin of Herbert Marsden Lloyd (1909). **Educ:** County School, St Asaph; Aldenham School. **Career:** Classics Master, Merchiston Castle School, Edinburgh; Captain, South Wales Borderers 1914–1919; Medical Missionary, Church of Scotland, Itu Leper Colony, Nigeria, and Santals, Tisri, Bihar, India 1933–1941; Captain, IMS, IAMC 1941–1945; Anatomy Department, Edinburgh Medical School 1945; Junior Medical Officer, Tropical Diseases Unit, Eastern General Hospital, Edinburgh 1947. **Awards:** Sizarship, SJC. Died 14 July 1987.

LLOYD, George Mark (1922) Born 1 August 1903, 80 Holland Road, Kensington, London; son of George William Aylmer Lloyd, RA, and Dorothy Hann. **Tutor(s):** E A Benians. **Educ:** Harrow School.

LLOYD, Henry Llewellyn (1933) Born 5 February 1913, Lea Hurst, Balmoral Road Grappenhall, Runcorn; son of Henry David Llewellyn Lloyd, Civil Engineer, and Amy Letitia Morgan; 1 son, 4 daughters. **Subject(s):** Mechanical Sciences; BA 1935. **Tutor(s):** J S Boys Smith. **Educ:** Packwood Haugh, Hockley Heath; Winchester College; RMA, Woolwich. **Career:** QVO Madras Sappers and Miners, Bangalore and NWFP India 1936–1940; SORE 1940–1941; OC, 275th (Highland) Field Company 1941–1943; Instructor, Staff College, Haifa 1943; Lieutenant Colonel, SORE, 8th Army Italy 1944–1945; CRE 8th Indian Division 1945–1946; SORE, Delhi 1947; Commanded the School of Military Engineering, Sialkot, Pakistan 1948–1952; Air Ministry 1953–1954; Ministry of Supply 1955–1957; General Manager and Director, Roballo Engineering 1958–1975; Antiquarian book business, London, then Winchester 1975–1994. **Awards:** Pollock Medal. **Honours:** OBE (Military); MC; King's Medal; Bar, African and Italian campaigns. Died 22 March 1998.

LLOYD, Herbert Marsden (1909) Born 5 October 1890, The Vicarage, St Asaph, Denbighshire, Wales; son of Thomas Lloyd, Clerk in Holy Orders, and Helen Jones; m May Burnand, 22 March 1922, St Thomas', Rhyl. **Subject(s):** Classics/Law; BA 1912; LLB 1912. **Tutor(s):** E E Sikes. **Johnian Relatives:** cousin of Ernest Llewellyn Lloyd (1912). **Educ:** Colet House Preparatory School, Rhyl; Rossal School, Fleetwood. **Career:** Political Officer, Nigeria 1914; West African Regiment; District Officer, Magistrate, Port Harcourt, Nigeria, WWI. **Awards:** Choral Studentship, SJC; Goldsmith Exhibition. Died 14 June 1929.

LLOYD, John Arthur (1946) Born 17 March 1927, Ione, Westfa Road, Swansea; son of Arthur Lloyd, Solicitor, and Sarah Isabella Davies; m Joyce Rees, 10 April 1952 (d 19 January 1992); 2 sons, 1 daughter. **Subject(s):** Law; BA 1948; MA 1952; LLB 1949; LLM 1985. **Tutor(s):** F Thistlethwaite. **Educ:** Oakleigh House School; Brynmill School, Swansea; Swansea Grammar School; Repton School. **Appointments:** JP, Swansea 1966–1997; Chairman, Swansea Magistrates 1981–1987; Deputy Lieutenant, County of West Glamorgan 1993; Chairman, West Glamorgan Magistrates Courts Committee 1995–1997. **Honours:** OBE 1997.

LLOYD, John Edward (1918) Born 23 June 1901, 21 Sprowston Road, Forest Gate, Essex; son of Charles Lloyd, Secretary of Public Companies/Lieutenant Colonel, RGA, and Louisa Sarah Threlford; m Mavis Wise, 1949; 1 son, 1 daughter. **Tutor(s):** E E Sikes. **Johnian Relatives:** godfather of John Thomas Naylor (1966). **Educ:** Alleyne Court Preparatory School, Westcliff-on-Sea, Essex; Wycliffe College, Stonehouse. **Career:** Chartered Accountant; Director, St Martin's Property; Vice-Chairman, John Govett & Co; Lieutenant Colonel, Essex Regiment, RA, WWII.

LLOYD, Kenneth Edward (1921) Born 31 August 1902, Woodstock House, Abergavenny, Monmouthshire; son of Thomas Edward Lloyd, Physician and Surgeon, and Annie Sophia Clark. **Tutor(s):** B F Armitage. **Educ:** King Henry VIII Grammar School, Abergavenny; Brynmelyn School, Weston-Super-Mare.

LLOYD, Michael Vernon (1949) Born 13 April 1929, 5 Barn Hill, Wembley, Middlesex; son of Vernon Edmund Lloyd, Medical Practitioner, and Margaret Hopper. **Subject(s):** History/Law; BA 1952; MA 1957. **Tutor(s):** A G Lee. **Educ:** Rokeby School, Wimbledon; King's College School, Wimbledon. **Career:** Solicitor. **Awards:** TD.

LLOYD, Murray Tenison (1908) Born 7 June 1889, Wilmington Hall, Wilmington, Dartford; son of John Buck Lloyd, Tea Broker, and Fanny Vincent; m Elizabeth Mary Rowe; 1 son (Charles Brian Murray b 11 March 1927). **Subject(s):** Classics; BA 1911. **Tutor(s):** E E Sikes. **Johnian Relatives:** father of Charles Brian Murray Lloyd (1947). **Educ:** Rose Hill School, Tunbridge Wells; Aldenham School. **Career:** Managing Director, Commonwealth Oil Refineries Ltd, Melbourne 1938. **Appointments:** Director, Petroleum Information Bureau, Australia 1951–1954; Chairman, Petroleum Pool. Died 1954.

LLOYD, The Revd Paul Medley (1947) Born 6 October 1923, Epworth House, Market Road, Chichester, Sussex; son of Alfred George Lloyd, Clerk in Holy Orders, and Sarah Gertrude Medley. **Subject(s):** English; BA 1949; MA 1954; PGCE (London). **Tutor(s):** F Thistlethwaite. **Educ:** County School, Gravesend; Kingswood School, Bath; Cuddesdon College. **Career:** Deacon 1953; Priest 1954; Curate, South Bank, Middlesbrough 1953–1956; Curate, St James, Piccadilly 1956–1958; Curate, St Stephen with St John, Westminster 1958–1959; Vicar, St Martin, Whinney Banks, Middlesbrough 1959–1960; Chaplain, Shrewsbury School 1961–1963; Curate, Long Buckby with Brington 1963–1965; Rector, Barnack with Ufford and Bainton, Northamptonshire 1965–1973; Vicar, St George's, Ramsgate 1973–1975; Vicar, St Mary the Virgin, Ringmer Diocese, Chichester, Sussex 1976–1983. Died 1 April 1984.

LLOYD, Canon Roger Bradshaigh (1919) Born 16 January 1901, 65 Half Edge Lane, Eccles, Lancashire; son of Walter Evans Lloyd, Lieutenant Colonel, Manchester Regiment, and Constance Jane Bentley; m Mildred Vera Frodsham Ward; 1 daughter (Rosemary). **Subject(s):** History; BA 1922; MA 1927. **Tutor(s):** E A Benians. **Educ:** Whitchurch Grammar School; Hildersham House, St Peters, Kent; Shrewsbury School; Courtenay Lodge, Sutton Courtenay, Berks; Egerton Hall, Manchester. **Career:** Ordained Deacon 1924; Curate, St Wilfred, Newton Heath 1924–1926; Ordained Priest 1925; Curate, St Mary, Crumpsall 1926–1929; Rector, St Stephen, Harpurhey 1929–1932; Rector, Great Harwood 1932–1937; Vicar, St Bartholomew and Examining Chaplain to Bishop of Blackburn 1933–1937; Canon, Winchester Cathedral and Diocesan Mission 1937. **Appointments:** Warden, Servants of Christ the King 1943–1963. **Publications:** Frequent contributor to the *Church Times*, and author of many books on Religion and Railways; *The Stricken Lute*, 1932; *Church of England in the Twentieth Century*; *Letters of Luke the Physician*; *Letters from the Early Church*; *Farewell to Steam*. Died 15 September 1966.

LLOYD OWEN, Dr Morus Wyn (1926) Born 4 June 1907, 132 Walm Lane, Cricklewood, London; son of Owen Lloyd Owen, Official of Insurance Company, and Helen Roberts; 1 son (Robin). BA 1929; MA 1946; BChir 1934; MB 1936; MRCS 1932; LRCP 1932. **Tutor(s):** M P Charlesworth. **Educ:** Brondesbury Kilburn High School; Peterborough Lodge School, Hampstead, Finchley Road; Mill Hill School. **Career:**

Consultant Anaesthetist, Croydon General Hospital and St Mary's Hospital Medical School, London 1959; Part time clinical teacher in Anaesthetics. Died 2 June 1998.

LOBB, Geoffrey Wilmot (1931) Born 8 February 1913, 33 St Austell Street, Truro; son of William Richard Lobb, Builder, and Wilmot Quick Wormington; m Roberta (Bobbie) Keith, St Paul's Church, Truro, 10 April 1943. **Subject(s):** Natural Sciences; BA 1934; MA 1938. **Tutor(s):** C W Guillebaud. **Educ:** Glenburnie Preparatory School, Truro; Truro College.

LOCK, Derrick James (1943) Born 4 April 1925, 61 Abbotts Park Road, Leyton; son of Frederick James Lock, Wholesale Furniture Manufacturer, and Hannah Ellen Davies. **Tutor(s):** C W Guillebaud. **Educ:** Oxford House School, Leytonstone; Chigwell School.

LOCKE, Cyril Stanley (1930) Born 2 November 1911, 51 Longland Road, Liscard, Wallasey, Cheshire; son of George Thomas Locke, Headmaster, Stand Grammar School, and Mabel Haydock. **Subject(s):** Mathematics. **Tutor(s):** J M Wordie. **Johnian Relatives:** son of George Thomas Locke (1894). **Educ:** Stand Preparatory School; Stand Grammar School; Bootham School, York.

LOCKE, Professor Michael (1949) Born 14 February 1929, 48 Lady Bay Road, West Bridgford, Nottingham; son of Robert Henry Locke, Director, GPO, and Kathleen Nellie Waite; m (1) Audrey Ashley, (2) Janet V Collins; (1) 3 sons (John, Timothy and Marius), 1 daughter (Vanessa). **Subject(s):** Natural Sciences; BA 1952; MA 1955; PhD 1956; ScD 1976. **Tutor(s):** W A Deer. **Educ:** Winchester House Preparatory School, Reading; St Edmund's Preparatory School, Felixstowe; Felixstowe County School; Drayton Manor County Grammar School, Ealing. **Career:** No 3 Medical Parachute Team, RAF 1947–1949; Anti Locust Research, British Museum 1952; Field Worker for Agriculture Canada, Norway 1953; Lecturer in Zoology, University of West Indies 1956–1961; Associate Professor of Biology 1961–1967, Professor of Biology 1967–1971, Case Western Reserve University; Raman Professor, University of Madras 1969; Chairman, Zoology Department 1971–1985, Professor of Zoology 1971–1994 (Emeritus 1994–), University of Western Ontario, Canada; Visiting Director of Research, ICIPE, Nairobi, Kenya 1977–1981. **Appointments:** Guest Investigator, K R Porter & G E Palade's Laboratory, The Rockerfeller Institute 1960; Symposium Editor, Society for Developmental Biology 1961–1969; Founding Member, Developmental Biology Center, Case Western Reserve University 1961–1971; Editorial Boards, *Tissue & Cell* 1968, and *Journal of Insect Physiology* 1978; Spencer Memorial Lecturer, University of British Columbia 1976; Chairman, Gordon Conference on Lysosomes 1976; Member, RSC 1980; Associate Editor for Developmental Biology, *Canadian Journal of Biochemistry* 1980–1982; Cell Biology and Genetics Panel, NSERC 1985–1988; FAAAS 1988; Killam Fellow 1988–1990; Honorary Fellow, American Society of Entomology 2000; Honorary Fellow, Royal Entomological Society 2000. **Awards:** Wright's Prize, SJC, Humphrey Prize, Sir Albert Howard Exhibition, SJC; Rockerfeller Foundation Award 1960; Carnegie Award 1961; Distinguished International Gold Medal in Morphology and Embryology 1988; Wigglesworth Medal from Royal Entomological Society, August 2000; Certificate of Distinction at the XXIst International Congress of Entomology; Hellmuth Prize, 2001. **Publications:** *Microscopic Anatomy of Invertebrates: Insecta*, Wiley-Liss, 1998; editor of 18 books; 150 research papers, including a citation classic; 220 short papers.

LOCKE, William Knight Herries (1919) Born 3 April 1901, Jaboticabal, São Paulo, Brazil; son of Robert Tod Locke, Civil Engineer, and Julia Carlim. **Subject(s):** Mechanical Sciences; BA 1922. **Tutor(s):** E A Benians. **Educ:** Wellington College.

LOCKWOOD, Arthur Frank (1922) Born 19 February 1905, Hainault, The Avenue, Grove Park, Wanstead, Essex; son of Henry John Lockwood, Secretary, Life Insurance Company, and Florence Elizabeth Simmons. **Tutor(s):** E Cunningham. **Johnian Relatives:** brother of Edward Harrington Lockwood (1919). **Educ:** Wanstead College, Snaresbrook; Caldicott School, Hitchin; The Leys School, Cambridge.

LOCKWOOD, Edward Harrington (1919) Born 7 June 1901, 109 Claremont Road, Forest Gate, East Ham; son of Henry John Lockwood, Secretary, National Mutual Assurance Office, and Florence Elizabeth Simmons. **Subject(s):** Mathematics; BA 1922; MA 1926. **Tutor(s):** E E Sikes. **Johnian Relatives:** brother of Arthur Frank Lockwood (1922). **Educ:** Wanstead College, Snaresbrook; Caldicott School, Hitchin; The Leys School, Cambridge. **Career:** Assistant Master, Clifton College 1923–1924; Mathematics Master, Felsted School 1924–1970. **Appointments:** Vice-president, Mathematical Association. **Awards:** Scholarship, SJC 1918. **Publications:** *A Book of Curves*, CUP, 1961; *Geometric Symmetry*, CUP, 1978. Died 19 August 1984.

LODGE, Stanley Perry (1936) Born 29 May 1918, The Hollies, St Austell, Cornwall; son of Harry Livingston Lodge, Schoolmaster, and Emily Maud Perry. **Subject(s):** Mechanical Sciences; BA 1939. **Tutor(s):** J S Boys Smith. **Educ:** The Lawn Preparatory School, St Austell; St Austell County School. **Career:** Pilot officer, RAF 1939–1940. Died 20 July 1940 (killed in a flying accident).

LOEWE, Professor Raphael James (1938) Born 16 April 1919, 4 Middleton Row, Calcutta, India; son of Herbert Martin James Loewe, Reader in Rabbinics, and Ethel Victoria Hyamson; m Chloe Klatzkin, 19 March 1952; 2 daughters. **Subject(s):** Classics; BA 1942; MA 1946; MA (by incorporation) (Oxon) 1949. **Tutor(s):** R L Howland. **Educ:** Dragon School, Oxford; The Leys School, Cambridge; Balliol College, Oxford. **Career:** War service, North Africa; James Mew School for Rabbinic Hebrew, Oxford University; Director, Institute of Jewish Studies; Lecturer in Hebrew, Leeds University 1949–1954; Bye-Fellow, Gonville & Caius College, Cambridge 1954; Lecturer in Hebrew, subsequently Reader and Goldsmid Professor, UCL 1965–1984. **Appointments:** President, Jewish Historical Society of England and Society for Old Testament Study. **Awards:** Major Scholarship, SJC 1937; John Stewart of Rannoch Scholarship in Hebrew, University of Cambridge 1939; Jeremie Septuagint Prize 1946; Seatonian Prize, University of Cambridge 2000. **Honours:** MC 1943. **Publications:** *The Rylands Haggadh*, 1985; *Solomon ibn Gabirol*, 1989; *Meshal ha-qadmoni, Fables from the Distant Past*, 2004.

LOEWENSTEIN, Max Otto Ludwig (LYNTON, Mark Oliver Lawrence) (1938) Born 16 April 1920, Stuttgart, Germany; son of Arthur J Loewenstein, Lawyer, and Martha Louise Kiefe; m Marion Sonnenberg, March 1957; 1 son (Michael b 1960), 1 daughter (Lili b 1961). **Subject(s):** Modern and Medieval Languages; BA 1941; MA 1945. **Tutor(s):** C W Guillebaud. **Educ:** Französisches Gymnasium, Berlin; Lycée Pasteur, Paris, France; Cheltenham College. **Career:** Major, Third Tank Regiment, Royal Armoured Corps; Ran Benelux Operations, Citroen (Brussels and Amsterdam) 1952–1957; Senior Executive, Hunter Douglas, Holland (remained on the board after retirement) 1957–1987. **Awards:** Major Scholarship, SJC 1937. **Publications:** *Accidental Journey: A Cambridge Internee's Memoir of World War II*, The Overlook Press, 1995. Died 1995.

LOFT, The Revd Edmund Martin Boswell (1946) Born 22 March 1925, The Vicarage, Great Carlton, Lincolnshire; son of Edmund William Boswell Loft, Clerk in Holy Orders, and Jane Western Johnson; m Valerie Jane Wills, 10 August 1963; 2 sons (Stephen Martin b 15 May 1965 and David William b 8 May 1967). **Subject(s):** Classics/Theology; BA 1949; MA 1955. **Tutor(s):** R L Howland. **Johnian Relatives:** stepson of Humphrey Phillips Walcot Burton (1907). **Educ:** King Edward VI Grammar School, Louth; St Edmund's School, Canterbury; Ely Theological College. **Career:** Royal Marines 1943–1946; Ordained Deacon, Carlisle Cathedral 1951; Assistant Curate, Holy Trinity, Carlisle 1951–1954; Ordained Priest, Carlisle Cathedral 1952; Assistant Curate, St George The Martyr, Barrow-in-Furness 1954–1956; Incumbent,

Allonby with Westnewton, Carlisle Diocese 1956–1962; Incumbent, Fillongley, Warwickshire, Coventry Diocese 1962–1977; Incumbent, St Barbara's, Earlsdon, Coventry 1977–1990. **Appointments:** Secretary, LMBC 1947–1948.

LOFTS, Robert John (1940) Born 9 March 1922, 1 London Road, Royston, Hertfordshire; son of John Francis Lofts, Bank Manager, and Katherine Jessie Pigg; m Anne Gillespie, 23 September 1950. **Subject(s):** Law; BA 1947; MA 1950. **Tutor(s):** J M Wordie. **Educ:** Harlow College; Felsted School. **Career:** Solicitor; Consultant to Nockolds, Bishop's Stortford. Died 27 July 1987.

LOMAX, William (1930) Born 25 November 1911, 83 Station Road, Kersley, Lancashire; son of Abraham Lomax, Director, Ainsworth Mercerising Company Ltd, and Florence Hollas; 1 son (John). **Subject(s):** Natural Sciences/Mechanical Sciences; BA 1933. **Tutor(s):** J M Wordie. **Educ:** C of E Elementary School, Ainsworth; The Municipal Secondary School, Ainsworth. Died March 1998.

LOMONOSSOFF, George (1926) Born 22 August 1908, Nikopol, Ekaterinoslav, Russia; son of George Vladimir Lomonossoff, Professor of Mechanics, Kiev University, and Raissa Rosen; m Peggy Winkworth; 2 sons (Nicholas b 17 October 1952 and George Peter b 15 August 1954). **Tutor(s):** J M Wordie. **Johnian Relatives:** father of Nicholas Lomonossoff (1971) and of George Peter Lomonossoff (1973). **Educ:** Francis Parker School, Chicago, USA; Leighton Park School, Reading; École Nouvelle, Lausanne. **Career:** Lieutenant Colonel, REME; Chief Inspector, Montreal Locomotive Works. Died 11 January 1954.

LONG, Albert Edward (1911) See SCHROEDER.

LONG, Archibald Percy (1908) Born 26 May 1889, King's Parade, Soham, Cambridgeshire; son of Reuben Long, Master Miller, and Ellen Crane; m Annie Hunt, 14 June 1916, St Peter's Church, Coton. **Subject(s):** Natural Sciences/Agriculture and Forestry; BA 1911. **Tutor(s):** J R Tanner. **Educ:** Soham Grammar School; Perse School, Cambridge. **Career:** Inspector, Board of Agriculture and Fisheries 1915; Divisional Officer, Timber Supplies Department, Board of Agriculture 1916–1919; Deputy Surveyor, Forest of Dean 1937–1940; Assistant Commissioner for Forestry for England and Wales 1940–1946; Director of Forestry for Wales 1946. **Honours:** OBE 1920; CBE 1952. Died 7 March 1959.

LONG, Geoffrey Wilson (1943) Born 27 August 1925, Church Farm, Wilsthorpe, Bourne, Lincolnshire; son of Wilson Cherrington Long, Warrant Officer, and Elsie Rushton. **Tutor(s):** C W Guillebaud. **Educ:** The Lickey Hills Preparatory School; Felsted School.

LONG, George Herbert (1902) Born 28 August 1883, 31 Robinson Road, Bethnal Green, Middlesex; son of William Thomas Long, Cabinet Maker, and Mary Louisa Stevenson. BA 1905; MA 1909. **Tutor(s):** D MacAlister. **Educ:** Parmiter's School, London. **Career:** Curate, All Saints, Leyton 1906–1912; Curate, St James, Hatcham 1912–1917; Vicar, Patshall 1917–1923; Vicar, Christ Church, Croydon 1923–1927. Died 1972.

LONG, Raleigh Seymour (1924) Born 14 April 1905, 43 Eldon Terrace, Leeds Road, Wakefield; son of Herbert England Long, Schoolmaster, and Mary Isabella Raleigh. **Subject(s):** Classics; BA 1929; MA 1937. **Tutor(s):** E E Sikes. **Johnian Relatives:** son of Herbert England Long (1890). **Educ:** Sowerby Bridge Secondary School. Died 5 June 1987.

LONG, William Casson (1941) Born 25 August 1923, 14 Greenhead Lane, Keighley, Yorkshire; son of Clifford Long, Chartered Accountant, and Bessie Casson; m Joan; 1 son (Duncan), 1 daughter (Jane). **Subject(s):** Economics. **Tutor(s):** C W Guillebaud. **Educ:** Drake and Tonson's School, Keighley; Keighley Grammar School; Sedbergh School. **Career:** Chartered Accountant. Died 20 October 1994.

LONG-BROWN, Kenneth (1922) See BROWN.

LONG-BROWN, Norman (1920) See BROWN.

LONGHURST, Edward Hubert Stooke (1919) Born 2 April 1900, The Vicarage, Rolleston, Nottinghamshire; son of Edward Salter Longhurst, Clerk in Holy Orders, and Jane Emma Sullock Stooke. BA 1922. **Tutor(s):** E A Benians. **Educ:** Newark Grammar School; Private Tuition; Glebe House School, Hunstanton; Malvern College; University College, Nottingham.

LONGMAN, Anthony Vivian (1949) Born 19 May 1931, 70 Woodberry Grove, Stoke Newington, London; son of Harry Longman, Candle Company's Overseas Sales Manager, and Leah Glassman. **Subject(s):** Mathematics; BA 1952; MA 1956. **Tutor(s):** J M Wordie. **Educ:** Canberra School, Hendon; City of London School.

LONGMORE, Thomas Robert William (1943) Born 24 July 1925, The Marish Cottage, Denham, Buckinghamshire; son of Charles Moorsom Longmore, Lieutenant Colonel, RA, and Jane Alexander Hammick; m Nancy Catherine Gatehouse, 1954. **Subject(s):** Classics/Archaeology and Anthropology; BA 1946; MA 1950. **Tutor(s):** C W Guillebaud. **Educ:** The Cathedral School, Salisbury; Hordle House, Milford on Sea; Wellington College, Crowthorne. **Career:** District Officer, HM Colonial Administrative Service, Northern Nigeria 1948–1960; Studied to be Solicitor 1960–1964; Partner (later Consultant), Messrs Anderson, Longmore and Higham Solicitors 1965–1990.

LONGMUIR, Professor Ian Stewart (1941) Born 12 March 1922, 184 Hyndland Road, Partick, Glasgow; son of John Bogie Longmuir, Engineer, and Rita Stewart; m Shirley Anne Wood, 24 March 1949, Church of St Edward King and Martyr, Cambridge; 1 son (Gavin); 3 daughters (Nicola, Diana and Karin). **Subject(s):** Natural Sciences; BA 1943; MA 1948; MB 1948; BChir 1948. **Tutor(s):** R L Howland. **Educ:** Jordanhill College School, Glasgow; Glasgow Academy. **Career:** House Physician, St Bartholomew's Hospital, London 1948; Assistant in Research, Department of Colloid Science, University of Cambridge 1948–1951; Senior, later Principal, Scientific Officer, Microbiological Research Department, Porton 1951–1954; Senior Lecturer in Biochemistry, Institute of Diseases of the Chest, University of London 1954–1965; Professor of Chemistry, North Carolina State University, Raleigh, North Carolina, USA 1965–1991. **Awards:** Scholarship, SJC. **Publications:** Approximately 100 papers on Biochemistry and related topics.

LOOSARARIAN, Armèn Barouyr (1945) Born 25 July 1923, New York, USA; son of Barouyr Loosararian, Designer, and Lucy Parseghian. **Tutor(s):** C W Guillebaud. **Educ:** Collège Arménien Samuel Moorat, Sèvres, France; School of Foreign Service, Georgetown University, Washington DC; Stuyvesant High School, New York City. **Career:** Technician, 4th Class, US Army.

LOOSEMORE, Thomas Gordon Evans (1936) Born 23 June 1918, Llwynon, St Martin's Road, Caerphilly; son of Percy Tom Loosemore, Clerk to Plympton District Council, and Gladys Evans; m Mary Michel Thompson, 4 October 1951; 1 daughter, 1 son. **Subject(s):** Natural Sciences; BA 1939; MA 1943; BChir 1943; MChir 1951. **Tutor(s):** R L Howland. **Educ:** Plymouth College Preparatory School; Plymouth College. **Career:** Airborne Field Ambulance Service; served in Ireland, Norway and India 1939–1945; London Cancer Hospital 1945–1949; Consultant Surgeon, Watford General Hospital 1953; Senior Surgeon, Watford General Hospital 1966–1976. Died 1976.

LOOSER, Richard Bernhardt (1945) Born 19 April 1919, Cleveland, Ohio, USA; son of Richard Francis Looser, General Manager, Ward's Baking Company, and Della Ruth Clark. **Tutor(s):** C W Guillebaud. **Educ:** Wayne University, Detroit; Western Reserve University, Cleveland; Garfield Heights High School. **Career:** Sergeant, US Army.

LOOSLEY, Stanley George Henry (1928) Born 18 July 1910, Ingleside, 36 Wellington Road, Maidenhead; son of Harold Downer Loosley, Bank Inspector, and Edith Maud Matthews; m Margaret Luker; 2 sons (John Richard and Robert George), 1 daughter (Elisabeth Jill). **Subject(s):** Geography/Mathematics; BA 1932; MA 1938. **Tutor(s):** J M Wordie. **Johnian Relatives:** brother-in-law of Cyril Tom Luker (1929); father of John Richard Loosley (1959). **Educ:** Mayville High School, Waverley Road, Southsea; Highland Road School, Southsea; St Helen's College, Southsea; Wycliffe College, Stonehouse. **Career:** RA 1939–1945; Headmaster, Wycliffe College, Stonehouse 1949–1967. **Awards:** Medal of Merit, Scout Association 1967. **Honours:** MC. **Publications:** *History of Wycliffe College*, 1982. Died 23 July 1991.

LORD, Alan (1947) Born 12 April 1929, Rochdale, Lancashire; son of Frederick Lord, Deputy General Manager, Rochdale Equitable Pioneers (Co-operative) Society, and Anne Whitworth; m Joan Ogden, 1953; 2 daughters (Hilary Margaret b 1958 and Rosemary Elizabeth b 1964). **Subject(s):** English/Archaeology and Anthropology; BA 1950; MA 1987. **Tutor(s):** F Thistlethwaite; R L Howland. **Educ:** Rochdale Municipal High School. **Career:** Inland Revenue 1950; Private Secretary to Deputy Chairman and to Chairman of the Board, Inland Revenue 1952–1954; HM Treasury 1959–1962; Principal Private Secretary to First Secretary of State 1962–1963; Inland Revenue 1963–1969; Commissioner 1969–1971, Deputy Chairman 1971–1973, Inland Revenue; Principal Finance Officer to DTI, subsequently to Departments of Industry, Trade, and Prices and Consumer Protection 1973–1975; Second Permanent Secretary (Domestic Economy), HM Treasury 1975–1977; Executive Director 1978–1984, Managing Director 1980–1982, Chief Executive 1983–1984, Dunlop Holdings; Managing Director 1978–1982, Chairman 1983–1984, Dunlop International AG; Chairman, Dunlop Limited 1983–1984; Non-Executive Director and Chairman, Dunlop Tire and Rubber Inc (USA) 1982–1984; Deputy Chairman and Chief Executive, Lloyd's of London 1986–1992. **Appointments:** Member, Council of Management, Henley Centre for Forecasting 1977–1982; Chairman, CBI Taxation Committee 1979–1981; Non-Executive Director, Allied-Lyons plc 1979–1986; Governor, NIESR; Trustee, Southern Africa Studies Trust 1982–1984; Non-Executive Director, Bank of England 1983–1986; Non-Executive Director, Johnson Matthey Bankers 1985–1986; President, Johnian Society 1985–1986; Member, Investments Committee, SJC 1993–2001. **Honours:** CB 1972. **Publications:** 'A Strategy for Industry', Sir Ellis Hunter Memorial Lecture, University of York, 1976; 'Earning an Industrial Living', Johnian Society Lecture, 1985.

LORD, Geoffrey Frank (1929) Born 9 May 1911, Lydstep, Grove Road, Cheam; son of Sydney Lord, Hosier and Outfitter, and Bessie Catton; m Margaret Scarf Theobald, 28 July 1948, London. **Tutor(s):** C W Guillebaud. **Educ:** Homefield School, Sutton; Sompting Abbots, Worthing; Shrewsbury School.

LORD, Geoffrey Fraser (1909) Born 14 June 1890, Kolhapur, Presidency of Bombay, India; son of Hugh Fraser Lord, Clerk in Holy Orders, and Alice Mary Shadwell. **Subject(s):** Classics; BA 1912. **Tutor(s):** E E Sikes. **Educ:** Tonbridge School. **Career:** Calcutta Volunteer Artillery, WWI; Burma Oil Company 1923. Died 20 February 1941.

LORD, George Geoffrey (1942) Born 15 August 1924, 108 Boothferry Road, Goole, Yorkshire; son of George Henry Lord, District Cartage Representative, and Elizabeth Laurie Hopley. **Subject(s):** Mechanical Sciences; BA 1945; MA 1949. **Tutor(s):** S J Bailey. **Educ:** Alexandra Street School, Goole; Goole Grammar School; Bridlington School.

LORD, Michael Hilton Joseph (1942) Born 6 September 1924, 227 Rochdale Road, Bury, Lancashire; son of Joseph Lord, Builder's Manager, and Kathleen Mary Hilton Brown. **Subject(s):** Modern and Medieval Languages; BA 1947; MA 1976. **Tutor(s):** C W Guillebaud. **Educ:** Hull High School for Girls; Hymers College, Hull. **Honours:** MBE.

LORD, Peter Herent (1943) Born 23 November 1925, 134 Werneth Hall Road, Oldham, Lancashire; son of Frank Lord, Master Builder, and Rosalie Jeanette Herent; m Florence Shirley Hirst, 1952; 2 sons (Frank Herent b 1954 and Peter Herent b 1960), 2 daughters (Rozanne Herent b 1953 and Janine Herent b 1957). **Subject(s):** Natural Sciences; BA 1946; MA 1956; MB 1949; BChir 1949; MChir 1961; FRCS. **Tutor(s):** S J Bailey. **Educ:** Werneth Council School; Manchester Grammar School. **Career:** Salford Royal Hospital, Christie Hospital, Manchester, St Margaret's, Epping, St George's Hospital 1949–1956; Captain, RAMC (National Service) 1953–1954; Senior Registrar, St George's Hospital 1956–1963; Consultant Surgeon, Wycombe General Hospital, High Wycombe 1964–1990. **Appointments:** H N Smith Research Fellow 1964, Penrose May Teacher 1970, Council Member 1978–1990, Vice-President 1986–1987, Senior Vice-President 1988, Royal College of Surgeons; Past Master, Worshipful Company of Barbers 1978. **Honours:** OBE 1991. **Publications:** *Cardiac Pacemakers*, 1964; *Pilonidal Sinus*, 1964; *Wound Healing*, 1966; *Haemorrhoids*, 1969; *Hydrocoele*, 1972; *Surgery in Old Age*, 1980.

LORDING, Robert Kenneth (1943) Born 8 August 1924, 6 North Common Road, Ealing; son of Frank Lording, Accountant, and Evelyn Madge Hastie. **Tutor(s):** C W Guillebaud. **Educ:** St Agnes College, Ealing; Rutland House School, Hanwell; Latymer Upper School, Hammersmith.

LORENZ, Hans Hugo Herbert (1907) Born 5 May 1888, 143 Devonshire Road, Forest Hill, Sydenham, Kent; son of Max Hugo Lorenz, Chemical Merchant, and Fanny Laura Joanna Hoffmeister; m Jessamy James, 6 November 1942, London. **Subject(s):** Natural Sciences; BA 1910; MA 1914. **Tutor(s):** J R Tanner. **Educ:** Dulwich College.

LORIMER, Guy (1929) Born 8 December 1909, 20 Fairview Road, Oxton, Tranmere; son of John Cyril Lorimer, Bank Cashier, and Alice Winifred Curwen; m Eileen Warleigh; 1 son (Alastair Cyril b 1 May 1946). **Subject(s):** Classics; BA 1932; MA 1939. **Tutor(s):** M P Charlesworth. **Johnian Relatives:** father of Alastair Cyril Lorimer (1964). **Educ:** Birkenhead Preparatory School; Birkenhead School; New College, Oxford; London School of Oriental Studies. **Career:** Cadet in Nigeria, Later Permanent Secretary for Northern Cameroons Affairs, Nigeria 1933, Cadet in Gambia 1939–1943, Colonial Office; Secretary, Derby Diocesan Board of Finance 1962. Died 31 January 1995.

LOTLIKAR, Vasant Mahadeo (1919) Born 23 October 1898, Poona, India; son of Mahadeo Dinkar Lotlikar, Secretary of Poona Municipality. BA (Bombay) 1919. **Tutor(s):** E A Benians. **Educ:** Municipal Vernacular School, No 4, Poona; New English School, Poona; Fergusson College, Poona.

LOUGH, Professor John (1931) Born 19 February 1913, 2 Holly Avenue West, Newcastle upon Tyne; son of Wilfred Gordon Lough, Meat Salesman, and Mary Turnbull Millican; m Muriel Barker, 1939 (d 1998); 1 daughter (Judith). **Subject(s):** Modern and Medieval Languages; BA 1934; MA 1938; PhD 1937; Honorary Doctor (Clermont) 1967; Honorary DLitt (Newcastle) 1972; FBA 1975. **Tutor(s):** C W Guillebaud. **Johnian Relatives:** brother of William Lough (1933). **Educ:** St Andrew's School, Jesmond; Royal Grammar School, Newcastle upon Tyne. **Career:** Assistant (later Lecturer), University of Aberdeen 1937–1946; Lecturer in French, University of Cambridge 1946–1952; Professor of French, University of Durham 1952–1978. **Appointments:** Leverhulme Resident Fellow 1973. **Awards:** Scholarship, SJC; Esmond Scholarship, British Institute, Paris 1935; Jebb Studentship, Cambridge 1936; Officier de l'Ordre National du Mérite 1973. **Publications:** *An Introduction to Eighteenth Century France*, 1960; *An Introduction to Nineteenth Century France*, 1978; *Writer and Public in France*, 1978; *Seventeenth Century French Drama: the Background*, 1979; *The Philosophes and Post–Revolutionary France*, 1982; *France Observed in the Seventeenth Century by British Travellers*, 1985; *France on the Eve of Revolution: Observations by British travellers 1763–1788*, 1987; *John*

Graham Lough (1798–1876), a Northumbrian Sculptor, 1987, (with E Merson); Articles on French literature and ideas in 17th and 18th centuries, in French and English learned journals. Died 21 June 2000.

LOUGH, William (1933) Born 15 September 1914, 2 Holly Avenue West, Newcastle upon Tyne; son of Wilfrid Gordon Lough, Master Butcher, and Mary Turnbull Millican; m Noreen Kelly; 2 sons (John b 1964 and Jeffrey b 1968), 1 daughter (Elizabeth b 1946). **Subject(s):** Modern and Medieval Languages; BA 1936; MA 1940. **Tutor(s):** C W Guillebaud. **Johnian Relatives:** brother of John Lough (1931). **Educ:** Royal Grammar School, Newcastle upon Tyne; Church High School, Newcastle upon Tyne. **Career:** Assistant Master, Royal Grammar School, Newcastle upon Tyne 1937–1939; War service, UK, India, Burma 1940–1946; Assistant Master, Lancing College 1940–1947; Head, Department of Languages, RMA, Sandhurst 1947–1974; Assistant Master, Christ's Hospital School 1974–1984. **Honours:** MBE 1946; OBE 1966. **Publications:** (ed) Erich Kästner, *Als ich ein kleiner Junge War*. Died 5 October 2000.

LOURIE, Arthur (1923) Born 10 March 1903, 90 Loveday Street, Johannesburg, South Africa; son of Harry Lourie, Wholesale Jeweller and Optician, and Regina Muller. **Subject(s):** Law; BA 1925; MA 1930; LLB 1925. **Tutor(s):** E A Benians. **Educ:** King Edward VII School, Johannesburg, South Africa; University of Capetown. **Career:** First Israel Consul-General in New York and Deputy Leader, Israel's Delegation to the UN; Israel's Ambassador to Canada; Choate Memorial Fellow, Harvard 1925–1926; Called to the Bar, the Inner Temple 1927; Secretary, Jewish Agency in London 1933–1940; Secretary, American Zionist Council 1940–1946; Head, United Nations Department, Jewish Agency 1946; Deputy Director-General, Israel's Foreign Ministry 1953; Israeli Ambassador in London 1960–1965. **Awards:** Scholarship, SJC. Died 1978.

LOVE, Professor Christopher Charles (1930) Born 1 September 1911, Uppingham, Rutland; son of John Joseph Love, Master Baker, and Mabel Helena Scott. **Subject(s):** Classics; BA 1933; MA 1937; PhD (Toronto) 1950; Honorary DLS (Victoria) 1990. **Tutor(s):** M P Charlesworth. **Educ:** Oakham School. **Career:** Classics Teacher, Victoria College, University of Toronto 1933; Classics Master, Bishop's College School, Lennoxville, Quebec 1933; Instructor in Navigation, Royal Canadian Navy 1941; Lecturer 1948, Assistant Professor 1954, Associate Professor 1960, Professor Emeritus 1977, English Faculty, Victoria College, University of Toronto. **Awards:** Sizarship, SJC; Commemorative Medal, 125th Anniversary of Canadian Confederation, 27 November 1992. Died 20 May 1998.

LOVE, Francis Stanley (1908) Born 10 June 1889, 97 South Street, Greenwich; son of Alfred Love, Vicar of St Paul's, Greenwich, and Julia Pugh. **Tutor(s):** J R Tanner. **Educ:** Weymouth College.

LOVERIDGE, Arthur John (1923) Born 24 August 1904, 3 Marine Parade, Sheerness, Kent; son of Charles William Loveridge, Admiralty Writer, Civil Service, and Alice Annie French; m Marjorie Gertrude Coleman, 1932, Shepperton; 1 daughter. **Subject(s):** Economics; BA 1926; MA 1930. **Tutor(s):** E A Benians. **Johnian Relatives:** brother of Charles Edward Loveridge (1925). **Educ:** St Mary's Elementary School, Balham; Emanuel School, Wandsworth Common. **Career:** Admitted to the Middle Temple 1927; Assistant Secretary, Institute of Industrial Psychology 1927; Called to the Bar 1932; Senior Judicial Adviser, Gold Coast 1947; Chief Commissioner, Gold Coast Colony 1950–1953; Chief Commissioner, Northern Territories 1953–1954; Chief Commissioner, Ashanti 1954–1956. **Appointments:** Member, Commission of Enquiry into Disturbances in Sierra Leone 1956, Uganda, 1960. **Honours:** OBE 1947; CMG 1954. **Publications:** *The Management of Education*, 1965. Died 11 August 1975.

LOVERIDGE, Charles Edward (1925) Born 11 April 1907, 19 Dagnan Road, Balham, Surrey; son of Charles William Loveridge, Civil Servant, and Alice Annie French. **Tutor(s):** J M Wordie. **Johnian Relatives:** brother of Arthur John Loveridge (1923). **Educ:** St Mary's Elementary School, Balham; Emanuel School, Wandsworth Common.

LOVERIDGE, Sir John Warren (1943) Born 9 September 1925, Hillburn, West Road, Bowdon, Cheshire; son of Claude Warren Loveridge, Civil Engineer, and Emilie Muriel Malone, College Principal; m Jean Marguerite Chivers, 12 June 1954; 3 sons (Michael, Steven and Robert), 2 daughters (Amanda and Emma). BA 1946; MA 1949; FRAS; FRAgS; ARBS 2001. **Tutor(s):** C W Guillebaud. **Johnian Relatives:** father of Emma Warren Loveridge (1984). **Educ:** Privately educated, London. **Career:** Painter; Modern Sculptor; Senior Partner of family businesses in agriculture, education and property; Principal, international residential college and schools 1956–; Member of Parliament (Conservative), Hornchurch 1970–1974; Member of Parliament (Conservative), Upminster 1974–1983. **Appointments:** Member, Hampstead Borough Council 1953–1959; Treasurer/Trustee, Hampstead Conservative Association 1959–1974; JP, West Central Division 1963; Vice-President, National Council for Civil Protection 1980–; Member, Guild of Freemen of the City of London; Vice-President 1984–1993 and 1996–, President 1993–1996, Greater London Area Conservatives; President, Hampstead and Highgate Conservative Association 1986–1991; President, Upminster Conservative Association 1992–2002; President, Dinosaurs Club 1999–2003. **Honours:** Kt 1988. **Publications:** *God Save the Queen, Sonnets of Elizabeth I*, 1981; (jointly) *Moving Forward: Small Businesses and The Economy*, 1983; *Hunter of the Moon*, 1983; *Hunter of the Sun*, 1984; *New Sculpture in Stone, Metal, Wood and Glass*, 2000.

LOW, Bevis Brunel (1914) Born 10 May 1896, 2 Mansfield Gardens, Ilford, Essex; son of David Allan Low, Professor of Engineering, and Eliza Jessie Miller; m Isabel Collier Shanks, 14 April 1923; 3 sons (Allan Andrew b 6 August 1924, d 17 April 1996, Edward David b 6 August 1924 and David Frank Bevis b 4 March 1926, d 25 May 1939). **Subject(s):** Mechanical Sciences; BA 1921; MA 1924; MIMechE 1944. **Tutor(s):** L H K Bushe-Fox. **Johnian Relatives:** father of Edward David Low (1942). **Educ:** Glenarm College, Ilford; Cranbrook College; Bancrofts School, Woodford. **Career:** Gunner, Second Lieutenant, MGC, Honourable Artillery Company 1917–1919; Demonstrator in Mechanical Engineering, Artillery College, Woolwich 1921–1922; Lecturer, Military College of Science (formerly Artillery College), Woolwich 1922–1945. **Publications:** *Mathematics*, 1931; *Strength of Materials*, 1949; *Theory of Machines*, 1954. Died 4 July 1959.

LOW, Edward David (1942) Born 6 August 1924, Stonefield, Kidbrooke Grove, London; son of Bevis Brunel Low, Lecturer in Mechanical Engineering, and Isabel Collier Shanks; m Joyce Marie Barrett, 5 August 1969. **Subject(s):** Mechanical Sciences; BA 1946; MA 1949; CEng; MIMechE. **Tutor(s):** S J Bailey. **Johnian Relatives:** son of Bevis Brunel Low (1914). **Educ:** Dartford Grammar School; The King's School, Macclesfield. **Career:** Flight Test Engineer, Bristol Aeroplane Company Limited 1945–1949; Graduate Apprentice 1949–1951, Mechanical Engineer 1951–1969, Chief Mechanical Engineer 1969–1971, George Kent Ltd, Luton, Bedfordshire; Founder Member and Director, Measurement Technology Ltd, Luton, Bedfordshire 1971–1985.

LOW, Kenneth Graham (1919) Born 1 November 1902, 8 Pembridge Villas, Kensington, London; son of Alexander Graham Low, Gentleman, Cement Manufacturer, and Annie Halley. **Tutor(s):** E E Sikes. **Johnian Relatives:** brother of Robert Fairweather Low (1919). **Educ:** Hildersham House, Broadstairs; Malvern College.

LOW, Robert Fairweather (1919) Born 15 April 1900, 8 Pembridge Villas, Kensington, London; son of Alexander Graham Low, Gentleman, Cement Manufacturer, and Annie Halley. BA 1923; MA 1926. **Tutor(s):** E E Sikes. **Johnian Relatives:** brother of Kenneth Graham Low (1919). **Educ:** Hildersham House, Broadstairs; Malvern College. **Career:** Royal College of Music; Headmaster, Gorselands School, Newbury, Berkshire. Died 14 January 1963.

LOWDEN, Gordon Stuart (1944) Born 22 May 1927, Bangkok, Siam; son of James Soutar Lowden, Chartered Accountant, and Jean Walker Watson Yule. **Subject(s):** Law; BA 1948; MA 1951. **Tutor(s):** S J Bailey. **Johnian Relatives:** brother of Victor Soutar Lowden (1940) and of James Stiven Lowden (1946). **Educ:** Dundee High School; Strathallan School. **Career:** Lecturer in Accountancy Law, Queen's College, Dundee, University of St Andrews.

LOWDEN, James Stiven (1946) Born 4 July 1925, Bangkok, Siam; son of James Soutar Lowden, Chartered Accountant, and Jean Walker Watson Yule; m Jean Scott Stiven, 10 September 1951; 3 daughters (Lesley, Morag and Heather). **Subject(s):** Mathematics; BA 1949; MA 1953. **Tutor(s):** J M Wordie. **Johnian Relatives:** brother of Victor Soutar Lowden (1940) and of Gordon Stuart Lowden (1944). **Educ:** Dundee High School; Strathallan School; University of St Andrews. **Awards:** Scholarship, SJC.

LOWDEN, Victor Soutar (1940) Born 13 September 1923, Bankok, Siam; son of James Soutar Lowden, Chartered Accountant, and Jean Walker Watson Yule; m Helen Richmond Hunter Bond, 11 December 1944; 1 son, 1 daughter. **Subject(s):** Economics; BA 1943; MA 1947. **Tutor(s):** S J Bailey. **Johnian Relatives:** brother of Gordon Stuart Lowden (1944) and of James Stiven Lowden (1946). **Educ:** High School, Dundee; Strathallan School. **Career:** Fleet Air Arm; Export Salesman 1946–1961, Export Manager 1961–1964, Special Director, and supervisor of subsidiary companies 1964–1969, Group Director 1969–1980, Low & Bonar (Group) Plc, Dundee; Business Consultant 1980–1988. **Honours:** DSC 1945. Died June 1998.

LOWE, Charles Frederick Peter (1920) Born 17 January 1903, Cornbrook, Legh Road, Knutsford, Cheshire; son of Clement Ward Lowe, Manufacturing Chemist, and Dora Lilian Bailey. BA 1924; MA 1969. **Tutor(s):** E E Sikes. **Educ:** The Old Hall School, Wellington, Salop; Charterhouse School.

LOWE, Robert Conyers (1940) Born 30 June 1922, 60 St Martin's, Stamford; son of Charles Conyers Lowe, Solicitor, and Marjorie Winifred Jones. **Subject(s):** Economics/Law; BA 1947; MA 1949. **Educ:** Stamford School. **Career:** Second Lieutenant, RA 1941–1942, Captain 1944, India and Burma, Major 1945; Consultant to Stapleton and Son, Stamford. Died 30 September 1988.

LUCAS, Ernest Charles (1904) Born 16 November 1870, Wiveliscombe, Somerset; son of Edwin Lucas, Schoolmaster, and Eliza Millett. **Subject(s):** Natural Sciences; BA 1907; MA 1911; LLB 1913. **Tutor(s):** D MacAlister. **Career:** Master, The Modern School, Leeds.

LUCAS, Walter Edward (1919) Born 4 December 1898, Richmond, Natal, South Africa; son of Edward Lucas, Captain, Army, and Maud Letitia Harte. **Subject(s):** History; BA 1920; MA 1927. **Tutor(s):** E A Benians. **Educ:** Wychwood School, Bournemouth; Winton House, Winchester; Wellington College. **Awards:** Exhibition, SJC 1917.

LUISI, Hector Angel Francisco (1944) Born 19 September 1919, Montevideo, Uruguay; son of Enrique Carlos Hector Luisi, Under-Secretary of National Defence, Uruguay, and Ines Berta Rodriguez Serpa. Doctor of Law and Civil Sciences (Montevideo) 1944. **Tutor(s):** C W Guillebaud. **Educ:** Liceo de Ensenanza Secundaria, Montevideo; Escuela Naval; University of Montevideo, Uruguay. **Career:** Teacher of Civic and Democratic Education, Military School.

LUKER, Cyril Tom (1931) Born 30 June 1913, Enfield, Graems Road, Madras; son of Arthur Tom Luker, Indian Import Merchant, and Mabel Gertrude Hoskins; m Jean Silvey; 4 daughters (Anne, Judith, Alison and Helen). **Subject(s):** Economics/Geography; BA 1934; MA 1938. **Tutor(s):** C W Guillebaud. **Johnian Relatives:** brother in law of Stanley George Henry Loosley (1928); uncle of John Richard Loosley (1959). **Educ:** Wycliffe College, Stonehouse. **Career:** Engineer, Joseph Lucas 1938–1953; Personnel Manager, Rotax 1953–1962. Died July 1962.

LUMB, Captain William (1907) Born 8 August 1886, 12 Boot Street, Burnley, Lancashire; son of Joseph Lumb, Tape Sizer, and Elizabeth Riley; m Mabel Elizabeth; 1 daughter (Angela). **Subject(s):** Modern and Medieval Languages; BA 1910. **Tutor(s):** E E Sikes. **Educ:** Burnley Wood Board School; Burnley Higher Grade School; Nelson Pupil Teacher Centre. **Career:** Master, Coatham Grammar School 1910–1911; Master, Wellington County School 1912–1913; Captain, RASC (Mentioned in Despatches), WWI; Master, Holloway County School 1926; Modern Language Master, King Edward VI Grammar School, Birmingham 1926. **Publications:** *Les Affaires*, Harrap. Died 7 November 1961.

LUND, Dr Guy Sefton (1913) Born 4 April 1894, Tydesley Vicarage, Atherton, Lancashire; son of John Lund, Clerk in Orders, and Susan Ramsden. BA 1919; MA 1925; LRCP; MRCS. **Tutor(s):** E E Sikes. **Johnian Relatives:** son of John Lund (1877). **Educ:** Denstone College. **Career:** Second Lieutenant, Manchester Regiment (TF), WWI; St Thomas' Hospital 1922 (House Physician, Children's Department, Clinical Assistant, Skin Department, Resident Orthopaedic House Surgeon); House Physician and House Surgeon, Addenbrooke's Hospital. **Publications:** Papers in *Biochemical Journal*.

LUND, Niels Theodore Walter (1919) Born 24 August 1897, Germiston, Transvaal, South Africa; son of Theodore Lund, Doctor of Medicine, and Emily Mary Heeley. BA 1923. **Tutor(s):** E A Benians. **Educ:** King Edward VII School, Johannesburg. Died 5 June 1986.

LUNN, John (1928) Born 26 December 1903, 26 Lower Green Lane, Astley, Leigh, Lancashire; son of John Lunn, Coal Merchant, and Annie Sanderson. **Tutor(s):** E A Benians. **Educ:** Leigh Grammar School; Victoria University, Manchester. **Awards:** Mullinger Scholarship, SJC 1928.

LUPTON, Kenneth Lofthouse (1942) Born 14 December 1922, 53 Windsor Terrace, Gosforth, Newcastle upon Tyne; son of George Cyril Lupton, Bank Cashier, and Ethel Waller Lofthouse. **Tutor(s):** S J Bailey. **Educ:** West Jesmond Council School, Newcastle upon Tyne; Baltic Street Council School, Hartlepool; Boys' High School, West Hartlepool; Royal Grammar School, Newcastle upon Tyne.

LUPTON, Neville Lloyd (1934) Born 7 March 1915, School House, Ffynnongynydd, Glasbury on Wye; son of Henry Kerr Lupton, Schoolmaster, and Sarah Jane Lloyd. **Subject(s):** English/History. **Tutor(s):** J S Boys Smith. **Educ:** Durham Cathedral Chorister School; Bacup Rawtenstall Grammar School; Pocklington School. **Awards:** Dowman Exhibition, SJC. Died September 1976.

LUSH, Jesse Hugh (1924) Born 20 October 1905, 2 Milburn Road, Gillingham, Kent; son of William Jesse Lush, Post Officer, RN, and Agnes Caroline Poland. **Subject(s):** English; BA 1927. **Tutor(s):** B F Armitage. **Educ:** Beacon Road LCC School, Hither Green, London; St Dunstan's College, London. **Career:** Assistant Master, Portsmouth Grammar School 1928–1929; Assistant Master, Marlborough College 1929–1930; Assistant Organist and Music Master, Trinity College, Glenalmond 1930–1932; Assistant Master, Ardingley 1933–1934; Assistant Master, Owen's School, Islington 1934; Army 1939–1945. **Awards:** John Stewart of Rannoch Scholarship in Sacred Music, University of Cambridge 1925. Died 24 December 1945.

LUSK, James (1902) Born 19 September 1878, Gowan Brae, Tollcross, Broomhouse, Lanarkshire; son of John Lusk, Master Baker, and Jessie Colville. **Subject(s):** Mechanical Sciences; BA 1905. **Tutor(s):** D MacAlister. **Educ:** Uddingston School; Glasgow and West Scotland Technical College. **Career:** Director, Colville & Sons Steel Works; Staff Captain, then Captain and Adjutant, 6th Cameronians (Scottish Rifles, TF) (Mentioned in Despatches) 1910–1915. **Honours:** Chevalier, Legion d'Honneur (France) 1915. **Publications:** *James Lusk: Letters and Memories*, 1916. Died 29 December 1915 (of wounds received in action 25 December 1915).

LUTLEY, The Revd Albert French (1919) Born 24 October 1900, Shanghai, China; son of Albert Lutley, Missionary, China Inland Mission, and Elizabeth Roberts; m Martha Davis Bullitt, 9 June 1925, Princeton, New Jersey, USA; 3 sons (James Bullitt b 21 March 1927, d 1935, John Herbert b 10 February 1935 and Albert Davis b 12 July 1940), 3 daughters (Mary Edith b 5 February 1929, Elizabeth Roberts b 26 April 1933 and Margaret Bullitt b 17 November 1936). **Subject(s):** Classics/Theology; BA 1922; MA 1926; ThM (Princeton Theological Seminary) 1925. **Tutor(s):** E E Sikes. **Johnian Relatives:** father of John Herbert Lutley (1955). **Educ:** China Inland Mission Schools, Chefoo, Shantung, North China; Dean Close School, Cheltenham. **Career:** Ordained Deacon 1930; Missionary, Church Missionary Society, Chengtu, Szechwan 1930–1944; Ordained Priest, West China 1933; Port Chaplain and Priest in Charge, Chefoo 1934–1937; Lecturer, Union Theological College, Chengtu 1939–1944; Cultural Fellow in Chinese Studies 1945–1946, Lecturer in Chinese 1946–1947, Columbia University; Priest in Charge, Great with Little Somerford, Wiltshire 1947–1949; Vicar, Charlton with Brokenborough, Malmesbury 1949–1952; Rector, Great with Little Somerford 1952–1966. **Awards:** Naden Studentship, SJC; Hughes Exhibition. Died 7 October 1975.

LYALL, David Ellis (1948) Born 14 September 1926, 81 Headingley Mount, Leeds; son of Horace Vernon Lyall, Accountant, and Constance Mary Ellis; m Jean Denham, 30 August 1952; 1 son (Andrew), 3 daughters (Helen, Claire and Sarah). **Subject(s):** Mathematics; BA 1951; MA 1955. **Tutor(s):** J M Wordie. **Educ:** Headingley Kindergarten; Leeds Grammar School. **Career:** West Yorkshire Regiment and Army Educational Corps 1946–1948; St Bees School, Cumbria 1952–1991 (Housemaster 1959–1981, Head of Mathematics 1959–1988, Deputy Head 1983–1988). **Appointments:** Member, Hawks Club 1949; Captain, Athletics Club, SJC 1950–1951; Honorary Freeman, Berwick-upon-Tweed 1968.

LYDALL, Edward Francis (1926) Born 4 August 1907, 16 Bedford Gardens, Kensington, London; son of Francis Lydall, Electrical Engineer, and Georgina Anne Day; m Norah Trevor Gell, 25 March 1961. **Subject(s):** Modern and Medieval Languages; BA 1929; MA 1937. **Tutor(s):** E A Benians. **Johnian Relatives:** son of Francis Lydall (1893). **Educ:** Ovingdean School, Brighton; Marlborough College; University of Munich, Bavaria, Germany. **Career:** Director, Christabel Foundation, Switzerland; Indian Civil Service 1931; Second Secretary, HM Legation at Kabul 1940–1941; President, Manipur State Council 1944; Assistant Commissioner, Assam; Called to the Bar, Inner Temple and practised at the Common Law Bar and the Midland Circuit 1970. **Publications:** *Enough of Action*, 1949 (autobiography, three volumes); *That's me, that was*, 1975; *Over the Hills*, 1993. Died 28 March 1998.

LYNCH, Thomas (1939) Born 27 September 1920, 36 Stanley Road, Barrow-in-Furness; son of Thomas Lynch, Draughtsman and Constructional Engineer, and Janet Balfour Baxter. **Tutor(s):** J M Wordie. **Educ:** Barrow Island School for Boys; Barrow Grammar School.

LYNN, Charles William (1927) Born 31 May 1908, 43 Wiverton Road, Sydenham, Beckenham, Kent; son of William Lynn, Civil Servant, Post Office, and Jemima Leggatt. DipAgr (Wye). **Tutor(s):** C W Guillebaud. **Educ:** St John's School, Penge; Clayesmore School, Enfield; Ingatestone House School; South Eastern Agricultural College, Wye. **Career:** Agricultural Officer, Gold Coast 1929–1942; Senior Agricultural Officer, Gold Coast 1942–1947; Imperial College of Tropical Agriculture 1947; Assistant Director of Agriculture, Gold Coast 1952; Director of Agriculture, Northern Rhodesia 1952. **Awards:** Scholarship from Empire Cotton-Growing Corporation.

LYNTON, Mark Oliver Lawrence (1938) See LOEWENSTEIN.

LYON, Dr Alexander Geoffrey (1947) Born 10 August 1918, 15 Richmondhill Place, Aberdeen; son of Alexander Lyon, Major, Gordon Highlanders, and Ruby Grant. PhD 1951; BSc (St Andrews) 1947. **Tutor(s):** G C L Bertram. **Educ:** Angusfield House, Aberdeen; Fettes College, Edinburgh; University of St Andrews. **Career:** Lecturer in Botany 1951–1964, Senior Lecturer in Botany 1964–1973, University College of Wales, Cardiff. Died 25 March 1999.

LYON, Francis John (1927) Born 24 February 1909, Beechwood, Thorn Park Road, Mannamead, Plymouth, Devon; son of Francis Howard Lyon, Engineer Commander, Royal Navy, and Evelyn Bayard Hall. **Subject(s):** Natural Sciences; BA 1930. **Tutor(s):** C W Guillebaud. **Educ:** Gresham's Junior School; Gresham's School, Holt. **Career:** Assistant Conservator of Forests, Colonial Forestry Service, Gold Coast 1933. Died 24 November 1933.

LYON, Dr Ian Barclay (1947) Born 17 May 1929, 198 Cromwell Road, Kensington, London; son of Alexander Barclay Lyon, Barrister-at-Law, and Margaret McLeod Henderson. **Subject(s):** Natural Sciences; BA 1950; MA 1991; BChir 1953; MB 1953. **Tutor(s):** G C L Bertram. **Johnian Relatives:** brother-in-law of Michael George Huxtable (1947). **Educ:** Willington School, Putney; Furzie Close, Barton on Sea; Clifton College. **Career:** GP.

LYON, Norman Geoffrey (1925) Born 2 July 1906, 97 Burley Lodge Road, Burley, Leeds, Yorkshire; son of James Lyon, School Master, and Sarah Martha Halliday; m Muriel Olive Rymer (née Silburn), 11 December 1943, Michaelhouse Chapel, Natal; 1 son (Richard Donald Halliday b January 1945), 1 stepson (Jolyon James Hugh b 4 October 1926). **Subject(s):** Classics; BA 1928; MA 1932. **Tutor(s):** M P Charlesworth. **Johnian Relatives:** stepfather of Jolyon James Hugh Rymer (1945). **Educ:** Queen's Road Council School, Leeds; The Grammar School, Leeds. **Career:** House Master, Michaelhouse, Balgowan, Natal. Died 20 November 1945.

LYON, William (1941) Born 13 April 1924, 25 Westfield Street, St Helens, Lancashire; son of William Lyon, Builder and Contractor, and Elizabeth Morvill Scowcroft. **Subject(s):** Law; BA 1947; MA 1949. **Tutor(s):** S J Bailey. **Educ:** St Luke's Church of England Elementary School, St Helens; Prescot Grammar School.

LYONS, Peter Stanley (1948) Born 6 December 1927, 16 Atherfold Road, Stockwell, London; son of Harold Leslie Lyons, Waiter, and Teresa Gadsden; m Bridget Webb-Jones, 31 July 1957, Wells Cathedral; 1 son (James Andrew b 8 December 1961), 2 daughters (Arabella Mary b 28 April 1958 and Virginia Clare b 12 September 1959). BA 1950; MA 1955. **Tutor(s):** C W Guillebaud. **Educ:** Haselrigge Road School; Alleyn's School, Dulwich. **Career:** Royal Signals; Director of Music, Royal Naval College, Greenwich 1950–1954; Deputy Headmaster and Director of Music, The Cathedral School, Wells 1954–1960; Headmaster, Witham Hall School 1961–1989.

LYONS, Richard Jenkins (1908) Born 14 March 1885, 26 Davy Street, Sydney, Australia; son of James Lyons, Gaol Warder, and Sarah Grace Jenkins. **Subject(s):** Mathematics; BA 1911; MA 1926. **Tutor(s):** L H K Bushe-Fox. **Educ:** Wollongong State School, Australia; Sydney Grammar School; University of Sydney. **Career:** Lecturer in Mathematics, University of Queensland 1911–1914; Lecturer in Mathematics, University of Sydney 1914–1938; Reader in Geometry, University of Sydney 1938–1951. **Appointments:** Elder of the Roseville Presbyterian Church. **Awards:** Barker Travelling Scholarship from Sydney 1908; Foundation Scholarship, SJC. Died 13 November 1951.

LYTHGOE, James Philip (1944) Born 10 November 1926, Kentraugh, Gravel Lane, Wilmslow, Cheshire; son of James Lythgoe, City Treasurer of Manchester, and Dorothy May Ashworth; m Anne Melvin, 1961; 1 son (James), 1 daughter (Alison). **Subject(s):** Natural Sciences; BA 1947; MB 1950; BChir 1950; MA 1951; FRCS. **Educ:** Wilmslow Preparatory School; Earnseat School, Arnside; Bootham School. **Career:** Research Fellow, Massachusetts General Hospital; Senior Surgical Registrar, Manchester Royal Infirmary; Consultant Surgeon, Preston and Chorley Hospitals 1964–1991. Died 14 March 1993.

LYTTLETON, Professor Raymond Arthur (1937) (admitted to Clare College 1930) Born 7 May 1911, 41 Galton Road, Oldbury, Worcestershire; son of William John Lyttleton, Civil Servant, and Agnes Kelly; m Meave Marguerite Hobden. BA (Clare) 1933; MA (Clare) 1937; PhD (Clare) 1937; FRS 1955. **Johnian Relatives:** brother-in-law of David Henry William Hobden (1940). **Educ:** Five Ways Grammar School, Birmingham; King Edward's School, Birmingham; Clare College, Cambridge; Princeton University, USA. **Career:** Title A Fellow, SJC 1937–1940; Experimental Officer, Ministry of Supply 1940–1942; Technical Assistant to Scientific Adviser to the Army Council, War Office, 1943–1945; Lecturer in Mathematics 1945–1954, Stokes Lecturer 1954–1959, Reader in Theoretical Astronomy 1959–1969, Professor of Theoretical Astronomy 1969–1978 (Emeritus 1978–1995), University of Cambridge; Lecturer 1949–1969, Title B Fellow 1949–1969, Title E Fellow 1969, Title C Fellow 1969–1971, Title D Fellow 1971–1995, SJC. **Appointments:** Jane Eliza Procter Visiting Fellow, Princeton University, USA 1935–1936; Geophysical Secretary 1949–1960, Council Member 1950–1961 and 1969–1972, Royal Astronomical Society; Council Member, Royal Society 1959–1961; Jacob Siskind Visiting Professor, Brandeis University, USA 1965–1966; Visiting Professor, Brown University, USA 1967–1968; Halley Lecturer, Oxford University 1970; Honorary Member, Mark Twain Society 1977; President, Milne Society 1977–1988; Milne Lecturer, Oxford 1978. **Awards:** Tyson Medal for Astronomy, University of Cambridge 1933; Smith's Prize, University of Cambridge 1935; Hopkins Prize, Cambridge Philosophical Society 1955; Gold Medal, Royal Astronomical Society; Royal Medal, Royal Society 1965. **Publications:** *The Stability of Rotating Liquid Masses*, 1953; *Man's View of the Universe*, 1961; *The Earth and its Mountains*, 1982; *The Comets and their Origin*, 1953; *The Modern Universe*, 1956; *Rival Theories of Cosmology*, 1960; *Mysteries of the Solar System*, 1968; *A Matter of Gravity*, 1968; (co-ed and contributor) *Cambridge Encyclopædia of Astronomy*, 1977; *The Gold Effect*, 1990; various papers. Died 16 May 1995.

LYWARD, George Aubrey (1917) Born 13 January 1894, 15 St John's Hill Grove, West Battersea, Surrey; son of George William Lyward, Mercantile Clerk, and Lilly Ethel Pain; m (1) Sarah Gladys Horn; (2) Sadie, 1932; (1) 1 son (John Martin b 22 September 1933). **Subject(s):** History; BA 1920; MA 1924. **Tutor(s):** E E Sikes. **Johnian Relatives:** father of John Martin Lyward (1954). **Educ:** Emanuel School, Wandsworth; KCL. **Career:** Master, Emanuel School 1916–1917 and 1921–1923; Master, Trinity College, Glenalmond 1923–1928; Founder and Headmaster, Finchden Manor School for emotionally disturbed boys 1929. **Awards:** Choral Scholarship, SJC 1917. **Honours:** OBE 1971. Died 23 June 1973.

M

MACALISTER, Donald (1928) Born 7 December 1910, Mavis House, Hills Road, Cherry Hinton, Cambridge; son of Alexander Paul MacAlister, Architect, and Agnes Mabel Cannon. **Tutor(s):** C W Guillebaud. **Educ:** Perse Preparatory School; Lynfield School, Hunstanton; County High School, Cambridge.

MACALLISTER, Hamilton (1948) Born 10 December 1922, 160 Prospecthill Road, Glasgow; son of John Gemmel Macallister, Railway Clerk, and Florence Annie Sutcliffe. **Tutor(s):** J M Wordie. **Educ:** Armthorpe Junior School; Thame Grammar School; Balliol College, Oxford.

MACAULAY, The Revd Donald (1903) Born 19 April 1884, 136 London Road, Leicester; son of Colin Alexander Macaulay, Land Agent, and Emily Stone; m Gladys Emily Fanshawe, 21 January 1913, St Mary's, Great Shelford. **Subject(s):** Classics; BA 1906. **Tutor(s):** E E Sikes. **Educ:** Colet House, Rhyl; Rugby School. **Career:** Ordained Deacon 1907; Ordained Priest 1908. Died 14 July 1941.

MCAULAY, Captain Francis Willmer (1909) Born 15 March 1891, Aylesby, Grimsby, Lincolnshire; son of Samuel McAulay, Farmer, and Maud Mary Pocock. **Subject(s):** Agriculture/Economics; BA 1912; MA

1916. **Tutor(s):** J R Tanner. **Educ:** The Leys School, Cambridge. **Career:** Commissioned 1910, Lieutenant 1913, Captain 1914–1916, 2nd Lincolnshire Battery, RFA. Died 21 May 1916 (killed in action).

MACBEAN, Alastair Henry Wilson (1937) Born 16 September 1918, Drew-y-Cord, Kotagiri, Coonoor Taluk, Nilgiri, Southern India; son of James Strong MacBean, Manager, J H Vavasseur & Co, and Dorothy Coles Wilson. **Subject(s):** Modern and Medieval Languages/Archaeology and Anthropology; BA 1940; MA 1944. **Tutor(s):** C W Guillebaud. **Educ:** Hill Brow School, Eastbourne; Clifton College; Bedford School. **Career:** Staff of Royal College, Nairobi; Senior Lecturer, College of Advanced Technology, Tripoli, Libya.

MCCALL, John Grice Armstrong (1935) Born 10 July 1913, The Rectory, Selkirk; son of James George McCall, Clerk in Holy Orders, and Mabel Lovat Armstrong; m Kathleen Mary Clarke, 29 September 1951. **Tutor(s):** J S Boys Smith. **Educ:** Glasgow Academy; Trinity College, Glenalmond; University of St Andrews. **Career:** Colonial Administrative Service, Nigeria. **Awards:** Colonial Probationer.

MCCALLUM, Archibald Duncan Dugald (1934) Born 26 November 1914, 4 Gladstone Terrace, Preston; son of Archibald Duncan McCallum, Medical Practitioner, and Marion Vassie Milne; m Rosemary Constance, 3 August 1950, Christ Church, Morningside, Edinburgh; 1 son (Ian). **Subject(s):** Classics/History; BA 1937; MA 1955. **Tutor(s):** R L Howland. **Educ:** The Leas School, Hoylake; Fettes College, Edinburgh. **Career:** Assistant Master, Fettes 1937–1939 and 1945–1951; 7th Battalion York and Lancashire Regiment, Mentioned in Despatches 1939–1945; Second Master, Strathallan School, Perthshire 1951–1956; Headmaster, Christ College, Brecon 1956–1962; Headmaster, Epsom College 1962–1970; Headmaster, Strathallan School, Perthshire 1970–1975. **Awards:** Classical Sizarship 1934. **Honours:** TD. Died 20 April 1993.

MCCALLUM, James Robert Henderson (1946) Born 7 August 1924, Altdoghal, Newtownstewart, County Tyrone; son of William McCallum, Farmer, and Ethel Mary Kerr Henderson. **Tutor(s):** G C L Bertram. **Educ:** Altdoghal Public Elementary School; Private School, Newtownstewart; Omagh Academy; Queen's University, Belfast. **Awards:** Colonial Agriculture Student.

MCCANN, Alastair Donald (1935) Born 28 April 1917, 8 South Bank, Oxton, Birkenhead; son of Frederick Donald McCann, Secretary, Shipping Federation Ltd, and Frances Gwendolen Cook. **Subject(s):** Classics. **Tutor(s):** R L Howland. **Educ:** Birkenhead School Preparatory Department; Birkenhead School Senior School. **Awards:** Scholarship, SJC 1936–1937. Died 25 September 1989.

MCCANN, Peter Orchard (1945) Born 29 October 1927, Denison House, Victoria Park, Rusholme, Manchester; son of William Thomson McCann, Bank Manager, and Vera Elsie Orchard. **Tutor(s):** J M Wordie. **Educ:** Broomhouse Law School, Pendleton; Sale High School, Cheshire; Manchester Grammar School.

MCCARTER, Ian Jamison (1941) Born 1 August 1923, 22 High View Avenue, Grays, Essex; son of William Harold Raphael McCarter, Medical Practitioner, and Margaret Wallace Jamison; m (2); (1) 1 son, 2 daughters, (2) 1 daughter. **Subject(s):** Mechanical Sciences; BA 1948; MA 1950. **Tutor(s):** S J Bailey. **Educ:** Streete Court Preparatory School, Westgate-on-Sea; Shrewsbury School. **Career:** Captain, REME 1942; Lecturer in Engineering, Brighton Technical College 1962.

MCCARTHY, Wilfrid Justin (1919) Born 12 August 1900, 11 Ellys Road, Coventry, Warwickshire; son of William Patrick McCarthy, Engineer Contractor, and Elizabeth Hennessey. BA 1922; MA 1926. **Tutor(s):** E A Benians. **Educ:** Douai Abbey, Woolhampton.

MCCAY, Francis Howard (1923) Born 6 October 1905, Puri, Calcutta, India; son of David McCay, Lieutenant Colonel, Indian Medical Service, and Florence Howard Hixson. **Subject(s):** Natural Sciences; BA 1926; MA 1932; BChir 1929; MB 1929; MD 1932. **Tutor(s):** B F Armitage. **Educ:** Gorse Cliff School, Boscombe; Rottingdean School, Brighton; Marlborough College. Died 28 June 1985.

MCCLARY, Andrew Bishop (1918) American Student.

MCCLOUGHIN, Darcy Kenelm (1936) Born 19 July 1916, Madras, India; son of Bertram Gordon McCloughin, Solicitor, and Kathleen Clewena Dawson; m Elisabeth Mary Masson Martin, 4 September 1943, London. **Subject(s):** Mechanical Sciences; BA 1938. **Tutor(s):** J S Boys Smith. **Educ:** Pembroke Lodge, Southbourne on Sea; Radley; RMA, Woolwich. **Career:** RE, retired as Major 1936–1957; Oakwell Park Restaurant 1962–1972.

MACCOBY, Ephraim Meyer (1910) Born 18 February 1892, 99 Rothschild's Buildings, Commercial Street, Spitalfields, London; son of Hyam Zundel Maccoby, Rabbi, and Hannah Bluma Blacher; m Fanny Rabinowitz, 1916; 2 sons (Hyam Zundel b 20 March 1924 and David b 6 March 1925), 3 daughters (Eva b 4 October 1916, Bertha Rachel (Bessie) b 25 February 1918 and Lorna b 18 November 1920). **Subject(s):** Mathematics; BA 1913; MA 1919; BSc (London) 1913. **Tutor(s):** L H K Bushe-Fox. **Johnian Relatives:** grandfather of Joseph Pearlman (1965) and of Chaim Zundel Pearlman (1967). **Educ:** London County Council School; Central Foundation School, London. **Career:** Master, Arrowsmith's Army School, Edinburgh 1914–1915; Head of Mathematics Department, Sunderland Bede Collegiate School (subsequently renamed Bede Grammar School for Boys) 1915–1957; Lecturer in Statistics, Armstrong College, Newcastle upon Tyne 1919. **Publications:** *Kol Ephraim* (original explanation of Ecclesiastes), Mevakshei Torah, Jerusalem, 1996 (published posthumously in Hebrew with notes and commentary by grandson Joseph Pearlman). Died 1 February 1957.

MCCOMBE, William Eric Mervyn (1919) Born 3 May 1900, 645 Anlaby Road, Hessle, Hull, Yorkshire; son of William James McCombe, Traffic Manager, and Caroline Maria Louise Allen. **Subject(s):** Classics; BA 1922; MA 1927. **Tutor(s):** E E Sikes. **Educ:** Hymers College, Hull. **Career:** Classics Master, King Edward VII School, Lytham 1922–1925; Teacher, Battersea Grammar School 1925. **Awards:** Exhibition, SJC 1918.

MACCONKEY, Charles Alexander Hamilton (1926) Born 23 July 1903, 97 Park Lane, Croydon, Surrey; son of Charles Edward MacConkey, Banker, and Julia Kenney Dixon. **Tutor(s):** J M Wordie. **Educ:** Shrewsbury School; Eidgenössische Technische Hochschule, Zurich, Switzerland.

MCCONNELL, Gerard Hamilton (1932) Born 22 January 1913, Riversdale, Middlewich Road, Church Hulme, Chester; son of Joseph McConnell, Wallpaper Engraver, and Ethel Jones. **Subject(s):** Modern and Medieval Languages; BA 1935; MA 1963. **Tutor(s):** C W Guillebaud. **Educ:** Holmes Chapel Elementary School; Sandbach Grammar School; Manchester Grammar School. **Career:** Assistant Under-Secretary of State, Home Office 1974. **Honours:** CB 1967.

MCCONNELL, Robert Melville Terence (1921) Born 7 February 1902, The Moat, Ballymaghan, Belfast, County Down, Ireland; son of Joseph McConnell, Auctioneer and Estate Agent, and Elizabeth McGown. **Tutor(s):** E A Benians. **Educ:** Bing's School, Rockport, Craigavad; Glenalmond School, Scotland.

MCCORMICK, Gregory David Pat (1938) Born 30 January 1920, 4 Sydenham Road, Croydon, Surrey; son of William Patrick Glyn McCormick, Vicar, St Martin in the Fields, and Ada Miriam Shelton. BA 1941; MA 1945. **Tutor(s):** J S Boys Smith. **Educ:** Crowthorne Towers; Loretto School. **Career:** Apprentice, British Aircraft Factory 1937–1938.

MCCORMICK, Canon Joseph Conybeare (1925) Born 23 September 1906, 3 Ullet Road, Liverpool; son of Joseph Gough McCormick, Dean of Manchester, and Alison Mary Conybeare. BA 1929; MA 1932.

Tutor(s): E E Sikes. **Johnian Relatives:** son of Joseph Gough McCormick (1893); nephew of Gregory Day McCormick (1894) and of William Patrick Glyn McCormick (1896); brother of Michael Edward McCormick (1927). **Educ:** The Old Malthouse, Langton Matravers; Marlborough College; Hoe Hall, East Dereham; Lincoln Theological College. **Career:** Ordained Deacon 1931; Curate, Bolton 1931–1933; Ordained Priest 1932; Curate, Warrington and Assistant Master, Boteler Grammar School 1933–1937; Vicar, St Paul, Monton, Lancashire 1937–1941; Vicar, Holy Trinity, Southport 1941–1946; Rector, St Matthew, Stretford (Rural Dean 1947) 1946–1955; Rural Dean, Stretford 1947; Rector, Willersey with Saintbury, Broadway, Gloucestershire 1955. **Appointments:** Chaplain, Actors' Church Union; Honorary Canon, Manchester 1953. Died 26 August 1960.

MCCORMICK, The Revd Michael Edward (1927) Born 26 May 1909, 10 Union Road, Cambridge; son of Joseph Gough McCormick, Clerk in Holy Orders, and Alison Mary Conybeare. BA 1930; MA 1934. **Tutor(s):** E A Benians. **Johnian Relatives:** son of Joseph Gough McCormick (1893); nephew of Gregory Day McCormick (1894) and of William Patrick Glyn McCormick (1896); brother of Joseph Conybeare McCormick (1925). **Educ:** The Old Malthouse, Langton Matravers; Marlborough College. **Career:** Lincoln Theological College; Ordained Deacon 1932; Curate, St Andrew, West Kirby 1932–1936; Ordained Priest 1933; Curate, St Mary and St James, Gromsby, in charge of St Barnabas 1936–1939; Rector, Bilsthorpe 1939–1946; Chaplain, RNVR 1941–1949; Chaplain, RNVR, HMS *Sheffield* 1946–1949; Chaplain, RN, HMS *St Vincent* 1949–1951; Chaplain, RN, HMS *Thunderer* 1951–1953; Chaplain, RN, HMS *Albion* 1953–1955; Chaplain, RN Hospital, Plymouth 1955–1957; Vicar, Dunster, Minehead, Somerset 1957–1966; Vicar, Flore, Northamptonshire 1966.

MCCOWAN, Hugh Wallace (1905) Born 15 December 1885, Water Street, Kingston, Georgetown, Demerara, British Guiana; son of William McCowan, Sergeant Major, Army, and Jane Corner; m Lucia Trail Simpson, 14 January 1914, Presbyterian Church, Wynberg, Cape Town. **Subject(s):** Mathematics; BA 1908; MA 1912. **Tutor(s):** J R Tanner. **Educ:** Queen's College, Demerara, British Guiana. **Career:** Assistant Master, Aldenham School 1909; Assistant Master, Wellingborough Grammar School 1910; Mathematics and Science Master, Boys' High School, Salisbury, Rhodesia 1911–1917 (Acting Principal 1913); Headmaster, Boys' School, Grenada, British West Indies 1917–1923; Inspector of Schools, Southern Province, Nigeria 1923–1927; Assistant Director of Education, Southern Province, Nigeria 1927; Chief Inspector 1929; Assistant Director-in-Chief 1930–1933.

MCCULLOCH, William (1911) Born 2 December 1891, 73 Melbourne Street, Stalybridge, Cheshire; son of Daniel Cooke McCulloch, Boot Dealer, and Mary Ann Abbott. **Subject(s):** Classics; BA 1914; MA 1935; DipEd. **Tutor(s):** E E Sikes. **Educ:** Manchester Grammar School. **Career:** Red Cross Ambulance Unit, WWI; Master, Kirkham Grammar School 1915–1919; Master, Caernarvon County School 1919–1920; Master, Stalybridge Technical School 1920–1923; Master, Ayr Academy 1923–1924; Master, Cowbridge Grammar School, Glamorganshire 1925; Master, Simon Langton School, Canterbury 1925–1956. **Appointments:** President, Old Langtonian Association. **Awards:** Scholarship, SJC. Died 26 November 1962.

MCCUTCHEON, Dr James Thomson (1930) Born 9 October 1911, 321 Cathedral Street, Glasgow; son of Joseph Glaister McCutcheon, Medical Practitioner, and Elizabeth McLaren Alexander; m Margaret (Margot) Hutchison, 28 March 1939, Glasgow; 1 son (John b 10 September 1940), 1 daughter (Gillian b 1 June 1942). BA 1935; MA 1944; LRCP (Edinburgh); LRCS (Edinburgh); LRFPS (Glasgow). **Tutor(s):** R L Howland. **Johnian Relatives:** father of John Joseph McCutcheon (1959). **Educ:** Glasgow Academy; Warriston School, Moffat; Loretto School, Musselburgh. **Career:** GP 1938–1950; Surgeon Lieutenant, RNVR 1939–1945; Assistant Scottish Secretary of the BMA 1950–1964; Scottish Secretary, BMA 1964. Died 9 June 1964.

MCDADE, Dr Robert Sinclair Charles (1923) Born 20 January 1905, 138 Lavender Hill, Battersea, London; son of Charles Edmund McDade, Medical Practitioner, and Frances Octavia Cluff Sinclair. BA 1927; MA 1933; BChir 1933; MB 1933; MRCS (St Thomas') 1931; LRCP (St Thomas') 1931. **Tutor(s):** B F Armitage. **Educ:** Manor House School, Clapham Common; St Paul's School, London; St Thomas' Hospital, London. **Career:** House Physician, Brompton Hospital; Deputy Medical Superintendent, Colindale Hospital; High Wood Hospital, Brentwood; Broomfield Hospital, Chelmsford. Died 4 June 1959.

MACDONALD, Alasdair (1924) Born 1 August 1905, National Bank House, Portree, Isle of Skye, Invernessshire, Scotland; son of Ronald Macdonald, Solicitor and Bank Agent, and Elizabeth Blair Coats; m Marjory Fordyce Millikin, 23 December 1931, Crookhill, Kilmalcolm; 2 daughters (Sheila and Catriona). **Subject(s):** Classics/English; BA 1928; MA 1933. **Tutor(s):** E E Sikes. **Johnian Relatives:** brother of Allan Ronald Macdonald (1926); uncle of Alasdair Blair Macdonald (1961). **Educ:** High School, Glasgow; Fettes College, Edinburgh. **Career:** Assistant Master, Fettes College, Edinburgh 1928–1931; Assistant Master, Housemaster of Chatham House, then Deputy Headmaster, Stowe School 1931. **Awards:** Scholarship, SJC 1923; Henry P Davison Scholarship, Yale 1926. Died 30 November 1993.

MACDONALD, Allan Ronald (1926) Born 21 December 1906, National Bank House, Portree, Invernessshire, Scotland; son of Ronald Macdonald, Solicitor, and Elizabeth Blair Coats; m (1) Katherine May Hodson, (2) Mary Shaw, 10 December 1954, Trinity Church, Bristol; (1) 2 sons (Keith Ronald and Alasdair Blair). **Subject(s):** History; BA 1929. **Tutor(s):** M P Charlesworth. **Johnian Relatives:** brother of Alasdair Macdonald (1924); father of Alasdair Blair Macdonald (1961). **Educ:** Portree Higher Grade School; Glasgow High School; Fettes College, Edinburgh. **Career:** Establishment Secretary, Uganda 1948–1951; Colonial Secretary, Sierra Leone 1951–1956; Chairman, Public Service Commission, Kenya 1956; Chairman, Public Service Commission, Aden 1966. **Awards:** Sizarship, SJC. **Honours:** CMG 1953. Died 21 April 1984.

MACDONALD, Andrew Sinclair (1948) Born 15 August 1928, Maternity Hospital, Glasgow, Scotland; son of Donald Andrew MacDonald, Farm Bailiff, and Catherine Christina McPherson Sinclair. BSc (Durham). **Tutor(s):** R L Howland. **Educ:** Pound Lane Junior School, Epsom; West Ewell Secondary School; King's College, Newcastle upon Tyne; University of Durham.

MCDONALD, Gordon Francis (1929) Born 15 April 1910, Kijabe, District of Kyambu, Province of Ukamba, East African Protectorate; son of Gordon James McDonald, Settler in British East Africa, and Marian Tomkins. BA 1932. **Tutor(s):** J M Wordie. **Educ:** Oxford High School; Private Tuition, Buckland; King's College, Taunton; Bedford School.

MACDONALD, Iain Alasdair (1942) Born 24 August 1909, South Lodge, Orton House, Rothes, Elgin; son of Thomas Fraser MacDonald, Head Gardener, and Jane Mann. **Subject(s):** Geography; BA 1944; MA 1948; MA 1931. **Tutor(s):** C W Guillebaud. **Educ:** Inchberry School, Morayshire; Milne's Secondary School, Fochabers; King's College, University of Aberdeen. **Career:** Flight Lieutenant, RAF; Instructor, Initial Training Wing.

MACDONALD, John Blair (1942) Born 10 April 1924, 183 Queen's Drive, Glasgow; son of Douglas MacDonald, Furniture Manufacturer, and Marion Blair. **Tutor(s):** S J Bailey. **Educ:** Glasgow Academy; Marr College, Troon.

MACDONALD, Patrick Donald (1927) Born 21 July 1909, Carnbrae House, Bellshill, Lanarkshire; son of Eric William Macdonald, Major, King's Own Scottish Borderers, and Amy Beatrice Cavalier; m Delia Edith Travers, 1937 (div); 2 daughters (Sally and Hilary). **Subject(s):** Geography/Archaeology and Anthropology; BA 1931. **Tutor(s):** J M Wordie. **Educ:** Parkfield Preparatory School, Haywards Heath;

Marlborough College. **Career:** Colonial Service, Gilbert and Ellice Islands 1932–1940; Assistant Secretary, Western Pacific High Commission 1940–1942; Assistant Colonial Secretary, Trinidad 1942–1946; Administrative Officer, Fiji 1946–1949; Chief Secretary, Leeward Islands 1949–1957; Colonial Secretary and Acting Governor of Fiji, later Chairman, Public and Police Service Commission 1957–1971. Died 15 June 1987.

MCDONALD, Thomas (1926) Born 16 January 1908, 14 Brunswick Square, Bristol, Gloucestershire; son of Donald McDonald, Draper, and Agnes Mary Howse. **Subject(s):** Natural Sciences; BA 1929. **Tutor(s):** C W Guillebaud. **Educ:** Merchant Venturers' School, Bristol; Cotham Secondary School, Bristol.

MACDONALD, Thomas John (1929) Born 27 December 1908, Brownlow Street, Comber, County Down; son of Thomas John Macdonald, Commercial Traveller, and Flora Anderson; 6 children. **Subject(s):** Mathematics; BA 1931; MA 1937; BSc (Belfast) 1929. **Tutor(s):** J M Wordie. **Educ:** Comber National School; Royal Belfast Academical Institution; Queen's University, Belfast. **Career:** Head of Mathematics, Ackham Hall School, Middlesbrough. Died March 1998.

MCDONNELL, Sir Michael Francis Joseph (1901) Born 15 June 1882, 5 Coleherne Road, Brompton, London; son of Francis McDonnell, Civil Servant, and Mary Josephine Ward; m Muriel Codrington Harvey, 8 September 1925, Church of San Girolamo, Italy. BA 1904; MA 1920. **Tutor(s):** D MacAlister. **Johnian Relatives:** brother of Thomas Francis Robert McDonnell (1895). **Educ:** St Paul's School, London. **Career:** Called to the Bar, Inner Temple 1908; Colonial Officer and Solicitor, West Africa 1911–1925; Chief Justice, Palestine 1927–1937. **Appointments:** Chairman, Tribunal on Conscientious Objectors. **Honours:** Commander, Order of St John of Jerusalem; Kt 1929; KBE 1949. **Publications:** *Ireland and the Home Rule Movement*; *A History of St Paul's School*; *The Laws of Sierra Leone*; *The Law Reports of Palestine*. Died 12 April 1956.

MCDONNELL, Peter Francis (1930) Born 1 July 1911, Fraser Road, Rangoon, Burma; son of Thomas Francis Robert McDonnell, Barrister-at-Law, and Emily Agatha Scott-Coward; m Nancy. **Subject(s):** History; BA 1933. **Tutor(s):** E A Benians. **Johnian Relatives:** son of Thomas Francis Robert McDonnell (1895). **Educ:** Downside School, Stratton-on-the-Fosse. Died 7 November 2000.

MACDOWALL, Joseph (1948) Born 14 August 1926, 11 Rullerton Road, Wallasey, Cheshire; son of Joseph MacDowall, Advertising Agent, and Nelly Hoadley Smith; m Oonagh Diana Bainbridge, 15 October 1955; 3 sons (Simon Charles b 1956, Thomas Patrick b 1960 and Peter William b 1961), 1 daughter (Josephine Catherine Hoadley b 1965). **Subject(s):** Mathematics/Natural Sciences; BA 1951; MA 1955; CPhys; MRAeS; PEng. **Tutor(s):** G C L Bertram. **Educ:** Liscard High School, Wallasey; Dronefield Grammar School, Derbyshire; Wallasey Grammar School; Rivington & Blackrod Grammar School. **Career:** Radar Mechanic, Royal Naval Air Arm 1945–1948; Scientific Officer/Senior Scientific Officer, Meteorological Office 1951–1956; Group Leader and Expedition Leader, Royal Society International Geophysical Year Antarctic Expedition to Hally Bay Antarctica 1956–1959; Systems Engineer, then Chief Engineering Physicist, British Aircraft Corporation, Stevenage, UK 1960–1966; General Manager, Research and Development Division, Barringer Research Ltd, Toronto, Canada 1966–1969; Canadian Government Scientific Co-ordinator, International Field Year for the Great Lakes 1969–1973; Chief, Applications Division, Canada Centre for Remote Sensing, Ottawa 1973–1975; Counsellor, Science, Canadian Embassy, Washington DC, USA 1975–1979; Counsellor, Science and Technology, Canadian Embassy, Tokyo, Japan 1979–1983; Senior Advisor on International Relations to Deputy Minister of Science and Technology 1983–1987; Technical Co-ordinator, Continuing Airworthiness, Transport Canada, Ottawa 1987–1997. **Appointments:** Associate Fellow, Institute of Physics, London 1964; Registered under

Professional Engineers Act of Ontario, Canada, in the Aeronautical Branch 1969; Associate Fellow, Royal Aeronautical Society, London 1969; Director, *Ottawa West Flyer* newspaper 1989, 1992–1996 and 2000–2002, Chief Executive Officer and Chairman of the Board 1994–1996 and 2000–2002. **Awards:** Bruce Medal of the Royal Society of Edinburgh 1960; Polar Medal 1961; NASA Awards 1969 and 1970; City of Ottawa Volunteer Appreciation Award 1998. **Honours:** OBE 1960. **Publications:** *Ben the Beaver*, *On Floating Ice: two years on an Antarctic Ice-Shelf*, The Pentland Press Ltd, 1999; various papers/articles.

MCDOWELL, John Muir (1927) Born 9 October 1909, Cromer, Cadogan Park, Belfast, County Antrim, Ireland; son of James Charley McDowell, Solicitor, and Jessie McMullan. **Subject(s):** Economics; BA 1930; MA 1947. **Tutor(s):** C W Guillebaud. **Johnian Relatives:** nephew of John Gaston Leathem (1891). **Educ:** Inch Marlo Preparatory School, Belfast; King William's College, Isle of Man; Shrewsbury School. **Career:** Articled to a London Firm 1931–1933; Stock Farming in Northern Ireland 1933–1938; Sergeant, RA 1939–1943; Royal West Africa Frontier Force, served in England, Africa and Sicily 1943–1945; Assistant Master, Branksome Hilders Preparatory School, Haslemere, Surrey 1946.

MACER, Dr Richard Charles Franklin (1949) Born 21 October 1928, Worthing, Sussex; son of Lionel William Macer, Mining Engineer and Surveyor, and Ada Elizabeth Franklin; m Vera G Jeapes, 1952, St George's Church, Worthing; 3 daughters (Valerie Anne b 1953, Diana Christine b 1954, and Gwendolen Mary b 1954). **Subject(s):** Natural Sciences; BA 1952; MA 1956; PhD 1955. **Tutor(s):** C W Guillebaud; W A Deer; E Miller. **Educ:** The High School for Boys, Worthing. **Career:** Military Service, The Royal Sussex Regiment 1947–1949; Scientific Officer 1955–1959, Head of Plant Pathology Section 1957–1966, Senior Scientific Officer 1959–1963, Principal Scientific Officer 1963–1966, Plant Breeding Institute, Cambridge; Plant Pathologist and Director 1966–1972, Director of Scientific Development 1967–1972, Rothwell Plant Breeders Limited, Rothwell, Lincolnshire; Technical Director, British Hybrid Cereals Ltd 1969–1972; Professor of Crop Production, University of Edinburgh 1972–1976; Director, Scottish Plant Breeding Station, Pentlandfield, Roslin, Midlothian 1976–1981; General Manager, The Plant Royalty Bureau Limited, Ely 1981–1985; Independent Consultant in Plant Pathology, Plant Breeding, Genetics, Genetic Research and Development, Biotechnology, and the organisation and administration of Biological Research 1985–1995. **Appointments:** Various appointments and related activities including: Member, Secretary, and President (1973–1974), British Mycology Society 1956–1988; Founder Member and Chairman, European and Mediterranean Cereal Rusts Foundation 1960–1973; Chairman, British Association of Plant Pathologists; Council Member, Association of Applied Biologists 1970–1973; FIBiol 1973–1986; Member and Chairman (1977–1980), Joint Consultative Organisation Arable Crops and Forage Board, Cereals Committee 1975–1980; Member, Research Advisory Panel, Home-grown Cereals Authority 1982–1987; Panel Member, Plant Varieties and Seeds Tribunal 1993–1996. **Awards:** Hutchinson Research Studentship 1952. **Publications:** 47 papers on fungal diseases of cereals and related topics.

MCFADYEAN, Dr Kenneth Michael (1944) Born 6 March 1926, 74 Herne Hill, London; son of Kenneth McFadyean, Medical Practitioner, and Elsie McCormick; m Barbara Marjorie Joan Cass, 3 March 1951; 3 sons (Gordon, Duncan and Gavin). **Subject(s):** Natural Sciences/ Clinical Medicine; BA 1947; MA 1951; MB 1950; BChir 1950; MRCS 1951; LRCP 1951; DObstRCOG 1953; MRCGP 1967. **Tutor(s):** S J Bailey. **Educ:** Glenshee House, Herne Hill; Dulwich College Preparatory School; University College School. **Career:** Medical Practitioner. **Appointments:** Licenced Lay Reader in the Church of England 1975; Fellow, Victoria College of Music.

MACFADYEN, Dr William Archibald (1912) Born 5 November 1893, 346 Oxford Street, Chorlton-upon-Medlock, Lancashire; son of Amelia Hill Johnson; m Margaret Mabel Grey Mayson, 1934; 1 son (Neil William). **Subject(s):** Natural Sciences; BA 1917; MA 1920; PhD 1928; ScD 1942. **Tutor(s):** R P Gregory. **Johnian Relatives:** father of Neil William Macfadyen (1962); grandfather of Robin Neil Macfadyen (1989). **Educ:** Bryn Derwyn; Rydal Mount. **Career:** Captain, The Buffs (East Kent Regiment, TF) (wounded, Mentioned in Despatches), then employed, Ministry of Munitions, WWI; Shell Oil Company 1929–1933; Iraq Government Geologist, Baghdad 1934–1939; Major, WWII; Government Geologist, British Somaliland 1949–1951; Chief Geologist, Nature Conservancy. **Honours:** MC 1917. Died 16 June 1985.

MCFADZEAN, Francis Scott (1937) Born 26 November 1915, 8 Fulbarton Terrace, Troon; son of Francis Findlay McFadzean, Secretary, and Annie Scott Smith. **Tutor(s):** C W Guillebaud. **Educ:** Higher Grade School, Troon; Glasgow University; LSE.

MCFARLANE, David (1942) Born 28 March 1915, 55 Randolph Gardens, Partick, Glasgow; son of William John McFarlane, Company Secretary and Director, and Helen Ure Weir. BSc (Glasgow); MRCVS. **Tutor(s):** C W Guillebaud. **Educ:** Glasgow Academy; Glasgow Veterinary College; Glasgow University.

MCGEOCH, Roy Burton (1943) Born 22 April 1926, 5 Mosslands Drive, Wallasey, Cheshire; son of Arthur Burton McGeoch, Civil Engineering Contractor, and Irene Biddulph Hilton. **Tutor(s):** S J Bailey. **Educ:** St Aidan's Preparatory School, Wallasey; Birkenhead School.

MCGHIE, Robert Frederick (1942) Born 7 April 1924, 28 Nicholas Road, Wallasey, Cheshire; son of Douglas McGhie, Company Director (tea merchants), and Susannah May Saxby. BA 1949; MA 1951. **Tutor(s):** C W Guillebaud. **Educ:** Birkenhead School; Rhyl County School.

MCGRADY, Samuel Hugh (1904) Born 20 December 1884, 2 Willow Avenue, Edgbaston, Birmingham; son of Hugh Henry McGrady, Commission Agent, and Matilda Napper (née Price). BA 1907; MA 1911. **Tutor(s):** D MacAlister. **Educ:** St Albans School; Lichfield Grammar School; St George's School, Harpenden. **Career:** Bombardier, RGA, WWI.

MCGREGOR, Dr Angus (1944) Born 26 December 1926, Glasfryn, Fidlas Road, Llanishen, Cardiff; son of William Hector Scot McGregor, Medical Practitioner, and Olwen May Richards, Medical Practitioner; m Mary Bridget Burke, 1951; 1 daughter (Catherine Helen b 1963). **Subject(s):** Natural Sciences; BA 1947; MB 1950; BChir 1950; MD 1958; MA 1958; FFCM; DPH; FRCP; MD. **Johnian Relatives:** brother of Charles Malcolm McGregor (1947). **Educ:** Harbourne College; Wellesbourne House School, Acocks Green; King Edward's High School, Birmingham; Solihull School. **Career:** Assistant Medical Officer of Health, Chester 1954–1956; Deputy Medical Officer of Health, Swindon 1957–1958; Deputy Medical Officer of Health, Hull 1958–1965; Medical Officer of Health and Port Medical Officer, Southampton 1964–1974; District Community Physician, East Dorset 1974–1979; Regional Medical Officer, West Midlands 1978–1988. **Appointments:** Visiting Professor, University of Keele 1988–1994. **Publications:** (with Tony Bunbury) *Disciplining and Dismissing Doctors in the NHS*, 1988.

MCGREGOR, Dr Charles Malcolm (1947) Born 11 December 1928, 23 Arlington Road, Porthcawl, Glamorganshire; son of William Hector Scott McGregor, Medical Practitioner, and Olwen May Richards. **Subject(s):** Natural Sciences; BA 1950; BChir 1953; MB 1954. **Tutor(s):** G C L Bertram. **Johnian Relatives:** brother of Angus McGregor (1944). **Educ:** Wellesbourne House School; Solihull School. **Career:** Assistant Medical Officer of Health and School Medical Officer, Wolverhampton 1960.

MCGUFFIE, James Carruthers Blair (BLAIR-MCGUFFIE) (1921) Born 2 June 1903, Isleworth, Chapel-en-le-Frith, Derbyshire; son of William Blair McGuffie, Wine Merchant, and Nora Mary Magrath. BA 1924; MA 1928. **Tutor(s):** E E Sikes. **Educ:** Ladycross, Seaford; Stonyhurst College. **Career:** General Manager, Granitese (Great Britain) Ltd 1937; Major, RE 21st Army Group 1945.

MCGUINNESS, Alexander Sellars (1928) Born 30 April 1910, 3 Buckingham Avenue, Claughton, Birkenhead, Cheshire; son of William McGuinness, Traffic Manager, Steamship Company, and Ethel Christina Sellars. **Tutor(s):** M P Charlesworth. **Educ:** Preparatory School, Birkenhead; Birkenhead School. Died 23 June 1995.

MCILWRAITH, Professor Thomas Forsyth (1919) Born 9 April 1899, Hamilton, Wentworth County, Ontario, Canada; son of Thomas Forsyth McIlwraith, Merchant, and Mary Stevens; 1 son, 2 daughters. **Subject(s):** Anthropology; BA 1921; MA 1925; FRSC. **Tutor(s):** E A Benians. **Educ:** Highfield School, Hamilton, Canada; McGill University. **Career:** University of Toronto Overseas Training Company 1917; Artists Rifles 1918, attached to No 2 Officer Cadet Battalion; Second Lieutenant, King's Own Scottish Borderers 1918–1919; Lecturer 1925–1960, Professor of Anthropology 1948, University of Toronto. Died 29 March 1964.

MCINNES, Dr Archibald Alastair (1942) Born 12 July 1924, Aberlour House, Raunds, Northamptonshire; son of Archibald McInnes, Medical Practitioner, and Ruth Annie Rose; 1 son, 1 daughter. **Subject(s):** Natural Sciences; BA 1945; MA 1965; BChir 1948; MB 1948; MRCGP. **Tutor(s):** S J Bailey. **Johnian Relatives:** brother-in-law of Frederick Brian Corby (1949); great uncle of Alistair James Baker (2002). **Educ:** King's College Choir School, Cambridge; Gadebridge Park Preparatory School, Hemel Hempstead; Oundle School. **Career:** Country GP, Northamptonshire, Bedfordshire, Cambridgeshire 1948–1994; RAF, Suez 1950–1953; Managing Director, Farming Company 1954–1988.

MACINNES, Dr Donald Gordon (1933) (admitted to Trinity College 1926) Born 7 June 1907, Ismailia Quarter, Cairo, Egypt; son of Rennie MacInnes, Clerk in Holy Orders, and Janet Waldegrave Carr. PhD 1927. **Tutor(s):** R L Howland. **Educ:** Windlesham House, Brighton; Harrow School; Trinity College, Cambridge. Died 7 May 1969.

MCINTIRE, George Shipley (1916) Born 18 December 1896, 171 Clayton Terrace, Westoe, South Shields, Durham; son of Laurence McIntire, Marine Engineer, and Jane Oswald Newton; m Doris Mabel Frampton, Croydon Parish Church, 9 April 1927. **Subject(s):** Economics/Law/Mathematics; BA 1922; MA 1949; LLB 1922. **Tutor(s):** E E Sikes. **Educ:** Westoe Boys' School; Westoe Senior School; Westoe Secondary School. **Career:** Solicitor 1924–1925; Assistant Town Clerk, Gloucester 1925; Town Clerk and Clerk of the Peace, Sunderland 1939. Died 18 March 1990.

MCINTOSH, Kenneth Alister (1929) Born 12 June 1909, Kotagiri, Nilgiri Hills, South India; son of Alexander McIntosh, Civil Engineer, and Annie Ethel May Gover. **Subject(s):** Mechanical Sciences; BA 1931. **Tutor(s):** J M Wordie. **Johnian Relatives:** brother of Robert Adrian McIntosh (1920). **Educ:** Bedford School; RMA, Woolwich.

MCINTOSH, Robert Adrian (1920) Born 18 June 1902, Cochin, Malabar Coast, South India; son of Alexander McIntosh, Executive Engineer, South Indian Railway, and Annie Ethel May Gover. **Subject(s):** Mechanical Sciences; BA 1924. **Tutor(s):** E E Sikes. **Johnian Relatives:** brother of Kenneth Alister McIntosh (1929). **Educ:** Preparatory School, Rokeby, The Downs, Wimbledon; Bedford Grammar School. **Career:** Assistant Engineer, Bengal-Nagpir Railway 1925. Died 20 January 1926.

MCINTYRE, David Graham (1944) Born 23 March 1926, Nursing Home, Hulme Hall Road, Cheadle Hulme; son of James Johnstone McIntyre, Bank Clerk, and Margaret Harvey Maitland. **Tutor(s):** J M Wordie. **Educ:** Macclesfield Grammar School; Oriel House Preparatory School; Kingswood School. **Appointments:** RAF Cadet, SJC.

MCINTYRE, Frederick Donald Livingstone (1924) Born 8 July 1905, 4 Queen's Road, Summer Hill, Bristol; son of Frederick William Jones, Commercial Traveller, and Marjorie Livingstone McIntyre. **Subject(s):** Law; BA 1927; LLB 1928. **Tutor(s):** E A Benians. **Educ:** Victoria School,

Penarth; Gladstone School, Cardiff; High School, Cardiff; Telferscot School, Balham; St Olave's School, Southwark. **Career:** Called to the Bar, Gray's Inn 1928; Flying Officer, RAFVR, WWII; Japanese POW, Java 1943; Judge, Bow County Court 1962. **Appointments:** General Council of the Bar 1961. **Awards:** Scholarship, SJC 1923.

MCINTYRE, Robert Billo (1936) Born 12 August 1913, Chinguacousy, Peel County, Ontario, Canada; son of Robert Manley McIntyre, Editorial Staff, *The Globe*, Toronto, and Carrie Elise Billo. **Subject(s):** Mechanical Sciences; BA 1938. **Tutor(s):** J S Boys Smith. **Educ:** Rawlinson Public School, Toronto; Vaughan Road Collegiate, Toronto; University of Toronto. Died 23 September 1985.

MACIVER, Andrew (1938) Born 8 February 1920, Beechfield, Heswall, Cheshire; son of Edward Squarey MacIver, Ship Owner, and Margaret Gostenhofer. **Subject(s):** Mechanical Sciences; BA 1941. **Tutor(s):** J S Boys Smith. **Johnian Relatives:** brother of John Edward MacIver (1942) and of Donald MacIver (1949). **Educ:** The Leas, Hoylake; Shrewsbury School. Died December 1999.

MACIVER, Donald (1949) Born 6 August 1929, Beechfield, Heswall, Cheshire; son of Edward Squarey MacIver, Ship Owner, and Margaret Gostenhofer. **Tutor(s):** C W Guillebaud. **Johnian Relatives:** brother of Andrew MacIver (1938) and of John Edward MacIver (1942). **Educ:** The Craig, Windermere; The Leas, Hoylake; Shrewsbury School. **Career:** Royal Artilley 1948–1949. **Awards:** Minor Scholarship, SJC 1947. Died 1993.

MACIVER, Dr John Edward (1942) Born 12 September 1923, Beechfield, Heswall, Cheshire; son of Edward Squarey MacIver, Ship Owner, and Margaret Gostenhofer; 5 children. **Subject(s):** Natural Sciences; BA 1945; BChir 1948; MB 1948; MD 1959; FRCP 1983. **Johnian Relatives:** brother of Andrew MacIver (1938) and of Donald MacIver (1949). **Educ:** St Fillans, Heswall; The Leas, Hoylake; Shrewsbury School. **Career:** Lecturer in Clinical Pathology, University College of the West Indies 1959; Consultant Haemotologist, Manchester Royal Infirmary 1963.

MCIVER, Leo (1942) Born 1 March 1915, 4 Cemetery Road, Padiham, Burnley; son of John Thomas McIver, Janitor, and Abigail Harrison. **Subject(s):** Geography; BA 1945; MA 1949. **Tutor(s):** C W Guillebaud. **Educ:** St John's Elementary School, Padiham; St Mary's College, Blackburn; Mount St Mary's, Milltown; St Mary's Hill, Paignton. **Career:** In Holy Orders, Roman Catholic Church.

MACKAY, Angus Newton (1948) Born 15 July 1926, 10 Blenheim Road, Moseley, Birmingham; son of James Mackay, Methodist Minister, and Bessie Newton. **Subject(s):** English; BA 1950. **Tutor(s):** F Thistlethwaite. **Educ:** Saugeen Preparatory School, Bournemouth; Gorse Cliff Preparatory School, Bournemouth; Kingswood School, Bath. **Career:** Actor.

MACKAY, Douglas Keith (1940) Born 25 September 1921, Calne Villa, Shortwood, Pucklechurch, Gloucestershire; son of Douglas Gordon Mackay, Insurance Official, and Florie Williams; m (1) Mej Landels (d 1976), (2) Betty Barbara Blake; 2 sons (James Douglas and Alistair Hugh), 1 daughter (Alison Jean). **Subject(s):** Mathematics/ Economics/Special RE Course; BA 1947; MA 1970. **Tutor(s):** S J Bailey. **Johnian Relatives:** brother of Graham Derek Mackay (1945); father of James Douglas Mackay (1968); uncle of Eleanor Sarah Mackay (1995). **Educ:** Richmond Collegiate School, Cardiff; Exeter School. **Career:** Managing Director, James Townsend & Sons Ltd, Printers, Exeter; Lieutenant, RE 1944. **Honours:** MC.

MACKAY, Eoin Vonde (1936) Born 23 September 1917, 40 Campbell Street, Greenock; son of Edward MacKay, Master Baker, and Agnes Jane Morrison. **Subject(s):** Natural Sciences; BA 1939; MA 1943. **Tutor(s):** R L Howland. **Educ:** Greenock Academy; Strathallen School. Died January 1995.

MACKAY, Graham Derek (1945) Born 17 March 1927, Whitchurch, Cardiff, Glamorganshire; son of Douglas Gordon Mackay, Insurance Manager, and Florie Williams. BA 1950; MA 1952. **Tutor(s):** J M Wordie. **Johnian Relatives:** brother of Douglas Keith Mackay (1940); uncle of James Douglas Mackay (1968) and of Eleanor Sarah Mackay (1995). **Educ:** Exeter School; Solihull Grammar School. **Career:** Solicitor. **Appointments:** RE Cadet, SJC. **Awards:** Vidal Exhibition, SJC 1945.

MCKAY, Horatio Malcolm (1920) Born 9 July 1898, 55 Merton Road, Bootle, Lancashire; son of Horatio McKay, Master Mariner, Merchant Services, and Elizabeth Mary Swan; m Mary Elizabeth Melhuish. BA 1921. **Tutor(s):** B F Armitage. **Johnian Relatives:** father of John Christopher McKay (1956). **Educ:** Brightlands, Newnham; HMS *Conway*; Royal Naval College, Osborne; Royal Naval College, Dartmouth.

MCKELLAR, Andrew William Ross (1919) Born 28 January 1901, Brighton Beach, Melbourne, Australia; son of Andrew Duncan McKellar, Director, Messrs Arthur & Co Ltd, and Margaret Sim. BA 1922. **Tutor(s):** E E Sikes. **Educ:** Kelvinside Academy; Lendrick, Bishopsteignton; The Leys School, Cambridge. Died 5 March 1944.

MCKENDRICK, Dr Charles Stewart (1937) Born 21 October 1919, 8 Clifton Avenue, Longbenton; son of James McKendrick, Chief General Manager, Martin's Bank Limited, and Blanche Miriam Blowman; m Olive Mary Bell, 3 June 1950; 1 son (Jamie b 27 October 1955), 3 daughters (Jennifer b 17 April 1951, Rosemary b 4 June 1953 and Helen b 14 June 1962). BA 1942; MA 1942; MB BChir 1943; MD 1955; MRCP 1948; FRCP 1967. **Tutor(s):** R L Howland. **Educ:** Duchess School, Alnwick; Earnseat Preparatory School, Arnside; Bootham School, York. **Career:** RAMC (North West Europe) and Commandos 1943–1947; Senior Physician, Liverpool Regional Cardiac Centre (major responsibility for establishment of the Centre); Consulting Physician (later Emeritus), Royal Liverpool Hospital; Honorary Director of Cardiological Studies, University of Liverpool; Consultant Physician, Sefton General Hospital, Liverpool. **Appointments:** TA 1948; Commanded 165 Western Casualty Clearing Station, RAMC, TA 1950–1954; Advisor in cardiology to WHO Europe 1960–1968; Member, Liverpool Regional Hospital Board 1961–1973; JP, Liverpool 1961–1987; Co-founder and Council Member, British Heart Foundation; Chairman, General Service Board, Alcoholics Anonymous 1987–1991; Chairman, Sick Doctors Trust 1997–2001. **Publications:** numerous articles on cardiology in medical journals and chapters in various textbooks of medicine.

MACKENZIE, Niel Allan Patrick Grant (1928) Born 8 May 1905, Longforgan, Perthshire, Scotland; son of Niel Kennedy Mackenzie, Parish Minister, and Edith Henrietta Frances Grant. **Tutor(s):** E A Benians. **Educ:** Dollar Academy; University of Edinburgh.

MACKENZIE, The Hon Norman Archibald MacRae (1924) Born 1 May 1894, Pugwash, Nova Scotia; son of James Arthur MacKenzie, Clergyman, and Elizabeth Catherine MacRae; m Margaret Roberts Thomas; 3 children. BA (Dalhousie); LLB (Dalhousie); LLM (Harvard); LLD; DCL (Whitman); Honorary LLD (Mount Allison, New Brunswick, Toronto, Ottawa, Bristol, Alberta and Glasgow); QC 1942; FRSC. **Tutor(s):** E A Benians. **Johnian Relatives:** father of Patrick Thomas Mackenzie (1954). **Educ:** Pictou Academy; Dalhousie University; Harvard University. **Career:** Called to the Bar, Gray's Inn 1924; Professor of International and Constitutional Law, Toronto University 1933; President, University of British Columbia, Vancouver; Legal Adviser, International Labour Office, Geneva; President, Canadian Institute of Public Affairs 1963; Senate of Canada 1966–1969. **Appointments:** Fellow, Carnegie Endowment for International Peace; Member, various committees on international affairs and labour problems 1932–1942; Chairman, Wartime Information Board of Canada; Chairman, National Conference of Canadian Universities;

Canadian Chairman, Save the Children Fund; Vice-President, Canadian YMCA; Honorary Fellow, SJC 1964. **Honours:** CMG 1946; MM and Bar; CC. Died 26 January 1986.

MACKENZIE ROSS, Ian Alexander Bruce (1946) Born 9 February 1928, Caer Gwent Nursing Home, Wykeham Road, Worthing, Sussex; son of Alexander Mackenzie Ross, Civil Servant, Air Ministry, and Margaret Marcia Simmonds; m Catherine Jane Tulloch, 16 May 1958, Fort Augustus, Invernessshire; 1 son (Alexander); 3 daughters (Anne, Jennifer and Catherine Marcia). **Subject(s):** Natural Sciences; BA 1949; MB ChB (Edinburgh) 1952. **Tutor(s):** E H F Baldwin; D V Davies; R H Winfield. **Johnian Relatives:** grandson of Arthur Simmonds (1870); nephew of Ronald John McLean Simmonds (1928); brother of Ronald Keith MacKenzie Ross (1954). **Educ:** St Cyprian's School, Eastbourne; Wellesley House, Rannoch Lodge, Loch Rannoch; Loretto School, Musselburgh. **Career:** GP, Kent; National Service, RMO, 5th Malay Regiment. **Appointments:** President, Village Cricket Team; Governor, Valence School.

MCKIBBIN, Frederick Malcolm (1928) Born 14 October 1910, 23 Chestnut Gardens, Cliftonville Road, Belfast; son of Frederick McKibbin, Estate Agent, and Mary Watt Wilson; 1 daughter. **Subject(s):** Mathematics/Law; BA 1932; MA 1936; ARICS 1936; FRICS. **Tutor(s):** J M Wordie. **Educ:** Royal Academical Institution, Belfast. **Career:** Surveyor. **Appointments:** JP; Member, Lands Tribunal for Northern Ireland 1964; Member, Lord Chief Justice's Board of Chartered Surveyors; Member, Court of the Lands Tribunal. Died 27 January 1998.

MACKINLAY, David Murray (1912) Born 23 November 1893, 40 Alleston Road, Stoke Newington, Middlesex; son of James Wait Mackinlay, Merchant, and Edith Harriet Sarah Harris; m Vera Marie May Frost, 16 July 1924, All Saints', Oakleigh Park. **Subject(s):** History; BA 1918; MA 1921. **Tutor(s):** E E Sikes. **Educ:** Fern Bank School; Mill Hill School. **Career:** Captain, King's Royal Rifle Corps (wounded), WWI.

MCKINNEY, Robert Lincoln (1918) American Student.

MACKINTOSH, Ian Brine (1944) Born 3 February 1926, Laurel Bank, Anstruther Easter, Fife; son of James Alexander Robertson Cowper Mackintosh, Medical Practitioner, and Emma Moss Booth-Tucker Ellis; m Hilary Lilian Hunt, 22 September 1962, Holy Trinity Church, Prince Consort Road, London; 1 son (John Sidney), 1 daughter (Catherine l'Anson). **Subject(s):** Mechanical Sciences; BA 1947; MA 1951; FICE 1965. **Tutor(s):** S J Bailey. **Educ:** Trinmore Kindergarten, Bristol; King Edward VI School, Bath; Private Tutor, Claverton; Epsom College. **Career:** Instructor in Mathematics, RMA Sandhurst 1947–1950; Sir William Halcrow and Partners, Consulting Civil Engineers 1950–1954; Niagara Mohawk Power Corporation, New York, and Morrison Knusden Co, Idaho 1954–1956; Taylor Woodrow Construction 1956–1965; Balfour Beatty Ltd 1965–1981; Teacher of Mathematics and IT, Cardinal Newman High School, Acton 1981–1985; Teacher of Mathematics and IT, Sacred Heart High School, Hammersmith 1985–1991; Lecturer in Computer Studies, Hammersmith Community Education 1991–1996. **Appointments:** Founder Secretary, Cambridge University and District Rugby Football Referees' Society. **Awards:** Goodwin Travelling Fellowship 1954–1955. **Publications:** Articles on dams and tunnels in *Water Power* and other technical publications, 1959–1965; (ed) *A Collection of Travels over 500 Years*.

MACKLIN, David Drury (1947) Born 1 September 1928, Brunswick Nursing Home, Cambridge; son of Laurence Hilary Macklin, Secretary, Associated Board of the Royal Schools of Music, and Alice Dumergue Tait; m Janet Smallwood, 23 July 1955; 4 sons (Alan Drury, Simon André, Alastair Jeremy and Adrian Roger). **Subject(s):** Classics/Law; BA 1950; MA 1955. **Tutor(s):** R L Howland. **Johnian Relatives:** grandson of Arthur James Tait (1891) and of Herbert Walter Macklin (1884); nephew of David Harold Macklin (1916); son of Laurence Hilary Macklin (1921); nephew of George Aidan Drury Tait (1921) and of

Cecil Wortley Tait (1925); cousin of Arthur Gordon Tait (1954); cousin of Richard Drury Tait (1956); father of Alan Drury Macklin (1976) and of Alastair Jeremy Macklin (1979); cousin of Celia Helen Gilbert Tait (1983); father of Adrian Roger Macklin (1986); cousin, once removed, of Helen Joanna Hendry (1996). **Educ:** Tormore School, Deal; Felsted School. **Career:** Baileys Shaw & Gillett, Solicitors 1951–1954; Assistant Solicitor, Coward Chance & Co 1954–1956; Warwickshire County Council 1956–1961; Devon County Council 1961–1969; Deputy Clerk, Derbyshire County Council 1969–1973; Chief Executive, Lincolnshire County Council 1973–1979; Chief Executive, Devon County Council 1979–1988. **Appointments:** Secretary, LMBC 1949–1950; Member, Cambridge University Appointments Board 1975–1980; Deputy Lieutenant, Devon 1990; Appointed Boundary Commission for England 1989; Chairman, Community Council of Devon 1992; Member, Devon and Cornwall Housing Association 1989–1998; Member, Village Retail Services Association. **Honours:** CBE 1989.

MACKLIN, David Harold (1916) Born 28 June 1897, Pidley Parsonage, Huntingdon; son of Herbert Walter Macklin, formerly Rector of Houghton Conquest, and Marian Moore Bridgman. **Tutor(s):** W D Sykes. **Johnian Relatives:** son of Herbert Walter Macklin (1884); brother of Laurence Hilary Macklin (1921); uncle of David Drury Macklin (1947); great uncle of Alan Drury Macklin (1976), Alastair Jeremy Macklin (1979) and of Adrian Roger Macklin (1986). **Educ:** Christ Church Cathedral School, Oxford; King's School, Rochester; University College, London. **Career:** 2nd Battalion, Artists' Rifles OTC 1916–1917; Second Lieutenant, 5th (Reserve) Bedfordshire Regiment; Brigade Bombing Instructor, Godstone; Intelligence Officer, 4th Battalion, Bedfordshire Regiment, France 1917–1918. **Awards:** Dowman Scholarship, SJC 1916. Died 27 March 1918 (killed in action near Albert, France).

MACKLIN, Laurence Hilary (1921) Born 18 August 1902, The Rectory, Houghton Conquest, Bedfordshire; son of Herbert Walter Macklin, Clerk in Holy Orders, and Marian Moore Bridgman; m Alice Dumergue Tait, 19 November 1926, St Paul's Cathedral, Calcutta; 1 son (David Drury b 1 September 1928), 1 daughter (Rosemary Jane b 15 October 1930). **Subject(s):** Classics/English; BA 1924; MA 1928; Hon FRAM. **Tutor(s):** E E Sikes. **Johnian Relatives:** son of Herbert Walter Macklin (1884); son-in-law of Arthur James Tait (1891); brother of David Harold Macklin (1916); brother-in-law of George Aidan Drury Tait (1921) and of Cecil Wortley Tait (1925); father of David Drury Macklin (1947); uncle of Arthur Gordon Tait (1954) and of Richard Drury Tait (1956); grandfather of Alan Drury Macklin (1976) and of Alastair Jeremy Macklin (1979); great uncle of Celia Helen Gilbert Tait (1983); grandfather of Adrian Roger Macklin (1986); great uncle of Helen Joanna Hendry (1996). **Educ:** Christ Church Cathedral Choir School, Oxford; Felsted School. **Career:** Principal Private Secretary to the Minister, Ministry of Shipping, Ministry of War Transport, WWII; Messers Mackinnon, Mackenzie and Co, Calcutta 1925–1935; Secretary, Associated Board of the Royal Schools of Music 1935–1963. **Appointments:** Secretary, Cambridge Preservation Society, 1965; Honorary Fellow, Royal Academy of Music; Secretary, Mendelssohn and Boise Foundations; Member, Committee of Management of UCL; Secretary, Committee on Higher Education in Music. **Awards:** Choral Studentship, SJC. **Honours:** OBE 1949. Died 18 November 1969.

MACKWORTH, Dr Norman Humphrey (1945) Born 2 December 1917, Bareilly, United Provinces, India; son of Norman Walter Mackworth, Lieutenant Colonel, Indian Medical Service, and Isabel Largie Anderson. PhD 1947; MB (Aberdeen); ChB (Aberdeen) 1939. **Tutor(s):** J M Wordie. **Educ:** Aberdeen Grammar School; University of Aberdeen. **Career:** Psychological Laboratory, Cambridge 1940; Title A Fellow, SJC 1949–1952; Director, Applied Psychology Research Unit, MRC, Cambridge 1953. **Awards:** Kenneth Craik Award, SJC 1946–1947.

MACLAREN, Archibald Shaw (1921) Born 18 September 1902, Corraith, Dundonald, Symington, Ayrshire, Scotland; son of John Finlay

Maclaren, Iron Founder, and Clara Louise Hillhouse; m Gladys Emily Godbold, 12 August 1931, St Saviour's, Claremont, Cape, South Africa; 1 son (Antony John Shaw). **Subject(s):** Mathematics/Mechanical Sciences; BA 1924; MA 1928; CEng; FICE. **Tutor(s):** E Cunningham. **Johnian Relatives:** father of Antony John Shaw Maclaren (1957). **Educ:** Bilton Grange, Rugby; Rugby School. **Career:** Chartered Civil Engineer. Died 21 March 1986.

MCLAREN, Colin Colby (1927) Born 7 March 1910, Portland Street, Aberystwyth, Cardigan; son of John Rattray McLaren, General Company Secretary, and Elizabeth Lucy Colby; m; 1 son (John T), 1 daughter (Ursula C). **Subject(s):** Mechanical Sciences; BA 1931; MA 1995. **Tutor(s):** J M Wordie. **Educ:** St Christopher's, Bath; Felsted School. **Career:** Student Apprentice, Walthamstow 1931–1932, Sales Engineer, London 1932–1938, ASEA Electric; Sales Engineer, English Electric, Stafford 1938–1942; Air Crew/Staff Pilot, RAF, South Africa 1942–1946; Sales Engineer, Brush Electrical, Loughborough 1947–1949; Head, Technical Section, Knowles & Foster, Brazil 1949–1954; Branch Manager, Winnipeg 1954–1961, Sales Engineer, Switzerland 1962–1967, Brown & Boveri; Night-staff Telephonist, GPO, Harrow 1967–1976; Self-employed Technical Translator from German, French and Portuguese 1967–1998. **Awards:** Exhibition, SJC; College Prize 1930. Died 13 December 2001.

MACLAURIN, Griffith Campbell (1932) Born 19 September 1909, Rark Road, Auckland, New Zealand; son of Kenneth Campbell Maclaurin, Headmaster, Ponsonby Public School, and Gwladys Rogers Jones. **Subject(s):** Mathematics; BA 1934; BA (New Zealand). **Tutor(s):** J M Wordie. **Johnian Relatives:** nephew of Richard Cockburn Maclaurin (1892). **Educ:** Te Awamutu Public (Primary) School; Whitiora Public Primary School, Hamilton; High School, Hamilton; Grammar School, Auckland; University College, Auckland. **Career:** Bookshop Proprietor, All Saints Passage, Cambridge 1934–1936. Died 16 November 1936.

MACLAY, Ebenezer (1909) Born 27 December 1891, 4 Park Terrace, Crosshill, Renfrewshire, Scotland; son of Joseph Paton Maclay, Shipowner, and Martha Strang. **Subject(s):** Economics; BA 1912. **Tutor(s):** E E Sikes. **Johnian Relatives:** brother of Walter Symington Maclay (1919); uncle of Walter Strang Symington Maclay (1949) and of John Lennox Sim Maclay (1957). **Educ:** Warriston School. **Career:** Father's shipping business; Lieutenant 1914, rising to rank of Captain, 5th Battalion, The Cameronians (Scottish Rifles) (invalided out after serving on the front); returned to father's shipping business; Lieutenant, Scots Guards until 1918. Died 11 April 1918 (of wounds received in action on 10 April).

MACLAY, Dr Walter Strang Symington (1949) Born 9 August 1931, Clarendon Nursing Home, Johannesburg, Transvaal, South Africa; son of Walter Symington Maclay, Medical Practitioner, and Dorothy Russell Lennox; m Elizabeth, 1956; 2 sons (Andrew and Christopher), 1 daughter (Janet). **Subject(s):** Natural Sciences; BA 1952; MA 1956; BChir 1955; MB 1956; MRCGP; DObstRCOG. **Tutor(s):** G C L Bertram. **Johnian Relatives:** nephew of Ebenezer Maclay (1909); son of Walter Symington Maclay (1919); brother-in-law of Robert David Ogden (1949); brother of John Lennox Sim Maclay (1957). **Educ:** Wagner's School, Queen's Gate, London; Dardunn School, Kilmacolm; Horris Hill Preparatory School, Newbury; Winchester College. **Career:** Commissioned, RAMC; Junior Specialist, Obstetrics and Gynaecology; GP, Whitley 1963. **Appointments:** Secretary and Chairman, Local Division, BMA. Died 23 April 1987.

MACLAY, The Hon Walter Symington (1919) Born 29 October 1901, 13 Park Terrace, Glasgow; son of Joseph Paton Maclay, Shipowner, and Martha Strang; m Dorothy Russell Lennox, 26 April 1928, Morningside Parish Church, Edinburgh; 3 sons, 2 daughters. BA 1922; MA 1928; MB 1928; BChir 1928; MD 1934; MRCP 1938; MRCS (St Bartholomew's) 1927; DTM&H 1928; LRCP (St Bartholomew's) 1927; FRCP 1952. **Tutor(s):** E E Sikes. **Johnian Relatives:** brother of Ebenezer Maclay

(1909); father of Walter Strang Symington Maclay (1949); father-in-law of Robert David Ogden (1949); father of John Lennox Sim Maclay (1957). **Educ:** Dardenne, Kilmacolm; Glasgow Academy; Fettes College, Edinburgh; St Bartholomew's Hospital. **Career:** King George Hospital, Ilford; House Surgeon and Physician, Royal Infirmary, Glasgow 1927–1928; Medical Officer, various hospitals in Kenya, Nyasaland and South Africa 1928–1931; Junior Staff, Hospital for Sick Children, Great Ormond Street 1931–1932; Maudsley Hospital 1932; Clinical Assistant, Royal Chest Hospital, City Road, and at Nose and Throat Department, St Bartholomew's; Head, Psychiatric Section, and Medical Superintendent, Mill Hill EMS Hospital 1939–1945; Senior Commissioner, Board of Control 1945–1954; Senior Medical Commissioner, Board of Control, and Senior Principal Medical Officer, Ministry of Health 1954–1961; Part-time help for Wessex Regional Hospital Board Psychiatric Services 1961. **Appointments:** Honorary Physician to the Queen; President, Royal Medico-Psychological Association; Fellow, Royal Society of Medicine and of the Royal Society of Tropical Medicine. **Honours:** OBE 1943; CB 1955. Died 27 April 1964.

MCLEAN, Hugh (1919) Born 3 June 1899, Glenhurst, Bishopton, Renfrew, Scotland; son of Hugh McLean, Sugar Broker, and Jeannie Brown. **Tutor(s):** E E Sikes. **Educ:** Greenock Academy; Loretto School, Musselburgh. **Career:** RFC then RAF 1917–1919 (Second Lieutenant, France 1918). **Honours:** DFC; Croix de Guerre.

MCLEAN, Professor Robert Colquhoun (1912) Born 18 July 1890, Kilcreggan, Dumbartonshire; son of Robert McLean, Presbyterian Minister, and Marion Cochrane; m Freda Marguerite Kilner, 30 July 1914 (d 8 January 1955); 3 sons (Denis b 28 May 1915, d 12 June 1969, David b 16 September 1917, and Roderick b 11 June 1921). **Subject(s):** Biology/Geology; BA 1916; MA 1919; BSc (London) 1910; DSc (London) 1917. **Tutor(s):** L H K Bushe-Fox. **Johnian Relatives:** father of Roderick MacLean (1946). **Educ:** Liverpool College; The Leys School, Cambridge; UCL. **Career:** Professor of Botany, University College of South Wales, Cardiff 1919–1955 (Emeritus 1955); Lecturer, University College, Reading; Pathologist, Military Hospital Reading, WWI; Group Warden, ARP, and fire-fighting, WWII. **Appointments:** Honorary Secretary, International University Conference 1934–1936; President, Association of University Teachers 1940; Member, National Parks Commission 1949; Member, Nature Conservancy 1949–1956; President, International Association of University Professors 1950; Fellow, Linnean Society. **Publications:** (with Ivimey Cooke) *Textbook of Botany* (4 vols). Died 7 April 1981.

MCLEAN, Robert Younger (1944) Born 5 February 1922, The Gables, Whitburn Road, Cleadon; son of James Younger McLean, Managing Director, Brewers, and Roberta Catherine Procter; m Kathleen Anne Foulis, 1950; 2 daughters. **Subject(s):** Mechanical Sciences; BA 1948; MA 1953; MIEE. **Tutor(s):** S J Bailey. **Educ:** Rock Lodge Preparatory School; Loretto School. **Career:** Lieutenant, RA 1940–1946; Parsons Peebles Power Transformers Ltd 1949–1985. **Appointments:** Founder Chairman, Wester Coates Amenity Society 1972–1984; Chairman, North Edinburgh Conservative Association 1976–1979.

MACLEAN, Roderick (1946) Born 11 June 1921, Berwyn, Mountain Road, Caerphilly, Glamorganshire; son of Robert Colquhoun McLean, Professor of Botany, University College, Cardiff, and Freda Marguerite Kilner, University Lecturer. **Subject(s):** History; BA 1948; MA 1953. **Tutor(s):** F Thistlethwaite. **Johnian Relatives:** son of Robert Colquhoun McLean (1912). **Educ:** St Pirans, Maidenhead; Oundle School. **Career:** War Service in British and Indian Armies 1940–1946; Administrator, Cocos Keeling Islands 1950–1951; Malayan Civil Service 1950–1963; North Borneo/Sabah Civil Service 1963–1969; Hong Kong Civil Service 1969–1975; Executive Director, Singapore International Chamber of Commerce 1976–1987. **Honours:** OBE 1968. **Publications:** *A Pattern of Change: The Singapore International Chamber of Commerce from 1837*, 2000.

MCLEISH, Alastair Campbell (1934) Born 17 November 1911, Ajmer, Rajputana, India; son of Alexander McLeish, Minister of the Church of Scotland, and Roberta Campbell. **Tutor(s):** J M Wordie. **Educ:** Larchfield, Helensburgh; St Mary's School, Melrose; Leighton Park, Reading; University of Glasgow.

MCLELLAN, John Hollingsworth (1921) Born 7 February 1903, Pinehurst, Gloucester Road, Cheltenham; son of Walter Daniel McLellan, Wine Merchants Manager, and Elsie Mary Ruddle. **Subject(s):** Mathematics; BA 1924; MA 1958. **Tutor(s):** E Cunningham. **Educ:** St Anne's School, Redhill; Pocklington School. **Awards:** Dowman Exhibition, SJC. Died 2 December 1978.

MACLENNAN, Donald James Henry (1921) Born 19 June 1904, Radnor Hall, Elstree, Hertfordshire; son of Donald Maclennan, Gentleman, and Alice Jane Davidge Cleminson; m Sybil Mary Sabine Pasley, 18 October 1930, All Saints', Ennismore Gardens. **Tutor(s):** E Cunningham. **Educ:** Private Tuition, Harrow; St Peter's School, Eastbourne; Harrow School.

MACLEOD, Alastair Leoid (1947) Born 2 November 1924, Glencairn, West Kilbride, Ayrshire; son of Robert Ure Macleod, Shipowner, and Mary Irving Smith; m Leonora Mary Symonds, 17 November 1956; 1 son (Robert), 1 daughter (Erica). **Subject(s):** Mechanical Sciences; BA 1950; MA 1954. **Tutor(s):** R L Howland. **Johnian Relatives:** son-in-law of Reginald Askwith Symonds (1925); brother of Kenneth Macallister Macleod (1934); brother-in-law of Robert Stobart Symonds (1958). **Educ:** Cambusdoon Preparatory School; Shrewsbury School; Royal Technical College, Glasgow. **Career:** Sub-Lieutenant, RNVR; Mechanical Engineer 1950; City firm of shipbrokers 1957. **Appointments:** President, CUBC; rowed for Great Britain, European Games, Milan 1950 and Helsinki Olympics 1952. Died 26 April 2002.

MACLEOD, Dr John William (1942) Born 7 June 1924, 52 Baxter Gate, Loughborough; son of Neil MacLeod, Medical Practitioner, and Ruth Hill; 4 children. **Subject(s):** Natural Sciences; BA 1945; MA 1966; BChir 1949; MB 1949. **Tutor(s):** S J Bailey. **Johnian Relatives:** brother of Hugh Roderick MacLeod (1950). **Educ:** Loughborough Junior High School; The Downs School, Colwall; Bryanston School.

MACLEOD, Kenneth Macallister (1934) Born 9 February 1916, Glencairn, West Kilbride, Ayrshire; son of Robert Ure Macleod, Shipbroker, and Mary Irving Smith; m Yvonne Moyra Graham Charlton, 18 December 1946, Takeley Parish Church; 2 children. BA 1937; MA 1945; MIMechE; FIMarE. **Tutor(s):** J M Wordie. **Johnian Relatives:** brother of Alastair Leoid Macleod (1947). **Educ:** Cambusdoon, Alloway; Shrewsbury School. **Career:** Sudan Civil Service (railways and dockyards); Director, Chinnor Cement and Lime Company, Oxon; Engineering Officer, RN 1939–1947; Director, Lloyd International Airway 1965–1970. **Honours:** DSC. Died 5 August 1995.

MCLEOD, Norman Chester (1923) Born 6 December 1901, Bilaspore, Central Provinces, India; son of Norman Chester McLeod, Conservator of Forests, and Margaret Isabel Schmid. **Tutor(s):** E A Benians. **Educ:** Colet Court, West Kensington; Eastbourne College. **Career:** Mexican Eagle Petroleum Company 1920–1923.

MACMAHON, Professor Percy Alexander (1904) Born 26 September 1854, Malta; son of Patrick William MacMahon, Brigadier General, and Ellen Curtis; m Grace Elizabeth Howard, 9 February 1907, St John the Evangelist, Kilburn. Honorary ScD 1904; Honorary Degree (Dublin, Aberdeen, St Andrews); FRS 1890. **Educ:** Cheltenham College; RMA, Woolwich. **Career:** RA 1872; Mathematics Instructor, RMA 1882–1890; Professor of Physics, Ordnance College 1890–1897; Deputy Warden of Standards, Board of Trade 1906–1920. **Appointments:** General Secretary, British Association 1902–1914; Vice-President, Royal Society 1917; President, Royal Astronomical Society 1917. **Awards:** Royal Society Medal 1900; Sylvester Medal, Royal Society 1919; De Morgan Medal of London Mathematical Society 1923. Died 25 September 1929.

MCMICKING, Ralph Gore (1918) Born 1 April 1897, Boycott Manor, Stowe, Buckingham; son of Gilbert McMicking, Major, RA, and MP for Kirkcudbrightshire, and Gertrude Rosabel Catherine Gore. **Tutor(s):** E E Sikes. **Educ:** St David's School, Reigate; Marlborough College. **Career:** Military and National Service.

MCMILLIN, Angus (1943) Born 14 June 1924, 16 Cornwall Road, St Albans; son of James McMillin, Tailor's Cutter, and Marion Rebecca Cox; m Ursula. **Subject(s):** Modern and Medieval Languages; BA 1948; MA 1950. **Tutor(s):** C W Guillebaud. **Educ:** Aylesford House School, St Albans; St Albans School. Died 20 September 1994.

MCMULLEN, Alexander Lawrence (1924) Born 2 September 1905, The Keep, Dartmouth, Devon; son of Alexander Percy McMullen, Adviser on Naval Education, Admiralty, and Catherine Maud Ashwell; m Muriel Felicite Sikes; 4 sons (William Alexander b 26 April 1937, Ian James and David Lawrence (twins) b 10 August 1939 and Michael Colin Geoffrey b 1942). BA 1927; MA 1931; FRIBA. **Tutor(s):** B F Armitage. **Johnian Relatives:** son-in-law of Edward Ernest Sikes (1886); brother of John Anthony McMullen (1929); father of William Alexander McMullen (1957), David Lawrence McMullen (1959) and of Ian James McMullen (1959). **Educ:** The Wells House Preparatory School; Sedbergh School. **Career:** Temporary Lecturer, School of Architecture, University of Cambridge; Major, London Scottish Regiment, WWII; Chartered Architect in private practice. **Awards:** Exhibition, SJC. Died 11 July 1982.

MCMULLEN, John Anthony (1929) Born 22 April 1911, The Keep, Dartmouth, Devon; son of Alexander Percy McMullen, Adviser on Naval Education, Admiralty, and Catherine Maud Ashwell. **Subject(s):** Mechanical Sciences; BA 1932; MA 1936. **Tutor(s):** J M Wordie. **Johnian Relatives:** brother of Alexander Lawrence McMullen (1924); uncle of William Alexander McMullen (1957), Ian James McMullen (1959) and of David Lawrence McMullen (1959). **Educ:** The Wells House, Malvern Wells; Sedbergh School. **Career:** Traffic Apprentice, London Midland and Scottish Railways; Lieutenant Colonel, Royal Signals, RE, BEF; Assistant Director of Transportation, HQ 21 Armoured Group, WWII; Assistant Controller, Lancaster, London Midland and Scottish Railways 1939; Passenger Assistant to the District Goods and Passenger Manager, Bristol 1945; Central Transport Department, ICI 1948; Transport Officer, ICI 1959. **Honours:** OBE 1944 (Military). Died 2 February 1983.

MCMULLEN, William Albert (1909) Born 8 March 1889, 13 St Albans Place, Blackburn, Lancashire; son of James McMullen, Assurance Director, and Hannah Morton. BA 1912. **Tutor(s):** L H K Bushe-Fox. **Educ:** Crediton Grammar School; Mercers' School, London. **Career:** Lieutenant, RASC (Mechanical Transport), WWI. **Honours:** MBE. Died 8 April 1930.

MCMURTRIE, Robert Peter Lax (1944) Born 24 March 1926, St Ibbs Bush, St Ippollitts, Hitchin, Hertfordshire; son of Donald Scott Anderson McMurtrie, Solicitor, and Margaret Isobel Stratton Amos; m Margaret Jane Wright, 12 September 1953, St John's Church, Woking. **Subject(s):** Economics; BA 1949; MA 1952. **Tutor(s):** J M Wordie. **Educ:** Pinewood, Farnborough; Heathmount, Hertford; Marlborough College. **Career:** RN Cadet. **Appointments:** Chairman, Hertfordshire Conservation Society; Qualified Mediator for Alternative Dispute Resolution through CEDR; Member, Solicitors Disciplinary Tribunal for England and Wales.

MCNEILL, Dr John Richard (1944) Born 13 April 1926, 4 Courtfield Gardens, Kensington; son of Neal McNeill, Civil Engineer, and Violet Ethel Taylor. **Subject(s):** Natural Sciences; BA 1947; MA 1951; BChir 1954; MB 1954. **Tutor(s):** J M Wordie. **Educ:** St Faith's School, Cambridge; Oundle School. **Appointments:** RN Cadet, SJC.

MACNICOLL, Douglas (1918) Born 25 July 1901, Derwas, Llanelian, Glan Conway, Denbighshire; son of Douglas H MacNicoll, JP, Land

Agent; and Susannah Anne Roberts. BA 1921; MA 1925. **Tutor(s):** E E Sikes. **Educ:** Repton School.

MACNISH, Dr James Martin (1924) Born 15 December 1905, 5049 Kensington Avenue, St Louis, Missouri USA; son of James Macnish, Mechanical Engineer, and Lucelle Martin. BA 1927; MA 1965. **Tutor(s):** B F Armitage. **Educ:** Hitchinson Central High School, Buffalo, USA; Washington University, St Louis, USA. **Career:** Lecturer in Urology, St Louis University; Lieutenant, USNR; Practice, St Louis, specialist in genito-urinary work; Licentiate, American Board of Urology 1938; Surgeon Commander, United States Navy, serving in the Pacific, New Hebrides, Solomons, the Philippines, Okinawa and Japan 1942–1946. **Publications:** (ed) *The Urologic and Cutaneous Review*. Died 26 February 1995.

MACPHERSON, Dr Ian William (1948) Born 10 August 1922, 9 Mosset Terrace, Forres, Morayshire, Scotland; son of William Lachlan Macpherson, Bank Accountant, and Janet Rose; m Gwendolyn Travers Lambert, 1956; twin sons (Robin Ian and Alan James b 1959). **Subject(s):** Classics; BA 1950; MA 1954; PhD 1959; MA (Aberdeen). **Tutor(s):** R L Howland. **Educ:** Rose's Academical Institution, Nairn; Aberdeen University; School of Slavonic Languages, London University. **Career:** First Secretary, FCO, served in Turkey, Switzerland, Hungary, Greece. Died 9 September 1993.

MACPHERSON, James Gordon (1942) Born 22 January 1924, 3 Reed Pond Walk, Gidea Park, Romford; son of Thomas Macpherson, Produce Merchant, and Lucy Butcher. **Tutor(s):** C W Guillebaud. **Educ:** Wells House, Malvern Wells; Loretto School; Kingussie School, Invernessshire.

MACRO, William Brindley (1929) Born 3 November 1911, 65 Fulham Park Gardens, Fulham, London; son of William Seaman Macro, Poultry Keeper, and Elizabeth Brindley Bond; m C Evelyn Stevenson, 16 August 1938 (d 1991); 2 sons (Raymond b 1941 and Robin b 1942), 1 daughter (Sylvia b 1942). **Subject(s):** Mathematics; BA 1932; MA 1936. **Tutor(s):** J M Wordie. **Educ:** New King's Road School, Fulham; Dickleborough Elementary School; Diss Secondary School. **Career:** Mathematics Teacher, Yarmouth Grammar School 1933–1936; Mathematics Teacher, Newcastle Royal Grammar School 1936–1962; Radar Research, TRE Malvern, Worcestershire 1941–1945; Head of Mathematics, Newcastle Rutherford School. **Awards:** Exhibition, SJC.

MACROBERT, Alexander Edgely (1948) Born 12 August 1927, 6 Lothian Gardens, Glasgow; son of Thomas Murray MacRobert, Professor of Mathematics, University of Glasgow, and Janet McGillivray Violet McIlreaith; m Irene Barbara Small, 10 June 1955, Glasgow; 2 sons (Alexander John b 10 April 1956 and Andrew Thomas b 29 May 1965), 1 daughter (Alison Barbara b 14 February 1958). **Subject(s):** History; BA 1951; MEd (Glasgow) 1967. **Tutor(s):** F Thistlethwaite. **Educ:** Glasgow Academy. **Career:** RA 1945–1948; Colonial Administrative Service, Uganda 1952–1962; Teacher and Principal Teacher, Glasgow 1963–1968; Assistant Director of Education, Dunbartonshire, subsequently Deputy Director and Senior Deputy Director 1968–1975; Senior Education Officer, Dunbarton Division 1975–1988. **Appointments:** Chairman, Scottish Central Committee on Religious Education 1983–1986. **Awards:** Exhibition, SJC 1945. **Publications:** *The Novels of Dumfries and Galloway*, 1992; *Mary's Flight to the Solway*, 1993; *To See Oursels – Visitors to Dumfries and Galloway from Medieval to Modern Times*, 2001; *Mary Queen of Scots and the Casket Letters*, 2002.

MACROBERT, Sir Iain Workman (1936) Born 19 April 1917, Carnousie House, Forglen, Aberdeenshire; son of Alexander MacRobert, Chairman, British India Corporation, and Rachel Workman. **Subject(s):** Economics/Geography; BA 1939. **Tutor(s):** J M Wordie. **Johnian Relatives:** brother of Roderic Alan MacRobert (1933). **Educ:** Cranleigh School. **Career:** Pilot Officer, Flying Corps, RAF 1939–1941. Died 30 June 1941.

MACROBERT, Sir Roderic Alan (1933) Born 8 May 1915, Douneside, Tarland, Aberdeenshire; son of Alexander MacRobert, Woollen Manufacturer, and Rachel Workman. **Subject(s):** Natural Sciences. **Tutor(s):** J M Wordie. **Johnian Relatives:** brother of Iain Workman MacRobert (1936). **Educ:** The Downs School, Colwall; The Dene School, Caterham; Bryanston School, Blandford; Cranleigh School. **Career:** Bomber Squadron, Palestine Command; Acting Pilot Officer 1938, then Flight Lieutenant, RAF. Died 22 May 1941 (killed in action at Mosul).

MCTURK, John (1933) Born 26 July 1914, 110 Tettenhall Road, Wolverhampton; son of John Norman McTurk, Physician and Surgeon, and Isabel Margaret Hall; m Sheila; 2 daughters (Amanda and Anthea). **Subject(s):** Law; BA 1936; MA 1948. **Tutor(s):** C W Guillebaud. **Educ:** The Wells House, Malvern Wells; Stowe School, Buckingham. **Career:** Colonial Administrative Service; Burma Civil Service 1937–1945; Assistant Secretary to the Governor of Burma 1940–1941; Commissioned, Burma Frontier Force 1941; Lieutenant Colonel, Burma Frontier Force 1945; Deputy Commissioner, Akyab District 1945–1946; Deputy Commissioner, Shwebo District 1947; Barrister-at-Law, Grays Inn 1949. Died 21 March 1990.

MCVEAN, John Duncan (1923) Born 9 November 1905, Blake House, 11 High Street, Lees, Oldham, Lancashire; son of John Duncan McVean, Physician and Surgeon, and Hilda May van Homrigh; m Ruth Swannack, June 1932, London; 1 son. BA 1926; MRCS; LRCP. **Tutor(s):** B F Armitage. **Johnian Relatives:** father of Richard Duncan McVean (1953). **Educ:** Wellington College, Salop; Clifton College, Bristol. **Career:** GP; Police Surgeon; Corps Surgeon, St John Ambulance Brigade. Died 4 January 1972.

MCWILLIAM, John Abram (1919) Born 31 July 1901, 19 Marlborough Road, Nether Hallam, Sheffield; son of Andrew McWilliam, Associate Professor of Metallurgy, University of Sheffield, and Consulting Metallurgist, and Georgina Elizabeth Beebee Croome; m Ethel Fenwick Van Wart, 29 June 1932; 1 son (John Andrew Clowes b 19 March 1937), 2 daughters (Anne Fenwick b 9 June 1941 and Mary Van Wart b 29 March 1943). **Subject(s):** Engineering; BA 1922; MA 1927. **Tutor(s):** E A Benians. **Educ:** E M Asterley's Preparatory School, Sheffield; King Edward VII School, Sheffield; Glasgow Academy; University of Glasgow. **Career:** Research Student, Sheffield University 1922–1924; Brown-Firth Research Laboratories 1924–1929 (Head, Pyrometric Laboratories 1925–1929); Travelling Advisor, Thomas Firth & Son Ltd, and Thomas Firth and John Brown Ltd 1929–1934; Firth-Vickers Stainless Steels Ltd 1934–1939; Lieutenant Colonel and CRE, 46th Division, BEF, France 1939–1941; work on the development of jet aircraft engines for Ministry of Aircraft Production, Firth Vickers Stainless Steels Ltd 1941. **Appointments:** Council Member, Sheffield Society of Engineers and Metallurgists. **Awards:** Hatfield Memorial Prize, Sheffield Metallurgical Association 1946. **Publications:** 'Welding of corrosion and heat-resisting steels', *Welding*, 1950. Died 8 March 1979.

MADAN, Michael Spencer (1944) Born 29 November 1927, Belgrano, Hartley Road, Altrincham, Cheshire; son of William Spencer Madan, Manager, Smith and Wellstood, and Janet Nellie Brown. **Tutor(s):** C W Guillebaud. **Educ:** Hurst Grange School, Stirling; Strathallan School; Dollar Academy, Clackmannanshire.

MADELOFF, Dr Stanley Michael (1948) Born 6 May 1930, 30 Harehills Avenue, Leeds; son of Ben Madeloff, House Furnisher, and Annie Levy. **Subject(s):** Natural Sciences; BA 1951; MA 1955; BChir 1956; MB 1956. **Tutor(s):** G C L Bertram. **Educ:** Ingledew College, Leeds; Grosvenor House School, Harrogate; Shrewsbury School. **Career:** Consulting Physician (Nephrology), Bethesda, Maryland; Teaching Fellow, Maryland University 1959–1961. Died December 1993.

MAGNAY, Harold Swindale (1922) Born 24 January 1904, 100 Audley Road, South Gosforth, Northumberland; son of Andrew Magnay, Barrister's Clerk, and Phoebe Elizabeth Swindale; m Meg, 1931; 1 son (Harold Huntley b 19 September 1932). **Subject(s):** History/Law; BA 1925; MA 1930; Honorary MA (Liverpool) 1959. **Tutor(s):** E A Benians. **Johnian Relatives:** father of Harold Huntley Magnay (1952); grandfather of Andrew Richard Magnay (1977). **Educ:** Elswick Road Council School, Newcastle upon Tyne; Royal Grammar School, Newcastle upon Tyne. **Career:** Director of Education, Barnsley 1934–1940; Director of Education, City of Leicester 1940–1946; Director of Education, City of Liverpool 1946–1964; Consultant to the OECD, Paris 1964. **Appointments:** Member, Department Committee, Board of Education 1944; Member, University Grants Committee 1946; President, Association of Education Officers; Chairman, Association of Art Institutions, BBC Northern Advisory Council. **Awards:** Exhibition, SJC 1921; Squire Scholarship 1922. Died 24 October 1971.

MAGNÚSSON, Magnús (1946) Born 19 October 1926, Reykjavík, Iceland; son of Magnús Skaftjeld Halldórsson and Steinunn Kristjánsdóttir; m Helga Alice Vilhjalmsson; 2 sons (Kjartan Guðmunder and Magnús Már), 1 daughter (Margrét Þorbjorg). **Subject(s):** Mathematics/Physics; BA 1949; MA 1952. **Tutor(s):** J M Wordie. **Educ:** Reykjavík Grammar School, Iceland; Princeton University, USA; Nordic Institute of Theoretical Physics (Nordita), Copenhagen, Denmark. **Career:** Professor of Physics 1960–1996, Director, University Computing Centre 1964–1972, Dean, Faculty of Engineering 1965–1967, Director and Chairman of the Board, University Science Institute 1966–1976, Dean, Faculty of Engineering and Science 1971–1973, University of Iceland. **Appointments:** Director, Iceland Nuclear Science Commission 1956–1960; Member, Steering Committee for Nuclear Energy of OECD (NEA) 1956–1976; Member, and Chairman, Executive Committee, National Research Council 1956–1976; Member, Nordic Committee for Atomic Energy 1956–1988; Representative of Ministry for Foreign Affairs to IAEA 1957–1997; Government Adviser on Atomic Energy 1960–1997; Board Member, Nordita 1972–1989 (Chairman 1982–1984); President, Icelandic Society of Sciences 1976–1979; Member, and Vice-Chairman, Icelandic Council of Science 1987–1993; Representative of Ministry for Foreign Affairs and Adviser, AEPS 1990–1994; Member, Executive Council, ESF 1990–1995; Member, Council and Regional Board, IASC 1990–1997; Representative of Ministry for the Environment, AMAP 1991–1994; President, IASC 1993–1997.

MAGOWAN, William Andrew (1941) Born 20 June 1923, British Consulate, Bremerhaven, Germany; son of John Hall Magowan, Civil Servant, Deputy Comptroller General, and Winifred Isabel Ray; m Mary Vivien Barbara Young, 6 December 1944, Culdaff Parish Church, County Donegal, Northern Ireland. **Subject(s):** Classics/Economics; BA 1944; MA 1947. **Educ:** American School, Port-au-Prince; Oyster School, Washington, USA; Mountnorris PE School, County Armagh; Royal School, Armagh.

MAGSON, The Revd Thomas Symmons (1928) Born 3 April 1909, 67 Pepys Road, Wimbledon, Surrey; son of Egbert Hockey Magson, Headmaster of Truro College, and Emily Laura Symmons, Housewife; m Rita, 1938; 1 son (Robert), 3 daughters (Celia, Jennifer and Mary). **Subject(s):** Natural Sciences; BA 1931; MA 1935. **Tutor(s):** C W Guillebaud. **Educ:** Richmond County Boys' School; Truro School; Ripon Hall Theological College, Oxford. **Career:** Science Master, Callington Grammar School, Cornwall 1944–1949; Headmaster, Headlands Grammar School, Swindon 1949–1974; Honorary Auxiliary Curate, St Michael's, Highworth with Hannington & Sevenhampton, Wiltshire 1974–1995. Died 1 August 1999.

MAGUIRE, Denis Richard (1940) Born 31 July 1922, Kuling, China; son of Cecil Edmund Maguire, Electrical Engineer, and Yvonne Caroline Pearl Ruffer; m Grace Mary Jane Bowen, 31 March 1949, London. **Subject(s):** Mechanical Sciences; BA 1943; MA 1947. **Tutor(s):** S J Bailey. **Educ:** Gunnersbury Preparatory School, Chiswick; Merchant Taylors' School. **Career:** RAF Pilot; Steam and Power Branch, Engineering Department, BP Ltd 1949–1952; Project Engineer, BP

Hamburg 1952–1954; Development Engineer/Project Engineer, BP Kent 1954–1960; Project Manager, various refineries 1960–1966, Project Manager, Grangemouth Expansion Project 1967–1969, Assistant Manager, Projects Division 1969–1970, Manager, Projects Division, Refineries Department 1970, BP.

MAHAJANI, Ganesh Sakharam (1921) Born 27 November 1898, Satara, Bombay, India; son of Sakharam Krishna Mahajani, Government Servant, and Durgabai Gopal Shirgavkar; m Indumati Paranjpye, 1948. **Subject(s):** Mathematics; BA 1924; MA 1930; PhD 1930; BA (Bombay) 1920. **Tutor(s):** E Cunningham. **Johnian Relatives:** brother of Vasudev Sakharam Mahajani (1926). **Educ:** The Government High School, Satara, India; Fergusson College, Poona, India. **Career:** Principal, Fergusson College, Poona 1929–1948; Dean, Faculty of Science, University of Bombay 1936–1938; Vice-Chancellor, University of Rajputana, Jaipur 1948–1953; Vice-Chancellor, Delhi University 1953–1957; Member, Union Public Service Commission 1957; First Vice-Chancellor, University of Udaipur, Rajasthan, India 1963. **Appointments:** Honorary Fellow, SJC 1973; Foundation Fellow, Indian National Sciences Academy; Foundation Fellow Indian Academy of Sciences. **Awards:** Smith's Prize, University of Cambridge 1926. **Publications:** *Lessons in Elementary Analysis; The Application of Moving Axis methods to the geometry of Curves and Surfaces; An Introduction to Pure Solid Geometry; The Liberal Outlook; Liberal and the Congress; The Problem of the minorities and constitutional democracy as its solution; Education and democracy; The Defence problem of India.* Died 26 July 1984.

MAHAJANI, Vasudev Sakharam (1926) Born 6 November 1904, Tarla Village, Kolhapur State, Bombay Presidency, India; son of Sakharam Krishna Mahajani, Government Servant, and Durgabai Gopal Shirgavkar. **Subject(s):** Mathematics; BA 1928; BA (Bombay) 1925. **Tutor(s):** J M Wordie. **Johnian Relatives:** brother of Ganesh Sakharam Mahajani (1921). **Educ:** Satara Municipal School, India; Fergusson College, Poona, India.

MAHÉ DE CHENAL DE LA BOURDONNAIS, HH Prince John Bryant Digby (1920) Born 9 July 1901, St Columb Major, Cornwall; son of HH Charles Mahé de Chenal de la Bourdonnais, Lieutenant Colonel, Reserve of Officers, and Jessie Ethel Wright; m Rachel Ursula Isolde Guiness, 26 November 1931, St Michael's Church, Chester Square. BA 1923; MA 1926. **Tutor(s):** E E Sikes. **Educ:** Private Tuition. Died 30 October 1996.

MAHER, Alfred Colin (1924) Born 4 November 1905, Maidens Green, Winkfield, Bracknell, Berkshire; son of Alfred Maher, Dairy Farmer, and Emma Minnie Sexton. **Subject(s):** Natural Sciences; BA 1927; MA 1932; DipAgr 1928; AICTA. **Tutor(s):** B F Armitage. **Educ:** Cranbourne Ranelagh School, Winkfield; Maidenhead County School; Holyport School. **Career:** Director, Central Treaty Organization Agricultural Machinery and Soil Conservation Training Centre, Karaj, Persia; Agricultural Officer 1930, Senior Soil Conservation Officer 1945, Colonial Service, Kenya. **Appointments:** Secretary, Board of Agriculture 1935–1936. Died 30 April 1979.

MAHINDRA, Kailash Chandra (1915) Born 3 March 1895, Lahore, India; son of Rai-Sahib Bishum Chandra Mahindra, Civil Engineer. **Subject(s):** Mathematics/Economics; BA 1918. **Tutor(s):** E E Sikes. **Educ:** Government College, Lahore. **Career:** Director, Steel Corporation of Bengal; Martin & Co, London and Calcutta (Junior Partner in 1933) 1918–1933; Worked in automobile and textile engineering industries in Bombay; Co-founder, Mahindra Group of companies 1945. **Appointments:** Chairman, India Supply Mission, Washington 1942; Chairman, Indian Coalfields Committee 1945. Died 31 October 1963.

MAJDALANY, Jameel (1923) Born 30 August 1906, 31 Moorland Road, Didsbury, Lancashire; son of Joakim Majdalany, Shipping Merchant, and Victoria Jureidini. BA 1926. **Tutor(s):** E A Benians. **Educ:** South Manchester Preparatory School; New College, Harrogate.

MAJOR, Derek Drew (1944) Born 10 March 1926, 40 Hilton Road, Wolborough, Newton Abbot; son of Cecil Major, Garage Proprietor, and Beatrice Mary Drew. **Tutor(s):** J M Wordie. **Educ:** All Saints Junior School, Newton Abbot; King Edward VI Grammar School, Totnes.

MAJOR, Donald (1943) Born 1 October 1924, 33 Grange Drive, Monton, Eccles, Yorkshire; son of Matthew Major, Foreign Correspondent, Shipping Agents, and Elizabeth Govan Dean; m Lilian Porter, 1948; 1 son (John b 1949); 1 daughter (Janet b 1952). **Subject(s):** Mathematics/Natural Sciences; BA 1947; MA 1994; MSc Medical Physics (Leeds) 1973. **Educ:** Sale High School; Manchester Grammar School. **Career:** Research Engineer and Physicist; Assistant Chief Engineer, Scientific Apparatus Department, AEI, Barton Works, Manchester 1959; Principal Physicist, Christie Hospital, Manchester 1976. **Awards:** Baylis Scholarship, SJC 1942.

MAJUMDAR, Hem Chandra (1903) Born August 1886, Pabna, Bengal, India; son of Mahima Chandra Majumdar, Pleader, and Bindu Bashini Debi. **Tutor(s):** D MacAlister. **Educ:** Pabna Zella School; Presidency College, Calcutta.

MAJUMDAR, Khagendra Nath (1903) Born 1886, Calcutta, India; son of Pratap Chandra Majumdar, Doctor of Medicine, and Barahini Debi. BA 1907; MA 1912. **Tutor(s):** D MacAlister. **Educ:** Metropolitan Institution; Presidency College, Calcutta. **Career:** Called to the Bar, Gray's Inn 1907.

MAKIN, John Langridge (1933) Born 3 May 1915, 3 Queen's Avenue, Whetstone, Friern Barnet, Middlesex; son of Walter Makin, Paper Merchant, and Frederica Katie Una von Pfistermeister. BA 1936; MA 1940. **Tutor(s):** J S Boys Smith. **Educ:** Tenterden Hall, Hendon; Tonbridge School.

MAKINSON, Donald Hindley (1938) Born 8 September 1920, 70 Worsley Road, Farnworth, Lancashire; son of Horace Makinson, Company Secretary, and Lily Hindley. **Subject(s):** Natural Sciences; BA 1941; MA 1945; BChir 1943; MB 1943; MB 1943; BChir 1943; MRCP (London) 1946; FRCP (London) 1971; MRCP 1946. **Tutor(s):** R L Howland. **Educ:** Worsley Road Council School; Farnworth Grammar School. **Career:** Senior Registrar Cardiology, Manchester 1949–1951; Consultant Physician, Caernarvonshire and Anglesey HMC 1951–1977; Director and Dean of Postgraduate Studies, University of Wales, College of Medicine 1977–1985. **Appointments:** Visiting Fellow in Therapeutic Research, University of Pennsylvania 1947–1948; Nuffield Foundation Fellow 1948–1949; Member, British Cardiac Society 1952.

MAKINSON, Canon Joseph Crowther (1910) Born 20 October 1884, 204 Great Clowes Street, Higher Broughton, Manchester; son of Joseph Makinson, Stipendiary Magistrate, and Florence Pickering; m Gladys Smart, 19 August 1914. BA 1913; MA 1917. **Tutor(s):** L H K Bushe-Fox. **Educ:** Brooklands School; Sale Grammar School; Haileybury College. **Career:** Admitted Solicitor 1908; Chaplain to the Actor Church Union, Derby; Deacon 1914; Curate, St Luke, Great Crosby 1914–1917; Priest 1915; Curate, Hitchin 1917–1920; Secretary, Sheffield Diocesan Board of Finance 1920–1926; Vicar, St Timothy, Crookes 1926–1931; Vicar, St Werburgh, Derby 1931–1953; Chaplain and Lecturer, Derby Training College 1932–1952; Rural Dean, Derby 1937–1955; Honorary Canon, Derby Cathedral 1939. **Appointments:** President, Derby Tigers Club; Vice-President, Derby Rowditch Bowls Club. Died 27 October 1955.

MAKINSON, Richard Elliss Bodenham (1935) Born 5 May 1913, Burwood, Sydney, Australia; son of Patrick Raymond Makinson, Bank Officer, and Kathleen Marian Bodenham; m Kathleen Rachel White, 16 August 1939. BA (Sydney) 1933; PhD 1939. **Tutor(s):** J M Wordie. **Educ:** Public School, Tenterfield; North Sydney High School; Sydney Church of England Grammar School; Sydney University. **Career:** Reader in Physics, University of Sydney 1940–1968; Associate Professor, University of Macquarie 1968. Died 15 January 1979.

MALCOLM, Andrew Moir (1931) Born 7 March 1914, Gildea Lodge, Reed Pond Walk, Romford, Essex; son of Henry William Malcolm, Doctor of Science, Chartered Electrical Engineer, and Helen Gray Connell. **Subject(s):** Natural Sciences; BA 1935; MA 1939. **Tutor(s):** J M Wordie. **Educ:** The Royal Liberty School, Hare Hall, Romford.

MALINS, Robert Edward (1938) Born 28 April 1920, 13 Gunnersbury Avenue, Ealing, London; son of Edward Sidney George Malins, General Merchant, and Ellen Wickham Jones; m Jean Mary Smith, 12 August 1954. BA 1948; MA 1950; FRICS. **Tutor(s):** J M Wordie. **Educ:** Hillside, Godalming; Radley College. **Career:** Chartered Surveyor.

MALLENDER, Peter Frederick (1938) Born 10 April 1919, Langham, Cullesden Road, Coulsdon, Surrey; son of William Frederick Mallender, Civil Engineer, and Dorothy Annie Edwards; m Brenda Mary Ord, 10 June 1944. **Tutor(s):** J S Boys Smith. **Educ:** The Dene School, Caterham; Ottershaw College. **Career:** Flight Lieutenant, RAFVR 1939–1945. **Honours:** DFC.

MALLETT, Alan Arthur (1943) Born 3 November 1924, 82 Garden Avenue, Mitcham, Surrey; son of Alfred Arthur Mallett, Manager, Leather Factory, and Edith May Ettridge. **Tutor(s):** C W Guillebaud. **Educ:** Streatham Grammar School; Dartford Grammar School.

MALLIK, Bimalendra Chandra (1924) Born 23 March 1903, Dattongang, Palamow, India; son of Satyendra Chandra Mallik, Indian Civil Service, and Kshanaprova Gupta. **Subject(s):** Natural Sciences; BA 1926. **Tutor(s):** B F Armitage. **Johnian Relatives:** son of Satyendra Chandra Mallik (1895). **Educ:** Krishnagare Collegiate School, India; Presidency College, Calcutta, India; Hughli Presidency College, Calcutta.

MALLIK, Suhrit Nath (DAEB) (1917) Born 16 September 1898, Bankipore, India; son of Devendra Náth Mallik, Professor, and Hemkushum Ghose. **Tutor(s):** E E Sikes. **Educ:** St Joseph's Convent; Taunton School; St Michael's High School; St Joseph's High School.

MALLOCH, Charles Edward (1939) Born 16 May 1921, Spa Terrace, Askern, Doncaster; son of Duncan Malloch, Medical Practitioner, and Mary Robertson Green. BA 1942; MA 1946. **Tutor(s):** R L Howland. **Educ:** Park Lane School, Doncaster; Hill House Preparatory School, Doncaster; Pocklington School. Died 6 October 1948.

MALONE, Patrick Oswald (1941) Born 4 August 1922, 12 Canterbury Road, Wallasey, Cheshire; son of Patrick Malone, Schoolmaster, and Angela Frances Mee. **Tutor(s):** S J Bailey. **Educ:** St Alban's School, Wallasey; St Francis Xavier's College, Liverpool.

MALONEY, Bernard Patrick (1948) Born 18 September 1927, 20 Shrewsbury Road, Oxton, Cheshire; son of Terence Maloney, Secretary, and Winifred Hynes. **Subject(s):** Natural Sciences; BA 1950. **Tutor(s):** G C L Bertram. **Educ:** Loreto College, Llandudno; Grace Dieu Manor Preparatory School; Ratcliffe College, Leicester.

MALTBY, Antony John (1947) Born 15 May 1928, 26 Lansdowne Road, Croydon, Surrey; son of Gerald Charles Maltby, Civil Servant, Ministry of Agriculture, and Emily Norah Kingsnorth; m (1) Jillian Winifred Burt, 4 April 1959, Dover (d 22 December 2000), (2) Elizabeth Mary Batin, 14 November 2001, Christchurch, New Zealand; 4 daughters (Claire b 1960, Anita b 1961, Katrina b 1965 and Lucy b 1968). **Subject(s):** History; BA 1950; MA 1954. **Johnian Relatives:** brother of Christopher Hugh Kingsnorth Maltby (1948). **Educ:** Kingshott Preparatory School, Hitchin; Whitgift School, Croydon; King Edward VI Grammar School, Evesham; Claysmore School. **Career:** Assistant Master, Dover College 1951–1958; Head of History and Housemaster, Pocklington School, York 1958–1968; Headmaster, Trent College 1968–1988; Field Officer, Rural Development Commission 1989–1994; Special Needs Teacher, Kent County Council 1994. **Appointments:**

President, SJC Athletics Club; Deputy Lieutenant, Derbyshire 1984–1991; Borough Councillor for Ashford Borough Council 1991; Chairman, Great Chart and Singleton Parish Council 1996; Member, Ashford Borough Council 1991; JP, Ilkeston, Derbyshire 1980; JP, Ashford 1992–1998.

MALTBY, Christopher Hugh Kingsnorth (1948) Born 3 May 1926, The Hollies, Elm Road, Evesham, Worcestershire; son of Gerald Charles Maltby, Civil Servant, and Emily Norah Kingsnorth; m Diana Mary Hadfield, 2 December 1961, Johannesburg; 3 daughters (Jennifer b 1963, Alison b 1965 and Katherine b 1967). BA 1950; MA 1955. **Tutor(s):** R L Howland. **Johnian Relatives:** brother of Antony John Maltby (1947). **Educ:** Kingshott Preparatory School, Hitchin; Whitgift School, Croydon; Claysmore School, Dorset. **Career:** Agricultural post with Fisons until 1976; Consultant on Agricultural Products and Pesticides 1976–1990. Died 23 September 1994.

MALTBY, Dr John Wingate (1948) Born 3 January 1928, 56 Rectory Road, West Hackney, London; son of Harry Wingate Maltby, Medical Practitioner, and Marjorie Francis; m (1) Margaret Mary Mitchell, 18 January 1958, St Peter's Church, (2) Sybil Dora Jones, 8 March 1980; 3 sons (Richard b 1958, James b 1960 and Robert b 1962); 1 daughter (Sarah b 1966). **Subject(s):** Natural Sciences; BA 1951; MA 1955; BChir 1955; MB 1955; FRCS (Eng) 1958; DObstRCOG. **Tutor(s):** G C L Bertram. **Educ:** Eastmans School, Southsea; Twyford School, Winchester; Trinity College School, Port Hope, Ontario, Canada; Marlborough College. **Career:** Medicine.

MANCE, Sir Henry Stenhouse (1930) Born 5 February 1913, Borough Field, Bricket Road, St Albans; son of Harry Osborne Mance, Brigadier General, and Elizabeth Hope Stenhouse; m Joan; 1 son (Jonathan), 3 daughters (Rosalind, Pippa and Carolyn). **Subject(s):** Economics; BA 1934; MA 1938. **Tutor(s):** C W Guillebaud. **Johnian Relatives:** brother of Herbert William Mance (1937). **Educ:** Charter Towers School, East Grinstead; Charterhouse. **Career:** Underwriting Member, Lloyds 1939; Marine Underwriter, Willis, Faber & Dumas Ltd 1956. **Appointments:** Committee Member 1966–1970, Deputy Chairman 1967, Lloyd's; President, Insurance Institute of London 1975–1976; President, Chartered Insurance Institute 1977–1978; John Maynard Keynes Political Economy Group; Committee Member, Lloyd's Register of Shipping; Treasurer, Church Missionary Society; Trustee, Ridley Hall, Cambridge; Trustee, Wycliffe Hall, Oxford; Chairman, Royal Foundation of St Katharine in Radcliff; Governor, Sutton's Hospital, Charterhouse. **Awards:** Lloyd's Gold Medal 1973. **Honours:** Kt 1971. Died 15 June 1981.

MANCE, The Revd Herbert William (1937) Born 15 June 1919, Firdale, Lower Bourne, Farnham; son of Harry Osborne Mance, Engineer and Company Director, and Elizabeth Hope Stenhouse; m Margaret Kate Anderson, 26 July 1957, St Leonard's Parish Church, Seaford; 2 sons (David and Christopher), 1 daughter (Susan). **Subject(s):** Natural Sciences/Metallurgy; BA 1940; MA 1944. **Tutor(s):** C W Guillebaud. **Johnian Relatives:** brother of Henry Stenhouse Mance (1930). **Educ:** Pinewood, Farnborough; Stowe School; Oak Hill Theological College. **Career:** Research in welding 1940–1947; Ordained Deacon 1949; Curate, St George's Church, Leeds, Ripon and Leeds Diocese 1949–1953; Ordained Priest 1950; CF, Egypt then Nigeria 1953–1957; Nigeria with CMS 1958–1971; Canon, Ibadan 1970–1971; Curate, Buckhurst Hill, Diocese of Chelmsford 1971–1975; Priest-in-Charge, Roydon 1975–1979; Vicar 1979–1985; Retired 1985; Permission to Officiate, Diocese of Lichfield 1985. Died 26 November 2003.

MANLEY, Herbert (1919) Born 29 June 1894, Allahabad, India; son of Henry Fleming Manley, Principal, Victoria College, and Emily Amelia Ball; m Dorothy Catherine Mary Reid, 16 February 1920, St James's, Piccadilly. BA 1924; MA 1928. **Tutor(s):** E E Sikes. **Johnian Relatives:** son of Henry Fleming Manley (1898). **Educ:** Perse School, Cambridge; St Edward's School, Oxford.

MANN, The Revd James Dennis (1919) Born 3 May 1900, The Firs, Queens Mead Road, Beckenham; son of Charles Bertram Mann, Banker's Clerk, and Sarah Walker Terry; m Marjory. **Subject(s):** Theology; BA 1922; MA 1926. **Tutor(s):** E E Sikes. **Educ:** Merchant Taylors' School, London. **Career:** Bishop's College, Cheshunt 1922; Ordained Deacon 1923; Curate, Wanstead 1923–1927; Ordained Priest, Chelmsford 1924; Curate, East Ham 1927–1932; Curate, St Paul, Goodmayes 1937–1943; Curate, St Alban the Martyr, Westcliff-on-Sea 1943; Honorary Canon, Chelmsford Cathedral 1964. **Awards:** Scholarship, SJC 1918; John Stewart of Rannoch Scholarship in Hebrew, University of Cambridge 1919. Died 24 May 1965.

MANN, John Colman (1917) Born 11 July 1898, Rockland All Saints with St Andrew, Attleborough, Norfolk; son of John Robert Mann, Farmer, and Sarah Alberta Colman. **Subject(s):** Natural Sciences; BA 1920; MA 1924; Diploma in Agriculture 1921. **Tutor(s):** E E Sikes. **Johnian Relatives:** brother of Thomas Eagling Mann (1906). **Educ:** Banham Grammar School; Thetford Grammar School. **Career:** Lecturer in Agricultural Chemistry, University of Leeds 1922; Member, Norfolk Agricultural Station. **Awards:** Drewitt Prize, University of Cambridge 1921. **Honours:** OBE. Died 26 February 1987.

MANN, Thomas Eagling (1906) Born 4 February 1888, Rockland All Saints, Attleborough, Norfolk; son of John Robert Mann, Farmer, and Sarah Alberta Colman. **Tutor(s):** L H K Bushe-Fox. **Johnian Relatives:** brother of John Colman Mann (1917). **Educ:** Rockland Board School; Banham Grammar School.

MANNING, The Revd Arthur Lionel (1935) Born 1 July 1916, The Parsonage, Hollingworth, Manchester; son of Henry Arthur Manning, Clerk in Holy Orders and Beatrice Ellen Kyle. **Subject(s):** Classics/Theology; BA 1938; MA 1944. **Tutor(s):** R L Howland. **Educ:** Birkenhead Preparatory School; Birkenhead School; Ridley Hall, Cambridge. **Career:** Ordained Deacon 1940; Curate of St Paul, Portwood, Stockport 1940–1942; Ordained Priest 1941; Vicar, Wrenbury with Baddiley, Cheshire 1948–1956; Vicar, Gatley, Cheadle, Cheshire 1952. **Appointments:** Permission to officiate at St Mary and St Paul, Birkenhead 1942; Honorary Canon of Chester Cathedral 1965–1992. Died 1992.

MANNING, Dr John Rowland (1943) Born 22 February 1925, 11 Manor Way, Onslow Village, Guildford, Surrey; son of Rowland Hill Manning, Newspaper Publisher, and Elsie Florence Ward; m Eileen Dorothy Garner; 1 son, 2 daughters. **Subject(s):** Mathematics/Natural Sciences; BA 1946; MA 1950; PhD (Loughborough) 1980. **Tutor(s):** C W Guillebaud. **Johnian Relatives:** father of Peter Toby Manning (1971). **Educ:** Hounslow Heath Council Schools; Latymer Upper School. Died 3 September 1998.

MANNING, Ronald Barrie (1940) Born 9 January 1922, 71 Newport Road, Chorlton-cum-Hardy, Lancashire; son of James Manning, Company Director and Manager, and Louisa Gertrude Barrie; m Margaret-Elisabeth Helen, 1970; 2 sons (James Eric and William Ronald). **Subject(s):** Mechanical Sciences; BA 1943; MA 1989; CEng; MIMechE. **Tutor(s):** S J Bailey. **Johnian Relatives:** father of James Eric Manning (1991). **Educ:** Amberleigh Private School, Chorlton-cum-Hardy; Manchester Grammar School. **Career:** Engineer Officer, RAF 1942–1947; Metropolitan Vickers Electrical Co Ltd, Manchester 1947–1952; Richardsons Westgarth Co Ltd, Wallsend 1952–1957; Senior Sales Manager, British Nuclear Fuels plc, Risley, Warrington 1957–1985.

MANSBRIDGE, Eric (1914) Born 27 September 1895, 25 Gap Road, Wimbledon, Surrey; son of George Frederick Mansbridge, Civil Servant, and Florence Guye; m Helen. **Tutor(s):** L H K Bushe-Fox. **Educ:** Limes School, Croydon; Dover College. **Career:** Captain, Aircraft Production Department, RFC/RAF 1914–1918. Died 30 June 1964.

MANSFIELD, Anthony Le Voir (1942) Born 1 October 1924, 30 Franklyn Road, Harlesden, London; son of Kenneth Arthur Mansfield, Deputy

Chief Accountant, Palestine Railways, and Margaret Anne Payne. **Tutor(s):** C W Guillebaud. **Educ:** German School, Haifa; Presentation School, Reading; Douai School, Reading. **Career:** Principal, Group Management Centre. Died 18 February 1986.

MANTON, Professor Guy Robert (1931) Born 13 February 1912, County Boys' School, Maidenhead; son of Joseph Manton, Headmaster, King Edward's Grammar School, and Mary Batchelor; m Barbara, 3 daughters (Jennifer, Susan and Elizabeth). **Subject(s):** Classics; BA 1934; MA 1938. **Tutor(s):** M P Charlesworth. **Educ:** The Grammar School, Sutton Coldfield; Edgbaston Preparatory School; King Edward's School, Birmingham. **Career:** Assistant Lecturer in Classics, London University 1934–1939; Woodhouse Classical Fellow, St Andrew's College and Lecturer in Greek, Sydney University 1939–1945; Senior Lecturer in Classics, Sydney University 1947; Professor of Classics, University of Otago 1948–1965; Dean, Faculty of Arts, Monash University, Australia 1965–1977. **Awards:** Whytehead Scholarship, SJC 1930; Porson Scholarship, University of Cambridge 1933. Died 6 June 1983.

MARCH, Juan (1926) Born 9 April 1906, Calle del Dodore Calafat, Santa Margarita, Mallorca, Baleares, Spain; son of Juan March, Banker, and Leonor Servera y Melis. **Tutor(s):** C W Guillebaud. **Educ:** Lycée, Palma de Mallorca; Colegio Comercial, Bonanova, Barcelona; Private Tuition, Antwerp; Private Tuition, Cambridge.

MARCHAND, Geoffrey Isidore Charles (1907) Born 26 June 1888, 4 Clarence Villas, Greyhound Lane, Streatham; son of Isidore Henri Alphonse Marchand, Manufacturer's Agent, and Annie Jane Heath; m (1) Elsie Mary Russell Smith, 30 December 1913, St Margaret's, Westminster (d 1945), (2) Mary Ursula Atkins, 30 December 1948. **Subject(s):** History; BA 1910; MA 1914. **Tutor(s):** J R Tanner. **Johnian Relatives:** brother-in-law of Humphrey Phillips Walcot Burton (1907). **Educ:** Aldenham School. **Career:** Captain, RFA, Brigade Major and Deputy Military Secretary to Viscount Allenby 1914–1918; Chairman, Restlight Ltd, and Kingsway Electrical Services; PA to Managing Director, British Glass Industries 1920; Founder and Director, Glass Manufacturer's Federation 1926–1949. **Appointments:** President, Society of Glass Technology 1946–1949; JP 1951; Vice-Chairman, National Dock Labour Board 1951–1953; Member, National Youth Employment Council; Council Member, Royal College of Art; Member, London and Home Counties Regional Advisory Council for Higher Technological Education. **Honours:** CBE 1949. Died 5 February 1965.

MARCHANT, Ernest Cecil (1921) Born 27 September 1902, 47 Montague Road, Chesterton, Cambridge; son of Ernest Joseph Marchant, Draper, and Gertrude Selina Saville. **Subject(s):** Geography/History; BA 1924; MA 1928. **Tutor(s):** B F Armitage. **Johnian Relatives:** brother of Herbert Stanley Marchant (1925). **Educ:** Higher Grade School, Cambridge; The Perse School, Cambridge. **Career:** Master, Oakham School 1925–1928; Geelong Grammar School, South Australia 1929–1930; Assistant Master, Marlborough College 1931. **Honours:** CIE. Died 13 September 1979.

MARCHANT, Sir Herbert Stanley (1925) Born 18 May 1906, 2 Melbourne Place, Cambridge; son of Ernest Joseph Marchant, Draper, and Gertrude Selina Saville; m Diana Selway, 1937; 1 son. **Subject(s):** Modern and Medieval Languages; BA 1928; MA 1933. **Tutor(s):** M P Charlesworth. **Johnian Relatives:** brother of Ernest Cecil Marchant (1921). **Educ:** Central School, Cambridge; Perse School, Cambridge. **Career:** Modern Languages Master, Harrow School 1928–1940; Foreign Office 1940; Bletchley Park, WWII; Consul, Denver 1946–1948; First Secretary (Information) 1948–1950; Counsellor, Embassy, Paris 1950–1952; Consul-General, Zagreb 1952–1954; Land Commissioner and Consul-General for North Rhine/Westphalia, Germany 1954–1957; Consul-General, San Francisco 1957–1960; Ambassador to Cuba 1960–1963; Ambassador to Tunisia 1963–1966. **Appointments:** British

Representative, UN Committee for Elimination of Racial Discrimination 1969–1973; Director, Institute of Race Relations 1966–1968; Chairman, British-Tunisian Society 1970–1974. **Awards:** Scholarship, SJC. **Honours:** OBE 1946; CMG 1957; KCMG 1963. **Publications:** *Scratch a Russian*, 1936; *His Excellency Regrets*, 1980. Died 8 August 1990.

MARCHANT, Professor Robert Brandwood (1934) Born 6 February 1916, Shirburn Avenue, Mansfield, Nottinghamshire; son of Harold Alfred Marchant, Master Tailor, Director of G Marchant & Sons Ltd, and Mary Brandwood. **Subject(s):** Classics; BA 1937; MA 1941; MusB 1939. **Tutor(s):** C W Guillebaud. **Educ:** Kindergarten Department, Queen Elizabeth's Girls' Grammar School; Queen Elizabeth's Boys' Grammar School, Mansfield. **Career:** Army dispatch rider and code-breaker at Bletchley Park 1939–1945; Director of Music, University College, Hull (later University of Hull) 1947–1976; Professor of Music, University of Hull 1976–1979 (Emeritus 1979). **Appointments:** President, Classical Association of Hull; President, Hull Chamber Music Club. **Awards:** Scholarship, SJC 1936–1937; Wright's Prize, SJC 1937; George Charles Winter Warr Scholarship, University of Cambridge 1937; Strathcona Studentship, SJC 1938. Died 4 July 1995.

MARCHBANK, Frank Havelock (1922) Born 26 November 1904, 104 Holly Avenue, Newcastle upon Tyne, Northumberland; son of William Marchbank, Coal Exporter, and Mary Elizabeth Havelock; m Phyllis Burnip, 19 August 1931, Jesmond Presbyterian Church; 1 son (Michael Havelock b 14 June 1932), 1 daughter (Judith Gillian b 19 March 1938). **Subject(s):** English/History; BA 1926; MA 1930. **Tutor(s):** E A Benians. **Johnian Relatives:** father of Michael Havelock Marchbank (1952). **Educ:** Ascham House Preparatory School, Gosforth; Fettes College, Edinburgh. **Career:** Headmaster and Founder, Mowden Hall School, Stocksfield, Northumberland until 1959. Died 12 July 1985.

MARCHINGTON, Trevor (1949) Born 13 December 1929, 2 Tetherdown, Muswell Hill, London; son of William Marchington, Draper, and Winifred May Hall; m Mary A Clarke, 7 August 1954; twin sons, 1 daughter. **Subject(s):** Geography; BA 1952; MA 1956; MA (London) 1961; Teaching Diploma 1953. **Tutor(s):** A G Lee. **Educ:** Priory School, Great Yarmouth; Kent's Bank School, Buxton; Buxton College. **Career:** Head of Geography, Wandsworth School 1956–1967; Senior Lecturer in Geography and Lecturer in University of London Education Department, Shoreditch College of Education 1967–1978; Senior Teacher, Wandsworth School 1978–1988. **Publications:** Various children's encyclopedias and geography text books.

MARDAN, Talpur Ali (1939) Born 26 January 1921, Khairpur Mirs, Sind, India; son of Talpur Mir Ghulam Reza and Bibi Chutan. **Tutor(s):** J S Boys Smith. **Educ:** Vernacular School, Khairpur; Naz High School, Khairpur; Aitchison College, Lahore; Muslim University, Aligarh.

MARDEN, Edwin David (1946) Born 25 December 1924, Overdale, Preston Road, Yeovil, Somerset; son of Albert Henry Down Marden, Food Manufacturer, and Madge Beatrice Rodway; m Marion Simpson, 5 September 1953, Bridlington. **Subject(s):** Mechanical Sciences; BA 1948. **Tutor(s):** R L Howland. **Educ:** Park School, Yeovil; Durlston Court Preparatory School, Swanage; Bradfield College. **Career:** Pilot, Fleet Air Arm, WWII; Civil Engineer, on water supply, motorway and other projects in UK, West Indies and Saudi Arabia. Died 25 October 1978.

MARDON, Gilbert Dennis Heber (1929) Born 14 December 1909, Ashwick House, Dulverton; son of Arthur Claude Mardon, of independent means, and Isabel Mary Deans. BA 1933; MA 1936. **Tutor(s):** M P Charlesworth. **Johnian Relatives:** brother of Noel Alexander Richard Mardon (1930). **Educ:** South Lodge, Enfield Chase; Private Tuition, Moor Hall, Ninfield; Private Tuition, Lilley Rectory. **Career:** Private, The Black Watch. Died 18 June 1942 (killed in action).

MARDON, Noel Alexander Richard (1930) Born 2 August 1912, Ashwick House, Dulverton; son of Arthur Claude Mardon, Lieutenant Colonel, and Isabel Mary Deans. **Subject(s):** Modern and Medieval Languages/English; BA 1934; MA 1939. **Tutor(s):** M P Charlesworth. **Johnian Relatives:** brother of Gilbert Dennis Heber Mardon (1929). **Educ:** Preparatory School, South Lodge, Enfield Chase; Harrow School.

MARGETSON, Sir John William Denys (1945) Born 9 October 1927, 15 Douglas Crescent, Edinburgh; son of the Very Revd William James Margetson and Constance Marion Lillian Jenoure; m Miranda Coldstream, 1963, St Saviour's Church, Hampstead; 1 son (Andrew b 19 February 1965), 1 daughter (Clare b 3 May 1967). **Subject(s):** Geography/Archaeology and Anthropology; BA 1949; MA 1978; Honorary RCM 1992; FRSCM 1994. **Tutor(s):** J M Wordie. **Educ:** West Hayes Preparatory School, Winchester; Kingwell Court Preparatory School, Bradford on Avon; Blundell's School, Tiverton. **Career:** Lieutenant, Life Guards 1947–1949; Colonial Service, District Officer, Tanganyika 1951–1960 (Private Secretary to Governor 1956–1957); Foreign (later Diplomatic) Service 1960–1987; Second Secretary, The Hague 1962–1964; Speech writer to Foreign Secretary, Rt Hon George Brown, MP 1966–1968; Head of Chancery, Saigon 1968–1970; Counsellor, seconded to Cabinet Secretariat 1971–1974; Head of Chancery, UK Delegation to NATO 1974–1978; Ambassador to Vietnam 1978–1980; Senior Civilian Instructor, RCDS, MOD 1981–1982; Ambassador and Deputy Permanent Representative to UN, New York, and President, UN Trusteeship Council 1983–1984; Ambassador to the Netherlands 1984–1987; Special Representative of the Secretary of State for Foreign and Commonwealth Affairs 1994–1998; Gentleman Usher of the Blue Rod, Order of St Michael and St George 1992–2002. **Appointments:** Director, John S Cohen Foundation 1988–1993; Chairman, Foster Parents Plan (UK) 1988–1990; Patron, Suffolk International Trade Group 1988–1990; Joint President, Suffolk and South East Cambridgeshire 1992 Club 1988–1990; Chairman, RSCM 1988–1994; Chairman, Joint Committee, London Royal Schools of Music 1991–1994; Yehudi Menuhin School 1990–1994; Trustee, Fitzwilliam Museum Trust 1990–1998; Trustee, Ouseley Trust 1991–1998; Trustee, Music in Country Churches 1993–2000. **Awards:** Choral Studentship, SJC. **Honours:** CMG 1979; KCMG 1986. **Publications:** *Gorty, Neville Gorton's Years at Blundell's 1934–42*, 1998.

MARGOLIS, Morris (1913) (migrated to St Catharine's College) Born 25 August 1894, Spitalfields, Middlesex; son of John Margolis, Manager, and Esther Diamond. **Subject(s):** Modern and Medieval Languages; BA 1916. **Tutor(s):** E E Sikes. **Educ:** Foundation School, Whitechapel; Aske's School, Hatcham. **Career:** Called to the Bar, Lincoln's Inn; Northern Circuit 1920. Died 9 August 1960.

MARGOLIS, Sydney (1941) Born 5 December 1923, 15 Mitchell Street, Manchester; son of Marcus Margolis, Furrier, and Doris Slifkin. **Subject(s):** Economics; BA 1947; MA 1949. **Tutor(s):** S J Bailey. **Educ:** Derby Street Elementary School; Manchester Grammar School.

MARINDIN, Francis Jocelyn de Vere (1922) Born 11 July 1904, Darjeeling, Bengal, India; son of Charles Randal Marindin, Indian Civil Service, and Edith Alice Atkinson; m Marcia; 1 daughter (Ann). **Subject(s):** History; BA 1925. **Tutor(s):** E A Benians. **Educ:** Kindergarten High School, Clifton; Ladies College, Jersey; Preparatory School, Jersey; Victoria College, Jersey; The School, Malvern Link; Shrewsbury School. **Career:** Asiatic Petroleum Company, India, later Burmah-Shell, Manager, Supplies and Distribution Department, Controller of Supplies 1926–1954. Died 15 May 1954.

MARK, Douglas Scott (1918) Born 10 October 1900, No 2 The Groves, Stockton-on-Tees, County Durham; son of Thomas Scott Mark, Hide Skin and Wool Merchant, and Elizabeth Thompson; m Mary Humphrey Hinton; 1 son (Peter). **Tutor(s):** E E Sikes. **Johnian Relatives:** father of Peter Hinton Mark (1949). **Educ:** New College, Harrogate.

MARK, Peter Hinton (1949) Born 13 December 1929, The Arches, Eaglescliffe, Stockton-on-Tees; son of Douglas Scott Mark, Hide and Skin Broker, and Mary Humphrey Hinton. **Subject(s):** Law; BA 1952; MA 1956; FCA. **Tutor(s):** C W Guillebaud. **Johnian Relatives:** son of Douglas Scott Mark (1918). **Educ:** Ragworth Hall School, Norton on Tees; Repton Preparatory School; Repton School.

MARKHAM, Ralph English (1933) Born 18 May 1913, 13 Rayleigh Grove, Bensham, Gateshead on Tyne; son of Thomas Henry English, Coal Miner, and Florence Emma Moore; m Patricia Morgan, 1939, Ghana; 1 daughter (Gillian). **Subject(s):** Geography/History; BA 1937. **Tutor(s):** E A Benians. **Johnian Relatives:** father-in-law of John Piers Recordon (1954). **Educ:** Preparatory School, Newcastle upon Tyne; Newcastle upon Tyne RGS. **Career:** Metropolitan Police Training College, Hendon 1937–1938; District Commissioner, the Gold Coast, Ghana 1938–1954. Died 13 May 2000.

MARKS, Peter Knell (1937) Born 11 March 1919, Seagrove, Somerville Gardens, Southend-on-Sea; son of Harold William Marks, Bank Manager, and Helen Buchan Crerar; m 1944; 4 children. **Subject(s):** Mathematics/Economics; BA 1940. **Tutor(s):** J M Wordie. **Educ:** Leigh Hall College, Leigh-on-Sea; Caterham School. **Career:** Part-time freelance writer, examiner and consultant, in monetary economics; Economics Department, Midland Bank. Died 31 May 2003.

MARLOW, Charles Christopher (1913) Born 22 January 1895, 5 Manor Road, Edgbaston, Worcestershire; son of Charles Frederick Marlow, Gentleman, and Catherine Mary List. **Subject(s):** English; BA 1918; MA 1921. **Tutor(s):** L H K Bushe-Fox. **Educ:** The Leys School, Cambridge; The Lizans, Malvern Link; Godesbergam, Germany. **Career:** Second Lieutenant, Royal Warwickshire Regiment, WWI. **Publications:** *The Fen Country*, 1925; *Legends of the Fenland People*, 1926; *People and Places in Marshland*, 1927.

MARMION, William Joseph (1939) Born 4 March 1921, 47 Langdale Road, Toxteth Park, Liverpool; son of William Henry Marmion, Civil Engineer, and Margaret Mary Hoare; m Frances Barbara; 1 son (James Oliver), 2 daughters (Sarah Frances and Katherine). **Subject(s):** Natural Sciences; BA 1958; FRSC 1981. **Tutor(s):** J M Wordie. **Educ:** Quarry Bank High School, Liverpool; St Benet's School, Ealing. **Career:** Anglo-Iranian Oil, Abadan Refinery 1941–1945; Managing Director, Mill Industries Ltd 1945–1948; London Sales Division 1948–1954, Department Manager 1954–1961, Shell Chemicals Ltd; Division Head, Shell International Chemical Company 1961–1967 and 1969–1972; Managing Director, Shorko Films Ltd 1967–1969; Chemical Industry Training Board, Manpower Research Projects 1972–1979.

MARMORSTEIN, Emile (1929) Born 7 June 1909, Vincovce, Slavonia; son of Arthur Marmorstein, Rabbi and Lecturer, Jew's College, London, and Antonia Gaster. **Subject(s):** Oriental Languages; BA 1933; MA 1936. **Tutor(s):** E A Benians. **Educ:** Warwick House School, Hampstead; St Paul's School, London. **Career:** BBC. **Awards:** Exhibition, SJC; Scholarship 1931; John Stewart of Rannoch Scholarship in Hebrew, University of Cambridge 1930. Died 1 March 1983.

MARPOLE, David Williams (1901) Born 23 October 1862, Maengwyn Street, Machynlleth, County Montgomery; son of Edward Marpole, Joiner and Builder, and Rachel Williams. **Tutor(s):** D MacAlister. **Educ:** Machynlleth Grammar School; Salop School, Oswestry.

MARR, Major Francis Alleyne (1913) Born 9 November 1893, 70 Huntingdon Road, Chesterton, Cambridgeshire; son of John Edward Marr, Fellow, SJC, and Amy Birkett Stubbs; m Margaret (Peggy) Agnes Cantrell, 3 October 1931, St Luke's Church, Maidenhead. **Tutor(s):** R P Gregory. **Johnian Relatives:** cousin of Charles John Geoffrey Stanley (1937). **Educ:** St Faith's, Cambridge; Oundle School. **Career:** Initially 1st Cambridgeshire Regiment, finally Brigade Major, 175 Infantry Brigade (twice Mentioned in Despatches) 1914–1918; Geologist, Burma

Oil Company 1919–1942. **Honours:** DSO; MC. Died 5 November 1942 (lost in SS *Cairo*).

MARRACK, Professor John Richardson (1905) Born 26 November 1886, Walton-in-Gordano, Somerset; son of John Read Marrack, Gentleman, and Mary Saunders; m (1) Bertha Ada Fitzgerald Whiddington, 1 August 1913, (2) Alice May Swaffield Milward, 18 March 1922; (1) 1 son, (2) 3 sons. **Subject(s):** Natural Sciences; BA 1908; MA 1915; MB 1912; BChir 1912; MD 1923. **Tutor(s):** D MacAlister. **Johnian Relatives:** son of John Read Marrack (1856); nephew of Richard Gubbs Marrack (1862). **Educ:** Blundell's School, Tiverton. **Career:** Captain, RAMC (wounded, Mentioned in Despatches), WWI; Medical Officer on Poison Gas 1914–1919; Lecturer in Pathological Chemistry, University of Cambridge 1919–1921; Professor of Chemical Pathology, London Hospital Medical School 1934–1952; Advisor to Ministry of Food 1939–1945; Department of Chemical Pathology, University of Cambridge 1952; Visiting Professor, University of Texas 1963–1966. **Appointments:** Beit Research Fellow, University of Cambridge; Vice-President, Blundell's Old Boys' Association. **Awards:** Minor Scholarship 1905; Price Entrance Scholarship, London Hospital Medical College 1909; John Lucas Walker Studentship, University of Cambridge 1913; Distinguished Service Award, International Congress of Immunology 1971. **Honours:** DSO; MC 1917. **Publications:** *The Chemistry of Antigens and Antibodies*, 1936; *Food and Planning*, 1942; *Clinical Pathology*, 1945; articles in *Biochemical Journal* and *British Journal of Experimental Pathology*; Editor, *Immunology* until 1961; Editor, *British Journal of Experimental Pathology*. Died 13 June 1976.

MARRIOTT, Sir John Brook (1941) Born 27 July 1922, 193 Urmston Lane, Stretford, Manchester; son of John Morley Marriott, Shipping Merchant's Buyer, and Maud Brook; m Mary Eleanor Norcliffe Thompson, 1952; 2 sons (Martin b 11 April 1954 and Andrew b 25 September 1955). **Subject(s):** Mathematics; BA 1944; MA 1948. **Tutor(s):** S J Bailey. **Johnian Relatives:** father of Martin John Marriott (1973). **Educ:** Rhos-on-Sea Preparatory School, North Wales; College School, Colwyn Bay; Merchant Taylors' School, Northwood. **Career:** Army Operational Research Group, Ministry of Supply 1943–1945; Foreign Office, Bletchley 1944–1945; Mathematics Master 1945–1982, Housemaster, Girdlestoneites House 1960–1975, Charterhouse; Keeper of the Royal Philatelic Collection 1969–1995. **Appointments:** Liveryman, Merchant Taylors' Company 1950; Council Member 1969, Vice-President 1979–1983, President 1983–1986, Honorary Fellow 1993, Royal Philatelic Society, London; Roll of Distinguished Philatelists, Philatelic Congress of Great Britain 1972; Governor, St Edmund's School, Hindhead 1979–1987; Member, National Postal Museum Board 1989. **Awards:** Major Scholarship, SJC 1941; Tilleard Medal 1968; Tapling Medal 1976; London Medal 1987; Alfred F Lichtenstein Award, Collectors Club, New York 1988; Lindenberg Medal, Berlin 1888 Philatelic Club 1988. **Honours:** LVO 1978; CVO 1991; KCVO 1995. **Publications:** *Philatelic History of Trinidad to 1862*, 1963; contributions to *London Philatelist*. Died 3 July 2001.

MARRIS, Frederick Alexander (1934) Born 1 May 1916, 10 Strathcona Road, Wallasey, Cheshire; son of Frederick Marris, Freight Manager, and Katie Moon. **Subject(s):** Natural Sciences; BA 1937. **Tutor(s):** C W Guillebaud. **Educ:** Somerville Preparatory School, New Brighton; Birkenhead School. **Career:** Pilot, Lieutenant, Fleet Air Arm, RNVR, HMS *Illustrious* and *Victorious* 1939–1945. Died April 1945 (killed in action).

MARSDEN, Dr Eric William (1947) Born 22 February 1926, 98 Manor House Lane, Preston, Lancashire; son of William Timbrell Marsden, Schoolmaster, and Elsie Victoria Rhodes; m 1954; 1 son, 2 daughters. **Subject(s):** Classics; BA 1950; MA 1954; PhD 1955. **Tutor(s):** R L Howland. **Educ:** Farnborough Road Council School, Southport; King George V School, Southport; Sedbergh School. **Career:** RA, WWII; Lecturer, then Reader, in Ancient History and Classical Archaeology, University of Liverpool 1959; Visiting Professor, University of British

Columbia 1967. **Publications:** *The Campaign of Gaugamela*, 1964; *Greek and Roman Artillery: Historical Development*, 1969; *Greek and Roman Artillery: Technical Treatises*, 1971. Died 2 October 1975.

MARSDEN, Sir John Denton (1932) Born 25 August 1913, Haverthwaite, Welholme Road, Grimsby; son of John Denton Marsden, 1st Bt, Managing Director of Fishing Companies, and Agnes Mary Ronald; m Hope Llewellyn, 1939; 2 sons, 2 daughters. BA 1935. **Tutor(s):** E A Benians. **Educ:** Downside School. **Career:** Lieutenant, RA 1939–1945; High Sheriff of Lincolnshire 1955–1956. **Appointments:** JP. Died 22 July 1985.

MARSH, Charles Donald (1940) Born 12 September 1921, Tetney, Lincolnshire; son of Charles Henry Marsh, Methodist Minister, and Sarah Davison. **Subject(s):** Natural Sciences; BA 1943; MA 1947. **Tutor(s):** J M Wordie. **Educ:** Lea Road Elementary School, Gainsborough; St George's Road Elementary School, Hull; Hull Grammar School; Coatham School, Redcar.

MARSH, Leon Robert (1940) Born 14 February 1922, 3 Embi Road, Kuala Lumpur, Selangor, Federated Malay; son of Thomas Duckworth Marsh, Agriculturalist, and Violet Frank. BA 1944; MA 1951. **Tutor(s):** C W Guillebaud. **Educ:** The Abbey School, Ramsgate; Ampleforth College. **Career:** Engineering and Management. Died 29 June 1991.

MARSH, Malcolm Charles (1923) Born 21 February 1904, All Saints Road, Peterborough, Northamptonshire; son of Frederick Stephen Marsh, District Valuer, Valuation Department, Inland Revenue, and Annie Tebbs; 1 son (David Malcolm). **Subject(s):** Natural Sciences (Physics); BA 1926; MA 1930. **Tutor(s):** B F Armitage. **Johnian Relatives:** father of David Malcolm Marsh (1951). **Educ:** Deacon's School, Peterborough; Northampton Town and County School. **Career:** Cambridge Scientific Instrument Company 1951.

MARSH, Richard Joseph (1912) Born 1 October 1893, Stoke on Tern, Hodnet, Shropshire; son of George Jennings Marsh, Gardener, and Sarah Ann Saville. **Subject(s):** History; BA 1915; MA 1919. **Tutor(s):** E E Sikes. **Educ:** Newport Grammar School. **Career:** Headmaster, Highbury County School, London; Master, Worksop College 1915–1921; Master, King Edward VII School, Sheffield 1921–1928.

MARSHALL, Frederick Stanley (1941) Born 5 November 1922, 142 Cartington Terrace, Heaton, Newcastle upon Tyne; son of Frederick Percy Marshall, Coach Painter, and Annie Dinning; m Margaret Sides, 6 July 1956, Belfast. **Subject(s):** Natural Sciences; BA 1944; MA 1948; BSc (London) 1948. **Tutor(s):** C W Guillebaud. **Educ:** North Heaton Council School; Chillingham Road Council School; Royal Grammar School, Newcastle upon Tyne. **Career:** Senior Physics Master, St Albans School 1948; Headmaster of Science Department, Royal Belfast Academical Institution 1962. Died 23 December 1979.

MARSHALL, Henry Ambler (1933) Born 15 July 1914, Thornleigh, Wath-on-Dearne, Rotherham; son of Arthur Rees Marshall, Colliery Sales Agent, and Edna Ambler Butterfield. **Subject(s):** Economics/Law; BA 1936; MA 1940. **Tutor(s):** C W Guillebaud. **Educ:** Epworth College, Rhyl; St Martin's School, York; Leeds Grammar School. **Career:** Crown Agent for the Colonies. Died 15 February 1942.

MARSHALL, Henry Hughes (1923) Born 11 June 1904, Milton, Norfolk, Massachusetts, USA; son of William Ainslie Marshall, Gentleman, and Emily Margaret Anna Hughes. **Subject(s):** Mathematics/Economics; BA 1926. **Tutor(s):** E Cunningham. **Educ:** Milton Preparatory School, USA; Milton Academy, USA; Munro College, Jamaica; Blundells School, Tiverton.

MARSHALL, Henry Leslie (1926) Born 2 August 1908, Lao Ling, Shantung, North China; son of Frederick William Marshall, Medical Practitioner, and Emily Gertrude Talent. **Subject(s):** Classics; BA 1929.

Tutor(s): M P Charlesworth. **Educ:** Pocklington Council School; Private Tuition; Yapham Cum Meltonby Church School; Pocklington School. **Awards:** Dowman Exhibition, SJC 1926.

MARSHALL, Ian Fraser (1926) Born 15 January 1907, 8 Lynedock Place, Glasgow, Scotland; son of Robert Cowan Marshall, Landowner, and Annabella Fraser. **Tutor(s):** M P Charlesworth. **Educ:** Lunehouse, Wetheral, Carlisle; Harrow.

MARSHALL, Professor John Stewart (1935) Born 18 July 1911, Welland, Ontario, Canada; son of John Wells Marshall, Inspector of Public Schools, and Catherine Amelia Stewart; m H Elizabeth R Scott; 2 daughters (Claire and Heather). **Subject(s):** Nuclear Physics; PhD 1941; BSc (Queen's University) 1931; MSc (Queen's University) 1933. **Tutor(s):** J M Wordie. **Educ:** Queen Street Public School, Welland, Canada; Welland High School; Niagara Falls Collegiate Institute; Queen's University, Kingston, Canada. **Career:** Radar Meteorologist; National Research Council and the Defence Research Board; Radar, Army Operational Research Group 1945; Professor of Physics, McGill University 1945–1979; Macdonald Professor of Physics, University of McGill 1960. **Appointments:** Founder, 'Stormy Weather' Group to investigate radar meteorology; Honorary Member, American Meteorology Society 1990. **Awards:** 1851 Exhibition Scholarship; Patterson Medal, Atmospheric Environment Service; Hugh Robert Mill Medal, Royal Meteorology Society; Prize in Applied Meteorology, Canadian Meteorology Society; Prize in Applied Meteorology, American Meteorology Society. **Publications:** Textbook on introductory physics. Died 20 March 1992.

MARSHALL, Kenneth (1927) Born 17 July 1908, 34 Ashfield Avenue, King's Heath, King's Norton, Worcestershire; son of Henry Herbert Marshall, Chemist and Druggist, and Edith Mary Marsh; m Cynthia Leach, 3 April 1943, St James' Church, Sussex Gardens, London; 2 sons (Robert b 25 May 1945 and Harold b 14 August 1948). **Subject(s):** Economics; BA 1930; MA 1936. **Tutor(s):** J M Wordie. **Educ:** King Edward's School, Birmingham. **Career:** Apprentice at United Steel Companies; Sales Staff, Brown Bayley's Steelworks 1936; Procurement of steel for Weapon and Wheeled Vehicle programmes, Ministry of Supply 1940–1946; Deputy Superintendent, Technical Applications of Metals 1943; Called to the Bar, Lincoln's Inn and joined Patent Chambers 1946; Director, Joint Iron Council 1948. **Appointments:** Fellow, Royal Economic Society; Associate Member, Institute of Industrial Administration; Member, Grand Council and the Home and Economic Policy Committee of the Federation of British Industries; Trustee, National Foundry Craft Training Centre; Council Member, British Cast Iron Research Association. Died 28 November 1995.

MARSHALL, Ronald (1923) Born 16 March 1905, 24 Boardman Street, Todmorden, Yorkshire; son of Barton Marshall, Butcher, and Lucy Sunderland. **Subject(s):** History; BA 1926; MA 1931. **Tutor(s):** E A Benians. **Educ:** Todmorden Secondary School. **Career:** Senior History Lecturer, Stranmillis Training College, Belfast 1947; Assistant Master, Methodist College, Belfast 1927. **Publications:** *Massimo D'Azeglio, an artist in politics 1798–1866.* Died 9 January 1993.

MARSHALL, Wilfred (1912) Born 15 November 1892, 55 Ebury Road, New Basford, Nottinghamshire; son of William Baldwin Marshall, Assistant Bank Manager, and Annie Selina Baldwin. **Subject(s):** Mathematics. **Tutor(s):** L H K Bushe-Fox. **Educ:** Nottingham High School. **Career:** Second Lieutenant, then Lieutenant, 10th Battalion, Leicester Regiment 1914; later attached to 1st Battalion, King's Own Scottish Borderers, Dardanelles 1915. Died 4 June 1915 (killed in action in Gallipoli).

MARS-JONES, The Hon Sir William Lloyd (1937) See JONES.

MARTIN, The Revd Canon Anthony Bluett (1949) Born 1 September 1929, Ingenio La Esperanza, Jujuy, Argentina; son of Arthur Cecil Martin, Accountant, and Joan Mary Rosamund Bluett; m Jean Arden

McLeod, 21 July 1992; 1 son (Stephen Bluett). **Subject(s):** Modern and Medieval Languages/Theology; BA 1952; MA 1956. **Tutor(s):** C W Guillebaud. **Educ:** St George's College, Argentina; Felsted School. **Career:** Curate, St Mary, Rushden, Northamptonshire 1954; Ordained Priest 1955; Curate, St George, Worthing 1957; Staff, Scripture Union in Schools 1959; Vicar, All Saints, Hoole, Diocese of Chester 1963; Vicar, Bowdon 1984–1994. **Appointments:** Honorary Canon, Chester Cathedral 1983; Canon Emeritus 1994.

MARTIN, Archibald Roy Hammond (1919) Born 18 June 1897, 21 Cranbrook Road, Chiswick, Middlesex; son of Edmund David Martin, Schoolmaster, and Elizabeth Jane Hammond; m Frances. **Subject(s):** Natural Sciences; BA 1921; MA 1926; Teacher's Diploma 1923. **Tutor(s):** E A Benians. **Educ:** Latymer Upper School, Hammersmith. **Career:** Rifleman, Queen's Westminster Rifles 1915–1919; Master, Worthing High School 1924; Master, Holloway School, London; Lecturer in Botany, University of Sydney; Lecturer in Botany, Rhodes University 1948–1960. Died 1969.

MARTIN, Desmond Levins Joseph (1930) Born 16 July 1906, Greenbank, Monkstown, Dublin, Ireland; son of Thomas Martin, Merchant and Director of Royal Bank of Ireland, and Mary Aloysius Moore; BA 1933. **Tutor(s):** C W Guillebaud. **Educ:** Downside School.

MARTIN, John Sinclair (1937) Born 28 March 1919, 5 North Parade, Belfast; son of John Martin, Merchant, and Mary Evelyn McDowell. **Subject(s):** Modern and Medieval Languages/Law; BA 1940. **Tutor(s):** C W Guillebaud. **Educ:** Richmond Lodge; Inchmarlo; Royal Academical Institution, Belfast. **Career:** Flying Officer, RAFVR, WWII. Died 29 October 1942 (missing from night operations in the Middle East, presumed killed).

MARTIN, Dr John Wilson (1944) Born 14 October 1926, 12 Parliament Street, Peterborough; son of Gilbert Algernon Martin, Engineer, and Glady Wilson; m Carol Marion Thompson, 1951; 1 son (Philip b 1957), 1 daughter (Janet b 1954). **Subject(s):** Natural Sciences; BA 1949; MA 1951; PhD 1953; ScD 1978; DPhil (Oxon); Chartered Engineer 1978; FIMMM. **Tutor(s):** C W Guillebaud; G C L Bertram; E Miller. **Educ:** King's School, Peterborough. **Career:** Title A Fellow, SJC 1954–1957; ICI Fellowship 1954–1956, Demonstrator, Department of Metallurgy 1956–1957, University of Cambridge; Lecturer in Metallurgy 1957–1990, Reader in Physical Metallurgy 1990–1994 (Emeritus 1994–), OCAMAC Senior Research Fellow 1994–, University of Oxford; Fellow 1960–1994 (Emeritus 1994–), St Catherine's College, Oxford. **Appointments:** RNR 1948–1971. **Awards:** Choral Studentship 1944–1945, 1948–1950; Scholarship 1950; Sidney Gilchrist Thomas Medal and Prize, Institute of Materials 1986; Platinum Medal, Institute of Materials 2001. **Honours:** VRD 1960. **Publications:** Over 220 papers in learned journals; 6 books.

MARTIN, Richard Neville (1921) Born 21 August 1904, Low Bank, Compstall, Hyde, Cheshire; son of Richard Martin, Chief Clerk and Secretary of an Ironworks, and Edith Johnston. **Subject(s):** English/History; BA 1925. **Tutor(s):** E E Sikes. **Educ:** Epworth College, Rhyl. Died 12 September 1929.

MARTINEAU, Charles (1926) Born 1 October 1908, 6 Rubislaw Place, Aberdeen, Scotland; son of Alfred Martineau, Solicitor and Notary Public, and Maud Helen Tapsfield. BA 1930; MA 1968. **Tutor(s):** M P Charlesworth. **Johnian Relatives:** brother of George Edward Martineau (1923). **Educ:** Cargillfield, Edinburgh; Uppingham School. Died 30 December 1978.

MARTINEAU, George Edward (1923) Born 18 January 1905, 6 Rubislaw Place, Aberdeen, Scotland; son of Alfred Martineau, Advocate, and Maud Helen Tapsfield; m (1) Christian (d 23 May 1957), (2) Hester; (1) 3 sons, 1 daughter. BA 1926; MA 1931. **Tutor(s):** E E Sikes. **Johnian Relatives:** brother of Charles Martineau (1926). **Educ:** Ardvreck, Crieff;

Uppingham School; Cuddesdon College. **Career:** Master, Ardvreck Preparatory School, Crieff 1926–1928; Ordained Deacon 1930; Curate, St Mary and All Saints, Chesterfield 1930–1933; Ordained Priest 1931; Curate, Old St Paul, Edinburgh 1933–1935; Perpetual Curate, New Mills, Derbyshire 1935–1939; Rector, Christ Church, Falkirk, with St Mary, Grangemouth and St Andrew, Dunmore 1944–1948; Rector, St John, Jedburgh 1948–1958; Rector, St Columba, Edinburgh, and Diocesan Missioner 1958; Honorary Canon, Edinburgh 1959; Dean, Edinburgh 1962–1969. Died 3 January 1969.

MARTIN-SPERRY, Anthony Douglas (1936) Born 21 February 1916, 130 Parade Street, Kingston Ward 1, Georgetown, British Guiana; son of Cecil Martin-Sperry, Director of Companies, and Cecile Irene Hodgson; m Judith Anne Pacey, 3 April 1957, London. **Subject(s):** Mechanical Sciences; BA 1938; MA 1942. **Tutor(s):** J S Boys Smith. **Educ:** Orley Farm School, Harrow; Shrewsbury School; RMA, Woolwich.

MARTLEW, David Leyland (1947) Born 26 March 1927, Maternity Home, Green Road, Ashbourne, Derbyshire; son of Thomas Martlew, Farm Inspector, and Muriel Bessie Goodale. **Subject(s):** Mechanical Sciences; BA 1949; MA 1953; BSc (London) 1947. **Tutor(s):** R L Howland. **Educ:** Perse School, Cambridge; Derby Technical College.

MARTYN, Padma Shri John Arthur King (1921) Born 15 August 1903, Main Street, Sedbergh, Yorkshire; son of Arthur John King Martyn, Clerk in Holy Orders and Schoolmaster, and Nora Anne Feaver King; m Mady. **Subject(s):** History; BA 1924; MA 1935. **Tutor(s):** E E Sikes. **Educ:** Sedbergh Preparatory School; Durham School. **Career:** Master, Harrow School 1925–1934; Headmaster, Doon School, Dehra Dun, India 1948–1966. **Appointments:** In Charge of Boys' Club, Harrow Mission, North Kensington 1931–1932. **Awards:** Baker Exhibition, SJC. **Honours:** OBE 1957; Padma Shri 1984. Died 29 June 1984.

MASON, Edmund William (1909) Born 15 February 1890, Abbey Lodge, Barking, Essex; son of Hugh Herbert Mason, Surgeon, and Susanna Louisa Roberta Johnson; m Una Slane, 4 September 1922, Holy Trinity, Richmond, Surrey. **Subject(s):** Natural Sciences; BA 1912; MA 1916. **Tutor(s):** J R Tanner. **Educ:** Oundle School. **Career:** Captain, Northumberland Fusiliers (wounded), WWI.

MASON, John (1926) Born 12 October 1907, 11 Neale Street, Sunderland, County Durham; son of Philip Mason, Bank Clerk, and Annie Emily Fall. **Subject(s):** Mathematics/Mechanical Sciences; BA 1929; AMICE; MIStructE; MInstW; MSAICE. **Tutor(s):** C W Guillebaud. **Educ:** Arlington House Preparatory School, Porthcawl; Bede Collegiate School, Sunderland. **Career:** Partner, Deane & Mason, Civil Engineering Consultants. **Appointments:** Deputy Mayor of Bexley; Chairman, Bexley Education Committee; Chairman, Bexley Finance and Plans Committees. Died 4 November 1992.

MASON, John Newby (1928) Born 10 March 1910, Allanfield, Workington, Cumberland; son of Daniel Johnston Mason, Solicitor, and Mary Isabel Newby. BA 1932; MA 1935. **Tutor(s):** C W Guillebaud. **Educ:** Denny School, Paris; Kingsland Grange Preparatory School, Shrewsbury; Shrewsbury School. Died 26 September 1977.

MASON, Peter (1915) Born 21 November 1895, Brooklands, Abergele, North Wales; son of William Tate Mason, Justice of the Peace, and Margaret Hilton. **Subject(s):** Classics. **Tutor(s):** E E Sikes. **Johnian Relatives:** grandson of Peter Mason (1819); nephew of Peter Hamnett Mason (1845); brother of William Tate Mason (1920). **Educ:** St Chad's College, Denstone; Perse Grammar School, Cambridge. **Career:** Second Lieutenant, King's Royal Rifle Corps 1915–1917. **Appointments:** Sergeant, OTC, Perse School, Cambridge. Died 17 February 1917 (killed in action at Miraumont).

MASON, Wilfred Bernard (1930) Born 8 April 1907, 29 Barrow Road, Streatham, Surrey; son of Francis Bernard Mason, Civil Engineer, and

Beatrice Binns. **Tutor(s):** C W Guillebaud. **Educ:** Dower House School, Wallington; Bishop's Stortford School; Andover Grammar School; South Eastern Agricultural College, Wye. **Awards:** Probationer/Colonial Agricultural Scholarship, Colonial Service Probationers Committee.

MASON, William Tate (1920) Born 1 December 1898, Abergele, North Wales; son of William Tate Mason, Tutor, Sidney Sussex College, Cambridge, and Margaret Hilton. BA 1922. **Tutor(s):** E E Sikes. **Johnian Relatives:** brother of Peter Mason (1915). **Educ:** Perse Grammar School, Cambridge. **Career:** Lieutenant, 2nd Battalion, MGC 1917–1918; Assistant Master, Beaudesert Park School, Minchinhampton, Gloucestershire 1923–1926; King's College School, Wimbledon 1926–1927; Shardlow High School, Derby 1927–1929; Private Tutor 1931–1936. **Honours:** MC. Died 6 October 1936.

MASSER, Ronald Thornton (1944) Born 2 December 1925, 35 Mapperley Hall Drive, Nottingham; son of Henry Thornton Masser, Solicitor, and Constance May Stevenson; m Heather Rust, 2 July 1949. **Tutor(s):** J M Wordie. **Educ:** Wyville School, Nottingham; Waverley School, Nottingham; St Peter's School, York.

MASSEY, Dr Paul Mackintosh Orgill (1947) Born 12 March 1929, Greenway, Ovingdean, Sussex; son of Stanley Orgill Massey, Medical Practitioner, and Winifred Bertha Mackintosh; m Constance Fay Waldron, 1 June 1956, Holy Trinity, Brompton, London; 2 sons (Simon Christopher Orgill b 14 December 1958 and Philip Wadham Orgill b 24 March 1967), 3 daughters (Fiona Jean Orgill b 2 October 1957, Henrietta Jayne Orgill b 30 June 1961 and Alice Mary Orgill b 27 March 1968). **Subject(s):** Natural Sciences; BA 1950; MA 1954; BChir 1953; MB 1953; MD 1958; MRCS (London) 1953; LRCP (London) 1953. **Tutor(s):** G C L Bertram. **Johnian Relatives:** brother of Michael Joseph Orgill Massey (1951). **Educ:** Wylde Green College; Bishop Vesy; Oundle School. **Career:** Scientist, Falkland Island Dependencies Survey 1954–1956; GP, Birmingham 1956. **Appointments:** Honorary Secretary, CUBC 1948; Captain, LMBC 1950; JP; Magistrate, City of Birmingham.

MASSIE, Frank Alan (1945) Born 12 May 1927, High Farm, Firby, Whitwell, Yorkshire; son of Frank Eric Massie, Farmer, and Edna Harrison. **Subject(s):** Natural Sciences; BA 1951; MA 1953. **Tutor(s):** C W Guillebaud. **Educ:** St Michael's School, Malton; Scarborough High School; Pocklington School. **Awards:** Exhibition, SJC. Died 14 March 2003.

MASSON SMITH, Dr David John (1948) (admitted to Downing College 1945) Born 21 March 1927, 18 Hampstead Way, Golders Green, Middlesex; son of Robert Masson Smith, Barrister-at-Law, Director of Land Companies, and Margaret Frazer Rae. **Subject(s):** Natural Sciences; BA 1951; PhD 1957. **Tutor(s):** G C L Bertram. **Educ:** Brunswick School, Haywards Heath; Haileybury College; Marlborough College.

MASTERMAN, Dr Ernest Bertram Zeller (1928) Born 5 March 1910, Jerusalem, Palestine; son of Ernest William Gurney Masterman, Surgeon, and Johanna Charlotte Hermene Zeller; m Mary K Davis, 10 April 1946, St Mary's Church, Goring-by-Sea (d 8 June 2000); 1 son (Timothy John), 3 daughters (Joanna Mary, Sally Margaret and Lucy Jane). **Subject(s):** Natural Sciences; BA 1931; MA 1936; BChir 1936; MD 1939; MRCS (Eng); LRCP 1934; FRCS (Edinburgh) 1947. **Tutor(s):** M P Charlesworth. **Johnian Relatives:** nephew of John Howard Bertram Masterman (1891); son of Ernest William Gurney Masterman (1898). **Educ:** Monkton Combe School, Junior and Senior. **Career:** Surgeon, Nottingham Group Hospitals (later Surgeon Emeritus).

MASTERS, Eric Henry (1941) Born 1 August 1922, 3 Langstone Road, Portsmouth; son of Henry George Masters, Civil Servant, and Winifred Nora Trowell. **Subject(s):** Mechanical Sciences; BA 1947; MA 1949; CEng; MBCS; MIMechE. **Tutor(s):** S J Bailey. **Educ:** King's School, Rochester; Plymouth College. **Career:** Operations Director, Humphreys & Glasgow Ltd, London. Died 24 March 1977.

MASTON, Charles James (1930) Born 15 May 1912, 13 Clarke Street, Westborough, Dewsbury, Yorkshire; son of James Maston, Accountant, and Amelia Clabour; m Eileen. **Subject(s):** History/Economics; BA 1933; MA 1937. **Tutor(s):** E A Benians. **Educ:** Orchard Street Council School, Guiseley; Yeadon and Guiseley Secondary School; The Grammar School, Bradford. **Career:** Under-Secretary, Department of Employment; Ministry of Labour 1934–1972. **Awards:** Scholarship, SJC 1932. Died 6 July 1986.

MATHER, Dr Harold Gordon (1939) Born 15 January 1921, 63 Havelock Square, Sheffield; son of Harold Mather, Osteopath, and Mary Alice Kober; m Frances Elisabeth Mather, 17 December 1949, All Saints' Church, Lindfield; 4 children. **Subject(s):** Natural Sciences; BA 1942; MA 1946; MB 1946; BChir 1946; MD 1954; MD (Western Reserve University) 1945; MRCP (London) 1950; FRCP 1965. **Tutor(s):** R L Howland. **Johnian Relatives:** father of William Gordon Mather (1969); grandfather of Tamsin Alice Mather (1995). **Educ:** Montessori School, Sheffield; King Edward VII School, Sheffield; Wycliffe College, Stonehouse. **Career:** Burney Yeo Scholar, King's College Hospital 1943; Consultant Physician, Bristol 1956–1986; Clinical Lecturer in Medicine, University of Bristol 1959–1986. **Appointments:** Captain, LMBC 1941; Chairman, Ski Bob Association of Great Britain 1983–1984; President, Hey Groves Medical Golfing Society 1984–1986; Chairman, Bristol Centre National Trust 1996–1999. **Awards:** Rockefeller Foundation Studentship 1943. **Publications:** Many papers including 'Acute MI, Home and Hospital Treatment', The Long Fox Memorial Lecture, University of Bristol, 1977.

MATHEWSON, Kenneth Douglas (1923) Born 12 February 1904, 6 Salisbury Road, Edinburgh, Scotland; son of James William Mathewson, Medical Practitioner, and Elizabeth Gertrude Cowan. **Subject(s):** Mechanical Sciences; BA 1926; CEng; FIStructE. **Tutor(s):** E Cunningham. **Educ:** Naish House, Burnham on Sea; Oundle School. Died 20 September 1997.

MATHIAS, Edward Lanfranc Morgan (1928) Born 27 June 1909, The Limes, East Street, Havant, Southampton; son of Edward Morgan Mathias, Civil Engineer, and Winifred Beatrice Gedge. **Tutor(s):** E A Benians. **Educ:** Perin's Grammar School, Arlesford; Christ's Hospital.

MATTAR, Fareed (1926) Born 8 March 1907, 20 Amhurst Street, Withington, Manchester, Lancashire; son of Amin Mattar, Shipping Merchant, and Salma Behamdouri. BA 1929. **Tutor(s):** E A Benians. **Educ:** New College, Harrogate.

MATTEI, Francis Bagshawe (1924) Born 24 February 1905, 33 Inverness Terrace, Paddington, London; son of Alfred Mattei, Advocate and Barrister, and Teresa Bagshawe; m Primrose Humphreys, 1 September 1932, St Michael's, Newcastle; 1 son (John). BA 1928; MA 1932; CEng; MIMechE. **Tutor(s):** J M Wordie. **Educ:** Beaumont College, Windsor; Private Tuition, Malta University. **Career:** RE. Died 13 January 1989.

MATTHEW, Patrick Chrichton (1926) Born 5 May 1908, Dray Cot Terrace, St Ives, Cornwall; son of Frederick Chrichton Matthew, Doctor, and Janie Marian Young. BA 1930. **Tutor(s):** M P Charlesworth. **Educ:** Lexden House School, Seaford; Clifton College.

MATTHEWS, Peter Thomas (1943) Born 11 July 1925, 60 Vicarage Road, Yardley, Birmingham; son of Edward Matthews, Engineer and Company Director, and Dorothy Groom. **Tutor(s):** C W Guillebaud. **Educ:** Lichfield Friary School; King Edward VI School, Lichfield.

MATTHEWS, Professor Robert Charles Oliver (1949) Born 16 June 1927, 18 Walker Street, Edinburgh; son of Oliver Harwood Matthews, WS, and Ida Finlay; m Joyce Hilda Lloyds, 1948. MA (by incorporation) 1951; BA (Oxon) 1947; Hon DLitt (Warwick) 1980; Hon DLitt (Abertay Dundee) 1996; FBA 1968. **Educ:** Rochester House, Edinburgh; Edinburgh Academy; Corpus Christi College, Oxford; Nuffield College, Oxford.

Career: Lecturer, Merton College, Oxford 1948–1949; Assistant Lecturer in Economics 1949–1951, Lecturer in Economics 1951–1965, University of Cambridge; Title B Fellow 1950–1965, Lecturer 1956–1965, SJC; Drummond Professor of Political Economy, University of Oxford 1965–1975; Fellow, All Souls College, Oxford 1965–1975; Master, Clare College, Cambridge 1975–1993 (Emeritus 1993–); Professor of Political Economy, University of Cambridge 1980–1991 (Emeritus 1991–). **Appointments:** Supervisor in Economics 1949–1956; Director of Studies in Economics 1957–1965, SJC; Visiting Professor, University of California, Berkeley 1961–1962; FIDE International Master of Chess Composition 1965; Chairman, Social Science Research Council 1972–1975; Member, OECD Expert Group on Non-inflationary Growth 1975–1977; Managing Trustee, Nuffield Foundation 1975–1996; Honorary Fellow, Corpus Christi College, Oxford 1976–; Chairman, Bank of England Panel of Academic Consultants 1977–1993; Trustee, Urwick Orr & Partners Ltd 1978–1986; President, Royal Economic Society 1984–1986. **Awards:** Foreign Honorary Member, American Academy of Arts & Sciences 1985; Honorary Member, American Economic Association 1993. **Honours:** CBE (1975). **Publications:** *A Study in Trade Cycle History*, 1954; *The Trade Cycle*, 1958; (with M Lipton and J M Rice) *Chess Problems: introduction to an art*, 1963; (with F H Hahn) *Théorie de la Croissance Economique*, 1972; (ed) *Economic Growth: trends and factors*, 1981; (with C H Feinstein and J C Odling-Smee) *British Economic Growth 1856–1973*, 1982; (ed, with G B Stafford) *The Grants Economy and Collective Consumption*, 1982; (ed) *Slower Growth in the Western World*, 1982; (ed, with J R Sargent) *Contemporary Problems of Economic Policy: essays from the CLARE Group*, 1983; (ed) *Economy and Democracy*, 1985; *Mostly Three-Movers: collected chess problems*, 1995; articles in learned journals.

MATTHEWS, Roy Anthony (1948) Born 1 July 1927, Mill Hill, Middlesex; son of Harold Marten Matthews, Auctioneer and Surveyor, and Hilda Jessie Heaney; m Rosemary Brunsdon, 26 November 1955, Toronto; 3 sons, 1 daughter. BA 1950; MA 1955. **Tutor(s):** G C L Bertram; R L Howland. **Educ:** University College School, Hampstead. **Career:** Market Research Analyst, Philips Electronics Industries, Toronto 1954–1956; Economic Studies Analyst, Canadian Industries Limited, Montreal 1956–1960; Chief Economist, Conference Board of Canada, Montreal 1960–1964; Director of Research, Private Planning Association of Canada, Montreal 1964–1971; Research Fellowship, International Development Research Centre, Ottawa 1972; Economic Council of Canada, Ottawa 1973–1986; seconded to Institute for Research on Public Policy, Ottawa 1980; Organisation for Economic Co-operation and Development, Paris 1984–1986. **Awards:** Ford Foundation Travel and Study Award 1969.

MAUNG, Percy Mya (1932) Born 7 August 1913, Rangoon, Burma; son of U Maung Maung, Barrister-at-Law, District and Sessions Judge, and Daw Thein Uga (Mya). **Subject(s):** History/Law; BA 1935. **Tutor(s):** E A Benians. **Educ:** Diocesan Boys High School, Rangoon, Burma.

MAVOR, Henry Alexander (1940) Born 27 December 1921, 23 Cranworth Street, Glasgow; son of John Bridie Mavor, Electrical Engineer, and Agnes Dickie Bowman Lindsay. BA 1947. **Tutor(s):** S J Bailey. **Johnian Relatives:** brother of John Osborne Mavor (1949). **Educ:** Laurel Bank Kindergarten, Glasgow; Glasgow Academy; Loretto School. Died 14 March 1996.

MAVOR, John Osborne (1949) Born 14 May 1930, 6 Kirklee Gardens, Glasgow; son of John Bridie Mavor, Mechanical Engineer, and Agnes Dickie Bowman Lindsay; m Anne Jennifer, 21 September 1957. **Subject(s):** Mechanical Sciences; BA 1952; MA 1956. **Tutor(s):** R L Howland. **Johnian Relatives:** brother of Henry Alexander Mavor (1940). **Educ:** Craigflower School, Fife; Loretto School. **Career:** Senior Management Consultant, PE International; Self-employed Management Consultant; Scottish Manager, 3i Enterprise Support; Part-time worker, Glasgow Development Agency. Died 3 April 1996.

MAW, Zali (1948) Born 14 April 1928, Rangoon, Burma; son of Ba Maw, Barrister-at-Law, Premier of Burma, and Kin Ma Ma Sein; 2 daughters. **Subject(s):** Economics; BA 1951; MA 1958; MA (Yale) 1954. **Tutor(s):** C W Guillebaud. **Educ:** St John's Convent, Rangoon; St Patrick's Preparatory School, Rangoon; St Paul's English High School, Rangoon; University of Rangoon; Yale University, New Haven, USA. **Career:** Partner, Associated Lawyers Limited, Bangkok, Thailand; Advocate of High Court, Rangoon, Burma; Barrister-at-Law; Called to the Bar, Gray's Inn 1958; Lecturer, Faculty of Law, Rangoon University 1960–1962. **Appointments:** Rotary International Foundation Fellowship 1953–1954.

MAWER, James (1934) Born 15 December 1915, 23 South Street, Louth, Lincolnshire; son of Francis Riggall Mawer, Butcher, and Emma Elizabeth Hillier; m Margot Mary Waite, 15 March 1946, Harrogate; 1 son (Richard James b 30 September 1949), 1 daughter (Hilary Margaret b 16 June 1947). **Subject(s):** Natural Sciences; BA 1938; MA 1941. **Tutor(s):** J M Wordie. **Johnian Relatives:** father of Richard James Mawer (1967). **Educ:** Ashville College, Harrogate; Wesleyan County Council School, Louth; Miss Surfleet's Preparatory School. **Career:** Teacher, Ashville College, Harrogate. Died 17 August 1993.

MAWLE, John Wetherall (1947) Born 24 June 1927, Six Hills, Cosby Road, Countesthorpe, Leicestershire; son of Norman William Reginald Mawle, Group Captain, RAF, and Lilian Louisa Griffin; m (1) Marion, 1950 (d 1975), (2) Miriam, 1982; (1) 1 son (Guy), 3 daughters (Alison, Iona and Caroline). **Subject(s):** Mechanical Sciences; BA 1950; MA 1969; MIMechE; MCIM; FIoD. **Tutor(s):** R L Howland. **Educ:** Portland House Preparatory School, Leicester; Handsworth Preparatory School, Birmingham; Leighton Park School, Reading. **Career:** Petty Officer, Submariner, RN 1944–1947; Graduate Trainee 1950–1952, Factory Manager 1952–1954, Hayward Tyler (pump manufacturer); Management Consultancy, TI 1954–1956; Director and General Manager, TI Plastics 1956–1959; Independent Management Consultant 1959–1964 and 1969–1980 (including assignments with Ransomes & Rapier, Cool Technology, ICFC); Managing Director, Bristol Pneumatic, National Enterprise Board, Wednesbury Tube, Weir Group (subsidiary), The Monotype Corporation and Yale Fork Trucks; Marketing Director, Redman Heenan; Production Director, Bristol Pneumatic and Andrew Valentine; Managing Director, Midland Steel Products and Steel Stampings, GEI International (engineering group) 1964–1969; Divisional Managing Director, The Monotype Corporation plc 1978–1990; Independent Management Consultant 1990–1998 (Director, Canterbury HRD Group, and assignments with Surrey TEC). **Appointments:** Captain, first XV, later President, Stourbridge Rugby Football Club. Died 7 September 2003.

MAXWELL, Ian Stanley (1936) Born 15 February 1917, Manor House School, North Side, Clapham Common, London; son of Stanley Maxwell, Schoolmaster, and Edith Marion Allen; m Margaret Joanna Pascoe, 31 December 1941, St Gerrans, Cornwall; 3 sons (Peter Stanley b 1946, Roger Stanley b 1949 and Nicholas Stanley b 1952); 1 daughter (Jennifer Stentiford b 1956). **Subject(s):** Geography; BA 1939; MA 1948. **Tutor(s):** J M Wordie. **Johnian Relatives:** grandson of Frederick Charles Maxwell (1866); son of Stanley Maxwell (1894); brother of Roland Stanley Maxwell (1920); cousin of Frank Stanley Allen (1938); brother of Malcolm Stanley Maxwell (1939); father of Nicholas Stanley Maxwell (1970). **Educ:** Manor House School, Clapham Common. **Career:** 10th LAA Training Regiment, RA 1940; Commissioned, RA 1941; Served in Ceylon, India and Burma 1942–1945; 43rd Light Anti-Aircraft Regiment, RA 1942–1945; demobilised 1946; Assistant Lecturer in Geography, Lecturer, Senior Lecturer, and Reader in Historical Geography, University of Sheffield 1946–1977. **Awards:** Scholarship, SJC 1939–1940. **Publications:** (joint ed and author) *The Domesday Geography of Northern England*, CUP, 1962; various publications mainly relating to the historical geography of Cornwall.

MAXWELL, Malcolm Stanley (1939) Born 2 April 1920, Manor House School, North Side, Clapham Common, London; son of Stanley Maxwell, Schoolmaster, and Edith Marion Allen. **Subject(s):**

Geography; BA 1947; MA 1949. **Tutor(s):** J M Wordie. **Johnian Relatives:** grandson of Frederick Charles Maxwell (1866); son of Stanley Maxwell (1894); brother of Roland Stanley Maxwell (1920) and of Ian Stanley Maxwell (1936); cousin of Frank Stanley Allen (1938); uncle of Nicholas Stanley Maxwell (1970). **Educ:** Manor House School, Clapham Common, London. **Career:** 13th Queen's Royal Regiment 1940; Commissioned, RE 1943; demobilised 1946; Schoolmaster. Died 21 August 1980.

MAXWELL, The Revd Roland Stanley (1919) Born 12 January 1902, Manor House School, Old Town, Clapham, Surrey; son of Stanley Maxwell, Schoolmaster, and Edith Marion Allen. **Subject(s):** Mathematics/Natural Sciences; BA 1924; MA 1927; BSc (London) 1924. **Tutor(s):** E A Benians. **Johnian Relatives:** grandson of Frederick Charles Maxwell (1866); son of Stanley Maxwell (1894); brother of Ian Stanley Maxwell (1936); cousin of Frank Stanley Allen (1938); brother of Malcolm Stanley Maxwell (1939); uncle of Nicholas Stanley Maxwell (1970). **Educ:** Manor House School; Battersea Polytechnic. **Career:** Lecturer, Westminster Training College 1925–1929; Deacon, St Stephen's House, Oxford 1929–1930; Curate, All Saints, Notting Hill 1930–1933; Priest, London 1930; Acting Headmaster, Manor House School, Clapham Common 1933; Acting Lecturer in Natural Philosophy, University of St Andrews 1933–1934; Curate, St Cyprian, Dorset Square, London 1934; Chaplain, RAF 1940–1946; Served in Singapore, Ceylon and India 1941–1945; Archdeacon, St Vincent and St Lucia, West Indies (later Emeritus); Archdeacon, Grenada, West Indies. **Publications:** (jointly) *A Text Book of Heat*, Macmillan, 1939. Died 13 September 1980.

MAXWELL-JACKSON, Ronald Emerson Maxwell (1920) See JACKSON.

MAY, George Harold (1941) Born 26 August 1922, Edson, Alberta, Canada; son of Harry May, Builder, and Dorothy Belle Thurston. **Tutor(s):** S J Bailey. **Educ:** Walter Moberly School, Vancouver, Canada; Bude County School, Cornwall; Henry Thornton School, Clapham. **Career:** 1st Airborne Division. Died 25 or 26 October 1944 (missing at Arnhem, The Netherlands).

MAY, Dr Harry Blight (1927) Born 12 November 1908, 25 Hamilton Street South, Devonport, Devon; son of John Thomas May, Police Inspector, and Isabel Blight. **Subject(s):** Natural Sciences (Pathology); BA 1930; MA 1934; BChir 1934; MB 1934; MD 1945; MRCS (London Hospital) 1934; LRCP (London Hospital) 1934; MRCP 1937; FRCP 1954. **Tutor(s):** C W Guillebaud. **Johnian Relatives:** brother of John Leslie May (1921). **Educ:** Johnston Terrace Council School, St Leonards; The High School, Devonport. **Career:** Assistant Lecturer in Bacteriology and Preventive Medicine, University of Manchester; Assistant, Bernhard Baron Institute of Bacteriology; Director, Clinical Laboratories at The London Hospital Medical College 1953–1968; Dean, Faculty of Medicine, London Hospital Medical College 1960–1964. **Awards:** Scholarship, SJC 1926. Died 21 June 1991.

MAY, John Leslie (1921) Born 10 April 1903, 8 Ocean Street West, Devonport, Devon; son of John Thomas May, Police Inspector, and Isabel Blight. **Subject(s):** Natural Sciences; BA 1924. **Tutor(s):** B F Armitage. **Johnian Relatives:** brother of Harry Blight May (1927). **Educ:** Johnston Terrace Council School; The High School, Devonport. **Awards:** Exhibition, SJC 1921.

MAY, John Otto (1932) Born 21 April 1913, 19 Well Walk, Hampstead, London; son of Otto May, Physician, and Gertrude Mabel Rose; m Maureen McNally, October 1939; 1 daughter (Sheila). **Subject(s):** Modern and Medieval Languages/Economics; BA 1936. **Tutor(s):** E A Benians. **Johnian Relatives:** son of Otto May (1897); nephew of Harry Cecil Rose (1902) and of Hubert Allan Rose (1905); cousin of Sidney Patrick Rose (1930); brother of Richard Percy May (1933); cousin of Michael Anthony Rose (1938). **Educ:** Heath Mount, Hampstead; St George's, Broadstairs; Sherborne School. **Career:** Department of

Overseas Trade 1937–1939; Private Secretary to Comptroller-General 1939; Assistant Commercial Secretary, Copenhagen 1939–1940; Assistant Commercial Secretary, Helsinki 1940–1942; Ministry of Economic Warfare (Representative in Caracas) 1942–1944; First Secretary (Commercial), Rome 1945–1948; First Secretary (Commercial), Bucharest 1948–1950; Foreign Office 1950–1953; First Secretary, Helsinki 1954–1957; Acting Chargé d'Affaires 1954–1957; Counsellor (Commercial) and Consul-General, HM Embassy, Athens 1957–1960; Consul-General, Genoa 1960–1965; Consul-General, Rotterdam 1965–1968; Consul-General, Gothenburg. **Awards:** Coronation Medal 1953. **Honours:** OBE 1949; CBE 1962. Died 27 November 2002.

MAY, The Revd Peter Dudfield (1931) Born 23 February 1912, Oaklands, Lee Common, Great Missenden, Buckinghamshire; son of Herbert Richard Dudfield May, Barrister-at-Law, and Mabel Sturdy; m Pattie Muriel Preston, 10 April 1937; 1 son (Hugh Preston b 1943), 2 daughters (Rosalind Susan b 1938 and Ruth Penelope b 1944). **Subject(s):** Law; BA 1934; LLB 1935; LLM 1985. **Tutor(s):** R L Howland; E A Benians. **Johnian Relatives:** nephew of Peter Langton May (1893) and of Frederick Sturdy May (1895); son of Herbert Richard Dudfield May (1897); cousin of Ivan Langton May (1922) and of Cecil Hugh Langton May (1927); brother of Richard Sturdy May (1928); brother-in-law of John Martyn Preston (1932). **Educ:** The Dene School, Caterham; Charterhouse School; Ripon Hall, Oxford 1938. **Career:** Barrister, Inner Temple 1935; Lay Reader 1937; Ordained Priest 1939; Deacon, Birmingham 1939; Assistant Curate, All Saints, Gravelly Hill 1939–1943; Assistant Curate, St James', Trowbridge 1943–1946; Vicar, Preshute, Salisbury 1946–1953; Vicar, Netherbury with Solway Ash 1954–1982; Priest, Netherbury with Solway Ash and Rector, Stoke Abbott 1957. **Awards:** Scholarship, SJC; MacMahon Studentship, SJC 1937–1938. Died 17 February 2001.

MAY, Richard Percy (1933) Born 26 March 1915, 19 Well Walk, Hampstead, London; son of Otto May, Doctor, and Gertrude Mabel Rose; m Caroline Rosemary Welby Jack, 10 May 1947. **Subject(s):** Classics/History; BA 1936; MA 1972. **Tutor(s):** R L Howland. **Johnian Relatives:** son of Otto May (1897); nephew of Harry Cecil Rose (1902) and of Hubert Allan Rose (1905); brother of John Otto May (1932); cousin of Sidney Patrick Rose (1930) and of Michael Anthony Rose (1938). **Educ:** Heathmount, Hampstead; St George's, Broadstairs; Sherborne School. **Career:** War service, Captain, RA, Member, HAC; Called to the Bar, Lincoln's Inn 1948; Solicitor 1953.

MAY, Richard Sturdy (1928) Born 20 April 1910, Oaklands, Lee Common, Great Missenden, Buckinghamshire; son of Richard Dudfield May, Barrister-at-Law, and Mabel Sturdy. **Subject(s):** Law; BA 1932; MA 1936. **Tutor(s):** E A Benians. **Johnian Relatives:** nephew of Peter Langton May (1893) and of Frederick Sturdy May (1895); son of Richard Dudfield May (1897); cousin of Ivan Langton May (1922) and of Cecil Hugh Langton May (1927); brother of Peter Dudfield May (1931). **Educ:** The Dene School, Caterham; Charterhouse. **Career:** Solicitor. Died 22 May 1955.

MAYALL, Dr Gordon Francis (1947) Born 19 December 1928, 36 Gidlow Avenue, Wigan, Lancashire; son of Harry Mayall, Lubricating Oil Manufacturer, and Mildred Heyes; m Elizabeth Thyne, 1960; 4 sons. **Subject(s):** Natural Sciences; BA 1950; MA 1953; BChir 1953; MB 1954. **Tutor(s):** G C L Bertram. **Educ:** St Michael's Church of England School, Wigan; Wigan Grammar School. **Career:** National Service, RAF 1954–1956; Consultant Radiologist, Royal Devon and Exeter Hospital 1965–1993. **Appointments:** Honorary Clinical Tutor, Exeter University.

MAYNE, Archibald Collier (1926) Born 13 July 1908, Betul, Central Provinces, India; son of Arthur John Mayne, Indian Civil Service, and Emily Bonnycastle Barnett. **Subject(s):** Economics; BA 1929. **Tutor(s):** E A Benians. **Johnian Relatives:** brother of Edward Bonnycastle Mayne (1920). **Educ:** Victoria College, Jersey.

MAYNE, Edward Bonnycastle (1920) Born 3 September 1902, Villa St Antoine, Boulevard Donville, St Servan, Ille et Vilaine, France; son of Arthur John Mayne, Indian Civil Service, and Emily Bonnycastle Barnett. **Subject(s):** Economics/History; BA 1923. **Tutor(s):** E E Sikes. **Johnian Relatives:** brother of Archibald Collier Mayne (1926). **Educ:** Nelson College, New Zealand; Clayesmore School, Pangbourne; The High School, Victoria, Canada; Clifton College, Bristol.

MAYNE, Leslie Samuel (1921) Born 11 October 1903, Mon Abri, Arthur Road, Winchester, Southampton; son of Bertie Victor Archibald Mayne, Portrait Painter, and Violet Helen Teague. BA 1924. **Tutor(s):** B F Armitage. **Educ:** Oakmount School, Highfield, Southampton; Harrow School. **Career:** President, California State Registered Professional Foresters; Forestry Service, Sarawak Government 1925. Died 12 April 1997.

MAYOU, Charles Alfred (1942) Born 21 September 1924, 14 Johnstone Street, Handsworth, London; son of Charles Mayou, Master Builder, and Louisa Spencer Hollier. **Subject(s):** Classics/Modern and Medieval Languages; BA 1947; MA 1949. **Tutor(s):** C W Guillebaud. **Educ:** Willenhall Road Council School, Wolverhampton; Gower Street Council School, Birmingham; King Edward's Grammar School, Aston; King Edward's High School, Birmingham.

MEAD, Arthur Frederick (1947) Born 29 February 1924, 33 Worthing Road, Southsea, Hampshire; son of Frederick John Mead, Grocer, and Lilla Gertrude Auston. **Tutor(s):** J M Wordie. **Educ:** Portsmouth Grammar School. **Career:** Colonial Service Course, Nigeria; Gunnery Control Officer, and officer in charge of radar, RNVR 1942–1946.

MEAD, Frederick Everitt Bruce (1919) Born 9 April 1899, 5 Beaumont Street, London; son of Frederick James Mead, Merchant, and Mary Bruce. **Subject(s):** Modern and Medieval Languages; BA 1921; MA 1926. **Tutor(s):** E E Sikes. **Educ:** Crowthorne Tower; Marlborough College. **Awards:** Scholarship, SJC 1916.

MEADOWS, The Revd John Michael (1948) Born 1 October 1927, Cochin, South India; son of Alfred Meadows, Merchant, and Margaret Adelaide Ives; m Dorothy Kathryn Stanbra, 7 August 1958, St Luke the Evangelist Church, Teluk Anson, Malaya. **Subject(s):** Modern and Medieval Languages; BA 1950; MA 1955. **Tutor(s):** C W Guillebaud. **Educ:** Bedford School; Ridley Hall, Cambridge. **Career:** Curate, St Mary's, Weymouth, Dorset; Ordained Deacon 1953; Curate, St George the Martyr, Daubhill 1953; Ordained Priest 1954; Overseas Missionary Fellowship, Malaya 1957–1961; Overseas Missionary Fellowship, Vietnam 1962–1975; Refugee Reception, Central Sopley 1979–1982; Non-Stipendiary Minister, Canford Magna 1986–1988; Curate, Radipole and Melcombe Regis 1989.

MEARES, Brigadier Cyril Denzil Nugent (1921) Born 18 November 1898, Bara Banki, United Provinces, India; son of Cecil Forlong Eddis Meares, India Civil Service, Opium Department, and Rachel Kelly; m Alecia. **Tutor(s):** B F Armitage. **Educ:** University School, Hastings; Bedford School; RMA, Woolwich. Died 15 December 1944.

MEARS, Joseph Henry Watt (1924) Born 20 January 1905, Oxford Lodge, Popes Grove, Twickenham, Middlesex; son of Joseph Theophilus Mears, Builder, and Henrietta Watt. **Tutor(s):** B F Armitage. **Educ:** Pembroke House School, Hampton; Malvern College. **Career:** Director, Stamford Bridge FC 1931; Chairman, Stamford Bridge FC 1940; Royal Marines, Crete, Egypt and Ceylon, WWII; Head of Security, Churchill's underground operation room, Whitehall; Chairman, Football Association 1963. Died 1 July 1966.

MEDLAND, John Aubrey (1933) Born 17 July 1910, Toronto, Canada; son of John Medland, Wholesale Grocer, and Mabel Millinet Van Horne. BA (Toronto) 1933. **Tutor(s):** C W Guillebaud. **Educ:** Howard Park Public School; University of Toronto Schools; University of Toronto.

MEEK, Richard Ombler (1927) Born 23 October 1908, Burnside, Tanglin Road, Singapore, Straits Settlements; son of Joseph Bertram Lloyd Meek, Civil Engineer, and Gladys Eleanora Rachel Strick. BA 1930; MA 1934; CEng; FICE. **Tutor(s):** J M Wordie. **Educ:** Brockhurst, Church Stretton; Rugby School. **Appointments:** Chairman, South Wales Association, Institute of Civil Engineers; President, University College of Swansea Engineering Society.

MEEK, Professor Ronald Lindley (1946) Born 27 July 1917, 128 Abel Smith Street, Wellington, New Zealand; son of Ernest William Meek, Accountant, and Matilda Isabel Williams; m (1) May Hyam, (2) Dorli; 1 son (Roger), 1 daughter (Alison). **Subject(s):** Economics; PhD 1949; LLB (New Zealand) 1938; LLM (New Zealand) 1939. **Tutor(s):** C W Guillebaud. **Educ:** Eastern Hutt School, Lower Hutt; Hutt Valley High School; Victoria University College, Wellington. **Career:** Lecturer in Political Economy, University of Glasgow 1950–1963; Tyler Professor of Economics, Leicester University 1963–1978. **Appointments:** East Midlands Regional Economic Planning Council 1967–1978; Royal Economic Society. **Awards:** Strathcona Studentship, SJC 1939. **Publications:** Various, including *Economics and Ideology and other essays: Studies in the Development of Economic Thought*, Chapman and Hall, 1967; *Figuring Out Society*, Fontana, 1971. Died 18 August 1978.

MEES, Gualtherus Hendrik (1922) Born 6 August 1903, Rotterdam, Holland; son of Abraham Cornelis Mees, Managing Director, International Credit & Trading Company, and Louisa Johanna Philippina Hen van Rijnberk. BA 1925; MA 1929; LLD (Leyden). **Tutor(s):** E A Benians. **Educ:** Commercial High School of Rotterdam, Holland. Died 5 June 1955.

MEES, Rudolf Pieter (1934) Born 19 February 1913, Vaassen (Comm Epe), Zutphen, Gelderland; son of Adriaan Rudolf Pieter Mees, Representative of Messrs R Mees & Sons, Bankers, and Pauline Caroline de Kuyper. **Tutor(s):** C W Guillebaud. **Educ:** ULO School, Vaassen; Gymnasium Apeldoorn.

MEESOOK, Boonyium (1934) Born 12 June 1914, Bangkok, Siam; son of Phra Bhasa Kosol, Royal State Railway Department; m KhunYing Amporn; 1 son (Palachai), 2 daughters (Astra and Kanitta). **Subject(s):** Natural Sciences; BA 1937; MA 1941. **Tutor(s):** J M Wordie. **Educ:** Suankularb College, Bangkok; Manchester Grammar School. **Career:** Director of the Bank Notes Printing Works, Bank of Thailand; Head, Thai Section, American Office of War Information 1947; Government Post, Bangkok 1947; Boonyium & Associates Limited. **Appointments:** President, Rotary Club of Bangkok 1968–1969; President, Thailand Management Association 1970–1972; President, Asian Association of Management Organisations 1983–1986; President, Engineering Institute of Thailand 1984–1985; Industrial and Engineering Research Division 1985–1995; Member, Board of Trustees, Thailand Management Association 1988; Chairman of Council, King Mongkut University of Technology Thonburi; Member, National Research Council of Thailand (Chairman); Member, Board of Professional Engineers of Thailand. **Awards:** Scholarship, SJC 1936–1937. Died 15 June 2001.

MEGAW, The Rt Hon Sir John (1928) Born 16 September 1909, 44 Northumberland Road, Donnybrook, Dublin, Ireland; son of Robert Dick Megaw, Barrister-at-law, and Annie McElderry; m Eleanor Grace Chapman, 1938; 1 son, 2 daughters. **Subject(s):** Classics/Law; BA 1931; MA 1935; LLB 1933; LLM 1985; Honorary LLD (Queen's, Belfast) 1968; Honorary DSc (Ulster) 1990; QC 1953; QC (Northern Ireland) 1954; PC 1969. **Tutor(s):** M P Charlesworth. **Educ:** St Andrew's College, Dublin; Royal Belfast Academical Institution; Harvard University Law School. **Career:** Barrister-at-Law, Gray's Inn 1934; Colonel, RA 1939–1945; Recorder, Middlesbrough 1957–1961; Bencher, Gray's Inn 1958; Judge, High Court of Justice, Queen's Bench Division 1961–1969; Lord Justice of Appeal 1969–1980; Treasurer, Gray's Inn 1976. **Appointments:** Joseph Hodge Choate Memorial Fellow, Harvard University Law School 1931; President, Restrictive Practices Court

1962–1968; Honorary Fellow, SJC 1967–1997; Visitor, New University of Ulster 1976; Chairman, Committee of Inquiry into Civil Service Pay 1981–1982; University of Ulster 1984–1989. **Awards:** Scholarship, SJC 1927; John Stewart of Rannoch Scholarship in Greek and Latin, University of Cambridge 1929; Legion of Merit (US) 1946. **Honours:** TD 1951; CBE 1956; Kt 1961. Died 27 December 1997.

MEHTA, Boman Hirjibhoy (1932) Born 17 September 1910, Mhow, Central India; son of Hirjibhoy Rustomji Mehta and Navazbai Franji Bhurakhan. **Subject(s):** English; BA (Nagpur). **Tutor(s):** J S Boys Smith. **Educ:** St Aloysius High School, Jubbulpore; Zoroastrian High School, Bombay; Imperial High School, Bombay; Morris College, Nagpur. Died 29 July 1973.

MEHTA, Jagat Singh (1946) Born 7 July 1922, Udaipur, Rajputana, India; son of Mohan Sinha Mehta, Chief Minister, Banswara State, and Hulas Kumari; m Rama (d 1978); 3 sons (Vikram b 30 October 1952, Ajay b 22 February 1954 and Uday b 4 June 1957), 1 daughter (Vijay b 4 June 1951). **Subject(s):** Economics; BA 1947; MA 1955. **Tutor(s):** C W Guillebaud. **Educ:** Modern High School, Delhi; Vidya Bhawan, Udaipur; Leighton Park School; Allahabad University. **Career:** Lecturer, Allahabad University 1944; RN 1945–1946; Indian Foreign Service 1947–1980; Head, Indian Embassy, China 1964–1966; High Commissioner, Tanzania 1970–1974; Foreign Secretary, India 1976–1979; Fellow, Harvard and Woodrow Wilson Centre 1980–1982; Professor, Lyndon B Johnson School, Austin, Texas 1983–1996. **Appointments:** President, Seva Mandir, Udaipur (Rural Development) 1985–1994; President, Vidya Bhawan (Educational Society) 1993–2000; President, Lake Protection Society, Udaipur. **Honours:** Padma Bhushan 2002.

MEIKLE, Ian Ormiston (1938) Born 15 August 1920, 24 Engayne Gardens, Upminster, Essex; son of Ormiston Meikle, Mechanical Engineer, and Phyllis Alma Adams. **Subject(s):** English; BA 1941. **Tutor(s):** J S Boys Smith. **Educ:** Gidea Hall; Brentwood Preparatory School; Hollingbury Court; Wycliffe College. **Career:** Lieutenant, First Airborne Division, RA 1939–1944. **Awards:** Minor Scholarship, SJC 1937. Died September 1944 (killed in action at Arnhem).

MELDRUM, Roy (1903) Born 26 October 1884, 15 Balmoral Road, Sherwood, Nottinghamshire; son of Thomas Meldrum, Lace Designer, and Anne Maria Keating; m Elise Marquerite Fraser. **Subject(s):** Classics; BA 1906; MA 1918. **Tutor(s):** J R Tanner; C E Graves. **Educ:** Nottingham High School. **Career:** Assistant Master, St Paul's School 1910; Lecturer in Education, University of Cambridge 1946–1950. **Appointments:** LMBC Coach 1936–1955. **Awards:** Minor Scholarship, SJC 1902; Browne Medal for Latin Ode, University of Cambridge 1905; Scholarship, SJC 1905; Members' Prize (English Essay), University of Cambridge 1906. Died 15 February 1955.

MELLIS, William Ranald Stuart (1927) Born 25 January 1909, 7 Carden Place, Aberdeen, Scotland; son of William Mellis, Manufacturer and Wholesale Merchant, and Beatrice Bertram Macrae; m Kathleen Winsome, 4 November 1931, St Michael's, Highgate. **Subject(s):** Economics; BA 1930. **Tutor(s):** J M Wordie. **Educ:** Angus Field House Preparatory School, Aberdeen; Tonbridge School.

MELLOR, Leonard (1927) Born 10 July 1908, 2 Carrington Road, Almondbury, Yorkshire; son of Thomas Edwin Mellor, Textile Pattern Weaver, and Lucy Jane Hall. **Subject(s):** Mathematics; BA 1930; MA 1936. **Tutor(s):** J M Wordie. **Educ:** Stile Common Council School; The Grammar School, Almondbury.

MELLOR, Philip Evert McIlvaine (1920) Born 5 February 1903, 14 Victoria Road, Kensington, London; son of Frank Mellor, Barrister-at-Law, and Elizabeth Markoe Camac. BA 1925. **Tutor(s):** E E Sikes. **Johnian Relatives:** son of Frank Mellor (1880). **Educ:** Kensington High School; Mr C H Gibbs' Preparatory School, London; Westminster

School. **Career:** Inspector, Sudan Plantations Syndicate Ltd 1925; Captain, AAC, WWII. **Publications:** 'The Cottage', *The Eagle* 43, 1924. Died February 1943 (killed in action in North Africa).

MELLOR, William John Rockfort (1929) Born 2 December 1905, Monghyr, Bihar, India; son of Arthur Mellor, Indian Civil Service, and Ivy Charity John. **Tutor(s):** C W Guillebaud. **Educ:** Sangeen School, Bournemouth; Sherborne School; RMC, Sandhurst. **Career:** Second Lieutenant 1925, Lieutenant 1927, West Yorkshire Regiment, 1st Battalion.

MELLORS, Peter Howard (1945) Born 30 December 1926, 202 Harrington Drive, Lenton, Nottingham; son of Bertram Mellors, Gentleman's Outfitter, and Agnes Edginton. **Subject(s):** History/Law; BA 1948; MA 1952; LLB 1952. **Tutor(s):** F Thistlethwaite. **Educ:** Westlake House School, Nottingham; Cavendish Road Junior School, Skegness; Skegness Grammar School; King's School, Peterborough. **Career:** Partner, Perry, Parr & Ford, Nottingham; Solicitor 1954; Registrar of the Diocese of Southwell and Bishop's Legal Secretary 1970. **Appointments:** Governor, Nottingham High School; Midlands Chairman of Winged Fellowship Trust; Vice-Chairman, Legal Advisory Commission of the Church of England; National Chairman, Ecclesiastical Law Association; President, Nottinghamshire Law Society 1984. **Awards:** Munsteven Exhibition, SJC 1945. Died 3 August 1990.

MELVILLE, William Patrick Stewart (1937) Born 4 June 1918, 46 Maxwell Drive, Glasgow; son of Alexander Melville, Civil Engineering Contractor, and Agnes Massey. **Tutor(s):** J S Boys Smith. **Educ:** Glasgow Academy; Dalhousie Castle School; Trinity College, Glenalmond.

MENENDEZ, Frank Treman Sibly (1914) Born 26 January 1896, St Matthew, Nassau, Bahamas; son of Frank Manuel Menendez, Planter, and Elizabeth Maud Sibly. **Tutor(s):** L H K Bushe-Fox. **Educ:** Nassau Grammar School; Preparatory School, Taunton; Wycliffe College, Stonehouse. **Career:** Lieutenant, York and Lancaster Regiment; Lieutenant, RAF. **Honours:** MC 1917.

MENON, Kizhakkepat Ramunny (1914) Born 2 June 1896, Srikrishnapuram, Amsam, Malabar, India; son of Kizhakkepat Palat Raman Menon, Additional Member, Madras Legislative Council. **Subject(s):** Mathematics/Natural Sciences; BA 1917; MA 1925. **Tutor(s):** R P Gregory. **Educ:** The Zammorin's College, Calicut; Madras Christian College.

MERCER, Professor Frank Verdun (1947) Born 15 April 1916, 194 Carrington Street, Young Ward, Adelaide, South Australia; son of Joseph Howard Mercer, Farmer, and Elsie May Edgar; m Marie. PhD 1951; BSc (Adelaide) 1942. **Tutor(s):** G C L Bertram. **Educ:** Crystal Brook Public School; Urrbrae Agricultural School; University of Adelaide. **Career:** Lecturer in Botany 1944–1947, Associate Professor of Plant Physiology 1950, University of Sydney; Professor of Biology and Head of the School, Macquarie University 1965. Died 4 December 1988.

MERIVALE, Bernard (1900) Born 15 July 1882, 2 Victoria Villas, Newcastle upon Tyne; son of John Herman Merivale, Mining Engineer, and Blanche Liddell; m Cicely Leila Stuckey, 22 July 1914, St Gilbert's, Kensington. **Subject(s):** Law; BA 1903. **Tutor(s):** D MacAlister. **Johnian Relatives:** great grandson of John Herman Merivale (1796); grandson of Charles Merivale (1826); great nephew of John Lewis Merivale (1834); nephew of Reginald Merivale (1870). **Educ:** Sedbergh Grammar School. **Career:** Qualified as Solicitor 1906; Dramatic Author 1913–1935. **Honours:** OBE 1920. **Publications:** 16 plays (some in collaboration). Died 10 May 1939.

MERRELL, Robert Maurice (1949) Born 1924; m Myra Fisher, 1951 (d 2000); 2 sons (James b 1953 and William b 1956). **Subject(s):** Mechanical Sciences; BA 1951; MA 1978. **Tutor(s):** R L Howland. **Educ:** Sevenoaks School. **Career:** Commissioned, RE 1943, retired as Brigadier

1979; Independent Highways Inquiries Inspector 1980–1994. **Honours:** MBE 1956.

MERRELLS, George Luen (1934) Born 14 December 1915, 43 Wimpole Road, Colchester; son of George Edward Merrells, Captain, RGA, and Winifred Alice Luen; m Wendy Gledhill; 1 son (Alan). **Subject(s):** Modern and Medieval Languages; BA 1937. **Tutor(s):** C W Guillebaud. **Educ:** The Gorgdon LCC Elementary School, Eltham, London; Colfe's Grammar School, Lewisham, London. **Career:** Burma Civil Service 1937; Served in Burma's military government in exile 1939–1945; Deputy Commissioner in Kyaukpyu and then Minbu 1945; HM Foreign (Diplomatic) Service, Oriental Secretary at British Embassy, Rangoon; British Consul, St Louis, USA and Western Pacific 1951; Lecturer in Burmese, SOAS, London. **Awards:** Scholarship, SJC 1936–1937. Died 16 September 1990.

MERRIMAN, Gabriel de Vesselitsky (1937) Born 12 May 1919, The Ark, 3 Montana Road, Wimbledon; son of Sergei de Vesselitsky Merriman, Examiner, War Office, and Aelfreda Edith Westall. **Subject(s):** Natural Sciences; BA 1940; MA 1944. **Tutor(s):** C W Guillebaud. **Educ:** Miss Nops' Private School, Surbiton; Shrewsbury House, Surbiton; Dover College.

MERRY, Douglas Cooper (1930) Born 10 April 1910, Southcote Road, Linslade, Buckinghamshire; son of Arthur Walker Merry, Surveyor and Auctioneer, and Alice Mary Haslam; m Una Evelyn Wallace 1934, Harpenden (d January 1990); 2 daughters. **Subject(s):** Mechanical Sciences; BA 1932; MA 1954; MIEE 1966; CEng. **Tutor(s):** J M Wordie. **Educ:** Berkhamsted School. **Career:** RMA, Woolwich; Commissioned, RE, retired as Lieutenant Colonel 1930–1958; Teacher of Electrical Engineering at Technical College level at Farnborough, Toronto and Reading. Died 22 June 1997.

MERRY, Frank (1945) Born 14 March 1927, 3 Davies Street, Oldham, Lancashire; son of Frank Merry, Warehouse Manager, and Ellen Smith; m; 3 daughters (Beverley b 1957, Ashley b 1958 and Phillipa b 1961). **Subject(s):** History; BA 1948; MA 1952. **Tutor(s):** F Thistlethwaite. **Educ:** Northmoor Council School, Oldham; Hulme Grammar School, Oldham. **Career:** Director, J Lyons & Co Ltd, 1961–1988; Director, Findus Ltd 1967–1971; Lyons Tea, Jersey 1971–1988; Chairman, Lyons Bakery Ltd 1972–1974; Chairman, Tetley Tea Co Ltd 1972–1988; Sole Café Ltd 1972–1988; Chairman, Glacier Foods Ltd 1973–1977; Assistant Managing Director, J Lyons 1982–1988. **Appointments:** Rotary Fellow, Columbia University, New York; Member, Food Manufacturers Federation; Council Member, British Nutrition Foundation; Chairman, Consumer Goods Study Group. **Awards:** Scholarship, SJC 1947; College Prize 1948.

MERSON, Ronald Leslie (1937) Born 4 August 1918, 42 Richmond Road, Lincoln; son of John Oswald Merson, Engineer, and Amy Constance Wesencraft; m Marjorie Blackwell, 1945; 2 daughters. **Subject(s):** Modern and Medieval Languages; BA 1940; MA 1944. **Tutor(s):** C W Guillebaud. **Educ:** The Royal Grammar School, Newcastle upon Tyne. **Career:** Principal Lecturer in French, Crewe and Alsager College of Higher Education 1965–1976. **Awards:** Sizarship, SJC 1937.

MERTON, Geoffrey Ralph (1941) Born 26 January 1922, 153 Banbury Road, Oxford; son of Thomas Ralph Merton, Treasurer, Royal Society, and Fellow of Balliol College, Oxford, and Violet Marjory Sawyer. **Tutor(s):** C W Guillebaud. **Educ:** Summer Fields, Oxford; Eton College; Balliol College, Oxford.

MERTON-JONES, Edmund Trevor (1926) Born 4 March 1908, Claverdale, Woodside Park Gardens, North Finchley, Middlesex; son of Merton Addleston Jones, Solicitor, and Winifred Haslehurst; m Betty Spaull, 20 January 1934, Holy Trinity, Brompton. BA 1929. **Tutor(s):** M P Charlesworth. **Educ:** Doone House School, Westgate-on-Sea; Oundle School.

MERTTENS, Fritz Roel (1917) Born 25 December 1898, Rothley Temple, Leicester; son of Frederick Merttens, Merchant, and Margaret Joanna Howell. **Tutor(s):** E E Sikes. **Educ:** Hillbrow, Rugby; Sidcot School; Down House, Westgate; Rugby School; Leighton Park School. Died June 1919.

MESTON, William (1900) Born 4 May 1871, 31 Constitution Street, Aberdeen; son of James Meston, Registrar, and Jane Grieg Scorgie. DD 1925; MA (Aberdeen) 1890; BD (Edinburgh) 1895. **Tutor(s):** D MacAlister. **Educ:** Grammar School, Aberdeen. **Career:** Missionary, Free Church of Scotland; Member, Madras Legislative Council 1921–1923, 1927 and 1928; Principal, Madras Christian College 1921–1928. **Appointments:** Fellow, University of Madras. **Awards:** Kaisar-I-Hind Medal (1st class), 1921. Died 12 January 1933.

METAXA, Count Andrea Dudly Richard (1921) Naval Officer.

METCALF, Henry Kenneth (1917) Born 17 August 1899, 13 Croxted Road, Herne Hill, Surrey; son of Henry Ernest Metcalf, Marine Engineer, and Edith Mary Crosland. **Tutor(s):** E E Sikes. **Educ:** St Winifred's School, Kenley; Oundle School. **Career:** Second Lieutenant, RGA.

METCALFE, Harry Francis (1942) Born 3 September 1924, Crescent Nursing Home, Rugby; son of Frank Walker Metcalfe, Mechanical Engineer, and Fanny Louise Lomax; m Joan Mary Wincott, 1948; 2 sons, 1 daughter. **Subject(s):** Mechanical Sciences; BA 1945; MA 1951. **Tutor(s):** S J Bailey. **Educ:** Lisvane, Scarborough; Bootham School, York; BTH Works, Rugby. **Career:** Computing, including the design and development of computing equipment with BTH, Ferranti and IBM, and later the development of systems for communications, banking and airlines.

METCALFE, Vincent (1939) Born 29 December 1921, Sutton-on-the-Forest, Yorkshire; son of Percy William Metcalfe, Farmer, and Beatrice Alcock; m (1) Maureen Devoy, (2) Margaret Kent; 3 sons (Andrew John, Raymond Hugh and Adrian Philip). BA 1942; MA 1946. **Tutor(s):** J M Wordie. **Educ:** Sutton-on-the-Forest Elementary School; Easingwold Grammar School. **Career:** Regular Army Officer, REME 1942–1976; Major General, REME Support Group, Woolwich 1974–1976; Colonel Commandant, REME 1977–1982.

METTERS, Thomas Lee (1921) Naval Officer.

MEWTON, Richard (1948) Born 26 August 1926, 53 Rodney Street, Liverpool; son of John Richard Mewton, Architect, and Zita Mary Hall; m Margaret; 1 son, 3 daughters. **Subject(s):** Agriculture; BA 1951; MA 1955; DipEd 1971. **Tutor(s):** R L Howland. **Educ:** Kingsley Preparatory School; Park High School, Birkenhead; Ellesmere College, Shropshire. **Career:** Teacher, Wells Secondary School 1971–1973; Corpusty School 1983; Brinton Primary School 1983–1984. **Appointments:** Churchwarden. Died April 1984.

MEYER, Richard (1904) Born 28 October 1883, 46 Colnische Strasse, Cassel, Germany; son of Paul Meyer, Railway Commissioner, and Helma Speyer. **Tutor(s):** D MacAlister. **Educ:** Elberfeld Gymnasium; Lessing Gymnasium; University of Geneva. Died 4 July 1955.

MIALL, Rowland Leonard (1933) Born 6 November 1914, 73 Corringham Road, Golders Green, London; son of Rowland Miall, Scientific Instrument Maker, and Sara Grace Dixon; m (1) Lorna Rackham, 1941 (d 1974), (2) Sally Bicknell (née Leith), 1975; (1) 3 sons, 1 daughter. **Subject(s):** Economics/Law; BA 1936; MA 1940; FRTS 1986. **Tutor(s):** C W Guillebaud. **Johnian Relatives:** nephew of Lawrence Miall (1897). **Educ:** Handside School, Welwyn Garden City; Ackworth School, Pontefract; Bootham School, York; Freiburg University. **Career:** Editor, *Cambridge Review* 1936; Lecturer in US 1937; Secretary, British-American Associates 1937–1939; BBC 1939–1984; BBC German Talks and Features Editor 1940–1942; Member, British Political Warfare Mission to US 1942–1944; Director of News, San Francisco, British Political Warfare Mission 1943; Personal Assistant to Deputy Director-General, Political Warfare Executive, London 1944; Head of New York Office, British Council Warfare Mission 1944; Acting Diplomatic Correspondent 1945; BBC Special Correspondent, Czechoslovakia 1945; Psychological Warfare Division, SHAEF, Luxembourg 1945; Chief Correspondent in US 1945–1953; Head of Television Talks 1954; Assistant Controller, Current Affairs and Talks, Television 1961; Special Assistant to Director of Television, planning start of BBC2 1962; Assistant Controller, Programme Services, Television, BBC 1963–1966; Advisor, Committee on Broadcasting, New Delhi 1965; BBC Representative in US 1966–1970; Delegate to Commonwealth Broadcasting Conference, Jamaica 1970; Controller, Overseas and Foreign Relations, BBC 1971–1974; Delegate to Commonwealth Broadcasting Conference, Kenya 1972; Delegate to Commonwealth Broadcasting Conference, Malta 1974; Director, Visnews Ltd 1974–1979; Overseas Director, BAFTA 1974–1979; Research Historian, BBC 1975–1984. **Appointments:** President, Cambridge Union 1936; Deputy Chairman, Visnews Ltd 1984–1985; Council Member, RTS 1984–1991. **Honours:** OBE 1961. **Publications:** *Richard Dimbleby, Broadcaster*, 1966; *Inside the BBC*, 1994; contributions to *Dictionary of National Biography* and various journals; obituaries for *The Independent*.

MIDDELBOE, Bernhard Ulrik (1947) Born 18 June 1929, Odense, Denmark; son of Hans Christian Middelboe, Farmer, and Ulla Agnete Willer Andersen. **Subject(s):** Economics; BA 1950. **Tutor(s):** C W Guillebaud. **Educ:** Kenton College, Nairobi; Prince of Wales School, Nairobi.

MIDDLEMISS, Hugh Percival (1922) Born 7 November 1903, 40 Eardley Crescent, Brompton, London; son of Charles Stewart Middlemiss, Superintendent, Mineralogical Survey, Kashmir, and Martha Frances Wheeler. **Tutor(s):** B F Armitage. **Johnian Relatives:** son of Charles Stewart Middlemiss (1878). **Educ:** St Bede's, Eastbourne; Haileybury College.

MIDDLETON, Christopher Basil (1903) Born 2 October 1884, Prissick House, Marton in Cleveland, Yorkshire; son of Christopher Middleton, Gentleman, and Elizabeth Hawdon; m Tempe Laura. **Subject(s):** Natural Sciences; BA 1906. **Tutor(s):** D MacAlister. **Educ:** Sedbergh School. **Career:** Government Survey Department 1906; Lieutenant, RFA, WWI. Died 22 August 1939.

MIDDLETON, Hugh Craigmyle (1940) Born 13 September 1921, 17 Bolton Road, Port Sunlight, Cheshire; son of Ralph Wardlaw Thompson Middleton, Congregational Minister, and Flora Blair Anderson. **Subject(s):** History; BA 1968. **Tutor(s):** C W Guillebaud. **Johnian Relatives:** nephew of William Blair Anderson (1936). **Educ:** Bebington Preparatory School, Birkenhead Institute; Dennis Road School, Birmingham; King Edward VI Grammar School, Birmingham; Sir Anthony Browne's School, Brentwood. **Awards:** Sizarship, SJC.

MIDDLETON, Sir Thomas Hudson (1903) Born 31 August 1863, Cromarty, Scotland; son of Alexander Allardyce Middleton, JP, Ross, Scotland, and Esther Murray Taylor; m Lydia Miller, 18 November 1890; 1 son, 1 daughter. MA 1902; MSc (Durham); BSc (Edinburgh); BSc (Glasgow); LLD (Aberdeen); LLD (Edinburgh); LLD (Wales); FRS 1936. **Educ:** Merchiston Castle School, Edinburgh. **Career:** Professor of Agriculture, Baroda College, India 1889–1896; Lecturer in Agriculture, University College of Wales 1896–1899; Professor of Agriculture, Durham College of Science 1899–1902; Drapers Professor of Agriculture, University of Cambridge 1902–1907; Assistant Secretary, Board of Agriculture 1906–1919; Deputy Director General, Food Production 1917–1919; Member, Royal Commission on Agriculture in India 1926–1928. **Appointments:** Commissioner under Development and Road Improvement Fund Acts 1919; Vice-Chairman 1929, Chairman 1938, Agricultural Research Council. **Awards:** Gold Medallist

and Honorary Member, Royal Agricultural Society. **Honours:** CB 1913; KBE 1918; KCIE 1929. Died 14 May 1943.

MILLAR, Bryan (1944) Born 8 May 1926, Cresswell, Bosdin Road, Flixton, Lancashire; son of Gilbert Hall Millar, Electrical Engineer, and Ethel Campbell. **Subject(s):** Mechanical Sciences; BA 1947. **Tutor(s):** S J Bailey. **Educ:** Flixton Junior Council School; Manchester Grammar School. **Career:** Research Trainee, Engineer, then sub-section Leader, AEI Research Laboratory, Aldermaston 1947–1962; Section Leader then Senior Engineer, AEI Automation Ltd 1962–1967; Senior Engineer, AEI Traction Division 1967–1968. Died 3 August 1972.

MILLAR, George Reid (1928) Born 19 September 1910, Boghall, Baldernock, Stirling; son of Thomas Andrew Millar, Architect, and Mary Reid Morton; m Isabel Beatriz Paske-Smith, 1945, London (d 1991). **Subject(s):** Architecture; BA 1932. **Tutor(s):** C W Guillebaud. **Johnian Relatives:** nephew of Fergus Dunlop Morton (1906); brother of James Broom Millar (1927). **Educ:** Kelvinside Academy, Glasgow; Loretto School, Musselburgh. **Career:** Architect 1930–1932; Journalist, *Daily Telegraph* and *Daily Express* 1934–1939; Paris Correspondent, *Daily Express* 1939; The Rifle Brigade, POW, then Agent in France 1939–1945; Tenant Farmer 1962. **Honours:** MC 1943; DSO 1944; Croix de Guerre avec Palmes 1944; Chevalier de la Legion d'Honneur 1944. **Publications:** *Maquis*, 1945; *Horned Pigeon*, 1946; *My Past was an Evil River*, 1946; *Isabel and the Sea*, 1948; *Through the Unicorn Gates*, 1950; *A White Boat from England*, 1951; *Siesta*, 1952; *Orellana*, 1954; *Oyster River*, 1963; *Horseman*, 1970; *The Bruneval Raid*, 1974; *Road to Resistance*, 1979.

MILLAR, James Broom (1927) Born 8 January 1909, Boghall, Baldernock, Stirling; son of Thomas Andrew Millar, Architect, and Mary Reid Morton; m (1) Countess Maria Lo Faro, 1949, (2) Margaret Room, 1956 (d 1984). **Subject(s):** Economics/History; BA 1930. **Tutor(s):** C W Guillebaud. **Johnian Relatives:** nephew of Fergus Dunlop Morton (1906); brother of George Reid Millar (1928). **Educ:** Kelvinside Academy, Glasgow; Loretto School, Musselburgh. **Career:** Television and Radio Broadcaster, Nigeria and Brunei; Consular Official, Berlin 1930s; Intelligence Corps, Middle East, Italy, Yugoslavia 1941–1946; Head, BBC Scotland 1962–1969; Head of Broadcasting, Sierra Leone 1969–1973. **Honours:** MBE; OBE. Died 19 August 1986.

MILLAR, Professor John Graham (1946) Born 30 September 1922, 11 Queens Avenue, Mount Eden, Auckland, New Zealand; son of Donald Millar, Shipping Agent, and Katharine Bernice Massey. **Subject(s):** Mathematics; BA 1948; BSc (New Zealand) 1942; MSc (New Zealand) 1943. **Tutor(s):** J M Wordie. **Educ:** Mount Albert Grammar School, Auckland; Auckland University College; Canterbury College, New Zealand. **Career:** Assistant Professor of Mathematics, University of Edmonton, Alberta 1948–1950. **Awards:** Cook Memorial Prize for Mathematics 1944; Shirtcliffe Fellowship 1944. Died December 1950.

MILLAR, Dr Sam Porter (1933) Born 28 November 1914, High Street, Omagh, Tyrone, Ireland; son of Samuel Millar, Hotel Proprietor, and Edith Olivia Porter; m 1941; 1 son (John), 2 daughters (Margaret and Maureen). **Subject(s):** Natural Sciences; BA 1936; MRCS 1940; LRCP 1940. **Tutor(s):** R L Howland. **Educ:** Campbell College, Belfast, Northern Ireland. **Career:** GP; RAFVR Medical 1941–1946.

MILLAR, William Donald (1944) Born 14 April 1926, 18 Bridle Road, Woodford, Cheshire; son of John William Millar, Cotton Salesman, and Elizabeth Williams; m June Cragg, 1958 (d 1994); 1 son (John b 1964), 1 daughter (Anne b 1965). **Subject(s):** Mechanical Sciences; BA 1947; MA 1951; MICE. **Tutor(s):** S J Bailey. **Educ:** King's School, Macclesfield; Helston County School, Cornwall. **Career:** Chartered Civil Engineer.

MILLARD, Anthony Walter Phipson (1922) Born 30 September 1902, Bombay, India; son of Walter Samuel Millard, Merchant, and Isabelle Caverhill Mackinlay. **Subject(s):** Natural Sciences. **Tutor(s):** E E Sikes.

Educ: Scaitcliffe, Egham; Malvern College; West Wratting Park, Cambridgeshire.

MILLARD, John Forster (1930) Born 8 March 1911, Herschel, Cape Province, South Africa; son of Philip Ernest Millard, Medical Practitioner, and Edith Ursula Forster; BA 1933; MA 1937. **Tutor(s):** C W Guillebaud. **Johnian Relatives:** grandson of Charles Sutton Millard (1854). **Educ:** St Andrew's Preparatory School, Grahamstown, South Africa; St Andrew's College, Grahamstown, South Africa.

MILLARD, John Franklin (1941) Born 12 May 1924, 77 Rochdale Road, Oldham, Lancashire; son of Harold Millard, Machine Operator, and Ellen Amelia Brown. BA 1944; MA 1948. **Tutor(s):** C W Guillebaud. **Educ:** Doctor Lane School, Scouthead, Oldham; Clarksfield Council School, Oldham; The Hulme Grammar School, Oldham. **Career:** Lieutenant, RE 1944.

MILLER, Alexander Lamont (1948) Born 8 February 1925, Grosvenor Nursing Home, 42 Forest Road, Nottingham; son of Campbell Lamont Miller, Medical Practitioner, and Helen McDowall. **Subject(s):** Modern and Medieval Languages; BA 1950; MA 1955. **Tutor(s):** C W Guillebaud. **Educ:** Primary School, Hucknall; Nottingham High School. **Career:** RAF.

MILLER, Derek (1949) Born 16 October 1929, 85 Montgomery Road, Sheffield; son of Bernard Mark Miller, Cutlery Manufacturer, and Sophia Miller. **Tutor(s):** A G Lee. **Educ:** Abbeydale Council School, Sheffield; King Edward VII School, Sheffield; Clifton College Preparatory School; Westmount High School, Montreal, Canada; Clifton College.

MILLER, Duncan McCorquodale (1944) Born 20 November 1925, 63 Nicholson Street, Greenock; son of James Miller, Warehouseman, and Isabella MacCorquodale. **Tutor(s):** J M Wordie. **Educ:** Sandbank Public School, Argyllshire; Dunoon Grammar School.

MILLER, Edward (1934) Born 16 July 1915, Acklington Park, Acklington, Morpeth; son of Edward Miller, Farm Steward, and Mary Lee Fowler; m Fanny Zara Salingar, 1941; 1 son (John). **Subject(s):** History; BA 1937; MA 1945; Hon LittD; Hon DLitt (Sheffield) 1972; FRHistS; FBA 1981. **Tutor(s):** J S Boys Smith. **Educ:** West Woodburn County School; Morpeth Grammar School. **Career:** Title A Fellow, SJC 1939–1947 (leave of absence while on war service 1940–1946); Major, Durham Light Infantry, RAC and Control Commission for Germany 1940–1945; Assistant Lecturer in History, University of Cambridge 1946–1949; Title B Fellow and College Lecturer 1947–1965, SJC; Lecturer, University of Cambridge 1948–1965; Warden, Madingley Hall, Cambridge 1961–1965; Professor of Medieval History, Sheffield University 1965–1971; Master, Fitzwilliam College, Cambridge 1971–1981. **Appointments:** Assistant Supervisor in History 1939–1940, Supervisor in History 1940–1941 and 1946–1947, Director of Studies in History 1946–1954, Tutor 1950–1956, Honorary Fellow 1974, SJC; Chairman, Victoria Company Histories Committee of Institute of Historical Research 1972–1979; Member, St Albans Research Committee; Chairman, Editorial Board, History of Parliament Trust 1975; Deputy Chairman, Committee to Review Local History 1978–1979; Honorary Fellow, Fitzwilliam College 1981. **Awards:** Scholarship, SJC 1936–1937; Exhibition, SJC; Hughes Prize, SJC 1937; Strathcona Travel Exhibition, SJC 1937; Strathcona Resident Studentship 1937–1939. **Publications:** *The Abbey and Bishopric of Ely*, 1951; *Portrait of a College*, 1961; (joint ed) *Cambridge Economic History of Europe*; *Historical Studies of the English Parliament*, 1970; (jointly) *Medieval England: Rural Society and Economic Change*, 1978; (ed) *Agrarian History of England and Wales*, 1991; (jointly) *Medieval England: towns, commerce and crafts*, 1995; Articles in Victoria County Histories of Cambridgeshire and York, *The Agrarian History of England and Wales*, *English History Review*, *Economic History Review*, *Transactions Royal Historical Society*, *Past and Present*. Died 21 December 2000.

MILLER, The Rev Edward Jeffery (1942) Born 25 May 1924, Pendeen, Okehampton, Devon; son of George Harold Miller, Bank Clerk, and Florence Elizabeth Jeffery; m Frances Sambell, 1953; 4 children. **Subject(s):** Engineering/Theology; BA 1948; MA 1950. **Tutor(s):** C W Guillebaud. **Educ:** Okehampton Grammar School; Upcott House Preparatory School, Okehampton; Exeter School; Wells Theological College. **Career:** Captain, RE 1942; Madras Sappers and Miners, India 1943; Ordained Deacon 1950; Ordained Priest 1951; Curate, St Luke's and St Philip's, Bath, Diocese of Bath and Wells; Missionary, Church Missionary Society, Krishna Diocese, Andhra Pradesh, Church of South India 1953–1967; Vicar, Timberscombe and Priest in Charge, Wootten Courtenay, Minehead, Diocese of Bath and Wells 1967; Rector, Selworthy, Timberscombe, Wootten Courtenay and Luccombe, Diocese of Bath and Wells 1980; Retired 1993. Died 30 September 2001.

MILLER, Dr Emanuel (1911) Born 26 August 1892, 30 Church Street, Spitalfields, London; son of Abraham Miller, Dealer in Furs, and Rebecca Fingelstein; m Betty Spiro (d 1965); 1 son (Jonathan Wolfe b 21 July 1934), 1 daughter (Sarah). **Subject(s):** Natural Sciences/Moral Sciences; BA 1914; MA 1922; DPM 1919; MRCS 1918; LRCP 1918; MRCP 1929; FRCP 1946; FBPsS. **Tutor(s):** J R Tanner. **Johnian Relatives:** father of Jonathan Wolfe Miller (1953). **Educ:** City of London School. **Career:** Captain, RAMC, Special Reserve, Military Hospital, Surgical Neurology, Tooting, WWI; Part-time Psychiatrist to the Surrey Child-Guidance Clinic; Honorary Clinical Psychologist and Director, Child Guidance Unit, West End Hospital for Nervous Diseases; Psychiatrist, later Honorary Director, East London Child Guidance Clinic; Neurological Specialist, Ministry of Pensions; Medical Officer, Ministry of Pensions Mental Deficiency Hospital, Roehampton; Lecturer to Medical Postgraduates, University of Cambridge 1924–1925; Psychiatrist, London Jewish Hospital; Honorary Physician in Child Psychiatry, St George's Hospital; Physician, later Emeritus, Maudsley Hospital; Co-Director, Institute for the Scientific Treatment of Delinquency; Lieutenant Colonel, RAMC, Army Psychiatrist, Directorate of Medical Research and Statistics, WWII. **Appointments:** Member, Child Guidance Council; Member, Home Office Council for the Treatment of Offenders; Chairman, Medical Section, British Psychological Association; President, Friends of Magen David Adom 1953; Honorary President, Fourth International Congress of Child Psychiatry, Lisbon 1958; Chairman, Association of Child Psychiatry and Child Development 1958; Chairman, Medical Friends of Magen David Adom in Britain. **Awards:** Conjoint Diploma, London Hospital. **Publications:** *Types of Mind and Body*, 1926; *Modern Psychotherapy*, 1931; 'Psychopathology of Childhood', *Recent Advances in Psychoneuroses*, 1931; 'Illusion and Hallucination', *Journal of Neurology*, 1927, 1931; *Insomnia and Disorders of Sleep*; (ed and part author) *Neurosis in War*, 1940; (founder and joint ed) *Journal of Child Psychology and Psychiatry*, 1959; (joint ed) *British Journal of Criminology*, 1948; (joint ed) *Library of Criminology*, 1960; (ed) *Foundations of Child Psychiatry*, 1967; (ed) *International Journal of Child Psychiatry*. Died 29 July 1970.

MILLER, Major Francis (1900) Born 7 November 1881, Colombo, Ceylon; son of Edward Francis Miller, Clerk in Holy Orders and Schoolmaster, and Caroline Louisa Ford; m Mollie. **Tutor(s):** C E Graves; J R Tanner. **Johnian Relatives:** grandson of William Hallowes Miller (1820); son of Edward Francis Miller (1867). **Educ:** The Grammar School, Bedford. **Career:** Second Lieutenant, Leicester Regiment 1902; Major, Indian Army. Died 23 January 1948.

MILLER, George James (1920) Born 2 January 1903, 3 Hillhead Gardens, Hillhead, Glasgow; son of James Miller, Architect, and Emelina Henrietta Crichton; m Margaret Isobel Kincaid. **Tutor(s):** E E Sikes. **Educ:** Stanley House, Bridge of Allan; Fettes College, Edinburgh.

MILLER, Professor Harold (1928) Born 14 September 1909, 1 Immingram Grove, Chesterfield Road, Staveley, Derbyshire; son of Ephraim Wheat Miller, Grocery Warehouseman, and Sarah Alice

Winter; m Mary Bacon, 1937; 3 sons (John b 4 February 1940, Robert b 29 August 1943 and Thomas Richard b 19 February 1947). **Subject(s):** Natural Sciences (Physics); BA 1931; MA 1935; PhD 1935; Honorary DSc (Sheffield) 1980. **Tutor(s):** C W Guillebaud. **Johnian Relatives:** father of John Miller (1959). **Educ:** Barrow Hill Council School; Staveley Netherthorpe Grammar School. **Career:** Commercial transmission of television, EMI 1934; Physicist, Sheffield National Centre for Radiotherapy 1942–1960; Chief Physicist, Sheffield Regional Hospital Authority 1960–1975; Consultant, International Atomic Energy Agency for work in Ghana 1965, for work in Thailand 1969; Associate Professor 1972, later Emeritus Professor, University of Sheffield; Consultant to the Overseas Development Agency for work in India 1980. **Appointments:** President, Hospital Physicists' Association 1957–1958; President, British Institute of Radiologists 1968–1969. **Awards:** Scholarship, SJC 1927. **Honours:** OBE 1972. **Publications:** (with J Walter) *A Short Textbook of Radiotherapy*, London, 1950; *A Brief History of Medical Physics in Sheffield, 1914–1982*; *History of the Hospital Physicists' Association, 1943–1983*, 1983; *Growing up with Primitive Methodism*, The Fifth (Methodist) Chapel Aid Lecture, 1995. Died 4 October 1995.

MILLER, Hugh Francis Ridley (1909) Born 11 March 1891, Llanbadare, Bush Hill Park, Enfield, Middlesex; son of Frank Campbell Miller, Deputy Principal, Bullion Office, Bank of England, and Milicent Hunter Hunter; m Marjorie Gertrude Kershaw, 8 June 1922; 2 sons (Geoffrey and Donald). **Subject(s):** Economics; BA 1912. **Tutor(s):** E E Sikes. **Educ:** St Catharine's School, Broxbourne. Died 12 November 1962.

MILLER, Joseph Irwin (1931) Born 26 May 1909, Columbus, Bartholomew, Indiana; son of Hugh Thomas Miller, Banker, and Nettie Irwin Sweeny. **Tutor(s):** C W Guillebaud. **Educ:** Columbus Public Schools; Taft School, Watertown; Yale University, New Haven.

MILLER, Thomas Harvey (1932) Born 29 October 1913, 4 Doune Terrace, Glasgow; son of Thomas Miller, Ship Owner/Broker, and Roberta Helen Harvey; m Kathleen Mary Murray, Dusseldorf, Germany, 25 March 1950. **Subject(s):** Law; BA 1935. **Tutor(s):** C W Guillebaud. **Educ:** Kelvinside Academy, Glasgow; Fettes College, Edinburgh.

MILLS, Donald Henry (1942) Born 26 September 1924, St Mary's Hospital, Paddington, London; son of Cephas Charles Mills, Grocery and Provision Merchant, and Lily Alice Ansell. **Tutor(s):** C W Guillebaud. **Educ:** St George's School, Hanover Square; Westminster City School; Twickenham Technical College.

MILLS, Edward Henry Fenwick (1910) See BLUMHARDT.

MILLS, Ernest James (1904) Born 6 February 1886, Stapenhill, Burton on Trent, Staffordshire; son of James Mills, Schoolmaster, and Emily Jane Wainwright. **Subject(s):** Mathematics; BA 1907; MA 1912. **Tutor(s):** D MacAlister. **Educ:** Burton Grammar School. **Career:** Lieutenant, Cheshire Regiment (TF), then Captain and Adjutant, MGC (Mentioned in Despatches), WWI; Mathematics Master, Sir William Turner's Grammar School, Coatham, Redcar 1907. **Awards:** Scholarship, SJC. **Honours:** OBE. Died May 1963.

MILLS, John (1944) Born 20 April 1927, Rydal House, Clarence Road, Hinckley, Lancashire; son of Roy Mills, Hosiery Factory Manager, and Annie Grace Jordan. **Tutor(s):** J M Wordie. **Educ:** Hinckley Church School; Hinckley Grammar School.

MILLS, John Yarnton (1921) Naval Officer.

MILLS, Joseph Frederick (1941) Born 1 May 1923, 47 Linden Road, Gosforth, Newcastle upon Tyne; son of Frederick Peter Mills, Mining Engineer, and Muriel Victoria Turnbull; m Pauline Lenore Ingham, 16 May 1953, Witherslack; 1 son (Simon Julian Felix). **Subject(s):** Natural Sciences and Metallurgy; BA 1944; MA 1947; FIM; CEng; FIEE.

Tutor(s): J M Wordie; C W Guillebaud. **Educ:** St Anne's School, Gosforth; Royal Grammar School, Newcastle upon Tyne. **Career:** Imperial Metal Industries Ltd, Birmingham 1950–1964; General Manager, Pyrotenax Ltd, Hebburn 1965–1978; Board Member, BICC Cables Ltd 1971–1981; Executive Director, BICC Metals 1978–1981. **Appointments:** BICC United Kingdom Cables Group Board 1971; General Commissioner of Income Tax, Salford and Manchester North Division 1982–1998.

MILLS, Dr Kenneth Frederick Thomas (1918) Born 28 August 1900, Smith Street, Durban, Natal, South Africa; son of Frederick William Mills, Electrical Engineer, and Margaret Ada Smith. **Subject(s):** Natural Sciences; BA 1921; BChir 1925; MB 1926. **Tutor(s):** E E Sikes. **Educ:** Highbury School, Hill Crest, Natal, South Africa; South African College, Cape Town; Bradfield College; UCL. **Career:** Superintendent, General Hospital, Johannesburg; Lecturer in Nursing and Hospital Administration, University of the Witwatersrand, Johannesburg 1959. Died 2 April 1964.

MILLS, Robert (1942) Born 9 September 1924, Edensor, 496 Manchester Road, Rochdale; son of Robert Mills, Woollen Manufacturer, and Sarah Ann Crabtree; m Elizabeth Eleanor Morton, 20 November 1948. BA 1944; MA 1949. **Tutor(s):** S J Bailey. **Educ:** Hamer House Preparatory School, Rochdale; Arnold School, Blackpool.

MILLS, Dr Ronald Hubert Bonfield (1941) Born 31 December 1921, 17 Norman Terrace, The Walk, Merthyr Tydfil; son of Lewis Mills, Chief Sanitary Inspector, and Margaret Ann Bonfield. **Subject(s):** Natural Sciences; BA 1944; MA 1947; MB 1959; MChir 1959; MD 1959; FRCS. **Tutor(s):** R L Howland. **Educ:** Merthyr Intermediate Secondary School; London Hospital Medical College. **Career:** Consultant in Traumatic and Orthopaedic Surgery, Pontypridd; Assistant Traumatic Surgeon, East Glamorgan Hospital 1956–1968; Rhonnda Hospital Group 1968. Died 21 August 1989.

MILLYARD, Thomas (1912) Born 21 December 1892, Little Bridge, Norton, Herefordshire; son of John William Millyard, Land Agent, and Jessie Bull. BA 1919. **Tutor(s):** E E Sikes. **Educ:** Hereford Cathedral School. **Career:** Captain, Herefordshire Regiment, then attached King's (Shropshire Light Infantry) (wounded), WWI. **Awards:** Somerset Exhibition, SJC. Died 21 June 1970.

MILNE, George (1907) Born 31 January 1886, 61 Woodmill Street, Dunfermline, Fifeshire; son of Thomas Milne, Commercial Traveller, and Helen Campbell. **Subject(s):** Mathematics; BA 1910; MA (St Andrews). **Tutor(s):** L H K Bushe-Fox. **Educ:** Morgan Academy, Dundee, Scotland; St Andrews University.

MILNE, James Malcolm (1934) Born 7 October 1915, Stanmore, 26 Frederick Road, Wylde Green, Sutton Coldfield; son of James Logie Milne, Chartered Surveyor, and Grace Thornton. **Subject(s):** Mathematics/Law; BA 1937; MA 1941. **Tutor(s):** J M Wordie. **Educ:** Miss Goldsack's Kindergarten, Sutton Coldfield; Wylde Green College; Arden House, Henley in Arden; Malvern College. **Career:** Barrister-at-Law; called to the Inner Temple 1938; Royal Tank Regiment 1939–1945; Deputy Chairman, Bradford Quarter Sessions 1965–1970. Died 23 December 1976.

MILNE, Robert Arthur (1923) Born 23 April 1899, Cressbrook, Queen's Road West, Aberdeen, Scotland; son of Arthur Pledge Milne, Managing Director, and Kate Bridget Mann. **Tutor(s):** E E Sikes. **Educ:** Aberdeen Grammar School; RMA, Woolwich.

MILNE, William Robert (1934) Born 10 August 1915, Fitzroy Terrace, Prospect, Adelaide, South Australia; son of Clive Gordon Milne, Wine and Spirit Merchant, and Mary Jessie Cotter; m Diana Lee Massie, 5 September 1963, St Mark's Church, Sydney. **Tutor(s):** J M Wordie. **Educ:** Wykeham School, Adelaide; Riverside School, Adelaide; Queen's School, Adelaide; Geelong C of E Grammar School, Victoria.

MILNER, Professor Christopher John (1930) Born 3 April 1912, 64 Wilkinson Street, Sheffield; son of Samuel Roslington Milner, Professor of Physics, University of Sheffield, and Winifred Esther Walker; m Eirene Joyce Thorburn 3 June 1937; 2 sons (Hugh and Francis), 2 daughters (Jocelyn and Jessica). **Subject(s):** Natural Sciences/Physics; BA 1933; MA 1937; PhD 1937; FInstP 1952. **Tutor(s):** C W Guillebaud. **Educ:** King Edward VII School, Sheffield; Worksop College, Nottinghamshire. **Career:** Physicist, The British Thomson-Houston Company Ltd, Research Laboratory, Rugby 1936–1952; UC Berkeley; Part of the Manhattan Project 1944; Head of Physics Section, The British Thomson-Houston Company Ltd, Research Laboratory, Rugby 1946; Professor of Applied Physics 1977 (later Emeritus), University of New South Wales, Sydney, Australia. **Awards:** Scholarship, SJC 1929. Died 20 February 1998.

MILNER, Fred (1924) Born 10 January 1905, 25 Whetley Hill Manningham, Bradford, Yorkshire; son of David Henry Milner, Furniture Dealer, and Louisa Webster; m Mina Pickles; 1 son (Anthony), 1 daughter (Shirley). **Subject(s):** History; BA 1927; MA 1931. **Tutor(s):** E A Benians. **Johnian Relatives:** father of Anthony David Milner (1957). **Educ:** Grange Road School, Infant and Elementary; Lidget Green Council School; Bradford Grammar School. **Career:** Assistant Director of Examinations, Civil Service Commission 1930–1939; Various posts, Ministries of Information and Home Security, and Home Office 1939–1944; Director of Examinations, Civil Service Commission 1944–1948; Assistant Secretary, Treasury 1948–1952; Financial Adviser and Treasury Representative in the Middle East 1952. **Awards:** Scholarship, SJC. **Honours:** CMG. Died 4 September 1957.

MILNES, Dr John Norman (1935) Born 4 October 1916, Oaklands, Lockerbie, Dumfries; son of John Milnes, Lecturer in Mathematics, and Mary Letitia Norman. **Subject(s):** Natural Sciences; BA 1938; MA 1954; MB 1942; BChir 1942; MD 1948; MRCP 1947; FRCP 1970. **Tutor(s):** R L Howland. **Educ:** Birkby Council School; Huddersfield College. **Career:** Consultant Neurologist, Queen Mary's Hospital for the East End; Consultant Neurologist Metropolitan Hospital, London; Physician, West End Hospital for Neurology and Neurosurgery 1954; Medical Officer, Sunlife Assurance Society 1966; Consultant Neurologist, Barnet General Hospital and Luton and Dunstable Hospital 1968; Consultant Neurologist, Royal Free Hospital, London; 1979–1982; Honorary Consultant Neurologist, Royal Free Hospital, London 1982–.

MINNS, Derek Stewart (1947) Born 24 August 1929, 8 Tullie Street, Carlisle; son of John Hodgson Minns, Caterer, and Dorothy May Stewart. **Subject(s):** Natural Sciences; BA 1952. **Tutor(s):** G C L Bertram. **Educ:** Norman Street Junior School, Carlisle; Carlisle Grammar School. Died 1984.

MIRFIN, Joseph Colin (1913) Born 9 July 1894, 142 Industry Road, Sheffield, Yorkshire; son of Joseph Mirfin, Spring Manager, and Florence Mary Jane Brook. **Subject(s):** Mathematics. **Tutor(s):** L H K Bushe-Fox. **Educ:** Pomona Street Council School, Sheffield; Central Secondary School, Sheffield. **Career:** Second Lieutenant, York and Lancaster Regiment 1915–1916. Died 17 August 1917 (of wounds received in action 7 December 1916).

MIRZA, Ali Akbar (1901) Born 3 November 1880, Bombay; son of Husein Khan Mirza, Solicitor, and Khatun Nisa Khanum; m; 3 sons. **Subject(s):** Moral Sciences; BA 1903; BA (Bombay). **Tutor(s):** D MacAlister. **Educ:** Wilson College, Bombay; University of Bombay. **Career:** Called to the Bar, Inner Temple 1904; Fellow, University of Bombay 1909; Principal and Chair in Jurisprudence, Government Law School 1914–1919; Vice Chancellor, University of Bombay 1930–1931. **Appointments:** Honorary Consul, Persia 1905–1922. Died 8 March 1934.

MITCHELL, Alec Burton (1942) Born 27 August 1924, 66 Chesham Road, Bury, Lancashire; son of Ronald Johnson Mitchell, Civil Servant, and Millicent Annie Burton, Teacher; m Barbara Florence Archer, 1952; 3 sons. **Subject(s):** Mechanical Sciences; BA 1945; MA 1949; CEng; FRINA; MIMechE. **Tutor(s):** S J Bailey. **Johnian Relatives:** brother of Neil Burton Mitchell (1947); father of Neil Archer Mitchell (1973); grandfather of Claire Elizabeth Teall Mitchell (1998). **Educ:** Crumpsall Lane Elementary School, Manchester; Purley County School. **Career:** Aeronautical Engineer with Rolls-Royce Ltd, Hucknall, Nottinghamshire 1944–1946; Graduate Apprentice, then Gas Turbine Design Engineer, English Electric Company, Rugby 1946–1948; research into hydro-acoustic aspects of ships and submarine design, Royal Naval Scientific Service 1948–1984; Director, Admiralty Research Laboratory 1974–1977; Director, Admiralty Marine Technology Establishment 1977–1984.

MITCHELL, John Edward (1949) Born 19 November 1928, 89a Watch House Lane, Bentley, Campsall, Yorkshire; son of John Alfred Mitchell, Engineer, and Alice Long; m Anne Cunnane, December 1955; 3 children. **Subject(s):** Mechanical Sciences; BA 1952; MA 1956; EurIng; FICE; FIWES; MCSCE. **Tutor(s):** R L Howland. **Educ:** St Peter's School, Doncaster; Doncaster Grammar School; Colne Grammar School. **Career:** Senior Engineer, Binnie & Partners 1952–1960; Construction Manager, Richard Costain Ltd 1960–1963; Senior Engineer, Sir Murdoch McDonald & Partners 1963–1967; Managing Engineer, Rendel, Palmer & Tritton 1967–1974; Vice President, SNC-Lavalin, Montreal, Canada 1974–1985; Director, Engineering & Power Development Co, Balfour Beatty Engineering 1985–1988; Divisional Director, Rendel, Palmer & Tritton 1988–1990; Consulting Engineer with own practice 1990. **Awards:** Townsend Scholarship, SJC 1946.

MITCHELL, John Stewart (1902) Born 2 March 1878, 22 King Street, Peterhead, Aberdeen; son of George Mitchell, Shipmaster, and Jessie Margaret Stewart. BSc (Glasgow). **Tutor(s):** D MacAlister. **Educ:** Glasgow High School; Glasgow University.

MITCHELL, Professor Joseph Stanley (1928) Born 22 July 1909, 211 Charles Road, Aston, Birmingham, Warwickshire; son of Joseph Brown Mitchell, Headmaster, and Ethel Maud Mary Arnold; m (Lilian) Mary Buxton, 1934 (d 13 January 1983); 1 son (Christopher), 1 daughter (Janet). **Subject(s):** Natural Sciences; BA 1931; MA 1935; BChir 1934; MB 1934; PhD 1937; MD 1957; DMR (London) 1943; Hon DSc (Birmingham) 1958; MRCP 1956; FRCP 1958; FFR 1954; FRS 1952. **Tutor(s):** M P Charlesworth. **Educ:** Yardley Road Council School, Birmingham; Camp Hill Grammar School; King Edward's School, Birmingham; Birmingham University. **Career:** House Physician, Birmingham General Hospital 1934; Beit Memorial Research Fellow, Colloid Science Laboratory, Cambridge; Title A Fellow 1936–1943, Supervisor in Physiology and Pathology 1938–1946, SJC; Resident Radiological Officer, Christie Hospital, Manchester 1937–1938; Director, Radiotherapeutic Unit, Addenbrooke's Hospital, Cambridge 1943; Title E Fellow, SJC 1943–1946 (leave of absence while on work of national importance in Canada 1944–1946); in charge of medical investigations, Montreal Laboratory of the British and Canadian Atomic Energy Plant 1944–1946; Professor of Radiotherapeutics 1946–1957, Regius Professor of Physic 1957–1975 (Emeritus 1975), Professor of Radiotherapeutics 1975–1976, University of Cambridge; Title C Fellow, SJC 1946–1976; Title D Fellow, SJC 1976–1987. **Appointments:** Honorary Consultant to the Ministry of Supply; President, British Section, Anglo-German Medical Society; Dunham Lecturer, Harvard 1958; Honorary Member, German Roentgen Society; Linacre Lecturer 1970; Foreign Fellow, Indian National Science Academy 1976; President, South East Cambridgeshire Liberal Association. **Awards:** Scholarship, SJC; Pirogoff Medal, USSR Academy of Medical Sciences 1967. **Honours:** CBE 1951. **Publications:** *Studies on Therapeutics*, 1961; *Cancer: If Curable, Why Not Cured?*, 1971. Died 22 February 1987.

MITCHELL, Lawrence John (1919) Born 15 September 1901, Oakville, Brockholes, Thurstonland, Yorkshire; son of Isaac Mitchell, Millwright, and Elizabeth Emma Dickinson. **Tutor(s):** E A Benians. **Educ:** New College, Harrogate. Died 1963.

MITCHELL, Neil Burton (1947) Born 22 November 1925, Bury, Lancashire; son of Ronald Johnson Mitchell, Civil Servant, HM Stationery Office, and Millicent Annie Burton; m Rosemary Margaret Naylor, 8 October 1960; 1 son (Ian Robert b 6 January 1966), 1 daughter (Susan Mary b 24 August 1963). **Subject(s):** Law; BA 1949; MA 1954; LLB 1949. **Tutor(s):** F Thistlethwaite. **Johnian Relatives:** brother of Alec Burton Mitchell (1942); uncle of Neil Archer Mitchell (1973); great uncle of Claire Elizabeth Teall Mitchell (1998). **Educ:** Purley County School; Law Society School of Law, Chancery Lane, London. **Career:** Army Service 1944–1947; Solicitor 1950. **Appointments:** Borough Secretary, London Borough of Sutton, until 1983.

MITCHELL, Robert (1932) Born 14 December 1913, 49 Crofton Road, Plaistow, Essex; son of Robert Mitchell, Marine Engineer, and Elizabeth (Lizzie) Snowdon; m Reinholda Thorretta L C Kettlitz, 1946; 2 sons, 1 stepson. **Subject(s):** Natural Sciences/Geography; BA 1935; MA 1946. **Tutor(s):** J M Wordie. **Johnian Relatives:** father of Robert Mitchell (1965). **Educ:** Holburn Road Elementary School; West Ham Municipal Secondary School, Stratford. **Career:** Councillor, Wanstead and Woodford Council 1958–1965; Chairman and Managing Director, R Mitchell & Co (Eng) Ltd 1959–1981; Deputy Mayor, Wanstead and Woodford Council 1960–1961; Councillor, Greater London Council 1964–1986. **Appointments:** London Representative, Cambridge University Swimming Club 1953–1975; Vice-Chairman, Wanstead and Woodford Conservative Association 1961–1965 (Chairman 1965–1968, Vice-President 1968); Member, Committee, Crystal Palace National Sports Centre 1965–1988; Governor, Chigwell School 1966–1996 (Vice-Chairman of Governors 1968–1988); Chairman, Fire Brigade and Ambulance Committees 1967–1971; Member, London and South-East Regional Council 1969–1979; Member, CBI Committee on State Intervention in Private Industry 1976–1978; Chairman, National Joint Negotiating Committee for Local Authority Fire Brigades 1970–1971; Chairman, GLC 1971–1972; Chairman, Covent Garden Joint Development Committee 1972–1973; Liveryman, Worshipful Company of Gardeners 1975; Chairman, Professional and General Services Committee 1977–1979; Chairman, Greater London Joint Supply Board 1977–1979; Member, Smaller Firms Council, 1977–1979; Member, Policy Committee, Association of Metropolitan Authorities 1978–1979; Verderer, Epping Forest 1978–1985; Member, Lea Valley Regional Park Authority 1982–1985; Governor, London Ecology Centre Trust 1985–1988; Chairman, London Ecology Centre Ltd 1986–1988. **Honours:** Grand Officer, Order of Orange Nassau (Holland) 1972; Order of Star (Afghanistan) 1971; OBE 1984. **Publications:** *Bob Mitchell's Epping Forest Companion*, 1991; newspaper and magazine articles mainly on countryside and political matters. Died 12 November 1996.

MITCHELL, The Revd William Augustine (1904) Born 2 August 1884, 7 White Post Lane, Little Ilford, Essex; son of John Waldo Mitchell, Indian Tea Buyer, and Sarah Emily Norton; m Gunhilda Isabel; 1 daughter (Margaret). **Tutor(s):** J R Tanner; C E Graves. **Educ:** The House of the Sacred Mission, Newark. **Career:** Vicar, Mumby, Lincolnshire. Died 27 July 1966.

MITCHELL SMITH, John Young (1919) See SMITH.

MITCHESON, Dr Victor Steele (1919) Born 10 November 1901, Hem Heath, Trentham, Staffordshire; son of George Arthur Mitcheson, Mining Engineer, and Sarah Bardsley Gardner; m Mildred Mary Walker, 16 November 1927, St Mary Abbots, Kensington; 1 son (Martin), 1 daughter (Barbara). **Subject(s):** Natural Sciences; BA 1922; MRCS 1925; LRCP 1925. **Tutor(s):** E A Benians. **Educ:** Leas Court Preparatory School, Folkestone; Downs Preparatory School, Colwall; Bootham School, York. **Career:** Resident Medical Officer, Children's Hospital, Birmingham; House Physician, General Hospital, Birmingham; Medical Officer, Folkestone and Elham Infirmary, Folkestone Cottage Homes, and Elham Rural District Council Sanatorium; Public Vaccinator, Elham District 1925–1968; Chairman, National Health Service

Executive Council for South East London and Kent 1968–1971. Died 4 September 1971.

MOFFAT, Barry John (1942) Born 26 October 1924, 50 Lightcliffe Road, Palmers Green, London; son of Rennie John Moffat, General Manager, Coal Mines Scheme, and Lottie May Mizen. **Tutor(s):** C W Guillebaud. **Educ:** Franklin House Preparatory School, London; Highgate School; King Edward VII School, Sheffield.

MOFFATT, Dr John Logan (1940) Born 19 July 1922, Holly House, Cadishead, Lancashire; son of Charles Moffatt, Medical Practitioner, and Amy Muller McKitrick; m Penelope Anne Tomlinson, 1950; 3 sons (James, Edward and Robert), 1 daughter (Elizabeth). **Subject(s):** Natural Sciences/Medicine; BA 1943; MA 1947; MB 1947; BChir 1947. **Tutor(s):** R L Howland; S J Bailey. **Educ:** St Fillan's School, Heswall; Willaston School, Nantwich; Wycliffe College, Stonehouse. **Career:** House Physician and House Surgeon, Guy's Hospital 1947–1948; general medical duties, RAF 1948–1950; Dermatological Registrar, Addenbrooke's Hospital, Cambridge 1951–1954; GP, Cambridge 1954–1987. **Publications:** Dermatological papers, 1951–1954.

MOFFOOT, Francis George Robertson (1944) Born 24 October 1925, 5 Glossop Terrace, Cardiff; son of George Robertson Moffoot, Dentist, and Doris Hilda Jobey. **Tutor(s):** J M Wordie. **Educ:** Eaglescliffe Council School; Yarm Grammar School.

MOGRIDGE, Basil Fullelove West (1915) Born 10 September 1896, Scalford Vicarage, Melton Mowbray, Leicestershire; son of Henry Twells Mogridge, Clerk in Holy Orders, and Fanny Collard. **Tutor(s):** E E Sikes. **Johnian Relatives:** brother of Henry Theodore Mogridge (1910). **Educ:** St Christopher's, Melton Mowbray; Oakham School. **Career:** Second Lieutenant, 4th Battalion, Leicester Regiment, WWI. **Awards:** Scholarship, SJC 1914; Johnson Exhibition, SJC 1915. Died October 1915 (killed in action in France).

MOGRIDGE, The Revd Henry Theodore (1910) Born 29 October 1891, The Vicarage, Loddington, Leicestershire; son of Henry Twells Mogridge, Clerk in Holy Orders, and Fanny Collard; m Constance Doudney, 6 February 1918, Ab Kettleby. **Subject(s):** Classics; BA 1913; MA 1917. **Tutor(s):** E E Sikes. **Johnian Relatives:** brother of Basil Fullelove West Mogridge (1915). **Educ:** Stoneygate School, Leicester; Haileybury College; Leeds Clergy School. **Career:** Deacon 1914; Curate, Christ Church, Northamptonshire 1914–1917; Priest 1915; Artists' Rifles, WWI; Curate, Melton Mowbray 1917–1920; Rector, Goadby Marwood 1920–1926; Rector, Aldrington, Hove, Sussex 1926–1955; Rural Dean of Hove 1942–1945; Senior Air-Raid Warden, WWII; Provincial Grand Chaplain, Sussex 1948; Prebendary, Chichester Cathedral 1951; Rector, Thakeham, Sussex 1955–1961; Rural Dean, Storrington 1961. **Appointments:** Member, Hove Rotary Club 1930–1942. **Awards:** Sizarship, SJC.

MOLINS, Desmond Walter (1928) Born 23 December 1910, 26 Fairholme Road, Fulham, Middlesex; son of Walter Everett Molins, Manufacturer of Cigarette Machinery, and Ethel Elizabeth Humphreys. **Tutor(s):** C W Guillebaud. **Educ:** Beechmont, Haywards Heath; Repton School.

MOLLAND, Ralph (1945) Born 7 September 1923, 45 Rosslyn Park Road, Peverell, Plymouth; son of Archibald Molland, Civil Servant, Post Office, and Ellen Mary Hooper; m Barbara Loveday Moyse; 1 son (Richard), 2 daughters (Clare and Jane). **Subject(s):** History; BA 1948; MA 1980. **Tutor(s):** F Thistlethwaite. **Educ:** Hyde Park Elementary School, Plymouth; Devonport High School, Plymouth. **Career:** Army 1943–1945; Research Fellow, Department of Economics, King's College, Aberdeen 1948–1950; Lecturer, Department of Adult Education and Assistant Warden, Urchfont Manor, University of Bristol 1950–1953; Head of Planning/Marketing Manager, Clarks Shoes Ltd 1953–1968; Managing Director, Braemar Knitwear 1968–1970; Director, C & J Clark

Retail Ltd 1970–1984. **Appointments:** Member, Knitwear Economic Development Committee 1969–1970; Member, Footwear Economic Development Committee 1972–1974; Chairman, Mendip District Council 1982–1984; President, Footwear Distributors Federation 1982–1984. **Awards:** Minor Scholarship, SJC 1941. **Publications:** 'Agriculture 1793–1870', *The Victoria History of the County of Wiltshire*, Vol IV, 1959; *From Making to Selling: The Politics of Change 1953–1984*, Monograph, C & J Clark Archives, 1985.

MOLLET, Gerald Geoffrey Holman (1931) Born 19 November 1911, 8 Kingscote Road, Acton, London; son of Horace George Holman Mollet, Headmaster, Derwentwater School, and May Noakes. **Subject(s):** Modern and Medieval Languages; BA 1933; MA 1938. **Educ:** Latymer Upper School, Hammersmith.

MOLLOY, Peter Edward (1942) Born 9 October 1924, 9 Tapton Crescent Road, Sheffield; son of Edward Molloy, Statistician, and Hilda Sanderson; 4 sons. **Subject(s):** Natural Sciences; BA 1949. **Tutor(s):** C W Guillebaud. **Educ:** The Leys School, Cambridge; King Edward VII School, Sheffield. Died 13 July 1997.

MOLYNEUX, Paul Stanley (1945) Born 14 November 1927, 28 Rue Jean Godefroy, La Rochelle, France; son of Arthur Ellis Molyneux, Steamship Manager, and Clara Denson; m Eleanor; 3 sons (Jonathan, Julian and Dominic). **Subject(s):** Mechanical Sciences; BA 1949; MA 1958. **Tutor(s):** S J Bailey; R L Howland. **Educ:** Lycée de La Rochelle; Sutton High School, Surrey; Calday Grange Grammar School. **Career:** Civil Engineer; Partner, Binnie and Partners; Assistant Engineer, Tai Lam Scheme, Hong Kong 1953. Died 2 February 1985.

MONAHAN, David (1938) Born 1 January 1920, 143 Coldershaw Road, Ealing, London; son of John Clarence Monahan, Civil Servant, and May Robson. **Subject(s):** Modern and Medieval Languages; BA 1941. **Tutor(s):** C W Guillebaud. **Educ:** Northfields Elementary School; County School for Boys, Ealing. **Career:** Lieutenant, Royal West Kent Regiment 1940–1944. **Awards:** Major Scholarship, SJC 1937. Died 8 June 1944 (killed in action in Italy).

MONCK-MASON, George Evelyn Arthur Cheyne (1908) Born 12 April 1886, 27 Brondesbury Villas, Kilburn, Middlesex; son of Gordon George Monck-Mason, Colonel, RA, and Millicent Rose Astell; m (1) Jeanne Antoinette Isabelle Szymenska-Lubicz (d 25 May 1927), (2) Violet Scudamore. **Tutor(s):** J R Tanner. **Educ:** Dover College. **Career:** Student Interpreter in the Levant 1910; Acting Vice-Consul, Uscub 1911; Adana 1911–1914; HM Vice-Consul, Diarkebir 1914; posts in Alexandria, Slonica and Cavalla 1914–1916; Acting Vice-Consul, Saffi 1916; Acting Vice-Consul, Laraiche 1917–1919; Acting Consul, Benghazi 1919–1920; Acting Consul-General, Salonica 1920–1921; Acting Vice-Consul, Suez 1921; later Vice-Consul 1921; Skoplje 1923; Cettinje 1924; Constantinople 1925; Mazagan 1925; Vice-Consul, Port Said 1925; Suez 1925–1926; Constantza 1927; In Charge of Consulate, Aleppo 1928; Consul, Aleppo 1929; Tetuan 1933; Mosul 1938. Died 4 April 1939.

MONCREIFF, The Revd Francis Hamilton (1923) Born 29 September 1906, Law View, Dirleton Avenue, North Berwick, Haddingtonshire, Scotland; son of James Hamilton Moncreiff, Bank of Bengal, India, and Elizabeth Lilian Harvey. BA 1927; MA 1931; Honorary DD (Glasgow) 1967. **Tutor(s):** E E Sikes. **Educ:** St Ninian's School, Moffat; Shrewsbury School; Cuddesdon Theological College. **Career:** Missions in Rhodesia and South Africa; Ordained Deacon 1930; Curate, St Giles, Cambridge 1930–1935; Ordained Priest 1931; Curate, St Augustine, Kilburn 1935–1941; Curate in charge, St Salvador, Edinburgh 1941–1947; Chaplain, HM Prison, Edinburgh 1942–1951; Rector in charge, St Salvador, Edinburgh 1947–1951; Canon, St Mary's Cathedral, Edinburgh 1950; Edinburgh Diocesan Missioner 1951–1952; Bishop, Glasgow and Galloway 1952–1974; Primate, Scottish Episcopal Church 1962–1974. Died 3 September 1984.

MONCRIEFF, The Revd Kenneth (1919) Born 5 June 1899, 39 Westmorland Road, Newcastle upon Tyne, Northumberland; son of John Mitchell Moncrieff, Consulting Civil Engineer, and Elizabeth Marsden Allan. **Subject(s):** Modern and Medieval Languages; BA 1921; MA 1925. **Tutor(s):** E E Sikes. **Educ:** Newcastle Preparatory School; The Abbey, Beckenham; Charterhouse; University of Durham College of Medicine. Died 16 July 1989.

MOND, Henry Ludwig (1915) Born 10 May 1898, 66 Lowndes Square, Chelsea, London; son of Alfred Moritz Mond, Baronet and MP, and Barrister-at-Law, and Violet Mabel Florence Gretze. **Tutor(s):** E E Sikes. **Educ:** Hawtrey's Preparatory, Broadstairs; Winchester, College.

MONEY, Rowland Cyril Kyrle (1935) Born 4 July 1915, 1 Morley Cottages, Chislehurst, Kent; son of Lieutenant Colonel Roland Money, Army Officer, and Constance Daisy Griffin. **Subject(s):** Mechanical Sciences; BA 1937; MA 1942. **Tutor(s):** J S Boys Smith. **Educ:** Stonyhurst College; Sefton Place, Arundel; Beaumont College; RMA Woolwich.

MONK, Robert Richardson (1939) Born 30 March 1921, 65 Dalmorton Road, Wallasey, Cheshire; son of Robert Chadderton Monk, Mersey Pilot, and Margaret Elizabeth Pearson; m Elizabeth Mary Usherwood, 1951; 2 sons, 3 daughters. **Subject(s):** Mechanical Sciences; BA 1942; MA 1946. **Tutor(s):** J S Boys Smith. **Educ:** Somerville Preparatory School, Wallasey; Denstone College, Uttoxeter. **Career:** RAF Pilot 1941–1946; Engineer ICI Ltd 1946–1977. **Honours:** DFC 1945.

MONRO, Dr Peter Alexander George (1937) Born 11 February 1919, 72a Lexham Gardens, Kensington; son of Alexander Edward Monro, Instructor Captain RN, and Sylvia Grace Alice Templer Dew; m Helen Sarah Booth, 2 January 1952, Church of the Holy Sepulchre, Cambridge; 1 son (Alexander b 1958), 1 daughter (Sophia b 1955). BA 1940; MB BChir 1943; MA 1950; MD 1954; MSc (London) 1951; MRCS 1943; LRCP 1943. **Tutor(s):** R L Howland. **Johnian Relatives:** son of Alexander Edward Monro (1886). **Educ:** Stubbington House, Fareham; Kelly College, Tavistock. **Career:** House Physician and House Surgeon, Hertford County Hospital 1943; Ship's Surgeon, Merchant Navy 1943–1946; House Surgeon, Harold Wood EMS Hospital 1946–1948; Demonstrator in Anatomy, London Hospital Medical College 1948–1951; Ship's Surgeon, Merchant Navy 1950–1951; Demonstrator in Anatomy 1951–1955, Lecturer in Anatomy 1955–1982, University of Cambridge; Title B Fellow 1966–1984, Lecturer in Anatomy 1967–1984, Title E Fellow 1984–1986, SJC. **Appointments:** Director of Medical Studies, Selwyn College, Cambridge 1951–1955; Eli Lilly Travelling Fellowship (MRC), National Institute of Health and University of Pennsylvania 1954–1955; Supervisor in Anatomy 1955–1967, Director of Studies in Anatomy 1973–1981 and 1982–1984, SJC; Honorary Member, President and Honorary Secretary, British Microcirculation Society; Honorary Member and former Treasurer, European Society for Microcirculation. **Awards:** Raymond Horton-Smith Prize, University of Cambridge 1954. **Publications:** *Sympathectomy, An Anatomical and Physiological Study with Clinical Applications*, 1959; *Early History of the British Microcirculation Society 1963–1984*, 1984; *The Professor's Daughter: An Essay on female conduct*, 1995; *Reminiscences of a Ship's Surgeon 1943–1951*, 2000.

MONTAGNON, Arthur (1912) Born 30 March 1893, 83 Malpas Road, Brockley, Kent; son of George Edward Montagnon, Engineer, and Ellen Penfold. **Subject(s):** Mathematics; BA 1915; MA 1919. **Tutor(s):** L H K Bushe-Fox. **Johnian Relatives:** uncle of Phillip Edward Montagnon (1936); great uncle of Christopher Edward Montagnon (1962), Timothy John Montagnon (1965) and Peter James Montagnon (1968). **Educ:** Mantle Road, London County Council School; City of London School. **Career:** Master, Cranleigh School 1915; Blackburn Grammar School; Taunton School; Mathematics Master, Head of Mathematics Department, Leeds Grammar School 1949. Died 25 July 1978.

MONTAGNON, Philip Edward (1936) Born 8 September 1917, 6 Ashmead Road, Deptford, London; son of Edward Langlois Montagnon, Civil Engineer, and Alice Eliza Potter; m (1) Barbara Elizabeth Hutton Shuttleworth (d 10 August 1950), (2) Mary Catherine Field (d 11 March 2002); (1) 3 sons (Christopher, Timothy and Peter), (2) 1 daughter (Catherine). **Subject(s):** Mathematics; BA 1939. **Tutor(s):** J M Wordie. **Johnian Relatives:** nephew of Arthur Montagnon (1912); father of Christopher Edward Montagnon (1962), Timothy John Montagnon (1965) and Peter James Montagnon (1968). **Educ:** Cherry Orchard School, Charlton; St Dunstan's College, Catford. **Career:** Scientific Officer, RAE, Farnborough; Senior Principal Scientific Officer, Ministry of Fuel; Deputy Chief Scientific Officer, Ministry of Power; Richard Costain (projects) Ltd; Director, F H Wheeler Ltd; Deputy Principal, Henley Administrative Staff College. **Appointments:** JP. **Awards:** Scholarship, SJC 1936–1937; Wright's Prize, SJC 1939. **Honours:** OBE 1954. Died 1995.

MONTAGUE, John Cook (1947) Born 20 June 1913, 10 Oak Drive, Rusholme, Manchester; son of Charles Edward Montague, Journalist, and Madeline Scott. BA (Oxon) 1934. **Educ:** The Leas Preparatory School, Hoylake; St Edward's School, Oxford; Balliol College, Oxford. **Career:** Secretary, School of Agriculture 1947.

MONTEITH, Alexander (1924) Born 16 December 1906, Stanleigh, Kirkstall Lane, Headingley, Leeds, Yorkshire; son of John Monteith, Director of Monteith, Hamilton and Monteith Ltd, and Rose Adeline Petty; m Denise Adams, 1931. BA 1928; MA 1932. **Tutor(s):** J M Wordie. **Educ:** Moorlands School, Headingley, Leeds; Mill Hill School. **Career:** Head, Property Department, Prices Tailors Ltd, Leeds; Commission in 54th Medium Brigade, RA 1928–1931. **Honours:** MBE; TD and Bar.

MONTGOMERIE, William Stirling (1905) Born 8 June 1886, 25 Montague Street, Rothesay, Bute, Scotland; son of William Barr Montgomerie, Master Baker, and Margaret Stirling. **Subject(s):** Modern and Medieval Languages; BA 1908. **Tutor(s):** J R Tanner. **Educ:** The Grammar School, Manchester.

MONTGOMERY, William (1906) Born 26 May 1871, Liverpool; son of James Rentoul Montgomery, Shipowner, Managing Director, Dominion Line to Canada, and Eliza Mary Reid. **Subject(s):** Theology; BA 1909; MA 1913; BA (London) 1902; BD (London) 1904. **Tutor(s):** J R Tanner. **Educ:** Private Tuition, Hamburg; University College, Liverpool; Presbyterian College, London; Institut Superieure de Commerce, Anvers; Merchant Taylors' School. **Career:** Censor's Department, then Admiralty 1916; Foreign Office 1918–1930. **Publications:** *Primitive Christianity* (translation of Otto Pfeiderer); other translations. Died 1930.

MOODIE, John Greenshields (1915) Born 4 June 1894, The Bank of Scotland House, Dumfries; son of John Alexander Moodie, Solicitor, and Susan Davidson; m Brenda Margaret; 1 daughter (Susan). **Subject(s):** Law; BA 1920; LLB 1920. **Tutor(s):** L H K Bushe-Fox. **Educ:** Dumfries Academy; St John's College, Johannesburg, South Africa; Transvaal University College.

MOODY, Basil (1908) Born 13 October 1889, The Vicarage, Frensham, Surrey; son of William Herbert Moody, Vicar of Frensham and Rural Dean of Farnham, and Rachel Deedes; m Eva Mary Evans, 20 December 1919, St Andrew's, Watford; 1 son (John), 1 daughter (Julia). **Subject(s):** Classics; BA 1911; MA 1929. **Tutor(s):** E E Sikes. **Educ:** Allen House, Guildford; Marlborough College. **Career:** Assistant Traffic Superintendent, Indian State Railways 1912–1922; Lieutenant, IARO, France 1915–1918; Major, DADGT, 1st Army and Army of the Rhine 1918; Assistant District Traffic Superintendent, North Western Railway 1922–1923; Officiating District Traffic Superintendent 1923–1926; Officiating Deputy Director of Traffic and Statistics, Railway Board 1926–1929; Divisional Commercial Officer, North Western Railway 1929; Divisional Superintendent, North Western Railway 1934–1935;

Officiating Secretary, Railway Board 1935–1936; Chief Operating Superintendent 1938. **Honours:** VD 1925. Died 11 October 1963.

MOODY, Bernard John (1945) Born 18 August 1927, 19 George Road, Hay Mills, Birmingham; son of William John Thomas Moody, Butcher's Shop Manager, and Gladys Annie Hands; m Rosemary, 2 sons (Edward and Richard), 2 daughters (Catherine and Sarah). **Subject(s):** Natural Sciences; BA 1948; MA 1952; CChem; PCE (Birmingham); FRIC. **Tutor(s):** G C L Bertram. **Educ:** Marsh Hill Council School, Erdington; Handsworth Grammar School. **Career:** Headmaster, Sandown High School; Master, Highgate Public School, London; Master, Latymer Grammar School, London; Head, Science Department, Bristol Grammar School 1956–1961; Headmaster, Preston Grammar School 1961–1966; Headmaster, Maidstone Grammar School 1966–1971; Director of Studies, RMA Sandhurst 1972.

MOONEY, Flight Lieutenant Edmund Frederick William (1936) Born 8 October 1918, 4 Upper Peanbrook Street, Dublin; son of Edmund William Mooney, Solicitor, and Rose Mary Harley. **Tutor(s):** J M Wordie. **Educ:** Sandford Park School, Dublin; Beaumont College, Berkshire. **Career:** Flight Lieutenant, RAF 1939–1942. Died 18 September 1942 (killed in action).

MOORE, James Inglis (1930) Born 18 September 1911, Mytholme, Wilsden, Bingley; son of Sydney Moore, Commission Woolcomber, and Charlotte Rosa Hall; m Frances Elizabeth. **Subject(s):** English/Modern and Medieval Languages; BA 1933. **Tutor(s):** J M Wordie. **Educ:** Preparatory School, Charney Hall, Grange-over-Sands; Shrewsbury School. **Career:** Member, British Graham Land Expedition in Antarctica 1934–1937. Died 8 March 1989.

MOORE, John Graham (1923) Born 22 April 1904, 13 Hillsborough Road, East Dulwich, Surrey; son of Thomas Moore, Schoolmaster, and Alice Elizabeth Matthews. **Subject(s):** English/Modern and Medieval Languages; BA 1927; MA 1930. **Tutor(s):** E E Sikes. **Educ:** Dulwich Hamlet Council School; Alleyns School, Dulwich. **Awards:** Exhibition, SJC 1922.

MOORE, John Roland (1905) Born 5 December 1887, 10 Adelaide Court, Hove, Brighton; son of Francis Moore, Member, Stock Exchange, and Evelyn Mary Harris; m Margaret; 2 daughters (Priscilla and Ann). **Tutor(s):** L H K Bushe-Fox. **Educ:** Sutherland House, Folkestone; Marlborough College. **Career:** Member, Stock Exchange 1913. Died 4 August 1958.

MOORE, Dr Martin Edward (1932) Born 29 April 1914, 22 Hamilton Terrace, Leamington Spa; son of Martin Stothart Moore, Manufacturing Confectioner, and Elizabeth Louise Elliott; m Helen Akenhead, 1940; 1 son (Michael b 1948). **Subject(s):** Medicine; BA 1935; MA 1939; MB 1939; BChir 1939; MD 1951. **Tutor(s):** R L Howland. **Johnian Relatives:** cousin of Geoffrey John Myers (1935). **Educ:** Arnold Lodge Preparatory School, Leamington Spa; Mill Hill School. **Career:** House Physician Royal Hampshire County Hospital, Winchester 1939–1940; RAMC, Middle East, Western Desert, Italy, Greece, Mentioned in Despatches in light field ambulance, Lieutenant Colonel on demobilisation 1940–1946; Medical Officer, Papworth Village Settlement 1946–1948; Medical Director, Mass Radiography Unit, Leicester 1948–1951; Consultant Chest Physician, Medical Director Mass Radiography Unit, Southampton 1951–1979. Died 29 May 2004.

MOORE, Dr Reginald Mark (1902) Born 10 October 1883, 266 High Street, Exeter, Devon; son of Reginald Bowerman Moore, Music Teacher, and Maria Frances Rowe; m Rene. **Subject(s):** Natural Sciences; BA 1905; MA 1911; MB 1910; BChir 1910; MRCS; LRCP 1908. **Tutor(s):** D MacAlister. **Educ:** Exeter School. **Career:** Lieutenant, RAMC, WWI; Medical Officer and Surgeon, Malmesbury; Clinical Assistant, East London Hospital for Children; House Surgeon, Westminster Hospital, North Devon Infirmary, Dorset County Hospital. Died 26 January 1947.

MOORE, Thomas Robert George (1920) Born 15 October 1901, Beech Road, Northwick, Cheshire; son of Thomas Moore, Merchant and Ship Owner, and Mary Cram. **Tutor(s):** E E Sikes. **Educ:** West Hill Preparatory School, Repton; Repton School.

MOORE, Dr William Keith Stevenson (1936) Born 16 January 1917, 14 St Nicholas Road, Wallesey, Cheshire; son of William Leysen Stevenson Moore, Marine Engineer, and Grace Dingwall Anderson Mitchell; m Dorothy Margaret Brown, 1946. **Subject(s):** Natural Sciences; BA 1939; MA 1952; MB 1942; BChir 1942; FFOMI 1977. **Tutor(s):** R L Howland. **Educ:** Birkenhead School; Wallasey Grammar School; Manchester Grammar School; Manchester University Medical School. **Career:** Registrar, Department of Haematology, Manchester; Military Service in India and Burma, RAMC 6th Field Ambulance, then OC 4th Field Ambulance 1942–1946; Chief Medical Officer, The Boots Company 1953–1977. **Appointments:** JP, City of Nottingham 1964–1974; Medical Director, Milton Keynes Occupational Health Service 1977–1981. Died 8 August 1992.

MOORE, William Patrick (1939) Born 2 January 1921, Pretoria, Transvaal, South Africa; son of Philip Alan Moore, Stockbroker, and Magdalena Elizabeth Beyers. **Subject(s):** Economics. **Tutor(s):** C W Guillebaud. **Educ:** Middleburg East School, Transvaal; King Edward VII School, Johannesburg; Diocesan College, Rondebosch, South Africa. **Career:** Air Force operations in Italy 1939–1944. Died May 1944.

MORAN, Professor Patrick Alfred Pearse (1937) Born 14 July 1917, St Elmo Flats, Billyard Avenue, Sydney, Australia; son of Herbert Michael Moran, Surgeon, and Eva Everill Augusta Mann. **Subject(s):** Mathematics; BA 1939; MA 1943. **Tutor(s):** J M Wordie. **Educ:** St Stanislaus College, Bathurst; University of Sydney. **Career:** Fellow, University House, Canberra; Staff Member, Oxford Institute of Statistics; Professor of Statistics, Research School of Social Science, Canberra. Died September 1988.

MORDELL, Professor Donald Louis (1939) Born 12 September 1920, 56 Elmbourne Road, Balham, London; son of Louis Joel Mordell, Professor of Mathematics, and Mabel Elizabeth Cambridge; m Mari Stuart Miller; 1 son (Jeremy), 2 daughters (Alison and Catriona). **Subject(s):** Mechanical Sciences; BA 1942; MA 1946; Honorary Degree (McGill University) 1973; FCASI 1960; FRAeS 1967. **Tutor(s):** J S Boys Smith. **Johnian Relatives:** son of Louis Joel Mordell (1907). **Educ:** Ladybarn House School; South Manchester School; Manchester Grammar School. **Career:** Rolls-Royce Ltd 1941–1947; Associate Professor of Engineering 1947–1951, Thomas Workman Professor of Mechanical Engineering 1951–1957, Dean, Faculty of Engineering 1957–1968, McGill University; President, Ryerson University 1970–1974. **Appointments:** Visiting Professor, Singapore Polytechnic 1969; President, Canadian Society of Mechanical Engineers 1971–1973; President, Engineering Institute of Canada 1974–1975; Chairman, Commonwealth Engineering Education and Training 1975–1987. **Awards:** Scholarship, SJC. Died 8 August 1988.

MORDELL, Professor Louis Joel (1907) Born 28 January 1888, Philadelphia, Pennsylvania, USA; son of Phineas Mordell, Teacher, and Anna Feller; m Mabel Elizabeth Cambridge; 1 son (Donald), 1 daughter (Kathleen). **Subject(s):** Mathematics; BA 1910; MA 1945; Honorary LLD (Glasgow) 1956, (Mount Allison University, New Brunswick) 1959, (University of Waterloo, Ontario) 1970. **Tutor(s):** L H K Bushe-Fox. **Johnian Relatives:** father of Donald Louis Mordell (1939). **Educ:** Central High School, Philadelphia, USA. **Career:** Ministry of Munitions 1916–1919; Fielden Professor of Mathematics, University of Manchester 1923–1945; Sadleirian Professor of Pure Mathematics 1945–1953 (Emeritus 1953), University of Cambridge; Title C Fellow 1945–1953, Title E Fellow 1953–1972, SJC. **Appointments:** President, London Mathematical Society 1943–1945; Visiting Professor, USA, Canada, Africa. **Awards:** Scholarship, SJC; Second Smith's Prize, University of Cambridge 1912; De Morgan Medal, London Mathematical Society 1941; Berwick Prize 1946; Sylvester Medal, Royal Society 1949. **Publications:** *Diophantine Equations*, Academic Press, 1969; 'Reminiscences of an Octogenarian Mathematician', *American Mathematical Monthly*; (ed) 'Acta Arithmetica', *Journal of Number Theory*; also some 270 pamphlets and papers. Died 12 March 1972.

MOREL, Jean (1910) Born 27 November 1881, Strasbourg, Alsace; son of Isidore Morel-Gentzbourger, Merchant, and Julia Saint-Imier Schmertzerl. **Educ:** Gymnasium, Strasbourg; University of Strasbourg; Sorbonne, Paris.

MORGAN, Eric (1940) Born 23 June 1916, 35 Glwyd Road, Cwaun cae Gurwen, Glamorganshire; son of John Morgan, Coal Grader, and Mary Thomas. BSc (Bangor) 1938. **Tutor(s):** C W Guillebaud. **Educ:** Cwmammam National School; Amman Valley County School; University College, Bangor. **Career:** Education Officer, RAF.

MORGAN, Glyn James (1938) Born 14 March 1920, 113 Queen's Road, Battersea, London; son of Hugh Robert Morgan, Wandsworth Borough Councillor, and Ellen Ann Roberts; m Mary Thomas, 1953. **Subject(s):** Law; BA 1941; MA 1945. **Tutor(s):** C W Guillebaud. **Educ:** Tennyson LCC School; Manor House School, Clapham. **Career:** Called to the Bar, Middle Temple 1947; Senior Legal Assistant, Department of Education and Science 1952–1974; Assistant Commissioner Charity Commission 1974–1978. **Awards:** George Long Prize for Jurisprudence 1941.

MORGAN, John Ross (1939) Born 31 July 1920, 4 Well Lane, Higher Bebington, Cheshire; son of John Morgan, Schoolmaster, and Louisa Emily Edwards. BA 1942; MA 1946. **Tutor(s):** S J Bailey. **Educ:** King Edward VI School, Bath; Kingswood School, Bath. **Awards:** Exhibition, SJC.

MORGAN, Joseph Charles (1940) Born 2 April 1921, 6 Coventry Street, Kidderminster; son of Joseph Morgan, Bootshop Manager, and Florence Jones; m Marna Mary Walker, 1948; 1 son (Christopher), 2 daughters (Caroline and Sarah). **Subject(s):** Classics; BA 1948; MA 1950; BSc Economics (London); PGCE (London); DipEd. **Tutor(s):** R L Howland. **Educ:** Brierley Hill RC School; Brockmoor Council School, Brierley Hill; King Edward VI Grammar School, Stourbridge. **Career:** Major, South Staffordshire Regiment, Malaya and India 1942–1947; Director of Antiquities, Tripolitania and Cyrenaica 1948–1951; Classics Master, Lawrence Sheriff School, Rugby 1952–1955; Senior Classics Master, St Olave's and St Saviour's Grammar School, Tooley Street, London 1955–1963; Senior Lecturer, Department of Education, University of Warwick 1988. **Awards:** Minor Scholarship, SJC.

MORGAN, Michael Clement (1948) Born 15 February 1928, Brookfield, Bradfield Gardens, West Kirby, Wirral, Cheshire; son of Clement Morgan, Schoolmaster, and Mabel Edwards; m Margaret Bryant, 16 August 1952, Halifax; 2 sons (Christopher b 21 November 1955 and Richard b 4 February 1961). **Subject(s):** Mathematics; BA 1950; MA 1955. **Tutor(s):** J M Wordie. **Educ:** Hoylake Church of England School; Calday Grange Grammar School. **Career:** Second Lieutenant, RA 1946–1948; Assistant Mathematics Master, St Dunstan's College, Catford 1952–1959; Assistant Mathematics Master, Fettes College, Edinburgh 1959–1962; Head, Mathematics Department, Worcester Royal Grammar School 1962–1967; Headmaster, St Albans Boys' Grammar School/Verulam School 1968–1988.

MORGAN, Dr Roger Harold (1947) Born 22 June 1929, Cottage Hospital, Eltham, London; son of Alfred Morgan, Naval Stores Supplier and West India Merchant, and Dorothy Agnes Barnett; m Valerie Flello, Eltham, 17 October 1953; 3 sons (Nicholas b 1957, Steven b 1959 and Roland b 1961). **Subject(s):** Natural Sciences; BA 1950; MA 1965; MB 1954; BChir 1954; MD 1966; LMSSA. **Tutor(s):** G C L Bertram. **Educ:** Eltham College; Taunton School. **Career:** National Service, RAF Hospital, Ely; GP, Aston, Birmingham; GP, Hurst Park Avenue, Cambridge 1965–1989. **Appointments:** Chairman, Cambridge University Real Tennis Club

1990–1995; Chairman, Johnian Society 1992–1999; JP, Cambridge Magistrate's Court. **Publications:** *Tennis, the Development of the European Ball Game*, 1995, and several papers on the subject; *Real Tennis in Cambridge – the first Six Hundred Years*, Cambridge University Real Tennis Club, 2000; *Tudor Tennis*, Ronaldson Publications, Oxford, 2001. Died 1 March 2003.

MORGAN, Dr Rowland Lloyd (1946) Born 11 March 1923, 7 Valley View, Aberdare; son of Samuel Rowland Morgan, Manager, Co-operative Society, and Sarah Lloyd. **Subject(s):** Natural Sciences; BA 1948; MA 1952; BChir 1952; MB 1952; BSc (Wales) 1943. **Tutor(s):** G C L Bertram. **Educ:** Aberdare County School; University College of Wales, Aberystwyth. **Career:** Hammersmith Postgraduate Medical School; Westminster Hospital 1949; Consultant Radiotherapist, Royal Marsden Hospital, Sussex 1964. Died December 1979.

MORGAN, Thomas Kirk (1942) Born 7 June 1924, 5 St Bride's Road, Glasgow; son of Andrew Morgan, Haulage Contractor, and Jean Houston Kirk. BA 1946. **Tutor(s):** C W Guillebaud. **Educ:** Belmont House Preparatory School, Newton Meacus; Loretto School. **Career:** Apprentice on a farm, Fifeshire.

MORGAN, William Glyn (1932) Born 10 January 1911, Bank House, Ystalyfera, Swansea Valley; son of Henry Morgan, Manager, Barclays Bank, Aberystwyth, and Sarah Olivia Lewis; m Mair Edwards. **Subject(s):** Law; BA 1934; MA 1939; LLB (Wales) 1932. **Tutor(s):** C W Guillebaud. **Educ:** Rhondda County School, Porth; Ardwyn School, Aberystwyth; University College of Wales, Aberystwyth. **Career:** Articled to Mr F Hubert Jessop, of Smith, Davies and Jessop, Aberystwyth; National Fire Service 1941–1944; Deputy Town Clerk, Bilston, Staffordshire 1945; Town Clerk, Scarborough 1945–1974. **Appointments:** Captain, Bilston Golf Club.

MORGENSTIERNE, (Wilhelm) Herman Ludvig (1910) Born 16 April 1892, 40 Lorne Street, Leith, Scotland; son of Christian Morgenstierne, Norwegian Consul, and Fredrikke Gruner. **Tutor(s):** J R Tanner. **Educ:** The Western College, Harrogate; Newcastle Grammar School.

MORISON, Dr Charles Rutherford (1929) Born 27 April 1910, 1 Claremont Place, Newcastle upon Tyne; son of James Rutherford Morison, Emeritus Professor of Surgery, Durham University, and Charlotte Marie Simonsen. BA 1932; MA 1938; MB 1937; BChir 1937; MD 1947. **Tutor(s):** J M Wordie. **Educ:** St Anselm's, Bakewell; Merchiston Castle School, Edinburgh.

MORLEY, Derek James (1941) Born 20 November 1923, 26 Woodlands Road, Reigate, Surrey; son of Frederick Morley, Station Master, and Dora May Head. **Tutor(s):** S J Bailey. **Educ:** Woodford House School; Midhurst Grammar School.

MORLEY, Gordon Harpur (1912) Born 8 May 1894, 48 Nottingham Street, Brightride, Bierlow, Sheffield, Yorkshire; son of Lancelot Arthur Morley, Registrar of Births and Deaths, and Louise Harpur Caldwell. **Subject(s):** Law. **Tutor(s):** E E Sikes. **Educ:** Wem Grammar School. **Career:** Second Lieutenant, Shropshire Light Infantry 1914, Far East and France 1914–1917. Died 30 December 1917 (killed in action).

MORLEY, John Austin (1942) Born 13 December 1924, 155 Ecclesall Road, South Sheffield; son of Austin Morley, Company Director, and Martha Bray. **Tutor(s):** C W Guillebaud. **Educ:** West House School, Millichope Park; Uppingham School. **Career:** Coldstream Guards Officer 1942–1946; Actor/writer. **Publications:** *The Magic of Houdini*, 1978; *The Performing Arts*, 1980. Died 16 July 1994.

MORLEY, Richard Brès (1936) Born 25 February 1917, Kent House, Falkland Road, Torquay; son of Cyril Savage Morley, Architect, and Hélène Adèle Brès; m Irene; 1 son (Vincent). **Subject(s):** English; BA

1939; MA 1946. **Tutor(s):** C W Guillebaud. **Educ:** Gunnersby Preparatory School; Bradfield College. **Career:** Education Officer, Mauritius 1946. Died 18 April 1987.

MORPETH, Geoffrey (1923) Born 10 July 1905, 10 Sanderson Road, Newcastle upon Tyne, Northumberland; son of Joseph Morpeth, Leather and Rubber Merchant, and Margaret Dawson; m Micheline; 2 daughters (Gay and Kit). **Subject(s):** Law; BA 1926; MA 1930. **Tutor(s):** E A Benians. **Educ:** Newcastle Modern School; Durham School. **Career:** Articled to Hedley Booth, Solicitor, Newcastle 1926; Solicitor, Watson, Burton, Booth and Robinson, Pilgrim House, Newcastle upon Tyne 1930; Second Lieutenant, RE, TA (later Major) 1930; Admitted Solicitor 1930. **Honours:** OBE. Died 17 January 1989.

MORREAU, Cecil Joseph (1924) Born 23 April 1905, 139 Lapwing Lane, Didsbury, Manchester; son of Marcus Morreau, Shipping Merchant, and Alice Weinmann; m Cecily. **Subject(s):** Mathematics/Mechanical Sciences; BA 1927; MA 1931. **Tutor(s):** J M Wordie. **Educ:** Moor Allerton School, Didsbury; Bilton Grange, Rugby; Marlborough College. **Career:** Assistant, Messrs Thomas Worthington & Sons, Manchester, Architects 1928–1933; Research, Building Research Station, Watford 1933–1937; Private Practice, Guildford 1937. **Awards:** Scholarship, SJC. Died 2 March 1939.

MORRELL, William Bowes (1931) Born 18 February 1913, Burton Croft, York; son of John Bowes Morrell, Director of Public Companies, and Bertha Watson; m Kate Lisa Probst, 1939; 3 sons. **Subject(s):** Economics/Law; BA 1934; MA 1938. **Tutor(s):** J M Wordie. **Educ:** Junior Mount School, York; The Downs School, Colwell; Bootham School, York. **Career:** Commissioned, RA 1939–1945; Manager, *Nottingham Journal* 1947–1957; Manager, *Birmingham Gazette* 1948; Director, Birmingham Post and Mail Ltd 1957; Director 1957–1978, Managing Director 1965–1976, Vice-Chairman 1976–1978, Westminster Press Provincial Newspapers Ltd. **Appointments:** Chairman, Press Association 1970–1971; Chairman, Rowntree Social Service Trust. Died 11 December 1981.

MORRIS, Arthur Russell (1931) Born 24 November 1913, 8 Belgrave Terrace, St Albans Crescent, Woodford Green, Essex; son of Arthur Sinclair Fleming Morris, Manager for group of US Manufacturers, and Agnes Gordon. **Subject(s):** Modern and Medieval Languages/ Economics; BA 1935. **Tutor(s):** C W Guillebaud. **Educ:** Old Wells Kindergarten, Woodford Wells; St Aubyn's School, Woodford Green; Wycliffe College, Stonehouse.

MORRIS, David Henry St Lawrence (1940) Born 25 November 1920, 12 Church Lane, Handsworth, Birmingham; son of John Henry Morris, Steel Structural Engineer, and Catherine Elizabeth Hackett. **Subject(s):** Economics. **Tutor(s):** C W Guillebaud. **Johnian Relatives:** brother of Ivor St Lawrence Morris (1937). **Educ:** Stamford House Preparatory School, Edgbaston; Hallfield Preparatory School, Edgbaston; Ellesmere College, Shropshire; Lausanne School of Languages.

MORRIS, Desmond Roy (1945) Born 22 May 1927, The Vicarage, Great Clacton, Essex; son of Arthur Harold Morris, Fitzwilliam House, Clerk in Holy Orders, and Evelyn Ethel Woods; m Monica George, 1959; 2 sons (Christopher George b 1960 and Simon Abrahall b 1962), 2 daughters (Elizabeth Anne b 1966 and Judith Monica b 1968). **Subject(s):** Modern and Medieval Languages; BA 1951; MA 1955. **Tutor(s):** C W Guillebaud. **Johnian Relatives:** father of Simon Abrahall Morris (1981). **Educ:** Arnold House Preparatory School, London; Northcliffe House, Bognor Regis; Westminster School. **Career:** National Service, Intelligence Corps 1946–1948; Assistant Master, Clifton College Preparatory School 1953–1956; Assistant Master, Brentwood School 1956–1958; Assistant Master, Housemaster, Assistant Headmaster, Deputy Headmaster, Royal Hospital School 1958–1991. **Awards:** Marquess of Salisbury Exhibition, SJC 1945. **Publications:** *The Royal Hospital School at Holbrook 1933–1993*, 1994.

MORRIS, Frank Mosedale (1910) Born 29 June 1891, 115 Hope Street, Dukinfield, Cheshire; son of Albert Morris, Schoolmaster, and Jane Elizabeth Mosedale. **Subject(s):** Mathematics/Natural Sciences; BA 1913. **Tutor(s):** L H K Bushe-Fox. **Educ:** Albion Higher Grade School, Ashton under Lyne; Secondary School, Ashton under Lyne; Manchester University. **Career:** Assistant Secretary in the Treasury. **Awards:** Minor Scholarship, SJC 1909; Scholarship, SJC 1912. Died 23 June 1937.

MORRIS, Ivor St Lawrence (1937) Born 31 December 1917, 217 Barclay Road, Oldbury; son of John Henry Morris, Inspecting Engineer, and Catherine Elizabeth Hackett. **Subject(s):** Medicine/Engineering; BA 1942; MA 1963. **Tutor(s):** R L Howland. **Johnian Relatives:** brother of David Henry St Lawrence Morris (1940). **Educ:** Stamford House School, Edgbaston; Edgbaston Preparatory School; Ellesmere College. **Career:** Chairman and Managing Director, George Lane and Sons Ltd. Died 17 March 1991.

MORRIS, James Noel Frederick (1918) Born 24 December 1896, 67 Wycliffe Road, Shipley, Yorkshire; son of James Morris, Excise Officer, and Frances Mudd. **Subject(s):** Mathematics/Natural Sciences; BA 1921; MA 1925. **Tutor(s):** E E Sikes. **Educ:** Merchant Taylors' School, Crosby. **Career:** Assistant Master, Tonbridge School 1921–1960. **Awards:** Exhibition, SJC 1915. Died January 1981.

MORRIS, Philip Enoch (1914) Born 4 January 1888, 57 Inverness Place, Roath, Glamorgan; son of John Richard Morris, Plasterer, and Elizabeth Enoch. **Subject(s):** Mathematics. **Tutor(s):** L H K Bushe-Fox. **Educ:** Shlott Board School, Cardiff; Municipal Secondary, Cardiff; University College of South Wales. **Career:** Private, Suffolk Regiment, WWI.

MORRIS, Samuel Derek Drake (1929) Born 23 December 1910, 40 Ashburton Road, Claughton, Birkenhead; son of James Morris, Works Manager, Paint and Varnish Company, and Edith Lilian Browse. **Subject(s):** Natural Sciences; BA 1932. **Tutor(s):** C W Guillebaud. **Educ:** Birkenhead Preparatory School; Birkenhead School. **Awards:** Exhibition, SJC 1929.

MORRIS, Thomas David (1928) Born 28 July 1909, Hill Farm, Llanishen, Trellick, Monmouthshire; son of Benjamin Morris, Farmer, and Sarah Thomas; m Jacqueline, 1 son (Peter), 1 daughter (Rosemary). **Subject(s):** Mathematics; BA 1931; MA 1935. **Tutor(s):** J M Wordie. **Educ:** The Grammar School, Monmouth. **Career:** Leader, Schools Mathematics Project of East Africa, and Consultant, Ministry of Education, Kenya; Assistant Master, Aldenham School 1931–1933; Assistant Master, Charterhouse 1949–1966. **Awards:** Sizarship, SJC. Died 1990.

MORRIS, Thomas Norman (1907) Born 24 January 1889, Haddenham, Cambridgeshire; son of Thomas Morris, Farmer, and Emma Norman; m May; 1 daughter. **Subject(s):** Natural Sciences/Agriculture; BA 1910; MA 1919. **Tutor(s):** J R Tanner. **Educ:** Cambridge and County School. **Career:** Bacteriologist for Acetone Production, HM Factory, King's Lynn, then chemist in charge of laboratory at Halifax producing picric acid, WWI; Research Chemist, Chivers and Sons, Histon, Cambridgeshire until 1927; Head, Canning Section, Low Temperature Research Station, Cambridge 1927. **Awards:** Scholarship, SJC. **Publications:** *Microscopic Analysis of Cattle-foods*, CUP, 1917. Died 21 May 1977.

MORRISON, Alexander Tupman (1922) Born 16 February 1903, Carisbrook, Helensburgh, Row, Dumbartonshire; son of William Morrison, Woollen Manufacturer and Merchant, and Selina Sarah Lawrence. **Tutor(s):** E E Sikes. **Educ:** St Clare, Walmer; The Limes, Croydon; Marlborough College.

MORRISS, Walter Slade (1924) Born 27 April 1905, Uffington, Lincolnshire; son of James Morriss, Schoolmaster, and Alice Slade. **Subject(s):** Natural Sciences; BA 1927; MA 1968. **Tutor(s):** B F Armitage. **Educ:** Uffington School; Stamford School. **Awards:** Sizarship; Marquess of Exeter Exhibition, SJC.

MORSE, Wilfred (1915) Born 1 January 1898, Shelford Vicarage, Nottinghamshire; son of Edward St John Morse, Clerk in Holy Orders, and Myra Reynolds. **Tutor(s):** E E Sikes. **Johnian Relatives:** son of Edward St John Morse (1871). **Educ:** Bruncote, Scarborough; Riber Castle, Matlock; Marlborough College.

MORTENSEN, Donald Van (1945) Born 22 March 1919, Gayville, South Dakota, USA; son of Christian Marinous Mortensen, Agriculturalist, and Hazel Dell Van Osdel. **Tutor(s):** C W Guillebaud. **Educ:** Union School, Gayville; Gayville High School; Yankton College, South Dakota. **Career:** Technician, Fifth Class, US Army.

MORTIMER-JONES, John Bracken (1949) Born 15 May 1924, The Vicarage, Hamilton Road, Cambridge, New Zealand; son of Clive Mortimer Mortimer-Jones, Clerk in Holy Orders, and Mildred Bracken Matthews. Bachelor of Commerce (New Zealand) 1948. **Tutor(s):** J M Wordie. **Educ:** Hastings West State School; Hereworth School, Havelock; Wanganui Collegiate School. **Career:** Colonial Service Course.

MORTON, Lord Fergus Dunlop (1906) Born 17 October 1887, Wilmore, Kelvinside, Partick, Lanarkshire, Scotland; son of George Morton, Stockbroker, and Janet Gray; m Margaret Greenlees, 17 December 1917, Troon Parish Church; 1 daughter (Anne). **Subject(s):** Classics/Law; BA 1909; MA 1913; LLB 1910; Honorary LLD (Glasgow) 1951; Honorary LLD (Cambridge) 1951; Honorary LLD (St Andrews) 1956; Honorary LLD (Sydney) 1957. **Tutor(s):** E E Sikes. **Johnian Relatives:** uncle of James Broom Millar (1927); uncle of George Reid Millar (1928); cousin, once removed, of Jock Hargrave Scott-Park (1949); grandfather of Nicholas Morton Viney (1966). **Educ:** Kelvinside Academy. **Career:** Called to the Bar, Inner Temple 1912; Captain, Highland Light Infantry, then employed, War Office, WWI; Lord Justice of Appeal 1944; Lord of Appeal in Ordinary 1947–1959. **Appointments:** Honorary Fellow, SJC 1940; Chairman, Commission of Inquiry into Laws of Divorce 1951. **Awards:** McMahon Law Studentship. **Honours:** MC WWI; Kt 1938; Privy Counsellor 1944; Life Peerage 1947. Died 18 July 1973.

MORTON, George (1934) Born 24 April 1914, The Gables, Troon, Ayrshire; son of William Wilson Morton, Stockbroker, and Annie Macgill; m Jane-Ohna Campbell, 14 June 1947, St Peter's, Vere Street, London. BA 1938. **Tutor(s):** C W Guillebaud. **Educ:** Kelvinside Academy; Loretto School.

MORTON, George Trestrail (1921) Born 5 January 1905, Hartley Manor, Hartley, Longfield, Kent; son of Thomas Morton, Stockbroker, and Edith Maude Trestrail; m Joan Stafford, 3 June 1930, St George's, Hanover Square. BA 1925; MA 1931. **Tutor(s):** E E Sikes. **Educ:** St Nicholas School, Chislehurst; St Hugh's School, Chislehurst; Hildersham House, Broadstairs; Bradfield College. Died April 1977.

MORTON, Henry Albert (1947) Born 20 July 1925, Gladstone, Manitoba, Canada; son of William Morton, Farmer, Cabinet Minister, and Mary Matilda Manwaring. **Subject(s):** History; BA 1948; MA 1953; MA (Manitoba) 1947. **Tutor(s):** F Thistlethwaite. **Educ:** Livingstone School; Gladstone High School; Kelvin High School; University of Manitoba. **Career:** Flying Officer, RCAF, WWII.

MORTON, The Revd Howard Knyvett (1948) Born 3 March 1930, Moorlands, West Fields, Richmond, Yorkshire; son of Francis Knyvett Morton, Royal Corps of Signals, and Hilda Charlotte Rosa McNeile. **Subject(s):** Mathematics; BA 1951; MA 1967. **Johnian Relatives:** grandson of Patrick McNeile (1892); brother of Alan McNeile Morton (1964). **Educ:** Farnborough Grammar School; Lincoln Theological College. **Career:** Ordained Deacon; Mathematics Teacher, St Stephen's College, Delhi, Cambridge Mission to Delhi 1951–1954; Head of Research, Indian Institute of Public Opinion, Delhi 1954–1955; Curate, Hatfield Hyde, Hertfordshire 1957–1960; Head of Religious Education, Heaton Grammar School, Newcastle 1960–1966; Church Missionary

Society 1966–1972; Chaplain and Head of Religious Education, Edwardes College, Peshawar, Pakistan 1967–1972; Head of Religious Education, Heaton School, Newcastle 1972–1975; Head of Year, Heworth Grange Comprehensive School, Gateshead 1975–1983; Computer Literacy (own business) 1984–1988; Regional Officer, Oxfam 1988–1991; World Development Officer, Diocese of Newcastle 1991–1995. **Awards:** Minor Scholarship, SJC.

MORTON, Professor Robert Kerford (1949) Born 7 August 1920, Cootamundra, New South Wales; son of John Wilson Morton, Sales Manager, and Catherine Elsie Harper; 2 sons. PhD 1953; BSc (Sydney) 1949; FAA. **Tutor(s):** J M Wordie. **Educ:** Sydney High School; Hawkesbury Agricultural College, Richmond; University of Sydney. **Career:** Lieutenant Commander, RN 1940–1945; Senior Lecturer in Plant Biochemistry, University of Melbourne 1954; Waite Professor of Agricultural Chemistry 1960, Professor of Biochemistry 1962, University of Adelaide. Died 27 September 1963.

MORTON, The Revd Victor Chalmers (1906) Born 5 June 1887, Fulshaw Cottage, Fulshaw, Wilmslow, Cheshire; son of John Morton, Estate Agent, and Marian Imray Jenkins. **Subject(s):** Classics/Theology; BA 1909; MA 1913. **Tutor(s):** J R Tanner. **Educ:** Manchester Grammar School. **Career:** Ordained Deacon 1910; Curate, St John, Walham Green 1910–1913; Ordained Priest 1911; Curate, St Peter, Streatham 1913–1927; Permission to Officiate, Diocese of Southwark 1927–1928; Minister, St John the Divine, Earlsfield 1928–1934; Vicar, St Peter, South Wimbledon 1934–1942; Rector, St Andrew by the Wardrobe with St Anne, Blackfriars 1942–1962. Died 1972.

MORTON, William Douglas (1942) Born 11 June 1924, Killamarsh, Derbyshire; son of William Douglas Morton, Electrical Engineer, and Emma Elizabeth Jowitt; m Beryl, 1949, 2 sons. **Subject(s):** Mechanical Sciences; BA 1945; MA 1949; FREng 1978. **Tutor(s):** S J Bailey. **Educ:** Bentley New Village Council School; Doncaster Grammar School. **Career:** Graduate Apprentice, English Electric, specialising in Traction Division, then General Manager, Witton Works; Managing Director, GEC Telecommunications Ltd 1958; Group Chief Executive, Aurora Plc 1983–1989. **Appointments:** Member, Engineering Employers Federation; Chairman, Coventry EEF; Chairman, Chesterfield Scout Association. Died 17 July 1995.

MORWOOD, Bryan (1946) Born 22 December 1922, Main Street, Larne, County Antrim, Northern Ireland; son of Thomas Morwood, Secretary, John Kelly Ltd, and Jane Magee; m Muriel Davison, 1 September 1950, Larne, County Antrim; 3 sons (Charles Ian b 4 August 1951, Michael Bryan b 26 September 1953 and Stuart Neil b 4 May 1959). **Subject(s):** Natural Sciences; BA 1949; MA 1955. **Educ:** Larne and Inver Public Elementary School; Larne Grammar School; Glasgow University. **Career:** University Department of Education 1949–1950; Clifton College 1950; HM Colonial Service, Kenya 1951–1964; Head of Biology and Housemaster, Portura Royal School, Enniskillen 1964–1985 (Second Master 1984–1985). **Awards:** Scholarship, SJC 1949. **Honours:** MC 1945.

MOSELY, Dr Frederick Maurice (1906) Born 20 July 1886, 40 Boundary Road, South Hampstead, London; son of Alfred Ezekiel Mosely, Diamond Merchant, and Florence Louisa Amelia Roberts; m Stella Margaret Spurr, 24 August 1926. BA 1913; MRCS; LRCP 1917. **Tutor(s):** E E Sikes. **Educ:** Clifton College; Hopkins Grammar School, New Haven; Black Hall School, Connecticut. **Career:** Clinical Assistant, Genito-Urinary Department, London Hospital; Surgeon Lieutenant, RN 1917–1919; Medical Officer, Wandsworth and District Gas Company 1934. Died 15 September 1958.

MOSS, Bernard (1942) Born 22 March 1924, 12 Albion Terrace, Grantham; son of John Moss, Barrister-at-Law, and Grace Elizabeth Bullard. **Subject(s):** Law; BA 1945; MA 1948; LLB 1945; LLM 1985. **Tutor(s):** S J Bailey. **Educ:** Hilden Oaks, Tonbridge; St George's School, Tunbridge Wells.

MOSS, John Kennedy (1943) Born 30 June 1924, Reader Cottage, Burton, Milnthorpe; son of Frederick Parker Moss, Market Gardener, and Catherine Mary Read; m (1) Myna Hunt, 20 August 1948, (2) Mary; 2 sons (Michael and Malcolm), 2 daughters (Margot and Miriam), 1 stepson (Dillon), 2 stepdaughters (Kate and Julia). **Subject(s):** History; BA 1946; MA 1950. **Tutor(s):** C W Guillebaud. **Educ:** Morewood School, Burton; Heversham Grammar School. Died 10 June 1989.

MOSS, Norman (JORDAN-MOSS) (1938) Born 5 February 1920, 72 Louisa Street, Openshaw, Manchester; son of Arthur Moss, Sanitary Inspector, and Ellen Jordan Round, Professional Pianist; m (1) Kathleen Lusmore, 1965, (2) Philippa Rands, 1976, (1) 1 son, 1 daughter, (2) 1 daughter. **Subject(s):** Classics; BA 1941; MA 1945. **Tutor(s):** R L Howland. **Educ:** Varna Street Municipal Elementary School, Manchester; South Manchester Grammar School; Manchester Grammar School. **Career:** Ministry of Economic Warfare 1940–1944; Assistant Representative of HM Treasury in Middle East 1945–1948; Principal of HM Treasury in Middle East 1948; First Secretary (Economic), Belgrade 1952–1955; Financial Counsellor, Washington 1956–1960; HM Treasury, Assistant Secretary 1956–1968; Counsellor, UK Permanent Delegation to OECD, Paris 1963–1966; HM Treasury, Under-Secretary 1968–1971; Deputy Under-Secretary of State, DHSS 1971–1976; Deputy Secretary, HM Treasury 1976–1980; Consultant, Hambros Bank 1981–1984; Director, Crown Financial Management 1984–1990. **Appointments:** Director, 1928 Investment Trust 1981–1984. **Awards:** Patchett Exhibition 1937; Scholarship, SJC 1940; College Prize, SJC. **Honours:** CMG 1965; CB 1972. **Publications:** *Don't Kill the Cuckoos*, Images, Hanley, Worcestershire 1991. Died 27 May 1998.

MOSS, William Donald (1917) Born 3 February 1900, 2 Bedford Road, Hitchin, Hertfordshire; son of Herbert John Moss, Managing Director, W B Moss & Co, and Gertrude Jane Agnes Fowler. BA 1920; MA 1924. **Tutor(s):** E E Sikes. **Educ:** Grammar School, Hitchin; Kent College, Canterbury.

MOSSÉRI, Henri Samuel (1924) Born 24 May 1905, Cairo, Egypt; son of Victor Maurice Mosséri, Agricultural Engineer, and Esther Mosséri. BA 1927; MA 1931. **Tutor(s):** B F Armitage. **Educ:** Courtenay Lodge School, Sutton Courtenay; École Pascal and Lycée Janson de Scilly, Paris. **Career:** Agricultural Consultant and Estates Manager, Egypt Board Member of various Egyptian Companies; Honorary Lecturer in Physiology, Zurich University 1955. Died 3 March 1960.

MOSSMAN, David James (1948) Born 10 September 1926, 268 Gloucester Terrace, Paddington, London; son of Cyril Vernon Mossman, Pilot Officer, RAF, and Mary Sproat Williamson, Secretary. **Subject(s):** History; BA 1950. **Tutor(s):** F Thistlethwaite. **Educ:** Princeton University; Colet Court Preparatory School; St Paul's School; Tutorial College, Eaton. **Career:** Freelance Journalist, Australia and Asia; Intelligence Corps, Greece 1945–1948; Journalist, *Daily Telegraph* 1950; Foreign Office 1952–1954; Reporter, *Panorama* 1959–1969; Editor and Presenter, *Review* 1969–1971. **Awards:** Commonwealth Fund Scholarship 1950; Major Scholarship, SJC. **Publications:** *Beggars on Horseback*; *The Thing Itself*; *Rebels in Paradise*; *Lifelines*. Died 5 April 1971.

MOSSOP, John Coubro (1931) Born 28 January 1915, West End, Holbeach; son of Samuel Septimus Mossop, Solicitor, and Grace Dorothy Coubro; m Mary Bowser; 2 sons, 2 daughters. **Subject(s):** Classics/Law; BA 1935; MA 1938. **Tutor(s):** M P Charlesworth. **Johnian Relatives:** father of Samuel Charles Mossop (1963) and of Patrick John Mossop (1966). **Educ:** The Glebe House, Hunstanton; Uppingham School. **Career:** Admitted Solicitor 1938; Solicitor, Mossop and Bowser, Holbeach, Lincolnshire 1938; Principal Officer, Admiralty 1941–1945. **Awards:** Scholarship, SJC 1930; Johnson Exhibition, SJC 1930. Died 1 September 1996.

MOTT, Charles Edward (1916) Born 24 July 1898, 12 Petherton Road, Islington, Middlesex; son of Herbert Major Mott, Accountant, and Maud Mary Hember. **Subject(s):** Oriental Languages; BA 1921. **Tutor(s):** E E Sikes. **Educ:** Highbury Park School; Merchant Taylors' School. **Awards:** Scholarship, SJC 1915.

MOTT, Professor Sir Nevill Francis (1924) Born 30 September 1905, 20 Clarendon Road, Leeds, Yorkshire; son of Charles Francis Mott, Director of Education for Liverpool, and Lilian Mary Reynolds; m Ruth Eleanor Horder, 24 March 1930; 2 daughters. **Subject(s):** Mathematics; BA 1927; ScD; MA (Caius) 1931; FRS 1936. **Tutor(s):** J M Wordie. **Educ:** Beswick House, Stafford; Clifton College. **Career:** Lecturer, Manchester University 1929–1930; Fellow, Gonville & Caius College, Cambridge 1930–1933; Lecturer in Mathematics, University of Cambridge 1932–1933; Melvill Wills Professor of Theoretical Physics 1933–1948, Henry Overton Wills Professor of Physics and Director of the Wills Laboratory 1948–1954, University of Bristol; Cavendish Professor of Physics 1954–1971 (Emeritus 1971), University of Cambridge; Fellow 1954–1966, Master 1959–1966, Gonville & Caius College, Cambridge; Senior Research Fellow, Imperial College, London 1971–1973. **Appointments:** President, International Union of Physics 1951–1957; President, Modern Languages Association 1955; President, Physical Society 1956–1958; Chairman, Nuffield Foundation's Committee on Physics Education 1961–1973; Honorary Fellow, SJC 1964–1996; Fellow, Imperial College, London 1978; Honorary Fellow, Darwin College, Cambridge. **Awards:** Scholarship, SJC 1923; Hughes Medal, Royal Society 1941; Royal Medal 1953; Copley Medal, Royal Society 1972; Faraday Medal, IEE 1973; Nobel Prize for Physics 1977. **Honours:** Kt 1962; CH 1995. **Publications:** *An Outline of Wave Mechanics*, 1930; *The Theory of Atomic Collisions*, 1933; *The Theory of the Properties of Metals and Alloys*, 1936; *Electronic Processes in Ionic Crystals*, 1940; *Wave Mechanics and its applications*, 1948; *Elements of Wave Mechanics*, 1952; *Atomic Structure and the Strength of Metals*, 1956; *Metal-Insulator Transitions*, 1970; *Electronic Processes in non-crystalline Materials*, 1971; *Elementary Quantum Mechanics*, 1972; *A Life in Science*, 1986; *Conduction in Non-Crystalline Materials*, 1986; *High Temperature Superconductors and other superfluids*, 1994. Died 8 August 1996.

MOTTERSHEAD, Frank William (1930) Born 7 September 1911, 108 Church Lane, Handsworth Wood, Birmingham; son of Thomas Hastings Mottershead and Adeline Townsend. **Subject(s):** Mathematics; BA 1933; MA 1973. **Tutor(s):** J M Wordie. **Educ:** Handsworth Wood School, Birmingham; King Edward's School, Birmingham; Imperial Defence College. **Career:** Secretary's Department, Admiralty 1934–1956; Principal Private Secretary to the First Lord 1944–1946; Under-Secretary 1956–1958, Deputy Secretary 1958–1965, Ministry of Defence; Deputy Secretary, Ministry of Health 1965–1971. **Awards:** Scholarship, SJC 1929. **Honours:** CB 1957.

MOTTRAM, Dr James Cecil (1905) Born 12 December 1879, Stody Lodge, Holt, Norfolk; son of James Alfred Mottram, Yeoman, and Clara Ellen Swanzy; m Rhoda Pritchard; 2 sons (Moti and Standish), 1 daughter (Ursula). MB (UCL) 1903; MRCS; LRCP 1903; DPH 1907. **Tutor(s):** D MacAlister. **Educ:** UCL. **Career:** Lieutenant, RNVR 1914–1918; Director, Research Department, Radium Institute, London and Mount Vernon Hospital 1918. **Publications:** *Controlled Natural Selection; Some New Arts and Mysteries; Sea Trout and Other Fishing Studies; Trout Fisheries, their Care and Preservation*, 1928. Died 4 October 1945.

MOUNSEY, Wilfred Edmund (1922) Born 8 December 1902, 9 West Lawn, Sunderland, County Durham; son of John Harold Mounsey, Managing Director of a Cafe Company, and Jessie Corder; m Muriel (Molly) Grace Dymond, 21 December 1926, Friends' Meeting House, Ilkley; 1 son (John Dymond), 1 daughter (Hester Anne Dymond). **Subject(s):** English/History; BA 1925; MA 1947. **Tutor(s):** E E Sikes. **Johnian Relatives:** father of John Dymond Mounsey (1950). **Educ:** Tonstall School, Sunderland; Bootham School, York. **Career:** Senior English Master, Doncaster Grammar School 1926–1948; Senior English Master, Kendal Grammar School 1948–1963. Died 2 September 1995.

MOUNTAIN, Ralph Howard (1943) Subject(s): Modern and Medieval Languages; BA 1948; MA 1952. **Tutor(s):** C W Guillebaud.

MOUNTFORD, Basil Wilfred (1938) Born 22 March 1920, 123 Newton Road, Bedworth, Warwickshire; son of Harry Roden Mountford, Schoolmaster, and Lilian Mary Moon; BA 1942; MA 1945. **Tutor(s):** J M Wordie. **Educ:** Bewdley Old Grammar School; King Charles I School, Kidderminster.

MOUNTJOY, Victor Ulric Allin (1901) Born 15 August 1883, 1 Stafford Road, Bow, London; son of Richard Allin Mountjoy, Clerk in Civil Service, and Eliza Beech. **Subject(s):** Natural Sciences; BA 1904; MA 1908. **Tutor(s):** D MacAlister. **Educ:** Coopers Company School, Bow. **Career:** Master, County Council Technical School, Hyde, Manchester 1906; Monoux School, Walthamstow 1919.

MOWAT, George Gordon (1923) Born 12 April 1905, 24 Higher Bridge Street, Bolton, Lancashire; son of George Mowat, Medical Practitioner, and Annie Darlington. BA 1929; MB 1933. **Tutor(s):** B F Armitage. **Educ:** Bolton School; Shrewsbury School. **Career:** Ear Nose and Throat Surgeon, Bolton Group Hospitals.

MOWAT, Ralph Gunn (1920) Naval Officer.

MOWBRAY, Eric Douglas Wharton (1919) Born 6 July 1899, The Rectory, Hinton Parva, Wiltshire; son of John Robert Wharton Mowbray, Clerk in Holy Orders, and Elizabeth Annie Beridge. **Subject(s):** History; BA 1924; MA 1933. **Tutor(s):** E E Sikes. **Johnian Relatives:** son of John Robert Wharton Mowbray (1884). **Educ:** Redland High School; Clifton College Preparatory School; Oundle School.

MOWTON, Walter Edward (1911) Born 7 December 1893, 8 Holland Street, Chesterton, Cambridge; son of Walter Mason Mowton, Solicitor's Clerk, and Annie Eliza Taylor. **Subject(s):** Natural Sciences; BA 1914; MA 1919; DipAgr 1914. **Tutor(s):** L H K Bushe-Fox. **Educ:** Cambridge County School. **Career:** Christ's Hospital, Horsham; Private, Suffolk Regiment, Palestine and France, WWI; Assistant Science Master, Reading School 1919. Died 26 October 1972.

MOXON, Gerald Richard (1930) Born 14 October 1911, 8 Vernon Place, Canterbury; son of Reginald Stewart Moxon, Clerk in Holy Orders, and Ina Mary Rowson; m Margaret Forster Mohun; 1 son (Edward Richard b 16 July 1941). **Subject(s):** History; BA 1933; MA 1960. **Tutor(s):** E A Benians. **Johnian Relatives:** nephew of Thomas Allen Moxon (1896); cousin of Roland James Moxon (1938); father of Edward Richard Moxon (1960); cousin of Anthony Peter Hobson (1971) and of David Godwin Hobson (1976). **Educ:** Lincoln School; Woodlands School, Deganwy; Shrewsbury School. **Career:** Director and President, Institute of Personnel Management, and Personnel Director to United Glass Ltd. Died 6 September 1980.

MOXON, Roland James (1938) Born 7 January 1920, Shakenhurst, Kingsland, Shrewsbury; son of Thomas Allen Moxon, Headmaster of Denstone College, and Evelyn Goodwin Stroyan. **Subject(s):** History; BA 1941; MA 1945. **Tutor(s):** J S Boys Smith. **Johnian Relatives:** son of Thomas Allen Moxon (1896); cousin of Gerald Richard Moxon (1930) and of Edward Richard Moxon (1960); uncle of Anthony Peter Hobson (1971) and of David Godwin Hobson (1976). **Educ:** Highfield, Liphook; Denstone College. **Career:** HM Colonial Political Administrative Service 1941; District Commissioner, Gold Coast Colony – Dodowa, Kpandu, Aburi, Accra 1942–1948; Mayor, Accra 1947–1948; Deputy Director, Ghana Information Service 1948–1954; Director, Ghana Information Service 1954–1960; Bookseller, Publisher, Poultry Farmer, Restaurateur 1957; Ghana Civil Service 1957–1967. **Appointments:** Beachcomber Society, SJC 1938; Chairman, Oxford and Cambridge Society of Ghana; Member, Ghana House of Chiefs with title Nana Kofi Obonyaa, Ankobea of Aburi 1963–1999. **Awards:** Ghana 1991 Book

Award; 30 Years of Elected Chief (Singular Honour) 1991. **Honours:** OBE 1957. **Publications:** *Volta – Man's Greatest Lake*, Andre Deutsch, 1969, 1984; *The Baden Powell Ashanti Diaries*, Leo Cooper, 1999. Died 24 August 1999.

MUIR, Dr Ian Douglas (1945) Born 6 February 1922, Dunedin, New Zealand; son of Louis Fairfax Muir, Clerk, and Mary Porter Glenn; m (1) Margaret H Atkins, 1947; (2) Maisie D Lee, 1996; 2 daughters (Anne and Liz). **Subject(s):** Natural Sciences; BA 1947; MA 1965; PhD 1950. **Tutor(s):** J M Wordie. **Educ:** Kaikorai School, Dunedin; Otago Boys' High School, Dunedin; University of Otago, Dunedin. **Career:** Control Chemist, Milburn Lime & Cement Co 1938–1942; RAF 1942–1945; Demonstrator in Mineralogy and Petrology 1950–1955, Lecturer 1955–1989, University of Cambridge; Fellow and College Lecturer in Natural Sciences 1962–1989, Class E Fellow 1989, Selwyn College, Cambridge. **Appointments:** Tutor, Selwyn College, Cambridge 1966–1989. **Awards:** Bonney Award, SJC; Henry Humphreys Award. **Publications:** *4 Axis universal stage*, Microscope Publications Ltd, 1981. Died 22 February 2004.

MUKHARJI, Rabindranath (1926) Born 23 December 1906, Utturhara, Hooghly, Bengal, India; son of (Rai Bahadur) Surendra Nath Mukharji, Subordinate Judge, and Suniti Banarji. **Subject(s):** Natural Sciences; BA 1928. **Tutor(s):** J M Wordie. **Educ:** Ram Mohun Roy Seminary; Patna College.

MUKTADAR, Khawja Abdul (1942) Born 15 January 1919, Hyderabad, Deccan, India; son of Khaja Abdul Aziz, Judge of the Hyderabad High Court, and Amina Begum. LLB (London). **Tutor(s):** S J Bailey. **Educ:** St George's Grammar School, Hyderabad; Private Tuition, England.

MULHOLLAND, William (1910) Born 30 June 1891, Christ Church Vicarage, Gateshead, County Durham; son of Thomas Cromwell Mulholland, Clerk in Holy Orders, and Edith Davison. **Subject(s):** Classics; BA 1913. **Tutor(s):** E E Sikes. **Educ:** Christ's Hospital; Sedbergh School. **Career:** Lieutenant, Manchester Regiment, WWI; Schoolmaster 1930; Assistant Commissioner, National Savings Committee 1951. **Honours:** MC.

MULLENDER, Dr Pieter (1947) Born 18 July 1917, Amsterdam, Holland; son of Klaas Mullender, Official, and Grietje Beugel; m Fina Maria Eilander, 17 July 1951, Amsterdam; 3 sons, 2 daughters. PhD 1949; Doctor in Mathematics (Vrije Universiteit, Amsterdam) 1945. **Tutor(s):** J M Wordie. **Educ:** Vrije Universiteit, Amsterdam. **Career:** Lecturer in Mathematics 1949–1952, Professor of Mathematics 1952–1981, Vrije Universiteit, Amsterdam.

MULLIGAN, Terence Elphinstone (1949) Born 5 June 1926, Zenana Mission Hospital, Bangalore, India; son of William Graham Mulligan, Missionary, and Enid Eleanora Sanger-Davies. BSc (TCD) 1947. **Tutor(s):** J M Wordie. **Educ:** Campbell College, Belfast; TCD.

MULLINS, Hugh Thomas (1906) Born 20 June 1887, The Mole House, Hirstham, Walton, Surrey; son of Alfred George Mullins, Manager, Bank of Africa, and Amy Vigers. **Tutor(s):** L H K Bushe-Fox. **Educ:** St Andrew's Preparatory School, Grahamstown, South Africa; Marlborough College.

MULRENAN, Richard John (1930) Born 7 September 1912, Marshfield, Maitland Crescent, Colombo, Ceylon; son of Henry John Mulrenan, Stockbroker, and Rose Mary Annie Brown. **Tutor(s):** C W Guillebaud. **Educ:** Angusfield, Aberdeen; Kite Hill, Purley; Whitgift School, Croydon; Bedford School.

MUMFORD, Dr William Bryant (1919) Born 16 January 1900, Gable Nook, Wilbraham Road, Chorlton-cum-Hardy; son of Alfred Alexander Mumford, Physician, and Edith Emily Read; m Grace; 3 sons (Peter, Edwin and David), 2 daughters (Barbara and Daphne). **Subject(s):** Mathematics; BA 1920; MA 1925; PhD (Toronto); Teacher's Diploma

(London) 1923. **Tutor(s):** E E Sikes. **Educ:** Manchester Grammar School; University of London. **Career:** Midshipman, RN 1918–1919; Assistant Master, Education Department, Tanganyika Territory 1923–1934; Head of Colonial Department, Institute of Education 1934–1941. **Publications:** Founder, *Colonial Review*. Died 28 January 1951.

MUNCEY, The Revd Edward Howard Parker (1905) Born 12 January 1886, 75 Victoria Road, Willesden, Middlesex; son of Frederick William Muncey, Auctioneer, and Gertrude Neale. **Subject(s):** Classics; BA 1908; MA 1912. **Tutor(s):** C E Graves; J R Tanner. **Educ:** Highgate School. **Career:** Ordained Deacon 1909; Curate, St Luke, Chelsea 1909–1910; Ordained Priest 1910; Minor Canon, Windsor 1910–1911; Priest Vicar, Chichester Cathedral and Master, Choir School 1911–1913; Chaplain, Magdalene College, Cambridge 1913–1915; Assistant Master, Wellington College 1915–1930; Headmaster, King's School, Gloucester and Precentor, Gloucester Cathedral 1930–1942; Licensed Preacher, Diocese of Gloucester 1942–1949; Vicar, Haresfield and Rector, Harescombe 1949–1954. **Appointments:** Choral Studentship, SJC. **Awards:** Second Winchester Reading Prize, University of Cambridge 1908; Choral Studentship, SJC. Died 12 December 1954.

MUNDY, Wilfrid Horace (1942) Born 21 January 1925, Fleming, Saskatchewan, Canada; son of Horace James Mundy, Clerk in Holy Orders, and Rosalind Arber. **Subject(s):** Economics/History; BA 1948. **Tutor(s):** C W Guillebaud. **Educ:** Garden Village Preparatory School, Hull; Hymers College, Hull.

MUNIR, The Hon Mr Mehmed Nedjati (1944) Born 7 December 1923, Nicosia, Cyprus; son of Sir Mehmed Munir Bey, Barrister-at-Law, and Vesime Hanum; m Hatice Osman Cemal, 24 October 1948; 1 son, 2 daughters. **Subject(s):** Law; BA 1946; MA 1950; Honorary Doctor of Public Administration (Ninth September University, Izmir, Turkey) 1989. **Tutor(s):** S J Bailey. **Johnian Relatives:** brother of Ali Ergun Munir (1952); father of Osman Erol Nedjati Munir Ertekun (1970). **Educ:** Froebel School, Kyrenia; Brentwood School. **Career:** Cyprus Volunteer Force and Attorney General's Office, Cyprus 1941–1943; Called to the Bar, Gray's Inn 1946; Solicitor General of Cyprus 1952; QC for Cyprus 1957; Coordinating Ambassador and Special Adviser on Political Affairs to His Excellency President Denktas, the President of the Turkish Republic of Northern Cyprus 1984–1999. **Honours:** OBE 1957. **Publications:** *Inter-Communal talks and the Cyprus Problem*, 1977; *Observations on UN General Assembly*, 1979; *In Search of a Negotiated Cyprus Settlement*, 1981; *The Cyprus Dispute and the Birth of the Turkish Republic of Northern Cyprus*, 1984; various other papers relating to Cyprus.

MUNNINGS, Frederick William (1925) Born 23 June 1907, Aswarby Lincolnshire; son of Frederick Charles Munnings, Gardener, and Lizzie Tindall. BA 1929. **Tutor(s):** J M Wordie. **Educ:** Carre's Grammar School, Sleaford.

MUNRO, John Gray (1930) Born 24 March 1913, 56 Polmuir Road, Aberdeen; son of John Donald Munro, Advocate, and Jane Gray; m Rita May. **Subject(s):** Mechanical Sciences; BA 1934; MA 1938. **Tutor(s):** J M Wordie. **Educ:** Albyn Place School, Aberdeen; The Grammar School, Aberdeen. **Career:** 47 Squadron, RAF 1935–1938; Research and Development Department, Air Ministry 1937–1940; Wing Commander, RAF 1939–1945; RAF, South East Asia and UK 1945–1949. Died 23 January 1951.

MUNSEY, David Thomas Foster (1929) Born 8 December 1911, 51 Bateman Street, Cambridge; son of Ellis Parker Munsey, Shopkeeper and Jeweller, and Katherine Maude Foster; m Sylvia Frances Sawyer, 6 August 1947; 2 sons (Nigel and Myles). **Subject(s):** Mathematics/Geography; BA 1933; MA 1937; FRICS. **Tutor(s):** C W Guillebaud. **Educ:** St Faith's School, Cambridge; Upton School, Walmer; Gresham's School, Holt. **Career:** Sudan Survey Department 1935–1959; Lecturer, Land Surveying, RMCS, Shrivenham 1959–1976. Died 10 December 1979.

MUNZ, Professor Peter (1946) Born 12 May 1921, 11 Zwickauer Strasse, Chemnitz, Germany; son of Leo Münz, Doctor of Medicine, and Agnes Lichtenstein; m Anne Vickerman, 21 September 1950; 1 son (Jacob). **Subject(s):** History; PhD 1949; MA (New Zealand). **Tutor(s):** F Thistlethwaite. **Educ:** Scuola Alpina Monte San Vigilio, Merano, Italy; Liceo Scientifico, Florence, Italy; Canterbury College, Christchurch, New Zealand. **Career:** Senior Lecturer and Associate Professor in History 1948–1968, Professor of History 1968–1986 (Emeritus 1986–), Victoria University, Wellington, New Zealand. **Publications:** *The Place of Hooker in the History of Thought*, 1952; *Problems of Religious Knowledge*, 1959; *The Origin of the Carolingian Empire*, 1960; *Relationship and Solitude: A Study of the Relationship between Ethics, Metaphysics and Myth*, 1964; *Frederick Barbarossa: a Study in Medieval Politics*, 1968; *Life in the Age of Charlemagne*, 1968; *When the Golden Bough Breaks*, 1973; (with G M Ellis) *Bose's Life of Alexander III*, 1973; *The Shapes of Time, A New Look at the Philosophy of History*, 1976; *Our Knowledge of the Growth of Knowledge*, 1985; *Philosophical Darwinism*, 1993; *Critique of Impure Reason*, 1999; *Beyond Wittgenstein's Poker: New Light on Popper and Wittgenstein*, 2004; many papers in learned journals; editor of several books; translator of several books from Italian and German.

MURDOCK, Dr Charles Rutherford (1932) Born 6 May 1914, Norwyn, Hampton Park, Belfast; son of John Murdock, Linen Merchant, and Norah Bland McDade; m Eirene Baird; 1 son. MB, BChir, BAO (Belfast) 1939; MD 1944. **Tutor(s):** J M Wordie. **Educ:** Ashleigh House School, Belfast; Royal Belfast Academical Institution. **Career:** House Physician and Resident Pathologist, Royal Victoria Hospital, Belfast 1939–1953; Pathologist, Emergency Hospital, Musgrave Park 1944; Bacteriologist, Northern Ireland Public Health Laboratory 1948; Consultant Pathologist, Belfast City Hospital 1953–1963; Director, Emergency Bed Service 1963–1968. **Appointments:** Musgrave Studentship 1942. Died 10 June 1968.

MURPHY, William Martin (1934) Born 25 April 1915, 75 Highfield Road, Dublin; son of Christopher Joseph Murphy, Newspaper Proprietor, and Mary Josephine Markey. **Tutor(s):** R L Howland. **Educ:** Sandford Park School, Dublin; St Gerard's School, Dublin; Ampleforth College, York.

MURRAY, Professor Albert Victor (1943) Born 1 September 1890, Choppington, Bedlington, Northumberland; son of John Ridley Murray, Grocer, and Elizabeth Lawther; m Winifred Seares, 1923; 2 sons, 2 daughters. BD 1945; MA (by incorporation); MA (Oxon) 1931; BLitt (Oxon) 1931. **Johnian Relatives:** father of John Seares Murray (1951). **Educ:** Choppington National School; Morpeth Grammar School; Magdalen College, Oxford; Mansfield College, Oxford. **Career:** Lecturer in Education, Selly Oak Colleges, Birmingham 1922; Professor of Education, University College, Hull 1933–1945; President, Cheshunt College, Cambridge 1945–1959. **Appointments:** Chairman, World Institute of Christian Education, Toronto. **Publications:** Several, including *The School in the Bush*, 1929; *Personal Experience and the Historic Faith*, 1939. Died 10 June 1967.

MURRAY, Bruce (1938) Born 21 July 1919, San José, Costa Rica; son of Alexander Murray, Coffee Exporter and British Vice Consul, and Adriana Quiros. **Subject(s):** Modern and Medieval Languages. **Educ:** St Mary's School, Roxburghshire; Sedbergh School. **Career:** Second Lieutenant, King's Own Scottish Borderers 1939–1940. **Awards:** Lupton and Hebblethwaite Exhibition, SJC. Died 1940 (killed in action).

MURRAY, Professor Hugh Alexander (1929) Born 13 April 1907, 6 Murray Terrace, St Machar, Aberdeen; son of Henry Murray, Fish Curer, and Jane Anne Grieg; m Gerda; 1 son, 2 daughters. **Subject(s):** Classics; BA 1931; MA (Aberdeen). **Tutor(s):** M P Charlesworth. **Educ:** Ferryhill Elementary School, Aberdeen; Aberdeen Grammar School; Aberdeen University. **Career:** Assistant Master, Aberdeen Grammar School; Assistant in the Greek Department, Aberdeen University 1934–1938; Lecturer in Classics, Durham University 1938; Professor of Classics,

Victoria University of Wellington, New Zealand 1946–1972. **Awards:** Craven Studentship, University of Cambridge 1931; Wright's Prize, SJC; Strathcona Studentship, SJC. Died 1973.

MURRAY, James Gibbes (1937) Born 2 November 1913, Commercial Bank House, Biggar; son of John Murray, Bank Agent, and Janet Murray; m (1) Joyce, (2) Marian; 2 sons, 2 daughters. MRCVS. **Tutor(s):** C W Guillebaud. **Educ:** Biggar Hill School; Kilmarnock Academy; George Watson's College; Glasgow Veterinary College; University of Manchester. **Career:** Department of Veterinary Pathology, University of Cambridge. Died 14 December 1990.

MURRAY, John Lamb Blackwood (1925) Born 12 December 1907, 92 Camperdown Road, Scotstown, Glasgow, Renfrewshire; son of Thomas Blackwood Murray, Chairman and Managing Director, Albion Motor Car Company Ltd, and Henrietta Wilhelmina Rusack. **Tutor(s):** J M Wordie. **Johnian Relatives:** brother of William Rusack Blackwood Murray (1928). **Educ:** Kelvinside Academy, Glasgow; Shrewsbury School.

MURRAY, Kenneth Walter (1927) Born 17 January 1909, 27 Pelham Road, Norwich, Norfolk; son of Walter Thomas Murray, Commercial Clerk and Manager, and May Elizabeth Steward. **Subject(s):** History; BA 1931. **Tutor(s):** E A Benians. **Johnian Relatives:** father of Ian Alan Kenneth Murray (1957). **Educ:** Angel Road Elementary School, Norwich; King Edward VI School, Norwich.

MURRAY, Michael Graeme (1941) Born 27 September 1923, 13b Earl's Court Square, London; son of David Charles Graeme Murray, in commerce, Major, RE and RFC, and Countess Elena Maia Sollohub; m Catherine Parker, 1949; 3 daughters. **Subject(s):** Architecture. BA 1947; MA 1949; ARIBA 1950; FRSA 1966; FRIBA 1970. **Tutor(s):** C W Guillebaud. **Educ:** Edinburgh Academy. **Career:** Private, Royal Scots (War Training Reserve) 1941–1942; RE (demobilised as Major) 1942–1947; Field Service with East Africa Engineers in Kenya, active service in Burma Campaign with 11th (East Africa) Division, (14th Army); Chartered Architect in salaried employment 1950–1956; Partner, Hening & Chitty, Architects, London 1956–1959; Partner, Lerche-Thomsen & Murray, Architects 1959–1977; Surveyor to the Honourable Society of The Middle Temple 1977–1988. **Appointments:** Liveryman, The Worshipful Company of Clockmakers 1968; Honorary Member of the Middle Temple 1988. **Publications:** *Middle Temple Hall – An Architectural Appreciation*, Middle Temple 1989.

MURRAY, Dr Ronald Ormiston (1932) Born 14 November 1912, 71 Wilson Street, Glasgow; son of John Murray, Master Grocer, and Elizabeth Ormiston McGibbon; m (1) Catherine Joan Suzette (Susan) Gauvain, 1940 (d 1980), (2) Jane Mathewson (née Tierney), 1981; (1) 1 son, 2 daughters. BA 1935; MA 1959; MB 1938; BChir 1938; MD 1959; FRCPE; DMR; FRCR. **Tutor(s):** R L Howland. **Educ:** Glasgow Academy; Loretto School, Musselburgh; Glasgow University. **Career:** Casualty Officer and Honorary Surgeon-Major, St Thomas' Hospital 1938–1939; RAMC (TA), MO 2nd Battalion The London Scottish, Honorary Lieutenant Colonel Associate 1939–1946; Professor, Radiology, American University Hospital, Beirut 1954–1956; Associate Editor, *British Journal of Radiology* 1959–1971; Senior Lecturer in Orthopaedic Radiology, Institute of Orthopaedics, London University 1963–1977. **Appointments:** Consultant Radiologist, Lord Mayor Treloar's Orthopaedic Hospital, Alton, and Heatherwood Hospital, Ascot 1951–1977; Consultant Radiologist, Royal National Orthopaedic Hospital 1956–1977; Honorary Member, Mexican and Peruvian Radiology Societies 1968; Honorary Fellow, American College of Radiology 1969; Robert Jones Lecturer, RCS 1973; Founder Vice-President, International Skeletal Society 1973 (President 1977–1978); Corresponding Member, American Roentgen Ray Society 1973; Baker Travelling Professor in Radiology, Australasia 1974; Caldwell Lecturer, American Roentgen Ray Society 1975; Honorary Member, Radiology Society of North America 1975; Honorary Member, Groupe d'Étude et de Travail en Radiologie Ostéo-Articulaire, France 1976; Fellow, RMS

(President, Radiology 1978–1979); Honorary Fellow, Royal Australasian College of Radiology 1979; Skinner Lecturer, RCR 1979; Honorary Fellow, Faculty of Radiologists, RCSI 1981; United Oxford and Cambridge University Club; Member, Hawks Club; Berkshire Golf Club, Rye Golf Club; Fellow, British Orthopaedic Association. **Honours:** MBE (Military) 1945. **Publications:** Chapters in: *Modern Trends in Diagnostic Radiology*, 1970; (ed D Sutton) *A Textbook of Radiology and Imaging*, 1969, 4th edition 1987; (jointly) *Radiology of Skeletal Disorders: Exercises in Diagnosis*, 1971, 3rd edition 1990; (jointly) *Orthopaedic Diagnosis*, 1984; papers in medical journals, mainly concerning radiological aspects of orthopaedics. Died 5 March 1995.

MURRAY, Thomas Prain Douglas (1918) Born 15 March 1901, Dryburgh, Lochee, Forfar; son of Joseph Murray, Estate Agent, and Susan Urquhart Prain. **Tutor(s):** E E Sikes. **Educ:** Dundee High School; Fettes College, Edinburgh.

MURRAY, William Rusack Blackwood (BLACKWOOD MURRAY) (1928) Born 31 March 1910, 92 Camperdown Road, Scotstown, Glasgow, Renfrewshire; son of Thomas Blackwood Murray, Chartered Civil and Mechanical Engineer, and Henrietta Wilhelmina Rusack; m Diana Mary Rawlins, 9 October 1948, St Mary and St Michael's, Trumpington; 2 sons (Michael and David), 1 daughter (Jane). **Subject(s):** Mechanical Sciences; BA 1932; MA 1936; MICE; FRGS. **Tutor(s):** J M Wordie. **Johnian Relatives:** brother of John Lamb Blackwood Murray (1925). **Educ:** Kelvinside Academy, Glasgow; Highfield Preparatory School, Liphook; Shrewsbury School. **Career:** Melville, Dundas and Whitson, Contractors 1937. Died 13 May 1989.

MURRAY-AYNSLEY, Sir Charles Murray (1913) Born 28 November 1893, 6 Uttoxter New Road, Derby; son of Alfred Evans Murray-Aynsley, Clerk in Holy Orders, and Alicia Harriett Murray-Aynsley; m (1) Elsa Marianova, 1920 (d 25 November 1951), (2) Annemaria Eleanor Curth, 20 November 1952, St Andrew's Cathedral, Singapore. **Subject(s):** Law; BA 1919. **Tutor(s):** L H K Bushe-Fox. **Educ:** Marlborough College; St Paul's School. **Career:** Lieutenant, King's Royal Rifle Corps, attached Army Cyclist Corps (wounded) 1914–1919; Called to the Bar, Inner Temple; Barrister 1920–1927; District Commissioner, Belize, British Honduras; acted as Attorney-General on several occasions 1927–1930; Chief Justice, Tonga 1930–1935; Chief Justice, Grenada 1935–1938; Judge, Ipoh, Federated Malay States; interned, WWII; Puisne Judge, Supreme Court of Straits Settlements 1938–1950; Chief Justice, Singapore 1946. **Awards:** Scholarship, SJC. Died 20 December 1952.

MUSGRAVE, Professor Peter William (1947) Born 9 April 1925, Kirkfield, Thornton, Bradford, Yorkshire; son of Frederick William Musgrave, Wool Merchant, and Emma Downs; m (1) Rosaline Symington, 1954 (d 1980), (2) Frances Mary Moran, 1984; (1) 1 son, 1 daughter. **Subject(s):** Economics; BA 1949; MA 1954; PhD (London) 1964; CertEd (Cantab) 1956. **Tutor(s):** C W Guillebaud. **Johnian Relatives:** nephew of James Downs (1917); cousin of John Patrick Downs (1944). **Educ:** Terra Nova, Birkdale, Southport; Loretto School. **Career:** Captain, 2nd Punjab Regiment, Indian Army 1944–1947; Woollen Textile Industry, UK and Australia 1949–1955; Secondary Teacher, Eltham College 1956–1961; Lecturer in Education, Homerton College, Cambridge 1962–1964; Principal Lecturer in Education, Bede College, Durham 1965; Lecturer, then Senior Lecturer in Sociology, University of Aberdeen 1965–1969; Professor of Education 1970–1985 (Emeritus 1986), Dean of Education 1977–1981, University of Monash. **Appointments:** Member, Australian Academy of Social Sciences 1972; Fellow, Academy of Social Sciences in Australia 1974; Visiting Scholar and Research Fellow, Corpus Christi College, Cambridge 1976. **Publications:** 16 books, including 5 monographs, 7 texts, and 4 readers.

MUSKER, Sir Harold John (1924) Born 25 January 1906, Shadwell Court, Rushford, Norfolk; son of Harold Taylor Musker, of independent means, and Margaret Gray McMonies; m (1) Elizabeth Loeffler, 1932, (2) Rosemary Pugh (née Beckwith-Smith), 1955, (3) Audrey Lucy (née

Paget), 1982; (1) 2 daughters. BA 1928. **Tutor(s):** B F Armitage. **Educ:** Privately educated. **Career:** Racehorse Breeder; Chairman of Cater & Co 1938–1960; Represented City of London, London County Council 1944–1949; Chairman, Cater Ryder & Co 1960–1971. **Appointments:** Chairman, Thoroughbred Breeders' Association 1968–1971. **Honours:** Kt 1952. Died 20 May 1992.

MYERS, Dr Geoffrey John (1935) Born 17 January 1917, Hillcroft, Hills Road, Cambridge; son of Norman Toller Myers, Architect, and Annie Isabella Moore; m Kathlene Margaret Cheale, 6 February 1943; 1 son (Michael b 1944), 1 daughter (Susan b 1947). **Subject(s):** Medicine; BA 1938; MRCS; LRCP. **Tutor(s):** R L Howland. **Johnian Relatives:** cousin of Martin Edward Moore (1932). **Educ:** St Faith's, Cambridge; The Leys School, Cambridge; Westminster Hospital, London. **Career:** House Physician, Westminster Hospital; RAFVR; BMA; GP, Cobham 1950–1982. **Appointments:** Council Medical Protection Society 1955–1989. Died June 2000.

MYERS, James Peter (1938) Born 8 October 1920, 4 Park Avenue, Harrogate; son of Joseph Ernest Myers, Director/Ladies Outfitter, and Rachel Lillian Myers; m Jill; 1 son (John), 1 daughter (Jane). **Subject(s):** Economics. **Tutor(s):** C W Guillebaud. **Educ:** Grosvenor House Preparatory School, Harrogate; Ashville College, Harrogate. Died 17 November 1989.

MYERS, Maurice John (1943) Born 28 August 1925, 73 Crouch Street, Colchester; son of Benjamin Myers, Branch Manager, and Fanny Cheek. BA 1948; MA 1950. **Tutor(s):** S J Bailey. **Educ:** Colchester Royal Grammar School.

MYLNE, Christopher Kenneth (1948) Born 29 April 1927, Dalhousie Castle, Cockpen, Midlothian; son of Kenneth Macnaughten Mylne, Schoolmaster, and Dorothy Susan Constance Parry-Okeden. **Subject(s):** Classics/English; BA 1951; FRPS 1965. **Tutor(s):** R L Howland. **Educ:** Cargilfield Preparatory School; Dalhousie Castle Preparatory School; Sedbergh School. **Awards:** Lupton and Hebblethwaite Exhibition, SJC.

N

NADARAJAH, Kandapoo Chinnathamby (1937) Born 19 June 1917, Karaveddy, Jaffna, Ceylon; son of Kandapoo Chinnathamby and Ponnammah; m Baby; 2 children (Priya and Kumar). **Subject(s):** Law. **Tutor(s):** C W Guillebaud. **Educ:** Vigueswara College, Karaveddy; St Joseph's College, Columbo; University College, Ceylon; KCL. Died 22 February 1985.

NAIFF, John Calverley (1932) Born 31 October 1913, 6 Lindley Road, Stoke-on-Trent; son of William Naiff, Clerk to Municipal Committee, and Alice Maude Hodder. **Subject(s):** Mathematics/Natural Sciences/Economics; BA 1935; MA 1978. **Tutor(s):** J M Wordie. **Educ:** Harpfield Preparatory School, Stoke-on-Trent; Harpfield Council School, Stoke-on-Trent; Hanley High School, Stoke-on-Trent. **Career:** Burmah Civil Service 1937–1947; Schoolmaster, Fettes College, Edinburgh 1947. **Awards:** Scholarship, SJC. Died 18 March 1991.

NAIRN, James Sword (1945) Born 18 July 1927, 532 Paisley Road, West Govan, Glasgow; son of James Sword Nairn, Cinema Circuit Supervisor, and Mary McCallum Black. **Tutor(s):** J M Wordie. **Educ:** Stirling High School; Inverness Royal Academy.

NAISBY, Tom (1928) Born 3 December 1909, 405 Audley Range, Blackburn, Lancashire; son of George William Naisby, Cotton Weaver, and Margaret Sharratt. **Subject(s):** History; BA 1931; MA 1935. **Tutor(s):** E A Benians. **Educ:** Accrington Road Council School, Blackburn; Queen Elizabeth's Grammar School, Blackburn. **Career:** English Teacher to Polish Squadrons, RAF, WWII; Announcer, BBC North 1946; Newsreader, BBC 1957–1962. Died 10 September 1972.

NANAVATI, Arvind Mohan Dhirajlal (1931) Born 10 November 1913, 21 Halpin Road, Kimendine, Rangoon; son of Dhirajlal Dayabhai Nanavati, Indian Civil Service, and Vidya Hargovindas. BA 1935; MA 1977. **Tutor(s):** C W Guillebaud. **Johnian Relatives:** son of Dhirajlal Dayabhai Nanavati (1905). **Educ:** Bishop's Home, Rangoon; Elphinstone High School, Bombay; The Grammar School, Quetta; Deccan College, Poona. **Career:** Lever Brothers (Indian) Ltd; Glaxo Laboratories (Indian) Ltd, until 1969 (retired as Personnel Director); Independent Management Consultant 1969. **Appointments:** Director, Capsulation Services Private Ltd. Died 1 August 1992.

NANAVATI, Dhirajlal Dayabhai (1905) Born 1 June 1885, Baroda, India; son of Dayabhai Harjiwandas Nanavati, British Indian Government Servant; m Vidya Hargovindas; 1 son (Arvind Mohan Dhirajlal b 10 November 1913). **Subject(s):** Natural Sciences; BA 1907. **Tutor(s):** J R Tanner. **Johnian Relatives:** father of Arvind Mohan Dhirajlal Nanavati (1931). **Educ:** Baroda College, India; St Xavier's College, Bombay. **Career:** Called to the Bar, Lincoln's Inn 1908; Assistant Commissioner, Burma 1908–1922; Officiating Legal Remembrancer and Secretary to the Governor of Burma 1922; District and Sessions Judge 1922–1923; Deputy Secretary to the Governor of Burma 1923–1925; Officiating and Sessions Judge, Bombay 1925–1929; Officiating Legal Remembrancer and Secretary to the Governor of Bombay 1929–1931; Officiating Judge, High Court 1931–1932.

NARASIMHAM, Maidavolu (1947) Born 3 June 1927, Bangalore, South India; son of Maidavolu Seshachelapathy, Advocate, and Sarvepalli Padmavathi; m Shanti Sundaresan; 1 son. **Subject(s):** Economics; BA 1949; MA 1983; Hon DLitt (Sri Krishnadevaraya University). **Tutor(s):** C W Guillebaud. **Educ:** PS High School, Madras; Presidency College, Madras. **Career:** Reserve Bank of India 1950–1972, Secretary 1967; Additional Secretary, Economic Affairs, Government of India 1972–1976; Secretary, Banking Department 1976–1977; Governor, Reserve Bank of India 1977–1978; India's Executive Director on the World Bank 1978–1980 and on International Monetary Fund 1980–1982; Secretary in Ministry of Finance and later Finance Secretary, Government of India 1982–1983; Principal, Administrative Staff College of India 1983–1985; Vice President, Asian Development Bank 1985–1988; Professor Emeritus and Chairman, Administrative Staff College of India 1992–. **Appointments:** Honorary Fellow, Indian Institute of Bankers; Honorary Fellow, All India Management Association; Associated as Member, Governing Boards of Centre for Policy Research, National Council of Applied Economic Research, among others; Chairman, Committee on Controls 1985; Chairman, Committee on the Financial System 1991; Chairman, Committee on Banking Sector Reforms 1998. **Honours:** Padma Vibhushan 2000. **Publications:** *World Economic Environment and Prospects for India*; *Economic Reforms: Development and Finance*; *From Reserve Bank to Finance Ministry and Beyond: Some Reminiscences*; articles in professional journals.

NASH, Charles Antony Marriott (1943) Born 28 May 1925, The Maternity Institute, Pottergate Street, Norwich; son of Richard Brettingham Nash, Electrical Engineer, and Adeline Jarvis. **Tutor(s):** S J Bailey. **Educ:** Pembroke House, Norwich; Quarry Bank, Liverpool; King's School, Chester.

NAUNTON, Dr William Johnson (1937) Born 31 October 1917, 44 Perrymead, Prestwich, Manchester; son of William Johnson Smith Naunton, Research Chemist, and Marion Louise Foster. BA 1940; MA 1945; MB, BChir 1945; MRCS; LRCP; DOMS. **Tutor(s):** R L Howland. **Johnian Relatives:** son of William Johnson Smith Naunton (1907). **Educ:** North Manchester School; Manchester Grammar School. **Career:** Surgeon Lieutenant, RNVR, Fleet Minesweepers; Senior Registrar, Manchester Royal Eye Hospital; Consultant Ophthalmic Surgeon, United Norwich Hospitals.

NAUNTON, Dr William Johnson Smith (1907) Born 22 March 1889, St John's Street, Woodbridge, Suffolk; son of William Johnson Naunton, Watchmaker and Jeweller, and Bessie Smith; m Marion Louise Foster; 1 son (William Johnson b 31 October 1917). **Subject(s):** Natural Sciences; BA 1910; MA 1914; BSc (London); MSc (London) 1917; PhD; FRIC; FIRI. **Tutor(s):** J R Tanner. **Johnian Relatives:** father of William Johnson Naunton (1937). **Educ:** Woodbridge School. **Career:** Chairman, Research Committee, Research Association of British Rubber Manufacturers; National Physical Laboratory; Head, Rubber Laboratories, Imperial Chemical Industries Ltd until 1952. **Appointments:** Council Member, Royal Institute of Chemistry; Vice President and Chairman, Institution of the Rubber Industry Council. **Awards:** Colwyn Gold Medal, Institution of the Rubber Industry. **Publications:** author of many papers and patents in the rubber field.

NAVARATNARAJAH, Paramanathan (1929) Born 16 December 1908, Puloly East, Point Pedro Division, Jaffna District, Ceylon; son of Kanapathyppillai Paramanathan, Clerk to the Ceylon Government, and Thaivanaippillai, daughter of Kanthapper. **Subject(s):** Mathematics; BA 1932; BSc (Ceylon) 1928. **Tutor(s):** J M Wordie. **Educ:** St Benedict's College, Ceylon; University College, Ceylon. **Awards:** University Scholarship, Ceylon.

NAYLOR, Guy Darnley (1924) Born 16 August 1906, 19 Lyndewode Road, Cambridge; son of Edward Woodall Naylor, Doctor of Music, and Susan Marion Wharton. **Subject(s):** English/Economics; BA 1927; MA 1956. **Tutor(s):** E E Sikes. **Educ:** Perse Preparatory School, Seafield, Collington, Bexhill; Radley College. **Career:** Called to the Bar, Gray's Inn 1952.

NAYLOR, Philip Edward (1939) Born 7 March 1921, 38 St Philip's Avenue, Worcester Park, Cheam, Surrey; son of Alexander James Naylor, Civil Servant, and Ethel Nellie Edwards. BA 1943; MA 1946. **Tutor(s):** J M Wordie. **Educ:** Umballa School, Worcester Park, Surrey; City of London Freeman's School, Ashstead Park; King's College School, Wimbledon. Died 28 February 2001.

NEALE, Harry Nelson (1937) Born 6 September 1917, Mon Repos, Park View Road, Berkhamsted; son of Nelson Neale, Steam Trawler Owner, and Eileen Florence Hoops. **Subject(s):** Modern and Medieval Languages; BA 1940; MA 1944. **Tutor(s):** C W Guillebaud. **Educ:** Dragon School, Oxford; Repton School. **Career:** Lieutenant, 3rd Carabiniers, India Command 1939–1944. Died 13 April 1944 (killed on active service in Burma).

NEALE, Humphrey Rossall (1917) Born 28 February 1899, Brockhall Rectory, Northamptonshire; son of John Neale, Clerk in Holy Orders, and Ada Rossall Sandford. BA 1921; MA 1926. **Tutor(s):** E E Sikes. **Johnian Relatives:** son of John Neale (1882). **Educ:** Hillbrow Preparatory School, Rugby; Marlborough College. **Career:** Lieutenant, KSLI, France and Belgium 1918.

NEAMTZU, Barbu (1925) Born 12 July 1906, 20 Ricrei Street, Craiova, Roumania; son of Constantin Neamtzu, Director of the Commercial Bank, Craiova, and Eugenia Albeanu. BA 1929; MA 1932. **Tutor(s):** M P Charlesworth. **Educ:** Lycée Carol I, Craiova, Roumania; Lycée G Lazar, Bucharest, Roumania. Died 1996.

NEASHAM, George (1938) Born 6 January 1917, Redworth, Darlington, Durham; son of George William Neasham, Lecturer, and Jane Elizabeth Gill; m Margaret. **Subject(s):** Modern and Medieval Languages; BA 1940; MA 1944; BA (London). **Tutor(s):** C W Guillebaud. **Educ:** Dean Bank School, Durham; High Coniscliffe Church of England School, Durham; Eastbourne Grammar School; Queen Mary College, London; KCL. **Career:** Head, Modern Languages Department, Wintringham Grammar School, Grimsby 1951; Assistant Education Officer, Middlesbrough 1951; Deputy Chief Education Officer, Gloucestershire 1980. Died 6 March 1992.

NEATE, Cyril Frank Caesar (1920) Naval Officer.

NEDDERMAN, John Midgley (1949) Born 16 April 1930, 33 Buxton Crescent, Rochdale, Lancashire; son of George Herbert Nedderman, Schoolmaster, Municipal High School, Rochdale, and Hannah Midgley; m Misa Saito, 21 March 1960. **Subject(s):** Mechanical Sciences; BA 1952; MA 1956; Diploma, Imperial College 1958; FIEE. **Tutor(s):** R L Howland. **Johnian Relatives:** brother of Ronald Midgley Nedderman (1953). **Educ:** High School, Rochdale; Spotland Junior Council School, Rochdale; Ackworth School; Leighton Park School. **Career:** Management of nuclear power plant construction and testing (mainly in Japan). **Awards:** Minor Scholarship, SJC 1947.

NEED, George Spofforth (1912) Born 18 December 1893, The Parks, Uttoxeter, Staffordshire; son of William George Need, Solicitor, and Lilla Caroline Ward. BA 1916. **Tutor(s):** R P Gregory. **Educ:** Parkfield School, Liverpool. **Career:** 88th Field Ambulance 1914 (Commended for Gallantry in Gallipoli); Sergeant, RAMC (TF), WWI.

NEEDHAM, Harry Lindley (1943) Born 28 June 1925, 242 Marlborough Avenue, Hull; son of Henry Needham, Civil Servant, and Gertrude Isabel Lindley. **Subject(s):** History; BA 1949 (Selwyn). **Tutor(s):** C W Guillebaud. **Educ:** Hull Grammar School.

NEILL, Norman Clark (CLARK-NEILL) (1902) Born 8 August 1883, Octavia Terrace, Greenock; son of William James Neill, Sugar Refiner, and Elizabeth Aitken Clark. **Subject(s):** Civil Engineering; BA 1905. **Tutor(s):** J R Tanner; C E Graves. **Educ:** Fettes College, Edinburgh. **Career:** Sub-Lieutenant, RNR, Lieutenant RNVR, then employed by Admiralty, WWI. **Appointments:** Council Member, Yacht Racing Association. Died 16 March 1935.

NELSON, The Revd Kenneth Edmund (1927) Born 10 December 1910, Elton, Nottinghamshire; son of Edmund Nelson, Clerk in Holy Orders, and Rose Bunting; m Barbara Jean Dye, 21 August 1950, Huddersfield Parish Church (d 29 November 2001); 1 son (Christopher Paul b 1954), 2 daughters (Elizabeth Mary b 1956 and Margaret Rosemary b 1958). **Subject(s):** Classics; BA 1933; MA 1936. **Tutor(s):** M P Charlesworth. **Educ:** Aysgarth Preparatory School, Yorkshire; Shrewsbury School. **Career:** Queen's College, Birmingham; Huddersfield Parish Church; Ordained Deacon, Huddersfield 1947; Ordained Priest 1948; Curate, Pocklington 1950–1952; Vicar, Brotton 1952–1958; Vicar, Sheriff Hutton, Diocese of York 1958–1964; Priest, St Peters, Little Aden, South Arabia 1965–1967; Rector, Crayke with Brandsby & Yearsley, Yorkshire 1967–1978; Curate (NSM), Wold Newton, Driffield 1978–1981. **Awards:** Hawksley Burberry Prize 1931.

NERY, Charles Albert (1920) Born 24 October 1902, 14 Cardinal Mansions, Carlisle Place, Westminster; son of Carlos de Oliveira Nery, Doctor of Medicine, late Consul General of Uruguay, and Carmen Luisa Cuestas. **Tutor(s):** E E Sikes. **Johnian Relatives:** brother of John Joseph Nery (1920). **Educ:** Leinster House School; The British School, Montevideo; Courtenay Lodge, Sutton Courtenay.

NERY, John Joseph (1920) Born 3 November 1901, 14 Cardinal Mansions, Carlisle Place, Westminster; son of Carlos de Oliveira Nery, Doctor of Medicine, late Consul General of Uruguay, and Carmen Luisa Cuestas. **Tutor(s):** E E Sikes. **Johnian Relatives:** brother of Charles Albert Nery (1920). **Educ:** Leinster House School; The British School, Montevideo; Courtenay Lodge, Sutton Courtenay.

NESBITT, Dr Philip (1947) Born 26 April 1929, 5 Barrack Square, Macclesfield; son of Frank Nesbitt, Railway Clerk, and Beatrice Mary Crook; m Brenda Frances Hill, 18 September 1954. **Subject(s):** Natural Sciences; BA 1950; MA 1954; PhD 1954. **Tutor(s):** G C L Bertram. **Educ:** Beech Lane School; The King's School, Macclesfield. **Awards:** Whytehead Scholarship, SJC.

NESS WALKER, Dr John (1913) Born 16 June 1895, Richmond, Yorkshire; son of William Ness Walker, Justice of the Peace, and Sarah

Plews. BA 1919; MA 1925; BChir 1925; MB 1925; MRCS; LRCP 1922. **Tutor(s):** R P Gregory. **Educ:** Sneaton Castle, Whitby; Merchiston Castle. **Career:** Lieutenant, RFA (TF Reserve), WWI; Doctor; House Surgeon, St Bartholomew's Hospital; Medical and Surgical Adviser, International Hospital, Kobe, Japan. Died 1977.

NEST, Hubert Clive (1919) Born 24 April 1900, 37 Midland Road, Gloucester; son of William Thomas Nest, Merchant, and Ellen Hobbs; m Marjorie Mabel Streatfield-James, 3 January 1941, St Stephen's Church, Cheltenham. **Subject(s):** Mathematics/Mechanical Sciences; BA 1922; MA 1926. **Tutor(s):** E E Sikes. **Educ:** Crypt Grammar School, Gloucester. **Career:** Assistant Master, Cranleigh School 1924–1925; Schoolmaster, Downside School 1926–1930; Schoolmaster, Marlborough College 1930. **Awards:** Exhibition, SJC 1918.

NEUMANN, Professor Maxwell Hermann Alexander (NEWMAN) (1915) Born 7 February 1897, 54 Lamont Road, Chelsea, London; son of Hermann Neumann, Secretary of Public Company, and Sarah Pike; m (1) Lyn Irvine (d 1973), (2) Margaret Penrose; (1) 2 sons (Edward b 20 October 1935 and William b 21 May 1939), (2) 3 stepsons (Oliver b 6 June 1929, Roger b 8 August 1931 and Jonathan b 7 October 1933), 1 stepdaughter (Shirley Victoria b 22 February 1945). **Subject(s):** Mathematics; BA 1921; MA 1924; Honorary DSc (Birmingham) 1967; FRS 1939. **Tutor(s):** L H K Bushe-Fox. **Johnian Relatives:** father of Edward Irvine Newman (1954) and William Maxwell Newman (1958); stepfather of Roger Penrose (1952). **Educ:** Goodrich Road Higher Grade London County Council School; City of London School; University of Vienna. **Career:** Beresford Fellow 1923–1926, Title A Fellow 1926–1931, Title B Fellow 1931–1945 (leave of absence on war service 1942–1945), Lecturer in Mathematics 1931–1945, SJC; Lecturer in Mathematics, University of Cambridge 1927–1945; Rockerfeller Research Fellowship, Princeton University 1928–1929; Government Code and Cipher School, Bletchley Park 1942–1945 (designed the Colossus machine, the world's first programmable electronic computer, which played a key part in deciphering the Lorenz code used by Hitler and his High Command); Fielden Professor of Mathematics, Manchester 1945–1964. **Appointments:** Supervisor in Mathematics, SJC 1929–1931; President, London Mathematical Society 1950–1951; President, Mathematical Association 1959. **Awards:** Scholarship, SJC 1914; Smith's Prize 1923; Rayleigh Prize, University of Cambridge 1923; De Morgan Medal, LMS 1962; Sylvester Medal, Royal Society 1958. **Publications:** *Topology of Plane Sets of Points*. Died 22 February 1984.

NEUMANN, Stephan Theodore (NORMAN) (1936) Born 21 April 1918, Vienna; son of Richard Neumann, Manufacturer, and Marguerita Herzl. **Subject(s):** Economics/Law; BA 1939. **Tutor(s):** J S Boys Smith. **Johnian Relatives:** nephew of Hans Herzl (1910). **Educ:** Paedagogium, Vienna; Theresianische Akademie, Vienna; Whittinghame College, Hove. **Career:** Representative, British Board of Trade 1946. Died 26 November 1946.

NEVILLE, Roland John (1935) Born 17 February 1916, Lincoln Lodge, Waldegrave Road, Twickenham; son of Charles William Neville, Director of Companies, and Dorothy Rochard. **Tutor(s):** C W Guillebaud. **Educ:** Arnold House, St John's Wood; Sherborne School.

NEWBERRY, George William (1923) Born 28 November 1904, Gardner Street, Hurstmonceux, Sussex; son of George William Newberry, Relieving Officer, and Henrietta Kate Gander; m Dorothy Coverdale Sharpe; 1 son (John Coverdale), 1 daughter (Ann Patricia). **Subject(s):** History; BA 1926; MA 1930. **Tutor(s):** E A Benians. **Johnian Relatives:** father of John Coverdale Newberry (1954). **Educ:** Gresham's School, Holt. **Career:** Schoolmaster, Christ's Hospital School, Horsham, Sussex 1927–1966. **Awards:** Scholarship, SJC 1926.

NEWBERY, John Alec (1930) Born 30 May 1911, 50 Grasmere Road, Muswell Hill, London; son of Robert Edwin Newbery, Solicitor, and Gertrude Eleanor Nicholson Bourner; m Ina Fairfax Knaston,

10 September 1941. **Johnian Relatives:** son of Robert Edwin Newbery (1903). **Educ:** Surrey House School, Margate; Sherborne School; Private Tuition, France.

NEWBERY, Robert Edwin (1903) Born 24 April 1884, 25 Wenlock Road, Hoxton, New Town, Middlesex; son of John Newbery, Yeoman, and Elizabeth Temperance Gravatt; m Gertrude Eleanor Nicholson Bourner. BA 1907; MA 1912. **Tutor(s):** E E Sikes. **Johnian Relatives:** father of John Alec Newbery (1930). **Educ:** Wellingborough Grammar School. **Career:** Second Lieutenant, MGC, WWI. **Honours:** MC 1919.

NEWELL, Adrian Nathaniel (1924) Born 17 December 1904, Calcutta, India; son of Alfred George Newell, Medical Practitioner, and Mary Wilhelmina Grennan; m Dorothy Wolff, 16 July 1932. **Subject(s):** Classics; BA 1928. **Tutor(s):** E E Sikes. **Educ:** Croxton Preparatory School; Epsom College; Merchant Taylors' School; Wrekin College; Perse School, Cambridge. **Career:** Lecturer in Latin, Leeds University. **Awards:** Scholarship, SJC. Died 22 June 1958.

NEWELL, Professor Martin Joseph (1930) Born 6 August 1910, Lombard Street, Galway, Ireland; son of Martin (Joseph) Newell, Merchant, and Annie (Maria) Corr; MSc (Ireland) 1930. **Tutor(s):** J M Wordie. **Educ:** St Joseph's Seminary, Galway; University College, Galway. **Career:** Professor of Mathematics, University College, Galway.

NEWEY, Clement John (1941) Born 14 August 1922, The Briars, Whitefields Road, Solihull, Warwickshire; son of James Clement Newey, Hook and Eye Manufacturer, and Madeline Jessie Fewings; m Lorraine King; 4 sons. **Subject(s):** Modern and Medieval Languages; BA 1947; MA 1949; MA Toronto University 1949. **Tutor(s):** C W Guillebaud. **Educ:** Caldicott School, Hitchin; The Leys School, Trumpington Road, Cambridge; School of Graduate Studies, Toronto University. **Career:** Personnel Administrator and Career Counsellor, Department of National Defence, Government of Canada; Cadet, SJC.

NEWIS, Kenneth (1935) Born 9 November 1916, 254 Walthall Street, Monks Coppenhall, Crewe; son of Herbert Thomas Newis, Schoolmaster, and Gladys Lindop; m Kathleen Barrow, 23 October 1943, Trinity Methodist Church, Stockport; 2 daughters (Gillian Mary and Sarah Margaret). **Subject(s):** Classics/History; BA 1938; MA 1942; FRSAMD 1995. **Tutor(s):** R L Howland. **Educ:** Brookdale Park School, Newton Heath; Alma Park School, Manchester; Manchester Grammar School. **Career:** Entered HM Office of Works 1938–1970; Private Secretary to Minister of Works (Right Honourable C W Key) 1948–1949; Assistant Secretary to Minister of Works 1949–1959; Under-Secretary to Minister of Works 1959–1970; Director of Management Services, Ministry of Public Building and Works 1969–1970; Under-Secretary, Scottish Development Department 1970–1973; Secretary, Scottish Development Department 1973–1976. **Appointments:** Conservator of Wimbledon and Putney Commons 1963–1970; Governor, Farrington's School 1964–1970; Governor, Richmond College 1964–1970; Board Member, RSAMD 1977–1988; Chairman, Queen's Hall (Edinburgh) 1977–1991; Board Member, Methodist Homes for the Aged 1977–1991; Vice-Chairman, MHA Housing Association 1977–1991; Member, Historic Buildings Council for Scotland 1978–1988; Member, Scottish Churches' Council 1984–1987; Chairman, Friends of Scottish Churches' Council 1984–1987; Vice-Chairman, Cockburn Association 1986–1994; RSAMD Trustee 1988–1992; Honorary President, Queen's Hall (Edinburgh) Ltd 1991. **Awards:** Patchett Scholarship, SJC 1934. **Honours:** CVO 1970; MVO 1958; CB 1967.

NEWMAN, Professor Barry George (1944) Born 23 May 1926, 232 Upper Chorlton Road, Stretford, Manchester, Lancashire; son of Frederick Challender Newman, Mechanical Engineer, and Dorothy Edna George; m Joan; 1 son, 2 daughters. **Subject(s):** Mechanical Sciences; BA 1947; MA 1951; PhD (Sydney) 1951; FRAeS 1964; FRSC 1982; FCASI; CEng. **Tutor(s):** S J Bailey. **Educ:** Forest School, Timperley; Beech Hall Preparatory School, Macclesfield; Manchester Grammar School.

Career: Research Officer, National Research Council of Canada 1953; Professor, Laval University, Quebec 1958; Canadair Professor of Aerodynamics, McGill University, Montreal 1959. **Appointments:** Chairman, Associate Committee for Aerodynamics, National Research Council of Canada 1968; Councillor, Canadian Aeronautics and Space Institute 1974; Member, Aeronautic Advisory Board, Department of Transport 1979; Fellow 1982, Vice-President 1985–1986, Academy of Science; Honorary Chairman, 11th Canadian Congress of Applied Mechanics 1987; Founding Fellow, Canadian Academy of Engineering 1987; Chairman, Committee for Mechanical Engineering in Aerospace Engineering 1989; Director of Applied Science, Royal Society of Canada 1992; President, Faculty Club 1993–1995. **Awards:** Strathcona Scholarship, SJC 1944; Edward Busk Memorial Prize, Royal Aeronautical Society 1961; McCurdy Award, Canadian Aeronautics and Space Institute 1997. Died 6 March 2000.

NEWMAN, Cyril Gordon (1930) Born 22 September 1911, 102 Queen's Avenue, Watford, Hertfordshire; son of Arthur Newman, Caterer, and Clara Jane Daniels; 2 sons (David Gordon and John Arthur). **Subject(s):** Natural Sciences; BA 1933. **Tutor(s):** C W Guillebaud. **Johnian Relatives:** father of John Arthur Newman (1964). **Educ:** Watford Grammar School; Farnham Grammar School. **Career:** Assistant Inspector of Taxes, rising to Principal Inspector, Inland Revenue Department 1934–1973; Tax Consultant (part-time) 1973–1999. **Awards:** Scholarship, SJC 1930.

NEWMAN, Edward Frederick George (1942) Born 30 March 1924, 7 Shafts Terrace, Bramford Road, Ipswich, Suffolk; son of Percy Robert Newman, Electrician, and Gertrude Parrish. **Tutor(s):** S J Bailey. **Educ:** Springfield County School, Ipswich; Northgate Secondary School, Ipswich.

NEWMAN, Harry (1946) Born 22 September 1921, St Ann's Hospital, St Louis, Missouri, USA; son of Harry Newman, Automobile Engineer, and Jean Fox; m (1) Mary Coltman, 12 March 1954, King's Weigh House Church, Grosvenor Square, London, (2) Anne; 1 son (Alan), 4 daughters (Felicity, Catherine, Elinor and Sara). MLitt 1949. **Educ:** St Louis Country Day School; Harvard College; Harvard Graduate School of Business Administration. **Career:** Commercial and Industrial Real Estate Developer, Newman Properties; Chairman, Newman Properties and Newman Northwest. **Appointments:** Chairman and Founder (1981), Long Beach Regional Arts Foundation; West Coast President 1969–1970, Trustee 1966–1968 and 1970–1975, International Council of Shopping Centers; Founder, British Case-Study Writers' Circle; Co-founder, Newman Neame Ltd; Founder (1961) and Chairman, Newman Properties. **Publications:** Author: *Poems for Executives and Other Addicts*, 1974; *Male Menopause and Other Cheerful Topics*, 1979; *Behind Pinstripes*, 1984; *Turning 21: A Businessman's Poetic Odyssey to the New Century*, Nine Muses Press 1999; (jointly) *Teaching Management*; (ed) *Partners in Production*. Died 19 October 2001.

NEWMAN, Dr James Fraser MacCallum (1948) Born 10 August 1927, Holme Lea, Bradford Road, Batley, Yorkshire; son of Samuel MacCallum Newman, Medical Practitioner, and Margaret Goldie Fraser; m Saliann; 2 daughters (Fiona and Helen). **Subject(s):** Natural Sciences; BA 1951; MA 1956; BChir 1955; MB 1956. **Tutor(s):** G C L Bertram. **Educ:** Batley Grammar School. **Career:** GP, Batley and Clinical Assistant, Dewsbury 1957–1990. **Appointments:** Chairman, Kirklees Local Medical Committee; Member, Kirklees Family Practitioner Committee; Member, Yorkshire Regional Health Authority Medical Committee; Chairman, Didsbury Division, BMA. Died 26 December 1990.

NEWMAN, Professor Maxwell Hermann Alexander (1915) See NEUMANN.

NEWTON, Horace Gerard Townsend (1904) Born 7 July 1885, Beechwood, Driffield, Yorkshire; son of Horace Newton, Canon of York, and Frances Jane Storrs. **Tutor(s):** E E Sikes. **Johnian Relatives:** son of

Horace Newton (1860). **Educ:** Arden House, Henley in Arden; Rugby School. **Career:** 13th Hussars 1906–1917 (Second Lieutenant 1908, Lieutenant 1910, Captain 1914–1917). Died 25 April 1917 (drowned on active service).

NEWTON, Richard James (1948) Born 17 November 1927, St Thomas' Hospital, London; son of Alfred Richard Newton, Professor of Music, Royal Academy of Music, London, and Rosamond Tunstill; m Elizabeth Seraphine Meuwissen, 1961 (d 1986); 4 sons. **Subject(s):** Classics; BA 1950; MA 1955. **Tutor(s):** R L Howland. **Educ:** South Kensington Preparatory School, London; Clifton College Preparatory School, Bristol; Clifton College, Bristol. **Career:** Courtaulds 1951–1958; Textile Marketing Manager, Midland Silicones Ltd 1959–1963; Manager, then Director of Sales, Chemstrand 1963–1966; Manager, Keith Shipton & Co 1967–1969; Managing Director, Bury & Masco (Holdings) 1970–1977; Fellow and Bursar, Trinity Hall, Cambridge 1977–1989. **Appointments:** Treasurer, The Royal Institute of Philosophy 1974–1998; Non-executive Director, Sketchley Plc 1978–1987 (Chairman 1983–1987); Non-executive Director, National & Provincial Building Society 1985–1993 (Chairman 1988–1993); Governor 1990, Council Member 1993–1998, Clifton College. **Awards:** Major Scholarship, SJC 1945.

NEWTON THOMPSON, Christopher Lawton (1937) Born 14 February 1919, 71 Ladbroke Grove, Kensington; son of Cyril Newton Thompson, Barrister-at-Law, and Joyce Nettlefold; m Philippa Bunn, 5 May 1951; 1 daughter (Charlotte). BA 1940; MA 1988. **Tutor(s):** J S Boys Smith. **Johnian Relatives:** son of Cyril Newton Thompson (1911). **Educ:** Diocesan College Preparatory School, Rondebosch; Diocesan College School, Rondebosch. **Career:** Major, Royal Armoured Corps, 1939–1945; Importer of goods from the UK, Johannesburg. **Appointments:** Wartime Rugby international; City Councillor, Johannesburg City Council; Member, Governing Council, Waterford Kamhlaba United World College of Southern Africa in Swaziland and Maru a Pula School, Gaborone, Botswana; JP. **Honours:** MC 1944. Died 29 January 2002.

NICHOLLS, Albert Charles (1907) Born 17 May 1886, Tilehouse Street, Hitchin, Hertfordshire; son of Albert Nicholls, Greengrocer and Farmer, and Elizabeth Gatward; m Kathleen Thornton; 1 son (Charles Geoffrey William b 10 October 1921), 2 daughters (Pamela Betty b 1924 and Patricia Mary Gillian b 1926). **Subject(s):** Law; BA 1910; MA 1931; LLB. **Tutor(s):** L H K Bushe-Fox. **Johnian Relatives:** father of Charles Geoffrey William Nicholls (1940). **Educ:** St Mary's National School, Hitchin; Hitchin Commercial School. **Career:** Lieutenant, Leicestershire Regiment and General List (wounded twice), WWI; Barrister-at-Law. Died 31 January 1947.

NICHOLLS, Professor Charles Geoffrey William (1940) Born 10 October 1921, Tilehouse Street, Hitchin, Hertfordshire; son of Albert Charles Nicholls, Barrister-at-law, and Kathleen Thornton; m Hilary McCallum, 1950; 1 son (Paul Charles Alexander b 1954), 2 daughters (Elizabeth Helen b 1951 and Felicity Kathleen Mary b 1962). **Subject(s):** Classics/Theology; BA 1947; MA 1949. **Tutor(s):** R L Howland. **Johnian Relatives:** son of Albert Charles Nicholls (1907). **Educ:** The Dower House School, Wallington; Whitgift School, Croydon; Wells Theological College. **Career:** Ordained Deacon, Wendover 1952; Ordained Priest 1953; Chaplain to Anglican Students in Edinburgh 1954–1960; Associate Professor of Systematic Theology and Church History, St John's College, University of Manitoba 1960–1961; Professor of Religious Studies 1961–1986 (Emeritus 1986), Head of Department 1964–1983, University of British Columbia. **Appointments:** Visiting Professor of Religious Studies, Hebrew University of Jerusalem 1984–1985. **Awards:** Major Scholarship in Classics, SJC; Norrisian Prize, University of Cambridge 1950. **Publications:** *Ecumenism and Catholicity* (The Norrisian Prize Essay for 1950), SCM Press, 1952; (ed) *Conflicting Images of Man*, The Seabury Press, 1966; *The Pelican Guide to Modern Theology, Volume 1: Systematic and Philosophical Theology*, Penguin Books, 1969; *Modernity and Religion*, Wilfrid Laurier University Press, 1987; *Christian Antisemitism: A history of hate*, Northvale, New Jersey, Jason Aronson, 1993.

NICHOLLS, Denys Raymond (1947) Born 16 September 1925, 82 Trevethan Road, Falmouth, Cornwall; son of Thomas Cecil Nicholls, Schoolmaster, and Gertrude Wilson Evans; m Maureen. **Subject(s):** History; BA 1949; MA 1954; Advanced Certificate in Education (Sheffield). **Tutor(s):** F Thistlethwaite. **Educ:** Trevethan Council School, Falmouth; Wellington Terrace School, Falmouth; Falmouth Grammar School. **Career:** Head of Careers and Vocational Guidance, Henry Faroham School, Sheffield. Died 16 October 1989.

NICHOLLS, Professor James John (1938) Born 10 May 1916, Glebe, Sydney, Australia; son of James Albert Nicholls, Foreman, Australian Gaslight Company, and Annie Mary Blackhall, Wardrobe Mistress, J C Williamson's; m Helen Rose Witney, 29 August 1942, 1 son (James Alfred b 29 March 1946), 3 daughters (Sue Spinks b 5 July 1944, Rosemary b 14 September 1948 and Brenda b 30 September 1950). **Subject(s):** Classics; BA 1940; MA 1946; BA (Sydney) 1938. **Tutor(s):** R L Howland. **Educ:** Forest Lodge Primary School, Sydney; Canterbury High School, Sydney; University of Sydney. **Career:** Master, Newington College, Sydney 1940–1945; Lecturer, Associate Professor of Latin, University of Sydney 1945–1981; Nuffield Foundation Travelling Fellow, SJC 1957. **Awards:** Foundation Scholarship 1940; Cooper Scholarship 1934; Cooper Graduate Scholarship 1938; University Medal for Classics, Sydney University, 1938; Graves Prize, SJC 1940; Wright's Prize, SJC 1940. Died 27 June 2001.

NICHOLS, Philip Peter Ross (1920) Born 28 June 1902, 58 Mill Hill Road, Heigham, Norwich, Norfolk; son of Frederick Peter Nichols, Lieutenant Colonel, RAMC, and Florence Mary Branson Ross. **Subject(s):** History; BA 1924; MA 1928. **Tutor(s):** E A Benians. **Educ:** County Council School, Bodmin; King's College, Taunton; Bloxham School. **Career:** Assistant Master, Barkston Preparatory School. **Appointments:** Chosen Chief, Order of Bards, Ovates and Druids. Died 30 April 1975.

NICHOLSON, Dr Bernard Clive (1922) Born 10 April 1904, 41 Filey Avenue, Upper Clapton, London; son of Ebenezer Bernard Nicholson, Surveyor and Estate Agent, and Frances Lilian Young; 1 son (Alick), 1 daughter. **Subject(s):** Natural Sciences; BA 1925; MA 1929; BChir 1930; MB 1932; MD 1936. **Tutor(s):** B F Armitage. **Educ:** Sutton Park School; Epsom College. **Career:** House Physician, Children's Department, and Medical Professorial Unit, St Bartholomew's Hospital. Died 11 January 1993.

NICHOLSON, David Hulme (1945) Born 21 February 1927, Acland, Billinge Road, Pemberton, Wigan, Lancashire; son of William Nicholson, Yarn Salesman, and Doris King; m Elsie Cheetham; 2 sons (Roger Timothy and Simon Jeremy). **Subject(s):** Modern and Medieval Languages/Law; BA 1948; MA 1952. **Tutor(s):** C W Guillebaud. **Johnian Relatives:** father of Roger Timothy Nicholson (1971). **Educ:** Highfield Church of England School, Wigan; Wigan Grammar School. **Career:** Solicitor.

NICHOLSON, Edgar Cyril (1910) Born 28 September 1891, 22 Balderton Gate, Newark, Nottinghamshire; son of Edward Henry Nicholson, Master Baker, and Emma Jane Atkinson. **Subject(s):** Natural Sciences. **Tutor(s):** J R Tanner. **Educ:** Magnus Grammar School, Newark. **Awards:** Sizarship, SJC.

NICHOLSON, Ernest Harvey (1944) Born 20 March 1926, Springfield Maternity Hospital, Rochdale, Lancashire; son of Ernest Nicholson, Wool Carboniser, and Winifred Blanche Holdsworth; 2 daughters (Judith and Helen). **Subject(s):** Mechanical Sciences; BA 1947; MA 1953; CEng; MIEE; MIMechE. **Tutor(s):** S J Bailey. **Educ:** Kirkheaton National School, Huddersfield; King James' School, Huddersfield. **Career:** Director and General Manager, Pye Connectors Ltd. Died 10 October 2000.

NICHOLSON, Harold Metcalfe (1934) Born 13 August 1915, Heighington, Durham; son of John Harold Nicholson, Schoolmaster, and Jane Anne Metcalfe. **Tutor(s):** J M Wordie. **Educ:** Heighington C of E School; Bishop Auckland Grammar School.

NICHOLSON, John (1921) Naval Officer.

NICHOLSON, Kenneth Fletcher (1930) Born 1 January 1910, Ackworth, Pontefract; son of William Fletcher Nicholson, Secretary to the Society of Friends, and Eliza Marion McCurdy; m Annis Bowman Strong, 22 December 1949; 1 son (Andrew). **Subject(s):** English/History; BA 1933; MA 1937. **Tutor(s):** M P Charlesworth. **Educ:** Ackworth School, Pontefract; Bootham School, York. **Career:** Recording Clerk, Society of Friends; Master, Leighton Park School 1935–1955 (Housemaster 1937); Senior English Master, Wadi Seidna School, Sudan; 1946–1947; Westtown School, Pennsylvania 1952; Headmaster, Saffron Walden School 1955. **Appointments:** Secretary, Reading Christian Council 1945; Secretary, Reading Christian Arts Festival; Chairman, Friends Guild of Teachers. Died 21 March 1969.

NICHOLSON, Peter (1933) Born 17 March 1915, 45 Wide Bargate, Boston, Lincolnshire; son of Edwin James Nicholson, Wholesale Tobacconist, and Lily Hansley Green; m Angela. **Subject(s):** Modern and Medieval Languages/English; BA 1936. **Tutor(s):** C W Guillebaud. **Educ:** Conway School, Boston; Boston Grammar School; Newark Magnus School; Spalding Grammar School. **Career:** Lieutenant, 5th battalion, Northamptonshire Regiment 1939–1943. Died January 1943 (killed in action in Tunisia).

NICHOLSON, Robert Keith (1945) Born 10 October 1927, 91 Alexandra Road, Kingston on Hull; son of Leonard Steff Nicholson, Schoolmaster, and Gertrude Jane Gleadhill. **Subject(s):** English; BA 1948; MA 1952. **Tutor(s):** F Thistlethwaite. **Educ:** Newland Avenue Elementary School, Hull; Middleton Street Elementary School, Hull; Hymers College, Hull.

NICHOLSON, Roydon Joseph (1927) Born 31 August 1909, 14 Eastern Road, Brockley, Kent; son of Hugh Stanley Nicholson, Maltster, and Florence Thérèse Goulding, Artist; m Evelyn Sophie Carlton Reader, 30 June 1934; 2 sons (George b 4 April 1936 and Peter b 6 March 1946), 3 daughters (Janet b 8 July 1939, Anne b 6 November 1951, d 23 May 1953 and Louise b 1 May 1954). **Subject(s):** Law; BA 1930. **Tutor(s):** C W Guillebaud. **Johnian Relatives:** brother-in-law of Arnold Daly Briscoe (1919); uncle of John Hubert Daly Briscoe (1951). **Educ:** Westerleigh School, St Leonards; Haileybury College. **Career:** Wartime Service Army Gunner; Solicitor; Consultant for Fladgate & Co. **Honours:** MBE. Died 16 August 1997.

NICKALLS, John Lawrence (1913) Born 5 November 1892, Tsou-Ping, Shantung, China; son of Edward Carey Nickalls, Missionary, and Mary Kirby. **Subject(s):** History/Economics; BA 1920. **Tutor(s):** L H K Bushe-Fox. **Educ:** China Inland Mission School; Bishop's Stortford College; University of Birmingham. **Career:** Assistant Librarian, Friends' Reference Library 1921.

NICKLIN, The Revd George Norman (1908) Born 2 December 1889, 36 High Street, Dorking, Surrey; son of George Tice Nicklin, Draper, and Fanny Softly; m Evelyn. **Subject(s):** Natural Sciences; BA 1911; MA 1920. **Tutor(s):** L H K Bushe-Fox. **Educ:** Dorking High School; Birkbeck College. **Career:** Bank of England 1912; Captain, IARO, attached 97th Deccan Infantry, WWI; Ordained Deacon 1938; Curate, Cobham 1938–1940; Priest 1939; Curate, Farnborough 1940–1943; Vicar, Beaulieu, Hampshire 1943–1949; Curate in charge, Elvetham, Hampshire 1952–1954; Curate, Dawlish, and in Charge, Holcombe 1954–1959. Died 30 December 1962.

NICKSON, Duncan (1944) Born 26 October 1926, 57 Cheltenham Street, Barrow-in-Furness, Lancashire; son of John Duncan Nickson, Pawnbroker, and Ethel Annie Hoggarth. **Subject(s):** History; BA 1950;

MA 1952; DipEd (Manchester). **Tutor(s):** J M Wordie. **Educ:** Oxford Street School, Barrow; Barrow Grammar School. **Career:** Teacher, Barrow Education Authority. **Appointments:** RAF Cadet, SJC.

NICOLL, John Malcolm (1943) Born 13 August 1925, 19 Lynedoch Place, Edinburgh; son of Frank Ewart Nicoll, Exchange Banker, and Isobel Mary Stuart; m Catherine Linden Hopkin, 17 September 1960. **Tutor(s):** C W Guillebaud. **Educ:** Craigflower, Torryburn; Trinity College, Glenalmond.

NICOLLE, Arthur Philip Ronald (1923) Born 10 September 1904, 76 Bath Road, Swindon, Wiltshire; son of Arthur John Nicolle, Bank Cashier, Lloyds Bank Ltd, Torquay, and Lilian Alexandra Jeffries. **Tutor(s):** B F Armitage. **Educ:** Newton College, Newton Abbot.

NIGHTINGALE, Neville Gascoyne (1930) Born 20 May 1911, Kimberley, South Africa; son of Lacy Gamaliel Nightingale, Barrister-at-Law, and Kate Harriet Wagner; 1 son (Tom). BA 1933; MA 1969. **Tutor(s):** C W Guillebaud. **Educ:** The Christian Brothers College, Pretoria; St John's College, Johannesburg; Diocesan College, Rondebosch. Died 29 September 1989.

NIKAM, Professor Narayan Rao Appu Rao (1931) Born 5 June 1903, Mysore, India; son of Appu Rao Nikam, Merchant, and Seetha Bai Nikam; 1 son (Jayasimha). **Subject(s):** Moral Sciences; BA 1933; MA 1938. **Tutor(s):** J S Boys Smith. **Educ:** Wesleyan Missions High School, Mysore; The Maharajah's Collegiate High School, Mysore; Mysore University. **Career:** Fulbright and Ford Foundation Scholar and Fellow, Yale University 1952–1953; Professor of Philosophy and Vice-Chancellor, Mysore University 1960–1962; Barclay Acheson Professor, Macalester College, St Paul, Minnesota, USA 1964–1965; Visiting Professor, California State College 1964–1965; Visiting Professor, Indian Institute of Advanced Study 1966. **Appointments:** Member, International Institute of Philosophy, Paris; General Secretary, 2nd Philosophical Congress 1949–1961; President, Indian Philosophical Congress 1965. **Awards:** Bhaba Memorial Gold Medal. Died 24 August 1974.

NIMMO, Johnston Robertson (1948) Born 15 April 1913, Vermont, Crookston, Paisley, Renfrewshire; son of Johnston Robertson Nimmo, Grocer, and Stuart Erskine Milne. **Tutor(s):** J M Wordie. **Educ:** Nairobi European School; Prince of Wales School, Kenya. **Career:** Farming in Kenya 1931–1934; Clerk in Treasury, Nairobi 1934–1939; Major, King's African Rifles 1939–1946; Administrative Officer, Kenya 1946. **Honours:** MC.

NISSIM, Joseph (1902) Born 18 June 1882, Bombay, India; son of Nissim Saleh Nissim, Manager, E D Sassoon & Co, and Reemah Isaacs; m Ena Joan Phillips, 9 May 1925, Spanish and Portuguese Synagogue, Maida Vale. **Subject(s):** History/Law; BA 1904; MA 1908; LLM 1906. **Tutor(s):** D MacAlister. **Johnian Relatives:** brother of Simon Nissim (1912). **Educ:** Scottish High School, Bombay; Elphinstone College, Bombay. **Career:** Admitted to Middle Temple 1902; Magistrate, Collector, Legislative Assistant, Indian Civil Service 1905–1918; Called to the Bar, Middle Temple 1906; Political Agent, Surgana 1910. **Publications:** *A Monograph on Wire and Tinsel in the Bombay Presidency*, 1909. Died 24 July 1972.

NISSIM, Simon (1912) Born 12 November 1889, Bombay, India; son of Nissim Silas Ezra Nissim, Manager, E D Sassoon & Co, and Reemah Isaacs. **Subject(s):** Economics/Law; BA 1915; MA 1919; LLB 1915. **Tutor(s):** L H K Bushe-Fox. **Johnian Relatives:** brother of Joseph Nissim (1902). **Educ:** Scottish High School, Bombay; Elphinstone College, Bombay. **Career:** Called to the Bar, Middle Temple 1916. Died 2 February 1968.

NIVEN, The Revd Hugh (1907) Born 31 May 1888, 15 Roseale Street, Langholm, Dumfriesshire; son of Thomas Niven, Timber Merchant, and Elizabeth Davidson. BA 1911; MA 1914. **Tutor(s):** E E Sikes. **Educ:** Higher Grade School, Carlisle; Grammar School, Carlisle. **Career:** Curate, Dalton-in-Furness 1905–1917; Ordained Deacon 1911; Curate, St Matthew, Barrow-in-Furness 1911–1915; Ordained Priest 1912; Vicar, All Souls', Netherton 1917–1930; Vicar, St Philip's, Mosser (Cockermouth) 1930–1937; Vicar, Christ Church, Penrith 1937. **Appointments:** Honorary Canon, Carlisle Cathedral 1947; Member, Cockermouth Rural Committee, and Chairman, Finance Committee. Died 8 July 1949.

NIX, Arthur Rupert (1920) Born 1 October 1901, 81 Guildhall Street, Bury St Edmunds, Suffolk; son of Rupert Edward Nix, Medical Practitioner, and Edith Mary Cooke; 2 sons. **Subject(s):** Classics; BA 1923; MA 1932. **Tutor(s):** E E Sikes. **Educ:** St Faith's School, Cambridge; Felsted School. **Career:** TA until WWII; 99th Field Regiment, RA in Palestine, Egypt and Transjordan (Mentioned in Despatches), WWII; Master, Private School, Little Horwood; Mathematics Master, Buckingham County Secondary School 1957. **Awards:** Scholarship, SJC 1919. Died 24 March 1976.

NIXON, St John (1936) Born 5 July 1917, 22a Oxford Avenue, Merton Park, London; son of Alfred Thornton Nixon, Trench Warfare Engineer's Representative, and Eva Gertrude Garrett. **Subject(s):** Modern and Medieval Languages; BA 1939; MA 1943. **Tutor(s):** C W Guillebaud. **Educ:** Denmark College, Wimbledon; Rutlish School, Merton. **Career:** Senior Lecturer in English, The Netherlands School of Business, Nijenrode, Breukelen; Tutor in English and Dean of Students, Nijenrode University, Netherlands. Died 4 October 1996.

NIXON, Wilfrid Earle (1934) Born 27 May 1916, 72 Pinehurst Cottages, Farnborough, Hampshire; son of Wilfrid Ernest Nixon, Chartered Secretary, and Bertha Eleanor Gregory; m Frankie Christainson; 1 daughter (Josephine b 1943). BA 1937; MA 1941. **Tutor(s):** J M Wordie. **Educ:** Grove Park Preparatory School, Kingsbury; Malvern College. **Career:** de Havilland Aircraft Company Ltd 1936–1938; RAFVR 1939–1944 (Pilot Officer 1940, Squadron Leader 1944). Died 5 August 1944 (killed on active service).

NOAKES, The Revd Harold Isaac (1924) Born 14 April 1905, 66 Edward Street, Canning Town, West Ham, Essex; son of Isaac Aaron Noakes, Builder, and Alys Jane Watts. BA 1928; MA 1931. **Tutor(s):** E A Benians. **Educ:** Eton House School, Southend; Private Tuition (Revd J S Bryers), Bowers Gifford Rectory. **Career:** Ordained Deacon 1931; Curate, Waltham Abbey 1931–1937; Ordained Priest 1932; CF, TA 1932; Officiated at Cathedral Church, Chelmsford 1937; Precentor 1938; Honorary Chaplain to Bishop of Chelmsford 1948. Died 28 September 1993.

NOBBS, Cyril Gordon (1921) Born 23 April 1903, Chesterton, Cambridge; son of James Alfred Nobbs, Schoolmaster, and Elizabeth Alice Brown. **Subject(s):** Mathematics; BA 1924; MA 1928. **Tutor(s):** E Cunningham. **Johnian Relatives:** brother of Douglas Nobbs (1927); father of David Gordon Nobbs (1955). **Educ:** Bridge Road School, Grays; Palmer's School, Grays. **Career:** Master, King Edward's School, Birmingham 1925–1928; Second Master, City of London School 1928. **Awards:** Hare Exhibition, SJC 1921; Scholarship, SJC 1923; College Prize, SJC 1923, 1924. Died 31 October 1968.

NOBBS, Douglas (1927) Born 29 June 1908, Fairfield, New Road, Grays, Essex; son of James Alfred Nobbs, Schoolmaster, and Elizabeth Alice Brown; m. **Subject(s):** History; BA 1930; MA 1934. **Tutor(s):** E A Benians. **Johnian Relatives:** brother of Cyril Gordon Nobbs (1921); uncle of David Gordon Nobbs (1955). **Educ:** Bridge Road School, Grays; Palmer's School, Grays. **Career:** Title A Fellow, SJC 1933–1936; Lecturer, later Reader in Political Science, University of Edinburgh 1947–1961. **Appointments:** Supervisor in History 1933–1935, SJC. **Awards:** Exhibition, SJC 1927; Scholarship, SJC 1929; Hughes Prize, SJC

1930; Essay Prize, SJC 1930. **Publications:** *Theocracy and Toleration*, 1938. Died 1 September 1973.

NOBLE, Alexander Hugh (1935) Born 10 February 1917, 43 Mansionhouse Road, Edinburgh; son of Alexander Bertram Noble, Writer to the Signet, and Agnes Alison Tod; m Norma Elizabeth Grant. **Subject(s):** Law; BA 1938; LLB (Edinburgh). **Tutor(s):** R L Howland. **Educ:** Edinburgh Academy; Dalhousie Castle; Fettes College, Edinburgh. **Career:** Writer to the Signet. **Awards:** Scholarship, SJC 1937. Died 10 March 1988.

NOBLE, Basil (1940) Born 11 October 1920, 36 Lancaster Road, Rugby; son of Kenneth John Noble, Consulting Engineer, and Anita Mary Harding; m Sheila Margaret Hesketh, April 1944; 1 son (Patrick b 5 June 1946), 2 daughters (Judith b 11 April 1948 and Katharine b 23 March 1953). **Subject(s):** Mathematics; BA 1943; MA 1949; PGCE (Birmingham) 1962. **Tutor(s):** S J Bailey. **Educ:** Dulwich College Preparatory School; Oundle School; City and Guilds College; Private Tuition, Bonn, Germany; Saltley Training College, Birmingham. **Career:** Industrial experience, hydro-electric power schemes, Atelier de Charmille, Geneva 1939; work on large diesel engine power generation, English Electric Co, Rugby; Commissioned Officer, Engineers Branch, RAF 1941–1946; Non-flying duties, crash inspection, retrieval and repair; Air Ministry Special Duties (development and provision of equipment for airbourne forces for D-Day Landings and later for conflict in the Far East); Graduate Apprentice, Steam Turbine Generation 1946–1948, Commercial Staff, preparing tenders for power generation equipment, negotiating orders and supervising subsequent contracts, notably the Wairakei Geothermal Project in New Zealand 1948–1959, BTH Co, Rugby; Sales Manager, Belliss & Morcom, Birmingham 1959–1961; Maths and Science Teacher, Queensbridge School, Moseley, Birmingham 1962–1964; Head of Maths, later Head of Maths and Science Faculty, Head of Middle School, Senior Tutor, Member of Birmingham Maths Teachers Panel for CSE, Dame Elizabeth Cadbury Bi-Lateral Art School 1964–1979. **Appointments:** (in retirement) voluntary work with swimming groups for blind and disabled elderly people; Co-ordinator, Outdoor Bowls Group, North Norfolk Branch, University of the Third Age.

NOBLE, Benjamin (1945) Born 1 May 1922, 87 College Bounds, Fraserburgh, Aberdeenshire, Scotland; son of John Noble, Cooper, and Elsie Young. **Subject(s):** Mathematics; BA 1947; MA 1953. **Educ:** Fraserburgh Central School; Fraserburgh Academy; Aberdeen University. **Career:** Head Scientist, Submarine Acoustic Experimental Station, Loch Goil, Admiralty Research Laboratory; Senior Lecturer in Mathematics, Royal College of Science and Technology, Glasgow; University of North Staffordshire, Keele 1953; Mathematics Research Centre, US Army 1964. **Publications:** *Numerical Methods* I and II, Oliver & Boyd, 1964.

NOBLE, Sir Peter Scott (1921) Born 17 October 1899, 33 School Street, Fraserburgh, Aberdeenshire, Scotland; son of Andrew Noble, Journeyman Cooper, and Margaret Trail; m Mary Stephen, 7 August 1928, Liverpool (d 1983); 2 sons (Andrew and Peter), 1 daughter (Isabel). **Subject(s):** Classics/Oriental Languages; BA 1923; MA 1928; MA (Aberdeen) 1921; Honorary LLD (Aberdeen) 1955. **Tutor(s):** E E Sikes. **Johnian Relatives:** father of Andrew Stephen Noble (1956) and of Peter Scott Noble (1960). **Educ:** Fraserburgh Academy; Aberdeen University. **Career:** Argyll and Sutherland Highlanders, and the Scottish Horse 1917–1919; Lecturer in Latin, Liverpool University 1926–1930; Title A Fellow, SJC 1927–1931; Professor of Latin Literature and Language, Leeds University 1930–1937; Regius Professor of Humanity, Aberdeen University 1937–1952; Principal, KCL 1952–1968. **Appointments:** Governor, Sedbergh School 1930; Member, University Grants Committee 1943–1953; Member, General Dental Council 1955; Member, Educational Trust, English-Speaking Union 1958; Governor, St Thomas' Hospital 1960; Vice-Chancellor, University of London 1961–1964; Member, Aberdeen Education Committee; Member,

Management Board, Aberdeen General Hospital. **Awards:** Hutchison Studentship 1925; Bendall Sanskrit Exhibition 1924, 1925. **Honours:** Kt 1967. **Publications:** (joint ed) *Kharosthi Inscriptions Vol III*; reviews, etc, in classical journals. Died 12 May 1987.

NOCK, William (1944) Born 13 April 1926, Lymore, Montgomery; son of William George Nock, Estate Clerk of Works, Apley Estates Company, and Effie Sarah Elizabeth Hillier. **Subject(s):** Natural Sciences; BA 1948; MA 1951. **Tutor(s):** C W Guillebaud. **Educ:** Elementary School, Norton, Shifnal; St Leonard's School, Bridgnorth; The Grammar School, Bridgnorth.

NOEL-TOD Geoffrey Noel (1927) See TOD.

NOONAN, Hon John Thomas (1946) Born 24 October 1926, Boston, Massachusetts, USA; son of John Thomas Noonan, Lawyer, and Marie Frances Shea; m Mary Lee Bennett, 27 December 1967; 1 son (John Kenneth), 2 daughters (Rebecca Lee and Susanna Bain). **Tutor(s):** F Thistlethwaite. **Educ:** Rivers Country Day School; Harvard College; Catholic University of America, Washington DC. **Career:** Teacher of Law, University of Notre Dame 1961–1966; Teacher of Law, University of California, Berkeley 1967–1992, Robbins Emeritus Professor of Law 1992, University of California; US Circuit Judge, Ninth Circuit Court of Appeals 1985–. **Appointments:** Visiting Professor of Law, Boston College, Harvard, Southern Methodist and Stanford; Oliver Wendell Holmes Jr Lecturer, Harvard Law School; Editor, *American Journal of Jurisprudence* 1960–1969. **Publications:** *Persons and Masks of the Law*; *Bribes*; *The Believer and the Powers That Are*; *The Responsible Judge*; *The Lustre Of Our Country: The American Experience of Religious Freedom*.

NOOTT, The Revd Eric Hervey Jenner (1917) Born 4 May 1899, St John's Vicarage, Pendlebury, Manchester; son of William Llewellyn Octavius Noott, Clerk in Holy Orders, and Maud Frances Parratt. BA 1920; MA 1924. **Tutor(s):** E E Sikes. **Johnian Relatives:** son of William Llewellyn Octavius Noott (1877). **Educ:** Manchester Grammar School. **Career:** Deacon 1922; Priest 1923; Curate, Christchurch, Malvern until 1927; Minor Canon, Gloucester Cathedral, and Assistant Master, King's School, Gloucester 1927–1936; Honorary Minor Canon, Gloucester Cathedral, and Vicar, Barnwood 1936–1948; Chaplain, Barnwood House, Gloucester 1937; Assistant Rural Dean, Gloucester 1940; Precentor, Gloucester Cathedral, and Headmaster, King's School, Gloucester 1948; Honorary Canon, Gloucester Cathedral; Rector, Withington, Gloucestershire 1950. Died 6 February 1987.

NORBURY, Francis Campbell (1901) Born 16 January 1882, Winton House, Stratford-on-Avon; son of Thomas William Norbury, Surgeon, and Eliza Theresa Fitzgerald. **Subject(s):** Classics; BA 1904; MA 1908. **Tutor(s):** J R Tanner; C E Graves. **Educ:** Oundle School. **Career:** Classics Master, Oundle School 1904; Captain, King's Royal Rifle Corps. Died 8 January 1915 (killed in action near Bethune).

NORMAN, Colonel Charles Richard Warrens (1931) Born 5 June 1913, The Coppice, Elmstead Lane, Chislehurst; son of Charles Frederick Norman, Architect, and Dorothy Edith Warrens; m Mary Patricia Timpson, 25 June 1949; 1 son, 1 daughter. BA 1934. **Tutor(s):** C W Guillebaud. **Educ:** Falconbury, Purley; Repton School, Derby. **Career:** Second Lieutenant, Durham Light Infantry 1933; Bombay 1936, Sudan 1937, Shanghai 1938, Tientsin and Peking 1939, Middle East 1940; Middle East Staff College, Haifa; Mentioned in Despatches 1942; Western Desert GHQ Middle East, Cairo 1943; War Office, London (Joint Planning Staff) 1944; HQ, Rhine Army 1945; Directing Staff, Middle East Staff College, Haifa 1946; General Staff Intelligence, Palestine and Transjordan, Jerusalem (Lieutenant Colonel) 1946–1948; Durham Light Infantry, Dortmund; Mentioned in Despatches 1949; Ministry of Defence (NATO) London 1950; Second-in-Command, 1 Durham Light Infantry, Berlin and Korea 1952–1953; OC 6 Durham Light Infantry, Bishop Auckland, County Durham 1953–1956; GSO1

(Intelligence) Suez Canal Expedition, Cyprus 1956; GSO1 Special Military Intelligence Staff, Hong Kong 1957–1959; RN Staff College, Greenwich 1960; NATO Defence College, Paris 1961; Colonel GS (intelligence) 1961–1963; Deputy Secretary, Joint Intelligence Committee, Cabinet Office, London 1963–1964. **Appointments:** Berkshire County Councillor 1965–1974; Oxfordshire County Councillor 1974–1981 (Vice-Chairman 1977–1979, Chairman 1979–1981); Founding Member, Oxfordshire Buildings Trust; Freeman and Liveryman, City of London (Worshipful Company of Coachmakers and Coach-Harness Makers). **Honours:** OBE (Military) 1948. Died 20 September 2002.

NORMAN, Stephan Theodore (1936) See NEUMANN.

NORMAN, Sydney (1919) Born 3 May 1899, 4 Clement Street, Gloucester; son of Isaiah Thomas Norman, Railway Goods Guard, and Agnes Robinson. **Subject(s):** Natural Sciences; BA 1921; MA 1926. **Tutor(s):** E E Sikes. **Educ:** The Crypt Grammar School, Gloucester. **Career:** Private, 34th Training Reserve Battalion 1917; Private, 4th Reserve Battalion, Somerset Light Infantry 1918–1919. Died March 1973.

NORRIS, John Henry (1922) Born 15 December 1903, The Vicarage, Loddington, Leicestershire; son of William Henry Norris, Clerk in Holy Orders, and Susan May Topliss. BA 1925; MA 1929. **Tutor(s):** E A Benians. **Johnian Relatives:** son of William Henry Norris (1891). **Educ:** Preston High School; Croxton Private School, Southport; Rossall School; Ridley Hall, Cambridge. **Career:** Ordained Deacon 1927; Curate, All Saints, Clayton le Moors 1927–1933; Ordained Priest 1929; Curate, Holy Trinity, Darwen 1933–1935; Vicar, St James, Darwen 1935–1956; Vicar, St John the Evangelist, Lund 1956–1972. Died 27 February 1984.

NORSE, Adrian Osborn (1918) American Student.

NORTH, Ernest Raymond (1937) Born 19 March 1918, Thorndale Farm, Wetwang; son of Ernest Coultas North, Farmer, and Alice Mary Stonehouse; m Elaine. **Subject(s):** Mathematics; BA 1941; MA 1944. **Tutor(s):** J M Wordie. **Educ:** Wetwang Church of England School; Bridlington School. **Awards:** Minor Scholarship, SJC 1936. Died 28 February 1986.

NORTHCOTT, Professor Douglas Geoffrey (1935) Born 31 December 1916, 5 Portland Road, Kensington, London; son of Geoffrey Douglas Spence Robertson, Electrical Engineer, and Clara Freda Behl (stepson of Arthur Hugh Kynaston Northcott, Civil Servant, and surname changed to Northcott in 1935); m Rose Hilda Austin, 1949 (d 1992); 2 daughters (Anne and Pamela). **Subject(s):** Mathematics; BA 1938; MA 1946; PhD 1949; FRS 1961. **Tutor(s):** J M Wordie. **Educ:** London County Council School, Roseberry Avenue; Christ's Hospital. **Career:** RA, POW, Far East 1939–1945; Commonwealth Fund Fellow, Princeton University 1946–1948; Title A Fellow, SJC 1947–1953; Assistant Lecturer 1949–1951, Lecturer 1951–1952, University of Cambridge; Town Trust Professor of Mathematics 1952–1982 (Emeritus 1982), University of Sheffield. **Awards:** Baylis Scholarship, SJC 1934; Wright's Prize, SJC 1936; Adams Memorial Prize 1938; Hughes Prize, SJC 1938. **Publications:** *Ideal Theory*, 1953; *An Introduction to Homological Algebra*, 1960; *Lessons on Rings, Modules and Multiplicities*, 1968; *A First Course of Homological Algebra*, 1973; *Finite Free Resolutions*, 1976; *Affine Sets and Affine Groups*, 1980; *Multilinear Algebra*, 1984.

NORTHCROFT, George Bernard (1929) Born 17 June 1911, 115 Harley Street, London; son of George Northcroft, Dentist, and Baroness Eva Schlotheim; m (1) Constance Mary Skey (d), (2) Vivien; 2 sons (Gavin and Adam), 3 daughters (Joanna b 3 June 1945, Lindi b 13 October 1948 and Sarah). BA 1932; MA 1936; LRCP 1937; FRCS 1958; MRCS. **Tutor(s):** J M Wordie. **Educ:** Warren Hill School, Eastbourne; Marlborough College. **Career:** Consultant Neurosurgeon,

South-East Metropolitan Regional Health Board; Mobile Neurosurgical Unit, 8th Army, North Africa, WWII; Neurosurgeon and Consultant, Joyce Green Hospital and Brook Hospital; Civilian Advisor to the British Army and Honorary Consultant to the Army's Royal Herbert Hospital. **Honours:** MBE 1943; Silver Jubilee Medal 1977. Died 17 February 1996.

NORTHORP, The Revd Frederic (1906) Born 28 September 1887, 42 Tindall Street, Scarborough, Yorkshire; son of William Thomas Northorp, Schoolmaster, and Elizabeth Parthenia Thorlby. BA 1909; MA 1921. **Tutor(s):** E E Sikes. **Educ:** Central Board School, Scarborough; Higher Grade School, Scarborough; St Martin's Grammar School, Scarborough. **Career:** Ordained Deacon 1911; Curate, Holy Trinity, Hull 1911–1914; Ordained Priest 1912; Curate, St Jude, South Kensington 1914–1915; Temporary CF, 4th Class, RACD (mentioned in Secretary of State's list, for valuable services in connection with the war) 1915–1920; Vicar, St Margaret, Methley, Leeds 1920–1947; Vicar, Great with Little Ouseburn, Ripon 1947.

NORWOOD, David Barry (1945) Born 16 December 1926, 4 Clifton Terrace, York; son of Denis Norwood, Schoolmaster, and Eileen Williams; m Sylvia Hunt, September 1972; 1 stepson (David), 1 stepdaughter (Sarah). **Subject(s):** Classics; BA 1948; MA 1952; PGCE 1954. **Tutor(s):** R L Howland; J M Wordie. **Educ:** Fairdays School, Harborne; West House School, Edgbaston; Manchester Grammar School. **Career:** RAF Education Branch, Flight Lieutenant 1948–1953; Schoolmaster, Bradfield College, Berkshire 1954–1987 (Housemaster 1963–1982); Squadron Leader, RAFVR(T) 1960–1966; Squadron Leader, OC, CCF 1960–1966; Bradfield College, Berkshire, Deputy Head 1983–1987. **Awards:** Patchett Scholarship, SJC 1945.

NOTCUTT, George Stanley (1929) Born 3 September 1910, Constitution Hill, Ipswich; son of Stephen Abbott Notcutt, Solicitor, and Constance Turner; m Sylvia Gibson, 24 November 1945. BA 1932; MA 1977. **Tutor(s):** E A Benians. **Johnian Relatives:** son of Stephen Abbott Notcutt (1883); brother of Stephen Abbott Notcutt (1926). **Educ:** The High School, Ipswich; Ipswich School. **Career:** Captain, RA; Second Master, Ipswich School until 1975.

NOTCUTT, Stephen Abbott (1926) Born 13 August 1908, Constitution Hill, Ipswich; son of Stephen Abbott Notcutt, Solicitor, and Constance Turner. **Subject(s):** Law; BA 1929; MA 1978. **Tutor(s):** E A Benians. **Johnian Relatives:** son of Stephen Abbott Notcutt (1883); brother of George Stanley Notcutt (1929). **Educ:** Mr Cawthorne's Preparatory School, Ipswich; Ipswich School. **Career:** Solicitor. Died 25 July 1979.

NOURSE, The Revd John (1940) Born 28 August 1922, Shute Vicarage, Axminster, Devon; son of Stanhope Mackie Nourse, Vicar, Shute, Devon, and Helena Isabel Pateman; m Helen Jane MacDonald Allison, 18 May 1945, St Margaret's, Newlands, Glasgow; 2 sons (Christopher Stuart b 1946 and Philip Stanhope b 1949). **Subject(s):** Economics; BA 1943; MA 1947. **Johnian Relatives:** descendent of Peter Nourse (1678) and of Edward Nourse (1700). **Tutor(s):** C W Guillebaud. **Educ:** St Wulfram's, Bournemouth; Sherborne School; Wells Theological College. **Career:** Lieutenant, RNVR 1942–1946; Assistant Master, Salisbury Cathedral Choir School 1946–1948; Lay Vicar, Salisbury Cathedral 1946–1948; Ordained Deacon 1949; Assistant Curate, St Augustin, Bournemouth 1949–1951; Ordained Priest 1951; Assistant Master, Hurstpierpoint College 1951–1952; Priest-in-charge, St Mark, Peaslake 1952–1957; Priest-in-charge, St John the Baptist, Eton Wick 1957–1962; Assistant Master, St George's Choir School 1957–1967; Minor Canon 1957–1967, Succentor 1961–1967, St George's Chapel, Windsor Castle; Vicar, Amesbury and Officiating Chaplain, RAF Boscombe Down 1967–1969; Precentor, Canterbury Cathedral 1969–1973; Vicar, Charing and Rector, Little Chart 1973–1988. **Awards:** Archbishops' Diploma in Church Music 1990.

NOWELL-ROSTRON, The Rev Sydney (1902) See ROSTRON.

NURSE, Samuel David (1908) Born 10 October 1889, Upper Robb Street, Georgetown, Demerara, British Guiana; son of Richard David Nurse, Builder and Contractor, and Francina McDonald. **Tutor(s):** L H K Bushe-Fox. **Educ:** The Middle School, Georgetown; The Queen's College, Georgetown.

NUTTALL, Charles Herbert (1924) Born 7 June 1905, Inglegarth, Bramhall Lane, Bramhall cum Hazelgrove, Cheshire; son of Charles Herbert Nuttall, Cotton Manufacturer, and Edith Helen Orr. BA 1927. **Tutor(s):** E A Benians. **Educ:** The Old College, Windermere; Malvern College.

NUTTALL, John Wardleworth (1944) Born 9 March 1926, 78 Rodney Street, Liverpool; son of Henry Clarence Wardleworth Nuttall, Surgeon, and Frances Lea Roberts; m (1) Mary Newcomb, 12 August 1950, Walberswick, Suffolk (div 1960), (2) Margaret Elizabeth Taylor, 26 November 1960. BA 1949; MA 1951. **Tutor(s):** S J Bailey. **Johnian Relatives:** descendant of James Wood (1778); brother of Richard Wardleworth Nuttall (1945). **Educ:** Grove Park School, Liverpool; Liverpool College; Marlborough College. **Career:** Competitions Manager, Smiths Motor Accessories Ltd until 1962; various printing firms, finally Garden House Press Ltd, London 1962–1985.

NUTTALL, Richard Wardleworth (1945) Born 20 October 1927, 78 Rodney Street, Liverpool; son of Henry Clarence Wardleworth Nuttall, Surgeon, and Frances Lea Roberts; m Veryll Sever, 21 March 1953. **Subject(s):** Natural Sciences; BA 1950; MA 1952. **Tutor(s):** C W Guillebaud. **Johnian Relatives:** descendant of James Wood (1778); brother of John Wardleworth Nuttall (1944). **Educ:** Grove Park School, Liverpool; Liverpool College; Marlborough College. **Career:** Chairman and Managing Director, Devon Boats Ltd, Exeter.

NUTTER, Jack Crossley (1943) Born 4 November 1925, Birch Hill House, Wardle, Lancashire; son of Horace Nutter, Electrical Engineer, and Gladys Margaret Crossley. **Subject(s):** Natural Sciences; BA 1946; MA 1956. **Tutor(s):** C W Guillebaud. **Educ:** Heybrook Council School, Rochdale; Hounslow Town School; Latymer Upper School, Hammersmith.

NYE, Ian William Beresford (1943) Born 7 May 1924, 47 Lavender Gardens, Battersea, London; son of George Vincent Nye, Chartered Surveyor, and Helen Long Fullerton; m Mary Evelyn Standley, 20 December 1952. **Tutor(s):** C W Guillebaud. **Educ:** St Christopher's School, Hove; Brighton, Hove and Sussex Grammar School; Brighton College. **Appointments:** RE Cadet, SJC.

NYE, John Tompsett (1944) Born 11 September 1927, Thrums, High Street, Cranbrook, Kent; son of Edward Nye, Solicitor's Clerk, and Mary Edith Tompsett; m (1) Audrey Enid Carpenter, 22 December 1951, (2) Stephanie Payn, 21 November 1961; (1) 1 son (Tony b 1952), (2) 2 daughters (Mandy b 1962 and Melanie b 1966). **Subject(s):** Natural Sciences; BA 1950; MA 1953. **Tutor(s):** C W Guillebaud; G C L Bertram; E Miller. **Johnian Relatives:** brother of Richard Tompsett Nye (1951). **Educ:** Horsmonden Grammar School; Cranbrook School. **Career:** Special Investigation Branch, RAF 1945–1948; Production Manager, Kent Mouldings 1952–1957; PA Management Consultants 1957–1959; Housemaster, Box Hill School 1960–1963; Chief Production Engineer, Kent Mouldings 1963–1964; Senior Master, Holmewood House 1965–1970; Independent Management Consultant 1968; Associate, Coverdale Plc 1970–2000. **Appointments:** Associate, Plastics Institute 1955; Associate Member, British Institute of Management 1957; Committee Member, Pioneer Health Centre 1980–1997; Trustee and Chairman, Weald of Kent Branch, Crossroads Caring for Carers 1996–2001; Young Enterprise 2001. **Publications:** Technical papers on plastics 1956–1970.

O

OADES, Reginald Charles (1926) Born 3 October 1907, 13 Park Road, Fremantle, Shirley, Southampton; son of Charles James Percival Oades, Civil Servant, and Harriett Hipwood Steele. **Subject(s):** Mathematics; BA 1929; MA 1949; FIS; FSS. **Tutor(s):** J M Wordie. **Educ:** King Edward VI School, Southampton. **Career:** Head, Statistical Department, Chamber of Shipping; Inland Revenue Department 1944. **Awards:** Sizarship, SJC 1926. **Honours:** MBE 1969.

OAKDEN, Dr George Frederic (1916) Born 26 February 1897, 33 Upper Talbot Street, Nottingham; son of Edward Oakden and Alice Fairbanks; m Isabel Mary Giles, 24 June 1931, All Saints Church, Milton. **Subject(s):** Mathematics/Mechanical Sciences; BA 1921; MA 1927; MB 1927; BChir 1927. **Tutor(s):** E E Sikes. **Educ:** Nottingham High School; Oundle School. **Career:** Anaesthetist, St Thomas' Hospital; Honorary Anaesthetist, Addenbrooke's Hospital; Senior Resident Medical Officer, House Surgeon and House Physician, Royal Infirmary, Chester.

OAKDEN, John Clarke (1918) Born 25 July 1900, 10 Pearson Street, Brierley Hill, Staffordshire; son of William Henry Oakden, Glass Decorator, and Rebecca Catherine Clarke; m Phyllis; 2 daughters (Elisabeth and Carolyn). **Subject(s):** Mathematics/Mechanical Sciences; BA 1921; MA 1925; MScTech (Manchester) 1934; FIMechE. **Tutor(s):** E E Sikes. **Educ:** Moor Street Council School, Brierley Hill; King Edward VI Grammar School, Stourbridge. **Career:** Assistant Lecturer in Mechanical Engineering, Faculty of Technology, University of Manchester 1925; Head, Department of Civil and Mechanical Engineering, Northampton Polytechnic (College of Advanced Technology) 1938–1966; Professor Emeritus, The City University, London 1966. Died 16 August 1989.

OAKLEY, Edgar Handel (1921) Born 21 July 1903, 22 Lawn Road, Portswood, Southampton; son of Alfred Henry Oakley, Shipping Contractor, and Bessie Brinton; m Nancy Doris Robinson, 4 April 1935, All Souls' Church, Langham Place, London; 2 sons (Michael Alfred b 1 January 1936 and Anthony Richard b 22 April 1940). BA 1924; MA 1944. **Tutor(s):** E E Sikes. **Johnian Relatives:** father of Michael Alfred Oakley (1956). **Educ:** Marlborough College. **Career:** Assistant Master, King's College Junior School, Wimbledon 1948–1956. Died 21 September 1976.

OAKLEY, The Revd Frederick Christian (1908) Born 27 September 1888, 4 Serington Street, Paddington, London; son of Edwin Henry Oakley, Clerk in Holy Orders, and Alice Harriet Anderson; m Olive Mary Raymond, 6 June 1919, Wickham St Paul's. **Subject(s):** Classics; BA 1911. **Tutor(s):** E E Sikes. **Educ:** Fauconbergh School, Beccles; Felsted School; Clergy Training School, Cambridge. **Career:** Ordained Deacon 1914; Curate, St Peter Mancroft, Norwich 1914–1918; Priest 1915; Temporary CF 1918–1919; Curate, Wymondham 1919–1924; Rector, Booton 1924–1926; Rector, Necton 1926–1945; Honorary Canon, Norwich 1941–1945; Curate, St John's Cathedral, Antigua, British West Indies (Registrar 1947) 1946. **Publications:** Various pieces for *The Eagle*.

OATLEY, Professor Sir Charles William (1922) Born 14 February 1904, 5A Badcox, Frome, Somerset; son of William Oatley, Baker and Grocer, and Ada Mary Dorrington, School Teacher; m (Dorothy) Enid West, 1930; 2 sons. **Subject(s):** Natural Sciences; BA 1925; MA 1931; Honorary DSc (Heriot-Watt University) 1974; Honorary DSc (Bath) 1977; FIEE; FEng; FRS 1969. **Tutor(s):** B F Armitage. **Educ:** Council School, Frome; Bedford Modern School. **Career:** Demonstrator, later Lecturer, Department of Physics, KCL 1927–1939; Air Defence Experimental Establishment (ADEE), Christchurch, Dorset, later located at Malvern as Radar Research and Development Establishment, Ministry of Supply 1939–1945; Acting Superintendent in charge of scientific work 1944–1945; Fellow, Trinity College, Cambridge 1945; Lecturer, later Reader, Department of Engineering 1945–1960, Professor of Electrical Engineering 1960–1971, University of Cambridge;

Director, English Electric Valve Company 1966–1985. **Appointments:** Foreign Associate, US National Academy of Engineering 1979. **Awards:** Exhibition, SJC 1922; Faraday Medal, Institute of Electrical Engineers 1970. **Honours:** OBE 1956; Kt 1974. **Publications:** *Wireless Receivers*, 1932; *The Scanning Electron Microscope*, 1972. Died 11 March 1996.

OBBARD, Harry Naismith (1921) Born 27 April 1898, Benares, India; son of Edward Naismith Obbard, Colonel, Army, and Florence Ella Molyneux Hutchinson. **Tutor(s):** E A Benians. **Educ:** Gisburne House, Watford; Inholmes School, Cheltenham; Haileybury College.

O'BRIEN, Charles Ian Milward (1948) Born 22 December 1927, 35 St George's Road, Edgbaston, Birmingham; son of John Francis Clare O'Brien, Senior Agricultural Officer, Tanganyika, and Esther Mary Milward; m Marion Ceinwedd Mary Lloyd, 19 October 1963, St Mark's, Surbiton. **Subject(s):** Geography; BA 1950. **Tutor(s):** J M Wordie. **Educ:** Bedales School; Dunhurst School, Petersfield. **Career:** RE 1946–1948; Directorate of Overseas Surveys 1953–1984 (Assistant Director 1963). **Awards:** Exhibition, SJC.

O'BRIEN, John Bernard (1942) Born 16 May 1924, Protestant Hospital, Salita San Rocchino, Genoa, Italy; son of Edward Joseph Harrington O'Brien, Author, and Florence Roma Muir Wilson. **Tutor(s):** S J Bailey. **Educ:** Dragon School, Oxford; Summerfields School, Oxford; Bedales School.

O'CONNELL, Peter (1944) Born 14 December 1918, Streatham Manor, Leigham Avenue, Streatham, Surrey; son of Henry O'Connell, Director and Secretary, Paper Company, and Grace Arnold; m Lea Kummer; 1 daughter (Suseli). **Subject(s):** History; BA 1946; MA 1956. **Tutor(s):** C W Guillebaud. **Educ:** Elmhurst Preparatory School, Croydon; Dulwich College. **Career:** Firm of East Indian rubber planters and tin miners; Officer, Royal Corps of Signals 1939; History Teacher, Boston, Massachusetts 1951–1955; Schoolmaster, St Paul's School 1955–1957; Founder Summer-only English Vacation School 1957; Founder, School of English Studies, Grimston Gardens, Folkestone 1960–1987; Launched Keyman Executive Course 1964; Studied the Suggestopedia method of language learning under its founder, Georgi Lozanov 1975; English Teacher, Beijing University 1977; Co-Founder, Society for Effective Affective Learning (SEAL) 1983. **Awards:** Best Business in Kent, School of English Studies, Grimston Gardens, Folkestone 1993. Died 5 September 1998.

O'CONNOR, Brian (1926) Born 23 January 1910, Allandale, Tarvin Road, Great Boughton, Cheshire; son of Peter Vincent O'Connor, Superintendent Clerk, Public Health Department, and Beatrice Coates. **Subject(s):** Classics; BA 1931; MA 1934. **Tutor(s):** M P Charlesworth. **Educ:** Chester Council School; The King's School, Chester. **Career:** Called to the Bar, Inner Temple 1946.

ODELL, William Norman (1929) Born 14 December 1910, Ferndale, Torquay; son of William Odell, Medical Practitioner, and Ruth Annie Moore; m Yolande Isa Upward, 10 April 1947, St Mary's Church, Motcombe, Dorset. **Subject(s):** History; BA 1932; MA 1936. **Tutor(s):** E A Benians. **Educ:** St Agnes School, Babbacome, Torquay; Park House School, Paignton; Epsom College. **Career:** Schoolmaster; RAC, Intelligence Corps 1940–1946; Licensed Reader, Diocese of Salisbury 1960. **Awards:** Sizarship, SJC 1929.

ODGERS, Lindsay Noel Blake (1911) Born 21 December 1892, 71 Fitzjohn's Avenue, London; son of William Blake Odgers, Barrister-at-Law, and Frances Hudson; m Constance Attneave, 6 September 1923, St John's Church, Groombridge. **Subject(s):** Mathematics; BA 1914; MA 1918. **Tutor(s):** J R Tanner. **Johnian Relatives:** brother of Robert Blake Odgers (1908). **Educ:** Rugby School. **Career:** Lieutenant, Middlesex Regiment, then Captain, RE; Assistant Under-Secretary of State, Fire Service Department, Home Office 1951. **Awards:** Scholarship, SJC. **Honours:** MC (WWI).

ODGERS, Robert Blake (1908) Born 26 February 1890, 71 Fitzjohn's Avenue, London; son of William Blake Odgers, Barrister-at-Law, and Frances Hudson; m Olive Asquith Brewerton, 10 June 1915, St Augustine's Church, Edgbaston. BA 1911; MIM 1917. **Tutor(s):** J R Tanner. **Johnian Relatives:** brother of Lindsay Noel Blake Odgers (1911). **Educ:** Sedbergh School. **Career:** Birmingham Metal and Munitions Company Ltd 1911 (Assistant to Head of Inspection Department 1914); Territorial RASC; Captain 1914; General Superintendent, Government Cartridge Factory 1916. Died 31 August 1917.

O'DONOVAN, Daniel (1930) Born 8 January 1912, 54 Stanmore Road, Tottenham; son of Jeremiah O'Donovan, Clerical Officer, and Julia Hurley; m Margaret Rawson, 1940; 3 sons, 2 daughters. **Subject(s):** Mathematics/Economics; BA 1933; MA 1937. **Tutor(s):** J M Wordie. **Johnian Relatives:** father of Robert Vincent O'Donovan (1970). **Educ:** St Ignatius College, Stamford Hill. **Career:** Civil Service 1933; Ministry of Information 1940–1945; Treasury 1945–1956; Secretary, Civil Service Commission 1956–1966; Assistant Secretary, Department of Education and Science 1966–1972; Mathematics Teacher 1972–1980. **Awards:** Baylis Scholarship, SJC. Died 14 April 1980.

OFFICER, Leonard Adrian (1948) Born 26 February 1928, The Vicarage, Barrow on Humber, Lincolnshire; son of Leonard Sydney Officer, Clerk in Holy Orders, and Gladys Eleanor Turner. **Subject(s):** Music; BA 1950; MA 1955; MusB 1951. **Tutor(s):** C W Guillebaud. **Educ:** St Hugh's Preparatory School, Woodhall Spa; Durham School. **Career:** National Service, RAF 1946–1948; Ernest Bailey Grammar School, Matlock 1952–1953; Southwell Minster Grammar School 1953–1960; Archbishop Holgate's Grammar School, York 1960–1965; Marine and Technical College, South Shields 1965–1983. **Publications:** *Who was Ernest Farrar? 1885–1918.*

OFFORD, Professor Albert Cyril (1934) Born 9 June 1906, 21 Braydon Road, Stamford Hill, London; son of Albert Edwin Offord, Printer's Manager, and Hester Louise Sexton; m Marguerite Yvonne Pickard, 4 August 1945; 1 daughter (Margaret Alison). PhD 1936; DSc (London) 1937; FRSE 1948; FRS 1952. **Tutor(s):** J M Wordie. **Educ:** Hackney Downs; UCL. **Career:** Title A Fellow, SJC 1937–1940; Lecturer, University College Wales, Bangor 1940–1941; Lecturer 1941–1945, Professor 1945–1948, King's College, Newcastle upon Tyne; Professor, Birkbeck College, University of London 1948–1966; Professor of Mathematics, LSE 1966–1973 (Emeritus 1973–2000). **Appointments:** Assistant Supervisor in Mathematics, SJC 1937–1938; Honorary Fellow, LSE 1978–2000. **Awards:** Strathcona Studentship, SJC 1935. **Publications:** Papers in various mathematical journals. Died 4 June 2000.

OGDEN, Guy William (1925) Born 13 June 1899, 15 West Hill Road, Wandsworth, London; son of Michael Guy Ogden, Architect and Surveyor, and Fanny Bridge. **Subject(s):** Mechanical Sciences; BA 1928; MA 1932. **Tutor(s):** J M Wordie. **Educ:** King's College School, Wimbledon; RMC, Camberley.

OGDEN, Leonard Dawson (1943) Born 19 March 1926, Davyhulme, Lancashire; son of Herbert William Ogden, Schoolmaster, and Mildred Elsie Dawson; m Valerie Anne Derrett, 1952; 1 son (Michael Gordon), 1 daughter (Elisabeth Anne). **Subject(s):** Mechanical Sciences; BA 1946; Diploma (Imperial) 1948; AMICE 1952; MICE 1968. **Educ:** Flixton Junior School; Manchester Grammar School; Imperial College, London. **Career:** Engineering Officer, RN, HMS *Zest* and HMS *Aurora* 1945–1947; Design Engineer, Site Engineer and Contracts Engineer, Peter Lind & Co, Civil Engineering Contractors 1948–1952; Chartered Civil Engineer 1952–1968; Project Engineer, Project Manager then Chief Engineer, Bombay Office, Sir Bruce White & Partners 1953–1964; Project Engineering and Project Management, Shell International Petroleum 1964–1984; Part-time Consultant to Enterprise Oil 1984–1994. **Awards:** State Bursary 1943.

OGDEN, Robert David (1949) Born 6 March 1930, Pent House, Almondbury, Yorkshire; son of Robert James Ogden, Medical Practitioner, and Frances Hirst; m Shirley Georgina Maclay, 25 June 1955; 3 sons (Nicholas, Jeremy and Ben), 1 daughter (Emma). **Subject(s):** Law; BA 1952; MA 1956. **Tutor(s):** A G Lee. **Johnian Relatives:** son-in-law of Walter Symington Maclay (1919); brother-in-law of Walter Strang Symington Maclay (1949) and of John Lennox Sim Maclay (1957). **Educ:** PNEU School, Huddersfield; St George's School, Windsor; Malsis Hall Preparatory School, Crosshills; Repton School. **Career:** Insurance Consultant. Died 1992.

OGILVIE, David Alexander (1948) Born 2 August 1927, 20 Murrayfield Gardens, Edinburgh; son of Frederick Wolff Ogilvie, Principal, Jesus College, Oxford, and Mary Helen Macaulay, Principal, St Anne's College, Oxford; m Hilary Hopkins, 31 July 1952; 3 sons, 1 daughter. **Subject(s):** Mechanical Sciences; BA 1950; MA 1955; BA (Open University) 1986; AMIMechE. **Tutor(s):** R L Howland. **Educ:** Packwood Haugh, Ruyton-XI-Towns; Rugby School. **Career:** RAC 1946–1948; District Officer Cadet, HM Colonial Service, Northern Rhodesia 1952–1954; Technical Manager and Director, Baker Perkins Ltd, Peterborough 1955–1966; Director, Small Business Division, Scottish Development Agency, Edinburgh 1966–1982; Head, Technical Operations Centre for the Development of Industry (ACP/EEC Lomé Convention), Brussels 1982–1986. **Appointments:** Member, Policy Board, then Volunteer Adviser, British Executive Service Overseas, London 1986–2002; Chairman, Graduate Association 1998–1999, Member of Senate 1999–2002, Open University. **Awards:** Major Scholarship, SJC 1945. **Publications:** Various publications on small businesses in *UNIDO* and other journals.

OGILVY, Kenneth Airlie (1943) Born 8 May 1925, 16 Trinity Road, Leith; son of Charles Ogilvy, Sales Manager, and Euphemia Laing; m Catriona McCance, 17 September 1949. **Tutor(s):** S J Bailey. **Educ:** Dulwich College.

OHM, Donald McKay (1904) Born 1 June 1884, The Grammar School House, Wigan, Lancashire; son of James Ohm, Principal, and Mary Gertrude McKay; m Gertrude Louisa Horobin; 1 daughter (Daphne d 1956). **Subject(s):** Mathematics; BA 1907; MA 1913. **Tutor(s):** D MacAlister. **Johnian Relatives:** son of James Ohm (1871); brother-in-law of George Charles Edward Simpson (1899). **Educ:** Wigan Grammar School. **Career:** Schoolmaster, Penarth Lodge, South Wales 1907–1908; Schoolmaster, Handel College, Southampton 1908–1909; Schoolmaster, Quernmore School 1909–1910; Second Master, Northwich Grammar School 1910–1917; Headmaster, Grace Ramsden's Grammar School, Elland and Lecturer, Huddersfield Technical College 1917–1919. Died 9 February 1967.

OKE, Balkrishna Yeshwant (1933) Born 14 February 1911, Akola, Berar, India; son of Yeshwant Ramchandra Oke, Pleader, and Yeshawadabai Phadake. MSc 1956; BSc (India) 1931; MSc (India) 1933. **Tutor(s):** J M Wordie. **Educ:** Government High School, Akola, India; Royal Institute of Science, University of Bombay. **Career:** Professor of Mathematics, Ramnarain Ruia College, Matunga, University of Bombay 1951.

OKELL, Dr Charles Cyril (1908) Born 10 December 1888, Primrose Avenue, Alexander Drive, Douglas, Isle of Man; son of Charles Percy Okell, Gentleman, Architect and Insurance Agent, and Marianne Kinley; m Dorothy Gladys Roberts, 2 January 1917; 2 daughters. **Subject(s):** Natural Sciences; BA 1911; MA 1936; BChir 1921; MB 1921; ScD 1937; MRCS; LRCP 1915; DPH 1923; Diploma in Tropical Medicine and Hygiene 1930; FRCP 1932. **Tutor(s):** L H K Bushe-Fox. **Educ:** Victoria College, Douglas; Douglas Grammar School. **Career:** Captain, RAMC, France, Palestine and Egypt, WWI; Wellcome Physiological Research Laboratories; Professor of Bacteriology, University College Hospital 1930. **Appointments:** Assistant Editor, *Journal of Pathology and Bacteriology*; Editor, *Journal of Hygiene*. **Awards:** Hichens Prize 1914; Wix Prize 1914; Brackenbury Scholarship in Medicine 1915; Milroy Lecturer 1932. **Honours:** MC. **Publications:** 'Titration of Diphtheria

Toxin and Antitoxin by Flocculation Methods', *Journal of Pathology and Bacteriology*, 1924; 'Rapid Control of Diphtheria Outbreak in Institutions', *Lancet*, 1924; 'Leptospiral Jaundice in Dogs', *Veterinary Journal*, 1925; 'The Role of the Haemolytic Streptococci in Infective Diseases' (Milroy Lecture), 1932. Died 8 February 1939.

OLDHAM, Frank (1925) Born 17 March 1903, 112 Harrow Road, Leicester; son of Charles Oldham, Investigation Officer, School Clinic, and Edith Sarah Hopkins. **Subject(s):** Natural Sciences; BA 1927; MA 1932; BSc (London) 1925. **Tutor(s):** J M Wordie. **Educ:** Alderman Newton's School, Leicester; KCL. **Career:** Physics Master, Manchester Grammar School 1927–1933; Headmaster, Hinckley Grammar School 1933–1963. **Appointments:** JP, Leicestershire 1943–1964; President, Midland Branch, Institute of Physics 1961–1963; President, Midland Branch, Association for Science 1963–1964; Chairman, Education Group and Member of Council, Institute of Physics 1963–1966; JP, Bournemouth 1964–1973; President, Bournemouth Natural Science Society 1976–1977; Chairman, Hinckley Branch of JPs. **Awards:** Jelf Medal, KCL; Scholarship, SJC 1927; Hockin Prize, SJC 1927. **Publications:** *Thomas Young, Philosopher and Physician*, 1933; *General Physics*, 1939; *Thomas Young, Natural Philosopher*, 1954; *Physics for Today*, 1963. Died 25 September 1989.

OLDHAM, John Hugh (1931) Born 30 July 1912, Martindale, Little Heath, North Mimms; son of James Edward Valentin Oldham, Wine Shipper, and Beatrice Mary Johnson. **Subject(s):** History/Law; BA 1934; MA 1938. **Tutor(s):** E A Benians. **Educ:** Inglemere, Enfield; Norman Court, Potters Bar; Haileybury College. Died 30 July 1993.

OLDROYD, James (1931) Born 13 October 1912, Dewsbury Gate Road, Staincliffe, Batley; son of George Willie Oldroyd, Meat Trader, and Mary Alice Oakland; m Mary Elizabeth Morgan (née Howard), 26 October 1991; 2 sons (James Robin Hawdon and Christopher, d 1982), 1 daughter (Elizabeth Joy Folland). **Subject(s):** History/Law; BA 1934; MA 1946; FCIS 1953. **Tutor(s):** J S Boys Smith; M P Charlesworth. **Educ:** Staincliffe Church of England School, Batley; Batley Grammar School. **Career:** TA 1936–1950 (commissioned Second Lieutenant, Tyne Electrical Engineers 1936); On active service 1939–1945 (France 1940, India 1943–1944, UK 1944–1945), demobilised rank of Major; Assistant Secretary, Croydon Gas Company Ltd 1946–1948; Assistant Secretary, Crosse and Blackwell Co Ltd 1949–1952; Secretary, British Electrical & Allied Manufacturers Association 1953–1963; Secretary, MK Electric Ltd 1964–1973. **Appointments:** Eagle, SJC; Chairman, Society of Yorkshiremen in London; Chairman, Yorkshire Society (Honorary Treasurer 1982); Vice-President, Surrey RFU; Vice-President, Warlingham RFC; Trustee, Ockham CC; MCC. **Honours:** TD 1948.

O'LEARY, Terence Daniel (1948) Born 18 August 1928, 40 Brunswick Court, Bermondsey, London; son of Daniel Hugh O'Leary, Engineer, and Mary Ellen Duggan; m Janet Douglas Berney, 1960; twin sons, 1 daughter. **Subject(s):** History; BA 1950; MA 1978. **Tutor(s):** F Thistlethwaite. **Educ:** St George's Roman Catholic School, Southwark; St Michael's Central School; Clapham College; Dulwich College. **Career:** Commissioned, Queen's Royal Regiment 1946–1948; Commerce 1951–1953; Assistant Principal, CRO 1953–1956; Second Secretary, British High Commission, Wellington 1956–1958; Principal, PSO's Department, CRO 1958–1960; First Secretary, New Delhi 1960–1963; First Secretary, Dar es Salaam 1963–1964; CRO 1964–1965; First Secretary and Defence Secretary, Canberra 1965–1968; Acting Head, South Asia Department, FCO 1969–1970; Assistant Secretary, Cabinet Office 1970–1972; Counsellor, Pretoria/Cape Town 1972–1974; Deputy High Commissioner, Wellington 1974–1978; Senior Civil Member, Directing Staff, National Defence College 1978–1981; High Commissioner, Sierra Leone 1981–1984; High Commissioner, New Zealand and Western Samoa, and Governor of Pitcairn 1984–1988. **Appointments:** Captain, TA 1946–1954; Chairman, Petworth Preservation 1989; Member and SBO, EC Monitoring Mission, Yugoslavia 1991–1992; Parish Councillor (Independent), Petworth 1993–1997. **Honours:** CMG 1982.

OLIPHANT, Sir Marcus Laurence Elwin (1934) (admitted to Trinity College 1927) Born 8 October 1901, Kent Town, Australia; son of Harold George Oliphant, Civil Servant and University Lecturer, and Beatice Fanny Tucker; m Rosa Wilbraham, 1925, Adelaide, Australia (d 1987); 1 son, 1 daughter (Vivien Wilson). PhD 1929 (Trinity); Honorary DSc (Toronto, Belfast, Melbourne, Birmingham, New South Wales, ANU, Adelaide); Honorary LLD (St Andrews); FRS 1937; FAA 1954; FTS 1976. **Educ:** Adelaide University, South Australia; Trinity College, Cambridge. **Career:** Manhattan Project; Title B Fellow, SJC 1934–1937; Assistant Director of Research, Cavendish Laboratory, University of Cambridge 1935; Poynting Professor of Physics, University of Birmingham 1937–1950; Director, Research School of Physical Sciences, ANU, Canberra 1950–1963; Professor of Physics of Ionised Gases, Institute of Advanced Studies, ANU 1964–1967; Governor of South Australia 1971–1976. **Appointments:** Messel Research Fellow, Royal Society 1931; Supervisor 1934–1937, Honorary Fellow 1952–2000, SJC; President, Australian Academy of Sciences 1954–1957; Chadwick Birth Centenary, Liverpool and Cambridge 1991; Patron, Funders University Medical Research Foundation; Patron, University of Adelaide Alumni Association. **Honours:** KBE 1959; KStJ 1972; AC 1977. **Publications:** *Recollections of the Cambridge Days*, 1972; various papers on electricity in gases, surface properties and nuclear physics. Died 14 July 2000.

OLIVER, Anthony Giles Gale (1941) Born 24 February 1923, 47 Marlborough Road, Hull; son of Cyril Henry Oliver, Dental Surgeon, and Olive Watt; m Elizabeth Ann Hooper, 12 July 1952. **Tutor(s):** S J Bailey. **Educ:** Froebel House, Hull; Hymers College, Hull.

OLIVER, Edward Spencer (1938) Born 3 December 1919, Lytham Cottage, Longmore Road, Shirley, Birmingham; son of Henry Hubert Oliver, Solicitor's Clerk, and Helen Elizabeth Spencer. **Subject(s):** Modern and Medieval Languages. **Tutor(s):** C W Guillebaud. **Educ:** Hall Green Elementary School, Birmingham; Solihull Roman Catholic Elementary School; Solihull School, Warwickshire. **Career:** War service. **Awards:** Exhibition, SJC 1937. Died 9 May 1940 (of wounds received in action).

OLIVER, Kenneth Raymond (1932) Born 4 February 1912, 11 London Road, Tunbridge Wells, Kent; son of Arthur John Oliver, Motor Engineer, and Edith Caroline Piper. **Subject(s):** Natural Sciences; BA 1935. **Tutor(s):** J M Wordie. **Educ:** Skinner's School, Tunbridge Wells; Tonbridge School.

OLIVER, Dr Tom Logan (1931) Born 27 October 1912, 7 Market Place, Thetford, Norfolk; son of Archibald Oliver, Medical Practitioner, and Helen Mary Dalgleish; m Constance Elizabeth Vincent; 1 son (Roderick Timothy Desmond b 4 August 1942). BA 1934; MA 1938; MB 1940; BChir 1940. **Tutor(s):** M P Charlesworth. **Johnian Relatives:** father of Roderick Timothy Desmond Oliver (1960). **Educ:** Lydgate House School, Hunstanton; Merchiston Castle School, Edinburgh.

OLIVER, William George (1932) Born 9 January 1913, Hope Terrace, Home End, Fulbourn, Cambridgeshire; son of William Thomas Oliver, Nurse, and Annie Cutler. **Subject(s):** Natural Sciences; BA 1935; MA 1955. **Tutor(s):** C W Guillebaud. **Educ:** C of E School, Fulbourn; Council School, Fulbourn; Cambridge and County High School for Boys. Died 10 March 1992.

OLLETT, Francis Arthur (1922) Born 12 May 1903, 50 Victoria Road, Clapham, London; son of Charles Edward Ollett, Schoolmaster, and Evelyn Margaret Syder; m Mary Louisa. **Subject(s):** History; BA 1925; MA 1929. **Tutor(s):** E A Benians. **Educ:** Bonneville Road School, London; Emanuel School, Wandsworth. **Career:** Tutor, Extra-Mural Department, University College, Leicester 1929–1936; Adult Education Tutor, Somerset 1936; Adult Education Tutor, Dorset, under Bristol and Southampton Universities, later Senior Tutor of Adult Education; Senior Lecturer, Bristol University. Died 11 December 1964.

O'MEARA, Julian Francis (1921) Born 3 January 1903, 6 Medora Road, Brixton Hill, Surrey; son of William Francis O'Meara, Foreign Correspondent, and Eva Mary Turner. **Subject(s):** History; BA 1924. **Tutor(s):** E A Benians. **Educ:** Madame Darnley's School, Thornton Heath; Winterborne Road School, Thornton Heath; Whitgift Middle School, Croydon; Whitgift Grammar School, Croydon. **Awards:** Exhibition, SJC.

O'NEILL, Hugh Cecil (1939) Born 28 February 1921, Clonony, Windsor Road, Saltburn-by-Sea; son of Cecil Arthur O'Neill, Director of Companies, and Irene Alexandrine Stewart; m France Mary Felicia Pascoe, 9 July 1955. **Subject(s):** Economics. **Tutor(s):** C W Guillebaud. **Educ:** Glenhow Preparatory School, Saltburn-by-Sea; Uppingham School.

OPENSHAW, James Frederick Melville (1928) Born 8 February 1909, 46 Leyland Road, Southport, Lancashire; son of James Openshaw, Barrister-at-Law, and Muriel Ellen Melville; m Heather Christine Seckham, 16 April 1935, Longdon Parish Church, Staffordshire. BA 1931; MA 1936. **Tutor(s):** C W Guillebaud. **Educ:** Stanmore Park; Harrow School. **Career:** King's Own Royal Regiment (Lancaster) 1931. Died 12 May 1965.

OPENSHAW, Norman (1932) Born 3 June 1913, 3 Holly Bank, Entwistle, Lancashire; son of Arnold Charles Openshaw, Yarn Salesman, and Clara Roscow. **Tutor(s):** C W Guillebaud. **Educ:** Bolton School; Sedbergh Preparatory School; Sedbergh School.

OPPENHEIMER, Dr Gordon (OSBORNE) (1932) Born 17 May 1914, 32 Cranfield Gardens, Hampstead; son of Michel Oppenheimer, Meat Importer, and Grace Evadne Michaelson; 2 daughters. BA 1935; MB 1939; BChir 1939; MD 1953; MRCP 1947; DMRD 1949. **Tutor(s):** R L Howland. **Educ:** The Hall Preparatory School, Hampstead; St Paul's School, Hammersmith. **Career:** RAF 1939–1946; Consultant Radiologist, Whittington Hospital, London 1954–1965. Died 6 November 1961.

ORCHARD, Anthony Clavis (1940) Born 29 May 1921, 1 Sefton Drive, Toxteth Park, Liverpool; son of John Orchard, Barrister-at-Law, and Miriam Emma Sumner; m Barbara Olive Eales White, 1 June 1946; 2 sons (Malcolm Anthony Edward b 1950 and Timothy John b 1951), 1 daughter (Sharan Ann b 1953). **Subject(s):** Mechanical and Electrical Engineering; BA 1944; MA 1947; AMICE; FICE 1969. **Tutor(s):** S J Bailey. **Johnian Relatives:** brother-in-law of Malcolm Edward Eales White (1940). **Educ:** St Christopher's, Liverpool; St Peter's, Exmouth; Exeter School. **Career:** Army 1942–1947, in India 1944–1946; Captain, IEME; Discharged Captain, REME 1947; Under Indentures, Wilton & Bell, consulting civil engineers 1947–1949; Worked with various civil engineering contractors including Scottish Hydro-Electric Scheme experience 1949–1953; Sir Murdoch MacDonald & Partners, consulting civil engineers, hydraulics, irrigation, groundwater design and construction 1953–1984.

ORCHARDSON, Ian Kipkerui (1949) Born 5 December 1929, Karatwet, Kericho, Kenya; son of Ian Quiller Orchardson, Tea Planter, and Taplule Chebkatam. **Subject(s):** History; BA 1952; MA 1961. **Tutor(s):** G C L Bertram. **Educ:** Dartington Hall, Devon; Kirkcudbright Academy; Kilquhanity School, Castle Douglas; St Christopher's School, Letchworth.

ORDE, Henry Leonard Shafto (1946) Born 13 January 1922, Burnaby Lodge, Ryton, Durham; son of Roden Horace Powlett Orde, Director, Joint Bureau of Hospital Information, and Augusta Isobel Amelia Law; m Micheline Grégoire, 9 November 1948, Huy, Belgium. **Subject(s):** Mathematics; BA 1948. **Tutor(s):** G C L Bertram. **Educ:** Mall School, Strawberry Hill; St Paul's School.

ORME, Donald Harrison (1945) Born 12 July 1927, 40 Ruskin Road, Congleton, Cheshire; son of Frank Orme, Commercial Traveller, and Mary Watkinson. **Subject(s):** Mechanical Sciences; BA 1948; MA 1952.

Tutor(s): S J Bailey; R L Howland. **Educ:** The Leys Preparatory School, Stockport; Stockport Grammar School; Solihull School.

ORME, Frank Leslie (1919) Born 10 May 1898, The Orchards, Buxton Road, Stockport; son of Edward Banks Orme, Cotton Merchant, and Kate Robinson; m (1) Margaret Clarke, 23 June 1927, Holy Trinity, Brompton, (2) Joan; 4 sons (Peter, Michael, Charles and Anthony). **Subject(s):** Economics; BA 1921. **Tutor(s):** E E Sikes. **Johnian Relatives:** brother of John Alexander Orme (1923); father of John Anthony Orme (1965). **Educ:** Braeside School, West Kirby; Charterhouse. **Career:** RMA, Woolwich 1915–1916; 2nd Brigade, RFA 1916; 19th Brigade RFA, Salonika 1916–1918; 27th Division Headquarters 1918–1919; Acting Captain, Army of the Black Sea 1919; Captain, Reserve of Officers 1919; Director, Thames and Mersey Marine Insurance Company Ltd, London Chambers, Liverpool and Vice-President, Liverpool Cotton Association Ltd 1921. **Honours:** OBE 1946. Died 25 December 1958.

ORME, John Alexander (1923) Born 3 February 1905, Glenmore, Oaklands Road, Hoylake cum West Kirby, Chester; son of Edward Banks Orme, Cotton Broker, and Kate Robinson; m Sheila. BA 1926; MA 1930. **Tutor(s):** B F Armitage. **Johnian Relatives:** brother of Frank Leslie Orme (1919); uncle of John Anthony Orme (1965). **Educ:** Braeside School, West Kirby; Oundle School. Died 10 July 1964.

ORMEROD, Arthur Hereward (1927) Born 9 February 1910, Elm Royd, Brighouse Wood Lane, Brighouse, Yorkshire; son of Charles Ormerod, Master Silk-Spinner, and Georgina Maude Mayfield Wilkinson. **Subject(s):** Law; BA 1930; MA 1934. **Tutor(s):** C W Guillebaud. **Educ:** Charney Hall, Grange-over-Sands; Rugby School. Died 1972.

ORMEROD, Peter Burton (1943) Born 1 October 1925, 57 Beaumont Street, Marylebone, London; son of Frank Cunliffe Ormerod, Surgeon, and Mary Burton. **Tutor(s):** S J Bailey. **Educ:** Open Air School, Regent's Park; The Hall School, Hampstead; Merchant Taylors' School.

ORMOND, Derek (1944) Born 16 December 1926, 122 Errwood Road, Burnage, Levenshulme, Manchester; son of Sydney Thomas Ormond, Commercial Traveller, and Lilian White. **Tutor(s):** J M Wordie. **Educ:** Alma Park Elementary School, Manchester; Burnage Municipal High School. **Appointments:** RAF Cadet, SJC.

ORPEN, Leslie D'Arcy (1930) Born 19 June 1910, Alpha, Claremont, District of Wynberg, Cape Colony, South Africa; son of Gerald Edward D'Arcy Orpen, Chartered Accountant, and Constance Maud Lawton. **Subject(s):** Economics; BA 1934; MA 1937. **Tutor(s):** C W Guillebaud. **Johnian Relatives:** brother of Neil Newton D'Arcy Orpen (1932). **Educ:** Private School, Kenilworth, South Africa; High School, Rondebosh, South Africa. Died 3 August 1997.

ORPEN, Neil Newton D'Arcy (1932) Born 6 October 1913, Cleveland Road, Claremont, District of Wynberg, Cape Colony, South Africa; son of Gerald Edward D'Arcy Orpen, Chartered Accountant, and Constance Maud Lawton. **Subject(s):** English/History; BA 1935; MA 1939. **Tutor(s):** C W Guillebaud. **Johnian Relatives:** brother of Leslie D'Arcy Orpen (1930). **Educ:** St John's College, Johannesburg, South Africa. **Career:** Served in heavy batteries, Simonstown, Durban and Libya, WWII. Died 1990.

ORR, Robert Graeme (1923) Born 22 August 1902, Cote Royal, Russell Street, Camberwell, Shire of Boroondara, Bourke, Victoria, Australia; son of William Francis Orr, Ophthalmic Surgeon, and Alice Elizabeth Smith. **Subject(s):** Natural Sciences; BA 1926; MA 1934; BChir 1931; MB 1946; MD 1956. **Tutor(s):** B F Armitage. **Educ:** Toorak Preparatory School, Australia; Church of England Grammar School, Melbourne; Trinity College, Melbourne University. **Career:** Honorary Ophthalmic Surgeon, Royal Children's Hospital, Melbourne; Honorary Senior Assistant Ophthalmic Surgeon, Victoria Eye and Ear Hospital, Melbourne. Died 1 October 1970.

ORR, Professor Robert (Robin) Kemsley (1938) (admitted to Pembroke College 1929) Born 2 June 1909, Brechin, Scotland; son of Robert Workman Orr and Florence Mary Kemsley; m (1) Margaret, 1937 (d 1979), (2) Doris Winny-Meyer, 1979; (1) 1 son (David Bodley), 2 daughters (Alison Braedine and Jean Kirsteen (d)), (2) 1 stepson (Daniel Leo), 2 stepdaughters (Caroline and Deborah). MusD 1950; BA (Pembroke) 1932; MA (Pembroke) 1938; MusB (Pembroke) 1932; Honorary DMus (Glasgow) 1972; Honorary LLD (Dundee) 1976; Honorary FRSAMD; Honorary RAM; FRCM. **Johnian Relatives:** father of David Bodley Orr (1959); stepfather of Daniel Leo Winny (1974). **Educ:** Loretto School; Royal College of Music, London; Pembroke College, Cambridge. **Career:** Director of Music, Sidcot School, Somerset 1933–1936; Assistant Lecturer in Music, University of Leeds 1936–1938; Organist 1938–1951, Title B Fellow 1948–1956, Title C Fellow 1965–1976, SJC; Flight Lieutenant, Photographic Intelligence, RAFVR 1940–1945; Lecturer in Music 1947–1956, Professor of Music 1965–1976 (Emeritus 1976), University of Cambridge; Professor of Theory and Composition, Royal College of Music 1950–1956; Gardiner Professor of Music, University of Glasgow 1956–1965. **Appointments:** Director of Studies in Music, SJC 1938–1951; Member, Carl Rosa Trust 1953–1970; Chairman, Scottish Opera 1962–1976; Director, Cambridge Arts Theatre 1970–1975; Director, Welsh National Opera 1977–1983; Honorary Fellow, SJC 1987–; Honorary Fellow, Pembroke College, Cambridge 1988. **Awards:** Silver Medal, Worshipful Company of Musicians 2002. **Honours:** CBE 1972. **Publications:** Compositions include: *Sonatina* for violin and piano, 1941; *Three Chinese Songs*, 1943; *Sonata* for viola and piano, 1947; *Winter's Tale* (Incidental Music), BBC, 1947; *Overture, The Prospect of Whitby*, 1948; *Oedipus at Colonus* (University of Cambridge Greek Play), 1950; *Four Romantic Songs* (for Peter Pears), 1950; *Festival Te Deum*, 1950; *Three Pastorals* for soprano, flute, viola and piano, 1951; *Italian Overture*, 1952; *Te Deum and Jubilate in C*, 1953; *Duo* for violin and cello, 1953; *I was glad*, 1955; *Spring Cantata*, 1955; *Sonata* for violin and clavier, 1956; *Rhapsody* for string orchestra, 1956; *3 Preludes on Scottish Psalm Tunes*, 1958; *Come and let yourselves be built*, 1961; *Symphony in one movement*, 1963; *Magnificat and Nunc Dimittis (Short Service)*, 1967; *Full Circle* (opera), 1968; *Sing aloud unto God*, 1968; *From the Book of Philip Sparrow*, 1969; *Symphony No 2*, 1970; *Journeys and Places* for mezzo–soprano and strings, 1971; *Hermiston* (opera), 1975; *Symphony No 3*, 1978; *Versus from Ogden Nash* for medium voice and strings, 1978; *Songs of Zion*, 1978; *On the Razzle* (opera), 1986; *Jesu, Sweet Son Dear*, a Carol, 1989; *Sinfonietta Helvetica*, 1990; *Rondeau des Oiseaux* for recorder, 1993; *Three Lyric Pieces* for piano, 1994; *O Gracious Light* for 8 voice choir, 1999; *A Carol for Christmas* for 8 voice choir, 2001.

ORR, William Edward Anderson (1920) Born 2 May 1903, 11 Windsor Quadrant, Kelvinside, Glasgow; son of Alexander Orr, Decorator, and Jessy Hardie Anderson. **Tutor(s):** E E Sikes. **Educ:** Fettes College, Edinburgh; Kelvinside Academy, Glasgow.

ORWIN, William Dickson (1940) Born 26 February 1921, Guildford, Kellfield Avenue, Gateshead; son of John Moses Orwin, Assistant Secretary to a Limited Company, and Elsie Dickson; m Barbara Isabelle van der Straaten, 27 September 1952. **Tutor(s):** J M Wordie. **Educ:** Musgrave Private School, Low Fell; Ascham House Preparatory School, Gosforth; Durham School.

OSBORN, Peter George Graeme (1949) Born 15 July 1929, Ashwood Grange, Heathfield Road, Woking, Surrey; son of Arthur John Osborn, Stockbroker, and Isabel Carnegie Thomson; m Mary Grace Keller, August 1954. **Subject(s):** English/History; BA 1952. **Tutor(s):** A G Lee. **Educ:** Brambletye School, East Grinstead; Sedbergh School; Lathallan School, Colinsburgh.

OSBORNE, Gerald Stanley (1944) Born 29 January 1926, 46 Ronald Road, Birmingham; son of Joseph Liggins Osborne, Solicitor's Managing Clerk, and Phoebe May Hiatt. **Subject(s):** Modern and Medieval Languages/English; BA 1947; MA 1962. **Tutor(s):** C W

Guillebaud. **Educ:** Colmore Road Elementary School, Birmingham; Solihull School; SOAS, London.

OSBORNE, Dr Gordon (1932) See OPPENHEIMER.

OTIS, Harrison Gray (1922) Born 28 February 1902, Winthrop, Massachusetts, USA; son of Harrison Gray Otis and Louisa McNamara. **Tutor(s):** E A Benians. **Educ:** Nobles School, Boston, USA; Middlesex School, Concord, USA.

OTTLEY, Warner Herbert Taylor (1908) Born 26 August 1889, Hilton, Malvern Link, Leigh, Worcestershire; son of Warner Ottley, Colonel, and Louisa Kilbey. **Subject(s):** Classics; BA 1911. **Tutor(s):** E E Sikes. **Educ:** Dartington House School, Eastbourne; Malvern College. **Career:** Home Civil Service 1913; War Office 1913; Director of Finance, War Office; Private Secretary and Parliamentary Under-Secretary. **Honours:** Chevalier de la Legion d'Honneur 1920; CB 1945.

OTTON, Sir Geoffrey John (1945) Born 10 June 1927, Holmlea, Sutton Lane, Banstead, Surrey; son of John George Alfred Otton, Chemical Broker, and Constance Alma Wilkie; m Hazel White, 1952; 1 son, 1 daughter. **Subject(s):** Classics; BA 1948; MA 1952. **Tutor(s):** R L Howland. **Educ:** Ewell Boys' School; City of London Freemen's School, Ashtead; Acton County School; Christ's Hospital. **Career:** Home Office 1950–1970; Principal Private Secretary to Home Secretary 1963–1965; DHSS 1970–1986; Chief Adviser to Supplementary Benefits Commission 1975–1979; Second Permanent Secretary, in charge of Social Security 1979–1986. **Appointments:** Chairman, Bromley Council for Voluntary Service 1986–1992; Chairman, St Piers Special School, Lingfield 1987–1994. **Awards:** Minor Scholarship, SJC 1945. **Honours:** CB (Civil) 1978; KCB 1981.

OUGHTON, William Lawson (1940) Born 28 August 1921, Stella View, Pelton Fell, Durham; son of Thomas Oughton, Boot and Shoe Repairer, and Edith Lawson. **Subject(s):** Natural Sciences; BA 1944; MA 1947. **Tutor(s):** J M Wordie. **Educ:** Pelton Roseberry Council Boys' School, Chester-le-Street Secondary School. **Career:** Senior Science Master, Friends' School, Yorkshire. Died March 1979.

OULSNAM, Sir Samuel Harrison Yardley (1919) Born 17 January 1898, 126 Newcastle Street, Burslem, Staffordshire; son of Samuel Oulsnam, Commercial Traveller, and Mary Ball. **Subject(s):** History; BA 1921. **Tutor(s):** E A Benians. **Educ:** The High School, Newcastle. **Career:** Lieutenant, No 2 RGA, Cadet School 1917; 462 Siege Battery 1917; 124th Heavy Battery 1917–1919; Half Lancashire Heavy Battery 1919; Indian Civil Service 1921; Assistant Commissioner, Central Provinces 1926; Officiating Deputy Commissioner 1928, 1932; Secretary to Government of India, Department of Health until 1947. **Awards:** Scholarship, SJC 1916. **Honours:** MC 1919; CIE 1937; CSI 1946; Kt 1948. Died 2 April 1972.

OUSELEY, John Aldrich (1931) Born 12 September 1913, 5 Press Lane, Norwich; son of Frank Balls Ouseley, Bank Clerk, and Kathleen Margaret Aldrich; m Winifred Matilda Grubb, 12 January 1946; 1 son (Christopher b 1949), 2 daughters (Cheryl b 1952 and Rachel b 1958). **Subject(s):** History; BA 1934; MA 1938. **Tutor(s):** E A Benians. **Educ:** Sunny House, Norwich; Norwich High School for Girls; Winton Preparatory School, Norwich; Gresham's, Holt. **Career:** Owen Owen Ltd, Liverpool (involving a year at LSE) 1934–1935; Assistant General Manager, Owen Owen, Coventry 1937–1939; Enlisted, RA 1939; Commissioned, 80 Medium Regiment (Scottish Horse) 1940; Staff Captain HQRA 1 BR Infantry Division 1942; Demobilised 1945; DAAG HQ 1 Division 1945; Rejoined Owen Owen Ltd 1946; General Manager, Mayes, Southampton 1953–1956; General Manager, TJ Hughes, Liverpool 1956–1969; Credit Controller 1969–1970; Manager, Chart & Lawrence, Horsham 1970–1972; Administration Officer, Redland Ltd, Horsham 1972–1981. **Awards:** Exhibition, SJC. **Honours:** MBE (Military) 1945. Died 28 July 2000.

OVERTON, David Roper (1947) Born 22 April 1926, Ashford, Agnes Road, Great Crosby, Lancashire; son of Charles Lockhart Overton, Cotton Merchant, and Helen Muriel Harpin. **Subject(s):** Classics; BA 1950; MA 1954. **Tutor(s):** R L Howland. **Educ:** Sandford School, Blundellsands; Trearddur House Preparatory School; Sedbergh School.

OWBRIDGE, Reginald Cyril Neville (1929) Born 3 March 1911, Cherry Garth, Cliff Drive, Canford Cliffs, Dorset; son of Cyril Smith Owbridge, of independent means, and Mary Elizabeth Ness; m Angela Knatchbull, April 1948, St Andrew's, Bournemouth. BA 1932; MA 1936. **Tutor(s):** J M Wordie. **Educ:** Mount Pleasant School; Marlborough College. **Career:** Family Firm, Messrs WT Owbridge Ltd; RAF, UK and Italy, WWII. Died 15 February 1975.

OWEN, Charles Brewster O'Maille (1925) Born 21 December 1906, 9 Pembroke Park, Donnybrook, Dublin, Ireland; son of Charles Ashley Owen, Architect, and Anna Grace Brewster. **Subject(s):** Natural Sciences; BA 1928; MA 1932. **Tutor(s):** J M Wordie. **Educ:** Castle Park, Dalkey, Dublin; Sedbergh School. **Career:** Master, Aldenham School 1929–1931; Master, Malvern College 1931–1937; Headmaster, English School, Cairo 1937. Died 20 April 1985.

OWEN, Canon David Hugh (1912) Born 7 August 1887, Alltgoch, Talybont, Cardiganshire; son of Owen Owen, Farmer, and Mary Evans. **Subject(s):** Economics; BA 1919; MA 1929; BA (Wales) 1911. **Tutor(s):** E E Sikes. **Educ:** Aberystwyth County School; University College of Wales, Aberystwyth. **Career:** Lieutenant, Welsh Horse and Royal Welsh Fusiliers, WWI; Deacon 1929; Curate, Christ Church, Albany Street 1929–1932; Priest 1930; Curate, St John the Evangelist, Ladbroke Grove, Kensington 1932–1934; Rector, Maidford and Vicar, Adstone, Northamptonshire 1934–1946; Vicar, Maxey with Deeping Gate, Rector, Northborough, and Rector, Barnack with Ufford and Bainton 1956; Non-residentiary Canon, Peterborough Cathedral 1958.

OWEN, Dr David Norman Howell (1943) Born 27 June 1925, Bryn-y-mor, Fishguard, Pembrokeshire; son of John Howard Owen, Medical Practitioner, and Mary Evelyn Davies. BA 1946; MA 1950; MB BChir 1952; MRCS LRCP 1949; DRCOG; DA. **Tutor(s):** S J Bailey. **Educ:** Hillstone School, Great Malvern; Epsom College. **Career:** GP, Fishguard; Anaesthetist, Haverfordwest Hospital.

OWEN, George (1942) Born 9 March 1923, 1 Laurel Grove, Selby, Yorkshire; son of George Owen, Schoolmaster, and Eveline Sherwood; m Kathleen Elsie Martin; 4 children. **Subject(s):** History; BA 1947; BSc Economics (London) 1951. **Tutor(s):** C W Guillebaud. **Educ:** Ulleskelf Church of England School; Craigend Park School, Edinburgh; Clayesmore School, Dorset; Pocklington School. **Career:** Lieutenant, RA and Royal Indian Artillery 1943–1946; Schoolmaster, Hatfield School, Hertfordshire; Schoolmaster, East Barnet Grammar School; Schoolmaster, Mexborough School, South Yorkshire. **Awards:** Minor Scholarship, SJC 1941. **Publications:** Articles in a variety of publications dealing with aspects of the history of Doncaster in the eighteenth and nineteenth centuries.

OWEN, Dr James Raymond (1927) Born 9 July 1909, Dunira, Harton, South Shields, County Durham; son of James William Owen, Timber Merchant, and Elizabeth Ellen Stephenson; m Dorothea Isabel Miller (d 19 January 2002); 2 sons (John Roger b 21 July 1938 and Peter Jeremy b 28 June 1941). BA 1931; MA 1937; BChir 1937; MB 1937. **Tutor(s):** M P Charlesworth. **Johnian Relatives:** father of John Roger Owen (1957) and of Peter Jeremy Owen (1961). **Educ:** Brighton College Preparatory School; Bedford School. **Career:** Consultant Gynaecologist, Hospital of St Cross, Rugby and St Mary's Hospital, Harborough Magna, Warwickshire 1938–1972. **Appointments:** Senior LMBC Coach. Died 15 December 1985.

OWEN, John Samuel (1933) Born 9 July 1914, St Augustine, Florida; son of Edward Owen, Colliery Agent, and Evelyn Stewart. **Subject(s):** Natural Sciences; BA 1936. **Tutor(s):** J M Wordie. **Educ:** St Christopher's,

British Columbia; St Ursula's, Grayshott; Private Tuition; Eton College. **Career:** Pilot Officer, AAF 1937; Flying Officer 1939; Acting Flight Lieutenant, RAF. Died 18 May 1940 (killed in action near Cambrai).

OWEN, Professor John Vallance (VALLANCE-OWEN) (1939) Born 31 October 1920, 26 Mount Park Road, Ealing, London; son of Edwin Augustine Owen, Professor of Physics, and Julia May Vallance; m Renee Thornton, 1950; 2 sons, 2 daughters. **Subject(s):** Natural Sciences; BA 1942; MA 1946; MB 1946; BChir 1946; MD 1951; FRCP 1962; Honorary FRCPI 1970; FRCPath 1971; FRCPI 1973; Honarary FHKCP 1996. **Tutor(s):** R L Howland. **Educ:** Friars Grammar School, Bangor; Epsom College. **Career:** Various appointments including Pathology Assistant and Medical First Assistant to Sir Horace Evans, London Hospital 1946–1951; Medical Tutor and Liaison Physician to Obstetrics Department, Royal Postgraduate Medical School, Hammersmith Hospital 1952–1955; Rockefeller Travelling Fellowship, George S Cox Medical Research Institute, University of Pennsylvania 1955–1956; Medical Tutor, Royal Postgraduate Medical School, Hammersmith Hospital 1956–1958; Consultant Physician and Lecturer in Medicine, University of Durham 1958–1964; Consultant Physician, Royal Victoria Infirmary, and Reader in Medicine, University of Newcastle upon Tyne 1964–1966; Consultant Physician, Royal Victoria Hospital, Belfast 1966–1982; Consultant Physician and Professor of Medicine, Queen's University of Belfast 1966–1982; Forster Green Hospital, Belfast 1975–1982; Director of Medical Services, Maltese Island 1981–1982; Foundation Professor and Chairman, Department of Medicine 1983–1988, Associate Dean, Faculty of Medicine 1984–1988, Chinese University of Hong Kong. **Appointments:** British Council Lecturer, Department of Medicine, Zurich University 1963; First Helen Martin Lecturer, Diabetic Association of South California; William H Mulberg Lecturer, Cincinnati Diabetes Association; Lecturer, Brookhaven National Laboratories, New York 1965; British Council Lecturer, Haile Selassie University, Makerere University College and South African Universities 1966; Guest Lecturer, Japan Endocrinological Society 1968; Guest Lecturer, Madrid University 1969; Guest Lecturer, Endocrine Society of Australia 1970; Member, Standing Medical Advisory Committee, Ministry of Health and Social Services, Northern Ireland 1970–1973; Regional Adviser to RCP, for Northern Ireland 1970–1975; Guest Lecturer, Bologna University 1976; Councillor, RCP 1976–1979; Member, Executive Committee, Association of Physicians of Great Britain and Ireland 1976–1979; Councillor, RCPI 1978–1982; Chairman, Medical Division, Belfast City Hospital 1979–1981; Chairman, Medical Staff Committee, Forster Green Hospital, Belfast 1979–1982; Honorary Consultant in Medicine to Hong Kong Government 1984–1988; Honorary Consultant in Medicine to the British Army in Hong Kong 1985–1988; Visiting Professor, Imperial College of Science, Technology and Medicine, Hammersmith Hospital 1988; Assessor for Clinical Complaints, North East Thames Regional Health Authority 1988–1996; Consultant Physician, London Independent Hospital 1988–1999; Medical Advisor on Clinical Complaints, North East Thames RHA 1989–1996; Medical Advisor on Clinical Complaints, South Thames RHA 1995–1996; Consultant Physician, Wellington Hospital, London 1999; Member, Specialist Advisory Committee (General Internal Medicine) to the Government; Member, Northern Health and Social Services Board, Department of Health and Society Services, Northern Ireland; Member Research Committee, British Diabetic Association. **Awards:** de Havilland Scholarship 1939–1943; Open Scholarship, London Hospital 1943–1946; Oliver-Sharpey Prize, RCP 1976. **Publications:** *Essentials of Cardiology*, 1961 (2nd edition 1968); *Diabetes: its physiological and biochemical basis*, 1976; papers in biochemistry, medical and scientific journals on carbohydrate and fat metabolism and aetiology of diabetes mellitus and related conditions, with special reference to insulin antagonism.

OWENS, Francis Henry (1912) Born 9 August 1892, 19 Coleridge Road, Crouch End, Middlesex; son of Henry Charles Owens, Private Secretary, and Jessie Mabel Clay; m Patti Mai Sweeney, 27 August 1930, All Saints' Church, Kingston on Thames. **Subject(s):** Natural Sciences; BA 1915;

MA 1919. **Tutor(s):** R P Gregory. **Educ:** Tollington School, Muswell Hill; Northern Polytechnic, Holloway. **Career:** Private, London Regiment (Artists Rifles), WWI.

OXLEY, Roderick Guy (1934) Born 20 April 1916, Brooklands, Clay Cross, Chesterfield; son of Robert Oxley, Draper, and Edith Sophia Simpkin; m Lorna. **Subject(s):** Economics; BA 1937; MA 1941. **Tutor(s):** J S Boys Smith. **Educ:** Clay Cross Council Elementary School; Clay Cross County Secondary School. **Career:** Senior Civil Servant. Died 23 August 1998.

P

PACEY, Hugh Edmund (1942) Born 10 June 1906, Sharnbrook, Bedfordshire; son of Edmund Charles Pacey, Builder's Foreman, and Helena Rose West. **Subject(s):** Geography; BA 1944; MA 1947; MSc (LSE) 1936. **Tutor(s):** C W Guillebaud. **Educ:** Sharnbrook Council School; Bedford Modern School; College of St Mark and St John, Chelsea; LSE. **Career:** Pilot Officer, RAF, Instructor, Initial Training Wing.

PACKARD, Richard Qu'Appelle (1946) Born 9 September 1920, 20 Marion Street, Wellington, New Zealand; son of Arthur White Packard, Journalist, and Tui Frances McKay. BSc (New Zealand) 1941. **Tutor(s):** G C L Bertram. **Educ:** Eltham Primary School, Taranaki; Christchurch High School; Canterbury University College, Christchurch.

PACKER, John Francis Smythe (1944) Born 12 May 1926, 15 Milton Street, Maidstone, Kent; son of Frank Herbert Packer, Lieutenant, Royal Army Pay Corps, and Frederica Lavinia Monica Smythe. **Subject(s):** Geography; BA 1948; MA 1950. **Tutor(s):** J M Wordie. **Educ:** St Francis Roman Catholic School, Maidstone; Maidstone Grammar School; Burnage High School, Manchester.

PADFIELD, John Edward (1936) Born 27 March 1917, 99 Belvedere Road, Penge, Croydon; son of Francis Joseph Padfield, Clerk in Holy Orders, and Winifred Parr Metcalfe. **Subject(s):** Oriental Languages/Theology; BA 1939; MA 1943. **Tutor(s):** J S Boys Smith. **Educ:** The Hall, Sydenham; Merchant Taylors' School. **Awards:** Scholarship, SJC; Rogerson Scholarship, SJC. Died December 1970.

PADLEY, The Revd Henry Wilson (1920) Born 22 June 1901, 92 Division Street, Sheffield; son of Henry Wilson Padley, Boot and Shoe Dealer, and Florence Mary Coates. **Subject(s):** English/Modern and Medieval Languages/Theology; BA 1923; MA 1927. **Tutor(s):** E A Benians. **Educ:** Carter Knowle Council School, Sheffield; Central Secondary School, Sheffield; Westcott House, Cambridge. **Career:** Lecturer in English, St Stephen's College, Delhi 1924–1928; Ordained Deacon 1928; Curate, St Barnabas, Sheffield 1928–1929; Ordained Priest 1929; Chaplain and Lecturer, St Stephen's College, Delhi 1929–1933; On the Staff of Sheffield Cathedral 1933–1934; Assistant Master, King's School, Canterbury 1934–1935. Died 25 March 1935.

PAGE, Arnold Thomas (1943) Born 22 November 1925, 20 Park Place, Mount Street, Birmingham; son of Harold Page, Gasmaker, and Annie Morteboys; m Joanna; 1 son (Julian b 1954), 2 daughters (Kate b 1956 and Susannah b 1958). **Subject(s):** Mechanical Sciences; BA 1949; MA 1951; MIMechE. **Tutor(s):** C W Guillebaud; R L Howland. **Educ:** Eliot Street Elementary School, Birmingham; Birchfield Road Elementary School, Birmingham; Handsworth Grammar School, Birmingham. **Career:** Chartered Engineer.

PAGET, Charles Edward Eden (1922) Born 18 May 1903, 12 Hyde Park Mansions, Marylebone, London; son of Eden Wilberforce Paget, Author, of independent means, and Gertrude Charnley. **Tutor(s):** B F Armitage. **Educ:** Parkfield, Haywards Heath; Bradfield College; Private Tuition. Died 14 October 1968.

PAIGE, Robert (1920) Born 26 April 1902, Rack Park, Kingsbridge & Dodbrooke, Devon; son of William Robert Paige, Manufacturer-Engineer, and Annie Caroline Savery. **Tutor(s):** E A Benians. **Educ:** High School, Sheffield; King Edward VII School, Sheffield; Aymestry House, Malvern; Loretto School, Musselburgh. **Career:** Chairman and Managing Director, Stalker Drill Works Ltd, Sheffield. Died 29 October 1969.

PAINE, David Baumann Easterbrook (1933) Born 23 May 1914, Epworth, Nassau, Bahamas; son of Frederick James Paine, Wesleyan Minister, and Helen Stranger. **Subject(s):** Modern and Medieval Languages; BA 1936; MA 1956. **Educ:** Deacons School, Peterborough; Wycliffe College, Stonehouse. **Career:** Gloucestershire Regiment 1939–1945; History and French Master, Wycliffe College 1975. **Awards:** Dowman Sizarship, SJC. Died 13 August 1979.

PAINE, The Revd David Stevens (1942) Born 20 February 1924, Tweedale Nursing Home, Tunbridge Wells; son of Robert Leslie Paine, Director, Departmental Store, and Hilda Elizabeth Stevens. **Subject(s):** Natural Sciences; BA 1945; MA 1953; BChir 1948; MB 1948. **Tutor(s):** S J Bailey. **Educ:** Tunbridge Wells High School; Eversleigh Preparatory School, Tunbridge Wells; Haileybury College. **Career:** Curate, Rowner 1954–1956; Curate, Freshwater, Isle of Wight, 1956; Vicar, South Cerney with Cerney Wick, Gloucestershire 1959–1964.

PALFREY, Dr Alec John (1945) Born 4 March 1928, 7 Fir Grove, Wollaston, Stourbridge; son of Harold Keith Palfrey, Skin Rug Manufacturer, and Hilda Cope Jones; m (1) Penelope Ann Hewetson (div), (2) Penelope Jane Haslam (née Morris); (1) 4 sons (Michael, Christopher, David and Neil), 3 daughters (Susan, Jane and Caroline). **Subject(s):** Natural Sciences; BA 1948; MA 1952; BChir 1951; MB 1951; MD 1975. **Tutor(s):** S J Bailey; G C L Bertram. **Educ:** Red Hill School, Stourbridge; King Edward VI Grammar School, Stourbridge; University College Hospital Medical School, London. **Career:** Various junior clinical appointments at University College Hospital (Paediatrics and Chest Medicine), the Brook Hospital (Chest Surgery) and Grove Park Hospital (Chest Medicine), London; Senior Registrar in Thoracic Surgery, Colombo General Hospital; National Service, RAF; Clinical post, Dreadnought Seamen's Hospital; Lecturer in Anatomy, University College, Ibadan; Lecturer and Senior Lecturer in Anatomy, St Thomas' Hospital Medical School; Director, Arthritis and Rheumatism Council's Electron Microscope Unit, St Thomas' Hospital Medical School; Senior Lecturer in Anatomy, then Reader in Functional Morphology (later Emeritus), Charing Cross and Westminster Medical School. **Appointments:** Member, various London University Committees; Secretary and Chairman, Board of Studies in Human Anatomy and Morphology; Chairman, Standing Medical Computing Committee; Examiner in Anatomy, London and Cambridge Universities, to the Royal College of Surgeons in London, Dublin etc, and to the Royal College of Surgeons in Ireland; Lecturer in Surgical Anatomy in London, Accra and Lusaka; Lecturer in Anatomy for Osteopaths in London and at Oxford Brookes University; Member, Guildford Diocesan Synod; Diocesan Stewardship Adviser; Member and Chairman, United Society for the Propagation of the Gospel; Lay Chairman, Emly Deanery Synod. **Awards:** Major Scholarship, SJC 1945. **Publications:** Papers on the Ultrastructure of Skeletal Tissues, the Rheology of Synovial Fluid and Human Pelvic Osteology.

PALLETT, Denis Edwin Henry (1949) Born 18 March 1930, Salisbury, Southern Rhodesia; son of Edwin Pallett, Architect, and Minnie Bowman. BA 1953; MA 1956. **Tutor(s):** R L Howland. **Educ:** Convent High School, Salisbury; St George's College, Salisbury.

PALLISTER, Dr Michael Alan (1949) Born 5 October 1930, Batu Gajah Hospital, Perak, Federated Malay States; son of Richard Alan Pallister, Colonial Medical Service, and Muriel Reay Hogg. **Subject(s):** Natural Sciences; BA 1952; MA 1992; BChir 1955; MB 1956. **Tutor(s):** G C L Bertram. **Educ:** Highlands School, Kaban Djahe, Indonesia; Guildford

Preparatory School, Perth, Western Australia; Hale School, Perth, Western Australia; Sedbergh School. **Career:** Officer Commanding, Princess Alexandra Hospital, RAF Wroughton 1989. **Honours:** Commander, Order of St John 1989.

PALMER, James Richard (1941) Born 1 July 1923, Newlands, Summerlands, Yeovil, Somerset; son of Wilfrid Ernest Palmer, Industrial Research Chemist, and Helen Margaret Webb; m Margaret Milne Carnegie, 1948; 2 sons (John and Michael). **Subject(s):** Mechanical Sciences; BA 1944; MA 1948; FRAeS; FIMA. **Tutor(s):** S J Bailey. **Johnian Relatives:** son of Wilfrid Ernest Palmer (1912); brother of Nigel Webb Palmer (1949); uncle of Simon David Palmer (1976). **Educ:** The Park School, Yeovil; St Nicholas' School, Yeovil; Bishop's Stortford College. **Career:** Commissioned RAF; Scientific Officer, RAE Farnborough; Research Assistant, Napiers (later Deputy Head, Combustion and Fuel Systems Section) 1947; Senior Lecturer (later Deputy Head of Aircraft Propulsion), Department of Aircraft Propulsion, Cranfield College of Aeronautics 1950–1988. **Appointments:** Member, Engine Aerodynamics Committee and Performance Committee, and Vice-Chairman, Turbomachinery Sub-committee, Aeronautical Research Council; External Examiner to a number of universities; Chairman, Scientific Advisory Committee, Mander College, Bedford; Member, Kempston Rotarians; Member, Bedford Samaritans 1965; Bedford Anti-drug Abuse Association; Chairman, Forum 71 (Dining Club) 1978. **Awards:** Exhibition, SJC 1940. Died 17 December 1997.

PALMER, John Bowden (1919) Born 26 June 1899, Bogotá, Columbia, South America; son of John William Goodier Palmer, Commercial Traveller, and Annie Christian Bowden; 1 son. **Subject(s):** Economics; BA 1921; MA 1926. **Tutor(s):** E A Benians. **Educ:** Elmfield College, York; The Schools, Cheadle Hulme; The County High School, Altrincham. **Career:** RNAS 1917; Lieutenant, 218 Squadron then 244 Squadron, RAF 1918; in commerce, Far East; Wing Commander, RAF, WWII. Died 28 April 1966.

PALMER, John Thomas Edward (1900) Born 27 July 1881, Wrockwardine, Shropshire; son of John Palmer, Schoolmaster, and Margaret Halford. BA 1903. **Tutor(s):** J E Sandys. **Educ:** Ludlow Grammar School.

PALMER, Mervyn Outlaw (1934) Born 10 October 1915, Brundall, Norfolk; son of Thomas Gordon Palmer, Milliner, and Hilda Sutton; m Mulca Marguerite Cohane, 1939; 4 sons (Michael, Jonathan, Adrian and Terence). **Subject(s):** History; BA 1937; MA 1945. **Tutor(s):** J S Boys Smith. **Johnian Relatives:** father of Jonathan Sutton Palmer (1969) and of Adrian Jeremy Palmer (1972). **Educ:** Newcastle Preparatory School; Bournemouth School; Solihull School; Durham School. **Career:** Senior History Master, George Dixon Grammar School, Birmingham 1938–1939; Major, HQ Eighth Army DAQMG, North Africa and Italy, Mentioned in Despatches 1940–1944; Lieutenant Colonel, HQ ALFSEA AQMG 1944–1945; Assistant Education Officer, Somerset 1945–1948; Deputy Director of Education, Leicestershire 1948–1958; Chief Education Officer, Hastings County Borough 1958–1974. **Appointments:** Chief Education Visiting Fellow, University of Sussex (Acting Director of Education 1975–1978); Senior Visiting Fellow 1976; Board Member, Food, Drink and Tobacco Training Board; Board Member, National Schools Sailing Association. **Awards:** Baker Exhibition, SJC 1934; Scholarship, SJC 1937. Died 8 June 1999.

PALMER, Nigel Webb (1949) Born 28 January 1930, Newlands, Summerlands, Yeovil, Somerset; son of Wilfrid Ernest Palmer, Glove Manufacturer, and Helen Margaret Webb; m Betty L Bradley, 1953; 1 son (Simon David b 1958), 2 daughters (Jane b 1956 and Clare b 1965). **Subject(s):** Natural Sciences; BA 1952; MA 1956; Diploma in Leather Science (London); FBIM; FSLTC 1993. **Tutor(s):** G C L Bertram. **Johnian Relatives:** son of Wilfrid Ernest Palmer (1912); brother of James Richard Palmer (1941); father of Simon David Palmer (1976). **Educ:** St Nicholas Preparatory School, Penn Hill; The College, Bishop's

Stortford; National Leathersellers' College, London. **Career:** Commissioned Army 1948–1949; Whitby Bros Ltd, Leather and Glove Manufacturers, Yeovil 1952–1954; C W Pittard & Co Ltd, Leather Manufacturers, Yeovil 1954–1959; Production Director, Pelts Products Ltd, Port Elizabeth 1959–1962; Technical Director, C W Pittard 1962–1971; Technical Director, Pittard Garner plc 1971–1978; Managing Director, R & A Kohnstamm Ltd, Kent 1978–1980; Managing Director, C W Pittard & Co Ltd 1980–1991; Consultant to Pittard Garner Plc 1991. **Appointments:** Rotary Club 1960; General Commissioner of Tax 1969; Council, British Leather Manufacturers' Association 1970–1991 (Chairman 1971); Chairman, CBI West of England Environmental Committee 1970–1991; Wessex Water Authority 1973–1979; JP 1981; Yeovil and District Housing Association 1981–1990; Member, Textiles and Other Manufacturers' Requirements Board 1984–1988; Chairman, South Somerset Education/Industry Group 1987; Magistrates' Courts Committee 1988; President, British Leather Confederation 1988–1990; Member, Liveryman, Worshipful Company of Glovers; President, Yeovil Branch, British Institute of Management 1989; Governor, Yeovil Tertiary College 1989; Advisory Committee on Business and the Environment 1991. **Honours:** OBE 1989. Died 24 December 1995.

PALMER, Canon Philip Nathaniel Hitchen (1921) Born 31 July 1902, 4 Doris Road, Heigham, Norwich, Norfolk; son of Thomas Joseph Mills Palmer, Solicitor, and Frances Lilian Girling; 2 sons, 1 daughter (Rosemary). **Subject(s):** Modern and Medieval Languages/Theology; BA 1924; MA 1928. **Tutor(s):** E E Sikes. **Johnian Relatives:** father of Philip Edward Hitchen Palmer (1957); grandfather of Caroline Laura Palmer (1989) and of Rebecca Sarah Palmer (1991). **Educ:** Pembroke House School, Norwich; Norwich High School; King Edward VII Grammar School, King's Lynn; Ridley Hall, Cambridge. **Career:** Vicar, St Osyth, Clacton; Ordained Deacon 1925; Ordained Priest 1926; Curate, St John, Lowestoft 1925–1931; Rector, Girton 1931–1937; Vicar, Swaffham, Norfolk 1937–1945; Rector, Great Oakley, Essex (later Rural Dean) 1945; Honorary Canon, Chelmsford Cathedral 1963. **Awards:** Exhibition, SJC; King George V Gold Medal. Died 10 August 1971.

PALMER, Wilfrid Ernest (1912) Born 22 May 1894, 32 Southtown Road, Gorleston, Great Yarmouth; son of Edward Ernest Palmer, Master Draper, and Laura Sarah Ashford; m Helen Margaret Webb; 2 sons (James (Jim) Richard b 1 July 1923 and Nigel Webb b 28 January 1930). **Subject(s):** Natural Sciences; BA 1918; MA 1921. **Tutor(s):** R P Gregory. **Johnian Relatives:** father of James (Jim) Richard Palmer (1941) and of Nigel Webb Palmer (1949); grandfather of Simon David Palmer (1976). **Educ:** Duncan House School, Great Yarmouth; Bishop's Stortford College. **Career:** Captain, Dorset Regiment and Training Reserve Battalion (Mentioned in Despatches), WWI; Postgraduate Industrial Research Chemist; Managing Director, Whitby Brothers Glove Manufacturer, Yeovil, Somerset. **Appointments:** Chairman of Governors, local Yeovil schools; Chairman, Yeovil Hospital Committee; President, Rotary Club, Yeovil. **Honours:** MBE. Died 23 March 1962.

PALMER, Dr William George (1911) Born 24 October 1892, Wolseley Road, Godalming, Surrey, son of Richard Mervyn Palmer, Schoolmaster, and Florence Emily Green; m Dorothy Muriel King, 7 June 1919, Cambridge; 1 son, 1 daughter. **Subject(s):** Natural Sciences; BA 1914; MA 1918; ScD 1937; BSc (London) 1914; DSc (London) 1925. **Tutor(s):** J R Tanner. **Educ:** Royal Grammar School, Guildford; UCL. **Career:** Ashton Fellow 1916–1926, Title A Fellow 1926–1931, Title B Fellow 1931–1960, Lecturer in Chemistry 1946–1960, Title D Fellow 1960–1969, SJC; Demonstrator in Chemistry 1924–1926, Lecturer in Chemistry 1926–1960, University of Cambridge. **Appointments:** Supervisor in Chemistry, SJC 1914–1947. **Awards:** Scholarship, SJC 1912; Hutchinson Studentship, SJC 1914; Allen Scholarship, University of Cambridge 1918. **Publications:** *Experimental Physical Chemistry*, 1941; *Experimental Inorganic Chemistry*, 1954; *Valency*; *History of Valency*; Various papers in *The Proceedings of the Royal Society*. Died 29 November 1969.

PARFIT, Arthur John Martindale (1932) Born 18 March 1912, Aris Anoub, Syria; son of Joseph Thomas Parfit, Clerk in Holy Orders, and Norah Caroline Stephens; m Mary Joyce Hudson, 9 November 1946, Old Fort Church, Durban. **Subject(s):** Geography/Moral Sciences; BA 1934; MA 1955. **Tutor(s):** E A Benians. **Johnian Relatives:** brother of Eric George Parfit (1929). **Educ:** Alleyn's School, Dulwich; The Grammar School, Newbury. Died 1985.

PARFIT, The Revd Eric George (1929) Born 11 March 1909, Church House, Beyrout, Syria; son of Joseph Thomas Parfit, Clerk in Holy Orders, Canon of Jerusalem, and Norah Caroline Stephens; m Dorothea Hagedorn, 10 August 1945, Machinac, Michigan, USA; 1 son (Michael). **Subject(s):** Natural Sciences; BA 1932; MA 1936. **Tutor(s):** E A Benians. **Johnian Relatives:** brother of Arthur John Martindale Parfit (1932). **Educ:** Private School, London; Alleyn's School, Dulwich; Ridley Hall, Cambridge. **Career:** Head, Photographic Department, King's College Hospital 1926–1928; Ordained Deacon 1936; Curate, St Mary, Bryanston Square, London 1936–1940; Ordained Priest 1937; Director, Gallery 113, Santa Barbara 1974–1991. **Appointments:** Member, Oxford Group (Moral Rearmament); Cartoonist, University Magazine, *Granta*; President, Santa Barbara Art Association 1975–1976.

PARIKH, Jitendra Ramaniklal (1939) Born 4 April 1921, Ahmedabad, India; son of Ramaniklal V Parikh, Mill Manager, and Ansuya Mangaldas Parikh. **Educ:** Ranchodlal Chhotalal High School, Ahmedabad; Gujarat College, University of Bombay.

PARISH, Charles Roy (1943) Born 6 July 1925, 246 Beeches Road, West Bromwich, Staffordshire; son of Charles Henry Parish, Works Manager, and Emma Bradbury; m Mary Hugill, April 1962 (d January 1991); 1 son (Andrew Hugill b March 1964, d 1996), 1 daughter (Alison Judith b 1969). **Subject(s):** Natural Sciences; BA 1946; MA 1950; PGCE 1948. **Tutor(s):** C W Guillebaud. **Educ:** Beeches Road Council School, West Bromwich; Handsworth Grammar School, Birmingham. **Career:** Sub-Lieutenant, RNVR (Special Branch), serving as Radar Officer 1945–1947; Head of Physics, Newport Grammar School, Essex 1948–1951; Head of Physics, Central Grammar School, Birmingham 1951–1954; long illness 1954–1958; Teacher, Alsager Secondary Modern School, Cheshire 1958–1960; Physics Department 1960–1981, Head of Physics 1982–1985, Sandbach School, Cheshire; Commanding Officer, Sandbach School CCF (retired as Honorary Squadron Leader, RAFVR(T)). **Appointments:** Licensed C of E Reader 1954–1995. **Awards:** Cadet Force Medal.

PARK, Cyril John (1926) Born 14 June 1909, 21 Roe Lane, Southport, Lancashire; son of Sidney Richmond Park, Forgemaster, and Minnie White; m Eileen Blackwood Rankin, 1937 (d 10 April 2000); 1 daughter (Maralyn Sylvia). BA 1931; MA 1935. **Tutor(s):** J M Wordie. **Educ:** Croxton; Terra Nova, Birkdale; Marlborough College. **Career:** Chairman, William Park and Company, Forgemasters, Wigan (family firm). **Appointments:** JP, Wigan; Worshipful Grand Master, County of Palatine Lodge, Wigan. Died 25 August 2003.

PARKER, Bernard Oliver (1943) Born 9 March 1926, The Brambles, Worlington, Suffolk; son of Donald Parker, Corn Miller, and Gladys Muriel Boyce; m Audrey Armitage, 7 July 1948, Rochester; 1 son (Michael), 3 daughters (Mary, Catherine and Judith). **Subject(s):** Mechanical Sciences; BA 1946; MA 1956. **Tutor(s):** S J Bailey. **Johnian Relatives:** brother of Christopher Parker (1949) and of Geoffrey Brian Parker (1955); father of Michael Bernard Parker (1969). **Educ:** Breckland School, Mildenhall; Bishop's Stortford College.

PARKER, Christopher (1949) Born 25 August 1931, Worlington, Mildenhall, Suffolk; son of Donald Parker, Corn Miller, and Gladys Muriel Boyce; m Helen Sinnett Davies, 25 August 1956; 3 children. **Subject(s):** Natural Sciences/Botany; BA 1952; MA 1956. **Tutor(s):** G C L Bertram. **Johnian Relatives:** brother of Bernard Oliver Parker (1943) and of Geoffrey Brian Parker (1955); uncle of Michael Bernard Parker (1969). **Educ:** Breckland School, Mildenhall; Bishop's Stortford

College Preparatory School; Bishop's Stortford College. **Career:** Agricultural Research, specialising in weed science for developing countries, continuing freelance work in retirement. **Publications:** *Parasitic Weeds of the World. Biology and Control*, 1993.

PARKER, Ernest Patrick (1937) Born 17 March 1919, Kymin, Newton, Porthcawl; son of Albert Ernest Parker, Engineer's Agent, and Gwynnaeth Mary Hooper. **Subject(s):** Mathematics/Economics; BA 1940. **Tutor(s):** J M Wordie. **Educ:** St John's School, Newton; Wycliffe College, Stonehouse. Died 1941 (torpedoed and drowned while on the way overseas to be trained as a Fleet Air Arm pilot or observer).

PARKER, Geoffrey Walter Austin (1946) Born 31 August 1915, 340 Fulham Road, South Kensington, London; son of Alfred Ernest Augustus Parker, Brewer's Manager, and Ada Mary Lamport; m Pauline Betty Bailey; 1 son (Max b 1960), 2 daughters (Cynthia b 1944 and Celia Ann b 1948). **Subject(s):** English; BA 1949; MA 1953. **Tutor(s):** F Thistlethwaite. **Johnian Relatives:** brother of Kenneth Alfred Lamport Parker (1930). **Educ:** Tottenham Grammar School. **Career:** Apprenticed to the Chief Engineer, Tottenham and District Gas Company 1931; Established Glove Manufacturing Company, Hertfordshire 1937–1941; RAF Pilot Training, California 1940–1941; Officer, RAF 1941–1946; Member of Pathfinder Squadron (promoted to Squadron Leader 1944) 1943–1946; Worked in Tanning Factory 1949; Ran Pig Breeding Unit 1953–1970; Managing Director, Hand Crafted Leather Goods Company 1958–1992. **Awards:** Scholarship, Hornsey School of Art 1931–1932. **Honours:** DFC 1944. **Publications:** 5 collections of English poetry books in miniature: Keats, Wordsworth, Tennyson, Shakespeare, and a book of English Verse (Donne, Milton, Blake and Swinburne). Died 27 December 2000.

PARKER, Herbert (1907) Born 17 April 1889, 27 Mansfield Road, Nottingham; son of Samuel Parker, Hosiery Warehouseman, and Annie Hall. **Subject(s):** Classics; BA 1910; MA 1921. **Tutor(s):** E E Sikes. **Educ:** Nottingham High School. **Career:** President of the Courts, British Military Administration, Cyrenaica; Burma Assistant Commissioner, Revenue and Agriculture Department, Government of India 1912; Assistant Rice Commissioner, Rangoon 1920; Officiating District and Sessions Judge 1924; Temporary Major, General List 1943; Civil Affairs Staff Centre, UK 1944; Senior Legal Assistant, Control Commission for Germany 1946; Temporary Judge, Central Commission Supreme Court 1947. **Awards:** Scholarship, SJC 1910. Died 8 December 1954.

PARKER, Kenneth Alfred Lamport (1930) Born 1 April 1912, 340 Fulham Road, South Kensington, London; son of Alfred Ernest Augustus Parker, Cinema Manager, and Ada Mary Lamport; m Freda Silcock; 1 son (Martin), 1 daughter (Hilary). **Subject(s):** History; BA 1933; MA 1937. **Tutor(s):** E A Benians. **Johnian Relatives:** brother of Geoffrey Walter Austin Parker (1946). **Educ:** Philip Lane School, Tottenham; Tottenham Grammar School. **Career:** Air-Raid Precautions Division (Ministry of Home Security); London Civil Defence Region; Assistant Principal, Home Office 1934; Head, Police Division 1948; Assistant Under-Secretary of State 1955; Head, Police Department 1961; Receiver, Metropolitan Police District 1967–1974. **Awards:** Exhibition, SJC 1929; Scholarship, SJC 1930–1934. **Honours:** CB 1959. Died 11 September 1995.

PARKER, Dr Ralph George Francis (1939) Born 14 December 1919, Durbanville, South Africa; son of Ralph George Parker, Farmer, and Daisy Pillar. **Subject(s):** Natural Sciences; BA 1942; MB 1944; BChir 1944; MD 1954. **Tutor(s):** R L Howland. **Johnian Relatives:** brother of William Stewart Parker (1946). **Educ:** Diocesan College, Rondebosch, South Africa; University of Cape Town, South Africa. **Career:** Consultant Pathologist, Birmingham Group of Hospitals. Died 4 January 1978.

PARKER, Robin Flint (1938) Born 12 December 1918, 19 Cleave Road, Gillingham, Kent; son of Jack Charles Parker, Army Officer, and Alice Evelyn Flint. **Tutor(s):** J S Boys Smith. **Educ:** Bedford School; RMA Woolwich.

PARKER, Ronald Henry George (1944) Born 2 January 1927, 202 Eardley Road, Streatham, London; son of George Henry Parker, Printer's Estimator, and Sarah Bowen. **Subject(s):** Natural Sciences; BA 1947; MA 1951. **Tutor(s):** C W Guillebaud. **Educ:** Granton Road Junior Elementary School, Streatham; Bushey Elementary School, Merton; Raynes Park County School. **Career:** Master, Rugby School. Died 4 January 1978.

PARKER, William Stewart (1946) Born 25 December 1920, Altydgedacht, Durbanville, Cape Province, South Africa; son of Ralph George Parker, Farmer, and Daisy Pillar. **Subject(s):** Economics; BA 1948; MA 1953. **Tutor(s):** F Thistlethwaite. **Johnian Relatives:** brother of Ralph George Francis Parker (1939). **Educ:** Diocesan College, Rondebosch, South Africa; University of Cape Town, South Africa. **Career:** South African Armed Forces 1940–1945; Commercial Service Department, Standard Bank 1948–1950; Colonial Administrative Service, Northern Rhodesia 1950.

PARKES, Alan Corson (1931) Born 10 February 1912, Kenwyn, Harboro Road; son of Sydney Parkes, General Manager, Lloyd's Bank Ltd, and Hilda Mary Corson; m Margery I Gordon, 14 February 1944. **Subject(s):** Modern and Medieval Languages. **Tutor(s):** C W Guillebaud. **Educ:** Holmfield Preparatory School, Sutton; The Leys School, Cambridge.

PARKES, Sir Edward Walter (1943) Born 19 May 1926, 29 Western Road, Wylde Green, Warwickshire; son of Walter Frederick Parkes, Jeweller, and Gladys Mabel Beeson; m Margaret Parr; 1 son (Christopher Edward), 1 daughter (Catherine). **Subject(s):** Mechanical Sciences; BA 1946; MA 1950; PhD 1952; ScD 1974; Honorary DTech (Loughborough) 1984; Honorary DSc (Leicester) 1984; Honorary LLD (Wales) 1984; Honorary DSc (City) 1988; FIMechE; FREng; Hon FIMechE 1992. **Tutor(s):** S J Bailey. **Johnian Relatives:** father of Christopher Edward Rupert Parkes (1973). **Educ:** Boldmere School, Wylde Green; Green Lanes School, Wylde Green; King Edward's High School, Birmingham. **Career:** RAE and aircraft industry 1945–1948; Fellow and Tutor, Gonville & Caius College, Cambridge 1945–1959; Lecturer in Engineering, University of Cambridge 1954–1960; Head of the Department of Engineering, University of Leicester 1960–1965; Professor of Mechanics, University of Cambridge 1965; Professorial Fellow, Gonville & Caius College 1965–1974; Vice-Chancellor, City University 1974–1978; Chairman, University Grants Committee 1978–1983; Vice Chancellor, University of Leeds 1983–1991. **Appointments:** Visiting Professor, Stanford University 1959–1960; Member, Brynmor Jones Committee 1964–1965; Advisory Board for Research Councils 1974–1983; University and Polytechnic Grants Committee for Hong Kong 1974–1997; Chairman, Advisory Panel on Limestone Workings in the West Midlands 1983–1994; Chairman, Clinical Academic Staff Salaries Committee 1985–1990, Vice-Chairman 1985–1989, Chairman 1989–1991, CVCP; DL, West Yorkshire 1990; Chairman, Academic Advisory Board, Asian University of Science and Technology, Thailand 1994–1999. **Awards:** Exhibition, SJC 1943. **Honours:** Kt 1983; Silver Bauhinia Star, Hong Kong 1999. **Publications:** *Braced Frameworks*, 1965, 2nd edition 1974; papers on elasticity, dynamic plasticity or thermal effects on structures in *Proceedings of the Royal Society*, *Philosophical Transactions of the Royal Society* and other journals.

PARKES, The Revd Dr James William (1936) Born 22 December 1896, St Andrews, Guernsey; son of Henry Parkes, Civil Engineer (Railways), and Annie Katherine Bell; m Dorothy Emily Wickings, 8 August 1942, St John's, Hildenborough. MA 1936; BA (Oxon) 1923; MA (Oxon) 1926; DPhil (Oxon) 1934. **Educ:** Elizabeth College, Guernsey; Hertford College, Oxford; Exeter College, Oxford; Ripon Hall, Oxford. **Career:** Private, Artists Rifles 1916; Second Lieutenant, Queen's Royal West Surrey Regiment 1917; Captain and Adjutant, 19th Queen's 1918; International Study Secretary, Student Christian Movement 1923–1926; Ordained Deacon 1925; Curate, St Stephen, Hampstead 1925–1928; Ordained Priest 1926; Warden, Student Movement House, London 1926–1928; Study Secretary, International Student Service, Geneva 1928–1934. **Appointments:** Charles William Eliot Lecturer, Jewish Institute of Religion, New York 1946–1947; President, Jewish Historical Society of England 1949–1951; Director, The Parkes Library, 1956–1964; Honorary Fellow, Hebrew University of Jerusalem 1970; Public Preacher. **Awards:** Open Classical Scholarship, Hertford College, Oxford; Buber-Rosenzweig Medal 1979. **Publications:** *The Jew and His Neighbour*, 1930; *International Conferences*, 1933; *The Conflict of the Church and the Synagogue*, 1934; *Jesus, Paul and the Jews*, 1936; *The Jew in the Medieval Community*, 1938; *The Jewish Problem in the Modern World*, 1939; *Oxford Pamphlets on World Affairs*; *Palestine*, 1940; *The Jewish Question*, 1941; *An Enemy of the People: Antisemitism*, 1945; *The Emergence of the Jewish Problem, 1878–1939*, 1946; *Judaism and Christianity*, 1948; *A History of Palestine from 135 AD to Modern Times*, 1949; *The Story of Jerusalem*, 1949; *God at Work*, 1952; *End of an Exile*, 1954; *The Foundations of Judaism and Christianity*, 1960; *A History of the Jewish People*, 1962; *Antisemitism*, 1963; *Prelude to Dialogue*, 1969; *Voyage of Discoveries: an autobiography*, 1969; *Whose Land? The Peoples of Palestine*, 1970; (as John Hadham) *Good God*, 1940; *God in a World at War*, 1940; *Between God and Man*, 1942; *God and Human Progress*, 1944; *Common Sense About Religion*, 1961. Died June 1981.

PARKES, Mathew Donald (1932) Born 17 June 1913, 34 Therapia Road, Honor Oak, London; son of Charles William Parkes, HM Inspector of Schools, and Janet Tannahill Anderson; 4 children. **Subject(s):** Mathematics; BA 1935; MA 1939. **Tutor(s):** J M Wordie. **Educ:** Forest Hill House School; Dulwich College Preparatory School; XIV School, Clifton; Clifton College. **Career:** Head of Mathematics and Housemaster, Wellington College 1935–1978; Rose to rank of Major 1939–1945. **Awards:** Scholarship, SJC; College Prize, SJC 1935. Died 18 January 1999.

PARKIN, Charles William (1946) Born 19 March 1924, 67 Wingrave Gardens, Newcastle upon Tyne; son of William Parkin, Engineering Clerk, and Julia Maude Hutchinson. **Subject(s):** History; BA 1951. **Tutor(s):** F Thistlethwaite. **Educ:** Newcastle City Council School; Royal Grammar School, Newcastle. **Career:** Fellow and Lecturer in History, Clare College, Cambridge 1955–1986. **Appointments:** Director of Studies and Tutor, Clare College, Cambridge 1955–1986. Died 22 October 1986.

PARKINSON, Desmond John (1932) Born 8 March 1913, Monghyr, Bengal, India; son of Frederick Arthur Parkinson, Merchant, and Mabel Graham; m (1) Leonor Hughes, 1940 (div 1954), (2) Lorna Mary Britton (née Wood), 1955. **Subject(s):** Classics; BA 1935. **Tutor(s):** R L Howland. **Educ:** British American School, Rio de Janeiro, Brazil; Hereford Cathedral School; Brasenose College, Oxford. **Career:** Colonial Administrative Service (Gold Coast, British Guiana, Nigeria) 1936–1960; MAFF 1960–1963; Agricultural Research Council 1963–1973 (Under-Secretary from 1971). **Awards:** Scholarship, SJC; College Prize, SJC. **Honours:** OBE 1950. Died 20 May 1996.

PARKINSON, Dr John (1901) Born 17 February 1872, Camden Road, London; son of Frederick John Parkinson, Civil Engineer, and Elizabeth; m Eleanor Fanny Whitlock, 1897; 1 son (Mark Mervyn Leofric b 4 June 1907), 1 daughter. **Subject(s):** Geology; BA 1903; MA 1906; ScD 1923; FRGS. **Tutor(s):** J R Tanner; C E Graves. **Johnian Relatives:** father of Mark Mervyn Leofric Parkinson (1924). **Educ:** Camden Road Collegiate School; UCL; Mason University College, Birmingham. **Career:** Lecturer in Geology and Geography, Harrow 1902–1903; Principal, Mineral Survey, Southern Nigeria 1903–1906; Geologist, Liberian Development Co, West Central Africa 1906–1907; Water Supply Geologist, Kenya 1914–1915; Economic Geologist in connection with petroleum, West Africa, Kenya, Trinidad, Venezuela, India, Burma and Tanganyika Territory; Leader, British Museum Expedition 1927–1928; Water Supply Geologist, Somaliland 1931–1932; Temporarily attached to Mining and Geology Department, Kenya Colony 1940; Ministry of Economic

Welfare, until 1942. **Awards:** Geological Society Lyell Fund Award 1915. **Publications:** *A Reformer by Proxy*, 1909; *Other Laws*, 1911; *The Dinosaur in East Africa*, 1930; many papers on petrology and field geology. Died 19 July 1947.

PARKINSON, Joseph Alfred (1919) Born 24 April 1899, Surfleet, Lincolnshire; son of Joseph Alfred Parkinson, Farmer and Grazier, and Mary Ann Fountain. BA 1921; MA 1926. **Tutor(s):** E E Sikes. **Educ:** Kirton Grammar School; Boston Grammar School. **Career:** RFC, serving in France, 1917. Died 27 January 1991.

PARKINSON, Kenneth Nuttall (1918) American Student.

PARKINSON, Mark Mervyn Leofric (1924) Born 4 June 1907, 30 Lensfield Road, Cambridge; son of John Parkinson, Geologist, and Eleanor Fanny Whitlock. BA 1929; MA 1969. **Tutor(s):** J M Wordie. **Johnian Relatives:** son of John Parkinson (1901). **Educ:** Upper Canada College, Toronto; Private Tuition, Littlehampton; Tonbridge School. **Career:** General Manager, Texaco Trinidad Inc; Assistant Manager, Texas Company, Iran, Limited 1958. Died 1996.

PARKINSON, William Hope (1934) Born 16 May 1915, Charnwood, Victoria Road, West Hartlepool; son of William Gerald Parkinson, Medical Practitioner, and Bessie Margaret Robson. **Subject(s):** Natural Sciences; BA 1937. **Tutor(s):** R L Howland. **Educ:** Brightlands Preparatory School, Gloucester; Marlborough College.

PARLOW, The Revd John Thomas Morgan (1940) Born 6 June 1921, 87 Grange Road, West Hartlepool; son of John Joseph Parlow, Primitive Methodist Minister, and Sarah Elizabeth Morgan. **Subject(s):** English/Theology; BA 1943; MA 1947. **Tutor(s):** C W Guillebaud. **Educ:** Scarborough School; Archbishop's School, York; Derby School; West Hartlepool Secondary School. **Career:** Ordained Deacon 1947; Ordained Priest 1948; Priest, Middleton-on-the-Wolds, North Dalton, Humberside 1978. Died 18 August 1978.

PARNELL, Charles Edward (1939) Born 1 June 1921, Kuching, Sarawak, Malaysia; son of Edward Parnell, Sarawak Civil Service, and Naka Lim. **Tutor(s):** C W Guillebaud. **Educ:** Hillstone, Malvern; Uppingham School.

PARNELL, Frederick Ivor (1933) Born 2 June 1914, Teluugapalayan Village, Agricultural College, Coimbatore, India; son of Frederick Richard Parnell, Government Botanist, and Eunice Elizabeth Hunt. **Subject(s):** Natural Sciences; BA 1937. **Tutor(s):** J M Wordie. **Johnian Relatives:** nephew of Thomas Parnell (1900); son of Frederick Richard Parnell (1905). **Educ:** Berkhamsted School; St John's College, Johannesburg, South Africa; Berkhamsted School.

PARNELL, Frederick Richard (1905) Born 6 April 1886, West Haddon, Northamptonshire; son of Richard Parnell, Farmer, Grazier and Cattle Salesman, and Kate Cotterell; m Eunice Elizabeth Hunt; 1 son (Frederick Ivor b 2 June 1914), 3 daughters. **Subject(s):** Natural Sciences; BA 1908. **Tutor(s):** D MacAlister. **Johnian Relatives:** brother of Thomas Parnell (1900); father of Frederick Ivor Parnell (1933). **Educ:** Northampton and County School. **Career:** Economic Botanist to the Madras Government, India 1913–1924; Empire Cotton Growing Corporation 1924. **Awards:** Scholarship, SJC 1904. Died 10 January 1971.

PARNELL, Professor Thomas (1900) Born 5 July 1881, West Haddon, Northamptonshire; son of Richard Parnell, Farmer and Meat Salesman, and Kate Cotterell. **Subject(s):** Natural Sciences; BA 1903; MA 1908. **Tutor(s):** J E Sandys. **Johnian Relatives:** brother of Frederick Richard Parnell (1905); uncle of Frederick Ivor Parnell (1933). **Educ:** Northampton County School. **Career:** Tutor, Trinity College, Melbourne 1904–1911; Lecturer in Physics, University of Queensland 1911–1919; Second Lieutenant, AIF, WWI; Professor of Physics 1919. **Awards:** Scholarship, SJC.

PARR, Thomas Thornton (1939) Born 28 July 1921, 30 Merches Gardens, Cardiff; son of Percy Parr, City Surveyor and Engineer, and Mary Elizabeth Thornton. **Subject(s):** Law; BA 1943; MA 1949; LLB 1950; LLM 1985. **Tutor(s):** S J Bailey. **Educ:** Rock Ferry High School, Birkenhead; Bishop Vesey's Grammar School, Sutton Coldfield; Whitgift School, Croydon.

PARRACK, Colin Arthur (1945) Born 1 October 1927, 33 Irvin Avenue, Saltburn, Yorkshire; son of John Charles Parrack, Schoolmaster, and Doris Nellie Crow; m Joan Canby, 27 December 1961, 1 son (Malcolm b 1963), 1 daughter (Ruth b 1966). **Subject(s):** Mathematics; BA 1948; MA 1952. **Tutor(s):** J M Wordie. **Johnian Relatives:** cousin of Robert William Crow (1961). **Educ:** Manchester Grammar School. **Career:** Master, Silcoates School, Wakefield; Head of Mathematics, Newcastle-under-Lyme High School, Staffordshire until 1987. **Appointments:** Secretary, Leek and District Civic Society; Vice-Chairman, Leek and Moorlands Historical Trust; Awarder for Step Further Maths B. **Awards:** Scholarship, SJC. Died 20 November 1999.

PARRY, Bernard King (1911) Born 14 June 1892, 139 Alma Road, Aston Manor, Warwickshire; son of Samuel Charles Parry, Attendance Officer, Aston Education Committee, and Martha Black; m Edith Emily Rew, 5 July 1921, Birmingham; 1 son (Douglas). **Subject(s):** Mathematics/ Natural Sciences; BA 1914; MA 1921. **Tutor(s):** J R Tanner. **Educ:** King Edward's School, Birmingham. **Career:** Assistant Commissioner, Central Provinces, Indian Civil Service; Sub-Judge, Indian Civil Service 1921; Officiating District and Sessions Judge, Indian Civil Service 1924–1928; Called to the Bar, Gray's Inn 1928. Died 2 December 1965.

PARRY, Hugh Meredith (1937) Born 31 March 1919, Penrhyn Dovey Pennal, Machynlleth; son of John Parry, Farmer, and Mary Davies; m Frances Mary Vodden; 1 son (John). **Subject(s):** Law; BA 1940; MA 1944. **Tutor(s):** C W Guillebaud. **Educ:** Machynlleth Elementary School; Machynlleth Intermediate School; Leighton Park School, Reading; University of Grenoble; University College of Wales, Aberystwyth. **Career:** Admitted Solicitor 1948. Died 14 March 1986.

PARRY, Dr James Hales (1908) Born 25 July 1890, Docking, King's Lynn; son of George Hales Parry, Physician and Surgeon, and Sarah Florence Howell; m Helen Stephens Hill, 12 June 1923. BA 1911; MRCS; LRCP 1914; Certificate in Tropical Medicine (London) 1920. **Tutor(s):** L H K Bushe-Fox. **Educ:** Epsom College; Banham Grammar School. **Career:** Captain, Indian Medical Service 1915–1919; Medical Officer, Tanganyika Territory 1919 (Senior Medical Officer 1928). Died 24 February 1947.

PARRY-WILLIAMS, Dr Henry Wyn (1948) Born 26 March 1930, North Road, Aberystwyth; son of John Oscar Parry-Williams, Secretary, Welsh Plant Breeding Station, and Dorothy Ellis. **Subject(s):** Natural Sciences; BA 1951; MA 1957; BChir 1955; MB 1956. **Tutor(s):** G C L Bertram. **Educ:** Alexandra Road School, Aberystwyth; Ardwyn County School, Aberystwyth.

PARSONS, Charles Wynford (1920) Born 22 July 1901, Redcliffe, Heathfield, Swansea, Glamorganshire; son of Tom Postlethwaite Parsons, Commercial Traveller, and Florence Williams; 2 sons, 2 daughters. **Subject(s):** Natural Sciences; BA 1923; MA 1933; FRSE 1933. **Tutor(s):** B F Armitage. **Educ:** Terrace Road School, Swansea; Swansea Grammar School; Bristol Grammar School. **Career:** Junior Assistant, later Lecturer, Zoology Department, University of Glasgow 1927–1950. **Appointments:** Member, Senate, University of Glasgow. **Publications:** Various. Died 26 August 1950.

PARSONS, Geoffrey Bonython Angas (1926) Born 1 February 1908, Adelaide, South Australia; son of Herbert Angas Parsons, Judge, Supreme Court, South Australia, and Mary Elsie Bonython. **Subject(s):** History/Law; BA 1929; MA 1933. **Tutor(s):** E A Benians. **Educ:** St Peter's Collegiate School, Adelaide. Died 16 October 1987.

PARSONS, George Samuel (1926) Born 6 February 1908, 103 Christchurch Road, Boscombe, Bournemouth; son of Frank Parsons, Managing Director, Dairy Company, and Rosa Beatrice Bigwood; m Mary. **Subject(s):** Economics/Law; BA 1929; MA 1933. **Tutor(s):** J M Wordie. **Educ:** Bournemouth School. Died March 1969.

PASCOE, Sir Frederick John (1912) Born 19 March 1893, Albany Road, Redruth, Cornwall; son of Frederick Richard Pascoe, Secretary, and Laura Augusta Tonkin; 1 son, 1 daughter (Belinda). **Subject(s):** Mechanical Sciences; BA 1919. **Tutor(s):** L H K Bushe-Fox. **Educ:** Exeter School. **Career:** Lieutenant, Duke of Cornwall's Light Infantry and MGC, WWI; Apprenticed to Leeds Forge; Secretary, Electric and Railway Finance Company until 1930; Board, later Chairman, British Timken Ltd (also later Chairman of Aberdare Holdings, Aberdare Cables, Aberdare Engineering and South Wales Switchgear) 1930. **Appointments:** Committee, Northamptonshire County Cricket Club; Various other Sporting appointments; Freeman, City of London; Liveryman, Worshipful Company of Tin Plate Workers; Liveryman, Fishmongers' Company; Chairman, London Committee, South Africa Foundation; Member, Council of Aims of Industry; Member, East Midlands Regional Advisory Council for the Organisation of Further Education. **Honours:** Kt 1957. Died 5 February 1963.

PASCOE, Kenneth John (1938) Born 14 May 1920, Three Mile Stone, Kenwyn, Truro, Cornwall; son of John Pascoe, Miller and Corn Merchant, and Enid Gwendoline Gatley; m Dorothy Betty Weldon, 5 March 1949, St Mary's, Putney; 5 children. **Subject(s):** Natural Sciences and Physics; BA 1941; MA 1945. **Tutor(s):** J M Wordie. **Educ:** Chyvelah Council School; Truro School. **Career:** Demonstrator in Engineering, University of Cambridge 1943–1953; Senior Scientific Officer, Royal Naval Scientific Service 1949; Lecturer in Engineering, University of Cambridge 1953–1984; Title B Fellow 1960–1984, Lecturer in Mechanical Sciences 1962–1984, Title D Fellow 1984–1994, SJC; Senior Proctor, University of Cambridge 1984–1985. **Appointments:** Tutor 1965–1980, Tutor for Graduate Admissions 1978–1980, Director of Studies in Engineering 1980–1984, Steward 1980–1982 and 1986–1987, SJC. **Awards:** Major Scholarship, SJC 1937. **Publications:** *The Properties of Engineering Materials.* Died 15 November 1994.

PASKIN, Sir Jesse John (1912) Born 15 November 1892, High Street, Quarry Bank, Staffordshire; son of John Edward Paskin, Gentleman, and Alice Avonia Brooks; m (1) Doris Blanche North, 1920, (2) Alice Marjorie (Eve) Ruston, 10 September 1947, London; (1) 1 son. **Subject(s):** Mathematics; BA 1918. **Tutor(s):** L H K Bushe-Fox. **Educ:** King Edward's School, Stourbridge. **Career:** Captain, 8th Battalion, Worcestershire Regiment and Major, MGC, France, Belgium, Germany, WWI; various private secretarial positions, Colonial Office 1920–1954. **Honours:** CMG 1944; KCMG 1954; MC; French Croix de Guerre. Died 16 September 1972.

PASLEY, Arthur Dalrymple Sabine (1922) Born 14 July 1903, Holbrook, Shooters Hill, Eltham, Kent; son of Richard Sydney Sabine Pasley, Harbour Master, and Mary Victoria Des Voeuse; m Doris. BA 1926. **Tutor(s):** B F Armitage. **Educ:** Little Appley School, Ryde; Shrewsbury School.

PASSMORE, Dudley Robert (1927) Born 27 March 1909, 50 Bishop's Mansions, Fulham, London; son of Stanley Joseph Passmore, Solicitor, and Jeanne Rose Russell. **Tutor(s):** E A Benians. **Educ:** Hawtreys, Birchington; Marlborough College.

PATEL, Behram Pestonji (1921) Born 2 July 1903, Bombay, India; son of Pestonji Dhunjibhoy Patel, Parsi Cotton Merchant, and Dosibai Meherwanji Polishwalla. **Subject(s):** Economics; BA 1924; MA 1928. **Tutor(s):** E A Benians. **Educ:** Imperial High School, Bombay; Private Tuition. **Career:** Partner, Patel Cotton Company Ltd, and Patel Brothers, Bombay. Died 8 October 1931.

PATERSON, Alan (1929) Born 31 December 1911, 13 Dean Road, Willesden Green, Middlesex; son of Herbert James Paterson, Accountant, and Catherine Ann Welch; m Betty, 1943 (d 1970); 4 children. **Subject(s):** Law; BA 1932; MA 1936; LLB 1933. **Tutor(s):** C W Guillebaud. **Educ:** Alleyn Court Preparatory School, Westcliff-on-Sea; Haileybury College. **Career:** Founder, Trustee and Administrator, the Cobden Trust; Partner, Birnberg and Paterson, London 1963; Company Secretary, War on Want 1970. **Appointments:** Legal Advisor, NCCL. **Publications:** *Legal Aid as a Social Service*, Cobden Trust 1970. Died 4 July 1999.

PATERSON, Sir George Mutlow (1924) Born 3 September 1906, The Gables, St George's, Grenada, British West Indies; son of George William Paterson, Medical Practitioner, and Olivia Hannah Mutlow-Williams; m Audrey Morris 1935; 1 son, 2 daughters. **Subject(s):** History/Law; BA 1927; MA 1945; LLB 1928; LLM 1985; QC 1950. **Tutor(s):** E A Benians. **Educ:** Grenada Secondary School. **Career:** Member, Colonial Service 1927; Nigerian Administration 1929; 6th King's African Rifles (reached rank of Lieutenant Colonel), WWII; Solicitor-General, Tanganyika 1946–1949; Attorney General, Sierra Leone 1949–1954; Attorney General 1954–1957; Chief Justice, Northern Rhodesia 1957–1961. **Appointments:** QC (Sierra Leone) 1950. **Awards:** Island Scholarship from Grenada. **Honours:** OBE 1946; Kt 1959. Died 24 January 1996.

PATERSON, Dr Matthew Wallace (1905) Born 3 September 1887, Tinsley, Rotherham, Yorkshire; son of William Paterson, Engineer, and Florence Nellie Smith; 1 son, 1 daughter. **Subject(s):** Natural Sciences; BA 1908; MRCS; LRCP 1913; BMA. **Tutor(s):** D MacAlister. **Educ:** The Grammar School, Blackburn; Manchester Grammar School. **Career:** House Surgeon, Alnwick Infirmary and Manchester Royal Infirmary; Senior Resident Medical Officer, Hope Hospital, Salford; Major, RAMC and Deputy Assistant Director of Medical Services (twice Mentioned in Despatches), WWI; GP, Hyde, Cheshire 1919–1947. **Appointments:** Chairman, BMA, Hyde Division 1930; Honorary Secretary, Association of Certifying Factory Surgeons 1930. **Honours:** MC 1917; OBE 1919; Medaille d'Honneur of French Government. Died 15 November 1958.

PATERSON, Noel Kennedy (1928) Born 25 December 1905, The Manse, Abercorn Road, Edinburgh; son of David Paterson, Minister of the United Free Church of Scotland, and Susannah Sampson Ralston Kennedy. **Tutor(s):** E A Benians. **Educ:** George Heriot's School, Edinburgh; University of Edinburgh.

PATERSON, Thomas (1939) Born 20 August 1915, Storetta, Jerviston Road, Motherwell; son of James Shirlaw Paterson, Commercial Traveller, and Maggie Storrie Denholm. **Subject(s):** Mathematics; BA 1941; MA (Glasgow) 1939. **Tutor(s):** J M Wordie. **Educ:** Calder Public High School, Motherwell; Dalziel High School, Motherwell; Glasgow University. **Awards:** Mayhew Prize, University of Cambridge 1941.

PATERSON, Lieutenant Colonel Victor James Ewing (1919) Born 24 May 1901, Manakau, Manewatu, Wellington Province, New Zealand; son of John Ewing Paterson, Captain, Intelligence Corps, British Army of the Rhine, and Enid Mary Barnard Brown; m Catherine. BA 1922; MA 1928. **Tutor(s):** E A Benians. **Educ:** Hurworth School, Wanganui; The Collegiate School, Wanganui. **Career:** Lieutenant Colonel, The Central India Horse. Died 26 December 1955.

PATON, John Miller (1942) Born 28 May 1924, Earlston, Bridge of Weir, Renfrewshire; son of James Shedden Paton, Manufacturer, and Mary Barclay Tweedale Lang. **Tutor(s):** C W Guillebaud. **Educ:** Warriston, Moffat; Rickerby House, Carlisle; Sedbergh School.

PATON, Valentine Stewart (1943) Born 14 March 1925, Perth Firs, Church Road, Hayling Island, Hampshire; son of Alexander Paton, Colonel, RA, and Sybil Isabella Grimwood Mears; m Jean Annette Comyn, 18 October 1952. **Tutor(s):** S J Bailey. **Educ:** Alleyn Court Preparatory School, Westcliff-on-Sea; Canford School.

PATTEN, Edward John Kelman (1939) Born 17 April 1920, 7 Park Road, Ipswich; son of John Alexander Patten, Congregational Minister, and Elsie Mary Lewis; m Monica Gatter, 4 June 1945, Calcutta. BA 1948; MA 1950. **Tutor(s):** J M Wordie. **Educ:** Ipswich High School; Ipswich School; Dulwich College Preparatory School; Belmont, Mill Hill; Mill Hill.

PATTERSON, Arthur (1926) Born 24 June 1906, 22 Landseer Street, Belfast, County Antrim, Ireland; son of Alexander Patterson, Clerical Officer, Imperial Civil Service, and Margaret Elizabeth Jackson; m Ann. **Subject(s):** Mathematics; BA 1929. **Tutor(s):** J M Wordie. **Educ:** St Jude's National School; The Model National School; Methodist College, Belfast; Queen's University, Belfast. **Awards:** Exhibition, SJC 1926; Scholarship, SJC 1927. **Honours:** CMG. Died 7 March 1996.

PATTERSON, Sir John Robert (1911) Born 27 August 1892, Bedlington, Northumberland; son of George Thomas Patterson, Outfitter, and Miriam Foggan; m Esther Margaret Sheldon; 2 sons (George and Hugh). BA 1914. **Tutor(s):** L H K Bushe-Fox. **Educ:** Whitley Memorial School Bedlington; Morpeth Grammar School. **Career:** Various administrative posts, Nigerian Civil Service 1915–1943; Chief Commissioner, Northern Province, Nigeria 1943–1947. **Honours:** CMG 1939; KBE 1945. **Publications:** *Kanuri songs*, 1925; *Stories of Abu Zeid*, in Shuwa Arabic, 1930.

PATTERSON, Joseph Lewis (1943) Born 29 April 1925, 116 Samuel Street, Woolwich; son of Henry William Charles Patterson, Police Constable, and Alice Edith Mary Brett. **Tutor(s):** S J Bailey. **Educ:** St Thomas' School, Woolwich; Wood Street School, Woolwich; Roan School, Maze Hill, Greenwich; Woolwich Polytechnic; Sir John Cass Technical Institute, Aldgate.

PATTERSON, Dr Richard Ferrar (1907) Born 29 January 1888, Kilmore, Holywood, Belfast, County Down; son of Richard Patterson, Merchant, and Clara Mulligan; 2 daughters. **Subject(s):** Classics/Modern and Medieval Languages; BA 1910; MA 1916; DLitt (Glasgow) 1922. **Tutor(s):** E E Sikes. **Educ:** Oundle School. **Career:** Senior Editor, Blackie & Sons; General Editor, the Scottish Text Society 1924. **Appointments:** Fellow, Society of Antiquaries of Scotland. **Awards:** Scholarship, SJC 1911. **Publications:** (ed) *Jonson's Conversations with Drummond of Hawthornden*; *The New Gresham Encyclopaedia*; *Six Centuries of English Literature*. Died 17 October 1948.

PATTINSON, George Norman (1905) (migrated to Emmanuel College) Born 14 August 1887, Elim Bank, Bowness, Ambleside, Westmorland; son of George Henry Pattinson, Builder and Contractor, and Sarah Agnes Thompson; m Mary. BA 1909 (Emmanuel). **Tutor(s):** D MacAlister. **Educ:** The Craig, Windermere; Sedbergh School. **Career:** Solicitor 1913; Captain, Army Service Corps, France, WWI; High Sheriff and JP 1941. Died 17 August 1966.

PATTINSON, Dr Tom Pickles (1934) Born 23 May 1916, 87 Grange Road, West Hartlepool; son of Joseph William Pattinson, Primitive Methodist Minister, and Mary Pickles. **Subject(s):** Natural Sciences; BA 1937; MA 1943; MB 1942; BChir 1942; MD 1949. **Tutor(s):** R L Howland. **Educ:** Elementary School, Stockton-on-Tees; Elementary School, Gilsden; Keighley Grammar School; Elmfield School, York; Ashville College, Harrogate. **Career:** Assistant Tuberculosis Officer, Somerset 1947. Died 7 April 1998.

PATTISON, George William (1946) Born 7 October 1921, Dorchester House, Beverley Road, Hull; son of Thomas Stanley Pattison, Director, T S Pouparts Ltd, and Blanche Sutton-Gardner. **Subject(s):** History; BA 1948; MA 1953; Diploma, Archaeology and Anthropology; PhD (London). **Tutor(s):** F Thistlethwaite. **Educ:** Glysegarth School; Dean Close School, Cheltenham. **Career:** Barman; Salesman, *Encyclopaedia Britannica*; Schoolmaster, Basildon, Essex 1962. **Appointments:** Tutor Organiser, Fenland Federation of the Workers' Educational Association 1949.

PATTON, Arnold Gordon (1912) Born 2 December 1892, Ivy Cottage, Friern Barnet, North Finchley, Middlesex; son of Horace Chmel Patton, Bookseller, and Mary Louisa Brooks. **Subject(s):** Classics; BA 1915. **Tutor(s):** E E Sikes. **Educ:** Higher Elementary School, East Finchley; Christ's College, Finchley; City of London School. **Career:** Various posts including Officiating Deputy Commissioner; Secretary, Finance and Revenue Department, Indian Civil Service 1916. **Awards:** Browne Medal for Greek Ode, University of Cambridge 1914; Browne Medal for Greek Epigram, University of Cambridge 1915. **Publications:** *The Proctor* (Greek); *The Strike* (Greek); 'D.I.D(ay)' (Latin) *The Eagle*, 35; 'Verse Translation of Catullus, Ode XLV', *The Eagle*, 35; 'Of Bedmakers', *The Eagle*, 35; 'Lines written below Grantchester Mill', *The Eagle*, 35. Died 27 April 1969.

PATUCK, Rustomjee Sorabjee (1905) Born 25 November 1884, Bombay, India; son of Sorabjee Kaikhusro Patuck and Mithibai Phirozeshah Pestonjee Meherjee. **Subject(s):** Natural Sciences; BA 1908. **Tutor(s):** L H K Bushe-Fox. **Educ:** Elphinstone College; The New High School, Bombay. **Career:** Indian Civil Service; Godfrey and Boyce Manufacturing Company, Calcutta 1950.

PATUCK, Sorab Pestonjee (1928) Born 15 April 1910, Bandra, Bombay Presidency, India; son of Pestonjee Sorabjee Patuck, Indian Civil Service, and Shirinbai. **Subject(s):** Mathematics/Mechanical Sciences; BA 1932. **Tutor(s):** J M Wordie. **Johnian Relatives:** son of Pestonjee Sorabjee Patuck (1895). **Educ:** Bedale's School, Petersfield.

PATWARDHAN, Madhukar Shankar (1947) Born 19 November 1927, Bombay, India; son of Shankar Ganesh Patwardhan, Pleader, High Court, Bombay, and Krishnabai Pandurang Kane; m Prabha Patwardhan Mudholkar, 11 April 1955, Bombay; 2 sons (Sanjeev Madhukar b 27 June 1957 and Ranjan Madhukar b 29 May 1959). **Subject(s):** Natural Sciences; BA 1950; MA 1954. **Tutor(s):** G C L Bertram. **Johnian Relatives:** brother of Vaman Shankar Patwardhan (1946); nephew of Prabhakar Pandurang Kane (1949); father of Ranjan Madhukar Patwardhan (1979). **Educ:** Charni Road Municipal Primary School; High School, Bombay; Elphinstone College, Bombay; Royal Institute of Science, Bombay. **Career:** Chief Executive, Burmah Shell Oil Storage and Distributing Company of India Ltd and Chairman of Burmah-Shell Refineries 1972–1976; Head, Chemicals Supply Economics and Operations, Shell International Chemical Company, London 1976–1978; Managing Director and Vice-Chairman, National Organic Chemical Industries Ltd, Bombay 1978–1993; Head, Patwardhan & Associates (Management Consultancy) and Chairman, Meridian Vat Reclaim (India) Ltd 1993–1996; Chairman, Castrol India Ltd and Neuland Laboratories Ltd 1994–1996. **Appointments:** Member, University of Bombay Senate 1970–1975; President, Bombay Chamber of Commerce and Industry 1980–1981; Member, Maharashtra State Planning Board 1980–1983; Director, Reserve Bank of India 1980–1985; President, Associated Chambers of Commerce and Industry 1984–1985. **Publications:** *Pride, Prejudice and Paradox in Indian Society*; *Oil and other Multinationals in India*; *Business and the Environment*; *Planning for Retirement*; *Managerial Evolution: Indian Experience*; *Bhagwad Gita for You and Me*. Died 24 March 1996.

PATWARDHAN, Vaman Shankar (1946) Born 19 May 1926, 156 Girgaum Road, Khetwadi, Bombay, India; son of Shankar Ganesh Patwardhan, Advocate, High Court, Bombay, and Krishnabai Pandurang Kane; m Anasuya Narayan Karandikar; 1 son (Madhav b 1954), 1 daughter (Mrinalini b 1957). **Subject(s):** Mechanical Sciences; BA 1949; MA 1953. **Tutor(s):** R L Howland. **Johnian Relatives:** brother of Madhukar Shankar Patwardhan (1947); nephew of Prabhakar Pandurang Kane (1949); uncle of Ranjan Madhukar Patwardhan (1979). **Educ:** Charni Road Municipal Primary School; CSS High School, Bombay; Elphinstone College, Bombay; Royal Institute of Science, Bombay. **Career:** Regional Manager (Western Region) Wimco Ltd, Bombay 1973–1978; General Manager, Phaltan Sugar Works Ltd 1978–1984; Honorary Worker, Students' Welfare Association, Pune 1986–1993.

PAUL, Air Commodore Gerard John Christopher (1926) Born 31 October 1907, 11 Wellington Circus, Nottingham; son of Edmund William Paul, Surgeon, and Florence Rose Meyrick; m (1) Rosemary Lane, 1937 (d), (2) Mollie Denise Samuels, 1987; (1) 2 sons (Simon and Timothy), 1 daughter (Azalea). **Subject(s):** Mechanical Sciences; BA 1929; MA 1966 CEng; FRAeS. **Tutor(s):** J M Wordie. **Educ:** Arden House Preparatory School, Henley in Arden; Cheltenham College. **Career:** OC, 90 Squadron, RAF; University of Cambridge Air Squadron, RAF Reserve of Officers 1927–1929; RAF 1929–1958; RNAS, HMS *Courageous*, HMS *Furious* 1931–1938; Bomber Command and Second Tactical Air Force 1939–1945; Commandant, Central Flying School, RAF 1946–1948; Air Commodore, RAF 1954. **Appointments:** CUAS 1925–1927; Secretary-General of the Air League, 1958–1975; President, Popular Flying Association, 1969–1978; Life Vice-President, RAF Gliding and Soaring Association; Fellow, Royal Aeronautical Society. **Awards:** Croix de Guerre avec Palme (Belgium) 1944; Military Cross (Czechoslovakia) 1945. **Honours:** DFC 1944; CB 1956. Died 11 January 2003.

PAULLEY, Christopher James Archibald (1939) Born 10 April 1920, Kingsland, King Street, Newcastle-under-Lyme; son of Harold Paulley, Principal, and Margaret Elspeth Douglas. **Tutor(s):** C W Guillebaud. **Johnian Relatives:** son of Harold Paulley (1907). **Educ:** The School, Malvern Link; St Edward's School, Oxford. **Career:** Lieutenant, Royal Inniskilling Fusiliers. Died 17 January 1944 (killed in action in Italy).

PAULLEY, Harold (1907) Born 14 December 1888, Pulham Market, Stratton, Norfolk; son of J N Legge Paulley, Surgeon, and Mary Elizabeth Fisher; m Margaret Elspeth (Rita) Douglas (d 21 July 1956); 2 sons, 1 daughter. **Subject(s):** Natural Sciences; BA 1910; MA 1919. **Tutor(s):** J R Tanner. **Johnian Relatives:** father of Christopher James Archibald Paulley (1939). **Educ:** Framlingham College. **Career:** Army Coach, Wyllies, Cuckfield, Sussex 1910–1912; Master, Brunswick Preparatory School, Haywards Heath 1913–1921; Captain, Norfolk Regiment, Middle East 1914–1919; Principal, Malvern Link Preparatory School 1921–1946. **Appointments:** Member, Malvern District Education Committee 1926–1953; Chairman, Malvern Link Coronation Committee 1953. Died 8 January 1973.

PAWANCHEE, Dr Abu (1948) See BAKAR.

PAXMAN, Edward Philip (1920) Born 2 August 1901, Brussels, Belgium; son of James Noah Paxman, Engineer, and Florence Muriel Sanders; m Dora Emilie Bowen, 27 April 1929, Hampstead Parish Church. BA 1923; MA 1927. **Tutor(s):** E E Sikes. **Johnian Relatives:** father of Philip John Paxman (1960). **Educ:** Rimpton, St Peter's, Thanet; Oundle School. **Career:** Trained with Vickers Electrical Company; Blackstone & Co; Chief Engineer, later Managing Director, Davey, Paxman & Co Ltd 1926. Died 25 March 1949.

PAXTON-PETTY, John Dennis (1928) Born 2 May 1908, 104 Kendrick Road, Reading, Berkshire; son of John Paxton-Petty, Master Printer, and Mabel Slater; 1 daughter. **Subject(s):** Mechanical Sciences; BA 1930. **Tutor(s):** J M Wordie. **Educ:** Crowthorne Towers Preparatory School; Haileybury College; RMA; School of Military Engineering, Chatham. Died 22 October 1996.

PAY, Dr Brian Wilfrid (1939) Born 25 September 1921, Swinderby, Claypole, Lincolnshire; son of Thomas Wilfrid Pay, Assistant Master, and Doris Amy Easton; m Nina. **Subject(s):** Natural Sciences; BA 1942; MA 1946 MRCP. **Tutor(s):** R L Howland. **Educ:** Pocklington School. **Career:** National Service, RAMC, Singapore and Malaya 1955; Senior Registrar, Royal Berkshire Hospital, Reading 1955–1965; Consultant Physician, Reading and District Hospital Group 1965–1983. Died 28 May 1983.

PAYNE, Alfred Leslie (1920) Born 25 December 1901, 5 Blockhouse Street, Peckham, Surrey; son of Alfred Henry Payne, Senior Rental Clerk, and Emily Eliza Hockey; m Olive J Kidd, March 1940, Cape Town; 2 sons (Kenneth b 18 August 1941 and Humphrey b 11 December 1943); 1 daughter (Anthea b 10 January 1948). **Subject(s):** Natural Sciences; BA 1923; MA 1927. **Tutor(s):** B F Armitage. **Johnian Relatives:** uncle of Anthony Charles Payne (1964). **Educ:** Haberdashers' Aske's School, Hatcham; London County Council School, Canterbury Road. **Career:** Assistant Master, Wellington College 1923–1935; Housemaster, School House, 1936–1951, Head of Science Department 1943–1966, temporary staff member 1969–1977, Bishops (Diocesan College), Cape Town, South Africa. **Appointments:** Fellow, Physical Society of London; Member, Science Masters' Association; Council Member, St Cyprian's School, Cape Town, South Africa 1957–1961; Inaugural Lecturer, Cape Town Planetarium 1958–1959. **Awards:** Scholarship, SJC 1919. Died 4 January 1985.

PAYNE, Professor Douglas Sutherland (1945) Born 29 July 1924, Aspen Villa, Whitehill Road, Gravesend, Kent; son of George Payne, Lieutenant Commander, RN, and Margaret Beer; m Grace Margaret, 21 June 1947; 3 children. PhD 1947; BSc (London) 1944. **Tutor(s):** J M Wordie. **Educ:** Wrotham Road Council School, Gravesend; Gravesend County School; King's School, Rochester; Sir John Cass Technical Institute, London; Imperial College of Science and Technology. **Career:** Assistant Lecturer, Imperial College 1947–1949; Lecturer, later Senior Lecturer, University of Glasgow 1949–1966; Professor of Chemistry, Hong Kong University 1966–1982; Fellowship Advisor, Croucher Foundation, Hong Kong 1982–1996; Consultant, Smiles Brewing Company, Bristol 1983–1991. **Honours:** MBE 1982. **Publications:** Various chemical journals and books.

PAYNE, George Peter Morgan (1930) Born 4 December 1911, Hadlow, Musgrave Road, Durban, Natal, South Africa; son of Harold William Payne, Director of Companies, and Gertrude Morgan Harvey; m Barbara M Elcome (d 1992); 1 son (John). **Subject(s):** Economics; BA 1933; MA 1937. **Tutor(s):** C W Guillebaud. **Educ:** Eversley Preparatory School, Tunbridge Wells; The Leys School, Cambridge. **Career:** Managing Director, Payne Bros Department Stores, South Africa; South African Navy, WWII; Property Developer, Western Canada 1954; Property Development, Guernsey 1965. **Appointments:** National Treasurer, British and Foreign Bible Society, States of Guernsey Ancient Monument Committee. Died 18 November 1999.

PAYNE, Richard Vaughan (1925) Born 16 July 1908, Northwood, Alton, Hampshire; son of Otto Vaughan Payne, Medical Practitioner, and Eleanor Beatrice Wise; 3 children. **Subject(s):** Natural Sciences; BA 1929; MA 1934; BChir 1934; MB 1934; MChir 1936; FRCS 1935. **Tutor(s):** M P Charlesworth. **Johnian Relatives:** son of Otto Vaughan Payne (1897). **Educ:** Edgeborough, Guildford; Sherborne School. **Career:** House Appointments, Guy's Hospital until 1936; Assistant Surgeon, King Edward VII Hospital, Windsor 1936–1939; Full Surgeon, King Edward VII Hospital, Windsor 1939–1947; Wing Commander and Adviser in Surgery, Air Headquarters, India 1946–1947; Surgeon, Canadian Red Cross Memorial Hospital, Taplow 1947. Died 10 December 1953.

PAYNE, Ronald John (1928) Born 12 June 1909, 9 Higher Terrace, Torquay, Devon; son of John Ernest Payne, Medical Practitioner, and Sylvia May Moore. **Subject(s):** History; BA 1931. **Tutor(s):** E A Benians. **Educ:** Cothill, Abingdon; Marlborough College; Private Tuition, West Wratting Park.

PEACOCK, Edward (1916) Born 24 August 1898, 32 Wales Street, Darlington, County Durham; son of Henry Peacock, Wood Pattern Maker, and Charlotte Pinkney. **Subject(s):** Modern and Medieval Languages; BA 1921; MA 1932. **Tutor(s):** E E Sikes. **Educ:** Darlington Grammar School; Albert Road Council School, Darlington.

PEACOCK, Hugh Myddleton (1924) Born 31 July 1905, 20 Devonshire Place, St Marylebone, London; son of Hugh Fenton Gilbert Peacock, Brewer, and Constance Fillingham Fletcher. **Tutor(s):** B F Armitage. **Educ:** Fonthill, East Grinstead; Harrow School.

PEACOCK, Robert Anderson (1938) Born 13 April 1920, 25 Montgomery Road, Glasgow, Scotland; son of John Peacock, Chartered Accountant, and Margaret Ferguson Anderson; m (1) N E Garrard, (2) N Walker, (3) J Willis; 1 son (John Gerrard), 2 daughters (Nina Ellen and Margaret Lesley). **Subject(s):** Economics. **Tutor(s):** C W Guillebaud. **Educ:** Dairsie House, Newlands; Cambusdoon School, Ayr; Belmont House School, Newton Mearns; Strathallan School, Forgandenny, Scotland. **Career:** RN 1938–1946; Partner in Chartered Accountants Firm 1950–1960; Chairman and Managing Director, Associated Bakeries & GI Co Ltd 1960–1966; Chairman, Walker Gowns (Partick) Ltd 1966–1976; Chairman, Devaco International Ltd 1985. **Appointments:** Member, Institute of Chartered Accountants of Scotland.

PEAR, Brian Hatherley (1938) Born 24 June 1919, 18 Chatham Grove, Withington, Manchester; son of Tom Hatherley Pear, Professor of Psychology, University of Manchester, and Catherine Robinson; m Betty Wallwork. **Subject(s):** Modern and Medieval Languages. **Tutor(s):** C W Guillebaud. **Educ:** Ladybarn House School; Manchester Grammar School. **Career:** Lieutenant, Westminster Dragoons 1939–1944. **Awards:** Sizarship, SJC. Died 3 November 1944 (killed in action in North-West Europe).

PEARCE, Eric George (1938) Born 1 July 1919, 45 Craven Walk, Stamford Hill, London; son of Leonard Roger Batten Pearce, Chemical Merchant, and Margaret Winifred Wilson; m Jean Amelia Mina Jenkins, 1953; 1 son (Clovis Roger Batten). **Subject(s):** Economics; BA 1941; MA 1945; FCI. **Tutor(s):** J M Wordie. **Educ:** Haileybury College, Hertford Heath; Hill School, Pottstown, USA. **Career:** Pilot, Fleet Air Arm, WWII; Chairman or Director of various companies. **Appointments:** Freeman, London; Liveryman, Worshipful Company of Shipwrights; Chairman, Institute of Commerce 1989; Member, Guinea Pig Club.

PEARCE, James Francis Stuart (1948) Born 31 March 1927, 2 The Broadway, Whetstone, Middlesex; son of William Pearce, Inspector, London and North Eastern Railway, and Doris Elsie Holmes; m Daphne May Rayner, 22 January 1955, St Andrew's Church, Orwell, Cambridgeshire; 1 son (Stephen Mark, b 31 May 1957), 2 daughters (Louise b 30 March 1961 and Virginia b 18 August 1962). **Subject(s):** Modern and Medieval Languages; BA 1950; MA 1955. **Tutor(s):** C W Guillebaud. **Educ:** Holy Trinity School, East Finchley; Haberdashers' Aske's Hampstead School, London. **Career:** Travel Industry; French Teacher, Weavers Road Secondary Technical School, Wellingborough 1958–1961; French and German Teacher, Head of Department, Stratton School, Biggleswade 1961–1987; Blue Badge Tourist Guide, Cambridge 1988–1999. Died 24 February 2002.

PEARSON, Cyril Edgar (1914) Born 7 May 1896, Corn Exchange House, Castle Gate, Newark, Nottingham; son of Walter Harry Pearson, Relieving Officer, and Elizabeth Garfield. **Tutor(s):** E E Sikes. **Educ:** Mount School, Newark; Magnus Grammar School, Newark. **Career:** Lieutenant, Durham Light Infantry 1914.

PEARSON, Desmond Lindon (1945) Born 26 June 1925, 48 Westgate, Guisborough, Yorkshire; son of John Lindon Pearson, Metallurgical and Chemical Engineer, and Clarice Brenda Goodyear. **Subject(s):** Mechanical Sciences; BA 1948; MA 1952. **Tutor(s):** S J Bailey; R L Howland. **Educ:** Ragworth Hall School, Norton-on-Tees; Durham School; Bournemouth Municipal College.

PEARSON, Professor James Douglas (1932) Born 17 December 1911, 163 Mill Road, Cambridge; son of William Henry Pearson, Builder's Labourer, and Elsie Edith Mary Hobbs, Dressmaker; m (1) Rose Betty Burden, (2) Hilda M Wilkinson; (1) 1 son, (2) 3 sons. **Subject(s):** Oriental Languages; BA 1935; MA 1939; Honorary FLA 1976. **Tutor(s):** J S Boys Smith. **Educ:** Linton C of E Elementary School; Cambridge and County High School. **Career:** Intelligence Corps, Germany, WWII; Assistant Under-Librarian, Cambridge University Library 1939–1950;

Librarian, School of Oriental and African Studies, University of London 1950–1972; Professor of Bibliography, with reference to Asia and Africa, School of Oriental and African Studies, University of London 1972–1979 (Emeritus 1979). **Awards:** Rogerson Scholarship, SJC 1931; Scholarship, SJC 1931; Scholarship, SJC 1934; Walford Award for lifelong achievement in bibliography 1992. **Publications:** *Index Islamicus, 1906–1955*, 1958; *Oriental and Asian Bibliography*, 1966; *Oriental Manuscripts in Europe and North America*, 1971; (joint ed) *Arab Islamic Bibliography*, 1977; (ed) *South Asia Bibliography*, 1978; *Creswell's Bibliography of the Architecture, Arts and Crafts of Islam, Supplement II*, 1984; *A Guide to Manuscripts and Documents in the British Isles relating to South and SE Asia*, Vol I, 1989, Vol II, 1990; *A Guide to Manuscripts and Documents in the British Isles relating to Africa*, Vol I, 1993, Vol II, 1994. Died 1 August 1997.

PEARSON, Michael (1936) Born 27 August 1918, Whitchurch, Oxfordshire; son of Mason Pearson, Brush Manufacturer, and Marie Josephe Genevieve Dutard; m Mary Cecilia Kemball, 14 December 1946, St Chad's, Cheadle, Cheshire; 1 son (Michael), 3 daughters (Genevieve, Audrey and Juliette). **Subject(s):** Economics; BA 1939; MA 1943. **Tutor(s):** J S Boys Smith. **Educ:** Our Lady's Convent, Amhurst Park; St Augustine's Abbey School, Ramsgate; Downside School. **Career:** Commissioned, RA (anti-aircraft) 1939; Mason Pearson Brothers, Brush Manufacturers (family firm), final position Chairman 1941–1965. **Appointments:** Life member, Cambridge University Cruising Club; Member, Cambridge University OTC (Signals). Died 23 July 2000.

PEARSON, Michael Geoffrey (1948) Born 12 July 1929, Santa Fé 899, Buenos Aires, Argentina; son of Alfred Marcus Worthington Pearson, Actuary, and Marie Therese Eileen Lamy. **Tutor(s):** J M Wordie. **Educ:** St George's Preparatory School, Buenos Aires; Ward College; St George's College.

PEARSON, Robert Scott Moncrieff (1940) Born 11 May 1922, Lovat Lodge, Albert Street, Nairn, Scotland; son of Norman Gillespie Pearson, Schoolmaster, and Lucy Catherine Ray. **Tutor(s):** S J Bailey. **Educ:** Alton Burn Preparatory School, Nairn; Loretto School. **Career:** Lieutenant, RE 1940–1943. Died 8 January 1943 (of wounds at El Agheila).

PEBERDY, John Rodney (1949) Born 23 June 1930, Clifton Villa, Hobson Road, Leicester; son of Philip Storer Peberdy, Museum Curator, and Amy Annie Barrow; m Monica Joplin Cutts, 10 September 1955, Machakos, Kenya; 1 son (John Richard Philip b 1958), 2 daughters (Joanna Elizabeth b 1957 and Sally Ann b 1961). **Subject(s):** Natural Sciences; BA 1952; MA 1956; DipAgr 1953; DipTropAgr (ICTA) 1954. **Tutor(s):** W A Deer. **Educ:** Mill Hill, Leicester; St Stanislaus College, Georgetown, British Guiana; Lodge School, Barbados; North Gloucestershire Technical College. **Career:** Colonial Service; training with ICTA; Agricultural Officer 1954, District Agricultural Officer 1955–1961, Machakos, Kenya; Provincial Agricultural Officer, Southern Province 1961; Personal Assistant to the Assistant Director of Agriculture, Central Province 1962–1963; Head of Range Management 1963–1966; Chief Agriculturalist 1966–1967; Head of Animal Production Division 1967–1970; Livestock Specialist, Agriculture Credit Division, World Bank 1971–1972; Agricultural Adviser, Southern Africa Development Division 1972–1974, Middle East Development Division 1974–1975, Ministry of Overseas Development, UK; Agriculturalist, East Africa Projects 1975–1976, Deputy Division Chief, Southern Africa Agriculture Projects 1976–1977, Division Chief, West Africa Agriculture Projects 1977–1987, Division Chief 1987–1991, Agriculture Adviser 1991–1992, West Africa Technical Department, World Bank, Washington. **Appointments:** Member, number of Kenyan National Boards, including Central Agriculture Board, Water Board, Kenya Dairy Board, Uplands Bacon Factory; Treasurer, Llangeinwen Church 1995–; Chairman, Anglesey Beekeepers Association 2002–. **Publications:** *Machakos Gazetteer*, 1958; *Notes on some aspects of Machakos District*, 1961; Chapter on Rangelands in ed W T W Morgan, *East Africa, Its Peoples and Resources*, 2nd edition, OUP, 1972; 'Rangeland Economics' in ed D J Pratt and M D Gwynne, *Rangeland Management and Ecology in East Africa*, Hodder & Stoughton, 1977; contributed papers to various specialist meetings on African Agriculture.

PECK, Michael (1945) Born 7 November 1927, 9 Flemingate, Beverley, Yorkshire; son of George Peck, Officer of Customs and Excise, and Lydia Ethel Jude. **Tutor(s):** S J Bailey. **Educ:** Beverley Minster School; Beverley Grammar School.

PEDDIE, James (1925) Born 22 June 1907, Elmbank, Church End, Finchley, Middlesex; son of James Peddie, Minister of the Presbyterian Church of England, and Elsie Mary Corby; m Daphne Marie-Therese Olliver, 24 April 1940, St Columba's Church, Pont Street, London; 3 daughters (Alison b 5 April 1941, Marigold b 5 December 1942 and Mary Rose b 11 August 1946). **Subject(s):** Economics; BA 1928; MA 1932. **Tutor(s):** E A Benians. **Johnian Relatives:** brother of Ronald Peddie (1923); uncle of Peter Charles Peddie (1951) and of James Barrie Peddie (1958). **Educ:** Glasgow Academy; Trinity College, Glenalmond. **Career:** TA Officer, London Scottish Regiment; Lieutenant Colonel, Gordon Highlanders 1939–1945; Partner, Corby, Palmer and Stewart, ladies' mantle manufacturers until 1975. **Appointments:** Committee Member and Trustee, OJHF; Chairman, Mantle Manufacturers Association. **Honours:** DSO 1944. Died 30 July 1982.

PEDDIE, Ronald (1923) Born 24 May 1905, Merlewood, Cyprus Road, Church End, Finchley, Middlesex; son of James Peddie, Presbyterian Minister, and Elsie Mary Corby; m Vera Nicklin, 2 June 1931, Holy Trinity Church, Bramley, Surrey; 3 sons (Peter Charles b 20 March 1932, David John b 11 June 1934 and James Barrie b 18 December 1937), 1 daughter (Kathrine Mary b 3 February 1946). BA 1926; MA 1977; CA 1930; Joint Diploma, Management Accounting 1967. **Tutor(s):** E A Benians. **Johnian Relatives:** brother of James Peddie (1925); father of Peter Charles Peddie (1951) and of James Barrie Peddie (1958). **Educ:** The Academy, Glasgow; The Leys School, Cambridge. **Career:** Chartered Accountant, McClelland, Ker & Co, Glasgow 1926–1931; Accountant and Assistant Secretary, C & J Clark Ltd, Street 1931–1943; Secretary, later Director, Finance and Administration, United Steel Companies Limited 1943–1967; Director, Finance and Administration, Midland Group 1967–1969, Managing Director, Administration 1969–1971, British Steel Corporation; Director, Iron Trade Employers' Insurance Association Ltd 1970–1975. **Appointments:** Secretary, Trevelyan Scholarships 1958; Member, Cambridge and Leeds University Appointments Board; JP, City of Sheffield 1964; Governor, Ashorne Hill Management College 1967–1971. **Honours:** CBE 1971. **Publications:** *The United Steel Companies: A History*, 1968; *The Trevelyan Scholarships*, 1975. Died 24 November 1986.

PEEL, Dr Michael John (1945) Born 11 July 1927, Sundor, Finchfield Gardens, Wolverhampton; son of Edward Percy Peel, Chartered Accountant, and Doris Mabel Gregory. **Subject(s):** Natural Sciences; BA 1948; MA 1964; BChir 1950; MB 1950. **Tutor(s):** S J Bailey. **Educ:** Westwood School, Bath; Kingswood School, Bath; Charterhouse. **Career:** GP.

PEERS, Dr Francis George (1944) Born 23 September 1926, Maternity Hospital, Birkenhead, Cheshire; son of George Peers, Boiler Fireman, and Margaret Bamber. **Subject(s):** Natural Sciences; BA 1948; MA 1951; PhD 1979. **Tutor(s):** C W Guillebaud. **Educ:** Cowie Street School; Birkenhead Institute.

PEET, Frank Antony (Tony) (1941) Born 5 May 1922, Naini Tal, United Provinces, India; son of Lionel Meredith Peet, Brigadier, Indian Army, and Eleanor Marian Hayward; m June Weall; 2 sons (John and Ronald), 1 daughter (Vanessa). **Tutor(s):** S J Bailey. **Johnian Relatives:** great grandson of Robert Baldwin Hayward (1846); grandson of Maurice Henry Weston Hayward (1886); nephew of Maurice John Hayward (1925). **Educ:** Swanbourne House, Buckinghamshire; Charterhouse; Brasenose College, Oxford. **Career:** Captain (final rank), RE, serving in

Africa, Italy and Austria (Mentioned in Despatches) 1941–1945; Colonial Service, Kenya 1949–1963; District Officer, Garissa, Embu, Wundanyi, Mombasa and Nairobi (seconded to Special Branch during Mau Mau rebellion); District Commissioner, Nakuru, Kiambu and Fort Hall 1957; Senior District Commissioner, Mombasa; Called to the Bar, Gray's Inn 1952; Solicitor, Marshall and Eldridge (later Marshall and Galpin), Oxford 1964–1988 (Partner from 1965). **Appointments:** Founder member, Pegasus; Church Treasurer 1964, later also Church Warden, St John the Baptist, Stadhampton; Under Sheriff of Oxfordshire 1986–1988; Field Officer, British Horse Society. Died 27 August 2003.

PEGG, Major David (1934) Born 19 March 1916, 26 Belsize Avenue, Hampstead; son of Harry George Pegg, South African Merchant, and Effie Barbara Stephen; m Margaret Morgan, 9 June 1945, St Paul's Church, Kandy, Ceylon; 3 daughters (Anne Patricia b 2 May 1948, Philippa Jane b 20 November 1950 and Gillian Mary b 25 December 1955). **Subject(s):** Classics; BA 1938; MA 1960; BA (Open University) 1988. **Tutor(s):** R L Howland. **Educ:** Summerfields, Oxford; Tonbridge School. **Career:** Army Officer, The Royal Signals, and Instructor, School of Signals, Catterick and Staff College, Quetta 1939–1960; Schoolmaster, Bedford School 1960–1985. **Appointments:** DL, Bedfordshire 1976. **Awards:** Scholarship, SJC; Exhibition, SJC 1936–1937. Died 9 November 2001.

PEIERLS, Sir Rudolf (1936) Born 5 June 1907, Berlin; son of Heinrich Peierls, Company Director, and Elisabeth Weigert; m Eugenia Kennegiesser, 1931 (d 1986); 1 son, 3 daughters. MA 1936; DPhil (Leipzig) 1929; DSc Manchester; Honorary DSc (Liverpool) 1960; Honorary DSc (Birmingham) 1967; Honorary DSc (Edinburgh) 1969; Honorary DSc (Sussex) 1978; Honorary DSc (Chicago) 1981; Honorary DSc (Coimbra) 1988; FRS 1945; FInstP. **Educ:** Humboldt School; Realgymnasium, Berlin Oberschöneweide, Germany; Berlin University; Munich University; Leipzig University. **Career:** Assistant, Federal Institute of Technology, Zürich 1929–1932; Rockefeller Fellow 1932–1933; Honorary Research Fellow, Manchester University 1933–1935; Assistant-in-Research, Royal Society Mond Laboratory 1935–1937; Professor of Mathematical Physics (formerly Applied Mathematics), University of Birmingham 1937–1963; worked on Atomic Energy Project in Birmingham 1940–1943; worked on Atomic Energy Project in USA 1943–1945; Wykeham Professor of Physics, University of Oxford 1963–1974; Fellow, New College, Oxford 1963–1974; Professor of Physics (part-time), University of Washington, Seattle 1974–1977. **Appointments:** Foreign Honorary Member, American Academy of Arts and Sciences 1962; Honorary Associate, College of Advanced Technology, Birmingham 1963; Foreign Associate, National Academy of Sciences, USA 1970; Honorary Member, French Physics Society 1979; Foreign Member, Royal Danish Academy 1980; Member, Leopoldina Academy, East Germany 1981; Corresponding Member, Yugoslav (later Croatian) Academy of Arts and Sciences 1983; Foreign Associate, French Academy of Sciences 1984; Foreign Member, USSR (later Russian) Academy of Sciences 1988; Corresponding Member, Lisbon Academy of Sciences 1988; Isotope Plant Design Committee; Consultant to Harwell's Theoretical Physics Division (Part-time Division Head, 1950–1951). **Awards:** Royal Society Royal Medal 1959; Lorentz Medal of Royal Netherlands Academy of Sciences 1962; Max Planck Medal, Association of German Physical Societies 1963; Guthrie Medal, IPPS 1968; Enrico Fermi Award, US Department of Energy 1980 (first British recipient); Royal Society Copley Medal 1986; Paul Dirac Medal 1991. **Honours:** CBE 1946; Kt 1968. **Publications:** *Quantum Theory of Solids*, 1955; *The Laws of Nature*, 1955; *Surprises in Theoretical Physics*, 1979; *Bird of Passage*, 1985; *More Surprises in Theoretical Physics*, 1991; Papers on quantum theory. Died 19 September 1995.

PEIRIS, Charles Jacob Harold (1923) Born 22 July 1905, Villa de Mel, Cinnamon Gardens, Colombo, Ceylon; son of Charles Thomas Peiris, Solicitor, Proctor of Supreme Court, and Agnes Georgiana Maude De Mel. **Subject(s):** Law; BA 1926; MA 1934. **Tutor(s):** E A Benians.

Johnian Relatives: nephew of James Peiris (1878); cousin of Leonard James Martinus Peiris (1911) and of Herbert Charles Jacob Peiris (1919). **Educ:** Royal College, Colombo, Ceylon; Training College, Colombo Ceylon.

PEIRIS, Herbert Charles Jacob (SENA, Devar Surya) (1919) Born 28 March 1899, St Leonards, Flower Road, Kollupitya Ward, Colombo, Ceylon; son of James Peiris, Barrister, and Amelia Louisa Grace De Mel. **Subject(s):** Law/History; BA 1923; MA 1946; LLB 1923; ARCM. **Tutor(s):** E E Sikes. **Johnian Relatives:** son of James Peiris (1878); brother of Leonard James Martinus Peiris (1911); cousin of Charles Jacob Harold Peiris (1923); great uncle of Remini Sharya de Soysa (Scharenguivel) (1993). **Educ:** Colet Court (St Paul's Preparatory School), London; Government Training College, Columbo, Ceylon; Tonbridge School. **Career:** Concert Singer and Broadcast Artist (BBC, India, Ceylon Broadcasting Corporation); Called to the Bar at Lincoln's Inn 1924. **Awards:** Choral Studentship, SJC; Winchester Reading Prize, University of Cambridge 1923. **Honours:** OBE. Died 11 November 1981.

PEIRIS, Leonard James Martinus (1911) Born 29 September 1892, Flower Road, Cinnamon Gardens, Colombo, Ceylon; son of James Peiris, Barrister, and Amelia Louisa Grace De Mel; m Isabel De Soysa, 1917; 1 daughter (Chloe). BA 1915. **Tutor(s):** J R Tanner. **Johnian Relatives:** son of James Peiris (1878); brother of Herbert Charles Jacob Peiris (1919); cousin of Charles Jacob Harold Peiris (1923); grandfather of Remini Sharya de Soysa (Scharenguivel) (1992). **Educ:** Tonbridge School. **Career:** Called to the Bar at Lincoln's Inn 1917; Social Worker, Visiting Agent and Valuer, Ceylon; Founder, LJM Peiris and Co. **Appointments:** Chairman, Ceylon Social Service League; Registrar, Anglican Church; Chairman, Deaf and Blind School; first President, Golf Union. Died 2 November 1955.

PEISER, Dr Herbert Steffen Albert Alexander (1936) Born 19 August 1917, Berlin-Grunewald; son of Herbert Peiser, Managing Director, and Nelly Berta Tarlau, Artist; m Primrose Elizabeth Elliot, 1949; 3 daughters (Primrose Clare, Georgina Jane and Alison Jeannie). **Subject(s):** Natural Sciences; BA 1939; MA 1944; DSc (Chungnam National University, Korea) 1979. **Tutor(s):** R L Howland. **Educ:** Maiden Erleigh School, Reading; Arndt Gymnasium, Berlin-Dahlem, Germany; St Paul's School, London. **Career:** Member of staff, Research Department, Imperial Chemical Industries 1941–1946; Senior Lecturer in Physics, Birkbeck College, London University 1946–1948; Messrs Hadfields Ltd, Steel Manufacturers, East Hecla Works, Sheffield 1948–1957; Metrology with the National Bureau of Standards, USA (renamed National Institute of Standards and Technology) 1957–1979; Research Fellow, Applied Physics, Harvard College, Cambridge, Massachusetts 1965–1966; National Bureau of Standards 1967–1979; Member, Commissions on the 'atomic weights' and isotope abundances of the chemical elements, International Union of Pure and Applied Chemistry 1967–2002; Scientific Consultant, National Institute of Standards and Technology 1979–2002; Advisor to several governments, UN Agencies, and international banks 1979–1989; Visiting Scientist, Central Bureau of Nuclear Measurements (renamed Institute for Reference Materials and Measurements) 1980–1998; Volunteer Scientist, US Geological Survey 1994–2002. **Awards:** Hutchison Research Scholarship, SJC 1941; Silver Medal, US Department of Commerce. **Honours:** National Medal of Honor (Order of the Camellia), Republic of Korea. **Publications:** In excess of 150, including (with A J C Wilson and H P Rooksby) *X-ray Diffraction by Polycrystalline Materials*, 1960; (ed) *Crystallography, Crystal Growth*, (3 volumes) 1967, 1968 and 1981, and several other books on industrialization in less developed countries.

PELHAM BROWNE, Joseph Byrne (1923) Born 6 June 1905, 58 West 68th Street, New York, USA; son of Joseph Byrne, Doctor of Medicine, and Cynthia Lilian Julia Webb. **Tutor(s):** E Cunningham. **Educ:** Gibbs' Preparatory School, Sloane Street; Mallam's Preparatory School, Heathfield; Epsom College; Beaumont College. Died 18 August 1923.

PELLING, Dr Henry Mathison (1939) Born 27 August 1920, 4 Curzon Road, Prenton, Cheshire; son of Douglas Langley Pelling, Stock and Share Broker, and Maud Mary Mathison. **Subject(s):** Classics/History; BA 1942; MA 1947; PhD 1950; MA (Oxon) 1949; Honorary DHL (New School for Social Research, New York) 1983; FBA 1992; LittD 1975. **Tutor(s):** R L Howland. **Educ:** Birkenhead School. **Career:** Commander, RE 1942; served NW Europe campaign 1944–1945; Fellow 1949–1965, Tutor 1950–1965, Dean 1963–1964, The Queen's College, Oxford; Smith-Mundt Scholar, University of Wisconsin, USA 1953–1954; Assistant Director of Research (History) 1966–1976, Reader in Recent British History 1976–1980 (Emeritus 1980–1997), University of Cambridge; Title B Fellow and Lecturer in History 1966–1980, Title E Fellow 1980–1997, SJC; Supernumerary Fellow, The Queen's College, Oxford 1980. **Appointments:** Fellow, Woodrow Wilson Center, Washington DC, 1983. **Awards:** Exhibition, SJC; Scholarship, SJC 1941. **Publications:** *Origins of the Labour Party*, 1954; *Challenge of Socialism*, 1954; *America and the British Left*, 1956; *British Communist Party*, 1958; (with Frank Bealey) *Labour and Politics*, 1958; *American Labor*, 1960; *Modern Britain, 1885–1955*, 1960; *Short History of the Labour Party*, 1961, 10th edition 1993; *History of British Trade Unionism*, 1963, 5th edition 1992; *Social Geography of British Elections*, 1967; *Popular Politics and Society in Late Victorian Britain*, 1968, 2nd edition 1979; *Britain and the Second World War*, 1970; *Winston Churchill*, 1974, 2nd edition 1989; *The Labour Governments 1945–51*, 1984; *Britain and the Marshall Plan*, 1988; articles and reviews in journals. Died 14 October 1997.

PEMBERTON, Ronald James (1928) Born 11 February 1910, Elveden, Suffolk; son of James Pemberton, Clerk to an Estate Agent, and Margaret Hannah McGowan. **Subject(s):** Natural Sciences; BA 1931; MA 1935. **Tutor(s):** J M Wordie. **Johnian Relatives:** father of Michael Ronald Pemberton (1957). **Educ:** Elveden Elementary School; The Grammar School, Thetford. **Career:** Foreign Office 1945. Died 7 April 1964.

PEMBERTON, The Revd Thomas Warwick Winstanley (1944) Born 21 February 1926, 15 Hasley Street, Chelsea, London; son of Warwick Geoffrey Travers Pemberton, Chartered Accountant, and Doris Shelley Winstanley; m Joyce Lilian Richardson, 5 March 1955; 1 son (Richard b 7 April 1957), 3 daughters (Julia b 20 July 1958, Lucy b 24 September 1961 and Catherine b 4 June 1967). **Subject(s):** Engineering; BA 1950; MA 1955; Chartered Mechanical Engineer. **Tutor(s):** J M Wordie. **Educ:** St Piram's School, Maidenhead; Eton. **Career:** Vickers Armstrongs Ltd, Elswick Works, Newcastle 1951; Vicar, Rickerscote, Stafford 1966–1973; Vicar, Titchfield 1973–1991. **Appointments:** RE Cadet, SJC. Died 9 April 1994.

PEÑA Y CAMUS, Oscar (1922) Born 8 January 1905, Santa Engracia 14, Madrid, Spain; son of Julio Peña y Martin, Colonel, Spanish Army, and Maria de los Angeles Camus de Peña. **Tutor(s):** E Cunningham. **Educ:** Instituto del Cardinal Cisneros, Madrid; Highgate School, London.

PENFOLD, Harold Lashmar (1906) Born 20 December 1885, Bendigo, Victoria, Australia; son of Oliver Penfold, Surgeon, and Mary Louisa Bayne; m (1) Erica Clarissa Blunden, April 1917, (2) Jean Mary Brett, 15 May 1937, London; (1) 1 daughter (Margery Eirene b 19 November 1918), (2) 1 son (Michael Lashmar b 3 December 1943), 3 daughters (Janet Elizabeth Mary b 20 November 1939, Barbara Helen b 14 November 1940 and Olivia Dorothy b 16 March 1948). **Subject(s):** Mechanical Sciences; BA 1909; MA 1926; MICE 1925; MIE (Aust) 1950. **Tutor(s):** L H K Bushe-Fox. **Johnian Relatives:** grandfather of John Penfold Knee (1968). **Educ:** Church of England Grammar School, Melbourne, Australia; University of Melbourne. **Career:** Civil Engineer for public works and road trace surveys, Federated Malay States (FMS) and Singapore 1910–1914; Captain, RE, 76th Field Company, Guards Division, France, then Ministry of Labour, WWI; Land Reclamation and Flood Prevention Works, Greece 1919–1922; Perak River Hydroelectric Power Company, Perak, Federated Malay States 1922 and 1926–1930; Consulting Engineer, London Passenger Transport Board 1931–1933;

Senior Assistant Resident Engineer for Stratford Extension, Central London Railways 1937–1939; Resident Engineer, adapting Chislehurst Caves for air raid shelter 1939–1943; Regional Land Restoration Officer, Department of Opencast Coal Production, Nottingham, Ministry of Fuel and Power 1943–1950; Chief Civil Engineer of Overseas Corporation (Aust) Ltd 1950–1952; Senior Engineer, Melbourne Harbour Trust 1952–1955. Died 27 December 1955.

PÉNIAKOFF, Lieutenant Colonel Vladimir (1915) Born 30 March 1897, Huy, Belgium; son of Dmitry Péniakoff, Ingenieur-chimiste, Docteur es Sciences, and Anna Brown; m Pamela Firth, Holy Trinity, London, 2 April 1948; 2 daughters (Olga and Anne). **Subject(s):** Mathematics. **Tutor(s):** R P Gregory. **Educ:** University of Brussels. **Career:** Gunner, French Army 1914–1918; Sugar Manufacturer, Egypt 1924–1939; British Army in Egypt, formed and led Popski's Private Army 1939–1945. **Honours:** Croix de Guerre 1940; MC 1942; DSO 1945. **Publications:** *Private Army.* Died 15 May 1951.

PENLINGTON, Dr Gilbert Napier (1947) Born 22 December 1928, Kingwell Road, Worsbrough Bridge, Yorkshire; son of Robert Napier Penlington, Civil Engineer, and Dorothy Beaumont; m Elizabeth Mendl, 10 February 1962; 3 sons (Robert b 1964, Charles b 1966 and Thomas b 1970). **Subject(s):** Natural Sciences; BA 1950; MA 1954; BChir 1953; MB 1954; FFARCS 1965; DA 1961; DRCOG 1961. **Tutor(s):** G C L Bertram. **Educ:** Merton School, Doncaster; Hill House Preparatory School, Doncaster; Worksop College; Middlesex Hospital Medical School; Birmingham University. **Career:** Flight Lieutenant, RAF Medical Branch, Malaya 1955–1958; GP, Singapore 1958–1959; Junior Posts at Guy's, King's, and Middlesex, Addenbrooke's Cambridge Hospitals (Registrar), and Massachusetts General Hospital, Boston, USA 1959–1969; Consultant Anaesthetist, Regional Cardiothoracic Unit, Walsgrave Hospital, Coventry 1970–1993; Vice-Chairman, Coventry Hospitals Cogwheel Executive Committee 1976–1978. **Appointments:** Treasurer, JB Shelton Memorial Committee 1981–; Treasurer, Stoneleigh Parochial Church Council 1981–1983; Lay Chairman, Kenilworth Deanery Synod, Diocese of Coventry (C of E) 1982–1987; Member, Coventry Diocesan Board of Finance 1982–1988; Chairman, Coventry and District Archaeological Society 1982–1985; Treasurer, Coventry SDP 1986–merger; President, Coventry Branch Historical Association 1989–1990; Chairman 1990–1991, President 1991–, Treasurer 1999, Coventry Liberal Democrats; Policy Chair, Liberal Democrats, West Midland Region 1991–1996; Member, Regional Finance and Internal Management and Organisation Committees; Liberal Democrat Parliamentary Candidate, South East Staffordshire 1992, Coventry NW 1997 and 2001; Returning Officer for several Constituencies 1993–.

PENNINGTON, Thomas Wilfrid (1922) Born 11 November 1902, Clovelly, Tower Road, Hereford; son of Thomas Seddon Pennington and Agnes Cater; m Jocelyn. **Subject(s):** Classics; BA 1925. **Tutor(s):** E E Sikes. **Educ:** Hereford Cathedral School. **Career:** Asiatic Petroleum Company, Ceylon, Malaya, Singapore 1925. **Awards:** Scholarship, SJC. Died 10 December 1973.

PENNY, Arthur Geoffrey (1927) Born 20 September 1908, Imperial Avenue, Kidderminster, Worcestershire; son of Arthur Henry Penny, Merchant and Shipper, and Emily Hanson. **Subject(s):** Modern and Medieval Languages/Economics; BA 1930. **Tutor(s):** M P Charlesworth. **Johnian Relatives:** brother of Henry Martin Penny (1930). **Educ:** The Grammar School, Wolverley, Kidderminster; King Edward's School, Birmingham.

PENNY, Henry Martin (1930) Born 25 May 1912, 21 Imperial Avenue, Kidderminster; son of Arthur Henry Penny, Carpet Merchant, and Emily Hanson. **Subject(s):** Modern and Medieval Languages; BA 1934; MA 1938; MusB 1934. **Tutor(s):** M P Charlesworth. **Johnian Relatives:** brother of Arthur Geoffrey Penny (1927). **Educ:** Wolverley Grammar School, Kidderminster; King Edward's School, Birmingham. **Career:** Composer and Musician. **Honours:** MBE 1987. Died 20 June 2000.

PENROSE, Lionel Sharples (1919) Born 11 June 1898, 44 Finchley Road, Marylebone, London; son of James Doyle Penrose, Artist, and Elizabeth Josephine Peckover; m Margaret Leathes, 17 October 1928; 3 sons (Oliver b 6 June 1929, Roger b 8 August 1931 and Jonathan b 7 October 1933), 1 daughter (Shirley Victoria b 22 February 1945). **Subject(s):** Moral Sciences; BA 1921; MA 1925; MD (St Thomas') 1930; MRCS 1928; LRCP 1928; FRS 1953; FRCP 1962; FRCPsych 1971; Honorary DSc (Sheffield) 1971. **Tutor(s):** E E Sikes. **Johnian Relatives:** father of Roger Penrose (1952); grandfather of Mathew David Penrose (1981) and of Christopher Shaun Penrose (1984). **Educ:** Downs School, Colwall; Leighton Park School, Reading; St Thomas' Hospital, London, 1928. **Career:** St John's Ambulance Corps, France 1918; Research Medical Officer, Royal Eastern Counties Institution, Colchester 1930–1939; Research Student, Cardiff City Mental Hospital; Ontario Hospital, Canada 1939–1945 (latterly Director of Psychiatric Research); Consultant Geneticist, UCH; Galton Professor of Human Genetics, University College London 1945–1965; deviser of intelligence tests, tests of musical skill, chess problems and mechanical puzzles. **Appointments:** Editor, *Annals of Human Genetics*, 1945–1965; Founder, Kennedy-Galton Centre for Mental Deficiency Research and Diagnosis, Harperbury Hospital, St Albans. **Awards:** Bristowe Medal, St Thomas' Hospital 1929; James Calvert Spence Memorial; Award made by the Joseph P Kennedy Foundation; Buckston Browne Prize; Albert Lasker Award for Basic Medical Research 1960. **Publications:** Various books and scientific articles, including 'Lysozyme Content of Saliva in Psychotics', *Lancet*, 1930; 'Case of Schizophrenia of Long Duration', *British Journal of Medical Psychology*, 1931; 'On the Interaction of Heredity and Environment', *Journal of Genetics*, 1932; *Mental defect*, Sidgwick & Jackson, 1933; *The Influence of Heredity on Disease*, H K Lewis & Co, 1934; *The Biology of Mental Defect*, Sidgwick & Jackson, 1949; *On the Objective Study of Crowd Behaviour*, H K Lewis & Co, 1952; *Outline of Human Genetics*, Heinemann, 1959. Died 12 May 1972.

PENTELOW, William Cyril Doughty (1922) Born 30 April 1903, 30 York Road, Northampton; son of Frederick Harris Pentelow, Master Tailor, and Harriet Elizabeth Doughty. **Subject(s):** Modern and Medieval Languages. **Tutor(s):** E E Sikes. **Educ:** Northampton School. **Awards:** Scholarship, SJC.

PENTLAND, Thomas Proctor (1919) Naval Officer.

PENTNEY, Richard George (1941) Born 17 August 1922, 120 Gold Street, Wellingborough, Northamptonshire; son of Albert Fred Pentney, Methodist Minister, and Ada Shelford; m Elisabeth Berthoud, 8 August 1953. **Subject(s):** Classics; BA 1947; MA 1952. **Tutor(s):** C W Guillebaud. **Educ:** Padstow Elementary School; Falmouth Grammar School; Northfields Elementary School; Kingswood School, Bath. **Career:** English Master, Oundle School; Headmaster, St Andrew's College, Minaki, Dar es Salaam; Headmaster, King's College, Taunton 1964. **Appointments:** Schoolmaster Fellow Commoner Michaelmas 1970. Died 19 May 1990.

PEPLER, Dr Richard Douglas (1942) Born 6 April 1923, Lyndhurst, George Lane, Marlborough, Wiltshire; son of Herbert Bartlett Pepler, Grocer's Traveller, and Una Cherry McKee. **Subject(s):** Moral Sciences; BA 1947; MA 1949; PhD 1956. **Tutor(s):** C W Guillebaud. **Educ:** Marlborough Grammar School. **Career:** MRC Unit of Applied Psychology, Cambridge 1947–1958; Research Scientist, Vice President, Director and Part Owner, Dunlop & Associates Inc (Research and Development Company), Connecticut, USA 1958–1987. **Awards:** Exhibitioner SJC.

PEPPER, John Edward (1923) Born 7 November 1903, 117 Lerchenfelder Strasse, Vienna VII, Austria; son of Sam Pepper, Lace Designer, and Rosa Schaufler; m Violet Irene Heath, 18 June 1932; 1 son (John Michael), 1 daughter (Jennifer Rose). **Subject(s):** Classics; BA 1927. **Tutor(s):** E E Sikes. **Educ:** Gymnasium, St Polten, Austria; Nottingham High School for Boys. **Career:** Cadet, Federated Malay States, Colonial Service 1928;

Class IV, District Officer, Tampin 1935; District Officer, Krian 1937; Class III, District Officer, Temerloh 1940; Treasury, Singapore 1941; Interned in Changi Jail, Singapore 1942–1945; Class II 1945; Class IB, Deputy Financial Secretary, Singapore 1948; Class IA, Secretary to the Treasury, Federation of Malaya 1951; Staff Grade A, Commissioner for Lands, Singapore 1953; Permanent Secretary, Ministry of Local Government, Lands and Housing, and Commissioner for Lands 1955–1958. **Awards:** Scholarship, SJC 1922. Died 17 August 1993.

PERASITCH, Nikola (1917) Born 21 November 1898, Cettigne, Montenegro; son of Bozhidar Perasitch, Doctor to the King of Montenegro, and Vidosava Poznanovich. **Tutor(s):** E E Sikes. **Educ:** Elementary School, Cettigne, Montenegro; Secondary School, Cettigne, Montenegro.

PERCEVAL, Dr Philip Edward (1933) Born 26 March 1915, 153 Church Street, Chelsea, London; son of Dudley Perceval, Landowner, and Mary Elizabeth Massey; m Joan Margaret Hacking, 20 November 1945, King's Chapel of the Savoy. **Subject(s):** Natural Sciences; BA 1936; MA 1940; MB 1940; BChir 1940; MD 1950. **Tutor(s):** R L Howland. **Educ:** Copthorne School; Radley College. **Career:** RAF 1939–1945; Consultant Physician. Died 23 May 1996.

PERCY, Dr Henry Gordon (1932) Born 14 September 1913, 7 Grange Road, Southport; son of Colin Stewart Percy, Engineer and Sales Manager, and Edith Annie Holland. BA 1935; MA 1946; MB 1946; BChir 1946; MRCS (Eng) 1938; LRCP (London) 1938. **Tutor(s):** R L Howland. **Educ:** Croxton School, Southport; Malvern College. **Career:** House Physician, St James's Hospital, London; House Surgeon St Mary's Hospital, London; Honorary Major, RAMC 1940–1945; GP, Parkhill, Birmingham (Senior Partner) 1973. **Honours:** MBE (Military). Died 20 June 1998.

PERCY, Hugh Harold (1938) Born 15 January 1920, Fernden Cottage, Fernhurst, Midhurst, Sussex; son of John Hugh Percy, Schoolmaster, and Josephine Bell. **Subject(s):** Classics. **Tutor(s):** R L Howland. **Educ:** Feltonfleet, Cobham; Taverham Hall, Norwich; Bradfield College. **Career:** Flight Lieutenant, RAF 1939–1944. Died May 1944 (killed in action).

PERCY, Josceline Richard (1914) Born 16 December 1894, 19 Bishop's Road, Highgate, Middlesex; son of Josceline Hugh Percy, Bank Clerk, and Ann Thompson; m Mary Nicholson. **Tutor(s):** E E Sikes. **Educ:** Highgate Junior School; St Bees School. **Career:** Lieutenant, Border Regiment, attached to RE (Signals) 1914–1918. **Awards:** Sizarship, SJC.

PERKES, William Anderson (1938) Born 24 October 1919, Claremont, Osterley Road, Heston, Middlesex; son of Emma Frances Monica Perkes. **Tutor(s):** R L Howland. **Educ:** Kingwell Hall Preparatory School; Charterhouse.

PERKINS, Professor Dexter (1945) Born 20 June 1889, Boston, Massachusetts, USA; son of Herbert William Perkins, Commission Merchant, and Cora Dexter Farmer; m Wilma Lord (d 1976); 1 son (Bradford). MA 1946; PhD (Harvard) 1914. **Educ:** Boston Latin School; Sanford School, Connecticut; Harvard University; École des Sciences Politiques, Paris. **Career:** Instructor in History, University of Cincinnati 1914–1915; Don Alonzo Watson Professor of American History, University of Rochester, New York 1925–1954; Professor of American History and Institutions, University of Cambridge 1945–1946; Title C Fellow, SJC 1945–1946; John L Senior Professor of American Civilization, Cornell University 1954–1959. **Appointments:** City Historian, Rochester 1936–1948; President, Rochester Association for the United Nations; President, American Historical Association 1959; Chairman, Rochester Branch, Foreign Policy Association. **Publications:** *Hands Off: The History of the Monroe Doctrine*; *America and Two Wars*; *The United States and the Caribbean*; *The Evolution of American Foreign Policy*; *The American Way*; *The United States and Latin America*. Died 12 May 1984.

PERKINS, John Bernard (1936) Born 25 August 1917, Hillmorton, The Park, Peterborough; son of Edward Christopher Perkins, Artist, and Agnes Berry Shaw. **Tutor(s):** J S Boys Smith. **Educ:** Wellington College, Wellington, New Zealand; Rotorua High School, New Zealand; King's School, Peterborough. **Awards:** Munsteven Exhibition, SJC.

PERKINS, Norman Charles (1948) Born 9 August 1914, Thornden, Dunkirk, Kent; son of Frederick George Perkins, Market Gardener, and Jane Maria Silk. BSc (London) 1936. **Tutor(s):** J M Wordie. **Educ:** Swalcliffe Church School; Oxford Street School, Whitstable; Simon Langton School, Canterbury; University College, Nottingham. **Career:** Import and Export Merchant 1937–1946; RA 1939–1946; Colonial Administrative Service, Nigeria 1946.

PERRATON, Christopher John (1947) Born 12 August 1928, 4 Brookleigh Road, Withington, Manchester; son of Leslie Harry Perraton, Schoolmaster, and Marjorie Alice Lingstrom, Teacher; m Olive Mary Rose, 1966, Newent, Gloucestershire. **Subject(s):** Natural Sciences; BA 1950; MA 1954; MIBiol. **Tutor(s):** G C L Bertram. **Educ:** Lee on Solent Council School; Churcher's College, Petersfield. **Career:** Biology Teacher 1951–1965; Education Officer, Schools Organisation and Planning, Wiltshire 1968–1974; Assistant Director of Education (Development and Planning), Wiltshire 1974–1988. **Appointments:** Council Member, Wiltshire Wildlife Trust; Council Member, Royal Society for Nature Conservation; Council Member, Wiltshire Archaeological and Natural History Society; Council Member, Ramblers' Association; Footpath Secretary, Ramblers' Association Wiltshire and Swindon Area. **Publications:** 'Salt Marshes of the Hampshire-Sussex Border', *Journal of Ecology*, 1953; 'Botanical Specimens', *Journal of the Association of Science Teachers of Jamaica*, 1960; 'The Biological Sciences Curriculum Study of the United States and its Implications for British Biology Teaching', *International Journal of Science Education*, 1966.

PERRET, Dr Cyril John (1946) Born 28 November 1919, Clevedon, Empress Avenue, Woodford Green, Essex; son of Arthur George Perret, Rubber Company's Buyer, and May Gertrude Sumner. **Subject(s):** Natural Sciences; BA 1950; MA 1953; PhD (London). **Tutor(s):** G C L Bertram. **Educ:** The Convent, Woodford Green; St Agnes' Convent, Erdington; St John's Convent, Erdington; St Philip's Grammar School, Birmingham; Birmingham Central Technical College; Aston Technical and Commercial College. **Career:** Lister Institute of Preventive Medicine; Royal Corps of Signals (prisoner at Singapore) 1940–1945; Senior Lecturer in Microbiology, University of Western Australia Medical School 1957. Died 2 March 1982.

PERRING, Hubert (1932) Born 8 April 1913, 33 West Street, Gillingham; son of Henry Richard Perring, Clerk of Works to War Department, and Edith Emma Welch. **Subject(s):** Mathematics/Mechanical Sciences; BA 1935; MA 1939. **Tutor(s):** J M Wordie. **Educ:** Practising School, Exeter; Exeter School. **Awards:** Vidal Exhibition, SJC; Scholarship, SJC 1935; College Prize, SJC 1935. Died February 1983.

PERRY, Arthur Leslie Roy (1940) Born 25 April 1921, Ivy House, Snedshill, Oakengates, Shropshire; son of Clifford Perry, Commercial Clerk, and Dorothea Robinson; m Margaret M Astbury (d July 2002); 3 children. **Subject(s):** Classics/History; BA 1947; MA 1949. **Tutor(s):** R L Howland. **Educ:** Priors Lee Church of England Elementary School; Wellington County High School, Shropshire. **Career:** Stockport Grammar School 1947–1951; Truro School 1951–1957; West Bromwich Grammar School 1957–1971; Worcester College for the Blind 1971–1986 (Deputy Headmaster 1972–1986). Died 20 September 2003.

PERRY, John Cyril (1907) Born 23 March 1888, Whiterow, Thrushelton, Devon; son of William Soper Perry, merchant, formerly farmer, and Anne Sargent Burnard; m Vera Annie Emma Coltman, 1926; 2 sons (John Leycester Coltman b 25 November 1928 and Anthony Joseph Burnard b 27 December 1929). BA 1910. **Tutor(s):** J R Tanner. **Johnian**

Relatives: father of John Leycester Coltman Perry (1948). **Educ:** Plymouth College. **Career:** Solicitor, Parson, Lee and Co 1913; Private, London Regiment (Queen Victoria's Rifles), Captain and Adjutant, RGA (wounded), WWI. Died 30 December 1948.

PERRY, John Leycester Coltman (1948) Born 25 November 1928, 19 Hendon Lane, Finchley, Middlesex; son of John Cyril Perry, Solicitor, and Vera Annie Emma Coltman; m (1) Doreen Patricia Smart, Chalfont St Giles, Buckinghamshire, 16 July 1956 (d 1989), (2) Ann Mary Gregg Le Fevre (née Coulson), 31 October 1999; 1 son (Timothy John b 20 May 1962), 2 daughters (Sara Jane b 16 September 1957 and Kathryn Ann b 18 June 1959). **Subject(s):** Law; BA 1951. **Tutor(s):** J M Wordie. **Johnian Relatives:** son of John Cyril Perry (1907). **Educ:** Blenheim House, Barnet; Beaufort Lodge, New Barnet; Aldenham School, Elstree. **Career:** RA 1947–1948; Solicitor, Senior Partner 1954–2000.

PESMAZOGLU, Dr John Stevens (Ioannis) (PESMAZOGLOU) (1945) Born 1 March 1918, Chios, Greece; son of Steven George Pesmazoglu, Banker, and Angeliki Stevens Lorentzou; m Miranda Oikonomou, 11 February 1945, Athens; 2 sons (Stefanos b 1949 and Vassilis b 1952). PhD 1949; Doctorate (Athens) 1945. **Tutor(s):** C W Guillebaud. **Johnian Relatives:** father of Stefanos Pesmazoglu (1968). **Educ:** Varvakion High School, Athens, Greece; University of Athens. **Career:** Military Service 1940–1941; Liberation of Greece 1944–1945; Lecturer in Political Economy 1950–1967, Professor 1967–1969, University of Athens; Director General, Greek Ministry of Coordination 1951–1955; Economic Adviser, Bank of Greece 1955–1960; Alternate Governor for Greece at the International Monetary Fund 1955–1967; Deputy Governor, Bank of Greece 1960–1967. **Appointments:** Leader of Greek Delegation in negotiations for Greece's Association with the European Economic Community 1959–1961; Chairman, Greek Interministerial Committee for European Cooperation 1962–1965; President, Delegation of the Greek Parliament in the Joint Parliamentary Commission, Greece-EEC 1975–1978; Honorary Fellow, SJC 1988; Honorary Member, European Parliament 1994; Full Member 1992, Vice-President 1995, President 1996, The Academy of Athens. **Awards:** First Prize in Penal Law, University of Athens 1938; First Prize in Political Economy, University of Athens 1939. **Honours:** Archon Megas Rhetor, Oecumenical Patriarchate; Grand Cross, Greek Order of the Phoenix; Commandeur de la Legion d'Honneur; Grand Commander German Order of Merit. **Publications:** Studies and articles on the international trade cycle, economic development and monetary policies and on European integration with special reference to Greece's membership of the European Community. Died 27 November 2003.

PETCH, Dr Charles Plowright (1928) Born 2 September 1909, North Wootton, Castle Rising, Norfolk; son of Tom Petch, Director of Tea Research, Government of Ceylon, and Edith Mary Plowright; m Margaret Stirling; 2 sons (Mike and Hugh). **Subject(s):** Natural Sciences; BA 1931; MA 1935; MB 1939; BChir 1939; MD 1948. **Tutor(s):** C W Guillebaud. **Johnian Relatives:** father of Michael Charles Petch (1959). **Educ:** Lynfield School, Hunstanton; Gresham's School, Holt. **Career:** Assistant Master, Stowe School 1934; RAF 1939–1945; Consultant Physician, St Helier Hospital 1948–1975. **Awards:** Scholarship, SJC. **Publications:** *Flora of Norfolk*. Died 8 December 1987.

PETERS, August Detlef (1911) Born 25 August 1892, Farrenwisch, Holstein, Germany; son of Georg Peters, Government Inspector, and Anna Maria Friederike Kruse; m (1) Helen MacGregor, (2) Margaret Lucy Mayne. **Subject(s):** Modern and Medieval Languages/Economics; BA 1914; MA 1960. **Tutor(s):** E E Sikes. **Educ:** Hilton Lodge School, Brighton; Horyshan's International College, London; Haberdashers' Aske's Hampstead School. **Career:** Accountant in a slate mine in Wales, then in a labour battalion 1919; Editor, *The World* 1919–1923; Dramatic Critic, *The Daily Chronicle* 1923–1924; Literary Agent 1924. Died 5 February 1973.

PETERS, David Robert (1949) Born 5 October 1928, London; son of Robert Douglas Peters and Winifred Mary; m Eileen Barnett, 1959; 3 sons (Andrew b 1961, Martin b 1967 and Kevin b 1969). **Subject(s):** Economics/Law; BA 1952; MA 1956; FRSA. **Tutor(s):** C W Guillebaud. **Educ:** Uppingham School. **Career:** Second Lieutenant, RA 1947–1949; Alcan Group Companies (UK and Canada) 1953–1974; Director, Alcan Industries Ltd 1964–1974; Chief Executive, Engineering Division, British Oxygen Company Ltd 1974–1981; Director, Fisons plc 1981–1992; Director-Chairman, Lazard Select Investment Trust 1981–2000; Chairman, Gartmore Growth Opportunities plc 1992. **Appointments:** Secretary, Law Society, SJC; Treasurer, May Ball Committee, SJC; Eagle, SJC; Founder Member, Swans, SJC; Director, London Enterprise Agency 1978–1982; Director 1981–1992, Vice President 1992–1998, Business in the Community; Director, London First 1992; Grants Committee, Church Urban Fund 1995; Director, London Sports Board 1994; Member, London Health Commission 2000; Member, All England Lawn Tennis Club. **Awards:** Sir Joseph Larmor Award, SJC.

PETERS, John Frederick Herbert (1935) Born 19 November 1917, Edendale, Station Road Llanishen, Cardiff; son of Sidney John Peters, Solicitor, and Essie Mills. **Educ:** St Ives Grammar School; Kimbolton School. **Career:** Pilot, RAF 1939–1945.

PETERS, Theophilus (1940) Born 7 August 1921, 10 Hills Court, Exeter, Devon; son of Mark Peters, Jeweller, and Dorothy Knapman; m Lucy Bailey Summers, 1953; 2 sons, 3 daughters. **Subject(s):** Modern Languages; BA 1947; MA 1949. **Tutor(s):** C W Guillebaud. **Educ:** Clyst St Mary Council School, Exeter; Exeter School. **Career:** Second Lieutenant, Intelligence Corps 1941–1942; Captain, 8 Corps HQ, Normandy, Holland (Mentioned in Despatches), Germany 1944–1946; Major, entered HM Foreign (subseqently Diplomatic) Service 1945–1946; Vice-Consul/Second Secretary, Peking 1948–1951; Foreign Office 1951–1952; Tripoli and Benghazi, Libya 1953; Foreign Office 1956; Deputy Secretary-General, CENTO 1960; Head of Chancery, Manila 1962; Counsellor (Commercial), Peking 1965; Director, Diplomatic Service Language Centre 1968–1971; Head of Training Department, Foreign and Commonwealth Office 1969–1971; Counsellor and Consul-General, Buenos Aires 1971–1973; Consul-General, Antwerp 1973–1978; Freelance Lecturer on Chinese History and Art, to art societies, schools, universities, NADFAS, the National Trust etc, UK and Europe 1978. **Appointments:** Director, Theophilus Knapman & Co 1979–1987; Choral Society; Ballet Club; President, Stamford and Peterborough National Trust Association 1995. **Awards:** Vidal Exhibition, SJC 1940. **Honours:** CMG 1967.

PETERSEN, Richard Courtenay (1941) Born 16 March 1923, 1 Kemerton Road, Beckenham, Kent; son of John Richard Sydney Petersen, Australian Merchant, and Stella Courtenay Dawson, Teacher; m Margaret Mary Rose, 5 January 1952, St Mary's, Banbury; 2 sons (John Richard Courtenay b 1953 and Anthony Edward James b 1954), 1 daughter (Stella Margaret Ann b 1954). **Subject(s):** Mechanical Sciences; BA 1944; MA 1948; Higher National Certificate Electrical Engineering (Borough Polytechnic) 1949; FIEE; Qualified Patent Agent 1953; CPA; EPA. **Tutor(s):** S J Bailey. **Educ:** St George's School, Windsor Castle; St Peter's College, Radley. **Career:** Temporary Experimental Assistant, Anti-Submarine Materiel Department, Admiralty 1943–1945; Temporary Experimental Officer, Boom Defence Department, Admiralty 1945–1946; Technical Assistant, Raworth Moss & Cook, Patent Agents 1946–1951; Technical Assistant, Page, White & Farrer, Patent Agents 1951–1953; Patent Section, General Motors 1953–1958; Patent Agent, De Havilland Propellers and Aircraft Companies 1958–1961; Patent Agent 1961–1963, Manager, Patent Department 1963–1974, Consulting Patent Attorney 1974–1983, IBM UK; European Patent Attorney 1978–1996; Self-employed 1983–1996. **Appointments:** Examiner 1963–1968, Member 1968–1991, Chairman 1970–1989, Board of Supervising Examiners, Council Member 1968–1995, Vice-President 1978–1979, President 1979–1980, Chartered Institute of Patent Agents; Council Member, European Patent Attorneys Institute 1978–1996; Secretary-

General, Committee of National Institutes of Patent Agents 1974–1989; Member, Examination Board, European Qualifying Examination European Patent Organisation 1978–1994. **Awards:** Andrews and Marples Sculling Prize, LMBC 1942; Chapel Lesson Reading Prize 1943. **Publications:** Numerous contributions to *CIPA*, the Journal of the Chartered Institute of Patent Agents and to *EPI Information*, the Journal of the European Patent Attorneys Institute, also to the *European Patents Handbook* and the *CIPA Guide to the Patents Act 1977*.

PETERSON, Edward Whittred Reed (1919) Born 14 July 1896, The Railway Hotel, Cranbrook, Kent; son of Edward Whittred Iltyd Peterson, Solicitor, and Gertrude Percy James. BA 1922; MA 1926. **Tutor(s):** E A Benians. **Educ:** Pitman's College; The Abbey, Beckenham, Kent. **Career:** Private, RASC 1915–1917; 29th Siege Battery, Ammunition Column, BEF 1917; Solicitor to Queen Anne's Bounty; In charge of the 'Latifa' 1945; Rear Commodore 1946–1949; Official Solicitor to Church Commissioners for England 1948. **Appointments:** First Organising Secretary, Johnian Society 1924; Honorary Secretary, Royal Ocean Racing Club 1940–1946; Secretary, Royal Motor Yacht Club 1961; President, Johnian Society 1974. Died 11 January 1983.

PETHERICK, Edward John (1940) Born 26 May 1921, Albany House, St Budeaux, Plymouth; son of Edward Petherick, Schoolmaster, and Eva Winifred Venning. **Subject(s):** Mechanical Sciences; BA 1943; MA 1947. **Tutor(s):** S J Bailey. **Educ:** Victoria Road School, St Budeaux; Plymouth College. **Career:** Head, development of special purpose computer using dekatrons to process supersonic wind tunnel instrumentation data (later known as RASCAL – RAE Sequence Calculator), Mathematical Services Department, RAE, Farnborough. Died 1970.

PETIT, Dr Dinshaw Jehangir (1925) Born 19 July 1905, Bombay, India; son of Jehangir Bomanjee Petit, Mill Agent and Proprietor, and Jaijee Sorabjee Patuck. **Subject(s):** Moral Sciences/Law; BA 1928; MA 1947; MRCS (UCH) 1943; DPM 1948; LRCP (UCH) 1943. **Tutor(s):** E A Benians. **Johnian Relatives:** nephew of Pestonji Sorabji Patuck (1895). **Educ:** St Xavier's School, Bombay; St Xavier's College, Bombay. **Career:** Staff positions at Netherne, Brookwood and Cefn Coed Hospitals, until 1950; Senior Hospital Medical Officer, Springfield Hospital 1950. Died 25 March 1969.

PETO, Major Basil Arthur John (1920) Born 13 December 1900, Dolly's Farm, Chobham, Surrey; son of Sir Basil Edward Peto, Director, Crucible Works, and Mary Matilda Annie Baird; m Patricia Geraldine Browne, 1934; 1 son, 3 daughters. **Subject(s):** History/Political Economy; BA 1923. **Tutor(s):** E E Sikes. **Educ:** Summerfields, St Leonards; Summerfields, Oxford; Harrow School; Army College, Farnham. **Career:** RA, King's Dragoon Guards 1924–1939; Served on the Rhine 1926–1927; ADC to Governor of Bombay 1929; ADC to Governor of India 1932–1935; Adjutant, Scottish Horse 1936–1937; Conservative MP, King's Norton Division, Birmingham and Parliamentary Private Secretary to Mr Geoffrey Lloyd, Chairman, Oil Control Board 1941–1945. **Publications:** *Escape from Now* (collection of verse). Died 3 February 1954.

PETRIE, Arthur Hill Kelvin (1927) Born 30 June 1903, York Street, District of Glebe, Sydney, Australia; son of James Matthew Petrie, Chemist, and Edith Maude Bradley. PhD 1929. **Tutor(s):** J M Wordie. **Educ:** Sydney Grammar School; University of Sydney; University of Melbourne. **Career:** Assistant Lecturer in Botany, University of Melbourne 1929–1931; Plant Physiologist, Waite Agricultural Research Institute, University of Adelaide 1931–1942. Died 1942.

PETSCHEK, Charles Ignaz (1939) Born 25 April 1922, Berlin, Germany; son of Karl Moritz Petschek, Kaufmann (Merchant), and Josefa de May; m Elaine Bloomberg; 1 son (Jay), 3 daughters (Carol, Nancy and Jill). **Subject(s):** Economics; MBA (Harvard). **Tutor(s):** C W Guillebaud. **Educ:** Lorber Schule, Berlin; Collège Français, Berlin; Rosenberg College, St Gallen, Switzerland; Harvard University Graduate School of

Business Administration. **Career:** Principal, Charles I Petschek Investments; Finance Staff, Harvard University Business School; Honorary Director of Engineering, Stevens Institute of Technology; Associate, Kuhn, Loeb & Co; Established the William Petschek Professorship in Mathematics at Harvard University 1984. **Appointments:** Board of Trustees, Medical Committee, Montefiore Medical Center; Board of Trustees, Investment Committee Chairman, Trustee Committee, Stevens Institute of Technology; Board of Directors, Development Committee, Investment Committee, Finance Committee, New York Philharmonic; Board of Governors, Investment Committee Chairman, American Jewish Committee; Board of Directors, UJA Federation; Vice-President, Investment Committee, International Board of Directors, National Advisory Council, Weizmann Institute of Science; Board of Directors, Investment Committee Chairman, Nominating Committee Chairman, FOJP Service Corporation; Board of Governors, Investment Committee Chairman, World Union for Progressive Judaism; Board of Trustees, Vice-President, Treasurer, Jewish Community Center (White Plains); Board of Governors, Treasurer, Sunningdale Country Club; President, Board of Governors, Vice-President, Harvard Business School Club; Board of Governors, Harvard Club of New York; Board of Governors, Harvard Business School Association; Board of Governors, Admissions Committee, Harmonie Club of New York; Board of Governors, Foreign Policy Association; Vice-President and Member, Board of Directors, Finance and Investment Committee, Israel Philharmonic Orchestra; Board of Directors, New York City Opera; Board of Directors, Terezin Museum.

PETTET, Ernest Charles (1932) Born 23 April 1913, 2 Charlotte Street, Camberwell, London; son of Charles Frederick Pettet, Engine Fitter, and Lottie Elizabeth Williams. **Subject(s):** History/English; BA 1935; MA 1939. **Tutor(s):** E A Benians. **Educ:** St Paul's Elementary School; The Grammar School, Maidstone. **Awards:** Exhibition, SJC; Scholarship, SJC 1935; College Prize, SJC 1935. Died 1983.

PETTIGREW, Andrew Hislop (1940) Born 7 July 1922, Creich, Fairlie, Largs, Ayrshire; son of Sir Andrew Hislop Pettigrew, Merchant, and Annie Abigail McLeod. **Subject(s):** Economics; BA 1946; MA 1949. **Tutor(s):** C W Guillebaud. **Educ:** Ardvreck, Crieff; Rugby School.

PETTIT, John Adrian (1941) Born 1 February 1924, Maternity Home, Colwyn Road, Northampton; son of John Thomas Herbert Pettit, Leather Manufacturer, and Mary Capell; m Patricia Campbell Preston, 30 June 1950. **Tutor(s):** C W Guillebaud. **Educ:** Waynflete House School, Northampton; Kimbolton School. **Career:** Captain in the Army; Leather Sellers' Technical College, London. Died 27 December 1951.

PETTOELLO, Leonardo Pierluigi (1941) Born 12 October 1922, Valperga Canavese, Aosta, Italy; son of Decio Egberto Saadi Pettoello, University Lecturer in Italian, Jesus College, Cambridge, and Antonietta Giovanna Regis. **Subject(s):** Classics/History; BA 1944; MA 1947. **Tutor(s):** R L Howland. **Educ:** Chesterton Preparatory School; King's College Choir School, Cambridge; The Leys School, Cambridge. **Career:** Master, grammar schools in Leeds and Daventry; Head, Classics Department, Bournemouth School 1954–1974. Died October 1974.

PETTUS, Bacon Page (1918) American Student.

PETTY, Archibald Dyke (1932) Born 21 September 1913, 1 Copland Road, Stanford-le-Hope, Essex; son of Archibald Dyke Petty, Labourer, Thames Haven Oil Works, and Amelia Sheed. **Subject(s):** Modern and Medieval Languages; BA 1935; MA 1946. **Tutor(s):** C W Guillebaud. **Educ:** The Council School, Stanford-le-Hope; Palmer's Endowed School, Grays; Southend High School. **Career:** Master, Southend High School. **Awards:** Kitchener Scholarship. Died 31 July 1993.

PEVIE, William Gray Gordon (1937) Born 27 April 1915, 58c King Street, Coatbridge; son of William James Henderson Pevie, Draper, and Martha Thompson. **Tutor(s):** R L Howland. **Educ:** Mount Vernon

Public School; Coatbridge Secondary School; Glasgow Veterinary College.

PFAFF, Philip Reynold (1932) Born 10 June 1914, 5 Firs Avenue, Ripon; son of Philip Reginald Theophilus Pfaff, Lay Clerk, Ripon Cathedral, and Elsie Grace Webb; m Angela Newitt, 7 December 1939; 2 sons (Malcolm Reynold b 1942 and Graham Reynold b 1948). **Subject(s):** Music; BA 1935; MA 1943; MusB 1935. **Tutor(s):** J S Boys Smith. **Educ:** Ripon Cathedral School; The Grammar School, Ripon; Royal College of Music. **Career:** Organist and Choirmaster, St Matthew's Church, Northampton 1936–1945; Technical Signals Officer, RAF 1940–1946; Director, Suffolk Rural Music School 1946–1948; Music Organiser, East Ham, London 1948–1960; Education Advisor, Chappell and Co Ltd 1958–1972; Head of Music, Trent Park College, Middlesex Polytechnic 1960–1975; Examiner, Royal Schools of Music 1972–1984. **Awards:** Choral Scholarship, SJC; McKenna Scholarship, Royal College of Music 1935–1936.

PFISTER, Bernhard (1931) Born 8 October 1900, Bütthard, Bavaria, Germany; son of August Pfister, Apothecary, and Dorothea Barth. **Tutor(s):** C W Guillebaud. **Educ:** Elementary School, Würzburg; Grammar School, Würzburg; University of Würzburg; University of Freiburg, Breisgau.

PHARAZYN, Peter Walter Johnston (1929) Born 20 December 1910, Highden, Awahuri, Palmerston North, New Zealand; son of Godfrey Norris Pharazyn, Sheep Farmer, and Ella Cecilia Johnston. **Subject(s):** Agriculture (Estate Management). **Tutor(s):** C W Guillebaud. **Johnian Relatives:** grandson of William Pharazyn (1860). **Educ:** Preparatory School, Eastbourne; Eton College. **Career:** RAFVR. Died 27 July 1932.

PHELPS, Gilbert Henry (1937) (admitted to Fitzwilliam House 1934) Born 23 January 1915, 7 Norfolk Terrace, Southgate Street, Gloucester; son of Gilbert Henry Phelps, Clerk, and Mary Moore Wilks; m (1) Dorothy Coad, 1939 (dis), (2) Kay Batchelor, 1972; (1) 1 son, 1 daughter, (2) 3 stepsons. **Subject(s):** English; MA 1941; BA (Fitzwilliam) 1937. **Tutor(s):** C W Guillebaud. **Educ:** National School, Gloucester; Crypt School, Gloucester; Fitzwilliam House, Cambridge. **Career:** Lecturer in English, British Institute of Portugal 1940–1942; Served in RAF (Signals) 1942–1943; Senior English Master, Blundell's School 1943–1945; Talks Producer, BBC Bristol 1945–1950; Supervisor of Educational Talks 1950–1952, Producer, the *Third Programme* 1950–1953, General Instructor, Staff Training Department 1953–1956, Chief Instructor, Staff Training Department 1956–1960, BBC; Author 1960–1993. **Appointments:** President, Cambridge University English Club; English Examiner, Oxford-Cambridge Joint Examinations Board 1937–1940. **Awards:** Strathcona Research Studentship, SJC 1937; Fellow, Royal Society of Literature 1978. **Publications:** Articles, poetry, and short stories; *The Centenarians*, 1958; Contributor to *Pelican Guide to Literature*; *The Last Horizon*, 1965; *The Dry Stone*; *A Man in his Prime*; *The Winter People*, 1963; *A Short History of English Literature*, 1964; *The Byronic Byron*, 1971; *The Love Before the First*; *The Tenants of the House*, 1971; *The Low Roads*, 1975; *The Russian novel in English Fiction*; *An Introduction to Fifty British Novels 1600–1900*, 1979; *The New Pelican Guide to English Literature*, 1981; *A Short Guide to the World Novel: from Myth to Modernism*, 1988; *The Cambridge Guide to the Arts in Britain*, 1988. Died 15 June 1993.

PHEMISTER, Professor Thomas Crawford (1925) Born 25 May 1902, 31 Hamilton Street, Govan, Lanarkshire, Scotland; son of John Clark Phemister, Mercantile Clerk, and Elizabeth Galbraith Crawford. PhD 1933; DSc (Glasgow); MSc (Chicago); Honorary Docteur (Rennes); FRSE. **Tutor(s):** J M Wordie. **Educ:** Allen Glen's High School of Science; University of Glasgow; University of Chicago. **Career:** Professor of Geology, Marischal College, Aberdeen; Associate Professor of Petrology, University of British Columbia 1927; Demonstrator in Mineralogy and Petrology, University of Cambridge 1933–1937; Kilgour Professor of Geology, University of Aberdeen 1937–1972; Principal and Vice-Chancellor, University of Aberdeen 1962. Died December 1982.

PHILBIN, John (1919) Born 13 February 1897, 8 Pratt Street, Newcastle-under-Lyme, Staffordshire; son of Andrew Philbin, Railway Platelayer, and Catherine Connolly. **Subject(s):** Natural Sciences; BA 1920. **Tutor(s):** E A Benians. **Educ:** St Patrick's Roman Catholic Elementary School, Newcastle; Newcastle High School, Newcastle-under-Lyme. **Awards:** Scholarship, SJC 1915.

PHILIP, John Simpson Paton (1943) Born 3 April 1926, Brunswick Nursing Home, Cambridge; son of Wilfrid Paton Philip, Tuberculosis Officer, Cambridgeshire County Council, and Mary Isabella Simpson; m Margaret Montgomery, 1952; 1 son, 3 daughters. **Subject(s):** Agriculture; BA 1946; MA 1950. **Tutor(s):** C W Guillebaud. **Johnian Relatives:** brother of Philip Paton Philip (1940). **Educ:** The Perse School, Cambridge. **Career:** Lecturer, later Vice-Principal, Chadacre Agricultural Institute, Bury St Edmunds, Suffolk 1946–1949; Resident Land Agent, Clandeboye Estate, Bangor, County Down 1949–1958; Principal, Chadacre Agricultural Institute 1958–1980. **Appointments:** President, University of Cambridge Agricultural Society 1946; President, CUBC 1946. **Honours:** MBE 1980. **Publications:** *Stock Husbandry*, Sir Isaac Pitman & Sons Ltd, 1953.

PHILIP, Philip Paton (PATON-PHILIP) (1940) Born 12 September 1922, 9 Brunswick Walk, Cambridge; son of Wilfrid Paton Philip, Physician, and Mary Isabel Simpson, Nursing Sister; 3 sons. **Subject(s):** Natural Sciences; BA 1944; MA 1961; MB 1946; BChir 1946; MChir 1959; MRCS; FRCS 1955. **Tutor(s):** R L Howland. **Johnian Relatives:** brother of John Simpson Paton Philip (1943). **Educ:** Perse Preparatory School; Perse School. **Career:** Surgeon Commander (Acting), RN 1947–1954; Consulting Urological Surgeon 1964–1988; Medico-legal work and Diving Office, RNVR 1988. **Honours:** VRD 1957.

PHILIPP, Dr Elliot Elias (1933) Born 20 July 1915, 202 Lordship Road, Stoke Newington, London; son of Oscar Isaac Philipp, Metal Refiner and Merchant, and Clarisse Weil; m Lucie Ruth Hackenbroch, 1939; 2 children (1 d 1998). **Subject(s):** Medical Sciences; BA 1936; MA 1942; MB 1947; BChir 1947; MRCS 1939; LRCP 1939; MRCOG 1947; FRCS England 1951; FRCOG 1962. **Tutor(s):** R L Howland. **Educ:** Warwick House School, Hampstead; St Paul's School, London. **Career:** Squadron Leader, RAFVR, twice Mentioned in Despatches 1940–1946; Consultant Gynaecologist, North London Group Hospitals and Harley Street 1952–1995. **Appointments:** Second Honorary Gynaecologist to the French Hospital, London 1952; Senior Consultant Gynaecologist, Royal Northern Hospital, London. **Honours:** Chevalier de la Legion D'Honneur, 1971. **Publications:** (co-author) *History of Obstetrics and Gynaecology*, Parthenon 1994, and 30 other books.

PHILLIPPS-WOLLEY, Clive John Fenwick (1929) Born 19 October 1910, Victoria, British Columbia, Canada; son of Clive Phillipps-Wolley, Lieutenant Commander, RN, and Laura Hide. BA 1932; MA 1936. **Tutor(s):** J M Wordie. **Educ:** The Manor House, Horsham; Stowe School, Buckingham; The Nautical College, Pangbourne.

PHILLIPS, Anthony Gordon (1943) Born 28 September 1925, 22 Church Lane, Prestwich, Lancashire; son of Gordon Phillips, Assistant Editor, Manchester Guardian, and Jessie Hall. **Subject(s):** Economics; BA 1948. **Tutor(s):** C W Guillebaud. **Educ:** Singleton Hill Preparatory School, Salford; Sedbergh School. **Career:** Lieutenant, RNVR. Died 20 July 1952.

PHILLIPS, Arnold Boyd (1943) Born 3 July 1925, Breedon Lodge, Breedon-on-the-Hill, Leicestershire; son of Sydney Edwin Phillips, Farmer, and Winifred Mary Arnold; m Erika Marie Johanne. **Subject(s):** Mechanical Sciences; BA 1946; MA 1950; MIL; MITI; MICE; MEng. **Tutor(s):** S J Bailey. **Educ:** Winchester House, Brackley; Marlborough College. **Career:** RE 1945–1970; Freelance Engineering and Technical Translator 1970. Died 3 October 1997.

PHILLIPS, Christopher Brian Michael (1940) Born 22 June 1921, 13 Park Avenue, Bush Hill Park, Enfield; son of Lewis Waight Phillips, Electrical Engineer and Lecturer in Physics, and Rebecca Williams. **Subject(s):** Mathematics/Economics; BA 1947; MA 1953; MIPM. **Tutor(s):** C W Guillebaud; J M Wordie. **Educ:** Friends' School, Saffron Walden; Bootham School, York. **Career:** Training and Development Officer, British Rail, York. Died 14 March 2003.

PHILLIPS, The Revd Edwin Albert (1905) (admitted to St Catharine's College 1904) Born 3 May 1874, Trevecca, Talgarth, Breconshire; son of John Phillips, Farm Labourer, and Margaret Williams; m (1) Angelique Blanche (d 1927), (2) Flora Elizabeth Freeman, 20 August 1929. **Subject(s):** Mathematics; BA (London) 1897; BA (Wales) 1898; FRAS 1902; FRAI 1915. **Tutor(s):** E E Sikes. **Educ:** University College of North Wales, Bangor. **Career:** Ordained Deacon 1901; Curate, Holy Trinity Exeter 1901–1904; Ordained Priest 1902; Curate, St Bene't, Cambridge 1904–1906; Curate, Chelton 1906–1910; Curate, Heanor 1910–1911; Vicar, Basildon 1911–1930; Assistant Master, Bradfield College 1917–1920; Tutor, Dorchester Missionary College 1925–1930; Rector, Gunthorpe with Bale, Norfolk 1930–1954. **Appointments:** Organising Secretary, Church of England Temperance Society, Norwich Diocese, 1933. Died 2 February 1954.

PHILLIPS, Harold Enoch (1913) Born 16 October 1894, 9 Sloane Street, London; son of Enoch Phillips, Merchant, and Elizabeth Marian Witham. **Tutor(s):** L H K Bushe-Fox. **Educ:** Broadstairs Preparatory School; Mill Hill School. **Career:** Provision Merchant; Lieutenant, Royal Welsh Fusiliers, Gallipoli and Macedonia 1914–1918. Died 26 September 1936.

PHILLIPS, Henry Wilfred Lewis (1913) Born 12 September 1894, 24 High Street, Leominster, Herefordshire; son of William Henry Phillips, Wholesale Fruiterer and Draper, and Margaret Emma Lewis. **Subject(s):** Natural Sciences (Chemistry); BA 1916; MA 1938. **Tutor(s):** R P Gregory. **Educ:** Bridgnorth Grammar School. **Career:** Metallurgist. **Awards:** Scholarship, SJC. Died March 1968.

PHILLIPS, John Dayton (1943) Born 20 April 1926, 42 West Hill, Tredegar, Monmouthshire; son of John Phillips, Headmaster, and Edith May Hodges, Schoolmistress; m Joan Gamble, 1975. **Subject(s):** Mechanical Sciences; BA 1946; MA 1950; CEng; MIMechE; MInstE. **Tutor(s):** S J Bailey. **Educ:** Earl Street Council School, Tredegar; Georgetown Boys' Central School, Tredegar; Lewis School, Pengam. **Career:** RAE, Farnborough 1945–1946; Dorman Long Steel 1946–1951; Lecturer 1952–1977, Head of Engineering Department 1978–1983, Isle of Wight College of Arts and Technology. **Awards:** Walter Hines Page Scholarship, English Speaking Union 1958.

PHILLIPS, The Revd Robert Stowell (1912) Born 5 April 1893, Nang-wa-kan, China; son of Hugh Stowell Phillips, Clerk in Holy Orders, and Minnie Mary Apperson; m Nonni; 2 sons (Ronald and John), 2 daughters (Celia and Pat). **Subject(s):** History; BA 1923; MA 1926. **Tutor(s):** E E Sikes. **Educ:** Elmhurst, Croydon; Trent College; Ridley Hall, Cambridge. **Career:** Lieutenant, 39th Garhwal Rifles, Indian Army, WWI; Deacon 1923; Curate, St Mary, Luton 1923–1926; Priest 1924; Curate, Holy Trinity, Cambridge 1926–1927; Perpetual Curate, St James, New Barnet 1927–1934; Vicar, St Peter, Hunslet Moor, Leeds 1934–1945; Rector, Darlaston, Staffordshire 1945–1952; Rector, Carlton Colville, Suffolk 1952–1960. Died 18 July 1967.

PHILLIPS, Sidney Hill (1900) Born 4 August 1882, Risca, Monmouthshire; son of Godfrey Hill Phillips, Ironmonger, and Annie Jane Ewing; m Isobel Gladys Custance, 20 June 1917, St Helen's, Wheathampstead; 1 son (John), 1 daughter (Joan). **Subject(s):** Mathematics/Natural Sciences; BA 1903; MA 1907. **Tutor(s):** D MacAlister. **Educ:** Risca Town School; St Loes School, Amberley; Cheltenham College. **Career:** Home Civil Service 1904; Principal Assistant Secretary, Admiralty 1936–1942. **Honours:** CB 1941. Died 28 February 1962.

PHILLIPS, William Richard (1908) Born 22 June 1885, 1 Blandy Terrace, Nantymoel, Llandyfodwy, Glamorgan; son of Jenkin Phillips, Building Contractor, and Mary Jones. **Subject(s):** Modern and Medieval Languages/Law; BA 1911; MA 1924; LLB 1912. **Tutor(s):** E E Sikes. **Educ:** Bridgend County School; University College, Cardiff; University College, Aberystwyth. **Career:** Master, St Mary's School, Melrose 1912–1913; Master 1913–1920, Lieutenant, OTC WWI, Royal Grammar School, Lancaster; Lieutenant, London Regiment, WWI; Assistant Master, Boys' High School, Newport, Monmouthshire 1920–1936. Died 29 March 1936.

PHILP, Arthur Leslie (1920) Born 22 February 1896, Morton House, Woodland Road, Bristol, Gloucestershire; son of Ernest Charles Philp, Lead Merchant, and Emma Jane Rowe; m Enid Marion Lee, 11 April 1928, All Saints, Wraxall. **Tutor(s):** R P Gregory. **Educ:** Clifton College. **Career:** Captain, SMRE, Royal Signals, France 1914.

PHILP, Claude Hastings George (1903) Born 17 December 1885, Albert Road, Romford, Essex; son of George Hastings Philp, Engineer, and Georgina Step; m Margaret Fussell; 1 son. **Subject(s):** Natural Sciences; BA 1907; MB 1912; BChir 1912. **Tutor(s):** D MacAlister. **Educ:** Falmouth Grammar School. **Career:** Resident Medical Officer, Herefordshire General Hospital; Captain, RAMC, India and France 1916–1918. Died 26 March 1918 (killed in action).

PHILPOT, Frederick Harold (1915) (admitted to Corpus Christi College 1914) Born 12 August 1894, Stanstead Abbotts, Ware, Hertfordshire; son of George Joseph Philpot, Civil Engineer, and Emily Elizabeth Weatherley; m Winifred Caroline Rock, 17 August 1921, St Barnabas Church, Plymouth; 1 son. **Subject(s):** Theology; BA 1918; MA 1930. **Tutor(s):** E E Sikes. **Educ:** Westminster Abbey Choir School; Westminster School. **Career:** Schoolmaster, RN 1916–1919; Assistant Master and House Master, Cheltenham College 1920; Headmaster, Stockport Grammar School 1941. **Awards:** Choral Studentship, SJC; Marquess of Salisbury Exhibition, SJC 1915. Died 9 December 1974.

PHILPOTT, Guy (1924) Born 19 April 1903, Little Appley, St Helens, Ryde, Isle of Wight; son of Richard William Philpott, Headmaster, and Jessie Marian Philpott. **Subject(s):** Modern and Medieval Languages; BA 1927. **Tutor(s):** E E Sikes. **Educ:** Little Appley School; Royal Naval Colleges, Osborne and Dartmouth; Imperial College of Science and Technology.

PHIPPS, Thomas Edward Donald (1919) Born 26 January 1900, 8 Spencer Parade, Northampton; son of Thomas Phipps, Consulting Brewer, and Ada Ruby Melville Bailey. **Subject(s):** Classics; BA 1921. **Tutor(s):** E E Sikes. **Educ:** Cambridge House School, Northampton; Avenue School, Bedford; Bedford School. **Career:** Managing Director, P Phipps & Co Ltd, brewers, wine and spirit merchants and hotel proprietors. **Awards:** Dowman Sizarship, SJC 1918. Died 21 December 1952.

PIAGGIO, Professor Henry Thomas Herbert (1903) Born 2 June 1884, 18 Lamb's Conduit Street, Holborn, London; son of Francis Piaggio, Dancing Teacher, and Mary Want. **Subject(s):** Mathematics; BA 1906; MA 1910; BSc (London) 1905; DSc (London) 1914. **Tutor(s):** E E Sikes. **Educ:** Medburn Street School; City of London School. **Career:** Mathematics Lecturer, University College, Nottingham 1909; Professor of Mathematics, University of Nottingham 1919–1950. **Appointments:** Council Member, Mathematical Association. **Awards:** Honourable Mention for Smith's Prize, University of Cambridge 1908. **Publications:** *Differential Equations*, 1920. Died 25 June 1967.

PICKERING, Edward Andrew (1919) Born 6 September 1901, 25 St Olave's Road, York; son of Octavius Parker Pickering, Commission Agent, and Eleanor Andrew. BA 1923. **Tutor(s):** E A Benians. **Johnian Relatives:** brother of Eric Stockdale Pickering (1921). **Educ:** Bedford School.

PICKERING, Eric Stockdale (1921) Born 27 February 1903, 25 St Olave's Road, York; son of Octavius Parker Pickering, Commission Agent, and Eleanor Andrew. **Tutor(s):** B F Armitage. **Johnian Relatives:** brother of Edward Andrew Pickering (1919). **Educ:** The Grammar School, Bedford.

PICKETT, Eric Samuel John (1941) Born 29 March 1924, 39 Gresham Road, Brentwood, Essex; son of Mark Pickett, Police Sergeant, and Alice Emily Allman; m Betty Buckingham, 1946; 1 son (b 1950), 1 daughter (b 1952). **Subject(s):** Mechanical Sciences; BA 1944; MA 1948; CEng. **Tutor(s):** S J Bailey. **Educ:** Brentwood Church of England School; Brentwood School. **Career:** Chartered Engineer.

PICKFORD, Frank (1936) Born 26 October 1917, 49 Minerva Street, Bulwell, Nottingham; son of Edwin Pickford, Railway Goods Guard, and Alice Dale. **Subject(s):** History; BA 1939. **Tutor(s):** J S Boys Smith. **Johnian Relatives:** father of Stephen John Pickford (1968). **Educ:** Bulwell Trust School; Albert Street Council School; Nottingham High School. **Career:** Under-Secretary, General Manpower Division, Department of Employment. **Awards:** Scholarship, SJC; Exhibition, SJC 1936–1937. Died 28 April 1984.

PIKE, Graham John Roger (1949) Born 20 February 1927, 192 The Rye, East Dulwich, London; son of John Reginald Pike, Assistant Chief Commercial Manager, and Marjory Constance Alice Webb. **Subject(s):** History. **Tutor(s):** A G Lee. **Educ:** Quainton Hall School, Harrow; Portland House School, Leicester; St John's School, Pinner; Merchant Taylors' School.

PILCHER, Richard Edward Montagu (1922) Born 30 July 1903, Liquorpond Street, Boston, Lincolnshire; son of Cecil Westland Pilcher, Medical Practitioner, and Evelyn Mary Southam; m Moira, 1933; 1 son, 2 daughters. **Subject(s):** Natural Sciences; BA 1925; MA 1941; BChir 1941; MB 1941; MRCS (St Thomas') 1928; FRCS (Edinburgh) 1931; LRCP (St Thomas') 1928. **Tutor(s):** B F Armitage. **Johnian Relatives:** father-in-law of John Nafford Brady (1954). **Educ:** Kingsland Grange, Shrewsbury; Shrewsbury School. **Career:** House Surgeon, House Physician and Senior Resident Medical Officer, Nottingham General Hospital; Honorary Surgeon, Boston Hospital; Surgeon for Tuberculosis, Lincolnshire County Council; Clinical Assistant, Tuberculosis Department, St Thomas'; GP, Boston, Lincolnshire. **Appointments:** Divisional Surgeon, St John Ambulance; Chairman, Lincolnshire and South Humberside Trust for Nature Conservation; Trustee and Council Member, Wildfowl Trust. **Honours:** Officer of the Order of St John. Died 30 December 1989.

PILKINGTON, Kenneth Reginald (1922) Born 10 May 1903, Bridgend House, Windygates, Fifeshire, Scotland; son of Reginald Murray Pilkington, Master Engineer, and Louisa Burns Mathieson. BA 1926. **Tutor(s):** E A Benians. **Educ:** Private Education, Crieff; Eton College; Lieutenant Colonel Phillips, Emberton Manor, Newport Pagnell.

PILLAI, Kokkat Sankara (1948) Born 20 July 1922, Travancore, India; son of Krishna Kurup, and Lekshmikutty Amma. BSc (Travancore) 1941. **Tutor(s):** J M Wordie. **Educ:** MM School, Olakettyampalam; EM School, Keerikkad; EH School, Quilon; University College, Trivandrum. **Career:** Indian Diplomatic Service.

PIM, Lieutenant Colonel Gerald Robert (1921) Born 9 April 1896, Newstead, St Julian's Road, Norwood, London; son of Robert Pim, Corn Broker, and Mary Elizabeth Belton; m Grace Magill Erskine; 2 sons (Michael and Pakenham). **Tutor(s):** E E Sikes. **Educ:** Hildersham House, St Peter's; Rugby School; RMA, Woolwich. **Career:** RE, France, WWI; Lieutenant Colonel, RE, WWII. **Honours:** MC (WWI). Died May 1940 (killed in action at Dunkirk).

PIMLOTT, Alan Kenneth (1941) Born 14 August 1923, Salterswall, Over, Cheshire; son of James Bertram Pimlott, Clothing Manufacturer, and Dorothy Mary Eaton; m Kathleen Fenwick-Smith, 26 August 1948; 3 sons (Graham Fenwick, David Bruce Fenwick and Christopher John). **Subject(s):** Economics; BA 1947; MA 1949. **Tutor(s):** C W Guillebaud. **Johnian Relatives:** brother-in-law of Peter Fenwick Smith (1941). **Educ:** Sir John Deane's Grammar School, Northwich. **Career:** Managing Director, Bradbury's, Clothing Manufacturer, Winsford, Cheshire; Director, Ben Williams and Co, Clothing Manufactuer, London. Died 12 April 1999.

PINDER, Geoffrey Peveril (1941) Born 6 June 1922, Woodsley Nursing Home, Leeds; son of Arthur Pinder, Consulting Motor Engineer, and Kate Irene Sutcliffe; m Enid Margaret McKenzie, 17 February 1951; 2 sons (Peter Leslie and Simon David), 1 daughter (Alison Peveril). **Subject(s):** Mechanical Sciences; BA 1944; MA 1947. **Tutor(s):** S J Bailey. **Educ:** Red House, Moor Monkton; Shrewsbury School. **Career:** Lieutenant, RNVR Fleet Air Arm, North Atlantic 1943–1946; Nestlé, Switzerland 1946–1970; Study of contribution of multinational companies to Third World 1971–1972; UN Food and Agriculture Organisation in South Korea 1972; Voluntary work aimed at improving quality of life 1972–. **Awards:** Wilson Reading Prize, SJC 1942.

PITEL, Adrien Philip (1919) Born 22 August 1898, Beachley, Chichester Road, Croydon; son of Aime Ferdinand Pitel, Stockbroker, and Mary Helen Barry; m Jane; 1 son (John), 2 daughters (Mary and Ann). **Tutor(s):** E A Benians. **Educ:** The Oratory School, Edgbaston; RMC, Sandhurst. **Career:** Second Lieutenant, 2nd Battalion, Queen's Regiment 1918; Member of the Stock Exchange. Died 26 June 1949.

PITMAN, John Henry Norton (1949) Born 29 October 1925, Tyndale Nursing Home, Clarence Square, Cheltenham; son of William Thomas Pitman, Assistant Paymaster, and Frances Christina Gastrell. **Tutor(s):** G C L Bertram. **Educ:** Christ Church Junior School, Cheltenham; Cheltenham Grammar School; Wadham College, Oxford. **Awards:** Agricultural Probationer, Colonial Service.

PITT, Dr Geoffrey John (1940) Born 11 May 1921, Bristol; son of George Howard Pitt, Civil Servant, and Winifred Flora Griffin; m Margaret Cole, 13 August 1949; 1 son (Antony John), 2 daughters (Angela Elizabeth and Helena Jane). **Subject(s):** Natural Sciences; BA 1943; MA 1947; BSc (London) 1945; PhD (London) 1949. **Tutor(s):** J M Wordie. **Johnian Relatives:** cousin of Michael John Pitt (1950); father of Antony John Pitt (1973). **Educ:** Merrywood (Southville) Elementary School, Bristol; Cotham Secondary School, Bristol; Birkbeck College, London. **Career:** Mullard Radio Valve Company, Mitcham, working on development of electronic valves 1942–1945; Research student with Professor J D Bernal, Crystallography Department, Birkbeck College, London 1945–1949; Research Assistant to Dr Dorothy Hodgkin, Department of Crystallography, Oxford (refinement of penicillin structure) 1949–1952; Research Scientist, National Coal Board, Coal Research Establishment, Cheltenham (responsibilities in Physics, Chemistry and Materials Science laboratories) 1952–1982; Retired, engaged in Local History Research 1982. **Awards:** Scholarship, SJC. **Publications:** (ed, with G R Millward) *Coal and Modern Coal Processing: An Introduction*, 1979; (contrib) ed D H Aldred, *Gotherington: The History of a Village*, 1993; sundry scientific papers in technical journals.

PITTOM, William Wynn Pratt (1908) Born 9 October 1888, Barby, Northamptonshire; son of Thomas Pittom, Farmer, and Mary Barker Wynn. **Subject(s):** Natural Sciences; BA 1911. **Tutor(s):** J R Tanner. **Educ:** Northampton and County School. **Career:** Government Scholarship, Animal Nutrition Institute, School of Agriculture, Cambridge. Died 10 October 1914.

PLACKETT, Geoffrey Pilkington (1923) Born 29 August 1905, 2 Middlewood Road, Sheffield, Yorkshire; son of Alfred Plackett, Bank Manager, and Bessie Pilkington. **Subject(s):** Geography/Mathematics; BA 1926. **Tutor(s):** J M Wordie. **Educ:** The High School, Chesterfield; The Home School, Grindleford; Wrekin College, Wellington. **Career:** Audit Department, Bombay, Baroda and Central Indian Railway 1927.

PLATT, Christopher James (1927) Born 24 May 1908, Brackenhoe, Ashley Road, Hale, Cheshire; son of Robert Matthew Platt, Bank Manager, and Ellen Sophie Paus; m Alma Muriel Collins, 1935; 2 daughters. **Subject(s):** Classics/Economics; BA 1930; MA 1937; FCA; ACMA. **Tutor(s):** M P Charlesworth. **Educ:** Wadham House School, Hale; St Cuthbert's School, Malvern; Shrewsbury School. **Career:** Clerk, Mellors, Basden & Mellors, Nottingham 1934–1938; Director and Secretary, Caxton Publishing Company Ltd 1938–1939; Major, RAPC, TA 1939–1945; Director and Secretary, Caxton Publishing Company Ltd 1945–1954; Company Secretary, Swain Group Ltd, London 1955–1960; Company Secretary, Heinemann Group of Publishers Ltd, Kingswood, London 1960–1964; Research Secretary, ICAEW 1964–1974; Part-time Author 1964–1980. **Awards:** Whytehead Scholarship, SJC 1927. **Publications:** Various publications on accountancy and tax.

PLATT, Frank Kenneth (1940) Born 13 April 1922, 162 Birmingham Road, Walsall; son of Frank Arthur Platt, Solicitor, and Dora May Devis. **Tutor(s):** R L Howland. **Educ:** Bridlemere Private School, Walsall; Queen Mary's Grammar School, Walsall; Denstone College. **Career:** Lieutenant, 13th Battery, 17th Field Regiment, RA 1940–1943. **Awards:** Scholarship, SJC. Died 24 April 1943 (killed in action in Tunisia).

PLATT, James (1948) Born 30 April 1928, 92 Barker Street, Oldham, Lancashire; son of Thomas Platt, Ironworks Labourer, and Elsie Race; m 1955; 1 daughter (b 1966). **Subject(s):** Modern and Medieval Languages; BA 1950; MA 1960. **Tutor(s):** C W Guillebaud. **Educ:** Henshaw's Blue Coat School, Oldham; The Hulme Grammar School, Oldham. **Career:** Indian Army 1946–1948; International Sports Correspondent, Reuters, and Orion Publicidade, São Paolo 1958–1962; Director, Courses and Studies, Lund University, Sweden 1959–1964; Director, Central Bureau for Educational Visits and Exchanges (UK Government Agency) 1964–1984; Chairman, Centre for International Sports Studies, and Centre for International Sports Exchange 1974–1984; Editor, *Sports International* 1974–1984; Chairman, Planning Committee, Olympic Solidarity Training Courses 1974–1984; Rector, Regent's College, London 1984–1986. **Appointments:** Adviser on International Strategies and Programmes to many Higher Education Institutions in Britain, Europe, USA, Canada and to 30 other countries; Co-ordinator, Academic Activities in the UK, US Sports Academy; Chairman, European Commission and Council of Europe Special Committees; President, FIOCES 1972–1984 (later Honorary President); Vice-President, Corinthian-Casuals FC; Honorary Fellow, Sheffield Hallam University; Honorary Citizen, City of Tel Aviv-Jaffa and Mobile, Alabama; UK Delegate, many international meetings and conferences including G7 Summit, USA, 16 Cultural Mixed Commissions, Council of Europe, European Commission; Chairman, UNESCO Regional Conferences, Jaipur, South East Asia, and Guadalajara, South America; Member, 23 International Associations and Committees concerned with international education. **Awards:** Distinguished Service Award, US Sports Academy. **Honours:** Ordre National du Merite (France); Order of the Crown (Belgium); Chevalier des Palmes Academique (France). **Publications:** (jointly) Swedish High School Textbook; (Publisher/Editor) *Working Holidays*; *School Travel & Adventure*; *Young Visitors to Britain*; *Study Abroad*; *Children's World of Art*; *Education International*; *Higher Education Exchange*.

PLATTEN, The Revd Thomas George (1919) Born 5 August 1899, 5 Broad Row, Great Yarmouth, Norfolk; son of George Platten, Draper and Outfitter, and Florence Smith; 3 children. **Subject(s):** Natural Sciences/Anthropology; BA 1922; MA 1926. **Tutor(s):** E A Benians. **Johnian Relatives:** father of Christopher John Platten (1954). **Educ:** The Grammar School, Great Yarmouth; Westcott House, Cambridge. **Career:** Ordained Deacon 1923; Curate, St John Chrysostom, Victoria Park, Manchester 1923–1927; Ordained Priest, Manchester 1924; Diocesan and Domestic Chaplain to the Bishop of Wakefield 1927–1928; Missionary, Trinity College, Kandy 1928–1932; Chaplain, College of St Mark and St John, Chelsea 1932–1935; Warden, Bishop Heber Hall and Professor in Madras College 1936–1947; Principal,

Saltley Training College, Birmingham, and Honorary Canon, Birmingham Cathedral 1947–1968. **Publications:** *The Growth of the Kingdom*, 1928; *Christianity and Mental Healing*, 1928; *The Odyssey of Israel*, 1936. Died 11 January 1986.

PLEVINS, St John Tempé (1920) Born 23 November 1900, Papillon Hall, Lubenham, Leicestershire; son of George Joseph Plevins, Landed Proprietor, and Ethel Louisa Tuck; m Virginia Tatters Byrne, 18 January 1928, St Paul's, Knightsbridge. **Tutor(s):** E E Sikes. **Educ:** Cottesmore School, Brighton; Eton College.

PLOWRIGHT, Colin Campbell (1903) Born 10 March 1884, 6 Cottingham Street, Allercliffe, Sheffield; son of Joseph Henry Plowright, Inspector of Buildings, and Janet Ramsden. BA 1906. **Tutor(s):** D MacAlister. **Educ:** Royal Grammar School, Sheffield. **Career:** Headmaster, Mitcham Singlegate School; Assistant Master, Bury St Edmunds County School 1907; Assistant Master, Walton on Thames Central School 1915; Headmaster, Gorringe Park School, Mitcham 1930–1950. **Appointments:** Chorister, His Majesty's Chapel Royal, Hampton Court Palace, for 30 years. **Awards:** Choral Studentship, SJC. Died 22 December 1952.

PLUMMER, Colin Vernon (1930) Born 26 March 1911, Armboth, Thorn Road, Hazel Grove cum Bramhall, Cheshire; son of Vernon Plummer, Insurance Clerk, and Elsie Jones; m Edna Dettmann, 13 July 1939, Kensington. BA 1933; MA 1943. **Tutor(s):** M P Charlesworth. **Educ:** Riley's Preparatory School, Alderley Edge; Sedbergh School. Died 23 January 1990.

PLUMPTON, Dr Charles (1938) Born 25 January 1920, 11 Grays Court, Louth, Lincolnshire; son of Sidney Plumpton, Poulterer, and Bertha Preston; m Joan Lee, 1948; 1 son, 1 daughter. **Subject(s):** Mathematics; BA 1941; MA 1945; PhD (London) 1959. **Tutor(s):** J M Wordie. **Educ:** Westgate Church of England School; Kidgate Council School, Louth; King Edward VI Grammar School, Louth. **Career:** Radar Officer, RNVR 1940; Chief Examiner, Joint Matriculations Board, the Oxford and Cambridge Board, and the London Schools Examination Board 1950; Lecturer, Battersea Polytechnic 1952; Queen Mary College, University of London 1952–1982 (Lecturer in Mathematics, Director of Engineering Mathematics and Reader in Applied Mathematics). **Awards:** Minor Scholarship, SJC 1937. Died January 1993.

PLUNKETT, Gerald Walter (1936) Born 3 February 1918, 89 Lower Baggott Street, Dublin; son of Oliver Plunkett, Judge, and Cordelia Edina Wheler; BA 1939. **Tutor(s):** C W Guillebaud. **Educ:** Claremont School; Ampleforth College. **Career:** Lieutenant, RA 1939–1943. Died April 1943 (killed in action in Tunisia).

PLUTTE, Charles Ernest Frederick (1926) Born 24 February 1908, 1 De Frene Road, Sydenham, Kent; son of Gottlieb Friedrich Plutte, Managing Director; and Helene Küpers. **Subject(s):** Modern and Medieval Languages; BA 1930. **Tutor(s):** M P Charlesworth. **Educ:** Lambourne House School, Forest Hill, London; Sydenham Hill School; Leighton Park School, Reading. Died 8 July 1953.

PLYMEN, John Cotterell (1931) Born 22 May 1912, Greenhill, Eddington; son of Francis Joseph Plymen, Director of Agriculture, Indian Agriculture Service, and Muriel Wacher; BA 1934; MA 1939. **Tutor(s):** C W Guillebaud. **Educ:** Herneville Preparatory School, Herne Bay; Herne Bay College; Tonbridge School. **Career:** Assistant Master, Ruzawi School, Southern Rhodesia 1935–1938; South African Artillery 1939–1945; Inspector of Schools, Basutoland Government 1939–1946; Education Officer, Mafeteng, Basutoland 1946. Died September 1965.

POCHIN, Sir Edward Eric (1928) Born 22 September 1909, Croyde, Priory Road, Sale, Cheshire; son of Charles Davenport Pochin, Mechanical Engineer, and Agnes Collier; m Margaret Julia Tilly, 1940 (d 1971); 1 son, 1 daughter. **Subject(s):** Natural Sciences; BA 1931; MA 1935; BChir 1936;

MB 1937; MD 1945; FRCP 1946. **Tutor(s):** M P Charlesworth. **Educ:** Brockhurst, Church Stretton; Repton School. **Career:** Scientific Staff, MRC 1941; Director, MRC Physiological Laboratory, Armoured Fighting Vehicles School Gunnery Wing, Lulworth 1941–1945; Director, Department of Clinical Research, University College Hospital 1946–1974. **Appointments:** UK Representative, UN Scientific Committee on Effects of Atomic Radiation 1956–1982; Chairman, International Commission on Radiological Protection 1962–1969; Councillor, Royal College of Physicians 1965–1968; Member, National Radiological Protection Board 1971–1982; Member, Physiological Society; Member, Association of Physicians; Member, International Radiation Protection Association; Member, British Institute of Radiology; Member, Medical Research Association; Member, Nippon Society Radiologica; Member, British Nuclear Medical Society; Member, Hospital Physicists' Association; Member, American Thyroid Association. **Awards:** Scholarship, SJC 1927; Michael Foster Studentship 1931; Strathcona Studentship, SJC 1931–1932; Gifford-Edmunds Prize, Ophthalmic Society 1940; Raymond Horton-Smith Prize, University of Cambridge 1945–1946. **Honours:** CBE 1959; Kt 1975. **Publications:** *An Index of Harm*, 1969; *Nuclear Radiation: Risks and Benefits*, 1984. Died 29 January 1990.

POLACK, Albert Isaac (1911) Born 4 April 1892, 1 Percival Road, Clifton, Bristol, Somerset; son of Joseph Polack, Schoolmaster, and Sophia Isaac; m Beatrice Cohen, 30 March 1922, Central Synagogue, Hallam Street; 2 sons, 2 daughters. **Subject(s):** Classics; BA 1914; MA 1920. **Tutor(s):** E E Sikes. **Johnian Relatives:** brother of Ernest Emanuel Polack (1912). **Educ:** Clifton College. **Career:** Lieutenant, RE, Gibraltar and Flanders, WWI; Master, Taunton School 1920–1923; Master, Clifton College 1923–1949; Education Officer, Council of Christians and Jews 1969–1971. **Awards:** Second John Stewart of Rannoch Scholarship in Greek and Latin, University of Cambridge 1912. **Publications:** *Tolerance: Can it be taught?* (pamphlet); (jointly with W W Simpson) *Jesus in the Background of History; Cup of Life: A Short History of Post-Biblical Judaism*. Died 3 July 1982.

POLACK, Alfred Philip (1931) Born 13 August 1922, 35 Westbere Road, Hampstead, Middlesex; son of Philip Nathan Polack, Hair and Bristle Merchant, and Violet Sophie Jackson; m Joanna Maud Salaman; 1 son, 2 daughters. **Subject(s):** Modern and Medieval Languages; BA 1934; MA 1938. **Tutor(s):** C W Guillebaud. **Johnian Relatives:** father of Michael Philip Polack (1965). **Educ:** Stanwell House School, London; University College School, Junior Branch; University College School, Senior Branch. **Career:** Teacher, Wycliffe College, Gloucestershire 1935–1939; Raynes Park County Secondary School 1939–1940; Captain Intelligence Corps, WWII; Clifton College, Bristol 1946–1965; Senior Lecturer in Spanish, University of Bristol 1965–1978. **Awards:** Scholarship, SJC. Died 24 November 2003.

POLACK, Ernest Emanuel (1912) Born 25 February 1893, Hamburg House, Percival Road, Clifton, Bristol, Somerset; son of Joseph Polack, Schoolmaster and Minister, and Sophia Isaac. **Tutor(s):** E E Sikes. **Johnian Relatives:** brother of Albert Isaac Polack (1911). **Educ:** Clifton College. **Career:** Lieutenant, 4th (City of Bristol) Battalion, Gloucestershire Regiment until 1916. **Awards:** First John Stewart of Rannoch Scholarship, University of Cambridge 1912. Died 17 July 1916 (killed in action).

POLLARD, Martin John (1923) Born 24 November 1903, 148 Court Road, Barry, Glamorganshire; son of Henry Martin Pollard, Assistant Superintendent, Post Office, and Jane Eliza Levers; 2 sons, 1 daughter. **Subject(s):** Mathematics; BA 1926; MA 1930; BSc (Wales). **Tutor(s):** E Cunningham. **Educ:** Highfield School, Cardiff; Clark's College, Cardiff; Academy, Cardiff; University College of South Wales and Monmouthshire. **Career:** Lecturer, KCL 1928–1930; Lecturer 1930–1954, Associate Professor 1954, Cape Town University. **Appointments:** Churchwarden, St George's Cathedral, Cape Town; Warden, College House, Cape Town. **Awards:** Scholarship, SJC. Died March 1960.

POLLARD, The Revd Samuel Lister (1932) Born 21 April 1903, 25 Winston Terrace, Horton, Bradford; son of Fred Pollard, Clerk in Holy Orders, and Ida Jane Feather; BA (Montreal) 1929; MA (Montreal) 1930; LTh (Montreal) 1932. **Tutor(s):** E A Benians. **Educ:** Lincoln School; KCL; McGill University, Montreal; Diocesan Theological College, Montreal. **Career:** Anglican Clergy Training Scheme, Canada. **Awards:** Strathcona Exhibition, SJC 1932.

POLLARD, Professor Spencer Drummond (1934) Born 3 December 1910, 3033–16th NW, Washington, Columbia, USA; son of Frank Drummond Pollard, Auditor, Railway System, and Violetta Spencer. **Subject(s):** Economics; AB (Harvard) 1932; BLitt (Oxon) 1935. **Tutor(s):** C W Guillebaud. **Educ:** Central High School, Washington; Harvard University; Balliol College, Oxford. **Career:** Lieutenant, US Army Reserve; Tutor in Economics, Harvard 1936–1939; Director, Educational Film Institute, New York University 1939–1940; Assistant Professor of Economics, University of California 1941; National War Labour Board, California 1942–1946; Associate Professor of Economics, 1946–1960, Professor 1960–1976 (Emeritus 1976), University of California. **Appointments:** Labour Dispute Arbitrator, California. **Awards:** Rhodes Scholarship. **Publications:** *Understanding Capitalism: Can It Succeed?*, W Foulsham & Co, 1967. Died 1989.

POLLARD, William Marcus Noel (1909) Born 1 January 1890, Kilglas, Abbeyshrule, County Longford, Ireland; son of William Pollard, Clerk in Holy Orders, and Annie Benner. **Subject(s):** Theology; BA 1912. **Tutor(s):** L H K Bushe-Fox. **Educ:** Denstone College. **Career:** Master, Denstone College 1912–1916; Second Lieutenant, North Staffordshire Regiment (TF), WWI. **Awards:** Exhibition, SJC. Died 10 April 1917 (killed in action).

POLWHELE, Thomas Cecil (1919) Naval Officer.

PONISOWSKY, Alexander (1920) Born 26 December 1901; son of Mathieu Ponisowsky, Director, Siberian Textiles Company Ltd, and Malia Wilenkin. **Subject(s):** Economics; BA 1923. **Tutor(s):** E A Benians. **Educ:** Flioroff's Classical Gymnasium, Moscow, Russia; KCL.

PONNIAH, Benedict (1935) Born 11 January 1915, Klang Selangor, Federated Malay States; son of Anthony Bastian Ponniah, Government Pensioner, Medical Department, and Victoria Innasipillary. **Subject(s):** Law; BA 1938. **Tutor(s):** C W Guillebaud. **Educ:** Anglo-Chinese School, Klang; St Paul's Institution, Seremban; St John's Institution, Kuala Lumpur. **Awards:** Scholarship, SJC 1937.

POOLE, The Revd John Twells (1900) Born 6 September 1879, 13 Croft Street, Deptford, Kent; son of John Gough Poole, Clerk in Holy Orders, and Hanna Maria Lockhart; m Rosamund Allen Hunt, 1906 (d 1957). BA 1903; MA 1931. **Tutor(s):** E E Sikes. **Educ:** St John's School, Leatherhead. **Career:** Assistant Master, Darwen House School, Streatham 1897–1898; Assistant Master, Malton House School 1898–1899; Ordained Deacon 1903; Ordained Priest 1904; Chaplain, Bletchingley 1909–1915; Rector, Wilby with Hargham, Norfolk 1922–1940; Chaplain, Wayland Union 1929; Rector, South with North Lopham 1940–1949. Died 21 December 1965.

POORE, Robert (1924) Born 8 January 1904, Hanslope Park, Hanslope, Olney, Buckinghamshire; son of Mark Saurin Poore, Managing Director, Lovibonds Brewery, Greenwich, and Irene Watts. BA 1927. **Tutor(s):** B F Armitage. **Educ:** Sandroyd School, Cobham; Harrow School. **Career:** Landed Gentleman.

POPE, Alan Thomas (1943) Born 10 December 1925, 44 Fairlands Avenue, Thornton Heath, Surrey; son of Benjamin Thomas Pope, Bank Clerk, and Agnes Frances Ridley. **Tutor(s):** C W Guillebaud. **Educ:** Winterbourne School, Thornton Heath; Whitgift Middle School, Croydon.

POPE, Henry Alfred (1933) Born 5 March 1914, Ravenscroft, Ansdell, Lytham, Lancaster; son of Arthur Henry Pope, Manager of Cotton Mill, and Mary Alice Vose; m Elizabeth Hunter, 2 April 1951, St Mary's Church, Rostherne, Cheshire. **Subject(s):** History/Geography; BA 1936. **Tutor(s):** E A Benians. **Educ:** Edenfield Preparatory School, Lytham; King Edward VII School, Lytham.

POPE, The Revd Norman Christopher (1901) Born 26 April 1882, Park Row, Nottingham; son of William Pope, Clerk in Holy Orders, and Elizabeth Emily Wybrow; m Catherine Una Sturrock, 30 June 1910, Radipole. **Subject(s):** Theology; BA 1904; MA 1908. **Tutor(s):** D MacAlister. **Educ:** Nottingham High School. **Career:** Ordained Deacon 1905; Ordained Priest 1906; St Andrew, Kowloon, South China 1912–1918. **Awards:** John Stewart of Rannoch Scholarship in Hebrew, University of Cambridge 1902. Died 14 February 1918.

POPE, Randall West (1926) Born 5 August 1907, 2 Wallbutton Road, Greenwich, Kent; son of Thomas Michael Pope, Journalist, and Olive Constance Helen Lamprey. **Subject(s):** Mathematics/Mechanical Sciences; BA 1929. **Tutor(s):** J M Wordie. **Educ:** The Grammar School, Ashford; Colet Court; St Paul's School, London. **Awards:** Exhibition, SJC. Died 7 January 1930.

POPPLE, Major William Geoffrey (1935) Born 26 September 1915, 485 Bolton Road, Pendlebury, Manchester; son of Thomas Mills Popple, Physician and Surgeon, and Mary Jane Higgs. **Tutor(s):** R L Howland. **Educ:** Wadham House, Hale; Tonbridge School. **Career:** Indian Army, Mentioned in Despatches in Eritrea 1939–1945; Police Cadet, Tanganyika 1947. **Honours:** MC.

PORRI, Charles Joseph (1920) Born 9 May 1902, Churchfield Terrace, Skipton, York; son of Baldisaro Porri, Merchant, and Maria Grace Margaret Kendall. **Tutor(s):** E A Benians. **Educ:** Bishop's Court Preparatory School, Liverpool; Ampleforth College, York.

PORTEOUS, George Herbert (1928) Born 20 March 1909, Casa Colon, Huelva, Spain; son of George William Porteous, Civil Engineer, and Eliza Wilkinson. BA 1932. **Tutor(s):** J M Wordie. **Educ:** King's College Junior School, Wimbledon; King's College School, Wimbledon.

PORTER, John Mason (1941) Born 26 August 1921, Lodore, Coronation Road, Hoylake, Cheshire; son of John Porter, Director of Food Factory, and Amelia Elizabeth Bibby; m Nora Limb, 1947; 1 son, 1 daughter. **Subject(s):** Economics/History; BA 1944. **Tutor(s):** C W Guillebaud. **Educ:** Braeside Preparatory School; Rydal School, Colwyn Bay. **Career:** Company Director, Nelsons of Aintree. **Appointments:** JP.

PORTER, Laurence Stevenson (1930) Born 28 April 1912, 162 Coventry Road, Ilford, Essex; son of Thomas Linton Daniel Porter, Science Master, Ilford County High School, and Emily Stevenson; m Marion Winfield, 11 June 1939; 2 sons (John Winfield b 8 January 1943 and Michael Winfield b 7 July 1945), 1 daughter (Anne Winfield b 26 August 1947). **Subject(s):** Natural Sciences; BA 1933; MA 1937; BSc (London) 1934. **Tutor(s):** C W Guillebaud. **Johnian Relatives:** father of John Winfield Porter (1961). **Educ:** The County High School, Ilford; City of London School. **Career:** Staff Sergeant, REME, WWII; Principal, Crops, Feedingstuffs and Subsidies Division, Ministry of Agriculture 1951; Clerk, Agricultural Research Council. **Appointments:** National President, Wesley Guild 1972. **Awards:** Scholarship, SJC 1929; Methodist Local Preachers' Long Service Certificate 1977. **Honours:** OBE 1964. Died 4 March 1993.

PORTER, Thomas Henry (1900) Born 24 January 1881, The Cottage, Dulwich Wood Park, Surrey; son of Thomas Porter, Architect, and Henrietta Eliza Banks. **Subject(s):** Classics; BA 1903. **Tutor(s):** E E Sikes. **Educ:** The Grammar School, Great Yarmouth; Hereford Cathedral School. **Career:** Teacher, Hereford Cathedral School 1903–1911. **Publications:** *A Maid of the Malverns.* Died 18 February 1916.

POSNETT, Sir Richard Neil (1938) Born 19 July 1919, Kotagiri, India; son of Revd Charles Walker Posnett, Minister of Religion, and Phyllis Barker; m (1) Elisabeth Stiebel, 1947, (2) Shirley Margaret Hudson, 1959; (1) 2 sons, 1 daughter, (2) 2 sons, 1 daughter. **Subject(s):** Mathematics/Law; BA 1941; MA 1947. **Tutor(s):** J M Wordie. **Educ:** Earnseat School, Arnside; Kingswood School, Bath. **Career:** HM Colonial Administrative Service, Uganda 1941–1962; Called to the Bar, Gray's Inn 1951; Colonial Office, London 1958–1960; Judicial Adviser, Buganda 1960–1961; Permanent Secretary for External Affairs, Uganda 1962–1963; Permanent Secretary for Trade and Industry 1963; Foreign (subsequently Diplomatic) Service 1964–1980; UK Mission to UN, NY 1967–1970; HM Commissioner, Anguilla 1969; Head of West Indian Department, FCO 1970–1971; Governor and Commander in Chief, Belize 1972–1976; Special Mission to Ocean Island 1977; Dependent Territories Adviser, FCO 1977–1979; UK Commissioner, British Phosphate Commissioners 1978–1981; British High Commissioner, Kampala 1979; Governor and Commander in Chief, Bermuda 1981–1983; Member, Lord Chancellor's Panel of Independent Inspectors 1983–1989. **Appointments:** Captain, Athletic Club, SJC 1939–1940; Member, Eagle's Club, SJC; first ascent of South Portal Peak, Ruwenzori 1942; Chairman, Uganda Olympic Committee 1954–1958; Life Member, Royal Institute of International Affairs 1985; Member, Royal Commonwealth Society; Member, Royal African Society; Member, Royal Forestry Society; Governor, Broadwater School 1985–1988; President, Godalming-Joigny Friendship Association 1985; Governor, Kingswood School 1986–1993. **Awards:** Winner, Marshall Hall Golf Trophy for Johnians 1990. **Honours:** OBE 1963; KStJ 1973; CMG 1976; KBE 1980. **Publications:** *The Scent of Eucalyptus*, 2001.

POTHECARY, Brian Peter (1942) Born 22 December 1923, Astley Cottage, The Glade, Letchworth, Hertfordshire; son of Herbert Martin Rixsen Pothecary, Solicitor, and Madeline Druce; m 6 December 1958; 3 daughters (Susan, Frances and Sarah). **Subject(s):** Mechanical Sciences; BA 1945; MA 1957; MSc (Durham) 1950; CEng; FIAgrE. **Tutor(s):** S J Bailey. **Educ:** New Beacon Preparatory School, Sevenoaks; Marlborough College; University of Durham. **Career:** Captain, REME, served in the Sudan and Egypt 1945–1947; Senior Agricultural Engineer, HM Overseas Civil Service, Gold Coast 1950–1956; Export Manager, Ransomes, Sims & Jefferies Ltd, Ipswich 1956–1963; Agricultural Engineering Adviser, Sudan Gezira Board 1964–1968; Consultant in Overseas Agricultural Development 1968–1988.

POTSIOS, George (1947) Born 17 June 1929, Rome; son of Constantin Potsios, Film Director and Producer, and Thetis Sekeris; m Monique Laraque, 27 October 1956, Rome; 2 sons (Gian Paolo b 22 November 1959 and Andrea b 9 January 1964). **Subject(s):** Economics; BA 1950; MA 1954. **Tutor(s):** C W Guillebaud. **Educ:** Lycée Chateaubriand, Rome. **Career:** Banker and Company Director.

POTT, Richard Holliday (1929) Born 9 February 1910, 15 Bellasis Avenue, Streatham Hill, London; son of William John Hallings Pott, Wholesale Ironmongers Clerk, and Emily Elsie Andrews; m Catherine; 3 sons (Andrew, Richard and Michael), 1 daughter (Margaret). **Subject(s):** Natural Sciences; BA 1933; MA 1937. **Tutor(s):** J M Wordie. **Educ:** Tonbridge School. **Career:** Member, London Stock Exchange; Assistant Master, Bradfield College 1934. **Honours:** OBE. Died 6 February 1968.

POTTER, Basil Robert Russell (1942) Born 15 June 1924, The Vicarage, Datchet, Buckinghamshire; son of Thomas Reginald Russell Potter, Clerk in Holy Orders, and Elizabeth Dorothy Villar; m Suzette Goodwin, 16 June 1956. **Subject(s):** Mechanical Sciences; BA 1945; MA 1957. **Tutor(s):** S J Bailey. **Educ:** Rimpton, Broadstairs; Upland House, Crawley; Marlborough College. Died 19 September 1977.

POTTER, Professor George Richard (1919) Born 6 August 1900, 259 Dereham Road, Heigham, Norwich; son of George Potter, Schoolmaster, and Ellen Olley; m Rachel Leon; 1 son, 1 daughter. **Subject(s):** History;

BA 1922; MA 1926; PhD 1926. **Tutor(s):** E A Benians. **Educ:** King Edward VI Grammar School, Norwich. **Career:** RNVR 1918–1919; Head of History Department, University College, Leicester 1925–1927; Lecturer, Queen's University, Belfast 1927–1931; Professor of Modern History, University of Sheffield 1931–1965; Cultural Attaché, British Embassy in Bonn 1955–1957. **Appointments:** Vice-chairman, Universities Council for Adult Education 1938–1964; Member, Royal Commission on Historical Manuscripts 1953; President, Historical Association 1961–1964. **Awards:** Scholarship, SJC 1918; College Prize, SJC; Wright's Prize, SJC; Lightfoot Scholarship, University of Cambridge 1921; Amy Mary Preston Read Scholarship 1924. **Honours:** CBE 1977. **Publications:** *Biography of Zwingli*, CUP, 1976. Died 17 May 1981.

POTTER, The Revd Guy Anthony (1937) Born 21 October 1918, 22 Redcliffe Gardens, Ilford; son of William Harry Potter, Clerk, Imperial and International Communications, and Kathleen Mary Cole; m Yvonne Demuth, 1943; 2 sons (Michael b 1944 and Timothy b 1949), 1 daughter (Mary b 1945). **Subject(s):** Theology; BA 1940; MA 1944. **Tutor(s):** J S Boys Smith. **Educ:** Cranbrook Park School, Ilford; Merchant Taylors' School; Cuddesdon College, Oxford. **Career:** Curate, St John the Baptist, Moordown, Bournemouth 1941–1946; Vicar, Marton cum Grafton, Yorkshire 1946–1954; Vicar, Aldborough, Yorkshire (in Plurality) 1952–1954; Vicar, All Saints, Alton, Hampshire 1955–1964; Rector, St Botolph, Heene, Sussex; Rector, Black Notley, Essex. **Appointments:** Liveryman, Merchant Taylors' Company; Freeman, City of London; Chaplain, Black Notley Hospital. Died 18 October 1996.

POTTER, James Eric (1921) Born 2 July 1902, 2 Bay View Villas, Manstone Road, St Laurence, Ramsgate, Kent; son of Robert Pead Potter, Schoolmaster, and Eunice Simpson; m Elizabeth Wilhelmina de Mueller; 1 son (Christopher Robert b 21 November 1935), 1 daughter (Ann Elizabeth b 21 December 1933). **Subject(s):** Mathematics/Geography; BA 1925; MA 1959. **Tutor(s):** E Cunningham. **Johnian Relatives:** father of Christopher Robert Potter (1957). **Educ:** Monkton Elementary School, Ramsgate; Opspringe Elementary School, Faversham; Henry Wright Secondary School, Faversham. Died 2 October 1989.

POTTER, Wilfrid Dennis (1918) Born 1 May 1900, 65 Palace Road, Tulse Hill Park, Streatham, Surrey; son of Frederick Ezra Potter, Advertising Agent and Contractor, and Jessie Metcalf. **Tutor(s):** E E Sikes. **Educ:** The Leys, Cambridge; St Winifred's, Kenley.

POTTS, Arthur Reginald (1944) Born 27 November 1926, 115 Barnsley Road, Stairfoot, Barnsley; son of John Leonard Potts, Company Secretary, and Elsie Mary Ambler; m Elizabeth Meryon Rushbrook Williams, 23 December 1950, Silchester. **Subject(s):** History; BA 1949; MA 1951. **Tutor(s):** J M Wordie. **Educ:** St Mary's School, Barnsley; Barnsley and District Holgate Grammar School. **Appointments:** RN Cadet, SJC. Died 2 June 1999.

POULTER, Dennis Ross (1944) Born 16 October 1926, Westleigh, Devonshire Road, Davenport Park, Stockport, Cheshire; son of Eric Seymour Poulter, Dental Surgeon, and Amy Phyllis Winder; m Patricia Doreen Payne, 16 August 1952, St Michael's Church, Broadway, Worcestershire; 1 son (Robert John b 1958), 1 daughter (Valerie Ann b 1955). **Subject(s):** Mechanical Sciences; BA 1947; MA 1951; CEng; MIMechE. **Tutor(s):** S J Bailey. **Educ:** Glenwood School, Stockport; Stockport Grammar School. **Career:** Graduate Apprentice, General Electric Company, Witton, Birmingham and Frazer and Chalmers, Erith, Kent 1947–1949; Estates Department, General Electric Company, Witton 1949–1952; Ministry of Supply (Department of Atomic Energy), UKAEA, later AEA Technology 1952–1991. **Publications:** *The Design of Gas-cooled Graphite-moderated Reactors*, OUP, 1963; several technical papers on various topics.

POWDRILL, Ernest Joseph (1937) Born 20 February 1918, Arnesby, Lutterworth; son of Walter Powdrill, Sports Groundsman, and Florence Helen Killingley; m Joyce Green, 1946; 2 daughters (Jane Susan b 1947 and Mary Helen b 1951). **Subject(s):** Natural Sciences/Geography; BA 1940; MA 1944. **Tutor(s):** J M Wordie. **Educ:** Braunstone Church School; Hinckley Road Council School, Leicester; Alderman Newton's Boys' School, Leicester. **Career:** Commissioned, RAFVR Signals (Radar) Branch 1941; various posts associated with Night Fighter Airbourne Radar, Fighter Command, until 1946; final rank Squadron Leader; Assistant Physics Teacher, Latymer Upper School, Hammersmith 1946–1949; Head of Physics, Percy Jackson Grammar School, Doncaster 1949–1953; Head of Physics and Head of Science, Gateway School, Leicester 1954–1972; Deputy Headmaster, Gateway School 1972–1979; Part-time Physics Teacher, Brooke House Independent Sixth Form College, Market Harborough 1979–1985. **Awards:** Exhibition, SJC 1936; Foundation Scholarship, SJC 1939.

POWELL, Anthony George (1941) Born 21 March 1923, 22 Church Road, Malvern Link, Worcestershire; son of Walter Powell, Schoolmaster, and Elsie Myra Henningham. **Subject(s):** Modern and Medieval Languages. **Tutor(s):** C W Guillebaud. **Educ:** Malvern Link Council School; Worcester Royal Grammar School. **Career:** Captain, KSLI, attached Intelligence Corps in France and Belgium 1944.

POWELL, Arthur Henry Stephen (1934) Born 26 December 1911, The Vicarage, St John's Road, Dudley; son of Charles Thomas Powell, Vicar, and Beatrice Mary Izard. **Tutor(s):** R L Howland. **Educ:** Worcester Cathedral King's School; UCL.

POWELL, Evan Caradoc (1911) Born 6 December 1892, Hendre, Grosvenor Road, Wrexham, Denbighshire; son of John Evan Powell, Master Ironmonger, and Martha Williams. **Subject(s):** Law; BA 1914; LLB 1914. **Tutor(s):** J R Tanner. **Johnian Relatives:** son of Charles Thomas Powell (1892); brother of Valence Charles Powell (1921). **Educ:** County School, Wrexham. **Career:** Captain, Royal Welsh Fusiliers (wounded), WWI.

POWELL, John Douglas (1922) Born 4 August 1903, 2 Gloucester Road, Bristol, Gloucestershire; son of John Joseph Powell, Physician and Surgeon, and Edith Elizabeth Barber. **Tutor(s):** B F Armitage. **Educ:** Redland House School; Clifton College Junior School; Wycliffe College, Stonehouse.

POWELL, Oliver (1919) Born 4 July 1899, 51 Torrington Square, London; son of Oswald Byrom Powell, Schoolmaster, and Winifred Marion Cobb. **Tutor(s):** E E Sikes. **Educ:** Bedale's School, Petersfield; Army College, Keyham. **Career:** Midshipman, HMS *Thunderer* 1918–1919.

POWELL, The Revd Valence Charles (1921) Born 23 August 1903, 3 College Yard, Worcester; son of Charles Thomas Powell, Clerk in Holy Orders, and Beatrice Mary Izard. BA 1925; MA 1932. **Tutor(s):** E E Sikes. **Johnian Relatives:** son of Charles Thomas Powell (1892); brother of Arthur Henry Stephen Powell (1934). **Educ:** Worcester Cathedral King's School; Sarum Theological College. **Career:** Ordained Deacon 1927; Curate, St John the Baptist, Kidderminster 1927–1934; Ordained Priest 1928; Curate in charge, St Francis, Dudley 1934–1935; Vicar in charge, St Francis, Dudley 1935–1940. Died 18 March 1940.

POWER, Basil Dixon (1937) Born 11 November 1918, St Mark's Vicarage, Newcastle upon Tyne; son of Walter Sandiford Power, Vicar of Erdington, and Winifred May Gill Dixon; m Lorna Mary Edwards, 4 September 1946, Erdington Parish Church, Birmingham; 3 sons (Richard b 1948, Basil b 1950 and Donald b 1954). **Subject(s):** Mechanical Sciences; BA 1940; MA 1949; CEng; FIMechE. **Tutor(s):** J S Boys Smith. **Educ:** Central High School, Newcastle upon Tyne; Stanley House School, Edgbaston; St John's School, Leatherhead. **Career:** Research Scientist, W Edwards & Co Ltd, London 1946–1964; Manager of Technical Division, Edwards High Vacuum, Crawley 1964–1970; Technical Director, Edwards High Vacuum (part of BOC Ltd) 1970–1978; Consultant to Edwards High Vacuum 1978–1985. **Publications:** *High Vacuum Pumping Equipment*, Chapman and Hall, 1966; numerous technical papers.

POWER, Brigadier Guy Stuart O'Neill (1927) Born 16 April 1898, Plymouth; son of Guy Francis Thomas Power, Indian Civil Service, and Annie Edith Stuart; m Joan; 1 daughter (Caroline). **Subject(s):** Mechanical Sciences; BA 1929; MA 1946. **Tutor(s):** J M Wordie. **Educ:** Charterhouse; RMA, Woolwich. **Career:** Second Lieutenant, RE 1917; Lieutenant, RE 1918; Lieutenant, Signals 1920; Brigadier. **Honours:** CBE. Died 9 February 1982.

POWLESLAND, John (1943) Born 21 May 1926, 6 St James Street, Okehampton, Devon; son of Arthur George Powlesland, HM Customs and Excise, and Hilda Annie Hill; (1) Rita (d); (2) Ulli (div), (3) Janet; 4 sons (Peter, Dominic, Gregory and Aidan), 2 stepchildren. **Subject(s):** Mechanical Sciences; BA 1946; DIC 1948; AMICE 1951; MConsE; MICE 1967. **Tutor(s):** S J Bailey. **Johnian Relatives:** uncle of Jonathan Powlesland (1985) and of Katherine Lucy Powlesland (1987). **Educ:** St Chad's School, Bury; Leiston Junior Elementary School; Leiston Secondary School; Framlingham College; Imperial College, London (City and Guilds College). **Career:** Engineering Officer, RN (National Service), served in the Mediterranean on HMS *Phoebe* and on Motor Torpedo Boats 1946–1947; Assistant Engineer, Peter Lind & Co Ltd, Civil Engineers 1948–1956; Consulting Civil Engineer (Private Practice), Colchester 1956 until retirement. Died 6 July 2004.

POWNALL, Alan Joseph (1944) Born 26 November 1926, Moss Cottage, Manchester Road, Ashton-under-Lyne, Lancashire; son of Henry Pownall, High Court Registrar, and Phyllis Kidd; m Hilary Margaret Law, 1951; 1 son (David James b 1956), 1 daughter (Josephine b 1953). **Subject(s):** Mechanical Sciences; BA 1947; MA 1951; CEng; MICE 1954. **Tutor(s):** S J Bailey. **Educ:** Oak Bank Preparatory School, Fairfield, Manchester; Audenshaw Grammar School, Manchester; Sedbergh School. **Career:** Commissioned in RE 1947–1949; Site Engineer 1949–1957, Measurement Engineer 1957–1967, Head of Contracts Department 1967–1990, Edmund Nuttall Ltd. **Awards:** Wilson Chapel Reading Prize 1946.

PRADO-UCHÔA, Affonso (1922) Born 18 October 1903, São Paulo, Brazil; son of Flavio de Menonea Uchôa, Civil Engineer, President and Director of various Companies, and Evangelina da Silva Prado. **Tutor(s):** B F Armitage. **Educ:** Gymnasio Lusitano.

PRALLE, Ludwig Rudolf Eric (1914) Born 20 December 1896, Finchley, Middlesex; son of Friedrich August Pralle, Colonial Produce Broker, and Martha Chemnitz. **Tutor(s):** L H K Bushe-Fox. **Educ:** Etchingham Park School; Mill Hill School. **Career:** Captain, RAF, WWI; Produce Broker. **Honours:** AFC 1918.

PRASAD, Kamta (1915) Born 11 February 1890, Hajipore, Dist Muzaffarpur, India; son of Achay Kumar, Pleader. **Subject(s):** Mathematics/Natural Sciences; BA 1918. **Tutor(s):** R P Gregory. **Educ:** Zila School; Patna College, India; Presidency College, Calcutta.

PRATT, Geoffrey Wyatt (1911) Born 21 June 1892, 89 Wellington Road North, Heaton Norris, Stockport, Lancashire; son of Richard Pratt, Clerk in Holy Orders, and Kate Andrew. **Subject(s):** Natural Sciences; BA 1914; MA 1920. **Tutor(s):** J R Tanner. **Educ:** Denstone College. **Career:** Surgeon Lieutenant, RN, WWI.

PRECIOUS, Clifford Maxwell (1915) Born 9 August 1896, 16 Elvin Road, East Dereham, Norfolk; son of Henry Thomas Precious, Solicitor's Managing Clerk, and Mary Boon. BA 1921; MA 1926. **Tutor(s):** R P Gregory. **Educ:** Paston Grammar School; King Edward VII School, King's Lynn. **Career:** Private, Middlesex Regiment, WWI. Died 9 April 1959.

PREECE, Dr John Fryer (1946) Born 29 April 1928, 8 Pinhoe Road, Heavitree, Exeter; son of Trevor Meyrick Preece, Medical Practitioner, and Ruby Colvin Fryer. **Subject(s):** Natural Sciences; BA 1949; MA 1966; MB 1952; BChir 1952; DObstRCOG; MRCGP 1995. **Tutor(s):**

G C L Bertram. **Johnian Relatives:** son of Trevor Meyrick Preece (1919). **Educ:** Exeter School; Norwood School, Exeter; Sherborne School. **Career:** Medical Practitioner. **Appointments:** Honorary Research Fellow, Exeter University; Editor, *Practice Computing* Magazine. **Awards:** Shuter Scholarship, St Bartholomew's Hospital, London; Prox Accessit Brackenbury Scholarship in Medicine, St Bartholomew's Hospital. **Publications:** *The Use of Computers in General Practice*, Harcourt Health Sciences, 2000; various musical compositions, such as: *The Seafarer's Carol*; *Holy Cross Anthem*; *Song of Moses* (Anthem for Choir of Magdalene College, Cambridge); *Suite for Harp*; *Suite for Flute, Clarinet & Piano*; *Cello Octet Suite*; *Woodwind Quintet Suite*.

PREECE, Dr Trevor Meyrick (1919) Born 16 September 1896, 76 Hannah Street, Porth, Ystradyfodwg, Glamorganshire; son of John Preece, Ironmonger, and Margaret John; m Ruby Colvin Fryer; 1 son (John Fryer b 29 April 1928). **Subject(s):** Natural Sciences; BChir 1928; MB 1928. **Tutor(s):** E E Sikes. **Johnian Relatives:** father of John Fryer Preece (1946). **Educ:** King's College, Taunton; Rhonda County School; University College, Cardiff. **Career:** GP, Exeter; Chief Medical Officer, Devon and Cornwall Constabulary; Medical Officer, Exeter Area Postal Services; Prison Medical Officer, Exeter. Died 15 June 1981.

PREEN, Thomas Owen Phillip (1948) Born 27 January 1928, Sun Cottage, Cusop, Bredwardine, Herefordshire; son of Edward Harding Preen, Farm Labourer, and Blanche Lilian Thirza Price. BA 1950; MA 1955. **Tutor(s):** R L Howland. **Educ:** Hay Council School; Lucton School.

PRENTIS, Avon Ramsay Combe (1920) Naval Officer.

PRESCOTT, William Robert Stanley (1932) Born 25 April 1912, Allington House, White Hart Lane, Tottenham; son of William Henry Prescott, Barrister-at-Law, and Bessie Smith Stanley; m (1) Hilda Gwendoline Aldridge, 1939 (div 1951), (2) Sheila Walker Hewitt, 22 June 1951; (1) 1 son. **Subject(s):** Law; BA 1934. **Tutor(s):** C W Guillebaud. **Educ:** The Grammar School, Tottenham. **Career:** Called to the Bar, Gray's Inn 1935–1939; Captain, Royal Corps of Signals, West Africa 1939–1943; Conservative MP for Darwen; Member, Court of Common Council, City of London 1943–1951. Died 6 June 1962.

PRESS, Kenneth Peter (ALLPRESS) (1937) Born 27 March 1917, Dandry, Constitution Hill, Woking; son of William Edward Press, Civil Engineer, and Emily Salome Foot; m Joyce Owen Evans; 3 daughters (Jennifer, Judy and Patricia). **Subject(s):** History; BA 1940; MA 1944. **Tutor(s):** R L Howland. **Educ:** Private tuition. **Career:** Captain, RA 1940–1946; POW Germany, WWII; Chairman, William Press & Sons 1949–1968. **Appointments:** Chairman, Director or President of over 13 companies. Died 24 March 1968.

PREST, Charles Parrington (1918) Born 29 November 1898, 5 Fell Road, Croydon, Surrey; son of Charles Parrington Prest, Chartered Accountant, and Ada Louise Salvage; m Muriel Irene Williams, 28 July 1925, St Paul's Church, Sketty; 2 sons (Charles George Osborne b 1927 and Hugh Godfrey b 1930). **Subject(s):** Natural Sciences; BA 1920; MA 1926. **Tutor(s):** E E Sikes. **Johnian Relatives:** nephew of Edward Ernest Prest (1893); second cousin of Durward William John Cruickshank (1947). **Educ:** The Limes School, Croydon; Whitgift Grammar School, Croydon. **Career:** HM Senior Inspector of Taxes; Army 1917–1918. Died 13 January 1989.

PRESTON, The Revd John Martyn (1932) Born 6 March 1913, 47 Leylands Lane, Heaton, Bradford; son of William Easterbrook Preston, Director, Corporation Art Gallery and Museum, Bradford, and Mary Whittingham. **Subject(s):** History/Theology and Religious Studies; BA 1935; MA 1942; Queen's College, Birmingham 1935. **Tutor(s):** E A Benians. **Johnian Relatives:** brother-in-law of Peter Dudfield May (1931). **Educ:** Rossefield Preparatory School, Heaton, Bradford; Private School, Bradford; The Grammar School, Bradford. **Career:** Ordained

Deacon, Diocese of Birmingham 1936; Curate, Langley, Birmingham 1936; Ordained Priest 1937; Inspector of Church Schools, Diocese of Sheffield 1968–1972. **Appointments:** Editor, *The Eagle*, for two years. **Awards:** Scholarship, SJC. Died 7 June 1995.

PRESTON, Dr Joseph Henry (1946) Born 1 March 1911, Swinescales, Hutton Soil, Greystoke, Cumberland; son of William Preston, Farmer, and Jean Dufton. MA 1946; BSc (London) 1932; PhD 1936; CEng; FRAeS. **Educ:** Bampton Endowed School; Queen Elizabeth Grammar School, Penrith; Queen Mary College, University of London. **Career:** University Lecturer in Aeronautics; Aero Division, National Physical Laboratory, Teddington 1938–1946; Reader in Aeronautics 1954; Professor of Fluid Mechanics, University of Liverpool 1955–1976. **Appointments:** Fellow, Queen Mary College, London. Died 28 July 1985.

PRESTT, Dr John (1942) Born 1 April 1924, 10 St Malo Road, Wigan, Lancashire; son of James Prestt, Provision Merchant, and Alice Ina Hesketh Wilkie. **Subject(s):** Natural Sciences; BA 1945; MA 1949; MB 1948; BChir 1948; MRCS, LRCP. **Tutor(s):** S J Bailey. **Johnian Relatives:** brother of Peter Prestt (1949); uncle of Karina Prestt (1992). **Educ:** Woodfield Preparatory School, Wigan; Huyton Hill Preparatory School, Liverpool; Oundle School. Died 23 September 1989.

PRESTT, Peter (1949) Born 1 June 1929, 20 Park Road, Southport, Lancashire; son of James Prestt, Grocer, and Alice Ina Hesketh Wilkie; m Christa Anna Kathe Skairies; 1 daughter (Karina b 24 August 1974). BA 1952. **Tutor(s):** C W Guillebaud. **Johnian Relatives:** brother of John Prestt (1942); father of Karina Prestt (1992). **Educ:** Wesleyan Secondary School; Wigan Grammar School; Oundle School. **Career:** Lance Corporal, Royal Marines; Company Director.

PRESTWICH, Professor Mark Fiennes (1929) Born 18 March 1911, 86 Steven Street, Stretford, Lancashire; son of Edgar Alfred Prestwich, Draughtsman to Constructional Engineers, and Mabel Alice Gibson; m Rose Vorster, 1948; 4 children. **Subject(s):** History; BA 1932; MA 1961. **Tutor(s):** E A Benians. **Educ:** Secondary School, Todmorden; Secondary School, Elland. **Career:** Lecturer in History, University of Natal 1938–1952; Lecturer in History, Department of Extra-Mural Studies, Queen's University, Belfast 1952–1953; Editor, *Natal Witness* 1953–1956 (continued to write leading articles for the newspaper until 1961); Senior Lecturer in History and Political Science 1957–1963, Professor, and Head of Department of History and Political Science 1963–1976, University of Natal. **Appointments:** Council Member, Natal Society Library. **Awards:** Scholarship, SJC; Sizarship, SJC; Naden Studentship, SJC 1933, 1934; Le Bas Prize, University of Cambridge 1935. Died 18 March 1985.

PRETHEROE, Edward Owen (1918) Born 23 March 1896, 17 Queen's Road, Bury St Edmunds, Suffolk; son of Edward Andress Pretheroe, Schoolmaster, and Mary Alice Douthwaite. **Subject(s):** Law; BA 1920; LLB 1920. **Tutor(s):** E E Sikes. **Educ:** Banham Grammar School; Thetford Grammar School. **Career:** Crown Council, Colonial Legal Service, Nigeria; Called to the Bar, Gray's Inn 1921; Puisne Judge, Federation of Malaya 1951. Died 4 August 1962.

PREVITÉ ORTON, Professor Charles William (1905) Born 16 January 1877, Arnesby, Leicestershire; son of William Previté Orton, Clerk in Holy Orders, and Eliza Shaffield Orton; m Ellery Swaffield Orton, 17 June 1913, Heen Parish Church; 1 daughter (Rosalind). **Subject(s):** History; BA 1908; MA 1912; LittD 1928; FBA 1929. **Tutor(s):** C E Graves; J R Tanner. **Johnian Relatives:** son of William Previté Orton (1856); brother of Kennedy Joseph Previté Orton (1891). **Educ:** Franklins Preparatory School, Stoneygate; UCL. **Career:** Beresford Fellow 1911–1917, Ashton Fellow 1925–1928, Librarian 1916–1937, Title E Fellow 1928–1932, Title B Fellow 1932–1937, Title C Fellow 1937–1942, Title E Fellow 1942–1947, SJC; Lecturer in History 1929–1937, First Professor of Medieval History 1937–1942, University

of Cambridge. **Appointments:** Praelector 1917–1926, Supervisor in History 1919–1937, Director of Studies in History 1933–1937, SJC; Editor, *The Eagle*; Editor, *English Historical Review* 1926–1938. **Awards:** Scholarship, SJC 1907–1909; Gladstone Memorial Prize, University of Cambridge 1907; Member's History Prize 1908. **Publications:** *Political Satire in English Poetry*, 1910; *The Early History of the House of Savoy*, 1912; *The Defensor Pacis of Marsilius of Padua*, 1928; *The History of Europe, 1198–1378*; Contributions to *Cambridge History of English Literature*, *Cambridge Medieval History* and *English Historical Review*. Died 11 March 1947.

PRICE, Arthur John Brownlow (1941) Born 26 October 1924, 31 Stamford Hill Mansions, Stamford Hill, London; son of Arthur Uvedale Brownlow Price, Civil Servant, and Marjorie Wynn Dyke. BA 1944; MA 1948. **Tutor(s):** S J Bailey. **Educ:** New College, Winchmore Hill; Mercers' School, Holborn; King's School, Ely. **Career:** Management Consultant. Died 28 May 1974.

PRICE, Dr Bernard Henry (1932) Born 27 January 1913, Calabar College, Slipe Pen Road, Kingston, Jamaica; son of Ernest Price, Headmaster, Calabar College, and Edith Letitia Woodward; BA 1935; BChir 1938; MB 1938; MRCS, LRCP. **Tutor(s):** R L Howland. **Johnian Relatives:** brother of Ernest Woodward Price (1926) and of Neville George Price (1928). **Educ:** The High School, Calabar, Jamaica. **Career:** Consultant Surgeon, Selly Oak Hospital, Birmingham; Major, RAMC; Lecturer in Anatomy, Birmingham University 1940–1943. **Honours:** MBE 1946.

PRICE, Edgar Hubert (1934) Born 12 October 1915, 8 Broadway Parade, Hornsey, Middlesex; son of Edgar Sydney Price, Assistant Paymaster, RN, and Gertrude Susan Barsted. **Subject(s):** History; BA 1937. **Tutor(s):** J S Boys Smith. **Educ:** Priory School, Hornsey; Taplow School; Christ's Hospital, Horsham. **Awards:** Sizarship, SJC.

PRICE, Dr Ernest Woodward (1926) Born 20 July 1907, 14 Steade Road, Ecclesall Bierlow, Sheffield, Yorkshire; son of Ernest Price, Baptist Minister and Headmaster, Calabar College, and Edith Letitia Woodward. **Subject(s):** Natural Sciences; BA 1929; MA 1933; BChir 1933; MB 1934; FRCSE 1947. **Tutor(s):** J M Wordie. **Johnian Relatives:** brother of Neville George Price (1928) and of Bernard Henry Price (1932). **Educ:** Mrs McHardy's Preparatory School, Kingston, Jamaica; Calabar High School, Jamaica; Wolmer's School, Kingston, Jamaica. **Career:** Consultant Bacteriologist, Birmingham Hospital Group 1959.

PRICE, Geoffrey Arthur (1936) Born 14 May 1918, Rose Bank, Chester Road, Northwich, Cheshire; son of William Price, Merchant, and Jessie Brockley; m Isobel Cecilia Fixter; 1 son, 2 daughters. **Subject(s):** Economics/Law; BA 1939; MA 1979. **Tutor(s):** J M Wordie. **Educ:** Heysoms College, Northwich; St Chad's, Prestatyn; Uppingham School. **Career:** Director, Firet NV (Holland) 1958–1969; Director, Tootal Broadhurst Lee Co Ltd 1959–1964; Director, Lantor Ltd 1963–1969; Chairman and Managing Director, Research and Industrial Property Division, Chairman Worsted Division, English Calico Ltd 1964–1969; Director of Corporate Legal Affairs, the Tootal Group plc 1969–1979.

PRICE, Neville George (1928) Born 26 May 1909, 37 Steade Road, Sheffield; son of Ernest Price, Baptist Minister and Schoolmaster, and Edith Letitia Woodward. **Subject(s):** Archaeology and Anthropology/Modern and Medieval Languages; BA 1933; MA 1936. **Tutor(s):** M P Charlesworth. **Johnian Relatives:** brother of Ernest Woodward Price (1926) and of Bernard Henry Price (1932). **Educ:** Calabar High School.

PRICE, Norman Jeredick (1908) Born 29 December 1888, 23 Stafford Street, Wednesbury, Staffordshire; son of Thomas Price, Schoolmaster, and Mary Ann Slater. **Subject(s):** Mathematics/Natural Sciences; BA 1911. **Tutor(s):** J R Tanner. **Educ:** King Edward's School. **Awards:** Scholarship, SJC.

PRICE SMITH, Roy David (1936) Born 23 November 1917, 11 Culverden Road, Balham, London; son of Roy Thomas Price Smith, Engineer, and Catharine Lloyd Dear. BA 1939; MA 1943. **Tutor(s):** R L Howland. **Educ:** St Paul's Cathedral Choir School; Haileybury College; Royal Academy of Music.

PRICHARD, The Revd Reginald Moreton (1914) (admitted to Selwyn College 1913) Born 25 July 1892, 31 London Road, Stoke-on-Trent, Staffordshire; son of Robert Moreton Prichard, Bank Manager, and Gertrude Malkin. BA 1916; MA 1920. **Tutor(s):** E E Sikes. **Educ:** Haverfordwest Grammar School; Wycliffe College, Stonehouse; The Leys School, Cambridge. **Career:** Second Lieutenant, Cheshire Regiment, WWI; Deacon, then Priest, Exeter 1917–1918; Curate, St Andrew, Plymouth 1917–1919; Curate, St Matthias, Torquay 1919–1921; Chaplain to the Bishop of St Edmundsbury and Ipswich 1922–1923; Secretary to the Bishop of Bradford, to the Diocesan Board of Finance, and Diocesan Inspector of Schools, Bradford 1923–1927; Vicar, St Wilfrid, Lidget Green, Bradford 1924–1927. Died 9 April 1927.

PRIDEAUX, Henry Sydney (1901) Born 16 December 1882, Basset Street, Camborne, Cornwall; son of Henry Prideaux, Gentleman, and Mary Maria Hick. BA 1907. **Tutor(s):** D MacAlister. **Educ:** Truro College. **Career:** Lieutenant, Duke of Cornwall's Light Infantry, WWI.

PRIDEAUX, John Kenneth Reginald (1935) Born 22 November 1916, 5 Vyvyan Terrace, Clifton, Bristol; son of William Reginald Bray Prideaux, Captain, 12th Royal Berkshire Regiment, Librarian, and Ruth Ford. **Subject(s):** Economics/Law; BA 1938. **Tutor(s):** C W Guillebaud. **Educ:** Horton School, Ickwell Bury, Biggleswade; Rugby School.

PRIESTLEY, Professor Charles Henry Brian (1934) Born 8 July 1915, 40 Southwood Avenue, Highgate; son of Thomas Gordon Priestley, Mantle Manufacturer, and Muriel Brown; m Constance Tweedy, 26 March 1946, Seghill, Northumberland; 1 son, 2 daughters. **Subject(s):** Mathematics/Economics; BA 1937; MA 1942; ScD 1953; Honorary DSc (Monash) 1981; FAA 1954; FRS 1967; FInstP. **Tutor(s):** J M Wordie. **Educ:** Beaumont House Preparatory School, Heronsgate; Mill Hill School, London. **Career:** Meteorological Office, Air Ministry 1939–1946; Chief, Division of Meteorological Physics 1946–1972; Chairman, CSIRO Environmental Physics Research Laboratories 1973–1977; Professor of Meteorology, Monash University, Australia 1978–1980; Chairman, La Trobe Valley Airshed Study 1980–1990. **Appointments:** Member Executive Committee, International Association of Meteorology 1954–1960; Vice-President, Australian Academy of Science 1959–1960; Member, Advisory Committee, World Meteorological Organisation 1964–1968 (Chairman 1967); Vice-President, International Association of Meteorology 1967–1975; Honorary Member, American Meteorological Society 1978; Honorary Life Fellow, Royal Meteorological Society 1978. **Awards:** Baylis Scholarship, SJC 1933; Adams Memorial Prize, SJC 1937; Mayhew Prize, University of Cambridge 1937; Hughes Prize, SJC 1937; David Syme Prize, University of Melbourne 1956; International Meteorological Organisation Prize 1973; Symons Medal, Royal Meteorological Society 1967; Buchan Prize, Royal Meteorological Society 1950; Rossby Medal, American Meteorological Society 1975. **Honours:** AO 1976. **Publications:** *Turbulent Transfer in the Lower Atmosphere*, 1959; around 60 papers in scientific journals. Died 18 May 1998.

PRIESTMAN, Professor Bryan (1920) Born 10 March 1897, 29 Beaufort Street, Chelsea, Middlesex; son of Bertram Priestman, Artist, and Grace Henwood. **Subject(s):** Mathematics/Natural Sciences; BA 1923; MA 1938; PhD. **Tutor(s):** B F Armitage. **Educ:** Norland Place School, London; Kensington Preparatory School; The Downs School, Colwall; Bootham School, York; UCL. **Career:** Professor of Physics, University of New Brunswick. Died 11 November 1945.

PRINCE, James Edmund (1928) Born 17 February 1909, Ivy Dene, Beverley Road, Hessle, Hull, Yorkshire; son of Stanley Prince, Mechanical Engineer, and Agnes Greening. **Subject(s):** Mathematics/

Mechanical Sciences; BA 1931. **Tutor(s):** J M Wordie. **Educ:** The Weir School; Hymers College, Hull.

PRINGLE, Air Marshal Sir Charles Norman Seton (1937) Born 6 June 1919, Irish Counties War Hospital, Glasnevin, Dublin; son of Seton Sydney Pringle, Surgeon, and Ethel Louisa McMunn, Nurse; m Margaret Elisabeth Sharp, 21 September 1946, St Barnabas Church, Heaton; 1 son (Andrew Charles Seton b 1949). BA 1940; MA 1947; CBIM; FRAeS 1963; CIMgt; FREng 1977; Hon FRAeS 1989. **Tutor(s):** J S Boys Smith. **Educ:** Castle Park School, Dalkey, Ireland; Repton School. **Career:** Commissioned into RAF 1941; Service in India and Ceylon 1942–1946; Air Ministry 1946–1948; RAE, Farnborough 1949–1950; Exchange Officer, US Air Force, Wright Patterson Air Force Base 1950–1952; Senior Technical Staff Officer No 3 Group, Bomber Command 1960–1962; Air Forces Middle East 1962–1964; Commandant, RAF St Athan and Air Officer, Wales 1964–1966; Ministry of Defence 1967; Imperial Defence College 1968; Director General of Engineering, RAF, Ministry of Defence 1969–1970; Air Officer Engineering, Strike Command 1970–1973; Controller, Engineering and Supply, RAF 1973–1976; Senior Executive, Rolls Royce Ltd 1976–1978; Director, Hunting Engineering Ltd 1976–1979; Director and Chief Executive, Society of British Aerospace Companies Ltd 1979–1984; Director, FR Group plc 1985–1989. **Appointments:** Honorary Secretary, Cambridge University Auto Club 1938–1940; President, Royal Aeronautical Society 1975–1976; Vice-Chairman, Council of Engineering Institutions 1976–1977; Chairman, Council of Engineering Institutions 1977–1978; Council Member, RSA 1978–1983 and 1986–1992; Council Member, CBI 1979–1984; Chairman of Governors, Repton School 1985–1992. **Honours:** CBE 1967; KBE 1973.

PRINGLE, John (1930) Born 20 August 1904, Cliffe House, Honley, Huddersfield; son of William Henderson Pringle, Barrister-at-Law, and Annie Nelson Forrest; m Jacqueline; 3 sons (Robin, Bill and Christopher). MA (Edinburgh) 1929. **Tutor(s):** E A Benians. **Educ:** Preparatory School, Harrow; City of London School; Otago High School, Dunedin, New Zealand; City of London School; University of Edinburgh. **Career:** Leader Writer, *Manchester Guardian*; Talks Producer, BBC; Deputy Editor, *The Listener* 1939–1945; Founder and President, National Schizophrenia Fellowship 1970. Died 29 March 1984.

PRINGLE, Norman Douglas (1902) Born 16 April 1883, Angeltown, Bridgend, Glamorgan; son of Henry Turnbull Pringle, Medical Superintendent, and Jessie Isabella Smith. **Tutor(s):** D MacAlister. **Educ:** I A E Tillyard's, May Place; James Hardie's, Holland Park.

PRIOR, Arthur Deane (1943) Born 17 May 1925, 17 Evelyn Terrace, Port Talbot, Glamorganshire; son of Arthur William Prior, Heating Engineer, and Jessie Bona. **Tutor(s):** S J Bailey. **Educ:** Corporation Road School, Newport; Sefton Park School, Bristol; Severn Road School, Cardiff; Canton High School, Cardiff.

PRIOR, Professor Oliver Herbert Phelps (1919) Born 6 September 1871, Vevey, Switzerland; son of William Phelps Prior, Clerk in Holy Orders, British Chaplain at Vevey, and Marie Louise de Laferrière; m Camille Mottu; 1 son. MA 1919; Docteur ès Lettres (Lausanne) 1913; Honorary DLitt (Durham). **Educ:** University of Lausanne, Switzerland; Collège St Michel, Fribourg, Switzerland. **Career:** Lecturer in Anglo-Norman, UCL; Assistant Master, Forest School 1892–1895; Schoolmaster, Berkhamsted School 1895–1897; Schoolmaster, Rugby School 1902–1919; Substitute for Professor of Romance Languages, University of London 1915–1919; Foundress Fellow, SJC 1919–1934; Drapers Professor of French, University of Cambridge 1919–1934. **Honours:** Chevalier de la Legion d'Honneur. **Publications:** *L'Image du monde de Maitre Gossuin*, 1913; *Caxton's Mirror of the World*, 1914; *French Studies and France*. Died 18 July 1934.

PROBERT, Eric Victor (1946) Born 16 November 1924, 10 Meldon Terrace, Newcastle upon Tyne; son of Ralph Ernest Probert,

Commercial Traveller, and Ada Olive Bulmer. **Subject(s):** Natural Sciences; BA 1949. **Tutor(s):** G C L Bertram. **Educ:** Chillingham Road Elementary School, Newcastle; West Jesmond Elementary School; Royal Grammar School, Newcastle upon Tyne.

PROCTER, John Tyndale (1930) Born 24 January 1913, Cherry Hill House, York; son of Tyndale Procter, Chemical Manufacturer and Agricultural Merchant, and Emily Vasie Adams; m Helen. **Subject(s):** Natural Sciences. **Tutor(s):** J M Wordie. **Educ:** Mount Junior High School, York; Terrington Preparatory School; Bootham School, York. Died 27 January 1989.

PROCTOR, Maurice Faraday (1920) Born 31 March 1901, 11 Caledonia Place, Clifton, Bristol; son of Harold Faraday Proctor, City Electrical Engineer and General Manager, and Amy Peckett. **Subject(s):** Natural Sciences; BA 1923; MA 1927. **Tutor(s):** B F Armitage. **Educ:** Clifton College, Preparatory School; Clifton College, Junior School; Clifton College, Upper School. **Awards:** Exhibition, SJC 1919.

PROSSER, John Michael (1945) Born 16 March 1927, 126 Bunbury Road, Northfield, Birmingham; son of Cyril Ernest Prosser, Sales Manager, Metal Company, and Elsie Florence Pendleton; m Rosemary Ann Hopper, 1955, Edgbaston Old Church, Birmingham; 2 sons (Richard Julian b 1956, d 1986 and Simon John b 1958), 1 daughter (Janet Louise b 1961). **Subject(s):** History; BA 1950; MA 1952; FCA. **Tutor(s):** J M Wordie. **Johnian Relatives:** father of Simon John Prosser (1977). **Educ:** Harborne Collegiate School, Birmingham; Uppingham School; AMP Harvard Business School. **Career:** Managing Director, Tucker Fasteners Ltd, Birmingham. **Appointments:** Honorary Secretary, JCR; President, Moseley Rugby Club 1981–1982. **Awards:** Major Scholarship, SJC; Johnson Exhibition, SJC 1944.

PROUD, Stanley (1932) Born 8 December 1913, Ameston Hall, Elwick Hall, Greatham, Durham; son of Herbert Hardy Proud, Officer of HM Customs and Excise, and Barbara Ethel Sanderson; m Ross. **Subject(s):** Mathematics; BA 1935. **Tutor(s):** J M Wordie. **Educ:** Temple School, Middlesex; The County School, Harrow; The County School, Stockton-on-Tees. **Career:** Meteorological Office; Meteorologist, Imperial Airways, in charge of staff at Foynes, later stationed at Hythe, Southampton 1935–1939; Flight Lieutenant, RAFVR 1939–1942. **Awards:** Sizarship, SJC. Died 1942 (lost at sea while on meteorological work).

PROUDLOCK, Robin (1911) Born 12 June 1892, Sawston, Cambridgeshire; son of William Proudlock, Engineer, and Agnes Marion Stewart. **Subject(s):** Modern and Medieval Languages; LLB 1914. **Tutor(s):** E E Sikes. **Educ:** Perse School. **Career:** Indian Railways 1914.

PROUTY, Professor Charles Tyler (1931) Born 30 May 1909, The Portner, 15th Street, Washington, USA; son of Ward Prouty, Clerk, and Claire Eleanor Streeter; m Ruth Patterson Belew. **Subject(s):** English; BA 1933; MA 1938; PhD 1939; BA (Dartmouth College) 1931. **Tutor(s):** E A Benians. **Educ:** Springfield Central High School, Massachusetts; Dartmouth College, New Hampshire. **Career:** Research Fellow, Folger and Member of English Faculty, Missouri 1939–1940; Research Analyst, War Department (Commendation for Meritorious Civilian Service) 1939–1945; Professor of English, Yale University 1948–1974. **Appointments:** Trustee, American Shakespeare Theater 1956; Fellow, Royal Society of Literature. **Publications:** General Editor, Yale Editions, Works of Shakespeare, 1954; (ed) *Much Ado About Nothing*, New York, 1948; *The Sources of Much Ado About Nothing: A Critical Study*, New Haven, 1950; *The Contention and Shakespeare's Two Henry VI's*, Oxford, 1954. Died 10 May 1974.

PROWDE, Gordon Longstaff (1941) Born 14 July 1922, 14 Azalea Avenue, Sunderland; son of Henry Gordon Prowde, Shipowner, and Ella Eliza Craighill. BA 1944. **Tutor(s):** S J Bailey. **Johnian Relatives:** nephew of Oswald Longstaff Prowde (1901). **Educ:** Polam Hall School,

Darlington; Grammar School, Darlington; Clifton House, Harrogate; Wedderburn, Harrogate. **Career:** Production Efficiency Staff, Messrs Rowntree, York 1950.

PROWDE, Oswald Longstaff (1901) Born 22 May 1882, Melsonby, Yorkshire; son of Edwin Longstaff Prowde, Bachelor of Medicine, and Elizabeth Porteous. **Subject(s):** Mechanical Sciences; BA 1904. **Tutor(s):** C E Graves; J R Tanner. **Johnian Relatives:** uncle of Gordon Longstaff Prowde (1941). **Educ:** Pocklington School. **Career:** worked on Gezira irrigation scheme on heightening of Aswan Dam, Egyptian Government Irrigation Service 1905–1925; Partner, Murdoch MacDonald and Partners, Civil Engineers; worked on Whitehaven Harbour, Brora hydro-electric works, River Great Ouse Flood Protection Scheme 1926. **Awards:** Telford Gold Medal (Civil Engineering Award) 1925. **Honours:** Order of the Nile; Order of Ismail; Order of Mejidieh; CMG. Died 5 November 1949.

PRYNNE, Major General Michael Whitworth (1932) Born 1 April 1912, The Secretary's Lodge, Bisley Camp, Pirbright, Guildford; son of Alan Lockyer Prynne, Lieutenant Colonel, Royal Marine Artillery, and Jeanette Annie Crosse; m Jean Violet Stewart, 1940; 1 son (Andrew), 3 daughters (Bridget, Caroline and Celia). BA 1934; MA 1964. **Tutor(s):** J S Boys Smith. **Educ:** St Edward's, Broadstairs; Bedford School; RMA, Woolwich. **Career:** Commissioned, RE 1932–1969; Military Attaché, Moscow 1951–1953; Deputy Director, War Office 1960; Chief of Staff, Headquarters, Southern Command 1969; Secretary, Association of Consulting Engineers 1969–1977. **Honours:** CB; CBE. Died 27 September 1977.

PRYTHERCH, Dr Robert Rees (1926) Born 17 January 1908, Monfa, Llangefni, Anglesey; son of John Rowland Prytherch, Physician, and Lowri Thomas; m Margaret; 2 daughters. BA 1929; MA 1937; MRCS (King's College Hospital) 1933; MRCGP; LRCP (King's College Hospital) 1933. **Tutor(s):** M P Charlesworth. **Educ:** Llangefni Council School; Friars School, Bangor. **Career:** GP, Criccieth 1937; Organiser, South Caernarvonshire Blood Transfusion Service, WWII. **Appointments:** High Sherriff, Caernarvonshire 1961–1962; Fellow, BMA 1968. Died 7 April 1976.

PUDDICOMBE, Donald Ramsay (1914) Born 12 November 1894, Regent House, 690 High Road, Leytonstone, Essex; son of Robert Westacott Puddicombe, Draper and Outfitter, and Isabella Reid Ramsay. **Tutor(s):** E E Sikes. **Johnian Relatives:** brother of William Ewart Puddicombe (1916). **Educ:** Wanstead College, Woodford; Scarborough College. **Career:** Second Lieutenant, East Yorkshire Regiment, Egypt then France, WWI. Died 26 July 1916 (of wounds received in action on the Somme 20 July 1916).

PUDDICOMBE, William Ewart (1916) Born 13 May 1898, Regent House, 690 High Road, Leytonstone, Essex; son of Robert Westacott Puddicombe, Draper and Outfitter, and Isabella Reid Ramsay; m Gwendoline. **Subject(s):** Economics/Law; BA 1921; MA 1978; LLB 1921. **Tutor(s):** E E Sikes. **Johnian Relatives:** brother of Donald Ramsay Puddicombe (1914). **Educ:** Scarborough College; Manshead College, Snaresbrook. **Career:** Partner, R W and I Puddicombe Ltd, Furriers and Milliners, Leytonstone. Died 28 August 1979.

PULLAN, Edward John McDonnell (1925) Born 19 June 1907, 38 Manor Park, Lee, Lewisham, Kent; son of Harry Pullan, Hotel Proprietor, and Matilda McDonnell. **Subject(s):** Moral Sciences, English; BA 1928; MA 1935. **Tutor(s):** E A Benians. **Johnian Relatives:** son of Harry Pullan (1887). **Educ:** Eastman's School, Portsmouth; Bembridge School, Isle of Wight.

PULLAN, Dr George Thomas (1946) Born 1 February 1929, Commercial Street, Tadcaster, Yorkshire; son of Thomas Noble Pullan, Brewer's Labourer, and Alice Leadley; m Audrey Lilian Abbott, 20 June 1953, St Paul's United Church, Toronto. **Subject(s):** Physics; BA 1949; MA

1953; PhD 1952. **Tutor(s):** G C L Bertram. **Educ:** Tadcaster Council School; Tadcaster Grammar School. **Career:** Research Fellow, National Research Council of Canada, University of Toronto 1952–1954; Senior Scientific Officer, National Physical Laboratory, Teddington 1954–1956; Sundry scientific appointments, Department of National Defence, Canada 1956–1984. **Awards:** Major Scholarship, SJC 1945; Wright's Prize, SJC 1947, 1948 and 1949; Hockin Prize, SJC 1949.

PULLIN, Captain Denis Herbert (1925) Born 8 January 1907, Alfriston, Hills Road, Cambridge; son of Albert Edward Pullin, Bank Manager, and Margaret Edith Erskine; m Margaret Eleanor Tanner, 2 June 1932, St Mary's Church, Shrewsbury; 1 son (Denis John b 21 March 1933), 1 daughter (Margaret Jane b 24 June 1935). **Subject(s):** Law; BA 1928; MA 1932; LLB 1929. **Tutor(s):** E A Benians. **Educ:** Kingsland Grange Preparatory School; Shrewsbury School. **Career:** Solicitor, Norfolk County Council 1932–1935, then Devon County Council 1935–1940; Royal Artillery, including service in North Africa and Sicily 1940–1944. Died 14 June 1944 (of wounds received in action in Normandy).

PULLIN, John Henton (1912) Born 16 December 1893, Elton House, Darlington, County Durham; son of William Henton Pullin, Pharmaceutical Chemist, and Emily Maria Smith. **Tutor(s):** E E Sikes. **Educ:** Bedford Grammar School. **Career:** Second Lieutenant, 8th Battalion, The King's Own Royal Lancashire Regiment, later transferred to Loyal North Lancashire Regiment 1914–1916. Died 21 January 1916 (of wounds received in action near Armentières 19 January 1916).

PURDY, Charles Edward (1924) Born 3 November 1905, 23 Intake Lane, Batley, Yorkshire; son of Erasmus Purdy, Property Owner, and Ann Gledhill. **Tutor(s):** B F Armitage. **Educ:** Brownhill School, Batley; The Grammar School, Batley.

PYBUS, Michael (1941) Born 27 March 1922, Longbenton, Northumberland; son of Robert Pybus, Commercial Representative, and Doris Kathleen Vickers. **Subject(s):** History; BA 1947; MA 1970; PGCE. **Tutor(s):** C W Guillebaud. **Educ:** Westgate Hill Council School, Newcastle upon Tyne; The Royal Grammar School, Newcastle upon Tyne. **Career:** Schoolteacher; Headmaster, Hassocks School. **Awards:** Minor Scholarship, SJC 1940. Died 15 February 1998.

PYE, Harold John (1920) Born 27 November 1901, 19 Humberstone Road, Chesterton, Cambridge; son of William George Pye, Scientific Instrument Manufacturer, and Annie Eliza Atkins; m Jennie Garner Milson, 1 March 1927, St James' Parish Church, Grimsby (d 2 May 1948). BA 1923; MA 1930. **Tutor(s):** E E Sikes. **Educ:** St Faith's, Cambridge; Oundle School. **Career:** Founder, Pye Radio 1929. Died 20 January 1986.

PYEFINCH, Kenneth Arthur (1930) Born 10 January 1911, 272 Newland Avenue, Sculcoates, Hull; son of Arthur Edward Hare Pyefinch, Merchant, and Ellen Susannah Roberts. **Subject(s):** Natural Sciences. **Tutor(s):** C W Guillebaud. **Educ:** Newland Church School; Hull Grammar School; Pocklington School. **Career:** Biologist. Died 1979.

Q

QUASS, Phineas (1910) Born 6 August 1891, 17 Lisson Grove, Marylebone, Middlesex; son of Michael Quass, Master Watchmaker, and Caroline Wollman; m Eleanor Ruth Grey, 1933; 1 son, 2 daughters. **Subject(s):** Mathematics/Natural Sciences/Law/History/Economics; BA 1913; MA 1917; QC 1952; FRSM. **Tutor(s):** J R Tanner. **Educ:** University College School. **Career:** Bencher of the Inner Temple; Called to the Bar, Inner Temple 1916. **Appointments:** Honorary Treasurer, Medico-Legal Association; Council Member, Institute for the Study and Treatment of Delinquency. **Awards:** Foundation Scholarship, SJC; McMahon Law Studentship, SJC; Whewell Scholarship in International Law, University of Cambridge 1913, 1915. **Honours:** OBE. Died 28 September 1961.

QUAYLE, Professor John Rodney (1949) Born 18 November 1926, 46 Birkenhead Road, Hoylake, Cheshire; son of John Martin Quayle, Chemist and Optician, and Mary Doris Thorp; m Yvonne Mabel Sanderson, 1951; 1 son, 1 daughter. PhD 1952; BSc (University College of North Wales, Bangor) 1946; PhD (University College of North Wales, Bangor) 1949; MA (Oxford) 1957; Honorary Dr (Göttingen) 1989; Honorary DSc (Bath) 1992; Honorary DSc (Sheffield) 1992; FRS 1978. **Tutor(s):** J M Wordie. **Educ:** Cilcain Elementary School; Alun Grammar School; University College of North Wales, Bangor. **Career:** Research Fellow, Radiation Laboratory, University of California 1953–1955; Senior Scientific Officer, Tropical Products Institute, London 1955–1956; Member of Scientific Staff, MRC Cell Metabolism Research Unit, University of Oxford 1956–1963; Lecturer, Oriel College, Oxford 1957–1963; Senior Lecturer in Biochemistry 1963–1965, West Riding Professor of Microbiology 1965–1983, University of Sheffield; Vice-Chancellor, University of Bath 1983–1992. **Appointments:** Visiting Research Professor of Gessellschaft für Strahlem und Umweltforschung, Institut für Mikrobiologie, Universität Göttingen 1973–1974; Walker Ames Visiting Professor, University of Washington, Seattle 1981; President, Society for General Microbiology 1990–1993. **Awards:** Ciba Medal, Biochemical Society. **Publications:** Articles in scientific journals.

QUIBELL, Ernest Philip (1928) Born 10 July 1910, Beaumond Cross House, London Road, Newark, Nottinghamshire; son of Ernest Hall Quibell, Agricultural Merchant, and Kate Amelia Chandler; m (1) Edmee Margaret Lane (d), (2) Doreen Patricia Roake; 2 sons, 1 daughter. **Subject(s):** Modern and Medieval Languages/Medicine; BA 1935; MRCS; LRCP; DCH. **Tutor(s):** M P Charlesworth. **Johnian Relatives:** father of Hugh Richard Quibell (1955). **Educ:** Forres Preparatory School, Swanage; The Leys School, Cambridge. **Career:** Consultant Paediatrician, Chailey Heritage 1950–1976; Consultant Paediatrician, Thalidomide Trust 1977–1980. **Awards:** Harding Award 1977. **Honours:** OBE 1976.

QUICK, The Revd Edward Keith (1907) Born 23 January 1889, 43 Telford Avenue, Streatham, Surrey; son of Edward Quick, Civil Engineer, and Emmeline Scott. **Subject(s):** Mathematics; BA 1910; MA 1914. **Tutor(s):** J R Tanner. **Educ:** Royal Asylum of St Anne's Society, Redhill; City of London School; Ridley Hall, Cambridge. **Career:** Master, Giggleswick 1911; Ordained Deacon 1914; Curate, St Leonards on Sea 1914–1919; Ordained Priest, Chichester 1915; Temporary CF, 4th Class, RACD (mentioned in Secretary of State's list for valuable services in connection with the war) 1915–1918; Private, London Rifle Brigade 1918; Master, Christ's Hospital 1920; Assistant Chaplain, Bedford School 1921–1922; Master and Assistant Chaplain, St Stephen's College, Hong Kong 1922–1926; Master, St Bees School 1926–1927; Licensed Preacher, Diocese of Carlisle 1926–1928; Headmaster, Cathedral School, Shanghai 1929–1936; Chaplain, Christ's Hospital, Horsham, Sussex 1937–1944; Rector, Monk Sherbourne with Pamber, Hampshire 1944–1948; Vicar, Long Sutton 1948; Rector, Ellisfield and Farleigh Wallop, Hampshire until 1960. **Awards:** Sizarship, SJC.

QUILTER, Leslie John (1932) Born 23 June 1913, Montreal, Canada; son of Frank Quilter, Accountant, and Ethel Mary Boyce. **Subject(s):** Law; BA 1936. **Tutor(s):** C W Guillebaud. **Educ:** Brooklyn and Bronxville Junior High School, New York; Lycée Jaccard, Lausanne; Bryanston School, Blandford. **Career:** Lieutenant, RA 1939–1945; Traffic Manager, Eastern National and Lincolnshire Road Car Companies 1946–1978.

QUIN, Basil Godfrey (1914) Born 2 February 1891, 30 Alexandra Place, Newcastle upon Tyne; son of Malcolm Quin, Minister and Author, and Frances Sarah Cookson. **Subject(s):** Mathematics; BSc (Durham) 1913. **Tutor(s):** L H K Bushe-Fox. **Educ:** Royal Grammar School, Newcastle upon Tyne; Armstrong College. **Career:** Captain, Cambridgeshire Regiment and Suffolk Regiment (TF), WWI; Mathematics Master, Rutherford College, Newcastle upon Tyne 1920. **Honours:** MC 1917.

QUINN, Edward (1918) American Student.

R

RAAD, The Revd Neone Nicholas Charles (1904) Born 4 March 1888, 12 Baker Street, London; son of Habib Amie Raad, Assyrian Correspondent, and Alice Annie Burton. BA 1910. **Tutor(s):** D MacAlister. **Educ:** Private Tuition. **Career:** Congregational Minister; Proprietor, Shaftesbury High School for Girls until 1962. Died 16 September 1962.

RABY, John Henry Muers (1929) Born 12 May 1910, Lynton, Corder Road, Ipswich, Suffolk; son of Andrew Raby, Clerk in Holy Orders, and Edythe Beatrice Muers. **Subject(s):** Law; BA 1932. **Tutor(s):** C W Guillebaud. **Johnian Relatives:** son of Andrew Raby (1898). **Educ:** Wyggeston Grammar School, Leicester; St Lawrence College, Ramsgate.

RABY, Kenneth Francis (1942) Born 29 November 1924, Broom Cottage Nursing Home, Broughton in Furness, Lancashire; son of Francis William Raby, Mineral Inspector and Surveyor, and Winifrid Lilian Whitehouse; m Margaret Anne Angus, 17 July 1948. **Subject(s):** Mechanical Sciences; BA 1945; MA 1949; FIEE. **Tutor(s):** S J Bailey. **Educ:** Broughton in Furness Church of England School; Ulverston Grammar School. **Career:** Engineering Director, GEC Machines Ltd; Demonstrator in Electrical Engineering, University of Cambridge 1944–1946; Graduate Apprentice, British Thomson-Houston Company, Rugby 1946–1948; Design Engineer 1948–1951; Section Engineer 1951–1958; Departmental Assistant Manager 1958. **Awards:** Charles Lamb Prize in Electrical Engineering; Rex Moir Prize. Died 5 September 1992.

RACKHAM, Harold Christopher (1936) Born 24 April 1917, 12 Thornton Avenue, Streatham, London; son of Bernard Rackham, Keeper, Victoria and Albert Museum, and Ruth Adams; m Elizabeth Smith, 17 August 1946, St Andrew the Great, Cambridge; 1 son (Bernard Douglas b 18 May 1953), 1 daughter (Sarah Ruth b 26 July 1949). **Subject(s):** Classics; BA 1939; MA 1945. **Tutor(s):** R L Howland. **Educ:** The Limes School, Croydon; St Paul's School, London. **Career:** Principal, Ministry of Education 1951–1960; Assistant Secretary, External Relations Branch 1960–1965; Secretary, Social Science Research Council 1965–1970; Assistant Secretary, Department of Education and Science, Teachers Branch (Training) 1970–1975; Assistant Secretary, Arts and Libraries Branch, DES 1975–1977. **Awards:** Exhibition, SJC 1936–1937.

RADCLIFFE, Sir Clifford Walter (1907) Born 18 December 1888, 4 Cambridge Place, Langfield, Todmorton, Yorkshire; son of Joseph Radcliffe, Professor, and Martha Smethurst; m Florence Eva Wright, 1915; 1 daughter (Joyce). BA 1911. **Tutor(s):** L H K Bushe-Fox. **Educ:** Private School, Rochdale; Municipal Secondary School, Rochdale; Municipal Secondary School, Manchester; School of Technology, Manchester. **Career:** Solicitor, articled to the Town Clerk, York 1916; Deputy Clerk of the Peace, Middlesex 1919; County Solicitor (Middlesex) 1923; Clerk, Middlesex County Council 1935; Assistant to the Town Clerk, Sunderland; Managing Clerk to Sarpe, Pritchard and Co, London; Assistant Solicitor, County Borough of Tynemouth; Solicitor to Fulham Borough Council. **Appointments:** Vice-President, Surbiton Cricket Club; Treasurer, Magistrates' Golfing Society; Honorary Secretary, Society of Chairmen and Deputy Chairmen of Quarter Sessions of England and Wales; Assistant Commissioner, Local Government Boundary Commission. **Honours:** CBE 1942; Kt 1953. **Publications:** *Middlesex: the Jubilee of the County Council*, 1939. Died 4 January 1965.

RADFORD, John Charles Victor (1945) Born 9 July 1926, 9 Minerva Road, Kingston on Thames, Surrey; son of Herbert Charles Taylor Radford, Insurance Clerk, and Miriam Alice Phillips. **Subject(s):** Modern and Medieval Languages; BA 1949; MA 1951; PGCE. **Tutor(s):** J M Wordie. **Educ:** Christ's Hospital, Horsham; Institute of Education, London. **Career:** Education Officer, Eastern Nigeria 1952–1955; English Language and Literature Master, Government Secondary Boarding School, Nigeria 1956–1957; Acting Principal, Government Teacher Training College and Senior Education Officer, Nigeria 1959–1960; Provincial Education Officer and Inspector of Education, Nigeria 1961–1962; Zonal Inspector of Education, Nigeria 1962–1964; Language Master and Housemaster, Government Secondary Boarding School, Nigeria 1964–1965. **Awards:** Scholarship, SJC. **Honours:** MBE. Died 20 February 1995.

RADFORD, Kenneth James (1940) Born 20 July 1922, Gattons, Hildaville Drive, Southend-on-Sea, Essex; son of George Leonard Radford, Headmaster, and Ethel Mary Hicks. **Subject(s):** Mathematics; BA 1943; MA 1947. **Tutor(s):** J M Wordie. **Johnian Relatives:** brother of Ronald Walter Radford (1934). **Educ:** Great Stambridge Council School; Laindon High Road Council School; Palmer's School, Grays.

RADFORD, Matthew Frederick (1949) Born 6 March 1929, Kia-Ora, Barton, Cambridgeshire; son of Matthew George Radford, Farmer, and Mary Eleanor Cardo; m Mary Deavin, 1956; 2 children. **Subject(s):** Mathematics; BA 1952; MA 1956; CEng; MIEE. **Tutor(s):** J M Wordie. **Educ:** Elsworth Church of England School; Abbotsley Church of England School; Kimbolton Grammar School. **Career:** Royal Signals, Signals Research & Development Establishment 1947–1949; Chief Engineer, Radar Research Laboratory, Marconi Company, Great Baddow 1988–1994; Admitted and licensed as a Reader by the Bishop of Bradwell 1990. **Awards:** Nelson Gold Medal for innovative technology 1987. **Publications:** HF section of *IEE Antenna Handbook*; various national and international conference papers.

RADFORD, Richard Arthur (1938) Born 16 June 1919, 67 Edward Road, West Bridgford, Nottingham; son of Arthur Radford, Professor of Social Administration, University of Nottingham, and Norah Frances Elliott, Analytical Chemist; m (1) Mary S Love, (2) Margaret E (Thompson) Baird; 2 sons (David William b 1947 and Arthur Hugh b 1951), 1 daughter (Emily Anne b 1950). **Subject(s):** History/Economics; BA 1946; MA 1983. **Tutor(s):** C W Guillebaud; J S Boys Smith. **Johnian Relatives:** nephew of Alfred Geary (1912); brother of Roger Nicholas Radford (1944). **Educ:** Nottingham High School. **Career:** RA, POW Italy 1939–1945; International Monetary Fund staff, Washington DC 1947–1980; Assistant Director, Fiscal Affairs Department. **Awards:** Minor Scholarship, SJC 1937. **Publications:** 'The Economic Organisation of a POW Camp', *Economica*, November 1945.

RADFORD, Roger Nicholas (1944) Born 15 December 1926, 41 Loughborough Road, West Bridgford, Nottingham; son of Arthur Radford, Professor of Social Administration, University of Nottingham, and Norah Frances Elliott, Analytical Chemist; m Jennifer Mary Hay, 19 December 1956; 2 sons (Simon John Elliott b 1957 and William Oliver b 1960). BA 1947; MA 1951; DipArch 1949; Associate RIBA 1949; MArch (Harvard) 1953. **Tutor(s):** C W Guillebaud. **Johnian Relatives:** nephew of Alfred Geary (1912); brother of Richard Arthur Radford (1938). **Educ:** West End Preparatory School, Beeston; Nottingham High School. **Career:** Architect; Messrs Hughes & Bicknell, Architects, Cambridge 1949–1950; Second Lieutenant, RE, Staff of Chief Engineer, Gibraltar 1950–1952; Skidmore, Owings & Merrill, Architects 1953–1990 (Associate, New York 1957–1960, Associate Partner, New York 1960–1986, Associate Partner, London 1986–1990). **Appointments:** Attended Salzburg Seminar 1949. **Awards:** Minor Scholarship, SJC 1944; Ashpitel Prizeman, RIBA 1949; Henry Fellowship, Harvard University (Graduate School of Design) 1952–1953.

RADFORD, Sir Ronald Walter (1934) Born 28 February 1916, Gattons, Hildaville Drive, Southend-on-Sea; son of George Leonard Radford, Schoolmaster, and Ethel Mary Hicks; m Alison Strange, 10 September 1949; 1 son, 1 daughter. **Subject(s):** Mathematics; BA 1937; MA 1947. **Tutor(s):** J M Wordie. **Johnian Relatives:** brother of Kenneth James Radford (1940). **Educ:** Westborough Council School, Southend-on-Sea; Great Stambridge Council School; High School for Boys, Southend-on-Sea. **Career:** Indian Civil Service 1939–1947; Assistant Principal,

Customs and Excise Department 1947–1948; Principal, Customs and Excise Department 1948–1953; Assistant Secretary, Customs and Excise Department 1953–1965; Commissioner, Customs and Excise Department 1965–1970; Deputy Chairman, Board of Customs and Excise 1970–1973; Chairman, HM Customs and Excise 1973–1977; Secretary General, Customs Co-operation Council 1978–1983. **Awards:** Scholarship, SJC 1936–1937; Wright's Prize, SJC 1937. **Honours:** MBE; KCB. Died 3 September 1995.

RAE, Robert (1948) Born 25 April 1927, Edgbaston; son of Harold Rae, Company Director, and Bessie Garnett. **Subject(s):** Mathematics; BA 1951; MA 1957. **Tutor(s):** J M Wordie. **Educ:** Shirley Preparatory School; Solihull School. **Career:** RAF 1945–1948; Mathematics Teacher, Clifton College, Bristol 1952–1953; Mathematics Teacher and Housemaster, then Deputy Head, Christ's Hospital, Horsham 1953–1990; RAFVR (Training Branch), retiring as Wing Commander, CCF 1955–1990. **Honours:** OBE 1990.

RAFFLE, David Lawrie (1940) Born 6 February 1922, 33 Surrey Street, Norwich, Norfolk; son of David James Raffle, Schoolmaster, and Elizabeth Georgina Lawrie; m Monica Mary Barton, 1949; 1 son (Timothy David b 1962), 3 daughters (Mary Susan b 1950, Hilary Monica b 1954 and Angela Elizabeth b 1956). **Subject(s):** Mechanical Sciences; BA 1943; MA 1965; CEng; FRAeS. **Tutor(s):** S J Bailey. **Johnian Relatives:** brother of John Andrew Raffle (1948). **Educ:** Colman Road Elementary School, Norwich; City of Norwich School. **Career:** Technical Department, Sir W G Armstrong Whitworth Aircraft Ltd, Coventry 1942–1956; Chief Performance Engineer, Armstrong Whitworth Aircraft 1956–1961; Chief Technical Officer, Hawker Siddeley Aviation, Whitworth Gloster Division 1961–1964; Chief Structural Engineer AW 681, Hawker Siddeley Aviation, Avro Whitworth Division 1964–1965; Deputy Chief Structural Engineer 1965–1966, Chief Performance and Weights Engineer 1966–1969, Hawker Siddeley Aviation, Manchester; Chief Aerodynamicist, British Aerospace, Manchester 1969–1985. **Honours:** MBE 1985.

RAFFLE, John Andrew (1948) Born 14 August 1926, Maternity Home, 3 Aspland Road, Norwich; son of David James Raffle, Schoolmaster, and Elizabeth Georgina Lawrie, School Teacher; m Tamsin Murray, 1953; 2 daughters (Carolyn Mary and Rosalind Jane). **Subject(s):** Geography; BA 1950; MA 1955; FRICS. **Tutor(s):** J M Wordie. **Johnian Relatives:** brother of David Lawrie Raffle (1940). **Educ:** Bignold Primary School, Norwich; City of Norwich School; Bristol University. **Career:** RE 1946–1948 (Second Lieutenant 1948); Registered Land Surveyor, Nyasaland 1960; Land Survey Division 1969; Land Surveyor, Republic of South Africa, and Republic of Botswana 1975. **Appointments:** Member, Botswana Institute of Development Professionals 1976. **Publications:** Various publications on Mapping and Remote Sensing in Southern Africa.

RAFFLE, Dr Wilfrid (1909) Born 5 December 1890, 4 Wood Terrace, Westoe, South Shields; son of William Raffle, Gentleman, and Elizabeth Ann Banks. **Subject(s):** Natural Sciences; BA 1912; BChir 1937; MB 1937; LRCP 1915. **Tutor(s):** L H K Bushe-Fox. **Educ:** The High School, South Shields. **Career:** Captain, RAMC (Mentioned in Despatches), WWI; St Mary's Hospital, Roehampton 1934.

RAFIQUE, Ahmed (1913) Born 15 September 1893, Delhi, India; son of Mohamed Rafique, Puisne Judge of the High Court of Judicature, Northwest Province, India. **Tutor(s):** L H K Bushe-Fox. **Educ:** Arnold School, Chester; Lincoln School; Ipswich Grammar School.

RAGG, The Revd Harry Richard (1908) Born 6 January 1889, 69 Wheeley's Road, Birmingham, Warwickshire; son of Frank Hugh Ragg, Bank Manager, and Priscilla Anne Butler; m Winifred; 3 sons (John, David and Ben), 2 daughters (Betty and Ruth). BA 1911; MA 1915; DD *jure dignitatis* (St John's College, Manitoba) 1939; Honorary DD (Saskatoon) 1944. **Tutor(s):** J R Tanner. **Johnian Relatives:** father of John Richard Groves Ragg (1935). **Educ:** Hereford Cathedral School;

Bishop's Hostel, Liverpool. **Career:** Deacon 1912; Curate, St Paul, Southport 1912–1914; Priest 1913; Vicar, Fruitvale, Canada 1914–1915; Rector, Trail 1915–1920; Rector, Chilliwack 1920–1925; Rural Dean, Yale 1921–1925; Rector, All Saints', Winnipeg, and Chaplain of the Provincial Jail 1925–1932; Associated Padre, Toc House 1926–1951; Rector, Church of the Redeemer, Calgary, and Dean, Calgary 1933–1945; Bishop, Calgary 1943–1951. **Appointments:** Executive Council, General Synod 1931; Prolocutor, Lower House 1939–1943. Died 15 August 1967.

RAGG, The Revd John Richard Groves (1935) Born 21 November 1915, Fruitvale, British Columbia, Canada; son of Harry Richard Ragg, Clerk in Holy Orders, and Winifred Mary Groves; m Gwen; 2 daughters (Elizabeth and Diana). **Subject(s):** History; BA 1938; MA 1943. **Tutor(s):** J S Boys Smith. **Johnian Relatives:** son of Harry Richard Ragg (1908). **Educ:** St John's College School, Winnipeg; Ridley College, Ontario; Mount Royal College, Calgary; Westcott House, Cambridge. **Career:** Ordained Deacon 1939; Curate, Bishop's Hatfield 1939–1941; Ordained Priest 1940; St Mary, Southampton 1941–1943; Ashstead, Surrey 1943; Commissary, Diocese of Calgary (for his father); Curate, St Martin in the Fields 1947–1950; Organising Secretary, SPCK 1948–1950; Curate in Charge, St Thomas, Bedminster, and Social and Industrial Adviser to the Bishop of Bristol 1950–1960; Head, Oxford House, Bethnal Green 1960–1966; Senior Chaplain, Portsmouth Polytechnic 1966–1970; Senior Lecturer, School of Management Studies 1966–1974; Canon Residentiary, Portsmouth Cathedral 1970. Died 29 April 1974.

RAGG, Theodore Frederick Arthur (1927) (migrated to Jesus College) Born 25 June 1909, The Cathedral School, Hereford; son of William Henry Murray Ragg, Clerk in Holy Orders, Prebendary of Hereford, and Florence Stead; m Mary Cecilia Stewart, 31 July 1935, St Peter's, Belfast. **Subject(s):** Classics/English; BA (Jesus) 1931; MA (Jesus) 1943. **Tutor(s):** M P Charlesworth. **Johnian Relatives:** brother of Thomas Murray Ragg (1919); uncle of Nicholas Murray Ragg (1951) and of William Giles Ragg (1955). **Educ:** St Michael's College, Tenbury; Bromsgrove School. **Career:** Assistant Master, Campbell College, Belfast 1931 (Librarian 1936, Housemaster 1946); OC, Air Training Corps 1941–1947. **Awards:** Rustat Scholarship, Jesus College 1928; Bell Exhibition 1928; Proximae Accessit, Chancellor's English Medal, University of Cambridge 1931.

RAGG, Thomas Murray (1919) Born 3 February 1897, The Grammar School, Trafalgar Road, Great Yarmouth; son of William Henry Murray Ragg, Clerk in Holy Orders, and Florence Stead; m Mollie Bashford, 12 April 1930, Fairbourne, North Wales; 2 sons (Nicholas and William), 1 daughter (Bridget). **Subject(s):** History; BA 1921. **Tutor(s):** E A Benians. **Johnian Relatives:** brother of Theodore Frederick Arthur Ragg (1927); father of Nicholas Murray Ragg (1951) and of William Giles Ragg (1955). **Educ:** The Cathedral School, Hereford. **Career:** Editor, Messrs G P Putnam's 1924–1935; Managing Director, Routledge & Kegan Paul 1936. Died 11 January 1953.

RAGHAVAN, Tandalam Narosimha Chariar Srinivasa (1922) Born 1 October 1901, Upper Anicut, Tanjore, Madras, India; son of Tandalam Raghaarachari Narosimha Chariar, Hindu Brahmin, Assistant Engineer, Public Works, and Ammani Ammal. **Subject(s):** Mathematics; BA 1924; MA 1934. **Tutor(s):** E Cunningham. **Educ:** Bhanadurai Secondary School, Kunbakonam; St Paul's High School, Vepery; Presidency College, Madras. **Career:** Various posts in the Indian Civil Service. **Awards:** Bhaonagar Medal, University of Cambridge 1925. Died 23 March 1988.

RAINBOW, Henry (1921) Born 23 January 1902, 116 Gosford Street, Coventry, Warwickshire; son of William Ballard Rainbow, Druggist/Drysalter, and Elizabeth Barr. **Subject(s):** Natural Sciences/Mathematics; BA 1924; MA 1926. **Tutor(s):** B F Armitage. **Educ:** John Gulson Elementary School, Coventry; Bablake Secondary School. **Awards:** Scholarship, SJC 1920.

RAJAGOPALACHARYA, Desikacharia (1920) Born 7 September 1900, Periyakulam, Madras Presidency, India; son of Valathur Krishnaiengar Desikachari, Sub-Judge, and Dorachi Ammal. **Subject(s):** History/Law; BA 1925; MA 1928; LLB 1925. **Tutor(s):** E A Benians. **Educ:** National High School, Negapatam; Victoria College, Palghat. **Publications:** 'Tagore: Poet Mystic and Teacher', *Sydney Herald*, 1920.

RAM, Chaudhri Jit (1931) Born 16 June 1907, Delhi Province, India; son of Chaudhri Shiva Chand, Agriculturalist, and Ram Kaur. **Subject(s):** Economics; BA 1933; MA (Delhi); BA (by incorporation) (Oxon) 1933. **Tutor(s):** C W Guillebaud. **Educ:** Villiage Ghiora, India; Jat HM High School, Rohtak, India; St Stephen's Mission College, Delhi.

RAMAGE, Hugh Pyesmith (1925) Born 7 October 1906, Ridgemont, Carrow Hill, City of Norwich; son of Hugh Ramage, Principal of Technical Institution, and Winifred Caroline Pye-Smith; m Catherine Meiklejohn Weddell, 21 December 1943, Cornwall. **Subject(s):** Natural Sciences (Zoology, Comparative Anatomy); BA 1928; MA 1932; FIBiol. **Tutor(s):** J M Wordie. **Johnian Relatives:** son of Hugh Ramage (1899). **Educ:** Bracondale School, Norwich; Mill Hill School. **Career:** Biology Master, Gresham's School, Holt 1933. **Appointments:** Officer, Science Masters' Association 1939–1963 (Chairman 1950); Officer, Association for Science Education (successor to the Science Masters' Association) 1963–1969. Died 14 April 1993.

RAMASWAMI AIYER, Palamaneri Narayanaswami Aiyer (1922) Born 5 May 1900, Tanjore, Madras, India; son of Palamaneri Narayanaswami Aiyer, Landowner, and Therapurasundari Ammal. **Tutor(s):** E A Benians. **Educ:** Kalyanasundaram High School, Tanjore, India; St Joseph's College, Trichinopoly.

RAMSAY, Hugh Baxter (1946) Born 29 December 1924, Poona, India; son of Arthur MacInnes Ramsay, Medical Practitioner, and Janet Baxter; m Isabel Ann Roper, 1961; 1 daughter (Elizabeth Christine). **Subject(s):** Natural Sciences; BA 1949; MA 1995; BSc (London) 1956; MSc (London) 1959. **Tutor(s):** G C L Bertram. **Educ:** The Ashe, Etwall; Giggleswick School; Derby Technical College. **Awards:** State Scholarship 1943; Open Exhibition, SJC 1943. **Career:** RAF, serving in Egypt 1944–1946; Researcher, GEC, London 1950–1959; Lecturer in Mathematics (Statistics), College of Advanced Technology, Salford, later Salford University 1959–1992. **Publications:** *The Use of Mathematics in the Electrical Industry*, Pitman, 1966. Died 4 November 1996.

RAMSDEN, John Fraser (1925) Born 21 December 1907, Dhoedam, Dum Duma, Assam, India; son of George Ramsden, Tea Planter and Director of Tea Companies, and Margaret Islay Florence Hannay. BA 1928. **Tutor(s):** J M Wordie. **Educ:** Norland House, Hove; Marlborough House, Hove; Sedbergh School.

RANDS, Ian Leslie (1943) Born 26 July 1925, Everest, Old Church Road, Isle of Wight; son of Edward George Rands, Manager, Stone Quarry, and Vera Annie Victoria Francis. **Tutor(s):** S J Bailey. **Educ:** Shanklin Church of England School; Newport Grammar School.

RANKIN, James Mottram Nasmith (1949) Born 22 December 1930, Little Stambridge Hall, Little Stambridge, Rochford, Essex; son of Harold Donaldson Rankin, Miller and Farmer, and Constance Winifred Martin; m Alex Laffan, 1963; 1 son, 2 daughters. BA 1952; MA 1991. **Tutor(s):** G C L Bertram. **Educ:** Sunningdale School, Berkshire; Eton College; Felsted School; Newcastle University. **Career:** Farmer 1952–; Director, Rankin Farms Ltd 1956–1994; Chairman and Managing Director 1994–.

RAO, Belthangadi Gopalakrishna (1932) Born 1 June 1909, Puttur, South Canara District, India; son of Belthangadi Mangesh Rao, Pleader, and Kodiyal Bhavani Bai; BA (Madras) 1930. **Tutor(s):** J M Wordie. **Educ:** Board High School, Puttur; Government College, Mangalore; Presidency College, Madras.

RAO, Professor Vinayek Ganpat (1909) Born 24 September 1888, Bombay, India; son of Ganpat Sadashid Rao, Acting Government Pleader, High Court, Bombay; m B R Kothare. **Subject(s):** History/Law; BA 1913; LLB 1913. **Tutor(s):** L H K Bushe-Fox. **Career:** Professor, Siddarth College, Bombay; Called to the Bar, Lincoln's Inn 1914; Professor of French, Elphinstone College, Bombay 1914–1917; Wilson College, Bombay 1914–1917; Wilson College, Bombay 1921–1923; Professor of Law, Government Law College 1923–1924.

RAPHAEL, George (1920) Born 7 August 1900, Galgorm House, Galgorm, Ballymena, County Antrim, Ireland; son of George Raphael, Linen Merchant, and Lilian Haslett Davidson; m Peggy Rosine Cohen, 30 March 1927, Trinity Presbyterian Church, Hampstead. BA 1923; MA 1928. **Tutor(s):** B F Armitage. **Johnian Relatives:** brother of Thomas Davison Raphael (1923). **Educ:** New College, Harrogate; Queen's University, Belfast. Died 13 August 1986.

RAPHAEL, Dr Thomas Davidson (1923) Born 16 April 1905, Galgorm House, Galgorm, Ballymena, County Antrim, Ireland; son of George Raphael, Linen Merchant, and Lilian Haslett Davidson. BA 1926; PhD 1932. **Tutor(s):** B F Armitage. **Johnian Relatives:** brother of George Raphael (1920). **Educ:** New College, Harrogate; Academical Institution, Coleraine. Died September 1987.

RAPLEY, Frederick (1922) Born 26 June 1904, 65 Ward Street, Sunderland, County Durham; son of Frederick Rapley, Marine Engineer, and Isabella Turnbull; m Gladys Pemberton, 1935. **Subject(s):** Mechanical Sciences/Mathematics; BA 1925; MA 1954; AMICE 1932. **Tutor(s):** E Cunningham. **Educ:** Hudson Road Council School, Sunderland; Cowan Terrace Council School, Sunderland; Bede Collegiate School, Sunderland. **Career:** Buenos Aires Great Southern Railway 1926; Superintendent, Bahia Blanca Waterworks Company 1945. **Awards:** Exhibition, SJC 1922.

RAPPAPORT, Charles David (1931) Born 12 May 1913, 6 Fontayne Road, Stoke Newington, Hackney; son of Harris Rappaport, Manufacturing Furrier, and Fanny Levenson; m Ruth A Cohen, 1954; 1 son (Jonathan b 14 January 1958), 1 daughter (Ann b 21 June 1961). **Subject(s):** Oriental Studies; BA 1934; MA 1939. **Tutor(s):** E A Benians. **Johnian Relatives:** second cousin of Norman Montague Bleehen (1976). **Educ:** Haberdashers' Aske's Hampstead School; KCL. **Career:** Intelligence Corps, Austria and Italy 1940–1945; Secretary, Palestine Committee, Board of Deputies of British Jews 1947–1949; Secretary, Israel and Foreign Affairs Committees of the Board of Deputies, and their Representative at the United Nations Commission for Human Rights 1958–1969; Education Secretary, Council of Christians and Jews 1969–1971; Deputy Director then Director, Jewish Colonisation Association Charitable Foundation 1971–1984. **Awards:** Rogerson Scholarship, SJC 1930; John Stewart of Rannoch Scholarship in Hebrew, University of Cambridge. Died 27 April 1999.

RATCLIFF, The Revd Edward Craddock (1915) Born 16 December 1896, 66 Barcombe Avenue, Streatham Hill, Surrey; son of John Adolphus Ratcliff, Member of London Stock Exchange, and Marie Louise Craddock. **Subject(s):** Oriental Languages/Theology; BA 1920; MA 1923. **Tutor(s):** E E Sikes. **Educ:** Streatham Hill College; Merchant Taylors' School. **Career:** YMCA, India 1916–1918; Ordained 1922; Curate, St Mary, Ely 1922–1924; Vice-Principal, Westcott House, Cambridge 1924–1930; Fellow and Chaplain, The Queen's College, Oxford 1930–1937; University Lecturer in Liturgiology, Oxford 1933–1939; Professor of Liturgical Theology, London 1945–1947; Ely Professor of Divinity 1947–1958, Regius Professor of Divinity 1958–1964, University of Cambridge; Title C Fellow 1950–1964, Title E Fellow 1964–1967, SJC. **Appointments:** Member, Archbishop's Commission to Consider Liturgical Questions 1956. **Awards:** Scholarship, SJC 1914; George Williams Prize, University of Cambridge 1922. Died 30 June 1967.

RATCLIFF, Dr Gerald Alfred (1944) Born 8 September 1926, Chesterton, Kimberley Road, Chingford, Essex; son of Alfred Jenner Ratcliff, Civil Servant, and Constance Agnes Jones; m Kennon 1954; 1 son (Kevin), 1 daughter (Heather). **Subject(s):** Natural Sciences; BA 1947; MA 1951; PhD (Cornell) 1954; FIChemE. **Tutor(s):** C W Guillebaud. **Educ:** Mornington Private School, Chingford; St Brandan's Preparatory School, Worthing; Worthing High School; Cornell University, USA. **Career:** Shell Oil 1948–1950 and 1954–1956; Lecturer in Chemical Engineering, University of Cambridge 1956–1964; Professor of Chemical Engineering and Chairman, Department of Chemical Engineering 1964–1976, Pro-Dean, Faculty of Graduate Studies and Research, McGill University. **Appointments:** Director, Canadian Society for Chemical Engineers. **Awards:** Goodwin Travelling Fellowship 1949. Died 19 July 1976.

RATCLIFF, Howard Dunbar (1917) Born 1 February 1898, Melbourne, Victoria, Australia; son of Joshua Ratcliff, Merchant, and Emily Moulder. **Tutor(s):** E E Sikes. **Educ:** Scotch College, Melbourne, Australia; Bootham School, York.

RATCLIFF, John Cooper (1949) Born 19 November 1928, 23 Carr Crofts, Armley, Leeds; son of Wilson Ratcliff, Engineer, and Gladys May Cooper; m Yvonne Jacqueline Sonia Faulder, 1957; 1 son (David). **Subject(s):** History/Law; BA 1952; MA 1956; FCA. **Tutor(s):** A G Lee. **Educ:** West Leeds High School; Leeds Grammar School; Pudsey Grammar School; Sedbergh School. **Career:** Royal Horse Artillery 1952–1954; Chartered Accountant 1955; Managing Director, Dobeckum 1961; Guthrie Corporation 1968; Managing Director and Chief Executive, Guthrie Corporation 1974; Chairman, John Ratcliff and Sons 1974. **Appointments:** Governor, Sedbergh School. **Awards:** Scholarship, SJC. Died 21 September 1978.

RATCLIFFE, Robert Arundel (1924) Born 29 April 1906, 77 Wellington Street, Nottingham; son of Thomas Snodgrass Ratcliffe, Company Director, and Mary Arundel; 1 son, 1 daughter. **Subject(s):** Law; BA 1927; MA 1931; LLB 1931. **Tutor(s):** E A Benians. **Johnian Relatives:** brother of Tom Arundel Ratcliffe (1927). **Educ:** Stanley Road Preparatory School, Nottingham; High Pavement Secondary School, Nottingham; High School, Nottingham. **Career:** Admitted Solicitor 1930; Solicitor, Herbert Hind, Belt and Ratcliffe, Nottingham; Squadron Leader, Administrative Division, RAF, WWII. Died 19 June 1963.

RATCLIFFE, Dr Tom Arundel (1927) Born 6 August 1910, 30 Milner Road, Nottingham; son of Thomas Snodgrass Ratcliffe, Director of Boots, and Mary Arundel; 1 daughter. **Subject(s):** Natural Sciences; BA 1931; MA 1947; MB 1934; BChir 1934; MRCS 1934; DPM; FRCPsych 1971; LRCP 1934; DCH. **Tutor(s):** J M Wordie. **Johnian Relatives:** brother of Robert Arundel Ratcliffe (1924). **Educ:** Mountford House Kindergarten; The High School, Nottingham. **Career:** Consulting Psychiatrist, Nottingham Children's Hospital; Director, Derby County Borough Child Guidance Clinic; House Appointments at Sheffield Children's Hospital, Sheffield Lodge Moor Hospital; Clinical Assistant, St Thomas' Hospital; Psychiatrist, St Andrew's Hospital, Norfolk, Saxondale and Mapperley Hospitals; Consultant Psychiatrist, RAMC, latterly Lieutenant Colonel, and Advisor in Psychiatry, Allied Land Forces, South-East Asia, WWII; Visiting Lecturer, Universities of Nottingham, Leicester and York; Consultant to National and Nottingham Marriage Guidance Councils; Consultant to Southwell House Probation Hostel, Nottingham; Consultant to the World Health Organisation and World Federation for Mental Health; Lecturer, Derby School of Occupational Therapy 1955. **Appointments:** Vice-Chairman, Education Committee, Institute for Scientific Treatment of Delinquency; Chairman, Clinical Services Committee; Member, Editorial Board, National Association for Mental Health; Committee, Association for Workers with Maladjusted Children; Association of Child Psychology and Psychiatry. **Awards:** Foundation Scholarship, SJC. **Publications:** *Parents under Stress*; *Discipline and the Child*; *The Child and Reality*; *The Development of Personality*, 1967. Died 4 February 1977.

RAŢIU, Dr Ioan Augustin Nicolae (1940) Born 6 June 1917, Turda, Romania; son of Augustin Nicolae Raţiu, Lawyer, and Eugenia Turcu; m Elisabeth Pilkington, 22 September 1945, Chapel of the Savoy, London; 2 sons (Nicolae and Indrei). **Subject(s):** Economics; BA 1943; MA 1947. **Tutor(s):** C W Guillebaud. **Johnian Relatives:** father of Indrei Stephen Pilkington Raţiu (1964); uncle of Martin Stephen Pilkington (1977). **Educ:** Lyceum Regele Ferdinand, Turda; Lyceum Gheorghe Baritiu, Cluj, Romania; Faculty of Law, University of Cluj, Romania. **Career:** Commissioned, Artillery Military Academy 1938; Diplomat, Romanian Legation, London 1940; Contributor for the BBC 1940; Founder, JR Shipping Company Limited 1957; British-Romanian Association 1965–1985; Founder and President, World Union of Free Romanians in Geneva 1984; MP for Turda, Romania 1990; National Peasant Party candidate for Presidency of Romania 1990; Journalist, broadcaster and author; Founder, *Cotidianul* newspaper, Bucharest 1990. **Publications:** *Policy for the West*, 1957; *Contemporary Romania*, 1975. Died 17 January 2000.

RATTENBURY, Arnold Foster (1940) Born 5 October 1921, Hankow, China; son of Harold Burgoyne Rattenbury, Methodist Minister, and Emily Mary Ewins; m Simonette Cooper-Willis, 3 April 1946. **Tutor(s):** C W Guillebaud. **Educ:** Hankow Private School; Quainton Hall Private School, Harrow; Kingswood School, Bath.

RAU, Benegal Sanjiva (1905) Born 12 December 1883, Mangalore, South Canara, India; son of Benegal Raghavendra Rau, Civil Apothecary, and Benegal Radha Bai. **Subject(s):** Natural Sciences/Mathematics; BA 1908; MA 1914. **Tutor(s):** D MacAlister. **Educ:** St Aloysius' College, Mangalore; Presidency College, Madras.

RAU, Kalle Kama Rau Sadashiva (1903) Born 16 July 1884, Mangalore, South Canara District, Madras; son of Kalle Subaran Rama Rau, Philosophy Lecturer, and Kalle Sutha Bai. **Subject(s):** Mathematics; BA 1906. **Tutor(s):** C E Graves; J R Tanner. **Educ:** Presidency College, Madras. **Career:** Assistant Accountant General, Madras 1908; Numerous posts in Accountancy and Audit, Madras and Bengal 1908–1939. Died September 1965.

RAVEN, The Revd Edward Earle (1909) Born 27 December 1889, 6 Kildare Terrace, Paddington; son of John Earle Raven, Barrister-at-Law, and Alice Comber; m Esther Margaret Brooks, December 1930; 1 son (John Martin Brooks Earle b 1 August 1936), 3 daughters (Anne b 22 February 1932, Joan b 25 July 1933 and Rosemary Esther Margaret b 17 May 1938). **Subject(s):** Classics/Theology; BA 1912; MA 1919. **Tutor(s):** E E Sikes. **Johnian Relatives:** brother-in-law of John Cowell Brooks (1928) and of Maxwell Peter Brooks (1933); father of John Martin Brooks Earle Raven (1956). **Educ:** Gloucester House School, London; Uppingham Lower School; Uppingham School. **Career:** Army 1914; Deacon 1914; Curate, St Mary, Hoxton 1914–1917; Priest 1915; Temporary CF, 4th Class, RACD, France 1917–1918; Head, Maurice Hostel, Hoxton 1918–1925; Chaplain 1921–1926, Ashton Fellow 1923–1926, Title A Fellow 1926, Title B Fellow 1926–1951, Dean 1926–1951, SJC; Canon Theologian, Liverpool Cathedral 1930–1935. **Appointments:** Examining Chaplain to the Bishop of Wakefield 1924–1928; Senior Proctor, University of Cambridge 1928–1929, 1944–1945; Praelector 1935–1951, SJC. **Awards:** Johnson Exhibition, SJC 1909; Scholarship, SJC 1910; College Prize, SJC 1910; Naden Studentship 1913, SJC. **Publications:** *The Heart of Christ's Religion*, 1933. Died 2 December 1951.

RAVENSCROFT, John Edward (1942) Born 20 July 1925, 245 Birchfield Road, Handsworth, Birmingham; son of Edward Henry Ravenscroft, Director, Ravenscroft Dairies, Birmingham, and Eva Magnay; m Kathleen Huntley, 15 September 1951; 4 sons (Nigel W, David S, Stephen E and Andrew R). **Subject(s):** Law; BA 1948; MA 1950. **Tutor(s):** S J Bailey. **Johnian Relatives:** father of Stephen Edward Ravenscroft (1979). **Educ:** Canterbury Road Council School, Birmingham; King Edward VI Grammar School, Birmingham; King

Edward VI High School, Birmingham; King Edward VI School, Lichfield. **Career:** Articled to Thomas Magnay & Co, Gateshead 1948–1950; Solicitor 1950–1980, Senior Partner 1980–1991, Thomas Magnay & Co, Gateshead.

RAWES, John (1930) Born 4 December 1910, Hunter House, Penrith; son of Isaac Rawes, Cattle Dealer, and Margaret Robinson. **Tutor(s):** E A Benians. **Educ:** Queen Elizabeth's Grammar School, Penrith; Seascale Preparatory School; Shrewsbury School.

RAWNSLEY, Lee (1919) Born 2 February 1895, 3 Marsh Street, Bradford, Yorkshire; son of John William Rawnsley, Assistant School Teacher, and Elizabeth Jane Holmes; m Hilda Morley, 15 October 1921, Hampstead. **Subject(s):** Natural Sciences; BA 1921; MA 1925. **Tutor(s):** E A Benians. **Educ:** Carlton Street Secondary School, Bradford; St John's College, Battersea, London. **Career:** Assistant Master, Haberdashers' Aske's School, Hampstead 1932.

RAWORTH, Edwin Llewellyn (1919) Born 21 April 1899, 5 South Park Road, Harrogate, Yorkshire; son of Edwin Raworth, Solicitor, and Mary Emma Galpine; 1 son, 3 daughters. **Tutor(s):** E A Benians. **Educ:** Clifton House School, Harrogate; Aldenham School. **Career:** Bomber Pilot, 27th Squadron, RFC, France (promoted to rank of Captain) 1917–1918; Founder and Director, McCall and Co Ltd, Steel Reinforcement Manufacturers, Sheffield 1922–1961. Died 18 February 1961.

RAWSON, Joseph Nadin (1912) Born 8 May 1880, 224 Aspley Terrace, Radford, Nottinghamshire; son of Joseph Rawson, Warehouseman, and Elizabeth Ross. BSc (London); BD (London). **Tutor(s):** E E Sikes. **Educ:** University College, Nottingham; UCL; Regent's Park College; Non Collegiate and Jesus College, Oxford.

RAY, John Norman Anthony (1920) Born 29 December 1901, Bridgham, Thetford, Norfolk; son of John Norman Charles Ray, Engineer and Contractor, and Kathleen Mary Ireland. BA 1923. **Tutor(s):** E E Sikes. **Educ:** Private School, Felixstowe; Oundle School.

RAYNER, Dr Laurence Stephen (1945) Born 9 October 1927, Dudley, Watergate Lane, Much Woolton, Liverpool; son of Stephen Rayner, Clerk, and Daisy Williams. **Subject(s):** Natural Sciences; BA 1948; MA 1952; PhD 1952. **Tutor(s):** G C L Bertram. **Educ:** Heatherlea Preparatory School; Quarry Bank High School.

RAYNS, Dr Frank (1919) Born 8 August 1894, Nether Broughton, Waltham, Leicestershire; son of Francis Edwin Rayns, Farrier and Publican, and Ada Willett; 5 daughters. **Subject(s):** Natural Sciences; BA 1921; MA 1926; Diploma in Agriculture 1922; Honorary DSc (Cantab) 1961. **Tutor(s):** E A Benians. **Educ:** The Grammar School, Barrow on Soar; The Midland Agricultural and Dairy College. **Career:** 309th Siege Battery, HAC 1915–1916; No 1 RGA Cadet School 1917–1918; 530th Siege Battery 1918; 309th Siege Battery, HAC 1918; Assistant Lecturer in Agriculture, Midland Agricultural College, Derbyshire; Director, Norfolk Agricultural Station, Sprowson 1924–1960; Executive Officer, Norfolk War Agricultural Committee 1939–1944. **Appointments:** Life Fellow, Royal Agricultural Society of England; President, Royal Norfolk Show 1962. **Awards:** Drewit Prize for Agricultural Chemistry 1922. **Honours:** OBE; CBE. Died 24 January 1976.

REA, James Taylor (1928) Born 19 October 1909, 83 Great Victoria Street, Belfast, Ireland; son of Martin Rea, Presbyterian Minister, and Mary Fisher; m Catharine Bleakney 1934 (d 1990); 2 sons (James Bleakney b 8 November 1935, d 15 May 1936 and William b 17 April 1947), 1 daughter (Mary Jane b 7 January 1950). **Subject(s):** Mathematics; BA 1930; MA 1935; BA (Queen's, Belfast) 1928. **Tutor(s):** J M Wordie. **Educ:** The Royal School, Dungannon; Queen's University, Belfast. **Career:** HM Colonial Administrative Service, Malaya and Singapore 1931–1958 (Assistant Secretary, Chinese Affairs, Federation of Malaya 1948–1949; Deputy Commander for Labour, Federation of Malaya 1949–1950; Deputy Malayan Establishment Officer 1950–1952; Deputy President 1952–1955, President 1955–1958, City Council, Singapore). **Appointments:** Nominated Member, General Dental Council 1961–1979; Chairman, Hotel Grants Advisory Committee, Northern Ireland 1963–1975; Chairman, Northern Ireland Training Executive 1972–1975; Chairman, Down District Committee, Eastern Health and Social Services Board 1974–1978; Member, Northern Ireland Housing Trust 1959–1971 (Vice-Chairman, 1970–1971); Independent Member, Catering Wages Council, Northern Ireland 1965–1982; Independent Member, Retail Bespoke Tailoring Wages Council 1965–1982; Independent Member, Laundry Wages Council 1965–1982; Independent Member, Shirtmaking Wages Council 1965–1982; Member, Downpatrick HMC 1966–1973 (Chairman 1971–1973). **Honours:** CMG 1958. Died 23 September 2001.

REA, Stanley Charles Walsh Wright (1920) Born 16 April 1901, 135 Glenfield Place, Belfast, County Antrim, Ireland; son of Thomas James Taylor Rea, Dental Surgeon, and Mary Eleanor Walsh. BA 1923; MA 1940. **Tutor(s):** B F Armitage. **Educ:** Clanrye School, Belfast; Cheltenham College. **Career:** Second Lieutenant, Essex Regiment 1920; Lieutenant, Essex Regiment 1924; Colonel, Essex Regiment. Died 8 October 1983.

REA, Thomas (1902) Born 4 November 1877, Drungorman, County Tyrone; son of Maxwell Rea, Farmer, and Ann Ruddy. **Subject(s):** Modern and Medieval Languages; BA 1903; MA 1909; MA (Royal University of Ireland). **Tutor(s):** D MacAlister. **Educ:** Royal School, Dungannon; Queen's College, Belfast; Queen's College, Galway. **Career:** Lecturer in German, University College of North Wales, Bangor 1904. **Publications:** *Schiller's Dramas and Poems in England*, 1906.

READ, Dr Arthur Hinton (1939) Born 12 October 1920, Montacute, Wentworth Road, Vaucluse, Sydney, Australia; son of John Read, Professor of Chemistry, University of St Andrews, and Ida Suddards; m Katherine Eaton, 1954; 1 son, 1 daughter. **Subject(s):** Mathematics; BA 1946; MA 1948; PhD (Harvard). **Tutor(s):** J M Wordie. **Educ:** St Salvators School, St Andrews; Lathallan School, Fife; Marlborough College. **Career:** Master, Marlborough 1945–1949; Lecturer in Mathematics, St Andrews 1949–1961. Died 2 December 1961.

READ, Arthur James (1903) Born 27 July 1884, 10 Prestonville Road, Brighton, Sussex; son of James Read, Bank Manager, and Catherine Swindells; m Ada Edith Maie Jolliffe, 24 June 1918; 1 son (James Jolliffe b 29 May 1926), 1 daughter (Mary Elizabeth b 9 March 1923, d 20 March 1998). BA 1906. **Tutor(s):** D MacAlister. **Johnian Relatives:** father of James Jolliffe Read (1947). **Educ:** Tonbridge School. **Career:** Mechanical Engineer, Buenos Aires and Pacific Railway 1906–1914; Lieutenant, Duke of Cornwall's Light Infantry (wounded at Ypres 1916), then with Ministry of Munitions, WWI; Meteorological Office 1919–1920; Audit Staff of Air Ministry 1920–1949. Died 13 September 1968.

READ, Bryan Colman (1943) Born 1 October 1925, 7 Mile End Road, Norwich; son of Lewes Hector Read, Flour Miller, and Ena Phyllis Colman; m Sheila Winter, 1949; 1 son (James), 3 daughters (Joanna, Susan and Rebecca). **Subject(s):** Mechanical Sciences; BA 1946; MA 1956; Honorary DCL (UEA) 1996. **Tutor(s):** S J Bailey. **Johnian Relatives:** nephew of Grantly Dick (Dick-Read) (1908); father of Jonathan James Read (1971). **Educ:** Unthank College, Norwich; Town Close House, Norwich; Bishop's Stortford College. **Career:** Miller. **Appointments:** Chairman, Norfolk and Norwich Festival; Deputy Lieutenant of Norfolk 1986; Member, UEA Council; JP. **Honours:** CBE.

READ, Dr Grantly Dick (DICK-READ) (1908) Born 26 January 1890, Ellough Road, Beccles, Suffolk; son of Robert John Read, Corn Merchant and Miller, and Frances Maria Sayer; m (1) Dorothea Cannon, 1921, (2) Jessica Winters, 1952; 2 sons, 2 daughters. **Subject(s):** Natural Sciences; BA 1911; MA 1916; MD 1920; MRCS; LRCP

(London Hospital) 1914. **Tutor(s):** J R Tanner. **Johnian Relatives:** uncle of Bryan Colman Read (1943); great uncle of Jonathan James Read (1971). **Educ:** Bishop's Stortford College. **Career:** Captain, RAMC 1914–1917; DADMS, Indian Cavalry Corps 1917–1919; House Physician, Junior Resident Accoucheur, Senior Resident Accoucheur, then Pathology Assistant, London Hospital 1919–1920; GP, Woking; Consulting work, Wimpole Street 1924–1928; Consulting work, Harley Street 1928–1941; GP, South Africa 1948–1953. **Publications:** *Natural Childbirth*, 1933; *Motherhood in the Post-war World*, 1943; *Childbirth without Fear* (alternative title – *Revelation of Childbirth*), 1944; *Birth of a Child*, 1947; *Antenatal Illustrated*, 1955; *No Time for Fear*, 1956. Died 11 June 1959.

READ, James Jolliffe (1947) Born 29 May 1926, Finchley, Middlesex; son of Arthur James Read, Civil Servant, Air Ministry, and Ada Edith Maie Jolliffe; m Margaret Janet Frances Saunders, 6 November 1954, Cardiff; 1 son (Duncan James b 16 June 1964), 2 daughters (Jane Mary b 9 March 1957 and Elizabeth Maie b 17 March 1959). **Subject(s):** Architecture; BA 1949; MA 1954; RIBA 1954; MRTPI 1957–1989; IHBC 1997. **Tutor(s):** C W Guillebaud. **Johnian Relatives:** son of Arthur James Read (1903). **Educ:** Henrietta Barnet School, Hampstead; University College School, Hampstead; Harrogate Grammar School; RWA School of Architecture, Bristol; Regent Street Polytechnic. **Career:** Army Signals, India/Pakistan 1944–1947; Nicholas and Dixon-Spain Architects 1950–1955; Deputy, Stepney/Poplar Division, London County Council Planning 1955–1960; Lecturer, Chelmsford Technical College 1958–1962; Planning, Town Centre South Division, Essex County Council 1960–1962; Deputy (Planning), Cumbernauld Development Corporation 1962–1967; Partner, Percy Johnson-Marshall and Partners, Edinburgh 1967–1969; Architectural Advisor, Department of Transport Bridge Department 1969–1977; Head, Conservation Division, English Heritage/Department of Environment 1977–1989. **Appointments:** Governor, Hemel Hempstead School 1974; Deputy Chairman, Hertfordshire Building Preservation Trust 1980–1999; Chairman, WEA Kings Langley 1993–1997; Chairman, Hertfordshire Building Preservation Trust 1999–2002.

READ, Lionel Frank (1949) Born 7 September 1929, 58 Queen's Road, Watford, Hertfordshire; son of Frank William Charles Read, Company Director, and Lilian Alberta Victoria Chatwin; m Shirley Greenhalgh, 1956; 2 sons, 1 daughter. **Subject(s):** Economics/Law; BA 1952; MA 1985. **Tutor(s):** C W Guillebaud. **Educ:** Ravensfield College, Hendon; Oundle School. **Career:** Commissioned, RHA 1949; Called to the Bar, Gray's Inn 1951; Recorder of the Crown Court 1974; General Commissioner of Income Tax, Gray's Inn Division 1986–1990; Deputy High Court Judge 1989. **Appointments:** Member, Senate of the Inns of Court and the Bar 1974–1977; Bencher 1981; Vice-Chairman 1986–1990, Chairman 1990–1994, Local Government and Planning Bar Association; Council on Tribunals 1990; Member, Bar Council 1990–1994; Treasurer, Gray's Inn 2001. **Awards:** QC 1973; Mons OCS Stick of Honour.

READE, George Lewis (1914) Born 25 October 1896, 38 Carlton Street, Cheltenham, Gloucestershire; son of John Reade, Bank Manager, and Alice Mary Wilson. **Subject(s):** History; BA 1921; MA 1926. **Tutor(s):** L H K Bushe-Fox. **Educ:** Wycliffe College, Stonehouse. **Career:** Captain, Rifle Brigade 1918; Master, Wycliffe College 1921. **Honours:** MC.

READER, Professor Desmond Harold (1946) Born 20 June 1920, 7 Woodland Road, Upper Norwood, London; son of Harold Norton Reader, Major, and Sarah Johanna Wasserfall; m Dolores; 4 sons (Nicholas, William, Howard and James). **Subject(s):** Moral Sciences/Archaeology and Anthropology; BA 1948; MA 1953; PhD 1953. **Tutor(s):** F Thistlethwaite. **Educ:** English School, Cairo; École Sacré Coeur, Mauritius. **Career:** Master, London Preparatory School; Professor, London University. **Appointments:** Anthony Wilkin Studentship in Ethnology and Archaeology, University of Cambridge 1949. Died 19 October 1983.

REAM, Charles Francis (1903) Born 21 August 1884, Doddington, Cambridgeshire; son of Charles William Ream, Harness Maker, and Mary Busby. **Subject(s):** Theology; BA 1906; MA 1910. **Tutor(s):** D MacAlister. **Educ:** King's School, Grantham. **Career:** Wesleyan Chaplain, RFA, Weedon, Northamptonshire 1906; Superintendent, West London Wesleyan Mission 1925; Four Ministry, Stockport; Ministry, Ilford, Highgate and Stratford, London. Died 16 January 1926.

REAY, Joseph (1922) Born 21 June 1902, 50 Bewick Road, Gateshead, County Durham; son of Joseph Reay, Shipowner and Colliery Owner, and Mary Eleanor Swallow. **Tutor(s):** B F Armitage. **Educ:** Wilkinson's Preparatory School, Newcastle; Oatlands, Harrogate; Aldenham School.

RECORDON, Dr Esmond Gareth (1922) Born 11 April 1904, Woodbury Cottage, Biggin Hill, Upper Norwood, Croydon, Surrey; son of David Recordon, General Merchant, and Hilda Mary Pike; m Frieda Robertson, 1933; 2 sons (Nigel and Piers). BA 1925; MA 1929; BChir 1928; MB 1929; MD 1936. **Tutor(s):** B F Armitage. **Johnian Relatives:** father of John Piers Recordon (1954) and of Nigel Esmond Recordon (1954). **Educ:** Berkhamsted School. **Career:** House Appointments, Norfolk and Norwich Hospital and St Bartholomew's Hospital; Senior Resident Officer, Moorfields Eye Hospital until 1933; Honorary Ophthalmic Surgeon, Addenbrooke's Hospital 1933; RAMC 1938–1943. **Appointments:** Vice-President, Ophthalmic Section, BMA. Died 23 August 1957.

REDDI, Cooduveli Venkata Krishna (1945) Born 17 October 1924, Rajahmundy, East Godavery District, India; son of Dewan Bahadu Cooduveli Viraswami Reddi, District and Sessions Judge, and Cooduveli Venkata Ramanamma. **Subject(s):** Mathematics; BA 1947; MA 1951; BA (Madras) 1945. **Educ:** Madras Christian College School; Madras Christian College.

REDDING, John Hubert (1942) Born 31 March 1924, 3 Shelfanger Road, Diss; son of Frederick Matthew Redding, Commercial Traveller, and Ellen Louisa Perry; m Margaret Joan Price, 10 September 1956, Timperley Parish Church, Cheshire; 2 sons (Michael Kenny and Steven Andrew), 2 daughters (Margaret Anne and Louise Julia). **Subject(s):** Mechanical Sciences; BA 1945; MA 1949; FIEE; FASCE; MPMI; MCIM; PEng. **Tutor(s):** S J Bailey. **Educ:** Eastholme Private School, Harleston; Bungay Grammar School; City of Norwich School. **Career:** Electrical Engineer, Metropolitan-Vickers Electrical Company Limited, Trafford Park, Manchester 1944–1953; Mechanical Engineer, Renold Chains Limited, Didsbury, Manchester 1953–1954; H G Acres and Company Ltd, Consulting Engineers, Niagara Falls, Ontario, Canada 1954–1961 (Resident Engineer, Maple Leaf Cement Plant, West Pakistan 1954–1956; Project Manager, Shadiwal Hydro-Electric Project, West Pakistan 1956–1961); Resident Engineer, Henry J Kaiser, Engineers and Contractors, Montreal 1961–1962; Resident Electrical Engineer, W P London & Partners, Consulting Engineers, Niagara Falls, Ontario 1963; Vice-President and General Manager, Pakistan, Asselin Benoit Boucher Ducharme Lapointe, Consulting Engineers, Montreal, Quebec, Canada 1964–1966; Director and Chief Thermal Engineer, Asselin Benoit Boucher Ducharme Lapointe, Consulting Engineers, Montreal 1966–1974; Ontario Regional Manager, Reid Crowther & Partners Limited, Consulting Engineers, Toronto 1974–1978; General Manager, C-Tran Development Corporation, Toronto 1978–1981; Project Manager, Kilborn Limited, Consulting Engineers, Toronto 1981–1996; Assistant Construction Manager, Bissett Gold Mining Company Ltd, Bissett, Manitoba 1996–1997; Project Manager, K-Line Maintenance & Construction Limited, Engineers and Contractors, Toronto 1998–1999; Project Manager, Hydro One Networks Inc, Toronto 1999. **Appointments:** CU Engineers Association.

REDDY, Cattamanchi Ramalingam (1902) Born 13 January 1881, Cattamanchi, Chitoor, India; son of Satrah Mania Reddiar, Landholder. **Subject(s):** History; BA 1905; MA 1909; Hon LittD 1936. **Tutor(s):** C E Graves; J R Tanner. **Educ:** Madras Christian College. **Career:** Professor of History 1909–1918, Principal 1916–1918, Maharajah's College, Mysore; Inspector-General of Education, Mysore 1918–1921; Vice-Chancellor, Andhra University 1926–1930 and 1936–1949; Pro-Chancellor, Mysore University 1949. **Appointments:** Vice-President, Cambridge Union Society 1906; Secretary, Cambridge University Liberal Club; Member, All-India Advisory Board of Education 1921 and 1940; Deputy Leader and Organiser, United Nationalist Party 1924; Member, Legislative Council of Madras 1935; nominated to Upper Chamber of New Provincial Legislature 1937; Member, All India Board of Scientific and Industrial Research 1941. **Awards:** Scholarship, Government of India; Madras University Prize for a work of modern interest in Telugu. **Honours:** Kt 1942 (relinquished 1947). **Publications:** *Speeches on University Reform; Political Economy in Telugu; Enquiry into the Principles of Poetry; Collected Poems and Collected Essays (Telugu); Congress in Office*, 1940; *Democracy in Contemporary India* (Madras University Endowment Lectures). Died 25 February 1951.

REDDY, Nayanivenkata Gopalakrishna (1927) Born 28 December 1905, Guntur, Madras, South India; son of Nayanivenkata Rango Rao, Zemindar of Mungala, and Buchamma; m Sarojini Devi; 1 son (Nayini Santosh Kumar b 22 October 1938). BA 1932. **Tutor(s):** J M Wordie. **Johnian Relatives:** father of Nayini Santosh Kumar Reddy (1958); grandfather of Neehara Reddy (1993). **Educ:** Toww High School, Guntur; Hindu High School, Triplicane; St Paul's College, Calcutta; St Xavier's College, Calcutta; Presidency College, Madras. Died 21 April 1997.

REDFERN, Philip (1940) Born 14 December 1922, The Hollies, Etwall, Derby; son of Robert Redfern, Timber Merchant, and Edith Florence Plant; m Gwendoline Mary Phillips, 1951; 3 daughters (Deborah b 1956, Dilys b 1959 and Clair b 1961). **Subject(s):** Mathematics; BA 1943; MA 1978. **Tutor(s):** J M Wordie; S J Bailey. **Educ:** Bemrose School, Derby. **Career:** Junior Scientific Officer, TRE, Malvern, working on 'OBOE' radar device 1942–1945; Assistant Statistician 1947–1950, Statistician 1950–1960, Central Statistical Office; Chief Statistician, Ministry of Education 1960–1967; Director of Statistics and Joint Head of Planning Branch, Department of Education and Science 1967–1970; Deputy Director, Office of Population Censuses and Surveys 1970–1982; Consultant to the Statistical Office of the European Communities 1983–1986. **Awards:** Scholarship, SJC 1940; Hughes Prize, SJC 1946. **Honours:** CB 1983. **Publications:** *A Study of the Future of the Census of Population: Alternative Approaches*, Luxembourg: Office for Official Publications of The European Communities, 1987.

REDMAN, Dudley Stewart (1922) Born 6 August 1903, Northcote, Laleham Road, Staines, Middlesex; son of Alfred John Redman, Brewer, and Minnie Jones; m Josephine (d 14 December 1952); 1 son (Timothy), 2 daughters (Desiree d January 1948 and Dawn). **Tutor(s):** E A Benians. **Educ:** Lindisfarne, Abberley Hall, Great Witley; Cheltenham College. **Career:** Chairman, Wells & Winch Ltd Brewers. **Appointments:** Chairman, Biggleswade Urban Council. Died 14 December 1960.

REDMAN, The Revd George Bertram (1910) (admitted to Jesus College 1905) Born 28 July 1886, Hyderabad, Sindh, India; son of Joseph Redman, Missionary, and Harriett Charlton; m Elinora Adelaide Staunton Batty, 18 September 1917, St Andrew's, Madulipatam. **Subject(s):** Classics/Theology; MA 1912; BA (Jesus) 1908. **Tutor(s):** J R Tanner. **Educ:** Repton School; Ridley Hall, Cambridge. **Career:** Priest 1914; Deacon 1912; CMS Missionary, Masulipatam 1913–1918; CMS Missionary, Khammamett 1918–1922 (on leave 1919–1920); Curate, St Paul, St Albans 1923–1926; Acting Secretary, Candidates' Department, CMS 1923–1926; Vicar, St Catherine, Leyton 1926–1933; Rector, Croft, with Vicarage, Yarpole 1933–1938; Rector, Whatfield, Suffolk 1938–1950. **Awards:** Naden Studentship, SJC; Bell Scholarship, University of Cambridge 1906; Rustat Scholarship, Jesus College. Died 20 November 1950.

REDMAN, Professor Roderick Oliver (1923) Born 17 July 1905, Bryans, Rodborough, Stroud, Gloucestershire; son of Roderick George Redman, Outfitter, and Elizabeth Miriam Annie Stone; m Kathleen Bancroft; 3 sons, 1 daughter. **Subject(s):** Mathematics; BA 1926; MA 1930; PhD 1930; FRS 1946. **Tutor(s):** E Cunningham. **Johnian Relatives:** father of David Roderick Redman (1957), Christopher Willard George Redman (1960) and of Richard Carlyle Redman (1964); grandfather of Nicholas David Roderick Redman (1995). **Educ:** Rodborough Council School, Stroud; Miss Newey's Private School, Stroud; Uplands Council School, Stroud; Marling School, Stroud. **Career:** Staff, Dominion Astrophysical Observatory, Victoria, British Columbia 1931; Assistant Director, Solar Physics Observatory, Cambridge 1931–1937; Title E Fellow, SJC 1931–1947; Chief Assistant, Radcliffe Observatory, Pretoria, South Africa 1937–1947; Professor of Astrophysics, University of Cambridge 1947–1972; Title C Fellow 1947–1972, Title D Fellow 1972–1975, SJC. **Appointments:** President, Royal Astronomical Society 1959–1961; Consultant, SRC. **Awards:** Isaac Newton Studentship, University of Cambridge 1927; Restricted John Stewart of Rannoch Scholarship in Sacred Music, University of Cambridge 1925; Sheepshanks Exhibition, University of Cambridge 1927. Died 6 March 1975.

REDPATH, Dr (Robert) Theodore Holmes (1937) (admitted to St Catharine's College 1931) Born 17 August 1913, 31 Arragon Gardens, Wandsworth, London; son of William Redpath, Engineer, and Kate Holmes; m Sarah Jane Campbell Taylor, 9 September 1964; 1 son, 2 daughters. **Subject(s):** English; MA 1938; PhD 1940; BA 1934 (St Catharine's); Final Bar Examination 1948. **Tutor(s):** J S Boys Smith. **Educ:** Oatlands School, Harrogate; The Leys School, Cambridge; St Catharine's College, Cambridge. **Career:** Assistant Lecturer in English 1951–1954, Lecturer in English 1954–1980, University of Cambridge; Fellow, Trinity College, Cambridge 1950–1997. **Appointments:** Pro-Proctor 1953–1954 and 1958, Senior Proctor 1955 and 1959, University of Cambridge; Tutor, Trinity College, Cambridge; Visiting Professor, Angers 1981; Visiting Professor, Heidleberg 1983; Visiting Professor, Daohisha University, Tokyo 1984; Visiting Professor, Tsuda College, Tokyo 1984; Visiting Professor, Davidson College, USA 1987. **Awards:** Charles Oldham Shakespeare Scholarship, University of Cambridge 1933; Strathcona Research Studentship for Philosophy, SJC 1937. **Publications:** *Songs and Sonnets of John Donne*, 1990; *Ludwig Wittgenstein: A Student's Memoir*. Died 1997.

RÉE, Harry Alfred (1933) Born 15 October 1914, 15 Mauldeth Road, Withington, South Manchester; son of Alfred Rée, Consultant, and Lavinia Elizabeth Dimmick; m Hettie (née Vine). **Subject(s):** Economics/Modern and Medieval Languages; BA 1936. **Tutor(s):** C W Guillebaud. **Educ:** The Craig, Windermere; Ladybarn House School, Withington; Shrewsbury School; Institute of Education, University of London. **Career:** Beckenham County School 1941; Civilian parachutist and organiser of sabotage for the Resistance; Talks Producer, BBC Forces Broadcast; Senior Modern Languages Master, Bradford Grammar School 1946–1951; Headmaster, Watford Grammar School 1951–1962; Professor of Education, University of York 1962–1974; Language Teacher, Woodberry Down Comprehensive 1974. **Awards:** Croix de Guerre; Medaille de la Resistance. **Honours:** DSO; OBE. **Publications:** *Educator Extraordinary, A Life of Henry Morris, Founder of Community Schools*. Died May 1991.

REECE, David Chalmer (1946) Born 14 February 1926, 1010 Jessie Avenue, Winnipeg, Manitoba, Canada; son of Rupert Camborne Reece, Grain Merchant, and Mary Gwendolen Marples; 3 children. **Subject(s):** Law; BA 1949; MA 1974. **Tutor(s):** F Thistlethwaite. **Johnian Relatives:** nephew of Francis Bertram Reece (1909). **Educ:** Grosvenor School; Ravenscourt School; University of Manitoba. **Career:** Called to the Bar, Inner Temple 1951; Department of External Affairs, Canada 1952; Minister and Deputy Permanent Representative to the United Nations 1969; High Commissioner to Trinidad & Tobago and Barbados 1972; High Commissioner to Ghana (and Ambassador to Dahomey & Togo) 1974–1976; Canadian Ambassador to the NATO Warsaw Pact Arms

Limitation talks, Vienna 1978; High Commissioner to Jamaica, Bahamas, Caymans, Belize 1982–1985; High Commissioner to Zambia and Malawi 1987–1990.

REECE, Francis Bertram (1909) Born 31 December 1888, The Rectory, Llanfwrog, Ruthin, Denbighshire; son of John Francis Reece, Clerk in Holy Orders, and Margaret Mary Paynter; m (1) Gladys Catherine Wood, 1914 (d 1939); (2) Dorothy Alice Macbeth, 1940; 1 daughter, 4 step-daughters. BA 1912. **Tutor(s):** L H K Bushe-Fox. **Johnian Relatives:** uncle of David Chalmer Reece (1946). **Educ:** Colet House School, Rhyl; Rossall School, Fleetwood. **Career:** Captain and Adjutant, RE, WWI; Called to the Bar, Inner Temple 1914; Recorder, Birkenhead 1935–1943; Metropolitan Magistrate 1943–1961 (at Bow Street 1948 onwards). **Appointments:** Chairman, Poisons Board 1946–1958. **Awards:** Squire Law Scholarship 1909. Died 4 April 1971.

REECE, Morris George Bernard (1901) Born 23 October 1882, Newport Road, Roath, Cardiff; son of Edmund Bernard Reece, Coroner, and Mary Pauline Long. **Subject(s):** History; BA 1904. **Tutor(s):** C E Graves; J R Tanner. **Educ:** Felsted School. **Career:** Assistant Commissioner, Karnal District, Indian Civil Service 1905–1909. Died 4 October 1909.

REED, Anthony Alfred (1923) Born 5 March 1904, Trenley, Mannamead, Plymouth, Devon; son of Anthony Alfred Sherwill Reed, Merchant or Commission Agent, and Mary Ann Ethel Martin. **Tutor(s):** B F Armitage. **Educ:** Sangeen Preparatory School, Bournemouth; Blundell's School, Tiverton; Stirling House School, Bournemouth. Died 11 January 1960.

REED, The Revd Denys Adrian (1942) Born 18 February 1925, 37 Grosvenor Drive, Whitley Bay, Northumberland; son of William Ernest Reed, Consulting Engineer, and Ethel Doreen Allard; 1 son (Paul). **Subject(s):** Modern and Medieval Languages, Economics; BA 1948; MA 1951. **Tutor(s):** C W Guillebaud. **Educ:** Newcastle upon Tyne Royal Grammar School. **Career:** Vicar, Starcross, Exeter; Curate, St Luke, West Hartlepool 1954–1956; Principal, Schlenker Secondary School, Port Loko, Sierra Leone 1956–1960; Rector, Berryharbour, Devon 1960; Warden, Jerome House, Students' Hostel, London 1968. Died 23 August 1982.

REEKIE, Dr James (1937) Born 4 February 1914, 11 Viewforth, Cockenzie, Tranent; son of Peter Reekie, Carpenter, and Agnes Plummer. PhD 1945. **Tutor(s):** J M Wordie. **Educ:** Adelaide Technical High School, Australia; University of Adelaide, Australia; University of Edinburgh.

REES, Arthur Carlyon (1918) Born 29 February 1888, Harrison's Terrace, Truro, Cornwall; son of Thomas Morgan Rees, Methodist Minister, and Louisa Walker. **Tutor(s):** E E Sikes. **Johnian Relatives:** brother of Francis Edward Rees (1914). **Educ:** Bradford Grammar School; KCL; Birkbeck College, London; United Methodist Theological College.

REES, Charles Owen Benwell (1924) Born 12 February 1906, Alexandria, Egypt; son of William Benwell Rees, Merchant and Shipowner, and Ethelreada Blanche Barker; m Elaine Trevitt Briggs, 26 April 1928, St Mark's, North Audley Street, London. BA 1927. **Tutor(s):** B F Armitage. **Educ:** St George's, Folkestone; King's School, Canterbury; Penfillican House, Folkestone. **Career:** Cotton Broker and Merchant, Rees & Co, Alexandria, Egypt 1932. Died 6 December 1982.

REES, David Hollingworth (1934) Born 27 February 1916, The Manse, Apperly Bridge, Rawdon, Yorkshire; son of Edward Rees, Wesleyan Minister, and Helen Elizabeth Jackson; m Dorothea. **Subject(s):** Classics; BA 1937; MA 1946; DipEd (Dunelm). **Tutor(s):** R L Howland. **Educ:** Harwich County Secondary School; Kingswood School, Bath. **Career:** Classics Master, Alsop High School 1947–1952; Senior Classical Master, Rochdale Municipal High School 1952–1953; Senior Classical Master, Dame Allan's School, Newcastle upon Tyne 1953–1959;

Headmaster, Carre's Grammar School, Sleaford, Lincolnshire 1959–1976. **Awards:** Scholarship, SJC. Died 18 July 1993.

REES, Francis Edward (1914) Born 20 November 1895, 6 Milton Place, Halifax, Yorkshire; son of Thomas Morgan Rees, Methodist Minister, and Louisa Walker. **Tutor(s):** E E Sikes. **Johnian Relatives:** brother of Arthur Carlyon Rees (1918). **Educ:** Stafford College, Forest Hill; Nottingham High School. **Career:** Sub-Lieutenant, Royal Naval Division 1915; Second Lieutenant (Aeroplane Officer), RFC/RAF 1916–1918. **Awards:** Exhibition, SJC. Died 22 August 1918 (killed in action).

REES, Hubert Leonard (1909) Born 10 November 1890, 7 Tennyson Street, Nottingham; son of Leonard Robert Rees, Journalist, and Mary Ellen Hollis. **Subject(s):** Mathematics; BA 1912. **Tutor(s):** J R Tanner. **Educ:** Merchant Taylors' School, London.

REES, John Idwal (1931) Born 25 July 1910, 15 Rosehill Terrace, Swansea; son of John Clarke Rees, Master Draper, and Jane Stephens; m Megan Davies, 1937 (d 2001); 1 son (Colin). **Subject(s):** Classics; BA 1933; MA 1939; BA (Swansea) 1931. **Tutor(s):** M P Charlesworth. **Educ:** Terrace Road Council School, Swansea; Swansea Grammar School; University College, Swansea. **Career:** Rugby International (14 caps) and sometime captain, Welsh Rugby Team; Headmaster, Cowbridge Grammar School 1938–1971. Died 31 August 1991.

REES, His Honour Richard Geraint (1929) Born 5 May 1907, Caradoc Road, Aberystwyth, Cardiganshire; son of Richard Jenkin Rees, Minister, Presbyterian Church of Wales, and Apphia Mary James; m (2) Peggy; 1 daughter (Victoria), 1 stepson (Paul), 1 stepdaughter (Felicity). **Subject(s):** Law; BA 1931; LLB (Wales). **Tutor(s):** C W Guillebaud. **Educ:** Secondary School, Aberystwyth; High School, Cardiff; University College of Wales, Aberystwyth. **Career:** Called to the Bar, Middle Temple 1932; Practised on the South Wales Circuit 1932–1956; Lieutenant Colonel, Welsh Guards 1939–1945; Metropolitan Magistrate, Old Street 1956–1961, Bow Street 1961–1972; Circuit Judge 1972–1981. **Awards:** Certificate of Honour, Middle Temple; US Bronze Star. Died 27 March 1986.

REESE, Clifford Raymond (1949) Born 24 October 1930, 3 Havelock Terrace, Welshpool, Powys, Wales; son of George Edward Reese, Tobacconist and Confectioner, and Gladys Marjorie Blockley; m Mary Frances Taylor, 18 November 1954; 2 sons (Gavin David b 1960 and Peter Barnes b 1967), 1 daughter (Lisa Georgina b 1962). **Subject(s):** Natural Sciences; BA 1952; MA 1956. **Tutor(s):** G C L Bertram. **Educ:** Berriew Council School, Welshpool; County School, Welshpool; King Edward VI School, Birmingham. **Career:** Radar Operator, RAF 1948–1949; Postgraduate Trainee, Standard Telephones and Cables 1952–1955; Development Engineer to Assistant Managing Director, GEC Avionics 1955–1993; Staff Executive, Marconi-Elliott Avionic Systems Ltd 1975–1979. **Awards:** Major Scholarship, SJC 1947.

REEVES, John Michael (1945) Born 1 December 1926, Merritt, British Columbia, Canada; son of Albert George Reeves, Clerk in Holy Orders, and Doris Helen Swinburn. **Subject(s):** Classics; BA 1948. **Tutor(s):** J M Wordie. **Educ:** St Hugh's School, Woodhall Spa; Marlborough College. **Career:** Lecturer in Classics, University of British Columbia 1948–1952; Producer and broadcaster, music, drama, documentary and religious programmes, CBC Radio 1952–1987; Freelance Producer 1987–; Composer and author. **Appointments:** Member, Canadian League of Composers. **Awards:** Choral Scholarship, SJC; Masaryk Award 1989; Canadian Music Council Award for best choral broadcast of 1982. **Publications:** Musical compositions including *Canons for String Orchestra, Op 7*, 1979; *For The Feast of All Hallows*, 1979; *Compline Cantata, Op 11*, 1980; *Advent Cantata, Op 17*, 1980; *Salvator Mundi, Op 20*, 1983; *Threnody for the People of Poland, Op 22*, 1984; *Veni Creator Spiritus, Op 31*, 1986; *Rossetti Prelude and Fugue, Op 33*, 1988; *Requiem Mass, Op 40*, 1990 and *Calendar, Op 41*, 1991; broadcast scripts including *A London Trio*, 1950 and *St Matthew Trio*, 1990; detective novels, *Murder by Microphone*, 1978; *Murder Before Matins*, 1984; *Murder with Muskets*, 1985.

REID, Ian Christie (1939) Born 14 June 1920, 13 Wellington Circus, Nottingham; son of Alexander Christie Reid, Ophthalmic Surgeon, and Ellen Jane Shaw Grant; m Barbara Herian, 27 December 1952; 1 son, 1 daughter. **Subject(s):** Geography; BA 1947; MA 1949. **Tutor(s):** R L Howland. **Educ:** Private Kindergarten School, Nottingham; Nottingham High School; Oakham School. **Career:** High School Teacher, Britain, Kenya, Canada, Australia. **Awards:** Award for Contributions to the Protection of the Environment.

REID, Raymond Warwick Harry (1942) Born 10 December 1923, The Orchard, Dundry, Avon; son of Harry Cyril Wilberforce Reid, Bank Accountant, and Muriel Adeline Palmer; m Melodie Brooke Peters, 10 October 1953, St Swithun's Church, Woodbury, Devon; 2 sons (Arthur Warwick Petre and Richard Harry). **Subject(s):** History; BA 1948; MA 1960. **Educ:** Weymouth College; Wellingborough School. **Career:** Entered Colonial Administration Service (later Overseas Civil Service) 1948, served in Malaya, Singapore, N Borneo 1948–1966; Administrator in an Industry Training Board 1966–1983; administrative positions, mainly connected with electronics 1983–1989.

REIDY, Dr Joseph Patrick Irwin (1926) Born 30 October 1907, 314 Commercial Road, St George's in the East, Middlesex; son of Jerome Joseph Reidy, GP, and Frances Warren Dawson; m (1) Anne Johnson, 1943 (d 1970), (2) Freda Clout (née Lowe), 1972; (1) 3 daughters. **Subject(s):** Natural Sciences; BA 1929; MA 1936; MB 1937; BChir 1937; MD 1959; FRCS; MRCS (London Hospital) 1932; LRCP (London Hospital) 1932. **Tutor(s):** M P Charlesworth. **Educ:** Stonyhurst College, Blackburn. **Career:** Metropolitan Police Surgeon 1930s; Albert Dock Hospital 1939–1940; St Andrew's Hospital, Billericay 1940–1942; Chief Assistant in Plastic Surgery, St Thomas' Hospital, London and Consultant Plastic Surgeon, Middlesex County Hospital 1947; Assistant to Professor Pomfret Kilner in Plastic Surgery, Stoke Mandeville Hospital until 1957; Director, Stoke Mandeville Plastic Surgery Unit and Consultant at Westminster Hospital 1957–1972; Lecturer in Surgery, Westminster Medical School 1959. **Appointments:** Twice Hunterian Professor, Royal College of Surgeons; President, British Association of Plastic Surgeons; Freeman, City of London. **Awards:** Gold Medal, Czechoslovak Academy of Sciences 1961. **Publications:** *Plastic Surgery and Psychotherapy*. Died 10 September 1991.

REILLY, Terence Callcott (1935) Born 5 August 1917, Madras, India; son of Terence Calcott Reilly, Assistant Accountant General, Indian Finance, and Laura Henrietta Winifred Copcutt. BA 1941; MA 1960. **Tutor(s):** J S Boys Smith. **Educ:** Breeks Memorial School, Ootacamund, India; Bradfield College.

REILY, Denis (1948) Born 14 December 1927, Royal Infirmary, Preston, Lancashire; son of Dennis Cyril Reily, Electrical Engineer, and Ellen Alice Taylor; m Joan Elizabet Davis Chapman, 16 May 1953, Welton; 1 son (Clive Michel b 4 August 1959), 1 daughter (Susan b 23 February 1954). **Subject(s):** Mechanical Sciences; BA 1950; MA 1974; MICE. **Tutor(s):** R L Howland. **Educ:** Leamington on Tyne Elementary School; Westhead Elementary School, Ormskirk; Birchfield Road Elementary School, Perry Barr; Handsworth Grammar School. **Career:** Civil Engineer. **Awards:** Strathcona Scholarship, SJC; Overseas Premium, ICE.

RENNIE, Donald Williamson (1904) Born 14 January 1885, 87 Park Road, Glasgow, Scotland; son of John Rennie, Electrical Engineer, and Agnes Balderston Williamson. **Subject(s):** Mechanical Sciences; BA 1907. **Tutor(s):** D MacAlister. **Educ:** St Mark's College School, Chelsea; City of London School. **Career:** Testing Assistant, Board of Trade Electrical Standards Laboratory 1907–1908; Pupil, Yarrow and Company 1908–1910; Second Lieutenant, 5th Battalion, Royal Fusiliers,

then attached, Royal Warwickshire Regiment, WWI. Died 11 November 1914 (killed in action).

RENSHAW, Robin Henry Leigh (1937) Born 6 November 1918, 392 Lea Bridge Road, Leyton; son of Isaac Renshaw, Clerk in Holy Orders, and Gwendoline Englefield Ford; m Olwen Renshaw. **Subject(s):** Economics; BA 1940; MA 1991. **Tutor(s):** J S Boys Smith. **Educ:** Gowan Lea Private School, London; Forest School, Walthamstead; Manchester Tutorial College, Manchester. **Career:** ICI. Died 12 March 2001.

REPARD, Hugo William Arbouin (1929) Born 15 May 1911, 4 Hatherley Road, Richmond; son of William John Repard, of independent means, and Grace Madeline Bigsby; m Rosemary. **Subject(s):** Law; BA 1932. **Tutor(s):** E A Benians. **Johnian Relatives:** stepbrother of Denis William Garstin Latimer Haviland (1929). **Educ:** Seafield School, Collington; Rugby School. Died 28 April 2002.

REUBEN, David Ezra (1914) Born 9 March 1893, Hassan, Mysore State, India; son of Ezra Reuben, Chief Judicial Officer, and Sarah Nagaokai. **Subject(s):** Mathematics; BA 1917. **Tutor(s):** L H K Bushe-Fox. **Educ:** St Joseph's College, Bangalore; Bishop's High School, Poona; Deccan College, Poona. **Career:** Assistant Magistrate and Collector, Bihar and Orissa 1919; Officiating Magistrate and Collector 1925–1926; Officiating Settlement Officer 1926–1928; Officiating District and Session Judge 1928–1932; District and Session Judge 1932–1944; Judge, Patna High Court 1944. **Awards:** Cama Prize 1918.

REUCHLIN, Jonkheer Henri (1925) Born 6 July 1906, Rotterdam, Holland; son of Johan George Reuchlin, Director, Holland-America Line, and Agatha Maria Elink Schuurman; m (1) Johanna Helena Jacola Lichtenbelt, 1967, (2) Emma Georgjovna Nedaba, 1995 (d); 3 sons, 3 daughters. **Subject(s):** Economics; BA 1928; MA 1932. **Tutor(s):** E E Sikes; M P Charlesworth; C W Guillebaud. **Educ:** Erasmianum Gymnasium, Rotterdam, Holland. **Career:** Department of Trade and Shipping, the Hague and later Amersfoort 1945; Executive Board, Holland-America Line, Rotterdam until 1971. **Appointments:** Chairman, Netherlands Institute of Transport 1971–1976; Member, Executive Board, Holland-America Line; Member, Board of Directors, Amsterdam-Rotterdam Bank. **Awards:** Foundation Scholarship, SJC 1928. **Honours:** Chevalier in the Order of the Netherlands Lion 1965. **Publications:** Books on Maritime History. Died 1 December 1998.

REYNOLDS, Arthur Rudolph (1926) Born 4 February 1906, 94 Brakespeare Road, Deptford, Kent; son of William Reynolds, Surgeon, and Florence Mary Tonkin. BA 1929; MA 1946. **Tutor(s):** M P Charlesworth. **Educ:** Durston House School, Ealing; The Ryley's School, Alderley Edge; Denston College; Harrow. **Career:** Assistant Secretary, Milk Marketing Board; Captain 1930, Major 1940, Lieutenant Colonel 1944, Sicily and Italy 1943–1945, TA; Twice Mentioned in Despatches; Called to the Bar, Lincoln's Inn 1931; Hudson's Bay Company 1946–1972 (Secretary 1948–1972). Died 22 July 1972.

REYNOLDS, The Revd Charles William (1900) Born 20 May 1881, Latchford, Warrington, Cheshire; son of John Pritchard Reynolds, Tanner, and Edith Mary Crossley. BA 1905. **Tutor(s):** D MacAlister. **Educ:** Preparatory School, Southport; Warrington Grammar School. **Career:** Ordained Deacon 1926; Ordained Priest 1927; Curate, Liverpool, Warrington, Farnworth 1927–1932.

REYNOLDS, Eric Vincent (1923) Born 30 April 1904, Cheapside, Sandridge, St Albans, Hertfordshire; son of Arthur John Reynolds, Farmer, and Lilly Barker. **Subject(s):** Modern and Medieval Languages; BA 1926; MA 1931. **Tutor(s):** E E Sikes. **Educ:** St Albans School; Haileybury College. **Career:** Lektor in English Language and Literature, University of Leipzig 1926–1927; Assistant Master, Rugby School 1927–1930; Assistant Master, Upper Canada College, Toronto, Canada 1931–1932; Head, JTC, Rugby School 1938–1944; Headmaster, Stowe School 1949–1958. **Honours:** TD. Died December 1992.

REYNOLDS, Oliver William (1926) Born 2 May 1908, Merdon, Surrey Road, Bournemouth; son of William Thomas Reynolds, Architect, and Alice Catherine Wood. **Subject(s):** Law; BA 1929; MA 1933. **Tutor(s):** M P Charlesworth. **Educ:** Henley School, Bournemouth; The College, Bishop's Stortford; RADA. **Career:** Dancer, Ballet Rambert; Actor; Drama Teacher, London Theatre Studio; Founder, own drama school; Teacher, Central School of Speech Training and Dramatic Art, until retirement in 1960s. Died 20 January 1998.

REYNOLDS, Canon Wilfrid James (1933) Born 27 May 1914, 31 Clark Street, Stourbridge, Worcester; son of Harry Arthur Reynolds, Journeyman Baker, and Louisa Hard; m Dorothy. **Subject(s):** Classics, Theology; BA 1936; MA 1940. **Tutor(s):** R L Howland. **Educ:** Wollaston C of E Elementary School; King Edward's School, Stourbridge; Ridley Hall, Cambridge. **Career:** Ordained Deacon 1938; Curate, Lower Milton 1938–1941; Ordained Priest 1939; Curate, St Nicholas with St Peter, Droitwich 1941–1942; Private Chaplain to Bishops of Worcester 1943; Licensed to officiate, Wollaston 1943–1946; Vicar, Whites Ladies Aston with Churchill and Spetchley 1946–1949; Vicar, Hallow, Worcester 1949–1979; Rural Dean, Martley and Worcester West 1972–1979. **Appointments:** Honorary Canon, Worcester Cathedral 1974–1979. Died 23 March 1986.

REYNOLDS, The Revd William Henry Robert (1910) Born 7 March 1888, 7 West Street, Grimsbury, Warkworth, Banbury, Northamptonshire; son of Henry Leonard Reynolds, Bookseller and Stationer, and Elizabeth Mary Marchant. **Subject(s):** History; BA 1913; MA 1919. **Tutor(s):** J R Tanner. **Educ:** Northampton and County School; Salisbury Theological College. **Career:** Schoolmaster 1904–1910; Deacon 1914; Curate, Kidderminster 1914–1919; Priest 1915; Temporary CF, 4th Class, RACD 1917–1919; Curate, St Paul, Burton on Trent 1919–1920; Assistant Master, St Andrew's School, Bloemfontein, South Africa 1920–1922; Assistant Master, Dale College, King Williams Town 1922–1928; Warden, Bishop's Hostel and Assistant Master, Boys' High School, Kimberley 1929–1943; Chaplain and Assistant Master, St Andrew's College, Grahamstown 1943–1947; Warden, Beda Hall, Fort Hare 1948–1949; English Master, St Matthew's College, Grahamstown 1949–1954; Assistant Priest, St James, Graaff Reinet 1957–1959. Died 16 September 1959.

RHOADES, George (1935) Born 27 April 1913, 2205 Broadway, New York, USA; son of Lyman Rhoades, Banker, and Carol Beardsley Nye. **Subject(s):** Economics; BA 1937. **Tutor(s):** C W Guillebaud. **Educ:** Hotchkiss School, Lakeville, USA; Los Alamos Ranch School, Otowi, New Mexico, USA; Williams College, Massachusetts, USA; University of North Carolina, USA. **Career:** Railroading, Banking, Financial Counselling; Publisher, *Municipal Bond Review*. Died 20 November 1972.

RHODEN, Harry George (1928) Born 27 July 1906, 10 Vine Street, Wigan, Lancashire; son of Joseph Rhoden, Chemist on Benzol Plant, and Margaret Smith; m (1) Olive (d 1 October 1949), (2) Ruth; 2 daughters (Margaret and Frances). **Subject(s):** Mathematics/Mechanical Sciences; BA 1930; MA 1939; BSc (London). **Tutor(s):** J M Wordie. **Educ:** Whelley Elementary School, Wigan; Wigan and District Mining and Technical College; London University. **Career:** Metropolitan-Vickers Electrical Company Ltd, Manchester 1930–1938; Demonstrator in Engineering 1938–1946, Lecturer in Engineering 1946–1955, Reader in Engineering 1955, University of Cambridge; Title B Fellow 1941–1972, Lecturer in Mechanical Sciences 1947–1972, SJC. **Appointments:** Supervisor in Mechanical Sciences 1939–1947, Director of Studies in Mechanical Sciences 1942–1969, SJC. **Awards:** Scholarship, SJC; Wright's Prize, SJC 1930; Ricardo Prize, University of Cambridge 1930; Whitworth Scholarship. Died 18 April 1972.

RHODES, Alan Naylor (1934) Born 25 April 1916, 85 Cross Flatts Street, Holbeck, Leeds; son of Arthur Rhodes, Commercial Traveller, and Annie Wilcock; 1 son. **Subject(s):** Law; BA 1937; MA 1941. **Tutor(s):** C W Guillebaud. **Educ:** Roundhay School, Leeds. **Career:** Solicitor; Captain, Army. **Honours:** MC.

RHODES, Charles Malcolm (1949) Born 2 November 1928, 183 Highgate, Heaton, Bradford, Yorkshire; son of Charles Rhodes, Bank Clerk, and Doris Isabel Rushworth. **Subject(s):** Geography; BA 1952. **Tutor(s):** J M Wordie. **Educ:** Bradford Grammar School. **Career:** Royal Army Ordnance Corps 1947–1949. **Publications:** 'UK Industries', *Geographical Review*.

RHODES, Donald Horsfall (1942) Born 6 January 1925, Huddersfield. **Subject(s):** Natural Sciences; BA 1945; MA 1948; CBiol; MIBiol; CertEd (Liverpool). **Tutor(s):** C W Guillebaud. **Educ:** Aireborough Grammar School, Yeadon. **Career:** Commissioned, Royal Indian Army Service Corp 1943–1947; Chief Fisheries Officer, Uganda Government 1949–1964; Head of Biology Department, Queen Elizabeth's Grammar School, Blackburn, Lancashire 1966–1985. **Honours:** MBE 1965. **Publications:** *Report to the Government of Kenya on Fisheries Development Possibilities*, Food and Agriculture Organisation of the United Nations, Rome 1965; *Uganda Government Fisheries Department Annual Reports, 1952–1964*, Government Printer, Entebbe, Uganda.

RHYS-LEWIS, Dr Rees Daniel Sidney (1934) See LEWIS.

RIACH, Donald James (1945) Born 2 April 1927, 22 Brompton Street, Oldham, Lancashire; son of George Alexander Riach, Railway Clerk, and Beatrice Maud Medley; m Agnes Barr (Nancy) Finlay, 17 December 1960; 1 son (Alastair b 1964), 1 daughter (Jeannie b 1962). **Subject(s):** Geography; BA 1948; MA 1952. **Tutor(s):** J M Wordie. **Educ:** Werneth Council School, Oldham; Oldham Hulme Grammar School. **Career:** Department of Education 1948–1949; RAF 1949–1953; Geography Assistant, Wellingborough Grammar School 1953–1959; Head of Geography and Housemaster, later Head of Middle School, Hinchingbrooke School, Huntingdon 1959–1983 (then part-time 1983–1987). **Publications:** (Contributor) *Field Excursions in Eastern England, Field Studies for Schools*, Vol 5, Rivingtons.

RIAD, Mohammed Abdel Moneim (1922) Born 3 September 1899, Cairo, Egypt; son of Mustafa Bey Riad and Anissa. **Tutor(s):** E A Benians. **Educ:** Egyptian Primary School; Egyptian Secondary School; Egyptian Royal School of Law.

RICE, Henry Goulding (1903) Born 24 July 1883, 12 Friar Gate, Derby; son of George Rice, Physician, and Constance Hardwick. **Subject(s):** Natural Sciences; BA 1906. **Tutor(s):** D MacAlister. **Educ:** St Olave's Grammar School, Southwark. **Career:** Captain, RAMC (wounded), WWI.

RICE, Leonard Cyril (1912) Born 14 January 1894, 47 Truro Street, Truro, Cornwall; son of Hugh Rice, Draper, and Emily Farley. **Subject(s):** Mathematics; BA 1917. **Tutor(s):** L H K Bushe-Fox. **Educ:** Truro College; The Leys School, Cambridge. **Career:** Captain, 6th Loyal North Lancashire Regiment, WWI; Accounts and Marketing, Strick, Scott and Co, Managing Agents 1919–1926; Manager, Khanaqin Oil Co, Baghdad 1926–1935; NAFT Chief Representative in Tehran 1935, in London 1946. **Honours:** CBE 1945.

RICE, Otis Radcliffe (1928) Born 18 August 1903, 1409 Hill Road, Reading, Pennsylvania, USA; son of Clarence Edgar Rice, Clergyman, and Mary Campbell Peckham. **Tutor(s):** E A Benians. **Educ:** Springfield Central High School; Harvard University; Graduate School, Episcopal Theological College, Harvard.

RICHARDS, David Rigby (1942) Born 27 September 1923, 4 Sydenham Road, Croydon; son of Darcy John Rigby Richards, Major General, RA, and Margaret Bridgwater. **Tutor(s):** S J Bailey. **Educ:** Nevill Holt Preparatory School, Leicestershire; Brighton College.

RICHARDS, Professor Elfyn John (1936) Born 28 December 1914, 93 Tynewydd Road, Barry, Glamorganshire; son of Edward James Richards, Schoolmaster, and Catherine Williams; m (1) Eluned Gwenddydd Jones (d 1978), (2) Olive Meakin, 1986 (d 1989), (3) Miriam Davidson Romsey, 1990; 3 daughters, 1 stepdaughter. **Subject(s):** Mathematics; BA 1938; MA 1943; DSc (Wales); Honorary DSc (Herriot Watt); Honorary DSc (Southampton); Honorary LLD (Wales); Honorary DTech (Loughborough); Hon FRAeS 1991. **Tutor(s):** J M Wordie. **Educ:** Gladstone School, Barry; Barry County School; University College, Aberystwyth. **Career:** Research Assistant, Bristol Aeroplane Company 1938–1939; Scientific Officer, National Physical Laboratory, Teddington 1939–1945; Chief Aerodynamicist and Assistant Chief Designer, Vickers Armstrong Ltd, Weybridge 1945–1950; Aeronautical Engineer; Professor of Aeronautics at Southampton University 1950–1961; Founding Director, Institute of Sound and Vibration Research 1961–1966; Vice-Chancellor, Loughborough University 1967–1975; Resident Professor, Florida Atlantic University 1983. **Appointments:** President, Society of Environmental Engineers 1971–1973. **Awards:** James Watt Medal, Institution of Civil Engineers; Taylor Gold Medal, Royal Aeronautical Society. **Honours:** OBE 1961. Died 7 September 1995.

RICHARDS, Dr Francis Alan (1922) Born 20 February 1904, Fellside, Sanderstead, Surrey; son of Roland Alfred Richards, Costume Manufacturer, and Frances Gregory Ison; m Mary Loveday Murray; 3 sons (Brian, John Murray and Martin). **Subject(s):** Natural Sciences; BA 1925; MA 1934; BChir 1930; MB 1930; MD 1934; MRCP. **Tutor(s):** E A Benians. **Johnian Relatives:** father of Brian Richards (1952), John Murray Richards (1957) and of Martin Richards (1959); grandfather of Vanessa Coral May Richards (1986) and of Tifanny Frances Caroline Richards (1992). **Educ:** Southover Preparatory School, Coulsdon; Whitgift Grammar School, Croydon. **Career:** Consultant Physician, St Bartholomew's Hospital, Rochester. Died 20 November 1978.

RICHARDS, Geoffrey Clement Thorneley (1937) Born 18 June 1918, 617 Stretford Road, Old Trafford; son of William David Richards, Clerk in Holy Orders, and Hilda Edmundson Thorneley; m Myola, 12 July 1944; 1 son (David b 1945), 1 daughter (Wendy b 1948). **Subject(s):** History/Archaeology and Anthropology; BA 1940; MA 1944. **Tutor(s):** J S Boys Smith. **Educ:** Rossall School; St Paul's Cathedral Choir School; Sedbergh School. **Career:** RAF, WWII; Master, Gresham's School 1946–1948; Wing Commander, RAF Education Branch 1948–1969; Lecturer, Norfolk College of Arts and Technology 1969–1979; Choirmaster, St Paul's Cathedral, Rockhampton 1985–1988. **Awards:** Sizarship, SJC 1937; Second Gordon Shephard Memorial Prize, RAF 1954. **Publications:** *A Life in Three Acts* (autobiography).

RICHARDS, Geoffrey John (1942) Born 6 June 1924, 6 Falkland Avenue, New Southgate, Middlesex; son of Frank Howe Richards, Accountant, and Mabel Lily Tull. **Educ:** New Malden Church of England Boys' School; Surbiton County Boys' School.

RICHARDS, John (1942) Born 21 January 1924, 27 Cressy Road, Cardiff; son of John Brinley Richards, Architect, and Sarah Jane Jenkins. **Subject(s):** Mechanical Sciences; BA 1945; MA 1949. **Tutor(s):** S J Bailey. **Educ:** Great Crosby Preparatory School; Merchant Taylors' School, Crosby.

RICHARDS, John Gilbert (1932) Born 28 March 1913, Jobs Well, Saint Peter, Carmarthen; son of John Richards, Medical Practitioner, and Gurladus Mary Brown. **Tutor(s):** R L Howland. **Educ:** The High School, Carmarthen; Preparatory School, Denstone College; Denstone College.

RICHARDS, Robert (1906) Born 7 May 1884, Tan-y-ffordd, Pencraig, Llangynog, Oswestry; son of John Richards, Foreman Quarryman, and Ellen Roberts; m Mary Myfanwy Owen, 1918 (d 1950). **Subject(s):** Economics; BA 1908. **Tutor(s):** E E Sikes. **Educ:** Llangynog Board School; Aberystwyth University College; Llangyllm County School.

Career: Lecturer, Glasgow University; Lecturer in Economics, University College Bangor 1922; Tutor in Economic and Political Science, Coleg Harlech 1922–1945; Labour MP for Wrexham 1922–1924, 1929–1931 and 1935–1954; Parliamentary Under-Secretary for India 1924. Died 22 December 1954.

RICHARDS, Thomas Clifford (1942) Born 8 January 1925, 4 Cunliffe Walk, Garden Village, Acton; son of Edward Thomas Richards, Colliery Fireman, and Susan Davies. **Tutor(s):** C W Guillebaud. **Educ:** Acton Park Council School; Grove Park County School.

RICHARDSON, Alexander Reginald Wakefield (1920) Born 17 November 1902, Ballydonaghy, Portadown, County Armagh, Ireland; son of Richard Henry Stephens Richardson, gentleman of independent means, and Ethel Johanna Richardson. **Tutor(s):** B F Armitage. **Educ:** Mourne Grange Preparatory School, Kilkeel; Leighton Park School, Reading.

RICHARDSON, Dr Alfred Henry (1903) Born 11 July 1884, 16 Lynwood Avenue, Lower Darwen, Lancashire; son of John Alfred Richardson, Schoolmaster, and Mary Anne Whitaker; m Olive. BA 1907; MA 1910; MB 1912; BChir 1912; MRCS; LRCP 1910; FRCS 1912. **Tutor(s):** J R Tanner; C E Graves. **Educ:** Durham School. **Career:** Surgeon Lieutenant, RN, WWI; Obstetric Surgeon, St Thomas' Hospital; Consulting Surgeon, Grosvenor Hospital for Women; Assistant Physician, General Lying-in Hospital. **Honours:** OBE. **Publications:** Medical texts. Died 20 August 1942.

RICHARDSON, Geoffrey Christian (1928) Born 8 September 1910, 19 Wingrove Road, Newcastle upon Tyne; son of Oswald Brown Richardson, Insurance Surveyor, and Margaret Ann Fatherley; m Sally; 2 sons (Joseph and Robert), 1 daughter (Jane). **Subject(s):** Law; BA 1932. **Tutor(s):** M P Charlesworth. **Educ:** Preparatory School, Eskdale Tower, Newcastle; Durham School. **Career:** Metropolitan Police, New Scotland Yard 1932; Higher Executive Officer, Metropolitan Police, New Scotland Yard 1938; Captain, 90th City of London Field Brigade, TA 1939. **Honours:** CBE. Died 1 July 1985.

RICHARDSON, George (1928) Born 10 May 1910, 5 North Parade, Batley, Yorkshire; son of Joseph Richardson, Coal Miner, and Annie Parkinson; 1 daughter (Ann). **Subject(s):** Mathematics; BA 1931; MA 1937. **Tutor(s):** J M Wordie. **Educ:** Purlwell Council School, Batley; The Grammar School, Batley. **Awards:** Miners Welfare National Scholarship. Died 11 December 1992.

RICHARDSON, Dr George Oglethorpe (1930) Born 31 January 1913, 6 Graingerville North, Newcastle upon Tyne; son of Ernest Yeoman Richardson, Dental Surgeon, and Emma Hanks; m Jean; 2 sons (Hugh and Ben), 1 daughter (Claire). BA 1934; MA 1942; BChir 1937; MB 1937; MD 1942; MRCP 1943; FRCP 1959. **Educ:** Thornton House School, Newcastle upon Tyne; Ascham House School, Gosforth; Durham School. **Career:** Clinical Teacher, King's College, Newcastle upon Tyne; Lecturer in Pathology, Newcastle 1937–1939; RAF, India 1939–1945; Senior Physician, Newcastle General Hospital 1945–1977. Died 27 March 1984.

RICHARDSON, Ian Jackson Herbert (1940) Born 9 December 1922, 69 London Road, Newark, Nottinghamshire; son of Cecil George Herbert Richardson, Mechanical Engineer, and Hilda Jackson; m Sheila G Rind, 18 November 1944, Hertfordshire. BA 1943. **Tutor(s):** S J Bailey. **Educ:** The Magnus Grammar School, Newark; The Preparation School, Sedbergh; Sedbergh School.

RICHARDSON, John Brown (1940) Born 7 June 1921, 76 Walmersley Road, Bury, Lancashire; son of Walter Richardson, Builder's Foreman, and Annie Cook; m Hazel Barratt Ward Manning, 30 October 1954, St Columba's Church, Scarborough, Yorks; 1 son (Neil Brown Kendal b 11 June 1957). **Subject(s):** History; BA 1946; MA 1949; ACII 1949; FCII 1952. **Tutor(s):** C W Guillebaud. **Educ:** Chesham School, Bury; Hope Park Council School, Prestwich; Bury Grammar School. **Career:**

Insurance company, Manchester, then (from 1948) Liverpool, 1946–1983 (including 6 months on loan to an agent in Nairobi 1950, employment in various Liverpool departments concerned with overseas business up to 1968, 3 months in London 1967–1968, work in publicity 1968–c1970, then management services until 1983). **Appointments:** Member, Ramblers' Association, Merseyside and North Wales Area Footpaths and Amenity Committee 1949–c1986 (Secretary c1959–1967, Footpath Secretary, West Lancashire 1967–c1984); Member, Ramblers' Association (Lancashire) Footpaths Council; Ramblers' Association Representative, General Council, Lancashire Branch, CPRE; Member, Executive Committee, Lancashire Branch, CPRE 1962–2004 (Chairman 1980–1989); Member, West Lancashire Conservation Areas Advisory Panel 1991–. **Awards:** Exhibition, SJC 1939; Award for Outstanding Service to the Countryside, CPRE 1997. **Publications:** Written representation in response to consultation document, reproduced in *2001–2016 Joint Lancashire Structure Plan Review: Challenges and Choices*, Joint Advisory Committee for Strategic Planning (Lancashire County Council, Blackpool Borough Council and Blackburn-with-Darwen Borough Council), 2001.

RICHARDSON, John Stanley (1929) Born 25 March 1911, Kirkby on Bain, Lincolnshire; son of John Robert Richardson, Farmer, and Annie Houldershaw. **Subject(s):** Modern and Medieval Languages; BA 1932; MA 1936; MRSL. **Tutor(s):** C W Guillebaud. **Educ:** C of E School, Kirkby on Bain; Queen Elizabeth Grammar School, Horncastle; KCL. **Career:** French Master, Mill Hill School; Translator to the Spanish Embassy in London 1936–1939; Lecture Tour, USA 1939–1940; RNVR, WWII. **Appointments:** Secretary, Arden Society of Artists and Writers Exiled in England 1938–1939. **Awards:** Jebb Research Studentship, 1933–1934; Strathcona Studentship, SJC 1934. Died March 1941.

RICHARDSON, Richard James (1943) Born 22 April 1925, 46 Ouseley Road, Balham, London; son of Alexander Richardson, Clerk, Ministry of Pensions, and Minnie Mann Farrant. **Tutor(s):** C W Guillebaud. **Educ:** Lavender Hill School; Henry Thornton School, Clapham Common.

RICHARDSON, Ruskin John Robert (1913) Born 14 April 1890, North Kensington, Middlesex; son of John James Richardson, gentleman of independent means, and Lucia Ellinor Freymuth. **Tutor(s):** L H K Bushe-Fox. **Educ:** Sydney Grammar School; Victoria College, Jersey; Bonn. **Career:** Enlisted in University and Public Schools Battalion 1914; gazetted Second Lieutenant, 3rd South Staffordshire Regiment; 2nd Battalion 1915 Lieutenant, 1st Battalion 1915. Died 25 September 1915 (killed in action in France).

RICHARDSON, William Eric (1946) Born 3 June 1925, 4 Benjamin Road, Wrexham, North Wales; son of William Richardson, Sales Representative, and Rose Hannah Rotchell; m Nancy Holmes, 1947; 1 son (Ian), 1 daughter (Susan). **Subject(s):** Geography; BA 1947; MA 1952; DipAnth; DipEd; MSc (Leeds) 1964. **Tutor(s):** J M Wordie. **Johnian Relatives:** father of Ian Michael Richardson (1970). **Educ:** Wrexham National School; Grove Park Grammar School, Wrexham; University of Edinburgh. **Career:** Teacher, Grove Park Grammar School, Wrexham; Thorne Grammar School, Yorkshire 1949; Samuel King's School, Alston, Cumberland; Lecturer in Geography, College of Commerce, Liverpool and Deputy Head, John Hamilton High School, Liverpool 1958–1964; Headmaster, Ellowes Hall Comprehensive School, Dudley 1964–1970; Headmaster, Four Dwellings Comprehensive School, Birmingham 1970–1982; Voluntary Parole Board (part time), Winson Green Prison. **Publications:** *Lost Canals of the Midlands*, 1996; *William Fowler, The Man and his Maps*, Kingswinford, 1999; *The Black Country as seen through Antique Maps*, 2000; Papers on climate (Cumberland and N Pennines).

RICHARDSON, The Revd William Thomas (1939) Born 2 April 1917, 17 Camden Road, Eastbourne; son of Samuel Wesley Richardson, Civil Engineer, and Ellen Theresa Phelan. BA 1942; MA 1946. **Tutor(s):** J S Boys Smith. **Educ:** St Augustine's Abbey School, Ramsgate; Douai School, Woolhampton. **Career:** Monk, St Augustine's Abbey.

RICHMOND, John (1926) Born 7 January 1903, 7 Southsea Terrace, Woodstock, Cape Town, South Africa; son of Frederick Walter Richmond, Ironmonger, British Manufacturers' Representative, and Jessie Josephine Isabella Turner. **Tutor(s):** J M Wordie. **Educ:** South African College, Junior School, Cape Town; South African College, High School, Cape Town; The University, Cape Town.

RICKARD, Frank Patrick (1935) Born 19 August 1912, Rangoon, Burma; son of Frederick Arthur Rickard, Bank Manager, and Ira Casement Smedley; m E M Barrett, 5 April 1945, Bedford. **Subject(s):** Mechanical Sciences; BA 1937; MA 1942. **Tutor(s):** J S Boys Smith. **Educ:** Oakfield, Rugby; Bedford School; RMA Woolwich.

RICKETTS, Henry Harcourt (1936) Born 1 August 1917, Rangoon, Burma; son of Alfred Arthur Hickman Ricketts, Civil Engineer, Public Works Department, Burma, and Annie Josephine Wells. **Subject(s):** Mechanical Sciences; BA 1939. **Tutor(s):** J S Boys Smith. **Educ:** Warwick School, Junior House; King Edward VI School, Bury St Edmunds; Warwick School. **Career:** RAF, WWII. Died 1940 (killed in the Battle of Britain).

RICKETTS, Malcolm (1937) Born 12 August 1917, The Grove, Penalt; son of William Shepherd Ricketts, Farmer, and Lizzie Robinson; 1 son. **Subject(s):** Classics/History; BA 1940; MA 1944. **Tutor(s):** R L Howland. **Educ:** Penalt School; Hereford Cathedral School. **Career:** War service (Mentioned in Despatches three times); Assistant Master, Dean Close School, Cheltenham 1946–1957; Schoolmaster, Manchester Grammar School 1957–1985. **Awards:** Sizarship, SJC 1937; Somerset Exhibition, SJC. Died 1 March 1997.

RIDDELL, David Adams (1919) Born 30 September 1899, 296 Renfrew Street, Glasgow, Scotland; son of William George Riddell, Engineer, and Jane Gibson Robb. **Subject(s):** History; BA 1922; MA 1934. **Tutor(s):** E A Benians. **Johnian Relatives:** brother of Thomas Cockburn Riddell (1922). **Educ:** St Mary's School, Melrose; Fettes College, Edinburgh.

RIDDELL, Thomas Cockburn (1922) Born 16 February 1903, Åbo, Finland; son of William George Riddell, Engineer, and Jane Gibson Robb. **Tutor(s):** E A Benians. **Johnian Relatives:** brother of David Adams Riddell (1919). **Educ:** St Mary's School, Melrose; Fettes College, Edinburgh.

RIDEAL, Guy St Clair (1924) Born 12 December 1905, Poplar Lodge, Twickenham, Middlesex; son of Arthur Henry Rideal, Doctor of Medicine, and Daisy Adeline Mead. BA 1927; MA 1931. **Tutor(s):** B F Armitage. **Educ:** St Hugh's Preparatory School, Chislehurst; St Andrew's Preparatory School, Eastbourne; Haileybury College. **Honours:** DSC. Died 20 April 1976.

RIDGWAY, David George (1933) Born 25 March 1915, 54 Baidsay Road, Walton, Liverpool; son of George Henry Ridgway, Flour Miller, and Mary Ann Young. **Subject(s):** Modern and Medieval Languages; BA 1936. **Tutor(s):** C W Guillebaud. **Educ:** Gladys Street Council School, Walton; Alsop High School, Walton.

RIDLEY, John Edward (1920) Born 31 July 1896, Lianchow, Kansuh, China; son of Henry French Ridley, Missionary, and Sarah Quéry; 1 son (David John). **Tutor(s):** E E Sikes. **Johnian Relatives:** father of David John Ridley (1951). **Educ:** China Inland Mission Boys' School, Chefoo, China; George Watson's College, Edinburgh; University of Edinburgh; RMA, Woolwich. **Career:** Lieutenant Colonel, RE; Fruit Farmer. **Awards:** Scholarship, SJC.

RIGBY, Donald Lang (1942) Born 17 September 1925, 72 Sandy Lane, Hindley, Lancashire; son of Joseph Rigby, Aircrew Inspector, and Lucy Lang. **Subject(s):** Mathematics; BA 1945; MA 1949. **Tutor(s):** C W Guillebaud. **Educ:** Castle Hill Church of England School, Hindley;

Hindley and Abram Grammar School. **Career:** Senior Scientist, British Scientific Instrument Research Association; RAE, Farnborough; Education and Training Officer, Development Engineering Group, UKAEA 1961; Assistant Secretary, North West Electricity Board 1961. Died 5 October 1982.

RIGG, Edward Comer (1944) Born 21 April 1926, Birch Hill House, Wardle, Rochdale, Lancashire; son of Charles Comer Rigg, Brewer's Outside Manager, and Annie Jeffrey. **Tutor(s):** J M Wordie. **Educ:** Lower Place Council School; Municipal High School, Rochdale. **Career:** RAF 1945–1976 (Pilot training, RAF College, Cranwell; test flying duties, mainly jet fighter aircraft, 1950s and 1960s; final rank, Wing Commander); Finance Industry, mainly dealing with British expatriates working abroad, for twenty years. **Appointments:** RAF Cadet, SJC. **Honours:** AFC 1957; MBE 1965.

RIGG, Dr John Michael (1946) Born 17 June 1928, 91 Fishergate Hill, Preston, Lancashire; son of Richard Phillip Anthony Rigg, Medical Practitioner, and Margery Bateman; m (1) Susan, 1958, (2) Alison Martin, 1997; (1) 3 sons (Philip, Andrew Michael and Christopher), 1 daughter (Caroline). **Subject(s):** Natural Sciences; BA 1949; MA 1955; BChir 1952; MB 1952; DCH (RCP) 1956; CRCP(C) 1961; FRCPC 1972. **Tutor(s):** G C L Bertram. **Johnian Relatives:** father of Andrew Michael Rigg (1985). **Educ:** Red House School, Moor Monkton, York; Sedbergh School. **Career:** Captain, RAMC 1953–1955; Clinical Professor of Paediatrics, University of British Columbia, Vancouver British Columbia, Canada 1974–1996; Examiner in Paediatrics, Royal College of Physicians and Surgeons of Canada 1978–1983; Consulting Paediatrician and Professor of Paediatrics, University of British Columbia 1980–1996 (Emeritus 1996). **Appointments:** President, Canadian Paediatric Society 1971–1972; Founding President, Canadian Paediatric Foundation 1973; Founding President, St George's School Foundation 1974; Trustee, Koerner Foundation 1984–1993; Honorary President, St George's School Foundation 1990.

RIGG, Theodore (1912) Born 6 April 1888, Settle, Yorkshire; son of John Rigg, Merchant and Importer, and Hannah Wilson. BA 1914; MA 1920. **Tutor(s):** R P Gregory. **Educ:** Newton School, Wellington, New Zealand; Wellington College, New Zealand; Victoria College, Wellington, New Zealand.

RIGHINI, Professor Guglielmo (1947) Born 16 January 1908, Castelfranco, Veneto, Treviso, Italy; son of Francesco Righini and Margherita Simoni. **Tutor(s):** J M Wordie. **Educ:** Università di Firenze; Instituto Tecnico, Padua. **Career:** Assistant, Astrophysical Observatory, Arcetri, Florence 1933–1937; Director, International Astronomical Station of Latitude, Carloforte 1937–1939; Professor of Astronomy and Physics, University of Cagliari 1938–1941; Professor of Spectroscopy, University of Florence 1941–1947; Professor of Astronomy, University of Bologna; Director, Astrophysical Observatory, Arcetri, Florence 1953–1978. **Publications:** Various, including *Radioastonomia solare*, N Zanichelli, 1960; 'New Light on Galileo's Lunar Observations', (eds) M L Righini Bonelli and William R Shea, *Reason, Experiment, and Mysticism in the Scientific Revolution*, Science History Publications, 1975; *Contributo alla interpretazione scientifica dell'opera astronomica di Galileo*, Istituto e museo di storia della scienza, 1978; (joint ed) *Padre Angelo Secchi nel centenario della morte, 1878–1978*, Accademia nazionale delle scienze, 1979. Died 29 May 1978.

RILEY, Keith Mcfarlane (1948) Born 15 February 1928, 24 Hornby Street, Oswaldtwistle, Lancashire; son of William Riley, Cotton Mill Salesman, and Audrey McFarlane Turner; m Joyce Ellen Wright, 25 August 1952, St Paul's Church, Oswaldtwistle; 5 daughters (Kathryn Elizabeth b 25 February 1953, Gillian Mary b 15 February 1954, Margaret Alison b 14 April 1955, Louise Anne b 11 January 1958 and Joanne b 26 November 1963). **Subject(s):** Natural Sciences; BA 1950. **Educ:** Mount Pleasant School; Accrington Grammar School; Sedbergh School. **Career:** Director in Textiles/Weaving.

RILEY, Peter (1949) Born 6 October 1930, Whitecross Nursing Home, Edgbaston, Birmingham; son of William Grimshaw Riley, Civil Engineer and Glass Manufacturer, and Catherine Walker. BA 1952. **Tutor(s):** R L Howland. **Johnian Relatives:** son of William Grimshaw Riley (1919). **Educ:** West Downs Preparatory School, Winchester; Old Hall Preparatory School, Wellington; Rugby School.

RILEY, Richard Woodburne (1949) Born 22 April 1930, Rough Lee Maternity Home, Accrington, Lancashire; son of Allan Woodburne Riley, Inspector of Schools, and Edith Margaret Ross; m Ruth Longworth Johnson, 31 March 1956; 1 son (Peter Ross Allan b 30 April 1966), 1 daughter (Alison Margaret b 11 October 1960). BA 1952; MA 1956; FICE 1964; FCIWEM 1970. **Tutor(s):** R L Howland. **Educ:** Uplands School, Stroud; Chuckery School, Walsall; Wolverhampton Grammar School. **Career:** Binnie, Deacon & Gourley (later Binnie and Partners, then Binnie, Black and Veatch) 1952–1995 (retired as Associate). **Awards:** Open Exhibition, SJC 1947; Scholarship, SJC 1952; James Forest Medal and Miller Prize, Institution of Civil Engineers 1956; Institution Medal, Chartered Institution of Water and Environmental Management 1978.

RILEY, William Grimshaw (1919) Born 5 March 1897, Stopes Brow, Blackburn, Lancashire; son of Timothy Riley, Draper, and Maria Grimshaw; m Catherine Walker, 28 July 1925, St Germain's, Edgbaston; 1 son (Peter). BA 1922; MA 1927. **Tutor(s):** E A Benians. **Johnian Relatives:** father of Peter Riley (1949). **Educ:** Stramongate School, Kendal.

RIMMER, Professor William Gordon (1947) (admitted to Sidney Sussex 1943) Born 7 October 1925, 5 Diana Street, Liverpool; son of William Rimmer, Whitesmith, and Florence Evelyn Marsh; m Sheila Davies, 24 June 1950; 3 daughters (Janet, Carolyn and Martine). **Subjects:** History; BA 1949; MA 1951; PhD 1968; MA (Harvard); FRHS. **Tutor(s):** F Thistlethwaite. **Educ:** Gladwys Street Council School, Liverpool; Liverpool Collegiate School; Harvard University. **Career:** Captain, RE 1943–1947; Lecturer in Economic and Social History, University of Leeds, until 1961; Professor of History, University College of the West Indies, Jamaica 1961–1964; Professor of History, University of Tasmania 1964–1969; Title B Fellow, SJC 1967–1968; Professor of Economic History, University of New South Wales 1969–1986. **Publications:** *Marshalls of Leeds: flax spinners, 1788–1886*, 1960; *Portrait of a Hospital: the Royal Hobart*, 1981; *In Time for War*, 1991. Died 29 June 1990.

RINGROSE, John Reginald (1922) See RINGROSE-VOASE.

RINGROSE, Dr Thomas Leonard (1945) Born 20 September 1927, 6 Arncliffe Road, Leeds; son of Henry Thomas Ringrose, Mechanical Engineer, and Doris Mary Hopps. **Subject(s):** Natural Sciences; BA 1948; MA 1962; MB 1952; BChir 1952; DMRT Eng 1961. **Tutor(s):** G C L Bertram. **Johnian Relatives:** cousin of Francis William Shepherd (1926); stepbrother of Michael Trevor Haslam (1952). **Educ:** Moorlands Preparatory School, Headingley; Old Hall Preparatory School, Wellington; Rugby School. **Career:** Middlesex Hospital; Assistant Radiotherapist, Mount Sinai Hospital, New York; Consultant Radiotherapist, Calgary, Canada.

RINGROSE, Thomas Sutcliffe (1937) Born 8 June 1918, Jamestown, New York State, USA; son of Thomas Hollingworth Ringrose, Company Director, and Florence Sutcliffe. BA 1940; MA 1944. **Tutor(s):** J S Boys Smith. **Educ:** St Peter's, Exmouth; Lickey Hills School, Redman; Oundle School.

RINGROSE-VOASE, John Reginald (RINGROSE) (1922) Born 27 October 1903, Anlaby House, Anlaby, Hull, Yorkshire; son of William Ringrose Ringrose-Voase, of independent means, and Isabel Watt; m Marjorie; 1 son (Christopher), 1 daughter (Elizabeth). **Tutor(s):** B F Armitage. **Educ:** Southcliffe School, Filey; Repton School; Home Place, Holt. Died October 1956.

RINGWOOD, Henry Hornby (1921) Born 11 April 1903, Ben Madigan, Fort William Park, Belfast, County Antrim, Ireland; son of Richard Frederic Ringwood, Solicitor, and Frances Dorothea Marriott. **Subject(s):** Law; BA 1924; LLB 1924. **Tutor(s):** E A Benians. **Educ:** Bilton Grange, Rugby; St Columba's College, Rathfarnham, Ireland.

RINTOUL, Andrew (1926) Born 21 June 1908, 62 Montgomerie Drive, Glasgow, Scotland; son of Peter Rintoul, Chartered Accountant, and Margaret Macdonald Tulloch; m Margaret Bell, 1936; 1 son, 1 daughter. BA 1929; CA. **Tutor(s):** J M Wordie. **Educ:** Allon Burn, Nairn; Merchiston Castle, Edinburgh. **Career:** Partner, Rintoul & Co, Chartered Accountants 1936; Chairman, Scottish National Trust Company Ltd 1938–1979; Chairman, Glasgow Stockholders' Trust Ltd 1938–1979; Chairman, Scottish Advisory Board, Legal & General Assurance Society 1967–1978; Member, Investment Advisory Committee, TSB Unit Trust 1969–1979; Chairman, Central Trustee Savings Bank 1979–1980; Honorary President, West of Scotland TSB 1980. **Appointments:** Trustee Savings Banks Association: Member, Executive Committee 1958–1967; Deputy Chairman 1961–1967; Vice-President 1968–1976; Chairman 1976–1980. Died 29 November 1984.

RIPPER, David William (1946) Born 16 November 1922, Kingsley, Eden Park, Lancaster; son of Charles Ripper, Art School Headmaster, and Ethel Snowden; m Pauline Wootton; 1 son (Martin Stephen b 5 May 1959), 1 daughter (Karen Mary b 11 August 1952). **Subject(s):** Natural Sciences; BA 1948; MA 1953; FIEE; CEng. **Tutor(s):** G C L Bertram. **Educ:** Scarborough College Preparatory School; Sherborne Preparatory School; King's School, Bruton; Brighton Technical College; Glasgow University (Military Technology). **Career:** Army Volunteer 1941; Second Lieutenant, RA 1942; Captain 1943–1946; Graduate Apprentice, J Lucas Ltd 1948–1950; Product Design Engineer, Section Leader, J Lucas Ltd 1950–1956; Product Chief Production Engineer, Plessey Ltd 1956–1958; Production Chief Development Engineer, Hoover Ltd 1958–1964; Product Manager, CAV Ltd 1964–1985. **Appointments:** Committee Member and Chairman, Ham Amenities Group 1986–1993; Ham Fair Organiser 1988–1995; Organising Executor and Trustee for three Family Trusts 1996.

RITCHIE, Alexander James Otway (1948) Born 5 May 1928, Edinburgh; son of Charles Henry Ritchie, Archdeacon of Northumberland, and Marjorie Alice Stewart; m Joanna Willink Fletcher, 12 September 1953, Fittleworth Church; 2 sons (Charles b 1957 and Andrew b 1961), 1 daughter (Susanna b 1954, d 1986). **Subject(s):** Modern and Medieval Languages/Economics; BA 1950; MA 1955. **Tutor(s):** C W Guillebaud. **Johnian Relatives:** nephew of John Neville Ritchie (1899) and of William Traill Ritchie (1901); son of Charles Henry Ritchie (1907); second cousin, once removed, of Graham Ward Bain (1910); cousin of James McLaren Ritchie (1927), Ian MacFarlane Ritchie (1932) and of Brian William Thomas Ritchie (1935); brother of Kenneth John Stewart Ritchie (1938); second cousin, once removed, of Joseph Bain (1949). **Educ:** Cargilfield School, Edinburgh; Stowe School, Buckingham. **Career:** Second Lieutenant, KRRC; Grindlays Bank plc, Deputy Chairman 1977–1983, Chief Executive 1980–1983; Glyn Mills and Co 1951–1970 (Director from 1964); Executive Director, Williams & Glyn's Bank 1970–1977; Chairman, Union Discount Company of London plc 1970–1990. **Appointments:** Member, London Committee, Ottoman Bank 1966; Governor, Stowe School 1971–1989; Member, Export Guarantees Advisory Council 1977–1982 (Deputy Chairman 1980–1981); Deputy Chairman, Grindlays Holdings 1978–1983; Chairman, Grindlays Bank 1984–1987; ANZ Holdings (UK) 1985–1987; Director 1986–1993, Deputy Chairman 1989–1993, Italian International Bank; Director, Australian and New Zealand Banking Group 1984–1987; Director, European Investment Bank 1986–1993; Chairman of Governors, Windlesham House School 1986–1993; Director, Debenham Tewson & Chinnocks Holdings plc 1987–1993; Director, Archdale Holdings 1991; Director, Bath Abbey Trust 1991; Chairman of Governors, Downe House School 1991–1995. Died 23 August 2000.

RITCHIE, Dr Brian William Thomas (1935) Born 30 October 1915, Cannington Cave, South Canterbury, New Zealand; son of William Traill Ritchie, Farmer, and Dorothy Cecil Dibbs; m (1) Jessie (Gillie) Carter (d 24 February 1951), (2) Prudence Blackley, 1954; (1) 1 son (Simon b 1948), 1 daughter (Julia b 1950, d 1990), (2) 2 sons (Johnathan b 1956 and James b 1959). **Subject(s):** Natural Sciences; BA 1938; MA 1946; MRCS; LRCP; DA; FFARCS. **Tutor(s):** R L Howland. **Johnian Relatives:** nephew of John Neville Ritchie (1899); son of William Traill Ritchie (1901); nephew of Charles Henry Ritchie (1907); second cousin, once removed, of Graham Ward Bain (1910); cousin of James McLaren Ritchie (1927); brother of Ian MacFarlane Ritchie (1932); cousin of Kenneth John Stewart Ritchie (1938) and of Alexander James Otway Ritchie (1948); second cousin, once removed, of Joseph Bain (1949). **Educ:** Timaru Boys' High School. **Career:** Consultant Anaesthetist, Newcastle AHA(T); Clinical Teacher in Anaesthetics, King's College, Newcastle upon Tyne 1959. Died 28 June 1992.

RITCHIE, Canon Charles Henry (1907) Born 28 May 1887, Balvraid, Dunedin, New Zealand; son of John MacFarlane Ritchie, Merchant, and Ella McLaren; m Marjorie Alice Stewart, 15 July 1915, St Michael's, Chester Square; 2 sons (Kenneth John Stewart b 1919, d 1989 and Alexander James Otway b 1928), 1 daughter (Jean b 1925, d 1951). BA 1910; MA 1914. **Tutor(s):** L H K Bushe-Fox. **Johnian Relatives:** brother of John Neville Ritchie (1899) and of William Traill Ritchie (1901); second cousin of Graham Ward Bain (1910); uncle of James McLaren Ritchie (1927), Ian MacFarlane Ritchie (1932) and of Brian William Thomas Ritchie (1935); father of Kenneth John Stewart Ritchie (1938) and of Alexander James Otway Ritchie (1948); second cousin of Joseph Bain (1949). **Educ:** Preparatory School, Dunedin, New Zealand; Collegiate School, Wanganui, New Zealand; Leeds Theological College. **Career:** Ordained Deacon 1911; Curate, St Michael, Chester Square 1911–1920; Ordained Priest 1912; Temporary Chaplain, RN 1914; Curate, All Saints, Dunedin, New Zealand 1921–1922; Curate, St Martin in the Fields, Westminster 1922–1927; Rector, St John the Evangelist, Edinburgh 1927–1939; Archdeacon, Northumberland, Canon, Newcastle upon Tyne, and Honorary Chaplain to Bishop of Newcastle 1939–1954; Chaplain to King George VI 1946–1952; Chaplain to HRH Queen Elizabeth II 1952–1958. Died 8 September 1958.

RITCHIE, Lieutenant Colonel George Lindsay (1909) Born 15 June 1888, Waltry, Milton of Campsie, Stirlingshire; son of William Ritchie, Owner of Calico Printing Works, and Edith Lamb; m Dorothy Beatrice Martyn. **Subject(s):** Classics; BA 1913. **Tutor(s):** E E Sikes. **Educ:** St Ninians Preparatory School, Moffat; Bedford Grammar School. **Career:** Articled to a Glasgow Shipbuilding Firm; Commissioned into Supplementary Reserve, then Captain, Royal Scots Fusiliers (wounded twice, Mentioned in Despatches), WWI; Royal Scots Fusiliers, WWII. **Awards:** Exhibition, SJC 1914. **Honours:** MC 1914. Died 24 March 1962.

RITCHIE, Ian MacFarlane (1932) Born 17 June 1913, Dunedin, New Zealand; son of William Traill Ritchie, Farmer, and Dorothy Cecil Dibbs; m Annette Gwendolene Orbell; 1 son (William Ian b 1941), 2 daughters (Pamela Gwendolene b 1943 and Suzanne b 1949). **Tutor(s):** E A Benians. **Johnian Relatives:** nephew of John Neville Ritchie (1899); son of William Traill Ritchie (1901); nephew of Charles Henry Ritchie (1907); second cousin, once removed, of Graham Ward Bain (1910); cousin of James McLaren Ritchie (1927); brother of Brian William Thomas Ritchie (1935); cousin of Kenneth John Stewart Ritchie (1938) and of Alexander James Otway Ritchie (1948); second cousin, once removed, of Joseph Bain (1949). **Educ:** Waihi Preparatory School, Winchester, New Zealand; Wanganui Collegiate School, New Zealand. Died 1998.

RITCHIE, James McLaren (1927) Born 23 November 1907, Dunedin, Otago, New Zealand; son of Russell Ian Ritchie, Medical Practitioner, and Lucy Bayley Rattray; m Nan Henrietta Orbell, 1936; 3 daughters (Judy Lyon b 1938, Wendy Diana b 1941 and Jane Catherine b 1945). BA 1930. **Tutor(s):** E A Benians. **Johnian Relatives:** nephew of John Neville

Ritchie (1899), William Traill Ritchie (1901) and of Charles Henry Ritchie (1907); second cousin, once removed, of Graham Ward Bain (1910); cousin of Ian MacFarlane Ritchie (1932), Brian William Thomas Ritchie (1935), Kenneth John Stewart Ritchie (1938) and of Alexander James Otway Ritchie (1948); second cousin, once removed, of Joseph Bain (1949). **Educ:** Waihi School, Winchester, New Zealand; Christ's College, Christchurch, New Zealand. **Career:** National Mortgage and Agency Company of New Zealand (Director 1953) 1935–1968. Died 18 August 1981.

RITCHIE, Kenneth John Stewart (1938) Born 30 April 1919, Torpoint, Cornwall; son of Charles Henry Ritchie, Clerk in Holy Orders, and Marjorie Alice Stewart; m Wanda Margaret Angela Bowlby, 7 July 1949, St Michael's, Chester Square; 2 sons (Ian b 1953 and Michael b 1956). **Subject(s):** Law; BA 1947; MA 1949. **Tutor(s):** R L Howland. **Johnian Relatives:** nephew of John Neville Ritchie (1899) and of William Traill Ritchie (1901); son of Charles Henry Ritchie (1907); second cousin, once removed, of Graham Ward Bain (1910); cousin of James McLaren Ritchie (1927), Ian MacFarlane Ritchie (1932) and of Brian William Thomas Ritchie (1935); brother of Alexander James Otway Ritchie (1948); second cousin, once removed, of Joseph Bain (1949). **Educ:** Cargilfield School; Stowe School. **Career:** Lieutenant, Durham Light Infantry, POW Germany, WWII; Called to the Bar, Inner Temple 1947; Legal Advisor to UKAEA 1977. Died 16 November 1989.

RITCHIE, William Traill (1901) Born 27 March 1882, Dunedin, New Zealand; son of John Macfarlane Ritchie, Merchant, and Ella McLaren; m Dorothy Cecil Dibbs, 28 April 1909, Sydney, New South Wales; 3 sons (Ian MacFarlane b 1913, d 1998, Brian William Thomas b 1915, d 1991 and Dennis Gordon Allright b 1923, d 1944), 1 daughter (Patricia Stuart b 1911). **Subject(s):** Mechanical Sciences; BA 1904. **Tutor(s):** D MacAlister. **Johnian Relatives:** brother of John Neville Ritchie (1899) and of Charles Henry Ritchie (1907); second cousin of Graham Ward Bain (1910); uncle of James McLaren Ritchie (1927); father of Ian MacFarlane Ritchie (1932) and of Brian William Thomas Ritchie (1935); uncle of Kenneth John Stewart Ritchie (1938) and of Alexander James Otway Ritchie (1948); second cousin of Joseph Bain (1949). **Educ:** Wanganui Collegiate School. **Career:** Quartermaster Sergeant (final rank), New Zealand Field Artillery 1914–1918; Farmer, Timaru, New Zealand. Died 22 May 1940.

RITTER, Laurence Wilbur (1946) Born 25 June 1922, New York City, USA; son of Harold Ritter, President, Norma-Hoffman Ball Bearings Company, and Esther Kinstler. **Subject(s):** History. **Tutor(s):** F Thistlethwaite. **Educ:** Julia A Stark Grammar School, Connecticut; Stamford High School; Dartmouth College, Hanover. **Career:** Staff Sergeant, US Army.

RIVETT, Dr Douglas Eric Arthur (1946) Born 27 June 1921, Cape Town, South Africa; son of Frank Norman Rivett, Bank Manager, Barclays Bank, and Susanna van Eeden; m Alletta Johanna Marais, 26 June 1954, Pretoria; 3 sons (Kelvin Norman b 15 October 1955, Malcolm John b 27 June 1957 and Alan Douglas b 5 September 1959). PhD 1948; MSc (South Africa) 1944. **Tutor(s):** G C L Bertram. **Educ:** Ceres High School, South Africa; Rhodes University College, Grahamstown. **Career:** South African Council for Scientific and Industrial Research, Pretoria, and Rhodes University, Grahamstown; Professor of Organic Chemistry, Rhodes University; President, South African Chemical Institute 1977–1978.

RIVLIN, Professor Ronald Samuel (1933) Born 6 May 1915, 39 Alderney Road, Mile End, Old Town, London; son of Israel Rivlin, Waste Rubber Merchant, and Bertha Aronsohn; m Violet Larusso, 16 June 1948; 1 son (John Michael b 1956). **Subject(s):** Mathematics/Physics; BA 1937; MA 1940; ScD 1952; Honorary Doctor of Science (Tulane) 1982; Honorary Doctor of Science (National Ireland) 1980; Honorary Doctor of Science (Nottingham) 1980; Honorary Doctor (Thessaloniki) 1984; AMIEE 1942; FInstP 1943. **Tutor(s):** J M Wordie. **Educ:** Dudley

House School; Hackney Downs School. **Career:** Research Physicist, Research Laboratories of The General Electric Company, Wembley 1937–1942; Scientific Officer, Telecommunications Research Establishment, Ministry of Aircraft Production, Malvern 1942–1944; Physicist, British Rubber Producers' Research Assocation, Welwyn Garden City 1944–1947; Guest Worker, National Bureau of Standards, Washington DC, and Consultant to the Office of the Rubber Reserve 1946–1947; Senior Physicist, British Rubber Producers' Research Association, Welwyn Garden City 1947–1950; Head of Research Group, Davy-Faraday Laboratory of the Royal Institution, London 1948–1952; Superintendent of Research, British Rubber Producers' Research Association, Welwyn Garden City 1950–1953; Head of Research Group, Mechanics Division, Naval Research Laboratory, Washington DC 1952–1953 (Lecturer, California Institute of Technology 1953); Professor of Applied Mathematics 1953–1963, Chairman, Division of Applied Mathematics 1958–1963, Professor of Applied Mathematics and Engineering Science and L Herbert Ballou University Professor 1963–1967, Brown University; Professor of Mathematics and Mechanics, Centennial University Professor and Director, Center for the Application of Mathematics 1967–1980, University Professor Emeritus 1980, Adjunct University Professor 1980–1990, Lehigh University; Consultant, Georgia Institute of Technology 1986–1987; Consultant, numerous industrial corporations; inventor and coinventor of nine patents. **Appointments:** Member, Editorial Committees, *Journal of Rational Mechanics and Analysis* 1952–1957; Member, Editorial Committees, *Archive for Rational Mechanics and Analysis* 1957–1972; Executive Committee, Society of Rheology 1957–1959 and 1971–1975 (Vice-President 1971–1973, President 1973–1975); Fellow, American Academy of Arts and Sciences 1958; Member, Editorial Committee, *Journal of Mathematical Physics* 1960; Member, Editorial Committee, *Journal of Applied Physics* 1960–1963; Guggenheim Fellow, University of Rome 1961–1962; Chairman, Society for Natural Philosophy 1962–1964; Member, Editorial Committee, *Rheologica Acta* 1963; Co-Chairman, Fourth International Congress of Rheology (Brown University) 1963; Member, Mechanics Advisory Committee, National Bureau of Standards 1965–1970; Professeur Associé, University of Paris 1966–1967; Member, Advisory Committee on the AIP Information Program, American Institute of Physics 1968–1974; Member, National Committee on Theoretical and Applied Mechanics 1972–1980, (Chairman 1976–1978, Vice-Chairman 1978–1980); Member, Editorial Committee, *Biorheology* 1972–1979; Member, Editorial Committee, *Mechanics Research Communications* 1974–; Board of Governors, Institute of Physics 1974–1975; Member, Committee of Scientific Society Presidents 1974–1977 (Executive Board 1975–1977, Secretary-Treasurer 1975–1976); Member, Editorial Committee, *Meccanica* 1975–1994; Representative of the International Committee on Rheology in the General Assembly, International Union of Theoretical and Applied Mechanics 1975–1980; Executive Committee, Applied Mechanics Division, ASME, 1975–1980, (Vice-Chairman and Secretary 1978–1979, Chairman 1979–1980); Member, Editorial Committee, *Journal of Non-Newtonian Fluid Mechanics* 1975–2001; Member, US Delegation to the General Assembly of the International Union of Theoretical and Applied Mechanics 1976–1978 (Chairman 1978); Russell Severance Springer Visiting Professor, University of California, Berkeley 1977; Honorary Member, Mexican Society of Rheology 1981; Member, Editorial Committee, *Journal de Mecanique Théorique et Appliquée* 1981–1989; Foreign Member, Accademia Nazionale dei Lincei 1982; Fellow, American Society of Mechanical Engineers 1983; Fellow, Institute for Advanced Study, Berlin 1984–1985; Distinguished Visiting Professor, University of Delaware 1985–1986; Member, National Academy of Engineering 1985; Honorary Member, RIA 1988; Member, Editorial Committee, *European Journal of Solids Mechanics* 1989–1991; Member, Editorial Committee, *International Journal of Solids and Structures* 1990–1995; Honorary Member, Editorial Committee, *Zeitschrift für Angewandte Mathematik und Mechanik* 1992–. **Awards:** Charles Goodyear Medal, American Chemical Society 1993; Theodore von Karman Medal, American Society of Civil Engineers 1993; Panetti Prize and Medal 1975; von Humboldt Senior Award 1981–1982;

Bingham Award Medal, Society of Rheology 1958; Timoshenko Medal, American Society of Mechanical Engineers 1987. **Publications:** (ed G I Barenblatt and D D Joseph) *Collected Papers of RS Rivlin* (2 volumes), Springer-Verlag New York Inc, 1996.

ROACH, William Francis (1918) Born 5 February 1898, Fennal Lodge, Harborne, Birmingham; son of Francis Handley Roach, Clerk in Holy Orders, and Mary Jessie Louisa Standerwick; m Doreen; 1 son (Peter). **Tutor(s):** E E Sikes. **Johnian Relatives:** uncle of Michael Lawrence Johnson (1952). **Educ:** St John's School, Leatherhead. **Honours:** MC. Died 25 January 1969.

ROB, Professor Charles Granville (1931) Born 4 May 1913, Hungerford Lodge, Oatlands Park, Weybridge, Surrey; son of Joseph William Rob, Medical Practitioner, and Alice Maud Granville-Smith; m Mary Dorothy Elaine Beazley, 23 July 1941; 2 sons (Joseph Michael and Peter James), 2 daughters (Caroline Mary and Sarah Rebecca). **Subject(s):** Natural Sciences; BA 1934; MA 1939; MB 1937; BChir 1937; MChir 1942; MD 1960; MChir (*Honoris Causa*) (TCD) 1961, Honorary DSc (Hartwick College, Oneonta, New York) 1967; Honorary MD (University of Ulm, Germany) 1985; FRCS 1939. **Tutor(s):** M P Charlesworth. **Johnian Relatives:** son of Joseph William Rob (1895); brother of John Vernon Rob (1934). **Educ:** Hordle House School, Milford-on-Sea, Hampshire; Oundle School. **Career:** Various Resident Medical and Surgical appointments, UK and Canada 1937–1942; Lieutenant Colonel, RAMC 1942–1946; Surgeon, St Thomas' Hospital 1946–1950; Reader in Surgery 1946–1950, Professor of Surgery 1950–1960, University of London; Consultant Vascular Surgeon, Royal National Orthopaedic Hospital; Consultant Vascular Surgeon to the Army 1949–1960; Surgeon in Chief, Strong Memorial Hospital; Professor of Surgery 1950–1960, Surgeon and Director, Surgical Professorial Unit 1950–1960, St Mary's Hospital; Professor and Chairman, Department of Surgery, The University of Rochester School of Medicine and Dentistry, New York State 1960–1978; Surgeon, Pitt Memorial Hospital; Professor of Surgery, University of East Carolina 1978–1983; Distinguished Professor of Surgery, Uniformed Services University of the Health Sciences, Bethesda, Washington DC 1983–2001. **Appointments:** Hunterian Professor, RCS 1946; Guest Surgeon, Australian and New Zealand Postgraduate Federation 1952; Surgeon in Chief Pro Tempore, Peter Bent Brigham Hospital, Boston 1952; Examiner for Doctorate of Medicine, University of Lund, Sweden 1955; Honorary Fellow, Venezuelen Surgical Society 1956, Cuban Society of Audiology 1956; Surgeon in Chief Pro Tempore, Presbyterian Hospital, New York City 1958; Visiting Surgeon in Chief, UCLA Medical Center, Los Angeles 1959; President, International Society of Cardiovascular Surgery 1961; Visiting Professor of Surgery, Walter Reed Army Hospital, Washington DC 1962, University of Michigan Medical School, Ann Arbor, Michigan 1963, University of Otago, Dunedin, New Zealand 1964, University of Manitoba, Winnipeg November 1965, Indiana University Medical Center, Indianapolis May 1966, Washington University, St Louis, Missouri and University of California, San Francisco 1967; Visiting Professor of Surgery and Honorary Fellow, University of Toronto 1970; Honorary Fellow, Australian Research Society 1970; President, International Cardiovascular Society, North American Chapter 1971; Honorary Fellow, Association of Surgeons of India 1972; Visiting Professor of Surgery, University of Cincinnati Medical Center 1973; Honorary Librarian, Royal Society of Medicine; Honorary Fellow and Secretary, Association of Surgeons of Great Britain and Ireland 1975; Honorary Fellow, Swedish Surgical Society 1978; Vice-President, American Surgical Association 1979; Honorary Fellow, Canadian Vascular Society 1983, Columbian Surgical Society 1986; Honorary Member, Israeli Society for Vascular Surgery 1986, West Coast Vascular Society 1986; Member, Court of Examiners, RCS. **Awards:** Rene Leriche Prize of the International Surgical Society 1975; Distinguished Community Service Award, Masons 1977; Roswell Park Medal, Buffalo Surgical Society 1981. **Honours:** MC 1943. **Publications:** (ed, with Rodney Smith) *Operative Surgery* (8 vols), 1956–1957, (14 vols), 1968–1969; more than 200 other papers and books. Died 26 July 2001.

ROB, John Vernon (1934) Born 17 December 1915, Hungerford Lodge, Oatlands Park, Weybridge, Surrey; son of Joseph William Rob, Physician and Surgeon, and Alice Maud Granville-Smith; m Bridget Anne Elizabeth Freeman, 1942 (div 1946); 1 daughter. **Subject(s):** Law; BA 1937; MA 1943. **Tutor(s):** R L Howland. **Johnian Relatives:** son of Joseph William Rob (1895); brother of Charles Granville Rob (1931). **Educ:** Hordle House School, Milford-on-Sea; Oundle School. **Career:** Probationer Vice-Consul, Paris 1939; Consulate, Liège 1939–1940; Army 1940–1945; Private Secretary to Parliamentary Under-Secretary (Foreign Service) 1945; First Secretary, Sofia 1949–1951; Attached to the Canadian National Defence College 1951–1952; Foreign Office 1952–1955; Counsellor, United Kingdom High Commission, New Delhi 1955–1958; Warsaw 1959–1960; British Ambassador to Republic of Congo, Gabon, the Central African Republic, and Chad Republic 1960–1962; HM Inspector of Foreign Service Establishments (Foreign Office) 1962–1965; British High Commissioner in Singapore 1965–1967; Foreign and Commonwealth Office (formerly Commonwealth Office). **Awards:** Munsteven Exhibition, SJC. **Honours:** CMG 1961. Died 7 March 1971.

ROBB, Alan Gardner (1944) Born 5 May 1926, Lodge Farm, Melton, Woodbridge, Suffolk; son of Campbell Robb, Captain, RAMC, and Marjorie Macneil Scott. **Tutor(s):** J M Wordie. **Educ:** Woodbridge School; Canford School.

ROBERTON, The Revd Spencer (1927) Born 1 May 1908, Craigielea, Heaton Road North, Newcastle upon Tyne; son of Edward Heton Roberton, Mining Engineer, and Florence Meek Lish. **Subject(s):** Classics; BA 1930; MA 1934; BD (London) 1938; MTh 1943. **Tutor(s):** M P Charlesworth. **Educ:** Denstone College; St John's School, Leatherhead; Exeter School. **Career:** Ordained Deacon 1931; Curate, St Andrew with St Catherine, Plymouth 1931–1934; Ordained Priest 1932; Curate, Old Radford 1934–1935; Curate, Rodbourne Cheney 1935–1936; Curate, Skipton in Craven 1936–1939; Rector, Norton Malreward 1939–1946; Perpetual Curate, Cudworth with Chillington 1946–1951; Vicar, Wroxton with Balscote, Oxon 1951–1969; Rector, St Creed, Cornwall 1960. **Awards:** Exhibition, SJC. Died 19 April 1986.

ROBERTS, Charles Edward (1910) Born 5 September 1891, East Haddon, Northamptonshire; son of Thomas Andrew Roberts, Shopkeeper and Sub Postmaster, and Abigail Smith. **Subject(s):** Natural Sciences; BA 1913; BSc (London) 1913. **Tutor(s):** L H K Bushe-Fox. **Educ:** East Haddon National School; Northampton and County School. **Career:** Merchants Marine Insurance Company 1940–1952. Died June 1957.

ROBERTS, His Honour David Ewart (1939) Born 18 February 1921, 843 Pershore Road, Selly Park, Birmingham; son of John Hobson Roberts, Manufacturing Confectioner, and Dorothy Rolason. **Subject(s):** Law; BA 1942; MA 1946; LLB 1947; LLM 1985. **Tutor(s):** S J Bailey; J M Wordie. **Educ:** West House School, Birmingham; Abingdon School. **Career:** Commissioned, RFA; service in Middle East, North Africa, Italy, Yugoslavia and Germany 1941–1946; Called to Bar, Middle Temple 1948; Assistant Recorder, Coventry QS 1966–1971; Recorder of the Crown Court 1978–1982; Circuit Judge 1982–1993. **Appointments:** Chairman, Midlands Branch, Johnian Society. Died 8 July 2002.

ROBERTS, David Wyn (1949) Born 12 February 1911, 5 Marmion Road, Toxteth Park, Liverpool; son of John Roberts, Presbyterian Minister, and Annie Jones Hughes; m Margaret MacDonald Baird; 1 son (Nicholas). **Subject(s):** Architecture; MA 1949; FRIBA. **Educ:** Elementary School, Cardiff; Cardiff High School; Welsh School of Architecture, Cardiff. **Career:** Lecturer, King's College, Newcastle 1936–1939; Captain, RE 1939–1945 (Mentioned in Despatches); Assistant Lecturer in Architecture, Faculty of Fine Arts 1946–1949, Lecturer in Fine Arts 1950–1978, University of Cambridge; Fellow, Magdalene College, Cambridge 1958; Practising Architect (designed buildings for Magdalene, Clare, Jesus, Churchill, Peterhouse and Girton). **Awards:** Sir John Sloane Medallion 1936. **Publications:** *The Town of Cambridge as it*

Ought to be Reformed: Plan of Nicholas Hawksmoor Interpreted in an Essay, CUP, 1955. Died 8 November 1982.

ROBERTS, Dr Donald James (1948) Born 9 November 1927, Moorlands Maternity Home, Dewsbury; son of Stanley Roberts, Accountant, and Eva Thompson; m Christine Margaret Lockyer, 24 August 1957, Hanover Street Congregational Church, Batley; 1 son (Jonathan Mark b 18 September 1961), 1 daughter (Elizabeth Anne b 20 October 1966). **Subject(s):** Natural Sciences; BA 1951; MA 1956; BChir 1956; MB 1956; DPH (Leeds) 1959; MRCS (England) 1954; LRCP (London) 1954; MFCM 1972; FFCM 1980; FFPHM 1989. **Tutor(s):** G C L Bertram. **Educ:** Haswell Council School; Wellfield Secondary School; Batley Grammar School; Guy's Hospital. **Career:** House Surgeon, House Physician, House Surgeon Obstetrics and Gynaecology, Victoria Hospital, Blackpool 1955–1956; GP, South Kirby, West Riding 1956–1957; Assistant County Medical Officer, West Riding Division 17 1957–1960; Deputy Medical Officer of Health, Deputy Principal School Medical Officer, Southport County Borough 1960–1963; Medical Officer of Health, Principal School Medical Officer and Port Medical Officer, Barrow-in-Furness County Borough 1963–1969; Medical Officer of Health, Principal School Medical Officer, City of Salford County Borough 1969–1974; Health Service Reorganisation, District Community Physician, South Manchester 1974–1976; Area Medical Officer, then District Medical Officer, St Helens and Knowsley Health Authority 1976–1986. **Appointments:** Member, BMA; FRSocMed; FRSH; FRIPHH. **Awards:** Arthur Newth Memorial Prize for year 1974–1975, Society of Community Medicine. **Publications:** Papers on Food Poisoning, Handicapped Children, and Cervical Cytology. Died January 2004.

ROBERTS, Donald Michael (1940) Born 2 June 1921, Lyndhurst, Farsley, Leeds; son of Donald Edward Roberts, Wholesale Clothier, and Mary Margaret Gaunt. **Tutor(s):** C W Guillebaud. **Educ:** Caldicott School, Hitchin; The Leys School, Cambridge. **Career:** Flying Officer, Bomber Command, RAFVR 1940–1945. **Awards:** Choral Scholarship, SJC. Died April 1945 (killed on air operations).

ROBERTS, Eldred Owen (1933) Born 4 May 1914, Thornaby, Ford Road, Upton, Cheshire; son of Owen Cadwalader Roberts, Company Director, and Florence Louisa Dawe. **Tutor(s):** C W Guillebaud. **Educ:** Birkenhead School; Liverpool College; Rydal School; LSE.

ROBERTS, Dr Ernest Theodore (1942) Born 29 January 1925, 121 Randolph Road, Glasgow; son of Theodore Ernest Roberts, Medical Practitioner, and Janet Pitcairn Hogg; m Maureen Milward, 3 September 1960; 2 sons (Graham b 1963 and Mark b 1970), 2 daughters (Jane b 1961 and Claire b 1966). **Subject(s):** Natural Sciences; BA 1945; MA 1949; BChir 1947; MB 1947. **Johnian Relatives:** father of Mark Theodore Milward Roberts (1988). **Educ:** Portsmouth Grammar School; Emmanuel School, Wandsworth (at Petersfield). **Career:** Casualty Officer and House Physician, St Thomas' Hospital 1947–1948; Flight Lieutenant and Medical Officer, RAF 1948–1950; GP, Portsmouth 1950–1990.

ROBERTS, Gwilym Henry Spooner (1926) Born 21 June 1907, Shop Foundry, 17 High Street, Llangefni, Anglesey; son of Robert Henry Roberts, Ironmonger, and Elizabeth Ann Gray-Owen. **Tutor(s):** J M Wordie. **Educ:** Council School, Llangefni; County Intermediate School, Llangefni.

ROBERTS, Harold Warlow (1926) Born 2 March 1908, Ethandune, St Helens Road, Ormskirk, Lancashire; son of Harold Heinekey Roberts, Miller and Merchant, and Amy Warlow; m Evelyn A Stone, 28 May 1938. **Subject(s):** Economics; BA 1929; MA 1934. **Tutor(s):** E A Benians. **Educ:** The High School, Ormskirk; Holmwood Preparatory School, Freshfield; Shrewsbury School. **Career:** Joseph Heap & Sons Ltd, Flour and Rice Millers, Liverpool; Civil Air Guard, Hooton 1938–1939; Auxiliary Fire Service 1940–1941. **Appointments:** Vicar's Warden,

Ormskirk Parish Church; First Secretary, Ormskirk Parochial Church Council. Died 27 March 1942.

ROBERTS, James Dearden (1948) Born 18 December 1926, Dunkerry, Longsight Road, Ramsbottom, Bury, Lancashire; son of William Roberts, Coal Merchant, and Ada Margaret Sharp; m Doreen May Billington, St Anne's Church, Tottington, Bury, 3 August 1977. BA 1950; MA 1955. **Educ:** The Grammar School, Bury; Mostyn House School, Parkgate; Oundle School. **Career:** Chairman, William Roberts & Son Ltd, Foundry Suppliers 1951; Chairman, Silver Street Building Company, Bury 1988. Died September 1998.

ROBERTS, John Bernard Parker (1921) Born 11 April 1902, Infield Park, Barrow-in-Furness; son of Harry Parker Roberts, Director of Finance, Ministry of Food, and Sarah Elizabeth Charles. BA 1924. **Tutor(s):** E A Benians. **Educ:** St Aubyn's, Barrow-in-Furness; Manor House School, Clapham Common.

ROBERTS, Philip Barker (1921) Born 7 December 1903, The Rectory, Tatham, Wennington, Lancashire; son of Arthur Senior Roberts, Clerk in Holy Orders, and Mary Jane Barker. BA 1925. **Tutor(s):** B F Armitage. **Johnian Relatives:** son of Arthur Senior Roberts (1887). **Educ:** St Annes-on-Sea; Lawrence House School, St Annes-on-Sea; Haileybury College; Sedbergh School.

ROBERTS, Robert John Michael (1944) Born 19 February 1926, Ellerslie, Longlands Park Road, Sidcup, Kent; son of Owen Morris Roberts, Civil Servant, and Dorothy Helen Roby. **Tutor(s):** J M Wordie. **Educ:** Merton Court School, Sidcup; Eastbourne College.

ROBERTS, Thomas Leslie Foulkes (1924) Born 17 April 1905, 1 Tower Road, Hereford; son of Thomas Mark Foulkes Roberts, Clerk in Holy Orders, and Grace Ethel Ireland. **Subject(s):** Classics; BA 1929. **Tutor(s):** E E Sikes. **Educ:** Hereford Cathedral School. **Career:** Master, Brandon House, Cheltenham 1927–1929; Master, Bandstead Hall Preparatory School, Surrey 1929; Master, Lockers Park Preparatory School, Hemel Hempstead. **Awards:** Exhibition, SJC. Died 8 September 1945.

ROBERTSON, Professor Alexander Provan (1947) Born 16 June 1925, 49 Tassie Street, Glasgow; son of Alexander Provan Robertson, Staff Inspector, LNER, and Hannah Cooper McLeish; m Wendy Sadie, 28 August 1951; 1 son (Philip), 4 daughters (Lorna, Clare, Rachel and Vivienne). **Subject(s):** Mathematics; BA 1949; PhD 1954; MA (Glasgow) 1946; FRSE; FIMA. **Tutor(s):** J M Wordie. **Educ:** Shawlands Secondary School; Glasgow University. **Career:** Assistant Lecturer in Mathematics, University of Glasgow 1946–1947; Lecturer in Mathematics 1951–1964, University of Glasgow; Title A Fellow, SJC 1954–1957; Lecturer, University of Western Australia 1963; Professor of Mathematics, University of Keele 1964–1972; Foundation Professor of Mathematics, Murdoch University, Western Australia 1973–1990 (Emeritus 1990). **Appointments:** Visiting Professor, University of Western Australia 1969; Member, Senate, Murdoch University. **Awards:** Prizes in Latin and Moral Philosophy, University of Glasgow; Ferguson Scholarship. **Publications:** (with Wendy Robertson) 'On the closed graph theorem', *Proceedings of the Glasgow Mathematical Association*, 3, 1956; 'On rearrangements of infinite series', *Proceedings of the Glasgow Mathematical Association*, 3(iv), 1958; (with Wendy Robertson) *Topological Vector Spaces*, CUP, 1964; (with Mike Thornett) 'On translation-bounded measures', *Journal of the Australian Mathematical Society (Series A)*, 37, 1984. Died 31 January 1995.

ROBERTSON, Professor Andrew John Blackford (1938) Born 21 February 1920, Bombay, India; son of David Robertson, Chief Accountant, and Anne Muriel Bagshaw. **Subject(s):** Natural Sciences; BA 1941; MA 1945; PhD 1946; DSc (London) 1967; CChem; FRIC. **Tutor(s):** J M Wordie. **Educ:** High School, Welwyn Garden City; Hertford Grammar School; St George's, Harpenden; St Christopher, Letchworth. **Career:** Reader and Professor in Physical Chemistry, KCL;

Title A Fellow, SJC 1946–1949; Junior Research Fellow, Royal Institution 1946–1949. **Awards:** Henry Humphries Prize, SJC 1946; Meldola Medal 1949. Died 29 April 1987.

ROBERTSON, Charles Goodwin (1926) Born 12 November 1907, The Lindens, Wesley Road, Armley, Leeds, Yorkshire; son of Maurice George Robertson, Physician and Surgeon, and Martha Mabel Goodwin. **Tutor(s):** M P Charlesworth. **Educ:** Lyddon Villa Preparatory School; Central High School, Leeds.

ROBERTSON, Charles James (1928) Born 10 February 1909, Belsize, Scott's Lane, Beckenham, Shortlands, Kent; son of David Robertson, Preserve Manufacturer, and Elizabeth Amalie Fischer; m Barbara Fry, 1935; 2 sons, 1 daughter. **Subject(s):** Mathematics/Economics; BA 1931; Chartered Accountant 1935; FSA. **Tutor(s):** J M Wordie. **Johnian Relatives:** brother of David Fischer Robertson (1928). **Educ:** Normandale School, Bexhill on Sea; Malvern College. **Career:** Chairman, Robertson's Jams; Lieutenant Colonel, RASC, WWII. **Appointments:** Council Member, Food Manufacturers' Association; Council Member, British Food Manufacturing Industries Research Association; Council Member, West Region, National Trust; Founder, Charles and Barbara Robertson Visiting Professorship, Courtauld Institute. **Publications:** *Guide to the Architecture of Bath.* Died 24 February 1983.

ROBERTSON, David Fischer (1928) Born 12 April 1911, Belsize, Scott's Lane, Beckenham, Shortlands, Kent; son of David Robertson, Preserve Manufacturer, and Elizabeth Amalie Fischer. BA 1932. **Tutor(s):** J M Wordie. **Johnian Relatives:** brother of Charles James Robertson (1928). **Educ:** Normandale School, Bexhill on Sea; Malvern College. Died 8 May 1986.

ROBERTSON, Donald William (1936) Born 13 May 1918, Oakholme, Old Station Road, Bickenhill, Warwickshire; son of Conrad James Robertson, Engineer, and Gertrude Catharine Fisher, School Teacher; m (Margaret) Elaine Macdonald, 7 November 1959. **Subject(s):** Mechanical Sciences; BA 1939; MA 1950; MICE; MIWEM. **Tutor(s):** J S Boys Smith. **Educ:** Hill School, Yardley; Solihull School. **Career:** Principal Engineer, Howard Humphreys & Sons, Consulting Civil Engineers; Binnie, Deacon and Gourley, Civil Engineers, Artillery Row, London 1951. Died 30 January 2001.

ROBERTSON, Professor James Duncan (1934) Born 16 January 1912, 27 Holyrood Quadrant, Glasgow; son of James Robertson, Schoolmaster, and Phemie Ellen Hunter Muir; PhD 1937; ScD 1962; BSc (Glasgow) 1933; FRSE. **Tutor(s):** C W Guillebaud. **Educ:** Rutherglen Academy; University of Glasgow. **Career:** Lieutenant, RAMC 1943; Specialist Entomologist, RAMC 1944–1948; Lecturer in Zoology 1948–1954, Professor of Comparative Physiology 1964, University of Glasgow. Died 22 December 1993.

ROBERTSON, John Archibald Campbell (1931) Born 21 November 1912, Lynswood, Roslin; son of Archibald Campbell Robertson, Bank Manager, and Marjory Ada Urquhart; m Diana von Cortland, 1941; 3 sons (Andrew, Nicholas and Alexander), 2 daughters (Frances and Amanda). **Subject(s):** History; BA 1934; MA 1938. **Tutor(s):** E A Benians. **Educ:** Brandon House Preparatory School; University College School, London. **Career:** Home Civil Service 1935–1954; Private Secretary to Financial Secretary 1939–1940; Private Secretary to the Permanent Secretary 1943–1945; Under-Secretary, HM Treasury 1951; Director of Personnel, United Nations, New York 1954–1957. **Honours:** CB 1961. Died 27 May 1962.

ROBERTSON, Dr Maurice Alexander (1924) Born 24 May 1906, 37 Wesley Road, Armley, Leeds; son of Maurice George Robertson, Physician and Surgeon, and Martha Mabel Goodwin. BA 1947; MA 1931. **Tutor(s):** B F Armitage. **Educ:** Miss Rowe, Armley; The Grammar School, Leeds. Died 1970.

ROBERTSON, Professor Sir Rutherford Ness (1936) Born 29 September 1913, Adam Street, South Yarra, Melbourne, Australia; son of Joshua Robertson, Clergyman, and Josephine Hogan; m Mary Helen Bruce Rogerson, 1937; 1 son (Robert James b 1944). **Subject(s):** Plant Physiology; PhD 1939; ScD (Honorary) 1969; DSc (Sydney) 1962; Honorary DSc (Tasmania, Monash, ANU, and Sydney); Honorary FRSE 1983; FRS 1961; FAA 1954. **Tutor(s):** C W Guillebaud. **Educ:** Carey Grammar School, Melbourne, Australia; St Andrew's College, Christchurch, New Zealand; University of Sydney. **Career:** Sydney University Science Research Scholar 1934–1935; Linnean Macleay Fellow 1935–1936; Exhibition of 1851 Research Scholar 1936–1939; Research at Botany School, Cambridge, in plant physiology 1936–1939; Assistant Lecturer, later Lecturer, Botany School, University of Sydney 1939–1946; Senior Research Officer, later Chief Research Officer, Division of Food Preservation, CSIRO 1946–1959; Plant Physiology Unit 1952–1959, Honorary Research Associate 1954–1959, Sydney University; Professor of Botany, University of Adelaide (later Emeritus) 1962–1969; Professor (Master, University House) 1969–1972, Pro-Chancellor 1984–1986, Director, Research School of Biological Sciences (later Emeritus) 1973–1978, ANU. **Appointments:** President, Linnean Society of NSW 1949; Honorary Secretary, Australian National Research Council 1951–1955; Corresponding Member, American Society of Plant Physiologists 1953; Secretary, Biological Sciences, Australian Academy of Science 1957–1958; Visiting Professor, University of California, Los Angeles 1958–1959; Kerney Foundation Lecturer, University of California, Berkeley 1959; Member Executive, CSIRO 1959–1962; Foreign Associate, US National Academy of Sciences 1962; President, Australian and New Zealand Association for the Advancement of Science 1964–1966; Chairman, Australian Research Grants Committee, 1965–1969; President, Australian Academy of Science 1970–1974; Honorary Member, Royal Society of New Zealand 1971; Foreign Member, American Philosophical Society 1971; Foreign Honorary Member, American Academy of Arts and Sciences 1973; Honorary Fellow, SJC 1973–2001; Deputy Chairman, Australian Science and Technology Council 1977–1981; Honorary Visitor, School of Biological Sciences, Sydney University 1979–1987; President, XIII International Botanical Congress, Sydney 1981; Three Societies Lecture 1988; Patron, Australia Committee of Cambridge Commonwealth Trust 1994. **Awards:** Scholarship, SJC; Clarke Memorial Medal, Royal Society of New South Wales 1955; Farrer Memorial Medal 1963; ANZAAS Medal 1968; Mueller Medal 1970; Burnet Medal 1975. **Honours:** CMG 1968; Kt 1972; AC 1980. **Publications:** (with G E Briggs and A B Hope) *Electrolytes and Plant Cells*, 1961; *Protons, Electrons, Phosphorylation and Active Transport*, 1968; *The Lively Membranes*, 1983; various scientific papers on plant physiology and biochemistry. Died 5 March 2001.

ROBERTSON, William David (1943) Born 2 October 1925, 1225 15th Avenue West, Calgary, Alberta, Canada; son of Ernest Victor Robertson, Barrister-at-law, and Miriam Jane Iredale. **Subject(s):** Natural Sciences; BA 1946; MA 1950. **Tutor(s):** C W Guillebaud. **Educ:** Connaught School, Calgary; Wilby Church Day School, Wellingborough; Wellingborough School; Northampton Town and County School.

ROBINSON, Dr Alfred (1948) Born 5 May 1930, 50 Roberts Street, Grimsby, Lincolnshire; son of Alfred Robinson, Wholesale Fish Merchant, and Kathleen Mary Hutton; m Audrey Denise Pask, 18 February 1956, Scartho, Grimsby; 2 sons (Guy b 17 February 1960 and Graham b 19 January 1972), 4 daughters (Louise b 24 August 1958, Hilary b 17 March 1961, Lindsey b 14 June 1962 and Sally b 15 March 1964). **Subject(s):** Natural Sciences; BA 1951; MA 1968; MB 1954; BChir 1954; DCH 1961; MRCP 1961; FRCP 1974. **Tutor(s):** G C L Bertram. **Educ:** Edward Elementary School, Grimsby; Corporation Grammar School, Grimsby; Wintringham Grammar School. **Career:** Surgeon Lieutenant, RN 1955–1958; Consultant Paediatrician, Chichester Health Authority and Worthing Health Authority 1965; Associate Post-Graduate Medical Dean, South West Thames 1991–1996. **Appointments:** Examiner, MRCP 1985–1997.

ROBINSON, Bevan Downing Gurth (1921) Born 2 September 1902, Knighton Road, Leicester; son of Charles Bernard Robinson, of independent means, and Lucy Kaye; m Phyllis Mary Law, 25 April 1929, All Saints', Branksome Park, Bournemouth. **Subject(s):** Natural Sciences; BA 1924; MA 1929. **Tutor(s):** B F Armitage. **Educ:** Suffolk Hall, Cheltenham; Cheltenham College Junior School; Clifton College. Died 20 December 1987.

ROBINSON, Dr Brian Hugh Bartlett (1948) Born 9 February 1930, 13 Winn Road, Lee, London; son of Percy Harry Bartlett Robinson, Headmaster, Archbishop Tenison's Grammar School, and Edith Margaret Mary Else; m Deirdre Monford, 1955; 1 son (b 1965), 1 daughter (b 1963). **Subject(s):** Natural Sciences; BA 1951; MA 1955; BChir 1954; MB 1954; MRCP; FRCP (London). **Tutor(s):** G C L Bertram. **Johnian Relatives:** cousin of Roger Christopher Lallemand (1954). **Educ:** Kingswood House School, Epsom; Archbishop Tenison's Grammar School, London; St Paul's School, West Kensington. **Career:** House Physician and Medical Registrar, Guy's Hospital 1954–1959; Registrar and Tutor, Royal Postgraduate Medical School 1959–1961; Research Fellow, Johns Hopkins Hospital, Baltimore, USA 1962; Senior Registrar, UCH 1962–1965; Consultant Physician, East Birmingham Hospital Group (later Birmingham Heartlands Hospital NHS Trust) 1965–1995; Consultant Nephrologist, Queen Elizabeth Hospital, Birmingham 1970–1990; Honorary Senior Clinical Lecturer, University of Birmingham 1970–1995. **Awards:** Major Scholarship, SJC 1947; Combined Hospitals War Memorial Scholarship, Guy's Hospital 1951; Treasurer's Medal and Prize in Clinical Medicine, Guy's Hospital 1953; Beaney Prize in Pathology, Guy's Hospital; Golding Bird Medal and Scholarship in Bacteriology, Guy's Hospital 1953; Fulbright Scholarship 1961–1962. **Publications:** Articles on Mineral Metabolism, Renal Disorders, Dialysis and Transplantation in various medical journals, including *Journal of Clinical Investigation, British Medical Journal, Lancet*; Editor, *Proceedings of European Renal Association*, 1976–1982.

ROBINSON, Ernest Harold (1910) (admitted as Non-Collegiate Student 1909) Born 12 January 1890, Stafford Road, Newport, Shropshire; son of James Robinson, Grocer, and Emma Jinks. **Subject(s):** Modern and Medieval Languages; BA 1912; MA 1932. **Tutor(s):** E E Sikes. **Educ:** Newport Grammar School. **Career:** Master, Magnus Grammar School, Newark 1912–1914; Major, King's Shropshire Light Infantry 1914–1919; Master, Magnus Grammar School, Newark 1919–1923; Headmaster, Moseley Secondary School, Birmingham 1923–1955; Colonel, Home Guard, WWII. **Honours:** DSO; MC with Bar. Died October 1968.

ROBINSON, Ernest Stanley (1921) Born 18 January 1905, Constant, Parish of St George, Barbados, British West Indies; son of Samuel Stanley Robinson, Sugar Planter, and Hannah Eliza Genever. **Tutor(s):** B F Armitage. **Educ:** Harrison College, Barbados; The King's School, Warwick.

ROBINSON, Frank Bright (1919) Born 8 October 1901, Chamber House, Heywood, Rochdale, Lancashire; son of Charles John Robinson, Engineer, and Helen Millicent Bright; m Margery. BA 1923; MA 1939. **Tutor(s):** E A Benians. **Johnian Relatives:** brother of John Cuthbert Robinson (1919). **Educ:** Private Tuition. **Career:** Thomas Robinson and Son, Railway Works, Rochdale. Died 1 December 1966.

ROBINSON, Geoffrey Hodgson (1942) Born 29 March 1924, Stillington, Yorkshire; son of John Robert Robinson, Agriculturalist, and Mabel Annie Cordukes; m Barbara M. **Subject(s):** History; BA 1948; MA 1950. **Tutor(s):** C W Guillebaud. **Educ:** Flaxton Parish School; New College, Harrogate; Ashville College, Harrogate. **Career:** Headmaster, Ridgeway School, Southborough 1969; Headmaster, Reed School, Strood, Kent 1969. Died 1 June 1996.

ROBINSON, George Hilary Alexander (1935) Born 27 June 1917, 173 Barnsley Road, Cudworth, Barnsley; son of Hilary Isaac Robinson, Clerk in Holy Orders, and Eileen Margaret Rose. BA 1939; MA 1943. **Tutor(s):**

R L Howland. **Educ:** Hill Cross School, Doncaster; Hill House School, Doncaster; Pocklington School, York.

ROBINSON, George Michael Moncrieff (1904) Born 14 July 1882, Ulgham, Bedlington, Northumberland; son of George Robinson, Clerk in Holy Orders, and Mary Hardy. **Tutor(s):** J R Tanner; C E Graves. **Johnian Relatives:** brother of Hilary Isaac Robinson (1903). **Educ:** Pocklington School. **Career:** Mining Surveyor's Assistant, Ashington, Morpeth 1901–1904; Rhodesian Police 1907.

ROBINSON, Major Gerald Barcroft (1927) Born 4 July 1908, The Crescent, Knaresborough, Yorkshire; son of George Christopher Robinson, Physician, and Olivia Eleanor Fayle; m Joy, 1939; 3 sons. BA 1930; MA 1934; MB (Leeds) 1937; ChB (Leeds) 1937. **Tutor(s):** E A Benians. **Johnian Relatives:** uncle of Derek Fayle Robinson (1952). **Educ:** Clifton House; St Peter's School, York; University of Leeds. **Career:** GP, Knaresborough 1937–1973; Army Medical Corps, Surgeon to General Auchinleck, Commander in Chief in India 1941–1945. Died 22 December 1999.

ROBINSON, Professor Gilbert de Beauregard (1927) Born 3 June 1906, Toronto, Ontario, Canada; son of Percy James Robinson, Classical Master, St Andrew's College, Toronto, and Esther Toutant de Beauregard. PhD 1931; BA (Toronto) 1927; FRSC. **Tutor(s):** J M Wordie. **Educ:** Rosedale Public School; St Andrew's College, Toronto, Canada; University of Toronto, Canada. **Career:** Associate Professor of Mathematics, University of Toronto 1948; Visiting Professor Michigan State University 1953; Professor of Mathematics, University of Toronto 1960; Visiting Professor, University of British Columbia 1963; Vice President (Research) 1964–1971; Visiting Professor, University of Christchurch, New Zealand 1968. **Awards:** Exhibition, SJC 1927. **Honours:** MBE 1948.

ROBINSON, The Revd Hilary Isaac (1903) Born 4 August 1883, Ulgham, Bedlington, Northumberland; son of George Robinson, Clerk in Holy Orders, and Mary Hardy. **Subject(s):** Mathematics; BA 1906; MA 1915. **Tutor(s):** J R Tanner; C E Graves. **Johnian Relatives:** brother of George Michael Moncrieff Robinson (1904). **Educ:** Pocklington School. **Career:** Ordained Deacon 1908; Curate, St Mary, Hull 1908–1911; Ordained Priest 1909; Curate, Buxton 1911–1912; Curate, Edwinstowe 1912–1913; Curate, Fulford 1913–1915; Curate, Cudworth, Yorkshire 1915–1918; Curate, Carlton Juxta Snaith 1918–1922; Vicar, Wadworth 1922–1930; Rector, Londesborough 1930–1946; Rural Dean, Weighton 1936–1946; Vicar, Sutton-on-the-Forest 1946–1954; Rural Dean, Easingwold 1950–1954.

ROBINSON, John Cuthbert (1919) Born 31 May 1899, Falinge Lawn, Rochdale, Lancaster; son of Charles John Robinson, Engineer, and Helen Millicent Bright. **Tutor(s):** E A Benians. **Johnian Relatives:** brother of Frank Bright Robinson (1919). **Educ:** Cordwallis, Maidenhead; Sandroyd, Cobham; Charterhouse.

ROBINSON, Louis Francis Woodward (1912) Born 17 December 1893, Buxar, Bengal, India; son of Francis Richard William Robinson, Superintendent, Rewah State, Central India, and Margaret Jane Woodward. **Tutor(s):** L H K Bushe-Fox. **Educ:** Roysse's School, Abingdon; Dane Court, Parkeston; Bedford School. **Career:** Lieutenant, RE 1914–1917. Died 26 May 1917 (killed in action).

ROBINSON, Luis Geoffrey (1931) Born 11 November 1910, 13 Drayton Road, Boreham Wood, Elstree; son of William Sutherland Robinson, Legal Patent Advisor, and Bartolina Anderson Brandstaetter. **Subject(s):** Mechanical Sciences; BA 1933. **Tutor(s):** J S Boys Smith. **Educ:** Christ's Hospital; RMA, Woolwich; School of Military Engineering, Chatham. **Career:** Gazetted Second Lieutenant, RE 1930.

ROBINSON, Maurice Allpress (1934) Born 15 February 1916, 187 Milton Road, Cambridge; son of Thomas Bertram Robinson, Solicitor's

Managing Clerk, and Florence Mary Ann Allpress; m (1) Marjorie D James, (2) Pamela Rosemary Margaret Allen (née Goss). **Subject(s):** Law; BA 1937; LLB 1938; MA 1941. **Tutor(s):** C W Guillebaud. **Educ:** King's College Choir School, Cambridge; The Leys School, Cambridge. **Career:** Solicitor, Barr Ellison of Cambridge; Under Sheriff for Cambridgeshire and Huntingdonshire 1960–1977; Member, Board of Directors, Solicitors Benevolent Association 1969. Died 24 August 1996.

ROBINSON, Percy Wilberforce (1918) Born 18 November 1893, Aldridge House, Aldridge Road, Perry Barr, Warwick; son of William Francis Robinson, Registrar, and Ellen Maria Pitt. **Tutor(s):** E E Sikes. **Educ:** Aston Preparatory School; King Edward's School, Birmingham.

ROBINSON, Richard Gruffydd (1914) Born 18 October 1895, 20 Albany Road, Roath, Cardiff; son of James Robinson, Physician and Surgeon, and Harriet Agnes Bevan. **Tutor(s):** E E Sikes. **Educ:** Cliff House School, Southborne on Sea; Sherborne School. **Career:** Commissioned in 20th and 14th Welsh Regiment, and MGC 1914–1918; Manager, Photoprinting Works; Orderly, Welch Hospital, Netley; Councillor, City of Cardiff 1928. **Appointments:** Alderman 1945; Lord Mayor of Cardiff 1947–1949; Chairman, Cardiff Education Committee 1949; Chairman, Cardiff Hospital Management Committee; Chairman, Bryn-y-Don Approved School; Chairman, Central Boys' Club, Cardiff; President, Association of Education Committee 1959; President, Welsh Amateur Gymnastic Association; President, Cardiff Aquarists Society; Life Vice-President, South Wales and Monmouthshire Budgerigar Society; variety of other appointments, particularly concerned with health and education.

ROBINSON, Professor Ronald Edward (1939) Born 3 September 1920, 18 Anhalt Road, Battersea, London; son of William Edward Robinson, Stock Keeper, and Aida Theresa Goldsmith; m Alice Josephine Denny, 1948; 2 sons, 2 daughters. **Subject(s):** History; BA 1946; MA 1949; PhD 1951. **Tutor(s):** C W Guillebaud. **Johnian Relatives:** father of Peter Denny Robinson (1972). **Educ:** Wix's Lane LCC Elementary School; Battersea Grammar School. **Career:** Flight Lieutenant, 58 Bomber Squadron, RAF 1942–1945; Research Officer, African Studies Branch, Colonial Office 1947–1949; Title A Fellow 1949–1953, Title B Fellow 1953–1971, Lecturer in History 1958–1971, SJC; Assistant Lecturer in History 1952–1954, Lecturer in History 1954–1966, Pro-Proctor 1954–1955, Smuts Reader in History of the British Commonwealth 1966–1971, University of Cambridge; Beit Professor of the History of the British Commonwealth, University of Oxford 1971–1987; Fellow, Balliol College, Oxford 1971–1987; Director, University of Oxford Development Records Project 1978–1987. **Appointments:** Supervisor in History 1953–1958, Tutor 1960–1966, Director of Studies in History 1967–1968, Secretary, College Council 1967–1969, SJC; Institute for Advanced Studies, Princeton 1959–1960; Member, Bridges Committee on Training in Public Administration 1961–1962; Chairman, Cambridge Conferences on Problems of Developing Countries 1961–1970; Chairman, Faculty Board of Modern History 1974–1976, Vice-Chairman, Faculty Board of Modern History 1979–1987, University of Oxford; UK observer, Zimbabwe election 1980. **Awards:** Major Scholarship in History 1938. **Honours:** DFC 1944; CBE 1970. **Publications:** (with J Gallagher) *Africa and the Victorians*, 1961; *Developing the Third World*, 1971; (joint ed) *Bismarck, Europe and Africa*, 1988; *Railway Imperialism*, 1991; articles in *Cambridge History of the British Empire*, Vol III, 1959, and *The New Cambridge Modern History*, Vol XI, 1963; reports on Problems of Developing Countries, 1963–1971; articles and reviews in journals. Died 19 June 1999.

ROBINSON, Slade Raymond Christopher (1945) Born 14 February 1927, Hill House, Lower Milton, Worcestershire; son of Philip Worth Robinson, Director, Messrs T B Worth & Sons, and Mary Katherina Baker-Stallard-Penoyre; m (1) Ursula Lessware, 4 August 1951, (2) Christine Elizabeth Verrier, 25 August 1967; (1) 1 son. **Tutor(s):** J M Wordie. **Educ:** The Link School, Malvern Link; Marlborough College. **Career:** Joint Managing Director, Thomas Bond Worth & Sons 1949.

ROBINSON, Professor Theodore Henry (1900) Born 9 August 1881, Katharine Villa, Edenbridge, Kent; son of William Venis Robinson, Baptist Minister, and Emily Jane Page; m Marie Helen Joseph, 1906 (d 1959); 1 daughter (Dorothy). **Subject(s):** Classics/History; BA 1903; MA 1907; LittD 1933; Honorary Degree (Aberdeen, Halle, Wales); BD (London) 1905. **Tutor(s):** C E Graves. **Educ:** Mill Hill School. **Career:** Lecturer in Semitic Languages 1915–1927, Professor of Semitic Languages 1927–1944, University College Cardiff. **Appointments:** Convenor of Old Testament Panel, New English Bible 1946–1956. **Awards:** British Academy Burkitt Bronze Medal for Biblical Studies 1946. **Publications:** *Studies of Old Testament Prophetic Literature*; textbooks of Hebrew and Syriac language; *History of the Old Testament*. Died 26 June 1964.

ROBINSON, Sir Wilfred Henry Frederick (1937) Born 24 December 1917, Johannesburg, Transvaal, South Africa; son of Wilfred Henry Robinson, Director of Randfontein Estates, and Eileen St Leger; m Margaret Alison Kathleen Mellish, 1946. **Subject(s):** History; BA 1940; MA 1944. **Tutor(s):** J S Boys Smith. **Johnian Relatives:** cousin of John Victor Lindbergh (1938) and Frederick Michael St Leger Lindbergh (1945); father of Peter Frank Robinson (1971). **Educ:** Diocesan College, Rondebosch, South Africa. **Career:** Devonshire and Parachute Regiments 1939–1946; Housemaster, Diocesan College, Rondebosch 1955–1969; Vice-Principal, Diocesan College, Rondebosch 1969–1977; Finance Officer, Society of Genealogists 1980–1992.

ROBINSON, William Eric Arnot (1927) Born 8 March 1909, 115 Norwood Road, Herne Hill, London; son of William Arnot Robinson, Managing Director, Anglo Continental Produce Company, and Ada Fraser. **Subject(s):** Economics; BA 1930. **Tutor(s):** E A Benians. **Educ:** Golden Parsonage, Hemel Hempstead; Courtenay Lodge, Sutton Courtenay.

ROBSON, Athol (1940) Born 14 January 1922, 3 Highbury, Monkseaton, Northumberland; son of John Paxton Robson, Coal Exporter, and Eleanor Pattie Pringle. **Tutor(s):** C W Guillebaud. **Educ:** Newcastle Preparatory School; Uppingham.

ROBSON, Richard Derek (1943) Born 26 January 1926, Claremont, Dudley Street, Grimsby, Lincolnshire; son of John Stanley Robson, Church Organist, and Ethel Jennings. BA 1947; MA 1953. **Tutor(s):** S J Bailey. **Johnian Relatives:** uncle of David Martin Tanton (1971). **Educ:** St James' Secondary School, Grimsby; Bridlington School. **Career:** Production Engineering Research Association; Enterprise Counsellor, Enterprise Initiative Consulting Scheme, DTI.

ROBSON, Dr Robert (1924) Born 24 June 1904, Beech Grove, Whickham, County Durham; son of Joseph Brunskill Robson, Schoolmaster, and Margaret Bell. **Subject(s):** Mathematics; BA 1926; MA 1931; BSc (Durham). **Tutor(s):** J M Wordie. **Educ:** Cornsay Colliery Council School; Johnstone Secondary School, Durham; Armstrong College, University of Durham. **Career:** Lecturer in Mathematics, Gordon Memorial College, Khartoum 1927. Died 15 April 1993.

RODD, Thomas Eric (1926) Born 25 January 1907, 33 Queen Street, Abertillery, Monmouthshire; son of John Rodd, Purveyor, and Elizabeth Florence Harris; m Evelyn M P Rodd. **Subject(s):** Natural Sciences (Geology); BA 1929; MA 1933; BSc (London) 1929. **Tutor(s):** J M Wordie. **Educ:** Clyst St Mary School; Hele's School, Exeter; Exeter School. **Career:** Chemistry Master, Merchiston Castle School, Edinburgh 1930–1933; Assistant Master, Durham School 1933–1938; Head of the Science Department and Commander, CCF, Eastbourne College 1939–1971. **Honours:** TD and Bar. Died 26 March 1994.

RODGER, William Rhodes (1948) Born 21 January 1928, 5 Cambridge Street, Edinburgh; son of John Wilfred Rodger, Managing Director, Electrical Engineering Company, and Emily Beatrice Rhodes; m Vilma Gartry, 1961; 2 daughters (Elizabeth Anne and Jane Louise b 20 January

1964). **Subject(s):** Natural Sciences/Chemical Engineering; BA 1950; MA 1955; MIChemE; CEng. **Tutor(s):** E Miller; G C L Bertram. **Johnian Relatives:** father-in-law of John Meurig Taylor Davies (1981); father of Jane Louise Rodger (1985). **Educ:** Rochester House, Edinburgh; Edinburgh Academy; Wellingborough School; Merchiston Castle, Edinburgh. **Career:** Management Trainee, Laporte Chemicals Ltd, Luton 1952–1956; Production (Acrylics), ICI Ltd, Runcorn and Billingham 1956–1985; Contract Design, ICD Ltd, Yarm, Cleveland 1985–1994.

RODGERS, John Malcolm (1922) Naval Officer.

RODWELL, Robert Hunter (1937) Born 10 September 1917, The Lodge, Holbrook, Suffolk; son of Kenneth Edward Hunter Rodwell, Company Director, and Margaret Grace Blain. **Tutor(s):** J M Wordie. **Educ:** Cheam School; Eton.

ROE, Dr Peter Frank (1949) Born 17 January 1931, Anglo-American Hospital, Cairo, Egypt; son of Harry Frank Roe, Missionary, and Ruth Isabella Sadler, Missionary; m Margaret Sapp, 9 August 1956, Croydon; 2 children. **Subject(s):** Natural Sciences/Moral Sciences; BA 1952; MA 1957; MB, BChir (Edinburgh) 1955; MD (Edinburgh) 1969; MRCP, RCPSG 1962; FRCP 1981. **Tutor(s):** G C L Bertram. **Educ:** British School, Suez; English Mission College, Cairo; Neville House, Eastbourne; Great Walstead, Haywards Heath; Taunton School; University of Edinburgh. **Career:** Short Service Commission, RAF 1956–1959; Senior Registrar, Adelaide Hospital; Tutor, TCD 1963–1966; Consultant Physician to Ugandan Government 1966–1967; Consultant Physician, Taunton and Somerset Hospital 1970–1996. **Appointments:** Licensed Reader, Church of England 1970–; Director, Somerset Care Ltd 1990–1993. **Publications:** Various medical papers.

ROEBUCK, Eric (1936) Born 17 January 1918, 19 Kawagudie, Osaka, Japan; son of Harold Roebuck, Textile Engineer, and Elizabeth Hannah Lyne. **Tutor(s):** R L Howland. **Educ:** Chartfield School, Oldham; Ashville College, Harrogate.

ROEDER, Professor Kenneth David (1926) Born 9 March 1908, 19 Richmond Bridge Mansions, Twickenham, Middlesex; son of Carl David Roeder, Company Secretary, and Grace Philips. **Subject(s):** Natural Sciences; BA 1929; MA 1933. **Tutor(s):** J M Wordie. **Educ:** Bembridge School, Isle of Wight. **Career:** Professor of Physiology (later Emeritus), Tufts University, Massachusetts. Died 28 September 1979.

ROGERS, Charles Hartley Delacourt (1922) Born 15 October 1901, Redcliffe, Durham Avenue, Beckenham, Kent; son of Herbert Malcolm Rogers, Consulting Marine Engineer and Naval Architect, and Emily Irene Cannington. **Tutor(s):** E E Sikes. **Johnian Relatives:** brother of Herbert Cannington Rogers (1920). **Educ:** Clare House School, Beckenham; Cheltenham College; Apprentice with Messrs Merryweather. **Career:** Swan, Hunter & Wigham Richardson, Neptune Works Shipyard 1924–1926; At sea with Blue Funnel Ships 1926–1927; Assistant Works Manager, Smiths Dock Company, North Shields 1927–1930; Assistant Consultant, later Partner, Burles, Gordon & Whiteford 1931. **Appointments:** Member, Society of Consulting Marine Engineers and Ship Surveyors (Council 1942–1952); Member, Institution of Naval Architects; Member, North East Coast Institution of Engineers and Shipbuilders; Member, Institute of Marine Engineers. Died October 1959.

ROGERS, Herbert Cannington (1920) Born 8 October 1899, Redcliffe, Durham Avenue, Beckenham, Kent; son of Herbert Malcolm Rogers, Civil Engineer, and Emily Irene Cannington; m Elsie Rose Frances Franck, 24 June 1931, Holy Trinity, Brompton (d 30 December 1960); 1 son (John), 1 daughter (Jill). BA 1923; MA 1928. **Tutor(s):** E E Sikes. **Johnian Relatives:** brother of Charles Hartley Delacourt Rogers (1922). **Educ:** Clare House School, Beckenham; Cheltenham College. **Career:** Engineer and Ship Surveyor, Lloyd's Register of Shipping 1929–1960. Died January 1979.

ROGERS, John Arthur (1937) Born 1 May 1914, Tyllwyd, Cilgerran, St Dogmalls; son of Arthur Henry Rogers, Minister of Religion, and Annie Jane Griffiths. **Subject(s):** English; BA 1939; MA 1943; University College of Wales, Aberystwyth, 1932–1937. **Tutor(s):** J S Boys Smith. **Educ:** Cilgerran School; Ammanfad Council School; Caruhedryn Council School; County School, Cardigan.

ROGERS, Samuel Philip Hugh (1921) Born 16 December 1903, 28 Goring Road, Llanelly, Carmarthenshire; son of Philip Rogers, Coal Exporter, and Cicely Hannah Williams; m Beryl Audrey Turpin, 15 October 1927, St Peter's Church, Cranley Gardens. BA 1924; MA 1931; Chartered Surveyor. **Tutor(s):** E A Benians. **Johnian Relatives:** father of Philip David Clark Rogers (1956). **Educ:** Kelvin School, Llanelly; Llanelly County School; Shrewsbury School. **Career:** Army Service, WWII; Chartered Surveyor, Cardiff.

ROGERSON, Walter Lohn Lancashire (1908) Born 3 May 1889, Chadsmoor, Cannock, Staffordshire; son of Thomas Rogerson, Clerk in Holy Orders, and Mary Agnes Lancashire; m Anne; 1 son (John), 1 daughter (Margaret). **Subject(s):** Classics; BA 1911. **Tutor(s):** L H K Bushe-Fox. **Educ:** St John's School, Leatherhead. **Career:** Cadet, Ceylon Civil Service 1912; Government Assistant in Anuradhapura, Kandy, and Badulla 1913–1914; Police Magistrate, Matale 1915–1917; Office Assistant, Kandy 1917–1921; Police Magistrate, Aviswella, then Kandy 1921–1922; District Judge, Kegalla 1922–1923; Police Magistrate, Colombo 1923–1925; Assistant Government Agent, Colombo, then North Western Province, then Nuwara Eliya 1925. Died 31 October 1966.

ROLFE, Robert Hugh Grandison (1936) Born 7 February 1918, 40 Loughborough Road, West Bridgford, Nottinghamshire; son of Frank Leslie Rolfe, Bank Manager, and Hilda Edith Morris. **Tutor(s):** J M Wordie. **Educ:** Radcliffe House School, West Bridgford; Alexandra Park School, Nottingham; Kimbolton School.

ROLLAND, John Lewis (1939) Born 20 June 1920, 30 Raeburn Terrace, Edinburgh; son of John Francis Rolland, Chartered Accountant, and Emily Louise Dawson; m Esme; 2 daughters (Deborah and Sheila). **Subject(s):** Modern and Medieval Languages; BA 1947; MA 1949. **Tutor(s):** C W Guillebaud. **Educ:** Oakley Hall School, Cirencester; Sedbergh School. **Career:** Commissioned Officer, Durham Light Infantry, India and Burma 1940–1945; Assistant Master, Downside School 1948–1955; Senior Modern Languages Master and Housemaster, Brighton College 1955–1964; Headmaster, Woodbridge School 1964. **Awards:** Lupton and Lupton and Hebblethwaite Exhibition, SJC. Died 30 January 1989.

ROLLS, Arthur Litton (1924) Born 10 November 1904, Kinnoull, Warlingham, Godstone, Surrey; son of Joseph Algernon Dawson Rolls, Colonial Broker, and Amanda Winifred Gabain; m Mary Service, 5 September 1947, St Mary's Church, Boxted, Essex. **Subject(s):** Modern and Medieval Languages; BA 1926. **Tutor(s):** B F Armitage. **Johnian Relatives:** cousin of Thomas Burnand Rolls (1928). **Educ:** King's Mead School, Seaford; Repton School; Home Place, Holt.

ROLLS, Thomas Burnand (1928) Born 6 September 1909, The Corner House, Merstham, Surrey; son of Norman Thomas Rolls, Colonial Broker, and Ella Janie Burnand; m June; 3 sons (Jonathan, Robert and Charles), 1 daughter (Caroline). **Subject(s):** Mechanical Sciences; BA 1931. **Tutor(s):** J M Wordie. **Johnian Relatives:** cousin of Arthur Litton Rolls (1924). **Educ:** Wykham House, Worthing; The Charterhouse, Godalming.

RONALDSON, Dr James Bruce (1902) Born 15 January 1886, Haddington, Scotland; son of James Bruce Ronaldson, Doctor, and Anne Macdonald; m Irene Constance Bird, 2 July 1915, Cromer Parish Church. **Subject(s):** Natural Sciences; BA 1906; MA 1928; MB 1910; BChir 1910; MD 1915; LRCP 1910; MRCS 1910. **Tutor(s):** D MacAlister.

Educ: Merchiston Castle, Edinburgh. **Career:** Resident Medical Officer, Royal Hospital for Sick Children, Edinburgh; House Surgeon, Resident Casualty Officer, Resident Obstetrical Officer, Charing Cross Hospital; Assistant Physician, King Edward VII Hospital, Windsor; Medical Officer, LCC Residential Deaf School, Rayners, Penn; Surgeon Captain, London Division, RNVR. **Appointments:** Honorary Physician to the King 1933–1936; Honorary Fellow, Edinburgh Obstetrical Society. Died 5 April 1952.

RONEY-DOUGAL, Richard Patrick (1929) Born 12 September 1907, Smallack, Egg Buckland, Plympton, Devon; son of George Bell Roney-Dougal, Major, Somerset Light Infantry, and Lettice Woodhouse. BA 1932. **Tutor(s):** C W Guillebaud. **Educ:** Alton, Burn, Nairn; Bradfield College; Aireman House, Sherborne; RMA, Woolwich. **Awards:** Kitchener Scholarship.

ROOD, Arthur Bryant (1948) Born 26 July 1928, Memorial Hospital, Brooklyn, New York, USA; son of Arthur Joseph Rood, Travel Manager, and Florence Beggs. **Subject(s):** Geography; BA 1950; MA 1968. **Tutor(s):** F Thistlethwaite. **Educ:** King Edward VI School, Bury St Edmunds. **Career:** European Representative, Morgan Crucible, London; Sales Manager, Ringsdorff, South Africa; Founded own company, Allotropic Carbon Products. **Awards:** Spalding and Symonds Exhibition 1946. Died 20 April 1999.

ROOD, Stephen Charles (1937) Born 24 December 1917, 67 Shaftesbury Road, Gosport; son of Charles William Rood, Clerk, and Isabella Maud Tailford. **Subject(s):** History; BA 1940; MA 1944. **Tutor(s):** J S Boys Smith. **Educ:** Kells Lane School, Gateshead; Chillingham Road School, Newcastle; Royal Grammar School, Newcastle. **Career:** Lieutenant, 8th Battalion, Durham Light Infantry, RA, WWII. **Awards:** Minor Scholarship, SJC 1936. Died 9 September 1944 (killed in action on the Albert Canal, Belgium).

ROOM, Eric Sydney (1947) Born 12 June 1926, East Cottingwith, Yorkshire; son of Sydney Wilson Room, Farmer, and Elsie Watson; m Patricia Mary Plant, September 1955, Tettenhall, Wolverhampton; 3 daughters (Helen Patricia b 1958, Katherine Elizabeth b 1962 and Judith Anne b 1964). **Subject(s):** Classics; BA 1949; MA 1954; BA (Open University). **Tutor(s):** R L Howland. **Educ:** East Cottingwith Council School; Pocklington School. **Career:** College Lecturer/Senior Tutor, Yale Sixth Form College. **Awards:** Dowman Exhibition, SJC.

ROOM, Professor Thomas Gerald (1920) Born 10 November 1902, Burtts Lime Works, Albany Road, Camberwell, Surrey; son of Ernest William Room, Manager of Whiting Works, and Emma Eliza Henry; m Jessie; 2 daughters (Rosemary and Geraldine). **Subject(s):** Mathematics; BA 1923; MA 1927; ScD 1955; FRS 1941. **Tutor(s):** E E Sikes. **Educ:** London County Council Higher Grade School, Goodrich Road; Alleyn's School, Dulwich. **Career:** Foundress Fellow 1925–1926, Title A Fellow 1926–1928, Supervisor in Mathematics 1928–1929, SJC; Lecturer in Mathematics, Liverpool University 1926; Lecturer in Mathematics, University of Cambridge 1928–1935; Professor of Mathematics, University of Sydney 1935. **Awards:** Exhibition, SJC; Scholarship SJC 1921; Smith's Prize, University of Cambridge 1925. **Publications:** *Geometry of Determinantal Loci.* Died 2 April 1986.

ROOTHAM, Jasper St John (1929) Born 21 November 1910, 4 Huntingdon Road, Chesterton, Cambridge; son of Cyril Bradley Rootham, Fellow, Lecturer and Organist of SJC, and Rosamond Margaret Lucas; m Joan McClelland, 25 September 1944; 1 son (John Daniel (Dan) b 15 February 1947), 1 daughter (Tutu Catherine Virginia b 1 November 1951). **Subject(s):** Classics; BA 1932; MA 1936. **Tutor(s):** M P Charlesworth. **Johnian Relatives:** son of Cyril Bradley Rootham (1894); father of John Daniel Rootham (1965). **Educ:** King's College School, Cambridge; Tonbridge School. **Career:** Served in the Ministry of Agriculture, the Colonial Office and the Treasury; Assistant Private

Secretary to the Prime Minister (Neville Chamberlain) 1938–1939; General Haining's Staff, Cairo 1943; Operative behind enemy lines, Serbia 1944; Lieutenant Colonel (later Colonel) 1939–1946; Bank of England 1946–1967 (Assistant Advisor 1951, Assistant to the Governor 1965); Senior Banking Director, Lazards 1967–1975. **Awards:** Scholarship, SJC. **Publications:** *Miss-Fire*, 1946; *Demi-Paradise*, 1960; *Verses 1928–72*, 1973; *Reflections from a Crag*, 1978; *Stand Fixed in Steadfast Gaze*, 1981; *Affirmation*, 1982; *Lament for a Dead Sculptor*, 1985. Died 30 May 1990.

ROPER, The Revd Lewis Hawkes (1936) Born 1 October 1918, 5 Camden Place, Cambridge; son of George Roper, Medical Practitioner, and Florence Mabel Hawkes; m Betty Pepper; 1 son (Mark), 2 daughters (Ann and Susan). **Subject(s):** English/Theology; BA 1939; MA 1943. **Tutor(s):** R L Howland. **Johnian Relatives:** brother of Richard Antony Lionel Roper (1939). **Educ:** St Faith's, Cambridge; The Leys School, Cambridge. **Career:** Ordained Deacon 1941; Curate, St James, Alperton 1941–1945; Ordained Priest 1942; Curate, St Mary Magdalene, Bermondsey 1945–1949; Perpetual Curate, Swanwick, Derbyshire 1949–1955; Vicar, Holy Trinity, Lyonsdown, Hertfordshire 1955; Vicar, Seaford, Diocese of Chichester 1971.

ROPER, Richard Antony Lionel (1939) Born 18 January 1921, 5 Regent Street, Cambridge; son of George Roper, Medical Practitioner, and Florence Mabel Hawkes; m Corina Benedettini, 21 June 1952; 1 son, 1 daughter. **Subject(s):** English/Music; BA 1942; MA 1946; MusB 1949; CertEd (Cambridge) 1957; ARCM 1952. **Tutor(s):** R L Howland. **Johnian Relatives:** brother of Lewis Hawkes Roper (1936). **Educ:** St Faith's School, Cambridge; The Leys School, Cambridge; Royal College of Music. **Career:** Composer. **Appointments:** Member, Composers Guild of Great Britain 1978; Performing Right Society 1991; Member, British Academy of Composers and Songwriters 1999; Member, Mechanical Copyright Protection Society. **Awards:** English Poetry and Song Society Prize. **Publications:** *Sonata for Euphonium*, Studio Music, 1996; *Vaughan Williams Charterhouse Suite*, arranged for wind quintet, Stainer and Bell Ltd, 1993.

ROPER, Surgeon Lieutenant Robert Dudley (1925) Born 4 September 1906, 6 Spencer Place, Leeds, Yorkshire; son of Herbert John Roper, Surgeon, and Mildred Elizabeth Coddington. BA 1928; MA 1932; BChir 1933; MB 1935; MRCS (St Bartholomew's) 1933; LRCP (St Bartholomew's) 1933. **Tutor(s):** M P Charlesworth. **Educ:** Chapel Allerton High School; Morelands School; Orleton School, Scarborough; St Edward's School, Oxford. **Career:** Casualty House Surgeon, St Bartholomew's Hospital; House Surgeon, Ear, Nose and Throat Department, Charing Cross (later Honorary Anaesthetist); Anaesthetist, Hospital of SS John and Elizabeth, and Connaught Hospital, Walthamstow; Private Practice; EMS, then Surgeon Lieutenant, RNVR, WWII. Died 2 February 1941.

ROSCOE, Canon John (1910) Born 25 August 1861, Kirkby, Liverpool; son of James Thomas Roscoe, and Ann Sixsmith; m Agnes Kate. MA 1910. **Educ:** Church Missionary College, Islington. **Career:** Rector, Ovington. Died 2 December 1932.

ROSE, Edward Michael (1932) Born 18 October 1913, 68 Wimpole Street, Marylebone, London; son of Frank Atcherley Rose, Surgeon, and Marion Elizabeth Darling Harris. **Subject(s):** History; BA 1935; MA 1959. **Tutor(s):** E A Benians. **Johnian Relatives:** son of Frank Atcherley Rose (1892). **Educ:** Oldfield, Swanage; Stubbington House; Rugby School. **Career:** Diplomatic Service 1937; Civilian Deputy to the British GOC 1952–1955; Minister in Bonn 1960–1963; Ambassador in Leopoldville (now Kinshasa) 1963–1965; Deputy Secretary in charge of foreign policy liaison in the Cabinet Office 1967–1968. **Appointments:** Director, East Africa and Mauritius Association; Chairman of the Board of International Affairs, The British Council of Churches. **Awards:** Exhibition, SJC; Scholarship, SJC; College Prize, SJC. **Honours:** CMG. Died 25 March 1986.

ROSE, Dr Frederic Gardiner (1904) Born 23 March 1885, East Street, South Cumingsbury, Demerara, British Guiana; son of James Frederick Rose, Schoolmaster, and Frances Bickford Savory. **Subject(s):** Natural Sciences; BA 1907; BChir 1913; MB 1914; MD 1926; MRCS; LRCP 1911. **Tutor(s):** D MacAlister. **Educ:** Grocers' Company's School, Hackney Downs; Queen's College, British Guiana. **Career:** Consulting Radiologist, Government of British Guiana; Leper Hospital, Mahaica, British Guiana; Government Pathologist, British Guiana 1915. **Publications:** 'Filiariasis in British Guiana', *Procedures of the Royal Society of Medicine*, 1921; 'Treatment of Leprosy at Mahaica Leper Hospital', *Transactions of the Royal Society of Tropical Medicine and Hygiene*, 1928.

ROSE, Harry Cecil (1902) Born 7 June 1883, 43 Overcliffe, Gravesend, Kent; son of Thomas Harry Rose, Master Draper, and Gertrude Elizabeth Blott; m Millicent Helena Gladys Dremel, 4 July 1912, St Stephen's Church, South Kensington. **Subject(s):** History/Law; BA 1905; MA 1909. **Tutor(s):** C E Graves; J R Tanner. **Johnian Relatives:** brother-in-law of Otto May (1897); brother of Hubert Allan Rose (1905); uncle of John Otto May (1932), Sidney Patrick Rose (1930), Richard Percy May (1933) and of Michael Anthony Rose (1938). **Educ:** Harrow School. **Career:** Major, RASC (Mentioned in Despatches), WWI; Solicitor, Crowdy and Rose, Faringdon, Berkshire 1908. **Appointments:** Clerk to the County Magistrates. Died 3 April 1966.

ROSE, Hubert Allan (1905) Born 21 December 1886, 43 Overcliffe, Gravesend, Kent; son of Thomas Harry Rose, Master Draper, and Gertrude Elizabeth Blott; m Patricia Burgoyne Laing, 1912; 3 sons, 1 daughter. **Subject(s):** Classics; BA 1908; MA 1914. **Tutor(s):** J R Tanner; C E Graves. **Johnian Relatives:** brother-in-law of Otto May (1897); brother of Harry Cecil Rose (1902); father of Sidney Patrick Rose (1930); uncle of John Otto May (1932) and of Richard Percy May (1933); father of Michael Anthony Rose (1938). **Educ:** Uppingham School. **Career:** Called to the Bar, Inner Temple 1912; Lieutenant, Royal Scots (Cyclist Battalion, TF) (wounded) 1914–1918; Equity Draughtsman and Conveyancer, Lincoln's Inn 1929–1957. **Appointments:** Member, Commission on Economic Position of Germans 1919. **Publications:** 'Conveyancing Precedents under the Property Statutes of 1925', 1925. Died 13 April 1968.

ROSE, Maurice Frederick (1926) Born 21 March 1908, Bisham Park Farm, Bisham, Berkshire; son of George Frederick Rose, Gardener, and Anna Lily Hewitt. **Subject(s):** Natural Sciences; BA 1929; MA 1934. **Tutor(s):** C W Guillebaud. **Educ:** Bisham School; Ellesborough School; Bourne End School; Sir William Borlase's School, Marlow. **Awards:** First Class Scholarship, Ministry of Agriculture and Fisheries.

ROSE, Michael Anthony (1938) Born 4 June 1920, 5 Court Downs Road, Beckenham, Kent; son of Hubert Allan Rose, Barrister-at-Law, and Patricia Burgoyne Laing. **Subject(s):** History; BA 1941. **Tutor(s):** J S Boys Smith. **Johnian Relatives:** nephew of Otto May (1897) and of Harry Cecil Rose (1902); son of Hubert Allan Rose (1905); brother of Sidney Patrick Rose (1930); cousin of John Otto May (1932) and of Richard Percy May (1933). **Educ:** Heathmount School, Hampstead; Aldro School, Eastbourne; Uppingham School. **Career:** Bandleader.

ROSE, Sidney Patrick (1930) Born 15 January 1914, Nurse Mathieson's Private Hospital, Royal Terrace, Dunedin, New Zealand; son of Hubert Allan Rose, Barrister, and Patricia Burgoyne Laing. **Subject(s):** Mechanical Sciences; BA 1935; MA 1957. **Tutor(s):** J M Wordie. **Johnian Relatives:** nephew of Otto May (1897) and of Harry Cecil Rose (1902); son of Hubert Allan Rose (1905); cousin of John Otto May (1932) and of Richard Percy May (1933); brother of Michael Anthony Rose (1938). **Educ:** Abbey School, Beckenham; Aldro School, Eastbourne; Uppingham School. **Career:** Consultant, Urwick, Orr and Partners 1973; Secretary, Society for Long Range Forecasting (or Planning) 1973.

ROSENBAUM, Robert Abraham (1936) Born 14 November 1915, 630 George Street, New Haven, Connecticut, USA; son of Joseph Rosenbaum, Teacher, and Goldey Rostow. **Tutor(s):** J M Wordie. **Educ:** Milford Grammar School; Milford High School; Yale University.

ROSENBERG, Abraham (ROSS, Arnold) (1933) Born 15 August 1914, 34 Hewitt Street, Cheetham, Manchester; son of Harold Rosenberg, Cap Cutter, and Rebecca Weintraub. **Subject(s):** Classics; BA 1936; MA 1953. **Tutor(s):** R L Howland. **Educ:** Jews School, Manchester; North Manchester School; The Grammar School, Manchester. **Career:** Classics Teacher, William Ellis School, Highgate; English Teacher; Lecturer in Mathematics, Kingsway College of Further Education, London. Died 1981.

ROSENBERG, Norman E (1911) Born 24 October 1888, Barkly East, Cape Colony, South Africa; son of Ellis Rosenberg, Property Owner, and Sarah Broude. **Subject(s):** Law; BA 1914. **Tutor(s):** L H K Bushe-Fox. **Educ:** South African College. **Career:** Called to the Bar, Inner Temple 1915. Died 12 March 1972.

ROSENHEAD, Professor Louis (1928) Born 1 January 1906, 4 Friendly Terrace, Leeds, Yorkshire; son of Abraham Rosenhead, Retail Butcher, and Ellen Nelson; m Esther Brostoff, 1932, Leeds; 2 sons. PhD 1930; BSc (Leeds) 1926; PhD (Leeds) 1928; DSc (Leeds) 1935; FRS 1946. **Tutor(s):** J M Wordie. **Johnian Relatives:** uncle of Daniel Victor Brostoff (1948); father of Martin David Rosenhead (1953) and of Jonathan Vivian Rosenhead (1956). **Educ:** Cross Stamford Street School, Leeds; Central High School, Leeds; Leeds University; Göttingen University. **Career:** Lecturer in Applied Mathematics, University of Swansea 1931–1933; Title A Fellow, SJC 1932–1935; Professor of Applied Mathematics 1933–1973 (Emeritus 1973), University of Liverpool; Ministry of Supply, WWII. **Awards:** Strathcona Research Studentship, SJC. **Honours:** CBE 1954. **Publications:** (ed, with A Fletcher and J C P Miller) *Index of Mathematical Tables*; (ed) *Laminar Boundary Layers*. Died 10 November 1984.

ROSENHEIM, Major Charles Leslie (1930) Born 25 August 1912, 13 Steeles Road, Hampstead; son of Ludwig Rosenheim, Stockbroker, and Martha Reichenbach; m Annelies Fromm. **Subject(s):** Economics; BA 1933; MA 1937. **Tutor(s):** C W Guillebaud. **Johnian Relatives:** brother of Max Leonard Rosenheim (1924). **Educ:** The Hall Preparatory School, Hampstead; Bromsgrove School. **Career:** Major, The Welch Regiment 1945. Died February 1945 (killed in action in Western Europe).

ROSENHEIM, Lord Max Leonard (1924) Born 15 March 1908, 13 Steeles Road, Haverstock Hill, London; son of Ludwig Rosenheim, Stockbroker, and Martha Reichenbach. **Subject(s):** Natural Sciences; BA 1929; MA 1933; BChir 1932; MB 1933; MD 1938; FRCP 1941; FRS 1972; Hon FRCGP 1970. **Tutor(s):** B F Armitage. **Johnian Relatives:** brother of Charles Leslie Rosenheim (1930). **Educ:** The Hall, Hampstead; Shrewsbury School. **Career:** Residential Appointments, UCH 1933; First Assistant, Medical Unit, UCH 1939; Colonel and OC Medical Division, RAMC, Middle East, North Africa, Sicily and Italy (later Consultant, SE Asia) 1941–1946; Professor of Medicine, London University and Director of Medical Unit, University College Hospital Medical School 1950–1971; President, Royal College of Physicians 1966–1972. **Appointments:** Member, Tropical Medicine Research Board 1960; Member, Joint Consultants Committee 1965–1972; Chairman, Medicines Commission 1971; Honorary Fellow, SJC 1970; Honorary Fellow, Ceylon College of Physicians. **Awards:** Raymond Horton-Smith Prize, University of Cambridge 1938; Sir Arthur Sims Commonwealth Professor 1958; Goldsmid and Filliter Exhibitions, UCH; Bilton Pollard Fellow to Massachussetts 1939. **Honours:** CBE 1955; KBE 1967; Baron Rosenheim of Camden 1970. Died 2 December 1972.

ROSENTHAL, Curt Arnold Otto (1905) Born 15 August 1885, Jena, Germany; son of Eduard Rosenthal, Professor, Jena University, and Fanny Clara Ellstätter. **Tutor(s):** D MacAlister. **Educ:** Gymnasium, Jena, Germany.

ROSEVEARE, Canon Edward (1919) Born 25 February 1901, The Rectory, Great Snoring, Norfolk; son of Richard Polgreen Roseveare, Clerk in Holy Orders, and Mary Isabel Skinner; 2 daughters. BA 1922; MA 1926. **Tutor(s):** E E Sikes. **Johnian Relatives:** nephew of William Nicholas Roseveare (1882); son of Richard Polgreen Roseveare (1885); nephew of Walter Harry Roseveare (1898); brother of Harold William Roseveare (1914) and of Martin Pearson Roseveare (1919); uncle of Robert Arthur Roseveare (1942); cousin, once removed, of Robert William Roseveare (1946); great uncle of Robert Edward Murray Roseveare (1967). **Educ:** Little Appley Preparatory School, Ryde; Fettes College, Edinburgh. **Career:** Bishop's College, Cheshunt 1922; Ordained Deacon 1924; Curate, St Paul's, Kings Cross, Halifax 1924–1929; Ordained Priest 1925; Sub-warden, St Paul's College, Grahamstown, South Africa 1929–1934; Warden, St Matthew's College, Grahamstown 1934–1940; Rector, St Philip, Cape Town 1940–1948; Rector, Holy Redeemer, Sea Point, Cape Province 1948–1954; Rector, Constantia, Cape Province, South Africa 1954–1958; Rector, Heene, Sussex 1958–1964. Died 7 May 1964.

ROSEVEARE, Harold William (1914) Born 18 March 1895, Monmouth; son of Richard Polgreen Roseveare, Clerk in Holy Orders, and Mary Isabel Skinner. **Tutor(s):** L H K Bushe-Fox. **Johnian Relatives:** nephew of William Nicholas Roseveare (1882); son of Richard Polgreen Roseveare (1885); nephew of Walter Harry Roseveare (1898); brother of Martin Pearson Roseveare (1919) and of Edward Roseveare (1919); uncle of Robert Arthur Roseveare (1942); cousin, once removed, of Robert William Roseveare (1946); great uncle of Robert Edward Murray Roseveare (1967). **Educ:** Little Appley Preparatory School; Marlborough College. **Career:** Second Lieutenant, Special Reserve of Officers, April 1914; called up August 1914, attached to Wiltshire Regiment. **Awards:** Scholarship, SJC 1913. Died 20 September 1914 (of wounds received in action in the Battle of the Aisne at Vailly, near Soissons).

ROSEVEARE, Henry Herbert (1901) Born 25 July 1868, Wiveliscombe, St Stephens, Saltash, Cornwall; son of Henry Roseveare, Farmer, and Mary Anne Adams; m Constance. BA 1904; MA 1908. **Tutor(s):** D MacAlister. **Educ:** Dunheved College, Launceston. **Career:** Modern Languages Master, Colchester Royal Grammar School; Headmaster, County School, Newquay, Cornwall 1910. Died 25 January 1941.

ROSEVEARE, Sir Martin Pearson (1919) Born 24 April 1898, Great Snoring, Norfolk; son of Richard Polgreen Roseveare, Clerk in Holy Orders, and Mary Isabel Skinner; m (1) Edith Mary Pearce, 10 August 1921, All Saints' Church, Foots Cray (dis 1958); (2) Olivia Margaret Montgomery, 1958; (1) 1 son (Robert Arthur b 25 May 1923), 4 daughters (Helen b 21 September 1925, Jean b 16 May 1927, Diana b 20 November 1932 and Frances b 20 September 1934). **Subject(s):** Mathematics; BA 1921; MA 1925. **Tutor(s):** E E Sikes. **Johnian Relatives:** nephew of William Nicholas Roseveare (1882); son of Richard Polgreen Roseveare (1885); nephew of Walter Harry Roseveare (1898); brother of Harold William Roseveare (1914) and of Edward Roseveare (1919); father of Robert Arthur Roseveare (1942); cousin, once removed, of Robert William Roseveare (1946); grandfather of Robert Edward Murray Roseveare (1967). **Educ:** Little Appley Preparatory School, Ryde, Isle of Wight; Marlborough College. **Career:** Royal Field Artillery 1916–1918; Assistant Master, Repton School 1921–1923; Assistant Master, Haileybury 1923–1926; HM Inspector of Schools; Staff Inspector of Mathematics 1926–1939; Ministry of Food (designed the Ration Book) 1939–1944; Senior Chief Inspector of Schools 1944–1957; Headmaster, Mzuzu School, Nyasaland 1957–1963; Principal, Soche Hill College, Malawi 1964–1967; Master, Marymount School, Mzuzu 1967–1970. **Appointments:** Honorary Fellow, SJC 1952–1985. **Awards:** Scholarship, SJC. **Honours:** Kt 1946. Died 30 March 1985.

ROSEVEARE, Robert Arthur (1942) Born 23 May 1923, Repton; son of Martin Pearson Roseveare, Inspector of Schools, Board of Education, and Edith Mary Pearse; m Katherine Ione Jay, 6 August 1947, the Church of St Lawrence, Herefordshire; 1 son (Robert Edward Murray b 1949). **Subject(s):** Mathematics; BA 1947; MA 1954. **Tutor(s):** S J Bailey.

Johnian Relatives: great nephew of William Nicholas Roseveare (1882); grandson of Richard Polgreen Roseveare (1885); great nephew of Walter Harry Roseveare (1898); nephew of Harold William Roseveare (1914); son of Martin Pearson Roseveare (1919); nephew of Edward Roseveare (1919); second cousin of Robert William Roseveare (1946); father of Robert Edward Murray Roseveare (1967). **Educ:** Red House School, Moor Monkton; Marlborough College. **Career:** War-time in Foreign Office (GCCS Bletchley) 1942–1945; John Lewis Partnership 1947–1948; Mathematics Master, Marlborough College 1949; Mathematics Master, Hilton College, Natal, SA 1949–1951; Mathematics Master, Michaelhouse, Natal 1952–1961; Mathematics Master, Marlborough College 1961–1962; Mathematics Master, St Martin's, Johannesburg 1962–1963; Mathematics Master, Waterford, Swaziland 1964–1965; Mathematics Master, Epsom College 1965–1970; Mathematics Master, Uppingham School 1970–1983; Mathematics Master, Monmouth Girls' School 1983–1984. **Awards:** Major Scholarship, SJC 1941.

ROSEVEARE, Robert William (1946) Born 23 August 1924, Mandalay, Burma; son of William Leonard Roseveare, Civil Engineer, and Marjory Constance Webb; m Patricia Thompson, 1954; 1 son, 3 daughters. **Subject(s):** Mechanical Sciences; BA 1948; MA 1967. **Tutor(s):** R L Howland. **Johnian Relatives:** grandson of William Nicholas Roseveare (1882); second cousin of Robert Arthur Roseveare (1942). **Educ:** Gresham's School, Holt; University College, Oxford (Naval Division). **Career:** Fleet Air Arm (Observer) 1943–1946; Ministry of Fuel and Power 1949–1962 (Assistant Private Secretary to Minister 1951–1954, Cabinet Office 1957–1959, British Embassy, Washington 1960–1962); Secretary 1967–1983, Managing Director, Administrative Affairs 1971–1983, British Steel Corporation; Director, Community Industry Ltd 1983–1991. **Honours:** CBE 1977. **Awards:** College Prize 1947.

ROSS, Alec Logie (1948) Born 26 April 1927, 18 Walker Street, Edinburgh; son of Alexander Ross, Civil Engineer, and Marjorie Elizabeth Logie; m Patricia; 1 son (Alex), 1 daughter (Mary). **Subject(s):** History; BA 1950. **Tutor(s):** F Thistlethwaite. **Educ:** Moreton End School, Harpenden; University College School, Hampstead. **Career:** Assistant Principal, Bank of England (Glasgow Branch). Died 15 June 1996.

ROSS, Archibald Douglas (1923) Born 11 January 1903, son of Douglas Gordon Ross, and Mabel Augusta MacNider; m Marjorie Evelyn Nancy Goodman, 2 May 1930, Christ Church, Mayfair. BA 1928; MA 1944. **Tutor(s):** E E Sikes. **Educ:** Shrewsbury School.

ROSS, Arnold (1933) See ROSENBERG, Abraham.

ROSS, Charles Gordon (1922) Born 8 June 1897, Gore's Lane, Formby, Lancashire; son of Frederic Gordon Ross, Cotton Broker, and Bessie Stripling Freeman; m Marie Zenou Albro Bent, 1921. **Tutor(s):** E E Sikes. **Johnian Relatives:** brother of Ronald Sterry Ross (1928); uncle of John Sterry Hawley Ross (1961); great uncle of David Alexander Ross (1988). **Educ:** Merchant Taylors' School, Great Crosby. Died 26 January 1930.

ROSS, Professor Donald Murray (1936) Born 21 May 1914, Sydney, Nova Scotia; son of Murdoch Willard Ross, Tailor, and Jennie Fail; m Ruth; 1 son (Andrew), 1 daughter (Mary). PhD 1941; BA (Dalhousie) 1934; MA (Dalhousie) 1936; ScD (Cantab) 1966; FRS 1964. **Tutor(s):** C W Guillebaud. **Educ:** Sydney Academy; Dalhousie University. **Career:** Research Officer, School of Agriculture, Cambridge; Demonstrator in Zoology 1945–1947, Lecturer in Zoology 1947–1961, UCL; Professor and Head of Department of Zoology 1961–1979 (Emeritus 1979–1986), Dean of Science 1964–1976, University of Alberta, Canada. **Appointments:** Member, Senate 1963–1966, Member, Board of Governors 1967–1969 and 1974–1977, Member, Campus Planning Committee, Academic Planning Committee and University Planning Committee, University of Alberta, Canada; Associate Editor, *Le*

Naturaliste Canadien 1968; Member, Canadian Physiological Society 1969–1974; Member, Unione Zoologica Italiana, 1972; Associate Editor, *Marine Behavior and Physiology*, 1974; Associate Editor, *Canadian Journal of Zoology* 1977; Member, American Society of Zoologists; Member, Canadian Society of Zoologists; Member, Zoological Society of London; Member, Society for Experimental Biology; Member, Animal Behavior Society. **Awards:** Governor-General's Gold Medal, Dalhousie University; Avery Prize, Dalhousie University; 1851 Exhibition Scholarship; various prizes for films on marine animal behaviour; Queen's Jubilee Medal 1977; Fry Medal, Canadian Society of Zoologists 1980. **Publications:** more than 80 on the subject of animal behaviour and marine biology. Died 13 February 1986.

ROSS, Eric Brockwell (1923) Born 24 July 1906, 4 Durand Gardens, Clapham Road, Kennington, Surrey; son of Edward Ross, Pharmaceutical Chemist, and Ida Emily Brockwell. **Subject(s):** Economics; BA 1927; MA 1931. **Tutor(s):** E Cunningham. **Educ:** Manor House School, Clapham.

ROSS, Graham (1949) Born 6 March 1930, Woodfield, Manchester Road, Oldham, Lancashire; son of George Ross, Headmaster, Hollins Secondary Modern School, Oldham, and Ida Haigh Taylor; m Christine Clucas, 7 April 1956, St Chad's Church, Saddleworth; 2 sons (Julian b 20 February 1960 and Joseph b 29 August 1966), 2 daughters (Jane b 5 February 1957 and Mary b 21 October 1958). BA 1952; DipAgr 1953; MA 1965; BSc (London) 1965. **Tutor(s):** G C L Bertram; E Miller. **Educ:** Friezland Council School, Grasscroft; Hulme Grammar School, Oldham. **Career:** Craftsman, REME 1948–1949; District Advisor, Natural Agricultural Advisory Service, Ministry of Agriculture in South Derbyshire 1953–1966; Lecturer in Agricultural Economics, University of Newcastle upon Tyne 1966–1983; Agricultural Consultant 1983–1990.

ROSS, Dr James Stirling (1928) Born 23 December 1909, 88 Morningside Drive, Edinburgh, Scotland; son of James Stirling Ross, Civil Servant, and Christina Macdonald Ross; 1 son (Euan M). BA 1931; MA 1935; BChir 1935; MB 1936; FBMA. **Tutor(s):** M P Charlesworth. **Educ:** Church End Finchley Preparatory School; Highgate School. **Career:** Department of Health and Social Security. **Appointments:** Member, Board of Governors, Royal National Orthopaedic Hospital. **Honours:** Queen's Silver Jubilee Medal 1977. Died 6 August 1992.

ROSS, The Revd John Estcourt Cresswell (1905) Born 26 January 1886, Pinkney House, Lansdowne Road, Bournemouth, Hampshire; son of Frederick John Ross, Clerk in Holy Orders, and Lucy Mary Coxwell Thomson. **Subject(s):** Mathematics; BA 1908. **Tutor(s):** D MacAlister. **Educ:** Rugby School. **Career:** Ordained Deacon 1909; Curate, St Mary, Luton 1909–1914; Ordained Priest 1910; Missionary, Jaffa, CMS 1914; Sergeant, 8th Battalion, Oxfordshire Light Infantry 1914–1919; Temporary CF, 4th Class, RACD 1915–1916; Permission to Officiate, St James, Holloway 1919–1920; Curate, All Saints, South Lambeth 1920–1926; Curate in Charge, New Ollerton Mission Church 1926–1929; Curate, St John, Worksop 1929–1930; Perpetual Curate, Belton in the Isle of Axholme 1930–1945.

ROSS, Professor Peter McGregor (1938) Born 25 June 1919, Nairobi, Kenya; son of William McGregor Ross, Civil Engineer, Colonial Civil Service, and Isabel Abraham; m Sylvia Robson Gripper; 2 sons (Christopher and Paul), 1 daughter (Alison). **Subject(s):** Mechanical Sciences; BA 1941; MA 1945. **Educ:** Montessori School, Nairobi; Montessori School, Purley; King Alfred School, London; Sidcot School, Winscombe; St Christopher's School, Letchworth; Ulverston Grammar School; Loughborough College of Engineering. **Career:** London Power Company; Head of Mechanical Research and Development, C A Parsons; Chief Development Engineer, Tube Investments Ltd 1941–1970; Professor of Engineering, University of Cambridge 1970–1974. **Awards:** Minor Scholarship, SJC 1937. Died 26 November 1974.

ROSS, The Revd Canon Philip James (1937) Born 10 April 1918, Carradale, Eastcote Road, Pinner; son of Robert Ross, Civil Servant, and Rosamond Jessie Turner; m Betty Ada Wilson, 14 June 1952, St Monica's College, Ogbunike, Nigeria; 1 son (David Anthony b 18 July 1955); 1 daughter (Rosamund Hilda Adora b 14 June 1952). **Subject(s):** Mathematics/Theology; BA 1940; MA 1944; DipEd (London) 1948. **Tutor(s):** J M Wordie. **Johnian Relatives:** brother of Robert Ross (1931); uncle of Robert John Ross (1967). **Educ:** Reddiford School, Pinner; Northwood Preparatory School; Merchant Taylors' School; Ridley Hall, Cambridge. **Career:** Ordained Deacon 1941; Ordained Priest 1942; Curate, St Mary, Islington 1941–1945; Mission Partner, Church Missionary Society, Nigeria 1945–1969, Sierra Leone 1969–1983; Canon Missioner, Diocese of Sierra Leone 1970–1983; Teacher, Dennis Memorial Grammar School, Onitsha, 1945–1946 and 1948–1953 (Principal 1950–1953); Principal, St Mark's Teacher Training College, Nibo-Nise 1953–1959; Member of Staff, Trinity College, Umuahia 1959–1969 (Principal 1960–1969); Canon, St Stephen's Cathedral, Bonny, Nigeria 1967–1970 (Emeritus 1970–1993); Member of Staff, Bo Bible Training Institute, Bo, Sierra Leone 1969–1975; Warden, Sierra Leone Theological Hall and Church Training Centre, Freetown 1975–1983; Canon, St George's Cathedral, Freetown, Sierra Leone 1970–1983 (Emeritus 1983–1993). Died 24 December 1993.

ROSS, Robert (1931) Born 14 August 1912, Ivybank, Headstone Lane, Pinner; son of Robert Ross, Civil Servant, Board of Agriculture, and Rosamond Jessie Turner; m Margaret Steadman; 1 son (Robert John b 26 July 1949), 3 daughters (Helen Mary b 28 December 1942, Anne Frances b 28 December 1942 and Isobel Margaret b 23 September 1946). **Subject(s):** Natural Sciences; BA 1934; MA 1938. **Tutor(s):** C W Guillebaud. **Johnian Relatives:** brother of Philip James Ross (1937); father of Robert John Ross (1967). **Educ:** Reddiford School, Pinner; Northwood Preparatory School; St Paul's School, London. **Career:** Member, Cambridge Botanical Expedition to West Africa 1935; Assistant Keeper, British Museum (Natural History) 1936–1950; Ministry of Aircraft Production 1940–1942; Operational Research Section, RAF Bomber Command 1942–1945; Principal Scientific Officer 1950–1962; Member, Ruwenzori Expedition 1952; Deputy Keeper 1962–1966; Keeper of Botany, British Museum (Natural History) 1966–1977. **Appointments:** Student Christian Movement 1933–1934; College Scientific Society; University Rover Scout Troop; University Boxing Team; The Round (University Country Dance Club); Cambridge Morris Men; Bagman, Morris Ring 1946–1950; Honorary Librarian, Royal Microscopical Society 1947–1951; Honorary Editor, RMS 1953–1971; Vice-President, RMS 1959–1960; Member of Council, Linnean Society 1963–1966; Administrator of Finances, International Association of Plant Taxonomy 1964–1969; Secretary, General Committee for Plant Nomenclature 1964–1969; Chairman, General Committee for Plant Nomenclature 1969–1981; President, British Phycological Society 1969–1971; President, Quekett Microscopical Club 1974–1976; President, International Society for Diatom Research 1994–1996 (Vice-President 1992–1994). **Awards:** Gold Medal, Royal Zoological Society of Antwerp 1978; Scholarship, SJC. **Publications:** Various papers in scientific journals on botanical subjects.

ROSS, Robert Dawes (1926) Born 8 October 1904, Orange, New Jersey, USA; son of Walter Willard Ross, Lawyer, and Jane Rose Ames. **Tutor(s):** M P Charlesworth. **Educ:** Ashville School; High School, Evanston; Laurenceville School; Harvard University.

ROSS, Ronald Sterry (1928) Born 18 July 1910, 25 Leopold Road, Waterloo, Blundellsands, Lancashire; son of Frederic Gordon Ross, Cotton Broker's Manager, and Bessie Stripling Freeman; m (1) Margaret Hawley, 1938 (d 1978), (2) Daphne Minton-Senhouse, 1980; 2 sons (Michael Gordon Ronald and John Sterry Hawley). **Subject(s):** Mechanical Sciences; BA 1932; MA 1936. **Tutor(s):** C W Guillebaud. **Johnian Relatives:** brother of Charles Gordon Ross (1922); father of John Sterry Hawley Ross (1961); grandfather of David Alexander Ross (1988). **Educ:** Lismore Private School; Merchant Taylors' School, Crosby. Died 13 November 1993.

ROSSER, Norman (1945) Born 2 December 1927, 3 Ethelbert Gardens, Ilford, Essex; son of Sydney John Rosser, Local Government Officer (Education), and Doris Agnes Shaw; m Myra Valerie Forster, 18 August 1951, Woodford Green; 1 son (Philip John b 1959), 1 daughter (Gillian Margaret b 1955). **Subject(s):** Mathematics/Geography; BA 1949; MA 1952; CertEd 1951; FRGS 1964. **Tutor(s):** J M Wordie. **Educ:** Redbridge School, Ilford; Brentwood School. **Career:** National Service, Second Lieutenant, RA 1946–1948; Master 1951–1988, Head of Geography Department 1955–1986, Housemaster 1962–1977, Archivist 1988–, Member of Governing Body 1991–2000, Malvern College. **Appointments:** JP 1972–97; Chairman, Malvern Hills Bench; Referee, European Squash Championships, Brussels 1976; President, Worcestershire Squash Rackets Association 1988–; Chairman of Governors, Hillstone Preparatory School 1988–2000; Rackets Correspondent, *Country Life*, 1998–.

ROSTRON, The Revd Sydney (NOWELL-ROSTRON) (1902) Born 10 August 1883, Mosley Street, Blackburn, Lancashire; son of Isaiah Rostron, Clerk in Holy Orders, and Sarah Jane Nowell; m Ella Vivian Davies, 1911. **Subject(s):** Theology; BA 1905; MA 1910; BD 1931. **Tutor(s):** D MacAlister. **Educ:** Middle School, Liverpool. **Career:** CF, 4th Class, RACD, WWI; Vicar, St Matthew, Bayswater 1922–1932; Whitehead Professor, London College of Divinity 1928–1942; Vicar, Paddington and Chaplain, St Mary's Hospital 1935–1941; Rector, Marston Morteyne, Bedfordshire 1944–1948. **Appointments:** Secretary, British and Foreign Bible Society 1918–1922. **Awards:** Hulsean Prize, University of Cambridge 1906. **Publications:** *The Christology of St Paul*, 1911; *Commentary on 1 and 2 Corinthians*, 1929; *The Challenge of Calamity*, 1939. Died 17 March 1948.

ROTHWELL, Professor Harry (1925) Born 8 September 1902, 213 Model Village, Cresswell, Derbyshire; son of Harry Rothwell, Coal Miner, and Emma Watson-Hewitt; m Martha Annabella Goedecke, 1935; 2 daughters (Margaret and Vivien). PhD 1930; BA (Manchester) 1925; FRHistS. **Tutor(s):** E A Benians. **Educ:** Holgate Grammar School, Barnsley; Manchester University. **Career:** Senior Assistant to Keeper of Western Manuscripts, Bodleian Library, Oxford 1928–1929; Lecturer in Medieval History, University of Toronto 1929–1931; Lecturer in Medieval and European History, Edinburgh University 1931–1945; Lieutenant, RNVR 1942–1945; Professor of History 1945–1968 (Emeritus 1968–1980), Dean of Faculty of Arts 1949–1952, University of Southampton. **Awards:** Mullinger Scholarship, SJC 1925–1928. **Publications:** (ed) *The Chronicle of Walter of Guisborough*, 1957; (ed) *English Historical Documents, 1189–1327*, 1975; articles and reviews in professional journals. Died 27 January 1980.

ROTHWELL, Richard William (1944) Born 8 July 1926, 171 Ashfield Road, Rochdale, Lancashire; son of Fred Rothwell, Bank Manager, and Gertrude Shepherd; 1 son (Michael), 1 daughter (Carolyn). **Subject(s):** Mechanical Sciences; BA 1947; MA 1951; FICE. **Tutor(s):** S J Bailey. **Educ:** Kingston-on-Thames Grammar School; Calday Grange Grammar School, West Kirby. **Career:** Radar Defence Projects 1952–1953, Sea and River Defence Projects 1953–1955, John Howard & Co Ltd; Contracts Engineer, specialising in Ports, Tunnels, Transportation and Defence Projects (contracts included ports on the River Tees, Port of Tema, Ghana, Port of Jeddah and Defence Projects in Saudi Arabia) 1955, Partner and Joint Secretary 1979, Chief Executive of Tunnels and Transportation Projects 1982–1987, Group Chief Executive 1987–1988, Group Chairman 1988–1991, Sir William Halcrow & Partners. **Appointments:** Member, Epsom and Ewell Borough Council 1973–1987; Member, Board of Hammersmith & West London College 1990–2000; Member, Surrey County Council 1993–2001.

ROUCHDY, Hassan (1926) Born 2 January 1908, Baghghala, Cairo, Egypt; son of Mohamed Ruchdi Bey, Controller of Female Education, Ministry of Education. BA 1929. **Tutor(s):** C W Guillebaud. **Educ:** Nasrich Primary School, Cairo; Saidia Secondary School, Giza; Royal Wakfs Secondary School, Cairo, Egypt.

ROUNDELL, Richard Henry Selborne (1920) Naval Officer.

ROUNTHWAITE, Denis Christopher (1940) Born 11 January 1922, Hillcroft South, Low Fell, Gateshead-on-Tyne; son of John Mawson Rounthwaite, Architect and Civil Engineer, and Evelyn Walker. **Tutor(s):** S J Bailey. **Educ:** Newcastle Preparatory School; Fettes College, Edinburgh. **Career:** Captain, RE 1940–1946; Administrative Officer, Nigeria 1947.

ROUTLEDGE, William Quentin Durward (1927) Born 26 December 1909, Ebrig, Eckstein Street Observatory, Johannesburg, South Africa; son of William Routledge, Solicitor, Notary Public and Conveyancer, and Flora Leslie Pithey. **Tutor(s):** E A Benians. **Educ:** St John's College, Johannesburg. Died 6 November 1991.

ROW, Vombatkere Pandrang (1901) Born 11 June 1881, Puttur, South Kanara District, Madras, India; son of Vombatkeri Naraini Row, Government Clerk, and Parvati Rai Vombatkeri. **Subject(s):** Natural Sciences; BA 1904. **Tutor(s):** D MacAlister. **Educ:** Presidency College, Madras; Government College, Bangalore. **Career:** Magistrate, Collector and Judge, Indian Civil Service 1903–1933; Called to the Bar, Gray's Inn 1904. **Awards:** Whewell Scholarship for International Law, University of Cambridge 1904.

ROWAN, Harry Bemersyde (1937) Born 4 December 1919, St Ronans, Kilmacolm, Renfrewshire; son of James George Rowan, Outfitter, and Christina Gray. **Subject(s):** Economics; BA 1941; MA 1944. **Tutor(s):** C W Guillebaud. **Educ:** West House Preparatory School, Birmingham; Strathallan School, Perthshire. **Career:** final rank of Captain, WWII; Chartered Accountant; in charge of BP Pension Funds until retirement. Died 17 January 2003.

ROWAN-ROBINSON, Arthur Ralph (1933) Born 9 July 1915, Water Lane House, Bisley, Gloucestershire; son of Leslie Charles Rowan-Robinson, Clerk in Holy Orders, and Francis Dorothea Eteson. **Subject(s):** History; BA 1936; MA 1940. **Tutor(s):** J S Boys Smith. **Educ:** Miss Morris' School, Ipswich; Ipswich Grammar School.

ROWE, John Bentley (1930) Born 29 June 1911, 210 Legsby Avenue, Grimsby, Lincolnshire; son of Joseph Ewart Rowe, Schoolmaster, and Edith Agnes Bentley. **Subject(s):** History; BA 1933; MA 1946. **Tutor(s):** E A Benians. **Educ:** The Bell School, Great Horton; The Grammar School, Bradford. **Awards:** Sizarship 1930. Died 30 December 1997.

ROWE, Peter Whitmill (1948) Born 12 February 1928, 144 Windmill Road, Headington, Oxford; son of Gerald Whitmill Leslie Rowe, Chartered Accountant, and Gladys Florence Hart, Secretary; m Bridget Ann Moyle, 4 April 1952, Allesley, Coventry; 2 sons (Crispin b 28 May 1955 and Patrick b 16 May 1958), 1 daughter (Clare b 29 June 1953). **Subject(s):** History; BA 1950; MA 1956. **Tutor(s):** F Thistlethwaite. **Educ:** Chigwell House, Birmingham; Bishop's Stortford College. **Career:** National Service 1946–1948; VI Form History Master, Brentwood School, Essex 1951–1954; Senior History Master, Repton School, Derbyshire 1954–1957; Headmaster, Bishop's Stortford College 1957–1970; Headmaster, Cranbrook School, Kent. 1970–1981; Teacher, Williston-Northampton School, Massachusetts, USA 1981–1983; Schoolmaster, Kent College, Canterbury 1983–1990. **Appointments:** JP, Bishop's Stortford 1968–1970; JP, Cranbrook 1971–1981. **Awards:** Minor Scholarship, SJC 1945; Hutton Prize, SJC 1949; Sir Joseph Larmor Prize, SJC 1950.

ROWELL, Sir Andrew Herrick (1909) Born 12 March 1890, Brigstock, Northamptonshire; son of Jabez Rowell, Fellmonger, and Eliza Tooke; m Olive Gwendoline Bessie Coles, 1922; 1 son (Oliver), 1 daughter (Jean). **Subject(s):** Mathematics; BA 1912; MA 1943; FIA 1922. **Tutor(s):** L H K Bushe-Fox. **Educ:** Wellingborough Grammar School. **Career:** Corporal, RE, WWI; General Manager, Clerical, Medical and General Life Assurance Society 1933–1950; Director 1950–1959; Deputy Chairman

1956–1967; Chairman, British United Provident Association (BUPA). **Appointments:** President, Institute of Actuaries 1946–1948. **Honours:** Kt 1948. Died 27 August 1973.

ROWETT, Dr Frederick Ernest (1912) Born 4 March 1889, 107 Charlotte Street, Morice Town, Devonport, Devon; son of James Rowett, Master Mariner, and Louisa Terrell. BA 1914; MA 1918; BSc (London) 1919; DSc (London) 1921. **Tutor(s):** L H K Bushe-Fox. **Educ:** HM Dockyard School, Chatham; East London College; Royal College of Science. **Career:** Flight Lieutenant, RNAS, WWI; Research Staff, Engineering Laboratory, Royal Naval College, Greenwich 1915; Principal, Medway Technical College, Gillingham 1918–1929; First Principal, North-Western Polytechnic 1929. **Awards:** Whitworth Scholarship; Whitworth Exhibition, IMechE. Died October 1935.

ROWLAND, David Herbert (1949) Born 1 February 1931, Ilford Maternity Home, Ilford, Essex; son of Herbert Standley Augustus Rowland, Schoolmaster, and Nellie Montrose Hambleton. **Subject(s):** Mathematics; BA 1952; MA 1956. **Educ:** St Angela's Preparatory School, Forest Gate; Milborne Port Church of England School, Somerset; Brentwood School. **Career:** Patent Office 1952. **Awards:** Major Scholarship, SJC.

ROWLAND, James Malcolm (1941) Born 23 April 1922, 13 Gotham Street, Leicester; son of Leonard Rowland, Mechanical Engineer, and Beatrice Lily Price. **Tutor(s):** C W Guillebaud. **Educ:** Wyggeston School, Leicester. Died 23 December 1942.

ROWLANDS, The Revd Evan Celyn (1925) Born 16 November 1906, The Rectory, St George super Ely, Cardiff, Glamorganshire; son of Robert Evan Rowlands, Clerk in Holy Orders, and Margaret Owen. **Subject(s):** Theology/Classics; BA 1929; MA 1934. **Tutor(s):** M P Charlesworth. **Educ:** Village School, St George super Ely; St John's School, Leatherhead. **Career:** Ordained Deacon 1930; Curate, St Andrew, Llwynpia 1930–1931; Ordained Priest 1931; Lecturer, St David's College, Lampeter 1931–1946; Examining Chaplain to the Bishop of Swansea 1939–1946; CF 1940–1945; Lecturer in West African Languages, SOAS, University of London 1946. **Awards:** Nunn Exhibition, SJC 1925. **Honours:** MBE 1956.

ROWNTREE, Thomas Whitworth (1934) Born 10 July 1916, 9 Upper Brook Street, London; son of Cecil William Rowntree, Surgeon; m Barbara Mary Sibbald, 17 April 1943, London; 1 son (Mark), 3 daughters (Sarah, Julia and Clare). **Subject(s):** Natural Sciences; BA 1937; MB 1941; BChir 1941; MChir 1958; MB (London) 1941; BS (London) 1941; MS (London) 1951; FRCS 1942. **Tutor(s):** R L Howland. **Johnian Relatives:** brother of William Henry Rowntree (1929); father of Mark Rowntree (1963). **Educ:** Radley College, Abingdon; University of Rome. **Career:** Second Lieutenant, Queens' Westminster Rifles 1938–1940; RAMC (Major from 1945) 1944–1946; Surgical Registrar Posts, Reading, St Mark's Hospital and The Royal Marsden Hospital 1946–1951; Consultant Surgeon, Southampton 1951–1981. **Honours:** Jubilee Medal. **Publications:** Various contributions to medical press, including anatomy of the nerve-supply of the hand, diverticular disease of the colon and surgery of the parathyroid glands.

ROWNTREE, William Henry (1929) Born 22 May 1912, 9 Upper Brook Street, London; son of Cecil William Rowntree, Consulting Surgeon; m Mary Erskine Ellis, 28 March 1942 (d 2000); 3 daughters (Ann b 1945, Margaret b 1949 and Elizabeth b 1951). **Subject(s):** Mechanical Sciences. **Tutor(s):** J M Wordie. **Johnian Relatives:** brother of Thomas Whitworth Rowntree (1934); uncle of Mark Rowntree (1963). **Educ:** Orley Farm School, Harrow; Radley College. **Career:** London Electric Supply Company 1933–1934; Military Service, TA Commission, Queen's Westminster 1935; Captain 1939; Major, Staff AFHQ 1944–1945; Engineer, Clesco, London 1946–1947; Manager, Courage & Co, Alton, Hampshire 1947–1952; Manager, ICL, London 1954–1975.

Appointments: Freedom of City of London and Freedom of Worshipful Company of Grocers 1934; Liveryman, Worshipful Company of Grocers 1959. **Honours:** MBE 1945; TD and Bar 1950. Died 23 May 2000.

ROWSELL, Francis Charles (1929) Born 8 March 1911, Ridge Green House, Nutfield, Surrey; son of Charles Frederick Rowsell, South African Merchant, and Olive Carterette Wright. **Subject(s):** Mechanical Sciences; BA 1933; MA 1964. **Tutor(s):** J M Wordie. **Educ:** Hillside, Reigate; Malvern College.

ROXBURGH, Thomas Cunningham (1948) Born 7 April 1928, Ardlui, Cabin Hill Gardens, Belfast; son of Thomas Peter Roxburgh, Principal Officer, Ministry of Education for Northern Ireland, and Sarah Cunningham. **Subject(s):** Modern and Medieval Languages; BA 1950. **Tutor(s):** C W Guillebaud. **Educ:** Bloomfield Collegiate School, Belfast; Methodist College, Belfast. **Career:** Corporal, Army Intelligence Corps. Died 19 February 1954.

ROYDS, George Herbert Alexander (1940) Born 11 December 1921, 59 Loughborough Park, Brixton, London; son of William Massy Royds, HBM's Consul General, and Doris Mary Todd; m Pamela Mary Maycock, 27 June 1952, Norwich. **Subject(s):** Economics; BA 1947; MA 1949. **Johnian Relatives:** son of William Massy Royds (1897). **Educ:** Abinger Hill; Haileybury College. **Awards:** Exhibition, SJC.

ROYLE, William Arthur Kirkcaldy (1928) Born 9 February 1909, Sutherland Road, Chatswood, District of Willoughby, New South Wales, Australia; son of Frederic Arthur Royle, Underwriter and Merchant, and Ethel Jessie Kirkcaldy. BA 1931; MA 1935. **Tutor(s):** M P Charlesworth. **Educ:** Edgecliffe Preparatory School; The King's School, Parramatta.

RUANE, John Davison (1937) Born 11 July 1919, Cambridge Road, Ely; son of William Ruane, Farmer, and Elsie Davison; m Mary Robin Phillips, 8 September 1948; 1 son. **Tutor(s):** R L Howland. **Educ:** King's School, Ely; Beaumont College, Old Windsor.

RUDD, Donald Henry (1945) Born 7 March 1926, Inglefield, Ormesby, Yorkshire; son of Walter Rudd, Coal Merchant, and Genevieve Henriette Germaine Hardy. **Subject(s):** English; BA 1950; MA 1955; DipEd 1952. **Tutor(s):** A G Lee; S J Bailey. **Educ:** Nunthorpe Preparatory School, Middlesbrough; Guisborough Grammar School. **Career:** Teacher. **Appointments:** Chairman, Teesside Music Society 1999. **Publications:** Several Plays, 1950–1970.

RUDDER, Brian Verge (1933) Born 1 January 1915, Albert Road, Strathfield, Burwood, Canterbury, Australia; son of Vincent Verge Rudder, Public Accountant, and Hilda Moses. **Subject(s):** Economics; BA 1936. **Tutor(s):** C W Guillebaud. **Educ:** Tudor House School, Moss Vale, New South Wales, Australia; Wrekin College, Wellington, Shropshire.

RUEDEMANN, Paul (1918) American Student.

RUGG, David Austen (1944) Born 14 August 1926, 22 Shaftesbury Street, Stockton-on-Tees; son of John Herbert Rugg, Post Office Clerk, and Matilda McTeer. BA 1947; MA 1951. **Tutor(s):** S J Bailey. **Educ:** Richard Hind Elementary School; Holy Trinity Higher Grade School; Stockton Grammar School; Pocklington School. **Awards:** Dowman Exhibition, SJC. Died July 1985.

RUGG-GUNN, Alexander Noel (GUNN) (1936) Born 3 October 1918, Kasauli Cantonment, Panjab, India; son of Andrew Rugg-Gunn, Opthalmic Surgeon, and Gertrude Martha Smith; m Bay White, September 1945; 2 sons (Simon b 1946 and Charles b 1949, d 1978). **Subject(s):** English/History; BA 1941; MA 1964. **Tutor(s):** J S Boys Smith. **Johnian Relatives:** brother of Mark Andrew Rugg-Gunn (1927). **Educ:** Norland Place, London; Dragon School, Oxford; Sherborne

School. **Career:** (final rank) Captain, RA 1939–1946; (as Alec Gunn) Actor, TV Executive 1946–1982. **Publications:** (as Alec Gunn) *The World Belongs to Charlie*, New Horizon; *The John Crabbe Trilogy:* (1) *The End of Summertime*, Regency Press; (2) *A Bridge Across the Arno*, Book Guild; (3) *Eager Madness*, Book Guild.

RUGG-GUNN, Dr Mark Andrew (1927) Born 2 August 1908, Ullapool, Lochbroom, Ross-shire, Scotland; son of Andrew Rugg-Gunn, Physician, and Gertrude Martha Smith; m (1) Hilda Mary Rowell, 1935 (d 1952), (2) Patricia Mary Elizabeth Cowan, 1 October 1952, St Mary & St Peter, Salcombe Regis, Devon; (1) 1 son (Andrew), 1 daughter (Bridget), (2) 1 son (Michael), 2 daughters (Naomi and Hilary). **Subject(s):** Natural Sciences; BA 1930; MA 1934; BChir 1934; MD 1947; MRCS (St George's) 1933; LRCP (St George's) 1933; MRCP. **Tutor(s):** M P Charlesworth. **Johnian Relatives:** brother of Alexander Noel Rugg-Gunn (Gunn) (1936). **Educ:** Dragon School, Oxford; Sherborne School; St George's Hospital. **Career:** Surgeon-Captain (final rank), RN 1934–1962; Director of Clinical Trials, May and Baker 1962. **Awards:** Entrance Scholarship to St George's 1930; Sir Benjamin Brodie Prize in Surgery and Thompson Medal in Medicine 1931. Died 7 March 1988.

RUMSEY, Professor Victor Henry (1938) Born 22 November 1919, Ivy House, The Green, Devizes, Wiltshire; son of Albert Victor Rumsey, Engineer, and Susan Mary Norman; m Doris Herring, 2 April 1942; 2 sons (John David and Peter Alan), 1 daughter (Catherine Anne). **Subject(s):** Mathematics; BA 1941; MA 1972; ScD 1973; DEng (Tohoku) 1962; FIEEE. **Tutor(s):** J M Wordie. **Educ:** Magdalene Street Boys', Colchester; Cowper Boys' School, Hertford; Esplanade Boys', Harwich; Henry Smith School, Hartlepool; Galleys Field, Hartlepool. **Career:** Professor Emeritus, University of California, San Diego. **Appointments:** Member, National Academy of Engineering, USA. **Awards:** Minor Scholarship, SJC 1937.

RUSCOE-POND, Malcolm George (1949) Born 22 May 1929, 3 Ellys Road, Coventry; son of Graham Ruscoe-Pond, Engineer, and Amy Elizabeth Hayes. **Subject(s):** Mathematics; BA 1952; MA 1956. **Tutor(s):** J M Wordie. **Educ:** St Margaret's Church of England School, Olton; Solihull School. **Career:** RAF 1947–1949.

RUSHALL, Richard Boswell (1929) Born 14 September 1911, 2 Park Road, Rugby; son of Richard Boswell Rushall, Stevedore, and Charlotte Sarah Trype; m (1) Helen Cruickshank (d 1984), (2) Ruby Letitia Brown (née Hills), 17 August 1991; 1 son (Richard John), 1 daughter (Andrea Mary). **Subject(s):** Law; BA 1933; MA 1939. **Tutor(s):** C W Guillebaud. **Educ:** Oakfield School, Rugby; Rugby School; Southampton University, Centre of Education. **Career:** Royal Indian Engineers, ABRO 1941–1946; Master Stevedores 1935–1957, Managing Director 1957–1967, Rushall & Co Ltd Shipping Agents, Rangoon; Assistant Master, New Milton Junior School, Hampshire 1967–1977. Died 13 January 2002.

RUSHBROOKE, Professor George Stanley (1933) Born 19 January 1915, 16 Crescent Road, Willenhall, Staffordshire; son of George Henry Rushbrooke, Miller and Baker, and Frances Isabel Wright; m Thelma Barbara Cox, 16 July 1949 (d 1977). **Subject(s):** Mathematics; BA 1936; MA 1945; PhD 1941; FRS 1982; FRSE. **Tutor(s):** J M Wordie. **Educ:** St Agnes Private School, Willenhall; The Grammar School, Wolverhampton. **Career:** Research Assistant, Bristol University 1938–1939; Senior DSIR Award and Carnegie Teaching Fellowship, University College Dundee, University of St Andrews 1939–1944; Lecturer in Mathematical Chemistry, Leeds University 1944–1948; Senior Lecturer in Theoretical Physics, Oxford University and Lecturer in Mathematics, University College, Oxford 1948–1951; Professor of Theoretical Physics 1951–1980, Head, Department of Theoretical Physics 1965–1980, Deputy Head, School of Physics 1972–1980, University of Newcastle upon Tyne. **Appointments:** Visiting Professor, Department of Chemistry, University of Oregon, USA 1962–63; Visiting

Professor of Physics and Chemistry, Rice University, Houston 1967; Leverhulme Emeritus Fellow 1981. **Awards:** Wright's Prize, SJC 1934; Mayhew Prize, University of Cambridge 1936; Rayleigh Prize, University of Cambridge 1938; Senior DSIR Award, University of St Andrews. **Publications:** *Introduction to Statistical Mechanics*, 1949; research papers in scientific journals. Died 14 December 1995.

RUSHTON, Donald Frederick Harvey (1942) Born 2 April 1924, 581 Stratford Road, Sparkhill, Birmingham; son of Donald Jack Rushton, Pharmaceutical Chemist, and Dora Margaret Kate Littlewood; m (1) Muriel Wyatt, 1948 (d 1993), (2) Lindsay Jenkinson, 18 March 1995; 2 daughters. **Subject(s):** Mechanical Sciences; BA 1945; MA 1949. **Tutor(s):** S J Bailey. **Johnian Relatives:** brother of Stanley John Rushton (1949). **Educ:** Yarwood High School, Hall Green, Birmingham; Wellesbourne House School, Acocks Green, Birmingham; Solihull School. **Career:** Consultant to manufacturing industry 1965–1991; Chairman, Coventry Section, Institution of Production Engineers 1983–1985; Director, Ingersoll Engineers, Rugby 1983–1988. **Appointments:** Chairman, Leamington Spa 41 Club 1983–1984; Chairman, Industrial Advisory Committee, School of Engineering, Coventry University 1989–1996; Visiting Lecturer, Department of Systems Science, City University, London; Council Member, IEE 1991–1993. **Publications:** Papers on manufacturing and management.

RUSHTON, John Atherton (1926) Born 21 May 1908, Arley, Egmont Road, Sutton, Surrey; son of Herbert George Rushton, Solicitor, and Florence Crampton. **Subject(s):** History; BA 1929. **Tutor(s):** E A Benians. **Educ:** The Leas, Hoylake; Shrewsbury School.

RUSHTON, Dr Peter Crampton (1930) Born 26 April 1912, 636 New Chester Road, Rock Ferry, Chester; son of Herbert George Rushton, Solicitor, and Florence Crampton; m Lorna; 3 sons (Tony, James and Michael), 1 daughter (Jane). BA 1933; MA 1946. **Tutor(s):** M P Charlesworth. **Educ:** Mill Mead Preparatory School, Shrewsbury; Shrewsbury School. **Career:** GP 1939; RAMC, Norway, Gibraltar, Normandy and India 1939–1945; ENT Consultant Surgeon, Worthing and Brighton 1945–1974. Died 31 August 1983.

RUSHTON, Philip Lawler (1942) Born 20 November 1923, Puebla, Mexico; son of Rupert Rushton, Clerk, and Marie Lawler; m Patricia Mary Pigot, August 1955; 1 son (Timothy Edward), 3 daughters (Elizabeth Susan, Sarah Julia and Nichola Jane). **Subject(s):** Engineering/Estate Management; BA 1949; MA 1953; FRICS. **Tutor(s):** S J Bailey. **Educ:** Penryn School; Stonyhurst College, Clitheroe. **Career:** RAF 1941–1946; Land Commissioner, Bury St Edmunds and subsequently served at Cambridge, Hertford, Chelmsford, Wolverhampton and Newcastle 1949–1981; Chief Regional Officer, South West Region Ministry of Agriculture Fisheries and Food 1981–1983. **Appointments:** RAF Cadet, SJC 1941.

RUSHTON, Stanley John (1949) Born 15 January 1929, Hall Green, Birmingham; son of Donald Jack Rushton, Pharmaceutical Chemist, and Dora Margaret Kate Littlewood; m Dorothy Rea, 1958, Manchester; 2 daughters (Elizabeth Anne b 1961 and Sally Alexandra b 1963). **Subject(s):** Mechanical Sciences; BA 1952; MA 1958; CEng; FIMechE; MCMI. **Tutor(s):** R L Howland. **Johnian Relatives:** brother of Donald Frederick Harvey Rushton (1942). **Educ:** Ruckleigh School, Solihull; Solihull School. **Career:** College Apprenticeship 1952–1954, Cost Investigation Engineer 1954–1955, Manufacturing Development Engineer 1955–1958, Metropolitan Vickers Electrical Co Ltd; Assistant Scientist, Research and Development 1958–1960, Assistant Engineer, Buckland Mill, Dover 1960–1963, Chief Engineer, Vegetable Parchment Mills, St Mary Cray 1963–1968, Deputy Chief Engineer, Wiggins Teape Converters 1968–1970, Senior Engineer, Project Engineering Division 1970–1972, Contract Manager, Project Engineering Division 1972–1973, Consultant Technical Services Division 1973–1975, Wiggins Teape Co Ltd Papermakers; Area Engineer, Lambeth, Southwark and Lewisham Area Health Authority (Teaching) 1976–1983.

RUSHWORTH, Louis Lionel Stuart (1926) Born 9 July 1907, Ahmedabad, India; son of Rendall Rushworth, and Beatrice Ellen Greaves. **Subject(s):** Modern and Medieval Languages; BA 1929; MA 1933. **Tutor(s):** M P Charlesworth. **Educ:** Langworthy Road Council School; Hallon Bank Council School, Salford; Manchester Grammar School. **Awards:** Scholarship, SJC 1925.

RUSSELL, Alexander Fraser (1932) Born 13 August 1913, Flowerdale, Liesbeck Road, Rosebank, Cape of Good Hope; son of Alexander Fraser Russell, Chief Justice, High Court of Southern Rhodesia, and Winifred Isobel Robertson; m Marjorie. **Tutor(s):** C W Guillebaud. **Johnian Relatives:** son of Alexander Fraser Russell (1897); brother of John James Fraser Russell (1927). **Educ:** Millin School, Bulawayo; The High School, Rondebosch. Died 10 April 1973.

RUSSELL, Captain John James Fraser (1927) Born 23 December 1906, Gairloch, Park Road, Mowbray, Wynberg, Cape of Good Hope; son of Alexander Fraser Russell, Judge, High Court of Southern Rhodesia, and Winifred Isobel Robertson; m Sheila Barker, February 1939. **Subject(s):** Natural Sciences; BA 1930; MB (Edinburgh) 1933; ChB (Edinburgh) 1933. **Tutor(s):** M P Charlesworth. **Johnian Relatives:** son of Alexander Fraser Russell (1897); brother of Alexander Fraser Russell (1932). **Educ:** Millin School, Bulawayo; Plumtree School, Southern Rhodesia; Merchiston Castle School, Edinburgh; University of Cape Town. **Career:** In medical practice, Claremont, Cape Town 1935–1939; Captain, South African Medical Corps 1939–1941. Died 2 December 1941 (killed in action in Libya).

RUSSELL, Ralph (1937) Born 21 May 1918, Master's Apartments, Hackney Union Workhouse, Homerton, London; son of Alfred Wood Russell, Clerical Assistant, London County Council, and Mildred Amos. **Subject(s):** Classics/Geography; BA 1940; BA (London). **Tutor(s):** R L Howland. **Educ:** Holme on Spalding Moor Council School, East Yorkshire; Loughton Council School; Chigwell School. **Career:** Lecturer, then Reader, in Urdu, School of Oriental and African Studies. **Awards:** Exhibition, SJC 1936. **Publications:** From 1969, a number of books and articles on, and translations from, Urdu literature.

RUSSELL-SMITH, Alan (1911) Born 20 March 1893, 1 Aubert Park, Highbury, Middlesex; son of Henry Russell-Smith, Analytical Chemist, and Ellen Goodman; m (1) Ethel Louisa Boys, 3 April 1919 (d 10 June 1920), (2) Bridget, 1927; (1) 1 son (John Francis b 8 June 1920), 1 daughter (Sylvia). BA 1914; MA 1918. **Tutor(s):** E E Sikes. **Johnian Relatives:** brother of Hugh Francis Russell-Smith (1906); uncle of Roy Sabine Russell-Smith (1933); father of John Francis Russell-Smith (1939); uncle of Rupert Hugh Russell-Smith (1950); great uncle of William Goodman Russell-Smith (1978). **Educ:** Rugby School. **Career:** Private, HAC 1914–1916; Partner, then Director, Fuller, Smith and Turner, Griffin Brewery, London. Died 12 March 1972.

RUSSELL-SMITH, Hugh Francis (1906) Born 11 August 1887, 1 Aubert Park, Highbury, Middlesex; son of Henry Russell-Smith, Analytical Chemist, and Ellen Goodman; m Dorothy Catherine Willett Tait, 31 March 1914, Westminster; 1 son (Roy Sabine b 1 July 1915). **Subject(s):** Classics/History; BA 1909; MA 1913. **Tutor(s):** E E Sikes. **Johnian Relatives:** brother of Alan Russell-Smith (1911); father of Roy Sabine Russell-Smith (1933); uncle of John Francis Russell-Smith (1939) and of Rupert Hugh Russell-Smith (1950); great uncle of William Goodman Russell-Smith (1978). **Educ:** Hildersham House, Broadstairs; Rugby School. **Career:** Bishop of Peterborough Fellow, SJC 1912–1916 (leave of absence for war service); Captain, 6th Battalion, Rifle Brigade 1915–1916. **Appointments:** Instructor, Training School for Officers, Pembroke College 1915. **Awards:** Allen Scholarship, University of Cambridge 1911; Second Winchester Reading Prize, University of Cambridge 1911; Thirlwall Prize, University of Cambridge 1911. **Publications:** 'Religious and Political Liberty Under Charles II and James II', *Cambridge Historical Essays, XXI*, Cambridge, 1911. Died 5 July 1916 (of wounds received in action during the Battle of the Somme).

RUSSELL-SMITH, John Francis (1939) Born 8 June 1920, Park View House, Leopold Road, Wimbledon; son of Alan Russell-Smith, Director of Public Company, and Ethel Louisa Boys; m (1) Cecilia Eleanor Forster, 23 March 1965 (d), (2) Gael, 2001. **Subject(s):** Architecture. **Tutor(s):** J M Wordie. **Johnian Relatives:** nephew of Hugh Francis Russell-Smith (1906); son of Alan Russell-Smith (1911); cousin of Roy Sabine Russell-Smith (1933) and of Rupert Hugh Russell-Smith (1950); uncle of William Goodman Russell-Smith (1978). **Educ:** Hildersham House School, Broadstairs; Bryanston School. **Career:** RNVR 1940–1946; Director and Life President, Fuller, Smith and Turner 1946–.

RUSSELL-SMITH, Dr Roy Sabine (1933) Born 1 July 1915, 48 Highbury Park, Islington, London; son of Hugh Francis Russell-Smith, University Lecturer and Fellow, SJC, and Dorothy Catherine Willett Tait; m (1) Dorothy Blanchford, (2) Angela Nicholson; 7 sons (Timothy, Michael, Charles, Andrew, Alistair, David and Robert). BA 1941; MA 1972; MRCS; LRCP. **Tutor(s):** J M Wordie. **Johnian Relatives:** son of Hugh Francis Russell-Smith (1906); nephew of Alan Russell-Smith (1911); cousin of John Francis Russell-Smith (1939), Humphrey James Oakley White (1950) and of Rupert Hugh Russell-Smith (1950); uncle of William Goodman Russell-Smith (1978). **Educ:** Arnold House, London; Hildersham House, Broadstairs; Rugby School; St Bartholomew's Hospital, London. **Career:** GP.

RUST, John Frederick (1947) Born 20 February 1921, 14 Queen's Terrace, Edgware, Middlesex; son of Harry Gurney Rust, Motor Engineer, and Lilian Rose Grove. **Subject(s):** Modern and Medieval Languages/Music; BA 1949; MA 1954; MusB 1950; ARAM; ARCM; ARSCM, LRAM. **Tutor(s):** C W Guillebaud. **Educ:** Burnt Oak School; Hendon County Grammar School; Royal Academy of Music. **Career:** Lieutenant, RNVR 1941–1946; Assistant Director of Music, Tonbridge School, Kent 1950–1957; Director of Music, Christ's Hospital, Sussex 1957–1961; Deputy Principal, Birmingham School of Music 1961–1969; Music Master, Victoria College Preparatory School, Jersey 1969–1981. **Awards:** Scholarship, College of St Nicholas, Canterbury 1946–1947; Choral Studentship, SJC 1947–1950. **Appointments:** Chorus Master, Hallé Choir 1966–1969.

RUTH, Anthony Barrons (1946) Born 20 April 1928, 178 Worple Road, Wimbledon, Surrey; son of William Richard Barrons Ruth, Schoolmaster, and Constance Phyllis Butterworth; m Beverly Ann Williams, 9 August 1958; 1 son (James William Barrons b 1962), 2 daughters (Joanna Caroline b 1961 and Amanda Jane b 1965). **Subject(s):** Natural Sciences (Physics); BA 1949; MA 1954. **Tutor(s):** G C L Bertram. **Educ:** King's College School, Wimbledon; Ruskin School, Wimbledon; Rokeby School, Wimbledon; Newcastle-under-Lyme High School. **Career:** Second Lieutenant, 2nd Regiment, Royal Horse Artillery 1950–1951; Assistant Master, Winchester College 1951–1966; Winchester College CCF 1951–1968, Major 1966–1968; Exchange Teacher, St Mark's School, Southborough, Massachusetts, USA 1966–1967; Assistant Master 1968–1990 (Housemaster 1968–1983), Winchester College. **Awards:** Major Scholarship, SJC 1945.

RUTHERFORD, Charles Ian (1937) Born 5 February 1919, Bingham Nottinghamshire; son of John Seymour Rutherford, Chartered Surveyor, and Hilda Vera Woods; m Yvonne Irene Boult, 14 June 1944, St Mary's Church, Parel, Bombay; 1 son, 1 daughter. **Subject(s):** Natural Sciences/Physics; BA 1940; MA 1948. **Tutor(s):** C W Guillebaud. **Educ:** St Piran's School, Maidenhead; Repton School. **Career:** Radar Officer, RAF 1940–1946; Process Control Research, ICI 1946–1949; Development and Manufacture, ICI Fibres 1950–1966; General Manager, Management Services, ICI 1966–1971. **Appointments:** Local Council 1972–1979; Member, Cheshire Wildlife Trust; Chairman, Cheshire Wildlife Trust; Past President, Lancashire and Cheshire Entomological Society. **Awards:** Minor Scholarship, SJC 1936. **Publications:** *Macro-Moths in Cheshire 1961–1993*.

RYAN, Arthur Healy (1920) Naval Officer.

RYCROFT, Dr Richard Noel (1934) Born 24 December 1915, Lucroft, Bentley Heath, Solihull; son of Alfred Thomas Rycroft, Dental Surgeon, and Edith Emily Cartwright; m Patricia Kitto, 25 May 1944, Salisbury. **Subject(s):** Natural Sciences; BA 1937; MA 1978; MRCS; LRCP 1940. **Tutor(s):** R L Howland. **Educ:** Etonhurst School, Weston-super-Mare; Tytenhanger Lodge School, Seaford; Rugby School. **Career:** Flight Lieutenant, RAF 1944. **Honours:** MC 1944. Died 12 February 1995.

RYDER, Archibald Stuart Dudley (1919) Naval Officer.

RYDINGS, Henry Anthony (1941) Born 20 August 1922, 15 Vodroffsplads, Copenhagen, Denmark; son of Douglas Gerald Rydings, British Consul at Panama, and Mary Dawe. BA 1948; MA 1955. **Tutor(s):** C W Guillebaud. **Educ:** Ravenscroft Preparatory School, Yelverton; Wycliffe College, Stonehouse. **Career:** Officer, RE 1939; Librarian, University College, Ghana; Librarian, Fourth Bay, Sierra Leone; Librarian, The University of Hong Kong 1961.

RYE, Ralph Walter (1926) Born 1 January 1908, Rosslyn Manse, 5 Pilgrims Lane, Hampstead, Middlesex; son of Frank Gibbs Rye, Solicitor and MP for Loughborough, and Ethal Mary Beloe; m Rosamund Copeman, 9 April 1936, St Andrew's, Norwich. BA 1929; MA 1933. **Tutor(s):** E A Benians. **Educ:** Elm House School, Surbiton; Winchester House School, Brackley; Bradfield College. Died 7 February 1983.

RYLE, Frederick Robert (1943) Born 17 February 1926, Bank House, Chester-le-Street, Durham; son of Frederick James Ryle, Bank Manager, and Lilian Welton; m; 6 children. **Subject(s):** Natural Sciences; BA 1946; MA 1950; BChir 1949; MB 1949; MRCGP. **Tutor(s):** S J Bailey. **Educ:** Red Rose Council School, Chester-le-Street; Royal Grammar School, Newcastle upon Tyne. **Career:** GP 1949–1991.

RYLEY, Donald Arthur George Buchanan (1912) Born 5 July 1893, Colorado Springs, Colorado, USA; son of Harold Buchanan Ryley, Headmaster, Emmanuel School, and Hughienna Lenny Florence Fraser. **Tutor(s):** E E Sikes. **Educ:** Sir R Marwood's School, Sandwich; St Olave's Grammar School. **Career:** Second Lieutenant, Manchester Regiment, then North Staffordshire Regiment 1914–1917. Died 11 February 1917 (killed in action at Hulluch).

RYMER, Dr Jolyon James Hugh (1945) Born 4 October 1926, 386 Loop Street, Pietermaritzburg, Natal; son of Hugh Thornton Rymer, Medical Practioner, and Muriel Olive Silburn; m (1) Sally Ann Sproles, 1952, (2) Margareta Hultenheim, 1962, (3) Nicole Dieu, 1987; (2) 1 son (James Hugh Gustaf b 11 August 1964), 2 daughters (Suzanne Emelie b 31 December 1962 and Mary Victoria b 14 June 1966). **Subject(s):** Natural Sciences (Medicine); BA 1947; MA 1952; BChir 1951; MB 1951; DMRD. **Tutor(s):** G C L Bertram. **Johnian Relatives:** stepson of Norman Geoffrey Lyon (1925). **Educ:** Preparatory High School, Durban; Michaelhouse, Natal; Rhodes University College, Grahamstown. **Career:** Middlesex Hospital Medical School 1947–1950; Clinical Fellow, Yale University, USA 1951; Fellow, Lahey Clinic, Boston, USA 1952; Radiology Department, Stanford University, USA 1953–1954; Senior Registrar, United Cambridge Hospitals 1962–1966; Consultant Radiologist, Bromley 1966–1986.

S

SABERTON, Frederick Rupert (1901) Born 27 May 1881, 13 Brunswick Street, Manchester; son of Frederick William Saberton, Surgeon, and Marian Ahenden. BA 1906. **Tutor(s):** D MacAlister. **Educ:** Private Tuition.

SABIN, Howard Westcott (1935) Born 19 October 1916, The Red House, School Road, Moseley, Worcestershire; son of John Howard Sabin, Stock and Share Broker, Captain, Royal Welsh Fusiliers, and Octavia Roads Scruby; m (1) Joan Eunice Noble, 1942 (div 1959), (2) Janet Eileen Baillie, 13 May 1959, St Columba's, Pont Street; 2 sons, 1 daughter.

Subject(s): History/Law; BA 1938; MA 1944. **Tutor(s):** J S Boys Smith. **Educ:** West House School, Edgbaston; Shrewsbury School. **Career:** Lieutenant Commander, RNVR 1939–1946; Called to the Bar, Middle Temple 1946; Counsel for Post Office (Midland Circuit) 1964; Prosecuting Counsel, Midland Circuit, appointed by the Attorney General; Assistant Recorder, Portsmouth 1966; Deputy Chairman, Bedfordshire QS 1968–1972; Legal Adviser to Associated Newspapers Group Ltd 1972–1984; Chairman, William Morris Rolling Mills Ltd (formerly William Morris & Son (Birmingham) Ltd) 1985. Died 9 February 1996.

SADDLER, Professor William (1911) Born 23 March 1892, 21 Green Street, Forfar; son of William Saddler, Merchant, and Margaret Crammond. **Subject(s):** Mathematics; BA 1914; MA (St Andrews) 1910. **Tutor(s):** E E Sikes. **Educ:** St Andrews University. **Career:** Lieutenant, RGA (Mentioned in Despatches), WWI; Professor of Mathematics, Canterbury University College, Christchurch, New Zealand 1930–1955. Died 1982.

SADICK, Ali (1939) Born 25 July 1919, Cairo, Egypt; son of Ali Bey Sadick, Landowner, and Fatma Naguib. **Subject(s):** Economics. **Tutor(s):** C W Guillebaud. **Educ:** Victoria College, Alexandria; Private Tuition, Felixstowe; Polytechnic, Regent Street.

SADLER, Eric John (1925) Born 16 June 1907, 93 Short Heath Road, Erdington, Birmingham, Warwickshire; son of John Sadler, Heraldic Engraver, and Maud Eliza Richards; m Marjorie Grey; 1 son (John Richard b 9 December 1937). **Subject(s):** Law; BA 1928; MA 1932; LLB 1929; LLM 1985. **Tutor(s):** J M Wordie. **Johnian Relatives:** father of John Richard Sadler (1958). **Educ:** King Edward's Grammar School, Aston, Birmingham; King Edward's School, Birmingham. **Career:** Solicitor. **Appointments:** Honorary Consul, Federal Republic of Germany. **Awards:** Scholarship, SJC 1924. **Honours:** TD; Officers Cross, 1st Class, Order of Merit of the Federal Republic of Germany, Bundes Verdienst Kreuz. Died 19 October 1993.

SADLER, John James Goode (1940) Born 18 December 1921, Gerrans, Barnt Green, Birmingham; son of Douglas James Goode Sadler, Farmer, and Ivy Louise Hitchcock. **Tutor(s):** R L Howland. **Educ:** The Lickey Hills Preparatory School; King Edward's High School, Birmingham. Died 13 May 1995.

SADLER, Samuel Aubrey (1945) Born 23 November 1926, Craigellon, Marton, Middlesbrough; son of Cecil Norman Sadler, Director of Colliery and Chemical Manufacturers, and Constance Evelyn Jones. **Tutor(s):** C W Guillebaud. **Educ:** Aysgarth School, Bedale; Charterhouse.

SÁENZ, Alfredo (1928) Born 6 September 1908, La Paz, Bolivia, South America; son of Jorge Sáenz, Minister of Bolivia to the Holy See in Rome, and Sara Garcia de Sáenz. BA 1931. **Tutor(s):** J M Wordie. **Educ:** The University School, Hastings.

SAID, Mohammad (1923) Born 16 June 1897, son of Mohammad Zaki Bey, Chief Government Official, Railways, Cairo, and Fatima Al Mashadiah. **Subject(s):** History; BA 1925; MA 1929. **Tutor(s):** E A Benians. **Educ:** Government Ackadeen School; Government Khadiviah School; Government School of Law.

SAINT, Henry Lancelot Basil (1933) Born 17 January 1911, 18 Clovelley Avenue, Oldham, Lancaster; son of Horace Victor Lawrence Saint, Colliery Fireman, and Ethel Bertha Hodgkinson. **Subject(s):** Mathematics; BA 1935; MA 1940; BSc (Liverpool) 1933. **Tutor(s):** J M Wordie. **Educ:** Hindley and Abram Grammar School; University of Liverpool. **Awards:** Exhibition, SJC 1934. Died 1 August 1996.

SAINT, Percy Johnston (1904) Born 27 June 1886, 29 Gladstone Place, Aberdeen, Scotland; son of James Saint, Draper, and Blanche Mary

Moffatt; m Clare Isabel McCulloch, 15 February 1915, St George's, Hanover Square; 2 daughters (Sandra and Jeanette). BA 1907; MA 1926; FRSM 1936. **Tutor(s):** D MacAlister. **Educ:** Rossall School. **Career:** Lieutenant, Pioneers, Indian Army, served in India, Egypt and France (wounded) 1908–1915; Wellcome Research Institute 1924; Assistant Director, Museum of Medical History 1934–1947. **Publications:** *Translations of Persian Poems*, 1924; *Outline of a History of Medicine in India*, 1927; *Green Hills and Golden Sands*, 1944; *Castanets and Carnations*, 1946. Died 1 July 1974.

ST CLAIR-THOMPSON, Guy Warren (1924) See THOMPSON.

ST JOHN, The Revd Father Fleming (1909) Born 30 January 1891, Coombe House, Westbury on Trym, Gloucestershire; son of Harris Fleming St John, Clerk in Holy Orders, and Gertrude Margaret Ward. **Subject(s):** History; BA 1912; MA 1933. **Tutor(s):** E E Sikes. **Educ:** Box House; Haileybury College; St Stephen's House, Oxford; Ely Theological College. **Career:** Priest 1915; Private, King's Royal Rifle Corps, France, WWI; Member, English Dominican Order; Founder of a school, Llanarth, Wales; Headmaster, Blackfriars School, Laxton, Northamptonshire 1932; Prior Provincial for England 1958. Died 9 March 1973.

SALAM, Professor Abdus (1946) Born 29 January 1926, Jhang, Punjab, Pakistan; son of Chauduri Muhammad Hussein, Clerk, Inspector of Schools' Office, and Hajira Begum; m (1) Hafiza Hussein, 1949, Pakistan, (2) Louise Napier Johnson, 1968, London; (1) 1 son (Ahmad b 9 July 1960), 3 daughters (Aziza b 8 June 1950, Bushra b 27 December 1956 and Asifa b 14 November 1954), (2) 1 son (Umar Ataus b 22 May 1974), 1 daughter (Sayyeda Hajira b 16 June 1982). **Subject(s):** Mathematics/Natural Sciences; BA 1948; MA 1952; PhD 1952; BA (Punjab) 1944; MA (Punjab) 1946; several honorary degrees, including Honorary ScD (Cambridge) 1985; FRS 1959. **Tutor(s):** J M Wordie. **Johnian Relatives:** father of Umar Ataus Salam (1992). **Educ:** Government College, Lahore, Pakistan; Punjab University. **Career:** Professor of Mathematics, Government College, Lahore 1951–1954; Title A Fellow 1951–1954, Title B Fellow 1954–1956, SJC; Lecturer in Mathematics, University of Cambridge 1954–1956; Professor of Theoretical Physics, Imperial College, London 1957–1993; Director and President, International Centre for Theoretical Physics, Trieste 1964–1994. **Appointments:** Supervisor in Mathematics and Physics, SJC 1954–1956; Scientific Secretary of the Geneva Conference on the Peaceful Uses of Atomic Energy 1955–1958; Scientific Adviser to President of Pakistan 1961–1974; Member, UN Advisory Committee on Science and Technology 1964–1975 (Chairman 1971–1972); Fellow, Royal Swedish Academy of Sciences 1970; Foreign Member, USSR Academy of Sciences 1971; Honorary Fellow, SJC 1972; Vice-President, IUPAP 1972–1978; Founding Member and President, Third World Academy of Sciences 1983; South Commission 1987; President, Third World Network of Scientific Organisations 1988; APS 1993; member of forty-seven academies/societies. **Awards:** Fourteen awards for contributions to peace and the promotion of international science, including the Atoms for Peace Prize 1968; Hopkins Prize, Cambridge Philosophical Society 1957; Hughes Medal, Royal Society 1964; Royal Medal, Royal Society 1978; John Torrence Tate Medal, American Institute of Physics 1978; Nobel Prize for Physics 1979; Einstein Medal, UNESCO, Paris 1979; Edinburgh Medal 1981; Lomonosov Gold Medal 1983; Catalunya Prize 1983; Royal Society's Copley Medal 1989. **Honours:** Order of Nishan-e-Imtiaz 1979; Honorary KBE 1989. **Publications:** (ed, with E P Wigner) *Aspects of Quantum Mechanics*, 1972; *Ideals and Realities: selected essays*, 1984; *Science and Education in Pakistan*, 1987; (with Ergin Sezgin) *Supergravity in Diverse Dimensions*, Vols I and II, 1988; (ed) *From a Life of Physics*, 1989; 'Unification of Fundamental Forces', 1988 Dirac Memorial Lecture, 1990; *Science and Technology: challenge for the South*, 1992; *Renaissance of Sciences in Islamic Countries*, 1994; papers on physics of elementary particles and on scientific and educational policies for developing countries and Pakistan. Died 21 November 1996.

SALE, The Revd David Morley (1921) Born 27 June 1902, Moor Cottage, Wirksworth, Derbyshire; son of Herbert William Sale, Merchant in Japanese Goods, and Alice Hannah Mawe; 1 daughter (Rosemary). BA 1924; MA 1928. **Tutor(s):** E A Benians. **Educ:** Preparatory School, Wallington; Mount Radford School, Exeter; Ebor School, Bexhill; Monkton Combe School, Bath; Ridley Hall, Cambridge. **Career:** Ordained Deacon 1926; Curate, St James, Tunbridge Wells 1926–1929; Ordained Priest 1927; Curate, St George, Tufnell Park 1929–1935; Vicar, Thornton with Bagworth and Stanton-under-Bardon, Leicestershire 1939–1945; Rector, Downe St Mary, Bow, Devon 1945–1955; Vicar, Holy Trinity, Southwell 1955–1967. **Publications:** *The Hymn Writers of Hampshire*, 1975; *Pilgrims Handbook*, 1977. Died 11 December 1979.

SALINGER, Cecil Gerald Furnivall (FURNIVALL) (1919) Born 1 November 1901, 5 Maze Hill, St Mary Magdalen, Hastings; son of Gustav Salinger, East India Merchant, and Emily Furnivall. **Subject(s):** Economics/Law; BA 1922; MA 1926; LLB 1922. **Tutor(s):** E A Benians. **Educ:** Lynchmore School, Eastbourne; Rugby School. **Career:** Lecturer and Author.

SALISBURY-ROWSWELL, Professor Richard Frank (1945) Born 8 December 1926, 67 Walton Street, Chelsea, London; son of Thomas Salisbury-Rowswell, Builders' Manager, and Marjorie Beatrice Smith; m Mary, 2 sons (Thomas and John), 1 daughter (Catherine). **Subject(s):** Modern and Medieval Languages; BA 1949; MA 1956. **Tutor(s):** J M Wordie. **Educ:** Preston Park Junior Mixed School, Wembley; University College School, Hampstead; Harvard University. **Career:** Professor of Anthropology 1962–1989, Dean, Faculty of Arts, 1986–1989, McGill University. **Appointments:** Canadian Human Rights Foundation. **Publications:** *From Stone to Steel*, 1962; *Vunamami*, 1969; *A Homeland for the Cree*, 1986. Died 18 June 1989.

SALMON, Peter Stanley (1949) Born 11 April 1926, 5 Hillbrook Road, Upper Tooting, London; son of Philip Ernest Salmon, Clerk, Royal Courts of Justice, and Edna May Spinks. BA 1951; MA 1956. **Tutor(s):** A G Lee. **Johnian Relatives:** cousin of Barry Sinclair Salmon (1953) and of Godfrey Nicholas Salmon (1961). **Educ:** Cheam Common Junior School; St Margaret's Westminster City School; Epsom County School; Cambridgeshire High School. **Career:** Worcester Cathedral Lay-Clerk and Schoolmaster 1952–1955; Vicar-Choral and Assistant Master, St Paul's Cathedral Choir School 1955–1988. Died 12 February 1998.

SALMON, Rider Gordon (1940) Born 13 December 1921, Streatham Manor, Leigham Avenue, Streatham; son of Charles Edgar Salmon, Architect, and Agnes Bowyer; m Pauline Amanda Dumas; 1 son (Patrick Charles b 16 July 1950). **Subject(s):** English; BA 1947; MA 1951. **Tutor(s):** C W Guillebaud. **Johnian Relatives:** father of Patrick Charles Salmon (1970). **Educ:** Hillsbrow School, Redhill; Leighton Park School; University of London Institute of Education.

SALMON, Sidney Herbert (1941) Born 25 March 1922, Noranside, Junction Road, Norton; son of Thomas Herbert Salmon, Borough Treasurer, and Jane Anne Curry; m Dorothy Mabel Hare (née Lishman). **Subject(s):** Mathematics. **Tutor(s):** J M Wordie. **Educ:** Ragworth Hall School, Norton-on-Tees; Durham School. **Career:** Chartered Surveyor; West African Army, served in Africa and India 1941–1946.

SALMOND, William Guthrie (1912) Born 8 June 1892, Temuka, New Zealand; son of John William Salmond, Solicitor-General of New Zealand, and Anne Bryham Guthrie. **Subject(s):** Law; BA 1917. **Tutor(s):** L H K Bushe-Fox. **Educ:** St Peter's Collegiate School, Adelaide, Australia; Wellington College, New Zealand; Victoria University College, Wellington. **Career:** Enlisted into 9th Lancers; Commissioned Second Lieutenant, North Somerset Yeomanry; transferred to 1st Wellington Battalion, New Zealand Forces; Lieutenant; acted as Adjutant, Acting Captain 1914–1918. Died 9 July 1918 (killed in action at Rossignol Wood).

SALOWAY, Sir Reginald Harry (1924) Born 26 October 1905, Victoria Grove, Bridport, Dorset; son of Henry Saloway, Schoolmaster, and Lily Courtney; m Betty Louisa Jenkins Cavill, 25 April 1930, Bombay Cathedral. **Subject(s):** History; BA 1927. **Tutor(s):** E A Benians. **Educ:** Bridport Secondary School; Exeter School. **Career:** Indian Civil Service 1928–1947; Secretary to the Board of Revenue, United Provinces 1936, Revenue and Finance Minister, Raupur 1937, Director General of Resettlement and Employment 1947, Indian Civil Service; Secretary of Rural Development 1947–1951, Chief Secretary and Minister of Defence and External Affairs 1951–1954, Often Acting Governor 1951–1954, Gold Coast, Civil Service; Controller of Operations, Colonial Development Corporation 1955. **Awards:** Exhibition, SJC. **Honours:** KBE 1954. Died 1 October 1959.

SALTER, Dr Clifford Edward (1947) Born 30 March 1929, 129 Bushey Road, Merton, Surrey; son of Edward Henry Salter, Sorter, General Post Office, and Hilda May Clifford. **Subject(s):** Natural Sciences; BA 1951; MA 1959; BChir 1954; MB 1955; MRCPsych; DPM. **Educ:** Bushey Junior Elementary School; Raynes Park County School. **Career:** Consultant in Mental Illness, East Cumbria Health District. **Appointments:** Vice-Chairman, National Council on Alcoholism; Member, Mental Health Group Sub-Committee, BMA; Executive Member, Medicines Control Agency. **Awards:** Freud Centenary Scholarship 1960. **Publications:** (with William Paul James and H George Thomas) *Alcohol and Drug Dependence – Treatment and Rehabilitation*, 1972.

SALTER, John Arthur Philip (1949) Born 27 June 1930, Veronique, Vicars Moor Lane, Southgate, London; son of Harold Philip Arthur Salter, Argentine Railway Company's Clerk, and Kathleen Vera Aldous; m Ruth Audrey Sunderland, 24 April 1954, St Michael's and All Angels, Cottingley, Yorkshire; 2 sons, 2 daughters. **Subject(s):** Mathematics; BA 1952; MA 1956; FCA. **Tutor(s):** J M Wordie. **Educ:** St Paul's Church of England School, London; Minchenden School, London; Highgate School, London. **Career:** Secretary, North Central Finance Ltd 1963–1970; Assistant Director, Lombard North Central Ltd 1970–1986.

SALTER, Lionel Paul Sydney (1932) Born 8 September 1914, 17 Ravenhill Road, Upton Park, West Ham, London; son of Morris Salter (originally Seltzer), Language Master, London County Council, and Jeanette Solomon; m Christine Fraser, 1939 (d 1989); 3 sons (Graham, Adrian and Brian). **Subject(s):** Modern and Medieval Languages/Music; BA 1935; MA 1939; MusB 1936. **Tutor(s):** C W Guillebaud. **Educ:** Burghley Road London County Council School; Owen's School, London; Royal College of Music. **Career:** Music Assistant in films 1936–1938; Staff Accompanist in the newly formed BBC Television Station 1937–1939; Intelligence Corps 1940; Warrant Officer 1943; Guest Conductor, Radio France Symphony Orchestra 1943–1944; Army Education Corps, Lieutenant 1944; Various BBC posts as Assistant Conductor with Theatre Orchestra 1945–1948; Music Supervisor, European Service, BBC 1948–1953; Artists' Manager 1953–1955; Head of Music Productions, BBC Television 1956–1963; Head of Opera, BBC, radio and television 1963–1967; Assistant Controller, Music at the BBC; Opera Co-ordinator and Producer, European Broadcasting Union 1972–1976. **Appointments:** Critic, *Gramophone* 1948; Programme Editor, Edinburgh International Festival 1951–1955; Chairman, Radio Music Group, European Broadcasting Union 1965–1974; Editor, BBC Music Guides 1967–1975; Programme Editor, BBC Promenade Concerts 1968–1974; Editor, Associated Board of Royal Schools of Music 1977–1995; Vice-Chairman, British Federation of Music Festivals 1984–1987; Associated Board Examiner; Festival and competition adjudicator. **Publications:** Numerous musical works; books and articles on music; 126 opera translations/musical scores. Died 1 March 2000.

SALTMARSH, Philip Cecil (1924) Born 18 February 1908, Raincliffe, New Barnet, East Barnet Valley, Hertfordshire; son of Sir Edward George Saltmarsh and Fanny Edith Priestley; m Ursula Mary Lane, 3 September 1936, St Peters in Eastgate, Lincoln; 3 sons, 1 daughter. **Subject(s):** Economics; BA 1929; FCA. **Tutor(s):** J M Wordie. **Johnian Relatives:** father of Philip David Saltmarsh (1959) and of Geoffrey Michael Saltmarsh (1960); grandfather of Jonathan Charles Saltmarsh (1986). **Educ:** Wootten Court, Canterbury; Repton School. **Career:** Deloitte, Plender, Griffiths & Co; Turner & Newall; Secretary and Accountant, London Cawder Company; Secretary, British Internal Combustion Engine Manufacturer's Association 1948–1951; Secretary and Director, W H Allen, Sons & Co 1951–1974. Died 8 December 1975.

SALTON, Professor Milton Robert James (1948) Born 29 April 1921, Glen Innes, New South Wales; son of Robert Alexander Bannerman Salton, Presbyterian Minister, and Stella Nellie Beatrice Goldthorpe; m Joy Marriott, 29 July 1951, St Edward's Church, Cambridge; 2 sons (Stephen Robert James b 1 September 1955 and Alastair Charles b 9 June 1961). PhD 1951; ScD 1967; BSc (Sydney) 1945; FRS 1979. **Tutor(s):** G C L Bertram. **Educ:** Newcastle High School; Sydney University. **Career:** Reader in Chemical Bacteriology, University of Manchester 1959; Professor and Chairman, Department of Microbiology 1964–1970, Professor Emeritus 1973–, New York University School of Medicine, New York, USA. **Awards:** Broodbank Fellowship 1953.

SALZ, Michael Heinz (1934) Born 1 May 1916, Kurassierstr 27, Breslau; son of Michael Jacob Salz, Lawyer, and Meta Wagner. **Subject(s):** Natural Sciences; BA 1937; MA 1943; FRCS. **Tutor(s):** R L Howland. **Educ:** Kleinberg Schule, Breslau; Johannes Gymnasium, Breslau.

SAMPSON, George (1920) Born 6 April 1873, London; son of Thomas Sampson, Mariner, London, and Sarah Howes; m Grace. MA 1920. **Educ:** Winchester College for Teachers; Southwark Pupil Teachers' School. Died 1 February 1950.

SAMPSON, Michael Treviskey (1914) Born 12 January 1896, 2 Mount Vernon Green, South Hornsey, Liverpool; son of John Sampson, University Librarian, Liverpool, and Jessie Margaret Sprunt; m Phyllis Seward, 17 April 1923, St Bene't's Church, Cambridge. **Subject(s):** Natural Sciences; BA 1920; MA 1926. **Tutor(s):** R P Gregory. **Johnian Relatives:** son-in-law of Albert Charles Seward (1883); brother-in-law of John Walton (1914). **Educ:** Beaconfield School, Runcorn; Greenbank School, Liverpool; Liverpool Institute. **Career:** Captain, later Major, King's Royal Rifle Corps, WWI. **Honours:** MC with Bar. Died 19 November 1956.

SAMPSON, Robert Frank Andrews (1922) Born 23 March 1903, Hill Top, Burntwood, Lichfield, Staffordshire; son of William Robert Sampson, Steward of County Mental Hospital, and Emily King. **Subject(s):** Natural Sciences; BA 1925. **Tutor(s):** E A Benians. **Educ:** Burntwood County Council School; Queen Mary's Grammar School, Walsall.

SANCEAU, Squadron Leader Reginald James (1910) Born 13 April 1892, Huelva, Spain; son of Reginald Constantine Sanceau, Industrialist, and Mary Elisabeth Morrison; m Marjorie Mary Rutherford, 9 February 1918, Reigate Parish Church. BA 1913. **Tutor(s):** L H K Bushe-Fox. **Educ:** Highbury School House, St Leonards on Sea. **Career:** RGA 1914; RFC 1916, France; Captain (Aeroplane Officer), RFC, then RAF (Mentioned in Despatches), WWI; Squadron Leader; Staff duties, Egypt; Record Office, Ruislip, until 1936.

SANDBACH, Richard Stainton Edward (1934) Born 13 June 1915, Greenwood, Wythenshawe Road, Sale; son of Frank Stainton Sandbach, Solicitor, and Beatrice Emmeline Clifton; m Brenda Mary (Wendy) Cleminson, 10 September 1949; 2 sons (John Christopher Stainton b 1950 and Richard Paul Stainton b 1956). **Subject(s):** Law; BA 1937; MA 1945; LLB 1938; LLM 1985. **Tutor(s):** C W Guillebaud. **Educ:** Sale Preparatory School; Sale High School; Manchester Grammar School. **Career:** Founder Chairman, Minster General Housing Association Ltd; Director, Gibbons Holdings Ltd; Director, Arcade Properties

(Peterborough) Ltd; Private, VR Suffolk Regiment 1939–1940; OCTU 1940; Second Lieutenant, 22 (Cheshire) Regiment 1940–1946; Junior Staff College 1941; Captain, 12 Corps District 1941–1943; Major, 1 Canadian Army 1943–1944; Airborne Corps 1944–1946; Admitted Solicitor 1946; Solicitor, Horwood & James, Aylesbury 1947–1950; Solicitor, Greenwoods, Peterborough 1950–1979 (Senior Partner 1970–1979); Clerk, Huntingdon Freemen 1968–1976; Chairman, DHSS Local Appeals Tribunal 1980–1988; Director and Chairman, Paten & Co Ltd 1988–1996; Chairman, Quatuor Coronati Correspondence Circle Ltd 1989–1997 and Quatuor Coronati Correspondence Circle (Sales) Ltd 1991–1997. **Appointments:** Member, Law Society 1947; Peterborough and District Law Society 1950–1979; Oxford & Cambridge Club, London 1950–; City and Counties Club, Peterborough 1950–1980; Victory Services Club 1945–; Royal Commonwealth Society 1949–; Member, Burgh Society, Peterborough 1965–1983, 1989– (President 1973–1974); Trustee, Peterborough Cathedral Preservation Trust 1994– (Member, Finance Advisory Committee and Investment Committee 1994–2000); Chairman, Peterborough Diocesan Board of Finance 1974–1984; Provincial Grand Master for Northamptonshire and Huntingdonshire, Ancient Free and Accepted Masons of England 1984–1990; Member, Quatuor Coronati Lodge 2076 1986– (Master 1992–1993); Member, Supreme Council of the Ancient and Accepted Rite for England and Wales and its Districts and Chapters Overseas 1989– (Sovereign Grand Commander 2000–). **Awards:** Foundation Scholarship, Manchester Grammar School; McMahon Law Studentship. **Publications:** *Priest and Freemason* (biography of Revd Dr G Oliver); *Peterborough Booklets* 1–5, 1988; articles in *Ars Quatuor Coronati*; *No Excuse* (autobiography).

SANDERS, Sir Harold George (1919) Born 9 October 1898, Wollaston, Wellingborough, Northamptonshire; son of Watkin Owen Sanders, Farmer, and Beatrice Alice Leete; m Kathleen Penson Plunkett, 1923 (d 1973); 1 son (Peter), 1 daughter (June). BA 1920; MA 1926; PhD 1928. **Tutor(s):** E E Sikes. **Johnian Relatives:** father of Peter Plunkett Sanders (Sanders-Rose) (1959); grandfather of Francesca Rose Gravely Sanders-Rose (Mills) (1984). **Educ:** Eaglehurst College, Northampton; Wellingborough School. **Career:** Second Lieutenant, RFA, France 1917–1919; Assistant (Physiology), Animal Nutrition Institute, School of Agriculture, Cambridge 1922–1929; Lecturer in Agriculture, University of Cambridge 1930–1944; Title B Fellow, SJC 1938–1944 (leave of absence for war service 1941–1944); Professor of Agriculture, Reading University 1945–1954. **Appointments:** Supervisor in Agriculture 1932–1944; Director of Studies in Agriculture 1939–1944, SJC; Executive Officer, Hertfordshire War Agricultural Executive Committee 1941–1944; Member 1949–1955, Chairman 1964–1967, University Grants Committee; Member, Central Advisory Council for Education 1952; Chief Scientific and Agricultural Adviser to MAFF 1955–1964; Adviser, Shellstar Ltd, London 1964. **Honours:** Kt 1963. **Publications:** *An Outline of British Crop Husbandry*, 1939; (with G Eley) *Farms of Britain*, 1946. Died 7 October 1985.

SANDERS, Theodorus Carlton (1942) Born 26 March 1924, Leiden, Holland; son of Anne Willem Sanders, Consulting Engineer, and Marjory Napier Stitt. **Subject(s):** Mechanical Sciences; BA 1945; MA 1951; CEng; MIMechE. **Tutor(s):** S J Bailey. **Educ:** Huyton Hill School, Liverpool; Brockhurst School, Church Stretton; Shrewsbury School. **Career:** Managing Director. Died 6 January 1993.

SANDERSON, Douglas Hamilton (1920) Born 12 July 1903, 10 Claremont Terrace, Newcastle upon Tyne, Northumberland; son of Thomas Sanderson, Engineer, and Margaret Dickinson; m Elsie Margaret Morpeth, 3 September 1927, Jesmond Parish Church; 1 son (John Stanley Hamilton b 29 December 1934), 1 daughter. BA 1924. **Tutor(s):** B F Armitage. **Johnian Relatives:** brother of Thomas Carton Hardman Sanderson (1919) and of Peter Howard Sanderson (1935); father of John Stanley Hamilton Sanderson (1955). **Educ:** Newcastle Preparatory School; Durham School. **Career:** Farmer 1939. **Appointments:** Chairman, Norfolk County Council. Died 11 March 1969.

SANDERSON, John Ernest Douglas (1946) Born 25 August 1925, Cadiz, Spain; son of Harold Wadsworth Sanderson, British Vice Consul, and Doris May Black. BA 1948; MA 1953; DA (Edinburgh); ARIAS; ARIBA. **Tutor(s):** C W Guillebaud. **Educ:** Morrison's Academy, Crieff. **Career:** Captain, Royal Marines 1943–1946.

SANDERSON, John Frederick Richard (1943) Born 14 July 1925, Houghton House, Crow Hill, Broadstairs, Kent; son of Leonard John Sanderson, Chemist, and Irene Alice Fear. **Tutor(s):** C W Guillebaud. **Educ:** King Edward VI School, Bath.

SANDERSON, Dr Peter Howard (1935) Born 30 November 1916, 3 Westfield Avenue, Gosforth, Newcastle upon Tyne; son of Thomas Sanderson, Engineer, and Margaret Dickinson; m Anne Patricia Bickford, 12 January 1943; 2 sons, 1 daughter. **Subject(s):** Natural Sciences; BA 1938; MA 1961; BChir 1943; MB 1943; MRCP 1944; FRCP 1964. **Tutor(s):** R L Howland. **Johnian Relatives:** brother of Thomas Carton Hardman Sanderson (1919) and of Douglas Hamilton Sanderson (1920); uncle of John Stanley Hamilton Sanderson (1955). **Educ:** Newcastle Preparatory School; South Gosforth Preparatory School; Fettes College, Edinburgh. **Career:** Commanding Officer, Dermatology Research Team, RAMC; Research Worker, MRC; Reader in Medicine, St Mary's Hospital Medical School, University of London. **Awards:** Exhibition, SJC 1937.

SANDERSON, Thomas Carton Hardman (1919) Born 24 March 1901, 12 Claremont Street, Newcastle upon Tyne; son of Thomas Sanderson, Engineer, and Margaret Dickinson. BA 1922. **Tutor(s):** E E Sikes. **Johnian Relatives:** brother of Douglas Hamilton Sanderson (1920) and of Peter Howard Sanderson (1935); uncle of John Stanley Hamilton Sanderson (1955). **Educ:** Newcastle Preparatory School; Durham School. Died 28 February 1978.

SANDFORD, Humphrey (1946) Born 12 June 1922, Brookfield, Shrewbridge Road, Nantwich, Cheshire; son of Humphrey Sandford, Farmer, and Marjorie Travers Pickmere. **Subject(s):** Agriculture; BA 1948; MA 1953. **Tutor(s):** G C L Bertram. **Educ:** Leas School, Hoylake; Shrewsbury School.

SANDISON, Gordon Ramsay (1931) Born 17 April 1913, 10 The Poplars, Gosforth; son of Gilbert Andrew Sandison, Manufacturer's Agent, and Hilda Armstrong; m Clare Michelle Longland; 1 son (Hamish), 3 daughters (Hilary, Jenifer and Jiffy). **Subject(s):** History/Law; BA 1934; MA 1938; LLB 1935. **Tutor(s):** E A Benians. **Educ:** St Margaret's High School; Newcastle Modern School; Royal Grammar School, Newcastle upon Tyne. **Career:** Called to the Bar, Gray's Inn; Lecturer in Law, University of London 1937–1945; National Fire Service 1939–1945; General Secretary, British Actors Equity Association 1947–1958. **Appointments:** President, International Federation of Actors. **Awards:** Scholarship, SJC 1934; Sizarship, SJC. Died 3 July 1958.

SANDS, Laurence Cowley (1929) Born 8 May 1910, 36 Cautley Avenue, Clapham, Surrey; son of Percy Cooper Sands, Headmaster, Pocklington School, and Olive Clara Cowley. **Subject(s):** Law; BA 1933; MA 1939. **Tutor(s):** E A Benians. **Johnian Relatives:** son of Percy Cooper Sands (1901). **Educ:** Pocklington School. **Career:** Solicitor, Powell & Young of Pocklington, York. **Awards:** Exhibition, SJC. Died 9 November 1986.

SANDS, Percy Cooper (1901) Born 3 February 1883, 56 Addison Street, Sherwood, Nottingham; son of John Sands, Printer, and Annie Maria Cooper; m Olive Clara Cowley; 1 son (Lawrence Cowley b 8 May 1910). **Subject(s):** Classics/History; BA 1904; MA 1908. **Tutor(s):** D MacAlister. **Johnian Relatives:** father of Lawrence Cowley Sands (1929). **Educ:** Nottingham High School. **Career:** Assistant Master, City of London School 1906–1914; Foundress Fellow, SJC 1907–1913; Headmaster, Pocklington School 1914–1944. **Appointments:** Magistrate, Pocklington 1936–1957. **Publications:** *Men of God*, 1950; *Client Princes of the Roman Empire*; *Literary Genius of the Old Testament*; *Gods and Heroes*. Died 15 March 1971.

SANG, Professor James Henderson (1937) (admitted to Fitzwilliam House 1936) Born 4 November 1912, 24 View Terrace, Aberdeen, Scotland; son of James Sang, Newsagent, and Helen George Wiseman Henderson. PhD 1942; BSc (Aberdeen) 1935; FRSE. **Tutor(s):** C W Guillebaud. **Educ:** Mile End Public School, Aberdeen; Robert Gordon's College, Aberdeen; University of Aberdeen; Fitzwilliam House, Cambridge. **Career:** Kilgou Research Scholar in Zoology, University of Aberdeen; Carnegie Senior Research Scholar and Assistant to the Professor of Natural History, University of Aberdeen; Ministry of Aircraft Production 1942–1948; Agricultural Research Council, Edinburgh; Professor, School of Biology, University of Sussex 1965. **Appointments:** Life Member, Genetical Society of Great Britain. **Awards:** Hutchison Research Scholarship. Died 10 February 2002.

SANGER, Dr Frederick (1936) Born 13 August 1918, The Old House, Rendcombe, Cirencester, Gloucestershire; son of Frederick Sanger, Medical Practitioner, and Cicely Crewdson; m Joan Howe, 1940; 2 sons, 1 daughter. **Subject(s):** Natural Sciences; BA 1939; PhD 1944; Honorary ScD (Cantab) 1983; Honorary DSc (Leicester) 1968; Honorary DSc (Oxon) 1970; Honorary DSc (Strasbourg) 1970; FRS 1954. **Tutor(s):** R L Howland. **Johnian Relatives:** son of Frederick Sanger (1894); nephew of Hubert Sanger (1899). **Educ:** Downs School, Colwall; Bryanston School. **Career:** Research in Biochemistry, University of Cambridge 1940–1961; Beit Memorial Fellowship for Medical Research 1944–1951; MRC Laboratory of Molecular Biology, Cambridge 1961–1983. **Appointments:** Foreign Honorary Member, American Academy of Arts and Sciences 1958; Honorary Member, American Society of Biological Chemists 1961; Foreign Associate, National Academy of Sciences 1967; Honorary Fellow, King's College 1983; Beit Memorial Fellowships; Millennium Fellow, Royal Society of Chemistry, Trinity College, Cambridge. **Awards:** Nobel Prize for Chemistry 1958 (for identifying the structure of insulin) and 1980 (for developing a method for determining the nucleotide sequences in DNA); Corday-Morgan Medal and Prize, Chemistry Society 1951; Alfred Benzon Prize 1966; Royal Medal, Royal Society 1969; Sir Frederick Gowland Hopkins Memorial Medal 1971; Gardiner Foundation Annual Award 1971, 1979; William Bate Hardy Prize, Cambridge Philosophical Society 1976; Hanbury Memorial Medal 1976; Copley Medal, Royal Society 1977; Horwitz Prize, Albert Lasker Award 1979; Biochemical Analysis Prize, German Society for Clinical Chemistry 1980; Gold Medal, RSM 1983. **Honours:** CBE 1963; CH 1981; OM 1986. **Publications:** Papers on Chemistry of Insulin and Nucleic Acid Structure in *Biochemical* and other journals.

SANGER-DAVIES, Peter (1934) Born 15 July 1915, 163 Robertson Road, Euston, Bristol; son of Hugh Joseph Turner Sanger-Davies, Clerk in Holy Orders, and Margery Nora Board; m Esmée. **Subject(s):** Geography; BA 1937; MA 1946. **Tutor(s):** J S Boys Smith. **Johnian Relatives:** brother of Vyvyan Joseph Sanger-Davies (1927). **Educ:** Etonhurst School, Weston-super-Mare; Bromsgrove School. Died 3 September 1997.

SANGER-DAVIES, Vyvyan Joseph (1927) Born 2 February 1908, 65 Warleigh Avenue, Devonport, Devon; son of Hugh Joseph Turner Sanger-Davies, Clerk in Holy Orders, and Margery Nora Board; 1 son. **Subject(s):** Natural Sciences; BA 1930; MA 1935. **Tutor(s):** C W Guillebaud. **Johnian Relatives:** brother of Peter Sanger-Davies (1934). **Educ:** Etonhurst, Weston-super-Mare; Marlborough College. **Career:** Assistant Master, Sedbergh School, Yorkshire 1930–1946; First Headmaster, Bathurst School of Science, Gambia 1946–1952; Headmaster, Queen's College, British Guyana 1952–1963; Assistant Master, Bloxham School 1963–1970; Editor, *Dasset Magna News* 1966–1994; Head of Geography Department, then Director of Humanities, Stratford-on-Avon Girls' High School 1970–1976. **Appointments:** Choral student; President, Anglican Young People's Association 1942–1945; Chairman, Oxfordshire Bridge Association; Member, Headmasters' Conference (UK). **Honours:** OBE 1963. **Publications:** *Gambia's First Teacher of Science*, Shotteswell, 1990. Died 16 December 1995.

SANSOM, Hugh Wilfred (1942) Born 11 May 1924, Kennel Moor, Milford, Surrey; son of George Samuel Sansom, Doctor of Science, UCL, and Dorothy Vivien Dodgson; m Susan Dove Ward, 1 December 1951, Nairobi; 4 daughters (Helen Vivien b 11 November 1952, Susan Mary b 15 September 1954, Ann Elizabeth b 17 October 1958 and Dorothy Joy b 18 October 1960). **Subject(s):** Natural Sciences; BA 1947; MA 1949. **Tutor(s):** C W Guillebaud. **Johnian Relatives:** brother of Kenneth John Sansom (1941); grandfather of Jonathan David Tuckwell (1996). **Educ:** Windlesham House School, Worthing; Stowe School. **Career:** Meteorologist.

SANSOM, Kenneth John (1941) Born 16 January 1922, Kennel Moor, Milford, Surrey; son of George Samuel Sansom, Doctor of Science, and Dorothy Vivien Dodgson; m Alison Elizabeth Anne Monroe, 14 May 1955, Weston Green; 1 son (Paul John b 31 January 1964), 2 daughters (Jane Elizabeth b 29 June 1959 and Vivien Kathleen b 27 September 1960). **Subject(s):** Geography. **Tutor(s):** C W Guillebaud. **Johnian Relatives:** brother of Hugh Wilfred Sansom (1942); great uncle of Jonathan David Tuckwell (1996). **Educ:** Windlesham House School, Worthing; Stowe School.

SANSOM, Thomas Keith Beck (1926) Born 7 December 1902, Manzana, Engcobo, Transkei, Cape Province, South Africa; son of Thomas Sansom, Farmer, and Ellen Mary Beck. **Tutor(s):** J M Wordie. **Educ:** St George's School, Bulawayo; Transvaal University College, Pretoria; Rhodes University College, Grahamstown.

SARABHAI, Dr Vikram Ambalal (1937) Born 12 August 1919, Shahibag Ahmedabad, India; son of Ambalal Sarabhai, Merchant, and Saraladevi G Gosalia; m Mrinalini; 1 son (Kartikeya), 1 daughter (Mallika). **Subject(s):** Natural Sciences; BA 1940; MA 1944; PhD 1947. **Tutor(s):** J M Wordie. **Johnian Relatives:** uncle of Kamal Mangaldas (1956) and of Anand Suhrid Sarabhai (1956); father of Kartikeya Vikram Sarabhai (1965); great uncle of Mischa Gorchov Brearley (1994). **Educ:** Retreat School, Ahmedabad; Gujarat College, Ahmedabad. **Career:** Indian Institute of Science, Bangalore 1940–1945; Professor then Director, Physical Research Laboratory, Ahmedabad 1947–1965. **Appointments:** Honorary Director, Ahmedabad Textile Industry's Research Association 1947–1955; Honorary Director, Indian Institute of Management, Ahmedabad; Chairman, Atomic Energy Commission, India; Chairman, Indian Space Research Organization; Director, Space Science Technology Centre, Thumba; Fellow, Cambridge Philosophical Society; Fellow, Institute of Advanced Studies; Fellow, MIT; Fellow, Indian Academy of Sciences; Fellow, National Institute of Sciences of India; Member, American Geophysical Union. **Awards:** Shanti Swarap Bhatnagar Memorial Award in Physics 1962; Padma Bhushan Award 1966. **Honours:** Padma Vibhushan 1972 (posthumously). Died 30 December 1971.

SARGAN, Professor John Denis (1941) Born 23 August 1924, Doncaster, Yorkshire; son of Harry Sargan, Police Constable, and Gertrude Amy Porter; m (Phyllis) Mary Millard, 1953; 2 sons, 1 daughter. **Subject(s):** Mathematics/Economics; BA (Mathematics) 1943; BA (Economics) 1946; MA 1948; Honorary Doctorate (University Carlos III, Madrid) 1993; FBA 1981; FAAAS 1987. **Tutor(s):** S J Bailey. **Johnian Relatives:** father of David Richard Sargan (1974). **Educ:** Doncaster Grammar School. **Career:** Assistant Lecturer, Lecturer and Reader, Leeds University 1948–1963; Reader, Professor of Econometrics 1963–1984, Tooke Professor of Economic Science and Statistics 1982–1984 (Emeritus 1984), LSE. **Appointments:** President, Econometrics Society 1980; Honorary Fellow, LSE 1990. **Awards:** Fulbright Scholarship to Universities of Minnesota and Chicago 1958. **Publications:** Seminal contributions to both theoretical and applied economics and economic modelling. Died 13 April 1996.

SARGANT, Dr William Walters (1925) Born 24 April 1907, Bryanston, The Bank, Highgate Hill, Middlesex; son of Norman Thomas Carr Sargant, Metal Broker and Rubber Merchant, and Alice Rose Walters; m

Peggy Glen. BA 1928; MA 1932; BChir 1932; MB 1933; MRCS (St Mary's) 1930; LRCP (St Mary's) 1930; MRCP 1933. **Tutor(s):** B F Armitage. **Educ:** Byron House School, Highgate; St Wilfrid's School, Seaford; The Leys School, Cambridge. **Career:** House Surgeon, House Physician, Head, Biochemistry Laboratory for the Medical Unit, Medical Superintendent in charge of admissions and nursing and junior medical staff, St Mary's Hospital; Hanwell Mental Hospital; GP, Nottingham; Maudsley Hospital; Rockerfeller Fellow, Harvard 1938; Assistant Clinical Director, Sutton Emergency Hospital, WWII; Physician in Charge, Department of Psychological Medicine, St Thomas' Hospital 1948–1972; Lecturer in Psychiatry, St Thomas' Medical School 1959; TV Psychiatrist. **Appointments:** Visiting Professor, Duke University; Assistant Secretary, World Psychiatric Association 1961–1966; President, Section of Psychiatry, Royal Society of Medicine; Registrar, Royal Medico-Psychological Association, later Royal College of Psychiatrists. **Awards:** Rockefeller Fellowship to Harvard 1938; Taylor Manor Hospital Award 1971; Starkey Memorial Prize, Royal Society of Health 1973. **Publications:** 'The Winnett Orr treatment of Osteomyletitis', *Clinical Journal*, 1931; 'The Treatment of Subacute Combined Degeneration of the Cord by Massive Iron Dosage', *Lancet*, 1932; *Battle for the Mind*, 1957; *The Unquiet Mind* (Autobiography) 1967; *The Mind Possessed*, 1973; *An Introduction to Physical Methods of Treatment in Psychiatry*. Died 27 August 1988.

SARGEANT, The Revd Hugh (1903) Born 31 October 1884, 24 Apple Street, Great Bolton, Lancashire; son of William Sargeant, Wheelwright, and Isabella Spencer. **Subject(s):** Theology; BA 1906; MA 1932. **Tutor(s):** D MacAlister. **Educ:** Pupil Teacher's Centre, Bolton. **Career:** Ordained Deacon 1927; Curate, St Luke, Weaste 1927–1931; Ordained Priest 1928; Curate, St Mary the Virgin, Bury 1931–1934; Rector, Heywood, Manchester 1934. **Appointments:** Honorary Canon, Manchester Cathedral 1947.

SARGENT, The Revd Edward Hewlett Gladstone (1906) Born 21 February 1887, Cornwall House, Osborne Road, Clifton, Bristol; son of Edward George Sargent, Bank Accountant, and Emily Grose. **Subject(s):** Classics; BA 1909; MA 1913. **Tutor(s):** J R Tanner. **Johnian Relatives:** brother of Percy William George Sargent (1891), Douglas Harry Grose Sargent (1897) and of Eric Lancelot Kingsley Sargent (1907); uncle of John Sargent (1928). **Educ:** Clifton College, Bristol. **Career:** Ordained Deacon 1913; Curate, St Johns, Hoxton 1913–1915; Ordained Priest 1914; Curate, Christ Church, Beckenham 1915–1918; Curate, St James, Hatcham 1918–1924; Vicar, St Peter, Upper Holloway 1924–1934; Vicar, Christ Church, Virginia Water, Surrey 1934–1952; Rector, St Michael with St Paul, Bath 1952–1965.

SARGENT, Dr Eric Lancelot Kingsley (1907) Born 13 June 1889, 80 Pembroke Road, Clifton, Bristol; son of Edward George Sargent, Bank Manager, and Emily Grose; m Margaret Mitchell, 27 May 1922, Wimbledon. **Subject(s):** Natural Sciences; BA 1910; MB 1913; BChir 1913; MRCS; LRCP 1913. **Tutor(s):** J R Tanner. **Johnian Relatives:** brother of Percy William George Sargent (1891), Douglas Harry Grose Sargent (1897) and of Edward Hewlett Gladstone Sargent (1906); uncle of John Sargent (1928). **Educ:** Clifton College. **Career:** Captain (specialist in advanced operative surgery), RAMC, India 1916–1919. **Appointments:** Honorary Medical Officer, Wimbledon Hospital; Honorary Surgeon, Nelson Hospital.

SARGENT, John (1928) Born 21 July 1910, 67a Harley Street, London; son of Sir Percy William George Sargent, Surgeon, and May Louise Ashman; 1 daughter (Sonia). **Tutor(s):** M P Charlesworth. **Johnian Relatives:** son of Percy William George Sargent (1891); nephew of Douglas Harry Grose Sargent (1897), Edward Hewlett Gladstone Sargent (1906) and of Eric Lancelot Kingsley Sargent (1907). **Educ:** Warren Hill, Eastbourne; Charterhouse. **Awards:** Paris Salon Silver Medal 1961; Paris Salon Gold Medal 1962. **Career:** Sculptor (pieces exhibited at the Royal Academy and Paris Salon, including *Sea Horse*, *Jibbing Horse*, and *Trotting Horse*). Died 24 January 1982.

SARGENTSON, James Kenneth (1930) Born 15 March 1911, Kent Villa, Hadfield, Glossop, Derbyshire; son of Percy Sargentson, Cotton Manufacturer, and Florence Brooks; BA 1933. **Tutor(s):** M P Charlesworth. **Educ:** Mostyn House School, Parkgate; Radley College.

SARKAR, Adit Kumar (1936) Born 30 September 1916, Simla, India; son of Rai Bahadur Akshay Kumar Sarkar, Assistant Secretary, Government of India, and Agnes Priothoma Chatterji. **Subject(s):** Economics; BA 1938. **Tutor(s):** J S Boys Smith. **Johnian Relatives:** brother of Karuna Moi Sarkar (1933). **Educ:** Sir Harcourt Butler School, Simla, India; St Stephen's College, Delhi, India.

SARKAR, Karuna Moi (1933) Born 13 June 1904, Simla, India; son of Rai Bahadur Akshay Kumar Sarkar, Assistant Secretary, Government of India, and Agnes Priothoma Chatterji. **Subject(s):** Indian History; MLitt 1937; BA (Punjab) 1924; MA (Punjab) 1926. **Tutor(s):** E A Benians. **Johnian Relatives:** brother of Adit Kumar Sarkar (1936). **Educ:** Government College, Lahore, India; Sir Harcourt Butler School, Simla, India; University of the Punjab, India. Died 13 August 1938.

SATHE, Dinker Dattatraya (1937) Born 23 September 1918, Mandleshwar, Central India; son of Dattatraya Laxman Sathe, Conservator of Forests, and Charumati Gole. **Subject(s):** Natural Sciences; BA 1939. **Tutor(s):** J M Wordie. **Educ:** Government High School, Nasik; St Joseph's European High School, Bangalore; Holkar College, Indore. **Career:** Joint Secretary to the Government of India, Ministry of Defence, New Delhi; Central Government, Ministry of Defence, New Delhi, 1969–1979; Chief Secretary, Maharashtra State; Chairman, Centre for Research and Development, Mumbai.

SATHE, Sir Jagannath Luxmon (1905) Born 20 April 1886, Jetpur, Kathiawar, India; son of Luxmon Vithal Sathe, Diwan of Sardargadh; m Rambai Agashe. **Subject(s):** Natural Sciences; BA 1907. **Tutor(s):** J R Tanner. **Educ:** Bahauddin College, Junagadh, India. **Career:** Magistrate and Collector, United Provinces 1910–1924; Officiating Excise Commissioner 1927–1932; Director, Bureau of Statistics and Economic Research 1932–1933; Secretary, Finance Department, United Provinces 1933–1936; Commissioner, Benares 1937–1939; Member, Board of Revenue 1940–1944; Advisor to the Governor, United Provinces 1944–1946; President, Sangli State Executive Council 1946. **Honours:** Kt 1946; CIE 1943.

SATTERLY, Professor John (1904) (admitted as Non-Collegiate Student 1903) Born 29 December 1879, North Street, Ashburton, Devon; son of John Satterly, Journeyman Carpenter, and Elizabeth Ann Skinner; m May Randall, 1905; 1 son, 1 daughter. BA 1908; MA 1911; BSc (London) 1901; DSc 1910; FRSC. **Tutor(s):** D MacAlister. **Educ:** Royal College of Science, London. **Career:** Cavendish Laboratory, Cambridge 1903–1912; Lecturer in Physics 1912–1921, Associate Professor 1921, Toronto University; Research, Admiralty, WWI. Died 1 October 1963.

SAUNDERS, Alan Douglas (1932) Born 14 June 1913, 25 Melbourne Road, Ilford, Essex; son of Albert Frederick Saunders, Chartered Accountant, and Alice Leathley. **Subject(s):** Modern and Medieval Languages; BA 1935. **Tutor(s):** C W Guillebaud. **Educ:** Homerfield Preparatory School, Sutton; Epsom College.

SAUNDERS, The Revd Edward George Humphrey (1941) Born 7 March 1923, Ootacamund, South India; son of George Musket Saunders, Civil Engineer, and Florence Elizabeth Mary Ryan; m Margaret Adair Talbot-Rice; 2 sons (Mark b 1964 and Jeremy b 1966); 1 daughter (Hilary b 1959). **Subject(s):** Theology; BA 1948; MA 1950. **Tutor(s):** S J Bailey. **Educ:** West Downs, Winchester; Charterhouse; Ridley Hall, Cambridge. **Career:** Ordained Deacon to the curacy of St Ebbe, Oxford 1950; Ordained Priest 1951; Candidates' Secretary 1952–1954, Clerical Assistant Secretary 1954–1958, Church Pastoral Aid Society; Vicar, Christ Church, Finchley 1958–1964; Secretary, Evangelical Churchmen's Ordination Council 1959–1964; Vicar, Chipping Campden,

Gloucestershire 1964–1969; Warden, Young People's Training Centre, Lindley Lodge, Nuneaton 1969–1971; Vicar, St Michael's Chester Square, London 1971–1984; Honorary Curate, St Andrew's Church, Oxford 1984–1989. **Appointments:** RAF Cadet, SJC. **Publications:** (with Hugh Sansom) *David Watson – a Biography*, 1942.

SAUNDERS, Kenneth Herbert (1918) Born 19 November 1892, 40A Gloucester Road, London; son of Charles Herbert Saunders, Architect and Surveyor, and Alice Maria Hawes; m Ione Heath Green, 15 July 1920, St Mary Abbots, Kensington. BA 1920; MA 1930; BSc (London) 1919. **Tutor(s):** E E Sikes. **Johnian Relatives:** brother of Leslie Gale Saunders (1921). **Educ:** Highgate School; City and Guilds of London Technical School, Finsbury; Nova Scotia Agricultural College; University of Toronto. **Career:** Fellow, Salter's Institute of Industrial Chemistry 1919–1920; Head, Catalytic Research Department, British Dyestuffs Corporation 1922.

SAUNDERS, Leslie Gale (1921) Born 3 December 1895, 21 Kingdon Road, West Hampstead, London; son of Charles Herbert Saunders, Auctioneer and Surveyor, and Alice Maria Hawes. **Subject(s):** Biology; PhD; MSc (McGill). **Tutor(s):** B F Armitage. **Johnian Relatives:** brother of Kenneth Herbert Saunders (1918). **Educ:** McGill University, Montreal, Canada; Macdonald College. **Career:** Professor of Biology, University of Saskatchewan 1948. Died 13 September 1968.

SAUNDERS, Peter (1947) Born 30 July 1926, Queen Victoria Hospital, Johannesburg, Transvaal; son of Philip Keith Saunders, Mechanical Engineer, and Edith de Smidt Bridges. BA 1949. **Tutor(s):** G C L Bertram. **Educ:** Thorpe's Preparatory School, George, South Africa; Tettenhall College, Wolverhampton; Blundell's School, Tiverton.

SAUNDERS-DAVIES, Arthur Owen (1920) Born 2 June 1901, Kilwendeage, Boncath, Pembrokeshire; son of Arthur Picton Saunders-Davies, Landed Proprietor, and Mabel Woodruff; m Mary Joyce Prioleau, 1923; 1 son, 1 daughter. **Tutor(s):** E E Sikes. **Educ:** Eton College; Courtenay Lodge, Sutton Courtenay. **Career:** Engineer, Slough; Farmer, Island Home Farm, Greatbridge and Lone Barn Farm, Romsey. **Appointments:** County Councillor, Mottisfont Division. Died 12 October 1959.

SAVAGE, Douglas Frederick (1945) Born 24 January 1927, 9 Brambledean Road, Portslade by Sea, Sussex; son of Frederick Ephraim John Savage, Fireman, and Mabel Alice Dyer. **Tutor(s):** G C L Bertram. **Educ:** St Andrew's Elementary School; East Hove Junior School; Hove County School; Croydon Polytechnic.

SAVORY, John Barwick Gaudern (1928) Born 25 March 1908, Cuxton, Baird's Hill, St Peter's, Thanet, Kent; son of Horace Edward Savory, Master Flour Miller, and Christine Bessie Hudson. **Tutor(s):** C W Guillebaud. **Johnian Relatives:** cousin of Theodore Horace Savory (1915). **Educ:** Doarn House, Westgate-on-Sea; Haileybury College; South Eastern Agricultural College, Wye.

SAVORY, Theodore Horace (1915) Born 28 April 1896, 18 Glen Eldon Road, Streatham, Surrey; son of Horace Reginald Savory, Manufacturer, and Eveline Gundred Besant; m Helen Mabel Walch, 1920, Much Hadham. **Subject(s):** Natural Sciences; BA 1918; MA 1927. **Tutor(s):** R P Gregory. **Johnian Relatives:** cousin of John Barwick Gaudern Savory (1928). **Educ:** Aldenham School. **Career:** Assistant Master, Aldenham 1918–1919; Assistant Master, Malvern College 1920; Stafford House Tutorial College, Kensington 1958. **Appointments:** Chairman, Malvern Library Committee 1949. **Awards:** Exhibition, SJC 1915. **Publications:** *British Spiders*, 1926; *The Arachnida*, 1935; *The Spiders and Allied Orders of the British Isles*, 1935; *Animals*, 1942; *Latin and Greek for the Use of Biologists*, 1946. Died 27 November 1980.

SAWYER, Professor Desmond Branson (1943) Born 12 September 1924, 11 Southsea Road, Woodhouse, Sheffield; son of Stanley Bernard Sawyer, Wholesale Textile Merchant, and Evelyn May Beevers; m Florence Pamela Clayton, July 1948; 2 daughters (Carolyn Mary b 1949 and Helen Ruth b 1955). **Subject(s):** Mathematics; BA 1947; MA 1949. **Tutor(s):** S J Bailey. **Educ:** Hazel Grove Council School; Sale High School; Manchester Grammar School. **Career:** Commissioned, RA; served in India with 1st Indian Survey Regiment, RIA 1943–1946; Lecturer in Mathematics, University of Otago, Dunedin, New Zealand 1948–1952; Lecturer, University College of the Gold Coast 1952–1954; Lecturer 1954–1956, Reader 1956–1957, Professor 1957–1965 and 1970–1985, University of Otago; Professor and Deputy Vice-Chancellor, University of Walkato, New Zealand 1965–1970. **Awards:** Major Scholarship, SJC 1942. **Honours:** MBE 1986. **Publications:** Various technical papers.

SAWYER, Professor Walter Warwick (1930) Born 5 April 1911, Osborne Cottage, St Ives; son of Walter Percy Sawyer, Surveyor of Taxes, and Elizabeth Whetnall d'Oultremont Stevens; m Hilda Elizabeth Crowther, 1940; 1 daughter (Anne Elizabeth). **Subject(s):** Mathematics; BA 1933; MA 1949. **Tutor(s):** J M Wordie. **Educ:** Tonstall School, Sunderland; Highgate School, London. **Career:** Assistant Lecturer, University College of Dundee 1935–1937; Assistant Lecturer, Manchester University 1937–1944; Lecturer in Mathematics, Leicester College of Technology (later Head of Mathematics Department) 1944–1946; Lecturer and First Head, Mathematics Department, University College of the Gold Coast 1948–1950; Lecturer, Canterbury College, New Zealand 1950–1956; Associate Professor, Mathematics Department, University of Illinois, USA 1957–1959; Professor of Mathematics, Wesleyan University, Connecticut, USA 1960–1966; Professor Emeritus jointly to the Departments of Mathematics and Education, University of Toronto, Canada 1966–1976. **Appointments:** Referent on Differential Equations for the journal *Fortschritte der Mathematik* 1947–1949. **Awards:** Baylis Scholarship, SJC 1928. **Publications:** *Mathematician's Delight*, Penguin Series 1943; *Mathematics in Theory and Practice*, Odhams, 1952; *Prelude to Mathematics*, Pelican Series, 1955; *Designing and Making*, Blackwell, 1957; *A Concrete Approach to Abstract Algebra*, W H Freeman Inc, 1959; *What is Calculus About?*, Yale University, 1961; *Vision in Elementary Mathematics*, Penguin, 1964; *A Path to Modern Mathematics*, Penguin, 1966; *The Search for Pattern*, Penguin, 1970; *An Engineering Approach to Linear Algebra*, CUP, 1972; *A First Look at Numerical Functional Analysis*, OUP, 1978; *In an Integrated Mathematics Scheme* (Books C, C2), Bell and Hyman, 1982–1985; numerous articles in journals.

SAXTON, William Eric (1947) Born 9 May 1925, 281 Stanstead Road, Forest Hill, Sydenham; son of William Herbert Saxton, Commercial Clerk, and Florence May Monk. **Subject(s):** History; BA 1949; MA 1954; PhD (Edinburgh) 1957. **Tutor(s):** F Thistlethwaite. **Johnian Relatives:** father of William Owen Saxton (1967); grandfather of Elizabeth Ann Saxton (1998). **Educ:** St Dunstan's College; University of Edinburgh. **Career:** RN and Indian Army 1943–1947; Lecturer in History, University College, Ibadan 1952–1959; Deputy Registrar, University of Durham 1959. Died 6 December 1991.

SAYER, Clinton (1933) Born 28 October 1914, 3 Lambert Street, Skipton; son of William Sayer, Master Baker, and May Griffin; m Margaret. **Subject(s):** Modern and Medieval Languages/History. **Tutor(s):** C W Guillebaud. **Educ:** C of E School, Barnoldswick; Ermysted's Grammar School, Skipton; The Grammar School, Batley. Died 13 July 1989.

SAYERS, Eldred Frank (1908) Born 28 September 1889, 26 Hamilton Road, Middlesex; son of Eldred Cubitt Sayers, Draper and JP for Middlesex, and Maude Mary Oetzmann. **Subject(s):** Law; BA 1911; LLB 1911. **Tutor(s):** L H K Bushe-Fox. **Educ:** Woodford House School, Birchington; King's College School, Wimbledon; Grenoble University. **Career:** Called to the Bar, Inner Temple 1913; Assistant Commissioner, Sierra Leone 1915; War Service, East Africa 1918; District Commissioner, Sierra Leone 1922.

SAYERS, Professor James (1937) Born 2 September 1912, Lishabon, Antrim, Ireland; son of James Sayers, Farmer, and Rachel Matthews; m Diana Ailsa Joan Montgomery, 1943; 2 sons, 1 daughter. PhD 1938; BSc, MSc (Belfast) 1930–1936. **Tutor(s):** J M Wordie. **Educ:** Ballymena Academy; Queen's University, Belfast. **Career:** Life Fellow, Franklin Institute of State of Pennsylvania; Research for Admiralty, University of Birmingham 1939–1943; Title A Fellow, SJC 1941–1948 (leave of absence on War Service 1941–1945); Member, British Group of Atomic Scientists transferred to work on US Manhattan Project 1943–1945; Professor of Electron Physics, University of Birmingham 1946–1972. **Appointments:** British Delegate, International Scientific Radio Union, Zurich 1950. **Awards:** Royal Commission Award to Inventors 1949. **Publications:** Papers in *Procedures of the Royal Society*, *Procedures of the Physical Society*, and in the reports of various international scientific conferences, on upper atmosphere physics and the physics of ionised gases. Died 13 March 1993.

SAYLES, Henry Sharrock (1924) Born 21 May 1905, 16 Walton Village, Walton on the Hill, Liverpool; son of Charles Philip Sayles, Schoolmaster, and Annie Elizabeth Sharrock. **Subject(s):** Mathematics/Mechanical Sciences; BA 1927; MA 1931; CEng; Honorary FIPlantE; FIMechE. **Tutor(s):** J M Wordie. **Educ:** Oakes Institute, Walton, Liverpool; Liverpool College, Sefton Park Road, Liverpool. Died 12 July 1990.

SCALE, Edmund Thomas (1919) Born 20 March 1893, 109 High Street, Bromsgrove, Worcester; son of Thomas Scale, Baker, and Sarah Jane Gwinnett. **Subject(s):** Mathematics. **Tutor(s):** E E Sikes. **Educ:** Stourbridge Road Council School, Bromsgrove; The Secondary School, Bromsgrove.

SCANTLEBURY, The Revd Raymond Marshall (1923) Born 11 March 1905, 19 Winifred Grove, Battersea, London; son of William Imlay Scantlebury, Hardware Merchant, and Alice Martha Marshall; m Margaret Norah Hicks, 5 June 1930, St Mark's, Barnet Vale, Hertfordshire; 4 sons (Lester, Peter, Julian and Stephen), 1 daughter (Judith). BA 1927; MA 1931. **Tutor(s):** E A Benians. **Educ:** Manor House School, Clapham Common; King's College School, Wimbledon; Ridley Hall, Cambridge. **Career:** Ordained Deacon 1928; Curate, Christ Church, Croydon 1928–1930; Chaplain, Cambridge Pastorate 1928–1942; Ordained Priest 1929; Curate, Southampton 1931–1933; Organising Secretary, CMS, Diocese of Winchester, Guildford, Portsmouth and Salisbury 1933; Secretary for Recruiting, CMS, Diocese of Winchester, Guildford, Portsmouth and Salisbury 1937; Chaplain, Christ's College 1940–1942; Rector, Gravesend 1942–1947; Residentiary Canon, Carlisle and Diocesan Missionary 1947–1958. **Appointments:** General Secretary, Colonial and Continental Church Society. Died 16 June 1958.

SCARTH, Robert Ewart (1913) Born 6 March 1894, Scarthingwell House, Morley, Leeds; son of Charles Scarth, Woollen Manufacturer, and Jessie Glendinning Watson. **Tutor(s):** L H K Bushe-Fox. **Educ:** Leeds Grammar School; Mill Hill School. **Career:** Second Lieutenant, Royal Field Artillery, WWI.

SCHARDT, Richard Geoffrey (1938) Born 31 July 1919, 286 East Park Road, Leicester; son of Charles Schardt, Dye Manufacturers Agent, and Emily Elizabeth Freeman, Teacher; m Elizabeth Ward, 1961 (d 1977). **Subject(s):** Natural Sciences; BA 1941; MA 1963. **Tutor(s):** C W Guillebaud. **Educ:** Micklefield School, Leicester; Wyggeston School, Leicester. **Career:** Biology Teacher, Leighton Park School, Reading 1941–1945; Teacher, Solihull School 1945–1950; Head of Biology, Leighton Park School, Reading 1950–1979. **Awards:** Scholarship, SJC; Exhibition, SJC 1937. Died 6 January 2004.

SCHEUER, Dr Peter August Georg (1948) Born 31 March 1930, Frankfurt am Main, Germany; son of Ernst Scheuer, Metallurgist, and Bertha Marie Helene Elisabeth Zindel; m Jane Elizabeth Morford, 1974;

1 daughter (Suzi). **Subject(s):** Natural Sciences; BA 1951; MA 1955; PhD 1955. **Tutor(s):** G C L Bertram. **Educ:** Miss Cossman's Private School, Frankfurt; Tower House College, Slough; Slough Grammar School; Aylesbury Grammar School. **Career:** Title A Fellow, SJC 1955–1958; National Service 1955–1956; Fellow, CSIRO, Australia 1959–1962; Assistant Director of Research in Physics 1963–1992, Reader in Radio Astronomy 1992–1997, University of Cambridge; Fellow and Lecturer in Natural Sciences, Peterhouse 1963–2001. **Awards:** Major Scholarship, SJC 1946; Hamilton Prize 1953. **Publications:** numerous papers and articles. Died 21 January 2001.

SCHLAPP, Dr Robert (1922) Born 18 July 1899, 9 Cluny Place, Edinburgh, Scotland; son of Otto Schlapp, Reader in German, University of Edinburgh, and Anna Elisabeth Lotze. PhD 1925; MA (Edinburgh) 1922. **Tutor(s):** E Cunningham. **Educ:** Trinity House Private School, Musselburgh; George Watson's College, Edinburgh; University of Edinburgh. **Career:** Lecturer in Mathematical Physics, University of Edinburgh until 1969. Died 1991.

SCHLESINGER, Wolfgang Wilhelm Otto (SLESSENGER) (1945) Born 15 March 1928, Bochum, Germany; son of Paul Schlesinger, Cloth Finisher, and Emma Riemenschneider; m Pat Thomas, 1957; 1 son (Peter b 1960), 1 daughter (Susan Nancy b 1959). **Subject(s):** Mathematics; BA 1948; MA 1952. **Tutor(s):** J M Wordie. **Educ:** Elementary School, Bochum; Almondbury Grammar School, Huddersfield. **Career:** Master, Bootham School 1948–1952; Assistant Master, Dulwich College 1952–1957; Longton High School, Stoke-on-Trent 1957–1961; Deputy Headmaster, Cavendish School, Hemel Hempstead 1961–1965; Headmaster, Grove Hill School/Astley Cooper School, Hemel Hempstead 1965–1987. **Appointments:** Holder of various offices in Head Masters' Association and Secondary Heads Association.

SCHNEIDER, Professor Ben Ross (1949) Born 7 July 1920, Bethesda Hospital, Cincinnati, Ohio, USA; son of Ben Ross Schneider, Civil Engineer, and Jean Kimball Taylor. **Tutor(s):** A G Lee. **Educ:** Winchester High School, Massachusetts; Williams College, Williamstown; Columbia University, New York. **Career:** Professor of English, Lawrence University. **Publications:** *Wordsworth's Cambridge Education*, CUP, 1958; *The Ethos of Restoration Comedy*, University of Chicago Press.

SCHOELLER, Ewald Georg (1913) Born 8 January 1893, Roth Lobendau, Kreis Goldberg-Hainau, Germany; son of Ewald Schoeller, Rittergutsbesitzer (Lord of the Manor), and Marianne Schoeller. **Tutor(s):** L H K Bushe-Fox. **Educ:** Realgymnasium aus Zwinger, Breslau.

SCHOELLER, Thomas Louis (1911) Born 2 March 1892, Schenkel Strasse, Düren, Germany; son of Leopold Schoeller, Manufacturer, and Christine Heimbach. **Tutor(s):** L H K Bushe-Fox. **Educ:** Real Gymnasium, Düren, Germany.

SCHOFIELD, Ernest (1934) Born 26 October 1916, 60 West Parade, Penistone, Yorkshire; son of Benjamin Schofield, Brewery Manager, and Alice Shaw; m Hattie Pritchard, 1940; 2 daughters (Elizabeth Helen b 1942 and Susan Caroline b 1946). **Subject(s):** Economics/History; BA 1937; MA 1941. **Tutor(s):** C W Guillebaud. **Educ:** Gerard Street Council School, Derby; Bemrose School, Derby. **Career:** Inland Revenue 1939–1976; RAF 1940–1945. **Awards:** Scholarship, SJC 1936–1937. **Honours:** DFC 1942. **Publications:** (with R C Nesbit) *Arctic Airmen – the RAF in Spitsbergen and North Russia 1942*, 1987.

SCHOFIELD, Harry (1929) Born 11 February 1911, 75 Wyatt Road, Forest Gate, West Ham; son of Arthur Edward Schofield, Engineer, and Maggie Simons; m Ethel Greenwood, 11 August 1937, Prestwich, Lancashire; 2 sons (Malcolm b 19 April 1942 and Rodney b 21 March 1944), 1 daughter (Margaret Anne b 4 June 1949). **Subject(s):** Mathematics; BA 1932; MA 1936. **Tutor(s):** J M Wordie. **Johnian Relatives:** father of Malcolm Schofield (1960) and of Rodney Schofield

(1961); uncle of Neil McCallum Schofield (1963). **Educ:** National School, Prestwich; Stand Grammar School, Whitefield. **Career:** Mathematics Master, then Senior Mathematics Master and Second Master, St Albans School 1932–1976. **Awards:** Scholarship, SJC. Died 5 January 1990.

SCHOLFIELD, Richard Denham (1910) Born 10 August 1891, Brunswick Terrace, Prestwich, Lancashire; son of Frank Scholfield, Manchester Warehouseman, and Emma Denham Walker. **Subject(s):** Law; BA 1913; LLB 1913. **Tutor(s):** L H K Bushe-Fox. **Educ:** Rivington School; Rossall School. **Career:** Articled to Town Clerk, Salford; Second Lieutenant, 6th Royal Lancashire Regiment until 1915. Died 10 August 1915 (killed in action at the Dardanelles).

SCHROEDER, Albert Edward (LONG) (1911) Born 8 May 1891, Clifton Garth, Yorkshire; son of Felix Gottlieb Ludwig Schroeder, Merchant, and Jane Thompson Long. **Subject(s):** Classics; BA 1914; MA 1919. **Tutor(s):** E E Sikes. **Educ:** St Peter's School, York. **Career:** Private, Training Reserve Battalion, WWI; Master, Royal Grammar School, Lancaster 1914–1915; Assistant Master, Copthorne School, Sussex 1915. **Awards:** Choral Scholarship, SJC. **Publications:** 'To a Camembert Cheese', *Eagle* 35 (German verse).

SCHUPBACH, Ernest Halley (1927) Born 19 May 1910, 46 Avondale Road, Croydon, Surrey; son of Charles Alexandri Schupbach, Bank Manager, and Louise Marguerite Ulliac; m Mavis Mark Wild, Holy Trinity Church, Leamington Spa, 17 July 1948. **Subject(s):** Economics; BA 1931; MA 1935. **Tutor(s):** C W Guillebaud. **Johnian Relatives:** father of William Mark Schupbach (1969). **Educ:** St Anselm's School, Croydon; Wycliffe College, Stonehouse. Died 11 January 1999.

SCHWAB, Dr Robert Sidney (1926) Born 6 December 1903, St Louis, Missouri, USA; son of Sidney Isaac Schwab, Neurologist, and Helen Dorothy Stix. **Subject(s):** Natural Sciences; BA 1928; MA 1929; MD (Harvard) 1931. **Tutor(s):** M P Charlesworth. **Educ:** Smith Academy, St Louis; Country Day School, St Louis; Harvard University; KCL. **Career:** Intern, Boston City Hospital; Neuropathology, University of Munich, Germany; Resident in Neurology, Massachusetts General Hospital, Boston; Resident in Psychiatry, Boston Psychopathic Hospital; US Navy, Pacific and Neurological Consultant to the US Navy in Boston, WWII; Neurological Consultant to the US Veterans' Bureau; Director of the Brain-Wave Laboratory, Massachusetts General Hospital 1937–1968; Emeritus Professor in Neurology, Harvard 1968. **Appointments:** Member, Harvard Ad Hoc Committee on Cerebral Death; President, American EEG Society; Vice-President, American Neurological Association; Honorary Member, EEG Society (GB). Died 6 April 1972.

SCOBLE, John Warren (1943) Born 4 August 1924, Hatfield Gardens, Upton, Torquay, Devon; son of Frank Sprague Scoble, Butcher, and Evelyn Minnie Harvey. **Tutor(s):** C W Guillebaud. **Educ:** Firswood Preparatory School; Newton College; Taunton School.

SCOTT, Alan Milne (1932) Born 5 July 1914, 8 Desswood Place, Aberdeen; son of James Scott, Contractor, and Helen Maitland Milne; BA 1935; MA 1939. **Tutor(s):** J S Boys Smith. **Educ:** Merchiston Preparatory School, Edinburgh; Merchiston Castle School, Edinburgh; The Grammar School, Aberdeen. **Career:** Director, Messrs James Scott and Son, Contractors, Aberdeen 1935–1939; Squadron Leader, RAF 1937–1940. Died 5 November 1940 (accidentally killed whilst on active service).

SCOTT, Angus Weatheritt (1945) Born 16 August 1927, 33 Fossdale Road, Sheffield; son of Charles Weatheritt Scott, HM Inspector of Mines, and Muriel Maud Leybourne; m Jean; 2 daughters (Elizabeth and Jane). **Subject(s):** Mechanical Sciences; BA 1949; MA 1960. **Tutor(s):** J M Wordie. **Educ:** Birkdale Preparatory School; Sedbergh School. **Career:** Housemaster, Gordonstoun School. Died 16 March 1990.

SCOTT, Brian Moore (1944) Born 24 April 1926, 97 Tenison Road, Cambridge; son of Charles Christopher Scott, Sub-Librarian, SJC, and Marian Fanny Moore; m Margaret Olga Rainsford, 4 July 1953, St Nicholas' Church, Wells-next-the-Sea; 1 son (John Christopher b 6 October 1960), 1 daughter (Jane Elizabeth b 29 May 1957). **Subject(s):** Natural Sciences; BA 1947; MA 1951; DipAgr 1948. **Tutor(s):** C W Guillebaud. **Educ:** Park Street Elementary School, Cambridge; Perse School, Cambridge. **Career:** Demonstrator in Agriculture, University of Nottingham 1949–1950; Assistant Field Trials Supervisor, Norfolk Agricultural Station, Sprowston, Norwich 1950–1952; Technical Assistant in charge of experimental work, Ministry of Agriculture Experimental Husbandry Farm, Preston Wynne, Hereford 1952–1956 and High Mowthorpe Experimental Husbandry Farm, Yorkshire 1956–1961; Assistant Director, Norfolk Agricultural Station 1961–1968; Meat Production Specialist, Agricultural Development and Advisory Service 1968–1981; Regional Livestock Husbandry Adviser 1981–1986. **Publications:** Various papers in livestock science journals.

SCOTT, Charles Russell (1919) Born 8 February 1898, 40 Graham Mansions, Graham Road, Hackney; son of Russell Scott, Professor, and Susanna Letitia Worthington; m Irene Keightley, 2 June 1923, Great Stambridge Parish Church; 3 sons (John Russell b 4 November 1924, Robert Prestwich b 25 October 1930 and Charles Geoffrey b 21 July 1932), 1 daughter (Delia Ann Russell b 1 July 1935). **Subject(s):** Natural Sciences; BA 1920; MA 1925. **Tutor(s):** E E Sikes. **Johnian Relatives:** father of Charles Geoffrey Scott (1951). **Educ:** Bedales Preparatory School; École de la Châtaigneraie, Geneva; École de L'Isle de France, Liancourt; Bedales School; Haileybury College. **Career:** RGA 1917–1919; Assistant Secretary for Education, Cambridgeshire 1922–1927; Assistant Master, Tonbridge School 1927–1929; Headmaster, Cranbrook School 1929–1960. **Appointments:** JP; Chairman, Juvenile Court; Chairman, Kent County Music Committee; Chairman, Kent Council of Social Service; Chairman, SE Conference of County Music Committees 1945–1962; Chairman, Standing Conference for Amateur Music 1947–1964; Chairman, Secretary or Member of numerous committees concerning amateur music, Social Service and Education. **Publications:** Author or editor of many articles on amateur music, Social Service and Education, including *Music and the Community*, 1933. Died 16 September 1979.

SCOTT, Dr David (1934) Born 7 August 1916, North Sunderland; son of George Scott, Butcher, and Mary Jane Murdue. **Subject(s):** Natural Sciences; BA 1937; MB 1940; BChir 1940; MA 1949; Diploma in Tropical Medicine (Liverpool) 1946. **Tutor(s):** R L Howland. **Educ:** North Sunderland School; Barnard Castle School. **Career:** RN 1939–1945; Medical Officer, Ministry of Health, Ghana 1947–1965; Epidemiologist, Ministry of Health, Ghana 1955; Director, Medical Field Units, Ministry of Health, Ghana 1962–1965; Consultant, World Health Organisation, Africa 1965; Lecturer, Liverpool School of Tropical Medicine 1965. **Honours:** OBE 1960. Died 6 April 1982.

SCOTT, David Angus George (1946) Born 2 April 1928, The Moorings, Bronshill Road, Torquay; son of James McAlpine Scott, Physician, and Elsie Dudley Richardson. **Tutor(s):** G C L Bertram. **Johnian Relatives:** brother of James Dudley Scott (1941). **Educ:** Mowden Hall School, Darlington; Leighton Park School.

SCOTT, David Gidley (1942) Born 3 January 1924, San Francisco, California; son of Bernard Wardlaw Habershon Scott, Architect, and Florence May Wheeler; m Elinor Anne Garthwaite, 1948; 2 sons, 2 daughters. **Subject(s):** Law; BA 1948; MA 1951; LLB 1950; LLM 1985. **Tutor(s):** C W Guillebaud; F Thistlethwaite. **Johnian Relatives:** brother of Paul Habershon Scott (1948). **Educ:** The Friary School, Whetstone; Oakleigh Park Preparatory School, Whetstone; Sutton Valence School. **Career:** RE 1942–1947; Acting Major, Palestine 1947; Called to the Bar, Lincoln's Inn 1951; Chancery Bar 1951–1984; Registrar of the High Court in Bankruptcy 1984–1996. **Awards:** Robins Exhibition 1942.

SCOTT, The Revd Canon Eric Walter (1935) Born 4 August 1916, 8 Greeb Villas, Barnack Road, St Martin Without, Stamford; son of Walter Scott, Commercial Traveller, and Marguerite Ethel Humphries; m Frances Winifred Strickson, 1940; 2 sons (Simon and Mark), 1 daughter (Anna). **Subject(s):** English; BA 1938; MA 1943. **Tutor(s):** J S Boys Smith. **Educ:** King's School, Peterborough. **Career:** Ridley Hall, Cambridge 1938–1940; Ordained Deacon 1940; Assistant Curate, St John's and St Stephen's, Reading, Diocese of Oxford 1940–1943; Ordained Priest 1941; Curate, Holy Trinity Church, Cambridge 1943–1945; Priest in Charge, St Mary Magdalen's, Tilehurst, Reading 1945–1949; Rector of Wasing with Brimpton 1949–1953; Diocese of Oxford, and Vicar, Midgham Diocese of Oxford (held in plurality) 1950–1953; Rector, Foothills Mission, Diocese of Calgary, Alberta, Canada 1953–1956; Rector, St George's Church, City and Diocese of Edmonton, British Columbia, Canada 1956–1957; Vicar, Midgham, Oxford 1957–1961 (Brimpton from 1959); Chaplain, Shawnigan Lake School, British Columbia, Canada 1961–1967; Rector, St John's, Courtenay, British Columbia and Honorary Canon of Christchurch Cathedral, Victoria, British Columbia 1967–1981; Permitted to Officiate, Ely 1990. **Awards:** Choral Scholarship, SJC.

SCOTT, Frank Munro (1919) Born 25 May 1897, Newbridge Crescent, Wolverhampton, Stafford; son of John William Scott, Surgeon, and Mary Babbage. **Tutor(s):** E E Sikes. **Educ:** Wolverhampton School; Bowdon College.

SCOTT, George (1933) Born 17 June 1914, North Sunderland, Sea Houses, Northumberland; son of George Scott, Master Butcher, North Sunderland, and Mary Jane Murdue. **Subject(s):** Natural Sciences; BA 1936; MA 1947. **Tutor(s):** J M Wordie. **Educ:** Sea Houses Council School; Barnard Castle School, Durham. **Career:** RAF Radar Branch (for five years); House Master, Nautical College, Pangbourne, Berkshire 1947.

SCOTT, Dr Gordon (1924) Born 9 December 1905, The Grove, Westoe, South Shields, County Durham; son of George Scott, Solicitor, and Gertrude Hannay; m Betty Noreen Fullerton; 1 son (Gordon (Sandy)); 3 daughters (Janet, Pauline and Clare). **Subject(s):** Natural Sciences; BA 1927; MA 1935; BChir 1935; MB 1935; MD 1957; MRCS (Middlesex Hospital); LRCP (Middlesex Hospital). **Tutor(s):** B F Armitage. **Johnian Relatives:** father of Gordon Scott (1962). **Educ:** Caldicott School, Hitchin; High School, South Shields; The Leys School, Cambridge. **Career:** HM Prison Medical Service 1933; DCH, Oxfordshire County Council 1947–1954. **Appointments:** Member, Board of Governors, United Oxford Hospitals; Chairman, Oxfordshire Association for Care of Old People. Died 27 June 1986.

SCOTT, Gordon Wood (1949) Born 26 April 1929, Allery, Reservoir Road North, Prenton, Cheshire; son of Thomas Scott, Director of a Produce Company, and Christina Bridgetower Wood; m 24 August 1955; 1 son, 1 daughter. BA 1952; MA 1957; FCA. **Tutor(s):** C W Guillebaud. **Educ:** Birkenhead School; Holmwood Preparatory School, Formby; Leighton Park School. **Career:** Farmer until 1996.

SCOTT, Herbert (1936) Born 10 January 1917, Hemplands Road, Stourbridge, Worcestershire; son of John Frederick Scott, Mechanic, Great Western Railway, and Rose Williams; m Joan M Potter, 1955; 3 daughters (Sally, Jane and Mary). **Subject(s):** Mathematics; BA 1939; MA 1947. **Tutor(s):** J M Wordie. **Educ:** Hill Street School, Stourbridge; Brook Street Senior School, Stourbridge; King Edward VI Grammar School, Stourbridge. **Career:** Enlisted, RA 1939; demobilised as major, 6th Indian Regiment, SEAC 1946; Head, Mathematics Department, Royal Grammar School, High Wycombe, Buckinghamshire until 1982. **Awards:** Open Exhibition, SJC 1935–1939.

SCOTT, Herbert Wyndham Fitzgerald (1930) Born 11 October 1911, Delhi, India; son of William Herbert Schroder Scott, Deputy Transport Superintendent, and Winifred Mary Watson. **Subject(s):** Ecomonics/

Law; BA 1933. **Tutor(s):** M P Charlesworth. **Educ:** Park House, Paignton; Sherborne School.

SCOTT, Dr James Dudley (1941) Born 8 July 1923, The Moorings, Bronshill Road, Torquay, Devon; son of James McAlpine Scott, Physician, and Elsie Dudley Richardson. **Subject(s):** Natural Sciences; BA 1944; BChir 1949; MB 1949. **Tutor(s):** S J Bailey. **Johnian Relatives:** brother of David Angus George Scott (1946). **Educ:** Orleton Preparatory School, Scarborough; Leighton Park School, Reading. **Career:** GP, Christchurch, Dorset 1978 until retirement. Died September 1993.

SCOTT, Kenneth (1936) Born 29 August 1917, 36 Arthur Road, Gainsborough; son of Thomas Scott, Bank Manager, and Eleanor Mabel Hanson; m (1) Barbara Mary Hills, 18 January 1947, Holne, Devon (dis 1952), (2) Joan Dorothy Pauline Nickells (née Abbis), 8 January 1953, Cambridge; (1) 1 son (John b 4 April 1948), (2) 1 son (Ian b 18 November 1954, d 21 October 1979), 1 daughter (Elizabeth Anne b 11 September 1953). **Subject(s):** History/Law; BA 1939; MA 1943; LLB 1940. **Tutor(s):** J S Boys Smith. **Educ:** Handel House School, Gainsborough; Queen Elizabeth's Grammar School, Gainsborough; King Edward VI Grammar School, East Retford. **Career:** Gunner, RA 1939; Temporary Captain, Officer Cadet Training Unit 1941; served in India/Burma 1945–1946; Captain, RA 1948; Title A Fellow 1943–1948 (suspended while on war service 1943–1946), Title B Fellow 1948–1977, Lecturer in Law 1957–1977, Title D Fellow 1977–1984, SJC; Called to the Bar, Middle Temple 1946; Assistant Lecturer in Law 1947–1949, Lecturer in Law 1949–1977, University of Cambridge. **Appointments:** Supervisor in Law 1948–1957, Junior and Tutorial Bursar 1949–1952, Director of Studies in Law 1961–1970, SJC; Treasurer, Cambridge Union Society 1951–1969; Major, Cambridgeshire Regiment, Territorial Army 1956–1968; Legal Advisor, *News of the World;* Chairman of Industrial Tribunals, England and Wales 1972. **Awards:** Exhibition, SJC 1937; Wright's Prize, SJC 1937; Notts County Senior Scholarship 1937; State Scholarship 1937; Scholarship, SJC 1938; McMahon Law Scholarship 1940. **Publications:** 'The Jewish Arcae', *Cambridge Law Journal,* 1950; contributions to books on the subject of law including (ed, with Bryan Clauson) Chapter 8, Chitty, Joseph, *Chitty on Contracts,* The Common Law Library Number 1, Twenty-first edition, Sweet and Maxwell, 1955. Died 19 August 1984.

SCOTT, Kenneth Alan (1937) Born 4 July 1919, Deswood, Barnt Green; son of Harold Seymour Scott, Architect and Surveyor, and Doris Bailey; m Ruth Storer Mason, 10 July 1947. **Subject(s):** Law; BA 1940; MA 1944. **Tutor(s):** C W Guillebaud. **Educ:** Lickey Hills School, Rednal; Aldenham School.

SCOTT, Mark (1940) Born 7 March 1922, Winchcombe, Gloucestershire; son of William Sibbald Scott, Medical Practitioner, and Kathleen Musgrave Gibson. **Tutor(s):** C W Guillebaud. **Educ:** Moorland House, Heswall; Shrewsbury.

SCOTT, Dr Paul Habershon (1948) Born 31 March 1927, Goodshelter, Oakleigh Avenue, Whetstone, Middlesex; son of Bernard Wardlaw Habershon Scott, Architect and Surveyor, and Florence May Wheeler; m Ursula Kay, 1958, Blackburn Cathedral; 3 sons (Martin b 1960, Giles b 1962 and Barnaby b 1967). **Subject(s):** Natural Sciences; BA 1951; BChir 1955; MB 1956. **Tutor(s):** G C L Bertram. **Johnian Relatives:** brother of David Gidley Scott (1942). **Educ:** Oakleigh Park Preparatory School; Sutton Valence School; Middlesex Hospital. **Career:** GP, Stevenage 1957–1987. **Awards:** Robins Exhibition 1945.

SCOTT, Peter (1943) Born 11 March 1926, Glenlyn, Newgate Street Road, Goff's Oak, Cheshunt, Hertfordshire; son of Rupert Scott, Schoolmaster, and Edna Townsend; m Dolores Maureen Beazley, 8 September 1952, Birmingham (d 1 July 2002). **Subject(s):** Mechanical Sciences; BA 1946; MA 1950. **Educ:** Chase Side Elementary School, Enfield; Enfield Grammar School. **Career:** Chief Engineer, NEI Peebles Projects. **Awards:** Strathcona Scholarship, SJC 1943.

SCOTT, Robert (1934) Born 7 July 1913, 13 Wingates Square, Westhoughton, Bolton; son of Harry Scott, Builder and General Contractor, and Frances Alice Pinkerton; m Dorothy M Howell, 1940, Westhoughton; 1 son, 1 daughter. **Subject(s):** Mathematics; BA 1936; MA 1946; BSc 1934 (Liverpool); DipEd (Liverpool) 1937; FIMA. **Tutor(s):** J M Wordie. **Educ:** Wingate's St Johns Elementary School; Hinley and Abram Grammar School; University of Liverpool. **Career:** Assistant Master, Newton-le-Willows Grammar School 1937–1941; Army and WO Staff 1941–1946; Scientific Civil Service, RMCS Shrivenham 1946–1954; Vice-Principal, Bolton Technical College 1954–1957; Principal, Wolverhampton and Staffordshire College of Technology 1958–1969; Director, Polytechnic, Wolverhampton. **Honours:** CBE 1976.

SCOTT, Stanley Henry (1901) Born 16 September 1882, Eardington, Bridgnorth, Shropshire; son of Thomas Scott, Gentleman, and Elizabeth Isabella Silver. BA 1904. **Tutor(s):** D MacAlister. **Educ:** Epsom College. **Career:** House Surgeon and Aural Clinical Assistant, Evelina Hospital for Sick Children; Surgeon, RNVR; Farmer and Horse Breeder 1925. Died 15 February 1938.

SCOTT, Thomas Torrance (1910) Born 13 January 1891, 253 Thorn Place, Dundee, Scotland; son of David Scott, Commercial Traveller, and Annie Torrance Scott. **Subject(s):** Classics; BA 1913. **Tutor(s):** E E Sikes. **Educ:** St Peter's Collegiate School, Wolverhampton; Wolverhampton Grammar School. **Career:** Lieutenant, Somerset Light Infantry; Captain, 52nd Sikhs, WWI; Labour Office, League of Nations, Geneva; Deputy Governor, Basra 1918; Assistant Master, Bradfield College 1919–1920.

SCOTT, William Hugh (1939) Born 19 March 1921, Welcot, Green Lane, Northwood, Middlesex; son of William Allan Scott, Solicitor, and Elizabeth Muriel Wells; m Diana Mary Malden, 1958; 2 sons (Alastair William and Richard Stewart). **Subject(s):** Geography; BA 1943; MA 1946; ARICS. **Tutor(s):** R L Howland. **Educ:** St Martin's Preparatory School, Northwood; Shrewsbury School. **Career:** Quantity Surveyor. **Honours:** MC.

SCOTT-MONCRIEFF, Ronald (1924) Born 22 October 1905, Montague House, Hoddesdon, Hertfordshire; son of William Elmsley Scott-Moncrieff, Indian Medical Service, and Margaret Vere Irving. BA 1928; MDCM (McGill) 1931. **Tutor(s):** B F Armitage. **Educ:** Victoria College; Brentwood College, Victoria, Canada. **Career:** St Mary's Hospital Medical School, London 1928; Otolaryngologist, Canadian General Hospital (rank of Major during WWII); Practised Otolaryngology in Montreal and Victoria, BC. Died 28 July 1995.

SCOTT-PARK, Jock Hargrave (1949) Born 21 July 1930, 4 Lochbrae Drive, Burnside, Rutherglen, Lanarkshire; son of Stanley Douglas Scott-Park, Medical Practitioner/Consultant Radiologist, and Meta Hargrave Wilson; m Myrtle Patricia Braithwaite Oxley, 1956; 2 sons, 1 daughter. **Subject(s):** Agriculture; BA 1952; MA 1961. **Tutor(s):** G C L Bertram. **Johnian Relatives:** cousin, once removed, of Fergus Dunlop Morton (1906). **Educ:** Glasgow Academy; Hurst Grange Preparatory School, Stirling; Eton College. **Career:** Farming, Portnellan 1952. **Appointments:** Council Member, Scottish National Farmers' Union (Legal and Commercial Committee); Member, Committee of Scottish Landowners Federation; Chairman, Kilmarnock Community Council; Member, Loch Lomond Park Authority; Playing Member, Royal Scottish Pipers Society; Active member, McCarrison Society, disseminating knowledge on the nutritional prevention of degenerative disease 1981–; Member, Health Promotion Steering Group of Argyll and Clyde Health Board.

SCOUGAL, Kenneth Hirst (1906) Born 13 June 1887, Brooklands, Gledholt, Huddersfield, Yorkshire; son of Edward Fowler Scougal, Doctor of Medicine, and Clara Hirst; m Cicely Marsden. **Subject(s):** Classics/Law; BA 1909; MA 1913; LLB 1909. **Tutor(s):** E E Sikes. **Educ:** Huddersfield College School; Rugby School. **Career:** Admitted Solicitor

1912; Procurator-General's Department, Naval Prize Work 1915–1919; Senior Legal Assistant, Treasury Solicitor's Department 1919–1939. Died 16 August 1959.

SCOUGALL, Dr Keith Harold Lauchlan (1937) Born 7 July 1918, Dinas Powis, St Andrews, Cardiff; son of James Somerville Scougall, Schoolmaster, and Lucy Beatrice Jago; m Betty; 3 children. BA 1941; MA 1955; MB, BChir 1949. **Tutor(s):** R L Howland. **Educ:** Brentwood; Hereford Cathedral School. **Career:** Captain, RAMC 1945–1946; Senior Medical Officer, Arab Legion 1946–1948; GP 1950–1985; Member, Texas Department of Mental Health. **Awards:** Somerset Exhibition (Wootton Rivers), SJC 1937. Died 14 March 2002.

SCOULAR, Alexander George (1926) Born 21 October 1907, 6 Hensingham Road, Whitehaven, Cumberland; son of Alexander Carlaw Scoular, Consulting Mining Engineer, and Margaret Evelyn Carrick; m Helen Yoma Johnston, 11 January 1945, Holy Trinity, Brompton, London. BA 1930; MA 1934. **Tutor(s):** J M Wordie. **Johnian Relatives:** son of Alexander Carlaw Scoular (1893); nephew of John Gladstone Scoular (1903). **Educ:** Little House Preparatory School, Wetheral; Cheltenham College.

SCOULAR, Major John Gladstone (1903) Born 17 September 1885, Hensingham, Whitehaven, Cumberland; son of George Scoular, Mining Engineer, and Janet Robb; m Annie Catherine Todd, 14 August 1917, Holy Saviour's Church, Tynemouth. BA 1907. **Tutor(s):** D MacAlister. **Johnian Relatives:** brother of Alexander Carlaw Scoular (1893); uncle of Alexander George Scoular (1926). **Educ:** Meadow House, St Bees; The Grammar School, St Bees. **Career:** Major, RGA, (wounded twice, Mentioned in Despatches), WWI; General Manager, North Eastern Divisional Coal Board, No 7 Area; Agent and Manager, Nostell Colliery Company, Nostell, Yorkshire 1925; Special Constabulary, WWII. Died 7 September 1953.

SCRASE, Squadron Leader George Edward Thomas (1930) Born 14 April 1911, Hillthorpe, Russell Hill, Beddington; son of Arthur George Scrase, Member, London Stock Exchange, and Violet Hamilton Whiteford. **Tutor(s):** J M Wordie. **Educ:** Holmleigh, Seaford; Aldwick Place, Bognor; Cheltenham College. **Career:** Flying Officer, AAF 1939, then Squadron Leader, RAF. Died September 1941 (killed in action).

SCREECH, Dr Guy (1946) Born 29 February 1928, Cranleigh, Caerleon, Monmouthshire; son of Eric Noble Screech, Dental Surgeon, and Ivy Isabel Wilson; m (1) Josephine Irene Gooch, February 1953, Spalding Parish Church, Spalding, Lincolnshire, (2) Sandra Alice Mitchell, 1968; (1) 2 sons (Martin and David), (2) 1 daughter (Jennifer). **Subject(s):** Natural Sciences; BA 1949; MA 1953; BChir 1957; MB 1957; FRCPC. **Tutor(s):** G C L Bertram. **Educ:** Beaufort Lodge Preparatory School; Kingswood School. **Career:** House Surgeon, South Devon and East Cornwall Hospital, Greenbank, Plymouth; Guy's Hospital; Staff Anaesthetist, Vancouver General Hospital 1961–1967; Anaesthetist, Royal Jubilee Hospital, Victoria, British Columbia 1968–1995.

SCRIVIN, Professor John William (1932) Born 17 August 1913, 4 Back, 11 College Street, Birmingham; son of Frank Scrivin, Railway Work Clerk, and Edith Wordley; m Muriel; 1 son (John), 1 daughter (Helen). **Subject(s):** Classics; BA 1935; MA 1947. **Tutor(s):** R L Howland. **Educ:** Camden Street Council School, Birmingham; Redcross Street Council School, Wolverhampton; Wolverhampton Grammar School. **Career:** Lecturer in Classics 1947–1953, Dean of Residence 1952, Trinity College, Toronto. **Awards:** Scholarship, SJC. Died 7 July 1953.

SCULLARD, Professor Howard Hayes (1922) Born 9 February 1903, 10 Albany Street, St Cuthbert, Bedford; son of Herbert Hayes Scullard, Professor at Hackney and New Colleges, London, and Barbara Louise Dodds. **Subject(s):** Classics; BA 1926; MA 1929; PhD (London); FBA 1955; FSA 1958. **Tutor(s):** E E Sikes. **Johnian Relatives:** son of Herbert Hayes Scullard (1885). **Educ:** Hendon Preparatory School; Highgate School. **Career:** Classics Tutor, New College, London 1926–1935;

Reader in Ancient History 1935–1959, Professor in Ancient History 1959–1970 (Emeritus 1970), Fellow 1970, KCL. **Appointments:** Acting Director, Institute of Classical Studies 1964; Vice President, Society for the Promotion of Roman Studies. **Awards:** Exhibition, SJC; Gladstone Memorial Prize and Thirlwall Prize, University of Cambridge 1929. **Publications:** *History of the Roman World from 753 to 146 BC*, 1933; (ed) *The Oxford Classical Dictionary*, 1949, 1967; *Roman Politics 220–150 BC*, 1951; *From the Gracchi to Nero*, 1959; *Aspects of Greek and Roman Life*, 1967; *Elephants in the Greek and Roman World*, 1974; *Festivals of the Roman Republic*, 1981; Articles in the *Encyclopaedia Britannica*. Died 31 March 1983.

SCURFIELD, George Bazeley (1938) Born 19 March 1920, 76 Clarkehouse Road, Sheffield; son of Harold Scurfield, Medical Practitioner, and Mary Louisa Bazeley; m Cecilia Robinson (née Hopkinson), 1946; 1 son, 4 daughters, 1 stepson, 1 stepdaughter. **Subject(s):** English; BA 1941; MA 1945. **Tutor(s):** J S Boys Smith. **Educ:** Seabrooke Lodge, Hythe; Oundle School. **Career:** Army Service, WWII; Postman, Shepreth 1950–1954; Baker and Shopkeeper 1954; Council Member, Cambridge City Council 1963–1966. **Awards:** Munsteven Exhibition, SJC 1938. **Honours:** MC. **Publications:** *The Bamboo House*, 1950; *Alone With Our Day*, 1952; *Home Baked*, 1956; *Cakes and Biscuits*, 1957; many poems. Died 15 December 1991.

SCUTT, The Revd John Alfred Homer (1910) Born 8 July 1891, 2 Albert House, Albion Road, Scarborough; son of Alfred Homer Scutt, Land Surveyor, and Annie Maria Gillard. BA 1913. **Tutor(s):** E E Sikes. **Educ:** Arnold College; Kelham Theological College. **Career:** Private, HAC; Lieutenant, Hampshire Regiment, WWI; Priest 1920; Deacon 1919; Curate, All Saints, South Acton 1919–1920; Assistant Tutor, House of the Sacred Mission, Kelham 1920–1936; Chaplain, St Helena's Home, West Ealing 1937–1940; Rector, Ufford with Ashton and Bainton 1940–1950; Chaplain, RAF 1942–1951; Assistant Tutor, Kelham 1951–1953; Vicar, St Cecilia, Parson Cross, Sheffield 1953–1954; Chaplain, St Edward's House, West Malvern 1954–1956; Perpetual Curate, Tresco with Bryher, Scilly Islands 1961. **Honours:** MC.

SEABROOK, Frederick James (1925) Born 9 January 1899, The Vicarage, Brockworth, Gloucestershire; son of James Herbert Seabrook, Clerk in Holy Orders, and Ethel Maud Power. **Subject(s):** Geography/History; BA 1927; MA 1946. **Tutor(s):** E E Sikes. **Educ:** Temple Grove Preparatory School, Eastbourne; Haileybury College. **Career:** Master, Clare House Preparatory School 1921–1924; Assistant Master, Radley 1928–1930; Assistant Master, Haileybury 1951. Died 7 August 1979.

SEALE, Dr George Hall (1939) Born 13 May 1921, 30 Minto Street, Edinburgh; son of James Fayle Seale, Medical Practitioner, and Anna Hall; m (1) Madeleine, 1953 (d 1973), (2) Gwen, 1977; (1) 2 sons (Clive and Patrick d 1971), 2 daughters (Isobel and Colette), (2) 1 son (Stephen), 1 daughter (Anna). BA 1942; MA 1946; MB 1945; BChir 1945. **Tutor(s):** R L Howland. **Johnian Relatives:** brother of James Lawrie Seale (1942) and of John Richard Seale (1945); father of Stephen George Seale (1998) and of Anna Catherine Seale (1999). **Educ:** Exeter School. **Career:** RAF, Coastal Command; Medical Practitioner, West Bromwich 1951–1952; Medical Practitioner, Leeds 1952–1954; Medical Practitioner, Rotunda Maternity Hospital, Dublin 1954; GP, Exeter 1954–1991; Member, Exeter City Council 1963; National Park Guide, Dartmoor 1991. **Awards:** Vidal Exhibition, SJC 1939. Died 3 December 1994.

SEALE, James Lawrie (1942) Born 25 September 1924, 30 Minto Street, Edinburgh; son of James Fayle Seale, Medical Practitioner, and Anna Hall; m Priscilla Harvey, 1958, Malacca; 1 son (Andrew b 1961). BA 1945; MA 1949; CEng; FICE; FIStructE; PEng; FIES. **Tutor(s):** S J Bailey. **Johnian Relatives:** brother of George Hall Seale (1939) and of John Richard Seale (1945); uncle of Stephen George Seale (1998) and of Anna Catherine Seale (1999). **Educ:** Exeter School. **Career:** Civil Engineer, Gammon (Malaya) Ltd (later renamed Bovis South East Asia Ltd) 1952–1980 (Chief Engineer 1965, Director 1967, Managing Director,

Bovis Singapore Ltd, until 1980); Founder, General Manager and Director, Lawrie Seale Project Consultants Ltd, Singapore 1980–1986. Died 27 June 2002.

SEALE, Dr John Richard (1945) Born 7 August 1927, The Firs, Denmark Road, Exeter; son of James Fayle Seale, Medical Practitioner, and Anna Hall; m (1) Elisabeth C Grillet, 22 October 1949 (div 1972), (2) Jane Blaydon, 3 December 1975; (2) 2 sons (Marc and Adam), 2 daughters (Charlotte and Victoria). **Subject(s):** Natural Sciences/Moral Sciences; BA 1948; MA 1952; MB 1951; BChir 1951; MD 1957; MRCP 1953. **Tutor(s):** S J Bailey. **Johnian Relatives:** brother of George Hall Seale (1939) and of James Lawrie Seale (1942); uncle of Stephen George Seale (1998) and of Anna Catherine Seale (1999). **Educ:** Exeter School; Sherborne School. **Career:** Senior Medical Registrar, St Mary's Hospital, London and the West Middlesex Hospital 1958–1961; Consultant Venereologist, St Thomas' Hospital, London 1966–1972; Consultant Genito-Urinary Physician, Middlesex Hospital 1966–1977. **Awards:** Scholarship, SJC 1947; Sir Joseph Larmor Award, SJC 1948; University Scholarship, St Thomas' Hospital, London 1948; Wainwright Prize (Medicine) 1951; Hadden Prize (Pathology) 1951; Toller Prize (Medicine) 1952; Research Scholarship, British Medical Association 1960. **Publications:** Various publications in medical journals on medical economics in the 1960s and on AIDS in the 1980s.

SEARLE, Cyril Theobald Roundell (1920) Naval Officer.

SEARLE, Harry John Mackenzie (1943) Born 27 April 1925, 32 Glenloch Road, Hampstead; son of Arthur Mackenzie Searle, Electrical Engineer, and Vera Catherine Young; m Mary Monica Dennis, 25 March 1949, St Mary's, Beverley (d 1997); 1 son (Christopher John Mackenzie b 6 July 1950), 2 daughters (Julia Charmian b 12 August 1951 and Penelope Mary b 16 June 1958). **Subject(s):** Mechanical Sciences; BA 1949; MA 1951. **Tutor(s):** C W Guillebaud. **Educ:** Friary Park Kindergarten; Oakleigh Park Preparatory School; Aldenham School; AMP, Harvard Business School. **Career:** Oil and Chemical Industry 1952; Senior Consultant, North West Regional Office, Associated Industrial Consultants 1961–1966; Manager, Commercial Department 1967–1973, Director 1973–1980, Storeys, Lancaster.

SEARLE, Malcolm Walter St Leger (1921) Naval Officer.

SEARS, The Revd Derek Lynford (1947) Born 15 March 1925, The Vicarage, Charnock Richard, Lancashire; son of Selwyn Edward Sears, Clerk in Holy Orders, and Elizabeth Stothert Maxwell; m Patricia Mary Trivitt, 3 September 1955, St Peter's Church, Rugby. **Subject(s):** History; BA 1949; MA 1953. **Tutor(s):** F Thistlethwaite. **Johnian Relatives:** son of Selwyn Edward Sears (1909). **Educ:** Hazelhurst, Frant, Tunbridge Wells; Felsted School. **Career:** Wycliffe Hall Theological College 1949–1951; Deacon, St Stephen's, Blackburn 1951–1953; Curate, St Paul, Preston 1953–1956; Vicar, St James, Burnley 1956–1962; Staff of St Peter's College, Kingston, Jamaica 1962–1966; Vicar, Holy Trinity, Freckleton, Lancashire 1966–1974; Rector, the Morant Bay Cure, Jamaica 1974–1978; Vicar, St Michael's, Ashton-on-Ribble, Preston 1978–1990; Priest-in-charge, Preston St Mark 1982–1990.

SEARS, Geoffrey Wadsworth (1941) Born 6 July 1922, 22 Gloucester Road, Teddington, Middlesex; son of John Edward Sears, Civil Servant, National Physical Laboratory, and Kathleen Lucy Wadsworth; m Linda Brenda Colette Wallis, 7 September 1944, London. **Subject(s):** Mechanical Sciences; BA 1944; MA 1948. **Tutor(s):** S J Bailey. **Johnian Relatives:** son of John Edward Sears (1902). **Educ:** Summerleigh, Teddington; Pembroke House School, Hampton; Belmont, Junior House, Mill Hill School. **Awards:** Minor Scholarship, SJC 1940.

SEARS, John Edward (1902) Born 18 September 1883, 90 Crofton Road, Camberwell, Surrey; son of John Edward Sears, Architect, and Selina Marianne Read; m Kathleen Lucy Wadsworth, 28 May 1919; 1 son (Geoffrey), 2 daughters (Daphne and Hilary). **Subject(s):** Mathematics/

Mechanical Sciences; BA 1905; MA 1910; AMICE; FRHS. **Tutor(s):** C E Graves; J R Tanner. **Johnian Relatives:** father of Geoffrey Wadsworth Sears (1941). **Educ:** Mill Hill School. **Career:** Chairman, Compendium Publishing Company; Principal Assistant, Metrology Department 1910, Deputy Warden of Standards 1921–1931, Superintendent, Metrology Division, until 1946, National Physical Laboratory. **Appointments:** President, International Committee of Weights and Measures. **Awards:** John Winbolt Prize in Civil Engineering, University of Cambridge 1907; Clayton Prize, IMechE 1947. **Honours:** CBE 1920. Died 21 December 1954.

SEARS, The Revd Selwyn Edward (1909) Born 27 November 1889, Manea, Cambridgeshire; son of Richard Henry Sears, Farmer, and Mary Elizabeth Giblin; m Elizabeth Stothert Maxwell, 1 June 1920, Atherton; 2 sons (Derek Lynford b 15 March 1925 and Philip Alan b 15 July 1932), 1 daughter (Pamela Jean Maxwell b 22 January 1922). **Subject(s):** Classics; BA 1912; MA 1916; BD (Manchester) 1915. **Tutor(s):** E E Sikes. **Johnian Relatives:** father of Derek Lynford Sears (1947). **Educ:** Sheffield School; Felsted School; Egerton Hall, Manchester. **Career:** Deacon 1914; Curate, St John the Baptist, Atherton 1914–1920; Priest 1915; Curate, St Mary the Virgin, Bury 1920–1922; Vicar, Charnock Richard 1922–1930; Vicar, Flitwick 1930–1937; Rector, Meppershall, Bedfordshire 1937–1942. Died 22 May 1942.

SEDDON, Richard Paul (1944) Born 8 January 1926, 58 Park Road, Kettering, Northamptonshire; son of Sidney Paul Seddon, Cardboard Box Manufacturer, and Violet Evelyn Wright; m Monica Lilian Mobbs, 18 July 1953, St Edward's Church, Kettering; 2 sons (Richard Charles Paul and David John). **Subject(s):** Engineering; BA 1947; MA 1951; FRSA. **Tutor(s):** S J Bailey. **Educ:** Kettering Grammar School; Kimbolton School. **Career:** Second Lieutenant, RE (National Service); Seddons & Arlidge, family box-making business; founder, own box-making business; Non-executive Chairman, Seddon Packaging & Print Ltd. **Appointments:** Chairman, Kettering Round Table; President, Rotary Club 1961–1962; Member, Appeal Committee for Nurses Recreation Hall, Kettering General Hospital 1965; Member, Kettering Health Authority 1966–1974; Vice-Chairman, Northamptonshire Health Authority 1974–1981; Chairman, Kettering Health Authority 1981–1989; JP 1971–1995; Member, Northampton Magistrates Court Committee 1976–1995 (Deputy Chairman 1981–1995); Captain, Kettering Golf Club 1977; Chairman of the Bench 1983–1995; High Sheriff, Northamptonshire 1992–1993; Deputy Lieutenant, Northamptonshire 1996. Died 7 February 2004.

SEELEY, The Revd Reginald Sidney Kingsley (1934) (admitted to Christ's College 1927) Born 12 June 1908, The Vicarage, Weston Beggard, Hereford; son of George Henry Seeley, Clerk in Holy Orders, and Hilda Constance Sidney Smith; m Marjorie. **Subject(s):** Classics/Theology; BA 1930; MA 1934. **Educ:** Marlborough College; Christ's College; Ridley Hall, Cambridge. **Career:** Deacon 1932; Priest, Coventry 1933; Curate, Rugby 1932–1934; Chaplain, SJC 1934–1938; Organising Secretary, Cambridge Mission to Delhi 1935–1938; Examining Chaplain to Bishop of Bristol 1936–1938; Professor of Exegetical Theology, St John's College, Winnipeg 1938; Canon, Winnipeg Cathedral 1938; Provost and Vice-Chancellor, Trinity College, Toronto 1945. **Appointments:** President, Canadian Welfare Council; Officer, Civil Liberties Association. **Awards:** Bell Exhibition 1927. **Publications:** *The Sign of the Cross*, 1945. Died 3 August 1957.

SEFTON-JONES, Felix William (1918) Born 18 October 1902, 47 Bedford Square, London; son of Herbert Sefton-Jones, Patent Agent, and Margaret Hughes. BA 1922; MA 1926. **Tutor(s):** E E Sikes. **Educ:** Oldfield Preparatory School, Swanage; Leighton Park School. Died 9 June 1929.

SELBY, Cedric Cree (1925) Born 2 February 1907, 2 Rue du Lac, Brussels, Belgium; son of Millin Selby, Engineer, and Margaret Nightingale. BA 1928; MA 1932. **Tutor(s):** J M Wordie. **Educ:** Wychwood Preparatory School, Bournemouth; Uppingham School.

SELLAR, Robert Milne (1942) Born 18 December 1923, Drumpark, Bridge of Allan, Stirlingshire; son of Robert Thomson Sellar, Agricultural Implement Maker, and Catherine Margery Milne; m Monica Mary Mott, 17 April 1948, St Peter in the East; 2 children. **Subject(s):** Modern and Medieval Languages; BA 1947; MA 1949. **Tutor(s):** C W Guillebaud. **Educ:** Huntly Gordon School; Angusfield House, Aberdeen; Loretto School. **Career:** J & P Coats Ltd, Sewing Thread Manufacturers; Production Manager 1957, Chief Production Manager 1965, Spirella Ltd, Letchworth. **Awards:** Major Scholarship, SJC 1941.

SELLERS, George Daniel (1938) Born 10 July 1920, Fadmoor, Kirbymoorside, Helmsley; son of George Sellers, Foreman Platelayer, and Annie Richardson. **Tutor(s):** J M Wordie. **Educ:** Gillamoor County School; Foggathorpe County School; Pocklington School. **Awards:** Dowman Exhibition, SJC.

SEMPLE, Professor John Greenlees (1925) Born 10 June 1904, 64 Kansas Avenue, Antrim Road, Belfast, Ireland; son of James Semple, Secretary, and Isabella Crowe; m Daphne Hummel; 2 children. **Subject(s):** Mathematics; BA 1927; PhD 1930. **Tutor(s):** J M Wordie. **Johnian Relatives:** brother of William Hugh Semple (1925) and of Robert Hugh Semple (1928); uncle of Andrew Greenlees Semple (1954). **Educ:** St Jude's National School, Belfast; Royal Academical Institution, Belfast; Queen's University, Belfast. **Career:** Title A Fellow, SJC 1930–1933; Professor of Mathematics, Queen's University, Belfast 1930–1936; Professor of Mathematics, KCL 1936–1969. **Awards:** Smith's Prize (Rayleigh), University of Cambridge 1929. Died 23 October 1985.

SEMPLE, Robert Hugh (1928) Born 23 February 1908, 214 Ravenhill Road, Belfast, Ireland; son of James Semple, Secretary, and Isabella Crowe. **Subject(s):** Classics/English; BA 1930; MA 1939; BA Belfast 1928. **Tutor(s):** M P Charlesworth. **Johnian Relatives:** brother of John Greenlees Semple (1925) and of William Hugh Semple (1925); uncle of Andrew Greenlees Semple (1954). **Educ:** Royal Academical Institution, Belfast; Queen's University, Belfast. **Career:** Classics and English Master, Roundhay School, Leeds 1930–1931; Master, All Hallows School, Honiton 1931; Lecturer and Director of Extra-Mural Studies, Queen's University, Belfast 1947.

SEMPLE, William Hugh (1925) Born 25 February 1900, 64 Kansas Avenue, Antrim Road, Belfast, Ireland; son of James Semple, Secretary, and Isabella Crowe; m Hilda Madeline Wood, 1932 (d 1978); 1 son (Andrew b 16 January 1934). **Subject(s):** Classics; BA (Queen's University, Belfast) 1921; PhD 1927. **Tutor(s):** E E Sikes. **Johnian Relatives:** brother of John Greenlees Semple (1925) and of Robert Hugh Semple (1928); father of Andrew Greenlees Semple (1954). **Educ:** Royal Academical Institution, Belfast; Queen's University, Belfast. **Career:** Lecturer in Classics, University of Reading 1927; Reader in Classics, University of Reading 1931; Hulme Professor of Latin, Manchester University 1937–1967. **Appointments:** Governor, John Rylands Library 1947–1972; Governor, Sedbergh School 1954–1975; Governor, Congregational College 1958–1981; Member, Bolton Educational Committee 1969–1975. **Publications:** PhD on Sidonius Apollinaris, *Cambridge Philological Society*, 1930. Died 10 March 1981.

SEN, Samarendra Chandra (1945) Born 15 February 1922, Calcutta; son of Susil Chandra Sen, Solicitor to Government of India in Bengal, and Ashalata Gooptu. **Tutor(s):** S J Bailey. **Johnian Relatives:** grandson of Romes Chunder Sen (1894). **Educ:** Nitra Institution, Calcutta; Presidency College, Calcutta; University Law College, Calcutta.

SEN, Dr Susanta Kumar (1926) Born 7 November 1906, Calcutta, India; son of Prasanto Kumar Sen, Barrister-at-Law, and Shushama Bose. BA 1929; MA 1933; BChir 1935; MB 1935; MD 1937; MRCS (St Bartholomew's) 1933; LRCP (St Bartholomew's) 1933; MRCP (London) 1935; FRCSE 1937. **Tutor(s):** M P Charlesworth. **Johnian Relatives:** son of Prasanto Kumar Sen (1899). **Educ:** Ram Mohan Roy

Seminary, Patna; Patna High School; Patna College. Died 24 December 1985.

SENIOR, The Revd Sam (1949) (admitted to St Catharine's College 1909) Born 3 November 1886, Prospect Place, Scholes Cleckheaton, Yorkshire; son of George Senior, Colliery Manager and Nancy Bolland; m Mildred Daisy (d 1948), 2 sons (Christopher and Martin). BA 1913 (St Catharine's); MA 1916 (St Catharine's). **Educ:** Scholes National School; Hanson Higher Grade School, Bradford; Carlton Street Pupil Teachers' Centre, Bradford; Cheltenham Training College; St Catharine's College, Cambridge. **Career:** Headmaster, St John's College Choir School 1912–1955; Deacon 1916; Curate, St Sepulchre, Cambridge 1916–1937; Priest 1917; Curate, Great St Mary, Cambridge 1937–1955; Precentor, SJC 1948–1955. **Appointments:** President, Cambridge Rotary Club. Died 25 February 1967.

SERJEANT, Richard Boddington (1929) Born 8 May 1911, Abbey Terrace, Ramsey; son of Richard Flowers Serjeant, Solicitor, and Beatrice Wilhelmina Samson; m Priscilla Amy (Pam) Stogdon, 15 October 1949, London. BA 1932; MA 1945. **Tutor(s):** E A Benians. **Educ:** St Christopher's School, Eastbourne; Radley College.

SEWELL, Arthur David (1943) Born 19 October 1925, Calcutta, India; son of Sydney Ewart Sewell, Civil Engineer, and Dorothea Marjorie Clyne. **Subject(s):** Mechanical Sciences; BA 1947. **Tutor(s):** S J Bailey. **Johnian Relatives:** son of Sydney Ewart Sewell (1906); cousin of Michael William Sewell (1940); brother of William Musgrave Sewell (1945) and of Anthony Philip Sewell (1952). **Educ:** Merton Court, Footscray; Wellingborough School. **Career:** Research Engineer, Vickers, Newcastle 1947–1950; Research Engineer, GEC Stanmore 1952–1962. Died 1 November 1993.

SEWELL, John Edward (1924) Born 11 August 1904, 263 Hampstead Road, St Pancras, Middlesex; son of John Wright Sewell, Silver Spoon and Fork Maker, and Emma Matilda Hill; m Eve. **Subject(s):** History/English; BA 1926. **Tutor(s):** E A Benians. **Educ:** Victoria London County Council Elementary School, London; Latymer Upper School, Hammersmith. **Career:** Lobby Correspondent, *Daily Telegraph.* **Awards:** Scholarship, SJC. **Publications:** *Parliament in the First Two Years of War*, 1942. Died 14 April 1957.

SEWELL, Michael William (1940) Born 1 February 1922, Kingarth, Whitburn, Durham; son of Thomas Reginald Sewell, Civil Engineer, and Hilda Margaret Dugdale; m Patricia Anne Haithwaite, 1953; 4 children. **Tutor(s):** J M Wordie. **Johnian Relatives:** nephew of Sydney Ewart Sewell (1906); cousin of Arthur David Sewell (1943), William Musgrave Sewell (1945) and of Anthony Philip Sewell (1952). **Educ:** Tonstal Preparatory School, Sunderland; Wellingborough School. **Career:** RA, WWII; Assistant Quarry Manager, rising to Managing Director, Sir Hedworth Williamson's Limeworks until 1982.

SEWELL, Sydney Ewart (1906) Born 28 April 1888, 35 Lansdowne Gardens, Kensington; son of William Sewell, Civil Engineer, and Elizabeth Jane Tait; m Dorothea Marjorie Clyne, 17 July 1924, St John's Church, Putney; 3 sons (Arthur David b 19 October 1925, William Musgrave b 20 August 1927 and Anthony Philip b 8 October 1933). **Subject(s):** Mechanical Sciences; BA 1909; MA 1930. **Tutor(s):** E E Sikes. **Johnian Relatives:** uncle of Michael William Sewell (1940); father of Arthur David Sewell (1943), William Musgrave Sewell (1945) and of Anthony Philip Sewell (1952). **Educ:** Wellingborough School. **Career:** Manager, Engineering Department, Messrs Best and Co Ltd, Madras, India 1911–1915 and 1919–1926; Captain, Volunteer Artillery Battery, Mesopotamia 1915–1916; Assistant Proof and Experimental Officer, Army HQ, India 1917–1919; Assistant Engineer, British Portland Cement Association 1929–1933. Died 14 April 1934.

SEWELL, William Musgrave (1945) Born 20 August 1927, Torquay, Devon; son of Sydney Ewart Sewell, Civil Engineer, and Dorothea

Marjorie Clyne; m Jill Tait, 28 July 1951, St Mary's Church, Whitburn, County Durham; 1 son (Iain Timothy Tait b 2 August 1953), 3 daughters (Elizabeth Jill b 7 February 1956, Alison Jane b 30 March 1960 and Katharine Judith 22 April 1962). **Subject(s):** Mechanical Sciences; BA 1949; MA 1985. **Tutor(s):** S J Bailey; J M Wordie. **Johnian Relatives:** son of Sydney Ewart Sewell (1906); cousin of Michael William Sewell (1940); brother of Arthur David Sewell (1943) and of Anthony Philip Sewell (1952). **Educ:** Merton Court School, Footscray; Wellingborough School. **Career:** Commissioned in Field Survey Regiment, RE 1948–1950; Professional training, British Transport Docks, Humber Ports, then Assistant Docks Engineer, Hull Docks 1950–1961; Director, GKN Foundations Ltd 1961–1969; Administrator, Haiste and Partners (consulting engineers) 1971–1984; Bursar, Chester Cathedral 1985–1991.

SHACKLETON, Clarence Francis (1927) Born 9 May 1909, Crossley Terrace, Hebden Bridge, Yorkshire; son of Francis Shackleton, Cotton Manufacturer, and Jessie Elizabeth Stafford. **Subject(s):** Economics; BA 1930; MA 1934. **Tutor(s):** C W Guillebaud. **Educ:** New College, Harrogate. Died 21 April 1992.

SHACKLETON, Patrick (1944) Born 13 May 1926, 40 Emboug Woengoe, Sourabaya, Java, East Indies; son of Charles Francis Shackleton, Merchant, and Rose Collins. **Tutor(s):** J M Wordie. **Appointments:** RE Cadet, SJC.

SHAHEEN, Medhat Hassan (1945) Born 14 December 1926, Maadi, Cairo, Egypt; son of Hassan Ibrahim Shaheen, Surgeon, and Samira Rifaat. BA 1948; MA 1952. **Tutor(s):** C W Guillebaud. **Educ:** English Private School, Maadi, Egypt; The English School, Cairo, Egypt; Woolwich Polytechnic.

SHAKESHAFT, Dr John Roland (1949) Born 9 December 1929, 53 Swiss Avenue, Chelmsford, Essex; son of Roland Stanley Shakeshaft, Congregational Minister, and Alice Eleanor Johnson. **Subject(s):** Natural Sciences; BA 1952; MA 1956; PhD 1957. **Tutor(s):** W A Deer. **Educ:** Eddington House Preparatory School, Herne Bay; Caterham School. **Career:** Title A Fellow, SJC 1957–1960; Fellow Librarian, St Catharine's College, Cambridge 1961; Assistant Director of Research, Department of Physics, University of Cambridge 1974. **Awards:** Minor Scholarship, SJC 1948.

SHAKESPEAR, John Harnby (1930) Born 12 August 1910, Langley Priory, Castle Donnington, Leicester; son of Charles Bowles Shakespear, Landed Proprietor, and May Foster. **Educ:** Fonthill, East Grinstead; Courtenay Lodge, Abingdon.

SHANLY, Herbert (1912) Born 9 September 1893, 78 Sumatra Road, Hampstead, Middlesex; son of Michael William Shanly, General Caterer, and Mathilde Russo; m Gladys Luke, 10 April 1920, St Edward the Confessor, Golders Green. **Subject(s):** Law; BA 1915; MA 1919. **Tutor(s):** L H K Bushe-Fox. **Educ:** University College School. **Career:** Captain, London Regiment (St Pancras Battalion), then Major, MGC (wounded, Mentioned in Despatches), WWI.

SHANNON, Gerald Cairns (1902) Born 17 October 1883, Kolhapur, Bombay; son of Robert James Shannon, Civil Engineer, and Jane Frances McDowell; m Eva Woods, 14 June 1923, All Saints' Church, Srinagar, Kashmir. **Subject(s):** Classics/History; BA 1905. **Tutor(s):** D MacAlister. **Educ:** High School, Dublin; Bath College. **Career:** Judge and Sessions Judge, Assistant Collector and Magistrate, Bombay 1906–1936; Called to the Bar, Inner Temple 1922. Died 29 December 1952.

SHANNON, Godfrey Eccleston Boyd (1926) Born 14 December 1907, 55 Argyll Road, Kensington, London; son of William Boyd Shannon, Major, Army, and Flora Gertrude Thompson. **Subject(s):** Classics; BA 1929; MA 1938. **Tutor(s):** M P Charlesworth. **Educ:** Radnor School, Redhill; Streete Court, Westgate-on-Sea; Wellington College. **Career:**

Dominions Office 1930; Official Secretary, UK High Commissioner's Office, New Zealand 1939–1941; UK Delegation to various international conferences in London, Geneva, New York, Chicago and Moscow 1944–1948; Deputy UK High Commissioner in Canada 1948–1950; Deputy UK High Commissioner in Calcutta 1952–1956; Assistant Under-Secretary of State, Commonwealth Office 1956–1968; Member, Committee for Exports to Canada 1964–1968; UK Delegation to Commonwealth Finance Ministers' Meetings, Jamica, Montreal and Trinidad 1965–1967; Member, Committee for Exports to Australia 1965–1968. **Appointments:** UK Delegation to UNCTAD 1964; Renter Warden, Dyers' Company 1967–1968; Prime Warden, Dyers' Company 1968–1969. **Awards:** Browne Medal for Greek Epigram, University of Cambridge 1928. **Honours:** CMG 1951. Died September 1989.

SHARDLOW, Ambrose John (1944) Born 27 January 1926, The Vicarage, Wairoa, New Zealand; son of John Ambrose Shardlow, Clerk in Holy Orders, and Joyce Stuhlman; m Janet R M Bisley, 10 September 1965. **Subject(s):** Mechanical Sciences; BA 1947. **Tutor(s):** S J Bailey. **Educ:** Lisvane School, Scarborough; St Peter's School, York.

SHARLAND, Charles Philip Abbott (1932) Born 24 April 1914, 80 Constable Road, Ipswich; son of Alan Abbott Sharland, Lieutenant, Lancashire Regiment, and Eleanor Edwards; m (1) Norma Hill-Spurr, 10 December 1943, Northern Rhodesia, (2) Anne Elizabeth Webb, 28 December 1956, Northern Rhodesia. **Subject(s):** Geography; BA 1936. **Tutor(s):** C W Guillebaud. **Educ:** Braidley, Clifton, Bristol; Repton School, Derby; Brentwood College, Vancouver Island.

SHARMAN, Herbert Guttridge (1919) Born 12 October 1901, Shanghai, China; son of Arthur Henley Sharman, Missionary, and Sarah Kate Herbert. **Tutor(s):** E E Sikes. **Educ:** Collegiate School, Reading; Leighton Park School, Reading.

SHARMAN, John Campton (1940) Born 5 August 1921, The Dingle, Wake Green Road, Moseley, Birmingham; son of William Stanley Sharman, Manufacturer, and Elsie Kate Jones; m Margaret Barham Johnson, 4 March 1946, St Chad's Church, Shrewsbury. **Subject(s):** Modern Languages; BA 1947; MA 1949; DLitt (South Africa), DPhil (South Africa) 1963. **Tutor(s):** C W Guillebaud. **Educ:** College Road Council School; King Edward's High School, Birmingham; University of South Africa.

SHARP, Clifford Graham (1903) Born 12 November 1883, Elmslea, Cheam Road, Sutton, Surrey; son of Harry Nugent Sharp, Stockbroker, and Annie Jenner Tooth; m Margaret Effie Statter; 1 son (Francis Richard b 4 July 1919). BA 1907; MA 1910. **Tutor(s):** C E Graves; J R Tanner. **Johnian Relatives:** son of Harry Nugent Sharp (1876); father of Francis Richard Sharp (1937). **Educ:** Private Tuition. **Career:** Second Lieutenant, The Queen's (Royal West Surrey Regiment) (wounded), WWI; Private Tutor. Died 7 March 1956.

SHARP, Francis Richard (1937) Born 4 July 1919, Shortlands, Seaton; son of Clifford Graham Sharp, Private Tutor, and Margaret Effie Statter. **Subject(s):** Law; BA 1940; MA 1945. **Tutor(s):** C W Guillebaud. **Johnian Relatives:** grandson of Harry Nugent Sharp (1876); son of Clifford Graham Sharp (1903). **Educ:** Leas Court, Canford Cliffs; Durlston Court, Swanage; Bradfield College.

SHARP, Sir Kenneth Johnston (1948) Born 29 December 1926, 1 Strand Road, Carlisle; son of Johnston Sharp, Chartered Accountant, and Ann Routledge; m Barbara Maud Keating, 1955; 1 son. **Subject(s):** Economics; BA 1950; MA 1955; ACA 1955; FCA 1960. **Tutor(s):** C W Guillebaud. **Educ:** Rickerby House, Carlisle; Shrewsbury School. **Career:** Indian Army 1945–1948; TA, 251st (Westmorland and Cumberland Yeomanry) Field Regiment, RA 1948–1962 (Second-in-Command 1959–1962); Partner, Armstrong, Watson & Co, Chartered Accountants 1955–1975; Head, Government Accountancy Service and Accountancy Advisor to DoI 1975–1983; Partner, Baker, Tilly & Co,

Chartered Accountants 1983–1989. **Appointments:** JP, Carlisle 1957–1973; Council Member 1966–1983, Vice-President 1972–1973, Deputy President 1973–1974, President 1974–1975, Institute of Chartered Accountants; Master, Company of Chartered Accountants in England and Wales 1979–1980; Member, Governing Body, Shrewsbury School 1976–1995. **Honours:** TD 1960; Kt 1984. **Publications:** *The Family Business and the Companies Act 1967*; articles in professional accountancy press.

SHARP, Thomas Hicks (1910) Born 4 August 1892, Brooklyn, May Pen, Clarendon, Jamaica; son of Francis Greenwich Sharp, Planter, and Florence Evelyn; m Kathleen Chandler, 1920 (d 1947); 2 daughters (Eileen and Prudence). **Subject(s):** Mathematics; BA 1913. **Tutor(s):** L H K Bushe-Fox. **Educ:** Potsdam School, Jamaica. **Career:** Founder, Central Jamaica Building Society; Lieutenant, Artists' Rifles 1914–1916; Admitted Solicitor, Supreme Court of Judicature, Jamaica 1917; Lawyer, Jamaica 1917–1964. Died 15 May 1964.

SHARP, William Henry Cartwright (CARTWRIGHT SHARP) (1902) Born 19 March 1883, 170 Bristol Road, Edgbaston, Birmingham; son of William George Graham Sharp, Confectioner, and Sarah Cartwright. **Subject(s):** Classics; BA 1905; MA 1909; LLB 1907; KC 1934. **Tutor(s):** C E Graves; J R Tanner. **Educ:** King Edward VI's School, Birmingham. **Career:** Called to the Bar, Inner Temple 1907; Recorder, Banbury 1936; Recorder, Wolverhampton 1938–1950. Died 20 December 1950.

SHARP, Lieutenant Colonel Wright Granville Maynard (1924) Born 5 January 1906, The Pygmalion, 3 Market Street, Cleckheaton, York; son of Walter Sharp, Clothier and Outfitter, and Adelina Gertrude Wright; m Margaret Vincent, 1935; 2 daughters. **Subject(s):** Economics; BA 1927; MA 1931. **Tutor(s):** E A Benians. **Educ:** Cleckheaton Secondary School; Ashville College, Harrogate. **Career:** Lecturer in Economics, West Riding Technical Institutes 1929–1934; Battery Captain, 68 Anti-Tank Regiment, RA 1939–1942; Staff Captain and DAQMG, Belfast Area 1942–1943; Senior British Staff Officer, Economics Section, Allied Control Commission, Italy 1943–1944; Chief Economics and Supply Officer, Military Government, Austria 1944–1945; MP for Spen Valley Division, West Riding, Yorkshire 1945–1950; Chairman, Select Committee of Estimates Sub-Committee 1946–1948; Parliamentary Private Secretary, Ministry of Civil Aviation 1946, and to Minister of Works 1947–1950. **Appointments:** Chairman, Spenborough Housing and Town Planning Committee 1935–1939; Honorary Secretary, Spen Valley Divisional Labour Party 1936–1939; Keymer Parish Councillor 1969–1983; County Council, East Sussex 1970–1974; Member, Cuckfield Rural District Council 1971–1974; Mid-Sussex District Council 1973–1976; County Council, West Sussex 1973–1985. Died 1997.

SHARPE, Eric Ellis (1926) Born 11 October 1907, West View, Gawthorpe, Ossett, Yorkshire; son of Hinchcliffe Sharpe, Master Baker, and Marian Ellis. **Subject(s):** History/Geography; BA 1929; MA 1933. **Tutor(s):** E A Benians. **Educ:** Southdale Council School, Ossett; Ossett Grammar School.

SHARPLEY, Roger Fielding Anthony (1949) Born 17 May 1929, The Martins, Chipping Campden, Gloucestershire; son of Reginald Sharpley, Landscape Artist, and Gladys Muriel Fielding. BA 1953. **Tutor(s):** G C L Bertram. **Educ:** Walton Lodge Preparatory School, Clevedon; Shrewsbury School. Died 12 February 1999.

SHAUGHNESSY, Charles Stephen (1918) American Student.

SHAW, Arthur (1915) Born 25 April 1896, 13 St Mark's Terrace, Moorlands Road, Dewsbury, Yorkshire; son of William Henry Shaw, Chartered Accountant, and Frances Hey; m Rosamund Taylor. **Subject(s):** History; BA 1922; MA 1926. **Tutor(s):** L H K Bushe-Fox. **Educ:** Wheelwright Grammar School; Sedbergh School. **Career:** Second Lieutenant, Yorkshire Light Infantry 1915–1918; Chartered Accountant; Partner, W H Shaw and

Son, Dewsbury 1923. **Awards:** Lupton and Hebblethwaite Exhibition, SJC 1915. **Honours:** MC 1917. Died June 1964.

SHAW, Brian Worsley Bolton (BOLTON SHAW) (1944) Born 22 February 1927, 3 Birch Polygon, Rusholme, Manchester; son of William Bolton Shaw, Consulting Engineer, and Maggie Worsley; m Delys Muriel Trestrail, 13 March 1965, Putley Methodist Church; 1 son (Michael b 28 November 1967). **Subject(s):** Mechanical Sciences; BA 1947; MA 1951; MSc (Cranfield) 1972; MIMechE; CEng; MRAeS. **Tutor(s):** C W Guillebaud. **Educ:** Birchfields Municipal School, Manchester; Manchester Grammar School; Cranfield Institute of Technology. **Career:** Engineering Officer, RAF 1952–1968; Research Scientist, Aeronautical Research Laboratories, Melbourne, Australia 1968–1991.

SHAW, Donald Curtis (1943) Born 8 July 1925, 25 Hillsborough Place, Hillsborough, Sheffield; son of Charles Shaw, Industrial Transport Manager, and Elsie Curtis. **Subject(s):** Mathematics; BA 1946; MA 1950. **Tutor(s):** S J Bailey. **Educ:** Fulwood Church of England School; Thurgoland Church of England School; Penistone Grammar School. **Awards:** Baylis Scholarship, SJC 1943.

SHAW, Douglas Jamieson (1946) Born 18 April 1926, 323 Loop Street, Pietermaritzburg, Natal, South Africa; son of Frank Routledge Shaw, Advocate, and Catherine Wallace Jamieson. **Subject(s):** Classics/Law; BA 1948; LLB 1949; LLM 1985; QC 1959. **Tutor(s):** R L Howland; F Thistlethwaite. **Educ:** Cordwalles Preparatory School, Pietermaritzburg; Michaelhouse, Balgowan, Natal; Natal University College, Pietermaritzburg. **Career:** South African Artillery 1944–1946; Called to the Bar, Inner Temple 1948; Admitted as an advocate in South Africa 1949; Barrister, South Africa. **Awards:** Certificate of Honour in the Bar Final 1948. **Publications:** *Admiralty Jurisdiction and Pravia.*

SHAW, The Revd Douglas William David (1945) Born 25 June 1928, 39 Palmerston Place, Edinburgh; son of William David Shaw, Wine Merchant, and Nansie Smart. **Subject(s):** Modern and Medieval Languages/Law; BA 1948; MA 1978; LLB (Edinburgh) 1951; BD (Edinburgh) 1960; Honorary DD (Glasgow) 1991; WS 1951; BD 1960. **Tutor(s):** C W Guillebaud. **Johnian Relatives:** uncle of Donald Hope Shaw (1969). **Educ:** Edinburgh Academy; Loretto School; Ashbury College, Ottawa, Canada; King's Collegiate School, Windsor, Nova Scotia. **Career:** Partner, Davidson & Syme, Solicitors 1953–1957; Ordained Minister, Church of Scotland 1960; Assistant Minister, St George's West Church, Edinburgh 1960–1963; Official Observer of World Alliance of Reformed Churches at Second Vatican Council, Rome 1962; Lecturer in Divinity 1963–1979, Dean, Faculty of Divinity, and Principal, New College 1974–1978, University of Edinburgh; Professor of Divinity, St Mary's College 1979–1991; Croall Lecturer, New College, Edinburgh 1983; Dean, Faculty of Divinity, University of St Andrews, University of Edinburgh 1983–1986; Principal, St Mary's College 1986–1992; Fraternal Delegate, Synod of Bishops of Europe, Rome 1991; Alexander Robertson Lecturer, University of Glasgow 1991–1992. **Appointments:** WS Edinburgh 1953–1957; Honorary Chaplain, Royal and Ancient Golf Club of St Andrews. **Publications:** *Who is God?*, SCM Press, London, 1968; *The Dissuaders*, SCM Press, London, 1978; *The Catholic Church from 1648 to 1870*, translated from German: F Heyer, 1969; (ed) *In Divers Manners – a St Mary's Miscellany*, 1990; (ed) *Dimensions – Literary and Theological*, 1992; (ed) *Theology in Scotland*, 1994 onwards; various articles in theological journals.

SHAW, George Douglas (1919) Born 9 September 1901, Albion House, Bath Street, Ilkeston, Derbyshire; son of John Vincent Shaw, Physician and Surgeon, and Edith Mary Blackburn. **Subject(s):** Law; BA 1923; MA 1927; LLB 1923. **Tutor(s):** E A Benians. **Educ:** Kindergarten School, Swadlincote; Kindergarten School, Nuneaton; King Edward VI Grammar School, Nuneaton; Coombe Hill School, Kings Langley; Wycliffe College, Stonehouse. **Career:** RA Officer Cadet School 1917; 6(A) Reserve Brigade, RFA, Glasgow 1917; Lieutenant, 218th Brigade, RFA 1917–1919.

SHAW, John (1935) Born 11 January 1916, 28 Wentworth Road, York; son of Frank Tunaley Shaw, Locomotive Engineer, and Mary Eliza Prescott. **Subject(s):** History; BA 1938; MA 1942. **Tutor(s):** J S Boys Smith. **Educ:** King's School, Peterborough. **Awards:** Exhibition, SJC 1934.

SHAW, Julius Brinkley (1901) Born 21 March 1882, 25 Orlando Road, Clapham, Surrey; son of James Shaw, Musician, and Charlotte Elizabeth James. **Tutor(s):** C E Graves; J R Tanner. **Educ:** St Paul's Cathedral Choir School, London; Sutton Valence School, Kent.

SHAW, Michael Mellodew (1945) Born 5 November 1927, Wynfield, High Grove, Greenfield, Saddleworth, Yorkshire; son of John Mellodew Shaw, Accountant and Branch Inspector, Cotton Combine, and Alice Holden Taylor, Librarian; m Barbara Downe, 1954; 2 sons (Tony b 1956 and David b 1958), 3 daughters (Gillian b 1955, Anne b 1955 and Elizabeth b 1958). **Subject(s):** Mathematics; BA 1948; MA 1973. **Tutor(s):** J M Wordie. **Educ:** Friezland Council School, Grasscroft; King Street Methodist School, Leigh; Leigh Grammar School. **Career:** Ministry of Defence 1948–1984; Civil Aviation Authority 1984–1987.

SHAW, Philip Malcolm (1939) Born 17 December 1921, 58 Thornhill Avenue, Huddersfield; son of Herbert Shaw, General Manager, Constructional Engineering Company, and Lilian Maude Senior; m Audrey. **Subject(s):** Natural Sciences; BA 1942; MA 1947; DipChemEng 1949; MBIM; FRIC; FIChemE. **Tutor(s):** J M Wordie. **Johnian Relatives:** father of Nicholas Alastair Shaw (1972). **Educ:** Oakes Elementary School, Huddersfield; Royds Hall Grammar School, Huddersfield; Manchester Grammar School; University College London. **Career:** Managing Director, William Blythe & Co Ltd; Director, Hickson & Welch (Holdings) Ltd. Died 2 August 2003.

SHAW, Ronald (1930) Born 1 August 1912, 12 Clarksfield Road, Oldham; son of Granville Shaw, Cotton Dealer, and Alice Maders; m Margaret; 3 children. BA 1934; MA 1937; FFARCS 1954. **Tutor(s):** M P Charlesworth. **Educ:** The University School, Southport; Sedbergh School; St Mary's Hospital, London. **Career:** Maxillofacial unit, Ranikhet, India, and mobile neurosurgical unit, Dirapur, WWII; GP, Leamington Spa; Consultant Anaesthetist, Warwick and Warneford Hospital. Died 30 March 2002.

SHAW, Wilfred (1916) Born 12 December 1897, Aston Manor, Warwickshire; son of Isaac Shaw, Metal Manufacturer, and Amelia Alice Pridey; m Frances Anne Grice, 30 June 1931, St Peter's Church, Caversham; 3 sons (John Humphrey Wilfred b 7 May 1932, Andrew Paul b 12 October 1938 and Peter Keith b 29 July 1941), 1 daughter (Jane Frances b 16 April 1935). **Subject(s):** Natural Sciences/Medicine; BA 1919; MA 1924; BChir 1921; MB 1924; MD 1928; LRCP 1921; MRCS 1921; FRCS 1923; FRCOG 1932. **Tutor(s):** R P Gregory. **Johnian Relatives:** father of John Humphrey Wilfred Shaw (1950) and of Andrew Paul Shaw (1958). **Educ:** Birchfield Road Council School; King Edward's School, Aston; King Edward's School, Birmingham; St Bartholomew's Hospital, London; Postgraduate study in Vienna, Berlin, Graz, Munich, and Dublin. **Career:** Surgeon-probationer on a destroyer, RN, WWI; Midwifery Intern; House Surgeon; Chief Assistant to the Department of Obstetrics and Gynaecology, St Bartholomew's Hospital, London; Resident Assistant Physician Accoucheur, St Bartholomew's Hospital 1926–1931 (first to hold this post), elected to Honorary staff from 1931; Berryfield House Maternity Hospital, Bradford-on-Avon, Wiltshire 1939–1945; Surgeon in charge of Gynaecological and Obstetrical Department, St Bartholomew's Hospital 1946–1953; Gynaecologist to St Andrew's Hospital, Dollis Hill, London 1946–1953. **Appointments:** Cattlin Research Fellow, St Bartholomew's Hospital; Arnott Demonstrator, RCS 1933; Member, Museum Committee, RCOG; Examiner in midwifery for Oxford, Cambridge, Central Midwives Board, London Conjoint Board, University of London and RCOG. **Awards:** Open Scholarship, SJC 1915; Foundation Scholarship, SJC 1918; Hare Exhibition, SJC 1918; Wright's Prize, SJC 1918; Shuter Scholarship; Matthews Duncan Prize and Gold Medal;

Lawrence Research Scholarship and Gold Medal; Raymond Horton-Smith Prize, University of Cambridge 1929; Jacksonian Prize, RCS 1931. **Publications:** *Textbook of Gynaecology*, 1936; *Textbook of Midwifery*, 1943; *Textbook for Midwives*, 1948; *Textbook of Operative Gynaecology*, 1954; numerous papers on obstetrics and gynaecology including pathology of ovarian tumours and prolapse surgery. Died 9 December 1953.

SHAWCROSS, Cyril Wilfred (1921) Born 16 July 1903, Oak Mount, Stockport Road, Cheadle Heath, Stockport, Cheshire; son of Frederick Wilfred Shawcross, Bank Manager, and Edith Annie Craig; m Irene Annie Catherine Smithson; 1 son (Francis Wilfred b 3 November 1936). **Subject(s):** Natural Sciences; BA 1924; MA 1928. **Tutor(s):** B F Armitage. **Johnian Relatives:** nephew of Herbert William Shawcross (1886); father of Francis Wilfred Shawcross (1957). **Educ:** Queen Elizabeth's Grammar School, Blackburn; Rossall School. **Career:** Commissioned, Welch Regiment 1939; Political Officer of Kufra Oasis during North African Campaign, then transferred to Iraqi Army; Senior Partner, Burt, Evans & Shawcross, Ross on Wye; Coroner, South Herefordshire. **Appointments:** President, Herefordshire, Breconshire, and Radnorshire Incorporated Law Society. Died 14 October 1969.

SHEARER, Ernest James Mollison (1931) Born 25 January 1910, 29 Broad Street, Kirkwall, Orkney; son of Ernest Shearer, Professor of Agriculture, and Jane Smith Tate; BSc (Edinburgh) 1931. **Tutor(s):** C W Guillebaud. **Educ:** Kirkwall Grammar School; Edinburgh Academy; University of Edinburgh. **Awards:** Scholarship, SJC.

SHEARME, John Cornwall (1944) Born 9 May 1926, 9 Trapps Lane, Luton, Bedfordshire; son of John Andrews Shearme, Manager, Westminster Bank, and Muriel Edith Moss. BA 1948; MA 1950. **Tutor(s):** J M Wordie. **Educ:** Mount House School, Plymouth; Blundell's School, Tiverton.

SHEEHAN, Maurice (1940) Born 18 January 1905, 2 The Crescent, Carlisle; son of Patrick Sheehan, Medical Practitioner, and Eliza Leeming. **Subject(s):** English; MB (Manchester) 1926. **Tutor(s):** C W Guillebaud. **Educ:** Carlisle High School; Carlisle Grammar School; Manchester University; London University. **Career:** Medical practice 1926–1939.

SHELTON, Laurence Hugh (1910) Born 17 November 1891, The Rectory, Taynton, Gloucestershire; son of Norman Wilfrid Shelton, Clerk in Holy Orders, and Mary Georgina Kirby; m Winifred. BA 1913; MA 1920. **Tutor(s):** J R Tanner. **Educ:** Hereford Cathedral School. **Career:** Barrister-at-Law; Nigerian Administration Services 1914. Died 2 May 1978.

SHEPHERD, Cyril George (1929) Born 5 September 1910, Boothby Pagnell, Grantham; son of James Shepherd, Chauffeur, and Agnes Louisa Vaughan. **Subject(s):** English/Modern and Medieval Languages; BA 1933. **Tutor(s):** M P Charlesworth. **Educ:** Boothby Pagnell School; Allington School; King's School, Grantham. **Awards:** Newcome Exhibition, SJC 1929.

SHEPHERD, The Revd Edward Hoskins (1909) Born 21 May 1890, Walford, Bedfordshire; son of William Richard Shepherd, Clerk in Holy Orders, and Catherine Josephine Lisle. BA 1912; MA 1916. **Tutor(s):** J R Tanner. **Educ:** Pocklington School. **Career:** Leeds Clergy School; Deacon 1914; Curate, Heckmondwike 1914–1918; Priest 1915; Temporary CF, 4th Class, RACD 1918–1922; Vicar, West Pinchbeck 1923–1925; Rector, Barberton, Transvaal, South Africa 1926–1932; Vicar, Illingworth, Yorkshire 1933–1934; Rector, Aliwal North, Diocese of Grahamstown (Rural Dean 1939–1940) 1934–1940; Rector, Graaff Reinet 1940–1942; CF, South Africa 1942–1946; Vicar, St Columba, Durban, Natal 1946.

SHEPHERD, Dr Francis William (1926) Born 6 December 1906, Cyprus Road, Magdala Road, Nottingham; son of William Shepherd, Bank Manager, and Martha Annie Ringrose; m Mary Hyde, 1965. **Subject(s):** Natural Sciences; BA 1929; MA 1933; BChir 1933; MB 1937; BSc (London) 1929; MRCS 1933; LRCP 1933; FRCS 1937. **Tutor(s):** M P Charlesworth. **Educ:** The High School, Nottingham. **Career:** House Posts, Hampstead, Ilford 1937–1938; Resident Surgical Officer, Huddersfield and Consultant in General Surgery 1938–1971; Honorary Assistant Surgeon, Huddersfield 1947. **Appointments:** President, Huddersfield Medical Society. Died 21 August 1978.

SHEPHERD, Leslie James Vaughan (1925) Born 15 November 1907, Boothby Pagnell, Grantham, Lincolnshire; son of James Shepherd, Mechanic, and Agnes Louisa Vaughan. **Subject(s):** History; BA 1928. **Tutor(s):** E A Benians. **Educ:** Allington Elementary School; The King's School, Grantham. **Awards:** Newcome Exhibition, SJC 1925.

SHEPHERD, Robert John (1934) Born 13 October 1915, 26 Ormidale Terrace, Edinburgh; son of Robert Francis Shepherd, WS, and Mabel Bedford Wilson; m Rhoda Stevenson, 15 June 1948, Edinburgh. BA 1937; LLB (Edinburgh). **Tutor(s):** C W Guillebaud. **Educ:** Edinburgh Academy. **Career:** Shepherd & Wedderburn WS (Solicitors). Died 20 March 1996.

SHEPHERD, Professor Ronald Malcolm Henry (1945) Born 21 December 1925, St Peter's Rectory, St Kitts, British West Indies; son of Henry Curll Shepherd, Clerk in Holy Orders, and Evelyn Isabel Smith; m Dorothy Henry, 1951; 1 son (David Henry), 1 daughter (Diana Evelyn). **Subject(s):** Classics; BA 1948; MA 1952. **Tutor(s):** J M Wordie; R L Howland. **Educ:** Harrison College, Barbados. **Career:** Lecturer in Greek, Department of Classics, University College 1949, Assistant Professor 1956, Associate Professor 1962, Professor of Classics 1965–1991 (Emeritus 1991), University of Toronto. **Appointments:** Registrar 1961–1970, Acting Principal 1980–1981, Speaker, Council 1989–1999, University College, University of Toronto; Chairman of Academic Board (Senate), Governing Council, University of Toronto 1971–1972 and 1979–1981. **Awards:** Barbados Government Scholarship 1944; John Stewart of Rannoch Scholarship in Greek and Latin, University of Cambridge 1946; Exhibition, SJC 1946; Major Foundation Scholarship, SJC 1947; Sesquicentennial Award for Distinguished Teaching and Service in University of Toronto 1977.

SHEPHERD, Roy Wootton (1946) Born 18 December 1924, Bourne Villas, Audlem, Nantwich, Cheshire; son of Richard Shepherd, Methodist Minister, and Emma Jane Beatrice Wootton. BA 1948; MA 1953; Diploma of Agriculture 1949. **Tutor(s):** G C L Bertram. **Educ:** Gilbert Heathcote's Council School, Chesterfield; Chesterfield Grammar School; Alford Grammar School; Kingswood School. **Career:** Sub-Lieutenant, RNVR 1943–1946; Norfolk Agricultural Station, Sprowston, Norwich 1949–1952; General Agriculture Advisory Officer, NAAS, Norfolk Agricultural Station 1952–1954; Bridgets Experimental Husbandry Farm 1954–1960; Farm Director, High Mowthorpe 1960–1963; Farmer, Allenford Farms, Damerham 1963–2000.

SHEPHERD, The Revd William Lisle (1906) Born 10 July 1887, Penyvan, Llandogo, Trelleck, Monmouthshire; son of William Richard Shepherd, Clerk in Holy Orders, and Catherine Josephine Lisle. **Subject(s):** Natural Sciences/Theology; BA 1909; MA 1913. **Tutor(s):** J R Tanner. **Johnian Relatives:** son of William Richard Shepherd (1879). **Educ:** Pocklington School. **Career:** Ordained Deacon 1911; Curate, Dewsbury Moor 1911–1913; Ordained Priest 1912; Curate, All Saints, Leeds 1913–1914; Curate, Scarborough 1914–1919; Rector, East Acklam 1919–1923; Vicar, Great Hormead and Rector, Little Hormead 1923–1930; Vicar, St Mary, Halifax 1930–1935; Vicar, Ripponden with Rishworth 1935–1941; Vicar, Holme on Spalding Moor, Yorkshire 1941–1953. Died 8 May 1953.

SHEPPARD, William George (1906) Born 16 January 1887, 6 Beatrice Road, St James', Bermondsey, Surrey; son of John Sheppard, Hatter, and Elizabeth Abigail Sullivan. **Subject(s):** Natural Sciences; BA 1909. **Tutor(s):** J R Tanner. **Educ:** Aske's School, Hatcham. **Career:** Science Master under London County Council 1909–1925; RAF Educational Service 1925–1947. Died 3 November 1952.

SHEPPERSON, Professor George Albert (1940) Born 7 January 1922, 3 Belham Road, Peterborough; son of Albert Edward Shepperson, Engineer's Fitter, and Bertha Agnes Jennings, Domestic Servant; m Joyce Irene Cooper, 1952; 1 daughter. **Subject(s):** English/History; BA 1943; MA 1948; CertEd (Cantab) 1948; Honorary Doctor (York) 1987, (Edinburgh) 1991; DLitt *honoris causa* (Malawi) 2002. **Tutor(s):** C W Guillebaud. **Educ:** Lincoln Road Council Boys' School, Peterborough; The King's School, Peterborough. **Career:** Commissioned, Northamptonshire Regiment; Seconded to the King's African Rifles, served in Kenya, Tanganyika, Ceylon, India and Burma 1943–1946; Lecturer in Imperial and American History 1948, Senior Lecturer in Imperial and American History 1960, Reader in Imperial and American History 1961, William Robertson Professor of Commonwealth and American History 1963–1986 (Emeritus 1986), Dean, Faculty of Arts 1974–1977, University of Edinburgh; Joint Editor, *Oxford Studies in African Affairs* 1969–1985. **Appointments:** Visiting Professor, Roosevelt and Chicago Universities 1959; Visiting Professor, Makerere College, Uganda 1962; Visiting Professor, Dalhousie University, Halifax, Nova Scotia 1968–1969; Chairman, Mungo Park Bicentenary Committee 1971; Chairman, British Association for American Studies 1971–1974; Chairman, David Livingstone Documentation Project 1973–1989; Chairman, Commonwealth Institute, Scotland 1973–1989; Member, Marshall Aid Commemoration Commission 1976–1988; Visiting Professor, Rhode Island College 1984; Visiting Scholar, WEB DuBois Institute for Afro-American Research, Harvard University 1986–1987; Honorary Fellow, Educational Institute of Scotland 1990. **Awards:** Munsteven Exhibition, SJC; Scholarship, SJC 1942. **Honours:** CBE 1989. **Publications:** (with T Price) *Independent African: John Chilembwe and the Nyasaland Rising of 1915*, Edinburgh University Press, 1958 (6th edn 1987); *David Livingstone and the Rovuma*, Edinburgh University Press, 1964; many articles and chapters in learned journals, collaborative volumes and encyclopaedias.

SHERRARD, Francis Raymond George Nason (1919) Born 20 August 1893, The Laurels, Hailsham, Sussex; son of David John Sherrard, Physician and Surgeon, and Sarah Faulconer. **Subject(s):** Natural Sciences; BA 1921. **Tutor(s):** E A Benians. **Educ:** Arlington House, Brighton; Brighton Grammar School.

SHEWELL, Captain Henry Anthony Lampen (1923) Born 15 March 1899, Padreda, Littleham, Exmouth, Devon; son of Harry Williamson McKan Shewell, Major, RA, and Ethel Frances Lampen; m Alda Evelyn Hoare, 29 January 1929, Crediton. **Tutor(s):** E E Sikes. **Educ:** Bramdean School, Exeter; Naish House, Burnham; Cheltenham College; RMA, Woolwich. **Career:** Commissioned, RE, served in France 1918; Lieutenant, RE 1919.

SHIACH, Gordon Leslie Kemp (1932) Born 31 August 1913, Llanishan, Glamorganshire; son of Samuel Allan Shiach, Medical Practitioner, and Catherine Leslie Kemp; m Lucie de Freitas. **Subject(s):** History/Law; BA 1935. **Tutor(s):** E A Benians. **Educ:** Wells House, Malvern; Chateau d'Oex; Brockhurst, Church Stretton; Haileybury College. Died 30 December 1948.

SHILLAN, Clement Archibald (1919) Born 22 April 1902, 65 Durham Road, Manor Park East Ham, Essex; son of Archibald William Shillan, Company Director, and Lizzie Osman Downes. **Subject(s):** Economics/Law; BA 1923; MA 1954; LLB 1923. **Tutor(s):** E A Benians. **Educ:** Central Secondary School, West Ham; The Leys School, Cambridge. Died 16 May 1968.

SHILLITO, Norman Wholey (Melbury) (1912) Born 26 July 1893, 2 Mayfield Road, Handsworth, Staffordshire; son of Henry Shillito, Medical Practitioner, and Elizabeth Wholey; m Alma Littlebury, 12 January 1918, Hampstead. **Subject(s):** History; BA 1919; MA 1922. **Tutor(s):** R P Gregory. **Educ:** Mill Hill School. **Career:** Second Lieutenant, RE, WWI; Central Insurance Company. **Honours:** MC 1917. Died 10 March 1968.

SHIPLEY, William Johnson (1943) Born 8 November 1925, 60 Westgate, Driffield, Yorkshire; son of Edwin Shipley, Grocer, and Bessie Johnson. **Subject(s):** Mechanical Sciences; BA 1946; MA 1978. **Tutor(s):** S J Bailey. **Educ:** Driffield Church of England School; Bridlington School. **Career:** Head of Examinations, Bridlington School.

SHIVDASAMI, Hassamal Baharmal (1911) Born 1 September 1891, Hyderabad, Bombay Presidency, India; son of Baharmal Lilaram Shivdasami, Judicial Officer, and Amolbai Jethmal Chandiramani. **Subject(s):** Mathematics; BA 1913; MA 1919. **Tutor(s):** E E Sikes. **Educ:** Elphistone College, Bombay, India. **Career:** Assistant Collector, Magistrate, and Cantonment Magistrate, Bombay, Indian Civil Service 1914–1922.

SHORE, Professor Lewis Rudall (1908) Born 16 February 1889, 13 Hill Side, Crouch Hill, Upper Holloway, Middlesex; son of Thomas William Shore, Physician, and Mary Elizabeth Sargent; m Christina McCallum, 29 June 1921, St Margaret's, Putney. **Subject(s):** Natural Sciences; BA 1911; MA 1919; MB 1919; BChir 1919; MD 1933; MRCS; LRCP 1913; MRCP 1921; DPH 1925; FRSM. **Tutor(s):** J R Tanner. **Johnian Relatives:** brother of Thomas Henry Gostwyck Shore (1906). **Educ:** Dulwich College; St Bartholomew's Hospital. **Career:** Captain, RAMC (wounded twice, Mentioned in Despatches) 1914–1919; Senior Lecturer in Anatomy, Witwatersrand University; Lecturer in Anatomy, House Surgeon and Casualty Physician, St Bartholomew's Hospital; University Demonstrator in Anatomy 1933–1936; Professor in Anatomy, University of Hong Kong 1939. **Awards:** Scholarship, SJC. **Honours:** MC. **Publications:** Medical texts in *Journal of Anatomy, British Journal of Surgery, St Bartholomew's Hospital Reports*. Died 9 February 1950.

SHORE, Dr Thomas Henry Gostwyck (1906) Born 21 June 1887, 13 Hill Side, Crouch Hill, Upper Holloway, Middlesex; son of Thomas William Shore, Physician, and Mary Elizabeth Sargent; m Viola Edith Hoare, 12 September 1925, St Bartholomew the Great, Smithfield. **Subject(s):** Natural Sciences; BA 1909; MB 1913; BChir 1913; MRCS; LRCP 1911; MRCP 1914; FRCP 1927. **Tutor(s):** J R Tanner. **Johnian Relatives:** brother of Lewis Rudall Shore (1908). **Educ:** Dulwich College. **Career:** House Physician, St Bartholomew's Hospital 1912–1913; Demonstrator in Pathology, St Bartholomew's Hospital 1914–1919; Captain, RAMC 1917–1919; Museum Curator 1919; Casualty Physician 1920–1922; Assistant Physician, Queen's Hospital for Children 1920–1923. **Awards:** Lawrence Research Scholarship, St Bartholomew's Hospital 1913. **Publications:** Articles in medical journals. Died 17 November 1961.

SHORE, Dr Thomas Leonard Hall (1927) Born 11 September 1909, Byron's Lodge, Grantchester, Cambridgeshire; son of Lewis Erle Shore, Fellow and Junior Bursar, SJC, and Agatha Catherine Hall; m Madeleine Pearce, 26 August 1939, Holy Trinity, Kingsway, London. **Subject(s):** Natural Sciences; BA 1931; MA 1936; BChir 1936; MB 1937; MRCS; LRCP. **Tutor(s):** M P Charlesworth. **Johnian Relatives:** son of Lewis Erle Shore (1882). **Educ:** Rugby School. **Career:** Physician, Taunton and Somerset, and Bridgwater and District General Hospitals; Consultant Physician, West Somerset Hospital Group; Major, RAMC 1942–1946. Died 2 June 1980.

SHORROCKS, Derek Martyn Marsh (1946) Born 31 December 1924, Hurst House, Heskin, Chorley, Lancashire; son of David Martyn Shorrocks, Schoolmaster, and Gertrude Jane Marsh; m Patricia, 1 son (Nicholas), 2 daughters (Sarah and Deborah). **Subject(s):** Classics; BA 1948; MA 1953; Diploma in Archive Administration (Liverpool); FSA 1982. **Tutor(s):** R L Howland. **Educ:** Walkden Moor School; Manchester Grammar School. **Career:** Deputy County Archivist 1957–1977, County Archivist 1978–1988, Somerset County Council. **Awards:** Patchett Scholarship, SJC 1942. **Publications:** *Visitation 1594* and *Smale Booke 1593–4*, Somerset Record Society. Died 10 April 2001.

SHORT, The Revd John Martin (1906) Born 25 July 1887, Bitchfield, Grantham, Lincolnshire; son of Martin Francis Short, Clerk in Holy Orders, and Alice Grummitt. **Subject(s):** Theology; BA 1909; MA 1913. **Tutor(s):** J R Tanner. **Educ:** The Grammar School, Grantham. **Career:** Ordained Deacon 1912; Curate, Redditch 1912–1918; Ordained Priest 1913; Temporary CF, 4th Class, RACD 1918–1920; Vicar, Gezina, Transvaal 1920–1923; Vicar, Nylstroom 1923–1928; Rector, St Paul, Port Elizabeth 1928–1933; Priest Associate, St Mary's Collegiate Church, Port Elizabeth 1928–1933; Rector, St Katherine, Uitenhage 1933–1942; Canon, Grahamstown Cathedral 1938–1942; Archdeacon and Rector, Cradock 1942–1946; Vicar, Leonard Stanley, Stonehouse, Gloucestershire 1947.

SHORTO, Harry Leonard (1937) Born 25 September 1919, 12 Hamfrith Road, Forest Gate; son of Charles Percival Shorto, Export Manager, and Mary Lockyer; m Joyce Lingford 1953; 1 son (Roderick), 1 daughter (Anna). **Subject(s):** Modern and Medieval Languages; BA 1940; MA 1948. **Tutor(s):** C W Guillebaud. **Educ:** Clark's College, Forest Gate Branch; Royal Masonic School, Bushey. **Career:** Army 1939–1945; Lecturer, Department of Languages and Cultures of South-East Asia and the Islands 1948–1964, Reader 1964–1971, SOAS; Professor of Mon-Khmer Studies, University of London 1971–1984. **Awards:** Major Scholarship, SJC 1936. **Publications:** *Dictionary of Modern Spoken Mon*, 1962; *Dictionary of the Mon Inscriptions from the Sixth to the Sixteenth Centuries*, 1971. Died 30 July 1995.

SHRUBBS, The Revd Eric Gordon (1923) Born 19 February 1904, 4 Emmanuel Road, Cambridge; son of Henry Shrubbs, Clerk in Holy Orders, and Maud Ellen Allen; m Billie; 1 son (Philip), 1 daughter (Lynette). BA 1926; MA 1936. **Tutor(s):** E A Benians. **Educ:** Merchant Taylors' School, London; Ripon Hall, Oxford. **Career:** Master, Brighton Preparatory School 1927; Colonial Service, Northern Rhodesia 1930; Principal, Government School, Aden 1946; Deacon 1956; Director of Education, Aden; Curate, Beccles 1956–1958; Rector, Lawshall, Suffolk 1958. **Appointments:** Chairman, Melford Rural District Council; Member, West Suffolk County Council. **Awards:** Exhibition, SJC. **Honours:** MBE 1950. Died 27 June 1964.

SHUKER, Henry Webb (1919) Born 2 February 1900, Tymawr, Towyn, Merionethshire; son of Herbert Henry Shuker, Gentleman Farmer, and Mary Isabel Jones; m Agnes Warden Frew, 7 September 1927, Westbourne Church, Glasgow; 1 son (Raymond). BA 1922. **Tutor(s):** E E Sikes. **Educ:** Mill Mead, Shrewsbury; Oundle School. Died 2 February 1977.

SIBLY, John (1938) Born 30 April 1920, Wycliffe College, Stonehouse, Gloucestershire; son of Thomas Mervyn Sibly, Schoolmaster, and Mary Shepherd; 3 sons (Richard b 1948, Paul b 1950 and Franklin b 1957). **Subject(s):** English; BA 1941; MA 1945. **Tutor(s):** C W Guillebaud. **Johnian Relatives:** son of Thomas Mervyn Sibly (1904); cousin of John Dawson Bulpin Williams (1940); cousin, once removed, of Alain Dominic Dawson Williams (1974). **Educ:** Wycliffe College, Stonehouse; Dauntsey's School, West Lavington. **Career:** Lecturer in English, Makerere College, Kampala, Uganda; Senior Lecturer, Birmingham Polytechnic. Died 25 May 1979.

SIBLY, Thomas Mervyn (1904) Born 21 February 1885, Stonehouse, Gloucestershire; son of George William Sibly, Schoolmaster, and Alice Kate Pillman; m Mary Shepherd; 1 son (John b 30 April 1920), 2 daughters (Mary b 1922 and Edith Mary b and d 1927). **Subject(s):** Natural Sciences; BA 1907; MA 1911. **Tutor(s):** C E Graves; J R Tanner. **Johnian Relatives:** father of John Sibly (1938); cousin, once removed, of John Dawson Bulpin Williams (1940); cousin, twice removed, of Alain Dominic Dawson Williams (1974). **Educ:** Wycliffe College. **Career:** Captain, Gloucestershire Regiment (Mentioned in Despatches), WWI; Master, Housemaster, and Scoutmaster, Wycliffe College 1910–1952. **Appointments:** Honorary Secretary, Gloucestershire Boy Scouts' Association 1931. Died 21 January 1967.

SIDDALL, The Revd Eric (1947) Born 17 July 1917, 80 Buxton Road, Stockport, Cheshire; son of George Harry Siddall, Joiner, and Annie Ellen Whittaker; 1 son (Nigel), 3 daughters (Carol, Anita and Monnica). BA 1949; MA 1957; BA (Durham) 1938; MA (Durham) 1947. **Tutor(s):** C W Guillebaud. **Johnian Relatives:** uncle of Richard Baynham Siddall (1966). **Educ:** St George's School, Stockport; Stockport Grammar School; St John's College, Durham. **Career:** Master, King's College (Church Missionary Society), Budo, Uganda 1938–1940; Kenya Regiment and Army Education Corps 1940–1942; CF 1943–1946; Curate, St Luke, Chesterton 1951; Vicar, Guyhirn with Rings End, Wisbech 1951; Vicar, Alexton with East Norton, and Loddington, Leicester 1954; Priest in Charge, Belton and Wardley, Rutland 1957; Vicar, Houghton-on-the-Hill with Keyham 1960; Priest in Charge, Thrussington, Leicester 1972. Died 1981.

SIDE, Dr David Erle (1948) Born 12 September 1927, 2 Lynton Road, Acton, Middlesex; son of Henry Walter Side, Textile Importer and Exporter, and Beatrice May Side; m 24 July 1957; 1 daughter (b 19 May 1960). **Subject(s):** Natural Sciences; BA 1951; MA 1958; BChir 1958; MB 1958; BA (Open University); LRCP; MRCS. **Tutor(s):** R L Howland. **Educ:** Lancaster House School, Acton; Milbourne Lodge, Esher; King's College School, Wimbledon. **Career:** GP, Basingstoke 1960–1987. **Appointments:** Captain of Boats, Westminster Medical School 1954–1955.

SIDGWICK, John Utrick (1949) Born 15 November 1928, The Sheilings, The Stray, Houghton-le-Skerne, County Durham; son of James Sidgwick, Upholsterer, and Amy Baty; m (1) Mavis Lawson Walker, 5 September 1950, Skipton Parish Church, West Riding, Yorkshire, (2) Jean MacDonald Schreider (née Scott), 7 July 1962, Mairie d'Hargeville, Seine-et-Oise, France, (3) Hildburg Erna Luise Williams (née Scholz), 26 November 1999, Barnet Register Office, Hertfordshire; 1 son (Renaud Marin b 26 February 1972). BA 1952; MA 1956. **Tutor(s):** C W Guillebaud. **Educ:** Monkseaton Grammar School; Choristers' School, Durham; Durham School; Paris Conservatoire. **Career:** Freelance Lecturer, Teacher and Musician, Paris (concerts, broadcasts and recordings) 1953–1962; Agricultural Attaché, British Embassy, Paris 1962–1985; Freelance Translator and Calligrapher 1985–. **Awards:** Baker Exhibition, SJC 1947. **Honours:** OBE.

SIFNEOS, Theodore (1937) Born 4 July 1919, Taganroy, Russia; son of Aristidis Sifneos, Industrialist, and Euridiki Kanaki; 2 daughters. **Subject(s):** Economics; BA 1940. **Tutor(s):** C W Guillebaud. **Educ:** Athens College, Greece. **Career:** Greek Navy 1942–1946; Operations Assistant, Rethymnis & Kulukundis Ltd, London 1947–1952; Company Director, Hadjilias & Co Ltd, London 1952–1978; Company Director, Kratigos Shipping Co, Piraeus, Greece 1978–1992. **Awards:** Naval Medal for Exceptional Services; Medal for Greek/German Italian War 1941–1945.

SILBY, Robert David Kerr (1924) Born 26 November 1905, Scott's Road, Singapore, Straits Settlements; son of Robert Passmore Silby, Engineer, and Mary Gibson Kerr. BA 1927; MA 1935. **Tutor(s):** E E Sikes. **Educ:** Holy Trinity Cathedral School, Shanghai; University School, Victoria, Canada; Brighton College.

SILK, The Revd George William (1914) Born 22 December 1895, 1 Handsworth Hill, Darnall, Sheffield; son of James Silk, Quarry Labourer, and Emma Turner; 2 sons (Eric and Peter), 1 daughter (Margaret). **Subject(s):** History; BA 1920; MA 1923. **Tutor(s):** E E Sikes. **Educ:** Darnall Church of England School, Sheffield; Sheffield Central Secondary School. **Career:** Lieutenant, East Yorkshire Regiment and General List (wounded) 1914–1918; Ordained by Bishop of Sheffield 1921; Curate, St Leonard's Church, Dinnington 1921–1926; Benoi, Transvaal 1926–1928; Protestant Cathedral, Johannesburg 1928–1929; Vicar, Standerton, Johannesburg 1930–1931; Curate in Charge, Moorends Conventional District, Thorne 1931–1939; Perpetual Curate, Drighlington 1939–1949; Vicar, Outwood, Yorkshire 1949–1957; Rector, Nigel, Transvaal 1958–1962. **Honours:** MC 1918. Died 16 January 1966.

SILLARS, Ronald William (1929) Born 1 August 1910, 84 Elwick Road, West Hartlepool, County Durham; son of Daniel Sillars, Steelworks Manager, and Mary Ellen Pool. **Subject(s):** Natural Sciences (Physics); BA 1932. **Tutor(s):** J M Wordie. **Educ:** Glenhow Preparatory School, Saltburn; Pocklington School. **Career:** College Apprentice, Research Department, Trafford Park, Metropolitan-Vickers 1932–1934; Metropolitan-Vickers Research Scholar, New College, Oxford 1935–1937; Section Leader (Semiconductors), Research Laboratory 1947, Group Leader, Physics Group 1950, Group Leader, Materials (Electrical) Group 1955, Metropolitan-Vickers. **Appointments:** Council Member, IEE 1946–1949; Board Member, Institute of Physics 1955–1960 (Vice-President 1958–1960). **Awards:** Dowman Exhibition, SJC 1929. **Publications:** Many papers, mostly on dielectrics and semiconductors.

SIMCOX, Lewis (1920) Naval Officer.

SIMEONE, Reginald Nicola (1944) Born 12 July 1927, 3 Calbourne Road, Balham, London; son of Nicola Francisco Simeone, Chartered Secretary, and Phyllis Iles; m Josephine Frances Hope, 2 April 1954; 2 sons (Nigel b 1956 and Robert b 1961). **Subject(s):** Geography; BA 1947; MA 1966; FRMetS 1993. **Tutor(s):** J M Wordie. **Educ:** Merton Park Junior Mixed School; Raynes Park Grammar School. **Career:** Instructor Lieutenant, RN 1947–1950; Assistant Principal 1950–1955, Principal 1955–1959, Admiralty; Finance Branch 1959–1961, Economics and Programmes Branch 1961–1965, Chief Personnel Officer AWRE 1965–1969, Principal Establishments Officer 1970–1976, Authority Personnel Officer 1976–1984, Comptroller of Finance and Administration 1984–1986, Board Member for Finance and Administration 1987–1988, Adviser to the Chairman 1988–1990, UKAEA; Adviser to the Chairman of Nuclear Electric plc 1990–1996. **Appointments:** Member, SJC Music Society 1944–1947; Member, SJC Yet Another Society 1944–1947; Member and office holder, University Geography Society 1944–1947; Co-founder and Dance Organiser, Inter-Varsity Club 1946–1947; Chairman, Atomic Energy Constabulary Police Committee 1986–1990; Executive Vice-President, European Atomic Energy Society 1987–1990. **Awards:** Minor Scholarship, SJC 1944. **Honours:** CBE 1985.

SIMISTER, Dr John Michael (1946) Born 16 May 1923, 10 Grange Park, Ealing, Middlesex; son of Sidney John Simister, Civil Servant, Staff Clerk, Ministry of Labour, and Blodwen Owen; m Margaret John, 1948; 1 son (John b 1954), 2 daughters (Miriam b 1949 and Jane b 1964). **Subject(s):** Natural Sciences; BA 1949; MA 1967; MB 1952; BChir 1952. **Tutor(s):** G C L Bertram. **Educ:** St Goar Preparatory School, Bristol; Bristol Grammar School. **Career:** Medical Director, W B Pharmaceuticals 1955–1974; Cancer Chemotherapist, Mount Vernon Hospital, Northwood, Middlesex 1961–1978; Medical Director, Lundbeck Ltd, Luton, Bedfordshire 1974–1987. **Publications:** *Cyclophosphamide*, 1963.

SIMKIN, Frederick (1919) Born 3 March 1895, Brisbane, Australia; son of George Seymour Simkin, Civil Engineer, and Ellen Josephine Merry. BA 1921. **Tutor(s):** E E Sikes. **Educ:** Bedford Modern School; Brisbane Grammar School; Private Tuition. **Career:** Second Lieutenant, King's Liverpool Regiment 1914 (wounded 1916), home service 1917–1919, WWI; Master, Winton House, Winchester.

SIMKINS, Rupert Mann (1917) Born 9 November 1899, 36 Argyle Road, Ealing, Middlesex; son of Arthur Richard Mann Simkins, Electrical Engineer, and Isabella Emma Hawkins. **Subject(s):** Classics; BA 1921; MA 1931. **Tutor(s):** E E Sikes. **Educ:** Hawthornden Preparatory School, London; Crypt Grammar School, Gloucester. **Career:** Classics Master, Manchester Grammar School 1921–1966. **Awards:** Scholarship, SJC; Wood and Hare Exhibition 1920; Hawksley Burbury Prize (Greek Verse) 1920; Wright's Prize, SJC 1920. Died 31 December 1990.

SIMM, Frank (1943) Born 20 June 1925, 111 Sidney Grove, Newcastle upon Tyne; son of Jonathan Simm, Motor Engineer, and Mabel Todd. **Subject(s):** Natural Sciences; BA 1946; MA 1950. **Tutor(s):** C W Guillebaud. **Educ:** Westgate Hill Council School, Newcastle upon Tyne; Newcastle Royal Grammar School.

SIMMONDS, Dr Frederick John (1933) Born 12 May 1915, 455 Green Lane, Goodmayes, Essex; son of Edgar John Simmonds, Boot-factor, and Florence Emily Ormrod. **Subject(s):** Natural Sciences; BA 1937; MA 1940; PhD 1947. **Tutor(s):** C W Guillebaud. **Educ:** Goodmayes Council School; Brentwood Grammar School. **Awards:** Scholarship, SJC 1934; Wright's Prize, SJC 1934.

SIMMONDS, Jack (1935) Born 27 August 1916, 22 Goodyere Street, Gloucester; son of Frederick Arthur John Simmonds, Building Contractor, and Sarah Jane Wood. **Subject(s):** Mathematics; BA 1938; MA 1946. **Tutor(s):** J M Wordie. **Educ:** Crypt School, Gloucester. **Career:** Civil Servant (Meteorological Office) 1939–1976. **Awards:** Scholarship, SJC 1936–1937.

SIMMONDS, Ronald John McLean (1928) Born 4 August 1908, St Mark's Vicarage, Reigate, Surrey; son of Arthur Simmonds, Clerk in Holy Orders, and Rosalie McLean. **Subject(s):** History; BA 1931. **Tutor(s):** E A Benians. **Johnian Relatives:** son of Arthur Simmonds (1870); uncle of Ian Alexander Bruce Mackenzie Ross (1946) and of Ronald Keith Mackenzie Ross (1954). **Educ:** Wykeham House School, Worthing; Thrings, Brunswick, Haywards Heath; Lancing College. **Career:** Second Lieutenant, Coldstream Guards. **Awards:** Sword of Honour, Sandhurst. Died 1933.

SIMMONS, George Martin (1923) Born 27 November 1904, 124 Hill Lane, Shirley, Southampton; son of Francis Ridsdill Simmons, Tailor's Cutter, and Martha Brightiff; m Thelma Alice Cecilia Howie; 1 son (John Richard b 20 March 1939). **Subject(s):** Modern and Medieval Languages; BA 1927. **Tutor(s):** E E Sikes. **Johnian Relatives:** father of John Richard Simmons (1959). **Educ:** Mill House Preparatory School, Sheffield; Taunton's Trade School, Southampton; Christ's Hospital, West Horsham. **Career:** Schoolmaster. Died 16 August 1990.

SIMMONS, Gerald Seymour (1919) Born 2 May 1902, Rio de Janeiro, Brazil; son of Charles Dowling Simmons, Banker, London and River Plate Bank, and Eleanora Cecile Smyth. BA 1923. **Tutor(s):** B F Armitage. **Educ:** Preparatory School, Brunswick, Haywards Heath; Malvern College. **Career:** Rio Flour Mills Ltd, Rio de Janeiro, Brazil. Died 26 May 1929.

SIMMONS, Dr Harold John Allpress (1920) Born 7 March 1903, Collipreest, Christchurch Road, Bournemouth, Hampshire; son of Harold Simmons, Medical Practitioner, and Mary Katherine Gertrude Wagstaffe. BA 1922; BChir 1928; MB 1928. **Tutor(s):** B F Armitage. **Educ:** Wychwood and Saugeen Schools, Bournemouth; Clifton College.

SIMMONS, John Richardson Mainwaring (1920) Born 19 March 1902, 52 Ward Place, Cinnamon Gardens, Colombo, Ceylon; son of Sidney Mainwaring Simmons, Clerk in Holy Orders, and Beatrice Margaret Reynolds; m Muriel Hare, 10 June 1926, St George's, Wilton, Taunton. **Subject(s):** Mathematics; BA 1923; MA 1952. **Tutor(s):** E E Sikes. **Educ:** Windlesham House School, Brighton; Brighton College. **Career:** Director and Chief Controller, J Lyons & Co Ltd until 1968. **Appointments:** Chairman, President, Institute of Administrative Management. **Awards:** Scholarship, SJC. Died 14 January 1985.

SIMMONS, Leonard Frederick George (1912) Born 13 August 1890, 58 Church Road, Gillingham, Kent; son of Frederick Charles Simmons, Engineer Manager, and Ada Lizzie Peckham; m Verena Baumgartner, 14 June 1927, Friends' Meeting House, Colthouse. **Subject(s):** Mathematics; BA 1914; MA 1925. **Tutor(s):** L H K Bushe-Fox. **Educ:** HM Dockyard, Chatham; Gillingham Technical School; Royal College of Science; Wesleyan Higher Grade School. **Career:** Principal Scientific Officer, Aerodynamics Division, National Physical Laboratory 1950. **Awards:** Whitworth Scholarship. Died 11 April 1954.

SIMPSON, Alistair Begg (1933) Born 10 August 1915, Little Pipers, Clay Hill, Enfield, Middlesex; son of William Begg Simpson, Architect, and Bessie Evelyn Cole. **Tutor(s):** C W Guillebaud. **Educ:** Hurst Court, Hastings; Gaveney House School, Hampstead; Camford School, Wimbourne. Died 28 October 1934.

SIMPSON, Charles Abercrombie (1943) Born 8 March 1926, 16 Cefn Park, Skewen, Neath, Glamorganshire; son of Charles Abercromie Simpson, Chartered Accountant, and Mary Russell Stevenson. BA 1946; MA 1950. **Tutor(s):** S J Bailey. **Educ:** Parc Wern Kindergarten, Swansea; Craig-y-nos Preparatory School; Oundle School.

SIMPSON, David (1944) Born 3 October 1926, St Mary's Hospital, Manchester; son of Leonard Simpson, Methodist Minister, and Bessie Snowdon. **Subject(s):** Modern and Medieval Languages; BA 1949; MA 1951. **Tutor(s):** J M Wordie. **Educ:** Farnseat Preparatory School, Arnside; Kingswood School. **Appointments:** RAF Cadet, SJC.

SIMPSON, Lieutenant Commander Denis Louis (1930) Born 26 February 1912, 61 Cambridge Road, Southport; son of Bernard Simpson, Cotton Spinner and Manufacturer, and Louise Blanche Potier; m Beattie; 1 son (Martin Bernard Carruthers b 25 October 1936). **Subject(s):** History; BA 1933. **Johnian Relatives:** brother of Geoffrey Bernard Albert Simpson (1924); father of Martin Bernard Carruthers Simpson (1954); uncle of Peter Bernard Simpson (1960). **Educ:** St Hugh's School, Bickley; Mr Malin's School, Freshfield; Claysmore School, Winchester; Harrow School. **Career:** Merchant, Cape Town. Died 5 February 1987.

SIMPSON, Derek William Alastair (1933) Born 5 January 1915, 36 Murivance, Shrewsbury, Salop; son of Archibald Simpson, Surgeon, and Honoria Sanderson. **Tutor(s):** R L Howland. **Educ:** Kingsland Grange School, Shrewsbury; Repton School.

SIMPSON, Geoffrey Bernard Albert (1924) Born 26 March 1906, Whitburn, Garstang Road, Preston, Lancashire; son of Bernard Simpson, Cotton Spinner and Manufacturer, and Louise Blanche Potier m Marjorie Alice Palmer; 1 son (Peter Bernard b 26 September 1941). BA 1927; MA 1935. **Tutor(s):** B F Armitage. **Johnian Relatives:** brother of Denis Louis Simpson (1930); uncle of Martin Bernard Carruthers Simpson (1954); father of Peter Bernard Simpson (1960). **Educ:** Croxton Preparatory School, Southport; Claysmore School, Winchester. Died 23 August 1985.

SIMPSON, James Wallace Skinner (1943) Born 20 January 1925, Dacca, India; son of Edward Skinner Simpson, Indian Civil Service, and Audrey Catherine Oatley. **Tutor(s):** C W Guillebaud. **Educ:** Milner Court, Sturry; King's School, Canterbury.

SIMPSON, Reginald James Laing (1930) Born 15 December 1911, Budleigh, Aliwal Road, Wynberg, Cape of Good Hope; son of Reginald Simpson, Solicitor, and Gladys Catherine Frances Miller. **Subject(s):** Law; BA 1933; MA 1964. **Tutor(s):** C W Guillebaud. **Educ:** Diocesan College Preparatory School, Grahamstown; St Andrew's College, Grahamstown. Died 20 October 1978.

SIMPSON, Robert Arthur (1929) Born 19 October 1907, Scotch Street, Dungannon, County Tyrone, Ireland; son of Robert Simpson, Public Elementary School Teacher, and Frances Havergal Sloan. **Subject(s):** Mathematics; BA 1931; MA 1936. **Tutor(s):** J M Wordie. **Educ:** Public Elementary School, Dungannon; Royal School, Dungannon; Queen's University, Belfast.

SIMPSON, Roger (1949) Born 25 September 1930, Murray Hospital, Benfieldside, Consett, County Durham; son of Thomas Simpson, Coal Hewer, and Lydia Smedley; m Jean Farbridge, 25 July 1956; 2 daughters (Helen b 1962 and Caroline b 1965). **Subject(s):** Geography; BA 1952; MA 1956; MSc (Durham) 1964; PGCE 1953. **Tutor(s):** J M Wordie. **Educ:** West Stanley Elementary School; Stanley Grammar School. **Career:** Geography Master, Annfield Plain Secondary School 1953–1955; Geography Master, Henry Smith School, Hartlepool 1956–1959; Head of Geography, West Hartlepool Grammar School 1959–1966; Deputy Head, Manor School, West Hartlepool 1966–1968;

Headmaster, Washington School 1968–1993. **Awards:** President's Award for Service to Chess, British Chess Federation 1997.

SIMPSON, William (1924) Born 7 August 1901, Tick Fen, Warboys, Huntingdonshire; son of William Simpson, Farmer, and Edith Hilda Sergeant; m Margaret. BA 1927; MA 1932. **Tutor(s):** B F Armitage. **Educ:** Eagle House, Sandhurst; Gresham's School, Holt. **Career:** Superintendent of Education 1927, Senior Education Officer 1938, Nigeria; Principal, Government College, Umuahia, Nigeria 1943. **Honours:** OBE. Died 27 December 1959.

SIMPSON, William Arthur (1941) Born 28 March 1923, Bugthorpe, Yorkshire; son of Charles Alfred Simpson, Rating Officer, and May Gillah. BA 1949; MA 1951. **Tutor(s):** C W Guillebaud. **Educ:** Fangfoss Elementary School; Pocklington School. **Appointments:** Member, The Institute of Careers Officers.

SIMPSON WHITE, John Nigel (1938) Born 13 October 1920, Pentre House, Andelm, Cheshire; son of John Simpson White, Medical Practitioner, and Elsie Mansbridge. **Tutor(s):** R L Howland. **Educ:** Branksome School, Godalming; Hailey School, Bournemouth; Charterhouse, Godalming; Wittington School, Somerset.

SIMS, Laurence George Cecil (1932) Born 28 November 1913, The Gables, Waddeston, Buckingham; son of Eustace Arthur Cecil Sims, Estate Agent, and Margaret Farmborough; m Laurena. BA 1935; MA 1939. **Tutor(s):** J M Wordie. **Educ:** Winchester House School, Brackley; Aldenham School. Died 10 January 1985.

SINCLAIR, Professor Thomas Alan (1919) Born 9 April 1899, 70 Eglantine Avenue, Belfast, Antrim; son of Samuel Sinclair, Merchant, and Edith Mary Darbishire; m Sally Dickson Ferguson, 19 August 1931; 1 son (Thomas Ferguson b 15 May 1936), 1 daughter (Frances b 8 September 1933). **Subject(s):** Classics; BA 1922; MA 1926; Hon DLitt (National University of Ireland, Dublin) 1956. **Tutor(s):** E E Sikes. **Johnian Relatives:** nephew of Herbert Dukinfield Darbishire (1884); father of Thomas Ferguson Sinclair (1955). **Educ:** Royal Belfast Academical Institution; Queen's University, Belfast. **Career:** Lecturer in Classics, University College, Southampton 1923–1926; Title A Fellow, SJC 1926–1929; Reader in Classics, Birkbeck College, University of London 1926–1934; Professor of Greek, Queen's University, Belfast 1934. **Appointments:** Chairman, Governing Body, Richmond Lodge School; Vice-Chairman, Governing Body, Royal Belfast Academical Institution; Secretary, Academic Council, and Pro-Vice-Chancellor, Queen's University, Belfast. **Publications:** (with Professor Frederic Adam Wright) *A History of Later Latin Literature*, Routledge, 1931; (ed) *Hesiod, Works and Days*, Macmillan, 1932; *A History of Classical Greek Literature*, Routledge, 1934; *A History of Greek Political Thought*, Routledge and Kegan Paul, 1951 (published, in translation, in French, Italian and Modern Greek); (translator) Aristotle, *The Politics*, Penguin, 1962. Died 10 October 1961.

SINGER, Abraham (1937) Born 15 September 1918, 102 City Road, London; son of Morris Singer, Capmaker, and Bessie Rosenberg. **Subject(s):** Classics/Law; BA 1940; MA 1946. **Tutor(s):** R L Howland. **Educ:** Malmesbury Road Council School, London; Southall Street Council School, Manchester; Manchester Grammar School. **Career:** Solicitor, Betesh, Singer & Co, Manchester 1948–1961. **Awards:** Patchett Scholarship, SJC 1936. Died 31 July 1989.

SINGH, Har Kishan (1900) Born 9 January 1882, Chiniot, Jhang District, Punjab, India; son of Sobha Ram, Respectable official class. **Subject(s):** Law/History; BA 1903; MA 1907; BA (Punjab). **Tutor(s):** C E Graves; J R Tanner. **Educ:** Government College, Lahore; Punjab University. **Career:** Called to the Bar, Lincoln's Inn 1904.

SINGH, Dr Nagendra (1934) Born 19 March 1914, Dungarpur, Southern Rajputana, India; son of HH Maharawal Sir Bijai Singhji, Ruler of

Dungarpur State, and Dewendra Kunwar, Her Highness the Senior Maji Sahiba of Dungarpur; m Pushpa Kumari Devi, 11 February 1940, Dungarpur. **Subject(s):** History; BA 1936; MA 1941; LLB (Cantab) 1953; LLM (Cantab) 1955; LLD (Cantab) 1965; BA (Agra) 1934; IDC 1950; BLitt (Dublin) 1954; DLitt (Bihar) 1954; DCL (Delhi); DSc (Moscow); DPhil (Calcutta); LLD (Dublin); numerous honorary degrees including Honorary LLD (Peking) 1986, (Cordoba, Argentina) 1987; Corresponding FBA 1986. **Tutor(s):** J S Boys Smith. **Educ:** Mayo College, Ajmer; Government College, Ajmer (Agra University). **Career:** Probationer 1937–1938, District Magistrate and Collector, Madhya Pradesh 1938–1946, Joint Secretary, Defence Ministry, India 1946–1956, Regional Commander, Eastern States 1948, Director-General, Shipping 1956–1964, Special Secretary, Ministry of Information and Broadcasting 1964, Secretary to Government of India, Ministry of Transport 1964–1965, Secretary to the President of India 1966–1972, Chief Election Commissioner 1972–1973, Indian Civil Service; Called to the Bar, Gray's Inn 1942; Honorary Bencher 1975; Bencher, King's Inn, Dublin 1985. **Appointments:** Member, Constituent Assembly of India 1947–1948; President, IMO 1963–1965; Member, International Law Commission 1967–1972; Chairman, Institute of United Nations Studies, Department of Indian Federation of United Nations Associations 1969; President, International Labour Conference 1970; Constitutional Advisor, Government of Bhutan 1970; Member, International Court of Justice, The Hague 1973–1988 (Vice-President 1976–1979, President 1985–1988); Chancellor, University of Goa 1985; President, UN International Law Commission; President, UNCITRAL; President, UN World Commission on Environment and Development; Deputy Chairman, IUCN Commission on Environmental Law; President, Indian Academy of Environmental Law; Honorary Member, American Society of International Law 1985; President, Indian Society of International Law; Professor of International Law, several universities; Freeman, City of Salta, Argentina; various lectureships; Member, Indian, European, American and other learned societies. **Awards:** Cama Prize 1938; Padma Vibushan 1973; Pinhey Medal, Agra University. **Publications:** *Termination of Membership of International Organisations*, Stevens, 1957; *Nuclear Weapons and International Law*, Stevens, 1959; *The Defence Mechanism of the Modern State: a study of the politico-military set-up*, India Publishing House, 1964; *Shipowners*, British Shipping Laws Series, Vol 8, 1967; *India and international law*, S Chand, 1969; *International Conventions of Merchant Shipping*, British Shipping Laws Series, Vol 13, 1973; *Commercial Law of India*, Thomson Press, 1975; *Maritime Flag and International Law*, Thomson Press, 1978; *Juristic Concepts of Ancient Indian Polity*, Vision Books, 1980; *International Maritime Law Conventions*, Stevens, 1983; *The Role and Record of the UN High Commissioner for Refugees*, Macmillan India, 1984; *Bhutan, a Kingdom in the Himalayas: a study of the land, its people and their government*, S Chand, 1985; *Enforcement of Human Rights in Peace and War and the Future of Humanity*, Nijhoff, 1986; (with Edward McWhinney) *Nuclear Weapons and Contemporary International Law*, Developments in International Law, Vol 11, Martinus Nijhoff, (2nd Revision edition) October 1988; *Role and Record of the International Court of Justice (1946–1988 – In Celebration of the 40th Anniversary)*, Martinus Nijhoff, 1990; various articles in law journals. Died 11 December 1988.

SINGH, Ram Dhan (1919) Born 1 May 1891, Kiloi, Rohtak District, Punjab, India; son of Chowdry Shankar Lal, Engaged in Agriculture, and Hans Kaur. **Subject(s):** Natural Sciences; BA 1922; MA 1926; BSc (Patna); LAg (Lyallpur). **Tutor(s):** E A Benians. **Educ:** Government High School, Rohtak; DAV College, Lahore; St Stephen's College, Delhi; Agricultural College, Lyallpur; Ravenshaw College, Cuttack; Patna University. **Career:** Assistant, Imperial Agricultural Research Institute, Pusa, Bihar. **Awards:** Scholarship, Government of India.

SINGLETON, David Ernest (1937) Born 18 July 1918, Parkside, Enm Lane, Heaton, Bradford; son of Walter Singleton, Wool Merchant, and Beatrice Sarah Shute; BA 1940; MA 1944. **Tutor(s):** R L Howland. **Educ:** Streete Court, Westgate-on-Sea; Shrewsbury.

SINHA, Professor Kumar Durganand (1947) Born 23 September 1922, Banaili, Bihar, India; son of Raja Kirtynand Sinha Bahadur, Zamindar, and Rani Shree Prabhavati Devi; 2 sons. MSc 1949; BA (Patna University) 1943; MA (Patna University) 1945. **Tutor(s):** C W Guillebaud. **Johnian Relatives:** cousin of Damodar Thakur (1948). **Educ:** Purhea Zila School; Patna Collegiate School; Patna University, India. **Career:** Junior Research Fellow 1949–1951, Lecturer in Applied Psychology 1951–1958, Patna University; Assistant Professor in Humanities and Social Sciences, Indian Institute of Technology, Kharagpur 1958–1961; Professor and Head of the Department of Psychology, Allahabad University 1961–1982; Director, A N Sinha Institute of Social Studies, Patna University 1982–1987; ICSSR National Fellow 1987–1989; Nehru Professor, Department of Human Development and Family Studies, Maharaja Sayajirao University of Baroda 1992; Visiting Professor, Department of Psychology, University of Hong Kong 1993. **Awards:** Jawaharlal Nehru National Award for Social Sciences, Madhya Pradesh Council for Science and Technology, Government of Madhya Pradesh, Bhopal, India 1996. **Publications:** 250 research papers, and many books.

SISSENER, John (1949) Born 17 March 1931, Oslo, Norway; son of John Sissener, Consulting Engineer, and Else Marie Hurum. BA 1951; MA 1955. **Tutor(s):** J M Wordie. **Educ:** Frogner Skole, Oslo.

SISSON, Marshall Arnott (1916) Born 14 February 1897, 27 Honyatt Road, Gloucester; son of Arthur White Sisson, Mechanical Engineer, and Ellen Mary Fox. **Subject(s):** Oriental Languages. **Tutor(s):** L H K Bushe-Fox. **Educ:** Beresford House, Gloucester; Crypt Grammar School, Gloucester; Leighton Park School.

S'JACOB, Frederick Bernhard (1927) Born 25 October 1907, Amsterdam, Holland; son of Frederick s'Jacob, Managing Director, Holland-America Line, and Jacoba Maria Loder. BA 1930. **Tutor(s):** C W Guillebaud. **Educ:** Amsterdam School Union; Amsterdam Lyceum; Rotterdam Municipal College; Courtenay Lodge, Sutton Courtenay. **Career:** Lieutenant, Netherlands Army, WWII. Died 14 May 1940 (killed at Dordrecht).

SKELTON, Allan Noel (1925) Born 25 December 1907, Woodham Lodge, Woodham Ferrers, Essex; son of Allan Skelton, Farmer and Stockbreeder, and Hilda Marie Rosewarne; m Mary P Hutchinson, 1931 (d 1991); 2 sons (John Noel b 21 September 1930, d 24 April 1934 and Ian Allan Noel b 3 June 1946), 1 daughter (Julie Mary b 21 June 1935). **Subject(s):** Agriculture/History; BA 1930; MA 1937. **Tutor(s):** E E Sikes. **Johnian Relatives:** cousin of John Chatto Skelton (1925); brother-in-law of Dennis Samuel Alfred Edward Jessop (1925). **Educ:** Westwood House, Maldon; Felsted School. **Career:** Junior Teacher, Brighton School, Mowden 1930; Head of Physical Education, South East Essex Technical College, Dagenham 1936; Crypt Grammar School, Gloucester; Teacher of Games and Mathematics, Kingston Grammar School, Surrey 1948–1973. Died 7 November 2003.

SKELTON, John Chatto (1925) Born 14 December 1907, Chathow, Loom Lane, Radlett, Aldenham, Hertfordshire; son of Reginald Albert Skelton, Iron and Steel Merchant, and Dorothea Chatto; m Moira Welberry, 23 June 1934, Christchurch, Southport (div 1951); 2 sons (David Barry b 16 July 1936 and Peter John b 17 February 1943). **Tutor(s):** J M Wordie. **Johnian Relatives:** cousin of Allan Noel Skelton (1925). **Educ:** Stanmore Park; Mill Hill School. **Career:** Apprentice, General Motors, Colindale 1926; R A Skelton & Co Limited, Steel and Engineering, London 1932–1959 (final position, Managing Director); RAF 1940–1946 (Pilot Officer 1940, Acting Squadron Leader 1945, twice Mentioned in Despatches 1943 and 1945). **Honours:** 1939–45 Star; Africa Star; Defence Medal; War Medal 1939–45. Died 14 April 1959.

SKENE, The Revd Claude Montague Benson (1903) Born 5 June 1884, 10 Rose Terrace, Kennington Park, London; son of Samuel Slinn Skene, Clerk in Holy Orders, and Charlotte Warren; m Charlotte Grace Judge, 12 July 1916, St John's, Hartley Wintney. BA 1906. **Tutor(s):** C E Graves;

J R Tanner. **Johnian Relatives:** brother of William Henry Skene (1890) and of Frederick Norman Skene (1896). **Educ:** Pocklington School. **Career:** Ordained Deacon 1907; Curate, St Mary, Walkley, Sheffield 1907–1909; Ordained Priest 1908; Curate, Darfield 1909–1911; Curate, Badby with Newnham 1911–1916; Temporary CF, 4th Class, RACD 1916–1917; Acting Rector, Heidelberg 1920–1921; Assistant Master, Western Province Preparatory School, Claremont, Cape Colony 1920–1921; Curate, All Saints, Dummer 1922–1923; Rector, Brown Candover with Chilton Candover 1923–1924; Curate, Sotby with Market Stainton 1924–1927; Vicar, Bitchfield and Basingthorpe with Westby 1927–1929; Vicar, Dalby on the Wolds 1929–1932; Rector, Braybrooke 1932–1937; Rector, Marwood, Devonshire 1937–1943. Died 8 July 1958.

SKINNER, Bruce Allan Maclean (1946) Born 29 August 1927, 39 Milton Road, Cambridge; son of John Adrian Dudley Skinner, Physician and Surgeon, and Nora Evelyn Goodchild. BA 1950. **Tutor(s):** C W Guillebaud. **Educ:** Taverham School; Yardley Court, Tonbridge; Rossall School. Died 21 December 2002.

SKINNER, Cyril Reed (1908) Born 3 September 1890, 5 Courtfield Road, Brompton, London; son of George William Skinner, Ship Owner, and Clara Morgan Reed; m Winifred Edith Martin, 17 June 1924, Paris. **Tutor(s):** L H K Bushe-Fox. **Educ:** Private Tuition.

SKINNER, Derek Rowland (1949) Born 20 December 1930, Purley Cottage Hospital, Croydon, Surrey; son of William James Ferdinand Skinner, Clerk, National Debt Office, and Catherine Emily Bradley. **Subject(s):** Mathematics; BA 1952; MA 1956; PGCE. **Tutor(s):** J M Wordie. **Educ:** Kenley Primary School, Whyteleafe; Caterham School. **Career:** Schoolmaster 1955–1988; Assistant Master, St Lawrence College, Ramsgate, Kent; Assistant Master, Caterham School, Surrey; Assistant Master, Abingdon School, Oxon; Assistant Master, Truro Cathedral School; Assistant Master, Duchy Grammar School, Cornwall.

SKINNER, Professor John (1903) Born 18 July 1851, Inverurie, Aberdeenshire; son of James Skinner and Agnes Niven; m Jessie Elizabeth. Honorary MA 1903; MA (Aberdeen) 1876; DD (Aberdeen) 1895; DD (St Andrews); Honorary DD (Oxford). **Career:** Professor of Old Testament History, Theological College of Presbyterian Church of England (later Westminster College); President, Westminster College, Cambridge 1908–1922. Died 20 March 1925.

SKINNER, Treves Irving (1921) Born 13 February 1903, Richmond Hill, Parish of St Peter, Barbados, British West Indies; son of Irving Seymour Skinner, Planter and Merchant, and Alice Maud Legall. BA 1924. **Tutor(s):** B F Armitage. **Educ:** Harrison College, Barbados, British West Indies.

SLACK, Arthur James (1933) Born 2 June 1915, The Poplars, Lymm, Cheshire; son of Arthur Slack, Company Director and Secretary, and Elsie Victoria Johnson. **Johnian Relatives:** brother of Roger Dutton Slack (1937). **Educ:** Woodlands School, Deganwy; Shrewsbury School. Died 23 April 1967.

SLACK, Dr Roger Dutton (1937) Born 22 February 1919, 25 Oxted Walton Road, Stockton Heath, Budworth; son of Arthur Slack, Company Director, and Elsie Victoria Johnson; m Janet Elizabeth Petter; 3 children. **Subject(s):** Anatomy/Physiology/Pharmacology; BA 1940; MB, BChir (Middlesex Hospital Medical School) 1943. **Tutor(s):** R L Howland. **Johnian Relatives:** brother of Arthur James Slack (1933). **Educ:** Woodlands School, Deganwy; Shrewsbury School. **Career:** GP, St Ives, Cornwall, 1947–1984.

SLATER, Alec Whitley (1933) Born 3 October 1914, 3 Watson Street, Morley, Yorkshire; son of Archibald Stockwell Slater, Schoolmaster, and Sarah Hodgson. **Subject(s):** Natural Sciences; BA 1936; MA 1940. **Tutor(s):** J M Wordie. **Educ:** Secondary School, Nunthorpe; Pocklington School.

SLATER, Dr Eliot Trevor Oakeshott (1922) Born 28 August 1904, 84 Eglington Road, Plumstead, Woolwich, Kent; son of Gilbert Slater, Professor of Indian Economics, University of Madras, and Violet Oakeshott; m (1) Lydia Pasternak, 1935, (2) Jean; (1) 4 children. **Subject(s):** Natural Sciences; BA 1925; MA 1940; PhD; MB 1931; MD 1940. **Tutor(s):** B F Armitage. **Johnian Relatives:** son of Gilbert Slater (1882). **Educ:** Dragon School, Oxford; Leighton Park School, Reading. **Career:** Maudsley Hospital 1931–1939; Rockefeller Foundation Fellowship, Munich 1934–1935; Clinical Director, Sutton Emergency Hospital 1939–1946; Physician in Psychological Medicine, National Hospital, Queen Square 1946–1964; MRC Psychiatric Genetics Unit, Maudsley Hospital 1959; Editor, *British Journal of Psychiatry* 1961–1972. **Appointments:** Member, Royal Commission on Capital Punishment 1949; Maudsley Lecturer 1960; Trustee, Shakespearean Authorship Trust; Member, Euthanasia Society; Honorary Fellow, Royal Society of Medicine; Honorary Fellow, Royal College of Psychiatrists; Honorary Fellow, American Psychiatric Association. **Awards:** Scholarship, SJC. **Honours:** CBE 1966. **Publications:** *Physical Methods of Treatment in Psychiatry*; *Psychotic and Neurotic Illnesses in Twins*, 1953; *Clinical Psychiatry*; *The Genetics of Mental Disorders*, 1971; *Mind, Matter and Heredity*, 1971; *Patterns of Marriage*; *Delinquency in Girls*. Died 15 May 1983.

SLATER, James Aubin (1948) Born 15 April 1927, 26 Victoria Street, Clitheroe, Lancashire; son of Robert Charnock Slater, Secretary, and Ethel Aubin; m Mary Sellers, 1 August 1953; 1 son (Ian b 1960), 1 daughter (Helen b 1962). **Subject(s):** Natural Sciences/Geography; BA 1950; MA 1955. **Tutor(s):** G C L Bertram. **Educ:** St James's School, Clitheroe; Clitheroe Royal Grammar School. **Career:** Biology Master, William Hulme Grammar School, Manchester 1952–1953; Head of Biology and Games Master, Bolton School 1953–1987. Died 13 May 1987.

SLATER, Stewart Beattie (1913) Born 7 October 1894, Windsor Terrace, Fairfield, Buxton, Derby; son of George Slater, Provision Merchant, and Sarah Beattie; m Nora Irene Norris, 1 March 1923; 1 son (George Norris Stewart b 22 June 1930), 1 daughter (Patricia Ann b 30 October 1926). **Subject(s):** Law. **Tutor(s):** L H K Bushe-Fox. **Johnian Relatives:** father of George Norris Stewart Slater (1950); grandfather of Judith Mary Slater (1983). **Educ:** Epworth College, Rhyl. **Career:** Captain, King's Royal Rifle Corps and Special List (Trench Mortar Battery) (Mentioned in Despatches), WWI; Solicitor. **Honours:** MC. Died 10 October 1958.

SLATER, William Rex (1941) Born 29 July 1923, The City Maternity Home, Westcotes Drive, Leicester; son of Cyril Slater, Architect, and Gladys Mary Porter; m Elizabeth Jean Milliken-Smith, 3 September 1960, St Catherine's Church, Blackwell, Worcestershire; 1 son (Timothy Rex b 15 December 1961), 2 daughters (Judith Mary b 20 August 1963 and Jennifer Elizabeth b 28 August 1965). **Subject(s):** Mechanical Sciences; BA 1944; MA 1948; CEng; MIMechE; MICE. **Tutor(s):** S J Bailey. **Johnian Relatives:** father of Timothy Rex Slater (1980). **Educ:** Granby Road Elementary School, Leicester; Hinckley Road Elementary School, Leicester; Wyggeston Grammar School, Leicester. **Career:** Production Director, Charles Winn Valves Ltd; Production-Engineering Ltd, London; ICI; Tube Investments; GEC; Central Wagon. Died 4 December 1996.

SLATTERY, Denis Peter (1943) Born 2 May 1925, Blennerville, Tralee, Kerry, Eire; son of Jerome Slattery, Merchant, and Adelaide Mary Wilmot. **Tutor(s):** C W Guillebaud. **Educ:** St Edmund's College, Ware.

SLAWIKOWSKI, Dr George Joseph Marian (1949) Born 26 August 1932, The Hospital of St Lazarus, Cracow, Poland; son of Zygmunt Joseph Slawikowski, Second Lieutenant, and Bronislawa Kurdziel; m Jennifer Cameron Smith, January 1963. **Subject(s):** Natural Sciences; BA 1952; MA 1956; MB (Edinburgh). **Tutor(s):** G C L Bertram. **Educ:** St Florian School, Cracow; King J Sobieski School, Cracow; Salesian College, Oxford; Gore Park Grammar School, Wrexham **Career:** Junior Resident in Surgery, Henrotin Hospital 1957–1959; Cancer Researcher, Walter Reed Army Institute of Research 1959–1961; Surgeon in Residence, Hines Veterans Hospital 1961; Director of Surgical Education, St Paul Medical Centre, St Paul, Minnesota 1964. Died 18 June 1964.

SLEIGHT, Albert Henry (1908) Born 2 May 1889, St Peter's Road, Cleethorpes, Lincolnshire; son of Henry Sleight, Fish Merchant, and Lucy Ann Chapman. **Subject(s):** Modern and Medieval Languages; BA 1911; MA 1919. **Tutor(s):** J R Tanner. **Educ:** Clee Grammar School; Wycliffe College. **Career:** Private, Royal Fusiliers (Public Schools Battalion), then Sergeant, attached Divisional HQ (Intelligence Branch), WWI. Died August 1971.

SLEIGHT, The Revd Arthur Blomefield (1900) Born 27 October 1881, The Vicarage, Swadlincote, Derbyshire; son of William Blomefield Sleight, Clerk in Holy Orders, and Ellen Jane Turner. **Subject(s):** History; BA 1903; MA 1926. **Tutor(s):** D MacAlister. **Educ:** Oakham School. **Career:** Ordained Deacon 1906; Parishes in Altringham, Egremont, St Columba 1906–1920; Ordained Priest 1907; Vicar, Ellesmere Port 1920–1934; Rector, Thurstaton, Cheshire 1934–1956. Died 11 March 1965.

SLESSENGER, Wolfgang Wilhelm Otto (1945) See SCHLESINGER.

SLINGSBY, David Bryan (1949) Born 16 June 1929, 29 Marfleet Lane, Sutton, Kingston-upon-Hull; son of Frank Decent Slingsby, Engineer, and Vera Winsall; m Patricia Watson, 11 December 1954, St John's, Lewisham; 2 sons (Merrick Henry Edgar b 18 August 1958, d 12 January 1960 and Daniel James b 24 November 1963), 2 daughters (Martha Jean b 24 June 1955 and Emma Julia b 22 October 1961). **Subject(s):** Mechanical Sciences/Chemical Engineering; BA 1952; MA 1962; MEng 1992; Diploma of Applied Economics (Hull) 1957. **Tutor(s):** R L Howland. **Educ:** Maybury Road Council School, Hull; The Willows High School, Hull; Cavendish Road Council School, Hull; Hornsea Council School; Pocklington School. **Career:** National Service, REME 1948–1949; Director 1952–1987, Managing Director 1974–1987, Chairman 1979–1987, G & A E Slingsby Ltd, tube and valve specialist suppliers; Magistrate, Hull Bench 1978–1996. **Appointments:** President, Hull Junior Chamber of Commerce and Shipping 1963–1964; International Marketing Institute, Harvard Business School 1967; Councillor, Kingston-upon-Hull County Borough Council 1970–1973; Governor of various Hull schools 1974–1992; Vice President, Hull Chamber of Commerce and Shipping 1978; Member, Hull Prison Board of Visitors 1987–1990; Vice-Chairman, Humberside Probation Committee 1992–1996; Chairman, Finance Committee Central Council of Probation Committees 1994. **Awards:** Dowman Exhibition, SJC 1947; State Scholarship 1947.

SLOLEY, Robert Walter (1901) Born 21 June 1879, 2 Oak Villas, Lewisham Road, Lewisham, Kent; son of Robert Hugh Sloley, Accountant, and Elizabeth Maxted. **Subject(s):** Mathematics; BA 1904; MA 1908; BSc (London) 1898. **Tutor(s):** D MacAlister. **Educ:** Colfe's Grammar School. **Career:** Teacher, Liverpool College 1904–1914; Air Ministry Instrument Inspection Section 1914–1918; Egyptologist and Archaeologist. **Publications:** Chapter on Science, *The Legacy of Egypt*, 1942. Died 18 August 1958.

SLOMAN, Robert (1944) Born 18 July 1926, 495 Lees Road, Oldham, Lancashire; son of Robert Sloman, Licensed Victualler, and Flossie Lilian Udy. **Tutor(s):** J M Wordie. **Educ:** Lockyer Street Private School; St James the Less Elementary School; Launceston College; St Boniface's College, Plymouth. **Appointments:** RAF Cadet, SJC.

SMALL, Fred (1949) Born 3 December 1928, Barnsley, Yorkshire; son of Fred Small, Licensed Victualler, and Ada Morris; m Sheila Waddington, 28 May 1955, Elsecar, Yorkshire; 1 son (Simon Jonathan b 28 August 1971), 1 daughter (Rachel Victoria b 17 November 1968). **Subject(s):** Mechanical Sciences; BA 1952; MA 1956; BEng (Sheffield) 1954; CEng;

MIMinE; Colliery Managers' Certificate of Competency. **Tutor(s):** R L Howland. **Educ:** Ardsley Oaks Junior School; Barnsley and District Holgate Grammar School. **Career:** Mining Engineer 1954–1989; Undermanager, Elsecar Main Colliery, South Yorkshire 1958–1961; Development Engineer 1961–1967, Technical Director 1967–1976, Managing Director, Special Products Group 1976–1989, Gullick Dobson Ltd, Wigan, Lancashire. **Awards:** Scholarship, SJC 1952.

SMALL, John Michael (1941) Born 30 September 1922, 9 Viewforth Terrace, Edinburgh; son of William Small, London Agent for Fireclay Manufacturers, and Joan Marie Clay. **Tutor(s):** S J Bailey. **Educ:** Sheen High School, Richmond; George Heriot's Hospital School, Edinburgh; William Ellis School, London.

SMART, Donovan Foster (1924) Born 4 July 1906, High Street, Chingford, Essex; son of Harry Casimir Smart, Director of Publicity Department, Australian Government, London, and Daisy Hope Foster. **Subject(s):** Law; BA 1927. **Tutor(s):** E A Benians. **Educ:** Bancroft's School; Brentwood School. Died 1 December 1934.

SMART, Geoffrey Edwin (1938) Born 30 August 1920, 36 Rustat Road, Cambridge; son of Edwin Smart, Accountant, and Beatrice Eleanor Stearn; m Joyce Christine Neal, 1950; 2 daughters (Christine Margaret b 1953 and Frances Jane b 1957). **Subject(s):** Economics/Law; BA 1941; MA 1945. **Tutor(s):** J M Wordie. **Educ:** Perse Preparatory School, Cambridge; Perse School, Cambridge. **Career:** Wireless Operator, RAF 1940–1945; POW, Far East 1942–1945; Partner, then Senior Partner, Ginn & Co Solicitors, Cambridge 1948–1989. **Appointments:** Deacon, St Andrew's Street Baptist Church, Cambridge. Died 17 August 2001.

SMEE, Cyril Walter (1911) Born 5 November 1892, Hornsey, Middlesex; son of Walter Wallis Smee, Commercial Traveller, and Ada Mary Drew; 1 daughter. **Subject(s):** Classics; BA 1914; FCA; ACIS. **Tutor(s):** E E Sikes. **Educ:** St Paul's Cathedral School; Grocers' Company's School; Dulwich College. **Career:** Second Lieutenant 1914, Lieutenant 1915, Captain 1916, Royal Fusiliers; Ministry of Shipping 1919; Inspector of Taxes, Inland Revenue 1920; Associate, London Association of Accountants 1925. Died 10 December 1990.

SMELLIE, James Wilton (1922) Born 4 January 1904, 39 Leigh Road, Prittlewell, Essex; son of John Clementson Smellie, Physician and Surgeon, and Lilian Fletcher. **Subject(s):** Natural Sciences; BA 1925. **Tutor(s):** B F Armitage. **Educ:** Alleyne Court Preparatory School, Westcliff-on-Sea; Felsted School. **Career:** Shell, Burma.

SMELLIE, Professor Kingsley Bryce Speakman (1916) Born 22 November 1897, 16 Fairmead Road, Islington; son of John Smellie, Theatrical Manager, and Elizabeth Speakman; m Stephanie Narlian, 28 March 1931, St John's Church, London. **Subject(s):** History; BA 1920. **Tutor(s):** E E Sikes. **Educ:** Private School, Hammersmith; Latymer Upper School. **Career:** London Scottish Regiment 1916–1918; LSE 1921–1965; Professor of Political Science, LSE 1949–1965; Ministry of Home Security and Board of Trade 1939–1945. **Appointments:** Rockerfeller Studentship, Harvard Law School 1925–1926. **Awards:** Scholarship, SJC 1915. **Publications:** *A Hundred Years of English Government*, 1930; *Reason in Politics*, 1939; *A History of Local Government*, 1946; *The British Way of Life*, 1955. Died 30 November 1987.

SMETHURST, Professor Stanley Eric (1934) Born 19 January 1915, 79 Goodman Street, Blackley, Manchester; son of Stanley Smethurst, Warehouseman, and Anna Linnert; m Viola. **Subject(s):** Classics; BA 1937; MA 1941. **Tutor(s):** R L Howland. **Educ:** Moston Lane Municipal School, Manchester; North Manchester School; Manchester Grammar School. **Career:** Professor in Classics, University of New Brunswick 1938–1947; Professor of Classics, Queen's University, Kingston, Ontario 1947–1980. **Awards:** Exhibition, SJC 1933; Somerset Exhibition, SJC 1934; Scholarship, SJC 1936–1937; Graves Prize, SJC 1937; Wright's Prize, SJC 1937. Died 2 February 1998.

SMITH, Alan Desmond (1943) Born 13 December 1925, 197 Hales Lane, Oldbury, Worcestershire; son of Ernest William Smith, Clerk in Iron and Steel Works, and Hilda Gladys Robbins. **Tutor(s):** S J Bailey. **Johnian Relatives:** brother of Vernon John Smith (1942). **Educ:** Nelson Street Elementary School; King Edward VI Grammar School, Birmingham.

SMITH, Albert Francis (1914) Born 29 December 1895, 23 Craven Park Road, Harlesden, Middlesex; son of George Thomas Smith, Manufacturing Chemist, and Hannah Candler Robinson. **Tutor(s):** E E Sikes. **Johnian Relatives:** uncle of John Henry Ford Ford (1932). **Educ:** Harlesden Preparatory School; Merchant Taylors'. **Career:** Second Lieutenant, Middlesex Regiment, then attached London Regiment (wounded), WWI.

SMITH, Arnold Nigel (1944) Born 14 July 1926, 80 Victoria Road, Headingley, Leeds; son of Arnold Thomas Noble Smith, Schoolmaster, and Doris Frances Chappel; m Moira Anne Robson, 22 October 1948; 2 sons (Nigel b 1949 and Christopher b 1954). **Subject(s):** Mathematics/Natural Sciences; BA 1947; MA 1951; Honorary FICeram 1984; Honorary FIM. **Tutor(s):** C W Guillebaud. **Johnian Relatives:** father of Nigel Hugh Hamilton Smith (1967). **Educ:** Chapeltown Council School, Leeds; Leeds Grammar School. **Career:** Director of Research, T & R Boote Ltd 1947–1956; Director of Research 1956–1959, Assistant Managing Director 1959–1961, Managing Director 1961–1986, Chairman 1972–1988, Pilkington's Tiles Ltd. **Appointments:** Natural Sciences Society; Chairman of Trustees, Clonter Farm Music Trust and Clonter Opera For All; Member, OJHF; Chairman, Poole Pottery Ltd and 12 other companies; President, British Ceramic Society 1972–1973; President, British Ceramic Manufacturers Federation 1974–1975; President, European Ceramic Manufacturers 1974–1977; President, Institute of Ceramics 1979–1981; President, British Ceramic Research Association 1984–1989; Deputy Chairman, Cheadle Royal Hospital Board 1994. **Awards:** Exhibition, SJC. **Publications:** Several papers in *Transactions and Journal of the British Ceramic Society*, 1949–1961.

SMITH, Cecil Furness (1909) Born 20 March 1890, 13 Oak Hill Road, Surbiton, Surrey; son of George Furness Smith, Clerk in Holy Orders, and Elizabeth Hayes. **Subject(s):** Mathematics; BA 1912; LLB 1913. **Tutor(s):** L H K Bushe-Fox. **Educ:** Birkenhead School. **Career:** Assistant District Commissioner, Gold Coast 1914–1921; Acting Circuit Judge, Gold Coast 1919–1932; District Commissioner, Gold Coast 1921–1925; Called to the Bar, Inner Temple 1922; Acting Solicitor General, Gold Coast 1927; Solicitor General, Tanganyika Territory 1932–1946; Chief Justice, Trinidad 1946.

SMITH, Christopher Jaffray (1948) Born 20 June 1928, Wandsworth, London; son of Norman Arthur Percival Smith, Indian Police, and Gladys Ivy Victoria. BA 1950. **Tutor(s):** F Thistlethwaite. **Educ:** Chelmsford Hall, Eastbourne; Sherborne School. **Career:** Underwriter, Lloyd's of London.

SMITH, Clive Gordon (1926) Born 28 October 1907, 41 Onslow Gardens, Highgate, Middlesex; son of Clive Bramwell Smith, Chartered Accountant, and Helen Katharine Brown; m Alison; 2 sons (Christopher and Paul). **Subject(s):** Mathematics/Mechanical Sciences; BA 1929; MA 1933. **Tutor(s):** J M Wordie. **Educ:** Highgate School. Died 1 September 1983.

SMITH, Cyril Randolph (1929) Born 10 December 1910, Eltonhurst, St Marys Road, Leeds; son of John Cyril Binns Smith, Merchant, and Eveline Oldroyd; m Kathleen Joan Ivimy, 17 February 1938; 2 daughters. BA 1932; MICE. **Tutor(s):** J M Wordie. **Educ:** Chapel Allerton Girls' High School, Leeds; Moorlands School, Headingley; Haileybury College.

SMITH, David Banister Lockhart (1946) Born 19 October 1921, Mountain Lodge, Hong Kong; son of Norman Lockhart Smith, Colonial Secretary, Hong Kong, and Maud Violet Banister. BA 1947; MA 1956.

Tutor(s): C W Guillebaud. **Johnian Relatives:** nephew of Thomas Roger Banister (1909). **Educ:** Sedbergh School; Christ Church, Oxford. **Career:** Royal Marines, WWII; Captain, Fleet Air Arm; Architect.

SMITH, David Henry Gould (GOULD SMITH) (1949) Born 16 March 1928, The Park, Donington, Lincolnshire; son of Francis Gould Smith, Solicitor, and Ada Catherine Grace Gleed; m Shirley Moore, 1957; 1 son (b 1958), 1 daughter (b 1961). **Subject(s):** Estate Management; BA 1952; MA 1972; ARICS 1954. **Tutor(s):** G C L Bertram. **Educ:** Orwell Park Preparatory School, Ipswich; Winchester College. **Career:** Land Agent, Rawlence & Squarey (Humberts), Sherborne, Dorset 1952–1954; Executive Land Agent, J Carter Jonas & Sons, Cambridge 1954–1959; Deputy Crown Estate Receiver (Agent), Somerset and Wiltshire, Marlborough 1959–1964; Inland Revenue Valuation Office, Bristol, Weston-Super-Mare and Taunton 1964–1988.

SMITH, David Hilbre (1949) Born 10 October 1929, Greylands, Bromley Cross, Lancashire; son of Hilbre Henry Smith, Cotton Bleacher and Dyer, and Catharine Beatrice Sharp; m (1) Carol Jean Nanette, 20 June 1953 (d), (2) Anne Jennifer, 24 April 1989; 1 son (Julian Hilbre), 2 daughters (Shan Amanda and Fiona Clare). **Subject(s):** Natural Sciences; BA 1952; MA 1956. **Tutor(s):** G C L Bertram. **Johnian Relatives:** grandson of William James Sharp (1882). **Educ:** Dumpton House, Broadstairs; Mill Mead, Shrewsbury; Sherborne School. **Career:** Family textile firm (became Chairman) 1953.

SMITH, David Hurst (1944) Born 11 April 1926, The Cedars, Carrington Barn, Marple, Cheshire; son of James Smith, Welfare Supervisor, and Dorothy Mary Johnson. **Subject(s):** Natural Sciences; BA 1947; MA 1955. **Tutor(s):** C W Guillebaud. **Johnian Relatives:** brother of Norman Johnson Smith (1940); uncle of David Kendall Smith (1968) and of Michael Denby Smith (1972). **Educ:** The King's School, Macclesfield. **Career:** Director, Meat and Livestock Commission, until 1989.

SMITH, The Revd Edward Harry (1908) Born 4 August 1889, 32 Cromwell Road, Hove, Sussex; son of Joseph Smith, Master Draper, and Laura Matilda Ward. **Subject(s):** Theology; BA 1911; MA 1915. **Tutor(s):** J R Tanner. **Educ:** Aldenham School; Ely Theological College. **Career:** Deacon 1913; Curate, Goole 1913–1915; Priest 1914; Curate, Wymondham 1915–1916; Curate, St Mary, Great Ildford 1916–1924; SPG Missionary, Bangalore 1924–1925; Principal, All Saints' College, Galle 1925–1926; Curate, St Matthew's, Custom House, Victoria Docks 1926–1929; Curate, St Saviour, Walthamstow 1929–1930; Curate, St Faith, Stoke Newington 1932–1934; Curate, St George, Netherfield 1934–1935; Chaplain, Home of Compassion, Thames Ditton 1935–1942; Chaplain, St Wilfrid's Convent 1943.

SMITH, Frederic Gordon (1929) Born 19 September 1910, 8 Florence Road, Stroud Green, Hornsey, Middlesex; son of Frederic Richards Smith, Municipal Officer, and Florence Minnie Tempest Keeping; 1 daughter. **Subject(s):** Mathematics; BA 1932; MA 1944. **Tutor(s):** J M Wordie. **Educ:** Stroud Green Council School; Owen's School, Islington. **Career:** Commissioned, Royal Signals, WWII; Civil Service 1947; Actuary, Government Actuary's Department 1951; Advisor: National Pension Scheme for Farmers, Zambia 1991. **Appointments:** Advisor, Social Security Scheme, Tanzanian Presidential Commission 1990; Advisor, IFAD. **Awards:** Scholarship, SJC 1928. **Honours:** CBE 1964. Died 23 April 1993.

SMITH, Frederick Arthur Lewis (1912) Born 22 January 1894, Everest Villa, Cambridge Road, Aldershot, Hampshire; son of Fred Smith, Major General, and Mary Ann Briggs. **Tutor(s):** E E Sikes. **Educ:** Blackheath; Public School, Wanskbek, Germany; Public School, Lausanne, Switzerland; Courtenay Lodge, Abingdon.

SMITH, Geoffrey Sheil (1940) Born 15 June 1921, 3 Devonshire Road, Birkenhead; son of Charles William Smith, Insurance Inspector, and Kathleen Leah Fletcher. **Subject(s):** Modern and Medieval Languages;

BA 1947; MA 1949. **Tutor(s):** C W Guillebaud. **Educ:** Upton Preparatory School; Ernest Bailey Secondary School; Birkenhead Institute.

SMITH, George Ernest (1912) Born 8 January 1893, 20 Lyndhurst Road, Camberwell, Surrey; son of George Stening Smith, Warehouseman, and Alice Ashton Salter. **Subject(s):** Natural Sciences/Mathematics; BA 1915. **Tutor(s):** R P Gregory. **Educ:** Lyndhurst Grove LCC School; Wilson's Grammar School, Camberwell. **Career:** Served in WWI; Schoolmaster, Wilson's Grammar School, Camberwell. **Awards:** Sizarship, SJC. **Honours:** Croix de Guerre. **Publications:** Chess Editor, *The Field.* Died 17 July 1946.

SMITH, George Perry (PERRY-SMITH) (1941) Born 10 October 1922, Widnes, Lancashire; son of Edward Smith, Wesleyan Methodist Minister, and Jane Ethel Oyston; m (1) Helen, (2) Ruth Jaine, 1954 (div 1961), (3) Mercedes (div 1970), (4) Heather Crosbie, 1990; 3 sons, 2 daughters, 4 stepsons (1 deceased), 1 stepdaughter. **Subject(s):** Modern and Medieval Languages; BA 1948; MA 1950; Diploma in Education (Bristol). **Tutor(s):** C W Guillebaud. **Educ:** Wychwood Preparatory School, Bournemouth; Silsden Elementary School; Brecon Elementary School; Callington Secondary School; Kingswood School, Bath; Bristol University. **Career:** Friends' Ambulance Unit, WWII; Exchange teacher, Lycée St Louis, Boulevard Saint-Michel, Paris; French teacher, Kingswood School, Bath; Chef and proprietor, Hole in the Wall Restaurant, George Street, Bath 1952–1972; Chef and proprietor, Riverside, Helford, Cornwall 1973–1986. **Appointments:** British Chef Laureate 1986. Died 1 October 2003.

SMITH, Gordon Henry Murray (1936) Born 6 May 1918, 160 King Henry's Road, Hampstead, London; son of James Gordon Murray Smith, Stockbroker, and Elsie Taylor. **Subject(s):** Mechanical Sciences; BA 1939. **Tutor(s):** C W Guillebaud. **Educ:** Norman Court, Potters Bar; Uppingham School. Died 29 August 1939.

SMITH, Graham Udale (1901) Born 20 January 1871, Laguna, Canary Islands; son of Derwent Henry Smith, Barrister, and Fanny Mary Underwood. **Tutor(s):** D MacAlister. **Educ:** Edinburgh Institution; KCL.

SMITH, Gregory Baird (1933) Born 3 December 1914, The Red House, Virginia Water, Egham, Surrey; son of George William Smith, Medical Practitioner, and Sylvia Rose Margaret Blackstone. BA 1936. **Tutor(s):** R L Howland. **Educ:** Gunnersby Preparatory School, Chiswick; Stowe School.

SMITH, Harry Graham (1948) Born 16 January 1930, Detroit, Michigan, USA; son of Joseph Henry Samuel Smith, Hotel Proprietor, and Doris Jane Harvey Rowe. **Subject(s):** Geography; BA 1951; MA 1955; FCA; FTII. **Tutor(s):** J M Wordie. **Educ:** Porthallow Elementary School; Illogan Elementary School; Redruth County Grammar School. **Career:** Accountant. **Appointments:** JP, Cornwall. Died 1992.

SMITH, Harry Percy (1926) Born 25 August 1908, 3 Ellerslie Road, Shepherd's Bush, Middlesex; son of George Edmund Smith, Schoolmaster, and Lavinia Augusta Jones. **Subject(s):** History; BA 1929; MA 1947. **Tutor(s):** E A Benians. **Educ:** Ellerslie Road London County Council School; Latymer Upper School, Hammersmith. **Awards:** Scholarship, SJC. Died 17 July 1983.

SMITH, Howard (1910) Born 16 December 1891, Waterloo Road, Wellington, Shropshire; son of Arthur Henry Smith, Bank Cashier, and Annie Waterhouse Hawkesford. **Subject(s):** Natural Sciences; BA 1913. **Tutor(s):** E E Sikes. **Educ:** Newport Grammar School. **Career:** Assistant, Forestry Department, Bombay Burma Corporation 1914.

SMITH, Hugh Fairfield (1928) Born 8 March 1904, Midsands, Ayr, Scotland; son of Hugh Fairfield Smith, Seed and Grain Merchant, and Agnes Matthieson Dobbie. BA (Edinburgh) 1926. **Tutor(s):** C W

Guillebaud. **Educ:** Trinity College, Glenalmond; Ayr Academy; University of Edinburgh; Cornell University, Ithaca; New York, USA. **Awards:** Vans Dunlop Scholarship, Edinburgh 1928–1929; Research Scholarship, Board of Agriculture for Scotland 1928–1930.

SMITH, Dr Ian McNicol (1937) Born 23 April 1920, 19 Sandholes, Paisley; son of Thomas Henry Smith, Master Butcher, and Helen McNicol Wilson; BA 1940; MB, BChir 1943. **Tutor(s):** R L Howland. **Johnian Relatives:** brother of James Anstruther Smith (1935). **Educ:** John Neilson Institution, Paisley; Strathallan School, Forgandenny.

SMITH, Dr James Anstruther (1935) Born 6 August 1917, 12 Townhead Terrace, Paisley; son of Thomas Henry Smith, Master Butcher, and Helen McNicol Wilson; m Wendy. **Subject(s):** Natural Sciences; BA 1938; BChir 1942; MB 1942; FFARCS. **Tutor(s):** R L Howland. **Johnian Relatives:** brother of Ian McNicol Smith (1937). **Educ:** John Neilson Institution, Paisley; Strathallan School, Forgandenny. **Career:** Senior Resident Anaesthetist, St Bartholomew's 1942–1944; Major, RAMC, served in India 1944–1946; Lecturer and Consultant in Anaesthetics, Royal Postgraduate Medical School, Hammersmith 1948–1953; Consultant Anaesthetist, Plymouth 1953. **Appointments:** President, Society of Anaesthetists, South-West region 1973. Died 18 December 1987.

SMITH, James Arthur Wilson (1926) Born 13 May 1907, Symcroft, Yeadon, Wharfedale, Leeds; son of Thomas William Smith, Solicitor, and Agnes Mary Williams; m Frances Elizabeth Smith, 13 September 1939; 1 daughter (Jean). **Subject(s):** Classics/Law; BA 1929; MA 1934. **Tutor(s):** M P Charlesworth. **Johnian Relatives:** grandson of James Reynold Williams (1849); uncle of Peter Nicholson Smith (1954) and of Brian Fenwick-Smith (1956). **Educ:** W Snow, The Craig, Windermere; Hereford Cathedral School. **Career:** Army 1939–1945; Solicitor until 1990. **Awards:** Somerset Exhibition, SJC 1926.

SMITH, Jeffrey Prowse (1938) Born 21 December 1919, Silverdale, Alderbrook Road, Solihull; son of Sidney Smith, Metal Manufacturer, and Hilda Prowse. **Subject(s):** Modern and Medieval Languages; BA 1941; MA 1945. **Tutor(s):** C W Guillebaud. **Educ:** Solihull Junior School; Manly Hall Cottage; Solihull School. **Career:** Called to the Bar, Inner Temple 1951.

SMITH, John Forbes (1905) Born 9 April 1886, Lynwood, Regent Street, Lancaster; son of Henry William Smith, Congregational Minister, and Jane Ellen Bliss; m Marjorie Helen Lawrence, 18 June 1919. **Subject(s):** History; BA 1908; LLB 1909. **Tutor(s):** C E Graves; J R Tanner. **Educ:** Mill Hill School. **Career:** Solicitor's Department, GPO 1911–1951.

SMITH, John Howard Marcus (1925) Born 28 June 1906, Nunlands, Great Stanmore, Middlesex; son of Marcus Smith, Dry Goods Merchant, and Dorothy Lydia Gregory Robinson; m (1) Alison Grace Gilkison, 1934, (2) Rubery Winifred Richards, 1940; 1 son (Richard Howard Marcus b 1954), 2 daughters (Susan Rubery b 1949 and Rosemary Jane b 1950). **Subject(s):** Economics/Engineering; BA 1928. **Tutor(s):** E A Benians. **Educ:** Heddon Court, Cockfosters, London; Shrewsbury School; Empire General Flying School. **Career:** Cook Strait Airways; Flying Instructor, Royal New Zealand Air Force Reserve; RAFVR, WWII; Mathematics and Physics Teacher, Southlands Boys' High School; Pilot and Ground Engineer, Douglas Mill, Auckland 1928–1929; MC McGregor's Hamilton Airways 1929–1931; Southland Aero Club 1931–1937; Car Salesman, Nelson 1950. **Honours:** AFC. Died 1 September 1971.

SMITH, John Philip (1933) Born 19 March 1915, 12 Seymour Road, Crumpsall, Manchester; son of Harold Smith, Electrical and Mechanical Engineer, and Florence Ruth Gamble; m (1) Sheila, (2) Marjorie; (1) 1 daughter. **Subject(s):** Modern and Medieval Languages. **Tutor(s):** J S Boys Smith. **Educ:** King's Lynn; Lynfield School, Hunstanton; Wellingborough School. **Career:** Design Staff, De Havilland Technical School 1934–1939; Military Aircraft Designer 1939–1945; Deputy Chief

Designer, de Haviland 1945; Director and Chief Engineer 1963; Chief Engineer, Hawker Siddeley Aviation 1968; Deputy Managing Director, British Aerospace 1977–1979. **Honours:** CBE 1978. Died 3 September 1995.

SMITH, John Young Mitchell (MITCHELL SMITH) (1919) Born 8 October 1901, St Monans, Cambuslang, Lanarkshire; son of John Young Smith, Merchant, and Mary Aitken. **Tutor(s):** E A Benians. **Educ:** Institution Nedoncelle, Roubaix, France; Wellington College.

SMITH, Professor Joseph Francis (1934) Born 20 June 1916, General Hospital, Bristol; son of Thomas Smith, Dairyman, and Ethel Maud Evans; m Hilda, 1 son, 1 daughter (Jennie Christie). **Subject(s):** Natural Sciences; BA 1937; BChir 1940; MB 1940. **Tutor(s):** R L Howland. **Educ:** Bristol Grammar School. **Career:** The London Hospital 1937–1940; Surgeon Lieutenant, RNVR 1941–1946; Senior Lecturer in Morbid Anatomy, University College Hospital Medical School 1949–1954; Assistant Professor, University of Cincinnati 1954; First Assistant to Sir Roy Cameron 1958, Reader in Morbid Anatomy 1959–1964, Professor of Morbid Anatomy 1964, University College Hospital Medical School. **Appointments:** Visiting Assistant Professor, State University of New York 1951–1952. **Awards:** Macloghlin Scholarship, RCS. **Publications:** Papers on the pathology of the kidney and the nervous system. Died September 2000.

SMITH, Joseph Marie William Lyle (1921) Born 3 January 1903, 22 Clovelly Road, Ealing, London; son of William Arrowsmith Lyle Smith, Civil Servant, and Frances Augusta Hamilton Leeming. BA 1924. **Tutor(s):** B F Armitage. **Educ:** Wimbledon College; Ampleforth College, Malton. **Publications:** 'Body No 19', *The Eagle*, 43, 1924.

SMITH, Kenneth Edward (1943) Born 17 September 1924, 80 Upper Medlock Street, Hulme, Manchester; son of Albert Edward Smith, Telephone Engineer, and Sarah Ellen Burgess; m Brenda Robinson, 28 March 1953; 1 son (Julian Kendal b 1960). **Subject(s):** Mechanical Sciences; BA 1949; MA 1965; CEng; MIMechE. **Tutor(s):** C W Guillebaud. **Educ:** Hanford Church of England School; Junior Technical School; North Staffordshire Technical College. **Career:** Principal Lecturer in Engineering, North Staffordshire Polytechnic. **Publications:** *Mechanical Engineering Principles*, 2 volumes, 1980.

SMITH, Leonard Danvers (1907) Born 27 August 1888, Holly Bank, Mount Pleasant, Ipsley, Redditch, Warwickshire; son of Charles Smith, Station Master, and Mary Anne Eliza Savage. **Subject(s):** Law; BA 1910; LLB 1910. **Tutor(s):** E E Sikes. **Educ:** Sutton Bridge School; Moulton School, Spalding; Bedford Grammar School.

SMITH, Marcus Cecil Forryan (1927) Born 30 September 1908, 93 Queen Street, Ordsall, East Retford, Nottinghamshire; son of George Archibald Smith, Journalist, and Jessie Venetia Hodges. **Subject(s):** English; BA 1930. **Tutor(s):** M P Charlesworth. **Educ:** King Edward VI Grammar School, East Retford; Royal Grammar School, High Wycombe; Chesterfield Grammar School. Died 7 November 1930.

SMITH, Norman Johnson (1940) Born 12 February 1922, Marple, Cheshire; son of James Smith, Personnel Manager, and Dorothy Mary Johnson, Classics Teacher; m Joan Elizabeth Kendall, 6 August 1949, St John's Church, Bilton; 3 sons (David, Michael and Andrew). **Subject(s):** Mathematics/Physics; BA 1943; MA 1947. **Tutor(s):** J M Wordie. **Johnian Relatives:** brother of David Hurst Smith (1944); father of David Kendall Smith (1968) and of Michael Denby Smith (1972). **Educ:** King's School, Macclesfield. **Career:** Senior Principal Scientific Officer, RSRE, Malvern, Worcestershire 1980. **Appointments:** Leader, Crusader Class, Malvern; Air Raid Warden, SJC. **Awards:** Scholarship, SJC. **Publications:** 'Data Handling and Displays for Air Traffic Control', *IEE Symposium*, 1960; (with B W Oakley) 'Methods of Extracting Radar Data for Automatic Processing'; (with P F Heggs) 'A Cathode Ray Labelling Plan-Display'; 'The Problems of Electronics',

Journal of the Royal Aeronautical Society, March 1966; various confidential Government reports. Died 3 November 2000.

SMITH, Norman Peter (1943) Born 29 August 1925, 5 Glencairn Road, West Derby, Liverpool; son of Samuel Smith, Clerk, Biscuit Factory, and Emma Done. **Subject(s):** Mathematics; BA 1947; MA 1950. **Tutor(s):** S J Bailey. **Educ:** Broadgreen Road Council School, Liverpool; Liverpool Institute High School. **Awards:** Minor Scholarship, SJC 1943.

SMITH, Oswald Carlton (1906) Born 30 May 1887, 14 Ingleby Road, Islington, Middlesex; son of Frederick Smith, Law Clerk, and Elizabeth Mercy Anne Blaxter. **Subject(s):** Natural Sciences/Mathematics; BA 1909; MA 1913; FCIS. **Tutor(s):** J R Tanner. **Educ:** Tollington Park College; Birkbeck College, London. **Career:** Assistant Master, Mill Hill School 1910–1913; Science Master, King Edward VII School, Lytham 1913–1916; Second Lieutenant, RGA (TF), WWI; W H Allen, Engineers, Bedford 1918–1919; Director and Secretary, Adamant Engineering Company, Luton 1919–1926. Died 8 June 1983.

SMITH, Paul Reynolds (1934) Born 15 August 1915, 163 Osborne Road, Newcastle upon Tyne; son of William Paul Smith, Master Printer, and Ada Spink. **Subject(s):** Mathematics/Economics; BA 1937; MA 1955; FIA 1948. **Tutor(s):** J M Wordie. **Educ:** West Jesmond Council School, Newcastle; Royal Grammar School, Newcastle. **Career:** Member 1937–1948, Assistant Actuary 1952–1954, Joint Actuary 1954–1966, Assistant Manager and Actuary 1966–1973, Director, Equity & Law Life Assurance Society; Chairman, Taxation Commission, Life Offices' Association 1967–1969. Died August 1993.

SMITH, Percy Chandler (1926) Born 14 June 1902, 54 Arundel Avenue, Toxteth Park, Liverpool; son of Frederick Elwell Smith, General Produce Broker and West African Merchant, and Nora Edith Chandler; m Annis Gillie; 1 son (Charles). BA 1929; MA 1944. **Tutor(s):** E A Benians. **Educ:** Holmwood Preparatory School, Freshfield; Radley College. **Career:** Architect.

SMITH, Peter Ernest Herbert (1942) Born 3 January 1924, 107 Maison Dieu Road, Dover, Kent; son of Ernest Thomas Cobley Smith, Colonel, and Marie Ann Hruby. **Tutor(s):** S J Bailey. **Educ:** St Peter's College, York; Belmont House, Blackheath; Beaumont College.

SMITH, Peter Fenwick (FENWICK-SMITH) (1941) Born 4 December 1923, Redlands, Midhurst Road, Longbenton, Newcastle upon Tyne; son of Bruce Fenwick Smith, Managing Director, Rope Manufacturing Company, and Margaret Muir Renton; m Jean Margaret Leatherland, February 1952. BA 1947; MA 1949; FCA; CCIM. **Tutor(s):** C W Guillebaud. **Educ:** Royal Grammar School, Newcastle upon Tyne; Fettes College, Edinburgh. **Career:** Finance Director, R Hood Haggie & Son Ltd, Rope Manufacturers, Newcastle upon Tyne; Chief Executive, Bridon plc, Doncaster. **Appointments:** JP; Freeman, London and Newcastle upon Tyne.

SMITH, Philip Burrows (1934) Born 29 May 1916, 20 Dunollie Road, Sale; son of Edwin Burrows Smith, Schoolmaster, and Annie Crewdson Metcalfe. **Subject(s):** Mechanical Sciences; BA 1937; MA 1941. **Tutor(s):** J S Boys Smith. **Educ:** Worthington Road Council School, Sale; Lyman Grammar School; Manchester Grammar School. **Awards:** Scholarship, SJC 1936–1937.

SMITH, Philip Lionel Forster (1947) Born 3 January 1924, Clarence Nursing Home, Tunbridge Wells, Kent; son of Hubert John Forster Smith, Land Agent, and Diana Watkins; m Alice Møller-Jensen 1951; 2 sons. **Subject(s):** Natural Sciences; BA 1949; MRCVS. **Tutor(s):** G C L Bertram. **Johnian Relatives:** brother of Robin Hugh Forster Smith (1950). **Educ:** Hall School, Hampstead; Blundell's School, Tiverton; Balliol College, Oxford; Royal Veterinary College, London. **Career:** Flying Instructor, RAF 1943–1947; Junior Partner, Veterinary Practice, St Columb Major, Cornwall 1952–1954; Partner, Practice in Melbury Osmond, Dorset 1954–1990. Died 28 September 2000.

SMITH, Reginald Edwin (1945) Born 14 June 1927, 14 Station Road, Frindsbury Intra, Rochester, Kent; son of Albert Dennis Smith, Superintendent, and Louisa Letley; m Isabel Murdoch Smith, 17 May 1954, Milngavie, Dunbartonshire; 2 daughters. **Subject(s):** Mechanical Sciences; BA 1948; MA 1952. **Tutor(s):** S J Bailey; R L Howland. **Educ:** Southend-on-Sea High School. **Career:** Engineer researching structural use of aluminium, Aluminium Laboratories Limited, Banbury, Oxon 1948–1988. **Publications:** 'Strength of aluminium single-angle tension members before and after corrosion', *The Structural Engineer*, September 1965. Died 18 October 1988.

SMITH, Reginald William (1923) Born 17 November 1904, Sturt Green, Bray, Maidenhead, Berkshire; son of Frederick Albert Smith, Agricultural Worker, and Gertrude Nutt. **Subject(s):** Natural Sciences; BA 1926. **Tutor(s):** B F Armitage. **Educ:** Church of England School, Holyport; County Boys' School, Maidenhead.

SMITH, Rex Stanley (1948) Born 20 February 1928, 53 Hahnemann Road, Walton, Liverpool; son of William Stanley Smith, Cabinet Maker, and Emilie Margaret Hawnaur. **Subject(s):** History; BA 1950; MA 1968. **Tutor(s):** F Thistlethwaite. **Educ:** Arnot Street Council School; Liverpool Collegiate School. **Awards:** Exhibition, SJC 1946.

SMITH, Richard Arthur Amyas (1940) Born 4 March 1922, Victoria Road, Karachi, India; son of Norman Percival Arthur Smith, Head of Indian Intelligence, and Gladys Ivy Victoria Martin; m (1) Margaret McLeod Panton, 25 November 1944, (3) Carol; 4 daughters. **Tutor(s):** J M Wordie. **Educ:** Temple Grove, Eastbourne; Tonbridge School. **Career:** Lieutenant, Oxford and Buckinghamshire Light Infantry, WWII; work in India and Pakistan 1946–1968; Personnel Director, Burmah Oil 1968. **Honours:** MC. Died 27 April 1993.

SMITH, Robert James (1922) Born 12 May 1902, Lochend, Troon, Ayrshire, Scotland; son of Robert Smith, Minister of Troon, and Janet Gilmore. **Subject(s):** Mechanical Sciences; BA 1924. **Tutor(s):** E Cunningham. **Educ:** Troon High Grade Public School; The Academy, Ayr; University of Edinburgh. **Awards:** John Winbolt Prize, University of Cambridge 1926.

SMITH, Roy (1928) Born 3 September 1911, 10 Beechfield Road, Birkby, Huddersfield; son of Sam Smith, Worsted Spinner, and Emma Parratt. **Subject(s):** Classics; BA 1933. **Tutor(s):** M P Charlesworth. **Educ:** Terra Nova, Birkdale; The Leys School, Cambridge. **Career:** Barrister, Middle Temple; Lieutenant Colonel, Mentioned in Despatches, WWII. **Awards:** Harmsworth Law Scholarship, Middle Temple. **Honours:** MC. Died 12 May 1984.

SMITH, Dr Russell Alexander (1948) Born 17 December 1925, Bent Street, Katoomba, New South Wales; son of George Malcolm Smith, Motor Body Builder, and Muriel Jean Robinson; m Katherine Mary Truman, 30 December 1954. **Subject(s):** Maths; BA 1950; MA 1954; PhD 1954; ScD 1986; BSc (Sydney) 1947. **Tutor(s):** J M Wordie. **Educ:** Taree High School; New England University College, University of Sydney. **Career:** Lecturer in Mathematics, University of Sydney 1953; Lecturer in Mathematics, University of Durham 1954. **Awards:** Rayleigh Prize, University of Cambridge 1952.

SMITH, Thomas (KNAPE SMITH) (1923) Born 5 August 1902, 2 Old Hall Street, Burnley, Lancashire; son of Walter Smith, Cashier, and Martha Ann Knape. **Subject(s):** Mathematics; BA 1926; MA 1930; BSc (Manchester) 1922; MSc (Manchester) 1924. **Tutor(s):** J M Wordie. **Educ:** Abel Street Elementary School, Burnley; Burnley Grammar School; University of Manchester. **Career:** Mathematics Master, Bancroft's School, Essex 1927; King Edward VI Grammar School, Retford 1927–1929; Heath School, Halifax 1929. Died 9 April 1989.

SMITH, Thomas Carl (1922) Born 2 June 1903, 8 Anne Street, Hull, Yorkshire; son of Thomas Smith, Master Chemist, and Betty Antoine

Anna Christine Bay. **Subject(s):** Mathematics; BA 1925; MA 1929. **Tutor(s):** E A Benians. **Educ:** Eton House School, Hull; The Grammar School, Wirksworth; Hymers College, Hull.

SMITH, The Revd Thomas Gregory (GREGORY-SMITH) (1927) Born 28 October 1908, 30 Byne Road, Sydenham, London; son of Gregory Smith, Clerk in the Bank of England, and Alice Jessie May; m Irene Emily Copeland, 1942 (d 1996); 2 sons (David Gregory and Robert Gregory), 1 daughter (Margaret). **Subject(s):** Mechanical Sciences; BA 1930; MA 1934. **Tutor(s):** C W Guillebaud. **Johnian Relatives:** father of David Gregory Gregory-Smith (1961); grandfather of Juliette Mary Leverment (1992). **Educ:** Convent School, Rickmansworth; The Grammar School, Watford. **Career:** Junior Civil Engineer, Charles Brand & Son, London 1930–1932; London College of Divinity 1933–1934; Ordained Deacon 1934; Curate, St Jude, Mildmay Park 1934–1936; Ordained Priest, London 1935; Curate, Emmanuel, South Croydon 1936–1938; Missionary, Church Missionary Society, Kabale, Uganda 1938–1947; Part-time Curate, St James, Shirley, Southampton 1948; Home Staff, Ruanda Mission (CMS) 1949–1952; Missionary, Church Missionary Society, Kabale and Fort Portal, Uganda 1952–1963; Home Staff, Ruanda Mission 1964–1971; Incumbent of Emmanuel, Wimbledon 1971–1976. **Awards:** Scholarship, SJC 1927. Died 26 April 2001.

SMITH, Vernon John (1942) Born 13 August 1924, Kelvin House, Edgbaston Road, Smethwick; son of Ernest William Smith, Clerk in Iron Works, and Hilda Gladys Robbins. **Subject(s):** Mechanical Sciences; BA 1945; MA 1949. **Tutor(s):** S J Bailey. **Johnian Relatives:** brother of Alan Desmond Smith (1943). **Educ:** Smethwick Hall Elementary; Nelson Street Elementary School, Birmingham; King Edward VI Grammar School, Birmingham.

SMITH, Vernon Sampson (1913) Born 11 July 1894, George Street, Horbury, Yorkshire; son of Colin Smith, Assistant Manager, Horbury Junction Iron Works, and Anne Sampson. BA 1919; MA 1943. **Tutor(s):** E E Sikes. **Johnian Relatives:** father of Colin Vernon-Smith (1958). **Educ:** Wakefield Grammar School. **Career:** Duke of Wellington's Regiment, later Indian Army; Captain, Mesopotamian Expeditionary Force; Mentioned in Despatches for gallantry and devotion to duty 1914–1918; Singapore Office, Shell 1920–1923; Branch Manager, Malay State of Perak 1923–1925; Branch Manager, Kuala Lumpur 1925–1927; Sales General Manager, Singapore 1927–1931; Assistant General Manager, Shell Company for Australia and New Zealand 1931; General Manager 1934. **Awards:** Exhibition, SJC. **Honours:** Kaisar-I-Hind Medal with Clasp. Died 28 February 1979.

SMITH, Victor St George (1919) Born 4 February 1898, 19 Killyon Road, Clapham, Surrey; son of William Alfred Smith, Clerk in Holy Orders, and Ellen Leah Selway Scott. BA 1922; MA 1926. **Tutor(s):** E E Sikes. **Educ:** Highbury New Park College, London; Merchant Taylors' School, London. **Career:** Private, Artists Rifles 1916; Cadet, No 2 Officer Cadet Battalion, Cambridge 1916–1917; Lieutenant, 7th Royal Sussex Regiment, France 1917–1919; Lieutenant, 4th Royal Sussex Regiment, Germany 1919. Died 12 April 1978.

SMITH, Wilfred Cantwell (1938) Born 21 July 1916, Toronto, Canada; son of Victor Arnold Smith, Insurance General Agent, and Sarah Cory Cantwell. **Tutor(s):** J S Boys Smith. **Educ:** Upper Canada College, Toronto; Lycée Campollion, Grenoble, France; Universidad de Madrid; Université de Grenoble, France; American University, Cairo, Egypt; University of Toronto.

SMITH, William Douglas (1945) Born 1 August 1927, Ellerston, Drumchapel, Dumbartonshire; son of William Sloan Smith, Iron Merchant, and Mary Campbell Inglis. **Subject(s):** Mechanical Sciences; BA 1948; MA 1952. **Tutor(s):** S J Bailey; R L Howland. **Educ:** Glasgow Academy. **Career:** Army, until 1949; Arnott Young Ltd 1949–1977 (Chairman and Chief Executive 1968–1977). **Appointments:** Founder and General Manager, Drumchapel Amateurs 1950–2004; Advisor to

European Community on use of scrap supplies; Consultant on marine salvage to Clyde Port Authority; President, British Scrap Federation; President, British Shipbreakers' Association; President, Scottish Scrap Association; Local Councillor, Cardross and Craigendoran, West Dunbartonshire; Captain, Boys' Brigade Company, Glasgow. Died 24 February 2004.

SMITH, William Edward (1949) Born 14 April 1929, Joseph Fraser Nursing Home, Columbo, Ceylon; son of Edward Henry Smith, Director, Fairey Aviation Company Ltd, and Barbara Cubitt. **Tutor(s):** G C L Bertram. **Educ:** Rutland House, Hanwell; Hurstpierpoint College; Oundle School. Died 1 June 1952.

SMITHIES, Dr Frank (1931) Born 10 March 1912, 33 Sciennes Road, Newington, Edinburgh; son of Frank Smithies, Courier, and Mary Brass Blakemore; m Nora Sophia Arone, 7 December 1945, Chelsea Registry Office (d 1 April 1987). **Subject(s):** Mathematics; BA 1933; PhD 1937; MA (Edinburgh) 1931; FRSE 1961. **Tutor(s):** J M Wordie. **Educ:** Sciennes School, Edinburgh; Outlook Tower, Edinburgh; University of Edinburgh. **Career:** Title A Fellow 1937–1945 (suspended 1940–1945 while on war service), Title B Fellow and Lecturer in Mathematics 1945–1979, Title D Fellow 1979–2002, SJC; Temporary Faculty Assistant Lecturer in Mathematics 1945–1947, Lecturer in Mathematics 1947–1962, Reader in Functional Analysis 1962–1979 (Emeritus 1979–2002), University of Cambridge. **Appointments:** Carnegie Fellowship 1936–1937; Leverhulme Research Fellowship 1952–1953; Director of Studies, SJC 1959–1971. **Awards:** Baylis Studentship, SJC 1934; Rayleigh Prize, University of Cambridge 1935; Studentship SJC 1935–1937. **Publications:** *Integral Equations*, CUP, 1958; *Cauchy and the Creation of Complex Function Theory*, CUP, 1997; about 30 articles and numerous book reviews in various periodicals; numerous abstracts in *Mathematical Reviews*. Died 16 November 2002.

SMITHSON, Thomas Alan (1948) Born 19 March 1928, 3 Holmlands Park, Chester-le-Street, Durham; son of Thomas Smithson, Bank Inspector, and Emily Stringer, Bank Clerk; m Ruth Fieldhouse, 16 October 1971. **Subject(s):** Maths; BA 1950; MA 1955. **Tutor(s):** J M Wordie. **Johnian Relatives:** brother of Robert Willis Smithson (1950). **Educ:** Dormie House, West Kirby; Newcastle Preparatory School; Bow School, Durham; Durham School. **Career:** RN 1946–1948; Operational Research Analyst, Mullard Ltd, Blackburn 1959–1965; Philips Industries Ltd, Croydon 1966–1969; Systems Designer, CRC Information Systems Ltd 1969–1980; Software Consultant, Alan Smithson Associates, London 1980–1989; Author 1989. **Awards:** Baker Exhibition, SJC 1946. **Publications:** *The Shape of the Whole*, 1990; *The Kairos Point*, 1997.

SMOUHA, Ellis Hay (1925) Born 11 July 1906, Middleton Road, Crumpsall, Manchester; son of Joseph Smouha, Merchant Shipper, and Rosa Acles; m Peggy; 1 daughter (Judy), 1 son (Derrick). BA 1928; MA 1931. **Tutor(s):** E A Benians. **Educ:** South Manchester Grammar School; Cheltenham College. Died 15 January 1986.

SMYTH, David (1943) Born 28 January 1925, 13 Veronica Road, Balham; son of Robert Smyth, Company Secretary, and Ethel Louisa Cole. **Subject(s):** Geography; BA 1948; MA 1950. **Tutor(s):** C W Guillebaud. **Educ:** Windsor House School, Slough; Northcliffe House School, Bognor Regis; Aldenham School. **Career:** Honorary Surveyor of the British School at Athens. Died 25 April 1995.

SMYTHE, The Revd Paul Rodney (1945) Born 4 June 1905, Wood Green, Middlesex; son of Herbert James Bevis Smythe, Civil Servant, and Ethel Mary Bradford. BA (Oxon) 1928; MA (Oxon) 1931, BD (Oxon) 1937. **Educ:** Bedford School; Merton College, Oxford. **Career:** Schoolmaster; Vicar, Horningsea; Deacon 1935; Curate, St Nicholas, Blundellsands 1935–1937; Priest 1936; Curate, St Giles, Oxford 1937.

SNEATH, Arthur (1903) Born 19 September 1876, 9 High Street, St Michael, Stamford, Lincolnshire; son of William Sneath, Fancy Goods

Warehouseman, and Sarah Emily Campbell; m Lena Sutton, 11 April 1917, Our Lady of Lourdes, London. BA 1906. **Tutor(s):** C E Graves; J R Tanner. **Johnian Relatives:** brother of Harry Sneath (1894) and of William Sneath (1897). **Educ:** Private Tuition. **Career:** Schoolmaster, Dover College Junior School 1900–1901; Master, Egyptian Government Schools 1906.

SNOW, Sir Harold Ernest (1919) Born 8 September 1897, 51 Shadwell Road, Horfield, Bristol; son of Ernest Alfred Snow, Shoe Store Manager, and Elizabeth Hannah May; m Nellie Dagmar Goodale, 1924; 1 son (John Brian b 19 July 1927), 1 daughter (Sonia Elizabeth b 25 August 1931). **Subject(s):** Mathematics; BA 1921; MA 1961. **Tutor(s):** E A Benians. **Johnian Relatives:** father of John Brian Snow (1945). **Educ:** Merchant Venturers' Technical College, Bristol; Faculty of Science, University of Bristol. **Career:** Technician RAMC, War Office & France 1915–1919; British Petroleum Company Ltd (then Anglo-Persian Oil Company Ltd) 1921–1932; Group Manager, Shell-Mex and BP Ltd 1932–1936; Manager, Distribution Department, Anglo-Iranian Oil Company 1936; Secretary, Petroleum Board 1939–1945; Deputy Director, Anglo-Iranian Oil Company Ltd 1946–1952; Director (later Deputy Chairman and Managing Director) British Petroleum Co Ltd 1952–1962; General Manager, Iranian Oil Participants Ltd 1954. **Awards:** Exhibition, SJC 1919. **Honours:** OBE 1946; CBE 1952; Kt 1961; Order of Homayoun (Class II), Iran 1963. Died 20 December 1971.

SNOW, John Brian (1945) Born 19 July 1927, Kenwood, Nower Hill, Pinner, Middlesex; son of Harold Ernest Snow, Anglo-Iranian Oil Company Ltd, and Nellie Dagmar Goodale; m Rosamund Elaine Surtees, 1958; 1 son (John William), 1 daughter (Rosamund Elisabeth). **Subject(s):** Mechanical Sciences; BA 1948; MA 1952; CEng; FIEE. **Tutor(s):** S J Bailey; R L Howland. **Johnian Relatives:** son of Harold Ernest Snow (1919). **Educ:** Sherborne School. **Career:** Sales Engineer, British Thomson-Houston Company Ltd 1948–1964; Commercial Manager, Associated Electrical Industries Ltd/GEC Switchgear Ltd 1964–1973; Sales Manager, Projects Manager, Projects Director, Commercial Director, GEC Transportation Projects Ltd 1973–1984; Commercial Director, GEC General Signal Ltd 1984–1990.

SNOWDEN, Joseph Stanley (1920) Born 16 October 1901, Fungarth, Heysham Road, Heysham, Lancashire; son of Joseph Snowden, Draper and House Furnisher, and Fanny Ruth Pickels; m Agnes Enid Mitchell, September 1938. **Subject(s):** Law; BA 1923; LLB 1923. **Tutor(s):** E E Sikes. **Educ:** Sefton College, Morcambe; Sedbergh School. **Career:** Called to the Bar, Inner Temple 1925; Barrister, North Eastern Circuit 1925–1973; Liberal Candidate for various Parliamentary Divisions. **Appointments:** Recorder of Scarborough 1951; Chairman, West Riding Quarter Sessions 1960–1973; Vice-President, Lancashire Liberal Association; Vice-President, Yorkshire Liberal Federation; Assistant Recorder, Leeds; Chairman, Agricultural Land Tribunal, Yorkshire and Lancashire Area.

SNUSHALL, David Bruce (1942) Born 16 January 1924, The Vicarage, Horsforth, Yorkshire; son of Claud Snushall, Clerk in Holy Orders, and Mary Bruce Haley; 1 son (Peter Bruce). **Subject(s):** Mechanical Sciences; BA 1945; MA 1949; CEng; FICE; MIWES; MACE. **Tutor(s):** S J Bailey. **Educ:** Clifton House School, Harrogate; Pocklington School, York. **Career:** Partner, Lemon and Blizard, Consulting Civil Engineers (in charge of Plymouth Office) 1962–1983. **Awards:** Dowman Exhibition, SJC 1942.

SOAR, Leonard Charles (1919) Born 26 February 1899, 20 Elgin Avenue, Paddington, London; son of William Edward Soar, Civil Servant, and Jane McMillen Breeze; m Margaret Mary Ellery; 2 sons (Peter Hale McMillan b 13 April 1928 and Geoffrey David Ellery b 4 August 1932). **Subject(s):** Mathematics; BA 1922; MA 1931. **Tutor(s):** E A Benians. **Johnian Relatives:** father of Peter Hale McMillan Soar (1949); father of Geoffrey David Ellery Soar (1951). **Educ:** Dulwich Hamlet London County Council School; Alleyn's School, Dulwich. **Career:** Master,

Whitgift Grammar School, Croydon 1923–1932; Headmaster, Royal Grammar School, Henley on Thames 1932–1934; Headmaster, Enfield Grammar School 1934–1964. **Appointments:** Assistant Examiner in Mathematics, School Certificate Examinations of University of London, Northern Universities' Joint Board & Cambridge Syndicate; Chairman, Enfield Youth Employment Committee; Member, Air Cadet Council. **Awards:** Exhibition, SJC 1917. Died 14 February 1969.

SOAR, Peter Hale McMillan (1949) Born 13 April 1928, 58 Ross Road, South Norwood, London; son of Leonard Charles Soar, Headmaster, Enfield Grammar School, and Margaret Mary Ellery, Teacher; m Kathleen Taylor (dis); 3 sons (Matthew, Timothy and Daniel). BA 1952; MA 1956. **Tutor(s):** A G Lee. **Johnian Relatives:** son of Leonard Charles Soar (1919); brother of Geoffrey David Ellery Soar (1951). **Educ:** Inglemere Preparatory School, Enfield; Enfield Grammar School. **Career:** Assistant Solicitor, Francis & Co, Cambridge 1957–1959; Assistant Solicitor, Leo Abse, Cardiff 1959–1960; Partner, Wild, Hewitson & Shaw 1960–1974; Principal, firm of Legal Aid Solicitors 1974–1995; Legal Aid Board 1988–1993; Consultant, Thomson & Co, Cambridge (later Thomson, Webb & Corfield) 1995–1997. **Appointments:** Remuneration Committee, Law Society 1980–1988. **Publications:** *The Solicitors Practice*, Butterworth, 1980; *Conveyancing after the Act*, Butterworth, 1986; *Houses of the Humbler Sort*, Cambridgeshire Cottage Housing Society Ltd, 2001; (ed) *The New International Directory of Legal Aid*, International Bar Association, 2002.

SOBEY, Wilfred Henry (1924) Born 1 April 1905, Pachuca, Mexico; son of Richard Thomas Sobey, Gentleman, and Katie Blight Noble; m Mary; 1 son, 1 daughter. BA 1927; MA 1932. **Tutor(s):** E A Benians. **Johnian Relatives:** father of Timothy John Sobey (1959). **Educ:** Collegiate School for Boys, Bournemouth; Mill Hill School. Died 27 February 1988.

SODEN, Dr Wilfred Scovil (1907) Born 26 December 1888, Salisbury, New Brunswick, Canada; son of Frank Holland Soden, Farmer, and Bertha Brown Flewelling; m Helen. **Subject(s):** Natural Sciences; BA 1910; MB 1920; BCh 1920; MRCS; LRCP 1913. **Tutor(s):** J R Tanner. **Educ:** Woodbridge School. **Career:** House Physician, House Surgeon, Pathologist and Registrar, Metropolitan Hospital 1913–1915; Captain, RAMC (TF) (Mentioned in Despatches) 1914–1918; Examiner in Medicine, Cairo School of Medicine 1919; Practice, Winchcombe 1921; Honorary Surgeon, Winchcombe District Hospital; Medical Officer and Public Vaccinator, Vale District. **Publications:** 'Case of Coexistent Suprarenal and Renal Disease of Uncertain Origin', *British Medical Journal*, 1919. Died 13 March 1941.

SOLLER, Maximilian Frederick (1941) Born 1 October 1923, Queen Mary Nursing Home, Derby; son of William Andrew Max Soller, Managing Director, British Celanese Ltd, and Louise Clowes. **Subject(s):** Economics; BA 1949; MA 1954. **Tutor(s):** C W Guillebaud. **Educ:** Repton School.

SOLOMON, Professor Arthur Kaskel (1937) Born 26 November 1912, Pittsburgh, Pennsylvania, USA; son of Mark Kaskel Solomon, Merchant, and Hortense Nattans; m; 1 son (Mark), 1 daughter (Susanna). PhD 1947; ScD 1964; BA (Princeton) 1934; MA (Harvard) 1935; PhD (Harvard) 1937; FAAAS. **Tutor(s):** J M Wordie. **Educ:** Wightman School, Pittsburgh; Shady Side Academy, Pittsburgh; Princeton University; Harvard University. **Career:** Research Associate in Physics and Chemistry, Harvard University 1939–1941; Ministry of Supply 1941–1943; British Admiralty 1943–1945; MIT 1945–1946; Assistant Professor of Physical Chemistry 1946, Professor of Biophysics 1968, Director, Biophysical Laboratory, Harvard Medical School. **Appointments:** Executive Committee, Committee on Growth, National Research Council 1954–1957; Executive Board, Biophysical Society 1958–1962; Radiation Study Division 1960–1963; Secretary General, International Union of Pure and Applied Biophysics 1961–1972; Biophysics Science Training Committee, National Institutes of Health 1963–1968 (Chairman 1966–1968); Executive Committee, International

Council of Scientific Unions 1966–1972; Representative to US National Commission for UNESCO 1968–1974; Harvard Committee on Higher Degrees in Biophysics (Chairman 1959–1981); member, American Chemical Society, American Physiological Society, Biophysics Society, Society of General Physiology. **Honours:** Order of Andres Bello, Government of Venezuela. Died 5 November 2002.

SOMERSET-THOMAS, Vyvyan John (1920) Naval Officer.

SOMERVILLE, Donald Murray (1918) Born 2 September 1896, Barden Villa, Springfield, Chelmsford, Essex; son of Frederick Hubert Somerville, Clerk in Holy Orders, and Laura Susannah Farrow; m Tinita Mary Christina Bridges, 15 September 1924; 1 daughter (Veronica). **Tutor(s):** E E Sikes. **Educ:** Caterham College. **Career:** RA, Gallipoli, France, and Italy 1914–1915; Manager, Devuli Ranch, Rhodesia 1935–1966; Commissioner, Cold Storage Commission 1947–1954. **Appointments:** MP for Umtali North 1933–1939; Member, Sir Godfrey Huggins' Reform Party; President, Victoria Stockowners Association. Died 16 October 1966.

SOMERVILLE, Sir Robert (1925) Born 5 June 1906, 82 James Street, Dunfermline, Fife, Scotland; son of Robert Somerville, Schoolmaster, and Jane Foggo; m (1) Marie-Louise Bergene, 1932 (d 1976), (2) Jessie Warburton, 1981; (1) 1 daughter. **Subject(s):** Classics; BA 1929; MA 1947. **Tutor(s):** M P Charlesworth. **Educ:** The High School, Dunfermline; Fettes College, Edinburgh. **Career:** Historian; Clerk to the Council of the Duchy of Lancaster; Office of the Duchy of Lancaster 1930; Ministry of Shipping, WWII; Chief Clerk 1945, Clerk of the Council and Keeper of Records 1952, Duchy of Lancaster; Chairman, London Record Society 1964–1984. **Appointments:** Honorary Secretary, Council, British Records Association 1947–1956; Member, Advisory Council on Public Records 1959; Chairman, London Record Society 1964–1984; Member, Royal Commission on Historical Manuscripts 1965. **Awards:** Sizarship, SJC. **Honours:** CVO 1953; KCVO 1961. **Publications:** *History of the Duchy of Lancaster*, Volume 1, 1953, Volume 2, 1970; *The Savoy*, 1960; *Duchy of Lancaster Office-Holders from 1603*, 1972. Died 16 July 1992.

SONN, Charles Douglas (1920) Born 30 August 1900, 7L Bickenhall Mansions, Marylebone, Middlesex; son of Gustav Sonn, Director of Companies, and Léonie Granichstaedten. BA 1922; MA 1928. **Tutor(s):** B F Armitage. **Educ:** St John's College, Johannesburg; Park Town Preparatory School, Johannesburg; Lancing College. **Career:** Captain, British Army Intelligence Corps 1939–1945.

SOTHERS, Edward Dudley (1911) Born 28 December 1891, 119 Cazenove Road, Stamford Hill, Middlesex; son of Harry Cove Sothers, Colonial Broker, and Mary Maria Wood; m Norah. **Subject(s):** Mathematics/Natural Sciences; BA 1914. **Tutor(s):** J R Tanner. **Educ:** Windermere Grammar School. **Career:** Second Lieutenant, London Rifle Brigade, WWI. Died 15 February 1965.

SOUTHERN, The Revd John Roy (1925) Born 11 August 1905, 367 Treton Road, Chatham, Kent; son of William John Southern, United Methodist Minister, and Esther Emma Le Rossignol. **Subject(s):** History; BA 1928; MA 1933. **Tutor(s):** E A Benians. **Educ:** Library School, Redruth; Sefton College, Morecambe; Manchester Grammar School; Egerton Hall, Manchester. **Career:** Ordained Deacon 1930; Curate, St James, Gorton 1930–1933; Ordained Priest 1931; Curate, St James, Birchin-Rusholme 1934–1936; Rector, St Laurence, Denton, Manchester 1936–1939; Rector, Black Notley, Essex 1939–1945; Vicar, East Ham 1945–1947; Rector, Holt 1947–1961; Rector, Felbrigge with Metton and Sustead, Norfolk 1961. **Awards:** Exhibition, SJC.

SOUTHWELL, Roy (1943) Born 26 January 1925, Church Farm, North Burton, Yorkshire; son of Benjamin Southwell, Farmer, and Elma Mary Conner. BA 1946; MA 1958. **Tutor(s):** S J Bailey. **Educ:** Burton Fleming Council School; Bridlington School.

SOUTHWOLD, Dr Martin (1949) Born 18 October 1929, 35 East Street, Braunton, Devon; son of Stephen Southwold, Author, and Edith Annie Sebra Bill. **Subject(s):** English/Archaeology and Anthropology; BA 1953; MA 1956; PhD 1959. **Tutor(s):** A G Lee. **Educ:** St Michael's Preparatory School, Seaford; Torquay Preparatory Grammar School; Hawthorn's Private School, Brixham; Totnes Grammar School; Blundell's School, Tiverton. **Career:** Assistant Lecturer in Social Anthropology 1962, Lecturer in Anthropology 1963, University of Manchester. **Awards:** Minor Scholarship, SJC 1946.

SPACKMAN, Canon Flower Stephen (1919) Born 15 September 1890, 7 Richmond Road, St Peter, Worcester; son of Flower Thomas Spackman, Secretary for Elementary Education, and Susan Mantle. BA 1921; MA 1925; FRGS 1931. **Tutor(s):** E A Benians. **Educ:** St Martin's Boys' School, Worcester; Victoria Institute, Worcester; Adeney Schoolmaster's Course, Aldershot; Emmanuel College, Saskatoon; Provincial University of Saskatchewan; Ridley Hall, Cambridge. **Career:** 2nd Volunteer Battalion, Worcester Regiment 1908–1913; Rose to CSM, Canadian Expeditionary Force, France; 1914–1919; Commissioned into Special Reserve, Worcestershire Regiment 1915; Ordained Deacon 1921; Incumbent of Meota 1921–1923; Ordained Priest, Saskatchewan 1922; Principal, Indian Reserve Schools, Alert Bay 1922–1926; Priest in Charge, Northern Mission, British Columbia 1924–1926; Curate, St Paul, Kersal 1927–1929; Vicar, All Saints, Marple, Cheshire (Surrogate 1931) 1929; Commissary for Uganda 1935; Musketry Officer and Chaplain, 37th Cheshire Battalion, Home Guard, and Chaplain, Army Cadet Force 1939–1945; Rural Dean, Stockport; Rector, St Peter, Chester; Honorary Canon, Chester Cathedral 1950; Vicar, Thornton Hough, Cheshire 1955–1962. **Appointments:** Member, Military Historical Society. Died December 1967.

SPACKMAN, Harry Maurice (1911) Born 31 July 1892, Penn Fields, Staffordshire; son of Harry Robert Spackman, Surgeon, and Sarah Henrietta Collis; m Mary Madeline Pinson, 7 September 1918, Codsall Parish Church, Staffordshire; 1 son (Michael). BA 1916; MA 1920. **Tutor(s):** J R Tanner. **Educ:** Dean Close School, Cheltenham. **Career:** Captain, Royal Field Artillery, then attached Mortar Trench Battery (wounded), WWI. Died 5 October 1984.

SPAFFORD, Dr Anthony John Howsin (1934) Born 6 July 1916, Southcroft, Carlisle Road, Fairfield, Buxton; son of Percy Lionel Spafford, Major, RASC, and Evelyn Mary Cox; m Jean Venables, 15 July 1942, St Mary's Church, Harrow on the Hill; 1 son, 1 daughter. MRCS; LRCP. **Tutor(s):** R L Howland. **Educ:** Cheam School, Surrey; Wellington College. **Career:** Captain, RAMC, Germany and India 1941–1946; GP, Whitchurch, Pangbourne, Berkshire 1946–1972. **Appointments:** Chairman, local Working Men's Club. Died 24 September 1978.

SPAFFORD, Douglas Harold (1942) Born 7 September 1922, 63 Cardigan Road, Leeds; son of Arthur Owen Spafford, Deputy Regional Director, and Winifred Alice Kerby. **Subject(s):** Modern and Medieval Languages. **Tutor(s):** C W Guillebaud. **Johnian Relatives:** brother-in-law of Hanns Ulrich Oskar Chester (1929). **Educ:** Norwood School, Pennsylvania Road, Exeter; Clifton College.

SPALDING, Thomas Ian (1949) Born 1 August 1928, Northwood, 56 Strathern Road, Broughty Ferry, Dundee; son of Thomas Spalding, Engineer-Captain, RN, and Gwendolen Beatrice Thomson; m Mary Julia Lawson, 11 October 1962; 2 sons (Christopher b 14 October 1967 and Michael b 2 July 1971), 3 daughters (Caroline b 10 August 1963, Julia b 24 August 1969 and Susanne b 12 August 1966). **Subject(s):** History/Law; BA 1952; CA. **Tutor(s):** A G Lee. **Educ:** Wellington House, Westgate-on-Sea; Clifton Hall, Kinloch House, Amulree; Sedbergh School. **Career:** Financial Director, J O Buchanan & Co Ltd, Specialist Oil Refiners, Renfrew; Councillor, Renfrew District Council 1988–1996; Deputy Provost 1992–1996.

SPARGO, Frederick Wilson (1907) Born 30 October 1888, Victoria Street East, Brunswick, County Bourke, Victoria, Australia; son of George Spargo, Clerk, and Harriett Vincent; m Lilian Julia Barnes; 2 sons (John Barnes b 13 July 1927 and David Frederick b 22 August 1932), 1 daughter (Mary Vincent b 9 May 1923). **Subject(s):** Mathematics; BA 1910. **Tutor(s):** J R Tanner. **Johnian Relatives:** father of John Barnes Spargo (1945); grandfather of Peter John Ralph Spargo (1970) and of Russell Howard Spargo (1986). **Educ:** William Ellis Endowed School. **Career:** Assistant Commissioner, Burma; Lieutenant, IARO, attached 70th Burma Rifles, WWI; Officiating District and Sessions Judge 1923; Officiating Judge, High Court, Rangoon 1936. Died 21 August 1969.

SPARGO, Dr John Barnes (1945) Born 13 July 1927, Maymyo Upper Burma; son of Frederick Wilson Spargo, Indian Civil Service, and Lilian Julia Barnes; m Patricia Wendy Madew, 1949, London; 2 sons (Peter John Ralph b 15 April 1952 and Paul Michael b 22 April 1954), 2 daughters (Jane Mary b 16 July 1950 and Kate Julia b 12 May 1961). **Subject(s):** Natural Sciences; BA 1948; MA 1952; MB 1950; BChir 1950. **Tutor(s):** S J Bailey. **Johnian Relatives:** son of Frederick Wilson Spargo (1907); father of Peter John Ralph Spargo (1970); uncle of Russell Howard Spargo (1986). **Educ:** Hillsborough School, Ealing; Wykeham House, Worthing; Earley Wood School, Ascot; Charterhouse. **Career:** GP 1955–1992.

SPARKS, Alexander Pratt (1949) Born 28 January 1931, Creebrae, High Pine Close, Weybridge, Surrey; son of Cedric Harold Sparks, Chief Engineer, Babcock & Wilcox Ltd, and Lilian Margaret Johnson; m Serena Evelyn Fairfax, 2 July 1976; 1 son (Hugo Fairfax Pratt b 1981), 1 daughter (Emma Louise Pratt b 1978). **Subject(s):** English/Law; BA 1953; MA 1956. **Tutor(s):** G C L Bertram; C W Guillebaud. **Johnian Relatives:** son of Cedric Harold Sparks (1911); nephew of John Victor Sparks (1915); cousin of Harry Hougham Sparks (1954). **Educ:** Wellesley House; Repton School. **Career:** Bateson and Payne (Insurance Brokers), London 1953–1956; James Howden (Engineers), Glasgow 1956–1960; Stewarts and Lloyds (Steel), Birmingham 1960–1963; Air Products (Industrial Gas), London 1963–1966; Coopers and Lybrand (Management Consultants) 1966–1975; C T Bowring (Insurance Brokers), London 1975–1993; Director, RAC Insurance Brokers Ltd; Director, RICS Insurance Services Ltd; Chairman, Bowring Financial Services Ltd; Director, Bowring London Ltd; Director, Bowring UK Ltd. **Appointments:** Governor of Oundle, Chairman 1985–1986; Master, Worshipful Company of Grocers 1985–1986; Friend of Royal College of Physicians; Director, Lomond Underwriting plc; Director, City and Guilds School of Art; Council Member, City and Guilds; Steward, Windsor Racecourse.

SPARKS, Cedric Harold (1911) Born 30 September 1892, Putney, Surrey; son of Charles Pratt Sparks, Consulting Engineer, and Mabel Florence Thacker; m Lilian Margaret Johnson; 1 son (Alexander Pratt b 28 January 1931), 2 daughters (b 1932 and 1939). **Subject(s):** Mechanical Sciences; BA 1914; MA 1922. **Tutor(s):** L H K Bushe-Fox. **Johnian Relatives:** brother of John Victor Sparks (1915); father of Alexander Pratt Sparks (1949); uncle of Harry Hougham Sparks (1954). **Educ:** Repton School; Faraday House, London. **Career:** Captain, RFA Guards Divisional Artillery, France, WWI, then RAF until 1920; Engineer 1920, Chief Engineer 1936, Main Board Director, then Deputy Chairman, Messrs Babcock and Wilcox, Renfrew. Died 30 May 1973.

SPARKS, Dr John Victor (1915) Born 28 October 1897, Ravenswood, Davenport, Cheshire; son of Charles Pratt Sparks, Consulting Engineer, and Mabel Florence Thacker; m Dorothy May Gudgeon, 4 January 1932, St James's, Picadilly; 1 son (Harry Hougham b 26 November 1933). BA 1918; DMRE 1924; MRCS; LRCP 1923; MRCP 1943. **Tutor(s):** L H K Bushe-Fox. **Johnian Relatives:** brother of Cedric Harold Sparks (1911); uncle of Alexander Pratt Sparks (1949); father of Harry Hougham Sparks (1954). **Educ:** Rottingdean; Repton School. **Career:** Radiologist, City of London Chest Hospital, and Alexandra Hospital, Swanley; Consultant Radiologist to Southmead Hospital and Frenchay Hospital,

Bristol; Surgeon Probationer, RNVR, Grand Fleet 1918; Assistant Radiologist, X-Ray Department, St Bartholomew's Hospital 1934; Assistant Director, X-Ray Department, Brompton Hospital 1934; Director, X-Ray Department, Royal Cancer Hospital 1934; Honorary Consulting Radiologist, Midhurst Sanitorium 1934; Emergency Medical Service, Royal Cancer Hospital, WWII; Honorary Radiologist, Bristol Royal Infirmary 1946. **Appointments:** Radiologists Group Committee, BMA. **Publications:** 'Analysis of Operative Findings Following X-Ray Examination of the Alimentary Tract at St Bartholomew's Hospital in 1925', *St Bartholomew's Hospital Journal*, 1926; 'Difficulties of Comparative Radiograms of the Chest', *British Journal of Radiology*, 1929; 'Pulmonary Asbestosis', *British Journal of Radiology*, 1931; 1932 (with F G Wood) 'Radiographic Appearances of the Lungs in Chronic Bronchitis and in Emphysema', *Lancet*. Died 14 March 1962.

SPARROW, The Revd Thomas William Francis (1926) Born 17 May 1907, The Vicarage, Luttons Ambo, Yorkshire; son of William Sparrow, Clerk in Holy Orders, and Maude Mary Chapman Griffith. **Subject(s):** Law; BA 1929; MA 1939. **Tutor(s):** M P Charlesworth. **Educ:** Pocklington School; Ripon Hall, Oxford. **Career:** Ordained Deacon 1934; Curate, St Barnabas, Linthorpe 1934–1937; Ordained Priest 1935; Curate, St Olave, York 1937–1939; Curate, St Mary, Kippax 1939–1942; CF 1942–1946; Curate in Charge, Brandesburton 1946–1947; Curate, Hornsea with Goxhill 1948–1949; Curate, Hornsea with Goxhill and Beverley 1949. **Awards:** Exhibition, SJC.

SPEAKMAN, Dennis (1946) Born 1 March 1925, Westminster, The Avenue, Leigh, Lancashire; son of Ernest Vernon Speakman, Director and Chief Executive Officer, Lancashire Associated Collieries, and Lydia Bourne Fish. **Subject(s):** Moral Sciences; BA 1949; MA 1953. **Tutor(s):** F Thistlethwaite. **Educ:** Chigwell School; St Chad's, Prestatyn, North Wales; Haileybury College.

SPEECHLY, William Grove (1927) Born 5 July 1906, Pilot Mound, Province of Manitoba, Canada; son of Harry Martindale Speechly, Physician and Surgeon, and Mary Barrett. BA 1930; MA 1934. **Tutor(s):** C W Guillebaud. **Johnian Relatives:** grandson of John Martindale Speechly (1855) and of William Fergusson Barrett (1863). **Educ:** Kelvin Secondary School, Winnipeg, Canada; University of Manitoba, Winnipeg, Canada.

SPELMAN, Sydney George Henry (1921) Born 1 September 1902, 46 London Street, St Andrews, Norwich, Norfolk; son of Gresham Henry Dutt Spelman, Grocer, and Louisa Barrett; m Nora Wilson Pank, 4 July 1927, Octagon Chapel, Norwich; 1 son (Michael John b 3 June 1940), 1 daughter (Sheila Mary b 25 July 1932, d 1984). **Subject(s):** Economics/History; BA 1924; MA 1929. **Tutor(s):** E A Benians. **Johnian Relatives:** father of Michael John Spelman (1959); grandfather of Daryl Martin Spelman (1996). **Educ:** King Edward VI School, Norwich. **Career:** Inland Revenue; Civil Service. **Awards:** Scholarship, SJC 1920. Died August 1992.

SPENCE, Andrew Macdonald (1924) Born 25 March 1907, Rangoon, Burma; son of Arthur Dunbar Spence, Physician and Surgeon, and May Arnold. **Tutor(s):** E A Benians. **Educ:** St Cyprian's School, Eastbourne; Fettes College, Edinburgh.

SPENCE, Charles Francis (1926) Born 6 February 1907, 41 Manning Road, Durban, Natal, South Africa; son of James Owen Spence, Merchant, and Emily Mabel Green. **Tutor(s):** J M Wordie. **Johnian Relatives:** brother of James Donald Spence (1923) and of Ralph William Spence (1928); father of Ian Michael Spence (1955); uncle of James Timothy Spence (1956). **Educ:** Merchiston Preparatory School; Pietermaritzburg College.

SPENCE, James Donald (1923) Born 11 February 1904, Moore Road, Durban, Natal, South Africa; son of James Owen Spence, Merchant, and Emily Mabel Green; m Muriel Cooper, 1 October 1929. BA 1928; MA

1946. **Tutor(s):** E A Benians. **Johnian Relatives:** brother of Charles Francis Spence (1926) and of Ralph William Spence (1928); uncle of Ian Michael Spence (1955); father of James Timothy Spence (1956). **Educ:** Merchiston Preparatory School, Maritzburg, South Africa; Pietermaritzburg College School, South Africa. **Career:** Auctioneer and Estate Agent, England; Messrs Armstrong Siddeley Motors Ltd 1939; Radar, RAF, Madagascar and Kenya, WWII. Died 26 January 1986.

SPENCE, Dr Magnus Peter (1942) Born 1 July 1923, 8 Colehill Gardens, Fulham, London; son of Magnus Thorfinn Spence, Meteorologist, and Violet Edith Williams; m Gillian Sara Squire, 1960 (d 1991); 2 sons (Magnus Andrew and Edward Tobias), 1 daughter (Katherine Emma). **Subject(s):** Natural Sciences; BA 1945; BChir 1947; MB 1947; MRCP 1948; FRCP 1975. **Tutor(s):** S J Bailey. **Educ:** Edinburgh Academy; St Paul's School, London. **Career:** Consultant Physician, Hospitals in Hertfordshire 1965–1988. **Awards:** Exhibition, SJC 1941.

SPENCE, Ralph William (1928) Born 25 June 1910, 21 Manning Road, Durban, Natal, South Africa; son of James Owen Spence, Merchant Importer, and Emily Mabel Green. **Tutor(s):** C W Guillebaud. **Johnian Relatives:** brother of James Donald Spence (1923) and of Charles Francis Spence (1926); uncle of Ian Michael Spence (1955) and of James Timothy Spence (1956). **Educ:** Merchiston School, Maritzburg; Pietermaritzburg College.

SPENCER, Cyril Charles (1931) Born 1 February 1912, Brampton Road, St Albans; son of Albert Edward Spencer, Colonial Civil Servant, and Elsie Maud Camp; m (1) 1938, (2) Catherine Dewar Robertson, 1949 (d 1995), (3) Phyllis Steele (née Rees), 1998 (d 1999); (1) 1 daughter (b 1939, d 1997). **Subject(s):** Mathematics/Economics; BA 1934. **Tutor(s):** J M Wordie. **Educ:** Wembley High School; Watford Grammar School; Royal Grammar School, Worcester. **Career:** Colonial Civil Servant, Uganda: Assistant Treasurer 1935–1937; Assistant District Officer 1937–1946; Assistant Financial Secretary 1946–1948; Economic Secretary, East Africa High Commission 1948; Financial Secretary 1948–1953; Acting Chief Secretary; Acting Governor; Commissioned on Special Duty 1953–1961; Secretary General, IACO, Paris 1961–1964; First Deputy Executive Director 1964–1968, Executive Director 1967–1968, ICO, London. **Appointments:** Chairman, Uganda Lint Marketing Board; Chairman, Uganda Coffee Marketing Board; Member, Uganda Electricity Board; Member, Uganda Development Corporation. **Honours:** CMG 1951; OM (Ivory Coast) 1985.

SPENCER, Dominick Evelyn Wellesley (1949) Born 21 July 1924, Arrow Road, Alcester, Warwickshire; son of Richard Henry Spencer, Royal University of Ireland, and Margaret Evelyn Purton; m Susan Lowe, 9 August 1956, St John's, Felbridge, East Grinstead; 3 sons (Robert b 30 May 1957, Michael b 15 June 1959 and Rupert b 16 April 1965). **Subject(s):** History; BA 1951; MA 1956. **Tutor(s):** A G Lee. **Educ:** The Grammar School, Alcester. **Career:** Army 1942–1947; Assistant Master, Repton Preparatory School 1947–1949, 1952–1962; Headmaster, Oswestry Junior School 1962–1970; Headmaster, Amesbury School, Hindhead, Surrey 1970–1989; Administrator, Somerleyton Hall, Suffolk 1989–1993; Tutor, University of the Third Age, Cambridge 1994–2000. **Publications:** Research on Nevile Henderson, HM Ambassador to Berlin 1937–1939.

SPENCER, Gordon Winstanley (1906) Born 22 August 1888, St James' Vicarage, Preston, Lancashire; son of Thomas Barton Spencer, Clerk in Holy Orders, and Eliza Isabella Winstanley; m Dorothy Webley, 25 March 1920, Garrison Church, Baghdad. **Subject(s):** Natural Sciences; BA 1910; MRCS; LRCP 1912. **Tutor(s):** J R Tanner. **Johnian Relatives:** son of Thomas Barton Spencer (1866). **Educ:** Grammar School, Preston. **Career:** Captain, RAMC, WWI; Ophthalmic Registrar, St Thomas' Hospital; Chief Ophthalmic Surgeon, Iraq Health Service 1934. **Publications:** 'Intrathecal Injection of Salvarsanized Serum', *Lancet*, 1914. Died 25 February 1947.

SPENCER, Marshall Macdonald (1936) Born 6 October 1916, 14 Hibbert Road, Barrow-in-Furness, Lancashire; son of Faraday Reginald Marshall Spencer, Master Stationer, and Elizabeth Shanks Macdonald Stewart; m Muriel. **Subject(s):** Geography; BA 1939; MA 1943; MA (by incorporation) (Oxon) 1948. **Tutor(s):** C W Guillebaud. **Educ:** Barrow Grammar School. **Career:** Tutor, Department of Education 1948–1951, Secretary, Institute of Education, later Secretary for Educational Studies 1951–1982, University of Oxford; Founding Fellow 1965–1981 (Emeritus 1981–1994), St Cross College, Oxford. Died 23 March 1994.

SPENCER, The Revd Peter Lane (1937) Born 15 August 1919, Farleigh, Dickinson Avenue, Ricksmanworth; son of Hubert Lane Spencer, Civil Servant, and Josephine Bella Coutts. **Subject(s):** Mathematics/ Theology; BA 1940; MA 1945. **Tutor(s):** J M Wordie. **Educ:** St Joan of Arc Convent School, Rickmansworth; Watford Grammar School; Merchant Taylors' School; Lincoln Theological College. **Career:** Curate, St Matthew, Oxney 1943–1948; Assistant Priest, Avondale, Salisbury, Rhodesia, later Rector Selukwe, Southern Rhodesia. **Awards:** Major Scholarship, SJC 1936. Died 1993.

SPENCER, Ralph Thornton Trevelyan (1921) Born 29 January 1903, Netherwitton Hall, Morpeth, Northumberland; son of Ralph Spencer, Steel Manufacturer, and Lilian Elizabeth Margaret Spencer Trevelyan. **Tutor(s):** B F Armitage. **Johnian Relatives:** son of Ralph Spencer (1879). **Educ:** Elstree School; Harrow School.

SPENCE-THOMAS, Richard Foulis (1921) Born 26 March 1902, Kazarma, Llanelly, Carmarthenshire; son of Hubert Spence-Thomas, Tin Plate Manufacturer, and Ruby Jean Foulis; m Eunice. **Tutor(s):** E A Benians. **Educ:** Shrewsbury School. Died 10 April 1953.

SPERRIN-JOHNSON, Professor John Charles (1913) See JOHNSON.

SPINK, Joseph Fenner (1901) Born 8 April 1882, Burnley Lodge, Alleyn Road, Dulwich, Surrey; son of Joseph Simon Spink, Bank of England Clerk, and Lucy Dorothea Critchett. **Subject(s):** Classics; BA 1904; MA 1908. **Tutor(s):** C E Graves; J R Tanner. **Educ:** Cranleigh School. **Career:** Ordained Deacon 1905; Curate, St John the Evangelist, Weymouth and Chaplain, Weymouth College 1905–1910; Ordained Priest 1906; Master, Bristol Cathedral School 1913–1916; Master, Fettes College, Edinburgh 1920–1926; Vicar, East Cowton 1926–1930; Vicar, Catterick 1930–1936; Rector, Forncett St Mary with St Peter, Norfolk 1936–1947. **Appointments:** Choral Studentship, SJC 1901. **Awards:** Second Winchester Reading Prize, University of Cambridge 1905. Died 3 July 1964.

SPITZER, Dr Lyman (1935) Born 26 June 1914, Toledo, Ohio; son of Lyman Spitzer, Paper box manufacturer, and Blanche Carey Brumbach; m Doreen Canaday, 29 June 1940, Toledo, Ohio; 1 son (Nicholas C), 3 daughters (Dionis S, Sarah S and Lydia S). BA (Yale) 1935; MA (Princeton) 1937; PhD (Princeton) 1938; Honorary DSc (Yale, Harvard, Case Institute of Technology); Honorary LLD (Toledo); MNAS; ARAS 1973. **Tutor(s):** J M Wordie. **Educ:** Warren School, Toledo, USA; École Pascal, Paris; Lycée Chateaubriand, Rome; Scott High School, Toledo; Phillips Academy, Andover; Yale University; Princeton University. **Career:** Postdoctoral Fellow, Harvard University 1938–1939; Instructor, Physics and Astronomy, Yale University 1939–1942; War Research 1942–1946; Director, Sonar Analysis Group, Columbia University (during which time he was the first to propose the development of a large space telescope, which became a reality with the launch of the Hubble Space Telescope in 1990) 1944–1946; Associate Professor of Astrophysics, Yale University 1946–1947; Professor and Chairman, Department of Astrophysical Sciences, Princeton University, and Director, Princeton University Observatory (led the group that developed the *Copernicus* satellite) 1947–1979; Charles A Young Professor of Astronomy, Princeton University 1952–1979; Founder and First Director of Project Matterhorn/Princeton Plasma Physics Laboratory 1953–1961. **Appointments:** President, American Astronomical Society 1959–1961; Chairman, University Research Board, Princeton, 1967–1972; Chairman, Space Telescope Scientific Institute Council 1981–1990; Foreign Member, Royal Society 1990; Member: American Philosophical Society; American Academy of Arts and Sciences; National Academy of Sciences; Royal Society of Sciences of Liège; Astronomical Society of the Pacific; Royal Astronomical Society; American Physical Society; American Geophysical Union; American Association of the University Professors. **Awards:** Henry Fellowship 1935; Henry Norris Russell Lectureship, American Astronomical Society 1953; Franklin Institute, David Rittenhouse Medal 1957; Bruce Medal, Astronomical Society of the Pacific 1973; Catherine Wolfe Bruce Gold Medal, Astronomical Society of the Pacific 1973; Jansky Prize, National Radio Astronomy Observatory 1974; Henry Draper Medal, National Academy of Sciences 1974; James Clerk Maxwell Prize for Plasma Physics, American Physical Society 1975; Karl Schwarzchild Medal 1975; NASA Distinguished Public Service Medal 1976; Gold Medal, Royal Astronomical Society 1978; National Medal of Science (presented by Jimmy Carter) 1979; Jules Janssen Medal of the Societé Astronomique de France 1980; Crafoord Prize, Royal Swedish Academy of Sciences 1985. **Publications:** *Physics of Fully Ionized Gases*, Wiley-Interscience, 1956, 1962; *Diffuse Matter in Space*, Wiley-Interscience, 1968; *Physical Processes in the Interstellar Medium*, Wiley, 1978; *Searching between the Stars*, Yale University Press, 1982; *Dynamical Evolution of Globular Clusters*, Princeton University Press, 1982; (ed with Jeremiah P Ostriker) *Dreams, Stars and Electrons: Selected Writings of Lyman Spitzer Jr*, Princeton University Press, 1997; various papers and articles in journals. Died 31 March 1997.

SPOONCER, Dr Ronald Clifford (1937) Born 8 August 1919, 23 Wellington Street, Moss Side; son of James Spooncer, Clerk, and Annie Edge; m Anne Patricia Mair, 13 April 1944, Priory Chapel, St Mary's Church, Birkenhead; 1 son (William Fraser), 3 daughters (Claire Elisabeth, Rachel Anne and Elaine). **Subject(s):** Mechanical Sciences; BA 1940; MA 1952; MSc (Manchester) 1980; PhD (Manchester) 1983. **Tutor(s):** J S Boys Smith. **Educ:** Seymour Road Council School, Clayton; Cavendish Municipal School, West Didsbury; Manchester Hulme Grammar School. **Career:** RAF 1941–1946; ICI 1946–1978; Director, Organics Division, ICI, 1964–1978; Professor Associate, Brunel University. **Awards:** Ricardo Prize, University of Cambridge 1940. **Publications:** more than 40 publications. Died 8 January 2000.

SPRAKE, Robert Rowland Hill (1919) Born 2 December 1900, Earsham Street, Bungay St Mary, Suffolk; son of Humphrey Jeans Sprake, Gentleman, and Harriet Reeve. **Tutor(s):** E E Sikes. **Educ:** University and Professional Preparatory College, Glasgow; Bungay Grammar School; Glasgow University. **Career:** Auctioneer, Valuer and Surveyor. **Appointments:** Member, Bungay Urban District Council; Representative of Earsham, Depwade Rural District Council; Vice-Chairman, Earsham Parish Council; Secretary, Bungay Race Committee; Clerk, Outney Common and Stow Fen Owners.

SPRIGG, Dr Richard Keith (1941) Born 31 March 1922, 20 Nottingham Road, Melton Mowbray, Leicestershire; son of Samuel Sprigg, Shoe Manufacturer, and Helen Cora Brown; m (1) Ray Margaret Williams, 1952, Melton Mowbray, (2) Elisabeth Ann Ransom, 2000, Crowborough; 1 son (David Edward MacDonald b 1957), 1 daughter (Eirene Maya b 1958). **Subject(s):** Classics; BA 1944; MA 1947; PhD (London) 1969; LittD 1982. **Tutor(s):** R L Howland. **Educ:** King Edward VII Grammar School, Melton Mowbray; Oakham School; University of London. **Career:** RAF, UK, India, Ceylon, Singapore, Japan 1943–1947; Lecturer in Phonetics, SOAS 1948; Reader in Phonetics, University of London 1968. **Appointments:** Honorary Member, Linguistic Society of Nepal. **Awards:** Johnson Exhibition, SJC 1940; Scholarship, SJC 1942. **Publications:** 'Festschrift', *Prosodic Analysis and Asian Linguistics: to Honour R K Sprigg*, Canberra: ANU, 1989; *Balti-English/English-Balti Dictionary*, Routledge/Curzon, London, 2002.

SPRUNT, Geoffrey Herbert (1927) Born 15 November 1909, Shortlands, Clairview Road, Streatham, Surrey; son of Herbert William Sprunt, General Manager of Public Utility Companies, and Mabel Shortlands Fisher; m Pamela Joy Fitch, 21 August 1947, St Mary's, Taunton. **Tutor(s):** J M Wordie. **Educ:** Shrewsbury House School, Surbiton; Aldro School, Eastbourne; Oundle School.

SPURDENS, Norman Arthur (1941) Born 24 October 1922, 32 Friern Road, East Dulwich; son of Arthur Amey Spurdens, Commercial Representative, and Lilian Mary Pays. **Tutor(s):** C W Guillebaud. **Educ:** Goodrich Road Elementary School; Heber Road Elementary School; Alleyn's School, East Dulwich.

SQUIRE, Sir John Collings (1903) Born 2 April 1884, 1 Princess Court, Plymouth, Devon; son of Jonas Squire, Veterinary Surgeon, and Elizabeth Rowe Collings; m Eileen Harriet Anstruther Wilkinson, 1908; 3 sons, 1 daughter. **Subject(s):** History; BA 1906; MA 1919; FSA; Honorary ARIBA; Honorary FRSL. **Tutor(s):** E E Sikes. **Johnian Relatives:** father of Raglan Hugh Anstruther Squire (1930); grandfather of Roger Maurice Squire (1962) and of Michael James Squire (1964). **Educ:** Plymouth Public School; Plymouth Corporation School; Blundell's School, Tiverton. **Career:** Literary Editor and Poet; Literary Editor, *New Statesman* (under name Solomon Eagle) 1914–1919; Columnist and Literary Critic, *Observer* and *Illustrated London News*; Acting Editor, *New Statesman* 1917–1918; Founder and Editor, *London Mercury*, and Chairman, London Mercury Ltd 1919–1934. **Appointments:** Honorary Member, Art Workers' Guild; Editor, *English Men of Letters* Series; Governor, Old Vic 1922–1926; Chairman, Architecture Club 1922–1928; Chairman, English Association 1926–1929; Honorary Secretary, Stonehenge Preservation Society; President, Devonshire Association 1934; Joint Editor, with Lord Lee of Fareham, *English Heritage* Series. **Awards:** Historical Scholarship, SJC 1903. **Honours:** Kt 1933. **Publications:** *Imaginary Speeches*, 1912; *Steps to Parnassus*, 1913; *The Three Hills, and other Poems*, 1913; *The Survival of the Fittest*, 1916; *Twelve Poems*, 1916; (ed) *The Collected Poems of James Elroy Flecker*, 1916; *Tricks of the Trade* (poetic parodies) 1917; *The Lily of Malud*, 1917; *The Gold Tree*, 1918; *Poems*, first series, 1918; *Books in General* (compilation of newspaper columns), 1918; *The Birds, and other Poems*, 1919; *Books in General*, second series, 1920; *The Moon, a poem*, 1920; *Life and Letters*, 1920; *Books in General*, third series, 1921; *Collected Parodies*, 1921; *Poems*, second series, 1922; *Essays at Large*, 1922; *Books Reviewed*, 1922; *American and other Poems*, 1923; *Essays on Poetry*, 1924; *Grub Street Nights*, 1924; *The Comic Muse*, 1925; *Poems in One Volume*, 1926; *Life at the Mermaid*, 1927; *The Cambridge Book of Lesser Poets*, 1927; *A London Reverie*, 1928; *Apes and Parrots*, 1928; *Sunday Mornings*, 1930; (ed) *If it had happened otherwise*, 1931; *A Face in Candlelight* (poems), 1933; *Outside Eden*, 1933; *Reflections and Memories*, 1935; *Shakespeare as a Dramatist*, 1935; *Flowers of Speech*, 1935; *Weepings and Wailings*, 1935; *The Honeysuckle and the Bee* (autobiography), 1937; *Water Music* (autobiography), 1939; *Selected Poems*, 1948; various anthologies and plays, including (with John L Balderston) three volumes of *Selections from Modern Poets and Berkeley Square*; *William the Silent*. Died 20 December 1958.

SQUIRE, Raglan Hugh Anstruther (1930) Born 30 January 1912, 10 Warltersville Road, Islington, London; son of John Collings Squire, Author, and Eileen Harriet Anstruther Wilkinson; m 1) Rachel Atkey, 1938 (d 1968), 2) Bridget (Delia) Lawless, 1968 (d 1977), 3) Mabel; 1) 2 sons (Michael James and Roger Maurice). **Subject(s):** Architecture. RIBA 1973; MSIA. **Tutor(s):** E A Benians. **Johnian Relatives:** son of John Collings Squire (1903); father of Roger Maurice Squire (1962) and of Michael James Squire (1964). **Educ:** Bigshotte School, Wokingham; Blundells School, Tiverton. **Career:** Private Architecture practice, London 1935; War Service, RE 1942–1945; Founder and Senior Partner, Raglan Squire & Partners, Architects, Engineers and Town Planners 1948–1981 (worked on projects ranging from prefabricated postwar housing 1945–1948 to Rangoon University Engineering College 1953–1956, a planning scheme for Mosul, Iraq 1955 and major hotels

across Asia 1955–1981); Consultant (retired from active practice), Raglan Squire & Partners 1981–2004. **Appointments:** Secretary, Architecture Club 1938–1939; Secretary, RIBA Postwar Reconstruction Committee 1941–1942; Guest Editor, *Architect's Journal*, 1947; Council Member, Architectural Association 1951–1952; Associated Architect, Transport Pavilion, Festival of Britain Exhibition 1951. **Publications:** *Portrait of an Architect*, 1985; articles in technical press on organisation of Building Industry, Architectural Education etc. Died 18 May 2004.

SQUIRES, Dr Gordon Leslie (1942) Born 2 July 1924, 391B Mile End Road, London; son of Barnett Squires, Ladies' Costumier, and Esther Levy. **Subject(s):** Natural Sciences; BA 1945; MA 1949; PhD 1953. **Tutor(s):** C W Guillebaud. **Educ:** Enfield Grammar School; Worthing High School. **Career:** Lecturer in Physics 1956 (Emeritus 1991), University of Cambridge; Fellow, Trinity College, Cambridge 1956.

STAFFORD, John (1949) Born 11 June 1929, Eastville, Jean Avenue, Leigh, Lancashire; son of Wesley Stafford, Letterpress Compositor, and Ada Hull. **Subject(s):** Mathematics; BA 1952; MA 1956; FBCS; FSS. **Tutor(s):** J M Wordie. **Johnian Relatives:** uncle of Mark Andrew Beckett (1985). **Educ:** King Street Methodist Elementary School, Leigh; Leigh Grammar School. **Career:** Mathematics Lecturer, University of Southampton, until 1991. **Awards:** Exhibition, SJC 1946.

STALKER, George Cameron (1935) Born 16 May 1914, 51 Dalhousie Street, Monifieth, Angus, Scotland; son of James Simpson Stalker, Schoolmaster, and Jessie Florence Robertson Stalker. **Subject(s):** Mathematics; BA 1937; MA 1942. **Tutor(s):** J M Wordie. **Educ:** Monifieth Public School; High School of Dundee; University of Edinburgh.

STALLARD, Francis William (1919) Born 11 July 1900, St John's House, Worcester; son of John Stallard, Solicitor, and Lilla Mary Thursfield; m Sadie Vance, 1934, Stoulton, Worcester; 1 son (William Brian b 15 March 1938), 1 daughter (Joan Mary b 2 September 1936). **Subject(s):** Law; BA 1922; LLB 1922. **Tutor(s):** E E Sikes. **Johnian Relatives:** father of William Brian Stallard (1958). **Educ:** Hill Side, West Malvern; Northwood Park; The Abbey, Beckenham; Shrewsbury School. **Career:** Admitted Solicitor 1925; Partner, John Stallard and Son, Solicitors, Worcester 1929–1948. **Appointments:** Clerk of the Peace, Worcester. **Awards:** Exhibition, SJC. Died 18 September 1948.

STAMMERS, Professor Arthur Dighton (1918) (Readmitted 1919) Born 5 May 1889, 92 Dresden Road, Islington, Middlesex; son of Frederick Dighton Stammers, Clerk in Holy Orders, and Charlotte Christina Noble. **Subject(s):** Natural Sciences; BA 1920; MA 1934; ScD. **Tutor(s):** E E Sikes. **Educ:** Perse School, Cambridge; Monoux Grammar School, Walthamstow; Dean Close School; UCL; London Hospital Medical College. **Career:** Director, Research Laboratory in Animal Nutrition, Lever Bros Ltd, Port Sunlight 1920–1921; Senior Lecturer in Physiology and Dean, Faculty of Medicine 1921–1949, Otto Beit Professor of Physiology 1927, University of the Witwatersrand. Died 21 October 1971.

STAMP, Professor Edward (1946) Born 11 November 1928, 23 Lance Lane, Liverpool; son of William Stamp, Public Health Officer, and Annie Wilson; m Peggy Higgins, 1 son (Philip), 3 daughters (Penny, Paddy and Shiobhan). **Subject(s):** Natural Sciences/Chemical Engineering; BA 1950; MA 1954; CA (Ontario); Honorary Doctor of Laws (Saskatchewan) 1984; FCA. **Tutor(s):** G C L Bertram. **Educ:** Mosspits Lane Council School; Booker Avenue Council School; Quarry Bank High School, Liverpool. **Career:** Partner, Messrs Clarkson, Gordon & Co, Toronto 1951–1963; Senior Lecturer 1963–1965, Professor of Accountancy 1965–1967, Victoria University of Wellington, New Zealand; Professor of Accounting and Business Method, University of Edinburgh 1967–1971; J Arthur Rank Research Professor and Director of the International Centre for Research in Accounting, University of Lancaster 1971. **Appointments:** Treasurer, New Zealand Institute of International Affairs; Member, New Zealand Government Commission of Inquiry into the Taxation System 1966–1967; Chairman, British

Accounting and Finance Association; Member, ARANZ. **Awards:** Fulbright and Smith-Mundt Scholarship. Died 10 January 1986.

STANDRING, William George (1919) Born 2 August 1899, 51 Kenmare Road, Toxteth Park, Liverpool, Lancashire; son of Herbert Wild Standring, Schoolmaster, and Kate Augusta White; m Ella. **Subject(s):** Mathematics/Mechanical Sciences; BA 1921; MA 1925. **Tutor(s):** E A Benians. **Educ:** Arnot Street Council School; Liverpool Collegiate School. **Career:** National Physical Laboratory, Teddington 1937; Principal Scientific Officer, Electrical Division 1951. **Awards:** Scholarship, SJC 1917. Died 13 January 1992.

STANFORD, Herbert Claude (1904) Born 9 January 1885, Saxmundham, Suffolk; son of Herbert Spencer Rabett Stanford, Auctioneer, Valuer and Estate Agent, and Clara Louisa Cooper; m Isabella Margaret Hotham-Newton, 19 April 1910 (d 1947), St Giles's, Cambridge. **Subject(s):** Classics; BA 1907; MA 1919. **Tutor(s):** E E Sikes. **Educ:** Yarmouth Grammar School; Hereford Cathedral School. **Career:** Second Lieutenant and Captain, Suffolk Regiment, and General List (Intelligence), WWI; Secretary, Cambridge University Library. **Honours:** MC. Died 17 July 1958.

STANHAM, Charles Taylor (1910) Born 30 November 1889, Belgrano, Buenos Aires, Argentina; son of George Graham Stanham, Private Gentleman, and Emma Gertrude Taylor. BA 1914; MA 1918. **Tutor(s):** E E Sikes. **Educ:** King's College Choir School, Cambridge; Belmont House School, Blackheath. **Career:** Navy 1904–1910; Lieutenant, The Buffs (East Kent Regiment, TF) and King's African Rifles, WWI. Died 1971.

STANIER, Harold (1912) Born 29 July 1893, Saverley Green, Stone, Staffordshire; son of Ralph Stanier, Gardener, and Harriet Bedson; m Margaret Elizabeth Martin; 1 son (Harold Meredith b 2 July 1922), 2 daughters (Elsie Margaret b 8 March 1925 and Mary Patricia b 18 April 1932). BA 1915; MA 1943. **Tutor(s):** L H K Bushe-Fox. **Johnian Relatives:** father of Harold Meredith Stanier (1940). **Educ:** Fulford Church of England School; Blythe Marsh Endowed School; Longton High School, Stoke-on-Trent. **Awards:** Scholarship, SJC 1912. **Career:** Chief Chemist, South East London Gas Board. Died 18 November 1973.

STANIER, Dr Harold Meredith (1940) Born 2 July 1922, 41 Finchley Road, Southend-on-Sea, Essex; son of Harold Stanier, Senior Chemist, South Metropolitan Gas Company, and Margaret Elizabeth Martin; m Joan Silcock, 1951; 1 daughter (Joy Margaret b 1954). **Subjects:** Mathematics/Physics; BA 1943; MA 1947; PhD 1951; MInstP; MIEE; CEng; FRAS. **Tutor(s):** J M Wordie. **Johnian Relatives:** son of Harold Stanier (1912). **Educ:** Chalkwell Towers Kindergarten, Westcliff-on-Sea; Glendale College (Preparatory), Westcliff-on-Sea; Westcliff High School for Boys, Westcliff-on-Sea. **Career:** ICI Research Associate. Died 1 December 2003.

STANIER, John Philip (1948) Born 26 July 1929, 32 Devon Gardens, Gateshead, County Durham; son of John Hamilton Stanier, Mechanical Engineer, and Elizabeth Davidson; m Margaret Black, 2 January 1952; 2 sons (John Hamilton b 1964, d 1988 and Julian Henry Douglas b 1969), 1 daughter (Mary Elizabeth b 1967). **Subject(s):** Natural Sciences (Zoology); BA 1951; MA 1955. **Tutor(s):** G C L Bertram; E Miller. **Educ:** Musgrave School, Low Fell, Gateshead; Royal Grammar School, Newcastle upon Tyne. **Career:** Research Assistant to J Z Young, UCL 1953–1955; Mechanical Engineer, Lumsden Machine Company, Gateshead 1955–1960; Assistant Master, teaching Biology, Chemistry and Physics, Corby Grammar School 1960–1966; Head of Biology, Preston Grammar School 1966–1974; Head, Science Department, Tuson College, Preston 1974–1988. Died 13 June 2002.

STANION, Gordon Stuart (1942) Born 13 April 1924, Lyncroft, King Edward's Road, Ruislip; son of Oliver Bernard Stanion, Spinner and Hosiery Manufacturer, and Gladys Stuart. **Tutor(s):** C W Guillebaud.

Educ: St Martin's Preparatory School, Northwood; Felsted School; Seafield Park School, Fareham.

STANLEY, Charles John Geoffrey (1937) Born 10 October 1918, Holwell, Huyton, Lancashire; son of Charles Douglas Stanley, Director of Omnibus Companies, and Adela Grace Walker-Jones; m Marjorie Laura Awdry Ball, 21 March 1942; 2 sons (Christopher Geoffrey Awdry b 1949 and Martin John Llewelyn b 1952). BA 1940; Fellow, Plastics Institute. **Tutor(s):** J S Boys Smith. **Johnian Relatives:** great nephew of John Edward Marr (1875); cousin of Francis Alleyne Marr (1913). **Educ:** Aldro School, Eastbourne; Eton. **Career:** BEF 1940; Lieutenant, 24th Lancers 1942–1944; Liaison Officer, HQ 11th Armoured Division 1944–1945; Various posts, British Plastics Federation 1947–1956; Chief Executive, British Plastics Federation, 1956–1974. **Appointments:** Captain, Lady Margaret Boat Club; Secretary, Area Group of Kent Trust for Nature Conservation; Member, Council and Executive Committee, Kent Trust for Nature Conservation. **Publications:** *The Moulding of an Industry*.

STANLEY, James Perham (1949) Born 7 February 1926, Trail-Tadanac Hospital, Trail, British Columbia, Canada; son of Oswald Stanley, Civil Engineer, and Bessie Blanche Diamond. BA (Toronto) 1948; MA 1948. **Tutor(s):** J M Wordie. **Educ:** Burlington Public School, Toronto, Canada; University of Toronto School; Queen Elizabeth's School, Crediton; Upper Canada College, Toronto, Canada; University of Toronto. **Career:** Computation Centre, McLennan Laboratory, University of Toronto; Mathematical Laboratory, University of Cambridge.

STANLEY, Philip John (1941) Born 4 July 1923, 19 Booth Street, Handsworth, Birmingham; son of Frank Stanley, Water Rate Collector, Corporation of Birmingham, and Maud Mary Clarke; m Beryl Hope, 1948; 2 sons (John b 1948 and David b 1964), 1 daughter (Susan b 1950). **Subject(s):** Mathematics; BA 1947; MA 1949. **Tutor(s):** S J Bailey. **Educ:** Rookery Road Elementary School, Handsworth; Handsworth Grammar School, Birmingham. **Career:** Advisory Service on Statistical Methods and Quality Control, Ministry of Supply 1942–1945; Joseph Lucas Ltd; Lecturer, Department of Aircraft Economics and Production, College of Aeronautics, Cranfield 1947–1953; Statistician, Glaxo Laboratories Ltd, Ulverton 1953–1956; Lecturer and Deputy Director, Sundridge Park Management Centre, Bromley 1956–1983.

STANNEY, Bernard Paul (1944) Born 17 May 1926, 4 Daffodil Street, Hammersmith; son of Bernard Philip Stanney, Civil Servant, and Ethel Mary Crowle; m Sylvia Joyce Parsons, 12 March 1947, Kensington; 1 son (Paul Anthony b 14 November 1949), 1 daughter (Sylvia Anne b 29 April 1948). **Subject(s):** Natural Sciences; BA 1947; MA 1951. **Tutor(s):** C W Guillebaud. **Educ:** Portobello Road LCC School; Buckingham Terrace LCC School; Latymer Upper School. **Career:** Schoolmaster 1949–1979.

STANSBURY, John Irvin (1943) Born 6 July 1924, Kenilworth, Cape Town, South Africa; son of Christopher Geoffrey Stansbury, Schoolmaster, and Christina Irvin; m Anne Hotblack, 12 September 1951, Calverleigh, Devon; 2 sons (Neill H D b 15 April 1958 and Peter M A b 14 September 1964), 2 daughters (D Elizabeth b 23 November 1952 and Nicola A b 5 April 1954). **Subject(s):** Classics/Geography; BA 1948; MA 1950. **Educ:** Western Province Preparatory School, Claremont, South Africa; Oundle School. **Career:** Teacher, various schools in Zimbabwe, for more than 30 years (various posts held, including Chief Assistant, Deputy Head and Head); Librarian and Archivist, St John's College, Harare, Zimbabwe. **Awards:** Munsteven Exhibition, SJC 1943.

STANSFELD, Dr Alfred Gimson (1935) Born 16 August 1916, 48 Bryanston Street, Portman Square, London; son of Alfred Ellington Stansfeld, Consulting Physician, and Helen Mary Squire; m Mary, 18

June 1949; 3 sons (Stephen, John and Andrew), 1 daughter (Jessica). **Subject(s):** Natural Sciences; BA 1938; MA 1942; MB 1941; BChir 1941; FRCPath. **Tutor(s):** R L Howland. **Educ:** Berkhamsted School; Epsom College. **Career:** Consultant in Histopathology to the RAF; Senior Lecturer in Morbid Anatomy, Royal Free Hospital School of Medicine 1952–1959; Lecturer in Pathology 1959–1970, Reader in Histopathology 1970–1981, St Bartholomew's Hospital Medical College. **Awards:** John Hunter Medal of the Royal College of Surgeons of England 1992. **Publications:** Several publications on lymphomas. Died 2 May 2002.

STANSFELD, Dr James Maryons (1935) Born 31 May 1917, Hardwyche, Hailsham, Sussex; son of Rex Stansfeld, Medicine, and Mable Fairbrother; m Lucy Chaundler, 1942 (d 1968); 1 son (Wyon b 1955), 2 daughters (Jane b 1945 and Elizabeth b 1947). **Subject(s):** Natural Sciences; BA 1938; MA 1942; MB 1941; BChir 1941; MD 1951; MRCS; LRCP 1941; FRCP 1975. **Tutor(s):** R L Howland. **Johnian Relatives:** son of Rex Stansfeld (1907). **Educ:** St Peter's School, Seaford; Oundle School. **Career:** Consultant Paediatrician, Durham and North-West Durham Hospital Group; Registrar in Child Health, King's College, Newcastle 1947–1952; Senior Lecturer, Pathology and Morbid Anatomy, Royal Free Hospital School of Medicine, London 1952–1959; Clinical Teacher in Child Health, King's College, Newcastle 1959–1961; Lecturer in Pathology 1961–1970, Reader in Histopathology 1970, St Bartholomew's Hospital Medical College; Associate Clinical Lecturer, Child Health Department, Royal Victoria Infirmary, Newcastle upon Tyne. Died 14 March 1998.

STANSFELD, Dr Rex (1907) Born 2 July 1888, 25 Agate Road, Hammersmith, Middlesex; son of Josiah Stansfeld, Staff Officer, Inland Revenue, and Florence Beatrice Beaven; m Mable Fairbrother, 31 March 1915, Hove; 1 son (James Maryons Stansfeld b 31 May 1917). **Subject(s):** Natural Sciences; BA 1910; MA 1920; BChir 1920; MA (incorporated) 1920; MRCS; LRCP. **Tutor(s):** E E Sikes. **Johnian Relatives:** father of James Maryons Stansfeld (1935). **Educ:** Westminster United School; City of London School; University Tutorial College. **Career:** St Bartholomew's Hospital 1913; Captain, RAMC, WWI. **Awards:** Choral Studentship, SJC; Senior Entrance Scholarship, St Bartholomew's 1910. Died 28 January 1958.

STANSFIELD, Dr Alfred Ellington (1902) Born 11 December 1882, 57 Bayston Road, West Hackney, Middlesex; son of Alfred Stansfield, Quantity Surveyor, and Harriette Louisa Ellington; m Helen Mary Squire, 3 July 1913, Holy Trinity Church, Leicester. **Subject(s):** Natural Sciences; BA 1905; MA 1911; BChir 1909; MB 1911; MD 1915; FRCP 1915. **Tutor(s):** E E Sikes. **Educ:** Central Foundation School, London. **Career:** Physician, Metropolitan Hospital, London; Senior Demonstrator in Pathology 1912. **Awards:** Kirkes Scholarship and Gold Medal 1908; Burrows Prize 1908; Brackenbury Medical Scholarship 1909; Lawrence Scholarship and Gold Medal 1910. Died 25 November 1918.

STANTON, James Vincent (1902) Born 16 August 1884, Grahamstown, Cape Colony, South Africa; son of James Stanton, Electrical Engineer, and Sarah Webber; m Edith Grace Masterman; 1 son (Royden James b 9 June 1922). AMIEE. **Tutor(s):** D MacAlister. **Johnian Relatives:** father of Royden James Stanton (1944); grandfather of Douglas Richard Stanton and Oliver James Stanton (1972). **Educ:** St Andrew's College, Grahamstown, South Africa. **Career:** Apprentice Engineer, then Sales Engineer (1910), Siemens Bros, Newcastle; Sales Engineer, Siemens Bros, Johannesburg 1912–1914; Owner, then Director, Engineering Business, until 1950. **Appointments:** President, Johannesburg Chamber of Commerce; President, South Africa Institute of Electrical Engineers.

STANTON, Dr John Bernard (1936) Born 14 October 1917, 19 Grove Park, Denmark Hill, London; son of Bernard Mackenzie Stanton, Colonial Civil Servant, and Nora Gordon Heslop; 1 son, 1 daughter. **Subject(s):** Natural Sciences; BA 1939; MA 1944; MB 1942; BChir 1942; FRCP; DPM; FRCPEd. **Tutor(s):** R L Howland. **Educ:** St Paul's School.

Career: First Assistant, Neurological Unit, London Hospital; Medical Officer, Merchant Navy 1942–1946; Senior Registrar in Psychiatry, Royal Victoria Infirmary 1954; Consultant Neurologist, Northern Group of Hospitals in Edinburgh 1954–1970. **Awards:** Scholarship, SJC 1935–1937; Wright's Prize, SJC 1937. Died 23 March 1970.

STANTON, Royden James (1944) Born 9 June 1922, 24 Mons Road, Bellevue, Johannesburg; son of James Vincent Stanton, Electrical Engineer, and Edith Grace Masterman, Housewife; m Dorothea Ruth Sloan, 2 September 1950, County Derry, Northern Ireland; twin sons (Douglas Richard and Oliver James b 25 November 1953), 1 daughter (Caroline Margaret b 7 May 1956). BA 1948; MA 1953. **Tutor(s):** S J Bailey. **Johnian Relatives:** son of James Vincent Stanton (1902); father of Douglas Richard Stanton (1972) and Oliver James Stanton (1972). **Educ:** St John's Preparatory School, Johannesburg; St John's College, Johannesburg. **Career:** Sergeant Instructor, Field Engineering, Lieutenant, 8th Army 1940–1945; Graduate Apprentice 1948, Engineer, Transformer Department 1949, Ferranti Ltd; Export Sales Area Manager, Ferranti, New Zealand, Australia and Far East 1951; Export Sales Manager, L A Mitchell Ltd; Lecturer, Oldham College of Further Education 1963; Principal Lecturer and Deputy Head of Engineering, Oldham College until 1982.

STAPLES, Edward George (1919) Born 6 July 1892, Cricklade Street, Cirencester, Gloucestershire; son of Edward Isaac Staples, Farmer, and Sarah Mary Lawrence. **Subject(s):** Natural Sciences; BA 1921; MA 1926; Diploma in Agriculture 1922. **Tutor(s):** E E Sikes. **Educ:** Cirencester Grammar School; Royal Agricultural College, Cirencester. **Career:** War service, near East, POW, Turkey, WWI; Agriculturalist, Agriculture Department, Nigeria; Colonial Service, Uganda and British Honduras 1922–1947. Died 15 July 1981.

STAPLETON, George Harold (1926) Born 29 November 1907, 21 Pearl Street, Starbeck, Harrogate, Yorkshire; son of George Arthur Stapleton, Confectioner, and Ella Mellor. **Subject(s):** Natural Sciences; BA 1929; MA 1934. **Tutor(s):** J M Wordie. **Educ:** Private School; The Grammar School, Leeds.

STARES, Michael John (1944) Born 21 July 1926, 2 Rutland Villas, Spitalfield Lane, Chichester; son of George Stares, Bootmaker, and Caroline Elizabeth Duke. **Tutor(s):** J M Wordie. **Educ:** Chichester Central School; Chichester High School. **Appointments:** RAF Cadet, SJC.

STARK, Robert Patrick Napier (1948) Born 2 August 1927, 29 Northmoor Road, Oxford; son of Robert Gordon Wienholt Stark, Furniture Designer, and Blanche Dunlop Anderson. **Tutor(s):** J M Wordie. **Educ:** Dragon School, Oxford; Kelly College, Tavistock. **Career:** Royal Armoured Corps 1946–1948.

STARNES, The Revd Peter Henry (1939) Born 16 August 1919, 9 Cromwell Road, Maidstone, Kent; son of Arthur George Starnes, Builders' Merchant, and Laura Busbridge. **Subject(s):** Classics/Theology; BA 1942; MA 1947; CertEd 1972; Advanced National Certificate in Agriculture, City & Guilds pass in Farm & Grassland Management, 1968; LTCL 1974. **Tutor(s):** R L Howland; J S Boys Smith. **Educ:** Maidstone Girls' Grammar School; Maidstone Grammar School; King's School, Canterbury. **Career:** CF; Ordained Deacon 1944; Curate, St Mary the Virgin, Gillingham, Dorset 1944; Ordained Priest 1945; Curate, St Peter's Church, St Peter-in-Thanet, Kent 1950–1952; Vicar, Westwell and Hothfield, Kent 1956; Rector, Eastwell with Boughton Aluph 1960–1965; Clarinet Teacher, licensed by Trinity College of Music, London 1974. **Appointments:** HCF 1954. **Awards:** Choral Studentship, SJC.

STARR, George Henderson (1937) Born 27 January 1914, Heath View, Freeford, Lichfield; son of William Henderson Starr, Army Officer, and Irene Constance Fox. **Subject(s):** Mechanical Sciences; BA 1939; MA

1943. **Tutor(s):** J S Boys Smith. **Educ:** Cliffe House School, Southbourne; Imperial Service College, Windsor. **Career:** Second Lieutenant, Royal Corps of Signals. Died 1989.

STATHAM, Allan Thomas (1943) Born 9 October 1924, 174 Beeches Road, West Bromwich; son of Thomas Albert Statham, Automobile Engineer, and Ruth Bull. **Tutor(s):** C W Guillebaud. **Educ:** Barnt Green School; Bromsgrove High School; Birmingham Central College. **Appointments:** RASC Cadet, SJC.

STATON, Robert Alan (1946) Born 21 August 1926, High Street, Clowne, Derbyshire; son of Rowland Staton, Steel Works Director, and Olive Woodhead; m Eileen May Froggatt, 2 April 1955, Millhouses Methodist Church, Sheffield; 1 son (Richard William b 28 May 1960), 1 daughter (Rosemary b 22 January 1962). **Subject(s):** English; BA 1948; MA 1954. **Tutor(s):** F Thistlethwaite. **Educ:** Carter Kowle Council School, Sheffield; King Edward VII School, Sheffield. **Career:** Journalist, *Keighley News, Telegraph and Argus*, Bradford, and the *Yorkshire Post*, Leeds; Art Desk, *Daily Express*, Manchester 1956–1964; Art Editor, *Daily Express*, Manchester 1964–1987. **Awards:** Minor Scholarship, SJC 1944.

STAVEACRE, Maurice Fleming (1926) Born 1 July 1909, 48 Davenport Crescent, Stockport, Cheshire; son of Wilson Bayley Staveacre, Stock and Share Broker, and Dora Ward; m (1) Joan Hadfield (d 1953), (2) Alice Mary Norton, 15 February 1965, St Thomas Becket Church at Chapel-en-le-Frith; 3 sons, 1 daughter. **Subject(s):** Law/Economics; BA 1930; MA 1939. **Tutor(s):** C W Guillebaud. **Educ:** Merton House School, Penmaenmawr; Shrewsbury School. **Career:** Chartered Accountant; Stockbroker, Manchester 1936; Lieutenant Colonel, WWII. **Honours:** OBE (WWII).

STEAD, The Revd William James Victor (1904) Born 14 February 1878, Bromborough, Cheshire; son of William Thomas Stead, Schoolmaster, and Frances Mary Barraclough; m Annie Mary. **Subject(s):** Classics; BA 1907; MA 1911. **Tutor(s):** D MacAlister. **Educ:** Crossley School, Halifax; Bradford Grammar School. **Career:** Ordained Deacon 1907; Ordained Priest 1908; Curate, Christ Church, Patricroft, Manchester 1908–1909; Curate, Rochdale 1909–1913; Curate, Littlehampton 1913–1914; Curate, Namaqualand 1914–1916; Warden, Bishop's Hostel, and Diocesan Director of Education, Kimberley 1916–1918; Curate, East Malling with Holy Trinity, New Hythe 1919–1923; Vicar, Mayland 1923–1930; Rector, Murston, Kent 1930; Rural Dean, Sittingbourne 1937. Died 5 December 1943.

STEDMAN, John Richard (1949) Born 24 January 1929, Elderslie, Burton Road, Melton Mowbray; son of Alfred Redvers Stedman, Headmaster, Marlborough Grammar School, and Ruth Nunn. **Subject(s):** History; BA 1952; MA 1956. **Tutor(s):** A G Lee. **Educ:** St Peter's School, Marlborough; Marlborough Grammar School; Marlborough College.

STEELE, Daniel Haines (1920) Born 22 June 1902, Saxonhurst, Northwood, Ruislip, Middlesex; son of Daniel Steele, Agriculturist, and Julia Katharine Wickes. **Subject(s):** Classics; BA 1923. **Tutor(s):** E E Sikes. **Educ:** Highgate Junior School; Bishop's Stortford College.

STEELE, Hugh Hepburn (1941) Born 22 January 1923, The Manse, Hedley Street, Blyth, Northumberland; son of John Steele, Minister, Presbyterian Church of England, and Elizabeth Hepburn. **Subject(s):** Law; BA 1947; MA 1949. **Tutor(s):** S J Bailey. **Educ:** Crofton Elementary School, Blyth; Plessey Road Elementary School, Blyth; Blyth Secondary School. **Career:** Articled to a solicitor in Newcastle; Partner, Maughan and Hall. **Awards:** James William Squire Scholarship, SJC 1941. Died 2 July 1966.

STEELE-PERKINS, Alfred Peter (1926) Born 30 June 1909, Westacott, Barnfield Road, Exeter, Devon; son of John Shirley Steele-Perkins, Medical Practitioner, and Elsie Charlotte Anne Harrild; m Betty; 1 son (David), 1 daughter (Shirley). **Subject(s):** Law; BA 1930; MA 1934; LLB

1931. **Tutor(s):** C W Guillebaud. **Johnian Relatives:** son of John Shirley Steele-Perkins (1894); brother of Guy Shirley Steele-Perkins (1926) and of Thomas Harrild Steele-Perkins (1930). **Educ:** Preparatory School, Norwood; Clifton College. **Career:** Solicitor; Major, RA 1939–1945. **Appointments:** Mayor of Exeter 1961. **Honours:** MC 1944. Died 16 August 1984.

STEELE-PERKINS, Dr Guy Shirley (1926) Born 28 February 1908, 47 Southernhay West, Exeter, Devon; son of John Shirley Steele-Perkins, Medical Practitioner, and Elsie Charlotte Anne Harrild. BA 1929; MA 1934; MB 1937; BChir 1937; DA 1946; FFARCS 1957. **Tutor(s):** M P Charlesworth. **Johnian Relatives:** son of John Shirley Steele-Perkins (1894); brother of Alfred Peter Steele-Perkins (1926) and of Thomas Harrild Steele-Perkins (1930). **Educ:** Norwood Preparatory School, Exeter; Clifton College. **Career:** Medical Practitioner, Exeter; Senior Consultant Anaesthetist, Royal Devon and Exeter Hospital. Died 20 February 1996.

STEELE-PERKINS, Peter Edward (1935) Born 25 July 1917, 5 Portland Terrace, Dawlish, South Devon; son of Arthur Edward Steele Steele-Perkins, Dental Surgeon, and Jessie Winifred Harris; m Joan Petts; 1 son (Anthony), 1 daughter (Gillian). **Subject(s):** Natural Sciences; BA 1938; MRCS London; LRCP England. **Tutor(s):** R L Howland. **Educ:** Gaisford House School, South Brent; Exeter School; Wellington School. **Career:** Medical Practitioner; Specialist Venereologist, RAMC.

STEELE-PERKINS, Thomas Harrild (1930) Born 6 October 1912, Westacott, Barnfield Road, Exeter; son of John Shirley Steele-Perkins, Medical Practitioner, and Elsie Charlotte Anne Harrild. **Tutor(s):** M P Charlesworth. **Johnian Relatives:** son of John Shirley Steele-Perkins (1894); brother of Guy Shirley Steele-Perkins (1926) and of Alfred Peter Steele-Perkins (1926). **Educ:** Preparatory School, Norwood; Clifton College.

STEEN, Frank Dunbar (1913) Born 4 January 1894, 13 Crawford Street, Wolverhampton, Staffordshire; son of John Jackson Dunbar Steen, Manufacturing Stationer, and Henrietta Maude Royston Crowe. **Tutor(s):** E E Sikes. **Educ:** Preparatory School, Oakfield, Rugby; Sedbergh School. **Career:** Progressed to rank of Captain, King's Royal Rifle Corps 1915–1918; Secretaries' Office, Somerset House 1918–1926. **Awards:** Exhibition, SJC. **Honours:** MC. Died 14 December 1926.

STEERS, Lieutenant Colonel Douglas Henry (1919) Born 11 December 1892, Park View, Foster Hill Road, Bedford; son of Henry Steers, Master Builder and Monumental Mason, and Annie Eliza Pearson. **Tutor(s):** E A Benians. **Educ:** St George's School, Harpenden; St Alban's School; Northampton Institute, London. Died 25 August 1958.

STEIMANN, Bernard Benjamin (1909) Born 15 September 1892, New York, USA; son of Osias Steimann, Merchant Shipper to South Africa, and Clara Salomon. **Subject(s):** Economics/Law. **Tutor(s):** L H K Bushe-Fox. **Educ:** St John's School, Bulawayo, Rhodesia; Grocers' School, Hackney Downs; Grammar School, 88 New York, USA; New York City College, USA; University College School, London.

STEPHENS, Professor Arthur Veryan (1927) Born 9 July 1908, Shirley, Kingsdown Road, Epsom, Surrey; son of Arthur John Stephens, Consulting Engineer and Chartered Patent Agent, and Mildred Sturge; m Jane Dow Lester, 30 December 1938, New York, USA. **Subject(s):** Mechanical Sciences/Mathematics; BA 1930; MA 1934; CEng; FRAeS. **Tutor(s):** J M Wordie. **Johnian Relatives:** father of Roger Somerville Stephens (1966); grandfather of Victoria Louise Ptarmigan Bishop (Kitcatt) (1987) and of Gisèle Anne Mireille Stephens (1996). **Educ:** St Cross, Walton on the Hill; Clifton College. **Career:** Scientific Officer, Royal Aircraft Establishment, Farnborough 1930–1934; Title A Fellow, SJC 1934–1940 (non-stipendiary 1939–1940); Demonstrator in Aeronautics, University of Cambridge 1937–1939; Professor of Aeronautical Engineering, University of Sydney 1939–1956; Professor of

Aeronautical Engineering 1956, Dean, Faculty of Engineering 1961–1964, Vice-President 1964–1967, Queen's University, Belfast. **Appointments:** Supervisor in Mechanical Sciences 1935–1940, Director of Studies in Mechanical Sciences, SJC 1937–1940; UK Aircraft Research Council. **Awards:** Scholarship, SJC 1926; John Bernard Seely Prize, University of Cambridge 1930; Wright's Prize, SJC 1930. Died 3 September 1992.

STEPHENS, Dr Cyril Joakim (1946) Born 8 October 1924, Rangoon, Burma; son of Joakim Stephens, Builder and Contractor, and Ella Catherine Martin. **Subject(s):** Natural Sciences; BA 1949; LRCP (London) 1953; MRCS; FFARCS 1962. **Tutor(s):** G C L Bertram. **Educ:** Methodist School, Rangoon; Diocesan School, Rangoon; Bishop's Stortford College. **Career:** Anaesthetist, Harlow Group Hospitals.

STEPHENS, George Stuart (1927) Born 21 May 1909, Rookwood, Merstham, Surrey; son of Peter Stuart Stephens, Insurance Broker and Member, Lloyds, and Adelaide Charlotte Edith Simpson. **Tutor(s):** M P Charlesworth. **Educ:** St Romans, West Worthing; Harrow School.

STEPHENS, John Christopher (1948) Born 24 April 1928, 42 Wheeley's Road, Edgbaston, Birmingham; son of John Sturge Stephens, Lecturer in History, University of Birmingham, and Helen Mary Rowat; m Alice Kendon, 6 September 1952, Friends' Meeting House, Jesus Lane, Cambridge; 3 sons (John Paul b 13 November 1953, William b 25 March 1956 and Mark b 24 March 1959), 1 daughter (Sarah Jane b 30 March 1963). **Subject(s):** Natural Sciences/Estate Management; BA 1951; MA 1955; QALAS 1954; ARICS. **Tutor(s):** R L Howland. **Johnian Relatives:** son of John Sturge Stephens (1910); son-in-law of Frank Samuel Herbert Kendon (1919); brother-in-law of Adam Kendon (1952). **Educ:** Edgbaston High School Preparatory Department; The Downs School, Colwall; Leighton Park School. **Career:** Served, Friends' Ambulance Unit 1946–1948; Assistant to J C P Langton, Agent to Burghley Estates, Stamford 1951–1955; Various posts in the Nyasaland and (post 1963) Malawi Government Service 1955–1974, including Leasehold Estates Officer, Agricultural Extension Officer, Regional Agricultural Officer, and Deputy, then Permanent, Secretary for Agricultural and Natural Resources. **Honours:** OBE 1974. Died 5 October 1975.

STEPHENS, John Gower (1925) Born 6 May 1898, Hazelbrook, New South Wales, Australia; son of Alfred George Stephens, Author and Journalist, and Constance Ivinsgbell Smith. **Tutor(s):** J M Wordie. **Educ:** The Technical High School, Sydney; St Andrews College, University of Sydney; Astrea College, Sydney.

STEPHENS, John Sturge (1910) Born 26 June 1891, The Cottage, Ashfield, Budock, Cornwall; son of John Gilbert Stephens, Rope Manufacturer, and Isabel Sturge; m Helen Mary Rowat, 30 March 1927, Friends' Meeting House, Falmouth; 2 sons (John Christopher b 24 April 1928 and Robert Nicholas b 2 June 1935), 1 daughter (Rachel Margaret b 22 March 1930). **Subject(s):** Classics; BA 1913; MA 1922. **Tutor(s):** J R Tanner. **Johnian Relatives:** father of John Christopher Stephens (1948). **Educ:** Leighton Park School. **Career:** Conscientious Objector with Friends' Ambulance Unit, then undertaking farm work, WWI; Lecturer, Heidelberg University; Lecturer in History, University of Birmingham. Died 12 June 1954.

STEPHENS, Michael William (1943) Born 4 November 1925, 46 Bounty Road, Basingstoke, Hampshire; son of Harold Nainby Stephens, Builder, and Frances Winifred Tigwell. **Subject(s):** History; BA 1948; MA 1950. **Tutor(s):** C W Guillebaud. **Johnian Relatives:** brother of Christopher Nainby Stephens (1950). **Educ:** Basingstoke Preparatory School; Claysmore Preparatory School; Bishop's Stortford College. **Career:** Navigator, RAF 1943–1947; Talks Assistant and Talks Producer, *Third Programme* 1949–1958, Representative, New Delhi, India 1958–1961, Assistant Head, Overseas Talks and Features 1961–1963, BBC; Secretary, Commonwealth Broadcasting Secretariat 1963–1968; Head of Further Education, BBC Radio 1969–1979. Died 19 March 1984.

STEPHENS, Professor Stanley George (1929) Born 2 September 1911, 135 Birmingham Road, Dudley; son of George Stephens, Manager of Engineering Works, and May Selwood. **Subject(s):** Natural Sciences; BA 1933; MA 1937. **Tutor(s):** M P Charlesworth. **Educ:** The Grammar School, Dudley; The Grammar School, Brewood. **Career:** State College of North Carolina, School of Agriculture; Head of Basic Genetics, Division of Biological Sciences.

STEPHENS, Thomas Anthony Stuart (1930) Born 27 June 1911, Rookwood, Merstham, Surrey; son of Peter Stuart Stephens, Insurance Broker, and Adelaide Charlotte Edith Simpson. **Tutor(s):** M P Charlesworth. **Educ:** St Romans, West Worthing; Harrow School.

STEPHENSON, Frederick (1915) Born 25 October 1896, 34 Cicely Street, West Derby, Liverpool; son of William Stephenson, Printer, and Alice Ann Laithwaite; m Gladys; 1 daughter. **Subject(s):** Classics; BA 1921; MA 1926; Honorary MA (Nottingham) 1956. **Tutor(s):** E E Sikes. **Educ:** Lawrence Road Council School, Liverpool; Liverpool Collegiate School. **Career:** Lieutenant, Loyal North Lancashire Regiment, then Captain, Special List (Brigade Signal Officer) (wounded), WWI; Master, St Paul's School 1921–1926; Assistant Secretary, Higher Education, Staffordshire 1926–1930; Deputy Director of Education, Staffordshire Education Committee 1930; Director of Education, Wallasey 1933–1938; Director of Education, Nottingham 1938–1956. **Awards:** Dowman Sizarship, SJC 1915; Scholarship, SJC. Died 18 May 1977.

STEPHENSON, Ian Stobbs (1949) Born 21 July 1926, The Gables, Elswick Road, Newcastle upon Tyne; son of William Herbert Stephenson, Farmer, and Lilian Victoria Stobbs. **Subject(s):** Law/English; BA 1952; MA 1957; LLB 1953; LLM 1985. **Tutor(s):** A G Lee. **Educ:** Queen Elizabeth School, Penrith; Durham School. **Career:** Lecturer in Law, University of Durham 1960.

STEPHENSON, John Lewis (1942) Born 28 May 1924, 204 High Street, Treorchy, Rhondda; son of Joseph Godolphin Stephenson, Pharmaceutical Chemist, and Lily Lydia Cossy Stokes. **Tutor(s):** C W Guillebaud. **Educ:** King Edward VI School, Stafford.

STERN, Professor (Joseph) Peter Maria (1941) Born 25 December 1920, Prague, Czechoslovakia; son of Gustav Stern, BBC Foreign Service and Economic and Social Council, United Nations, and Luisa Bondyová; m Sheila McMullan, 1944; 2 sons, 2 daughters. **Subject(s):** Modern Languages; BA 1945; MA 1947; PhD 1950; LittD 1975; FBA 1990. **Tutor(s):** C W Guillebaud. **Johnian Relatives:** father of Anthony McMullan Stern (1963). **Educ:** Elementary School, Prague, Czechoslovakia; Elementary School, Vordehindelang, Allgäu; Secondary School, Prague; Comenius (Czech) School, Vienna; Barry Secondary School, Glamorganshire; LSE; University of Göttingen. **Career:** Czech Army, then Rear Gunner, Czech Squadron, RAF (VR), WWII; Assistant Lecturer, Bedford College, London 1950–1952; Assistant Lecturer in German 1952–1957, Lecturer in German 1957–1972, University of Cambridge; Title B Fellow 1955–1972, Lecturer in German 1960–1972, SJC; Professor of German and Head of Department, UCL 1972–1986; Professor Emeritus, University of London 1986. **Appointments:** Supervisor in German 1952–1962, Director of Studies in Modern Languages 1960–1972, Tutor 1963–1969, Honorary Fellow 1990–1991, SJC; Visiting Professor, City College, New York 1959; Visiting Professor, Berkeley 1964 and 1967; Visiting Professor, University of Virginia, Charlottesville 1972; Visiting Scholar, Villa Serbelloni, Bellagio 1975; Chairman of Board, Germanic Languages and Literature 1978–1979, Honorary Director, Institute of Germanic Studies 1981–1985, Fellow, Institute of Germanic Studies 1986, University of London; Andrew D White Professor, Cornell University 1979–1982; Deutsche Forschungsgemeinschaft 1979–1985; Corresponding Member, Göttingen Academy of Arts and Sciences 1985; Bernhard Visiting Professor, Williams College, Williamstown, Massachusetts 1986–1987; Visiting Professor, University of California, Irvine 1988; Visiting Professor, Hochschule für angewandte Kunst, University of Vienna 1988. **Awards:**

Goethe Medal, Goethe Institute 1980; Alexander von Humboldt Research Prize 1980. **Publications:** *Ernst Jünger: a writer of our time*, 1952; (trans) R W Meyer, *Leibnitz and the seventeenth–century revolution*, 1952; (trans) H–E Holthusen, *R M Rilke: a study of his later poetry*, 1952; *G C Lichtenberg: a doctrine of scattered occasions*, 1959; *Re–Interpretations: seven studies in nineteenth–century German literature*, 1964, reprint 1981; (ed) *Arthur Schnitzler: three works*, 1966; *Idylls and Realities: studies in nineteenth–century German literature*, 1971; *On Realism*, 1973, revised German version, 1982; *Hitler: the Führer and the People*, 1975 (3rd edn 1990, German version 1978, French trans revised by S F Stern, 1985, Czech version, 1987); *Nietzsche* (Fontana Modern Masters), 1978; *A Study of Nietzsche*, 1979, revised German version, 1982; (with Michael Silk) *Nietzsche on Tragedy*, 1981 (J G Robertson Prize, 1988); (ed) *The World of Franz Kafka*, 1981; (ed) *London German Studies* II, 1984, III, 1986; (ed) *Paths and Labyrinths: a Kafka symposium*, 1985; contributions (including 42 Poems from the Czech, trans with S F Stern) and articles in English and foreign journals and newspapers; (general ed) *Landmarks of World Literature*, CUP, 1986–1987; posthumous publications: *The Heart of Europe: essays on literature and ideology*, 1992; ed Sheila Stern et al, *The Dear Purchase, a theme in German Modernism*, 1995. Died 18 November 1991.

STERN, Nathan (1901) Born 12 February 1878, No 223 West 33rd Street, New York, USA; son of Julius Stern, Confectioner, and Jeanette Joung. **Tutor(s):** D MacAlister. **Educ:** Columbia University, New York.

STERNDALE BENNETT, James Bury (1907) Born 10 November 1889, St Helen's House, Derby; son of James Robert Sterndale Bennett, Schoolmaster, and Mabel Agnes Gaskell; m Athene Seyler, 1915; 1 daughter (Jane Ann b 17 April 1917). **Tutor(s):** J R Tanner. **Johnian Relatives:** grandson of William Sterndale Bennett (1856); son of James Robert Sterndale Bennett (1865); brother of John Sterndale Bennett (1897) and of Robert Sterndale Bennett (1901); grandfather of Gareth David Jones (1969). **Educ:** St Paul's School. **Career:** Private, HAC, then Captain, South Wales Borderers (POW, mentioned in the Secretary of State's list, for valuable services in connection with the war), WWI. **Honours:** MC 1918. Died 13 March 1941.

STERNDALE BENNETT, Robert (1901) Born 12 September 1880, Southwold, Suffolk; son of James Robert Sterndale Bennett, Lecturer, KCL, and Mabel Agnes Gaskell; m Gwendolen Dorothy Risch Miller, 20 April 1912, St Mary Abbot's, Kensington; 1 son (Robin b 1915), 2 daughters (Elizabeth b 1913 and Anne b 1918). BA 1904; MA 1908; ARCM 1900; ARCO 1906. **Tutor(s):** C E Graves; J R Tanner. **Johnian Relatives:** grandson of William Sterndale Bennett (1856); son of James Robert Sterndale Bennett (1865); brother of John Sterndale Bennett (1897) and of James Bury Sterndale Bennett (1907); great uncle of Gareth David Jones (1969). **Educ:** Derby School. **Career:** Music Master, Fettes College, Edinburgh 1905–1908; Director of Music, Organist and Choirmaster, Uppingham School 1908; Major, Uppingham School OTC, WWI. **Appointments:** President, Music Masters' Association 1923. **Awards:** John Stewart of Rannoch Scholarship in Sacred Music, University of Cambridge 1901; ARCO Cart Prize 1906. Died 27 August 1963.

STEVENS, Dr Bernard George (1934) Born 2 March 1916, 82 Holmleigh Road, Stamford Hill, London; son of George Stevens, Art Metal Manufacturer, and Nellie Louise Martin; m Bertha; 1 daughter (Cathy). **Subject(s):** English; BA 1937; MA 1946; MusB 1939; MusD 1969; Fellow, Royal College of Music. **Tutor(s):** C W Guillebaud. **Educ:** Dudley House School, Stoke Newington; Thorpe Boys' Secondary School; Southend High School. **Career:** Professor of Composition, Royal College of Music 1948–1981. **Appointments:** Honorary Member, Royal Academy of Music; Founder Member, CND. Died 2 January 1983.

STEVENS, Derek Scott (1940) Born 21 May 1922, 2 Overcombe, The Shrubbery, Weston-Super-Mare; son of Herbert Leslie Stevens, District Auditor, Ministry of Health, and Isabella Jane Ross Taylor; 3 children.

Subject(s): Economics/Law; BA 1947; MA 1949. **Tutor(s):** S J Bailey. **Johnian Relatives:** father of Anthony Nigel Stevens (1971). **Educ:** Petergate Pre-Preparatory School, Weston-Super-Mare; Westbourne Preparatory School, Sheffield; Strathallan School, Forgandenny. **Career:** Bank of England pensioner 1972.

STEVENS, John Kelland (1911) Born 11 September 1892, Cambridge; son of William Henry Kelland Stevens, Grocer, and Elizabeth Harriet Mills; m Ruby Mary Collier, 7 November 1917, St Andrew the Great, Cambridge. **Subject(s):** Classics; BA 1914; MA 1927. **Tutor(s):** E E Sikes. **Educ:** Lyndwode House; Perse School. **Career:** Second Lieutenant, Royal Fusiliers, then Lieutenant, Special List (RTO) (wounded), WWI. Died 18 November 1930.

STEVENS, John Richard (1929) Born 28 June 1910, South View, East Barnet Road, Enfield; son of Nicholas Richard Stevens, Chartered Surveyor and Valuer, Inland Revenue, and Mabel Winifred Troughton. **Subject(s):** Classics/Geography; BA 1932; MA 1937. **Tutor(s):** M P Charlesworth. **Educ:** Lyndale, Hillside Road, St Albans; The Grange, Stevenage; Aldenham School. **Career:** Headmaster, Summerfold House, Burgess Hill, Sussex. Died 14 January 1996.

STEVENS, Robert Hilary (1930) Born 15 August 1912, Ashleigh, Shortlands Road, Beckenham, Kent; son of Walter Beckwith Stevens, Law Book Publisher, and Florence Helen Ashton. **Tutor(s):** C W Guillebaud. **Educ:** Abbey School, Beckenham; St Andrew's School, Eastbourne; Blundell's School, Tiverton; Le Val Changis, France.

STEVENSON, James (1920) Born 29 September 1901, Schoolhouse, Cockburnspath, Berwickshire, Scotland; son of James Stevenson, Schoolmaster, and Agnes Falconer Robertson; 2 sons (James Falconer and Mark Maclaren), 1 daughter (Catharine). **Subject(s):** Classics; BA 1923; MA 1929. **Tutor(s):** E E Sikes. **Johnian Relatives:** father of James Falconer Stevenson (1958) and of Mark Maclaren Stevenson (1962). **Educ:** Cockburnspath Public School; Fettes College, Edinburgh. **Career:** Lecturer, McMaster University, Toronto 1925–1927; Lecturer in Classics, University College, Swansea 1928; Lecturer in Divinity 1936, Senior Proctor 1941, Junior Proctor 1946, Special Pro-Proctor for Motor Vehicles and Aircraft 1949–1951, University of Cambridge; Fellow, Downing College, Cambridge 1951–1968. **Appointments:** Jane Eliza Proctor Visiting Fellow, Princeton 1923; Tutor 1951–1962, Praelector 1951–1968, Downing College, Cambridge. **Awards:** Thirlwall Prize, University of Cambridge 1927; Scholarship, SJC. Died 22 May 1983.

STEVENSON, Kenneth Malcolm (1945) Born 18 May 1927, 27 Welbeck Street, Marylebone; son of Arthur Stevenson, Paper Manufacturer, and Mercia Constance Doris Daniels. **Subject(s):** Mechanical Sciences; BA 1948; MA 1969; MBA (Harvard) 1951. **Tutor(s):** S J Bailey; R L Howland. **Educ:** Hampstead Garden Suburb Elementary School; University College School. **Career:** Managing Director, Hugh Stevenson and Sons. Died June 1987.

STEVENSON, Peter Verran (1929) Born 26 May 1911, 237 Chesterton Road, Cambridge; son of Claude Maberly Stevenson, Physician, and Dorothy Thirza Verran; m Mary Christina Webb, 23 March 1940, Roath Park Congregational Church; 1 son (David Webb b 7 December 1947). **Subject(s):** History/Economics; BA 1933; MA 1936; FCA. **Tutor(s):** E A Benians. **Johnian Relatives:** son of Claude Maberly Stevenson (1898); father of David Webb Stevenson (1966). **Educ:** Mr Henry's Lower School, Chesterton, Cambridge; The Leys School, Cambridge. **Career:** Incorporated Accountant, Liverpool 1950. Died 2 September 1987.

STEVENSON, Robert Edward (1924) Born 31 March 1905, Devonshire House, Corbar Road, Fairfield, Derbyshire; son of Hugh Hunter Stevenson, Box Manufacturer, and Clementina Louise Johnson; 1 daughter (Venetia). **Subject(s):** Mechanical Sciences; BA 1927; MA 1931. **Tutor(s):** J M Wordie. **Educ:** Observatory House School, Westgate-on-Sea; Shrewsbury School. **Career:** Gaumont British Picture

Corporation. **Appointments:** President, Cambridge Union Society Easter Term 1928. **Awards:** Scholarship, SJC 1923; John Bernard Seely Prize, University of Cambridge 1926.

STEWARDSON, John Rennie (1942) Born 31 December 1923, Dr Fearn's Sanatorium, Shanghai, China; son of Robert Ernest Stewardson, Architect, and Ray Tipple; m (1) Donny Bellinger 1951, (2) Bridget Hill (née Footner), 1977; (1) 3 children. **Subject(s):** Law; BA 1947; MA 1985. **Tutor(s):** C W Guillebaud. **Educ:** Birklehof, Hinterzarten, Germany; St Cyprian's, Eastbourne; The English School, Château d'Oex, Switzerland; Charterhouse. **Career:** Lieutenant, RNVR, Battle of the Atlantic, RN 1942–1946; Barrister, Called by the Inner Temple 1949–1951; Solicitor 1954–1979; Legal Adviser, Imperial Tobacco Company, Bristol 1957–1959; Group Company Secretary, Consolidated Gold Fields Plc 1969–1979; Secretary, Advertising Association 1980–1989. **Publications:** *The Ratchet: A Cool Look at the European Union*, The June Press; articles in *The European Union*.

STEWART, Dr Andrew Wendover (1931) Born 22 January 1913, Cathcart, Cape Province, South Africa; son of Andrew Stewart, Opthalmic Surgeon, and Dorothy Kathleen Mary Wendover. **Subject(s):** Natural Sciences; BA 1934; MB 1939; BChir 1939. **Tutor(s):** M P Charlesworth. **Educ:** St Andrew's Preparatory School, Grahamstown, South Africa; St Andrew's College, Grahamstown, South Africa. Died 1989.

STEWART, Cyril Malcolm Halley (1920) Born 10 November 1900, The Tower, Hart Hill, Luton, Bedfordshire; son of Percy Malcolm Stewart, Cement Manufacturer, and Cordelia Rickett. **Tutor(s):** E E Sikes. **Educ:** Preparatory School, Leas Court, Folkestone; Malvern College.

STEWART, Douglas Martin (1904) Born 14 August 1885, 13 Westfield Grove, Stanley, Wakefield, Yorkshire; son of Martin Stewart, Solicitor, and Bertha Wigglesworth; m Eleanor Margaret Wynne, Minera, Wrexham, 26 April 1921; 1 son (Hugh Martin b 8 December 1924). **Subject(s):** Classics/Law; BA 1907; MA 1912; LLB 1908; Solicitor 1911. **Tutor(s):** C E Graves; J R Tanner. **Johnian Relatives:** son of Martin Stewart (1872); nephew of Walter Edward Stewart (1877); father of Hugh Martin Stewart (1947). **Educ:** Orleton School, Scarborough; Shrewsbury School. **Career:** Articled Clerk and Solicitor, Munby & Scott, Solicitors 1908–1915; Lieutenant, later Captain, Welsh Regiment (Cardiff Pals), Balkan Front (Mentioned in Despatches) 1915–1919; Secretary, Jersey Canning and Preserving Company 1920–1922; Articled Clerk, Lea & Whitfield, Chartered Accountants, Leeds 1922–1927; Secretary, Stanley Holmes, Leeds (clothing company) 1927–1937; Royal Observer Corps, York 1940–1950. **Appointments:** Treasurer, York Diocesan Ordination Candidates' Fund (1940s). **Awards:** Scholarship, SJC. Died 27 October 1963.

STEWART, The Revd Dr Hugh Fraser (1907) (admitted to Trinity College 1883) Born 27 October 1863, Aldershot, Hampshire; son of Ludovick Charles Stewart, Army Surgeon, and Emma Ray; m Jessie Graham Crum, 8 April 1902, St Marylebone, London (d 1966); 1 son, 4 daughters. DD 1916; BA 1886 (Trinity); MA 1891 (Trinity); BD (Trinity) 1906. **Educ:** Rugby School. **Career:** Assistant Master, Marlborough 1889–1895; Ordained Deacon 1894; Ordained Priest 1895; Vice-Principal, Salisbury Theological College 1895–1899; Precentor/Chaplain, Trinity College 1899–1907; Platt Fellow, Dean, and Lecturer in French, SJC 1907–1918; Curate, St Mary the Great, Cambridge 1901–1902; Fellow 1918, Praelector in French 1918, Dean of Chapel 1923, Trinity College, Cambridge; Fellow, Eton College 1919–1948; Reader in French, University of Cambridge 1922–1944 (Emeritus 1944–1948). **Appointments:** President, Cambridge University Music Society; Birkbeck Lecturer in Ecclesiastical History, Trinity College, Cambridge 1927; Senior Proctor, University of Cambridge 1910–1911; Hulsean Lecturer, University of Cambridge 1914; University of Cambridge correspondent, *The Guardian*. **Awards:** Hulsean Prize 1888; Buchanan Prize. **Honours:** Chevalier de la Legion d'Honneur. **Publications:** *Boethius: an essay*, 1891; (trans and notes) *Thirteen Homilies of St Augustine*, 1900; *Doctrina Romanensium de Invocantione Sanctorum*, 1907; (ed, with Arthur Tilley) *The romantic movement in French literature*, 1910; *The Holiness of Pascal: the Hulsean Lectures, 1914–15*, 1915; (ed) Pascal, Blaise, *Les Lettres provincials*, 1920; (with Paul Desjardins) *French patriotism in the nineteenth century*, 1923; *Francis Jenkinson: a memoir*, 1926; *The Secret of Pascal*, 1941; (trans and notes) Pascal, Blaise, *Pensées*, 1950; various sermons, lectures and translations from French and Latin. Died 23 January 1948.

STEWART, Hugh Martin (1947) Born 8 December 1924, Harrogate, Yorkshire; son of Douglas Martin Stewart, Solicitor, and Eleanor Margaret Wynne; m Margaret Adams, 8 September 1962, St Bartholomew the Great, London. **Subject(s):** Maths; BA 1950; MA 1955; FIA 1959. **Tutor(s):** J M Wordie. **Johnian Relatives:** grandson of Martin Stewart (1872); great nephew of Walter Edward Stewart (1877); son of Douglas Martin Stewart (1904). **Educ:** Clifton School, York; Orleton School, Scarborough; Shrewsbury School. **Career:** Signalman, Royal Corps of Signals 1943–1946; Serjeant Instructor, RAEC 1946–1947; Equity & Law Life Assurance Society plc 1951–1985 (Assistant Group Business Secretary 1960–1966, Assistant Accountant 1966–1968, Chief Accountant 1968–1970, Company Secretary 1970–1985). **Appointments:** Junior Treasurer, LMBC 1948–1950; Johnian Society Committee 1950s; OJHF Committee 1952–1990 (Secretary 1968–1978, Treasurer 1968–1986). **Awards:** Scholarship, Shrewsbury School. **Publications:** 'Notes on the Word Blazer', *Cambridge Review*, 1950; Translation of Agathias, *The Eagle*, 1951; (ed with W C B Tunstall) *The History of the Lady Margaret Boat Club Volume II 1926–1956*, 1957; 'Pyrrha', *Greece and Rome*, 1959; (with C J Brockson) 'The Taxation of Life Assurance Companies in the United Kingdom', *Journal of the Institute of Actuaries Students' Society*, 1971; 'A Founding Vice-President of the Institute of Actuaries – James Joseph Sylvester (1814–1897)', *Transactions of the 26th International Congress of Actuaries*, 1998.

STEWART, Hugh St Clair (1929) Born 14 December 1910, 7 Stratton Terrace, Falmouth, Cornwall; son of Mervyn James Stewart, Clerk in Holy Orders, and Margaret Emma Steuart; m Frances Henley Curl, 31 July 1934, St Jude's, Kensington; 2 sons (Andrew Mervyn b 1943 and Michael Henley b 1949), 2 daughters (Penelope Agnes b 1939 and Trottie b 1949). **Subject(s):** English; BA 1932; MA 1948. **Tutor(s):** M P Charlesworth. **Educ:** Belmont School, Falmouth; Claysmore School, Winchester. **Career:** Film production 1932; Army Service 1939–1944; Film Producer 1945–1967; Teacher of English Literature, College of Further Education 1968–1986; Teacher, Uxbridge College 1998–2001. **Appointments:** Restarted Nash Society 1931; Member, *Granta* Staff; Member, Mummers. **Honours:** MBE 1945 (Military).

STEWART, John Eachus (1941) Born 31 August 1923, Eden Hospital Calcutta, India; son of John Anderson Stewart, Deputy Chief Engineer, and Kathleen Isabel Eachus. **Tutor(s):** S J Bailey. **Educ:** Berkhamsted School.

STEWART, Malcolm Geoffrey (1928) Born 7 December 1908, Fort Stewart, Ramelton, County Donegal, Ireland; son of Sir Harry Jocelyn Urquhart Stewart, Baronet, and Isabel Mary Mansfield; m Beatrice Joan Cox, 21 December 1946, RMA Chapel, Sandhurst. **Subject(s):** History/Classics; BA 1931. **Tutor(s):** M P Charlesworth. **Educ:** Aravon School, Bray; Durham School. **Career:** Master, Mourne Grange Preparatory School, County Down 1932–1935; Master, Wellington House, Westgate 1935–1937; Master, Durlstone Court, Swanage 1938. **Awards:** Baker Exhibition, SJC 1928.

STEWART, Robert Penman (1932) Born 26 March 1914, 3 George Street, Germiston; son of Robert Stewart, Building Contractor, and Lina Ingram. **Tutor(s):** J S Boys Smith. **Educ:** Central School, Germiston; St John's College, Johannesburg; Merchiston Castle, Edinburgh. Died 2 June 1935.

STEWART, Professor Robert William (1947) Born 21 August 1923, Smoky Lake, Alberta, Canada; son of Robert Edward Stewart, Schoolmaster, and Florence May Berry; m (1) Vera Brand, 1948–1967, (2) Anne-Marie Robert, 1973; (1) 2 sons (Brian b 1952 and Philip b 1966), 1 daughter (Anne b 1949), (2) 1 son (Colin b 1975). **Subject(s):** PhD 1952; BSc (Queen's) 1945; MSc (Queen's) 1947; DSc (McGill); DPhil (Dalhousie); DSc (Victoria). **Tutor(s):** J M Wordie. **Educ:** Olds Public School, Canada; Rideau Park Public School, Calgary, Canada; Bow View Public School, Calgary, Canada; Hillhurst Junior High School, Calgary, Canada; Crescent Heights High School, Calgary, Canada; Queen's University, Ontario, Canada; McGill University, Dalhousie University, University of Victoria. **Career:** Associate Professor of Physics 1955–1962, Professor of Physics 1962–1970, University of British Columbia; Adjunct Professor, University of Victoria 1993–2001. **Appointments:** Science Officer, International Council of Scientific Unions; President, Alberta Research Council; Deputy Minister of Universities, Science and Communications, British Columbia; Director, Institute of Ocean Sciences, Patricia Bay 1970–1980. **Awards:** Career Achievement Award, Science Council of British Columbia 1991. **Publications:** Numerous.

STEWART, Thomas George (1900) Born 19 July 1876, 5 Clifton Villas, Putney; son of Thomas Stewart, Bank Accountant, and Mary Ann Miller. BA 1913; MA 1916. **Tutor(s):** D MacAlister. **Educ:** Private Schools; St Dunstan's College, Catford. **Career:** Ordained Deacon (Chelmsford) 1914; Curate, All Saints, Leyton, Essex 1914–1916; Priest 1915; Curate, St James, West Ealing, Middlesex 1916–1918; Curate, Wandsworth, Surrey 1919–1920; Deputation Secretary, Dr Barnardo's Homes, Bristol area 1920–1922; Curate, Wembley, Middlesex 1922–1926; Curate, St Marylebone 1926–1927; Rector, Quinton with Preston Deanery, Northamptonshire 1927–1945.

STEYN, Johannes Roelof (1945) Born 19 December 1922, Onze Rust, Bloemfontein, Orange Free State; son of Colin Fraser Steyn, Minister of Justice, South Africa, and Rachel Maria Eksteen. BSc (Cape Town) 1944. **Tutor(s):** J M Wordie. **Educ:** Meisieskool Oranje, Bloemfontein; Grey College School, Bloemfontein; University of Cape Town. **Career:** Signaller in South African Army 1944–1945.

STIBBARD, Wilfred Stanley (1933) Born 25 June 1914, 48 Cambridge Street, Norwich; son of Alfred David Stibbard, Company Secretary, and Elizabeth Williamson; m Olive Rosalie Campling, 8 May 1948, Sprowston Parish Church. **Subject(s):** History; BA 1936; MA 1940. **Tutor(s):** E A Benians. **Educ:** Avenue Road Elementary School; City of Norwich School. **Career:** Solicitor, Blyth & Robinson, Cromer 1941. **Awards:** Exhibition, SJC; Scholarship, SJC; College Prize, SJC; Special Essay Prize, SJC 1935. Died 16 February 1986.

STILES, Dr Walter Stanley (1922) Born 15 June 1901, 135 Cavendish Buildings, Holborn, London; son of Walter Stiles, Superintendent of Metropolitan Police, and Elizabeth Catherine Smith; m Pauline Frida Octavia, 1928. **Subject(s):** Mathematics; BSc (London) 1920; PhD (London) 1929; DSc (London) 1939; FRS 1957. **Tutor(s):** E Cunningham. **Educ:** Commercial Secondary School, Regent Street Polytechnic; Birkbeck College, London; UCL. **Career:** Demonstrator in Physics, University College London 1920–1922; Technical Officer, RN Signal School 1923–1925; Scientific Officer and Chief Scientific Officer, National Physical Laboratory 1925–1961. **Appointments:** General Secretary, International Commission on Illumination 1928–1931; Vice President, Physical Society 1948–1949; Chairman, Colour Group, Physical Society 1949–1951; Thomas Young Orator, Physical Society 1955; President, Illuminating Engineering Society 1960; Regent's Lecturer, UCLA 1964; Newton Lecturer 1967. **Awards:** Carpenter Medallist, London University 1944; Gold Medal, Illuminating Engineering Society 1967; Tillyer Medal, Optical Society of America 1965; Finsen Medallist, International Congress on Photobiology 1968. **Honours:** OBE 1946. **Publications:** *Thermionic Emission*, 1932; *Colour Science*, 1967; *Mechanisms of Colour Vision*, 1978. Died 15 December 1985.

STILL, Dr Hereford Crossfield (1937) Born 10 November 1918, 29 Northumberland Square, Tynemouth; son of William Herbert Still, Clerk in Holy Orders, and Frances Annie Happold; 1 son (John), 2 daughters (Janet and Susan). BA 1940; MA 1944; MB BChir (Guy's Hospital) 1943; CCFP; FCFP. **Tutor(s):** R L Howland. **Educ:** Earnseat School, Arnside; Exeter School. **Career:** Associate Professor of Family Medicine, Dalhousie University, Halifax, Canada (later Emeritus). **Awards:** Vidal Exhibition, SJC 1937; Family Physician of the Year 1990. Died 18 May 2001.

STIMPSON, Robert (1914) Born 24 October 1895, Norwich Street, East Dereham, Norfolk; son of Thomas Stimpson, Butcher and Farmer, and Leila Barley. **Tutor(s):** L H K Bushe-Fox. **Educ:** East Dereham Grammar School; East Dereham Church School; Banham Grammar School; Thetford Grammar School. **Career:** Private, London Regiment (Rangers) 1914–1918.

STIRLING-GILCHRIST, John (1918) See GILCHRIST.

STOCK, Peter Duguid Heath (1930) Born 8 June 1912, 34 Swinburne Road, Darlington, Durham; son of Cyril Joseph Heath Stock, Public Analyst and Analytical Chemist, and Constance Walker; m Margaret Evelyn Winters, 22 May 1947. **Tutor(s):** C W Guillebaud. **Educ:** The Grammar School, Darlington; Sedbergh School.

STOCKS, Dr Arthur Vernon (1907) Born 6 July 1888, 23 Ellesmere Avenue, Eccles, Lancashire; son of John Stocks, Wholesale Provision Merchant, and Margaret Ann Mead; m Elsie; 3 sons. **Subject(s):** Natural Sciences; BA 1910; MA 1914; BChir 1914; Diploma in Public Health 1920. **Tutor(s):** J R Tanner. **Educ:** Manchester Grammar School. **Career:** House Physician and House Surgeon, Manchester Royal Infirmary; RAMC, WWI; First Divisional Medical Officer for Eccles, Swinton, Worsley and Irlam areas; Assistant School Medical Officer, Cheshire County Council 1920–1929; Medical Staff, Lancashire County Council, Medical Officer of Health for Urmston, and Divisional School Medical Officer for Worsley and Irlam 1929–1948; First Divisional Medical Officer for Middleton, Chadderton, Failsworth and Royston 1948–1950. **Appointments:** President, and Honorary Secretary, North-Western Branch, Society of Medical Officers of Health; Lay Preacher, Altrincham Area; Society Steward and Circuit Steward, Methodist Church Sunday-School Superintendent; Assistant Commissioner for Handicapped Scouts. **Awards:** Silver Acorn (Scouts). Died 25 September 1961.

STOCKWOOD, Illtyd Henry (1911) Born 29 July 1892, Silver Mere, Porthcawl, Glamorganshire; son of Samuel Henry Stockwood, Solicitor, and Alice Emma Taylor; m Kathleen Taylor, 19 September 1919, St Illtyd's Church, Newcastle, Bridgend. **Subject(s):** Law; BA 1914; MA 1947; LLB 1914. **Tutor(s):** L H K Bushe-Fox. **Educ:** Penarth Lodge; Bradfield College. **Career:** Lieutenant, South Wales Borderers, Captain, Tank Corps, then Honorary Captain (Observer Officer), RAF, WWI; Senior Partner, Stockwood & Williams, Bridgend. **Appointments:** President, Bridgend Law Society. Died 6 August 1970.

STODDARD, Thomas Leslie (1929) Born 20 January 1910, 10 Haley Street, Cheetham, North Manchester; son of William Stoddard, Municipal Official, and May Hammersley. **Subject(s):** Classics; BA 1932; MA 1937. **Tutor(s):** M P Charlesworth. **Johnian Relatives:** father of Antony Leslie Stoddard (1960). **Educ:** Manchester Grammar School, Preparatory Department; Manchester Grammar School. **Career:** Second Master and Housemaster, Kelly College, Tavistock, until 1972. **Awards:** Patchett Scholarship, SJC. Died 26 June 1994.

STODDART, James Roylance (1906) Born 20 June 1888, 5 Brunswick Terrace, Chester Road, Stretford, Lancashire; son of William Viner Stoddart, Oil Merchant, and Margaret. **Tutor(s):** L H K Bushe-Fox. **Educ:** Commercial School, Stretford; Rossal School. **Career:** Studied Medicine, St Bartholomew's. Died 29 December 1933.

STOKES, Christopher William (1919) Born 18 January 1898, 25 Mount Pleasant Road, St Mary in the Castle, Hastings; son of Samuel Stokes, Luggage Porter, and Polly Burrows; m Hilda Mary Sly; 1 son (Michael Christopher b 26 March 1933). **Subject(s):** Mathematics; BA 1922; MA 1926. **Tutor(s):** E E Sikes. **Johnian Relatives:** father of Michael Christopher Stokes (1951). **Educ:** Aylsham House School; Priory Road School; Holy Trinity School; The Grammar School, Hastings. **Career:** Assistant Master, Shrewsbury School 1922–1923; Senior Mathematics Master, Worcester Royal Grammar School 1923–1930; Headmaster, Clitheroe Royal Grammar School, Lancashire 1930–1934; HM Inspector of Schools, Kent 1935–1939; Seconded for War Service to Ministry of Information and then Admiralty 1939–1943; Secretary, Oxford Local Examinations Delegacy 1939–1962; Tutor in Mathematics, Wolsey Hall, Oxford 1964–1968. **Appointments:** Deputy Director, Organizing Secretary for the launch of Samaritans in Bedford. **Awards:** Scholarship, SJC. **Publications:** *Queen Mary's Grammar School, Clitheroe, Part 1, The 16th & 17th Centuries*, Manchester, for the Chetham Society, 1934. Died 22 February 1981.

STOKES, John Whitley Gabriel (1905) Born 15 April 1886, 12 Hanover Street, Hanover Square, London; son of John Whitley Stokes, of independent means, and Mary Beach Coates. BA 1908. **Tutor(s):** E E Sikes. **Johnian Relatives:** brother of Josiah Stokes (1900). **Educ:** Lyroell House, Llandudno; Uppingham School. **Career:** Lieutenant, RGA, WWI.

STOKES, Josiah (1900) Born 7 June 1881, Bodynfoel Hall, Llanfechain, Montgomeryshire; son of John Whitley Stokes, of independent means, and Mary Beach Coates. BA 1905. **Tutor(s):** E E Sikes. **Johnian Relatives:** brother of John Whitley Gabriel Stokes (1905). **Educ:** Private Tuition.

STOKES, Richard Albert Gordon (1934) Born 17 July 1915, 41 Powerful Street, Walney, Barrow-in-Furness; son of Richard Albert William Stokes, Engineer, and Rose Taylor; m Kathleen Mary Goddard, 1939; 2 sons (Richard b 1943 and Christopher b 1947). **Subject(s):** Natural Sciences; BA 1937; MA 1946; CBiol; MIBiol. **Tutor(s):** C W Guillebaud. **Johnian Relatives:** father of Christopher John Stokes (1967). **Educ:** North End High School, Portsmouth; Colet Court, London; St Paul's School, London. **Career:** Assistant Master, Portsmouth Grammar School 1938–1946; Commissioned Royal Signals, Italian Campaign (Mentioned in Despatches), final rank of Major 1939–1945; Assistant Master 1946–1970, Senior Master 1970–1977, Merchant Taylors' School, Northwood; Senior Master, Sir James Henderson School, Milan, Italy 1977–1979. **Appointments:** Assistant Examiner and Chief Examiner, UCLES; Assistant Examiner, A-level Biology, Joint Matriculation Board; Chief Examiner for overseas candidates. **Publications:** *Elementary Practical Chemistry*, 1959; articles in various journals. Died 11 September 2002.

STOKES, Robert Ian (1944) Born 3 August 1925, White Cottage, Lonsdale Road, Bournemouth; son of Norman Stokes, Tea and Coffee Merchant, and Elsye Truslove; m Hazel Joan Lidstone, 17 August 1949, Harrow Congregational Church; 3 sons, 1 daughter. **Subject(s):** Modern and Medieval Languages; BA 1947; MA 1951. **Tutor(s):** C W Guillebaud. **Educ:** Cathedral School, Salisbury; Felsted School. **Career:** Master, Junior School, Felsted 1944; Master, Sedbergh School 1947–1949; Master, Aldenham School 1949–1983 (Careers Master 1953–1983, Housemaster 1959–1974, Head of Modern Languages Department 1959–1983). **Appointments:** Regional Secretary, Independent Schools Careers Organisation 1983–1990.

STOKOE, William Geoffrey (1942) Born 12 October 1924, Eggleston, Barnard Castle, County Durham; son of John William Stokoe, Headmaster, St John's School, Darlington, and Emma Adamson. **Subject(s):** Natural Sciences/Physics; BA 1947; MA 1949; CertEd. **Tutor(s):** C W Guillebaud. **Educ:** Eggleston Church of England School; St John's Church of England School, Darlington; The Grammar School, Darlington. **Career:** Teacher.

STONE, Leonard (1948) Born 6 February 1928, 15 Carr Street, Birstall, Yorkshire; son of Teddy Stone, Foreman Blender, and Ethel Kitchingman. **Subject(s):** Natural Sciences; BA 1951; MA 1958. **Tutor(s):** G C L Bertram. **Educ:** Birstall Council School; Healey Senior School; Batley Grammar School.

STONELEY, Dr Robert (1912) Born 14 May 1894, 92 Almack Road, Hackney, Middlesex; son of Robert Stoneley, House Decorator, and Fanny Bradley; m Dorothy Minn, 28 March 1927, Ilford Parish Church; 2 sons (Robert and Anthony). **Subject(s):** Mathematics/Natural Sciences; BA 1915; MA 1921; ScD 1931; FRS 1935. **Tutor(s):** R P Gregory. **Educ:** Parmiter's School; City of London School. **Career:** Assistant Lecturer in Mathematics, Sheffield University 1920–1923; Assistant Mathematics Lecturer, later full Lecturer and Reader in Geophysics, Leeds University 1923–1934; University Lecturer in Mathematics 1934–1949, Reader in Theoretical Geophysics 1949–1961 (Emeritus 1961), University of Cambridge; Fellow, Pembroke College, Cambridge 1943. **Appointments:** Chairman, British Association Seismological Committee 1946; President, International Seismological Association 1948–1951; Chairman, National Committee for Geodesy and Geophysics 1949–1954; National Correspondent, International Geophysical Year 1953–1960; Director, International Seismological Summary 1957–1963; Senior Consultant, International Institute of Seismology and Earthquake Engineering, Tokyo 1963; Fellow, American Geophysical Union; Honorary Member, Seismological Society of America; Visiting Professorships, University of California, California Institute of Technology, American University of Washington, and University of Pittsburgh. **Awards:** Taylor Research Studentship, SJC 1916. Died 2 February 1976.

STOPES-ROE, Dr Harry Verdon (1947) Born 27 March 1924, 25 Dorset Square, London; son of Humphrey Verdon Roe, Landed Proprietor, and Marie Carmichael Stopes; m Mary Eyre Wallis, 27 July 1948; 2 sons (Jonathan b 1951 and Christopher b 1958), 2 daughters (Catherine b 1953 and Helena b 1956). MSc 1950; PhD 1957; BSc (London) 1944. **Tutor(s):** J M Wordie. **Educ:** Charterhouse; Imperial College of Science. **Career:** Senior Lecturer, Science Studies, Department of Extra-Mural Studies, University of Birmingham 1959–1983. **Appointments:** Chairman (1974–1976 and 1977) and Vice-President, British Humanist Association. **Publications:** Articles in various philosophical and humanist periodicals.

STOPFORD, The Revd James Stanley Bird (1917) Born 9 January 1900, 15 St Albans Street, Rochdale, Lancashire; son of John Bird Stopford, Clerk in Holy Orders, and Ada Fletcher; m Florence Cook, 26 February 1930, Manchester Cathedral. BA 1923; MA 1926. **Tutor(s):** E E Sikes. **Johnian Relatives:** son of John Bird Stopford (1879); brother of John Stopford (1910). **Educ:** Hulme Grammar School, Oldham; Manchester Grammar School. **Career:** Deacon 1926; Curate, Rothbury 1926–1929; Priest 1928; Curate, Earlsfield 1929–1932; Vicar, Coppul, Chorley 1932.

STOPFORD, John (1910) Born 20 September 1890, Lower Mill Cottage, Wuerdle, Littleborough, Lancashire; son of John Bird Stopford, Clerk in Holy Orders, and Ada Fletcher; m E Mary Yates, 15 October 1931, Osaka, Japan; 1 son (David). BA 1913; MA 1921. **Tutor(s):** E E Sikes. **Johnian Relatives:** son of John Bird Stopford (1879); brother of James Stanley Bird Stopford (1917). **Educ:** Hulme Grammar School, Oldham. **Career:** Lieutenant, Lancashire Fusiliers, MGC, Mesopotamia, WWI; Teacher of English Business Practice, Hikone Higher Commercial College, Japan 1930–1934; Army Pay Corps 1939–1942; Ministry of Pensions 1942–1950. Died 22 March 1955.

STORER, David George (1949) Born 27 June 1929, Carterton, Oxford; son of Herbert Edwards Storer, Hide and Skin Merchant's Agent, and Edith Anne Quaif, Nursing Sister; m Jean Mary Isobel Jenkin, 14 May 1960, Morden, Surrey; 1 son, 2 daughters. **Subject(s):** Modern and Medieval Languages; BA 1952; MA 1956. **Tutor(s):** C W Guillebaud. **Educ:** Rutlish School, Merton; Monmouth School. **Career:**

Administrative Branch, Home Civil Service 1952–1989; Under-Secretary, Manpower Services Commission, London 1977–1984. **Awards:** Exhibition, SJC 1947.

STORER, Walter Owen (1932) Born 23 February 1914, Glanhesbin, Stoney Road, Coventry; son of Walter Charles Storer, House Agent and Rent Collector, and Alice Mary Owen; m Helen Mary Passmore, 1940; 1 son (Michael), 1 daughter (Susan). **Subject(s):** Mathematics; BA 1935; MA 1946. **Tutor(s):** J M Wordie. **Educ:** Frederick Bird Elementary School, Coventry; Bablake School, Coventry. **Career:** Senior Lecturer, University of Aston; Lecturer, University of Southampton 1937–1939; Meteorologist with RAF, stationed in East Anglia 1939–1945; Mathematics Master, Highgate School 1946–1953; Lecturer, Department of Education, University of Birmingham 1953–1979. **Appointments:** President, Midlands Branch of the Mathematics Association. **Awards:** Scholarship, SJC; Exhibition, SJC. Died 4 February 1999.

STORK, François Gerard (1925) Born 20 January 1905, Hengelo, Overijssel, Holland; son of Coenraad Frederik Stork, Engineer, and Helene Albertine Waller; m Anna Helena van der Meer; 1 son (François Gerard b 15 November 1945). BA 1928; MA 1932. **Tutor(s):** J M Wordie. **Johnian Relatives:** father of François Gerard Stork (1965). **Educ:** Gymnasium, Hengelo, Overijssel, Holland. **Career:** Works Manager 1932, Managing Director 1947, Stork Brothers, Holland. Died January 1977.

STORR, Christopher William (1949) (Admitted to Christ's College 1944) Born 15 February 1926, 27 Cecil Court, Kensington, London; son of Charles Felix Stoehr, Lieutenant Colonel, RE, and Winifred Wake Twining; m (1) Mary Irene Phillips (d), (2) Peggy Joyce Evelyn Weatherfield; 1 son (Peter Nicholas b 1959), 1 daughter (Judith Margaret b 1956). **Subject(s):** Mechanical Sciences; BA 1951. MICE. **Tutor(s):** R L Howland. **Educ:** Chafyn Grove School, Salisbury; Wellington College. **Career:** Regular Army Officer; Major, RE.

STOUT, The Revd Alan (1925) Born 8 February 1906, 50 Acresfield Road, Pendleton, Salford, Lancashire; son of Harry Stout, Chemist, and Emily Gill; m Elsie Fernandez, 1932; 2 daughters (Eileen and Dorothy). **Subject(s):** Classics/Theology; BA 1928; MA 1934. **Tutor(s):** E E Sikes. **Johnian Relatives:** brother of Harry Prentice Stout (1933). **Educ:** Pendleton Grammar School; Manchester Grammar School; Ridley Hall, Cambridge. **Career:** Part-time Master, Ormskirk Grammar School; Assistant Examiner for Northern Universities Matriculation Board; Master, Merchant Taylors' School for Girls, Crosby; Ordained Deacon 1929; Curate, St George, Everton 1929–1930; Ordained Priest 1930; Curate, Christ Church, Ince-in-Makerfield 1930–1934; Vicar, St Ann, Warrington 1934–1937; Vicar, Newburgh, Wigan 1937–1952; Vicar, St Philip, Southport 1952–1963; Vicar, St James, Sutton, Macclesfield 1963. **Awards:** Scholarship, SJC. Died 5 May 1972.

STOUT, Dr Harry Prentice (1933) Born 23 July 1914, Seedley Road, Pendleton, Salford; son of Harry Stout, Chemist, and Emily Gill; m Heather Ford, 1948; 1 son (Hamish), 1 daughter (Helen). **Subject(s):** Natural Sciences; BA 1936; PhD 1940; FTI; MInstP. **Tutor(s):** J M Wordie. **Johnian Relatives:** brother of Alan Stout (1925). **Educ:** Pendleton High School; Pendleton Grammar School; Manchester Grammar School. **Career:** Research Department, Explosives Division, ICI, Ardeer, WWII; Senior Physicist 1948, Director of Research 1959, British Jute Trade Research Association, Dundee; Senior Researcher, Department of Management, Science and Technology Studies, Stirling University 1972–1981. **Appointments:** Noise Advisory Council 1972–1978; UNEDO Consultant 1979–1985. **Awards:** S G Smith Medal 1963. **Honours:** OBE 1978. Died 26 December 2003.

STRAIN, Thomas Greer (1902) Born 8 May 1878, The Manse, Dromore, County Down; son of James Kirker Strain, Presbyterian Minister, and Maria Mossom Greer. **Subject(s):** Mathematics/Natural Sciences; BA

1905; MA 1912. **Tutor(s):** D MacAlister. **Educ:** Lurgan College; Queen's College, Galway. **Career:** Mathematics Teacher, Chesterfield Grammar School 1907; Lecturer, South Western Polytechnic Institute 1909. Died 20 March 1949.

STRAKER, Dr Thomas William (1946) Born 2 October 1915, Granity, Westland, New Zealand; son of Donald Matthew Straker, Mining Engineer, and Hannah Smith; m Helen Dorothy Goldfinch; 2 daughters (Antoinette Elizabeth Louise and Rosalind Helen Blanch). PhD 1950; MSc (New Zealand) 1938. **Tutor(s):** J M Wordie. **Educ:** Terrace End Primary School, Palmerston North, New Zealand; Nelson College, New Zealand; Canterbury College, Christchurch University, New Zealand. **Career:** New Zealand Division, Middle East 1939–1941; POW, Italy 1941–1943; Lecturer in Physics, University of Geneva 1944; Lecturer in Physics, Christchurch University, New Zealand 1945–1946; Canadian Defence Research Board, Canada 1950–1954; Canadian Joint Staff, London 1954–1957; The Marconi Company, Chelmsford 1957–1970; Marconi Italiana Company, Genoa, Italy 1970–1973; Marconi/GEC Process Control, Chelmsford 1973–1980.

STRANG, Colonel John Braithwaite (1929) Born 4 July 1911, 3 Norfolk Street, Caversham, Dunedin, New Zealand; son of William Rankin Strang, Company Director, and Kathleen Minnie Braithwaite; m Margaret Kimberley Laird, 24 July 1937; 2 daughters (Diana and Susan). BA 1933; MA 1937; CEng; MIEE; FIMechE. **Tutor(s):** C W Guillebaud. **Johnian Relatives:** brother of William Braithwaite Strang (1931). **Educ:** Primary School, New Zealand; Bickley Hall, Kent; Eastbourne College. **Career:** Colonel. Died 3 August 1988.

STRANG, William Braithwaite (1931) (migrated to Trinity Hall) Born 6 May 1913, 3 Norfolk Street, Caversham, Dunedin; son of William Rankin Strang, Director of Shipping Agents, and Kathleen Minnie Braithwaite; m Jean; 2 sons (William and Ronald), 1 daughter (Kathleen). **Subject(s):** Mechanical Sciences; BA 1936. **Tutor(s):** J M Wordie. **Johnian Relatives:** brother of John Braithwaite Strang (1929). **Educ:** Bickley Hall, Kent; Eastbourne College. Died c1949.

STRATFORD, Francis Joseph (1931) Born 11 February 1913, 11 Ashen Grove, Wimbledon; son of Edward Joseph Stratford, Postmaster, and Hettie Francis Stringer. **Subject(s):** Mathematics; BA 1934; MA 1938. **Tutor(s):** J M Wordie. **Educ:** Ashley Lodge Private School, London; Battersea Grammar School, London. **Awards:** Scholarship, SJC; Adams Memorial Prize, SJC 1934.

STREATFIELD, Terence Ernest (1924) Born 18 February 1906, Pettridge, Bower Mount Road, Maidstone, Kent; son of Ernest Warton Streatfield, Corn Merchant, and Ella Lovelace Wagon. **Subject(s):** History; BA 1927; MA 1978. **Tutor(s):** E A Benians. **Educ:** Maidstone Grammar School; Sutton Valence School. **Career:** Indian Civil Service 1927; Assistant Collector, Bombay 1928; Officiating Under-Secretary to Government, Revenue Department, Bombay 1934–1947; Officiating Collector 1935. **Awards:** Sizarship, SJC.

STREET, Professor Reginald Owen (1908) Born 1 January 1890, 4 Castle Street, Christ Church, Hampshire; son of Alfred James Street, Ironmonger, and Christiana Jane Owen; m Alice. **Subject(s):** Mathematics; BA 1911; MA 1915. **Tutor(s):** L H K Bushe-Fox. **Educ:** Christ Church Congregational Church; Christ Church High School; Bournemouth School. **Career:** RFC, Meteorological Section, Air Ministry, and Second Lieutenant (TF), RAF, WWI; Lupton Fellow, SJC 1920–1922; Chief Assistant, Department of Applied Mathematics, Liverpool University until 1934; Professor of Mathematics 1934–1953 (Emeritus 1953), Royal Technical College, Glasgow (now Strathclyde University). **Awards:** Rayleigh Prize, University of Cambridge 1913. Died 24 August 1967.

STREETEN, The Revd Basil Robert (1908) Born 26 May 1889, Summerhill, Kingswinford, Staffordshire; son of Robert Henry Streeten,

Clerk in Holy Orders, and Mary Frances Crauford. **Subject(s):** Theology; BA 1911. **Tutor(s):** E E Sikes. **Educ:** The Elms, Colwall, Malvern; Hereford Cathedral School; Wells Theological College. **Career:** Curate, Gedling 1912; Ordained Deacon 1912; Priest 1913; Temporary CF, 4th Class, RACD, WWI. Died 1 November 1918 (died of pneumonia in France).

STRETTON, Lionel James (1942) Born 18 February 1924, Sunnyside, Franche Road, Kidderminster; son of John Weston Stretton, Consulting Surgeon, and Mary Smellie. **Tutor(s):** S J Bailey. **Educ:** Denstone College Preparatory School; Sebright School, Wolverley.

STRICKLAND, The Revd Douglas John (1932) Born 11 May 1913, Ashfield, Station Road, Kettering; son of William Frederick Strickland, Journalist, Conservative MP for Coventry, and Annie Lucretia Storton. **Subject(s):** History/Theology; BA 1935; MA 1939. **Tutor(s):** J S Boys Smith. **Educ:** St Nicholas Preparatory School, Sutton Coldfield; Bishop Vesey Grammar School, Sutton Coldfield; University of Birmingham; Westcott House, Cambridge. **Career:** Ordained Deacon 1937; Curate, Aston-juxta-Birmingham 1937–1943; Ordained Priest 1938; Curate in Charge, Conventual District of Dorridge 1943–1947; Vicar, St James, Handsworth 1947–1953; Rector, Sheldon 1953–1966; Rural Dean, Coleshill 1958; Honorary Canon, Birmingham Cathedral 1964; Vicar, Wimborne Minster, Dorset 1966; Canon and Prebendary, Salisbury Cathedral 1970. Died 7 April 1987.

STRINGER, Professor John (1943) Born 29 May 1925, Brendon, Hinckes Road, Tettenhall, Staffordshire; son of Philip Charles Brian Stringer, Architect and Surveyor, and Mary Elizabeth Richardson; m (1) Josephine Legge, (2) Norma Goldsmith; 2 sons. **Subject(s):** Engineering (Mechanical Sciences); BA 1946; MA 1951. **Tutor(s):** S J Bailey. **Educ:** Ely House Preparatory School, Wolverhampton; St Jude's Church of England School, Wolverhampton; Wolverhampton Grammar School. **Career:** Marine Aircraft Experimental Establishment, Ministry of Supply 1945–1948; British Iron and Steel Research Association 1948–1950; Operational Research, London Transport 1950–1955; Head of Operational Research, Central Electricity Generating Board 1950–1962; Operational Research Manager, BOC 1962–1964; Institute for Operational Research, Tavistock Institute of Human Relations, London 1964–1976 (Director from 1969); Foundation Professor, Australian Graduate School of Management, University of New South Wales 1976–1986. **Appointments:** Chairman, Energy Research Development and Information Centre, University of New South Wales; Board Member, New South Wales Energy Authority. **Awards:** Minor Scholarship, SJC 1942.

STRONG, Samuel Digby (1914) Born 21 June 1896, Percival House, Great Baddow, Essex; son of John Warrington Strong, Clerk in Holy Orders, and Rosamond Marion Wingfield-Digby. BA 1919; MA 1922. **Tutor(s):** E E Sikes. **Educ:** King's School, Worcester. **Career:** Lieutenant, Royal Field Artillery, WWI; Master, King's School, Worcester 1932–1933. **Awards:** Choral Studentship, SJC.

STROSS, Robert Adolf Franz (1931) Born 10 January 1913, Alexandria, Egypt; son of Walter Stross, Austrian Consul General, and Laura Strehblow. **Tutor(s):** C W Guillebaud. **Educ:** Schotten Gymnasium, Vienna, Austria.

STROUD, Ernest Gordon (1919) Born 18 November 1897, Trinity View, Parish of St Philip, Barbados; son of George Leopold Augustus Stroud, Chemist and Druggist, and Eugenie Bolton Connell. **Tutor(s):** E A Benians. **Educ:** Lodge School, Barbados; Harrison College, Barbados. **Career:** Lecturer, Harrison College 1917–1919. **Awards:** Barbados English Scholarship in Science 1917. Died 24 April 1921.

STROUTS, Bernard Murton (1928) Born 22 October 1910, 28 Palace Street, Westminster; son of Edward Murton Strouts, Brewer, and Milicent Fawcus; m Rosalind; 3 sons (John, Edward and Robert).

Subject(s): Modern and Medieval Languages; BA 1931. **Tutor(s):** J M Wordie. **Johnian Relatives:** brother of Edward Allen Strouts (1919). **Educ:** Mr Gladstone's Preparatory School, London; Aldenham School. **Career:** Traffic Apprentice, Relief Station Master, Manchester District 1931, Assistant to Industrial Agent 1935, LNER; Joint Secretary to Indian Railway Enquiry Committee 1936; Chief General Manager's Office, LNER 1937; Assistant to District Goods Manager, King's Cross 1938; Lieutenant, RE, Persia and Middle East, WWII; Assistant District Superintendent, Manchester 1945–1946, Assistant Passenger Manager (General), Southern Area 1946–1949, Rates, Fares and Development Assistant, Passenger Commercial Section, Railway Executive Headquarters 1948–1949, LNER; Coordination Officer, Inland Transport, Road Haulage Executive 1949–1953; Deputy General Manager, Nyasaland Railways Ltd, and Zambesia Railway Company Ltd 1953–1962. Died 3 January 1988.

STROUTS, Edward Allen (1919) Born 26 July 1901, 2 Langley House, Long Acre, London; son of Edward Murton Strouts, Brewer, and Milicent Fawcus. **Subject(s):** Natural Sciences; BA 1922. **Tutor(s):** E E Sikes. **Johnian Relatives:** brother of Bernard Murton Strouts (1928). **Educ:** Mr Gladstone's Preparatory School, Eaton Square, London; Aldenham School. **Career:** Assistant Conservator, Indian Forest Service 1923; Assistant Conservator, Pahang, Malay Straits 1933.

STRUDWICK, John Philip (1933) Born 30 May 1914, Nesfield, Green Lane, Eltham, London; son of Philip Strudwick, Quantity Surveyor, and Marjorie Alice Clements; m Elizabeth Marion Stemson, 1942; 2 sons, 4 daughters. **Subject(s):** Mathematics; BA 1936; MA 1973. **Tutor(s):** J M Wordie. **Johnian Relatives:** grandfather of Rupert Joseph Strudwick (1989). **Educ:** Christ Church Preparatory School, Eltham; Eltham College. **Career:** Assistant Principal, Inland Revenue Department 1937–1942; Principal, Board of Inland Revenue 1942–1951; Secretary, Millard Tucker Committee on Taxation Treatment of Provisions for Retirement 1951–1953; Assistant Secretary, Stamps and Taxes Division, Board of Inland Revenue 1951–1974; Chairman, University of Sussex Catholic Chaplaincy Association 1972–1976. **Awards:** Scholarship, SJC. **Honours:** CBE 1970; CVO 1973; Papal Medal; Papal Knighthood (KSG) 1977. Died 18 May 1994.

STRUTHERS, Dr James Arthur (1914) Born 16 June 1895, 5 Grove Terrace, Handcroft Road, Croydon; son of John Struthers, Tradesman and Author, and Harriet Rebecca Ann Westeraway; m Edith Mary Langford, 6 June 1925, St Bartholomew the Great; 1 son, 1 daughter. **Subject(s):** Natural Sciences; BA 1920; MB; BChir 1923; MD 1930; Conjoint Diploma 1922; MRCP; DPH. **Tutor(s):** E E Sikes. **Educ:** Kindergarten School, Harlesden; Holloway College; Marylebone Central School; City of London School. **Career:** Lecturer on Public Health; Lieutenant, Durham Light Infantry (wounded) 1914–1916, then employed, Ministry of Labour, WWI; St Bartholomew's Hospital 1922–1926; Called to the Bar 1926; Medical Officer of Health to Holborn (and in 1953 to Westminster) 1933–1960. **Appointments:** General Medical Services Committee 1948–1951. **Awards:** Scholarship, SJC. **Publications:** *Aids to Sanitary Science and Law.* Died 21 November 1971.

STRUTHERS, John (1930) Born 2 April 1902, Montgomery Street, Larkhall; son of James Barr Struthers, Tailor, and Agnes Brown; MA (New Zealand); BSc (New Zealand); MA (London). **Educ:** Larkhall Academy, Scotland; Elmwood Primary School, New Zealand; Christchurch High School, New Zealand; Christchurch West District High School, New Zealand; University College Canterbury, New Zealand. **Career:** Master, Thames Valley Grammar School, Twickenham 1932–1946; Lecturer in Mathematics, Emergency Teacher's Colleges, Lancaster and Wandsworth 1947–1952; Malayan Teacher's College, Liverpool 1953–1962; Officer for School Mathematics for New Zealand, Curriculum Development Unit 1963–1969. **Publications:** *Mirimar Peninsula.*

STRUTT, Gordon Knowles (1935) Born 6 April 1916, 24 High Street, Dodworth, Barnsley, Yorkshire; son of Herbert Strutt, Surveyor and Sanitary Inspector, and Martha Alice Knowles, Teacher; m Emily Roebuck, April 1941, Ingbirchworth, Nr Huddersfield; 1 son (Andrew b 23 December 1946), 6 daughters (Rachel b 28 April 1942, Elizabeth b 25 September 1943, Katherine b 21 September 1945, Elaine b 29 January 1950, Rosalind b 14 January 1954 and Lorna b 18 March 1962). **Subject(s):** Natural Sciences; BA 1938; MA 1942; Diploma in Agriculture 1939. **Tutor(s):** C W Guillebaud. **Johnian Relatives:** brother-in-law of Stuart Max Walters (1938). **Educ:** Church of England School, Dodworth; Penistone Grammar School. **Career:** Agricultural Officer to War Agricultural Committee, Norfolk and North Devon 1938–1944; Farmer, South Devon 1945–1964; Biology Teacher, Totnes and Bracknell 1964–1981. **Awards:** Exhibition, SJC 1934. **Publications:** Translations from German, including: H Ellenberg, *Vegetation Ecology of Central Europe*, CUP, 1988. Died 12 December 1998.

STUART, The Revd Cyril Edgar (1911) Born 27 November 1892, 116 Grosvenor Road, Holloway, Middlesex; son of Edward Alexander Stuart, Canon of Canterbury, and Emily Ada Guy; m Mary Summerhayes, 30 December 1924, St Peter's Limpsfield. BA 1914; MA 1920. **Tutor(s):** J R Tanner. **Johnian Relatives:** son of Edward Alexander Stuart (1872); brother of Herbert Edward Stuart (1905). **Educ:** Repton School. **Career:** Lieutenant, North Staffordshire Regiment, then attached to Hampshire Regiment (wounded), WWI; Ordained Deacon 1920; Curate, St Mary, Hornsey Rise 1920–1921; Ordained Priest 1921; Chaplain and Lecturer, Ridley Hall, Cambridge 1921–1925; Assistant Master, Government College, Achimota, with licence to officiate in the diocese of Accra 1931–1932; Missionary, Diocese of Uganda, Church Missionary Society 1931–1932; Assistant Bishop, Diocese of Uganda 1932–1934; Bishop of Uganda 1934–1952; Assistant Bishop of Worcester, Honorary Canon of Worcester 1953–1965. Died 23 September 1982.

STUART, Donald Harry (1919) Born 10 November 1900, St Dunstan's College, Catford, Lewisham, Kent; son of Charles Maddock Stuart, Headmaster, and Bertha Marion Coghill; m Marion Liddell; 1 son (Alasdair b 31 August 1948, d 2 September 1948). BA 1922; MA 1927. **Tutor(s):** E A Benians. **Educ:** Little Appley Ryde; Rugby School; Eastbourne College.

STUART, The Revd Herbert (1909) Born 15 October 1889, 23 Belgrave Crescent, Edinburgh; son of Robert Laidlaw Stuart, Writer to the Signet, and Marie Louise Treloar. **Subject(s):** History; BA 1912; MA 1918. **Tutor(s):** J R Tanner. **Educ:** Edinburgh Academy; Edinburgh Theological College. **Career:** On Staff, Church Missionary Society's College, Allahabad 1914; Deacon 1920; Chaplain, Edinburgh Cathedral (in charge of St Luke's Mission, Dalry) 1920–1925; Priest 1921; Rector, Comrie (with Church of the Holy Spirit, St Fillans, from 1937) 1928–1943. Died 30 January 1943.

STUART, The Revd Herbert Edward (1905) Born 9 August 1883, 52 Highbury Hill, Highbury, Middlesex; son of Edward Alexander Stuart, Clerk in Holy Orders, and Emily Ada Guy; m Katherine Frances Haynes, 20 April 1911, Northwood Parish Church. **Subject(s):** Theology; BA 1908; MA 1913. **Tutor(s):** J R Tanner; C E Graves. **Johnian Relatives:** son of Edward Alexander Stuart (1872); brother of Cyril Edgar Stuart (1911). **Educ:** Harrow School. **Career:** Ordained Deacon 1909; Curate, St James the Less, Bethnal Green 1909–1912; Ordained Priest 1911; Curate, Christ Church, Croydon 1912–1914; Curate, Stoke-on-Trent 1914–1916; Curate, St Mary, Swansea 1917–1918; Vicar, St James, Holloway 1918–1930; Vicar, Danehill 1930–1932; Curate, St Peter, Harrow 1937.

STUART, Ian Charles (1940) Born 15 January 1923, 16 Wolverton Gardens, Ealing; son of Edward John Stuart, Mechanical Engineer, and Eva Christine Jenkins; m Emilie Louise Bichard, 1 June 1948; 2 sons (Nicholas and William), 2 daughters (Christina and Mary). **Subject(s):** Mechanical Sciences; BA 1943; Chartered Civil Engineer 1958; MICE. **Tutor(s):** S J Bailey. **Educ:** Peterborough Lodge, Swiss Cottage; Downsend, Leatherhead; Bryanston School, Blandford Forum; Victoria Tutorial College. **Career:** Corps of RE, retired as Major 1942–1961; Overseas service in North West Europe, Palestine, Korea and Nepal 1944–1960; States of Guernsey Civil Service, Technical Services Department 1961–1983. **Appointments:** States Engineer, States of Guernsey 1974.

STUART, Ian David (1945) Born 29 May 1928, Willowbrae, Ferry-Port on Craig, Fifeshire; son of Charles Egerton Stuart, Chartered Accountant, and Elizabeth Maud Pagan. **Subject(s):** Economics; BA 1949; MA 1952; LLB (St Andrews) 1953; CA 1952. **Tutor(s):** C W Guillebaud. **Educ:** St Fillan's School, Newport; High School, Dundee; Higher Grade School, Kingussie; Strathallan School. **Career:** Secretary and Treasurer, Representative Church Council, Episcopal Church in Scotland. Died 18 February 1985.

STUART, Innes (1924) Born 17 August 1905, 21 Palmerston Place, St George's, Edinburgh, Scotland; son of William Stuart, Net Manufacturer, and Sue Campbell Williams; m Audrey Ruston Spencer, March 1939; 1 son (John Spencer Innes b 20 May 1940, d 12 July 2003). BA 1928. **Tutor(s):** E A Benians. **Johnian Relatives:** father of John Spencer Innes Stuart (1959). **Educ:** Courtenay Lodge, Sutton Courtenay; Beckhythe, Overstrand. **Career:** Captain, Lovat Scouts; Standard Life Insurance.

STUART, Kenneth Charles (1931) Born 7 July 1912, 8 East Park Avenue, Kingston Upon Hull; son of John Charles Stuart, Confidential Clerk, and Elsie Kate Strachan; m W Mary. **Subject(s):** Modern and Medieval Languages; BA 1934; MA 1938. **Tutor(s):** C W Guillebaud. **Educ:** Hull Education Committee School; Hymers College, Hull. **Career:** Headmaster, The Grammar School, Maldon, Essex 1948. Died 26 May 1967.

STUART, Malcolm Moncrieff (1921) Born 21 May 1903, 19 Lyndoch Place, Edinburgh, Scotland; son of George Malcolm Stuart, Writer to His Majesty's Signet, and Mary Elizabeth Scott-Moncrieff. **Subject(s):** History; BA 1924; Honorary MA (Edinburgh) 1978. **Tutor(s):** B F Armitage. **Johnian Relatives:** father of Jonathan Balfour Stuart (1953). **Educ:** Edinburgh Academy; Cargillfield; Sedbergh School. **Career:** Indian Civil Service 1927–1947; Assistant Magistrate and Collector, Bengal; Officiating Magistrate and Collector 1932; Commissioner, Dacca Division, Bengal; Recorder to the Lord High Commissioners; Government of Pakistan, Dacca 1947–1950. **Appointments:** Honorary, Secretary, Scottish Text Society; Reporter to Secretary of State in Planning; Researcher of historical records, South Asian Studies Centre, Cambridge. **Awards:** Lupton and Hebblethwaite Exhibition, SJC. **Honours:** OBE; CIE 1948. Died 1991.

STUART, Thomas (1901) Born 3 November 1872, Roosky, Gortlin, County Tyrone, Ireland; son of Thomas Stuart, Assistant Surveyor, and Maria Nathery. **Subject(s):** Mathematics; BA 1902. **Tutor(s):** D MacAlister. **Educ:** Queen's College, Galway. **Career:** Junior Fellow, Royal University of Ireland 1902; Lecturer in Mathematics, University College, Cardiff 1903.

STURGE, Philip Arthur Joseph (1936) Born 4 March 1919, 19 Carpenter Road, Edgbaston, Birmingham; son of Philip Maximillian Sturge, Paint and Varnish Manufacturer, and Florence Maude Stammers; m Anne; 2 sons, 2 daughters. **Subject(s):** Natural Sciences; BA 1939; MA 1969. **Tutor(s):** R L Howland. **Johnian Relatives:** father of David Philip Sturge (1966); grandfather of Joseph Edward Lewis-Bowen (1990). **Educ:** Park Hill Kindergarten School; West House Preparatory School, Edgbaston; Shrewsbury School. **Career:** Lieutenant, RNVR, WWII (Mentioned in Despatches); Director in Charge of Export Trade and Board Member, later Managing Director, Arthur Holden and Sons Ltd, Birmingham 1948–1982. Died 20 March 1995.

STURROCK, George Stuart (1925) Born 4 December 1905, Shima, Malta; son of George Stephen Sturrock, Eastern Telegraph Company, and Flora Mitchell. **Subject(s):** Mathematics/Mechanical Sciences; BA 1928; MA 1932. **Tutor(s):** J M Wordie. **Educ:** Abingdon School, Berkshire. Died 15 March 1986.

STURROCK, Professor Peter Andrew (1942) Born 20 March 1924, 99 London Road, South Stifford, Grays, Essex; son of Albert Edward Sturrock, Lime Plant Foreman, and Mabel Minnie Payne; m (2) Marilyn Fern Stenson, 1963; (1) 1 daughter (Myra), (2) 1 son (Colin); 1 daughter (Deirdre). **Subject(s):** Mathematics; BA 1945; MA 1948; PhD 1952. **Tutor(s):** S J Bailey; J M Wordie. **Educ:** Stifford Council School; Palmer's Endowed School, Grays. **Career:** Radar Engineer, TRE, Malvern 1943–1946; Physicist, National Bureau of Standards, Washington 1949–1950; CNRS Fellow, University of Paris 1950–1951; Harwell Fellow, AERE 1951–1953; Title A Fellow, SJC 1952–1955; Research Associate, Microwave Laboratory 1955–1961, Professor of Applied Physics 1961–1999, Stanford University; Ford Foundation Fellow, CERN 1957–1958. **Awards:** Rayleigh Prize, University of Cambridge 1949; Gravity Prize, Gravity Foundation 1967; Lindsay Award, Goddard Space Flight Center 1977; Hale Medal, American Astronomical Society 1986; Arctowski Medal, National Academy of Sciences 1990; Space Science Award, American Institute of Aeronautics and Astronautics 1992. **Publications:** *Electron Optics*, CUP 1955; *Plasma Astrophysics*, Academic Press 1967; *Physics of the Sun*, Reidel 1986; *Plasma Physics*, CUP 1994; *The UFO Enigma*, Warner 1999.

STURT, John Edward (1929) Born 19 June 1910, Longdown Lodge, Epsom; son of Francis Edward Sturt, Stock Jobber, London Stock Exchange, and Zara Beatrice Irene Alcock. BA 1932. **Tutor(s):** C W Guillebaud. **Educ:** Hill Brow, Meads, Eastbourne; Haileybury College. **Career:** Lieutenant, 1st Indian HAA Regiment, RA, POW, WWII.

STURTON, Dr Clement (1917) Born 21 January 1900, 6 Park Terrace, Cambridge; son of Richard Sturton, Chemist, and Mary Emma Sturton; m Mary Ellen Pratt Brookes, 17 October 1925, Clapton Hall, Stoke Newington; 3 children. **Subject(s):** Natural Sciences; BA 1920; MA 1925; BChir 1923; MB 1923; LRCP; MRCS; FRCS; Diploma in Tropical Medicine 1925. **Tutor(s):** E E Sikes. **Educ:** Miss Hutt's School; Perse School, Cambridge. **Career:** House Surgeon, Salisbury General Infirmary; Medical Officer, West Africa Medical Staff, Nigeria; in Practice, Kettering; Assistant Medical Officer, Kettering and District General Hospital. **Awards:** Joint Shuter Scholarship, St Bartholomew's 1920. Died 4 September 1936.

SUBBARAO, Nanjangud Subbarao (1905) Born 13 March 1885, Seringapatam, India; son of Nanjangud Subbarao, Pleader. **Subject(s):** History/Economics; BA 1908; MA 1912. **Tutor(s):** J R Tanner. **Educ:** Maharajah's College, Mysore; Central College, Bangalore; Christian College, Madras. **Career:** Called to the Bar, Inner Temple 1909; History Lecturer, Maharajah's College, Mysore 1910. **Awards:** Le Bas Prize, University of Cambridge 1909. **Publications:** 'Economic and Political Conditions in Ancient India as described in the Jatakas', *Mysore*, 1911 (Le Bas Prize Essay).

SUCKLING, Peter Gordon (1944) Born 12 April 1927, 38 Prospect Road, Moseley, Birmingham; son of Sydney Clarence Suckling, Metal Salesman, and Rhoda Barnfield; m (2) Betty, December 1984; (1) 1 daughter (Anne Caroline). **Subject(s):** Natural Sciences; BA 1949; MA 1951. **Tutor(s):** C W Guillebaud. **Educ:** Solihull Tree School; Solihull School. **Career:** Suckling & Thomas Ltd 1950–1992 (Director 1958–1965, Managing Director, 1965–1992). **Appointments:** President, Old Silhillians Rugby Union Football Club 1963–1964; President, Rotary Club of Solihull St Alphege 1994–1995.

SUFI, Mohammed Husain (1938) Born 13 February 1914, Village Kot Isháq, Gujranwala, Punjab, India; son of M Ghulam Mohammed, Agriculturalist, and Fatima Bibi. **Tutor(s):** R L Howland. **Educ:**

Government High School, Gujranwala; East College, Lahore. **Awards:** International Colonial Service.

SUGDEN, Dr David Bertram (1941) Born 26 January 1923, 10 Ealand Crescent, Batley, Yorkshire; son of John Bertram Sugden, Woollen Mill Manager, and Hilda Thornton; m Mary. **Subject(s):** Natural Sciences; BA 1944; MA 1948; MB 1948; BChir 1948; DIH 1967. **Tutor(s):** S J Bailey. **Educ:** Carlinghow Council School; Dewsbury Wheelwright Grammar School; Batley Grammar School. Died 27 January 1998.

SUGDEN, Henry Thackeray (1944) Born 30 January 1926, Braemar, Snelsins Lane, Cleckheaton, Yorkshire; son of Henry Ellison Sugden, Manufacturing Chemist, and Laura Margaret Calverley. **Tutor(s):** J M Wordie. **Educ:** Oatlands School, Harrogate; Uppingham School.

SUGGITT, Leslie (1928) Born 25 January 1909, 9 Victoria Avenue, Ripon, Yorkshire; son of John Suggitt, Manager in a Grocery Store, and Hetty Cust; m Laura Parker, 1936. BA 1931; MA 1948; MusB 1931. **Tutor(s):** E A Benians. **Educ:** Westholme School, Ripon; North Eastern County School, Barnard Castle; Ripon Grammar School. **Career:** Music Master, Bridlington School 1932–1977; Organist and Choirmaster, Emmanuel Church, Bridlington; Instructor, Signals 1941–1945; Sergeant-instructor, Army Educational Corps 1945–1946. Died August 1988.

SUKTHANKAR, Vishna Sitaram (1903) Born 4 May 1887, Bombay, India; son of Sitaram Vishna Sukthankar, Civil Servant, Indian Government, and Dhaklibai Shantaram Narayan. **Subject(s):** Mathematics; BA 1906; MA 1912. **Tutor(s):** D MacAlister. **Educ:** St Xavier's College, Bombay.

SUMMERHILL, Dr James Hugh Everett (1926) Born 12 August 1908, Clark Road, Wolverhampton, Staffordshire; son of James Summerhill, Company Director, Fruit Farmer, and Emma Crosbie Browne. **Subject(s):** Natural Sciences; BA 1930; MA 1935; MRCS 1935; LRCP 1935. **Tutor(s):** M P Charlesworth. **Educ:** University School, Victoria; St Michael's School, Victoria; Berkhamsted School. **Career:** Ear, Nose & Throat Surgeon, University College Hospital; Resident Medical Officer, City of London Maternity Hospital; House Physician and Officer, Miller General Hospital, Greenwich. Died 26 January 1957.

SUMNER, Professor Donovan Bradshaw (1934) Born 11 August 1910, District Cathcart, Cape Province, South Africa; son of George Henry Sumner, Farmer, and Johanna Elizabeth Maria van Heerden. **Subject(s):** Mathematics; MSc 1940; MA (Witwatersrand); DPhil (Witwatersrand). **Tutor(s):** J M Wordie. **Educ:** Booysens, Traffontein and Germiston Intermediate Schools, South Africa; Germiston High School, South Africa; Witwatersrand University, South Africa; Johannesburg Normal College, South Africa. **Career:** Associate Professor of Mathematics, McMaster University, Hamilton College, Hamilton, Ontario 1953–1960; Professor of Mathematics, McMaster University 1960–1968; Professor, University of Waterloo, Canada 1968.

SUTCLIFFE, Dr John (1931) Born 27 June 1913, 9 Arnold Avenue, Gee Cross, Hyde; son of James Sutcliffe, Director, Sutcliffe, Bird & Co, and Frances Smith. **Subject(s):** Natural Sciences; BA 1934; MB 1938; BChir 1938; MRCP 1947; FRCR; FRCP. **Tutor(s):** M P Charlesworth. **Educ:** Gee Cross School; The County School, Hyde. **Career:** RAF, Far East 1939–1945; Senior Registrar, X-ray Diagnostic Department, St Thomas' Hospital 1950; Consultant Radiologist, Great Ormond Street Hospital 1950–1978. **Appointments:** Founder Vice-President, European Society of Paediatric Radiology; Medical Representative, NSPCC Committee on Non-accidental Injuries. **Awards:** Scholarship, SJC. Died 15 October 1980.

SUTCLIFFE, John Herbert Holman (1919) Born 15 July 1902, Sydney House, Horncastle Road, Boston, Lincolnshire; son of John Bell Sutcliffe, Ship Owner, and Elizabeth Brook; m Sheila Doreen Frowd, 1 May 1943, St George's Church, Hanover; 2 sons (John b 7 July 1944 and

Charles b 23 August 1950). **Subject(s):** Law; BA 1924; MA 1927; FICS; FSA 1971. **Tutor(s):** E A Benians. **Johnian Relatives:** brother of Richard Brook Sutcliffe (1921); uncle of David Brook Sutcliffe (1953); father of John Haddon Frowd Holman Sutcliffe (1962). **Educ:** Ingelow House Kindergarten, Boston; Kirton Grammar School; Pannal Ash College, Harrogate; Sedbergh School. **Career:** Family Shipping Business, Boston, Lincolnshire; Called to the Bar, Inner Temple 1925. **Appointments:** JP 1939; Deputy Chairman, Holland Quarter Sessions 1950–1972; Founder Member, Council of the Georgian Group; Chairman, North Holland Petty Sessions Division. **Publications:** Various Historical articles. Died 8 October 1982.

SUTCLIFFE, John William Robert (1942) Born 25 September 1923, 15 Ivy Grove, Shipley, Bradford, Yorkshire; son of Harry Sutcliffe, Textile Manager, and Leonora Pearson. **Subject(s):** Economics; BA 1947. **Tutor(s):** C W Guillebaud. **Educ:** St Paul's School, Buttershaw; Bradford Grammar School. **Awards:** Minor Scholarship, SJC 1941.

SUTCLIFFE, Norman (1922) Born 2 February 1902, Brearley House, Mytholmroyd, Luddenham Foot, Yorkshire; son of William Henry Sutcliffe and Mary Helena Greenwood. **Tutor(s):** E E Sikes. **Educ:** Oatlands, Harrogate; Harrow School; Courtenay Lodge, Sutton.

SUTCLIFFE, Peter Hoyle (1943) Born 1 March 1926, 16 Elmfield Road, Davenport, Stockport; son of Fred Sutcliffe, Wholesale Hosier, and May Hoyle. **Subject(s):** History/English; BA 1949; MA 1957. **Tutor(s):** C W Guillebaud. **Educ:** Oriel Bank School; Stockport Grammar School. **Publications:** *The Blindness of Richard Blake*, Cresset Press, 1951.

SUTCLIFFE, Richard Brook (1921) Born 26 April 1904, Sydney House, Horncastle Road, Boston, Lincolnshire; son of John Bell Sutcliffe, Shipowner and Broker, and Elizabeth Brook; m Eileen Constance Tuxford; 1 son (David Brook b 26 November 1934). **Tutor(s):** B F Armitage. **Johnian Relatives:** brother of John Herbert Holman Sutcliffe (1919); father of David Brook Sutcliffe (1953); uncle of John Haddon Frowd Holman Sutcliffe (1962). **Educ:** The Grammar School, Kirton; Pannal Ash College, Harrogate; Sedbergh School.

SUTCLIFFE, Roy (1949) Born 16 October 1929, 21 Mills Hill Road, Middleton, Manchester; son of Orlando James Sutcliffe, Skip Manufacturer, and Jessie Mary Daniels; m Margaret H Wallbank, 20 December 1952; 2 sons (Anthony J and Ian T). **Subject(s):** Mathematics; BA 1952; MA 1978. **Tutor(s):** J M Wordie. **Educ:** Mills Hill Council School, Chadderton; Chadderton Grammar School. **Career:** Royal Signals 1948–1949; Reed Paper Group 1952–1955; Kimberly-Clark Corporation 1955–1990 (Product Manager, Kleenex Tissues 1957; UK Marketing Manager 1960; UK Business Management and Development 1967; European Business, Engineering and Research Development Manager 1980). **Appointments:** Member, Eagles; Member, Hawks; Member, Pegasus 1950–1960; Captain, Football Club, SJC 1951–1952.

SUTHERLAND, George Arthur (1911) Born 6 February 1891, School House, New Deer, Aberdeenshire; son of John Sutherland, Schoolmaster, and Hannah Ironside; m (1) Mabel Christine Bell, 1 May 1916 (d 1941); (2) Mary Sanders Lakeman, 10 September 1943; (1) 1 son (Ian). **Subject(s):** Mathematics; BA 1913; MA 1921. **Tutor(s):** L H K Bushe-Fox. **Johnian Relatives:** father of Ian Sutherland (1939). **Educ:** Muir High School; Rhodes University College, Grahamstown; Glasgow University. **Career:** Acoustic Consultant, Wembley Exhibition Hall, Legislative Chamber, New Delhi, Friends' House, London and Central Hall, Manchester; Lecturer in Physics, University of the Cape, South Africa 1913–1915; Assistant Master, Harrow School 1915; Lecturer in Physics, University College London 1919–1924; Principal, Dalton Hall, Manchester 1924–1958; Special Lecturer in Physics, University of Manchester 1927–1958. **Appointments:** Member, Court of Governors, University of Manchester; President, Acoustics Section, 12th International Congress of Architects 1930; Clerk to Meeting for

Sufferings (Society of Friends). **Publications:** *Dalton Hall – a Quaker Venture*, 1963. Died 1 March 1970.

SUTHERLAND, Dr Ian (1939) Born 30 June 1921, Hampstead, London; son of George Arthur Sutherland, University Lecturer, and Mabel Christine Bell; m Susanne Lederer, 30 March 1946 (d 1997); 2 sons (Alastair Timothy b 1950 and Steven Andrew b 1955). **Subject(s):** Mathematics; BA 1945; MA 1947; DPhil (Oxford) 1948. **Tutor(s):** J M Wordie. **Johnian Relatives:** son of George Arthur Sutherland (1911). **Educ:** Ladybarn House School; South Manchester School; Manchester Grammar School. **Career:** Assistant Statistician, Institute of Social Medicine, Oxford 1945–1952; Member, MRC Statistical Research Unit, London School of Hygiene and Tropical Medicine 1952–1969; Director, MRC Statistical Research and Services Unit, University College Hospital Medical School, London (renamed and relocated in 1980 as MRC Biostatistics Unit, Cambridge) 1969–1986. **Appointments:** WHO Consultant, Tuberculosis Chemotherapy Centre, Madras; Member, Tuberculosis Surveillance Research Unit, International Union Against Tuberculosis, The Hague; Member, Toxicity and Clinical Trials Subcommittee, Committee on Safety of Medicines; Member, WHO Expert Panel on Tuberculosis. **Awards:** Open Minor Scholarship 1938; Weber-Parkes Prize and Medal, Royal College of Physicians 1984. **Honours:** The Queen's Silver Jubilee Medal 1977. **Publications:** Many research studies, mostly on prevention and epidemiology of tuberculosis; *Stillbirths*, Oxford, 1949; 'When was the Great Plague?', *Population and Social Change*, Glass and Revelle, London, 1972.

SUTOR, John Allan (1928) Born 1 July 1909, Maescourt, Knighton-on-Teme, Worcester; son of Robert Macdonald Sutor, Farmer, Flight Lieutenant, RNR, and Gertrude Maesmon Morris, formerly Willmott. BA 1931. **Tutor(s):** M P Charlesworth. **Educ:** Bengeo School, Hertford; Uppingham School. **Career:** Singapore, WWII. Died 1 December 1966.

SUTTON, Geoffrey Robert (1920) Born 24 February 1901, 4 Sanderson Road, Newcastle upon Tyne; son of Robert Morton Sutton, Shipowner, and Mary Denton Price. BA 1923; MA 1927. **Tutor(s):** E A Benians. **Educ:** Newcastle Preparatory School; Aysgarth School, Yorkshire; Uppingham School. Died 6 April 1979.

SWAIN, Paul Bryan (1936) Born 11 June 1918, 38 Nevern Square, South Kensington, London; son of Leo Harry Swain, Civil Engineer and Eileen Francis Edith O'Brian; BA 1939; MA 1947. **Tutor(s):** C W Guillebaud. **Educ:** Thring's, Haywards Heath; Marlborough College. Died 29 October 1985.

SWAINE, Kenneth Bruce (1925) Born 13 September 1906, 8 Cross, Edinburgh Street, Goole, Yorkshire; son of Wilfred Bennett Swaine, Civil Servant, and Kate Bruce. **Subject(s):** Mathematics; BA 1928; MA 1935. **Tutor(s):** J M Wordie. **Educ:** Thoresby Street Council School, Hull; Hessle National School; Hymers College, Hull. **Awards:** Scholarship, SJC. Died November 1974.

SWALLOW, Dr John Crossley (1941) Born 11 October 1923, 4 Merehouse Terrace, New Mill, Huddersfield, Yorkshire; son of Alfred Swallow, Sawyer and Woodturner, and Elizabeth Crossley; m Mary Morgan (née McKenzie), 1958; 1 stepdaughter (Lucy). **Subject(s):** Mathematics and Natural Sciences; BA 1945; MA 1948; PhD 1955; FRS 1968. **Tutor(s):** C W Guillebaud. **Educ:** Hepworth Council School; Holme Valley Grammar School, Honley. **Career:** Admiralty Signal Establishment 1943–1947; research in marine geophysics, Cambridge and HMS *Challenger* 1948–1954; Physical Oceanographer, Institute of Oceanographic Sciences 1954–1983; work on ocean circulation, in RRS *Discovery II*, and in RRS *Discovery*, and other vessels 1954–1983; Rossby Fellow, Woods Hole Oceanographic Institute 1973–1974. **Appointments:** Murchison Grant, RGS 1965. Foreign Honorary Member, American Academy of Arts and Sciences 1975. **Awards:** Exhibition, SJC 1940; Commemorative Medal of Prince Albert I; Four American awards in oceanography. **Publications:** Papers on physical oceanography. Died 3 December 1994.

SWEENEY, Hubert Douglas (1932) Born 14 December 1913, 102 Crouch Hill, Hornsey, Middlesex; son of Hubert Joseph Peter Sweeney, Barrister-at-Law, and Mary Douglas Power. **Subject(s):** Natural Sciences; BA 1935. **Tutor(s):** R L Howland. **Educ:** Bembridge School, Isle of Wight; Highgate Junior School; City of London School. **Awards:** Exhibition, SJC. Died 28 June 1936.

SWEETMAN, James George (1933) Born 7 November 1914, 61 Lower Baggot Street, Dublin, Ireland; son of James Michael Sweetman, Barrister-at-Law, and Agnes Mary Fottrell. **Subject(s):** Mathematics/Economics; BA 1936. **Tutor(s):** J M Wordie. **Educ:** St John's Beaumont Preparatory School; Beaumont College, Old Windsor. **Career:** Private, Suffolk Regiment; rose to Lieutenant Colonel on General Staff; Secretary to Field Marshal Alexander, Supreme Allied Commander in the Mediterranean; Mentioned in Despatches 1939–1945; Assistant to Chairman, Sales Director, then Chairman, D & W Gibbs 1945–1954; Marketing Adviser, Unilever's Continental Europe Group; Member, Directorate, Unilever (Germany) 1954–1961; Director, Unilever Ltd; Member, Chief Executive 1961–1974; Vice-Chairman, Unilever Ltd; Member of Chief Executive 1974–1978; Deputy Chairman, Price Commission 1977–1979. **Appointments:** Trustee, Leverhulme Trust; Director, Commonwealth Finance Company; Non-executive Director, Mercedez-Benz UK. **Honours:** MBE. Died 1 February 1985.

SWIFT, Alan Herbert Illingworth (1932) Born 18 August 1913, 29 Falsgrave Road, Scarborough; son of Herbert Swift, Manufacturer, and Agnes Maud Illingworth; m Betty, 1938; 2 daughters. **Subject(s):** Law; BA 1935; MA 1939; LLB 1936. **Tutor(s):** C W Guillebaud. **Educ:** Hillside Preparatory School, Scarborough; Holmwood Private School, West Ayton; The College, Scarborough; The Grammar School, Leeds. **Career:** Assistant Solicitor, Heston and Isleworth, York 1938–1945; Deputy Town Clerk, Heston 1945–1948; Town Clerk, Cambridge 1949–1962. **Awards:** McMahon Studentship, SJC 1937. Died 27 November 1962.

SWIFT, Professor Herbert Walker (1914) Born 15 December 1894, Deptford, Kent; son of Thomas Walker Swift, Civil Engineer, and Sarah Lydia Hill; m Maisie; 2 daughters (Mary and Joan). **Subject(s):** Mechanical Sciences; BA 1920; MA 1924; DSc (London) 1936; MIMechE. **Tutor(s):** L H K Bushe-Fox. **Educ:** West Hill London County Council School; Christ's Hospital. **Career:** Captain, London Regiment (QVR) (wounded, Mentioned in Despatches), WWI; Chief Engineer, William Hollins Ltd 1920–1922; Assistant Lecturer, Leeds University 1922; Head, Mechanical Engineering Department, Bradford College of Technology 1926–1936; Professor of Engineering, University of Sheffield 1936–1955. **Awards:** Barnes Scholarship 1915; Thomas Hawksley Medal, Institution of Mechanical Engineers. Died 14 October 1960.

SWIFT, The Revd John McIntosh (1905) Born 1 February 1886, 11 Windle Street, St Helens, Lancashire; son of Henry Swift, Colliery Secretary, and Wilhemina Sawyers; m Marion Walley, 29 April 1931, Chester Cathedral; 3 sons (John Michael b 10 October 1936, David Walley b 31 March 1938 and Stephen Maxwell b 28 December 1945). **Subject(s):** Theology; BA 1908; MA 1912. **Tutor(s):** J R Tanner; C E Graves. **Johnian Relatives:** father of David Walley Swift (1957). **Educ:** Huyton College School, Liverpool; Ridley Hall, Cambridge. **Career:** Ordained Deacon 1909; Assistant Chaplain and Tutor, St Aidan's College, Birkenhead 1909–1912; Ordained Priest 1910; Assistant Chaplain and Assistant Master, St Edmund's School, Canterbury 1912–1913; Chaplain, Training Ship *Indefatigable* 1913–1916; Temporary CF, 4th Class, RACD 1916–1920; Chaplain and Assistant Master, Epsom College 1920–1923; Assistant Master, Liverpool College 1923–1929; Licensed to Officiate, St Bridget, Wavertree 1924–1929; Vicar, Garston, Liverpool 1929–1943; Canon Diocesan, Liverpool Cathedral 1943–1944; Vicar, St Augustine with St Andrew, Bexhill 1944–1949. **Appointments:** Press and Information Secretary, Diocese of Chichester; Editor, Chichester Diocesan Gazette 1945. **Publications:** *The Story of Garston and its Church*, 1937; *Editing a Parish Magazine* (handbook for clergy). Died 25 April 1949.

SWINGLER, Revd Prebendary Jack Howell (1938) Born 4 November 1919, 123 Ivor Road, Sparkhill, Birmingham; son of Samuel Swingler, Manufacturer, and Jessie Louisa Howell; m Elsie Elizabeth Ellen McDowell, 10 June 1950, Fontmell Magna, Dorset. **Subject(s):** Classics; BA 1941; MA 1947. **Educ:** Dennis Road Council School, Birmingham; King Edward's Grammar School, Camphill, Birmingham; King Edward's High School, Birmingham; Ridley Hall, Cambridge. **Career:** Ordained Deacon 1948–1949; Curate, Yeovil Parish Church 1948–1953; Ordained Priest 1949; Vicar, Henstridge 1953–1979; Rural Dean, Merston, Diocese of Bath and Wells 1974–1985; Priest in Charge, Charlton Horethorne with Stowell 1978–1979; Rector, Henstridge and Charlton Horethorne with Stowell 1979–1985. **Appointments:** Prebendary, Wells Cathedral 1979. **Awards:** Minor Scholarship, SJC 1937; College Prize 1941.

SWORDS, William Francis (1906) (admitted as a Non-Collegiate Student 1905) Born 16 November 1873, Cranham Street, Oxford; son of John George Swords, Schoolmaster, and Eliza Thomas; 1 daughter (Molly). **Subject(s):** Law; BA 1908; LLB 1908; BSc (London) 1897. **Tutor(s):** L H K Bushe-Fox. **Educ:** Taunton's School, Southampton; Hartley College, Southampton; Royal College of Science, London. **Career:** First Master, Middle Temple 1905; Bishop's School, Salisbury 1905. **Appointments:** KC 1930. **Awards:** Middle Temple Prize 1905; McMahon Law Studentship 1909. Died 4 March 1964.

SYKES, The Revd David Thomas (1918) Born 27 February 1894, 57 Bright Street, Attercliffe, Sheffield; son of William Sykes, Clerk in Holy Orders, and Annie Jane Dodgson; 2 daughters (Angela and Anne). BA 1922; MA 1925. **Tutor(s):** E E Sikes. **Johnian Relatives:** brother of William Dodgson Sykes (1908); uncle of Richard Dodgson Sykes (1952) and of Stephen Whitefield Sykes (1958). **Educ:** Private Tuition; Westcott House, Cambridge. **Career:** Deacon 1922; Curate, St Mary, Sheffield 1922–1924; Priest 1923; Permission to Officiate at St Giles, Willenhall 1924–1925; Curate, Sheffield Cathedral 1925–1926; Vicar, Dunston with Coppenhall 1926–1930; Vicar, St Catherine, Hatcham 1930–1937; Officiating Chaplain, South Eastern Hospital, New Cross 1933–1937; Commisionary for Mombasa, Kenya 1936; St Antholin Lecturer, St Mary Aldermary, London, and Vicar of All Saints', Stoke Newington 1937; Secretary, Kenya Church Aid Association 1937–1938. **Appointments:** Publications Secretary, London Diocesan Fund 1961. Died 7 August 1975.

SYKES, George Dennis (1938) Born 19 August 1920, 24 Mountjoy Road, Huddersfield; son of Edward George Ramsden Sykes, Auctioneer, Valuer and Estate Agent, and Gertrude Lawford; m (1) Mary B Reeder, 1954 (d 1958), (2) Penelope Hamilton Jack, 1960; 1 son (Edward Ramsden b 1965), 1 daughter (Philippa b 1963). **Subject(s):** Classics; BA 1941; MA 1945; FRIBA; FRICS. **Tutor(s):** R L Howland. **Educ:** Gledhow Preparatory School, Huddersfield; Oatlands Preparatory School, Harrogate; Uppingham School. **Career:** RA 1940; Fighter Pilot, RAF 1943; Chartered Surveyor and Consulting Architect, Private Practice 1951–1985. **Awards:** RAF Air Efficiency Award. Died 14 May 2001.

SYKES, The Revd Maurice Gaskell (1902) Born 10 December 1879, Lucknow, India; son of Thomas Gaskell Sykes, Principal, La Martiniere College, and Mary Elizabeth Burrows; m Constance Mary Lilian Roberts, 4 September 1919, St Jude's on the Hill, Golder's Green. **Tutor(s):** D MacAlister. **Educ:** Rydal Mount, Colwyn Bay. **Career:** Indian Civil Service 1902–1925; Lieutenant (Observer Officer), RAF, WWI; Rector, Hadstock 1932–1936; Rector, Huggate, Yorkshire 1936–1947; Vicar, Rendham with Sweffling, Suffolk 1948–1957.

SYKES, Neil Winn (1945) Born 10 April 1927, Holly Bank, Netherton, Huddersfield, Yorkshire; son of Arthur Sykes, Professional Engineer, and Mabel Elsie Winn, Secretary; m Dorothy May White, 1 September 1951; 1 son (Alan), 3 daughters (Rosamund, Catherine and Virginia). **Subject(s):** Mechanical Sciences; BA 1948; MA 1952; BSc (Eng) (London); CEng; FIEE; FIMechE. **Tutor(s):** S J Bailey; R L Howland. **Johnian Relatives:**

brother-in-law of Geoffrey White (1949). **Educ:** Netherton Council School; South Crosland Church of England School; Holmfirth Holme Valley Grammar School. **Career:** Graduate Apprentice, English Electric/Marconi 1948–1950; Research Engineer, English Electric Company 1950–1954; Management Assistant 1954–1956, Chief Electronics Engineer, Special Purpose Machines 1956–1963, Technical Manager, R&D Components Division 1963–1968, Fluidics Manager 1968–1971, Plessey Company; Managing Director, British Fluidics and Controls Ltd 1971–1990. **Awards:** Exhibition, SJC; Scholarship, SJC; Hockin Prize, SJC. **Publications:** Various technical papers.

SYKES, Dr Peter (1948) (admitted to Clare College 1944) Born 19 February 1923, 67 Upper Chorlton Road, Moss Side, Manchester; son of Charles Hyde Sykes, Chartered Accountant, and Alice Booth; m Joyce. **Subject(s):** PhD (Clare) 1947; BSc (Manchester) 1943; MSc (Manchester) 1944. **Educ:** Singleton Hill School, Manchester; Rydal School; Manchester University; Clare College, Cambridge. **Career:** Demonstrator in Organic and Inorganic Chemistry 1947–1955, University Lecturer 1955–1982, University of Cambridge; Title A Fellow, SJC 1948–1951; Fellow 1956–1982, Life Fellow 1982–2003, Vice-Master 1984–1988, Christ's College, Cambridge. **Appointments:** Member, International Union of Pure and Applied Chemistry Commission on the Teaching of Chemistry 1963–1975, Secretary 1963–1966; Member, Nuffield Committee for A Level Physical Sciences 1964–1971; Member, British Committee on Chemical Education 1965–1967 and 1973–1975; Visiting Professor, College of William and Mary, Williamsburg, Virginia 1970–1971 and 1977–1978, University of Cape Town 1974 and 1980, Universities of São Paulo and Campinas, Brazil 1976, University of Melbourne 1982–1983; Member, Cambridge Board of Extra-Mural Studies (now Continuing Education) for 33 years, ultimately Chairman; Seconded to Sri Lankan Ministry of Education 1975; Syndic, Local Examinations Syndicate 1976–1992; Syndic, CUP 1978–1992. **Awards:** Mellor Medal, University of New South Wales 1982. **Publications:** *A guidebook to Mechanisms in Organic Chemistry*, 1961; *The Search for Organic Reaction Pathways*, 1978; *Primer to Mechanism in Organic Chemistry*, 1995. Died 24 October 2003.

SYKES, The Revd William Dodgson (1908) Born 11 April 1888, 30 Windsor Street, Birkenhead, Cheshire; son of William Sykes, Clerk in Holy Orders, and Annie Jane Dodgson; 2 sons (Richard Dodgson b 12 September 1932 and Stephen Whitefield b 1 August 1939). **Subject(s):** Theology; BA 1911; MA 1915. **Tutor(s):** J R Tanner. **Johnian Relatives:** brother of David Thomas Sykes (1918); father of Richard Dodgson Sykes (1952) and of Stephen Whitefield Sykes (1958). **Educ:** Sheffield Grammar School and Private Study. **Career:** Ordained Priest 1913; Tutor 1912–1913, Dean 1913–1923, Acting Principal 1925–1926, Vice-Principal 1923–1932, McNeile Professor of Biblical Exegesis 1926–1932, London College of Divinity; Principal, Bible Churchmen's College, Bristol 1932; Rector, St John the Baptist with St Mary le Port, Bristol 1933–1962; Examining Chaplain to the Bishop in Northern Africa 1936. **Awards:** Carus New Testament Prize 1910; Crosse Scholarship, University of Cambridge 1911. Died 24 February 1975.

SYMON, John Parker (1940) Born 30 November 1921, 43 Midmills Road, Inverness; son of James Alexander Symon, Civil Servant, and Marion Rae Parker. **Tutor(s):** S J Bailey. **Educ:** Inverness Royal Academy; Edinburgh Academy. **Career:** Lieutenant, RE 1940–1944. Died June 1944 (killed in action in France).

SYMONDS, Frederick Michael (1930) Born 21 September 1911, 14 de Parys Avenue, St Peter, Bedford; son of Noel Parry Vic Symonds, Vice-Master, Bedford School, and Mabel Alloway Askwith; m Bridget (d 1995). **Subject(s):** Classics; BA 1933; MA 1960. **Tutor(s):** M P Charlesworth. **Johnian Relatives:** son of Noel Parry Vic Symonds (1883); brother of Reginald Askwith Symonds (1925), Ronald Henry Humfrys Symonds (1928) and of Robert Vincent Symonds (1934); uncle of Robert Stobart Symonds (1958). **Educ:** Bedford School. Died 1 October 1996.

SYMONDS, Reginald Askwith (1925) Born 30 September 1906, 14 de Parys Avenue, St Peter, Bedford; son of Noel Parry Vic Symonds, Vice-Master, Bedford School, and Mabel Alloway Askwith; m Olivia Margaret Stobart; 1 son (Robert (Robin) Stobart b 20 July 1938), 1 daughter (Leonora (Lorna) Mary). **Subject(s):** Classics/Law; BA 1928; MA 1933. **Tutor(s):** M P Charlesworth. **Johnian Relatives:** son of Noel Parry Vic Symonds (1883); brother of Ronald Henry Humfrys Symonds (1928), Frederick Michael Symonds (1930) and of Robert Vincent Symonds (1934); father-in-law of Alastair Leoid Macleod (1947); father of Robert Stobart Symonds (1958). **Educ:** Bedford School. Died 30 March 1976.

SYMONDS, Robert Vincent (1934) Born 22 January 1915, 14 de Parys Avenue, St Peter, Bedford; son of Noel Parry Vic Symonds, Schoolmaster, and Mabel Alloway Askwith. **Subject(s):** Classics/English; BA 1937; MA 1942. **Tutor(s):** R L Howland. **Johnian Relatives:** son of Noel Parry Vic Symonds (1883); brother of Reginald Askwith Symonds (1925), Ronald Henry Humfrys Symonds (1928) and of Frederick Michael Symonds (1930); uncle of Robert Stobart Symonds (1958). **Educ:** Bedford School. **Awards:** Minor Scholarship, SJC 1933.

SYMONDS, Ronald Henry Humfrys (1928) Born 15 October 1909, 14 de Parys Avenue, Bedford; son of Noel Parry Vic Symonds, Vice-Master, Bedford School, and Mabel Alloway Askwith. **Tutor(s):** J M Wordie. **Johnian Relatives:** son of Noel Parry Vic Symonds (1883); brother of Reginald Askwith Symonds (1925), Frederick Michael Symonds (1930) and of Robert Vincent Symonds (1934); uncle of Robert Stobart Symonds (1958). **Educ:** Bedford School. **Career:** Army 1939–1945 (POW from 1940). **Appointments:** Coach, LMBC 1945 (also later of CUBC). Died 26 June 1956.

SYMONS, Humphrey (1942) Born 3 October 1924; son of Arthur Denis Symons, Medical Officer, and Phyllis Maude Alexander. **Tutor(s):** C W Guillebaud. **Johnian Relatives:** descendent of Robert Housman (1780), Thomas Housman (1814), Basil Williams (1836), and of Herbert Williams (1841); brother of Michael Symons (1939). **Educ:** Parents' Union School, Shrewsbury; Kingsland Grange School, Shrewsbury; Shrewsbury School.

SYMONS, Dr Michael (1939) Born 10 August 1920, St John's Vicarage, Clifton, Bristol; son of Arthur Denis Symons, Medical Officer of Health, and Phyllis Maude Alexander; m Mary Rowland, 1944 (d 1996); 1 son (Richard), 2 daughters (Heather and Susan). BA 1942; MA 1946; MB 1944; BChir 1944; MRCP 1946; FRCPath 1963; FRCP London 1975. **Tutor(s):** R L Howland. **Johnian Relatives:** descendent of Robert Housman (1780), Thomas Housman (1814), Basil Williams (1836), and of Herbert Williams (1841); brother of Humphrey Symons (1942). **Educ:** Union School, Shrewsbury; Kingsland Grange School, Shrewsbury; Shrewsbury School. **Career:** Assistant Lecturer in Pathology, University of Bristol 1945–1947; Consultant Histopathologist 1949–1985. **Appointments:** Vice-President of the Housman Society 1986.

T

TABBUSH, Victor Emmanuel (1932) Born 10 April 1913, Rue Henri, Seekabini, Cairo; son of Abraham Joseph Tabbush, Merchant, and Judith Forté. **Subject(s):** Mathematics/Economics; LLB (London) 1953. **Tutor(s):** J M Wordie. **Educ:** Elementary School; Manchester Grammar School. **Career:** Called to the Bar, Middle Temple, 1954; Paz Oil Company, Israel 1956; Hotel and Property Business. **Appointments:** Lawyer Member, London Rent Assessment Panel. **Awards:** Somerset Exhibition, SJC. Died 20 November 1995.

TACHMINDJI, Michel Alexander (1925) Born 17 November 1905, Smyrna, Turkey; son of Alexander Tachmindji, Banker and Merchant, and Eftichia George Michalinos. **Subject(s):** Economics; BA 1928; MA 1932. **Tutor(s):** M P Charlesworth. **Educ:** Captain Fox, Courtenay Lodge, Sutton Courtenay; Lycie Greco Français, Aronia, Smyrna, Turkey.

Career: Director: Michalinos & Co; Michalinos Investments Ltd; Overseas & General Chartering Ltd; United Merchants Shipping Company Ltd. Died 22 November 1985.

TAFT, Hulbert (1930) Born 27 August 1907, La Fayette Avenue, Cincinnati; son of Hulbert Taft, Editor, and Nellie Phillips Leaman. **Tutor(s):** E A Benians. **Educ:** Franklin School, Cincinnati; The Taft School, Watertown; Yale University.

TAIT, (Cecil) Wortley (1925) Born 2 October 1906, St Aidan's College, Forest Road, Claughton, Cheshire; son of Arthur James Tait, Clerk in Holy Orders, and Jane Dumergue Drury; m Jo. **Subject(s):** Classics; BA 1928. **Tutor(s):** E E Sikes. **Johnian Relatives:** son of Arthur James Tait (1891); brother of George Aidan Drury Tait (1921); brother-in-law of Laurence Hilary Macklin (1921); uncle of David Drury Macklin (1947), Arthur Gordon Tait (1954) and of Richard Drury Tait (1956); great uncle of Alan Drury Macklin (1976), Alastair Jeremy Macklin (1979), Celia Helen Gilbert Tait (1983) and of Adrian Roger Macklin (1986). **Educ:** King's College Choir School, Cambridge; Marlborough College. **Career:** Interpreter for the British Forces in Burma, WWII; Shell International Petroleum Company, Japan and the Far East, then London Head Office. **Awards:** Scholarship, SJC 1924.

TAIT, George Aidan Drury (1921) Born 9 June 1902, The Lodge, St Aidan's College, Forest Road, Claughton, Birkenhead, Cheshire; son of Arthur James Tait, Clerk in Holy Orders, and Principal, Ridley Hall, Cambridge, and Jane Dumergue Drury; m Margaret Evelyn Gray, 11 August 1933; 2 sons (Arthur Gordon b 28 July 1934 and Richard Drury b 15 May 1936), 2 daughters (Eleanor Gillian b 15 June 1939 and Diana Ruth b 18 August 1944). **Subject(s):** Classics; BA 1925; MA 1932. **Tutor(s):** E E Sikes. **Johnian Relatives:** son of Arthur James Tait (1891); brother-in-law of Laurence Hilary Macklin (1921); brother of Cecil Wortley Tait (1925); uncle of David Drury Macklin (1947); father of Arthur Gordon Tait (1954) and of Richard Drury Tait (1956); great uncle of Alan Drury Macklin (1976) and of Alastair Jeremy Macklin (1979); grandfather of Celia Helen Gilbert Tait (1983); great uncle of Adrian Roger Macklin (1986); grandfather of Helen Joanna Hendry (1996). **Educ:** King's College School, Cambridge; Haileybury College; British School of Archaeology, Athens. **Career:** Assistant Professor of Classics and Fine Arts, Oberlin College, USA 1926–1927; Classics Master, Eton College 1927–1962 (Housemaster 1942–1957); Curator, Myers Museum. **Appointments:** Coach, Eton Rowing Eight. **Awards:** Scholarship, SJC. **Publications:** 'The Egyptian Relief Chalice', *Journal of Egyptian Archaeology* 49, 1963. Died 22 November 1970.

TAIT, Hugh Nimmo (1907) Born 25 April 1888, Castle Eden, County Durham; son of Thomas Slater Tait, Principal, Baroda College, India, and Margaret Nimmo. **Subject(s):** Mathematics/Natural Sciences; BA 1910. **Tutor(s):** L H K Bushe-Fox. **Johnian Relatives:** son of Thomas Slater Tait (1873). **Educ:** Harrogate College; Clifton College. **Career:** Clerk in Chief Secretary's Office, Ireland 1911; 2nd Class Clerk, Colonial Office 1912; Acting 1st Class Clerk 1917; Military Service 1918; Secretary, Rhodesian Commission 1919–1920; Acting Assistant Secretary, Dominions Office 1929; Assistant Secretary 1930; Assistant Secretary, Commonwealth Relations Office 1950. **Awards:** Scholarship, SJC. Died 10 May 1960.

TAIT, John Collins (1926) Born 24 December 1907, 89 Walker Road, Newcastle upon Tyne, Northumberland; son of Henry Tait, of independent means, and Margaret Bowes Hall. **Subject(s):** Law; BA 1930; MA 1933. **Tutor(s):** E A Benians. **Educ:** Dame Allen's School, Newcastle upon Tyne; Royal Grammar School, Newcastle upon Tyne.

TALBOT, Dr Clifford Heyworth (1943) Born 22 April 1925, 2 Falkland Road, Southport, Lancashire; son of Frank Heyworth Talbot, Barrister-at-Law, and Mabel Jane Williams; m Margaret Hilda Hooper, 17 June 1950, St Luke's Church, Wimbledon Park. **Subject(s):** Natural Sciences; BA 1946; MA 1950; MB 1948; BChir 1948; MChir 1957. **Tutor(s):** S J

Bailey. **Educ:** The Downs School, Malvern; Leighton Park School, Reading. **Career:** Consultant Surgeon, United Sheffield Hospitals.

TAN, Thoon Lip (1930) Born 22 February 1910, 4 Mount Elizabeth, Singapore; son of Tan Kwee Swee, General Broker and Estate Agent, and Leong Loy The. **Subject(s):** Law; BA 1933; LLB 1934. **Tutor(s):** C W Guillebaud. **Educ:** Anglo Chinese School, Singapore; Raffles Institution, Singapore.

TANNAHILL, John Allan (1936) Born 7 February 1918, 12 Carriagehill Drive, Paisley, Renfrewshire, Scotland; son of James Tannahill, Officer of HM Customs and Excise, and Mary Graham Allan. **Subject(s):** History; BA 1939; MA 1947. **Tutor(s):** J S Boys Smith. **Educ:** King's School, Ely. **Career:** Suffolk Regiment 1939–1943; Board of Trade 1943–1948; Department of Employment (Assistant Secretary), Health and Safety Executive 1948–1978; Research Fellow, Manchester University 1956–1957. **Awards:** Exhibition, SJC 1935–1937. **Publications:** *European Volunteer Workers in Britain*, Manchester University Press, 1958.

TANNER, Donald Vaughan (1920) Born 18 August 1901, The Chestnuts, Frome, Somerset; son of Lanfear Robson Tanner, Master Printer and Bookbinder, and Ellen Trotman. **Tutor(s):** E A Benians. **Educ:** Wells House, Malvern; Cheltenham College.

TANNER, Guy Montague (1920) Born 5 November 1902, 2 Pretoria Terrace, Enfield, Middlesex; son of Percy Barrett Tanner, Postmaster of Blackpool, and Annie May Ratcliff. **Subject(s):** Natural Sciences; BA 1923; MA 1927. **Tutor(s):** B F Armitage. **Johnian Relatives:** brother of Howard Barrett Tanner (1926). **Educ:** High School, Walham Cross; St Catherine's School, Bishop's Stortford; Bishop's Stortford College; Horsham Grammar School. **Career:** Surgeon Commander, RNVR. **Honours:** VRD. Died 18 November 1986.

TANNER, Howard Barrett (1926) Born 16 February 1907, 39 Eleanor Cross Road, Waltham Cross, Hertfordshire; son of Percy Barrett Tanner, Postmaster of Liverpool, and Annie May Ratcliff. **Subject(s):** History/Law; BA 1929; MA 1934. **Tutor(s):** M P Charlesworth. **Johnian Relatives:** brother of Guy Montague Tanner (1920). **Educ:** St Catherine's School, Bishop's Stortford; Gringley School, Horsham; Collegers School, Horsham; Hereford Cathedral School. **Career:** Editorial Staff, *Huddersfield Examiner, Yorkshire Evening News, Daily Telegraph*; Liberal Candidate, Leeds North; Called to the Bar, Gray's Inn 1937; North-Eastern Circuit 1939; Captain, Dorset Regiment. **Awards:** Somerset Exhibition, SJC. Died 13 June 1943 (died in hospital after a motor cycle accident on duty).

TANNER, Jesse Ossawa (1921) Born 25 September 1903, Sloane Maternity Hospital, New York, USA; son of Henry Ossawa Tanner, Artist, and Jessie Macauley Olsson; 1 son (Jacques). **Subject(s):** Natural Sciences; BA 1924; MA 1955. **Tutor(s):** B F Armitage. **Educ:** Hill Crest School, Folkestone; Denny School, Boulogne sur Seine, Paris. Died 10 May 1985.

TANNER, Laurance Edgar (1910) Born 8 May 1891, 26 Rosehill Road, Wandsworth, Surrey; son of Edgar Robson Tanner, Solicitor, and Marian Button; m Gwladys Marjorie Day, 5 December 1916, The Free Church, St Ives, Huntingdonshire. BA 1913; MA 1919. **Tutor(s):** J R Tanner. **Johnian Relatives:** son-in-law of George Dennis Day (1879); brother-in-law of George Lewis Day (1910), Dennis Ivor Day (1911) and of Miles Jeffrey Game Day (1915). **Educ:** Charterhouse. **Career:** Captain, Gloucestershire Regiment (TF), then with Ministry of Munitions (wounded), WWI; Admitted Solicitor 1920. **Awards:** Winchester Reading Prize, University of Cambridge 1912. **Publications:** *The Child of the Moor*, 1917; *Mischief, My Spaniel*; 'Caleb the Carpenter', *The Eagle*, 33, 1912; 'Songs of Exmoor', *The Eagle*, 34, 1913. Died June 1941.

TAPHOUSE, Frank Goodwin (1921) Born 16 August 1902, 64B Fulham Park Gardens, Fulham, Middlesex; son of Frank Taphouse, Ladies' Tailor, and Sarah Goodwin; m Doris Mary Byrne, 22 December 1928,

St John the Baptist, Belmont. **Subject(s):** Classics; BA 1924; MA 1930. **Tutor(s):** E E Sikes. **Educ:** Southfield London County Council School; Emanuel School, Wandsworth Common. **Career:** Master, Whitgift Grammar School, Croydon; Classics Master, Hertford Grammar School; Master, Bromley County School 1924–1927. **Awards:** Sizarship, SJC. Died 1971.

TARN, Thomas Cresswell Butson (1924) Born 30 May 1907, 12 Church Street, Shildon, Bishop Auckland, County Durham; son of Frederick Butson Tarn, Master Draper, and Hannah Lance Boddy. **Subject(s):** Law; BA 1928; MA 1932; LLB 1932. **Tutor(s):** E A Benians. **Educ:** New College, Harrogate.

TATTERSALL, John Lloyd (1929) Born 22 June 1909, 56 Lancaster Place, Blackburn; son of Walton Tattersall, Company Director, and Edith Gwendolen Lloyd Jones; m Kathleen; 2 daughters (Anne and Susan). **Subject(s):** Economics; BA 1932; MA 1936. **Tutor(s):** C W Guillebaud. **Educ:** The Grammar School, Blackburn; Caldicott School, Hitchin; The Leys School, Cambridge. Died 23 January 1989.

TAYLOR, The Revd Arnold Douglas (1904) Born 24 November 1885, Parsonage Farm, Wood Ditton, Cambridge; son of Sidney Augustus Taylor, Farmer, and Georgina Bowyer. BA 1907; MA 1921. **Tutor(s):** D MacAlister. **Educ:** King Edward's School, Bury St Edmunds. **Career:** Ordained Deacon 1910; Curate, Coleford 1910–1913; Ordained Priest 1911; Vicar, Wood Ditton 1913–1921; Temporary CF 1917–1919; Rector, Cheveley 1921–1930; Rector, Mistley with Bradfield 1930–1933; Vicar, Budbrooke, Warwickshire 1933–1945; Rector, Icklingham, Suffolk 1945–1955; Rector, Lackford 1947–1948. Died 3 April 1967.

TAYLOR, Christopher Beech (1921) Born 28 October 1904, 18 Rosslyn Hill, Hampstead, Middlesex; son of Edwin Claude Taylor, Doctor of Medicine, and Huldah Rebecca Southall. **Tutor(s):** E A Benians. **Educ:** Hampstead Kindergarten; Leighton Park School, Reading; Heath Mount Preparatory School, Hampstead.

TAYLOR, David Gladstone (1901) Born 27 November 1879, 364 Govan Street, Glasgow, Lanarkshire, Scotland; son of David Taylor, Master Grocer, and Marion Brown. **Subject(s):** Mathematics; BA 1904; MA 1908. **Tutor(s):** D MacAlister. **Educ:** Glasgow University; Allen Glen's School, Glasgow. **Career:** Assistant Lecturer in Mathematics, University College of South Wales, Cardiff 1904. Died June 1961.

TAYLOR, Dr Edward McKenzie (1925) Born 11 August 1889, 13 Walter Street, Nottingham; son of John George Taylor, Schoolmaster, and Joanna Margaret McKenzie; m Marjory Tiver Basnett, 1914. DSc (Durham). **Tutor(s):** J M Wordie. **Educ:** The Grammar School, Stockton; Armstrong College, Durham University. **Career:** Demonstrator in Agricultural Chemistry, University of Durham; Lecturer in Agricultural Science, Harper-Adams Agricultural College; Head, Chemistry Department, East Anglian Institute of Agriculture; Senior Chemist, Cotton Research Board, Egyptian Ministry of Agriculture; University Lecturer in Agricultural Chemistry, Cambridge 1926–1930; Director, Irrigation Research Institute, Lahore 1930–1944; Director, Military Engineer Research Station, Lahore Cantonment; Brigadier 1941; Agronomist to Rotary Hoes Ltd 1952. Died 17 October 1961.

TAYLOR, Frank Robert Forbes (1926) Born 25 September 1908, Salvation Army Maternity Hospital, Cape Town, South Africa; son of Harry Langford Taylor, Director, ESYA Robinson Ltd, and Amy Catherine Yeldham Mackay; m Caroline, 1935. **Subject(s):** Mechanical Sciences; BA 1930; FIMechE 1979. **Tutor(s):** J M Wordie. **Educ:** Fairleigh Preparatory School, Weston-Super-Mare; Clifton College. **Career:** Crane Designer and Builder, Bristol; RAF, Sierra Leone, WWII. **Publications:** 'Heavy Goods Handling Prior to the 19th Century', *Transactions of the Newcomen Society*. Died 1979.

TAYLOR, Abbot Frederick Lewis (1911) Born 28 March 1892, 88 Palatine Road, Stoke Newingon, Middlesex; son of Lewis Charles Taylor, Compositor, and Camille Victorie Soulard. **Subject(s):** History; BA 1914; MA 1918. **Tutor(s):** J R Tanner. **Educ:** Hackney Downs School. **Career:** Captain, Royal Fusiliers, later in the Ministry of Labour, WWI; Novice, St Augustine's Abbey 1920; Headmaster, Ramsgate Abbey School 1924–1934; Abbot, Ramsgate 1934–1954; Superior, Supiaco Congregation Community, Farnborough Abbey, Hampshire. **Awards:** Prince Consort Prize, University of Cambridge 1920; Gladstone Memorial Prize, University of Cambridge 1920. **Honours:** MC 1917. **Publications:** 'The Art of War in Italy, 1494–1529', 1921 (Prize Essay). Died 31 July 1961.

TAYLOR, Frederick William (1933) Born 8 March 1909, Dale Cottage, Plymouth Street, Merthyr Tydfil; son of James Edward Taylor, Solicitor, and Emily Beatrice Price; m Muriel Vera Markreed, 1938; 2 daughters. **Subject(s):** Law; BA 1935; MA 1951; LLB (Wales); LLM (Wales) 1954. **Tutor(s):** C W Guillebaud. **Educ:** Twynyrodyn School, Merthyr Tydfil; Cyfarthfa Secondary School; University College of Wales. **Career:** Articled to Solicitor 1925–1930; Assistant Lecturer in Law, University College, Hull 1935–1940; Assistant Lecturer in Law, Southampton University College 1940; Assistant Lecturer in Law 1941, Lecturer in Law 1948–1974, Head of Law Department 1951, Professor of Law 1956, University of Hull. Died 8 May 1989.

TAYLOR, Geoffrey Walton (1944) Born 1926, Accrington, Lancashire; son of Percy Warley Taylor, Bank Manager, and Annie Walton; m Maureen Hazel Jacques, 10 July 1954, Great St Mary's Church, Sawbridgeworth; 3 sons (David, Michael and Peter). **Subject(s):** Mechanical Sciences; BA 1947; MA 1951; CEng; FICE. **Tutor(s):** S J Bailey. **Johnian Relatives:** father of Michael John Taylor (1974) and of Peter Gordon Taylor (1977). **Educ:** Hyndburn Park School, Accrington; Heywood Grammar School. **Career:** C S Allott & Son, Consulting Engineers 1947–1950; Managing Director, R G Horton (Engineers) Ltd and Associated Civil Engineering Companies 1960–1985; Director, Hoskins & Horton Plc 1966–1985.

TAYLOR, Gerald Phillips (1943) Born 31 May 1925, 58 Hamilton Square, Birkenhead, Cheshire; son of George Edward Taylor, Assistant Clerk to Justices, and Florence Edwards. **Tutor(s):** C W Guillebaud. **Educ:** Claughton Preparatory School, Birkenhead; Birkenhead School.

TAYLOR, Godfrey Midgley Chassereau (1904) Born 7 November 1885, Hopefield, Fasset Road, Kingston, Surrey; son of Gotfred Midgley Taylor, Civil Engineer, and Frances Isabel Chassereau; m (1) Edith Granger (d 1958), (2) Violet Gale (d 1972); 2 sons (Oliver Midgley b 28 February 1916 and Jerry Granger b 3 September 1917). **Subject(s):** Mechanical Sciences; BA 1907; MA 1911; RIBA; MInstCE; MConsE; FRSanI. **Tutor(s):** C E Graves; J R Tanner. **Johnian Relatives:** father of Oliver Midgley Taylor (1934) and Jerry Granger Taylor (1937); great-grandfather of Susanna Margaret Grant (2000). **Educ:** Cranleigh School. **Career:** Architect, DoE; Lieutenant, Royal Marines; Captain, RE; Partner 1912–1942, Senior Partner 1942–1965, John Taylor and Sons, Caxton House, Westminster (specialist in waterworks, sewerage and sewage disposal). **Appointments:** President, Institution of Public Health Engineers 1934; Chairman, Association of Consulting Engineers 1941; President, Institution of Water Engineers 1946; Director, several water companies, including Lee Valley Water Company. **Honours:** MC; OBE. Died 25 January 1983.

TAYLOR, Graham Sinclair (1934) Born 27 July 1915, Shanghai; son of Claude Sinclair Taylor, Consulting Engineer, and Irene Spicer; BA 1937. **Educ:** Stancliffe Hall, Matlock; Uppingham. **Career:** Pilot Officer, RAF 1939–1940. Died 26 January 1940 (killed in action).

TAYLOR, Guy Arthur (1909) (migrated to Corpus Christi College) Born 6 April 1890, 22 Hornton Street, Kensington, London; son of Arthur Taylor, Civil and Mining Engineer, and Emilie Nancy Bontoux;

m Margaret Ellen Heath, 24 November 1917, Winchmore Hill Wesleyan Chapel. **Subject(s):** Natural Sciences; BA 1912 (Corpus Christi). **Tutor(s):** L H K Bushe-Fox. **Educ:** Colet Court School; St Paul's School, London. **Career:** Northern Rhodesia Administrative Service.

TAYLOR, Captain Harold Charles Norman (1911) Born 26 October 1892, 20 Wimpole Street, Cavendish Square, London; son of Frederick Taylor, Physician, and Helen Mary Manby. **Subject(s):** Classics; BA 1914. **Tutor(s):** E E Sikes. **Educ:** Charterhouse School. **Career:** Captain, London Regiment (Blackheath and Woolwich Battalion) 1914–1916. **Publications:** 'Innocents Abroad', *The Eagle*, 35; 'Some Fragments of Plato', *The Eagle*, 35. Died 21 May 1916 (killed in action on Vimy Ridge).

TAYLOR, Harold Midgley (1919) Born 8 May 1893, Ambleside, Upperton Road, Eastbourne; son of John Taylor, Gentleman of independent means, and Sarah Midgley. **Tutor(s):** E E Sikes. **Johnian Relatives:** brother of John Norman Taylor (1902). **Educ:** Felsted School; Université de Lausanne.

TAYLOR, Dr Henry Dennis (1944) Born 19 January 1925, Military Families Hospital, Brompton, Kent; son of Harry Dennis Taylor, Colonial Civil Servant, and Helen Jessie Smith. **Subject(s):** Natural Sciences; BA 1947; MA 1953. **Tutor(s):** C W Guillebaud. **Educ:** Magdalen College School, Brackley. **Career:** Radio Officer, Merchant Service 1941–1944; BCURA 1947–1953; Imperial College 1953–1957; Esso 1957–1959; CEGB 1959–1962; Fire Protection Association 1962–1973; Bowrings 1973–1977; Independent forensic investigator of marine fires and explosions 1977–1997.

TAYLOR, Hermon (1922) Born 11 May 1905, 36 Guard Street, Workington, Cumberland; son of Enoch Oliver Taylor, Director of Education, Edmonton Education Committee, and Frances Louisa Harrison, Teacher; m (1) Marie Amelie Pearson, 17 September 1932 (d 1981), (2) Noreen Cooke, 19 March 1983, Sidlesham Methodist Church; 3 sons (John b 16 October 1936, Richard James Hermon b 18 November 1941 and Christopher b 10 April 1945), 2 daughters (Judith b 12 September 1934 and Jennifer b 23 June 1938). **Subject(s):** Natural Sciences; BA 1926; MA 1931; MB 1931; BChir 1931; MD 1934; MRCS; LRCP 1929; FRCS 1930. **Tutor(s):** B F Armitage. **Johnian Relatives:** father of John Hermon-Taylor (1954) and of Richard James Hermon-Taylor (1960). **Educ:** Cowley Secondary School, St Helens; Latymer Secondary School, Edmonton. **Career:** House Surgeon, Orthopaedic House Surgeon, later Demonstrator in Pathology, St Bartholomew's Hospital; Resident Surgical Officer, Hertford and Lincoln County Hospitals; Honorary Surgical Registrar, Prince of Wales General Hospital, Tottenham; Consultant Surgeon, King George Hospital, Ilford; Consultant Surgeon, Royal London Hospital 1939–1970; Part-time Lecturer in Surgery, London Hospital Medical College 1959. **Appointments:** President, British Society of Gastroenterology. **Awards:** Entrance Scholarship, St Bartholomew's Hospital 1926; Willet Medal for operative surgery, St Bartholomew's Hospital, 1929; Luther Holden Research Scholarship in surgery 1932; Raymond Horton-Smith Prize, University of Cambridge 1934; Waltham Prize for surgical pathology and proximae accessit Brackenbury Surgical Scholarship. **Publications:** Various, on gastric endoscopy, conservative treatments for perforated duodenal ulcer and breast cancer, and on stomach surgery for ulcers with reduced side-effects. Died 10 January 2001.

TAYLOR, James Alexander Simson (1935) Born 19 June 1917, 9 Albert Quadrant, Weston-Super-Mare; son of George Taylor, Physician, and Evelyn Anna Simson. **Subject(s):** Classics/History; BA 1938; MA 1942; Diploma of Physical Education (Leeds). **Tutor(s):** R L Howland. **Educ:** St George's School, Leicester; Wyggeston Grammar School, Leicester; Oakham School; Carnegie College, Leeds. **Career:** Schoolmaster, Loretto School, Mussleburgh, Midlothian; Part-time Teacher, Loretto School and Stewart's/Melvill College; Strathallan School 1948. **Honours:** TD. Died 16 May 1993.

TAYLOR, Jerry Granger (GRANGER-TAYLOR) (1937) Born 3 September 1917, Little Milton, Oxfordshire; son of Godfrey Midgley Chassereau Taylor, Chartered Civil Engineer, Lieutenant, RN Division, RE, and Edith Granger; m (1) Barbara Brunskill Reid, 1940, (2) Jacqueline Roger, 1960; (1) 2 daughters (Claudia and Hero), (2) 2 sons (Peter and Nicolas). **Subject(s):** Architecture; BA 1940; MA 1978; RIBA. **Tutor(s):** J S Boys Smith. **Johnian Relatives:** son of Godfrey Midgley Chassereau Taylor (1904); brother of Oliver Midgley Taylor (1934). **Educ:** The Old Malthouse, Langton; Radley College; Slade School of Art, University of London. **Career:** RE, WWII; Architect, DoE 1969–1982. Died 27 July 1999.

TAYLOR, John (1948) Born 30 August 1927, 12 Alwinton Terrace, Gosforth, Northumberland; son of Jeffrey Taylor, Chartered Accountant, and Ellen Bertha Futty. **Tutor(s):** C W Guillebaud. **Educ:** PNEU School, Gosforth; Newcastle Preparatory School; Earnseat, Arnside; Sedbergh School. **Career:** Commissioned, Durham Light Infantry.

TAYLOR, John Norman (1902) Born 4 December 1882, Old Rowney, Southill, Bedfordshire; son of John Taylor, gentleman of independent means, and Sarah Midgley; m Agnes Irene Hederstedt, 13 October 1915, Calcutta Cathedral. **Subject(s):** Classics/Law; BA 1905; MA 1909; LLB 1905. **Tutor(s):** D MacAlister. **Johnian Relatives:** brother of Harold Midgley Taylor (1919). **Educ:** Rossall School. **Career:** Solicitor, Jeffreys and Powell, Brecon 1908–1939; Lieutenant, Calcutta Light Horse, Indian Defence Force, WWI; Partner, Crawford, Bayley and Co Bombay 1923. **Appointments:** President, Breconshire and Radnor Incorporated Law Society. Died 29 May 1966.

TAYLOR, Oliver Midgley (1934) Born 28 February 1916, Little Milton, Oxfordshire; son of Godfrey Midgley Chassereau Taylor, Chartered Civil Engineer, Lieutenant, RN Division, RE, and Edith Granger, Artist; m Margaret Marion Doll, 24 November 1945, St Richard's Church, Haywards Heath (d 1999); 3 sons (Antony Midgley, Jonathan Ernest and Charles Godfrey), 2 daughters (Mary Honor and Hilary Beatrice). **Subject(s):** Mechanical Sciences; BA 1937; MA 1941; FICE; FIWES. **Tutor(s):** J S Boys Smith. **Johnian Relatives:** son of Godfrey Midgley Chassereau Taylor (1904); brother of Jerry Granger Taylor (1937); grandfather of Susanna Margaret Grant (2000). **Educ:** The Old Malthouse, Langton Matravers; Radley College. **Career:** Second Lieutenant, RE, N Africa and Greece (POW for four years), WWII; John Taylor & Sons, Chartered Civil Engineers 1937–1973; Engineer on Boards of several Water Companies 1973–retirement. Died 15 March 2002.

TAYLOR, The Revd Canon Paul Aloysius (1933) Born 28 June 1915, 42 Florentine Road, West Derby, Liverpool; son of Charles Santley Taylor, Schoolmaster, and Johanna Lacy, Teacher. **Subject(s):** Natural Sciences; BA 1936; MA 1946; DD (Fribourg) 1945. **Tutor(s):** J M Wordie. **Educ:** St Francis Xavier's College, Liverpool; University of Fribourg. **Career:** Ordained Roman Catholic Priest 1943; Curate, Roman Catholic Cathedral, Northampton 1946–1955; Parish Priest, All Souls, Peterborough 1955–1968; Parish Priest, Our Lady and The English Martyrs, Cambridge 1968–1980; Chancellor, Diocese of East Anglia 1976–1992; Parish Priest, St Etheldreda's, Ely 1980–1993. **Appointments:** Chapter Canon, Northampton 1967–1976; Honorary Canon, Northampton 1976. **Awards:** Scholarship, SJC. **Honours:** Prelate of Honour 1984.

TAYLOR, Peter Royston (1945) Born 29 February 1928, 42 Monument Street, Peterborough; son of John William Edward Taylor, Chief Petty Officer, RN, Gunner's Mate, HMS Woolwich, and Violet London. **Subject(s):** History; BA 1948; MA 1952; BD (London) 1956. **Tutor(s):** F Thistlethwaite. **Educ:** Boundary Road Private School, Chatham; Queen's Drive West School, Peterborough; Ordnance Street School, Chatham; King's School, Peterborough. **Career:** Headmaster, Chingford Senior High School 1970.

TAYLOR, Philip Tetlow (1930) Born 17 June 1911, 34 Derby Road, Heaton Chapel, Stockport, Lancashire; son of Gladstone Taylor, Textile Engineer, and Ellen Tetlow; 2 children. **Subject(s):** Classics; BA 1933; MA 1945. **Tutor(s):** M P Charlesworth. **Educ:** Denton Lane Elementary School, Chadderton; Manchester Grammar School. **Career:** Head of Classics, Thornton Grammar School, Bradford 1934–1938; RAF 1939–1945; Head of Classics, Nottingham Grammar School 1951; Headmaster, Maldon Grammar School 1951–1971. Died 16 October 1971.

TAYLOR, Sidney Barr (1920) Born 10 October 1901, 26 Napier Road, Tottenham, Middlesex; son of Frank Barr Taylor, and Ellen Constance Pearson. **Subject(s):** Mathematics/Natural Sciences (Physics); BA 1923. **Tutor(s):** E A Benians. **Johnian Relatives:** father of Nicholas Barr Taylor (1956). **Educ:** Royal British Orphan Schools; Highgate School. **Career:** Command Instruction Officer, HMS *Drake*, on staff of the Commander in Chief, Plymouth, and Port Librarian; Instructor Captain, RN 1952. **Awards:** Scholarship, SJC 1919.

TAYLOR, Theo Mallinson (1931) Born 14 August 1913, Swainelly, Beeches Avenue, Carshalton, Surrey; son of John Whitaker Taylor, Mechanical Engineer and Edith Maude Mallinson; m Ruth; 1 son (Nigel). **Subject(s):** Natural Sciences; BA 1935. **Tutor(s):** J M Wordie. **Educ:** The Grammar School, Stockton-on-Tees; Ashville College, Harrogate. Died 3 January 1990.

TAYLOR, Thomas (1930) Born 18 April 1911, 42 Wellington Road, Blackburn; son of William Taylor, Grocer, and Margaret Harrison; m Lydia. **Subject(s):** Mathematics; BA 1933; MA 1937. **Tutor(s):** J M Wordie. **Educ:** All Saints' School, Blackburn; Queen Elizabeth's Grammar School, Blackburn. Died 13 March 1975.

TAYLOR, Thomas Charles (1926) Born 21 November 1907, Rock Road, Oundle, Northamptonshire; son of Thomas Stephen Taylor, Motor Mechanic, and Ambrosine Harrison Cave. **Subject(s):** Natural Sciences; BA 1929; MA 1962. **Tutor(s):** C W Guillebaud. **Educ:** Stamford School. **Awards:** Sizarship, SJC 1926. Died 1997.

TAYLOR, William (1923) Born 25 July 1903, 16 Greenbank Street, Galashiels, Selkirkshire, Scotland; son of William Taylor, Organist, and Lucy Ann Birch; m. **Subject(s):** Mathematics; BA 1925; MA (Edinburgh) 1923. **Tutor(s):** J M Wordie. **Educ:** Episcopal School, Galashiels; Gala High School, Galashiels; University of Edinburgh. **Career:** Assistant Lecturer, Department of Physics, Manchester University 1925–1929; Senior Mathematics Master, Wolverhampton Grammar School 1929; Headmaster, Wigan Grammar School 1939; Deputy Director of Education, Leeds 1947; Chief Inspector of Schools, Leeds 1948.

TAYLOR, William Smalley (1930) Born 1 June 1911, 38 Windermere Road, Muswell Hill, Middlesex; son of William Percy Taylor, Hair and Feather Merchant, and Elizabeth Hannah Smalley; BA 1933. **Tutor(s):** C W Guillebaud. **Educ:** Merton Court School, Sidcup; Pocklington School. **Career:** Lieutenant, The Queen's Bays 1942. Died 27 June 1942 (killed in action in Libya).

TEAGUE, Derek Michael (1943) Born 11 May 1925, 54 Montalt Road, Walthamstow, Essex; son of Frederick Herbert Teague, Supervisor, Cable & Wireless, and Mary Ross Campbell. **Tutor(s):** C W Guillebaud. **Educ:** Eureka Preparatory School, Highams Park, London; Park Street Elementary School, St Albans; Watford Grammar School.

TEALE, Donald Eric (1934) Born 14 November 1915, Maternity Hospital, Singapore; son of George Eric Teale, Rubber Estates Agent, and May Yorston. **Tutor(s):** R L Howland. **Educ:** Terra Nova, Southport; Clifton College; Manchester Technical Institute.

TEALL, Major George Harris (1900) Born 24 October 1880, 9 All Saints Street, Nottingham; son of Jethro Justinian Harris Teall, HM Geological Survey, and Harriet Moore Cowen; m Josephine Burrell, 11 March 1919.

Tutor(s): D MacAlister. **Johnian Relatives:** son of Jethro Justinian Harris Teall (1869). **Educ:** Dulwich College; Oundle School; Guy's Hospital. **Career:** Second Lieutenant, Royal Garrison Regiment 1903; Lieutenant, Lincoln Regiment 1906; Captain 1914; Major, Lincolnshire Regiment, Deputy Assistant Adjutant-General (Mentioned in Despatches five times, wounded) 1914–1919; Called to the Bar, Gray's Inn 1925. **Honours:** DSO, WWI; French Croix de Guerre, WWI. Died 21 June 1939.

TEARLE, James Francis (1947) Born 6 May 1927, Stone Field, Kidbrooke Grove, Charlton, Kent; son of Francis John Enoch Tearle, Mechanical Engineer, and Nettie Liddell McLean; m Peggy Urmston, 23 August 1958 (d 1996); 1 son (John), 2 daughters (Elizabeth and Katherine). BA 1950; MA 1954; CEng; MIMechE. **Tutor(s):** R L Howland. **Educ:** Edge Grove Preparatory School, Aldenham; Shrewsbury School. **Career:** Metropolitan-Vickers Electrical Company Ltd; AEI – John Thompson Nuclear Energy Group; The Nuclear Power Group Ltd; The National Nuclear Corporation Ltd. **Appointments:** Master, Worshipful Company of Broderers 1985–1986.

TEBBS, Reginald (1927) Born 8 May 1908, 19 Thornvill Crescent, Burley, Leeds, Yorkshire; son of William Tebbs, Chief Clerk in a Fire Insurance Company, and Nellie Farrow. **Tutor(s):** M P Charlesworth. **Educ:** Miss Christie's School, Headlingley; Headingley Kindergarten School; The Grammar School, Leeds.

TEESDALE, Edmund Brinsley (1937) Born 30 September 1915, Shanghai, China; son of John Herman Teesdale, Solicitor, and Winifred Mary Gull; m Joyce Thunder 22 May 1947. **Tutor(s):** R L Howland. **Educ:** Wellington House, Westgate; Lancing College; Trinity College, Oxford.

TELFER, Douglas Ross (1946) Born 1 September 1921, 34 Prince's Avenue, Great Crosby, Lancashire; son of Matthew Ross Telfer, Timber Merchant, and Winifred Johnstone (née Fisher); m Hedy Lehner, 23 August 1949; 2 sons (Mark and Nicholas), 1 daughter (Susan). **Subject(s):** Economics; BA 1948; MA 1953. **Tutor(s):** C W Guillebaud. **Educ:** Holmwood Preparatory School, Formby; Shrewsbury School. **Career:** Captain, RE; Secretary 1950, Director 1959, Vincent Murphy & Co Ltd, Timber Importers, Liverpool. **Appointments:** Captain, West Lancashire Golf Club. Died 19 August 1966.

TELFER, Ian Edmund (1949) Born 20 September 1930, 11 Chelsea Villas, Newcastle upon Tyne; son of Edmund Victor Telfer, Professor of Naval Architecture, and Edith Louisa Smedley. BA 1952; MA 1956. **Tutor(s):** R L Howland. **Educ:** St Ronan's School, Newcastle; Ewell Elementary School; Downs Lodge School, Sutton; Repton School.

TELFER-SMOLLETT, Patrick Tobias (1947) Born 26 December 1914, Makeney House, Milford, Derbyshire; son of Alexander Drummond Telfer-Smollett, Major-General, and Marion Lucy Strutt. **Tutor(s):** C W Guillebaud. **Educ:** Canford School. **Career:** Commissioned in Highland Light Infantry. **Honours:** MC.

TEMPEST, Robert Kershaw (1948) Born 6 November 1925, Northwich, Cheshire; son of Frederick Dickens (stepfather) and Dorothy Tempest. BSc (Liverpool) 1945; MSc 1947. **Tutor(s):** J M Wordie. **Educ:** Danebridge Church of England School, Northwich; Sir John Deane's Grammar School, Northwich; Liverpool University.

TEMPLE, James Muir (1949) Born 24 January 1929, 993 Scott Hall Road, Leeds; son of Leslie Temple, Dental Surgeon, and Gladys Isabel Forsyth; m Margaret Macdonald, 30 December 1953; 1 son (Richard b 18 March 1955), 1 daughter (Nicola b 29 November 1956). **Subject(s):** Modern and Medieval Languages/Archaeology and Anthropology; BA 1952; MA 1956. **Tutor(s):** C W Guillebaud. **Educ:** Ingledew College, Leeds; Leeds Grammar School; Terrington Hall Preparatory School; Sedbergh School. **Career:** Assistant Master, Liverpool College 1953–1958;

Assistant Master, Housemaster and Second Master, Stowe School 1958–1988. **Awards:** Exhibition, SJC 1947.

TEMPLEMAN, Rt Hon the Lord Sydney William (1938) Born 3 March 1920, 41 Bracewell Road, Hammersmith, London; son of Herbert William Templeman, Coal Merchant, and Lilian Pheasant; m (1) Margaret Joan Rowles, 1946, (2) Sheila Barton Edworthy, 1996; (1) 2 sons. **Subject(s):** History/Law; BA 1941; MA 1945; Honorary DLitt (Reading) 1980; Honorary LLD (Birmingham) 1986, (CNAA) 1990, (Exeter) 1991, (West of England) 1993, (National Law School of India) 1994; QC 1964; PC 1978. **Tutor(s):** J S Boys Smith. **Johnian Relatives:** father of Peter Morton Templeman (1979). **Educ:** Alexandra Road School, Hounslow; Southall County School. **Career:** Commander, 4/1st Gurka Rifles 1941; North West Frontier 1942; Arakan 1943; Imphal 1944; Burma with 7th Indian and 17th Indian Division 1945; Final rank Major; Mentioned in Despatches; Called to the Bar 1947; Attorney General, Duchy of Lancaster 1970–1972; Judge of the High Court of Justice, Chancery Division 1972–1978; Lord Justice of Appeal 1978–1982; Lord of Appeal in Ordinary 1982–1994. **Appointments:** Honorary Fellow, SJC 1982; Member, Middle Temple and Lincoln's Inn; Member, Bar Council 1961–1965, 1970–1972; Bencher, Middle Temple 1969; Member, Tribunal concerning the Vehicle and General Insurance Company 1971; Member, Advisory Committee on Legal Education 1972–1974; Treasurer, Senate of the Four Inns 1972–1974; President, Senate of the Inns of Court and the Bar 1974–1976; Honorary Member, Canadian Bar Association 1976; Honorary Member, American Bar Association 1976; Member, Royal Commission on Legal Services 1976–1979; President, Bar Association for Commerce, Finance and Industry 1982–1985; President, Holdsworth Club 1983–1984; Honorary Member, Newfoundland Law Society 1984; Treasurer, Middle Temple 1987; President, Bar European Group 1987–1995; Member, Chairman, Bishop of London's Commission on City Churches 1992–1994; President, Association of Law Teachers 1997–2001. **Awards:** Major Scholarship, SJC 1937; Whytehead Scholarship, SJC 1937; Harmsworth and MacMahon Scholarship. **Honours:** MBE 1946; Kt 1972.

TEMPLEMAN, William Henry (1902) Born 18 July 1883, 59 Spring Street, Myton, Kingston upon Hull; son of William Henry Templeman, Grocer, and Margaret Ann Fairweather. **Subject(s):** Natural Sciences; BA 1906; MA 1919; LLM 1908. **Tutor(s):** D MacAlister. **Educ:** Hymers College, Hull. **Career:** Captain, RAOC, WWI; Master, King's School, Canterbury 1915; Master, Tonbridge School 1919. **Awards:** Scholarship, SJC 1901. Died 11 March 1919.

TEMPLETON, Malcolm Clark (1948) Born 25 February 1928, The Dingle, Wake Green Road, Moseley, Birmingham; son of James Clark Templeton, Consulting Geologist, and Edith Florence Williams; m Hazel. BA 1951. **Tutor(s):** R L Howland. **Educ:** St John's School, Pinner; Oundle School. Died 20 October 1991.

TENNENT, Hugh Patrick Lorraine (1920) Naval Officer.

TENNENT, James Short (1925) Born 6 January 1907, 1 Freehold Terrace, Guide Port, Bedlington, Northumberland; son of Matthew Tennent, Master Grocer, and Jane Elizabeth Short. **Subject(s):** English/Modern and Medieval Languages; BA 1928. **Tutor(s):** E E Sikes. **Educ:** Choppington Church of England School, Morpeth; The Grammar School, Morpeth.

TERRETT, James Anthony (1949) Born 6 May 1930, Surbiton, Surrey; son of Alexander Terrett, Inspector of Taxes, and Kathleen Bertha Proom. **Subject(s):** History; BA 1952. **Tutor(s):** A G Lee. **Educ:** The Limes Preparatory School, Sudbury; Kings Road School, Chelmsford; King Edward VI Grammar School, Chelmsford; Cheltenham Grammar School; Worcester Royal Grammar School. **Awards:** Mullinger Exhibition, SJC.

TERRY, John (1921) Naval Officer.

TETLEY, John Lewis (1924) Born 27 June 1904, 50 West Street, Scarborough, Yorkshire; son of Alfred Samuel Tetley, Headmaster, and Ellen Norah Lewis. **Subject(s):** Natural Sciences; BA 1927; MA 1936. **Tutor(s):** B F Armitage. **Johnian Relatives:** son of Alfred Samuel Tetley (1887). **Educ:** The Municipal Secondary School, Scarborough; Bootham School, York. **Career:** Government Laboratory, Hong Kong. Died 1942 (Missing, presumed killed in Malaya).

TETSTALL, Reginald George (1941) Born 5 July 1922, 47 Broad Street, Worcester; son of George Emmanuel Tetstall, Workshop Clerk, and Winifred Smith, Teacher; m Patricia Morris, 1950; 1 son (Roger), 1 daughter (Philippa). **Subject(s):** Classics; BA 1944; MA 1948; Certificate of Competent Knowledge in Modern Greek (Cambridge). **Tutor(s):** R L Howland, C W Guillebaud. **Educ:** British Infants' School, Worcester; St Martin's Boys' School, Worcester; Broughton Green School, Hanbury; King Edward VI School, Stourbridge. **Career:** Senior Adviser of Studies in the Faculty of Arts, University College, Cardiff; Senior Examiner in Latin for the Joint Matriculation Board; Commissioned, Army Intelligence 1942–1946; Lecturer in Classics, University College, Cardiff 1950–1987. **Appointments:** Senior Examiner in Latin, Joint Matriculation Board; Council Member, Classical Association. **Awards:** Exhibition, SJC 1940. **Publications:** Various articles in Classical journals on aspects of Greek drama.

TEVERSON, Henry Walter Samuel (1946) Born 30 April 1928, Hall Farm, East Winch, King's Lynn, Norfolk; son of Harry Gordon Teverson, Farmer, and Hilda Mary Cross; m Elizabeth; 1 son (Stephen), 2 daughters (Helen and Rachel). **Tutor(s):** F Thistlethwaite. **Johnian Relatives:** father of Stephen Charles Teverson (1978). **Educ:** Downham Market Secondary School. **Career:** Farmer, Agricultural Broadcaster and Ringside Commentator; Chivers & Sons Farms, Cambridgeshire 1944–1945. Died 8 June 1986.

TEW, David Healy (1942) Born 6 April 1924, St Aubin's, Headley Close, Great Warley, Essex; son of Arthur Healy Tew, Foreign Exchange Broker, and Millicent Kathrine Haywood Smith. **Tutor(s):** S J Bailey. **Educ:** Highclere; St Felix School; Culford School.

THAKUR, Damodar (1948) Born 28 December 1924, Singhwara, Darbhanga, Bihar, India; son of Pushkar Thakur, District Magistrate, Bihar Civil Service, and Sureshwari Thakur; m Kishori Jha, 9 March 1947; 2 sons (Manohar and Sudarshan), 3 daughters (Rupa, Kanchan and Bhamati). **Subject(s):** English; BA 1950; BA (Patna) 1944; MA (Allahabad) 1946. **Tutor(s):** F Thistlethwaite. **Johnian Relatives:** cousin of Kumar Durganand Sinha (1947). **Educ:** Patna Collegiate School, India; Bisheswar Seminary, Chapra; Williams High English School, Supaul; George Coronation High English School, Nawadah; Patna College, India; Allahabad University, India. **Career:** University Professor and Head of English Department, Bhagalpur University; Lecturer in English, Patna College 1946–1948; Professor of English, Bihar Education Service, Langat Singh College, Muzaffarpur 1951–1957; University Professor of English, Kathmandu, under the Colombo Plan 1957–1963; Padma Kanya College, Trichandra College, Tribhubhan University 1963–1966; Professor of English, Patna University 1966–1972; Principal, Ranchi College 1972–1974; Principal, Patna College 1974; Director, Higher Education, Government of Bihar, Patna 1974–1983; President, Regional Recruitment Board, State Bank of India, Patna 1983–1987. **Publications:** *The Constant Pursuit*, 1964; a number of papers in University Journals of India.

'T HART, Jacob (1939) Born 19 July 1921, The Hague, Holland; son of Jacob 't Hart, Marine Superintendent, and Johanna van der Toorn. **Tutor(s):** C W Guillebaud. **Educ:** Municipal School, Amsterdam; Private School, Singapore; Municipal School, Haarlem; Hogere Burgerschool, Haarlem; Technical High School, Delft.

THATCHER, Arthur Roger (1944) Born 22 October 1926, 315 Hagley Road, Edgbaston, Birmingham; son of Arthur Thatcher, Borough

Treasurer, and Edith Mary Ruth Dobson; m Mary Audrey Betty Street, 1950; 2 daughters. **Subject(s):** Mathematics/Economics; BA 1947; MA 1952. **Tutor(s):** J M Wordie. **Educ:** Wilmslow Preparatory School; Harden House Preparatory School, Alderley Edge; The Leys School, Cambridge. **Career:** Meteorological Officer, RN 1947–1949; Statistician, North Western Gas Board 1949–1952; Admiralty 1952–1961; Cabinet Office 1961–1963; Ministry of Labour 1963–1968; Department of Employment 1968–1978 (Director of Statistics 1968–1978, Deputy Secretary 1972–1978); Director, Office of Population Censuses and Surveys, Registrar General for England and Wales 1978–1986. **Honours:** CB 1974. **Publications:** (jointly) *The Force of Mortality at Ages 80 to 120*, Odense University Press, 1998; many articles and papers, mostly in official publications, statistical and demographic journals.

THEOBALD, Raymond Walter (1920) Born 19 November 1897, 36 Southtown Road, Southtown, Gorleston, Great Yarmouth, Norfolk; son of William Mann Theobald, Missionary, School Principal, and Mary Ann Forder; m Irene. **Tutor(s):** E A Benians. **Educ:** Hebron Preparatory School, Coonoor, India; Stanes European High School, Coonoor, India; Bristol Grammar School. Died 4 June 1950.

THEOPHILUS, Reginald Arthur (1900) Born 18 October 1880, Port Elizabeth, South Africa; son of John Theophilus, Farmer, and Emily Augusta Birch. **Subject(s):** Classics; BA 1903. **Tutor(s):** E E Sikes. **Educ:** Bedford Grammar School. **Career:** Solicitor, Port Elizabeth 1906.

THISTLETHWAITE, Professor Frank (1934) Born 24 July 1915, 11 Powell Street, Burnley; son of Lee Thistlethwaite, Cotton Cloth Salesman, and Florence Nightingale Thornber; m Jane Hosford, 1940 (d 1992); 2 sons, 3 daughters. **Subject(s):** History/English; BA 1938; MA 1941; Honorary LHD (Colorado) 1972; Honorary DCL (UEA) 1980; Honorary DSc (Minnesota) 1994; Honorary FRIBA 1985; FRHistS. **Tutor(s):** J S Boys Smith. **Johnian Relatives:** father of Miles Thistlethwaite (1966). **Educ:** Coal Clough Council School; Burnley Grammar School; Bootham School. **Career:** Commonwealth Fund Fellow, University of Minnesota 1938–1940; British Press Service, New York 1940–1941; RAF 1941–1945; Seconded to Office of War Cabinet (Joint-American Secretariat) 1942–1945; Title B Fellow 1945–1961, College Lecturer in History 1949–1961, SJC; Lecturer, Faculty of Economics and Politics, University of Cambridge 1949–1961; Founding Vice-Chancellor 1961–1980, Emeritus Professor 1980, UEA. **Appointments:** Editor, *The Cambridge Review* 1937; Tutor 1945–1949, Supervisor in History 1948–1950, Praelector 1952–1956, Steward 1958–1961, SJC; Member, Institute for Advanced Study, Princeton 1954–1955; Chairman, British Association for American Studies 1955–1959; Visiting Professor of American Civilization, University of Pennsylvania 1956; Governor, Sedbergh School 1958–1973; Member, IUPC 1962–1981 (Chairman 1977–1981); US-UK Educational (Fulbright) Commission 1964–1979; Marshall Aid Commemoration Commission 1964–1980; Member, Provisional Council, University of Zambia 1965–1969; Chairman, Committee of Management, Institute of US Studies, University of London 1966–1980; Adviser to National Council of Higher Education, Ceylon 1967; European Advisory Council, Salzburg Seminar in American Studies 1969–1974; Member, Academic Advisory Committee, Open University 1969–1974; Member, Provisional Council, University of Malawi 1971–1975; Board, British Council 1971–1982; Visiting Fellow, Henry E Huntington Library, California 1973; British Committee of Award, Harkness Fellowships 1974–1980; Member, Provisional Council, University of Mauritius 1974–1984; Honorary Fellow, SJC 1974; Leverhulme Emeritus Fellow 1981; President, Friends of Cambridge University Library 1983–1995; Honorary Professor of History, University of Mauritius 1981; Hill Visiting Professor, University of Minnesota 1986. **Awards:** Exhibition, SJC 1933; Scholarship, SJC 1936–1937. **Honours:** CBE 1979. **Publications:** *The Great Experiment: An Introduction to the History of the American People*, 1955; *The Anglo–American Connection in the Early Nineteenth Century*, 1958; *Dorset Pilgrims: the story of West Country pilgrims who went to New England in the 17th century*, 1989; 'Migration from Europe Overseas in the Nineteenth and Twentieth

Centuries', (ed Rudolph J Vecoli and Suzanne M Sinke), *A Century of European Migrations 1830–1930*, 1991; *A Lancashire Family Inheritance*, 1996; *Our War 1938–45*, 1997; *Cambridge Years 1945–61*, 1999; *Origins: A Personal Reminiscence of the Founding of the University of East Anglia*, 2000; *A Reminiscence of Undergraduate Life*, 2001; contributions to *New Cambridge Modern History* and other historical works and journals; contribution to (ed M G Ross) *New Universities in the Modern World*. Died 17 February 2003.

THODAY, David Robert Gabriel (1928) Born 16 March 1911, 25 Halifax Road, Chesterton, Cambridgeshire; son of David Thoday, Professor of Botany, and Mary Gladys Sykes; m Margaret Kellock Durrell. **Subject(s):** Natural Sciences; BA 1933; MA 1940. **Tutor(s):** C W Guillebaud. **Educ:** Ladybarn House School, Manchester; South African College School, Cape Town; Friars School, Bangor; Bootham School, York. **Career:** Housemaster, Worksop College. Died 8 June 1983.

THOM, Alan Watson (1941) Born 11 July 1923, Thalassa, Dunlop, Ayrshire; son of Alexander Thom, Lecturer in Engineering, and Jeanie Boyd Kirkwood. **Subject(s):** Mechanical Sciences; BA 1944. **Tutor(s):** S J Bailey. **Educ:** Dunlop Public School; Kilmarnock Academy; University of Glasgow. **Career:** RAE, Farnborough. **Appointments:** Cadet, SJC. **Awards:** Ricardo Prize in Thermodynamics, University of Cambridge; John Bernard Seely Prize, University of Cambridge 1943. Died 27 April 1945.

THOM, Robert Wilson (1931) Born 14 June 1912, Buckingham Terrace, Glasgow; son of Robert Thom, Merchant, and Mary Muir Wilson. **Subject(s):** Geography; BA 1935. **Educ:** Glasgow Academy.

THOMAS, Adin Bryn (1938) Born 18 December 1919, 9 Pavillion Terrace, Wood Lane, Hammersmith; son of David Thomas, Science Teacher, and Florence Eleanor Lock. **Subject(s):** Mathematics/Mechanical Sciences; BA 1941; MA 1945; FIEE. **Tutor(s):** J S Boys Smith. **Johnian Relatives:** father of David Thomas (1967). **Educ:** Islwyn Elementary School, Porth; Porth Boys' County School; Barry County School; University of Cardiff. **Career:** Radio Department, RAE 1941–1945; Research Officer, Radiophysics Division, Council for Scientific and Industrial Research, Sydney 1966.

THOMAS, Alfred Llewelyn (1919) Born 10 December 1894, Weedon, Northamptonshire; son of John Thomas, Farmer and Grazier, and Mary Selina Adams; m (1) Brenda Mary Champion, 21 April 1927, St Nicholas's Church, Luton, (2) Mary Birkbeck Wooldridge, 14 January 1954; 1 son (David Llewelyn b 17 October 1930). **Subject(s):** Natural Sciences; BA 1921; MA 1926; Diploma in Agriculture (Cambridge) 1922. **Tutor(s):** E A Benians. **Johnian Relatives:** father of David Llewelyn Thomas (1951). **Educ:** University of Birmingham; Rugby Lower School; Wellingborough Grammar School. **Career:** Oxford and Bucks Light Infantry 1914–1919, including active service in France and Solonika (wounded 1916, Mentioned in Despatches 1918); Master, Sutton Valence School 1923–1928; Biology Master, Tonbridge School 1928. Died 18 October 1979.

THOMAS, Alwyne Bell Wyndham (1920) Born 8 January 1899, Maindee Hall, Newport, Monmouthshire; son of Wyndham Partridge Thomas, Ironmaster, and Margaret Gairdner Shankland Bell; m Gladys Blain, 8 June 1923, St Margaret's, Warnham, Sussex. **Tutor(s):** E E Sikes. **Educ:** Llanyre Hall, Llandrindod Wells; Harrow School; Army College, Heath End, Farnham. **Career:** Lieutenant, 4th Royal Sussex Regiment.

THOMAS, Andrew Rowland Benedick (1923) Born 11 October 1904, 9 Princes Avenue, Great Crosby, Lancashire; son of William Rowland Thomas, Schoolmaster, and Ellen Myfanwy Phillips; m Elizabeth Ann Levo, 1967; 1 daughter. **Subject(s):** Mathematics; BA 1926; MA 1931. **Tutor(s):** J M Wordie. **Career:** Mathematics Master, Blundell's School, Tiverton 1926–1969 (Housemaster 1940–1955). **Publications:** *Chess for the Love of it*, 1973; *Chess Techniques*. Died 18 May 1985.

THOMAS, Cecil Holt (1922) Naval Officer.

THOMAS, David Biron (1925) Born 7 March 1907, 418 Streatham High Road, Streatham, Surrey; son of Cyril Meurig Thomas, Schoolmaster, and Marion Biron. **Subject(s):** Moral Sciences/Classics; BA 1928. **Tutor(s):** M P Charlesworth. **Educ:** Burlington House, Richmond; Cheltonia College, Streatham; Pocklington School. **Career:** Honorary Research Associate in English, UCL 1959. **Awards:** Dowman Exhibition, SJC 1925.

THOMAS, David Ian (1944) Born 17 December 1924, 1 Carden Terrace, Aberdeen; son of William Thomas, HM Inspector of Schools, and Elizabeth Morgan. **Subject(s):** Law; BA 1946. **Tutor(s):** S J Bailey. **Educ:** Worcester School for the Blind; University College of Wales, Aberystwyth. Died 9 August 1962.

THOMAS, David Llewelyn (1922) Born 14 January 1904, Bank House, 315 Kentish Town Road, St Pancras, London; son of David Rice Thomas, Bank Accountant, and Isabella Hutchison. **Subject(s):** History; BA 1925; MA 1929. **Tutor(s):** E A Benians. **Educ:** Forest School, Walthamstow; Mill Hill School. Died 16 March 1979.

THOMAS, David Llewelyn (1936) Born 1 March 1918, Pontypridd, Glamorganshire; son of Robert William Thomas, Bank Sub-Manager, and Myfanwy Llewelyn. **Subject(s):** Law; BA 1939; MA 1943. **Johnian Relatives:** brother of Robert Edgar Thomas (1940). **Educ:** Oystermouth Council School, Swansea; Swansea Grammar School; Newport Boys' High School. **Career:** 132nd Field Regiment, North Africa 1939–1945; Collins, Woods & Vaughan Jones, Solicitors, Swansea 1946. Died 22 March 1979.

THOMAS, Donald Gomer Cobden (1924) Born 8 February 1906, 5 Courtland Terrace, Merthyr Tydfil, Glamorgan; son of Gomer Llewellyn Thomas, Colliery Proprietor, and Isobel Erie Wenonah Johnson. BA 1927; MA 1959. **Tutor(s):** E A Benians. **Johnian Relatives:** brother of Robert Llewellyn Thomas (1913), Wendell William Thomas (1914), and of Mervyn Lincoln Thomas (1922). **Educ:** Mill Hill School.

THOMAS, Edward William (1927) Born 8 December 1909, 4 Bilton Road, Rugby, Warwickshire; son of Edgar Holmes Thomas, Bank Manager, and Elizabeth Eleanor Bickley; m Elizabeth Murray Ward, 17 August 1939; 4 sons (Howard b 20 October 1940, Martin b 27 April 1942, Nigel b 20 September 1944 and Giles b 31 August 1946). **Subject(s):** Classics/History; BA 1931; MA 1935. **Tutor(s):** M P Charlesworth. **Johnian Relatives:** cousin of Howard Reginald Thomas (1928); father of Martin William Thomas (1960). **Educ:** Lindley Lodge School; Rugby School. **Career:** Schoolmaster, University College School 1932–1933; Schoolmaster, King Edward VII School, Sheffield 1933–1939; Schoolmaster, Haberdashers' Aske's Hatcham Boys' School 1939–1965. Died 28 October 1965.

THOMAS, Eric Leslie Vivian (1917) Born 2 September 1899, Carbis Bay, Cornwall; son of Joseph Vivian Thomas, Solicitor, and Edith Mary Craze. **Subject(s):** Law; BA 1921; LLB 1921. **Tutor(s):** E E Sikes. **Educ:** West Cornwall College, Penzance; Wycliffe College. **Career:** Second Lieutenant, RGA 1918; Solicitor 1923; Borough Coroner 1926–1927; Partner, Vivian Thomas & Jervis 1946–1961. **Appointments:** President, Cornwall Law Society 1952–1953. Died 6 July 1962.

THOMAS, Eric Lionel (1944) Born 7 November 1919, 6 Salop Road, Oswestry, Shropshire; son of Rowland Thomas, Newspaper Proprietor, and Elizabeth Parry. LLB (Wales) 1940. **Educ:** Leighton Park School; University College of Wales, Aberystwyth. **Career:** Captain, REME.

THOMAS, Frank Basil (1915) Born 24 June 1891, 20 Treharris Street, Roath, Cardiff; son of David Terry Thomas, Headmaster, and Mary Ann Walton. **Tutor(s):** R P Gregory. **Johnian Relatives:** brother of Terry Thomas (1913). **Educ:** Municipal Secondary School, Cardiff; University of London. **Career:** Master, St Matthew's School, Cambridge 1914.

THOMAS, George (1937) Born 27 February 1919, 42 Chapel Street, Lye, Stourbridge; son of William Richard Thomas, Commercial Traveller, and Phoebe Collins; m Elizabeth. **Subject(s):** Classics; BA 1940; MA 1944. **Tutor(s):** R L Howland. **Educ:** Station Road Elementary School, Witton, Birmingham; Cemetery Road Infant's School, Lye; Orchard Lane Elementary School, Lye; King Edward VI School, Stourbridge. **Career:** Technical College Principal. **Awards:** Minor Scholarship, SJC 1936. Died 14 December 1994.

THOMAS, The Revd Harold Augustus (1905) (admitted as a Non-Collegiate Student 1904) Born 10 September 1876, The Vicarage, Beguildy, Radnorshire; son of Abraham Thomas, Clerk in Holy Orders, and Elizabeth Margaret Hamer. **Subject(s):** Law; BA 1907; MA 1948; LLB 1907. **Tutor(s):** E E Sikes. **Educ:** Christ's College, Brecon. **Career:** Deacon 1908; Curate, Leesfield 1908–1912; Priest 1909; Curate, Lancaster 1912–1916; Vicar, Dobcross, Oldham, Lancashire 1916–1963.

THOMAS, Howard Reginald (1928) Born 7 September 1909, 13 Charlotte Street, Leamington, Warwickshire; son of Basil Lewis Thomas, Chartered Accountant, and Effie Susan Assinder; m Dorothy Pike; 6 daughters (Susan, Rachel, Esther, Joanna, Penina and Thomasina). **Subject(s):** Geography/Archaeology and Anthropology; BA 1931; MA 30 June 1935. **Tutor(s):** M P Charlesworth. **Johnian Relatives:** cousin of Edward William Thomas (1927); cousin, once removed, of Martin William Thomas (1960). **Educ:** Mount Radford School, Exeter; Perse School, Cambridge.

THOMAS, Keith (Colwinston) (1946) Born 11 August 1928, Greystones, Graigwen, Pontypridd, Glamorganshire; son of Edward Percival Thomas, Schoolmaster, and Vernie John. **Subject(s):** English/Law; BA 1949; MA 1953. **Tutor(s):** F Thistlethwaite. **Educ:** Herbert Thompson Elementary School; Canton High School. **Career:** Colonial Administrative Service 1950–1953; Ministry of Defence 1954–1987; Consultant, MOD and FCO 1988–1997.

THOMAS, Leonard Cameron (1923) Born 25 August 1904, 43 Willows Crescent, Balsall Heath, Birmingham; son of Leonard Kirkby Thomas, Surgeon, Medical Practitioner and Anaesthetist, and Annie Hay Cameron. **Tutor(s):** B F Armitage. **Educ:** Greenhill School, Moseley; King Edwards High School, Birmingham.

THOMAS, Mervyn Lincoln (1922) Born 9 April 1903, 5 Courtland Terrace, Merthyr Tydfil, Glamorgan; son of Gomer Llewellyn Thomas, Colliery Proprietor, and Isobel Erie Wenonah Johnson; m Joan Lavinia Gotzler, 27 August 1955. BA 1926; MA 1935. **Tutor(s):** E A Benians. **Johnian Relatives:** brother of Robert Llewellyn Thomas (1913), Wendell William Thomas (1914) and of Donald Gomer Cobden Thomas (1924). **Educ:** Wycliffe College; Mill Hill School. Died 3 April 1972.

THOMAS, Norman (1945) Born 3 April 1927, 7 Parker Street, Gorton, Manchester; son of Fred Thomas, Clerk, and Marion Stokes. **Tutor(s):** J M Wordie. **Educ:** Beaver Road School, Manchester; William Hulme's Grammar School, Manchester; Stockport Grammar School.

THOMAS, Major Norman Henry (1930) Born 14 March 1911, Maple Street, Blackpool; son of Lewis Charles Thomas, Laundry Proprietor, and Beatrice Elizabeth Taylor; 2 sons (David and Nigel). **Subject(s):** Law; BA 1933; MA 1937. **Tutor(s):** C W Guillebaud. **Educ:** Palatine Road School, Blackpool; C of E School, Clitheroe; Royal Grammar School, Clitheroe. **Career:** Major, RE (TA and War Service); Clerk and Solicitor, Northumbrian River Authority 1937–1974. Died 30 June 1989.

THOMAS, Richard Charles Clement (1947) Born 28 January 1929, 160 Donald Street, Cardiff; son of David John Richard Thomas, Depot Manager, and Edna Madeline Dodd. **Tutor(s):** G C L Bertram. **Educ:** Bryntirion School, Bridgend; Blundell's School, Tiverton.

THOMAS, Richard Keay (1941) Born 27 January 1923, Redditch, Worcestershire; son of William George Thomas, Solicitor, and Ethel Neason. **Tutor(s):** S J Bailey. **Educ:** Finstall Park, Bromsgrove; Dean Close School, Cheltenham.

THOMAS, Richard Victor (1921) (Migrated to Gonville & Caius College 1921) Born 15 November 1903, Bygrave Park, Bygrave, Baldock, Hertfordshire; son of Richard Frederick Hill Thomas, Colonial Service, and Emily Stapleton. **Subject(s):** Natural Sciences; BA (Caius) 1925; MA (Caius) 1936. **Tutor(s):** E Cunningham. **Educ:** Grove House School, Baldock; Private Tuition (The Revd H P Waller), Radwell Rectory; The Grammar School, Portsmouth; Gonville & Caius College, Cambridge. **Awards:** Scholarship, Gonville & Caius 1921.

THOMAS, Robert Bernard Hobson (1913) Born 25 June 1894, 1 Erddig Terrace, Wrexham, Denbighshire; son of John Hobson Thomas, Baptist Minister, and Margaret Jane McLean; m Dora Nicholson Lapthorn, 2 April 1927, Christ Church, Southsea. **Subject(s):** Classics/Law; BA 1916; MA 1920. **Tutor(s):** E E Sikes. **Educ:** Bedford Modern School; Portsmouth Grammar School. **Career:** Second Lieutenant, RGA, WWI. **Publications:** 'Aeschylus and Marlowe', *The Eagle*, 37, 1916. **Awards:** Scholarship, SJC; Hawksley Burbury Prize, SJC 1916. Died 16 March 1928.

THOMAS, Robert Edgar (1940) Born 15 May 1920, Bronyglyn, Vicarage Road, Penygraig, Glamorganshire; son of Robert William Thomas, Bank Manager, and Myfanwy Llewelyn; m Nesta. **Subject(s):** Law; BA 1943; MA 1947; LLB 1944. **Tutor(s):** C W Guillebaud. **Johnian Relatives:** brother of David Llewelyn Thomas (1936). **Educ:** Oystermouth Council School, Mumbles; Swansea Grammar School; Newport High School. **Career:** Solicitor; co-founder (with brother), David & Roy Thomas Solicitors, Swansea 1948. Died 30 April 1996.

THOMAS, Robert Llewellyn (1913) Born 31 July 1894, 2 Somerset Place, Merthyr Tydfil, Glamorgan; son of Gomer Llewellyn Thomas, Colliery Proprietor, and Isobel Erie Wenonah Johnson. **Tutor(s):** L H K Bushe-Fox. **Johnian Relatives:** brother of Wendell William Thomas (1914), Mervyn Lincoln Thomas (1922) and of Donald Gomer Cobden Thomas (1924). **Educ:** Court School, Merthyr; Wycliffe College. **Career:** Second Lieutenant, Welsh Regiment, WWI.

THOMAS, Dr Ronald (1943) Born 22 February 1926, 4 Garth Villas, Merthyr Tydfil; son of Harold Edwin Thomas, Medical Practitioner, and Phyllis May Griffiths. **Subject(s):** Natural Sciences; BA 1946; MA 1950; MB 1950; BChir 1950. **Tutor(s):** S J Bailey. **Educ:** Dixton House School, Monmouth; Monmouth School. **Career:** House Physician, Royal Southampton Hospital; GP 1963. Died 4 April 1963.

THOMAS, Dr Terry (1913) (Admitted as a Non-Collegiate student 1911) Born 19 October 1888, 40 Sapphire Street, Roath, Cardiff, Wales; son of David Terry Thomas, Schoolmaster, and Mary Ann Walton; m Mair Davies, 1915; 2 daughters (Jean and Eryl). **Subject(s):** Mathematics/Natural Sciences/Law; BA 1913; LLB 1914; MA 1919; BSc (Wales); BSc (London) 1908; PhD (London) 1922; Honorary LLD (Leeds) 1948. **Tutor(s):** L H K Bushe-Fox. **Johnian Relatives:** brother of Frank Basil Thomas (1915). **Educ:** Cardiff Municipal School; University College, Cardiff. **Career:** Lecturer and Demonstrator, Glamorgan Summer School 1906–1914; Chief Science Master, The Academy, Inverurie, Aberdeen 1909–1914; Head, Military and Engineering Side 1914–1922, Lieutenant, OTC, WWI, Haileybury College; Headmaster, Leeds Grammar School 1923–1953. **Appointments:** Member, Headmasters' Conference Committee; Captain OTC; President, Incorporated Association of Headmasters 1936; Member, Norwood Committee; Member, Court of Leeds University; JP, Leeds 1937; Chairman, Leeds Bench of Magistrates 1957; Chairman, Psychiatry and Law Committee; Deputy Chairman, Leeds Group B Hospital Management Committee 1948–1954 (Chairman, Finance Committee); Chairman, Visiting Magistrates, Leeds Prison

1948–1963; Chairman, Leeds Juvenile Court; Chairman, Leeds Bench of Magistrates 1950–1963; President, West Riding Branch, Magistrates' Association 1956–1958; President, Leeds Literary and Philosophical Society 1952–1953; Member, National Association Board Tribunal; Education Adviser, RAF Benevolent Fund. **Awards:** Isaac Roberts Science Scholarship, University College, Cardiff; Foundation Scholarship, SJC. **Publications:** Mathematical and Science papers for Army Candidates; *Revision Arithmetic, Logarithms, Slide Rule, Mensuration, Specific Gravity and Density*, Crosby Lockwood & Son, 1919 (second revised edition 1920); *Notes on Dynamics*, Crosby Lockwood & Son, 1920; *Outlines of the Calculus for Science and Engineering Students*, Mills & Boon, 1922; *Revision Arithmetic and Mensuration*, Mills & Boon, 1924 (third revised edition); *Outlines of Dynamics*, Mills & Boon, 1927 (third revised edition) *The Leeds Intelligence Test*, Bell & Sons, 1930; *The Science of Marking*, John Murray, 1930. Died 22 July 1978.

THOMAS, Theodore Lynam (1919) Born 17 September 1900, 19 Folly Lane, Warrington, Lancashire; son of Llewelyn Wynn Thomas, Clerk in Holy Orders, and Helen Penelope Lynam; m Margaret Evelyn Astbury, 8 April 1931, Church of St Philip and St James, Oxford; 2 sons (Nigel Eric Lynam b 18 February 1933 and Michael Gavin Lynam b 14 August 1936). **Subject(s):** Geography; BA 1922; MA 1935. **Tutor(s):** E E Sikes. **Johnian Relatives:** son of Llewelyn Wynn Thomas (1886); father of Nigel Eric Lynam Thomas (1953). **Educ:** Preparatory School, Bowden, Cheshire; St John's School, Leatherhead; Oxford Preparatory School; King William's College, Isle of Man. **Career:** Master, King William's College, Isle of Man 1922–1923; Master, Rugby School 1923–1944; Headmaster, Repton School 1944–1961. **Appointments:** Governor, Dartington Hall School; First Ombudsman for the Law Society. **Awards:** Sizarship, SJC 1919. Died 15 May 1976.

THOMAS, Wendell William (1914) Born 21 April 1896, 2 Somerset Place, Merthyr Tydfil, Glamorgan; son of Gomer Llewellyn Thomas, Colliery Proprietor, and Isobel Erie Wenonah Johnson. **Subject(s):** Modern and Medieval Languages. **Tutor(s):** L H K Bushe-Fox. **Johnian Relatives:** brother of Robert Llewellyn Thomas (1913), Mervyn Lincoln Thomas (1922) and of Donald Gomer Cobden Thomas (1924). **Educ:** Court School, Merthyr Tydfil; Wycliffe College. **Career:** Lieutenant, South Wales Borderers, then Captain, Special List (Trench Mortar Battery), WWI.

THOMAS, William Harvey Evelyn (1921) Born 25 April 1898, 23 Carlisle Mansions, Westminster, London; son of Harvey Thomas, Journalist, and Evelyn Frances Ogle Moore; m Eileen Cook, 6 August 1946, Devizes. **Tutor(s):** B F Armitage. **Educ:** Earlywood School, Ascot; Wellington College.

THOMASSON, John Walker (1941) Born 25 July 1923, 75 Manchester Road, Audenshaw, Manchester; son of John Thomasson, Schoolmaster, and Marion Rain Walker. **Tutor(s):** S J Bailey. **Educ:** Manchester Road Council School; Manchester Grammar School.

THOMLINSON, William Francis Kirk (1915) Born 30 September 1893, The Green, Seaton Carew, Durham; son of William Thomlinson, Colonel, and Hannah Kirk. **Tutor(s):** E E Sikes. **Educ:** Courtenay Lodge School, Sutton Courtenay.

THOMPSON, Alexander Challis (1904) Born 18 December 1884, Skipsea, Yorkshire; son of Robert Thompson, Clerk in Holy Orders, and Caroline Alice Alpe. BA 1911. **Tutor(s):** D MacAlister. **Educ:** The Grammar School, St Bees.

THOMPSON, Alfred Ross (1906) Born 31 October 1886, The School House, Charlwood, Horley, Surrey; son of Lionel Thompson, Secretary to West Sussex Education Committee, and Clara Jane Davey; m Kathleen Oliver Ling (d 1967); 4 sons (John, Philip, Roger and Peter), 1 daughter (Mary). **Subject(s):** Mathematics; BA 1909; MA 1913.

Tutor(s): L H K Bushe-Fox. **Johnian Relatives:** brother of Sidney Lionel Thompson (1907); father of John Ross Thompson (1937), Roger Ross Thompson (1943) and of Peter Ross Thompson (1944). **Educ:** King Edward VI Middle School, Norwich; Horsham Grammar School. **Career:** Master 1911–1919, Lieutenant, OTC, WWI, Berkhamsted School; Master, Bedford Modern School 1919–1921; Headmaster, Ashton Grammar School, Dunstable 1921–1927; Headmaster, Solihull School, Warwickshire 1927–1947. **Awards:** Exhibition, SJC 1907. Died 26 November 1972.

THOMPSON, Arthur Denys Halstead (1927) Born 15 February 1907, 16 Fife Street, Darlington, County Durham; son of Arthur Stanley Thompson, Clerk in Holy Orders, and Emma Jane Cousthope; m (1) Rosemary (d), (2) Betty; 1 son, 1 daughter (d 1984), 1 stepson. **Subject(s):** Classics/English; BA 1930; MA 1937. **Tutor(s):** M P Charlesworth. **Educ:** Darlington Grammar School; St John's School, Leatherhead. **Career:** English Master, Gresham's School, Holt 1942; Air Ministry 1942–1945; Headmaster, Yeovil Grammar School 1945. **Appointments:** Founder, National Association for the Teaching of English. **Publications:** *The Uses of Poetry*, 1978; *Distant Voices*, 1978; *Reading and Discrimination*; *Rhyme and Reason*; *Between the Lines*; *Change and Tradition in Rural England*; (ed) *Scrutiny*; (ed) *Recollections and Impressions*; (with F R Leavis) *Culture and Environment*; Founder, *English in Schools*, which became *The Use of English*. Died 28 February 1988.

THOMPSON, Bruce Logan (1925) Born 17 January 1907, Westbourne, Bowness, Windermere, Westmorland; son of Charles Edward Kayss Thompson, Colliery Agent, and Agnes Logan. **Subject(s):** English; BA 1928. **Tutor(s):** E E Sikes. **Johnian Relatives:** nephew of Arthur James Kayss Thompson (1891). **Educ:** Preparatory School, Windermere; Private Tuition. **Career:** Assistant Secretary, National Trust. Died 10 March 1977.

THOMPSON, Charles Brodrick (1908) Born 15 April 1889, 12 Archbold Terrace, Newcastle Upon Tyne, Northumberland; son of Henry Brodrick Thompson, Solicitor, and Elizabeth Georgina Morgan. **Subject(s):** Classics; BA 1911. **Tutor(s):** E E Sikes. **Educ:** Newcastle Preparatory School; Shrewsbury School. **Career:** Assistant District Commissioner, East Africa Protectorate 1911; First Grade Administrative Officer, Kenya 1924. Died 29 June 1954.

THOMPSON, Christopher Lawton (1937) See NEWTON THOMPSON.

THOMPSON, Cyril Newton (1911) Born 24 June 1891, Butterworth, Transkei, South Africa; son of Newton Ogilvie Thompson, Resident Magistrate, Civil Service, and Jessie Blanche Lawton; m Joyce Nettlefold, 21 February 1917, Christ Church, Lancaster Gate, London; 3 sons (Mark, Christopher and Oswald). **Subject(s):** Law; BA 1914; MA 1919; LLB 1914; KC 1938. **Tutor(s):** L H K Bushe-Fox. **Johnian Relatives:** father of Christopher Lawton Newton Thompson (1937). **Educ:** Rhodes University College, Grahamstown, South Africa. **Career:** Captain, Rifle Brigade (final rank, Major), later employed Officer Cadet Battalion (wounded twice) WWI; Admitted to the Cape Bar 1917; Lecturer in Criminal Law, University of Cape Town 1944; President, Cape Bar Council 1944; Appointed to the Bench 1944; Acting Judge of Appeal 1952. **Appointments:** President, Western Province Lawn Tennis Association. **Awards:** Porter Scholarship, University of South Africa. Died 21 February 1958.

THOMPSON, Eric Clifford (1939) Born 30 July 1921, Port Sunlight, Bebington, Wirral, Cheshire; son of William Thompson, Commercial Clerk, and Beatrice Jane Cliffe; m Gwenda. BA 1942; MA 1946. **Tutor(s):** C W Guillebaud. **Educ:** New Chester Road County School, Port Sunlight; Wirral Grammar School, Bebington. **Career:** Intelligence Corps 1941–1945; Officer, House of Commons; Junior Library Clerk, later Assistant Librarian 1946–1977. **Awards:** Exhibition, SJC. Died 20 August 1977.

THOMPSON, Ernest Edward (1903) Born 17 January 1884, East Haddon, Northamptonshire; son of Edward Thompson, Schoolmaster, and Emily May. **Subject(s):** Natural Sciences; BA 1906; MA 1910. **Tutor(s):** D MacAlister. **Educ:** East Haddon National School; Northampton Modern Technical School. **Career:** Master, Banham School, Norfolk 1906–1909; Master, Thetford Grammar School 1909–1914; Headmaster, Diss Secondary School 1914; Second Lieutenant, RGA. **Awards:** Foundation Scholarship, SJC. Died 16 October 1918 (killed in action).

THOMPSON, Frank William (1924) Born 19 September 1906, 175 Palgrave Road, Great Yarmouth, Norfolk; son of William Thompson, Commercial Traveller, and Florence Leeson. **Subject(s):** Natural Sciences (Chemistry); BA 1927. **Tutor(s):** B F Armitage. **Johnian Relatives:** brother of Ralph Herbert Thompson (1928). **Educ:** Northgate Street School, Great Yarmouth; Edward Worledge School, Great Yarmouth; The Grammar School, Great Yarmouth. **Awards:** Exhibition, SJC 1924.

THOMPSON, Guy Warren St Clair (ST CLAIR-THOMPSON) (1924) Born 23 March 1906, Glasfryn Towyn, County Merioneth; son of Stephen John Thompson, of independent means, and Lily Caroline Patti Wright Warren; m Katharine Honor Spender, 1938; 1 son (Stephen John b 17 December 1948). BA 1927. **Tutor(s):** J M Wordie. **Johnian Relatives:** father of Stephen John St Clair-Thompson (1967). **Educ:** Windlesham House School, Brighton; Southern Cross, Brighton & Nevill House, Eastbourne; Malvern College. **Career:** Botanist, Tsetse Research Department, Tanganyika 1927–1932; Cambridge Forestry Department 1932–1934; Oxford 'Refresher Course' 1934–1936; Gold Coast Forestry Service 1936–1938; Uganda Forestry Service (Provincial Forest Officer at retirement) 1938–1955; Timber Pest Consultant 1955–1965. **Publications:** *The Protection of Woodlands*, 1927. Died 25 April 1970.

THOMPSON, Harold Lenox (1923) Born 18 January 1904, 28 Kingswood Road, Clapham, London; son of Harry Thompson, Optician, and Edith Marie Offer; m Helen Mary; 2 sons (Richard and Edward). BA 1927; MA 1931. **Tutor(s):** B F Armitage. **Educ:** Royal Chapel Savoy School; Emanuel School, Wandsworth. Died 26 March 1966.

THOMPSON, Harry Kayss (1902) Born 12 April 1880, Lauder Villa, Preston, Lancashire; son of Thomas Thompson, Bank Manager, and Ann Bambridge Kayss. BA 1905. **Tutor(s):** J R Tanner; C E Graves. **Educ:** Lancaster Grammar School.

THOMPSON, John Ross (1937) Born 10 May 1918, The Limes, Berkhampsted; son of Alfred Ross Thompson, Schoolmaster, and Kathleen Oliver Ling; m Alison Patricia Blows, 29 December 1960; 1 son (David Ross b 1962), 1 daughter (Joanna Ross b 1964). **Subject(s):** Natural Sciences; BA 1941; MA 1988. **Tutor(s):** J M Wordie. **Johnian Relatives:** son of Alfred Ross Thompson (1906); nephew of Sidney Lionel Thompson (1907); brother of Roger Ross Thompson (1943) and of Peter Ross Thompson (1944). **Educ:** Yardley Court, Tonbridge; Tonbridge School. **Career:** RA 1940–1946; Schoolmaster 1946–1978, Housemaster 1954–1970, Registrar 1972–1978, Marlborough College. **Appointments:** Secretary, Marlborough Club 1978–1988; Rackets correspondent, *Country Life* 1983–1998.

THOMPSON, John William (1919) Born 8 April 1895, 16 Gill Street, West Hartlepool, Durham; son of George Donkin Thompson, Railway Traffic Official, and Mary Elizabeth Martin; m (1) Joan Harriett Peckett Holden, (2) Nancy Archdale, 17 August 1948; (1) 1 son (Richard Martin Holden b 30 April 1934). **Tutor(s):** E A Benians. **Johnian Relatives:** father of Richard Martin Holden Thompson (1954). **Educ:** Secondary School, West Hartlepool; Private Tuition. **Career:** 20th Hussars 1914; 7th Cameron Highlanders 1915 (wounded and gassed); Second Lieutenant, King's Own Scottish Borderers 1917; Acting Captain, attached to 52nd Gordon Highlanders 1918; Merchant. Died 5 May 1956.

THOMPSON, The Revd Canon Dr Peter Ross (1944) Born 19 December 1926, The Grammar School, Dunstable, Bedfordshire; son of Alfred Ross Thompson, Schoolmaster, and Kathleen Oliver Ling. **Subject(s):** Natural Sciences; BA 1947; MB 1950; BChir 1950; DObstRCOG 1952; DTM&H (London) 1953. **Johnian Relatives:** son of Alfred Ross Thompson (1906); nephew of Sidney Lionel Thompson (1907); brother of John Ross Thompson (1937) and of Roger Ross Thompson (1943). **Educ:** Eversfield Preparatory School, Solihull; Yardley Court Preparatory School, Tonbridge; Oundle School; Tyndall Hall. **Career:** Missionary, Bible Churchmen's Missionary Society, Burma 1954–1966; Ordained Deacon, New Malden and Coombe 1960; Ordained Priest 1961; Rector, Slaugham, Sussex 1966–1972; Vicar, Polegate, East Sussex 1972–1992; Canon and Prebendary, Chichester Cathedral 1991–1992.

THOMPSON, Ralph Herbert (1928) Born 18 October 1909, 175 Palgrave Road, Great Yarmouth, Norfolk; son of William Thompson, Commercial Traveller, and Florence Leeson. **Subject(s):** Natural Sciences; BA 1931. **Tutor(s):** J M Wordie. **Johnian Relatives:** brother of Frank William Thompson (1924). **Educ:** Edward Worlledge School; The Grammar School, Great Yarmouth.

THOMPSON, Roger Ross (1943) Born 17 May 1925, School House, High Street, North Dunstable; son of Alfred Ross Thompson, Schoolmaster, and Kathleen Oliver Ling. **Subject(s):** Natural Sciences; BA 1946; MA 1950; CEng, FIEE. **Tutor(s):** C W Guillebaud. **Johnian Relatives:** son of Alfred Ross Thompson (1906); nephew of Sidney Lionel Thompson (1907); brother of John Ross Thompson (1937) and of Peter Ross Thompson (1944). **Educ:** Solihull School; Oundle School. **Career:** Science Master, Worksop School 1949–1952; Science Master, Cranleigh School, Surrey 1952–1956; English Electric Valve Company, Chelmsford 1956–1969; Group Research and Development Manager, Dexion Comino International Ltd, Hemel Hempstead, Hertfordshire 1969–1979; Belling Lee Inter Ltd, Enfield 1979–1987.

THOMPSON, Ronald Massicks (1917) Born 12 July 1899, 264 Abbey Road, Barrow-in-Furness, Lancaster; son of Robert Thompson, Major, The King's Own, and Christine Huartson; m Olive Kathleen Cox; 1 son (Richard Brian Massicks b 15 February 1931). **Tutor(s):** E E Sikes. **Johnian Relatives:** father of Richard Brian Massicks Thompson (1950). **Educ:** St Aubyns Preparatory School, Barrow-in-Furness; Sedbergh Preparatory School; Sedbergh School; Courtenay Lodge School.

THOMPSON, Lieutenant Colonel Sidney Lionel (1907) Born 29 June 1888, 190 Lee Bank Road, Edgbaston, Birmingham; son of Lionel Thompson, Secretary to West Sussex Education Committee, and Clara Jane Davey; m Gwynneth Wallece Moncrieff. BA 1910. **Tutor(s):** L H K Bushe-Fox. **Johnian Relatives:** brother of Alfred Ross Thompson (1906); uncle of John Ross Thompson (1937), Roger Ross Thompson (1943) and of Peter Ross Thompson (1944). **Educ:** Edward VI Middle School, Norwich; Horsham Grammar School. **Career:** Captain, 113th Infantry, Indian Army, WWI; Lieutenant Colonel, Rajputana Rifles.

THOMPSON, Wilfrid Jansen (1923) Born 15 January 1904, Clovelly, Lynwood Road, Redhill, Surrey; son of Frank Wilfrid Thompson, HM Inspector of Schools, and Laura Winifred Davies; m Gladys Mary Fyson, 9 April 1930, St Paul's Church, Cambridge. **Subject(s):** Mathematics; BA 1926; MA 1930; Diploma, Oxford Education Course. **Tutor(s):** E Cunningham. **Johnian Relatives:** brother-in-law of Joseph Frank Jackson (1934); uncle of Richard Andrew Jackson (1966). **Educ:** King Edward VI School, Bury St Edmunds; Oakham School. **Career:** Assistant Master, Calday Grange Grammar School, West Kirby; Master, Radley College 1926–1931. **Awards:** Johnson Exhibition, SJC 1923. Died 19 February 1996.

THOMPSON, The Revd William Brian (1919) Born 22 April 1898, 13 Quernmore Road, Lancaster; son of Thomas Bainbridge Kayss Thompson, Colliery Agent and Mechanical Engineer, and Emily Agnes Bell. BA 1922; MA 1925. **Tutor(s):** E A Benians. **Educ:** Aylwyn College,

Arnside; Melbourne Church of England Grammar School; Ordination Test School, France.

THOMPSON, William Cyril (1904) Born 16 February 1885, Barwickstead, Beckermet, St John's, Cumberland; son of John Dixon Thompson, Gentleman, and Josephine Connell; m Nora; 1 son (Michael). BA 1907. **Tutor(s):** D MacAlister. **Educ:** The Grammar School, St Bees. **Career:** Solicitor, Wilkins and Thompson, Uttoxeter (later Senior Partner) 1912. **Appointments:** President, Clifton Cricket Club; Member, Parochial Church Council; Chairman, Ex-Servicemen's Association. Died 16 March 1951.

THOMSON, Arthur James (1937) Born 4 July 1919, 45 Stanhope Avenue, Finchley; son of Edward Allan Thomson, Marine Engineer, and Jane Shaw Blaikley; m Janet (Nettie) Davidson Girvan, 1946, Tyndrum, Perthshire; 2 sons (William Allan b 5 November 1946 and Peter James b 31 March 1948), 2 daughters (Margaret Jane b 1 May 1950 and Sylvia Janet b 14 March 1952). **Subject(s):** Mechanical Sciences; BA 1940; MA 1944. **Tutor(s):** J S Boys Smith. **Johnian Relatives:** cousin of David James Blaikley (1932) and Robert Marcel Blaikley (1935). **Educ:** Miss Brimer's Kindergarten and Preparatory School, London; University College School, London. **Career:** RAF 1940–1946; Dairy Farmer. Died 1 May 1977.

THOMSON, Dr Christopher Bruce (1949) Born 9 June 1929, 56 Overstrand Mansions, Battersea, London; son of Ian Stewart Thomson, Deputy Medical Officer of Health, City of Westminster, and Sarah Bruce Rennet. **Subject(s):** Natural Sciences; BA 1952; MA 1960; MRCS, LRCP 1956; DIH (Dundee) 1970; FFOM, RCP 1983. **Tutor(s):** G C L Bertram. **Educ:** Cumnor House School, South Croydon; Whitgift School, Croydon; Cranleigh School. **Career:** GP, South Devon 1957–1967; Company Medical Officer, Qatar Petroleum Company 1967–1972; Employment Medical Advisory Service (UK) (part of the Health and Safety Executive from 1974) 1972–1992; Employment Medical Adviser, Plymouth 1972–1979; Senior Employment Medical Adviser, Bristol 1979–1992. **Appointments:** Regional Specialty Adviser to the Joint Committee for Higher Medical Education; Honorary Clinical Lecturer in Occupational Medicine, Bristol University.

THOMSON, Donald Einar (1943) Born 2 October 1924, 6 Kingscote Road, Acton; son of John Thomson, Schoolmaster, and Margit Olsen. **Subject(s):** Modern and Medieval Languages/Economics; BA 1948; MA 1978. **Tutor(s):** C W Guillebaud. **Educ:** Greenhill Council School, Harrow; University College School. **Career:** Bank of England, Adviser in the Overseas Department; Seconded to Malawi as Governor, Reserve Bank of Malawi 1968–1971. **Appointments:** Council Member, National Trust for Scotland; Treasurer, Diocese of Moray, Ross and Caithness and with other charitable bodies. Died 10 December 1996.

THOMSON, Professor James Leonard (1932) Born 9 August 1905, 43 Isabella Street, Stretford, Lancashire; son of James Thomson, Marine Engineer, and Jessie Lumb. **Subject(s):** Mechanical Sciences; BA 1934; MA 1939; BSc (Manchester). **Tutor(s):** J S Boys Smith. **Educ:** Victoria Road and Balfour Road Schools, Runcorn; County Secondary School, Runcorn; College of Technology, Manchester; University of Manchester. **Career:** Mather & Platt Ltd, Manchester 1923–1926; Lecturer, Technical College, Horwich 1930–1932; Research Engineer, ICI Billingham-on-Tees 1934–1938; Lecturer, Department of Civil and Mechanical Engineering, University of London, King's College 1938; Managing Engineer, HM Royal Ordnance Factory, Pembrey, Carmarthenshire 1940–1942; Principal Technical Officer, School of Tank Technology 1942–1946; Professor of Mechanical Engineering, RMCS, Shrivenham 1946–1961; Seconded to Middle East Technical University, Ankara, Turkey 1961–1965; Professor of Civil Engineering 1965–1970 (Emeritus 1970), Head of Department of Civil Engineering 1965–1970, RMCS. **Awards:** Whitworth Senior Scholarship 1931. **Honours:** CBE 1955. **Publications:** Various scientific papers dealing with high pressure techniques. Died 12 January 1997.

THOMSON, Kenneth Roy (Lord Thomson of Fleet) (1945) Born 1 September 1923, Toronto, Canada; son of Roy Herbert Thomson, Publisher of Daily Newspapers, and Edna Annis Irvine; m Nora Marilyn Lavis, 1956; 2 sons (David Kenneth Roy and Peter John), 1 daughter (Lesley Lynne). **Subject(s):** Modern Languages/Law; BA 1947; MA 1952. **Tutor(s):** C W Guillebaud. **Educ:** North Bay Public School; Upper Canada College; Keele Street School, Toronto; Cantab College, Canada; University of Toronto, Canada. **Career:** Royal Canadian Air Force 1942–1945; Editorial Department, *Timmins Daily Press*, Timmins, Ontario, Canada 1947; Advertising Department 1948–1950, General Manager 1950–1953, *Galt Reporter*, Cambridge, Ontario, Canada; Director, Canadian and American Operations, Head Office, Thomson Newspapers, Toronto; Deputy Chairman 1966–1967, Chairman 1968–1970, Co-President (with Lord Astor) 1971–1981, Times Newspapers Ltd; Chairman of the Board, President, CEO and Director, Thomson Newspapers Ltd; Chairman, The Thomson Corporation 1976–2002. **Appointments:** President, Thomson Works of Art Ltd; Chairman, The Woodbridge Company Ltd.

THOMSON, Kenneth Sinclair (1906) Born 7 October 1886, Wellington, New Zealand; son of John Sinclair Thomson, Bank Manager, and Annie Gould. **Subject(s):** Natural Sciences; BA 1909. **Tutor(s):** E E Sikes. **Educ:** Collegiate School, Wanganui, New Zealand. **Career:** Second Lieutenant, King's Colonial Yeomanry 1910; Lieutenant, 21st Cavalry, Indian Army, then attached to 16th Cavalry. Died 3 March 1915 (killed in action near the Persian Gulf).

THOMSON, Kenneth Taylor (1930) Born 25 October 1911, Rockholme, Elmete Avenue, Rounday, Leeds; son of Robert Greig Thomson, Engineer, and Rose Clayton. **Subject(s):** Mathematics; BA 1933. **Tutor(s):** J M Wordie. **Educ:** Edinburgh Academy. **Career:** War Service 1943–1945; Patons & Baldwins Ltd, Alloa 1958. **Appointments:** Board Member, Patons and Baldwins 1951; Fellow, Textile Institute 1964; President, Worsted Spinners' Federation 1971.

THOMSON, Robert Charles Muirhead (1930) Born 2 May 1914, The Manse, Kilmaurs, Ayrshire; son of John Knox Thomson, Minister, Church of Scotland, and Marion Forrest Risk. **Tutor(s):** C W Guillebaud. **Educ:** The Edinburgh Academy; Kelvinside Academy, Glasgow.

THORNBERY, Derek Russell Wallis (1948) Born 15 June 1927, Arran Bank, Hayesden Lane, Tonbridge, Kent; son of Harold Todd Thornbery, Paint Manufacturer, and Margaret Caroline Wallis; m Juliet Pryke, 1978; 1 adopted child. **Subject(s):** English/Moral Sciences; BA 1950; MA 1977. **Tutor(s):** F Thistlethwaite. **Educ:** Bickley Hall; Bassetts, Farnborough; Clayesmore School. **Career:** Assistant Master, Ipswich School 1952–1958; Housemaster, Woolverstone Hall School 1958–1984; Assistant Master, Orwell Park Preparatory School 1984–1992. **Appointments:** Guide, Norwich Cathedral; Lecturer on Literature, History and Travel.

THORNE, The Revd Clifford Graham (1935) Born 10 March 1916, The Retreat, Summerhill Avenue, Newport; son of Godfrey Strong Thorne, Provision Merchant, and Margaretta Evans; m Dorothy; 1 son (David), 2 daughters (Elizabeth and Mary). **Subject(s):** History; BA 1938; MA 1950; FHA. **Tutor(s):** J S Boys Smith. **Educ:** St Piran's, Maidenhead; Bryanston School. **Career:** Regular Army Major 1939–1949; Regional Supplies Officer, Northern Regional Health Authority 1968–1978; Ordained Anglican Priest 1978; Honorary Curate, Ponteland, Hayton and Cumwitton, Cumbria 1978–1993. Died September 1999.

THORNELOE, Alfred Hubert (1919) Born 22 September 1899, 13 Sheep Street, Northampton; son of Alfred Edward Thorneloe, Master Tailor, and Elizabeth Annie Cole. **Subject(s):** Natural Sciences (Chemistry); BA 1922; MA 1926; BSc (London) 1922. **Tutor(s):** E E Sikes. **Educ:** Campbell Square Council School, Northampton; Moulton Council School, Northampton; Northampton Town and County School. **Awards:** Scholarship, SJC 1917.

THORNE WAITE, Arnold (1905) Born 2 December 1886, Kentish Town, Middlesex; son of Robert Thorne Waite, Water Colour Painter, and Marian Parkman; m Gwendoline Cecile Griffiths, 22 December 1941, All Saints, Llangorwen. **Subject(s):** Law/History; BA 1908; MA 1912. **Tutor(s):** C E Graves; J R Tanner. **Educ:** Mill Hill School. **Career:** University of Paris 1909–1910; Artists' Rifles 1914–1915; Lieutenant, Second Battalion KSLI 1915–1919; Military Secretary to General Cooke-Collis, Military Governor, Batoum, Trans-Caucasia 1919; Joint Headmaster, Boxgrove Preparatory School, Guildford 1932; Schoolmaster, Bournemouth, Guildford, Hampstead, Plymouth and Walmer. Died 28 September 1963.

THORNTON, George Lawrence (1932) Born 18 July 1913, 4 Binn Villas, Marsden, Staithwaite, West Riding, Yorkshire; son of Herbert Dyson Thornton, Schoolmaster, and Ann Bottomley. **Subject(s):** History; BA 1935. **Tutor(s):** E A Benians. **Educ:** Marsden Council School; Royston National School; Holgate Grammar School, Barnsley. **Awards:** Scholarship, SJC 1934; College Prize, SJC.

THORNTON, Leonard Cyril (1924) Born 20 December 1903, Alderley, Elliotdale, Cape Province, South Africa; son of Charles Harold Thornton, Merchant, and Alice Minnie Barbour. **Subject(s):** Natural Sciences; BA 1926. **Tutor(s):** J M Wordie. **Educ:** De Hoct School, Ida, South Africa; Diocesan Grammar School, St James' Road, East London, South Africa; Rhodes University College, Grahamstown. Died 1930.

THORNTON, Dr Robert Ribblesdale (1929) Born 2 April 1913, 16 Arncliffe Road, Leeds; son of Thomas Thornton, Solicitor, Town Clerk of Leeds, and Florence Gatenby; m Ruth Eleonore Tuckson, 27 January 1940; 1 son (Peter Ribblesdale b 1946), 1 daughter (Ann b 1941). **Subject(s):** Law; BA 1935; MA 1939; LLB 1936; LLM 1985; Honorary LLD (Leicester) 1987. **Tutor(s):** C W Guillebaud. **Johnian Relatives:** father of Peter Ribblesdale Thornton (1965). **Educ:** Leeds Grammar School. **Career:** Assistant Solicitor, Leeds 1938–1940; War service, RA 1940–1946; Assistant Solicitor, Leeds 1946–1947; Assistant Solicitor, Bristol 1947–1953; Deputy Town Clerk, Southampton 1953–1954; Town Clerk, Salford 1954–1966; Town Clerk, Leicester 1966–1973; Chief Executive, Leicestershire County Council 1973–1976. **Appointments:** President, Society of Town Clerks 1971; DL, Leicestershire 1974–1985; Treasurer, University of Leicester 1980–1985; Member 1976–1982, Deputy Chairman 1982, Local Government Boundary Commission for England. **Awards:** Scholarship, SJC 1936; McMahon Law Studentship 1937. **Honours:** Croix de Guerre 1945; CBE 1973.

THOROLD, Montague (1925) Born 27 March 1906, Sandon Lodge, Sandon, Stone, Staffordshire; son of James Ernest Thorold, Landowner, and Katharine Isabel Mary Tindal-Atkinson; m Helen Moye Stone, 23 November 1946, St Mary at the Wall, Colchester. BA 1928. **Tutor(s):** E A Benians. **Educ:** Hill House School, St Leonards on Sea; Lancing College. **Career:** Lieutenant Colonel, Leicestershire Regiment, WWII.

THORP, Peter Dixon (1941) Born 16 March 1924, 18 West Wells Road, Ossett, Yorkshire; son of Arthur Thorp, Solicitor's Managing Clerk, and Alice Dixon; m Doreen, 1 son (Jeremy), 1 daughter (Amanda); 1 stepdaughter (Linda). **Subject(s):** Law; BA 1947; MA 1949; LLB 1948; LLM 1985. **Tutor(s):** C W Guillebaud. **Educ:** Southdale Council School, Ossett; Batley Grammar School. **Career:** Involved in the Italy landings; Articled to a solicitor in Ossett; Consultant Solicitor, Chadwick Lawrence. **Awards:** Minor Scholarship, SJC 1940. Died 13 February 1995.

THORP, Ralph Roland (1944) Born 15 March 1926, 46 Church Street, Horwich, Lancashire; son of Herbert Thorp, Finished Work Inspector, and Mary Alice Dickinson; m Margaret Mary Mounter, 20 August 1955, St Mary's Church, Surrenden Road, Brighton; 4 sons (Richard Michael b 28 May 1956, Robert Anthony b 10 September 1957, Rodney Phillip b 3 June 1959 and Roger Simon b 19 November 1964), 1 daughter

(Katherine Margaret b 20 February 1967). **Subject(s):** Natural Sciences; BA 1947; MA 1951; MIEE; CEng. **Tutor(s):** C W Guillebaud. **Educ:** Horwich National School; Horwich Old Boys' School; Rivington and Blackrod Grammar School. **Career:** National Service, REME 1947–1949; Scientific Officer, GEC Research Laboratory, Stanmore 1950–1955; Chief Engineer and Deputy Head, Marshall of Cambridge Electronics 1955–1962; Electronics Design Engineer 1962–1972, Senior Design Engineer 1972–1993, part-time Demonstrator (in retirement) 1993, University of Cambridge Engineering Department.

THORPE, Chun (1906) Born 20 May 1886, Shanghai, China. **Tutor(s):** J R Tanner. **Educ:** University of Peking, China; Nangyang College, Shanghai, China.

THORPE, John Knowles (1920) Born 22 February 1903, Wyton, Ross on Wye, Herefordshire; son of William Thorpe, Solicitor, and Amy Gertrude Arnold. **Subject(s):** Mechanical Sciences; BA 1924; MA 1928; AMICE; AMIMechE. **Tutor(s):** E E Sikes. **Educ:** Pudleston Rectory, Herefordshire; Monmouth Grammar School; HMS *Conway* School Ship, Rock Ferry; Royal Naval College, Dartmouth. **Career:** Public Works Department, Ibadan, Southern Nigeria, 1937; Clerk to the Justices of the Peace of Ross; Admitted Solicitor, Thorpe and Thorpe, Ross, Herefordshire 1938. **Appointments:** President, Herefordshire Incorporated Law Society. Died 29 October 1957.

THORS, Thor (1926) Born 26 November 1903, Reykjavik, Iceland; son of Thor Jenson, Merchant and Company Director, and Margjet Thorbjorg Kristjansdottir; m Augusta Ingolsdottir. **Tutor(s):** E A Benians. **Educ:** Grammar School, Reykjavik, Iceland; University of Iceland; University of Paris, Sorbonne. **Career:** Ambassador to the USA and Permanent Delegate to the UN; Managing Director, Kveldulfur Fisheries and Fish Exporters 1927–1934; MP, Iceland 1933–1942; Consul General of Iceland in New York 1940–1941; Minister to the USA 1941. **Publications:** *A Report on South America*, 1935.

THRES, Douglas Philip (1920) Born 14 March 1901, 71 High Street, Ilford, Essex; son of Henry Walter Thres, Caterer, and Kate Radford; m Dr Grace Veronica Andrew, 18 September 1953, London. BA 1923; MA 1928. **Tutor(s):** E E Sikes. **Educ:** Ardingley College; Cranleigh School. **Awards:** Exhibition, SJC. Died July 1976.

THURMAN, Arthur Leslie (1922) Born 14 September 1903, Holwell, Melton Mowbray, Leics; son of William Bonser Thurman, Farmer and Farm Manager, and Ida Loverseed. **Subject(s):** Mathematics; BA 1926; MA 1930. **Tutor(s):** E Cunningham. **Educ:** The King's School, Grantham. **Awards:** Newcome Exhibition, SJC. Died 31 December 1975.

THURSBY, John Harvey (1921) Born 6 January 1903, 33 Eccleston Square, Belgravia, London; son of Harvey William Gustavies Thursby, Clerk in Holy Orders, and Margaret Emily (or Elizabeth) Mount. **Tutor(s):** E E Sikes. **Educ:** Evelyn's, near Uxbridge; Eton College.

THURSBY, Major Patrick Dehany Francis (1940) Born 29 December 1922, 13 Claremont Street, Belfast; son of Francis Dehany Victor Thursby, Army Officer (Major), and Marjorie Frances Ralph Barrow; m Gabrielle Odette Newman, 22 April 1946. **Tutor(s):** S J Bailey. **Educ:** Walton Lodge Preparatory School, Clevedon; Cheltenham College.

THURSBY, Walter (1908) Born 29 June 1890, Tretower House, Cwmdu, Crickhowell, County Brecon; son of Herbert Edward Thursby, Clerk in Holy Orders, and Elinor Eulalia Martyn. **Tutor(s):** L H K Bushe-Fox. **Educ:** Sedbergh School.

THURSFIELD, The Revd Gerald Arthur Richard (1905) Born 13 April 1886, Short Heath, Kidderminster, Worcestershire; son of Alfred Spencer Thursfield, Solicitor, and Mary Stallard; m Margaret Ethel Elliott-Taylor, 18 December 1919, St Wilfrid's, Haywards Heath. BA

1908; MA 1912; 1 son (Robert Hugh b 22 December 1928). **Tutor(s):** E E Sikes. **Johnian Relatives:** father of Robert Hugh Thursfield (1947); grandfather of Roger Lidderdale Scarlett-Smith (1978). **Educ:** Hereford Cathedral School. **Career:** Ordained Deacon 1909; Curate, St John with St Paul, Battersea 1909–1912; Ordained Priest 1910; Chaplain, Additional Clergy Society, Bassein and Aykab 1913–1917; Temporary CF, 4th Class, RACD (Mentioned in Despatches) 1917–1919; Chaplain, Dagshai 1920–1921; Chaplain, Waziristan Field Force 1921; Chaplain, Rangoon Cantonments 1921–1924 and 1930–1931; Chaplain, Maymo 1924–1928; Chaplain, Aykab 1929–1930; Chaplain, Mandalay 1931–1934; Cathedral Chaplain, Rangoon 1934–1936; Acting Archdeacon and Commissary, Rangoon 1935; Examining Chaplain to Bishop of Rangoon 1935–1936; Vicar, Sunninghill, Berkshire 1936. Died 6 February 1970.

THURSFIELD, Robert Hugh (1947) Born 22 December 1928, 78 Buckingham Road, Brighton; son of Gerald Arthur Richard Thursfield, Clerk in Holy Orders, and Margaret Ethel Taylor. **Subject(s):** Natural Sciences; BA 1950; MA 1954. **Tutor(s):** G C L Bertram. **Johnian Relatives:** son of Gerald Arthur Richard Thursfield (1905); uncle of Roger Lidderdale Scarlett-Smith (1978). **Educ:** Earleywood School, Ascot; Marlborough College.

TIARKS, The Revd Geoffrey Lewis (1926) Born 8 October 1909, 4 St Andrew's Villas, New Road, Clewer Without, Berkshire; son of Lewis Hermann Tiarks, Clerk in Holy Orders, and Edith Margaret Stokes; m Betty; 1 son, 1 daughter (d). **Subject(s):** English; BA 1931; MA 1935. **Tutor(s):** M P Charlesworth. **Johnian Relatives:** son of Lewis Hermann Tiarks (1889). **Educ:** Hawtrey's, Westgate-on-Sea; Marlborough College; Westcott House, Cambridge. **Career:** Ordained Deacon 1932; Curate, St Saviour with St Peter, Southwark 1932–1933; Ordained Priest 1933; Chaplain, HMS *London*, RN 1933–1937; Assistant Chaplain, Royal Hospital School, Holbrook 1937–1939; HMS *Repulse* and HMS *St George*, RN 1939–1943; Royal Naval College, Eaton, Cheshire 1943–1945; HMS *Vanguard*, RN 1945–1947; Assistant Chaplain, Diocesan College, Rondebosch, Cape Province 1948–1950; Rector, St Paul, Rondebosch 1950–1953; Vicar, Lyme Regis 1954–1961; Archdeacon, Isle of Wight 1961–1964; Archdeacon, Portsmouth 1964–1968; Chaplain to Lord Ramsey, Archbishop of Canterbury 1969–1974; Bishop Suffragan, Maidstone 1969–1976. Died 14 January 1987.

TICEHURST, Dr Claud Buchanan (1900) Born 1 August 1881, 1 Pevensey Road, St Leonards on Sea, Sussex; son of Augustus Rowland Ticehurst, Surgeon, and Amy Sophia Venables. **Subject(s):** Natural Sciences; BA 1903; MA 1908; BChir 1908; MRCS; LRCP 1907. **Tutor(s):** D MacAlister. **Johnian Relatives:** brother of Gerald Augustus Ticehurst (1897); uncle of Rowland Gerald Ticehurst (1931). **Educ:** Tonbridge School. **Career:** Consulting Surgeon, North Suffolk Hospital; House Physician and Resident Obstetrician, Guy's Hospital; Medical Practice, St Leonards on Sea, Sussex 1928; Ornithologist. **Appointments:** President, Norfolk and Norwich Natural History Society. **Publications:** *A History of the Birds of Suffolk*, Gurney & Jackson, 1932; *A Systematic Review of the Genus Phylloscopus, Willow-Warblers or Leaf-Warblers*, 1938. Died 17 February 1941.

TICEHURST, Dr Rowland Gerald (1931) Born 27 April 1912, 54 London Road, St Leonards on Sea; son of Gerald Augustus Ticehurst, Medical Practitioner, and Henrietta Elizabeth Taylor; m 5 July 1941 (d 23 October 1996); 2 sons (b 1944 and 1947). **Subject(s):** Natural Sciences; BA 1934; LMSSA 1939. **Tutor(s):** M P Charlesworth. **Johnian Relatives:** son of Gerald Augustus Ticehurst (1897); nephew of Claud Buchanan Ticehurst (1900). **Educ:** Tonbridge School. **Career:** RMO, Queen Mary's Hospital, Roehampton 1939; Hospital of St Cross, Rugby 1940–1941; MO, 70th East Surrey Regiment 1941–1943; Commissioned into RAMC 1941–1946; MO, 9th Indian Field Regiment, Indian Artillery 1944–1946; GP, Wells-next-the-Sea, Norfolk 1947–1977.

TIDDY, Claude Winstanley Elliott (1901) Born 5 February 1882, Margate, Kent; son of William Elliott Tiddy, Naval Instructor, China, and Ellen Willett; m Hilda Constance Ogden, 25 October 1919, Our Lady and St Joseph, Ealing. **Subject(s):** Classics; BA 1904. **Tutor(s):** D MacAlister. **Educ:** Oundle School. **Career:** Egyptian Civil Service 1919.

TIDY, George (1941) Born 14 September 1922, 13 Middlesbro Road, Edmonton; son of James Tidy, Bread Baker, and Elizabeth Hannah Maddison. **Subject(s):** Mechanical Sciences; BA 1944; MA 1948; Certificate of Advanced Engineering 1955; MICE 1950. **Tutor(s):** S J Bailey. **Educ:** Raynham Road School, Edmonton; Latymer's School, Edmonton. **Career:** RN 1943–1947; Civil Engineer 1947–1967, Management Consultant 1967–1982, British Rail. Died 10 January 2004.

TILLARD, Lawrence Berkley (1906) Born 11 August 1888, 1 St Chad's Gardens, Headingley, Leeds, Yorkshire; son of John Tillard, HM Inspector of Schools, and Mabel Katherine Berkley; m Aline Dickerson Elliott, 1 June 1922, St Paul's, Knightsbridge. **Subject(s):** Classics; BA 1909. **Tutor(s):** E E Sikes. **Educ:** King Edward VI Grammar School, Norwich; Aldenham School; British School, Athens. **Career:** Called to the Bar, Inner Temple 1914; Captain, 6th (City of London) Regiment 1914–1918. **Publications:** *The Fortifications of Phokis*, 1911. Died 12 February 1943.

TILNEY, Richard (1933) Born 1 June 1915, Bray, Mildred Avenue, Watford, Hertfordshire; son of Max James Eccles Tilney, Consulting Electrical Engineer, and Elaine Amy Muriel Griffin. **Subject(s):** Mechanical Sciences; BA 1936; MA 1981; Chartered Mechanical Engineer. **Tutor(s):** J S Boys Smith. **Educ:** Bilton Grange School, Rugby; Clifton College, Bristol. **Career:** London, Midland and Scottish Railway Company, Derby 1937; Lieutenant Colonel, Innage House, Stratford, Watford 1951.

TIMBRELL, David Yorke (1948) Born 20 June 1928, 15 Cardigan Road, Richmond, Surrey; son of Vincent Yorke Timbrell, Inspector of Taxes, and Christine Mary Williams. **Subject(s):** English; BA 1950; MA 1967. **Tutor(s):** F Thistlethwaite. **Educ:** Colet Court, Kensington; Richmond Hill School; John Bright County School, Llandudno; Thames Valley Grammar School, Twickenham. **Career:** Chartered Accountant, Canada. **Awards:** Minor Scholarship, SJC. Died 5 November 1990.

TIMMS, Dr Geoffrey (1925) Born 16 February 1903, 166 Lister Avenue, Bowling, Bradford, Yorkshire; son of Frederick Timms, Rope Manufacturer, and Clara Louisa Barraclough. PhD 1928. **Tutor(s):** J M Wordie. **Educ:** Woodhouse Grove School, Apperley Bridge; University of Leeds.

TIN, Maung Han (1940) Born 24 June 1915, Rangoon, Burma; son of U Ba Tin, District Magistrate, and Daw Tin Tin. **Tutor(s):** C W Guillebaud. **Educ:** Baptist English High School, Rangoon; St Paul's English High School, Rangoon; Rangoon University College.

TINKLER, John Eric (1935) Born 9 November 1916, 10 Out Cast, Ulverston, Lancashire; son of Alfred Tinkler, Shipyard Clerk, and Rachel Annie Duston. **Subject(s):** Natural Sciences; BA 1938; MA 1942; Diploma in Administrative Law and Practice (Edinburgh) 1951. **Tutor(s):** J M Wordie. **Educ:** St Martin's School, Scarborough; Scarborough High School. **Career:** Secretary, Central Midwives Board for Scotland; Assistant Secretary, Scottish Home and Health Department 1977. **Awards:** Scholarship, SJC. Died 30 April 1996.

TINSLEY, Michael (1946) Born 9 May 1920, 39 Bath Road, Swindon, Wiltshire; son of Joseph Tinsley, Chief Clerk, Swindon Electricity Department, and Ethel Annie Twine; m Evelyn. **Subject(s):** Mechanical Sciences; BA 1948; MA 1953. **Tutor(s):** R L Howland. **Educ:** King William Street Church of England School, Swindon; The Commonweal Secondary School, Swindon; The College Technical Department, Swindon. Died 9 January 1994.

TITLEY, Alfred Eric (1919) Born 14 January 1898, Fern Cottage, Craig-y-Don, Llandudno; son of John Titley, Civil Servant, and Flora Sarah Painter; m Betty; 1 son (Colin), 1 daughter (Jessica). **Subject(s):** Modern and Medieval Languages; BA 1921; MA 1927. **Tutor(s):** E E Sikes. **Johnian Relatives:** father of Colin Richard Eric Titley (1959). **Educ:** Emanuel School, Wandsworth. **Career:** Devonshire Regiment (Mentioned in Despatches) 1916–1918; Assistant Master, Marlborough College (later Head, Modern Languages Department and Housemaster) 1921–1950; Lieutenant Colonel, in charge of training team, Devonshire Regiment 1939–1945; Staff Inspector, Ministry of Education 1950. **Honours:** MC. Died 11 March 1961.

TITTERINGTON, Edward John Goodall (1903) Born 8 September 1884, 4 College Terrace, Cambridge; son of Edward Thomas Titterington, Post Office Telegraph Engineer, and Helen Baker. **Subject(s):** Mathematics; BA 1906; MA 1910. **Tutor(s):** E E Sikes. **Johnian Relatives:** half-brother of Eric Titterington (1919). **Educ:** Perse Grammar School, Cambridge. **Career:** Clerk, Local Government Board 1908; British Vice-Consul, Vardo, Norway 1916–1919.

TITTERINGTON, Major Eric (1919) Born 7 January 1892, 13 Lyndewoode Road, Cambridge; son of Edward Thomas Titterington, Sectional Engineer, Post Office Telegraphs, and Alice Eliza Cross. **Tutor(s):** E E Sikes. **Johnian Relatives:** half-brother of Edward John Goodall Titterington (1903). **Educ:** Perse Grammar School, Cambridge; South Western Polytechnic Institute, University of London. **Career:** Lieutenant, Worcester Regiment, WW1; Private Chemist to HH King Faud of Egypt 1920; Intelligence Corps, Claims Commission 1946–1951. **Appointments:** Secretary, Cairo Scientific Society 1926–1952. **Honours:** Chevalier of the French Legion of Honour; Commander of the Order of Leopold II; Grand Officer, Order of the Crown of Italy; Order of the Nile (4th Class) 1921; Order of Ismail (4th Class) 1923; Order of the Nile (3rd Class) 1936. Died 1 November 1971.

TITTERTON, Lewis Henry (1920) Born 22 December 1900, The Hollies, Acomb, Yorkshire; son of Charles Henry Titterton, Clerk in Holy Orders, and Anna Louise Maitland. **Subject(s):** Oriental Languages; BA 1923. **Tutor(s):** E A Benians. **Educ:** Highgate School; KCL.

TOASE, The Revd Edward James (1908) Born 8 September 1889, 11 Bath Street, Huddersfield; son of Edward Barton Toase, Clerk in Holy Orders, and Janet Paterson; m Ruth Mary Paris; 1 son (Robert Christopher b 8 February 1937). BA 1911; MA 1915. **Tutor(s):** J R Tanner. **Johnian Relatives:** father of Robert Christopher Toase (1955). **Educ:** Denstone College; Leeds Clergy Training School. **Career:** Deacon 1912; Curate, All Saints', Dewsbury 1912–1915; Priest 1913; Curate, Brighouse 1915–1919; Curate, St Andrew, Rugby 1919–1926; Vicar, Marham 1926–1933; Rector, Benwick 1933–1941; Rector, Ashill 1941–1962. Died 26 May 1965.

TOBIN, Thomas Victor (1926) Born 30 January 1906, 7 Belvedere Road, Sunderland, County Durham; son of Thomas Charles Tobin, Naval Architect, and Isabel May Rawlinson. BA 1930; MA 1934. **Tutor(s):** J M Wordie. **Johnian Relatives:** son of Thomas Charles Tobin (1894). **Educ:** Clanryi Preparatory School, Belfast; Aldenham School; College of Technology, Belfast. **Career:** Premium Pupil, Marine Engineering Shops, Messrs Harland and Wolff Limited, Belfast.

TOD, Geoffrey Noel (NOEL-TOD) (1927) Born 8 September 1908, Peeters Road, Rayapat, Fallowfield, Madras, India; son of Wilfred Hugh Tod, Broker, and Eva Muriel Helen Lake. **Subject(s):** History; BA 1930; MA 1955. **Tutor(s):** M P Charlesworth. **Johnian Relatives:** brother of John Dudley Hugh Tod (1933). **Educ:** Willesden House Preparatory School, London; Dunchurch Hall, Rugby; Uppingham School. **Career:** Chairman, Parry & Co, Madras; Director, East India Distilleries & Sugar Factories Ltd. **Awards:** Exhibition, SJC. **Honours:** OBE (Military) 1946; CBE 1963. Died 26 March 1983.

TOD, John Dudley Hugh (1933) Born 13 September 1915, Madras, India; son of Wilfred Hugh Tod, Broker, and Eva Muriel Helen Lake; m Marguerite Irene Hope Fawkes, 3 March 1945, London. **Subject(s):** Economics; BA 1936. **Tutor(s):** C W Guillebaud. **Johnian Relatives:** brother of Geoffrey Noel Tod (Noel-Tod) (1927). **Educ:** Seafield, Bexhill-on-Sea; Uppingham School. Died 26 December 1991.

TODD, Douglas Brian (1948) Born 6 November 1926, 47 Pleasant View, Compstall, Cheshire; son of Wright Tymm Douglas Todd, Engineer, and Eveline Carr. **Subject(s):** History; BA 1950; MA 1955. **Tutor(s):** F Thistlethwaite. **Educ:** St Paul's School, Compstall; Romiley Church School; King's School, Macclesfield. **Career:** Royal Insurance Group Ltd, London West End Branch. Died November 1982.

TODD, The Revd Hugh Wilfred (1908) Born 7 October 1888, 46 Stapleton Hall Road, Stroud Green, Hornsey, Middlesex; son of Thomas Todd, Assistant Master, City of London School, and Emma Louisa Emberly. **Subject(s):** Classics/Theology; BA 1911; MA 1932. **Tutor(s):** E E Sikes. **Educ:** City of London School; Ridley Hall, Cambridge. **Career:** Deacon 1913; Curate, St Paul, Winchmore Hill 1913–1916; Priest 1914; CF, 4th Class, RACD (Mentioned in Despatches) WWI; CF, serving at Bourdon 1920–1923; Aldershot 1923–1926; with the Rhine Army 1926–1927; in Egypt 1927–1929; Woolwich 1930–1932; Millbank Hospital 1932–1937; Singapore 1937–1940; Southern Command 1942–1943; Vicar, St Mabe, Cornwall 1943–1946; Permission to Officiate in the Diocese of St Edmundsbury 1947. **Awards:** Wood Exhibition; Reading Prize 1910. **Honours:** MC.

TODD, Professor John (1931) Born 16 May 1911, Carnacally; son of William Robert Todd, Elementary School Teacher, and Catherine Elizabeth Stewart; m Olga Taussky, 29 September 1938 (d October 1995). **Subject(s):** Mathematics. **Tutor(s):** J M Wordie. **Educ:** Methodist College, Belfast; Queen's University, Belfast. **Career:** Lecturer, Queen's University 1933–1937; Lecturer, KCL 1937–1949; Chief Computation Laboratory, then Chief Numerical Analysis, National Bureau of Standards 1947–1957; Professor of Mathematics, California Institute of Technology 1957; Fulbright Professor, Vienna, Austria 1965. **Appointments:** Member, American Mathematical Society; Member, Society of Industrial and Applied Mathematics; Member, Mathematical Association of America. **Awards:** Research Exhibition, SJC 1931–1932; Strathcona Research Studentship, SJC 1932–1933. **Publications:** Author and Editor, books on numerical analysis and tables; Editor in Chief, *Numerische Mathematik* 1959; Associate Editor, *Acquationes Mathematicae* 1967–1985, 1989–1995; Associate Editor, *Journal of Approximation Theory* 1967–1993.

TODD, Colonel Walter John Cambridge (1929) Born 2 October 1910, Hindscarth, Park Road, West Hartlepool; son of Ralph Todd, Headmaster, and Florence Mary Tomlinson; m Sheila Gertrude Macbeth, 1950 (d); 1 daughter (Griselda Christian Macbeth Davies b 1959). **Subject(s):** Science; BA 1932; MA 1936. **Tutor(s):** J M Wordie. **Educ:** Mr Scott's Preparatory School, West Hartlepool; West Hartlepool Secondary School; Durham School. **Career:** Durham Heavy Regiment RA, served in India, Persia and Iraq 1930–1952; Articled to the Clerk of the Peace, Northumberland 1932–1934; Town Clerk, West Hartlepool 1934–1935; In Practice, Chester 1937; Lieutenant Colonel, RA, TA 1945; Commandant, Cheshire Army Cadet Force 1959; DL, County of Cheshire 1975; Solicitor, Cheshire County Council, until 1977. **Appointments:** Royal Chester Rowing Club (Captain 1939 and 1946–1949); Chairman, Chester Regatta Committee 1977–1988. **Honours:** OBE 1953 (Military); TA Decoration with two clasps. Died 27 November 2000.

TOLLES, Raymond Pardee (1918) American Student.

TOLLIT, Christopher Charles (1920) Born 9 September 1899, The School House, Derby; son of Percy Kitto Tollit, Senior Mathematical Master, Brighton College, and Mildred Steer; m (1) Dorothy Beryl Bishop, 18 August 1926, St Mark's Church, Kemp Town, (2) Marjorie. **Subject(s):**

Economics; BA 1921; MA 1935. **Tutor(s):** E A Benians. **Educ:** Junior School, Brighton College; St Cross, Walton on the Hill; Brighton College. **Career:** Second Lieutenant, RE 1918–1919. Died 1 June 1951.

TOLMER, Guy Stedman Foster (1939) Born 28 January 1916, The Sanatorium, Durban, Natal; son of Horace Foster Tolmer, Farmer, and Hilda Mary Sparrow. **Tutor(s):** J S Boys Smith. **Educ:** Highbury Preparatory School; Rhodes University College, Grahamstown; Michaelhouse, Balgowan, Natal.

TOMLINSON, Brian (1949) Born 18 September 1928, Royal Free Hospital, St Pancras, London; son of George Arthur Tomlinson, Research Scientist, and Evelyn Margaret Kirk. **Subject(s):** Modern and Medieval Languages; BA 1952; MA 1956; Diploma in Education (Oxford) 1953. **Tutor(s):** C W Guillebaud. **Educ:** Hampton Hill Council School; King's College Junior School, Wimbledon; Glaston Tor School, Glastonbury; Bedales School, Petersfield. **Career:** Army Intelligence Corps 1947–1949.

TOMLINSON, George Arthur (1906) Born 7 January 1885, 145 Nicholson Road, Heeley, Sheffield, Yorkshire; son of George Tomlinson, Draper, and Elizabeth Cutts Beech. BSc (London). **Tutor(s):** L H K Bushe-Fox. **Educ:** Cavendish School, Matlock; Nottingham High School; UCL. **Career:** Lecturer in Electrical Engineering, Rutherford Technical College, Newcastle; National Physical Laboratory, then Principal Scientific Officer, Metrology Division 1915. Died 1 December 1944.

TOMLINSON, Professor Rolfe Cartwright (1943) Born 1 September 1925, 48 Carlton Avenue, Kenton, Wealdstone, Middlesex; son of Arthur Tomlinson, Establishments Officer, Ministry of Pensions, and Kate Phyllis Faulkner; m (1) Jill Griffiths, 1952 (d 1976), (2) Helen Williams, 1978 (d 1993), (3) Margaret Adcock, 1995; 2 sons (Philip and Andrew), 1 daughter (Kate). **Subject(s):** Mathematics; BA 1946; MA 1950; DIC (Aeronautics) 1946; CEng. **Tutor(s):** S J Bailey. **Johnian Relatives:** father of Andrew David Tomlinson (1977). **Educ:** Quainton Hall School, Harrow; Merchant Taylors' School, Sandy Lodge. **Career:** Director, Operational Research Executive, National Coal Board 1965–1977; Chairman, Management and Technology Area, International Institute of Applied Systems Analysis 1977–1980; Professor of Systems and Operational Research, Warwick Business School, University of Warwick 1980–1990. **Appointments:** Member, Institute of Fuel; Fellow, Institute of Statistics; President, Operational Research Society 1972–1973; President, European Federation of Operational Research Societies 1982–1985; Member, Coventry Health Authority 1984–1995. **Awards:** Major Scholarship, SJC 1943; Companion of Operational Research 1991. **Publications:** (ed) *OR Comes of Age*, Tavistock, 1971; over 50 papers in learned journals.

TOMPSON, Frank Gordon (1900) Born 5 September 1880, 12 Camden Square, Kentish Town, London; son of Frederick James Tompson, Brewery Manager, and Eliza Harvey Thompson. BA 1903; MA 1907. **Tutor(s):** C E Graves; J R Tanner. **Educ:** Uppingham School.

TONG, Robert Percy (1932) Born 29 December 1911, 10 Wyles Road, Chatham; son of Percy Tong, Engine Room Artificer, and Sophy Fox; m Constance Snape, 23 August 1941, Oxford. **Subject(s):** Geography; BA 1935; MA 1939; University Certificate of Education. **Tutor(s):** J S Boys Smith. **Educ:** Cathedral Choir School, Rochester; King's School, Rochester. **Career:** Major, The Queen's Own Regiment; Housemaster and Director of Music, King's School, Canterbury; Chairman, Board of Governors, Chelmsford College of Technology; Registrar, Queen Mary College, University of London 1946–1978; JP 1960; Deputy Chairman, UCCA 1970; Fellow, Queen Mary and Westfield College 1978. **Awards:** Scholarship, SJC. Died 17 December 1994.

TOOLIS, James Hollingworth (1912) (admitted to Clare College 1912) Born 22 July 1893, Woods House, Dobcross, Saddleworth, Yorkshire; son of Thomas Smith Toolis, Clerk in Holy Orders, and Mary Ann

Hollingworth. **Tutor(s):** L H K Bushe-Fox. **Educ:** The Grange, Stevenage; The Perse School, Cambridge.

TOONE, Charles Gilbert (1903) Born 22 September 1884, 27 Freehold Street, Liverpool; son of Charles Samuel Toone, Fruit Salesman, and Sarah Widdowson; m Cynthia Copley Jones. **Subject(s):** Mathematics; BA 1906; MA 1910. **Tutor(s):** J R Tanner; C E Graves. **Educ:** Christ's Hospital. **Career:** Baptist Minister, Norwich 1909–1910; Baptist Minister, St Albans 1910–1913; Baptist Minister, Sale 1913–1918; Baptist Minister, Skegness 1918–1924; Baptist Minister, St Leonards 1924–1930; Unitarian Minister, Lytham St Annes 1931–1936; Unitarian Minister, Moreton Hampstead and Newton Abbot 1936. Died August 1960.

TOOTH, Dr Geoffrey Cuthbert (1926) Born 1 September 1908, 34 Harley Street, London; son of Howard Henry Tooth, Physician, and Helen Katharine Chilver; m (1) Princess Olga Galitzine, 1934 (d 1955), (2) HSH Princess Xenia of Russia, 1958. BA 1930; MA 1935; BChir 1935; MB 1937; MD 1946; MRCS 1934; LRCP 1934; DPM 1944; MRCP 1965. **Tutor(s):** M P Charlesworth. **Johnian Relatives:** son of Howard Henry Tooth (1873); nephew of Percy Ernest Tooth (1882). **Educ:** Horris Hill School, Newbury; Rugby School. **Career:** Assistant Psychiatrist, Maudsley Hospital 1937–1939; Surgeon Lieutenant Commander, RNVR, Neuropsychiatric Specialist 1939–1945; Colonial Social Science Research Fellow 1946–1953; Commissioner, Board of Control 1954–1960; Principal Medical Officer, Senior Principal Medical Officer, then Head, Mental Health Section, Medical Division, until 1968, Ministry of Health; Visiting Scientist, National Institute of Mental Health, USA 1968–1971. **Appointments:** Member, Expert Advisory Panel (Mental Health), WHO. **Publications:** *Studies in Mental Illness in the Gold Coast*, 1950; various reports to learned societies; articles and papers in medical journals. Died 18 February 1998.

TOOVEY, Francis William (1933) Born 5 February 1911, 32 Nansen Road, Battersea; son of Francis Joseph Toovey, Tram Conductor, and Lily Hannah Emily Smith. BSc (London) 1933. **Tutor(s):** E A Benians. **Educ:** Riversdale School, London; Battersea Grammar School; Imperial College of Science and Technology, London. **Awards:** Colonial Probationer; Colonial Agricultural Scholarship.

TOPLEY, Dr William Whiteman Carlton (1904) Born 19 January 1886, Brockley, London; son of Ebenezer Topley, Managing Director, and Elizabeth Whiteman; m Kate Amsden, 1912; 2 daughters. **Subject(s):** Natural Sciences; BA 1907; MA 1919; BChir 1911; MB 1911; MD 1919; LRCP; MRCS 1909. **Tutor(s):** D MacAlister. **Educ:** City of London School. **Career:** Lecturer in Bacteriology, Charing Cross Hospital 1911–1922; Captain, RAMC, Serbia, WWI; Professor of Bacteriology, University of Manchester 1922–1927; Director of Bacteriology and Immunology, London School of Hygiene and Tropical Medicine 1927–1941; Member, MRC 1928–1941; Secretary, Agricultural Research Council 1941–1944. **Appointments:** Honorary Physician to the King; Harben Lecturer 1926; Linacre Lecturer, SJC 1940; Croonian Lecturer, Royal Society 1941. **Awards:** Scholarship, SJC 1906; Royal Society Medal for work on epidemiology and immunity. **Honours:** Order of St Sava, 4th Class (Serbia) 1916. **Publications:** *Outbreak of Immunity*, 1933; *Principles of Bacteriology and Immunity*, 1936. Died 21 January 1944.

TORRY, Arthur James Dashwood (1905) Born 18 May 1887, Marwood Rectory, Devon; son of Alfred Freer Torry, Clerk in Holy Orders and Fellow, SJC, and Elizabeth Georgina Goldie. **Subject(s):** Mechanical Sciences; BA 1908. **Tutor(s):** C E Graves; J R Tanner. **Johnian Relatives:** grandson of Charles Dashwood Goldie (1843); son of Alfred Freer Torry (1858); nephew of Laurence Stephenson (1858), John Haviland Dashwood Goldie (1868) and of Charles James Dashwood Goldie (1871). **Educ:** Bedford Grammar School. **Career:** Shop Student, Royal Arsenal, Woolwich 1908–1911; Drawing Office, Vickers' Works, Barrow-in-Furness 1911–1913; Canadian Explosives Factory, Montreal 1913–1914; Lieutenant, RGA, then attached RFC (wounded) 1915–1917. **Honours:** MC 1916. Died 9 October 1917 (killed in action).

TOTHILL, Alec Norman (1925) Born 29 September 1900, 78 Trinity Road, Wimbledon, Surrey; son of John Tothill, Publisher, and Mary Beer. **Tutor(s):** J M Wordie. **Johnian Relatives:** brother of Reginald John Tothill (1925) and of Richard Fleming Tothill (1930). **Educ:** Rokeby School, Wimbledon; St Francis Xavier's College, Bruges, Belgium; St Francis Xavier's College, Clapham; London Polytechnic School of Engineering; Manchester College of Technology. Died 21 January 1926.

TOTHILL, Reginald John (1925) Born 23 May 1908, 10 Merton Hall Road, Wimbledon, Surrey; son of John Tothill, Director and General Manager, Geographical and Map Publisher, and Mary Beer. BA 1929; MA 1937. **Tutor(s):** J M Wordie. **Johnian Relatives:** brother of Alec Norman Tothill (1925) and of Richard Fleming Tothill (1930). **Educ:** Blakesley House, Merton; Bickley Hall School; Tonbridge School. Died 1973.

TOTHILL, Richard Fleming (1930) Born 19 January 1911, 32 Wilton Crescent, Wimbledon; son of John Tothill, Director and General Manager of Publishers, and Mary Beer; m Joyce Evelyn Garland; 1 daughter (Sandra Mary Gillian b 1938). BA 1933; MA 1937. **Tutor(s):** J M Wordie. **Johnian Relatives:** brother of Alec Norman Tothill (1925) and of Reginald John Tothill (1925). **Educ:** Bickley Hall Preparatory School, Bickley; Tonbridge School. **Career:** Hotellier.

TOTTY, Peter Harland (1940) Born 9 September 1921, 11 Undercliffe Lane, Bradford, Yorkshire; son of Ernest Arthur Totty, Builder and Contractor, and Florence Mary Schofield. BSc (London) 1940. **Tutor(s):** S J Bailey. **Educ:** Bradford Grammar School; Bradford Technical College. **Career:** Director, Totty of Bradford. Died 1966.

TOUCHE, John Edgeworth David (1931) Born 9 December 1913, 14 Strathearn Road, Edinburgh; son of John Edward Touche, Consulting Engineer, and Sarah Minns Ware. **Subject(s):** Mechanical Sciences; BA 1935; MA 1939; MRAeS; CEng. **Tutor(s):** J M Wordie. **Educ:** Merchiston Castle Preparatory School, Edinburgh; Merchiston Castle School, Edinburgh.

TOULMIN, John Heaton (1928) Born 29 August 1909, 35 Highgate Avenue, Fulwood, Lancashire; son of George Fisher Toulmin, Chartered Accountant and Company Managing Director, and Isabella Annie Brown. BA 1931. **Tutor(s):** E A Benians. **Educ:** Preston Grammar School; Norwood School, Exeter; Clifton College, Bristol.

TOWERS, Dr Malcolm Kinsey (1940) Born 1 May 1921, 38 Laburnum Avenue, Wallsend, Northumberland; son of Arthur Kinsey Towers, General Medical Practitioner, and Marion Malcolm; m Margaret Joyce Williams, 24 February 1951; 2 sons (David and John), 2 daughters (Sarah and Jenny). **Subject(s):** Natural Sciences; BA 1943; MA 1947; MB 1946; BChir 1946; MRCP 1951; FRCP 1970. **Tutor(s):** R L Howland. **Educ:** Newcastle Preparatory School; Durham School; Cornell University Medical College; London Hospital; National Heart Hospital. **Career:** House Physician, London Hospital 1946–1947; RAMC 1947–1949; Registrar, London Hospital 1950–1954; Lecturer, National Heart Hospital 1955–1961; Consultant in Cardiometrics, Brompton Hospital 1962–1965; Consultant Cardiologist, Harefield Hospital 1965–1987. **Awards:** Rockefeller Studentship 1943; Entrance Scholarship, London Hospital 1943; Baker Exhibition, SJC.

TOWERS, Thomas Dundas (1936) Born 1 August 1914, 99 Bo'ness Road, Grangemouth, Stirlingshire; son of Walter Towers, Artist Etcher, and Georgina West; m Dorothy; 2 sons (Christopher and Nigel). **Subject(s):** Mathematics; BA 1938; MA 1958; MA (Glasgow) 1936; BSc (London) 1954; CEng; MIERE. **Tutor(s):** J M Wordie. **Johnian Relatives:** father of Christopher Dundas Towers (1966). **Educ:** Grangemouth Infant School; Dundas Public School, Grangemouth; Queen's Park Secondary School; University of Glasgow. **Career:** Colonial Audit Service, Kenya 1940–1945; Colonial Audit Service, Nigeria 1945–1947; Colonial Audit

Service, London 1947–1949; Principal Auditor, Windward Islands 1949–1952; Finance trouble shooter, Sarawak, Brunei 1952–1959; Sales Director, Pye's Newmarket Transistors Factory 1959. **Awards:** Ferguson Scholarship, SJC; Scholarship, SJC 1937; Wright's Prize, SJC 1937. **Honours:** MBE 1952. Died 9 March 1987.

TOWNEND, Charles Russell Balme (1938) Born 30 March 1920, Hazelmere, St Albans Road, Halifax; son of Charles Lowe Townend, Incorporated Accountant, and Mabel Balme. **Subject(s):** Economics/Law; BA 1941; MA 1945; FCA. **Tutor(s):** R L Howland. **Educ:** Crossley and Porter, Halifax; Oakmount Arnside; Shrewsbury. **Career:** Chartered Accountant. **Appointments:** Commercial Directorship.

TOWNEND, Merton Vincent (1905) Born 10 March 1885, Steart House, Cutcombe, Somerset; son of William Vincent Townend, Gentleman, and Myra Vincent Smith. **Tutor(s):** J R Tanner; C E Graves. **Educ:** Western School, St Marychurch. Died 3 June 1939.

TOWNEND, Peter Lawson (1949) Born 10 February 1928, Denison House, Victoria Park, Rusholme, Manchester; son of Percy Lawson Townend, Methodist Minister, and Gladys Amy Pain; m Jeanne Anne Bates, 2 August 1956, Leigh Memorial Chapel, Milton, Staffordshire; 1 son (Michael Jonathan b 5 April 1959), 1 daughter (Elizabeth Anne b 9 July 1957). **Subject(s):** Modern and Medieval Languages; BA 1954; MA 1959; PGCE (London) 1955. **Tutor(s):** C W Guillebaud. **Educ:** Ashburton Elementary School, Croydon; Westwood Preparatory School; Kingswood School; Westminster College, University of London. **Career:** RAF, UK, Egypt, Iraq and Aden 1947–1949; Head of French, Woodhouse Grove School, Apperley Bridge, West Yorkshire 1955–1959; Head of German, Wallasey Boys' Grammar School, Merseyside 1959–1963; Head of Modern Languages, Goole Grammar School, West Yorkshire 1963–1967; Head of Modern Languages, Exmouth School, Devon 1967–1998. **Appointments:** voluntary work for The Samaritans and the Citizens' Advice Bureau in retirement.

TOWNSEND, Hugh Hamilton Massey (1927) Born 9 September 1908, Portobello House, Dublin, Ireland; son of George Hugh Chetwood Townend, Estate Agent to Lord Barrymore, and Geraldine Massey. **Subject(s):** Natural Sciences; BA 1930. **Tutor(s):** J M Wordie. **Johnian Relatives:** nephew of Crewe Armand Hamilton Townsend (1893). **Educ:** Mourne Grange, Kilkeel, Ireland; Sherbourne School.

TOWNSEND, Professor Peter Brereton (1948) Born 6 April 1928, Nursing Home, The Avenue, Middlesbrough; son of Philip Brereton Townsend, Commercial Traveller, and Alice Mary Southcote; m (1) Ruth Pearce, 1949, (2) Joy Skegg, 1977, (3) Jean Ann Corston, 1985; (1) 4 sons, (2) 1 daughter, (3) 1 stepson, 1 stepdaughter. **Subject(s):** Moral Sciences/Archaeology and Anthropology; BA 1950; DU (Essex) 1990; DLitt (Teesside) 1994; DUniv (Open) 1995; DSc (Edinburgh) 1996; DUniv (Lincolnshire and Humberside) 1997; DUniv (York) 2000; DUniv (Stirling) 2002; FBA 2004. **Tutor(s):** C W Guillebaud. **Educ:** Fleet Road School, Hampstead; University College School, London; Free University, Berlin. **Career:** National Service, Army 1946–1948; Research Secretary, Political and Economic Planning 1952–1954; Research Officer, Institute of Community Studies 1954–1957; Research Fellow, then Lecturer in Social Administration, LSE 1957–1963; Professor of Sociology 1963–1981, Pro-Vice-Chancellor (Social Policy) 1975–1978, Visiting Professor of Sociology 1982–1986, University of Essex; Professor of Social Policy 1982–1993 (Emeritus 1993), Director, School of Applied Social Studies 1983–1985 and 1988–1993, Senior Research Fellow 1993–, University of Bristol; Centennial Professor of International Social Policy, LSE 1998–. **Appointments:** Chairman 1965–1966, Vice President 1989–, Chairman, Social Policy Committee 1970–1982, Chairman, Research and Publications Committee 1983–1986, Fabian Society; President, Psychiatric Rehabilitation Association 1968–1983; Chairman 1969–1989, Life President 1989–, Child Poverty Action Group; Chairman 1974–1999, President 1999–, Disability Alliance; Member, Chief Scientist's Committee, DHSS

1976–1978; Government Working Group on Inequalities and Health 1977–1980; UNESCO Consultant on poverty and development 1978–1980; Manpower Services Commission Working Group on Quota Scheme for Disabled 1983–1985; Consultant to Northern RHA on Inequalities of Health 1985–1986; Consultant to GLC on poverty and the labour market in London 1985–1986; Consultant to a consortium of 7 metropolitan boroughs on deprivation and shopping centres in Greater Manchester 1987–1988; Consultant to Islington Borough Council on deprivation and living standards 1987–1988; South-west Region, Mencap 1989–1993; Michael Harrington Distinguished Visiting Professor of Social Science, CUNY 1991–1992; Consultant to UNDP on social safety net in Georgia 1994; Consultant to UNDP and IILS on patterns and causes of social exclusion 1994; Consultant to UN for world summit on social development 1994–1995; Consultant to Department of Foreign Affairs, Denmark 1997–2000; Visiting Professor of Social Policy, LSE 1998; Visiting Professor of International Social Policy, University of Wales 1998. **Publications:** *The Family Life of Old People*, 1957; (jointly) *National Superannuation*, 1957; (jointly) *Nursing Homes in England and Wales*, 1961; *The Last Refuge: a survey of Residential Institutions and Homes for the Aged in England and Wales*, 1962; (jointly) *The Aged in the Welfare State*, 1965; (jointly) *The Poor and the Poorest*, 1965; (jointly) *Old People in Three Industrial Societies*, 1968; (ed) *The Concept of Poverty*, 1970; (ed) *Labour and Inequality*, 1972; *The Social Minority*, 1973; *Sociology and Social Policy*, 1975; *Poverty in the United Kingdom: a Survey of Household Resources and Standards of Living*, 1979; (ed) *Labour and Equality*, 1980; (jointly) *Inequalities in Health*, 1980; (jointly) *Manifesto*, 1981; (ed jointly) *Disability in Britain*, 1981; *The Family and Later Life*, 1981; (ed jointly) *Responses to Poverty: lessons from Europe*, 1984; (jointly) *Inequalities of Health in the Northern Region*, 1986; *Poverty and Labour in London*, 1987; (jointly) *Health and Deprivation: Inequalities and the North*, 1987; (jointly) *Service Provision and Living Standards in Islington*, 1988; (jointly) *Inequalities in Health: the Black Report and the Health Divide*, 1988, 3rd edn 1993; *The International Analysis of Poverty*, 1993; (jointly) *Poverty and Social Exclusion in Britain*, 2000, Joseph Rowntree Foundation, 2000; (ed jointly) *Breadline Europe: The Measurement of Poverty*, Policy Press, 2001; *Targeting Poor Health: Professor Townsend's Report of the Welsh Assembly's National Steering Group on the Allocation of NHS Resources*, Volume 1, The National Assembly for Wales, 2001; (ed jointly) *World Poverty: New Policies to Defeat an Old Enemy*, 2002; (jointly) *The Distribution of Child Poverty in the Developing World*, UNICEF, 2003.

TOWNSEND, Robert Wilfred (1910) Born 1 June 1891, 4 Southernham West, Exeter, Devon; son of James Townsend, Master Printer, and Mary Ann Gadd; m Judith Ann Wolton, 23 April 1924, St Mary Stoke Church, Ipswich. **Subject(s):** Mathematics/Economics; BA 1913; MA 1919. **Tutor(s):** L H K Bushe-Fox. **Educ:** Exeter School. **Career:** Captain, Devon Regiment (twice Mentioned in Despatches), WWI. **Honours:** MC. Died 11 March 1982.

TOZER, The Revd Ernest Francis (1905) Born 17 January 1886, Curzon School House, Mayfair, London; son of Henry Tozer, Scripture Reader, and Susan Prout. BA 1908; MA 1915. **Tutor(s):** D MacAlister. **Johnian Relatives:** brother of Sydney Prout Tozer (1914). **Educ:** City of London School; Mile End Pupil Teachers' School. **Career:** Ordained Deacon 1911; Curate, All Saints, Lower Brixham 1911–1914; CF, 4th Class, RACD, WWI; Curate, Ottery St Mary 1915–1923; Rector, St Paul with St Pancras and All Hallows, Exeter 1923–1924; Incumbent of Emmanuel, Exeter 1924–1963. Died January 1963.

TOZER, Sydney Prout (1914) Born 17 February 1895, 161 Stepney Green, Mile End, London; son of Henry Tozer, Lay Minister, and Susan Prout. **Subject(s):** Mathematics. **Tutor(s):** L H K Bushe-Fox. **Johnian Relatives:** brother of Ernest Francis Tozer (1905). **Educ:** Dudley Grammar School; Central Foundation School. **Career:** Lieutenant, Devon Regiment until 1918. Died 8 October 1918 (killed in action near St Quentin).

TRACEY, Christopher Birdwood (1919) Born 9 May 1898, The Gables, Willand, Devon; son of Henry Eugene Tracey, Physician and Surgeon, and Emily Alice Martin; m Eileen Bowen Cooke, 27 July 1932; 1 son (Richard); 2 daughters (Belinda and Mary). **Subject(s):** Classics; BA 1921; MA 1926. **Tutor(s):** E E Sikes. **Johnian Relatives:** brother of John Brodrick Tracey (1924). **Educ:** Blundell's School, Tiverton; St Lawrence College, Ramsgate; Monkton Combe School, Bath. **Career:** Second Lieutenant, RGA (anti-aircraft) 1917; Assistant District Commissioner, Sudan Civil Service 1922–1944; Governor, Northern Province, Sudan 1944–1948; British Administration in Libya 1948–1952. **Appointments:** Director, The Builder (publishers of *Building*). **Awards:** Exhibition, SJC 1916; Foundation Scholarship, SJC 1922. Died 24 January 1984.

TRACEY, Dr John Brodrick (1924) Born 17 July 1906, The Gables, Willand, Devon; son of Henry Eugene Tracey, Surgeon, and Emily Alice Martin. BA 1928; BChir 1932; MB 1936. **Tutor(s):** B F Armitage. **Johnian Relatives:** brother of Christopher Birdwood Tracey (1919). **Educ:** Monkton Combe Junior School; Monkton Combe Senior School. Died 7 October 1995.

TRACHTENBERG, Mendel Isidore (1901) Born 30 June 1882, 22 Woburn Place, Bloomsbury, London; son of Israel Mendel Trachtenberg, Commercial Traveller, and Eve Lyons; m Jennie Luxenburg, 4 November 1913. **Subject(s):** Mathematics; BA 1904. **Tutor(s):** C E Graves; J R Tanner. **Educ:** The Latymer School, Hammersmith. **Career:** Statistician, Tariff Commission 1906–1918; Lance Corporal, 9th Battalion, Royal Fusiliers, Jewish Regiment, Egypt and Palestine 1918. **Awards:** Exhibition, SJC 1900. Died 12 October 1918 (died of malaria at Jerusalem).

TRAPNELL, Dr Barry Maurice Waller (1942) Born 18 May 1924, Manor House, St John's Wood Park, London; son of Waller Bertram Trapnell, Diamond Merchant, and Rachel Posthumus; m Dorothy Joan Kerr, 1951; 2 daughters (Linda and Marguerita). **Subject(s):** Natural Sciences; BA 1945; MA 1949; PhD 1949; MA, DPhil (by incorporation) (Worcester College, Oxford) 1951. **Tutor(s):** C W Guillebaud. **Educ:** Chester College, Harrow; University College School, Hampstead. **Career:** Lecturer in Physical and Inorganic Chemistry, Worcester College, Oxford 1951–1954; Lecturer in Physical and Inorganic Chemistry, University of Liverpool 1954–1957; Headmaster, Denstone College 1957–1968; Headmaster, Oundle School, Peterborough 1968–1984; Director, Southend Estates Group 1984–1986; Director, Thomas Wall Trust 1984–1990; Chairman, Cambridge Occupational Analysts 1986. **Appointments:** Deputy Lieutenant, Staffordshire and Northamptonshire; Honorary Fellow, College of Preceptors; President, Independent Schools Association 1984–1995; Honorary Liveryman, Worshipful Company of Grocers. **Honours:** CBE 1982. **Publications:** *Chemisorption*, Butterworths 1955, 2nd edition 1964, Russian edition, Moscow 1958; *Learning and discerning in higher education*, SPCK, 1966.

TRAVERS, Robert Morris William (1935) Born 16 October 1913, Bangalore, India; son of Morris William Travers, Professor, University of Bristol, and Dorothy Gray. **Tutor(s):** J M Wordie. **Educ:** Canford School; University of Bristol; UCL; Hilltop Court School, Seaford; Lycée Malherbe Caen; Musterschule Real Gymnasium, Frankfurt am Main.

TRAXLER, Joseph Frank (1918) Born 28 June 1900, 86 Brailsford Road, Brixton, Surrey; son of Joseph Traxler, Manager of Public Company, and Thirza Jane Hartnoll. **Tutor(s):** E E Sikes. **Educ:** Melville College, Purley; Purley Preparatory School; Whitgift, Croydon.

TREACY, Professor Peter Bradley (1948) Born 30 June 1925, Sydney, New South Wales; son of Roy Hugh Treacy, Company Director, and Anne Isabel Ritchie; m Grace Barbara Mills, 25 August 1951; 3 sons (Richard b 21 July 1955, James and John (twins) b 25 September 1959), 1 daughter (Ann b 10 July 1952). **Subject(s):** Natural Sciences; PhD 1952; ScD 1981; BSc (Sydney) 1946; MSc (Sydney) 1947. **Tutor(s):** J M

Wordie. **Educ:** The Scots College, Sydney; Sydney University. **Career:** Research Fellow 1952–1956, Fellow 1958–1962, Professor of Physics 1962–1990 (Emeritus 1990), Research School of Physical Sciences, ANU. **Appointments:** Fellow, Australian Institute of Physics, ACT Chair 1979–1981; Australian Representative, International Committee of Atomic Collisions in Solids 1981–1989; Honorary Secretary, Australian Committee, Cambridge Commonwealth Trust 1986–1992; Foundation Secretary, Cambridge Australia Trust 1986–1995; Visiting Fellow, Physics, The Faculties, ANU 1991–1997; Honorary Registrar, Cambridge Australia Trust 1995–. **Awards:** 1851 Commission Overseas Scholarship 1948–1951. **Publications:** Research papers on Experimental Nuclear Physics, Theories of Nuclear Reactions, Beam-foil X-ray Spectroscopy, Atomic Collisions in Solids.

TREGEAR, George Herbert Benjamin (1944) Born 27 January 1926, Ashland, Wolsey Road, East Molesey, Surrey; son of George Herbert Tregear, Civil Servant, Ministry of Labour, and Emma Frances Harnsberger; m (1) Elisabeth Bridget Brennan, 1952 (d 1990), (2) Elsie Wright, 1994; (1) 1 son (Francis Benedict William b 1957), 3 daughters (Sara Catherine Charlotte b 1953, d 1988, Penelope Margaret Clare b 1959 and Alice Rachel Caroline b 1963). **Subject(s):** Mechanical Sciences; BA 1947; MA 1951; MITMA; CPA 1958; EPA. **Johnian Relatives:** father of Francis Benedict William Tregear (1975); father-in-law of Alan Charles Baldwin (1981); father of Alice Rachel Caroline Tregear (Baldwin) (1982). **Educ:** Roxbury School, Kingston-on-Thames; King's College School. **Career:** Page, White & Farrer 1949–1951; P S Allam, Allam and Tregear 1951–1958; Partner, Allam & Tregear 1959–1962; Partner, Tregear Thiemann & Bleach 1962–1979; Partner, Lloyd Wise Tregear 1979–1991.

TREHARNE, Dr Philip Gordon (1941) Born 22 January 1924, Bridgend, Glamorganshire; son of Samuel Thomas Treharne and Margaret Mona Edwards; m Hermione Merwood, 21 June 1958; 2 sons (Timothy b 1962 and Andrew b 1964), 1 daughter (Philippa b 1967). **Subject(s):** Natural Sciences; BA 1944; MA 1948; BChir 1947; MB 1947. **Tutor(s):** S J Bailey. **Educ:** Cowbridge Grammar School. **Career:** House Surgeon, St Bartholomew's Hospital 1948; Captain, RAMC 1950; General Medical Practitioner, Portsmouth, Hampshire 1954–1994.

TRELEAVEN, The Revd Woodman (1906) Born 17 October 1886, Burgersdorp, Cape Colony, South Africa; son of William Woodman Treleaven, Wesleyan Minister, and Joan Selina Quick. BA 1909; MA 1913. **Tutor(s):** J R Tanner. **Educ:** Kingswood School, Bath. **Career:** Corporal, RAMC, then CF, 4th Class, RACD, WWI.

TREMEARNE, The Revd Allen Riddle (1906) (admitted as a Non-Collegiate Student 1905) Born 26 August 1881, 1 Welford Terrace, West Hackney, Middlesex; son of Allen Shirley Tremearne, Clerk, and Rose Riddle. BA 1908; MA 1920. **Tutor(s):** J R Tanner. **Educ:** Ipswich Middle School. **Career:** Ordained Deacon 1908; Curate, St Mark, Marylebone 1908–1910; Ordained Priest 1909; Curate, St Paul, Bow Common 1911–1914; Curate, St Barnabas, Marylebone 1914–1916; Permission to Officiate, St Mary, Vincent Square 1916–1917; Curate, St John, Hendon 1917–1919; Curate, St Mary Magdalene, Paddington 1920–1922; Permission to Officiate, St Peter, Eaton Square 1922–1923; St Stephen, Gloucester Road 1923; St Philip, Earls Court 1923–1925; St Ethelred, Fulham 1925–1927; St Jude on the Hill, Hampstead 1927–1928; Curate, St Mary Boltons, South Kensington 1928–1931; Vicar, Rebourne, Lincolnshire 1931–1946. Died 16 August 1981.

TREMELLEN, Kenneth (1921) Born 14 February 1903, 136 Cathedral Road, St John, Cardiff, Glamorganshire; son of Henry Josiah Tremellen, Shipowner, and Elizabeth Davies. **Tutor(s):** E E Sikes. **Educ:** Highgate School; Tonbridge School. **Career:** Coal and Shipping Trade.

TRENCH, Peter Edward (1938) Born 16 June 1918, 61 The Avenue, Wood Green, Edmonton, London; son of James Knight Trench, Managing Director, Sandar Chemical Company Ltd, and Grace Mary

Sim. **Tutor(s):** C W Guillebaud. **Educ:** Eddington House; Herne Bay College; École de Commerce, Neuchâtel; LSE. **Career:** Managing Director, Peter Trench Associates. **Honours:** CBE.

TREPTE, George Wyndham Macdonnell (1923) Born 23 May 1904, Sundhope, Waterhouse Lane, Shirley, Southampton; son of George Herbert Trepte, Clerk in Holy Orders, and Emily Charlotte Evanson. **Subject(s):** Classics/History; BA 1926; MA 1930. **Tutor(s):** E E Sikes. **Educ:** St John's School, Leatherhead. **Career:** Assistant Master, Fettes College, Edinburgh 1926–1933. **Awards:** Sizarship, SJC. Died 12 July 1933.

TREVALDWYN, John Reginald (1932) Born 10 April 1914, Marldon Vicarage, Paignton, Devon; son of Reginald Francis Holiocke Trevaldwyn, Clerk in Holy Orders, and Gertrude Edith Harper; m Mehala. **Subject(s):** Mathematics; BA 1935. **Tutor(s):** J M Wordie. **Educ:** Park House School, Paignton; Marlborough College. **Career:** Civil Servant, War Office and Treasury 1936–1950. **Awards:** Scholarship, SJC. Died 3 October 1950.

TREVES, Dr Piero (1938) Born 27 November 1911, Milan; son of Claudio Guiseppe Treves, Member of Parliament, and Olga Levi; m Janet M Dutton, 27 July 1953. **Tutor(s):** R L Howland. **Educ:** Milano Gymnasio; Universities of Turin, Rome and Milan. **Career:** Professor, University of Florence; London Correspondent, *Corriere della Sera*, Italian Section, BBC 1941. **Appointments:** Chairman, Faculty of Arts, University of Florence. **Awards:** Strathcona Studentship, SJC 1938.

TROMP, Felix Johan (1913) Born 27 November 1893, Bethulie, Orange Free State, South Africa; son of Jacobus Johan Tromp, General Dealer, and Johanna Catherina McDonald. **Subject(s):** Natural Sciences (Chemistry); BA 1915. **Tutor(s):** R P Gregory. **Educ:** Government School, Bethulie; Grey University College, Bloemfontein. **Career:** Lecturer in Chemistry, Transvaal University College, Pretoria 1917.

TROTT, Alan Charles (1913) Born 26 March 1895, 1 Midway Terrace, Heavitree, Exeter, Devon; son of John Trott, Science Tutor, and Dorothea Eliza Robinson; m Hester Dorothy Richardson, 18 June 1927, Canford Church; 2 sons (John Michael b 21 July 1929 and Peter Alan b 30 December 1934), 1 daughter (Rachel Dorothea b 1 May 1928). **Subject(s):** Mathematics/Economics/Oriental Languages; BA 1921; MA 1925. **Tutor(s):** R P Gregory. **Johnian Relatives:** brother of Francis William Trott (1912); father of John Michael Trott (1949); father of Peter Alan Trott (1953). **Educ:** St John's Hospital School, Exeter; Hele's School, Exeter; Exeter School. **Career:** Lieutenant, 4th Battalion, Devon Regiment, Egypt and Mesopotamia, then Captain, Special List 1915–1919 (Mentioned in Despatches); Levant Consular Service, Casablanca 1921; Acting Vice-Consul, Tehran 1923; Called to Bar, Gray's Inn 1925; Consul General, Jeddah, Saudi Arabia 1940–1945; Consul General, Ahwaz, Persia 1945–1947; Consul and Ambassador, Saudi Arabia 1947–1951; Director, Middle East Centre for Arabic Studies, Beirut 1953–1957. **Awards:** Minor Scholarship 1912; Devon County Scholarship 1913; Stevens & Acland Scholarship 1913; Vidal Scholarship, SJC 1913. **Honours:** OBE 1941; CMG 1948. **Publications:** 'From Astara to Ardabil', *The Eagle* XLI, 1920. Died 6 July 1959.

TROTT, Francis William (1912) Born 19 December 1892, 1 Richmond Villas, North Avenue, Padstoe Road, Heavitree, Exeter, Devon; son of John Trott, Teacher in the School of Science, Albert Memorial Museum (later University of Exeter), and Dorothea Eliza Robinson; m Lilian Gladys Jerman; 1 son (Christopher b 1934), 2 daughters (Sylvia b 1920 and Una b 1922). **Subject(s):** Mathematics; BA 1919. **Tutor(s):** L H K Bushe-Fox. **Johnian Relatives:** brother of Alan Charles Trott (1913); uncle of John Michael Trott (1949) and of Peter Alan Trott (1953). **Educ:** St John's Hospital School, Exeter; Hele's School, Exeter; Exeter School. **Career:** Captain, Devonshire Regiment (wounded twice, twice Mentioned in Despatches) 1914–1918; Staff Officer, RAF 1918; in charge of Officer Training, Cranwell; posting to Kohat and the North

West Frontier, India; First Commanding Officer, No 1 Air Armament School, Manby, Lincolnshire (Group Captain 1939); Head, Air Mission Washington, then liaison with US Army, London 1940–1945; Head, P5, Air Ministry; Teacher in retirement. **Awards:** Vidal Scholarship, SJC 1912. **Honours:** OBE 1919; MC; two Medals of Honor from the USA. Died 3 August 1975.

TROTT, John Michael (1949) Born 21 July 1929, St Audrey's, Colehill, Wimborne, Dorset; son of Alan Charles Trott, HM Ambassador, Jeddah, Saudi Arabia, and Hester Dorothy Richardson; m Joan Doris Wills, 15 March 1958; 1 son (Stephen Alan), 1 daughter (Frances Gael). **Subject(s):** Economics/Law; BA 1952; MA 1956. **Tutor(s):** C W Guillebaud. **Johnian Relatives:** nephew of Francis William Trott (1912); son of Alan Charles Trott (1913); brother of Peter Alan Trott (1953). **Educ:** Winchester House School, Brackley; University School, Montreal, Canada; Repton School. **Career:** Solicitor 1956–1990. **Appointments:** President, Cornwall Rugby Football Union 1990–1991.

TROUBRIDGE, James Lewis (1905) Born 28 June 1882, 21 London Road, Northfleet, Kent; son of Lewis James Troubridge, Schoolmaster, and Mary Ann Eavis; m Lucy May Prescott (d 1969); 1 son (John). BA 1908. **Tutor(s):** J R Tanner. **Educ:** City of London School; St Mark's College, Chelsea; École Normale, Rouen. **Career:** Assistant Master, Manchester Grammar School 1908–1909; Assistant Master, Cheltenham College 1909–1910; Master, City of London School 1911–1924. Died 1924.

TROUGHT, Thomas Edmund Trevor (1947) Born 30 November 1922, Gezira, Sudan; son of Trevor Trought, Agriculturalist/Botanist, and Elsa Kathleen Butler; 2 sons, 2 daughters. BA 1949; MA 1954. **Tutor(s):** G C L Bertram. **Johnian Relatives:** son of Trevor Trought (1910); brother of Vincent Paul Trevor Trought (1938). **Career:** Entomologist, Ugandan Government 1951–1954; Entomological Pest Control Research, Shell Chemical Company 1955–1966; Entomological Pest Control Research, Ministry of Agriculture and Fisheries, New Zealand 1966–1982.

TROUGHT, Trevor (1910) Born 17 March 1891, 57 Summerfield Crescent, Lady Wood, Birmingham; son of Thomas Wilson Trought, Schoolmaster, and Helena Maud Windle; m Elsa Kathleen Butler, 30 April 1919, Christ Church, Summerfield (d 1961); 2 sons (Vincent Paul Trevor b 18 February 1920 and Thomas Edmund Trevor b 30 November 1922), 1 daughter. **Subject(s):** Natural Sciences; BA 1913; MA 1925. **Tutor(s):** J R Tanner. **Johnian Relatives:** father of Vincent Paul Trevor Trought (1938) and of Thomas Edmund Trevor Trought (1947). **Educ:** King Edward's School, Birmingham. **Career:** Assistant Director of Agriculture, Central Provinces, India 1914; Captain, Queen's Own (Royal West Kent Regiment, TF), WWI; Cotton Botanist, Egypt 1920–1923; Assistant Director of Agriculture Central Provinces, India 1924; Director, Gezira Research, Ministry of Agriculture, Amman, Jordan. Died 23 July 1970.

TROUGHT, Vincent Paul Trevor (1938) Born 18 February 1920, Cairo, Egypt; son of Trevor Trought, Botanist, and Elsa Kathleen Butler. BA 1941; MA 1945; BSc (Edinburgh) 1951; MRCVS. **Tutor(s):** M P Charlesworth. **Johnian Relatives:** son of Trevor Trought (1910); brother of Thomas Edmund Trevor Trought (1947). **Educ:** Dragon School, Oxford; Dauntsey's School, West Lavington. **Career:** Veterinary Surgeon, Rochester, Kent. **Honours:** OBE 1961.

TROUP, Harold James Gardiner (1946) Born 3 December 1922, 23 Cluny Drive, Edinburgh; son of George Elmslie Troup, Minister, United Free Church, and Agnes Dorothy Cowan; m Sheelagh Elizabeth Anne McLeod Simpson, June 1947, St Margaret's, Northam; 2 daughters (Helen Agnes Catriona Franklin and Mary Elizabeth). **Subject(s):** Theology; BA 1948; MA 1952. **Tutor(s):** R L Howland. **Educ:** Cargilfield School, Edinburgh; Sedbergh School. **Career:** Lieutenant, RNVR, Far East 1941–1946; Parish Minister, St John's Church, Leven, Fife 1951–1963; Parish Minister, St John's Church, Inverkeithing and North Queensferry, Fife 1963–1970; Parish Minister, Garelochnead Church,

Argyll 1970–1980. **Appointments:** JP. **Awards:** Star 1939–1945; The Atlantic Star; The Burma Star; The Defence Medal; The Medal 1939–1945.

TROWELL, Dr Oswald Arthur (1926) Born 19 May 1909, 67 Norfolk Road, Erdington, Birmingham; son of Alfred Arthur Trowell, Company Director, and Jessie Newbold. **Subject(s):** Natural Sciences; BA 1929; MA 1933; MB 1933; BChir 1933; MD 1940; FRSE. **Tutor(s):** M P Charlesworth. **Johnian Relatives:** father of Timothy Martin Trowell (1959). **Educ:** Bishop Vesey's Grammar School, Sutton Coldfield; Lincoln School; King Edward's School, Birmingham. **Career:** Demonstrator in Physiology, University of Liverpool 1933–1934; Title B Fellow, SJC 1934–1937; Demonstrator in Physiology, University of Cambridge 1934–1937; Lecturer in Physiology, University of Edinburgh until 1946; Reader in Physiology, University of Bristol 1946–1948; Staff, MRC Radio-Biological Research Unit, Harwell 1948. **Appointments:** Director of Medical Studies and Supervisor in Physiology, SJC 1934–1937. **Awards:** Open Exhibition, SJC; Scholarship, SJC 1928; Raymond Horton-Smith Prize, University of Cambridge 1940. **Publications:** Chapters in *Cells and Tissues in Cultures* and numerous articles in scientific journals. Died 17 November 1967.

TRUMPER, John Henry Walwyn (1904) Born 8 January 1885, The Parsonage, Colne, St Ives, Huntingdonshire; son of John Frederick Walwyn Trumper, Clerk in Holy Orders, and Evelyn Greswell; m Marjorie Cicely Scobie, 30 January 1915, St Thomas', Rhyl; 2 sons (John and Peter). BA 1907. **Tutor(s):** E E Sikes. **Johnian Relatives:** son of John Frederick Walwyn Trumper (1869). **Educ:** Hereford Cathedral School. **Career:** Educational work, India 1909–1911; Schoolmaster, Scartcliffe, Englefield Green, Surrey 1911–1913; Educational work, St Petersburg 1913–1914; Second Lieutenant, 1st Monmouthshire Regiment (wounded) 1914–1916; Foreign Office 1916–1919. **Honours:** OBE 1920. Died 6 April 1965.

TUCKER, Dennis Henry Maine (1914) Born 28 October 1895, 35 Westbourne Road, Penarth; son of William Henry Maine Tucker, Merchant, and Minna Sarah Lane Hall. **Tutor(s):** E E Sikes. **Educ:** Miss Herbert's School, Penarth; Penarth Lodge; Llandaff Cathedral School; Marlborough College. **Career:** Lieutenant, Manchester Regiment 1914–1918.

TUCKETT, Dr Ronald Francis (1935) Born 5 June 1917, 26 Waterloo Road, Devonport; son of Edward Francis Tuckett, Engineer, Lieutenant Commander, RN, and Mildred Fitzgerald Perryman; m Elizabeth Mary Frith, 21 March 1944, Rogate, Sussex (d 1976); 5 sons (David, Christopher, John, Richard and Roger). **Subject(s):** Natural Sciences; BA 1938; PhD 1941. **Tutor(s):** C W Guillebaud. **Educ:** Kindergarten School, Sydney; Somerset Place Council School, Devonport; Plymouth College. **Awards:** Exhibition, SJC 1936–1937. **Publications:** *Linear Polymers*, Longman, 1951.

TUNKS, Donald Russell (1926) Born 16 November 1908, Roundstone, Dene Road, Guildford, Surrey; son of Frederick Russell Tunks, Chemical Engineer, and Lilian Payne; m Daphne Merton, 9 July 1932, St Mary's-at-Finchley. BA 1929. **Tutor(s):** J M Wordie. **Educ:** Yardley Court, Tonbridge; Clifton College.

TUNSTALL, William Cuthbert Brian (1918) Born 23 April 1900, 88 Palace Gardens Terrace, Kensington, London; son of Frederick William Whitelock Tunstall and Isabel Agnes Renny; m Gillean Elizabeth Corbett, 31 March 1928, Danehill Parish Church; 2 sons (Cuthbert Jeremy b 14 October 1934 and Julian Brian b 14 June 1931, d 12 July 1983). **Subject(s):** History; BA 1921; MA 1926. **Tutor(s):** E E Sikes. **Johnian Relatives:** son of Frederick William Whitelock Tunstall (1879); father of Julian Brian Tunstall (1951) and of Cuthbert Jeremy Tunstall (1955). **Educ:** Harrow View School, Ealing; Haileybury College. **Career:** Master, Oundle School 1922–1925; Lecturer in History, Royal Naval College, Greenwich 1925–1947; Senior Lecturer in International Relations, LSE 1959. **Appointments:** Secretary, Navy Record Society.

Publications: (ed with H M Stewart) *The History of the Lady Margaret Boat Club Volume II 1926–1956*, 1957. Died 27 September 1970.

TURNBULL, Dennis Etherington (1949) Born 2 August 1929, 4 Station Street, Waterhouses, Brandon; son of George Turnbull, Civil Servant, and Gladys Etherington. **Subject(s):** Economics; BA 1952. **Tutor(s):** C W Guillebaud. **Educ:** Waterhouses Junior School; Chester-le-Street Red Rose Junior School; Chester-le-Street Grammar School.

TURNBULL, Derwent Greville (1940) Born 4 January 1922, 29 Henley Road, Ipswich, Suffolk; son of Herbert Westren Turnbull, Professor of Mathematics, and Ella Drummond Williamson; m (1) Morna Jean Gauld, 1947, (2) Gennifer Vorgan, 1973; (1) 1 son, 1 daughter, (2) 2 daughters. **Subject(s):** Mechanical Sciences; BA 1943; MA 1947; MSc (Cranfield) 1954; CEng; ARCM. **Tutor(s):** J M Wordie. **Educ:** The Rectory, St Andrews; Lathallan Preparatory School; Rugby School. **Career:** Aeronautical Engineer, RNVR 1942–1945; Instructor Branch, RN, retired as Commander 1945–1968; Lecturer in Mechanical Engineering 1969–1983, Music Advisor 1976–1983, Dundee University. **Awards:** Scholarship, SJC.

TURNBULL, Gerald William (1927) Born 29 April 1910, Brantwood Newall, Otley, Yorkshire; son of Arthur Turnbull, Solicitor, and Annie Wildblood; 1 son, 1 daughter. **Subject(s):** Law; BA 1931; MA 1938; LLB 1934; BSc (London). **Tutor(s):** C W Guillebaud. **Educ:** Moorlands School, Headingley, Leeds; The Leys School, Cambridge. **Career:** Solicitor. **Awards:** Postgraduate Studentship, Empire Cotton Growing Corporation. Died 14 December 1980.

TURNER, Donald Reginald Stuart (1935) Born 1 January 1917, 100 Wilbraham Road, Chorlton-cum-Hardy, Manchester; son of Percy Stuart Turner, Electrical Engineer, and Laura Beatrice Cowley. **Subject(s):** Mechanical Sciences; BA 1938; Higher National Certificate in Electrical and Mechanical Engineering. **Tutor(s):** J S Boys Smith. **Johnian Relatives:** brother of Roland Harold Stuart Turner (1926). **Educ:** King's College School, Wimbledon; Oundle School. **Career:** Graduate Apprenticeship, British Thomson-Houston Co, Rugby; Sales Manager, then General Manager, Turbo-Alternator Factory, Larne, Northern Ireland; General Manager, Sorocco, Belfast; Turbine Sales Department British Thompson Houston Company 1945. Died 1 August 1994.

TURNER, Geoffrey Redman (1928) Born 21 September 1910, 71 Cecil Avenue, Horton, Bradford, Yorkshire; son of William Arthur Turner, Incorporated Accountant, and Geraldine Eliza Hargreaves. **Subject(s):** Economics/Law; BA 1931; MA 1935; ICA 1935. **Tutor(s):** E A Benians. **Johnian Relatives:** uncle of Anthony Hugh Benson Turner (1958). **Educ:** Malsis Hall Preparatory School; The Leys School, Cambridge. **Career:** Articled in Price Waterhouse & Co, Chartered Accountants, until 1938; Partner, WA Turner & Co 1938–1964; TA, RE, later RA, Major 1939–1945; Partner, Claridge Turner 1964–1976; Partner, Russan Claridge Turner 1976–1980; President, Bradford Permanent Building Society. **Appointments:** President, Leeds and Bradford District Society of Chartered Accountants. Died 21 November 1987.

TURNER, George Michael (1943) Born 21 July 1925, 7 Woodlands, Highgate Road, Dewsbury; son of George Turner, Silk Merchant, and Phyllis Augusta Thornton, Housewife; m Zara Coats, 1952, Paisley; 2 daughters (Zara Caroline and Jeniffer Ann). **Subject(s):** Mechanical Engineering; BA 1946; MA 1950. **Tutor(s):** S J Bailey. **Educ:** Gledhow Preparatory School, Huddersfield; Elland Grammar School; Wellingborough School. **Career:** Graduate Engineer, Apprentice, then Project Engineer, Babcock & Wilcox, Renfrew and London 1945–1950; Senior Design Engineer, then Chief Mechanical Engineer, John Brown Land Boilers, Clydebank 1951–1959; Chief Designer, then General Manager and Director, Yarrow Engineers Ltd, Glasgow 1959–1972; Principal Consultant, Yarrow Admiralty Research Department Ltd, Glasgow 1972–1983; Consulting Engineer, Hancox & Partners, Glasgow 1983–1984; Information Control Leader, Yarrow Admiralty Research

Department Ltd, Glasgow 1984–1990. **Publications:** (with P D Pepe) IMechE paper 'Design of the First Large UK Power producing Refuse Incineration Plant', 1969.

TURNER, Godfrey Michael (1928) Born 17 August 1910, Beightons, Rochdale, Lancashire; son of Frank Turner, Director of Companies, and Helen Peters. BA 1931. **Tutor(s):** C W Guillebaud. **Johnian Relatives:** brother of John Dennis Turner (1922). **Educ:** Sandroyd School, Cobham; Charterhouse.

TURNER, Guy Elliot (1926) Born 5 November 1907, Nasik, Bombay Presidency, India; son of Ernest George Turner, Civil Servant, and Edith Mary Hand. **Subject(s):** History; BA 1929; MA 1977; PGCE 1964. **Tutor(s):** E A Benians. **Johnian Relatives:** son of Ernest George Turner (1893). **Educ:** Lake House Preparatory School, Bexhill on Sea; Haileybury College. **Career:** Malayan Civil Service 1931; Deputy Commissioner of Labour, Department of Labour, Perak, until 1957; Teacher 1957–1968. Died 1984.

TURNER, John Dennis (1922) Born 16 January 1904, Brotherod Hall, Rochdale, Lancashire; son of Frank Turner, Rubber Manufacturer, and Helen Peters; m Rosemary. **Tutor(s):** B F Armitage. **Johnian Relatives:** brother of Godfrey Michael Turner (1928). **Educ:** Sandroyd School, Cobham; Charterhouse. Died 9 September 1925.

TURNER, John Moore (1924) Born 19 December 1905, The Pavement, St Ives, Huntingdonshire; son of Harold Strange Turner, Chemist and Druggist, and Alice Rinder Gibbon. **Tutor(s):** B F Armitage. **Educ:** The Modern School, Bedford.

TURNER, Professor John Stewart (1949) (admitted to Selwyn College 1927) Born 9 September 1908, Middlesbrough, Yorkshire; son of Thomas Stewart Turner, Admirality Overseer, and Ellen Spice; m Kathleen; 1 son (Peter), 1 daughter (Susan). BA 1930 (Selwyn); MA 1934 (Selwyn); PhD 1935 (Selwyn). **Educ:** Central Secondary School, Sheffield; Selwyn College, Cambridge. **Career:** University Demonstrator in Botany 1934–1938; Professor of Botany & Plant Pathology 1938–1973, Dean, Faculty of Science 1944–1947, University of Melbourne; Title B Fellow, SJC 1949–1950; Visiting Fellow, Clare College, Cambridge 1964. **Awards:** Frank Smart Studentship, University of Cambridge 1932; Allen Scholarship, University of Cambridge 1933; Gedge Prize, University of Cambridge 1934. **Honours:** OBE 1973. Died 9 May 1991.

TURNER, Robert (1936) Born 4 August 1918, 2 Astley Street, Tyldesley, Lancashire; son of Arthur Turner, Railway Clerk, and Alice Farnworth; m Doris Vera Thompson, 6 May 1950; 1 son (Martin b 1957), 1 daughter (Susan b 1953). **Subject(s):** Mathematics; BA 1939; MA 1947; FSS. **Tutor(s):** J M Wordie. **Johnian Relatives:** father of Martin Guy Turner (1976). **Educ:** Tyldesley St George's C of E School; Manchester Grammar School. **Career:** RA 1939–1946; Commissioned 1940; HQ125 Infantry Brigade and 11 Corps Home Forces 1940–1942; Graduated Staff College, Camberley 1942; HQ 102 Beach Brigade and 30 Corps, Eighth Army, Middle East and Central Mediterranean 1943; Force 133 and Force 136, Special Operations Executive, Middle East and South East Asia 1943–1946; Lieutenant Colonel 1945; Assistant Principal, Ministry of Labour and National Service 1946; Assistant Private Secretary to Minister of Labour 1948–1949; Principal Private Secretary to Minister of Labour 1949; Loaned to Colonial Office 1950–1954; Regraded Statistician 1961; Chief Statistician 1965; Deputy Director of Statistics 1968–1972. **Awards:** Baylis Scholarship, SJC 1935; Scholarship, SJC 1936–1937; Wright's Prize, SJC 1937. Died 25 September 1989.

TURNER, Roland (1902) Born 28 March 1883, Board School House, Newmarket, Suffolk; son of John Turner, Schoolmaster, and Elizabeth Martha Haslewood. BA 1906. **Tutor(s):** J R Tanner; C E Graves. **Educ:** Glenwood Collegiate School, Newmarket; Guildhall Middle School, Bury St Edmunds. **Career:** Lieutenant, York and Lancaster Regiment, WWI. **Honours:** MC.

TURNER, Roland Harold Stuart (1926) Born 14 August 1907, 57 Ryebank Road, Chorlton-cum-Hardy, Lancashire; son of Percy John Duncan Stuart Turner, Electrical Engineer, and Laura Beatrice Cowley. BA 1929; MA 1933; CEng; FIProdE. **Tutor(s):** J M Wordie. **Johnian Relatives:** brother of Donald Reginald Stuart Turner (1935). **Educ:** King's College School, Wimbledon. **Career:** Director of Personnel, GEC Power Engineering Ltd; Metropolitan-Vickers Ltd 1930 (Superintendent of Plant Department 1948, Works Manager 1952, Director of Manufacture and Board Member 1955). **Appointments:** Chairman 1961–1963, National President 1965–1967, Institution of Production Engineers; Governor, Royal Technical College, Salford; Member, Education UK Advisory Council Committee on Education for Management. Died 21 June 1972.

TURNER, Ronald (1948) Born 14 June 1928, Briarcliffe, Clitheroe, Lancashire; son of Walter Turner, Cotton Mill Secretary, and Gladys Annie Brennand. **Tutor(s):** F Thistlethwaite. **Educ:** Pendle Junior School, Clitheroe; Clitheroe Royal Grammar School.

TURNER, Roy (1940) Born 18 July 1922, 32 Cecil Road, Rochester, Kent; son of Herbert Alfred Turner, Acting Constructor, HM Admiralty, and Hetty Ariadne Braybrooke; m Helen Mary Row, 1954; 3 sons (John b 1956, Robert b 1959 and Andrew b 1961). **Subject(s):** Natural Sciences; BA 1943; BA (Open) 1994. **Tutor(s):** J M Wordie. **Educ:** Glencoe Road Elementary School, Chatham; Mathematical School, Rochester. **Career:** Captain, RE, Middle East and India 1943–1947; Research Chemist, BP 1947–1975; Manager, BP Research Centre, Sunbury 1976–1979; Assistant General Manager, BP Research and Development Department 1979–1982. **Awards:** Minor Scholarship, SJC 1939. Died 28 January 2004.

TURNER, William Aylmer Laws (1932) Born 9 November 1913, 7 Kingswood Avenue, Newcastle upon Tyne; son of William Gilbert Turner, Electrical Engineer, and Katherine Annie Laws; m (1) Phyllis Mary Dwelly, 19 June 1943, Liverpool Cathedral, (2) Barbara. **Subject(s):** Mechanical Sciences; BA 1935; MA 1944. **Tutor(s):** J S Boys Smith. **Educ:** St Winifred's, Kenley; Bradfield College. **Career:** British Thomson-Houston Company, Rugby 1937; Commercial Manager, Atomic Power Constructions 1957; Manager, English Electric Company 1965. Died 3 January 1994.

TURNER, William Leslie (1909) Born 25 July 1890, 30 Camden Road, South Town, Great Yarmouth; son of William Hindhaugh Turner, Accountant, and Adelaide Blackley. **Subject(s):** Natural Sciences; BA 1912. **Tutor(s):** L H K Bushe-Fox. **Educ:** St Catherine's School, New Cross; Haberdashers' Aske's Hatcham Boys' School.

TURNEY, Frederick Donald d'Avray (1929) Born 22 February 1910, Phoenix, Plaines Wilhelms, Mauritius; son of Fred Turney, Civil Engineer, and Claire Blanche d'Avray. BA 1932; MA 1945. **Tutor(s):** C W Guillebaud. **Johnian Relatives:** cousin of Austin James Wilson (1926) and of Frank Albert Wilson (1932). **Educ:** Clifton College; Seafield Park, Fareham. **Career:** Manager, Sugar Factory, Kenya; Estate Manager, Ceylon; Senior Science Master, Victoria College, Egypt; Education Officer, Iraq; Captain, Indian Army, Served in North Africa and Italy.

TURNEY, Roy Frederick (1944) Born 10 December 1925, 17 Wellington Road, Raunds, Northamptonshire; son of Ralph Turney, Shoe Finisher, and Edith Marjorie Jeffkins. **Tutor(s):** J M Wordie. **Educ:** Raunds Council School; Raunds Church of England Junior School; Wellingborough Grammar School.

TURPITT, Walter George (1931) Born 20 June 1912, South Radworthy, North Molton; son of Edward William Turpitt, Farm Labourer, and Thirza Slee. **Subject(s):** Natural Sciences; BA 1934; MA 1938. **Tutor(s):** C W Guillebaud. **Educ:** Heasley Mill Elementary School; West Buckland School. **Awards:** Scholarship, Ministry of Agriculture and Fisheries.

TURQUET, Pierre Maurice (1932) Born 13 December 1913, 59 Loxley Road, Wandsworth; son of André Turquet, Director, Coaching School for Diplomatic Service, and Gladys Milnes; m Ellen Clare Hunter, 12 October 1940, St Joan of Arc Church, Farnham; 2 sons, 1 daughter. **Subject(s):** Natural Sciences; BA 1935; MA 1939; MRCS; DPM; FRCPsych; LRCP. **Tutor(s):** E A Benians. **Educ:** Westminster School. **Career:** Lieutenant, special personnel selection work with the French forces 1939–1945; Psychoanalyst; Consultant, Tavistock Clinic, London 1952–1975. Died 27 December 1976.

TWENTYMAN, Captain Denzil Clive Tate (1909) Born 27 June 1890, Shanghai, China; son of James Robert Twentyman, Engineer, and Ada Minns; m Sybil Josephine Hall, 20 June 1915, Bushey Parish Church, Hertfordshire. BA 1913. **Tutor(s):** J R Tanner. **Educ:** Bromsgrove School. **Career:** Hong Kong and Shanghai Banking Corporation; Second Lieutenant, 10th York and Lancashire Regiment 1914; Lieutenant 1914; Captain 1915–1916. Died 1 July 1916 (killed in action).

TWIGG, Dr George Hilton (1935) Born 3 April 1913, 41 Balfour Street, Alloa, Clackmannan; son of George Twigg, Architect, and Sarah Hilton; m Anna Morton Brown; 1 son (Robert Douglas Hilton), 1 daughter (Julia Morton). PhD 1939; Honorary DSc (St Andrews) 1970. **Tutor(s):** J M Wordie. **Johnian Relatives:** father of Robert Douglas Hilton Twigg (1963). **Educ:** Alloa Academy; Dollar Academy; University of St Andrews. **Career:** Laboratory of Colloid Science, Cambridge 1936–1947; Research Manager, Distillers Co Ltd, Epsom (subsequently BP Chemicals) from 1947. **Appointments:** Honorary Secretary and Treasurer 1936 and 1937, Vice President 1938, SJC Chess Club; Member, Faraday Club; Council Member, Faraday Society; Member, Parliamentary and Scientific Committee; Visiting Professor, Chemical Sciences, University of East Anglia 1968; Member, SRC 1970. **Awards:** Strathcona Exhibition, SJC. Died 22 October 1970.

TWINN, Frank Charles George (1904) Born 1 September 1885, Mile End, London; son of George Twinn, Railway Worker, and Mary Brown. **Subject(s):** Classics/Economics; BA 1907. **Tutor(s):** E E Sikes. **Educ:** Fair Street Board School; St Olave's Elementary School; St Olave's Grammar School. **Career:** Post Office 1909.

TYLER, Dr Geoffrey James (1945) Born 16 March 1928, 21 Berkeley Street, Stone, Staffordshire; son of Bernard Tyler, Insurance Agent, and Emily Ada Andrews, Teacher; m Mollie Brook, 1951; 1 son (David), 2 daughters (Vivien and Helen). **Subject(s):** Natural Sciences; BA 1948; MA 1952; PhD 1953; BPharm (Welsh School of Pharmacy, Cardiff) 1977; FChemSoc; MRPharmS 1978. **Tutor(s):** G C L Bertram. **Educ:** Christ Church School, Stone; Alleynes Grammar School, Stone. **Career:** Research Chemist and Section Manager, Research and Development, ICI Fibres, Pontypool 1952–1974; Locum Pharmacist, South East Wales 1978–2001. **Appointments:** Founder, Cwmbran Baroque Singers 1971. **Awards:** Scholarship, SJC 1947. **Publications:** (with R Brown, A W Johnson and E Robinson) 'The 'Striga' Germination Factor 2', *Biochemical Journal*, 1952; (with K Butler and P R Thomas) 'Some New Benziminazole Derivatives', *Journal of the Chemical Society*, May 1957; 'Stereospecific Polymerisation of Some Polar Vinyl Monomers', *Journal of Polymer Science*, 1960; *Cwmbran Baroque Singers 1971–1996 – The Story in Music and Words* (3CDs and booklet), compiled and published privately, 2000.

TYREMAN, Anthony Carlisle (1948) Born 15 December 1927, West Hartlepool, Durham; son of Ernest Tyreman, Journalist, and Mary Olive Mowbray; m Margaret. **Subject(s):** Classics; BA 1950; MA 1955. **Tutor(s):** R L Howland. **Educ:** Elwick Road Elementary School, West Hartlepool; Brinkburn Secondary School, West Hartlepool; Pocklington School. **Career:** Commodity Broker. **Appointments:** Associate of major London museums 1994. Died 14 September 1994.

TYSON, Harold Edward (1924) Born 24 April 1905, 14 Diamond Terrace, Weymouth, Dorset; son of Thomas Jardine Tyson, Chief Engine Room Artificer, RN, and Kate Beck. **Subject(s):** Natural Sciences; BA 1927; MA 1931; CEng; FIMinE. **Tutor(s):** B F Armitage. **Educ:** George Street Elementary Council School, Portsmouth; The Grammar School, Portsmouth. **Career:** Ashington Coal Company, Limited; Undermanager, Seghill Colliery and Bowburn Colliery; Manager, Burnhope and Auckland Park Collieries; Area Safety Engineer, St Helens Area, North-Western Divisional Coal Board; Manager, Cronton Colliery 1943. **Appointments:** President, Junior Section, North of England Institute of Mining and Mechanical Engineers; President 1950, Honorary Secretary 1954, National Vice-President 1957, National President 1959, Lancashire Branch, National Association of Colliery Managers. **Awards:** Scholarship, SJC 1923. Died 1995.

U

UDALL, The Revd Geoffrey Sturt (1936) Born 16 January 1917, 25 Cecil Road, Muswell Hill, London; son of Ernest Alexander Udall, Director of Companies, and Ethel Winifred Sturt; m Eleanore Brighouse Mason, 27 July 1946, Hanover Square (d 1982). **Subject(s):** Natural Sciences; BA 1939; MA 1943; BChir 1943; MB 1943. **Tutor(s):** R L Howland. **Educ:** Downs School, Colwall, Malvern; Bryanston School. **Career:** Qualified at St Thomas' Hospital 1943; Army Medical Corps, Burma 1945; Senior Assistant Medical Officer, Brentford and Chiswick, Heston and Isleworth and Southall 1959–1960; Deputy Area Medical Officer for Hornsey and Tottenham 1960; Reader/Consultant Paediatrician, St Bartholomew's Hospital 1962–1981; Founding Member, Horticultural Therapy 1978–1989; Ordained Deacon 1982–1983; Non-Stipendary Minister, St Matthew's, Reading 1982–1986; Ordained Priest 1983; Assistant Rural Dean, Reading 1985–1994; Christ Church, Whitley 1986–1994. **Appointments:** Chairman of Governors, Bryanston School. Died 22 March 1994.

UDALL, Humfrey Nicholas (1949) Born 26 January 1929, Dairan, Meaford Road, Barlaston, Stoke-on-Trent; son of John Sheppard Udall, Chartered Accountant, and Joyce Mary Grace Addyman. **Subject(s):** Mechanical Sciences; BA 1952; MA 1957; CEng; AWS; ASM; ASME; MIMechE. **Tutor(s):** R L Howland. **Educ:** Chaucer House, Dresden; Ryeford Hall, Stonehouse; Wycliffe College. Died 13 November 1990.

ULLYOTT, Henry Wilson (1942) Born 14 June 1924, Lissett, Driffield, Yorkshire; son of Raymond Wilson Ullyott, Farmer, and Kate Broumpton. **Tutor(s):** S J Bailey. **Educ:** Lissett Church of England School; Bridlington School.

URABE, Tosio (1938) Born 4 May 1912, 773 Kuriyamacho Kakutamura; son of Eitarow Urabe, Businessman, and Toyo Ikami. **Educ:** First High School, Tokyo; Tokyo Imperial University.

URIE, Robert Wallace (1913) Born 20 September 1894, Ravenswood, Caledonia Road, Saltcoats, Ayrshire; son of Robert Wallace Urie, Engineer, and Jeanie Chalmers. **Tutor(s):** R P Gregory. **Educ:** Wilson Grammar School, Camberwell; King Edward VI School, Southampton; Hartley College, Southampton. **Career:** Captain, RFA (wounded, Mentioned in Despatches), WWI.

URLING-SMITH, Alban (1922) Born 20 February 1904, 73 Alexandra Road, Southport, Lancashire; son of Alban Urling-Smith, Clerk in Holy Orders, and Alice Josephine Smith. BA 1925. **Tutor(s):** E E Sikes. **Educ:** St Michael's Preparatory School, Buxton; Normanton School, Buxton; Holm Leigh School, Buxton; St Edward's School, Oxford.

URQUHART, Major Ian Alexander Norfolk (1938) Born 19 December 1919, The Court, Acomb, York; son of Alexander Urquhart, Civil Engineer, and Jessie Norfolk; m Beatrice Soulsby, 19 January 1957. **Educ:** Fisher Institute, Montreux, Switzerland; Dover College Junior School; Dover College. **Career:** Commissioned in Border Regiment, India, then Instructor, Army Gas School 1939–1946; Colonial Service, Kuching, Sarawak; Cadet Officer, Sibu 1947. **Honours:** MC 1944.

USHERWOOD, Kenneth Ascough (1922) Born 19 August 1904, Jesmond, Compton Road, Winchmore Hill, Southgate, Middlesex; son of Herbert Thomas Usherwood, Assurance Clerk, and Lettie Humphries Ascough; m Mary Louise Reepmaker d'Orville, 20 December 1946, London. **Subject(s):** Mathematics; BA 1925; MA 1930. **Tutor(s):** E Cunningham. **Educ:** Winchmore Hill Collegiate School; City of London School. **Career:** Prudential Assurance 1925–1931; Prudential Assurance, South Africa 1931–1947; Director of Statistics, Ministry of Supply, WWII; Deputy General Manager 1947–1960, Chief General Manager 1961–1967, Director 1968–1979, Chairman 1970–1975, President 1979–1982, Prudential Assurance. **Appointments:** Chairman, Industrial Life Offices Association 1961–1962; President, Institute of Actuaries 1962–1964; Member, Gaming Board 1968–1972. **Honours:** CBE 1964. Died 5 December 1988.

USSHER, Percival Arland (1919) Born 9 September 1899, 19 Overstrand Mansions, Prince of Wales Road, Battersea; son of Beverley Grant Ussher, Landowner, and Emily Horsley Jebb; m (1) Emily Atkinson Whitehead, 1925 (d 1974), (2) Peggy, 1975; (1) 1 daughter (Henrietta). **Tutor(s):** E E Sikes. **Educ:** High School, Shrewsbury; King Alfred Co-educational School; Gore Court, Sittingbourne; Abbotsholme, Staffordshire; TCD. **Career:** Writer, Essayist, Philosopher and Scholar. **Appointments:** President, Irish Academy of Letters. **Awards:** 13th Gregory Medal, Irish Academy of Letters. **Publications:** *Caint an tSean-Shaoghail*, 1942; *Cúrsaí an tSean Shaoil*, 1942; *The Face and Mind of Ireland*, 1949; *A Journey Through Dread*, 1955; *The Magic People*, 1952; *Three Great Irishmen*, 1952; *Spanish Mercy*, 1959; *Sages and Schoolmen*, 1967; *The Twenty Two Keys of the Tarot*, 1976; *From a Dark Lantern*, 1978; *The Juggler*, 1982. Died 24 December 1980.

UTTLEY, John Corin Taylor (1933) Born 12 September 1914, Sidcot, South Downs Road, Hale; son of James Arthur Uttley, Civil Engineer, and Alice Jane Taylor. **Subject(s):** Classics/History; BA 1936; MA 1956. **Tutor(s):** R L Howland. **Educ:** Tarlet Hall Preparatory School; Sedbergh School. **Career:** Captain, Royal Devon Yeomanry (Artillery), POW Germany WWII. **Awards:** Exhibition, SJC.

V

VAIDYA, Shridhar Balkrishna (1908) Born 25 February 1890, Sangli, Sangli State, Bombay Presidency, India; son of Balkrishna Narayan Vaidya, Deputy Collector, Bombay Presidency, India, and Kamlabai Balkrishna Vaidya. **Subject(s):** Mathematics/Natural Sciences/History; BA 1911. **Tutor(s):** L H K Bushe-Fox. **Educ:** Elphinstone College, Bombay, India. **Career:** Called to the Bar, Gray's Inn 1914.

VALE, Henry Edmund Theodoric (1909) Born 9 September 1888, Greenfield Hall, Holywell, Flintshire; son of William Theodoric Vale, Clerk in Holy Orders, and Catherine Emma Buxton; m Ruth Madeleine Hutchings, 9 June 1924, Sherborne Abbey; 1 son (Bob), 2 daughters (Richenda and Anna-Mary). BA 1913; MA 1920. **Tutor(s):** L H K Bushe-Fox. **Educ:** Moorland House School, Heswall. **Career:** Captain, General List, attached RE (Signals), WWI. **Publications:** *The Mail Coach Men of the Late 18th Century*; Various contributions to *The Eagle*. Died 15 March 1969.

VALENTINE, Dr Anthony Seymour (1948) Born 4 February 1928, Women's Hospital, Sparkhill, Birmingham; son of Lionel Valentine, Flight Lieutenant, RAF, and Sarah Barbash; m Catherine Mary Birtles, 1958; 2 sons (Michael Paul and David Simon), 2 daughters (Alison Mary and Pamela Jane). **Subject(s):** Natural Sciences/Medicine; BA 1951; MA 1978; MB 1954; BChir 1954; Certification, College of Family Physicians of Canada 1971. **Tutor(s):** G C L Bertram. **Johnian Relatives:** nephew of Hezekiah Barbash (1914). **Educ:** Four Oaks Preparatory School, Sutton Coldfield, Bishop Vesey's Grammar School, Sutton Coldfield; Rugby School. **Career:** National Service, RAF 1946; Medical Officer, Sierra Leone 1956; GP, Nottingham 1960; Family Practice, Winnipeg, Manitoba, Canada 1969; Assistant Professor, Department of Family

Medicine, University of Manitoba 1985; Family and General Practice, Gillam, Manitoba 1987; Family Practice, Winnipeg 1991. **Appointments:** President, Manitoba College of Family Physicians 1976; Fellow, College of Family Physicians of Canada 1980; Council Member, College of Physicians and Surgeons of Manitoba 1990. **Awards:** Manitoba Family Physician of the Year 1991.

VALENTINE, The Rt Revd Barry (1945) Born 26 September 1927, Shenfield, Essex; son of Henry John Valentine, Liaison Officer, Lloyds, and Ethel Margaret Purkiss; m (1) Mary Currell Hayes, 1952, (2) Shirley Carolyn Shean Evans, 1984; 3 sons, 1 daughter. **Subject(s):** History; BA 1949; MA 1952; Honorary DD (University of Manitoba, Winnipeg) 1969, (Montreal Diocesan College); BD (McGill); LTh (Montreal). **Tutor(s):** F Thistlethwaite. **Educ:** Brentwood School. **Career:** Bishop of Rupert's Land 1969–1982; Assistant Bishop of Maryland 1986–1989. **Publications:** *The Gift that is in you*, 1984.

VALENTINE, Professor David Henriques (1930) Born 16 February 1912, 29 Bowker Street, Higher Broughton, Salford; son of Emanuel Henriques Valentine, Brewer's Traveller, and Dora Deborah Besso; m Joan Winifred Todd, 1938; 2 sons, 3 daughters. **Subject(s):** Natural Sciences; BA 1933; MA 1937; PhD 1937. **Tutor(s):** C W Guillebaud. **Educ:** North Manchester Preparatory School; Manchester Grammar School. **Career:** University Demonstrator and Curator, Herbarium and Museum, Botany School, University of Cambridge 1938–1945; Title A Fellow, SJC 1938–1946 (suspended during leave of absence on War Service); War Service 1940–1945; Temporary Officer, Ministry of Food 1939–1945; Reader of Botany 1945–1950, Professor of Botany 1950–1966, University of Durham; George Harrison Professor of Botany and Director of the Experimental Grounds, University of Manchester 1966. **Appointments:** Assistant Supervisor in Botany, SJC 1938–1946; President, Botanical Section; Vice-President, Cambridge Natural History Society 1940. **Awards:** Frank Smart Prize for Botany, University of Cambridge 1932; Frank Smart Studentship, University of Cambridge 1935. **Publications:** *Flora Europa*, 5 volumes, 1964–1980. Died 10 April 1987.

VALENTINE, Dr Wilfrid Henry (1929) Born 9 February 1912, 103 Magdalen Yard Road, Dundee; son of Charles Wilfrid Valentine, Professor of Education, University of Birmingham, and Margaret Ethel Rothwell Jackson. **Subject(s):** Natural Sciences; BA 1933; MA 1942; MB 1936; BChir 1936; MD 1942. **Tutor(s):** M P Charlesworth. **Educ:** Preparatory School, Edgbaston; King Edward's School, Birmingham. **Career:** Lieutenant Colonel, RAMC 1943–1945; GP 1946–1965; Regional Medical Officer, DHSS 1965–1975. **Awards:** ERD; Lister Scholarship, SJC 1930. **Honours:** OBE.

VALERO, Haim Aron (1932) Born 3 August 1914, Jerusalem, Palestine; son of Joseph Moses Valero, Judge of the District Court, Jerusalem, and Lea Batia Schaikewitsch. **Subject(s):** Law; BA 1935; MA 1939; LLB 1936; LLM 1936. **Tutor(s):** C W Guillebaud. **Educ:** Hebrew Grammar School, Jerusalem; The Perse School, Cambridge. **Career:** Public Member, Civil Service Commission; Landlord and Tenant Government Commission; Public District Governor, Lions International and various other government and public committees; Barrister-at-Law, Advocate and Notary in Israel.

VALLANCE-OWEN, Professor John (1939) See OWEN.

VAN DEN BERGH, Edward Arthur Roderick (1942) Born 30 April 1924, 1 St Oswald's Terrace, York; son of Arthur Felix Charles Van den Bergh, Managing Director, Diamond Fertiliser & Chemical Company, and Hilda Hirst; m Theresa Anne Voelcker, 22 December 1956, Johannesburg. **Subject(s):** Mechanical Sciences; BA 1947; MA 1952. **Tutor(s):** C W Guillebaud. **Johnian Relatives:** brother of Frank Asquith Van den Bergh (1943). **Educ:** Bickley Hall Preparatory School; Aldenham School. **Career:** Director of Companies and Deputy Chairman, Diamond Fertiliser Chemical Company.

VAN DEN BERGH, Frank Asquith (1943) Born 3 November 1925, 1 St Oswald's Terrace, York; son of Arthur Felix Charles Van den Bergh, Managing Director, Fertiliser Company, and Hilda Hirst. **Subject(s):** Mechanical Sciences; BA 1946; MA 1967. **Tutor(s):** S J Bailey. **Johnian Relatives:** brother of Edward Arthur Roderick Van den Bergh (1942). **Educ:** Bickley Hall Preparatory School; Alpine College, Villars, Switzerland; Aldenham School. **Career:** Managing Director, Diamond, Fertiliser and Chemical Company. Died 8 January 1993.

VAN DER LEE, Jacob Jan (1949) Born 5 February 1918, Rotterdam, Netherlands; son of Jacob Jan van der Lee, Naval Officer, and Gurtje Vink; m Johanna Alexandrine Boers, 16 March 1962, Brussels (d 26 December 1992). MLitt 1951; Doctorate of Law (Amsterdam Free University) 1945. **Tutor(s):** C W Guillebaud. **Educ:** Elementary School, Leyden; Latin Grammar School, Leyden; Latin Grammar School, Zwolle; Latin Grammar School, Apeldoorn; Faculty of Law, Sorbonne, France; Amsterdam University; Amsterdam Free University. **Career:** Secretary to the Dutch Minister of Agriculture and Food 1947–1949; Director, Ministry of Agriculture 1951–1958; Chief of Cabinet/Director, European Commission, Brussels 1958–1966; Burgomaster, Dordrecht 1966–1973; Burgomaster, Eindhoven 1973–1979; Member, Council of State (Raad van State), the Netherlands 1979–1988. **Honours:** Knighthood, Order of the Lion of the Netherlands; Officer, Legion d'Honneur, France 1954; Officer, Ordre Dannebrog, Denmark 1959; Commander in the Order of Orange-Nassau 1987.

VAN DRUTEN, Captain Henry John (1911) Born 13 October 1893, 41 Heathland Road, Stoke Newington, Middlesex; son of Wilhelmus van Druten, Banker, and Eva Benedictus; m (1) Margot Cinquevalli, 26 April 1921, (2) Gladys. **Subject(s):** Law; BA 1914; MA 1919. **Tutor(s):** L H K Bushe-Fox. **Educ:** Haberdashers' School; University College School. **Career:** Captain, Middlesex Regiment (wounded), WWI; Captain, RASC, WWII. Died 3 June 1946.

VAN DULKEN, Geoffrey Theodore Hicks (1947) Born 22 February 1924, 14 Purley Oaks Road, Sanderstead, Surrey; son of Frederick Theodore van Dulken, Bank Clerk, and Isabella Hicks Morley. **Subject(s):** Law; BA 1949. **Tutor(s):** F Thistlethwaite. **Educ:** Sanderstead Junior School; Cumnor House School, South Croydon; Canford School. **Career:** Captain, Royal Indian Artillery 1943–1946; Called to the Bar, Inner Temple 1957; Legal Work, International Air Transport Association (IATA) 1953–1983.

VAN GEYZEL, Frederick Christopher William (1920) Born 30 May 1901, Caledon House, Barnes Place, Cinnamon Gardens, Colombo, Ceylon; son of Colvin Thomas van Geyzel, Doctor of Medicine, and Antoinette Aileen Beling. **Tutor(s):** B F Armitage. **Johnian Relatives:** brother of Leonard Colvin van Geysel (1924). **Educ:** Government Training College, Ceylon; Royal College, Colombo.

VAN GEYZEL, Leonard Colvin (1924) Born 4 September 1905, Barnes Place, Cinnamon Gardens, Colombo, Ceylon; son of Colvin Thomas van Geyzel, Doctor of Medicine, and Antoinette Aileen Beling. **Subject(s):** Law/English; BA 1928. **Tutor(s):** E A Benians. **Johnian Relatives:** brother of Frederick Christopher William van Geyzel (1920). **Educ:** Royal College, Colombo, Ceylon.

VAN GEYZEL, Vivian Allan (1914) Born 21 September 1894, The Grange, Union Place, Slave Island, Western Province, Colombo, Ceylon; son of Charles Walter van Geyzel, Doctor of Medicine, and Emma Eliza Ferdinands. **Tutor(s):** L H K Bushe-Fox. **Educ:** Royal College, Colombo.

VAN HEES, Albert Strancham Marsh (1903) Born 24 April 1883, Kimberley, Cape Colony, South Africa; son of George Young van Hees, Merchant, and Sarah Adrianna Sophia Ford. **Subject(s):** Law; BA 1906; MA 1910; LLB 1906. **Tutor(s):** D MacAlister. **Educ:** South African College School, Cape Town. **Career:** Called to the Bar, Inner Temple 1906.

VAN MILLINGEN, Evelyn Francis Mackenzie (1920) Born 24 June 1901, Roumeli Hissar, Constantinople; son of Alexander van Millingen, Professor of History, Constantinople, and Frances Elizabeth Hope Mackenzie; m Kathleen Maud Jackson, 31 October 1929, St George's, Penang. BA 1923; MA 1927. **Tutor(s):** E A Benians. **Educ:** Eagle House, Sandhurst; Uppingham School. **Career:** Timber Merchant 1932; Bombay Burma Trading Company, Siam 1939; Lieutenant Colonel, Cambridgeshire Regiment 1921–1950. Died 15 October 1957.

VAN PALLANDT, Baron Hugh Pope Alexander (1911) Born 30 May 1891, Rosendaal, Arnhern, Gelderland, Netherlands; son of Baron Frederick Jacob Willem van Pallandt van Rosendaal, and Constantia Alexine London. **Tutor(s):** J R Tanner. **Educ:** Walbury School, Arhern, Holland.

VAN ZWANENBERG, Hugh Arnold (1935) Born 5 November 1916, 6 Fitzgeorge Avenue, Kensington, London; son of Isaac van Zwanenberg, Director of Public Companies, and Dorothy Lydia Sax; m Suzanne Bridget Holdron, 13 June 1953; 2 sons (Guy and Nicholas), 1 daughter (Gillian). BA 1938. **Tutor(s):** J M Wordie. **Educ:** Heath Mount, Hampstead; Shrewsbury School. Died 1 September 1984.

VANSTONE, The Revd Canon William Hubert (1948) Born 9 May 1923, 4 Derby Street, Mossley, Manchester; son of Richard Bartlett Vanstone, Clerk in Holy Orders, and Susannah Florence Davies. BA 1950; BA (Oxon) 1948. **Tutor(s):** C W Guillebaud. **Educ:** Bradford Grammar School; Balliol College, Oxford. **Career:** Theological Chaplain to the Bishop of Chester; Union Theological Seminary, New York 1950; Curate, Halliwell St Thomas 1950–1955; Ordained Priest 1951; Curate (then Vicar 1964), Kirkholt 1955–1976; Examining Chaplain to the Bishop of Manchester 1959; Honorary Canon, Manchester Cathedral 1968–1976; Vicar, Hattersley, Chester 1977–1978; Canon, Chester Cathedral 1978–1990; Six Preacher, Canterbury Cathedral 1983–1991. **Appointments:** Hulsean Lecturer 1983. **Awards:** Senior Scholefield Prize, University of Cambridge 1949.

VARWELL, Ralph Peter (1901) Born 13 February 1883, 3 Sydney Place, Alphington Road, St Thomas, Exeter, Devon; son of Hawkins Blake Varwell, Merchant, and Emma Mortimer Heron. BA 1906. **Tutor(s):** D MacAlister. **Educ:** Exeter School. **Career:** Army 1907; Captain, Royal Irish Rifles (wounded, Mentioned in Despatches three times), then Major, DAAG, WWI; Lieutenant-Colonel, Royal Ulster Rifles. **Honours:** MC; French Croix de Guerre. Died 23 December 1956.

VAUGHAN, Commodore Douglas Brian (1942) Born 15 July 1925, The Nursing Home, Ruabon, Denbighshire; son of Douglas Cyril Vaughan, Medical Practitioner, and Annie Vera Parton; 3 daughters. **Subject(s):** Mechanical Sciences; BA 1945. **Tutor(s):** S J Bailey. **Johnian Relatives:** brother of Geoffrey Parton Vaughan (1947) and of Selwyn Michael Vaughan (1958). **Educ:** Lucton School, Herefordshire. **Career:** RN, specialising in nuclear physics. **Appointments:** Honorary Manager, British Lions Tour to South Africa. Died April 1977.

VAUGHAN, Dr Geoffrey Parton (1947) Born 26 June 1929, Maelor View, Rhos, Denbighshire; son of Douglas Cyril Vaughan, Medical Practitioner, and Annie Vera Parton; m Ailleen Mary Caldwell, 4 August 1954; 3 sons (Paul, Mark and Justin), 1 daughter (Gaye). **Subject(s):** Natural Sciences; BA 1950; MA 1958; BChir 1953; MB 1954. **Tutor(s):** G C L Bertram. **Johnian Relatives:** brother of Douglas Brian Vaughan (1942) and of Selwyn Michael Vaughan (1958). **Educ:** Lucton School, Herefordshire. **Career:** Medical Officer, RAF Staff College 1955–1958; Medical Practice, Herefordshire 1958–1968; Medical Practice, Auckland, New Zealand 1968–1998.

VAUGHAN, Dr James Rodney Mitchell (1940) Born 2 May 1921, 1 Cliffside, Fifth Avenue, Margate, Kent; son of James Vaughan, General Manager, and Dulcie Gysberta Chiesman; m Anne Blyth, 18 December 1948, 2 sons (Peter J and Timothy M), 1 daughter (Caroline H).

Subject(s): Mathematics; BA 1948; MA 1957; PhD 1973; FIEEE 1982. **Tutor(s):** J M Wordie. **Educ:** St Clare, Upper Walmer; Aldenham School. **Career:** Captain, Royal Signals, North Africa, Italy and the Middle East, WWII; Research Engineer, EMI 1957; General Electric Company, New York 1957–1968; Researcher, Litton Industries, USA 1968–1989; President, Rodney Vaughan Associates 1989. **Awards:** Litton Advanced Technology Achievement Award 1988. Died 9 February 1995.

VAUGHAN, John Paul (1937) Born 2 October 1912, City of London Lying-in Hospital, London; son of Paul Martin Kuoefel, Motor Car Company Director, and Edith Evelyn Mary Vaughan; m Edith; 2 sons (Michael and Paul). BA 1947; MA 1949. **Tutor(s):** J S Boys Smith. **Educ:** Queen Elizabeth's Grammar School, Tamworth; Bethany School, Goudhurst. **Career:** Master, King Edward VI School, Birmingham; Headmaster, Hillscourt School. Died 16 February 1985.

VAUSE, Thomas Christopher (1904) Born 12 November 1882, 17 Hall Grove, Kirkstall, Leeds, Yorkshire; son of Thomas Orlando Vause, Mungo Manufacturer, and Margaret Gardam; m Maud Rosamond Helmsley; 1 son (Thomas Robert b 11 October 1908). **Subject(s):** History; BA 1907; MA 1911; LLB 1913. **Tutor(s):** C E Graves; J R Tanner. **Johnian Relatives:** father of Thomas Rupert Vause (1926). **Educ:** Leeds Modern School; New College, Harrogate. **Career:** Master, Harrogate Modern School 1907–1910; Master, Leeds Central High School 1910–1914; Master, Cleckheaton Secondary School 1914; Inns of Court OTC 1914; Second Lieutenant, West Yorkshire Regiment (TF) 1914–1916. Died 3 September 1916 (killed in action near Albert).

VAUSE, Thomas Rupert (1926) Born 11 October 1908, 23 St George's Road, Harrogate, Yorkshire; son of Thomas Christopher Vause, Schoolmaster, and Maud Rosamond Helmsley. **Subject(s):** History/Geography; BA 1930; MA 1934. **Tutor(s):** E A Benians. **Johnian Relatives:** son of Thomas Christopher Vause (1904). **Educ:** New College, Harrogate.

VEEVERS, William (1905) Born 16 October 1883, Green Boat House, Alnwick, Northumberland; son of William Robinson Veevers, Timber Merchant, and Sarah Crauford; m Viola K A Judge, 27 July 1937, Winchester Cathedral. **Subject(s):** Law; BA 1908; LLB 1908. **Tutor(s):** D MacAlister. **Educ:** Grammar School, Alnwick; Royal High School, Edinburgh; University of Edinburgh. **Career:** Second Lieutenant, RGA, WWI.

VEITCH, James Malcolm Mitford (1944) Born 24 March 1926, The Gables, Elswick Road, Newcastle upon Tyne; son of Arnold Ernest Veitch, Company Secretary, and Elizabeth Mitford Rowell. BA 1947; MA 1951. **Tutor(s):** C W Guillebaud. **Educ:** Monkseaton Infants Council School; Whitley Bay North Council School; Royal Grammar School, Newcastle upon Tyne.

VENOSTA, Dr Guido (1930) Born 4 October 1911, Milan, Italy; son of Giuseppe Venosta, General Manager, Societa Italiana Pirelli Tyres, and Carolina Argia Neri; m Carla Fossati Bellani. **Subject(s):** Economics; BA 1934; MA 1937. **Tutor(s):** C W Guillebaud. **Educ:** Instituto Vittoria Colonna, Milan; Instituto Salvoni, Milan, Italy; Regio Ginnasio e Liceo Parini, Milan, Italy; Universita degli studi di Pavia. **Career:** Manager, Pirelli 1965; AIRC 1965–1996 (President 1967–1994, Honorary President 1994–1998); President, FIRC 1979–1996 (Honorary President 1996–1998). **Awards:** Medaglia D'Oro Della Sanita. **Honours:** Grand Ufficiale Repubblica Italiana. **Publications:** *From Profit to Non-profit – one experience*. Died 4 February 1998.

VERCOE, Dr Richard Herbert (1903) Born 24 August 1884, Bodmin, Cornwall; son of Richard Vercoe, Master Draper, and Eliza Littleton; m Celie. **Subject(s):** Natural Sciences; BA 1906; MRCS; LRCP 1910. **Tutor(s):** D MacAlister. **Educ:** Exeter School. **Career:** Clinical Assistant, Brompton Hospital; Casualty House Surgeon and Senior House Physician, Prince of Wales' Hospital, Tottenham. Died 22 March 1930.

VERINDER, David (1943) Born 13 March 1925, 142 Upper Clapton Road, Upper Clapton, London; son of Arthur Verinder, Clerk, Ministry of Labour, and Lilian Elizabeth Spittle. **Tutor(s):** C W Guillebaud. **Educ:** Alleyn Court Preparatory School; Felsted School.

VERNON, Bryan Tom Jackson (1943) Born 15 November 1925, Dollisfield, Totteridge, Hertfordshire; son of Herbert Wallace Vernon, Flour Miller, and Gertrude Mary Jackson. **Tutor(s):** C W Guillebaud. **Educ:** Oakleigh Park Preparatory School; Bilton Grange, Rugby; Loretto School.

VERNON, Cecil Heygate (1911) Born 15 April 1892, Drayton, Christchurch Road, Boscombe, Hampshire; son of Arthur Heygate Vernon, Surgeon, and Elizabeth Agnes Dence; m Edith; 2 sons (Peter and Hugh), 2 daughters (Judith and Milenka). **Subject(s):** Natural Sciences; BA 1914; BChir 1918; MB 1918; MRCS; LRCP 1918; FRCS 1920. **Tutor(s):** J R Tanner. **Johnian Relatives:** father of Peter Heygate Vernon (1939). **Educ:** Oundle School. **Career:** Lieutenant, Hampshire Regiment (TF), then, Captain (Medical), RFC (wounded, mentioned in Secretary of State's list, for valuable services in connection with the war), WWI; Senior Consultant Obstetrician, Royal Victoria Hospital, Bournemouth. **Appointments:** Honorary Secretary, Obstetrics and Gynaecology Section, BMA 1934; Chairman, Bournemouth Division 1950. **Awards:** King's Prize, Bisley 1924. **Honours:** CStJ 1956; KStJ 1966. Died 10 March 1968.

VERNON, Peter Heygate (1939) Born 18 September 1920, 1 The Crescent, Boscombe, Bournemouth; son of Cecil Heygate Vernon, Surgeon, and Edith Abel; BA 1942. **Tutor(s):** R L Howland. **Johnian Relatives:** son of Cecil Heygate Vernon (1911). **Educ:** Pembroke Lodge Preparatory School, Southbourne; Canford School.

VERNON, Professor Philip Ewart (1924) Born 6 June 1905, 3 Bevington Road, St Giles, Oxford; son of Horace Middleton Vernon, Investigator for MRC, and Katherine Dorothea Ewart; m (1) Annie Craig Gray, 1938 (d 22 November 1946), (2) Dorothy Anne Fairley Lawson, 22 September 1947, St John's, Greenock; (2) 1 son (Philip). **Subject(s):** Natural Sciences/Moral Sciences; BA 1927; MA 1931; PhD 1932; DSc (London) 1952; Honorary LLD (Calgary) 1980. **Tutor(s):** B F Armitage. **Educ:** Oxford Preparatory School; Oundle School; Yale University; Harvard University. **Career:** Rockefeller Fellow, Harvard 1930–1931; Title A Fellow 1931–1933, Supervisor in Moral Science 1932–1934, SJC; Psychologist, London County Council, Maudsley Hospital Child Guidance Clinic 1933–1935; Head, Psychology Department, Jordanhill Training Centre (for teachers), Glasgow 1935–1938; Head, Psychology Department, University of Glasgow 1938–1947; Psychological Research Adviser to Admiralty and War Office 1942–1945; Professor of Educational Psychology 1949–1964, Professor of Psychology 1964–1968 (later Emeritus) Institute of Education, University of London; Professor of Educational Psychology, Calgary, Canada 1968–1978 (Emeritus 1979). **Appointments:** President, Psychology Section, BAAS 1952; numerous international educational consultancies and lecture tours for British Council 1953–1968; Visiting Professor, Princeton University and Educational Testing Service 1957; Fellow, Centre for Advanced Studies in Behavioural Sciences, Stanford, California 1961–1962; President, BPsS 1954–1955; Fellow, American Psychological Association; Member, American Academy of Education; Council Member, International Association of Applied Psychology; Visiting Professor, Teachers' College, Sydney 1977; Life Fellow, Canadian Psychology Association. **Awards:** Open John Stewart of Rannoch Scholarship in Sacred Music, University of Cambridge 1925; Strathcona Research Studentship, SJC 1927–1929; Laura Spelman Rockefeller Fellowship in Social Sciences 1929–1931; Pinsent-Darwin Studentship in Mental Pathology, University of Cambridge 1934–1936; Government of Alberta Achievement Award 1972. **Publications:** (with G W Allport) *Studies in Expressive Movement*, 1933; *The Measure of Abilities*, 1940, 2nd edition 1956; (with J B Parry) *Personnel Selection in the British Forces*, 1949; *The Structure of Human Abilities*, 1950, 2nd edition 1961; *Personality Assessment: A Critical*

Survey, 1963; (ed) *British Journal of Educational Psychology*, 1956–1961; *Intelligence and Cultural Environment*, 1969; *Readings in Creativity*, 1971; (with G Adamson and Dorothy F Vernon) *Psychology and Education of Gifted Children*, 1977; *Intelligence: Heredity and Environment*, 1979; *The Abilities and Achievements of Orientals in North America*, 1982; numerous papers in British and American psychological journals. Died 28 July 1987.

VESTEY, John Derek (1932) Born 4 June 1914, Gedhow, Highfield Road, Beddington, Surrey; son of John Joseph Vestey, Shipping Manager, and Dorothy Mary Beaver. **Tutor(s):** E A Benians. **Educ:** Oatlands School, Harrogate; The Leys School, Cambridge.

VICKERMAN, Allan Dodson (1927) Born 28 May 1909, 28 Wakefield Road, Dalton, Huddersfield, Yorkshire; son of William Vickerman, Master Wheelwright, and Lily Jackson; m Margaret Bennett. **Subject(s):** History; BA 1930; MA 1934. **Tutor(s):** E A Benians. **Educ:** Palatine School, Blackpool; Secondary School, Blackpool. **Career:** Admitted Solicitor 1934; Assistant Solicitor, Middlesbrough Corporation, later Deputy Town Clerk of Bebington, then Town Clerk of Congleton 1945; Town Clerk, Whitehaven 1945. **Awards:** McMahon Law Scholarship. Died 17 July 1950.

VIGERS, Brian Edmund Allen (1919) Born 4 June 1900, 1 Earl's Terrace, Kensington, London; son of Allan Francis Vigers, Architect, and Mary Ethel Allen; m Norah Malley, 14 June 1928, Parish Church, Wimbledon. **Subject(s):** Mathematics/Mechanical Sciences; BA 1922; MA 1950; AMInstCE 1927. **Tutor(s):** E E Sikes. **Educ:** Doon House School, Westgate; Tonbridge School. **Career:** Civil Engineer; B Laporte Ltd, Chemical Manufacturers, Luton 1937. **Awards:** Judd Exhibition 1918. Died 5 February 1986.

VILLARD, Henry Hilgard (1932) Born 18 January 1911, 145 West 58th Street, New York; son of Oswald Garrison Villard, Editor, *The New York Nation*, and Julia Breckinridge Sandford. **Subject(s):** Economics; BA 1934; MA 1939. **Tutor(s):** E A Benians. **Educ:** The Fay School, Massachusetts; The Taft School, Conneticut; Yale University, New Haven. Died 28 December 1983.

VINCENT, Basil Walter (1925) Born 22 April 1907, 12 Abbotstone Road, Putney, Surrey; son of Joseph Walter Vincent, Chartered Accountant, and Eleanor Eliza Osment; m Kathleen Gibson, 11 July 1933; 4 sons (Patrick James b 26 April 1934, John Antony b 23 March 1936, Nicholas b 24 April 1940 and Christopher b 24 April 1940, d 5 August 1961). **Subject(s):** Economics/Law; BA 1928; MA 1932; ACA 1931; FCA 1938. **Tutor(s):** J M Wordie. **Johnian Relatives:** brother of Stanley Ralph Vincent (1928); father of Patrick James Vincent (1954), John Antony Vincent (1956), Nicholas Vincent (1959) and of Christopher Vincent (1959); uncle of Stephen Hereward Vincent (1961). **Educ:** Leinster House School, Putney; Brentwood School. **Career:** Farrow Middleton (father's firm); General Commissioner of Taxes, Brentwood Division for 27 years, including 15 years as Chairman; JP, Brentwood Magistrates Bench 1951; Chairman, Main Bench 1962–1977; Senior Partner, Farrow Middleton 1971–1972. **Appointments:** Governor, Brentwood School 1952–1986; Vice-President and Committee Member, Essex County Hockey Club and Brentwood Hockey and Cricket Clubs; Prime Warden, Worshipful Company of Basketmakers, City of London. Died 23 September 1997.

VINCENT, Paul Howard (1942) Born 9 April 1924, 33 Crofton Park, Yeovil; son of Stanley Howard Vincent, Motor Engineer, and Dorothy Violet Ficken. **Tutor(s):** C W Guillebaud. **Educ:** St Nicholas's School, Yeovil; Bishop's Stortford College.

VINCENT, Richard (1930) Born 31 March 1912, White Hall, Witham, Essex; son of Augustus Robert Vincent Dimmer, Barrister, and Helen Christabel Nalder; m Marie Louise Guitard, 6 May 1950, London. **Subject(s):** History/Law; BA 1933; LLB 1935. **Tutor(s):** E A Benians.

Educ: Shirley House School, Blackheath; Highfield School, Liphook; Shrewsbury School.

VINCENT, Stanley Ralph (1928) Born 12 February 1910, 12 Abbotstone Road, Putney, Surrey; son of Joseph Walter Vincent, Chartered Accountant, and Eleanor Eliza Osment; m Joan Ashworth Richardson (d 16 August 1994); 1 son (Stephen Hereward), 1 daughter. **Subject(s):** Law; BA 1931; MA 1935; LLB 1932; LLM 1985. **Tutor(s):** E A Benians. **Johnian Relatives:** brother of Basil Walter Vincent (1925); uncle of Patrick James Vincent (1954), John Antony Vincent (1956), Nicholas Vincent (1959) and of Christopher Vincent (1959); father of Stephen Hereward Vincent (1961). **Educ:** Leinster House School, Putney; Brentwood School. **Career:** Admitted Solicitor 1934; from Sapper to Major, TA (including War Service) 1938–1946; Liell Partner, Attwater & Liell, Solicitors, City of London 1938–1952, Brentwood, Essex 1952–1985; General Commissioner of Taxes, Brentwood District 1969–1985. **Appointments:** Life Fellow, Royal Geographical Society 1947; Assistant, Worshipful Company of Basketmakers, City of London; Secretary, Brentwood Hockey Club. **Awards:** Efficiency Decoration, TA.

VINE, Bernard Theodore (1906) Born 13 September 1887, Eversley, Hartley Road, Littleham, Exmouth, Devon; son of Edwin John Vine, Solicitor, and Eliza Anne Davey. BA 1910; MA 1920. **Tutor(s):** J R Tanner. **Educ:** Exeter School.

VINES, Jack Harold (1942) Born 28 June 1924, 6 Radford Road, Lewisham; son of Harold Albert Vines, Compositor, and Edith Gladys Lewis. **Tutor(s):** C W Guillebaud. **Educ:** Morden Terrace School; Torridon Road School; Brockley County Secondary School. **Career:** Flying Officer and Navigator, RAF 1942–1945. Died 26 April 1945 (killed in action over Hamburg).

VINNICOMBE, John (1949) Born 17 January 1930, 1 Lampton Road, Hounslow, Middlesex; son of Francis William Vinnicombe, Export Agent (Hosiery), and Marjorie Florence Shuff; m Diana Mary Swan, 1958; 3 daughters (Sarah b 1959, Amanda b 1961 and Jane b 1964). **Subject(s):** Natural Sciences; BA 1952; MA 1956; BChir 1955; MB 1956; MChir 1966; FRCS 1958. **Tutor(s):** G C L Bertram. **Educ:** St Hilary's Elementary School, Godalming; Branksome-Hilders Preparatory School, Haslemere; Godalming County Secondary School. **Career:** Medical Training, St Thomas' Hospital 1952–1966; Consultant Urological Surgeon, Portsmouth Hospitals 1966–1995; Consultant Urological Surgeon, King Edward VII Hospital, Midhurst 1970–1995; Senior Surgeon, Portsmouth Hospital 1990–1995. **Appointments:** Member, Hawks Club; Research Fellow, Stanford University, California 1963; Past Secretary and Treasurer, later Honorary Member, BAUS; Past President, later Honorary Member, Section of Urology, RSM.

VINT, James (1914) Born 15 August 1892, Muckamore, Antrim; son of William Vint, Linen Bleacher, and Frances Strain. MA (Belfast). **Tutor(s):** L H K Bushe-Fox. **Educ:** Model School, Ballymena; Queen's University of Belfast. **Career:** Lieutenant, RGA, WWI; Lecturer in Pure Mathematics, University of Bristol 1958. **Honours:** MC.

VINYCOMB, Thomas Bernard (1903) Born 2 November 1878, Seaview, Holywood, Belfast, Ireland; son of John Vinycomb, Artist, and Dora Thorpe; m Emily Katherine Adams, 1908. **Tutor(s):** D MacAlister. **Educ:** Queen's College, Belfast. **Career:** Chief Assistant, Physics Department, Woolwich Polytechnic 1907. **Appointments:** Junior Fellow, Royal University of Ireland 1903; Purser Assistant to Professor of Mathematics 1906. Died 23 June 1943.

VIVIAN, The Revd Thomas Keith (1945) Born 19 February 1927, 40 Condurrow Road, Beacon, Camborne, Cornwall; son of William Vivian, Mining Engineer, Kolar Goldfields, and Gladys Irene Thomas; m Audrey Cowan; 1 son (Jonathan b 1954), 1 daughter (Jennifer b 1956). **Subject(s):** Natural Sciences/Moral Sciences; BA 1948; MA 1952; PGCE. **Tutor(s):** J M Wordie. **Johnian Relatives:** father of Jonathan Mark

Vivian (1973). **Educ:** Beacon Elementary School, Camborne; Roskear Elementary School, Camborne; Truro School. **Career:** Master, Christ's Hospital 1949–1954; Master, Rugby School 1954–1962; Headmaster, Lucton School, Leominster 1962–1984; Ordained Deacon; Priest, Chew Stoke, Diocese of Bath & Wells 1985–1988; Rector and Priest, Chew Stoke 1988–1997; Rural Dean, Chew Magna 1992–1997. **Appointments:** Governor of various schools 1985; Parish Councillor; Director of charities.

VOKES, The Revd Frederick Ercolo (1929) Born 12 August 1910, Ringwood Road, Totton, Eling, Southampton; son of William Arthur Vokes, Railway Clerk, and Emma Maude Whitfield; m Edith Halliday Jung (d 1991); 1 son (David), 2 daughters (Elizabeth and Mary). **Subject(s):** Classics/Theology; BA 1933; MA 1946; BD 1953; MA (Dublin) 1967. **Tutor(s):** M P Charlesworth. **Educ:** Freemantle C of E School; King Edward VI School, Southampton; Westcott House, Cambridge. **Career:** Ordained Deacon 1934; Curate, St James, East Cowes 1934–1937; Ordained Priest 1935; Assistant Master, Cranbrook School, and Licensed Preacher, Diocese of Canterbury 1937–1942; Assistant Master, Stamford School 1942–1943; Assistant Master, King Edward VI School, Retford 1943–1944; Rector, Thornhaugh with Wanseford, Peterborough 1944–1947; Rector, Forncet St Peter with Forncet St Mary 1947–1955; Professor of Theology and Hebrew, St David's College, Lampeter 1955–1957; Archbishop King's Professor of Divinity, TCD 1957–1980. **Appointments:** Fellow, TCD 1974. **Awards:** Sizarship, SJC; Foundation Scholarship, SJC 1931; Carus Greek Testament Prize, University of Cambridge 1933; Junior Scholefield Prize, University of Cambridge 1933; Jeremie Hellenistic Prize; George Williams Prize, University of Cambridge 1934. **Publications:** *The Riddle of Didache*, 1938; numerous papers in learned journals. Died 8 April 2000.

VUNIVALU, Ravuama (1948) Born 20 November 1921, Draiba, Levuka, Fiji; son of Eminoni Vunivalu, Clerk, Union Steamship Company, and Mere Tuisalato. **Subject(s):** Economics; BA (New Zealand) 1947. **Tutor(s):** C W Guillebaud. **Educ:** Convent School, Levuka; Methodist School, Suva; Auckland University College, New Zealand. **Awards:** Morris, Hedstrom Ltd, University Scholarship 1944; Colonial Development and Welfare Scheme Scholarship.

VYVYAN, Lieutenant Colonel Philip Henry Nugent Norris (1900) Born 30 August 1881, 6 Portland Street, St Giles, Bootham, York; son of Henry Vyvyan, Clerk in Holy Orders, and Lucy Nugent Grattan; m Mary Caroline Flynn, 11 November 1917, St Mary's, Bryanston Square. **Tutor(s):** D MacAlister. **Johnian Relatives:** son of Henry Vyvyan (1873). **Educ:** Exeter School. **Career:** Second Lieutenant, York and Lancaster Regiment 1902; Lieutenant 1906; Captain 1913; Major, Army Service Corps, WWI; Brevet Lieutenant Colonel 1928. **Honours:** Italian Croce de Guerra; Croix de Guerre 1918; OBE (Military) 1919. Died 16 July 1967.

W

WACE, Geoffrey Richard (1947) Born 24 November 1924, Gloucester House, Uxbridge Road, Hampton Hill; son of Oliver Richard Wace, Commander, RN, and Elizabeth Lavinia Mackie; m Ann Elizabeth King, 10 August 1963, St Cuthbert, Ormesby; 1 daughter (Joanna Caroline b 2 June 1972). **Subject(s):** Engineering; BA 1949. **Tutor(s):** R L Howland. **Educ:** Birchington House, Kent; Prestefelde, Shrewsbury; Mill Mead, Shrewsbury; Shrewsbury School; Trinity College, Oxford. **Career:** Lieutenant, RNVR, served North Atlantic and Far East; Electrical Engineer; Press and Publicity Officer. **Appointments:** Freeman, Shrewsbury. Died 7 June 2004.

WADDELL, John Kennedy (1946) Born 2 October 1924, Foochow, China; son of John Waddell, Musician, and Margaret Helen Manson Christie. **Subject(s):** Classics; BA 1948; MA 1959; PGCE 1950. **Tutor(s):** R L Howland. **Johnian Relatives:** brother of David Charles Manson Waddell (1951). **Educ:** Wavertree School, Horley; Aldenham School, Elstree. **Career:** Assistant Master, The King's School, Canterbury

1950–1953; Schoolmaster, Aldenham School 1954–1986. **Appointments:** SJC Choir; Co-founder, Lady Margaret Singers; Joint Honorary Secretary 1956, Editor, *Aldenhamiana* newsletter 1986, Old Aldenhamian Society; organiser of many musical events. **Awards:** Major Scholarship, SJC 1942. **Publications:** (ed) *The History and Register of Aldenham School*, 9th, 10th and 11th editions, 1959, 1969 and 1986. Died 12 November 1998.

WADE, Professor Emlyn Capel Stewart (1928) (admitted to Gonville & Caius College 1917) Born 31 August 1895, Saffron Walden, Essex; son of Charles Stewart Douglas Wade, Solicitor, and Ethel Lofft Holden; m Mary Esme Cardew, 1924; 4 daughters. **Subject(s):** Law; BA 1920 (Caius); MA 1925 (Caius); Honorary DCL (Durham); FBA; QC 1959. **Educ:** St Faith's School, Cambridge; St Lawrence College; Gonville & Caius College, Cambridge. **Career:** Barrister-at-Law; Called to the Bar, Inner Temple; Captain, RGA, British Salonika Force, and in France 1916–1919; Lecturer, Armstrong College 1923–1924; Vice-Principal, Society School of Law, 1924–1928 (Principal 1926); Title B Fellow and Lecturer, SJC 1928–1931; Lecturer in Law, University of Cambridge 1928–1945; Fellow and Lecturer, Gonville & Caius College, Cambridge; Temporary Major, TA until 1942, Brigade Major, London Anti-Aircraft Defences, War Cabinet Secretariat, Home Office 1939–1945; Downing Professor of the Laws of England, University of Cambridge 1945–1962 (Emeritus 1966); Reader in Constitutional Law, Council of Legal Education 1945–1966. **Appointments:** Tutor, Gonville & Caius College, Cambridge 1931; Honorary Master of the Bench, Inner Temple 1951; Committee on Electoral Reform 1944–1945; Lord Chancellor's Committee on Law of Defamation and on Limitation of Actions; The Law Reform Committee 1952; Secretary and President, Society of Public Teachers of Law; Council Member, University of Cambridge Senate; Chairman, Faculty Board of Law; Hinkley Visiting Professor, John Hopkins University, Baltimore 1962–1963. **Awards:** Whewell Scholarship, University of Cambridge 1922. **Publications:** *Constitutional Law*, 1931; *Dicey's Law and Conventions of the Constitution*, 1939 and 1959; *The History of Law Legislation, 1939–1945*; numerous articles in *The Law Quarterly Review, Cambridge Law Journal*, and elsewhere. Died 28 April 1978.

WADE, Peter George (1942) Born 5 December 1924, 60 Cole Park Road, Twickenham; son of Ernest Wentworth Wade, Brigadier, RAMC, and Winifred Alexander; m Rosemary Vanda Wylie, 30 April 1960, Holy Trinity Church, Northwood; 2 sons. **Subject(s):** Mechanical Sciences; BA 1949; MA 1951. **Tutor(s):** S J Bailey. **Educ:** Warren Hill, Eastbourne; Hill Brow, Eastbourne; Sherborne School. **Career:** Lieutenant, RE 1944; Captain 1946; Paratrooper, RE 1952–1960; Major 1958; Parachute Regiment 1960–1965; Teacher 1965–1987.

WADHAM, Giles Anthony (1920) Born 6 October 1901, Thamesfield, Lower Halliford, Shepperton, Middlesex; son of Henry Davison Wadham, Member, London Stock Exchange, and Mabel Emily Beeching. **Tutor(s):** E E Sikes. **Educ:** Hillside, Godalming; Marlborough College; Courtenay Lodge.

WADIA, Nowroji Jehangir (1904) Born 27 August 1884, Bombay, India; son of Jehangir Pestomjee Wadia, Doctor, Government Service. **Subject(s):** History; BA 1907. **Tutor(s):** C E Graves; J R Tanner. **Educ:** Deccan College, Poona, India. **Career:** Called to the Bar, Lincoln's Inn 1909; Assistant Collector, Magistrate, and Assistant Judge, Bombay, India 1909–1923; Acting Judge and Sessions Judge 1923–1925; Deputy Secretary, Legal Department of Bombay Government 1925; Reforms Secretary 1927; Judge, Bombay High Court 1928–1933. **Appointments:** Chairman, Bombay Provincial Delimitation Committee 1935.

WADIA, Siavax Hirji (1910) Born 15 August 1890, Bombay, India; son of Hirji Pestonji Wadia, District Judge, and Sirinbai Kaikhoshna Mehta. **Subject(s):** Natural Sciences; BA 1913. **Tutor(s):** E E Sikes. **Educ:** St Xavier's High School, Bombay, India; St Xavier's College, Bombay, India. **Career:** Various posts including District Judge, Acting

Commissioner of Local Government, Police Magistrate, Assistant Controller of Revenue, Ceylon Civil Service from 1914.

WADSWORTH, Peter (1941) Born 1 April 1923, 328 Wellington Road North, Heaton Chapel, Stockport, Cheshire; son of William Caubon Wadsworth, Clothing Company Proprietor, and Ida Lister; 1 son. BA 1944; MA 1947. **Tutor(s):** S J Bailey. **Educ:** Arnold School, Blackpool; Uppingham School.

WAGSTAFF, Professor John Edward Pretty (1911) Born 11 August 1890, 11 Infirmary Square, Leicester; son of Daniel Wagstaff, Shoe Riveter, and Sarah Maria Pretty; m Dorothy Margaret McRobie; 1 son (David), 1 daughter (Dorothea Primrose). **Subject(s):** Mathematics/Natural Sciences; BA 1915; MA 1920. **Tutor(s):** L H K Bushe-Fox. **Johnian Relatives:** father-in-law of Ivor William Broomhead (1942). **Educ:** Newton's School, Leicester. **Career:** Research Physicist, Ministry of Munitions, Woolwich 1916–1919; Junior Demonstrator, Cavendish Laboratory, University of Cambridge 1919; Lecturer in Physics, University of Leeds 1920; Foundress Fellow, SJC 1922–1925; Professor of Physics 1924–1955 (Emeritus 1955–1963), Durham University. **Awards:** Foundation Scholarship, SJC. Died 2 August 1963.

WAGSTAFF, Raymond Claude (1940) Born 8 November 1914, 33 Hartlepool Road, Coventry; son of Amos Wagstaff, Tool Hardener, and Ellen Elizabeth Gorsuch. BSc (London) 1938. **Tutor(s):** C W Guillebaud. **Educ:** Bablake Secondary School, Coventry; Birmingham Central Technical College. **Career:** Pilot Officer, RAF, WWII.

WAILES, Reginald (1919) Born 6 March 1901, Sandyford, Hadley Wood, Enfield, Middlesex; son of Reginald Percy Wailes, Engineer, and Florence Peach. **Tutor(s):** E A Benians. **Educ:** Private Tuition, Kent; Oundle School.

WAIN, The Revd Frank Lonsdale (1919) Born 30 September 1900, Ponthill, Wolstanton, Staffordshire; son of Frank Wooliscroft Wain, Solicitor, and Jane Maude Lonsdale. **Subject(s):** Natural Sciences/Theology; BA 1922; MA 1926. **Tutor(s):** E A Benians. **Educ:** The High School, Newcastle; Cuddesdon College. **Career:** Ordained Deacon 1923; Curate, South Bank, Middlesbrough 1923–1929; Ordained Priest 1924; Curate, All Saints, Middlesbrough 1929–1931; Mission Priest, Society of St John the Evangelist, Mazagon, Bombay 1934–1937; Mission Priest, Poona 1937–1950; Mission Priest, Lonavia 1950–1953; Archdeacon, Poona 1953–1957. **Awards:** Scholarship, SJC 1918. Died 2 June 1990.

WAINWRIGHT, Dr John Hilditch (1921) Born 23 April 1904, Stapeley House, Knighton, Radnorshire; son of Arthur Hilditch Wainwright, Master Clothier, and Helen Stubbs. BA 1925; MRCS; LRCP. **Tutor(s):** B F Armitage. **Educ:** The Grange, Shrewsbury; Wycliffe College, Stonehouse. **Career:** Surgeon Lieutenant, RNVR. Died 18 July 1943 (killed at sea).

WAINWRIGHT, John Tillotson (1922) Born 8 October 1898, Rye, New York, USA; son of John Tillotson Wainwright, Broker and Banker, and Anna Rutherford Peabody. **Subject(s):** English/History; BA 1924. **Tutor(s):** E E Sikes. **Educ:** Chestnut Hall Academy, Philadelphia, USA; St Paul's School, Concord; Princeton University. Died 2 November 1930.

WAITE-BROWNE, Henry Franklyn (1900) Born 19 April 1882, Langton Manor, Wragby, Lincolnshire; son of Edward Waite Browne, Farmer, and Edith Alethea Franklyn. BA 1903. **Tutor(s):** J E Sandys. **Educ:** Buxton School; Repton School. **Career:** Served with Naval Division, Egypt; Director, Geographia Ltd, London 1922.

WAKELY, Herbert Denning (1901) Born 6 February 1882, 36 Glengall Road, Camberwell, Surrey; son of Charles Wakely, Secretary, Band of Hope Union, and Elizabeth Knight; m Florence Dean Titley; 1 son (William Hugh Denning b 20 February 1912). **Subject(s):** Classics; BA

1904. **Tutor(s):** E E Sikes. **Johnian Relatives:** brother of Leonard Day Wakely (1898); uncle of William Hugh Denning Wakely (1932). **Educ:** St Olave's Grammar School, Southwark. **Career:** Secretary's Office, General Post Office 1905; Assistant Private Secretary to Postmaster-General 1910. **Awards:** Powis Prize 1902, 1903. Died 18 August 1963.

WAKELY, William Hugh Denning (1932) Born 20 February 1912, 34 Lancaster Road, Wimbledon; son of Leonard Day Wakely, Civil Servant, India Office, and Florence Dean Titley. **Subject(s):** Mechanical Sciences; BA 1934. **Tutor(s):** J S Boys Smith. **Johnian Relatives:** son of Leonard Day Wakely (1898); nephew of Herbert Denning Wakely (1901). **Educ:** Rokeby School, Wimbledon; Westminster School; RMA, Woolwich. **Career:** Engineer Officer; Major, RE 1952. **Awards:** Marquess of Salisbury Exhibition, SJC.

WALDRON, Eric Brind (1920) Born 11 August 1902, Dolgarda, Parklands, Surbiton, Surrey; son of Walter George Waldron, Ship Broker, and Louisa Constance Trengrowse. **Tutor(s):** B F Armitage. **Educ:** Hurst Court, Ore; Repton School.

WALES, Harold Robert (1914) Born 2 May 1895, 242 Moorfields, Sheffield; son of Horace Wales, Cutlery Manager, and Ada Clements. **Subject(s):** Mathematics. **Tutor(s):** L H K Bushe-Fox. **Educ:** Sharrow Lane Council School, Sheffield; Central Secondary School, Sheffield. **Career:** Second Lieutenant, East Yorkshire Regiment, WWI. **Awards:** Scholarship, SJC. Died 14 July 1916 (killed in action).

WALKER, Dr Alick Donald (1943) Born 26 October 1925, The Rectory, Skirpenback, Yorkshire; son of John Kenworthy Walker, Clerk in Holy Orders, and Kathleen Woodcock. BSc (Bristol) 1951, PhD (Durham) 1957. **Tutor(s):** S J Bailey. **Educ:** Skirpenbeck School; Pocklington School. **Career:** Researcher in Vertebrate Palaeontology 1951–1954, Lecturer, Department of Geology 1954–1957, King's College, Newcastle. **Awards:** Dowman Exhibition, SJC.

WALKER, Archibald Galbraith (1900) Born 13 July 1881, 43 Rodney Street, Mount Pleasant, Liverpool; son of George Edmund Walker, Surgeon, and Louisa Nimmo; m Madeline. **Subject(s):** Mechanical Sciences; BA 1903; MICE 1942. **Tutor(s):** D MacAlister. **Educ:** Liverpool College. **Career:** Captain, RE, WWI; Managing Director, Walker Bros (Wigan) Ltd 1937. **Appointments:** Associate Member, ICE 1920. Died 24 September 1943.

WALKER, Arthur Stephen (1928) Born 2 September 1910, Sacksfield House, Redmarley; son of Charles Francis Walker, Farmer, and Mabel Blunt; m (Alberta) May Thomson. **Subject(s):** Natural Sciences; BA 1932; MA 1936. **Tutor(s):** C W Guillebaud. **Educ:** Colchester House School, Clifton; Oakham School. **Career:** Lecturer, Chiswick Polytechnic 1972. Died 13 September 1998.

WALKER, Dr Clement Willoughby (1919) Born 19 March 1903, Ningpo, China; son of Alfred James Walker, Dean of Shanghai, and Edith Middleton; m Margery Alys Eveline Elton, 27 April 1932, St Katherine's Church, Merstham. **Subject(s):** Natural Sciences; BA 1924; MA 1934; MRCS (St Thomas') 1927; LRCP (St Thomas') 1927; Fellow, BMA. **Tutor(s):** B F Armitage. **Johnian Relatives:** son of Alfred James Walker (1892); father of Peter Elton Walker (1954). **Educ:** Cathedral Choir School, Shanghai, China; Windlesham House School; Rugby School. **Career:** Practice in Cambridge; County Surgeon (Cambridge). **Appointments:** Member, Board of Governors, United Cambridge Hospitals; Local Chairman, Cystic Fibrosis Society; Vice-President, Medical Defence Union; Medical Advisor to the John Hilton Bureau; Honorary Secretary, Cambridge and Huntingdon Branch, BMA. Died 16 January 1974.

WALKER, Dr David (1941) Born 7 September 1923, Kuliang, Foochow, China; son of Ronald Ralph Walker, Medical Practitioner, and Margaret Conyers Kirby; m Rosemary Colman, 18 January 1947. BA 1944; MA

1948. **Tutor(s):** S J Bailey. **Johnian Relatives:** cousin of Richard Geoffrey Watkinson (1943). **Educ:** Abberley Hall School, Worcestershire; Stowe School.

WALKER, David Littlejohn (1918) Born 27 January 1901, The Rectory, Partney, Lincolnshire; son of Gilbert George Walker, Clerk in Holy Orders, and Margaret Littlejohn; m Catriona MacMillan White, 9 October 1930, St Mary at the Walls. BA 1922. **Tutor(s):** E E Sikes. **Educ:** King's School, Grantham.

WALKER, Donald Clemson (1946) Born 12 February 1920, Wembley, Middlesex; son of Charles Clemson Walker, Engineer, and Elsie Dean; m Margaret Jean Hemmin. **Educ:** Northfields Elementary School, Ealing; Lincoln School. **Career:** Colonial Service Course; Middlesex Yeomanry, commissioned, Royal Corps of Signals; served in Norway, Madagascar and Burma 1939–1945; Private Secretary to the Governor, Colonial Administrative Service, Sarawak 1950.

WALKER, Edward Gowan (1934) Born 25 May 1916, 2 Segrave Place, Cheltenham; son of Edward Walker, Artist, and Beatrice Mary Gowan. **Tutor(s):** C W Guillebaud. **Johnian Relatives:** brother of Neville Gowan Weybourne Walker (1931). **Educ:** Private Tuition.

WALKER, Sir Edward Ronald (1931) Born 26 January 1907, Coban, New South Wales, Australia; son of Frederick Thomas Walker, Methodist Minister, and Mary Melvina Annie King; m Louise Clementine Donckers; 1 son (Ronald Alfred b 11 April 1937). PhD 1933; LittD 1949; BA (Sydney) 1927; MA (Sydney) 1930; Honorary DSc 1973. **Tutor(s):** C W Guillebaud. **Johnian Relatives:** father of Ronald Alfred Walker (1956). **Educ:** Fort Street High School, Sydney, Australia; University of Sydney, Australia. **Career:** Acting Dean, Department of Economics, Sydney University; Rockefeller Research Fellowship in Economics, University of Cambridge; Lecturer in Economics, Sydney University 1927–1939; Professor of Economics, University of Tasmania 1939–1946; Australian Ambassador to Japan 1952–1955, to United Nations 1956–1959, to France 1959–1968, to Germany 1968–1971; OECD 1971–1973. **Honours:** CBE 1956; Kt 1963. **Publications:** *From Economic Theory to Policy*, Chicago, 1943. Died 1988.

WALKER, Professor Eric Anderson (1936) Born 6 September 1886, Craig-mor, Polworth Road, Streatham; son of William Walker, Secretary to Steamship Company, and Jessie Goodman; m Lucy Stapleton, 1913; 2 daughters. MA (by incorporation) 1936; Honorary DLitt (Witwatersrand) 1952; Honorary DLitt (Cape Town) 1968. **Educ:** Mill Hill School; Merton College, Oxford. **Career:** Lecturer in History, Bristol University; King George V Professor of History, Cape Town 1908–1936; Vere Harmsworth Professor of Imperial and Naval History, University of Cambridge 1936–1951 (Emeritus 1951); Title C Fellow 1936–1951, Title E Fellow 1951–1968, SJC. **Publications:** *History of South Africa*, 1928; *The Great Trek*, 1934. Died 23 February 1973.

WALKER, Geoffrey Howard (1926) Born 3 April 1908, Kexborough, Barnsley, Yorkshire; son of Henry Milnes Walker, Solicitor, and Ellen Ollerenshaw; m (1) Enid Boston Walker (d), (2) Cynthia; 2 sons, 2 daughters. **Subject(s):** Law; BA 1930; MA 1934; LLB 1931. **Tutor(s):** E A Benians. **Johnian Relatives:** brother of Philip Ollerenshaw Walker (1922), Stephen Walker (1922) and of Michael Milnes Walker (1932); uncle of Michael John Milnes Walker (1956). **Educ:** Scarborough Preparatory School; Mill Hill School. **Career:** Partner, Bury & Walkers (solicitors) 1933–1962; JP, West Riding 1962. **Appointments:** County Commissioner, South Yorkshire District Scouting Association 1969; President, Barnsley Liberal Association; DL. **Awards:** Silver Acorn Award (Scouting) 1951. **Honours:** MC (El Alamein) 1942. Died 15 March 1983.

WALKER, George Elliot (1925) Born 27 November 1906, Gleneva, North Park Grove, Leeds, Yorkshire; son of Herbert Almond Hinchcliffe Walker, Draper/Milliner, and Emily Verity; m Elisabeth Helene Jenny Hitchen, 31 October 1938, Cochin. **Subject(s):** Law; BA 1928; MA 1961.

Tutor(s): E A Benians. **Educ:** Willaston School, Nantwich. **Career:** Practised in Nyasaland 1930–1934; Secretary, Madras Chamber of Commerce 1934–1941; Member, Legislative Assembly, Madras 1937–1941; Commander, RINVR and Judge Advocate 1941–1946; Secretary, later Director, Associated Electrical Industries 1946–1967. **Honours:** OBE 1946.

WALKER, John Eric (1905) Born 7 October 1886, 18 Claremont Road, Childs Hill, Hendon, Middlesex; son of Robert William Walker, Commission Agent, and Elizabeth Fellows Pickard. BA 1910; MA 1914. **Tutor(s):** J R Tanner; C E Graves. **Educ:** Harrow School. **Career:** Private, East Yorkshire Regiment 1914; Assistant Master, Wolverhampton Grammar School 1919–1933.

WALKER, John Henry (1933) Born 14 May 1915, 35 Water Street, Nelson, Lancashire; son of Edwin Walker, Master Grocer, and Sarah Ellen Nutter. **Subject(s):** Modern and Medieval Languages; BA 1936. **Tutor(s):** J S Boys Smith. **Educ:** Bradshaw Street Council School, Nelson; Whitefield Council School, Nelson; Secondary School, Nelson.

WALKER, Dr Michael Milnes (1932) Born 18 April 1914, Kexborough House, Barnsley; son of Henry Milnes Walker, Solicitor, and Ellen Ollerenshaw; 2 sons, 2 daughters. **Subject(s):** Classics; BA 1936. **Tutor(s):** R L Howland. **Johnian Relatives:** brother of Philip Ollerenshaw Walker (1922), Stephen Walker (1922) and of Geoffrey Howard Walker (1926); uncle of Michael John Milnes Walker (1956). **Educ:** Mostyn House School, Parkgate; Mill Hill School. **Career:** House Officer, Hillingdon County Hospital 1938; RN 1939–1946; GP, Cawthorne and Barnsley 1946–1977. **Appointments:** Founder Member, RCGP; Trustee, Treasurer and Organist, Kexborough Methodist Chapel; Samaritan. Died 26 January 1977.

WALKER, Nevil Gowan Weybourne (1931) Born 24 September 1913, 2 Segrave Place, Cheltenham; son of Edward Walker, Headmaster, Scarborough School of Art, and Beatrice Mary Gowan; BA 1934; MA 1938. **Tutor(s):** J M Wordie. **Johnian Relatives:** brother of Edward Gowan Walker (1934). **Educ:** Educated at home. **Career:** Engineer, Esso Petroleum. Died 15 August 1991.

WALKER, Philip Ollerenshaw (1922) Born 23 April 1903, Victoria Avenue, Barnsley, Yorkshire; son of Henry Milnes Walker, Solicitor, and Ellen Ollerenshaw. **Subject(s):** Law; BA 1925; MA 1929; LLB 1927; LLM 1985. **Tutor(s):** E A Benians. **Johnian Relatives:** brother of Stephen Walker (1922), Geoffrey Howard Walker (1926) and of Michael Milnes Walker (1932); father of Michael John Milnes Walker (1956). **Educ:** Orelton School, Scarborough; Mill Hill School. **Career:** Admitted Solicitor 1927; Partner, Bury and Walkers, Barnsley 1927. **Appointments:** Council Member, Yorkshire Archaeological Society 1946; JP, Barnsley. **Awards:** Clements Inn Prize 1927. Died 22 May 1993.

WALKER, Dr Ralph James (1936) Born 15 January 1918, Hing-hua, Fukhien, China; son of Ronald Ralph Walker, Medical Missionary, and Margaret Conyers Kirby; 1 son, 1 daughter. **Subject(s):** Natural Sciences; BA 1939; MA 1943; MB 1942; BChir 1942. **Tutor(s):** R L Howland. **Educ:** Brockhurst Church, Stretton; Templehouse Stowe School. **Career:** GP, Presteigne, Radnorshire. Died 10 February 1972.

WALKER, The Revd Richard George (1936) Born 28 January 1918, 22 Fell Croft, Dalton-in-Furness, Lancashire; son of George Adams Walker, Motor Engineer, and Eleanor Mary Johnston; m Olive Shaw, 3 November 1942, Barrow-in-Furness; 1 son (Christopher John b 1951), 1 daughter (Anne Hilary b 1957). **Subject(s):** History/English; BA 1939; MA 1943. **Tutor(s):** J S Boys Smith. **Educ:** Barrow Grammar School, Barrow-in-Furness; Westminster College, Cambridge. **Career:** Minister of Religion, Presbyterian Church of England; Ordained 1942; St James's Presbyterian Church, Sheffield, Yorkshire 1942–1947; Jarrow Presbyterian Church 1947–1958; Moderator, Newcastle Presbytery 1956–1957; Low Fell Presbyterian Church, Gateshead 1958–1971;

Allerton Presbyterian Church, Liverpool 1971–1983; Hoylake, United Reformed Church 1983–1986. **Appointments:** Chairman, Yorkshire Presbytery Fellowship of Youth Council 1946; Assistant Clerk, General Assembly of Presbyterian Church of England; Presbytery Clerk, Newcastle Presbytery 1962–1971; Presbytery Clerk, Liverpool Presbytery 1971–1972; Synod Clerk, Mersey Province of United Reformed Church 1972–1983; Trust Officer and Secretary of United Reformed Church (Mersey Province) Trust Ltd 1983–2000.

WALKER, Stephen (1922) Born 4 March 1902, Victoria Road, Barnsley, Yorkshire; son of Henry Milnes Walker, Solicitor, and Ellen Ollerenshaw. **Subject(s):** Law; BA 1925. **Tutor(s):** E A Benians. **Johnian Relatives:** brother of Philip Ollerenshaw Walker (1922), Geoffrey Howard Walker (1926) and of Michael Milnes Walker (1932); uncle of Michael John Milnes Walker (1956). **Educ:** Wakefield Grammar School; Mill Hill School. Died 31 August 1926.

WALKER, The Revd William George (1929) Born 26 February 1911, 10 Richmond Terrace, Aberdare, Glamorganshire; son of Thomas Walker, Schoolmaster, and Mary Brown Nicholas; m Marguerite, 1 daughter (Helen). **Subject(s):** Classics/Theology; BA 1932; MA 1936. **Tutor(s):** M P Charlesworth. **Educ:** C of E School, Aberdare; St Fagan's C of E School; Hereford Cathedral School; St Michael's Theological College, Llandaff. **Career:** Ordained Deacon 1934; Curate, Cyfarthfa 1934–1936; Ordained Priest 1935; Curate, Glyntaff 1936–1938; Curate, Griffithstown 1938–1942; Curate, St Luke, Cardiff 1942–1945; Curate, Ystrad Mynach, Glamorganshire 1945; Vicar of Panydarren, Llandaff 1955; Vicar, Llanover, Monmouth 1955–1977; Rural Dean, Raglan 1972; Rector, Llanfair Kilgeddin 1972. **Awards:** Exhibition, SJC. Died 12 August 1988.

WALL, Thomas Charlton (1928) Born 21 December 1909, Rectory Farm, Ogbourne St George, Marlborough, Wiltshire; son of Thomas Wall, Farmer, and Margaret Lucas. **Tutor(s):** M P Charlesworth. **Educ:** Berkhamsted School.

WALLACE, Gerald Louis (1940) See WALLACH.

WALLACE, William Dugald (1942) Born 24 July 1924, 55 Forsyth Road, Newcastle upon Tyne; son of William Reid Wallace, Insurance Engineer's Surveyor, and Rachel Wright; m Hilda Simpson, 1949; 1 daughter (Julia Clare b 1960). **Subject(s):** Mechanical Sciences; BA 1945; MA 1979. **Tutor(s):** S J Bailey. **Educ:** Hoylake Church of England School; Calday Grange Grammar School. **Career:** Constructor Lieutenant, Probationer to Royal Corps of Naval Constructors 1944–1948; Assistant Constructor, Submarine Design 1948–1951; Contructor, Hydrodynamic design of warship hulls and propellers, Admiralty Experiment Works, Haslar 1951–1955; Constructor Commander, Staff of Flag Officer Submarines 1955–1958; Constructor, HM Dockyard Portsmouth 1958–1960; Assistant Professor of Naval Architecture, RN College Greenwich 1960–1963; Constructor, Aircraft Carrier Design, MOD Bath 1963–1966; Chief Constructor, Submarine Design 1966–1971; Assistant Director of Naval Construction, Future Projects 1971–1972; Project Manager, 'Hunt' Class Mine Countermeasure Vessels 1972–1977; Assistant Director Design for Contract Build and Design Warships 1977–1980. **Awards:** Minor Scholarship, SJC 1943; Ricardo Prize for Thermodynamics, University of Cambridge 1944.

WALLACH, Gerd Ludwig (WALLACE, Gerald Louis) (1940) Born 23 September 1920, Berlin, Germany; son of Eugen Karl Adolf Wallach, Managing Director, Hirsch Kupfer und Messingwerke, and Edith Geiger. **Subject(s):** Mechanical Sciences; BA 1943; MA 1947. **Tutor(s):** S J Bailey. **Educ:** Collège Français, Berlin; Goldschmidt School, Berlin; Lyceum Alpinum Zuoz, Switzerland. Died 11 July 1987.

WALLER, Robin Daniel (1902) Born 1 August 1882, High Street, Hoddesdon, Hertfordshire; son of Herbert Pretyman Waller, Clerk in Holy Orders, and Sarah Mary Anne Barker. **Tutor(s):** E E Sikes. **Johnian Relatives:** son of Herbert Pretyman Waller (1870); brother of Bertram Pretyman Waller (1898). **Educ:** St Catherine's School, Broxbourne. **Career:** Master, Stratford-on-Avon Grammar School 1907.

WALLIS, Brian Kenneth (1942) Born 21 July 1924, 15 Alexandra Road, Kingston, Surrey; son of Charles Frank Wallis, Schoolmaster, and Kathleen Alice Ermine Ilsley. **Tutor(s):** C W Guillebaud. **Educ:** Richmond Road School, Kingston; Long Ditton Church of England School; Surbiton County School.

WALLIS, Major Charles Braithwaite (1918) Born 25 June 1873, Muswell Hill, Middlesex; son of Charles Woodward Wallis, Barrister-at-Law, and Gertrude Edmonds; m Bessie Agnes Laird, 1913. BA 1919; MA 1924; LLB 1920; MLitt 1939. **Tutor(s):** E E Sikes. **Educ:** Shrewsbury House, Surbiton; Military College, Oxford. **Career:** Commissioned in 4th Battalion, Manchester Regiment 1894; Captain 1898; seconded to Sierra Leone Frontier Force, Mentioned in Despatches 1894–1899; Cameronians (Scottish Rifles) 1899; served in India until 1901; Assistant Commissioner, Sierra Leone 1901; Commissioner 1906; Took part in operations in Liberian Hinterland and Consul for Liberia 1906–1908; Consul General for French Western Africa, Dakar 1909–1920; served in France and Flanders 1914–1918; Called to the Bar, Middle Temple 1917; Consul General, New Orleans 1920–1923; Envoy Extraordinary and Minister Plenipotentiary, then Consul General, Republics of Panama and Costa Rica 1923–1931. **Awards:** Silver Medal and Certificate, Royal Humane Society 1901; Coronation Medal 1911. **Honours:** Bronze Star 1914–1915; African Medal and Clasp. Died 4 August 1945.

WALMSLEY, Canon Alfred Moss (1904) (admitted as Non-Collegiate Student 1903) Born 16 April 1881, 12 Blakelow Road, Macclesfield, Cheshire; son of David Walmsley, HM Inspector of Factories, and Sarah Moss; m Alice Jane. BA 1906; MA 1910. **Tutor(s):** D MacAlister. **Educ:** Stockport Technical School; Borough Road College, Isleworth. **Career:** Ordained Deacon 1906; Assistant Master, Trinity College, Kandy, Ceylon 1906–1911; Ordained Priest 1907; Second Lieutenant, IARO, attached Supply and Transport Corps, WWI; Itinerant Missionary, Diocese of Columbo 1917–1925; Mesopotamia Expeditionary Force 1918; Missionary, Kegalle 1927–1931; Superintendent Missionary, Tamil Coolie Mission, Kandy 1931–1940; Honorary Canon, Henry Martyn, Christ Church Cathedral, Colombo 1939–1940; Permission to Officiate, Diocese of Gloucester 1946–1947; Rector, Westcote, Oxfordshire 1947–1950. **Appointments:** Honorary Canon, Christ Church Cathedral, Colombo 1939. Died 3 July 1967.

WALMSLEY, Ernest Roland (1948) Born 25 October 1927, Springfield Maternity Home, Blackburn, Lancashire; son of Ernest William Walmsley, Photographer's Assistant, and Elsie Dickinson; m Dorothy Coultous, 23 December 1963, Bradford, Yorkshire. **Subject(s):** French and Spanish/Theology; BA 1951; MA 1960. **Tutor(s):** C W Guillebaud. **Johnian Relatives:** brother-in-law of Frederick David Coultous (1944). **Educ:** Roe Lee Park School, Blackburn; St Francis Church of England School, Blackburn; The John Gulson School, Coventry; Bablake School, Coventry; Bradford Grammar School. **Career:** Coventry Cathedral Choir 1937–1941; Lay Clerk, Bradford Cathedral 1943–1946; RN 1946–1948; Royal Insurance, Leeds 1952–1955; Royal Insurance, Venezuela 1955–1960; Bradford Education Authority 1960–1961; Head, Spanish Department, St Bede's Grammar School, Bradford 1961–1978; General Manager, Headrow Housing Group, Leeds 1978–1991. **Appointments:** JP, City of Bradford 1972; Magistrate Member, West Yorkshire Police Authority 1975.

WALSH, Herbert (1919) Born 20 February 1897, 57 Ranger Street, Accrington, Lancashire; son of John William Walsh, Engineer, and Sarah Thompson. **Subject(s):** Economics/Law; BA 1922. **Tutor(s):** E A Benians. **Educ:** Accrington Municipal Secondary School. **Career:** Royal Fusiliers 1915–1916; RE 1916–1919.

WALTERS, Geoffrey Alfred (1934) Born 20 February 1916, 15 Albert Road, Handsworth; son of Alfred Walters, Designer of Machine Tools, and Daisy Lizzie Boden. **Subject(s):** Modern and Medieval Languages; BA 1937; MA 1941. **Tutor(s):** C W Guillebaud. **Educ:** Grove Lane Council School; King Edward's Grammar School, Aston; King Edward's High School, Birmingham. **Career:** Headmaster, Pinewood School, Swindon. Died 31 January 1987.

WALTERS, Dr Stuart Max (1938) Born 23 May 1920, Wharncliffe View, Oughtibridge, Sheffield; son of Bernard Walters, Steel Rolling Mill Furnace Foreman, and Ivy Dane; m Lorna Mary Strutt, 1948; 2 sons (Philip Max and Martin Gordon), 1 daughter (Stella Mary). **Subject(s):** Natural Sciences/Botany; BA 1941; MA 1947; PhD 1950; ScD 1980. **Tutor(s):** J M Wordie. **Johnian Relatives:** brother-in-law of Gordon Knowles Strutt (1935). **Educ:** National School, Stocksbridge; Council School, Stocksbridge; Penistone Grammar School, Penistone. **Career:** Civilian hospital work (conscientious objector to military service) 1940–1945; Curator of Herbarium, Botany School 1948–1973, Lecturer in Botany 1962–1973, Director, Botanic Garden 1973–1983, University of Cambridge; Title A Fellow, SJC 1949–1952; Fellow, King's College, Cambridge 1964–1984. **Awards:** Linnean Medal of Botany 1995; The Victoria Medal of Honour in Horticulture (Royal Horticultural Society) 1984. **Publications:** (with J S L Gilmour) *Wild Flowers*, 1954; (with J Raven) *Mountain Flowers*, 1956; (ed with F H Perring) *Atlas of the British Flora*, 1962; (with F H Perring, P D Sell and H L K Whitehouse) *A Flora of Cambridgeshire*, 1964; (with D Briggs) *Plant Variation and Evolution*, 1969, 3rd edn 1997; *The Shaping of Cambridge Botany*, 1981; *Wild and Garden Plants*, 1993; (with E A Stow) *Darwin's Mentor: John Stevens Henslow 1796–1861*, 2001.

WALTON, Professor John (1914) Born 14 May 1895, 22 West Cromwell Road, Brompton, Middlesex; son of Edward Arthur Walton, Artist, and Helen Henderson; m Dorothy Seward, 10 August 1918, St Bene't's, Cambridge; 1 son, 1 daughter. **Subject(s):** Natural Sciences/Botany; BA 1920; MA 1923; ScD 1948; DSc (Manchester); Docteur es Sciences (Montpellier); LLD (McMaster); FRSE 1931. **Tutor(s):** R P Gregory. **Johnian Relatives:** son-in-law of Albert Charles Seward (1883); brother-in-law of Michael Treviskey Sampson (1914). **Educ:** Daniel Stewart's College, Edinburgh. **Career:** Lecturer in Botany, University of Manchester 1923; Regius Professor of Botany, University of Glasgow 1930–1962; Forestry Commissioner 1949–1953. **Appointments:** President, Botanical Society of Edinburgh 1962. **Awards:** Neill Prize, Royal Society of Edinburgh 1947–1949. Died 13 February 1971.

WALTON, Sydney Russell (1932) Born 29 September 1913, 17 Lyndhurst Avenue, West Jesmond, Newcastle upon Tyne; son of Sydney Hepworth Walton, General Merchant, and Jessie Gertrude Elliott; m Vera; 1 son (Neville). **Subject(s):** Mathematics/Economics; BA 1936; MA 1972. **Tutor(s):** J M Wordie. **Johnian Relatives:** father of Neville Russell Walton (1971). **Educ:** Newcastle Modern School, Newcastle; Royal Grammar School, Newcastle. **Career:** Civil Servant 1935–1949; Ministry of Transport Representative in the US 1949. **Awards:** Baylis Scholarship, SJC. Died 16 September 1994.

WALTON, William George (1920) Born 13 February 1902, Marinpol, South Russia; son of William Sherington Walton, British Vice-Consul, Rostov on Don, South Russia, and Marie Ronomarenko. BA 1923; MA 1951. **Tutor(s):** B F Armitage. **Educ:** Golizino Jakovlev Gymnasium, Golizino, Russia; Sedbergh School.

WALWORTH, George (1911) Born 5 August 1892, 266 Girlington Road, Manningham, Bradford, Yorkshire; son of Harry Walworth, Journeyman Joiner, and Mary Ann Mowe; m Gladys Rebecca. **Subject(s):** Natural Sciences/Agriculture; BA 1914; MA 1919; DipAgr 1914. **Tutor(s):** J R Tanner. **Educ:** Belle Vue Secondary School, Bradford. **Career:** Head Research Bio-Chemist, Messrs Cadbury Brothers Ltd, Bourneville; Lecturer in Agricultural Chemistry, Agricultural College, Newport, Shropshire 1914–1916; Chemist, then Acid Manager,

Explosive Works, Messrs Chance and Hunt Ltd, Oldbury 1916–1918; Demonstrator in Agricultural Chemistry, Botany and Agriculture, and Ministry of Agriculture Research Scholar, University of Cambridge 1919; Lecturer in Agricultural Chemistry, University of Bangor, North Wales, and Head, Animal Nutrition Department 1919. **Appointments:** Member, Council of the Duchy of Lancaster; Agricultural Advisor, the Cooperative Union; Organising Secretary, Cooperative Union Meat and Milk Trade Associations. **Awards:** Holden Scholarship of the City. **Publications:** *Modern Dairy Management*; (with T Ellison) *Salesmanship in the Dairy Department*; (with T Ellison) *Feeding the Nation in Peace and War*. Died 27 November 1956.

WAN, Dr Yik Shing (1912) Born 20 June 1894, Canton, South China; son of Tün Mo Wan and Au; m D Jarret. **Subject(s):** Natural Sciences; BA 1915; MA 1919; BChir 1921; MB 1924. **Tutor(s):** L H K Bushe-Fox. **Educ:** St Stephen's College, Hong Kong; Weymouth College; University College School, London. **Career:** Lieutenant Colonel (final rank), RAMC, WWII. Died 14 June 1976.

WANDLESS, Keith Forrester (1935) Born 26 October 1911, Oatwan, Windmill Street, Gravesend, Kent; son of William Oscar Wandless, Trinity House Channel Pilot, and Olive Beatrice Oates. **Subject(s):** Natural Sciences/English; BA 1938. **Tutor(s):** J M Wordie. **Educ:** Gravesend County School; Bishop's Stortford College. **Career:** Pilot Officer, RAFVR 1939–1943. Died 17 February 1943 (killed in action).

WARBRICK, Allan James (1943) Born 8 January 1925, 53 Ellesmere Street, Bolton; son of Robert Warbrick, Secretary, Bleach Works, and Frances Howarth. **Educ:** Brandwood Street Elementary School, Bolton; Bolton Church Institute. **Appointments:** RE Cadet, SJC.

WARD, Charles Herbert John (1925) Born 5 November 1907, 43 Grantham Road, Stockwell, London; son of Frederick John Ward, Proprietor of Residential Hotels, and Edith Ann Kinns. **Subject(s):** Modern and Medieval Languages/Law; BA 1929; MA 1934. **Tutor(s):** M P Charlesworth. **Educ:** St Mary's School, Balham, London; Bedford Modern School.

WARD, Denis Hugh (1941) Born 9 April 1924, Southlands, Chapel Road, Warlingham, Surrey; son of Arnold Richard Ward, Insurance Clerk, and Gertrude Amy Bennett; m Audrey Josephine Hosier, 23 April 1949; 1 son (Timothy John); 3 daughters (Margaret Anne, Elizabeth Grace and Amanda Mary). **Subject(s):** Mathematics; BA 1944; MA 1948; FSS. **Tutor(s):** S J Bailey. **Educ:** Gracedieu School, Warlingham; Caterham School. **Career:** Experimental Officer, Ministry of Supply, Advisory Service on Statistical Methods 1943–1945; Ironworks Statistician, Appleby-Frodingham Steel Company, Scunthorpe, Lincolnshire 1945–1950; Divisional Mathematician, North West Division, National Coal Board 1950–1959; Industrial Statistician, Birds Eye Foods Ltd, Walton-on-Thames 1959; Organisation Division, Unilever; Company Statistician, Birds Eye Foods Ltd, Walton-on-Thames; Statistician, Home Office 1975–1987; Statistician, Department of the Environment 1987–1989. **Appointments:** Council Member, Vice President, Royal Statistical Society; Fellow, Council Member, Institute of Statisticians; Member, International Statistical Institute. **Publications:** numerous articles and reports in various journals including *Applied Statistics*, *The Statistician*, *The Journal of the Royal Statistical Society*.

WARD, Dudley William (1904) Born 23 September 1885, 20 Upper Bainbridge Street, Derby; son of Frederick William Ward, Railway Clerk, and Edith Welch Bardill; m Anne Marie Elisabeth Clothilde von der Planitz, 15 May 1912, Munich; 1 son (Peter Dudley b 7 February 1913), 2 daughters (Clothilde d 2002 and Elisabeth). **Subject(s):** History/ Economics; BA 1907; MA 1911. **Tutor(s):** C E Graves; J R Tanner. **Johnian Relatives:** father of Peter Dudley Ward (1932). **Educ:** Derby School. **Career:** Gregson Fellow, SJC 1909–1915; Assistant Editor, *The Economist* 1910–1912; Research, Germany 1913–1914; Department of the Treasury 1914–1919 (Officer in Charge of Statistics 1916–1919);

Attached to British Delegations, Peace Conference 1919, and Brussels Conference 1920; Director and Manager, British Overseas Bank 1920–1939; Ministry of Economic Warfare, WWII; General Counsel to the European Office of UNRRA 1944–1948; London Representative of UNICEF 1948–1957. **Awards:** Scholarship, SJC 1904–1908; Gladstone Memorial Prize for Economics, University of Cambridge 1906; Whewell Scholarship for International Law, University of Cambridge 1907; MacMahon Law Studentship 1908. **Honours:** CBE 1922. Died 8 February 1957.

WARD, Humphrey David (1939) Born 10 June 1921, 4 Myrtle Grove, Penwortham, Preston, Lancashire; son of Frank Ward, Local Government Officer, and Elizabeth Turnbull-Smith; m Dorothy Louise Taylor, 1951. **Subject(s):** Engineering; BA 1942; MA 1946; MIEE. **Tutor(s):** J S Boys Smith. **Educ:** Holmwood School, Formby; Shrewsbury School. **Career:** Electrical Research Department 1942–1946, Guided Weapons Department 1946–1948 RAE, Farnborough, Hampshire; Ironmaking Research, Process and Practice Field Trials, subsequently Divisional Technical Secretary, British Iron and Steel Research Association, later part of British Steel Corporation 1948–1981.

WARD, John Derek (1945) Born 26 May 1927, 23 St Mary's, York; son of John Ward, Fruiterer, and Hannah Mary Breckon; m Judith Sparkes, 1 September 1954, The Church of St Philip and St James, Clifton, York; 1 son (Nigel Mark b 3 April 1961), 1 daughter (Susan Jane b 17 March 1958). BA 1949; MA 1951. **Tutor(s):** J M Wordie. **Educ:** Haughton School; Tanghall School; St Peter's School, York. **Career:** Sub-Lieutenant, HMS *Hound*, RNVR 1946–1948; Solicitor 1952–1989. **Appointments:** RN Cadet, SJC. Died 23 March 2001.

WARD, John Hamilton Mackenzie (1927) Born 23 December 1908, 102 Elgin Crescent, Kensington, London; son of John Frederick Ward, Analytical Chemist, and Anna Mackenzie. **Tutor(s):** C W Guillebaud. **Educ:** Colet Court; St Paul's School, West Kensington.

WARD, Peter Dudley (1932) Born 7 February 1913, 63 Augsburger Strasse, Charlottenburg, Berlin; son of Dudley William Ward, Bank Director, and Anne Marie Elisabeth Clothilde von der Planitz. **Subject(s):** Modern and Medieval Languages/Economics; BA 1935; MA 1951. **Tutor(s):** E A Benians. **Johnian Relatives:** son of Dudley William Ward (1904). **Educ:** St Faith's School, Cambridge; Stowe School. **Career:** Ran for England in Olympic Games 1936 and in Empire Games. **Appointments:** Captain, Cambridge University Cross Country Team 1935.

WARDLE, Dr Derek Basil James (1942) Born 4 October 1924, 150 White Cross Road, Hereford; son of Harry Wardle, Schoolmaster, and Elsie Clarkson. **Subject(s):** Natural Sciences; BA 1945; MB 1948; BChir 1948. **Tutor(s):** S J Bailey. **Educ:** Hereford Cathedral Preparatory School; Hereford Cathedral School.

WARDMAN, Professor Alan Edgar (1947) Born 28 April 1926, 51 Crane Avenue, Isleworth, Middlesex; son of Oswald Wardman, Headmaster, and Kate Louise Rayner; m Judith. **Subject(s):** Classics; BA 1949; MA 1957. **Tutor(s):** R L Howland. **Educ:** Isleworth Town School; Isleworth County School. **Career:** Lecturer in Classics 1951–1974, Reader in Classics 1974–1983, Head of Classics Department 1979, Professor of Classics 1983–1986, University of Reading. **Awards:** Henry Arthur Thomas Scholarship, University of Cambridge 1950; Porson Scholarship, University of Cambridge 1950. **Publications:** *Plutarch's Lives*, 1974; *Rome's Debt to Greece*, 1976; *Religion and Statecraft among the Romans*, 1982. Died 21 October 1986.

WARING, Donald Arthur (HORNBY-WARING) (1922) Born 29 March 1903, Long Riston Parsonage, Skirlaugh, Hull, Yorkshire; son of Arthur Waring, Clerk in Holy Orders, and Jane Hornby. BA 1925; MA 1978. **Tutor(s):** E E Sikes. **Educ:** Pocklington School. Died 29 January 1981.

WARNER, Charles Randall Mallet (1936) Born 18 August 1917, 70 Addison Street, Nottingham; son of Charles Horne Warner, Doctor of Medicine, and Rafna Mallet. **Subject(s):** Natural Sciences; BA 1939. **Tutor(s):** R L Howland. **Educ:** Broadgate School, Nottingham; Seacroft School, Skegness; Gresham's School, Holt.

WARNER, Gilbert Patrick (1933) Born 12 July 1914, Lulworth, Woodlands Road, Sparkhill, Birmingham; son of John Henry Warner, Clerk in Holy Orders, and Lilian Mary Bufton. **Subject(s):** Classics/ English; BA 1936; MA 1943. **Tutor(s):** R L Howland. **Johnian Relatives:** brother of Wilfred John Nicholas Warner (1926). **Educ:** Bradford Grammar School.

WARNER, Wilfrid John Nicholas (1926) Born 12 October 1907, Ilmington, Warwickshire; son of John Henry Warner, Clerk in Holy Orders, and Lilian Mary Bufton. **Subject(s):** Classics/Moral Sciences; BA 1929; MA 1946. **Tutor(s):** M P Charlesworth. **Johnian Relatives:** brother of Gilbert Patrick Warner (1933). **Educ:** King Edward VI School, Birmingham; Derby School; Bradford Grammar School. **Career:** Squadron Leader, RAF; Welfare Officer for University Assistants 1946, Senior Assistant Registrary, Secretary of the Assistant Staff Board 1961–1972, University of Cambridge. **Awards:** Exhibition, SJC; Bell Scholarship, University of Cambridge 1927. Died 28 September 1987.

WARREN, Herbert Moffat (1920) Born 13 October 1902, Belgrano, Mendoza, Argentina; son of George Charles Warren, Agriculturalist and Wine Maker, and Margaret Louisa Moffat. **Tutor(s):** B F Armitage. **Educ:** Horton School, Ickwell; St George's College, Quilnes, Buenos Aires, Argentina.

WARREN, James Lionel East (1913) Born 4 January 1895, Jabalpor, Central Provinces, India; son of John Alexander Faris Warren, Clerk in Holy Orders, and Mary Kathleen East. **Tutor(s):** E E Sikes. **Educ:** Monkstown Park School, County Dublin; Dean Close School, Cheltenham. **Career:** Second Lieutenant, Lieutenant, then Captain, Welsh Regiment 1915. **Awards:** Exhibition, SJC. Died 1 or 2 October 1915 (wounded and missing, presumed killed in action, at the Hohenzollern Redoubt).

WARREN, John Anthony Crosby (1931) Born 20 March 1911, 15 Upper Belgrave Road, Clifton; son of Crosby Noel Maurice Warren, Metal Manufacturer, and Ellen Winifred Annie Cook; m Nell. BA 1934; MA 1938. **Tutor(s):** J M Wordie. **Educ:** Private Tuition; Clifton College, Bristol. **Career:** Test Pilot, jet-propelled planes, Gloster Aircraft Company 1934–1944 (posthumously commended for valuable service in the air). Died 27 April 1944 (killed in an air crash).

WARRINER, Robert Peverell (1920) Born 1 August 1898, 37 Park Place, Leyton, Essex; son of Robert Warriner, Chief Engineer, Bethlehem Shipbuilding Corporation, and Eleanor Peverell. **Tutor(s):** E A Benians. **Educ:** Malvern House School, Lewisham; Dulwich College; Stones School, Boston, USA; MIT, Cambridge, USA.

WARRINGTON, Paul (1927) Born 18 November 1909, Springhead, Woodlesford Lane, Rothwell, Yorkshire; son of Austin Warrington, Colliery Proprietor, and Isabella Winpenny. **Subject(s):** Natural Sciences; BA 1930; MA 1934. **Tutor(s):** J M Wordie. **Educ:** Grosvenor House School, Harrogate; Ushaw College, Durham. Died 28 December 1992.

WARTERS, Colonel Reginald Arthur (1908) Born 1 January 1890, Greenhill Lane, Alfreton, Derbyshire; son of William Alexander Warters, Surgeon, and Mary Beatrice Earp; m Doreen Pritchard, 4 July 1930, St John the Evangelist, Bromley, Kent. BA 1911; MA 1919; MB (Edinburgh)1915; ChB (Edinburgh) 1915. **Tutor(s):** J R Tanner. **Educ:** Oakham School. **Career:** Temporary Lieutenant, RAMC 1916; Temporary Captain 1917–1920; Indian Medical Service 1920; Major, Indian Medical Service 1928. Died 16 March 1962.

WASHBURN, Louis Mumford (1918) American Student.

WASKETT, Dennis (1937) Born 12 January 1915, 94 Richmond Road, Ilford; son of Frederick George Waskett, Clerk, and Mary Ann Driscoll. **Tutor(s):** J S Boys Smith. **Educ:** Bute Road Elementary School, Wellington; West Leigh Elementary School, Leigh-on-Sea; Southend Municipal School of Art; Southend Evening Technical Institute; Polytechnic, Regent Street; Northampton Polytechnic, London.

WASS, Sir Douglas William Gretton (1941) Born 15 April 1923, 40 Norwood Road, Wallasey, Cheshire; son of Arthur William Wass, Surveyor of Customs and Excise, and Winifred Elsie Gretton; m Milica Pavicic, 1954; 1 son, 1 daughter. **Subject(s):** Mathematics; BA 1944; MA 1948; Hon DLitt (University of Bath). **Tutor(s):** S J Bailey. **Educ:** Colmore Road Elementary School, Birmingham; Cottesmore Central School, Nottingham; Nottingham High School. **Career:** Scientific research with the Admiralty, at home and in the Far East 1943–1946; Assistant Principal 1946, Principal 1951, HM Treasury; Private Secretary to the Chancellor of the Exchequer 1959–1961; Chief Secretary 1961–1962, Assistant Secretary 1962, HM Treasury; Alternate Executive Director, International Monetary Fund and Financial Counsellor, British Embassy, Washington DC 1965–1967; Under-Secretary 1968, Deputy Secretary 1970–1973, Second Permanent Secretary 1973–1974, Permanent Secretary 1974–1983, HM Treasury; Joint Head of the Home Civil Service 1981–1983; Senior Adviser and Chairman, Nomura International plc 1986–1998. **Appointments:** Commonwealth Fund Fellow in USA, 1958–1959; Visiting Fellow, Brookings Institution, Washington DC 1959; Chairman, British Selection Committee of Harkness Fellowships 1981–1984; Honorary Fellow, SJC 1982; Council Member, Centre for Economic Policy Research 1983–1990; Director then Chairman, AXA Equity & Law 1984–1995; Director, Barclays Bank 1984–1987; UN Advisory Group on Financial Flows for Africa 1987–1988; President, Market Research Society 1987–1991; Chairman, University Syndicate to Advise on Constitutional Matters 1988–1989. **Awards:** Major Scholarship, SJC 1940. **Honours:** CB 1971; KCB 1975; GCB 1980. **Publications:** *Government and the governed*, 1984; articles in newspapers and journals.

WATERFALL, Charles Richard (1943) Born 21 February 1925, St Winifred's Nursing Home, Babbacombe, Torquay, Devon; son of Charles Francis Waterfall, Indian Civil Service, and Ada Duckworth; m Joan Aldyth Malkinson, 9 April 1949. **Subject(s):** Mechanical Sciences; BA 1946; MA 1950. **Tutor(s):** S J Bailey. **Educ:** St Catherine's School; Exeter School. **Career:** Member, Institute of Engineers and Shipbuilders in Scotland; Fellow, Institution of Industrial Managers 1990.

WATERHOUSE, Deryck Frank (1945) Born 13 August 1927, 210 Bristnall Hall Road, Oldbury, Birmingham; son of Wilfred Edward Waterhouse, Cashier, Gas Works, and Doris Mabel Greaves; 3 children. **Subject(s):** Natural Sciences; BA 1948; MA 1952. **Tutor(s):** J M Wordie. **Educ:** Bristnall Hall Junior School; Oldbury County High School, Oldbury. **Career:** RAF 1948–1950; Tube Investments Ltd 1950–1967; UKAEA 1954–1960; Sales Director, Firth Brown Ltd 1967–1974; British Steel Producers 1974–1988.

WATERHOUSE, Professor Gilbert (1907) Born 15 July 1888, 2 Mayfield, Hipperholme, Halifax, Yorkshire; son of Harold Waterhouse, Railway Storekeeper, and Sarah Ellen Jackson; m Mary Elizabeth Woods, 30 August 1920, Killiney Parish Church, County Dublin; 3 daughters (Margaret b 14 August 1921, Elizabeth b 30 May 1926 and Dorothy b 21 June 1929). **Subject(s):** Modern and Medieval Languages; BA 1910; MA 1914; LittD (Dublin) 1917; FRGS 1913. **Tutor(s):** E E Sikes. **Johnian Relatives:** brother of Hugh Waterhouse (1914); grandfather of Gilbert John Dunlop (1979) and of Hugh Christopher Dunlop (1980). **Educ:** Manchester Grammar School. **Career:** English Lecturer, Leipzig 1911–1914; Master, Manchester Grammar School 1914–1915; Professor of German, TCD 1915–1932; Lieutenant, Dublin University OTC (Easter Rising 1916); Lieutenant, RNVR 1918; Professor of German,

Queen's University, Belfast 1933–1953. **Awards:** Tiarks German Scholarship, University of Cambridge 1910. **Publications:** *The Literary Relations of England and Germany in the Seventeenth Century*, 1914; *The War and the Study of German*, 1917; *History of German Literature*, 1928. Died 25 July 1977.

WATERHOUSE, Hugh (1914) Born 17 November 1891, 25 Charles Street, Pendleton, Lancashire; son of Harold Waterhouse, Railway Storekeeper, and Sarah Ellen Jackson; m Betty Crabtree, 22 August 1929, Fairhaven Congregational Church, Lytham St Annes; 1 son (Edward). **Subject(s):** Modern and Medieval Languages; BA 1920; MA 1926. **Tutor(s):** E E Sikes. **Johnian Relatives:** brother of Gilbert Waterhouse (1907); great uncle of Gilbert John Dunlop (1979) and of Hugh Christopher Dunlop (1980). **Educ:** Pendleton Grammar School; Manchester Grammar School; University of London. **Career:** Captain, Lancashire Fusiliers; Master, Retford Grammar School; Master, Rugby School; Master, Edward VII School, Lytham; Headmaster, Chorley Grammar School 1933. **Honours:** MC 1918. Died 26 April 1981.

WATERHOUSE, Dr John Alfred Humphrey (1938) Born 30 December 1918, 60 Hagley Road, Edgbaston, Birmingham; son of Thomas Alfred Foster Waterhouse, Commercial Traveller, and Kate Elizabeth Humphreys; m Rachel Elizabeth Franklin, 1947; 2 sons (Matthew John Franklin b 21 September 1950 and Edmund Hugh Foster b 4 February 1952), 2 daughters (Deborah Mary Rachel b 11 March 1956 and Rebecca Susan Kate b 20 October 1958). **Subject(s):** Mathematics; BA 1941; MA 1959; PhD (Birmingham). **Tutor(s):** J M Wordie. **Johnian Relatives:** father of Edmund Hugh Foster Waterhouse (1970). **Educ:** Edgbaston Church of England School; West House Preparatory School; King Edward's School, Birmingham; University of Birmingham. **Career:** Senior Lecturer in Human Genetics, Department of Medical Statistics, Birmingham Medical School 1947–1953; Reader in Medical Statistics 1953–1961, Reader in Epidemiology 1961–1985, University of Birmingham; International Agency for Research into Cancer, Lyons 1981–1982. **Appointments:** Director, Birmingham (later the West Midlands) Cancer Registry; Founder Member and Second President, International Association of Cancer Registries 1957; Honorary Fellow, Faculty of Occupational Medicine, Royal College of Physicians. **Awards:** Exhibition, SJC 1937. **Publications:** (ed, first five volumes) *Cancer Incidence in Five Continents*, 1981–82. Died 7 October 2000.

WATERHOUSE, The Hon Sir Ronald Gough (1944) Born 8 May 1926, Holywell, Flintshire; son of Thomas Waterhouse, Company Chairman, and Doris Helena Gough; m Sarah Selina Ingram, 16 July 1960; 1 son (Thomas Hugh Ingram b 1962), 2 daughters (Sophie Alexandra b 1966 and Laura Diana b 1974). **Subject(s):** Economics/Law; BA 1949; MA 1951; LLB 1951; LLM 1985; Honorary LLD (Wales) 1986. **Tutor(s):** G C L Bertram; J M Wordie. **Johnian Relatives:** father of Sophie Alexandra Waterhouse (1985). **Educ:** Holywell County Grammar School, Flintshire. **Career:** RAFVR 1944–1948; Called to the Bar, Middle Temple 1952; Deputy Chairman, Cheshire QS 1964–1971; Deputy Chairman, Flintshire QS 1966–1971; QC 1969–1978; Recorder, Crown Court 1972–1977; Bencher, Middle Temple 1977; Circuit Leader, Wales and Chester 1978; Judge, High Court of Justice, Family Division 1978–1988; Judge, Employment Appeal Tribunal 1979–1987; Presiding Judge, Wales and Chester Circuit 1980–1984; Judge, High Court of Justice, Queen's Bench Division 1988–1996. **Appointments:** President, Cambridge Union Society, Michaelmas 1950; Member, Bar Council 1961–1965; Chairman, Interdepartmental Committee of Inquiry into Rabies 1970–1971; Vice-President and Council Member, Zoological Society of London (intermittently) 1972–1993; Chairman, Local Government Boundary Commission for Wales 1974–1978; President, Llangollen International Music Eisteddfod 1994–1997; Treasurer, Honourable Society of the Middle Temple 1995; Chairman, Tribunal of Inquiry into Child Abuse in North Wales 1996–2000; Chairman, Independent Supervisory Authority for Hunting 1999–. **Awards:** McMahon Studentship, SJC; Harmsworth Scholarship 1953–1956. **Honours:** Kt 1978; GBE 2002.

WATERS, Henry Jones (1932) Born 13 April 1913, 139 Gladstone Street, Abertillery; son of Walter Waters, Headmaster of an Elementary School, and Kate Jones. **Subject(s):** Classics; BA 1935. **Tutor(s):** R L Howland. **Educ:** The Cathedral School, Hereford. **Awards:** Somerset Exhibition, SJC.

WATERS, John David (1943) Born 15 July 1925, 103 Wimbledon Park Road, Wandsworth; son of Maurice William Waters, Railway Clerk, and Edith Alice Danells; m Mary Pamela Liddell, 1974 (d 1994). **Subject(s):** Mechanical Sciences; BA 1946; FBCS. **Tutor(s):** S J Bailey. **Educ:** Durham House Preparatory School, Putney; St Paul's School. **Career:** Sub-Lieutenant, RN 1945–1947; British Timken, Duston 1947; Green Size and Heat Treatment Engineer 1949; Head, Quality Control Department, Duston 1952; Green Size Engineer 1954; Computing Engineer 1955; Data Processing Manager, Renton-Bucyrus, Lincoln 1959–1972; Computer Consultant, Fraser-Williams, Sheffield 1972–1987.

WATERS, Kenneth Selby (1909) Born 18 June 1890, School House, Nuneaton, Warwickshire; son of Samuel George Waters, Clerk in Holy Orders, and Ellen Selby. **Subject(s):** Mathematics; BA 1912. **Tutor(s):** L H K Bushe-Fox. **Educ:** King Edward VI School, Nuneaton; King's School, Warwick; King's School, Grantham. **Career:** Turner, Morrison and Co (shipping firm), Calcutta Branch 1912–1914; Port Defence Corps, Calcutta 1914; Second Lieutenant, No 1 British Mountain Battery, RGA, North West Frontier Provinces, WWI. Died 30 May 1917 (killed in action at Bara Gali).

WATERS, Roy William (1949) Born 26 June 1928, 40 Hanover Road, Kensal Rise, Willesden, Middlesex; son of William Joseph Waters, Motor Mechanic, and Florence Amy Walker. **Subject(s):** English; BA 1952; MA 1956. **Tutor(s):** A G Lee. **Educ:** Harvist Road School; Kilburn Grammar School. **Career:** Teacher and Headteacher in London comprehensive schools 1954–1988; Divisional Inspector for Lambeth, Inner London Education Authority 1968–1988. **Awards:** Exhibition, SJC.

WATHES, Richard Sidney (1934) Born 10 August 1915, 11 St Albans Road, Moseley, Birmingham; son of Thomas Sidney Wathes, Dairyman Master and Captain, 216th Battalion, Warwick Regiment, and Doris Collins; m Rosemary. **Subject(s):** Natural Sciences; BA 1937; MRCS; LRCP. **Tutor(s):** R L Howland. **Educ:** Elms School, Colwall; Wrekin College, Wellington. **Career:** GP, Bromsgrove, then Axbridge, Somerset; RAMC 1939. Died 13 November 1989.

WATKIN, Dr John Emrys (1949) Born 19 March 1929, North Parade, Aberystwyth; son of Edward Emrys Watkin, Lecturer in Zoology, University College of Wales, and Lilian Louisa Evans; m Gwyneth Benjamin, 1955; 2 daughters (Sian b 1950 and Cara b 1960). **Subject(s):** Natural Sciences; BA 1952; MA 1957; PhD (Wales) 1955. **Tutor(s):** E Miller. **Educ:** St Padarn's Convent School, Aberystwyth; Alexandra Road Board School, Aberystwyth; Ardwyn County School, Aberystwyth. **Career:** National Research Council of Canada 1955–1988; Consultant to Royal Canadian Mounted Police 1988–1995. **Publications:** Various publications in fields of Plant Biochemistry and Fingerprint Science.

WATKINS, Allen (1908) Born 2 March 1889, Broomy Hill, Hereford; son of Alfred Watkins, Miller, and JP for Hereford, and Marion Mendham Cross; m Isabelle Glyn Marnock, 1 October 1955, Stroud. **Subject(s):** History/Economics; BA 1912; MA 1917; Chartered Accountants Exams 1922. **Tutor(s):** E E Sikes. **Educ:** Hereford Cathedral School. **Career:** Chartered Accountant 1925; Chief Accountant and Internal Auditor, University Correspondence College, Cambridge 1930. **Publications:** 'Chess Shorthand', *British Chess Magazine*, 1916; *Economics for Examinees*, 1928. Died 7 January 1977.

WATKINS, Arthur Ernest (1916) Born 23 April 1898, 27 Bolingbroke Road, West Kensington; son of Alfred Charles Watkins, Departmental Manager, J Lyons & Co, and Edith Isabel Thomas; m Amy Marjorie.

Subject(s): Mathematics/Natural Sciences; BA 1920; MA 1925. **Tutor(s):** L H K Bushe-Fox. **Educ:** Frobel Institute; Latymer Upper School. **Career:** Plant Breeding Institute, School of Agriculture, Cambridge 1924–1931; Fellow, SJC 1924–1931; Lecturer in Cytology 1931–1948, Lecturer in Agriculture 1948, University of Cambridge. **Awards:** Scholarship, SJC 1915. Died 3 January 1967.

WATKINSON, George (1923) Born 19 March 1904, Newlands, Northowram, Halifax, Yorkshire; son of George Watkinson, Clerk in Holy Orders, and Lucy Walsh. BA 1926; MA 1930. **Tutor(s):** B F Armitage. **Educ:** Stancliffe Hall, near Matlock; Uppingham School.

WATKINSON, Dr Richard Geoffrey (1943) Born 3 June 1925, Silverdale, The Mount, Heswall, Cheshire; son of Arthur Stanley Watkinson, Shipyard Manager, and Marjorie Leslie Roberts; m (1) Dr Ellen Veldhuyzen, 15 July 1950, St James's, Garlickhythe, London, (2) Patricia Plunkett, 16 May 1970; (1) 1 son (Hugh b 1955), 1 daughter (Alice b 1947), (2) 1 son (Tom b 1971). **Subject(s):** Medicine; MB 1949; BChir 1949. **Tutor(s):** S J Bailey. **Johnian Relatives:** cousin of David Walker (1941). **Educ:** Braeside School, West Kirby; Oundle School. **Career:** GP. Died 14 January 2001.

WATON, John Howard (1941) Born 6 August 1923, 26 Weltje Road, Hammersmith, London; son of David Waton, Chartered Secretary, and Gertrude Winifred Osborn. **Subject(s):** Natural Sciences; BA 1944; MA 1948; BSc (London) 1946; Teacher's Diploma (London) 1947; MPhil (London) 1979; ARIC 1946; AIL Fr 1950; FRIC 1955 (later FRSC); MIL 1966. **Tutor(s):** C W Guillebaud. **Educ:** Palmer's Endowed School, Grays; KCL. **Career:** Chemist, Metallurgical Analysis Laboratory, Murex, Rainham, Essex 1943–1946; Assistant Lecturer, Wolverhampton and Staffordshire Technical College 1947–1949; Assistant Lecturer in Inorganic Chemistry, Brighton Technical College 1949–1952; Lecturer 1952–1960, Senior Lecturer 1960–1988, in Inorganic Chemistry, Kingston Technical College (later Polytechnic).

WATSON, Arthur Lockhart (1901) Born 29 June 1883, Starston, Norfolk; son of Frederick Watson, Clerk in Holy Orders and Fellow, SJC, and Margaret Lockhart; m Mary Frances Olive Courtenay, 25 June 1908, St Martin's, East Horsley. BA 1904; MA 1913. **Tutor(s):** J R Tanner; C E Graves. **Johnian Relatives:** son of Frederick Watson (1864); brother of Henry Adam Watson (1900) and of Basil Lockhart Watson (1908). **Educ:** All Saints' School, Bloxham. **Career:** Ordained Deacon 1907; Curate, Plumstead 1907–1909; Ordained Priest 1908; Curate, Wantage 1909–1913; Curate, Cranham 1913–1915; Vicar, Aldworth 1918–1936; Vicar, Ufford with Ashton and Bainton 1936–1940. Died 19 March 1940.

WATSON, Basil Lockhart (1908) Born 7 June 1889, Stow cum Quy, Cambridge; son of Frederick Watson, Clerk in Holy Orders and Fellow, SJC, and Margaret Lockhart; m Dorothy Joan Chaffer. BA 1911. **Tutor(s):** L H K Bushe-Fox. **Johnian Relatives:** son of Frederick Watson (1864); brother of Henry Adam Watson (1900) and of Arthur Lockhart Watson (1901). **Educ:** St Faith's School, Cambridge; Cranleigh School. **Career:** Captain, General List, attached RE (Signals) (Mentioned in Despatches), WWI. Died 4 August 1923.

WATSON, Bernard Angus (1924) Born 17 January 1906, 14 Sunbury Avenue, Newcastle upon Tyne; son of James Angus Watson, Canned Goods Importer, and Ethel Reid. BA 1927. **Tutor(s):** E A Benians. **Johnian Relatives:** brother of Graham Angus Watson (1931). **Educ:** Old College, Windermere; Mill Hill School. **Career:** Principal, Admiralty. Died 19 August 1965.

WATSON, Charles Reginald (1922) Born 2 May 1906, 2 Marlborough Terrace, Stockton-on-Tees, County Durham; son of Arthur James Watson, Timber Merchant, and Adele Mary Wood. **Subject(s):** Law; BA 1927; MA 1931; LLB 1928. **Tutor(s):** E A Benians. **Educ:** Queen Victoria High School, Stockton; New College, Harrogate. **Career:** Admitted Solicitor 1930. Died 11 June 1960.

WATSON, Sir Francis John Bagott (1926) Born 24 August 1907, St James's Road, Dudley, Worcestershire; son of Hugh Watson, Headmaster, Dudley Grammar School, and Ellen Marian Bagott; m Mary Rosalie Gray, 1941 (d 1969); 1 son (adopted). **Subject(s):** English/Mathematics; BA 1929; FSA; FBA. **Tutor(s):** J M Wordie. **Educ:** Stone Grammar School; Shrewsbury School. **Career:** Registrar, Courtauld Institute of Art 1934–1938; Assistant Keeper (later Deputy Director) 1938–1963, Director 1963–1974, Wallace Collection; Slade Professor of Fine Art, University of Oxford 1969–1970; Wrightsman Professor, New York University 1970–1971; Kress Professor, National Gallery, Washington DC 1975–1976. **Appointments:** Deputy Surveyor of the King's Works of Art 1947–1952; Deputy Surveyor of The Queen's Works of Art 1952–1963; Surveyor of The Queen's Works of Art 1963–1972; Trustee, Whitechapel Art Gallery 1949–1974; Chairman, Furniture History Society 1966–1974; Chairman, Walpole Society 1970–1976; Visiting Lecturer, University of California 1970; Regent Fellow, Smithsonian Institution 1982–1984. **Awards:** Ufficiale del Ordine al Merito della Repubblica Italiana 1961; New York University Gold Medal 1966. **Honours:** KCVO. **Publications:** Canaletto, 1949; (jointly) Southill, A Regency House, 1951; Wallace Collection: Catalogue of Furniture, 1956; Louis XVI Furniture, 1959; The Choiseul Gold Box (Charlton Lecture), 1963; (jointly) Great Family Collections, 1965; The Guardi Family of Painters (Fred Cook Memorial Lecture), 1966; (jointly) Eighteenth Century Gold Boxes, 1966; (jointly) The Wrightsman Collection Catalogue (Volume 1: Furniture, 1966, Volume 2: Furniture, Gilt Bronzes, Carpets, 1966, Volumes 3 and 4: Furniture, Snuffboxes, Silver, Porcelain, 1970, Volume 5: Paintings and Sculpture, 1974); Giambattista Tiepolo, 1966; Fragonard, 1967; Chinese Porcelains in European Mounts, 1980; (jointly) Catalogue of the Mounted Oriental Porcelains in the J Paul Getty Museum, 1983; (contributor) Vergoldete Bronzen–Die Bronzearbeiten des Spätbarok zu Klassizmus: Einfurung, 1985; Oriental Porcelains in European Mounts, 1986; Systematic Catalogue of Seventeenth and Eighteenth Century French Furniture, National Gallery, Washington, 1992; numerous contributions to learned journals in Europe, America and Asia. Died 27 September 1992.

WATSON, Graham Angus (1931) Born 8 June 1913, Whitewell Lodge, Adderstone Crescent, Newcastle upon Tyne; son of James Angus Watson, Food-preserver, and Ethel Reid; m Dorothy Vasey, 1946; 2 daughters (Julia and Sophie). **Subjects:** English/History; BA 1934. **Tutor(s):** E A Benians. **Johnian Relatives:** brother of Bernard Angus Watson (1924). **Educ:** Preparatory School, Newcastle; The Old College, Windermere; Repton School. **Career:** Nicholson and Watson, publishers (family firm) 1934; Gunner, Royal Horse Artillery 1940–1942; Officer, RASC (twice Mentioned in Despatches) 1942–1946; Director and Chairman, Curtis Brown Ltd, Literary Agents 1947–1980 (Managing Director 1966–1980, Chairman 1970–1980). **Publications:** Book Society, 1980; Echoes from a War, 2003 (published posthumously). Died 14 November 2002.

WATSON, Henry Adam (1900) Born 7 October 1881, The Rectory, Starston, Norfolk; son of Frederick Watson, Clerk in Holy Orders and Fellow, SJC, and Margaret Lockhart; m Hannah Mary Millicent, 1922; 1 son (Peter), 1 daughter (Catherine). **Tutor(s):** C E Graves. **Johnian Relatives:** son of Frederick Watson (1864); brother of Arthur Lockhart Watson (1901) and of Basil Lockhart Watson (1908). **Educ:** Mr Goodchild's Preparatory School, Cambridge; St Edward's School, Oxford. **Career:** Fruit Grower; War Service, Boer War 1901; in Canada 1904–1915; Inland Water Transport, France, WWI.

WATSON, John Donald Mackenzie (1939) Born 21 August 1921, 43 Fountainhall Road, Edinburgh; son of John Thomas Sherriff Watson, Chartered Accountant, and Ethel Lucy Mackenzie. **Tutor(s):** S J Bailey. **Educ:** St Colm's Kindergarten, Edinburgh; Edinburgh Academy; Loretto School, Edinburgh.

WATSON, John Stewart Ferra (1929) Born 14 July 1912, High Street, Wootton Bassett; son of John Nuthall Watson, Physician and Surgeon, and Eleanor Gordon Macfarlane. BA 1934. **Tutor(s):** M P Charlesworth. **Educ:** Mowden School, Brighton; Marlborough College.

WATSON, Peter Bartlett Collier (1926) Born 22 September 1907, 77 Kirkstall Road, Streatham Hill, Surrey; son of Harold Collier Watson, Solicitor, and Mary Judith Bartlett; m Marjorie Clare Richards, 21 November 1945, Grosvenor Chapel. **Subject(s):** Law; BA 1929; MA 1938. **Tutor(s):** E A Benians. **Johnian Relatives:** nephew of Percy William Felton (1909); cousin of William Fowler Felton (1936). **Educ:** Miss Wallis, Mount View, Streatham; Dulwich College Preparatory School; Dulwich College. **Career:** Senior Partner, Watson Sons and Room. Died 25 November 1970.

WATSON, Roy Stuart (1944) Born 18 April 1926, 2 Barton Road, West Derby, Lancashire; son of Henry Watson, Director, Hardware Merchants, and Gladys Smith Bradley. **Tutor(s):** J M Wordie. **Educ:** Hulme Hall, Cheadle Hulme; Cheadle Hulme School. **Appointments:** RAF Cadet, SJC.

WATSON, Thomas William (1908) Born 18 March 1889, Marsden's Lane, Wollaston, Stourbridge; son of Thomas Watson, Journeyman Glassmaker, and Sarah Bonnington; 2 daughters (Mildred and Anne). **Subject(s):** Mathematics/Natural Sciences; BA 1911; MA 1919. **Tutor(s):** L H K Bushe-Fox. **Educ:** Wollaston National Boys' School; King Edward VI School, Stourbridge. **Career:** Temporary Master, Merchant Taylors' School 1912; Mathematics and Form Master, Highgate School 1913–1914; Artists' Rifles, WWI; Ministry of Munitions until 1922; Senior Mathematics and Physics Master and Housemaster, Pocklington School 1922–1925; Headmaster, King Edward VI Grammar School, Camp Hill, Birmingham 1925–1930; Headmaster, Dudley Grammar School 1931–1934; Headmaster, Stourbridge King Edward VI School 1934–1951. **Honours:** MC. Died 19 January 1957.

WATSON, William Vernon Crowther (1915) Born 16 November 1896, Swincliffe Villa, Birkenshaw, Yorkshire; son of Joseph Watson, Colliery Director, and Polly Crowther. **Tutor(s):** R P Gregory. **Educ:** The Girls' Grammar School, Bradford; Grammar School, Bradford. **Career:** West Yorkshire Regiment 1915; Second Lieutenant 1916; Active Service, France 1917. **Awards:** Exhibition, SJC 1915. Died October 1917 (killed in action near Ypres).

WATSON, Woodland Ronald Harry (1939) Born 26 December 1920, Ipswich, Suffolk; son of Harry Frederick Watson, Bank Manager, and Winifred Grace Maskelyne Smith. **Subject(s):** Economics/Law; BA 1947; MA 1959. **Tutor(s):** C W Guillebaud. **Educ:** St Felix School, Felixstowe; Uppingham School. **Career:** Articled to a solicitor. Died 12 March 1974.

WATT, The Revd Father Christopher Eugene (1943) Born 16 December 1922, Furnarobert, Armoy, Antrim, Northern Ireland; son of Joseph Watt, Flesher, and Isabella Miller. **Subject(s):** English; BA 1946; MA 1950. **Educ:** St John's College, Kintbury. **Career:** Roman Catholic Priest.

WATT, Cyril Stanley (1946) Born 19 April 1916, Belle Vue, Linace, Dugannon; son of Samuel James Watt, Mineral Water Manufacturer, and Myra Hall. BSc Chemistry 1938, Physics 1939 (Belfast); MSc (Belfast) 1940. **Tutor(s):** J M Wordie. **Educ:** Union Place School, Dugannon; Dugannon Royal School; Queen's University, Belfast.

WATT, Professor Ian Pierre (1935) Born 9 March 1917, Craig Cottage, Craig Walk, Bowness on Windermere; son of Thomas Watt, Schoolmaster, and René Gabrielle Jeanne Guitton; m Ruth Alma Mellinkoff, 22 November 1947, Boston, Massachusetts, USA; 1 son (George), 1 daughter (Josephine). **Subject(s):** English; BA 1938; MA 1946; FAAAS 1971. **Educ:** Boyne House, Dover; Dover County School; University of California, Los Angeles; Harvard University. **Career:** Lieutenant, 5th Suffolk Regiment 1939–1946, POW in Japanese hands, Malaya 1942–1945; Title A Fellow, SJC 1948–1952; Assistant Professor, Department of English, University of California, Berkeley, USA 1952–1962; Professor of English Literature and Dean, School of English

Studies, University of East Anglia 1962–1964; Jackson Eli Reynolds Professor of English 1964 (later Emeritus), Chairman, English Department 1968–1971, Founding Director, Stanford Humanities Center 1980–1985, Stanford University, California, USA. **Appointments:** Member, Advisory Board of Victorian Studies and Nineteenth Century Fiction 1962. **Awards:** Exhibition, SJC 1934; Scholarship, SJC 1937; Strathcona Research and Travel Exhibition, SJC 1938; Commonwealth Fund Fellowships, University of California then Harvard 1946–1948; Guggenheim Fellowship 1959 and 1972. **Publications:** *The Rise of the Novel*, 1957; (ed) *Jane Austen, a collection of critical essays*, 1963; *The Augustan Age*, 1968; (ed) *The Victorian Novel: Modern Essays in Criticism*, 1971; (ed) *Conrad, The Secret Agent, A Casebook*, 1973; *The British Novel: Scott Through Hardy*, 1973; *Conrad in the Nineteenth Century*, 1980; *Myths of Modern Individualism*, 1996; many other books and articles. Died 13 December 1999.

WATT, William Warnock (1933) Born 28 May 1915, 152 Craigpark, Glasgow; son of Alexander Watt, Flesher, and Anna Maclaren Lang Leithhead Liddell; m Joan Finlay Strathairn, 25 September 1943, Crieff South Church. **Subject(s):** Law; BA 1936; MA 1940. **Tutor(s):** C W Guillebaud. **Educ:** Glasgow High School; Strathallan School. **Career:** Articled Clerk, London; Ross and Liddell, Glasgow (family Estate Agency). Died 5 November 1968.

WATTS, Bertram Tom (1902) Born 28 August 1883, Cranford St Andrew, Northamptonshire; son of Thomas Robert Watts, Farmer, and Mary Everett; m Grace Arnold-Larsen, 21 December 1913; 2 sons (Eric Arnold Larsen b 1 July 1915 and Tom Andrew b 13 November 1920), 1 daughter (Joan). **Subject(s):** Mathematics; BA 1905. **Tutor(s):** E E Sikes. **Johnian Relatives:** father of Eric Arnold Larsen Watts (1933). **Educ:** Wellingborough Grammar School. **Career:** Special Irrigation Surveys, Sudan; Inspector, Egyptian Government Survey 1905–1908 and 1912; Director, Special Irrigation Surveys for the Turkish Government, Mesopotamia 1908–1911; Assistant Director, Surveys, Cyprus 1912–1920; Acting Registrar General 1913, 1918, 1919, 1920; Acting British Delegate, Evkaf (Pious Foundations), Cyprus 1919, 1923 and 1926; Registrar General, Cyprus 1920–1929 (title altered to Director, Land Registration and Surveys 1927); Director of Surveys, Land Officer and Commissioner of Mines, Uganda 1930–1938. **Appointments:** General Survey of Egypt, 1905. **Honours:** OBE. Died 11 May 1955.

WATTS, Eric Arnold Larsen (1933) Born 1 July 1915, Nicosia, Cyprus; son of Bertram Tom Watts, Director of Surveys, Uganda Government, and Grace Arnold-Larsen; m Alexandra Grizel Budge, April 1947; 3 daughters (Frances Mary, Lucinda Margaret Grizel (d) and Jeanetta Helen Christine). **Subject(s):** History/Law; BA 1936. **Tutor(s):** E A Benians. **Johnian Relatives:** son of Bertram Tom Watts (1902). **Educ:** The Grange, Stevenage; The King's School, Canterbury. **Career:** Colonial Administrative Officer, Uganda (final appointment, Permanent Secretary, Animal Industries, Game & Fisheries) 1936–1963; General Secretary, London Marriage Guidance Council 1963–1980. **Appointments:** Member, Hawks Club; Captain, Hockey Club, SJC.

WATTS, Michael (1942) Born 5 April 1924, 26 Market Street, Haverfordwest, Pembrokeshire; son of Thomas Williams Watts, Pharmaceutical Chemist, and Winifred Mary Morgan. **Subject(s):** History; BA 1947; MA 1949. **Tutor(s):** C W Guillebaud. **Educ:** Hill House College, Haverfordwest; Barn Street Council School, Haverfordwest; Llandaff Cathedral School; Ellesmere College, Shropshire. Died 2 July 1996.

WATTS, Dr Percival Stuart (1932) Born 7 October 1908, Waverley, Bensham Manor Road, Croydon; son of Percival Stuart Watts, Civil Servant, and Edith Violet Boulter; 3 sons. PhD 1936; BSc 1930 (London); MRCVS. **Tutor(s):** C W Guillebaud. **Educ:** Whitgift Grammar School, Croydon; University of London, Royal Veterinary College; School of Hygiene and Tropical Medicine. **Career:** Assistant Pathologist, Institute of Animal Pathology, Cambridge 1936–1938;

Veterinary Pathologist, Hannah Dairy Research Institute 1938–1950; Head, Veterinary Section, Institute of Medical and Veterinary Science, Adelaide, Australia 1950. **Appointments:** Council Member, National Veterinary Medical Association; Member, Agricultural Research Council; Member, Ayr and District Beekeepers' Association. **Awards:** Scholarship in Animal Pathology, Ministry of Agriculture; Colonial Service Probationer. Died 8 January 1987.

WATTS, Raymond John (1914) Born 18 December 1895, 54 Belmont Road, Bristol, Somerset; son of Edwin Watts, Solicitor, and Kate Osbourne Littledike. **Subject(s):** Law; BA 1920. **Tutor(s):** L H K Bushe-Fox. **Educ:** Lord Weymouth's Grammar School, Warminster; Clifton College.

WATTS, Robert Newell Crawford (1947) Born 30 April 1923, 13 Claremont Street, Belfast; son of Robert Watts, Solicitor, and Lydia Norah Humphreys; m Margaret Anderson, 31 July 1951; 3 sons (Alan Robert, Charles Roger and Jonathan), 1 daughter (Jane). **Subject(s):** Law; LLB 1948; LLM 1985; BA (TDC) 1947. **Tutor(s):** F Thistlethwaite. **Educ:** Cabin Hill Preparatory School, Belfast; Campbell College, Belfast; TCD. **Career:** Sub-Lieutenant, RNVR; RN 1943–1946; Articled to a solicitor in Northern Ireland 1950; Solicitor in family firm, Belfast 1950–1996 (Senior Partner 1980–1996); Solicitor to Presbyterian Church in Ireland 1966–1993.

WATTS, Ronald George Henry (1932) Born 15 May 1914, 3 Bury Villas, Southbury Road, Enfield; son of Frederick Thomas Watts, Chief Clerk, and Mabel Lucy Pilbrow; m Ruth Hanson, 1940. **Subject(s):** Modern and Medieval Languages/History; BA 1936. **Tutor(s):** C W Guillebaud. **Educ:** Public Elementary School; The Grammar School, Enfield; Latymer School, Edmonton. **Career:** Probationer Vice-Consul, Tokyo 1937–1940; Served at Nanking 1940–1941; Ministry of Information 1941–1942; Vice-Consul, HM Consular Service 1943; Vice-Consul, Foreign Office 1943–1945; Consul (Grade II) 1945–1946; Attached to United Kingdom Liaison Mission for Japan 1945–1946; Foreign Service Officer (Grade 7) 1946–1949; Transferred to Bucharest 1949; Foreign Office 1951. **Honours:** CBE 1962.

WAWN, Middlemost (1938) Born 3 May 1920, 10 Thornhill Terrace, Sunderland; son of Edgar Allan Wawn, Consulting Marine Engineer, and Barbara Annie Wigham. BA 1947; MA 1949. **Tutor(s):** J S Boys Smith. **Educ:** Colchester School, Corbridge; Oundle School.

WAY, Derek John (1947) Born 22 April 1929, 62 Crocker Street, Newport, Isle of Wight; son of Wilfrid John Way, Solicitor's Clerk, and Beatrice Hargreaves; m Mildred McCorduck, 12 September 1959, Monkstown Parish Church, County Dublin. **Subject(s):** History; BA 1950; MA 1954; FLA 1956. **Tutor(s):** F Thistlethwaite. **Educ:** The National School, Newport; Newport Grammar School; Oundle School. **Career:** Librarian, Birmingham Law Society 1958–1965; Law Librarian, University of Liverpool 1965–1994. **Appointments:** Vice-President (and founder Member), The British and Irish Association of Law Librarians 1997–2001. **Awards:** Exhibition, SJC 1946. **Publications:** *The Student's Guide to Law Libraries*, 1967; contributions to: *The Manual of Law Librarianship*, 1976, 1987; *Information Sources in Law*, 1997; *History of the British and Irish Association of Law Librarians*, 2000.

WAYTE, Alan Wymont (1923) Born 14 June 1905, 1 Brinton Terrace, Halifax, Yorkshire; son of Frank Edward Wayte, Physician and Surgeon, and Lizzie Flockton Macdonald. **Tutor(s):** B F Armitage. **Educ:** Halifax New School; Halifax Grammar School; Mill Mead Preparatory School, Shrewsbury; Malvern College.

WEATHERILT, Charles Geoffrey Bellew (1931) Born 16 October 1912, 179 du Toitspan Road, Kimberley, South Africa; son of Henry Charles Weatherilt, Rancher, and Maude Boyne Bellew. **Tutor(s):** C W Guillebaud. **Educ:** St Andrew's Preparatory School, Grahamstown; St Andrew's College, Grahamstown. **Career:** Rancher. Died 16 November 1957.

WEAVER, Albert Paul (1946) Born 25 November 1925, 11 Johnston Terrace, Devonport; son of William Thomas Weaver, Chief Gunner's Mate, RN, and Veronica Agnes Kirby; 1 daughter. **Subject(s):** History/Archaeology and Anthropology; BA 1948; MA 1953. **Educ:** Keyham Barton Elementary School; St Boniface's College, Plymouth. **Career:** British Council Representative, Ghana. Died 9 September 1993.

WEAVER, Dr Derek Bargrave (BARGRAVE-WEAVER) (1941) Born 18 October 1922, 117 High Road, Streatham, London; son of Alfred Neil Weaver, Leather Merchant, and Vera Cross. **Subject(s):** Classics; BA 1947; MA 1949. **Tutor(s):** C W Guillebaud. **Educ:** Fidelis Convent; Dulwich College Preparatory School; Dulwich College. **Awards:** Scholarship, SJC. Died 15 May 1998.

WEAVING, Michael Reginald Vernon (1943) Born 13 June 1925, St Chad's Hospital, Edgbaston, Birmingham; son of Archibald Arthur Weaving, Departmental Works Manager, ICI, and Helena Rosalie Vernon Harriss. **Subject(s):** Classics; BA 1948; MA 1953. **Tutor(s):** C W Guillebaud. **Educ:** Chigwell House, Birmingham; High School, Welwyn Garden City; Wellingborough School; Aldenham School. **Awards:** Scholarship, SJC. Died 28 September 1972.

WEBB, Alan Howard (1925) Born 7 July 1907, 21 North Road, Hertford; son of Frederick Howard Webb, Managing Director, Private Company, and Margaret Elizabeth Broad; 1 son (Peter), 2 daughters (Mary and Katherine). **Subject(s):** Natural Sciences/Economics; BA 1928; MA 1932. **Tutor(s):** J M Wordie. **Educ:** Hertford Grammar School; Bedford Modern School. Died 11 March 1990.

WEBB, Geoffrey Owen Davies (1930) Born 31 January 1911, Cavendish Road, Johannesburg, South Africa; son of Clement Davies Webb, Solicitor and Newspaper Proprietor, and Georgina Elizabeth Pretorius; m Stella Favier, 19 November 1936, Marylebone Town Hall. **Subject(s):** Medicine; BA 1935; MA 1945. **Tutor(s):** M P Charlesworth. **Educ:** St John's College, Johannesburg, South Africa.

WEBB, Harry Howard (1923) Born 26 April 1898, Johannesburg, South Africa; son of Harry Howard Webb, Consulting Mining Engineer, and Virginia Morton. **Tutor(s):** E A Benians. **Educ:** Columbia University, New York, USA; University of California, USA.

WEBB, John Herbert (1932) Born 14 March 1913, Park House, Hagley, Worcester; son of Charles Walter Herbert Webb, Glass Manufacturer, and Dorothy Mary Fisher. **Tutor(s):** C W Guillebaud. **Educ:** The Wells House, Malvern Wells; Shrewsbury School.

WEBB, John Marshall (1940) Born 8 September 1921, Le Touquet Paris Plage, France; son of Henry Marshall Webb, Bacteriologist, Civil Service, and Evelyn Francis Robinson. **Tutor(s):** J M Wordie. **Educ:** Woodlands School, Deganwy; Aldenham School.

WEBBER, Dr Harold Norris (1900) Born 9 July 1881, 1 Argyle Villas, Preston, Brighton; son of William Henry Webber Jr, Builder, and Hepzibah Close; m Madeline Mary, 22 December 1924, St Simon Stock, Putney. **Subject(s):** Natural Sciences; BA 1903; MA 1919; BChir 1928; MRCS; LRCP 1912. **Tutor(s):** C E Graves. **Educ:** Brighton Grammar School. **Career:** Anaesthetist and Surgeon, University College Hospital; Visiting Medical Officer, Hostel of St Luke (after retirement) 1946. **Appointments:** Fellow, Faculty of Anaesthetists, RCS 1948. **Publications:** *Anaesthesia and Anaesthetics*, 1930. Died 24 December 1954.

WEBBER, Harry Edwin (1918) American Student.

WEBBER, John Francis (1927) Born 26 April 1909, 8 Wonford Road, Exeter, Devon; son of John Owen Webber, Sports Outfitter, and Agnes Jerred. **Subject(s):** Natural Sciences; BA 1930. **Tutor(s):** J M Wordie. **Educ:** Exeter School.

WEBBER, John Phillips (1936) Born 1 April 1918, St Columb, Bloomfield Road, Chelmsford, Essex; son of William Grose Webber, Jeweller, and Ethel Violet Dench; m Bunty. BA 1939; MA 1943. **Tutor(s):** C W Guillebaud. **Educ:** Chelmsford Grammar School; Ashville College, Harrogate. **Career:** Called to the Bar, Gray's Inn 1947; Private Practice 1947–1951; Magistrate, Kenya Colony 1951–1952; Crown Counsel, Attorney General's Chambers 1953–1957; Senior Crown Counsel 1957–1959; Deputy Public Prosecutor, then Solicitor-General and Permanent Secretary for Legal Affairs 1959–1962; Attorney-General for Gilbratar 1962. Died 29 December 1991.

WEBER, Dr Gregorio (1944) Born 4 July 1916, 325 Calle San Lorenzo, Buenos Aires, Argentina; son of Leon Weber, Clerk, and Rosa Gerchunoff; m Shirley Roxana Nixon, 1 March 1947. PhD 1947; FAAAS. **Tutor(s):** C W Guillebaud. **Educ:** College Manuel Belgruo, Buenos Aires; University of Buenos Aires. **Career:** Laboratory Assistant, Instituto de Fisiologia, Buenos Aires 1938–1944; Senior Lecturer in Biochemistry 1959, Reader in Biophysics 1961–1962, University of Sheffield; Univeristy of Illinois 1962. **Appointments:** Member, National Academy of Sciences. Died 18 July 1997.

WEBSTER, Paul Michael (1941) Born 29 September 1922, 188 Hatfield Road, St Albans, Hertfordshire; son of Samuel Henry Webster, Schoolmaster, and Gwen Hayward Dobbs; m Pamela Bell, 16 February 1957, St Albans (d 11 August 1997); 3 sons, 1 daughter. **Subject(s):** History; BA 1947; MA 1949. **Tutor(s):** C W Guillebaud; F Thistlethwaite. **Educ:** St Albans School. **Career:** RAC and Sudan Defence Force, commanded No 6 Mounted Infantry Company of the Western Arab Corps (attained rank of Major) 1942–1946; Purchasing Assistant, London Transport 1947–1951; Construction Department 1951–1959, Group Contracts Officer, Southern Project Group 1959–1974, CEGB; Company Secretary, Redpath Dorman Long Ltd, Steel Fabricators, Civil Engineering Contractors 1974–1978; Deputy Director and Secretary, EEA 1978–88; Secretary, ECTEL 1988–1995. **Awards:** Open Exhibition, SJC 1940.

WEBSTER, Ralph Osler (1941) Born 20 October 1922, Poona, India; son of William Joseph Webster, Indian Medical Service, and Janet Hay. **Tutor(s):** S J Bailey. **Educ:** Angusfield Preparatory School, Aberdeen; Albyn School, Aberdeen; Aberdeen Grammar School; Trinity College, Glenalmond. **Career:** Flight Lieutenant, RAF 1940–1945. Died February 1945 (killed in a flying accident).

WEBSTER, Robert Chilion Peter (1923) Born 25 December 1900, Ottawa, Ontario, Canada; son of Robert Edward Webster, Surgeon, and Annie Irene Jones. **Subject(s):** Mathematics. **Tutor(s):** J M Wordie. **Educ:** Ottawa Collegiate Institute; RMC, Kingston; McGill University.

WEDD, George Morton (1948) Born 30 March 1930, Maternity Hospital, Green Road, Ashbourne, Derbyshire; son of Albert Edward Wedd, Police Constable, and Dora Morton; m Kate Pullin, 1953; 2 sons, 1 daughter. **Subject(s):** History; BA 1951. **Tutor(s):** F Thistlethwaite. **Educ:** Loscoe Church of England School; Matlock Council School; Ernest Bailey Grammar School, Nottingham. **Career:** Home Civil Service, Ministry of Housing and Local Government (later Department of Environment) 1951–1990 (Principal 1957–1966, Assistant Secretary 1966–1976, Under-Secretary 1976–1990); South-West Regional Director, Departments of the Environment and Transport, Bristol 1983–1990; Planning Consultant and Inspector 1990. **Awards:** McAulay Scholarship, SJC 1947. **Honours:** CB 1989. **Publications:** HMSO publications; contributions to various publications including *Contemporary Review*.

WEE, Hon Mr Justice Chong Jin (1935) Born 28 September 1917, 1 Light Street, Penang, Straits Settlements; son of Wee Gim Puoy, Merchant, and Lim Paik Yew; m Cecilia Mary Henderson; 3 sons, 1 daughter. **Subject(s):** Law; BA 1938; MA 1979; Hon DCL (Oxon) 1987. **Tutor(s):** C W Guillebaud. **Johnian Relatives:** brother-in-law of Leonard Dale Bonsall (1938); uncle of Christopher John Bonsall (1970) and of David

Charles Bonsall (1974). **Educ:** Penang Free School, Penang. **Career:** Called to Bar, Middle Temple 1938; Admitted Advocate and Solicitor of Straits Settlement 1940; Practised in Penang and Singapore 1940–1957; Puisne Judge, Singapore 1957; Chief Justice of the Supreme Court, Singapore 1963–1990. **Awards:** McMahon Studentship, SJC.

WEIGHTMAN, William Henry (1906) Born 24 March 1887, Septon Road, Litherland, Lancashire; son of Henry Herbert Weightman, Architect, and Mary Fernie. **Subject(s):** Mathematics/Law; BA 1909; LLB 1910. **Tutor(s):** L H K Bushe-Fox. **Educ:** Liverpool College. **Career:** Civil Servant, Post Office. Died 3 November 1971.

WEIR-RHODES, David Edward (1942) Born 27 October 1923, Ellerslie, Farnham Road, Guildford; son of Edward Henry Weir-Rhodes, Tailor and Outfitter, and Edith Bell. **Tutor(s):** C W Guillebaud. **Educ:** Lanesborough Preparatory School; Guildford Royal Grammar School.

WELCH, David Henry (1935) Born 11 November 1913, Breezynook, Richmond Road, Huntly, Aberdeenshire; son of William Beadie Welch, Science Teacher, and Isabella Corr. **Tutor(s):** C W Guillebaud. **Educ:** Shepton Mallet Grammar School; Bristol Grammar School; University of St Andrews. **Awards:** Colonial Agricultural Scholarship.

WELFORD, The Revd Alan Traviss (1932) Born 27 January 1914, 39 Lewisham Road, St Pancras, Middlesex; son of Edward Welford, Company Director, and Dorothy Marguerite Traviss; m Ruth Ada Brown, 28 March 1951, Cambridge. **Subject(s):** Natural Sciences/Theology/Moral Sciences; BA 1937; MA 1939; ScD 1964; MA (Princeton) 1946; DSc (Adelaide) 1969; FBPsS. **Tutor(s):** J S Boys Smith. **Johnian Relatives:** brother of Norman Traviss Welford (1938). **Educ:** St Christopher's School, Hampstead, London; University College School, London. **Career:** Chaplain, SJC 1938–1945; University Lecturer in Experimental Psychology, University of Cambridge 1947–1968; Title B Fellow 1956–1968, Lecturer in Natural Sciences 1967–1968, SJC; Professor of Psychology 1968–1979, Head, Department of Psychology 1969–1974, University of Adelaide. **Appointments:** Junior Bursar 1940–1945, Supervisor in Psychology 1947–1968, Tutor 1956–1968, Director of Studies in Natural Sciences 1964–1968, SJC; Commonwealth Visiting Professor 1964, University of Adelaide; Distinguished Visiting Professor, New Mexico State University 1979; Fellow, Academy of Social Sciences in Australia. **Awards:** Scholarship, SJC 1934–1936; Wright's Prize, SJC 1937. **Publications:** Many articles; *Ageing and Human Skill*, 1958; (ed) *Society: Problems and Methods of Study*, 1962; (with J Birren) *Behaviour, Ageing and the Nervous System*, 1965; *Fundamentals of Skill*, 1968. Died 16 June 1995.

WELFORD, Michael Trevor (1948) Born 13 September 1927, The Mount, Brook Street Hill, South Weald, Brentwood, Essex; son of Clement Rockwell Welford, Manufacturer of Ladies Wear, and Maude Emily Nash; 2 sons (Robert and Mark), 2 daughters (Emma and Lucy). **Subject(s):** Economics; BA 1950. **Tutor(s):** C W Guillebaud. **Educ:** Brentwood School. **Career:** Managing Director, Family Business 1950–1998.

WELFORD, Dr Norman Traviss (1938) Born 5 February 1921, 34 Glenilla Road, Hampstead; son of Edward Welford, Company Director, and Dorothy Marguerite Traviss; m Muriel Janet Mooring Aldridge, 30 December 1944, Richmond Hill Congregational Church, Bournemouth; 1 son (Edward John), 2 daughters (Helen Frances and Angela Mary). **Subject(s):** Natural Sciences/Theology/Moral Sciences; BA 1941; MA 1945; MB 1945; BChir 1945; MA (London); Certified Clinical Engineer. **Tutor(s):** R L Howland. **Johnian Relatives:** brother of Alan Traviss Welford (1932). **Educ:** St Christopher's School, Hampstead; University College School; Middlesex Hospital Medical School. **Career:** Biomedical Engineer. Died 20 June 2000.

WELLARD, Francis Albert Leon (1920) Born 10 April 1902, Rambla Cataluña, 99 Barcelona, Spain; son of James Herbert Wellard, Merchant Shipper to the Far East, and Maria Giraudier. **Subject(s):** Mechanical Sciences; BA 1923; MA 1927. **Tutor(s):** B F Armitage. **Educ:** Bishop's Court Preparatory School, Freshfield; Stonyhurst College. Died 8 March 1975.

WELLS, James Simpson (1926) Born 10 September 1907, 56 Orange Street, Cape Town, South Africa; son of Alexander Simpson Wells, Medical Practitioner, and Edith Boyd Henderson. **Subject(s):** Law; BA 1928. **Tutor(s):** E A Benians. **Educ:** South African College School, Cape Town; St Andrew's College, Grahamstown; University of Cape Town. Died 23 November 1931.

WELLS, Patrick Habershon (1947) Born 26 April 1925, Greenways, Christchurch, Hampshire; son of Philip Wynyard Wells and Norah Notlay Mosedale; m Jean 1960; 2 sons (Adrian b 1961 and Nicholas b 1963). **Subject(s):** Agriculture; BA 1949; MA 1954. **Tutor(s):** G C L Bertram. **Johnian Relatives:** son of Philip Wynyard Wells (1919). **Educ:** Durlston Court, Swanage; Bradfield College. **Career:** RA (National Service); Lecturer, Shuttleworth College, Biggleswade 1950–1953; Agricultural Advisory Office, Ministry of Agriculture 1953–1973; Senior Lecturer in Farm Management, Seale Hayne College, Newton Abbot, Devon 1991. **Appointments:** Parish Councillor; Founder Member, Devon Branch, CPRE; Chairman, Village Conservation Society. Died 22 May 1996.

WELLS, Philip Wynyard (1919) Born 20 November 1899, Mosbrough Hall, Eckington, Derbyshire; son of George Edwin Wells, Solicitor, and Ada Stead Booth; m Norah Notlay Mosedale; 1 son (Patrick b 26 April 1925). BA 1922; MA 1926. **Tutor(s):** E E Sikes. **Johnian Relatives:** father of Patrick Habershon Wells (1947). **Educ:** Claysmore School, Pangbourne; Wellington College, Berkshire; Sutton Courtenay. Died 3 October 1963.

WELLS, Walter Douglas (1908) Born 10 August 1889, 16 Sach Road, Upper Clapton, Essex; son of Walter Wells, Schoolmaster, and Maria Sisley Austin. **Subject(s):** Modern and Medieval Languages; BA 1911; MA 1922. **Tutor(s):** E E Sikes. **Johnian Relatives:** son of Walter Wells (1879). **Educ:** Grocers' Company's School, Hackney Downs; Real Gymnasium Schwerin Mecklenburg; Lycée Malherbe, Caen. **Career:** Master, Clifton College 1911–1912; Master, Friar's School, Bangor 1912; Master, Hillbrow School, Rugby 1913–1914; Master, St Neot's School, Eversley 1914–1915; Master, Chigwell School 1915; Lieutenant, Chigwell School OTC, WWI. **Awards:** Scholarship, SJC. Died 1 April 1938.

WELSH, Robert Cullen-Kerr (1946) Born 4 November 1926, 11 Maybeck Road, Mount Albert, Auckland, New Zealand; son of Henry Welsh, Deputy Director of Demobilisation for South Africa, and Vida Reid. BA 1949; MA 1953. **Tutor(s):** G C L Bertram. **Educ:** Hillbrow School, Eastbourne; Rhodes University College, Grahamstown; Michaelhouse, Natal; Witwatersrand University, Johannesburg.

WELTMAN, Joseph (1929) Born 19 October 1910, 60 Cheetham Hill Road, Cheetham, Manchester; son of Charles Weltman, Decorator, and Sophia Myers; m Margery Barnard (d 1983); 2 daughters (Sarah b 1940 and Judith b 1941). **Subject(s):** Modern and Medieval Languages; BA 1932; MA 1936. **Tutor(s):** C W Guillebaud. **Educ:** Bowker Street Elementary School, Salford; Grecian Street Elementary School, Salford; Manchester Grammar School. **Career:** Languages Teacher, Scarborough, Liverpool and the City of London School 1933–1940; RAF Intelligence 1940–1946; Producer, BBC Schools Department 1946; BBC Talks Department 1958–1959; Television production training 1959–1960; Educational Programme Department, Granada TV 1961–1963; National Educational TV Service, Independent Television Authority 1963–1967; Head of Programme Services, Independent Broadcasting Authority 1967–1975; Chairman, Founding Committee, York University of the Third Age; German Teacher, York University of the Third Age. **Appointments:** Freeman, City of London 1938. **Awards:** Scholarship, SJC 1928; Tiarks German Scholarship to Tübingen University, University of Cambridge 1932. **Honours:** OBE 1967.

WENDT, Henry Lorenz (1921) Born 24 February 1904, son of Henry Lorenz Wendt, Senior Puisne Justice, Ceylon, and Amelia de Saram. **Subject(s):** Law; BA 1925. **Tutor(s):** E A Benians. **Educ:** Government Training College; St Thomas' College, Colombo. **Career:** Called to the Bar, Inner Temple 1927.

WERNHAM, James Chrystall Stephen (1943) Born 14 April 1921, 18 Mitchell Street, Kirkcaldy, Fife; son of Archibald Garden Wernham, Manager, Charles Helmrich & Son, Stationers, and Christina Noble. **Subject(s):** Theology; BA 1945; MA 1949; MA (Aberdeen). **Tutor(s):** C W Guillebaud. **Educ:** Dunnikier Primary School, Kirkcaldy; Old Aberdeen Primary School; Sunnybank Intermediate School, Aberdeen; Aberdeen Central Secondary School; Aberdeen University. **Career:** Lecturer in Philosophy, University of Toronto 1953; Professor of Philosophy, Carleton University, Ottawa 1960. **Appointments:** Master of Theology, Union Theological Seminary, New York.

WERTH-REGENDANZ, Hubert (1927) Born 6 January 1910, Kiel, Germany; son of Fritz Willy Ernst Alexander Werth, Admiral, and Carmen Herrman. **Tutor(s):** C W Guillebaud. **Educ:** Kiel; Arndt Gymnasium, Berlin-Dahlen.

WESCOMBE, Anthony Willingdon (1949) Born 11 January 1930, King Edward Hospital, Paget, Bermuda; son of William Wescombe, Civil Servant, and Lily Jane Blandford; 1 son, 1 daughter. **Subject(s):** English; BA 1952; MA 1956. **Tutor(s):** A G Lee. **Educ:** Byron Road School, Gillingham; St Mark's School, Widcome; City of Bath School; Taunton School. **Career:** Assistant Manager, Barclays Bank, Fenchurch Street, London 1962–1965; Deputy Manager, Barclays Bank, Preston 1965–1969; Deputy Manager, Barclays Bank, Regent Street, London 1969–1972; Manager, Barclays Bank, Curzon Street, London 1972.

WESSON, Leonard Joynson (1937) Born 3 April 1919, Netherleigh Bilston; son of Alfred John Wesson, Iron Master, and Elsie Cash Joynson; m Aliette El Sawy 9 May 1943. **Subject(s):** Modern and Medieval Languages. **Tutor(s):** C W Guillebaud. **Educ:** Baswick House, Stafford; Shrewsbury School.

WEST, Cyril (1919) Born 16 December 1887, 7 Colfe Road, Forest Hill, Sydenham, Kent; son of John Stapylton West, Tea Salesman, and Ellen Eliza Humphreys. BA 1921; MA 1926; BSc (London) 1911; DSc (London) 1918. **Tutor(s):** E E Sikes. **Educ:** Imperial College of Science, London. **Career:** Low Temperature Research Station, Cambridge; Netherlands Society for Cooling Technique 1963. **Awards:** Kamerlingh-Onnes Medal.

WEST, Cyril Ernest (1935) Born 6 September 1916, 99 Bromley Road, Beckenham, Kent; son of Percy Camidge West, Bank Manager, and Elsie Marion Clarke. **Tutor(s):** R L Howland. **Educ:** Clare House School, Beckenham; Sydenham Hill School; Packwood Hough Preparatory School; The Leys School, Cambridge.

WEST, Frederick Charles (1920) Born 5 March 1896, 40 Byrne Road, Balham, Surrey; son of Charles Albert West, Civil Servant, Education Department, and Ida Maria Loin. **Tutor(s):** E E Sikes. **Educ:** Alleyn's School, Dulwich; London University; RMA, Woolwich. **Awards:** Exhibition, SJC.

WEST, Ronald Leonard (1948) Born 15 December 1927, 286 Union Grove, Aberdeen; son of Frederick James West, Departmental Store Manager, and Annie Alexander Love; m Amelia Bell, 1951, Longtown, Cumbria; 2 sons (Charles and Peter), 1 daughter (Caroline). BA 1950. **Tutor(s):** R L Howland. **Educ:** Dumfries Academy; Sedbergh School. **Career:** Military Service, Scottish Regiment 1946; Second Lieutenant, RAOC; Rolls-Royce, Crewe 1951–1982, final position, Chief Development Engineer (Car Division). Died 1987.

WEST, Professor William Dixon (1920) Born 27 January 1901, 6 Madeira Rise, Bournemouth, Hampshire; son of Arthur Joseph West, Civil Engineer, and Mary Louisa Dixon. **Subject(s):** Natural Sciences (Geology); BA 1923; MA 1929; ScD 1944; FGS, FNA. **Tutor(s):** B F Armitage. **Educ:** Mount View School, Streatham Hill, London; King's School, Canterbury. **Career:** Assistant Superintendent 1923, Director 1945–1951, Geological Survey of India; Professor of Applied Geology 1959, Vice-Chancellor 1971–1973, first Professor Emeritus, University of Sagar, Madhya Pradesh, India. **Appointments:** Founder member and Fellow, National Institute of Sciences, India; Founder member, several geological societies and organisations in India; General President, Indian Science Congress 1972. **Awards:** Wiltshire Prize, University of Cambridge 1922; Harkness Scholarship, University of Cambridge 1923; Lyell Medal, Geological Society 1951; P N Bose Medal, Asiatic Society of Bengal. **Honours:** Star of Afaghanistan; CIE 1948; MBE 1990. Died 23 July 1994.

WESTLAKE, Dr Aubrey Thomas (1913) Born 1 July 1893, 2 Ridgeway Road, Redhill, Reigate, Surrey; son of Ernest Westlake, Gentleman, and Lucy Anne Rutter; m Marjorie Gladys Harrod; 1 son (Ernest Keith b 21 November 1924). **Subject(s):** Medicine; BA 1916; MRCS; LRCP (St Bartholomew's). **Tutor(s):** R P Gregory. **Johnian Relatives:** father of Ernest Keith Westlake (1943). **Educ:** Sidcot School. **Career:** GP, Bermondsey. **Publications:** *The Pattern of Health*, 1961; (ed) *Woodcraft Way* Series.

WESTLAKE, Dr Ernest Keith (1943) Born 21 November 1924, 92 Southwark Park Road, Bermondsey, London; son of Aubrey Thomas Westlake, Medical Practitioner, and Marjorie Gladys Harrod; 2 daughters. **Subject(s):** Natural Sciences; BA 1946; MA 1953; MB 1949; BChir 1949; MD 1953; MRCP. **Tutor(s):** S J Bailey. **Johnian Relatives:** son of Aubrey Thomas Westlake (1913). **Educ:** Forest School, Godshill; Kingsmoor School, Glossop; Leighton Park School. **Career:** House Physician, Poole General Hospital; Senior House Physician, Chase Farm Hospital; House Physician, Brompton Hospital; Senior Medical Registrar, Middlesex Hospital. **Awards:** Raymond Horton-Smith Prize, University of Cambridge 1953; Ernest Hart Memorial Scholarship, BMA 1952. Died 18 June 1958.

WESTLAKE, Professor Henry Dickinson (1925) Born 4 September 1906, Glencairn, Chase Green Avenue, Enfield, Middlesex; son of Charles Arthur Westlake, Managing Director, Coal and Iron Company, and Charlotte Maud Manlove; m Mary Helen Sayers, 1940; 1 son, 1 daughter. **Subject(s):** Classics/History; BA 1929; MA 1932; MA (Manchester) 1953. **Tutor(s):** E E Sikes. **Educ:** Stancliffe Hall, near Matlock; Uppingham School. **Career:** Assistant Lecturer, University College, Swansea 1930–1932; Title A Fellow, SJC 1932–1935; Assistant Lecturer, University of Bristol 1936–1937; Lecturer, King's College, Newcastle 1937–1946; Administration Assistant, Ministry of Home Security 1941–1944; Reader in Greek, University of Durham 1946–1949; Hulme Professor of Greek 1949–1972 (Emeritus 1972), Dean of Faculty of Arts 1960–1961, Dean of Faculty of Music, Pro-Vice-Chancellor 1965–1968, University of Manchester. **Appointments:** Secretary, Northumberland and Durham Classical Association. **Awards:** Scholarship 1924; Strathcona Research Studentship, SJC 1929. **Publications:** *Thessaly in the Fourth Century BC*, 1935; *Timoleon and His Relations with Tyrants*, 1952; *Individuals in Thucydides*, 1968; *Essays on the Greek Historians and Greek History*, 1969; *Studies in Thucydides and Greek History*, 1989. Died 23 July 1992.

WESTON, Arthur Ralph Kingsley (1934) Born 7 February 1914, Barrackpore, Bengal, India; son of Arthur Thomas Weston, Director of Industries, and Millicent Phoebe Cheetham. **Subject(s):** Mechanical Sciences; BA 1936. **Tutor(s):** J S Boys Smith. **Educ:** Oxford House School, St Annes-on-Sea; County School, Abergele; Bedford Modern School; RMA.

WESTON, Sir Eric (1911) Born 8 December 1892, 26 Winchester Street, South Shields, County Durham; son of William John Weston, Schoolmaster, and Katherine Sarah Wells; m Georgina Cork, 1919;

3 daughters (Beryl, Daphne and Christine). **Subject(s):** Mathematics; BA 1914. **Tutor(s):** L H K Bushe-Fox. **Educ:** Baring Street Elementary School, South Shields; High School, South Shields. **Career:** Various legal posts, Indian Civil Service 1915–1952, including Judge 1929, Chief Justice 1950–1952. **Honours:** Kt 1954. Died 20 October 1976.

WESTON, Dr Thomas Alexander (1902) Born 23 August 1883, 38 Booth Street, Handsworth, Staffordshire; son of Samuel Thomas Darby Weston, Surgeon, and Annie David; m Muriel Zica Murray, 14 November 1919, All Souls', Langham Place. **Subject(s):** Natural Sciences; BA 1905; MChir 1910; MB 1910; MRCS; LRCP 1908; FRCS (Edinburgh) 1926. **Tutor(s):** D MacAlister. **Educ:** Falmouth Grammar School. **Career:** House Physician, Brompton Hospital for Diseases of the Chest; House Surgeon, Addenbrooke's Hospital 1909; Captain, RAMC, WWI. **Publications:** Medical papers on anaesthesia, 1916, and appendix tumours, 1921.

WESTON, William Guy (1928) Born 30 January 1907, 113 Thorpe Road, Melton Mowbray, Leicestershire; son of William Harry Weston, Departmental Manager, and Gertrude Etty Goodman. **Subject(s):** History; BA 1933. **Tutor(s):** E A Benians. **Educ:** The Grammar School, Melton Mowbray; Manchester University. **Career:** Assistant Principal, Board of Trade 1929; Private Secretary, Secretary of the Department of Overseas Trade 1932; Principal, Mercantile Marine Department, Board of Trade 1934; Ministry of Shipping 1939; Ministry of War Transport (in charge of Foreign Shipping Relations Divisions) 1941–1945; Deputy Secretary 1946, Under-Secretary 1946, Ministry of Transport; United Kingdom Delegate, Inter-Governmental Maritime Consultative Organisation, Geneva 1948. **Awards:** Scholarship, SJC 1927; Lightfoot Scholarship, University of Cambridge 1929. **Honours:** CMG 1945.

WETHERLEY-MEIN, Dr Gordon (1936) Born 30 June 1918, 2 Portsdown Avenue, Drayton, Farlington; son of William Archibald Mein, Consulting Surgeon, and Betty Allan Taylor; m Elizabeth; 1 son (Colin), 1 daughter (Karen). **Subject(s):** Natural Sciences; BA 1939; MB 1942; BChir 1942; MD 1953; FRCP. **Tutor(s):** R L Howland. **Educ:** Wychwood School, Bournemouth; Loretto School, Edinburgh; Forres School, Swanage. **Career:** Regimental Medical Officer, North Africa, Sicily and Normandy Landings 1942–1945; Clinical Pathology Laboratory, St Thomas' Hospital 1945–1954; Physician 1954; Professor of Haematology, St Thomas' 1964–1983. **Appointments:** Wolfson Research Fellow, RCP 1983. Died 24 March 1987.

WHATMAN, Major Amherst Barrow (1933) Born 1 November 1909, 4 Manston Terrace, Heavitree, Devon; son of Amherst Blunt Whatman, Major, Somerset Light Infantry, and Myrtle Elen Waller Barrow. **Subject(s):** Mechanical Sciences; BA 1935; MA 1942; FIEE. **Tutor(s):** J S Boys Smith. **Educ:** Twyford School; Winchester College; RMA, Woolwich. **Career:** Chief Engineer, Rediffusion Ltd, Preston, Lancashire; Major, Royal Corps of Signals 1954. **Honours:** MBE. Died 4 October 1984.

WHEATLEY, Kenneth William (1934) Born 2 November 1915, 45 Chalk Hill, Oxhey, Watford; son of Edward John Wheatley, Warehouseman, and Violet Ada Good; m G Joan Ridley, 6 August 1949 (d 8 October 1989); 1 son (Peter Kenneth b 1952), 1 daughter (Janet Rachel b 1954). **Subject(s):** Mathematics; BA 1937; PGCE (London Institute of Education) 1947. **Tutor(s):** J M Wordie. **Johnian Relatives:** father of Peter Kenneth Wheatley (1971). **Educ:** Oxhey Council School; London Road Council School; Watford Grammar School. **Career:** Senior Mathematics Master, Borden Grammar School, Sittingbourne 1947–1967; Senior Mathematics Master, Queen Elizabeth's Grammar School, Faversham 1968–1981. **Awards:** Whytehead Scholarship, SJC 1933. Died 8 February 2003.

WHEELER, Geoffrey (1928) Born 22 November 1909, 8 Back Row, Morton, Derbyshire; son of Albert Edward Wheeler, Coal Miner, and Harriet Wilson. **Subject(s):** History; BA 1931. **Tutor(s):** E A Benians.

Educ: County Secondary School, Clay Cross. **Career:** Under-Secretary, Ministry of Defence; Assistant Under-Secretary of State; Assistant Director, Civil Service Selection Board. **Appointments:** Chairman, London Derbyshire Society. **Awards:** Exhibition, SJC; Scholarship, SJC 1930; College Prize, SJC. **Honours:** CB 1952. Died 27 June 1987.

WHEELER, Peter Hayden (1945) Born 29 March 1928, Perrymead, St Andrew's Road, Henley-on-Thames; son of William Albert Wheeler, Draper, and Ethel Elizabeth Patterson. **Subject(s):** Natural Sciences. **Tutor(s):** G C L Bertram. **Educ:** Nevill Holt Preparatory School; Shrewsbury School.

WHELDON, Sir Wynn Powell (1900) Born 22 December 1879, Bronygraig, Festiniog, Merionethshire; son of Thomas Jones Wheldon, Calvinist Minister, and Mary Ellinor Powell; m Megan Edwards, 31 July 1915; 2 sons, 2 daughters. **Subject(s):** Law; BA 1903; MA 1920; Honorary Doctor of Law (University of Wales). **Tutor(s):** D MacAlister. **Educ:** Festiniog Elementary and Higher Grade School; Oswestry High School; University College of North Wales. **Career:** Solicitor, Lloyd George, Roberts & Co 1905–1914; Royal Welsh Fusiliers 1914–1919; Secretary and Registrar, Bangor University College 1920–1933; Permanent Secretary, Welsh Department, Board of Education 1933–1945. **Appointments:** Deputy Chairman, Boundary Commission for Wales; Member, BBC Wales Advisory Council. **Honours:** DSO 1917; Kt 1939; KBE 1952. Died 10 November 1961.

WHEWELL, The Revd Herbert (1906) Born 20 September 1887, 309 Guide, Lower Darwen, Blackburn, Lancashire; son of William Whewell, Insurance Agent, and Betsy Ann Holden; 1 daughter (Dorothy). **Subject(s):** Mathematics; BA 1909; MA 1913. **Tutor(s):** L H K Bushe-Fox. **Educ:** Guide National School; Blackburn Grammar School. **Career:** Ordained Deacon 1910; Curate, St John, Higher Broughton 1910–1913; Ordained Priest 1912; Curate, Victoria Avenue Mission Church, Blackley 1913–1915; Curate, Holy Trinity, Prestolee 1915–1916; Rector, St Philip, Bradford Road, Manchester 1916–1920; Vicar, Birch in Hopwood 1920–1925; Vicar, Castleton Moor 1925–1935; Surrogate and Rural Dean, Ashton 1935; Rector, Ashton under Lyne 1935–1950; Chaplain, Darnton House and Lake Hospital 1937–1939. **Appointments:** Honorary Canon, Manchester 1939–1950 (Emeritus 1950). Died 9 July 1967.

WHIDBY, Frank (1948) Born 8 May 1928, 37 Annie Street, Sunderland; son of Fred Whidby, Clerk, and Edith Mary Williams. **Subject(s):** History; BA 1951; MA 1955. **Tutor(s):** C W Guillebaud. **Educ:** Fulwell Elementary School, Sunderland; Bede Collegiate School, Sunderland. **Career:** Sergeant, RAEC. **Awards:** Exhibition, SJC.

WHIDDINGTON, Professor Richard (1905) Born 25 November 1885, Upper Holloway, Middlesex; son of Richard Whiddington, Schoolmaster, and Ada Anne Fitzgerald; m Katherine Grant, 9 April 1919, Hendon; 1 son (Richard Harcourt b 3 March 1928), 1 daughter. **Subject(s):** Natural Sciences/Mathematics; BA 1908; MA 1912; FRS 1926. **Tutor(s):** C E Graves; J R Tanner. **Johnian Relatives:** father of Richard Harcourt Whiddington (1949). **Educ:** William Ellis Endowed School. **Career:** Researcher, Cavendish Laboratory, Cambridge 1908–1914; Foundress Fellow 1911–1919 (absent on war work 1914–1918), SJC; Captain, RFC, Royal Aircraft Factory, Farnborough (work on radio telegraphy and telephony research and design), then Major (TF), RAF (Mentioned in Despatches three times), WWI; Cavendish Professor of Physics 1919–1951 (absent on war work 1940–1945), Pro-Vice-Chancellor 1949–1951, University of Leeds; Department of Scientific Research, Admiralty (development of radar equipment for the navy) 1940–1942; Deputy Director of Scientific Research, Ministry of Supply 1942–1945. **Appointments:** Supervisor in Physics 1914–1918, Director of Studies in Physics 1918–1919, SJC; Honorary Wing Commander, RAFVR, WWII; Member, Joint Recruiting Board, University of Leeds, WWII; Honorary Editor, *Proceedings of Leeds Philosophical and Literary Society*, 1925; Scientific Advisor to

CENTO (Foreign Office). **Awards:** Hutchinson Research Studentship 1909; Allen Scholarship, University of Cambridge 1910. **Honours:** CBE 1946. **Publications:** *Science at War*. Died 7 June 1970.

WHIDDINGTON, Richard Harcourt (1949) Born 3 March 1928, 36 Moor Road, Leeds; son of Richard Whiddington, Cavendish Professor of Physics, Leeds, and Katherine Grant; m Elizabeth Jean Middlebro', 1954. **Subject(s):** Natural Sciences; BA 1952; MA 1956. **Tutor(s):** G C L Bertram. **Johnian Relatives:** son of Richard Whiddington (1905). **Educ:** Dragon School, Oxford; Owen Sound College, Canada; Harrow. Died 1992.

WHILE, Dennis Aubrey (1935) Born 15 June 1916, Abbotsfield Barrow, Lancashire; son of Augustus While, Ironmaster, and Sarah Armstrong. **Tutor(s):** J M Wordie. **Educ:** Meadowcroft, Windermere; Harrow.

WHIPP, Dr Brian (1927) Born 15 September 1909, 131 Edenfield Road, Rochdale, Lancashire; son of William Whipp, Architect's Assistant, and Mabel Brierley. **Subject(s):** Natural Sciences; BA 1930; MA 1934; PhD 1934. **Tutor(s):** J M Wordie. **Educ:** Central School, Rochdale; Manchester Grammar School. **Awards:** Somerset Exhibition, SJC 1927.

WHITAKER, Edgar Haddon (1927) Born 30 August 1908, The Cottage, Diss, Norfolk; son of Leonard Edgar Whitaker, Publisher (proprietor of *Whitaker's Almanack*), and Edith Olave Cox; m Molly Marion Seely. **Subject(s):** Economics; BA 1930; MA 1944. **Tutor(s):** C W Guillebaud. **Johnian Relatives:** father of David Haddon Whitaker (1951). **Educ:** Hurworth Preparatory School, Wanganui, New Zealand; Lancing College; Brentwood School. **Career:** J Whitaker & Sons Ltd Publishers (later Chairman & Director) 1932. **Honours:** OBE. Died 5 January 1982.

WHITAKER, The Revd Philip Randle Kerr (1928) Born 25 March 1907, The Lodge, Bedworth, Warwickshire; son of Alexander Kerr Whitaker, Clerk in Holy Orders, and Blanche Tudor Denniston Sword. BA 1931. **Tutor(s):** J M Wordie. **Johnian Relatives:** son of Alexander Kerr Whitaker (1896). **Educ:** Hailey Preparatory School, Bournemouth; Hill House Preparatory School, Doncaster; St John's School, Leatherhead; Wycliffe Hall, Oxford. **Career:** Ordained Deacon 1933; Curate, Owlerton, Sheffield 1933–1936; Ordained Priest 1934; Vicar, Loversall 1937–1949; CF 1940–1945; Chaplain, St Catherine's Hospital and Infectious Diseases Hospital, Doncaster 1946–1949; Vicar, Masbrough 1949–1951; Rector, Burough Green and Brinkley, Suffolk 1951; Rural Dean, Cheveley 1965. Died 20 April 1969.

WHITBY, Ralph Preece (1948) Born 27 September 1924, 2 Lewlands Street, Barry, Glamorganshire; son of Francis Alfred Whitby, Cycle and Radio Dealer, and Gwen Preece. BA (Manchester) 1944. **Tutor(s):** J M Wordie. **Educ:** Holton Road Elementary School, Barry; Barry County School; Manchester University. **Career:** Colonial Administrative Service, Malaya; Captain, Gurkha Regiment 1944–1947.

WHITE, Francis Alfred (1903) Born 18 June 1881, 15 Mount Pleasant Square, Ranelagh, Rathmines, Dublin; son of Charles Leonard Jackson White, Civil Engineer, and Nina Emily Baynes. **Subject(s):** Economics. **Tutor(s):** D MacAlister. **Educ:** Belgrano English School, Buenos Aires, Argentina; Sutton Preparatory School; Norfolk House School, Bognor; Boys' High School, Harcourt Street; Middle School, Ipswich. **Career:** Second Lieutenant, Suffolk Regiment, South Africa 1901–1903. **Appointments:** President, University of Cambridge Cruising Club. Died 7 August 1905.

WHITE, Francis Puryer (1912) Born 26 October 1893, 100 College Place, Camden Town, Middlesex; son of John Francis White, Schoolmaster, and Emily Jane Puryer; m Alice Barbara Dale, 1934. **Subject(s):** Mathematics; BA 1915; MA 1919. **Tutor(s):** L H K Bushe-Fox. **Educ:** Stanley Higher Elementary School; Owen's School, Islington. **Career:** Foundress Fellow 1919–1926, Title B Fellow 1926–1961, Lecturer 1923–1961, Deputy Librarian 1939–1945, Librarian

1948–1961, Deputy Librarian 1966–1967, Title D Fellow 1961–1969, SJC; Lecturer in Mathematics, University of Cambridge 1926–1961. **Appointments:** Praelector 1931–1935, Tutorial Bursar 1935–1946, Director of Studies in Mathematics 1945–1959, Keeper of the College Records 1961–1969, SJC; Council Member, LMS 1923. **Awards:** Isaac Newton Studentship, University of Cambridge 1916. Died 11 July 1969.

WHITE, Dr Frank (1945) Born 6 March 1927, 2 Stanley Street, Sunderland; son of Frank White, Flour Miller's Clerk, and Violet Alexandra Livingstone. **Subject(s):** Natural Sciences; BA 1948; MA 1952; ScD 1992. **Tutor(s):** G C L Bertram. **Educ:** Redby Council School; Bede Collegiate School, Sunderland. **Career:** Curator, Fielding-Druce and Forest Herbaria; Demonstrator in Forest Botany 1948–1955, Lecturer in Botany, Plant Sciences Department 1955–1994, University of Oxford; Curator, Forest Herbarium 1961–1992; Curator, Fielding-Druce Herbarium 1971–1992; Distinguished Research Curator, Oxford University Herbarium 1992–1994. **Awards:** Frank Smart Prize for Botany, University of Cambridge. Died 12 September 1994.

WHITE, Sir Frederick William George (1929) Born 26 May 1905, Johnsonville, Wellington, New Zealand; son of William Henry White, Chief Steward, and Wilhelmina Dunlop; m Elizabeth Cooper, September 1932, Fitzroy Square, London; 1 son (John Peter White b 8 October 1937), 1 daughter (Jane Elizabeth White b 8 December 1939). PhD 1934; MSc (New Zealand) 1929; Honorary DSc (Australian National) 1969, (Monash) 1969, (Papua New Guinea) 1970; FAA 1960; FRS 1966. **Tutor(s):** J M Wordie. **Johnian Relatives:** father of John Peter White (1961). **Educ:** Te Aro School, Wellington; Victoria University College; Wellington College. **Career:** Assistant Lecturer in Physics 1932–1934, Lecturer in Physics 1934–1937, KCL; Professor of Physics, Canterbury University College, New Zealand 1937–1941; Chief, Division of Radiophysics 1941, Executive, Division of Radiophysics 1946, CSIR; Executive 1949–1970, Deputy Chairman 1957, Chairman 1959, CSIRO. **Appointments:** President, ANZAAS 1963–64. **Awards:** Strathcona Studentship, SJC 1929; ANZAAS Medal 1975. **Honours:** CBE 1954; KBE 1962. Died 17 August 1994.

WHITE, Geoffrey (1949) Born 7 September 1931, West End, Skelmanthorpe, Huddersfield, Yorkshire; son of Owen White, Butcher, and Alice Hepworth. **Subject(s):** Natural Sciences; BA 1952; MA 1956; VetMB 1955. **Tutor(s):** G C L Bertram. **Johnian Relatives:** brother-in-law of Neil Winn Sykes (1945). **Educ:** Skelmanthorpe Church of England School; Holme Valley Grammar School. **Career:** Veterinary Surgeon.

WHITE, James George Charles (1947) Born 14 December 1921, Moss of Ellon, Ellon, Aberdeenshire; son of James Samuel Michie White, Schoolmaster, and Sophia Mortimer; m Kim. **Subject(s):** Classics; BA 1949; MA (Aberdeen) 1942; Honorary DLitt (Herriot-Watt) 1986. **Tutor(s):** R L Howland. **Educ:** Ellon Primary School; Craigievar Primary School; Robert Gordon's College, Aberdeen; University of Aberdeen. **Career:** Chairman, Scottish Equitable Life Assurance Company; Major, Army Intelligence, WWII; Baillie, Gifford & Co, Investment Managers, Edinburgh (Partner since 1955) 1949–1984; Chairman, Scottish Equitable Unit Trust 1974. **Appointments:** Board Member, Claverhouse Investment Trust, Winterbottom Trust, Scottish Equitable Life Assurance Society; Governor, Morrison's Academy, Crieff; Member, Investment Committee of the Carnegie Trust for the Universities of Scotland; Deputy Chairman, Association of Investment Trusts. Died 29 May 1989.

WHITE, John Hylas (1946) Born 15 September 1922, Royal Free Hospital, St Pancras, London; son of Ernest Edwin White, Headmaster, The Thomas Coram School, Berkhamsted, and Nellie Elizabeth Adams; 2 sons, 1 daughter. **Subject(s):** Classics; BA 1948. **Tutor(s):** R L Howland. **Educ:** St Andrew's Church School; Woodmansterne Road LCC School; Battersea Grammar School.

WHITE, Malcolm Edward Eales (1940) Born 20 April 1922, The Nursing Home, 23 Arragon Road, Twickenham, Middlesex; son of Edward Albert White, Insurance Broker, and Olive Decima Eales. **Subject(s):** Natural Sciences; BA 1943; MA 1981; BChir 1947; MB 1947; FRCS. **Tutor(s):** R L Howland. **Johnian Relatives:** brother-in-law of Anthony Clavis Orchard (1940). **Educ:** Orleans School, Twickenham; Reigate Grammar School. **Career:** Consultant Surgeon, Coventry Hospital Group.

WHITE, Neville Hall (1941) Born 13 September 1922, Fern Villa, High Street, Holbeach, Lincolnshire; son of Arthur White, County Court Clerk, and Edith Susannah Hall. **Subject(s):** Modern and Medieval Languages; BA 1947; MA 1949. **Tutor(s):** C W Guillebaud. **Educ:** Infants' School, Holbeach; Boys' Council School Holbeach; Grammar School, Moulton.

WHITE, Dr Norman Lewis (1917) Born 8 September 1898, St Declans Place, Waterford, Ireland; son of Robert Eaton White, Chemist and Oil Merchant, and Edith Elizabeth Whieldon; m Sylvia Mary Quilter, 2 December 1931, St John's Church, Crowborough (d 28 July 1967); 3 sons (Michael Robert b 13 April 1937, Peter Wilfrid b 6 May 1940 and Jeremy Rowland b 6 February 1943). **Subject(s):** Natural Sciences; BA 1920; MA 1929; BChir 1929; MD 1933; MRCS; LRCP; FRCS; MRCOG; FRCOG. **Tutor(s):** E E Sikes. **Johnian Relatives:** father of Michael Robert White (1958). **Educ:** Newtown School, Waterford; Sidcot School, Somerset; Leighton Park School. **Career:** House Physician, University College Hospital Medical School 1921–1943 (Obstetric Registrar 1928); Honorary Consultant Obstetric Surgeon, University College Hospital and Royal Northern Hospital 1943. **Awards:** Wood and Hare Exhibition; Scholarship, SJC 1920; College Prize, SJC 1920. Died 3 October 1978.

WHITE, Richard Henry (1915) Born 22 December 1896, 16 The Limes, Armoury Road, Small Heath, Birmingham, Warwickshire; son of Richard Alfred White, Travelling Inspector, Army Inspection Department, and Alice Maud Stockwin. **Tutor(s):** R P Gregory. **Educ:** St Margaret's Church School, Olton; Chesterfield Road Church School; Enfield Grammar School. **Career:** Commissioned London Regiment 1915–1917. **Awards:** Minor Scholarship, SJC 1915. **Honours:** MC. Died 5 August 1917 (killed in action).

WHITE, Richard Loughnan (1934) Born 27 June 1913, 70 Yale Court, Honeybourne Road, Hampstead; son of Richard Pratt White, Solicitor, and Mary Helen Britten; m Hazel Robarts, 1 March 1945, Sherborne. **Subject(s):** Mechanical Sciences; BA 1936; MA 1941; CEng; FICE; MIStructE. **Tutor(s):** J S Boys Smith. **Educ:** Sherborne Preparatory School; Downside; RMA. **Career:** RE 1933–1960; Senior Civil Engineer, MPBW, DoE, PSA 1960–1962; Superintending Civil Engineer, MPBW, DoE, PSA 1962–1977. Died 19 October 1992.

WHITE, William Rogers (1945) Born 22 July 1927, 11 Vivian Terrace, Truro, Cornwall; son of William Lloyd White, Bank Manager, and Agnes Mary Rogers; m Barbara Wentworth 1950; 1 son (Rodger b 1952), 2 daughters (Gillian b 1953 and Judith b 1955). **Subject(s):** Mechanical Sciences; BA 1948; MA 1952; CEng; MIEE. **Tutor(s):** S J Bailey; R L Howland. **Educ:** Strangways Terrace School, Truro; Truro School. **Career:** Senior Engineer, PTO I UKAEA Operations/Maintenance Low Power Reactors Group; Engineer, English Electric Company, Stafford, Brush E E Company, Loughborough and Atomic Energy Establishment, Winfrith Heath, Dorset 1948–1960; PTO I UKAEA Winfrith Section Leader Workshops 1960–1979; PTO I UKAEA Productivity Group Leader 1979–1981.

WHITEFIELD, John Reginald (1941) Born 20 April 1923, 64 Broxash Road, Battersea; son of George Reid Whitefield, Bank Clerk, and Ella May Routledge. **Subject(s):** Natural Sciences; BA 1944; MA 1948. **Tutor(s):** C W Guillebaud. **Educ:** Radley House School, Wandsworth; Edgware Council School; Christ's College, Finchley. **Career:** General

Manager, Proctor & Gamble, Indonesia 1960–1963; Staff Distribution Manager, Proctor & Gamble, Europe 1982–1985. **Appointments:** Life Member, International Wine and Food Society 1972. Died 19 November 1996.

WHITEHEAD, The Revd Canon Derek (1948) Born 13 December 1927, 138 Whitegate Lane, Chadderton, Lancashire; son of Andrew Hardman Whitehead, Spinning Master, and Fanny Beaumont. **Subject(s):** Modern and Medieval Languages/Economics; BA 1950; MA 1955; BD (London) 1960; PhD (Lancaster) 1973. **Tutor(s):** C W Guillebaud. **Educ:** Denton Lane Church of England School; Chadderton Grammar School. **Career:** Sergeant, RAEC; Wells Theological College 1955–1956; Ordained Deacon, Manchester Diocese 1956; Curate, Church of the Ascension, Lower Broughton 1956–1959; Ordained Priest 1957; Divinity Master and Chaplain, Lichfield Grammar School, and Lecturer, Lichfield Theological College 1959–1963; Chaplain, Highgate School, London 1963–1965; Divinity Lecturer, Preston Polytechnic 1965–1979; Director of Education to the Diocese of Chichester 1979–1994; Canon, Chichester 1982; NSM 1993, Priest-in-Charge 1994, Parish of Fletching, Diocese of Chichester 1994.

WHITEHEAD, Harold Norman (1931) Born 6 November 1912, 27 Carlton Road, Ashton-upon-Mersey; son of Arthur Whitehead, Electrical Engineer, and Lucy Beckett. **Subject(s):** Modern and Medieval Languages; BA 1934; MA 1938. **Tutor(s):** C W Guillebaud. **Educ:** All Saints School, Ashton-on-Mersey; Sale High School; Manchester Grammar School. **Awards:** Scholarship, SJC 1930.

WHITEHEAD, Richard Bertram (1922) Born 6 November 1879, 156 Canning Street, Liverpool; son of Robert Whitehead, Clerk in Holy Orders, Schoolmaster, and Isabel Grimshaw; m Margaret Elizabeth. MA 1925; LittD 1940; BA (Oxon) 1901. **Tutor(s):** E A Benians. **Educ:** Liverpool College; Exeter College, Oxford. **Career:** Assistant Commissioner, Indian Civil Service, Punjab 1903–1922; Settlement Officer, Indian Civil Service, Punjab 1915–1917; Deputy Commissioner, Indian Civil Service, Punjab 1917–1922. **Appointments:** Fellow Commoner, SJC. Died 4 March 1967.

WHITEHOUSE, The Revd Alfred (1902) Born 19 January 1872, 13 High Street, Prince's End, Sedgeley, Staffordshire; son of Alfred Whitehouse, Boot and Shoe Dealer, and Elizabeth Pugh. BA 1905; MA 1909. **Tutor(s):** D MacAlister. **Educ:** Higher Grade School, Barrow-in-Furness; Church Missionary College. **Career:** Ordained Deacon 1905; Priest 1906; Rector, Christ Church, Port Antonio, Jamaica 1906–1912; Curate, St Mary Magdalene, Broughton in Furness 1912–1914; Curate, All Saints, Leyton 1915–1916.

WHITEHOUSE, Bertram Reginald (1910) Born 28 August 1891, Arundel Villa, Paddock Road, Bushey, Hertfordshire; son of Percy James Whitehouse, Tailor, and Henrietta Florence Lones. **Subject(s):** Classics; BA 1913. **Tutor(s):** E E Sikes. **Educ:** King Edward's School, Birmingham; King Edward's High School, Birmingham. **Career:** Various posts including District Officer; Acting Registrar, District Judge and First Magistrate, Civil Service in the Straits Settlements, Singapore. Died 30 September 1977.

WHITEHOUSE, Dr Frederick William (1922) Born 20 December 1900, Ipswich, Queensland, Australia; son of Frederick William Whitehouse, Tradesman, and Florence Amelia Terrey. PhD Geology 1925; BSc (Queensland); DSc (Queensland) 1939. **Tutor(s):** B F Armitage. **Educ:** The Grammar School, Ipswich; University of Queensland. **Career:** Geological Survey, Queensland; Lecturer in Geology and Mineralogy, University of Queensland, Brisbane 1926–1955 (Associate Professor 1949); Lieutenant Colonel, Engineering Intelligence Section, Advanced Headquarters, Australian Military Force 1940–1945. **Appointments:** President, Queensland Naturalists' Club. **Awards:** Walter Burfitt Prize, Royal Society of New South Wales 1941; University of Queensland Gold Medal. Died 22 March 1973.

WHITEHOUSE, Geoffrey (1938) Born 11 December 1919, Elder House, Shelley; son of Walter Whitehouse, Worker in Woollen Mill, and Clara Berry; m Norah Goldthorpe, 24 August 1946, Shelley Parish Church; 1 son (Andrew), 2 daughters (Susan and Rachel). **Subject(s):** Mathematics; BA 1941; MA 1946. **Tutor(s):** J M Wordie. **Johnian Relatives:** brother of Walter Alexander Whitehouse (1933). **Educ:** Shelley Council School; Penistone Grammar School. **Career:** Mathematics Master, Durham School 1946–1950; Mathematics Master, Penistone Grammar School 1950–1957; Headmaster, Berwick-upon-Tweed Grammar School 1957–1964; Headmaster, Queen Elizabeth Grammar School, Hexham 1964–1980; Headmaster, Queen Elizabeth High School, Hexham 1976–1980. **Appointments:** Chairman, Hexham Hospital Management Committee 1970–1974; Chairman, Northumberland Community Health Council 1974–1977; Chairman, Northumberland Health Authority 1981–1986.

WHITEHOUSE, The Revd John James (1900) Born 3 December 1879, 151 Dalton Road, Barrow-in-Furness, Lancashire; son of Alfred Whitehouse, Boiler Maker, and Elizabeth Pugh; m Agnes Marsh; 1 son (John James Garth b 21 August 1912). BA 1903; MA 1908. **Tutor(s):** D MacAlister. **Johnian Relatives:** father of John James Garth Whitehouse (1931). **Educ:** Commercial School, Barrow-in-Furness; Higher Grade School, Barrow-in-Furness. **Career:** Ordained Deacon 1903; Ordained Priest 1904; Warden, Jamaica Church Theological College, and Examining Chaplain to Bishop of Jamaica 1906–1913; Vicar, All Saints, Leyton 1913–1918; Vicar, St John the Baptist, Southend 1918–1951.

WHITEHOUSE, John James Garth (1931) Born 21 August 1912, Bank End, Broughton in Furness; son of John James Whitehouse, Clerk in Holy Orders, and Agnes Marsh; 1 daughter (Margaret). **Subject(s):** Geography; BA 1934; MA 1938. **Tutor(s):** J M Wordie. **Johnian Relatives:** son of John James Whitehouse (1900). **Educ:** Alleyn Court Preparatory School, Westcliff on Sea; The High School, Westcliff on Sea. **Career:** Deputy Headmaster, The Judd School, Tonbridge 1966. Died 3 August 1994.

WHITEHOUSE, The Revd Walter Alexander (1933) Born 27 February 1915, Far Bank, Shelley; son of Walter Whitehouse, Teazer in Woollen Mill, and Clara Berry; m (1) Beatrice Mary Kent Smith (d 1971), (2) Audrey Ethel Lemmon, 1974. **Subject(s):** Mathematics; BA 1936; MA 1940; MA (Oxon) 1940; BLitt (Oxon) 1940; Honorary DD (Edinburgh) 1960. **Tutor(s):** J M Wordie. **Johnian Relatives:** brother of Geoffrey Whitehouse (1938). **Educ:** Shelley Council School; Penistone Grammar School. **Career:** Minister, Elland Congregational Church 1940–1944; Chaplain and Tutor, Mansfield College, Oxford 1944–1947; Reader in Divinity, University of Durham 1947–1965; Principal, St Cuthbert's Society, University of Durham 1955–1960; Pro-Vice-Chancellor and Sub-Warden, University of Durham 1961–1964; Master, Eliot College, University of Kent 1965–1969; Professor of Theology, University of Kent 1965–1977; Master, Eliot College, University of Kent 1973–1975; Minister at High Chapel, Ravenstonedale 1977–1982. **Appointments:** Member, Gloucester County Council, 1989–1993; Co-Chairman, Police Authority. **Publications:** *Christian Faith and the Scientific Attitude*, 1952; *Order, Goodness, Glory* (Riddell Memorial Lectures), 1959; *The Authority of Grace*, 1981. Died 11 April 2003.

WHITELAW, Dr Alan Dunlop (1915) Born 7 February 1898, son of Robert Whitelaw, Medical Practitioner, and Elizabeth Wilhelmina Dunlop; m Isobel; 1 son (Robert), 1 daughter (Joan). **Subject(s):** Medicine; BA 1918; MA 1924; MD 1928; LRCP (London); MRCS. **Tutor(s):** R P Gregory. **Educ:** Clifton College, Harrogate. Died 6 May 1992.

WHITELEY, Joseph Edward (1927) Born 29 July 1909, 34 Halifax Road, Brighouse, Yorkshire; son of Thomas William Whiteley, Master Cotton Doubler, and Sarah Hannah Peel. **Subject(s):** History/Law; BA 1930. **Tutor(s):** E A Benians. **Educ:** The Grammar School, Rastrick; King Edward VII School, Rytham.

WHITEMAN, William Meredith (1923) Born 29 May 1905, 36 Harpenden Road, West Norwood, Surrey; son of George Frederick Francis Carl Whiteman, Publisher, and Emily Brown; m (1) Patricia Eileen Thornton, 1931 (d 1954), (2) Mary (Mimmo) Moore (née Hall); (1) 3 daughters (Miranda, Gillian and Philippa). BA 1926; MA 1930; FRSA. **Tutor(s):** E E Sikes. **Educ:** Belmont College, Streatham Hill; Arlington Park College, Turnham Green; St Alban's School. **Career:** Writer on local history, caravanning and the countryside; Director, Caravan Club 1938–1960; Editor, *The Caravan* 1938–1961; Managing Editor, Link House Publications Ltd 1942–1970. **Appointments:** Founder and Honorary Secretary 1939–1949, Honorary Director 1949–1952, National Caravan Council; Organiser, Moveable Dwelling Conference 1947–1949; UK Member 1947–1970, President 1957–1970, International Caravan Commission; Vice-President, British Caravanners Club 1948–1977; Countryside Commission Transit Site Study Group 1969–1970; Member, Executive Committee, Hampshire Council of Community Service 1971–1983; Life Vice-President, Petersfield Society 1986; Honorary Life Member, Caravan Club; Honorary Member, Fédération Internationale de Camping et de Caravanning; Vice-President, Camping and Caravanning Club. **Publications:** Books on camping and caravanning. Died 11 December 1989.

WHITESIDE, Charles Edward (1933) Born 25 May 1914, Brookside, Waddington, Yorkshire; son of Dennis Whiteside, Master House Decorator, and Susannah Sarah Broughton. **Subject(s):** History/ English; BA 1936. **Tutor(s):** J S Boys Smith. **Educ:** Waddington Elementary School; Church of England School, Clitheroe; Royal Grammar School, Clitheroe. Died August 1943.

WHITFIELD, Edward Hilliard Day (1910) Born 19 December 1892, The Point Farm, Sealand, Chester, Cheshire; son of Edward Hilliard Whitfield, Farmer, and Eleanor Jane Hankey. **Subject(s):** Mathematics; BA 1913. **Tutor(s):** L H K Bushe-Fox. **Educ:** St Paul's School, Boughton, Chester; The King's School, Chester. **Career:** Lecturer in Mathematics, St David's College, Lampeter 1913; Second Lieutenant, York and Lancaster Regiment 1914–1915. Died 30 August 1915 (missing presumed killed at Gallipoli).

WHITFIELD, Dr Gerald Arthur Wadsworth (1925) Born 9 September 1906, 21 Bentinck Street, Marylebone, Middlesex; son of Arthur Whitfield, Physician, and Margaret Wadsworth Tuttle; m Annie Llewelyn Jones; 1 son (John Martin b 15 April 1938). **Subject(s):** Natural Sciences; BA 1928; MA 1933; MB 1933; BChir 1933. **Tutor(s):** B F Armitage. **Johnian Relatives:** father of John Martin Whitfield (1958). **Educ:** Norfolk House School, Beaconsfield; Oundle School.

WHITFIELD, John Wesley (1936) Born 30 May 1917, Wester Craggs, Stanley, Durham; son of Robert Whitfield, General Manager and Secretary, and Mary Jane Brown. **Subject(s):** Natural Sciences/Moral Sciences; BA 1939; MA 1943. **Tutor(s):** J M Wordie. **Educ:** West Stanley Council School; Alderman Wood Secondary School, Stanley; Sunderland Bede Collegiate School. **Career:** Reader in Psychology, University College London 1950–1979. **Appointments:** Honorary Deputy Director, MRC Industrial Psychology Research Group 1951. **Awards:** Thornton Medallist 1956. **Publications:** *A Severity Rate for Industrial Accidents*, 1943; *Notes on the Causes of Accidents*, 1950; *Individual Differences in Accident Susceptibility among Coal Miners*, 1954. Died 21 July 1979.

WHITING, Walter Frederick (1919) Born 8 August 1900, Highbury, Hitchin; son of Walter Whiting, Bank Manager, and Marion Pepper. **Tutor(s):** E A Benians. **Educ:** Saffron Walden Preparatory School; Aldenham School. **Appointments:** Aldenham OTC 1915–1919. **Career:** Cadet, RFA 1918.

WHITLEY, Edward Gordon (1919) Born 24 September 1901, Beech House, Greenbank Road, Allerton, Bradford; son of Edward Bairstow Whitley, Mohair Merchant and Woolcomber, and Alice Maud

Whittingham; m Alice Mary Bland, 9 September 1924, St Mark's, North Audley Street. BA 1922; MA 1926. **Tutor(s):** E A Benians. **Educ:** Oatlands School, Harrogate; Sedbergh School. **Career:** Principal, Greenwood, Whiteley and Co Ltd, Woolcombers, Bradford. Died 27 August 1961.

WHITLEY, George (1900) Born 10 May 1882, Holland Lodge, Edmonton, Middlesex; son of George Whitley, Manager, Floor Cloth Works, and Elizabeth Moncaster Mitcheson. BA 1904. **Tutor(s):** C E Graves. **Educ:** Mill Hill School. **Career:** Linoleum Manufacturer, New York 1926.

WHITLOCK, Professor Percy Oddie (1907) Born 15 March 1884, High Street, Brackley, Northamptonshire; son of Frederick Whitlock, Grocer, and Rachel Oddie. **Subject(s):** Modern and Medieval Languages; BA 1910; BA (Manchester) 1904. **Tutor(s):** E E Sikes. **Educ:** Friends' School, Sebford Ferris, Banbury; Yorkshire College, Leeds; University of Manchester. **Career:** Assistant Master, Sibford School, Banbury 1904–1906; Assistant Master, Ackworth School 1906–1907; Master, Stramongate School 1910; Professor, Indian Educational Service 1914; Inspector of Schools, Bihar and Orissa 1925; Professor of English, Ravenshaw College, Cuttack 1926; Deputy Director of Public Instruction, Bihar and Orissa 1929; Officiating Principal, Patna College 1932; Professor of English, Patna College 1933–1935.

WHITMORE, Dr David Noel (1948) Born 25 December 1929, 16 Reporto Avenue, Grimsby, Lincolnshire; son of Frank Stanley Whitmore, Assistant Master, Wintringham Secondary School, and Evelyn Dixon; m Elizabeth Anne Cumming, 17 September 1955, Hove, Sussex; 3 sons (John Keith b 16 October 1959, Richard Martin b 10 May 1961 and Michael David b 28 October 1964). **Subject(s):** Natural Sciences; BA 1951; MA 1955; MB 1955; BChir 1955; MRCP 1958; FRCPath 1976; FRCP 1979. **Tutor(s):** G C L Bertram. **Educ:** Welholme Council School, Grimsby; Wintringham Secondary School, Grimsby. **Career:** Consultant Pathologist, Lewisham Hospital Group 1964; Consultant Haemotologist, Lewisham University Hospital 1981–1991. **Appointments:** Consultant Member, District Management Team; Consultant Member, Lewisham and North Southwark Health Authority; Chairman, South East Region, Haemotology Committee; Examiner in Haemotology, Royal College of Pathology. **Awards:** Lister Scholarship, SJC 1947.

WHITNEY, Alan (1948) Born 11 June 1930, Doncaster; son of Albert Ashton Whitney and Lilian Barraclough; m Shirley Jean Makey, 24 July 1954, St Mary Magdalene Church, Gillingham, Kent; 1 son (David John b 1963), 1 daughter (Philippa Jane b 1956). **Subject(s):** History/English; BA 1951; MA 1994. **Tutor(s):** F Thistlethwaite. **Educ:** Doncaster Grammar School. **Career:** Training and Industrial Relations, Lucas and Mitchell Construction; Personnel Director, Lucas Aerospace 1974–1985; Independent Consultant in Industrial Relations 1985–1990. **Awards:** Choral Studentship, SJC.

WHITTAKER, Charles Richard (1949) Born 25 October 1929, Wesleyan High School, Secunderabad, India; son of Frank Whittaker, Methodist Minister, and Constance Snowden. **Subject(s):** Classics; BA 1952; MA 1956. **Tutor(s):** R L Howland. **Johnian Relatives:** son of Frank Whittaker (1913). **Educ:** Hebron School, Conoor; Woodstock School, Mussoorie; Kingswood School, Bath. **Career:** Fellow, Churchill College, Cambridge 1971; Lecturer, University of Cambridge 1971–1993. **Appointments:** Director of Studies in Classics 1971, Churchill College, Cambridge. **Publications:** (ed, with Peter Garnsey and Keith Hopkins) *Trade in the Ancient Economy*, Chatto & Windus: Hogarth Press, 1983; (ed, with Peter Garnsey) *Trade and Famine in Classical Antiquity*, Cambridge Philological Society, Supplementary Volume No 8, 1983; (ed) *Pastoral Economies in Classical Antiquity*, Cambridge Philological Society, Supplementary Volume No 14, 1988; *Land, City and Trade in the Roman Empire*, Variorum, 1993; *Frontiers of the Roman Empire: a social and economic study*, Johns Hopkins University Press, 1994.

WHITTAKER, Duncan (1924) Born 6 April 1906, Winthrop, Ansdell, Lytham, Lancashire; son of Christopher Joseph Whittaker, Mechanical Engineer, and Polly Mitchell; 1 daughter. BA 1929; MA 1942; MRCS (St Thomas') 1934; DPM 1942. **Tutor(s):** B F Armitage. **Educ:** Kingsland Grange; Shrewsbury School. **Career:** Psychiatrist, Portman Clinic; Chief Assistant, Department of Psychological Medicine, St Thomas' Hospital; Consultant Psychiatrist, Woolwich and Bromley Hospital Groups; Senior Assistant Physician, Bethlem Royal Hospital 1945. Died 25 January 1969.

WHITTAKER, The Rt Hon Frank (1913) Born 14 December 1894, 234 Rochdale Road, Oldham, Lancashire; son of Henry Whittaker, Pork Butcher, and Mary Hannah Shaw; m Constance Snowden; 1 son (Charles Richard). **Subject(s):** Theology/Classics; BA 1919; MA 1922. **Tutor(s):** E E Sikes. **Johnian Relatives:** father of Charles Richard Whittaker (1949). **Educ:** Coldhurst National School; Waterloo Elementary School; Hulme Grammar School, Oldham. **Career:** Tutor, Didsbury College, Manchester; served with the YMCA, Basara and Bangalore 1914–1918; Principal, Wesleyan Training College, Hyderabad 1922; Missionary, National Christian Council, India 1923; Consecrated as Bishop 1947; Methodist Minister. Died December 1961.

WHITTAKER, Roy (1944) Born 16 July 1926, Wesley Terrace, Greenfield, Saddleworth, Yorkshire; son of Clifford Whittaker, Master Printer, and Mary Pilling; m Elsie Kathleen, 2 September 1950 (d 2001); twin daughters (Elizabeth Jane and Susan Mary b 1954). **Subject(s):** Natural Sciences; BA 1947; MA 1951; CEng; MIChemE. **Tutor(s):** C W Guillebaud. **Educ:** Greenfield Council School; Hulme Grammar School, Oldham. **Career:** Paint Maker, Jenson & Nicholson 1949–1951; Managing Director, Cookson Industrial Materials (formerly Associated Lead Manufacturers) 1981–1988; Deputy Divisional Director, Cookson Group 1984–1988; Managing Director, Newcastle University Ventures Ltd (Nuventures) 1989–1992. **Appointments:** Magistrate, Bootle; General Commissioner for Taxation, Liverpool.

WHITTINGHAM, Professor Charles Percival (1940) Born 7 September 1922, The Royal Free Hospital, St Pancras, London; son of Herbert Joseph Whittingham, Caterer, and Alice Lavinia Russell; m Janet Alison Phillips; 2 daughters (Christine and Susan Lucy). **Subject(s):** Natural Sciences; BA 1943; PhD Botany 1950. **Tutor(s):** J M Wordie. **Educ:** Owen's School, Islington, London; Grafton Road LCC (Infants) School, Holloway, London; Bush Hill Park Junior School, Enfield; Manchester Street LCC School, Kings Cross, London. **Career:** Research (under Professor G E Blackman) on field trials and herbicides 1943; Research Fellow, University of Illinois, including time at Stanford University 1950; Botany School, Cambridge 1950; Senior Research Assistant in Botany 1952; Assistant Director of Research 1957; Professor of Botany, Queen Mary College, University of London 1958; Professor of Plant Physiology, Imperial College, London 1964; Head, Department of Botany, Rothamsted Experimental Station 1971–1982. **Appointments:** Visiting Lecturer with Professor A H Brown, University of Minnesota 1953–1954; Member, Technical Committees of Ministry of Agriculture, Potato Marketing Board, Reseach and Education Committee for Sugar Beet; Visiting Summer Professor, Calouste Gulbenkian Institute of Science, Oeiras, Portugal 1967–1973. **Awards:** Exhibition, SJC; Hughes Prize, SJC; Frank Smart Prize for Botany, University of Cambridge 1943. **Publications:** Various, including (with Dr Robin Hill) *Photosynthesis*, 1955.

WHITTINGTON, Dr Alan MacRae (1940) Born 13 August 1920, Heston Lodge, London Road, Isleworth; son of Arthur George Whittington, Farmer, and Ada Jessie Law; m Ann Leslie Smith, 22 May 1947, Holy Trinity, Brompton, London; 2 sons (Richard Gordon b 28 January 1950 and John MacRae b 14 April 1952). **Tutor(s):** R L Howland. **Educ:** Hounslow Court; Colet Court, West Kensington; St Paul's School, London; Middlesex Hospital. **Career:** ENT, Middlesex Hospital; RAF, National Service; GP, Longridge, Lancashire; GP, Ascot, Berkshire 1950–1983. Died 4 August 2002.

WHITTLE, Geoffrey Alan (1943) Born 2 April 1924, 59 Bradgate Road, Nottingham; son of Edward Whittle, Departmental Manager, and Gertrude Mitchell. **Subject(s):** Natural Sciences; BA 1946. **Tutor(s):** S J Bailey. **Educ:** Nottingham High Pavement Secondary School.

WHITWORTH, Martin Dysart (1943) Born 25 October 1925, Quetta, Baluchistan, Pakistan; son of Dysart Edward Whitworth, Brigadier, Indian Army, and Helena Margherita Powell; m Elizabeth Ruth Goldney; 1 son, 1 daughter. **Subject(s):** Mechanical Sciences; BA 1948; Postgraduate Nuclear Engineering Course (Manchester) 1955; CEng; FIMechE; MIMarEST. **Tutor(s):** S J Bailey. **Johnian Relatives:** father of David Paul Dysart Whitworth (1972). **Educ:** St Piran's on the Hill, Maidenhead; Shrewsbury School; Manchester University. **Career:** Chartered Mechanical and Marine Engineer.

WHYE, John William (1903) (admitted as a Non-Collegiate Student 1902) Born 23 March 1879, West End, March, Cambridgeshire; son of John William Whye, Builder, and Mary Ann Hodson. BA 1905. **Tutor(s):** J R Tanner; C E Graves. **Educ:** March Elementary School. **Career:** Lieutenant, Leicestershire Regiment, WWI. **Awards:** Choral Studentship, SJC. **Honours:** MC 1917.

WICKENS, Robert (1944) Born 26 February 1926, 13 Bridge Street, Olney, Buckinghamshire; son of Arthur Thomas Wickens, Gardener, and Lily Perkins. **Subject(s):** Natural Sciences; BA 1947; MA 1953; DipAgr; DTA. **Tutor(s):** C W Guillebaud. **Educ:** Church School, Rothersthorpe; Town and County School, Northampton. **Career:** Agronomist, West African Cocoa Research Institute 1950–1957; Agricultural Adviser 1957–1968; Director, Arthur Rickwood 1968–1982; Director, Experimental Centres, Agricultural Development and Advisory Service 1982–1986.

WICKHAM, Bernard William Theodore (1913) Born 23 October 1894, St Andrew's Vicarage, Wigan, Lancashire; son of William Arthur Wickham, Clerk in Orders, and Clara Peck. **Tutor(s):** E E Sikes. **Educ:** Millmead, Shrewsbury; Christ's Hospital. **Career:** Second Lieutenant, South Staffordshire Regiment 1914–1917. **Honours:** MC. Died 14 April 1917 (killed by a sniper near Ypres).

WICKHAM, Peter Guy (1949) Born 19 February 1929, 6 Lansdowne Road, Bedford; son of Guy Vivyan Wickham, Indian Political Service, and Joyce Frances Lloyd; m Janet Treweeks, 1963; 2 daughters. **Subject(s):** Mathematics; BA 1952; MA 1960; FRMetS. **Tutor(s):** J M Wordie. **Educ:** Rushmoor School, Bedford; Durham School. **Career:** RA 1947–1949; Meteorological Office 1952–1989; Chief Instructor, Meteorological Office College 1978–1989. **Honours:** Imperial Service Order 1989. **Publications:** *The Practice of Weather Forecasting*, HMSO, 1970; *Directory of Meteorological Satellite Applications*, EUMETSAT, 1993; (jointly) *Images in Weather Forecasting*, CUP, 1995.

WICKSTEAD, Henry Arthur (1932) Born 2 May 1913, 20 Pargeter Road, Oldbury, Worcestershire; son of Thomas Henry Wickstead, Schoolmaster, and Lilian Ray Pett; m Margaret Goodrich, 22 August 1953, Lincolnshire; 4 sons (Timothy, Peter, Mark and David). **Subject(s):** Classics; BA 1935; MA 1939. **Tutor(s):** R L Howland. **Johnian Relatives:** son-in-law of Harold Spencer Goodrich (1912); brother-in-law of Philip Harold Ernest Goodrich (1949); father of Arthur Timothy John Wickstead (1973). **Educ:** Clewer House School, Birmingham; King Edward's School, Birmingham. **Career:** Henry Fellow, Yale; Teacher, Phillips Academy, Massachusetts; Assistant Master, Bedford School 1938; Major (final rank), SOE, served in North Africa, Greece and Palestine (Mentioned in Despatches), WWII; Education Officer, Shropshire County Council, then Cornwall County Council; Deputy Director of Education, Lindsey County Council 1952–1974. **Awards:** Browne Medal for Greek Epigram, University of Cambridge 1934; Scholarship, SJC. Died 26 July 1989.

WIDDAS, Frank (1947) Born 25 March 1929, Ryton, Mainsforth, Ferryhill, Durham; son of Frank Widdas, Mining Engineer, and Frieda Blaiklock; m Marjorie Graeme Barron (née Dickson). **Subject(s):** Natural Sciences; BA 1950; MA 1954. **Tutor(s):** G C L Bertram. **Educ:** Polam Hall, Darlington; Ascham House, Gosforth; Sedbergh School.

WIDDELL, Joseph William (1946) Born 8 October 1922, 34 Sickle Street, Oldham, Lancashire; son of Leonard Widdell, Textile Machine Fitter, and Ella Kenning. **Subject(s):** History; BA 1947; MA 1952. **Tutor(s):** F Thistlethwaite. **Educ:** St Anne's National School; Uppermill Central School; Hulme Grammar School, Oldham. **Career:** Colonial Service, Nigeria.

WIDE, Nicholas Scott (1941) Born 7 May 1923, Nottingham; son of Leonard Alfred Wide, CF, overseas, and Kathleen Irene Allender; m Ruth M N Bird, 17 November 1945, London Road Congregational Church, Kettering; 3 sons (Marcus Allender, Charles Thomas and Adam George). BA 1948; MA 1950. **Tutor(s):** C W Guillebaud; G C L Bertram. **Educ:** Mrs Ramsden's Private School, Burnley; Silcoates School, Wakefield. **Career:** Farm Pupil 1940–1941; 4th/7th Royal Dragoon Guards (Northwest Europe and Middle East) 1942–1947; Assistant Land Commissioner, Ministry of Agriculture and Fisheries 1949–1950; Executive and Manager, Thomas Bird and Son, Shoe Manufacturers 1950–1955; Managing Director, Glover Norton Ltd, Shoe Manufacturers 1956–1968; Chairman and Managing Director, Kids & Co (Footwear) Ltd 1969–1985. **Honours:** MC 1944.

WIGGINS, Dr Arthur Edward Michael (ASH) (1935) Born 21 October 1916, The Hall, Dallinghoo, Woodbridge; son of Edward Cecil Magnus Ash, Farmer and Second Lieutenant, RFA, and Judith Nora Pratt. **Subject(s):** Natural Sciences; BA 1938; MA 1943; MRCS; LRCP. **Tutor(s):** R L Howland. **Educ:** Bedford School.

WIGGINS, Hugh Sidney (1948) Born 15 June 1928, 78 Herne Hill Road, Herne Hill, London; son of Sidney William Robert Wiggins, Chartered Accountant's Clerk, and Marjorie Annie May Baldrey. BA 1951. **Tutor(s):** G C L Bertram. **Educ:** Cheam Common School; Raynes Park County School.

WIGGINS, Norman Ewart (1919) Born 5 May 1901, 6 Kingsley Road, Northampton; son of Robert Wiggins, Coal Merchant, and Frances Payne; m Phyllis Diana Priestley, 7 March 1930, London; 2 sons (David and Peter). **Subject(s):** Law; BA 1923; MA 1937; LLB 1923; LLM 1985. **Tutor(s):** E A Benians. **Johnian Relatives:** father of Francis Peter Temple Wiggins (1957). **Educ:** Waynefleete House School, Northampton; Northampton Town and County School; Wycliffe College, Stonehouse. **Career:** Called to the Bar, Inner Temple 1925. **Honours:** OBE. Died 29 June 1989.

WIGLESWORTH, Reginald Thomas (1929) Born 8 December 1907, Danedale Lodge, Minster, Kent; son of Thomas Ridler Wiglesworth, General Medical Practitioner, and Elsie Emma Ladd. **Tutor(s):** C W Guillebaud. **Educ:** Warden House, Upper Deal; St Lawrence College, Ramsgate; Harper Adams Agricultural College, Newport.

WILD, Alfred Crabtree (1928) Born 10 October 1910, 67 Greyswood Street, Streatham, London; son of Alfred Crabtree Wild, Consulting Engineer, and Rachel Alcock. **Subject(s):** Mathematics; BA 1931; MA 1935. **Tutor(s):** J M Wordie. **Educ:** St Chad's Church of England School, Bury; The Grammar School, Manchester. **Awards:** Scholarship, SJC 1927.

WILD, Peter Dickinson (1936) Born 1 June 1918, Sheffield; son of Frank Dickinson Wild, Company Director, and Dorothy Parkin; m Helen Good, 21 January 1942; 2 sons (Maxwell and Simon); 1 daughter (Rosalind). **Subject(s):** Economics/Law; BA 1939; MA 1943. **Tutor(s):** J S Boys Smith; C W Guillebaud. **Educ:** Fernden School, Haslemere; Rugby School. **Career:** Major, The Green Howards; Director, A G Wild & Co Ltd; Fundraiser, Aston University; Probation Officer, South Yorkshire; Social Worker, Cambridgeshire. Died 22 January 2003.

WILD, William Ferris (1926) Born 11 April 1908, 1 King's Buildings, Chester, Cheshire; son of William Wild, Farmer, and Mary Margaretta Boffey. **Tutor(s):** M P Charlesworth. **Educ:** The King's School, Chester.

WILDEN-HART, Kenneth Gordon (1942) Born 15 January 1923, 44 Clifton Gardens, London; son of Bernard John Wilden-Hart, Emeritus Professor, Imperial Japanese University, and Gladys Marion Wheeler; m Monica Morgan, 9 August 1947. **Subject(s):** Modern and Medieval Languages; BA 1945; MA 1956. **Tutor(s):** C W Guillebaud. **Educ:** St John's School, Leatherhead. **Career:** Master, Wycliffe College, Stonehouse 1949.

WILDERS, Dr John Simpson (1948) Born 30 July 1927, Brookfield, Nottingham Road, Mansfield, Nottinghamshire; son of Charles Alban Wilders, Architect and Surveyor, and Emily Ida Starr Simpson; m Benedikte. **Subject(s):** English; BA 1951; MA 1955; PhD 1956; DPhil (Oxon, by incorporation). **Tutor(s):** F Thistlethwaite. **Educ:** Sutton-in-Ashfield C of E School; Queen Elizabeth's Grammar School, Mansfield. **Career:** RN 1945–1948; Tutorial Fellow in English, Worcester College, Oxford; Lecturer in English, Princeton University; Lecturer in English, Bristol University; Literary Consultant to BBC for its major production of the complete cycle of Shakespeare's plays; Emeritus Fellow, Worcester College, Oxford 1987; Professor of the Humanities, Middlebury College, Vermont, USA 1987. **Appointments:** Visiting Professor, University of California, Santa Barbara; Visiting Senior Researcher, ANU; Governor, Royal Shakespeare Company. **Awards:** Jane Eliza Proctor Scholarship, Princeton University. **Publications:** (ed) William Shakespeare, *Antony & Cleopatra*, New Arden Edition, Routledge; *The Lost Garden*, London, 1978; *New Prefaces to Shakespeare*, Blackwell; *Shakespeare in Production: Macbeth*, Cambridge.

WILGAR, Professor William Percy (1934) Born 15 May 1912, Port Arthur, Ontario, Canada; son of William Percy Wilgar, Professor of Civil Engineering, and Emmelie Stewart Low. **Subject(s):** English; BA 1936; MA 1945. **Tutor(s):** J S Boys Smith. **Educ:** Victoria School, Ontario; Kingston Collegiate Institute; Queen's University, Kingston. **Career:** Professor of English, Carlton College; Lecturer in English, University of Texas 1937–1941; Associate Professor of English, Mount Allison University, Canada 1941–1950. Died 7 September 1950.

WILKES, Kenneth William (1947) Born 23 October 1928, 455 Park Road, Birmingham; son of Samuel Cecil Wilkes, Warehouseman, and Ivy Evelyn Newey. **Subject(s):** Natural Sciences; BA 1950; MA 1954. **Tutor(s):** G C L Bertram. **Educ:** Benson Road Council School, Birmingham; Handsworth Grammar School, Birmingham. **Career:** National Service, RAF Education Branch 1951–1953; Assistant Master, Harrow School 1953–1961; Headmaster, Borehamwood Grammar School 1962–1965; Principal then Assistant Secretary, Ministry of Agriculture, Fisheries and Food 1965–1988; Consultant, British Veterinary Association 1989–1994; Consultant, Royal College of Veterinary Surgeons 1994–1996. **Awards:** Major Scholarship, SJC 1946.

WILKES, Professor Sir Maurice Vincent (1931) Born 26 June 1913, 24 Gammage Street, Dudley; son of Vincent Joseph Wilkes, Company Director, and Ellen Malone; m Nina Twyman, 1947; 1 son, 2 daughters. **Subject(s):** Mathematics; BA 1934; MA 1938; PhD 1938; ScD 1993; Honorary DTech (Linköping) 1975; Honorary DSc (Newcastle upon Tyne) 1972, (Hull) 1974, (Kent) 1975, (City) 1975, (Amsterdam) 1978, (Munich) 1978, (Bath) 1987, (Pennsylvania) 1996; FRS 1956; FREng 1976; FIEE; FBCS. **Tutor(s):** J M Wordie. **Educ:** King Edward VI School, Stourbridge. **Career:** Physics Research, Cavendish Laboratory 1934–1937; University Demonstrator in Mathematics 1937–1946; University of Cambridge; Radar and Operational Research 1939–1945; Acting Director 1945, Lecturer 1946, Director 1946–1970, Mathematical Laboratory, University of Cambridge; Title E Fellow 1950–1965, Title C Fellow 1965–, SJC; Professor of Computer Technology 1965–1980 (Emeritus 1980–), Head, Computer Laboratory (formerly Mathematical Laboratory) 1970–1980, University of Cambridge; Computer Engineer,

Digital Equipment Corporation, USA 1980–1986; Adjunct Professor of Computer Science and Electrical Engineering, MIT 1981–1985; Member for Research Strategy, Olivetti Research Board 1986–1996; Staff Advisor on Research Strategy, Olivetti and Oracle Research Laboratory, Cambridge 1996–1999; Staff Consultant, AT&T Laboratories, Cambridge 1999–2002. **Appointments:** Member, Measurement and Control Section Committee, IEE 1956–1959; Member and First President, BCS 1957–1960; Council Member, IFIP 1960–1963; Turing Lecturer, Association for Computing Machinery 1967; Chairman, IEE East Anglia Sub-Centre 1969–1970; Distinguished Fellow, BCS 1973; Council Member, IEE 1973–1976; Foreign Honorary Member, American Academy of Arts and Sciences 1974; Foreign Associate, US National Academy of Engineering 1977; Foreign Corresponding Member, Royal Spanish Academy of Sciences 1979; Foreign Associate, US National Academy of Sciences 1980. **Awards:** Hughes Prize, SJC 1934; Hockin Prize, SJC 1934; Harry Goode Award, American Federation of Information Processing Societies 1968; Eckert-Mauchly Award, Association for Computing Machinery and IEEE Computer Society 1980; Faraday Medal, IEE 1981; McDowell Award, IEEE Computer Society 1981; Pender Award, University of Pennsylvania 1982; C & C Prize, Foundation for C & C Promotions, Tokyo 1988; Italgas Prize for Research and Innovation, Turin 1991; Kyoto Prize, Inamori Foundation 1992; John von Neumann Medal, IEEE 1997. **Honours:** Kt 2000. **Publications:** *Oscillations of the Earth's Atmosphere*, 1949; (jointly) *Preparations of Programs for an Electronic Digital Computer*, 1951; *Automatic Digital Computers*, 1956; *A Short Introduction to Numerical Analysis*, 1966; *Time–sharing Computer System*, 1968; (jointly) *The Cambridge CAP Computer and its Operating System*, 1979; *Memoirs of a Computer Pioneer*, 1985; *Computing Perspectives*, 1995; papers in scientific journals.

WILKIE, Professor John Ritchie (1943) Born 24 May 1921, Hill of Forest, Rathen, Aberdeenshire; son of John Christie Wilkie, Schoolmaster, and Mary Penny Ritchie; m Sheila. **Subject(s):** Modern and Medieval Languages; BA 1945; MA 1972; MA (Aberdeen) 1943. **Tutor(s):** C W Guillebaud. **Educ:** Ellon Secondary School, Aberdeenshire; Crudie Public School, Aberdeenshire; The Academy, Banff; Aberdeen University. **Career:** Lecturer in German 1952–1972, Professor of German and Head, German Department 1972, University of Leeds. Died 30 August 1991.

WILKIN, Allan Whiteley (1937) Born 5 September 1918, Providence Villa, Welholme Road, Grimsby; son of John Wilkin, Estate Agent, and Edith Mary Smith. **Tutor(s):** J M Wordie. **Educ:** Oaklands, Harrogate; The Leys School, Cambridge. **Career:** Engineer.

WILKIN, Dr John Marmaduke (1932) Born 16 May 1913, Touraine, Park Drive, Grimsby, Lincolnshire; son of John Wilkin, Estate Agent, and Edith Mary Smith; m Dorothy May, 1941; 1 son (David), 2 daughters (Jean and Catherine). **Subject(s):** Natural Sciences; BA 1935; MA 1939; MB 1939; BChir 1939. **Tutor(s):** R L Howland. **Educ:** Oatlands, Harrogate; The Leys School, Cambridge; St Mary's Hospital, London. **Career:** Squadron Leader, RAF, WWII; Medical Practitioner, Grimsby 1938–1984. **Appointments:** Honorary Member, Trinity College of Music; JP 1960–1983; Chairman, Local Medical Council; Secretary, local branch, BMA. Died 4 March 2002.

WILKINS, Arnold Frederick (1928) Born 20 February 1907, 26 Linden Road, Levenshulme, Manchester, Lancashire; son of John Knowles Wilkins, Headmaster, and Louisa Jones. **Tutor(s):** J M Wordie. **Educ:** Manchester College of Technology; King's School, Chester; City and Council School, Chester; Hulme Hall, Manchester.

WILKINS, Professor Maurice Hugh Frederick (1935) Born 15 December 1916, Pongaroa, New Zealand; son of Elgar Henry Wilkins, Assistant School Medical Officer, Birmingham, and Eveline Constance Jane Whittaker; m Patricia Ann Chigley; 2 sons, 2 daughters. **Subject(s):** Natural Sciences; BA 1938; MA 1942; PhD (Birmingham) 1940;

Honorary LLD (Glasgow) 1972; Honorary ScD (TCD) 1992; Honorary ScD (Birmingham) 1992; FRS 1959. **Tutor(s):** J M Wordie. **Educ:** Wylde Green College; King Edward's High School, Birmingham. **Career:** Research for Ministry of Home Security and Aircraft Production, Physics Department, Birmingham University 1938; Manhattan Project, University of California 1944; Lecturer in Physics, St Andrews University 1945; Deputy Director 1955–1970, Director 1970–1972 and 1974–1980, MRC Biophysics Unit, Physics Department, KCL; Director, MRC Neurobiology Unit 1972–1974; Honorary Lecturer 1958, Professor of Molecular Biology 1963–1970, Professor of Biophysics 1970–1981 (Emeritus 1981), Fellow 1973, KCL. **Appointments:** Honorary Member, American Society of Biological Chemists 1964; President, British Society for Social Responsibility in Science 1969–1991; Foreign Honorary Member, American Academy of Arts and Sciences 1970; Honorary Fellow, SJC 1972; President, Food and Disarmament International 1984. **Awards:** Albert Lasker Award, American Public Health Association 1960; (Joint) Nobel Prize for Medicine 1962. **Honours:** CBE 1963. **Publications:** Papers in scientific journals on luminescence and topics in biophysics, such as molecular structure of nucleic acids and structure of nerve membranes.

WILKINS, Walter Gordon (1902) Born 21 July 1884, 118 London Road, Wotton, Kingsholme, Gloucester; son of Edward Weedon Wilkins, Stock and Share Broker, and Emmeline Bruce George. **Tutor(s):** D MacAlister. **Educ:** Cheltenham College; Leighton Park, Reading. **Career:** Lieutenant, Canadian Field Artillery, WWI. **Honours:** MC.

WILKINSON, Albert (1947) Born 3 November 1928, 19 Clarkson Street, Dale, Worsbrough, Yorkshire; son of Joseph Wilkinson, Coal Miner, and Elizabeth Shepherd; m Beryl Midgley, 1956; 4 daughters (Susan Jane b 1959, Janet Diane b 1960, Debra Ruth b 1963 and Caroline Adele b 1969). **Subject(s):** History; BA 1950; MA 1954. **Tutor(s):** F Thistlethwaite; A G Lee. **Educ:** Worsbrough Dale Council School; Barnsley and District Holgate Grammar School. **Career:** Head of Lower School, then Upper School, Worsbrough High School 1958–1968; Senior Deputy Head, Willowgarth High School 1968–1985. **Appointments:** Secretary 1948–1949, Captain 1949–1950, SJC Table Tennis Club.

WILKINSON, Bernard Harold (1920) Naval Officer.

WILKINSON, Edward Neville (1907) Born 5 May 1888, Blyth Spital, Hodsock, Nottinghamshire; son of Frank Booth Wilkinson, Farmer, and Clara Clater. **Tutor(s):** E E Sikes. **Educ:** East Retford Grammar School; Reading School; Bath College.

WILKINSON, The Revd Ernest Roland (1901) Born 24 July 1882, 14 Front Street, Tynemouth, Northumberland; son of Auburn Wilkinson, Doctor of Medicine, and Henrietta Featherstone. **Subject(s):** History; BA 1904; MA 1909. **Tutor(s):** E E Sikes. **Educ:** Epsom College. **Career:** Ordained Deacon 1907; Parishes in Liverpool 1907–1913; Ordained Priest 1908; Parishes in Calcutta, Darjeeling 1918–1933; Vicar, Slaley, Hexham-on-Tyne 1934–1953. Died 15 March 1973.

WILKINSON, Frederick (1948) Born 27 April 1927, 23 Bridge Street, Swinton, Yorkshire; son of Thomas Albert Wilkinson, Pharmacist, and Margaret Crompton; m Margaret Jean White, 24 July 1954, St Chrysostom's Church, Rusholme, Manchester; 3 sons (David Lindon b 1956, Robert Stephen b 1958 and James Frederick b 7 December 1963). **Subject(s):** History; BA 1950; MA 1955; PGCE 1952. **Tutor(s):** F Thistlethwaite; A G Lee. **Johnian Relatives:** father of James Frederick Wilkinson (1983). **Educ:** Barrow Grammar School, Barrow-in-Furness. **Career:** Assistant Master, Latymer Upper School, London 1953–1960; Head of History, Priory School, Shrewsbury 1960–1966; Deputy Headmaster, High Pavement School, Nottingham 1966–1970; Headmaster, Dame Allan's School (HMC), Newcastle upon Tyne 1970–1988. **Appointments:** Chairman, North East Division, Headmasters' Conference 1986–1988; College Representative Governor

at meetings of the University Court, University of Hull 1984–2002; Chairman, House of Laity, Diocesan Synod, Newcastle Diocese 1982–1994; Chairman, Northumbrian Industrial Mission 1990–1997; Member, Bishops Council, Chairman, Board for Mission and Social Responsibility, Diocese of Newcastle. Died 4 May 2002.

WILKINSON, Harry Clifford (1938) Born 25 September 1915, 48 Keswick Street, West Hartlepool; son of Henry Wilkinson, Joiner, and Lillian May Webber. **Subject(s):** Mechanical Sciences; BA 1941; MA 1949; BSc (Newcastle) 1938. **Tutor(s):** S J Bailey; J S Boys Smith. **Educ:** West Hartlepool Secondary School; West Hartlepool Technical College; King's College, Newcastle upon Tyne. **Career:** Technical Assistant to Director, Parsons and Marine Engineering Research and Development Association, Wallsend 1945–1968; Deputy Head, Marine Engineering Department 1968–1977, Manager, Management Services 1977–1979, British Ship Research Association, Wallsend. **Awards:** Wright's Prize, SJC 1939; Scholarship, SJC 1939; Ricardo Prize in Thermodynamics, University of Cambridge. Died 8 May 2000.

WILKINSON, Hermann Denis Darrell (1927) Born 19 June 1909, 29 Eastcourt Terrace, Headingley, Leeds, Yorkshire; son of George Ernest Wilkinson, Schoolmaster, and Alison Hermine Söhns. **Subject(s):** Law; BA 1931; MA 1935. **Tutor(s):** C W Guillebaud. **Educ:** Leeds Grammar School; Woodhouse Grove School, Apperley Bridge, near Bradford. **Career:** Assistant Auditor, Mauritius; Assistant Auditor, Nigeria 1939.

WILKINSON, Dr Lawrence (1945) Born 2 March 1927, 38 Princes Road, Mexborough, Yorkshire; son of John Herbert Alfred Wilkinson, Electrical Engineer, and Stella Ward. **Subject(s):** Natural Sciences; BA 1953; MB 1954; BChir 1954. **Tutor(s):** G C L Bertram. **Educ:** Sandy Elementary School; Bedford School.

WILKINSON, Louis Umfreville (1902) Born 17 December 1881, Aldeburgh, Suffolk; son of Walter George Wilkinson, Clerk in Holy Orders, and Charlotte Elizabeth Emra; m (1) Frances Josefa Gregg, 10 April 1912, Philadelphia, USA, (2) Ann Alexander Reid, (3) Diana Bryn (4) Joan Lamburn; (1) 1 son, (2) 1 daughter. **Subject(s):** History; BA 1905; MA 1909; LittD (Annapolis) 1914. **Tutor(s):** C E Graves; J R Tanner. **Educ:** Eaton House, Aldeburgh; Radley College; St John's College, Annapolis; Pembroke College, Oxford. **Career:** Lecturer in Literature, American University Extension Society 1905–1909; Lecturer in Literature, Oxford University Extension Society 1909; Lecturer in Literature, London University Extension 1919; Novelist (under name of Louis Barlow) and Biographer. **Awards:** Scholarship, Pembroke College, Oxford. **Publications:** *The Puppet's Dallying*, 1905; *The Buffoon*, 1916; *Swan's Milk*, 1934; *Welsh Ambassadors*, 1936; *The Devil in Crystal*, 1944; *Forth Beast!*, 1946; (ed) *The Letters of John Cowper Powys to Louis Wilkinson*, 1958. Died 12 September 1966.

WILKS, Thomas Grenfell (1938) Born 1 April 1920, The Hurtles, Torton, Hartlebury, Kidderminster; son of Thomas Nellist Wilks, Farmer, and Jessie Ballard. **Subject(s):** Natural Sciences; BA 1941; MA 1945. **Tutor(s):** C W Guillebaud. **Educ:** Bewdley Old Grammar School; Bridgnorth Grammar School.

WILLANS, Gordon Jeune (1904) Born 23 April 1885, The Palace, Much Hadham, Hertfordshire; son of William Blundell Willans, Physician and Surgeon, and Henrietta Amelia Jeune. BA 1908; MA 1940. **Tutor(s):** D MacAlister. **Educ:** Framlingham College. **Career:** Schoolmaster 1908–1914; Civil Servant, Admiralty; Acting Principal Clerk, Ministry of Pensions; Registrar, St Bartholomew's Hospital 1923–1945. Died 24 September 1963.

WILLCOCK, Dr Richard Mellor (1941) Born 28 June 1923, Devonshire House, Davenport Park, Stockport, Cheshire; son of Harold Willcock, Civil Servant, and Edith Mellor, Head Teacher; m Mavis Jones, 15 June 1957; 1 son (David Richard Mellor b 13 July 1958), 1 daughter (Barbara

Ann b 10 January 1961). **Subject(s):** Mechanical Sciences; BA 1944; MA 1948; PhD (Birmingham) 1973; FICE. **Tutor(s):** S J Bailey. **Educ:** St Saviour's School, Stockport; Stockport Grammar School; University of Birmingham. **Career:** Aero-engine research at RAE, Farnborough 1943–1946; Chartered Civil Engineer on hydro-electric schemes: Lochalsh, Scotland 1947–1948, Owen Falls, Uganda 1950–1953, Breadalbane and Shin, Scotland 1953–1957, Columbia, Fraser and Saskatchewan Rivers, Canada 1957–1961, Kainji, Nigeria 1961–1965, British Columbia, Canada 1977–1985; Senior Lecturer, Civil Engineering, University of Birmingham 1965–1977. **Awards:** Scholarship, SJC.

WILLCOX, William Bradford (1926) Born 29 October 1907, Ithaca, New York, USA; son of Walter Francis Willcox, Professor of Economics and Statistics, Cornell University, and Alice Eloise Work. **Tutor(s):** E A Benians. **Educ:** Ithaca High School; The Hill School, Pottstown; Cornell University.

WILLEMSTYN, Jan Willem Diederik (1934) Born 27 October 1915, Oud en Nieuw, Gastel, Holland; son of Hendrik Aegidius Willemstyn, General Manager, and Clasina Petronella Magdalena Opstelten; m Phyllis Marjorie Coombe, 4 May 1946. BA 1937; MA 1941. **Tutor(s):** J S Boys Smith. **Educ:** Standaarbinten, Holland; Private Tuition, Ely; King's School, Ely.

WILLETT, Everard William (1905) Born 1 August 1885, 27 Cromwell Road, Hove, Sussex; son of Everard John Willett, Builder's Manager, and Rebecca Neal; m Elizabeth Ann Williamson, 24 September 1919, St Mary's, Wimbledon. **Subject(s):** Law; BA 1908; MA 1912; LLB 1908. **Tutor(s):** J R Tanner; C E Graves. **Educ:** Dean Close School, Cheltenham. **Career:** Called to the Bar, Inner Temple 1909; Second Lieutenant, RASC (Mechanical Transport), WWI; Solicitor 1923; Solicitor, Maddison, Stirling, Humm and Willett 1939. Died 17 November 1964.

WILLETT, John Arnold (1913) Born 10 February 1895, Banwell, Somerset; son of John James Willett, Corn Merchant, and Eliza Ann Coster. **Tutor(s):** E E Sikes. **Educ:** Clarence School, Weston-Super-Mare; Wycliffe College. **Career:** Private, Gloucestershire Regiment 1914; Second Lieutenant, Prince Albert's Somerset Light Infantry 1914; Lieutenant, Royal Fusiliers 1915. Died 28 June 1915 (missing presumed killed in action in the Dardanelles).

WILLEY, Dr Eric John Baxter (1925) Born 5 June 1901, 23 David Street, Grimsby, Lincolnshire; son of George Willey, Schoolmaster, and Mary Heaton Baxter; m Marjorie. **Subject(s):** Natural Sciences; PhD 1926; MSc (Durham); DSc (London); FRIC. **Tutor(s):** J M Wordie. **Educ:** The Municipal College, Grimsby; Armstrong College, Newcastle upon Tyne. **Career:** Lincolnshire Regiment, WWI; Member, Davy-Faraday Laboratory, Royal Institution of Great Britain; Master, Exeter School 1941; Research Manager, Climax Rock Drill and Engineering Works Ltd 1943; Science Tutor for O and A level pupils, and for University Entrance 1949. **Appointments:** Honorary Scientific Adviser and Chief Technical Reconnaissance Officer (Civil Defence) to Cornwall County Council 1952; Member, Cornwall Organists' Association; Member, Choir of St Mary's Parish Church, Penzance. **Publications:** *Collisions of the second kind: their role in physics and chemistry*, Edward Arnold, 1937; 'The Electrical Measurement of Pressures and Indicator Diagrams', *Journal of Scientific Instruments*, 1946; articles in *Journal of the Chemical Society*. Died 7 August 1967.

WILLEY, Frederick Thomas (1930) Born 13 November 1910, Rose Acre, Shincliffe, Durham; son of Frederick Willey, Architect, and Mary Emma Thompson; m Eleanor Snowdon, 1939; 2 sons, 1 daughter. **Subject(s):** Law; BA 1933; LLB 1935. **Tutor(s):** C W Guillebaud. **Johnian Relatives:** father of Frederick Richard Willey (1964). **Educ:** Preparatory School, Durham; Neville's Cross School, Durham; Johnston School, Durham. **Career:** Parliamentary Private Secretary to the Home Secretary;

Chairman, Select Committee on Estimates; Secretary, Northern Group of Labour MPs; Called to the Bar, Middle Temple 1936; London Fire Service 1939–1945; Labour MP 1945–1981; Parliamentary Secretary to Ministry of Food 1950; Front Bench Spokesman on Education 1961; Minister of Land and Natural Resources 1964; Housing Minister 1967; Chairman, Parliamentary Labour Party 1979. **Appointments:** Member, Fire Brigade's Union; Member, Clerical and Administrative Worker's Union; Member, Haldane Society; Member, Fabian Society; Member, Wood and Green Southgate Divisional Labour Party; Member, Archbishop's Commission 1962. **Publications:** *The Honourable Member*, Sheldon Press, 1974. Died 13 December 1987.

WILLIAMS, Anthony Leonard Stuart (1940) Born 24 February 1921, 16 Earl's Terrace, Kensington, London; son of Leonard Williams, Motor Engineer, and Sybil Ann Smyth. **Tutor(s):** S J Bailey. **Educ:** Seafield School, Bexhill on Sea; Charterhouse. **Career:** Engineering works, J N Napier & Son, Acton.

WILLIAMS, Arthur Hilton (1932) Born 19 September 1913, 46 Elizabeth Street, Ashton-under-Lyne; son of Harold Williams, Railway Clerk, and Ethel Pendlebury. **Subject(s):** Mathematics/Natural Sciences; BA 1935; MA 1939. **Tutor(s):** J M Wordie. **Educ:** Christ Church School, Ashton-under-Lyne; The Secondary School, Ashton-under-Lyne; Bemrose School, Derby. **Career:** Assistant to the District Operating Superintendent, Stoke; Assistant District Operating Superintendent, Barrow; London Midland and Scottish Railway 1935–1942; Army, Transport Division, Control Commission 1942–1946; Assistant District Traffic Superintendent, Barrow 1958; Traffic Assistant to the Divisional Traffic Manager, Merseyside and North Wales Division 1958–1961. **Honours:** MBE 1946.

WILLIAMS, Dr Arthur Warriner (1923) Born 28 August 1905, Hawthorn House, Haltwhistle, Northumberland; son of George James Williams, GP, and Joanna Meyler; m Florence Mary McConnell; 3 sons (John Francis Meyler, Martin James and Andrew Edward), 2 daughters. **Subject(s):** Medicine; BA 1926; MA 1934; MB 1931; MD 1938; MRCP 1946; FRCP 1955; DTM&H 1931. **Tutor(s):** B F Armitage; M P Charlesworth. **Johnian Relatives:** cousin of Walter James Philipps Williams (1927); father of John Francis Meyler Williams (1953) and of Martin James Williams (1958); cousin of John Tabram Hay (1960). **Educ:** Alnmouth Preparatory School; Oundle School; Westminster Hospital Medical School. **Career:** Medical Officer, Colonial Medical Service, Uganda 1931–1946; Physician Specialist, Tanganyika 1947–1949; Physician and Medical Superintendent, Mulago Hospital, Uganda 1949–1951; Head, Department of Medicine 1951–1961, Professor, Department of Medicine 1953–1961, Vice-Principal 1957–1960, Makerere College, University of East Africa; Director, Post-Graduate Medical Studies, University of Oxford 1961–1971. **Appointments:** Titmus Commission on Future Tanganyika Health Services 1962–1964; Fellow, St Cross College, Oxford 1965–1971; Advisory Committee on Low-Price Books for Developing Countries 1966–1974; Member, Board of Governors, United Oxford Hospitals; MRC Tuberculosis Research Committee. **Honours:** CBE 1961. **Publications:** (with R Titmuss et al) *The Health Services of Tanganyika*, 1964; papers on Heart Disease, Tuberculosis, Medical Education and other topics.

WILLIAMS, Coleman Shaler (1926) Born 18 October 1903, 31 West 12th Street, New York, USA; son of Roger Henry Williams, Banker, and Frances Coleman. **Subject(s):** Natural Sciences; BA 1929; MA 1936. **Tutor(s):** J M Wordie. **Educ:** Lawrenceville School; Cornell University. **Career:** Assistant, American Museum of Natural History 1923–1925. Died August 1985.

WILLIAMS, Colin Pascoe (1929) Born 27 June 1910, 28 Alban Road, Llanelly; son of Joseph Pascoe Williams, Secretary and Works Manager, Tinplate Works, and Ethel Alice Dewsberry. **Tutor(s):** C W Guillebaud. **Educ:** Kingsland Grange, Shrewsbury; Shrewsbury School.

WILLIAMS, David Sims (1942) Born 21 May 1925, 9 St Albans Road, Swansea; son of John Williams, Schoolmaster, and Hannah Jenkins. **Subject(s):** Natural Sciences; BA 1945; MA 1974. **Tutor(s):** C W Guillebaud. **Educ:** Deeside Preparatory School, West Kirby; Calday Grange Grammar School, West Kirby.

WILLIAMS, Professor Ernest Frank (1946) Born 18 February 1909, 103 Granville Road, Wood Green, London; son of Bertram John Williams, Works Superintendent, UCL, and Louisa May Collins; m Phil. MA 1946; FRIC; FIFST; FRIPHH. **Educ:** Bounds Green Elementary School; Northern Polytechnic, London. **Career:** Laboratory Assistant, UCL 1924–1930; Laboratory Assistant, Imperial College, London 1930; Research Assistant, Biochemistry Department, University of Cambridge 1943–1945; Senior Principal Scientific Officer, Food Science Advisors' Division, Ministry of Agriculture, Fisheries and Food 1950–1953; Chief Chemist, then Director of Research, J Sainsbury Ltd 1953–1972; Special Professor of Food Hygiene, University of Nottingham 1971–1982. **Appointments:** Chairman, Advisory Board, Food Research Institute, AFRC 1975–1980; Member, Food Additives and Contaminants Committee, Ministry of Agriculture. **Honours:** OBE 1964. Died 7 July 1994.

WILLIAMS, Francis Dillon Mountford (1928) Born 24 March 1911, Victoria Hospital, Hong Kong; son of Ernest Alfred Mountford Williams, Accountant, and Lilian Dillon Smith. BA 1933. **Tutor(s):** J M Wordie. **Educ:** Peak School, Hong Kong; Soulhey Hall, Worthing; Shawnigan Lake Preparatory School, Vancouver Island; Brentwood College, Victoria, Canada.

WILLIAMS, Dr George (1936) Born 6 August 1917, Shrewton, Wiltshire; son of Charles Henry Williams, Farmer, and Thirza Ann Chamings; m Margaret Jean Hoyle; 1 daughter. **Subject(s):** Natural Sciences; BA 1939; MA 1943; Honorary DSc (Heriot-Watt University) 1979; FInstPet; FGS. **Tutor(s):** R L Howland. **Educ:** St Probus School, Salisbury; Truro School. **Career:** Pilot, RAF 1939–1946 (Wing Commander 1943–1946); Chief Executive Shell Companies, British Borneo 1963–1964; Managing Director, Shell UK, Exploration and Production 1964–1973; Director General UK Offshore Operators Association 1975–1984. **Appointments:** Honorary Fellow, Society of Underwater Technology 1989. **Honours:** Commander of the Most Honourable Order of the Crown of Brunei 1965; OBE 1968; CBE 1983.

WILLIAMS, Professor Glanville Llewelyn (1931) Born 15 February 1911, Tremayne, Cowbridge Road, Bridgend, Glamorgan; son of Benjamin Elwey Williams, Tailor, and Gwladys Llewelyn; m Lorna Margaret Lawfield, 1939; 1 son (Rendel Brian Glanville b 11 September 1941). **Subject(s):** Law; BA 1933; MA 1937; PhD 1936; Litt D 1995; LLB (Wales) 1931; LLD (Nottingham) 1963; FBA 1957; QC 1968. **Tutor(s):** C W Guillebaud. **Johnian Relatives:** father of Rendel Brian Glanville Williams (1960). **Educ:** Oldcastle Elementary School, Bridgend; Cowbridge Grammar School; University College of Wales, Aberystwyth. **Career:** Called to the Bar, Middle Temple 1935; Title A Fellow, SJC 1936–1942; Reader in English Law, then Professor of Public Law and Quain Professor of Jurisprudence, London University 1945–1955; Professor of Public Law, LSE 1948; Fellow, Jesus College, Cambridge 1955–1997; Reader in Law 1957–1965, Professor of English Law 1966–1968, Rouse Ball Professor of English Law 1968–1978, University of Cambridge. **Appointments:** Supervisor in Law, SJC 1935–1945; Honorary Master of the Bench, Middle Temple 1966. **Publications:** *Liability for Animals*, 1939; *The Law Reform (Frustrated Contracts) Acts*, 1943; (ed) *Salmon's Jurisprudence*, 1947; *Crown Proceedings*, 1948; *Joint Obligations*, 1949; *Joint Torts and Contributory Negligence*, 1950; *Criminal Law: The General Part*, 1953; *The Proof of Guilt*, 1955; *The Sanctity of Life and The Criminal Law*, 1958; *Textbook of Criminal Law*, 1978; many articles. Died 10 April 1997.

WILLIAMS, Professor Gwyn (1927) Born 27 November 1904, 42 Rutland Park Mansions, Willesden Green, Middlesex; son of William Jones Williams, Secretary to Kodak Ltd, and Mary Williams. PhD 1931.

Tutor(s): J M Wordie. **Educ:** Lady Margaret School, London; University College School, Hampstead; University College of North Wales, Bangor. **Career:** Fellow, University of Wales 1929–1931; Researcher, Department of Colloid Science, Cambridge 1931–1936; Researcher, Research Laboratories, Eastman Kodak Company, Rochester, USA 1936–1937; Lecturer in Chemistry, KCL 1939–1946; Professor of Chemistry, Royal Holloway College, University of London 1946. **Awards:** Strathcona Research Studentship, SJC 1927–1929. Died 6 April 1955.

WILLIAMS, Harry Ben (1913) Born 8 April 1894, 6 Kingsmead Road South, Oxton, Birkenhead, Cheshire; son of Harry Ben Williams, Marine Insurance Broker, and Gertrude Maberley Hassal. **Tutor(s):** E E Sikes. **Educ:** Birkenhead School. Friends' War Victims Relief Expedition, France 1914–1915; Second Lieutenant, The King's Liverpool Regiment 1915–1917. **Honours:** MC. Died 3 May 1917 (killed in action in the Battle of Arras).

WILLIAMS, Henry William Knowlson (1915) Born 4 May 1896, 160 Marylebone Road, London; son of Henry William Williams, Gentleman, and Phoebe Mathilda Griffin. **Tutor(s):** E E Sikes. **Educ:** Preparatory School, Clifton; Clifton College, Harrogate. **Career:** RFC/RAF, WWI. Died 11 July 1917.

WILLIAMS, The Revd Canon Howard (1936) Born 18 March 1908, Rose Villa, Llanwrtyd Wells, Breconshire; son of Benjamin Evan Williams, Baptist Minister, and Hannah Thomas; 2 children. MLitt 1945; BA (Swansea) 1929; Honours (Aberystwyth) 1930; MA 1932. **Tutor(s):** J S Boys Smith. **Educ:** Llanwrtyd Wells Council School; Builth Wells County School; Swansea Grammar School; University College, Swansea; University College, Aberystwyth; St Stephen's House, Oxford. **Career:** Associate, London College of Music 1927; Ordained Deacon 1931–1932; Curate, St Michael, Aberystwyth 1931–1936; Ordained Priest, St David's 1932; Vicar, Llannon 1938–1949; Diocesan Inspector of Schools, St David's 1940–1957; Vicar, Bettws with Ammanford, Carmarthenshire 1949–1957; Lecturer, University of Wales 1950–1970; Vicar, Llanelli 1957–1975; Chaplain, Llanelli Hospitals, Bishop's Examining Chaplain 1957–1975; Canon Residentiary, St David's 1960–1975; Canon Treasurer 1973–1975. **Awards:** Welsh Church Scholarship; Powis Exhibition.

WILLIAMS, Dr Ifor Pennant (1940) Born 1 February 1922, Fairholme, Hereford Road, Abergavenny; son of Thomas Lewis Williams, Schoolmaster, and Rosa Mabel Lee. **Subject(s):** Natural Sciences; BA 1943; MA 1962; BChir 1945; MB 1945; MRCP 1947. **Tutor(s):** R L Howland. **Educ:** Castle Street Infants' School, Abergavenny; Hereford Road Boys' School, Abergavenny; Hereford Cathedral School. **Career:** Consultant Radiologist, Newmarket General Hospitals and Saffron Walden General Hospital 1955–1984. **Awards:** Somerset Exhibition (Wootton Rivers), SJC.

WILLIAMS, Dr Jocelyn Trevor Newcombe (1948) Born 10 February 1928, 1 Westville Road, Newport, Monmouthshire; son of Trevor Williams, Corn Merchant, and Kathleen May Newcombe; m (1) Betty Howell, 5 March 1955, St Woolos Cathedral, Newport (div 1978), (2) Brenda Janet Guyatt (née Lagdon), 25 June 1981, Malvern Registry Office; (1) 1 son (David Guilym b 26 January 1959), 3 daughters (Ann Elizabeth b 18 September 1956, Jennifer Mary b 6 October 1963 and Gillian Myra b 29 May 1967). **Subject(s):** Natural Sciences; BA 1951; MA 1955; MB 1955; BChir 1955; DObstRCOG 1955. **Tutor(s):** G C L Bertram. **Educ:** St Woolos Preparatory School; Newport High School; Felsted School. **Career:** Guy's Hospital 1951–1955; GP, High Wycombe 1956–1966; GP, Stourport-on-Severn 1966–1991.

WILLIAMS, John Brynmor (1936) Born 22 July 1917, Pentwyn, The Parade, Pontypridd; son of Llewelyn Williams, Draper, and May Elizabeth Protheroe. **Subject(s):** Classics/History; BA 1939; MA 1955. **Tutor(s):** R L Howland. **Educ:** Nympsfield C of E School, near Stonehouse; Pontypridd Council School; Whitchurch (Cardiff) Council School; Hereford Cathedral School. **Career:** Teacher Training

1939–1940; OCTU, Plymouth; 504 Coast Regiment, Forth, later Battery Commander and Captain, 368 Coast Battery, Fishguard 1940–1945; Adjutant, OC, 4th Indian Coast Regiment, RA 1945–1946; Schoolmaster and Housemaster, Berkhamsted School 1946–1974. **Awards:** Somerset Exhibition, SJC 1936. Died 13 October 1998.

WILLIAMS, John Dawson Bulpin (1940) Born 17 May 1922, 30 Cumberland Terrace, London, NW1; son of Ernest Ulysses Williams, Physician and Radiologist, and Emma Christine Pillman, Physician and Pathologist; m Fernande Marie Liétard, 1952; 1 son (Alain), 2 daughters (Anne and Susan). **Subject(s):** Economics/Law; BA 1947; MA 1949. **Tutor(s):** R L Howland, C W Guillebaud. **Johnian Relatives:** cousin, once removed, of Thomas Mervyn Sibly (1904); cousin of John Sibly (1938); father of Alain Dominic Dawson Williams (1974). **Educ:** Ryeford Hall Preparatory School; Wycliffe College. **Career:** Captain, RA 1941–1946; Audit Staff member, Peat, Marwick, Mitchell & Co 1947–1955; Consultant, Robson Morrow & Co 1955–1958; Consultant, Robson, Morrow, Nixon & Co (Sydney) 1958–1961; Financial Controller, United Breweries Ltd, Hedges & Butler Ltd, Bass Ltd, Director of Financial Services, Bass Ltd 1962–1982. **Appointments:** Member, ICAS 1952.

WILLIAMS, The Revd John Elwyn Askew (1929) Born 27 November 1909, The Parsonage, Hucknall Torkard, Nottinghamshire; son of James Williams, Clerk in Holy Orders, and Mary Griffiths, Secretary; m Kathleen Ella Ferris Bearder (d 6 July 2002); 4 children. **Subject(s):** History/Theology; BA 1932; MA 1936. **Tutor(s):** M P Charlesworth. **Johnian Relatives:** son of James Williams (1897). **Educ:** Lincoln School; Oswestry Grammar School; Cheltenham College Junior School; Cheltenham College; Lampeter College; Ridley Hall, Cambridge. **Career:** Ordained Deacon 1934; Curate, St Margaret, Rochester 1934–1937; Ordained Priest 1935; Curate, Lenton, Nottinghamshire 1937–1940; CF 1940–1946; Curate, Eakring 1946–1947; Rector, Eakring, Nottinghamshire 1947–1955; Vicar, Winkburn, Nottinghamshire 1947–1955; Vicar, Sutton on the Forest, Yorkshire 1955–1961; Vicar, Whitchurch, Buckinghamshire 1961–1981. **Appointments:** Honorary Chaplain to Stoke Mandville Hospital 1981–1990.

WILLIAMS, The Revd John Howard (1948) Born 23 June 1922, 27 Well Place, Aberdare, Glamorganshire; son of Evan John Williams, Civil Servant, and Elizabeth Mary Florence Newcombe. BA 1950; MA 1954; BA (Wales) 1948. **Tutor(s):** C W Guillebaud. **Educ:** Cwmbach Elementary School; Aberdare Town Elementary School; Aberdare Grammar School; University College, Cardiff. **Awards:** Lewis and Gibson Scholarship, Westminster College, Cambridge.

WILLIAMS, John Ratcliffe (1939) Born 24 September 1920, 5 Cwmdonkin Terrace, Swansea, Wales; son of Percival Ratcliffe Williams, Draper and Furrier, and Violet Mary Gamage; m (1) Valerie Trimble, 3 May 1945 (d 1980), (2) Barbara Nias, 1984; (1) 2 sons, 2 daughters. **Subject(s):** History/Music; BA 1942; MA 1946; MusB 1942; FRSA 1991; FRCO. **Tutor(s):** C W Guillebaud. **Johnian Relatives:** father of Gareth Patrick Williams (1973). **Educ:** All Saints' Choir School, Margaret Street, London; King's School, Canterbury. **Career:** Organist and Choirmaster, All Saints', Margaret Street, London 1948–1952; Organist and Choirmaster, St Mark's, Hamilton Terrace, London 1954–1964; Professor, Royal College of Music 1960–1989; Director of Music, Chapel Royal, HM Tower of London 1965–1988. **Appointments:** Choral Studentship, SJC. Died 17 October 2002.

WILLIAMS, Dr John Vivian (1949) Born 7 February 1931, 44 Abbey Road, Port Talbot, Glamorganshire; son of Thomas Williams, Corporation Inspector of Shops, and Mary Henry; m Audrey Una Anne Taylor, 1963; 1 son (Iain Henry), 1 daughter (Lorna Mary). **Subject(s):** Natural Sciences; BA 1952; MA 1967; BChir 1955; MB 1956; MD 1963; MRCP 1959; FRCP 1969; FCCP 1970. **Tutor(s):** G C L Bertram. **Educ:** Port Talbot Central School; Port Talbot Secondary School. **Career:** Consultant in General Medicine, Pontypridd and Rhondda Hospital

Group 1965–1969; Internal Medicine Specialist and Clinical Professor of Medicine, University of Alberta 1969–1996. **Publications:** Papers on Farmer's Lung and Pulmonary Physiology.

WILLIAMS, Kenneth Sydney (1944) Born 5 June 1927, 19 Bolingbroke Grove, Battersea, London; son of Sydney Williams, Linotype Operator, and Annie Topping; m Ena Hugill, 1954; 1 son, 1 daughter. **Subject(s):** Mechanical Sciences; BA 1947; MA 1951. **Tutor(s):** S J Bailey. **Educ:** Bushey Junior School, Raynes Park; Raynes Park County School; Sorbonne, Paris. **Career:** Director, American plastics manufacturing industry in England and Scotland. **Appointments:** Labour Councillor, Bridgwater (Somerset) Town Council 1956; Council Leader 1958; Chairman, Water Committee, Bridgwater Town Council.

WILLIAMS, Percy Malcolm Wykeham (1908) Born 20 July 1889, 6 St Boniface Road, Ventnor, Isle of Wight; son of David Wykeham Williams, Headmaster, and Lilian Aldridge. **Subject(s):** Mathematics/ Natural Sciences; BA 1911. **Tutor(s):** L H K Bushe-Fox. **Educ:** St Anne's School, Redhill; City of London School. Died 18 April 1962.

WILLIAMS, Peter Henry (1949) Born 29 May 1930, 43 Mill Street, Hereford; son of Henry Williams, Corn Merchant, and Mildred Victoria Beavan; m Alison Christine Williams; 2 sons (Adam Peter and Dominic Ross). **Subject(s):** Classics; BA 1952; MA 1956; Diploma of Classical Archaeology 1953; ARPS 2002. **Tutor(s):** R L Howland. **Educ:** St James' School, Hereford; St Owen's School, Hereford; Cathedral School, Hereford. **Career:** Company Director. **Appointments:** JP 1978–2000; Governor, Hereford Cathedral School 1993–2000. **Awards:** Somerset Exhibition, SJC 1947; First Prize, Lockwood West Award (national open competition for Poetry Speaking) 2002. **Publications:** Poetry in *From the Heart.*

WILLIAMS, Dr Peter Orchard (1944) Born 23 September 1925, Knaggs Hill, Port of Spain, Trinidad; son of Robert Orchard Williams, Deputy Director of Agriculture, Trinidad, and Agnes Annie Birkinshaw; m Billie Innes Brown, 1949; 2 daughters. **Subject(s):** Natural Sciences; BA 1947; MA 1951; BChir 1950; MB 1950; Honorary DSc (Birmingham) 1989, (University of the West Indies) 1991, (Glasgow) 1992; Honorary DM (Nottingham) 1990, (Oxford) 1993; MRCP 1952; FRCP 1970. **Educ:** Caterham School; Queen's Royal College, Trinidad; St Mary's Hospital Medical School. **Career:** House Physician, St Mary's Hospital 1950–1951; Registrar, Royal Free Hospital 1951–1952; Medical Specialist, RAMC, BMH Iserlohn 1954–1955; Medical Officer, Headquarters, MRC 1955–1960; Assistant and Deputy Scientific Secretary 1960–1964, Scientific Secretary 1964–1965, Director 1965–1991, Wellcome Trust. **Appointments:** Member, Committee of Enquiry into Charity Law and Practice, National Council of Social Services 1974–1976; Chairman, Association of Medical Research Charities 1974–1976 and 1979–1983; Vice-President, Royal Society of Tropical Medicine and Hygiene 1975–1977; Chairman, Foundations Forum 1977–1979; Member, BBC/IBA Central Appeals Advisory Committee 1978–1983; Chairman, Hague Club (European Foundations) 1981–1983; Director, Wellcome Institute for the History of Medicine 1981–1983; DHSS Joint Planning Advisory Committee 1986; President, Royal Society of Tropical Medicine and Hygiene 1991–1993; Honorary Visiting Fellow, Green College, Oxford 1993; Honorary Fellow LSHTM 1986. **Awards:** Mary Kingsley Medal for Services to Tropical Medicine, Liverpool School of Tropical Medicine 1983. **Honours:** CBE 1991. **Publications:** *Careers in Medicine*, 1952; papers in scientific journals; memoirs.

WILLIAMS, Professor Phillip (1944) Born 30 August 1926, Brynteg, Heol-y-Bunsey, Pontypridd, Glamorganshire; son of Edward Watkin Williams, Schoolmaster, and Ceinwen James; m Glenys Lodwick Davies, 1950; 2 sons, 1 daughter. **Subject(s):** Natural Sciences; BA 1948; MA 1951; BSc (London); PhD (London) 1959; Teacher's Diploma (London) 1949; Educational Psychology Qualification (Tavistock Clinic) 1953; FBPsS. **Tutor(s):** C W Guillebaud. **Educ:** Pontypridd County School;

The Leys School, Cambridge. **Career:** Teacher and Educational Psychologist 1949–1961; Lecturer, then Senior Lecturer in Education, University of Wales, Swansea 1961–1970; Professor, latterly Dean of Educational Studies, Open University 1970–1979; Professor and Dean of Education 1979–1983, Emeritus Professor 1983, University of Wales, Bangor. **Appointments:** President, National Council for Special Education; Chairman, Schools Council Committee for Wales; Member of various Government Committees and professional bodies including Summerfield Committee, Warnock Committee, Social Science Research Council Psychology Committee, University Grants Committee, Education Sub-Committee, Schools Council, Welsh Advisory Board for Higher Education, Schools Broadcasting Council for Wales. **Awards:** Leverhulme Emeritus Fellowship. **Publications:** *Children and Psychologists*, Hodder and Stoughton, London, 1977; *A Glossary of Special Education*, 1988; *The Special Education Handbook*, 1991; *The Edge of Death* (novel), 2003; author and contributor, various books, articles and other publications.

WILLIAMS, Philip Gresham (1919) Born 18 May 1898, Rooksbury, Gombards Road, St Albans, Hertfordshire; son of Edward James Williams, Member, London Stock Exchange, and Ethel Hunt. BA 1921. **Tutor(s):** E E Sikes. **Educ:** Allen House Preparatory School, Hook Heath; St Bees School.

WILLIAMS, Ralph Norman Haile (1921) Born 12 January 1903, Wellmeadow, Bream, Newland, Gloucestershire; son of Ralph Williams, Master Draper and Grocer, and Alice Evaline Haile. **Tutor(s):** B F Armitage. **Educ:** Bream Infant School; Sydney Secondary School; Wycliffe College, Stonehouse.

WILLIAMS, Raymond Howel (1944) Born 19 October 1927, Oakdene, Wrea Green, Kirkham, Lancashire; son of Evan John Williams, Schoolmaster, and Emily Gertrude Smith. **Subject(s):** Geography/English; BA 1947; MA 1951. **Tutor(s):** C W Guillebaud. **Educ:** Kirkham Grammar School. **Career:** Schoolmaster 1973; Auxiliary Minister, St Peter's Church, Derby 1973–1975; Priest in Charge, St Paul's Church, Hadley Wood 1975. **Awards:** Exhibition, SJC 1944.

WILLIAMS, Reginald Arnold Forrest (1924) Born 7 April 1906, 37 Quai de la Tournelle, Paris, France; son of Tom Alfred Williams, Physician, and Minnie Forrest; m Phoebe; 1 daughter (Jacqueline), 1 stepson (Peter), 1 stepdaughter (Anne). BA 1927. **Tutor(s):** E E Sikes. **Educ:** Highfield School, Liphook; Harrow School. Died 25 July 1989.

WILLIAMS, Reginald John Cyril (1919) Born 17 September 1899, 44 Bridget Street, Rugby, Warwickshire; son of John Williams, Factory Manager, and Elizabeth Nicholls. **Subject(s):** Natural Sciences; BA 1922. **Tutor(s):** E E Sikes. **Educ:** The King's School, Peterborough. **Career:** Wireless Operator in charge, HMT *Phoebe* 1916–1919. **Awards:** Munsteven Exhibition, SJC 1918.

WILLIAMS, Richard Derrick (1943) Born 30 March 1926, Whitchurch, Shropshire; son of Richard Leslie Williams, Clerk with Railway Clearing House, and Elizabeth Paddington; m Beryl Newbury Stonebanks, 1949; 4 sons. **Subject(s):** History; BA 1949; MA 1953. **Tutor(s):** C W Guillebaud; F Thistlethwaite. **Educ:** Whitchurch Council School; Whitchurch Grammar School. **Career:** Chief Education Officer, County of Avon 1972–1977; Principal, Gloucestershire College of Arts and Technology 1977–1989; President, Educational Centres Association 1979–1989.

WILLIAMS, The Revd Richard Lloyd (1910) Born 22 August 1890, 203 Albion Road, Stoke Newington, Middlesex; son of John Railton Williams, gentleman of independent means, and Esther Jones. BA 1913; MA 1917. **Tutor(s):** J R Tanner. **Educ:** Paradise House School, Stoke Newington; Wells Theological College. **Career:** Deacon 1914; Curate, Bridgwater with Chilton 1914–1917; Priest 1916; War Service 1917–1919; Curate, Dunster 1919–1927; Vicar, Leigh on Mendip 1927–1954; In Charge, St Michael, Alcombe 1929–1954. Died 20 May 1954.

WILLIAMS, Professor Robert Deryck (1936) Born 27 November 1917, 3 Paradise Lane, Hall Green, Birmingham; son of Robert Williams, Solicitor, and Eileen Gertrude Parkin; m Grace (d 1979); 3 daughters (Jane, Susan and Elizabeth). **Subject(s):** Classics; BA 1939; MA 1946. **Tutor(s):** R L Howland. **Educ:** Yorks House School, Birmingham; King Edward VI High School, Birmingham. **Career:** International teaching: Chicago, Pennsylvania, Ottawa, Victoria, Canberra, Perth, Melbourne, Otago; Officer, RAF Special Duties Branch, Persia and Middle East 1939–1945; Lecturer in Classics 1945, Senior Lecturer, Reader, Professor in Classics 1974, University of Reading. **Appointments:** President, Virgil Society 1975; President, Classical Association 1981. **Awards:** Scholarship, SJC 1936–1937; Wright's Prize, SJC 1939; Graves Prize, SJC 1939. **Publications:** (ed) *The Aeneid of Virgil, Books I–VI*, 1972, *Books VII–XII*, 1973; *Aeneas and the Roman Hero*, 1973; (with T S Pattie) *Virgil: His Poetry Through the Ages*, 1982. Died 9 July 1986.

WILLIAMS, Dr Robert Martin (1945) Born 30 March 1919, Opawa, Christchurch, New Zealand; son of Henry Williams, Clerk in Holy Orders, and Ethel Florence Martin; m Mary Constance Thorpe, 1944; 1 son (Anthony Martin b 1949), 2 daughters (Elizabeth Janet b 1946 and Bridget Rosamund b 1948). **Subject(s):** Mathematics; BA 1947; PhD 1950; MA (New Zealand) 1940; Honorary LLD (Otago) 1972. **Tutor(s):** J M Wordie. **Educ:** St Mark's School, Christchurch; Dunelm, Christchurch; Christ's College, Christchurch; Canterbury University College, Christchurch. **Career:** Researcher, Radio Development Laboratory, DSIR, Wellington, New Zealand 1940–1944; Researcher, Berkeley, California Manhattan Project, USA 1944–1945; Director, Applied Mathematics Laboratories, DSIR 1953–1962; Member 1963–1966, Chairman 1979–1981, State Services Commission, New Zealand; Vice Chancellor, University of Otago, New Zealand 1967–1972; Vice Chancellor, ANU 1973–1974. **Appointments:** President, New Zealand Statistical Association; President, New Zealand Book Council; President, National Library Society; Member, International Statistical Institute; Chairman, Policy Committee of the *Dictionary of New Zealand Biography*. **Awards:** Shirtcliffe Travelling Fellow. **Honours:** CBE 1973; CB 1981. **Publications:** Several papers, mainly in Mathematical Statistics.

WILLIAMS, Sir Robin Philip (1948) Born 27 May 1928, 125 Howards Lane, Putney, London; son of Sir Herbert Geraint Williams, MP, Civil Engineer, and Dorothy Frances Burton-Jones; m Wendy Adele Marguerite Alexander, 19 February 1955; 2 sons (Anthony Geraint and Stephen Robin Alexander). **Subject(s):** Law/Economics; BA 1950; MA 1955. **Tutor(s):** J M Wordie. **Johnian Relatives:** nephew of Richard McNair Jones (1905); son-in-law of Felix Alexander Joseph (1913); father of Anthony Geraint Williams (1977). **Educ:** Eaton House School, Eaton Gate; St Andrew's School, Eastbourne; Eton College. **Career:** Second Lieutenant, RA 1947; Called to the Bar, Middle Temple 1954; Lloyd's Underwriter 1961–1999; Insurance Broker 1972–1991. **Appointments:** Vice-Chairman, Federation of University Conservative and Unionist Associations 1951–1952; Chairman, Bow Group (Conservative Research Society) 1954; Councillor, Haringey 1968–1974; Chairman, Anti-Common Market League 1969–1984; Director, Common Market Safeguards Campaign 1973–1976; Honorary Secretary, Safeguard Britain Campaign 1976–1989; Honorary Secretary, Campaign for an Independent Britain 1989. **Publications:** *Whose Public Schools?*, 1957.

WILLIAMS, Dr Roger Lester (1914) Born 8 September 1896, 36 Spelman Street, Carmarthen; son of Edward Richard Williams, Surgeon, and Laura Elizabeth Lester. BA 1917; MD 1923; MRCS; LRCP 1919; FRCS 1923. **Tutor(s):** R P Gregory. **Educ:** Carmarthen High School; Carmarthen Grammar School; Epsom College. **Career:** Resident Surgeon, Sheffield Royal Infirmary; Clinical Assistant, St Peter's Hospital for Stone; Surgeon in charge of out-patients, Seaman's Hospital, Greenwich; Honorary Surgeon, Passmore Edwards Hospital, Wood Green, and London Lock Hospital; Assistant Surgical Officer, Royal Northern Hospital; Clinical Assistant, Great Ormond Street

Children's Hospital; Senior House Surgeon, St Bartholomew's Hospital and Metropolitan Hospital.

WILLIAMS, Rowland James (1938) Born 19 July 1919, 1 Hanover Street, Merthyr Tydfil, Wales; son of William James Williams, Director of Education, City of Cardiff, and Margaret Ann Simons, Schoolteacher; m Margaret Beulah Blake, 1945; 1 daughter (Margaret Jill b 1947). **Subject(s):** Natural Sciences; BA 1941; MA 1946; MB 1946; BChir 1946; FRCS; LRCP (London). **Tutor(s):** R L Howland. **Educ:** Kirby Preparatory School, Middlesbrough; Middlesbrough High School; Cardiff High School; University College, Cardiff; University College Hospital London. **Career:** Consultant Surgeon, Merthyr and Aberdare HMC 1953–1959; Consultant General Surgeon, Pontypridd and Rhondda Hospital Management Committee Group 1959–1983; Chairman, Cardiac Project Team, University Hospital of Wales 1986–1989; Chairman, Welsh Heart Programme 1985–1989; Medical Officer, Complaints, Welsh Office, Cardiff, Wales 1986–1989. **Awards:** Goldsmid Entrance Scholarship, UCH 1941. **Honours:** OBE 1985.

WILLIAMS, Samuel Dudley (1921) Born 25 June 1903, 2 Mina Street, Llanelly, Carmarthenshire; son of Joseph Howell Williams, Timber Merchant, and Charlotte Eleanor Evans. BA 1924; MA 1942. **Tutor(s):** B F Armitage. **Educ:** Llanelly School; Shrewsbury School. **Career:** Works Manager, Tinplate Manufacturers; TA, WWII (invalided out 1941); Ministry of Aircraft Production. Died 27 February 1947.

WILLIAMS, Thomas Hewett (1933) Born 12 February 1915, 6 Johnson Street, Pendlebury, Lancashire; son of Thomas Williams, Colliery Winding Engineer, and Margaret Softley; m Dorothy Reed, 27 August 1942, Methodist Chapel, Alford, Lincs; 1 daughter (Ann). **Subject(s):** Modern and Medieval Languages; BA 1936. **Tutor(s):** C W Guillebaud. **Educ:** Halton Bank Council School, Pendleton; Manchester Grammar School. **Career:** Head of Modern Languages 1939–1977, Deputy Headmaster 1964–1977, Acting Headmaster Autumn Term 1974, Queen Elizabeth I Grammar School, Alford, Lincs; RA, Gunner, then First Airborne, Languages Instructor and Motorcycle Courier, served in NW Europe, N Africa, Italy and Norway 1940–1946. Died 4 January 1999.

WILLIAMS, Walter James Philipps (1927) Born 11 November 1903, Cefn-y-dre, Fishguard, Pembrokeshire; son of Walter Levi Williams, Solicitor, and Martha Philipps Harries; 2 sons (Dafydd and Owen), 2 daughters (Susan and Rachel). LLB 1929; LLB (London) 1926. **Tutor(s):** C W Guillebaud. **Johnian Relatives:** cousin of Arthur Warriner Williams (1923), John Francis Meyler Williams (1953), Martin James Williams (1958) and of John Tabram Hay (1960). **Educ:** County School, Fishguard; Cheltenham College. **Career:** Senior Partner, Phillips, Williams & Co (Solicitors), Haverfordwest. **Appointments:** Chairman, Pembrokeshire County Council; Council and Court of University of Wales; Member, Welsh Books Council. **Honours:** OBE 1974. Died 10 August 1987.

WILLIAMS, William (1924) Born 10 March 1905, 21 Picton Terrace, Carmarthen; son of William Jenkins Williams, Tin Plate Manufacturer, and Annie Margery Evans. **Tutor(s):** B F Armitage. **Educ:** St Andrew's, Tenby; Harper Adams College, Newport.

WILLIAMS, Lieutenant Colonel William Henry (1913) Born 21 January 1893, Langstone Rectory, Newport, Monmouthshire; son of William Henry Williams, Clerk in Holy Orders, and Gertrude Martha Butler. **Tutor(s):** E E Sikes. **Educ:** Stancliffe Hall, Matlock; Hereford Cathedral School. **Career:** RMC, Camberley 1914; Commissioned RASC 1914; Commander, 23rd Division Ammunition Park 1916; Adjutant, 10th Corps, Siege Park 1917–1918; Adjutant, RASC, Cork 1920–1922; Commander, 9 Mechanical Transport Company to Turkey, General Military Service 1922–1930; Life Underwriter for Manufacturers' Life Insurance Company of Canada 1930. **Honours:** MBE; MC. Died 15 December 1960.

WILLIAMS, Sir William Law (1926) Born 1 May 1907, Pabble, Girtin, District of Omagh, County Tyrone, Ireland; son of Sir Frederick Law Williams, Captain, Dorset Regiment, and Emily Reid; m Betty Kathleen Taylor, 22 May 1950. BA 1930. **Tutor(s):** E A Benians. **Educ:** Sherborne School; Crouch House, Crouch, Borough Green; Hopedene, Hillingdon, Eastbourne. **Career:** Captain, Royal Welch Fusiliers. Died 1 July 1960.

WILLIAMS, The Revd William Troth (1910) Born 4 July 1892, Causewayside, Linthwaite, Yorkshire; son of William Thomas Williams, Clerk in Holy Orders, and Florence Troth. **Subject(s):** Theology; BA 1914; MA 1918. **Tutor(s):** J R Tanner. **Educ:** The Grammar School, Bury St Edmunds; Westcott House, Cambridge. **Career:** Cambridge Mission to Delhi 1914–1922; Deacon 1919; Priest 1920; SPG Missionary, Gurgaon, Punjab 1922–1945; Furlough 1945; Vicar, Shudy Camos, and Rector, Castle Camps 1952–1958. Died 27 March 1958.

WILLIAMSON, John Christopher (1942) Born 28 March 1924, Queen Mary Nursing Home, Derby; son of John Hibberd Williamson, Manager, Oil Company, and Marjorie Davidson. **Tutor(s):** C W Guillebaud. **Educ:** Hymers College, Hull; Whitehaven County Secondary School.

WILLIS, George Geoffrey Lightly (1925) Born 16 May 1908, 122 Inverness Terrace, Paddington, London; son of John Willis, Member, London Stock Exchange, and Hester Catharine Lewis; m Peggy; 1 son (Michael). BA 1930. **Tutor(s):** B F Armitage. **Educ:** Arnold House School, London; Tonbridge School. **Career:** Lieutenant Colonel, 3rd County of London Yeomanry (Sharpshooters), WWII. **Honours:** DSO (WWII). Died 17 July 1943 (killed in Sicily).

WILLMER, Professor Edward Nevill (1930) Born 15 August 1902, 66 Park Road, West Claughton, Birkenhead, Cheshire; son of Arthur Washington Willmer, Cotton Broker, and Janet Mary Cooper; m Henrietta (Penny) Noreen Rowlatt, 11 March 1939 (d 1998); 2 sons (Patrick and Hugh), 2 daughters (Janet and Erica). **Subject(s):** Zoology; MA 1929; ScD (Clare) 1944; BA (Oxon); MSc (Manchester) 1960; FRS. **Educ:** Birkenhead Preparatory School; Birkenhead School; Corpus Christi College, Oxford. **Career:** Assistant Lecturer and Demonstrator, University of Manchester 1924–1929; Lecturer in Physiology 1929–1948, Reader in Histology 1948, Professor of Histology 1966–1969 (Emeritus 1969), University of Cambridge; Fellow, Clare College, Cambridge 1936. **Appointments:** Member, Botanic Garden Syndicate. **Publications:** *Tissue Culture*, 1935; *Retinal Structure and Colour Vision*, 1946; *Cytology and Evolution*, 1960; *Cells and tissues in culture: Methods, biology and physiology*, 3 Volumes, 1965–1966; *Old Grantchester*, 1967; *The River Cam*, 1979; *The New Heritage Grantchester*, 1981; *Waen and the Willmers*, 1988; (introduction and illustrations) *What the poet saw: an illustrated edition of 'The Old Vicarage, Grantchester'*, 1993; *The Sallow Bush*, 1999. Died 8 April 2001.

WILLMORE, Dr Patrick Lever (1939) Born 20 February 1921, Royton House, Mount Sion, Tonbridge Wells; son of Alfred Willmore, Traveller for an Oil Company, and Hilda Mary Lever. **Subject(s):** Natural Sciences; BA 1942; MA 1946; PhD 1950. **Tutor(s):** C W Guillebaud. **Educ:** Homefield Preparatory School, Worthing; High School for Boys, Worthing. **Career:** Title A Fellow 1946–1949, Title E Fellow 1949–1952, SJC; Seismologist to the Government of Canada 1952. **Appointments:** Imperial Chemical Industries Fellow, University of Cambridge 1948–1951. **Awards:** Scholarship, SJC. Died 2 March 1994.

WILLS, Eric Foulger (1908) Born 1 February 1890, 11 Upper Belgrave Street, Clifton, Bristol; son of Samuel Day Wills, Magistrate, Bristol, and Eva Blanche Tubbs; m Helen Irene Ridges; 1 son (John Brian b 12 September 1928). **Subject(s):** History; BA 1911; MA 1919. **Tutor(s):** J R Tanner. **Johnian Relatives:** father of John Brian Wills (1948); grandfather of Susannah Helen Wills (1988). **Educ:** Clifton College; Leighton Park School, Reading. **Career:** Schoolmaster; Settlement Warden. Died 4 May 1961.

WILLS, George Saunders (1940) Born 1 May 1921, Wesley Manse, Pocklington, Yorkshire; son of Verrant Wills, Methodist Minister, and Laura Helen Stone. **Subject(s):** Modern Languages. **Tutor(s):** C W Guillebaud. **Educ:** Williton Elementary School, Somerset; Tiverton Elementary School, Devon; St Hilary Elementary School, Cornwall; Kingswood School, Bath. **Career:** Flight Lieutenant, RAF 1940–1945. Died 8 December 1946.

WILLS, Gerald Alfred (1919) Naval Officer.

WILLS, John Brian (1948) Born 12 September 1928, Rockleaze, Dousland, Walkhampton, Devon; son of Eric Foulger Wills, Settlement Warden, and Helen Irene Ridges; m Patricia Margaret Ann Alford; 1 daughter (Susannah Helen b 17 December 1968). **Subject(s):** Economics/Geography; BA 1950; MA 1955. **Tutor(s):** C W Guillebaud. **Johnian Relatives:** son of Eric Foulger Wills (1908); father of Susannah Helen Wills (1988). **Career:** Compilation Officer, Department of Soil and Land Use Survey, Ghana; Editor, *Ghana Crop Science Journal*; Ministry of Overseas Development, 1966.

WILLS, Dr Lancelot Kenneth (1920) Born 6 February 1902, 59 Apsley Road, Clifton, Gloucestershire; son of Walter Kenneth Wills, Dermatologist, and Kathleen Isabella Tubbs; 1 daughter. BA 1924; MA 1927; BChir 1933; MB 1933. **Tutor(s):** E E Sikes. **Johnian Relatives:** son of Walter Kenneth Wills (1891). **Educ:** Clifton College. **Career:** GP, Neasden; RAMC, WWII. **Appointments:** Divisional Surgeon and Examiner to the Red Cross and St John's Ambulance; Honorary Physician, Willesden General Hospital; Honorary Dermatologist, Central Middlesex Hospital. Died 20 December 1970.

WILMERS, Charles Kossman (1927) Born 6 January 1909, 14 Hall Road, St Marylebone, London; son of Ernest Wilmers and Julia Szkolny. **Subject(s):** Modern and Medieval Languages; BA 1930. **Tutor(s):** M P Charlesworth. **Educ:** School for Children of British Officers, Cologne; Bootham School, York. **Awards:** Scholarship, SJC 1926.

WILMERS, John Geoffrey (1938) See WILMERSDOERFFER.

WILMERSDOERFFER, Hans Max (WILMERS, John Geoffrey) (1938) Born 27 December 1920, Munich; son of Ernst Wilmersdoerffer, Referender Doktor der Staatswissenschaften, and Martha Schimmelburg; m June Mecredy, 1946; 1 son, 2 daughters. **Subject(s):** Law; BA 1941; QC 1965. **Tutor(s):** C W Guillebaud. **Educ:** Primary State School, Munich, Germany; Gymnasium, Munich, Germany; Gymnasium, Bienne, Switzerland; Leighton Park School, Reading. **Career:** Commando, Army and SAS, WWII; Called to the Bar, Inner Temple 1948; Deputy Chairman, Hampshire Quarter Sessions 1970–1978; Recorder, then Bencher, Inner Temple 1972–1978; Judge, Appeal Court of Jersey and Guernsey 1978. **Appointments:** Bencher, Inner Temple; Recorder, Crown Court; Governor, Leighton Park School. Died 17 December 1984.

WILMORE, Albert Nelson (1908) Born 16 April 1889, Gladstone Terrace, Trawden, Colne, Lancashire; son of Albert Wilmore, Schoolmaster, and Hannah Wormwell. **Tutor(s):** J R Tanner. **Educ:** Colne Municipal Secondary Day School; Manchester Grammar School.

WILMOT-DEAR, Peter William (1943) Born 15 August 1925, 85 Dalberg Road, Brixton; son of Arthur Ernest Dear, Property Manager, and Mabel Wilmot; m Jean Thompson, 1949; 1 son (Michael Raymond b 1961), 2 daughters (Ann Patricia b 1950 and Christine Melanie b 1952). **Subject(s):** Natural Sciences; BA 1946; CertEd 1949. **Tutor(s):** C W Guillebaud. **Johnian Relatives:** father of Michael Raymond Wilmot-Dear (1980). **Educ:** Clapham High School, Kindergarten; Dulwich College Preparatory School; Dulwich College. **Career:** Sub-Lieutenant, RNVR 1945–1947; Research Department, Mullard Radio Valve 1947–1948; Teacher, Westminster City School 1949–1951; Teacher, Dulwich College 1951–1952; Head of Biology, King's School, Peterborough 1953–1959; Head of Sciences, Girls' Grammar School,

Stevenage 1959–1966; Head of Chemistry, Wyndham School, Egremont 1966–1973.

WILMOTT, Alfred James (1906) Born 31 December 1888, Tottenham, Middlesex; son of Alfred John Wilmott, Schoolmaster, and Hannah Butler; m 1914; 1 son. **Subject(s):** Natural Sciences; BA 1909; MA 1936. **Tutor(s):** J R Tanner. **Educ:** Cambridge and County School. **Career:** Natural History Museum 1911; Deputy Keeper, Botany Department, Natural History Museum 1931–1950. **Awards:** Frank Smart Prize, University of Cambridge 1910. **Publications:** Papers on Taxonomy of British plants; papers for *Journal of Botany*. Died 27 January 1950.

WILSON, Alan Sydney (1913) Born 15 February 1894, 53 Waverley Road, Redland, Bristol, Gloucestershire; son of William Wilson, Higher Education Secretary, and Elizabeth Finnie. **Subject(s):** Medicine. **Tutor(s):** R P Gregory. **Educ:** Manchester Grammar School. **Career:** Private, Royal Scots 1914; Second Lieutenant, Lancashire Fusiliers 1914, transferred to South Lancashire Regiment, then MGC 1914–1917. Died 23 April 1917 (missing, presumed killed, in Scarpe Valley, France).

WILSON, Dr Alasdair Robertson (1931) Born 3 October 1909, Trafford House, Liscard, Wallasey, Cheshire; son of Andrew Robertson Wilson, Medical Practitioner, and Alice Owen; 4 sons. PhD 1936; BSc (Edinburgh) 1931. **Tutor(s):** C W Guillebaud. **Educ:** Somerville School, New Brighton; Bois Gentil, Chateau d'Oex, Switzerland; Down House School, Sussex; University of Edinburgh. **Career:** Deputy Director, Scottish Crops Research Institute. **Awards:** Scholarship, Ministry of Agriculture. Died 10 April 1984.

WILSON, Allan Curtis (1947) Born 3 April 1925, 23 Millicent Road, West Bridgford, Nottingham; son of Arthur Wilson, Sales Manager; m Pamela Kilner, 9 June 1951; 1 son (Nicholas), 2 daughters (Diana and Helen). **Subject(s):** Modern and Medieval Languages; BA 1949; MA 1954; ACII; FCIB, FInstD. **Tutor(s):** C W Guillebaud. **Educ:** Royal Grammar School, Newcastle upon Tyne. **Career:** Lieutenant, RA and Royal Indian Artillery 1943–1947; London Insurance Market 1950–1985 (Director of Lowndes Lambert UK Ltd, Lloyd's Brokers, and predecessor Companies 1963–1985). **Appointments:** Freeman, City of London 1959; Liveryman, Worshipful Company of Pattenmakers 1959; Underwriting Member of Lloyd's 1976–1996; General Commissioner of Income Tax 1987–1996. **Awards:** Bain Prize for Foreign Languages, Chartered Insurance Institute 1951.

WILSON, Andrew Thomas (1947) Born 21 June 1926, Mount Pleasant Farm, Newton Road, St Helens, Lancashire; son of John Wilson, Farmer, and Gertrude Lucas. **Subject(s):** Agriculture; BSc (Leeds) 1947. **Educ:** Parr Flat Junior School; Cowley School; University of Leeds. **Awards:** Colonial Agricultural Scholarship.

WILSON, Professor Arthur James Cochran (1938) Born 28 November 1914, Springhill, Nova Scotia, Canada; son of Arthur Augustine Cuthbert Wilson, Physician, and Hildegarde Gretchen Geldert; m Harriett Charlotte Friedeberg; 2 sons, 1 daughter. PhD 1942; BSc (Dalhousie) 1934; MSc (Dalhousie) 1936; PhD (MIT) 1938; LLD (Dalhousie) 1991; FRS 1963; FIM; FInstP; FRS. **Tutor(s):** J M Wordie. **Educ:** Springhill Public Schools, Halifax; King's Collegiate School, Windsor; King's College, Dalhousie University, Canada; Massachusetts Institute of Technology, USA. **Career:** Research Assistant, Cavendish Laboratory, University of Cambridge 1940–1945; Lecturer in Physics, University College, Cardiff 1945; Senior Lecturer 1946, Professor of Physics 1954–1965, University of Cambridge; Professor of Crystallography, Department of Physics, Birmingham University 1965–1982. **Appointments:** Editor, *Acta Crystallographica* 1960–1977. Died 1 July 1995.

WILSON, Arthur Wesley (1915) Born 25 March 1897, 26 Sydney Avenue, Blackrock, County Dublin, Ireland; son of Samuel Wesley Wilson, Physician and Surgeon, and Annie Elizabeth Jones-Lloyd. **Tutor(s):** R P

Gregory. **Educ:** Stanley House School, Margate; Denstone College. **Career:** Second Lieutenant, Scots Guards, Machine Gun Company, WWI. Died 30 July 1917 (killed in action).

WILSON, Austin James (1926) Born 20 July 1908, Vacoas, Plaines Wilhelms, Mauritius; son of Alfred James Wilson, Planter, and Anna Marie d'Avray. **Tutor(s):** E A Benians. **Johnian Relatives:** cousin of Frederick Donald d'Avray Turney (1929); brother of Frank Albert Wilson (1932); uncle of Austin Raymond Wilson (1957). **Educ:** Seafield Park, Fareham; Royal College, Mauritius; Brighton College. Died 18 November 1930.

WILSON, Campbell Aubrey Kenneth (1926) Born 20 June 1905, 41 Maison Dieu Road, Dover, Kent; son of Raleigh Alban Kenneth Wilson, Lieutenant, Shropshire Light Infantry, and Mary Angela Walker. **Tutor(s):** J M Wordie. **Educ:** Belvedere, Hove; Fettes College, Edinburgh; RMA, Woolwich.

WILSON, David Arthur Calder (1901) Born 24 September 1882, Felix House, Brixton Rise, Brixton, Surrey; son of David Henry Wilson, Barrister, and Rosalie Rendle. **Tutor(s):** D MacAlister. **Educ:** Private Tuition.

WILSON, David Binnie (1941) Born 8 February 1923, 10 Coates Crescent, Edinburgh; son of George David Wilson, Chartered Accountant, and Margaret Dorothy Carrington-Smith; m Rosalie Winifred Nicolls, 27 March 1947; 1 daughter (Anne Yvonne). **Subject(s):** Modern Languages. **Tutor(s):** C W Guillebaud. **Educ:** Manor House, Horsham; Shrewsbury School. **Career:** Fleet Air Arm and Royal Marines Captain, WWII; TA Major, post WWII; Export Executive. **Appointments:** Fellow, Institute of Directors. **Honours:** TD.

WILSON, Edward Raynold (1920) Naval Officer.

WILSON, Frank Albert (1932) Born 5 May 1914, Vacoas, Plaines Wilhelms, Mauritius; son of Albert James Wilson, Planter, and Anna Marie d'Avray. **Subject(s):** Natural Sciences; BA 1938; MA 1944. **Tutor(s):** C W Guillebaud. **Johnian Relatives:** brother of Austin James Wilson (1926); cousin of Frederick Donald d'Avray Turney (1929); father of Austin Raymond Wilson (1957). **Educ:** St Christopher's School, Eastbourne; Royal College, Mauritius; Brighton College; Private Tuition. **Career:** Nutrition Officer, Mauritius; Research on the vitamin content of local foodstuffs 1944.

WILSON, Gardiner (1901) Born 17 December 1882, The Park, Alpeston, Hendon, Middlesex; son of John Strange Wilson, Gentleman, and Elizabeth Makins. **Subject(s):** Classics; BA 1904; MA 1908. **Tutor(s):** E E Sikes. **Educ:** Yarmouth Grammar School; Hereford Cathedral School. **Career:** Master, Mr Littlejohn's Naval School, Greenwich 1904; Master, Loughborough Grammar School 1908; Lieutenant, Norfolk Regiment, WWI. Died 7 April 1972.

WILSON, Geoffrey Malcolm (1948) Born 17 September 1928, Singapore; son of Henry Ernest Wilson, Insurance Agent, and Winifred Woodcock; m Rachel; 4 children. **Subject(s):** History; BA 1950. **Tutor(s):** F Thistlethwaite. **Educ:** Terrington Hall Preparatory School; Sedbergh School. **Career:** Reckitt & Colman, Hull, then transferred to Cape Town. Died December 2002.

WILSON, George James (1903) Born 26 March 1885, Maguiresbridge, Fermanagh, Ireland; son of William Wilson, Travelling Methodist Minister, Australia, and Elizabeth Payne. **Tutor(s):** D MacAlister. **Educ:** Campbell College, Belfast. **Awards:** Scholarship, SJC. Died 11 October 1905.

WILSON, George Thomas Jamieson (1931) Born 5 September 1907, Kumara, New Zealand; son of George Wilson, Dredge Master, and Edith Alice Jamieson. **Subject(s):** History; BA 1933; MA 1947; MA (New Zealand) 1930. **Tutor(s):** E A Benians. **Educ:** Greymouth District High School, New Zealand; Canterbury College, University of New Zealand. **Career:** Teacher, Christchurch Schools; Lecturer in History and Political Science, Canterbury College, University of New Zealand; Meteorologist, Air Force, WWII; Lecturer in History 1945–1946, Senior Lecturer in History 1947–1972, Warden, Hytten Hall 1960–1974, University of Tasmania. **Appointments:** Fellow, National University of Australia 1949; President, Staff Association, University of Tasmania 1960s; marriage celebrant. **Publications:** *The Golden Grey: an historical treatise on the Grey district during the provincial period, 1854–1876* (MA Thesis), 1930; *A Report on Local Government*, 1944; 'A History of Canterbury' (manuscripts), c1957. Died 1991.

WILSON, Gordon (1926) Born 15 February 1907, 49 Rubislaw Den, South Aberdeen, Scotland; son of James Adam Wilson, Science Master, Robert Gordon's College, Aberdeen, and Elizabeth Taylor Riddall Henderson; m Jean; 2 daughters (Margaret and Elizabeth). **Subject(s):** Classics/English; BA 1929; MA 1957. **Tutor(s):** M P Charlesworth. **Educ:** Aberdeen Grammar School; Robert Gordon's College, Aberdeen; Fettes College, Edinburgh. **Career:** Cadet, Nigerian Administrative Service, Colonial Office; Gaskiya Corporation, 1945; Institute of Administration, Colonial Office, Zaria, Northern Nigeria. **Publications:** (ed) *Gaskiya Ta Fi Kwabo*, 1944. Died 20 September 1985.

WILSON, Harris (1930) Born 18 January 1911, Manchester, Lancashire; son of Richard Wilson, Schoolmaster, and Gertrude Harris; m Kathleen Mabel Smith; 1 son, 1 daughter. **Subject(s):** Classics; BA 1933; MA 1937. **Tutor(s):** M P Charlesworth. **Johnian Relatives:** father of Richard Harris Wilson (1960). **Educ:** Hague Street Municipal School; Manchester Grammar School. **Career:** Ministry of Labour, Manchester 1933; Juvenile Department, Employment Exchange, Bolton 1936; Ministry of National Insurance 1948–1950; Manager, Salford Office 1950, Manager, Bolton Office 1954, Ministry of National Insurance; Controller, Northern Region, Department of Health and Social Security. **Awards:** Patchett Scholarship, SJC 1929. Died 5 April 1996.

WILSON, Ian Hume (1943) Born 15 November 1925, 30 Hilldrop Road, London; son of John Wilson, Motor Engineer, and Margaret Hume Aitken. **Subject(s):** Mathematics; BA 1948; MA 1950. **Tutor(s):** S J Bailey. **Educ:** Raglan School, Enfield; Latymer's School, Edmonton. Died 27 February 1986.

WILSON, Jacob (1937) Born 20 November 1913, 309 Stanhope Road, South Shields; son of Jacob Wilson, Schoolmaster, and Mary Edith Blenkinsop Blackie. **Tutor(s):** C W Guillebaud. **Educ:** Westoe Secondary School, South Shields; Armstrong College, Durham University. **Career:** RA 1939–1945; Chief Economic Botanist, Burma; Senior Lecturer in Botany, Imperial College of Tropical Agriculture, Trinidad; Head, Plant Quarantine Station, Trinidad; Director, Sugar Experiment Station, Mount Edgcumbe. **Awards:** Ministry of Agriculture Research Scholarship.

WILSON, James (1940) Born 12 March 1922, Norwood, Bank Street, Irvine, Ayrshire; son of Alexander Robertson Wilson, Solicitor, and Elizabeth Wyllie Murray. **Tutor(s):** J M Wordie. **Johnian Relatives:** brother of Norval Murray Wilson (1936). **Educ:** Irvine Academy; Edinburgh Academy. **Career:** Major, RA.

WILSON, James Boyd (1921) Born 19 October 1903, Johannesburg, Transvaal, South Africa; son of Nathaniel Wilson, Consulting Mechanical Engineer, and Mabel Hadfield; m Alice Yvonne Juanita Voisin, 20 March 1932, Anglo-American Church, Lima, Peru. BA 1924. **Tutor(s):** E E Sikes. **Educ:** Berkhamsted School. **Career:** Duncan, Fox and Company, merchants, sent to South America 1925.

WILSON, Dr James Maxwell Glover (1931) Born 31 August 1913, Edinburgh, Scotland; son of James Thomas Wilson, Fellow, SJC and Professor of Anatomy, University of Cambridge, and Mabel Mildred

Millicent Salomons; m (1) Wilhelmina (Vilma) Mehner, (2) Lallie Methley; (2) 3 sons. **Subject(s):** Natural Science; BA 1934; MA 1938; MB 1938; BChir 1938; FRCP; FFCM; FRCPE; FFPHM. **Tutor(s):** R L Howland. **Johnian Relatives:** son of James Thomas Wilson (1920); brother of Thomas Douglas Glover Wilson (1924) and of John Julian Glover Wilson (1927). **Educ:** King's College Choir School; Oundle School. **Career:** Clinical Appointments, London and Cambridge 1937–1939; Major, 6th Airborne Division, RAMC 1939–1945; Hospital Appointments, London and Edinburgh 1945–1954; Medical Work, Tea Estates in India 1954–1957; Medical Staff, Ministry of Health (later DHSS) 1957–1976; Lecturer (part-time), Public Health Department, London School of Hygiene and Tropical Medicine 1968–1972; Senior Principal Medical Officer, Department of Health and Social Security 1972–1976; Senior Research Fellow, Information Services Division, Common Services Agency, Scottish Health Service 1976–1981. **Appointments:** Research Fellow, Scottish Health Service. **Publications:** (with G Jungner) *Principles and Practice of Screening for Disease*, WHO, 1968; contributions to medical journals, mainly on screening for disease.

WILSON, James Morton (1934) Born 10 July 1917, Dromore, Majors Loan, Falkirk; son of William Wilson, Gas Engineer, and Elizabeth Jane Morton. **Subject(s):** Natural Sciences; BA 1937; MA 1943. **Tutor(s):** R L Howland. **Educ:** Burton Grammar School; Strathallan School, Perth. Died 1972.

WILSON, Professor James Thomas (1920) Born 14 April 1861, Ayr Street, Moniaive, Glencairn, Dumfries; son of Thomas Wilson, Schoolmaster, and Helen Brown; m (1) Jane Elizabeth Smith, (2) Mabel Mildred Millicent Salomons (d 1944); (1) 1 daughter (Jane), (2) 3 sons, 3 daughters. MA 1920; MB (Edinburgh) 1883; MChir (Edinburgh) 1883; LLD (Edinburgh). **Johnian Relatives:** father of Thomas Douglas Glover Wilson (1924), John Julian Glover Wilson (1927) and of James Maxwell Glover Wilson (1931). **Educ:** Moniaive School. **Career:** Challis Professor of Anatomy, University of Sydney; Professor of Anatomy 1920–1934 (Emeritus 1934–1945), University of Cambridge; Foundress Fellow 1920–1934, Title E Fellow 1934–1945, SJC. **Appointments:** Council Member, Royal Society 1922–1923; President, Cambridge Philosophical Society 1924–1925; President, Anatomical Society of Great Britain 1924–1925. Died 2 September 1945.

WILSON, John Asquith (1933) Born 17 August 1915, The Grange, Kilham, Driffield, East Yorkshire; son of Richard Lamplugh Wilson, Farmer, and Gertrude Middlewood. **Subject(s):** History; BA 1937; MA 1941. **Tutor(s):** E A Benians. **Educ:** Woodhouse Grove School, Apperly Bridge, near Bradford. **Career:** Squadron Leader, RAF. **Honours:** OBE 1957. Died 29 January 1998.

WILSON, John Julian Glover (1927) Born 19 November 1909, Nelson Street, Woollahra, New South Wales, Australia; son of James Thomas Wilson, Fellow, SJC and Professor of Anatomy, University of Cambridge, and Mabel Mildred Millicent Salomons; m Anne Mackintosh Colvin, 31 July 1937; 1 son (Mark), 2 daughters (Katharine and Joanna). **Subject(s):** Law; BA 1931; MA 1935; LLB 1932; LLM 1985. **Tutor(s):** C W Guillebaud. **Johnian Relatives:** son of James Thomas Wilson (1920); brother of Thomas Douglas Glover Wilson (1924) and of James Maxwell Glover Wilson (1931). **Educ:** Edgecliff Preparatory School, Sydney; King's College Choir School, Cambridge; Oundle School. **Career:** Solicitor, London. Died 6 January 2004.

WILSON, Professor John Tuzo (1930) Born 24 October 1908, Carleton County, Ottawa, Ontario; son of John Armitstead Wilson, Dominion Civil Servant, and Henrietta Loetitia Tuzo. **Subject(s):** Natural Sciences; BA 1932; MA 1940; ScD 1958; BA (Toronto) 1930; PhD (Princeton) 1936; LLD (Carleton); Eight Honorary Degrees; FRSC. **Tutor(s):** J M Wordie. **Educ:** Rockliffe Preparatory School; Ashbury College, Ottawa; Ottawa Collegiate Institute; Trinity College, University of Toronto. **Career:** Director General, Ontario Science Centre, Toronto; Professor of

Geophysics, University of Toronto 1948. **Appointments:** Overseas Fellow, Churchill College, Cambridge 1965; Honorary Fellow, SJC 1981–1993. **Awards:** Wollaston Medal, Geological Society of London 1978; Columbia University's Vetlesen Prize 1978. **Honours:** OBE. **Publications:** 'Hypothesis of Earth's Behaviour', *Nature*, 8 June 1963. Died 15 April 1993.

WILSON, Lancelot Elce (1919) Born 25 November 1879, 2 Hall Bank, Buxton, Derbyshire; son of Matthew Bacon Wilson, Engineer, and Elizabeth Elce. BA 1921; MA 1925. **Tutor(s):** E A Benians. **Educ:** The College, Buxton; Yorkshire College Engineering Laboratory. **Career:** Engineer, Cambridge Drainage Committee; Consulting Engineer to City of Ely Water Supply Extension; Surveyor, four years articled pupil with J Thropp, MICE; various drainage and engineering commissions, including Resident Engineer in charge of Vancouver and District Joint Sewerage and Drainage Scheme 1903–1919. Died 15 November 1970.

WILSON, Leslie (1945) Born 24 December 1926, Morley, Yorkshire; son of Bernard Wilson, Company Secretary, and Gladys E Webster, Teacher; m Glenys Mary Jacob, 10 June 1950, Trumpington Church; 2 sons (Trevor John and Brian Richard). **Subject(s):** Engineering; BA 1948; MA 1952. **Tutor(s):** S J Bailey; R L Howland. **Educ:** Cross Hall Junior School, Morley; Batley Grammar School. **Career:** Flying Officer, RAF; Engineering Staff, Central Gunnery School, Leconfield 1948–1950; Graduate Apprentice 1950–1951, Research Staff 1951–1954, Mather & Platt Ltd; Managerial Staff (Sales, then Contracts Department), Spooner Industries Ltd 1954–1988.

WILSON, Captain Norval Murray (1936) Born 11 December 1917, Norwood, Bank Street, Irvine, Ayrshire; son of Alexander Robertson Wilson, Solicitor, and Elizabeth Wyllie Murray. BA 1939. **Tutor(s):** C W Guillebaud. **Johnian Relatives:** brother of James Wilson (1940). **Educ:** Irvine Royal Academy; Edinburgh Academy. **Career:** Captain, 122 Battery, RA 1939–1945, serving with 36th Division in the Burma Campaign. Died 26 February 1945 (of wounds received in action in Burma on 25 February).

WILSON, Dr Peter Audaer Overend (1937) Born 18 July 1918, 11 St Michael's Crescent, Leeds; son of Walter Audaer Wilson, Gas Engineer, and Gertrude Mary Sinclair. **Subject(s):** Natural Sciences; BA 1940; MA 1944; MB BChir 1943; MRCP; FRCP. **Tutor(s):** R L Howland. **Educ:** Moorlands School, Far Headingley; Clifton College Preparatory School; Clifton College. **Career:** Senior Registrar, National Heart Hospital, London; Thoracic Surgery Department, General Infirmary, Leeds; Consultant in Cardiology, Iraq. Died 11 December 1981.

WILSON, Richard William Russell (1921) Born 13 August 1905, The Green House, Tettenhall, Wolverhampton, Staffordshire; son of William Robert Wilson, Brewer, and Alice Mary Benson Russell; m Nancy Openshaw Coupe, 29 December 1943, St Chad's, Stockton; 1 son (Christopher Richard William b 14 October 1944), 1 daughter (Vivian Ann Veronica Lord b 26 April 1948). BA 1926. **Tutor(s):** B F Armitage. **Johnian Relatives:** brother-in-law of Gordon Ian Brand Dick (1924); uncle of Robert Ian Dick (1958), John Brand Dick (1964) and of Charles Richard Dick (1969). **Educ:** Ashdown House, Forrest Row; Rugby School. **Career:** Special Constable in the General Strike 1926; W Butler & Co Ltd, Brewers, of Wolverhampton (Managing Director at the time of his death) 1929–1953; Lieutenant Colonel, TA 1939–1945. **Honours:** OBE (military). Died 11 March 1953.

WILSON, Dr Robert Hugh (1926) Born 19 July 1908, 13 Prospect Place, Newcastle upon Tyne, Northumberland; son of Edward James Wilson, Clerk in Railway Company, and Eleanor Barbara Brewis. **Subject(s):** Natural Sciences; BA 1929; MA 1933; PhD 1933. **Tutor(s):** J M Wordie. **Educ:** Chillingham Road School, Newcastle upon Tyne; Barnard Castle School. **Awards:** Scholarship, SJC 1925.

WILSON, Professor Robert McLachlan (1942) Born 13 February 1916, Gateside Avenue, Gourock, Renfrewshire; son of Hugh Jack McLachlan Wilson, Insurance Manager, and Janet Nicol Struthers; m Enid Mary Bomford, 1945; 2 sons. PhD 1945; MA (Edinburgh) 1939; BD (Edinburgh) 1942; FBA 1977; Hon DD (Aberdeen) 1982. **Tutor(s):** C W Guillebaud. **Educ:** Greenock Academy; Royal High School, Edinburgh; University of Edinburgh. **Career:** Head Office, Standard Life Assurance Company 1935; Minister, Rankin Church, Strathaven, Lanarkshire 1946–1954; Lecturer in New Testament 1954–1964, Senior Lecturer in New Testament 1964–1969, Professor of New Testament Language and Literature 1969–1978, Professor of Biblical Criticism 1978–1983, University of St Andrews. **Appointments:** Visiting Professor, Vanderbilt Divinity School, Nashville 1964–1965; Associate Editor 1967–1977, Editor 1977–1983, *New Testament Studies*; Honorary Member, SBL 1972; President, SNTS 1981–1982; Member, International Committee for Publication of Nag Hammadi Codices, and of Editorial Board of *Nag Hammadi Studies* monograph series. **Awards:** Burkitt Medal for Biblical Studies, British Academy 1990. **Publications:** *The Gnostic Problem*, 1958; *Studies in the Gospel of Thomas*, 1960; *The Gospel of Philip*, 1962; *Gnosis and the New Testament*, 1968; (ed) English trans, Hennecke–Schneemelcher, *NT Apocrypha*, vol 1, 1963 (3rd edition, completely revised, 1991), vol 2, 1965 (3rd edition 1993); (ed and trans, jointly) *Jung Codex treatises: De Resurrectione*, 1963, *Epistula Jacobi Apocrypha*, 1968, *Tractatus Tripartitus*, pars I, 1973, partes II et III, 1975; (ed) English trans, Haenchen, *The Acts of the Apostles*, 1971; (ed) English trans, Foerster, *Gnosis*, vol 1, 1972, vol. 2, 1974; (ed) *Nag Hammadi and Gnosis*, 1978; (ed) *The Future of Coptology*, 1978; (ed jointly) *Text and Interpretation*, 1979; (ed) English trans, Rudolph, *Gnosis*, 1983; *Commentary on Hebrews*, 1987; articles in British, American and European journals.

WILSON, Major General Ronald Dare (1938) Born 3 August 1919, Priestfield Lodge, Burnopfield, Newcastle upon Tyne; son of Sydney Erskine Dare Wilson, Coal Owner, and Dorothea Grace Burgess; m Sarah Stallard, 14 July 1973; 2 sons. **Subject(s):** Economics/Land Economy; BA 1972; MA 1974; FRGS. **Tutor(s):** R L Howland; G C L Bertram. **Educ:** Harecroft Hall, Gosforth; Orleton, Scarborough; Shrewsbury School. **Career:** Commissioned into Royal Northumberland Fusiliers 1939; BEF 1940; Middle East, Italy and North West Europe 1944–1945; 6th Airborne Division, Palestine 1945–1948; 1st Battalion Parachute Regiment 1949; Ministry of Defence 1950; Royal Northumberland Fusiliers: Korea 1951; Kenya 1953; Directing Staff (Instructor), Staff College, Camberley 1954–1956; Assistant Adjutant and Quartermaster-General, 3rd Division 1958–1959; Commander, 22 Special Air Service Regiment 1960–1962; Canadian National Defence College 1962–1963; Colonel General Staff, 1 (BR) Corps, British Army of the Rhine 1963–1965; Brigadier 1966; Commander, 149 Infantry Brigade (TA), 1966–1967; Brigadier Adjutant/Quartermaster, Middle East Command 1967; Major-General 1968; Director, Land/Air Warfare, Ministry of Defence 1968–1969; Director, Army Aviation, Ministry of Defence 1970–1971; Exmoor National Park Officer 1974–1978. **Appointments:** Member, Army Cresta Run Team and Army Rifle VIII; Captain, British Free-Fall Parachute Team 1962–1965; Consultant to Federation of Nature and National Parks of Europe; Speaker for English-Speaking Union in USA; DL, Somerset 1979–1996; Church Warden, Church of St George, Morebath, Devon 1980–1993; Chairman, British Parachute Association 1962–1965; Council Member, Cambridge Society 1989–2002; President, Somerset Branch, Cambridge Society 1999–. **Awards:** Royal Humane Society Award 1953; Royal Aero Club Silver Medal 1967. **Honours:** MC 1945; MBE 1949; CBE 1968. **Publications:** *Cordon and Search*, 1948, reissued USA, 1984; contributions to military journals.

WILSON, Dr Thomas Douglas Glover (1924) Born 10 December 1906, Apheta, Nelson Street, Woollahra, Sydney, Australia; son of Professor James Thomas Wilson, Fellow, SJC and Professor of Anatomy, University of Cambridge, and Mabel Mildred Millicent Salomons; m (1) Hazel Constance Fulton, 26 September 1931, St Paul's, Knightsbridge, (2)

Audrey 1980; (1) 1 son (Jamie). **Subject(s):** Natural Sciences; BA 1927; MA 1933; BChir 1933; MB 1933; MRCS (University College Hospital) 1931; LRCP (University College Hospital) 1931. **Tutor(s):** B F Armitage. **Johnian Relatives:** son of James Thomas Wilson (1920); brother of John Julian Glover Wilson (1927) and of James Maxwell Glover Wilson (1931). **Educ:** Scots College, Sydney, Australia; Oundle School. **Career:** House Physician, Westminster Hospital; GP, London, Okehampton and Dulverton. Died 20 November 1990.

WILSON, Thomas George (1934) Born 15 January 1915, Greenwood, Maghull, Liverpool; son of George Algernon Wilson, Farmer, and Amy Milbourn. **Subject(s):** History/English; BA 1937; MA 1960. **Tutor(s):** J S Boys Smith. **Educ:** Private School, Ormskirk; Kendal Grammar School; Wycliffe College. **Career:** Army 1937. **Honours:** OBE 1945. Died 15 November 1990.

WILSON, Thomas Sydney (1936) Born 24 April 1913, Nafferton, Duffield, Yorkshire; son of Thomas Wilson, Builder, and Jane Sissons Davison. **Subject(s):** Mathematics; BA 1938. **Tutor(s):** J M Wordie. **Educ:** Nafferton Church of England School, Nafferton; Bridlington School; University College, Hull. Died 1 August 1998.

WILSON, Wilfrid (1922) Born 28 May 1890, Goody Hills, Holme St Cuthberts, Wigton, Cumberland; son of William Osmotherly Wilson, Yeoman and Farmer, and Isabella Ewart. **Tutor(s):** E Cunningham. **Educ:** Carlisle Grammar School; KCL.

WILSON, William John Fleetwood Seddon (1920) Born 3 October 1902, 3 Lathom Road, Southport, Lancashire; son of John Elphinstone Fleeming Jordan Wilson, Engineer, and Elizabeth Seddon. BA 1923. **Tutor(s):** B F Armitage. **Educ:** Cherwell House School, Bexhill-on-Sea; St Oswald's School, Clifton; Clifton College.

WIMBUSH, The Revd James Christopher (1919) Born 5 April 1901, Bulawayo, Southern Rhodesia, South Africa; son of James Sedgwick Wimbush, Clerk in Holy Orders, and Judith Isabel Fox. BA 1923; MA 1926. **Tutor(s):** E A Benians. **Educ:** Aysgarth School, Newton le Willows; Haileybury College; Westcott House, Cambridge. **Career:** Assistant Master, Bishop Cotton School; Assistant Master, St Andrew's School, Eastbourne 1922; Schoolmaster, Mount House, Plymouth 1923; Schoolmaster, The Leas, Hoylake 1926; Ordained Deacon 1927; Curate, St Maurice, York 1927–1929; Ordained Priest 1928; Chaplain, St Matthew, Bangalore 1929–1941; Chaplain, St Paul, Moradabad 1941–1942; CF, India and Assam 1942–1943; Permission to Officiate, Diocese of Oxford 1944–1950; Master, Old Hall, Wellington 1947; Diocese of London 1951. Died 21 April 1959.

WINCH, Dr Eric William (1919) Born 18 May 1901, High House, Sheering Road, Harlow, Essex; son of Walter William Winch, Builder, and Minnie Coleman; m Jessie Kathleen Jeanette Garrould, 1925, 3 sons (Jeremy Neville William b 2 January 1929, Thomas Beverley Charles b 8 April 1930 and Anthony George b 14 April 1939), 1 daughter (Penelope Anne Jeannette b 13 February 1934). **Subject(s):** Natural Sciences; BA 1923; MA 1927; MRCS 1928; LRCP 1928. **Tutor(s):** B F Armitage. **Johnian Relatives:** brother-in-law of Ivor George Bayes Garrould (1920); father of Thomas Beverley Charles Winch (1950). **Educ:** Churchgate Street School, Harlow; St Mary's College, Harlow; Bishop's Stortford College. **Career:** Casualty Officer, House Surgeon, House Physician, ENT House Surgeon, St George's Hospital; Honorary Anaesthetist, Southend Victoria Hospital; Practice, Essex; Practice, Wiltshire 1938–1950. Died 25 September 1964.

WINDER, Alexander John Henry (1940) Born 23 October 1921, 133 Church Street, Chelsea, London; son of Alexander Stuart Monck Winder, Lieutenant Colonel, RAMC, and Helen Mary Swayne. **Tutor(s):** S J Bailey. **Educ:** St George's Preparatory School, Folkestone; Shrewsbury School.

WINDER, The Revd Reginald McDonnell (1908) Born 1 June 1889, 25 Bournevale Road, Streatham, Surrey; son of Thomas Winder, Secretary to and Director of Public Companies, and Edith Wilson. BA 1911. **Tutor(s):** E E Sikes. **Educ:** Cranleigh School; Abbey School, Beckenham; Ely Theological College. **Career:** Deacon 1912; Curate, St Luke's, Chelsea 1912–1913; Lieutenant, Royal Marine Artillery 1915–1918.

WINFIELD, Dr Bernard James Oliver (1932) Born 24 May 1914, 1 White Gables, Millington Road, Cambridge; son of Percy Henry Winfield, Rouse Ball Professor of English Law, University of Cambridge, and Helena Chapman Scruby. **Subject(s):** Natural Sciences; BA 1935; BChir 1938; MB 1938; MD 1947. **Tutor(s):** R L Howland. **Johnian Relatives:** son of Percy Henry Winfield (1896); brother of Roland Henry Winfield (1928). **Educ:** Kings College School, Cambridge; Shrewsbury School. **Career:** Squadron Leader, RAF, WWII. **Honours:** AFC.

WINFIELD, Dr Roland Henry (1928) Born 20 December 1910, 57 Chesterton Road, Cambridge; son of Percy Henry Winfield, Rouse Ball Professor of English Law, University of Cambridge, and Helena Chapman Scruby; m (1) Frances Macmillan, 1938 (div 1946), (2) Christine Munro, 1947 (d 1999); (1) 2 daughters (Joan b 1939 and Christine b 1942). BA 1931; MA 1950; MB 1938; BChir 1938; MB (Edinburgh) 1931. **Tutor(s):** M P Charlesworth. **Johnian Relatives:** son of Percy Henry Winfield (1896); brother of Bernard James Oliver Winfield (1932). **Educ:** King's College Choir School, Cambridge; Shrewsbury School. **Career:** Chief Assistant to the Consultant in Applied Physiology, RAF 1939–1947; Wing Commander, RAFVR; Commanding Officer, RAF Institute of Aviation Medicine, Farnborough, Hampshire (ADC 1942) 1942–1946; Title B Fellow and Lecturer, SJC 1946–1954; Demonstrator in Physiology, University of Cambridge 1953–1956; GP 1954. **Appointments:** Director of Medical Studies, SJC 1949–1954; Honorary Medical Adviser to the Guild of Air Pilots and Air Navigators. **Honours:** AFC 1942 (entitled to wear the ribbon of the 1939–1943 Star); DFC 1944. **Publications:** article on air sickness in *Journal of Otolaryngology*, 1942; 'The Royal Airforce North Polar Research Flights, 1945' in *The Polar Record*, 33–34, 1947; *The sky belongs to them*, Kimber, 1976. Died 1 November 1970.

WINLAW, Ashley William Edgell (1933) Born 8 February 1914, 54 Longton Grove, Sydenham, Kent; son of George Preston Kelsall Winlaw, Clerk in Holy Orders, and Minnie Ashley. **Subject(s):** Modern and Medieval Languages/History; BA 1936; MA 1953. **Tutor(s):** J S Boys Smith. **Johnian Relatives:** son of George Preston Kelsall Winlaw (1891); brother of Roger de Winton Kelsall Winlaw (1931). **Educ:** St Peter's School, Seaford; Clifton Junior School; Winchester College. **Career:** Assistant Master, Aldenham School 1936–1939; Intelligence Corps, WWII; Assistant Master, Rugby School 1946–1954; Headmaster, Achimota School, Gold Coast 1954–1959; Headmaster, Government Cadet College, Hassan Abdal, West Pakistan 1959–1966; Headmaster, Federal Government College, Nigeria 1966–1969. **Awards:** Sizarship, SJC. Died 13 February 1988.

WINLAW, Roger de Winton Kelsall (1931) Born 28 March 1912, The Rectory, Morden, Surrey; son of George Preston Kelsall Winlaw, Clerk in Holy Orders, and Minnie Ashley; m Marsali, 1 son (Anthony), 1 daughter (Juliet). **Subject(s):** Classics/History; BA 1934. **Tutor(s):** M P Charlesworth. **Johnian Relatives:** son of George Preston Kelsall Winlaw (1891); brother of Ashley William Edgell Winlaw (1933). **Educ:** St Peter's School, Seaford; Winchester College. **Career:** Master, Harrow 1939; Squadron Leader, RAF 1939–1942. Died October 1942 (killed on active service).

WINTER, John Leslie Haywood (1925) Born 14 November 1905, 13 Eastbourne Street, Lincoln; son of Joseph Winter, Mechanical Engineer's Clerk, and Emmeline Heywood. **Subject(s):** History; BA 1928; MA 1944. **Tutor(s):** E A Benians. **Educ:** Lincoln School; Wellingborough School.

WINTER, Dr John Openshaw (1946) Born 11 June 1928, 143 Campbell Street, Farnworth, Lancashire; son of Samuel Hugh Winter, Estimating Clerk and Foreign Correspondent, and Gladys Openshaw; m Gillian; 2 sons (Hugh and Leigh). **Subject(s):** Natural Sciences; BA 1949; MA 1961; MB 1952; BChir 1952. **Tutor(s):** G C L Bertram. **Educ:** Plodder Lane Council School, Farnworth; Bolton School; St Thomas' Hospital. **Career:** House Surgeon, St Mary's Hospital, Portsmouth 1952; GP, Portsmouth 1959–1990. Died 15 May 1991.

WINTER, Robert Llewellyn (1948) Born 19 July 1930, Dar-es-Salaam, Tanganyika; son of Arthur Llewellyn Winter, Bank Manager, and Lily Sim; m Gwenyth Anne Banbury, 30 June 1963; 1 son (Charles). **Subject(s):** Law; BA 1951; MA 1956. **Tutor(s):** J M Wordie. **Educ:** Dar-es-Salaam Government School; Grosvenor House, Harrogate; Etonhurst Preparatory School, Weston-Super-Mare; St Mary's School, Nairobi. Died 24 October 1988.

WINTRINGHAM, Charles Richard Fildes (1927) Born 23 April 1909, The Garden House, Humberston, Great Grimsby, Lincolnshire; son of John Fildes Wintringham, Solicitor, and Eliza Mapson Workman. BA 1930. **Tutor(s):** C W Guillebaud. **Educ:** Arnold House School, London; Old School House, Gresham's School House; Gresham's School, Holt. **Career:** Flying Officer, RAF. Died 17 March 1931.

WIRZ, Eduard Wilhelm (1910) Born 21 December 1890, Gerbergasse 38, Basel, Switzerland; son of Wilhelm Wirz, Merchant, and Lina Wirz. **Tutor(s):** J R Tanner. **Educ:** Kantonale Obere Realschule, Basel, Switzerland; University of Zurich, Switzerland.

WISDEN, John Patrick (1920) Naval Officer.

WISE, Dr David (1947) Born 20 July 1928, 43 Brixton Hill, Norwood, London; son of Cuthbert Edward Wise, Medical Practitioner, and Phyllis Decima Dixon. **Subject(s):** Natural Sciences; BA 1949; MB 1952; BChir 1952; MD 1960; MRCP 1954. **Tutor(s):** G C L Bertram. **Educ:** Dulwich College Preparatory School; The Craig, Windermere; Oundle School. **Career:** Consultant in General Medicine, Dartford and Darenth Hospital Groups.

WITHERS, Hartley (1938) Born 15 July 1867, Aigburth, Liverpool; son of Henry Hartley Withers, Banker, and Jane Livingstone Lowndes; m Alice Elliott, 1921; 1 daughter (Elizabeth). MA 1939. **Educ:** St Peter's College, Westminster; Christ Church, Oxford. **Career:** Assistant Master, Clifton College 1890; Stock Exchange Clerk 1891–1893; City Office, *The Times* 1894; City Editor, *The Times* 1905–1910; City Editor, *Morning Post* 1910–1911; Merchant Banker, Seligman Brothers 1911; Director of Financial Enquiries, Treasury 1915–1916; Editor, *Economist* 1916–1921; Editor, Financial Supplement, *Saturday Review* 1921–1923. **Appointments:** Director Allied Investors' Trusts. **Publications:** *The Meaning of Money*, 1909; *Stocks and Shares*, 1910; *Money Changing*, 1913; *Poverty and Waste*, 1914; *War and Lombard Street*, 1915; *International Finance*, 1916; *Our Money and the State*, 1917; *The Business of Finance*, 1918; *War-Time Financial Problems*, 1919; *The Case for Capitalism*, 1920; *Bankers and Credit*, 1924; *Hints about Investments*, 1926; *Money*, 1927; *Quicksands of the City, and a Way Through for Investors*, 1930; *Everybody's Business*, 1931; *Money in the Melting Pot*, 1932; *National Provincial Bank, 1833 to 1933*, 1933; *Investing Simplified*, 1934; *The Way to Wealth*, 1935; *The Defeat of Poverty*, 1939; *Archiepiscopal Economics*, 1942. Died 21 March 1950.

WITHEY, William Henry (1902) Born 28 August 1883, 55 High Street, Stroud, Gloucester; son of William Butt Withey, Grocer, and Elizabeth Roberts. **Subject(s):** Natural Sciences; BA 1905. **Tutor(s):** D MacAlister. **Educ:** Marling School, Stroud; Cotteswold School, Cirencester.

WITNEY, Peter Norman (1931) Born 31 March 1913, Cromwell House, Oxford Street, Whitstable; son of Ernest William Witney, Medical Practitioner, and Lottie May Lamprey; BA 1934; LRCP; MRCS.

Tutor(s): M P Charlesworth. **Educ:** Junior King's School, Canterbury; Yardley Court School, Tonbridge; Tonbridge School. **Career:** Captain, RAMC 1939–1941. Died 25 December 1941 (killed in Hong Kong).

WOELCK, Hans Ulrich Carl Otto (1933) Born 9 January 1914, 9 Wildenbruch Strasse, Frankfurt Oder, Germany; son of Kurt Fritz Woelck, General Director, Federation of Master Printers, and Gertrude Maria Luise Helmin Stöve. **Tutor(s):** C W Guillebaud. **Educ:** Gymnasium Spandau; Höhere Töchterschule, Leipzig; Höhere Töchterschule, Berlin; Prinz Heinrich Gymnasium, Berlin-Schöneberg; Gymnasium Zehlendorf.

WOLFE, Bernard William (1935) Born 19 June 1916, 54 Halifax Road, Chesterton, Cambridge; son of William Ernest Wolfe, Bursar's Clerk, SJC, and Mabel Priscilla Watson; m Norah Elizabeth Beaumont, 14 April 1939. **Subject(s):** Natural Sciences; BA 1938; MA 1942. **Tutor(s):** J M Wordie. **Educ:** Perse School, Cambridge.

WOLFER, Dr Heinrich Herbert (1934) Born 19 August 1909, Winterthur, Switzerland; son of Leo Heinrich Wolfer, Managing Director, Sulzer Bros Ltd, and Lucie Sulzer; m Charlotte De Armas, 9 March 1944; 3 sons (Thomas b 1945, Martin b 1945 and Albert b 1949), 1 daughter (Margaret b 1948). **Subject(s):** Engineering; PhD 1937; Diploma in Mechanical Engineering (ETH) 1933. **Tutor(s):** J S Boys Smith. **Educ:** Primar Schule, Winterthur; Gymnasium, Winterthur; Eidgenössische Technische Hochschule, Zurich. **Career:** Sulzer Bros Ltd, Winterthur 1936–1982 (Joint Managing Director 1948–1975, Deputy Chairman, Board of Directors 1959–1982). **Appointments:** President, Employees Federation of the Swiss Engineering Industry 1964–1971.

WOLFES, Franz (1914) Born 24 May 1896, 13 Oeltzen Strasse, Hanover, Germany; son of Joseph Wolfes, Doctor of Laws, and Elsa Magnus. **Tutor(s):** L H K Bushe-Fox. **Educ:** Goethe Gymnasium, Hanover; Kaiser Wilhelms Gymnasium, Hanover.

WOLFF, Professor Michael Jonas (1945) Born 2 July 1927, 24 Lodge Parade Mansions, Green Lanes, Southgate, Middlesex; son of Joel Wolff, Antique Dealer, and Phyllis Goldhill; m Sara Starr, Washington DC, 18 December 1955; 1 son (Jeremy b 1959), 2 daughters (Jessica b 1957 and Judith b 1960). **Subject(s):** Moral Sciences/English; BA 1948; MA 1955; MA (Princeton) 1955; PhD (Princeton) 1958. **Tutor(s):** F Thistlethwaite. **Educ:** The Hall School, Hampstead; Hunter College Model School, New York; St Edward's School, Oxford. **Career:** Procter Fellow, Princeton University 1954; Lecturer in English 1955–1959, Instructor in English and History 1959–1969, Director, Summer Institute for Teachers of English from Negro Colleges (Rockefeller and Carnegie grants) 1964–, Chairman, Victorian Studies Graduate Program 1966–1969, Secretary, Faculty Council 1967–1969, Professor of English and Victorian Studies 1968–1970, Indiana University; Professor of English 1970–1992 (Emeritus 1992), University of Massachusetts. **Appointments:** Council Member, Victorian Society; Board Member, Victorian Studies Centre, Leicester University; Co-founder/Co-editor 1955–1963, Editor 1963–1970, Chairman, Editorial Board 1970–1975, Advisory Board 1975, *Victorian Studies*; Founding President, Research Society for Victorian Periodicals 1969–; Director, Summer Seminar, Trinity College, Oxford 1987; Michael Wolff Lecture Series 2000–. **Awards:** Minor Scholarship, SJC 1945. **Publications:** Various books, articles and editorships, including: (co-editor) *1859: Entering an Age of Crisis, Indiana and Oxford University Presses*, 1959; 'Victorian Reviewers and Cultural Responsibility', *1859*; 'Critics' Poll: 1859', *Saturday Review*, October 17 1959; 'The Rubaiyat's Neglected Reviewer: A Centennial Recovery', *Victorian Newsletter*, Spring 1960; (Advisory editor) *Wellesley Index to Victorian Periodicals*, Vols I-IV, 1963; 'Victorian Study: An Interdisciplinary Essay', *Victorian Studies*, September 1964; (with H J Dyos) *The Victorian City*, 1972, 2nd edition 1999; (ed, with Joanne Shattock) *The Victorian Periodical Press: Samplings and Soundings*, University of Leicester Press, 1982; (ed, with Miles Taylor) *The Victorians since 1901*, Manchester University Press, 2004.

WOLSTENCROFT, Alfred Stratten (1912) Born 25 January 1894, Roseleigh, Hullgate, Cottingham, Yorkshire; son of James Samuel Wolstencroft, Congregational Minister, and Charlotte Blyth Westerdale; m L Dorothy M Flokes, 1941. **Subject(s):** Modern and Medieval Languages; BA 1915; MA 1947. **Tutor(s):** E E Sikes. **Educ:** Silcoates Northern Congregational School, Wakefield. **Career:** Assistant Master, Silcoates School, Wakefield 1915–1916; Friends' Ambulance Unit 1916–1919; Assistant Master, High School, Wellington, Shropshire 1919–1921; Assistant Master, Warwick School 1922. Died 16 December 1964.

WOLSTENCROFT, Professor John Hollas (1940) Born 23 November 1922, 10 Spendmore Lane, Coppull, Lancashire; son of Ernest Wolstencroft, Cotton Yarn Salesman, and Alice Hollas; m Hisako Ikeda; 3 children (Alan, Helen and Utako). **Subject(s):** Natural Sciences; BA 1943; MA 1947; PhD 1952. **Tutor(s):** J M Wordie. **Educ:** Woodfield Preparatory School, Wigan; Coppull Council School; Chorley Grammar School. **Career:** Lecturer in Physiology 1966, later Professor of Physiology, University of Birmingham. **Publications:** Articles in *The Journal of Physiology, Journal of Neurophysiology, British Journal of Pharmacology, Nature, British Medical Bulletin, Brain Research, Pain, Neuroscience, Life Sciences, Neuroscience Letters, Neuropharmacology, Archives Italiennes de Biologie, The Journal of Pharmacy and Pharmacology, The Journal of Comparative Neurology, International Journal of Neuropharmacology, Experientia*. Died 3 May 1983.

WOLSTENHOLME, Allan Grant (1937) Born 21 January 1917, Sunny Bank, Bury; son of John Wolstenholme, Papermaker's Engineer, and Hilda Parks. LMSSA (London) 1943. **Tutor(s):** R L Howland. **Educ:** Aldro School, Eastbourne; Harrow School; Guy's Hospital, London. **Career:** House Surgeon, West Kent Hospital, Maidstone 1943–1944; House Surgeon, Charing Cross Hospital, London 1944–1947; King's African Rifles, RAMC, Kenya 1944; House Surgeon and Orthopaedic Registrar, Prince of Wales' Hospital, Tottenham 1947–1953; GP, Mayfield 1953–1987.

WOMACK, Harold Athelstan (1923) Born 2 August 1902, 2 Greencroft Gardens, South Hampstead, London; son of Frederick Womack, Lecturer in Physics, St Bartholomew's Medical School, and Ada Christmas. BA 1926; MA 1932. **Tutor(s):** E Cunningham. **Educ:** Arnold House Preparatory School, St John's Wood; University College School, Frognal, Hampstead. Died 10 July 1987.

WONG, Dr Man (1913) Born 9 May 1895, 1 McDonald Road, Tsim Shatsui, Hong Kong, China; son of Kam Fuk Wong, Compradore, and Tim Ho; m Uk Chi, 31 May 1924. **Subject(s):** Natural Sciences; BA 1916; MA 1920; BChir 1921; MB 1924; MD 1947; MRCS; LRCP 1919. **Tutor(s):** R P Gregory. **Educ:** Dulwich Preparatory School; Dulwich College. **Career:** Dean, Sun Yat-Sen Medical College, Canton; Director of Health, Kwangtung Province and Canton City; Surgeon, Sacred Heart Hospital; Teacher in Surgery, Anatomy and Special Senses, Hackett Medical College, Canton. **Publications:** 'Common Diseases of Eye, Ear, Nose and Throat', *National Medical Journal of China*, 1924; (trans) *Poems from China*, Creation Books, 1950; *Between Two Worlds*, Student Book Store, 1956; (trans and annotated) *The Poems of Mao Tse-Tung*, Eastern Horizon Press, 1966. Died 21 September 1963.

WOO, Ching Sung (1906) Born 13 September 1885, Honan, China. **Tutor(s):** J R Tanner. **Educ:** University of Peking.

WOOD, Andrew (1931) Born 27 June 1913, Dalehead, Broomley, Northumberland; son of Andrew Selby Wood, Paint Manufacturer, and Ruth Swan. **Subject(s):** Economics/Law. **Tutor(s):** C W Guillebaud. **Educ:** Corchester School; Shrewsbury School.

WOOD, Ernest (1900) Born 9 February 1881, 46 Strawberry Street, Southcoates, Hull; son of George Henry Wood, Tailor, and Eliza Bowes. **Subject(s):** Mathematics/Natural Sciences; BA 1903; London Diploma of Pedagogy 1910. **Tutor(s):** J E Sandys. **Educ:** Hymers College, Hull. **Career:** Master, Tettenhall College 1904–1910; Wilson's Grammar School 1912–1933. Died 20 June 1933.

WOOD, Francis Hugo (1926) Born 4 July 1908, 99 Doncaster Road, Barnsley, Yorkshire; son of William Francis John Wood, Glass Manufacturer, and Eliza Beatrice Haslam; m Elizabeth Rosemary Athron, 23 October 1945, Church of St Martin, Scarborough. BA 1930; MA 1934. **Tutor(s):** J M Wordie. **Educ:** Orleton Park School, Scarborough; Oundle School.

WOOD, Frank Eugène (1932) Born 29 October 1914, Onglewood, Bath Road, Reading; son of Thomas Eugène Wood, Solicitor, and Ethel Blatch. **Subject(s):** Modern and Medieval Languages; BA 1935; MA 1939. **Tutor(s):** C W Guillebaud. **Johnian Relatives:** son of Thomas Eugene Wood (1905). **Educ:** Hailey Preparatory School, Bournemouth; Canford School, Wimborne.

WOOD, The Revd James Edward Hathorn (1910) Born 2 December 1891, Stonewall, Manitoba, Canada; son of James Hathorn Roworth Wood, Clerk in Holy Orders, and Edith Elizabeth Smith. **Subject(s):** Classics; BA 1913; MA 1919. **Tutor(s):** J R Tanner. **Johnian Relatives:** brother of Reginald Sydney Carruthers Hathorn Wood (1897). **Educ:** St John's School, Leatherhead; Sarum Theological College. **Career:** Deacon 1917; Curate, Heath, Derbyshire 1917–1919; Priest 1918; Curate, South Scarle with Beesthorpe and Girton, Nottinghamshire 1919–1920; Vicar, Tythby with Cropwell-Butler, Nottinghamshire 1920–1923; Vicar, South Scarle with Beesthorpe and Girton, Nottinghamshire 1920–1924; Vicar, Cropwell Bishop 1924–1936; Perpetual Curate, Owlthorpe, Nottinghamshire 1928–1936; Rector, Knipton with Harston, Leicestershire 1936–1962. **Awards:** Sizarship, SJC. Died 11 January 1962.

WOOD, Norman Wright (1915) Born 10 August 1896, Holly Bank, Dukinfield, Cheshire; son of William Edward Wood, JP, and Emily Moss. **Tutor(s):** E E Sikes. **Educ:** Moravian Ely School, Dukinfield; Willaston School. **Career:** Private, Cheshire Regiment, WWI.

WOOD, Patrick Ronald Oliver (1944) Born 24 January 1927, Woodsley Nursing Home, 158 Woodsley Road, Leeds; son of Ronald Wood, Medical Practitioner, and Winifred Blanche Johnston; m Marjorie Richardson, 11 August 1949; 1 daughter (Gillian Margaret b 25 March 1953). **Subject(s):** Natural Sciences; BA 1947; MA 1951. **Tutor(s):** C W Guillebaud. **Johnian Relatives:** brother of Timothy George Wood (1949). **Educ:** Headingley Kindergarten; Leeds Grammar School; Sedbergh School. **Career:** Schoolmaster, Glenalmond 1947–1949; Usher, Master, House Master, Chapel Warden, Deputy Head, Registrar, Bedford School 1949–1987. **Appointments:** Secretary, LMBC. Died 20 June 2001.

WOOD, The Revd Richard Calvert (1932) Born 17 February 1914, York House, Beaconsfield Road, Greenwich, Kent; son of Herbert Wood, Congregational Minister, and Edith Ella Jacquest; 3 daughters (Suzanne, Amanda and Carolyn). **Subject(s):** Modern and Medieval Languages/Economics; BA 1935; MA 1939; MA (Oxon); FRAS. **Tutor(s):** C W Guillebaud. **Johnian Relatives:** nephew of Samuel Percy Jacquest (1907). **Educ:** Council School, Handsworth; The Grammar School, Handsworth; Westcliffe High School. **Career:** National Secretary, Fellowship of the Reconciliation 1938–1941; Minister, Hertford Congregational Church 1941; Minister, Kingston on Thames Congregational Church 1950; Minister, Bexhill Congregational Church 1965. Died 24 July 1974.

WOOD, Ronald Ernest (1922) Born 14 June 1897, King Edward's School, Witley, Surrey; son of Jonas Wood, Schoolmaster, and Caroline Hannah Holmes. **Tutor(s):** E E Sikes. **Educ:** Royal Grammar School, Guildford.

WOOD, Thomas Albert Victor (1912) Born 22 May 1893, Oxley House, Bushbury, Staffordshire; son of Albert Edward Wood, Brewery Agent, and Gertrude Annie Hunter; m Rosamond Louise Armitage; 1 daughter

(June). BA 1919. **Tutor(s):** R P Gregory. **Educ:** Wolverhampton Grammar School; Guy's Hospital Medical School. **Career:** Captain, Duke of Cornwall's Light Infantry, WWI.

WOOD, Thomas Eugène (1905) Born 21 June 1887, Osborne House, Doncaster Road, Barnsley; son of Alphonse Wood, Glass Manufacturer, and Annie Wood; m Ethel Blatch; 1 son (Frank Eugène b 29 October 1914). **Subject(s):** Law; BA 1908; MA 1912; LLB 1908. **Tutor(s):** C E Graves. **Johnian Relatives:** father of Frank Eugène Wood (1932). **Educ:** New College, Harrogate. **Career:** Partner, Piecy & Wood, Bournemouth 1937; Solicitor, SJC. Died 16 January 1972.

WOOD, Timothy George (1949) Born 12 July 1929, 12 Kepstorn Road, Leeds; son of Ronald Wood, Medical Practitioner, and Winifred Blanche Johnston. BA 1952; MA 1957. **Johnian Relatives:** brother of Patrick Ronald Oliver Wood (1944). **Educ:** Headingley Kindergarten; Leeds Grammar School; Sedbergh School. **Career:** Draughtsman, Aston Martin; Schoolmaster, Cheltenham College; Senior Lecturer, Britannia Royal Naval College, Dartmouth 1960–1989.

WOOD, William Levi (1905) Born 29 August 1879, Old Ford, Standerwick, Frome, Somerset; son of William Browning Wood, Woollen Manufacturer, and Martha Martin. **Tutor(s):** J R Tanner. **Educ:** St Anne's School, Redhill. **Career:** Editor, *Vogue*, English Edition 1916–1923; Editor, *Architect and Building News* 1926–1946. Died 9 October 1958.

WOOD, William Ronald (1924) Born 15 April 1906, 90 Clough Road, Rotherham, Yorkshire; son of William Chapman Wood, Journalist, and Gertrude Brudenell. **Subject(s):** Classics; BA 1927. **Tutor(s):** E E Sikes. **Educ:** Bishop Fox's School, Taunton; Wellington Road School, Taunton; Sherborne School. **Career:** Burma-Shell, Madras, until 1958. Died 1981.

WOODALL, Frank Ewart (1908) Born 10 November 1889, 62 Adswood Lane East, Stockport, Cheshire; son of Edward Woodall, Company Manager, and Hilda Gosnay; m Nora Holden; 2 daughters (Rosemary and Pat). **Subject(s):** Classics; BA 1911; MA 1919; FRGS 1920. **Tutor(s):** E E Sikes. **Educ:** Brentnall Street Higher Grade School, Stockport; Manchester Grammar School. **Career:** Master, Greenbank Preparatory School, Liverpool 1911–1912; Master, Oundle School 1912–1920; Lieutenant, Guards Machine Gun Regiment, WWI; Headmaster, Lady Manners School, Bakewell 1920–1923; Headmaster, Churcher's College, Petersfield 1924–1927; Headmaster, Preparatory School, The Stroud, Grayswood, Haslemere. Died 29 September 1967.

WOODCOCK, Brian (1943) Born 27 September 1924, Newfield, Haslingden, Lancashire; son of Thomas Woodcock, Solicitor, and Beryl Duckworth. **Subject(s):** Law; BA 1948; MA 1950; LLB 1949; LLM 1985. **Tutor(s):** C W Guillebaud. **Johnian Relatives:** descendant of Robert Holden (1673); brother of Graham Woodcock (1939) and of Samuel Richard Woodcock (1945). **Educ:** Clough End School, Haslingden; Stancliffe Hall, Darley Dale; Uppingham School. **Career:** Flying Officer, RAF 1943–1947; Solicitor 1952; Partner, Woodcock & Sons (family firm).

WOODCOCK, Cleever Ralph (1925) Born 24 December 1906, 20 Hutton Avenue, Wellingborough, Northamptonshire; son of Cleever Woodcock, Bank Manager, and Eleanor Mabel Nunneley. **Tutor(s):** E A Benians. **Educ:** Hilcott, Godalming; Courtenay Lodge, Sutton Courtenay, Abingdon.

WOODCOCK, Professor Eric Charles (1923) Born 20 May 1904, 18 Turville Road, Handsworth, Birmingham; son of Charles Thomas Woodcock, Sanitary Engineer, and Mary Elizabeth Ball; m Ruth Mary Ball, 1933; 2 sons. **Subject(s):** Classics; BA 1927; MA 1930. **Tutor(s):** E E Sikes. **Johnian Relatives:** father of John Gordon Woodcock (1953). **Educ:** King Edward VI School, Birmingham; King Edward VI High School, Birmingham. **Career:** Instructor, Department of Ancient Languages,

Harvard 1927–1928; Assistant Lecturer, University of Reading 1928–1930; Assistant Lecturer in Latin 1930–1932, Lecturer in Latin 1932–1947, Senior Lecturer in Latin 1947–1948, University of Manchester; Professor of Latin 1948–1966 (Emeritus 1966), Durham University. **Awards:** Scholarship, SJC. **Publications:** (ed) *The Annals of Tacitus, Book XIV*, 1939; *A New Latin Syntax*, 1959. Died 6 November 1978.

WOODCOCK, Graham (1939) Born 25 July 1920, Newfield, Haslingden, Lancashire; son of Thomas Woodcock, Solicitor, and Beryl Duckworth. **Subject(s):** Law; BA 1947; MA 1954. **Tutor(s):** C W Guillebaud. **Johnian Relatives:** descendant of Robert Holden (1673); brother of Brian Woodcock (1943) and of Samuel Richard Woodcock (1945). **Educ:** Clough End School, Haslingden; Stancliffe Hall, Darley Dale; Uppingham School. **Career:** Captain, RA 1940–1946; Solicitor 1949; Chairman, Greater Manchester and Lancashire Rent Assessment Panel 1982–1985. **Appointments:** Lancashire County Councillor 1969–1981; Member, General Purposes and Executive Committees of National Union of Conservative and Unionist Associations 1975–1997; Treasurer 1985–1989, Chairman 1989–1992, Patron 1992–1997, North West Area Conservative Council; Founder Chairman 1967–, Higher Mill Textile Museum Trust, Helmshore, Lancashire; President, Rossendale & Pendle Mountain Rescue Team 1976–; Honorary Legal Adviser to the Royal Regiment of Fusiliers 1980–2002. **Honours:** OBE 1980; CBE 1992.

WOODCOCK, Samuel Richard (1945) Born 2 March 1927, Newfield, Haslingden, Lancashire; son of Thomas Woodcock, Solicitor, and Beryl Duckworth. **Tutor(s):** J M Wordie. **Johnian Relatives:** descendant of Robert Holden (1673); brother of Graham Woodcock (1939) and of Brian Woodcock (1943). **Educ:** Clough End House, Haslingden; Stancliffe Hall, Darley Vale; Uppingham School. **Appointments:** RE Cadet, SJC. Died 14 March 1975.

WOODCOCK, Thomas Graham (1919) Born 21 June 1897, 29 College Avenue, Gillingham, Kent; son of Harry Graham Woodcock, Army and Navy Contractor, and Gladys Kathleen Clegg. **Tutor(s):** E A Benians. **Educ:** Mathematical School, Rochester; Thames Nautical Training College. **Career:** Midshipman, RNR 1916–1919 (HMS *Duncan* 1916–1917, HMS *Patia* 1917–1918, HMS *Pembroke* 1918, HMS *Tay and Tyne* 1918). **Honours:** The Order of the Redeemer (Greece), WWI.

WOODCOCK, William Watson (1919) Born 15 October 1899, Knowle Road, Golcar, Huddersfield, Yorkshire; son of John Henry Woodcock, Commercial Traveller, and Emma Jane Watson. **Subject(s):** Modern and Medieval Languages; BA 1921; MA 1925. **Tutor(s):** E E Sikes. **Educ:** The Grammar School, Manchester. **Awards:** Scholarship, SJC 1917.

WOODFORD, Alan John (1942) Born 15 August 1924, Mount Pleasant, High Street, Wanstead; son of Edward Woodford, Contracts Officer, Ministry of Aircraft Production, and Daisy Maud Swinton. **Subject(s):** Mathematics/Economics; BA 1947. **Tutor(s):** S J Bailey. **Educ:** Gearies Elementary School; Ilford County High School; St Paul's School.

WOODHEAD, Andrew (1947) Born 27 May 1928, St John's Avenue, Bridlington, Yorkshire; son of Wilfrid Saxe Woodhead, Seed Merchant, and Nancy Sibylla Vincent Wickham. **Subject(s):** Classics; BA 1949; MA 1966; ALA. **Tutor(s):** R L Howland. **Educ:** Baswich House, Weeping Cross, Stafford; Nevill Holt, Market Harborough; Uppingham School. **Career:** Director, Woodheads Seeds Ltd 1958–1995; Senior Library Assistant, then Principal Library Assistant, University of Essex 1967–1989. **Awards:** Johnson Exhibition, SJC.

WOODHOUSE, Lionel Clayton (1921) Born 10 May 1903, 17 Palace Gardens Terrace, Kensington, London; son of Alfred Edward Clayton Woodhouse, Dental Surgeon, and Susanna Mary Pugsley. **Subject(s):** Mechanical Sciences; BA 1924; MA 1928. **Tutor(s):** E E Sikes. **Johnian Relatives:** brother of Michael Clayton Woodhouse (1926); uncle of Robin Clayton Woodhouse (1954). **Educ:** Mr Chadwick's, Forres, Northwold; Rugby School. Died 1986.

WOODHOUSE, Dr Michael Clayton (1926) Born 9 September 1910, St Helena, Dene Road, Ruislip, Northwood, Middlesex; son of Alfred Edward Clayton Woodhouse, Dental Surgeon, and Susanna Mary Pugsley. **Subject(s):** Natural Sciences; BA 1931; MA 1940; BChir 1940; MB 1940. **Tutor(s):** M P Charlesworth. **Johnian Relatives:** brother of Lionel Clayton Woodhouse (1921); uncle of Robin Clayton Woodhouse (1954). **Educ:** St Dunstan's, Burnham on Sea; Rugby School. **Career:** Chief Assistant in Orthopaedics, St Thomas' Hospital, London; Consulting Physician, St Mary's Hospital, London 1972.

WOODLAND, Percy (1922) Born 5 September 1903, 56 Baker Street, Heavitree, Devon; son of William Woodland, Plumber and Electrician, and Mary Bowden Cook; m Eve. **Subject(s):** Natural Sciences; BA 1925; MA 1929; DipEd (Oxford). **Tutor(s):** B F Armitage. **Educ:** Ladysmith Road School, Exeter; Hele's School, Exeter; Exeter School. **Career:** Assistant Master, Bedford School; Bedford Technical Institute 1925–1944 (Principal 1935–1944); Headmaster, Dursley Secondary School and Technical Institute 1945–1969. Died 9 August 1987.

WOODMAN, John Geoffrey Wootten (1924) Born 23 March 1907, Dunsden House, Dunsden, Oxon; son of Captain Leonard Cecil Woodman, of independent means, and Mary Dorothea Borwick; m Irene Marie Price (née Courtin), 7 May 1949, St George's, Hanover Square. **Subject(s):** Law; BA 1928. **Tutor(s):** J M Wordie. **Johnian Relatives:** stepfather of Peter Henry Mabille Price (1956). **Educ:** St Cyprian's School, Eastbourne; St Andrew's School, Eastbourne; Wellington College. **Career:** Called to the Bar, Inner Temple 1929; Farmer of 1000 acres. **Appointments:** President, Shorthorn Society 1958–1959. Died 12 December 1959.

WOODMAN, John Vere (1930) Born 25 December 1911, Gordleton Mill, Hordle, Lymington, Hampshire; son of Leslie Woodman, Miller and Corn Merchant, and Dorothy Margaret Taylor; m Hildegard Maria Gerlach, 1940; 1 son (Dennis b 1940), 1 daughter (Joanna b 1946). **Subject(s):** Natural Sciences; BA 1933; MA 1945; Chartered Member, Institute of Gas Engineers. **Tutor(s):** C W Guillebaud. **Johnian Relatives:** step-grandson of Frederick Thomas Huntley (1881); father of Dennis Vere Woodman (1960). **Educ:** Milton Abbas Grammar School, Blandford; Weymouth College. **Career:** Trainee, Canons Glue Works 1934; Laboratory Assistant, War Department Chemist, Woolwich 1934; Salesman, Edmundsons Electric 1935; Chemist, ICI/Alfloc Water Treatment 1936–1939; Development Chemist, BP Swansea and Iran 1939–1944; Technical Sales Engineer, Whessoe Foundry and Engineering Company Ltd 1945–1965; Gas Consultant 1965–1975. **Appointments:** Member, Royal Horticultural Society; Member, International Camellia Society; Member, Ikebana International.

WOODMANSEY, The Revd Geoffrey Erskine (1910) Born 24 December 1891, 33 Whitehall Park, Islington, Middlesex; son of John Henry Woodmansey, Solicitor, and Florence Ada Culver; m Helen Mary Haswell, 26 April 1927, All Saints' Church, Hull; 3 children. **Subject(s):** History; BA 1913; MA 1917. **Tutor(s):** E E Sikes. **Educ:** Wynyard House School, Watford; Winchester House School, Deal; Aldenham School. **Career:** Deacon 1914; Priest 1915; CF, 4th Class, RACD, WWI; Vicar, St Matthias, Sheffield 1927–1935; Vicar, St Mark, Barrow-in-Furness 1935–1942; Rector, Walcot, Bath 1942. Died 27 April 1942 (killed in an air raid).

WOODROFFE, Squadron Leader Charles Peter (1943) Born 28 February 1925, Durian Daun Hospital, Malacca, Straits Settlements; son of Arthur Stanley Woodroffe, Rubber Planter, and Elizabeth Ellen Isabella Townley; m Barbara Scott Taylor; 2 sons (Nick and Guy), 1 daughter (Fiona). **Subject(s):** Mechanical Sciences; BA 1946; MA 1950. **Tutor(s):** S J Bailey. **Educ:** Hillmorton Kindergarten School, Worthing; Caterham School. **Career:** Oil Company; Whaling Station; Gold Mine; Instructor, RAF College, Cranwell; OC Aberdeen University Air Squadron; RAF 1950; Staff Officer, RAF, Singapore 1961. Died 16 June 1980.

WOODROOFFE, Thomas Borries Ralph (1920) Naval Officer.

WOODWARD, The Revd Geoffrey Wallace (1941) Born 4 March 1923, Foundry House, Linden Road, Brownhills, Walsall; son of Samuel Arthur Woodward, Engineer and Ironfounder, and Eleanor Woodhouse Mansfield; 1 daughter. **Subject(s):** History; BA 1947; MA 1950. **Tutor(s):** C W Guillebaud. **Educ:** Queen Mary's Grammar School, Walsall; Denstone College; Westcott House, Cambridge. **Career:** Ordained Deacon, to the curacy of St John, Middlesbrough 1949; Ordained Priest 1950; Curate, Rugeley, Staffordshire 1952–1954; Curate, Edgmond 1954–1955; Vicar, Whorlton, Yorkshire 1955; Vicar, St Thomas, Middlesbrough 1965; Vicar, Nunthorpe in Cleveland 1965; Anglican Chaplain, East Netherlands 1990–1993; Anglican Chaplain, Holy Trinity, Malta 1993–1994. Died September 1998.

WOODWARK, Dr George Millington (1941) Born 27 April 1923, 4 Harley Street, London; son of Arthur Stanley Woodwark, Consulting Physician, and Hilda Mary Robinson; m (1) Carol Mary Jenkins, 21 February 1948, St James' Church, Sussex Gardens, (2) Sheila Mary Wise, 1983; 1 son (William), 3 daughters (Sara, Penelope and Lorraine). **Subject(s):** Medical Sciences; BA 1944; MA 1948; BChir 1947; MB 1947; MRCP London 1953; FRCPC Canada 1960; MRCS (London); LRCP (London) 1947. **Tutor(s):** S J Bailey. **Johnian Relatives:** brother of Richard Graham Woodwark (1939). **Educ:** Arnold House, London and Langley Place; Westminster School. **Career:** House Physician and Surgical House Officer, Westminster Hospital 1947; Surgeon Lieutenant, RNVR 1948–1949; House Physician, Brompton Hospital 1950; Medical Registrar, Westminster Hospital 1951–1952; Resident Medical Officer, National Heart Hospital 1953; Cardiologist, Salisbury, Southern Rhodesia 1953–1958; Lecturer in Cardiology, University of Colorado, USA 1959; Cardiologist, Victoria, BC, Canada 1960–1998. **Appointments:** Fellow, American College of Cardiology; Fellow, American Heart Association.

WOODWARK, Richard Graham (1939) Born 11 April 1921, 4 Harley Street, London; son of Arthur Stanley Woodwark, Consulting Physician, and Hilda Mary Robinson; m Elizabeth Janet Glendinning, 2 April 1949; 1 son, 3 daughters. **Subject(s):** Mechanical Sciences; BA 1942; MA 1946; AMIEE; FIEE. **Tutor(s):** J M Wordie. **Johnian Relatives:** brother of George Millington Woodwark (1941). **Educ:** Arnold House School, St John's Wood; Westminster School. **Career:** Lieutenant, RNVR 1941–1946; British Iron and Steel Research Association; Principal Scientific Officer, Ministry of Defence; MI6 1946–1955; J L Eve Construction Ltd 1955–1985 (Managing Director 1970–1985). **Appointments:** Liveryman 1943, Master 1960 and 1972, Clerk 1985–1996, The Worshipful Company of Turners. **Honours:** DSC 1942. Died 25 December 2001.

WOOLDRIDGE, Duncan Wakeman (1908) Born 25 April 1889, Stourbridge Road, Lye, Worcestershire; son of Henry Wooldridge, Nail Manufacturer, and Elizabeth Wakeman. BA 1911. **Tutor(s):** L H K Bushe-Fox. **Educ:** St John's Parish Schools, Stourbridge; Hill Street Board Schools, Stourbridge; Edward VI Grammar School, Stourbridge; Falmouth Grammar School.

WOOLER, Charles Armytage (1914) Born 16 March 1895, Elsdon House, Wortley, Yorkshire; son of Ernest Octavius Wooler, Solicitor, and Tabitha Louisa Nowell. **Tutor(s):** E E Sikes. **Johnian Relatives:** brother of Herbert Sykes Wooler (1911). **Educ:** Sedbergh School. **Career:** Second Lieutenant, West Yorkshire Regiment, WWI. **Awards:** Lupton and Hebblethwaite Exhibition, SJC. Died 20 July 1916 (of wounds received in action on 1 July 1916).

WOOLER, Cyril Upton (1905) Born 9 March 1886, Thurgoland, Sheffield, Yorkshire; son of William Upton Wooler, Vicar, Thurgoland, and Jane Eliza Price. **Subject(s):** Theology; BA 1908. **Tutor(s):** E E Sikes. **Johnian Relatives:** son of William Upton Wooler (1867). **Educ:** Archbishop Holgate's School, Barnsley; Denstone College. **Career:**

Ordained Deacon 1914; Curate, St George, Camberwell 1914–1917; Curate, West Wycombe 1917–1920; Curate, Worsborough 1924–1927.

WOOLER, Herbert Sykes (1911) Born 28 November 1892, 5 Gladstone Terrace, Morley, Leeds; son of Ernest Octavius Wooler, Solicitor, and Tabitha Louisa Nowell. **Subject(s):** Classics; BA 1914. **Tutor(s):** E E Sikes. **Johnian Relatives:** brother of Charles Armytage Wooler (1914). **Educ:** Sedbergh School. **Career:** Second Lieutenant, 12th Battalion, West Yorkshire Regiment, WWI. **Awards:** Lupton Scholarship. Died 28 March 1916 (of wounds received in action at St Eloi).

WOOLLEN, Wilfrid Henry (1906) Born 27 December 1887, 74 Leathwaite Road, Clapham Common, London; son of Henry Woollen, Civil Servant, and Sarah Hastings; 2 daughters (Joan and Truda). **Subject(s):** Mathematics; BA 1909; MA 1927. **Tutor(s):** L H K Bushe-Fox. **Educ:** Lavender Hill Elementary School; Ipswich Higher Elementary School; Ipswich School. **Career:** Master, Wellesley House, Broadstairs 1909–1910; Ordained Deacon 1911; Master, Mount St Benedict, Gorey, County Wexford 1915–1918; Master, St Gerard's, Bray, County Wicklow 1918–1921; Master, Downside School 1921–1927; Master, Ealing Priory School 1927. **Appointments:** Appeals Secretary, Oxford and Cambridge Catholic Education Board 1930; Member, Executive Committee, Converts' Aid Society 1950. **Publications:** *St Gertrude*; *Father Faber*, 1929; *The Earlier History of Catholic Emancipation*, 1929; *The Layman in the Parish*, 1931. Died 22 July 1960.

WOOLLETT, Major General John Castle (1935) Born 5 November 1915, 53 Ritherdon Road, Wandsworth, London; son of John Castle Woollett, Schoolmaster, and Lily Bradley Penny, Schoolmistress; m (1) Joan Eileen Stranks, 1941 (div 1958), (2) Helen Wendy Willis, 1959; (1) 3 sons, (2) 2 stepsons. **Subject(s):** Mechanical Sciences; BA 1937; MA 1966; CEng; FICE. **Tutor(s):** J S Boys Smith. **Johnian Relatives:** cousin of Michael Francis Castle Woollett (1951). **Educ:** Ealing Priory School; RMA Woolwich. **Career:** Joined RE 1935; 23 Field Company 1938–1940 (BEF 1939–1940); 6 Commando (raids to Norway) 1940–1942; Major Commanding, 16 Field Squadron and 16 Assault Squadron, RE 1942–1945 (BLA 1944–1945); Student, Staff College, Camberley 1946; DAAG and GSO2, British Service Mission to Burma 1947–1950; Major Commanding, 51 Port Squadron RE 1950; Instructor, Staff College, Camberley 1950–1953; Lieutenant Colonel Commanding, 28 Field Engineer Regiment (Korea) 1954–1955; Brevet Lieutenant Colonel 1955; Commander, Christmas Island 1956–1957; H Bomb Trials, GSO1, Northern Army Group 1957–1959; Colonel, British Instructor, US Army Staff College, Fort Leavenworth 1959–1961; DQMG (Movements), BAOR 1962–1964; Brigadier Commanding, Hampshire Sub District and Transportation Centre, RE 1964–1965; School of Transport 1965–1966; Deputy Engineer-in-Chief 1966–1967; Major-General, Chief Engineer, BAOR 1967–1970; Retired 1970; Planning Inspector, DoE 1971; Principal Planning Inspector, DoE 1975; Panel of Independent Inspectors 1981–1985. **Appointments:** Colonel Commandant, RE 1973–1978; President, Institution of RE 1974–1979; President, Brockenhurst Branch Royal British Legion 1992–; President, Normandy Veterans Association (South East Branch) 1993–. **Honours:** MC 1945; OBE 1955; CBE 1957.

WOOLNOUGH, Hector Thomas (1945) Born 16 April 1927, 2 Symington Street, Northampton; son of George Arthur Benjamin Woolnough, Painter and Decorator, and Hilda Louise Smith. **Tutor(s):** J M Wordie. **Educ:** Northampton Town and County School; Bloxham School, Oxfordshire.

WOOLRICH, Dr William Grant (1912) Born 5 December 1893, 24 Trossacks Road, East Dulwich, Surrey; son of William John Woolrich, Bank Manager, and Pennel McAndrew Grant; m Lorna Ballard, 3 March 1921, All Saints', Sanderstead, Surrey. BA 1915; MA 1921; MRCS; LRCP 1917. **Tutor(s):** R P Gregory. **Educ:** Whitgift Grammar School. **Career:** Captain, RAMC, WWI; Honorary Anaesthetist, Croydon General Hospital; Assistant Resident, Medical Officer, London Fever Hospital;

House Physician, Casualty Officer, and Resident Anaesthetist, St Thomas' Hospital. Died Spring 1973.

WOOTTON, Professor Ian David Phimester (1939) Born 5 March 1921, 75 Church Lane, Tipton, Staffordshire; son of David Wootton, Schoolmaster, and Charlotte Phimester; m Veryan Mary Walshe, 1946; 2 sons, 2 daughters. **Subject(s):** Natural Sciences; BA 1942; MA 1946; MB 1945; BChir 1945; PhD (London); FRSC; FRCPath; FRCP; FRIC. **Tutor(s):** R L Howland. **Educ:** Lodmoor High School; Weymouth Grammar School. **Career:** Research Assistant, Postgraduate Medical School 1945; Lecturer, Postgraduate Medical School 1949; Major, RAMC 1949; Smith-Mundt Fellow, Memorial Hospital, New York 1951; Consultant Pathologist, Hammersmith Hospital 1952; Senior Lecturer 1959, Reader 1961, Professor of Chemical Pathology 1963–1982, Royal Postgraduate Medical School, University of London. **Appointments:** President, Athletic Union, SJC; Member, MRC Unit, Cairo 1947–1948. **Publications:** *Microanalysis in Medical Biochemistry*, 1964; *Biochemical Disorders in Human Disease*, 1970; papers in medical and scientific journals on biochemistry and pathology.

WORDEN, Professor Alastair Norman (1940) Born 23 April 1916, 9 Raikes Parade, Blackpool, Lancashire; son of Charles Norman Worden, Schoolmaster, and Elizabeth Cameron; m Mary, 1950; 2 sons (Blair and Mark), 1 daughter (Sarah), 1 stepson (Robert Peel). **Subject(s):** Natural Sciences; BA 1942; MA 1946; PhD 1970; MB 1983; BChir 1983; BSc (London) 1939; DVetMed (London) 1969; DMedVet (Zurich) 1972; FRCPath; FRCVS; FRIC; FIBiol; FACVT. **Tutor(s):** J M Wordie. **Johnian Relatives:** stepfather of Robert Peel Worden (1965). **Educ:** Queen Elizabeth's School, Barnet; Royal Veterinary College, London; Lister Institute of Preventative Medicine; Veterinary Laboratory, Ministry of Agriculture, Weybridge. **Career:** Institute of Animal Pathology, Cambridge; Milford Research Professor of Animal Health, University College of Wales, Aberystwyth 1944; Founder and Chairman, Nutritional Research Unit (later renamed the Huntingdon Research Centre) 1951–1978; Professor of Toxicology, University of Bath 1973–1985; Fellow and Co-ordinator of Environmental Studies, Wolfson College, Cambridge; Founder, Cantab Group. **Appointments:** Honorary Professor of Toxicology, University of Surrey 1978; Expert pharmacologue toxicologue speciale, Ministere de la Sante et de la Securite Sociale, France 1981–1986; various positions of authority on many committees. **Publications:** (with Michael Balls and Rosemary J Riddle) *Animals and Alternatives in Toxicity Testing*, Academic Press, 1943; (ed) *The UFAW Handbook on the Care and Management of Laboratory Animals*, Bailliere, Tindall and Cox, 1947; (with Harry Vassie Thompson) *The Rabbit*, New Naturalist Special Volume, Collins, 1956; *Functional Anatomy of Birds*, Cage Birds, 1956; (ed, with Kenneth Charles Sellers, Derek Edward Tribe, and with the collaboration of Donald Whewell Jolly) *Animal Health, Production and Pasture*, Longmans, 1963; (ed, with Michael Balls and Rosemary J Riddell) *Animals and alternatives in toxicity testing* (Proceedings of a meeting held in London in 1982 to discuss the report of the Fund for the Replacement of Animals in Medical Experiments Toxicity Committee), Academic Press, 1983; (ed, with Dennis V Parke and John Marks) *The future of predictive safety evaluation*, Volumes 1 and 2, MTP Press, 1986, 1987; many scientific papers. Died 10 August 1987.

WORDIE, George Thompson (1948) Born 12 July 1927, 63 Grange Road, Cambridge; son of James Mann Wordie, Fellow and Tutor, SJC, and Gertrude Mary Henderson; m Mina Reid Ellis, 10 February 1958, Grey Friars Church, Aberdeen. BA 1950; MA 1955. **Tutor(s):** R L Howland. **Johnian Relatives:** son of James Mann Wordie (1910); brother of John Stewart Wordie (1945) and of Peter Jeffrey Wordie (1952). **Educ:** Bramcote, Scarborough; Winchester College.

WORDIE, Sir James Mann (1910) Born 26 April 1889, 4 Buckingham Terrace, Hillhead, Partick, Lanarkshire, Scotland; son of John Wordie, Carting Contractor, and Jane Catherine Mann; m Gertrude Mary Henderson, 21 March 1923, St Columba's, Pont Street, London; 3 sons

(Peter Jeffrey b 30 May 1932, John Stewart b 15 January 1924 and George Thompson b 12 July 1927), 2 daughters (Elizabeth Stephen b 14 October 1925 and Alison Fotheringham b 24 February 1929). **Subject(s):** Geology; BA 1912; MA 1919; BA (Glasgow) 1906; Hon LLD (Hull) 1957; Hon LLD (Glasgow) 1954. **Tutor(s):** J R Tanner. **Johnian Relatives:** father of John Stewart Wordie (1945), George Thompson Wordie (1948) and of Peter Jeffrey Wordie (1952). **Educ:** Glasgow Academy; Glasgow University. **Career:** Chief of Scientific Staff, Shackleton Antarctic Expedition 1914–1917; Demonstrator in Petrology, University of Cambridge 1914–1917 and 1919–1923; Lieutenant, RA (TF) (wounded), served in France 1917–1918; Foundress Fellow 1921–1926, Title B Fellow 1926–1952, Lecturer in Geography 1946–1952, Master 1952–1959, Title D Fellow 1959–1962, SJC. **Appointments:** Geologist and Second in Command in the Scottish Spitzbergen Expeditions 1919 and 1920; Expeditions to Jan Mayen and East Greenland 1921, 1923, 1926 and 1929; Supervisor in Geography 1921–1948, Director of Studies in Geography 1921–1952, Tutor 1923–1952, Senior Tutor 1933–1952, President 1950–1952, SJC; Junior Proctor, University of Cambridge 1923–1924; Discovery Committee Member, Colonial Office 1923–1949; Expeditions to North West Greenland, Ellesmere Island and Baffin Island 1934 and 1937; Chairman, Cambridge Scott Polar Research Institute 1937–1955; Expedition to South Orkneys, South Shetlands and Graham Land, Antarctica 1947; Member, Council of the Senate, University of Cambridge 1948–1950; Chairman, British-Norwegian Antarctic Expedition; President, Royal Geographical Society 1951–1954; Chairman, British Mountaineering Council 1953–1956; Honorary Fellow, TCD 1954; Vice President, Alpine Club; Chairman, British National Committee of the International Geophysical Year 1954–1958; Chairman, Discovery Committee of the Colonial Office; Member, Committee of the Trans-Antarctic Expedition; Chairman, Administrative Committee of the Mount Everest Foundation; Vice-President, International Commission on Snow and Ice. **Awards:** Polar Medal 1917; Harkness Scholarship, University of Cambridge; Back Grant 1920; Bruce Medal, Royal Society of Edinburgh 1926; Founder's Medal, Royal Geographic Society 1933; Gold Medal, Royal Scottish Geographic Society 1944; Charles P Daly Medal, American Geographical Society of New York 1952. **Honours:** CBE 1947; Kt 1957; Commander of the Order of St Olaf of Norway. Died 16 January 1962.

WORDIE, Sir John Stewart (1945) Born 15 January 1924, 3 Wordsworth Grove, Cambridge; son of James Mann Wordie, Fellow and Tutor, SJC, and Gertrude Mary Henderson; m Patricia Gladys Kynoch, 11 August 1955; 4 sons. **Subject(s):** Law; BA 1948; MA 1953; LLB 1949; LLM 1985. **Tutor(s):** S J Bailey. **Johnian Relatives:** son of James Mann Wordie (1910); brother of George Thompson Wordie (1948) and of Peter Jeffrey Wordie (1952). **Educ:** Bramcote, Scarborough; Winchester College. **Career:** RNVR 1942–1946; Called to the Bar, Inner Temple, then in practice at the Bar 1950–1986; Commander, London Division, RNR 1969–1971. **Appointments:** Chairman, Wages Councils 1956–1993; Chairman, Soulbury Committee 1966; Chairman, Burnham and Pelham Committees 1966–1987; Member 1971, Master 1975, Court of Assistants, Salters' Company; Member, Agricultural Wages Board for England and Wales 1974–1995; Deputy Chairman and Member, Central Arbitration Committee 1976–1991; Chairman, National Joint Council for Lectures in Further Education 1980–1993; Council Member, ACAS 1986–1990. **Honours:** VRD 1963; CBE 1975; Kt 1981. Died 21 January 1997.

WORLIDGE, Edward John (1948) Born 31 May 1928, Little Croft, Draycott Road, Wanstead, Essex; son of Robert Leonard Worlidge, Coal Factor, and Kathleen Frances Bonallack; m Margaret Elizabeth Murray, 8 January 1955, Aberdeen; 3 sons (David John b 19 August 1956, Nigel James b 4 July 1960 and Mark Gregor Murray b 30 October 1963). **Subject(s):** Mechanical Sciences; BA 1950; MA 1976; FRSA. **Tutor(s):** R L Howland. **Johnian Relatives:** father of David John Worlidge (1975). **Educ:** St Aubyn's Preparatory School, Woodford; Northcliffe House Preparatory School, Bognor Regis; Marlborough College. **Career:** Executive Director, BAT Industries plc 1980–1989; Chairman, Wiggins Teape Group 1984–1989; Non-executive Director, Thames Water plc and the Rugby Group plc 1987–1997. **Appointments:** Secretary, LMBC 1950–1951; Secretary, May Ball Committee, SJC 1951; Member, Hawks; Member, Eagles; Council Member and Chairman of Finance Committee, Marlborough College 1988–1998; Governor, Westbourne House School 1990–; Governor, Woolmer Hill (LEA) School, Haslemere 1992–2000. **Awards:** Sir Joseph Larmor Award 1951; Grand Challenge Cup (with LMBC), Henley Royal Regatta 1951; Grand Challenge Cup (with Leander), Henley Royal Regatta 1952.

WORMALD, Brian Harvey Goodwin (1936) (admitted to Peterhouse 1931) Born 24 July 1912, All Saints' Parsonage, Four Oaks, Sutton Coldfield, Birmingham; son of Charles Octavius Richard Wormald, Clerk in Holy Orders, and Ada Wynifred Coulson Brooks; m Rosemary Lloyd, 1946, Little St Mary's, Cambridge; 4 sons. **Subject(s):** History; BA 1934; MA 1938. **Tutor(s):** J S Boys Smith. **Educ:** Harrow School, London; Peterhouse, Cambridge. **Career:** Fellow 1938–1979 (Emeritus 1979), Chaplain and Catechist 1940–1948, Dean 1941–1944, Peterhouse, Cambridge; Lecturer in History 1948–1979, Junior Proctor 1951–1952, University of Cambridge. **Appointments:** Tutor, Peterhouse, Cambridge 1952–1962; Select Preacher, Cambridge 1954. **Awards:** Scholarship, SJC; Strathcona Research Studentship, SJC 1936–1938; Members' Prize (English Essay) 1935; Prince Consort Prize, University of Cambridge 1938. **Publications:** *Clarendon: Politics, History and Religion, 1640–1660*, CUP, 1951; *Francis Bacon: History, Politics and Science, 1561–1626*, CUP, 1993.

WORMELL, Professor Donald Ernest Wilson (1926) Born 5 January 1908, 38 Theresa Avenue, Bristol, Gloucestershire; son of Thomas Wilson Wormell, Schoolmaster, and Florence Pickles; m Daphne; 3 sons, 1 daughter. **Subject(s):** Classics; BA 1930; MA 1933. **Tutor(s):** M P Charlesworth. **Johnian Relatives:** brother of Thomas Wilson Wormell (1922). **Educ:** The Perse School, Cambridge. **Career:** Title A Fellow, SJC 1933–1936; Fellow 1939, Professor of Latin 1942, Senior Lecturer and Public Orator 1952, TCD. **Appointments:** Member, RIA 1955. **Awards:** Scholarship, SJC 1925; Browne Medal, University of Cambridge 1929; Porson Prize, University of Cambridge 1929; Sandys Studentship, University of Cambridge 1930; Strathcona Studentship, SJC 1930. **Publications:** *The Delphic Oracle*, 1956; (ed with E H Alton and E Courtney) *P Ovidi Nasonis Fastorum libri sex*, 1978. Died 15 July 1990.

WORMELL, Dr Thomas Wilson (1922) Born 28 November 1903, 22 Nevil Road, Bristol, Gloucestershire; son of Thomas Wilson Wormell, Schoolmaster, and Florence Pickles. **Subject(s):** Natural Sciences; BA 1925; MA 1929. **Tutor(s):** B F Armitage. **Johnian Relatives:** brother of Donald Ernest Wilson Wormell (1926). **Educ:** Wigan Grammar School; Manchester Grammar School; Perse School, Cambridge. **Career:** Observer in Meteorological Physics 1926–1950, Lecturer in Meteorological Physics 1950–1971, University of Cambridge; Fellow, Fitzwilliam House, Cambridge 1963. **Appointments:** Supervisor in Physics, SJC 1943–1963; Secretary 1953–1954, Vice-President, 1953–1955, Royal Meteorological Society; Editor, *Journal of the Royal Meteorological Society.* **Awards:** Scholarship, SJC. Died 3 January 1985.

WORRALL, Newton (1903) Born 22 March 1884, 20 Talbot Place, Sheffield, Yorkshire; son of Joseph Worrall, Merchant, and Annie Newton. **Subject(s):** Modern and Medieval Languages; BA 1906; MA 1919. **Tutor(s):** E E Sikes. **Educ:** Wesley College, Sheffield. **Career:** Acting Vice-Consul, Bushire 1910–1912; Vice-Consul, Diarbekir 1912; Head, Vice-Consulate, Resht 1912–1913; Vice-Consul, Ispahan 1913.

WORSLEY, Thomas Cuthbert (1926) Born 10 December 1907, 23 North Bailey, Durham; son of Frederick William Worsley, Dean of Llandaff, and Catherine Ethel Payne. **Subject(s):** Classics; BA 1929. **Tutor(s):** M P Charlesworth. **Educ:** Llandaff Cathedral School; Brightlands, Newnham; Marlborough College. **Career:** Assistant Master, Wellington College 1929–1934; Private tutor; Master, Gordonstoun School; Freelance writer and theatre reviewer, articles appearing in *Britain Today* and *Nation;* Writer and reviewer, *New Statesman* 1939; Education

Officer, Initial Training Wing, starting at Torquay Training Command, RAF 1940; Literary Editor and Drama Critic, *New Statesman* 1946–1952; Drama Critic 1952–1964, Television Critic 1965–1972, *Financial Times.* **Awards:** IPC Critic of the Year 1972. **Publications:** *Behind the Battle*, 1939; (with W H Auden) *Education Today & Tomorrow*, 1939; *Barbarians and Philistines*, 1940; *The Fugitive Art*, 1952; (with J Dover Wilson) *Shakespeare's Histories at Stratford 1951*, 1952; *Flannelled Fool*, 1967; *Five Minutes, Sir Matthew*, 1969; *Television: the Ephemeral Art*, 1970; *Fellow Travellers*, 1971. Died 23 February 1977.

WORSTENHOLM, John (1916) Born 16 December 1897, Eaglescliffe, Durham; son of Luther Worstenholm, Editor, *The Northern Echo*, Darlington, and Margaret Hemsley. **Tutor(s):** E E Sikes. **Educ:** Darlington Grammar School. **Career:** Artist's Rifles, then Second Lieutenant (Observer Officer), RFC, WWI. Died 25 September 1917 (killed in action).

WORTHINGTON, The Revd John Clare (1936) Born 3 August 1917, 50d, Clanricarde Gardens, Kensington, London; son of Frank Worthington, Lieutenant Colonel, RAMC, and Ella Marion Skardon Burney; m Rosemary Gerard, 1950; 2 sons (David b 1956 and Peter b 1962), 1 daughter (Anne b 1954). **Subject(s):** Economics; BA 1939; MA 1946. **Tutor(s):** J S Boys Smith. **Johnian Relatives:** son of Frank Worthington (1898). **Educ:** Temple Grove School, Eastbourne; Rossall School; Westcott House, Cambridge. **Career:** Captain, Northumberland Fusiliers 2nd Battalion 1939–1945; Deacon, Rotherham Parish Church 1948–1951; Priest 1949–2000; CF, RACD 1951–1965; Vicar, Ellingham and Harbridge, Diocese of Winchester 1965–1985; Rural Dean of Christchurch 1979–1982; Vicar, Ibsley; Permission to Officiate, Winchester 1985–1995. Died 25 October 2000.

WORTHY, William Digby (1941) Born 29 March 1923, Fernlea, Cleveland Road, West Hartlepool; son of John William Worthy, Schoolmaster, and Ethel May Johnson; 2 children. **Subject(s):** Mechanical Sciences; BA 1944; MA 1948. **Tutor(s):** S J Bailey. **Educ:** Brougham School, West Hartlepool; Pocklington School. **Career:** Mechanical Engineer. **Awards:** Open Exhibition, SJC 1940; Dowman Exhibition, SJC 1941; IEE Major Annual Award in Electronic Engineering 1973. Died 26 January 2004.

WOYKA, Dr John Graham (1947) Born 10 May 1922, 11 Myrtle Park, Glasgow; son of John Graham Woyka, Chartered Accountant, Managing Director, John Woyka & Co Ltd, and Marion Dorothea Forrest. BA 1948; MA 1957. **Tutor(s):** G C L Bertram. **Educ:** Glasgow High School.

WRAGG, Norman (1919) Born 6 June 1897, 23 Station Road, Coatham, Kirkleatham, Yorkshire; son of Edward Wragg, Grocer, and Mary Tyerman. **Subject(s):** Mathematics; BA 1921; MA 1925. **Tutor(s):** E A Benians. **Educ:** Durham Technical School; Bournemouth School. **Career:** Lieutenant, Dorset Regiment 1914; Master, Stowe School 1924. **Awards:** Scholarship, SJC 1915. **Honours:** MC 1919.

WRAITH, James Osborn Barker (1931) Born 25 November 1912, 21 Strawberry Hill Road, Twickenham; son of Herbert Osborn Wraith, Electrical Engineer, and Louise Marian Barker. **Subject(s):** Classics/Law; BA 1934; MA 1938. **Tutor(s):** M P Charlesworth. **Educ:** Ovingdean Preparatory School; Winchester College. **Career:** Pilot Officer, RAF 1939–1942. Died 5 October 1942 (killed during operational flying duties).

WRAITH, Louis Charles (1919) Born 4 February 1902, 40 Headingley Road, Handsworth, Staffordshire; son of Louis Frederic Carl Fürstenau, Colliery Agent, and Dora Wraith. **Tutor(s):** E E Sikes. **Educ:** Westholme School, Hunstanton; Brighton College.

WREN, Thomas Lancaster (1908) Born 18 April 1889, 32 Paddenswick Road, Hammersmith; son of Thomas Wren, Schoolmaster, and Amy Elizabeth Lancaster. **Subject(s):** Mathematics; BA 1911; MA 1915. **Tutor(s):** L H K Bushe-Fox. **Educ:** Latymer Upper School. **Career:**

Assistant in Mathematics, Bedford College, London 1913–1914; Foundress Fellow 1913–1919, Lecturer in Mathematics 1914–1919 (on war service 1915–1918), SJC; Lieutenant, RASC 1915; Anti-Aircraft Experimental Section, Munitions Inventions Department 1917; Reader in Geometry, University of London 1919–1954. **Appointments:** Vice-President, London Mathematical Society 1931–1933. **Awards:** Rayleigh Prize, University of Cambridge 1913; Foundation Scholarship 1908. **Publications:** 'Some Applications of the Two-Three Birational Space Transformation', *Procedures of the London Mathematical Society*, 15, 1916; 'Involutory Point-Pairs in the Quadro-Quadric Cremona Space Transformation', *Procedures of the London Mathematical Society*, 24, 1926; 'The Correspondence between Lines in Threefold Space and Points of a Quadric Fourfold in Fivefold Space, Established by a Geometrical Construction', *Procedures of the Cambridge Philosophical Society*, 23, 1926; 'The Sets of 27 Points in which a Plane Cubic Curve is Met by the Lines on Cubic Surfaces', *Journal of the London Mathematical Society*, 6, 1931. Died 14 June 1972.

WRIGHT, Charles Alban (1902) Born 18 October 1882, Codrington College, St John's Parish, Barbados; son of Alban Henry Wright, Clerk in Holy Orders, and Martha Jane Moore. BA 1904. **Tutor(s):** J R Tanner; C E Graves. **Educ:** Bedford Modern School.

WRIGHT, Charles William Brydon (1921) Born 22 June 1882, Waterloo Place, Cranbrook, Kent; son of Peter Halliday Wright, Teacher, and Caroline Rosita Chilton; m Kathleen Amy (d 9 March 1951); 2 daughters (Peggy and Diana). **Subject(s):** Horticulture; MA 1921. **Johnian Relatives:** son of Peter Halliday Wright (1875). **Educ:** Moorland House, Heswell; Liverpool College. **Appointments:** Honorary Life Councillor, Lawn Tennis Association 1962. Died 8 April 1964.

WRIGHT, Edmund (1945) Born 18 October 1927, 20 Vermont Street, Hull; son of George Kelsey Wright, Signwriter, Decorator and Violinist, and Harriet Ann Clark; m (2) Ursula; (1) 1 son, 1 daughter, (2) 1 son (Dominic), 1 daughter (Berenice). **Subject(s):** Natural Sciences; BA 1949; MA 1963; DPhil (Oxon) 1959. **Tutor(s):** J M Wordie. **Educ:** St Vincent's Roman Catholic School; The Marist College, Hull; Balliol College, Oxford. **Career:** Prospecting for bauxite, New Guinea, and for gold, Australia 1952–1953; Mapping, Red Sea Hills and Equatorial Province for Geological Survey of Sudan 1954–1955; Mapping, Botswana 1955–1958; Supervisor, mapping basement complex rocks of the Jos Plateau with Geological Survey of Nigeria 1960; UK Nature Conservancy 1963; Geology Teacher, University of Saskatoon 1965; Hydrogeology Group, British Geological Survey 1966; Head of Overseas Hydrogeology, British Geological Survey, and Adviser to Overseas Development Administration on Hydrogeology and Geothermal Energy 1973–1987; Water Resources Associated Ltd 1995–1998. **Appointments:** Independent Consultant, Overseas Development Administration, United Nations Development Programme, the World Bank, WaterAid, bilateral aid agencies and consulting firms 1987; Visiting Professor in Hydrogeology, UCL 1994. Died July 1998.

WRIGHT, Frank Burnet (1936) Born 23 May 1917, Bemersyde, Kilmacolm, Renfrewshire; son of Thomas Brown Wright, Electrical Contractor, and Annie Ure Primrose Burnet. BA 1939. **Tutor(s):** J S Boys Smith. **Educ:** Warriston, Moffat; Loretto School, Musselburgh. **Career:** Pilot Officer, RAF. Died 6 January 1941 (killed in action).

WRIGHT, Geoffrey Richard Hodgson (1918) Born 13 October 1900, 4 Park Road, Halifax, Yorkshire; son of John Crossley Wright, Major, RAMC, and Florence Le Motte. **Tutor(s):** R P Gregory. **Johnian Relatives:** son of John Crossley Wright (1884). **Educ:** Southcliffe School; Marlborough College.

WRIGHT, Harry Albert (1942) Born 25 September 1924, Crown Farm, Moulton Marsh, Spalding; son of Albert Wright, Farmer, and Edith Manton; m Audrey; 2 daughters (Christine and Pauline). **Subject(s):** Natural Sciences; BA 1947; MA 1953; DipAgr 1949. **Tutor(s):** C W

Guillebaud. **Educ:** Moulton Grammar School; Spalding Grammar School. **Career:** Pilot, Fleet Air Arm 1943; Deputy County Advisory Officer for Herefordshire, National Agricultural Advisory Service 1964. Died 29 September 1988.

WRIGHT, Professor Henry Myles (1927) Born 9 June 1908, 2 Jesmond Gardens, Newcastle upon Tyne; son of Henry Thomas Wright, Architect, and Gertrude Emma Blair; m Catharine Noble, 1939 (d 1981); 2 daughters. **Subject(s):** Architecture; BA 1930; MA 1937. **Tutor(s):** C W Guillebaud. **Educ:** Newcastle Preparatory School; Fettes College, Edinburgh; Royal Institute of British Architects. **Career:** Assistant in various private offices 1930–1935; Assistant Editor, *The Architects' Journal*, and in private practice 1935–1940; Partner in firm of Sir William Holford 1948–1954; Lever Professor of Civic Design, University of Liverpool 1954–1975 (Emeritus 1975); University Planning Consultant 1957–1977. **Appointments:** Member, British Caribbean Federal Capital Commission 1956. **Publications:** *The Planner's Notebook*, 1948; (with Lord Holford) *Cambridge Planning Proposals*, 1950; (with Lord Holford) *Corby New Town*, 1952; (ed and contributor) *Land Use in an Urban Environment*, 1961; *The Dublin Region: Preliminary and Final Reports*, 1965 and 1967; *Lord Leverhulme's Unknown Venture*, 1982; other technical publications.

WRIGHT, James Brown (1921) Naval Officer.

WRIGHT, James Faulkner (1941) Born 24 April 1923, Kislingbury, Northamptonshire; son of Christopher Edmund Wright, Secretary, NFU, and Ivy Stella Payne; m Marie Hurditch Stephens, 15 July 1954, St Lawrence's Church, Towcester; 1 son (Charles Edmund Faulkner b 8 May 1957). **Subject(s):** Law; BA 1948; MA 1950; LLB 1949. **Tutor(s):** S J Bailey. **Johnian Relatives:** father of Charles Edmund Faulkner Wright (1976). **Educ:** Wayneflete House Preparatory School; Kimbolton School. **Career:** Captain, RA, India 1947; Articled to Messrs Hensman, Jackson and Chamberlain, Northampton (Partner 1954).

WRIGHT, Captain John Walker (1940) Born 12 April 1922, Beaumont Lodge, Paignton, Devon; son of Thomas Wright, Secretary to the Chairman of the London County Council, and Hilda Mary Walker; m Jenny Macmillan (née Richardson), 1971; 2 stepchildren. **Subject(s):** Engineering; BA 1943; MA 1949. **Tutor(s):** S J Bailey. **Educ:** Colet Court, London; Thrings Brunswick, Haywards Heath; St Paul's School. **Career:** RE 1940–1946; 1st Battalion King George V's Bengal Sappers and Miners; Lieutenant, 2nd Field Company Indian Engineers; 291 Field Company; 70 Field Company; Public Works Department, Malaya; World Bank; Civil Engineering posts on United Nations development projects, Far East (latterly State Engineer of Jahore); Consultancy work with various engineers including work in the UK, India, Central Africa, and Papua New Guinea; Howard Humphreys, Consulting Engineers; Lecturer in Industrial Administration, University of Manchester 1959. **Awards:** Post-war winner, Malaysian Grand Prix. **Honours:** MC 1944; AMN. Died 31 May 2002.

WRIGHT, Keith William (1944) Born 18 March 1926, 158 Queens Road, Wimbledon, Surrey; son of William Joseph Wright, Company Secretary, and Edith Phyllis Curgenven; m Pamela Margaret Vaissière, 1955; 2 daughters (Susan Diana b 1958 and Jane Sylvia b 1960). **Subject(s):** Mathematics; BA 1949; MA 1960; FIA 1955. **Tutor(s):** J M Wordie. **Johnian Relatives:** uncle of Anthony John Purnell (1983). **Educ:** Bushey Junior School, Merton; Raynes Park County School. **Career:** Actuarial Student, Equity & Law Life Assurance Society 1950–1962; Partner, Gilbert Eliott & Co 1962–1964; Partner, L Messel & Co 1964–1986. **Appointments:** Parish Church Treasurer.

WRIGHT, Norman Mackay (1926) Born 9 June 1904, Victoria Road, Aldershot, Southampton; son of Thomas Wright, Medical Practitioner, and Mabel Mary Galway. BA 1930; MA 1934. **Tutor(s):** J M Wordie. **Johnian Relatives:** brother of Thomas Wright (1926). **Educ:** Edinburgh House School, Lee-on-Solent; St Edward's School, Oxford. **Career:**

Stockbroker 1922–1923; Assistant Master, Witon House Preparatory School, Winchester 1923–1924; Assistant Master, School in Enfield 1924–1925.

WRIGHT, Norman Parker (1925) Born 25 July 1906, 29 Wesley Crescent, Shildon, County Durham; son of James Wright, Inspector of Schools, and Frances Margaret Parker; m; 1 son (Peter), 2 daughters (Celia and Alison). **Subject(s):** English/Modern and Medieval Languages; BA 1929; MA 1932. **Tutor(s):** E E Sikes. **Educ:** Council School, New Shildon; Barnard Castle School; University of Paris. **Career:** Secretary, Department of Education 1966–1973. Died 25 June 2002.

WRIGHT, Richard Adair (1933) Born 24 March 1915, 101 Castle Road, Scarborough; son of William Lord Wright, Master Draper, and Helen Stevenson Adair. **Subject(s):** Mathematics; BA 1936; PGCE. **Tutor(s):** J M Wordie. **Educ:** The Downs School, Colwall, Malvern; Bootham School, York. **Career:** Teacher, Brummana High School, Lebanon; Teacher, Leighton Park School 1945–1946; Head of Mathematics and Senior Master, Friends' School, Saffron Walden 1946–1978. Died February 2002.

WRIGHT, Theodore (1912) Born 20 February 1893, Flowergate Cross, Ruswark, Whitby, Yorkshire; son of William Wright, Gentleman, and Kate Colenutt; m Cecilia Ray, 26 October 1921, St Columba's, Nairn, Scotland; 1 son. **Subject(s):** Mathematics; BA 1915. **Tutor(s):** L H K Bushe-Fox. **Educ:** Sneaton Castle School, Whitby; Sedbergh School. **Career:** Captain, Yorkshire Regiment, WWI; Egyptian Civil Service 1925; served in WWII; Mathematics Master, Newpark School for Boys, St Andrews. **Honours:** Order of the Nile. Died July 1972.

WRIGHT, Colonel Thomas (1926) Born 10 November 1906, Victoria Road, Aldershot, Southampton; son of Thomas Wright, Medical Practitioner, and Mabel Mary Galway; m Joyce; 2 sons (John and Robert), 1 daughter (Ann). **Subject(s):** Mechanical Sciences; BA 1928. **Tutor(s):** J M Wordie. **Johnian Relatives:** brother of Norman Mackay Wright (1926). **Educ:** Edinburgh House School, Lee on the Solent; Dover College; RMA, Woolwich. **Career:** RE. Died 7 January 1989.

WRIGHT, Thomas Grieve (1928) Born 30 May 1911, 21 Falkland Mansions, Glasgow, Scotland; son of Thomas Grieve Wright, Writer and Professor of Law, Glasgow University, and Isabella Gilmour Forsyth. **Tutor(s):** C W Guillebaud. **Educ:** Kelvinside Academy; Merchiston Castle Preparatory School; Merchiston Castle, Edinburgh.

WRIGHT, The Revd William Roland Henry (1907) (admitted as a Non-Collegiate Student 1906) Born 19 January 1886, 75 Bradshawgate, Pennington, Leigh, Lancashire; son of William Wright, Schoolmaster, and Rebecca Shuttleworth. BA 1911; MA 1930. **Tutor(s):** J R Tanner. **Educ:** University School, Southport. **Career:** Leeds Clergy School 1913; Ordained Deacon 1914; Curate, Mirfield 1914; Army 1914–1917; RFC/RAF 1917–1920; Curate, Leeds 1923; Priest 1923; CF, TA 1928–1939; Vicar, Pateley Bridge 1931–1949; Vicar, Greenhow Hill 1931–1949; Surrogate from 1940; Rural Dean, Nidderdale 1947–1949; Perpetual Curate, Bothenham with Walditch, Dorset 1949–1962. Died 9 October 1965.

WU, Yuan Luang (1929) Born 16 January 1909, Peking, China; son of Din Chang Wu, President, Yienyieh Commercial Bank, and Shing Rue Chun. BA 1935. **Tutor(s):** J M Wordie. **Educ:** UCL; Berlitz School of Languages, London; Cheng Ta Middle School, Peking, China.

WYATT, Professor Michael (1949) Born 19 February 1929, Denison House, Victoria Park, Rusholme; son of Stanley Wyatt, Director of Research Unit, MRC, and Maria Catharina Rahusen. BSc (Manchester) 1949; FGS. **Tutor(s):** J M Wordie. **Educ:** Kingsmoor School, Glossop; Manchester University. **Career:** Assistant Professor of Mineralogy, Stanford University. Died 16 September 1956.

WYCHERLEY, Ronald Fowke (1923) Born 30 June 1904, Corbet Arms Hotel, Market Drayton, Salop; son of Alfred Ernest Wycherley, Wine and Spirit Merchant, and Gertrude Ellen Fowke. BA 1926. **Tutor(s):** J M Wordie. **Educ:** The Grammar School, Market Drayton; Denstone College.

WYLIE, Colin St Aubyn (1938) Born 16 July 1918, Barrackpore, India; son of David Angus Wylie, Jute Broker, W F Ducat & Co, and Helen St Aubyn Nixon; m (1) Claudia, 1940, (2) Diana, 1989; (1) 1 daughter (Tessa b 1941). **Subject(s):** Mechanical Sciences; BA 1947; ARICS. **Tutor(s):** J S Boys Smith. **Johnian Relatives:** brother of Kenneth Neil Wylie (1932). **Educ:** Bedford School; RMA Woolwich. **Career:** RE 1938–1962.

WYLIE, Colonel Kenneth Neil (1932) Born 7 September 1911, Calcutta, India; son of David Angus Wylie, Merchant, and Helen St Aubyn Nixon; m Leonie Quarry, 16 June 1945. **Subject(s):** Mechanical Sciences; BA 1934; MA 1958. **Tutor(s):** J S Boys Smith. **Johnian Relatives:** brother of Colin St Aubyn Wylie (1938). **Educ:** Radley College; Bedford School; RMA, Woolwich. **Career:** RE; Cambridge University Careers Service. **Appointments:** Vice Commodore, Royal Ocean Racing Club; Senior Treasurer, LMBC. **Honours:** DSO; MBE. Died 23 October 1991.

WYLLIE, Herbert Ian Campbell (1924) Born 20 March 1906, 108 St Mary's Mansions, Paddington, London; son of John Algernon Wyllie, Insurance Broker, and Ethel Bertha Horatia Goodwin; m Edith Mary Burridge, 21 June 1939. **Subject(s):** Natural Sciences; BA 1927; MA 1947. **Tutor(s):** J M Wordie. **Educ:** Flydneye House, Baldslow; Marlborough College. **Career:** Sales Manager, Sterilizair Ltd; British Reinforced Concrete Engineering Company 1934; Squadron Leader, RAF, Burma 1940–1945. Died 11 June 1988.

WYMAN, Jeffries (1924) Born 21 June 1901, West Newton, Massachusetts, USA; son of Jeffries Wyman and Helen Mackay. **Tutor(s):** B F Armitage. **Educ:** Harvard College; Graduate School of Arts and Sciences, Harvard.

WYNNE WILLSON, The Revd Archdall Alexander (1927) Born 20 June 1908, Thornbury, Whitecross Road, Hereford; son of Archdall Beaumont Wynne Willson, Clerk in Holy Orders, and Andrina Jardine; m Beryl Sturt; 1 daughter. **Subject(s):** Mathematics/Moral Sciences; BA 1930; MA 1934. **Tutor(s):** J M Wordie. **Educ:** Hereford Cathedral Preparatory School; Bengeo School, Hereford; Marlborough College; Lincoln Theological College. **Career:** Ordained Deacon 1932; Curate, Norton on Tees, Durham 1932–1935; Ordained Priest 1933; Curate in Charge, St Cuthbert Conventional District, Monk Wearmouth 1935–1936; Perpetual Curate, Benfieldside, Shotley Bridge 1936. **Awards:** Scholarship, SJC. Died 26 June 1938.

Y

YARDLEY, Georges Emile (1927) Born 2 January 1909, 7 Quai Asnières, Asnières, Seine, France; son of Wilfred Yardley, Employé de Commerce, and Denise Pauline Leontine Louise Perdriau; m Mollie; 2 sons (Peter and Simon). **Subject(s):** Law/Modern and Medieval Languages; BA 1930; MA 1935; MB 1937; BChir 1937; MRCS (Guy's Hospital) 1937; LRCP (Guy's Hospital) 1937. **Tutor(s):** C W Guillebaud. **Educ:** Caldicott School, Hitchin; The Leys School, Cambridge. **Career:** Assistant House Surgeon, Out-patients Officer, and House Physician, Guy's Hospital; Captain, RAMC, 12th Field Ambulance, North Africa and Italy 1941–1944. Died 19 May 1944 (of wounds received on active service).

YARDLEY, Norman Walter Dransfield (1934) Born 19 March 1915, 12 Gawber Road, Barnsley, Yorkshire; son of Percy Dransfield Yardley, Master Grocer, and Alice Hephzibah Smith; m Toni; 3 sons, 1 daughter. BA 1937. **Tutor(s):** J M Wordie. **Educ:** Wakefield Grammar School (Preparatory); St Peter's, York. **Career:** Green Howards, Western Desert (wounded) WWII; Cricketer, Yorkshire 1936–1955 (Captain 1948–1955); England Test Cricketer 1938–1950 (Vice-Captain 1946–1947, Captain 1947–1950); England Test Selector 1951–1954 (Chairman 1951–1952); Journalist and Broadcaster 1954. **Appointments:** President, Yorkshire County Cricket Club 1981–1984 (subsequently Vice-President); Member, BBC North Regional Advisory Council. **Publications:** *Cricket Campaigns*, 1950; (with J M Kilburn) *Homes of Sport*, 1952. Died 3 October 1989.

YARROW, John Alfred Forrest (1935) Born 30 July 1916, Victoria, British Columbia, Canada; son of Norman Alfred Yarrow, Shipbuilder and Engineer, and Ada Hope Leeder. **Tutor(s):** J S Boys Smith. **Educ:** St Michael's School, Victoria; Kingsley School, Vancouver; Brentwood College, Vancouver. Died 11 February 1938.

YARROW, Ronald (1923) Born 27 June 1904, Cauldhams, Roseberry Avenue, Harpenden, Hertfordshire; son of Thomas Alexander Yarrow, Export Coal Merchant, and Annabella Lamb. **Tutor(s):** B F Armitage. **Educ:** Amesbury Hall, Bickley; Temple Grove, Eastbourne; Repton School.

YATES, David Wallace (1929) Born 28 March 1912, 25 Lambolle Road, Hampstead; son of Ernest George Yates, Estate Agent, and Doris Sybil Neal. **Subject(s):** Law; BA 1933; MA 1974. **Tutor(s):** C W Guillebaud. **Educ:** Wellesley House, Broadstairs; Repton School. **Career:** Called to the Bar, Inner Temple 1925.

YATES, Dr Edward Leighton (1935) Born 24 August 1910, 40 Worcester Drive, West Derby, Liverpool; son of Edward Yates, French Polisher, and Mary Agnes Leighton. PhD 1939. **Tutor(s):** J M Wordie. **Educ:** Victoria Council School, Wrexham; Grove Park County School, Wrexham; University College of North Wales, Bangor. **Career:** Senior Lecturer in Physics, University of Sheffield 1938–1955; Professor of Physics, University College of Rhodesia and Nyasaland; Professor of Science Education, University of Zambia; Acting Professor of Physics, Botswana 1955. Died 14 September 1988.

YATES, Dr Frank (1921) Born 12 May 1902, Fog Lane, Didsbury, Withington, Lancashire; son of Percy Yates, Seed Merchant, and Edith Wright; m (1) Pauline (d 1976), (2) Ruth. **Subject(s):** Mathematics; BA 1924; MA 1935; ScD 1938; FRS 1947. **Tutor(s):** E E Sikes. **Educ:** High School, Hale; Wadham House, Hale; Clifton College. **Career:** Mathematics Advisor to the Gold Coast (now Ghana); Chief Statistician, Rothamsted Experimental Station; Member, UN sub-commission on statistical sampling 1947–1952; Senior Research Fellow 1959–1964, Senior Visiting Fellow 1974–1977, Imperial College. **Awards:** Scholarship, SJC 1920; Weldon Memorial Prize, University of Oxford 1953; Royal Medal, Royal Society 1966. **Honours:** CBE 1963. **Publications:** *Design and Analysis of Factorial Experiments*, 1937; (with R A Fisher) *Statistical Tables for Biological, Medical and Agricultural Research*, 1938; *Sampling Methods for Censuses and Surveys*, 1949; *Experimental Design: Selected Papers*, 1970. Died 17 June 1994.

YATES, George Alfred (1927) Born 2 November 1908, 20 Sefton Drive, Liverpool; son of Ellis Keyser Yates, Tobacco Merchant, and Julia Moseley. **Subject(s):** Oriental Languages; BA 1931; MA 1934. **Tutor(s):** M P Charlesworth. **Educ:** Preparatory School, Liverpool; Liverpool College; Clifton College. **Awards:** Rogerson Scholarship, SJC 1926; John Stewart of Rannoch Open Scholarship in Hebrew, University of Cambridge 1927. Died 20 June 1949.

YATES, James Garrett (1947) Born 22 October 1915, Ardmore Mell, Drogheda, Louth, Ireland; son of James Yates, Assistant Secretary, Ministry of Education, and Ethel Thrift; m Jean. **Subject(s):** Mechanical Sciences; MA (by incorporation) 1941. **Educ:** High School, Dublin; Methodist College, Belfast; TCD. **Career:** Demonstrator in Engineering 1945–1948, Lecturer in Engineering 1948–1957, University of Cambridge; Fellow, Trinity College, Cambridge 1954–1957. Died 1 November 1957.

YATES, John Keith (1943) Born 17 October 1926, 336 Waterloo Road, Blackpool, Lancashire; son of Harold Yates, Solicitor, and Annie Whittle; m Joan Parry. **Subject(s):** Mechanical Sciences; BA 1946; MA 1950; Final Examination of Law Society 1952. **Tutor(s):** S J Bailey. **Educ:** Garville School, Blackpool; College of St Joseph, Blackpool; Arnold School, Blackpool. **Career:** Aeronautical Engineering Company, Middlesex; Partner, Blackhurst Parker Yates Solicitors, Blackpool. Died 23 April 1991.

YATES, Paul Lamartine (LAMARTINE YATES) (1927) Born 19 June 1908, Dorset Hall, Merton, Surrey; son of Thomas Lamartine Yates, Solicitor, and Rose Janau. **Subject(s):** History/Economics; BA 1930; MA 1936. **Tutor(s):** E A Benians. **Educ:** The Hall School, Weybridge; Sidcot School, Winscombe. **Career:** Senior Economist, United Nations Food and Agriculture Organization 1951; Director, Joint Agriculture Division, Economic Commission for Europe 1961.

YATES, Robert Eric Burton (1946) Born 6 May 1922, Families Hospital, Meerut, United Provinces, India; son of George Dougal Yates, Lieutenant Colonel, RAMC, and Ruby Emily Elizabeth Reaney. BA 1948; MA 1953; FRICS. **Tutor(s):** G C L Bertram. **Educ:** Lime House, Wetheral; Sedbergh School.

YEADON, Roy Stephenson (1938) Born 10 October 1920, Woodlands, Farsley, Leeds; son of Nathaniel James Yeadon, Company Director, and Gladys May Stephenson. **Subject(s):** Economics. **Tutor(s):** J S Boys Smith. **Educ:** Fulbeck School, Pudsey; Ashville College, Harrogate.

YEARSLEY, Claude Blakesley Lancelot (1903) Born 18 July 1885, Sutton Bonington, Nottinghamshire; son of Ralph Owen Yearsley, Clerk in Holy Orders, and Caroline Jane Blakesley; m Stella de Murinelly; 1 son (John). **Tutor(s):** J R Tanner; C E Graves. **Educ:** Bradfield College. **Career:** Director of Music, King Edward VI Grammar School, Stratford on Avon; Composer and Musical Director; Manager, Prince of Wales Theatre 1921. **Awards:** Choral Studentship, SJC; Sizarship, SJC. Died 31 December 1961.

YEATS, George Francis Walker (1901) Born 27 June 1882, Lyonsdown Vicarage, East Barnet, Hertfordshire; son of George Yeats, Clerk in Holy Orders, and Rosa Bertha Walker. BA 1904; MA 1910. **Tutor(s):** E E Sikes. **Johnian Relatives:** son of George Yeats (1851). **Educ:** St Peter's School, York. **Career:** Master, Sunnydown, Guildford 1904; Private, Middlesex Regiment, WWI.

YEO, The Revd John Haydon (1912) Born 27 December 1888, 92 Yarburgh Street, Moss Side, Lancaster; son of George Christopher Yeo, Linen Manufacturer, and Emma Mary Perry. **Subject(s):** Theology; BA 1915; MA 1919. **Tutor(s):** E E Sikes. **Educ:** Fettes College, Edinburgh; Bishops' College, Cheshunt. **Career:** Deacon 1916; Curate, Lady Margaret's, Walworth 1916–1921; Priest 1917; Curate, St Anne's, Wandsworth 1921–1926; Curate, St Paul's with St Mark's, Deptford 1926–1929; Vicar, St Paul's, Bermondsey 1929–1937; Vicar, Somerford Keynes with Sharncote, Cirencester 1937–1948; Vicar, Rownhams, Southampton 1948–1959 (with Nursling 1955). **Publications:** 'Children of the Dead End', *The Eagle*, 36. Died 1 May 1973.

YEOH, Guan Seok (1901) Born 10 October 1883, China Street, Penang, Straits Settlements; son of Heng Goo Yeoh and Choo Cheed Ho. **Subject(s):** Law/History; BA 1904; LLB 1904. **Tutor(s):** J R Tanner; C E Graves. **Educ:** Penang School. **Career:** Called to the Bar, Gray's Inn 1906. **Awards:** Certificate of Honour, Council of Legal Education 1906.

YEOMAN, Dr John Harbottle (1949) Born 31 August 1930, 10 Fernwood Road, Newcastle upon Tyne; son of John Campbell Yeoman, Medical Practitioner, and Isabel Harbottle; 4 sons. **Subject(s):** Natural Sciences; BA 1952; MB (Edinburgh); BChir (Edinburgh) 1955. **Tutor(s):** G C L Bertram. **Educ:** Tynemouth School; Newton Hall Preparatory School; Bow School, Durham; Loretto School. **Career:** GP in partnership at Whitley Bay Health Centre.

YERBURGH-BONSEY, Robert Harold (1927) Born 9 May 1908, Upton House, Ifield, Crawley, Sussex; son of Harold Robert Yerburgh-Bonsey, Barrister-at-Law, and Henrietta Mary Finch. **Tutor(s):** C W Guillebaud. **Educ:** Forest School, Walthamstow; Rottingdean School; Forest School, Walthamstow. Died 15 December 1945.

YONGE, The Revd Gilbert Vernon (1904) Born 21 March 1885, Rackam, Amberley, Sussex; son of Vernon Cave Yonge, Land Agent, and Alice Sharp; m Marion Beswick, 7 September 1915, St John's, Chester; 3 daughters. BA 1910. **Tutor(s):** E E Sikes. **Johnian Relatives:** grandson of Vernon George Yonge (1841). **Educ:** Oakham School. **Career:** Ordained Deacon 1911; Curate, St Oswald, Chester 1911–1914; Ordained Priest 1912; Curate, St John the Baptist, Chester 1914–1915; Curate, St Mark, New Ferry 1915–1922; Temporary CF 1917–1919; Curate, Minehead 1922–1923; Rector, Horwood with Newton Tracey 1923–1926; Rector, Whitewell, Flintshire 1926–1937; Rector, Old Cleeve, Somerset 1937–1955. Died 8 February 1973.

YORK, Joseph Bernard (1935) Born 14 May 1916, Blue House Farm, Great Barr, Birmingham; son of Sidney York, Farmer, and Mary Jessie Robinson. **Subject(s):** History; BA 1938. **Tutor(s):** J S Boys Smith. **Educ:** Great Barr Church Schools; Walsall Blue Coat School; Queen Mary's Grammar School, Walsall.

YORKE, Alfred Rose (1905) Born 18 December 1885, 90 Harley Street, London; son of William Abbey Yorke, Gentleman, and Catherine Rose. **Tutor(s):** D MacAlister. **Educ:** Aldenham School.

YOUATT, Brian Dinsdale (1919) Naval Officer.

YOUNG, Andrew Blackwood Stewart (1919) Born 13 May 1902, Altdarroch, Toward, Dunoon, Argyllshire; son of Thomas Charles Young, Solicitor, and Isabella Stewart; m Winifred Laura Blacklock, 6 April 1932, Hillhead Parish Church; 2 sons (Donald Stewart b 2 February 1933 and Kenneth Charles Stewart b 28 January 1935), 1 daughter (Ann b 18 January 1937). BA 1922. **Tutor(s):** E E Sikes. **Johnian Relatives:** brother of Thomas Charles Young (1918); father of Kenneth Charles Stewart Young (1953). **Educ:** Kelvinside Academy, Glasgow; Fettes College, Edinburgh. **Career:** Sub-Lieutenant, RNVR; Chairman and Managing Director, Mechans Ltd, Iron and Steel Works, Glasgow until 1957. **Appointments:** Deacon Convenor of the Hammermen, a Glasgow Trades House; Member, The Royal and Ancient Golf Club of St Andrews, Troon, Prestwick, Elie, Glasgow Golf Club. Died 7 November 1984.

YOUNG, Dr Archibald (1932) Born 26 September 1913, 34 Berkeley Terrace, Glasgow; son of Archibald Young, Regius Professor of Surgery, University of Glasgow, and Anna Stuart. **Subject(s):** Natural Sciences; BA 1935; MA 1943; MB (Glasgow); BChir (Glasgow); FRCS (Glasgow). **Tutor(s):** R L Howland. **Educ:** High School of Glasgow. **Career:** Lieutenant Colonel, RAMC; Lecturer in Anatomy, University of Glasgow 1952. **Honours:** TD. Died 2 November 1996.

YOUNG, Colin Arthur MacKenzie (1942) Born 3 November 1924, 53 Burnt Ash Road, Lee, Lewisham, Kent; son of Arthur Frederick Young, Chartered Accountant, and Muriel Alicia Southern; m Phoebe Curtis Brown, 30 September 1950. **Subject(s):** Economics/History; BA 1948; MA 1952. **Tutor(s):** C W Guillebaud. **Educ:** Shirley House Preparatory School, Watford; The Knoll Preparatory School, Woburn Sands; Charterhouse; Upper Canada College, Toronto. **Career:** Curtis Brown Ltd, Literary Agents. Died 19 November 1954.

YOUNG, Ivan Laurence (1932) Born 3 April 1914, 3 East Savile Road, Edinburgh; son of Andrew Laurence Francis Young, Distiller, Broker, Wine and Cigar Agent, and Mary Malcolm Ormiston; m Elizabeth Moir Gartshore, 16 October 1952, Toronto; 1 son (Andrew), 1 daughter (Mary). **Subject(s):** Economics/Law; BA 1935; LLB (Edinburgh) 1938. **Tutor(s):** C W Guillebaud. **Educ:** The Academy, Edinburgh. **Career:**

Lawyer; Senior Partner, Messrs Blair Cadell & Macmillan, Edinburgh 1947. **Honours:** TD. Died 10 December 1995.

YOUNG, Kenneth Gibson (1932) Born 22 June 1913, 169 Glencairn Crescent, Edinburgh; son of Thomas Edwin Young, WS, and Agnes McDougal Turnbull; m Veronica; 3 sons (David, John and William). **Subject(s):** Law; BA 1935; LLB (Edinburgh) 1938. **Tutor(s):** C W Guillebaud. **Educ:** Warriston School, Moffat; Edinburgh Academy. **Career:** Qualified, Notary Public 1939; Apprenticed to Todds Murray WS, Edinburgh 1938; 71 and 108 HAA Regiment, RA 1939–1945; Senior Partner, Young & Kennaway WS, Auchterarder 1945–1984. **Appointments:** Admitted to the Writers of the Signetry 1939; Burgh Chamberlain and Town Clerk, Royal Burgh of Auchterarder 1950–1975; Elder, Church of Scotland for thirty years; Founder, Auchterarder History Association. Died 6 February 2000.

YOUNG, Dr Leopold (1943) See JUNG.

YOUNG, Dr Lindsay Menzies (1945) Born 3 March 1919, 58 Claribel Road, Durban, Natal; son of John Alexander Young, Clerk, South African Railways, and Margaret Jane Menzies. PhD 1947; BA (South Africa) 1938; MA (South Africa) 1941. **Tutor(s):** F Thistlethwaite. **Educ:** Durban Preparatory High School; Durban High School; Natal University College, Pietermaritzburg; University of South Africa. **Career:** Assistant Master, Maritzburg College, Natal, South Africa 1942–1945; Lecturer, then Senior Lecturer, in History, University of Natal 1947–1966; Secretary to the Provisional Council, then first Registrar, University of East Africa 1961–1965; Secretary to the Provisional Council, then first Registrar, University of Zambia 1965–1970; Sub Dean (administration), Faculty of Social Sciences, Open University, Walton Hall, Milton Keynes, retiring as Senior Assistant in the office of the Vice-Chancellor 1976–1982. **Awards:** Boden Scholarship. Died 9 May 1992.

YOUNG, Dr Maurice Durward (1930) Born 20 September 1912, North Vancouver, British Columbia, Canada; son of Ernest Vanderpoel Young, Manager of Iron Works, and Emily Frances Wood Bainbridge. BA 1933; MA 1938; MB 1938; BChir 1938; MRCP 1944; FRCP 1948; FRCPC. **Tutor(s):** M P Charlesworth. **Educ:** Chesterfield Preparatory School, North Vancouver; Brentwood College, near Victoria. **Career:** Associate Dean, Faculty of Medicine; Professor of Paediatrics, University of British Columbia 1953–1960. **Appointments:** Honorary Surgeon to HM Queen Elizabeth II 1958–1960. Died 29 July 1990.

YOUNG, Michael (1944) Born 24 October 1925, 311 Cemetery Road, Broomhall, Sheffield; son of Frederick Cass Young, Chartered Accountant, and Shirley Pexton; m Winifred Mary Darby, 1959; 3 sons (Nicholas b 1960, Simon b 1962 and Alexander b 1964). **Subject(s):** Economics; BA 1948; MA 1950; DipEd 1957. **Tutor(s):** J M Wordie. **Johnian Relatives:** father of Nicholas Andrew Young (1979) and of Simon Richard Young (1981). **Educ:** Dore and Totley High School, Sheffield; King Edward VII School, Sheffield; Wycliffe College. **Career:** Management Trainee, Cadbury's 1949–1956; Head of Economics, Ilford County High School 1957–1970; Head of Economics, King Edward VI Five Ways School, Birmingham 1970–1971; Head of Economics, King's School, Worcester 1971–1990.

YOUNG, Peter Stuart (1927) Born 21 March 1910, Eskdale, Baring Road, Grove Park, Lee, Kent; son of Walter Stuart Young, Solicitor, and Lilian Carrie Williams; m Heather Jane Bell, 21 August 1947, Hampstead; 1 son. **Subject(s):** Mathematics; BA 1931; MA 1943. **Tutor(s):** J M Wordie. **Educ:** Cransbrook Grammar School; Bedales School; St Christopher's School, Letchworth.

YOUNG, The Revd Philip Norton Frushard (1903) Born 17 March 1885, 5 Rutland Terrace, Stamford, Lincolnshire; son of Philip Young, Clerk in Holy Orders, and Elizabeth Norton Handson; m Marguerite Winifred Maude Tidmarsh, 27 May 1927; 1 daughter (Ruth).

Subject(s): History/Theology; BA 1906; MA 1910. **Tutor(s):** J R Tanner; C E Graves. **Educ:** Derby School; Clergy Training School, Cambridge. **Career:** Deacon 1908; Curate, St Stephen, Portsmouth 1908–1911; Priest 1909; Chaplain, SJC 1911–1913; Professor, St Stephen's College and Member, University of Cambridge Mission Brotherhood, Delhi 1913–1924; Missionary, University of Cambridge Mission, Delhi 1924–1927; Chaplain, Additional Clergy Society 1927–1930; On the Ecclesiastical Establishment 1930; Chaplain, Simla 1932–1936; On Furlough 1930 and 1936; Delhi 1936; Vicar, St Augustin's, Bournemouth 1939–1945; Warden, College of the Ascension, Selly Oak, Birmingham 1945. **Awards:** Naden Studentship. **Publications:** 'A Summer Camp' (Swanwick), *The Eagle*, 34, 1913; *The Good News of Luke the Physician*, 1934. Died 10 January 1975.

YOUNG, Dr Samuel Knibb (1945) Born 23 May 1927, The Orchard, Chester le Street, Durham; son of Samuel Knibb Young, Medical Practitioner, and Margaret Barkes; m Jean Carr; 2 sons (Thomas and Nicholas), 1 daughter (Margaret). **Subject(s):** Natural Sciences; BA 1948; MA 1959; LMSSA (London) 1954. **Tutor(s):** S J Bailey; G C L Bertram. **Educ:** High School, Durham; Bow School, Durham; Sedbergh School. **Career:** Captain, Brigade of Gurkhas, RAMC 1955–1957; Senior Partner in General Practice, retired 1987. **Honours:** SBStJ 1990.

YOUNG, Stuart (1936) Born 13 January 1918, 34 Berkeley Terrace, Glasgow, Scotland; son of Archibald Young, Regius Professor of Surgery, University of Glasgow, and Anna Stuart; m (1) Joyce Watson, 1940s (d 1984), (2) Ann Gardner, 1986; (1) 1 son (Jonathan), 3 daughters (Joanna, Penny and Cynthia). **Subject(s):** Natural Sciences; BA 1939; MA 1943; MB ChB (Glasgow) 1942; FRCS (Glasgow) 1947; FRCS (Edinburgh) 1956. **Tutor(s):** R L Howland. **Educ:** High School, Glasgow. **Career:** RAF Medical Services in UK and India 1942–1945; Consultant Surgeon, Stobhill Hospital, Greater Glasgow Health Board. **Appointments:** Honorary Registrar for Surgical Examinations, Royal College of Physicians and Surgeons of Glasgow. Died 5 August 1998.

YOUNG, Terence Charles John (1928) Born 23 August 1903, 8 Shanklin Terrace, Downs Road, Walmer, Kent; son of John Young, Quartermaster Sergeant, Royal Marines, and Mary Letitia Hayes. **Subject(s):** Economics; BA 1931; MA 1945; FIS; FSS; FRES. **Tutor(s):** C W Guillebaud. **Educ:** Private School, Deal; Wesleyan Elementary School, Deal; County School for Boys, Dover; Islington Tutorial Class; Toynbee Hall (advanced tutorial class). **Career:** Acting Government Statistician, Nigeria, Colonial Service 1947; Economic Adviser for Industrial Development, South Wales. **Appointments:** Class Secretary, Secretary of the Islington Branch, Workers' Educational Association; Branch Correspondence Secretary, National Union of Clerks. **Awards:** Bursary for Extra Mural Studies, University of Cambridge. Died 10 January 1994.

YOUNG, Thomas Charles (1918) Born 20 November 1900, Partick, Lanarkshire; son of Thomas Charles Young, Solicitor, and Isabella Stewart; m Winifred Jean McKellar, 7 October 1925, Westbourne Church, Glasgow. **Subject(s):** Law; BA 1921; LLB 1922. **Tutor(s):** E E Sikes. **Johnian Relatives:** brother of Andrew Blackwood Stewart Young (1919); uncle of Kenneth Charles Stewart Young (1953). **Educ:** Kelvinside Academy; Fettes College, Edinburgh. **Career:** Solicitor, T C Young & Son, Glasgow.

YULE, George Udny (1913) Born 18 February 1871, Haddington, Midlothian; son of George Udny Yule, Indian Civil Servant, and Henrietta Peach Pemberton; m May Winifred Cummings, 1899 (annulled 1912). MA 1913; FSS 1895; FRS 1921. **Educ:** Winchester College; UCL. **Career:** Pupil at Engineering Works 1890–1892; Research into electric waves, University of Bonn 1892–1893; Demonstrator 1893–1896, Assistant Professor of Applied Mathematics 1896–1899, UCL; Secretary to the Examination Board, City and Guilds of London Institute 1899–1912; Lecturer in Statistics 1912–1930, Reader in Statistics 1931, University of Cambridge; Statistician, Army Contracts Department, War Office 1915–1917; Director of Requirements, Ministry of Food 1917–1918; Foundress Fellow 1922–1926, Title B Fellow 1926–1940, Lecturer in Statistics 1932–1940, Title E Fellow 1940–1951, SJC. **Appointments:** Newmarch Lecturer in Statistics, UCL 1901–1913; Secretary 1907–1919, President 1924–1926, Royal Statistical Society; Director of Studies in Natural Sciences 1923–1935, SJC; President, Cambridge Philosophical Society 1928–1929. **Awards:** Guy Medal in Gold, Royal Statistical Society 1911. **Honours:** CBE 1918. **Publications:** *An Introduction to the Theory of Statistics*, 1911; *The Statistical Study of Literary Vocabulary*, 1944; many papers. Died 26 June 1951.

Z

ZACKON, Jack (1924) Born 2 August 1902, 17 Warrenville Terrace, Wesley Street, Cape Town, South Africa; son of Solomon Zackon, General Merchant, and Gertrude Rosenberg. **Subject(s):** Law; BA 1926. **Tutor(s):** E A Benians. **Educ:** South African College School, Cape Town; University of Cape Town.

ZECY, Theodore (1945) Born 15 October 1921, Marlboro, Massachusetts, USA; son of Harry Cosmos Zecy, Food Store Proprietor, and Agorou Gatzouis. **Tutor(s):** C W Guillebaud. **Educ:** Marlboro High School; Boston University, Massachusetts. **Career:** Technician, Fifth Class, US Army.

ZIMMERN, Richard Frederick (1944) Born 18 December 1925, 8 Kinnaird Road, Withington, Manchester; son of Norman Harold Zimmern, Director, BBC Latin American Service, and Frances Olive Rennie Dixon. **Subject(s):** History. **Tutor(s):** J M Wordie. **Educ:** Ladybarn House School, Manchester; Moor Allerton Preparatory School; Manchester Grammar School. **Career:** Marketing Director, Mobil Plastics Europe UK, Mobil Oil; Business, ICI 1979. **Appointments:** RAF cadet, SJC.

ZOLLER, Kenneth Norman (1943) Born 7 January 1924, The Hermitage, Donnington Road, Cuddington, Surrey; son of Sydney Zoller, Engineering Draughtsman, and Gertrude Jessie McLean. **Tutor(s):** C W Guillebaud. **Educ:** Malden Parochial School; Epsom County School. **Appointments:** RE Cadet, SJC.

ZUKMANN–BIZONY, Michael Thomas (1942) Born 3 February 1924, Vienna, Austria; son of Béla Zukmann-Bizony, Violinist and Conductor, and Johanna Cecilie Stöckel. BA 1947. **Tutor(s):** C W Guillebaud. **Educ:** Letzlingen Castle; St Paul's School. **Career:** Lieutenant, RN.

Members of College listed by year of admission

1900

Allen, Francis Williams
Argyle, Frank Wilkinson
Arnold, John Corry
Aspin, Albert
Atkins, Hugh Leslie
Bachert, Louis Richard Arthur
Balls, William Lawrence
Barradell-Smith, Walter
Baxter, Arthur Harold Young
Beacall, Thomas
Bennett, George Anselm
Bernard, George Henry Brian
Booker, Edward
Briggs, William Arthur
Caddick, Sydney David
Canham, Edwin Dillon Frank
Carlyll, Hildred Bertram (Carlill)
Clarke, Roderick Ernest
Corbett, Arthur Edward
Cunningham, John Arthur
Davies, David Richard
Dawes, Herbert Edwin Tonge
Densham, Arnold Thomas
de Souza, Edouardo Valentine
Draper, John Robert
Evans, Jenkin
Evatt, George Raleigh Kerr
Frean, Henry George
French, Reginald Thomas George
Fryer, Sydney Ernest
Garcia, Leopold Basil Ronald
Garle-Browne, John Babington
Gaze, Edwin Howard
Gaze, Geoffrey Atkinson
Ghosh, Mahim Chandra
Gill, Gordon Harry
Gold, Ernest
Harding, William Iliff
Hardingham, John
Hatten, Arthur William
Hawkes, William John
Hockey, Harold Hibbet Hubert
Horne, John William
Horowitz, Solomon
How, John Charles Halland
Humfrey, John Charles Willis
James, Gwilym
Jarratt, George Lansdell
Jenkins, Hammond Beaconsfield
Johnston, Sydney
Kershaw, Arthur
Laidlaw, Patrick Playfair

Lal, Manohar
Lewis, Henry Godfrey
Linnell, Robert McCheyne
Merivale, Bernard
Meston, William
Miller, Francis
Palmer, John Thomas Edward
Parnell, Thomas
Phillips, Sidney Hill
Poole, John Twells
Porter, Thomas Henry
Reynolds, Charles William
Robinson, Theodore Henry
Singh, Har Kishan
Sleight, Arthur Blomefield
Stewart, Thomas George
Stokes, Josiah
Teall, George Harris
Theophilus, Reginald Arthur
Ticehurst, Claud Buchanan
Tompson, Frank Gordon
Vyvyan, Philip Henry Nugent Norris
Waite-Browne, Henry Franklyn
Walker, Archibald Galbraith
Watson, Henry Adam
Webber, Harold Norris
Wheldon, Wynn Powell
Whitehouse, John James
Whitley, George
Wood, Ernest

1901

Allan, Douglas
Allen, Albert William
Allen, James Edmund Percival
Bagchi, Satis Chandra
Beckett, John Norton
Beith, Gilbert
Broad, Percival Gordon
Bruce, Oswald
Chapple, Harold
Clarke, Herbert Lovell
Collins, John Stratford
Cox, Horace Beresford
Crees, James Harold Edward
Cutting, Ernest Melville
de Souza, Aniceto Emmanuel
Dhavle, Shankar Balaji
Dutta, Indu Bhushan
Evans, Edgar David
Fewings, Percy James
Figueiredo, José Borges

Franklin, Thomas Bedford
Fraser, James
Grigson, Pawlet St John Baseley
Hamilton, Arthur James Stanley
Henderson, Mervyn
Henderson, Percival
Hiron, John Bennett
Hori, Timothy Keishi
Horton, Frank
Jenkins, Albert Ernest
Joce, John Burden Dunn
Johnson, Ernest William
Johnston, Donald Vaughan
Jolly, Leonard John Parker
Jones, David Treborth
Keyworth, Frederick Munday
Khan, Mahomed Ismail
Kirkness, Lewis Hawker
Kitto, John Lemon
Kraemer, Adolf Ernst
Lamplugh, Alfred Amoz Fletcher
Laws, Samuel Charles
Leadman, Wilfrid Morley
Leathem, George
Lee, Harry
Lipkind, Goodman
McDonnell, Michael Francis Joseph
Marpole, David Williams
Mirza, Ali Akbar
Mountjoy, Victor Ulric Allin
Norbury, Francis Campbell
Parkinson, John
Pope, Norman Christopher
Prideaux, Henry Sydney
Prowde, Oswald Longstaff
Reece, Morris George Bernard
Ritchie, William Traill
Roseveare, Henry Herbert
Row, Vombatkere Pandrang
Saberton, Frederick Rupert
Sands, Percy Cooper
Scott, Stanley Henry
Shaw, Julius Brinkley
Sloley, Robert Walter
Smith, Graham Udale
Spink, Joseph Fenner
Stern, Nathan
Sterndale Bennett, Robert
Stuart, Thomas
Taylor, David Gladstone
Tiddy, Claude Winstanley Elliott
Trachtenberg, Mendel Isidore
Varwell, Ralph Peter

Wakely, Herbert Denning
Watson, Arthur Lockhart
Wilkinson, Ernest Roland
Wilson, David Arthur Calder
Wilson, Gardiner
Yeats, George Francis Walker
Yeoh, Guan Seok

1902

Arnott, Edward Whinstone
Ashby, Norman
Baker, Martyn Wilfred
Balcomb, Herbert Francis George
Barlow, Percival Smith
Bell, Richard Eardley Thomas
Best, Isaac James
Boyle, David Harrop
Brooke, Zachary Nugent
Brownson, Roger Dawson Dawson-Duffield
Carter, Charles Christopher
Checkland, Montmorency Beaumont
Cheese, William Gerard
Coad, Claude Norman
Coop, Wilfrid
Craggs, George Craggs
Crowther, James Arnold
Cullen, Alfred Edgar
Cullis, Leonard
Cummins, Cresswell Arthur
Davidge, Henry Thomas
Drysdale, George Frederick
Easton, Frank Reginald James
Edmonds, Harold
Evans, Howell Thomas
Fergusson, Louis Roy
Finch, Henry Kingsley
Fisher, Charley
Foster, William Henry
Gathorne, Christopher
Gough, Henry Joseph
Grant, Francis Henry Symons
Green, Ernest William
Grimes, Gerald Hubert
Grimes, Henry Sydney King
Hamilton, Kismet Leland Brewer
Hardy, Gordon Sidey
Harris, Henry Wilson
Hill, John Robertshaw
Hulme, Thomas Ernest
Hunt, Alfred Garrod Leedes
Hyams, Alexander
Jones, Pendril Charles Varier
Jones, William Havercroft
Khan, Fazl Muhammed
Kingdon, Donald
Knight, Charles
Koh, Kheng Seng
Linnell, Charles Darby
Long, George Herbert
Lusk, James
Mitchell, John Stewart

Moore, Reginald Mark
Neill, Norman Clark (Clark-Neill)
Nissim, Joseph
Pringle, Norman Douglas
Rea, Thomas
Reddy, Cattamanchi Ramalingam
Ronaldson, James Bruce
Rose, Harry Cecil
Rostron, Sydney (Nowell-Rostron)
Sears, John Edward
Shannon, Gerald Cairns
Sharp, William Henry Cartwright
   (Cartwright Sharp)
Stansfield, Alfred Ellington
Stanton, James Vincent
Strain, Thomas Greer
Sykes, Maurice Gaskell
Taylor, John Norman
Templeman, William Henry
Thompson, Harry Kayss
Turner, Roland
Waller, Robin Daniel
Watts, Bertram Tom
Weston, Thomas Alexander
Whitehouse, Alfred
Wilkins, Walter Gordon
Wilkinson, Louis Umfreville
Withey, William Henry
Wright, Charles Alban

1903

Airey, John Robinson
Barber, Cyril Arthur
Barritt, William Vernon
Belgrave, Arthur Cyril
Bentley, John Henry
Beresford, Hans Aden
Bosworth, Thomas Owen
Brady, Frank
Brayshay, Sidney
Brockbank, Birkett
Brown, Arthur Edward
Castle, Graham Hunt
Clissold, William
Cole, Ralph Turney
Coombs, Arthur George
Cort, John Leonard Patchett
Crole-Rees, Herbert Stanley
Dé, Birendra Nath
Dewick, Edward Chisholm
Dyer, Charles Henry
Edmonds, Sydney Arthur
Ellis, Arthur Isaac
Evans, Albert Ernest
Fleet, William Walter Strong
Gibbins, Thomas William Horn
Gill, Reginald George
Gorringe, Allan Lindsay
Hassé, Henry Ronald
Higgins, Frederick Alfred Raymond
Hodges, Charles Frederic

Honeybourne, Harry Cecil
Irwin, William Livingstone
Jackson, Charles Albert
Johnston, Alec Bowman
Johnston, Frank
Keeble, Cyril Francis Allan
Knight, Hugh Frederick Parker
Lewis, Percy James
Macaulay, Donald
Majumdar, Hem Chandra
Majumdar, Khagendra Nath
Meldrum, Roy
Middleton, Christopher Basil
Middleton, Thomas Hudson
Newbery, Robert Edwin
Philp, Claude Hastings George
Piaggio, Henry Thomas Herbert
Plowright, Colin Campbell
Rau, Kalle Kama Rau Sadashiva
Read, Arthur James
Ream, Charles Francis
Rice, Henry Goulding
Richardson, Alfred Henry
Robinson, Hilary Isaac
Sargeant, Hugh
Scoular, John Gladstone
Sharp, Clifford Graham
Skene, Claude Montague Benson
Skinner, John
Sneath, Arthur
Squire, John Collings
Sukthankar, Vishna Sitaram
Thompson, Ernest Edward
Titterington, Edward John Goodall
Toone, Charles Gilbert
van Hees, Albert Strancham Marsh
Vercoe, Richard Herbert
Vinycomb, Thomas Bernard
White, Francis Alfred
Whye, John William
Wilson, George James
Worrall, Newton
Yearsley, Claude Blakesley Lancelot
Young, Philip Norton Frushard

1904

Adams, Frank
Ard, Horace Herbert William
Atkinson, Myles
Bass, Roger Arthur
Bhide, Mahadeva Vishnu
Bolderston, William Northcott
Byron-Scott, Wallace
Campbell, Archibald Young
Coates, David Wilson
Collins, Edward Lawrence
Cooper, Thomas
Crauford, Leonard George
Cripps, Richard Seymour
Darwin, John Henry
Dawson, Reginald Thomas

Druce, Cyril Lemuel
Edridge-Green, Frederick William
Every, John Morris
Fayerman, Alec George Percy
Gandy, Henry
Geake, Anthony
Gledstone, Frederick Farrar
Habich, Leopold Sylvester Morrice
Hakim, Meherban Hormasjee
Hallack, William Collin
Hay, William King
Hogan, Reginald Victor John Somervill
Hume, Percy John
Hutchinson, Francis Downes
Jarvis, Charles Hooper
Jenkins, Frederick
Jolly, Evelyn Hugh Parker
Jones, Robert Francis
Khong, Kam Tak
Laidlaw, Hugh Alexander Lyon
Láll, Panna
Lamplugh, Lancelot John
Lim, Guan Cheng
Lincoln, Norman
Lucas, Ernest Charles
McGrady, Samuel Hugh
MacMahon, Percy Alexander
Meyer, Richard
Mills, Ernest James
Mitchell, William Augustine
Newton, Horace Gerard Townsend
Ohm, Donald McKay
Raad, Neone Nicholas Charles
Rennie, Donald Williamson
Robinson, George Michael Moncrieff
Rose, Frederic Gardiner
Saint, Percy Johnston
Satterly, John
Sibly, Thomas Mervyn
Stanford, Herbert Claude
Stead, William James Victor
Stewart, Douglas Martin
Taylor, Arnold Douglas
Taylor, Godfrey Midgley Chassereau
Thompson, Alexander Challis
Thompson, William Cyril
Topley, William Whiteman Carlton
Trumper, John Henry Walwyn
Twinn, Frank Charles George
Vause, Thomas Christopher
Wadia, Nowroji Jehangir
Walmsley, Alfred Moss
Ward, Dudley William
Willans, Gordon Jeune
Yonge, Gilbert Vernon

1905

Adeney, Eric Leonard
Alexander, Philip George
Alexander, Ralph Cleave
Allen, Alexander Drake

Allen, Geoffrey Austin
Allott, Cecil Bertram Scott
Anderson, Laurence Robert Dacre
Arnold, John Henry
Averill, Charles Edward
Barnes, Geoffrey George
Bell, Thomas Osmond
Boddington, Vincent Coke
Brice-Smith, Rollo
Campbell, Colin Guy Hirst
Churchward, Arthur Cyril
Corney, Leonard George
Cruickshank, George Malcolm
Dalál, Ardeshir Rustomji
Dawson, Ambrose Middleton
Deane, James Killen
Dodd, Rowland Pocock
Dollman, John Guy
Dunkley, Herbert Francis
Hawcridge, Robert Stuart
Henslow, Cyril John Wall
Hicks, Francis William
Hobbs, Victor William John
Hogan, Claude Douglas Devereux
Hughes, John Evans
Hull, Gordon Ferrie
Iremonger, Edward Victor
Jackson, John Edward Norman
James, Francis Arthur
Jones, Richard McNair
Kraus, Martin
Leonard, Percy James
McCowan, Hugh Wallace
Marrack, John Richardson
Montgomerie, William Stirling
Moore, John Roland
Mottram, James Cecil
Muncey, Edward Howard Parker
Nanavati, Dhirajlal Dayabhai
Parnell, Frederick Richard
Paterson, Matthew Wallace
Pattinson, George Norman
Patuck, Rustomjee Sorabjee
Phillips, Edwin Albert
Previté Orton, Charles William
Rau, Benegal Sanjiva
Rose, Hubert Allan
Rosenthal, Curt Arnold Otto
Ross, John Estcourt Cresswell
Sathe, Jagannath Luxmon
Smith, John Forbes
Stokes, John Whitley Gabriel
Stuart, Herbert Edward
Subbarao, Nanjangud Subbarao
Swift, John McIntosh
Thomas, Harold Augustus
Thorne Waite, Arnold
Thursfield, Gerald Arthur Richard
Torry, Arthur James Dashwood
Townend, Merton Vincent
Tozer, Ernest Francis
Troubridge, James Lewis

Veevers, William
Walker, John Eric
Whiddington, Richard
Willett, Everard William
Wood, Thomas Eugene
Wood, William Levi
Wooler, Cyril Upton
Yorke, Alfred Rose

1906

Allen, Charles Richards
Arnell, Oliver Roach
Barrett, Hugh Scott
Bilsland, James Alexander
Calvert, Edward
Cheshire, Francis Moreton
Clough, Thomas
Constable, William George
Cruickshank, Donald Edward
Dalvi, Vishvanath Ganpat
Dixon, Cuthbert
Easton, James William
Fewings, John Albert
Fleet, Charles Stanley
Fletcher, John Norman
Fraser, Donald Stuart
Freke, Cecil George
Gonehalli, Venkanna Hosnabaik
Green, Norman
Guest-Williams, Warren Kirkham
Hall, Alfred Francis
Harding, Walter Harry
Haslam, Victor Kingdon
Heaton, Frederick Alphonse Arthur Will
Hill, William Edward
Holthouse, Cuthbert Lempriere
Hughes, Arnold
Hurst, Ronald Francis
Ireland, William Francis
Irving, Percy Alexander
Jeffreys, Robert Sydney
Kirloskar, Vinayak Ganesh
Lane, Henry Clarence Horsburgh
Lees, Samuel
Levy, Leslie Charles
Lewis, Edmund Oliver
Lillie, Denis Gascoigne
Lister, Tom
Mann, Thomas Eagling
Montgomery, William
Morton, Fergus Dunlop
Morton, Victor Chalmers
Mosely, Frederick Maurice
Mullins, Hugh Thomas
Northorp, Frederic
Penfold, Harold Lashmar
Richards, Robert
Russell-Smith, Hugh Francis
Sargent, Edward Hewlett Gladstone
Scougal, Kenneth Hirst
Sewell, Sydney Ewart

Shepherd, William Lisle
Sheppard, William George
Shore, Thomas Henry Gostwyck
Short, John Martin
Smith, Oswald Carlton
Spencer, Gordon Winstanley
Stoddart, James Roylance
Swords, William Francis
Thompson, Alfred Ross
Thomson, Kenneth Sinclair
Thorpe, Chun
Tillard, Lawrence Berkley
Tomlinson, George Arthur
Treleaven, Woodman
Tremearne, Allen Riddle
Vine, Bernard Theodore
Weightman, William Henry
Whewell, Herbert
Wilmott, Alfred James
Woo, Ching Sung
Woollen, Wilfrid Henry

1907

Allen, Lucien Arthur
Arias, Harmodio
Askey, Stephen Grange
Beale, Cyril (Elmes Beale)
Bentley, Arthur James
Bentley, Reginald Arthur
Beresford, Gilbert Adrian
Bonser, Geoffrey Alwyn Gershom
Bowen, Leslie Harold
Brash, Edward John Yelverton
Burton, Humphrey Phillips Walcot
Butt, Sam
Cassels, John Samuel de Oliveira
Chasteney, Howard Everson
Cleland, John Robert
Dale, Frank
Doggart, William Edward
Dollman, Hereward Chune
Donne, Reginald Felix
Donovan, Edmund Lawrence
Dutton, Harold
Evans, Percy Edwin
Everatt, Reginald William
Ferris, William Edward
Fisher, Frederic Browell
Green, Stuart Montague
Guest-Williams, Alyn Arthur
Halsey, Reginald Tom
Hellings, Geoffrey Stuart
Ho, Shai Leung
Holtzapffel, John George Holtzapffel (Budd)
Hughes-Jones, Oswald
Hyde, Ronald William
Irving, John Christopher
Jackson, Harley Douglas
Jacquest, Samuel Percy
Khan, Mohamed Islam-ullah
Laidlaw, Charles Glass Playfair

Leeser, Herbert
Lorenz, Hans Hugo Herbert
Lumb, William
Marchand, Geoffrey Isidore Charles
Milne, George
Mordell, Louis Joel
Morris, Thomas Norman
Naunton, William Johnson Smith
Nicholls, Albert Charles
Niven, Hugh
Parker, Herbert
Patterson, Richard Ferrar
Paulley, Harold
Perry, John Cyril
Quick, Edward Keith
Radcliffe, Clifford Walter
Ritchie, Charles Henry
Sargent, Eric Lancelot Kingsley
Smith, Leonard Danvers
Soden, Wilfred Scovil
Spargo, Frederick Wilson
Stansfeld, Rex
Sterndale Bennett, James Bury
Stewart, Hugh Fraser
Stocks, Arthur Vernon
Tait, Hugh Nimmo
Thompson, Sidney Lionel
Waterhouse, Gilbert
Whitlock, Percy Oddie
Wilkinson, Edward Neville
Wright, William Roland Henry

1908

Adamson, Edward Blythman
Alexander, Aaron
Anthony, Arthur Lawrence
Aschaffenburg, Wilhelm Arthur
Atkinson, Henry Noel
Aubry, Carl Paul
Auler, Kurt Max Friedrich Robert
Bilsland, William Blair
Braunholtz, Hermann Justus
Brice-Smith, Harold Francis
Brownson, Thomas Kerfoot
Burr, Frederick Godfrey
Button, Arnold Elliot
Cardwell, Alfred George
Carpenter, Charles Gordon
Carter, William Herbert
Chadwick, Morley
Chell, Harold
Conder, John Marmaduke
Cooper, Harold
Cotton, Robert Hugh Alban
Crellin, Douglas
Cullen, Augustus Pountney
Davies, Eric
Davis, Harold James
de Dirsztay, Gedeon
Denham, Joseph Percival
Dixon, Douglas Gilbert

Dodd, Walter Prichard
Durant, William Maitland
Earle, George Foster
Eastick, Frederick Charles
Edwards, Arthur Tudor
Ferris, Samuel Bernard Clutton
Fryers, John Lawrence
Gale, Cuthbert Courtenay
Garabedian, Dikran Garabed
Gillson, Albert Henry Steward
Goode, Reginald Henry
Griffiths, George Arthur Mence
Hattersley, William Hanchett
Higgins, Frank Edmund
Hirjee, Rustom
Hutton, Robert Jermyn
Jackson, Gilbert Edward
Jerusalem, Georg
Knox, Robert Uchtred Eyre
Lloyd, Murray Tenison
Long, Archibald Percy
Love, Francis Stanley
Lyons, Richard Jenkins
Monck-Mason, George Evelyn Arthur
   Cheyne
Moody, Basil
Nicklin, George Norman
Nurse, Samuel David
Oakley, Frederick Christian
Odgers, Robert Blake
Okell, Charles Cyril
Ottley, Warner Herbert Taylor
Parry, James Hales
Phillips, William Richard
Pittom, William Wynn Pratt
Price, Norman Jeredick
Ragg, Harry Richard
Read, Grantly Dick (Dick-Read)
Rogerson, Walter Lohn Lancashire
Sayers, Eldred Frank
Shore, Lewis Rudall
Skinner, Cyril Reed
Sleight, Albert Henry
Smith, Edward Harry
Street, Reginald Owen
Streeten, Basil Robert
Sykes, William Dodgson
Thompson, Charles Brodrick
Thursby, Walter
Toase, Edward James
Todd, Hugh Wilfred
Vaidya, Shridhar Balkrishna
Warters, Reginald Arthur
Watkins, Allen
Watson, Basil Lockhart
Watson, Thomas William
Wells, Walter Douglas
Williams, Penry Malcolm Wykeham
Wills, Eric Foulger
Wilmore, Albert Nelson
Winder, Reginald McDonnell
Woodall, Frank Ewart

Wooldridge, Duncan Wakeman
Wren, Thomas Lancaster

1909

Acton, Henry
Adams, John Bernard Pye
Andrews, James Collingwood
Antia, Merwanji Jamshedji
Applewhaite, Charles Trueman
Armitage, Bernard William Francis
Averill, Thomas Henry
Banister, Thomas Roger
Beard, Edwin Cyril
Belgrave, William Norman Cummins
Bellman, Alexander Frederick
Bevan, Guy Theodore Molesworth
Bunt, Arthur Percival
Bush, Richard Eldon
Carruthers, Kenneth St Clare
Cavalier, Francis Bernard
Chatterji, Amulya Kumar
Cheetham, Frederic Philip
Clarke, Robert Shuttleworth
Clow, Andrew Gourlay
Cole, James Humphrey
Coles, Victor John Hulbert
Cushing, William Ewart Whitrick
Darlington, William Aubrey Cecil
Davis, Herbert
Douglas, William Ewart
Ennos, Frederick Raine
Evans, Herbert Clyde
Felton, Percy William
Gardiner, Kenneth John Rattray
Gleave, John Wallace
Grail, Clifford George
Gregory, Arthur Reginald
Griffiths, Hugh Peregrine
Grigg, Percy James
Guillebaud, Claude William
Guillebaud, Walter Henry
Halliwell, Wilfred Newbold
Hanson, James
Haslam, Reginald Kingdon
Hedgecock, Arthur Thomas
Henry, William David Murray
Holden, Norman Victor
Hunter, John Bowman
James, Reginald William
Jopson, Norman Brooke
Kidd, Franklin
Kirk, John Haydn
Laidlaw, Walter Sibbald
Leakey, Herbert Nettleton
Levy, Stanley Isaac
Lloyd, Herbert Marsden
Lord, Geoffrey Fraser
McAulay, Francis Willmer
Maclay, Ebenezer
McMullen, William Albert
Mason, Edmund William

Miller, Hugh Francis Ridley
Pollard, William Marcus Noel
Raffle, Wilfrid
Rao, Vinayek Ganpat
Raven, Edward Earle
Reece, Francis Bertram
Rees, Hubert Leonard
Ritchie, George Lindsay
Rowell, Andrew Herrick
St John, Fleming
Sears, Selwyn Edward
Shepherd, Edward Hoskins
Smith, Cecil Furness
Steimann, Bernard Benjamin
Stuart, Herbert
Taylor, Guy Arthur
Turner, William Leslie
Twentyman, Denzil Clive Tate
Vale, Henry Edmund Theodoric
Waters, Kenneth Selby

1910

Adamson, Francis Douglas
Antrobus, Harvey
Bain, Graham Ward
Bilsland, Alexander Steven
    (Lord Bilsland of Kinrara)
Black, Stuart Gordon
Blaxter, Augustus Pearce Llewellyn
Blumhardt, Edward Henry Fenwick (Mills)
Browne, Barrington
Chadwick, Brian Lloyd
Chaudhry, Girdhari Lal
Clark, Henry Robert Ernest
Cliff, Arnold Pearse
Coggin, Maurice Edward Henry
Coleman, Noel Dolben
Colson, Charles Gordon Tulloch
Crick, Louis Graham Minden
Day, George Lewis
Dunlop, John Kinninmont
Earp, John Rosslyn
Eberlie, (Wilhelm, later William) Felix
Edwards, Geoffrey Richard
Engledow, Frank Leonard
Englefield, Frederick Ronald Hastings
Fernando, Charles Herbert Zuleski
Fison, Alexander Key
Foster, Robert Douglas
Giesecke, Ernest Franz Rudolph Hans
Gilbert, Bernard William
Goldie, Archibald Hayman Robertson
Grear, Ernest John Lantsbery
Hall, George Noel Lankester
Harris, John Frederick
Heimann, Herman Paul
Herzl, Hans
Honeyball, Frederick Ralph
Hughes, John Lawrence
Hunter, John Adams
Jeffreys, Harold

Johnson, Vernon Yate
Kemp, Percy Vickerman
Laird, Andrew John
La Touche, Hugh Norman Digues
Maccoby, Ephraim Meyer
Makinson, Joseph Crowther
Mogridge, Henry Theodore
Morel, Jean
Morgenstierne, (Wilhelm) Herman Ludvig
Morris, Frank Mosedale
Mulholland, William
Nicholson, Edgar Cyril
Quass, Phineas
Redman, George Bertram
Reynolds, William Henry Robert
Roberts, Charles Edward
Robinson, Ernest Harold
Roscoe, John
Sanceau, Reginald James
Scholfield, Richard Denham
Scott, Thomas Torrance
Scutt, John Alfred Homer
Sharp, Thomas Hicks
Shelton, Laurence Hugh
Smith, Howard
Stanham, Charles Taylor
Stephens, John Sturge
Stopford, John
Tanner, Laurance Edgar
Townsend, Robert Wilfred
Trought, Trevor
Wadia, Siavax Hirji
Whitehouse, Bertram Reginald
Whitfield, Edward Hilliard Day
Williams, Richard Lloyd
Williams, William Troth
Wirz, Eduard Wilhelm
Wood, James Edward Hathorn
Woodmansey, Geoffrey Erskine
Wordie, James Mann

1911

Appleton, Edward Victor
Atkinson, Gerald
Bethell, Alexander Duke
Billinger, Hector Fussell
Bingley, Gerald Arthur
Binns, Arthur Lennon
Blanshard, Herbert Lewis
Brock, Eric George
Bromfield, Joseph Dicken
Brown, Christopher Wilkinson
Bullen, Frederick John
Care, Henry Clifford
Carter, Henry Robison
Clouts, Philip
Davies, Richard Morgan
Day, Dennis Ivor
de Silva, Lucien Macull Dominic
Dunkerley, Cecil Lawrence
Edwards, William Griffith

English, Frederick Hubert
Evans, William Emrys
Fletcher, Thomas Charles
Foden, William Bertram
Garner, Henry (Harry) Mason
Gottstein, Kurd Felix Waldemar
Gwynne, Hubert Llewelyn
Hanson, Richard Harold
Hardisty, Charles William
Harris, Henry Lyn
Hearn, Robert Cecil
Herrmann, Paul Millington
Herzog, Albert Ludwig Ewald
Ho, Shai Chuen
Holden, Frank
Holden, John Railton
Hook, Charles Wilfrid Theodore
Howe, George Arthur
Jacklin, James Valentine
Johnson, Leslie
Jones, Frank Butler
Kalé, Vithal Dhondo
Kendall, Guy Melville
Kingdom, William Alexander
Lacson, Domingo W
Lee Warner, Roland Paul
Lindsell, John
McCulloch, William
Miller, Emanuel
Mowton, Walter Edward
Odgers, Lindsay Noel Blake
Palmer, William George
Parry, Bernard King
Patterson, John Robert
Peiris, Leonard James Martinus
Peters, August Detlef
Polack, Albert Isaac
Powell, Evan Caradoc
Pratt, Geoffrey Wyatt
Proudlock, Robin
Rosenberg, Norman E
Russell-Smith, Alan
Saddler, William
Schoeller, Thomas Louis
Schroeder, Albert Edward (Long)
Shivdasani, Hassamal Baharmal
Smee, Cyril Walter
Sothers, Edward Dudley
Spackman, Harry Maurice
Sparks, Cedric Harold
Stevens, John Kelland
Stockwood, Illtyd Henry
Stuart, Cyril Edgar
Sutherland, George Arthur
Taylor, Frederick Lewis
Taylor, Harold Charles Norman
Thompson, Cyril Newton
van Druten, Henry John
van Pallandt, Hugh Pope Alexander
Vernon, Cecil Heygate
Wagstaff, John Edward Pretty
Walworth, George

Weston, Eric
Wooler, Herbert Sykes

1912

Allen, Francis
Barbour, George Brown
Barrett, Sidney Thomas
Bartlett, Frederic Charles
Beard, Arthur John
Bernard, Henry Claude
Bird, Douglas Joseph
Brian, Frederick Reginald Hugh
Briggs, George Edward
Brown, Eric Metcalfe
Bruford, Walter Horace
Burling, Edward James Poynter
Burrell, John Hugh
Bushell, Herbert Donald
Callender, Reginald Henry
Cheetham, Ernest Mark
Clarke, John Harrison
Cobbold, Robert Henry Wanklyn
Corder, Philip
Cubbon, Henry Thomas
Davies, Arthur Thomas
Davies, Ivor Glyndwr
Earp, Freeling Oswald Millns
Evans, Rhys David
Every, Austin Rimmington
Frederick, Thomas
Gaussen, John MacCulloch
Geary, Alfred
Goodrich, Harold Spencer
Goolden, Hugh Joseph
Gordon, Edward Francis Strathearn
Greenstreet, Norman Bernard de Medina
Grice, Norman
Guruswami, Krishnaswamireddiar
Hagger, Norman Watson
Hall, James Griffith
Hand, Henry Sheerman
Hibberd, Andrew Stuart
Higginton, John Martin
Higgs, Sydney Limbrey
Highfield-Jones, Philip
Higson, Leslie Arthur
Hilary, Robert Jephson
Howard, Horace Reginald
Hoyland, Geoffrey
Hurry, Arthur Gordon
Jacob, Anstey Ross
Langton, Harold McKee
Latif, Sarhan Carnrudin
Lloyd, Ernest Llewelyn
Macfadyen, William Archibald
Mackinlay, David Murray
McLean, Robert Colquhoun
Marsh, Richard Joseph
Marshall, Wilfred
Millyard, Thomas
Montagnon, Arthur

Morley, Gordon Harpur
Need, George Spofforth
Nissim, Simon
Owen, David Hugh
Owens, Francis Henry
Palmer, Wilfred Ernest
Pascoe, Frederick John
Paskin, Jesse John
Patton, Arnold Gordon
Phillips, Robert Stowell
Polack, Ernest Emanuel
Pullin, John Henton
Rawson, Joseph Nadin
Rice, Leonard Cyril
Rigg, Theodore
Robinson, Louis Francis Woodward
Rowett, Frederick Ernest
Ryley, Donald Arthur George Buchanan
Salmond, William Guthrie
Shanly, Herbert
Shillito, Norman Wholey (Melbury)
Simmons, Leonard Frederick George
Smith, Frederick Arthur Lewis
Smith, George Ernest
Stanier, Harold
Stoneley, Robert
Toolis, James Hollingworth
Trott, Francis William
Wan, Yik Shing
White, Francis Puryer
Wolstencroft, Alfred Stratten
Wood, Thomas Albert Victor
Woolrich, William Grant
Wright, Theodore
Yeo, John Haydon

1913

Ainley, Kendrick Edward Denison
Badcock, Arthur Lawrence
Barrett-Greene, Alan Henry
Belgrave, Herbert Alan
Bennett, George Macdonald
Benoy, James Francis
Benson, George Enoch
Bisdee, Jame Sutherland Mitchell
Bladwell, Ernest Wilfrid
Bond, Brian Willoughby
Booth, Ernest
Brackett, Arthur William Keith
Brookes, Ralph Caldecott
Brownson, George Stephen
Burt, Cyril Lodovic
Cadle, Harry Sidney
Cassels, Wilfrid Gardiner
Chapman, Alfred Reginald Bewes
Clarke, Donald
Collins, Ernest Jacob
Curzon-Siggers, William Arthur
Doderet, William
Douglas, John
Dumas, Arthur Blair

Eves, Ralph Shakespeare
Filmer, Walter George Harry
Fleck, Fritz
Galt, Robert Brownlie
Gardner, Jack Montfort Stanley
Gleave, Thomas Reginald
Glyn, Charles Reginald
Grabham, George Wallington
Hardman, Wilfrid Henry
Heald, William Margetson
Hiller, Alan Menzies
Hillier, Thomas Lucas
Hobbs, Alan Victor
Hofmann, Johannes Alfred Franz Georg
Horlington, Frank
Jayawardana, Andrew Cyril Joseph Perera
    Wijeratna
Jenkins, Herbert Riches
Johnson, John Charles (Sperrin-Johnson)
Jones, Isaac Ernest
Joseph, Felix Alexander
Keeley, Thomas Clews
Knowles, Joseph Albert
Lawe, Francis Walsham
Lund, Guy Sefton
Margolis, Morris
Marlow, Charles Christopher
Marr, Francis Alleyne
Mirfin, Joseph Colin
Murray-Aynsley, Charles Murray
Ness Walker, John
Nickalls, John Lawrence
Phillips, Harold Enoch
Phillips, Henry Wilfred Lewis
Rafique, Ahmed
Richardson, Ruskin John Robert
Scarth, Robert Ewart
Schoeller, Ewald Georg
Slater, Stewart Beattie
Smith, Vernon Sampson
Steen, Frank Dunbar
Thomas, Robert Bernard Hobson
Thomas, Robert Llewellyn
Thomas, Terry
Tromp, Felix Johan
Trott, Alan Charles
Urie, Robert Wallace
Warren, James Lionel East
Westlake, Aubrey Thomas
Whittaker, Frank
Wickham, Bernard William Theodore
Willett, John Arnold
Williams, Harry Ben
Williams, William Henry
Wilson, Alan Sydney
Wong, Man
Yule, George Udny

1914

Archer-Hind, Laurence
Baker, Ralph Homfield

Baldry, Robert Ashley
Barbash, Hezekiah (Hedley)
Barnes, James Haydn
Barton, Frederick Sherbrooke
Beckley, Verey Alfred
Benstead, Alfred Sydney
Bevan, Eric James
Blakeley, Frank Roland
Brown, Edward Richardson
Buckingham, John
Buckley, William Howell
Cadbury, Paul Strangman
Castle, Cecil Wells
Chidson, Lawrence Drury
Cummins, Francis John
Davis, Harold
Davis, Victor Samuel England
Davy, Clifton Lionel
Drummond, John Berney
Duffield, Henry William
Dyke Marsh, Henry St George
Fairbank, James
Gasper, Philip Arnold
George, John Trevor
Gill, Cecil Gervase Hope
Gill, George Austin
Gobbitt, Reginald Henry Sutton
Goldwater, Harry Gerald
Harris, Edward Sewell
Holden, Henry Francis
Holttum, Richard Eric
Howell, Maurice Ives Berthon
Hutchinson, Richard Wyatt
Jacobsohn, Arthur
Johnson, Eric Finnis
Johnston, Malcolm Charteris
Kelders, Theodor Carl
Laughlin, Philip Herbert
Lee, Eric Hanson
Lees, George Thomas
Leonard, John Gifford
Lewis, John Morgan
Low, Bevis Brunel
Mansbridge, Eric
Menendez, Frank Treman Sibly
Menon, Kizhakkepat Ramunny
Morris, Philip Enoch
Pearson, Cyril Edgar
Percy, Josceline Richard
Pralle, Ludwig Rudolf Eric
Prichard, Reginald Moreton
Puddicombe, Donald Ramsay
Quin, Basil Godfrey
Reade, George Lewis
Rees, Francis Edward
Reuben, David Ezra
Robinson, Richard Gruffydd
Roseveare, Harold William
Sampson, Michael Treviskey
Silk, George William
Smith, Albert Francis
Stimpson, Robert

Strong, Samuel Digby
Struthers, James Arthur
Swift, Herbert Walker
Thomas, Wendell William
Tozer, Sydney Prout
Tucker, Dennis Henry Maine
van Geyzel, Vivian Allan
Vint, James
Wales, Harold Robert
Walton, John
Waterhouse, Hugh
Watts, Raymond John
Williams, Roger Lester
Wolfes, Franz
Wooler, Charles Armytage

1915

Adamson, Cuthbert
Alldred, Reginald Alan
Aris, Douglas Heath
Bentall, William Douglas
Brice-Smith, John Kenneth
Callender, Thomas Ormiston
Chadwick, Norman Ellis
Crowther, Herbert Arnold
Davenport, Arthur
Day, Cyril Rupert
Day, Miles Jeffrey Game
Denyer, Charles Leonard
Franklin, Harold Walter
Gale, Conrad Arthur Lewis
Glyn, John Westray Wilson
Grayson, John Richard
Green, Henry Edward Beck
Hartree, Douglas Rayner
Hitching, Wilfrid Wallace
Horton-Smith-Hartley, Percival Hubert
    Graham
Hughes, Basil Frederick Murray
Hurdman, Cyril
Hutton, Percy Granville
Johnson, Martin Christopher
Littleboy, Gerald
Mahindra, Kailash Chandra
Mason, Peter
Mogridge, Basil Fullelove West
Mond, Henry Ludwig
Moodie, John Greenshields
Morse, Wilfred
Neumann, Maxwell Hermann Alexander
    (Newman)
Péniakoff, Vladimir
Philpot, Frederick Harold
Prasad, Kamta
Precious, Clifford Maxwell
Ratcliff, Edward Craddock
Savory, Theodore Horace
Shaw, Arthur
Sparks, John Victor
Stephenson, Frederick
Thomas, Frank Basil

Thomlinson, William Francis Kirk
Watson, William Vernon Crowther
White, Richard Henry
Whitelaw, Alan Dunlop
Williams, Henry William Knowlson
Wilson, Arthur Wesley
Wood, Norman Wright

1916

Bhansali, Mansen Damoder
Brooke, Sidney
Buckingham, Raymond
Burn, Ernest William
Cocker, Thomas Bernard
Dalzell, Donald Percy
Ellis, Oliver Bernard
Gerson, Guillaume Hubert Auguste
Gleave, George Eric
Grange, George William Keith
Greaves, William Michael Herbert
Kitto, Humphrey Davy Findley
Lawn, Lawrence
McIntire, George Shipley
Macklin, David Harold
Mott, Charles Edward
Oakden, George Frederic
Peacock, Edward
Puddicombe, William Ewart
Shaw, Wilfred
Sisson, Marshall Arnott
Smellie, Kingsley Bryce Speakman
Watkins, Arthur Ernest
Worstenholm, John

1917

Allsopp, Herbert Leslie
Barker, Philip Townsend
Brown, Alec John Charles
Buchanan, Robert Donald
Chapman, Cecil Anstis Bewes
Collins, Henry Stanley
David, Illtyd
Downs, James
Evans, Theophilus Islwyn
Godjevatz, Dragutin
Gould, Douglas Harold Mellor
Gray, Sydney Joseph Pereira
Guttridge, George Herbert
Hedley, Percy Little
Heward, Arthur Brian Augustus
Lyward, George Aubrey
Mallik, Suhrit Nath (Daeb)
Mann, John Colman
Merttens, Fritz Roel
Metcalf, Henry Kenneth
Moss, William Donald
Neale, Humphrey Rossall
Noott, Eric Hervey Jenner
Perasitch, Nikola
Ratcliff, Howard Dunbar

Simkins, Rupert Mann
Stopford, James Stanley Bird
Sturton, Clement
Thomas, Eric Leslie Vivian
Thompson, Ronald Massicks
White, Norman Lewis

1918

Aarons, Frank Lewis Frankel
Adamson, James Henry
Baker, Frank Bernard
Ball, Charles Olin
Bartlett, John Shirley
Barton, James Edward
Bateson, Martin
Blanche, Eugene Hornby
Bloomer, Leonard
Briscoe, Arnold Daly
Broadbent, Bernard
Colwill, Charles Kingsley
Darling, Ralph McIntire
Dymond, Edmund Gilbert
Edwardes, Eric Grant
Foster, William Roy
French, William Arthur Liveing
Gilchrist, John Stirling (Stirling-Gilchrist)
Girling, John Robert
Glidden, Herbert Harrison
Head, James Lawrence
Hoggan, Ralph Walter
Holmes, John
Howard, Jack Wesley
Huston, Frank Edward
Iyengar, Omeo
Jago, Jack Alexander
Kant, Frederick William
Kiddle, Frederick Edward
Kinney, Raymond Harold
Knowles, John Clapham
Koontz, Patrick Duffy
Lathrop, Julian Langson
Layman, Felix Herbert
Le Maitre, Alfred Sutherland
Lindsay, Robert James Forsythe
Little, Bryce
Lloyd, John Edward
McClary, Andrew Bishop
McKinney, Robert Lincoln
McMicking, Ralph Gore
MacNicoll, Douglas
Mark, Douglas Scott
Mills, Kenneth Frederick Thomas
Morris, James Noel Frederick
Murray, Thomas Prain Douglas
Norse, Adrian Osborn
Oakden, John Clarke
Parkinson, Kenneth Nuttall
Pettus, Bacon Page
Potter, Wilfrid Dennis
Prest, Charles Parrington
Pretheroe, Edward Owen

Quinn, Edward
Rees, Arthur Carlyon
Roach, William Francis
Robinson, Percy Wilberforce
Ruedemann, Paul
Saunders, Kenneth Herbert
Sefton-Jones, Felix William
Shaughnessy, Charles Stephen
Somerville, Donald Murray
Stammers, Arthur Dighton
Sykes, David Thomas
Tolles, Raymond Pardee
Traxler, Joseph Frank
Tunstall, William Cuthbert Brian
Walker, David Littlejohn
Wallis, Charles Braithwaite
Washburn, Louis Mumford
Webber, Harry Edwin
Wright, Geoffrey Richard Hodgson
Young, Thomas Charles

1919

Abeyewardena, Charles Christopher Patrick
  Perera
Adeney, Noel Frederick
Aldcroft, James Stuart
Alldred, Stanley Douglas
Allen, William Ruskin
Anderson, Alexander Bruce
Arnold, Erik Stennett
Arnott, Ronald Whiston John
Arundel, Dennis Drew (Arundell)
Avery, Ernest Victor
Bailey, Stanley John
Baker, Derek Collingwood
Ball, Edward Fernley Gawen
Bamber, John Reginald
Barclay, Cuthbert
Barnard, Henry Benjamin
Barnard, John Marles Sedgwick
Barrett, Hugh Tremearne
Bassett, Stephen James
Bates, Kingsley Darwin
Bell, Ivan Crosland
Belshaw, Stanley Ainscow
Bevan, Rupert Charles Molesworth
Bingham, Francis Denis
Bird, Charles Kellam
Bliss, Alfred Howard
Bond, Ralph Norman
Bootheway, George Hartley
Bowden, Harold Treacher
Boys Smith, John Sandwith
Brasher, William Kenneth
Breffit, Reginald Ernest
Brodie, Ian Eustace
Broome, Frank Milnes
Brotherton, Clifford
Brown, Alexander Carnegie
Brown, George Colin Woods
Brown, Sidney Kemp

Bryan, John Lindsay
Buckley, John
Bushell, William
Butler, Francis Herbert Culverhouse
Butler, Rupert Donovan Weeden
Buttle, Gladwin Albert Hurst
Cameron, Noël Roy Scott
Carslaw, Ronald McGregor
Chalke, Herbert Davis
Chapman, Edward Nowel Bewes
Clarke, Christopher Garrard
Clarke, Desmond Frederick Aubrey
Cohen, Leon Gaston
Cole, Geoffrey Bruce
Cole, Reginald Alexander Lister
Combridge, John Theodore
Comrie, Leslie John
Copley, Arthur Charles
Coulton, George Gordon
Cowper, Joseph Herbert
Crafer, Charles Thomas
Craggs, Ernest Wade Foxton (Hall-Craggs)
Crawford, William Glasgow
Creed, John Martin
Crone, Gerald Roe
Croome, John Capel
Curtler, Ernest Alfred
Darlington, Alfred Frankland Dean
Davidson, Alan Salisbury
Davies, Arthur Lloyd
Davison, Edward Lewis
Dawson, Ralph Sigismund
Dearden, John Robert Biffin
D'Elboux, Raymond Herbert
Dennis, Stratford Hercules
de Trafford, Cuthbert Henry
Dinsmore, John Francis
Dobbs, Sealey Patrick
Dockray, John Vernon
Dower, John Gordon
Duchesne, Charles Samuel Collier
Dunkerley, Lionel Ernest Brooke
Dunlop, Andrew Fergus
Dunn, John Stanley
Dynes, Max Russell
Eagles, Jack Mortimer
Eddowes, Alfred Bowman
Edgar, Samuel Gairdner Gibson
Ellis, George Rayner
El-Ricaby, Mohammed Akram
Eméleus, Karl George
Epps, Stanley Moorcroft
Evans-Atkinson, Norman
Ewbank, Alan Maurice
Field, Hubert Astley
Finlay, James Stimpson
Ford, Richard Brutton
Francis, Clement Alexander
Francis, John Harvey
Freme, Herbert Michael More
Gallimore, Alfred Smithson
Girling, Frank Aldous

Golden, Harold Arthur
Gray, Oliver
Green, Reginald Kersey
Griffith, William Graham Allix
Gurney, Maurice Patrick
Halford, Richard Frederick
Harker, Maurice John
Harris, William Anderton
Hartree, Colin William
Haseler, Digby Bertram
Hayward, John Ralph Goodwin
Heath, Ernest Alfred John
Hemmings, Henry
Hensman, John Cyril
Hervey, Maurice William Bethell
Hewlett, Alfred Lionel
Hinton, William Kirtland
Holmes, Lockhart Eastwood
Horsfall, Thomas Mendelssohn
Howell, Illtyd Mark
Hunt, George William
Jefferson, John Launcelot
Johnson, Cyril Jossé
Jones, John Sharpley
Kendon, Frank Samuel Herbert
Kershaw, Cecil Aubrey
Kikuchi, Taiji
King, Dennis Hoare
Knight, Leslie Cartwright
Lacey, Horace Marsden
Laming, Eric Laird
Langton, Frederick Edward Palmer
Laski, Norman
Law, Frank William
Layard, Arthur Frank Capel
Leakey, Richard John Montague
Lean, Leslie John Lawrance
Leslie, William
Lewis, Hugh Gething
Lloyd, Roger Bradshaigh
Locke, William Knight Herries
Lockwood, Edward Harrington
Longhurst, Edward Hubert Stooke
Lotlikar, Vasant Mahadeo
Low, Kenneth Graham
Low, Robert Fairweather
Lucas, Walter Edward
Lund, Niels Theodore Walter
Lutley, Albert French
McCarthy, Wilfrid Justin
McCombe, William Eric Mervyn
McIlwraith, Thomas Forsyth
McKellar, Andrew William Ross
Maclay, Walter Symington
McLean, Hugh
McWilliam, John Abram
Manley, Herbert
Mann, James Dennis
Martin, Archibald Roy Hammond
Maxwell, Roland Stanley
Mead, Frederick Everitt Bruce
Mitchell, Lawrence John

Mitcheson, Victor Steele
Moncrieff, Kenneth
Mowbray, Eric Douglas Wharton
Mumford, William Bryant
Nest, Hubert Clive
Norman, Sydney
Orme, Frank Leslie
Oulsnam, Samuel Harrison Yardley
Palmer, John Bowden
Parkinson, Joseph Alfred
Paterson, Victor James Ewing
Peiris, Herbert Charles Jacob
    (Sena, Devar Surya)
Penrose, Lionel Sharples
Pentland, Thomas Proctor
Peterson, Edward Whitred Reed
Philbin, John
Phipps, Thomas Edward Donald
Pickering, Edward Andrew
Pitel, Adrien Philip
Platten, Thomas George
Polwhele, Thomas Cecil
Potter, George Richard
Powell, Oliver
Preece, Trevor Meyrick
Prior, Oliver Herbert Phelps
Ragg, Thomas Murray
Rawnsley, Lee
Raworth, Edwin Llewellyn
Rayns, Frank
Rees, Arthur Carlyon
Riddell, David Adams
Riley, William Grimshaw
Robinson, Frank Bright
Robinson, John Cuthbert
Roseveare, Edward
Roseveare, Martin Pearson
Ryder, Archibald Stuart Dudley
Salinger, Cecil Gerald Furnivall (Furnivall)
Sanders, Harold George
Sanderson, Thomas Carton Hardman
Scale, Edmund Thomas
Scott, Charles Russell
Scott, Frank Munro
Sharman, Herbert Guttridge
Shaw, George Douglas
Sherrard, Francis Raymond George Nason
Shillan, Clement Archibald
Shuker, Henry Webb
Simkin, Frederick
Simmons, Gerald Seymour
Sinclair, Thomas Alan
Singh, Ram Dhan
Smith, John Young Mitchell
    (Mitchell Smith)
Smith, Victor St George
Snow, Harold Ernest
Soar, Leonard Charles
Spackman, Flower Stephen
Sprake, Robert Rowland Hill
Stallard, Francis William
Standring, William George

Staples, Edward George
Steers, Douglas Henry
Stokes, Christopher William
Stroud, Ernest Gordon
Strouts, Edward Allen
Stuart, Donald Harry
Sutcliffe, John Herbert Holman
Taylor, Harold Midgley
Thomas, Alfred Llewelyn
Thomas, Theodore Lynam
Thompson, John William
Thompson, William Brian
Thorneloe, Alfred Hubert
Titley, Alfred Eric
Titterington, Eric
Tracey, Christopher Birdwood
Ussher, Percival Arland
Vigers, Brian Edmund Allen
Wailes, Reginald
Wain, Frank Lonsdale
Walker, Clement Willoughby
Walsh, Herbert
Wells, Philip Wynyard
West, Cyril
Whiting, Walter Frederick
Whitley, Edward Gordon
Wiggins, Norman Ewart
Williams, Philip Gresham
Williams, Reginald John Cyril
Wills, Gerald Alfred
Wilson, Lancelot Elce
Wimbush, James Christopher
Winch, Eric William
Woodcock, Thomas Graham
Woodcock, William Watson
Wragg, Norman
Wraith, Louis Charles
Youatt, Brian Dinsdale
Young, Andrew Blackwood Stewart

1920

Acworth, Donald George William
Akroyd, Peter Swainson
Arnott, Trevor
Barlow, Christopher Matthew
Barlow, Harold Ernest
Barnett, Alec
Bateson, Stuart Latham
Bathe, Denys
Bayley, Cornelius Felix
Bennett, Hilary Romaine
Bewley, Edward Clibborn
Birbeck, Harold Leslie
Black, Robert Andrew Stransham
Blake, John Raymond
Blick, Harry Moffat
Bowman, James Eric
Braddock, Joseph Edward
Brewer, Cyril Griffith
Brown, Norman Long (Long-Brown)
Buckley, William

Butterworth, Albert Wilson
Cann, Denis Moore
Chapman, Arthur Salisbury
Chappell, Peter Stanley
Charnock, William Henry
Chaudhuri, Shiva Kumar
Clark, Albert Edward
Cole, Geoffrey Alfred
Constable, Frederick Hurn
Cosgrove, Edward Cecil
Cradock, Leonard
Currie, James Donald Maxwell
Curry, Basil John Elmitt
Davies, Bernard Sydney
de la Motte, Edward Septimus George
Dicks, Henry Victor
Dobbs, Leonard George
Dobson, Robert Arthur
Edwards-Taylor, Sherwood
el-Bakri, Essayid (El-sayid) Ahmed Morad
Ely, Trevor Howorth Anthony
Entwistle, Roy
Evans, Albert Dan
Evans, Ifor Leslie
Fisher, William Alexander Penton
Fleming, David Johnstone
Flemming, Arthur Adrian Greig
Foster, Thomas Hartley
Fulljames, Owen Ralph
Garrould, Ivor George Bayes
Gilchrist, Robert Munn
Glen, William Burns Cowan
Gracie, Henry Stewart
Gray, Richard Anthony Pereira
Griffiths, David Thomas
Guinness, Gordon Meyer
Halsey, Edward James
Hampton, Sidney
Hatton-Ellis, Alfred Willmott Balfour
Heesom, Dudley Stone
Herbage, Deryk Livingston
Hillyer, Reginald Arthur Nicholas
Holt, James Garfield
Hovil, Guy Oscar
Hulme, Sidney
Hutchinson, Joseph Burtt
Ispahani, Mirza Abol Hassan
Jackson, Ronald Emerson Maxwell
   (Maxwell-Johnson)
Jenkins, Cecil
Jenks, George Bernard
Jewell, Edward Basil
Jones, William Percival
Kavanagh, George Charles MacMorrough
Khanna, Nand Lal
Laing, Rodney Ninian Warrington
Langhorne, George Wilmot
Layton, Ronald Allinson
Lazenby, Eric Walter
Lefèvre, Edward
Leigh-Sarney, Harvey Frederick
Lowe, Charles Frederick Peter

McIntosh, Robert Adrian
McKay, Horatio Malcolm
Mahé de Chenal de la Bourdonnais, John
   Bryant Digby
Mason, William Tate
Mayne, Edward Bonnycastle
Mellor, Philip Evert McIlvaine
Miller, George James
Moore, Thomas Robert George
Mowat, Ralph Gunn
Neate, Cyril Frank Caesar
Nery, Charles Albert
Nery, John Joseph
Nichols, Philip Peter Ross
Nix, Arthur Rupert
Orr, William Edward Anderson
Padley, Henry Wilson
Paige, Robert
Parsons, Charles Wynford
Paxman, Edward Philip
Payne, Alfred Leslie
Peto, Basil Arthur John
Philp, Arthur Leslie
Plevins, St John Tempé
Ponisowsky, Alexander
Porri, Charles Joseph
Prentis, Avon Ramsay Combe
Priestman, Bryan
Proctor, Maurice Faraday
Pye, Harold John
Rajagopalacharya, Desikacharia
Raphael, George
Ray, John Norman Anthony
Rea, Stanley Charles Walsh Wright
Richardson, Alexander Reginald Wakefield
Ridley, John Edward
Rogers, Herbert Cannington
Room, Thomas Gerald
Roundell, Richard Henry Selborne
Ryan, Arthur Healy
Sampson, George
Sanderson, Douglas Hamilton
Saunders-Davies, Arthur Owen
Searle, Cyril Theobald Roundell
Simcox, Lewis
Simmons, Harold John Allpress
Simmons, John Richardson Mainwaring
Snowden, Joseph Stanley
Somerset-Thomas, Vyvyan John
Sonn, Charles Douglas
Steele, Daniel Haines
Stevenson, James
Stewart, Cyril Malcolm Halley
Sutton, Geoffrey Robert
Tanner, Donald Vaughan
Tanner, Guy Montague
Taylor, Sidney Barr
Tennent, Hugh Patrick Lorraine
Theobald, Raymond Walter
Thomas, Alwyne Bell Wyndham
Thorpe, John Knowles
Thres, Douglas Philip

Titterton, Lewis Henry
Tollit, Christopher Charles
van Geyzel, Frederick Christopher William
van Millingen, Evelyn Francis Mackenzie
Wadham, Giles Anthony
Waldron, Eric Brind
Walton, William George
Warren, Herbert Moffat
Warriner, Robert Peverell
Wellard, Francis Albert Leon
West, Frederick Charles
West, William Dixon
Wilkinson, Bernard Harold
Wills, Lancelot Kenneth
Wilson, Edward Raynold
Wilson, James Thomas
Wilson, William John Fleetwood Seddon
Wisden, John Patrick
Woodrooffe, Thomas Borries Ralph

1921

Armstrong, Bernard
Ashe, Percy
Axford, Ernest Coleman
Barbour, Robert Freeland
Barker, John Townsend
Benson, Theodore Ernest
Berridge, Evan Denys
Bingemann, Alfred Mervyn
Blackman, Geoffrey Emett
Blaxter, Cyril Glyndwr
Brewer, Godfrey Noel
Brewster, Leslie George
Brittain, Percival Bernard
Broad, Philip
Broadbent, Thomas Arthur Alan
Burnett, Reginald Penrith
Cameron, Alexander Maurice
Capron, Evelyn Charles
Charters, Alan Dumergue
Colegrave, Edward Henry Manby
Colley, David Bayley
Cox, Henry Talbot
Cox, Robert Mundy
Craig, Terence Vincent
Cranley, John Desmond
Dalby, Robert
Davidson, Percy Maurice
Dearden, John Royds
Dew, William Harold
Dirac, Paul Adrien Maurice
Dobbie, Joseph Hume Leslie
Eagles, Frank Mortimer
Edinger, John Philip
Fagnani, Henry Hutchinson
Ferriday, Thomas Bennett
Field, George Arthur Charles
Fleming, John
Gaccon, William Edward
Gann, Henry Charles
Gardiner, Henry Rolf

Gatty, Philip Vincent
George, William Ewart
Gillespie, Charles Bainbridge
Graham, Graeme Scott (Scott Graham)
Grant, Cecil Charles l'Estrange
Gregory, John Henry
Gunston, David
Hale, James Leonard Ramsay
Hardern, Leslie Harry
Harkness, Kenneth Lanyon
Harmer, John William
Harris, Noël Hedley Vicars
Hesselgreaves, John Wainwright
Hinton, Arthur Russell
Holden, William Richard
Hudson, Wilfred Faraday
Hutchinson, Henry Procter
Hyslop, James
Ives, Arthur Lionel
Ives, John Bapty
Jackson, Richard Meredith
Jaquet, Brian Sidney
John, Basil Joseph
Johnston, James Entwisle
Kefford, Harry Kingsley
Koettlitz, Maurice
Lee, Hau Shik
Leyland, Robert Clive
Lightfoot, Arthur Wilfrid
Llewellyn, David William Alun
Lloyd, Kenneth Edward
McConnell, Robert Melville Terence
McGuffie, James Carruthers Blair
   (Blair-McGuffie)
Macklin, Laurence Hilary
Maclaren, Archibald Shaw
McLellan, John Hollingsworth
Maclennan, Donald James Henry
Mahajani, Ganesh Sakharam
Marchant, Ernest Cecil
Martin, Richard Neville
Martyn, John Arthur King
May, John Leslie
Mayne, Leslie Samuel
Meares, Cyril Denzil Nugent
Metaxa, Andrea Dudly Richard
Metters, Thomas Lee
Mills, John Yarnton
Morton, George Trestrail
Nicholson, John
Nobbs, Cyril Gordon
Noble, Peter Scott
O'Meara, Julian Francis
Oakley, Edgar Handel
Obbard, Harry Naismith
Palmer, Philip Nathaniel Hitchen
Patel, Behram Pestonji
Pickering, Eric Stockdale
Pim, Gerald Robert
Potter, James Eric
Powell, Valence Charles
Rainbow, Henry

Ringwood, Henry Hornby
Roberts, John Bernard Parker
Roberts, Philip Barker
Robinson, Bevan Downing Gurth
Robinson, Ernest Stanley
Rogers, Samuel Philip Hugh
Sale, David Morley
Saunders, Leslie Gale
Searle, Malcolm Walter St Leger
Shawcross, Cyril Wilfred
Skinner, Treves Irving
Smith, Joseph Marie William Lyle
Spelman, Sydney George Henry
Spencer, Ralph Thornton Trevelyan
Spence-Thomas, Richard Foulis
Stuart, Malcolm Moncrieff
Sutcliffe, Richard Brook
Tait, George Aidan Drury
Tanner, Jesse Ossawa
Taphouse, Frank Goodwin
Taylor, Christopher Beech
Terry, John
Thomas, Richard Victor
Thomas, William Harvey Evelyn
Thursby, John Harvey
Tremellen, Kenneth
Wainwright, John Hilditch
Wendt, Henry Lorenz
Williams, Ralph Norman Haile
Williams, Samuel Dudley
Wilson, James Boyd
Wilson, Richard William Russell
Woodhouse, Lionel Clayton
Wright, Charles William Brydon
Wright, James Brown
Yates, Frank

1922

Alessandrini, Goffredo
Ashby, Francis Cyril
Banister, Harry
Barlow, Charles Gerald
Barnes, James Albert
Bateson, Gregory
Beaton, Cecil Walter Hardy
Bell, Joseph Howard
Bland, Ernest John
Bone, Cyril Cornelius
Brooke, Edward Newton
Brown, Kenneth Long (Long-Brown)
Cann, Charles Alfred
Carson, Brian Hardy
Carus, Alexander
Claridge, Marcus William
Clay, Reginald Eustace
Cockcroft, John Douglas
Colvin, Gilbert Russell
Connell, Ernest Oldham
Craggs, Richard Berthold Trechmann
   (Hall-Craggs)
Craig, Thomas Bird

Craven, William Anthony Hubert
Davison, Jack Gunn
de Landa, Francis Joseph
de Yarburgh-Bateson, Stephen Nicholas
　(Lord Deramore)
Edwards, Arthur Bertie Duncan
Elliot Smith, Grafton Latimer
Elliott, John Dickerson
Elliott-Smith, John
Ellis, Rowland
Escandon y Salamanca, Manuel
Falcon, Michael
Feather, Peter Kelk
Field, Thomas Richard Owen
Finnegan, Thomas
Fletcher, Frank Cecil
Fletcher, Philip
Fraser, Keith
Fyzee, Asif (Asaf) Ali Ashgar
Gamgee, Joseph Leonard
Gibby, David
Gilchrist, Ronald Renshaw
Goldstein, Sydney
Gower, Dudley George
Graetz, Gerhard Hermann Arnold
Harris, John Corbett
Harrison, Wilfred Hugh Lane
Hartwell, Charles Herbert
Harvey, John Allen
Herbage, Julian Livingston
Hey, William Rennie
Hirst, Geoffrey Audus Nicholson
Howard, Richard Samuel
Hurll, John Patrick
Inaba, Naomichi
Ives, James
Jenks, William Corfield
Jennings, John Rannard
Keen, Maxwell Frederick Arthur
Kellock, Joseph Grigg
Kin, Harry Myo
Lakshnakara, Mom Chao
Landa y Osio, José de
Lang-Anderson, William Grant
Langton May, Ivan
Layton, Paul Henry
Leakey, Louis Seymour Bazett
Lloyd, George Mark
Lockwood, Arthur Frank
Magnay, Harold Swindale
Marchbank, Frank Havelock
Marindin, Francis Jocelyn de Vere
Mees, Gualtherus Hendrik
Middlemiss, Hugh Percival
Millard, Anthony Walter Phipson
Morrison, Alexander Tupman
Mounsey, Wilfred Edmund
Nicholson, Bernard Clive
Norris, John Henry
Oatley, Charles William
Ollett, Francis Arthur
Otis, Harrison Gray

Paget, Charles Edward Eden
Pasley, Arthur Dalrymple Sabine
Peña y Camus, Oscar
Pennington, Thomas Wilfrid
Pentelow, William Cyril Doughty
Pilcher, Richard Edward Montagu
Pilkington, Kenneth Reginald
Powell, John Douglas
Prado-Uchôa, Affonso
Raghavan, Tandalam Narosimha Chariar
　Srinivasa
Ramaswami Aiyer, Palamaneri Narayanaswami
　Aiyer
Rapley, Frederick
Reay, Joseph
Recordon, Esmond Gareth
Redman, Dudley Stewart
Riad, Mohammed Abdel Moneim
Richards, Francis Alan
Riddell, Thomas Cockburn
Ringrose-Voase, John Reginald (Ringrose)
Rodgers, John Malcolm
Rogers, Charles Hartley Delacourt
Ross, Charles Gordon
Sampson, Robert Frank Andrews
Schlapp, Robert
Scullard, Howard Hayes
Slater, Eliot Trevor Oakeshott
Smellie, James Wilton
Smith, Robert James
Smith, Thomas Carl
Stiles, Walter Stanley
Sutcliffe, Norman
Taylor, Hermon
Thomas, Cecil Holt
Thomas, David Llewelyn
Thomas, Mervyn Lincoln
Thurman, Arthur Leslie
Turner, John Dennis
Urling-Smith, Alban
Usherwood, Kenneth Ascough
Wainwright, John Tillotson
Walker, Philip Ollerenshaw
Walker, Stephen
Waring, Donald Arthur (Hornby-Waring)
Watson, Charles Reginald
Whitehead, Richard Bertram
Whitehouse, Frederick William
Wilson, Wilfrid
Wood, Ronald Ernest
Woodland, Percy
Wormell, Thomas Wilson

1923

Aalders, Willem Jan Goossen
Alexander, Archibald Corbet Fleming
Armstrong, Alfred Elliott
Ball, Ernest Frederick
Bambawale, Bhargao Amrit
Bazeley, Henry Paulle
Beauchamp, Guy Evelyn Louis Beachim

Bevan, Llewelyn Vaughan
Biggs, Charles Edward James
Blair, Alexander Tritton
Booth, John Charles Hedley
Brennand, Arthur Fynes
Brooke, William Aspinall Newton
Bruce-Johnston, Roy Grego
Burley, Percival Leslie
Burstall, Aubrey Frederic
Butterworth, John
Campion, Donald
Carse, William
Carter, Henry Stewart
Charlesworth, Martin Percival
Clarke, Brian Aylmer
Clegg, Harry James Rowland
Cooper, Cyril George
Cowper, Alfred William Noel
Crosby, John
Cunningham, Thomas Sheriff
d'Aguiar, John Edward
Denny, George Andrew Willert
Dunnicliff, Harry
Durley, Thomas Clifford
Edmunds, Paul Roberts
Eley, Alan John
Elizaga y Romero Rubio, Lorenzo Manuel
　Porfirio
Engelbrecht, Petrus Albertus
Fell, Arnold
Foottit, Raymond Langdon Carter
France, Norman Hoole
Francis, Reginald Harvey
Galbraith, Alexander Henderson
Garnett, Philip Robert Mauleverer
Ghey, Geoffrey William Essington
Gnau, Howarth Widman
Goodman, William Wolf
Greene, Edward Reginald
Greenwood, Alan Frederic
Harden, Charles George Stuart
Harper, Wallace Russell
Harrison, Milton
Hawton, John Malcolm Kenneth
Haynes, Philip Francis
Hayter, William Duncan Cary
Henderson, James Lomas
Herrick, Herbert John Charles
Herridge, Geoffrey Howard
Hignett, Reginald Arthur
Hill, Eric Desmond Hume Darley
Hodge, William Vallance Douglas
Hollingworth, Henry Neville
Howard, Henry Fraser
Hyde, Edgar Stanley
Imam, Syed Naqui
Jackson, John Eric
Jackson, Kenneth Greer
Jenks, Walter Henry
Jessop, Harry Victor Edwards
Jones, Thomas Lovel
Kingston, John Samuel

Kousmichoff, Constantine
Larmuth, Reginald Stone Ashley
Leversedge, Leslie Frank
Lewis, Cecil Jack
Lewis, Charles Cedric Carr
Lewis, Frank Stanley
Light, Lovell Hillier Benjamin
Lourie, Arthur
Loveridge, Arthur John
McCay, Francis Howard
McDade, Robert Sinclair Charles
McLeod, Norman Chester
McVean, John Duncan
Majdalany, Jameel
Marsh, Malcolm Charles
Marshall, Henry Hughes
Marshall, Ronald
Martineau, George Edward
Mathewson, Kenneth Douglas
Milne, Robert Arthur
Moncreiff, Francis Hamilton
Moore, John Graham
Morpeth, Geoffrey
Mowat, George Gordon
Newberry, George William
Nicolle, Arthur Philip Ronald
Orme, John Alexander
Orr, Robert Graeme
Peddie, Ronald
Peiris, Charles Jacob Harold
Pelham Browne, Joseph Byrne
Pepper, John Edward
Plackett, Geoffrey Pilkington
Pollard, Martin John
Raphael, Thomas Davidson
Redman, Roderick Oliver
Reed, Anthony Alfred
Reynolds, Eric Vincent
Ross, Archibald Douglas
Ross, Eric Brockwell
Said, Mohammad
Scantlebury, Raymond Marshall
Shewell, Henry Anthony Lampen
Shrubbs, Eric Gordon
Simmons, George Martin
Smith, Reginald William
Smith, Thomas (Knape Smith)
Spence, James Donald
Taylor, William
Thomas, Andrew Rowland Benedick
Thomas, Leonard Cameron
Thompson, Harold Lenox
Thompson, Wilfrid Jansen
Trepte, George Wyndham Macdonnell
Watkinson, George
Wayte, Alan Wymont
Webb, Harry Howard
Webster, Robert Chilion Peter
Whiteman, William Meredith
Williams, Arthur Warriner
Womack, Harold Athelstan
Woodcock, Eric Charles

Wycherley, Ronald Fowke
Yarrow, Ronald

1924

Acosta, George Alfred
Archer, Geoffrey Clifford
Bagshawe, John Leslie
Baillie, John Gilroy
Barrett, Wilfred Phillips
Beale, John Montagu
Bentall, Reginald George
Blaxter, Royston
Bradley, Rupert Stevenson
Brailowsky, Vadime
Brain, Kenneth Roy
Bramwell, Eric Arundell
Bridgeford, George Macrae
Brodie, Douglas Spencer
Cairns, Richard
Caro, John Everard (Jack)
Carter, Derrick Hunton
Cave, Richard
Charlton, William Hartley Denys
Concannon, Edmond James Blake
Cooke, Arthur Hunt (Hunt Cooke)
Cowen, Harold Wolfe
Craig, Norman Vincent
Crawford, Maurice Paterson
Crossley, Alan Francis
Davidson, James Johnston
de Romero y Dorrego, Manuel
de Watteville, Kenneth William
Denning, Gordon Masey
Dick, Gordon Ian Brand
Eastick, Douglas Martineau
Edsall, John Tileston
Farewell, John Freke
Fisher, Graham Russel (Russel-Fisher)
Freeman, Jack Greenfield
Fuchs, Vivian Ernest
Fyson, Harold
Gardiner, Gilbert Claydon
Gent, Harold Arthur
Glover, Roderick Lewis
Green, Donald Cecil
Griffiths, Gordon Craven
Hannah, Gerald Rainsford
Harding, James William
Harris, Colin Spurge
Hencken, Hugh O'Neill
Henry, Howard Francis
Holden, Arthur Alfred
Howland, Robert Leslie
Husain, Akhter
Ince, Ralph Edward
James, William Owen
Jennings, Jan McIlwraith
Jones, Sydney
Kefford, Edward Kingsley
Kenchington, Francis Ernest
Kenny, Ronald Edmond

Lamb, George Liston
Leftwich, Richard Alfred
Lewis-Bowen, Gerard Arthur
Liebert, Geoffrey Rex
Lincoln, René
Liversidge, Charles
Long, Raleigh Seymour
Lush, Jesse Hugh
Macdonald, Alasdair
McIntyre, Frederick Donald Livingstone
Mackenzie, Norman Archibald MacRae
McMullen, Alexander Lawrence
Macnish, James Martin
Maher, Alfred Colin
Mallik, Bimalendra Chandra
Mattei, Francis Bagshawe
Mears, Joseph Henry Watt
Milner, Fred
Monteith, Alexander
Morreau, Cecil Joseph
Morriss, Walter Slade
Mosséri, Henri Samuel
Mott, Nevill Francis
Musker, Harold John
Naylor, Guy Darnley
Newell, Adrian Nathaniel
Noakes, Harold Isaac
Nuttall, Charles Herbert
Parkinson, Mark Mervyn Leofric
Paterson, George Mutlow
Peacock, Hugh Myddleton
Philpott, Guy
Poore, Robert
Purdy, Charles Edward
Ratcliffe, Robert Arundel
Rees, Charles Owen Benwell
Rideal, Guy St Clair
Roberts, Thomas Leslie Foulkes
Robertson, Maurice Alexander
Robson, Robert
Rolls, Arthur Litton
Rosenheim, Max Leonard
Saloway, Reginald Harry
Saltmarsh, Philip Cecil
Sayles, Henry Sharrock
Scott, Gordon
Scott-Moncrieff, Ronald
Sewell, John Edward
Sharp, Wright Granville Maynard
Silby, Robert David Kerr
Simpson, Geoffrey Bernard Albert
Simpson, William
Smart, Donovan Foster
Sobey, Wilfred Henry
Spence, Andrew Macdonald
Stevenson, Robert Edward
Streatfield, Terence Ernest
Stuart, Innes
Tarn, Thomas Cresswell Butson
Tetley, John Lewis
Thomas, Donald Gomer Cobden
Thompson, Frank William

Thompson, Guy Warren St Clair
   (St Clair-Thompson)
Thornton, Leonard Cyril
Tracey, John Brodrick
Turner, John Moore
Tyson, Harold Edward
Van Geyzel, Leonard Colvin
Vernon, Philip Ewart
Watson, Bernard Angus
Whittaker, Duncan
Williams, Reginald Arnold Forrest
Williams, William
Wilson, Thomas Douglas Glover
Wood, William Ronald
Woodman, John Geoffrey Wootten
Wyllie, Herbert Ian Campbell
Wyman, Jeffries
Zackon, Jack

1925

Allen, Douglas Geoffrey Glenn
Arnold, William Aubrey
Babb, Burland Arthur
Baines, Roger Holford
Bell, George Alexander
Bickford, Nicholas
Bird, Francis George
Blackman, John Vernon
Bowle, Brian Edward
Brightman, Geoffrey
Britton, Roland Henfrey Glanville
Broome, Philip Gordon
Brown, George Carnegie (Carnegie Brown)
Brown, Herbert Harris
Bryson, Robert
Buchanan, Donald Batts
Burch, William Edward Victor
Burdon-Cooper, Alick McLaurin Monteath
Bushe-Fox, Patrick Loftus
Butler, Felix John
Cadman, Samuel Parkes Hubert
Campbell, Donald John
Chamberlain, James Russell
Chapman, Frederick Spencer
Clark, Robert Edward David
Cole, William Arthur Stewart
Connell, William John Ramsay
Cooke, Anthony Eskrigg
Cosserat, Eric Cyril
Crawford, John Aikman
Croft, Eric David
Crofts, John Raymond
Currant, Eric James
Davies, Frank
Davies, David Richard Seaborne
Davison, Bruce Munro
Dias, Ponnahannodigey Christopher Edward
   Arnold
Drayson, Harold Percy
Emms, Geoffrey Donald
England, Arthur Francis John

Evelyn-Jones, Lorence
Filmer, William Edmund
Finch, Peter Charles
Foot, Hugh Mackintosh (Lord Caradon)
Foster, Laurence Edward Anderton
Foxworthy, Alfred William
Franklin, Eric Stanley
Gatty, Hugh Percival Wharton
Genge, Donald Sealy Gilbert
Gibson, Humphrey Graeme
Gillespie, Robert Pollock
Goode, John Basil
Grubb, John Burlingham
Hall-Smith, George Waldo
Hancock, Charles Magin Coulter
Hanmer, Stephen Henry
Harbinson, William Kenneth
Harris, Brian Kempster
Harrison, William
Hayburn, Edward Francis
Hayward, Maurice John
Hedley, Charles Stephens
Hibbert, Francis Dennis
Hill, Ivan Conrad
Hipps, Nathaniel
Hockin, John Russell Ayscoghe
Hosmer, Henry Barnes
Iles, John Bird
Jacob, Bernard Binyon
Jarratt, Thomas
Jessop, Dennis Samuel Alfred Edwards
Keast, John Harris
Kellock, John Denis Gilbert
Kennedy, Edward Gilbert
King, Raymond
Kitchin, Finlay Tower
Leathem, John Gaston
Lewis, David Lincoln (Lincoln-Lewis)
Lincoln, Louis John
Loveridge, Charles Edward
Lyon, Norman Geoffrey
McCormick, Joseph Conybeare
Marchant, Herbert Stanley
Munnings, Frederick William
Murray, John Lamb Blackwood
Neamtzu, Barbu
Ogden, Guy William
Oldham, Frank
Owen, Charles Brewster O'Maille
Payne, Richard Vaughan
Peddie, James
Petit, Dinshaw Jehangir
Phemister, Thomas Crawford
Pullan, Edward John Mcdonnell
Pullin, Denis Herbert
Ramage, Hugh Pyesmith
Ramsden, John Fraser
Reuchlin, Henri
Roper, Robert Dudley
Rothwell, Harry
Rowlands, Evan Celyn
Sadler, Eric John

Sargant, William Walters
Seabrook, Frederick James
Selby, Cedric Cree
Semple, John Greenlees
Semple, William Hugh
Shepherd, Leslie James Vaughan
Skelton, Allan Noel
Skelton, John Chatto
Smith, John Howard Marcus
Smouha, Ellis Hay
Somerville, Robert
Southern, John Roy
Stephens, John Gower
Stork, Francois Gerard
Stout, Alan
Sturrock, George Stuart
Swaine, Kenneth Bruce
Symonds, Reginald Askwith
Tachmindji, Michel Alexander
Tait, (Cecil) Wortley
Taylor, Edward McKenzie
Tennent, James Short
Thomas, David Biron
Thompson, Bruce Logan
Thorold, Montague
Timms, Geoffrey
Tothill, Alec Norman
Tothill, Reginald John
Vincent, Basil Walter
Walker, George Elliot
Ward, Charles Herbert John
Webb, Alan Howard
Westlake, Henry Dickinson
Whitfield, Gerald Arthur Wadsworth
Willey, Eric John Baxter
Willis, George Geoffrey Lightly
Winter, John Leslie Haywood
Woodcock, Cleever Ralph
Wright, Norman Parker

1926

Adam, Kenneth
Adcock, Cecil Milton
Alexander, George Baker
Anderson, Godfrey Alard
Archbold, John William
Arrow, John William Frederick
Astbury, Norman Frederick
Avery, Eric Nugent
Bancroft, George Charles
Barber, James Bertram
Barber, Wilfred Carlisle
Beavan, John Allan
Bence, Ronald Ivor
Berry, Oscar Keith de la Tour (de Berry)
Binning, Rex Austin
Blenkinsop, John Rowell
Boatman, John Herbert
Booth, Norleigh
Bucknell, Douglas Wentworth
Burgess, Thomas Charles

Campbell, James Duncan Donald
Cash, Francis William
Cater, Ian Barwys Reid
Champion, Frank Clive
Chapman-Andrews, Edwin Arthur
Chew, Frederick Robert Gansel
Childs, Patrick
Clements, Clement Lisle
Coll y Serna, Charles Arthur
Colman, Edwin Woodruff
Cooper, Thomas Bruce
Corcuera, Carlos Loizaga
Craig, James Alan
Crompton, John William Richardson
Crossley, Frank Leggo
Crouch, Bernard Cyril
Cule, Eric William
Delgado, Gregorio Alexander
De Silva, Harry Reginald
Dimock, Eric John
Dunkley, Kenneth Lawrance
Earl, Lionel Richard Franklyn
Eddy, Spencer
Everett, Leslie Scott
Finkelstein, Maurice Moores Behr
Fitzherbert, Henry
Foster, Andrew Brisbin
Fraser, Kenneth
Gardiner, John David
George, Thomas Neville
Gilbert, Thomas
Glen, Robert Muir
Gordon, Ernest Harold
Goupille, Joseph Philippe
Green, Horace Norman
Grimsdell, Eric Hedley McKenzie
Hadland, John Kynaston Phipps
Haigh, Frederick Thomas Stretton
Harman, John Bishop
Harwood, Herbert Clifton Fairfax
Hay, David
Hesse, Ernst Paul
Hill, Rowland
Howell, Trevor Henry
Hoyland, William Frazer
Hunter, Oscar Geldert
Hutton, Herman Gardner
Ives, Edward Kenneth
Ives, Francis Wilson Ernest
Jackson, Myles Allen Maxwell
Johnstone, John Robert Maxwell
Jones, Ernest Gibson
Jones, Ernest Loveday
Jones, Merlin Hywel
Judge, Edward Thomas
Kamath, Hundi Srinivasa
Kendall, Maurice George
Larmour, James
Lascelles, Daniel Richard
Lewis, Isaiah Leonard
Lewis, Roland Swaine
Lilley, James

Lloyd Owen, Morus Wyn
Lomonossoff, George
Lydall, Edward Francis
MacConkey, Charles Alexander Hamilton
Macdonald, Allan Ronald
McDonald, Thomas
Mahajani, Vasudev Sakharam
March, Juan
Marshall, Henry Leslie
Marshall, Ian Fraser
Martineau, Charles
Mason, John
Mattar, Fareed
Matthew, Patrick Chrichton
Mayne, Archibald Collier
Merton-Jones, Edmund Trevor
Mukharji, Rabindranath
Notcutt, Stephen Abbott
Oades, Reginald Charles
O'Connor, Brian
Park, Cyril John
Parsons, Geoffrey Bonython Angas
Parsons, George Samuel
Patterson, Arthur
Paul, Gerard John Christopher
Plutte, Charles Ernest Frederick
Pope, Randall West
Price, Ernest Woodward
Prytherch, Robert Rees
Reidy, Joseph Patrick Irwin
Reynolds, Arthur Rudolph
Reynolds, Oliver William
Richmond, John
Rintoul, Andrew
Roberts, Gwilym Henry Spooner
Roberts, Harold Warlow
Robertson, Charles Goodwin
Rodd, Thomas Eric
Roeder, Kenneth David
Rose, Maurice Frederick
Ross, Robert Dawes
Rouchdy, Hassan
Rushton, John Atherton
Rushworth, Louis Lionel Stuart
Rye, Ralph Walter
Sansom, Thomas Keith Beck
Schwab, Robert Sidney
Scoular, Alexander George
Sen, Susanta Kumar
Shannon, Godfrey Eccleston Boyd
Sharpe, Eric Ellis
Shepherd, Francis William
Smith, Clive Gordon
Smith, Harry Percy
Smith, James Arthur Wilson
Smith, Percy Chandler
Sparrow, Thomas William Francis
Spence, Charles Francis
Stapleton, George Harold
Staveacre, Maurice Fleming
Steele-Perkins, Alfred Peter
Steele-Perkins, Guy Shirley

Summerhill, James Hugh Everett
Tait, John Collins
Tanner, Howard Barrett
Taylor, Frank Robert Forbes
Taylor, Thomas Charles
Thors, Thor
Tiarks, Geoffrey Lewis
Tobin, Thomas Victor
Tooth, Geoffrey Cuthbert
Trowell, Oswald Arthur
Tunks, Donald Russell
Turner, Guy Elliot
Turner, Roland Harold Stuart
Vause, Thomas Rupert
Walker, Geoffrey Howard
Warner, Wilfrid John Nicholas
Watson, Francis John Bagott
Watson, Peter Bartlett Collier
Wells, James Simpson
Wild, William Ferris
Willcox, William Bradford
Williams, Coleman Shaler
Williams, William Law
Wilson, Austin James
Wilson, Campbell Aubrey Kenneth
Wilson, Gordon
Wilson, Robert Hugh
Wood, Francis Hugo
Woodhouse, Michael Clayton
Wormell, Donald Ernest Wilson
Worsley, Thomas Cuthbert
Wright, Norman Mackay
Wright, Thomas

1927

Alcock, Robert Saxelby
Allen, Ronald Charles Tucker
Anabtawi, Wasfi Sadeq
Ashby, Richard Thompson
Aylett, Arthur Denis
Bairstow, John Holroyd
Banks, Kenneth Charles
Barbour, Thomas Lawson
Barkby, Joseph Ewart
Baxter, Arthur Douglas
Behrend, Stanley William Emile
Bentley, John Hardy
Bilsby, Herbert
Bishop, William Douglas
Blanch, Joseph William
Blunt, William Gwyn
Bradlow, Emanuel Percy
Brereton, John Jerningham
Bretherton, Leonard Francis
Brief, Morris
Brightman, John Anson
Broad, Stephen
Broome, Richard Neville
Bruce, George
Caldwell, John
Carris, Harold Edward

Caswell, Francis Emil George
Chamberlain, Ralph
Chapman, Maurice Boswell
Chapman, Robert Geoffrey
Chotzner, John Raymond (Colchester)
Cleary, Denis Mackrow
Colby, John Bothway
Coleman, Francis Hayling
Collison, Lewis Herbert
Connell, Frank James
Cooke, George Edward
Crawley-Boevey, Richard Martin
Crothers, John Clemens
Crowther, Joseph Stanley
Davidson, Stephen Moriarty
Duell, Charles Halliwell
Duncan, Arthur Bryce
Eberhart, Richard Ghormley
Edwards, Anderson Colin Talbot
Edwards, Robert Cleveland
Elsworth, Walter Leslie
Evans, David Hubert Raymond
Forbes, Alastair
Fosbrooke, Henry Albert
Foster, Herbert Frederick Brudenell
Fountain, Christopher Osborn
Gardner, John Bardsley
Ghey, Philip Henry Ratcliffe
Gilchrist, Reginald Thomas
Greenup, Basil William
Griffin, Ewart Maxse
Hall, Richard de Zouche
Harbinson, George Chamberlain
Harrison, Beverley Thelwall
Harriss, Kendal Bushe
Holbard, Cyril Arthur
Hunter, William Clayton
Huntley, John Guy Henderson
Hutchison, Denis Charles
Iles, Gordon Butler
Inaba, Viscount Masayashi
Jackson, Richard Hoyle
Jaúregui, Julio Ventura
Johnston, John Worthington
Jones, Lawrence Charles Kennedy Vaughan
Joshi, Surendra Vinayak
Keen, Alfred Stewart
Kefford, Richard William Kingsley
Ker, Robert Dermot Paton
Key, Samuel
Kirkwood, Thomas Miller
Knight, Robert Lanier
Kyle, David
Langton May, Cecil Hugh
Laycock, Handley Theodore
Layton, Frank Michael
Leakey, Douglas Gray Bazett
Lendon, Nelson Courtney
Lynn, Charles William
Lyon, Francis John
McCormick, Michael Edward
Macdonald, Patrick Donald

McDowell, John Muir
McLaren, Colin Colby
Marshall, Kenneth
May, Harry Blight
Meek, Richard Ombler
Mellis, William Ranald Stuart
Mellor, Leonard
Millar, James Broom
Murray, Kenneth Walter
Nelson, Kenneth Edmund
Nicholson, Roydon Joseph
Nobbs, Douglas
Ormerod, Arthur Hereward
Owen, James Raymond
Passmore, Dudley Robert
Penny, Arthur Geoffrey
Petrie, Arthur Hill Kelvin
Platt, Christopher James
Power, Guy Stuart O'Neill
Ragg, Theodore Frederick Arthur
Ratcliffe, Tom Arundel
Reddy, Nayanivenkata Gopalakrishna
Ritchie, James McLaren
Roberton, Spencer
Robinson, Gerald Barcroft
Robinson, Gilbert de Beauregard
Robinson, William Eric Arnot
Routledge, William Quentin Durward
Rugg-Gunn, Mark Andrew
Russell, John James Fraser
Sanger-Davies, Vyvyan Joseph
Schupbach, Ernest Halley
Shackleton, Clarence Francis
Shore, Thomas Leonard Hall
s'Jacob, Frederick Bernhard
Smith, Marcus Cecil Forryan
Smith, Thomas Gregory (Gregory-Smith)
Speechly, William Grove
Sprunt, Geoffrey Herbert
Stephens, Arthur Veryan
Stephens, George Stuart
Tebbs, Reginald
Thomas, Edward William
Thompson, Arthur Denys Halstead
Tod, Geoffrey Noel (Noel-Tod)
Townsend, Hugh Hamilton Massey
Turnbull, Gerald William
Vickerman, Allan Dodson
Ward, John Hamilton Mackenzie
Warrington, Paul
Webber, John Francis
Werth-Regendanz, Hubert
Whipp, Brian
Whitaker, Edgar Haddon
Whiteley, Joseph Edward
Wilkinson, Hermann Denis Darrell
Williams, Gwyn
Williams, Walter James Philipps
Wilmers, Charles Kossman
Wilson, John Julian Glover
Wintringham, Charles Richard Fildes
Wright, Henry Myles

Wynne Willson, Archdall Alexander
Yardley, Georges Emile
Yates, George Alfred
Yates, Paul Lamartine (Lamartine Yates)
Yerburgh-Bonsey, Robert Harold
Young, Peter Stuart

1928

Abhayaratna, Walter Patrick Leopold
Airey, George William Edwin
Andrews, Ronald Alford
Astle, Edward William Browne
Bailey, George Herbert
Baldwin, Ernest Hubert Francis
Bane-Sinhji, Kumar Shri
Barbor, Ronald Charles Blair
Bate, William Kendal
Bearcroft, John Fortescue
Bevan, Owen Vaughan
Beveridge, William John Morton
Binns, Howard Reed (Rees)
Brearley, Joseph
Brock, Byron Britton
Brooke, John Claude
Brooks, John Cowell
Burton, Dennis Arthur Edward
Burton, John Henry Montagu
Cameron, Donald Ian
Carter, Geoffrey William
Casson, Hugh Maxwell
Champness, John Alec
Clothier, Peter Thompson
Coggan, (Frederick) Donald
Cohen, Jacob
Collier, Frank Kenneth Gerald
Collings, Hubert Dennis
Collins, Leslie Arthur
Cornwall, Ian Wolfran
Corsellis, Henry Alexander
Cowburn, Richard Edridge
Creek, Ernest George
Culpin, Claude
Culshaw, Frank Hubert
David, John Ernest Awelrydd
Davies, Denis Laidlaw
Davies, Hugh Sykes (Sykes Davies)
Denholm, George Lovell
Drayton, William John
Drinkwater, Allen Paul
Dudley, Donald Reynolds
Easten, Guthrie Philip
Elliott, William Alexander
Fergusson, John Douglas
Foottit, Edward Hall
Forgan, Thomas Adrian
Forster, Oliver Matthew
Fraser, Gordon
Gale, Alexander John
Garton, Arthur Ernest James
Getty, Robert John
Gleadow, Edward Purdy

Goffe, Reginald
Goodall, John Francis
Goode, Robert Charles Jeffrey
Green, Frederick Arthur
Greenhalgh, Arthur Ward
Haig-Thomas, David
Harrison, Michael Beverley Leeds
Heatley, Norman George
Hilton, Philip Trevor
Himely, Luis Sigismund
Hunt, Sidney Robert
Innes, Alexander
Jackson, Frank Storer
Jackson, Kenneth Hurlstone
Jehu, Ivor Stewart
Jenkyn, Thomas Richard
Johnson, Maurice Alexander
Jones, Ronald Morgan
Kerkham, Robin Kingsford
Kimber, John Cowley Britton
King, John Ernest
Kirkness, James Michael Percy
Laing, Kenneth Macrae
Lapwood, Ernest Ralph
Lazier, Morley John Campbell
Legg, Francis Benjamin Stuart
Lim, Kheng Kooi
Loosley, Stanley George Henry
Lunn, John
MacAlister, Donald
McGuinness, Alexander Sellars
Mackenzie, Niel Allan Patrick Grant
McKibbin, Frederick Malcolm
Magson, Thomas Symmons
Mason, John Newby
Masterman, Ernest Bertram Zeller
Mathias, Edward Lanfranc Morgan
May, Richard Sturdy
Megaw, John
Millar, George Reid
Miller, Harold
Mitchell, Joseph Stanley
Molins, Desmond Walter
Morris, Thomas David
Murray, William Rusack Blackwood
　(Blackwood Murray)
Naisby, Tom
Openshaw, James Frederick Melville
Paterson, Noel Kennedy
Patuck, Sorab Pestonjee
Paxton-Petty, John Dennis
Payne, Ronald John
Pemberton, Ronald James
Petch, Charles Plowright
Pochin, Edward Eric
Porteous, George Herbert
Price, Neville George
Prince, James Edmund
Quibell, Ernest Philip
Rea, James Taylor
Rhoden, Harry George
Rice, Otis Radcliffe

Richardson, Geoffrey Christian
Richardson, George
Robertson, Charles James
Robertson, David Fischer
Rolls, Thomas Burnand
Rosenhead, Louis
Ross, James Stirling
Ross, Ronald Sterry
Royle, William Arthur Kirkcaldy
Sáenz, Alfredo
Sargent, John
Savory, John Barwick Gaudern
Semple, Robert Hugh
Simmonds, Ronald John McLean
Smith, Hugh Fairfield
Smith, Roy
Spence, Ralph William
Stewart, Malcolm Geoffrey
Strouts, Bernard Murton
Suggitt, Leslie
Sutor, John Allan
Symonds, Ronald Henry Humfrys
Thoday, David Robert Gabriel
Thomas, Howard Reginald
Thompson, Ralph Herbert
Toulmin, John Heaton
Turner, Geoffrey Redman
Turner, Godfrey Michael
Vincent, Stanley Ralph
Wade, Emlyn Capel Stewart
Walker, Arthur Stephen
Wall, Thomas Charlton
Weston, William Guy
Wheeler, Geoffrey
Whitaker, Philip Randle Kerr
Wild, Alfred Crabtree
Wilkins, Arnold Frederick
Williams, Francis Dillon Mountford
Winfield, Roland Henry
Wright, Thomas Grieve
Young, Terence Charles John

1929

Alderson, Denis Fordred
Amin, Mahmoud Loutfy
Anderson, William Thomas
Appleby, Mark
Arnison, Thomas Mitchell
Ashby, Hugh King
Austin, William Norman
Avery, Richard Francis
Baker, James Alison
Barbour, Gavin Butler
Barry, William Henry
Batterbury, George Anthony
Bayley, Arthur Desmond Charles
Beggs, Robert David Irving
Benson, Henry Frederick Hamlyn
Bertram, George Colin Lawder
Bowley, John Lindsay William
Bradford, John Eric

Brain, Michael Benjamin
Brown, Frederick (Freddie) Richard
Buckingham, Richard Arthur
Butterworth, George Neville
Bythell, Denis William Prestwich
Carter, Douglas
Chambers, Oliver Ronald
Clay, Ralston Nelson Hope
Clementi, Dennis Montagu
Clements, John Selby
Cosh, Frederick Sydney
Coutinho, Fritz Herbert
Crowther, Edward Ramsden
Cutts, Anson Bailey
Daniels, Cyril Ernest
Davie, Geoffrey Bowcher
Davies, Noel Gordon
de Silva, Neil Marcus
de Styrcea, Jonel
de Winton, Charles Francis Seton
de Yarburgh-Bateson, Richard Arthur
　(Lord Deramore)
Diggle, William Mellalieu
Dixon, Foster Hickman
Dow, James Findlay
Escritt, George Stanley
Eve, Stephen Theodore
Farrar, John Evelyn
Field, Arthur Michael Cary
Francis, Hugh Elvet
Gamble, John Christopher
Glover, Colin Merriam
Gonzalez, Alphonso
Grant, Robert Sturge
Green, William Otis
Hadingham, Frank Edward
Harbour, Harold Ernest
Harman, Roger Chamberlain
Haviland, Denis William Garstin Latimer
Hay, Alexander Charles de Prudrik
Hay, James Foulis
Hay, Michael
Higginson, Herbert Walmsley
Hill, Philip Eustace Lionel
Hobson, Stanley Wakefield
Hollick, Frank Samuel Jennings
Horne, Roderick Rees Kimball
Hudspith, Hubert Corot
Hunt, Richard Swinton
Hussey-Freke, Ambrose Frederick
Hynes, Martin
Jagger, John Greenwood
Jarchow, Frederick Carl
Jones, Brynmor
Kennedy, John Reid
Kennedy, William Hall
Khan, Sahibzada Rashid Ali
Khosla, Krishna Kumar
Knopp, Alexander Edward Robert
Kuester, Hanns Ulrich Oskar (Chester)
Lait, John
Lane, Edward Arthur

Law, William Alexander
Lawrenson, Alexander Cameron
Litherland, Geoffrey
Lord, Geoffrey Frank
Lorimer, Guy
McDonald, Gordon Francis
Macdonald, Thomas John
McIntosh, Kenneth Alister
McMullen, John Anthony
Macro, William Brindley
Mardon, Gilbert Dennis Heber
Marmorstein, Emile
Mellor, William John Rockfort
Morison, Charles Rutherford
Morris, Samuel Derek Drake
Munsey, David Thomas Foster
Murray, Hugh Alexander
Navaratnarajah, Paramanathan
Northcroft, George Bernard
Notcutt, George Stanley
Odell, William Norman
Owbridge, Reginald Cyril Neville
Parfit, Eric George
Paterson, Alan
Pharazyn, Peter Walter Johnston
Phillipps-Wolley, Clive John Fenwick
Pott, Richard Holliday
Prestwich, Mark Fiennes
Raby, John Henry Muers
Rees, Richard Geraint
Repard, Hugo William Arbouin
Richardson, John Stanley
Roney-Dougal, Richard Patrick
Rootham, Jasper St John
Rowntree, William Henry
Rowsell, Francis Charles
Rushall, Richard Boswell
Sands, Laurence Cowley
Schofield, Harry
Serjeant, Richard Boddington
Shepherd, Cyril George
Sillars, Ronald William
Simpson, Robert Arthur
Smith, Cyril Randolph
Smith, Frederic Gordon
Stephens, Stanley George
Stevens, John Richard
Stevenson, Peter Verran
Stewart, Hugh St Clair
Stoddard, Thomas Leslie
Strang, John Braithwaite
Sturt, John Edward
Tattersall, John Lloyd
Thornton, Robert Ribblesdale
Todd, Walter John Cambridge
Turney, Frederick Donald d'Avray
Valentine, Wilfrid Henry
Vokes, Frederick Ercolo
Walker, William George
Watson, John Stewart Ferra
Weltman, Joseph
White, Frederick William George

Wiglesworth, Reginald Thomas
Williams, Colin Pascoe
Williams, John Elwyn Askew
Wu, Yuan Luang
Yates, David Wallace

1930

Adcock, Reginald
Allen, John Francis
Allen, John Piers
Aspinall, William Briant Philip Pryce
Athanassoff, Vladimir
Atkinson, James Arthur Lionel
Atkinson, Myles Birkett
Baines, Guy Harrison
Barran, Arthur Haworth
Barton, John Percival
Bartrum, Peter Clement
Battcock, Whalley Vowe
Beaumont, Kenneth
Bell, George Trafford
Bhandari, Dharm Pal
Blackburn, Julian Murray
Blakstad, Gabriel Clifford Clark
Bonsey, William
Bowen, William Henry
Boyd, Leslie Stanthorne
Boyes, William Edward
Braithwaite, Bernard Sedgwick
Brooke, Donald Guest
Brown, Edward Walter William
Brown, John Gordon Leonard
Browne, Alan Chapman Lloyd
Bryers, Richard Hugh Castellain
Burgess, Frederick William
Butzer, Heinrich Wilhelm Viktor
Buxton, Gurney Harry Lionel
Calvert, Sidney Denis
Carnes, Gerald Lambton
Carter, James Roger
Cleave, William Paul Oke
Clemow, John
Common, Francis Graeme
Connell, Reginald Morton
Corbett, Andrew James Gerald
Coulson, Bernard William Harrison
Crittall, Richard Guy Berrington
Daniel, Peter Maxwell
d'Antal, Andrew Louis
Davey, John
Davies, David Idwal
Davies, Jack Gale Wilmot
Dawson, Sidney Cooper
Dé, Debi Kumar
Dehn, Stanley Gustav
de Mel, Louis Hilton Vere
Diver, John
Dunlop, Thomas
Eden, Alfred
Elliot Smith, Stephen
Evans, George Clifford

Fairweather, David Armstead
French, Edward Brodie
Genge, James Robert
Gibbons, Thomas James
Gibbs, John Morel
Gibson, Ronald George
Goodlet, Brian Laidlaw
Gregory, Donald Leonard
Grice, Dennis Neve
Grimsdell, Richard Lucian
Guthrie-Jones, Edward
Gutsell, Leslie Charles
Harding, Douglas Arthur
Hart, Edward Watson
Hart, Richard William Kennett
Hepworth, Arthur Jackson
Howard, John
Hulme, Alfred Cresswell
Irvin, Charles Watkinson
Jehangir, Jehangir Cowasji
Johnson, William Arthur
Jones, Harry Ernest
Jones, Ronald Montague
   (Montague-Jones)
Kater, Gregory Blaxland
Kater, Norman Herman Murchison
Keidan, Joshua Marcus
Kenyon, Harold Frederick
Kershaw, Geoffrey
Knight, Astley Chadborn
Landells, John Wingrave
Latifi, Komair
Laycock, John Dixon
Leathem, Terence Robert
Lewis, Dudley George
Locke, Cyril Stanley
Lomax, William
Love, Christopher Charles
McCutcheon, James Thomson
McDonnell, Peter Francis
Mance, Henry Stenhouse
Mardon, Noel Alexander Richard
Martin, Desmond Levins Joseph
Mason, Wilfred Bernard
Maston, Charles James
Merry, Douglas Cooper
Millard, John Forster
Milner, Christopher John
Moore, James Inglis
Mottershead, Frank William
Moxon, Gerald Richard
Mulrenan, Richard John
Munro, John Gray
Newbery, John Alec
Newell, Martin Joseph
Newman, Cyril Gordon
Nicholson, Kenneth Fletcher
Nightingale, Neville Gascoyne
O'Donovan, Daniel
Orpen, Leslie D'Arcy
Parker, Kenneth Alfred Lamport
Payne, George Peter Morgan

Penny, Henry Martin
Plummer, Colin Vernon
Porter, Laurence Stevenson
Pringle, John
Procter, John Tyndale
Pyefinch, Kenneth Arthur
Rawes, John
Richardson, George Oglethorpe
Rose, Sidney Patrick
Rosenheim, Charles Leslie
Rowe, John Bentley
Rushton, Peter Crampton
Sargentson, James Kenneth
Sawyer, Walter Warwick
Scott, Herbert Wyndham Fitzgerald
Scrase, George Edward Thomas
Shakespear, John Harnby
Shaw, Ronald
Simpson, Denis Louis
Simpson, Reginald James Laing
Squire, Raglan Hugh Anstruther
Steele-Perkins, Thomas Harrild
Stephens, Thomas Anthony Stuart
Stevens, Robert Hilary
Stock, Peter Duguid Heath
Struthers, John
Symonds, Frederick Michael
Taft, Hulbert
Tan, Thoon Lip
Taylor, Philip Tetlow
Taylor, Thomas
Taylor, William Smalley
Thomas, Norman Henry
Thomson, Kenneth Taylor
Thomson, Robert Charles Muirhead
Tothill, Richard Fleming
Valentine, David Henriques
Venosta, Guido
Vincent, Richard
Webb, Geoffrey Owen Davies
Willey, Frederick Thomas
Willmer, Edward Nevill
Wilson, Harris
Wilson, John Tuzo
Woodman, John Vere
Young, Maurice Durward

1931

Adkins, Edward William Orton
Ahmed, Mohamed Mursi
Akeroyd, Frederick Bromley
Barrett, John Henry
Bell, Henry Esmond
Bennett, Albert Joseph
Blanford, Edward Oliver Trenchard
Bolster, Richard Vary Campbell
Bootheway, Kenneth Charles Hartley
Box, Antony William
Braithwaite, John Vernon
Branch, Newton Kemal
Brookes, Alexis Michael Panther

Buchanan, John MacAlister
Budd, Bernard Wilfred
Bullen, Keith Edward
Burnett, Donald Fenn
Burns, Ian Forrest
Burton, Charles Alan
Calvin, Archibald Augustus
Campbell, Robert
Clark, George Edward
Clementson, Peter George Alfred
Cochran, William Gemmell
Cockerton, John Penn
Collins, Francis Geoffrey
Collins, James Frederick
Cousen, Cecil
Crowley, John Yarborough
Dark, Geoffrey Fairfax
Davison, Robert
Dickens, John Raymond
Dunant, Charles Edward
Edwards, George Hewlett Dawes
Egner, William Edward
Ellis, John Matthew
Espley, Gilbert Thornber
Evans, Roland Thompson
Everett, John Frederick
Faulkner, John Herbert
Fell, Eric Whineray
Foster, Edward James Graham
Franklin, Mervin Clarence
Fraser, Donald
Gardiner, Richard Aylmer
Gardner, Eric Kay
Gaskell, William Harriman Craig
Haigh, Harry
Hales, Anton Linder
Harbinson, Gerald Edward
Hart, Henry St John
Hassan, Tengku Abdullah
Haworth, Christopher Matthew
Heffernan, Herbert Nesbitt
Hetherington, Robert Newett
Hicks, Arthur Lionel
Highet, Hugh Campbell
Hill, Stanley
Hoare, Henry George Wishart
Hornak, Hermann Bernhardt
Hunter, Ernest John
Husband, Anthony Dearden
Hyde, Ronald Harry Picton
Jerrome, Ronald Henry
Johnson, Ronald Ernest Charles
Johnston, Vivian Dale
Kemp, James Herbert
Lack, Christofer Cheyne
Langdon, Augustus John
Lawless, Michael
Lewis, David Henry
Lewis, Edward Axford
Lieu, Nyam Nyi
Llewellyn, William John Michael
Lloyd, David Demarest

Lobb, Geoffrey Wilmot
Lough, John
Luker, Cyril Tom
Malcolm, Andrew Moir
Manton, Guy Robert
May, Peter Dudfield
Miller, Joseph Irwin
Mollet, Gerald Geoffrey Holman
Morrell, William Bowes
Morris, Arthur Russell
Mossop, John Coubro
Nanavati, Arvind Mohan Dhirajlal
Nikam, Narayan Rao Appu Rao
Norman, Charles Richard Warrens
Oldham, John Hugh
Oldroyd, James
Oliver, Tom Logan
Ouseley, John Aldrich
Parkes, Alan Corson
Pfister, Bernhard
Plymen, John Cotterell
Polack, Alfred Philip
Prouty, Charles Tyler
Ram, Chaudhri Jit
Rappaport, Charles David
Rees, John Idwal
Rob, Charles Granville
Robertson, John Archibald Campbell
Robinson, Luis Geoffrey
Ross, Robert
Sandison, Gordon Ramsay
Shearer, Ernest James Mollison
Smithies, Frank
Spencer, Cyril Charles
Stewart, Andrew Wendover
Strang, William Braithwaite
Stratford, Francis Joseph
Stross, Robert Adolf Franz
Stuart, Kenneth Charles
Sutcliffe, John
Taylor, Theo Mallinson
Thom, Robert Wilson
Ticehurst, Rowland Gerald
Todd, John
Touche, John Edgeworth David
Turpitt, Walter George
Walker, Edward Ronald
Walker, Nevil Gowan Weybourne
Warren, John Anthony Crosby
Watson, Graham Angus
Weatherilt, Charles Geoffrey Bellew
Whitehead, Harold Norman
Whitehouse, John James Garth
Wilkes, Maurice Vincent
Williams, Glanville Llewelyn
Wilson, Alasdair Robertson
Wilson, George Thomas Jamieson
Wilson, James Maxwell Glover
Winlaw, Roger de Winton Kelsall
Witney, Peter Norman
Wood, Andrew
Wraith, James Osborn Barker

1932

Absalom, Harold John
Alcock, Alfred Samuel Mackenzie
Alexander, Donald William
Armstrong, Edmund Clarence Charles
Balls, Jack Lawrence
Bentley, John Brian
Bignall, John Reginald
Blaikley, David James
Bray, Basil Richard
Briggs, James Hillsdon
Bryce, Robert Broughton
Buchanan, Alexander Maclaurin
Burkitt, Henry Gale Stewart
Butler, Cuthbert Hilary
Callard, Eric John
Caunce, Fred
Christie, John Belford Wilson
Chua, Seng Chew
Clarke, Roy Rainbird
Coates, Peter John Hurst
Collis, Henry John Gurney
Cox, David
Crane, James Alfred
Crawford, Arthur Dennis Benjamin
Crawford, Robert
Crosthwaite, Charles Noel
Daniel, Glyn Edmund
Davis, Paul John Reginald
de Quincey, William Bertram
Diamond, John Gilbert
Drever, James
Drewe, Brian Sydney
Duncan, Frank Alan
Flack, Alan William
Ford, John Henry Ford
Forrester, Basil Holden
Forse, William Arthur
Fynes-Clinton, Hugh Arthur
Gamble, William
Gaminara, Albert William
Genders, William Roy
Gillett, Anthony Walter
Green, Charles Norman
Guillebaud, Peter Delabere
Guise, Charles Alexander Leonard
Gunn, Sidney George
Hamblin, Henry Joel
Harding, Harold Frederick
Heywood, Henry Thomas
Holdich, Cyril Leslie
Hoskyn, Charles Henry
Hunter, Robert Stuart
Hutton, Thomas Blythe
Jones, John Kenneth Trevor
Jones, Leslie Edwin (Godfrey-Jones)
Jowett, Edward Pearse
Kaestlin, John Paul
Kemp, Ralph
Kenchington, Noel Scott
Kenrick, Cecil John
King, John Norman

Lawrence, Eustace Henry
Laws, Gilbert James
Lawson, Thomas Campbell
McConnell, Gerard Hamilton
Maclaurin, Griffith Campbell
Marsden, John Denton
Maung, Percy Mya
May, John Otto
Mehta, Boman Hirjibhoy
Miller, Thomas Harvey
Mitchell, Robert
Moore, Martin Edward
Morgan, William Glyn
Murdock, Charles Rutherford
Murray, Ronald Ormiston
Naiff, John Calverley
Oliver, Kenneth Raymond
Oliver, William George
Openshaw, Norman
Oppenheimer, Gordon (Osborne)
Orpen, Neil Newton D'Arcy
Parfit, Arthur John Martindale
Parkes, Mathew Donald
Parkinson, Desmond John
Pearson, James Douglas
Percy, Henry Gordon
Perring, Hubert
Pettet, Ernest Charles
Petty, Archibald Dyke
Pfaff, Philip Reynold
Pollard, Samuel Lister
Prescott, William Robert Stanley
Preston, John Martyn
Price, Bernard Henry
Proud, Stanley
Prynne, Michael Whitworth
Quilter, Leslie John
Rao, Belthangadi Gopalakrishna
Richards, John Gilbert
Ritchie, Ian MacFarlane
Rose, Edward Michael
Russell, Alexander Fraser
Salter, Lionel Paul Sydney
Saunders, Alan Douglas
Scott, Alan Milne
Scrivin, John William
Sharland, Charles Philip Abbott
Shiach, Gordon Leslie Kemp
Sims, Laurence George Cecil
Stewart, Robert Penman
Storer, Walter Owen
Strickland, Douglas John
Sweeney, Hubert Douglas
Swift, Alan Herbert Illingworth
Tabbush, Victor Emmanuel
Thomson, James Leonard
Thornton, George Lawrence
Tong, Robert Percy
Trevaldwyn, John Reginald
Turner, William Aylmer Laws
Turquet, Pierre Maurice
Valero, Haim Aron

Vestey, John Derek
Villard, Henry Hilgard
Wakely, William Hugh Denning
Walker, Michael Milnes
Walton, Sydney Russell
Ward, Peter Dudley
Waters, Henry Jones
Watts, Percival Stuart
Watts, Ronald George Henry
Webb, John Herbert
Welford, Alan Traviss
Wickstead, Henry Arthur
Wilkin, John Marmaduke
Williams, Arthur Hilton
Wilson, Frank Albert
Winfield, Bernard James Oliver
Wood, Frank Eugène
Wood, Richard Calvert
Wylie, Kenneth Neil
Young, Archibald
Young, Ivan Laurence
Young, Kenneth Gibson

1933

Addison, Cecil James Sim
Allen, Robert Willoughby John
Arulanandom, Victor Ross
Baldwin, John Anthony Ingthorpe
Barnard, George Alfred
Barnett, Anthony Michael
Barton, John Holland
Bassett, Eric George
Baumann, Francis Edgar
Beale, Norman Bewsey
Boag, John Wilson
Bowen, Evan Roderic
Bower, Thomas Henry
Bown, John Henry Edgar
Bratt, John Bernard
Brooks, Maxwell Peter
Brown, Bernard Henry Kingsmill
Brown, Cyril Maitland Ash
Budden, Kenneth George
Bullerwell, Robert Alexander Finlay
Burrow, Felix George Marton
Button, John Carr
Calvert, James Michael
Carmichael, Hugh
Chilton, Cecil William
Clarke, Denis Horace Hilary
Claxton, Patrick Fisher
Clementi, Kenneth John
Close, Hubert Michael
Cook, Raymond Baker
Corsellis, John Arthur Nicholas
Cosh, John Arthur
Coverley, Leonard James
Cunliffe, Herbert
Del Mar, Ronald Henry
Dunk, Harry Wormald
Dunlop, William Beckett

Emery, John Nicholas
Espley, Herbert Noel
Farmer, Frank Reginald
Faulks, Philip James
Fawkes, Marmaduke Ayscough
Fidler, John Carter
Fuchs, Wolfgang Heinrich Johannes
Gale, Ernest Frederick
Gilbert, Keith Reginald
Graveson, George Stanley
Greatorex, Thomas William
Habakkuk, Hrothgar John
Hambridge, Rhodes
Harman, Michael Boys
Hastie, John Williams
Healey, Robert Geoffrey
Henton, Richard
Hibbert, Richard Oswald
Holgate, James William
Hopkin, William Aylsham Bryan
Horberry, Winston Robert
Howles, Ralph
Jackson, Frederic Sinclair
Jacobs, William Ernest Walter (Carpenter-Jacobs)
Johnston, George Arthur Patrick
Jones, Douglass Gordon
Kauntze, John Travis
Keysell, Francis Paul
Knox, Bernard McGregor Walker
Lamballe, Oliver Ward
Leeson, Patrick George
Levy, Cecil Herbert (Lindsey)
Lewis, George Matthews
Lewis, John Cecil Wyn
Lingford, Kenneth
Linnell, Maurice Edward
Lloyd, Henry Llewellyn
Lough, William
MacInnes, Donald Gordon
MacRobert, Roderic Alan
McTurk, John
Makin, John Langridge
Markham, Ralph English
Marshall, Henry Ambler
May, Richard Percy
Medland, John Aubrey
Miall, Rowland Leonard
Millar, Sam Porter
Nicholson, Peter
Oke, Balkrishna Yeshwant
Owen, John Samuel
Paine, David Baumann Easterbrook
Parnell, Frederick Ivor
Perceval, Philip Edward
Philipp, Elliot Elias
Pope, Henry Alfred
Rée, Harry Alfred
Reynolds, Wilfrid James
Ridgway, David George
Rivlin, Ronald Samuel
Roberts, Eldred Owen
Rosenberg, Abraham (Ross, Arnold)

Rowan-Robinson, Arthur Ralph
Rudder, Brian Verge
Rushbrooke, George Stanley
Russell-Smith, Roy Sabine
Saint, Henry Lancelot Basil
Sarkar, Karuna Moi
Sayer, Clinton
Scott, George
Simmonds, Frederick John
Simpson, Alistair Begg
Simpson, Derek William Alastair
Slack, Arthur James
Slater, Alec Whitley
Smith, Gregory Baird
Smith, John Philip
Stibbard, Wilfred Stanley
Stout, Harry Prentice
Strudwick, John Philip
Sweetman, James George
Taylor, Frederick William
Taylor, Paul Aloysius
Tilney, Richard
Tod, John Dudley Hugh
Toovey, Francis William
Uttley, John Corin Taylor
Walker, John Henry
Warner, Gilbert Patrick
Watt, William Warnock
Watts, Eric Arnold Larsen
Whatman, Amherst Barrow
Whitehouse, Walter Alexander
Whiteside, Charles Edward
Williams, Thomas Hewett
Wilson, John Asquith
Winlaw, Ashley William Edgell
Woelck, Hans Ulrich Carl Otto
Wright, Richard Adair

1934

Ashe, Francis Patrick Bellesme
Atkinson, William
Ayton, George Edward
Ballantyne, John Andrew
Barrett, Laurence Ambrose
Barve, Sadashiv Govind
Beatty, Richard Alan
Bell, George Raymond
Benians, Richard Gore
Blood, Terence Fitzgerald
Bromwich, John I'Anson
Brown, Alastair Houghton
Buchanan, Angus Batts
Burling, Philip Cecil George
Cantopher, John Keily
Constant, Michael Brancovan
Cowper, Michael Roy
Cripps, Cyril Humphrey
Deer, William Alexander
Diggle, James
Doyle, Harold John
Drever, Harald Irving

Duff, William Leslie Gordon
Duncombe, Eliot
Eddy, Lambert Wellington
Enderby, George Edward Hale
Eugenides, Eustathuis
Farmer, Bertram Hughes
Faulkner, Donald
Feather, Clive Edward
Fettes, Peter
Fisher, John Derbyshire
Gajendra Singh, Bhanwar
Garrett, Edward John
Gooderson, Richard Norman
Green, Daniel Ezra
Green, Harry Norman
Hall, Hedley Walter
Halliday, Ernest
Hamilton, John Dennys
Harper, David Neale
Harris, Edward Brian
Haupt, Alden Morgan
Hayman, Perceval Ecroyd Cobham
Hemmings, William Oliver Chambers
Henderson, John Anthony
Hendry, James Frank Williamson
Henry, Norman Fordyce McKerron
Hibbert, John Desmond
Hollings, Peter Shaw
Hone, Arthur Robert
Hosie, James Findlay
Huck, Richard James
Hughes, John Victor
Hyde, Ernest William
Inksetter, James Gibson
Jackson, Joseph Frank
Jenkins, Gwilym John
Johnson, Arthur Hazel Lionel
Keiller, Patrick Lewis Laurence
Kells, John Henry McKnight
Kelynack, Hilary Clifton
Kemball-Cook, Richard Bertie
Keong, Siew Tong
Kidd, Douglas Alexander
Kirkwood, Tristram Guy Hammett
Lambah, Paul
Langstadt, Erich
Leuchars, John Noel
Lewis, Rees Daniel Sidney (Rhys-Lewis)
Litler-Jones, Robert Clouston Martland
Lupton, Neville Lloyd
McCallum, Archibald Duncan Dugald
McLeish, Alastair Campbell
Macleod, Kenneth Macallister
Marchant, Robert Brandwood
Marris, Frederick Alexander
Mawer, James
Mees, Rudolf Pieter
Meesook, Boonyium
Merrells, George Luen
Miller, Edward
Milne, James Malcolm
Milne, William Robert

Morton, George
Murphy, William Martin
Nicholson, Harold Metcalfe
Nixon, Wilfrid Earle
Offord, Albert Cyril
Oliphant, Marcus Laurence Elwin
Oxley, Roderick Guy
Palmer, Mervyn Outlaw
Parkinson, William Hope
Pattinson, Tom Pickles
Pegg, David
Pollard, Spencer Drummond
Powell, Arthur Henry Stephen
Price, Edgar Hubert
Priestley, Charles Henry Brian
Radford, Ronald Walter
Rees, David Hollingworth
Rhodes, Alan Naylor
Rob, John Vernon
Robertson, James Duncan
Robinson, Maurice Allpress
Rowntree, Thomas Whitworth
Rycroft, Richard Noel
Salz, Michael Heinz
Sandbach, Richard Stainton Edward
Sanger-Davies, Peter
Schofield, Ernest
Scott, David
Scott, Robert
Seeley, Reginald Sidney Kingsley
Shepherd, Robert John
Singh, Nagendra
Smethurst, Stanley Eric
Smith, Joseph Francis
Smith, Paul Reynolds
Smith, Philip Burrows
Spafford, Anthony John Howsin
Stevens, Bernard George
Stokes, Richard Albert Gordon
Sumner, Donovan Bradshaw
Symonds, Robert Vincent
Taylor, Graham Sinclair
Taylor, Oliver Midgley
Teale, Donald Eric
Thistlethwaite, Frank
Walker, Edward Gowan
Walters, Geoffrey Alfred
Wathes, Richard Sidney
Weston, Arthur Ralph Kingsley
Wheatley, Kenneth William
White, Richard Loughnan
Wilgar, William Percy
Willemstyn, Jan Willem Diederik
Wilson, James Morton
Wilson, Thomas George
Wolfer, Heinrich Herbert
Yardley, Norman Walter Dransfield

1935

Adams, Alexander Francis Lucas
Allsop, Raymond

Andrews, Philip Kenneth Aylmer
Arias, Harmodio
Arias, Roberto Emilio
Arnott, Hugh Whitehorn
Atkinson, James Robert
Banks, James Dallaway
Blaikley, Robert Marcel
Bode, Karl Ernst Franz
Bowen, Leslie Harold
Brewster, John
Broadhead, Denis Lumb
Brocklehurst, Frederick
Burden, Donald Fletcher
Burkett, Richard Southern
Burkitt, William Gale
Burnett, David Humphery
Burney, Christopher Arthur Geoffrey
Burton, Arnold James
Cadman, Donald Spencer
Cambridge, Harold William George
Campbell, Hugh
Carnegie, James
Carr, John Wooltorton
Carswell, Alexander
Casson, Geoffrey Norman
Chadwick, William Owen
Challis, James Dobb
Clarke, Denis Lowther Lovell
Coutts, Walter Fleming
Cowan, John
Crowley-Milling, Michael Crowley
Crowther, Denys James
Cunningham, Morris Anskar
Dalvi, Ganpat Vishvanath
Darwall, Michael Theodore Dyott
Davidson, Alexander Craig Lennox
Davidson, John Peter Archibald
Dear, John Colin
Dehn, Harold Bruce
Diamond, Jack
Doley, John Oliver
Douglas, Brian Kirkbride
Dowell, Keith Walton
Drane, Arthur Benjamin
Duncan, Cyril John
Durham, Peter Walter
Earle, Francis John Wansford
Eason, Thomas William
Eastick, Bernard Charles Douglas
Edgar, John David
Ellison, Michael John
Eschelbacher, Hermann Friedrich (Ashbrook)
Evans, Horace Wynne
Fenn, Charles Henry
Fink, Frederick William
Foster, Kenneth John
France, Kenneth Robertson
Frowde, Russell
Garrett, Henry Hamilton
Gatty, Oliver
Gebhard, John Leslie (Bowen)
Gerrard, Raymond Ormesher

Gibson, Charles Edward Dehany
Gilani, Abdulla
Glassow, Francis Solomon
Glover, Eric Charles
Greenwood, William Henry
Guppy, Ronald James
Guthrie-Jones, David
Guthrie-Jones, Griffith Winston
Hall, Leonard Graham
Harrison, Gilbert Henry
Heath, Karl Edwin
Hill, Ernest Gordon
Hills, Walter Hyde
Holmes, Cecil Ewart
Hore, Henry (Harry) Sinclair
Hudson, Robert Lindsay
Hughes, Arthur
Hunnybun, Kenneth Gresham
Huxley, Herbert Henry
Ince, Cecil Raymond Sidney
James, David Elidyn Howell
Johnston, George Robert Arthur McGarel
Johnstone, Alastair Ian Campbell
Johnstone, James Arthur
Keogh, John Denis
Kilford, William Kenneth
Knight, Bartholomew Francis
Kuipers, John Dennis
Laslett, Thomas Peter Ruffell
Lauriston, Richard Basil
Ledgard, Thomas Callinan
Lewin, Richard
Lillis, Francis Barry
McCall, John Grice Armstrong
McCann, Alastair Donald
Makinson, Richard Elliss Bodenham
Manning, Arthur Lionel
Marshall, John Stewart
Milnes, John Norman
Money, Rowland Cyril Kyrle
Myers, Geoffrey John
Neville, Roland John
Newis, Kenneth
Noble, Alexander Hugh
Northcott, Douglas Geoffrey
Peters, John Frederick Herbert
Ponniah, Benedict
Popple, William Geoffrey
Prideaux, John Kenneth Reginald
Ragg, John Richard Groves
Reilly, Terence Callcott
Rhoades, George
Rickard, Frank Patrick
Ritchie, Brian William Thomas
Robinson, George Hilary Alexander
Sabin, Howard Westcott
Sanderson, Peter Howard
Scott, Eric Walter
Shaw, John
Simmonds, Jack
Smith, James Anstruther
Spitzer, Lyman

Stalker, George Cameron
Stansfeld, Alfred Gimson
Stansfeld, James Maryons
Steele-Perkins, Peter Edward
Strutt, Gordon Knowles
Taylor, James Alexander Simson
Thorne, Clifford Graham
Tinkler, John Eric
Travers, Robert Morris William
Tuckett, Ronald Francis
Turner, Donald Reginald Stuart
Twigg, George Hilton
van Zwanenberg, Hugh Arnold
Wandless, Keith Forrester
Watt, Ian Pierre
Wee, Chong Jin
Welch, David Henry
West, Cyril Ernest
While, Dennis Aubrey
Wiggins, Arthur Edward Michael (Ash)
Wilkins, Maurice Hugh Frederick
Wolfe, Bernard William
Woollett, John Castle
Yarrow, John Alfred Forrest
Yates, Edward Leighton
York, Joseph Bernard

1936

Allan, Derek Scott
Allen, Richard de Courcy
Anderson, William Blair
Argyle, Douglas Causer
Attlee, Wilfred Ormiston
Badr-El-Din, Abd El Latif Mohammed
Baldwin, Philip Harold
Ballinger, Maurice
Barker, Roland Richard Sinclair
Barnes, George Victor
Barnes, John Arundel
Barraclough, Geoffrey
Bartholomew, Walter
Bennett, Peter Luddington
Bibby, Howard Morton
Blake, John Philip
Booty, Bernard Kenneth
Bowen, Thomas Jim
Boyce, Peter McConnell
Braddell, Lionel Henry
Braybrook, Clifford Herbert
Buxton, Peter Howroyd
Bywaters, Bruce William Draper
Carmichael, Donald Macaulay
Carris, Bertram Dudley
Chambers, John Frank
Collison, Victor Edward
Connell, James Archibald
Corby, Harold Douglas Lane
Coulson, Douglas Joseph
Cowen, Painton Sydney
Cowley, Ralph Alexander
Cragg, Francis Talbot

Craik, Kenneth James William
Crosthwait, Michael Leland
Culpin, Stanley
Davies, Laurence Hector
Dawson, Ernest John
Dhenin, Geoffrey Howard
Donald, James Mackie
Dow, John Alexander
Ennals, John Arthur Ford
Fairless, Thomas Arnold Ashbridge
Felton, William Fowler
Fewings, John Atkinson
Fisher, George Walter Peter
Forbes, Richard Lumsden
Fudge, Harry Vincent
Gamblen, Frank
Genders, Antony Clive
Gilbert, William Hamish
Greig, Murray Thomson
Hall, Kenneth
Hall, Michael Lindsay Bracebridge
Hall, Reginald John Ratcliff
Hansen, Erwin Gunther
Hansford, Richard Norman
Haygarth, Harold John
Hayman, Henry John Godfrey
Herd, Thomas Brodie
Heron, Michael
Hicks, Ernest Philip
Hilton, Herbert Geoffrey
Ho, Maung Kway Foung
Holmberg, Eric Robert Reginald
Hulme, Allan
Hume, Peter Joseph
Hutton, John Henry
Ibrahim, Ahmad bin Mohamed
Ingram, William Mark
Jefferis, Robert Stephen
Johnston, Robert Smith (Kincraig)
Jones, Cecil Henry Douglas
Jones, Cyril Greenslade
Jukes, John Andrew
Kemp-King, Paul Robert
Khan, Sirdar Abdussamad
Kingdon, Richard Donald
Kittel, Jerome Charles
Koinange, Peter Mbiyu
Lawrance, Norman Macleod
Lees, Roland James
Lilley, Samuel
Lodge, Stanley Perry
Loosemore, Thomas Gordon Evans
McCloughin, Darcy Kenelm
McIntyre, Robert Billo
MacKay, Eoin Vonde
MacRobert, Iain Workman
Martin-Sperry, Anthony Douglas
Maxwell, Ian Stanley
Montagnon, Philip Edward
Mooney, Edmund Frederick William
Moore, William Keith Stevenson
Morley, Richard Brès

Neumann, Stephan Theodore (Norman)
Nixon, St John
Padfield, John Edward
Parkes, James William
Pearson, Michael
Peierls, Rudolf
Peiser, Herbert Steffen Albert Alexander
Perkins, John Bernard
Pickford, Frank
Plunkett, Gerald Walter
Price, Geoffrey Arthur
Price Smith, Roy David
Rackham, Harold Christopher
Richards, Elfyn John
Ricketts, Henry Harcourt
Robertson, Donald William
Robertson, Rutherford Ness
Roebuck, Eric
Rolfe, Robert Hugh Grandison
Roper, Lewis Hawkes
Rosenbaum, Robert Abraham
Ross, Donald Murray
Rugg-Gunn, Alexander Noel (Gunn)
Sanger, Frederick
Sarkar, Adit Kumar
Scott, Herbert
Scott, Kenneth
Smith, Gordon Henry Murray
Spencer, Marshall Macdonald
Stanton, John Bernard
Sturge, Philip Arthur Joseph
Swain, Paul Bryan
Tannahill, John Allan
Thomas, David Llewelyn
Towers, Thomas Dundas
Turner, Robert
Udall, Geoffrey Sturt
Walker, Eric Anderson
Walker, Ralph James
Walker, Richard George
Warner, Charles Randall Mallet
Webber, John Phillips
Wetherley-Mein, Gordon
Whitfield, John Wesley
Wild, Peter Dickinson
Williams, George
Williams, Howard
Williams, John Brynmor
Williams, Robert Deryck
Wilson, Norval Murray
Wilson, Thomas Sydney
Wormald, Brian Harvey Goodwin
Worthington, John Clare
Wright, Frank Burnet
Young, Stuart

1937

Allen, Anthony Kenway
Argyle, Robert Murray
Armitage, Edward John
Ashton-Cross, Desmond Ian Cyril

Atkinson, Terence Wickham
Bailey, Joseph Eric
Barnes, Robert Searle
Barron, Donald Henry
Beckett, Peter Henry Robert Osborne
Berkowitz, Sidney Maschelle
Blaxter, Peter Llewellyn
Borchardt, Roger John
Brewster, Alan Roulston
Brook, Alexis
Brownlee, Kenneth Alexander
Bury, Patrick James
Buttle, William Roland
Calvert, John Harold Knowles
Campbell, Frank William Argyll
Campbell, John Macleod
Carmichael, Donald Dewar
Carnell, Geoffrey Gordon
Carroll, Patrick Milne
Carson, James Eric Rutherford
Cartwright, Harry
Case, Humphrey John
Cheers, Francis
Chong, Frederick
Christie, Dan Edwin
Cole, Robert Templeman
Cornwell, Derek John
Craven, Arthur
Curran, Samuel Crowe
de Silva, Hettihewagé Benedict
de Wet, Jacobus Stephanus
Dickson, Edward Chambre
Dunlop, John Ralph Renton
Edwards, David St John
Fearnside, Kenneth
Filtness, Donald Dunstan
Forrester, Robert Michael
Frankland, Edward Raven Percy
Fraser, Ian Richardson
French, Thomas Worden
Galbraith, Ian Robertson
Gorringe, John Allan Lindsay
Gunn, John Currie
Hall, Bruce
Harris, Henry Albert
Hart, Eric Leslie
Harvey, Donald George Robert
Hayman, Christopher Hartley
Hayman, John David Woodburn
Hendry, Joseph McInnes
Hicks, Anthony Rayner Harvey
Hinsley, Francis Harry
Hinton, John
Hobson, Antony John
Hodgetts, Robert Bartley
Hughes, Percival Tryfen Maurice
Hurst, Donald Geoffrey
Inns, Frederic Cutts
James, Thomas Cecil Garside
Johnstone, Ronald David
Jones, Arthur Emrys
Jones, Roland Norman

Jones, William Lloyd (Mars-Jones)
Keeble, Thomas Whitfield
Kemsley, John Edward Timothy
Keyte, Douglas Joseph Henry
Kirby, Frank
Kirby, Harold
Koch, Otto Erich Alfred
Lee, Arthur Guy
Lewis, Frederick Victor
Lewis, Raymond Wilfred Logan
Lickerish, Leslie Arthur
Lyttleton, Raymond Arthur
MacBean, Alastair Henry Wilson
McFadzean, Francis Scott
McKendrick, Charles Stewart
Mance, Herbert William
Marks, Peter Knell
Martin, John Sinclair
Melville, William Patrick Stewart
Merriman, Gabriel de Vesselitsky
Merson, Ronald Leslie
Monro, Peter Alexander George
Moran, Patrick Alfred Pearse
Morris, Ivor St Lawrence
Murray, James Gibbes
Nadarajah, Kandapoo Chinnathamby
Naunton, William Johnson
Neale, Harry Nelson
Newton Thompson, Christopher Lawton
North, Ernest Raymond
Parker, Ernest Patrick
Parry, Hugh Meredith
Pevie, William Gray Gordon
Phelps, Gilbert Henry
Potter, Guy Anthony
Powdrill, Ernest Joseph
Power, Basil Dixon
Press, Kenneth Peter (Allpress)
Pringle, Charles Norman Seton
Redpath, Robert Theodore Holmes
Reekie, James
Renshaw, Robin Henry Leigh
Richards, Geoffrey Clement Thorneley
Ricketts, Malcolm
Ringrose, Thomas Sutcliffe
Robinson, Wilfred Henry Frederick
Rodwell, Robert Hunter
Rogers, John Arthur
Rood, Stephen Charles
Ross, Philip James
Rowan, Harry Bemersyde
Ruane, John Davison
Russell, Ralph
Rutherford, Charles Ian
Sang, James Henderson
Sarabhai, Vikram Ambalal
Sathe, Dinker Dattatraya
Sayers, James
Scott, Kenneth Alan
Scougall, Keith Harold Lauchlan
Sharp, Francis Richard
Shorto, Harry Leonard

Sifneos, Theodore
Singer, Abraham
Singleton, David Ernest
Slack, Roger Dutton
Smith, Ian McNicol
Solomon, Arthur Kaskel
Spencer, Peter Lane
Spooncer, Ronald Clifford
Stanley, Charles John Geoffrey
Starr, George Henderson
Still, Hereford Crossfield
Taylor, Jerry Granger (Granger-Taylor)
Teesdale, Edmund Brinsley
Thomas, George
Thompson, John Ross
Thomson, Arthur James
Vaughan, John Paul
Waskett, Dennis
Wesson, Leonard Joynson
Wilkin, Allan Whiteley
Wilson, Jacob
Wilson, Peter Audaer Overend
Wolstenholme, Allan Grant

1938

Abbott, John Cave
Agarwal, Prem Prakash
Allan, Gilbert Francis
Allen, Frank Stanley
Allen, John Frank
Allnatt, John Edward
Ames, George Ernest
Ashton, Cyril Lea
Baligh, Amrullah Nafez
Barnett, Stephen Frank
Barron, John Reginald Bernard
Bates, Martin Vernon
Beard, Trevor Cory
Beevers, Thomas
Benians, Martin Ackland
Blackman, Peter Francis
Bocks, Shirley John
Bonner, Colin Abbott
Bonsall, Leonard Dale
Bower, Alan John
Bradley, David John
Brandenburger, Peter Hugh
Bratherton, David Georges
Briggs, Arthur John
Bruce Jones, Thomas Dunlop
Buchanan, Ian Batts
Bullock, Albert Holden
Butcher, Harold John
Byrne, Patrick Charles
Cameron, John Alexander
Campbell, Donald
Cannell, Anthony John
Cardno, James Alexander
Carter, Charles Frederick
Chan, Shu-Fung
Chapple, Peter Arbuthnot Lane

Clapin, Basil Philip Waterlow
Combs, Willis Ide
Cooke, John Caister
Crane, Charles David
Crauford, Clive Lane
Croston, Arthur Kenneth
Curtis, Geoffrey Carew
Daniels, John Michael Ewan
Davidson, Angus Garth
Davidson, James Wightman
de Souza Santos, Marcello Damy
Dewar, Thomas Wright
Dichmont, Ian Alexander
Dickinson, Patrick John
Doherty, Michael Verran
Dohoo, Roy McGregor
Dupont, Jack Norman
Dyson, Alan
Earle, Thomas Jeffrey
Edwards, James (Jimmy) Keith O'Neill
Eley, Daniel Douglas
Espley, Frank Alan
Farley, John Robert
Fowler, John Anthony
Gabriel, Philip Llewelyn
Gibson, George
Goody, John Rankine
Gordin, Peter
Goward, Frank Kenneth
Green, Charles John Sanders
Gribbin, Kenneth David
Grose, Richard John Hicks
Grove, Leslie Stevenson
Gwynn, Brian Purnell
Hall, Denys James Nicholas
Halliday, Philip James
Haresign, Arthur Sneath
Harris, Henry Stephen Lyn
Hartridge, Gerald
Hodge, James
Hodges, Henry Woolmington Mackenzie
Hodgson, Thomas Riley
Holley, Geoffrey Evelyn Windham
Homan, George Maxwell
Howarth, Ronald Matthews
Howe, Bruce
Howell, Malcolm Bardsley Warbeck
Jesty, John Bedford
Kapur, Shikandhi
Kidd, Fred
Launder, Geoffrey William
Le Couteur, Kenneth James
Lean, James Hugh John
Lewis, Owen Calder
Leyland, Eric
Lindbergh, John Victor
Lister, John
Loewe, Raphael James
Loewenstein, Mark Oliver Lawrence
  (Lynton, Mark Oliver Lawrence)
McCormick, Gregory David Pat
MacIver, Andrew

Makinson, Donald Hindley
Malins, Robert Edward
Mallender, Peter Frederick
Meikle, Ian Ormiston
Monahan, David
Morgan, Glyn James
Moss, Norman (Jordan-Moss)
Mountford, Basil Wilfred
Moxon, Roland James
Murray, Bruce
Myers, James Peter
Neasham, George
Nicholls, James John
Oliver, Edward Spencer
Orr, Robert (Robin) Kemsley
Parker, Robin Flint
Pascoe, Kenneth John
Peacock, Robert Anderson
Pear, Brian Hatherley
Pearce, Eric George
Percy, Hugh Harold
Perkes, William Anderson
Plumpton, Charles
Posnett, Richard Neil
Radford, Richard Arthur
Ritchie, Kenneth John Stewart
Robertson, Andrew John Blackford
Rose, Michael Anthony
Ross, Peter McGregor
Rumsey, Victor Henry
Schardt, Richard Geoffrey
Scurfield, George Bazeley
Sellers, George Daniel
Sibly, John
Simpson White, John Nigel
Smart, Geoffrey Edwin
Smith, Jeffrey Prowse
Smith, Wilfred Cantwell
Sufi, Mohammed Husain
Swingler, Jack Howell
Sykes, George Dennis
Templeman, Sydney William
Thomas, Adin Bryn
Townend, Charles Russell Balme
Trench, Peter Edward
Treves, Piero
Trought, Vincent Paul Trevor
Urabe, Tosio
Urquhart, Ian Alexander Norfolk
Walters, Stuart Max
Waterhouse, John Alfred Humphrey
Wawn, Middlemost
Welford, Norman Traviss
Whitehouse, Geoffrey
Wilkinson, Harry Clifford
Wilks, Thomas Grenfell
Williams, Rowland James
Wilmersdoerffer, Hans Max
  (Wilmers, John Geoffrey)
Wilson, Arthur James Cochran
Wilson, Ronald Dare
Withers, Hartley

Wylie, Colin St Aubyn
Yeadon, Roy Stephenson

1939

Addey, John Michael
Allebone, Philip
Amsden, Richard Sidney
Bagley, James Harold
Bakar, Abu (bin Tamin)
Bansall, Ian Aitken
Barber, Bernard Anson
Barbosa da Silva, Edmundo Penna
Beale, John Elmes
Beattie, Hugh Ronald Montgomerie
Bell, William Rupert Graham
Benstead, John Gordon
Bertin, Reginald James Edmund
Binnie, Mark
Blackwell, Basil Davenport
Bompas, William Michael Gwynnett
Branford, Robert Richard
Brock, Werner Gottfried
Brockbank, James Tyrrell
Brough, John
Brown, David Eric
Burkitt, Harold Gale
Burton, William Glynn
Bywaters, Keith Robertson
Caughley, James Gilfillan
Cave, George Charles Montague Major
Charlesworth, Geoffrey Brown
Cheshire, Albert White
Christie, Alexander Kenneth
Cockburn, Ian George Colin
Cooper, John Napier
Crisp, Edmund Theodore
Crook, John Anthony
Davidson, Donald Georges
de Boer, George
Dolby, Arthur
Dowell, Peter Derrick
Dowling, Edmund John
Dudley, John George
Eberlie, (William) John Dymoke
Farr, Peter James
Fenton, Richard Coote
Ferguson, John
Fergusson, Sydney George
Forrester, William Herbert
Foxall, Dennis Arthur
Freeman, Eric John
Furness, John Bernard
Goddard, Laurence Stanley
Goldie, Alfred William
Goldie-Scot, William Norton Longman
Goody, Richard Mead
Green, Arthur Norman
Green, Charles Roger Heyden
Gregorowski, William Reinhold
Gregory, Frank
Gwyn, John David

Harcourt, Robert Albert Foyson
Harris, David Burnsall
Harrison, Francis Burton
Hart, Kenneth Forster
Hartree, Edward Francis
Hendry, John Robin Napier
Hereward, Hugh Gordon
Hewlett, Donald Marland
Hines, James Wilfred
Holt, Peter Fox
Horne, Michael Rex
Howorth, Roland Heslop
Hoyle, Fred
Hudson, George
Hunter, Brian Vincent
Hutchinson, George William
Hutton, Thomas Edward
Ivory, James Harvey Trevithick
Jackson, Robert Flinders
Jeavons, Peter Machin
Jeejeebhoy, Phiroze Jamshedji
Jiménez, Manuel
Johnson, John Aylmer
Johnston, David Kenneth
Jones, Frederick Charles Dudley
   (Dudley-Jones)
Jones, Robert Peter Neil
Jucys, Adolfas
Kale, Dhundiraj Govind
Knight, David Arthur
Krause, Eric Sutherland
Lapworth, Harold John
Lees, Ronald Samuel Mann
Lewis, Gerald Brassington
Lewis, Ian Alexander Darroch
Lynch, Thomas
Malloch, Charles Edward
Mardan, Talpur Ali
Marmion, William Joseph
Mather, Harold Gordon
Maxwell, Malcolm Stanley
Metcalfe, Vincent
Monk, Robert Richardson
Moore, William Patrick
Mordell, Donald Louis
Morgan, John Ross
Naylor, Philip Edward
O'Neill, Hugh Cecil
Owen, John Vallance (Vallance-Owen)
Parikh, Jitendra Ramaniklal
Parker, Ralph George Francis
Parnell, Charles Edward
Parr, Thomas Thornton
Paterson, Thomas
Patten, Edward John Kelman
Paulley, Christopher James Archibald
Pay, Brian Wilfrid
Pelling, Henry Mathison
Petschek, Charles Ignaz
Read, Arthur Hinton
Reid, Ian Christie
Richardson, William Thomas

Roberts, David Ewart
Robinson, Ronald Edward
Rolland, John Lewis
Roper, Richard Antony Lionel
Russell-Smith, John Francis
Sadick, Ali
Scott, William Hugh
Seale, George Hall
Shaw, Philip Malcolm
Starnes, Peter Henry
Sutherland, Ian
Symons, Michael
't Hart, Jacob
Thompson, Eric Clifford
Tolmer, Guy Stedman Foster
Vernon, Peter Heygate
Ward, Humphrey David
Watson, John Donald Mackenzie
Watson, Woodland Ronald Harry
Williams, John Ratcliffe
Willmore, Patrick Lever
Woodcock, Graham
Woodwark, Richard Graham
Wootton, Ian David Phimester

1940

Arthur, Allan Charles
Barber, John Stuart
Beharrell, George David
Bennett, Philip Roger Luddington
Bowes, John Foster Lyon
Boxall, Randolph Leonard
Boyes, Albert Edgar
Brown, Vivian Fox
Bruce Lockhart, Logie
Butler, John David
Butson, Arthur Richard Cecil
Bygate, Noel
Coates, Michael Antony Wilson
Coldwell, Alan
Collins, Martyn
Colson, Alexander Francis Lionel
Conder, James Edward Bevill
Connelly, George Fredrick
Cooksley, George Antony Hawkes
Crookshank, Alexander Oldfield
Curtis, Ronald Edgar
da Cunha, John Wilfrid
Dain, John
Darling, Thomas Young
Davidson, Malcolm Norman
Davies, Idris John
Davis, Peter Sidney
Donoghue, Matthew James
Draper, Philip Johnson
Evans, Hugh Everard
Fairhurst, Jack
Finucan, Henry Maurice
Fogg, Gordon Elliott (Tony)
Forestier-Walker, Edmond Annesley
Forse, John

Garner, Henry Clifford
Gaskell, Peter Monks
Glover, Michael Alison
Graham-Martin, Hugh Noël
Grint, Leslie Alfred
Hackett, George Reginald
Hansford, John Talbot
Harington, John Berkeley
Harris, Nicholas King
Harrison, Eric
Harrison, John Dashwood St Clair
Harvey, Gordon Columba
Hobden, David Henry William
Howson, Thomas Leslie
Jackson, Reginald
Jarvis, Philip Charles
Jones, Ivon Lewis Lloyd
Kerrod, Norman
Laidlaw, Christophor Charles Fraser
Landin, Dennis Mould
Leaper, Robert Anthony Bernard
Littlewood, James
Livesey, Derek Leonard
Lofts, Robert John
Lowden, Victor Soutar
Lowe, Robert Conyers
Mackay, Douglas Keith
Maguire, Denis Richard
Manning, Ronald Barrie
Marsh, Charles Donald
Marsh, Leon Robert
Mavor, Henry Alexander
Middleton, Hugh Craigmyle
Moffatt, John Logan
Morgan, Eric
Morgan, Joseph Charles
Morris, David Henry St Lawrence
Nicholls, Charles Geoffrey William
Noble, Basil
Nourse, John
Orchard, Anthony Clavis
Orwin, William Dickson
Oughton, William Lawson
Parlow, John Thomas Morgan
Pearson, Robert Scott Moncrieff
Perry, Arthur Leslie Roy
Peters, Theophilus
Petherick, Edward John
Pettigrew, Andrew Hislop
Philip, Philip Paton (Paton-Philip)
Phillips, Christopher Brian Michael
Pitt, Geoffrey John
Platt, Frank Kenneth
Radford, Kenneth James
Raffle, David Lawrie
Rațiu, Ioan Augustin Nicolae
Rattenbury, Arnold Foster
Redfern, Philip
Richardson, Ian Jackson Herbert
Richardson, John Brown
Roberts, Donald Michael
Robson, Athol

Rounthwaite, Denis Christopher
Royds, George Herbert Alexander
Sadler, John James Goode
Salmon, Rider Gordon
Scott, Mark
Sewell, Michael William
Sharman, John Campton
Sheehan, Maurice
Shepperson, George Albert
Smith, Geoffrey Sheil
Smith, Norman Johnson
Smith, Richard Arthur Amyas
Stanier, Harold Meredith
Stevens, Derek Scott
Stuart, Ian Charles
Symon, John Parker
Thomas, Robert Edgar
Thursby, Patrick Dehany Francis
Tin, Maung Han
Totty, Peter Harland
Towers, Malcolm Kinsey
Turnbull, Derwent Greville
Turner, Roy
Vaughan, James Rodney Mitchell
Wagstaff, Raymond Claude
Wallach, Gerd Ludwig (Wallace, Gerald Louis)
Webb, John Marshall
White, Malcolm Edward Eales
Whittingham, Charles Percival
Whittington, Alan MacRae
Williams, Anthony Leonard Stuart
Williams, Ifor Pennant
Williams, John Dawson Bulpin
Wills, George Saunders
Wilson, James
Winder, Alexander John Henry
Wolstencroft, John Hollas
Worden, Alastair Norman
Wright, John Walker

1941

Aitchison, David Ridsdale
Aitken, William McCrae
Alexander, Charles Gundry
Allon, John Philip Hilton
Andrews, John Henry
Angel, Joseph Harold
Angelbeck, Edward Norman James
Armstrong, Gerard Bruce
Armstrong, John Barton (Barton-Armstrong)
Ashworth, Thomas Holmes Evelyn Battersby
Atkinson, Peter Doughton
Attwood, Cyril
Baldwin, Nelson Mills
Barlow, Peter Gordon Rigby
Barnes, John Down
Bartlett, Hugh Frederic
Berlescu-Beza, Constantin (Beza-Daponte)
Booth, Guy Herman
Boyns, Richard Wallis Harley
Bramwell, Hartley

Brander, Michael William
Brayshaw, John Derwent
Brierley, Alan Corns
Briggs, Peter George
Bright, Peter Hayne
Brown, James Clifford
Bunce, John Victor
Burn, Macdonald
Burns, Robert James
Byrne, James John
Campbell, Adrian Hugh Ward
Campbell, John Charles Kenneth
Chant, William Morton
Corney, John Victor
Craig, Douglas Stuart
Crick, Anthony Frederick
Criddle, Sidney James
Croft, Kenneth Stuart Bayne
Curnow, John Michael
Curtis, Allan Raymond
Danielli, James Frederic
Denton, Eric James
Dianderas, Roberto
Dixon, James Neville
Dorward, Adam Paterson
Edwards, Edward John Paul
Elgood, John Lawson Alsager
Elliott-Binns, Michael Ferrars Elliott (Binns)
Ellison, Roger John
Evans, David Dunston Silian
Field, Derek Harold
Foden, Raymond Davidson
Foggon, James Joseph
Foster, Eric
Galbraith, Walter Anderson
George, Bryan Henry
Gibbs, Alan Edward Russell
Gillett, Kenneth Arthur
Glen, John Douglas
Gorman, Patrick
Green, Stewart
Gugenheim, Peter Gerhard Arthur Fritz
Haggard, Michael Verner
Haswell, Anthony James Darley
Hay, Robert Malcolm
Heap, Alan
Hemmings, John
Henstock, Ralph
Holdsworth, John Alexander Philip
Hollings, John Shaw
Hood, Alastair Moar
Horsford, Eric John
Howl, Oliver Brian
James, Geoffrey Sargood
James, Horace Meredith
Johnson, Colin Aylmer
Joy, David Victor
Kilner, John Goff
Kirby, Frederick Neville
Lankester, John Ernest
Lawson, John David
Long, William Casson

Longmuir, Ian Stewart
Lyon, William
McCarter, Ian Jamison
Magowan, William Andrew
Malone, Patrick Oswald
Margolis, Sydney
Marriott, John Brook
Marshall, Frederick Stanley
Masters, Eric Henry
May, George Harold
Merton, Geoffrey Ralph
Millard, John Franklin
Mills, Joseph Frederick
Mills, Ronald Hubert Bonfield
Morley, Derek James
Murray, Michael Graeme
Newey, Clement John
Oliver, Anthony Giles Gale
Palmer, James Richard
Peet, Frank Anthony
Pentney, Richard George
Petersen, Richard Courtenay
Pettit, John Adrian
Pettoello, Leonardo Pierluigi
Pickett, Eric Samuel John
Pimlott, Alan Kenneth
Pinder, Geoffrey Peveril
Porter, John Mason
Powell, Anthony George
Price, Arthur John Brownlow
Prowde, Gordon Longstaff
Pybus, Michael
Rowland, James Malcolm
Rydings, Henry Anthony
Salmon, Sidney Herbert
Sansom, Kenneth John
Sargan, John Denis
Saunders, Edward George Humphrey
Scott, James Dudley
Sears, Geoffrey Wadsworth
Simpson, William Arthur
Slater, William Rex
Small, John Michael
Smith, George Perry
Smith, Peter Fenwick (Fenwick-Smith)
Soller, Maximilian Frederick
Sprigg, Richard Keith
Spurdens, Norman Arthur
Stanley, Philip John
Steele, Hugh Hepburn
Stern, (Joseph) Peter Maria
Stewart, John Eachus
Sugden, David Bertram
Swallow, John Crossley
Tetstall, Reginald George
Thom, Alan Watson
Thomas, Richard Keay
Thomasson, John Walker
Thorp, Peter Dixon
Tidy, George
Treharne, Philip Gordon
Wadsworth, Peter

Walker, David
Ward, Denis Hugh
Wass, Douglas William Gretton
Waton, John Howard
Weaver, Derek Bargrave (Bargrave-Weaver)
Webster, Paul Michael
Webster, Ralph Osler
White, Neville Hall
Whitefield, John Reginald
Wide, Nicholas Scott
Willcock, Richard Mellor
Wilson, David Binnie
Woodward, Geoffrey Wallace
Woodwark, George Millington
Worthy, William Digby
Wright, James Faulkner

1942

Andrews, Peter Searell
Ashbee, John Michael Neville
Ashbrooke, Philip Biden Derwent
Astorga, Eduardo Antonio
Attrill, James Bernard
Babbage, Iver Reginald
Bailey, David Earle
Barker, Paul Stuart
Barraclough, Peter
Batchelor, Robert
Beatty, Anthony Carlyle
Bell, Gordon John
Benians, Peter Roy
Bennett, John Antony
Binns, George
Blake, Anthony Roger Morley
Blanchard, Paul Harwood
Booth, Nathaniel Barton
Booth, Stephen Dion
Bristow, George
Broadbent, Ewen
Bromhead, Michael Bernard
Broomhead, Ivor William
Bryden, John Whitfield
Bullard, Jack Alfred Arthur
Burrow, Geoffrey Robert France
Butler, George
Byrne, Douglas Norman
Campbell, Colin
Campbell, John Hope
Chivers, William Douglas
Clay, Michael Nelson
Coburn, Donald
Constable, William Briggs (Briggs Constable)
Corbett, George Ernest
Cox, David Roxbee
Crofts, John James
Crosthwaite, Hugh
Darmon, Stanley Edward
Davies, Ian Leonard
Davies, Norman Frederick
Davis, Colin Geoffrey
Davis, Michael Gerard

Denman, George Roy
Dent, John Chisholm
de Potier, Adrian
Dirac, Gabriel Andrew
Douglas, Ian Kenneth Hamilton
Dow, James Crown
Durbin, James
Elms, Charles Francis
English, Michael
Evans, Vincent
Farrar, Reginald Hodson
Finch, Frank Richard
Fleet, George
Forge, Geoffrey Baynton
Forster, Charles Arthur
Freeman, Alan Douglas
Fry, Percival John Margrie
Gifford, David Ross
Gilchrist, Ronald Reid
Giles, Sidney Herbert
Gill, Alan
Gillespie, John Ronald
Gilman, Edgar Ivan
Glasgow, Eric Lawrence Harper
Godwin, William Henry
Goodall, Peter Bentley
Goode, John
Goodram, Alan James Sloman
Goodwin, Eric Anthony
Gordon, Ian Robert
Gordon, William Roger
Gould, Lionel John
Grant, Geoffrey John Cardross
Green, Gilbert Wilson
Greenwood, Roger Paul
Griffiths, William Hugh
Hall, Edgar Bernard
Hall, John Kenneth
Hardy, Douglas
Harrocks, Donald Raymond
Hinde, Robert Aubrey
Hine, Francis Jopson
Hine, Peter Ewan
Hodgess, Frederick Henry
Hodgson, Oliver Ernest Fenner
Holden, Brian Astbury
Howarth, John Lee
Hpa, Sao Hseng
Hurrell, Arthur
Hutchings, Raymond Francis Dudley
Ince, Charles Augustus
Jackson, Arthur David
James, Leslie Hollins Prideaux
Jarman, Ronald Arthur
Johns, Ewart Morien
Johns, John Gordon Peter Owen
Johnson, Howard William
Jollans, William Mallinson
Jones, Evan John
Joslin, David Maelgwyn
Kempson, Gerald Peter
Kent, Alan

Khanna, Amrit Kumar
Laing, Charles William
Lang, David Marshall
Langton, Ernest William
Lethbridge, John Anthony
Lewis, David
Lewis, Dennis Stanley
Lindars, Frederick Chevallier (Barnabas)
Lord, George Geoffrey
Lord, Michael Hilton Joseph
Low, Edward David
Lupton, Kenneth Lofthouse
MacDonald, Iain Alasdair
MacDonald, John Blair
McFarlane, David
McGhie, Robert Frederick
McInnes, Archibald Alastair
MacIver, John Edward
McIver, Leo
MacLeod, John William
Macpherson, James Gordon
Mansfield, Anthony Le Voir
Mayou, Charles Alfred
Metcalfe, Harry Francis
Miller, Edward Jeffery
Mills, Donald Henry
Mills, Robert
Mitchell, Alec Burton
Moffat, Barry John
Molloy, Peter Edward
Morgan, Thomas Kirk
Morley, John Austin
Morton, William Douglas
Moss, Bernard
Muktadar, Khawja Abdul
Mundy, Wilfrid Horace
Newman, Edward Frederick George
O'Brien, John Bernard
Owen, George
Pacey, Hugh Edmund
Paine, David Stevens
Paton, John Miller
Pepler, Richard Douglas
Pothecary, Brian Peter
Potter, Basil Robert Russell
Prestt, John
Raby, Kenneth Francis
Ravenscroft, John Edward
Redding, John Hubert
Reed, Denys Adrian
Reid, Raymond Warwick Harry
Rhodes, Donald Horsfall
Richards, David Rigby
Richards, Geoffrey John
Richards, John
Richards, Thomas Clifford
Rigby, Donald Lang
Roberts, Ernest Theodore
Robinson, Geoffrey Hodgson
Roseveare, Robert Arthur
Rushton, Donald Frederick Harvey
Rushton, Philip Lawler

Sanders, Theodorus Carlton
Sansom, Hugh Wilfred
Scott, David Gidley
Seale, James Lawrie
Sellar, Robert Milne
Smith, Peter Ernest Herbert
Smith, Vernon John
Snushall, David Bruce
Spafford, Douglas Harold
Spence, Magnus Peter
Squires, Gordon Leslie
Stanion, Gordon Stuart
Stephenson, John Lewis
Stewardson, John Rennie
Stokoe, William Geoffrey
Stretton, Lionel James
Sturrock, Peter Andrew
Sutcliffe, John William Robert
Symons, Humphrey
Tew, David Healy
Trapnell, Barry Maurice Waller
Ullyott, Henry Wilson
Van den Bergh, Edward Arthur Roderick
Vaughan, Douglas Brian
Vincent, Paul Howard
Vines, Jack Harold
Wade, Peter George
Wallace, William Dugald
Wallis, Brian Kenneth
Wardle, Derek Basil James
Watts, Michael
Weir-Rhodes, David Edward
Wilden-Hart, Kenneth Gordon
Williams, David Sims
Williamson, John Christopher
Wilson, Robert McLachlan
Woodford, Alan John
Wright, Harry Albert
Young, Colin Arthur MacKenzie
Zukmann-Bizony, Michael Thomas

1943

Abel, John Percival
Acteson, Henry William Alec
Allen, Francis Donald
Allitt, Peter James
Andrews, Bernard Keith
Appleton, Anthony
Armstrong, John Dickson
Asem, Alfred Kofi
Attwooll, Victor William
Aylmer, Michael Leycester
Balmain, Graham Coumbe
Barclay, Norman Veitch Lothian
Bargh, George Edward Norman
Barrett, Peter Thomas
Barton, Brian Austin
Batchelor, Richard Ernest
Batting, Frank Merlin
Benians, Hubert Michael
Bickerton, Derek

Birtles, George Duncan
Blake, David Eustace
Blanshard, Gerald Phoenix
Bottero, Victor William Kenneth
Brandhendler, Boris Peter Conradin Frederick
    Anatole (Brand, Boris Peter)
Bray, George James
Brazier, Leslie Frederick
Brieger, Ernest Oskar (Blake, Ernest Oscar)
Briggs, Geoffrey Hugh
Broom, Trevor
Broome, Kenneth Reginald
Bunt, John Percival
Burton, Thomas Edmund
Cattrell, Victor Gordon
Cawthorne, Donald Ernest
Chang, Tse-Chun
Cheston, John Anthony
Clarke, Harold John
Cleveland, James Brian
Cockayne, Alan Harry
Croft, Peter Gardom
Cunningham, Cyril
Davies, Denys Martin Owen
Davison, Deryck Porter
Denison, Norman
Dewey, Leonard
Dickinson, Alan
Dingle, Robert Balson
Dorward, Arthur Fairgrieve
Downer, Edward George
Downsbrough, Frank Keith
Dunkerley, Gerald
Elgood, Ronald Lloyd
Elliott-Binns, Christopher Plunkett Elliott
Ellis, David Edmund
Espley, William Arthur
Farr, Peter John
Ffrench Mullen, Christopher Richard
Fletcher, William Bruce
Fredjohn, Dennis
Freke, John Henry
Gardiner, Dennis Malcolm
Gaudie, Martyn
Gill, Stanley
Govier, Leonard John
Haggis, Bernard Murray
Hair, Paul Edward Hedley
Hardman, John Alan
Harris, Alfred Stanley
Haymann, Walter Kurt (Hayman)
Hearle, John William Stanley
Hemmings, Robert Frederick
Heptonstall, Cyril Philip
Hill, Roger Frank
Hobbs, Leonard Paul
Horrell, John Ernest Bryant
Horsfield, John
Howells, James Bletsoe
Hughes, Harold
Hughes, John Morgan
Hunt, Leonard Bryan

Hunter, Michael James
Ireson, Norman Wilfred
Johnson, Desmond Sidney
Jollans, John Lewis
Jones, Anthony Humphrey Lewis
Julian, Desmond Gareth
Jung, Leopold (Young)
Kendall, William Clarke
Kendon, Richard Donald
Kermode, Terence Lucas
Kettlewell, Geoffrey Wade
King, Roy Favell
Kragh, Alan Mackenzie
Lacey, Egerton Jeffery
Lacey, Thomas Lewis Guthrie
Lake, Malcolm George
Lamb, George Manners
Laverack, Frederick Cyril
Lavery, Hugh
Law, Kenneth Kitson
Layton, David
Legh-Jones, Peter Edward Legh
Lethbridge, Christopher John
Lewis, William Peter
Littman, Niculae (Lawrie)
Livesey, Harry Talboys
Llewellyn, Nathaniel James (Bentley- Llewellyn)
Lock, Derrick James
Long, Geoffrey Wilson
Longmore, Thomas Robert William
Lord, Peter Herent
Lording, Robert Kenneth
Loveridge, John Warren
McGeoch, Roy Burton
McMillin, Angus
Major, Donald
Mallett, Alan Arthur
Manning, John Rowland
Matthews, Peter Thomas
Moss, John Kennedy
Mountain, Ralph Howard
Murray, Albert Victor
Myers, Maurice John
Nash, Charles Antony Marriott
Needham, Harry Lindley
Nicoll, John Malcolm
Nutter, Jack Crossley
Nye, Ian William Beresford
Ogden, Leonard Dawson
Ogilvy, Kenneth Airlie
Ormerod, Peter Burton
Owen, David Norman Howell
Page, Arnold Thomas
Parish, Charles Roy
Parker, Bernard Oliver
Parkes, Edward Walter
Paton, Valentine Stewart
Patterson, Joseph Lewis
Philip, John Simpson Paton
Phillips, Anthony Gordon
Phillips, Arnold Boyd
Phillips, John Dayton

Pope, Alan Thomas
Powlesland, John
Prior, Arthur Deane
Rands, Ian Leslie
Read, Bryan Colman
Richardson, Richard James
Robertson, William David
Robson, Richard Derek
Ryle, Frederick Robert
Sanderson, John Frederick Richard
Sawyer, Desmond Branson
Scoble, John Warren
Scott, Peter
Searle, Harry John Mackenzie
Sewell, Arthur David
Shaw, Donald Curtis
Shipley, William Johnson
Simm, Frank
Simpson, Charles Abercrombie
Simpson, James Wallace Skinner
Slattery, Denis Peter
Smith, Alan Desmond
Smith, Kenneth Edward
Smith, Norman Peter
Smyth, David
Southwell, Roy
Stansbury, John Irvin
Statham, Allan Thomas
Stephens, Michael William
Stringer, John
Sutcliffe, Peter Hoyle
Talbot, Clifford Heyworth
Taylor, Gerald Phillips
Teague, Derek Michael
Thomas, Ronald
Thompson, Roger Ross
Thomson, Donald Einar
Tomlinson, Rolfe Cartwright
Turner, George Michael
Van den Bergh, Frank Asquith
Verinder, David
Vernon, Bryan Tom Jackson
Walker, Alick Donald
Warbrick, Allan James
Waterfall, Charles Richard
Waters, John David
Watkinson, Richard Geoffrey
Watt, Christopher Eugene
Weaving, Michael Reginald Vernon
Wernham, James Chrystall Stephen
Westlake, Ernest Keith
Whittle, Geoffrey Alan
Whitworth, Martin Dysart
Wilkie, John Ritchie
Williams, Richard Derrick
Wilmot-Dear, Peter William
Wilson, Ian Hume
Woodcock, Brian
Woodroffe, Charles Peter
Yates, John Keith
Young, Leopold (see Jung)
Zoller, Kenneth Norman

1944

Adye, Alan Michael
Allan, Peter Gerald
Allen, Geoffrey Reginald Cowley
Anderson, William Douglas Laing
Baker, David King
Barber, Denis Ian
Barrett, Leonard Middleton
Barron, John
Bartlett, Denis James
Bates, Eric William
Bayly, Denis Gibson
Beaumont, William Hugh
Belsham, Ian Rollo Bernard
Berwin, Stanley Jack
Birkett, Alan Abbott
Brading, George Thomas Robert
Bright, Gerald Emery
Brind, Arthur Henry
Brown, Ian Michael
Buller, Christopher Anson
Burke, Anthony Edgerton
Butler, Richard Francis Culverhouse
Cadbury, Charles Lloyd
Cartwright, Edgar David Beverley
Catford, John Robin
Chapman, Henry Bryan Parry
Clandillon, Edmund John
Clarke, Brian Lawson
Clarke, Donald Hugh
Collinson, Michael
Costello, Kevin
Coultous, Frederick David
Court, Kenneth Frank
Cragg, John Norman
Cribb, Robert James Preston
Cross, David Anderson
Crossman, Edward Robert Francis Ward
Culton, John Greenwood
Cussins, Wilfred Denys
Das Gupta, Charu Chandra
Davies, David Edgar
Davies, David Vaughan
Davis, Edward Derek
Davis, Peter Brian
Dawes, Alan
Daws, Hubert Gordon
De, Debesh Chandra
de Garis, Leslie
Dickinson, Alan
Dickinson, Allan William
Dixon, William Maxwell
Donovan, Philip Anthony
Downs, John Patrick
Drake, Brian John
Duce, Alan Godfrey
Edwards, John Llewelyn Jones
Elias, Charles Frederick
Evans, Geoffrey David
Fairhead, Russell Wale
Forster, Kenneth
Franklin, Roland Arthur Ellis

Garrood, John Francis
Gay, Michael Algar Parrish
Gibson, Alan Calvert
Gibson, John Milne
Gittins, Peter Robert
Goudy, Alexander Porter
Gough, John Richard
Greener, Paul
Griffiths, John David
Hall, John
Hall, John Frank Austin
Hall-Craggs, Ernest Christopher Bernard
Hamilton, Lester Dewie Goodchild
Harpur, Richard Latimer
Harrap, Michael Leslie
Haskett, Ronald Walter
Haughton, Michael Frederick
Haws, Edward Thomas
Hewitt, Charles Geoffrey
Higginson, Graham Kenrick
Higgs, Geoffrey William Hawley (Hawley-Higgs)
Hill, Richard Baird
Hogg, Denis Broadbery
Holmes, Eusebius
Horsfield, William Donald
Howe, James Turner
Hurst, Dennis George
Hutchinson, Miles
Jahn, Richard Edgar
Janes, Geoffrey Gilbert
Jarman, Maurice Vernon
Jenkins, David Philip
Johnson, Brian Gordon
Jones, David Pritchard
Jones, Richard Granville
Kennedy, Hewat Munro
Knowles, Alan Keith
Laing, Peter Elston
Lake, Neville Robert Norris
Langford, David
Laskey, Raymond John
Lavers, Norman Henry Stewart
Lines, Alfred James
Livesley, Robert Kenneth
Lowden, Gordon Stuart
Luisi, Hector Angel Francisco
Lythgoe, James Philip
McFadyean, Kenneth Michael
McGregor, Angus
McIntyre, David Graham
Mackintosh, Ian Brine
McLean, Robert Younger
McMurtrie, Robert Peter Lax
McNeill, John Richard
Madan, Michael Spencer
Major, Derek Drew
Martin, John Wilson
Masser, Ronald Thornton
Millar, Bryan
Millar, William Donald
Miller, Duncan McCorquodale
Mills, John

Moffoot, Francis George Robertson
Munir, Mehmed Nedjati
Newman, Barry George
Nicholson, Ernest Harvey
Nickson, Duncan
Nock, William
Nuttall, John Wardleworth
Nye, John Tompsett
O'Connell, Peter
Ormond, Derek
Osborne, Gerald Stanley
Packer, John Francis Smythe
Parker, Ronald Henry George
Peers, Francis George
Pemberton, Thomas Warwick Winstanley
Potts, Arthur Reginald
Poulter, Dennis Ross
Pownall, Alan Joseph
Radford, Roger Nicholas
Ratcliff, Gerald Alfred
Rigg, Edward Comer
Robb, Alan Gardner
Roberts, Robert John Michael
Rothwell, Richard William
Rugg, David Austen
Scott, Brian Moore
Seddon, Richard Paul
Shackleton, Patrick
Shardlow, Ambrose John
Shaw, Brian Worsley Bolton (Bolton Shaw)
Shearme, John Cornwall
Simeone, Reginald Nicola
Simpson, David
Sloman, Robert
Smith, Arnold Nigel
Smith, David Hurst
Stanney, Bernard Paul
Stanton, Royden James
Stares, Michael John
Stokes, Robert Ian
Suckling, Peter Gordon
Sugden, Henry Thackeray
Taylor, Geoffrey Walton
Taylor, Henry Dennis
Thatcher, Arthur Roger
Thomas, David Ian
Thomas, Eric Lionel
Thompson, Peter Ross
Thorp, Ralph Roland
Tregear, George Herbert Benjamin
Turney, Roy Frederick
Veitch, James Malcolm Mitford
Waterhouse, Ronald Gough
Watson, Roy Stuart
Weber, Gregorio
Whittaker, Roy
Wickens, Robert
Williams, Kenneth Sydney
Williams, Peter Orchard
Williams, Phillip
Williams, Raymond Howel
Wood, Patrick Ronald Oliver

Wright, Keith William
Young, Michael
Zimmern, Richard Frederick

1945

Aitchison, Alastair Gordon
Alexander, John Amyas
Anstey, Roger Thomas
Ashby, Michael Louis
Ballance, Michael Heudebourck
Bambrough, John Renford
Banks, Arthur Ashton
Bender, Eugene Jacob
Black, Peter Robert
Blackwood, John Barry
Bloch, Arnold
Bodington, George Christopher
Bourne, Charles Beresford
Bradbeer, John Wyatt
Braithwaite, John Geden North
Branford, William Richard Grenville
Bray, John Clive Russell
Brown, Kenneth Douglas
Bruce, Victor Walter
Bursill, Claude
Cardenas, Martin
Carpenter, Bernard Linley
Chapman, John Brian
Chapman, Rodney Harold Benbow
Chirgwin, Eric Graham
Chivers, John
Clement, Thomas Roy
Cobb, Peter Graham
Cochrane, Robert Hope
Collinge, Neville Edgar
Collinson, Roy Gladwin
Common, Donald Keith
Cook, Charles William
Cooper, John Sydney
Cooper, Michael George
Cooper, Peter Brian
Corlett, David Ernest
Cross, John Arthur
Crowder, Norman Harry
Davies, Ben
Dewes, John Gordon
Dressler, Patrick Edward
Edwards, John Martin Baskerville
Fahey, Edmund Joseph Francis
Ferguson, Thomas Barker
Fisher, Kenneth John
Forward, Nigel Stewart
Foster, Brian Stanley
Fraser, Simon Barron
Frazer, Andrew Keith
Gale, Ian Walter Valence
George, John Key Durancé
Gerrard, John Anthony Fraser
Gibson, John Nevill
Gillespie, John Kenneth
Goodchild, Arthur James Poulton

Gray, Frank Truan
Green, Martin Burgess
Gregory, Eric
Hall, John Challice
Harding, George William
Harris, Peter Medley John
Harris-Jones, Frank
Hayward, Roger Kendrick
Head, Kenneth Harold
Hepburn, Fred
Hill, Arthur David Frank
Hill, John McGregor
Hills, Kenneth Arthur
Hilton, Joseph Raymond
Hoffman, Wallace Benjamin
Holding, Daniel John
Holmes, George Arthur
Howarth, Leslie
Hutchins, Philip Frank
Instance, Michael Courage
Jardin, Dennis William
Jewell, Peter Arundel
Johnson, Anthony Alfred
Jones, Clement Workman
Kellar, James Noel
Kerruish, Norman
Kneel, Jack Alexander Charles
Lang, Ian Newcomb
Leeming, John Coates
Lees, John Francis
Lindbergh, Frederick Michael St Leger
Loosararian, Armèn Barouyr
Looser, Richard Bernhardt
McCann, Peter Orchard
Mackay, Graham Derek
Mackworth, Norman Humphrey
Margetson, John William Denys
Massie, Frank Alan
Mellors, Peter Howard
Merry, Frank
Molland, Ralph
Molyneux, Paul Stanley
Moody, Bernard John
Morris, Desmond Roy
Mortensen, Donald Van
Muir, Ian Douglas
Nairn, James Sword
Nicholson, David Hulme
Nicholson, Robert Keith
Noble, Benjamin
Norwood, David Barry
Nuttall, Richard Wardleworth
Orme, Donald Harrison
Otton, Geoffrey John
Palfrey, Alec John
Parrack, Colin Arthur
Payne, Douglas Sutherland
Pearson, Desmond Lindon
Peck, Michael
Peel, Michael John
Perkins, Dexter
Pesmazoglu, John Stevens (Pesmazoglou)

Prosser, John Michael
Radford, John Charles Victor
Rayner, Laurence Stephen
Reddi, Cooduveli Venkata Krishna
Reeves, John Michael
Riach, Donald James
Ringrose, Thomas Leonard
Robinson, Slade Raymond Christopher
Rosser, Norman
Rudd, Donald Henry
Rymer, Jolyon James Hugh
Sadler, Samuel Aubrey
Salisbury-Rowswell, Richard Frank
Savage, Douglas Frederick
Schlesinger, Wolfgang Wilhelm Otto
    (Slessenger)
Scott, Angus Weatheritt
Seale, John Richard
Sen, Samarenda Chandra
Sewell, William Musgrave
Shaheen, Medhat Hassan
Shaw, Douglas William David
Shaw, Michael Mellodew
Shepherd, Ronald Malcolm Henry
Smith, Reginald Edwin
Smith, William Douglas
Smythe, Paul Rodney
Snow, John Brian
Spargo, John Barnes
Stevenson, Kenneth Malcolm
Steyn, Johannes Roelof
Stuart, Ian David
Sykes, Neil Winn
Taylor, Peter Royston
Thomas, Norman
Thomson, Kenneth Roy
    (Lord Thomson of Fleet)
Tyler, Geoffrey James
Valentine, Barry
Vivian, Thomas Keith
Ward, John Derek
Waterhouse, Deryck Frank
Wheeler, Peter Hayden
White, Frank
White, William Rogers
Wilkinson, Lawrence
Williams, Robert Martin
Wilson, Leslie
Wolff, Michael Jonas
Woodcock, Samuel Richard
Woolnough, Hector Thomas
Wordie, John Stewart
Wright, Edmund
Young, Lindsay Menzies
Young, Samuel Knibb
Zecy, Theodore

1946

Ainscow, Nigel Richard
Allen, William Francis Atwell
Ashenden, Michael Roy Edward

Ashworth, Nigel Whittaker
Avis, Anthony Charles
Bailey, Trevor Edward
Baker, Berkeley Edward
Bansall, Harry Allan
Bardsley, Edwin Roy
Bell, Thomas Edward
Bennett, John Seabrook
Bennett, Michael Haynes
Bishop, Laurence Jack
Blow, Roland John
Bott, John David (Constance)
Bridge, James Haslam Newham
Buckland, Mervyn William Lancelot
Bullen, John Jaques
Butler, Ronald Crossley
Campbell, Merville O'Neale
Carr, Harold
Charlton, John Maxwell Town
Clark, Donald
Clarke, William Edward
Clews, Charles John Birkett
Clifton, Henry Tilden
Cole, Brian Wilson
Cole, William Frederick
Coster, Hendrik Paulus
Cowen, Roderick
Cradock, Percy
Creed, John Leslie
Custance, Richard Martin
Davis, Richard James Lance
de Nobriga, Alexander Percy
de Vos, Pieter Jacobus Gerhard
Ditcham, Anthony Greville Fox
Dixon, Brian Fenton
Drummond, Octavio Almeida
Duckworth, John Noel
Eastman, Hugh Leonard
Forbes, Peter Ronald Anthony
Foster, Reginald John
Fox, Donald Douglas
Freeman, Ronald Walter
Gilbert, Robert Greenway
Goodwin, John Charles Hill
Gough, Gordon
Greeves, John Anthony de Maine
Gregory, Alan Thomas
Gregson, Howard Davenport
Griffiths, Peter
Gunson, Gerald
Gwilt, George David
Hamilton, Michael Brewer
Harris, George Henry Gordon
Hassan, Salvador
Haworth, Fred
Henry, David
Heuston, Robert Francis Vere
Hill, Charles Kenneth
Hill, Robert William McLeavy
Horlock, John Harold
Horridge, George Adrian
Howe, Peter William Herbert

Howells, Herbert Norman
Hughes, Philip
Hutchinson, Arthur Lockwood
Ilitch, Milorad
Jeffery, David Schofield
Jelley, John Valentine
Jonas, Harry Oliver John Carter
Jones, Hywel Francis
Kellett, John Reginald
Kew, Norman Henry
Khong, Kit Soon
Kronheimer, Erwin Heinz
Lash, John Noel de Warrenne
Lennon, Derek Carlton
Lewis, John Scott
Lloyd, John Arthur
Loft, Edmund Martin Boswell
Lowden, James Stiven
McCallum, James Robert Henderson
Mackenzie Ross, Ian Alexander Bruce
MacLean, Roderick
Magnússon, Magnús
Marden, Edwin David
Meek, Ronald Lindley
Mehta, Jagat Singh
Millar, John Graham
Morgan, Rowland Lloyd
Morwood, Bryan
Munz, Peter
Newman, Harry
Noonan, John Thomas
Orde, Henry Leonard Shafto
Packard, Richard Qu'Appelle
Parker, Geoffrey Walter Austin
Parker, William Stewart
Parkin, Charles William
Pattison, George William
Patwardhan, Vaman Shankar
Perret, Cyril John
Preece, John Fryer
Preston, Joseph Henry
Probert, Eric Victor
Pullan, George Thomas
Ramsay, Hugh Baxter
Reader, Desmond Harold
Reece, David Chalmer
Richardson, William Eric
Rigg, John Michael
Ripper, David William
Ritter, Laurence Wilbur
Rivett, Douglas Eric Arthur
Roseveare, Robert William
Ruth, Anthony Barrons
Salam, Abdus
Sanderson, John Ernest Douglas
Sandford, Humphrey
Scott, David Angus George
Screech, Guy
Shaw, Douglas Jamieson
Shepherd, Roy Wootton
Shorrocks, Derek Martyn Marsh
Simister, John Michael

Skinner, Bruce Allan Maclean
Smith, David Bannister Lockhart
Speakman, Dennis
Stamp, Edward
Staton, Robert Alan
Stephens, Cyril Joakim
Straker, Thomas William
Telfer, Douglas Ross
Teverson, Henry Walter Samuel
Thomas, Keith (Colwinston)
Tinsley, Michael
Troup, Harold James Gardiner
Waddell, John Kennedy
Walker, Donald Clemson
Watt, Cyril Stanley
Weaver, Albert Paul
Welsh, Robert Cullen-Kerr
White, John Hylas
Widdell, Joseph William
Williams, Ernest Frank
Winter, John Openshaw
Yates, Robert Eric Burton

1947

Adams, Norman Stuart
Aitchison, Timothy John
Akiwumi, Akilano Molade
Alexander, Arthur Louis Lionel
Allen, Frank
Argyle, Geoffrey Vaughan
Armstrong, George Trevor
Arthur, William Todd
Ashby, Peter James
Bailey, Ronald Headley
Barr-Sim, Albert Derek
Beaumont, Henry Francis
Bell, Hubert Graham
Benians, Robin Christopher
Bishop, Terence Alan Martyn
Blackwell, Michael James
Blench, John Wheatley
Bonsall, Geoffrey Weatherill
Booth, Paul Rupert
Booth-Jones, Charles Ellison
Bower, Anthony Hugh Brian
Boyns, Martin Laurence Harley
Brasher, Christopher William
Brown, Andrew Torrance
Bruckland, Norman Ernest
Bruckner, Edgar Thomas
Burns, John Carlyle
Callander, Henry Ronald Burn
Callaway, Archibald Charles
Campbell, John Murray Martin
Cannell, Michael Frederick
Catherwood, Robert Ernest Frederick
Chapman, George Critchett
Clark, Peter Kenneth
Clarke, Philip Holmes
Clifford, Dudley Ronald
Coffey, Michael

Cole, Kenneth Edward
Coles, John Patrick
Collins, Derek Wilfred
Collins, Neville Clarence
Cormack, Allan MacLeod
Costain, Cecil Clifford
Crichton, John Wallis
Crick, John Louis Mingaye
Crook, John
Cross, Barry Albert
Cross, John Stanley
Cruickshank, Durward William John
Dannatt, Peter Conrad
Davies, John Howard
Davy, Arthur
Dawson, John Kenneth Nettleton
Domville, Alan Ratcliffe
Doubleday, John Gordon
Dunn, Peter MacNaughton
Dunston, Arthur John
Eden, John Forbes
Elsley, Jack Leslie
Evans, Michael David Thompson
Fairhurst, Harry
Field, William Patrick McDonnell
Fielding, Raymond
Finlayson, John Richard Terrell
Finnie, John
Fournier d'Albe, Eugene Robert
Fox, Basil Norman
Gent, Derek Frederick
Graaff, Johannes de Villiers
Green, James Alexander
Green, Reginald Arthur
Greenwood, Guy Kenneth
Gregory, William Charles Edward
Gross, Dauve
Guest, George Howell
Hacking, Peter Michael
Hague, Michael Taylor
Hall, George Garfield
Harker, Robert Ian
Harries, David John
Harry, John
Hartley, Anthony Vivian
Henderson, Ian Montrose
Heywood-Waddington, Michael Broke
Hobson, Patrick James
Hodgson, John Richard Patrick
Hollings, John Carter
Hosier, John
Humphrey, George
Hunter, John
Huxtable, Michael George
Jacobsen, Ronald Norman
Jefferies, John Trevor
Jones, Anthony Lewis
Jones, James Dennis
Joshi, Atmaram Bhairav
Kier, Hans Harold
Kittermaster, Arthur Richard
Laws, John Richard Harwood

Leach, Donald Anthony
Lewis, Dyfed
Lewis, William Russell
Lindsey, Peter Kenneth John
Linney, Duncan Stuart
Lloyd, Charles Brian Murray
Lloyd, Paul Medley
Lord, Alan
Lyon, Alexander Geoffrey
Lyon, Ian Barclay
McGregor, Charles Malcolm
Macklin, David Drury
Macleod, Alastair Leoid
Maltby, Antony John
Marsden, Eric William
Martlew, David Leyland
Massey, Paul Mackintosh Orgill
Mawle, John Wetherall
Mayall, Gordon Francis
Mead, Arthur Frederick
Mercer, Frank Verdun
Middelboe, Bernhard Ulrik
Minns, Derek Stewart
Mitchell, Neil Burton
Montague, John Cook
Morgan, Roger Harold
Morton, Henry Albert
Mullender, Pieter
Musgrave, Peter William
Narasimham, Maidavolu
Nesbitt, Philip
Nicholls, Denys Raymond
Overton, David Roper
Patwardhan, Madhukar Shankar
Penlington, Gilbert Napier
Perraton, Christopher John
Potsios, George
Read, James Jolliffe
Righini, Guglielmo
Rimmer, William Gordon
Robertson, Alexander Provan
Room, Eric Sydney
Rust, John Frederick
Salter, Clifford Edward
Saunders, Peter
Saxton, William Eric
Sears, Derek Lynford
Siddall, Eric
Sinha, Kumar Durganand
Smith, Philip Lionel Forster
Stewart, Hugh Martin
Stewart, Robert William
Stopes-Roe, Harry Verdon
Tearle, James Francis
Telfer-Smollett, Patrick Tobias
Thomas, Richard Charles Clement
Thursfield, Robert Hugh
Trought, Thomas Edmund Trevor
van Dulken, Geoffrey Theodore Hicks
Vaughan, Geoffrey Parton
Wace, Geoffrey Richard
Wardman, Alan Edgar

Watts, Robert Newell Crawford
Way, Derek John
Wells, Patrick Habershon
White, James George Charles
Widdas, Frank
Wilkes, Kenneth William
Wilkinson, Albert
Wilson, Allan Curtis
Wilson, Andrew Thomas
Wise, David
Woodhead, Andrew
Woyka, John Graham
Yates, James Garrett

1948

Absolon, Peter Chambers
Allison, Harold
Almond, Harry Hudson
Anand, Nitya
Anderson, John Dacre
Appleby, Brian John
Armitage, Brian
Armstrong, David John
Bakar, Abu (Pawanchee)
Bambah, Ram Prakash
Bardsley, Richard Geoffrey
Barnes, Frederick George
Barnes, Hugh Michael Francis
   (Barnes-Yallowley)
Barnett, Richard David
Barton, George Paterson
Beer, John Bernard
Beers, Robert Stewart Ross
Bellis, Bertram Thomas
Berry, Donald
Berry, Gerard John
Bertschinger, Max
Bolt, David Dingley
Bond, Derek Arthur
Boumphrey, John Michael Howorth
Boydell, James Stephen
Bradshaw, Peter Malcolm Clark
Brickstock, Alan
Brostoff, Daniel Victor
Brough, James Nuttall
Brown, Michael Evelyn
Bryan, Patrick John
Burnett, Donald Stuart
Bury, Henry Philip Roberts
Butcher, George Laidman
Carlisle, Raymond
Carter, Edmund Brian
Chaumeton, John Bryan
Cockburn, William Derrick
Cotton, John Horace Brazel
Crawshaw, Derek Anthony John
Cullen, Patrick Arthur Augustus
d'Assis-Fonseca, Honorio Bingham (Fonseca)
Dakin, Robert Humphrey
Danckwerts, Peter Victor
Darling, William Hunter

David, John
Davidson, Francis Stanley
Davies, Jack
Davies, Patrick Taylor
Day, Neville John
Denman, Eric Edward
Denney, Anthony Howe
Denson, John Boyd
Dewhurst, Arthur
Dickinson, James Stanley
Donaldson, William Anderson
Dorman, Richard Bostock
Dukes, Maurice Nelson Graham
Edwards, Norman Henry
Elliot, Anthony Russel Pontifex
Ellis, Keith Stanley
Emery, Richard Seabrook
Finlay, David Thornton
Flint, John Edgar
Freundlich, Herbert Frederick
Galloway, Antony Lennox
Garbett, Peter
Gardner, John Edmund
Gilbert, Roger Key
Goldstein, David John
Goodhand, Ian Frank
Grant, Malcolm Leith
Griffith, George Hugh Clarence
Halket, Peter Buchanan
Hambling, Andrew
Harris, Desmond John
Hawkins, Michael Oliver Slade
Hay, Andrew Mackenzie
Hay, William
Henton, Guy Robin Plenderleith
Hill, Henry Gordon
Hodgkiss, Derek Saunders
Hodgson, James
Holland, Graham Lambert
Hood, Edwin John
Hopper, Michael Thompson
Hotchin, Philip Lowther
Howe, David Randall
Hunt, John Christopher Noel
Ivill, John
Jeeves, Malcolm Alexander
Jenks, Robin Eric
Johnson, Derek
Jolly, Keith
King, Alan Brasher
King, Arthur David Newton
Kipping, Stanley Arnold Brian
Kirk, Peter John Daniels
Laxton, Harold Raymond Wentworth
Leaton, Esmond Harold
Leigh, Philip Mark
Lindon, Denis Norman
Line, Timothy Charles
Linfoot, Edward Hubert
Linney, George
Lyall, David Ellis
Lyons, Peter Stanley

Macallister, Hamilton
MacDonald, Andrew Sinclair
MacDowall, Joseph
Mackay, Angus Newton
Macpherson, Ian William
MacRobert, Alexander Edgely
Madeloff, Stanley Michael
Maloney, Bernard Patrick
Maltby, Christopher Hugh Kingsnorth
Maltby, John Wingate
Masson Smith, David John
Matthews, Roy Anthony
Maw, Zali
Meadows, John Michael
Mewton, Richard
Miller, Alexander Lamont
Morgan, Michael Clement
Morton, Howard Knyvett
Mossman, David James
Mylne, Christopher Kenneth
Newman, James Fraser MacCallum
Newton, Richard James
Nimmo, Johnston Robertson
O'Brien, Charles Ian Milward
O'Leary, Terence Daniel
Officer, Leonard Adrian
Ogilvie, David Alexander
Parry-Williams, Henry Wyn
Pearce, James Francis Stuart
Pearson, Michael Geoffrey
Perkins, Norman Charles
Perry, John Leycester Coltman
Pillai, Kokkat Sankara
Platt, James
Preen, Thomas Owen Phillip
Rae, Robert
Raffle, John Andrew
Reily, Denis
Riley, Keith Mcfarlane
Ritchie, Alexander James Otway
Roberts, Donald James
Roberts, James Dearden
Robinson, Alfred
Robinson, Brian Hugh Bartlett
Rodger, William Rhodes
Rood, Arthur Bryant
Ross, Alec Logie
Rowe, Peter Whitmill
Roxburgh, Thomas Cunningham
Salton, Milton Robert James
Scheuer, Peter August Georg
Scott, Paul Habershon
Sharp, Kenneth Johnston
Side, David Erle
Slater, James Aubin
Smith, Christopher Jaffray
Smith, Harry Graham
Smith, Rex Stanley
Smith, Russell Alexander
Smithson, Thomas Alan
Stanier, John Philip
Stark, Robert Patrick Napier

Stephens, John Christopher
Stone, Leonard
Sykes, Peter
Taylor, John
Tempest, Robert Kershaw
Templeton, Malcolm Clark
Thakur, Damodar
Thornbery, Derek Russell Wallis
Timbrell, David Yorke
Todd, Douglas Brian
Townsend, Peter Brereton
Treacy, Peter Bradley
Turner, Ronald
Tyreman, Anthony Carlisle
Valentine, Anthony Seymour
Vanstone, William Hubert
Vunivalu, Ravuama
Walmsley, Ernest Roland
Wedd, George Morton
Welford, Michael Trevor
West, Ronald Leonard
Whidby, Frank
Whitby, Ralph Preece
Whitehead, Derek
Whitmore, David Noel
Whitney, Alan
Wiggins, Hugh Sidney
Wilders, John Simpson
Wilkinson, Frederick
Williams, Jocelyn Trevor Newcombe
Williams, John Howard
Williams, Robin Philip
Wills, John Brian
Wilson, Geoffrey Malcolm
Winter, Robert Llewellyn
Wordie, George Thompson
Worlidge, Edward John

1949

Ackery, Duncan Melville
Adams, Christopher Douglas
Alexander, Anthony Victor
Anderson, Thomas Bruce
Andrewartha, Kenneth
Andrews, David Mark
Ashforth, John Vincent
Austin, Kingsley David
Bain, Joseph
Baker, Richard Geoffrey
Ball, David Hamilton
Bamber, John
Barker, Stuart John
Barker, William Thomas
Bartholomew, Alick Nairne
Baxter, Jeremy Richard
Beaumont, John Robert
Beckley, Verey Robert Sidley
Bennett, Donald Edward
Bewick, William Alfred Malcolm
Binnian, James Anthony
Birtles, Gordon Padfield

Blick, John David
Breddy, Denis Charles George
Brooks, Edwin
Brown, Frederick Bamford
Brown, Michael John Hilton
Bruce, Harold Trefusis
Buckatzsch, Erich John Metius
Burgin, David Harding
Busvine, Robert Lewis
Butler, Basil Richard Ryland
Butler, Ian Edward
Calviou, Peter Michael
Campbell, Alexander Elmslie
Cannon, Brian Norris
Canny, Martin Joseph Patrick
Carr, Charles Raymond
Cellan-Jones, Alan James Gwynne
Charters, John Dumergue
Cheers, Brian
Cheng, Chao-tsung
Clack, Nicholas Barry Menzies
Clark, Harold Edward
Clarke, Charles Richard
Combridge, Anthony Theodore
Conway, John Seymour
Cooper, Michael John Richardson
Corby, Frederick Brian
Coutie, George Angus
Craggs, James Wilkinson
Crawley-Boevey, Thomas Michael Blake
D'Arcy, John Robert
Davison, Peter Hubert
Dee, Robert John
Dehn, Michael Harold
de la Torre, Fernando
Dexter, John Alfred
Dickinson, Michael George Heneage
Dingle, John Rodney
Dixon, John Lindley
Douglas, David Hamilton
Duncan, Angus Henry
Dunlop, Robert Fergus
Earnshaw, David Anthony
Elliott, John Sinclair
Embleton, Clifford
Erickson, John
Fairbairn, Walter McArthur
Faulks, John Michael
Fayle, Brian William Knott
Fisher, Michael George Penton
Fitzherbert, Basil Francis Nicholas
    (Lord Stafford)
Ford, Dennis Howard
Fuad, Kutlu Tekin
Gardiner, James Aitken
Gavins, Raymond Cedric
Geddes, Archibald
Gilbert, David Hew
Gilbert, David Martyn
Gilmore, Paul Carl
Girling, Michael Stuart
Goldsmith, Colin Cecil

Goode, James Edward
Goodrich, Philip Harold Ernest
Green, Gordon Leonard
Greenstreet, Anthony John
Gregory, Geoffrey
Guthrie, Colin Bain
Gwynne-Timothy, Kenneth Gordon Rupert
Hagon, David Olaf
Hakki, Ahmed
Halson, Geoffrey Robert
Hammond, John Edwin
Harley, James Macgregor Bruce
Harris, David Russell
Harvey, Henry Norman Martin
Haslam, Richard Alleyn Kingdon
Hearn, Harry Robert
Hebditch, Gerald Edward William
Helliwell, Leslie
Heughan, Donald Malcolm
Higgins, Larratt Tinsley
Hill, Eric Grenville
Hirst, William Henry
Hollings, Christopher Ingham
Holmes, John Maxwell Wilson
Hosking, Anthony John
Hudson, George Alexander
Hunt, David Edward
Hutton, Patrick Hamilton
Hyatt, John Hampden
Iliffe, John Kenneth
Ispahani, Mirza Mohamed
Ispahani, Mirza Mohamed Ali
Jackson, Francis William David
Jackson, Graeme Clark
Jenkins, Henry John
Johnson, Malcolm MacDonald
Jones, Dewi Roland
Kane, Prabhakar Pandurang
Lardner, Thomas Harry Afolabi
Lees, George Milne
Littleboy, Michael Francis
Lloyd, Michael Vernon
Locke, Michael
Longman, Anthony Vivian
Macer, Richard Charles Franklin
MacIver, Donald
Maclay, Walter Strang Symington
Marchington, Trevor
Mark, Peter Hinton
Martin, Anthony Bluett
Matthews, Robert Charles Oliver
Mavor, John Osborne
Merrell, Robert Maurice
Miller, Derek
Mitchell, John Edward
Mortimer-Jones, John Bracken
Morton, Robert Kerford
Mulligan, Terence Elphinstone
Nedderman, John Midgley
Ogden, Robert David
Orchardson, Ian Kipkerui
Osborn, Peter George Graeme

Pallett, Denis Edwin Henry

Pallister, Michael Alan

Palmer, Nigel Webb

Parker, Christopher

Peberdy, John Rodney

Peters, David Robert

Pike, Graham John Roger

Pitman, John Henry Norton

Prestt, Peter

Quayle, John Rodney

Radford, Matthew Frederick

Rankin, James Mottram Nasmith

Ratcliff, John Cooper

Read, Lionel Frank

Reese, Clifford Raymond

Rhodes, Charles Malcolm

Riley, Peter

Riley, Richard Woodburne

Roberts, David Wyn

Roe, Peter Frank

Ross, Graham

Rowland, David Herbert

Ruscoe-Pond, Malcolm George

Rushton, Stanley John

Salmon, Peter Stanley

Salter, John Arthur Philip

Schneider, Ben Ross

Scott, Gordon Wood

Scott-Park, Jock Hargrave

Senior, Sam

Shakeshaft, John Roland

Sharpley, Roger Fielding Anthony

Sidgwick, John Utrick

Simpson, Roger

Sissener, John

Skinner, Derek Rowland

Slawikowski, George Joseph Marian

Slingsby, David Bryan

Small, Fred

Smith, David Henry Gould (Gould Smith)

Smith, David Hilbre

Smith, William Edward

Soar, Peter Hale McMillan

Southwold, Martin

Spalding, Thomas Ian

Sparks, Alexander Pratt

Spencer, Dominick Evelyn Wellesley

Stafford, John

Stanley, James Perham

Stedman, John Richard

Stephenson, Ian Stobbs

Storer, David George

Storr, Christopher William

Sutcliffe, Roy

Telfer, Ian Edmund

Temple, James Muir

Terrett, James Anthony

Thomson, Christopher Bruce

Tomlinson, Brian

Townend, Peter Lawson

Trott, John Michael

Turnbull, Dennis Etherington

Turner, John Stewart

Udall, Humfrey Nicholas

van der Lee, Jacob Jan

Vinnicombe, John

Waters, Roy William

Watkin, John Emrys

Wescombe, Anthony Willingdon

Whiddington, Richard Harcourt

White, Geoffrey

Whittaker, Charles Richard

Wickham, Peter Guy

Williams, John Vivian

Williams, Peter Henry

Wood, Timothy George

Wyatt, Michael

Yeoman, John Harbottle